GENEALOGIES IN THE LIBRARY OF CONGRESS

A BIBLIOGRAPHY

GENEALOGIES

IN THE

LIBRARY OF CONGRESS

A BIBLIOGRAPHY

Edited by

MARION J. KAMINKOW

VOL. II

K - Z

MAGNA CARTA BOOK COMPANY
BALTIMORE, MD.
U.S.A.
1972

Library of Congress catalog card number: 74-187078

ISBN: 0-910946-15-9

PREFACE

As explained in the Editor's Note which follows, this bibliography lists genealogical books and other related materials in the collections of the Library of Congress. Books on genealogy, heraldry, and U. S. local and State history must be used at the Library of Congress because the Library does not circulate them on interlibrary loan. It is advisable to ascertain the hours of public service before coming to the library.

In general, books on genealogy and U. S. local history may be consulted only in the Local History and Genealogy Room. In addition to works on local history and genealogy in the Library's general collections, there is an extensive reference collection in the room, comprising indexes, guides, and other works, conveniently arranged for the use of the reader, and special card catalogs, most of which are organized by family name.

The reference staff on duty in the Local History and Genealogy Room assists users in identifying publications that relate to the subjects of their research, chiefly by explaining the use of the indexes and catalogs in the collection. The staff of the Library cannot undertake research in family history or heraldry. In order to perform work of this nature satisfactorily, it is necessary to identify the particular branch of a family concerned; because of the time and effort involved, searches for this type of information usually require the services of a professional genealogist or heraldic searcher; normally such research is undertaken for a fee.

The Library does not have copies of genealogies for sale. Dealers in books, including out-of-print materials, may be able to assist in securing copies of needed publications. It may be possible, however, to purchase photocopies of out-of-print items from the Library. The specific pages and material to be copied must be cited, and provided no copyright restrictions apply, photocopies may be obtained in accordance with conditions indicated in an order form available from the Library of Congress, Photoduplication Service, Washington, D. C. 20540.

EDITOR'S NOTE

This bibliography brings up to date similar printed works published in 1910 and 1919 under the title AMERICAN AND ENGLISH GENEALOGIES IN THE LIBRARY OF CONGRESS, as well as the microcard edition which appeared in 1954. The present compilation lists not only American and English works but also holdings of Canadian, Irish, Welsh, Scottish, Australian, Latin American, Polish, German, Dutch, Scandinavian, French, Spanish, Italian, Portuguese, and Asian sources. It includes all the entries from the Family Name Index, the 60-drawer card catalog located in the Local History and Genealogy Room of the Library of Congress.

The cards of the Index refer to printed books and to genealogies in diverse formats, such as typescripts and handwritten materials. In addition, there are cards for genealogies in works on local history, periodicals, and many unlikely sources, probably not referred to elsewhere in a genealogical sense, such as Izaac Walton's THE COMPLEAT ANGLER which includes his pedigree.

As would be expected, much of the information presented here is not in the 1919 edition. New materials listed include not only works produced since that year but also many items published before 1919 and acquired by the Library after that date. This new edition can therefore be considered as three tools in one: a guide to genealogical monographs which may be found in the Library of Congress and in other libraries; the Library's own particular index to genealogies in sources not primarily genealogical in nature; and a guide to the unique collection of nonprinted genealogies held by the Library, other than those in its Manuscript Division. Some of the genealogical material contained in the collections of the latter is listed in THE NATIONAL UNION CATALOG OF MANUSCRIPT COLLECTIONS and in other guides which show Manuscript Division holdings.

Although there are some variations, the Index places family names together which are pronounced alike, or almost alike, even though there are differences in spelling. The entries under these names are then grouped in chronological order. This system has been retained by the publishers, since it simplifies the finding of a name that is spelled in one of any number of ways; it is still advisable, however, to check variant spellings (e. g., Alsop, Allsop) in their proper alphabetical locations.

There are cross-references for genealogical sources which have sections referring to a family whose name does not appear in the title of the work cited. An example is "Andrus. See also: Dixon, 1922." This leads the reader to look under the name Dixon for a 1922 publication which includes information about the Andrus family. Other cross-references cite entry numbers for works that have no family name in the title.

In a compilation of this size it is impossible to avoid all inconsistencies. The omission of an entry number may indicate that a duplicate card has been eliminated. An item omitted from the main list may be found in the addenda at the end of each volume, together with publications which have appeared since work on this bibliography began. A reference to a missing item that is not included in the addenda is to a card not located in the catalog of the Local History and Genealogy Room but rather in the Library's Main Catalog.

A book of additions and corrections is kept in the Local History and Genealogy Room and added to from time to time as errors and omissions are discovered in genealogical sources. References to these additions and corrections appear in the volumes affected or in some cases (i. e. when a volume is on microfilm), on the catalog card describing the volume.

Library of Congress call numbers are provided for all cataloged items in the Library's collections.

EDITOR'S NOTE

Abbreviations used for bibliographic details include the following:

l.	leaf or leaves
p.	page or pages
n. p.	no place of publication
pl.	plate
c	copyright (usually preceding date)
t. - p.	title page
port.	portrait

The call number E171.A53, which is cross referenced many times, refers to the publication Americana.

The publishers wish to express their gratitude to the Library of Congress for graciously permitting publication of this bibliography for the use of genealogists all over the world. Thanks are also due to all the librarians who have had a hand in compiling the Family Name Index over the years, and particularly to the present staff of the Local History and Genealogy Room, without whose unfailing help and courtesy the present work could not have been accomplished.

Marion J. Kaminkow

K

KACHLEIN.   See: EYERMAN, 1898
                        EYERMAN, 1902

KACHLIN.   In vertical file under PRANKE family.   Ask reference librarian for this material.

KAGARISE.   See SNOWBERGER, 1964

9476   KAHN.   The story of Estate; another chapter of the romance of business in the land of oppor-
tunity, by Melodia and Walter S. Rowe.   (Hamilton, O., The Hill-Brown printing co., c.1937)
45 p. illus. (mounted ports.) 20 cm.   A history of the Estate stove company and an account of the accomplishments of the Kahn family. cf. Pref.
37-4117.   TS425. R6

9477   KAHN.   Die Familie Kahn von Sulzburg/Baden, ihre Geschichte und Genealogie.   By Ludwig
David Kahn.   (Basel) 1963.   206 p. illus., maps, ports. 25 cm. Bibliography: p. 11-16. 64-5243.   CS629.K32   1963

KAIGHN.   See COOPER, 1931

KAIL.   See No. 1547 - Cabell county.

9478   KAINE.   A letter from Mrs. Thomas Morris, to her nephew the Hon. Judge John K. Kane, regarding the Kane and Kent families ... (New York, c.1889)   cover-title, 27 p. 23½ cm. 9-11468.
                                                                              CS71.K13   1889

KAINE.   See also: TODD, 1867
                                VAN RENSSELAER, R171.A53 vol. 14

9479   KAISER.   The Swiss family Kaiser.   By Roland Glenn Kaiser.   (Salt Lake City, 1962)
151 p. illus. 29 cm. 62-41039.   CS71.K135   1962

KAISER.   In vertical file under PRANKE family.   Ask reference librarian for this material.

9480   KALBFLEISCH.   A genealogical record of the descendants of Reinhardt Kalbfleisch, born 12
August 1812 in Germany, died 27 June 1894 near Elmira, Ontario.   By Raymond Winfield Kalbfleisch.
Private limited ed.   Levering, Mich. (1956)   107 p. illus. 24 cm. Two fold. geneal. tables, dated May, 1960, inserted.
60-38619.   CS71.K14   1956

KAMLAH.   See CHRYSLER, 1959

KAMM.   See GRAY, 1925

KAMPE.   See BECHTEL, 1936

KAMPHUIS.   See KOLE, 1962

9481   KAMPMANN.   History of Texas and Texans ... By Francis W. Johnson.   Chicago & New York,
The American Historical Society, 1914.   v. 3, p. 1251.   F386J66

KANE.   See KAINE.

9482   KAPP.   History of the Kapp family.   By Webster Wayne Kapp.   (ed. by Numer M. Kapp. Harrisville, Pa., 1948)   32 p. illus., coat of arms.   23 cm.   Cover title.   48-23451*.   CS71.K15   1948

9483   KAPROV.   The B'nai Khaim in America; a study of cultural change in a Jewish group, by Joseph M. Gillman in collaboration with Etta C. Gillman.   Philadelphia, Dorrance (c. 1969)   xviii, 168 p. illus., geneal. tables, map, ports. 22 cm.   Includes bibliographical references.   69-19899 MARC.   CS71.K16   1969

9484   KARAJAN, de.   A daughter of Firenze; an account of my mother's childhood in Italy, by Rosamond Swan Hammer.   New Haven, The Tuttle, Morehouse & Taylor press, 1924.   7 p. l., 98 p. front., pl., ports.   21 cm.   Genealogical notes: p. 73-79.   Music: p. (81)-98.   25-24872.   DG735.6.H3

KARI.   See CARY.

9485   KASE.   Reminiscences of the Kase family.   (Flemington? 18 -?)   1 l. front. 25 cm. Caption title. Signed Elias Vosseller.   3-4825.   CS71.K19   18 -

9486   KASPER.   Some of Lewis P. Kasper's kin, compiled by A.M. Prichard ... Staunton, Va. (Campfield printing co.) 1946.   30 p., 1 l. front. (port.) 23 cm.   46-16963.   CS71.K192   1946

KASSEL.   See CASSEL.

9487   KASSON.   Genealogy of a part of the Kasson family, in the United States and Ireland.   By George M. Kasson.   Woodbury, Conn., A.E.Knox, 1882.   51 p. 18½ cm. 10-31152.   CS71.K193   1882

9488   KATHAN.   ... History of Captain John Kathan, the first settler of Dummerston, Vt. and his associates and family descendants, and the Moores, the Frosts, the Willards, allied by marriage to the Kathans.   Also a partial account of William French and Daniel Houghton the first martyrs of the revolution; by David L. Mansfield ... Brattleboro, E.L.Hildreth & co., 1902.   xii, 147 p. incl. front. plates, ports., fold. map. 23½ cm. 3-26849.   CS71.K196   1902

KATZENMAIER.   See KATZENMEIER.

KATZENMEYER.   See KATZENMEIER.

9489   KATZENMEIER.   Genealogy of the Katzenmaier family by Lawrence and Myrtle Katzenmeier. Colby, Kan., Prairie Printers (c. 1963)   1 v. (unpaged) ports.   25 cm.   Cover title: Katzenmaier family history, 1658-1962.   64-55037.   CS71.K1996   1963

KAUFFMANN.   See KAUFMAN.

9490   KAUFHOLZ.   The Kaufholz families of America and Europe ... Genealogies compiled by Charles Frederick Kaufholz, jr. ... Canton, O. (1940)   3 p. l., 28 numb. l. 32½ cm.   Type-written.   41-31424.   CS71.K2   1940

9491   KAUFMAN.   The Peter Kaufman and Freni Strausz Kaufman family record, 1844-1963, by Ed. G. Kaufman with assistance of committee: Peter R. Kaufman (and others.   North Newton, Kan.) 1963.   vi, 100 p. illus., ports., maps, facsims., geneal. table.   24 cm.   64-871.   CS71.K21   1963

9492   KAUFMAN.   Lineages of the Murray M. Kauffman and Daniel Hollinger families of Adams and Franklin Counties, Pennsylvania, 1696-1963.   By Robert Terry Kauffman.   (Harrisburg? Pa., 1963)   26, 25 p. ports.   31 cm.   Cover title.   64-1215.   CS71.K21   1963a

9493   KAUFMAN.   The Kauffman family of Adams and Franklin Counties, Pennsylvania, since 1800 A.D.; a brief lineage of the children, grandchildren and great-grandchildren of Leonard M. Kauffman, and his wife, Polly M. Carbaugh through their son Isaac Martin Kauffman, and his wife, Christina Naomi Baker and their children Elmira, Samantha, Clara, Ida, Nettie, Murray, Harvey, Edward, Albert and George.   Harrisburg, Pa., 1963.   31 cm.   64-54777.   CS71.K21   1963b

9494 KAUFMAN. A genealogy and history of the Kauffman-Coffman families of North America, 1584 to 1937; including brief outlines of allied Swiss and Palatine families who were among the pioneer settlers in Lancaster and York counties of Pennsylvania from 1717 on; viz., Becker, Baer, Correll, Erisman, Fahs, Kuntz, Kneisley, Hershey, Hiestand, Meyers, Musselman, Neff, Martin, Ruby, Snavely, Shenk, Shirk, Sprenkle, Witmer, and others. Compiled by Charles Fahs Kauffman. York, Pa., The author (c. 1940)   xxi, 775 p. front., illus. (incl. plans, facsim., coats of arms.) pl., ports. 23½ cm. 40-32503.

CS71.K21   1940

KAUFMAN. See also: CAUFFMAN, 1892 (addenda)
CLAUSER, 1959
GRABER, 1948
KIESSEL, 1948
STRICKLER, 1925

KAUFMANN. See KAUFMAN.

KAUP. See BORNEMAN, 1881

9495 KAVANAUGH. Lineage of Sophia Elizabeth Kavanaugh-Bear in (Argall-Filmer), Green, Clay, Bruce, and Palmer ancestry (maternal) Loftus, (Woods-Wallace), (Miller-Dulaney), Kavanaugh (paternal); a loving tribute to her memory by her daughter, Sophia Elizabeth Bear-Sherlock ... (Lexington, Ky., Commercial printing company) 1929.   189 p., 1 l. illus. (coats of arms) port. 18½ cm. 30-4544.

CS71.K215   1929

KAVANAGH. See KAVANAUGH.

KAVANAUGH. See also: MILLER, 1907
O'CONNOR, 1941

9496 KAY. Pedigree of Kay. (By Charles Jackson. Worksop, R. White, 1881)   geneal. tab. 25½ x 38½ cm. Excerpt from the author's Doncaster charities, past and present, Worksop, 1881. 25-17991.   CS439.K3

9497 KAY. Documentary notes relating to the district of Turton. Ed. and comp. by Jas. C. Scholes ... Bolton, "Evening news" & "Journal" offices, 1882.   1 p. l., 161 p. fold. facsim., 2 fold. geneal. tab. 19½ cm. "Pedigree of the Kays of Entwisle and Turton Tower." "Pedigree of the Taylors and Barlows of Turton and Entwisle." 15-22371.

DA690.T93S3

KAY. See also COOK, HV250.D6J3

9498 KAYSER. Familie Kayser, Bilder and Gestalten aus dem Leben einer deutschen Familie. Ed. Johanne Kayser. Dresden, O. Günther (19 -)   232 p. ports., geneal. table. 22 cm. "Literatur und Quellen": p. 232. 49-58278 *   CS679.K3   1900z

9499 KAZUKI. In Japanese. Title romanized: Watakushi wa Nintoku Tennō no Kōei da. By Aiki Oka.   202 p. illus., geneal. tables, map, ports. 18 cm. Bibliography: p. 201-202. 76-807745.

CS1309.K3   1967
Orien. Japan.

9500 KEAGY. A history of the Kägy relationship in America, from 1715 to 1900, by Franklin Keagy of Chambersburg, Pa. ... Harrisburg, Pa., Harrisburg publishing company, 1899.   675 p. incl. front., plates, ports. 24 cm. 20-17037.   CS71.K22   1899

KEAGY. See also ESPENSCHIED, 1949

KEAN. See KEEN.

KEARFOTT. See KERFOOT.

KEARNEY. See: ALSTON, 1901
PARKER, 1925

9501   KEARL.   Kearl family history; biographies of James Kearl, 1833-1902, his wives and posterity.   Editor: Alley V. Johnson Taylor.   1st ed.   Provo, Utah, Printed by J. G. Stevenson (1963?-
v. 25 cm. 65-67224.   CS71. K226   1963

9502   KEARL.   Proud to remember; genealogy and history on four ancestral lines of Lula Barzilla
Humphrey Kearl: paternal, Humphrey-Thames; maternal, Brunson-Marshall.   By Vera Lee (Kearl)
Marshall.   Provo, Utah, Brigham Young University Press, 1964.   vii, 137 p. ports. 28 cm. 67-9212.
                                                                        CS71. K226   1964

9503   KEARNS.   A family history and a list of the descendants of John Kearns and his wife Margaret.
Issued ... by Miss Ruth Kearns.   Mount Vernon, Ia., The Hawk-eye press, 1911.   57 l. front. (2 port.)
15½ cm.   All leaves but one printed one side only.   13-13974.   CS71. K23   1911

9504   KEARNY.   The Kearnys of Perth Amboy.   By William Carroll McGinnis.   (Perth Amboy, N. J.)
City of Perth Amboy, 1956.   13 p. illus. 22 cm. 59-43213.   CS71. K235   1956

        KEARNY.   See also PARKER, 1925

9505   KEARSLEY.   The descendants of Jonathan Kearsley, 1718-1782, and his wife Jane Kearsley,
1720-1801, (from Scotland) who settled at Carlisle, Penn'a.   Died at Shippensburg, Pa. and are buried
at Middle Spring church yard, Cumberland county, Pa.   (By Elmer L. White.   Pittsburgh? Pa.) 1900.
75, (1) p. 5 facsim. , fold. geneal. tab.   23 cm.   Compiled by Elmer L. White from data mainly collected by Maj. Edmund Roberts Kearsley.
Explanatory note signed Elmer M. White.   Type-written additions to 1926 supplied by George T. Kearsley, inserted after p. 20 and p. 28.   10-22836.
                                                                        CS71. K24   1900

9506   KEARSLEY.   The Kearsley family in America.   Maternal side.   Comp. by Geo. T. Kearsley.
(Radford, Va. ?) 1911.   14 (i. e. 15) numb. l.   33 x 22 cm.   Two leaves are numbered 10.   "Gleanings from English parish registers,
in Library of Congress Comp. by G. T. Kearsley": 1 leaf, 1915 inserted at end.   20-23927.   CS71. K24   1911

9507   KEATING.   Keating and Forbes families and reminiscences of C. A. Keating, A. D. 1758-1920.
Dallas, Tex. (Wilkinson printing co.) 1920.   175 p. illus. (incl. ports.) fold. geneal. tab.   23 cm.   20-10512.
                                                                        CS71. K25   1920

9508   KEATOR.   Three centuries of the Keator family in America.   By Alfred Decker Keator.   New
York, American Historical Co., 1955.   351 p. 24 cm.   CS71. K252   1955
        —— Keator family in America.   Addenda et corrigenda.   Harrisburg, Pa., 1961.
unpaged. 23 cm.   55-30093 rev.   CS71. K252   1955a

9509   KEATS.   John Keats and his family; a series of portraits.   (By Maurice Buxton Forman)
Edinburgh, Printed at the Dunedin press limited, 1933.   10 l. 6 port. 20½ cm.   "Note" signed: M. Buxton Forman.
"Edition limited to one hundred copies. "   34-3713.   PR4836. F6
                                                                        Rare book room.

        KEATS.   See also PITMAN, 1920

        KEAYNE.   See KEENEY.

        KEBLE.   See HOLBROW, 1901

9510   KECK.   The Keck family, with special reference to the descendants of Michael Keck, who
came to Ohio in 1806 ... Compiled and edited by John Melvin Keck ... (n. p.) 1926.   71 p. illus. (ports.)
19½ cm.   Nine pages at end left blank for "Memorandum".   27-3868.   CS71. K255   1926

9511   KECK.   History of the Keck family.   By Joseph A. Keck.   (n. p., 1901?)   51 p. illus. 23 cm.
                                                                        CS71. K255   1901
        —— Supplement, compiled by Kathryn Keck Kipper.   Rocky Ford, Colo., 1965.   18 l. 28 cm.
Typescript (carbon copy) 53-56122 rev.   CS71. K255   1901
                                                                        Suppl.

9512   KEEFER.   Memoirs of the Keefer family, by Rev. Robert Keefer ... Norwood, Ont., The Norwood register press, 1935.   3 p. 1., (9)-26, (4) p. illus. (coat of arms) plates, ports. 23½ cm. Blank pages for "Births, marriages, deaths" (4) at end. 35-16213.   CS90.K4   1935

9513   KEELER.   Genealogical record of the Keeler family, 1726-1924, by Joseph Brigham Keeler ... Provo, Utah, Post publishing company, 1924.   79 p. 23 cm. 36-24702.   CS71.K26   1924

9514   KEELER.   Ancestors of Evelyn Wood Keeler, wife of Willard Underhill Taylor, compiled for their children, Mary Morgan Taylor, Willard Underhill Taylor, jr. (and) Annette Evelyn Taylor, by Josephine C. Frost (Mrs. Samuel Knapp Frost) ... (Brooklyn? N.Y.) Priv. pub., 1939.   4 p. 1., 630 p. front. (col. coat of arms) 25 cm. Running title: Keeler-Wood genealogy. Includes bibliography. 40-5546.   CS71.K26   1939

> KEELER.   See also: BENEDICT, F129.S697.V33
>   ROCKWELL, 1903
>   STRANGE, 1915

> KEELING.   See: FLETCHER, CS439.F53
>   GIBBON, 1918

> KEAN.   See MERRYWEATHER, 1899

9515   KEEN.   The descendants of Jöran Kyn of New Sweden, by Gregory B. Keen ... Philadelphia, The Swedish colonial society, 1913.   318, (16) p. front. (map) 26 cm. The Swedish colonial society. (List of officers and members: (16) p. at end. 14-5099.   CS71.K264   1913

9516   KEEN.   Keene family history and genealogy, by Elias Jones ... Baltimore, Md., Press of Kohn and Pollock, inc., 1923.   343 p. plates, ports., facsims., coats of arms. 24 cm. 24-1715.   CS71.K264   1923

> KEEN.   See also: BUTLER, 1919
>   DAY, 1923
>   FLETCHER, CS439.F53
>   JOHNSON, 1924
>   MERRYWEATHER, 1897
>   ROBINSON, 1952

> KEENE.   See KEEN.

9517   KEENER.   The Keeners and allied families.   A memorial to Ann Maria Keener.   Compiled by Letitia Pinnell Wilson.   Baltimore, Md., 1923.   17, (1), 70 (i.e. 76) numb. 1. 22½ cm. Extra numbered leaves: 28½, 28¾ 41 A-C, 65A. 23-18591.   CS71.K265   1923

9518   KEENER.   The descendants of William and Rachel Keener.   Compiled by Lawson Keener Lacy (Mrs. Rogers Lacy).   Longview, Tex., 1964.   154 1. facsims. 29 cm. 67-46982.   CS71.K265   1964

9519   KEENER.   The Keayne, Keen(e), Keeney, Kinne(y) Kenny and allied families, by Florence Loveless Keeney Robertson ... (Los Angeles, Haynes corporation, printers, 1942 -   v. front., illus. ports., coat of arms) 20½ cm. Includes bibliographies. 42-18886.   CS71.K2654   1942

> KEENEY.   See KINNEY and KENNEY.

> KEENY.   See KEENEY.

9520   KEEP.   John Keep of Longmeadow, Massachusetts, 1660-1676, and his descendants; compiled by Frank E. Best; in which is incorporated an unpublished Keep genealogy prepared by W.J. Keep in 1866; a record of ancestry by Helen E. Keep; and the extended ancestry of Sallie Keep Best. Chicago, Ill., F. E. Best, 1899.   263 p. front., pl., fold. geneal. tab. 23 cm. 99-2876.   CS71.K266   1899

9521   KEEPER.   In vertical file.   Ask reference librarian for this material.

> KEESE.   See KEYES.

9522 KEESEE. A book of poems, by Lulu Evarts. (Oklahoma City, Printed by H. R. Stephens, c. 1917) cover-title, (24) p. 19½ cm. Introduction: William Keesee and his descendants. (4) p. 17-30265.

PS3509.V445B7 1917

9523 KEFFER. The Keffers of the Conewago Valley. By John Poist Keffer. Trenton, MacCrellish & Quigley, printers, 1960. 187 p. illus., ports., maps, coat of arms, facsims. 23 cm. Bibliography: p. 185-187. 61-34759.

CS71.K268 1960

KEHL. See WEISER, 1960

KEHOE. See STARKWEATHER, 1925

KEIGWIN. See BLACKMAN, 1928

9524 KEIM. An account of the Keim family. By Henry May Keim. Reading, Pa., Print. priv. (Press of B. F. Owen) 1874. 26 p. front. (port.) 23½ cm. Title vignette: coat of arms. One hundred copies. no. 49. 9-11466.

CS71.K27 1874

9525 KEIM. The Keim and allied families in America and Europe ... a monthly serial of history, biography, genealogy and folklore, illustrating the causes, circumstances and consequences of the German, French and Swiss emigrations to America during the 17th, 18th and 19th centuries. De B. Randolph Keim, editor ... v. 1-2 (no. 1-24); Dec. 1898-Nov. 1900. Harrisburg, Pa., 1899-(1900) 768 p. illus., plates, ports., facsims. 25 cm. Published by the editor for subscribers only. 7-3953.   CS71.K27 1899-1900

9526 KEIR. Sketch of the life of James Keir, esq., F. R. S., with selection from his correspondence ... London, Printed by R. E. Taylor (1868) 164 p. 22½ cm. Printed for private circulation. Preface (p. (37)-38) signed: J. Keir Moilliet. 1868. "The imperfect tribute of a daughter to the memory of a beloved and revered father" (p. (11)-16) signed: Amelia Moilliet. "The genealogy of the family of James Keir. esq., F. R. S.": p. (27)-34. 14-22789.   QD22.K4A3

KEISTER. See CLEEK, 1957

KEITER. See ENDERS, 1960

9527 KEITH. An historical and authentic account of the ancient and noble family of Keith, earls marischal of Scotland, from their origin in Germany, down to 1778 ... Also a full ... account of all the attainted Scottish noblemen who lost their titles and estates in 1715 and 1745, for their adherence to the Stuart cause. By P. Buchan ... Peterhead, Printed by P. Buchan, 1820. 2 p. l., (ix)-xii. (13)-128 p. 19½ cm. "Attainted noblemen of Scotland": p. (98)-128. 15-18507.   CS479.K3

9528 KEITH. Memoir of Royal Keith, together with the annals of the Keith family of Scotland, and the writings of Charles Edward Keith. Boston, C. E. Keith & co., 1873. 24 p. 24½ cm. (With his Works ... Centennial ed. Boston, 1876) 9-25106.   AC8.K32

9529 KEITH. A genealogy of the descendants of Benjamin Keith through Timothy, son of Rev. James Keith, together with an historical sketch of the early family and personal reminiscences of recent generations. By Ziba C. Keith. Brockton, G. A. Goodall, printer, 1889. 111. (3) p. plates, ports., map. 27½ cm. Title vignette: Coat of arms. 9-11465.   CS71.K28 1889

9530 KEITH. ... The Keith genealogy, by J. Montgomery Seaver. Philadelphia, Pa., 1930. 146 p. front. (coat of arms) plates (incl. ports.) 29 cm. Mimeographed with printed t. p. "References": p. 143. 40-18355.

CS71.K28 1930

9531 KEITH. The Keith book, compiled by Adelaide Keith Merrill. Minneapolis, Minn., 1934. 2 p. l., vii-xii p., 1 l., 187 p. front. (map) illus. (coat of arms) plates, ports. 23½ cm. Song with music: p. 84-87. 35-5792.

CS479.K3 1934

9532 KEITH. (Family tree of the descendants of Rev. James Keith of Va.) By Keith (Frazier) Somerville. Cleveland, Miss., c. 1947. geneal. table. coat of arms. 80 x 142 cm. 47-29251*.

CS71.K28 1947

9533   KEITH.   Chart of the Samuel Larned Keith family (descendants of the Rev. James Keith) showing the allied lines of Ward-Pell, Larned, and Starkey.   By Laurence Prescott Keith.   Chicago, 1950.   geneal. table.   57 x 64 cm. fold. to 41 x 31 cm.   52-20622.   CS71.K28   1950

9534   KEITH.   Alexander Keith.   Data on the Keith family.   Pos. and neg.   7432
                                                                            Microfilm reading room.

KEITH.   See also: BYRD, E159.G55   LA RUE, 1921
                     DOUGLAS, DA758.3.A1T2   MARTIN, 1949
                     DUNNOTTAR, 1925   RANDLEMAN, 1965
                     KEY, 1931   TILSON, 1916

9535   KELKER.   Genealogisches verzeichniss der familie Kölloker von Herrliberg, bezirk Meilen, kanton Zurich in der Schweitz, abgefast in sommer 1849, durch John Jacob Hess ... (Translation of above) Genealogical record of the family of Koelliker of Herrliburg, district of Meilen, canton Zurich, Switzerland, completed in summer of 1849 ... Added a record of the family of Kelker, since their arrival in this country in 1743, comp. from authentic sources, for the use of the members of the family, by Rudolph F. Kelker.   Harrisburg, L.S.Hart, printer, 1883.   132 p., 1 l.   27½ cm.   Lettered on publisher's binding: Kelker family register.   Memorandum copied from the "Wappen buch," 1860, inserted after p. 8.   "Mrs. Rudolph F. Kelker"; 2 p. inserted at end.   15-27877.   CS71.K285   1883

KELLAND.   See GUERIN, 1890

9536   KELLER.   History of the Keller family, by the Rev. Eli Keller ... Tiffin, O., Press of W.H. Good, 1905.   192 p.   front., plates. ports. map. fold. geneal. tab.   22 cm.   23-14463.   CS71.K287   1905

9537   KELLER.   The Kellers of Hamilton Township; a study in democracy, by David Henry Keller ... Alexandria, La., The Wall printing co., 1922.   vii, 133, (5) p.   front., plates. ports., maps, facsims.   27 cm.   Blank pages for "The family record" 4 at end)   "225 copies of this have book have been printed, of which this is no. 225."   Includes contributions by Horatio G. Shull, Rev. William H. Brong, Rev. Charles A. Butz, Robert E. Keller and Charles R. Roberts.   Contains also the Bossard, Butz, Dill and Drach families.   23-877.   CS71.K287   1922

9538   KELLER.   Descendants of Henry Keller of York County, Pennsylvania and Fairfield County, Ohio.   Rev. E. S. Shumaker, D.D., editor; Amos Keller, associate editor; Zarel (Lulie) Jones, assistant editor.   Indianapolis, Ind., E.S.Shumaker (c.1924)   594 p. incl. illus., ports., coat of arms. fold. facsim.   23½ cm.   24-31166.   CS71.K287   1924

9539   KELLER.   Keller family.   (By Thomas John Hall)   page 279.   CS71.H177   1941

9540   KELLER.   The descendants of Conrad Keller; a genealogy, with notes on Gwinn, Newsome, Ripley, Slagle, Speece, Vanden, Wiseman (and) Wright.   Compiled from research and data gathered from the descendants during the years 1932 to 1951, and supplemented by data furnished by Earl A. Ross.   By Bennie De Forset Keller.   (n.p.) 1951.   iv, 229 p.   29 cm.   52-24873.   CS71.K287   1951

KELLER.   See also LOPER, 1969

9541   KELLEY.   A genealogical account of the descendants of John Kelly of Newbury, Massachusetts, U.S.A., by Giles M. Kelly.   (Albany, J. Munsell's sons) 1886.   178 p.   ports., coat of arms.   23 cm.   Imprint from label mounted on t.-p.   1-1848 rev.   CS71.K29   1886

9542   KELLEY.   Reminiscences of New Hampton, N.H.; also a genealogical sketch of the Kelley and and Simpson families, and an autobiography by Frank H. Kelley ... Worcester, Mass., Printed by C. Hamilton, 1889.   2 p. l., ix, (11)-147 p.   front., pl., port.   28 cm.   3-13313.   F44.N66K3

9543   KELLEY.   Genealogical gleanings relating to the Kelleys of Brentwood, N.H., and kindred families of Edgerly, Shute, Robinson, Hancock, and Cleveland.   By William Henry Kelley ... Saint Paul, Minn.   (Press of D. Ramaley & son) 1892.   48 p.   port.   23 cm.   The portrait is a mounted photograph.   20-12154.   CS71.K29   1892

9544   KELLEY.   A genealogical history of the Kelley family descended from Joseph Kelley of Norwich, Connecticut, with much biographical matter concerning the first four generations and notes of inflowing female lines.   Comp. by Hermon Alfred Kelley.   Cleveland, O., Priv. print., 1897. 122, xv p. front., plates, ports. 21 cm. 13 blank leaves inserted. 11-22489.   CS71.K29   1897

9545   KELLEY.   History of James and Catherine Kelly and their descendants.   Written by Richard T. Kelly (great-grandson of James Kelly), Springfield, Ohio.   Edited by Clifton M. Nichols.   Published by Oliver S. Kelly (grandson of James Kelly) ... (Springfield) Printed by the Springfield publishing company, 1900.   114 p. 1 l. illus., ports. 23½ cm. 1-3008.   CS71.K29   1900

9546   KELLEY.   A genealogy of the Kelly family, by Thomas McAdory Owen.   Carrollton, Ala., West Alabamian print, 1900.   7 p. 24½ cm. 2-14242.   CS71.K29   1900a

9547   KELLEY.   The Kelly clan, published by Richmond Kelly ... Portland, Ore., 1901.   78 p. front., illus. (coat of arms) 22½ cm. 27-25100.   CS71.K29   1901

9548   KELLEY.   Kelly, Kelley, Killey, O'Killia, descendants of David O'Killia who took the oath of fidelity as an inhabitant of Yarmouth, Barnstable county, Plymouth colony (Massachusetts Bay province after 1692) 1657, by Alice L. Priest.   Brookline, Mass., 1937.   1 p. l., 9 numb. l. 28 cm. Type-written. 37-10353.   CS71.K29   1937

9549   KELLEY.   The American ancestors and descendants of Seth Kelly, 1762-1850, of Blackstone, Mass.   Compiled by William P. Kelly.   (n. p.) 1937.   60, (11) p. 23 cm. 37-38450.
                                                                                                       CS71.K29   1937a

9550   KELLEY.   Imprints on the sands of time left by certain Kelly's, Lampman's, Craig's (and) Ferguson's, by Henry R. Kelly.   (n. p.) 1939.   1 p. l., 45 numb. l. 2 fold. geneal. tab. 28 cm. Mimeographed. 39-32314.   CS71.K29   1939

9551   KELLEY.   Imprints on the sands of time left by certain Kelly's, Lampman's, Craig's (and) Ferguson's.   2d ed.   (n. p.) 1955.   94 l. 20 cm. 57-16264.   CS71.K29   1955a

9552   KELLEY.   That Kelly family.   By John Dennis McCallum.   New York, Barnes (1957) 229 p. illus. 22 cm. 56-10859.   CS71.K29   1957

9553   KELLEY.   The family history of Virginia L. Kelly.   (Longview? Tex., 19 -)   185 p. illus. 30 cm. 61-45113.   CS71.K29

9554   KELLEY.   The Charles Kelly family (1769-1963) by Lloyd E. Kelly.   (n. p., 1963) 37, 2, 28 l. 29 cm. Caption title. "Supplement" (dated 1965): 28 l. at end. 66-98558.   CS71.K29   1963

> KELLEY.   See also: CAMPBELL, 1921
>   WALKER, 1964
>   WOODRUFF, 1925
>
> KELLIE, Earls of.   See MAR.

9555   KELLOGG.   Family meeting of the descendants of Charles Kellogg, of Kelloggsville, N.Y., with some genealogical items of the Kellogg family.   Reprinted from the New England historical and genealogical register for July, 1858.   Boston, H.W.Dutton and son, printers, 1858.   cover-title. 8 p. 23 cm. "Family meeting ..." signed: D.K.L.; "Genealogical items ..." by D.O.Kellogg. 9-15609.   CS71.K291   1858

9556   KELLOGG.   Family records of George Clark and Daniel Kellogg: with their descendants. Also, family record in part of Edward Nash.   Compiled by the late Albert Clark, of Washington. Washington, D.C., A.C.Patterson, 1877.   39, (25) p. 22 cm. 24 blank pages at end for additions. 40-37483.
                                                                                                       CS71.C6   1877

9557   KELLOGG.   Notes on some of the descendants of Joseph Kellogg of Hadley ... (London, Printed by T. Moring) 1898.   26 p., 1 l. fold. geneal. tab. 24½ cm. Comp. by Justin Perkins Kellogg. For private circulation only. 3-468.   CS71.K291   1898

9558   KELLOGG.   A supplement to Notes on Joseph Kellogg of Hadley, containing notes on the families of Terry, White, and Woodbury, by Justin P. Kellogg.   (n.p.) (For private circulation only) 1899.   45 p. 24½ cm.   17-15778.   CS71.K291   1898a

9559   KELLOGG.   The Kelloggs in the Old world and the New; by Timothy Hopkins ... San Francisco, Cal., Sunset press and photo engraving co., 1903.   3 v. double fronts., plates, plan, facsim. 27½ cm. Paged continuously.   Vol. 3: Index.   3-17744.   CS71.K291   1903

9560   KELLOGG.   Ancestry, life and descendants of Martin Kellogg, "The Centenarian," of Bronson, Huron Co., Ohio, 1786-1892.   By Dale Cosnett Kellogg.   Elyria, 1954.   86 p. illus. 23 cm. 55-36306.
                                                                                      CS71.K291   1954

        KELLOGG.   See also: CALLENDER, 1911
                                CLARK, 1877
                                FIELD, 1877
                                FOOT, 1922
                                ROSS, 1959
                                VANREIN, E171.A53 vol.16

        KELLY.   See KELLEY.

9561   KELSEY.   A genealogy of the descendants of William Kelsey who settled at Cambridge, Mass., in 1632, at Hartford, Conn., in 1636, and at Killingworth, Conn., in 1663, by Edward A. Claypool and Azalea Clizbee and concluded by Earl Leland Kelsey from data collected by Leroy Huron Kelsey ... and many others.   (New Haven, Tuttle, Morehouse & Taylor Co.) 1928-47.   3 v. illus., 2 ports., maps, col. coats of arms.   24 cm.   "Printed for private distribution."   28-29808 rev. 2.   CS71.K296   1928

        KELSEY.   See also: BASSETT, 1926
                               RANNEY, F104C8A2

9562   KELSO.   Andrew Foster Kelso; history and descendants.   By Marie (Arrington) Davidson.   Twin Falls, Idaho, 1957.   52 l. illus. 29 cm. 58-16148.   CS71.K297   1957

        KELSO.   See also HARLOE, 1943

9563   KELTON.   Kelton family items.   By Dwight H. Kelton ... (Montpelier? 1895?)   caption title.   14 p. 23½ cm.   One hundred copies printed.   1-1850.   CS71.K3   1895

        KELTON.   See No. 516 - Notable southern families vol.2

        KEMBLE.   See: KIMBALL.
                        Addenda.

9564   KEMEYS.   Baronia de Kemeys.   From the original documents at Bronwydd.   Ed. Sir Thomas Davies Lloyd.   Cambrian archaeological association.   London, J.R.Smith;   (etc., etc., 1862)   4 p. l., (3)-136 p. fold. map, fold. geneal. tab. 22 cm.   The various documents referring to the Lordship of Kemeys are preserved in the muniment room at Bronwydd by the present owner of the manor, Thomas Davies Lloyd, and by him communicated to the Cambrian archaeological association. cf. Pref. Pedigree of Thomas Davies Lloyd. based on the original pedigree of 1677, was prepared and brought down to 1861 by Sir Thomas Phillipps. fold. geneal. tab. 22-24633.   CS459.K3   1862

9565   KEMEYS.   Welsh royalists.   Sir Nicholas Kemeys, bart., Cefn Mably, the captor and defender of Chepstow castle, with the family history and pedigree, deduced from pedigrees and mss.   By J. Rowlands (!) (Giraldus).   Also prize epic poems, Cardiff eisteddfod, 1879, prize given by Mr. Lewis Jones (Gorswg) Cardiff, South Wales printing work (1881)   39 p., 1 l., IV, 23 p., 1 l., III, (25)-60 p. 22 cm.

9565 continued: Lettered on cover: The Kemeys of Cefn Mably.   "An epic poem on Sir Nicholas Kemeys, the captor and defender of Chepstow castle, Cardiff, South Wales printing works, 1881." (1 1., IV, 23 p.) has special t.-p., and preface signed: Osric (i. e. Rhys D. Morgan). "Arwregerdd Sir Nichol s Kemeys, gorchrygwr ac amddiffynwr Casgwent. Jan Dafydd Morganwg (i. e. David William Jones) ... Caerdydd. Gweith-feydd argraffyddol Deheudir Cymru, 1881" (1 1., III (25)-60 p.) has special t. p.   19-6529.

CS459.K3

9567   KEMMERER.   Two centuries of Kemmerer family history, 1730-1929, compiled by the Kemmerer family association ... Allentown, Pa., Searle & Bachman co., 1929.   152, (8) p. front. (col. coat of arms) plates, ports. 24 cm.   Preface signed: William A. Backenstoe.   Blank pages for "Memoranda" (8 at end) 30-5234.

CS71.K318   1929

9568   KEMP.   The Kempes of Suffolk.   Extracted from "The visitation of Suffolke." (By William Harvey) Edited by Joseph Jackson Howard ... Lowestoft (Eng.) Printed by S. Tymms, 1867.   10 p., 1 1. illus. (coat of arms) 27½ x 22 cm. 9-16892 rev.   CS439.K44

9569   KEMP.   A general history of the Kemp and Kempe families of Great Britain and her colonies, with arms, pedigrees, portraits, illustrations of seats, foundations, chantries, monuments, docu-ments, old jewels, curios, etc.; by Fred. Hitchin-Kemp, assisted by Daniel Wm. Kemp ... and John Tabor Kemp ... and with illustrations by Miss Lucy E. Kemp-Welch and others.   London, The Leadenhall press; New York, C. Scribner's sons (1902)   6 pt. in 1 v. front., illus. (incl. facsims.) ports., fold. geneal. tables. 28½ cm.   Contents. - (section I) The Kemp and Kempe families of Kent. - section II. The ... families of Norfolk and Suffolk. - section III. The ... families of Essex. Middlesex and surrounding counties. - section IV. The ... families of Cornwall, Sussex and the south of England. - section V. The ... families of the Midlands, western counties and north of England. - section VI. The ... families of Scotland, Ireland, the British empire & United States.   3-17494.

CS439.K4
Microfilm 10309 CS

9570   KEMP.   Kemps of Ollantigh and Kemps of Poole; being a brief outline of the ancient Kemp family of Ollantigh manor, Wye, Kent county, and a brief history of the Kemp family of Poole, Dorset county, England, and some of the descendants in the United States.   By George Edward Kemp (usually called G. Ward Kemp) ... Seattle, Wash.   (McKay printing co.) c.1939.   xi, 80, (1) p. incl. front., illus., ports., coat of arms.   23 cm.   Bibliography: (1) p. at end.   39-12980.   CS71.K32   1939

KEMP.   See also: BOOHER, 1956
                             CAMP.
                             DOBYN, 1908
                             GAMBLE, 1906
                             HARLLEE, 1934-37
                             ZIMMERMAN, 19 -

KEMPE.   See KEMP.

9571   KEMPER.   Genealogy of the Kemper family in the United States, descendants of John Kemper of Virginia; with a short historical sketch of his family and of the German reformed colony at Germanna and Germantown, Va.   Compiled and edited by Willis Miller Kemper and Harry Linn Wright.   Chicago, G.K.Hazlitt & co., printers, 1899.   248 xix p. 26½ cm. 0-2257 rev.   CS71.K321   1899

9572   KEMPER.   Kemper records (1946) A supplement to The Kemper family (1899)   (By Virginia Mary McComb.   Chambersburg? Pa., 1946)   240 p. ports., coats of arms. 24 cm.   Errata slip inserted. 47-27058*.
CS71.K321   1946

9573   KEMPER.   The descendants of Dr. George Whitfield Kemper, Jr., Port Republic, Virginia. By George Frederick Switzer.   Harrisonburg (1951)   30 1. illus., ports. 29 cm.   "Copy number 39, Library of Congress." Bibliography: leaf 1. 51-27717.   CS71.K321   1951

9574   KEMPER.   The Kemper book.   By Clarence Cannon.   (Elsberry? Mo.) 1957.   129 p. 29 cm. 58-40725.   CS71.K321   1957

KEMPSON.   See LONG, 1956

KEMPT.   See FORRESTER, 1905

KEN.   See WALTON, 1875

9575   KENAN.   The Kenan family and some allied families of the compiler and publisher.   States-
boro, Ga., J. S. Kenan II, 1967.   xxii, 294 p. illus., col. coat of arms, geneal. tables, ports. 24 cm.   Bibliography: p. 259-263.
68-2437.   CS71.K326   1967

KENASTON.   See KENNESTON.

9576   KENDALL.   Memorial of Josiah Kendall, one of the first settlers of Sterling, Mass., and of
some of his ancestors, and of his descendants.   By Oliver Kendall.   Providence (R. I.) Printed by the
author, 1884.   1 p. l., xvi, (2), 135 p. front., illus., plates.   25½ cm.   One hundred and twenty copies printed.   9-11464.
                                                                                            CS71.K33   1884

9577   KENDALL.   The Kendalls of Austrey, Twycross and Smithsby.   A family history.   Illustrated.
(London, W. P. Griffith & sons, ltd., 1909)   64 p. incl. illus., geneal. tab. front. (col. coat of arms) plates. ports.,
facsims. 28 cm.   : "This ed. is limited and issued for private circulation by Henry John Broughton Kendall." Preface dated 1909.   11-14118.
                                                                                            CS439.K47

9578   KENDALL.   The Kendall family in America, ed. by William Montgomery Clemens ...
Hackensack, N. J., W. M. Clemens, 1919.   24 p. 23 cm.   "Limited edition of three hundred copies." 20-9244.
                                                                                            CS71.K33   1919

9579   KENDALL.   Kendalls in the revolution.   (By William Montgomery Clemens)   (In Genealogy; a
monthly magazine of American ancestry. edited by William Montgomery Clemens ... Hackensack, N. J., 1919.   23 cm.   vol. VIII. p. 33-35)
37-16961.   CS42.G7 vol. 7
        —— Separate   CS71.K33   1919a

9580   KENDALL.   Kendall genealogy; the descendants of Thomas and Francis Kendall of Charlestown
and Woburn, Mass.; set forth in rhyme by Anstis Kendall Miles in 1855; now reprinted and rendered
in prose with many additions.   By Irma A. Rich.   Boston, C. E. Goodspeed & co., 1920.   38 p. 21½ cm.
20-7236.   CS71.K33   1920

9581   KENDALL.   The Kendall journal, by Norman F. Kendall.   Grafton, W. Va. (1930)   4 p. illus.
(ports.) 43 cm. 31-19489.   CS71.K33   1930

9582   KENDALL.   Kendall family and connections.   (n. p., 193-?)   186-481 p. 27 cm. 53-55539.
                                                                                            CS71.K33

9583   KENDALL.   A landsman's voyage to California; being the account, compiled from letters and
the journal of Joseph Kendall, of the voyage 'round the Horn of the bark Canton, from New York harbor
to San Francisco bay in the year 1849, with two letters from his wife, Charlotte Kendall.   San
Francisco (Printed by Taylor & Taylor) 1935.   xiv, 137 p. front., ports., facsim., fold. geneal. tab. 21 cm.   Title
vignette.   "Privately published in an edition of 200 copies."   The letters of Joseph Kendall are addressed to his daughter, Lucy (Mrs. W. F. Herrick)
Edited by Wilbur Hall.   cf. Introd.   35-4379.   F865.K34

9584   KENDALL.   Memorial of Samuel Reed and Matilda Thomas Kendall, and of some of their
ancestors and of their descendants, by Ralph R. Kendall.   Worcester, Mass., 1936.   45 p. ports. 23 cm.
37-21331.   CS71.K33   1936

9585   KENDALL.   Genealogy of the Kendall family in Virginia, Kentucky, Louisiana and Texas; with
notes on allied families, particularly those connected with the Louisiana branch, compiled by J. S.
Kendall.   Washington, D. C., 1939.   1 p. l., 19, 21-98 (i.e. 99) numb. l. 28 cm. 40M3511T.
                                                                                            CS71.K33   1939

9586   KENDALL.   (Genealogical chart of Elias Kendall and Isabel Snodgrass, his wife, prepared by
Will Davis) Sutton, W. Va., 1939.   geneal. tab. 45 x 59 cm. 40M1942T.   CS71.K33   1939a

9587   KENDALL.   Kendall family, data collected by Mrs. Laura Kendall Thomas, 1907 to 1941.
(Elmhurst, Ill., 1941)   13 l. 28 cm. In manuscript. Leaves variously numbered. 42-4210.   CS71.K33   1941

9588 KENDALL. History and genealogy, Kendalls, Cunninghams, Snodgrasses... by Norman Festus Kendall ... Grafton, W. Va., Printed by the Grafton sentinel publishing company (1942) 160 p. illus. (incl. ports.) 29½ x 23 cm. Errata slip and other miscellaneous matter inserted. "Sources of information"; p. 2. 44-4219.
CS71.K33   1942

9589 KENDALL. Kendall family of Virginia, Kentucky and Louisiana. (By John Smith Kendall. Berkeley, Calif., 1945) 24 numb. 1. 27½ x 21½ cm. Caption title. Type-written (carbon) 46-23130. CS71.K33   1945

9590 KENDALL. The Kendall family of Kentucky. Sketches found in history of Todd & Christian counties. (By John Smith Kendall. Berkeley? Calif., 1945) 12 1. 28 x 21½ cm. Caption title. Type-written (carbon copy) "First Baptist evangel. Kendall memorial number" (4 p.) and newspaper clipping inserted. 48-14049.
CS71.K33   1945a

9591 KENDALL. (A collection of notes, letters, and genealogical tables of the Kendall family of Virginia, Maryland and Kentucky. By John Smith Kendall. Berkeley, Calif., 1945) (38) 1. 28 cm. Typewritten. 49-42928 *. CS71.K33   1945b

9592 KENDALL. The storied Kendalls; with historical and genealogical records of Scottish and allied families. By Anne Kendrick Walker. Richmond, Dietz Press, 1947. ix. 163 p. illus. (part col.) ports., col. coats of arms, facsim. geneal. tables. 28 cm. 48-15395 *. CS71.K33   1947

9593 KENDALL. Descendants of William Kendall of Ashford, Conn.; a genealogy. By Kendall Laughlin. (n. p.) 1953. 20 p. 23 cm. 54-29256. CS71.K33   1953

9594 KENDALL. Descendants of William Kendall of Ashford, Connecticut, and Caledonia County, Vermont; a genealogy. By Kendall Laughlin. 2d ed. (Chicago?) 1955. 36 p. 23 cm. 55-37773.
CS71.K33   1955

KENDALL. See also: CHAFFEE, 1911   REMINGTON, 1960
                     CROCKER, 1923   TODD, 1909
                     DIXON, 1922   WASHINGTON, CS69.W5
                     GAMBLE, 1906

9595 KENDERDINE. Kenderdine family. Paper read by Thaddeus Kenderdine, of Newtown ... (at the May meeting of the Bucks County historical society, 1902) (n. p., 1902?) (4) p. 27 cm. Caption title. 9-15622. CS71.K331   1902

9596 KENDRICK. ... Memoir of William Kendrick. Born, February 11, 1819. Died, March 16, 1880. (Louisville, Ky., Printed by E. H. Welburn, 1881) 126 p. front. (port.) 18½ cm. By Drummond Welburn. 14-790. CS71.K335   1881

9597 KENDRICK. Kenrick. Kendrick. Kindrick. Some of the descendents of John Kenrick, the immigrant, with historical matter connected therewith. Comp. by John Kenrick's great grandson's (Benjamin⁴) daughter's (Abigail⁵) grandson, Isaac Brooks Dodge ... Milford, N. H., 1894. 30 numb. 1. incl. facsims. plates, ports., fold. plan. 27 cm. On cover: Historical genealogy. Kenrick, Brooks, Dodge. 19-2004.
CS71.K335   1894

KENDRICK. See also: COX, 1870
                      DINKINS, 1908
                      KENRICK.

KENERSON. See KENNESTON.

KENISON. See KENNESTON.

KENMARE. See BROWN, 1942

9598 KENNAMER. The Kennamer family, by John Robert Kennamer ... and Lorrin Garfield Kennamer ... Nashville, Tenn., McQuiddy printing company, 1924. 375 p. incl. front., illus., ports. 23½ cm. 35-20355. CS71.K338   1924

9599   KENNAN.   Genealogy of the Kennan family, by Thomas Lathrop Kennan ... Milwaukee, Cannon printing co., 1907.   121, (12) p. incl. front. plates, ports.   23½ cm.   8-23725.   CS71.K34   1907

9600   KENNARD.   The genealogy and the family tree of Owen Clay Kennard and wife Sarah Meiser Kennard.   By Ella Kennard.   (Santa Cruz, Calif., 1968)   9 p.   30 cm.   Title from the first lines of the preface.   71-3173 MARC.   CS71.K344   1968

KENNASTONE.   See KENNESTON.

9601   KENNEDY.   Historical and genealogical account of the principal families of the name of Kennedy.   From an original ms.   With notes and illustrations, &c.   By Robert Pitcairn ... Edinburgh, W. Tait and J. Stevenson; (etc., etc.,) 1830.   ix p., 1 l., 218 p.   facsim., fold. geneal. tab.   27½ cm.   14-11658.
                    CS479.K4

9602   KENNEDY.   History of the descendants of William Kennedy and his wife Mary or Marian Henderson, from 1730 to 1880, carried down by numbers.   To which is added the meaning of the name Kennedy, with some facts connected with their history in Scotland and Ireland.   Comp. by Elias Davidson Kennedy, for private use.   Philadelphia, Press of H. B. Ashmead, 1881.   86 p.   26 cm.   23-14861.
                    CS71.K35   1881

9603   KENNEDY.   Genealogical descendants of David and Jane Greacen Kennedy.   By Russell Kennedy.   1783-1919.   2d ed.   Pittsburgh, Pa. (1919?)   geneal. tab.   102 x 46 cm.   fold. to 35 cm.   Signed: Russell Kennedy.   21-2964.   CS71.K35   1919

9604   KENNEDY.   Thx. Kennedy family records, by J. Montgomery Seaver.   Philadelphia, Pa., American historical-genealogical society, 1929.   1 p. l., 5-34 p.   23 cm.   Coat of arms on cover.   "References": p. 31.
30-8671.   CS71.K35   1929

9605   KENNEDY.   The Kennedy clan and Tierra Redonda (by) Alice Clare Lynch.   (San Francisco, Marnell & company, c. 1935)   3 p. l., 264 p.   29 cm.   A history of the author's family.   35-2038.
                    CS71.K35   1935

9606   KENNEDY.   A family of Kennedy of Clogher and Londonderry c. 1600-1938, by Major Francis M. E. Kennedy, C. B.   Taunton (Eng., Printed for private circulation by Barnkotts) 1938.   4 p. l., 136 p. front., pl., ports.   20½ cm.   Alternate pages blank, except 129-132, 135-136 which are blank leaves.   Accompanied by two folded genealogical tables in portfolio.   Bibliography: p. 128.   38-38141.   CS439.K48

9607   KENNEDY.   Schoolmaster of yesterday; a three-generation story, 1820-1919, by Millard Fillmore Kennedy, in collaboration with Alvin F. Harlow; illustrated by Howard Simon.   New York, Whittlesey house, McGraw-Hill book company, inc. (c. 1940)   viii, 359 p. incl. front. (5 port.) illus.   22½ cm.   "First edition."   Illustrated t.-p.   40-31823.   LA2317.K4A3

9608   KENNEDY.   The American ancestry of Yvonne Odette Kennedy, by Glenn A. Kennedy.   (Stockton, Calif.) 1942.   27 l.   22½ cm.   Type-written (carbon copy) 43-6122.   CS71.K35   1942

9609   KENNEDY.   The seven sons of the Provost; a family chronicle of the eighteenth century compiled from original letters, 1692 to 1761.   London, New York, T. Nelson, 1949.   viii, 236 p. plates, ports.   25 cm.   49-6933*.   CS479.K4   1949

9610   KENNEDY.   The Kennedys; "Twixt Wigton and the town of Ayr."   With tartan and chief's arms in colour, and a map.   Edinburgh, W. & A. K. Johnston & G. W. Bacon (1958)   32 p. illus. (part col.) map, coat of arms.   19 cm.   (W. & A.K. Johnston's clan histories)   Bibliography: p. (4) Bibliographical footnotes.   59-38561.
                    CS479.K4   1958

9611   KENNEDY.   The Kennedy family; a brief record of the Kennedy family of Lenoir and Wayne Counties, North Carolina.   By John Thomas Kennedy.   Columbia, S. C., 1963.   v, 97 p. illus., ports., maps (on lining papers) 24 cm.   63-23817.   CS71.K35   1963

9612   KENNEDY.   A family chronicle.   By Melville T. Kennedy.   Norwich, Town, Conn., 1963.
164 p. illus., ports.   26 cm.   "Limited edition of 100 copies."   64-1167.   CS71.K35   1963a

9613   KENNEDY.   The clan Kennedy, by Crawford H. Kennedy.   (Beaver? Pa.) c.1964.   802 p. illus.,
ports. 22 cm. 65-2682.   CS71.K35   1964

9614   KENNEDY.   The evolution of Everyman: ancestral lineage of John F. Kennedy, by J. F. Brennan.
Dundalk, Dundalgan P., 1968.   xix, 259 p. 26 plates, illus., maps, ports. 23 cm. Bibliography: p. 245-247. 68-140006.
                                                                               CS479.K4   1968

        KENNEDY.   See also: AGNEW, 1926   SAMPSON, 1922
                              BURGESS, 1961   SELDEN, 1911
                              HUME, 1916   WARNER, 1956
                              HUME, 1926

9615   KENNER.   Kenner; a compilation of family letters and data pertaining to the Kenner and related families, their early life in Virginia and subsequent years after migration to Ohio.   By Paul Wood
Cleveland.   (Erie, Pa.) 1966.   187 l. 30 cm. 66-5183.   CS71.K356   1966

9616   KENNESTON.   The Kenison story and allied families, Esselsteyn, Sweet, Green, McCallum,
Heath, Box, Rapp.   By Mable Azeltine Rapp.   (Shenandoah, Iowa) 1968.   98 p. illus., coats of arms, ports.
23 cm. 72-3168 MARC.   CS71.K357   1968

9617   KENNETT.   Kennett pedigree.   (London, 1877)   (2) p. pl. 26½ cm. Communicated by
Francis Bayley.   Reprinted from Miscellanea genealogica et heraldica. n.s. v.2, p.287-288. 9-18135.   CS439.K49

9618   KENNEY.   Pedigree of the family of Kenney of Kilclogher, (or Kenne-Court,) co. Galway.
(And Clogher house, co. Mayo) Extracted from Sir Bernard Burke's "Dictionary of the landed gentry
of Great Britain and Ireland."   With additions of some notes, by J. C. Fitzgerald Kenney ... Dublin
(Printed by M. Davis, 1868)   1 p. l., 5 (i.e. 7) p. front. (coat of arms) 25 cm. 2 pages of "additional notes" containing data to
1870 inserted after p. 4. 9-11823.   CS499.K5

9619   KENNEY.   The Kenney genealogy.   By Alfred A. Doane ... (Yarmouth, N.S., 1909)   13 p.
21 cm. Caption title. "Reprinted from the Yarmouth herald, August 17, 1909." 15-5256.   CS71.K36   1909

9620   KENNEY.   Israel Kenny, his children and their families, by Edwin Wallace Bell ... Edited by
Lilian M. B. Maxwell.   (Vancouver, B.C.) 1944.   3 p. l., 111 p. fold. maps, facsim. 22 cm. Additions and corrections
in manuscript. 46-15314.   CS71.K36   1944

        KENNEY.   See also KEENEY.

        KENNING.   See DUNHAM, 1956

        KENNISON.   See KENNESTON.

        KENNISTON.   See KENNESTON.

        KENNON.   See: BASKERVILLE, 1917
                        CHAMBERS, 1957
                        COLBERT, 1956

        KENNY.   See KENNEY.

        KENNYSTONE.   See KENNESTON.

9621   KENRICK.   ... Edward Kenwrick, the ancestor of the Kenricks or Kendricks of Barnstable
County and Nova Scotia, and his descendants.   Yarmouthport, Mass., C. W. Swift, 1915.   cover-title,
20 p. 24½ cm. (Library of Cape Cod history & genealogy. no. 35) Comp. by Josiah Paine. 15-19858.   CS71.K335   1915

        See also: DE CLARE, 1921
                   KENDRICK.

9622   KENT.   Genealogies of the different families bearing the name of Kent in the United States together with their possible English ancestry A. D. 1295-1898.   By L. Vernon Briggs ... Boston, Rockwell & Churchill press, 1898.   vii, 339 p. front. (coats of arms) plates, ports. 24 cm. 9-15624.
CS71.K37   1898

9623   KENT.   History and genealogy of the Kent family.   Decendants (!) of Richard Kent, sen. who came to America in 1633.   By Edward Irving Dale.   (Spencer, Mass., E. E. Dickerman, 1899)
143 p., (2) 1 l. ports., plan. 24 cm.   By E. I. Dale and Edward E. Kent.   1-18210 rev.   CS71.K37   1899

9624   KENT.   Royal ancestry of Daniel Kent, of Worcester, and his descent from three Magna charta sureties.   (n. p.) 1918.   geneal. tab. 50 x 60 cm. fold. to 26 x 17 cm. Blu-print. 19-3964.   CS71.K37   1918

9625   KENT.   Kent genealogy, by Arthur Scott Kent.   (n. p.) Priv. print., 1933.   2 p. l., 101 p. 23½ cm.
33-14356.   CS71.K37   1933

9626   KENT.   Notes on Deacon Horner.   Ancestors of Justin Kent of Portland, Maine.   (By Helen (Richardson) Kluegel.   (Honolulu? 1961)   unpaged. 29 cm. 62-36807.   CS71.K37   1961

9627   KENT.   Kent, Gibson, Jeans; pioneer families of the Oregon Territory.   Compiled by Frances E. Caldwell.   (Veneta? Or., c. 1968)   69 l. 28 cm. 72-6675 MARC.   CS71.K37   1968

KENT.   See also: BOSS, E171. A53 vol. 18
CORNER, DA670. S95S9 vol. 22
KAINE, 1889
TENNEY, 1875
TODD, 1909

KENWRICK.   See KENDRICK.

9628   KENYON.   American Kenyons; history of Kenyons and English connections of American Kenyons, genealogy of the American Kenyons of Rhode Island, miscellaneous Kenyon material, by Captain Howard N. Kenyon.   Rutland, Vt., The Tuttle company, 1935.   285 p. illus. (incl. map, 2 coats of arms) pl., ports. 24 cm.   Portrait group facing p. 189 accompanied by leaf with key to names of persons, not included in paging. 35-10150.
CS71.K375   1935

9629   KENYON.   William Squire Kenyon and the Kenyon, Duncombe, Williams, Squire family histories, by Howard Eldred Kershner.   (New York) National Americana society, 1935.   7 p. l., 158 p. plates, ports., 2 col. coats of arms. 35 cm.   Bibliography: p. 157-158. 35-6105.   E748.K39K4

9630   KENYON.   A house that was loved, by Katharine M. R. Kenyon, with 12 plates and endpaper map.   London, Methuen & co., ltd. (1941)   xi p., 1 l., 253, (1) p. 1 illus. (music) plates, ports., facsim. 22 cm.
"First published in 1941."   The story of a Shropshire home in nineteenth century England. 43-5861.   CS439.K498   1941

9631   KEOGH.   The lineage of my children.   The historical, genealogical and topographical records of the Keogh, Benjamin, Knapp and Bellinger families, by Chester Henry Keogh ... Chicago, Ill., 1926.
50 p., 2 l. illus. (incl. maps) 25 cm.   "Privately printed for the author."   Two blank leaves at end for "Memorandum", and three genealogical tables, and facsimile map in pocket on back cover. 27-2028.   CS71.K38   1926

9632   KEPHART.   Danish royal Skiöldung genealogy of Zincke (Zinck, Zinke, Zink, Zingg) and certain Gebhardt (Kephart, Capehart) families.   By Calvin Kephart.   Shadyside, Md., 1950.   2. 20 p.
geneal. tab. 27 cm.   Cover title.   Bibliography: p. 19-20. 51-17351.   CS71.K384   1950

9633   KEPLER.   The Peter Kepler family of Erie and Crawford Counties, Pennsylvania.   By Frank Roy Kepler.   Detroit, 1953.   168 l. illus. 29 cm. 55-44918.   CS71.K385   1953

KEPNER.   See WEISER, 1960

9634   KEPPEL.   Fifty years of my life, by George Thomas, earl of Albemarle ... London, Macmillan and co., 1876.   2 v. front. (port.) fold. geneal. tab. 25 cm.   Title vignettes.   "The Keppels of Guelderland and the Keppels of England": v. 1, p. 1-215. 17-20509.   DA68.22.A3A2   1876

9635   KEPPEL.   Fifty years of my life, by George Thomas, earl of Albemarle.   New York, H. Holt and company, 1876.   ix, 420 p. 20½ cm.   Appendix. "The Keppels of Guelderland," and "The Keppels of England": p. (303)-398. 17-20508.   DA68. 22. A3A2   1876a

9636   KEPPEL.   Some early Keppel families: Keppel's of Pennsylvania, Maryland, North Carolina. Various spellings: Keppel, Keppele, Kepple, Kappel, Koeppel, Köppel, Copple, Coppel, etc.   Hollis, N.Y. (1952?)   unpaged. 28 cm.   53-15507.   CS71.K387   1952

9637   KEPPEL.   Keppel family history, Holland to America.   By Helen Marie (Keppel) Toal. (Stockton? Calif., 1964)   iv, 65 l. ports. 30 cm. 64-5542.   CS71.K387   1964

      KEPNER.   See SEIDNER, 1961

9638   KER.   Pedigree of the family of Ker of Cessford, Greenhead and Pryonsidelock ... etc.   By Christian Leopold Reid.   CS479.K5   1914

      KER.   See also: KERR.
                         LEWEN, 1919
                         READ.

      KERCHEVAL.   See POUND, 1904

9639   KERFOOT.   Kerfoot, Kearfott, and allied families, in America.   Illustrated with many photos. and genealogical charts and with drawings by the author.   By Robert Ryland Kearfott.   (Mamaroneck? N.Y.) Priv. published by members of the family, 1948.   ix, 169 p. illus., ports., tables. 23 cm.   "Errata": 1 p. inserted. 58-28651.   CS71.K389   1948

9640   KERFOOT.   A Kerfoot history, Canadian branch.   By John M. Morris.   London, Ont., Watt Letter Service (1953)   187 p. illus. 29 cm. 55-29769.   CS90.K45   1953

      KERLER.   See FRANK, F575.G3F8

      KERLEY.   See CONRAD, 1957

9641   KERN.   The Kern genealogy, by P.E.Kern ... (El Paso? Tex., 1917)   368 p. front., illus., plates, ports. 25½ cm.   This edition is limited to 150 numbered copies of which this copy is not numbered.   Dedicated to the descendants of Francis Xavier Kern, 1785-1835. 26-16561.   CS71.K39   1917

9642   KERN.   Kern family history, descendants of Abraham Kern, Wurtemberg to United States, 1731; complete genealogy of Lt. William Kern, Jr., and Catharine Hoover Kern and their descendants. By Tilden H. Kern.   (Normalville? Pa.) 1960.   75 p. illus. 23 cm. 64-40392.   CS71.K39   1960

9643   KERN.   The Kern family of Rowan County, North Carolina, Nicholas County, Kentucky, Boone, Clinton, Lawrence, Monroe Counties, Indiana, Hancock County, Illinois, Lee County, Iowa.   Compiled by Mary Margaret Kern Garrad, in collaboration with Stanley Kern, Jr.   (Noblesville? Ind.) 1968.   53 p. illus., geneal. table, map. 24 cm.   Caption title.   Cover title: The family of Conrad Kern. Limited ed. 74-2174.   CS71.K3893   1968

      KERN.   See also: GIFT, 1909
                          STRASSBURGER, 1922

9644   KERNAN.   Notes on the descendants of John Kernan of Ned, County Cavan, Ireland, and of Jane Brady his wife.   Englewood, N.J., 1949.   58 p. port. 24 cm. Cover title. 50-19618.
                                                                                    CS71.K3915   1949

9645   KERNAN.   The Utica Kernans; descendants of Bryan Kernan, gentleman, of the townland of Ned in the parish of Killeshandra, barony of Tullyhunco, county of Cavan, Province of Ulster, Kingdom of Ireland.   By John Devereux Kernan.   (Hamden, Conn., Kernan Enterprises) 1969.   101 p. col. coat of arms, facsims., ports. 27 cm. 1949 ed. published under title: Notes on the descendants of John Kernan of Ned. 68-58952 MARC.
                                                                                    CS71.K3915   1969

      KERNER.   See KÖRNER.

16

9646   KERNS.   Genealogical narrative; a history of three pioneer families: the Kerns, Popes, and Gibsons, by Edith Kerns Chambers.   Limited ed.   Eugene, Or.   (Portland, Or., Printed by Binfords & Mort) 1943.   93 p., 1 l. front., ports.   24 cm.   43-18538.   CS71.K392   1943

9647   KERR.   Correspondence of Sir Robert Kerr, first earl of Ancram, and his son William, third earl of Lothian ... Edinburgh (Printed by R. & R. Clark) 1875.   2 v. illus. (incl. facsims.) pl., ports. 26½ x 21 cm.   Edited by David Laing.   Geneal. tab. in vol. 1.   11-12217.   PR1105. R7   1875
                                                                                                                                                   Office.

9648   KERR.   Kerr of Abbotrule.   (London, 1877)   1 l. 28½ cm.   Reprinted from "Miscellanea genealogica et heraldica," 1877, n. s. v. 2, p. 382.   9-25109.   CS479.K5

9649   KERR.   Notices of the families of Kerr of Kerrisland and Monfode of that ilk.   (By Robert Malcolm Kerr) (n. p.) 1880.   3 p. l., (5)-99 p. 21 cm.   The accounts of these families are founded on the genealogy in Robertson's Ayrshire families, and other mss. of the late James Dobie, ed. by John Shedden Dobie. 20-18083.   CS479.K54

9650   KERR.   Pedigree of the family of Ker of Cessford, Greenhead and Pryonsidelock (including Hoselaw) and later of Hoselaw, Roxburghshire; Ker-Reid, of Hoselaw, Roxburghshire; and later of Newcastle-upon-Tyne and London, England; Australia and United States of America, comp. by Christian Leopold Reid, Newcastle-upon-Tyne (1890-1914) Newcastle-upon-Tyne, A. Reid & company, limited, 1914.   3 p. l., (9)-33 p., 13 l. front. (coat of arms)   XIII pl., fold. geneal. tab. 29 cm.   Each plate preceded by leaf with descriptive letterpress. "Imprint of 150 copies ... No. thirteen." 16-14965.   CS479.K5   1914

9651   KERR.   Brief history of Kerrs and kin, 1730 to 1930.   (By Vincent Brown Kerr) Staunton, Va., 1930.   36 p. illus. 33½ cm. "Revercomb, Hogshead. Forrer. et al. ", added to title in manuscript, and additions and corrections in manuscript throughout text.   Type-written foot-note inserted at p. 15.   34-42436.   CS71.K395   1930

9652   KERR.   The Kerr clan of New Jersey beginning with Walter Ker of Freehold and including other related lines, compiled by William C. Armstrong.   Morrison, Ill., The Shawver publishing co., 1931 -   v. ports. 17 cm. 35-14587.   CS71.K395   1931

9653   KERR.   The Kerr family and related lines, 1806-1949.   By Chester Lincoln Somers.   Rev., 1954.   (Hamilton? Mass., 1955)   11 l. 29 cm. 56-19339.   CS71.K395   1955

9654   KERR.   Kerr family records, compiled and arr, by Margaret Ingraham.   (San Antonio, Tex., Stallings Co.) 1964.   1 v. (various pagings) ports. 28 cm. Cover title. 64-5331.   CS71.K395   1964

9655   KERR.   Kerr family genealogy: James Dinsmore Kerr, his American ancestors and descendants, 1782-1968.   By Ralph L. Kerr.   (Denver? 1968)   50 p. 23 cm. Cover title. An extension and updating of James Kerr of Washington County, Pennsylvania and his descendants, 1782-1909, compiled by Thomas B. Kerr.   68-4320.
                                                                                                                                                   CS71.K395   1968

9656   KERR.   In vertical file.   Ask reference librarian for this material.

     KERR.   See also: BENZ, 1931   KER.
                         BOGARDUS, 1900   LEWEN, CS439. L52
                         BRUMBACH, 1961   REID, 1960
                         DAVIS, 1939   RUDDIMAN, 1901

KER-REID.   See KERR, 1914

KERRICH.   See CLARK, 1921

KERSEY.   See WHITE, 1951a

KERSHAW.   See SALISBURY, 1961

KERSHNER.   See BOOHER, 1956

KERWIN.   See LAWSON, 1903

KESSLER.   See BRUMBACH, 1961

KESTER.   See POUND, 1904

9657   KETCHAM.   Genealogy of the Ketcham and Kutch families, twelve and eight generations respectively.   Reproduction of plant and animal life, by Melcherd H. Kutch ... A brief autobiography of
the author written in third person and a few reminiscences in pictures ... (Pasadena, Calif., Wood &
Jones, printers, c.1939)   2 p. l., 7-207, (6) p.   illus. (incl. ports., coat of arms) 28¼ cm.   Blank pages for "Notes" (6 at end)
39-2697.   CS71.K4   1939

9658   KETCHAM.   Ketcham family history; the descendants of John Ketcham and his wife Sarah
Matthews of Mt. Hope Township (one time knwon as Deerpark, later Calhoun, and finally Mt. Hope)
Orange County, N.Y. (By Electa (Ketcham) Penney.   (n.p.) W.J.Coulter, 1954.   62. 48 l. 29 cm.
60-38922.   CS71.K4   1954

          KETCHAM.   See also: BATTEY, 1940a
                                 DUNHAM, 1956
                                 LINDLEY, 1950

      KETCHELL.   See KITCHELL.

      KETCHUM.   See KETCHAM.

      KETEL.   See KITTELLE.

      KETELHUYN.   See SWARTWOUT, 1899

9659   KETT.   The Ketts of Norfolk, a yeoman family.   Comp. by L.M.Kett.   London, Mitchell,
Hughes and Clarke, 1921.   v, 154 p. VII double geneal. tab. 28½ cm.   Compiled from material collected by Mr. George Kett.
22-7113.   CS439.K5

      KETTELLE.   See SWARTWOUT, 1899

9660   KETTENRING.   Kettenring family in America.   By Henry Hardy Catron.   (Springfield? Ill.,
1956 or 7)   237 p. 25 cm. 58-29669.   CS71.K42   1956

      KETTERING.   See KETTENRING.

9661   KEVE.   History of the Keve family.   Also short histories of the following families: the Coles,
the Fullwoods, the Latourettes, the Floreys, the Whipples, the Longs.   Written by J.F.Keve ...
(Arlington? Ia., 1914?)   71, (1) p., 1 l. illus. (ports.) 18½ cm.   15 blank leaves at end for additional records.   Colored coats of
arms inserted at p. 8.   Appendix: p. !-IV inserted at end.   14-20950.   CS71.K43   1914

9662   KEWLEY.   The name Kewley (by D.K.Martin.   West Chazy, N.Y., 196 -)   (35) l. 28 cm.
65-430.   CS71.K435

9663   KEY.   Key and allied families, by Mrs. Julian C. Lane ... Macon, Ga., Press of the J.W.
Burke company, 1931.   495 p. incl. illus. ports., facsims., coats of arms. front. 23½ cm.   Blank pages for "Family records"
(394-402) Allied families: Waller, Garrett, Cantelou, Keith, Randolph, Marshall, White, Kilpatrick, Bell, Clarke, Martin, Tandy, Terrell, and
Bibb. 31-19245.   CS71.K438   1931

9664   KEY.   The Keys in Texas, and related families; the genealogy and history of the Key family,
Groves family, Burrow family, McGehee, Potts and others.   By Della (Tyler) Key.   Amarillo, Texas,
L.M.Key, 1965.   vi, 96 l. ports. 29 cm. 65-71320.   CS71.K438   1965

9665   KEY.   By my strong hand; the motto of Clan MacKay of Southerland, Scotland; an account of
some of the lives and adventures of the Key family of Prince George County, Maryland, and Marshall,
Texas from the earliest times to the present.   Compiled and illustrated from material in the family
records, by Hobart Key, Jr.   Marshall, Tex., Port Caddo Press, 1965. xv. 166 p. illus., ports. 27 cm.
Bibliography: p. xi. 67-3664.   CS71.K438   1965a

KEY.   See also: KEYES.
No. 516 - Notable southern families, vol. 1

9666   KEYES.   A brief notice of the late Thomas Keyes, of West Boylston, together with a short historical account of his descendants, and also of his ancestry; with some incidents and circumstances connected therewith.   Worcester, H.J.Howland, 1857.   15 p. 18 cm. 1-18199.   CS71.K44   1857

9667   KEYES.   Genealogy of C.W.Keyes ... (Des Moines, 1875)   10 p. 20 cm. 3-678.
CS71.K44   1875

9668   KEYES.   Genealogy.   Robert Keyes of Watertown, Mass., 1633.   Solomon Keyes of Newbury and Chelmsford, Mass., 1653.   And their descendants: also, others of the name, by Asa Keyes.   Brattleboro, G.E.Selleck, 1880.   10 l. iv, 319 p. front. (port.) coat of arms. 23 cm. 3-5662.
CS71.K44   1880

9669   KEYES.   Genealogy.   Solomon Keyes of Newbury and Chelmsford, Mass., and his descendants, 1653-1880.   By Asa Keyes.   Brattleboro, G.E.Selleck, printer, 1880.   3 p. l., (3)-188, (177)-180 p. front. (port.) coat of arms. 23½ cm. Pages (177)-180 repeated in numbering. "Forms second part of the 'Genealogy of the Keyes family.'" 2-26727.
CS71.K44   1880a

9670   KEYES.   Keese family history and genealogy, from 1690 to 1911.   By W.T.Keese.   Dedicated to the descendants of John and Elizabeth Titus Keese.   By Willis T. Keese.   Cardington, O., Independent printing co., 1911.   3 p. l., (9)-48 p., 3 l. plates, ports. 23 cm. Blank leaves for "Births, Marriages, Deaths" (3 at end) 28-29666.   CS71.K44   1911

9671   KEYES.   Keese family history; southern branch.   By William Shelton Keese.   (Chattanooga?) 1950.   26 p. illus., ports., coat of arms. 23 cm. Bound with Keese, W.T.   Keese family history and genealogy. Cardington, Ohio. 1911. 51-24362.   CS71.K44   1911
copy 2

9672   KEYES.   Genealogy and history of the related Keyes, North and Cruzen families, with a sketch of the early Norths of England, by Millard Fillmore Stipes.   Jamesport, Mo., The author, 1914.   321 p. illus. (coat of arms) pl., ports. 22½ cm. 20-12158.   CS71.K44   1914

9673   KEYES.   (Ancestral charts of Fredelle Carolyn Keyes and her brother George Bacon Keyes, and description of the persons mentioned, by Charles Hubbard Keyes.   Barrington? R.I., 1931)   2 p. l., 55, 66 numb. l. map, coat of arms. 29 cm. Type-written. No title-page; title from preface. 31-18260.
CS71.K44   1931

KEYES.   See also FLAGG, 1920

KEYLOR.   See MACGINNIS, 1891

9674   KEYSER.   ... The Keyser family; descendants of Dirck Keyser of Amsterdam.   Compiled by Charles S. Keyser.   Philadelphia (Press of W. F. Fell & co.) 1889.   1 p. l., 161 p. illus., plates (ports.) facsims., coat of arms. 28 cm. The Genealogy has special t.-p.   Contents. - The bicentennial reunion of the Keyser family. 1688-1888. - The genealogy of the Keyser family. 1688-1888. 2-8717.   CS71.K442   1889

9675   KEYSER.   Keyser ... copyright ... (by) C.L.Turner.   (Philadelphia) c.1936.   geneal. tab. 35 cm. "This genealogy is a record transcribed from a transcript from the Keyser Holland Bible some years after death of Michael Keyser." Blueprint. 40-18938.   CS71.K442   1936

KEYSER.   See also MEAD, 1933

9676   KIBBE.   Kibbe genealogical notes on some descendants of Edward Kibbe and his wife Mary Partridge Kibbe.   By Doreen (Potter) Hanna.   (Skowhegan? M.) 1967.   i. 285 p. 28 cm. 67-31974.
CS71.K447   1967

9677   KIBLING.   Kiblinger family, later spelled Kibling, data collected by Mrs. Laura Kendall Thomas.   Elmhurst, Ill. (1931?)   1 p. l., 11 numb. l. 28 cm. In manuscript. 42-4569.
CS71.K45   1931

KIBLINGER. See KIBLING.

9678 KICHLINE. The Kichlines in America, prepared by Thomas J. Kichline, president of the Kichline family association and read by him before the Northampton County historical and genealogical society at Easton, Pa., under date of January 15, 1926, at 8 p.m., at the home of Frank C. Williams ... (Easton? 1926) 2 p. l., 29 p. illus. (port.) 23 cm. 26-16569. CS71.K46 1926

9679 KIDD. The Kidd, Oder, Parks, Stone, Boone, Logan, Moore, Miller, Paxson, Carter, Wasson, Landon, Bellamy, Hartley, McMillin, Maugridge pedigree, by Ephraim Stout Lillard ... (Washington, Court of Neptune press, 1944) 1 p. l., geneal. tab. 24 cm. 44-29933. CS71.K4616 1944

9680 KIDD. Reuben Vaughan Kidd, soldier of the Confederacy. By Alice V. Pierrepont. Petersburg, Va. (1947) xii, 462 p. illus., ports., map. 24 cm. 48-1006*. E605.K5P5

KIDD. See also BAX, 1936

9681 KIDDER. History and records of the Kidder family. 1876. (By Samuel Theodore Kidder) Chicago, Culver, Page, Hoyne & co., printers, 1876. 32 p. front. (port.) illus. incl. coat of arms. 23 cm. On cover: 1492. Kidder. 1876. "Sources of information": p. (2) 34-19794. CS71.K462 1876

9682 KIDDER. Kidder (family. By Thomas Bellows Wyman. Boston, D. Clapp and son, 1879) 3 p. 25½ cm. 39M421T. CS71.K462 1879

9683 KIDDER. A history of the Kidder family from A.D.1320 to 1676, including the biography of our emigrant ancestor, James Kidder, also a genealogy of his descendants through his son, John Kidder, who settled in Chelmsford, Mass., about 1681. Allston, Mass., F.E.Kidder, 1886. iv. 175 p. front., plates, ports., facsims., coats of arms. 24 cm. Comp. by Frank Eugene Kidder. 9-11463. CS71.K462 1886

9684 KIDDER. A genealogy of the Kidder family comprising the descendants in the male line of Ensign James Kidder, 1626-1676, of Cambridge and Billerica in the colony of Massachusetts Bay, by Morgan Hewitt Stafford ... Rutland, Vt., The Tuttle publishing co., inc. (1941) xxxiii, (1), 749, (7) p. front., plates. ports., coats of arms (part col.) fold. geneal. tables. 26½ cm. Maps on lining-papers. Six pages at end for "Births," "Marriages," and "Deaths." 42-23196. CS71.K462 1941

KIDDER. See also: BRAYTON, 1922
FUNSTEN, 1926
MEAD, 1921
PAGE, 1887
WHITING, 1952

KIDSTON. See FORRESTER, 1905

9685 KIEHL. Pedigree charts of Kiehl/Grinnell and related families of Onondaga County, N.Y.; a preliminary genealogical work. By Ralph Adam Kiehl. El. Cajon, Calif., 1959. 1 v. 22 x 36 cm. 59-54042. CS71.K465 1959

KIENE. See KÜHNE.

KIER. See KIAER.

KIERSTED-SMEDES. SEBOR, 1923

KIESEL. See KIESSEL.

9686 KIESS. Some descendants of Johann Friederich Kiess. By Carl Clarence Kiess. Washington, 1958. 28 p. 23 cm. 59-33176. CS71.K466 1958

9687 KIESSEL. (The history of the Kiessel family, with allied families; By William Carl Kiessel. Kaufmann, Beck and Fleck. Tenafly, N.J., 1948) (95) l. coat of arms, geneal. table. 29 cm. Includes bibliographies. 48-14878*. CS71.K468 1948

KIESZEL.   See KIESSEL.

KIGHT.   See HAMLETT, 1958

KIHS.   In vertical file under PRANKE family.   Ask reference librarian for this material.

9688   KILBORN.   The family memorial.   A history and genealogy of the Kilbourn family, in the
United States and Canada, from the year 1635 to the present time ... by Payne Kenyon Kilbourn ...
Hartford, Brown & Parsons, 1845.   3 p. 1., (3)-151 p. front., illus., port., coats of arms. 23 cm. "Advertisement" dated
November, 1847.   Kilbourn historical and genealogical society, founded 15th of April, 1848; p. 149-151.   18-2198.

CS71.K48   1845

9689   KILBOURN.   Kilbourn historical and genealogical society.   Proceedings.   1854.   (New Haven?
1854)   16 p. 23½ cm. Caption title. 9-15048.   CS71.K48   1854

9690   KILBOURN.   The history and antiquities of the name and family of Kilbourn (in its varied orthography) by Payne Kenyon Kilbourne ...   New Haven, Durrie & Peck, 1856.   444 (i. e. 484). (8) p. front., illus.
(incl. coats of arms) plates, ports., geneal. tables.   23½ cm.   Pages 33-72 repeated in numbering as 33*- 72*.   The 8 pages at end left blank
for "Family record."   9-11462.   CS71.K48   1856

9691   KILBORN.   The Kilbourn family history.   By George Darius Kilborn.   (n. p., K. W. Kilborn,
1957)   462 p. port., coat of arms. 26 cm. 62-33617.   CS71.K48   1957

KILBURN.   See KILBORN.

KILDARE, Earls of.   See FITZGERALD.

KILE.   See: KYLE.
          SMITH, 1964a

9692   KILGORE.   Charles Kilgore of King's mountain, by Hugh M. Addington; a new history of the
Kilgore family.   By Hugh Milburn Addington.   Nickelsville, Va., Service printery, 1935.   2 p. 1., v.
154p. front., plates, ports. 18½ cm. 35-29164 rev.   CS71.K482   1935

KILGORE.   See also: DINWIDDIE, 1957
                       No. 1547 - Cabell county.

9693   KILHAM.   The early Kilhams.   By William Stowell Mills ... (In New England historical and
genealogical register.   Boston, 1902.   24 cm.   v. 56, p. 344-346)   2-8370.   F1.N561 vol. 56

KILHOLM.   See SMITH, 1878a

9694   KILLEGREW.   Memorabilia of the family of Killegrew.   By the Rev. Mark Noble ... (n. p.)
1825.   2 p. 1., 30 p., 1 l. 26 cm. In manuscript. 25-19808.   CS439.K57N6

9695   KILLIAN.   The Killian family, and particularly the ancestors & descendants of Andreas Killian,
1702-1788, arrived in America 23 September 1732.   Compiled by George W. Killian.   (Rochester?
N. Y., 1969)   1 v. (unpaged) 29 cm. Cover title: Andreas Killian, 1702-1788, his ancestors and descendants.   Contents. - Introduction and
dedication, by G. W. Killian. - The history of the Killian family in North Carolina, by J. Y. Killian. - Killians in Europe, by C. H. Killian. - Account
of talk at the unveiling of the Andreas Killian memorial on 19 October 1952, by C. H. Killian. - Colonial Killians and their families. by C. H. Killian.
- An essay about Philip Killian, a grandson of Andreas through John, by C. H. Killian. - Andreas Killian and some of his descendants in Georgia. by
T. D. Killian. - Killians and the Mormon Church from 1942 minutes. by G. W. Killian. - Wills and miscellaneous. - Cletus Killian's comments after
reading the history of the Killian family in North Carolina, by C. H. Killian.   71-8914 MARC.

CS71.K484   1969

KILLOUGH.   See HOOPES, 1948

KILLUM.   See BRUCE, 1914

9696   KILMER.   History of the Kilmer family in America.   Comp. and ed. by Rev. C. H. Kilmer. With original chart.   Pub. by the author.   Elmira, N. Y., Advertiser association, printers, 1897. 214 p. ports., fold. geneal. tab.   25 x 20 cm.   9-17834.   CS71.K485   1897

9697   KILNER.   The descendants of James & Ann Kilner, formerly of Mansergh, Westmoreland. (London, 1862)   14 p. 24½ cm.   Preface signed: James Kilner.   8-29438.   CS439.K6

9698   KILNER.   Decendents (sic) of Thomas Kilner believed to be a brother of James Kilner.   By Charles Frances Thomas Kilner.   (Arlington, Va., 1949)   5 l. 28 cm.   Caption title.   50-21398. CS71.K486   1949

9699   KILPATRICK.   The Kilpatrick family; ancestors and descendants of Marian Douglas Jones and Robert Jackson Kilpatrick, with related families, by Marian Douglas (Jones) Kilpatrick; compiled from genealogical notes which she assembled but had not put in book form when the Reaper came.   (Beatrice, Neb.)   R. J. Kilpatrick, 1930.   xv, 311 p. incl. geneal. tables.   20 cm.   30-18837.   CS71.K487   1930

KILPATRICK.   See also KEY, 1931

KILTZ.   Family of John and Louesa Kiltz (by) Burton F. Kiltz.   (Arlington, Va., 1969?) 40 p. port.   28 cm.   Cover title.   79-8549.   CS71.K488   1969

9700   KIMBALL.   The Joseph Kimball family: a genealogical memoir of the ascendants and descendants of Joseph Kimball, of Canterbury, N. H.   Ten generations: 1634-1885.   Comp. by John Kimball ... Concord, N. H., Printed by the Republican press association, 1885.   1 p. l., 103 p. front (coat of arms) ports.   24 cm.   9-11461.   CS71.K49   1885

9701   KIMBALL.   History of the Kimball family in America, from 1634 to 1897, and of its ancestors the Kemballs or Kemboldes of England, with an account of the Kembles of Boston, Massachusetts.   By Leonard Allison Morrison ... and Stephen Paschall Sharples ... Boston, Damrell & Upham, 1897. 2 v.   illus., plates, ports., coat of arms.   23 cm.   Paged continuously.   9-11459.   CS71.K49   1897

9702   KIMBALL.   The Kimball family news; being supplemental to Kimball family history.   v. 1-5, v. 6, no. 1-2; Jan. 1898-Feb. 1903.   Topeka, Kan., G. F. Kimball, 1898-1903.   6 v. in 3. illus., plates. ports. 23 cm.   monthly.   Cover-title.   No more published.   5-7996.   CS71.K49   1898

9703   KIMBALL.   The Kimball family news, being supplementary to the History of the Kimball family in America.   Consisting of the regular monthly parts for the years 1898 and 1899.   With additional illustrations.   Topeka, Kan., G. F. Kimball, 1900.   2 v. in 1. illus., ports. 22 cm.   Paged continuously.   5-5647. CS71.K49   1900

9704   KIMBALL.   The genealogy of Charles, and his wife Edith Chase, Kimball.   Burlington, Vt. (Printed at the shop of P. C. Dodge) 1901.   16 p.   25½ cm.   12-31010.   CS71.K49   1901

9705   KIMBALL.   Kimball-Weston memorial.   The American ancestry and descendants of Alonzo and Sarah (Weston) Kimball of Green Bay, Wisconsin, comp. by William Herbert Hobbs.   Madison, Wis., Priv. print., 1902.   103, (6) p.   1 pl., 3 ports. (incl. front.) 1 fold. geneal. tab.   25 cm.   "The descendants of Alonzo and Sarah Weston Kimball.   (Compiled by Mary Cornelia Kimball Walker)": p. (90)-92.   3-17719.   CS71.K49   1902

9706   KIMBALL.   Record of the family of Levi Kimball and some of his descendants, comp. by his grandson, Levi Darbee, 1861, rev. and extended 1913 by Robert M. Darbee.   (Brooklyn, Brooklyn eagle press, 1913)   119, 54 p., 1 l. 23 cm.   Appendix: Record of the family of Jedediah Darbee and some of his descendants: 54 p. at end.   15-21819.   CS71.K49   1913

9707   KIMBALL.   Kimball ancestry of my mother Eureka Kimball Goddard, compiled by Charles Austin Goddard.   Fayetteville, W. Va., 1937.   7 numb. l., 1 l.   28½ cm.   Caption title.   Type-written.   "References": 1 leaf at end.   37-38452.   CS71.K49   1937

9708   KIMBALL.   The Lt. Moses and Jemima Clement Kimball family, by Pauline Kimball Skinner. Wilmington, Del., Press of W. N. Cann, inc. (1941)   5 p. l., 3-152 p. illus. (incl. ports.) 24 cm.   "250 copies only have been printed."   Pages 139-152 blank for "Family notes."   42-5165.   CS71.K49   1941

9709   KIMBALL.   Genealogy of Jacob Kimble of the Paupack settlement, Wayne and Pike County (sic) Pa., and his descendants with information on the allied families of Ridgway and Ansley.   Prepared by Mr. and Mrs. John H. Schneider, and Howard Kimble.   (n.p.) Accurate Law Print. Co., 1952.
53 p.   24 cm.   55-57897.   CS71.K49   1952

9710   KIMBALL.   Genealogies of George West and James R. Kimble and their descendants through Samuel and Elizabeth (Kimble) West, researched and prepared 1953-1963, by Austin L. Pino.   Ann Arbor, Mich., Printed by University Microfilms, 1964.   64 p.   map, group port. 23 cm.   Includes mounted errata and addenda slips.   Bibliography: p. 6.   65-9641.   CS71.W52   1964

> KIMBALL.   See also: ANDREWS, 1890   EATON, 1890
> CARPENTER, 1930   TODD, 1909
> DRIVER, 1889   WHITE, 1900

9711   KIMBER.   The descendants of Richard Kimber.   A genealogical history of the descendants of Richard Kimber, of Grove, near Wantage, Berkshire, England. - Comp. by Sidney A. Kimber. - Containing the families in the United States from the settlements in Pennsylvania and New York, the families in England, and the descendants in Australia.   Boston, S.A.Kimber, 1894.   3 p. 1., 9-76, (6) p. front. (coat of arms) plates, facsim.   25 cm.   9-11442.   CS71.K491   1894

9712   KIMBER.   The descendants of Thomas Kimber; a genealogical history of the descendants of Thomas Kimber of Down Ampney, near Cirencester, Gloucester, England. (By Sidney Arthur Kimber) Cambridge, Mass., S.A.Kimber, 1923.   3 p. 1., 34 p. front. (coat of arms) illus., plates, ports. 24 cm.   "Acknowledgment" signed: Sidney A. Kimber.   "Seventy-five copies have been made."   23-8250.   CS71.K491   1923

9713   KIMBERLY.   Thomas Kimberly, New Haven, Conn. 1638.   (New Haven, The Tuttle, Morehouse & Taylor press, 1896)   cover-title, fold. geneal. tab. (30½ x 60 cm.) 21 cm.   "This record to the sixth generation was prepared by Hon. Dennis Kimberly ... The record of Gilead and Mary (Brocket) Kimberly was prepared by Martha Kimberly, wife of Augustus Lines ..." 2-25216.   CS71.K492   1896

> KIMBERLY.   See also PRINDLE, 1906

> KIMES.   See MAXWELL.

9715   KIMBROUGH.   Kim & Hite: their grandparents, Hite-McLean-Hardy-Kimbrough.   By Lenore McLean.   (n.p.) c.1960.   unpaged. 30 cm.   61-28841.   CS71.K493   1960

> KIMBROUGH.   See also HITE, 1960

> KIMSEY.   See: KIMZEY.
> TIPPIN, 1939

9716   KIMZEY.   Chart of the Kimzey family, compiled 1945 ... By Herbert Bennett Kimzey. Cornelia, Ga., 1947.   geneal. tab. 46 x 59 cm.   Photocopy (negative) 47-3939.   CS71.K495   1947

9717   KIMZEY.   Kimzey and Kimsey ... revised chart of the Kimzey family.   By Herbert Bennett Kimzey.   Comp. March 1947.   Cornelia, Ga. (1947)   geneal. table. 51 x 23 cm.   Caption title.   Photocopy (positive) 47-29918.   CS71.K495   1947a

9718   KIMZEY.   Kimzey family history; Kimzey and Kimsey family records.   By Herbert Bennett Kimzey.   Cornelia, Ga., 1949.   A-G, 28 p. 30 cm.   49-15595*.   CS71.K495   1949

9719   KIMZEY.   Kimzey family history (by) Cecile Kimzey Tackman (and) Edith Kimzey Manuel. (n.p.) 1963.   62 1. illus. 28 cm.   66-54206.   CS71.K495   1963

9720   KINCAID.   Kincaid genealogy, by G. L. Kincaid.   Sardinia, O., Sardinia news press, 1922.
44 p. 15 cm. 28-9893.   CS71.K52   1922

9721   KINCAID.   The Kinkeads of Delaware as pioneers in Minnesota, 1856 - 1868.   Contemporary
account of experiences in the Sioux uprising, 1862, by Clara Janvier Kinkead.   Some genealogical
history of the Kinkead and Janvier families.   Research and editing by Jeannette Eckman.   Wilmington, Del., G. W. Butz, Jr., 1949.   95 p. illus., ports., maps (1 fold.) geneal. tables. 23 cm. 50-968.
                                                                                              CS71.K52   1949

          KINCAID.   See also: BRUMBACH, 1961
                                 CLEEK, 1957
                                 KINKADE.

          KINCANNON.   See KINNISON, 1956

9722   KINCHANT.   Quienchant v. Quinchant v. Kinchant.   (v. = vel, or)   Family notes, by Major-
General John Charlton Kinchant ... (London?) 1917.   3 p. l., 3-31 numb. l. pl. 33 cm.   "Sixty-five copies printed for
private circulation."   "Chart for desk use" and "Family notes" in pocket at end. 40-16310.
                                                                                              CS439.K65   1917

9723   KINCHELOE.   Kincheloe, McPherson, and related families: their genealogies and biographies.
By Lewin Dwinell McPherson.   (Washington) c. 1951.   505 p. ports., col. coats of arms. 29 cm. Caption title.
51-40859.   CS71.K524   1951

9724   KINDLEY.   The William Kindley family genealogy: his nine sons and their descendants.   By
Bessie Jewel Mayes Wimberly.   (Arlington, Va., Arlington Printers, 1967)   xi, 309 p. illus., ports. 28 cm.
67-27969.   CS71.K527   1967

          KINDRICK.   See KENDRICK.

9725   KING.   (Descendants of Ruth Hyde and Thomas King   By Reuben Hyde Walworth)   (In his Hyde
genealogy. Albany, 1864. 24 cm. v. 1, p. 285-286) 4-25642 rev.   CS71.H993 vol. 1
          —— Copy 2, detached.   CS71.K53   1864

9726   KING.   Genealogy of the families of Kings, who lived in Raynham, from 1680, to the present,
1865.   By E. Sanford, A.M. ...   Taunton, C.A. Hack & son, printers, 1866.   28 p. 22 cm. 9-15603.
                                                                                              CS71.K53   1866

9727   KING.   King pedigree. - The pedigree of the family and collateral descendants of the Most
Reverend William King, D. D., lord archbishop of Dublin, 1703-1729.   (n. p., 1870?)   5 l. 22½ cm.
Caption title.   "The King pedigree was printed for insertion in the quarterly series of the Miscellanea genealogica.   The compiler, Sir C. S. King,
however, requested that it should not be published.   The type was consequently distributed after 3 proofs had been struck off." - Ms. not on fly leaf,
signed J. J. Howard   Grants of arms, notes and coats of arms in ms., and correspondence concerning the pedigree, inserted at end.   Correspondence
signed: Charles S. King. 21-18017.   CS499.K6

9728   KING.   Children of William and Dorothy King of Salem.   By Henry F. Waters.   (From the
Historical collections of the Essex institute, vol. XVI, p. 114)   Salem, Printed at the Salem press,
1880.   8 p. 24½ cm. 4-25648.   CS71.K53   1880

9729   KING.   ... King family of New York.   By Wm. H. Smith.   (In The Maine historical and genealogical recorder.
Portland, 1884. 23 cm. v. 1, p. 182-186) 4-25645.   F16.M18 vol. 1
          —— Detached copy.   CS71.K53   1884

9730   KING.   David King, of Saco, and some of his descendants.   Comp. by S. M. Watson.   (In The
Maine historical and genealogical recorder. Portland, 1886. 23 cm. v. 3, p. 118-125)
                                                                                              F16.M18 vol. 3
          —— Detached copy.   Contains portrait of James G. King, taken from the Maine historical and genealogical recorder, v. 1.
4-25643.   CS71.K53   1886

9731   KING.   Pedigree of King, of Salem, Essex County, Mass., 1595-1887.   Five lines of descent traced by Rufus King ... (New York, 1888)   geneal. tab.   56 x 71½ cm. fold. to 25½ cm.   "One hundred copies printed. no. 24." 9-12292.
CS71.K53   1888

9732   KING.   Pedigree of King, of Lynn, Essex County, Mass.   1602-1891.   Five lines of descent traced by Rufus King ... (New York, 1891)   geneal. tab.   56 x 71 cm. fold. to 22½ cm. 9-12326.
CS71.K53   1891

9733   KING.   The King family of Suffield, Conn.   By Edmund Janes Cleveland.   Boston, D. Clapp & son, printers, 1892.   7 p. 24½ cm.   Edition, 100 copies.   Reprinted from the New Eng. hist. and geneal. register for October. 1892. 9-10189.
CS71.K53   1892

9734   KING.   The King genealogy, and its branches, Moulton, Sedgwicks and Shaws, and their descendants, bearing other names.   A record of the descendants of William King, of Monson, Mass., 1770, both male and female lines being carried out complete to 1897.   Also, a complete record of the ancestry of William King, and of his wife Hannah Lamphear King, from the sixteenth century ... By Harvey B. King.   Hartford, Conn.   (Plimpton mfg. co. print.) 1897.   142 p. front., ports., plates, map, tab. 23½ cm.   Appendix, p. 114-118, contains early records of many other King families, the early settlers of New England. 9-10190.
CS71.K53   1897

9735   KING.   The genealogy of the New York branch of the King family of Suffield, Connecticut, beginning with William King of Ugborough, Devonshire, England, the father of James King, the founder of the Suffield family, and extending to and including the descendants ... of Roger King who removed from Suffield to Troy, N.Y., in the year 1795; to which is added an appendix containing historical information concerning the family, and also genealogies of some of the maternal ancestors.   Comp. by Harvey James King.   Troy, N.Y. (Saratoga Springs, N.Y., Printed by E. P. Howe & son) 1897.   2 p. l., (3)-56 p. incl. front. (mounted facsim.) 32 x 25 cm.   "A limited edition of fifty copies of which this is no. 16."   "Addenda, relative to the Devotion family": p. (51)-56.   Postal and letter in manuscript inserted.   4-29748 rev.
CS71.K53   1897a

9736   KING.   King genealogy.   Clement King of Marshfield, Mass., 1668, and his descendants.   Compiled by George Austin Morrison, jr. ... Albany, J. Munsell's sons, 1898.   65 p. 29 cm.   Limited edition.   9-15594.
CS71.K53   1898

9737   KING.   A genealogical record of the families of King and Henham, in the county of Kent.   Containing pedigrees of Cox, Knowles, Hopwood, Thornton, Peckham, Sex, Hicks, Hughes, Alexander, Woodhams, Larkin, Wild, Coveney, Boorman, Gore, Hatch, Vine, Plane, Iden, etc. etc.   Comp. and collected by William Louis King ... With two illustrations and a photogravure ... London, Mitchell and Hughes, 1899.   39, (1) p. front., illus., plates, geneal. tab.   33 cm.   "Memoranda referring to the will of John Iden of Hadlow, esquire," 1 leaf inserted before p. 23.   Forty copies privately printed.   "Errata" and "Boorman, Henham, Martyr and Wild alliance," 1 leaf inserted before p. 3.   11-5262.
CS439.K7

9738   KING.   The King family of Southold, Suffolk County, New York, 1595-1901.   Comp. from public records, family papers and the manuscript King genealogy of Mr. Rufus King of Yonkers, N.Y., by Lucy Dubois Akerly ... Edition of one hundred copies.   Privately printed.   (New York, Press of T. A. Wright) 1901.   20 p. illus. (facsims.) plates. 27½ cm.   Contents. - Records of the King family of Southold, Suffolk County, New York.   Communicated by Mr. Rufus King of Yonkers, New York; p. (5)-9.   Reprinted from the New York genealogical and biographical record for April, 1901. - William and Dorothy King, of Salem, Mass., and three generations of their Long Island descendants.   Comp. by Lucy D. Akerly from the manuscript genealogy of Rufus King of Yonkers, N.Y.; p. (11)-20.   Reprinted from the New York genealogical and biographical record for April, 1902.   16-27490.
CS71.K53   1901

9739   KING.   The King family, by W. W. Spooner.   (In American historical magazine.   New York. 1907.   24½ cm. v. 2, no. 4. p. 261-273.   port.)   CA9-3906 unrev.
E171.A53
—— Copy 2
CS71.K53   1907

9740   KING. The King family of Suffield, Connecticut, its English ancestry, A. D. 1389 - 1662, and American descendants, A. D., 1662-1908, comprising numerous branches in many states of the United States, also appendices containing information concerning some of its maternal ancestors, comp. by Cameron Haight King.   San Francisco (Press of the Walter N. Brunt co.) 1908.   592 p., 1 l., lxiii p. front., illus., plates, ports., map, facsims., coats of arms (1 col.) 24 cm.   15-23149.
CS71.K53   1908

9741   KING.   The "King" family heraldry.   A brief history of the origin of the families of this name in old and New England entitled to bear coat armor, by George Austin Morrison ... New York, New York genealogical and biographical society, 1910.   35 p.   VII coats of arms (incl. front.) 27 cm.   "Edition of one hundred copies."   "Reprinted from the New York genealogical and biographical record. for October, 1910."   18-16650.

CS439.K7   1910

9742   KING.   Descendants of Vincent King - Jane Gay Stevenson.   Jane Holesclaw.   Data collected and arranged by William Harrison King - Roy Stevenson King.   (n. p.) 1914.   geneal. tab.   58 x 73½ cm.   "Registered number 45."   Blue print.   15-2144.

CS71.K53   1914

9743   KING.   A genealogy of the King family.   Buffalo, N. Y., American heraldic society, 1930.   2 p. l., 9-199 p.   col. coat of arms.   21 cm.   31-18246.

CS71.K53   1930

9744   KING.   Our family history.   By Faith (Whitaker) Stucker.   (New London, Iowa) 1930.   (20) p.   22 cm.   Cover title.   48-35390*.

CS71.K53   1930a

9745   KING.   Ancestry of Catherine King who married Robert R. Herron, September 2, 1856 at Worthington, Armstrong county, Pennsylvania, compiled by Ella Foy O'Gorman (Mrs. Michael Martin O'Gorman) (n. p.) 1933.   34 l. 28 cm. Typewritten. "References." Contains also Buffington, Mendenhall, Smedley, Williamson families.   38M3358T.

CS71.K53   1933

9746   KING.   The family tree of Nina Todd King ... (by) George Fuller Green ... Kansas City, Mo., 1937.   geneal. tab. illus. (coats of arms) 77 x 45 cm.   In manuscript.   "References." 38-32669.

CS71.K53   1937

9748   KING.   Genealogy: King, Watts.   (Comp. by Ida Hunt Branyon and Odessa Hunt.   Atlanta, 1948)   (25) l. 29 cm. Cover title. Typewritten. 49-26960*.

CS71.K53   1948

9749   KING.   Genealogy: Jacob King (König) and Matheus King (König) of Northampton County, Pennsylvania.   By Wilbur Lewis King.   Bethlehem, Pa., 1951 (i.e. 1952)   119 p. 23 cm. 53-19697.

CS71.K53   1952

9750   KING.   An interim tracing of the ancestry of Valerie Daly King.   By Charles Daly King.   (Richmond?) 1956.   iv, 240 p. 25 cm. Cover title: Ancestry of Valerie Daly King. Contains the ancestry of Charles Daly King. compiled and arr. by E. B. D. King, and the ancestry of Mildred Sisson King, compiled by E. G. Sison. Includes bibliographical references. 57-37600.

CS71.K53   1956

9751   KING.   King-Boardman family tree.   (By Gervase James Patterson Barger)   (Washington?) 1958.   4 geneal. tables. ports. 60 cm. 59-28591.

CS71.K53   1958

9752   KING.   United King book, 1820 to 1960.   By Guy Laster King.   (Alhambra? Calif., 1959)   141 p. 22 cm. 60-37079.

CS71.K53   1959a

9753   KING.   The Kings of York County: pioneers, patriots, and paper-makers.   By Richard Shue.   (York? Pa., 1959-1960)   4 pts. 19 cm. 60-32759.

CS71.K53   1959

9754   KING.   Family history; ancestors of Cathy Lynn King.   By Edward Johnson Ladd.   Fort Payne, Ala., 1965.   1 v. (unpaged) illus., geneal. tables. ports. 30 cm. 65-9227.

CS71.K53   1965

KING.   See also:

AMES, 1889	CRAIG, 1960a	KETCHAM, 1954
BACKHOUSE, DA690.M74C3	FOSTER, 1889	KLING, 1924
BACKHOUSE, CS439.B18	GALLOWAY, 1939	McCLARY. E171.A53 v.13
BARD, F128.25V27	GRIFFIN, F129.S74G8	McHARG, 1905
BARNES, 1961	HABERSHAM, 1901	McILHENNY, 1916
BARNES, 1964	HALL, 1943	MINNS, 1925
CLARK, 1917	JOHNSON, 1893a	MULLIKEN, 1936

cont. p. 27

KING continued:

RANDOLPH, 1961 VAN RENSSELAER, 1907 WARNER, 1956
SHEFFIELD, 1929   VENN, 1904   WILSON, 1957
SODEN, 1959

9755 KING-HALL. Sea saga, edited by L. King-Hall; being the naval diaries of four generations of the King-Hall family ... By Louise King-Hall. London, V. Gollancz, ltd., 1935. 541 p. plates, ports. 22 cm. Errata slip inserted before p. (265) 36-4930.   DA88.1.K48K5 1935

9756 KINGDON. Arms and pedigree of Kingdon-Gould. of New York and Georgian court, Lakewood, New Jersey, showing descent from John Kingdon of Coleridge, county Devon, England, esquire (1596), a cadet of the house of Kyngdon of Trehunsey, Quethiock, county Cornwall (12th century) Compiled with proofs and references to authorities from the results of researches made by the Genealogical department of the Grafton press and published in the year 1906. New York, The Grafton press, 1906. 25 p. col. pl. (coat of arms) 30 cm. "Authorities": p. (19)-25. 6-42439.   CS71.K54 1906

9757 KINGMAN. The Kingman memorial. Genealogical memoirs of the descendants of Henry and Joanna Kingman of Weymouth, Mass., U.S.A., together with a brief history of the family, in England, 1635-1898, by Bradford Kingman ... Brookline, New England illustrated historical publishing co., 1898. 1 p. l., 96 p. 24 cm. 37-21321.   CS71.K546 1898

9758 KINGMAN. The Kingman and Ordronaux families. Some records of the descendants of Henry Kingman, an Englishman, who settled at Weymouth, Mass., in 1635, and of Capt. John Ordronaux, a Frenchman, a privateer in the war of 1812, who settled in New York city in 1816, obtained from various sources and comp. by Leroy Wilson Kingman. Oswego, N.Y., Gazette printing office, 1911. 45 p., 1 l. 23½ cm. "Only seventy-five copies of this work have been printed... no. 69. L. W. K." 11-14783. CS71.K546 1911

9759 KINGMAN. Descendants of Henry Kingman. Some early generations of the Kingman family by Bradford Kingman. Boston, Press of David Clapp & son, 1912. 3 p. l., 96 p. 25 cm. Caption and running title: Kingman memorial. A sketch of the life of the author reprinted from the "Memoirs of the New England historic genealogical society" for 1904. 1 prelim. leaf. 13-12341.   CS71.K546 1912

KINGMAN. See also ISBELL, 1889

9760 KINGSBURY. Henry Kingsbury and his descendants. (By John Ward Dean of Boston) (Boston, 1859?) 4 p. 25 cm. Caption title. Reprinted from New Eng. hist. and geneal. register for April, 1859. 5-14279.   CS71.K551 1859

9761 KINGSBURY. ... A pendulous edition of Kingsbury genealogy, gathered by Rev. Addison Kingsbury ... Compiled by Joseph Addison Kingsbury ... Pittsburgh, Murdoch-Kerr press, 1901. 4 p. l., (iii)-xlviii, 5-258 p. front., illus. (coats of arms) plates. ports., facsim. 27½ cm. "Of an edition of one hundred, this is no. 63." Colored coat of arms on cover. 1-27662.   CS71.K551 1901

9762 KINGSBURY. A genealogical record comprising the early English ancestor to America, and the line of descent to Nathaniel Kingsbury of Keene, N.H., and the descendants of three daughters, viz.: Abigail Kingsbury White, Hannah Kingsbury Clark, Chloe Kingsbury Sumner. Comp. by Frank Burnside Kingsbury. Keene, N.H., Darling & company, 1904. 3 p. l., (11)-63 p. front., ports. 20½ cm. 4-22355.   CS71.K551 1904

9763 KINGSBURY. The Kingsbury directory (upward of 1600 names) Comp. by the historian of the association of Kingsbury and kindred. Northampton, Mass., Printed for the Bureau of Kingsbury ancestry by the Kingsbury box & printing co., 1904. 31 p. 24½ cm. 9-29650.   CS71.K551 1904a

9764 KINGSBURY. The genealogy of the descendants of Henry Kingsbury, of Ipswich and Haverhill, Mass.; from collections made by Frederick John Kingsbury, LL.D., ed. with extensive additions by Mary Kingsbury Talcott. (Hartford, Conn.) Hartford press: The Case, Lockwood & Brainard company, 1905. 732 p. front., illus., plates, ports., maps (1 fold.) fold. geneal. tab., facsims. 24 cm. "Three hundred copies printed." This copy not numbered. 5-35770.   CS71.K551 1905

9765 KINGSBURY. Kingsbury and allied families, a genealogical study with biographical notes, compiled and privately printed for Miss Alice E. Kingsbury by the American historical society, inc. New York, 1934. 280 p. ports., facsim., col. coats of arms. geneal. tables. 32½ cm. Title-page, dedication, initials, and tailpieces in colors. Some of the coats of arms are accompanied by guard sheets with descriptive letterpress. Bound in blue levant, gold tooled and inlaid, with leather doublures. Allied families: Scovill, Peck, Davies, Foote, Hotchkiss, Lamson and Booth. 35-14591 rev.

CS71.K551   1934

9766 KINGSBURY. Kingsbury, Scovill, Davies and allied families, genealogical, biographical. Hartford, Conn., States historical society, inc., 1937. 1 p. l., 267, (22) p. plates. ports., facsims., col. coats of arms. 28½ cm. 40-2272.

CS71.K551   1937

9767 KINGSBURY. Kingsbury-Bush, American ancestry of Wayland Briggs Kingsbury, son of Joseph B. and Hannah Brown Kingsbury, of Windham Co. Vt. and Osage, Iowa, and Flora Jane Bush Kingsbury, daughter of Alva and Eliza Moore Bush of Chautauqua Co. N.Y. and Osage, Iowa ... Redlands, Calif., 1958. 72 p. 28 cm. 58-4800.

CS71.K551   1958

9768 KINGSBURY. Kingsbury genealogy, the genealogy of the descendants of Joseph Kingsbury of Dedham, Massachusetts, together with the descendants in several lines of Henry Kingsbury of Ipswich, Massachusetts, and our Canadian cousins. Minneapolis, Printers: Burgess-Beckwith, 1962. vii, 371 p. illus., ports., col. coat of arms. 29 cm. 61-17650.

CS71.K551   1962

KINGSBURY.   See also: BASSETT, 1926
                         BENTON, 1901
                         CORLISS, 1875
                         McCOLLUM, 1936

9769 KINGSLEY. Kingsley genelogy (!) with a brief history of Joseph Kingsley and family, with records and sketches of his ancestry and descendants; by Leroy Brown ... (St. Paul? 1907) 40 p. illus. (port.) 17 cm. 7-21167.

CS71.K553   1907

9770 KINGSLEY. Kingsleys. With Christmas greetings from Richard Walden Hale. 1934. (Boston, A.C. Getchell & son, printers, 1934) 21 p. 24½ cm. "My Christmas pamphlets": p. 21. A sketch of the Kingsleys as authors, including a short discursive bibliography and a brief Kingsley anthology. 35-11381.

PR4839.K9H3

9771 KINGSLEY. Kingsley and other ancestry of the Espenscheid-Kingsley family of New York city, by Lloyd Espenschied ... New York city, 1944. 2 p. l., 8 numb. l., 3 l. fold. geneal. tables. 29 x 23 cm. Biographical sketch of the author mounted on fly-leaf. Bibliographical references: 3 leaves at end. 45-13965.

CS71.K553   1944

9772 KINGSLEY. Amos Kingsley, 1768-1847; a biography and genealogy from ancestor John Kingsley of Dorchester, 1635, to descendants in 1960. By Edna Hartshorn Deane using notes compiled by Maretta Hartshorn. Utica, N.Y., Printed by Fort Schuyler Press (c. 1961) 162 p. illus., ports. 24 cm. Bibliography: p. 147-148. 63-25435.

CS71.K553   1961

KINGSLEY.   See also: LEONARD, CS71.L58
                        RUGGLES, 1901
                        RUGGLES, 1917

9773 KINGSTON. Miramichi woodsman, by George Brooks Johnson. Richmond, Va., Press of Whittet & Shepperson (1945) 102 p. front., plates, ports., map, facsim. 24 cm. "One hundred and fifty copies ... No. 110." 47-25346.

CT275.K577J6

KINGSTONE.   See also: OLIPHANT, CS439.O6
                         TWEEDIE, 1956

9774 KINKADE. The Kinkade family in Clark county, Mo. A postscript to "Our book," 1932. By Ben F. Dixon. San Diego, Calif. (1939) 2 p. l., 7 numb. l. 26½ cm. Type-written. 42-4310.

CS71.K554   1939

KINKADE.   See also: DIXON, 1932
                       KINCAID.

KINLEY.   See KINDLEY.

9775   KINNAIRD.   The silver wedding of Lord and Lady Kinnaird, and the coming of age of the master of Kinnaird, August 1900, with a sketch of the history of the barons of Kinnaird.   Rossie Priory, Perthshire.   (Dundee, Printed by J. Leng & co.) 1900.   vi p., 1 l., (9)-116 p. front., illus., plates, ports. 19 cm.   Coat of arms on publisher's binding.   Signed: J. M. L.   15-25135.   DA816.K5S5

9776   KINNEAR.   The Kinnears and their kin; a memorial volume of history, biography and genealogy, with revolutionary and civil and Spanish war records; including manuscript of Rev. David Kinnear (1840).   Comp. by Emma Siggins White, assisted by Martha Humphreys Maltby ... Kansas City, Mo., Tiernan-Dart printing co., 1916.   xviii, 578 p. front., illus., plates, ports., col. coats of arms. 24 cm. "Authorities referred to in this volume": p. (vii) - (viii) 16-15602.   CS71.K559   1916

9777   KINNEY.   History and genealogy of a branch of the family of Kinne.   By Emerson Kinne. Syracuse, N.Y., Masters & Stone, printers, 1881.   96 p. 22 cm.   Descendants of Cyrus Kinne of Onondaga Co., N.Y. 1-1870.   CS71.K557   1881

9778   KINNEY.   Some Virginia families; being genealogies of the Kinney, Stribling, Trout, McIlhany, Milton, Rogers, Tate, Snickers, Taylor, McCormick and other families of Virginia, by Hugh Milton McIlhany, jr. ... Staunton, Va., Stoneburner & Prufer, printers, 1903.   3 p. l., 274 numb. l. 23 port. (incl. front.) 24 cm.   Printed on one side of leaf only.   3-22491.   F225.M15

9779   KINNEY.   The genealogy of Henry and Ann Kinne, pioneers of Salem, Massachusetts, by Florance Keeney Robertson, M.A.   Los Angeles, Calif., Wetzel publishing co., inc. (1947) xiii, 218 p. incl. front. (port.) 23½ cm. 47-19558.   CS71.K557   1947

9780   KINNEY.   The Kinney family.   By Edwin Warfield Beitzell.   Washington, 1948.   15 p. 28 cm. Caption title.   50-22859.   CS71.K557   1948

KINNEY.   See also: KEENEY.
                      No. 553 - Goodhue county.

KINNICUM.   See CUNNINGHAM.

9781   KINNICK.   The Kinnick family, a genealogical history of the Kinnick family of America; descendants of John Kinnick and Ann Kinnick of Davie County, North Carolina.   By Nettie Edna Waggener. Franklin, Ind., 1953.   xix, 355 p. illus., ports., maps. 24 cm. 53-34775.   CS71.K5575 1953

9782   KINNICUTT.   Record of Daniel Kinnicutt's family.   (By Field Dalee) (n. p., n. d.) geneal. tab. 56 x 43 cm. In manuscript. "Copy of record written by Field Dalee, 1808 (i. e. 1880?)" 41-41196.   CS71.K558

9783   KINNISON.   Genealogical history of William Henry Kinnison, 1853-1933, of Angus, Nuckolls County, Nebraska.   Related families: Kincannon, Day, Dykes, Norwood, Taylor, Palmer.   By Don E. Kinnison.   (Casper? Wyo.) 1956.   74 l. port., coat of arms. 28 cm. 58-29865.   CS71.K5583 1956

9784   KINSEY.   A history of Jacob Kinsey (Jacob Kintzy) and his descendants, by Wm. Kinsey ... Union Bridge, Md., The Pilot publishing company, 1934.   174, 191-202 p. illus. (incl. ports.) fold. geneal. tab. 21½ cm. 36-1635.   CS71.K559   1934

9785   KINSEY.   Kinsey, Jones County, North Carolina.   By Sybil Hyatt.   Kinston, 1948.   8 l. 28 cm. Caption title.   Typewritten.   49-13500*.   CS71.K559   1948

9786   KINSLER.   The Kinslers of South Carolina.   By William Kinsler Beckham.   (Columbia? S. C., 1964)   90 p. facsims., map. 22 cm. 65-389.   CS71.K5595   1964

9787   KINSMAN.   The Kinsman family.   Genealogical record of the descendants of Robert Kinsman, of Ipswich, Mass. from 1634 to 1875.   Comp. for Frederick Kinsman by Lucy W. Stickney.   Boston, Printed by A. Mudge & son, 1876.   vi, 258 p. front. (coat of arms) port., fold. geneal. tab. 23½ cm. Portrait mounted on verso of frontispiece.   English record and "Pedigree" comp. by Mrs. Harriet A. De Salis.   9-11458.

CS71.K56   1876

9788   KINSMAN.   ... Candlewood, an ancient neighborhood in Ipswich; with genealogies of John Brown, William Fellows, Robert Kinsman, by T. Frank Waters;   proceedings at the annual meeting December 1, 1908.   Salem, Mass., Salem press, 1909.   1 p. 1., 161 p. front., plates, maps. 23½ cm. (Publications of the Ipswich historical society.   XVI-XVII of the Proceedings of the Ipswich historical society.   10-15750.

F74.I618 v. 16-17

KINSMAN.   See also BROWN, F74.I618 v. 16

9789   KINSOLVING.   Early history of Virginia and Maryland and seven centuries of lines (by) Wythe Leigh Kinsolving ... Studies in pre-American and early American colonial times ... (Halifax? Va., pref. 1935)   54 p. 21½ cm. 36-25771 rev.   F225.K56

KINTON.   See KENTON.

9790   KINZIE.   ... Narrative of the massacre at Chicago (Saturday), August 15, 1812, and of some preceding events.   (By Juliette Augusta (Magill) Kinzie)   2d ed., with illustrations, additional notes, and index ... Chicago, Fergus printing company, 1914.   2 p. 1., 7-71 p. 1 illus., plates. 21 cm. (Fergus' historical series, no. 30)   Foreword signed: G. H. F. (i. e. George Harris Fergus)   First edition, Chicago, 1844.   "The Kinzie family in America": p. 45-54.   "John Kinzie, a sketch, by Eleanor Lytle Kinzie Gordon": p. 55-64.   15-19631 rev.   F536.F35 no. 30

9791   KIP.   (Kipp family tree.   The descendants of Jacobus Kipp, 1632 to 1807)   (n. p. 18 -?)   geneal. tab.   50 x 45 cm.   Photostat reproduction (positive) of pen and ink drawing.   38M1901T.   CS71.K57   18 -

9792   KIP.   Historical notes of the family of Kip of Kipsburg and Kip's Bay, New York.   (By William Ingraham Kip) (Albany) Priv. print. (J. Munsell) 1871.   49 p. 22½ cm.   Title vignette (coat of arms) 9-11443.

CS71.K57   1871

9793   KIP.   Contributions to the history of the Kip family of New York and New Jersey.   By Edwin R. Purple ... New York, Priv. print., 1877.   24 p. front. (port.) 27½ cm. Reprinted with additions from "Contributions to the history of the ancient families in New York."   "Edition 75 copies.   no. 46."   9-11457.   CS71.K57   1877

9794   KIP.   Abstract of title of Kip's Bay farm in the city of New York, with all known maps relating thereto ... Also, the early history of the Kip family and the genealogy as refers to the title.   By John J. Post ... New York, S. V. Constant, 1894.   2 p. 1., x, 2056 p. front., fold. maps. 26½ cm. 9-11455.

CS71.K57   1894

9795   KIP.   History of the Kip family in America, by Frederic Ellsworth Kip ... assisted by Margarita Lansing Hawley ... (Boston, Hudson printing co., c. 1928)   4 p. 1., (13)-440, xxii p. illus., col. plates, ports., maps (1 fold.) facsims., 3 col. coats of arms (incl. front.) 27 cm.   29-13558.   CS71.K57   1928

9796   KIP.   Six generations of the Kip family in California.   By Carroll Peeke.   (San Francisco)   1969 (c. 1968)   6 p. 23 cm. Bibliography: p. (iv) 77-1254.   CS71.K57   1969

KIP.   See also: CHIPP, 1933
RAPALJE, CS69.H7
VAN NORDEN, 1923
WASHINGTON, CS69.W5

KIPLING.   See: MACDONALD, 1960
POWELL, 1891a

KIPP.   See KIP.

KIRACOFE.   See BAKER, 1964a

9797   KIRBY.   The Kirbys of New England; a history of the descendants of John Kirby of Middletown, Conn. and of Joseph Kirby of Hartford, Conn., and of Richard Kirby of Sandwich, Mass. together with genealogies of the Burgis, White and Maclaren families, and the ancestry of John Drake, of Windsor, Conn.   By Melatiah Everett Dwight.   New York, The Trow print, 1898.   4 p. l., 451 p. front. (coat of arms) plates, ports.   25 cm.   No. 151 of an edition of 185 copies.   Portrait facing p. 148 wanting.   9-11454.

CS71.K58   1898

KIRBY.   See also: ABBOT, 1926
RANNEY, F104.C8A2

KIRCHER.   See GRIM, 1934

KIRCHMAYER.   In vertical file under PRANKE family.   Ask reference librarian for this material.

9798   KIRK.   Historic-genealogy of the Kirk family, as established by Roger Kirk, who settled in Nottingham, Chester County, province of Pennsylvania, about the year 1714 ... By Charles H. Stubbs, M. D. ... Lancaster, Pa., Wylie & Griest, 1872.   xxxv. (1) p., 2 l., 252 p. 19½ cm.   2-4013.

CS71.K59   1872

9799   KIRK.   Genealogy of the descendants of John Kirk,   Born 1660, at Alfreton, in Derbyshire, England.   Died 1705, in Darby Township, Chester (now Delaware) County, Pennsylvania.   Comp. by Miranda S. Roberts ... Ed. by Gilbert Cope ... Doylestown, Pa., Press of the Intelligencer company, 1912-13.   viii, 721 p. front., plates, ports., facsim., coat of arms.   28 cm.   13-24652.   CS71.K59   1912

9800   KIRK.   The Kirk and Wilson family tree, by Clarence K. Wilson.   Cincinnati, O., The Hobson press, incorporated, 1943.   ix, (1) p., 1 l., 128 p. incl. front. (port.) 22 cm.   Reproduced from type-written copy.   Includes also the Garrison and Hobday families.   43-17336.   CS71.K59   1943

9801   KIRK.   The Kirk and Wilson family tree.   2d ed.   By Clarence Kirk Wilson.   (Baltimore, Deford, 1967)   xiv, 240 p. illus., ports. 24 cm.   Pages 238-249 blank for "Notes and dates."   Includes bibliographical references. 68-798.   CS71.K59   1967

KIRK.   See also: BARTON, 1941
HALL, 1908-9
TRUESDELL, 1960

9802   KIRKALDY.   A short history of the family of Kirkaldy of Grange, Monkwearmouth and London.   Comp. from various sources by James Kirkaldy ... For private circulation only.   London, Crowther & Goodman, printers, 1903.   31 p. illus. (coats of arms) 2 fold. geneal. tab. 31 cm.   "List of authorities": p. (3) 17-23919.

CS479.K55

9803   KIRKBRIDE.   A brief history of the Kirkbride family; with special reference to the descendants of David Kirkbride, 1775-1830, prepared by Sherman A. Kirkbride.   (Alliance, O., Alliance leader print) 1913.   64 p. illus. (incl. ports.) 23½ cm.   This history is based on a little booklet entitled "Domestic portraiture of the Kirkbride family, published in 1824.   Blank pages for "The Kirkbride family" records (16 at end) 25-19249.   CS71.K592   1913

9804   KIRKLAND.   The Kirkland of Kirtland family.   By V. C. Sanborn.   Reprinted from N. England historical and genealogical register for Jan., 1894.   Boston, Press of D. Clapp & son, 1894.   8 p. 23½ cm.   17-31804.   CS71.K593   1894

9805   KIRKLAND.   The genealogy of certain descendants of Nathaniel Kirtland of Lynn, Mass., 1635. By Edwin Simpson Hartshorn.   (Washington) 1948.   7, (1) l. 28 cm.   Typewritten.   Bibliography: leaf (8) 50-21690.

CS71.K593   1948

KIRKLAND.   See also: BATES, CS439.B35
CRAIG, 1891
SANBORN, 1894
SOUTHWORTH, 1903
STEWART, 1960

9806   KIRKPATRICK.   The Kirkpatrick memorial; or, Biographical sketches of father and son, and a selection from the sermons of the Rev. Jacob Kirkpatrick, jr., the sketches by the Rev. George Hale, D. D.   Ed. by the Rev. Wm. M. Blackburn.   Philadelphia, Westcott & Thompson, 1867.   312 p. 2 port. (incl. front.) 20 cm.   "The Kirkpatrick family": p. 13-32.   3-31337.   BX9225.K6B6

9807   KIRKPATRICK.   Chronicles of the Kirkpatrick family, by Alexander de Lapere Kirkpatrick. (Privately printed) (London, Printed by T. Moring, De La More press, 189-?)   64 p. 28½ cm.   Title vignette (coat of arms) Blank pages for "Births, Marriages, Deaths and Our records" (57-64) 19-3668.
                                                                                                CS499.K7

9808   KIRKPATRICK.   Major Abraham Kirkpatrick and his descendants.   Comp. by one of the descendants.   (Pittsburgh, J. P. Durbin, printer, 1911)   2 p. l., (7)-48 p. 23½ cm.   Dedication signed: Kirk Q. Bigham. Contains sketches of the Oldham, Shaler, Cowan, Lewis, and Bigham families.   13-12768.
                                                                                    CS71.K595   1911

9809   KIRKPATRICK.   ... The Kirkpatricks, by John L. Shawver; origin of the family and the name, as given by old family records long in possession of the family, together with a sketch of Sir Roger Kirkpatrick and his times.   Morrison, Ill., The Shawver publishing co., 1926.   (23) p. 17 cm. (American families series) 36-22552.   CS479.K56   1926

9810   KIRKPATRICK.   Capt. John Kirkpatrick of New Jersey, 1739-1822, and his sisters, Mrs. Joseph Linn, and Mrs. Stephen Roy, a genealogy by William Clinton Armstrong ... New Brunswick, N. J., J. Heidingsfeld company, 1927.   81 p. front., plates, ports., map, facsim. 24 cm.   Bibliography: p. 76-77. 28-18808.
                                                                                    CS71.K595   1927

9811   KIRKPATRICK.   ... Kirkpatrick family genealogy, compiled by John L. Shawver.   Morrison, Ill., The Shawver publishing co., 1930.   (134) p. 17 cm. (American families series) 35-14588.
                                                                                    CS71.K595   1930

9812   KIRKPATRICK.   John Kirkpatrick of East Tennessee.   By Elkana Spears McCollough. (Knoxville, Tenn., 1938)   6 numb. l. 28 cm.   Type-written. Signed: E. Spears McCollough.   "Paper ... read at the unveiling and dedication of the government memorial to John Kirkpatrick ... in Bent Creek cemetary near Whitesburg, Tenn., on Sunday, Sept. 18, 1938." Accompanied by newspaper clipping, type-written account and 4 photographs of the Memorial. 38M5852T.   CS71.K595   1938

9813   KIRKPATRICK.   John Kirkpatrick of East Tennessee, by E. Spears McCollough.   (In The Lookout. Zella Armstrong, publisher. Chattanooga, Tenn., 1938. 30 cm.   vol. lv, no. 10) 38M5851T.
                                                                                    CS71.K595   1938a

9814   KIRKPATRICK.   David Kirkpatrick of Missouri.   (Knoxville, Tenn., 1938)   By Elkana Spears McCollough.   4 numb. l. 28 cm.   Type-written. Signed: E. Spears McCollough. 38M5853T.   CS71.K595   1938b

9815   KIRKPATRICK.   James Kirpatrick of Alabama.   By Elkana Spears McCollough.   (Knoxville, Tenn., 1938)   5 numb. l. 28 cm.   Type-written. Signed E. Spears McCollough. 38M5854T.
                                                                                    CS71.K595   1938c

9816   KIRKPATRICK.   William Kirkpatrick, died November 20, 1838: immigrant ancestor from Ireland to America, Clermont County, Ohio, and Edgar County, Illinois; a directory of his descendants.   By Ellen (Kirkpatrick) Korbitz.   (Burlington? Iowa, 1958)   30 p. illus. 22 cm. 58-36403.
                                                                                    CS71.K595   1958

9817   KIRKPATRICK.   John and Priscilla Kirkpatrick of Prince William County, Va., and their descendants; records.   By Martin Glen Kirkpatrick.   Skyland? N. C., 1959.   68 l. 29 cm. 60-24620.
                                                                                    CS71.K595   1959

        KIRKPATRICK.   See also: BARCKLEY, 1931
                                   HYNES, 1941-2
                                   SHOBE, 1919
                                   SHOBE, 1950

        KIRNER.   See KÖRNER.

KIRTLAND.   See KIRKLAND.

KIS.   In vertical file under PRANKE family.   Ask reference librarian for this material.

KISCH.   In vertical file under PRANKE family.   Ask reference librarian for this material.

KISE.   See JARRATT, 1957

KISEL.   See KIESSEL.

KISHMAN.   See GOODLOCK, 1951

9818   KISLING.   The Kisling and Mauzey families.   By Richard Mauzey.   CS71.M453   1911

      KISLING.   See also: GRIM, 1934
                            MAUZY, 1911

      KISS.   In vertical file under PRANKE family.   Ask reference librarian for this material.

9819   KISSAM.   The Kissam family in America from 1644 to 1825.   By Edward Kissam.   New York, Dempsey & Carroll's art press, 1892.   94 p. front. (coat of arms) 18½ cm. 9-11452.
                                                          CS71.K615   1892

      KISSAM.   See also STRANG, 1915

      KISSEL.   See KIESSEL.

9820   KISTLER.   Kistler families descended from George Kistler, jr., of Berks county, Pennsylvania, by Mrs. Floride Kistler Sprague.   Chauncey, O.   (Ann Arbor, Mich., Lithoprinted by Edwards brothers, inc.) 1944.   2 p. l., 46 p. incl. illus. (ports.) coats of arms) geneal. tab. 28 x 22 cm. 44-35431.
                                                          CS71.K616   1944

      KITCAT.   See HUGHES, CS439.H768

9821   KITCHEL.   Robert Kitchel, and his descendants.   From 1604 to 1879.   Compiled by H. D. Kitchel.   New York, J. P. Prall, printer, 1879.   80 p. 23½ cm. 24-12326.
                                                          CS71.K63   1879

9822   KITCHEL.   Robert Kitchel and his descendants.   From 1604 to 1879.   Compiled by H. D. Kitchel.   New York, J. P. Prall, printer, 1879.   80 numb. l. 23½ cm. Photostat (negative) Imperfect: leaf 1-6 including t. -p. missing. 39M4506T.
                                                            CS71.K63   1879a

9823   KITCHEL.   Genealogical memoranda relating to the family of Kitchell.   London, Mitchell and Hughes, 1883.   8 p. coats of arms. 29 x 22 cm. Published also in the Miscellanea genealogica et heraldica. London, 1884. n. s., v. 2. p. 398-400, 405-407. 17-21458.
                                                            CS439.K73   1883

9824   KITCHEL.   John Kitchel and Esther Peck, their ancestors, descendants and some kindred families, comp. in 1912 by George Chalmers McCormick ... Fort Collins, Col., Press of the Fort Collins express, 1913.   134. (2) p. incl. front. (port. group) ports. 20½ cm. 13-2453.
                                                            CS71.K63   1913

      KITCHEL.   See also: CARMAN, 1935
                              CORY, 1937a
                              WHALLON, 1934

      KITCHELL.   See: CORY, 1937
                         KITCHEL.

9825   KITCHEN.   Tucson, Tubac, Tumacacori, Tohell.   A 1st limited ed.   By Gil Procter.
Tucson, Arizona Silhouettes, 1956.   110 p. illus. 24 cm. 56-42535.   F811.P76

KITCHING.   See ROBSON, 1892

9826   KITE.   The Kite family.   A fragmentary sketch of the family from its origin in the 9th century
to the present day.   (n. p., 1908?)   122 p. incl. coat of arms. plates. 20 cm. Dedication signed: Virginia A. Kite. 24-12334.
                                                                          CS71.K635   1908

        KITE.   See also: CONRAD, 1957
                            KIGHT.

    KITSON.   See PITMAN, CS439.P62

9827   KITTELLE.   The Ketel family, also (Ketele, Kettele, Kettel, Kittelle and Kittle) by Sumner
Ely Wetmore Kittelle ... Washington, D. C., 1946.   67 p. front. (coat of arms) ports. 23½ cm. "References": p. 66.
46-18938.   CS71.K637   1946

9828   KITTLE.   Some descendants of Edward Kittle and his wife Susanna Godfrey of Taunton,
Massachusetts, compiled by Ella Foy O'Gorman (Mrs. Michael Martin O'Gorman) 1934.   (Washington, D.C., 1935)   2 p. l., 17 numb. l. 28 cm. Type-written. References: Leaf (!) 28 cm. 38M3359T.
                                                                          CS71.K638   1935

9829   KITTREDGE.   The Kittredge family in America, by Mable T. Kittredge.   Rutland, Vt., The
Tuttle publishing company, inc. (1936)   iv p., 1 l., 215 p. front. (col. coat of arms) pl., ports. 24 cm. 37-10367.
                                                                          CS71.K6385   1936

9830   KITTRELL.   Kittrell family, by Edythe Rucker Whitley.   Nashville, Tenn., 1936.   cover-title.
12 numb. l. 19 cm. Mimeographed. 36-30610.   CS71.K639   1936

9831   KITTRELL.   Our family mosaic; (the Kittrells, the Earls, the Joneses, Gills, Ellingtons,
Rowland, Mitchells, Fullers, Youngs, and others, written by Mrs. U. B. Alexander.   Kittrell, N.C.,
1959)   (40) p. 16 cm. Cover title. Pages (39) - (40) blank for "other data." "A second postscript" (3 p. in MS) inserted. 68-35396 rev.
                                                                          CS71.K639   1959

    KITTS.   See also NEWLIN, 1942

9832   KLAPP.   The lineage of the brothers, John Ludwig and George Valentine Klapp.   By Richard E.
Clapp.   (Denville? N.J.) 1963.   83 l. 29 cm. 63-5341.   CS71.K6392   1963

        KLAPP.   See also CLAPP.

        KLAPPER.   See SNYDER, 1958

9833   KLECKNER.   The Kleckner Fessler families in Berk's, Schuylkill, Northampton, and Lancaster Counties, Pennsylvania.   By David Spurgeon Jenkins.   (Annapolis? Md., 1957?)   54 l. 30 cm.
Includes bibliography. 59-34529.   CS71.K3694   1957

9834   KLEE.   A genealogy and history of some of the descendants of Johan Nicholas Klee of Bern
Township, Berks County, Pennsylvania; Clays of Pennsylvania Dutch ancestry.   Compiled and written
by Don C. Shaw.   Chicago, 1968.   ix, 229 p. illus., facsims., ports. 28 cm. Bibliography: p. 204. 72-1285.
                                                                          CS71.K6395   1968

        KLEIN.   In vertical file under PRANKE family.   Ask reference librarian for this material.

        KLEIN.   See also: JOHNSON, 1956
                            KLINE.

    KLEINGINNA.   See KLEINJENNI.

9835   KLEINJENNI. Johannes Kleinjenni (Kleinginna) of Berks County, Pa., and some of his descendants. By Ralph Marion Seeley. Candor, N.Y., 1959.   21 p. 22 cm. 65-49783.
CS71.K6397   1959

KLEISER. See LEWIS, 1901

9836   KLEPPINGER. Kleppinger-Clippinger family history, by Stanley J. Kleppinger. Bethlehem, Pa., Bethlehem printing company, 1928.   209 p. illus. (incl. ports.) 23½ cm. 29-4869.
CS71.K64   1928

9837   KLEPPINGER. Kleppinger, Clippinger, Klepinger family history. By Stanley Jeremiah Kleppinger. Allentown, Pa., Printed by G. P. Schlicher, 1956.   351 p. illus., ports., coat of arms, geneal. table. 24 cm. 57-42220.
CS71.K64   1956

KLICKNER. See KLECKNER.

9838   KLINE. The descendants of Hans (Johannus) Klein, by John M. Kline ... assisted by Thomas K. Vincent ... (Washington, D.C., c.1939)   1 p. l., 22 p. port. 18½ cm. 39-22761.   CS71.K647   1939

9839   KLINE. Kline and Young families of the Mohawk valley, by Roscoe L. Whitman. (Westfield, N.J.) 1941.   1 v. plates. 29 cm. Loose-leaf. Reproduced from type-written copy. "Authorities consulted": p. 59. 42-16082.
CS71.K647   1941

9840   KLINE. The Kline klan, compiled by Helen Kline, M. P. Whitenight (and) Mrs. Henry Stoll. Wauseon, Ohio, Gilson Lithographing Co., 1960.   173 p. illus. 24 cm. 60-44550.   CS71.K647   1960

9841   KLING. Genealogical history of John Ludwig Kling and his descendants, 1755-1924. (By Margaret E. Kling) (Amsterdam, N.Y., Printed by Wm. J. Kline & son, inc., c.1924)   145 p. front. (port.) 23 cm. 24-16307.   CS71.K65   1924

KLINGER. See WEISER, 1960

9842   KLINGLER. Klingler family (tree) in vertical file.   Ask reference librarian for this material.

9843   KLOCK. Klock-Clock (family.) By Helen Laura (Clock) Williams. (Euclid, Ohio, 1949)   a-c, 40, 10, (22) l. 29 cm. Cover title. Supplement, with index: 22 leaves at end. 51-29688.   CS71.K657   1949

9844   KLOCK. Klock-Clock (genealogy) By Helen Laura (Clock) Williams. (Euclid, Ohio, 1952?)   a-c, 103, 40 p. 30 cm. Title from label mounted on cover. 53-15175 rev.   CS71.K657   1952
—— Supplement. Euclid, Ohio.   no. 29 cm.   CS71.K657

9845   KLOCK. Klock-Clock (genealogy) Rev. By Helen Laura (Clock) Williams. (Euclid, Ohio) 1960.   1 v. (loose-leaf) 29 cm. 61-39892.   CS71.K657   1960

KLOCK. See also NELLIS, F129.P15M17

KLÖCKNER. See KLECKNER.

9846   KLOPFENSTEIN. Klopfenstein family record; the chronology of the descendants of Michael Klopfenstein, 1757-1925, compiled and published by John Henry Klopfenstein. Grabill, Ind. (c.1926)   68 p. 28 cm. 26-15031.   CS71.K66   1926

KLOPPER. See CLOPPER.

KLOSKY. See LEDLIE, 1961

9847   KLOTZ. The story of Hackettstown, New Jersey, 1754-1955. Hackettstown, Hackettstown National Bank (1955)   199 p. illus. 29 cm. 55-28895.   F144.H14N8

9848   KLUMPH. Klumph genealogy and early Klumph history. By Richard Amidon Klumph. 2d and rev. ed. (Kalamazoo, Mich.) 1960.   68 p. 23 cm. 61-39251.   CS71.K665   1961

9849   KLUMPH.   Descendants, 1763-1966 of John Thomas Klumph (no. 1) 1729-1818 and early Klumph history.   By Richard Amidon Klumph.   (Kalamazoo, Mich., 1967)   383 p. port. 24 cm.   Second ed. published in 1960 under title: Klumph genealogy and early Klumph history.   67-5296.   CS71.K665   1967

KLUPPELBERG.   See No. 9847 - Hackettstown.

KLUPPER.   See CLOPPER.

9850   KNAGGS.   History of the Knaggs family of Ohio and Michigan.   Historical, biographical and genealogical.   Ed. by Robert B. Ross.   Detroit, C. M. Burton, 1902.   56 p. illus. (incl. ports., maps) 31 cm.   In triple columns.   3-14589.   CS71.K67   1902

9851   KNAPP.   Pedigree of Mathew Grenville Samwell Knapp, of Little Linford, Bucks, and of Arthur John Knapp, of Llanfoist house, Clifton Down, Bristol.   Privately printed.   London, Mitchell and Hughes, printers, 1879.   6 p. 28 cm.   Reprinted from "Miscellanea genealogica et heraldica," vol. III, new series, 1880.   p. 261-264.   17-23924.   CS439.K75   1879

9852   KNAPP.   The Knapp family in America.   A genealogy of the descendants of William Knapp who settled in Watertown, Mass., in 1630.   Including also a tabulated pedigree, paternal and maternal, of Hiram Knapp, by Arthur Mason Knapp ... Boston, Mass.   (Fort Hill press) 1909.   76 p. front. (port.)   2 fold. geneal. tab. 24 cm.   Edited by George B. and Katharine Knapp.   12-23782.   CS71.K675   1909

9853   KNAPP.   A history of the chief English families bearing the name of Knapp.   Comp. by Oswald Greenwaye Knapp ... Illustrated with portraits, views, etc.   (London) Priv. print, for the author by the St. Catherine press, 1911.   2 p. l., x, 288 p. front., plates, ports. 29 cm.   The American family: p. 189-234. 13-10098.   CS439.K75   1911

9854   KNAPP.   A Knapp line back to Adam with Huguenot, Crusade, and Magna charta connections.   By Alfred Averill Knapp.   (Winter Park, Fla., 1960)   10 l. 29 cm. 62-59757.   CS71.K675   1960

9855   KNAPP.   ... Bulletin.   Knapp family association.   v. 1 -   (New York?) 1937 -   v. 23 cm. Caption title. Editor: 1937 -   Mrs. F. K. Dickinson. 37-16846.   CS71.K675   1937

9856   KNAPP.   We Knapps thought it was nice, by Edward Spring Knapp.   New York, Priv. print., 1940.   211 p., 2 l. incl. front., plates, ports. 27 cm.   "The edition ... is strictly limited to two hundred numbered copies for private distribution ... It has been printed at the Marchbanks press in New York.   This is copy number 152." 42-2483.   CT275.K63A3

9857   KNAPP.   Family memories, by Shepherd Knapp.   (Worcester? Mass.)   Priv. print., 1946.   1 p. l., 73 p. fold. geneal. tab. 29 x 22½ cm. Errata slips inserted. 47-15735.   CS71.K675   1946

9858   KNAPP.   The ancestral lines of Mary Lenore Knapp.   By Alfred Averill Knapp.   Peoria, Ill., 1947 (i.e. 1948)   181 p. 24 cm. 48-9963*.   CS71.K675   1948

9859   KNAPP.   George Knapp, of England, and some of his descendants in America.   By Alfred Averill Knapp.   Winter Park, Fla., 1952.   16 l. 28 cm. 52-67542.   CS71.K675   1952

9860   KNAPP.   Job Knapp and some of his descendants.   By Alfred Averill Knapp.   Winter Park, Fla., 1952.   11 l. 28 cm. 52-68603.   CS71.K675   1952a

9861   KNAPP.   Nicholas Knapp genealogy.   By Alfred Averill Knapp.   Winter Park, Fla., 1953.   xiii, 900 p. illus., ports., col. coat of arms, facsims. 29 cm. 53-4353 rev.   CS71.K675   1953
—— Supplement.   Winter Park, Fla., 1956.   105 l. 28 cm.   CS71.K675   1953 Suppl.

9862   KNAPP.   Roger Knapp of New Haven, Conn., 1638-1647, and some of his descendants; a genealogy founded upon research of, and material collected by, Charles Ruggles Knapp (and others) By Alfred Averill Knapp.   Winter Park, Fla., 1959.   38 l. 29 cm. 60-3683.   CS71.K675   1959

KNAPP.   See also: BRUMBACH, 1961
KEOGH, 1926
LINDLEY, 1950
REYNOLDS, 1959

9863   KNARR.   Daniel Knarr and Lucinda Ault.   By Nellie Wallace Reeser.   (York? Pa., c.1955)
106 p. illus. 29 cm. 56-31614.   CS71.K676   1955

9864   KNARR.   A charted record of the Abraham Knerr family in America.   By Nellie Wallace
Reeser.   (Indianapolis, 1969)   636 p. 23 x 37 cm. Title page, foreword, and index in typescript; records in MS. on printed
geneal. forms entitled: One family group records. 78-10621 MARC.   CS71.K676   1969

9865   KNATCHBULL.   Kentish family.   By Sir Hughe Montgomery Knatchbull Hugessen.   London,
Methuen (1960)   xvi, 269 p. illus., ports., fold. geneal. tables. 26 cm. Includes bibliographical references. 60-51963.
CS439.K76   1960

KNATCHBULL.   See also BRYDGES, 1834

9866   KNAUSS.   History and genealogy of the Knauss family in America, tracing back the records to
Ludwig Knauss to the year 1723, comp. and arranged by James Owen Knauss ... and Tilghman John
Knauss ... Emaus, Pa., Knauss family association, inc., 1915.   242 p. front., plates, ports., col. coat of arms.
24 cm. 15-18261.   CS71.K678   1915

9867   KNAUSS.   Knauss genealogy; Luke Knauss (1633-1713) of Düdelsheim, Germany, and his
American descendants, compiled by Wilbur Lewis King ... Bethlehem, Priv. print., 1930.
v, 239 p., 1 l. front. (col. coat of arms) plates, ports. 23½ cm   30-27677.   CS71.K678   1930

9868   KNEASS.   ... Memorials of the Kneass family of Philadelphia.   Contributed by Miss Anna J.
Magee.   (In Genealogical society of Pennsylvania. Publications. Philadelphia, 1920. 25 cm. v. 7, p. 107-126). Compiled by J.
Granville Leach. 21-8414.   F146.G32 vol. 7

9869   KNEELAND.   Some royal, noble, and colonial ancestors.   Augusta, Me., Printed by the Kennebec
journal, c. 1959.   149 p. 27 cm. 59-46892.   CS71.D26   1959

KNEELAND.   See also MASON, E171.A53 vol. 19 p. 379-86

9870   KNEISLY.   Kneisly genealogy, copyright ... by Harry Loren Kneisly ... Including the names
of 685 descendants, and relatives of the earliest residents in America of whom records have been obtained, and references to 150 others believed to be related ... (Reading, Pa., Miller printing and
lithographing co., c. 1932)   46 p. 23 cm. 32-10157.   CS71.K69   1932

KNERR.   See KNARR.

KNEVET.   See CLOPTON, 1939

9871   KNICKERBOCKER.   The Knickerbacker or Knickerbocker family, by George Castor Martin
from mss. notes by Mrs. Alfred H. Massey.   Frankford, Philadelphia, Martin & Allardyce, 1912.
cover-title, 7 p. 19½ cm. Edition of twenty copies. 12-975.   CS71.K70   1912

9872   KNICKERBOCKER.   Sketches of allied families Knickerbacker-Viele, historical and genealogical, to which is added an appendix containing family data, by Kathlyne Knickerbacker Viele.   New
York, T. A. Wright, 1916.   5 p. l., 9-134 p. front. (facsim.) plates, ports. 24½ cm. "Limited edition of seventy-five copies of
which this is no. 27." Contents. - pt. I. The Knickerbackers of Schaghticoke. - pt. II. Cornelis Volkertszen (Velius), director of the New
Netherland company and ancestor of the Viele family of New York state. 16-17969.   CS71.K70   1916

9873   KNIGHT.   Chawton manor and its owners; a family history, by William Austen Leigh ... and
Montagu George Knight ... London, Smith, Elder & co., 1911.   4 p. l., 219 p. incl. illus., plans, facsims.,
v geneal. tab. front., plates, ports. 27 cm. 12-4496.   DA690.C47A8

9874 KNIGHT. The Knight family, by Joseph C. Martindale, M. D. Frankford, Phila., Martin & Allardyce, 1911. cover-title, 16 p. 19½ cm. 12-25489. CS71.K725 1911

9875 KNIGHT. Genealogy of the Knight, Walton, Woodson, Lamar, Daniel, Benning, Cobb, Jackson, Grant and other Georgia families. Including biographies of many distinguished members. By Lucien Lamar Knight ... (n. p., 193-) 3 p. l., 242 numb. l. 28 cm. Type-written. 37-7888. CS71.K725 193-

9876 KNIGHT. Knight and allied families, genealogical and biographical, prepared and privately printed for Nancy J. (Knight) Wyeth by the American historical society, inc. New York, 1932. 105 p. port., col. coats of arms. 33 cm. Alternate pages blank. Title-page ornamented in colors; initials; tail-pieces. Allied families: Brock, Brackett, Thomes and Ingersoll. Bound in blue levant, gold tooled and inlaid, with leather doublures. 33-1911 rev.
CS71.K725 1932

9877 KNIGHT. The Knight family in Dallas, with the descendants of Obediah (!) W. Knight, compiled by E. B. Comstock, and V. S. Albertson. (Dallas?) 1932. 3 p. l., ii-iii numb. l., 39 numb. l., 9 l. ports., fold. plan. 25½ cm. Typewritten, with printed t. -p. Imprint date on cover: 1933. Two unnumbered leaves inserted between 7-8 and 36-37 respectively. Plan of "The Obadiah Knight farm" is a blue-print. 34-8467. CS71.K725 1932a

9878 KNIGHT. The Jesse Knight family; Jesse Knight, his forebears and family, by Jesse William Knight ... (Salt Lake City) The Deseret news press, 1940. 139 p. front., plates, ports. 20½ cm. 41-1646.
CS71.K725 1940

9879 KNIGHT. The Knight family. By Augusta Charlotte (Dixon) Clarendon. (n. p., 1946?) 10 l. 28 cm. Caption title. Typewritten (carbon copy) 48-19710*. CS71.K725 1946

9880 KNIGHT. Knight family records. (A history of the long ago, to the present time, 640-1951) By Sarah Ann Knight. (Bellefontaine, Ohio, 1952, c.1951) unpaged. illus. 28 cm. 52-24872.
CS71.K725 1952

9881 KNIGHT. Knight family; (also) Albertson, Bennett, Gardner, Harding, Schultz, Thorn (and) Wisner (families. By Ray Roberts Knight. Minneapolis, 1952?) 1 v. 28 cm. 54-19893.
CS71.K725 1952a

9882 KNIGHT. Geneology (sic) of Knight family, prior to 1682 to 1957, et seq. By Edward Hussey Knight. (Indianapolis, 1957) 10 l. 31 cm. 61-40556. CS71.K725 1957

KNIGHT. See also: BARBER, DA690. L982C6
GILMAN, 1929
LLOYD, 1912
MOORE, 1918
ROBINSON, 1894
THIGPEN, 1961

9883 KNIGHTLY. Stemmata et propagationes antique familiae de Knightley. Copied from the original roll in the possession of Sir Rainald Knightly, bart., of Fawsley. (London) Priv. print., 1867. 20, (1) p. front., illus. (coats of arms) 32 cm. An edition of twenty-five copies printed. "Reprinted from "Miscellanea genealogica et heraldica.' " 16-8328. CS439.K8

9884 KNIPE. Early Knipe families of Pennsylvania (including the male line of descent to the present generation) By James Lloyd Knipe. Lancaster, Pa., 1949. Microfilm copy (positive) of typescript. Collation of the original, as determined from the film: 593 l. Mic 58-6230. Microfilm 4341 CS
Microfilm reading room

9885 KNISKERN. Some of the descendants of Johann Peter Kniskern of Schoharie County, New York, born circa 1685, died November 11, 1759. Petersburg, Va., Plummer Print. Co., 1960. 470 p. 24 cm. 60-39972. CS71.K728 1960

9886 KNISS. Kniss and allied families, by Frederic P. Van Duzee. Burlington, Vt., Chedwato Service, 1965. 55 p. 28 cm. 66-40178. CS71.K7283 1965

9887   KNOLLYS.   A treatise on the law of adulterine bastardy, with a report of the Banbury case, and of all other cases bearing upon the subject.   By Sir Harris Nicolas ... London, W. Pickering, 1836.   xvi, 288, 288b-288c, 289-588 p. 22 cm. "List of authorities and cases stated": p. (xv)-xvi. "Case of the earldom of Banbury (proceedings before the Committee for privileges of the House of lords. 1808-1813, on the petition of William Knollys, claiming to be Earl of Banbury)": p. 289-554. 38-13244.   LAW

      KNOLLYS.   See also KNOWLES.

9888   KNOTT.   A sketch of the Knott family from researches made by John O. Knott ... (n. p., 19 -) cover-title, (3) p. illus. (port.) 22½ cm. 38-14710.   CS71.K729   19 -

      KNOWLES.   See: BROWN, 1929   MAUNSELL, CS439.M37
                        EVERTON, 1942   PETTY, BX5195.T5B6
                        KING, CS439.K7   SHERIDAN, 1875
                        LLOYD, 1912   WILBUR, 1936

9889   KNOWLTON.   Statue of Colonel Thomas Knowlton: ceremonies at the unveiling.   Hartford, Conn., Press of the Case, Lockwood & Brainerd co., 1895.   53 p. front., illus. (map) 23½ cm. "Historical address by P. Henry Woodward": p. 9-40. "Paternal lineage of Col. Thomas Knowlton, by Dr. Ashbel Woodward": p. 45-53. 9-23198.
                                                      E263.C5S7

9890   KNOWLTON.   The history and genealogy of the Knowltons of England and America.   By the Rev. Charles Henry Wright Stocking ... New York, The Knickerbocker press, 1897.   xi, 1 l., 597 p. front., plates, ports., facsim., coat of arms. 24½ cm. 9-11449.   CS71.K73   1897

9891   KNOWLTON.   Prospectus and year book containing the history, constitution, by-laws, list of officers and members of the Knowlton association of America from its organization, with an account of the first and second reunions.   Compiled and edited by William Herrick Griffith ... published under the auspices of Miner Rockwell Knowlton ... and William Herrick Griffith ... and presented by them to association members.   Albany, N.Y., S.H.Wentworth, printer, 1897.   88 p. 22½ cm. 15-2147.
                                                      CS71.K73   1897a

9892   KNOWLTON.   Errata and addenda to Dr. Stocking's History and genealogy of the Knowltons of England and America, together with a complete index to both books and a supplement with copies of old wills, administration records, etc.   With the approval of Rev. Charles Henry Wright Stocking, D.D., comp. for the Knowlton association of America, by George Henry Knowlton ... Boston, The Everett press company, 1903.   3 p. l., 234 p. ports. 24½ cm. 5-14809.   CS71.K73   1903

      KNOWLTON.   See also: FLAGG, 1903
                              SHAW, 1920
                              WHITNEY, 1925

9893   KNOX.   Genealogical tree of the Knoxes.   Edinburgh, J. Menzies (1858)   geneal. tab. 76 x 51 cm. A copy of the "Genealogical account of the Knoxes", which was in the family of the late James Knox, minister of Scone, with additions to the present period, collected by the Rev. David Crawford of Edinburgh.   22-13853.   CS479.K6   1858

9894   KNOX.   Genealogical memoirs of John Knox and of the family of Knox, by the Rev. Charles Rogers ... London, The Grampian club, 1879.   iv, 5-184 p. front. (port.) 23½ cm. 2-5219.
                                                      CS479.K6
                                                      Microfilm 8721

9895   KNOX.   Thomas (Nock) Knox, of Dover, N.H., in 1652, and some of his descendants.   Comp. by W.B.Lapham ... August (Me.) Press of the Maine farmer, 1890.   34 p. 24 cm. Privately printed. 9-11448.
                                                      CS71.K74   1890

9896   KNOX.   Reminiscences of the Knox and Soutter families of Virginia, written for her children by Emily Woolsey Dix.   New-York, The De Vinne press, 1895.   2 p. l., 107, (1) p. front., ports. 23½ cm. "The Alexander family of Scotland and America": p. 91-107. 38-36166.   CS71.K74   1895

9897   KNOX.   Knox genealogy; descendants of William Knox and John Knox the reformer, by a lineal descendant.   Edinburgh, G. P. Johnston, 1896.   3 p. l., 21 p. 2 double geneal. tab. 22 cm. Edited from material mainly collected by the late Rev. David Crawford to 1857. and brought down to the present time by his elder son. - Pref. signed: Wm Crawford Table I. The descendants of John Knox. Table II. The descendants of William Knox. in three parts. 16-17296.   CS479.K6   1896

9898   KNOX.   General Henry Knox; his family, his manor, his manor house, and his guests.   A paper read before the 12mo club, Rockland, Maine, March 3, 1902, by Lewis Frederick Starrett. (Rockland, Me., Huston's bookstore, 1902)   2 p. l. (9)-34 p. incl. pl. port. 20½ cm. "Books and articles consulted in preparation": 2d prelim. leaf. 4-22363.   E207.K74S7

9899   KNOX.   The Knox family; a genealogical and biographical sketch of the descendants of John Knox of Rowan County, North Carolina, and other Knoxes, by Hattie S. Goodman ... Richmond, Va., Whittet & Shepperson, 1905.   2 p. l., 266 p. front., plates. ports. 23 cm. 20-20510.   CS71.K74   1905

9900   KNOX.   William Knox of Blandford, Mass.; a record of the births, marriages and deaths of some of his descendants, by Nathaniel Foote ... Rochester, N. Y., 1926.   v. 297 p. 23½ cm. 27-686.
                    CS71.K74   1926

KNOX.   See also: CUNNINGHAM, 1946
                    FITZHUGH, 1932
                    No. 2070 - Memories of ... eastern N. C.

KNOYLE.   See: KNOWLES.
                    MAUNSELL, CS439.M37

9901   KNUDSEN.   Slaegten Knudson fram Billum.   Om Knud Christian Neilsen, født 1812, og hustru, deres forfaedre og efterkommere.   Skals, Bredegard, 1968.   (123) l. illus., facsim., ports. 30 cm. N. T. Four geneal. tables in plastic cover inserted. 77-421539.   CS919.K765   1968

KOBER.   See COOVER.

9902   KOCH.   Thirty ancestors of Richard Henry Koch, 1939.   Pottsville, Pa., J. F. Seiders-printing (1939)   327 p. front., ports. 23½ cm. Limited edition of 100 copies. Blank pages for genealogical data at end. Includes the Neufang. Bock. Bolich. Beck and Le Fevre families. 39-12233.   CS71.K77   1939

9903   KOCH.   Lüdwig Koch.   In vertical file.   Ask reference librarian for this material.

KOEHM.   See DECKER.

9904   KOGER.   The house of Koger, by A. B. Koger.   (Baltimore? 1938)   cover-title. 11. (1) p. ports. 22½ cm. 39-7640   E185.97.K65

9905   KOHL.   Kohl genealogy.   By Edwin Phillips Kohl.   (1st ed.   Milwaukee?) 1961.   56 l. 28 cm. 62-36494.   CS71.K79   1961

9906   KOINER.   A historical sketch of Michael Keinadt and Margaret Diller, his wife.   The history and genealogy of their numerous posterity in the American states, up to the year 1893.   Prepared by a committee appointed for that purpose by the "Michael Koiner memorial association" ... Staunton, Va., Stoneburner & Prufer, 1893.   v. (1). 171 p. front., 22 cm. 2-24814.   CS71.K8   1893

9907   KOINER.   Other names than Koiner in the Keinadt Koiner book, indexed by a Coyner descendant, Pearl Ghormley Ingle.   (Bondurant, Ia., 1939?)   cover-title. 12 numb. l. 18 x 22 cm. Type-written (carbon copy) An index to "A historical sketch of Michael Keinadt and Margaret Diller. his wife, prepared by the Michael Koiner memorial association, 1893." 41-22226.   CS71.K8   1893a

KOLB.   See KULP.

9908   KOLE.   The Kole and Kamphuis families.   By Carrie Louise Lartigue.   (Spokane, Wash.) 125 p. illus., group ports., map. 30 cm. Leaves 123-125 blank for marriages. births, and deaths after Aug. 1962. 64-2489.
                    CS71.K84   1962

9909   KOLLER.   Some notes relative to the Culler family; descendants of Jacob and Mary Culler (Koller).   By Millard Milburn Rice.   (Walkersville, Md.) 1969.   22 l. geneal. tables. 30 cm. Cover title. 72-10625 MARC.   CS71.K845   1969

KÖLLIKER.   See KELKER.

KOLLOCH.   See JAQUETT, 1922

9910   KOLLOCK.   Genealogy of the Kollock family of Sussex County, Delaware, 1657-1897; by Edwin Jaquett Sellers.   Philadelphia (Press of J. B. Lippincott co.) 1897.   1 p. l., 72 p. 25½ cm. Edition limited to two hundred copies, of which this is no. 5. 9-11447.   CS71.K81   1897

KOLLOCK.   See also JAQUETT, 1922

KOLSHORN.   See No. 553- Goodhue county.

9911   KÖNIG.   The Koenig album; biographies, photographs, genealogy charts and impressions from here and there.   The history of the Robert F. Koenig family through the blood line of the Koenigs, Metzs, Rawleighs and Trevillians, 1804-1950.   (Freeport, Ill., Priv. print., 1949)   xxi. 330 p. illus. (part col.) ports . maps (on lining papers) 24 cm. 50-16813.   CS71.K78   1949

KÖNIG.   See also ACHELIS, 1938

9912   KOOGLER.   The Koogler family of Virginia and allied families of Austin, Good, Hahn, Heatwole, Hemp, Knicely, Martin, Rhodes, Rodes, Showalter, Snead, Taylor and Witmer.   By Virginia Koogler Whitney.   (Aztec, N. M.) c. 1968.   85 l. 29 cm. 68-59556 MARC.   CS71.K83   1968

KOOL.   See COLE.

KOON   See KUHN.

KOONTZ.   See CONRAD, 1957

KOPPEL.   See No. 553 - Goodhue county.

9913   KOPPEMHAFER.   Genealogy of a branch of the Koppenhafer family from Germany which settled in Vermilion Township, Erie Co., Ohio.   By Claude Charles Hamel.   Amherst, 1948. 10 l. 27 cm. Typewritten. "References": leaf 10. 50-25320.   CS71.K84   1948

KOPPENHAVER.   See WEISER, 1960

KOPPENHEFFER.   See WEISER, 1960

9914   KORB.   Prairie days, by Nettie Korb Bryson.   Los Angeles, Times-mirror (c. 1939) 5 p. l., 171. (3) p. front.. ports. 20½ cm. illustrated t.-p. An account of the Korb family. 39-8607.   CS71.K86   1939

9915   KÖRNER.   Joseph of Kernersville, being the stories of the families: Körner-Kerner, Kastner, Spach, Gardner, Pike and Wiesner and their descendants in the town of Kernersville, North Carolina, by Jules Gilmer Körner, Jr.   Durham, N. C., Seeman Printery, 1958.   xxii, 215 p. illus., facsims., maps. ports. 24 cm. Bibliographical footnotes. 65-53303.   CS71.K863   1958

9916   KORNMAN.   Genealogical record of descendants of Ludwig Kornman, Sr., in America.   By Charles Albert Cornman.   Carlisle, Pa., The Sentinel, 1916.   155 p. illus. 24 cm. 56-54574. CS71.K864   1916

KORSTED.   See No. 553 - Goodhue county.

KORTRIGHT.   See COURTRIGHT.

KOSEC.—See No. 553 - Goodhue county.

KOSTNER.   In vertical file under PRANKE family.   Ask reference librarian for this material.

KOSTNERIN.   In vertical file under PRANKE family.   Ask reference librarian for this material.

9917   KOTHMANN.   The Kothmanns of Texas, 1845-1931, by Selma Metzenthin Raunick and Margaret Schade; original compiler Mrs. E. Marschall.   Austin, Tex., Press of Von Boeckmann-Jones company (1931)   5 p. l., 163 p. incl. plates, ports., col. coat of arms.   23½ cm.   33-14352.   CS71.K87   1931

9918   KOZACIK.   John and Susan Kozacik; a biography.   By Mary Kozacik.   East Chicago, Ind., 1965.   16 p. geneal. table, map, port. 24 cm.   Additions and corrections in MS.   77-3476 MARC.   CS71.K88   1965

9919   KOZIK.   Kozik family in vertical file.   Ask reference librarian for this material.

KRAEHENBUEHL.   See KREHBIEL.

9920   KRAMER.   The Kramer clan; a geanealogical (sic) and biographical record of its families in the State of Pennsylvania, beginning in the year 1732, with the first German Kramer pioneers, by William E. Kramer (and) Joseph J. Kramer.   (n. p., 1961 -   v. ports. 22 cm.   62-2225.   CS71.K89   1961

9921   KRAMER.   Johann Baltasar Kramer, or "Baltzer" Kramer, pioneer American glass blower; a record of his known descendants and relatives.   (Chicago, American printers and stationers, 1939)   4 p. l., 62 p. plates, ports. 24 cm.   "Compiled and privately printed by Le Roy Kramer."   39-32315.   CS71.K89   1939

9922   KRATZ.   A brief history of John Valentine Kratz, and a complete genealogical family register, with biographies of his descendants from the earliest available records to the present time ... By Rev. A. J. Fretz ... With an introduction by R. W. Kratz ... Elkhart, Ind., Mennonite pub. c., 1892.   ix, (10)-314 p., 1 l. front., plates, ports. 20½ cm.   9-11446.   CS71.K9   1892

KRAUSS.   See: FLAGG, 1903
                           GOODLOCK, 1951

KRAYBILL.   See GRAYBILL.

9923   KREBS.   Bedstemoder's erindringer (af) Ebba Victoria Krebs.   (Wilmington, Del., G. A. Wolf, 1920)   6 p. l., 11-104 p. front., illus., plates,ports. 29 cm.   In English.   Illustrated by Geo. A. Wolf.   26-7741.   CT275.K87A3

9924   KREBS.   Since coming to America, by Ebba Victoria Krebs.   From 1880 to 1924.   Phila- delphia, J. B. Lippincott company (1924)   7 p. l., 7-199, (3) p. front., plates, ports. 28½ cm.   Some of the plates are printed on both sides.   26-7740.   CT275.K87A5

KREBS.   See also KRUSE, 1924

KRECKELER.   See KREKLER.

9925   KREGEL.   Genealogy of Peter Kregel of Grambow, province of Pommern, Germany, and his descendants who came to America in 1857 and settled in Wisconsin, prepared by John H. Schneider ... Winnetka, Ill. (1941)   1 p. l., 52 p. 23½ cm.   Includes also the Dobberpuhl family.   41-21919.   CS71.K915   1941

KREHBIED.   See GRABER, 1948

9926   KREHBIEL.   History of one branch of the Krehbiel family, compiled and published by W. J. Krehbiel.   McPherson, Kan., 1950.   100 p. 24 cm.   65-5609.   CS71.K917   1950

KREHBUEHL.   See KREHBIEL.

9927   KREISCHE.   The story of the Kreische family, 1849-1952, by Alton A. Appelt.   Yoakum, Tex., Yoakum Herald-Times (1967)   52 p. illus., ports. 21 cm.   Cover title: The life story of the Kreische family.   67-5542.
CS71.K9155   1967

KREKELER.   See KREKLER.

9928   KREKLER.   Krekler and related families, compiled by Bessie K. Schafer.   (Oxford? Ohio) 1963.   35 p. 23 cm.   65-88879.
CS71.K916   1963

9929   KRESS.   Kress family history, compiled, written and published by Karl Friedrich von Frank zu Döfering ... The genealogical material concerning the American line of the Kress family was contributed by Charles Rhoads Roberts ... Vienna, Austria, 1930.   2 p. l., v, 770 p. col. front., illus. (incl. ports., facsims., coats of arms) geneal. tables (2 fold. in pocket) 33½ cm.   "This publication is not for sale but only for private circulation."   "This copy no. 700."   "Register of sources": p. 735-740.   31-2765.
CS71.K92   1930

KREUGER.   See DAVIS, 1956b

KREUSSLER.   SNYDER, 1958

KREZEK.   See INECK, 1965

KRIEBIEL.   See GRAYBILL.

KRIEGLER.   See CRIGLER.

9930   KRIJGER.   Het geslacht Krijger, 1668-1958.   By Adriaan Willem Eliza Dek.   's-Gravenhage, 1958.   44 p. illus. 25 cm.   59-33544.
CS829.K6   1958

KRINGLE.   See HELLAND, 1967

KRISE.   See No. 553 - Goodhue county.

9931   KRISTIANSSON.   Kristiansson.   (Compiled and edited by J. Henry Benson.   Arcadia, Calif., 1962)   8 l. 29 cm.   Caption title.   79-211561.
CS71.K925   1962

9932   KROH.   Chronological record of the descendants of Henry Kroh.   By James Henry Franklin Kroh.   Indianapolis? 1908.   29 l. 30 cm.   Photocopy of typescript. 45 cm.   64-58324.
CS71.K93   1908a

9933   KROLL.   Our family (by) Eleanor Kroll.   (Chicago, Ill., Bankers print, c.1940)   cover-title, iii, 24 p. incl. geneal. tab.   illus. (coats of arms) 22½ cm.   Includes bibliographies.   40-32942.
CS71.K94   1940

9934   KROM.   Krom-Krum genealogy, descendants of Gysbert Crom (1650 - ?) of Marbletown, New York, compiled by Louise Hasbrouck Zimm ... Woodstock, N.Y., 1941 -   v. 28 cm.   Type-written.
Contents - v. 1. First four generations carried down in male lines. - v. 2. Fifth generation carried down in male line with notes on later Kroms.
42-16472 rev.
CS71.K95   1941

9935   KROUPA.   The Kroupa genealogy ... a history of the Kroupa, Lada, Zitka, Schrader, Santovsky, and Marcelbetts families.   By Robert Ellis Schrader.   Los Angeles (1957?)   276 l. illus. 29 cm.   60-145.
CS71.K953   1957

KROUSKOP.   See McCOLLUM, 1936

KROWNSKY.   See CROUNSE.

KRUM.   See KROM.

9936   KRUPP   ... Alfred Krupp und sein geschlecht; 150 jahre Kruppgeschichte, 1787-1937, nach den quellen der familie und des werks, von Wilhelm Berdrow.   Mit über 100 bildern im text und auf 32 tiefdrucktafeln.   Berlin, P. Schmidt, 1937.   229, (3) p. incl. front., illus., plates, ports., facsims., geneal. tab. 24½ cm. (Vergangenheit und gegenwart; länder, menschen, wirtschaft) 38-35400.
DD205.K7B42

9937   KRUPP.   The Krupps; 150 years Krupp history, 1787-1937, based on documents from the family and works archives, by Wilhelm Berdrow.   Translated by Fritz Homann.   Berlin, Verlag für sozialpolitik, wirtschaft und statistik, P. Schmidt, 1937.   325, (1) p. front. (facsim.) plates, ports. 21 cm. Errata slip laid in.   Frontispiece accompanied by guard sheet with English translation.   38-32336.

DD205.K7B425

9938   KRUPP.   Krupp; or, The lords of Essen, by Bernhard Menne.   London (etc.) W. Hodge and company limited, 1937.   vi p., 1 l., 406 p. 22½ cm.   "Translated by G.H. Smith."   38-9699.   UF537.K76   1937

9939   KRUPP.   Blood and steel; the rise of the house of Krupp, by Bernhard Menne.   New York, L. Furman, inc., 1938.   viii, 424 p. plates, ports., maps. 22 cm.   "Translated from the German by G.H. Smith."   "Published in England under the title: Krupp, the lords of Essen."   Bibliography: p. 409-413.   38-19903.   UF537.K76   1938

9940   KRUSE.   Family sketches, by Ebba Victoria Krebs.   Philadelphia, London, Printed for private circulation by J. B. Lippincott company, 1924.   4 p. l., 3-57, (1) p. front., plates, ports. 28½ cm.   Some of the plates are printed on both sides.   Contains some Kruse, Roed, Sonnin and Krebs family history.   26-7742.   CT275.K87A4

KRÜTZ.   See CREUTZ.

9941   KUHL.   Genealogy of the family of Charles Fred and Alice Caroline (Baatz) Kuhl, of Erie County, Ohio.   By Claude Charles Hamel.   Amherst, 1951.   4 l. 27 cm.   52-20692.

CS71.K957   1951

9942   KUHN.   Notes on the Kuhns family.   (By Ezra McFall Kuhns.   Dayton? O.)   Priv. print., 1934.   1 p. l., 35 p. illus. (incl. ports. facsim) 23½ cm.   34-42437.   CS71.K96   1934

9943   KUHN.   Koon and Coons families of eastern New York; a history of the descendants of Matthias Kuntz and Samuel Kuhn (two distinct families) who came with the Palatine immigration from Germany and settled on the Hudson river in New York in 1710, compiled by William Solyman Coons, aided by Kate Koon Bovey, Leon C. Hills (and) C. Carroll Koon ... Rutland, Vt., The Tuttle publishing company, inc. (1937)   xxiii, 268, (10), (269)-480, (12) p. front., pl., ports., facsims., geneal. tables (part fold.) 26 x 20 cm.   39-32324.

CS71.K96   1937

9944   KUHN.   Kuhns, a genealogy.   By Philip Harmon Shaub.   (Jefferson? Ia., pref. 1941)   22 p. 22½ cm.   "The original Kuhns genealogy was published in 1910 by the late Philip H. Shaub ... The author of this revised edition has collected additional family history and endeavored to bring the genealogy down to date." - Pref., signed John R. Black.   41-28034.

CS71.K96   1941

9945   KUHN.   Family history: Kuhn, Dittmeier, compiled by Kathryne Kuhn Krouse.   Falls Church, Va., 1964.   1, 27 l. illus. 28 cm.   64-55132.   CS71.K96   1964

KUHN.   See also: CALVERT, 1905-8
                          COONS.

KUHNS.   See: COONS, CS71.C776
                       KUHN.
                       MORRIS, 1905

9946   KULP.   A genealogical history of the Kolb, Kulp or Culp family, and its branches in America, with biographical sketches of their descendants, from the earliest available records from 1707 to the present time, including Dielman Kolb in Germany ... By Daniel Kolb Cassel ... Norristown, Pa., M. R. Wills, 1895.   584 p. front., ports. 24 cm.   9-11444.   CS71.K965   1895

9947   KULP.   Andrew Egger and William Bond Kolb: the lives and heritage of Mississippi brothers, compiled by Avery E. Kolb.   Springfield, Va., 1969.   vii, 135 p. illus., facsims., ports. 28 cm.   74-7477 MARC.

CS71.K965   1969

KULP.   See also: CUSTER, 1937
                          STRASSBURGER, 1922

KUMP. See RUDOLPH, 1962

KUNDERS. See CONRAD.

KUNGEL. See KUNKEL.

9948 KUNKEL. The Kunkel family of Frederick, Maryland. By Mildred (Hoge) Richards. (Tucson? Ariz., 1954)   unpaged. illus. 28 cm. 60-35385.   CS71.K8   1954

KUNTZ. See COONS.

KUNZ. See COONS.

KÜRNER. See KÖRNER.

9949 KURTZ. Johann Nicolaus Kurtz, life and genealogy. (By Benjamin Kurtz Miller. Oconomowoc (Wis.) Priv. print. at the Enterprise office, 1925)   cover-title, 106 p., 1 l., (5) p. plates, facsims. 30 cm. "Life of Johann Nicolaus Kurtz (missionary, clergyman, president of the Lutheran ministerium ...). With notes of his brother Johann Wilhelm Kurtz, Lutheran clergyman (from a manuscript by) Margaret A. Cruikshank, edited by Benjamin Kurtz Miller": p. (1)-35. "Descendants of Johann Georg Kurtz, for 25 years schoolmaster at Lutzellinden (near Giesen) Kreis Wetzlar, Nassau-Weilberg, Germany. By Benjamin Kurtz Miller": p. (37) - 98. Appendix, p.(99)-106 contains Giibs, Holden, Miller, Peckham, Peterson, Smyser, Williams and Chester genealogies. 26-20739.

CS71.K97   1925

9950 KURTZ. Ascending and descending genealogy of the children of Joseph Kurtz and Lydia Zook, by Alta Kurtz Christophel ... Mishawaka, Ind. (The author, 1940?)   (20) p. illus., vi geneal. tab. on 3 l. 20 cm. Page (20) blank for "Additional records". 41-3513.   CS71.K97   1940

KUSTER. See CUSTER.

KUTCH. See KETCHAM, 1939

9951 KUYKENDALL. History of the Kuykendall family since its settlement in Dutch New York in 1646, with genealogy as found in early Dutch church records, state and government documents, together with sketches of colonial times, old log cabin days, Indian wars, pioneer hardships, social customs, dress and mode of living of the early forefathers ... by George Benson Kuykendall, M. D. Portland, Or., Kilham stationery & printing co., 1919.   11 p. l., 645, (20) p. front., illus., ports., fold. geneal. tab. 23½ cm. 19-18600.   CS71.K98   1919

KUYKENDALL. See also MILLER, 1923

KYES. See FRIMEMOOD, 1923

9952 KYLE. A partial history of the Kyle, Kile, Coyle family in America with some Scotch, Irish, and English background. By Orville Merton Kile. Baltimore, Printed by Waverly Press, 1958. 186 p. illus., map, coats of arms (1 col.) geneal. tables. 24 cm. Pages 173-186 blank for "Supplementary family data." 58-49301.   CS71.K99   1958

KYLE. See also: JACKSON, 1890
                  McINTOSH, F129.C36M2
                  No. 1547 - Cabell county.

9953 KYME. Kyme family of Lewes, by W. H. Challen. (Worthing? Eng., 1963?) 112-136 p. 22 cm. Caption title. 65-56434.   CS439.K87   1963

KYME. See also MARMION, 1817

KYMPTON. See BACKHOUSE, DA690.M74C3

KYN. See KEEN.

9954   KYTSON.   The Kytsons and Gages of Hengrave, Suffolk.   Extracted from "The visitation of Suffolke."   (By William Harvey)   Ed. by Joseph Jackson Howard ... Lowestoft, Printed by S. Tymms, 1867.   28 p.   illus. (coats of arms) 28 cm.   20-18091.   CS439.K9

L

9955   LA BAU (LABAW)   Information in vertical file.   Ask reference librarian for this material.

LABBADIE.   See CHOUTEAU, 1893

LACEY.   See LACY.

LA CHESNELAYE.   See DU BOISBAUDRY, 1958

9956   LACKEY.   A history of the Lackey family, by Mrs. Jay Lackey and Mrs. H. G. Duncan. (Wilkesboro? N. C.) c. 1962.   59 p. illus. 28 cm. 63-28853.   CS71. L14   1962

LACOCK.   See LINTON, 1887

9957   LACY.   The Blazon Of Gentrie: Deuided into two parts.   The first named The Glorie of Gen-erositie.   The second, Lacyes Nobilitie.   Comprehending discourses of Armes and of Gentry. Wherein is treated of the beginning, parts, and degrees of Gentlenesse, with her lawes: Of the Bearing, and Blazon of Cote-armors: Of the Lawes of Armes, and of Combats.   Compiled by Iohn Ferne Gentle-man, for the instruction of all Gentlemen bearers of Armes, whome and none other this worke concern-eth.   (Band)   At London, Printed by John Windet, for Toby Cooke, 1586.   10 p. 1., 341, 130 p. illus. (coat of arms) 19½ cm. "The second part intituled, Lacies Nobilitie" has separate paging. On t.-p. in manuscript: Sir Tho. FitzGerald   . . . . . Binding by Rivière, full red morocco, with gold tooling; gilt edges. Book-plates: (1) Sir Henry Hope Edwardes. (2) Clarence S. Bement. 24-18041.   CR19. F4

9958   LACY.   A genealogy of the Lacey family, by Thomas McAdory Owen.   Carrollton, Ala., West Alabamian print, 1900.   1 p. 1., 4 p. 24½ cm. 2-13777.   CS71. L151   1900

9959   LACY.   History of General Edward Lacey and some of his descendants.   (By Robert Alexander Lacey) (Montgomery, Ala., 1935?)   28 1. 30 cm. Mimeographed. "Extract from the Gulf states historical magazine. - July 1902. General Edward Lacey of the Revolution and some of his descendants": leaves 1-4. 38-14730.   CS71. L151   1902

9960   LACY.   The Walter Garner Lacy branch of the Lacy family of colonial Virginia.   Compiled by Harriet E. N. Chace, genealogist, from the results of her research among original and published records and from family data gathered and preserved by Mrs. Walter Garner Lacy and Mrs. Frank Lorenzo Miller.   (Washington, D. C., Press of C. H. Potter & co., inc., 1925)   1 p. 1., 54 p. 2 port. (incl. front.) fold. map. 16½ cm. "Privately printed for Walter Garner Lacy of Waco, Texas." 26-5597 rev.   CS71. L151   1925

9961   LACY.   ... The roll of the house of Lacy; pedigrees, military memoirs and synoptical history of the ancient and illustrious family of De Lacy, from the earliest times, in all its branches, to the present day.   Full notices on allied families and a memoir of the Brownes (Camas) collected and com-piled by De Lacy-Bellingari ... Baltimore, 1928.   viii, 409 p. illus. (incl. maps, facsims.) plates, ports., coats of arms. 23½ cm. 28-10534 rev.   CS439. L17D4

9963   LACY.   General Edward Lacey and his descendants.   (By Robert Alexander Lacey.   Washing-ton, 1943)   25 numb. 1. 32 x 20½ cm. Caption title. Repr. from type-written copy. 44-1933.   CS71. L151   1943

9964   LACY.   General Edward Lacey and his descendants, compiled by Robert Alexander Lacey. (Washington) 1944.   2 p. l., 40 numb. l., 1 l. 32 x 20½ cm. Reproduced from type-written copy. 45-8323.

CS71. L151   1944

9965   LACY.   The Lacy family in England and Normandy, 1066-1194, by W. E. Wightman.   Oxford, Clarendon P., 1966.   xi, 274 p. 2 plates (diagrs.) 5 maps. 22½ cm. Bibliographical footnotes. 66-70205.

CS439. L17W5

LACY.   See also: BATEMAN, 1952
                   FITZ RANDOLPH, 1958
                   GEORGE, 1940
                   GOODNER, 1960
                   HALE, 1948
                   ROQUEMORE, 1942

LADA.   See KROUPA, 1957

9966   LADD.   The generations of a New-England family.   (By Alexander Ladd Hayes) Cambridge, Printed for private distribution at the University press (1885)   22 p. 30½ cm. Introductory note signed: A. L. H. "Verses recited at the house of Mr. Charles E. Wentworth, in Cambridge, Mass., Christmas evening, 1885. Written by a descendant of all the ancestors named in the early generations and accompanied by scenes acted by other descendants. Includes the Ladd, Wentworth, Dudley, Glover and Haven families. 20-7228.

CS71. L154   1885

9967   LADD.   The Ladd family.   A genealogical and biographical memoir of the descendants of Daniel Ladd, of Haverhill, Mass., Joseph Ladd, of Portsmouth, R. I., John Ladd, of Burlington, N. J., John Ladd, of Charles City Co., Va.   Comp. by Warren Ladd ... New Bedford, Mass., Printed for the author by E. Anthony & sons, 1890.   1 p. l., xii, 413 p. front. (port.) 23½ cm. 9-11923.

CS71. L154   1890

9968   LADD.   History of the Ladds and the descendants of Mordica Ladd to 1915, comp. by Earl C. L. Van Wert.   (n. p.) 1915.   geneal. tab. illus. (coat of arms) 32½ x 36 cm. 16-2609.

CS71. L154   1915

9969   LADD.   Ancestral chart of George Edgar Ladd.   (n. p., 1919?)   geneal. tab. 65½ x 112 cm. fold. to 26 x 17 cm. 21-12153.

CS71. L154   1919

9970   LADD.   A genealogical record of Samuel Greenleaf Ladd ... and Caroline de Olivier Vinal Ladd, his wife, by Horatio Oliver Ladd ... Limited ed.   (Boston, The Alpine press) 1927. 24 p. incl. front., illus. (ports., coat of arms) 18½ cm. 28-699.

CS71. L154   1927

9971   LADD.   The Ladd family, a genealogy.   By Thomas Mifflin Ladd.   Norfolk, Va., Printed by the H. C. Young Press, 1964.   x, 73 p. illus., coat of arms, ports. 24 cm. 64-55216.

CS71. L154   1964

LADD.   See also: CORLISS, 1875
                   DAMERON, 1953
                   HOWELL, 1897
                   RICE, 1915
                   RUGGLES, 1896

LADTURNER.   See LADURNER.

9972   LA FAYETTE.   ... Madam de Lafayette en ménage, d'après des documents inédits.   By Emile Magne.   Paris, Émile-Paul frères, 1926.   3 p. l., (ix)-xi, (1), ,293 p., 1 l. front., plates, ports., plans, facsim. 19 cm. Continued by the author's Le coeur et l'esprit de Madame de Lafayette. "Appendice: Titre et actes inedits concernant les familles de Lafayette, Pioche et Péna (Résumés)": p. (245)-293. Genealogical table of the Péna family: p. 14. Bibliographical foot-notes. 30-5877.

DC130. L2M3   1926

9973   LA FAYETTE.   Tableau de filiation de la maison du Motier de La Fayette avec l'état présent de la descendance du général de La Fayette publié d'après les titres et documents originaux et les actes de l'état civil par les soins du comte Georges de Morant ... Paris, L'International college of heraldry, 1928.   cover-title, fold. geneal. tab. illus. (incl. coats of arms) 92 x 59 cm. fold. to 35 x 28 cm. "Sources à consulter." 37-21309.

CS599. I11   1928

9974 LA FITTE. Some Huguenot families of South Carolina and Georgia, Peter Lafitte, Andre
Verdier, Samuel Montague, Henri Francois Bourquin, Jean Bapiste (!) Bourquin, Peter Papot, Benjamin
Godin, by Harry Alexander Davis of the Huguenot society of South Carolina. (Washington) 1926.
1 p. l., 59 numb. l., 1 l. mounted port. 26½ cm. Reproduced from type-written copy. 26-17543 rev.   F268.D37   1926

9975 LA FITTE. Some Huguenot families of South Carolina and Georgia, Peter Lafitte, Andre
Verdier, Samuel Montague, Henri Francois Bourquin, Jean Baptiste Bourquin, Peter Papot, Benjamin
Godin, Peter Morel, by Harry Alexander Davis of the Huguenot society of South Carolina. (Washington,
D. C., 1927)   1 p. l., 78 (i.e. 85 numb. l. 2 port. (incl. front.) 26 cm. Extra numbered leaves: 34 a-b, 48 a-c. 54 a. 58 a. "Second
edition, revised and enlarged." Autographed from type-written copy. 27-11169.   F268.D37   1927

    LAFFITTE. See BROYLES, 1959

9976 LAFLIN.   Laflin genealogy, compiled from the manuscript of Louis Ellsworth Laflin, with
additions, by Alfred L. Holman ... Chicago, Priv. print. for Mrs. Louis E. Laflin, 1930.
3 p. l., 142 p. front., ports. 23½ cm. 30-13436.   CS71.L17   1930

9977 LA FOLLETTE. History of the La Follette family in America.   Compiled by John H. La
Follette, edited by Will La Follette. Ottumwa, Ia., C. F. Lang, 1898. 1 p. l., vii, ii, iii, iii, 84 p. 27 port.
14½ cm. Contains also the Henton family. 31-19480.   CS71.L18   1898

9978 LA FOLLETTE. Early LaFollette history. By Robert E. LaFollette. (New Albany? Ind.,
1961?)   13 l. 27 cm. 62-36818.   CS71.L18   1961

    LA FOLLETTE. See LINCOLN, 1929

9979 LA FORCE. Notes on the lineage of the Force family of Hunterdon and Warren Counties, New
Jersey. Washington, 1958.   11 l. 33 cm. 59-34525.   CS71.L182   1958

    LA FORCE. See also: CAUMONT.
                           FORCE.

    LĀHĀ. See LAW.

    LAHIFF. See LONG, 1954

    LAICON. See LYCAN.

    LAIDLAW. See ELIOT, 1907

    LAIDLEY. See No. 1520 - Cabell county.

9980 LAIN. Descendants of William Lain and Keziah Mather with her lineage from Reverend
Richard Mather. By Beatrice (Linskill) Sheehan. Brooklyn, N. Y., T. Gaus' Sons, 1957. 310 p. illus.
24 cm. 57-12193.   CS71.L183   1957

    LAING. See: MALCOLM, 1950
                  THOM, 1957
                  WILSON, 1960

9981 LAIR. Lair, a Huguenot family from near Lyons, France, 1752, landed in New York and
settled in New Jersey, by Alice L. Priest. Brookline, Mass., 1937. 1 p. l., 6 numb. l. 28 cm. Type-written.
37-10357.   CS71.L185   1937

9982 LAIR. Background of the Lair family, 1738-1958, by Maude Ward Lafferty (and) Helen Lafferty
Nisbet. Lexington, Ky., 1958. 62 p. illus. 22 cm. 58-39301.   CS71.L185   1958

9983 LAIRD. Laird family, by Forrest E. Brouhard. Harland, Iowa, Economy Print. Co., 1964.
(36) p. coat of arms, ports. 23 cm. 64-55040.   CS71.L187   1964

9984 LAITHWAITE. The Laithwaites; some records of a Lancashire family. Rev. and amplified ed. By Sir Gilbert Laithwaite. Karachi, 1961. 225 p. 26 cm. 62-38839. CS439.L18 1961

9985 LAKE. Descendants of Thomas Lake of Stratford, Connecticut. By David Minor Lake ... Albert Edward Lake, and Arthur Crawford Lake ... Chicago (Fergus printing company) 1908. 16 p. 24½ cm. 10-6530. CS71.L19 1908

9986 LAKE. A genealogy of the Lake family of Great Egg Harbour in Old Gloucester County in New Jersey. Comp. by Arthur Adams and Sarah A. Risley. (Hartford, Conn.) Priv. print., 1912. iv, (5)-26 p. 23½ cm. 12-22808. CS71.L19 1912

9987 LAKE. A genealogy of the Lake family of Great Egg Harbour in Old Gloucester County in New Jersey, descended from John Lake of Gravesend, Long Island; with notes on the Gravesend and Staten Island branches of the family, by Arthur Adams and Sarah A. Risley ... (Hartford) Priv, print., 1915. x, 376 p. front. (col. coat of arms) plates, ports., 2 fold. genealogical tab. 25 cm. Ancestral register of Esther Steelman Adams: p. 254. 15-21639. CS71.L19 1915

9988 LAKE. A personal narrative of some branches of the Lake family in America with particular reference to the antecedents and descendants of Richard Lake, Georgia pioneer, by Devereux Lake. (Lorain, O.) Priv. pub. (The Lorain printing company) 1937. 8 p. l., 131, (1), 132-256 p. incl. illus., ports. 24½ cm. 38-793. CS71.L19 1937

9989 LAKE. Facts regarding one Joseph Lake of Staten island, New York, compiled by Elmer G. Van Name. (Revised April 5, 1940) Haddonfield, N.J. (1940) 6 l. 28 cm. Caption title. Type-written (carbon copy) 43-35965. CS71.L19 1940

9990 LAKE. Facts regarding one Joseph Lake of Staten Island, N.Y. By Elmer Garfield Van Name. Rev. Nov. 18, 1954 (Haddonfield? N.J., 1954) 7 p. 23 cm. 55-22500. CS71.L19 1954

9991 LAKE. A history of my people and yours, including the families of Nicholas Lake (and others. n.p.) 1956. x, 822 p. illus., ports., col. coat of arms. 25 cm. 57-393. CS71.L19 1956

LAKE. (Martha Carson Lake Mayo, Civil War nurse and cousin of Kit Carson. See MAYO family folder in vertical file. Ask reference librarian for this material.

LAKE. See also MONNET, 1911

9992 LAKIN. Lakin family. By Hon, Samuel A. Green ... (Boston, 1894) 3 p. 24½ cm. Caption title. "Reprinted from the New England historical and genealogical register for Oct., 1894": v. 48, p.444-446. 3-16105. CS71.L192 1894

9993 LAKIN. The Lakin family of Groton, Mass. By William H. Manning. Boston, New England historic genealogical society, 1909. 11 p. 22 cm. Reprinted from the New England historical and genealogical register for October, 1909. 17-6157. CS71.L192 1909

LALAIN. See MINNS, 1925

LALIME. See RAVENELLE-LALIME, F1054.R5.D3

LALINE. See CHOQUETTE, F1054.R5D3

LALOR. See BROPHY, 1940

LA MANCE. See WALTMAN, 1928

9994 LAMAR. Thomas Lamar of the province of Maryland, and a part of his descendants. By William Harmong Lamar. (In Southern history association. Publications. Washington, D.C., 1897. 25 cm. v. 1, p. (203)-210) 15-21027. F206.S73 v.1

9995   LAMAR.   Genealogy and history, a branch of the family of Lamar, with it's related families of Urquhart, Reynolds, Bird, Williamson, Gilliam, Garratt, Thompson, Herman, Empson, and others; compiled and written for the private information of his own children by Edward Mays ... (Hattiesburg, Miss., The Southern library service, 1935)   74 p. 23 cm. On cover: 53 copies issued. "Important notice ... In a family copy the following corrections were found, and have been printed here ... (signed) Charles R. Knight": 2 p. inserted before t. - p. 39-32313.

CS71. L2   1935

9996   LAMAR.   History of the Lamar or Lemar family in America, by Harold Dihel LeMar ... Omaha, Neb., Cockle printing company, c. 1941.   2 p. l., 337, (24), 86 p. 24 cm. Includes twenty-four blank pages for additional records.   41-18205.

CS71. L2   1941

LAMAR.   See also: KNIGHT, 193-
MAY, 1928

LAMASTER.   See LEMASTER.

9998   LAMB.   Family records.   Lamb, Savory, Harriman.   Collected and compiled by F. W. Lamb, a descendant.   (n. p.) A. Caldwell, 1900.   24 p. 23 cm. 1-1941.

CS71. L218   1900

9999   LAMB.   Genealogical sketch of the Lamb family; compiled by Fred W. Lamb (a descendant) 2d ed. rev. and enl. ... Manchester, N. H., Printed by the J. B. Clarke company, 1903.   7 p. front. (port.) 24½ cm. 4-24193.

CS71. L218   1903

10000   LAMB.   Genealogy of Lamb, Rose and others; compiled by Daniel Smith Lamb ... Washington, D. C., Beresford, printer, 1904.   xiii, 61, 20, (83)-109 p. front. (port.) 23½ cm. "In making up the index, the paging of part II has been changed from 1 to 20, to 63 to 82.   4-36357.

CS71. L218   1904

10001   ... Early marriage records of the Lamb family in the United States; official and authoritative records of Lamb marriages in the original states and colonies from 1628 to 1865, ed. by William Montgomery Clemens.   1st ed. (limited) N(ew) Y(ork) W. M. Clemens, 1916.   39 p. 23 cm. (The Clemens American marriage records, v. 4) 16-11120.

CS71. L218   1916

10002   LAMB.   Early Lamb marriages (In Genealogy; a monthly magazine of American ancestry, edited by William Montgomery Clemens ... New York, N. Y., 1917.)   23 cm. vol. vii, p. 1-7) 39M2427T.

CS42. G7 vol. 7

—— Separate.

CS71. I218   1917

10003   LAMB.   Some annals of the Lambs: a border family.   (By Edmund George Lamb.   London) Priv. print. (The Westminster press) 1926.   xvi, 137 p., 2 l. 1 illus., plates, ports., facsims., fold. geneal. tab. (in pocket) 26 x 20 cm. Coat of arms on cover and t. - p. Preface signed: Mabel Lamb. 44-38678.

CS439. L19   1926

10004   LAMB.   Nathan Lamb of Leicester, Massachusetts, his ancestors and descendants, compiled by Charles Francis Lamb ... (Madison, Wis.) 1930.   92 p. plates, facsims. 22½ cm. 31-19473.

CS71. L218   1930

10005   LAMB.   Thomas Lambe of Roxbury, English Puritan, founder of an American lineage in the colony of the Massachusetts bay, and some of his descendants, 1630-1932 ... compiled by Albert Roswell Lamb ... Washington, D. C. (1932)   2 p. l., 82 numb. l., 4 l. 27½ cm. Bibliographical foot-notes. 41-41199.

CS71. L218   1932

10006   LAMB.   William Lamb of Delaware County, New York, and his descendants.   By Eldon P. Gundry.   Flint, Mich., 1957.   46 p. 24 cm. 58-19120.

CS71. L218   1957

10007   LAMB.   Lamb-Parker-Richardson families.   A collection of MSS, genealogical notes, deeds, etc.   In vertical file.   Ask reference librarian for this material.

LAMB.   See also: ATWOOD.
DEAN, 1940

LAMBART.   See LAMBERT.

10008   LAMBDIN.   Geneology (sic) of the Georgia branch of the Lambdin family and its Maryland forebears.   By Charles Edwin Lambdin.   (Hobart? Ind., 1960)   44 l. illus. 30 cm. 60-34868.
CS71.L2185   1960

10009   LAMBERT.   A concise account of some natural curiosities, in the environs of Malham, in Craven, Yorkshire.   By Thomas Hurtley ... London, Printed at the Logographic press, by J. Walter, 1786.   68, 199, (1) p. 3 pl. (1 fold.) 22½ cm.   "Appendix no. III containing a pedigree of the Lambert family, and especially some memoirs of John Lambert, esq., major-general of the parliamentary forces": p. (13)-199.   3-15606.   DA690.M24H9

10010   LAMBERT.   History of the colony of New Haven, before and after the union with Connecticut. ... By Edward R. Lambert.   New Haven, Hitchcock & Stafford, 1838.   216 p. front. (map) illus., plates, plans. 19 cm.   "A genealogical sketch of the Lambert family of Milford, Conn.": p. (205)-216.   1-Rc3184.
F98.L2

10011   LAMBERT.   Leaves from a family tree, by Edgar Lambart.   London, Printed for private circulation by Messrs. Hatchard, 1902.   2 p. l., 56 p. illus. (incl. coats of arms) plates, ports. 29½ cm. 15-16269.
CS439.L2

10012   LAMBERT.   The Lambert family of Salem, Massachusetts, by Henry W. Belknap ... Salem, Mass., Essex institute, 1918.   1 p. l., 45 p. front. (ports.) 24½ cm.   Fifty copies reprinted from the Historical collections of the Essex institute, vol. LIV. 18-3028.   CS71.L219   1918

10013   LAMBERT.   Roger Lambert and his descendants ... Compiled by Ira C. Lambert.   Toms River, N.J., 1933.   61 p. illus. (coat of arms) plates, ports. 24 cm.   On cover: History of Rudolph De Lombard and descendants, 1066-1933.   34-23201.   CS71.L219   1933

10014   LAMBERT.   Reverend James Franklin Lambert, pioneer minister in Georgia, and descendants.   By Susan (Lambert) Martin.   (Atlanta? 1963)   74 p. illus., ports., coat of arms, facsims. 23 cm. 64-425.
CS71.L2188   1963

LAMBERT.   See also: CARY, DA690.M73A5
                        HEBERT-LAMBERT, F1054.R5D3

LAMBETH.   See No. 2070 - Memories ... of eastern N.C.

10015   LAMBING.   Michael Anthony and Anne Shields-Lambing; their ancestors and their descendants.   By a member of the family.   Pittsburgh, Pa., Printed for the family by Fahey & co., 1896.   42 p. front. (port.) 22½ cm. 13-16552.   CS71.L222   1896

10016   LAMBORN.   The genealogy of the Lamborn family, with extracts from history, biographies, anecdotes, etc.   Comp. by Samuel Lamborn ... Philadelphia, Press of M. L. Marion, 1894.   486 p., 1 l. front., plates, ports., facsims., coats of arms. 23 cm.   Blank leaves at end: "Births, marriages, deaths." 9-11922.
CS71.L225   1894

LAMBSON.   See LAMSON.

10017   LA MOILLE.   Poke O'Moonshine, by Latham Cornell Strong ... New York, G. P. Putnam's sons, 1878.   117 p. 17½ cm.   In verse. 31-2637.   PS2959.S535

10018   LAMONT.   An account of the re-union of the descendants of the late Thomas W. La Monte, of Charlotteville, N.Y. at the residence of his son, George La Monte, Bound Brook, N.J.   November 22nd and 23rd.   New York, J. W. Pratt, printer, 1877.   cover-title, 16 p. 23½ cm.   "Historical sketch by Rev. Thomas La Monte": p. 3-14. 9-11921.   CS71.L233   1877

10019   LAMONT.   Clan Lamont society.   Report of the 1st, 3d general meetings ... 1897-1899. (Glasgow, 1897?-1899)   2 v. in 1. 21 cm. 9-19335.   CS479.L2

10020   LAMONT.   The Lamont Tartan.   An address delivered to the Clan Lamont society at their annual general meeting in Glasgow on 6th May, 1910, by Wm. Lamont, C.A., Glasgow.   (Glasgow, 1910)   2 p. l., 18 p. 8 mounted samples. 23 cm.   Each sample accompanied by guard sheet with descriptive letterpress.   "200 copies, of which this is no. 195." 11-16489.   DA880.H76L2

GENEALOGIES IN THE LIBRARY OF CONGRESS

10021   LAMONT.   Clan Lamont journal ... v. 1 -   (no. 1 -   Oct. 1912 -
(Hereford, Eng., Wilson & Phillips, 1912 -   v. plates (1 fold.) ports. 25½ cm.   quarterly. Caption title. Editor:
Oct. 1912 -   A. H. Lamont. Cover-title of no. 1: Clan Lamont society journal. 42-35229.   CS479. L19

10022   LAMONT.   An inventory of Lamont papers (1231 - 1897), collected, ed., and presented to
the Scottish record society, by Sir Norman Lamont of Knockdow, baronet, F. S. A. Scot.   Edinburgh,
Printed by J. Skinner & company, ltd., 1914.   xi, 495 p. 26 cm. The index and some additional matter (p. 423-495) were
issued in 1918 with cover-title: Further additions (1442-1859) and corrections to An inventory of Lamont papers with an index; compiled and presented to the Scottish record society ... 19-9468.   CS479. L2   1914

10023   LAMONT.   A brief account of the life at Charlotteville of Thomas William Lamont and of his
family; together with a record of his ancestors, of their origin in Scotland, and of their first coming
to America about 1750, by his son, Thomas Lamont.   New York, Duffield & company, 1915.
vi, 133, (2) p. 21½ cm. 15-24248.   CS71. L233   1915

10024   LAMONT.   The Lamont clan 1235-1935; seven centuries of clan history from record
evidence, by Hector McKechnie ... with 27 pedigrees and 36 plates.   Edinburgh, Printed for the Clan
Lamont society by Neill & co., ltd., 1938.   xxii p., 1 l., 602 p., 1 l. xxxvi pl. (incl. col. front., ports., facsim., col.
coats of arms, music, sample) 26 cm. Maps on lining-papers. The sample "pattern of Lamont tarton", is inserted between two leaves, the first
with descriptive letterpress. "This edition is limited to 400 copies of which this is no. 250." "Abbreviations in reference notes": p. xxi-xxii.
"Reference notes": p. 491-594. 40-1339.   CS479. L2   1938

10025   LAMONT.   La Mont-Eldredge family records.   By Belle La Mont.   Albion, N. Y., 1948.
334 p. group port. 24 cm. addenda slip inserted. 50-39107.   CS71. L233   1948

10026   LAMONT.   The Thomas Lamont famly, by Thomas Lamont (and others)   With recollections
and poems by John Masefield.   Edited by Corliss Lamont.   New York, Horizon Press, 1962.
ix, 276 p. illus., ports., map (on lining papers) coat of arms, geneal. tables. 24 cm. 63-993.   CS71. L233   1962

LAMONT.   See also BOSS, 1948

LA MONTE.   See LAMONT.

10027   LAMPERT.   A genealogical record of the Lampert family, compiled by Margaret Lampert
Wiesenberg.   (Lakewood? N. J.) 1939.   3 p. l., 47 p. 24½ cm. "Printed for private circulation." 41-194.
CS71. L2355   1939

LAMPHEAR.   See LANPHEAR.

LAMPHERE.   See LANPHEAR.

LAMPLUGH.   See YATES, 1939

LAMPMAN.   See: KELLEY, 1939
                        KELLEY, 1955a

LAMPREY.   See DRAKE, 1962

LAMPSON.   See LAMSON.

10028   LAMPTON.   Sketch of the Lampton family in America, 1740-1914.   (n. p., 1914)
cover-title, 59 p. front. (port.) 23 cm. Dedication signed: C. K. (i. e. Clayton Keith) 15-1500.   CS71. L236   1914

10029   LAMSON.   Memorial of Elder Ebenezer Lamson of Concord, Mass., his ancestry and de-
scendants, 1635-1908; originally comp. by Otis E. Lamson ... rev. and extended by Frank B. Lamson
... (Delanot, Minn., Press of the Eagle printing co., 1908?)   2 p. l., 121 p. plates, ports., facsim. 24½ cm.'
Comp. and pub. 1876 by O. E. Lamson under title: Genealogy of the Lamson name and blood from 1741 to 1876. 10-15500.
CS71. L237   1908

10030 LAMSON. Descendants of William Lamson of Ipswich, Mass. 1634-1917. By William J. Lamson ... New York, T.A.Wright, 1917. 414 p. front., plates, ports. 24½ cm. No. 64. 18-2449.
CS71.L237 1917

LAMSON. See also: GREEN, 1904
KINGSBURY, 1934

10031 LANCASTER. Memoirs of the rival houses of York and Lancaster, historical and biographical: embracing a period of English history from the accession of Richard II. to the death of Henry VII. By Emma Roberts ... London, Harding and Lepard (etc.) 1827. 2 v. front. (port.) 22 cm. 2-18557.
DA245.R644

10032 LANCASTER. The story of the house of Lancaster. By Henry Hartwright ... London, E. Stock, 1897. 5 p. l., 322 p. 23½ cm. 1-1009. DA245.H337

10033 LANCASTER. The Lancaster family. A history of Thomas and Phebe Lancaster, of Bucks County, Pennsylvania, and their descendants, from 1711 to 1902. Also a sketch on the origin of the name and family in England ... Comp. by Harry Fred Lancaster ... (Huntington, Ind., A.J.Hoover printing co.) 1902. 291, (11) p. front., plates, ports., plans, facsims., coat of arms. 22 cm. 3-469.
CS71.L245 1902

10034 LANCASTER. The Lancaster genealogy, record of Joseph Lancaster of Amesbury, Massachusetts, and some of his descendants. Compiled for Alston Howard Lancaster, M.D., by Josephine S. Ware (Mrs. Henry F. Ware) ... (Rutland, Vt., The Tuttle company, 1934) 3 p. l., 5-125 p. front. (port.) 23½ cm. "Printed for private distribution." "Authorities": 3d prelim leaf. 34-32139. CS71.L245 1934

LANCASTER. See also: CLARK, 1904
ROBERTS, F159.R48R6
SEMMES, 1956
TONGUE, 1949

LANCE. See FENDER, 1942

LANDAFF. See LLANDAFF, Earls of.

10035 LANDEFELD. Landefeld-Howell-Clemons. By Ella (Foy) O'Gorman. 1956. sheet. A genealogical table consisting of a printed form filled out in MS. Photocopy. 39 x 59 cm. 70-230294 MARC. CS71.L256 1956a

10036 LANDER. A brief history of Rev. Samuel Lander, senior, and his wife Eliza Ann (Miller) Lander ... their two sons William Lander and Samuel Lander, and their grandson Samuel A. Weber, by William Lander Sherrill. (Greensboro, N.C., The Advocate press, 1918) 63, (1) p. plates, ports. 23 cm. On cover: A brief history of the Lander family. 1918. 33-29129. CS71.L255 1918

LANDERS. See: DANIEL, 1959
JOHNSTON, 1964

LANDFAIR. See JOHNSON, 1961

10037 LANDIS. The Landis family of Lancaster county, a comprehensive history of the Landis folk from the martyrs' era to the arrival of the first Swiss settlers, giving their numerous lineal descendants; also, an accurate record of members in the rebellion, with a sketch of the start and subsequent growth of Landisville and Landis valley, and a complete dictionary of living Landis adults ... By D.B. Landis ... Lancaster, Pa., Pub. and printed by the author, 1888. 90 p. 21 cm. 9-11919.
CS71.L257 1888

10038 LANDIS. Reunion of the Landis families. 1st - 1911 - Landis Family Reunion Association. Lancaster, Pa. (etc.) v. illus., ports., maps (part fold.) fold. geneal. chart. 23-26 cm. Annual, 1911-17, 1929 - biennial, 1919-27. No reunions were held 1942-45. Reports for the 27th (1946) and 29th (1948) reunions erroneously called 26th and 27th, respectively. Title varies slightly. 35-32271 rev. CS71.L257

10039   LANDIS.   Partial genealogy of the Landis family, with some historical notes embracing the direct lineal descendants of Abraham Landis.   By Beulah F. Mumma.   (Waynesboro? Pa., 1925)
58 p.   20 cm.   50-49674.   CS71. L257   1925

10040   LANDIS.   The Landis genealogy, compiled by Norman A. Landis and H.K. Stoner, with an historical outline by James B. Landis.   Berlin, Pa., Berlin Pub. Co., 1935.   51 p.   22 cm.   53-54277.
                                                                             CS71. L257   1935

10041   LANDIS.   Descendants of Jacob Landes of Salford Township, Montgomery Co., Pennsylvania.
By Henry S. Landes.   Souderton, 1943.   24 p.   24 cm.   54-49805.   CS71. L257   1943

10042   LANDIS.   The Landis family book.   By Ira David Landis.   Lancaster, Pa., 1950 -
v.   illus., ports.   27 cm.   Place of imprint on cover: Lititz, Pa.   51-24208.   CS71. L257   1950

10043   LANDIS.   Landis family, 1751-1951.   (Canton, Kan., Arthur D. Diener family) 1951.
14 p.   16 cm.   Additions and corrections in ms.   53-34071.   CS71. L257   1951

LANDIS.   See also STRASSBURGER, 1922

10044   LANDON.   Account of the family of Landon of Monnington and Credenhill, co. Hereford.
Comp. from notes and information collected by some members of the family.   (n. p.) 1912.
18 p.   illus. (coat of arms)   30 cm.   20-15247.   CS439. L22

10045   LANDON.   Landon genealogy; the French and English home and ancestry, with some account of the descendants of James and Mary Vaill Landon in America.   Part II. Boardman genealogy, the English home and ancestry of Samuel Boreman and Thomas Boreman, now called Boardman, with some account of their descendants in America, by James Orville Landon.   New York, N.Y., South Hero, Vt., C. Boardman co., ltd., 1928.   2 p. l., iii-xvi, 385 p.   illus. (coat of arms)   26 cm.   29-18100.
                                                                             CS71. L259   1928

10046   LANDOR.   Pedigree of the paternal ancestry of Walter Savage Landor, with evidences.   Compiled by Rev. Rashleigh E. H. Duke ... London, Mitchell, Hughes and Clarke, 1912.   1 p. l., 16 p. fold.
col. pl.   28 cm.   Reprinted from "Miscellanea genealogical et heraldica".   4th ser., v. 5, 1912.   The plate is a reproduction of the illuminated grant of arms to Walter Landor by the College of arms.   "Pedigree of Taylor": p. 6.   23-14538.   CS439. L225

10047   LANE.   Memoranda relating to the Lane, Reyner, and Whipple families, Yorkshire and Massachusetts ... By W. H. Whitmore.   Boston, H. W. Dutton, printers, 1857.   24 p.   facsims., fold.
geneal. tab.   23½ cm.   "Reprinted from the New England historical and genealogical register, for April and July, 1857."   9-11920.
                                                                             CS71. L266   1857

10048   LANE.   Hampton Lane family memorial.   A re-print of the address at the funeral of Dea.
Joshua Lane, of Hampton, N.H. (who was killed by lightning June 14, 1766) By his son, Dea. Jeremiah Lane of Hampton Falls.   With sketches of his ancestry and families to the fourth generation from William Lane of Boston, Mass., 1651.   By Rev. James P. Lane.   Norton, Mass., Printed by Lane brothers, 1885.   2 p. l., 16 p., 2 l. (11) p.   17 cm.   Reprint of original t. - p.: A memorial and tear of lamentation, with the improvement of the death of pious friends, Hampton Falls, July 17, 1766.   Portsmouth, in New Hampshire; Printed by D. & R. Fowle, 1766.   9-11918.
                                                                             CS71. L266   1885

10049   LANE.   Lane families of the Massachusetts Bay colony.   Memorial address at the reunion of descendants and kindred of William Lane, Boston, 1651, William Lane, Hampton, 1685.   Dea. Joshua Lane, Hampton, who was killed by lightning, June 14, 1766.   In the Congregational church, Hampton, N.H.   Wednesday, Sept. 1, 1886.   By Rev. James P. Lane.   (Norton, Mass., Printed by Lane Brothers, 1886)   58 p.   illus.   23 cm.   Printed by request.   9-11917.   CS71. L266   1886

10050   LANE.   James Lane of North Yarmouth, Me., and his descendants.   Communicated by Rev.
James P. Lane ... (Boston, 1888)   12 p.   25 cm.   Caption title.   "Reprinted from the N. E. historical and genealogical register for April, 1888."   9-11916.   CS71. L266   1888

10051   LANE.   Lane genealogies ... Exeter, N.H., The News-letter press, 1891-1902.   3 v. fronts., plates, ports. 23 cm.   Volume 1 compiled by Rev. Jacob Chapman and Rev. James H. Fitts; v.2-3, by James Hill Fitts.   Volume 1 has manuscript notes inserted.   Contents. -v.1. William Lane of Boston, Mass., 1648, including the records of Edmund J. Lane and James P. Lane.   Capt. John Lane of York county, Maine, 1693; Capt. John Lane of Fishersfield, N.H., 1737. - v.2. William Lane, Dorchester, Mass., 1635. Robert Lane, Stratford, Conn., 1660; John Lane, Milford, Conn., 1642; John Merrifield Lane, Boston, Mass., 1752; Daniel Lane, New London, Conn., 1651; George Lane, Rye, New York, 1664. - v.3. English family. Rickmansworth, Hertfordshire, 1542-1758; Job Lane, Malden, Mass., 1649; James Lane, Casco Bay, Maine, 1650; Edward Lane, Boston, Mass., 1657.   3-20073 rev.

CS71.L266   1891-1902

10052   LANE.   Genealogical notes on the families of Daniel Lane 2d and Mary Griswold Lane, of Killingworth and Wolcott, in Connecticut, (married at Killingworth, July 14th, A.D. 1763) Comp. by four of their descendants (Hiram W. Lane, Mrs. Elisha R. Newell, Mrs. Joseph F. Smith, Albert C. Beckwith) Elkhorn, Wis. (The Independent print) 1899.   64 p. 21½ cm. 99-1571.

CS71.L266   1899

10053   LANE.   Joel Lane, pioneer and patriot.   A biographical sketch, including notes about the Lane family and the colonial and revolutionary history of Wake county, North Carolina.   By Marshall De Lancey Haywood ... Raleigh, N.C., Alford, Bynum & Christophers, 1900.   23 p. 20½ cm. 0-2623 rev.

F258.L26

10054   LANE.   A biographical sketch of Hannah Lane Usher of Buxton and Hollis, Maine, with historical and genealogical facts relating to the Lane family of Buxton; by her grandson, Ellis Baker Usher ... (La Crosse? Wis.) Priv. print., 1903.   21 p. front., pl., ports. 21½ cm. "Of this volume twenty-five copies have been printed." 4-2396.

CS71.L266   1903

10055   LANE.   Lane of Bentley hall (now of King's Bromley manor) co. Stafford, by Henry Murray Lane ... London, E. Stock, 1910.   45, (1) p. front., illus., plates. 26½ cm. 16-19782.

CS439.L23

10056   LANE.   Captain Daniel Lane and his wife, Molly Woodman ... (Milwaukee? 1912)   (10) p. illus. 19½ cm. "Of this pamphlet 100 copies were printed." "This statement was prepared by Ellis Baker Usher, 2nd, Milwaukee, Wisconsin, January 1, 1912." References: p. (9) - (10) 12-5615.

F29.B96U8

10057   LANE.   Joel Lane, pioneer and patriot; a biographical sketch including notes about the Lane family, and the colonial and revolutionary history of Wake County, North Carolina.   2d ed. revised by the author.   By Marhsall De Lancey Haywood ... Raleigh, N.C., A. Williams & company, 1925.   30 p. 19½ cm. An illustration of the Joel Lane home mounted on p. (5) 25-21351.

F258.L262

10058   LANE.   Lane, Hughey and allied families; a genealogical study with biographical notes, privately printed for Lulie H. Lane by the American historical company, inc.   New York, 1941.   165 p. plates, ports., col. coats of arms, col. geneal. tables. 32 cm. Some of the plates are accompanied by guard sheets with descripttive letterpress. Title-page, dedication, initials and genealogical tables decorated in colors. Bound in blue crushed levant, gold tooled. Allied families: Allen, Peters, Cavet, Hill, Strong and Pettus. Bibliographical notes throughout text. 42-3262.

CS71.L266   1941

LANE.   See also: AVERY, 1925   PENDEREL, DA446.H89
                      CHICKERING, 1919   SELDEN, 1911
                      DRAKE, 1962   STEARNS, 1898
                      LAYNE.   No. 1547 - Cabell county.
                      McCULLOUGH, 1918

10059   LANG.   A genealogy of the first five generations in America of the Lang family, descendants of Robert Lang, fisherman, of the isles of Shoals ... with some notices of allied Sagamore creek and other Portsmouth families, Williams, Walford, Brooking, Wallis, Staples, Peverly, Sherburne, Jones, Savage, Moses, Jeffry, Beck, Banfield, etc.   A chart of the first four generations, a chart of the first seven generations of adult male Langs, a map of Sagamore creek family homesteads, by Howard Parker Moore ... (Rutland, Vt., The Tuttle company, 1935)   4 p. l., (7)-98 p. map, 2 geneal. tab. (1 fold.) 24 cm. 35-28834.

CS71.L27   1935

LANG.   In vertical file under PRANKE family.   Ask reference librarian for this material.

LANG.   See also: GIRDLESTONE, CS439.G53
                   LONG.
                   No. 579 - Monroe, N.H.

10060   LANGDALE.   The pedigree of the Langdale family.   (London, G. Beridge and co., printers,
187-?)   26 p.   7 coats of arms.   22½ cm.   Interleaved.   19-3634.   CS439.L24

LANGDALE.   See also STOURTON, 1899

10061   LANGDON.   From one generation to another ... (Brooklyn, N.Y., H.N. Langdon and A.M.
Smith, 1906)   2 p. l., (7) - 80 p.   illus. (incl. ports., facsims.)   3 geneal. tab. (2 fold.)   22 cm.   Dedication signed: Harriet Langdon
Williams, Elam Chester Langdon.   "Printed for private distribution December 20th, 1906 to commemorate the one hundredth anniversary of the
arrival overland from Vershire, Vermont, of the Langdon family at Columbia, afterwards Cincinnati, Ohio.   Ed. and pub. by Harriet Nash Langdon
and Annie Morrill Smith ... "   Contents. - Our family. - Our father. - Home and customs. - Schools. - Churches. - Amusements. - Roads and
highways.   14-19996.   CS71.L273   1906

10062   LANGDON.   Memory pictures, by Harriet Langdon Williams.   Printed for private distribu-
tion ... (Brooklyn) 1908.   89 p. incl. fold. pl., ports.   22½ cm.   "Edited and published by Annie Morrill Smith." - ms. note on t.-p.
Contents. - Henry Archer Langdon - To the memory of my brother John Phelps Langdon. - To the memory of my brother Elam Chester Langdon. -
Memory pictures of my angel sister Cynthia Langdon Morrill. - Memories of my life 1825-1908.   Harriet Langdon Williams.   16-17953.

                                                                  CS71.L273   1908

10063   LANGDON.   Robert Bruce Langdon and his descendants, by Caroline Langdon Brooks.
Minneapolis, Minn., The Miller publishing co., 1926.   3 p. l., (23) p., 1 l.   front. (port.)   24½ cm.   Bibliography:
1 leaf at end.   27-3962.   CS71.L273   1926

10064   LANGDON.   Thomas Langdon of Hempstead, Long island, and some of his descendants, by
Henry Alanson Tredwell, jr. ... Brooklyn, N.Y.)1945?)   2 p. l., 14 numb. l., 1 l.   28 x 22 cm.   Type-written
(carbon copy)   Bibliography: 2d prelim. leaf.   45-9546.   CS71.L273   1945

10065   LANGDON.   Geneology (i.e. Genealogy) of the Langdon family, 1950.   By Buel Amos Langdon.
(Wilmette? Ill., 1950)   61-90 p.   22 cm.   63-25437.   CS71.L273   1950

LANGDON.   See also: CHURCHILL, 1935
                       LAYTON, 1885
                       TODD, 1867
                       VAN NORDEN, 1923
                       VAN RENSSELAER, CS69.S7

LANGE.   See FLAGG, 1903

LANGEMO.   See No. 553 - Goodhue county.

LANGENBERGER.   In vertical file under PRANKE family.   Ask reference librarian for this material.

LANGENECKER.   See LONGENECKER.

LANGENSTEIN.   See: BELL, 1959
                     BELL, 1960

LANGEVIN.   See LANGEVIN-LACROIX.

10066   LANGEVIN-LACROIX.   La famille Langevin-Lacroix 1653-1916, par l'abbé Edmond Langevin
dit Lacroix ... Montréal, Imprimé au "Devoir" (1916?)   2 p. l., (7)-52 p. incl. plates, 2 port. on 1 l., facsim.
20½ cm.   47-39014.   CS90.L23

10067   LANGFORD.   Genealogy of Langford and the allied families of Sweeting, Robertson, Bell (by)
George Langford.   Joliet, Ill., 1936.   4 v. in 1.   Blue-print.   Paged continuously.   Includes bibliography.   "I have been
assisted by information accumulated over a long period of time by Mrs. Charles L. Alden ... whose maiden name was Mary Langford Taylor.   The
results of her researches form a considerable part of each of volumes I, II and IV," - Foreword.   37-7889.

                                                                  CS71.L274   1936

10068   LANGFORD.   The descendants of John Frederick Langford of Great Britain, Indiana, and Illinois and his wife, Mary Adams, of Kentucky and Illinois, to the sixth generation, by Virginia Ingles Maes.   (Rushville, Ill.) 1942.   14 l. 28 x 21½ cm.   Reproduced from type-written copy.   45-32373.

CS71.L274   1942

LANGHIRT.   In vertical file under PRANKE family.   Ask reference librarian for this material.

10069   LANGLADE.   Langlade papers - 1737-1800.   Compiled by Morgan Lewis Martin.
(In Wisconsin. State historical society.   Report and collections ... 1877-1879. Madison, 1879. 23 cm. v. 8, p. (209)-223) A collection of documents relating to the Langlade fam. of Green Bay, Wis. Introd. signed: M. L. Martin. 20-16691.   F576.W81 vol. 8

LANGLEY.   See: LONGLEY.
No. 553, Goodhue county.

10070   LANGLOIS.   The Langlois family history.   By Eileen Risley Heitzman.   (n. p.) c. 1966.
28 l. 22 x 36 cm.   Caption title.   Bibliography: leaf 28.   67-8833.   CS71.L2745   1966

10071   LANGS.   The descendants of Jacob Langs and Elizabeth Fowler.   Data collected and arranged by Dr. W. O. A. Langs; with an introductory sketch, "The Langs family of Pennsylvania," by John Pierce Langs.   (n. p.) 1941.   32 p. 23 cm.   Date of imprint in ms. on t. -p.   43-49609.   CS71.L2746   1941

10072   LANGSTAFF.   The Langstaffs of Teesdale and Weardale: materials for a history of a yeoman family gathered together by George Blundell Longstaff ... London, Mitchell, Hughes and Clarke, 1906.   (742) p. incl. geneal. tables.   2 pl., port., facsim. 28½ cm.   8-17887.   CS439.L25

10073   LANGSTAFF.   The Langstaffs of Teesdale and Weardale: materials for a history of a yeoman family gathered together by George Blundell Longstaff ... Rev. ed   London, M. Hughes and Clarke, 1919.   2 v. fold. front. (map) geneal. tables. 32½ x 26 cm.   Paged continuously. 45-25181 rev.   CS439.L25   1919

10074   LANGSTAFF.   War services of the Longstaffs and allied families, compiled by Mary L. Longstaff.   Printed privately.   London, H. Rees, ltd., 1922.   23 p. 32 x 27 cm.   (With, as issued: Longstaff, G. B. The Langstaffs of Teesdale and Weardale ... London, 1923) 46-28406.   CS439.L25   1923

10075   LANGSTAFF.   The Langstaffs of Teesdale and Weardale: materials for a history of a yeoman family, gathered together by Geoge Blundell Longstaff ... Rev. ed.   London, Mitchell, Hughes and Clarke, 1923.   xiii p., 1 l., 574 p., 1 l. incl. geneal. tables.   front. (port.) fold. map. 32 x 27 cm.   With this is bound, as issued: Longstaff, Mary L. S.   War service of the Longstaffs and allied families ... London, 1922. 46-28167.   CS439.L25   1923

10076   LANGSTON.   Descendants of Solomon Langston of Laurens county, South Carolina, through his son, Bennett. (By Carroll Spencer Langston.) (Williamsville, Ill.) 1942.   1 p. l., 46 (i. e. 47) numb. l.   28 x 21½ cm.   Includes extra numbered leaf 41 a.   Reproduced from type-written copy.   "Sources of information": leaves 2-3. 44-1941.   CS71.L2747   1942

LANGSTON.   See also POOL, 1931

10077   LANGTON.   The story of our family.   By Anne Langton.   (Printed for private circulation.)   Manchester, T. Sowler & co., printers, 1881.   2 p. l., 204 p. front., plates, fold. map. 21 cm. 21-21740.   CS439.L255

LANGTON.   See also CRALL, 1908

10078   LANGWORTHY.   Memorandum and reminiscences; personal sketches and memoirs of the family Langworthy, 1707 to 1849, '52-'60.   By Lyman Barker Langworthy.   (Rochester, N. Y., 1869)   101 numb. l. 20 x 27 cm.   Type-written copy.   Coat of arms attached to p. 5.   Presented by Charles Ford Langworthy. 24-25460.   CS71.L275   1869

10079   LANGWORTHY.   The Langworthy chronicle.   18th - 46th   Aug. 1908 - Aug. 1936.   Hamilton, N. Y., 1908-36.   28 no's. illus. (incl. ports.) 21 - 27 cm.   annual.   Title varies: 18th-36th Langworthy family reunion (or Langworthy reunion.   Annual reunionof the Langworthy family, Reunion of the Langworthy family) 37th - The Langworthy chronicle.   Earlier reports of the reunion were published in the Utica newspapers. 37-16819.   CS71.L275   1908

10080   LANGWORTHY.   The Langworthys of early Dubuque and their contributions to local history.
(In Iowa journal of history and politics. Iowa City, Ia., 1910. 26½ cm. v. 8, p. (315)-422) Contents. - Introduction, by J. C. Parish. - Autobiographical sketch of Lucius H. Langworthy. - Autobiographical sketch of Solon M. Langworthy. - Sketch of Edward Langworthy. - Autobiographical
sketch of Edward Langworthy. - Sketches of the early settlement of the West, by L. H. Langworthy. - Dubuque; its history, mines, Indian legends, etc.
by L. H. Langworthy. 18-8372.   F616. I5 vol. 8

——— Copy 2, detached.   F629. D8P23

10081   LANGWORTHY.   The Langworthy family; some descendants of Andrew and Rachel (Hubbard)
Langworthy who were married at Newport, Rhode Island, November 3, 1658, compiled by William
Franklin Langworthy ... Hamilton, N. Y., W. F. and O. S. Langworthy (1940)   x, 403 p. front. (coat of arms)
plates, ports. 23½ cm. 40-34268.   CS71. L275   1940

10082   LANIER.   Sketch of the life of J. F. D. Lanier.   (Printed for the use of his family only)   New
York (Hosford & sons, printers) 1871.   62 p. front., port. (mounted phot.) 22 cm. 12-19111.
                                                                              F526. L29

10083   LANIER.   Sketch of the life of J. F. D. Lanier.   (Printed for the use of his family only.)   2d ed.
(New York?) 1877.   87 p. front. (port.) 24 cm. "The late Richard H. Winslow": p. 65-68. Appendix: Letter from Sidney Lanier
containing a short genealogy of the Lanier family: p. 75-87. 16-10379.   F526. L295

10084   LANIER.   Lanier, her name, in memoriam, Elizabeth Lanier Clement, May 19, 1904 -
December 24, 1927.   (Danville, Va., 1954)   55 p. illus. 23 cm. 56-52177. CS71. L276   1954

        LANIER.   See also JEFFERSON, E159. G56

10085   LANING.   History of the Laning family.   By Robert Laning Clifford.   (Princeton, N. J.)
1967.   10 l. 32 cm. Caption title. 68-5473.   CS71. L277   1967

        LANNING.   See LANING.

10086   LANPHEAR.   History and genealogy of the Lanpheres and the Pierces, Halls, Martins, Pikes,
Achermans, and many others.   By Frances Lanphere Elder (and) Edward Everett Lanphere.   (Evanston? Ill.) 1958.   1 v. illus. 30 cm. 61-33970.   CS71. L278   1958

        LANPHERE.   See LANPHEAR.

        LANPHIER.   See LANPHEAR.

10087   LANSING.   The Lansing family.   A genealogy of the descendants of Gerrit Frederickse
Lansing who came to America from Hasselt, province of Overijssell, Holland, 1640.   Eight generations.   By Claude G. Munsell.   (New York) Priv. print., 1916.   3 p. l., 103, (10) p. front. (coat of arms)
30 cm. 16-14527.   CS71. L28   1916

        LANTERMAN.   See ROBB, 1902

        LANTMAN.   See SNYDER, 1958

10088   LANTZ.   The Lantz family record, being a brief account of the Lantz family in the United
States of America, by Jacob W. Lantz ... (Cedar Springs? Va., 1931)   vii, 265 p. plates, ports., facsims.
23 cm. 31-20880.   CS71. L29   1931

10089   LAPE.   Some descendants of Gottleib Lape and his wife Carolina Jacobs of Zanesville, Ohio.
Compiled by Charles Frederick Lape and Ella Foy O'Gorman (Mrs. Michael Martin O'Gorman) (n. p.)
1935.   1 p. l., 6 numb. l. 28 cm. 38M2011T.   CS71. L3   1935

10090   LAPHAM.   Lapham family register, or Records of some of the descendants of Thomas
Lapham of Scituate, Mass., in 1635.   By William B. Lapham ... Augusta (Me.) Sprague, Owen &
Nash, printers, 1873.   1 p. l., 31 p. 23½ cm. 9-11915.   CS71. L312   1873

10091 LAPHAM. Concerning John Lapham and some of his descendants; a copy of an article published in 1948 in the American genealogist, with corrections and additions. By Mary W. Peckham. (Santa Barbara? Calif., 1948?) 70 l. (l. 68-70 blank) 25 cm. Cover title: John Lapham of Dartmouth, Mass. Includes bibliographies. 50-32105. CS71.L312 1948

10092 LAPHAM. Laphams in America; thirteen thousand descendents including descendents of John from Devonshire, England, to Providence, R.I., 1673, Thomas from Kent, England, to Scituate, Mass., 1634, and genealogical notes of other Lapham families. By Bertha (Bortle) Beal Aldridge. (Victor? N.Y., 1953) 552 p. port. 24 cm. 54-36430. CS71.L312 1953

LAPHAM. See also: KELLEY, 1939
SANBORN, 1928

LAREW. See DOBYNS, 1908

10093 LARICHELIERE. Généalogie de la famille Richard-Lavallée-Larichelière, par Gérard Malchelosse ... Montréal, G. Ducharme, 1928. 2 p. l., (9)-43 p., 2 l. incl. front. (port.) 23½ cm. A 33-63. CS90.L25

10094 LARIMER. The Larimer, McMasters and allied families, comp. and ed. by Rachel H. L. Mellon. Philadelphia, Printed for private circulation by J. B. Lippincott company, 1903. 196 p. front., illus., plates, ports., facsims., fold. geneal. tab., coats of arms. 25 cm. Title vignette (coat of arms) Allied families: Sheakley, McCurdy, Creighton, Hughey, King, McLaughlin, and Irwin. 3-32810. CS71.L322 1903

LARIMORE. See ADAMS, 1958

10095 LARISON. The Larisun famili: a biografic scetch ev the descendants ev Jen Larisun, the Dan, thru hiz sun Jamz Larisun, and hiz grandsun Andru Larisun. Bi C.W. Larisun ... Ringos, N.J., Fonic publishin heus, 1888. 472 p. photos. 20 cm. Phonetic type. CA9-2575. CS71.L323 1888

LARISON. See also GARDINER, 1929

LARISUN. See LARISON.

10096 LARKIN. Chronicle of the Larkin family of the town of Westerlie and colony of Rhoad Island in New England. La Porte, Ind., Pub. for the Larkin family association by W.H. Larkin, jr., 1908 - v. fold. geneal. tab. 21 cm. 11-7227 rev. CS71.L325 1908

10097 LARKIN. Genealogy of Belinda Amy Guess Larkins, by Linnie Florilla Larkins. (Washington) 1913. 31 l. fold. geneal. tab. 23½ cm. A manuscript copy of the Buck, Goodrich, Treat and Bulkeley ancestry of Mrs. Larkins, and a photostat copy of a manuscript genealogical table. 24-20933. CS71.L325 1913

10098 LARKIN. Larkin - Nicholson. (1964?) (23) l. 28 cm. Caption title. Typescript (carbon copy) 78-218622 MARC. CS71.L325 1964

10099 LARKIN. A Larkins genealogy; Eldridge Larkins and Elizabeth Bledsoe, and their descendants, by Winniferd Eyrich Perrigo and Lyle Donovan Perrigo. Richard, Wash. (1969) xii, 63 p. illus., maps, port. 29 cm. 79-108249 MARC. CS71.L325 1969

LARKIN. See also: KING, CS439.K7
LINCOLN, 1930

LARKINS. See LARKIN.

LARNED. See LEARNED.

LARNETT. See LEARNED.

LAROE. See LA RUE.

10100   LARRAIN.   ... Los de Larrain en Chile.   By Guillermo de la Cuadra Gormez   Trabajo pub. en la Revista chilena de historia y geografia.   Santiago de Chile, Imprenta universitaria, 1917
19 p. 26 cm. 20-8417.   CS319.L3

10101   LARREATEGUI.   La casa solariega de los Larreategui (1878-1895) Dibujos i reproducciones del sr. Teobaldo Constante.   Miguel M. Luna.   (Guayaquil) Lib. e imp. Gutenberg de E. A. Uzcategui,
1943.   80 p. incl. front., illus. (ports., plan, coats of arms) 15 x 22 cm. 48-32227.   CS379.L3   1943

        LARSEN.   See: LARISON.
                           SALISBURY, 1961

        LARSON.   See: No. 553 - Goodhue county.
                           No. 5536 - The sloopers.

10102   LA RUE.   Six generations of La Rues and allied families: containing sketch of Isaac La Rue, senior, who died in Frederick County, Virginia, in 1795, and some account of his American ancestors and three generations of his descendants and families who were connected by intermarriage, among others, Carman, Hodgen, Helm, Buzan, Rust, McDonald, Castleman, Walters, Alexander, Medley, McMahon, Vertrees, Keith, Wintersmith, Clay, Neill, Grantham, Vanmeter and Enlow; copies of six old wills and other old documents; various incidents connected with the settlement of the Nolynn Valley in Kentucky; also a chapter on the La Rue family and the child Abraham Lincoln.   By Otis M. Mather ... Hodgenville, Ky., 1921.   xiii, 198 p. front., illus. (incl. ports., facsim., geneal. tab.) 21 cm. 21-11584.
                                                                        CS71.L328   1921

10103   LA RUE.   Jacques Le Roux; the French Huguenot and some of his descendants, LeRoux, Laroe, LaRue, by Emojene Demarest Champine.   (Minneapolis, Printed by Augsberg publishing house)
1939.   100, (8) p. front., plates, ports. 20½ cm. Blank pages for "Records" (8 at end) "First edition." "References: Le Roux-Laroe-La Rue": p. 75-77. 40-3759.   CS71.L328   1939

10104   LARWOOD.   Morphology of Larwood genealogy: being a prefatory tabulation of the relation- ships and descents of members of the Larwood family in America since circa 1720; preparatory to a full account of the history and nomenclature of the name in England since circa 1300, with its trans- itions through De La Wode, Larwode (Delawood) Larawode, Larrawood to Larwood.   By James Larwood.   (n. p.) 1933.   1 p. l., ii, 15 (i.e.14) numb. l. 28 cm. Type-written. No. 13 omitted in pagination. "Compiled for private circulation." 38-14723.   CS71.L336   1933

10105   LARZELERE.   Larzelere family and collateral lines of Elkinton, Stockton, Brigham, Carpenter.   By Alexander Du Bin.   Philadelphia, Historical Publication Society, 1950.
20 l. 26 cm. 51-4633.   CS71.L338   1950

10106   LASCELLES.   The history and antiquities of Harewood, in the county of York, with topograph- ical notices of its parish & neighbourhood; by John Jones.   London, Simpkin, Marshall, & co.; (etc., etc.) 1859.   2 p. l., viii, (9)-312 p. front., illus., 9 pl., plan. 23 cm. Some of the plates are from Whitaker's History of Leeds. cf. Boyne, The Yorkshire library. 3-15898.   DA690.H27J7

10107   LASCELLES.   Pedigrees of Lascelles of Brakenburgh, Hinderskelf, and Eryholme, in the county of York.   Copied from the original roll, in the possession of Robert Morley Lascelles, esquire, of Slingsby, and from the Heraldic visitation of Yorkshire, 1584-5.   (London) Printed by Taylor and co., 1869.   1 p. l., 7 p. illus. (coats of arms) 29 cm. Reprinted from the Miscellanea genealogica et heraldica. London, 1876. vol. II, p. 123-129. 19-3636.   CS439.L26

10108   LASELL.   ... John Lazell of Hingham and some of his descendants, compiled by Theodore Studley Lazell.   (Haverhill, Mass.) Priv. print. (The Record publishing company) 1936. 130 p. 24½ cm. At head of title: Lassell, Lasell, Lazell. "Reprinted with corrections from the New England historical and genealogical register, vols. 88 and 89." 38-32666.   CS71.L34   1936

        LASELL.   See also: McKAY, 1950
                                MILLER, 1939

10109   LASHER. Lasher genealogy... New York, C. S. Williams, 1904.   270 p. plates, ports. , map. 24 cm.
"Edition of two hundred copies." "The compiling of this genealogy was started through the active co-operation of George W. Lasher ... Alfred P.
Lasher ... Hazard Lasher ... and Thomas J. Lasher ... of whom Alfred P. Lasher ... took the lead. " - Pref.   Contents. - pt. 1. Descendants of
Francois Le Seur. - pt. 2. Descendants of Sebastian Loescher. - pt. 3. Descendants of John Lejere. 4-21918.   CS71. L343   1904

         LASSELL.   See LASELL.

10110   LATANÉ.   Parson Latané, 1672-1732, by Lucy Temple Latané.   Charlottesville, Va., The
Michie company, printers, 1936.   3 p. l., 162, (2) p. front. (coat of arms) 24½ cm.   "Genealogy" (p. (91)-102) followed
by 2 blank pages for "genealogical notes". Bibliography: p. (83)-86. 36-22996.
                                                                                      CS71. L347   1936

         LATANE.   See JONES, 1891

10111   LATERRIÈRE.   La famille de Sales Laterrière, par M. l'abbé H. R. Casgrain.   Quebec,
Atelier typographique de L. Brousseau, 1870.   63 p. 13½ cm. 12-2849.   CS90. L3

         LATHAM.   See: AUSTIN, F78. A93
                           AUSTIN, F78. A94
                           READ, 1957
                           READING, 1898
                           SOUTHERLAND, 1931

         LATHAN.   See WASHBURN in vertical file.   Ask reference librarian for this material.

         LATHOM.   See NORRES, 1856

         LATHROP.   See LOTHROP.

         LATHURNER.   See LADURNER.

10112   LATIMER.   The history and antiquities of the parish of Hammersmith, interspersed with
biographical notices of illustrious and eminent persons, who have been born, or who have resided in
the parish, during the three preceding centuries.   By Thomas Faulkner ... London, Nicholas & son
(etc.) 1839.   xiv, (2), 446 p. front. (port.) illus., pl., fold. maps. 22 cm. Title vignette. Contains pedigree of the Latimer family.
3-11546.   DA685. H2F2

10113   LATIMER.   Memorials of St. John at Hackney.   Compiled by R. Simpson.   Part III. Guild-
ford, Printed by J. Billing and sons, 1882.   viii, 301 p., 1 l. 21 cm. Extracts from the Minutes of the Select vestry: p. (60)
- 195. Ms. note on cover after pt. III: "Complete in itself. The Latimer pedigree: p. (209)-301. 17-432.
                                                                                      DA690. H1S5

10114   LATIMER.   Jonathan Latimer, by Arthur B. Wells.   (Marblehead, Mass., Printed by the
N. A. Lindsey co., inc., 1929?)   1 p. l., 24 p. 21 cm.   Type-written and manuscript additions throughout text. "Authorities":
p. 22. 33-312.   CS71. L35   1929

         LATIMER.   See also: ALNO, CS419. P3
                                BENSON, 1932
                                MOUNSEY, 1947
                                SMALL, 1905

         LATON.   See MOORE, 1918

         LATOUR.   See CASTELBERG, 1959

10115   LATROBE.   John H. B. Latrobe and his times, 1803-1891, by John E. Semmes; with thirty-
eight illustrations in color and black and white.   Baltimore, Md., The Norman, Remington co. (c. 1917)
viii, 601 p. plates (part col.) ports. (2 col., incl. front.) coat of arms, facsim. 24½ cm. Latrobe genealogy: p. 574-580. 18-2814.
                                                                                      CT275. L277S4

LATSON.   See No. 9385 - Twiggs county, Ga.

10116   LATTA.   Crowned in palm-land.   A story of African mission life ... (By Robert Hamill Nassau)   Philadelphia, J.B. Lippincott & co., 1874.   390 p. front. (port.) plates, map.   19 cm.   A memoir of Mrs. Mary Cloyd Nassau.   Genealogy of Latta family: p. 13-14.   33-18572.   BV3542. N3N3

10117   LATTA.   Following out branches of his family tree gives retired publisher (Robert H. Latta) absorbing hobby.   By Editha L. Watson.   Chicago, 1934.   1 l. 27 cm. 39M118T.
CS71. L36   1934

10118   LATTA.   Robert H. Latta family collection.   (manuscripts, letters, etc.)
CS71. L36
Rare book room.

10119   LATTA.   American descendants of Samuel Latta.   (By Mrs. Enid M. (Dickinson) Collins) (Jamaica, N.Y., 1940?)   7 numb. l. 28 cm. Signed: Enid D. Collins. Caption title. Type-written. 41-15225.
CS71. L36   1940

10120   LATTIMORE.   Our family, by Alida Lattimore ... (Pultneyville, N.Y.) 1936.   6 numb. l. 33 x 21½ cm. Caption title. Type-written; corrections in manuscript. 44-26059.   CS71. L365   1936

LATTURNER.   See LADURNER.

10121   LAUBACH.   Eleven generations of Laubachs, the ancestry and descendants of John Laubach and Anna Kline Laubach.   By Merit Lees Laubach.   Terre Haute, Ind., 1958.   63 l. 29 cm. 59-28590.
CS71. L368   1958

10122   LAUDER.   Notes on historical references to the Scottish family of Lauder, ed. by James Young.   Glasgow, Printed by T. Duncan, 1884.   102, lxii p. plates (coats of arms) 27½ cm. "Only forty two copies printed for sale, of which this is no. 36": ms. note on book. 16-20934.   CS479. L3

LAUDER.   See also DICK, DA890. E4S18

10123   LAUDERDALE.   The Lauderdales of Scotland and America, 1056-1936 ... by Charles J. Lauderdale.   Joplin, Mo., Gahagan printing co. (c.1937)   6 p. l., 91 p. illus. (coat of arms) pl., ports. 21 cm. 37-4782.   CS71. L37   1937

LAUER.   See LOWER.

LAUFER.   See: BECHTEL, 1936
            LAUFFER.

10124   LAUFFER.   The Lauffer history.   A genealogical chart of the descendants of Christian Lauffer, the pioneer, with a few biographical sketches.   September, 1905 ... Publication committee, Joseph A. Lauffer ... chairman.   Dr. Chas. A. Lauffer ... secretary.   Henry Z. Lauffer ... treasurer.   (Jeannette, Pa., Press of the Westmoreland journal, 1906)   4 p. l., 180 p. plates, ports. 23 cm. "The matter of this volume exclusive of the John Lauffer division of the Henry Lauffer branch was arranged for the printer by Dr. Chas. A. Lauffer." 6-34016.   CS71. L373   1906

10125   LAUGHLIN.   ... Laughlin history prepared for the centennial reunion, held at Lore City, Ohio, Thursday, August 22, 1907, by John W. Laughlin.   Barnesville, O. (1907)   64 p. port. 19 cm. At head of title: 1807-1907. 25-12668.   CS71. L374   1907

10126   LAUGHLIN.   ... Laughlin history, prepared for the re-union held at Bellecenter, Ohio, Thursday, August twenty-second, nineteen hundred and twelve by John W. Laughlin.   Barnesville, O. (1912)   104 p., 10 l. front., ports. 22½ cm. At head of title: 1807-1912. "Revised edition." 41-41200.   CS71. L374   1912

LAUGHLIN.   See also: KING, 1930
                        LEDLIE, 1961

10127   LAUNCE.   A memorable note wherein is conteyned the names in part of the cheefest kendred of Robert Launce, late of Mettfeild in the county of Suff.   Deceased, collected faithfully out of an old booke of his own handewriting by Thomas Fella of Hallisworth.   And in this p'sent writing spesified as heere followeth.   Privately printed.   (n. p., 188-?)   (14) p., 1 l.   illus.   30 cm.   Title within ornamental border.   Grant of arms to John Launce of Halesworth, 1580 (1 leaf)   A facsimile reproduction of the note copied from a folio manuscript volume in the Halesworth church chest by Thomas Fella, about 1611.   It is in the handwriting of Fella and has on verso of p. (3) an elaborate full-page pen and ink drawing, representing "a tree of divers fruits."   The merchants' mark of Thomas Fella, the writer, occurs twice in the volume.   20-15248.
CS439. L265

LAUNDER.   See MASTER, CS439. M36

LAURENS.   See DU LAURENS.

LAURENZ.   See LORENTZ.

10128   LAURIE.   Sir Peter Laurie.   A family memoir by Peter G. Laurie.   (Printed for private circulation.)   Brentwood, Wilson and Whitworth, limited, 1901.   4 p. l., (5)-349 (i. e. 351), (1) p. incl. illus., fold. geneal. tables. front., ports. 22 cm.   Includes extra numbered pages 330 a - 330 b.   "The family of Peter Thomson of 'Makerston,' near Kelso" (genealogical table) : p. 337.   16-20955.
DA536. L31L3

LAURIE.   See also LOWRY.

10129   LAUSON.   De la famille des Lauson.   (In Societe historique de Montreal.   Memoires.   Montreal, 1859.   25 cm.
2. livr., p. 65-96)   Signed L. H. L., i. e. (Sir Louis Hypolite Lafontaine.   1-6690.
F1051. S67
         —— Copy 2, detached.
CS90. L388   1859

LAUSON.   See also LAWSON.

10130   LAUSTRUP.   Slaegtsbogen Laustrup.   By Aage Laustrup.   (Farm) 1968.   97 l.   illus.   26 cm.
N. T.   "Anetavie": leaf (in pocket)   77-422205.
CS909. L333

10131   LAUTERBACH.   Chronicle of the Lauterbach family.   By Leo Lauterbach.   3d rev.   Jeru-
salem, 1955.   xxxiii l., 90 p., 91-110 l.   27 cm.   56-41042 rev.
CS39. L33   1955
         —— Supplement containing personal recollections of members of the family by members of the family.   Jerusalem, 1957.   22 p.   28 cm.
CS39. L33   1955
Suppl.
         —— Additions and amendments.   Jerusalem.   v.   28 cm.
CS39. L33   1955
Add.

10132   LAUZON.   Un pionnier de Ville-Marie, Gilles Lauzon et sa postérité.   Éd. de famille.
Québec, L'Action sociale, 1926.   248 p.   front., facsim.   24 cm.   27-25196 rev. *
CS90. L27

10132a   LAVARELLO.   Ask reference librarian for the D'OBRENOVITCH LAVARELLO folder in vertical file.

10133   LAVARS.   ... Family of Lavars.   Cornwall.   Comp. by John Lavars, Bristol, 1874.
(Bristol? 1874?)   7 p.   22 cm.   Caption title.   Printed for private circulation.   "Additions and alterations" in ms. at end.   17-23914.
CS439. L27

10134   LA VEILLE.   La Veille and allied families, genealogical records and biographical notes, prepared and privately printed for Josephine L. Perkins by the American historical society, inc.   New York, 1933.   131 p.   plates, ports., facsims., col. coat of arms, col. geneal. tab.   33 cm.   Alternate pages blank.   Title-page and dedication in colors.   Allied families: Perkins, Beckwith and Leach.   34-5040 rev.
CS71. L412   1933

10135   LA VELLE.   Genealogy of the nine Leavell brothers of Oxford, Mississippi.   By Charlotte (Henry) Leavell.   (Charlottesville? Va., c. 1957)   185 p.   illus., ports., coats of arms, geneal. tables.   28 cm.
Includes bibliographies.   58-17985.
CS71. L4125   1957

10136   LA VERENDRYE.   Verendrye.   (In South Dakota historical collections. Pierre, S.D., 1914. 23½ cm. v.7, p. (89) -402) Contents. - Editorial note (and) Verendrye calendar, by Doane Robinson. - The Verendrye explorations and discoveries, by C.E. De Land. - Journal of La Verendrye, 1738-39. - The Chevalier Verendry's journal, 1742-3. - Correspondence with M. Jusserand. - Parkman's story of the Verendryes. 15-1502 rev.
                                                                                                           F646.S76 vol. 7

10137   LAVOCAT.   The Lavocat family in America, from 1845 to 1929, as compiled by Matilda V. Baillif.   (Minneapolis, c.1929)   6 p. l., 153 p. ports. 16½ cm. "Edition of 250 copies providing a copy for each individual of the present family." 29-13687.
                                                                                                           CS71. L413   1929

10138   LAVOIE.   Notice historique sur la famille de René de la Voye (Canada) par J. Edmond Roy. Lévis, Imprimerie de l'auteur, 1899.   198, ii p., 1 l. illus., facsims. 22 cm. "Ouvrage tiré à 100 exemplaires." Head-pieces. 24-6060.
                                                                                                           CS90. L36   1899

10139   LAVOIE.   ... La famille Lavoie au Canada, de 1650 à 1921; préface de l'hon. Thomas Chapais ... Quebec, 1922.   3 p. l., v-xiii, 403 p. 27 cm. 24-15931.   CS90. L36   1922

        LAVOYE.   See LAVOIE.

10140   LAW.   The antient and modern state of the parish of Cramond.   To which are added, biographical and genealogical collections, respecting some of the most considerable families and individuals connected with that district; comprehending a sketch of the life and projects of John Law of Lauriston ... Edinburgh, Printed by J. Paterson and sold by P. Hill: (etc., etc.) 1794.   vii, 291 p., 1 l. 7 pl., port., map, 3 geneal. tab. 27½ cm. Introduction signed: John Philp (!) Wood. Contains the genealogies of the Law, Loch, Inglis, and Howison families. 3-30367.
                                                                                                           DA890. C88W8

10141   LAW.   The Law family of Calcutta, by Kumud Lal Dey.   Calcutta (R. N. Seal) 1932. x, 190 p. ports. 18½ cm. Completed by Dr. Nalinaksha Dutt, cf. Introductory note. 42-51674.   CT1507. B4D47

10142   LAW.   The kinsmen of John Law (1636-1708) of Acton, Mass., by Adolph Law Voge ... Washington, D. C., 1942.   65 l. 29 x 22½ cm. Type-written. Bibliographical foot-notes. 46-41898.   CS71. L417   1942

        LAW.   See also: ADGER, 1936
                          WATERS, 1928

        LAWDER.   See JOHNSON, 1963

10143   LAWLESS.   The history of the descendants of John and Margaret (Skirvin) Lawless. Quincy, Ill., Printed by Jost & Kiefer printing co., 1927.   89, (8) p. 21 cm. Compiled by a committee of the descendants. Eight pages at end left blank for "Additional history". 27-25085.   CS71. L418   1927

10144   LAWLESS.   The History of the descendants of John Lawless II and Margaret Skirvin Lawless. (Rev. ed., compiled by Helen Lawless Wickliffe and others) Quincy, Ill., Printed by Jost & Kiefer Print. Co., 1968.   203 p. illus., col. coat of arms, facsim., ports. 22 cm. 70-6286 MARC.   CS71. L418   1968

10145   LAWLOR.   The life and struggles of an Irish boy in America; an autobiography, by David S. Lawlor.   Newton, Mass., Carroll publishing company (c.1936)   274 p. incl. front. (port.) 20 cm. Coat of arms on t.-p. 36-9524.
                                                                                                           CT275. L278A3

        LAWLOR.   See also CAIRNS, CS479. C16

        LAWRANCE.   See LAWRENCE.

10146   LAWRENCE.   A genealogical memoir of the family of John Lawrence, of Watertown, 1636; with brief notices of others of the name in England and America. ... (Boston, Press of Coolidge & Wiley) 1847.   64 p. 25 cm. Preface signed: John Lawrence. 9-11912.   CS71. L42   1847

10147   LAWRENCE.   Genealogy of the ancestors and posterity of Isaac Lawrence.   By Frederick S. Pease ... Albany, Printed by J. Munsell, 1848.   20 p. 22½ cm. 9-11910.   CS71. L42   1848

10148   LAWRENCE.   Genealogy of the ancestry and posterity of Isaac Lawrence, and Centennial meeting of his descendants, November 27, 1851. (2d ed.) Albany, J. Munsell, 1853. 76 p. illus. 20 cm. By Frederick Salmon Pease. p. 71-76 left blank for "Births, marriages, deaths." 17-6130.   CS71.L42   1853

10149   LAWRENCE.   Pedigree of Lawrence. Compiled from heralds' visitations, inquisitions post mortem, deeds, charters, wills, parish registers, and other original manuscripts. (Boston, 1856) Comp. by H.G.Somerby. 1 sheet. 40 x 43 cm. Reprinted from N.E. hist. and gen. register, v.10, 1856, p. 296a. 4-27606.   CS71.L42   1856

10150   LAWRENCE.   Pedigree of Lawrence. Compiled ... by H.G.Somerby. (Boston, 1856) 1 sheet. 35½ x 43½ fold. to 22 x 10½ cm.   Reprinted from N.E. hist. and gen. register, v.10, 1856 p. 296 a. 3-4813.   CS71.L42   1856a

10151   LAWRENCE.   A genealogical memoir of the families of Lawrences, with a direct male line from Sir Robert Lawrence of Lancashire, A.D.1190; down to Robert Lawrence of Watertown, A.D. 1636: with notices of others of same name in different states. By Mercy Hale, Stowe, Mass. Boston, Printed for the author, 1856. 20 p. 21½ cm. 17-6151.   CS71.L42   1856b

10152   LAWRENCE.   The genealogy of the family of John Lawrence, of Wisset, in Suffolk, England, and of Watertown and Groton, Massachusetts. Boston, Pub. for the author (John Lawrence) by S.K. Whipple and company, 1857.   4 p. l., 191 p. coat of arms. 26 cm. Title vignette: coat of arms.   p. 171-174 left blank for family record. 9-11636.   CS71.L42   1857

10153   LAWRENCE.   Historical genealogy of the Lawrence family, from their first landing in this country, A.D.1635, to the present date, July 4th, 1858. By Thomas Lawrence ... New York, Printed by E.O. Jenkins, 1858.   240 p. 23 cm. p. 7-16, 72-82, 125-134, 163-172, 235-240 left blank for memoranda. Genealogy of the ancestry and posterity of Isaac Lawrence, and centennial meeting of his descendants, Nov. 27, 1851, p. (177)-234. 9-11635.   CS71.L42   1858

10154   LAWRENCE.   The genealogy of the family of John Lawrence of Wisset, in Suffolk, England, and of Watertown and Groton, Massachusetts ... Boston, Pub. for the author (John Lawrence) by Nichols & Noyes, 1869.   3 p. l., (9)-332 p. coats of arms. 24½ cm. Title vignette: coat of arms. p. 291-294 left blank for family record. 9-11911.   CS71.L42   1869

10155   LAWRENCE.   The genealogy of the family of John Lawrence, of Wisset in Suffolk, England, and of Watertown and Groton, Massachusetts, continued to the present year ... (Cambridge, Mass.) Printed for the author (John Lawrence by H.O.Houghton and company) 1876.   74 p. front., coats of arms. 23½ cm. Title vignette: coat of arms. p. 59-62 left for family record. 9-11469.   CS71.L42   1876

10156   LAWRENCE.   In memoriam. The family of John Lawrence (continued). The family of Philip Goss, of Lancaster, Mass., and Winchester, N.H. The family of Selah Pomroy, of Stanstead P., Quebec. By Rev. John Lawrence ... Albany, N.Y., Munsell, printer, 1881. 2 p. l., 92 p. 23 cm. p. 83-88 left for family record. 9-11633.   CS71.L42   1881

10157   LAWRENCE.   Memorials of Robert Lawrence, Robert Bartlett, and their descendants.   By Hiram Bartlett Lawrence. (Holyoke? 1888) 223, (1) p. 24 cm. Contents. - pt. I. Lawrence memorials, with indexes. - pt. II-III. Bartlett memorials, with indexes. - pt. IV. Genealogical register of Plymouth Bartletts. 3-6531.   CS71.L42   1888

10158   LAWRENCE.   Historical sketches of some members of the Lawrence family.   With an appendix. By Robert M. Lawrence ... Boston, Rand Avery co., printers, 1888. 215 p. front., plates, ports. 24 cm. p. (157-162) left for family record. 9-11634.   CS71.L42   1888a

10159   LAWRENCE.   The divine covenant fulfilled in the ancestral family history of the Lawrence-Hughes and Eldredge generations of Cape May county, New Jersey. By the Rev. Daniel Lawrence Hughes ... Cape May City, N.J., J.L.Landis, Printer, 1891. (3)-161 p. illus., front., plates, ports. 23½ cm. 1-13541.   CS71.L42   1891

10160   LAWRENCE.   The descendants of Major Samuel Lawrence of Groton, Massachusetts, with some mention of allied families, by Robert Means Lawrence, M.D. Cambridge, Printed at the River-side press, 1904.   viii p., 1 l., 344 p., 1 l. front., pl. 24 cm. "Sequel to the compiler's 'Historical sketches of some members of the Lawrence family,' issued in 1888." - Pref. 5-18117.   CS71.L42   1904

10161   LAWRENCE.   Ancestry of Hannah Lawrence.   (n. p., n. d.)   geneal. table.   27 x 41 cm. fold. to
27 x 21 cm.   Reproduction of original ms.   53-50281.   CS71. L42

10162   LAWRENCE.   The Lawrence family of Groton, Mass., by Hon. Samuel A. Green ... Boston,
Press of David Clapp & son, 1907.   4 p. 24½ cm.   Reprinted from the New-England Historical and genealogical register,
July, 1907.   11-28975.   CS71. L42   1907

10163   LAWRENCE.   The Lawrence kin.   (By Anson Titus.   Boston? 1909?)   cover-title, 8 p. 18½ cm.
"The Lawrence kin appeared as a signed article on the editorial page of the Boston evening transcript of January 16, 1909. "   31-18517.
CS71. L42   1909

10164   LAWRENCE.   The pedigree of the Aberdeenshire Lawrances.   (By Robert Murdoch Lawrance)
Aberdeen, W. Smith & sons, 1912.   2 p. l., fold. geneal. tab.   33 cm.   Additions in manuscript.   24-29117.
CS479. L35

10165   LAWRENCE.   Family history of the Lawrences of Cornwall.   (By Edith Jane (Smith)
Durning-Lawrence.   West Norwood, S. E., Priv. print. by Truslove & Bray, ltd., 1915)   6 p. l., 80,
xxiv p.   xlv pl. (part double; incl. front., ports.) vii fold. geneal. tab.   22½ cm.   Preface signed: Edith J. Durning-Lawrence.   "Sir Edwin
Durning-Lawrence": p. 49-75.   "Bibliography of Sir Edwin's writings": p. 76-80.   "Sir Edwin as a patron of science.   By Sir Ronald Ross":
Appendix, p. xix-xxiv.   20-16926.   CS439. L275

10166   LAWRENCE.   Geneology (!) of the Lawrence family from 1700 to 1917.   Branch of Joseph
William, sr., comp. by Henry North Lawrence.   (n. p.) 1917.   38, (2) p. ports. 24 cm.   23-14872.
CS71. L42   1917

10167   LAWRENCE.   (Long Island, N. Y., family cemetery inscriptions from the following named
cemeteries: the Lawrence cemetery, Steinway, Long Island City; the Riker and Luyster cemeteries,
North Beach; and the Moore cemetery, Woodside.   New York, New York genealogical and biographical
society, 1923)   1 p. l., 19 numb. l. 28 cm.   24-6101.   F127. L8N5

10168   LAWRENCE.   An echo of the battle of Plattsburgh, by Mrs. Milo H. Marshall, set down by
Mrs. Charles H. Signor and George Stephenson Bixby ... Champlain, Priv. print. at the Moorsfield
press, 1929.   14 p. incl. pl. front. (port.) 24½ cm.   "Printed in the Plattsburgh daily republican, June 20th, 1927, and reprinted for the
Saranac chapter, Daughters of the American revolution. "   "One hundred fifty-six copies printed from the original metal by Hugh McLellan ...
... no. 101. "   "The Lawrence lineage": p. 10-14.   29-13341.   E356. P7M3

10169   LAWRENCE.   The genealogy of Charles Lawrence, governor of Nova Scotia, by James F.
Kenney ... Ottawa, F. A. Acland, printer to the King's Most Excellent Majesty, 1932.   8 p. 25 cm.
"Reprinted from the Annual report of the Canadian historical association, 1932. "   33-18735.   CS90. L37K4

10170   LAWRENCE.   Lawrence, by Gladys Wilkinson Lawrence.   (Los Angeles, c. 1932)   12 p.
illus., plates, ports. 22 cm.   Genealogy of descendants of Jacob Lawrence of New York.   32-34644.
CS71. L42   1932

10171   LAWRENCE.   Descendants of Amos A. and Sarah E. Lawrence.   (By William Lawrence.
n. p.) 1932.   fold. geneal. tab.   40 x 54 cm. fold. to 23 x 19 cm.   Title from cover.   Signed: William Lawrence, 1933.   Photograph
of a manuscript chart, limited to 150 copies.   34-5039.   CS71. L42   1932a

10172   LAWRENCE.   A genealogical bibliography of the Lawrence family, by Schuyler Lawrence ...
(New York) 1935.   5 p. l., 2-5 (i. e. 4) numb. l. 28 x 21½ cm.   (Lawrence family genealogy series.   Part 1)   No. 4 omitted in paging.
"50 copies of this ms. have been mimeographed and prepared at Columbia university ... no. 17. "   Title-page and introductory matter type-written.
CS36-326 unrev.   CS439. L2748 pt. 1

10173   LAWRENCE.   A history of the Church of Our Saviour, Protestant Episcopal, in Longwood,
Massachusetts, from its founding in 1868 to 1936, written and compiled at the request of the Parish
council of the church. by Herbert H. Fletcher ... Brookline, Mass., Parish council of the church, 1936.
xvi, 173 p. front., plates, ports. 21½ cm.   "Acknowledgment": p. (vii) 37-1466.   BX5980. B74C5

10174   LAWRENCE.   The Lawrences: squires of Ashton, Lancs.   By Schuyler Lawrence ... (New
York) Columbia university, 1936.   3 p. l., vi numb. l. 28½ cm.   (The Lawrence family records series.   II)   Type-written;
additions in manuscript.   "About ten copies of this paper will be prepared ... "   Bibliography: 2d prelim l. 36-12016.   CS439. L275   1936

10175   LAWRENCE.   Lawrence of Newtown, being a genealogical record of one branch of the Lawrence family from Thomas Lawrence, the emigrant, through his son, Jonathan.   Compiled by Patia Havens L'Hommedieu.   Port Washington, N.Y., 1937.   59 l. fold. geneal. tab., coat of arms. 29 cm. Type-written.   Blank leaf for notes at end.   "Authorities and references (with key)": 44th-46th leaves. 38-36155 rev.   CS71.L42   1937

10176   LAWRENCE.   ... Daughters of Thomas Lawrence, Newtown, L.I., compiled by Robert Furman ... (New Haven, 1940)   p. (74)-78 23 cm. Caption title. "From the American genealogist, vol. XVII, October, 1940." 41-1457.   CS71.L42   1940

10177   LAWRENCE.   History of the Lawrence family in England, Virginia, and North Carolina, with historical sketches and genealogical outlines of the Lawrence family in Connecticut, Maryland, Massachusetts, New Jersey, New York, and South Carolina.   Also including genealogical records of other families coverging with the Lawrence family of Virginia-North Carolina: Vaughan with Lawrence 1805, Rea with Lawrence 1836, Jordan with Darden, 1825, Darden with Pruden 1844, Pruden with Lawrence 1870, Moorman with Lawrence 1901.   Bristol, Va., 1964.   1 v. (various pagings) mounted col. coat of arms. 29 cm. Addenda inserted.   65-41940.   CS71.L42   1964

10178   LAWRENCE.   Rosman Lawrence family; embracing the descendants as far as known of Rosman Lawrence of Middletown, Connecticut, and his descendants of other names, by Mrs. A. Lawrence Jinks.   Dalton, N.Y., Burt's Print. Service (1965)   156 p. illus., ports. 24 cm. 66-7269.   CS71.L42   1965

LAWRENCE.   See also:

BENEDICT, F129.S697 v.33   STARKEY, 1892   THOMAS, 1883
COLLIER, 1951a   STARKEY, 1910   TOWNLEY, 1883
DANIEL, 1959   STUART, 1961   TOWNLEY, 1888
DOTY, 1942   TALLMAN, 190 - WETHERILL, 1882
GOODCHILD, CS439.G575   THOMAS, 1878   No. 3939 - Colebrook.
PAGE, 1953

10179   LAWSON.   The Lawson-Irwin-Kendall line.   (n.p., n.d.)   8 p. 28 x 21½ cm. Caption title. Type-written. 46-42059.   CS71.L425

10180   LAWSON.   Family genealogy: Baird, Blair, Butler, Cook, Childs, Clark, Cole, Crane, De Kruyft, Edwards, Finney, Fleming, Graves, Gandine, Haney, Hitchcock, Kerwin, Lawson, Lowry, McAlpin, Peper, Richardson, Rittenhouse, Southwood, Stolp, Williams and Wright.   By Publius V. Lawson ... (Menasha, Wis., P.V.Lawson) 1903.   5 p. l., 304 p. 8 port. 20½ cm. 3-31016.   CS71.L425   1903

10181   LAWSON.   History and genealogy of the descendants of John Lawson, of Scotland and Union, Connecticut, by Rev. Harvey M. Lawson, M.A.   Southbridge, Mass., Central Massachusetts printing co. (1931)   195 p. illus. (ports.) 23 cm. 32-3314.   CS71.L425   1931

10182   LAWSON.   Lawson-Chester genealogy, compiled and edited by Altshuler genealogical service.   Boston, Mass. (Concord, N.H., The Rumford press) 1946.   6 p. l., 50 p. ports., fold. geneal. tables. 23½ cm. "Privately printed." Some paged left blank for memoranda. A 47-961.   CS71.L425   1946

10183   LAWSON.   Genealogy of the descendants of Anthony Lawson of Northumberland, England.   By Robert Runyon.   (Brownsville, Tex., 1952.   52 p. illus. 22 cm. 52-23552.   CS71.L425   1952

LAWSON.   See also: BRENT, 1936
                       CORN, 1959

LAWTHER.   See No. 553 - Goodhue county.

10184   LAWTON.   A saga of the South, by Edward P. Lawton.   Ft. Myers Beach, Fla., Island Press (1965)   318 p. illus., map, ports. 23 cm. Bibliographical references included in "Notes" (p.303-304) 65-19041.   CS71.L4254   1965

LAWTON.   See also: BRAYTON, 1922
SMITH, 1931
SMITH, 1957a

10185   LAY.   The descendants of Robert Lay of Saybrook, Conn.   By Edwin A. Hill.   Boston, New England historic genealogical society, 1908.   10 p. 23 cm.   "Reprinted from the New England historical and genealogical register," v. 62, 1908, p. 172-178, 238-241. 17-19200.   CS71. L427   1908

LAY.   See also: JAMES, 1912
SALISBURY, 1892

10186   LAYMAN.   Garrett county history of pioneer families ... The Layman family, by Charles E. Hoye.   (Oakland, Md., 1937)   mounted l. 26 cm.   Newspaper clipping.   No. XCVII of a series of articles contributed to the Mountain democrat. 41M3021T.   CS71. L428   1937

10187   LAYNE.   Layne genealogy.   By Floyd Benjamin Layne.   Los Angeles, 1958.   250 p. illus. 24 cm.   54-31929.   CS71. L4283   1953

10188   LAYNE.   Layne-Lain-Lane genealogy; being a compilation of names and historical informa- tion of male descendants of sixteen branches of the Layne-Lain-Lane family in the United States, gathered from legal records and other available sources.   Los Angelse (1962)   336 p. illus. 24 cm. 63-35481.   CS71. L4283   1962

10189   LAYNE.   Descendants of John Layne of Goochland County, Virginia, (1685-1963)   By Ralph Hoover Lane.   Edited 1964 by John P. Landers.   Washington, M.O. Lane, 1965.   388 p. 28 cm. 65-6354.   CS71. L4283   1965

LAYNE.   See: DUNHAM, 1956
LANE.

10190   LAYTON.   Leighton genealogy.   An account of the descendants of Capt. William Leighton, of Kittery, Maine.   With collateral notes relating to the Frost, Hill, Bane, Wentworth, Langdon, Brag- don, Parsons, Pepperrell, Fernald, Nason, and other families of York county and its vicinity.   By Tristram Frost Jordan ...   To which are added, brief memoirs of Major Charles Frost, of Kittery, and Captain John Hill, of Berwick.   Albany, N.Y., Press of J. Munsell's sons, 1885.   127 p. 25 cm. Memoirs of Major Charles Frost, of York county, Maine, and of Capt. John Hill, by Usher Parsons: p. (77)-113.   "Wm. Pepperrell's descendants": p. (115)-120. 9-11632.   CS71. L429   1885

10191   LAYTON.   A genealogical sketch of a Dover, N.H., branch of the Leighton family, by Walter L. Leighton, PH. D.   Newton Center, Mass., Priv. print. (Cambridge, Mass., University press) 1940. 3 p. l., 31, (1) p., 1 l. pl., 2 port. (incl. front.) 21 cm.   Includes bibliographies. 40-34269.   CS71. L429   1940

10192   LAYTON.   Records of the Ward and Layton families, together with those of the O'Neal, Lodge, and Lacey families.   (Washington, 1942)   cover-title, 1 p. l., 22 numb. l. 20 cm.   Reproduced from type- written copy.   Foreword signed: Florence W. Layton. 45-33715.   CS71. W26   1942a

10193   LAYTON.   Layton of western Maryland, compiled by Mrs. Mary Turpin Layton ... (Washing- ton, 1944)   10 l. 28 x 22 cm.   Type-written. 45-10116.   CS71. L429   1944

10194   LAYTON.   (Bible records of the Layton family.   n. p., 1948?)   sheet 57 x 46 cm. fold. to 30 x 23 cm. 50-32399.   CS71. L429   1948

LAYTON.   See also: EATON, CS90. E2
WARD, 1942

LAZELL.   See LASELL.

10195   LAZENBY.   Lazenby, being such account as I have been able to collect of the families in the United States bearing the name.   Copyright ... by Mary Elinor Lazenby.   Washington, D. C., c. 1938. 3 p. l., 2-59, 5 p. pl., 6 port. on 1 pl., map, coat of arms.   31 cm.   Text corr. in ms.   Mimeo. 39-14333.   CS71. L43   1939

10196   LAZENBY.   Lazenby, some account of families in the United States which bear the name.
By Mary Elinor/Lazenby ... 2d ed., 1942 ... Washington, D.C., Old neighborhoods press, 1942.
82 1. pl., 6 port. on 1 1., map, coat of arms. 30 cm.   Mimeographed.   42-22190.   CS71.L43   1942

      LAZIER.   See BOGART, 1918

      LEA.   See: LEE.
            No. 516 - Notable southern families vol. 3 p. 69

10197   LEACH.   Leach family record.   Descendants of Lawrence Leach of Salem, Mass., 1629.
Through his son Giles, of Bridgewater, Mass., 1665.   Comp. by Samuel Chessman.   Albany, N.Y.,
J. Munsell's sons, 1898.   41 p., 1 1. pl. 30 x 22½ cm. Title in red and black. 3-13301.
                                                                                                  CS71.L433   1898

10198   LEACH.   Leach: a genealogy (by Owen Glenn Leach, Jr.   Greenwich, Conn.) 1968.
x, 137 p. illus., maps, ports. 23 cm. "A first edition limited to 100 copies ... number 16." Bibliography: p. 119-120. 77-8551 MARC.
                                                                                                  CS71.L433   1968

10199   LEACH.   Leach family chart of West Virginia, compiled by Mrs. E. Camden Jones.   (Smithton? W. Va.) 1910.   (1) 1. 43 cm. Manuscript; typed title page supplied. 54-50859.   CS71.L433   1910

10200   LEACH.   Lawrence Leach of Salem, Massachusetts, and some of his descendants, by F.
Phelps Leach ... East Highgate, Vt., F.P. Leach, 1924-26.   3 v. plates, ports. 22 cm. 24-21363 rev.
                                                                                                  CS71.L433   1924

10201   LEACH.   Lawrence Leach of Salem, Massachusetts and some of his descendants; being the
descendants of Jabez Leach in particular.   (East Highgate, Vt., introd. 1941)   1 v. (loose-leaf) mounted
illus., coat of arms. 29 cm. (New England Historic Genealogical Society. Pilgrim tercentenary no. 58) 62-55438.   CS71.L433   1941

      LEACH.   See also: HOLDEN, 19 -
                        LA VEILLE, 1933
                        RICHARDSON, 1960
                        VANDERPYL, 1933
                        VEILLE, 1933
                        YERKES, 1904

      LEADBEATER.   See LEADBETTER.

10202   LEADBETTER. Leadbetter records (by) J. E. Ames.   (n. p.) 1917.   317 p. plates, ports. 23½ cm.
Coat of arms in color on cover. 19-8161.   CS71.L435   1917

10203   LEADBETTER. Ledbetters from Virginia, by Roy C. Ledbetter (and others. Dallas? 1964)
xvi, 369 p. fold. map (in pocket) ports. 24 cm. 64-23709.   CS71.L435   1964

      LEADBETTER.   See also BLAKE, 1948

10204   LEAGER.   The family of Jacob Leager of Hadleigh and Kersey co., Suffolk, England, and
Boston, Massachusetts, by John Insley Coddington ... (New Haven, 1943)   cover-title, 5 p. 24 cm. "Reprinted
from "The American genealogist,' April 1943." Bibliographical foot-notes. 44-49820.   CS71.L436   1943

10205   LEAHY.   A family book of memories by the Mike Leahy family.   Comp. by Vina Mary
(Fortin) Leahy.   (Seattle? 1948?)   1 v. (unpaged) ports., map. 28 cm. Cover-title. 49-24024*.
                                                                                                  CS71.L4363   1948

      LEAK.   See LEEKE.

      LEAKE.   See: JOHNSON, 1961
                        LEEKE.
                        LINDLEY, 1950

10206   LEAMING.   The ancestry of the Romney Leamings, compiled in commemoration of the one hundredth anniversary of the founding of the Leaming family at Romney, Indiana, in July, 1844.   Prepared for the 12th annual reunion of the descendants of Furman Leaming, 1786-1832, held at Hazelwood, Romney, Indiana, July 23, 1944.   (By Ruby (Zion) Leaming)   (Romney, 1944)   1 p. l., 31 p. front., illus. (incl. ports.) 24½ cm. Cover-title: Leaming centennial, 1844-1944. Romney, Indiana. Prepared by the committee: Ruby Zion Leaming, Mary Austin Simison and Emma Leaming Waters. cf. Foreword. 45-12866.   CS71.L4365   1944

10207   LEAMING.   Leming family history and geneology (!) By Samuel Kellough Leming.   Waldron, Ark., 1947.   138 p. ports. 24 cm. 48-14255 *.   CS71.L4365   1947

LEAMON.   See LEHMAN.

10208   LEARNED.   The Learned family (Learned, Larned, Learnard and Lerned) being descendants of William Learned who was of Charlestown, Massachusetts, in 1632.   Comp. by William Law Learned, in part from the papers of the late Joseph Gay Eaton Larned.   Albany, J. Munsell's sons, 1882.   v, 346 p. 23 cm. 20-11357.   CS71.L437   1882

10209   LEARNED.   The Learned family (Learned, Larned, Learnard, Larnard and Lerned) being descendants of William Learned who was of Charlestown, Mass., in 1632.   Comp. by William Law Learned in part from the papers of the late Josepn Gay Eaton Larned.   2d ed., enl.   Albany, Weed-Parsons printing co., 1898.   v, 505 p. facsims. 23½ cm. 9-11470.
                                                                       CS71.L437   1898

10210   LEARNED.   The Learned family in America, 1630-1967.   By Eugenia Learned James.   (St. Louis?) Setco Print. Co., 1967.   ix, 406 p. col. coat of arms, forms. 23 cm. Revised and updated ed. of The Learned family, by William Law Learned, first published in 1882. 68-306.   CS71.L437   1967

LEARNED.   See also: KING, 1956
                             LEONARD.

10211   LEAS.   Leas genealogy, by Fay W. Leas.   (Fort Wayne, The Lincoln press, printers, 1930?)
53 p. incl. illus. (ports.) 22½ cm. 32-19218.   CS71.L4373   1930

10212   LEAS.   Leas genealogy.   By Fay Willis Leas.   (2d ed.   Waterloo? Ind.) 1950.
166 p. illus. 23 cm.   CS71.L4373   1950
————— (Index of surnames) indexed for H. Leslie Leas Foundation by Clara Haberichter, Marguerite Pettie Krohn (and) Karen Leas.   (n. p.) 1958.   35 p. 21 cm. 56-43806 rev.   CS71.L4373   1950
                                                                                       Index.

LEATHAM.   See SALISBURY, 1961

10213   LEATHERMAN.   All Leatherman kin history; a brief history and a partial genealogical record of Leatherman families and their descendants in the North American continent, with records of wills, transfers of real estate, and special activities in the lives of some of the subjects, with portraits and other illustrations, compiled by Rev. I. John Letherman ... in collaboration with Emma Leatherman Candler ... Nappanee, Ind., E. V. publishing house, 1940.   xv, 1152 (i. e. 1153) p. incl. front., illus. (incl. ports., facsims.) 24 cm. Includes extra numbered leaf 978 a. Pages 1147-1152 blank for "Addenda." 41-903.
                                                                       CS71.L4374   1940

10214   LEATHERS.   Edward Leathers, and his descendants.   By Rev. Dr. A. H. Quint.   Reprinted from the Dover enquirer.   (Dover, N. H.) 1891.   (13) p. 22 cm. 15-220.   CS71.L4375   1891

LEATHERWOOD.   See ALBAUGH, 1949

LEAVELL.   See LA VELLE, 1957

10215   LEAVENS.   The Leavens name, its origin and its track through New England to northern Vermont.   By the Rev. P. F. Leavens ... Passaic, N. J., Thurston & Barker, printers, 1889.
25, 2 p. 19½ cm. On cover: 1632-1889. 46-41896.   CS71.L438   1889

10216   LEAVENS.   The Leavens name including Levings; an account of the posterity descending from emigrant John Levins: 1632-1903, by Philo French Leavens.   Passaic, N.J., Passaic daily news print, 1903.   3 p. l., 137, xv p. pl., 3 port. 23½ cm. 7-22902.   CS71.L438   1903

10217   LEAVENWORTH.   A genealogy of the Leavenworth family in the United States, with historical introduction, etc., by Elias Warner Leavenworth ... Being a revision and extension of the genealogical tree comp. by William and Elias W. Leavenworth, then of Great Barrington, Mass., in 1827 ... Syracuse, N.Y., S.G.Hitchcock & co., 1873.   376 p. front. (coat of arms, and facsims.) plates, ports. 22½ cm. 9-11631.
                                                                               CS71.L439   1873

        LEAVENWORTH.   See also SWEET, 1940

10218   LEAVITT.   Thomas Levitt of Exeter and Hampton, in New Hampshire: his English connect-ions.   Wentworth, Hutchinson, Wheelwright ... Kenilworth, Ills., Priv. print. by V.C.Sanborn, 1904.
8 p. 23 cm.   By Victor C. Sanborn.   9-11599.   CS71.L4394   1904

10219   LEAVITT.   Thomas Levet of Exeter and Hampton; reprinted from the New England historical and genealogical register; with notes on the English and American families of Levett and Leavitt, by Victor C. Sanborn, Kenilworth, Illinois.   (Boston?) 1913.   21 p. front. (coat of arms) 24½ cm. 13-378.
                                                                               CS71.L4394   1913

10220   LEAVITT.   The Leavitts of America, a compilation of five branches and gleanings from New England to California and Canada, published by Mr. Jane Jennings Eldredge ... for the Leavitt family association, 1924.   Salt Lake city, Utah (1924)   cover-title, (16), 254 p. 23 cm.   "How to use this book", signed: Cecilia G. Steed, genealogist.   38-14742.   CS71.L4394   1924

10221   LEAVITT.   Leavitt.   Tilton, N.H., 1941 - By Emily Florence (Leavitt) Noyes.   1941 -
      v. illus., ports. 24 cm.   On spine, v.1: Genealogy. Dudley and Leavitt.   Contents. - (v.1) Descendants of John, the immigrant, through his son Moses. - v.2. Descendants of John Leavitt, the immigrant, through his son Israel and Lydia Jackson.   41-21615 rev. *
                                                                               CS71.L4394   1941

10222   LEAVITT.   History of Josiah Leavitt and Mary Ann Bowler and family.   By Rose (Leavitt) McAllister.   (n.p., c.1965)   x, 366 p. illus., ports. 29 cm. 66-7259.   CS71.L4394   1965

        LEAVITT.   See also SANBORN, 1894

10223   LE BARON.   ... Descendants of Francis Le Baron of Plymouth, Mass.   Comp. by Mary Le Baron Stockwell.   Boston, T. R. Marvin & son, printers, 1904.   521 p. front., plates, ports., facsims. 25 cm. 4-8088.   CS71.L44   1904

        LEBARON.   See JOHNSON, 1956

10224   LEBBY.   Nathaniel Lebby, patriot, and some of his descendants, by E. Detreville Ellis. (Chevy Chase? Md.) 1967.   xi, 553 p. illus., map (on p. (2)-(3) of cover), ports. 28 cm. Bibliography: p. 506-519.   76-4359.
                                                                               CS71.L443   1967

        LE BLANC.   See collection of correspondence etc. relating to ALLAIN and LE BLANC families under ALLAIN in vertical file.   Ask reference librarian for this material.

        LE BLOUT.   See CROKE.

        LEBO.   See ENDERS, 1960

        LE BOSQUET.   See CHAFEE, 1955

        LE BOURDIEU.   See DuBOURDIEU.

        LE BRUEN.   See SAMPSON, 1922

10225   LE CATO.   A record of the LeCato family; 300 years in America, 1650-1950.   By Charles Beauregard LeCato.   (Haddonfield? N.J., 1965)   21 l.   geneal. tables.   30 cm.   Cover title.   66-40185.
CS71.L45   1965

LECATT.   See LECATO.

10226   LECHMERE.   Hanley and the house of Lechmere.   London, Pickering and co., 1883.
viii, (9)-79 p.   front., illus. (coats of arms) pl.   23 cm.   Dedication signed: Evelyn Philip Shirley.   15-23247.   CS439.L3

10227   LECKIE.   Leckie of Leckie, by R.G.E.L.   (Robert Gilmour Edwards Leckie)   Vancouver, British Columbia, 1913.   2 p. l., (3)-157, xxv p.   front., plates.   23 cm.   Coat of arms on cover.   24-6504.
CS479.L4

LEDBETTER.   See LEADBETTER.

LEDDRAUGH.   See LEDERACH.

LEDERACH.   See STRASSBURGER, 1922

10228   LEDLIE.   Joseph Ledlie and William Moody, early Pittsburgh residents; their background and some of their descendants.   By Ledlie Irwin Laughlin.   (Pittsburgh) University of Pittsburgh Press (1961)   x, 208 p.   illus., ports., geneal. tables (4 fold. in pocket) 24 cm.   Bibliography: p. 172-177.   60-53564.
CS71.L465   1961

10229   LEDYARD.   Ledyard-Cass biographical records; Benjamin Ledyard, Benjamin Ledyard, 2d., Henry Ledyard, Henry Brockholst Ledyard, Lewis Cass Ledyard, Jonathan Cass, Lewis Cass.   New York, The Press association, 1924.   (57) p. incl. mounted col. front. (coat of arms) mounted ports.   31½ cm.   25-2146 rev.
CS71.L467   1924

10230   LEE.   Magazine.   Society of the Lees of Virginia.   (Charlottesville, Ca., The Michie company)   v.   24½ cm.   40-18932.   CS71.L48

10231   LEE.   Lee of Loughton.   Notes illustrative of the pedigree in the Visitation of Essex 1664-1668.   By James Henry Lea.   (London, 18 -)   3 p.   31 cm.   "Communicated by J. Henry Lea, esq. of Cedarhurst, Fairhaven, Mass., to Miscellanea genealogica et heraldica."   38M2062T.   CS439.L35

10232   LEE.   Genealogical table of the Lee family from the first emigration to America in 1641.   Brought down to the year 1851.   Comp. from information furnished by Hon. Martin Lee ... By the Rev. William H. Hill ... Albany, Weed, Parsons & co.'s print., 1851.   31 p. 23 cm.   Printed for private circulation only.   14-778.   CS71.L48   1851

10233   LEE.   AEdes Hartwellianae; or, Notices of the manor and mansion of Hartwell.   By Captain W. H. Smyth ... London, Printed for private circulation, by J. B. Nichols and son, 1851.   vii, 414 p., 1 l.   illus., XIII pl. (1 col.) incl. port., map, 2 plans.   31 cm.   "Genealogical table of the family of Lee, of Hartwell": p. 96.   10-12636.
N5245.H4

10234   LEE.   A parochial history of Enstone, in the county of Oxford; being an attempt to exemplify the compilation of parochial histories from antiquarian remains, ecclesiastical structures and monuments, ancient and modern documents, manorial records ... &c., &c., by the Rev. John Jordan ... London, J. R. Smith; (etc., etc.,) 1857.   xvi, 465 p.   19½ cm.   Memorials of the noble families of Lee and Dillon, now Lee-Dillon of Ditchley: p. 59-140.   2-21780 rev.   DA690.E5J8

10235   LEE.   History and pedigree of the Lee Jortin family.   (n.p.) 1858.   20 p. illus. 19 cm.
58-54450.   CS439.L35   1858

10236   LEE.   Genealogical history of the Lee family of Virginia and Maryland, from A.D. 1300 to A.D. 1866.   With notes and illustrations.   Edited by Edward C. Mead.   New York, Richardson & co., 1868.   114 p. plates, ports., coats of arms. 24 cm.   9-11630.   CS71.L48   1868
Microfilm 8644

10237   LEE.   Genealogical history of the Lee family of Virginia and Maryland from A. D. 1300 to A. D. 1866, with notes and illustrations, ed. by Edward C. Mead.   New York, University publishing co., 1871.   114 (i.e. 109) p. front., illus., pl., ports., col. coats of arms. 24 cm.   Pages 16 to 20 omitted in numbering.   L. C. COPY REPLACED BY MICROFILM.   17-19196.   CS71. L48   1871
                                                                                                                                Microfilm 8645 CS

10238   LEE.   Genealogy of the descendants of John Lee.   Communicated to the Historical and genea- logical register for October, 1874, by the Rev. Samuel Lee ... (Boston, 1874)   8 p. 25½ cm.   Caption title. 5-14688 rev.   CS71. L48   1874

10239   LEE.   Genealogy of the descendants of John Lee.   By the Rev. Samuel Lee.   (In The New-England historical and genealogical register.   Boston, 1874.   24 cm.   Vol. XXVIII, p. 394-401) 5-14689 rev.   F1. N56 vol. 28
          —— Copy 2, detached.   CS71. L48   1874a

10240   LEE.   Memoir of Benjamin Lee.   Addressed to his grandchildren by his son Alfred Lee ... (Philadelphia, Press of J. B. Lippincott & co., 1875)   65, (1), xxiv p. 2 facsim. 31 cm.   Title-page and title of "Family record" illuminated.   "Family record": XXIV p. at end.   10-2789.   CS71. L48   1875

10241   LEE.   Contributions towards a history of the ancient parish of Prestbury, in Cheshire.   By Frank Renaud, M. D.   (Manchester) Printed for the Chetham society, 1876.   4 p. l., (v)-viii, 244 p. plates, map, facsim., fold. tab., geneal. tables (1 fold.) 22½ x 18 cm.   (Added t.-p.: Remains, historical & literary, connected with the palatine counties of Lancaster and Chester. Pub. by the Chetham society. vol. XCVII) 18-5570.   DA670. L19C5 vol. 97

10242   LEE.   A history of the house of Lyme (in Cheshire), compiled from documents of the Legh family of that house, and from other sources, by W. Beamont ... Warrington, P. Pearse, 1876. 2 p. l., 205, (2) p. 22½ cm. 2-20281.   CS439. L9

10243   LEE.   Notices of the family of Leigh of Addington.   By Granville Leveson-Gower ... London, Wyman & sons, 1878.   49 p. 2 pl., coats of arms, 2 fold. geneal. tab. 22½ cm.   Reprinted from the Surrey archaeological collections, v. 7, p. 77-123. 15-21496.   CS439. L35   1878

10244   LEE.   John Lee, of Farmington, Hartford County, Conn., and his descendants, arranged by Sarah Marsh Lee ... Norwich, Press of the Bulletin company, 1878.   149 p., 1 l., xxxi p. front. 25½ cm. 14-785.   CS71. L48   1878

10245   LEE.   Memorial of John Clarke Lee.   Communicated by Rev. E. B. Willson.   (In Essex institute, Salem, Mass. Historical collections.   Salem, 1879.   24½ cm. v. 15, p. 35-62) 15-25662.   F72. E7E81 v. 15

10246   LEE.   The descent of General Robert E. Lee, from King Robert the Bruce, of Scotland.   A paper read before the Southern historical association, of Louisville, Ky., March 29, 1881, by Wm. Winston Fontaine, A. M., principal of Holyoke academy.   (n. p., 1881?)   cover-title, 6 p., 1 l. 25½ cm. "Descendants of Gov. Spotswood and his wife": 1 leaf at end.   26-19564.   CS71. S765   1881

10247   LEE.   Genealogy of the family of Lee of Chester, Bucks, and Oxon, shewing the lineal de- scent of the late General Robert E. Lee of Virginia, America, from Sir John Lee, knot.   With arms, notes, etc.   Comp. by the Rev. Frederick George Lee ... London, Mitchell and Hughes, 1884. 17 p. front., illus., plates, facsims. 28 cm.   Issued also in "Miscellanea genealogica et heraldica", London, 1886, 2d ser., v. 1.   L. C. COPY REPLACED BY MICROFILM.   10-1183.   CS439. L35
                                                                                                                                Microfilm 10310 CS

10248   LEE.   Lee family quarter-millennial gathering of the descendants and kinsmen of John Lee, one of the early settlers of Farmington, Conn., held in Hartford, Conn., Tues. & Wed., Aug. 5th & 6th, 1884.   (Comp. by W. W. Lee) Meriden, Republican steam print., 1885.   3 p. l., vi, 116 p. ports., fold. map. 23½ cm.   p. (87)-116: Appendix containing interesting matter relating to the Lee family, collected ... from the Connecticut state library, at Hartford and other sources; also contibutions concerning various branches of the family ... 9-11471.   CS71. L48   1885

10249   LEE.   Genealogy (of the) Lee family of Virginia and Maryland ... an original drawing.   (n. p.) c. 1886.   geneal. table. 84 x 65 cm. fold. to 42 x 65 cm.   "This tree, with its 460 limbs, contains the genealogy of the Lee family - descended from Col. Richard Lee of Virginia." 59-56125.   CS71. L48   1886

10250   LEE.   John Leigh of Agawam (Ipswich) Massachusetts, 1634-1671, and his descendants of the name of Lee, with genealogical notes and biographical sketches of all his descendants, so far as can be obtained; including notes on collateral branches, comp. by William Lee ... Albany, N.Y., J. Munsell's sons, 1888.   1 p. l., vii, (3)-499 p. pl., map, facsims. 23 cm. 9-11628.
CS71.L48   1888

10251   LEE.   Lee of Virginia.   Genealogical notes proving the error of the previously accepted pedigree.   Coomunicated by J. Henry Lea, Cedarhurst, Fairhaven, Mass.   (Boston, 1890)
11 p. fold. geneal. tab. 23 cm. Caption title. Reprinted from the New England historical and genealogical register for January, 1890.
18-365.
CS71.L48   1890

10252   LEE.   Lee of Virginia, by J. Henry Lea ... (Boston? 1892)   23 p. illus. 24 cm. Caption title. Reprinted from the New Eng. hist. and geneal. register for January, 1892. 9-11627.
CS71.L48   1892

10253   LEE.   The Lee family, relating especially to Samuel Lee, of Watertown, Mass., and some of his descendants.   By O.P. Allen ... Newport, R.I., R.H. Tilley, 1893.   14 p. front. (port.) 24 cm. Reprinted from the Magazine of New England history. 1-17384.
CS71.L48   1893

10254   LEE.   Lee of Virginia.   By W.B. Lee, esq. of Seend, Melksham, Wilts, England.   (Boston, 1893)   3, (1) p. 25 cm. Caption title. "Reprinted from N. England historical and genealogical register for Jan., 1893." 31-19488.
CS71.L48   1893a

10255   LEE.   Lee of Virginia, 1642-1892; biographical and genealogical sketches of the descendants of Colonel Richard Lee, with brief notices of the related families ... Edited and published by Edmund Jennings Lee.   Philadelphia, 1895.   586 p. plates, ports,, fold. map, coats of arms, facsims. 27 cm. 9-11626 rev. *
CS71.L48   1895
——— Supplement.   (n.p., 1950?)   2 v. 30 cm. Title from spine. Photocopies of applications for membership in the Society of the Lees of Virginia.   Contents. - (1) Alexander - Laird. - (2) Lee-Wyche.
CS71.L48   1895
Suppl.

10256   LEE.   Lee of Pocklington.   A rejoinder, by J. Henry Lea.   Reprinted from Genealogist, April, 1895.   Exeter, W. Pollard & co., printers, 1895.   1 p. l., 9 p. 23½ cm. An answer to G. Ambrose Lee's criticism in the July number of "The Genealogist," of the author's article on the Lees of Quarrendon, in "The Genealogist," April 1894. 17-9521.
CS439.L35   1895

10257   LEE.   Re-union of the descendants of John Lee, of Farmington.   Held at Farmington ... August 12 and 13, 1896.   Ed. from minutes of the meeting by Leonard Lee.   Pub. by the Lee association.   Meriden, Republican pub co., 1896.   lxv p., 1 l. 23 cm. 1-3473.   CS71.L48   1896

10258   LEE.   John Lee of Farmington, Hartford Co., Conn., and his descendants.   Containing over 4,000 names.   1634.   2d ed. 1897.   1st ed. by Sarah Marsh Lee, of Norwich, Conn., 1878.   With much miscellaneous history of the family - brief notes of other Lee families of New England - biographical notices - valuable data collected by William Wallace Lee - military records - to which is added a "roll of honor," of two hundred who have served in the various wars of the country.   Comp. by Leonard Lee and Sarah Fiske Lee.   Pub. by the 'Lee association."   Meriden, Conn., Republican-Record book print, 1897.   527 p. illus., ports., fold. plans (incl. front.) 23½ cm. 4 blank leaves inserted for memoranda.
4-29776.
CS71.L48   1897

10259   LEE.   Memoranda of the Lees and cognate families.   For three hundred years back, gathered chiefly from family sources, by J.N. Lee ... Waukegan, Ill., De Kay bros., printers, 1898.
2 p. l., 47 p. illus. 18½ cm. 9-11625.   CS71.L48   1898
——— Supplement ... 1634.   1900.   Containing corrections, changes, births, marriages, deaths, etc., reported since the publication - new discoveries, with an addition of nearly 1000 names ... Comp. by Leonard Lee.   Pub. by the "Lee association."   Meriden, Conn., Record-Republican print, 1900.   xii, 13-176 p. front., illus., ports. 23½ cm. 4-29777.   CS71.L48   1900

10260   LEE.   The ancestry and posterity of John Lea, of Christian Malford, Wiltshire, England, and of Pennsylvania in America, 1503-1906, by James Henry Lea and George Henry Lea.   Philadelphia and New York, Lea brothers & co., 1906.   xv, 611 p. col. front., illus., plates, ports., map, facsim. 27 cm. English section, by James Henry Lea; American section, by George Henry Lee. 6-2088.
CS71.L48   1906

10261   LEE.   Stratford hall and the Lees connected with its history; biographical, genealogical and historical, comp. ... by Frederick Warren Alexander ... Oak Grove, Va., F. W. Alexander, 1912.
2 p. l., 9-332 p. illus. (incl. ports.) pl. 24 cm. 12-16569.   CS71. L48   1912

10262   LEE.   Brevet-Brigadier General William Raymond Lee ... by Thomas Amory Lee ... (Reprint from Colonial families of the United States of America." vol. v) (Baltimore, Seaforth press, 1915)   cover-title, p. 344-353. 25½ cm. 16-5351.   CS71. L48   1915

10263   LEE.   Colonel William Raymond Lee of the revolution, by Thomas Amory Lee ... Salem, Mass., The Essex institute, 1917.   29 p. pl., 4 port. (incl. front.) 24½ cm. "Reprinted from Essex institute historical collections, v. 53; with additions." 17-20842.   E263. M4L45

10264   LEE.   Colonel Jeremiah Lee, patriot, by Thomas Amory Lee ... Salem, Mass., The Essex institute, 1916.   1 p. l., 23 p. pl., 3 port. (incl. front.) 24½ cm. "Reprinted from the Essex institute historical collections, vol. 52 with additions." 17-9571.   E263. M4L4

10265   LEE.   Lee marriages in Connecticut.   (By William Montgomery Clemens)   (In Genealogy; a monthly magazine of American ancestry, edited by William Montgomery Clemens ... Hackensack, N. J., 1919.   23 cm.   vol. VII, p. 145-152) 37-16966.   CS42. G7 vol. 7
——— Separate.   CS71. L48   1917

10266   LEE.   Lincoln and Lee; a patriotic story, by Smith D. Fry ... (Washington, D. C., Model printing co., 1922)   xi, 160 p. 23 cm. 23-1174.   E457. 15F94

10267   LEE.   Henry and Mary Lee, letters and journals, with other family letters, 1802-1860, prepared by their granddaughter, Frances Rollins Morse.   Boston, Mass. (T. Todd company, printers) 1926.   xix, 423 p. front., plates, ports. 23½ cm. "Privately printed." "Errata" (1 leaf) inserted at end. "Prepared ... with the ... help of ... Ellen Hale." - Errata.   Bibliography: p. vii-viii. 34-32586.   CS71. L48   1926

10268   LEE.   The genealogy and history of the John Keysar Smith family of Valley Rest, Florence, Nebraska, by Angeline Smith Pickering Crane and Cora Phebe Smith Mullin.   (Omaha, Citizen printing co., 1924)   4 p. l., 243 p., 2 l. 21½ cm. "Genealogy of Smith, Douglas, Crane, Baxter, Denison, Stanton, Gardiner, Griswold, Tracy, Nehemiah Smith, Bourne, Lord, Lee, Browne, Hyde, Wolcott, Hough, Brewster, Mayflower line, etc. 24-30876. CS71. S643   1924

10269   LEE.   Stratford on the Potomac, by Ethel Armes, and address on Robert E. Lee, by Sidney Lanier; maps and line drawings by Catherine Claiborne Armes.   Greenwich, Conn., William Alexander jr. chapter, United daughters of the confederacy, 1928.   40, (4) p. incl. front., illus. 22 cm. "Authorities consulted": p. 40. 28-28982.   CS71. L48   1928

10270   LEE.   ... Lee family records, by J. Montgomery Seaver.   Philadelphia, American historical-genealogical society (1929)   63 p. front. (4 port.) coat of arms. 29 cm. Coat of arms of the Lee family on recto of frontispiece.   Pages 62-63 blank for "Family record". "References": p. 60-61. 40-18912.   CS71. L48   1929

10271   LEE.   Arlington house and its associations.   Washington, Custis, Lee.   (1st ed., 1932) (Fort Humphreys, 1932)   3 p. l., 45 p., 1 l. illus., plates, ports., plans. 28 cm. "Arlington house was restored by Act of Congress and is maintained by the Quartermaster corps, under the direction of the secretary of war." - 3d prelim. leaf. "Illustrations in the catalogue by the Signal corps, U. S. A., and the Construction division, Office of the quartermaster general." - 2d prelim. leaf. 33-26386.
                                    F234. A7L48

10272   LEE.   The Lee family, relating especially to Thomas Lee of Lyme, Connecticut, and some of his descendants ... (New York, Printed by B. H. Tyrrel, 1933)   1 p. l., 3-22 numb. l. 20 cm. "This record of one branch of the descendants of Thomas Lee was assembled from data collected by Samuel Orlando Lee (8th generation) of Huntington, New York." "Edited and privately published in 1933 by Irving Call Lee (10th generation)" Bibliography: p. 3. 34-5042. CS71. L48   1933

10273   LEE.   The Lees of Virginia; biography of a family, by Burton J. Hendrick ... Boston, Little, Brown, and company, 1935.   3 p. l., (v)-xii p., 2 l., (3)-455 p. front., pl., ports., fold. geneal. tab. 25 cm. "Of this edition three hundred copies have been autographed, printed and bound wholly uncut with paper label." 35-18228.   E467. 1. L4H35

10274   LEE.   Stratford hall, the great house of the Lees, by Ethel Armes; with an introduction by Franklin D. Roosevelt.   Richmond, Va., Garrett and Massie, incorporated, 1936.   xxiv p., 2 l., 575 p. incl. front., illus. (incl. ports., maps, plans, facsims., coats of arms) 28 cm. Bibliography: p. (549)-558. 37-294. CS71. L48   1936

10275   LEE.   The Lees of Virginia; biography of a family, by Burton J. Hendrick ... New York, Halcyon house (1937)   2 p. l., (v)-xii p., 2 l., (3)-455 p. front., pl., ports., fold. genealogical tab. 22½ cm. 38-15114.
E467.1.L4H353

10276   LEE.   Garrett county history of pioneer families, by Chas, E. Hoye ... The Dudley Lee family.   (Oakland, Md., 1937)   mounted l. 33 x 27 cm. Newspaper clipping. No. xcvi of a series of articles contributed to the Mountain democrat. 41M3014.
CS71.L48   1937

10277   LEE.   The Jacksons and the Lees; two generations of Massachusetts merchants, 1765-1844, by Kenneth Wiggins Porter ... Cambridge, Mass., Harvard university press, 1937.   2 v. fronts., plates, ports., 2 geneal. tab. (1 double) facsims. (1 double) 2 diagr. 22 cm. (Half-title: Harvard studies in business history. III. Ed. by N. S. B. Gras) Paged continuously. "The plan has been to present the texts of the various documents, almost wholly letters, and to append to each an introduction which assists the reader to understand the document in question and its relationship to the whole ... Into the long general introduction ... has been put a body of facts concerning the business history elucidated by the records." - Editor's introd. "List of manuscripts reproduced": vol. II, P. (1537) - 1573, "List of manuscript collections": vol. II, p. (1575)-1585. 37-35641.
HF3161.M4P6

10278   LEE.   Stratford, colonial home and plantation, Westmoreland county, Virginia; birthplace of Robert E. Lee and of two signers of the Declaration of Independence, Richard Henry Lee, Francis Lightfoot Lee.   (Robert E. Lee memorial foundation, inc.) (Washington, D.C., Press of B.S. Adams, c. 1940)   (16) p. illus. (incl. ports., map, plans) 30½ cm. 40-11635 rev.
F234.S865R6

10279   LEE.   The Lee family of Hounsfield, N.Y., and related families, by Walter John Coates, LITT.D.   North Montpelier, Vt., The Driftwind press, 1941.   102 p. 21½ cm. Bibliographical foot-notes. 43-5992.
CS71.L48   1941

10280   LEE.   Happy heritage; genealogies of seven southern families, by Lyndon Lee Cannon (Mrs. R. B. Cannon) Columbia, S.C., The State company, 1943.   203 p. illus., plates, ports., coats of arms. 20 cm. 43-14331.
CS71.L48   1943

10281   LEE.   Genealogy of William Lee I of England and of Virginia and his descendants, 900-1945. Compiled by Elizabeth Hoyle Rucker ... (Miami, Fla., Printed by the Franklin press, inc., 1945)   115 p. 2 port. (incl. front.) col. coat of arms. 26½ cm. 46-12549.
CS71.L48   1945

10282   LEE.   Stratford; the Lees of Virginia and their contemporaries; a loan exhibition of their portraits ... April 29 through May 18, 1946. New York, Knoedler galleries, (1946)   47, (1) p. incl. front., illus. (incl. ports., map) geneal. tab. 28 cm. 46-6067.
ND1311.K5

10283   LEE.   The family tree of Caroline Jackson Lee (1864-1947) by George Harrison Sanford King. (Fredericksburg? Va.) 1954.   140 p. 28 cm. 56-45688.
CS71.L48   1954

10284   LEE.   Lee chronicle, studies of the early generations of the Lees of Virginia.   Compiled and edited by Dorothy Mills Parker. New York, New York University Press, 1957.   411p. illus., ports., maps, coats of arms, geneal. tables. 25 cm. Includes bibliographical references. 56-10782 rev.
CS71.L48   1957

10285   LEE.   Threads of gold. By Myrtie (Lee) Powers. (1st ed.) New York, Vantage Press (1957)   189 p. illus. 21 cm. Reminiscences. 56-12840.
CS71.L48   1957a

10286   LEE.   The descendants of Thomas Lee of Charleston, South Carolina, 1710-1769; a genealogical, biographical compilation. By Thomas Carpenter Read. (Columbia? S.C.) 1964.   xxv, 465 p. illus., coat of arms, ports. 24 cm. Bibliographical footnotes. 65-408.
CS71.L48   1964

10287   LEE.   The Sidney S. Lee family, 1825-1959, by Lloyd E. Kelly. (n.p., 1964)   10 l. 29 cm. Cover title. 66-99121.
CS71.L48   1964a

10288   LEE.   The Lees of Virginia. Descendents of Richard Lee and Anna Constable, who came to Jamestown in 1639. Arlington, Va., Society of the Lees of Virginia, 1967.   iv, 13 p. illus. 28 cm. 67-29916.
CS71.L48   1967

10289   LEE.   Descendants of Isaac and Elizabeth Pruitt Lee. By Develand Flowers. Fort Worth, Tex., A.B.C. Print. Co. (1967)   97 p. 23 x 29 cm. 68-2711.
CS71.L48   1967b

10290   LEE.   Society of the Lees of Va.   Applications for Membership.   Microfilm 1502

10291   LEE.   "The Queen of England's American Ancestry and Cousinship to Washington and Lee,"
New York Genealogical and biographical record v. 70 (July 2939) p. 201-205.   F116. N28 v. 70
                                                                                                Ref.

10292   LEE.   Lee family (Stephen Lee, ca. 1710-91) In vertical file.   Ask reference assistant for this material.

        LEE.   See also

ARMSTRONG, CS61. A6 v. 3	JACKSON, HF 3161. M4P6	
BEAL, 1956	LEIGH.	ROBERTSON, 1936
BARROW, 1941	LI.	RUCKER, 1927
BOYKIN, 1935	LINCOLN, E457.32T98	STEVENS, 1956
COLLIER, 1951a	McCURDY, 1892	STOUT, 1960
FUNSTEN, 1926	MACKEY, 1957	TAYLOR, 1898
HAMPTON, 1893	MASSIE, 1942	VAN HOOK, 1957
HUTCHINSON, CS439. H795	PETTY, BX5195. T5B6	VAN RENSSELAER, CS69. S7

10293   LEE-WARNER.   The life of John Warner, bishop of Rochester, 1637-1666.   With appendix,
containing some account of his successors, the Lee-Warner family.   By Edward Lee-Warner.   London, Mitchell and Hughes, 1901.   vi p., 1 l., 95 p.   col. front., illus., plates, ports., coats of arms.   28½ x 22 cm.   2-12136.
                                                                                                BX5199. W37L4

        LEECH.   See also YERKES, 1904

10294   LEEDOM.   Leedom genealogy; descendants of John Leedom and Elizabeth Potts of Pennsylvania, from 1824 to 1953.   By Arthur Francis Lefferts.   (Jenkintown? Pa.) c. 1953.   geneal. table.
61 x 39 cm.   53-36243.   CS71. L4815   1953

10295   LEEDS.   (Thomas Leeds, an Englishman, settled at Shrewsbury, N.J., probably 1677.   By
Benjamin Franklin Leeds.   Philadelphia, 1886)   geneal. tab.   56 x 43½ cm. fold. to 21½ x 28 cm.   9-11624.
                                                                                                CS71. L482   1886

10296   LEEDS.   Leeds: a New Jersey family, its beginning and a branchlet.   By Clara Louise
Humeston.   Los Angeles, Cal., California voice print.   (1900)   2 p. l., 17 p.   23 cm.   Issued by B. F. Leeds,
Philadelphia.   Descendants of Thomas Leeds of Shrewsbury, N.J.   1-13540.   CS71. L482   1900

        LEEDS.   See also BEVILLE, 1917

        LEEDY.   See FALL, 1961

10297   LEEKE.   The family of Leck of Bedlington in the county of Durham, and the charity of John
George Leake in New York, United States.   (Compiled from the printed reports of the Legislature of
the state of New York, and other sources.   Communicated by John William Bury, esq.   Newcastle,
Printed by M. A. Richardson, 1845)   14 p., 1 l.   illus.   25½ cm.   Inserted is a manuscript copy of the will of the late John G.
Leake; and a clipping from the N. Y. Daily herald, Sept. 28, 1882: The Leake-Watts orphan home.   History of the founder and his family.   The
strange will.   Litigations prior to the establishment of the home.   9-15599.   CS71. L485   1845

10298   LEEKE.   A brief memoir of the life and writings of the late Lieutenant-Colonel William
Martin Leake ...   London, Printed by Whittingham and Wilkins for private circulation only, 1864.
2 p. l., 43, (1) p.   29 cm.   Folded genealogical table in manuscript inserted as frontispiece.   14-6369.   DF212. L4M3

10299   LEEKE.   ... The Leake family and connecting lines (by) George Warren Chappelear ...
Dayton, Va., The Shenandoah press, 1932.   3 p. l., 84 p.   front. (coat of arms) pl., 23½ cm.   (Families of Virginia.
Vol. I)   32-20641.   CS71. L485   1932

10300   LEEKE.   The descendents (!) of Philip Leek.   From Dover, Kent county, England, to New
England, about the year 1638.   One of the first settlers of New Haven, Ct.   Compiled by H. R. Coles
... (n. p., 1936?)   2 p. l., 9 numb. l.   28 x 21½ cm.   Type-written.   Mounted facsim. on l. 2.   36-30614.   CS71. L485   1936

LEEKE.   See also: CRAWFORD, 1924
                     SCRUGGS, 1912

LEEMASTER.   See LEMASTER.

10301   LEEPER.   Genealogy of Alexander Leeper.   By Laura Alnetta Leeper.   (Akron) 1926
59 p. ports., coat of arms (on cover) 24 cm.   Cover title: The Alexander Leeper family history.   49-38079*.   CS71.L4854   1926
———— Supplement to The Alexander Leeper family history.   (Akron, 1948?)   44 p.   23 cm.   Bound
with the main work.   49-38079*.
                                                                                          CS71.L4854   1926

10302   LEEPER.   The kith and kin of Captain James Leeper and Susan Drake, his wife, by Nell
McNish Gambill.   New York, The National historical society (1946)   196, (2) p. illus. (incl. facsims.) ports.,
fold. geneal. tab.   24 cm.   46-4592.   CS71.L4854   1946

10303   LEESE.   The Lawrence Leese family history; two centuries in America (1741-1941); a
biographical and genealogical history of Lawrence Leese and his descendants from the time of his
arrival in the city of Philadelphia through a period of two hundred years down to the ninth generation.
By Charles Leese ... Frankfort, Ky., Printed by Roberts printing co., 1941.   214 p. ports., coat of arms.
23½ cm.   42-14894.   CS71.L4857   1941

10304   LEETE.   The family of Leete: with special reference to the genealogy of Joseph Leete ...
Collected by the late Charles Bridger ... and ed. by J. Corbet Anderson.   (London, Wertheimer, Lea
& co., printers) printed for private circulation, 1881.   xxii, 113, (1) p. front. (port.) tables (part fold.) 24½ cm.
9-11620.   CS439.L4   1881

10305   LEETE.   The family of William Leete, one of the first settlers of Guildford, Conn., and
governor of New Haven and Connecticut colonies.   Compiled by Edward L. Leete ... New Haven,
Tuttle, Morehouse & Taylor, printers, 1884.   168 p. illus. (coat of arms) 24 cm.   Edited, with some additions and a few
notes, by Alvan Talcott.   Errata slip inserted.   2-24898.rev.   CS71.L486   1884

10306   LEETE.   The family of Leete, by Joseph Leete ... in conjunction with John Corbet Anderson
... 2d ed., rev. and enl.   London (Blades, East & Blades, printers) 1906.   xxviii p., 1 l., 211 p. illus.,
xxix pl. (incl. front., ports., map, facsims.) tables (part fold.) coats of arms.   28½ cm.   The American branch of the family of Leete: p. (161)
-177.   First edition published in 1881.   7-1953.   CS439.L4   1906

10307   LEETE.   The descendants of William Leete, one of the founders of Guilford, Conn., president of the Federation of colonies and governor of New Haven and Connecticut colonies, compiled by
Edward L. Leete ... 2d ed. ... New Haven, The Tuttle, Morehouse & Taylor co., printers (c.1934)
x p., 1 l., 398 p. front., port., col. coat of arms.   24 cm.   Published in 1884 under title "The family of William Leete".   This earlier edition
was edited by Dr. Alvan Talcott due to the death of the compiler Edward L. Leete before its completion.   This second edition has been edited by
Edith Raymond and has been arranged as nearly as possible to conform with the original volume.   cf. Note, signed: Edith Raymond.   35-1658

                                                                                     CS71.L486   1934
         LEETE.   See also WALWORTH, E171.A53 v.20

10308   LEETHAM.   The origin and lineage of the Leetham family, with some personal notes.   (By)
Lieut. Colonel Sir Arthur Leetham ... "Corrected and enlarged.   September 1st.   London, 1919.
cover-title, 2 p. l., 7-60 p. illus. (1 col.) plates, ports., fold. geneal. tab.   25 cm.   Author's coat of arms on cover.   "Additions to next
edition.   Appendix II" (typewritten) in pocket at end.   40-280.   CS439.L38   1919

10309   LEEVES.   A family memorial.   Dedicated to a beloved mother.   (Brighton) Printed for
private circulation, 1872.   3 p. l., 42, 6, 43-187, 3 p. front, plates, ports. 22 cm.   The plates are mounted photographs.   Preface
signed: A.M.Moon (nee Elsdale)   Contents. - Stray thoughts in verse in early years. - A few literary remains and notices of the life of my grandfather the Rev. William Leeves. - A few brief incidents in the life of the Rev. H.D.Leeves. - Lines by Miss E. Leeves. - A brief sketch of the life of
the Rev. Robinson Elsdale, D.D. - Appendix.   15-14151.   CS439.L415   1872

10310   LEEVES.   In memoriam.   The Rev. W. Leeves, author of the air of "Auld Robin Gray. '
With a few notices of other members of the family.   (Ed. Mrs. Anna Maria (Elsdale)Moon.   (Brighton)
Printed for private circulation, 1873.   5 p. l., 31, (ix)-xvi, (35)-42, 6, 43-187, (3) p. front., plates, ports. 22 cm.
Half-title: A family memorial.   15-14150.   CS439.L415   1873

LEFANU. See SHERDIAN, 1875

10311   LE FANU.   Memoir of the Le Fanu family, by T.P. Le Fanu; largely from materials collected by W.J.H. Le Fanu.   Privately printed.   (Manchester, Sherratt and Hughes, printers, 1924)
4 p. l., 80 p. front., ports., 2 geneal. tab.   26 cm.   Title vignette (coat of arms) "One hundred and fifty copies only of his Memoir have been
printed.   number 137."   "List of works by members of the Le Fanu family": p. 75-80.   The portraits are reproductions from original paintings by
Emery Walker.   25-3768.   CS439. L417

LE FEVRE.   See KOCH, 1939

10312   LEFEVRE.   En marge de troi siècles d'histoire domestique, la descendance de Pierre
Lefèvre, 1646-1694, de Rouen, marié à Laprairie en 1673, à Marguerite Gagné, 1653-1720.   Mont-
réal, 1947.   33 p. coat of arms. 26 cm.   "Il a été tiré de ce mémoire 500 exemplaires sur papier ivoire numérotés 1 à 500.   Exemplaire
no. 74."   "Extrait de la Revue de l'Université d'Ottawa, juillet-septembre 1947."   48-43030*.   CS90. L375   1947

10313   LEFEVRE.   The Pennsylvania Le Fevres, compiled by George Newton Le Fevre.   Co-com-
piler, Franklin D. Le Fevre. Strasburg, Pa.,   Le Fevre Cemetery and Historical Association, 1952.
xix, 256 p. illus., port., col. coat of arms, facsims., geneal. table. 24 cm.   52-39276.   CS71. L4956   1952

LEFFEL.   See: BILLINGS, 1931
                    CROFT, 1964   (addenda)

10314   LEFFERTS.   Abstracts of the title of the Lefferts farm, in the city of Brooklyn, known as
the New Bedford farm, situate on the north side of the Jamaica turnpike about seventeen chains, or
eleven hundred and twenty-two feet easterly from the Hunterfly road, and estimated to contain about
ninty-seven (!) or one hundred acres, and represented on the accompanying diagram.   Compiled by
A.S. Wheeler.   Brooklyn, 1870.   New York, Eckler (1870?)   cover-title, 5 numb. l. geneal. tab. 21 x 35 cm.
A genealogical table of the Lefferts family showing the chain of title to the New Bedford farm.   2-8935.   CS71. L492   1870

10315   LEFFERTS.   Genealogy of the Lefferts family, 1650-1878, by Teunis G. Bergen ... Albany,
J. Munsell.   1878.   v. (6)-172 p. pl., facsim., coats of arms. 23 cm.   9-11472.   CS71. L492   1878

10316   LEFFERTS.   American ancestry of Marshall Lefferts and Mary Allen... By Marshall Clifford
Lefferts.   New York, N.Y., 1905.   geneal. tab. 73 x 73 cm.   "This chart has been issued to members of the family in its
present incomplete state as a convenience in the work of compiling a final edition ..." 35-16392.   CS71. L492   1905

LEFFERTS.   See also DOWNING, 1901

LEFFERTS-HAUGHWOUT.   See HAUGHAWOUT.

10317   LEFFINGWELL.   1637-1897.   The Leffingwell record.   A genealogy of the descendants of
Lieut. Thomas Leffingwell, one of the founders of Norwich, Conn.   By Albert Leffingwell ... and
Charles Wesley Leffingwell ... Aurora, N.Y., Leffingwell pub. co., 1897.   v, (1), 256 p. front., plates,
ports., facsims. 26 cm.   9-11623.   CS71. L493   1897

10318   LEFFLER.   Leffler, Genealogical notes collected in Oct., Nov., & Dec. 1919, from public
records, wills, administrations, land records and other sources in Pa., Ky., Ill., Ind., by Henrietta
E. Bromwell.   Denver, Col., 1920.   1 p. l., 44, (9) p., 1 l. illus. (map) 30 cm. Type-written.   "Additional unindexed
notes collected after 1919": 1 leaf at end.   Supplementing the Leffler family in the author's Bromwell genealogy, 1910.   23-18600.
                                                                                                                  CS71. L495   1920

10319   LEFROY.   Notes and documents relating to the family of Loffroy, of Cambray prior to 1587,
of Canterbury 1587-1779, now chiefly represented by the families of Lefroy of Carriglass, co. Long-
ford, Ireland, and of Itchel, Hants; with branches in Australia and Canada.   Being a contribution to
the history of foreign Protestant refugees, by a cadet.   Woolwich, Printed at the press of the Royal
artillery institution.   For private circulation, 1868.   lvi p., 13 numb. l., 14-233, (4) p. illus. (coats of arms) plates,
fold. geneal. tables. 24 cm.   Preface signed: J.H. Lefroy.   Eight pages left blank, and 4 pages inserted for additional data.   Text within
ornamental borders.   Letters and notes in ms., and newspaper clippings inserted; also marginal notes in ms.   21-17134.
                                                                                                                  CS439. L42

LEFTURCH.   In HUNTER family folder (William Edward Graham Hunter) in vertical file.
Ask reference librarian for this material.

10320   LEFTWICH.   Leftwich-Turner families of Virginia and their connections, by Walter Lee
Hopkins ... Richmond, Va., J. W. Fergusson & sons, printers, 1931.   xvii, 351 p. pl., ports., fold. geneal.
tab., coat of arms. 23½ cm. 31-13352.   CS71. L4957   1931

        LEFTWICH.   See also: GLASSCOCK, 195 -
                               THROCKMORTON, 1939

10321   LEFVENDAHL.   Lefvendahl, Smoak and related family records, by Georgie I. Adams
Lefvendahl. (Orangeburg, S. C.) 1966.   74 1. illus., ports. 28 cm. 66-7443.   CS71. L49573   1966

10322   LEGARD.   The Legards of Anlaby & Ganton: their neighbours & neighbourhood,   By Colonel
Sir James Digby Legard, K. C. B.   London, Simpkin, Marshall, Hamilton, Kent & co., 1926.
xix, 244 p. front., plates, ports., facsims., geneal. tab. 25½ cm. Bibliographical foot-notes. 46-34068.   CS439. L44   1926

        LEGARD.   See JOHNSON, 1934

10323   LEGARE.   Biographical sketches of the Huguenot Solomon Legare and of his family, extending
down to the fourth generation of his descendants.   Also, Reminiscences of the revolutionary struggle
with Great Britain, including incidents and scenes which occurred in Charleston, on John's Island, and
in the surrounding country of South Carolina during the war.   Comp. and written by one of his great-
great-grand-daughters, Mrs. Eliza C. K. Fludd, and printed by subscription.   Charleston, S. C.,
E. Perry & co., printers and stationers, 1886.   142 p. 21 cm. 9-24035.   E263. S7F6

        LEGERTON.   See ADAMS, 1950

10324   LE GEYT.   A short account of the Le Geyt-dit-Rauvet family of St. Saviour's, Jersey. Comp.
September, 1906, by Charles A. Bernau ... St. Saviour's, Jersey, Priv. print. at the expense of Miss
R. A. Le Geyt, 1906.   1 p. 1., 22 p. front. (coat of arms) 25½ cm. ... 100 copies. 15-19651.   CS439. L45

10325   LE GEYT.   The descendants of John and Elizabeth Newton LeGeyt, compiled by Mary LeGeyt
Frantz and Dorothy J. LeGeyt Valois, N. Y., 1957.   38 1. 28 cm. 59-27844.   CS71. L4958   1957

10326   LEGGE.   Notes and documents relating to the family of da Lezze.   An heraldic, historical,
and genealogical study, by Giovanni de Pellegrini & co., Venice ... Translated from the Italian by
J. A. Herbert ... Norwich, A. H. Goose, 1900.   2 p. 1., v, (4), 141, (1) p. front. (port.) illus., pl., col. coats of arms.
28½ cm. Imperfect: the frontispiece and two plates wanting.   Introduction signed: A. G. L. (i. e. Augustus George Legge) An attempt to establish
the Italian ancestry of the Legge family.   The heraldic, historical and genealogical study (p. 1-18) was compiled from the "Libri d'oro".   "A
history of the noble Venetian families with whom the family of Traversari della Legge conracted matrimonial alliances.   Taken from the Cronica
veneta di tutte le famiglie nobili della iclita citta de Venetia cominciando di nostra salute l'anno CCCCXXI (British museum: add. mss. 22,500)
Translated from the Italian by Florence Lucy Legge": p. (19)-100.   24-8354.   CS769. L4A3

10327   LEGGE.   Genealogy of the Legge family; data from memorial tablets in St. Botolphe's church,
London, of the Legge and Washington families.   History of origin of stars and stripes, deciphered
from the Legge and Washington coat of arms quartered together ... Compiled by Mrs. Etta Legg(ə)
Galloway ... (Baltimore, 1926)   17 1. 3 pl. 27 cm. Index contributed by Maryland Daughters of the American revolution.   A
photostat copy (positive) of the type-written copy and of the photographs in possession of the Maryland historical society and Mrs. Etta Legge
Galloway, Baltimore, Md. 27-25105.   CS71. L496   1926

        LEGGE.   See also EVELYN, DA690. B631. H3

10328   LEGGETT.   Early settlers of West Farms, Westchester County, N. Y.   Copied from the
manuscript record of the late Rev. Theodore A. Leggett, with additions by A. Hatfield, jr. ... New
York, 1913.   2 p. 1., 117 p. 26½ cm. Edition of one hundred copies. Reprinted from the New York genealogical and biographical
record, July, 1913 -   17.1607.   CS71. L497   1913

        LEGGETT.   See also GUSTIN, 1900

10329 LEGH. Warrington in M.CCCC.LXV. As described in a contemporary rent roll of the Legh family, in the possession of Thomas Legh, esquire, of Lyme park. Ed. by William Beamont ... (Manchester) Printed for the Chetham society, 1849. 3 p. l., (iii)-lxxviii p., 1 l., 151 p. front. (fold. plan) facsim. 23 x 18 cm. (Added t.-p.: Remains, historical & literary, connected with the palatine counties of Lancaster and Chester, pub. by the Chetham society. vol. XVII) Latin text and English translation on opposite pages. 18-5239. DA670.L19C5 vol. 17

10330 LEGH. Contributions towards a history of the ancient parish of Prestbury, in Cheshire. By Frank Renaud, M.D. (Manchester) Printed for the Chetham society, 1876. 4 p. l., (v)-viii, 244 p. plates, map, facsim., fold. tab., geneal. tables (1 fold.) 22½ x 18 cm. (Added t.-p.: Remains, historical & literary, connected with the palatine counties of Lancaster and Chester. Pub. by the Chetham society. vol. XCVII) 18-5570. DA670.L19C5 v.97

10331 LEGH. A history of the house of Lyme (in Cheshire), compiled from documents of the Legh family of that house, and from other sources. By William Beamont ... Warrington, P. Pearse, 1876. 2 p. l., 205, (2) p. 22½ cm. 2-20281. CS439.L9

10332 LEGH. The house of Lyme from its foundation to the end of the eighteenth century, by the Lady Newton ... London, W. Heinemann, 1917. xvi, 422, (1) p. front., plates, ports., fold. map, facsim., fold. geneal. tab. 24 cm. 18-1254. DA306.L8N4

10333 LEGH. Lyme letters, 1660-1760, by the Lady Newton ... London, W. Heinemann, ltd., 1925. xii, 341, (1) p. front. plates, ports., fold. geneal. tab. 24½ cm. 26-14297. DA306.L8N43

LE HEUP. See WITTEWRONGE, CS439.W65

10334 LEHMAN. Short history of the Lehman family in Maryland, by Samuel A. Lehman. (Baltimore, Md., Printed by Hess printing company) 1935. 64 p. 23 cm. 35-20347. CS71.L5 1935

10335 LEHMAN. Lehmann of Neuchatel, by Elizabeth Dwight Garrison Shepard and Charles Shepard. Rochester, N.Y., C. Shepard, 1949. geneal. table. 37 x 50 cm. fold. to 20 x 18 cm. (Shepard genealogical series, no. 20) "Limited edition. Copy no. 9." 50-990. CS71.L5 1949

10336 LEHMAN. Ancestors and friends. By John Lehmann. London, Eyre & Spottiswoode, 1962. 287 p. ports. 23 cm. 64-4903. CS439.L46 1962

LEHMAN. See also: BOOHER, 1956
WALLBRIDGE, 1898

LEHMANN. See LEMANN.

LEIB. See HARRISON, 1910a

LEIBELSPERGER. See LEIBENSPERGER.

LEIBENGUTH. See LEVEGOOD.

10337 LEIBENSPERGER. History and genealogy of the Leibensperger family, descendants of John George Leipersberger and Catherine, compiled by Elmer I. Leibensperger ... (Kutztown, Pa.) Leibensperger family association (1943) 256, xxxii, 257-564 p. illus. (incl. ports.) 23½ cm. 44-24408. CS71.L513 1943

LEIBS. See HARRISON, 1932

LEIBUNDGUT. See LEVEGOOD.

10338 LEIBY. The Leiby-Lambert lineage. By Margaret Leiby (Glanding) Rupp. (York, Pa.) 1952 pts. 28 cm. 52-67539 rev. CS71.L514 1952

10339 LEIBY. Leiby genealogy; the ancestors and descendants of Daniel L. and Mary Steigerwalt Leiby. Published by a committee for the preparation of a brief genealogy. Tamaqua, Pa., 1956. 64 p. illus. 24 cm. 57-20952. CS71.L514 1956

10340   LEIDHEISER.   Genealogy of the Werner Leidheiser descendants of Lorain County and Erie County, Ohio.   By Claude Charles Hamel.   Amherst, 1951.   11 l. 27 cm. 52-20695.

CS71.L515   1951

10341   LEIDY.   Lieut. Col. Jacob Reed; proceedings at the dedication of the monument erected to his memory in Franconia Township, Pennsylvania, under the auspices of the Historical society of Montgomery County, Pennsylvania, October 8, 1901.   Norristown, Pa., 1905.   xvi, 198 p. front., illus. (incl. facsims.) plates, ports. 26 cm. Contents. - Reed, W.H. Lieutenant Colonel Jacob Reed. - Luckenbill, B.F. Dedicatory address. - Braden, Mrs. F. He fought with Washington (poem) - Reed, W.H. The Leidy family. - Proctor, J. History of Leidy's church - Reiter, D.H. Address of welcome. - Hackman, Miss A.T. Ancestral home (poem) - Souder, J.D. Private burying grounds of Franconia Township. - Reed, W.H. Indian Creek Reformed church. - Mathews, E. Hatfield Township. 5-24243.

F159.F8R3

10342   LEIGH.   Minutes of evidence taken before the Committee for privileges, to whom the petition of George Leigh, esquire, to His Majesty, claiming to be Baron Leigh of Stoneley, in the county of Warwick, was referred ... (London) 1828-29.   441, 157 p. illus. (coats of arms) fold. geneal. tab. 34 cm. (Parliament, 1828-1829. House of lords. Papers and bills 117, 59) Genealogical table of the Cotton family: p. 141, 2d pt. Book-plate of George Chetwynd. 24-22159 rev.

CS423.L4A5

10343   LEIGH.   Stoneleigh abbey, thirty four years ago, containing a short history of the claims to the peerage and estates, and a catalogue of the confessed and suspected crimes, &c. &c. &c. by Charles Griffin.   Leamington Spa, C. Griffin; Brimingham, Printed by R.J. Salter (pref. 1848)   vi, (7)-90, (2) p. 16½ cm.   Ms. note on fly leaf: Suppressed and bought up by the (Leigh) family. 2-18006.

CS439.L35   1848

10344   LEIGH.   The Cistercian abbey of Stoneley-in-Arden, Warwickshire; and its occupants ...   Ashby-de-la-Zouche, W. and J. Hextall, 1854.   vi, 44 p. front., plates, plan, fold. geneal. tab. 23 cm.   Armorial book-plate of Charles Gresley of Lichfield.   "At first intended for publication in a periodical as a review of the interesting volume (Stoneleigh abbey, from its foundation to the present time, by F.L. Colville.   Warwick, 1850) ... but outgrowing the limits usually allowed for such communications, the writer enlarged it ... and has had a few copies of it printed." - Pref. note, signed J.M. Gresley. "The Leigh family": p. 23-31. 17-2873.

DA690.S87G7

10345   LEIGH.   Notices of the family of Leigh of Addington.   By Granville Leveson-Gower ...   London, Wyman & sons, 1878.   49 p. 2 pl., coats of arms, 2 fold. geneal. tab. 22½ cm. Reprinted from the Surrey archaeological collections, v. 7, p. 77-123. 15-21496.

CS439.L47   1878

10346   LEIGH.   A genealogical memoir of the ancient, honourable, and extinct family of Leigh of Addington, by H.S. Sweetman, B.A. ... 1860.   North Devon, Priv. print, for Mrs. Halliday, 1887.   2 p. l. (3)-46 p., 1 l. plates, port., fold. geneal. tab. 23 cm. Ed. by Maria Halliday. "50 copies printed for private circulation." 9-14906 rev.

CS439.L47   1887

10347   LEIGH.   Memorials of a Warwickshire family by the Rev. Bridgeman G.F.C.W.-Boughton-Leigh ... With prefatory note by Sir Hugh Gilzean-Reid ... London, H. Frowde, 1906.   xvi, 208 p. front., illus., plates, ports., 2 geneal. tab. (1 fold.) 23 cm. 11-4476.

CS439.L35   1906

10348   LEIGH.   The Leigh history; descendents of George W. Leigh.   By Ruth C. Pennington.   West Covina, Calif., 1957.   21 l. illus. 36 cm. 57-31379.

CS71.L517   1957

10349   LEIGH.   Leigh family (also variant spellings) in vertical file.   Ask reference librarin for this material.

LEIGH.   See also: HUTCHINSON, 1902
                          LEE.

LEIGHTON.   See: BOTFIELD, CS439.B78
                          LAYTON.

LEINAU.   See LIGNAUD.

LEIPERSBERGER.   See LEIBENSPERGER.

10350   LEIPHAM.   History and genealogy of the family of Peter Leipham and his wife Catherine Berger of Russell Hill, Penn'a, and Vacation reminiscences.   By William Henry Stang.   (Wilkes-Barre, Pa., c. 1927)   x, 65 p. illus., ports., fold. map. 24 cm. "Leipham reunion at Vose, Pa., August 11, 1928" (2 l.) inserted.

CS71. L52   1927

—— Supplement.   no. 1 -   Aug. 1952 -   (Palmyra, N.J., etc.)   v. 22 cm.

CS71. L52   1927
Suppl.

10351   LEIS.   The Leis family; M. Louis Leis, Charlotte Meir, married in Germany, 1844, settled north of Greenville, 1847.   By Florence Louise (Clark) Lease.   Greenville, Ohio, C. Runke, 1948.
1 v. (unpaged) ports. 22 cm. 53-23407.   CS71. L528   1948

10352   LEISLER.   Genealogical notes relating to Lieut-Gov. Jacob Leisler, and his family connect-ions in New York.   By Edwin R. Purple ... New York, Priv. print., 1877.   24 p. 27½ cm. "Reprinted from the New York genealogical and biographical record: with additions.   Edition, 75 copies." 3-17362.   CS71. L531   1877

10353   LEIST.   Leist family.   A true copy of Leist family record taken from original documents written about 1802 and now in the archives of the Ross County Historical Society museum at Chillicothe, Ohio (by David K. Webb.   (n. p., 19 -)   1 l. 28 cm. 53-33630.   CS71. L535

LEITER.   See FOX, 1924

10354   LEITH.   The Leiths of Harthill, the story of some turbulent lairds and a royalist martyr, by Francis Bickley, with an architectural description of Harthill castle by W. Douglas Simpson ... London, A. Maclehose & co., 1937.   3 p. l., 120 p. front. (plan) plates, fold. geneal. tab. 19 cm. 37-29921.

CS479. L44   1937

10355   LEITH.   Trustie to the end; the story of the Leith Hall family, by Henrietta Leith-Hay and Marion Lochhead.   Edinburgh, Oliver and Boyd (1957)   152 p. illus. 23 cm. 58-19374.

CS479. L44   1957

LEITH.   See also FORBES, 1839

10356   LELAND.   The Leland magazine; or, A genealogical record of Henry Leland, and his de-scendants ... embracing nearly every person of the name of Leland in America, from 1653 to 1850. By Sherman Leland.   Boston, Printed by Wier & White, 1850.   1 p. l., 278 p., 1 l. ports. 24½ cm. 9-25090.

CS71. L538   1850

LE MAISTRE.   See LEMASTER.

LE MAITRE.   See: DELAMATER.
                                    LEMASTER.

LEMAN.   See LEMON.

10357   LEMANN.   The Lemann family of Louisiana; an account compiled from diaries, correspond-ence and personal reminiscences.   By Bernard Lemann.   (Donaldsonville? La., 1965)   180, (22) p. illus., facsims., map, ports. 27 cm. "The Lemann family tree, edited by Arthur A. Lemann, III": (22) p. 65-51583.

CS71. L539   1965

LEMANN.   See also LEHMAN.

LEMAR.   See LAMAR.

10358   LEMASTER.   Lemaster family, U.S.A., 1960, by many interested members of the family as listed herein.   Compiled by Howard Marshall Lemaster, assisted by Margaret Nelson Herberger. Carlinville, Ill., 1960.   117 p. illus. 21 cm. 61-29002.   CS71. L685   1960

LEMASTER.   See also DELAMATER.

LEMASTERS.   See LEMASTER.

10359   LE MAY.   Records of the Le May family in England, 1630-1950.   By Reginald Stuart Le May.   (London) 1958.   65 p. illus. 23 cm. 58-41924.   CS439.L483   1958

LEMEN.   See LEMON.

10360   LEMERT.   The Lemert family in America; the story of Lewis Lemert and his descendants. By Amy Lemert Hake.   (Schenectady, N.Y., 1968)   87, A-O p. illus., facsims., geneal. table, ports. 29 cm. Bibliography: p. O. 73-3641 MARC.   CS71.L5397   1968

10361   LE MIEUX.   Lucius Augustus Le Mieux, Seymout, Outagamie County, Wisconsin.   (Chicago, J.H. Beers & co.) 1895.   2 p. l., 5-25 l. 21 cm. Prepared for the "Commemorative biographical record of the Fox River Valley, Wisconsin." Inserted are two folded leaves in ms. of the ancestry of the author's wife Fannie Edith (Fox) Le Mieux. 13-9628.
CS71.L54   1895

LEMING.   See LEAMING.

LEMLEY.   See BRUMBACH, 1961

LEMMING.   See LEAMING.

LEMMON.   See LEHMAN.

LEMMOND.   See LEMOND.

10362   LEMON.   (A collection of deeds relating to the Leman family from 1607 to 1704.   19 manuscripts on vellum. CA 30-1018 unrev.   LAW

10363   LEMON.   Lithographed pedigree of Leman family of Norfolk and Suffolk.   (n.p.) 184 - geneal. tab. 42½ x 255 cm.   CS439.L48

10364   LEMON.   ... History of the Lemen family, of Illinois, Virginia, and elsewhere ... By Frank B. Lemen.   Collinsville, Ill. (1898)   644 p. plates, ports., facsim. 20 cm. At head of title: 1656-1898. Contents. - pt. I. Illinois branch. - pt. II. Virginia branch. 98-2281 rev.   CS71.L555   1898

LEMON.   See also YEAGER, 1912

10365   LEMOND.   Genealogy of the families of Milas and Mary Means Lemond and of their brothers and sisters, by Marcus Monroe Lemond.   Brooklyn, New York city, 1937.   2 p. l., (11)-162 p., 1 l. 2 port. (incl. front.) 22 cm. Blank leaves at end for additions. 39-14787.   CS71.L557   1937

10366   LE MOYNE.   ... Les Machabées de la Nouvelle-France; histoire d'une famille canadienne, 1641-1768.   By Joseph Marmette.   Québec, Impr. de L. Brousseau, 1878.   180 p. 17 cm. "Sources": p. (11)-12. 38-37765.   F1030.M35

10367   LE MOYNE.   Le Moyne des Pins genealogies from 1655 to 1930, with historical notes, biographical sketches, and with particular attention paid to the descent of the families of Benjamin Le Moine and William Henri Le Moine, by Edith Le Moyne White.   (n.p.) Priv. print., 1930. viii, (9)-110 p. coat of arms. 25 cm. "1st edition 100 copies; no. 64." 31-20703.   CS90.L38

10368   LEMPRIERE.   A monograph of the house of Lempriere, recording, by tabular pedigrees, biographical notices, and other illustrative data, its history from A.D.970 to 1862.   By J. Bertrand Payne ... With illustrations from designs by the author.   London, Priv. print., 1862.   3 p. l., 30 p. front., illus., coats of arms, fold. geneal. tab. 35 cm. "Comparative pedigree, showing the connection of the family of Lempriere with the ducal house of Normandy, and with several of the noble families of the kingdom": fold. geneal. tab. 17-2878.   CS439.L49

10369   LE NEVE.   Calendar of correspondence and documents relating to the family of Oliver Le Neve, of Witchingham, Norfolk, 1675-1743. By the late Francis Rye, completed by his widow, Mrs. Amy Rye. (Uniform with Report on the manuscripts of the family of Gawdy, formerly of Norfolk) Ed., with an introduction, by Walter Rye. Norwich, A.H. Goose, 1895.   1 p. l., xxi, 222 p. 25 cm. 21-16268. CS439.L493

10370   LENFEST.   Genealogy of the Lenfest family in America (by) Bertram A. Lenfest.   (n. p., 1931?)   cover-title, 22 1. 32 x 24 cm. Blue-print. 33-316.   CS71. L558   1931

10372   LENFEST.   Genealogy of the Lenfest-Lenfestey family in Guernsey, arranged by B. A. Lenfest, Brooklyn, N. Y.   Well attested church and other records in Guernsey bring the earliest dates back to 1475 A. D., while one of the six genealgies shows that Lenfesteys were living in Guernsey before 1400 A. D.   Much credit should be given to Mr. Fred Priaulx, St. Saviour's, Guernsey, for his expert cooperation.   Data collected Sept. & Oct. 1938.   (Brooklyn, 1938)   cover-title, 4 fold. geneal. tab. 28 x 41 cm. fold. to 28½ x 22½ cm. Blue-prints. Title from label mounted on cover. "Genealogy of Lenfesteys and others from Miss Edith F. Carey's notes": 1st geneal. tab. 40-21849.   CS439. L4933   1938

10373   LENFEST.   Lenfests in probate records in counties of Essex, Middlesex, Norfolk and Suffolk, commonwealth of Massachusetts.   Abstracted by Dr. Bertram A. Lenfest ... (n. p.) 1941.   cover-title, 5 numb. 1. 28½ cm. Blue-print. 43-1843.   CS71. L558   1941

10374   LENFEST.   Lenfests in Massachusetts registry of deeds in the counties of Essex, Middlesex, Norfolk and Suffolk.   Collected and abstracted by Dr. Bertram A. Lenfest ... (n. p.) 1941.   cover-title, 10 numb. 1. 28½ cm. Leaves 1-7 blue-print; 8-10 type-written (carbon copy) 43-1844.   CS71. L558   1941a

10375   LENFEST.   Lenfests in probate records in all sixteen counties of the state of Maine.   Abstracted by Dr. Bertram A. Lenfest.   (n. p.) 1941.   cover-title, 6 numb. 1. 28½ cm. Blue-print. 43-1845.   CS71. L558   1941b

10376   LENFEST.   Lenfests in state of Maine registry of deeds in all sixteen counties.   Collected and abstracted by Dr. Bertram A. Lenfest ... (n. p.) 1941.   cover-title, 3 p. 1., 58 numb. 1. 28½ cm. Part of the leaves are blue-print, part type-written (carbon copy) 43-1846.   CS71. L558   1941c

LENFESTY.   See LENFEST.

10377   LENHART.   The Lenhart family of Greenwich and Albany Twps., Berks County, and York County, Pa.   (n. p.) 1937.   20 1. illus. 29 cm. 61-57042.   CS71. L56   1937

10378   LENHER.   The Lenher family, a genealogy compiled by Sarah Marion Lenher ... (Elizabeth? N. J.) 1903.   24 p. 23½ cm. 9-11473.   CS71. L566   1903

LENHER.   See also LUNDY, 1902

10379   LENNARD.   More about Stifford and its neighbourhood, past and present ... By William Palin ... Printed for private circulation.   (London, Printed by Taylor and co.) 1872.   xi, 167 p. plates. 27½ cm. Title vignette. A supplementary volume to the author's "Stifford and its neighbourhood, past and present," London, 1871. History of the Lennard family: p. 13-22. 15-7451.   DA690. S835P4

10380   LENNARD.   An account of the families of Lennard and Barrett.   Compiled largely from original documents, by Thomas Barrett-Lennard.   With portraits.   (London, etc., Printed by Spottiswoode & co. ltd.) 1908.   xvii, (1), 681 p. front., illus. (facsims.) ports., plates. 23½ cm. "Printed for private circulation." "This work is limited to 250 copies, each copy being numbered. no. 173. " Compiled from family papers and documents, first collected by Thomas Barrett Lennard, 29th baron Dacre, and later arranged in four volumes under title The Lennard papers, by the late Henry Barrett Lennard. Contains also Fynes and Dacre families. 25-127.   CS439. L494

LENNARD.   See also LEONARD.

LENNELL.   See LINNELL.

10381   LENNOX.   Cartularium comitatus de Levenax ab initio seculi decimi tertii usque ad annum M. CCC. XCVIII.   Ad fidem apographi in Bibliotheca Facultatis juridicae edinensis servati cum aliis m. s. s. collati.   Impressum Edinburgi, 1833.   xxiv p., 1 1., 125 p. 27 x 21½ cm. (Maitland club. Publications. no. 24) 90 copies printed. Ed. James Dennistoun; presented to the club by Alexander Campbell. 18-14165.   DA750. M3 no. 24

10382   LENNOX.   Additional remarks upon the question of the Lennox or Rusky representation, and other topics, in answer to the author of "History of the partition of the Lennox," &c.   With an éclaircissement as to the discussion about Richard II.   By John Riddell ... Edinburgh, T. Clark, 1835.
xxvii, (1), 151 p. 23 cm. 8-30548.   DA758.3.L6R5

10383   LENNOX.   History of the partition of the Lennox.   By Mark Napier ... Edinburgh, W. Blackwood and sons; (etc., etc.) 1835.   xvi, 256 p. illus. 23 cm. Title vignette. 6-36772.   DA758.3.L6N2

10384   LENNOX.   The family of Lennox.   (In The great governing families of England, by John Langton Sanford and Meredith Townsend ... Edinburgh (etc.) 1865. 23 cm. vol. 2, p. 287 -) 4-24748.   DA305.S2

10385   LENNOX.   The Lennox, by William Fraser ... Edinburgh (T. & A. Constable) 1874.
2 v. plates, ports., facsims. 26 cm. Title vignette in colors. Impression, 150 copies. 8-22929.   DA758.3.L6F8

10386   LENNOX.   "The Lanox of Auld."   An epistolary review of "The Lennox, by William Fraser," by Mark Napier.   Edinburgh, D. Douglas, 1880.   2 p. l., xxii, 153 p. illus. (incl. coats of arms) plates, geneal. tab.
29 cm. "Note" signed: Francis Napier. 17-23083.   DA758.3.L6N3

          LENNOX.   See also: BANKS, 1938
                              NAPIER, 1885

          LENOIR.   See GWINN, 1940

10387   LENOX-CONYNGHAM.   An old Ulster house and the people who lived in it, by Mina Lenox-Conyngham.   Dundalk, W. Tempest, 1946.   8 p. l., 254 p. front., illus. (incl. coat of arms) plates, ports., fold. geneal.
tab. 26½ x 21 cm. 47-20054.   CS499.L4   1946

10388   LENT.   History of the Lent (van Lent) family in the United States, genealogical and biographical, from the time they left their native soil in Holland, 1638-1902, by Nelson Burton Lent ... Newburgh, N.Y., Newburgh journal printing house and book-bindery, 1903.   171 p. front., plates, port. 25½ cm.
3-26623.   CS71.L573   1903

          LENT.   See also BLAUVELT, 1957

10389   LENTHALL.   The Lenthall houses and their owners.   By Maud Burr Morris.   (In Columbia historical society. Records. Washington, 1930. 23½ cm. v. 31-32, p.1-35, pl. I-II (incl. port.) "Read before the society, January 18, 1927."
W 31 -1.   F191.C72 vol.31

          LENTHALL.   See also EELLS, 1903

10390   LENTILHON.   The Lentilhons and their kinsmen of Forez, France & the United States, by Eugène Lentilhon.   Paris (Printed by Bishop and Garrett) 1931.   1 p. l., 103 p. front., plates, ports., fold. maps,
fold. genal. tab., coats of arms. 24 cm. "This edition is limited to fifty copies, numbered 1 to 50, for private circulation." This copy not
numbered. English and French on opposite pages. "Authorities": p. 2-3. 32-35717.   CS599.L46

          LENTZ.   See ENDERS, 1960

10391   LENZ.   The Lenz family; history of the American branch, established at Stone Arabia, N.Y., in 1854, by Friedrich Konrad Lenz, of Werdorf, Germany, compiled by Ella Elizabeth Lenz (Mrs. Albert William Patten) ... (St. Johnsville, N.Y.) Printed by the Enterprise and news, 1937.
x, 187 p. incl. front., illus., ports., coat of arms. 23½ cm. 38-2524.   CS71.L575   1937

10392   LEONARD.   A genealogical memoir of the Leonard family; containing a full account of the first three generations of the family of James Leonard, who was an early settler of Taunton, Ms., with incidental notices of later descendants ... By Wm. R. Deane, ... Boston, Office of the New England historic-genealogical register, 1851.   20 p. 24½ cm. "Prepared for the New England historic-genealogical register."
5-13624.   CS71.L58   1851

10393   LEONARD.   A genealogical memoir of the Leonard family; containing a full account of the first three generations of the family of James Leonard, was an early settler of Taunton, Ms., with incidental notices of later descendants ... By Wm. R. Deane ... Boston, Office of the New England historic-genealogical register, 1851 (1853)   23, (1) p. 24 cm. "Prepared for the New England historic-genealogical register." "Appendix. - Notice of Major Zephaniah Leonard" (From the N. E. hist. and gen. reg., Jan., 1853): p. (21)-23. 5-13621.

CS71.L58   1853

10394   LEONARD.   Major Thomas Leonard.   (Communicated by Wm. R. Deane.   Boston, 1868) (25)-28 p. 26 cm. "From the N. Eng. hist. and genealogical reg., April, 1868." "Continuation of A. genealogical memoir of the Leonard family ... By Wm. R. Dean ... Boston, 1851." An elegy ... Major Thomas Leonard": p. 26-27. 5-13622.   CS71.L58   1868

10395   LEONARD.   Biographical sketch of the centenarian, Mrs. Abigail Alden Leonard, of Raynham, Mass., by Rev. Enoch Sanford ... Raynham, Mass., 1887.   40 p. 25 cm. 16-7847.

CS71.L58   1887

10396   LEONARD.   Emily J. Leonard, by Georgia Louise Leonard.   Privately printed.   New York, The Knickerbocker press, 1889.   160 p. front., pl., ports. 24 cm. 22-6214.

CT275.L3665L4

10397   LEONARD.   Memorial: genealogical, historical and biographical of Solomon Leonard, 1637, of Duxbury and Bridgewater, Massachusetts, and some of his descendants ... By Manning Leonard ... (Auburn, N. Y., Knapp, Peck & Thomson, 1896)   452, (2) p. front., plates, ports., coat of arms. 24½ cm. Three hundred copies. No. 119. 9-11622.   CS71.L58   1896

10398   LEONARD.   Stephen Banks Leonard of Owego, Tioga county, New York, prepared by his grandson William Andrew Leonard.   (n. p.) Printed for private circulation, 1909.   4 p. 1., 13-342 p. plates, ports., coat of arms. 24 cm. "This work is limited to 200 copies, each copy being numbered. no. 40." "References to consult": p. 323-327. 35-16388.   CS71.L58   1909

10399   LEONARD.   Annals of the Leonard family ... Comp. by Fanny Leonard Koster ... (New York, The C.H. Koster co.) 1911.   xviii, 208 p., 7 1. front., plates, ports., facsim., coats of arms, 3 fold. geneal. tab. 22½ cm. "Chart of English ancestry" (in pocket of front cover) "Chart of descendants of James Leonard" (in pocket of back cover) Blank leaves at end for "Memoranda". "This work is limited to 200 copies." no. 16." 14-16975.   CS71.L58   1911

10400   LEONARD.   Memoirs of the Leonard, Thompson, and Haskell families, with their collateral families   of Alden, Andrews, Bell ... and many others, by Caroline Leonard Goodenough ... ... published by the author.   (Yellow Springs, O., The Antioch press) 1928.   5 p. 1., 3-344 p. front., illus., plates, ports., coats of arms. 22½ cm. "Of this book one thousand copies have been printed of which this is no. 24." 28-6743.

CS71.L58   1928

10401   LEONARD.   John Leonard of Springfield, Mass., and some of his descendants, compiled by Constance Leonard, b. 1785, d. 1855.   The original compilation and several later ones are now in the possession of Mrs. Alice M. (Leonard) Hathaway, of Springfield, Mass. and with her consent were copied, with no attempt at verification of statements or of dates, by Mrs. Kate W. Barney.   Springfield, Mass., 1929.   1 p. 1., 62 numb. 1., 16 1. 22½ cm. Type-written (carbon copy) CA 31-349 unrev. CS71.L58   1929

10402   LEONARD.   Legends, loves and loyalties of old New England, by Caroline Leonard Goodenough ... Rochester, Mass., The author (1930)   5 p. 1., (3)-344p. front., illus., plates, ports., coats of arms. 22½ cm. "Of this book one thousand copies have been printed." This copy not numbered. Half-title: Memoirs of the Leonard, Thompson, and Haskell families. The work was first published, 1928, under this title. 31-22890.   CS71.L58   1930

10403   LEONARD.   Some ancestors and descendants of Avery Leonard of Seneca county, Ohio, by Harry S. Blaine.   Toledo, O., Press of G. A. Blaine, 1933.   2 p. 1., 42 numb. 1. front., illus. (plan) pl. (incl. ports.) 27½ cm. Mimeographed. "Books and authorities consulted in the compilation of this work": leaf 42. 39-16901.

CS71.L58   1933

10404   LEONARD.   100 years, 1834-1934 ... (London, Ont., E. Leonard & sons, ltd., 1934) 25 p. incl. front., illus. (incl. ports., facsims.) 23 cm. Introductory material signed: Fred Landon. Contains biographical sketches. A35-64

TS304.C2L4

LEONARD.　See also:　DILLON, 1909　　PAINE, 1913
　　　　　　　　　　　　GILES, 1864　　　PARSONS, 1867
　　　　　　　　　　　　HUNT, 1946　　　TAYLOR, 1886
　　　　　　　　　　　　JENNINGS, 1899　WHITAKER, 1935
　　　　　　　　　　　　LEARNED, 1898

LEOPOLD.　See LUBOLD, 1937

10406　LEPELL.　Molly Lepell, lady Hervey, by Dorothy Margaret Stuart ... London (etc.) G. G. Harrap & co., ltd. (1936)　375, (1) p. front., plates, ports., facsim., double geneal. tab. 22½ cm. 36-17667.
　　　　　　　　　　　　　　　　　　　　　　　　　　　　　　DA501. H5S8

LE PELLETIER.　See DU PONT, 1923

LE PLASTRIER.　See DU PONT, 1923

LE PORTE DE LOUVIGNY.　See LOUVIGNY.

LERCEDKNE.　See COLLOW, 1877

10407　LERIGÉ.　... Clément Lerigé, sieur de La Plante, officier des troupes de la marine;　ancêtre des familles Leriger, Dériger, de La Plante, La Plante et Laplante-Courville.　Son origine et sa famille en France.　By Roger D. Parent.　Montrel (G. Ducharme) 1942.　16 p. 23 cm. 43-234.
　　　　　　　　　　　　　　　　　　　　　　　　　　　　　　F1030. L55

10408　LERIGÉ.　... Clément Lerigé de la Plante et sa descendance; généalogie d'une famille canadienne.　By Roger D. Parent.　Montreal, G. Ducharme, 1942.　28 p. incl. pl. 22 cm. 43-46623.
　　　　　　　　　　　　　　　　　　　　CS90. L39　　　　1942

LE ROTER.　See RUTTER.

LEROUX.　See LA RUE.

10409　LE ROY.　Le Roy family and collateral lines of Cornell-Edgar-Goodridge-Jones, Newbold-Otis-Rutgers-Van den Bergh, edited by Alexander Du Bin.　Philadelphia, The Historical publication society (c. 1941)　32 p. 25½ cm. Pages 29-32 blank for "Family record." 41-18206.
　　　　　　　　　　　　　　　　　　　　CS71. L6　　　　1941

10410　LÉRY.　La famille C. de Lery.　(By Francois Daniel)　(In his Nos gloires nationales.　Montréal, E. Senécal, 1867. 22 cm. t.2, p. (67)-240. front., ports., coat of arms) Also issued, with additions, under title: Le vicomte C. de Léry, lieutenant-général de l'Empire français, ingénieur en chef de la grande armée et sa famille ...　9-19129.　F1005. D19 t. 2

10411　LÉRY.　Le vicomte C. de Léry, lieutenant-général de l'empire français, ingénieur en chef de la grande armée, et sa famille.　Montréal, E. Senécal, 1867.　iv, 44, 299 p. front., plates, ports., facsims., coat of arms. 22½ cm. By François Daniel. 9-19128.　CS90. L4
　　　　——— Copy 2.　(In Nos gloires nationales, Montreal, 1867. 22½ cm. v.2, p.67-240) 9-19129.　F1005. D19

10412　LE SAGE.　Mémorial de familles divisé en trois parties.　Généalogie Le Sage avec annexe Hudon dit Beaulieu & Beland.　Généalogies Martin & Hamelin y compris l'historique de chaque famille.　Préface de Messire J. F. Béland, Ptre ... Introduction de "Colette" Mlle. E. Lesage.　Lettre de M. l'abbé L. M. Hamelin, C. S. V.　Documents et Actes authentiques soigneusement compilés et reunis par Madame Caroline Hamelin née Martin.　(Montreal, Imprimerie du "Devoir") 1910.　1 p. l., ii, vii, iii p. 1 l., 227, (1) p. ports. 21½ cm. 14-5215.　CS89. H3

LE SAGE.　See also No. 1547 - Cabell county.

LE SEUR.　See LOZIER.

10413   LESH.   A collection of over six hundred names, descendants of Balthaser and Susanna Phillipina Loesch, Palatines from Gernsheim, near Worms, Germany; with historical notes, comp. by William W. Lesh (Loesch) ... (Washington, D. C., National capital press, inc., c.1914)
47 p. front. (port.) illus. (coat of arms) pl. 24 cm. 14-14615 rev.   CS71.L629   1914
—— Supplemental list, descendants of Balthaser and Susanna Phillipina Loesch, of Gernsheim, near Worms, Germany, who emigrated to America in 1710, comp. by William W. Lesh (Loesch). (Washington, D. C., National capital press, inc., c.1916)   21 p. 23 cm. 14-14615, rev.
CS71. CS71. L629

LESIER.   See LOZIER.

LESLEY.   See L. C. additions and corrections no. 3

10414   LESLIE.   Historical records of the family of Leslie from 1067 to 1868-9, collected from public records and authentic private sources by Colonel Leslie, K.H., of Balquhain.   Edinburgh, Edmonston and Douglas, 1869.   3 v. 23½ cm. 7-36797.   DA758.3L7L6

10415   LESLIE.   James Lesslie of Topsfield, Massachusetts, and some of his descendants, including biographical sketches of Rev. George Lesslie and Rev. David Lesslie, D. D.   By M.V.B.Perley. (One hundred copies reprinted from the Historical collections of the Essex institute, volume LI) Salem, Mass., Essex institute, 1915.   cover-title, 56 p. ports., facsims. 24½ cm. 24-581.
CS71. L6295   1915

10416   LESLIE.   An historical record of the family of Leslie, a famous family of Scotland, and their descendants, compiled and abranged (!) by Mrs. I. R. Marsh ... (Dearborn? Mich., 192-?)
5 p. l., 116 numb. l. 28 x 21½ cm. Type-written (carbon copy) 44-26034.   CS71.L6295   1920

10417   LESLIE.   Lesley, Leslie; William Robert Lesley and Elizabeth Buchanan Lesley and their descendants.   A history of two hundred years in America, 1755-1955.   By Ruth Cleveland Leslie. (Washington? 1956)   412 p. illus. 24 cm. 56-42827.   CS71.L6295   1956

LESLIE.   See also: DOUGLAS, DA758.3.A1T2
                      MELVILLE, DA758.3.M42F7

10418   LESNETT.   Genealogy, Christian Lesnett ... Compiled and published by Daniel M. Bennett ... Bridgeville, Pa. (1931)   112 p. incl. front., illus. (plan) 23½ cm. Contains also the Rowley, Boyce and Neal families. Blank pages for "Memorandum" (102-112) 36-12556.   CS71.L63   1931

L'ESPENARD.   See LISPENARD.

LESSLIE.   See LESLIE.

LESIEUR.   See SMITH, 1962

10419   LESTER.   Bryant Lester, of Lunenburg Co., Va., and his descendants.   By Thomas McAdory Owen.   (In Southern history association. Publications. Washington, D.C. 1897. 25 cm. v. 1, p. (127) - 137) 15-21026.
F206.S73 v.1

10420   LESTER.   Bryant Lester of Lunenburg County, Virginia, and his descendants, by Thomas McAdory Owen.   Baltimore, Md., The Friedenwald company, 1897.   13 p. 24½ cm. From Publications of the Southern history association, April, 1897. 2-14240.   CS71.L641   1897

10421   LESTER.   The Andrew Lester line of America, 1642-1925 (by) James W. Lester ... (From "The Lester line") (Gary, Ind., 1925)   1 l., 4 numb. l. 28 x 21½ cm. Type-written. Contents. - Ten generations of Lesters. - The Andrew Lester line. - War records. 25-19242.   CS71.L641   1925

10422   LESTER.   The Lesters; a brief history and genealogy of the Lesters of the Massachusetts and Connecticut colonies, with biographical sketches of members of kindred families, 1926, by J. William Lester ... Gary, Ind., Printed by Calumet press, 1926.   2 p. l., 9-34 p. illus. (port.) 24 cm. "Family letter to the Lesters": 1 leaf inserted at end. 27-3241.   CS71.L641   1926

10423   LESTER.   The royal origin of an American line, lineage from King Egbert I, by J. William
Lester ... Davenport, Ia. (1938)   cover-title, (5) p. 23 cm. 38-14166.   CS71.L641   1938

      LESTER.   See also: HARKNESS, 1958
                           ROBERTS, F159.R48R6

10424   LE STRANGE.   History of Hunstanton, Norfolk: with which is incorporated a narrative of the
life of St. Edmund, king & martyr.   By John Storer Cobb ... London, Jarrold & sons (1868)
viii, 148 p. 16 cm.   "Genealogical history of the Le Strange family": p. 32-82.   21-1476.   DA690.H92C6

10425   LE STRANGE.   Le Strange records; a chronicle of the early Le Stranges of Norfolk and the
March of Wales, A.D. 1100-1310, with the lines of Knockin and Blackmere continued to their extinction
... by Hamon Le Strange ... London, New York (etc.) Longmans, Green and co., 1916.   xii p., 1 l.,
407 p. x numb. pl. (incl. plan facsims.) 26 cm.   17-61.   CS439.L495

10426   LE STRANGE.   ... Observations on the Le Stranges, with some corrections of prevalent
genealogical errors.   By C. L'Estrange Ewen ... Paignton, Devon, C.L. Ewen, 1946. cover-title, 8 p.
geneal. tab. 21½ cm. 47-17678.   CS71.L642   1946

10427   LESTRE.   Une famille de l'Auxois sous l'Ancien Regime: Les Lestre.   By Robert Miron
d'Aussy.   (Dijon, 1964)   180, v, 8 p. 27 cm.   Cover title. 67-35667.   CS71.L6412   1964

      LETCHER.   See HYNES, 1941-2

10428   LETCHWORTH.   The life and work of William Pryor Letchworth, student and minister of
public benevolence, by J.N. Larned ... Boston and New York, Houghton Mifflin company, 1912.
viii p., 1 l., 472 p., 1 l. front., plates, ports., map. 20½ cm. 12-9984.   HV98.N7L3

      LE TEYNTERER.   See TAINTER.

10429   LETHAM.   The Letham of Leatham family book of remembrance; the story of Robert Letham
and his wife Janet Urquhart, with historical-genealogical and biographical data on their ancestry and
descendants.   Ann Arbor, (Mich.) Edwards Bros., 1955.   xiii, 1072 p. illus., ports., maps, facsims., geneal.
tables. 29 cm. 55-6431.   CS71.L643   1955

10430   LETTON.   Some Lettons and Willetts of Maryland and a few descendants and allied families
(Layton, Leighton, Letten, Leyton, Liten, Litten, Litton, Lytton) By Estelle Osborn Watson.
(Louisville?) 1955.   43 p. 28 cm. 56-44909.   CS71.L6435   1955

10431   LETTSOM.   Lettsom, his life, times, friends and descendants, by James Johnston Abraham
... London, W. Heinemann, ltd., 1933.   xx, 498 p. incl. front., illus. (incl. ports., maps, facsims.) fold. geneal. tab.
25½ cm. 33-35649.   R489.L6A35

10432   LEUTWYLER.   Leutwyler von Lupfig, 1693-1947.   By Paul Leutwyler.   Reinach (Aargau)
Buchdr. E. & H. Tenger, 1948.   140 l. illus., ports. 25 cm. Continues the author's Leutwyler von Reinach, Sigristen, 1749-
1947. Includes Genealogy of the Luitwieler family, compiled by Clarence S. Luitwieler. 49-22968.
                                                 CS999.L46   1948

10433   LEUTZ.   Important descendants from the innkeeper-family (inn of "lion") Joh. Leonhard
Leutz & Marie Elisabeth, maiden name Bussemer (out of the family-book "Leutz") (n.p., 19 -)
1 l. 30 cm. 52-21866.   CS71.L644

10434   LeVAN.   Genealogical record of the LeVan family, descendants of Daniel LeVan and Marie
Beau (Huguenots) natives of Picardy, France, who settled in Amsterdam, Holland; 1650 to 1927,
compiled by Warren Patten Coon ... (Newark? 1927?) 2 p. l., 3-356 p. 23½ cm. 29-6044. CS71.L645   1927

10435   LE VASSEUR.   Histoire de notre famille: Pierre Levasseur dit l'Espérance, Jeanne de
Chanverlange, Pierre Levasseur dit l'Espérance, Anne Mesnage, Denis-Joseph Levasseur, Marie-
Charlotte couturier, François Levasseur dit Vigoureux, Marie-Charlotte Gailloux, François Levasseur,
Josephte Provencher, Joseph Levasseur, Judith Rivard dit Lavigne, David Levasseur, Victorine Beau-
chesne.   By Gérard Levasseur. (n.p., 1955) 33 l. 28 cm. 64-30581.   CS90.L45   1955

10436   LE VASSEUR.   Les pioneers (sic) Le Vasseur-Vasseur et allied (sic) familles.   The
pionerrs (sic) Le Vasseur, Vasseur and allied familys (sic) n. p., 1956 -   2v . (loose-leaf) mounted illus.
29 cm.   Title from label mounted on cover.   Typescript (carbon copy) 62-38961.   CS90. L45

10437   LEVEGOOD.   ... The Levegood, Levergood, Levengood, Livingood family, "Americans for
over two centuries".   By Lynne L. Levegood.   Long Island City, N. Y., 1934.   1 p. 1., 38 numb. 1., 3 1.
5 pl. (mounted photos) 26½ cm.   At head of title: American genealogy - The Pennsylvania Germans, from the Palatinate, Alsace & Switzerland.
Type-written.   34-35336.   CS71. L65   1934

10438   LEVEGOOD.   ... Genealogy of the Levegood, Levergood, Levengood, Livergood, Livengood,
Livingood family.   "Americans for over two centuries." By Lynne L. Levegood.   Floral Park, N. Y.,
1935.   cover-title, 54 numb. 1. 28 cm.   At head of title: ... The Pennsylvania Germans from the Palatinate, Alsace and Switzerland.
"Revised 1935." Mimeographed.   35-28833.   CS71. L65   1935

10439   LEVEGOOD.   Descendants of Henry Livergood and Salome Ruby-Livergood.   By Ethyl Eolia
(Livergood) McDonald.   (Eagle Grove, Ia., 1938)   cover-title, 42 numb. 1., 1 1. pl. 29 cm.   Mimeographed.   Plate,
printed on both sides, has 7 portraits on recto.   Introduction signed: Ethyl L. McDonald.   39-9239.
CS71. L779   1938

LEVENGOOD.   See LEVEGOOD.

LEVERGOOD.   See LEVEGOOD.

10440   LEVERETT.   A genealogical memoir of the family of Elder Thomas Leverett, of Boston.   By
Nathaniel B. Shurtleff ... Boston, Printed for the author, 1850.   20 p. front. (port.) 21½ cm. 10-9967.
CS71. L66   1850

10441   LEVERETT.   A memoir biographical and genealogical, of Sir John Leverett, knt., governor
of Massachusetts, 1673-79; of Hon. John Leverett, F. R. S., judge of the Supreme court, and president
of Harvard college; and of the family generally ... By Charles Edward Leverett.   Boston, Crosby,
Nichols & co., 1856.   203 p. front., plates, ports., fold. geneal. tab. 24½ cm.   Title vignette: coat of arms. 9-11618.
CS71. L66   1856

10442   LEVERETT.   Pedigree of the Leverett family.   (Boston, Crosby, Nicholas and company,
1856)   geneal. tab. 28½ x 35½ cm. fold. to 13½ x 20½ cm.   Detached from the Memoir ... of Sir John Leverett ... by Charles Edward
Leverett.   Boston, 1856.   9-11619.   CS71. L66   1856a

10443   LEVERING.   The Levering family; or, A genealogical account of Wigard Levering and
Gerhard Levering, two of the pioneer settlers of Roxborough township, Philadelphia County ... and
their descendants; and an appendix, containing brief sketches of Roxborough and Manayunk, by Horatio
Gates Jones ... Philadelphia, Printed for the author, by King & Baird, 1858.   x, 193 p. front., plates, ports.,
facsims. 24 cm. 9-11617.   CS71. L661   1858

10444   LEVERING.   Proceedings of the Levering family reunion ... Vol. 1.   Columbus, O., 1892 -
1 v. 23 cm.   Published by order of the Levering family historical association. 9-11474.   CS71. L661   1892

10445   LEVERING.   Levering family; history and genealogy.   By Col. John Levering ... (Indianapolis?) Levering historical association (1897)   975 p. front., illus., plates, ports., facsims. 23½ cm.   Title vignette:
coat of arms. 9-11616.   CS71. L661   1897

LEVERING.   See also: BREWER, 1947
                              PASTORIUS, 1926

10446   LEVESON-GOWER.   Lord Granville Leveson Gower (first earl Granville): private correspondence, 1781 to 1821, ed. by his daughter-in-law, Castalia, countess Granville ... London, J.
Murray, 1916.   2 v. fronts., 1 illus., plates, ports., fold. facsim., fold. geneal. tables. 23 cm.   "Lord Granville's principal
correspondent (was) Henrietta, countess of Bessborough." - Introd. 16-15697.   DA536. G68A2

LEVESON-GOWER.   See also GOWER.

LEVET. See: LEAVITT.
SANBORN, 1894

10447 LEVETT. (Publications. Portland, Me., Printed for the Gorges society, 1884)-
v. plates (part fold.) ports., fold. maps, plans (part fold.) facsims. (Part fold.) fold. geneal. tables. 22 x 18½ cm. Part V. contains: - Christopher Levett, of York, the pioneer colonist in Casco Bay. 1893. 5-39197.

F16.G66

LEVIN. See JOHNSON, 1960

10448 LEVINGE. Jottings for early history of the Levinge family. By Sir Richard G. A. Levinge, bart. Part I. Dublin, Printed for private circulation by Browne & Nolan, 1873. 2 p. l., (iii)-v, 78 p. 21½ cm. No more published in this edition. A complete edition appeared in 1877 under title: Jottings of the Levinge family. 19-6527.

CS439.L497

LEVINGER. See LOEVINGER.

LEVINGS. See LEAVENS.

LEVINS. See: DODDRIDGE, 1961
LEAVENS.

10449 LEVIS. Catalogue of engraved portraits, views, etc., connected with the name of Levis. London, Printed for the author for private distribution only at the Chiswick press, 1914. xx, 113, (1) p. incl. illus., port. front. 22½ cm. Front., title, within ornamental border; illus., port. called "Plate I (-XXXII)" "Only fifty copies printed." "Introductory note" signed: H.C.Levis. 15-8484.

CS439.L5

LEVITT. See: DRAKE, 1962
LEAVITT, .L4394

LEVY. See MOISE, 1961

LEWALLEN. See CORN, 1959

10450. LEWEN. History and pedigree of the family of Lewen of Durham, Northumberland, and Scarborough. With pedigrees of their connections Fulwood, Ker, Rutherfurd, Radcliffe, and Watson of Ingleby Greenhow and Newport, Mon., and pedigrees of other families called Lewen, Lewin, Levinge, etc., with extracts from wills, public records etc. London, Mitchell Hughes and Clarke, 1919. xi, 354 p., 1 l. front., plates, ports., plans (1 fold.) facsims. 29 cm. Preface signed: T.E.Watson. 20-11874.

CS439.L52

10451 LEWIS. Brief memoir of Dr. Winslow Lewis. By John H. Sheppard ... Albany, N.Y., J. Munsell, 1863. 33, (1) p. front. (port.) 22 cm. "From the New Eng. hist. and genealogical register." "Genealogy of the Winslow family," p. 20-23; "Genealogy of the Lewis family," p. 24-29; "Genealogy of the Greenough family," p. 30-33. 35M1187.

R154.L43S5

—— Copy 2

Taner coll.

10452 LEWIS. The adventures of my grandfather. With extracts from his letters, and other family documents, prepared for the press with notes and biographical sketches of himself and his son John Howe Peyton, esq., by John Lewis Peyton ... London, J. Wilson, 1867. x, 249 p. 22 cm. Narrative of the circumstances connected with the settlement of M. Jean Louis or John Lewis and his family in Virginia, p. 215-224; Correspondence relating to Braddock's campaign, p. 225-249. 3-471.

F229.P51

10453 LEWIS. Radial charts of the Winslow and Lewis families, showing the patronymic line of Rev. Isaiah Lewis, of Wellfleet, and Abigail Winslow, of Marshfield, Mass. (New York) c. 1877. geneal. chart. coat of arms. 48 x 76 cm. Signed: David Parsons Holton. 14-11909.

CS71.L675 1877

10454 LEWIS. Genealogies of the Lewis and kindred families, edited by John Meriwether McAllister ... and Lura Boulton Tandy ... Columbia, Mo., Printed by W.W.Stephens publishing company, 1906. 416 p. front., port., coats of arms. 22 cm.

CS71.L675 1906

—— Supplement, edited January 1, 1943 by Ruth Tandy Royse ... (n.p., 1943?)
1 p. l., 5 numb. l. 28 x 21½ cm. Manuscript note on t.-p.: Revised Jan. 1947. 6-19078 rev. Suppl. CS71.L675 1906

10455　LEWIS.　Edmund Lewis, of Lynn, Massachusetts, and some of his descendants, by George Harlan Lewis ... Salem, Mass., Essex institute, 1908.　1 p. l., ii. 179 p. 23½ cm.　"Addenda": p. 151-179.　"one hundred and twenty-five copies reprinted from the Historical collections of the Essex institute, volumes XLII and XLIV."　9-21013.

CS71.L675　　1908

10456　LEWIS.　Lewis, with collateral lines: Andrews, Belden, Bronson, Butler, Gillett, Newell, Peck, Stanley, Wright, and others; ancestral record of Henry Martyn Lewis, compiled and prepared by Harriet Southworth (Lewis) Barnes.　Philadelphia, 1910.　73 p. front. (port.) 19½ cm.　10-13930.

CS71.L675　　1910

10457　LEWIS.　A genealogical history of my ancestors and the story of my life (by) Ladd J. Lewis. Adrian, Mich., Printed by S. F. Finch printing company, 1921.　124 p. incl. front. plates, ports., fold. geneal. tab. 22½ cm.　Running title: Family history of Ladd J. Lewis.　35-17576.

CS71.L675　　1921

10458　LEWIS.　Lucy Jefferson Lewis, sister of President Thomas Jefferson; Virginia, 1752 - Kentucky, 1811 (by) Martha Grassham Purcell.　(n.p., 1924)　cover-title, 16 p., 1 l.　23 cm.　Caption title: The Sage of Monticello's sister sleeps in Kentucky soil.　30-5662.

CS71.L675　　1924

10459　LEWIS.　History of Eli Lewis and family, given in a speech by Ellis S. Lewis, at Lewisberry home-coming service.　Tells of Welsh race.　Sunday, October 4, 1925.　(York? Pa., 1925)　1 p. l., 5 p.　22 cm.　Reprint from "The Gazette & daily, York, Pa., 10/5/25."　26-17564.

CS71.L675　　1925

10460　LEWIS.　Lewis family, pioneers of eastern Tennessee and Indiana Territory; being an account of the revolutionary record of Nathan Lewis of Wales, some of his descendants, and the Lewis family history written by his great-grandson, William G. Lewis of Fairmount, Indiana ... Compiled and edited by Mrs. Maunta G. Miller ... (Marion, Ind., Arnold-Barr printing co.) c.1928.　55, (1) p.　illus. (incl. ports.) 22 cm.　28-17792.

CS71.L675　　1928

10461　LEWIS.　Randall Lewis of Hopkinton, Rhode Island, and Delaware County, New York, and some of his descendants; a biographical and genealogical record by Frank Pardee Lewis, and Edward Chester Lewis ... Seattle, The Argus press, 1929.　200 p. incl. illus., ports. 23½ cm.　Blank pages for additions and corrections (185-200) "Edition 300 copies."　29-6442.

CS71.L683　　1929

10462　LEWIS.　1602 - William Lewis - 1671, of Stoke-by-Nayland, England, and some of his ancestors and descendants, by Isaac Newton Lewis ... Walpole (Mass.) 1932.　xix, 87 p. front., 1 illus., plates, ports., facsims. 23½ cm.　32-14684.

CS71.L675　　1932

10463　LEWIS.　James Lewis and Ann Elizabeth Stewart Lewis of North Carolina and Missouri. Their ancestry and descendants.　By P. Loyd Lewis.　(Ferguson, Mo., 1934)　5 p. l., 23 p.　29 cm. Type-written.　35-20364.

CS71.L675　　1934

10464　LEWIS.　Garrett county history Lewis family, by Chas. E. Hoye.　(Oakland, Md.) 1935　1 l.　39 cm.　Detached from the Mountain democrat.　February 28th, 1935.　38M1238T.

CS71.L675　　1935

10465　LEWIS.　Lewis of Warner hall: the history of a family including the genealogy of descendants in both the male and female lines, biographical sketches of its members, and their descent from other Virginia families, compiled by Merrow Egerton Sorley ... 1935.　(Columbia, Mo., Printing and binding by E. W. Stephens company, c.1937)　887 p.　front., plates, ports., fold. geneal. tab., coat of arms. 23½ cm. 37-17643.

CS71.L675　　1937

10466　LEWIS.　Lewises, Meriwethers and their kin; Lewises and Meriwethers with their tracings through the families whose records are herein contained, compiled from family papers and from reliable sources by Sarah Travers Lewis (Scott) Anderson ... Richmond, Va., The Dietz press, 1938. 6 p. l., 652, (1) p. front., plates, port., map. 23½ cm.　Blank pages for "Notes" (509-511) "Copyright ... by Mrs. Sarah Anderson Gordon." Includes bibliographies.　38-22938.

CS71.L675　　1938

10467　LEWIS.　(Descendants of) William Lewis, emigrated from Wales and settled in Northumberland County, Virginia, married Elizabeth Markham ... By Andrew Aldridge Lewis.　(Fredericksburg? 194 -?)　geneal. table.　51 x 97 cm. fold. to 49 x 37 cm.　Reproduction of original ms.　Compiled in 1940, with additions dated 1941-46. 50-39113.

CS71.L675

10468   LEWIS.   Ancestry of Thomas Lewis and his wife, Elizabeth Marshall, of Saco, Maine.   By Walter Goodwin Davis.   (Boston, 1947)   33 p. illus. 23 cm. "Reprinted from The New England historical and genealogical register, vol. cl, January and April, 1947." 47-27250.   CS71.L675   1947

10469   LEWIS.   A footnote to a history of the Lewis family, being a partial list of the descendants of William Henry Lewis (1799-1879) of Jackson County, Alabama.   By Robert Martin McBride.   Nashville, 1954.   57 l. illus. 29 cm. 54-27870.   CS71.L675   1954

10470   LEWIS.   William Lewis of Horry County, South Carolina.   By Mary (Lewis) Stevenson.   Columbia, S.C., Printed by R.L.Bryan Co., c.1960.   181 p. illus. 24 cm. 60-43294.
CS71.L675   1960

10471   LEWIS.   The family of John Lewis, pioneer.   By Irvin Frazier.   (San Marino, Calif., 1960)   108 p. illus., 3 fold. geneal. tables (in pocket) 36 cm. Cover title. Bibliography: p. 106-108. 61-20151.   CS71.L675   1960a

10472   LEWIS.   Lewis of Warner Hall, by Mrs. Wm. (Opal) Dyess.   Washington, A.W.Burns (1966)   28 l. 29 cm. 66-52940.   CS71.L675   1966

10473   LEWIS.   Ancestors: a personal exploration into the past, by Michael Lewis.   London, Hodder & Stoughton (1966)   224 p. 4 plates (incl. ports.) diagrs. 22½ cm. Diagr. on endpapers. 66-71359.
CS439.L524

LEWIS.   See also addenda and:

BASSETT, 1926	HENDRICKS, 1963	SWINK, 1940
BEAL, 1956	HIGHLAND, 1936	TAYLOR, 1898
BENSON, 1920	HOWARD, 1929	VAN METER, F225.V26
BOARMAN, 1934	JONES, 1891	VAWTER, 1905
BROWN, 1931	KIRKPATRICK, 1911	WASHINGTON, 1879
BUCKNER, 1907	LIGON, 1947	WATSON, 1910
CARD, E171.A53 v.20	PATTERSON, 1917	WEIS, 1922
COLEMAN, 1962	PATTERSON, 1948	WILLIAMS, F592.W672, 1936
CROCKER, 1923	PEYTON, F230.P51	WILLIS, 1898
EUBANK, 1938	POCAHONTAS, 1887	WINSLOW, CT99.L677S4
GLASSELL, 1890	RIVES, F230.K53	No. 553 - Goodhue county.
GREENOUGH, CT99.L677S4	ROBERTS, 1960	No. 1459 - Early families of
HABERSHAM, CS71.H114 19 -	SMITH, 1910	.... Kentucky.
HALEY, 1916		

10474   LEWKENOR.   Denham parish registers, 1539-1850, with historical notes and notices.   Bury St. Edmund's, Paul & Mathew, 1904.   xii, 339 p. front. (map) illus., plates, port. 22 cm. (Suffolk green books, no. VIII) Contains Lewkenor wills ... Six Edward Lewkenors. 11-5062 rev.
CS436.D25

LEWKENOR.   See also KNIGHT, DA690.C47A8

LEYBORNE.   See LEYBURN.

LEYBORNE-POPHAM.   See CALSTON, 1900

10475   LEYBURN.   A description of the heart-shrine in Leybourne church, with some account of Sir Roger de Leyburn, kt., and his connection with the wars of the barons in the thirteenth century.   A letter to Thomas Godfrey Faussett ... London, Printed by J.E.Taylor, 1864.   2 p. l., 76 p. illus., plates. 32 cm. Signed: L.B.L. (i.e. Lambert Blackwell Larking) "Reprinted, with additional notes, from 'Archaeologia cantiana', vol. v." Seventy-five copies only, for presentation. "Pedigree of De Leyburn" ... p. (75) 21-21736.   DA228.L4L3

10476   LEYBURN.   Laybourn, Laiburn, Laibrun, Leyburn, Leybourne, Leborne (and) Leyborne (families. n.p., 1945?)   1 v. 28 cm. 53-33629.   CS71.L68   1945

LEYBURN.   See also: CALSTON, 1900
                      YARKER, 1894

10477　L'HOMMEDIEU.　L'Hommedieu genealogy.　(Chicago? 1951)　2 v. (930 p.) illus., ports., facsims.
26 cm.　Title from spine.　Includes bibliographical references.　52-28215.　　　CS71.L69　　1951

L'HOMMEDIEU.　See also: HOMMEDIEU.
VAIL, 1894

LIBBEY.　See LIBBY.

10478　LIBBY.　The Libby family in America.　1602-1881.　Prepared and pub. by Charles T. Libby.
Portland, Me., Printed by B. Thurston & co., 1882.　628 p front., ports. 23½ cm.　Blank leaves at back for record.
L. C. COPY REPLACED BY MICROFILM.　9-11614　　　CS71.L694　　1882
Microfilm 10067 CS

10479　LIBERTAT.　De Libertat: a historical & genealogical review, comprising an account of the
submission of the city of Marseilles, in 1596, to the authority of Henry of Navarre: and the lineage of
the family de Libertat, from the XIVth to the XVIIIth century.　Compiled from historical manuscripts
and other authentic records.　London, T. Pettitt & co., 1888.　4 p. l., 85 p. front., 2 illus., fold. map, fold.
geneal. tab.　29 cm.　Introduction signed: A. Lasenby Liberty.　"Edition ... limited to 250 copies, of which this is no. 43."　8-37481.
CS599.L5

LIBERTY.　See also LIBERTAT, CS599.L5

LICHTENFELS.　See BRENDLINGER, 1941

10480　LICHTENSTEIN.　The Virginia Lichtensteins; amplified by historical and biographical data,
by Gaston Lichtenstein.　Richmond, Va., H.T.Ezekiel, printer, 1912.　16 numb. l. front. (port.) 22 cm.
12-15737.　　　CS71.L697　　1912

LIDDELL.　See: TRAILL, 1902
WALLACE, 1930

10481　LIDDLE.　Genealogy of the Liddle family, Martha (Liddle) Gifford, Vineland, N.J., author.
Designed and arranged by Raymond M. Sides.　(n. p., 1922?)　72 p. front., illus., ports., col. coat of arms. 20 cm.
Some of the plates are printed on both sides.　24-6789.　　　CS71.L698　　1922

LIEBENGUTH.　See LEVEGOOD.

LIEBMAN.　See McAFEE, 1929

LIEBMANN.　See McAFEE, 1929

10482　LIEN.　A brief history of the Lien family, Norwegian pioneers of East Koshkonong, Dane
county, Wisconsin.　By Abel E. Lien.　Portland, N. D., 1930.　71 p. illus. (incl. ports.) 23 cm.　33-6838.
CS71.L716　　1930

LIENAU.　See LIGNAUD.

LIEVERSE.　See SNYDER, 1958

LIGHT.　See LÜDERS, CS439.L87

10483　LIGHTBOURNE.　Lightbourne family in vertical file.　Ask reference librarian for this material.

LIGHTFOOT.　See BASS, E171.A53 v.19

LIGHTNER.　See CLEEK, 1957

10484　LIGNAUD.　The history of the family De Lignaud (Lienau-Leinau)　(n.p., 18 -)
33 l. col. coat of arms. 23½ cm.　36-12562.　　　CS71.L72　　18 -

10485   LIGON.   The Madresfield muniments, with an account of the family and the estates.   (By William Lygon. 7th earl Beauchamp) Worcester (Eng.) Printed at the Echo office, 1929. cover-title, iii, 138 p. 21 cm. 38-29281.   CS438. B4

10486   LIGON.   Ligon family and kinsmen association.   Proceedings .... v. 1 -   Oct. 1937 -   New York, N. Y., 1937 -   v. 24 cm. annual. Cover-title. Editor: Oct. 1937 -   W. D. Ligon, jr. 37-38436.   CS71. L724   1937

10487   LIGON.   The Ligon family and connections.   By William Daniel Ligon.   (New York?) 1947 - 57.   2 v. illus. , ports. , coats of arms. 25 cm. Vol. 2 published in Shipman, Va. Includes bibliographies. 48-572 rev.*
                                                                                  CS71. L724   1947

10488   LIGON.   Ligon pioneers in Kentucky.   Compiled and published by Marvin J. Pearce, Sr.   El Cerrito, Calif. (1967)   104 p. illus. , coat of arms, ports. 28 cm. 68-307.   CS71. L724   1967

       LILE.   See LILES.

10489   LILES.   The Liles family with variations of Lile, Lyles, Lisle, Lyell, Lyle, de Lisle; a partial history.   By Parker Liles.   (Stone Mountain? Ga.) 1968.   212 l. illus. , coats of arms, geneal. tables. 30 cm. 68-1134.   CS71. L726   1968

       LILES.   See also: LISLE.
                           LYLE.

10490   LILIENTHAL.   Ernest Reuben Lilienthal and his family; prepared from family histories, documents and interviews.   By Frederic Gordon O'Neill.   (n. p.) 1949.   xiv, 176 p. illus. , ports. , geneal. tables. 28 cm. On spine: ERL. 50-16282.   CT275. L43805

10491   LILLARD.   Lillard; a family of colonial Virginia, by Jacques Ephraim Stout Lillard.   1415 to 1928; including authentic revolutionary service references, early marriage records, wills, deeds, legal documents, original family letters of early American Lillards, etc.   Richmond, Va., Williams printing company (c. 1928)   348 p. front. , pl. , ports. , facsims. , fold. geneal. tab. 23½ cm. 29-456 rev.
                                                                                  CS71. L727   1928

10492   LILLARD.   A compilation of the known descendants of Thomas and Rhoda (Patterson) Lillard, a pioneer family of Missouri, Illinois, and Iowa.   By Gerald Francis Lillard.   (Arlington? Va.) 1950. vii, 44 l. 29 cm. Includes bibliographies. 50-31892.   CS71. L727   1950

       LILLARD.   See ADAMS, 1939

10493   LILLIBRIDGE.   Thomas Lillibridge of Newport, R. I., and his descendants.   By Joel N. Eno, A. M.   Boston, Press of D. Clapp & son, 1909.   11 p. 24½ cm. (Register reprints, series A, no. 26) "Reprinted from the New England historical and genealogical register for January, 1909." 9-25860.   CS71. L728   1909

10494   LILLIBRIDGE.   The Lillibridge family, and its branches in the United States, by Joel N. Eno, A. M.   Rutland, Vt., The Tuttle company, printers, 1915.   50 p. front. , ports. 23½ cm. Publisher's lettering: Lillibridge genealogy, 1662-1915.   Typewritten note, mounted on t. - p. : "Published by the author: 815 Macy ave. , Brooklyn, N. Y. " 15-23034.
                                                                                  CS71. L728   1915

       LILLIBRIDGE.   See also: McINTOSH, 1888
                                 MULFORD, 1920

       LILLIE.   See LILLY . L729

10495   LILLY.   Major John Lillie, 1755-1801.   The Lillie family of Boston, 1663-1896.   By Edward Lillie Pierce.   Rev. ed. Cambridge (Mass.) J. Wilson and son, 1896.   122 p. front. (port.) 22½ cm. 9-11613.
                                                                                  CS71. L729   1896

10496   LILLY.   Genealogy of the southern Lilly family.   From the year 1566, county of Staffordshire, England.   By Julius Whiting Lilly ... Elmhurst, N. Y. (1916)   11 l. 29 cm. Autographed from type-written copy. 19-7926.   CS71. L729   1916

10497   LILLY.   Foundation of a genealogy of the northern Lilly family.   By Julius Whiting Lilly ...
1640-1923.   Los Angeles, Calif., 1923.   10 l. 28 cm. Autographed from type-written copy. 23-1887.

CS71.L729   1923

10498   LILLY.   A genealogical and biographical record concerning Mehitable (Reed) Lilly and George
Lilly and all of their descendants to January 1, 1958.   Mehitable Reed and George Lilly were married
in 1762 in Woolwich, Maine.   Mehitable Reed was a daughter of Jonathan Reed and Keziah Converse
Reed.   (New York?) 1959.   vii, 644 p. illus., ports. 29 cm. 59-4229.   CS71.L729   1959

LILY.   See LILLY .L729

10499   LIMA.   Cuatro grandes dinastias mexicanas en los descendientes de los hermanos Fernández
de Lima y Barragán.   By Matilde Cabrera e Ypiña de Corsi.   San Luis Potosi, México, 1956.
181 p. port., geneal. tables. 24 cm. 59-48299.   CS110.L5   1956

LIMA Y BARRAGAN.   See LIMA.

LIMESI.   See LINDSAY, 1917

LINCH.   See BAVIS, 1880

10500   LINCOLN.   A sermon preached after the funeral of Noah Lincoln, who died in Boston, July 31,
1856, aged eighty-four.   By Chandler Robbins ... With genealogical and biographical notes.   Boston,
Printed by J. Wilson and son, 1856.   49 p. 24 cm. 9-13125.   CS71.L74   1856

10501   LINCOLN.   Notes on the Lincoln families of Massachusetts, with some account of the family
of Abraham Lincoln, late president of the U. States.   By Solomon Lincoln ... Boston, D. Clapp & son,
printers, 1865.   10 p. 24½ cm. "Reprinted from the Hist. and gen. reg. for Oct., 1865." 9-11611.   CS71.L74   1865
F1.N56 vol.19

10502   LINCOLN.   The lineage of President Abraham Lincoln.   By Samuel Shackford, of Chicago,
Ill.   (Boston, 1887)   7 p. 24½ cm. "Reprinted from the New-England historical and genealogical register for April, 1887." 5-11386.
E457.32.S52
F1.N56 v.41

10503   LINCOLN.   The Lincolns of Fayette County, by John S. Ritenour.   (n. p.) C. Lincoln (189-)
cover-title, 27 p. 23 cm. Reprinted from the Genius of liberty, Uniontown, Pa., 189-? 14-15303.   CS71.L74   189-

10504   LINCOLN.   The family of Lincoln.   (London, 1890)   11 p. 24½ cm. Caption title. Signed: R. E. G. Kirk.
Reprinted from "The Genealogist," January 1890, vol. VI, p. 129-139. 17-9498.   CS439.L53

10505   LINCOLN.   Stephen Lincoln of Oakham, Massachusetts, his ancestry and descendants.
Comp. by John E. Morris.   Hartford, Conn., Press of the Case, Lockwood & Brainard company, 1895.
109 p. front., illus., port. 24 cm. 9-11612.   CS71.L74   1895

10506   LINCOLN.   The Lincoln family and branches, of Wareham, Mass.   Comp. by James Minor
Lincoln.   (Cambridge, Mass., The Riverside press) 1899.   iv p., 2 l., 124 p. facsims. 22½ cm. Descendants
of Rufus Lincoln and his ancestry traced to Thomas Lincoln of Hingham. 90-1147.   CS71.L74   1899

10507   LINCOLN.   The Lincoln, Hanks and Boone families, by H. E. Robinson ... (Columbia, Mo.,
1906)   cover-title, p. (72)-84. 23 cm. A paper read at the fourth annual meeting of the Missouri historical society, December 9, 1904.
Reprinted from Missouri historical review, vol. I no. 1, October, 1906. 18-879.   CS71.L74   1906

10508   LINCOLN.   The ancestry of Abraham Lincoln (by) J. Henry Lea and J. R. Hutchinson.   Boston
and New York, Houghton Mifflin company, 1909.   xvi, 212 p., 1 l. front., plates, port., map, facsims. 29 cm. 9-5537.
CS71.L74   1909

10509   LINCOLN.   Abraham Lincoln, an American migration; family English not German; with
photographic illustrations, by Marion Dexter Learned ... Philadelphia, W. J. Campbell, 1909.
xii, 149 p. front. (port.) plates, maps, facsims. 25 cm. "Only 500 copies of this work have been printed...no. 2. 9-31062.
CS71.L74   1909a

10510   LINCOLN.   Under the search-light; address delivered March 5, 1914, before the Command-
ery of the state of Illinois Military order of the loyal legion of the United States, by Wilber Gorton
Bentley, lt. colonel 9th New York cavalry.   (Chicago, The Libby company, printers, 1914)
23, (1) p.   24 cm.   Notes on the genealogy of Abraham Lincoln: p. 13-14.   Copy of marriage license of Lincoln's parents, inserted.   20.18477.

E649.B49

10511   LINCOLN.   The Lincoln family magazine; genealogical, historical and biographical.   Edited
by William Montgomery Clemens.   v. 1, v. 2, no. 1-2; Jan. 1916 - Apr. 1917.   New York city, N.Y.,
W. M. Clemens, 1916-17.   2 v. in 1.   23 cm.   quarterly.   No more published.   16-2767 rev.   CS71.L74   1916

10512   LINCOLN.   The man who married Lincoln's parents, an address by Rev. William E. Barton
... Delivered at the dedication of a monument at the grave of Rev. Jesse Head and Jane Ramsey Head,
his wife, in Spring Hill cemetery, Harrodsburg, Kentucky, Thursday, November 2, 1922.   Harrodsburg, Ky., The Harrodsburg herald, 1922.   (16) p.   illus.   (incl. port.)   27½ cm.   24-17112.   E457.32.B24

10513   LINCOLN.   The parents of Abraham Lincoln, an address by William E. Barton ... Delivered
at the grave of Thomas Lincoln, Goose Nest Prairie, near Janesville, Illinois, September 18, 1922.
Charleston, Ill., The Charleston daily courier, 1922.   8 p.   23 cm.   24-17105.   E457.32.B26

10514   LINCOLN.   Sarah Bush Lincoln, the beloved foster mother of Abraham Lincoln;   a memorial.
Elizabethtown, Ky., Elizabethtown woman's club (1922)   cover-title, (8) p.   1 illus., fold. facsim.   24 cm.   24-5633.
E457.32.W87

10515   LINCOLN.   The Lincolns in their old Kentucky home;   an address delivered before the Filson
club, Louisville, Kentucky, December 4, 1922, by William E. Barton ... Berea, Ky., Berea college
press, 1923.   24 p.   29 x 23½ cm.   "This edition is limited to three hundred copies, of which this is no. 42."   Signed by the author.
24-13564.   E457.8.B328

10516   LINCOLN.   "Old theories upset", being the brief report of an address on Abraham Lincoln's
lost grandmother, by William E. Barton ... This address was delivered before ... the Chicago historical society.   (Chicago, 1923)   30 (4) p.   21½ cm.   "Reprint from the Chicago daily news, Feb. 3, 1923."   25-3680.
E457.8.B33

10517   LINCOLN.   History of the Lincoln family;   an account of the descendants of Samuel Lincoln
of Hingham, Massachusetts, 1637-1920, comp. by Waldo Lincoln ... Worcester, Mass., Commonwealth press, 1923.   x, 718 p.   front., plates, ports.   24½ cm.   23-10111.   CS71.L74   1923

10518   LINCOLN.   In the footsteps of the Lincolns, by Ida M. Tarbell ... New York and London,
Harper & brothers, 1924.   xi, (2), 418 p.   front., illus.   (map, facsims.)   plates, ports.   24½ cm.   24-3279.
E457.3.T175

10519   LINCOLN.   The Lincoln family in America.   (By William Eleazar Barton)   (In The Magazine of
history, with notes and queries.   Tarrytown, N.Y., 1925.   26½ cm.   Extra number.   no. 113 (v. 29 no. 1)   Rare Lincolniana no. 26, p. (52)-61)
Signed: William E. Barton.   25-25232.   E173.M24 no. 113

10520   LINCOLN.   The lineage of Lincoln (by) William E. Barton ... Indianapolis, The Bobbs-Merrill
company (c. 1929)   14 p. 1., 419 p.   front., illus.   (maps) plates, ports., facsims.   24½ cm.   "A critical bibliography": p. (393)-397.
29-9284.   E457.32.B23
———— Copy 3.   Stearne coll.   Rare book room.

10521   LINCOLN.   Hananiah Lincoln in revolution and pioneer history, by Louis A. Warren ...
(Bloomington, Ind., University press, 1929?)   1 p. 1., 29-39 p.   25½ cm.   "Copyrighted reprint from Indiana magazine of
history, March, 1929."   34-29299.   E457.32.W275

10522   LINCOLN.   Contemporary kindred of Abraham Lincoln;   a paper read at a meeting of the
Weymouth historical society, March 29, 1928, by Clarence W. Fearing ... Weymouth, Mass. (c. 1929)
53 p., 3 1.   front. (mounted port.)   24 cm.   29-30438.   E457.32.F28

10523   LINCOLN.   The Lincoln and La Follette families in pioneer drama, by Louis A. Warren ...
(Menasha? Wisc., 1929)   23 p.   1 illus.   24½ cm.   "Reprint from the Wisconsin magazine of history, June, 1929."   34-40408.
E457.32.W276

10524   LINCOLN.   Memoirs of Lincoln, by Herring Chrisman.   (Mapleton, Ia., Pub. by his son
W. H. Chrisman, 1930.   5 p. l., 97 p. ports., fold. geneal. tab. coat of arms. 21 cm. 31-5578.   E457.15.C55

10525   LINCOLN.   Barton and the lineage of Lincoln, claim that Lincoln was related to Lee refuted
... by Lyon Gardiner Tyler ... 2d ed.   (n. p., 1930?)   12 p. 15½ x 8½ cm. ca 30-1220 unrev.
E457.32.T98

10526   LINCOLN.   Some descendants of Stephen Lincoln of Wymondham, England, Edward Larkin
from England, Thomas Oliver of Bristol, England, Michael Pearce of London, England, Robert Wheaton
of Swansea, Wales, George Burrill of Boston, England, John Porter of Dorset, England, John Ayer of
Norwich, England, and notes of related families ... New York, Printed for William Ensign Lincoln,
Pittsburgh, Penna., by the Knickerbocker press, 1930.   v, (1), 322 p. illus. (incl. ports.) 24 cm. 30-11181.
errata and addenda slip mounted on p. 322.   CS71.L74   1930

10527   LINCOLN.   Lincoln and the Lincolns, by Harvey H. Smith ... Memorial ed.   (New York)
Pioneer publications, inc. (1931)   xxiii, 482 p. front., illus., plates, ports. 24½ cm. 31-33610.
E457.S66

10528   LINCOLN.   The Lincolns in Elizabethtown, Kentucky, by R. Gerald McMurtry ... Fort
Wayne, Ind., Lincolniana publishers, 1932.   (16) p. illus. (map) 23 cm. "First thousand." 33-2229.
CS71.L74   1932

10529   LINCOLN.   The Moultrie county Lincolns, privately published by Herbert Wells Fay, custod-
ian Lincoln's tomb.   (Springfield, Ill.) 1933.   (4) p. 20 cm. Reprinted from Week by week, October 28, 1933. 34-1603.
CS71.L74   1933

10530   LINCOLN.   The Lincolns in their old Kentucky home; an address delivered before the Filson
club, Louisville, Kentucky, December 4, 1922, by William E. Barton ... Berea, Ky., Berea college
press, 1923.   (New York, N. Y., Reprinted, W. Abbatt, 1934)   (In The Magazine of history, with notes and queries.
New York, N. Y., 1934. 26½ cm. Extra number. no. 193 (v. 49, no. 1) Rare Lincolniana no. 46, p. (3)-30) 34-10422.
E173.M24 no. 193

10531   LINCOLN.   Pilgrimage conducted June 20-30, 1937, by Louis A. Warren ... on the 300th
anniversary of the Lincolns landing in America; inclduing the meeting at Long run Baptist church,
Jefferson county, near the site of the home of pioneer Abraham Lincoln; sponsored by the Filson club,
Louisville, Kentucky, incorporated, June 25, 1937.   (Louisville, Ky., Press of J. P. Morton & company, incorporated, c. 1937)   1 p. l., 16 p. illus. (incl. maps, facsims.) port. 25 cm. Contents. - Lincoln tercentenary
programs memorializing the ancestors of Abraham Lincoln, June 20-30, 1937. - The Lincolns in Jefferson county, Kentucky, by R. C. B. Thruston. -
The Long run Baptist church, by T. C. Fisher. 37-20452.   E457.32.P55

10532   LINCOLN.   The Lincoln kinsman. no. 1 -   July 1938 -   Fort Wayne, Ind.
(Lincolniana publishers) 1938 -   v. 22½ cm. monthly. Editor: July, 1938 -   L. A. Warren. 38-36149.
CS71.L74   1938

10533   LINCOLN.   A series of monographs concerning the Lincolns and Hardin county, Kentucky, by
R. Gerald McMurtry ... Elizabethtown, Ky., The Enterprise press, 1938.   4 p. l., 133 p. illus. (incl. map)
23½ cm. "First printing, March 15, 1938, one thousand copies." "First published in the Hardin county enterprise, November 28, 1935 to April
29, 1937." - Foreword. 38-12569.   E457.32.M23

10534   LINCOLN.   Our kin; descendants of Joshua Lincoln and Elizabeth Seekins Lincoln of Taunton,
Massachusetts, compiled by William Simpson Lincoln.   (Olympia, Wash., The Olympia news, 1942)
4 p. l., 128 p., 1 l., (5) p. pl., ports. 23½ cm. 43-3382.   CS71.L74   1942

10535   LINCOLN.   The Lincolns and Tennessee, by Samuel C. Williams ... Revised edition of
articles appearing in Lincoln herald, vol. XLIII, no. 3 and 4, 1941, and vol. XLIV, no. 1, 1942.
Harrogate, Tenn., Dept. of Lincolniana, Lincoln memorial university, 1942.   33 p. illus. (incl. map)
26 cm. Bibliographical references included in "Notes" (p. 31-33) 42-25849.   E457.32.W73 1942

10536 LINCOLN. The Lincolns and Tennessee, by Samuel C. Williams ... Revised edition of articles appearing in Lincoln herald, vol. XLIII, no. 3 and 4, 1941, and vol. XLIV, no. 1, 1942. Johnson City, Tenn., The Watauga press, 1942. 33 p. illus. (incl. map) 26 cm. "This de luxe edition is limited to 100 copies." Issued by the Department of Lincolniana, Lincoln memorial university. Bibliographical references included in "Notes" (p. 31-33) 42-25850 rev. E457.32.W73 1942a

10537 LINCOLN. Lincoln, descendant of first family Americans, by Ralph G. Lindstrom, with foreword by F. Ray Risdon. (n. p.) Lincoln fellowship of Southern California, 1943. 14 p., 1 l. incl. mounted front. (port.) 24 cm. Reprinted from the Los Angeles times' Home of February 7, 1943. cf. Foreword. "One hundred two copies ... printed by the Institute press ... at Los Angeles." 43-10571. E457.32.L43

10538 LINCOLN. Legends that libel Lincoln, by Montgomery S. Lewis. New York, Toronto, Rinehart & company inc. (1946) xiii, 239 p. 21 cm. "Sources": p. (225)-231. 46-6962. E457.L67

10539 LINCOLN. The Lincolns in Virginia, by John W. Wayland ... Staunton, Va., Printed for the author by the McClure printing company, 1946. 299, (1) p. incl. front., illus. (incl. ports., maps, facsims.) 23½ cm. "Five hundred copies printed." 46-23124. CS71.L74 1946

10540 LINCOLN. Howell, Lincoln, and allied families; a genealogical study with biographical notes. Compiled and priv. print. for Fannie Esther Lincoln Howell. American Historical Company, inc. New York, 1949. 179 p. ports., col. coats of arms. 33 cm. Includes bibliographies. 50-3684. CS71.H858 1949

10541 LINCOLN. Abraham Lincoln. By Howard Leavitt Horton. (Boston? 1950) (25) l. plates, group ports., facsims. 28 cm. (His New England chronicle no. 1) Bibliography: leaf (25) 50-8501. CS71.L74 1950

10542 LINCOLN. Genealogy of the allied families of Lincoln, Morris, Mann, Morrison, Compher, Jobusch, Barr, Linde, and Menold. By Virginia Lee (Mann) Jobusch. Ann Arbor, Mich., Lithographed by Edwards Letter Shop, 1961. 105 p. illus. 24 cm. 61-41378. CS71.L74 1961

10543 LINCOLN. Lincoln family in vertical file. Ask reference librarian for this material.

LINCOLN. See also: BOONE, 1922 HOWELL, 1949
BOYDEN, 1949 LEONARD, 1928
BURR, E171.A53 v.16 PASTORIUS, 1926
CROCKER, 1923 PIRTIE, 1936
FOSTER, 1898

LINDALL. See GILES, 1864

10544 LINBERGH. ... The Lindberghs. By Lynn Haines. New York, The Vanguard press (c. 1931) 4 p. l., 3-307 p. front. (ports.) 21½ cm. At head of title: Lynn and Dora B. Haines. Chiefly a biography of Charles August Lindbergh, member of Congress 1907-1917. 32-1354. E748.L74H2

10545 LINDBERGH. The Lindberghs; the story of a distinguished family, by P. J. O'Brien ... (Philadelphia) International press, 1935. 352 p. incl. front., illus. (incl. map) plates, ports., facsims. 21½ cm. 35-5832. HV6603.L503

10546 LINDENBERG. ... A familia Lindenberg na Alemanha e no Brasil ... By Karl Fouquet. Sao Paulo, Empreza graphica de "Revista dos tribunaes," 1941. 20 p. incl. pl., ports. 23½ cm. At head of title: C. Fouquet. Seal of Sociedade Hans Staden, Sao Paulo, on t.-p. "Separata de 'Revista genealogica brasileira,' ano 1, n.° 1 e 2, 1940. Publicačo do 'Instituto genealogico brasileiro'". "Bibliographia": p. 20. 47-34587. CS309.L5 1941

LINDESEIE. See LINDSAY .L753

10547 LINDEVIG. A tree that flourished; or, The story of the Lindevig family of Telemarken in Norway and America. By Borghild (Lindevig) Olson. (La Cross? Wis.) 1958. 150 p. illus. 23 cm. 59-23111. CS71.L743 1958

10548 · LINDLEY. The history of the Lindley-Lindsley-Linsley families in America, 1639-1930, by John M. Lindly ... Winfield, Ia., 1924 -   v. illus. (incl. ports., facsims.) 24 cm. Vol. 1, c.1930; v.2, 1924. Vol. 2 has title: The history of the Lindley-Lindsley-Linsley families in America, 1639-1924. 31-10488.   CS71.L746   1924

10549 LINDLEY. The genealogy of John Lindsley (1845-1909) and his wife Virginia Thayer Payne (1856-1941) of Boston, Massachusetts. By Herbert Armstrong Poole. Milton, Mass., 1950. 532, 111 p. 30 cm. 57-37598.   CS71.L746   1950

LINDLEY. See also: CORN, 1959
TRUEBLOOD, 1964

LINDLY. See LINDLEY.

10550 LINDSAY. Lives of the Lindsays; or, A memoir of the houses of Crawford and Balcarres, by Lord Lindsay. To which are added, extracts from the official correspondence of Alexander, sixth earl of Balcarres, during the Maroon war; together with personal narratives by his brothers, the Hon. Robert Colin, James, John, and Hugh Lindsay; and by his sister, Lady Anne Barnard ... London, J. Murray, 1849. 3 v. front. (geneal. tab.) 2 pl., 4 facsim. 22 cm. 8-23791.   DA758.3.L8C7

10551 LINDSAY. Report of the speeches of counsel, and of the lord chancellor and Lord St. Leonards in moving the resolution, upon the claim of James, earl of Crawford and Balcarres to the original dukedom of Montrose (created in 1488) ... preceded by an address to Her Majesty ... and by an analysis of the argument as between the claimant and the officers representing the crown ... and followed by an appendix, containing the leading documents adduced and referred to ... by Lord Lindsay ... London, J. Murray, 1855. 2 p. l., (iii)-xli, xcv, cxlv, 593, (1) p. fold. facsim., fold. geneal. tab. 34 cm. 37-20522.   CS476.M7C7

10552 LINDSAY. Lives of the Lindsays; or, A memoir of the houses of Crawford and Balcarres, by Lord Lindsay. To which are added extracts from the official correspondence of Alexander sixth earl of Balcarres, during the Maroon war; together with personal narratives by his brothers, the Hon. Robert, Colin, James, John, and Hugh Lindsay; and by his sister, Lady Anne Barnard. 2d ed. London, J. Murray, 1858. 3 v. front. (fold. geneal. tab.) 2 pl., 2 fold. facsim. 22 cm. 14-21098.   DA758.3.L8C7   1858

10553 The history and traditions of the land of the Lindsays in Angus and Mearns, with notices of Alyth and Meigle, by the late Andrew Jervise ... To which is added an appendix containing extracts from an old rental-book of Edzell and Lethnot, notices of the ravages of the Marquis of Montrose in Forfarshire, and other interesting documents. Rewritten and corrected by James Gammack ... 2d ed. Edinburgh, D. Douglas, 1882. xxv, (1) 468 p. front., illus., plates. 23 cm. "List of authors": p. xxi-xxv. 3-29085.   DA880.A5J4   1882

10554 LINDSAY. The Lindsays of America. A genealogical narrative, and family record beginning with the family of the earliest settler in the mother state, Virginia. By Margaret Isabella Lindsay ... Albany, N.Y., J. Munsell's sons, 1889. xv, (1), 275, (5) p. plates, geneal. tables (part fold.) 22 x 18½ cm. 9-11621.   CS71.L753   1889

10555 LINDSAY. Publications. Clan Lindsay society. v.1 -   (n. 1 -   ); 1901 - Edinburgh (1901)   v. in   illus., plates, ports. 22½ cm. 7-6349 rev.   CS479.L6

10556 LINDSAY. Annual report. Lindsay family association of America. 1st -   1904 - (Boston? 1904 -   nos. in v. 23 cm. Report for 1904 issued without title. 6-16039 rev.   CS71.L753   1904

10557 LINDSAY. David Lindsay and the reunion of his descendants, at Pebbly beach, Oconomowoc Lake, July 4, 1916. Seventy-fifth anniversary of arrival in the United States. (n. p., 1916) 1 p. l., 5-52 p. illus., plates, port., fold. geneal. tab. 23½ cm. 25-11795.   CS71.L753   1916

10558 LINDSAY. The Lindeseie and Limesi families of Great Britain, including the probates at Somerset house, London, England, of all spellings of the name Lindeseie from 1300 to 1800, with the sincere regards of the author, John William Linzee ... Boston, Mass., Priv. print. (The Fort Hill press) 1917. 2 v. front., illus. (coats of arms) plates, ports. 25½ cm. 17-30248.   CS71.L753   1917

10559   LINDSAY.   Early settlers in Campbell County, Ky.   Lindsey - McPike - Noble.   By Helen Bradley Lindsey, Newport, Ky.   (n.p., 1927?)   p. 9-22. 25½ cm.   CA 29-28 unrev.   CS71.L753   1927

10560   LINDSAY.   Hawaiian pedigree chart, compiled by Corporal Jessie M. (Higbee) Lindsey ... (n.p.) 1943.   geneal. tab.   36¼ x 59½. Photostat reproduction (positive)   The Hawaiian ancestry of the Lindsey family, descended from James Fay and Kaipukai Lauia Kahahana.   Includes a bibliography.   44-31797.   CS2209.L5

10561   LINDSAY.   The Lindesays of Loughry, County Tyrone; a genealogical history.   By Ernest H. Godfrey.   London, H.H.Greaves, 1949.   119 p. illus., ports., geneal. table.   22 cm.   Errata slip inserted.   50-32798.   CS499.L18   1949

10562   LINDSAY.   (Documents relating to the Lindsay family) Ed.Smythe H. Lindsay.   In vertical file.   Ask reference librarian for this material.

        LINDSAY.   See also: DINGWALL, CS410.M8 4th ser. vol.5
                               LINDSEY.
                               SELDEN, 1911

10563   LINDSEY.   Lindsey; (book of remembrance; golden memories.   By Retha Vaughn (Hamberlin) Rowley.   Winona? Tex., 1963)   248 p. illus. 29 cm.   63-20054.   CS71.L7533   1963

        LINDSEY.   See also LINDSAY.

        LINDSLEY.   See: LINDLEY, 1924
                            MULFORD, 1920

        LINEBARGER.   See LEYENBERGER.

        LINEBERGER.   See HOFFMAN, 1915

10564   LINENBERGER.   The Linenberger genealogy, by Amy Toepfer and Agnes C. Dreiling. (Carthagena? Ohio, 1956, c.1955)   432 p. illus. 23 x 29 cm.   56-29862 rev.   CS71.L754   1956

10565   LINES.   The Lines family, by Donald Lines Jacobus of New Haven, Connecticut.   (Hartford, Conn., 1905)   15 p. 23½ cm.   Reprinted from the Connecticut magazine, April, 1905.   24-5155.   CS71.L755   1905

        LINES.   See also WELLMAN, 1954

10566   LINFORD.   An autobiography of James Henry Linford, Sr., patriarch of the Church of Jesus Christ of Latter-day Saints of Kaysville, Utah.   (Logan, Utah) John Linford Family Organization, 1947.   vi, 104 p. ports. 25 cm.   "For this new printing the genealogy of the Linford family has been compiled as completely and accurately as possible as of June 30, 1947."   47-7101*.   F826.L55   1947

10567   LINGARD.   The Lingards of Huncoat, and their descendants.   By Richard Ainsworth. Accrington, Wardleworth, 1930.   51 p. illus. 21 cm.   61-58061.   CS439.L54   1930

        LINGLEY.   See LINLEY.

        LINGO.   See TALIAFERRO, 1926 and 1960

10568   LININGER.   The Liningers, genealogical register of the descendants of Henry Lininger, compiled and published by William H. Lininger.   Chicago, Ill., 1930.   23 (1) p. illus. (incl. ports., map, double facsim.) 24 cm.   32-30555.   CS71.L756   1930

10569   LINK.   The Link family; antecedents and descendants of John Jacob Link, 1417-1951, with much history about the Stoner, Crowell, Demory, Remsburg, Thraves, Ropp, Boyer, Fuchs (Fox), Beard (Bart), Miller, Filler, Hanger, Wayland, Osbourn, Hendricks, Reinhart, Stone, Burrier, Root, Houff, Stover, Turner, La Grange, Smith, Kneiple, Shank, Grove, Cale, Palmer, Lewis, Woodward, Burnett, McChesney, Baylor, Freer, Garrett, Girdner, Creager, Burckhardt, and Eisenhower families. (Paris? Ill.) 1951.   xiv, 872 p. illus., ports., maps. 24 cm.   53-22402.   CS71.L7563   1951

10570   LINLEY.   The Linleys of Bath, by Clementina Black.   London, M. Secker (1911)
11, 339, (1) p. front., ports. 24 cm. 11-26468.   DA506. L6B6

LINLEY.   See also: LINDLEY.
MYERS, 1906

LINN.   See LYNN .L989

10571   LINNELL.   The genealogy of Joseph Linnell, a soldier of the American Revolution.   By Mary
Belle Linnell.   (Sylvania? Ohio, 1963?)   108 1. mounted col. illus. 29 cm. 65-3402.
CS71. L7564   1963

10572   LINSLEY.   Connecticut Linsleys, the six Johns, being the history, so far as known, of the
descendents of the first of the name in Connecticut.   By Ray Keyes Linsley.   (Bristol? Conn., 1949)
144 1. 29 cm. 50-38418.   CS71. L7565   1949

LINSLEY.   See also LINDLEY, 1924

10573   LINT.   (The Lint-Gorby family, by Frank Stuart Lint)   (Los Angeles, 1943)   1 v. mounted
photos., facsim., geneal. tables. 23 x 35½ cm. Loose-leaf. Includes mounted clippings. The genealogical data is type-written on forms.
Includes bibliographical references. 43-16362.   CS71. L7567   1943

10574   LINTHICUM.   Genealogy of the Linthicum and allied families ... compiled and edited by
Matilda P. Badger ... Baltimore, Md. (1936)   189 p. front., illus. (coats of arms) plates, ports. 24 cm. Two
type-written leaves on the Wells family, numbered 138-138a inserted after p. (138) and four leaves of "Additions and corrections" at end.
36-12590.   CS71. L757   1936

10575   LINTON.   Linton-Lacock, 1831-1881.   (Philadelphia, 1881)   15 p. 19 cm. Caption title. Signed:
James M. Swank.   A sketch of the Linton family, traced to John, who came from Ireland and settled in Pennsylvania in 1695, prepared for the
celebration of the golden wedding of John Linton and Adelaide Lacock. 17-9755.   CS71. L758   1881

10576   LINTON.   The allied families of Linton, Chichester (and) Ulle.   By Wiliam C. Linton.
Washington, 1963.   37 1. col. coats of arms, port. 28 cm. Cover title: A family of Lintons. 63-23796.
CS71. L7568   1963

LINTON.   See also HORTON, CS439. H754

LINVILLE.   See: ADAMS, 1958
BOONE, 1922

LINZEE.   See LINDSAY.

LIONBERGER.   See LEYENBERGER.

10577   LIPPINCOTT.   A genealogical tree of the Lippincott family in America, from the ancestors
of Richard and Abigail ... Constructed and published by Charles Lippincott, Cinnaminson.... New
Jersey. (Philadelphia, J. LSmith) 1880.   col. geneal. tab. coat of arms in colors. 198 x 114 cm. Fold. to 39½ x 40 cm.
3-17337.   CS71. L765   1880

10578   LIPPINCOTT.   The Lippincotts in England and America: edited from the genealogical papers
of the late James S. Lippincott.   Philadelphia, 1909.   42 p. 24½ cm. 24-5649.   CS71. L765   1909

LIPPINCOTT.   See also: CHRYSLER, 1959
CLEMENTS, 1934
GILMAN, 1919
NOYES, 1907

10579   LIPPITT.   The Lippitt family; a collection of notes and items of interest by one of its
members.   Los Angeles, 1959.   13 p., 148 1., (82) p. illus., ports., map, facsims. 30 cm. "Limited edition of 250 copies
... Number 144." Includes bibliographies. 60-50831.   CS71. L767   1959

LIPSCOMBE. See DEVERELL, 1945

LISLE. See: CARR, 1899
              LILES.

10580 LISPENARD. Antoine L'Espenard, the French Huguenot, of New Rochelle. By Gen. Charles W. Darling ... (Utica, N.Y., 1893?) cover-title, 20 p. front., illus., ports., coats of arms. 27 cm. Reprinted from the New York biographical and genealogical record, July, 1893. 9-11475. CS71.L771 1893

10581 LISPERGUER. Los Lisperguer y la Quintrala (doña Catalina de los Rios); episodio historico-social, con numerosos documentos inéditos, por B. Vicuña Mackenna. 2. ed. estensamente aum. i corr. Valparaiso, Impr. del Mercurio, 1877. 285 p. 24 cm. 33-21205. F3091.R57

10582 LISPERGUER. ... Los Lisperguer y la Quintrala (Doña Catalina de los Rios). Episodio histórico-social con numerosos documentos inéditos, por B. Vicuña Mackenna. Ed. estensamente aumentada i correjida conforme al orijinal. 3. ed. Santiago de Chile, F. Becerra M., 1908. 278 p. 19 cm. (Biblioteca de autores chilenos. 2 ser.) 18-13222. F3051B582 v.1.

10583 LISTER. Memorials of an ancient house: a history of the family of Lister or Lyster, by the Rev. Henry Lyttelton Lyster Denny ... Illustrated. Edinburgh, Printed for the author by Ballantyne, Hanson & co., 1913. xvi, 384 p. front., plates, ports., fold. geneal. tables. 29 cm. Appendix: p. 255-378. Title vignette. A 13-1897. CS439.L56

        LISTER. See also: CURZON, AC901.M5V200 no.6
                            ROBSON, 1892

        LISTON. See: McCALL, CS479.M17
                       POUND, CS71.P876 1904

10584 LISZT. Franz Liszt; abstammung, familie, begebenheiten, von universitätsprofessor dr. Eduard ritter von Liszt. Mit 61 abbildungen. Wien-Leipzig, W. Braumüller, 1937. xiv, 111 p., 1 l. front., illus. (incl. facsims.) 18 pl. (incl. ports.) on 9 l., geneal. tab. 24½ cm. "Literatur": p. xi-xiv. Anhang: 1. Zwel briefe Franz Liszts an meinen vater. 2. Franz Liszts diener. 3. Einige worte über Franz-Liszt anekdoten. 38-228. ML410.L7L57

10585 LITCHARD. See GERNHARDT.

10586 LITCHFIELD. The descendants of Lawrence Litchfield, the Puritan (n. p., 1899?) geneal. chart. 61 x 77 cm. Compiled by Alvin A. Vinal. 15-12364. CS71.L776 1899

10587 LITCHFIELD. The Litchfield family in America. Pt. 1, no. 1-5. (Southbridge, Mass., W. J. Litchfield) 1901-1906. 5 v. 25 cm. Compiled by Wilford Jacob Litchfield. CA9-3909. CS71.L776 1901-6

        LITHGOW. See BRIDGE, 1924

10588 LITTELL. Descendants of William Littell of Essex County, N. J., who served in the revolutionary war in Captain Benjamin Laing's company, First regiment, Essex county militia (1757-1819) (Compiled by Miss Doreen Haight Littell) (Bridgeport, Conn., 1933) 4 l. 28 cm. Type-written. 38M2251T. CS71.L7765 1933

        LITTELL. See also UNGRICH, E171.A53 v.13

10589 LITTLE. Descendants of George Little, who came to Newbury, Massachusetts, in 1640. Comp. by George T. Little. Cambridge, Printed at the University Press by C.J. Little, 1877. 82 p. incl. front., illus. 20 cm. 1-15069. CS71.L777 1877

10590 LITTLE. The descendants of George Little, who came to Newbury, Massachusetts, in 1640. By George Thomas Little ... Auburn, Me., The author, 1882. xiv, 2, 620, 2 p. front. (col. coat of arms) illus., 5 pl., 19 port. 26½ cm. No. A of the edition. Two pages of addenda which follow p. 620 are also inserted between p. 514 and 515. Imperfect: 2 plates, 4 portraits wanting. Five additional portraits inserted. 1-15070 rev. CS71.L777 1882

10591   LITTLE.   (Genealogical chart of the Lytle family; descendants of Christopher Lytle)   By Leonard Lytle.   Detroit, Mich., 1921.   geneal. tab.   22 ½ x 56 ½ cm.   "Prepared from data furnished by Chas. J. Livingood." 21-14451.   CS71.L777   1921

10592   LITTLE.   Stephen Little of New York, his background and family; also short sketches of the MacMahon, Elliotte, Knox and Little lines of north Ireland, by Maryella R. Little.   (n. p., 1932?) 35 p. 17½ cm.   "One hundred copies privately printed.   No. 34."   A33-352.   CS71.L77   1932?

10593   LITTLE.   The Littles and Youngmans of Peterborough, New Hampshire and their descendants; family facts as compiled by Fred W. Cheney.   Albuquerque, N.M., 1940.   23 p.   22 cm.   Leaf of "Errata" mounted on p. (3) of cover.   Includes also the Reed family.   41-5559.   CS71.L777   1940

10594   LITTLE.   Descendants of Thomas Lytle ... and Polly (Mary) Wilson ... by Herschel B. Rochelle ... Battle Creek, Mich., 1943.   geneal. tab.   illus. (incl. ports., coats of arms) 20½ x 25½ cm.   Photostat reproduction (positive) 44-1906.   CS71.L777   1943

10595   LITTLE.   Descendants of Col. John Little, Esq., of Shrewsbury Township, Monmouth County, New Jersey.   By Donald Campbell Little.   (Edwardsville? Kan.) 1951.   123 p.   coat of arms, facsims.   24 cm. 52-24605.   CS71.L777   1951

10596   LITTLE.   The history of Monroe, New Hamsphire, 1761-1954.   By Frances Ann Johnson. (Littleton, N.H.) 1955.   638 p.   illus., ports., maps, facsims.   24 cm.   "Genealogy records": p. 402-618.   68-22312.
                                                                                                                              F44.M8J6

10597   LITTLE.   Descendants of William Little, Jr., and allied families.   By Harriet (Fredericksen) Little.   (Provo? Utah) James Little and Susannah Young Family Association, 1958.   785 p. illus. 29 cm. 58-49596.   CS71.L777   1958

LITTLE.   See also: ALLEN, 1921   NELSON, 1938
                        AVERY, 1919   NELSON, 1967
                        AVERY, 1925   POOR, 1881
                        HORNE, 1936   POOR, 1881a
                        JOHNSON, 1938   POOR, 1881b
                        LYTLE.   THIGPEN, 1961

LITTLEDALE.   See ROYD, CS439.R75

10598   LITTLEFIELD.   Anthony Littlefield of New York and Michigan and his descendants.   Compiled by Eldon P. Gundry.   Rev. Flint, Mich., 1965.   iv, 103 p.   illus., maps, ports.   29 cm.   67-38074.
                                                                                                                              CS71.L779   1965

10599   LITTLEHALE.   A complete history and genealogy of the Littlehale family in America from 1633 to 1889.   Collated and compiled by Frederick H. Littlehale, of Boston, Mass. ... Boston, Mass., A.W. & F.H. Littlehale, 1889.   vi, 128 p.   plates, ports., coat of arms, geneal. tables.   24 cm.   A 25-568.
                                                                                                                              CS71.L78   1889

10600   LITTLEJOHN.   Littlejohn genealogy; Oliver Littlejohn's descendants.   By Iris (Littlejohn) McKown.   (Gaffney, S.C.) Gaffney Ledger, 1953.   1109 p. illus. 24 cm.   53-34776.
                                                                                                                              CS71.L7813   1953

LITTLEPAGE.   See: GLASSELL, F225.H141
                       WINSTON, 1927

LITTLER.   See ALLEN, 1921

LITTLETON.   See No. 430 - Adventurers of purse and person.

10601   LITZENBERG.   The Litzenbergs in America; a biographical record of George Litzenberg and his wife, Grace Coates, with a preview of their ancestors and a genealogical and biographical record of their descendants. By John Elmer Litzenberg. Centerberg, Ohio, 1948.   xvii, 629 p.   port., map.   23 cm. 49-377 *.   CS71.L782   1948

LIVERGOOD. See LEVEGOOD.

10602   LIVERMORE.   Report to the Livermore association, U.S.A., made by Josiah Q. Hawkins, agent, A.D. 1865.   Containing information already collected in America and England relative to the Livermore property in England: the crest and coat of arms of the family, likewise a genealogy of the Livermore family in England and America, so far collected ... Rutland, Livermore association, 1865.   38 p.   22 cm.   9-15602.   CS71.L785   1865

10603   LIVERMORE.   The Livermore family of America, by Walter Eliot Thwing ... Boston, W.B. Clarke company, 1902.   479 p. front., plates, ports. 24½ cm. 2-30082.
                                                                          CS71.L785   1902

        LIVERMORE.   See also: BENJAMIN, 1900
                                 DOW, 1939
                                 JOHNSON, 1938

LIVESAY.   See BRUMBACH, 1961

10604   LIVEZEY.   The Livezey family, a genealogical and historical record, assembled for the Livezey association, by Charles Harper Smith.   Philadelphia, Pa.   (George H. Buchanan company) 1934.   3 p. l., 440 p. front. (col. coat of arms) plates, fold. plan. 23½ cm. "Limited to 250 copies ... Number 207." 35-13998 rev.
                                                                          CS71.L7855   1934
        ——— Supplement ... 1934-1944.   Jenkintown, Pa., Printed by Times chronicle co., inc. (1945)
2 p. l., 55 p.   23 cm.   CS71.L7855   1934
                                                                          Suppl.

LIVINGOOD.   See LEVEGOOD.

10605   LIVINGS.   Genealogy of Richard and Rachael Livings, American premogenitors, Sarah Livings and David R. Moulton branch, compiled by Earl Alexander MacLennan.   Morrison, Ill., 1927.
14 p. 21½ cm.   One page left blank at end for Memorandum.   28-5830.   CS71.L786   1927

10606   LIVINGSTON.   Memoirs of the Rev. John Henry Livingston ... Prepared in compliance with a request of the General synod of the Reformed Dutch church in North America, by Alexander Gunn ... New York, W.A.Mercein, printer, 1829.   540 p. front. (port.) 22 cm. Genealogy: p. 13-35. 17-6165.
                                                                          BX9543.L55G8   1829

10607   LIVINGSTON.   Memoirs of the Rev. John Henry Livingston ... by the late Rev. Alexander Gunn ... New ed, cor. and condensed, with the addition of some new matter.   New York, Board of publication of the Reformed Protestant Dutch church, 1856.   x, (11)-405 p. front. (port.) 18 cm. 17-6166.
                                                                          BX9543.L55G8   1856

10608   LIVINGSTON.   The Livingstons of Callendar, and their principal cadets.   A family history by Edwin Brockholst Livingston ... (Edinburgh, Scott & Ferguson) 1887- (92)   xviii, 656 cix p. front., plates, ports., facsims. (1 fold.) coats of arms (part col.) fold. geneal. tab. 31 cm.   Title vignette: colored coat of arms. "Privately printed for Clermont and Edwin Brockholst Livingston.   Impression: seventy-five copies, of which this is no. 58." Issued in 5 numbers, in portfolios; number 6 to contain Addenda and corrigenda, errata, index, &c., not published.   Bound in two volumes.   Pedigree showing the American ancestry of the author's family: p. 476.   Contents. - pt. I, no. I-IV. Scotland.   section I. The Livingstons of Livingston and the Livingstons, lords of Callendar.   section II. The earls of Linlithgow.   section III. The earls of Callendar.   section IV. The earls of Newburgh.   section V. The viscounts of Kilsyth.   section VI. The Livingstones of Jerviswood and Newbigging and Sir Thomas Livingston, viscount of Teviot.   section VII. The Livingstons in France. - pt. II, no.v. America, section I. The manor of Livingston, and of the Livingstons of New York, during colonial and revolutionary times.   section III. Clermont.   20-20492.
                                                                          CS71.L787   1887

10609   LIVINGSTON.   The Livingston manor; address written for the New York branch of the Order of colonial lords of manors in America, by John Henry Livingston ... (Baltimore? 191-?)   37 p. incl. illus., col. pl., ports., facsim. 23½ cm.   (Order of colonial lords of manors in America.   New York branch.   Publications.)   20-16023.
                                                                          E186.99.O6N5
        —— Copy 2.   F127.C8L78

10610   LIVINGSTON.   The Livingstons of Livingston manor; being the history of that branch of the Scottish house of Callendar which settled in the English province of New York during the reign of Charles the Second; and also including an account of Robert Livingston of Albany, "The nephew," a settler in the same province, and his principal descendants, by Edwin Brockholst Livingston ... (New York, The Knickerbocker press) 1910.   xxxiii, 590 p. plates (partly col.) ports., map, facsims. (partly fold.) 2 fold. geneal. tab. (incl. front.) 24½ cm. "275 copies only printed by private subscription." "List of authorities": p. 564-575. 10-5281.

CS71.L787   1910

10611   LIVINGSTON.   Chancellor Robert R. Livingston of New York and his family; by Joseph Livingston Delafield ... (Albany) Printed by J. B. Lyon company (1911)   1 p. l., p. 313-356. 23 cm. Reprinted from the Report of the American scenic and historic preservation society for 1911. 11-30210.

CS71.L787   1911

10612   LIVINGSTON.   The Livingstons of Callendar, and their principal cadets; the history of an old Stirlingshire family, by Edwin Brockholst Livingston ... New ed., entirely rewritten and greatly enl. ... Edinburgh, Printed at the University press of the author, 1920.   xix, 511 p. front. (fold. facsim.) plates, ports., col. coats of arms. 26½ cm. "Contains a set of coloured heraldic plates from drawings specially executed for this new edition by Mr. Graham Johnston, heraldic artist to the Lyon court." "A chronology of the most notable events in the history of the Livingstons of Callendar": p. xv-xviii. "Notes and references": p. 139-143. 20-22842.

CS479.L7   1920

10613   LIVINGSTON.   Ancestral line of Rev. John Livingston, father of Robert Livingston, first lord of the manor.   Compiled by Rev. George B. Kinkead ... Washington, D.C., 1936.   geneal. tab. 46 x 77 cm. fold. to 37 x 30 cm. Photostat copy (positive) 36-11412.

CS71.L787   1936

10614   LIVINGSTON.   The ancestry of Edward Livingston of Louisiana, by James A. Padgett.   (New Orleans) 1936.   40 p. 26½ cm. "Reprinted from the Louisiana historical quarterly, vol. 19, no. 4, October, 1936." Bibliographical foot-notes. 37-5920.

CS71.L787   1936a

10615   LIVINGSTON.   Material relating to the Livingston, Nicholson, Clark, Wheelock, Hamilton, Steele and Schuyler families, copied from various sources by Robert Livingston Nicholson.   Kansas City, 1939.   67 l. 28 cm. Type-written (carbon copy) 40-37503.

CS71.L787   1939

10616   LIVINGSTON.   Notes on the ancestry of David Livingstone, for the Library of Congress, by Frank Grant Lewis .., (Canisteo, N.Y., 1939)   2 l. 28 cm. Caption title. Type-written. 39M4606T.

CS71.L787   1939a

10617   LIVINGSTON.   Lines composing the pedigree of Master John Livingston, D.D., 1603-1673 (!) of Monyabroch, Ancrum and Stranraer, Scotland, and who had the parish of Killinchy, County Down, Ireland, and of his descendants in America.   (n.p.) 1945.   79 l. 29 cm. Photocopy (positive) from manuscript. 48-16848*.

CS71.L787   1945

10618   LIVINGSTON.   The Livingston family in America and its Scottish origins.   By Florence Van Rensselaer.   Arr. by William Laimbeer.   New York, 1949.   413 p. 25 cm. "Lines composing the pedigree of Master John Livingston, D.D., 1603-1673 (sic)" (p. (1)-77) previously issued in 1945. "Authorities and references": p. 363-364. 50-220.

CS71.L787   1949

10619   LIVINGSTON.   Genealogical records.   By Minnie (Livingston) Radcliffe.   1912, rev. 1925 and 1946.   (Tacoma? Wash.) Priv. print. (1950)   141 p. coats of arms, geneal. tables. 25 cm. 50-33119.

CS71.L787   1950

10620   LIVINGSTON.   Notes on the Livingstone family of Lanark, Scotland, and Detroit, Michigan, and related families.   By David Sanders Clark.   Washington, 1966.   1 v. (various pagings) 29 cm. Bibliographical footnotes. 67-7767.

CS71.L787   1966

10621   LIVINGSTON.   Livingston family in vertical file.   Ask reference librarian for this material.

LIVINGSTON.   See also: BYRD, E159.G55
CLARKSON, 1876
EDGCUMBE, CS438.E4
PIERCE, 1895
REPALJE, CS69.H7

ROBINSON, 1907
SEWALL, 1924
SHIPPEN, E302.6.L67L6
TAYLOR, F486.O51 v.13

LIVINGSTONE.　See LIVINGSTON.

LLANDAFF, Earls of.　See MATTHEW, CS499. L2

10622　LLEWELLYN.　Morris Llewellyn of Haverford, 1647 (!)-1730.　By Morris Llewellyn Cooke ... Philadelphia, 1935.　19 p. plates, map, facsims. 23 cm.　"A paper delivered at a meeting of the historical society of Montgomery county, April 30, 1921." 36-11427.
F159. H43L65

LLEWELLYN.　See also No. 430 - Adventurers of purse and person.

10623　LLOYD.　Baronia de Kemeys.　From the original documents at Bronwydd. (Ed. Sir Thomas Davies Lloyd)　Printed for the Cambrian archaeological association.　London, J. R. Smith; (etc., etc., 1862)　4 p. l., (3)-136 p. fold. map, fold. geneal. tab. 22 cm.　The various documents referring to the Lordship of Kemeys are preserved in the muniment room at Bronwydd by the present owner of the manor, Thomas Davies Lloyd, and by him communicated to the Cambrian archaeological association.　cf. Pref.　Pedigree of Thomas Davies Lloyd, based on the original pedigree of 1677, was prepared and brought down to 1861 by Sir Thomas Philipps. fold. geneal. tab. 22-24633.
CS459. K3　　1862

10624　LLOYD.　Lineage of the Lloyd and Carpenter family.　Comp. from authentic sources by Charles Perrin Smith ...　For circulation among the branches of the family interested.　Camden, Printed by S. Chew, 1870.　88 (i. e. 94) p. illus. (coats of arms) pl. 31 x 24 cm. 9-15017.
CS71. L792　　1870
—— (Addenda)　Trenton, Printed by W. S. Sharp, 1873.　cover-title, 19, 6, (1) p. illus. 30½ x 23½ cm. 9-1508.
CS71. L792　　1873

10625　LLOYD.　Farm and its inhabitants.　With some account of the Lloyds of Dolobran.　By Rachel J. Lowe ...　Privately printed (London, Chiswick press) 1883.　2 p. l., 117, (2) p. front. (coat of arms) illus. 23 cm.　Initials and head-pieces.　Printer's mark at end. 16-20944.
CS439. L6　　1883

10626　LLOYD.　The pedigrees of Lloyd of Dolobran, Montgomeryshire, the Wordsworth family ... Foster, late of Le Court, Hants ... Hanbury of Holfield grange, Essex ... Wakefield of Sedgwick house, Kendal ... Wakefield of New Zealand and So. Australia ... by Sandys B. Foster. (London) Printed for private circulation (by W. H. and L. Collingridge) 1890.　2 p. l., (1), 188-214 p. 32 x 26 cm. Interleaved.　Extracted from the Pedigree of Wilson of High Wray of Kendal ... by Joseph Foster ... 2d ed., by S. B. Foster, 1890. 25-12937.
CS439. L6　　1890

10627　LLOYD.　Genealogical notes relating to the families of Lloyd, Pemberton, Hutchinson, Hudson and Parke, and to others connected directly or remotely with them from the original manuscript of James P. Parke and Townsend Ward, with notes, additions and corrections, ed. at the request of Charles Hare Hutchinson ... by Thomas Allen Glenn.　Philadelphia, Printed for private distribution (on the press of E. Stern & co., inc.) 1898.　89 p. 1 illus., coat of arms. 29 cm.　"300 copies of this book were privately printed." 4-24202.
CS71. L792　　1898

10628　LLOYD.　Charles Lamb & the Lloyds; comprising newly discovered letters of Charles Lamb, Samuel Taylor Coleridge, the Lloyds, etc.　Ed. by E. V. Lucas ...　Philadelphia, J. B. Lippincott company, 1899.　324 p. front., ports., fold. facsim. 19½ cm.　"Story of a notable family," the Lloyds; includes more than 20 new letters of Lamb, mainly to Robert Lloyd. 98-1583.
PR4863. L7

10629　LLOYD.　The Lloyds of Brimingham, with some account of the founding of Lloyds bank, by Samuel Lloyd.　2d ed.　Birmingham, Cornish brothers, limited; (etc., etc.) 1907.　xvi, 246 p. 25 pl. (incl. front., ports., plan, facsims.) fold. geneal. tab. 23½ cm.　Introduction signed: E. V. Lucas. 8-9082.
CS439. L6　　1907

10630　LLOYD.　Lloyd manuscripts.　Genealogies of the families of Awbrey-Vaughan, Blunston, Burbeck, Garrett, Gibbons, Heacock, Hodge, Houlston, Howard, Hunt, Jarman, Jenkin-Griffith, Jones, Knight, Knowles, Lloyd, Newman, Paschall, Paul, Pearson, Pennell, Pott, Pyle, Reed, Sellers, Smith, Thomas, Till, Williams, Wood.　Welsh records from the collections of the late Howard Williams Lloyd.　Lancaster, Pa., Press of the New era printing company, 1912.　vii p., 2 l., 3-437 p. fold. geneal. tab. 25½ cm.　Preface signed: Thomas Allen Glenn. 13-4158.
CS71. L792　　1912

10631   LLOYD.   Some family records & pedigrees of the Lloyds of Allt yr Odyn, Castell Hywel, Ffos-y bleiddiaid, Gilfach wen, Llan llyr and Waun ifor.   Comp. and ed. by Lucy E. Lloyd Theakston & John Davies.   With an introduction by George Eyre Evans.   Oxford, Fox, Jones & company, 1913.   4 p. l., 119 p., 1 l., 30 p., 1 l., xlv p. 30½ cm. "One hundred copies only of this book have been printed for issue to subscribers. The number of this signed copy is XXVII." "Some pedigrees of the Lloyds of Allt yr Odyn, Castell Hywell, Fios y bleiddiaid, Gilfach wen, Llan Hyr and Waun ifor" ... has special t.-p and separate pagination. "Appendix to the Lloyd family records" has special t.-p. and separate pagination with imprint date 1912. Title vignette: coat of arms. 13-22309.

CS459.L6T5

10632   LLOYD.   Loyd family of New York, Kentucky and Ohio.   Compiled and written by Emma Rouse Lloyd.   (available for consultation at Lloyd library, 309 West Court St., Cincinnati 2, Ohio.

10633   LLOYD.   Lloyd family in vertical file.   Ask reference librarian for this material.

LLOYD.   See also: CHAMBERLAIN, 1880   OSWELL, CS439.O67
                            CROSSLEY, CS439.C835   REIFSNYDER, 1902
                            FOSTER, 1871   TILGHMAN, 1937
                            HARRISON, 1932   VAUGHAN, CS459.V3
                            HILL, 1854   WILSON, 1890
                            KEMYS, 1862   No. 430 - Adventurers of purse and
                                                          person.

10634   LOAR.   Garrett county history of the Loar family.   By Charles E. Hoye.   Oakland, Md., 1935. 1 l. 48 cm. Detached from the Mountain democrat, August 1, 1935. 38M1252T.   CS71.L795   1935

10635   LOAR.   The Loar genealogy, with cognate branches, 1774-1947.   By Emma Frances (Loar) Gaddis.   xi, 388 p. illus., ports., coat of arms (on cover) 29 cm. 49-54123*.   CS71.L795   1949

10636   LOBB.   The Lobb family from the sixteenth century.   By G. Eland.   Oxford, Printed for Yda Cory-Wright at the University Press, 1955.   103 p. illus. 23 cm. 56-17920.   CS439.L62   1955

LOBB.   See also HIGHBAUGH, 1961

10637   LOBDELL.   ... Simon Lobdell - 1646 of Milford, Conn., and his descendants.   Compiled and published by Julia Harrison Lobdell.   Nicholas Lobden (Lobdell) - 1635 of Hingham, Mass., and some of his descendants.   Chicago, The Windermere press (1907?)   2 p. l., vi p., 2 l., 9-374 p., 1 l., xlvii p. ports., map. 24 cm. At head of title: 1907. 9-8069.   CS71.L796   1907

LOBDELL.   See also JOHNSON, 1938

LOBINGIER.   See BEATTY, 1886

10638   LOCH.   The family of Loch by Gordon Loch.   Edinburgh, Priv. print. by T. and A. Constable ltd., 1934.   xxviii, 517 p. plates, ports., fold. plan, map, facsims. (part double) fold. geneal. tables, col. coats of arms. 29 cm. "This edition is limited to 111 copies, of which this copy is no. 70." Plates accompanied by guard sheets with descriptive letter-press. 34-35185.

CS479.L73

LOCH.   See also LAW, DA890.C88W8

LOCHRIDGE.   See CHASTAIN, DC111.C47

LOCHRY.   See LOUGHRY.

10639   LOCKE.   Book of the Lockes.   A genealogical and historical record of the descendants of William Locke, of Woburn.   With an appendix containing a history of the Lockes in England, also of the family of John Locke, of Hampton, N.H., and kindred families and individuals.   By John Goodwin Locke ... Boston, J. Munroe & co., 1853.   406 p. front., illus., ports., facsims., coat of arms. 24½ cm. 9-11610.

CS71.L813   1853

10640   LOCKE.   The descendants of Calvin Locke, of Sullivan, N.H., who was of the fifth generation from Dea. William Locke, of Woburn, Mass. (1628-1720).   Compiled by Rev. Samuel L. Gerould. Lebanon, N.H., H.E.Waite & co., 1900.   23, (1) p. 23 cm. 1-9346.   CS71.L813   1900

10641   LOCKE.   A history and genealogy of Captain John Locke (1627-1696) of Portsmouth and Rye, N.H., and his descendants; also of Nathaniel Locke of Portsmouth, and a short account of the history of the Lockes in England, by Arthur H. Locke ... (Concord, N.H., The Rumford press, 1916?) ix, 720 p. pl., ports., map, coats of arms.   24 cm.   "Historical account of the Locke family in England": p. 570-586.   16-24581.
CS71.L813   1916

10642   LOCKE.   The Locks of Norbury; the story of a remarkable family in the XVIIIth and XIXth centuries, by the Duchess of Sermoneta.   London, J. Murray (1940)   xii, 390 p. front., plates, ports., double geneal. tab. 22½ cm. "First edition 1940." Bibliography: p. 379. A 41-2789.   CS439.L63   1940

        LOCKE.   See also: BREAUX, 1947
                              HANAFORD, 1915
                              LUCK, 1900
                              SALISBURY, 1892

10643   LOCKER.   My confidences.   An autobiographical sketch addressed to my descendants.   By Frederick Locker-Lampson ... 2d ed.   London, Smith, Elder, & co., 1896.   x p., 1 l., 440 p. 2 port. (incl. front.) 28 cm. Edited by Augustine Birrell. 4-22765.   PR4891.L2A83 1896

        LOCKERY.   See LOUGHRY.

10644   LOCKETT.   Lockett family ... by Ashworth P. Burke.   London, Harrison and sons, printers, 1896.   cover-title, 4 p. illus. (coat of arms) 27½ cm. Reprint from "Family records." 19-3637.   CS439.L65

10645   LOCKETT.   Thomas Lockett of Virginia; genealogical memoir by Katherine Dixon Carter Blankenburg.   San Diego, Calif., The Arts & crafts press, 1940.   2 p. l., vii-xv, 131 p. incl. pl., ports. 23 cm. "The object of this memoir is to complete the work begun by my mother, Mary Katherine Lockett Carter." - Introd. 41-6685.
CS71.L815   1940

        LOCKETT.   See also SCARBOROUGH, 1951

10646   LOCKHART.   The Lockhart papers: containing memoirs and commentaries upon the affairs of Scotland from 1702 to 1715, by George Lockhart ... his secret correspondence with the son of King James the Second from 1718 to 1728, and his other political writings; also, journals and memoirs of the Young Pretender's expedition in 1745, by Highland officers in his army.   Pub. from original manuscripts in the possession of Anthony Aufrere ... London, Printed by R. and A. Taylor, for W. Anderson, 1817.   2 v. 28½ cm. 3-28445.   DA805.L83

10647   LOCKHART.   The Lockhart ancestry and known descendants of H(oratio?) James Lockhart. By Oliver Cary Lockhart.   Washington, 1964.   23 l. coat of arms. 28 cm. Bibliographical footnotes. 65-1151.
CS71.L816   1964

10648   LOCKHEAD.   A reach of the river; a family chronicle, 1880-1954.   (Gillingham) Dorset, Priv. print, at the Blackmore Press (1955)   470 p. illus. 23 cm. 56-25333.   CS439.L627   1955

        LOCKIN.   See No. 553 - Goodhue county.

10649   LOCKMAN.   The Lockman and Flaacke families of early New York; genealogical and bio-graphical data from 1628 to 1965, by Frances Flaacke Donaldson.   Washington, Printed (by) the F. Foster Co., 1965.   103 p. 19 cm. "Sources of research": p. 11-12. 65-27825.   CS71.L8164   1965

        LOCKRIDGE.   See CLEEK, 1957

10650   LOCKWOOD.   Descendants of Robert Lockwood.   Colonial and revolutionary history of the Lockwood family in America, from A.D.1630.   Comp. by Frederic A. Holden and E. Dunbar Lockwood.   Philadelphia, Print. priv. by the family, 1889.   xxv, 708 p., 2 1., 50, 31, 35, (831)-884 p. front., illus., plates, ports., maps, facsims., coat of arms. 26 cm.   Between pages 708 and 831 are three sermons by James Lockwood, with separate pagination and reprints of original title-pages.   9-11608.   CS71.L817   1889

10651   LOCKWOOD.   Rev. Clark Lockwood, 1805-1892, his descendants.   By Arthur Channing Downs.   (Primos? Pa., 195 -)   58 p.   illus. 22 cm.   56-45187.   CS71.L817

LOCKWOOD.   See also: BARLOW, 1891
NOYES, 1900
DANIELSON, E171.A53 vol. 13

10652   LODGE.   A record of the descendents (!) of Robert and Elizabeth Lodge (English Quakers) 1682-1903, by William Jacob Lodge, M.D.   Geneva, W.F.Humphrey press inc., 1942.   2 p. 1., 150 p. front., 2 port. on 1 1. 23½ cm.   Preface signed: G.L. (i.e.Gonzalez Lodge)   42-18890.   CS71.L818   1942

LODGE.   See also O'NEILL, 1944

10653   LOENNECKER.   Slekten Loennecker, Lönnecker.   Samlet, skrevet og utg. av Sigurd H. Loennecker.   Oslo, Børsum, 19   v. illus. 31 cm.   Contents. - 2. bok. Johann Christian Loennecker og hans forfedre. 72-421551.   CS919.L59   1968

LOESCH.   See LESH.

10654   LOEVINGER.   The Loevinger family of Laupheim, Pioneers in South Dakota.   Its history and genealogy.   Compiled by Ludwig D. Kahn.   (Basle, in Selbstverlag,) 1967.   xii, 83 p. 25 cm. 67-97728.   CS71.L8183   1967

10655   LOEVINGER.   Loevinger family folder in vertical file.   Ask reference librarian for this material.

10656   LOEWEN.   The descendants of Isaak Loewen.   By Solomon Leppke Loewen.   Hillsboro, Kan,, 1961.   1 v. illus. 29 cm.   63-4608.   CS71.L8184

10658   LOGAN.   The Logans of Knockshinnoch ... (By James M'Adam Hyslop)   Rev. and cor. (Edinburgh, Printed by R. & R. Clark) 1885.   2 p. 1., 32 p. 22½ cm.   Dedication signed J.H.M. (i.e.James M'Adam Hyslop)   21-21734.   CS479.L75   1885

10659   LOGAN.   The Logans·   (In Historic families of Kentucky ... By Thomas Marshall Green ... 1st series.   Cincinnati, 1889. 23½ cm.   p. 117-229)   4-11454.   F450.G79

10660   LOGAN.   Memoir of Dr. George Logan of Stenton, by his widow Deborah Norris Logan, with selections from his correspondence, ed. by their great-granddaughter, Frances A. Logan; with an introduction by Charles J. Stillé.   Illustrations from photographs by C.S. Bradford.   Philadelphia, The Historical society of Pennsylvania, 1899.   207 p. 3 pl., 2 port. (incl. front.) facsim. 26½ cm.   99-3378.   E302.6.L8L8

10661   LOGAN.   A record of the Logan family of Charleston, South Carolina, by George William Logan, Richmond, Virginia, 1874.   New edition with preface, biographical additions and tables, by Lily Logan Morrill.   Cincinnati, O., 1923.   70 p. 22 cm.   With reproduction of t.-p. of original edition, Sacramento, 1874.   31-18490.   CS71.L82   1923

10662   LOGAN.   History of the Logan family, by Major G.J.N.Logan Home ...   Edinburgh, G. Waterston & sons ltd., 1934.   xii,250 p. illus.,plates,ports.,facsims., col. coats arms. 25½ cm. 34-39658.   CS479.L75   1934

10663   LOGAN.   Logans of Pennsylvania.   Logan family, some items of family history concerning a number of early settlers of Pennsylvania named Logan.   Compiled by Harry Willard Mills and associate compilers ... Washington, D.C., Mills lettergram (1942)   22 l., 3 numb. l., 1 l.   map.   28 cm. (Logan family series, no. 1)   Type-written.   42-10565.   CS71.L82   1942

10664   LOGAN.   ... Logan family; some items of family history and family papers concerning a number of early settlers of Maryland named Logan.   Compiled by Harry Willard Mills ... and associate compilers: Rev. James Allen Logan ... and others.   Washington, D.C., Mills' Lettergram, 1942.   16 l. incl. forms.   coat of arms.   28 x 21½ cm.   At head of title: ... Logans of Maryland.   Reproduced from type-written copy. Bibliography: leaf 15.   44-25544.   CS71.L82   1942a

10665   LOGAN.   The ancestry and posterity of Thomas S. Logan of Burlington County, New Jersey. Research by Thomas L. Gaskill.   Compilation by Nelson B. Gaskill.   (Camden? N.J.) 1956. 9 l.   group ports.   28 cm.   cover title.   66-56586.   CS71.L82   1956

10666   LOGAN.   Our Logan history, 1803-1966.   Compiled and edited by Ora Ellen (Logan) and Marshall Wayne Doyle.   (Greensburg? Kan., 1966?)   167 l.   coat of arms.   28 cm.   67-4235.
                                                                                CS71.L82   1966

          LOGAN.   See also: FISHER, 1839
                              IRVINE, 1916
                              JENKINS, 1904
                              McDOWELL, F450.G79
                              POCAHONTAS, 1887
                              WALKER, 1902

10667   LOGSDON.   A historical sketch and a genealogical record of the endless line of the Logsdon and Kelly families, compiled by Harry C. Logsdon.   Millersburg, Ohio, 1965.   76 p.   illus., ports.   29 cm. 65-8493.   CS71.L823   1965

10668   LOGUE.   The Logues in America, and related families.   Part I by Mabel Logue Hopkins; part II by Leona Logue Schneiter.   Edited by Albert Marion Logue.   (San Leandro? Calif., 1955) 77, xlix l.   28 cm.   55-44923.   CS71.L825   1955

10669   LOKERSON.   A forest of family trees, by John T. Lokerson ... Chevy Chase, Md., J.T. Lokerson, c.1942.   1 p. l., iii numb. l., 1 l., 141 (i.e.145) numb. l. incl. map.   28 cm.   Includes extra numbered leaves 36a, 46a, 61a,126a.   Reproduced from type-written copy.   42-25332.   CS71.L814   1942

10670   LOMAX.   Genealogical and historical sketches of the Lomax family, by Joseph Lomax ... Grand Rapids, Mich., The Rookus printing house, 1894.   264, (60) p. illus., ports., coats of arms.   23½ cm. 9-11606.   CS71.L839   1894

10671   LOMAX.   Genealogy of the Virginia family of Lomax ... by one of the seventh generation in the direct line; with references to the Lunsford, Wormeley, Micou, Roy, Carobin, Eltonhead, Tayloe, Plater, Addison, Tasker, Burford, Wilkinson, Griffin, Gywnn, Lindsay, Payne, Presley, Thornton, Savage, Wellford, Randolph, Isham, Yates, and other prominent families of Virginia and Maryland. Chicago, Rand, McNally & co., 1913.   79, (6) p. incl. ports., facsim., coats of arms.   28½ x 21 cm.   Compiled by Edward Lloyd Lomax.   6 blank pages at end for "Family record of births, marriages, and deaths."   13-17130.   CS71.L839   1913

10672   LOMAX.   The Lomax family.   By Quintin Wentworth Lomax.   Cherryvale, Kan., 1947. 55 p.   ports., coat of arms.   22 x 28 cm.   49-21031*.   CS71.L839   1947

10673   LOMBARD.   A genealogical sketch of the early Lombards, with verses.   By Albert E. Lombard ... Lowell, Mass., The Franklin press, 1883.   71, (1) p.   17 cm. 9-11604.   CS71.L84   1883

10674   LOMBARD.   ... The Lombards of Truro.   Yarmouthport, Mass., C.W.Swift, 1912. cover-title, 7 p.   25 cm.   (Library of Cape Cod history & genealogy, no.76)   Comp. by Shebnah Rich.   Ed. by C.W.Swift.   12-30945.
                                                                                CS71.L84   1912

10675 LOMBARD. The Lumbert or Lombard family, by Amos Otis. Yarmouthport, Mass., C.W. Swift, 1914. cover-title, 12 p. 24½ cm. (Library of Cape Cod history & genealogy, no. 54) 14-13435.

CS71. L84   1914

LOMBARD. See also: MURRAY, 1938
                          VICKERS, 1864

10676 LOMEN. Genealogies of the Lomen (Ringstad), Brandt and Joys families, compiled by G. J. Lomen. Northfield, Minn., Mohn printing company, 1929. 1 p. l., 361 p. front., illus. (incl. ports.) 20½ cm. Blank pages throughout text for additions. "Supplements to 'Genealogies of the Lomen, Brandt, and Joys families'": genealogical tables in pocket. Edited by the Mohn printing company. cf. Publisher's note. 33-6859.   CS71. L845   1929

LOMPSON. See LAMSON, . L127

10677 LONDON. A genealogical history of one branch of the London family in America; ancestors and descendants of Charles Marion Henry London. By Hoyt H. London. Columbia, Mo., University of Missouri, 1957. 52 p. illus. 23 cm. 58-62573.   CS71. L847   1957

10678 LONDONDERRY. Londonderry house and its pictures, by H. Montgomery Hyde, D. LITT., with a foreword by the Most Hon. the Marquess of Londonderry. London, The Cresset press, ltd. (1937) xi, 61 p. front., xxviii pl. (incl. ports.) 25½ cm. 39-16129.   DA687. L7H9

10679 LONEY. Loney family. (by Thomas John Hall) Page 251.   CS71. H177   1941

10680 LONG. Historical account of the family of Long of Wiltshire; by Walter Chitty. (London) Printed for private circulation (Gilbert and Rivington, limited) 1889. 2 p. l., 63 p. incl. 3 geneal. tables. 23½ cm. 3-1403.   CS439. L7

10681 LONG. Genealogy of Benjamin Long, late of Tonawanda, Erie County, N. Y., deceased. Compiled by his grandson, Benjamin F. Thomas. Rochester, N. Y., 1897. 8 p. 21 cm. 9-11607.   CS71. L849   1897

10682 LONG. Genealogy of Benjamin Long ... late of Tonawanda, Erie County, N. Y. Rev. illustrated, enlarged by ... Benjamin F. Thomas ... Rochester, N. Y. (R. W. Lace) 1898. 10 p. front., 24½ cm. Sept. 7, 98-86.   CS71. L849   1898

10683 LONG. Long family of Drumore Township, Lancaster County, Pennsylvania. By Warren Smedley Ely. (Doylestown? Pa.) 1909. 51 l. map. 27 cm. Typescript with additions and corrections in ms. 52-52868.   CS71. L849   1909

10684 LONG. Long family; charts of Drumore Township, Lancaster County, about seventeen hundred twenty-five (1725) By Warren Smedley Ely. (n. p.) 1910. 2 geneal. tables. 278 x 44 cm. fold. to 32 x 44 cm. Manuscript. The chart containing the children and their descendants of Robert Long, born 8-16-1774, and Jean Harah, born 4-19-1782, made by R. L. Brownfield, Jr. and Rex Newlon Brownfield. 55-55831.   CS71. L849   1910

10685 LONG. Records and letters of the family of the Longs of Longville, Jamaica, and Hampton lodge, Surrey; edited by Robert Mowbray Howard ... with 62 full-page illustrations and 15 full-page pedigrees ... London, Simpkin, Marshall, Hamilton, Kent & co., ltd. (1925) 2 v. front., plates, ports., fold. geneal. tables. 22½ cm. Paged continuously. Contains also the families of Byndloss, Morgan, Polnitz, Gregory, Beckford, Ballard and Howard. 25-23233.

CS439. L7   1925

10686 LONG. A Long genealogy. A partial genealogy of the Longs of Charlestown and Nantucket, Massachusetts, by Hallock P. Long ... Washington, D. C., 1926. 20 p. 24 cm. 26-18774.   CS71. L849   1926

10687 LONG. John Long and Tennessee, sketch of a pioneer and his progeny, by his great-great-granddaughter, Caroline Grantland Candler Branan. (New Orleans? 1930?) 2 p. l., (7)-101, xiii p., 1 l. incl. diagrs., geneal. tab. 24 cm. Bibliography: p. 8-9.   CS71. L849   1930

10688   LONG.   History of the Long family of Pennsylvania, published by the Long family organization of Pennsylvania, William Gabriel Long, historian ... Huntington, W. Va., Printed by the Huntington publishing company, 1930.   1 p. l., vii, 3-365 p. illus. (incl. ports., plans, facsims.) fold. pl., fold. facsims., fold. geneal. tables.   29 cm.   33-8508.   CS71.L849   1930a

10689   LONG.   Family history: Atchley, Griffith, Long, Maples, Scoggin, etc. ... compiled, printed, published ... by Mrs. Maud Horn ... Houston, Tex., 1937.   2 p. l., 529 p., 2 l.   maps, plan.   29 cm. Part of the leaves are printed on one side only and are numbered as one page.   Mimeographed.   "References and sketches": p. 483-492.   Ruled leaves for memoranda (2 at end)   37-4730.   CS71.L849   1937

10690   LONG.   Notes for a Long genealogy.   A partial genealogy of the Longs of eastern Massachusetts and New Hampshire (revised 1937) by Hallock P. Long.   Washington, D.C. (1937) cover-title, 28 p.   23 cm.   38-32683.   CS71.L849   1937a

10691   LONG.   A Long genealogy; a partial genealogy of the Long family of Cass county, Michigan, traced maternally through Lydia Nash Long, covering a period of 300 years.   Data collected from history of Nash family, genaology (!) dictionary of New England, vol. XI of Massachusetts soldiers and sailors of the revolutionary war, and data compiled by the Media research bureau and Hallock P. Long, of Washington, D.C.   (By) T.W. Long ... Boonville, Mo., 1937.   14 p.   21½ cm.   Facsimile mounted on p. (2) of cover.   39-12236.   CS71.L849   1937b

10692   LONG.   Pertinent biographical and geneological (!) data concerning the descendants of Christian Long and Hannah Ellen Atkinson, assembled for submission to William Gabriel Long, historian, for culling material in future editions of the Long history of Pennsylvania including some briefed data from the (1) to (6) generation.   (By Nellie Viola (Geiger) Royer)   (Chambersburg? Penna., 1940) 1 p. l., 10 numb. l.   29 cm.   Printed on one side of leaf only.   Foreword signed: Nellie G. Royer.   41-1458.
                                                                                       CS71.L849   1940

10693   LONG.   Emigré saga, a tale of early America, by Theodore K. Long.   New Bloomfield, Pa., Carson Long institue, 1943.   4 p. l., 78 (i.e. 80) p.   21 cm.   Bibliography: p. 76-78.   44-1733.
                                                                                       CS71.L849   1943

10694   LONG.   Our nation builders, by Mrs. Marshall Martin (née Lula Long)   Americus, Ga., Printed by Gammage print shop, c.1947.   142 p.   illus. (1 col.; incl. ports.)   24 cm.   "The ancestors and descendants of Captain Abram Heath Long and Isabella Slappey, his wife." - p. 5.   47-1376.
                                                                                       CS71.L849   1947

10695   LONG.   Long family records, Lancaster County, Pennsylvania, by Robert L. Brownfield, Jr. (and) Rex Newlon Brownfield.   (n.p., 1951)   3 l.   36 cm.   Typescript.   Holograph and typewritten letters inserted. 52-35762.   CS71.L849   1951

10696   LONG.   Long family; a chart thereof, 1910.   By Adda (Long) Nichols.   (n.p., 1951?) 23, (19) l.   36 cm.   Typescript; the chart (19 l.) in ms.   Holograph material and a certified copy of "The will and codicil of James Long" inserted.   52-35765.   CS71.L849   1951a

10697   LONG.   Long and Lahiff biblibyography (sic) as a compliment to the relatives of Joshua or John Mary (Logan) Long.   By Dora Elvin (Breiner) Vought.   Thor, Iowa (1954) c.1953.   104 p.   29 cm. 55-15419.   CS71.L849   1954

10698   LONG.   A documented history of the Long family, Switzerland to South Carolina, 1578-1956, including allied families; a documentary record of the Long (Lang) family of Newberry, Edgefield and Saluda Counties, South Carolina, inclduing many allied families.   By Eytive (Long) Evans.   (Atlanta, 1956)   xii, 316 p.   illus., maps.   24 cm.   Bibliography: p. 283-285.   56-11873.   CS71.L849   1956

10699   LONG.   The Long-Jackson family, 1782-1958.   Compiled by Ruth Jane Long and Gladys Long Griffith.   (n.p., 1958)   48 p.   22 cm.   58-3994.   CS71.L849   1958

10700   LONG.   The Longs of Louisiana.   By Stan Opotowsky.   (1st ed.)   New York, Dutton, 1960. 271 p.   ports.   21 cm.   60-6001.   E748.L8606

10701   LONG.   Maud Horn's Atchley family history, including Long, Maples, Scoggin, and Griffith families.   2d ed. by Paul L. Atchley and Mary Ann Morris Thompson.   Knoxville, Tenn., 1965.
xiii, 530 p. illus., map, ports. 24 cm.   Except for additions, a reprint of the original ed. by Maud Horn, published under title: Family history: Atchley, Griffith, Long, Maples, Scoggin, etc.   67-4016.   CS71.L849   1965

LONG.   See also: ALDEN, 1925   HOLSINGER, 1959
                       DEVOL, 1942   LANG.
                       GRIM, 1934   OWEN, 1929a
                       HARAH, 1910   No. 1547 - Cabell county.
                                                   No. 9385 - Twiggs county.

LONGACRE.   See LONGENECKER.

LONGAKER.   See LONGENECKER.

10702   LONGENECKER.   History of the Longacre-Longaker-Longenecker family.   Published for the committee (of the) family re-union association.   Philadelphia, Lutheran publication society (1902?)
viii, 9-310 p. 20½ cm.   5-10319.   CS71.L852   1902

10703   LONGENECKER.   Genealogical diagram dedicatory to the lineal descendants of Daniel Langenecker, through his son David and grandson Peter Langenecker to the fifth generation ... Prepared by John Longenecker.   Wilmot, O., 1903.   geneal. tab. 35 x 35 cm. 25-7744.   CS71.L852   1903

LONGENECKER.   See also: ALBAUGH, 1949
                             REIFSNYER, 1902

10704   LONGESPÉE.   Annals and antiquities of Lacock abbey, in the county of Wilts; with memorials of the foundress, Ela, countess of Salisbury, and of the earls of Salisbury of the houses of Sarisbury and Longespe; including notices of the monasteries of Bradenstoke, Hinton, and Farley.   By the Rev. W. L. Bowles ... and John Gough Nichols ... London, J. B. Nichols and son, 1835.   xvi, 374 (i.e. 386), lxiii, (1) p. front., illus., plates, plans, geneal. tables (part fold.) 22 cm.   Extra numbered pages: 77* - 80*, 87* - 90*, 263* - 266*.   Contains pedigrees of the Romera and Vitré families.   18-4070.   DA690.L15B6

10705   LONGFELLOW.   Genealogy of the Longfellow family.   Being a record of the ancestors in America of Nathan Longfellow (born Dec. 26, 1773, died Oct. 26, 1840,) and of his descendants of the Longfellow name.   Byfield, Mass., The Old=Byfield press, 1898.   14 p. 14 cm. 39-16917.
                                                                                       CS71.L853   1898

10706   LONGFELLOW.   Genealogy of the Longfellow family.   Being a record of the ancestors in America of Nathan Longfellow (born Dec. 26, 1773, died Oct. 26, 1840,) and of his descendants of the Longfellow name.   Byfield, Mass., the Old-Byfield press, 1898.   (Boston, Reprinted by Goodspeed's book shop, inc., 1939)   14 p. 14 cm.   "Only 50 copies printed."   39-16918.   CS71.L853   1898a

LONGFELLOW.   See also ELLIS, F3T61

LONGINO.   See BATSON, 1959

10707   LONGLEY.   Elijah Longley and his descendants; a contribution toward a Longley genealogy, by Arthur Willis Stanford.   (Kobe, Japan) Printed by the Fukium printing co., ltd., Kobe branch, 1909.
3 p. l., 31 p. front. (port.) 22 cm.   10-18970.   CS71.L856   1909

10708   LONGLEY.   Descendants of William Longley of Lynn, Mass., in 1635.   Compiled from family records and revised by Alice Longley.   Priv. print. (Boston, T. R. Marvin & son, printers)
1916.   10 p. 24½ cm.   "Forty copies printed from type."   16-23265.   CS71.L856   1916

10709   LONGLEY.   Longley family.   Some descendants of William Longley, born in England 1614; a land grantee of Lynn, Mass., 1638; died at Groton, Mass., 1680.   Containing a complete list of the descendants of Isaac Longley, 1823-1914, up to Jan. 17, 1952.   North Anson, Me., Ideal Print Shop, 1952.   39 p. illus. 21 cm. 52-31478.   CS71.L856   1952

LONGLEY.   See also: BENT, 1903
POLLOCK, 1932

10710   LONGRIDGE.   Genealogical notes of the kindred families of Longridge, Fletcher, and Hawkes. Collected and arranged by Robert Edmond Chester Waters ... (Printed for private circulation) (London? 1872?)   3 p. l., 14 p., 1 l., 15-21 p., 1 l., (23)-37 p. illus. (coats of arms) 3 fold. geneal. tab.   24½ cm.   13-25839.
CS439.L8

LONGSHORE.   See WILSON, 1929

LONGSTAFF.   See LANGSTAFF.

LONGSTREET.   See MAY, 1928

10711   LONGSTRETH.   The Longstreth family records, rev. and enl. by Agnes Longstreth Taylor ... Philadelphia, Press of Ferris & Leach, 1909.   804 p. front., plates, ports., facsims., col. coat of arms. 23½ cm. 350 copies. No. 47." Rev. and enl. from genealogical records of Bartholomew Longstreth in the "Dawton family records, by Charles C. Dawson." 1874. Blank pages at end for "Additions."   17-28714-5
CS71.L858   1909
———— Supplement of The Longstreth family records, comp. by Agnes Longstreth Taylor. (Philadelphia) 1914.   1 p. l., 16 p. 23½ cm.

LONGSTRETH.   See also: HALLOWELL, 1893
PARRISH, 1927

10712   LONGSWORTH.   Longsworth family history; descendants of Solomon Longsworth, Sr., of Maryland.   By Mary Esther (Longsworth) Breese.   (Lima, Ohio) 1951.   225 p. illus., ports., map, coat of arms. 24 cm. 52-23969.
CS71.L859   1951

10713   LONGTIN.   Material in vertical file.   Ask reference librarian for this material.

10714   LONGWORTH.   The making of Nicholas Longworth; annals of an American family, by Clara Longworth de Chambrun.   New York, R. Long & R. R. Smith, inc., 1933.   6 p. l., 3-322 p. front., plates, ports. 22 cm. 33-3183 rev.
E748.L88C4

LONGWORTH.   See also SULLENS, 1942

10715   LONGYEAR.   The descendants of Jacob Longyear of Ulster county, New York, compiled by Edmund J. Longyear ... (New Haven, Conn.) Priv. print. for the compiler (The Tuttle Morehouse & Taylor company, 1942)   xvii, 622 p. 24½ cm. 42-2481.
CS71.L86   1942

LONSDALE.   See FELL.

10716   LOOBY.   A short history of the Looby family, Ireland-Canada-U.S.A., by Arthur Looby, CSB. (Windsor, 1967)   86 p. illus., maps, ports. 28 cm. 68-117115.
CS499.L56   1967

LOOCKERMANS.   See DUPUY, 1910

LOOFBOURROW.   See BROWN, 1959

LOOKABAUGH.   See LUCKENBACH.

LOOKE.   See TOWNE, 1927

10718   LOOMER.   The Loomer family ancestry of Addie E. Loomer-Shepard and her descendants. With an appendix giving the descendants of her parents, Philip and Lucretia (Cass) Loomer.   Des Moines, Printed by the Globe Pub. Co. (1946?)   61 p. illus., ports. 23 cm. 51-27332.
CS71.L8616   1946

10719   LOOMER.   The descendants of Stephen Loomer of New London, Connecticut, comprising the first to and including the ninth generation.   By Addie Eugenia (Loomer) Shepard.   Allison, Iowa (1960 or 61)   unpaged. 30 cm. 61-39249.
CS71.L8616   1961

10720   LOOMIS.   The descendants of Joseph Loomis, who came from Braintree, England, in the year 1638, and settled in Windsor, Connecticut, in 1639.   By Elias Loomis ... New Haven, Tuttle, Morehouse & Taylor, 1870.   vii, 5-292 p. front. (coats of arms) 23½ cm. 9-11602.

CS71.L863   1870

10721   LOOMIS.   The descendants of Joseph Loomis, who came from Braintree, England, in the year 1638, and settled in Windsor, Connecticut, in 1639.   By Elias Loomis ... 2d ed., rev. and enl. New Haven, Tuttle, Morehouse and Taylor, 1875.   viii, 9-611 p. front. (coats of arms) ports. 23½ cm. 3-7919.

CS71.L863   1875

10722   LOOMIS.   The descendants (by the female branches) of Joseph Loomis, who came from Braintree, England, in the year 1638, and settled in Windsor, Connecticut, in 1639.   By Elias Loomis ... New Haven, Tuttle, Morehouse & Taylor, 1880.   2 v. front. 23½ cm. Paged continuously. 9-11603.

CS71.L863   1880

10723   LOOMIS.   Descendants of James Robinson Loomis.   By William Raymond Loomis.   Washington (1906)   3 l. 27 cm. Caption title. Manuscript. 48-33995 *.   CS71.L862   1906

10724   LOOMIS.   The Loomis family in America, a brochure.   Addresses delivered at the reunion of the Loomis family asscoiation, at Hartford, Connecticut, September twenty-seventh, nineteen hundred and five, and including the official record of the business transacted.   (Hartford) Press of the Connecticut magazine, 1906.   1 p. l., (5)-46 p. plates. 25½ cm. Title vignette (coat of arms) 23-18599.

CS71.L863   1906

10725   LOOMIS.   Descendants of Joseph Loomis in America, and his antecedents in the Old world; the original pub. by Elias Loomis, 1875, rev. by Elisha S. Loomis, PH. D., 1908.   (Bera? O., 1909) 4 p. l., (xiii)-xiv, (15)-859, (8) p. plates, ports.. maps, facsims. 27 cm. Title in red within blue ornamental border. "This edition is limited to 700 numbered copies of which this book is no. 22." 8 blank pages at end for "Family register." "The Loomis family in the Old world ... by Charles A. Hoppin, jr." p. (53)-114. 9-29641.

CS71.L863   1909

10726   LOOMIS.   ... Family of Loomis ... Compiled by Frances M. Smith.   (New York, F. Allaben genealogical company, 1909?)   8 p. incl. coat of arms. 20 cm. (Colonial families of America) Title from slip mounted on cover. 38M4605T.

CS71.L863   1909a

10727   LOOMIS.   Edward Lumas, of Ipswich, Massachusetts, and some of his descendants.   Comp. by George Harlan Lewis, from the notes of Elisha S. Loomis, PH. D., with additions by Charles A. Lummus.   (One hundred copies reprinted from the Historical collections of the Essex institute, volume LIII.) Salem, Mass., Essex institute, 1917.   1 p. l., 43 p. 24½ cm. 21-17504.   CS71.L863   1917

LOOMIS.   See also: BASSETT, 1926
DAVIS, 1929
PECK, 1925

10728   LOOS.   The Loos family genealogy, 1535-1958.   By Sila Lydia Bast.   (Milwaukee? 1959) 234 p. illus. 29 cm. 59-29193.   CS71.L865   1959

10729   LOPER.   Loper, Keller, Van Meter (and) allied lines.   By Melba Wood.   (Godfrey, Ill.) 1969.   54 p. 29 cm. Cover title. 76-8918 MARC.   CS71.L87   1969

10730   LOPEZ.   The story of the Lopez family, a page from the history of the war in the Philippines; ed. and with an introduction by Canning Eyot ... Boston, J. H. West company, 1904.   217 p. front., plates, ports. 20½ cm. 4-2996.   DS676.8.L8E9

LOPEZ.   See also MOISE, 1961

10731   LORAINE.   ... Pedigree and memoirs of the family of Loraine of Kirkharle. (By Sir Lambton Loraine) (London, Printed by J. B. Nichols and sons) 1902.   xi, 428 p. illus. (facsims., coats of arms) plates, ports., plan, 2 geneal. tab. (1 double) coat of arms on fold. 1. 27 cm. Introduction signed: L. L. (i.e. Lambton Loraine) "For private circulation." "Addenda and corrigenda" inserted at p. (1) Pages 349-370 blank "For manuscript biographical notes". Contains also pedigrees of the Del Strother, Bowes, Maddison, Fenwick, Lambton, Millot, Campart, Elkins and Broke families. 39-23103.

CS439.L83   1902

10732   L'ORANGE.   Anetavle for oberst Johan Ingolf Koren l'Orange og hans søsken.   2. utg. supplert og revid.   V. Aker, 1947.   19 p. fold. diagr. 26 cm. 49-21654*.   CS919. L67   1947

10733   LORCK.   Die Chronik der Familie Lorck; Schicksale und Genealogie einer Flensburger Kaufmannsfamilie aus vier Jahrhunderten.   Neumünster, K. Wachholtz, 1949.   205 p. illus., ports., geneal. tables. 25 cm. Pages 193-205 numb. as leaves. Bibliography: p. 169-170. 50-33291.   CS629. L67   1949

10734   LORD.   Genealogy of the Lord family which removed from Colchester, Conn., to Hanover, N. H., and then to Norwich, Vt.   By Rev. John M. Lord.   Concord, N. H., I. C. Evans co., printers, 1903.   116 p. 19 cm. 10-23158.   CS71. L873   1903

10735   LORD.   A history of the descendants of Nathan Lord of ancient Kittery, Me.   Compiled by C. C. Lord, arranged for publication by George E. Lord.   Concord, N. H., The Rumford press, 1912. v, 218 p. front. (port.) coat of arms. 24 cm. 24-582.   CS71. L873   1912

10736   LORD.   The ancestors and descendants of Lieutenant Tobias Lord.   By Charles Edward Lord. (Boston) Priv. print, *T. R. Marvin & son, printers) 1913.   263 p. front., plates, ports., 2 fold. maps, facsims. 25 cm. "Two hundred and ten copies of this book have been printed. no. 79." 13-10558.   CS71. L873   1913

10737   LORD.   Certain members of the Lord family who settled in New York city in the early 1800's, descendants of Thomas Lord of Hartford, Connecticut, by Kenneth Lord.   (Concord) Priv. print. (Rumford press) 1945.   xi, (1), 90, (4) p., 1 l. incl. front. (coat of arms) illus. (incl. ports., maps) geneal. tab. 29 x 21 cm. Additions and corrections in manuscript. 46-531.   CS71. L873   1945

10738   LORD.   Genealogy of the descendants of Thomas Lord, an original proprietor and founder of Hartford, Conn., in 1636, compiled by Kenneth Lord.   New York, 1946.   vi p., 2 l., 482 p., 1 l. front. (col. coat of arms) pl., ports., maps, facsim., geneal. tab. 26½ cm. 46-6882.   CS71. L873   1946

10739   LORD.   Lord family in vertical file.   Ask reference librarian for this material.

LORD.   See also: BLACK, 1966   SMITH, 1924
                          FOSTER, 1897   SNYDER, 1958
                          McCORMICK, 1957   TODD, 1909
                          McCURDY, 1892   TRACY, 1895a
                          NOYES, 1900   WELLS, 1927a
                          NOYES, 1907   YVERY, CS439. Y9A5

LOREE.   See WELLES, F116. N28 vol. 53

LORENCE.   See LORENTZ.

10740   LORENTZ.   Lest we forget.   By Bess Lorentz Wade.   (White Plains, N. Y., Printed by Murphy Print. Co., 1968)   134 p. facsim., ports. 25 cm. Cover title. Chronicles of the Lorentz family. 68-6402.   CS71. L874   1968

LORENZ.   See LORENTZ.

10741   LORILLARD.   (The wills of George Lorillard, of the city of New York, tobacco manufacturer.   New York, 1831)   14 p. 24 cm. Marginal notes in ms. 17-9565.   CS71. L875   1831

10742   LORIMER.   Lorimer, Scotland.   (London, Hamilton, Adams & co., 1877)   4 p. front. (coat of arms) 27 cm. Comp. by R. R. Stodart. Caption title. Reprinted from "Miscellanea genealogica et heraldica," n.s., 1877, v.2, p.421-423. 9-19119.   CS479. L8

10743   LORING.   Loring genealogy, comp. from "The chronicles or ancestral records" of James Speare Loring, from his original manuscript in possession of the New England historic genealogical society, by permission; from the manuscripts of John Arthur Loring, and from many other sources, by Charles Henry Pope, assisted by Katharine Peabody Loring.   Cambridge, Mass., Murray and Emery company, 1917.   xix, 424 p. front., plates, ports., coats of arms (1 col.) 24 cm. 17-25785.   CS71. L878   1917

LORIO. See MOSS, 1964a

LORRENCE. See LORENTZ.

LORRENTZ. See LORENTZ.

10744   LORY.   The Lorys of Cornwall.   By Letta (Lory) Shepherd.   (Platteville? Wis., 1962)
348 p. illus. 23 cm. 62-68150.   CS71. L879   1962

10745   LOTBINIERE, De.   The De Lotbinieres.   A bit of Canadian romance and history.   By I. J.
Greenwood.   (Boston, D. Clapp & son, printers, 1896)   8 p. 24½ cm.   "Reprinted from the New-England hist, and
gen. register for January, 1896."   9-19130.   CS90. L6

10746   LOTBINIERE.   The seigneurie of Alainville on lake Cahmplain; address read at the annual
meeting of the New York branch of the Order of colonial lords of manors in America, held in the city
of New York, April 19th, 1929, by A. de Lery Macdonald.   Baltimore, 1929.   36 p. col. front., illus. (incl.
ports., map) 23½ cm.   (On cover: (Order of colonial lords of manors in America.   New York branch.   Publications) no. 20)   34-5029.
                                                                        E186. 99. O6N5 no. 20
—— Copy 2.   F127. C6M2

10747   LOTHROP.   A genealogical memoir of the Lo-Lathrop family in this country, embracing the
descendants, as far as known, of the Rev. John Lothropp, of Scituate, and Barnstable, Mass., and
Mark Lothrop, of Salem and Bridgewater, Mass., and the first generation of descendants of other
names.   By the Rev. E. B. Huntington, A. M.   Ridgefield, Conn., Mrs. Julia M. Huntington, 1884.
3 p. l., 457 p., 1 l. front., ports. 25 cm. 9-11609.   CS71. L882   1884
                                                                        Microfilm 8655 CS

10748   LOTHROP.   Ancestors and descendants of Daniel Lothrop sr., 1545 to 1901 ... Comp. and
pub. by George David Read Hubbard ... Brooklyn, N. Y. (1901?)   37 p. front., pl., ports. 29 cm.   Ward family
history: p. (30-31) 19-14391.   CS71. L882   1901

10749   LOTHROP.   History of the Lathrop family, by Irma Lathrop Moorman.   (Swanton, O.) 1940.
(32) p. 22 cm.   Title vignette (Lathrop coat of arms) Pages (27) - (32) blank for "Notes and clippings."   42-4025.
                                                                        CS71. L882   1940

10750   LOTHROP.   Lothrop family in vertical file.   Ask reference librarian for this material.

LOTHROP.   See also: ALCOTT, PS255. C6L6   JENNINGS, 1923
                      AVERY, 1925   NORTON, 1935
                      BARTLETT, 1951   VANREIN, E171. A53 vol. 16
                      CROCKER, 1923   WHITING, 1952
                      HYDE, 1864   WOOLSEY, 1900

10751   LOTT.   The Lott family in America, including the allied families: Cassell, Davis, Graybeal,
Haring, Hegeman, Hogg, Kerley, Phillips, Thompson, Walter, and others.   By A. V. Phillips ...
Trenton, N. J., Sold by Traver's book store, 1942.   x, 179 p. incl. front., illus. (map) plates, ports., facsims. coat of
arms. 28 cm.   "Lithoprinted."   "Key to references": p. 159-160.   A42-5054 Rev.   CS71. L8825   1942

LOTT.   See also GABRISKIE.

10752   LOTTER.   The silversmiths and goldsmiths of the cape of Good Hope, 1652-1850, by Mollie
N. Morrison.   Published by the author with the assistance of a grant from the Carnegie corporation of
New York, through the Research grant board of the Union of South Africa.   (Johannesburg, 1936)
xv, 84 p. illus., 16 pl. on 8 l., geneal. tab. 27 x 21 cm.   The "Placaat" (an ordinance to control the gold and silversmithing industry) issued on
the 31st July, 1715 by Governor de Chavonnes (original Dutch and translation): p. 22-35.   Genealogical table of the descendants of Matthias Lotter:
p. 77.   "Chronological list of commanders and governors of the cape of Good Hope": p. 78-79.   37-17521.   NK7189. C3M6

10753   LOTTINVILLE.   The Lottinville family, by Armand J. Lottinville.   Washington, D. C.
(Murray & Heister) 1942.   105 p. ports. 23½ cm.   Coat of arms of Lottinville fam. on cover.   43-20381.   CS71. L883   1942

10755   LOUCKS.   Genealogy of the Loucks family, beginning with Johann Dietrich Loucks, and his descendants in direct line to Joseph Loucks, fourth generation, and all his known and traceable descendants to date.   By Edwin Merton McBrier.   New York, John S. Swift co., inc., 1940.   xxii, 294 p. incl. col. front. (coat of arms) illus. (incl. ports.) fold. map. 25 cm.   Excerpts from "The history of Montgomery classis, R. C. A.," by W. N. P. Dailey: p. 195-234.   41-21917.   CS71. L884   1940

10754   LOUD.   Genealogical record of the descendants of Caleb Loud, 1st., 13th child of Francis Loud jr., and Onner Prince Loud.   Compiled by Watson Loud ... and published by H. M. Loud ... 1889.   Detroit, Winn & Hammond, printers, 1889.   70 p. 23½ cm. 9-11476.
                                                                                                          CS71. L885   1889

10756   LOUGHER.   The Loughers of Glamorgan, their descent and connections.   By John Lougher. (Cardiff, 1952)   54 p. 25 cm.   52-34704.   CS459. L68   1952

LOUGHERY.   See LOUGHRY.

10757   LOUGHLAND.   History of the family of Lofland in America and related families; their settlements, migrations, marriages (and) military achievement, compiled from published and documentary records.   By Jewell (Lofland) Crow.   (Dallas?) c. 1956.   133, 21 p. illus., ports., col. coat of arms, geneal. tables. 29 cm.   Cover title: The Lofland family, 1667-1955.   56-29861.   CS71. L886   1956

10758   LOUGHRY.   A brief genealogy of the Loughry family of Pennsylvania, compiled by Julia A. Jewett.   St. Louis, Mo., 1923.   3 p. l., 85, xxviii p. 22½ cm.   24-7522.
                                                                                                          CS71. L887   1923

LOUNDSBURY.   See LOUNSBERRY.

LOUNSBERRY.   See: DAVENPORT, 1960
                             HILL, 1907
                             MINER, 1928

LOUNSBERY.   See DAVENPORT, 1960

LOURIE.   See LOWRY

LOUTREL.   See BARLOW, 1891

10759   LOVAT.   The Lovat Peerage.   Newspaper clippings from the London Times, May 6, 11, 19, 20, 1885.   In vertical file.   Ask reference librarian for this material.

10760   LOVE.   History of the Love family.   (n. p. 18 -)   8 numb. l. 27 cm.   Photostat copy (positive).   "Copied from one made by Edith Love Stockder of Hartford, Conn.   The history written by a Rev. Love of Hartford.   Died before completing and having published."   38M1172T.   CS71. L895   18 -

10761   LOVE.   Love - A partial history of the families of Joseph Love, of Augusta county, Virginia, and his brother, Samuel Love, originally from Ireland.   (By Mary Virginia (Brown) Connally) (Atlanta? 190)   4 l. 23 cm.   Title taken from beginning of first column.   Ms. note at top of page: Love record written by Mrs. E. L. Connally ...   7-9222.   CS71. L895   190-

10762   LOVE.   Love history and genealogy, by George W. Allen.   (La Porte, Ind.)   Allen press, 1937.   1 p. l., (4)-82 (i. e. 85) p. incl. illus., pl. plates, ports. 21 cm.   Nos. 62 and 69 repeated in paging; one plate numbered as p. 48. Blank pages for births, marriages, deaths (69-74)   38-32682.   CS71. L895   1937

10763   LOVE.   The Love family of Gadsden county, Florida, descendants of Alexander Love ... Also other allied families ... Compiled by Pearle Trogdon Love.   (n. p.) 1941.   A-D, 75 (i. e. 76), 33 numb. l. 28 cm.   Includes extra numbered leaf 32A.   Type-written.   42-50341.   CS71. L895   1941

10764   LOVE.   (Love family tree)   By Pearle Golden (Trogdon) Love.   (Quincy, Fla.) 1947. geneal. tables.   95 x 102 cm. fold. to 50 x 50 cm.   Photocopy (negative)   48-14032 ♣.   CS71. L895   1947

121

10765   LOVE.   Love family history.   From the first draft (ms) of "The ancestry of William De Loss Love, DD. " (Hartford, 195-?)   17 1. 28 cm. 55-19920.   CS71.L895

10766   LOVE.   General Thomas Love of western North Carolina and western Tennessee and his brothers Robert and James. 2d ed., with addenda and corrections. By Robert Abner Love. (St. Petersburg? Fla., 195-)   43 1. 29 cm. 59-33189.   CS71.L895

10767   LOVE.   The descendants of William De Loss, 1819-1898, and Matilda Longworth Love, 1820-1906, as of December 1951; together with the record of the Love family in Hamilton College. Also some data on collateral relatives of William De Loss Love. (Berkeley, Calif., 1951)   26 1. illus. 29 cm. 53-32481.   CS71.L895   1951

10768   LOVE.   The Love family historical and genealogical quarterly. v. 1 -   Sept. 1953 -   (Camden, S.C., etc., Love Family Historical and Genealogical Association)   v. in illus. 27 cm. Published Sept. 1953 by R.A. Love. Current issues in vertical file. 59-31684.   CS71.L895   1953

10769   LOVE.   Our ancestors, the Love family of Trezevant, Carroll County, Tennessee. By Albert Gallatin Love. Washington, 1953.   130 1. 29 cm. 54-27074.   CS71.L895   1953a

10770   LOVE.   Love's Valley. By Jolee Love. Nashville, Printed by Ambrose Print.Co. (1954)   556 p. illus., ports., maps, coats of arms, facsims. 24 cm. 55-17244.   CS71.L895   1954

          LOVE.   See also: MEIGS, 1906
                               SMITH, 1960
                               No. 1547 - Cabell county.

10771   LOVEDAY.   ... A collection of charters relating to Goring, Streatley and the neighborhood, 1181-1546, preserved in the Bodleian library, with a supplement.   Edited by T. R. Gambier-Parry ... Oxford, Issued for the Society, 1931-32.   2 v. fronts., pl., fold. map. 23 cm. (Half-title: The Oxfordshire record society ... Oxfordshire record series - vol. XIII-XIV) At head of title: Oxfordshire record society. Running title: The Goring charters. Paged continuously. 32-30612.   DA670.O9A3 v.13-14

10772   LOVEJOY.   Genealogical record of John Lovejoy (1622-1917) of Andover, Massachusetts, and of his wife Mary Osgood of Ipswich, Massachusetts, also of their descendants unto the tenth generation, prepared and published by Annie Givin Jacskon. Denver, Col., 1917.   28 p. front., ports. 23 cm. Additions and corrections in manuscript. 31-9476.   CS71.L896   1917

10773   LOVEJOY.   The Lovejoy genealogy, with biographies and history, 1460-1930, especially recording the American descendants and the English ancestry of John Lovejoy (1622-1690) of Andover, Mass., and of Joseph Lovejoy (1684-1748) of Prince George County, Md., but also embracing all known data on other persons bearing the Lovejoy name, whether or not identified with the emigrant ancestors. Compiled, written, edited and published by Clarence Earle Lovejoy ... (New York) c.1930.   4 p. l., 5-466 p. front., plates, ports., map, facsims., 2 col. coats of arms on 1 pl. 23½ cm. "This is copy no. 93 of an edition of 300." Signed: C.E.Lovejoy.   30-18836.   CS71.L896   1930

10774   LOVEJOY.   Genealogy, ancestry of Joseph Lovejoy of Westminster, Vt.   By Ella Fontenelle (Jones) Tafe.   In Calif. state soc. Sons of the Revolution. Bulletin. Los Angeles, 1934. vol. xi, no.4. p. 13-14) Signed E.F.J.T. (i.e. Ella Fontenelle Jones Tafe) 38M5036T.   CS71.L896   1934

          LOVEKYN.   See LUKIN.

          LOVEL.   See LOVELL.

10775   LOVELACE.   The Lovelace-Loveless and allied families.   By Florance Alice Loveless (Keeney) Robertson. (Los Angeles? 1952)   xi, 203 p. illus., ports., coats of arms. 21 cm. Bibliography: p.xi. 52-42739.   CS71.L897   1952

10776   LOVELACE.   The American ancestry of Kenneth John Loveless (by) Richard W. Loveless. (Oshkosh, Wis.) Oshkosh Press, 1969.   x, 10 1. ports. 29 cm. 71-4418 MARC.   CS71.L897   1969

LOVELACE.   See also: REED, 1963
                        WINSTON, 1927

LOVELACE-GORSUCH.   See No. 430 - Adventurers of purse and person.

10777   LOVELAND.   Genealogy of the Loveland family in the United States of America, from 1635 to 1892, containing the descendants of Thomas Loveland, of Wethersfield, now Glastonbury, Conn. ... By J. B. Loveland ... and George Loveland ... (Fremont, O., I. M. Keeler & son, printers, 1892-95)   3 v. illus., ports., coats of arms. 22½ cm.   9-11605.   CS71. L898   1892-5

LOVELAND.   See also: CLARK, John E.   By E. A. Crawford.
                        WITTER, 1929

10778   LOVELL.   The ancestry of Thomas Lovell and his wife Mary Ellen Ricker, by Frederick W. Lovell and Eva G. Lovell.   Rutland, Vt., The Tuttle publishing company, inc. (1940)   172, (4) p. plates, ports, map. 23½ cm.   Four blank pages for "Family records" at end.   "Morrill family sources": p. 78.   Includes also the Ricker, Wentworth, Perkins, Morrill, Johnson, Whittemore and Weston families.   41-6686.   CS71. L890   1940

LOVELL.   See also: REMINGTON, 1960
                      STAWELL, CS439. S89
                      SUNDERLAND, 1914
                      YVERY, 1742

LOVET.   See SANBORN, 1894

10779   LOVETT.   Ecclesiastical memorials of the Lovett family, by R. J. Arden Lovett ... Ostend (Belgium) Printed by E. Van de Water (1897)   (61) p. front. 35 cm.   24-20422.   CS439. L84   1897

10780   LOVETT.   Lovett of Buckinghamshire.   (By Robert Jonathan Arden Lovett) 1066-1912. (n. p., Priv. print., 1913)   61 p. plates, ports., coat of arms. 34 cm.   Compiled by R. J. Arden Lovett and Rev. Ernest Neville Lovett.   24-6057.   CS439. L84

LOVETT.   See also SHIRLEY, CS439. S485

LOVICK.   See NORWOOD, 1944

LOVING.   See: HAMLETT, 1958
                 WHITAKER, 1930

LOVINGER.   See LOEVINGER.

LOW.   See LOWE.

10781   LOWDERMILK.   Garret county history of Lowdermilk family.   By Charles Edward Hoye. (Oakland, Md.) 1934.   1 l. 39 cm.   Detached from the Mountain democrat, November 22, 1934.   35-13986.   CS71. L91   1934

10782   LOWE.   ... Descendants of William Low, of Boston, Massachusetts.   Compiled by Edmund D. Barbour, January 1, 1890.   (Boston?) 1890.   cover-title, fold. geneal. tab. 64½ x 40 cm. fold. to 11 x 20 cm.   0-7139 rev.   CS71. L912   1890

10783   LOWE.   ... Some account of the family of Lowe, formerly of Hartford, and elsewhere in the county of Chester, subsequently of Highfield in the county of Nottingham, and now of Shirenewton hall in the county of Monmouth.   Comp. from the papers left by the late Lieutenant-Colonel Alfred Edward Lawson Lowe ... by Otto-William Braunsdorff ... Dresden, 1896.   4 p. l., 63 p. front., illus., plates, ports., facsims., coats of arms. fold. geneal. tables. 39 cm.   16-8306.   CS439. L85

10784   LOWE.   The ancestors of the John Lowe family circle and their descendants.   Fitchburg, Printed by the Sentinel printing company, 1901.   189 p. front., plates, ports., facsims. 24 cm.   "Comp. by Ellen M. Merriam for the John Lowe family circle."   11-30204.   CS71. L912   1901

10785   LOWE.   A genealogical quest, by Wm. G. Low.   (n. p.) 1908-(15)   2 v. 23½ cm. Cover-title.
The ancestry of Thomas Low of Ipswich, Mass.   20-22876.   CS71. L912   1908

10786   LOWE.   Family notes (by) Wm. G. Low.   (n. p.) 1918.   cover-title, 15 p. 23 cm. 20-17036.
                                                                    CS71. L912   1918

10787   LOWE.   A genealogical quest, and Family notes.   By William Gilman Low.   (2d ed.   n. p.,
1928)   21, 8 p., 14 l. 23 cm. 62-55439.   CS71. L912   1928

10788   LOWE.   Low genealogy; the descendants of Seth Low and Mary Porter.   (By Abbot Low
Moffat)   (n. p.) 1932.   1 p. l., 60, 14 numb. l. 30 cm. Introduction signed: Abbot Low Moffat. Type-written. 32-19219.
                                                                    CS71. L912   1932

10789   LOWE.   Alexander Low and his descendants in America; includes genealogical data on the
Barkalow, Borden, McClees and Moreau lines, compiled by Ann Augusta McClees.   Freehold, N. J.,
1939 (i. e. 1940)   cover-title, 8 p. 23½ cm. "200 copies printed by D. H. Moreau, Flemington, N. J., 1940." 41-6095.
                                                                    CS71. L912   1940

10790   LOWE.   The Low family of New York city, publishers, 1795-1829, by Sanford A. Moss,
PH. D.   (New York, The New York public library, 1943)   4 p. 25 cm. Caption title. "Reprinted from the Bulletin
of the New York public library of February 1943. " A43-1127.   Z473. L85M6

10791   LOWE.   Tall ships to Cathay.   By Helen Augur.   (1st ed.)   Garden City, N. Y., Doubleday
(1951)   255 p. illus., ports. 21 cm. 51-9289 rev.   CS71. L912   1951

10792   LOWE.   Low genealogy, old Low, old Low's son; the descendants of Seth Low and Mary
Porter, 1807-1956.   By Abbot Low Moffat.   (Washington?) 1956.   78 p. illus. 24 cm. Cover-title: Old Low,
old Low's son.   61-33825 rev.   CS71. L912   1956

10793   LOWELL.   The one hundred and fiftieth anniversary of the foundation of the First religious
society of Newburyport, originally the Third parish of Newbury.   Celebrated October 20th, 1875.
Newburyport, W. H. Huse & co., printers, 1876.   72 p. 22½ cm. Note signed by the compiler: C. J. B. Genealogy of
the Lowell family, compiled by Amos Noyes: p. 70-72.   10-6786.   F74. N55N493

10794   LOWELL.   The historic genealogy of the Lowells of America from 1639 to 1899.   Compiled
and edited by Delmar R. Lowell ... Pub. by the author.   Rutland, Vt., The Tuttle co,, printers, 1899.
iii, 826 p. plates, ports., coats of arms. 24½ cm. 9-11598.   CS71. L915   1899

10795   LOWELL.   The Lowells and their seven worlds ... By Ferris Greenslet.   Boston, Houghton
Mifflin company, 1946.   xi, 442 p. plates, ports., geneal. tab. 23½ cm. 46-25260.   CS71. L915   1946

        LOWELL.   See also: LYMAN, 1932
                               WYMAN, 1941

        LOWENSTEIN.   See PRICE, 1967

10796   LOWER.   Some account of the Lower family in America, principally of the descendants of
Adam Lower, who settled in Williamsburg, Pa., in 1779.   Compiled by Rev. Joseph Leaney Lower ...
(Cincinnati, Monfort & co., typographers, 1913)   144 p. incl. front., illus. (part ports.) 20 cm. 13-17675.
                                                                    CS71. L917   1913

10797   LOWJEE.   A memorial of the descendants and representatives of Monackjee Lowjee and
Bomanjee Lowjee, deceased, formerly master builders in the Bombay dock-yard, dated 25th January,
1840; to the Honorable court of directors of the East India company.   With an appendix.   (London,
Printed by J. Wilson, 1840)   1 p. l., 49 p. 22 cm. Signed: Nowrojee Jamsetjee, and others. Relative to the exemption from tax
of the date and brab trees on the Enam estate, granted to the Lowjee family.   17-23923.   CS1209. L7

10798   LOWMAN.   The Lowmans in Chemung county, compiled by Seymour Lowman.   Elmira, N. Y.
(Printed by the Commercial press) 1938 (i. e. 1939)   5 p. l., (13)-237 p. plates, ports., facsims. 24 cm. "Copyright
1939. "   41-5824.   CS71. L918   1938

LOWREY. See LOWRY.

10799   LOWNDES.   Lowndes of South Carolina, and historical and genealogical memoir.   By George B. Chase ... Boston, A. Williams & co., 1876.   1 p. l., 81 p. front. (port.) coat of arms. 25 cm. 9-11601.

CS71. L919   1876

10800   LOWRY.   The history of the two Ulster manors of Finagh, in the county of Tyrone, and Coole, otherwise manor Atkinson, in the county of Fermanagh, and of their owners.   By the Earl of Belmore, M. R. I. A.   London, Longmans, Green & co.: (etc., etc.,) 1881.   xi, 383, (1) p. 22½ cm. 4-2454.

DA990. M46B3

10801   LOWRY.   Historico-genealogical sketch of Col. Thomas Lowrey, and Esther Fleming, his wife.   By Henry Race, M. D.   Flemington, N. J., H. E. Deats, 1892.   16 p. incl. ports. 23½ cm. 10-14372.

CS71. L93   1892

10802   LOWRY.   The history of two Ulster manors and of their owners, by the Earl of Belmore ... Re-issue, rev. and enl.   London, New York (etc.) Longmans, Green, and co.; (etc., etc.) 1903.   iv, (iii)-xiv, 456, iv, 8 p. front., pl., ports., facsims. 22½ cm. "Errata" (1 leaf) mounted on p. (iii) The 1st edition (1881) has title: The history of the two Ulster manors of Finagh, in the county of Tyrone, and Coole, otherwise manor Atkinson, in the county of Fermanagh, and of their owners. 21-1504.

DA990. U46B3 1903

10803   LOWRY.   The Lowrys; Robert and Mary Lowry and their children (six generations) ... (By Lucian Hezekiah Emmett Lowry) (Carlsbad, N. M., Printed in the book and job office of Carlsbad current, 1921)   1 p. l., 2-118 p. incl. facsims. 25 cm. Explanation signed: L. H. E. Lowry. Edited by Houston W. Lowry. 23-18587.

CS71. L93   1921

LOWRY.   See also: CORRY, 1903   ROBINSON, 1907
                      GREER, 1897   SMITH, 189-
                      LAWSON, 1903   WARD, 1940
                      RHEES, 1899   WILSON, 1898a

10804   LOWTHER.   Some notes on the Lowthers who held judicial office in Ireland, in the seventeenth century.   By Sir Edmund T. Bewley ... (Reprinted from the Cumberland and Westmorland antiquarian and archaeological society's Transactions, vol. II - new series.) Kendal, Printed by T. Wilson, 1902.   cover-title, 28, (1) p. pl. 23 cm. 21-19039.   CS499. L6

LOWTHER.   See also YERBURGH, 1912

LOXLEY.   See RHEES, 1899

LOY.   See: SHARP, 1953
              TRESSLER, 1949

LOZIER.   See OUTWATER, 1924

LUBBERTSEN.   See REICHNER, 1918

10805   LUBBOCK.   Notes on the history and genealogy of the family of Lubbock, by Robert Birkbeck, F. S. A.   (London, Mitchell and Hughes, printers) 1891.   4 p. l., 55, (1) p. illus. (facsim.) fold. geneal. tab., col. coats of arms. 22 cm. "Sketch pedigree shewing the descent of Sir John Lubbock, bart.": geneal. tab. 23-14533.

CS439. L855

10806   LUBOLD.   Lubold, Lupold, Leopold, and related families, by Daniel G. Lubold ... (Reading, Pa., E. S. Smtih, printer, 1937?)   2 p. l., 3-22 p., 1 l. 21½ cm. Edited by his children, Helen Lubold Fittro, and William Ralph Lubold. 40-34270.   CS71. L935   1937

10807   LUCAS.   The Lucases of Suffolk.   Extracted from "The visitation of Suffolk," by Joseph Jackson Howard ... Lowestoft, Printed by S. Tymms, 1867.   20 p., 1 l. illus. (coat of arms) 28 cm. 20-18089.

CS439. L86

10808   LUCAS.   Little Saxham parish registers.   Baptisms, marriages, and burials, with append-ices, biographies, &c. 1559 to 1850.   Woodbridge, G. Booth, 1901.   xiv, (2), 264 p. front., illus., 2 pl. 22 x 18 cm.   (Suffolk green books no. v) Preface signed: S.H.A.H. (i.e. Sydenham Henry Augustus Hervey) Contents. - Preface ... (etc.) - Baptisms. - Marriages. - Burials. - Appendix I-XXII. - Lucas family. - Crofts family. - Crofts of Bardwell. - Little Saxham in 1638. - Short notes. - (indices) 5-4688.   CS436.S45

10809   LUCAS.   Lucas genealogy.   Compiled by Annabelle Kemp.   Hollywood, Calif., 1964. viii, 495 p. facsim., port. 24 cm.   65-3403.   CS71.L9355   1964

            LUCAS.   See also: CHANCE, 1892
                                   DE BLOIS, 1950
                                   DODSON, 1959

10810   LUCÉ.   Jean de Lucé family and origin.   In vertical file.   Ask reference librarian for this material.

10811   LUCK.   A pedigree of the families of Luck, and Lock, comp. by Edward John Luck ... London, Printed by the Army & navy co-operative society, ltd., 1900.   46 p. front. (port.) 19½ cm. "Authorit-ies quoted": p.4.   The portrait is a mounted photograph.   Mounted on cover: coat of arms.   21-9655.
                                                                                                    CS439.L865

            LUCK.   See also HALE, 1948

            LÜCK.   In vertical file under PRANKE family.   Ask reference librarian for this material.

            LUCKEN.   See: LUKENS.
                               PASTORIUS, 1926

10812   LUCKENBACH.   Descendants of John Gerradt Luckenbach & Conrad Hawk, 1740-1958.   Com-piled by Helen H. King, Erwin M. King (and) D. Walter Hawk.   Warren, Ohio, Manufactured by Riffle Photography (1958)   100 p. illus., ports., facsims. 25 cm. Cover title: Family history of Lookabaughs and Hawks. Bibliography: p. 71-72.   63-25759.   CS71.L936   1958

            LUCKENBACH.   See also CLEWELL, 1907

            LUCKENBAUGH.   See LUCKENBACH.

10813   LUCKETT.   The Lucketts of Portobacco; a genealogical history of Samuel Luckett, gent., of Port Tobacco, Charles county, Maryland, and some of his descendants, with a sketch of the allied family of Offutt, of Prince Georges county, Maryland, by Harry Wright Newman.   Washington, D.C., The author, 1938.   1 p. l., (v)-viii, 108 p. coat of arms. 24 cm. "This printing was limited to 100 copies." 39-14784.
                                                                                                    CS71.L937   1938

            LUCKETT.   See also SEMMES, 1956

            LUCKEY.   See ARNOLD, 1931

            LUCKYN.   See LUKIN.

10814   LUCY.   Lineal descendants of Major Samuel Kelly Lucy, native of Brunswick county, Virginia, born February 7, 1801 ... died November 2, 1876 ... Compiled by Calvin Tompkins Lucy. (Richmond) 1937.   2 p. l., (3)-47 p. illus. (facsims.) pl., port. 15½ cm. Genealogical table inserted before title-page. Lucy coat of arms in color on cover. 38-32678.   CS71.L94   1937

10815   LUCY.   Charlecote and the Lucys; the chronicle of an English family.   By Alice Fairfax-Lucy.   London, Oxford University Press, 1958.   327 p. illus. 23 cm. 58-4273.   CS439.L866   1958

10816   LUCY.   History and genealogy of the Lucy family in America.   By Gregory Ramsey Lucy. Mountain Home, Ark., W.K.Lucy, c.1959.   205 p. col. coat of arms. 21 cm. 59-31692.
                                                                                                    CS71.L94   1959

LUCY.   See also EYRE, CS459.E96

LUDEMAN.   See CLAYTON, 1960

LUDFORD.   See CHANCE, CS439.C515

10817   LUDINGTON.   The Ludington family, the first of the name in America, by Lewis S. Patrick. Marinette, Wis., The Independent press, 1886.   (4) p.   23 cm.   12-18980.   CS71.L945   1886

10818   LUDINGTON.   William Luddington of Malden, Mass., and East Haven, Conn., and his descendants.   By James Shepard.   Boston, Press of D. Clapp & son, 1904.   13 p.   25 cm.   "Reprinted from New-Eng. historical and genealogical register, for Jan., 1904."   "Register re-prints, series A, no.4."   20-9261.   CS71.L945   1904

10819   LUDINGTON.   Genealogical record of William Luddington, of Malden, Mass., and East Haven, Conn., and his descendants, comp. by H.T.Cory.   May 1916.   (n.p., 1916)   26 1. 28½ cm.   Type-written.   "Part of chapter I - 'Genealogy', of the book 'Colonel Henry Ludington, a memoir' by W.F.Johnson ... cf. Pref.   21-9020.   CS71.L945   1916

10820   LUDINGTON.   Ludington-Saltus records, originally collected by Ethel Saltus Ludington, edited by Louis Effingham de Forest ... (New Haven, The Tuttle, Morehouse & Taylor company) 1925.   287 p. front., plates, ports., facsims., fold. geneal. tables. 24 cm. Contains bibliographies. 26-11995.   CS71.L945   1925

LUDLAM.   See MESSINGER, 1916

10821   LUDLOW. Proceedings at the laying of the corner-stone of the Ludlow and Willink hall of St. Stephen's college, Annandale, N.Y., on Wednesday, June 13, A.D.1866.   Published by order of the trustees.   Cambridge, Printed at the Riverside press, 1866.   2 p. l., (7)-46 p. illus. 22½ cm.   Contents. - Introductory narrative. - Historical notice of St. Stephen's college. - The genealogy of the Ludlow family. - Address by Rev. S.R.Johnson. - Address by Rev. Francis Vinton. 3-24698 rev.   LD331.B56749 1866

10822   LUDLOW.   ... A genealogical history of the Ludlow family.   By N.M.Ludlow.   St. Louis, Riverside printing house, 1884.   32 p. front. (port.) illus. (coat of arms) 22 cm.   Printed for private circulation only.   17-2862.   CS71.L946   1884

10823   LUDLOW.   ... Gabriel Ludlow (1663-1736) and his descendants, by William Seton Gordon ... (New York, 1919)   44 p. front., pl., ports. 26 cm.   Caption title.   "Reprinted from the New York genealogical and biographical record." 20-2616.   CS71.L946   1919

10824   LUDLOW.   The ancestry of Roger Ludlow, with connections to the peerages and royal families of England, Ireland, Scotland, and France.   Including a critical study of the ancestry of Sancha (de Ayala) Blount of Toledo, Spain, by Milton Rubincam.   By Herbert Furman Seversmith.   Chevy Chase, Md., 1958 -   v. 29 cm.   (His Colonial families of Long Island, New York and Connecticut, v.5) 66-54182.   CS71.S499   1944   vol. 5

10825   LUDLOW.   Roger Ludlow (1590-1666) By Herbert F. Seversmith. Reprinted from the N.G.S. Quarterly, vol.51, 1963.   In vertical file.   Ask reference librarian for this material.

10826   LUDLOW.   Genealogical research in medieval English records: a case history, ancestry of Roger Ludlow.   By Herbert S. Seversmith.   In vertical file.   Ask reference librarian for this material.

10827   LUDLOW.   The ancestry of Roger Ludlow, with connections to the peerages and royal families of England, Ireland, Scotland, and France, including a critical study of the ancestry of Sancha (De Ayala) Blount of Toledo, Spain.   By Herbert Furman Seversmith.   Chevy Chase, Md. (n.d.)   2,051-2,248 p. 28 cm.   Issued also as v. 5 of the author's Colonial families of Long Island, New York and Connecticut, and continues the pagination of that work. 62-49060.   CS71.L946

LUDLOW.   See also   CHAMBERS, F497.R59
                    FOWLER, 1888
                    POWELL, 1829

CS71.L954

LUDWELL. See FUNSTEN, 1926

10828 LUDWIG. Ludwig genealogy. Sketch of Joseph Ludwig, who was born in Germany in 1699, and his wife and family, who settled at "Broad Bay," Waldoboro', 1753. By M. R. Ludwig ... Augusta, Kennebec journal, 1866. 223 p. front., pl., port. 21½ cm. 3-7937. CS71.L948 1866

LUDWIG. See also MONNET, 1911

10829 LÜDERS. Annals of two extinct families of the eighteenth century (Von Lüders and Light) with some account of their vicissitudes in Hamburg, Bath, and East Indies, British Guiana, and Canada, by John Alexander Temple ... with twenty-two illustrations (two in colour) and two sheet pedigrees. London, F. U. White & co., ltd., 1910. xii, 152 p. plates, ports., coats of arms (part col.) 2 fold. geneal. tab. 22 cm. 17-29949. CS439.L87

LUGG. See also BASSETT, 1926

10830 LUITWIELER. Genealogy of the Luitwieler family, compiled by Clarence Luitwieler. (Abington, Mass.) 1942. 31 p. incl. front. (port.) 24½ cm. 43-14995. CS71.L952 1942

LUKEN. See LUKENS.

10831 LUKENS. Descendants of John Lukens of Horshan, Montgomery County, Pa. Collated by Theodore Cooper. New York, 1900. geneal. tab. 56 x 71 cm. 4-541. CS71.L954 1900

10832 LUKENS. American ancestors and descendants of Abraham Tennis Lukens. By William Lukens Edwards. (Washington?) 1957. (26) l. 28 cm. 59-41750. CS71.L954 1957

LUKENS. See also: ADAMS, 1963a
HALLOWELL, 1924
LUKIN.
ROBERTS, 1940

10833 LUKER. Luker family historical society newsletter. In vertical file. Ask reference librarian for this material.

10834 LUKIN. The romance of Melusine and de Lusignan together with genealogical notes and pedigrees of Lovekyn of London, Lovekyn of Lovekynsmede, and of Luckyn of Little Waltham, and Lukyn of Mashbery, all in the county of Essex, and of Lukin of Felbrigg, co. Norfolk. Compiled and arranged by Sir Algernon Tudor Tudor-Craig ... London, The Century house, 1932. 3 p. l., vi, 58 p. col. front., illus., pl., ports., col. coats of arms. 26½ cm. On cover: Melusine and the Lukin family. "One hundred and twenty-five copies only have been printed ... This copy is no. 51." 40-21850. CS439.L873 1932

LUKIN. See also LUKENS.

LUKIN-PAGE. See No. 430 - Adventurers of purse and person.

LUKIS. See GUÉRIN, 1890

LUKYN. See LUKIN.

10835 LULL. The Lull book ... compiled by Hilah Violet Eddy. Detroit, Mich., 1926. 84 p. illus. 19 cm. 26-15195. CS71.L955 1926

10836 LUM. Genealogy of the Lum family, compiled by Edward H. Lum ... Somerville, N.J., Unionist-gazette association (c. 1927) 270 p. illus. (coat of arms) 23½ cm. 27-16091. CS71.L957 1927

10837 LUM. Sylvanus Lum family, 1307-1930. Other families: Van de Bogurt, Bean, Gary, Fuller, Paine. (By Elmour Denton Lum. n. p.. 1930) cover-title, 4 p. l., 42, 43a, 44-53, (7) p. ports. 23½ cm. Blank pages throughout text for additions. Preface signed: Elmour D. Lum. "Supplement: The Lum family in England": 2d - 4th prelim. leaves. 33-8510. CS71.L957 1930

LUM. See also CAMP, 1961

LUMAS. See LOOMIS .L863

LUMBERT. See LOMBARD.

LUMISDEN. See LUMSDEN.

10838   LUMLEY. Records of the Lumleys of Lumley castle, by Edith Milner; ed. by Edith Benham. London, G. Bell and sons, 1904. xii, 380 p. incl. geneal. tables. front., pl., 11 port., geneal. tab. 29½ cm. Title in red and black. 5-6758. DA28.35.L8M6

10839   LUMNOR. Mannington hall and its owners. By Charles S. Tomes ... Norwich, Goose & son, ltd., 1916. 2 p. l., 66 p. illus., plates, fold. plans, fold. geneal. tab. 22½ cm. "The history of the manor of Mannington extends back to the period of the Norman conquest, whilst during the 850 years which have since elapsed it has passed through the hands of only four families, the Tyrels, the Lumnors, the Potts and the Walpoles." - p.2. "Arms of some of the families mentioned": p. 64-66. 28-19376. DA664.M3T6

10840   LUMPKIN. The Lumpkin family of Georgia, by L. L. Cody. Macon, Ga., 1928. 63 p. 22½ cm. On cover: Lumpkin lore. "The Cody family of Ireland and America": p. (48)-63. 28-21523. CS71.L958   1928

10841   LUMPKIN. Wilson Lumpkin, governor of Georgia, and his Virginia ancestry, with notes on in-laws of the Lumpkin family of Halifax county, Virginia, including Hendricks, Hurts, Smiths, by George Magruder Battey III ... (Washington, 1944) 1 p. l., 9 numb. l. 28 x 22 cm. Type-written (carbon copy) 44-25014. CS71.L958   1944

10842   LUMPKIN. Ancestors and descendants of Robert Lumpkin and his wife Elizabeth Forrest Lumpkin, compiled by Ira W. Hepperly. Smith Center, Kan., Robert Lumpkin Family Association (1969?) 240 p. illus., facsims. 24 cm. 70-79787. CS71.L958   1969

            LUMPKIN. See: RAND, 1936
                             RAND, 1940
                             WILSON, 1929a

10843   LUMSDEN. Memorials of the families of Lumsdaine, Lumisden or Lumsden, by Lieut-Col. H.W.Lumsden ... Edinburgh, D. Douglas, 1889. x p., 1 l., 116 p. front., illus., plates, ports., facsim., fold. geneal. tab. 26 cm. "Eighty copies printed, of which this is no. 75." 17-2876. CS479.L85

            LUMSDEN. See also STRANGE, NE642.S8D4

            LUNSFORD. See: CLOPTON, 1939
                             LOMAX, 1913

            LUND. See No. 5536 - The sloopers.

10844   LUNDBERG. Lundberg-Thoorsell family genealogy (by John A. Lundberg. Portland, Or.) 1967. 12 l. 29 cm. Cover title. 76-5400 MARC. CS71.L96   1967

10845   LUNDY. The Lundy family and their descendants of whatsoever surname, with a biographical sketch of Benjamin Lundy, by William Clinton Armstrong, A.M. New Brunswick, N.J., J. Heidingsfeld, printer, 1902. 485 p. front., illus., plates, ports., facsim. 24½ cm. 3-22580. CS71.L962   1902

            LUNDY. See also: WILSON, 1959
                             No. 9847 - story of Hackettstown.

            LUNT. See REMINGTON, 1960

10847   LUPFER. A family record (ancestors of Elizabeth Baker Lupfer, Baker, Miller, Dickinson, Melyn, Shellabarger, Morgan, Lupfer) Compiled by Robert N. Lupfer. Springfield, Ohio, 1963. 67, S-10, A-4 l. illus., geneal. tables. 29 cm. Bibliographical footnotes. 78-10751 MARC. CS71.L966   1963

LUPO. See LEWIS, 1960

LUPOLD. See LUBOLD, 1937

LUPTON. See: FOSTER, 1953
            PETTY, BX5195.T5B6

LURIE. See LURIA.

LUSCOMB. See DRIVER, 1889

LUSH. See DICKERSON, 1919

LUSHINGTON. See STORY, 1920

10848   LUSIGNAN. Recital concerning the sweet land of Cyprus, entitled 'Chronicle', edited with a translation and notes by R.M. Dawkins ... Oxford, The Clarendon press, 1932. 2 v. fold. map, fold. geneal. tab. 23 cm. At head of title: Leontios Makhairas. Greek and English on opposite pages. "The text is printed from the Venice manuscript (Class VII, cod. XVI, in the Libreria nazionale, the old Library of St. Mark) with no alterations beyond a very few emendations." - Introductory note, v.1, p. (xv); Introd., v.2, p. (1) "Genealogical tree of the Lusignan kings of Cyprus": fold. leaf at end of v.2. "Bibliographical note": v.2, p. (25) -30. 32-35352.
                                                                        DS54.6.M185

    LUSIGNAN. See also LUKIN, 1932

10849   LUSK. The Lusk family; a record of the ancestors and descendants of Willard Clayton Lusk. (By Alma Victoria (Davies) Lusk. n.p.) 1938. 123 p. incl. illus., ports. 21½ cm. "Largely compiled by Alma Victoria Davies Lusk ... completed and published by ... Martin Willard Lusk." - Dedication. 40-18330.   CS71.L97   1938

    LUSK. See also CORAY, 1968

    LUSS. See CROSSLEY, CS439.C835

10850   LUTER. The Luter-Davis and allied families: Luter-Davis-Burkhalter-Smart-Perkins, and others. By Marie (Luter) Upton. (Madison? Miss.) 1959. 141 p. 27 cm. 60-24618. CS71.L972   1959

10851   LUTHER. The Luther family, devoted to the interests of the descendants of Captain John Luther of the Massachusetts Bay Colony. v.1-6 (no.1-20); July 1945-Apr.1950. (Moravia, N.Y., L.L. and B.K. Luther) 6 v. in 1. ports. 28 cm. quarterly. No more published? Also on microfilm in microfilm reading room. 57-48963.   CS71.L973   1950

10852   LUTHER. The descendants of Captain John Luther, c.1600-1645, of the Massachusetts Bay Colony; a genealogy. By Leslie Leon Luther. Moravia, N.Y., 1952. Microfilm copy of typescript. Made by the Frederic Luther Company, Indianapolis. Positive. Collation of the original, as determined from the film: 1709 l. illus., ports., map, facsim. Mic 56-4276.   Microfilm 4528 CS

    LUTTRELL. See: ARMSTRONG, CS61.A6 vol.1
                     MOHUN, DA690.D85L75
                     MOHUN, DA690.D85L8
                     READ, 1930
                     No. 516 - Notable southern families.

10853   LUTZ. The third reunion of the children of Jacob D. Lutz ... (Circleville, O., 1874) 4 p. 24 cm.   CS71.L975   1874

10854   LUTZ. The Lutz damily of central North Carolina, by Margaret D. Lutes. Boise, Idaho (1969)   32, (65) l. facsims. 30 cm. 70-7674 MARC.   CS71.L975   1969

10855   LUTZ. Lutz family in vertical file. Ask reference assistant for this material.

    LUTZ. See also WALTMAN, 1928

LUVEL.   See YVERY, 1742

10856   LUXMORE.   The family of Luxmoore, by Chas. F. C. Luxmore ... Exeter and London, W. Pollard & co., printers, 1909.   3 p. l., (3)-135 p. front., illus. (incl. facsims.) plates, ports., coats of arms. 32½ cm. Contains also pedigrees of the families of Moore, Cuningham, Coryndon, Parr, Hiern, Lethbridge, Merrifield, Brooke, Bouverie, Sheppard, Logan, Putt, Ommanney, Arscott and Cartwright of Okehampton, Stonehouse, and Carpenter. 21-15208.   CS439. L89

LUYSTER.   See LAWRENCE, 1923

10857   LYBARGER.   A brief history of the Lybarger family, compiled by Donald F. Lybarger ... and Jesse J. Lybarger ... Reading, Penna., 1915.   cover-title, (8) p. 18 cm. 15-15745.   CS71.L98   1915

10858   History of the Lybarger family, by Donald Fisher Lybarger.   Cleveland, O., 1921. 101 p. 21 cm.   Blank pages at end for "Additional records." 21-18199.   CS71.L98   1921

10859   LYBARGER.   History of the Lybarger family.   By Donald Fisher Lybarger.   Cleveland, 1959.   122 l.. 30 cm. 60-43308.   CS71.L98   1959

10860   LYBARGER.   The story of the Dowler-Hartshorn, Fisher-Lybarger families.   Written for Cornelia Marie Lybarger (and others) by their father (Donald Fisher Lybarger) Cleveland, 1938 (i.e.1962)   63 l. geneal. table. 29 cm. 63-1392.   CS69. L9

10861   LYCAN.   Historical and genealogical notes of and about the family Lycan, gathered and written by Harold John Dane, assisted by Gilbert L. Lycan.   (Boca Raton? Fla., 1958)   49 l. 28 cm. 58-40714.   CS71.L982   1958

LYDE.   See AMES, 1889

LYDECKER.   See: ANDERSON, 1916
                                BLAUVELT, 1957

LYELL.   See LILES.

10862   LYFORD.   Francis Lyford of Boston and Exeter, and some of his descendants; by William Lewis Welch ... Salem, Printed for the Essex institute, 1902.   1 p. l., 88 p. 24½ cm. From the Historical collections of the Essex institute, vol. XXXVII and XXXVIII. 3-4170.   CS71.L984   1902

10863   LYLE.   Daniel Lyle, immigrant; one of the Lyle family who emigrated from Ireland to America and settled in the valley of Virginia in 1840 (i.e.1740) By Daniel Lyle.   Peck, Idaho, 1946.   60 p. illus. 23 cm. 65-48677.   CS71.L985   1946

10864   LYLE.   Samuel Lyle, William Lyle, James Ramsey, and John Montgomery, trustees: William McClung, and many alumni; or, The Lyle chapter in the history of Washington and Lee university. By William Henry Ruffner.   (In Washington and Lee university, Lexington, Va. Historical papers. Baltimore, 1892. 23 cm. no. 3, p. 129-167) Caption title. 6-10194.   LD5873.A2 no.3

10865   LYLE.   Lyle family, the ancestry and posterity of Matthew, John, Daniel and Samuel Lyle, pioneer settlers in Virginia ... By Oscar K. Lyle.   New York city, Printed by Lecouver press company, 1912.   2 p. l., (3)-361 p. front. (port.) plates, col. coat of arms. 27½ cm. 13-5631.   CS71.L985   1912

10866   LYLE.   The Lyles of Washington county, Pennsylvania, being an account of the origin, migrations and generations of the family, compiled by Alvin Dinsmore White, with the collaboration of numerous members of the clan ... Carlisle, Pa., Baker & Gussman (1934)   (5)-157 p. incl. ports. front., col. coat of arms. 23 cm. "Printed for private distribution." 38-14724.   CS71.L985   1934

LYLE.   See also: LILES.
                        No. 516 - Notable southern families.

LYLES.   See LILES.

10867   LYMAN.   Genealogies of the Lymans of Middlefield, of the Dickinson of Montreal, and of the Partridges of Hatfield.   Boston, D. Clapp & son, printers, 1865.   29 p., 1 l. incl. geneal. tables. 24½ cm.
Comp. by James Taylor Dickinson.   The "Genealogy of the Partridges of Hatfield" was compiled by S. D. Partridge. 3-486.

CS71. L986   1865

10868   LYMAN.   Lyman anniversary.   Proceedings at the reunion of the Lyman family, held at Mt. Tom and Springfield, Mass., August 30th and 31st, 1871.   Albany, N. Y., J. Munsell, 1871.
59, (1) p. 23½ cm.   Addresses by Hon. Lyman Tremain and Rev. Lyman Coleman, D. D. 9-11600.   CS71. L986   1871

10869   LYMAN.   Genealogy of the Lyman family, in Great Britain and America; the ancestors and descendants of Richard Lyman, from High Ongar in England, 1631.   By Lyman Coleman ... Albany, N. Y., J. Munsell, 1872.   xvi, (9)-533 p. front. (col. coat of arms) ports., fold. geneal. tab. 23 cm. p. 343-344 duplicated.
L. C. COPY REPLACED BY MICROFILM. 10-2213.   CS71. L986   1872
                                                                      Microfilm 1636 CS

10870   LYMAN.   Memoir of the life of Mrs. Anne Jean Lyman ... (By Susan Inches (Lyman) Lesley) Privately printed.   Cambridge, Mass. (Press of J. Wilson & son) 1876.   4 p. l., 543 p. front., plates, ports.
26 cm.   Reprinted in 1899 under title: Recollections of my mother, Mrs. Anne Jean Lyman of Northampton ... by Susan I. Lesley. 17-22135.
CT275. L85L3

10871   LYMAN.   The upright and useful citizen.   A discourse commemorative of Dea. Samuel Lyman, preached in Southampton, Mass., by Rev. Myron A. Munson, January 7, 1877.   Springfield, Mass., Weaver, Shipman and company, printers, 1877.   33 p. 23 cm. 14-1308.   CT275. L853M8

10872   LYMAN.   Recollections of my mother, Mrs, Anne Jean Lyman, of Northampton; being a picture of domestic and social life in New England in the first half of the nineteenth century; by Susan I. Lesley ... Boston and New York, Houghton, Mifflin and company, 1899.   vi, 505, (1) p. front., plates, ports.
21 cm.   Reprint of the author's Memoir of the life of Mrs. Anne Jean Lyman. 0-58 rev.   CT275. L85R3 1899

10873   LYMAN.   A sketch of the record of the descendants of Daniel Lyman and Sally Clapp, of Easthampton, Mass., by Eunice A. Lyman.   Privately published for the family. (Fall River, Mass., The Munroe press, 1923?)   68, (2) p. illus. (incl. ports.) 23 cm. "Corrections": 1 leaf inserted at end. 24-6779.
CS71. L986   1923

10874   LYMAN.   Sketch of Elias Lyman, 3rd., of Hartford, Vermont, by his grand-daughter, Louise Homer Lyman.   (White River Junction, Vt., The Vermonter press, 1925)   3 p. l., 64 p. plates. 21½ cm.
"Reference section": p. 61. Genealogy: p. 62-64. 31-18100.   CT275. L852L8

10875   LYMAN.   Arthur Theodore Lyman and Ella Lyman; letters and journals with an account of those they loved and were descended from, prepared by their daughter, Ella Lyman Cabot. (Menasha, Wis.) Priv. print. (George Banta publishing company) 1932.   3 v. front. (v. 1) plates, ports., map, 2 col. coats
of arms. 23½ cm. 33-8255.   CS71. L986   1932

10876   LYMAN.   A record of the descendants of David Belden Lyman and Sarah Joiner Lyman of Hawaii, 1832-1933.   With some account of their antecedents in America, England and Europe.   Compiled by Ellen Goodale Lyman and Elsie Hart Wilcox.   Honolulu, Hawaii (Honolulu Star-bulletin) 1933.
(7)-94 p. incl. illus., plates, ports., col. coats of arms. front. 24 cm. "Genealogical record" (p. 35-85) printed on one side of leaf only.
A34-637.   CS71. L986   1933

            LYMAN.   See also: COOPER, 1906
                              HOLTON, 1881
                              WANTON, F76. R52 vol. 3
                              WARNER, 1956

            LYME.   See LEE, CS439. L9

10878   LYNCH.   Genealogical memoranda relating to the family of Lynch.   London, Mitchell and Hughes, 1883.   15 p. front. 29½ cm. Reprinted from Miscellanea et heraldica. London, 1874. 27 cm. N. S. v. 4. 10-11538.
CS439. L92

10879   LYNCH.   Lynch record containing biographical sketches of men of the name, Lynch, 16th to 20th century, together with information regarding the origin of the name ... Compiled by Elizabeth C. Lynch.   New York, N.Y., W.J.Hirten co., inc. (c.1925)   154 p. 20½ cm. "List of works consulted": p. 153-154. 37-21348.   CS71.L987   1925

10880   LYNCH.   Lynch: brothers William Lynch (1790?-1840) and Anderson Lynch (12-27-1795/8-28-1863) and their descendants.   By Fannie Belle (Taylor) Richardson.   Greenwood, Ind., 1958.
            110 1. 30 cm. 59-43208.   CS71.L987   1958

10881   LYNCH.   Lynch families of the Southern States; lineages and court records.   By Lois Davidson Hines.   Edited and published by Dorothy Ford Wulfeck.   Naugatuck, Conn., 1966.
v, 373 p. port. 29 cm. 68-2157.   CS71.L987   1966

        LYNCH.   See also BARD, F128.26 v.27

        LYNCHARD.   See HAMLETT, 1958

10882   LYNDE.   The diaries of Benjamin Lynde and of Benjamin Lynde, jr.; with an appendix.   Boston, Priv. print. (Cambridge, Riverside press) 1880.   xvi, 251 p. front., ports., facsim., geneal. tab. 22 cm.
Ed. by Fitch Edward Oliver.   "Family of Lynde": p. (iii)-xvi.   Pedigree of Browne and Lynde.   3-4167.
                                                                                                            F67.L98

        LYNDE.   See also: BOWDOIN, 1887
                             BOWDOIN, 1894
                             McCURDY, 1892

        LYNLEY.   See LINLEY.

10883   LYNN.   A history of a fragment of the clan Linn and a genealogy of the Linn and related families, by Dr. George Wilds Linn ... (Lebanon, Pa., Report print) 1905.   204, (13) p. 3 port. (incl. front.)
22½ cm. 13 blank pages at end, for records of marriages, births and deaths. 6-20341.   CS71.L989   1905

10884   LYNN.   Genealogy of Colonel Andrew Lynn, jr. and Mary Ashercraft Johnson and their descendants, by Eliza B. Lynn ... Uniontown, Pa., The Uniontown printing compay, 1912.   54, 3 p. front.
(mounted fold. facsim.) mounted photos,, mounted ports., fold. geneal. tables, mounted coat of arms. 23½ cm. 12-25212.
                                                                                                            CS71.L989   1912

10885   LYNN.   Genealogical history of the family of William Linn who came from Belfast, Ireland, in 1771, by Margarett Virginia Hull ... Scottdale, Pa., Mennonite publishing house, 1932.   xii, 146 p.
incl. front., illus. (incl. ports., coat of arms) 19¾ cm. 37-38446.   CS71.L989   1932

10886   LYNN.   Descendants of George Linn, by Evangeline Linne Halleck ... (Ann Arbor, Mich., Lithoprinted by Edwards brothers, inc., 1941)   xiii, 220 p. incl. illus. (ports.) facsim.) pl., coat of arms. 24 cm.
41-27340.   CS71.L989   1941

        LYNN.   See also: KIRKPATRICK, 1927
                            MOULTON, 1922

10887   LYON.   Life of General Nathaniel Lyon.   By Ashbel Woodward, M.D.   Hartford, Case, Lockwood & co., 1862.   xii, (13)-360 p. front. (port.) plates, plan. 18½ cm. Genealogy, p. 349-356. 4-6837.
                                                                                                            E467.1.L9W8

10888   LYON.   Lyon of Ogil ... (London, Field & Tuer, printers, 1869?)   1 p. l., 10 p., 1 l., incl. pl.
28½ cm.   Compiled by William Lyon, 10th laird of Ogil.   Caption title.   Seven sheets of additions and corrections in manuscript inserted.   "Copy of a genealogical ms. lent by Walter F. Lyon, esq., London, in January, 1869, the property of Mr. John Lyon ... "   Manuscript note concerning William Lyon who emigrated to America in 1635, is inserted.   10-59.   CS479.L9

10889   LYON.   The Lyons of Cossins and Wester Ogil, cadets of Glamis, by Andrew Ross ... Edinburgh, G. Waterston & son, 1901.   6 p. l., 150 p. 26 cm. 15-23253.   CS479.L9   1901

GENEALOGIES IN THE LIBRARY OF CONGRESS

10890   LYON.   Lyon memorial.   Massachusetts families, including descendants of the immigrants
William Lyon, of Roxbury, Peter Lyon, of Dorchester, George Lyon, of Dorchester, with introd.
treating of the English ancestry of the American families.   Editors: A. B. Lyon(s), G. W. A. Lyon.
Associate editor: Eugene F. McPike.   Detroit, W. Graham Print. Co., 1905.   491 p. illus., ports. 21 cm.
Editor's copy; holograph material, clippings, etc., inserted, additions and corrections in ms.   the 1st vol. of the Lyon memorial, the 2d of which
is Families of Connecticut and New Jersey, edited by S. E. Lyon, and the 3d of which is New York families, edited by R. B. Miller.   6-1360 rev. *
                                                                                                CS71. L99   1905

10891   LYON.   Lyon memorial.   Families of Connecticut and New Jersey, including records of the
descendants of the immigrants, Richard Lyon, of Fairfield, Henry Lyon, of Fairfield, with a sketch of
"Lyons farms" by S. R. Winans, jr.   Illustrated with maps.   Editor: Sidney Elizabeth Lyon ... associate editors, Louise Lyon Johnson ... A. B. Lyons ... Detroit, Mich., W. Graham printing co., 1907.
1 p. l., (5)-453 p. illus. (maps) plates, ports., plan. 21 cm. Lettered: Lyon memorial **. 7-30467 rev.
                                                                                                CS71. L99   1907

10892   LYON.   Lyon memorial.   New York families descended from the immigrant Thomas Lyon,
of Rye, with introductory chapter by Dr. G. W. A. Lyon on the English Lyon families; with maps and
facsimile reproduction of interesting ancient manuscripts.   Editor: Robert B. Miller ... associate
editor: A. B. Lyons ... Detroit, Mich., Press of W. Graham printing co., 1907.   1 p. l., (5)-539 p. illus.,
plates, ports., fold. facsims. 21½ cm. Lettered: Lyon memorial *** 8-17282.   CS71. L99   1907a

10893   LYON.   William Penn Lyon, by Clara Lyon Hayes.   (Madison) State historical society of
Wisconsin, 1926.   6 p. l., (7)-210 p. front., ports. 26 cm. "Five hundred copies printed." First published in serial form in v. 9 of the
Wisconsin magazine of history.   cf. Foreword.   "Part II. Illustrative documents": p. (95)-210. 27-18747.
                                                                                                LAW.

10894   LYON.   In memoriam.   (By Louise Antoinette (Lyon) Johnson.   Minneapolis? 1928)
cover-title, 40 numb. l. illus. (incl. ports.) 31 cm.   The illustrations are photographs.   Dedication: To the memory of Walter Lyon and his
wife Maria Antoinette (Giddings) Lyon, by their daughter Louise Antoinette (Lyon) Johnson ... Aprtil, 1928.   Descendants of Walter Lyon and his
wife. 29-12049.
                                                                                                CS71. L99   1928

10895   LYON.   Lyon, Wells, Shurtlett, Fairfield, Thurber, Wardwell families.   Assembled by
Eugene Farifield MacPike ... Chicago, 1934.   43 l. 7 port. (incl. front.) 3 facsim. 30 cm.   Photostat (positive) Includes
letters, magazine articles, etc. 34-10426.   CS71. L99   1934

10896   LYON.   The Hiram Wesley Lyons family.   A memorial.   By A. W. Lyons.   Salt Lake City,
Utah (Printed by the Western hotel register company) 1943.   208 p. incl. illus., plates, ports. 21 cm. 44-30849.
                                                                                                CS71. L99   1943

            LYON.   See also: DOBYNS, 1908   PAGE, 1953
                                McPIKE, 1930   WASHINGTON, CS69. W5 vol. 2
                                MERRILL, 1949   No. 1547 - Cabell county.
                                MESSINGER, 1934

            LYONS.   See LYON.

10897   LYTE.   Lytes Cary manor house, Somerset, and its literary association; with notices of
authors of the Lyte family, from Queen Elizabeth to the present time.   By William George.   Bristol
(Eng.) W. George (1879)   14 p. front., phot. 23½ cm. 3-13435.   DA664. L8G5

10898   LYTE.   The Lytes of Lytescary, by H. C. Maxwell Lyte, C. B., with a description of Lytescary by Edmund Buckle, M. A.   Yaunton, Printed by Barnicott & Pearce, 1895.   2 p. l., 127 p. illus. (incl.
facsim., coats of arms) plates, plans, fold. geneal. tab. 25 cm.   Title vignette: coat of arms.   "Reprinted from Proceedints of the Somersetshire archaeological and natural history society, vol. XXXVIII, with addenda and index. 21-21735.   CS439. L925

10899   LYTLE.   Descendants of Thomas Lytle ... and Polly (Mary) Wilson ... by Herschel B.
Rochelle ... Battle Creek, Mich., 1943.   geneal. tab. illus. (incl. ports., coats of arms) 20½ x 25½ cm.   Photostat reproduction (positive) 44-1906.   CS71. L777   1943

LYTLE.   See also: LITTLE.
                    WALTMAN, 1928

10900   LYTTELTON.   Descriptive catalogue of the charters & muniments of the Lyttelton family in the possession of the Rt. Hon. Viscount Cobham, at Hagley hall, Worcestershire.   Comp. with introduction, notes, and index, by Isaac Herbert Jeayes.   London, C.J. Clark, 1893.   xvi, 154 p. 26 cm.
Running title: The Lyttelton charters.   21-19044.   CS439.L93

10901   LYTTELTON.   Chronicles of the eighteenth century, founded on the correspondence of Sir Thomas Lyttelton and his family, by Maud Wyndham ... London, Hodder and Stoughton, limited, 1924.
2 v. pl., ports., plans.   23 cm.   Bibliography: v.1, p. viii-ix.   24-18776.   DA483.L8L4

M

MAAR. See MARR.

10902   MABERRY.   The Maberry Clan.   By Lois Glenn Maberry Willingham.   Dallas, Tex. (1969?)
155 p. illus., ports. 29 cm. 72-7116 MARC.   CS71.M105   1969

10903   McADAMS.   Some ancestors of Eugene Perrot McAdams and Mary Elizabeth Pope McAdams
of Hawesville, Kentucky, edited by Pope McAdams.   Shively, Ky., Mimeographed by Lockard letter
shop, 1936.   (443) p. incl. illus., coats of arms. ports. 28 cm. "Sources of information" at end of most of the chapters. 40-8609.
                                                                                       CS71.M11   1936

10904   McADAMS.   William Rufus McAdams family history;   other family names included:
Hutchinson and Tutor.   By Mrs. H. M. McAdams.   Hobbs, N.M., 1960 (i.e. 1961) 6 l. illus. 29 cm.
63-6217.   CS71.M11   1961

McADOO.   See No. 516 - Notable southern families.   vol. 1

McADORY.   See PRUDE, 1939

10905   McAFEE.   ... The McAfee-Skiles-Liebmann memorial;   the history of the lives and times of
three American soldiers and their families and connections ... By August George Liebmann.   Chicago,
Ill., A.G. Liebmann, c. 1929.   3 p. l., 93, (7) p., 1 l. front. (port.) illus. (incl. maps, facsim.) 23½ cm. At head of title: (For
private circulation only) "First edition limited to five hundred copies." "Compiled by the private research of August George Liebmann."
Bibliography: p. 91-92. 29-18039.   CS71.M112   1929

McAFEE.   See also: AMES, 1959
                      WOODS, 1905   (addenda)

10906   McALEER.   A study in the origin and signification of the surname McAleer and a contirbution
to McAleer genealogy.   Comp. ... by George McAleer, M.D.   Worcester, Mass., G. McAleer, 1909.
103 p. 2 port. (incl. front.) fold. geneal. tab. (in pocket) 23 cm. 9-14498.   CS71.M113   1909

McALISTER.   See McALLISTER.

10907   McALLISTER.   Descendants of Archibald McAllister, of West Pennsboro township, Cumberland county, Pa.   1730-1898.   By Mary Catharine McAllister.   Harrisburg, Pa., Scheffer's printing
and bookbinding house, 1898.   85, 93, (14) p. 2 mounted phot. (incl. front.) 25 cm. 98-1586 rev.
                                                                                       CS71.M114   1898

10908   McALLISTER.   Genealogical record of the descendants of Col. Alexander McAllister, of
Cumberland County, N.C.;   also of Mary and Isabella McAllister.   By Rev. D.S. McAllister.   Richmond, Va., Whittet & Shepperson, 1900.   244 p. front. (port.) coats of arms. 19½ cm. Jan 10, 1901-58.
                                                                                       CS71.M114   1900

10909   McALLISTER.   Family records, comp. for the descendants of Abraham Addams McAllister
and his wife Julia Ellen (Stratton) McAllister, of Covington, Virginia, containing a sketch of A. A.
McAllister, prepared and published by the conspiracy and co-operation of his sons, and related data,
which will answer some of the questions our grandchildren are sure to ask, by J. Gray McAllister.
(Easton, Pa., Press of the Chemical publishing company) 1912.   88 p. front., illus. (incl.. ports., facsims.)
23½ cm. 16-5068.   CS71.M114   1912

10910   McALLISTER.   The Clan McAllister; family centenary, 1852-1952.   (n. p., 1952?)
30 p. illus. 22 cm. 55-19917.   CS71.M114   1952

McALLISTER.   See also MACMILLAN, CS477.K6M3

McALPIN.   See LAWSON, 1903

10911   McAMIS.   Notes on the McAmis, Johnson, Register (and) Rankin families.   By Robert F.
McAmis.   (n. p.) 1948.   7 l. 28 cm.   Typewritten (carbon copy) 50-21399.   CS71.M115   1948

10912   McARTHUR.   McArthur family record.   Columbus, Ga., Gilbert printing co., 1911.
vii, 95 p. front., ports. 17 cm.   Introduction signed: Thomas Eugene Sikes. 27-25027.   CS71.M116   1911

10913   MacARTHUR.   Story and who's who of the MacArthur family.   By Edith Tunnell.   (New
York) 1946.   10 l. map. 30 cm.   Title from label mounted on cover. 48-16647*.   CS71.M116   1946

10914   McARTHUR.   McArthur-Barnes ancestral lines.   By Selim Walker McArthur.   Portland,
Me., Anthoensen Press, 1964.   vii, 221 p. 26 cm. 65-6807.   CS71.M116   1964

10915   MacARTHUR.   MacArthur family in vertical file.   Ask reference librarian for this material.

McARTHUR.   See also ANDERSON, 190-

10916   MACAULAY.   ... Memoirs of the clan "Aulay" with recent notes of interest, extracted from
public sources and family papers.   Carmarthen, W. J. Morgan, "Welshman" printing and publishing
offices, 1881.   5 p. l., 264 p. 25½ cm.   "Printed strictly for private circulation."   Edited by Joseph Babington Macaulay.   Contents. -
book I. Memoirs. - book II. Recollections by a sister of T. B. Macaulay. 24-1367.

CS479.M15

10917   MACAULAY.   Ardincaple castle and its lairds, by Edward Randolph Welles.   Glasgow,
Jackson, Wylie & co., 1930.   x p., 3 l., 200, (2) p. front., plates, fold. map, fold. plan. 26 cm.   Each plates accompanied by
guard sheet with descriptive letterpress.   "Two hundred and fifty copies of this book have been printed." 30-22855.

DA890.A55W4

MACAUSLANE.   See McCAUSLAND.

10918   MACBETH.   An abstract of a genealogical collection, by Malcolm Macbeth ... Vol. 1.   St.
Louis (Printed by Nixon-Jones printing co.) 1907 -   1 v. illus. (facsims.) ports. 26½ cm.   Cover-title.
CA9-1632.   CS71.M118   1907

McBETH.   See MAGINET, 1961

10919   MACBRAIRE.   The Brier family; a collection of data tracing this family from its earliest
beginnings in Dumfriesshire, Scotland to the present day in the New World.   Ed. Charles Templeton
Brier.   Sacramento, Calif., 1956.   ii, 106 p. illus., ports., fold. map coats of arms, facsims., geneal. tables. 28 cm.
57-44901.   CS71.M1186   1956

McBRAYER.   See ROBERTS, 1960

McBRIDE.   See HOGG, 1921

10920   McBRIER.   Genealogy of the descendants of Henry McBrier and Kezia Sloan McBrier who
migrated to the United States in 1827, by Edwin Merton McBrier ... (New York?) Priv. print., 1941.
xxviii, 284 p. incl. illus., ports., facsims. col. front. (coat of arms) 25 cm.   Part II has special t.-p.: The origin of the 5 and 10 cent store
... Brief historical sketches of Frank Winfield Woolworth, Charles Sumner Woolworth, Seymour Horace Knox ... 42-3726.

CS71.M1188   1941

10921   MACBRYDE.   MacBryde (McBryde - Macbride) of Auchinnie, parish of Port Montgomerie
(Portpatrick) co. of Wigton, Galloway, Scotland ... Genealogy by David Caldwell MacBryde, chart by
Genealogical bureau of Virginia.   Richmond, Va., 1931.   geneal. chart. illus. (coats of arms) 53 x 43 cm.
31-33661.   CS71.M119   1931

10922   MACBRYDE.   ... A McBride chronology, with a perspective view of the findings, a series of notices on "McBride" from the public records of early Virginia and Kentucky, chronologically arranged, with an interpretation of their evidence.   A preliminary survey of McBride records, by Ben F. Dixon ..   Washington, D.C., 1941.   3 p. l., 11 numb. l. 27 cm.   Type-written.   Bibliography: leaf 1.   42-4311.

CS71.M119   1941

10923   MACBRYDE.   The story of James McBride of Whitehall, Illinois; a report of a genealogical search undertaken for Coral Joyce McBride.   By Robert Abner Love.   (Arlington, Va., 1949)   20, 47 l. 35 cm.   Typewritten (carbon copy)   "Some sources of information found in the report": leaves 46-47.   49-52812 rev. *.

CS71.M119   1949

McBRYDE.   See MACBRYDE.

McCABE.   See JENNINGS, 1899

10924   McCAHAN.   Burdsall, Shull, McCahan, Stockton and allied family histories; genealogical and biographical.   Compiled under the direction of Thomas H. Bateman.   New York, National Americana Publications, 1952.   2 v. (804 p.) plates, ports., col. coats of arms, facsims., col. geneal. tables.   36 cm.   Includes bibliographies.   53-1575.

CS71.M12   1952

10925   McCALL.   One branch of the family tree of the McCall family.   Descendants of James and Anna McCall, of Marshfield, Mass.   By A. J. McCall.   Bath, N. Y., Underhill, printer, 1884.   geneal. tab.   27½ x 21½ cm. fold. to 21½ x 14 cm.   10-8907.

CS71.M122   1884

10926   McCALL.   Memoirs of my ancestors.   A collection of genealogical memoranda respecting several old Scottish families.   With an appendix consisting of a genealogy of the McCall family.   By Hardy Bertram McCall.   Birmingham, Priv. print. by Watson & Hall, 1884.   6 p. l., 119 p. front., 2 col. pl. coats of arms) fold. geneal. tab.   28½ cm.   "One hundred and fifty copies of this work are printed for private circulation, of which this is no. 53."   Contains genealogies of the Adam, Liston, Scott, Hardie, Halkerston and Young families.   Inserted at end are 2 leaves, 39½ x 25½ cm, containing reproduction of t.-p. of the New Testament of 1707, with three pages of ms. notes relating to the family.   12-31626.   CS479.M17

10927   McCALL.   Some old families: a contribution to the genealogical history of Scotland, with an appendix of illustrative documents by H. B. McCall ... Birmingham, Printed for private circulation, Watson & Ball, 1890.   xxvii, (1), 290 p., 1 l., lxiii, (1) p. front., illus., plates, ports., fold. geneal. tables, facsims. (part double) coats of arms.   29 cm.   Added t.-p., engr.   The plates are engraved by Geo. Bailey and J. B. Obernetter.   "Impression: one hundred copies of which this is no. 34."   The ancestry of Vida Mary McCall.   Includes the Allan, Dalrymple, Halkerston, Hardy, Liston, Orr, Ranken, Scott, Wilkie and Young families.   List of authorities: p. xx.   25-5044.

CS478.M15

10928   McCALL.   McCall-Tidwell and allied families, compiled by Ettie Tidwell McCall ... Atlanta, Ga., The author, 1931.   ix, 663 p. illus., col. coats of arms.   24 cm.   Allied families: Hale, Judson, Shelton, Benedict, Coates and others.   Includes "References".   31-16767.

CS71.M122   1931

10929   McCALL.   A short history of the Mackall family of Calvert co., Md. ... by ... Louis C. Mackall ... Garden City, N.Y., c.1946.   52 (i. e. 58) numb. l. incl. illus., coat of arms.   31 x 23½ cm.   Includes extra numbered leaves.   Reproduced from type-written copy.   46-16740.

CS71.M1525   1946

McCALL.   See also: HOWE, 1960   PATE, 19 -
                    McCONNELL, 19 -   WINGFIELD, 1958

10930   McCALLUM.   McCallums; Daniel McCallum, Isabel Sellars, their antecedents, descendants and collateral relatives, a compilation by Louis Farrell ... (and) Flora Janie Hamer Hooker ... (Nashville) Pub. by the compilers for private distribution, 1946.   234 p. illus. (coat of arms) plates, ports. 23½ cm.   47-15733 rev.

CS71.M1224   1946

MACCALLUM-MORE.   See ARGYLL.

10931   McCAMPBELL.   Samuel Shannon McCampbell, Sarah Prudence Smith McCampbell, ancestors and descendants, by Nellie Pearl McCampbell assisted by Marian W. McCampbell (and) David Babelay.   Knoxville, Tenn., 1965.   166 l. illus., facsims., ports. 29 cm.   68-5169.   CS71.M12445 1965

McCAMPBELL.   See also IRVINE, 1916

10932   McCANDLESS.   The McCandless families of Center and Franklin townships, Butler County, Pennsylvania, 1929.   Compiled by Olive Jane McCandless Morgan.   (Bridgeville, Pa., c. 1929)
95 p. 23½ cm. The Fish family: p. (9)-15. 29-19078.   CS71.M1225   1929

10933   McCANDLISH.   McCandlish-Black family history, compiled by Elisabeth Black.   Worthington, O. (c. 1935)   160, (45) p. 22 cm. "The genealogical history of William McCandlish, of County Ayr, Scotland, and his descendants, and also ... of William Black, of Ballymoney, County Antrim, Ireland, and his descendants." - Pref.   35-14531.
CS71.M1227   1935

10934   McCANN.   McCann-Alley (genealogy) Descendants of Thomas N. & Margaret N. (Alley) McCann of Nantucket & Randolph, Mass., with ancestral record of Margaret Nuns Alley (including notices on allied lines of Alley, Butler, Hood, Ingalls, Fisher) By Kenneth Sutherland McCann.
(Glen Burnie, Md.) 1954.   70 l. illus. 28 cm. 55-30542.   CS71.M1228   1954

10935   McCANN.   McCann-Gilman (genealogy) an account of the family of Thomas Nash & Sarah Elizabeth Gilman McCann and their descendants.   By Kenneth Sutherland McCann.   (Glen Burnie, Md.)
1954.   92 l. ports. 28 cm. "Genealogy of Niels A. N. & Karen S.(Andersen) Bruns. showing descent of Anna Marie (Bruns) McCann, being Supplement no. 2 (revised) to McCann-Gilman genealogy, 1954. Glen Burnie, Md., 1963" (55-70 l.) supersedes and replaces old pages 55-70. "Notes, additions & corrections (1963)" (vi-xv l.) inserted after leaf v. "Complete index" (14 l.) inserted at end. 55-30540 rev.
CS71.M1228 1954a

10936   McCANN.   Some descendants of John Keand of Whithorn, Scotland, many of whom lived and died in Paris, Bourbon County, Kentucky, and were known as McCanns (by W. R. & R. L. McCann. n. p., 1955?)   1 v. illus. 30 cm. 57-40151.   CS71.M1228   1955

10937   McCANN.   Family of Wesley D. McCann; Bourbon County, Kentucky; Adams County, Illinois. With index. (By R. Lee McCann amd William R. McCann. Hopewell? Va., 1962?)   12 p. 29 cm. 64-56617.
CS71.M1228   1962

10938   McCANN.   Family of Eliza R. McCann who married Lytle Griffing; Bourbon County, Kentucky; Adams County, Illinois. With index. (By Robert Lee McCann and William Ray McCann. Hopewell? Va., 1963?)   75 p. geneal. table. 28 cm. 64-56540.   CS71.M1228   1963

10939   McCANN.   Ancestral lineage: Mildred Olive Bates McCann, Adair County, Iowa; Prince George County, Virginia. Wiht index. (By Virginia Wilhelm Graham and William Ray McCann. Hopewell?, Va., 1964)   32, (13) p. 28 cm. Includes reproduction (p. (33) - (43)) of The Shaker harvest in Kentucky, by R. J. Randles from the Filson Club history quarterly, v. 37, 1963, p. (38)-57. Bibliographical footnotes. 64-56539.
CS71.M1228   1964

10940   McCARTHY.   A historical pedigree of the Sliochd Feidhlimidh the MacCarthys of Gleannacroim, from Carthach, twenty-fourth in descent from Oilioll Olum, this day, by Daniel MacCarthy (Glas) ... Exeter, Printed for the author by W. Pollard (1880?)   4 p. l., xv, 216 p. 23 cm. 16-18075.
CS499.M15

10941   MACCARTHY.   The McCarthys in early American history, by Michael J. O'Brien ... New York, Dodd, Mead and company, 1921.   xxii p., 2 l., 322 p. front. (col. coat of arms) 21½ cm. Bibliographical footnotes. 21-4322.   CS71.M123   1921

10942   MACCARTHY.   The MacCarthys of Munster; the story of a great Irish sept, by Samuel Trant McCarthy ... Dundalk, The Dundalgan press, 1922.   4 p. l., 399 p. front., plates, ports., maps, geneal. tables. 19 cm. "Authorities": 1 p. preceding p. (1) 24-10833.   DA916.3.M12M3

10943   MACCARTHY.   Gleanings from Irish history, by William F. T. Butler ... with 9 maps and a pedigree. London, New York (etc.) Longmans, Green and co., 1925.   xv, 335 p., 1 l. IX maps (1 fold.) fold. geneal. tab. 22½ cm. "Sources for the lordship of MacCarthy Mor": p. (297) Contents. - The lordship of MacCarthy Mor. - The lordship of MacCarthy Reagh. - The policy of surrender and regrant. - The Cromwellian confiscation in Muskerry. 25-25300.   DA905.B8

10944   McCARTHY.   Work and play, the ancestry and experience of Richard Justin McCarty. (Kansas City, Mo., Press of Joseph D. Havens co., c. 1925)   2 p. l., 253 p. ports. (incl. front.) 20 cm. 26-1191.
CT275. M35A3

10945   MACCARTHY.   Work and play: an autobiography; the ancestry and experience of Richard Justin McCarty, 1851-1934 ... (Kansas City, Mo., Press of Empire printing co., 1934?)   3 p. l., 273 p. front., ports. 20 cm. The first edition appeared in 1925. 36-7199.
CT275. M35A3   1934

10946   McCARTHY.   Garrett county history of the McCarty family, by Charles E. Hoye.   (Oakland? Md., 1935?)   1 l. 47 cm.   Accompanied by portrait of "The McCarty's." 38M1253T.
CS71. M123   1935

10947   McCARTNEY.   The family of Charles McCartney of Madison County, Alabama, in Madison County by 1809.   By Mary Bivins Geron Countess.   (Huntsville? Ala., 196 -)   12 l. 28 cm. Bibliographical footnotes. 68-1767.
CS71. M1235

   MACCARTHY.   See also: JOHNSON, 1938
                           LANCASTER, 1902

   McCARTY.   See: BEAL, 1956
                    DAY, 1916
                    McCARTHY.

   McCARVER.   See CONKLING, 1909

   McCASKIE.   See CASKIE.

   McCAUGHEY.   See JACKSON, 189-

10948   McCAUSLAND.   The McCauslands of Donaghanie and allied families.   (Compiled by Miss) Marvin.   (Shenandoah? Ia., 1911)   66, (36) p incl. illus., ports., map. 23½ cm. Title on cover. Pages (8-36) at end, left blank for "Family record." 12-4938.
CS71. M124   1911

   MACCAUSLAND.   See CROSSLEY, CS439. C835

10949   MACEO.   La familia Maceo.   Carta a Elena.   Conversaciones patrioticas al calor del hogar, por la dra.   Maria Julia de Lara Mena ... La Habana, Editorial selecta (1945)   141 p., 1 l. illus. (facsim.) 2 col. port. 20½ cm. On cover: 1845 - centenario de Maceo - 1945. " 'Los ancianitos.' Ejercicios" (music for physcial exercises): p. 58. "Bibliografia": p. (135) A 46-5664.
F1755. M3L3

10950   McCHESNEY.   Family tree of David and John McChesney, by W. H. McChesney.   (New Orleans, 1903)   19 p. 15 cm. Caption title. 12-34876.
CS71. M125   1903

   McCHESNEY.   See also PORTER, 1897

10951   McCHORD.   The McChords of Kentucky and some related families: the Hynes, Caldwell, Wickliffe, Hardin, McElroy, Shuck and Irvine families (by) J. H. McChord ... Louisville, Ky. (Printed by Westerfield-Bonte co.) 1941.   cover-title, ii p., 1 l., 56 p. 23 cm. 42-5162.
CS71. M1255   1941

   McCLAIN.   See: CRAIG, 1960
                    WASHINGTON, 1932

10952   McCLANAHAN.   The McClanahans.   (Roanoke, Va.) The Stone printing and manufacturing company, 1894)   43 p. fold. geneal. tab. 15½ cm. Pref. signed: H. M. White. 8-2766.
CS71. M126   1894

   McCLANAHAN.   See also SAMPSON, 1922

McCLAREN.   See MARBLE, 1959

McCLARTY.   See GLASSELL, F225.H41

10953   McCLARY.   A sketch covering four generaions of the McClary family.   Beginning with the immigration of Andrew McClary from Ulster in 1726, and ending with the death of Andrew McClary, of Peacham, Vt., in 1869.   (By Horace P. McClary.   Windsor, Vt., 1896)   cover-title, 35, (1) p. 23½ cm.
9-17612.   CS71.M127   1896
          Copy 2.   52 p. illus. 23½ cm.   "The Smith family": p. (43)-52.   27-15869.   CS71.M127   1896a

10954   McCLAUGHRY.   Genealogy of the MacClaughry family; a Scoto-Irish family, originally from Galloway, Scotland, appearing in Ireland about 1600, and emigrants to New York in 1765.   Comp. by Charles C. McClaughry ... Anamosa, Ia., 1913.   7 p. l., 462 p. coats of arms. 24 cm. Pages 445-462 left blank for
"Additional genealogical data."   Contains also the Savage, Clark, Leal, Douglas, Rose, Riggs, Spence, Madden, Struthers, Swift, Montgomery, Hume and Parish families.   21-16579.   CS71.M1275   1913

          McCLEARY.   See: HAYNES, 1940
                            McCLARY.

          McCLEES.   See LOWE, 1939

10955   McCLELLAN   Descendants of William Brownlow McClellan.   By Aubrey Lester McClellan.
Shreveport, La.   (1946)   26 p. 30 cm. 63-51251.   CS71.M12786

10956   McCLELLAN.   Descendants of William Brownlow McClellan.   By Aubrey Lester McClellan.
2d ed.   Wolfe City, Tex., Printed by Henington Pub. Co., 1966.   109 p. illus., ports. 23 cm. 67-3239.
                                                                                 CS71.M12786   1966

          McCLELLAN.   See also: DOUGLAS, DA758.3 A1T2
                                  WATTS, 1947

          McCLELLAND.   See McCLELLAN.

10957   McCLENAHAN.   The John McClenahan folk, by Johh McClenahan Henderson.   Pittsburgh,
Pa., The United Presbyterian board of publication, 1912.   vi p., 1 l., 125 p. ports. 20 cm. 37-16851.
                                                                                 CS71.M1279   1912

10958   McCLENAHEN.   The McClenahen family (with some Dorman notes)   By Raymond Martin Bell.
Washington, Pa., 1963.   9 l. 28 cm. Cover title. 64-2295.   CS71.M12794 1963

10959   McCLESKEY.   McCleskey-Robinson descendents (by) George F. and Marian Housley Bott.
1st ed.   Alameda, Calif., 1968.   51 l. 28 cm. Includes bibliographical references. 77-10436 MARC.
                                                                                 CS71.M12795 1968

          McCLINTOCK.   See McKEE, 1900

10960   McCLOUD.   (Genealogy of the McCollum and allied families.   By Charles Leroy McCollum.
Richland Center, Wis., 1936)   60 l. 28½ cm. Preface signed: C. L. McCollum. Part type-written and part mimeographed. Blank
leaves throughout text.   Includes the Krouskop, McCloud and Kingsbury families.   37-7875.   CS71.M1286   1936

10961   McCLOUD.   A charted history of the Thomas McCloud family in America.   By Nellie Wallace
Reeser.   (Indianapolis? 1968 or 9)   306 p. 24 x 36 cm. 76-3063 MARC.   CS71.M12796 1968

          McCLOUD.   See also McCOLLUM, 1936

          McCLUNG.   See McELREATH, 1941

10962   McCLURE.   Diary of David McCLURE, doctor of divinity, 1748-1820, with notes by Franklin B. Dexter, M.A.   Privately printed.   New York, The Knickernocker press, 1899.   2 p. l., iii-vi p., 1 l., 219 p.   front. (port.) 25½ cm.   "Of this limited letterpress edition, two hundred and fifty copies have been printed for William Richmond Peters."   11-19495.

F516.M165

10963   McCLURE.   The McClure family.   By James Alexander McClure.   Limited ed.   Petersburg, Va., Presses of F.A. Owen, 1914.   2 p. l., 232 p.   front., pl., ports. 24 cm.   The appendix contains an account of the Alexander, Baxter, Bumgardner, Mitchel, McCown, Pilson, Draper, Ingles, Gilkeson, Humphreys, Steele, Tate, and Wallace families: p. 184-220.   15-18263.

CS71.M1285   1914

10964   McCLURE.   McClure family records.   An account of the first American settlers and colonial families of the name of McClure, and other genealogical and historical data, mostly new and original material, including early wills and marriages, heretofore unpublished.   By William M. Clemens.   Limited ed.   New York, W.M. Clemens, 1914.   13 p. 22½ cm.   15-19443.

CS71.M1285   1914a

10965   McCLURE.   Pioneer McClure families of the Monongahela valley, their origins and their descendants, by Cicero Pangburn McClure and Roy Fleming McClure.   (Akron, O., Press of the Superior printing co., 1924)   171 p. front., pl. 19½ cm.   Title-vignette: coat of arms of "Macleod".   35-28843.

CS71.M1285   1924

10966   McCLURE.   The McClures, the Kennedys, the Tennants, the Gays, compiled by Mable B. McClure.   Enid, Okla., Baer's printery, 1934.   71. (2) p. incl. front. (coat of arms) illus. (incl. ports.) 20½ cm.   On cover: The McClure clan.   34-8484.

CS71.M1285   1934

10967   McCLURE.   Archibald McClure and Elizabeth Craigmiles, his wife.   Notes regarding their ancestors and a record of the descendants of their sons James and Archibald McClure.   (New York, N.Y., Press of B. H. Tyrrel) 1938.   2 p. l., 38 p. 25 cm.   Blank pages for "Memoranda" (33-36) 38-36176.

CS71.M1285   1938

10968   McClure.   The McClure family of the line from Richard McClure, sr. ... (By George Ross McClure) (McPherson, Kan., 1938)   1 p. l., 6 numb. l. 35 x 21½ cm.   Caption title.   Mimeographed.   "Secured and printed by G. R. McClure."   Additions in manuscript to 1939.   41-1459.

CS71.M1285   1938a

10969   McCLURE.   McClure (McLure) family of Kentucky.   By Emma Rouse Lloyd.   (Available for consultation at Lloyd library, 309 West Court Street, Cincinnati 2, Ohio)

            McCLURE.   See also: CLEEK, 1957
                                    CLOUD, 1965
                                    PECK, 1955
                                    ROUSE, 1932
                                    ZORBAUGH, 1941

        McCOLLEY.   See HART, 1923

10970   McCOLLUM.   (Genealogy of the McCollum and allied families.   (By Charles Leroy McCollum) Richland Center, Wis., 1936)   60 l. 28½ cm.   Preface signed: C.L. McCollum.   Part type-written and part mimeographed.   Blank leaves throughout text.   Includes the Krouskop, McCloud and Kingsbury families.   37-7875.

CS71.M1286   1936

10971   McCOMAS.   The McComas saga; a family history down to the year 1950, compiled by Henry Clay McComas, assisted by Mary Winona McComas.   (n. p., 1950)   1 v. (unpaged) coats of arms (part col.) photos.   30 cm.   "The McComas tartan" (sample) and 4 envelopes, containing photo-copies of wills, inventories, etc., of Daniel Macomus, Alexander, Daniel, John, and William Maccomas, in pockets.   51-24209.

CS71.M12864   1950

        McCOMAS.   See also No. 1547 - Cabell county.

10972   McCOMB.   A genealogical register of the McComb family in America, comp. from records furnished by the individual families, and public records, etc.   By P.H.K.McComb.   Indianapolis, Ind., 1913.   121 p. illus. (coat of arms) 23½ cm.   21-2417.

CS71.M1287   1913

10973   McCOMB.   A genealogical register of the McComb family in America, compiled from records furnished by the individual families, and public records, etc., by P.H.K.McComb, Indianapolis, Ind., 1913.   1912-1942 record and notes compiled by Virginia M. McComb.   (Chambersburg, Pa., 1942)
331 p. illus. (coat of arms) 24 cm.   Cover-title: The McComb family.   "Sources": p.317.   44-30851.   CS71.M1287   1942

MACOMB.   See HALL, 1892

10974   MACOMBER.   Macomber genealogy, by Everett S. Stackpole ... (Lewiston, Me., Press of the Journal company (1908?)   1 p. 1., (5)-252 p. 23½ cm. 9-14471.   CS71.M171   1908

10975   M'COMBIE.   Memoir of the families of M'Combie and Thomas, originally M'Intosh and M'Thomas, comp. from history and tradition by William M'Combie Smith.   New ed.   Edinburgh and London, W. Blackwood and sons, 1890.   xiv, 224 p. front., ports. 24 cm. 14-6986.
CS479.M18

10976   McCONNELL.   Genealogical history of the families of McConnells, Martins, Barbers, Wilsons, Bairds, McCalls and Morris'.   The histories of the Sctoch-Irish and of the Presbyterians in the Revolutionary war.   The battles of King's mountain and the Cowpens, together with an autobiographical sketch by Newton Whitfield McConnell.   (n. p., 19 -)   2 p. 1., 3-399, (4) p. front., plates, ports., facsim.   23 cm.   36-14636.   CS71.M1288   19 -

10977   McCONNELL.   McConnell marriage genealogy; ancesters, descendants, marriages of an illustrious family of Virginia, by Hugh M. Addington and Mattie E. Addington.   Nichelsville, Va., Service printer, 1929.   3 p. 1., 36 p. 15½ x 10½ cm. 29-9419 rev.   CS71.M1288   1929

10978   McCONNELL.   Who am I? A brief sketch of the McConnell and related families in southwest Virginia by John Preston McConnell ... (East Radford, Va., 1929)   1 p. 1., 192 numb. 1., 1 1. 28 cm.   Mimeographed.   An unnumbered leaf between 183 and (184)   Part of the leaves are blank.   33-1913.
CS71.M1288   1929a

10979   McCONNELL.   Letters of McConnell family.   (London? Ont., 1943?)   1 p. 1., 126 numb. 1.
29 x 23½ cm.   Type-written (carbon) copy made by Edwin Seaborn from the originals.   43-22830.
CS499.M155

McCONNELL.   See also STARK, 1961

McCONNICO.   See PUCKETT, 1931

10980   McCOOK.   A brief historical sketch of the "Fighting McCooks" ... New York, The J. Kempster printing company (1903)   cover-title, 28 p. incl. pl. 25½ cm.   Comp. by Henry Howe.   "Reprinted from the Proceedings of the Scotch-Irish society of America (v. 6, p.161-171)" 6-3331.
CS71.M129   1903

10981   McCORD.   David McCord, Ann Shipley McCord and Alexander Elder family records, compiled by William Oscar McCord and Minnie Connelly McCord; edited by Edwin N. Canine, 1942, with records of related families.   (Terre Haute? Ind., 1942)   1 p. 1., 137 numb. 1. 28½ x 22½ cm.   Type-written (carbon copy) "Sources of information": leaf 3.   43-7282.   CS71.M1296   1942

McCORD.   See also: McKINNEY, 1905
ROBINSON, 1867

10982   McCORMICK.   Family record and biography.   Comp. by Leander James McCormick. Chicago, 1896.   478, (16) p. plates, ports. 26 cm. 9-11937.   CS71.M13   1896

10983   McCORMICK.   Scotch-Irish in Ireland and in America, as shown in sketches of the pioneer Scotch-Irish families McCormick, Stevenson, McKenzie, and Bell, in North Carolina, Kentucky, Missouri and Texas.   By Andrew Phelps McCormick ... (New Orleans) 1897.   2 p. 1., 174, 72 p., 1 1. 24 cm.   Printed, not published.   2-8203.   E184.S4M2

10984   McCORMICK.   Point au Pelee island.   A historical sketch of and an account of the McCormick family, who were the first white owners on the island.   (By Thaddeus Smith)   Amherstburg, The Echo printing company, limited, 1899.   4 p. l., 43 p. 24 cm. 1-19550 rev.   CS71.M13   1899

10985   McCORMICK.   Genealogical tables of the descendants of Robert McCormick of "Walnut grove," Rockbridge county, Virginia, born 1780 - died 1846.   (Strasburg, Va., Shenandoah publishing house, inc., 1934)   xii, 42, (2) p. incl. fold. geneal. tables. plates, ports. 23½ cm. "Privately printed 1934." Foreword signed: L. McC-G. (i. e. Leander McCormick-Goodhart) These genealogical tables bring up to date the information collected by Mr. Leander J. McCormick in his "Family record and biography," published in 1896.   35-14596 rev.   CS71.M13   1934

——— Genealogical line of Leander James McCormick of Chicago.   Descent to June 1, 1946.   To be used in substitution for the tree included in the author's "(Genealogical tables of the) descendants of Robert McCormick ... 1934."   (n. p., 1946)   cover-title, geneal. tab.   144½ x 23½ cm. fold. to 23½ x 15½ cm.   35-14596 rev.   CS71.M13   1934   Table.

10986   McCORMICK.   McCormick-Hamilton, Lord-Day ancestral lines.   Compiled for Elizabeth Day McCormick and Robert Hall McCormick, III.   (n. p.) 1957.   1165, lix p. ports., col. coats of arms, facsims. 28 cm. Bibliography: p. 1137 - 1165. 58-3350.   CS71.M13   1957

10987   McCORMICK.   William McCormick 1732-1812; a soldier in the American Revolution: his ancestors and descendants 1570-1969.   Compiled (by) Roma C. Harlan (and) Hazel S. Wright.   (Washington) 1969.   a-c, 25 l. 30 cm. 78-3148 MARC.   CS71.M13   1969

McCORMICK.   History of the McCormick family.   By Mrs. T. F. Crissell.   In vertical file.   Ask reference librarian for this material.

McCORMICK.   See also: CARSON, 195 -   PORTER, 1897
                      FLEWELLEN, 1958   WEITZEL, 1883
                      KINNEY, F225.M15   No. 1547 - Cabell county.
                      McDILL, PN.4899.C4T83

10988   McCORT.   Family history of James and Anne McCort, 1760-1921.   (n. p., 1921?)   cover-title, (29) p. illus. (ports.) 23½ cm. Signed: Cora M. Hough, author and associate editor; Emerson Capper, historian and editor; Charles T. McCort, publisher. 37-38431.   CS71.M1313   1921

——— Supplement.   1st -   April 1, 1928 -   (n. p.) 1923 -   no. 24½ cm.   CS71.M1313   1921   Suppl.

McCOSKEY.   See POUND, 1904

10989   McCOURTIE.   Genealogical chart of the McCourtie family.   Minneapolis, 1908)   geneal. tab. illus. (port.) 185 x 103½ cm. fold. to 53 cm. Signed: W.H.L.McCourtie. 17-17345-6.   CS71.M1314   1908

——— (Supplement.   Minneapolis, 1914)   27 p. front. (port.) 24 cm. Cover-title: "McCourtie genealogy."   CS71.M1314   1908   Suppl.

10990   McCOWN.   The McCown family of the Peedee section of South Carolina, by Louise McCown Clement.   Columbia, S. C., Printed by R. L. Bryan Co. (c. 1966)   xi, 246 p. illus. (part col.) 24 cm. Bibliography: p. 223-225. 67-14052.   CS71.M13145   1966

10991   McCOWN.   McCown family in vertical file under Perry Co., Pa., fams.   Ask ref. librarian for this.

McCOWN.   See also: CROSS, 1932
                   MITCHELL, 1914
                   TOWLES, 1957

10992   McCOY.   William McCoy and his descendants; a genealogical history of the family of William McCoy, one of the Scotch families coming to America before the revolutionary war, who died in Kentucky about the year 1818.   Also a history of the family of Alexander McCoy, a Scotchman who served through the revolutionary war, and died in Ohio in the year 1820.   By Lycurgus McCoy.   Battle Creek, Mich., The author, 1904.   204 p. front., ports. 21½ cm. 20-7239.   CS71.M1315   1904

10993   McCOY.   Notes on the McCoy family, by William H. McCoy, 1915.   Edited by Elizabeth Hayward.   Rutland, Vt., The Tuttle publishing company, inc., 1939.   1 p. l., 5-23 p. 23 cm.   40-1204.
CS71.M1315   1939

McCOY.   See also POUND, 1904

McCRACKEN.   See No. 9847 - Hackettstown.

10994   McCRAE.   The McCrase of Guelph, by A. E. Byerly ... (Elora, Ont.)   Printed (by) Elora express, 1932.   cover-title, 13 p. incl. facsim. pl. 22 cm.   Portrait on cover.   "The contents of this booklet were contributed by me to the Elora express, and the London, Ontario, free press, in August and September 1931." - Foreword.   35-13705.
CS90.M14B9

McCREA.   See McCRAE

10995   McCREADY.   The Robert McCready family, compiled by Robert J. McCready, M. D.   Pittsburgh, Pa., Priv. print. (Horner-Doyle-Wright company) 1931.   6 p. l., 3-44 p., 1 l., 65 p., 3 l. front., illus. (map) plates, ports., facsim. 26½ cm.   Blank leaves for "Notes" (3 at end) 31-11193.   CS71.M1318   1931

10996   McCRILLIS.   Records of the McCrillis families in America.   Compiled and arranged by H. O. McCrillis ... Taunton, Printed at the office of J. S. Sampson, 1882.   42 p. 22½ cm.   On cover: McCrillis family records.   1882.   43-28826.   CS71.M1319   1882

McCRILLIS.   See also FOSS, F44.S2R4

10997   MacCRIMMON.   A history of the clan MacCrimmon, compiled by G. C. B. Poulter ... (Camberley, Eng.)   The Clan MacCrimmon society, 1928 -   v. front. (port.) 21 cm. 40-288.
CS479.M19   1938

McCRONE.   See WHEELER, 1920

10998   McCRUM.   Genealogy of the McCrum family, 1909?   By Ephraim Banks McCrum.   With notes by Foster McCrum Palmer.   (Watertown? Mass.)   1965.   19 l. geneal. tables. 29 cm.   Bibliographical footnotes.   66-38223.   CS71.M13195   1965

McCUAN.   See WILFORD, 1959

10999   McCUBBIN.   I licked the platter clean; the true story of Louis McCubbin.   By Kelman Frost. Dundee (Scot.) Oberon Press (1947)   193 p. 23 cm.   48-24357*.   CT788.M132F7

11000   McCUE.   The McCues of the Old Dominion.   Supplemented with brief charts of the Steele, Arbuckle and Cunningham families.   Compiled by John N. McCue ... Mexico, Mo., Missouri ptg. & pub. co., 1912.   2 p. l., (3)-272, (15) p. front., illus., plates, ports. 23½ cm.   13-1119.
CS71.M132   1912

McCUISTON.   See McQUISTON.

11001   McCULLEY.   The McCulley family tree; a history of Solomon and Sarah McCulley and some of their descendants to the eigth generation, compiled by William Straight McCulley with the assistance of Frances J. Baldwin (and others) (Bryan? Tex.) 1968.   1 v. (various pagings) 22 cm.   Cover title.   79-7087 MARC.
CS71.M1328   1968

McCULLOCH.   See McCULLOUGH.

McCULLOH.   See McCULLOUGH.

11002   McCULLOUGH.   Genealogy of the McCullough family and other sketches.   Comp. by John McCullough, III.   Harrisburgh, Pa., The Telegraph printing company, 1912.   100 p. front., pl., ports. 20 cm.   "Life with the aborigines ... by John McCullough I": p. (29)-82.   "A sketch of Captain James Paull McCullough, by J. Howard Wert": p. 85-91.   19-11627.   CS71.M1325   1912

11003   McCULLOUGH.   Fragmentary records of the McCullough and connected families.   (Kearny, N.J., 1918)   54 1. 30 cm.   Caption title.   Autographed from type-written copy.   Introduction signed.   George G. McCullough.   Containes also records of the Hine, Bamford, Lane and Doherty families.   19-3959.   CS71.M1325   1918

11004   McCULLOUGH.   Genealogy of the McCullough and related families, compiled by J. R. McCullough ... Supplemental to the "Captain Ambrose Hine" record published by him previously the same year.   Glen Rock, N.J., 1928.   (4) p. 28 cm.   31-18264.   CS71.M1325   1928

11005   McCULLOUGH.   A history of the McCulloch family.   (Compiled by Charlotte McCulloch Steenbergen and Janet McCulloch Byers, with the able assistance of John G. Aten, Jr.   Point Pleasant? W. Va., 1963)   76 p. illus. 24 cm.   64-3736.   CS71.M1325   1963

       McCULLOUGH.   See also: EASLEY, 1947
                               EWING, 1957
                               HOGG, 1921
                               MAXWELL, 1916

11006   McCUNE.   Memorial to Elizabeth Claridge McCune, missionary, philadnthropist, architect.   By Susa Young Gates.   Salt Lake City, 1924.   117 p., 1 l. incl. front. illus. (inco. ports.) 25 cm.   Contains also accounts of the McCune, Claridge, and Hopkins families.   25-11811.   CS71.M1328   1924

11007   McCUNE.   Some of the descendants of Robert and Jane (——) McCune of Bourbon and Nicholas County, Kentucky.   Comp. by Alfred Averill Knapp and Mrs. Amy Edna (Ramey) McCune, (Mrs. Lewis O.)   Winter Park, Fla., The College Press (1947?)   57 p. 23 cm.   47-27366*.   CS71.M1328   1947

       McCURDA.   See: HILTON, 1905
                         McCURDY.

11008   McCURDY.   Family histories and genealogies.   A series of genealogical and biographical monographs on the families of MacCurdy, Mitchell, Lord, Lynde, Digby, Newdigate, Hoo, Willoughby, Griswold, Wolcott, Pitkin, Ogden, Johnson, Diodati, Lee and Marvin, and notes on the families of Buchanan, Parmelee, Boardman, Lay, Locke, Cole, De Wolf, Drake, Bond and Swayne, Dunbar and Clarke, and a notice of Chief Justice Morrison Remick Waite.   With twenty-nine pedigree charts and two charts of combined descents ... By Edward Elbridge Salisbury and Evelyn McCurdy Salisbury.   Privately printed.   (New Haven, Press of Tuttle, Morehouse & Taylor) 1892.   3 v. in 5. port., fold. geneal. tables, coats of arms.   31½ cm.   "The edition consists of fifty copies on large paper and two hundred and fifty of this size of which this is no. 136."   Contents. - v.1, pt. 1.   Genealogical and biographical monographs on the families of MacCurdy, Mitchell and Lord and notes on the families of Buchanan, Parmelee, Boardman and Lay and a notice of Chief Justice Morrison Remick Waite. - v.1, pt.2. Genealogical and biographical monographs on the families of Lynde, Digby, Newdigate, Hoo and Willoughby and notes on the families of Locke and Cole. - v.2. Genealogical and biographical monographs on the families of Griswold, Wolcott, Pitkin, Ogden, Johnson and Diodati and notes on the families of De Wolf, Drake, Bond and Swayne, and Dunbar. - v.3. Genealogical and biographical monographs on the families of Lee and Marvin and Clarke (or Clark) notes. - v.3, supplement.   Twenty-nine pedigree-charts with two charts of combined descents.   L. C. COPY REPLACED BY MICROFILM.   9-14118.

                                              CS71.S167   1892
                                              Microfilm 8686 CS

11009   McCURDY.   Historical geneology (!) of the McCurdy family; a concise history of the McCurdy's dating from 1489, including a record of their ancestry to Gilkrist Makurerdy, a Scottish chief, and to Robert II, king of Scotland, compiled by D. E. McCurdy.   Dennison, O., W. D. McCurdy (1915?)   3 p. 1., (9)-76 p. 20 cm.   This work has been completed by W. D. McCurdy.   cf. "Publisher's explanations."   35-21362.
                                                CS71.M133   1915

11010   McCURDY.   The ancestral McCurdys, their origin and remote history, by H. Percy Blanchard.   London, The Covenant publishing company, 1930.   xi, 42 p. fold. map. 25 cm.   Portrait of the author inserted.   30-14813.   CS71.M133   1930

11011   McCURDY.   Genealogical record & biographical sketches of the McCurdys of Nova Scotia, compiled and edited by H. Percy Blanchard.   Published for the Hon. F. B. McCurdy ... London, The Covenant publishing company, 1930.   xxi, 228 p. illus. (coat of arms) ports., facsims. 25 cm.   Red line borders.   Includes the Archibald family.   33-25908.   CS90.M15B5

11012   McCURDY.   Genealogical history of James Winslow McCurdy and Neil Barclay McCurdy. Genealogical research by Brian Llewellyn Young.   Edited by Gordon Newell.   Seattle, Superior Pub. Co. (1963)   95 p. illus., ports., map, col. coats of arms, geneal. tables. 23 cm. Bibliography: p. 95. 63-18496.

CS71.M133   1963

McCURDY.   See also: HILTON, 1905
SALISBURY, 1885
SALISBURY, 1892

11013   McCutchen.   The McCutchen trace.   By Hildegard Smith.   (Little Rock, Ark., 1963?)
313 p. illus. 23 cm. 64-56209.

CS71.M1335   1963

McCUTCHEN.   See also MAY, 1969

11014   McCUTCHEON.   The McCutcheon (Cutcheon) family records, allied families of McClary, Tripp, Brown and Critchett; also Mayflower line of Marie Amnie Warner (Mrs. Byron M. Cutcheon) through Warner, Cooper, Rockwell, Foote, Whitney, Treat, Canfield, Clark, Willoughby, Hotchkiss, Ives, Cook, Buell, Fitch to Governor Bradford.   And ancestry of Betsey Webster Carr (Mrs. Lewis M. Cutcheon) to George Carr, founder of Salisbury, Massachusetts, and to Aquila Chase of Hampton, New Hampshire, through Carr, Webster, Stuart, Brewer, Hudson, Ford, Edwards, Morrill, Waldo, Cogswell, Morse, Perley, Chase.   Compiled by Florence McCutcheon McKee, (Mrs. S. W.)   Grand Rapids, Mich., Commonwealth printing company, 1931.   316, xxxxvi, (8) p. incl. plates, ports. 21½ cm. Includes blank pages for "Ancestry and descendants' record". 31-23671.

CS71.M1335   1931

McCUTCHEON.   See also BRUMBACH, 1961

11015   McDANIEL.   McDaniel family record; family of Stephen McDaniel, sr., compiled by Charles G. Harris ... assisted by Miss Hettie C. O'Connor ... Louisville, Ky., The Franklin printing company, incorporated (1929)   1 p. l., 5-179 p. incl. ports. 22 cm. Blank pages for "Birth record, Marriage record, Death record" (162-179) 30-15025.

CS71.M1337   1929

McDANIEL.   See also: LEWIS, 1960
LIGON, 1947
STEVENS, 1956

11016   McDAVID.   McDavid-Dorroh families (by) Rose McDavid Munger.   (n. p., 1964?)
121 p. 23 cm. Cover title. Addenda slip inserted at p. 63. 64-57089.

CS71.M13377   1964

11017   McDILL   McDills in America; a history of the descendants of John McDill and Janet Leslie of county Antrim, Ireland.   Also a partial record of other branches of the McDill, MacDill, Medill and Madill families, compiled by Robert McDill Woods and Iva Godfrey Woods ... Ann Arbor, Mich., Edwards brothers, inc., 1940.   xiv, 210 p. incl. front., illus. (incl. ports., maps) 24 cm. Photoprinted. "Information concerning the earlier generations had been gathered many years ago by Mr. Jennie Agnes McDill Woods." - Foreword. 40-13578.

CS71.M1338   1940

11018   McDILL.   ... An American dynasty, by John Tebbel.   Garden City, New York, Doubleday & company, inc., 1947.   x p., 1 l., 363 p. pl., ports., double geneal. tab. 22 cm. At head of title: The story of the McCormicks, Medills and Pattersons. "First edition." 47-30087.

PN4899.C4T83

11019   MACDONALD.   A Keppoch song: a poem in five cantos: being the origin and history of the family, alias Donald, Lord of the Isles, carried down to its extinction, with a continuation of the family of Keppoch; the whole combined with the history of Scotland, with notes and references, and concluding with an analysis of the Scotch acts of Parliament, relative to the Douglas association; and an address to His Royal Highness the prince regent, &c. &c., by John Paul Macdonald ... Montrose, Printed for the author by J. Watt, 1815.   viii p., 1 l., (19)-263, (1) p. 23 cm. 14-21097.

CS479.M2   1815

11020   MACDONALD.   Vindication of the "Clanronald of Glengarry" against the attacks made upon them in the Inverness journal and some recent printed performances.   With remarks as to the descent of the family who style themselves "of Clanronald" ... Edinburgh, W. & C. Tait, 1821.   3 p. l., 97, xxx p. fold. geneal. tab. 23½ cm. By John Riddell. Engr. t.-p. 4-107.

CS479.R8

11021   MACDONALD.   Historical, genealogical and miscellaneous tracts, by Alexander Sinclair. Printed for private circulation.   (Edinburgh, 1860?)   2 p. l., (218) p. incl. geneal. tables. 22½ cm.   Contents. - Sketch of the history of the Macdonalds of the Isles. - Sketch of the succession of the ancient historical earldom of March, till it was confiscated in 1434 ... - Remarks on the tables of the heirs of the royal house of Baliol ... - Vindication ... as to "heirs-male" in peerages, and wives' and widows' names. - The crowned heart of Douglas. - (The dukedom of Gordon. - Earl and Marquis of Huntly and Duke of Gordon. - Chronological abstract of the charters of Huntly. - Notes on the case of the Earl of Perth, to prove his right to succeed to the ancient estates of his family as heir-male. - On the inheritance of Scottish peerages by designation. - A succinct account of the long feud between the earls of Glencairn and Eglinton on account of the bailliary of Kilwinning, and controverted precedency of their earldoms. - On peculiarties in names of old ... - "The clan Campbell and the Marquess of Lorne" (etc.) - Anecdotes of the Cavendishes. - Sketch of the dukes of Devonshire.   The great difficulty in selection. - Appendix: Latter portion of the speech at Lewes, with a few miscellaneous remarks. - More Percy anecdotes, old and new. - Curious case of two cotemporary lords Dacre, deriving from the same creation, commencing with after summonses of the same date. - Case of the succession to the dukedom of Somerset in 1750. - France and the French.   Part II. National charactersistic differences. - Notes on crops and harvest.   Let not the cap fit. - Harvest. - (Anecdotes) - Summary of the six cases of succession by propinquity against representation.   16-19784.   CS464.S4

11022   MACDONALD.   Genealogy of the MacDonald family.   Ed. B.   Comprising all names obtained up to February, 1876.   (New Haven, Conn., Press Tuttle, Morehouse & Taylor, 1876)   6 p. l., 123 p. 20½ x 33 cm.   "Greeting" signed: F. V. McDonald.   9-11936.   CS71.M134   1876

11023   MACDONALD.   Contributions to the early history of Bryan McDonald and family, settlers in 1689, on Red Clay Creek, Mill Creek Hundred (or Township) Newcastle County, Delaware.   Together with a few biographical sketches and other statistics of general interest to their lineal descendants. By Frank V. McDonald ... San Francisco, Winterburn & co., printers and electro-typers, 1879.   64, (1) p. front. (port.) 28 cm.   9-18741.   CS71.M134   1879

11024   MACDONALD.   Supplement no. 1 to edition B of the MacDonald genealogy.   Containing records of the descendants of Jesse Peter, on of the pioneer settlers near Mackville, Washington County, Kentucky; together with a few remarks on the early history of the Peter family, and whatever other information of value concerning this branch of the name could be collected up to Feb. 25, 1880. Compiled and edited by Frank V. McDonald ... Cambridge, University press, J. Wilson and son, 1880.   72 p. front., pl., ports. 31½ cm.   9-18739.   CS71.M134   1880

11025   MACDONALD.   Notes preparatory to a biography of Richard Hayes McDonald of San Francisco, California.   Compiled and edited by his eldest child, Frank V. McDonald.   v. 1 ... Cambridge, University press, 1881.   xix, (1) p., 3 l., (29)-95, 119 p. front., illus., plates, ports. 34 x 25 cm.   No. 53 of 150 copies printed.   "Ancestral line of Richard Hayes McDonald": p. xii-xix.   "Appendix E. Descendants of Colonel James and Martha Shepard McDonald of Mackville, Washington County, Ky.": p. 21-39.   3-5666.   F865.M15

11026   MACDONALD.   History of the Macdonalds and Lords of the Isles; with genealogies of the principal families of the name.   By Alexander Mackenzie ... Inverness, A. & W, Mackenzie, 1881.   xxiv, 534 p. 23½ cm.   3-9292.   CS479.M2   1881

11027   MACDONALD.   The Macdonalds of Clanranald.   By Alexander Mackenzie ... Inverness, A. & W. Mackenzie, 1881.   v, 108 (i.e. 106) p. 22 cm.   Numbers 3-4 omitted in paging.   34-35186.

CS479.M2   1881a

11028   MACDONALD.   A family memoir of the Macdonalds of Keppoch, by Angus Macdonald ... written from 1800 to 1820, for his niece, Mrs. Stanley Constable.   Edited by Clements R. Markham, C.B.; with some notes by the late Charles Edward Stuart, comte d'Albanie.   (London, Whiting and co., limited) 1885.   xii, 153 p. 23 cm.   "Impression limited to 150 copies: no. 126."   40-16311.   CS479.M2   1885

11029   MACDONALD.   Moidart; or, Among the Clanranalds.   By the Rev. Charles MacDonald ... Oban, D. Cameron, 1889.   vii, 264 p. front. 18 cm.   18-3327.   DA758.3.C5M3

11030   MACDONALD.   The last Macdonalds of Isla: chiefly selected from original bonds and documents, sometime belonging to Sir James Macdonald, the last of his race, now in the possession of Charles Fraser-Mackintosh ... Glasgow, "Celtic monthly" office, 1895.   xvi, 99 p. illus. 26 cm.   "Documents ... reprinted from the pages of the Celtic monthly - some of them in extenso, with abstracts of other." - p. (1)   25-14582.

CS479.M2   1895

11031   MACDONALD.   The clan Donald, by the Rev. A. Macdonald, minister of Killearnan, and the Rev. A. Macdonald, minister of Kiltarlity ... Inverness, The Northern counties publishing company ltd., 1896-1904.   3 v. front. (v. 3) illus., plates, ports., facsims. (part fold.) 25½ cm. 15-18508.   DA758.3.M25M3

11032   MACDONALD.   The Macdonald collection of Gaelic poetry, by the Rev. A. Macdonald, minister of Killearnan ... and Rev. A. McDonald, minister of Kiltarlity ... Inverness, The Northern counties newspaper and printing and publishing company, limited, 1911.   xcii, 408 p. 26 cm. Consists almost entirely of poems which have not hitherto been published, many of them by Macdonald bards or relating to the clan. cf. Pref. Annotated contents: p. (vii)-lxxi. 21-3543.   PB1633.M25

11033   MACDONALD.   The Glengarry McDonalds of Virginia. By Mrs. Flora McDonald Williams; with an introductory sketch of the early history of the Glengarry clan. Louisville, G. G. Fetter company, 1911.   340 p. plates, ports. (1 col.) 24 cm. 12-13463.   CS71.M134   1911

11034   MACDONALD.   Macdonald of the Isles; a romance of the past and present, by A.M.W. Stirling ... New York, The John Lane company, 1914.   xii, 295, (1) p. incl. geneal. tables. col. front., plates, ports. 23 cm. 14-9542.   CS479.M2   1914

11035   MACDONALD.   Highland papers ... ed. by J.R.N.Macphail, K.C. vol. I, II.   Edinburgh, Printed by T. and A. Constable for the Scottish history society, 1914-34.   4 v. fronts., fold. facsims. 23 cm. (Half-title Publications of the Scottish history society. 2d ser. vol. v, xii   3d ser. v. 22.   Contents. - vol. I. History of the Macdonalds. Macnaughton of that ilk. A sufficient account of the family of Calder. Papers relating to the murder of the Laird of Calder. Genealogy of the Macras. Papers relating to the Macleans of Duart, 1670-1680. - vol. II. The genealogie of the surname of M'Kenzie since ther coming into Scotland. Ane accompt of the genealogie of the Campbells. Writs relating chiefly to the lands of Glassarie and their early possessors. Documents relating to the massacre of Dunavertie. The ewill trowbles of the Lewes, and how the Macleoid of the Lewes was with his whol tribe destroyed and put from the possession of the Lewes. Papers relating to the estates of the Chisholm and the Earl of Seaforth forfeited in 1716.   DA750.S25
14-11585.
2d ser. vol. 5, 12
3d ser. v. 22

11036   MACDONALD.   ... History of the clan Donald, the families of MacDonald, McDonald and McDonnell, by Henry Lee. New York, R.L.Polk and company, inc. (1920)   138 p. 20½ cm. (The Maxwell series. Famous old families) 35-11241.   DA758.3.D55L4

11037   MACDONALD.   The house of the Isles, by Lady Macdonald of the Isles.   Edinburgh, Priv. print, by T. and A. Constable, ltd. (1925)   6 p. l., 168 p. front. (ports.) plates. 20½ cm. "Authorities": 6th prelim. leaf. Pedigree: p. 141-157. 27-15275.   DA758.3.M25M28

11038   MACDONALD.   ... MacDonald, McDonald family records, by J. Montgomery Seaver.   Philadelphia, Pa., American historical-genealogical society (1929)   51, (3) p. front. (4 port.) coat of arms. 29 cm. Coat of arms of the McDonald family on recto of frontispiece. Three blank pages at end for "Family records". "References": p. 51. 40-18913.   CS71.M134   1929

11039   MACDONALD.   Alexander McDonald of New Inverness, Georgia, and his descendants.   By Daniel Huntley Redfearn. Miami, 1954.   177 p. illus. 23 cm. 54-31955.   CS71.M134   1954

11040   MACDONALD.   Our pioneer heritage. By Clarinda Pauline McDonald.   (Dallas? c. 1961)   vii, 202 p. illus., ports., facsims. 26 cm. 63-25881.   CS71.M134   1961

11041   MACDONALD.   Notes on the house of Macdonald of Kingsburgh and Castle Camus.   By Reginald Henry Macdonald. (Pittsburgh?, label: 1962)   50 p. illus. 28 cm. 63-26919.   CS479.M2   1962

11042   MACDONALD.   James McDonald-Sarah Ferguson; their progenitors and their posterity.   By Ila May (Fisher) Maughan. (Salt Lake City, 1964)   viii, 150 p. illus., facsims., geneal. tables, maps, ports. 29 cm. Includes bibliographies. 65-2956.   CS71.M134   1964

11043   MACDONALD.   One small branch of the old MacDonald tree, by Herbert S. MacDonald.   (North Haven? Conn.) 1968.   xi, 113 p. illus., geneal. table (in pocket), ports. 24 cm. 68-8723 MARC.   CS71.M134   1968

11044   MACDONALD.   Descendants and ancestors of William McDonald, 1822-1910 and Christian Wallace, 1826-1879.   By Leona McDonald Smith.   (Provo, Utah, J.G. Stevenson, 1968)   xii, 343 p. illus., coat of arms, facsims., geneal. tables, maps, ports. 25 cm. 79-7777 MARC.   CS71.M134   1968b

      MACDONALD. See also: BLACK, 1954
                                 HORNE, 1936
                                 LA RUE, 1921
                                 McKEAN, CS479.M3
                                 ROBINSON, 1907

11045   MACDONNELL.   An historical account of the Macdonnells of Antrim: including notices of some other septs, Irish and Scottish.   By Rev. George Hill ... Belfast, Archer & sons, 1873. 4 p. l., 510 p., 1 l. 24 cm. 22-642.   CS499.M16

11046   MACDONELL.   A sketch of the life of the Honourable and Right Reverend Alexander Macdonell, chaplain of the Glengarry fencible or British Highland regiment, first Catholic bishop of Upper Canada, and a member of the legislative council of the province.   By J. A. Macdonell, of Greenfield.   Alexandria, Printed at the office of the Glengarrian, 1890.   2 p. l., (3)-86 p. 22 cm. 21-17182 rev.
                                                     BX4705.M17M2

11047   McDONNELL.   The ancient Franciscan friary of Bun-na-margie, Bally castle, on the north coast/of Antrim: being a descriptive and historical notice of this once celebrated friary, so intimately associated with the family of Macdonnell, earls of Antrim.   By Francis Joseph Bigger ... With plans drawings by William J. Fennell ... Belfast, New York (etc.)   M. Ward & co., limited (1898) 45 p. incl. front., illus. 25 cm. Special volume of Ulster journal of archaeology. 6-9629.
                                                 DA990.U45U4

11048   McDONNELL.   McDonnell and allied families.   By Lina Vandergrift (Denison) Cherry.   (St. Louis) C. V. C. McDonnell, 1959.   108 p. illus. 22 cm. 61-46688.   CS71.M135   1959

11049   MACDONNELL.   Irish chiefs and leaders.   By Paul Walsh.   Edited by Colm O Lochlainn. Dublin, Sign of the Three Candles (1960)   334 p. 23 cm. 61-66526.   DA916.4.W3

      McDONNELL.   See also MACDONALD, 1920

      MACDONELL.   See MACDONNELL.

11050   McDONOUGH.   The olographic will of John McDonough, of Louisiana, formerly a citizen of Baltimore.   Baltimore, Printed by J. Lucas, 1850.   cover-title, (3)-28 p. 23 cm. 17-22129.
                                                     CT275.M434A3

11051   McDONOUGH.   The Macdonough-Hackstaff ancestry, by Rodney Macdonough.   Boston, Press of S. Usher, 1901.   1 p. l., xii, 526 p. plates, ports., facsims. 24½ cm. "A limited edition of three hundred copies, printed from type." 1-25831.   CS71.M136   1901

      MACDOUGAL.   See MACDOUGALL.

11052   MACDOUGALL.   McDougal genealogy (1748-1954); the known descendants in the United States of America of Robert McDougal of western Scotland (1748-1832)   (.n. p., 1954)   55 l. illus. 30 cm. 55-19919.   CS71.M137   1954

      MACDOUGALL.   See also: ARGYLL, DA880.A6C1
                                   BRISBANE, 1840
                                   CAMPBELL, 1882
                                   ROBINSON, 1907

      McDOUGAL.   See PEDEN, 1961

11053   McDOWELL.   Historic families of Kentucky.   With special reference to stocks immediately derived from the valley of Virginia; tracing in detail their various genealogical connexions and illustrating from historic sources their influence upon the political and social development of Kentucky and the states of the South and West.   By Thomas Marshall Green ... 1st series.   Cincinnati, R. Clarke & co., 1889.   iv, 304 p. front. (port.) 23½ cm. 4-11454.   F450.G79

11054   McDOWELL.   ... Historic homes in North Carolina - Quaker Meadows, by Judge A. C. Avery ... (Raleigh, E.M.Uzzell & co., printers, 1904)   cover-title, 24 p. pl. 19 x 14 cm. (The North Carolina booklet; great events in North Carolina history, vol. IV, no. 3, July, 1904) Title-page reads: ... The North Carolina booklet.   Contains biographical notices of the McDowell family, owners of Pleasant Gardens and Quaker Meadows in Burke co., N.C.   21-8431 rev.

F251.N86 v. 4 no. 3
—— Copy 2   F258.A95

11055   McDOWELL.   History of the McDowells and connections (being a compilation from various sources) by Hon. John Hugh McDowell.   Memphis, C. B. Johnston & co., 1918.   5 p. l., (13) - 680, (2) p. incl. illus., ports., coats of arms. 22½ cm. Lettered on cover: McDowells, Erwins, Irwins & connections. 18-22262.
CS71.M138   1918

11056   McDOWELL.   References to persons named McDowell in the 1850 Baltimore, Md. federal census.   2 mimeographed pages. In vertical file. Ask reference librarian for this material.

McDOWELL.   See also: ATWOOD, CS439.A8   PEDEN, 1961
                        BUFORD, 1903   SAMPSON, CS71.S189
                        GREENLEE, 1908   SHELBY, 1933
                        HARRISON, 1893   TORRENCE, 1894
                        HAYNES, 1940

11057   McDUFFIE.   John and Flora McDonald McDuffie of the Isle of Skye, Scotland, and a record of their descendants who settled in North Carolina, Mississippi, and Louisiana.   By Eva (Loe) McDuffie.   (Oak Ridge? La., 195-)   91 l. 28 cm. 59-24056.   CS71.M1384

11058   MACE.   Brice Martin Mace and Ella Cook, their ancestors and descendants, by the children. Editor: Brice Martin Mace, Jr.   (New York, 1968)   53 l. coats of arms, 2 fold. geneal. tables. 30 cm. 73-3739 MARC.
CS71.M1388   1968

McEACHERN.   See McELREATH, 1941   and McEATHRON, 1941

McEACHRAN.   See McEATHRON.

McEACHRON.   See McEATHRON.

11059   McEATHRON.   McEathron (McEachron, McEachran, McEachern) family ... (By Ellsworth Dudley McEathron.   (San Pedro? Calif., 1941)   8 p. 32½ x 21½ cm. Caption title. Text runs parallel with back of cover. 42-16473.   CS71.M139   1941

11060   McELREATH.   My folks, by Walter McElreath ... (Atlanta, J.T.Hancock, 1941)
4 p. l., (7)-124, (2) p. 24 cm. Includes the McElreath, McClung & McEachern families. 42-5163.   CS71.M14   1941

11061   McELROY.   The Scotch-Irish McElroys in America, A.D.1717 - A.D.1900, by Rev. John M. McElroy, D.D.   Albany, N.Y., Fort Orange press, Brandow printing company, 1901.
183 p. ports. 23½ cm. 24-584.   CS71.M141   1901

McELROY.   See also McCHORD, 1941

McELVE.   See McKELVEY.

11062   McELWEE.   Geneology (sic) of William McElwee, II, of Clarks Fork of Bullocks Creek of York County, South Carolina.   By Pinckney Glasgow McElwee.   Washington, 1959.   227 p. 28 cm.
61-22310 rev.   CS71.M1412   1959

11062 cont.: —— (Supplement, i.e. Chapter 7); genealogy of Mary McElwee Enloe ... Washington, 1964.
a-j, 52 p. 28 cm.   CS71.M1412
                                                                                     Suppl.

McELWEE.   See also REID, 1960

McEWEN.   See: DIXON, 1946
                 EWEN, 1904

11063   McFADDIN.   The McFaddin dedication, Sardinia, S.C. ... (Clinton, S.C., Jacobs and company, 1937)   98 p. illus. (incl. ports.) 23 cm. 39M4803T.   CS71.M1413   1937

11064   McFADIN.   Macfadin family in vertical file.   Ask reference librarian for this material.

11065   McFALL.   Notes on the McFall and allied families. (By Ezra McFall Kuhns)   (Dayton? O.)
Priv. print. (1936)   39 p. illus. (incl. ports.) 23 cm. Errata slip inserted. Foreword signed: Ezra McFall Kuhns. 37-16823.
                                                                                     CS71.M1415   1936

McFALL.   See also MERSHON, 1946

11066   McFARLAND.   Our kindred.   The McFarlan and Stern families, of Chester County, Pa.,
and New Castle County, Del. In two parts ... By Cyrus Stern.   Edited by Lizzie M. Marshall.   Introduction by Jacob Taggart Stern.   (West Chester, Pa., F.S.Hickman) 1885.   5 p. l., 179 (4) p. front.,
plates, ports., facsims. 26 cm. 9-15613.   CS71.M142   1885

11067   MACFARLAND.   History of the clan MacFarlane, (Marfarlane) MacFarlan, MacFarland,
MacFarlin.   By Mrs. C.M. Little.   Tottenville, N.Y., Mrs. C.N. Little, 1893.   viii, (9)-252, (2) p. front.,
illus., plates, ports. 23 cm. For private circulation. 9-11931.   CS71.M142   1893

11068   McFARLAND.   Descendants of Daniel McFarland one of the Scotch Presbyterians who settled
in Worcester, Massachusetts.   Compiled by Ellery B. Crane for the Worcester society of antiquity.
Worcester, Mass., The Blanchard press, 1907.   28 p. pl., ports. 24½ cm. 9-13261.   CS71.M142   1907

11069   McFARLAND.   Genealogy of the McFarland family of Hancock County, Maine.   By Daniel Y.
McFarland.   Middlebury, Vt., Press of Seymour brothers, 1910.   58 p. front., plates, ports. 22 cm. 11-6711.
                                                                                     CS71.M142   1910

11070   MACFARLAN.   The Red fox; a story of the clan Macfarlan.   By James Macfarlane.   London,
R.T.Lang, limited, 1912.   xv, 207 p. front., plates, mounted map. 19½ cm. 12-24687.   PZ3.M1645R

11071   MACFARLAND.   The book of the generations of William McFarland and Nancy Kilgore,
1740-1912.   Historian, Joseph McFarland ... Editor and publisher, Edward Norton Cantwell ...
Elgin, Ill., Press of Elgin courier (1913)   110 p. front. 22 cm. "Some additional items": 1 p. inserted at end. 13-17706.
                                                                                     CS71.M142   1913

11072   McFARLAND.   Genealogy of Daniel McFarland, sr., d. 1738 ... compiled by Clara Emerson.
(n. p.) 1930.   geneal. tab. 96 x 61 cm. 31-19482.   CS71.M142   1930

11073   McFARLAND.   Genealogy of Daniel McFarland, sr., d. 1738 ... Compiled by Clara Emerson.
Petersburg, Ill., 1930.   geneal. tab. 97 x 61 cm. "This chart is a supplement to the other Daniel McFarland, sr., genealogical
chart, and is taken almost entirely from the book by Ellery Crane." 31-31268.   CS71.M142   1930a

11074   McFARLAND.   ·Three central Pennsylvania families: McFarland of Blair Co., Weston of
Huntingdon Co. (and) Gates-Getz of Centre Co. By Raymond Martin Bell.   Washington, Pa., 1948.
5 l. 28 cm. 48-17904*.   CS71.M142   1948

11075   McFARLAND.   (The ancestors of Earl McFarland. By Mary Jo Forbes. 1965)   geneal. table.
45 x 60 cm. "The original of the chart was prepared by Mary Jo Forbes about 1950, and preserved by Earl McFarland, redrawn 1965 by Jos. G.
Ferrier." Photocopy of MS. 67-123181.   CS71.M142   1965

MACFARLAND.　See also: BARKSDALE, 1922
　　　　　　　　　　　　CLEEK, 1957
　　　　　　　　　　　　DEPEW, 1959
　　　　　　　　　　　　McKENNEY, 1905
　　　　　　　　　　　　McNAIR, 1914

MACFARLAN.　See McFARLAND.

McFARLANE.　See McFARLAND.

11076　MACFARLANE.　History of clan MacFarlane, by James MacFarlane ... published under the auspices of the clan MacFarlane society ... Glasgow, D.J. Clark limited, 1922.　171 p. plates (part col., part fold.; incl. music) port., map, facsims., coats of arms. 18½ cm.　31-17785.　CS479.M23

McFARLANE.　See also McFARLAND.

MACFARLIN.　See McFARLAND.

11077　McFATRIDGE.　The McFatridge, Holmes and Wilson families of Mercer Co., Penna., by Ralph E. K. Jones ... Data also by Mabel McCloskey.　(Warren? O., 1935)　4 p. 28 cm.　Type-written. 38M1708T.　CS71.M143　1935

11078　McFATRIDGE.　The McFatridge clan, from Ireland to the United States of America, for the past 200 years, by Charley Merritt McFatridge.　Moravia, Ia. (1942)　iv, 66 (i.e.71) numb. 1., 1 1. 36 x 23 cm.　Text runs parallel with back of cover.　42-50344.　CS71.M143　1942

11079　McFERRIN.　John B. McFerrin.　A biography.　By O. P. Fitzgerald ... Nashville, Tenn., Publishing house of the M. E. church, South, 1888.　448 p. front. (port.) 20½ cm.　"A genealogical glance": p. 15-21. 12-32194.　BX8495.M23F5

MACFIRBIS.　See FIACHRACH, 1844a

11080　McGAVOCK.　The McGavock family.　A genealogical history of James McGavock and his descendants from 1760 to 1903, by Rev. Robert Gray ... Richmond, W. E. Jones, 1903.　175 p. 23½ cm. 5-2289.　CS71.M144　1903

11081　McGEE.　Hall McGee and his descendants, compiled by his descendants.　(Columbia? S. C., 1962)　63 p. illus. 24 cm.　63-34850.　CS71.M14414　1962

McGEE.　See also: BURRUS, 1941
　　　　　　　　　　MACPHERSON, 1949
　　　　　　　　　　MILLER, 1923
　　　　　　　　　　No. 516 - Notable southern families vol. 1

11082　McGIFFIN.　The McGiffin story.　By James Quail McGiffin.　(Baytown, Tex.) 1952. 174 1. 22 x 36 cm.　52-39277.　CS71.M1442　1952

11083　McGILL.　The McGills, Celts, Scots, Ulstermen and American pioneers; history, heraldry and tradition, by Capt. A. McGill.　Saint Paul, McGill-Warner company, 1910.　345 p. plates, ports. 23 cm.　Contains biography of Andrew Ryan McGill, tenth governor of Minnesota.　12-8813.　CS71.M1445　1910

11084　McGILL.　The Macgill-McGill family of Maryland; a genealogical record of over 400 years beginning 1537, ending 1948.　By John McGill.　Washington, c. 1948.　vi, 262 p. illus., ports., col. coat of arms. 25 cm.　48-21691*.　CS71.M1445　1948

MAGILL.　See also No. 516 - Notable southern families, vol. 2

11085 McGILLYCUDDY.   The McGillycuddy papers: a selection from the family archives of "the McGillycuddy of the Reeks," with an introductory memoir; being a contribution to the history of the county of Kerry.   By W. Maziere Brady ... London, Longmans, Green, and co., 1867.   xxxiii, 209, (1) p. 29 x 23 cm.   Errata slip inserted.   4-34660 rev.   DA916.3.M16B8

McGINNESS.   See MAGGINISS.

11086 MACGINNIS.   Notes on the family of Magennis; formerly lords of Iveagh, Newry and Mourne, in the kingdom of Ulidia, Ireland.   Collected from varioys authentic sources, by Edmund Francis Dunne ... Salt Lake City, Utah, Printed at the Star printing office, 1878.   1 p. l., 17 p. 22 cm. 8-4666.   DA916.3.M3D9

11087 MACGINNIS.   Origin and history of the Magennis family, with sketches of the Keylor, Swisher, Marchbank and Bryan families ... By John F. Meginness. ... Williamsport, Pa., Heller bros. ' printing house, 1891.   1 p. l., 245, iii p. front., ports. 24 cm. 9-11935.
                                                                     CS71.M145   1891

11088 MACGINNIS.   McGinness and Scott families and their branches.   Genealogical notes.   By Samuel W. McGinness and Mary R. Ford ... Pittsburgh, Press of Murdoch, Kerr & co., 1892. 299 p. 2 port. (incl. front.) 23½ cm. 3-5668 rev.   CS71.M145   1892

11089 MACGINNIS.   Pedigree of the Magennis (Guinness) family of New Zealand, and of Dublin, Ireland ... Comp. by Richard Linn ... Christchurch, New Zealand, Caygill and Maclaren, 1897. 58, (1) p. incl. front., illus. (coat of arms) pl., ports. 18½ cm. Half-title: The Guinness family. 18-2164.
                                                                             CS499.M18

MACGINNIS.   See also No. 1547 - Cabell county.

McGLAUGHLIN.   See CLEEK, 1957

McGLOCKLIN.   See MITCHELL, 1940

11090 McGOWAN.   Proceedings of the reunion of the McGowan family, held at Liberty Springs church (Presbyterian) ... August 3, 1915.   Cross Hill, S.C., 1915.   51 p. 23 cm. 23-6172.
                                                                     CS71.M1475   1915

11091 McGRADY.   Daniel Hugh McGrady and his descendants, b. 1852 - d. 1935, compiled by L. J. McGrady.   Toledo? 1964.   1 sheet (geneal. table) 73 x 58 cm. 64-55032.   CS71.M1476   1964

McGRATH.   See: GALE, 1957
                  OSTRANDER, 1936

11092 MACGREGOR.   Historical memoirs of Rob Roy and the clan Macgregor; including original notices of Lady Grange.   With an introductory sketch illustrative of the condition of the Highlands, prior to the year 1745.   By K. Macleay ... Glasgow, W. Turnbull; (etc., etc.) 1818.   xi, (9)-403 p. front. (port.) 19½ cm. 18-3663.   DA810.M3M2

11093 MACGREGOR.   The life and surprising exploits of Rob Roy Macgregor; with an historical sketch of the celebrated clan Macgregor.   By D. Stewart ... New York, Printed for S. King, 1821. 38 p. 19½ cm. 5-27274.   DA810.M3S7

11094 MACGREGOR.   History of the clan Gregor, from public records and private collections; comp. at the request of the Clan Gregor society by one of its vice-presidents, Amelia Georgiana Murray MacGregor ... Edinburgh, W. Brown, 1898-1901.   2 v. col. front. (coat of arms) 26½ cm. Front. of v. 2: Old Mac Gregor weapons & flag. 2-8876.   CS479.M24
                                                                        Microfilm 10068

11095 MACGREGOR.   ... Rules and regulations, 1910, officers, council, committee on membership, entolled members.   Washington, D.C., The Law reporter printing company, 1911.   4 p. l., 7-26 p. 23 cm.   At head of title: American clan Gregor.   11-20878 rev.   CS71.G8178   1911

11096　MACGREGOR.　"Royal is my race."　Three probable origins of the Clan-gregor.　By Olive Smith Pope.　(Atlanta? 1943?)　geneal. table.　153 x 60 cm. to 42 x 61 cm.　Photocopy (negative) 48-32072*.
CS71.M1477　1943

11097　MACGREGOR.　Highland constable; the life and times of Rob Roy MacGregor.　By Hamilton Howlett.　Edinburgh, Blackwood, 1950.　xii, 292 p. ports., maps. geneal. table.　23 cm.　51-24354.
DA810.M3H6

11098　MACGREGOR.　The clan MacGregor (clan Gregor); the nameless clan.　By William Ramsay Kermack.　Edinburgh, W. & A. K. Johnston & G. W. Bacon (1953)　32 p. col. illus., map, col. coat of arms, geneal. tables.　19 cm.　(A. & A. K. Johnston's clan histories)　61-42050.
CS479.M24　1953

11099　MACGREGOR.　Macgregor family in vertical file.　Ask reference librarian for this material.

MACGREGOR.　See also GREGOR.

McGREW.　See BIGGS, 1963

McGROUTHER.　See MACGREGOR.

McGRUDER.　See MAGRUDER.

11100　MAGRUDER.　Magruder family in vertical file.　Ask reference librarian for this material.

11101　McGUFFEY.　The story of the McGuffeys.　By Alice McGuffey (Morrill) Ruggles.　New York, American Book Co. (1950)　viii, 133 p. illus., ports. 21 cm.　51-9191.
CS71.M1479　1950

11102　McGUFFIN.　Samuel McGuffin, copyright ... by Howard B. Grant ... Philippi, W. Va., H. B. Grant, c.1935.　1 1. 28½ x 23 cm.　Caption title.　Text runs parallel with back of cover.　Mimeographed.　38M831T.
CS71.M148　1935

11103　McGUIRE.　The McGuire family in Virginia, with notices of its Irish ancestry and some connected Virginia families.　Compiled by William G. Stanard ... Richmond, Va., Old Dominion press, 1926.　126 p., 1 1. incl. front. (coat of arms) 24 cm.　"Printed for private distribution."　Compiled from material collected by Dr. Edward McGuire.　27-3869.
CS71.M148　1926

11104　McGUIRE.　Lineage of Elisha Whipple McGuire.　(Windham, Conn., Printed at Hawthorn house, 1938)　(20) p. 22 cm.　Includes bibliography.　40-2258.
CS71.M1482　1938

11105　McGUIRE.　Pioneer families: McGuire, Berry, Hughes.　By Bruna Luella McGuire.　Hardin, Mo., c.1954.　unpaged. illus. 28 cm.　55-16317.
CS71.M1482　1954

McGUIRE.　See also GRAY, 1938

11106　McHARG.　Notes for a family record, 1604-May 1, 1905, Webster, Ingersoll, Moss, King, Hawley, McHarg, by William N. McHarg.　New York, Priv. print. (The Lotus press) 1905.　2 p. 1., 7-46 p. 16 cm.　"Of this book 100 copies were printed.　22-13259.
CS71.M1485　1905

11107　McHARG.　Family record of John P. McHarg of Bethlehem, Albany county, New York.　By Ernest J. McHarg.　(Binghamton? N. Y.) 1933.　3-30 p. incl. front., illus., ports. fold. geneal. tab.　26 cm.　"Foreword" signed: Ernest J. McHarg.　36-30624.
CS71.M1485　1933

11108　McHARG.　History and genealogy, the family of McHargue in America, compiled by Barbara Sue McHargue ... Corbin, Ky., Westbrook printing co., 1938.　2 p. 1., 58 p. pl., ports. 21 cm.　39-3174.
CS71.M1485　1938

11109　MACHELL.　The Machells of Crackenthorpe.　By F. Bellasis ... (Reprinted from the Transactions of the Cumberland and Westmorland antiquarian and archaeological society.)　Kendal, Printed by T. Wilson, 1886.　cover-title, p. 416-466. 2 fold. geneal. tab., coats of arms. 21 cm. 24-8028.　CS439.M15

11110   McHENCH.   The McHench family in America, being some descendants of John McHench, 1755-1833, who emigrated to America before 1788.   San Diego, Calif., 1958.   20 l. illus. 33 cm.   61-42034.
CS71.M14857 1958

11111   McHENRY.   Garrett county history of the McHenry family, by Charles E. Hoye ... (Oakland, Md., 19 -?)   1 l. 49 cm.   Reprinted from the Mountain democrat.   38M1254T.   CS71.M1486   19 -

11112   Machir.   Genealogical history of the decendants of Machir of Scotland.   Based on material compiled by Machirs and Machir descendants and by Mae R. Crummel & James L. Pyles, both of whom married Machir descendants.   Researched and rev. by Mrs. Lewis W. (Dolores) Machir and Mrs. William F. (Violette) Machir.   Pt. Pleasant, W. Va., Mattox Print. Service, 1964.   164 p. (p.163-164 blank) illus., ports. 23 cm.   On cover: 1699-1964. Additions and corrections in MS.   "Corrections" slip stapled on p. 7.   Bibliography: p. 151-153.   64-5544.
CS71.M14864 1964

McHUGH.   See: GOODMAN, 1968
                JOHNSON, 1961

MACIEL.   See ANTUNES MACIEL.

11113   McILHENNY.   The McIlhenny family genealogical chart; investigations of court house records, churches, etc. , by Warren S. Ely.   Prepared for and by R. L. Brownfield, Jr. and Rex Newlon Brownfield.   (n. p., n. d.)   geneal. table. 53 x 41 cm. fold. to 27 x 41 cm.   Manuscript. Includes "Newcomer family chart, no. 2, of Lancaster County, Penna., about seventeen hundred twenty (1720)" 55-55826.
CS71.M1487

11114   McILHENNY.   The McIlhenny family genealogical chart; investigations of court house records, churches, etc., by Warren S. Ely.   Prepared for and by R. L. Brownfield, Jr. and Rex Newlon Brownfield.   (n. p.) 1909.   geneal. table. 53 x 41 cm. fold. to 27 x 41 cm.   Manuscript. " McIlhenny family chart of Lancaster County, Penna., about seventeen hundred twenty (1720) Chart number one (1)" 55-55829.
CS71.M1487   1909

11115   McILHENNY.   History of the McIlhenny-King families of Adams County, Pennsylvania.   By John Andrew Himes.   (Gettysburg? 1916?)   144 p. illus. 22 cm.   McIlhenny family compiled by J. A. Himes; King family compiled by W. A. McClean.   54-48412.   CS71.M1487   1916

11116   McILHENNY.   Descendants of Ezekiel McIlhenny.   By Samuel Alfred McIlhenny.   (n. p., 1943)   (5) l. 29 cm.   53-55957.   CS71.M1487   1943

11117   McILHENNY.   The family and descendants of Edward Avery McIlhenny.   By Pauline (McIlhenny) Simmons.   (Avery Island? La., 1948?)   (1) l. 23 cm.   Typed title page supplied. 53-36204.
CS71.M1487   1948

11118   McILHENNY.   McIlhenny families of Lancaster County, Pennsylvania, compiled by Robert L. Brownfield, Jr., and Rex Newlon Brownfield.   (n. p.) 1952.   19 p. 36 cm.   Typed title page supplied. 53-32478.
CS71.M1487   1952

McILHENNY.   See also: KINNEY, 1903
                         NEWCOMER, 1910

McILHANY.   See also KINNEY, F225.M15

McILVAINE.   See TORRENCE, 1958

McILWRAITH.   See McELREATH.

11119   McINTIRE.   The McIntire family, descendents (!) of Micum Mecantire of York county, Maine; compiled by Harry Alexander Davis ... (Washington, D. C.)   McIntire clan (of) York county, Me., 1939.   viii 243 numb. l. front., plates, port. 28 cm.   Reproduced from type-written copy. 40-34271.   CS71.M1488   1939

11120   McINTIRE.   Descendants of Micum McIntire, a Scottish Highlander, deported by Oliver Cromwell after the battle of Dunbar, September 3, 1650, and settled at York, Maine, about 1668, compiled and published by Robert Harry McIntire ... Rutland, Vt., The Tuttle publishing company, inc., 1940.   158, (2) p. front. (coat of arms) illus. (map) 2 pl. on 1 l. 23½ cm. "This edition is limited to three hundred copies of which this is number 51." Two pages at end for "Owner's lineage." 41-371.   CS71.M1488   1940

11121   McINTIRE.   Descendants of Philip McIntire, a Scottish Highlander who was deported by Oliver Cromwell following the battle of Dunbar, September 3, 1650, and settled at Reading, Mass., about 1660, compiled and published by Robert Harry McIntire ... Lancaster, Pa., Lancaster press., inc., 1941.   218, (2) p. front. (coat of arms) illus. (map) ports. 23½ cm. Two pages at end for "Owner's lineage." "This edition is limited to three hundred copies of which this is number 42." 42-450.   CS71.M1488   1941

11122   McINTIRE.   The MacIntyre, McIntyre and McIntire clan of Scotland, Ireland, Canada, and New England.   By Robert Harry McIntire.   (n. p.) 1949.   372 p. 27 cm. 52-32361.   CS71.M1488   1949

11123   McINTIRE.   Ancestry of Robert Harry McIntire and of Helen Annette McIntire, his wife. Norfolk, Va., 1950.   447 l. 27 cm. 52-32556.   CS71.M1488   1950

11124   McINTIRE.   Tombstone inscriptions of Cherry Fork Cemetery, Adams County, Ohio, and genealogical gleanings, compiled by Lillian Colletta and Leslie E. Puckett.   Denville, N.J., 1964. viii, 91 p. illus., map. 28 cm. 65-3529.   F499.C38C6

McINTIRE.   See also: FLAGG, 1903
                                        McINTYRE.
                                        McLEAN, 1942
                                        ZANE, F495.M33

11125   McINTOSH.   A genealogical record of the descendants of Andrew McIntosh of Willington, Conn. ... with a sketch of the family of David Lillibridge ... By J. C. McIntosh ... Springfield, Mass., C. W. Bryan & co., printers, 1888.   51 p. 22 cm. 3-490.   CS71.M15   1888

11126   McINTOSH.   History of Cayuga village, compiled and written by Florence Pharis McIntosh ... Syracuse and New York, Mason printing corporation, 1927.   2 p. l., 7-112 p. fold. front., illus. (incl. ports., map) 23½ cm. "Genealogy record of the first families, 1798-1927": p. (89)-112. 27-13339.   F129.C37M2

11127   McINTOSH.   McIntosh family history through the line of Charles, David and James Wesley, by S. A. McIntosh.   (n. p., 1937?)   3 p. l., 101 numb. l. incl. illus. (mounted photos.) fold. geneal. tab. 28 cm. Typewritten. 37-21346.   CS71.M15   1937

11128   McINTOSH.   The Clan Mackintosh and the Clan Chattan.   By Margaret Elizabeth Mackintosh. Foreword by Donald Cameron of Lochiel.   Edinburgh, W. & A. K. Johnston, 1948.   xiv, 130 p. plates (part col.) ports., maps, facsim., coats of arms (part col.) 23 cm. 48-23965*.   CS479.M33   1948

11129   McINTOSH.   McIntosh family in vertical file.   Ask reference librarian for this material.

McINTOSH.   See also: BAILLIE, 1898
                                          BUFORD, 1903
                                          GUNTHER, CS629.G8
                                          HYNES, 1957
                                          VANDERPYL, 1933

11130   McINTYRE.   The McIntyres of Montgomery County, North Carolina, 1836-1965 (by) Lucy E. McIntyre.   Red Oak, N. C., 1965.   1 v. (unpaged) ports., facsim. 21 cm. Cover title. 66-96552.   CS71.M1512   1965

McINTYRE.   See also McINTIRE.

11131   McIVER.   Account of the Clan-Iver.   Aberdeen (W. Bennett, printer) 1873.   3 p. l., 111 p. 25 cm. By Peter Colin Campbell. Edition limited to 150 copies. 6-8684.   CS479.M26

11132   McIVER.   Genealogy of the McIver family, by Helen H. McIver.   (Monterey, Cal., 1910)
26 p. 22 cm. Cover-title. Manuscript notes throughout text. 16-10508.   CS71.M1515   1910

11133   McIVER.   Genealogy of the McIver family of North Carolina, compiled by Helen M. McIver.
Richmond, Va., Whittet & Shepperson, 1943 -   v. 23½ cm.   44-1908.   CS71.M1515   1943

11134   McIVER.   McIver family of North Carolina, by Kenneth L. Kelly.   Washington, McIver Art
and Publications (c. 1964)   382 p. illus., ports. 27 cm. Revision and extension of Genealogy of the McIver family of North
Carolina, by Helen H. McIver, published in 1922. 64-24754.   CS71.M1515   1964

11135   MACK.   Mack genealogy.   The descendants of John Mack of Lyme, Conn., with appendix
containing genealogy of allied families, etc.   By Mrs. Sophia (Smith) Martin ... Rutland, Vt., The
Tuttle company, printers, 1903-04.   2 v. 24 cm. Paged continuously. 4-33874.   CS71.M152 1903-4

11136   MACK.   Alexander Mack, the Tunker, and descendants, by Rev. Freeman Ankrum, A.B.
Scottdale, Pa., Pub. by the Herald press for F. Ankrum, Masontown, Pa., 1943.   xvi, 352 p. incl. front.,
illus. (incl. ports., facsim.) 20 cm. 43-14382.   CS71.M152   1943

11137   MACK.   The Mack and Sine families.   By Harry Wilson Mack.   (Detroit? 195-?)
74 p. illus. 28 cm. 56-44906.   CS71.M152

11138   MACK.   Mack family: the ancestors and some other relatives of the grandchildren of Charles
Samuel Mack (1856-1930) and Laura Gordon (Test) Mack (1871-1962) through their children Francis
Test Mack, Edward Ely Mack, senior, Gordon Charles Mack, Cornelia Rebecca Mack, Julian Ellis
Mack and David Mack, by J.E.M. (Julian Ellis Mack) with the help of L.T.M. and others.   Chicago,
Printed under the direction of C.S. Mack, 1961 -   1 v. (loose-leaf) illus. 29 cm. 63-37031.
                                                                                    CS71.M152   1961

          MACK.   See also: SMITH, 1908
                                        TREMAN, 1901

11139   MACKAY.   History of the house and clan of Mackay, containing for connection and elucidation,
besides accounts of many other Scottish families, a variety of historical notices, more particularly of
those relating to the northern division of Scotland during the most critical and interesting periods; with
a genealogical table of the clan.   By Robert Mackay, writer, Thurso.   Edinburgh, Printed for the
author by A. Jack & Co., 1829.   viii, 592 p. 29½ cm. 16-25575.   DA758.6.M27M3

11140   McKAY.   The genealogy of Hugh McKay and his lineal descendants. 1788-1895. (Boston, 1895)
76 p. 20½ cm. Signed William L. Kean. 1-1821.   CS71.M153   1895

11141   MACKAY.   Genealogy of the family of Mackay, sometime of Sandwood and Kinlochberire, but
anciently of Kirkiboll, Ribigill and Lettermore, with an account of the clan Mackay.   By Angus
Mackay ... and ed. by W.P.W. Phillimore ... London, Printed for private circulation and issued by
Phillimore and co., 1904.   2 p. l., 27, (1) p. 28½ cm. 15-16631.   CS479.M28   1904

11142   MACKAY.   The book of Mackay, by Angus Mackay ... Edinburgh, N. Macleod; Madoc, Ont.,
E. Mackay, 1906.   x, 499, (1) p. illus., 4 pl. (2 col.) 12 port. (incl. front.) map. 26 cm. "The edition is limited to five hundred
copies, of which this is no. 31, signed by the author." 6-36624.   CS479.M28   1906

11143   MACKAYE.   Annals of an era; Percy MacKaye and the MacKaye family, 1826-1932; a record
of biography and history, in commentaries and bibliography, edited, with an introduction, by Edwin
Osgood Grover ... Comprising records chiefly included in the MacKaye collection at the Dartmouth
college library.   Prefatory note by Gamaliel Bradford.   Published under the auspices of Dartmouth
college.   Washington, D.C., The Pioneer press, 1932.   3 p. l., v-xxiii, 72 p., 2 l., xxix-xliv p., 2 l., 77-534 p.,
1 l., xlvii-lxxviii p. front. (4 port.) 22½ cm. "The Mackaye collection; a supplemental bibliography, 1761-1931, of material preserved at
Dartmouth college library ... compiled chiefly from original sources in the archives of Steele MacKaye and Percy MacKaye, by Marion Morse
MacKaye": p. (299)-534. 32-35594.   Z8534.8.G88
          —— Copy 2.   xvi pl. (incl. ports., facsims.) on 8 l. 26 cm. 33-6605.   Z8534.8.G881

11144   McKAY.   A sketch of the family of Richard McKay, compiled by Oscar Reed McKay.   Rev.
ed. Indianapolis, Ind., 1934.   16, (3) p. illus. (incl. ports.) geneal. tables. 29 cm.   Blank pages for "Additions and corrections"
(3 at end)   35-14613.   CS71.M153   1934

11145   McKAY.   McKay, Tucker, Douglass (and) Lazelle families, by Joseph W. McKay; with
sketches of Douglass and Lazelle families, by Lillian D. McKay.   (Shreveport, La., 1950)
101 p. 21 cm. 50-30810.   CS71.M153   1950

11146   MACKAY.   The clan Mackay; a Celtic resistance to feudal superiority.   By Margaret O.
MacDougall.   Edinburgh, W. & A.K.Johnston & G.W.Bacon (1953)   32 p. illus. 19 cm. (W. & A.K. Johnston's
clan histories 6) 55-38570.   CS479.M28   1953

11147   McKAY.   The McKoy family of North Carolina and other ancestors including Ancrum, Berry,
Halling, Hasell (and) Usher.   By Henry Bacon McKoy.   Greenville, S.C., 1955.   198 p. illus., ports.,
coats of arms. 24 cm. 56-20196.   CS71.M153   1955

11148   MACKAY.   Descendants of Thomas Mackay, Utah pioneer.   Murray, Utah pioneer.   By
Thomas Mackay Family Organization.   Utah (1964 -   v. illus., ports., facsims., geneal. tables. 24 cm.
64-3380.   CS71.M153   1964

11149   McKAY.   Joseph McKay - Martha Blair; their progenitors, posterity and lineal lines, a documented history, 1135-1967.   By Ila May (Fisher) Maughan.   (n.p., c.1967)   x, 254 p. illus., coat of arms,
forms, maps, ports. 29 cm. Includes bibliographies. 68-3495.   CS71.M153   1967

MACKAY.   See also : FUNSTEN, 1926
                      MACKOY.
                      WANNAMAKER, 1937

MACKAYE.   See MACKAY.

11150   McKEAN.   Genealogy of the McKean family of Pennsylvania, with a biography of the Hon.
Thomas McKean, LL.D. ... By Roberdeau Buchanan.   With an introductory letter by the Hon.
Thomas F. Bayard, LL.D.   Lancaster, Pa., Inquirer printing company, 1890.   xiv, 273 p. front. (port.)
facsims. 23 cm. 9-11934.   CS71.M154   1890

11151   McKEAN.   McKean genealogies, from the early settlement of McKeans or McKeens in
America to the present time, 1902; with portraits representing the different branches of the family.
By Cornelius McKean ... Des Moines, The Kenyon printing & mfg. co., 1902.   213 p. front., illus., pl.,
ports., geneal. tab. 23½ cm. 3-24079.   CS71.M154   1902

11152   McKEAN.   McKean historical notes, being quotations from historical and other records, relating chiefly to MacIain-MacDonalds, many calling themselves McCain, McCane, McEan, MacIan,
McIan, McKean, MacKane, McKane, McKeehan, McKeen, McKeon, etc.   Arranged and mostly comp.
by Fred G.McKean, U.S.N.   Washington, D.C.   (Press of Gibson bros.) 1906.   250 p. illus. (incl. ports.,
maps, facsims.) pl. 24 cm. Mounted pattern of MacKeane tartan. Contains music. Supplements "McKean genealogies," by Cornelius McKean,
published, 1902. cf. Introd. 7-2575.   CS479.M3

11153   McKEAN.   See also: DINSMORE, D919.M87
                             DINSMORE, 1898

11154   McKEE.   The McKees of Virginia and Kentucky, By George Wilson McKee ... (Pittsburgh,
Pa., Press of J.B. Richards, 1891)   2 p. l., 3-196 p. front. (port.) 21 cm. 26-392.   CS71.M156   1891

11155   McKEE.   American genealogy of the allied families McKee, McClintock, Mills, Stipp and
Stewart.   Compiled by James Robert McKee.   Los Angeles, Cal., 1900.   sheet. 107½ x 71½ cm. 5-34160.
                                                                                                          CS71.M156   1900

11156   McKEE.   McKee and allied families; a genealogical study with biographical notes.   Compiled and priv. print. for Mrs. J. Langdon McKee.   American Historical Company, inc., New York,
1949.   141 p. ports., col. coats of arms. 33 cm. Alternate pages blank. 50-1661.   CS71.M1443   1949

McKEE. See also: HOGG, 1921
 HYNES, 1941-2
 WALLACE, 1930

McKEEHAN. See WILLIAMS, 1928

McKEEL. See WHITFIELD, 1965

McKEEN. See McKEAN.

11157   McKEEVER. McKeever history, with allied families of West Middletown, Washington County, Pennsylvania. By Bernice (Bartley) Bushfield. (Toronto? Ohio, 1959)   160 p. 28 cm. 60-36362.
CS71.M1563   1959

McKELVEY. See WILBUR, 1961

11158   McKENNEY. Some descendants of Mordecai McKinney, edited by Gerald McKinney Petty and Eular McKinney Ridgway. (n.p.) 1953.   185 p. illus. 23 cm. 55-19400.   CS71.M158   1953

McKENNEY. See also: McKINNEY.
 SMALL, 1910
 SMALL, 1934

11159   MACKENZIE.   The genealogie of the Mackenzies, preceeding ye years M. DC. LXI.   Wreattin in ye year M. DC. LXIX. by a persone of qualitie.   Edinburgh, University press, 1829.   2 p. l., 16 p. 29 cm. "Only 50 copies printed." "Printed from a ms. written by Sir George Mackenzie, of Rosehaugh, afterwards Earl of Cromarty, Viscount Tarbat ... The editor was J.W. Mackenzie, esq. ..." - Martin, Privately printed books, 1834. 2-27570.   CS479.M32   1829

11160   MACKENZIE.   The earls of Cromartie; their kindred, country, and correspondence, by William Fraser ... Edinburgh, 1876.   2 v. illus., plates (partly col.) ports., facsims. 26 cm. 11-21773.
DA758.3.C7F7

11161   MACKENZIE.   History of the clan Mackenzie; with genealogies of the principal families. By Alexander Mackenzie ... Inverness, A. & W. Mackenzie, 1879.   xv, 463, (1) p. fold. geneal. tab., 22½ cm. 8-37483.   CS479.M32   1879

11162   MACKENZIE.   History of the Mackenzie, with genealogies of the principal families of the name.   New, revised and extended edition.   By Alexander Mackenzie ... Inverness, A. & W. Mackenzie, 1894.   xv, 648 p. front. (port.) col. pl. 22½ cm. 14-15285.   CS479.M32   1894

11163   MACKENZIE.   The genealogy of the stem of the family of Mackenzie, marquesses and earls of Seaforth.   Mentioning also the cadet branches of the family: from which chief each is descended: and such hereditary honours as have been conferred upon them by the Crown.   By Sir E. Mackenzie Mackenzie, bart. ... (Melbourne, Australia, 1904)   61 l. front. 22 cm. Tail-pieces. 15-21510.
CS479.M32   1904

11164   MACKENZIE.   Ancient deeds and other writs in the Mackenzie-Wharncliffe charter-chest, with short notices of Sir George Mackenzie of Rosehaugh; the first earls of Cromarty; the Right Honourable James Stewart Mackenzie, lord privy seal of Scotland; and others.   Prepared on the instructions of the Right Hon. Francis John, earl of Wharncliffe, by J. W. Barty, LL.D.   Edinburgh, Priv. print. by T. and A. Constable, 1906.   5 p. l., 142 p. front. (port.) illus., plates, facsims. (part fold.) 29 cm. "Only 100 copies printed, of which this is no. 47." Title vignette. 21-9662.   CS479.M32   1906

MACKENZIE. See also: BELLAIRS, 1899   McINTOSH, CS477.H5M2
 COULTHART, 1855   McCORMICK, E184.S4M2
 DOUGLAS, DA758.3.A1T2   TRAILL, 1902
 LAW, DA890.C88W8

11165   McKERREN.   The McKerren family of the United States of America, with their collateral and correlative kinfolk ... by Charles Joseph Aloysius McKerren ... Chicago„ Ill., c. 1939.
1 v. geneal. tables. 29 cm.   Mimeographed; loose-leaf.   Text runs parallel with back of cover.   40-3762.   CS71.M1568   1939

11166   McKESSON.   The descendants of John and Jean McKesson.   By Harley D. McKesson.   Miami, Fla. (Willard's Kopy Kat, 1966)   iv, 283 p. geneal. tables, ports. 22 cm.   67-287.   CS71.M15683 1966

McKESSON.   See also SAMPSON, 1922

11167   MACKEY.   The Mackeys (variously spelled) and allied families.   By Beatrice (Mackey) Doughtie.   (Decatur? Ga., 1957)   1002 p. illus. 24 cm.   57-1182.   CS71.M1569   1957

MACKEY.   See also GRANT, CS479.G7

MACKIE.   See TELFORD, 1956

McKIE.   See BACON, 1958

11168   McKIM.   In memoriam Sarah A. McKim, 1813-1891 ... New York, Priv, print., at the De Vinne press, 1891.   23 p. ports. 20 cm.   Title vignette (portrait) "Genealogical memoranda": p. 22-3   26-21696.
CT275.M436G3

MACKINETT.   See MAGINET.

MACKINLAY.   See McKINLEY.

11169   McKINLEY.   The clan MacKinlay ... (Chicago?) 1893 -   20 cm.   Cover-title: Scotland 1745
America 1893.   The (first) -   gathering of the clan MacKinlay ... September 13, 1893 -   Minutes of the gatherings.   Coat of
arms on cover.   Additions in manuscript.   4-24206 rev.   CS71.M157   1893-

11170   McKINLEY.   The Scotch ancestors of William McKinley, president of the United States. Compiled by Edward A. Claypool ... Chicago (Printed by Schulkins & co.) 1897.   1 p. l., 9-45, (1) p.
front. (port.) illus. 19½ cm.   9-11932.   CS71.M157   1897

11171   McKINLEY.   The life of William McKinley, including a genealogical record of the McKinley family and copious extracts from the late President's public speeches, messages to Congress, proclamations, and other state papers ... Illustrated with nearly two hundred photographs and four full pages in color.   New York, P. F. Collier & son, 1901.   iv, (2), 128 p. col. front., illus., 3 col. pl., ports. 26½ cm.
By Oscar K. Davis and John K. Mumford.   10-1238.   E711.6.D26

11172   McKINLEY.   Genealogy of William McKinley.   By Rev. A. Stapleton.   (In Ohio archaeological and
historical quarterly.   Columbus, 1901.   23 cm.   v. 10, p. 236-242) 17-31373.   F486.O51 v. 10

McKINLEY.   See also: DEPEW, 1959
No. 553 - Goodhue county.

11173   McKINNEY.   History of the families of McKinney - Brady - Quigley, by Belle McKinney Hays Swope ... Newville, Penna., 1905.   289, xvi, (20) p. col. front., 17 pl. (3 col.) port. 24 cm.   7-42109.
CS71.M158   1905

11174   McKINNEY.   Some descendants of Mordecai McKinney, edited by Gerald McKinney Petty and Eylah McKinney Ridgway.   (n.p.) 1953.   185 p. illus. 23 cm.   55-19400.   CS71.M158   1953

11175   McKINNEY.   A record of my maternal ancestors, compiled by Robert B. Powers.   Delaware, Ohio, 1966 (c. 1967)   366 p. illus., ports. 29 cm.   Bibliography: p. 328-329.   68-918.   CS71.M158   1967

McKINNEY.   See also: GOLSON, 1959
GRAYDON, 1909

11176   McKINNIE.   The descendants of Lewis McKinnie.   (Washington? 194-)   9 l. 27 cm. Typewritten,
with additions in ms.   50-25464.   CS71.M1586   1940

11177   MACKINNON.   Memoirs of the clan Fingon.   For private circulation.   By Rev. Donald D. Mackinnon, M.A.   Tunbridge Wells, Printed by L. Hepworth (1884)   viii p., 2 l., 221 p. plates, fold. geneal. tables. 22 cm.   Genealogical table of the clan Mackinnon has coat of arms and the clan tartan in color.   "List of authorities consulted and works alluded to in this memoir": p. 211-212.   18-2155.   DA758.3.M28M4

MACKINNON.   See also: GORDON, 1933
                                           TORRENCE, 1938

11178   McKINSTRY.   Genealogy of the McKinstry family, with a preliminary essay on the Scotch-Irish immigrations to America.   By William Willis ... Boston, H.W. Dutton & son, printers, 1858. 28 p. 23½ cm. 9-11933.   CS71.M159   1858

11179   McKINSTRY.   Additional notes on the McKinstry family (supplementing certain lines in the genealogy of that family by William Willis) compiled by Mabel L. White.   Starkville, Miss., 1940. 4 l. 28 cm. Type-written. 41-38330.   CS71.M159   1940

11180   McKINSTRY.   Genealogy of the descendants of Perseus and Grace (Williams) McKinstry, of Chicopee, Massachusetts, continuing The genealogy of the McKinstry family, by William Willis.   Compiled by Ruth Everard McKinstry, assisted by Mabel Louise White.   Chicopee, Mass., 1942. 1 p. l., 21 numb. l. 28½ cm. Type-written. "Sources": leaf 2. 43-2039.   CS71.M159   1942

11181   McKINSTRY.   Genealogy of the descendants of Perseus and Grace (Williams) McKinstry of Chicopee, Massachusetts, continuing the Genealogy of the McKinstry family, by William Willis; 2d ed. 1866.   p. 15-16.   Compiled by Ruth Everard McKinstry, assisted by Mable Louise White.   Revised November, 1943.   Chicopee, Mass. (1943)   1 p. l., 21 (i.e. 22) p. 23 cm. Reproduced from type-written copy. "Sources": p.2. 44-26065.   CS71.M159   1943

11182   MACKINTOSH.   Historical and traditional sketches of Highland families, and of the Highlands. By John Maclean, the Inverness centenarian ... Dingwall, Printed at the Advertiser office, 1848. vii, (9)-128 p. 18 cm. Dedication and preface signed: F. Maclean. Contents. - The Mackintoshes of Borlum, &c. - Historical and traditional sketches of Simon, lord Lovat. - Historical and traditional sketches of Lord President Forbes. - Historical and traditional sketches of Sir Geo. Mackenzie of Rosehaugh. - Historical and traditional sketches of the family of Chisholm, &c. - Historical and traditional sketches of the Mackenzies of Redcastle. - The Black Watch, or Forty-second Royal Highlanders, &c. - Donald Gruimach, the Black-isle cattle lifter. - Highland robbers and cattle-lifters. 16-2834.   CS477.H5M2

11183   MACKINTOSH.   Historical memoirs of the house and clan of Mackintosh and of the clan Chattan, by Alexander Mackintosh Shaw ... London, Printed for the author by R. Clay, sons, and Taylor, 1880.   2 v. fronts. (v.2, port.) 30 cm. "Large paper edition. 50 copies only printed." no. 45. "List of authors, books, records, etc. referred to or quoted": p. (xxiii) - xxvii. 20-19563.   CS479.M33   1880

11184   MACKINTOSH.   The Mackintoshes and clan Chattan, by A.M. Mackintosh.   Edinburgh, Printed for the author, 1903.   xxiv, (2), 566 p. 2 pl. 22½ cm. Title vignette. "The number of copies of this book printed is 250 octavo and 25 quarto size." "List of authors, books, records, etc. referred to or quoted": p. xiii - xviii. 14-15286.   CS479.M33   1903

11185   McKISSICK.   The McKissicks of South Carolina; the stories of a Piedmont family and related lines.   Compiled and edited by Nell S. Graydon, Augustus T. Graydon and Margaret McKissick Davis. (Columbia, S.C.? 1965)   xv, 485 p. illus., coats of arms, ports. 26 cm. Bibliography: p. 471. 66-7276.   CS71.M1595   1965

McKISSON.   See McKESSON.

McKITRICK.   See WILLIAMS, 1916

11186   McKNIGHT.   Genealogical record of Thomas and Harriet Clapp McKnight, Charles and Almira Clapp McKnight, and descendants, here styled the McKnight family circle.   This book relates to but one branch of the family name.   Compiled from authentic sources by William S. Brockway ... (Milwaukee, Swain & Tate, printers) 1889.   98 p. geneal. tab. 24 cm. 3-480.   CS71.M16   1889

McKNIGHT.   See also COULTHART, CS479.C85

MACKOY, McKOY,   See McKAY.

11187   MACLACHLAN.   Memorial history of the family of Campbell-Maclachlan by Archibald Neil Campbell-Maclachlan ... London, Printed by S. Golbourn, 1883.   x p., 2 l., (3) - 275 p. fold. geneal. tab. 22½ cm. 18-2166.   CS479.M335

MACLACHLAN.   See also: ARGYLL, DA880.A6C1
CAMPBELL, 1882

MACLACHLEN.   See MACLACHLAN.

11188   MACLAGAN.   The clan of the bell of St. Fillan.   A contribution to Gaelic clan etymology. By Robert Craig Maclagan ... (Edinburgh) Printed for private circulation (by Lorimer and Gillies, 1879)   36 p. col. front. 22 cm. "List of works referred to": p. (35)-36. 20-2222.   CS479.M337

McLANE.   See WALTMAN, 1928

11189   McLAREN.   The MacLarens; a history of Clan Labhran.   By Margaret MacLaren.   Stirling (Scotland) E. MacKay, 1960.   xxi, 147 p. plates (part col.) 3 maps (2 fold.) col. coats of arms, facsim., geneal. table. 23 cm. Bibliography: p. 142-144. 61-34401.   CS479.M338   1960

11190   McLAREN.   Clan McLaren Society, U.S.A.   Quarterly.   v.1 -   Mar.1969 - (Dallas)   v. 28 cm. 72-2049.   CS71.M1613

MACLAREN.   See also: BARTON, 1941
FALLASS, 1929
KIRBY, 1898

11191   MACLAUGHLIN.   The MacLaughlins of clan Owen.   A study in Irish history.   By John Patrick Brown ... Boston, W.J.Schofield, 1879.   v, (1) p., 1 l., 87 p. 17½ cm. 9-19107.
CS499.M2

11192   MACLAUGHLIN.   McLaughlin.   By Margaret Grace (McLaughlin) Cary.   (n.p.) 1957 (i.e.1961)   30 l. 31 cm. Bibliographical footnotes. 66-39688.   CS71.M1617   1961

McLAURIN.   See CROSLAND, 1958

11193   MACLAY.   Maclay memorial: sketching the lineage, life and obsequies of Hon. William B. Maclay, by Orrin B. Judd, LL.D.   Published for the friends of the deceased.   Edition limited.   New York, Printed by E.D.Croker, 1884.   192 p. front., ports. 21 cm. Sketch of the life of Rev. Archibald Maclay: p. 18-40. 3-24607.   E415.9.M16J9

11194   MACLAY.   The Maclays of Lurgan.   Being a biographical sketch of the descendants of Charles and John Maclay who came to America in the year 1734.   By Edgar S. Maclay, M.A.   Brooklyn, N.Y. (Ogilvie print) 1889.   6, (2), 7-80 p. 30½ cm. Text within ornamental borders. Blank leaves interspersed. 9-15014.
CS71.M162   1889

11195   MACLAY.   The genealogy of Samuel Maclay, 1741-1811.   A brief sketch of a prominent citizen and public official and a genealogy of the Maclay family in America from the year 1734, by A. Monroe Aurand, jr.   Harrisburg, Pa., Priv. print., the Aurand press, 1938.   22 p. 22 cm. "Bibliography of the clan Maclay": p. 22. 39-1625.   CS71.M162   1938

MACLAY.   See also HUNTER, 1934

11196   MACLEAN.   An historical and genealogical account of the clan Maclean from its first settlement at Castle Duart in the Isle of Mull, to the present period.   By a Seneachie ... London, Smith, Elder & co.; Edinburgh, Laing & Forbes, 1838.   10 p. l., xvi, 358 p. 22 cm. Compiled by Lachlan Maclean. 9-19337.   CS479.M34

11197   MACLEAN.   A history of the clan MacLean from its first settlement at Duart Castle in the Isle of Mull, to the present period; including a genealogical account of some of the principal families, together with their heraldry, legends, superstitions, etc.   By J.P.MacLean ... Limited ed.   Cincinnati, R. Clarke & co., 1889.   480 p. front. (map) illus., port. 26 cm. 1-18885.   CS71.M163   1889

11198   MACLEAN.   The clan MacLean.   Instituted 1892 ... Glasgow, J. Thomlinson, 1893.   64 p. illus. 21½ cm.   List of members: p. (59)-64. 8-16630.   CS479.M34   1893

11199   MACLEAN.   A brief history of the ancestry and posterity of Doctor Neil McLean, of Hartford, Conn. U.S.A.   (By) John J. McLean.   Palmyra, N.Y., 1900.   iv, (5)-36 p. 22 cm. 3-4169.   CS71.M163   1900

11200   MACLEAN.   A brief history of the ancestry and posterity of Allan MacLean, 1715-1786, Vernon, colony of Connecticut ... by Mary McLean Hardy.   Berkeley, Cal., Marquand printing co., 1905.   80 p. coat of arms. 23½ cm. 15-22433.   CS71.M163   1905

11201   MACLEAN.   Clan Maclean association.   Instituted 1892.   List of members and office-bearers, &c., &c.   1908-1909.   Glasgow, Printed by D.M.Goudielock (1908)   32 p. front. (port.) 18 cm.   Comp. by John Maclean. 10-13890.   CS479.M34   1908

11202   MACLEAN.   Renaissance of the clan MacLean, comprising also a history of Dubhaird Caisteal and the great gathering on August 24, 1912.   Together with an appendix containing letters of Gen'l Allan MacLean, narrative of an American party, a MacLean bibliography.   By J.P.MacLean, PH. D.   Columbus, O., The F.J.Heer printing co., 1913.   208 p. incl. front., illus., plates, ports., plans. 23 cm.   Bibliography: p. (183)-192. 13-8301.   CS71.M163   1913

11203.   An account of the surname of Maclean, or Macghillean, from the manuscript of 1751, and A sketch of the life and writings of Lachlan MacLean, with other information pertaining to the clan Maclean, ed. by J.P.MacLean.   Xenia, O., The Aldine publishing house, 1914.   48 p. illus. (incl. ports.) 23½ cm.   Crest and coat of arms on verso of t.-p.   Lettered on cover: Lachlan MacLean of Arnabost. 15-19892.   CS479.M34   1914

11204   MACLEAN.   The family of Maclean, ed. from the manuscript entitled, A brief genealogical account of the family of Maclean, from its first settling in the island of Mull, and parts adjacent, in the year 1716, now in the Advocates' library, Edinburgh.   By J.P. Maclean.   Toronto, The Maclean publishing co., limited, 1915.   29 p. pl. 23½ cm.   Title vignette: coat of arms.   Lettered on cover: "MacLean ms. of 1716." 15-19663.   CS479.M34   1915

11205   McLEAN.   Maclean bibliography, copied from the catalogue of books in the British museum, July, 1918.   (n. p., 1918?)   2 p. l., 57 numb. l. 24½ x 18½ cm.   Manuscript. CA 27-372 unrev.   Z8536.M16

11206   MACLEAN.   A Mac Lean souvenir, by J.P.Mac Lean ... Franklin, Ohio, The News book & job print, 1918.   (55) p. incl. illus., plates, ports., maps. 23 cm.   MacLean bibliography: p. (51) - (53) 19-19096.   CS479.M34   1918

11207   MACLEAN.   Mull and Iona peoms including How the Macleans came back to Duart, by Sir George Rowley Hill, bart.   Bunessan, Mull, The author (1933)   53, (1) p. 19 cm.   Title vignette (Maclean coat of arms) "First cheap edition 1933." 33-13829.   PR6015.I.474M8 1933

11208   McLEAN.   Lumber river Scots and their descendants; the McLeans, the Torreys, the Purcells, the McIntyres, the Gilchrists, by Angus Wilton McLean ... John Edwin Purcell I ... Archibald Gilchrist Singletary ... (and) John Edwin Purcell II ... (Richmond, The William Byrd press, inc.) 1942.   xxx, 839 p. port. 24½ cm. 42-14522.   CS71.M163   1942

11209   MACLEAN.   The clan Maclean; a Gaelic sea power.   Edinburgh, W. & A. K. Johnston & G. W. Bacon (1954)   32 p. col. illus., map, col. coats of arms, geneal. tables. 19 cm.   (W.. & A. K. Johnston's clan histories) 61-42049.   CS479.M34   1954

11210   MACLEAN.   A brief historic account of Angus and Rebecca (MacMillan) MacLean, pioneers, their descendants and married relations the Kennedys of Glen Road and Ohio (by) A. Kennedy MacLean. (n. p.) 1963.   84 p. illus. 23 cm. 65-89151.   CS71.M163   1963

MACLEAN.　See also:　GILLEAN, 1899　　　　　MACDONALD, DA750.S25
　　　　　　　　　　　　　HITE, 1960　　　　　　　　　　　2d ser. v.1
　　　　　　　　　　　　　KIMBROUGH, 1960　　　　　　　McKEAN, CS479.M3
　　　　　　　　　　　　　MACDONALD, DA750.S25 v.5,12　SINCLAIR, 1879
　　　　　　　　　　　　　　　　　　　　　　　　　　　　WHIPPLE, 1917

MACLELLAN.　See LANDEFELD, 1954

11211　McLENDON.　The McLendons of Anson County (1696-1957.　Wadesboro, N.C., 1958)
112 p.　coat of arms, ports.　24 cm.　Pages 109-112 blank for "Notes."　68-5320.　　　CS71.M1633　1958

McLENDON.　See also JOHN, 1959

11212　MACLEOD.　History of the Macleods with genealogies of the principal families of the name.
By Alexander Mackenzie ... Inverness, A. & W. Mackenzie, 1889.　xv, 463 p.　23 cm.　9-26239.
　　　　　　　　　　　　　　　　　　　　　　　　　　　　　　　　CS479.M36　1889

11213　MACLEOD.　... The Macleods: a short sketch of their clan, history, folk-lore, tales and
biographical notices of some eminent clansmen.　By the Rev. R. C. Macleod of Macloed.　Edinburgh,
The Clan Macleod society, 1906.　118 p., 1 l.　front., 6 port.　19 cm.　(Clan Macleod publications.　no. 1) Errata slip.
9-9556.　　　　　　　　　　　　　　　　　　　　　　　　　　　CS479.M36　1906

11214　MACLEOD.　The MacLeods of Dunvegan from the time of Leod to the end of the seventeenth
century, based upon the Bannatyne ms. and on the papers preserved in the Dunvegan charter chest, by
the Rev. Canon R. C. MacLeod of MacLeod.　(Edinburgh) Priv. print. for the Clan MacLeod society,
1927.　xx, 220 p.　plates, 2 port.　(incl. front.) plan, coats of arms.　22 cm.　30-13750.　　DA758.3.M285M3

11215　MACLEOD.　The book of Dunvegan, being documents from the muniment room of the Mac-
Leods of MacLeod at Dunvegan castle, isle of Skye, edited by the late Rev. Canon R. C. MacLeod of
MacLeod ... Aberdeen, Printed for the Third Spalding club, 1938 -　v.　front., plates, plans (1 fold.)
facsims.　18 cm.　Contents. - v.1. 1340-1700. -　38-24168.　　　　　　CS479.M36　1938

11216　MACLEOD.　Our Macleod ancestry, by Claude Alford McLeod.　(n.p.) Priv. print. (1942)
9 p. l., 3-59 p.　fold. geneal. tab.　20½ cm.　Bibliographical references included in preface.　43-3008.　CS71.M1635　1942

11217　MACLEOD.　The MacLeods; the history of a clan, 1200-1956.　London, Faber & Faber
(1959)　653 p.　illus.　23 cm.　59-39677.　　　　　　　　　　　　DA758.3.M285G72

11218　McLEOD.　Neal McLeod, emigrant from the Isle of Skye, Scotland, 1774-1961, his genealogy.
Written by Grover S. McLeod and compiled by Ophelia McLeod Wright.　(Wedowee, Ala.)　120 p.　illus.
22 cm.　62-34129 rev.　　　　　　　　　　　　　　　　　　　CS71.M1635　1962

MACLEOD.　See also MACDONALD, DA750.S25 vol. 5,12

11219　MACLIN.　The family chronicle and kinship book of Maclin, Clack, Cocke, Carter, Taylor,
Cross, Gordon and other related American lineages, by Octavia Zollicoffer Bond ... (Nashville,
McDaniel printing co., c.1928)　7 p. l., 663, (10) p.　24 cm.　29-5263.　　CS71.M164　1928

MACLYSAGHT.　See BROWN, 1942

11221　MACMAHON.　Some account of the territory or dominion of Farney, in the province and
earldom of Vlster.　By Evelyn Philip Shirley ... London, W. Pickering, 1845.　viii, 211 (1) p.　illus. (incl.
facsims.) 29 cm.　Title vignette.　21-3226.　　　　　　　　　DA990.F3S5

McMAHON.　See also:　LA RUE, 1921
　　　　　　　　　　　　REID, 1960

11222　MACMANUS.　The ancient family of MacManus of McManus.　London, 1920.　8 p.　20½ cm.
Title vignette: coats of arms.　"Extracted by Sir John Bernard Burke ... from the Record in Ulster's office, Dublin castle."　20-23516.
　　　　　　　　　　　　　　　　　　　　　　　　　　　　CS499.M23

McMANUS.   See also: DUNHAM, 1956
                        SOTHERON, CS439.S7

11223   McMASTER.   The history of MacMaster - McMaster family.   Columbia, S.C., The State
company (c. 1926)   142 p. front., illus. (coat of arms) ports., fold. map. 19½ cm. Preface signed: Fitz Hugh McMaster. 26-20899.
                                                                    CS71.M165   1926

11224   McMASTER.   The McMasters family; it's (sic) Scottish background and clan connections.
1st proof ed.   By M.H.McMasters.   Dallas, 1961.   30 l. illus. 29 cm. 62-40440.
                                                                    CS479.M363   1961

        McMASTER.   See also LARIMER, 1903

        McMASTERS.   See McMASTER.

11225   McMATH.   Memorials of the McMath family; including a genealogical account of the descendants of Archibald McMath, who was born in Scotland about the year 1700 ... Compiled by Frank M.
McMath ... Detroit, Speaker printing company, 1898-1937.   2 v. fronts., plates, ports., coats of arms (1 col.)
23 cm.   Volume II has title: Collections for a history of the ancient family of McMath, by Frank Mortimer McMath ... Memphis, Tenn., Press of
C. A. Davis printing company, inc., 1937.   Vol. II is an "Edition (of) 200 copies." 1-10271 rev.   CS71.M167   1898

11226   McMECHEN.   Chart of the descendants of Jas. McMechen, who with his father, Capt. Wm.
McMechen, settled on Ohio river before the revolutionary war, prepared from notes of Sidney
McMechen van Wijck, jr., & of many members of the family by Elizabeth Whitney Putnam ... Brook-
lyn, N.Y., c.1938.   geneal. tab. 70 x 70½ cm. fold. to 18½ x 19 cm. 38-25888.   CS71.M1672   1938

11227   McMICHAEL.   The Harris prairie, Indiana, McMichaels.   (South Bend? Ind., Printed by
A.L.Beardsley, 1938)   (4) p. 28 cm.   "Written ... by Carl V. Johnson from data gathered by Mr. and Mrs. David Bacon and Miss
Mae McMichael." 40-2255 rev.   CS71.M1673   1938

11228   McMICHAEL.   Descendants of James McMichael (1772-1821) and Rosanna De Mott (1785-
1856) (New York, 1942)   3 p. l., 23 numb. l., 31. 28½ x 21½ cm. Reproduced from type-written copy. Compiled by H. Lyman
Hooker. cf. Foreword. No. 21 of 60 copies. 45-31785.   CS71.M1673   1942

        McMICHAEL.   See also LANCASTER, 1902

11229   McMILLAN.   McMilland genealogy & history; a record of the descendants of John McMillan
and Mary Arnott, his wife, who were born and married in Scotland, removed to the north of Ireland
and thence to Washington County, New York, about the middle of the eighteenth century, by W. F.
McMillan and C.E.McMillan.   (St. Paul? Minn., 1908?)   353 p. front. (col. coat of arms) plates, ports. 25 cm.
26-1618.   CS71.M1675   1908

11230   McMILLAN.   Genealogy of the McMillen and Gilliland families (by) Alonzo B. McMillen.
Albuquerque, N.M., 1927.   52 p. 19½ cm. 27-18283.   CS71.M1675   1927

11231   McMILLAN.   Life and work of Rev. John McMillan, D.D., pioneer, preacher, educator,
patriot, of western Pennsylvania.   Collected, compiled and published by Daniel M. Bennett.   Bridgeville, Pa., 1935.   xvi, 525, (3) p. incl. front., illus., ports., map, facsim. 24 cm.   Blank pages for "Memorandum" (3 at end)
36-3981.   BX9225.M28B4
        —— Copy 2.   CS71.M1675   1935

11232   McMILLAN.   Notes on Hugh and Christiana McMillen of Loch Eil, Scotland and Stony
Creek, N.Y., by Anna Allen Wright (Mrs. A. H. Wright) Ithaca, N.Y. (1939?)   cover-title, 48 l. incl.
maps, geneal. tables. pl. (ports.) 37 cm. Mimeographed. 40-32943.   CS71.M1675   1939

11233   McMILLAN.   Descendants of Hugh McMillen and Lydian Southwick, 1774 to 1940.   Data collected by Nellie May Wall Grant, Robert Dudley McMillan, Reginald Ray Stuart, Anna Allen Wright.
Chart prepared by Lester Allen Eggleston ... (n.p.) 1940.   geneal. tab. illus. (ports.) 248 x 35 cm. fold. to 35 x
25½ cm. Includes index. 41-1460.   CS71.M1675   1940

11234   McMILLAN.   Historical notes and speculations on the activities of the six sons of David McMillin during the Civil War.   By Lamar McMillin.   (n. p., 195-?)   13 p. 23 cm. 56-29662.

CS71.M1675

11235   McMILLAN.   The McMillans, 1750-1907; a record of the descendants of Hugh McMillan and Jane Harvey from Scotland through Ireland to America, by James Henry Cooper, assisted by his daughter, Martha Gertrude Cooper.   Revised by Historical Committee of the Clan McMillan, 1937-1951.   Fairborn, Ohio, Printed by the Miami Valley Pub. Co. (1951?)   96 p. coat of arms, geneal. table. 23 cm. 52-23548.

CS71.M1675   1951

11236   MACMILLAN.   The MacMillans and their septs.   By Somerled MacMillan.   Glasgow, K. and R. Davidson, printers, 1952.   126 p. plates, port., geneal. table. 22 cm. Errata slip inserted. 54-31926.

CS479.M365

11237   MACMILLAN.   Families of Knapdale, their history and their place-names: being a compendium of information on the MacMillans, the MacSweens, the Campbells, the MacNeills, the Mac-Allisters, the MacTavishes, the MacIlvernocks or Grahams, and others of Knapdale.   By Somerled MacMillan.   Cover design and maps by Hugh J. Collins.   Ipswich, Mass., Priv. print. by E. B. Mc-Millan, c. 1960.   68 p. illus. 22 cm. 61-24103.   CS477.K6M3

11238.   MACMILLAN.   Clan MacMillan Society of North America.   Newsletter.   Bells, 'Baxters, McBaxters, MacMillans, McMillans, 'Millans, McMillens, McMillins, McMullans, 'Mullins, McMullins, 'Mullens, McMullens, etc.   In vertical file.   Ask reference librarian for this material.

MACMILLAN.   See also: DUNHAM, 1956
                                            LAKE, 1956
                                            PATE, 19 -
                                            No. 516 - Notable southern families.

McMILLEN.   See McMILLAN.

McMONIGLE.   See BOWMAN, 1940

McMULLEN.   See: BROWNING, 1935
                                    McMILLAN.
                                    RYLE, 1961

11239   McMURTRIE.   One McMurtrie family.   Compiled by Ira Smith Brown, 1942.   Edited and published by Marion Brown Preston.   (Hackettstown? N. J.) 1968.   1 v. (unpaged) illus., coat of arms, geneal. tables. 28 cm. 79-6473 MARC.   CS71.M1678   1968

11240   MACNAB.   The clan Macnab, a short sketch by John McNab ... Edinburgh, Pub. by the Clan Macnab association, 1907.   2 p. l., 27 p. col. front. (coat of arms) col. pl., ports. 22 cm. 17-29938.

CS479.M37

McNAB.   See also FORRESTER, 1905

11241   McNAIR.   A genealogical record of the descendants of John McNair and Christiana Walker ... Dansville, N. Y., Woodruff & Knapp, printer, 1880.   cover-title, 1 p. l., 6 numb. l. 26½ x 40 cm. 23-6173.

CS71.M168   1880

11242   McNAIR.   The clan MacFarlane; the division of the clan.   Ancestry of David D. McNair, by Mary Wilson MacNair.   Hartford, Conn., The Case, Lockwood & Brainard co., printers, 1914.   24 p. front. (coat of arms) 24 cm. Bibliography: p. 22-24. 15-1688.   CS71.M168   1914

11243   McNAIR.   McNair, McNear, and McNeir genealogies.   By James Birtley McNair.   Chicago, 1923.   vii, 315 p. ports., facsim., coats of arms. 23 cm. Bibliography: p. 17-18. 23-8159 rev. 3*   CS71.M168   1923
———— Supplement, 1928 -   Los Angeles (etc.)   v. illus., ports., coats of arms, facsims. 23 cm.

CS71.M168   1923
Suppl.

11244   McNAIR.   Descendants of Daniel McNair of Georgia, Jacob Miller of South Carolina, James Nisbet of Georgia and Robert Jones of South Carolina, by Mrs. John D. Humphries.   (Atlanta? 1935)
65 p. 19 cm. 35-14615.
CS71.M168   1935

McNAIR.   See also: COVINGTON, 1956
STEWART, 1960
WHITING, 1912

11245   MACNAMARA.   The story of an Irish sept, their character & struggle to maintain their lands in Clare, by a member of the sept.   London, J. M. Dent & co., 1896.   xv, (1), 339 p. front., plates (1 double) ports., plans, maps, fold. geneal. tab. 23 cm. "Prefatory note" signed: N. C. Macnamara. 22-643.
CS499.M25   1896

11246   MACNAMARA.   The pedigree of John Macnamara, esquire, with some family reminiscences. Compiled by R. W. Twigge, F.S.A.   (n. p.) 1908.   3 p. l., (5)-84, (2) p. pl., ports., fold. facsim., fold. geneal. tab., 22½ cm. Added t. - p.: The pedigrees of MacConmara of Moin-ui-g Cianachta (parish of Cill-iubrain, co. Claire) and later of England and Wales: of MacConmara of Madhmatalmhuin (parish of Cluain-laogh, co. Clare): and of Macnemara, counts of France. A chapter from the history of Clann-Cullein, by R. W. Twigge ... 19-2311.
CS499.M25   1908

MACNAMARA.   See also SMITH, 1915b

11247   McNARY.   McNary family with trees and history.   Pittsburgh, Pa., McNary & Simpson, printers (1907?)   175 p. illus. (incl. ports.) fold. geneal. tables. 23½ cm. Preface signed" The publishing committee. 32-2625.
CS71.M169   1907

11248   McNARY.   The clan McNary of the U.S.A., the McNary-Reed sept; probable ethnic origin, clan traditions and time of immigration, by Joseph Rea McNary.   Pub. for private distribution.   Pittsburgh, James N. Simpson printing co., 1914.   4 p. l., 11-144 p. ports. 18½ cm. p. 143-144 blank. 14-13273.
CS71.M169   1914

McNARY.   See also LA RUE, 1921

11249   McNAUGHT.   McNaught-Franklin-Bartholomew families, by Virginia Eliza (Hodge) McNaught. (n. p., 1934?)   9 p. l., 103 numb. l. 28½ cm. Mimeographed. Blank pages throughout text. Edited by Helen Fairfax McNaught Geary. cf. Foreword. Includes bibliography. 37-7878.
CS71.M17   1934

McNAUGHTEN.   See McNAUGHTON.

11250   MACNAUGHTON.   The MacNauchtan saga, a story-book history of an ancient clan and its branches; with illus. and biographies.   Written and priv. print. for the entertainment of clan members. Palmer, Mass., 1951.   2 v. illus., ports. 26 cm. "Postscript and promise": (2) p. inserted. 51-5664.
CS479.M372   1951

11251   MACNAUGHTON.   The chiefs of clan Macnachtan and their descendants.   By Angus Derek Iain Jacques Macnaghten.   Windsor (Eng.) Priv. print. by Oxley, 1951.   176 p. plates (part col.) ports. 23 cm. Bibliography: p. 166-167. 55-22533.
CS479.M372   1951a

11252   MACNAUGHTON.   Family roundabout.   By Angus Derek Iain Jacques Macnaghten.   Edinburgh, Oliver and Boyd, 1955.   124 p. illus. 19 cm. 56-22754.
CS479.M372   1955

McNAUGHTON.   See also : MACDONALD, DA750.325 2d ser. v. 5,12
ROBINSON, 1907

McNEAL.   See McNEIL.

McNEAR.   See McNAIR, 1923

11253   McNEEL.   The McNeel family record; descendants of pioneer John McNeel and Martha Davis of Pocahontas County, West Virginia, 1765-1967.   By Betsy (Jordan) Edgar. Parsons, W. Va., McClain Print. Co., 1967.   496 p. illus. 22 cm. 67-25901.
CS71.M1705   1967

McNEEL.   See also McNEIL.

MCNEELEY.   See HOBBS, 1964

11254   MACNEIL.   The clan Macneil; clann Niall of Scotland, by the Macneil of Barra ... with an introduction by the Duke of Argyll ... New York, The Caledonian publishing company, 1923.
2 p. l., iii-xi p., 1 l., 227 p.   front., col. mounted pl., ports., col. coat of arms, geneal. tabs. 24½ cm.   24-6908.   DA758.3.M29M3

McNEIL.   See also: HOOK, 1925
                              McMILLAN, 1960
                              POLK, 1939

McNETT.   See MAGINET.

McNIEL.   See McNEIL.

MACNISH.   See: LEEPER, 1946
                          Addenda.

McNULTY.   See FELT, 1921

McNUTT.   See PORTER, 1897

MACOCK.   See No. 430 - Adventurers of purse and person.

MACOMB.   See GUSTIN, 1900

11255   MACOMBER.   Macomber genealogy, by Everett S. Stackpole ... Lewiston, Me., Press of the Journal company (1908?)   1 p. l., (5) - 252 p. 23½ cm. 9-14471.   CS71.M171   1903

MACOMBER.   See also: FLAGG, 1903
                                  PIERCE, 1874

11256   MACON.   Gideon Macon of Virginia and some of his descendants.   By Alethea Jane Macon. Allied families, Macon, Ga., Press of the J.W.Burke Co.   (1956)   267 p. illus. 24 cm. 57-17605.
                                                                                                          CS71.M1713   1956

MACON.   See also: MAJOR, 1913
                            SELDON, 1911
                            No. 3509 - Orange county.

11257   McPEAK.   The William McPeak family history (by) Hugh McPeak.   (Cope, Colo., 1967)
132 p. ports. 23 cm. 67-6902.   CS71.M1715   1967

McPEAKE. See McPEAK.

11258   McPHAIL.   Daniel Alexander McPhail and his descendants.   (Compiled by Fannie Vann Simmons.   Raleigh, N.C., Print by Litho Industries, 1968)   xi, 242 p. illus., col. coat of arms, map, ports.
24 cm. 76-7937 MARC.   CS71.M17156   1968

11259   McPHAIL.   Daniel McPhail and his descendants.   Compiled by Fannie Vann Simmons. (Raleigh, N.C., Print. by Litho Industries) 1968.   x, 148 p. illus., col. coat of arms, map, ports. 24 cm.
70-7922 MARC.   CS71.M17156 1968b

McPHAIL.   See also GEDDIE, 1959

11260   McPHEETERS.   The McPheeters family.   By Helen McPheeters Rice.   Winter Park, Fla.,
1956.   182 l. 28 cm. 56-44908.   CS71.M1716   1956

McPHEETERS.   See also: SCISM, 1942
                                WALKER, 1902

11261   McPHERSON.   List of the descendants of Robert and Janet McPherson, the former of whom died near Gettysburg, Pennsylvania, December 25, 1749, aged 60 years, and the latter September 23, 1767, aged 78 years.   Prepared by Edward McPherson.   Gettysburg, Pa., 1869.   geneal. tab. 95 x 60 cm. 43-32623.

CS71.M1718   1869

11262   McPHERSON.   McPherson and allied families, genealogical and biographical, prepared and privately printed for Nettie and Kate McPherson ... New York, The American historical society, inc., 1929.   153 p., 2 l. plates, ports. (1 col.) col. coats of arms. 32cm.   Dedication signed: Nettie and Kate McPherson.   Alternate pages blank.   Part of the plates accompanied by guard sheets with descriptive letterpress.   Bound in blue levant, gold. tooled.   Allied families: Winsor, Hardings, Gregg.   29-11633.

CS71.M1718   1929

11263   McPHERSON.   MacPherson family; some of the descendants of Adam McPherson.   By Elsie M. Cameron.   (Ann Arbor? Mich., 1958)   87 p. illus. 23 cm. 58-31373.   CS71.M1718   1958

McPHERSON.   See also: BYRD, E159.G56
CHATTAN, DA750.S25 vol. 41
DICKEY, 1935
KINCHELOE, 1951
Le MOYNE, 1930
REID, 1960

11264   McPIKE.   Tales of our forefathers and biographical annals of families allied to those of McPike, Guest and Dumont.   Compiled from authentic sources.   Edited by Eugene F. McPike. Albany, J. Munsell's sons, 1898.   181 p. 30 cm. A11-153.   CS71.M172   1898

11265   McPIKE.   The direct ancestry of Elizabeth & Helen McPike, of Chicago, Illinois.   (Including families of Allen, Arnaud, Babcock, Brabbs, Clark, Colburn, Curtis, Denton, Dumont, Fairfield, Forman, Guest, Halley, Leland, Lowe, Lyon, McPike, Mountain, Pike, Polley, Ranney, Rezeau, Ruggles, Shirtliff, Thurber, Tooke, Traverrier, Vechte, Vechten, Veghte, Waddingham, Wells.) With a reference list of published articles, notes, etc., by Eugene Fairfield McPike, Chicago, Illinois. (Chicago, 1906)   (16) l. 26½ cm. Typewritten copy, in cover. 30 cm. 6-34313.   CS71.M172   1906

11266   McPIKE.   Romance of genealogy, by Eugene F. McPike.   (New York, 1911-12)   1 p. l., 21 p. l., 23-41, 8 p. 25½ cm. Half-title. Two parts in 1 vol; pt. II has special t.-p. with imprint. Reprinted from the Magazine of history. 1912. "Addenda et agenda": 8 p. added at end as chapter XI. 12-8812 rev.   CS71.M172   1912

11267   McPIKE.   McPike family notes, by Eugene F. McPike.   Reprinted from the Transactions of the Illinois state historical society, 1926.   Danville, Ill., Illinois printing co., 1926.   9 p. 23 cm. "Ky to sources": p. 9. 28-9892.   CS71.M172   1926

11268   McPIKE.   Pyke and MacPike families, by Eugene Fairfield MacPike.   Aberdeen, Printers, Milne and Hutchison (1927)   6 p. 22 cm. "Continued from 2nd series, Scottish notes and queries, vol. VII, p.119." 28-5862.

CS71.M172   1927

11269   MACPIKE.   (Photostat reproductions of the charts of the MacPike, Pyke, Halley, Lyon and Dumont families)   Compiled by Eugene F. MacPike, Chicago, 1930.   10 geneal. tab. 49 x 36 cm. Two of the charts are unsigned. 31-30052.   CS71.M172   1930

11270   McPIKE.   The ancestry and descendants of James MacPike (1751? - 1825)   Compiled by Eugene Fairfield MacPike ... Chicago, 1931.   3 p. l., 40 (i.e. 44) numb. l., 11 l. front. (ports.) pl., 7 facsim. 34½ cm. Photostat reproduction (positive) of type-written manuscript, letters, magazine articles, t.-p. and plates.   The following pamphlets have been inserted: Pyke and MacPike families by Eugene Fairfield MacPike.   Aberdeen (1927); 1 leaf "reprinted from the Pennsylvania magazine of history and biography, January, 1918"; McPike family notes, by Eugene F. McPike.   Danville, Ill., 1926.   Reprinted from the Transactions of the Illinois state historical society; Notes, queries and corrections.   Notes on the Mountain Drake and MacPike families.   By Eugene Fairfield MacPike. (Reprinted from the Publications of the Genealogical society of Pennsylvania, March 1928)   Appendix II - III wanting.   Contents. - pt. 1. The Halley and Stuart traditions in the MacPike family. - pt. II. MacPike family genealogy. - Appendix: I. Signature: "John MacPike's, June 5th, 1821."   II. Letters, in 1829, 1840, 1841 and 1843, from John M'Pike.   III. Letter, dated April 28th, 1847, from Henry G. McPike.   IV. Copy of manuscript, dated January 1, 1888, signed: Henry G. M'Pike.   V. Four revolutionary soldiers (The Magazine of history with notes and queries, March, 1908)   VI. Sources (3 l. at end)   31-35125.

CS71.M172   1931

11271   McPIKE.   ... Bibliographical reference to the families of Pike, Pyke, MacPike, McPike in Great Britain and America.   Compiled by E. F. MacPike.   San Diego, Calif., 1938.   11 l.   29 cm.   At head of title: First draft only.   Type-written.   40-2259.
CS71.M172   1938

>   McPIKE.   See also: GUEST, 1928
>   PIKE.

>   MACQUARRIE.   See HATTIE, 1936

11272   MACQUEEN.   The Macqueens of Queensdale; a biography of Col. James MacQueen and his descendants, by Mrs. Annabella Bunting MacElyea; with an introduction containing a history of the origin of the clan MacQueen by Hon. A. W. MacLean, and the proceedings of the first Clan MacQueen meeting, at Maxton, N.C., June 3 to 5, 1913.   (Charlotte, N.C., Observer printing house, 1916)
6 p. l., (9)-261 p. incl. front., illus.   (ports., coat of arms, facsim.) pl. 24 cm.   Bound in the plaid of the clan.   16-23615.
CS71.M174   1916

11273   MACQUEEN.   The MacQueens; being a brief history of the origin of the MacQueen family, with special reference to the MacQueens of Corrybrough, by James Archibald Nydegger ... (Baltimore, Meyer & Thalheimer, 1928)   98, xiii p.   20½ cm.   28-30436.
CS479.M375

>   MACQUEEN.   See also CALDWELL, 1959

>   McQUESTON.   See McQUISTON.

>   MACQUILLAN.   See MACQUILLIN.

>   MACQUILLEN.   See MACQUILLIN.

>   MACQUILLIAN.   See MACQUILLIN.

11274   MACQUILLIN.   The Quillin (MacQuillin) family: The MacQuillins in Ireland, by Claude MacQuillin.   The Quillins in America, compiled by Milligan Wood Quillen and Mary Kinser Brown.   Gate City, Va., Quillin Clan (1961)   viii, 398 p.   illus., col. coat of arms.   24 cm.   61-38327.
CS71.M17415 1961

11275   MACQUILLIN.   The Quillen family, an Ohio branch.   By Mary Quillen Honeywell.   (n.p.)   1966.   32 l.   coat of arms, geneal. charts.   28 cm.   In manuscript: 100 copies printed, no. 11.   66-31540.
CS71.M17415 1966

11276   MCQUISTON.   The McQuiston, McCuiston and McQuesten families 1620 - 1937, compiled by Leona Bean McQuiston ... Louisville, Ky., The Standard press, 1937.   xx, 750 p.   illus. (maps) ports., facsims.   24 cm.   Facsimile on lining-papers.   "Source books": p. 685-686.
CS71.M1742   1937

>   MACRA.   See CROSLAND, 1958

11277   MACRAE.   History of the clan Macrae, with genealogies, by the Rev. Alexander MacRae.   Dingwall, A.M. Ross & company, 1899.   xxiv, 442 p., 1 l.   pl., map, facsim. 22½ cm.   2-12142.
CS479.M38

11278   MACRAE.   Duncan MacRae, Anne Cameron (his wife) and their descendants, Fayetteville, N.C. 1773, compiled by Lawrence MacRae.   Greensboro, N.C., 1927.   cover-title, 1 p. l., 23 numb. l.   20 cm.   Type-written.   27-18505.
CS71.M1745   1927

11279   MACRAE.   Descendants of Duncan & Ann (Cameron) MacRae of Scotland and North Carolina.   Compiled by Lawrence MacRae ... (Greensboro? N.C., 1928)   cover-title, 62 p.   27 cm.   Stamped on cover: Compiled by Lawrence MacRae, Greensboro, N.C.   Two pages of type-written "Addenda" at end.   29-7567.
CS71.M1745   1928

>   MACRAE.   See: PATE, 19-
>   POCAHONTAS, 1887

11280   McREA.   The name and family of McCrea, (193-)   11 l. 28 cm. On t.-p: Washington, D.C. Typescript (carbon copy) Bibliography: leaf 11.   78-9255 MARC.   CS71.M1745 1930z

MACRO.   See GIBBS, CS436.W53

11281   McROBERT.   Prince Edward County, Virginia; Archibald McRobert, patriot, scholar, man of God; an address before the Daughters of the American revolution, chapter of Farmville, February 1928, by Dr. J. D. Eggleston.   (Farmville, Va., 1928)   15 p. illus. 19½ cm. "Reprint from the Farmville herald, April 20, 1928." 28-13953.   F232.P83E3

11282   McROBERTS.   McRoberts family; some notes on: McRoberts' in Pennsylvania, Virginia and Kentucky; McRoberts family of Lincoln county, Ky.   A Family history miniature.   (By Harry Willard Mills)   Washington, D.C., Mills' Lettergram (1943)   cover-title, 5 l. 28 x 21½ cm. Notes originally published in the August, 1943, issue of Mills' Lettergram as the first of its new section Family history miniatures. cf. 1st leaf. "Compiled principally with family papers contributed by Mrs. A. S. Frye, sr." 44-18443.   CS71.M1746   1943

McSPADDEN.   See MEIGS, 1906

11283   MACSWEENEY.   Genealogy of the MacSweeny family.   (By John M. Sweeney)   Syracuse, N.Y., J.M.Sweeney (n.d.)   23 p. illus. (port.) 22 cm. Colored coat of arms of the MacSweeneys on cover. Signed: John M. Sweeney. 39-12255.   CS71.M1747

McTAGGART.   See MONTGOMERY, 1925

McVETTA.   See GOODLOCK, 1951

11284   McVICAR.   Memoranda relating to the McVickar family in America.   (New York, 1906)   22 l. 22½ cm. Introductory note signed Edward McVicker, William Constable Breed. 9-21010.   CS71.M175   1906

McVICAR.   See also BARD, F128.25.V27

McVICKAR.   See McVICAR.

MACWETHY.   See WITHEY.

McWHORTER.   See WARD, 1966

11285   McWILLIAMS.   McWilliams papers.   (Washington, 1940)   35 l. 59 cm. Binder's title. Photostat reproduction (positive) made by the Library of Congress from the original in Georgetown university. Contains papers relating to St. Clement's manor, Md., granted to Thomas Gerard, miscellaneous papers of the McWilliams family, and a list of deaths in St. Mary's county, 1806-1844. 42-49730.   F187.S2M3

11286   McWILLIE.   Genealogy of the McWillie and Cunningham families.   By Robert Brown Johnson.   Columbia, S.C., R.L.Bryan co., 1914 (i.e.)1938.   iv, 219 p. 24 cm. 50-45220.   CS71.M176   1938

11287   MACY.   Genealogy of the Macy family fron 1635-1868.   Compiled by Silvanus J. Macy ...   Albany, J. Munsell, 1868.   1 p. l., 457 p. front., ports., facsims. (part fold.) 25 cm. 9-11930.   CS71.M177   1868

11288   MACY.   The Macy family in America, 1635-1950 (Rooks County Kansas line) By Elbert Bonebrake Macy.   (Manhattan, 1952)   24 l. 28 cm. 52-34009.   CS71.M177   1952

MACY.   See also: FOY, 1931-2
                  FOY, 1933
                  TEETOR, CS71 T
                  THOMAS, 1926
                  WOODRUFF, 1934 a

11289 MADAN. The Madan family and Maddens in Ireland and England; a historical account with notes and pedigrees of connections by marriage, Spanish branches, and the Maddens, by Falconer Madan ... Oxford, Printed for subscribers at the University press by J. Johnson, 1933. x p., 2 l., (3)-325 p. 25½ cm. Title vignette: coat of arms. Bibliographies of Judith Madan and the Rev. Martin Madan; and Notes of authorities: p.264 - 304. 34-6745. CS439.M17

MADAN. See also GRESLEY, CS439.G75

MADDEN. See O'MADDEN.

MADDISON. See MADISON.

11290 MADDOX. The Maddox family of Maryland, with Webster and related families. By Fredonia (Maddox) Webster. (Atlanta?) c.1957. vii, 340 p. illus., ports., maps, coats of arms, facsims., geneal. tables. 22 cm. "Limited to 300 copies... Number 14." - Label mounted on inside front cover. 57-38394. CS71.M18 1957

MADILL. See McDILL.

MADISON. See: LEWIS, 1893 (addenda)
LONG, 1956
TAYLOR, 1898
WILLIS, 1909
WINSTON, 1927

MADLAND. See No.5536 - The sloopers.

MAES. See MAAS.

MAGANET. See MAGINET.

11291 MAGEE. A title to heritage. Compiled, typed, and edited by the writer. Alma Dell (Magee) Clawson. New Orleans (1964) 103 l. 28 cm. Bibliography: leaf 102. 65-1148. CS71.M182 1964

11292 MAGEE. Genealogy of Patrick Magee and his wife Rosanna (McCullar) Magee. By Clarence Elbert Moore. Fort Worth, Tex., 1967. 150 l. 30 cm. 67-9481. CS71.M182 1967

11293 MAGEE. The Magee family; a history of the family in America. By Robert Ashley Stevenson. Rev. and enl. Boulder, Colo., Johnson Pub. Co. (1968) ix, 631 p. illus., coat of arms, facsims., ports. 23 cm. 68-8387. CS71.M182 1968

MAGEE. See also LUTER, 1959

MAGENNIS. See MACGINNIS.

MAGERT. See MAGGARD.

11294 MAGGARD. Maggard family history. By Victor N. Phillips. (Clarksville? Ark., 1958?) 20 p. illus. 23 cm. 59-43498. CS71.M183 1958

MAGGERT. See MAGGARD.

11295 MAGILL. Magill family record. By Robert M. Magill ... Richmond, Va., R.E.Magill, 1907. 244 p. fronts., illus. (coats of arms) plates, ports. 24 cm. 17-31797. CS71.M185 1907

11296 MAGILL. Descendants of James Boyd Magill, 1799-1880, emigrant from Ireland to Chester Co., S.C. in 1823; a biographical and historical genealogy, including allied families. By Hazel (Parker) Jones. (Kershaw, S.C., c.1963) 195 p. illus., ports. 24 cm. Bibliography: p. 167-168. 64-1083. CS71.M185 1963

MAGILL.   See also: ARMSTRONG, CS61. R6 v. 2.
                                      JONES, 1961
                                      POWELL, 1928

11297   MAGINET.   Ancestors of George McNett and Susan Armentrout with their known descendants and some related families.   By Thomas A. Ebaugh.   (New Orleans? 1961)   218, xxxiv p. illus., ports., col. coat of arms, facsims. 24 cm. "Limited to 200 copies." 61-39890.   CS71. M187   1961

MAGINNISS. See BASKERVILLE, 1930

11298   MAGNAN.   La famille Magnan, établie à Charlesbourg en 1665.   Quelques notes sur la famille Magnan établie à Saint-Cuthbert en 1775, puis à Sainte-Ursule en 1852.   Les familles alliées: Beland, Bruneau, Lemieux, Paquet, Cloutier et Tardivel.   Par Hormisdas Magnan.   Québec, 1925.   100 p. pl., ports., plan. 23½ cm. Blank pages for "Memorandum" (94-98) 25-14874.   CS90. M2

MAGNET.   See MAGINET.

11299   MAGOON.   The Magoon family.   By Leonard Webster Ellinwood.   Washington, 1960.   17 l. illus. 22 cm. 60-44430.   CS71. M22   1960

11300   MAGOUN.   Descendants of Aaron and Mary (Church) Magoun, of Pembroke, Mass.   (n. p., 1890?)   (3)-14 p. illus. (ports.) 23 cm. 29-7564.   CS71. M21   1890

11301   MAGOUN.   Descendants of Aaron and Mary (Church) Magoun, of Pembroke, Mass. ... 3d ed. By Samuel Breck ... Washington, D.C., R. H. Darby, book and job printer, 1891.   28, v, 14 p. illus. (ports.) 23 cm. "Supplement to the Magoun memorial ... Descendants of John and Rebecka Magoun ...": 14 p. at end. p. 25-28 blank for additional records. 9-11929.   CS71. M21   1891

11302   MAGRUDER.   John Magruder of "Dunblane," by Caleb Clarke Magruder, jr.   Baltimore, The Waverly press, 1913.   (81) - 95 p. 2 pl., fold. facsim. 23 cm. Extracted from the year book of the American clan Gregor society, 1913. 13-33799.   CS71. M225   1913

11303   MAGRUDER.   Nathan Magruder of "Knave's dispute," by Caleb Clarke Magruder.   Reprinted from Year book of American clan Gregor society.   (Charlottesville, Va., The Michie company) 1915.   cover-title, 11 p. front., fold. facsim. 23 cm. 16-7845.   CS71. M225   1915

11304   MAGRUDER.   Nathaniel Magruder of "Dunblane."   By Caleb Clarke Magruder, jr. ... Richmond, Va., Appeals press, inc., 1917.   29 p. 23 cm. "Reprinted from Year book of the American Clan Gregor society, 1916." 18-15857.   CS71. M225   1917

11305   MAGRUDER.   Descendants of Isaac Magruder, revolutionary soldier, by Caleb Clarke Magruder.   (Charlottesville, Va.) 1929.   7, 7 p. 23 cm. "Reprint from the Year book of the American clan Gregor society." 29-30093.   CS71. M225   1929

11306   MAGRUDER.   Vital statistics of George Milton Magruder family of Near Appling, Columbia county, Ga. ... (Washington, D.C., 1940)   1 p. l., 3 numb. l. 28 cm. "Furnished by George Milton Magruder, II." - Caption title. Type-written (carbon copy) 41-38331.   CS71. M225   1940

11307   MAGRUDER.   Royal pedigree of Alexander Magruder, B.C. 2349 - 1610 A.D.   By Olive Smith Pope.   Atlanta, 1943.   geneal. table. illus. 360 x 45 cm. fold. to 54 x 45 cm. Photocopy (negative) 48-31753*.   CS71. M225   1943

11308   MAGRUDER.   Early kings of Gaul, ancestors of Alexander Magruder, 1610-1677.   (n. p., n. d.)   geneal. table. 194 x 46 cm. fold. to 50 x 46 cm. Photocopy (negative) 48-31754*.   CS71. M225

11309   MAGRUDER.   Our Viking fathers from Odin to Alexander Magruder.   By Olive Smith Pope. (n. p., n. d.)   geneal. table. illus. 437 x 84 cm. fold. to 54 x 84 cm. Photocopy (negative) 48-31752.   CS71. M225

11310   MAGRUDER.   Ancestry from Alexander Magruder through Samuel Magruder and Sarah Beall ... Washington (195 -)   (6) l.   42 cm.   Photocopy (negative)   54-29026.   CS71.M225
          —— Ancestry from Alexander Magruder.   Washington (1954?)   1 geneal. table.   46 x 61 cm.   fold. to 33 x 22 cm.   Caption title.   CS71.M225   1954

          MAGRUDER.   See also: BATTEY, 1940
                                   GREGOR.
                                   McGREGOR, 1943
                                   ZIMMERMANN, 19 -

11311   MAGUIRE.   The history of Enniskillen with reference to some manors in co. Fermanagh, and other local subjects, by W. Copeland Trimble ... Enniskillen, W. Trimbe, 1919-21.   3 v.   fronts. (plans, fold. map) illus., plates, ports., facsims. (part fold.) 22 cm.   Part of the plates are printed on both sides.   "Chief authorities": vol. I, p. (xxi)   Contents. - I. The plantation, before and after. - II. The commonwealth, restoration and revolution. - III. From 18th century onward. 26-23808.   DA995. E6T7

          MAHANNAH.   See LITZENBURG, 1948

          MAHER.   See O'MEAGHER.

11312   MAHONE.   William Mahone of Virginia, soldier and political insurgent, by Nelson Morehouse Blake, PH. D.   Richmond, Garrett & Massie, 1935.   xv, (1). 323 p. incl. geneal. tab. front., plates, ports., maps, facsims. 23½ cm.   Bibliography: p. (277) - 284.   36-164.   F231.M25

          MAHONY.   See O'MAHONY.

          MAHR.   See MARR.

11313   MAHURIN.   The Mahurin family; a family history and genealogical record of Stephen Mahurin (1774-1849) of Grayson County, Kentucky: his descendants ot date and his an(c)estors to Hugh Mahurin (1690? - 1718) of Tauunton (sic) Massachusetts.   (Bethesda? Md.) 1959.   91 p. illus. 23 cm. 59-2574.   CS71.M227   1959

          MAILLER.   See RING, 1935

11314   MAILLY.   Extrait de la généalogie de la maison de Mailly, suivi de l'histoire de la branche des comtes de Mailly, marquis d'Haucourt, et de celle des marquis du Quesnoy.   Dressé sur les titres originaux, sous les yeux de m. de Clairambaut ... et pour l'histoire, par m*** ... (father Simplicien) (Paris) Impr. de Ballard, 1757.   5 pts. in 1 v. illus., fold. geneal. tab., coats of arms (part fold.) 32½ cm. Engraved t. - p.   45-45190.   CS599.M36   1757

11315   MAILLY.   Recueil de différentes pièces concernant l'histoire généalogique de la branche des comtes de Mailly, marquis d'Haucourt, et des marquis du Quesnoy, en Flandres, qui en sont issus.   Imprimé en 1757.   (Paris?) 1763.   2 pts. in 1 v. illus., fold. geneal. tab., coats of arms (part fold.) 28½ cm. Engraved t. - p.   45-45192.   CS599.M36   1763

11316   MAIN.   The descendants of Ezekiel Maine of Stonington, Conn.   By Algernon Aikin Aspinwall. Washington, 1905.   161, 18 l.   30 cm.   55-45310.   CS71.M23   1905

11317   MAIN.   Genealogical record of Nathaniel Babcock, Simeon Main, Isaac Miner, Ezekiel Main. Boston, The Everett press, 1909.   362 p. front., plates, ports. 23½ cm. 11-4149.   CS71.B118   1909

          MAIN.   See: BABCOCK, 1909
                          COOK, 1967
                          CARD, E171.A53 vol. 20
                          FISH, 1941
                          FORRESTER, 1905

          MAINS.   See MAIN.

11318   MAINWARING.   Tracts written in the controversy respecting the legitimacy of Amicia, daughter of Hugh Cyveliok, earl of Chester, A. D. 1673-1679.   By Sir Peter Leycester, bart., and Sir Thomas Mainwaring, bart.   Reprinted from the collection at Peover.   Ed., with an introduction, by William Beaumont, esq.   (Manchester) Printed for the Chetham society, 1869.   3 v.   fronts. (incl. 2 port.) 1 illus. 23 x 18 cm. (Added t.-p: Remains, historical & literary, connected with the palatine counties of Lancaster and Chester. Pub. by the Chetham society.   vol. LXXVIII - LXXX) Paged continuously.   Cover-title: The Amicia tracts.   With reproductions of original title-pages. 18-5443.

DA670. L19C5 vols. 78-80

11319   MAINWARING. ... A short history of the Mainwaring family, by R. Mainwaring Finley ... London, G. F. Okeden & Welsh (1890)   91, (2) p. incl. front. (coat of arms) pl. 20 cm. "For private circulation only." 17-23913.

CS439. M23

MAINWARING.   See also: BUCK, 1909
CAULKINS, CT99. C3725H3

MAIRE.   See ROBSON, 1892

11320   MAISSEN.   In RADIOSCOLA (Cuera 1958).   Written in Swiss-Romansh.   In vertical file. Ask reference librarian for this material.

11321   MAISSEN.   La genealogia de Clan Maissen.   1 p. Note: American descendants are the Rensch (Rensh), Showell, and Harpst families of Toledo, Ohio.   Written in Swiss-Romansh.   In vertical file.   Ask librarian for this material.

11322   MAITLAND.   Short genealogy of the family of Maitland, earl of Lauderdale.   Edinburgh, 1785. (Reprint, n. p., 186-)   32 p. 18 x 24½ cm. Reprinted with additions to 1868. By Andrew Dalzel. 15-22367.

CS479. M385   1868

11323   MAITLAND.   A genealogical and historical account of the Maitland family.   Compiled from charters, deeds, parish registers, wills, and other authentic evidences, by George Harrison Rogers-Harrison, Windsor herald.   London, Priv. print., 1860.   11 p. 29 cm. Issued also in Miscellanea genealogica et heraldica, v. 2, p. 205-213. 9-18129.

CS439. M25

11324   MAITLAND.   The pedigree of the Maitland family of Dundrennan, N. B. & Otago, N. Z., by G. H. Rogers-Harrison ... Privately printed.   London, H. Gray, Genealogical record office, 1905. 1 p. l., 10 p. front. (col. coats of arms) 22 x 28½ cm. Reprinted from the 1869 ed., with a few corrections and additions by Henry Gray, 1905. 15-19682.

CS479. M385   1905

11325   MAITLAND.   Fort Maitland; its origin and history, by Alfred Jackson Hanna.   Maitland, Fla., The Fort Maitland committee, 1936.   xxi, (1), 92 p., incl. front. (coat of arms) illus. maps (1 double) 21½ cm. Illustrated lining-papers. "Chronology": p. (1)-43. 36-17823.

F319. M35H26

11326   MAITLAND.   The saga of a pioneer family; the Maitlands, Mettlens, and Metlens.   By Gertrude (Metlen) Wolfram.   Zarephath, N. J., Reproduced by Pillar of Fire, c. 1956.   80 l. 29 cm. 56-14669.

CS71. M2314   1956

MAITLAND.   See also: DOUGLAS, DA758. 3. A1T2
JAMES, 1913a
MOORE, 1918
PYOTT, CS479. P9

11327   MAJOR.   The Majors and their marriages, by James Branch Cabell, with collateral accounts of the allied families of Aston, Ballard, Christian, Dancy, Hartwell, Hubard, Macon, Marable, Mason, Patteson, Piersey, Seawell, Stephens, Waddill, and others ... Richmond, Va., The W. C. Hill printing co. (c. 1915)   4 p. l., 13-188 p. 24 cm. On cover: The Roxbury edition. 16-3942.   CS71. M232   1915

11328   MAKEPIECE.   The genealogy of the Makepeace families in the United States.   From 1637 to 1857.   By William Makepeace ... Boston, Printed by D. Clapp, 1858.   v. p., 1 l., (9)-107 p. coat of arms. 19 cm. Autograph letter of author inserted. 9-11928.   CS71. M234   1858

MAKEPEACE. See also: GUSTIN, 1900
TAPPAN, 1959

MAKINET. See MAGINET.

11329 MALASPINA. La falsa genealogia dei Malaspina di Corsica. By Geo. Pistarino. Bordighera, Instituto internazionale di studi liguri, Sezione lunense, 1958. 107 p. plate, map, facsims., geneal. tables. 25 cm. (Collana storica della Liguria orientale, 1) Bibliography: p. 87-92. 60-30684. CS599.M375 1958

11330 MALCHELOSSE. Généalogie de famille Machelosse, par Gérard Malchelosse ... Letter-preface de m. Benjamin Sulte ... Montreal, Le Pays laurentien, 1918. 31 p. 25 cm. 34-39659.
CS90.M23

11331 MALCOM. The history and genealogy of the Malcolm family of the United States and Canada. By John Karl Malcolm. Ann Arbor, Mich., 1950. 238 p. illus. 24 cm. 61-45643.
CS71.M24 1950

MALET. See MALLET.

11332 MALHIOT. The Sarran-Malhiot family tree. Compiled by Ule A. Malhiot. (Sun City, Ariz., 1965) 1 v. (variously paged) illus., facsim., ports. 28 cm. 68-33790. CS71.M243 1965

MALICK. See MELLICK.

11333 MALL. Ancestry Mall. (A history and genealogy of the descendants of Hans Wendel Mall of Söllingen, near Karlsruhe, Baden, Germany, and much information of the Alsace Malls and several other tribes of Malls) Edited by Lydia Mall Gates and Jesse M. Mall. (Hoisington, Kan., J.M.Mall, 1954) 241 p. illus., ports., coat of arms, geneal. table. 27 cm. 54-25569. CS71.M25 1954

11334 MALLARD. History of the Mallard family; an account of their ancestors and descendants, with the allied families of Sturdivant, McWatty, Fairbank, and Poe; also Holland, Rees, McGhee, and Crawford. By Eula Mae (Priscilla) Sturdivant Fairbank. (Richmond?) 1960. 28 p. 23 cm. 61-25849.
CS71.M2515 1960

MALLERY. See MALLORY.

MALLET. See MALLETT.

11335 MALLETT. Notices of an English branch of the Malet family. Compiled from family papers and other authentic sources by Arthur Malet ... London, Harrison & sons, printers, 1885. viii, 158 p., 1 l. fold. geneal. tab. 26 cm. "For private circulation only." "Sources of information": p. (vii)-viii. 18-20835.
CS439.M255

11336 MALLETT. John Mallet, the Huguenot, and his descendants, 1694-1894. Compiled by Anna S. Mallett. Harrisburg, Pa., Harrisburg publishing company, 1895. xx, 342 p. col. front. (coat of arms) facsims. 27 cm. 9-11927. CS71.M252 1895

11337 MALLETT. Historical notes and biographical sketches regarding the American branch of the Mallet family, 1794-1930. Compiled by Severo Mallet-Prevost. New York (1930) 2 p. l., 91 p., 2 l., 85 p. incl. ports. (1 col.) facsims., fold. geneal. tab. front., double pl. 33 cm. and atlas of 3 fold. geneal. charts. 33 x 31½ cm. Title vignette: coat of arms. "This edition is limited to one hundred and fifty copies of which this is number 72." "This volume ... deals exclusively with deceased persons." "Facsimile reproductions: Seventy-five selected pages of a diary, kept in 1831 by Andre Mallet-Prevost. - Certificate of British consul in Philadelphia, 1826. - Address on letter to Paul Henri Mallet-Prevost, dated Mallet-Prevost' as postmaster at Alexandria. - Certificate of death of Henry Mallet, dated at Geneva, April 13, 1812. - Genealogical tree of the Mallet family, 1530 - 1753. Genealogical tables (in atlas): Ancestral chart of Paul Henri Mallet-Prevost. Genealogical tree of the descendants of Paul Henri Mallet-Prevost. - Genealogical tree of the Prevost family. 31-19476.
CS71.M252 1930

11338 MALLETT. Some Huguenot families of South Carolina and Georgia; supplement number 2: David Huguenin, Gideon Mallet, François Gabriel Ravot. Compiled by Harry Alexander Davis ... Washington, D.C., 1937. 1 p. l., 85 numb. l. front. (coat of arms) 28½ cm. Mimeographed. Letter containing additional material inserted at end. 38-11585. F268.D372

MALLETT.   See also: HILL, E171.A53 v.13
HUGUENIN, F268.D372
ROWLAND, CS439.R7

11339   MALLOCK.   Ballads and songs, by David Mallet.   A new ed., with notes and illustrations and a memoir of the author, by Frederick Dinsdale ... London, Bell and Daldy; (etc., etc.) 1857.
ix p., 1 1., 325 (i.e. 342), 2 p. illus., plates, port., fold. facsims. 20 cm. Starred pages, 69*-82*. 121* - 123* inserted. Contains genealogical of the Malloch, Elstob, Railton and Wrightson families. Includes music. 16-25492 rev.   PR3545.M4A6 1857

MALLON.   See NEALE, 1915

11340   MALLORY.   Mallery.   By C. C. Baldwin ... (Cleveland, Leader printing company, 1882)
1 p. 1., p. (159)-165. 23½ cm. From the author's Candee genealogy, Cleveland, 1882. 14-11912.   CS71.M255   1882

11341   MALLORY.   American lineage of the Mallery family of Wayne county, Pa., by Ira D. Mallery and Mildred Mallery Tewksbury.   (Windsor, N.Y., Press of the Windsor standard, 1940.   39 p. illus.
(coat of arms) pl., fold. geneal. tab. 23 cm. 42-14897.   CS71.M255   1940

11342   MALLORY.   Some descendants of Peter Mallory, 1607-1698.   Washington (1964?)
26, A-R 1. geneal. tables. 29 cm. 64-3457.   CS71.M255   1964

11343   MALLORY.   Ophelia Mallory, her ancestors & her descendants.   By Floyd Mallory Shumway. New York, 1964.   ii, 74 1. 29 cm. Bibliography: leaves 64-74. 64-3604.   CS71.M255   1964a

11344   MALLORY.   The probably ancestry of Peter Mallory of Otsego County, N.Y.   By Floyd Mallory Shumway.   New York, 1964.   9 1. 30 cm. Bibliography: leaves 8-9. 64-3605.
CS71.M255   1964b

11345   MALLORY.   Some descendants of Peter Mallory, 1607-1698 (by) L. D. Mallory.   Rev. Panama? 1967.   42 (1), A-C 1. geneal. table. 30 cm. Caption title. Bibliography: leaf (43) 68-1708.   CS71.M255   1967

MALLORY.   See also: BUNNELL, 1937
CANDEE, 1882

11346   MALONE.   The Malone genealogy.   By Edwin Scott Malone.   (n.p., 1959)   (15) 1. map, col.
coat of arms. 29 cm. 59-9916.   CS71.M257   1959

MALONE.   See also PARISH, 1935

MALONEY.   See FLECK, 1958

MALPAS.   See MALPASS.

11347   MALPASS.   The James Malpas family; a history of the descendants of James Malpass of the Moore's Creek Bridge community in New Hanover now Pender County near Currie, N.C., with the line of lineage of Cholmondeley Malpas of England as taken from Burke's Peerage as found further along in this expose covering the period from William Le Belward, Lord of the moity of the Barony of Malpas including Calmundelai.   With as complete history as was possible to find from 1760 to 1964.   Wilmington, N.C. (c.1966)   216 p. illus. 24 cm. 67-8817.   CS71.M258   1966

11348   MALPICA.   Bosquejo del árbol genealógico de la familia Malpica, por León Malpica Hidalgo ... de donde viene su origen y descendencia según datos de sus antepasados.   2. ed., aumentada con datos genealógicos recopilados por el doctor A, M. Capriles M.   Valencia (Venezuela) Tipografia Minerva, 1945.   5 p. 1., 7-141 p. 24½ cm. 47-15221.   CS399.M3   1945

MALSBY.   See MAULSBY.

MALTBIE.   See MALTBY.

11349   MALTBY.   Family record of the Maltby-Morehouse family.   A list of pedigrees with genealogical notes, arranged for the convenience of the children of George Ellsworth Maltby and Georgia
Lord (Morehouse) Maltby by their mother.   (New Haven, Conn., The Tuttle, Morehouse & Taylor
press, c. 1895)   iv p., 1 l., (5)-157 p. 26½ cm. "A limited edition privately printed." 9-11926.   CS71.M26   1895

11350   MALTBY.   The Maltby association compiled by the secretary ... (Forman, N. Dak., Press
of J. H. Maltby) 1909.   v.   illus. incl. ports. 19½ cm. 39M4838T.   CS71.M26   1909

11351   MALTBY.   Maltby-Maltbie family history; compiled and edited by Dorothy Maltby Verrill.
Newark, N.J., B.L.Maltbie, by the authority of the Maltby association (1916)   435 p. front. (coat of arms)
illus. (incl. ports.) 24 cm.   The expense of the publication was borne by Mr. B. L. Maltbie.   17-30090.
                                                                                        CS71.M26   1916

       MALTBY.   See also MAULSBY.

11352   MALTHUS.   Collections for a history of the family of Malthus, by John Orlebar Payne ...
(Priv. print.) London (Burns and Oats, ld., printers) 1890.   xii, (13) - 154 p. fold. geneal. tab. 29½ cm. 16-18074.
                                                                        CS439.M26

       MALTMAN.   See COMEY, 1896

       MAN.   See MANN.

       MANBECK.   See GRIM, 1934

       MANCHESTER.   See GUITERAS, 1926

       MANDEVILLE.   See: GUSTIN, 1900
                                    PETTY. BX5195.T5B6

       MANDT.   See FELLAND, 1940

       MANDUIT.   See ALNO, CS419.P3

       MANDELL.   See MENDELL.

       MANER.   See SMITH, 1931

       MANEVAL.   See OZIAS, 1943

11353   MANGAS.   The William O. Mangas family (by William O. Mangas, Minnie Coby Mangas, and
Gladys Mangas Pate.   Union City, Ind.?   1951)   44 p. illus., ports., geneal. table (mounted on p. (3) of cover)
31 cm.   Pages (35) - (44) blank for "Family records." 51-26595.   CS71.M264   1951

11354   MANGOLD.   Mangold and allied families, a genealogical and biographical memoir, compiled
and privately printed for Anna Mangold by the American historical society, inc.   New York, 1937
51 p. plates, ports., col. coat of arms. 32 cm. Alternate pages blank. Title-page and dedication in colors; initials in colors. Bound in blue
levant, gold tooled. Includes also the Weber family. Includes bibliographical notes. 38-2255 rev.   CS71.M265   1937

11355   MANGOLD.   Mangold and allied families, a genealogical and biographical memoir, compiled
and privately printed for Anna Mangold by the American historical company, inc.   New York, 1939.
51 p. plates, ports., col. coat of arms. 32 cm. Alternate pages blank. Includes the Weber family. Includes bibliographical notes. 39-16897.
                                                                                        CS71.M265   1939

11356   MANIFOLD.   The story of Benjamin and Annabel Manifold and their environments and descendants.   By Jesse Benjamin Manifold.   (E. Washington? Wash., 1953)   79 p. facsims. 28 cm. 54-19235.
                                                                                        CS71.M267   1953

11357   MANLEY.   The Manly family; an account of the descendants of Captain Basil Manly of the revolution, and related families, compiled by Louise Manly.   Greenville, S.C. (Keys printing company) 1930.   xv p., 2 l., 351 p., 1 l. front. (fold. geneal. tab.) ports. 19½ cm. Contents. - Captain Basil Manly and his four children: Governor Charles Manly, Rev. Basil Manly, Judge Matthias Evans Manly, Mrs. Louisa Manly Thompson-Powell. - Syng, Murray and Rudulph lines, and descendants of Rev. Basil Manly, sr. 30-23877.   CS71.M27   1930

11358   MANLEY.   The Manley family of Easton, Mass. ... Compiled, executed and distributed by Fannie Smith Spurling.   Delavan, Wis. (1938)   4 p.l., 52 numb. l., 1 l. front. (mounted port.) 29 cm. Autographic reproduction of type-written copy. Paging irregular. Contents. - pt. I. William Manley of Easton, Mass. First five generations in America. Rev. war soldiers. 1790 census. - pt. II. Thomas, David and William Manley (and descendants) who settled in Rutland county, Vermont. 1797/8 - pt. III. Allied families. Swift, Warren, Jackson, Patten, Jenkins, Bond, Biscoe, Spring, Cutting, Smith, Mead, Burton, Herrick, Whedon. 40-2180.   CS71.M27   1938

11359   MANLEY.   Manley family; New England and New York, 1650-1950, by Henry S. Manley. (Strykersville? N.Y.) 1965.   42 p. 24 cm. 66-50153.   CS71.M27   1965

11360   MANLEY.   Tales of the Old Lord Nelson Inn: a family story which tells how Marsden became Nelson.   By Gertrude Victoria Wilson.   Nelson (Lancs.) Nelson Local History Society, 1966.   36 p. illus. (incl. ports.) diagr. 22 cm. 67-78694.   CS439.M26   1966

MANLEY.   See also BREREWOOD, DA690.C5E2

MANLOVE.   See WILSON, 1961

MANLY.   See MANLEY.

11361   MANN.   Genealogy of the Mann family, by Rev. Joel Mann.   (n.p., 1873)   cover-title, 24 p. 19½ cm. 3-2817.   CS71.M28   1873

11362   MANN.   Chronological record of the English Manns, by J.B.Mann.   Rochester, N.Y., E.R. Andrews' book and job printing house, 1874.   95 p. fold. front. (coat of arms) 15 cm. 39-16924.   CS71.M28   1874

11363   MANN.   Record of the Man, Needles, (Nedels) and Hambleton families, with others affiliated thereunto.   A.D.1495 to A.D.1876, et seq.   Revised, enlarged, and the modern records copied by Samuel Hambleton Needles ... Philadelphia, Printed for the subscribers by E. Deacon, 1876.   54, viii, 55-124 p. front. 25½ x 21 cm. Blank leaves inserted for "Memoranda." 9-15615.   CS71.M28   1876   Office.

11364   MANN.   Mann memorial.   A record of the Mann family in America.   Genealogy of the descendants of Richard Mann, of Scituate, Mass.   Preceded by English family records, and an account of the Wentham, Rehoboth, Boston, Lexington, Virginia, and other branches of the Manns who settled in this country.   By George S. Mann.   Boston, Press of D. Clapp & son, 1884.   251 p. front. (coats of arms) ports., geneal. tables. 23½ cm. 9-12297.   CS71.M28   1884

11365   MANN.   The autobiography of Robert Mann, with reminiscences of the Mann family in the counties of Centre, Mifflin, and Clinton, Pennsylvania.   Philadelphia, J.B.Lippincott company, 1897.   83 p. 2 port. (incl. front.) 24½ cm. 17-18582.   CT275.M456A3

11366   MANN.   Wir waren fünf; Bildnis der Familie Mann.   By Viktor Mann.   Konstanz, Südverlag (1949)   612, (4) p. illus., ports., facsims., geneal. table. 21 cm. Erratum slip inserted. "Das Werk Thomas Manns": p. 611-612. "Das Werk Heinrich Manns": p. 612 - (613) 50-21950.   CS662.M3

11367   MANN.   Man - Peters - Mann: ancestors and descendants of John Man and his wife Margaret Peters of Hebron, Connecticut.   By Charles Richard Ammerman.   St. Petersburg, Fla., 1958.   51 p., 30 columns. map (on cover) coats of arms, geneal. tables. 29 cm. Cover title. 58-49332.   CS71.M28   1958

MANN.   See also: HAWES, E171.A53 v.14
                LINCOLN, 1961

11367a MANNEN. The John Mannen genealogy. By Mabel Irene Huggins. (Topeka, Kan., foreword
1968) iii, 53 1. 28 cm. 71-5703 MARC.   CS71.M282   1968

MANNEN. See MANNING.

11368 MANNERS. The history of Belvoir castle, from the Norman conquest to the nineteenth century.... by the Rev. Irvin Eller ... London, R. Tyas; (etc., etc.) 1841. 1 p. l., 410 p. front., illus. (coats of
arms) pl., port., plans, fold. geneal. tab. 23 cm. Added t.-p., engr. "Geneal. tab. of the noble and distinguished family of Manners, duke
of Rutland, &c. " 16-19779.   DA664.B4E5

11369 MANNERS. The Manners family. (In The great governing families of England, by John Langton Sanford and Meredith
Townsend ... Edinburgh, 1865. 23 cm. vol. 1, p.290-302) 4-24748.   DA305.S2

MANNERS. See also: CALL, 1920
VERNON, 1871
VERNON, 1924

11370 MANNING. Manning family of Salem and Ipswich, Massachusetts. Maternal pedigree of
Nathaniel Hawthorne. (By James Arthur Emmerton. Salem, 1880) geneal. tab. 22 x 28 cm. Detached
from "Gleanings from English records about New England families. Communicated by James A. Ammerton and Henry F. Waters. " Salem, 1880.
Published also in Essex institute. Historical collections, vol. XVII, 1880. 17-6139.   CS71.M283   1880

11371 MANNING. Pedigree of Manning and allied families. By Henry F. Waters, A.M. (Boston,
1897) broadside, 24 x 30½ cm. Reprinted from the New-England historical and genealogical register, 1897, vol. LI. 3-27369.
CS71.M283   1897

11372 MANNING. Notes on the Manning family of co. Kent, England. With additional notes on the
Waters, Proctor and Whitfield families. By Henry F. Waters, A.M. Boston, Printed for private dis-
tribution, 1897. 35 p. fold. geneal. tab. 25 cm. Reprinted from Waters's gleanings in the Historical and genealogical register for July
1897. 18-9196.   CS71.M283   1897a

11373 MANNING. Jacob Warren Mannin ... (Boston? Graves & Steinbarger?) 1901. 13 p. port.
21 cm. Title vignette. "From the Massachusetts edition of the American series of biographies. " 10-34466.
SB63.M3J3

11374 MANNING. The genealogical and biographical history of the Manning families of New
England and descendants, from the settlement in America to present time. I. The William Manning
family, of Cambridge, Mass. II. The Richard and Anstice Manning families of Salem-Ipswich, Mass.
III. Miscellaneous families ... By William H. Manning. Salem, The Salem press co., 1902.
v, 857 p. front., pl., port., facsim. 23½ cm. 3-3809.   CS71.M283   1902

11375 MANNING. Overflow letters from the Genealogical and biographical history of the Manning
families of New England. For the use of later compilers. By William H. Manning, 1902. (n.p.)
1924. 1 p. l., 77 numb. l. 28 cm. Type-written from original manuscript, May 1924. 24-20307.   CS71.M282   1902a

11376 MANNING. We should not forget, by Egbert Hans. Cambridge, Mass., Manning association,
1924. 22 p. pl. (coats of arms) 19½ cm. 24-20306.   CS71.M283   1924

11377 MANNING. In loving memory of Frank Leary Manning; family letters, 1881-1932, compiled by Mrs. E. Magawly Banon (Agnes Manning) his sister. New York, N.Y., Priv. print. by the
Paulist press, 1933. 147 p. incl. front., illus., ports. 23½ cm. 33-19784.   CS71.M283   1933

11378 MANNING. The Manning family. The Te Roller family. By Scott Lee Boyd. (Santa
Barbara? Calif.) 1954. 14, 29 1. 29 cm. 55-20151.   CS71.M283   1954

11379 MANNING. Manning and allied families. By Elizabeth Ann Wright. (Dallas? Tex.) c.1956.
116 p. ports., col. coat of arms, facsims. 28 cm. 57-17606.   CS71.M283   1956

11380 MANNING. Our kin, by W.H.Manning, Jr., and Edna Anderson Manning. Augusta, Ga.,
Walton Print. Co., 1958. 1601 p. illus. 24 cm. 59-35714.   CS71.M283   1958

MANNING.   See also BROWN, 1937

MANNSPERG.   See MANSPERGER.

MANNSPERGER.   See MANSPERGER.

MANSBERGER.   See MANSPERGER.

MANSEL.   See MAUNSELL.

MANSER.   See MANSUN.

11382   MANSFIELD.   The descendants of Richard and Gillian Mansfield who settled in New Haven, 1639; with sketches of some of the most distinguished.   Also, of connections of other names.   Comp. and pub. bu H. Mansfield.   New Haven, 1885.   2 p. l., 198 p., 1 l. front., ports., facsims. 23½ cm. 17-6128.
CS71.M285   1885

11383   MANSFIELD.   History of the Samuel Mansfield family, collected by Zola Mansfield Hoyt ... and Harry O. Mansfield ... (n. p.) 1933.   cover-title, 23, (1) p. 21 cm. "The Mansfield family, by J. Clark Mansfield": p. 3-4. "References": p. 4. 36-30607.
CS71.M285   1933

MANSFIELD.   See also: CLARK, 1934
MINNS, 1925

MANSHIP.   See PATE, 19 -

MANSON.   See MONSON.

11384   MANSPERGER.   Descendants of the Mannspergs; a genealogy of the Mansperger family in Germany and America ... by Martin Matheny Mansperger, sr. ... (New York, Chambers printing company, inc., c. 1939)   v. front., illus. (coat of arms) plates, ports., facsims. 23 ½ cm. "Mannsperg coat of arms" on t. - p. of v. 1. Includes blank pages for memoranda. 39-5237.
CS71.M2857   1939

11385   MANSPERGER.   (Coat of arms of the Mansberger family, accompanied by a photostat copy (negative) of a letter to the Library of Congress, describing it, from Charles Mansberger.   Zanesville? O., 1939?)   plate (coat of arms) 28 cm. 41-38332.
CS71.M2857 1939a

11386   MANSUR.   A partial record of the Mansur family.   By John H. Mansur.   (Royersford, Pa. ?) 1901.   2 p. l., 59 p. 22½ cm. Reprinted from the Genealogical quarterly magazine, Burlington, Vt., 1901. 1-19653.
CS71.M286   1901

11387   MANSUR.   The house of Mansur, published by Mary Rebecca Ellis ... Jefferson City, Mo., The Hugh Stephens press, 1926.   243 p. plates, ports., coats of arms. 23½ cm. 26-21719.
CS71.M286   1926

11388   MANTON.   Records of the Manton family, 1750-1914, by Edward Manton ... Chicago, W. S. Parker, printer, 1914.   3 p. l., 3-46 (i. e. 48) p. illus., plates, ports. 26½ cm. "Memory," a poem, (2) p. between p. 40 and 41. "James A. Garfield, Williams college, 1856, in his senior year," written in ms. at end of poem. 17-15676.   CS71.M29   1914

MANWARING.   See MAINWARING.

11389   MANY.   41 first cousins, a history of some descendants of Jean Many, French Huguenot. West Hartford, Conn., 1961.   71 p. 23 cm. 62-38090.   CS71.M293   1961

11390   MAPES.   A tentative correction of the Mapes family line, by Lester Dunbar Mapes ... (New York, J. S. Swift co.) c. 1941.   1 p. l., 21 p. 28 cm. Reproduced from type-written copy. "References": p. 21. 41-6961.
CS71.M295   1941

11391   MAPES.   Some south Jersey descendants of Joseph Mapes, a Quaker, of Southold, Long island, and subsequent marriages of his son's widow Mary.   By Lester Dunbar Mapes ... (Brooklyn) 1944.   5 numb. l. 35½ x 21½ cm. Reproduced from type-written copy. "References": leaf 5. 45-20358.   CS71.M295   1944

11392   MAPES.   The Mapes family in America.   Compiled by the registrars of the Mapes Family Association of New York and edited by Frank Mapes Ham.   (Bridgeport? Conn.) 1962.   513 p. coat of arms. 28 cm. Errata and addenda sheets inserted.   64-1702 rev.

CS71.M295   1962

—— 1964 addenda.   Bridgeport, Conn., 1964.   88 l. 28 cm. Intended for insertion in the original work.

CS71.M295   1962
Addenda

MAPES.   See also: CONKLING, 1909
SACKETT, 1897

11393   MAPLES.   A Maples leaf.   By Mary Ford Southworth.   (Orange? Calif., 1968)   52 p. map. 28 cm.   74-218656 MARC.

CS71.M296   1968

MAPLES.   See also: LONG, 1937
LONG, 1965

11394   MAPPIN.   Pedigree of Mappin.   (London, 1923)   cover-title, geneal. tab. col. coat of arms. 42½ x 32 cm. "Extracted from the records of the College of arms, London."   46-30513.

CS439.M28   1923

MAQUINET.   See MAGINET.

11395   MAR.   The earldom of Mar in sunshine and in shade during five hundred years.   With incidental notices of the leading cases of Scottish dignities from the reign of King Charles I. till now. In reply to an address to the peers of Scotland by Walter Henry, earl of Kellie, May 1879.   Letters to the lord clerk register of Scotland (George Frederick earl of Glasgow, lord Boyle, etc.) by the late Alexander earl of Crawford and Balcarres, lord Lindsay, etc. ... Edinburgh, D. Douglas, 1882. 2 v. 23 cm. 5-2685.

DA758.3.M3C9

MAR.   See also: DOUGLAS, DA758.3.A1T2
ERSKINE, 1875a

MAR.   See also MARR.

MARABLE.   See also MAJOR, 1915

11396   MARBLE.   Family history, by Miriam Maclaren Marble.   Compiled by Miriam Marble Hinrichs.   (n. p.) 1959.   31 l. illus. 28 cm. 60-38918.

CS71.M298   1959

MARBLE.   See also BOTSFORD, 1933

11397   MARBURY.   The English ancestry of Anne Marbury Hutchinson and Katherine Marbury Scott, including their descent and that of John Dryden, poet-laureate, from Magna charta sureties with notes on the English connections of the settlers William Wentworth and Christopher Lawson of New Hampshire and Francis Marbury of Maryland, by Meredith B.Colket, jr.; with the collaboration of Edward N. Dunlap ... Philadelphia, The Magee press, 1936.   60 p. incl. front. (geneal. tab.) 23½ cm. Running title: The Marbury ancestry.   "First edition."   36-36470.

CS71.M3   1936

11398   MARBURY.   Key to the ancestry of Anne (Marbury) Hutchinson and Katherine (Marbury) Scott, who landed at Boston, Massachusetts, September 18, 1634, compiled from the manuscripts of Anne Bartlett Coddington, by Edward N. Dunlap, foreword by Geoffrey Wardle Stafford ... (Seattle, 1934)   16 p. 23 cm. (Pacific northwest foundation for genealogical research. Publication no.1) Coat of arms on cover. 37-9453.

CS71.M3   1936a

MARBURY.   See also WILBUR, 1936

11399   MARCELUS.   A chart showing the ancestors and descendants of Nicholas A. Marcellus of Amsterdam, N.Y., and John N. Marselus of Schenectady, N.Y., compiled and drawn by J. Lawrence Marcellus ... Brooklyn, 1881.   geneal. tab. 61 x 47½ cm. fold. to 31½ x 25½ cm. 9-18738.

CS71.M314   1881

11400   MARCH.   March genealogy, by Ellen Gates March.   (n. p.) 1899.   cover-title, 4 p. 23½ cm. 21-6659.

CS71.M318   1899

11401   MARCHAND.   The house of Marchand.   By Sidney Albert Marchand.   Donaldsonville, La.,
c. 1952.   106 p. illus. 24 cm. 53-15954.   CS71.M319   1952

11402   MARCHAND.   Marchands on the Mississippi and the St. Lawrence (by) Sidney A. Marchand.
Donaldsonville, La. (1968)   183 p. illus., ports. 23 cm. 79-1276.   CS71.M319   1968

   MANCHAND.   See also BARTON, 1941

   MARCHBANK.   See MACGINNIS, 1891

   MARCHMONT.   See HUME, Earls of.

   MARCOUILLER.   See DUGUAY, 1916-23

   MARCUM.   See No. 1547 - Cabell county.

11403   MARCY.   Record of the Marcy family.   Communicated to the N. E. hist. and gen. register
for July, 1875, by Prof. Oliver Marcy ... (Boston, 1875?)   14 p. 24 cm. Caption title. 9-11939.
                                                                          CS71.M322   1875

11404   MARCY.   Moses Marcy and his descendants.   (By Oliver Marcy.   Evanston? Ill., 1897)
cover-title, 15 p. 24½ cm. 2-28225.   CS71.M322   1897

   MARCY.   See also HILL, 1904

11405   MARENCHES.   Histoire de la maison de Marenches en France-Comté.   By Jaques Pierre
Meurgey Tupigny.   Préf. de La Varende.   Paris, 1948.   xl, 190 p. ports., facsims.. geneal. tables. 23 cm.
"Sources": p. (xxxi)-xl. 49-20076*.   CS599.M42   1948

   MARET DE LA RIVE.   See COLLOT D'ESCURY.

11406   MARGADANT.   De Nederlandsche tak van het geslacht Margadant.   The Netherland branch
of the generation Margadant.   By Steven Willem Floris Margadant.   (Denver? 1956)   72 p. ports., coat
of arms, geneal. tables. 29 cm. "Translation of the original book ... published in Gravenhage in 1910." 61-35011.
                                                                          CS829.M27   1956

11407   MARGANE DE LAVALTRIE.   La famille Margane de Lavaltrie, par Pierre Georges Roy.
Lévis, 1917.   1 p. l., (5) - 40 p. 25 cm. Tiré à 125 exemplaires." 24-8345.   CS90.M25

   MARGARETEN.   See HOROWITZ, 1955

   MARIARTE.   See: MONNET, 1911
                     MULLIKIN, 1936

11408   MARIAUCHAU D'ESGLY.   La famille Mariauchau D'Esgly, par Pierre George Roy.   Lévis,
1908.   13 p. 23 cm. Tiré à 100 exemplaires." 24-8347.   CS90.M27

   MARINER.   See: SMALL, 1910
                     SMALL, 1934

   MARING.   See MERING.

11409   MARIS.   The Maris family in the United States.   A record of the descendants of George and
Alice Maris.   1683-1885.   Compiled for the family by George L. and Annie M. Maris.   West
Chester, Pa.   (F. S. Hickman) 1885.   xxxiii, 279 p. front., plates, ports. 27 cm. 9-15614.
                                                                          CS71.M342   1885
                                                                          Microfilm 10069

   MARK.   See MARKS.

   MARKE.   See MARKS.

11410   MARKEY.   Genealogy and history of the Jacob Markey family of York County, Pennsylvania, 1750-1961.   (n. p., 1961?)   124 p. illus., ports., col. coat of arms. 28 cm. Bibliography: p. 124. 62-6846.

CS71.M344   1961

MARKEY.   See also FALL, 1961

11411   MARKHAM.   A history of the Markham family.   By the Rev. David Frederick Markham. London, Printed by J. B. Nichols and sons, 1854.   xi, 116 p. fronts. (mounted port., coat of arms) illus., geneal. tables (part double) 22 cm. Preface signed: C. R. M. (i. e. Sir Clements Robert Markham) 4-9658 rev.   CS439.M3

11412   MARKHAM.   History of the Markhams of Northamptonshire.   By Christopher A. Markham, F. S. A. ... Privately printed.   Northampton, The Dryden press, Taylor & son, 1890.   4 p. l., 108 p. front. (2 port.) illus. (coat of arms, part mounted) plates (1 fold.) fold. geneal. tab. 22½ cm. Frontispiece is a mounted photograph. Blank pages at end for additional records. "Of this work not more than one hundred copies have been printed, of which this is no. 93." "The pedigree drawn up by the late Arthur Bayley Markham, forms the foundation of this narrative." cf. Pref. 16-2711.   CS439.M3   1890

11413   MARKHAM.   Genealogical memoranda relating to the family of Markham.   (n. p.) Priv. print., 1903.   2 p. l., 21 p. illus., pl., fold. geneal. tab. 30 cm. Pedigree signed: Christopher A. Markham. 21-21732.
CS439.M3   1903

MARKHAM.   See also: POCAHONTAS, 1887
                                    REMINGTON, 1960

MARKIE.   See BOYD, 1935

MARKLE.   See: BOYD, 1935
                             MARKEL.

11414   MARKLEY.   Descendants of Jacob Markley of Skippack, Montgomery County, Pennsylvania ... (By Henry Sarsaman Dotterer.   Norristown) The Markley freundschaft, 1884.   36 p. 23½ cm.
9-12288.   CS71.M345   1884

11415   MARKLEY.   Stammtafel der familie Merkle, nach den kirchenbüchern zu Bonfeld, oberamts Heilbronn, königreich Wurttemberg, und denen zu Wimpfen, grossherzogtum Hessen.   (n. p.) Markley freundschaft of Montgomery Co. , Pa. , 1886.   geneal. tab. 22x66 cm. fold. to 24 cm. 1-22676.
CS71.M345   1886

11416   MARKLEY.   Genealogy of John and Mary Markley.   Compiled by Alonzo Markley Johnson ... La Junta, Col., Daily Democrat print., 1924.   37 p. 25½ cm. 25-20714.   CS71.M345   1924

MARKLEY.   See also: DOTTERER, 1903
                                     FRICK, 1934
                                     STRASSBURGER, 1922
                                     ZERBE, F157.S3E9

11416a MARKOES.   Markoes family.   By R. H. Spencer.   In Thomas family book, CS71.T46 1914 page 134.

11417   MARKS.   Genealogy of the family of Mark, or Marke; county of Cumberland.   Pedigree and arms of the Bowscale branch of the family, from which is descended John Mark, esquire; now residing at Greystoke, West Didsbury, near Manchester ... To which is added a copy of an old vellum roll; compiled in 1746, for Jacob Mark, of Dublin ... Also a collection of biographical excerpts and Appendix of genealogical notes, compiled by John Yarker.   Manchester, Priv. print., Palmer, Howe & co., 1898.   xii, 274 p. front., plates, ports., 2 fold. facsim., fold geneal. tab. 28½ cm. "Some quaint wills discovered since the publication": 4 p. inserted after p. 22.   History of Manchester during the mayoralty of John Marks, 1889-91. p. (49)-210. 15-25119. CS439.M3115 1898

11418   MARKS.   Marks-Platt ancestry, comp. by Eliza J. Lines ... Sound Beach, Conn., Pub. by request of A. A. Marks, 1902.   2 p. l., (3)-98, (16) p. front., plates, ports., geneal. tables. 24½ cm. 16 blank pages at end for "descendants' record."   The ancestral record of Amasa Abraham Marks and Lucy Ann Platt Marks. 3-9126.   CS71.M346   1902

11419 MARKS. Marks-Barnett families and their kin, including Anderson, Bennett, Bernard, Cargile, Crawford, Eubanks, Gaines, Harvie, Jamison, Matthews, Meriwether, Stark, Tomkins, also royal lines on many branches, embracing the finest families of the old world nobility. Notes on numerous other families of prominence in America with which they are allied. War records, deeds, wills, marriages and random notes, gleaned from southern history, court records, family Bibles, family letters, etc., compiled and edited by Marion Dewoody Pettigrew, (Mrs. Clarence W.) ... Macon, Ga., The J. W. Burke company, 1939. x, 441 p. incl. front., illus. (incl. ports.,) coats of arms) fold. geneal. tables. 23½ cm. On cover: Colonial pioneers. Includes bibliographies. 39-9234. CS71.M346 1939

11420 MARKS. Brief biographical sketch and history of William S. Marks, together with data as to some of his ancestors and relatives, compiled and arranged by William S. Marks. (n. p.) Priv. print., 1939. cover-title, 19 numb. 1. 28 cm. Mimeographed. 40-2261. CS71.M346 1939a

11421 MARKS. The genealogy of the Mark family. By Gordon St. George Mark. (n. p.) 1953. unpaged. illus. 28 cm. 54-31925. CS71.M346 1953

11422 MARLETT. Gideon Marlett, Gedeon Merlet; a Huguenot of Staten Island, N. Y. With some account of his descendants in the United States and Canada, 1662-1907. Burlington, Vt., 1907. 293 1. 29 cm. 61-57029. CS71.M348 1907

11423 MARLEY. The Marleys of Langton, Ingleton, Hilton and Houghton-le-Side in co. Durham. By Thomas W. Marley. (2d de.) (London) Mitchell, Hughes and Clarke, 1921. cover-title, 23 p. 32 cm. 23-14534. CS439.M312 1921

MARLEY. See CROW, 1961

11424 MARMION. History of the ancient noble family of Marmyun; their singular office of King's champion, by the tenure of the baronial manor of Scrivelsby, in the county of Lincoln: also other dignitorial tenures, and the services of London, Oxford, &c. on the coronation-day. The whole collected at a great expense from the public records ... By T. C. Banks, esq. London, H. K. Causton, 1817. 2 p. 1., viii, (4), 204 p. VI fold. pl. (incl. front. (port.) coat of arms) fold. geneal. tables. 23½ cm. Contains also genealogical tables of the Dymoke, Welles, and Kyme families. 16-2837. CS439.M313 1817

11425 MARMION. History of the baronial family of Marmion, lords of the castle of Tamworth, in the county of Warwick, between the Norman conquest and the close of the thirteenth century. By Charles Ferrers R. Palmer, O. P. Tamworth, J. Thompson, printer; London, Simpkin, Marshall & co., 1875. vi, 126, xi p. 21½ cm. 15-13924. CS439.M313 1875

11426 MARMION. Scrivelsby, the home of the champions. With some account of the Marmion and Dymoke families. Illustrated. By the Rev. Samuel Lodge ... London, S. Stock; (etc., etc.) 1893. xv, (1), 199, (1) p. col. front., 13 pl., 3 port. 25½ x 19½ cm. 6-22734. DA690.S42L8

11427 MARMION. Scrivelsby, the home of the champions, with some account of the Marmion and Dymoke families ... By the Rev. Samuel Lodge ... 2d ed. ... London, E. Stock; (etc., etc.) 1894. xix, (1) 216 p. col. front. (coat of arms) plates, ports., fold. geneal. tab. 25 cm. 35-17121. DA690.S42L8 1894

MARQUAND. See MONROE, E171.A53 v. 14

11428 MARQUIS. ... La famille Canac-Marquis et familles alliées, dictionnaire généalogique ... By Paul Victor Charland. Québec, Imp. de l"Action sociale, ltée., 1918. 4 p. 1., (3)-414 p. front., illus. (incl. plan, facsims.) plates, ports. 27 cm. 35-21354. CS90.C23C5

11429 MARR. (Marr family of Pennsylvania, charted by W. P. Marr. Racine, Wis., 1918) geneal. tab. 60 x 47 cm. fold. to 15 x 23 cm. Blue-print. "Charted by W. P. Marr" added in ms. 20-22871. CS71.M35 1918

11430 MARR. The Marr family. Compiled by Warren Marr, II. (n. p., 1967?) 39 1. illus., map 29 cm. Cover title. 68-2222. CS71.M35 1967

MARR. See also MAR.

MARRIOTT. See HALL, 1908

11431   MARROTT.   A genealogy of William Marrott and Louisa Fowlke, Latter Day Saint pioneers, by Kenneth C. Bullock.   Provo, Utah, 1965.   ix l., 277 p. illus., geneal. tables, ports. 28 cm. On spine: William Marrott (and) Louisa Fowlke. 68-5197.   CS71.M355   1965

11432   MARROW.   The records of King Edward's school, Birmingham ... London, Pub. for the Dugdale society by H. Milford, Oxford university press, 1924 -   v. front., coats of arms. 25 cm. (Half-title: Publications of the Dugdale society ... vol. IV.   Contents. - I. The miscellany volume, with an introduction by William Fowler Carter. 1924. 25-9059.   DA670.W3D9

MARRS.   See ROGERS, 1958

11433   MARSDEN.   George Marsden, Revolutionary patriot: his family, friends, and descendants. By Kenneth L. Marsden.   (New Rochelle, N. Y., 1961)   56 p. illus. 24 cm. 61-39981.   CS71.M36   1961

MARSDEN.   See also HALL, 1908

11434   MARSH.   Genealogy of the Marsh family.   Outline for five generations of the families of John of Salem, 1633. John of Hartford, 1636.   Samuel of New Haven, 1646.   Alexander of Braintree, 1654 John of Boston, 1669, and William of Plainfield, 1675.   With accounts of the Third family reunion at Lake Pleasant in 1886, edited by D. W. Marsh, of the gen. com., and printed, for additions and correct- ions by the Marsh family association.   Amherst, Press of J. E. Williams, 1886.   cover-title, 59 (1) p. 23½ cm. 17-24551.   CS71.M365   1886
Microfilm 8648

11435   MARSH.   Genealogy of the family of George Marsh, who came from England in 1635 and settled in Hingham, Mass.   By E. J. Marsh.   Leominster, Press of F. N. Boutwell, 1887.   vii, (9)-197, 197, xxxii p. 23½ cm.   9-8511.   CS71.M365   1887

11436   MARSH.   The genealogy of John Marsh of Salem and his descendants, 1633-1888.   Collected and published by Col. Lucius B. Marsh ... Revised and edited by Rev. Dwight W. Marsh ... Amherst, Mass., J. E. Williams, book and job printer, 1888.   283 p. 23½ cm. 6-869.   CS71.M365   1888

11437   MARSH.   Marsh genealogy.   Giving several thousand descendants of John Marsh of Hartford, Ct.   1636-1895.   Also including some account of English Marshes, and a sketch of the Marsh family association of America.   Comp., ed. and pub. by Dwight Whitney Marsh ... Amherst, Mass., Press of Carpenter & Morehouse, 1895.   lxvii, (1), 516 p., 1 l. pl., ports., diagrs., coat of arms. 24 cm. p. 469 - (476) blank for memoranda. 9-12295.   CS71.M365   1895

11438   MARSH.   Some notice of various families of the name of Marsh,   Compiled by G. E. C. Exeter, W. Pollard & co., ltd., printers, 1900.   3 p. l., 56 p. 24 cm. Supplement to the Genealogist. Probably by G. E. Cokayne. 9-24156. rev.   CS439.M315

11439   MARSH.   Marsh, Smith, Willard and allied families, a genealogical study with biographical notes, compiled and privately printed for Bertha S. Marsh, by the American historical society, inc. New York, 1935.   318 p. plates, ports., col. coats of arms. 30 cm. The coats of arms, and the pictures of the mosaic of Charlemagne are accompanied by guard sheets with descriptive letterpress. Bibliography throughout text. 35-13984 rev.   CS71.M365   1935

11440   MARSH.   The Marsh family of southern Indiana ... (by) William E. Marsh.   Oklahoma City, Okla., Southwestern engraving co. (1936)   (7) p. illus. (incl. ports.) 47 x 27½ cm. "The work was begun ten years ago by my father James Newton Marsh, who left his data to me with the request that I would complete and publish it." 37-16833.   CS71.M365   1936

11441   MARSH.   Marsh family bulletin.   v. 1 -   Jan. 1955 -   Williamsport, Pa. v.   22 cm. bimonthly. Editor: 1955 -   W. L. Marsh. 67-3719.   CS71.M3644

11442   MARSH.   Genealogy of the Marsh family of Maryland.   By Edward Everett Marsh.   (Balti-more? 1957)   unpaged. illus. 30 cm. 59-27023.   CS71.M365   1957

11443   MARSH.   The plantation Marshes; the colony of Edgefield County Marshes and the account of their lineage, by Lillian Marsh Harmon.   (Edgefield, S. C.)   Edgefield Advertiser, 1964.   153 p. illus., coats of arms, ports. 24 cm. 65-2526.   CS71.M365   1964

11444   MARSH.   Marsh genealogy.   Giving several thousand descendants of John Marsh of Hartford, Ct. 1636-1895.   Also including some account of English Marshes, and a sketch of the Marsh family association of America.   Comp., ed. and pub. by Dwight Whitney Marsh ... Amherst, Mass., Press of Carpenter & Morehouse, 1895.   lxvii, (1), 516 p., 1 l. pl., ports., diagrs., coat of arms. 24 cm. p. 469 - (476) blank for memoranda. 9-12295.   CS71.M365   1895

11445   MARSH.   Marsh family in vertical file.   Ask reference librarian for this material.

MARSH.   See also: EASTERBROOK, 1959
                                JERNEGAN, 1967
                                PEARSON, 1945
                                THOMPSON, 1915
                                WILLIARD, CS71.M365
                                WINDECKER.

11446   MARSHALL.   Miscellanea Marescalliana, being genealogical notes on the surname of Marshall.   Collected by George William Marshall, LL.D. ... (Worksop, Eng., R. White, printer, 1883-88)   2 v. fold. geneal. tables. 23½ cm. "Fifty copies for private distribution." This copy was made up by the author as the 51st copy, for one of his colleagues at the Herald's college and is vouched for by him as complete. A few of the original pages had run out, so he repaged the substituted ones, from the Yrokshire archaeological and topographical journal, in his own handwriting. 16-23489.   CS439.M318

11447   MARSHALL.   The Marshall family, or A genealogical chart of the descendants of John Marshall and Elizabeth Markham, his wife, sketches of individuals and notices of families connected with them.   By William McClung Paxton.   Cincinnati, R. Clarke & co., 1885.   415 p. front. (port.) 21½ cm. Folded "Genealogical chart of the Marshall family" and typewritten notes on "Some of the Marshall-Smiths ... "bound at end. 9-12296.   CS71.M367   1885

11448   MARSHALL.   John Marshall, of Billerica, and his descendants.   (By Grace Merle Marshall. Rutherford, N.J., 19 -)   (11) l. 28 cm. 50-21257.   CS71.M367

11449   MARSHALL.   Marshall family record, with Haskell, Boutwell, Barrett, Wadsworth, White, Read, Maurice, Kingsbury, Holbrooke, Stevens, Carpenter, and allied families ... Dedicated to mother, Ellen Maria (Carpenter) Kingsbury ... By Mr. and Mrs. Frank Burnside Kingsbury.   Keene, N.H., Press of Walter R. Nims, 1913.   103 p. incl. front., illus. 23 cm. Of an edition of 200 copies this book is no. 68. 13-25976.   CS71.M367   1913

11450   MARSHALL.   "The old house on the hill"; a brief historical sketch issued as a souvenir, by Coleman Randoph.   Morristown, N.J., 1921.   (23) p. front., plates, ports., map. 33 cm. "Necrology" of the Marshall family: p. (23) 21-15268.   F459.W3R2

11451   MARSHALL.   A history of the Marshall and related families, by Wallace Marshall; ed. by Fannie Spaits Merwin.   (La Fayette, Ind., Haywood publishing co.) 1922.   374 p. illus. (ports.) fold. geneal. tables. 23½ cm. "Family photographs": p. 321 - 374. 22-18420.   CS71.M367   1922

11452   MARSHALL.   ... Marshall family records, by J. Montgomery Seaver.   Philadelphia, American historical-genealogical society (1929)   44 p. front. (port.) coat of arms. 29 cm. Coat of arms of the Marshall family on recto of frontispiece. Pages 43-44 blank for "Family Record." "References": p. 41-42. 40-18914. CS71.M367   1929

11453   MARSHALL.   The Marshall family tree; Rufus Marshall and Suzanna George branch ... (By Grace Merle Marshall) Rutherford, N.J. (1940)   18 numb. l. 28½ cm. Caption title. Reproduced from type-written copy. "Compiled by Grace M. Marshall and Gertrude P. Marshall." - Leaf 1. 42-4208.   CS71.M367   1940

11454 MARSHALL. Ancestry charts of Rufus Marshall and Suzanna George ... (By Grace Merle Marshall) Rutherford, N.J., 1940) 11 l. 28½ cm. Caption title. Reproduced from type-written copy. "References": leaf 1. 42-4207. CS71.M367 1940a

11455 MARSHALL. The Marshalls ... descendants of John Marshall of Billerica, Mass., chiefly in the line of Joseph Marshall of Weare, N.H., compiled by Grace Merle Marshall, from records of Gertrude Pearl Marshall ... Rutherford, N.J., 1943. 2 p. l., 11 numb. l., 6 l. mounted illus. (incl. port., facsim.) 30 x 23 cm. Type-written (carbon copy) 44-10623. CS71.M367 1943

11456 MARSHALL. Joseph Williams Marshall and Mary Allen, their ancestors and descendants together with some related families. By James G. Marshall. (Niagara Falls? N.Y., 1948) 207 p. ports., facsims. 24 cm. On cover: The Marshall family of Bellefonte, Pa. Addenda slips inserted. 50-1532. CS71.M367 1948

11457 MARSHALL. The Daniel Marshall family, with a sketch of the Aaron Marshall family. By George Sidney Marshall. (Columbus? Ohio) 1949. 74 p. ports. 24 cm. 50-56727. CS71.M367 1949

11458 MARSHALL. Marshall family of Pennsylvania, records: 1650-1952. By Joseph Bowman Marshall. Wilmette, Ill., c.1952. 33 l. 30 cm. 52-36939. CS71.M367 1952

11459 MARSHALL. Descendants of Moses and Mary (Adams) Marshall of Columbiana County, Ohio, with reference to the Adams, Aleshire, Clark, Darst and Edmundson families. By Sanford Charles Gladden. (Boulder? Colo.) 1965. 152 p. group ports. 29 cm. Limited to 100 copies. No. 9. Includes bibliographical references. 65-5560. CS71.M367 1965

MARSHALL. See also: COLLIER, 1951a KENDALL, 1947
ANDERSON, 19 - KEY, 1931
GARDINER, 1929 NEWLIN, 1942
GILES, 1864 ROSS, 1908
HASKELL, 1887 SMITH, 1904

11460 MARSHAM. Register of the Marshams of Kent down to the end of the year 1902. By the Hon, Robert Marsham-Townshend ... London, Mitchell, Hughes and Clarke, 1903. 15 l. 35 x 43½ cm. 8-28721. CS439.M32

11461 MARSOLET. La famille Marsolet de St-Aignan, par Pierre-Georges Roy. Levis, 1934. 1 p. l., (5) - 29 p. 24½ cm. 35-14026. CS599.M43 1934

MARSOLET. See also D'Amours, 1961

11462 MARSTELLER. Seven Marstellers and their lineal descendants, compiled by John Andrew Thompson Marsteller. (Fincastle, Va., C.C.Hedrick, printer, 1938) 32 p. incl. plates, port., coat of arms. 23½ cm. 38-14721. CS71.M37 1938

MARSTERS. See BRAYTON, 1922

11463 MARSTON. Memoirs of the Marstons of Salem, with a brief genealogy of some of their descendants ... Reprinted from the New-England historical and genealogical register. vol. XXVII, 1873. Boston, Press of D. Clapp & son, 1873. 1 p. l., 48 p. illus. 26 cm. "Two hundred copies." "Prefatory note" signed: John L. Watson. "Appendix. Containing brief genealogies of some of the descendants of Benjamin Marston and Elizabeth Winslow": p. (37) - 48. 9-11924. CS71.M373 1873

11464 MARSTON. The Marston genealogy. In two parts. Compiled by Nathan Washington Marston, esq. ... South Lubec, Me., 1888. xii, 594 p., 1 l. plates, ports. 23½ cm. 9-12294. CS71.M373 1888

11465 MARSTON. Genealogical chart of a Marston family; Salem, Mass., Hampton, Moultonboro' and Sandwich, N.H. Compiled by Enoch Quimby Marston, M.D. Centre Sandwich, N.H. (Exeter, N.H., The News-letter press) 1898. geneal. tab. 31 x 55½ cm. fold. to 22½ cm. Cover-title. On back of cover: Chart of American ancestry of John Marston and his wife Nancy (Anna) Moulton with their children and their husbands and wives. 9-12293. CS71.M373 1898

190

11466   MARSTON.   Ralph Fitz John or Ralph de Merston, by G. Andrews Moriarty ... London, Mitchell, Hughes and Clarke, 1924.   1 p. l., 6 p. 25½ cm.   "Reprinted from 'Misc. gen. et her.', March, 1924."   38-14083.

CS439.M33M6

11467   MARSTON.   Marston English ancestry, with some account of the American immigrants of the name, by Mary Lovering Holman ... Boston, Mass., T. R. Marvin & son, 1929.   2 p. l., (3)-41 p. fold. geneal. tab. 24 cm.   "English records edited and arranged by George R. Marvin."   "200 copies printed from type."   29-6681.

CS71.M373   1929

MARSTON.   See also: BLAKE, 1948
DAY, 1916
DRAKE, 1962
THAYER, 1948

11468   MARTENS.   Stamtavle over slaegten Martens i Bergen med dens grene paa kvindesiden 1698-1897, samt "spredte" personer af samme navn i Norge, samlet, ordnet og udg. af Johan Martens, jr. ... Trykt som manuskript.   Bergen, J. Griegs bogtrykkeri, 1898.   147, (4) p. incl. illus., ports., fold. geneal. tab.   25½ cm.   13-22719.   CS919.M4

MARTENSE.   See RYERSON, 1916

11469   MARTIAU.   Nicolas Martiau, the adventurous Huguenot, the military engineer, and the earliest American ancestor of George Washington, by John Baer Stoudt.   Norristown, Pa. (The Norristown press) 1932.   xvii p., 1 l., 103, (1) p. front., illus. (incl. ports., maps) plates, facsims., coat of arms. 24½ cm. Contents. - Nicolas Martiau, the Huguenot. - Nicolas Martiau and the Earl of Huntington. - Nicolas Martiau, the military engineer. - Silkworms and grapes. - Nicolas Martiau, burgess and justice. - Jane Martiau. - The Read family. - The Warner family . - The Lewis family. - The Washington family. - The Nelson family. - The Colonial national monument. 32-31736.   F229.M32

MARTIAU.   See also No. 430 - Adventurers of purse and person.

11470   MARTIN.   The genealogy of the family of Martins.   (By Martin Wheeler.   Providence, R. I., Hugh H. Brown, printer, 1816)   12 p. 26 cm.   Caption title.   Dedication signed: Wheeler Martin.   Imperfect: pages 1-2 wanting, supplied by photostats from the copy in the New England historical and genealogical society library.   For a description and reprint of this pamphlet, of which only 125 copies were printed, see Henry J. Martin's "Notices genealogical and historical of the Martin family in New England, Boston, 1880", p. 133, (186)-208.   35-21372.   CS71.M35   1816

11471   MARTIN.   Genealogical record of the Martin family.   (Pine Grove? Ky., 1857)   8 p. 23½ cm. Caption title.   Signed: Sam'l D. Martin, near Pine Grove, Clark County, Ky.   April 1857.   9-12291.

CS71.M38   1857

11472   MARTIN.   Genealogical memoranda relating to the family of Martyn.   Comp. by Michael Williams ... Privately printed.   London, Mitchell & Hughes, 1873.   14 p. illus. (coats of arms) 28½ cm. 9-18130.   CS439.M35

11473   MARTIN.   Notices: genealogical and historical, of the Martin family, of New England, who settled at Weymouth and Hingham in 1635, and were among the first planters of Rehoboth (in 1644), and Swansea (in 1667), with some account of their descendants.   By Henry J. Martin.   Boston, Lee and Shepard; New York, C. T. Dillingham, 1880.   358 p. front., ports. 23 cm.   "Three hundred copies of this work are printed for private circulation among the family, of which this is no. 1."   9-12290.   CS71.M38   1880

11474   MARTIN.   Genealogy of the family of Martin of Ballinahinch castle, in the county of Galway, Ireland.   A copy of the original emblazoned parchment deposited in the Office of arms, Dublin castle. By Archer E. S. Martin ... (Printed for private circulation)   Winnipeg, The Stovel company, 1890. geneal. tab. illus. (coat of arms) 50 x 70 cm. fold. to 23 x 13 cm..   21-19031.   CS499.M3

11475   MARTIN.   William Martin, esq., representative from North Yarmouth to the General court of Massachusetts, 1792-5, 7.   By Edward Payson Payson.   Boston, Printed by D. Clapp & son, 1900. 9 p. 2 pl. 24½ cm.   The two plates have the coats of arms and two miniatures of Mr. & Mrs. Martin.   "Reprinted from the New-England historical and genealogical register for Jan. 1900."   18-418.   CS71.M38   1900

11476   MARTIN.   An account of some of the later generations of the Martin family in America, by Richard A. Martin.   New York, 1902.   (6) p.   17 cm.   "150 numbered copies ... No. 60."   5-37333 rev.

CS71.M38   1902

11477   MARTIN.   The house of Martin: being chapters in the history of the west of England branch of that family.   By W.G. Willis Watson ... with an introduction by H. Tapley Soper ... Exeter, W. Pollard & co., ltd., 1906.   xii, 46 p. front., plates, coat of arms. 25½ cm. 20-16681.

CS439.M34   1906

11478   MARTIN.   The Martin family, descendants of Thomas Martin of Goochland Co., Virginia, by Irene Dabney Gallaway.   Fayetteville, Ark., Sentinel print, 1906.   (28) p. 20½ x 17½ cm. 10-5042.

CS71.M38   1906

11479   MARTIN.   History of the Martin family.   By Stapleton Martin ... (n.p., 1908)   2 p. l., (7)-104 p. 23 cm.   Blank pages for "History of the Martin family" (71-104) 19-3357.

CS439.M34   1908

11480   MARTIN.   The Martin family, compiled by George Castor Martin.   vol. I -   Frankford, Philadelphia, Martin & Allardyce, 1911 -   1 v. plates, ports., coats of arms. 14½ cm. 11-27505.

CS71.M38   1911

11481   MARTIN.   Martin genealogy.   Descendants of Lieutenant Samuel Martin of Wethersfield, Conn., showing descent from royalty; also giving brief histories of, and descent from, the following colonial families: Nichols, Bradstreet, Marsh, Cotton, Squire, Webster, Ward, Chamberlain, Stoddard, Chipman, Dudley, Bliss, Williams, Stratton, Dodge; showing "Mayflower" descent, signer of Declaration of independence, revolutionary war records. Comp. by Thomas Arthur Hay.   (New York? 1911 -   v. front. (col. coat of arms) illus. 20½ cm. 12-4939.   CS71.M38   1911

11482   MARTIN.   Old Irish life, by J.M. Callwell.   Edinburgh and London, W. Blackwood and sons, 1912.   viii p., 1 l., 380 p. 2 pl., 2 port. (incl. front.) 22½ cm. 13-1827.   DA925.C2

11483   MARTIN.   Some old colonial families of Virginia, by Cynthia Martin Polk.   Memphis, Tenn., Paul & Douglass company, 1915.   147 p. illus. (incl. coat of arms) 20½ cm.   Contents. - Genealogies: Martin. Payne-Pillow. Payne-Fleming. Woodson-Fleming. Payne of Virginia. Fleming family. Steptoe family. Cro'Martin of Ireland. Payne of England. Americans of royal descent.   Col. William and Gideon Pillow, sr. 16-14144.   CS71.M38   1915

11484   MARTIN.   Genealogy of the Martin family.   By Charles William Francis.   (La Porte? Ind., 1918-58)   2 v. illus., ports., coat of arms. 23 cm.   Cover title: Martin history and genealogy. Vol. 2 by A.B. Shedd. 25-4511 rev.   CS71.M38   1918

11485   MARTIN.   The Martin family of Ipswich, Massachusetts; four generations of descendants of George Martin of Salisbury through his son George, by Charles Shepard.   Albany, N.Y., 1921.   geneal. tab. 29 x 42½ cm.   Blue-print. 21-6213.   CS71.M38   1921

11486   MARTIN.   George Martin of Salisbury, Mass., and his descendants.   Also of the probably related lines of Samuel Martin of Francestown, N.H., his brother Jesse Martin of Francestown, N.H.; of Richard Martyn of Portsmouth, N.H., and Ephraim Martin of Goffstown, N.H., and Bradford, Vt. By Elliot Burnham Watson, M.D., and Rev. Alven Martyn Smith ... So. Pasadena, Calif., A.M. Smith, 1929.   (1), xxiii, 293 p. 27½ cm.   Autographic reproduction of type-written copy.   32-2320.   CS71.M38   1929

11487   MARTIN.   ... Martin family records, by J. Montgomery Seaver.   Philadelphia, Pa., American historical-genealogical society (1929)   60 p. front. (ports.) 28 cm.   Colored coat of arms on recto of frontispiece. References: p. 56 - 57. Forms for additional "Family records": p. 58-59. 35-21364.   CS71.M38   1929a

11488   MARTIN.   Martin family history.   (By William John Coulter) Sussex, N.J., Wantage recorder press, 1931 -   2 v. illus (coat of arms) 23½ cm.   "This edition is limited to three hundred copies, all of which are personally signed by the author, of which this one is no. 69. W.J. Coulter, author." 33-14357.   CS71.M38   1931

11489   MARTIN.   The great matriarchs.   (By George Whitney Martin.   New York, Printed by Stratford press. c. 1933)   cover-title, 8 p. port. 20½ cm.   Page 8 signed G. W. M.   Running title: Willow brook.   An account of family stocks involved in life at Willow brook during the author's boyhood, 1892-1902.   38M2551T.   CS71.M38   1933

11490   MARTIN.   The history of the Martyn or Martin family, by Bryan I'Anson ... London, Janson & co., 1935 -   v. front., illus., plates (part col.) ports., fold. geneal. tab., coats of arms. 28 cm.   36-14477.   CS439.M34   1935

11491   MARTIN.   The Martin family, 1680-1934, by Anne C. Porcher.   (Brooklyn) c. 1935.   52 (i. e. 74) numb. l. coat of arms. 28½ cm.   Extra numbered leaves inserted.   Mimeographed.   "Errata": numb. leaf 52.   Originally published in 1857, by Dr. Samuel Davies Martin under title Genealogical record of the Martin family; republished in 1886 by Hon. Alfred M. Martin; rewritten, corrected and added to by Anne Carrington Martin Porcher in 1933 and 1934. cf. numb. leaf 1.   35-4564.   CS71.M38   1935

11492   MARTIN.   Genealogy; Daniel Martin, his parents, five sisters, eleven children (two died young) forty-one grand children, ninety-seven great grandchildren, one hundred seven great great grand children, fifteen great great great grand c.   (By George Ross McClure. McPherson, Kan., 1939)   19 numb. l. 35 cm.   Caption title.   Introduction (numbered leaf 1) signed: G. R. McClure.   Reproduced from type-written copy.   40-18331.   CS71.M38   1939

11493   MARTIN.   Some Ohio pioneers; Martin-Cresap descendants who helped make a typical American community.   McComb, Miss., The Cresap society, 1941.   cover-title, 44 (i. e. 48), (3) p. illus., plates, ports., fold. facsims. 23 cm.   43-3509.   CS71.M38   1941

11494   MARTIN.   Distaff descent.   (By Marion Willis (Martin) Rivinus.   Phoenixville, Pa., 1943)   iv, 433 (i. e. 444) numb. l. illus., plates, ports., geneal. tables. 28½ x 23 cm.   Coats of arms of the Martin and Price families on t. -p.   An account of the Martin and Price families.   Bibliography: leaves 415-420.   44-36699.   CS71.M38   1943

11495   MARTIN.   The Martin family.   (By James Calvin Tinkey.   Mt. Vernon, O., 1945)   23 p. illus. (incl. ports.) 26½ cm.   Compiled by J. Calvin Tinkey.   cf. Pref.   46-15313.   CS71.M38   1945

11496   MARTIN.   Martin and allied families; Martin, Bogan, Farrar, Truitt, Smith, Saxon, Hay, Cheney, Grubbs, Pope, Curry, Watson, Swann, Birch, King, Pruett (and) other branches ... Compiled and edited by: Lillie Martin Grubbs (Mrs. Clifford) Columbus, Ga. (1946)   xii, 306, (2) p. incl. front., illus. (incl. ports., coats of arms) fold. geneal. tables. 24 cm.   Bibliography: p. ix.   46-5007.   CS71.M38   1946

11497   MARTIN.   An inquiry into the American ancestry of Jasper Newton Martin, 1847-1929 of ... Tennessee, and of his wife, Tabitha Frances Keith, 1863-1910 ... together with a partial list of their collateral descendants and a complete list of their children, grandchildren and great-grandchildren as of April 1949.   By Robert Martin McBride.   Washington, 1949.   Washington, 1949. 44 l. 29 cm.   "Copy no. 71 of 100 copies."   49-22660.   CS71.M38   1949

11498   MARTIN.   Ancestors and descendants of George Castor Martin.   San Antonio, 1950.   unpaged. illus. 27 cm.   52-22228.   CS71.M38   1950

11499   MARTIN.   Martin (also Martyn)   By David Kendall Martin.   West Chazy, N.Y. (1962)   unpaged. 28 cm.   62-59979.   CS71.M38   1962

11500   MARTIN.   Some of the descendants of Daniel Martin (1745-1829) of Laurens County, South Carolina, and the allied families of Hudgens, McNeese, Rodgers, and Saxon.   By Christine (South) Gee.   (Greenwood? S. C.; printed privately by Keys Print. Co., Greenville, S. C., 1963.   v, 97 p. 24 cm.   63-25667.   CS71.M38   1963

11501   MARTIN.   Some Martin, Jeffries, and Wayman families and connections of Virginia, Maryland, Kentucky, and Indiana, compiled by Estelle Clark Watson.   Skokie, Ill., Guild Press, 1965.   xii, 273 p. geneal. tables, port. 28 cm.   Bibliography: p. 193-194.   65-5591.   CS71.M38   1965

11502   MARTIN.   Genealogy of the Martin, Shaw, Pate and Story families.   Compiled by Mrs. Chester E. (Susie) Martin.   (Atlanta) 1966.   40 p. coats of arms, facsims., ports. 24 cm.   66-24018.   CS71.M38   1966

11503   MARTIN.   The descendants of Samuel Martin, 1775-1842, of Mifflin County, Pennsylvania, by Raymond Martin Bell and John Martin Stroup.   Washington, Pa., 1967.   22 l. maps. 28 cm. 67-6149.

CS71.M38   1967

11504   MARTIN.   Martin family in vertical file.   Ask reference librarian for this material.

MARTIN.   See also:

ARNOLD, 1960	KEY, 1931	RUCKER, 1927
BOOHER, 1956	KNIGHT, DA690.C47A8	ST. LEGER, DA690.L39M3
BUGH, 1943	LE SAGE, CS89.H3	TELFORD, 1956
CLARK, 1934	LEWIS, 1893 (addenda)	THROOP, 1933
ENDERS, 1960	LUTER, 1959	TODD, 1960
FLAGG, 1903	McCONNELL, 19 -	WARD, 1926
GUILD, 1891	PEARSON, F129.A96B3	WASHINGTON, CS69.W5
HAIRSTON, 1940	PEDEN, 1961	WEINGARTH, 1943
HAYNES, 1940	POUND, 1904	WITHERSPOON, 1922
HOLSINGER, 1959	PYRTLE, 1930	No. 1547 - Cabell county.
HUGHES, 1922	REED, 1963	

11505   MARTINDALE.   Autobiography and sermons of Elder Elijah Martindale, also Pioneer history of the Boyd family, by Belle Stanford.   Indianapolis, Carlon & Hollenbeck, 1892.   vii, 173 p. front., port. 20 cm. 1-4226.

BX7343M3A3

11506   MARTINDALE.   John Martindell (or Martindale) Cordwainter, of Philadelphia, and some of his descendants.   Compiled from material collected by Harry H. Martindale.   Edited and arranged by Marjorie Seward Cleveland and Charles Harvey Roe.   (Tarreytown? N.Y.) 1953.   103 p. 30 cm. 56-43787.

CS71.M384   1953

MARTINDALE.   See also HALL, 1959

11507   MARTLING.   Martling family genealogy.   By Ida Dudley Dale.   7391   Positive. 1 reel.   Microfilm reading room.

MARTO.   See POUND, 1904

MARTYN.   See MARTIN.

MARVEL.   See PEPPER, 1960

11508   MARVIN.   Genealogical sketch of the descendants of Reinold and Matthew Marvin, who came to New England in 1635.   Comp. from authentic sources, by T. R. Marvin.   Boston, 1848.   56 p. 19½ cm. 18-13528.

CS71.M39   1848

11509   MARVIN.   The English ancestry of Reinold and Matthew Marvin, of Hartford, Ct., 1638; their homes and parish churches.   By William T. R. Marvin ... Boston, Priv. print. (T. R. Marvin & son, printers) 1900.   184 p. front., pl., maps (part fold.) 23½ cm. 0-2030.   CS71.M39   1900

11510   MARVIN.   Descendants of Reinold and Matthew Marvin of Hartford, Ct., 1638 and 1635, sons of Edward Marvin, of Great Bentley, England, by George Franklin Marvin ... and William T. R. Marvin ... Boston, T. R. Marvin & son, 1904.   658 p., 1 l. front., plates, ports., 2 maps, facsims. 24½ cm. 4-37010.

CS71.M39   1904

11511   MARVIN.   A portion of the war record of the Marvin family, 1775-1921; comp. by Sylvester S. Marvin, assisted by Mrs. Mary E. Rumsey.   (Boston, Mass., T. R. Marvin & son, printers) 1921.   2 p. l., (3) - 36 p. front. 26 cm. Privately printed; 150 copies. Running title: Marvin war record. Blank pages interspersed. 22-519.

CS71.M39   1921

11512   MARVIN.   The genealogical directory, 1931, George Ritchie Marvin, M.A., compiler.   Boston, Mass., The Federation of American family associations (1931)   2 p. l., 62 p. front. (port.) 24 cm.   Advertising matter: p. 55-62. 31-31145.

CS44.M3

11513   MARVIN.   Biography of John Huston Marvin.   By Francis M. Marvin.   (Bartonsville, Pa.,
194-?)   24 p. plate, ports., col. coat of arms. 23 cm.   49-38528 *.   CT275.M46M35

11514   MARVIN.   Notes on the ancestry of Reinold and Matthew Marvin, by John Insley Coddington ...
(New Haven, 1941)   cover-title, 13 p. 23½ cm.   "Reprinted from 'The American genealogist' July, 1941." 42-4026.
                                                                                    CS71.M39   1941

        MARVIN.   See also: BASSETT, 1926   MERVYN.
                              DEERING, 1929   SALISBURY, 1892
                              HALL, 1943a   McCURDY, 1892

        MARYE.   See FONTAINE, 1886

11515   MARYON.   Records and pedigree of the family of Maryon of Essex and Herts.   By John
Ernest Maryon.   (n. p.) 1895.   10 p. 26 cm.   "Maryon family, by John E. C. Maryon": leaf inserted. 60-55130.
                                                                                    CS439.M352   1895

11516   MARYON.   Maryon family.   (A supplement to the pedigree of the Maryon family published
in (1895) By John E. Maryon.   Perth, Western Australia, 1924.   1 l. 25 cm. Typewritten. 39M4888T.
                                                                                    CS439.M352   1924

11517   MASCY.   The descent of the Mascys of Rixton, in the county of Lancaster.   From original
documents.   By Mrs. Arthur Cecil Tempest ... Liverpool, T. Barkell, printer, 1889.   102 p. front.
(double geneal. tab.) plates. 22 cm.   "From vol. 39 of the Transactions of the Historic society of Lancashire and Cheshire." 29-2766.
                                                                                    CS439.M353

11518   MASKELL.   Thomas Maskell of Simsbury, Connecticut; his son Thomas Maskell of Greenwich, New Jersey and some of their descendants, compiled by Frank D. Andrews ... Vineland, N.J.,
1927.   2 p. l., (3)-15, 15a, 16, 16a, 17-38 p. 23½ cm.   "Privately printed, 61 copies .. no. 2." 27-18281.   CS71.M397   1927

11519   MASKELYNE.   White magic; the story of Maskelynes, by Jasper Maskelyne.   With twenty-
five illustrations.   London, S. Paul & co. Ltd.   (1936)   287 p. front., plates, ports. 24 cm. 37-19296.
                                                                                    GV1545.M3W45

11520   MASKELYNE.   Basset Down, an old country house.   By Mary Lucy (Story-Maskelyne)
Arnold-Forster.   Foreword by Charles Morgan.   London, Country Life (1949)   175 p. plates, ports.,
geneal. tables. 26 cm.   50-25983.   CS439.M354   1949

11521   MASON.   Mason lineage and arms.   By Jane Griffith Keys.   In Michigan Historical Commission Historical
Collections vol. xxxv p. 602.   F561.M47 v. 35

11522   MASON.   A legacy to my children, including family history, autobiography, and original
essays.   By Dr. Philip Mason ... Cincinnati, Moore, Wilstach & Baldwin, printers, 1868.   610 p. front.,
(port.) 25 cm.   13-26804.   CS71.M41   1868

11523   MASON.   Capt. John Mason, the founder of New Hampshire.   Including his tract on Newfoundland, 1620; the American charters in which he was a grantee; with letters and other historical
documents.   Together with a memoir by Charles Wesley Tuttle, PH. D.   Edited with historical illustrations by John Ward Dean, A.M.   Boston, The Prince society, 1887.   xii p., 1 l., 492 p. illus. (facsims.)
2 pl. (1 fold.) fold. map, geneal. tab. 22 x 18 cm. (Added t.-p: The publications of the Prince society ... (v. 17) "250 copies." Contents. -
Preface. - Memoir of Captain John Mason. - The family of Captain John Mason. - Captain John Mason's patent of Mariana, by C.L. Woodbury. -
Captain Mason's plantations on the Pascataqua. - Introduction to Captain John Mason's "Brief discourse." - A briefe discourse of the New-found-land
(by John Mason), Edinburgh, Andro Hart, 1620. - Early English works on Newfoundland. - A grant of Cape Anne in New England from the president
and Councill of New England to John Mason, esqr. (March 9, 1621-2) - A grant of the province of Maine to Sr. Ferdinando Gorges, and
John Mason, esqr. 10th of August, 1622. - Grant of New Hampshire, November 7, 1629. By the Council of New-England to Captain John
Mason. The grant of the province of Laconia to Sr. Fernandino Gorges & Capt. John Mason, November. 1629. - Grant of Piscataway, November 3,
1631. - Grant of New-Hampshire and Massonia to Captain John Mason (April 22, 1635). Letters and documents, 1615-1661. Charter from Charles I
to Capt. John Mason August 19, 1635. - Lease from the Council of New England to Wollaston, April 18, 1635. - Deed of Wollaston to Mason, June 11,
1635. Deed from Gorges to Mason, Sept. 17, 1635. - Will of Captain John Mason. - Memorial to Capt. John Mason, at Portsmouth, England.
3-24569.   E186.P85 v. 17
                                                                                   F37.M4
———— Copy 2

11524   MASON.   A record of the descendants of Robert Mason, of Roxbury, Mass. ... Edited by William L. Mason.   Milwaukee (Burdick, Armitage & Allen, printers) 1891.   8 p., 9-35 l., 36-39 p. 24 cm. 9-12289.   CS71.M41   1891

11525   MASON.   The life of George Mason, 1725-1792, by Kate Mason Rowland, including his speeches, public papers, and correspondence; with an introduction by General Fitzhugh Lee ... New York, London, G. P. Putnam's son, 1892.   2 v. front. (port.) 2 facsims. 23½ cm. Bibliography: v. 1, p.xvii. 12-36679.
E302.6.M45R3

11526   MASON.   Mason chart, Capt. John Mason, grantee of N.H.   (n.p., 1894?)   geneal. tab.
40 x 33 cm. fold to 22½ x 17 cm.   In manuscript.   Title from slip mounted on cover. 38M2567T.   CS71.M41   1894

11527   MASON.   Preliminary notes on the genealogy of the Sampson Mason family, printed and published by Alverdo H. Mason.   East Brainstree, Mass., 1897.   3 p. l., 122 (i.e.131) p. 22½ cm. Nine additional leaves inserted numbered 30 a (2 l.) 60 a (3 l.) 84 a (2 l.) 84 b and 97 a. "Miss Asenath W. Cole of Warren, R.I. ... placed at the disposal of the compiler, materials for nearly two-thirds of the present volume." - Compiler's note. 33-29114. L.C.COPY REPLACED BY MICROFILM.
CS71.M41   1897
Microfilm 8744 CS

11528   MASON.   George Mason of Virginia; an address by Lewis H. Machen, presenting a portrait to Fairfax County, May 20th, 1901.   (Washington, D.C., Press of B. S. Adams, 1901)   35 p. front. (port.) 24 cm. Appendix, Genealogy: p. 31-33. 1-23740.
E302.6.M45M14

11529   MASON.   Genealogy of the Sampson Mason family.   Compiled by Alverdo Hayward Mason. (Part I) East Braintree, Mass., Printed by A. H. Mason, 1902.   1 v. front. (map) 25½ cm. "This edition is limited to three hundred and fifty copies, of which this copy is no. 193." 9-11940.   CS71.M41   1902

11530   MASON.   Family record in our line of descent from Major John Mason of Norwich, Connecticut, by Theodore West Mason ... New York, The Grafton press, 1909.   59, 8, (4) p. front. 24½ cm. "Limited edition for private distribution." 9-31827.   CS71.M41   1909

11531   MASON.   ... Enoch and Elizabeth Mason, their ancestry and descendants ... Comp. and arranged by S. S. Mason.   Kingsley, Ia., Printed by J. H. Beardsley, 1911.   90 p., 2 l. illus., ports., coat of arms. 19½ cm. Interleaved. 11-31994.   CS71.M41   1911

11532   MASON.   ... Sir John Mason; and the Masons of Hampshire.   By V.C. Sanborn ... (London and Exeter, 1917)   6 p. 24 cm. Caption title. "Reprinted from the Genealogist, n.d., vol. xxxiv, July, 1917." 38M4283T.
CS439.M357   1917

11533   MASON.   Archibald Dale Mason; his life, ancestry and descendants, collected and ed. by Harrison D. Mason.   Pittsburgh, Pa., Priv, print., 1921.   v, 46 p. front., ports. 24 cm. "Edition limited to 200 copies printed from type. For private distribution." 22-2317.   CS71.M41   1921

11534   MASON.   Genealogy and history; the family of Hugh Mason, William Mason and allied families, by Mary Eliza Mason ... (Parkersburg, W. Va., Baptist banner publishing co., 1930)   351 p. illus., plates, port. 23½ cm. Committee on publication: Miss Addie C. Irish, Miss Bertha E. White, Mrs. Harley Frye, Mrs. Ada Nau. 32-30547.   CS71.M41   1930

11535   MASON.   A double Mason line from Major John Mason, deputy-governor of Connecticut to new cadet John Mason Kemper, West Point, 1931.   (By Caroline (Kemper) Bulkley.   n.p., 1932)   3 p. l., 2-9 numb. l., 1 l. 29 cm. Signed: Caroline Kemper Bulkley. Type-written. Foot-notes. 32-20374.   CS71.M41   1932

11536   MASON.   The ancestors and descendants of Joseph Mason and Debby Ann Palmer.   Compiled and written by Kirk Bentley Barb ... (Camden, N.J.) 1932.   9 p. l., 2-103 numb. l. 27½ cm. Multigraphed.
CS71.M41   1932a

11537   MASON.   Descendants of Capt. Hugh Mason in America, by Edna Warren Mason (Mrs. Mason Pfizenmayer) New Haven, Conn., The Tuttle, Morehouse & Taylor company, 1937.   2 p. l., iii, 867 p. front., ports. 27 cm. 37-1853.   CS71.M41   1937

11538   MASON.   The Mason family (1590-1949; a brief history of the ancestors and descendants of Lyman Gates Mason I, 1829-1898, and Ella Louise Mason, 1851-1932) Los Angeles, 1949. 24 p. ports., geneal. tables. 23 cm. Cover title. 50-26115.   CS71.M41   1949

11539   MASON.   The Mason family (1590-1949; a brief history of the ancestors and descendants of Lyman Gates Mason I, 1829-1898, and Ella Louise Mason, 1851-1932) By George Abbott Mason. Los Angeles, 1949.   24 p. ports., geneal. tables. 23 cm. Cover title. 50-26115.   CS71.M41   1949

11540   MASON.   Mason-Parsons genealogy.   By John Frederick Preston.   (Washington? 1964?) 1 v. (various pagings) geneal. table. 28 cm. Cover title. 65-67712.   CS71.M41   1964

11541   MASON.   The William Mason family of Casey County, Kentucky, Edgar County, Illinois, Knox County, Missouri. (n.p.) 1968.   10 l. 28 cm. 78-4102 MARC.   CS71.M41   1968

11542   MASON.   Mason family in vertical file.   Ask reference librarian for this material.

       MASON.   See also:

BAILEY, 1908	HERNDON, 1930	SELDEN, 1911
BAKER, 1896	HESTER, 1905	SMITH, 1915
BOARDMAN, 1849	JONES, 1913	THROOP, 1934
BORTON, 1908	MAJOR, 1915	TORRENCE, 1938
CHAFEE, 1911	MYERS, 1908	TUTT, 1925
CRISPIN, 1901	POOL, 1931	No. 430 - Adventurers of purse
GUTHRIE, 1953	REMEY, 1923	and person.

11543   MASSASOIT.   Descendants of Massasoit.   Indian history, biography and genealogy: pertaining to the good sachem Massasoit of the Wampanoag tribe, and his descendants.   With an appendix. By Ebenezer W. Peirce ... North Abington, Mass., Z. G. Mitchell, 1878.   261 p. front., plates, ports. 19½ cm. 2-15071.   E90.M4P3

       MASSENGALE.   See MASSENGILL.

11544   MASSENGILL.   The Massengills, Massengales and variants, 1472-1931, by Samuel Evans Massengill ... Bristol, Tenn., The King printing compay, 1931.   908 p., 1 l. illus. (facsims.) plates, ports. 24½ cm. "Addenda" slips mounted on p. 97 and 745.   Appendices: A. The Cobbs. - B. The Tiptons. - C. The Jobes, including the Fain, Ensor and McMahon connections. - D. The Dysarts and Bradens, including the Rhea connection. - E. The Evanses, including the Vance and Colville connections. - F. The Smiths, including the Humphreys connection.   31-34705.   CS71.M42   1931

11545   MASSENGILL.   Records on the Henry Massengill memorial and directory near Johnson City, Tennessee... (By Samuel Evans Massengill) (Bristol? Tenn., 1940?)   10 l. 32 - x 21½ cm. Mimeographed. 41-4325.   CS71.M42   1940

11546   MASSENGILL.   A sketch of medicine and pharmacy and a view of its progress by the Massengill family from the fifteenth to the twentieth century, by Samuel Evans Massengill, M.D. (Bristol, Tenn.-Va., The S.E.Massengill company, 1940)   144 p. illus., 3 pl. (1 col.) on double l. 25 cm. 41-8614.   R131.M28

11547   MASSENGILL.   A sketch of medicine and pharmacy and a view of its progress by the Massengill family from the fifteenth to the twentieth century.   By Samuel Evans Massengill, M.D. (Bristol, Tenn., The S.E.Massengill company, c.1942)   6 p. l., 11-445 p. illus., 3 pl. (1 col.) on double l. 24 cm. "Second edition." 43-3798.   R131.M28   1942

11548   MASSEY.   A brief genealogical research with references relating to Hamo de Masci, first baron of Dunham Massey (circ. 1047-1100) Cheshire.   (By George Massey.   New York? 1910?) (8) p. 24 cm. Signed: G.M. (i.e. George Massey) 37-31880.   CS439.M358

11549   MASSEY.   Massey, Lea (and) Heckscher families.   By Alexander Du Bin.   Philadelphia, Historical Publ. Society, 1948.   25 p. 26 cm. 49-2931 *.   CS71.M422   1948

11550   MASSEY.   The Masseys, founding family.   By Mollie Gillen.   Toronto, Ryerson Press (1965)   174 p. illus., geneal. table, ports. 22 cm. 70-3809.   CS90.M297   1965

MASSEY.   See also MASSIE.

11551   MASSICOTTE.   La famille Massicotte.   Histoire - Généalogie - portrait, par E. Z. Massicotte ... Montréal, Imprimé pour l'auteur, 1904.   150, (2) p. front., ports. 22 cm. "Cet ouvrage est tiré à cent exemplaires ... no. 97." 23-1275.   CS90.M3

11552   MASSIE.   What does America mean to you?   History and genealogy ... (By) Evelyn Jeanette (Miller) Ownbey ... Chicago, 1942.   (201) p. front., plates, port. 27½ cm. Reproduced from type-written copy. Includes bibliographies. Contents. - The tradition of Mary Dabney Winston Massie. - Biographical outline of the author. - pt. I. Rankin, Clendenin, Huston, and genealogical material on the Eckles and Creighs. - pt. II. Massie, Hart, Dabney (d'Aubigne), Barret, Lee, and genealogical material on the allied families of Winston and Chiswell. 42-50296.   CS71.M423   1942

MASSIE.   See also: MASSY.
THOMPSON, CS479.T5

11553   MASSINGBERD.   History of the parish of Ormsby-cum-Ketsby, in the hundred of Hill and county of Lincoln, compiled from original sources; by W. O. Massingberd ... Lincoln, J. Williamson, printer (1893)   viii p., 2 l., 454 p. front., fold. geneal. tables. 23 cm. Extracts from the parish registers: p. 354-386. 13-3149.   DA690.O6M3

MASSY.   See: EVELYN, CS439.E9
MASSIE.

11554   MAST.   A brief history of Bishop Jacob Mast and other Mast pioneers; and a complete genealogical family register and those related by inter-marraige, with biographies of their descendants from the earliest available records to the present time; with portraits and other illustrations.   By C. Z. Mast.   Elverson, Penna.   (Scottdale, Pa., Menonite publishing house press, c.1911)   2 p. l., (9)-822 p. front., illus. (incl. ports.) 22½ cm. 11-32200.   CS71.M425   1911

MAST.   See also DIXON, 1922

11555   MASTER.   Some notices of the family of Master, of East Langdon and Yotes in Kent, New Hall and Croston in Lancashire, and Barrow Green in Surrey.   With appendices of abstracts of parish registers, monumental inscriptions, original documents and wills.   Together with notices of the families of Streynsham, Wightman, Launder, Hoskins, and Whalley, now represented by that of Master. By the Rev. George Streynsham Master ... (London) Printed for private circulation only by Mitchell and Hughes, 1874.   iv, 104 p. front., illus. (incl. facsims., coats of arms) plates, ports., 2 geneal. tab. (1 fold.) 27 cm. 15-15273.   CS439.M36

11556   MASTERMAN.   The pedigree of the Masterman family of Little and Great Ayton in Cleveland, Yorkshire.   Accompanied by a descriptive and explanatory memorandum of its descent and history down to modern times.   Newcastle-upon-Tyne, Printed by M. S. Dodds, 1914.   59 p. front. (port.) double geneal. tables. 31½ cm. Preface signed: Cleveland Masterman. Cyril Ravenhill Everett. Pages left blank at end for additional record. 20-18039.   CS439.M365

MASTERMAN.   See also: DOWSE, 1890
HARRIS, CS439.H29
HEATH, 1914

MASTERS.   See: CONNER, 1963
JENKINS, 1904

MASTERSON.   See ABELL, 1928

11557   MASTERTON.   A critical examination of the genealogy of Masterton of that ilk, Parkmill, etc.   Pub. in Douglas's 'Baronage of Scotland,' and Crawfurd's 'Memorials of Alloa.'   Priv. print. London, Mitchell and Hughes, 1878.   7 p. 27 cm. Published also in "Miscellanea genealogica et heraldica." London, 1880. n.s., vol. III, p.135-136, 141-143. 20-20605, or 20-20605 rev. *.   CS479.M395   1878

11558   MATHER.   The Mather family.   By Enoch Pond ... Boston, Massachusetts Sabbath school society, 1844.   viii, (9)-180 p. front. (port.) 16 cm. 9-12980.   CS71.M427   1844

11559   MATHER.   Genealogy of the Mather family, from about 1500 to 1847; with sundry biographical notices ... Hartford, Press of E. Geer, 1848.   vi, (7)-76 p. incl. front. (coat of arms) 17 cm. Preface signed: John Mather. 24-16089.   CS71.M427   1848

11560   MATHER.   ... Journal of Richard Mather.   1635.   His life and death, 1670.   Boston, D. Clapp, 1850.   iv. (5)-108 p. 19 cm. (Collections of the Dorchester antiquarian and historical society. no. 3) Pedigree of the Mather Cotton-Lake-Gookin family: p. 97-98.   p. (35-36) blank. 1-11344.   F74.D5D5 no.3

11561   MATHER.   A memoir of the Rev. Cotton Mather, D. D., with a genealogy of the family of Mather.   By Samuel G. Drake.   Boston, C. C. P. Moody, printer, 1851.   16 p. front., ports., geneal. tab. 24 cm.   Title vignette: coat of arms. 9-11946.   CS71.M427   1851

11562   MATHER.   Pedigree of the family of Mather.   (Boston, C. C. P. Moody, printer, 1851)   geneal. tab. 42 x 34 cm. fold. to 22 x 18½ cm.   Reprinted from the Memoir of the Rev. Cotton Mather, D. D. By Samuel Gardner Drake. 1851. 9-12287.   CS71.M427   1851a

11563   MATHER.   Lineage of Rev. Richard Mather, by Horace E. Mather ... Hartford, Conn., Press of the Case, Lockwood & Brainard company, 1890.   539 p., 1 l. front., illus., plates, ports. 23 cm. 9-11945.   CS71.M427   1890

11564   MATHER.   Abstracts of the wills of the Mather family, proved in the Consistory court at Chester from 1573 to 1650; by J. Paul Rylands ... Boston, Priv. print. (D. Clapp & son) 1893.   38 p. 1 pl. 23½ cm.   Reprinted from the New-Eng. hist, and geneal. register for January, 1893. 3-4181.   CS71.M427   1893

11565   MATHER.   The services of the Mathers in New England religious development, by Williston Walker ...   (In American society of church history. Papers. New York and London, 1893. 24½ cm. vol. v. p. 61-85) A35-2965.   BR140.A4 vol.5)

11566   MATHER.   Ten fac-simile reproductions relating to various subjects, by Samuel Abbott Green.   Boston, Mass., 1903.   4 p. 1., 36 p. 23 facsim. 37 x 27½ cm.   "One hundred and twenty-five copies printed." Contents. - Some engraved portraits of the Mather family. - The south and north batteries, - An early Boston imprint, 1681 - The Boston news-letter, 1704. - Reprintes of early Boston newspapers. - Panorama of Boston, 1775. - The midnight ride of Paul Revere. - The battle of Bunker hill. - The crossed swords. - Lawrence academy, Groton, Massachusetts. 3-31448.   F67.G82

11567   MATHER.   The Mather family of Cheltenham, Pennsylvania; being an account of the descendants of Joseph Mather, compiled from the records of Charles Mather of Jenkintown.   By Horace Mather Lippincott, PH. B.   Philadelphia, L. J. Levick, 1910.   2 p. 1., 150, (16) p., 1 l. front., illus. (coats of arms) plates, facsim. 25 cm. 11-27482.   CS71.M427   1910

11568   MATHER.   The libraries of the Mathers, by Julius Herbert Tuttle ... Worcester, Mass., The Davis press, 1919.   90 p. 2 facsim. on 1 pl., diagr. 25½ x 15 cm.   Reprinted from Proceedings of the American Antiquarian society at the semi-annual meeting, April, 1910. "A catalogue of books belonging unto Mr. Increase Mather. 8. 18. 1664": p. 14-24. - "Mather books in the Massachusetts historical society": p. 35-39. - "Mather books in other libraries": p. 39-44. - "Catalogue of Dr. Cotton Mather's library purchased by Isaiah Thomas and given by him to the American antiquarian society": p. 47-90. 14-22949.   Z989.M28T8

11569   MATHER.   The Mather bibliography, by Thomas J. Holmes.   (In The papers of the Bibliographical society of America. Chicago, Ill., 1937) 24½ cm. v. 31, pt. 1, 1937, pt. 57-76) CD38-167.   Z1008.B51P v. 31 pt.1

11570   MATHER.   The minor Mathers, a list of their works, by Thomas James Holmes.   Cambridge, Mass., Harvard university press, 1940.   xxx, 218 p. incl. front. (geneal. tab.) facsims. 23 cm. "Two hundred copies printed." "Appendix: Manuscripts of the minor Mathers, by William Sanford Piper": p. 189-204. 40-34769.   Z8554.H76

MATHER.   See also: GOULD, 1897
LAIN, 1957
SHARP, 1948
WALKER, 1968

11571   MATHESON.   History of the Mathesons, with genealogies of the various families, by Alexander Mackenzie ... 2d ed.   Edited, largely re-written, and added to, by Alexander Macbain ... Stirling, E. Mackey; London, Gibbings & Coy, ltd., 1900.   xi, (1) p., 2 l., (3)-162 p. front. (port.) illus., plates (1 col.) coats of arms. 23 cm.   L. C. COPY REPLACED BY MICROFILM.   4-4171.   CS479.M4

11572   MATHESON.   The Mattesons in America, 1646-1940.   Genealogical data re the descendants of Henry and Hannah Parsons Matteson.   (n. p., 1940?)   1 v. (various pagings) 28 cm.   Cover title.   52-48366.   CS71.M43   1940

11573   MATHESON.   A Mathewson lineage, including the descendants of John and Lois (Hicks) Mathewson, collected and compiled by Louie Clark Mathewson ... (Hanover, N. H.) c. 1941.   1 p. l., 29 numb. l. incl. facsim. pl., 8 port. on 1 l. 29 x 22½ cm.   Reproduced from type-written copy. "Sources" p. 29. 41-27341.   CS71.M43   1941

11574   MATHESON.   William Matheson, watchmaker, Lucan, Ontario.   (London? Ont., 1942?)   1 p. l., 32 numb. l. 29 cm.   Introductory remarks signed: Elena B. Matheson-Moorehouse.   Type-written copy (carbon) made by Edwin Seaborn from the original.   Includes material on the Matheson family.   43-3679.   CT310.M37M66

MATHESON.   See also: CURTIS, 1912
FOSTER, 1912
HURLBURT, 1938
MATTESON.
SHARP, 1948
SUTTON, 1935

MATHEW.   See MATTHEWS.

11575   MATHEWS.   The Mathews family of Virginia and allied families.   Compiled by Anne D. Montgomery.   (n. p.) 1968.   52 l. map. 31 cm.   On cover: Mathews family of Virginia and Tennessee.   75-5676MARC.   CS71.M44   1968b

MATHEWS.   See also: MATTHEWS.
MATTESON, 1938 (addenda)
No. 430 - Adventurers of purse and person.

MATHEWSON.   See MATHESON, 1941

MATHIASON.   See HOUGEN, 1957

11576   MATILE.   Histoire généalogique des différents branches de la famille Matile, par J. C. H. Matile ... Amsterdam, 1914.   411, (1) p., 1 l. col. coat of arms. 24 cm. 20-15858.   CS409.M3   1914

11577   MATLACK.   Col. Timothy Matlack, patriot and soldier, a paper read before the Gloucester County historical society at the Old tavern house, Haddonfield, N. J., April 14, 1908, by Dr. A. M. Stackhouse.   (n. p.) Priv. print., 1910.   2 p. l., 105 p. front., port., fold. facsim. 23 cm.   An oration delivered March 16, 1780, before the ... American philosophical society ... By Timothy Matlack ... : p. (29)-58.   Genealogical notes of the family of Timothy Matlack: p. 71- (100)   The Varnall family: p. 103-105. 11-1406.   E263.P4M3

MATLACK.   See also LAMB, 1904

MATSON.   See PATTERSON, 1917

MATTER.   See ENDERS, 1960

MATTESON.   See addenda.

MATTHEW.   See MATTHEWS.

11578   MATTHEWS.   The family of Mathews of Castell-y-Mynach in Wales; of northern Ireland; of Australia and England.   (n. p., n. d.)   (4) p. illus. 25 cm. 40M3035T.

CS439. M366

11579   MATTHEWS.   Genealogy of the earls of Landaff of Thomastown, county Tipperary, Ireland ... (n. p., 189-?)   106 p. incl. plates, ports. 23½ cm. Ancestry of Arnold Harris Mathew.   Appendix: The ancestors and relatives of the 1st earl of Llandaff's mother, Mary Matthew's by the Rev. Murray A. Mathew, p. (65)-104. 19-1544.

CS499. L2

11580   MATTHEWS.   Family history (of Matthews and Denman families) Compiled by Mary Rebekah Matthews ... Newton, N.J., Press of W. H. Nicholls, 1897.   cover-title, 1 p. 1., 16 p. 22½ cm. 5-24594.

CS71.M44   1897

11581   MATTHEWS.   ... The Matthews family of Yarmouth.   Yarmouthport, Mass., C. W. Swift, 1912.   cover-title, 8 p. 25 cm. (Library of Cape Cod history & genealogy, no. 81) Arranged by W. P. Davis and ed. by C. W. Swift. 12-30938.

CS71.M44   1912

11582   MATTHEWS.   Y Mathiaid, the Mathews of Llandaff, by Gregory M. Mathews ... London, H. F. & G. Witherby, 1924.   2 p. 1., iii, (1), 40 p. front., illus. (coat of arms) plates. 26 cm. 39-6922.

CS459.M27   1924

11583   MATTHEWS.   The Mathews (Mathes) family in America, by I. C. Van Deventer ...(Kansas City, Mo., Alexander printing company, 1925)   2 p. 1., (3)-105 p. front., pl., ports. 24½ cm. 27-24782.

CS71.M44   1925

11584   MATTHEWS.   Garrett county history of pioneer families, by Chas. E. Hoye ... The Matthews family.   (Oakland, Md.) 1935.   1 l. 23 cm. Detached from the Mountain democrat, November 7th, 1935. 38M1240T.

CS71.M44   1935

11585   MATTHEWS.   Luke Matthews of Brunswick county, Virginia, 1739-1788, and his descendants, by William Kennon Matthews.   Kobe, Japan, H. Kodama, printer (1937?)   4 p. 1., iv p., 1 l., 150 p. 19½ cm. "Three hundred and twenty copies." 38-2526.

CS71.M44   1937

11586   MATTHEWS.   The Matthews and Mitchell families of Mayslick, Ky., and the Power and Dudley families of Flemingsburg, Ky., compiled by Mitchell Dudley Matthews.   (Pearl harbor, T. H., 1940)   1 v. 27 cm. Title from label mounted on cover. Reproduced from type-written copy. Includes also the Shotwell, Hull, and Bruce families. Includes bibliographical references. 42-11472.

CS71.M44   1940

11587   MATTHEWS.   The descendents (!) of William Mathews and Martha McConnell.   By John Pratt Nesbit.   (n. p., 194-)   32 l. port. 19 cm. Cover title. Typewritten. 49-39360 *.

CS71.M44

11588   MATTHEWS.   Matthews and Greer families; genealogical records with biographical notes, prepared and privately printed for Eleanor B. Matthews by the American historical company, inc. New York, 1942.   3 p. 1., 5-59 p. plates, ports., col. coat of arms. 28½ cm. Alternate pages blank. Title-page and dedication ornamented in colors; colored initials. Bound in blue levant, gold tooled, with coat of arms of the Matthews family on covers. Includes bibliographical notes. 43-7603.

CS71.M44   1942

11589   MATTHEWS.   The world and Virginia, by Wythe Leigh Kinsolving, M. A.   Charlottesville, Va., 1943.   1 p. 1., 174 p. 23 cm. "The story of man" (narrative poem): p. (1)-76. 43-15889.

F229. K5

11590   MATTHEWS.   The Matthews magazine. v. 1 -   1951 -   Knoxville, Ill., (Mathews Family Association)   v. 28 cm. annual. Vol. 1 complete in one no. 52-31945.

CS71. M438

11591   MATTHEWS.   Mathews family record; descendants of John and Sarah Mathews of County Tyrone, Northern Ireland.   By James Ray Bowman.   Washington, 1953.   92 p. 23 cm. 53-11205.

CS71.M44   1953

MATTHEWS.   See also: JEWETT, 1914   SEMMES, 1918
KINSOLVING, 1935   SEMMES, 1956
MARSDEN, 1961   STUART, 1961
MATHEWS.

MATTHEWSON.   See MATHESON.

MATTIAC.   See MATTICE.

11592   MATTICE.   Mattice family history, 1709-1961; Palatine emigration.   By Rex George
Mattice.   Provo, Utah, J.G.Stevenson, c.1962.   xxiv, 1092 p. illus., ports., maps, coat of arms. 25 cm. 62-48872.
CS71.M442   1962

11593   MATTINGLY.   Garrett county history of pioneer families, by Charles E. Hoye ... The
Mattingly family.   (Oakland, Md., 1936)   mounted l. 38 x 32 cm. Newspaper clipping. No. LXXX of a series of articles
contributed to the Mountain democrat. 41M3024T.
CS71.M443   1936

11594   MATTINGLY.   The descendants of Henry Mattingly, c.1750-1823; progenitor of Western
Maryland, Ohio, Indiana, Illinois, and many other Mattingly families (by) Herman E. Mattingly.   (n. p.)
1969.   vi, 236 p. 23 cm. 77-5951 MARC.
CS71.M443   1969

MATTISON.   See: MATHESON.
MATTESON.
SUTTON, 1935

11595   MATTOON.   Mary Matton and her hero of the revolution (General Ebenzer Mattoon) by Alice
M. Walker.   Cover design by Martha Genung.   Amherst, Mass. (Press of Carpenter & Morehouse)
1902.   83, (1) p. front., plates, ports. 18 cm. Contains genealogy of the Mattoon and Dickinson families. 3-5965.
F74.A5M44   1890

11596   MATTOON.   A genealogy of the descendants of Philip Mattoon of Deerfield, Massachusetts.
Researchers and compilers: Lillian G. Mattoon (and) Donald P. Mattoon.   (Littleton, N.H., 1965)
1 v. (various pagings) col. coat of arms, maps, ports. 24 cm. On cover and spine: Mattoon family genealogy. "Mattoon family genealogy"
(13 fold. p. in pocket) 67-123920.
CS71.M445   1965

11597   MAUDE.   History of some of the ancestors & descendants of Sir Robert Maude, bart., who
was born A.D.1676, and died August 4th, 1750.   Comp. by his grandson Captain Francis Maude, R.N.,
May 1886 ... London (Middlesex printing works) 1886.   29, (3) p. 21 cm. 21-3211.
CS439.M373

MAUDE.   See also FOSTER, 1871

11598   MAUDUIT.   Genealogical memoranda of the family of Ames.   By Reginald Ames, M.A.
Privately printed.   London, Mitchell and Hughes, 1889.   xxii p., 1 l., 96, 3-12 p. front., plates, ports., facsims.,
geneal. tables (6 fold., 5 double) coats of arms. 29 cm. Tudor pedigrees I, II: 2 fold. geneal. tab. Contains also pedigrees of the Chauncy,
Collins, Lyde, Mortimer, Darby, Gouge, King, Mauduit families, and others. 24-5031.   CS439.A56

MAUGHAN.   See SALISBURY, 1961

MAUGER.   See GUÉRIN, 1890

11599   MAULE.   Genealogy of the Maule family, with a brief account of Thomas Maule, of Salem,
Massachusetts ... (Comp. by Richard L. Nicholson.   Philadelphia, 1868)   15 p. illus. (coat of arms)
23 cm. Caption title. Cover-title: M., A.D.996. A.D.1868 (with coat of arms) 10-6582.   CS71.M449   1868

11600   MAULE.   Registrum de Panmure; records of the families of Maule, de Valoniis, Brechin,
and Brechin-Barclay, united in the line of the barons and earls of Panmure. Compiled by the Hon. Harry
Maule of Kelly, A.D.1733.   Edited by John Stuart ... Edinburgh, 1874.   2 v. front., illus. (part col.) plates
(part col.) ports., facsims., 2 col. coats of arms. 29 cm. "One hundred and fifty copies printed for private distribution by Fox Maule-Ramsay,
earl of Dalhousie, no. 45." Signed: H. Panmure-Gordon. 15-22368.   CS479.P3

11601   MAULE.   The Panmure papers; being a selection from the correspondence of Fox Maule, second baron Panmure, afterwards eleventh earl of Dalhousie, K. T., G. C. B., edited by Sir George Douglas ... and Sir George Dalhousie Ramsay... With a supplementary chapter by the late Rev. Principal Rainy, D. D.   London, Hodder and Stoughton, 1908.   2 v. fronts. (v.1, port.) 1 illus. 25 cm. "First edition printed September 1908; second edition printed October, 1908. " "Lord Dalhousie and the Free church of Scotland," by Rev. Principal Rainy: v.2, p.500-520.   9-3530.

DA68. 22. D25D6

11602   MAULE.   Genealogy of the Maule family, with a brief account of Thomas Maule, of Salem, Massachusetts, the ancestor of the family in the United States.   (By Richard L. Nicholson.   San Antonio? Tex., 1925?)   15, (1) p. illus (coat of arms) 23 cm.   Caption title.   On cover: M. A.D. 996, A.D. 1924 (with coat of arms)   A reprint of the first edition, A. D 996 - A.D. 1868, Philadelphia, 1868, with the addition of a record of the descendants of Caleb Maule (p. 15) and a genealogical table of the Wendell family (1 p. at end)   32-3312.

CS71. M449   1925

MAULE. See also: DOUGLAS, DA758.3. A1T2
HOLBROW, CS439. H6
MAULL.

11603   MAULL.   John Maull (1714-1753) of Lewes, Delaware, a genealogy of his descendants in all branches, by Baldwin Maull; edited by Rosalie Fellows Bailey ... New York, The Corporate press, 1941.   2 p. 1., 241, xxxix p. 23½ cm.   "References": p. 2-3.   41-21918.

CS71. M4495   1941

MAULL.   See also MAULE.

MAULEVERER.   See INGRAM, 1901

11604   MAULSBY.   Genealogy of the Maulsby family for five generations, 1699-1902; compiled by careful research among Quaker, government and family records by Cora M. (Patty) Payne ... Des Moines, Ia., G. A. Miller press, 1902.   4 p. 1., 142 p., 1 1., (2) p. front., illus. (incl. ports.) plates, fold. map, fold. facsim. 24 cm.   Ten leaves before the index left blank for addition.   3-3828.

CS71. M45   1902

11605   MAULSBY.   Early Maltby, with some Roades history and that of the Maulsby family in America, descendants of William and Mary Maltby, emigrants from Nottinghamshire, England, to Pennsylvania.   By Ella K. Barnard.   Baltimore, 1909.   7 p., 1 1., ii, 388 p., 1 1. front., illus., plates, port., facsims. (1 fold.) 24½ cm. 9-12868.

CS71. M45   1909

MAULSBY.   See also MALTBY.

MAULTHROP.   See MOULTHROP, 1925

MAUNDY.   See HUGHES, CS439. H768

11606   MAUNEY.   Three Mauney families, by Bonnie Mauney Summers (Mrs. F. R.).   Kings Mountain? N.C., 1967.   23, 54, 46, 31 1. coats of arms. 28 cm.   67-6760.

CS71. M4515   1967

11607   MAUNSELL.   A descriptive catalogue of the Penrice and Margam abbey manuscripts in the possession of Miss Talbot of Margam; by Walter de Grey Birch ... London, Priv. print., 1903-05.   3 v. 25½ cm.   Contents. - Fourth series (pt. I) group 1 General and personal. group 2. Margam abbey. - pt. II. group 2 (continu.) Aberavon and other places in the vicinity of the abbey and the western part of the county, to 1750. group 3. Gower, to 1750. - pt. III. group 4. Eastern Glamorgan. Appendix of misc. documents. group 5. Misc. counties. General index of subjects.   8-2483.

DA740. G5T3

11608   MAUNSELL.   History of Maunsell, or Mansel, and of Crayford, Gabbett, Knoyle, Persse, Toler, Waller, Castletown; Waller, Priot park; Warren, White, Winthrop, and Mansell of Guernsey. Compiled by Robert George Maunswell.   Cork, Guy and company, limited.   1903.   6 p. 1., 185 i. e. 186 p. front. (port.) plates, facsim. 25½ cm.   Blank leaves interspersed.   10-11182.

CS439. M37

11609   MAUNSELL.   History of the family of Maunsell (Mansell, Mansel), comp. chiefly from data collected during many years by Colonel Charles A. Maunsell, written by Edward Phillips Statham ... London, K. Paul, Trench & co., limited, 1917-20.   2 v. in 3. col. fronts., plates, ports. (part col.) plan, facsim., double geneal. tab. coats of arms. 30 cm.   17-27691 rev.

CS439. M37   1917

MAUNSELL. See also: GUÉRIN, 1890
MUNSELL.

11610 MAUPIN. The Maupin family with allied branches of Miller, Harris, Martin, Ballard, Mitchie, Dabney, White, Jarman, Mullins, McKenzie, Adkins, Waltrip, Jones, Neal, Hall, Rea families. Peoria, Ill., c1962. 114, 30 p. illus. 22 cm. 62-35611.   CS71.M452   1962

MAUPIN. See also: MILLER, 1907
No. 1547 - Cabell county.

11611 MAURAN. Memorials of the Mauran family. Collected in part by James Eddy Mauran. Compiled by John C. Stockbridge. Providence (Snow & Farnham, printers) 1893. 4 p. l., 171 p. incl. ports. front. (coat of arms) pl. 23½ cm. Interleaved. 9-11944.   CS71.M453   1893

11612 MAURER. The Maurer family, Pennsylvania pioneers; a brief history of the family, with records of all known descendants of Jacob Maurer, 1791-1863, and his wife, Maria Polly Hilbisch, 1793-1861, of Snyder County, Pennsylvania. Compiled by George Franklin Dunkelberger and Enid Eleanor Adams. (1st ed.) Seattle, 1954. 242 p. 29 cm. 55-33607.   CS71.M454   1954

11613 MAURICE. Pedigree of the families of Maurice, Owen, etc., of Clenenney in the county of Carnarvon, and of Porkington (now Brogyntyn) in the county of Salop; shewing the descent of the estates in England and Wales, of John Ralph, lord Harlech. Privately printed. London, 1876. 1 p. l., 8 p. coat of arms. 28½ cm. Compiled by William Watkins Edward Wynne. Issued also in Miscellanea genealogica et heraldica, new series, vol. II, p. 289-296. 9-19349.   CS459.M3

MAURICE. See also MARSHALL, 1913

11614 MAURY. John Walker Maury; his lineage and life. A sketch by his son William A. Maury. Washington (Press of W. F. Roberts) 1916. 18, (1) p. front. (port.) 25 cm. 16-6747.   CS71.M456   1916

11615 MAURY. Intimate Virginiana; a century of Maury travels by land and sea, edited by Anne Fontaine Maury. Richmond, Va., The Dietz press, 1941. ix p., 2 l., 342 p. front., plates, ports., facsims. (incl. music) coats of arms. 23½ cm. Chart on lining-papers. "Biographical notes": p. (311) - 331. Bibliography: p. (335) - 336. A44-832.   F230.M43

11616 MAURY. Une famille française; la province au siècle dernier. Notes et souvenirs. By Lucien Mary. Paris, Stock, Delamain et Boutelleau, 1942 (c. 1941) 215 p. port. 19 cm. Bibliography: p. (209)-211. 50-50485.   CS599.M44   1942

MAURY. See also: FONTAINE, 18 -   JAMES, 1913a
FONTAINE, 1886   POSTON, 1959
FONTAINE, 1967   TAYLOR, 1898

11617 MAUS. History & genealogy of the Maus family, U.S.A., A.D.1762-1954. By Alban Fruth. Ogema, Minn. (1954) 18 p. illus. 32 cm. Caption title. 72-6667 MARC.   CS71.M457   1954

11618 MAUZY. Genealogical record of the descendants of Henry Mauzy, a Huguenot refugee, the ancestor of the Mauzys of Virginia and other states, from 1685 to 1910, and of the descendants of Jacob Kisling from 1760 to 1910, by Richard Mauzy ... Harrisonburg, Va., Press of the Daily news, 1911. 127 p. incl. front. (port.) 21 cm. 14-4607.   CS71.M459   1911

11619 MAUZEY-MAUZY family in The Virginia Magazine of History and Biography. vol. 58, 1950. Pages 112 - 119.   F221.V91 v.58

11620 MAVERICK. Remarks on the Maverick family and the ancestry of Gov. Simon Bradstreet. By Isaac J. Greenwood. Boston, Press of D. Clapp & son, 1894. 8 p. 24½ cm. Cover-title. "Reprinted from the N.E. historical and genealogical register for April, 1894." 9-3048.   CS71.M461   1894

11621   MAVERICK.   The Mavericks of Devonshire and Massachusetts, by Beatrix F. Creswell. Exeter, J.G.Commin, 1929.   64 p. front., plates, facsim. 23 cm. 32-9008.   CS71.M461   1929

11622   MAVERICK.   The Mavericks, by Frederick C. Chabot on the occasion of Maury Maverick for Congress. (n.p.) 1934.   8 p. 23 cm. 34-32108.   CS71.M461   1934

11623   MAVERICK.   Maverick family notes in vertical file.   Ask reference librarian for this material.

11624   MAVITY.   The Mavity family.   By Norman Bloss Mavity.   (French Lick? Ind., 1954)   270 p. illus. 29 cm. 55-24856.   CS71.M463   1954

MAW.   See NOURSE, 195 -

MAXEY.   See HYNES, 1957

11625   MAXSON.   The Maxson family; descendants of John Maxson and wife Mary Mosher of Westerly, Rhode Island.   By Walter Le Roy Brown.   (Albion? N.Y.) 1954.   247 p. 24 cm. 55-30284.   CS71.M464   1954

MAXSON.   See also SMITH, 1968

11626   MASTONE.   The Maxtones of Cultoquhey, by E. Maxtone Graham.   Ediburgh & London, The Moray press (1935)   240 p. front., ports., map, fold. geneal. tables. 23½ x 18½ cm. "First published 1935." 44-17059.   CS479.M43   1935

11627   MAXWELL.   ... The seize quartiers of the Right Honourable Henry Maxwell, seventh baron Farnham, K.P., and of his brothers and sisters.   (n.p., 18 -)   geneal. tab. 38 x 56½ cm. fold. to 38 x 28½ cm. 40-21851.   CS439.M373

11628   MAXWELL.   ... Herries peerage.   Supplement to the case of William Constable Maxwell esq., claiming to be Lord Herries of Terregles in the peerage of Scotland. (London, G. & T.W. Webster, 1853)   3 p. 1., 23 p. 34 cm. 27-10164.   CS479.M45   1853

11629   MAXWELL.   Memoirs of the Maxwells of Pollok, by William Fraser ... Edinburgh, 1863.   2 v. illus., plates, ports., facsims. 29½ cm. Engr. t.-p.; plates printed on both sides. 8-22936.   DA758.3.M4F8

11630   MAXWELL.   The book of Carlaverock; memoirs of the Maxwells, earls of Nithsdale, lords Maxwell & Herries, by William Fraser ... Edinburgh, 1873.   2 v. illus., plates (partly col.) ports., facsims. in colors. 29 cm.   Title within ornamental border; added t.-p., illus. "Privately printed for William lord Herries ... Impression one hundred and fifty copies. no. 50." Contents. - I. Memoirs. - II. Correspondence & charters. 11-21777.   DA758.3.M4F67

11631   MAXWELL.   The cartulary of Pollok-Maxwell.   By William Fraser.   Edinburgh (T. & A. Constable) 1875.   xiv, 421, (1) p. illus., facsim. 29 cm. Illus. t.-p. in colors. This impression consists of only 20 copies, privately printed for Sir Wm. Stirling Maxwell. 8-22935.   DA758.3.M4F7

11632   MAXWELL.   Pedigree of the family of Maxwell of Springkell, county Dumfries, now head of the Clydesdale branch of the house of Maxwell ... Compiled by Michael John Maxwell Shaw Stewart (and) printed at the charge of Edward Heron Maxwell Blair.   Worksop, Notts., 1890.   geneal. tab. 64½ x 56½ cm. fold. to 34 cm. Additions and corrections in manuscript. 16-20941.   CS479.M45   1890

11633   MAXWELL.   The Maxwell family.   Descendants of John and Ann Maxwell, 1701-1894.   With appendix containing sketch of the Maxwell family and biographical sketches.   Comp. by Henry D. Maxwell ... Easton, Pa. (Easton express print) 1895.   2 p. 1., 85 numb. 1. coat of arms. 26 cm. 9-11943 rev.   CS71.M465   1895

11634   MAXWELL.   Maxwell history and genealogy, including the allied families of Alexander, Allen, Bachiler, Batterton, Beveridge, Blaine, Brewster, Brown, Callender, Campbell, Carey, Clark, Cowan, Fox, Dinwiddie, Dunn, Eylar, Garretson, Gentry, Guthrie, Houston, Howard, Howe, Hughes, Hussey, Irvine, Johnson, Kimes, McCullough, Moore, Pemberton, Rosenmüller, Smith, Stapp, Teter,

11634 continued.   Tilford, Uzzell, Vawter, Ver Planck, Walker, Wiley, Wilson.   By Florence Wilson Houston, Laura Cowan Blaine, Ella Dunn Mellette.   Also baptismal record of the Rev. John Craig, D.D., of Augusta County, Virginia, 1740-1749, containing one thousand four hundred and seventy four names. (First publication of the original record) Indianapolis, Ind., Press of C.E. Pauley & co., Indianapolis engraving co. (c.1916)   8 p. l., 642 p. front., plates, ports., coat of arms. 24 cm. 16-11225.

CS71.M465   1916

11635   MAXWELL.   The Maxwell family from the Story of Connecticut, by Col. Charles W. Burpee. Rockville, Conn., Priv. print. (at the sign of the Stone book, by the Case, Lockwood & Brainard co., Hartford) 1939.   3 p. l., 15 p. illus. (col. coat of arms) 21 cm. A page of the Rockville journal of August 3, 1939, containing an account of William Maxwell, in pocket at end. 40-2244.

CS71.M465   1939

11636   MAXWELL.   Thomas Maxwell of Virginia and Georgia and his descendants.   (Compiled by Annie Norman, Helen Maxwell Longino, and Annie Lou Maxwell) Macon, Ga., Press of the J.W. Burke Co. (1956)   x, 477 p. illus., port. 24 cm. 57-16752.

CS71.M465   1956

11637   MAXWELL.   The annals of one branch of the Maxwell family in Ulster.   By Sir William George Maxwell. (2d ed. Kuala Lumpur, Federation of Malaya, 1959)   68 p. illus. 26 cm. 59-41350.

CS499.M45   1959

MAXWELL.   See also: AMES, 1959
                       CARPENTER, 1959
                       CROSSLEY, CS439.C835
                       DOUGLAS, DA758.3.A1T2
                       HERBERT, 1939
                       STRONG, 1912

11638   MAY.   Memoir of Col. Joseph May, 1760-1841.   By Samuel May, of Leicester ... Boston, D. Clapp & son, 1873.   12 p. front. (port.) 23½ cm. Reprinted from the New-England historical and genealogical register for April, 1873. Genealogical sketch: p. 3-5. 12-23857.

F73.44.M43

11639   MAY.   A genealogy of the descendants of John May, who came from England to Roxbury, in America, 1640.   Boston, Franklin press: Rand, Avery & co., 1878.   1 p. l., xxxv p., 1 l., 175 p. 25 cm. The first suggestion of the work came from Richard S. Eden. p. 171-172 omitted. Introduction signed: Samuel May ... John Wilder May ... John Joseph May. Indexed. 9-11942.

CS71.M467   1878

11640   MAY.   The Mays of Basingstoke, with special reference to Lieut-Colonel John May ... By F. Ray ... London, Simpkin and co., ltd.; (etc., etc.) 1904.   x, 60 p. front., plates, ports. 26 cm. 12-31633.

CS439.M375

11641   MAY.   Genealogical notes on the family of Mays, and reminiscences of the war between the states, from notes written around the campfires by Samuel Elias Mays, born in South Carolina, Nov. 12th, 1834; died at Plant City, Florida, Nov. 27th, 1906; and some references to the Earle family. (Plant City, Printed by Plant City enterprise, 1927)   324 p. 2 port. (incl. front.) 23½ cm. "Compiler's note" signed: Samuel E. Mays. 28-18063.

E605.M46

11642   MAY.   Genealogical notes on a branch of the family of Mayes and on the related families of Chappell, Bannister, Jones, Peterson, Locke, Hardaway, Thweatt and others, by Edward Mayes ... (Jackson, Miss., Printed by Hederman bros., 1928?)   99, b-160, D-168, C-74 p. 24 cm. Cover-title: Genealogy of the families of Mayes, Rigg, Lamar and Longstreet and related families. L.C. copy imperfect: p. D-35 - D49, D-68 - D-120, D-137 - D-152 wanting. Additions and corrections in manuscript. 28-12170.

CS71.M467   1928

11643   MAY.   Our ancestors, a record of these families: May, Hanson, Pollard, Philips ... Written by Homer Eiler ... Grenola, Kan., Printed by J.S. Dancy, 1929.   36, (1) p. illus. (incl. port.) 21½ cm. 31-19470.

CS71.M467   1929

11644   MAY.   Genealogy of the Mays family and related families to 1929 inclusive.   By Samuel Edward Mays. Plant City, Fla. (1929)   4 p. l., (3)-288 p. plates, ports., coats of arms (1 col.) 23 cm. Cover-title: The Mays family. "(The author's) father, Samuel Elias Mays ... assembled the foundation data for the genealogy." - Pref. 30-9799.

CS71.M467   1929a

11645   MAY.   The Mayes book.   By Clarence Cannon.   (Elsberry? Mo.) 1957.   121 p. 29 cm.
58-40724.
CS71.M467   1957

11646   MAY.   The May family of Kingston, Ohio; a genealogy of Henry and Susannah McCutchen May and their descendants, with sections on the McCutchen and Taylor families and related lines. (Washington) 1969.   72 p. illus., geneal. tables, ports. 26 cm. Bibliography: p. 48-50. 78-7845 MARC.
CS71.M467   1969

MAY.   See also: EDWARDS, 1931
                   KNIGHT, DA690.C47A8
                   MAYES.
                   PAINE, 1914
                   SNYDER, 1958
                   STEEN, 1959

MAYBERRY.   See: BOONE, 1922
                   HOWARD, 1961

MAYDSTONE.   See CLOPTON, 1939

11647   MAYER.   Memoir and genealogy of the Maryland and Pennsylvania family of Mayer which originated in the free imperial city of Ulm, Würtemberg: 1495-1878.   By Brantz Mayer. (Baltimore, Md., Priv. print. for the family by W. K. Boyle & son, 1878)   1 p. l., (5)-179 p. front., illus., pl. 25½ cm.
9-11941.
CS71.M468   1878

11648   MAYER.   The Mayer family by Harriet Hyatt Mayer ... (Annisquam, Mass., 1911)
(8) p. incl. illus., geneal. tables. 30½ cm. Caption title: The Mayer family, 1604-1911. Edition of 150 copies. "This pamphlet is designed to supplement the 'Memoirs and genealogy of the Maryland and Pennsylvania family of Mayer,' by Brantz Mayer, Baltimore, 1878." 11-30061.
CS71.M468   1911

11649   MAYER.   Material in vertical file.   Ask reference librarian for this material.

MAYER.   See also MEYER.

11650   MAYES.   See MAY.

11651   MAYFIELD.   Memorabilia of Albert and Ann Mayfield and their descendants, 1850-1969. By Fay Hicks Mayfield. (Abilene? Tex., 1969)   114 p. illus., col. coat of arms, facsims., ports. 24 cm. On cover: Memorabilia, 1850-1969. 75-10430 MARC.
CS71.M4684   1969

MAYFIELD.   See also: BOONE, 1902
                        MILLER, 1923
                        TIPPIN, 1939

11652   MAYHAM.   1937 Mayham family reunion.   Mayham family directory, with names, addresses and family lines of present members of family. (n. p., 1937)   1 p. l., 24 p. illus. (ports.) 28 cm. "Collected by the family historian, Mrs. Percy E. Raymond." 38-32679.
CS71.M4687   1937

11653   MAYHAM.   The family of Henry Maham of Blenheim Hill, Schoharie County, New York. By Eva Grace Mayham (Goodenough) Raymond.   (Lexington? Mass.) Mayham Family Reunion Committee, 1950.   64 p. 28 cm. Cover title: The Mayham family, 1795-1950. 52-25730.   CS71.M4687   1950

11654   MAHEW.   (The Mayhew family tree.   Descendants of Thomas Mayhew) (n. p., n. d.) mounted geneal. tab. illus (port., coat of arms) 30 x 39 cm. A phtog. repro. of the Mayhew geneal. tab., ...1855. 42-41456.   CS71.M469

11655   MAHEW.   Indian converts: or, Some account of the lives and dying speeches of a considerable number of the Christianized Indians of Martha's Vineyard, in New-England ... By Experience Mayhew ... To which is added, Some account of those English minsters who have successively presided over the Indian work in that and the adjacent islands. By Mr. Prince ... London, Printed for S. Gerrish, bookseller in Boston in New-England; and sold by J. Osborn (etc.) 1727.   7, ix-xxiv, 310 p. 19 cm. The narrative of Thomas Prince (p. (277)-310) has separate t.-p. 6-19809.
E78.M4M64

11656   MAYHEW.   The Mayhew family tree.   Descendants of Thomas Mayhew.   Buffalo, Lith.
Compton, 1855.   geneal. tab. port., coat of arms. 87 x 103 cm. (fold. to 22½ cm.) 17-19209.

CS71.M469   1855

11657   MAYHEW.   The venerable Mayhews and the aboriginal Indians of Martha's Vineyard.   Condensed from Rev. Experience Mayhew's history printed in London in 1727, and brought down to the
present century.   By William A. Hallock ... New York, American tract society (c. 1874)   190 p. front.
15½ cm.   From Mayhew's "Indian converts: or, Some accounts of the lives and dying speeches of a considerable number of the Christianized
Indians of Martha's Vineyard." 5-10337.   E78.M4H2

11658   MAYHEW.   The English ancestry of Gov. Thomas Mayhew of Martha's Vineyard 1593-1682,
by Charles Edward Banks, M. D.   Cambridge, Mass., Lucy H. Greenlaw, 1901.   10 p. front. (coat of
arms) geneal. tab. 24½ cm. 4-24926.   Reprinted from the Genealogical advertiser, Cambridge, 1901 v. 4 p. 1-8.   4-24926.

CS71.M469   1901

———— Copy 2.   Photostat of above.   Negative.   41M2754T-2   CS71.M469   1901a

11659   MAYHEW.   (Record of the ancestry of Richard Nelson Mayhew)   (n. p., 1935?)   2 p. 1., 62 geneal.
tab. ports., coats of arms. 55 cm. Blue print. Dedication signed: W. Nelson Mayhew. 38M2597T.

CS71.M469   1935

11660   MAYHEW.   Material in vertical file.   Ask reference librarian for this material.

MAYHEW.   See also: HALL.
STRONG, 1912

11661   MAYLAM.   Maylam family records.   First series.   Gravtestone inscriptions.   Compiled
by Percy Maylam ... Canterbury (Priv. print., Cross & Jackman) 1932.   4 p. 1., xii p., 76 numb. 1., 77-88 p.
xv pl., 2 double geneal. tab. 30 cm. 40-282.   CS439.M378   1932

11662   MAYLE.   Garrett county history of pioneer families, by Charles E. Hoye ... The Mayle
family.   (Oakland, Md., 1936)   mounted 1. 38 x 32 cm. Newspaper clipping. No. LXXVII of a series of articles contributed
to the Mountain democrat, April 16, 1936. 41M3023T.   CS71.M4694   1936

MAYN.   See MAIN.

MAYNE.   See MAIN.   ·

MAYNARD.   See: CRANMER, 1965
HILL, 1961
WILLIAMSON, 1962

11663   MAYO.   A genealogical account of the Mayo and Elton families of the counties of Wilts and
Hereford; with an appendix, containing genealogies, for the most part not hitherto published, of
certain families allied by marriage to the family of Mayo; to which is added a large tabular pedigree
set in type by Theodore Mayo.   London, Priv. print. by C. Whittingham, 1882.   177 p. illus. 27 cm.
59-55237.   CS439.M38   1882

11664   MAYO.   A genealogical account of the Mayo & Elton families of Wilts and Herefordshire and
some other adjoining counties, together with numerous biographical sketches; to which are added many
genealogies for the most part not hitherto published of families allied by marriage to the family of
Mayo and a history of the manors of Andrewes and Le Mote, in Cheshunt, Hertfordshire.   By Charles
Herbert Mayo ... 2d and greatly enl. ed. with many illustrations.   London, Priv. print. at the
Chiswick press by C. Whittingham and company, 1908.   xix, (1) p., 1 1., 628 p. front., illus., plates, ports., facsims.
30 cm.   Allied families: Adeane, Alderne, Chase, Druitt, Dyer, Gibbs, Hare, Hayes, Ogilvie, Perrott, Prichard, Reynolds, Willim, Woodward.
11-14206.   CS439.M38

11665   MAYO.   ... The Mayo family of Truro, by Shebnah Rich.   Yarmouthport, Mass., C. W.
Swift, 1914.   cover-title, 2 p. 24½ cm. (Library of Cape Cod history & genealogy, no. 50) 17-6142.

CS71.M47   1914

11666   MAYO.   The Mayo family in the United States ... by Chester Garst Mayo.   (n. p. 1927)
2 v. 28½ cm.   Type-written.   Contents - v. 1. John Mayo of Roxbury, Mass., the first Mayo to land in America, and the genealogical and biographical record of all his descendants bearing the name of Mayo. -v. 2. John Mayo of Barnstable, Mass., and the genealogical and biographical
record of all his descendants bearing the name of Mayo.   27-14692.   CS71.M47   1927

11667   MAYO.   Descent of Edward Leonard Mayo from Rev. John Mayo, by Winifred Lovering
Holman ... compiled by the author for Harriet (Elwood) Mayo.   (Watertown, Mass., 1932)   2 p. l.,
86 numb. l., 12 l.   15 cm.   Type-written.   "Principal sources consulted": p. 85-86.   33-9642.   CS71.M47   1932

11668   MAYO.   Mayos of Virginia and kinsmen, Smiths of Virginia and others of the connection.   By
their relative, George Magruder Battey III ... (Washington, D. C., 1940)   1 p. l., 4 l.   28 cm.   Type-written
(carbon copy) 41M182T.   CS71.M47   1940

11669   MAYO.   Rev. John Mayo and his descendants, by E. Jean Mayo.   (2d ed.   Pueblo? Colo.,
1965)   iv, 176 l.   map.   29 cm.   Cover title.   Bibliography: leaves 162-163.   66-52933.   CS71.M47   1965

11670   MAYO.   John Mayo of Roxbury, Massachusetts, 1630-1688; a genealogical and biographical
record of his descendants.   By Chester Garst Mayo.   Huntington, Vt., 1965 (cover 1966)
304 p.   illus., col. coat of arms, facsims., ports. (part col.) 32 cm.   64-19684.   CS71.M47   1966

11671   MAYO.   Mayo family (Martha Caron Lake Mayo, Civil war nurse and cousin of Kit Carson.
In vertical file.   Ask reference librarian for this material.

        MAYO.   See also: HOWES, 1917
                           TAYLOR, 1875

        MAYOR.   See RANDALL.

        MAYS.   See MAY.

        MAYSON.   See SMITH.

11672   MAYTAG.   Fred L. Maytag, a biography, by A. B. Funk.   Cedar Rapids, Ia., Priv, print. by
the Torch press (c. 1936)   226 p.   front., plates, ports.   24½ cm.   36-15580.   CT275.M4653E8

        MAZYCK.   See HARRIS, 1941

11673   MEACHAM.   Family book of remembrance and genealogy, with allied lines.   By Leonidas De
Von Mecham.   (Salt Lake City?) 1952 (cover 1953)   1010 p.   illus., ports., coats of arms.   28 cm.   Cover title:
Meacham-Mecham family, book of remembrance and genealogy, with allied lines.   55-26413.
CS71.M476   1953

11674   MEAD.   History and genealogy of the Mead family of Fairfield County, Connecticut, eastern
New York, western Vermont and western Pennsylvania from A. D. 1180 to 1900; by Spencer P. Mead
... New York, The Knickerbocker press, 1901.   vii p., 1., 471 p.   col. front., pl., ports.   25 cm.
CS71.M48   1901

        —— Genealogical index to the Genealogy of the Mead family published in 1901, by Spencer P.
Mead ... N(ew) Y(ork) The Knickerbocker press, 1907.   1 p. l., 73 p.   24½ cm.   1-27748 additions.
CS71.M48   1901a

11675   MEAD.   Genealogy of a branch of the Mead family, with a history of the family in England
and in America and appendixes of the Rogers and Denton families, by Lucius Egbert Weaver.   Rochester, N. Y., 1917.   63 p.   23½ cm.   19-11625.   CS71.M48   1917

11676   MEAD.   Andrew Meade of Ireland and Virginia; his ancestors, and some of his descendants and
ther connections, including sketches of the following fanilies: Meade, Everard, Hardaway, Segar, Pettus,
and Overton ... By P. Hamilton Baskervill ... chiefly from letters, papers, and other material furnished
by Mrs. Elise Meade (Skelton) Baskervill and from other sources.   Richmond, Va., Old dominion press,
inc., printers, 1921.   xv, 170 p.   col. front. (coat of arms) illus., plates, ports., geneal. tables (1 fold.) 24½ cm.   "Authorities":
p. (xi)-xii.   21-13991 rev.   CS71.M48   1921

11677   MEAD.   Mead relations; Mead, Brown, Powell, Keyser, Kelly, Trumbo, Austin, Toler, Prichard.   Virginia, Kentucky.   Compiled by A. M. Prichard.   Staunton, Va., 1933.   3 p. l., (9)-265 p. ports.   23½ cm.   34-8481.   CS71.M48   1933

11678   MEAD.   Our two centuries in North Greenwich, Connecticut, 1728-1924.   By Louise Celestia (Mead) Feltus.   (n. p.) 1945.   135 p. illus., ports., coat of arms, geneal. tables. 23 cm.   CS71.M48   1945

——— A supplement of addenda and corrigenda.   (Troy, N.Y., R.H. Prout Co.) 1948.   74 p. 23 cm.   47-60 rev*   CS71.M48   1945   Suppl.

11679   MEAD.   Mead-Clark genealogy, compiled by Eva Mead Firestone ... (Ann Arbor, Mich., Lithoprinted by Edwards brothers, inc.) 1946.   1 p. l., vii, 84 (i.e. 88), 9, viii, 88 (i.e. 98) p. port. 21 cm.   Includes extra numbered pages.   Additions in manuscript.   Includes bibliographies.   46-19643.   CS71.M48   1946

11680   MEAD.   Lineage of Jeremiah Mead, Jr., of Greenwich, Connecticut, soldier of the American Revolution.   By Mary Beller Sawers.   Middletown, Conn., 1958.   50 l. 28 cm.   Includes bibliography. 58-31374.   CS71.M48   1958

11681   MEAD.   The Meade genealogy, by George P. Meade.   New Orleans, 1966.   10 p. 23 cm.   Bibliography: p.10.   67-4213.   CS71.M48   1966

11682   MEAD.   The Mead family of Connecticut.   Compiled by C. E. Parker.   Santa Ana, Calif., 1968.   68, (4) l. 30 cm.   Label mounted on cover: Part of the Ebenezer Mead branch.   Bibliography: p. (69) - (71) 68-7401.   CS71.M48   1968

MEAD.   See also: BENEDICT, F129.S697YO3   POCAHONTAS, 1887
BUCK, 1917 suppl.   POOL, 1958
FUNSTEN, 1926   SMITH, 1939
MANLEY, 1938   No. 1459 - Early families of ... Ky.

MEADE.   See MEAD.

11683   MEADOR.   The Meadors and the Meadows, compiled by Edward Kirby Meador ... Boston, Meador publishing company, 1941.   57 p. incl. front. (coat of arms) 20½ cm.   Bibliography: p. 23, 57.   41-26562.   CS71.M483   1941

11684   MEADOR.   The Meadors of Virginia, by Edward Kirby Meador.   A play in three acts ... Boston, Meador publishing company, 1941.   40 p. diagr. 19½ cm.   42-626.   PN6120.A5M36755

11685   MEADOR.   Genealogical records of some members of the Meador family who are descendants of Thomas Meador of Virginia.   By Daniel Burton Meador.   (North Newton, Kan., Printed by the Mennonite Press, 1968)   248 p. coat of arms. 24 cm.   68-55079.   CS71.M483   1968

MEADOWCRAFT.   See ROYD, CS439.R75

11686   MEADOWS.   The Suffolk Bartholomeans: a memoir of the ministerial and domestic history of John Meadows ... ejected under the act of uniformity from the rectory of Ousden in Suffolk.   By the late Edgar Taylor, F.S.A., one of his descendants, with a prefatory notice by his sister.   Printed by Arthur Taylor.   London, W. Pickering, 1840.   viii, 165, (2) p. illus., 2 port. (incl. front.) 2 fold. geneal. tab. 25 cm.   "To the reader" signed: Emily Taylor.   "Pedigree of Fairfax of Norfolk and Suffolk": folded genealogical table following p. 64.   "Mr. Fairfax's letters, and extract from sermon.   Mrs. Sarah Meadows's reflections on the education of her children": p. (121)-150.   14-19507 rev.   BX9225.M395T3

11687   MEADOWS.   Sketch of the Meadows family.   By Simeon Joseph Meadows.   In vertical file.   Ask reference librarian for this material.

MEADOWS.   See also HILL, 1961

MEAGHER.   See O'MEAGHER.

11688   MEAKES. See MIX.

11689   MEANS. History of the Means family in America and Great Britain.   Comp. by the Rev. Chas. N. Sinnett. Brainerd, Minn. (191 -?)   1 p. l., 198 numb. l. 23 cm. Type-written. 21-9023.
CS71.M485   191-

11690   MEANS.   Amherst and our family tree, by Anne M. Means.   Boston, Priv. print., 1921.
4 p. l., iv, 414 p. front., plates, ports., 4 geneal. tab. (in pocket) 21½ cm. 22-10470.   CS71.M485   1921

MEANS.   See also LEMOND, 1937

MEARING.   See MERING.

MEARS.   See AMES, 1967

MEAUTYS.   See CORNWALLIS, DA396.C6A3

MEDBERY.   See MEDBURY.

11691   MEDBURY.   History and genealogy of the Medbury-Medbery-Medberry family descendants of John Medbury, Swansea, Mass., 1680.   Compiled by Mrs. James F. Medbery.   Silver Spring, Md., 1965.   127 l. 30 cm. Bibliography: leaf 116. 66-35185.   CS71.M486   1965

MEDBURY.   See also WILCOX, 1902

11692   MEDEARIS.   Biography of the Medearis family (compiled by Mrs. Frank Medearis) (Richmond, Ind., 1925)   7, (1) p. 11½ cm. Caption title. 32-1223.   CS71.M487   1925

MEDEARIS.   See also YANCEY, 1958

11693   MEDICI.   History of Florence from the founding of the city through the renaissance, by Ferdinand Schevill ... New York, Harcourt, Brace and company (c.1936)   3 p. l., iii-xxxiv, 536 p. incl. geneal. tab. front., plates, maps (1 double) 24½ cm. "First edition." 36-21463.   DG736.S3

MEDILL.   See McDILL.

11694   MEDLEY.   The history of the parish of Hailsham, the abbey of Otham, and the priory of Michelham.   By L. F. Salzmann ... Lewes, Farncombe & company, limited, printers, 1901.
1 p. l., ix, 308 p. pl., fold. map, plans, fold. geneal. tab. 23 cm. "Pedigree of Medley": fold. geneal. tab. 2-23018.
DA690.H14S2

MEDLEY.   See also: HUNTER, 1959
LA RUE, 1921

11695   MEDSKER.   Descendants of Rev. Jehu Cain Madsker and Josinah Dodd Medsker ... (By Eugene Studebaker Wierbach) (Muncie? Ind., 1941)   3 l. 28 cm. Caption title. Type-written. 42-4211.
CS71.M4875   1941

11696   MEDWIN.   Memoirs of William West Medwin, with a few poems, written by him.   Also some poems by his eldes son.   Together with addenda, by James Medwin, by whom this volume is compiled for the use of the family.   London, 1882.   2 p. l., 267 p. front., plates, ports., coat of arms. 21½ cm. The plates are mounted photographs. 21-11412.   CT788.M35A3

MEECH. See WALBRIDGE, 1898

11697   MEEDS.   The descendants of James Meeds (c.1760 - c.1795) and his wife Diana Bingley-Orrey (c.1765 - c.1815) William Pusey (1779-1839) and his wife Ann Hill (1798-1822) (by) Benjamin N. Meeds, jr. ... and William P. Meeds, jr. ... (n.p.) 1936.   2 p. l., 16 p. 26½ cm. Mimeographed. 37-21345.
CS71.M488   1936

11698   MEEK.   Voices of the past, with partial history and genealogy of the Meek and Galloway families, by Georgia May L. V. Meek.   (Springfield, Mo., 1929)   69 p. incl. illus., ports. 23½ cm. 29-10727.
CS71.M49   1929

11699   MEEK.   Meek genealogy, 1640-1954.   By Carleton Lee Meek.   (Lincoln? Neb.) c. 1954.
1 v. 27 cm. 54-35802.
CS71.M49   1954

11700   MEEK.   Meek genealogy, 1640-1962.   By Carleton Lee Meek.   (Lincoln? Neb.) c. 1962.
62, 44 p. map, coat of arms. 27 cm. 63-32602.
CS71.M49   1962

MEEK.   See also: ODELL, 1960a
PECK, 1955
No. 1547 - Cabell county.

MEEKER.   See COLEMAN, 1937

11701   MEEKS.   Murder of the Meeks family, or, Crimes of the Taylor brothers.   The full and authentic story of the midnight massacre, by Bill and George Taylor, of the Meeks family, father, mother, and three little children ... The gruesome story of little Nellie Meeks, sole survivor of the massacre ... By E. A. McDonald.   Kansas City, Mo., R. Walker (1896)   58 p. illus. 19 cm. CA25-1153 unrev.
HV6534.B8A6 1894c

11702   MEEM.   John G. Meem, Lynchburg, Virginia.   (Lynchburg? 1869?)   48 p. 23 cm. Compilation of newspaper articles, etc., concerning the Meem family and its estate, Mr. Airy, near Lynchburg, Va.   41-38737.
CT275.M46558J6

MEET.   See CRALL, 1908

11703   MEGEE.   Kith and kin of the John Megee family and descendants of Indian River Hundred, Sussex County, Delaware.   (Washington? 1963)   A-B, iv, 331, (59) p. illus., ports. 29 cm. Cover title. "Copy number 78 of 110 copies." 64-4318.
CS71.M4926   1963

11704   MEGGINSON.   History of Ralph Megginson and his descendants.   By Cecil Elmer Megginson. (n. p.) c. 1952.   1 v. illus. 30 cm. 52-34366.
CS71.M493   1952

MEGGS.   See CASE, DA690.B23C3

MEGINNES.   See MACGINNIS.

11705   MEGREW.   The Megrew's, genealogy and history, by Rowena Megrew McFatridge ... (Moravia, Ia., 1943)   ii numb. l., 1 l., 20 numb. l., 1 l. 23 x 36 cm. Cover-title: Megrews, the agrarians. Text runs parallel with back of cover; reproduced from type-written copy. 43-14675.
CS71.M495   1943

11706   MEHARRY.   History of the Meharry family in America, descendants of Alexander Meharry I, who fled during the reign of Mary Stuart, queen of Scots, on account of religious persecution, from near Ayr, Scotland, to Ballyjamesduff, Cavan county, Ireland, and whose descendants, Alexander Meharry III emigrated to America in 1794.   (Meharry history publishing committee) (Lafayette, Ind., Lafayette printing company, 1925)   5 p. l., (9)-384 p. front., illus. (incl. facsims.) ports. 23 cm. 29-19080.
CS71.M497   1925

MEHURIN.   See MAHURIN.

MEIER.   See: MEYER.
MYERS.
STARKWEATHER, 1925

11707   MEIGS.   Record of the descendants of Vincent Meigs, who came from Dorsetshire, England, to America about 1635 ... By Henry B. Meigs.   (Baltimore, Md., J. S. Bridges & co., 1901)   374 p. front., (port.) illus., pl. 28½ cm. Blank pages inserted for genealogical data. 2-11712.
CS71.M511   1901

11708   MEIGS.   Meigs chart of American ancestry.   By Henry Benjamin Meigs.   Baltimore, 1902.
geneal. tab.   41½ x 71 cm. fold. to 22 x 15½ cm.   Includes "References."   3-3193 rev.   CS71.M511   1902

11709   MEIGS.   The Meigs tribe, 346 yrs: 1559-1905 A.D. ... table made by Captain Joe Vincent
Meigs in April 1905.   (Boston?) 1905.   blue-print geneal. tab.   61 x 49½ cm. fold. to 25 x 15½ cm.   CA6-2655.
CS71.M511   1905

11710   MEIGS.   The Meigs tribe, 346 yrs.: 1559 to 1905 A.D.   Comp. by Joe Vincent Meigs.
Boston, 1905.   blue-print geneal. tab.   61½ x 48½ fold. to 24 x 15½ cm.   Dated August, 1905. 1st edition, April, 1905.   CA6-2654.
CS71.M511   1905a

11711   MEIGS.   The commixtion of the tribes in the United States of America, of McSpadden - Love -
Meigs - Clendinen - Van Bibber - Pope and others is here shown: an effort, to know myself, and to
inform my sons - grand children, and many others, from whence their individualtiy came - Most of
this matter came from Bible records - from my own papers and letters of my father - The Clendinen
matter from Mrs. Delia A. McCulloch and Mrs. Edith Clendinen Miller Stephens of W. Va. - The names
of data furnishers are all given below - Joe Vincent Meigs.   (Boston) 1906.   geneal. tab. 54½ x 80 cm. fold.
to 20 x 14 cm.   Blue-print.   6-46416.   CS71.M511   1906

11712   MEIGS.   Record of the descendants of Vincent Meigs who came from Dorestshire, England,
to America about 1635 ... By Henry Benjamin Meigs.   (Westfield, N.J.) c.1935.   2 p. l., 230 p. illus.
(coat of arms) 29½ cm.   "The first edition of this record was prepared by Henry B. Meigs, was copyrighted by him in 1901, and published in 1902.
This (1934) edition has been prepared by Return Jonathan Meigs, 9th."   Includes blank pages for genealogical data.   Mimeographed.   On cover:
The Meigs family in America.   35-9676.   CS71.M511   1935

11713   MEIGS.   The line of the Returns.   No. 1, Vincent Meigs, the American founder (by) R.J.
Meigs.   (n.p.) 1936.   geneal. tab.   30 x 44½ cm.   "Note: Numbers are as given in "The Meigs family in America" (by H.B. Meigs,
1935)"   37-16854.   CS71.M511   1936

11714   MEIGS.   The line of the Returns.   No. 1, Vincent Meigs, the American founder, 1583-1658.
(By) R.J.Meigs.   (Westfield, N.J.) c.1939.   geneal. tab.   26½ x 41 cm.   Photoprinted.   "Numbers are as given in "The
Meigs family in America" (by H.B. Meigs, 1935)"   40-18334.   CS71.M511   1939

    MEIGS.   See also: CLENDINEN, 1905
                         WILCOX, 1893
                         WILCOX, 1938

11715   MEISENHOLDER.   Gottlieb Meisenholder, John Schmierer, and their descendants.   By
Thomas Jules Schmierer.   (Vermillion? S.D.) c.1959.   unpaged. illus. 29 cm.   59-51849.
CS71.M513   1959

    MEISENHOLDER.   See SCHMIERER, 1961

    MEISER.   See MEISSER.

    MEISINGER.   See MESSINGER, 1962

11716   MEISSER.   A genealogy of the Meisser family (Meiser, Miser, Mizer, Myser) from the
founding in America by immigrant ancestors to the present time.   Compiled and edited by Lloyd E.
Mizer and the Meisser Genealogy Association.   Index by Gladys McDonald.   Lancaster, Pa., Printed
by Forry and Hacker (1966)   xi, 631 p. illus., col. coat of arms, maps, ports. 24 cm.   Cover-title: The Meisser family
genealogy.   67-314.   CS71.M5145   1966

11717   MEISTER.   A history of the "Meister-Allion" families, their emigration to and settlement in
America, compiled by H.D. Meister.   Wauseon, O., 1917.   cover-title, (60) p. 20½ cm.   Interleaved. 28-15343.
CS71.M515   1917

    MEIXELL.   See MIKESELL.

11718   MELBOURNE.   The history of Melbourne, in the county of Derby, including biographical
notices of the Coke, Melbourne, and Hardinge families: by John Joseph Briggs.   2d ed.   Derby,
Bemrose and son; London, Whittaker and co. (1852)   8 p. l., (9)-205 p. front., 6 pl., 2 port., 2 plans. 25½ cm.
3-14497.   DA690.M55B8

MELDRIM.   See MELDRUM.

11719   MELDRUM.   Meldrum family history, by Earl T. Meldrim.   (Richmond, Calif.) 1967.
1 v. (various pagings) illus. col. coat of arms, maps, ports. 29 cm.   "Edition limited to 50 copies ... number 21."   68-20632.
CS71.M52   1967

MELHUS.   See No. 553 - Goodhue county.

MELICK.   See MELLICK.

11720   MELL.   The genealogy of the Mell family in the southern states.   By Dr. and Mrs. P. H.
Mell ... (Albany, N.Y., J. Munsell's sons) 1897.   61, xxviii p. incl. coat of arms, front., pl., port. 20½ cm.   Blank
leaves inserted. 1-11967.
CS71.M523   1897

11721   MELL.   The Mell families, 1679-1938.   (By Ned Burton Smith.   Youngstown, O., 1938)
3 l. 27½ cm. Caption title. Mimeographed. Signed: Ned Smith. 41-38333.
CS71.M523   1938

11722   MELLARD.   The Mellards & their descendants, inclduing the Bibbys of Liverpool with memoirs of Dinah Maria Mulock & Thomas Mellard Reade, by Aleyn Lyell Reade ... London, Priv. print.
for the author at the Arden press, 1915.   xii p., 1 l., 227, xxii p. front., plates, ports., 4 fold. geneal. tab. 30 cm.   Contains also accounts of the Jenkinson and Bucknall families. "List of scientific communications" of Thomas Mellard Reade: p. 174-180. "Evidences
in proof of pedigrees": p. (181) - 197. 16-6572.
CS439.M387

11723   MELLICK.   The story of an old farm; or, Life in New Jersey in the eighteenth century, by
Andrew D. Mellick, jr.   With a genealogical appendix.   Somerville, N.J., The Unionist-Gazette,
1889.   xxiv, (2), 743, (1) p. front., plates. 25 cm.   "Moelich-Malick-Melick-Mellick genealogy": p. (627)-713. 1-13406.
F142.S6M7

11724   MELLON.   Thomas Mellon and his times ... Printed for his family and descendants exclusively.   Pittsburgh, W.G.Johnston & co., printers, 1885.   1 p. l., 648, viii p. plates, 2 port. (incl. front.) coat
of arms. 24 cm.   Contents. - pt.I. Family history. - pt. II. Autobiography. 37-38459.
CS71.M525   1885

11725   MELLON.   Mellon's millions, the biography of a fortune; the life and times of Andrew W.
Mellon, by Harvey O'Connor ... New York, The John Day company (1933)   xv p., 1 l., 443, (1) p. front., pl.,
ports. 21 cm.   "Copyright, 1933 ... Third printing, August, 1933." 34-1604.
E748.M52O23

11726   MELLON.   Judge Mellon's son, by William Larimer Mellon; Boyden Sparkes, collaborator.
(Pittsburgh?) Priv. print., 1948.   x, 570 p. illus., ports. 25 cm. 48-1887*.
CS71.M525   1948

11727   MELLON.   The Mellons of Pittsburgh.   By Frank Richard Denton.   New York, Newcomen
Society of England, American Branch, 1948.   32 p. illus., port. 23 cm.   "Address ... delivered during the '1948
Pittsburgh dinner' of the Newcomen Society of England ... May 13, 1948." 48-3176*.
CS71.M525   1948a

MELOWN.   See NITZEL, 1941

MELOY.   See DAWSON, 1874a

MELVILL.   See MELVILLE.

11728   MELVILLE.   The Melvilles, earl of Melville, and the Leslies, earls of Leven; by Sir
William Fraser ... Edinburgh, 1890.   3 v. fronts., illus., plates, ports., facsims. (partly fold.) 26 cm.   "Impression: one
hundred and fifty copies. No. 76." Contents. - v.1. Memoirs. - v.2. Correspondence. - v.3. Charters. 11-19838.
DA758.3.M42F7

11729   MELVILLE.   The Melvill book of roundels, ed., with an introduction, by Granville Bantock
and H. Orsmond Anderton.   London, Priv. print. for presentation to the members of the Roxburghe
club, 1916.   xxviii p., 2 l., 57 (i.e.115) p., 1 l.; 204 p. (music) front., facsims. 32 x 27½ cm.   Presented to the Roxburghe club by
Michael Tomkinson, owner of the manuscript. ... Old and modernised texts on opposite pages, paged in duplicate; includes some Latin;
modern version by Miss Margaret E. Thompson. 22-21714 rev.
PR1105.R7   1916c

11730   MELVILLE.   The Melvill family, a roll of honour of the descendants of Captain Philip Melvill, lieut-governor of Pendennis castle, and their immediate connections by marriage, in the years of the world war, 1914-1918.   By E. J. Joubert de la Ferté ... London, A. L. Humphreys, 1920.
150 p.   front. (coat of arms) ports.   26½ cm.   21-10458.   CS439.M388

MELVIN.   See PALMER, 1905

MELVYN.   See ACKLEY, 1960

MENDALL.   See MENDELL.

11731   MENDELL.   Mendell family genealogy, an account of the ancestors and descendants of Isaac Mendell and Patience Harlow, also some descendants of John Mendall ... compiled by Mary Porter Smith and Sidney Dean Smith, edited by Sidney Dean Smith.   (Mason City, Ia., Klipto loose leaf company) 1943.   127 p. incl. front., illus. (ports.) 22½ cm.   "Edition of one hundred and twenty-five copies ... Number 101." 45-13966.
                                                                CS71.M537   1943

11732   MENDENHALL.   History, correspondence, and pedigrees of the Mendenhalls of England and the United States, relative to their common origin and ancestry, methodically arranged and elucidated, after many years of diligent inquiry and research, by William Mendenhall ... Extended by the addition of authentic documents, and the compilation of tables of pedigrees of the American family, by his son Edward Mendenhall ... Cincinnati, Moore, Wilstach & Baldwin, printers, 1865.   63 p.   map, 3 fold. facsim., 5 fold. geneal. tab.   24 cm.   Folded deed inserted.   12-1825.   CS71.M54   1865

11733   MENDENHALL.   History, correspondence and pedigrees of the Mendenhalls of England, the United States and Africa relative to their common origin and ancestry, methodically arranged and elucidated, after many years of diligent inquiry and research, by William Mendenhall ... extended by the addition of authentic documents, and the compilation of tables of pedigrees of the American family by his son, Edward Mendenhall ... until the year eighteen hundred and sixty-four, continued and revised by Thomas A. Mendenhall ... Greenville, O., C. R. Kemble press, 1912.   299 p. front., illus. (incl. ports., map, facsims., geneal. tables) 28 cm.   On cover: History of the Mendenhall family by T. A. Mendenhall.   Blank pages for additions throughout text.   36-24706.   CS71.M54   1912

11734   MENDENHALL.   Our branch of the Mendenhall tree.   By Ruth Mendenhall Kornitz.   (n. p.) 1966.   (7) p. 30 cm. Bibliography: p. (7) 68-833.   CS71.M542   1966

MENDENHALL.   See also KING, 1933

11735   MENDOZA.   Historia genealógica de la casa de Mendoza.   Ed., prólogo e indice de Angel González Palencia.   (Madrid) Instituto Jerónimo Zurita del Consejo Superior de Investigaciones Científicas, 1946.   2 v. (631 p.) 25 cm. (Biblioteca conquense, 3-4) 50-54738.   CS959.M42   1946

MENEFIE.   See No. 430 - Adventurers of purse and person.

11736   MENHINICK.   The Menhinick family; Meneghy Nyot.   The history and genealogy of a Cornish family.   By Thomas Shaw.   Rogherham, Yorks., 1950.   123 p. illus., coats of arms. 26 cm. 51-27696.
                                                                CS439.M3885 1950

MENIFEE.   See DULIN, 1961

11737   MENTEITH.   The lake of Menteith: its islands and vicinity, with historical accounts of the priory of Inchmahome and the earldom of Menteith; by A. F. Hutchison, M. A.   Illustrated with pen and ink drawings by Walter Bain.   Stirling, E. Mackay, 1899.   xxxiv, 368 p. incl. illus., plates, plans, facsims. 25 x 19 cm.   "Alphabetical list of ... authorities": p. (xvii)-xxii.   3-4128.
                                                                DA880.M5H9

MENTIETH, Earls of.   See: ALLARDICE, CS478.N5
                                   ATHOLL, DA775.C75
                                   GRAHAM, DA758.3.M45F7

11738   MENZIES.   The Menzies clan society ... Its history, objects, biographies, members, etc. By D. P. Menzies ... Glasgow, Laird, McIntyre & co. (1897)   1 p. l., 28 p. 16 cm. Title vignette: coat of arms. 9-19340.   CS479.M5   1897

11739   MENZIES.   The Lanark manse family; narrative found in the repositories of the late Miss Elizabeth Bailie Menzies, of 31 Windsor street, Edinburgh.   With notes and appendices by Thomas Reid ... Printed for private distribution.   Lanark, Printed by D. A. V. Thomson, 1901.   54 p. front. (port.) illus., plates. 21½ cm. 20-15865.   CS479.M5   1901

11740   MENZIES.   The Red and white book of Menzies; a review.   By C. Poyntz Stewart ... Exeter, W. Pollard & co., ltd., printers, 1906.   20 p. 24 cm. Reprinted from the Genealogist, n.s. vol. xxii, October, 1905. 6-43478.   CS479.M5   1906

11741   MENZIES.   The "Red and white" book of Menzies ... by D. P. Menzies ... 2d ed., priv. printed.   Plean castle, Mengieston, Balmeinnarigh, Plean, Stirlingshire, 1908.   1 p. l., xxiv, (4), 529 (i.e. 563), (1) p. front., illus., plates (partly col.) ports. 26 cm. The first ed. with extra pages inserted. Contains also the original t.-p., with imprint: Glasgow, Banks & co., printers, 1894. 8-32483.   CS479.M5   1908

11742   MENZIES.   The long inheritance of the Menzies family.   (By Anne (Menzies) Spears)   (n.p., 1930)   61 p. 23½ cm. 43-18869.   CS71.M543   1930

11743   MERCER.   Some account of Lieut.-Colonel William Mercer, author of "Angliae speculum .." London, 1646.   By David Laing, esq. ... (Edinburgh, 1860)   19 p. incl. geneal. tab. 21½ cm. (Hazlitt tracts, v. 6 no. 6)   Caption title.   Reprinted from the Proceedings of the Society of antiquaries of Scotland. 1860. 23-1823.

AC911.H3 vol. 6 no. 6
Rare book.

11744   MERCER.   The life of General Hugh Mercer; with brief sketches of General George Washington, John Paul Jones, General George Weedon, James Monroe and Mrs. Mary Ball Washington, who were friends and associates of General Mercer at Fredericksburg; also a sketch of Lodge no. 4, A.F. and A.M., of which Generals Washington and Mercer were members; and a genealogical table of the Mercer family.   By John T. Goolrick ... New York & Washington, The Neale publishing company, 1906.   140 p. 11 pl., 4 port. (incl. front.) 20½ cm. 6-24130.   E207.M5G6

11745   MERCER.   Descendants of Noah Mercer and wife Sarah, born in Jones County, N.C. about 1773, died 1823 in Jones County, Gray, Ga.   (by Joseph J. Mercer.   Gray, 1964, c. 1967) iii, 58 p. illus., ports. 28 cm. Cover title. 76-4028.   CS71.M548   1967

MERCER.   See also: FARLEY, 1932
GARNETT, 1910
SELDEN, 1911

MERCHANT.   See JARRATT, 1957

MERCIER.   See: BUTLER, 1919
FANEUIL, 1851

11746   MEREDITH.   The ancient families of the Meredyths and the Eustaces ... (By Eustace Meredyth Martin)   London, Remington & co., 1887.   3 p. l., 53 p. 17 cm. 44-49968.   CS439.M389   1887

MEREDITH.   See also: ROSS, 1908
TWEEDIE, 1956

MEREDYTH.   See MEREDITH.

MERES.   See DEACON, 1898

11747   MERGENTHALER.   Die Mergenthaler, der ahnen- und sippenkreis des württembergischen ministerpräsidenten.   Die Hohenacker Mergenthaler.   Der erfinder Ottmar Mergenthaler.   Mit 11 bildseiten.   Bearbeitet von dr. jur. Wilhelm Bauder ... Leipzig, Zentralstelle für deutsche personen- und familiengeschichte, 1939.   171 p. incl. illus., plates, ports., map, facsim., geneal. tables. 34½ cm. (Half-title: Stamm- und ahnentafelwerk der Zentralstelle fur deutsche personen- und familiengeschichte ... bd. xx) AF48-4591.   CS719.M4B3

MERIAM.   See MERRIAM.

MERIEL.   See MURIEL.

11748   MERIET.   Genealogy of the Somersetshire family of Meriet, traced in an unbroken line from the reign of the Confessor, to its extinction in the reign of King Henry V., compiled from public record cords and other authentic sources, with notes and references, by B. W. Greenfield, barrister at law, 1883.   Taunton; printed by J. F. Hammond ... With additions and corrections by Douglas Merritt. New York (T. A. Wright) 1914.   131, (1) p. front. (col. coats of arms) fold. geneal. tab. 22 cm. 14-18299.
CS439.M39   1914

MERIHEL.   See MURIEL.

MERIHIL.   See MURIEL.

11749   MERING.   The "Mering" family.   (By Warren Mering) Sussex, N. J., Wantage recorder press, 1929.   50 p. 24 cm. Foreword signed: Warren Mering. 30-5058.   CS71.M55   1929

11750   MERION.   Genealogy of the Merion, Kienzle, and allied families.   (Compiled by Mary Martha Merion Pedlar, and others.   Columbus? Ohio) 1956.   84 p. 28 cm. 57-49141.
CS71.M555   1956

11751   MERIVALE.   Family memorials.   Comp. by Anna W. Merivale.   Printed for private circu- lation.   Exeter, T. Upward, printer, 1884.   xii, 392 p. 20 cm. Preface signed: Charles Merivale. 20-18077.
CS439.M394

11752   MERIVALE.   Autobiography & letters of Charles Merivale, dean of Ely, edited by Judith Anne Merivale ... Oxford, Printed for private circulation by H. Hart, 1898.   4 p. l., 499, (1) p. front. (port.) fold. geneal. tables. 23 cm. Includes genealogical tables of the Merivale, Drury and Frere families. 2-9186.
BX5199.M4A3

MERIWEATHER.   See MERRYWEATHER.

MERKLE.   See GRIM, 1934

11753   MERKEL.   Merkel - Markle genealogy, 1458-1965; John Christian Merkel, emigrant from Metz, Alsace-Lorraine, his nine children and one line traced to 1965, by Evelyn Martz Guldner. (Cedar Grove? N. J., 1965)   81 l. 30 cm. 65-89993.   CS71.M558   1965

11754   MERLE D'AUBIGNE.   ... La vie américaine de Guillaume Merle d'Aubigné; extraits de son journal de voyage et de sa correspondance inedite, 1809-1817; avec une introduction et des notes par Gilbert Chinard.   Paris, E. Droz; Baltimore, The Johns Hopkins press; (etc., etc.,) 1935.   152 p., 2 l. incl. front. (port.) illus. (facsims.) 27 cm. (Historical documents. Institut francais de Washington. cahier IX) 36-6733.
E165.M57

MERLET.   See MARLETT.

MERREFIELD.   See MERRIFIELD.

MERRELL.   See REMINGTON, 1960

11755   MERRIAM.   Some Meriams and their connection with other families.   By Rufus N. Meriam ... Worcester, Mass., Private press of F. P. Rice, 1888.   52 p. 24½ cm. Reprinted from the Proceedings of the Worcester society of antiquity for 1887. 9-12306.   CS71.M567   1888

11756   MERRIAM.   The family of Merriam of Massachusetts.   By W. S. Appleton.   Boston, D. Clapp & son, 1892.   1 p. l., 15 p. 15½ cm.   "Corrected and enlarged from the New-England historical and genealogical register for April, 1868, and April, 1870." 9-12517.   CS71.M567   1892

11757   MERRIAM.   Genealogical memoranda relating to the family of Merriam by Charles Pierce Merriam and C. E. Gildersome-Dickinson.   London, Priv. print. at the Chiswick press, 1900.
1 p. l., viii, 99, (1) p., 1 l. plates, fold. geneal. tables.   30 cm.   Limited edition of 112 copies.   1-3420.
                                                                                          CS439.M4

11758   MERRIAM.   Merriam genealogy in England and America, including the "Genealogical memoranda of Charles Pierce Merriam, the collections of James Shelton Merriam, etc.   Compiled by Charles Henry Pope.   Boston, C. H. Pope, 1906.   xv, 500 p. plates, ports., facsim., geneal. tables. 25 cm.   Includes a reprint of the larger part of "Genealogical memoranda" by C. P. Merriam and C. E. Gildersome-Dickinson.   Appendix: Massachusetts soldiers and sailors in the war of the revolution. 6-37961.   CS71.M567   1906

11759   MERRIAM.   Col. Jonathan Merriam and family, compiled by Ralph Merriam; edited by Frank White Conley and Henry Jonathan Merriam.   Chicago, Print. priv. (Chicago law printing company) 1940.   253 p. incl. front., illus. (incl. ports.) 24 cm.   "Two hundred copies have been printed." Pages 239-240 blank for "Births, marriages, deaths". 40-29603.   CS71.M567   1940

MERRIAM.   See also: FLAGG, 1903
                                      LINDLEY, 1950
                                      PEABODY, 1929

11760   MERRICK.   Genealogy of the Merrick - Mirick - Myrick family of Massachusetts, 1636-1902, by George Byron Merrick.   Madison, Wis., Tracy, Gibbs & company, 1902.   vi, (2), 494 p. 3 pl. (1 col.) 12 port. (incl. front.) 23 cm.   3-18026.
                                                                                          CS71.M568   1902

11761   MERRICK.   The story of the Myricks.   By Allie Goodwin (Myrick) Bowden.   Macon, Ga., Press of the J. W. Burke Co., 1952.   x, 254 p. illus., ports., coat of arms. 24 cm.   Includes bibliographical references. 53-15952.   CS71.M568   1952

MERRICK.   See also: CORLISS, 1875
                                      LEONARD, 1928
                                      POLLOCK, 1932
                                      PORTER, 1937

11762   MERRIFIELD.   The Merrififeld family in America, with special attention to the descendants of Francis Elliot Merrifield and Sarah Cook Kimball Merrifield.   Compiled by Flora Lincoln Merrifield, Charles Chester Merrifield (and) Richard Henry Merrifield.   (n. p., The Merrifield Cousins) 1967.   108 p., illus., coat of arms, ports. 29 cm.   Includes bibliographies. 68-5599.   CS71.M569   1967

11763   MERRILL.   My wife and my mother. (By Heman Humphrey Barbour) Hartford, Press of Williams, Wiley & Waterman, 1864.   x, (11)-312, 84 p. 2 geneal. tab. 19½ cm.   Preface signed: H. H. B (i. e. Heman Humphrey Barbour) "Genealogy (of the Merrill and Humphrey families)": 84 p. at end. 37-16948.   CS71.M57   1864

11764   MERRILL.   Genealogy prepared and published in 1864, by Heman H. Barbour as an appendix to his book entitled, My wife and my mother.   Hartford, Press of Wiley, Waterman & Eaton, 1885.
1 p. l., 84 p. 2 diagr. 20 cm.   9-11938 rev.   CS71.M57   1885

11765   MERRILL.   The Merrill family, by William M. Sargent, esq.   Reprint from the Maine historical and genealogical recorder.   Portland Me., S. M. Watson, 1886.   1 p. l., 4 p. illus., 23 cm.   Title vignette: coat of arms. 1-2602.   CS71.M57   1886

11766   MERRILL.   A memorial for Rev. Moses Merrill, and his wife, Eliza (Wilcox) Merrill, missionaries of the American Baptist missionary union, to the Otoes, in Indian Territory (now Nebraska), at Bellevue and the Platte River, six miles from its mouth, from 1833 to 1840. (Rochester, N. Y., 1888)   10 p. 18 cm.   By Samuel Pearce Merrill.   Caption title. 9-12304.   PM2082.O8M43
                                                                                          Office.

11767   MERRILL.   Joshua Merrill and family.   A family record.   (By Stephen Mason Merrill)
(Mediapolis, Ia., Printed by J. W. Merrill) 1899.   64 p.   23 cm.   Blank pages for "Family record" (14 at end)   "Introductory notice" signed: S. M. Merrill, J. W. Merrill.   36-29805.
CS71.M57   1899

11768   MERRILL.   A contribution to the genealogy of the Merrill family in America; being a particular record of the ancestry of Hamilton Wilcox Merrill, by his son Frederick J. H. Merrill.   Albany, Printed privately for the writer and for his friends, 1899.   20 p.   23½ cm.   Title vignette (coat of arms)   With this book are two genealogical tables entitled: "A genealogical chart of the ancestry of Frederick J. H. Merrill.   Albany, N. Y., 1898." - "A genealogical chart of the ancestry of Abigail Phelps by her great-grandson Frederick J. H. Merrill.   Albany, 1898."   4-24961.
CS71.M57   1899

11769   MERRILL.   The American ancestors of George W. Merrill of Saginaw, Michigan, with other family records compiled by his son, William Merrill.   Saginaw, Mich., 1903.   1 p. l., 25 p.   illus. (coat of arms)   21 cm.   4-24947.
CS71.M57   1903

11770   MERRILL.   Merrill genealogy; descendants of Barzilla Merrill, 1764-1850.   (Cooperstown, N. Y., Crist, Scott & Parshall, 1907)   50, (1) p.   plates, 19 cm.   Introduction signed: Mary Thrasher.   14-4711.
CS71.M57   1907

11771   MERRILL.   A contribution to the genealogy of the Merrill family in America; being a particular record of the ancestry of Edward Henry Merrill, by his son, Cyrus Strong Merrill, M. D.   Albany, N. Y., Priv. print., 1920.   18 p.   ports.   24 cm.   Title vignette (coat of arms)   21-16575.
CS71.M57   1920

11772   MERRILL.   Adrian Merrill and his descendants ... (By Arthur McEwen Merrill)   Rogers, Ark., A. M. Merrill, 1925.   (93) p.   illus. (incl. ports.)   28½ cm.   "Published privately."   33-14351.
CS71.M57   1925

11773   MERRILL.   A Merrill memorial; an account of the descendants of Nathaniel Merrill, an early settler of Newbury, Massachusetts, by Samuel Merrill ... Cambridge, Mass., 1917-28.   2 v.   illus. (incl. maps, facsims., coats of arms) facsim. 28 cm.   "This copy is number twelve."   Autographed from type-written copy.   Additions in manuscript.   28-12500.
CS71.M57   1928

11774   MERRILL.   Captain Benjamin Merrill and the Merrill family of North Carolina, by William Ernest Merrill, M.S.   (Penrose, N. C., 1935)   1 p. l., 90 p.   22½ cm.   "Private publication."   36-5181.
CS71.M57   1935

11775   MERRILL.   Utah pioneer and apostle; Marriner Wood Merrill and his family; material obtained from the autobiography, diaries, and notes of Marriner Wood Merrill and from record data and textual contributions by members of the family, edited by Melvin Clarence Merrill.   (Salt Lake City, Deseret news) 1937.   527 p. incl. illus., port.   22½ cm.   37-18571.
F826.M57

11776   MERRILL.   Descendants of Marriner Wood Merrill; material obtained from various sources - mainly from questionnaires and letters written by members of the family, September 1937 to June 1938.   Compiled by Joseph F. Merrill.   (Salt Lake City, Deseret news press) 1938.   240 p. incl. ports. 20 cm.   "This little book is the second volume of the story of Marriner Wood Merrill and his family (by Melvin Clarence Merrill) which began with the publication of the first volume in July 1937."   "A few errata": 1 leaf mounted on p. (5)   39-3069.
CS71.M57   1938

11777   MERRILL.   Merrill family history, one branch from 1633 to 1949, in conjunction with allied families of the Lyon and Sisson lines.   By Alice Louise (Merrill) Hunt.   Ithaca, N.Y., 1949.   90, 4 l.   col. coat of arms, geneal. tables.   28 cm.   Typewritten.   50-30781.
CS71.M57   1949

11778   MERRILL.   The Merrill family; a genealogical sketch of one line of one branch of the Merrill family, traced by "family units" in America directly descendent from Nathaniel Merrill, immigrant progenitor of this branch of the Merrill family within the United States, May 4, 1601 to December 1, 1958.   By Frank Peiro Randolph.   Washington, 1958.   9 l.   31 cm.   "Corrected to May 1959."   60-245.
CS71.M57   1958

11779   MERRILL.   The Daniel Ford Merrill family: the vital statistics.   Collected by C. M. Merwin.   (Washington? 1955)   12 l.   28 cm.   Caption title.   Typescript (carbon copy)   76-2259.   CS71.M57   1955

MERRILL.   See also: BARTON, 1941   JOHNSON, 1962
                         BASSETT, 1926   SINCLAIR, 1896
                         HENDRICKS, 1963   SMITH, 1962
                         HILDRETH, 1950

11780   MERRIMAN.   Walter Merryman of Harpswell, Maine, and his descendants, by Rev. Charles Nelson Sinnett.   Concord, N.H., Rumford printing co., 1905.   123 p. 23 cm.   Cover-title: Merryman genealogy, 1905.   6-28554.
CS71.M571   1905

11781   MERRIMAN.   Nathaniel Merriman, one of the founders of Wallingford in the state of Connecticut.   By Mansfield Merriman ... New York, 1913.   24 p. 23 cm.   13-12045.
CS71.M571   1913

11782   MERRIMAN.   Reunion of descendants of Nathaniel Merriman at Wallingford, Conn.   June 4, 1913, with a Merriman genealogy for five generations.   New Haven, Conn., D.L.Jacobus, 1914   187 p. front. 19 cm.   Parts I and II, containing the proceedings of the reunion, comp. by Mansfield Merriman.   Part III, a Merriman genealogy comp. by Donald L. Jacobus.   cf. Pref.   Preface signed: George B. Merriman, chairman of general committee.   Merriman bulletin, March 4, 1915; June 4, 1917: (8) o. inserted at end.   14-7901.
CS71.M571   1914

11783   MERRIMAN.   Merriman bulletin (no. 1,   New York, 1915.   v. 17 cm.   M. Merriman, editor.   "This bulletin records facts regarding the ancestors and descendants of Nathaniel Merriman which have come to light since the publication of the book Merriman reunion and genealogy in April 1914."   38M2685T.
CS71.M571   1914a

MERRIMAN.   See also: ADAMS, 1894a
                         BEACH, 1960
                         PARISH, 1935

MERRIN.   See MERING.

MERRING.   See MERING.

11784   MERRITT.   (Merritt records.   Rhinebeck, N.Y., 1908?)   cover-title, (14) p. 24½ cm.   First two leaves, 27½ cm.   Comp. by Douglas Merritt.   Contents. - Early records of English Merritts. - Early American Merritts. - Thomas Merritt of Rye, N.Y., and first three generations of his descendants.   10-5267.
CS71.M572   1908

11785   MERRITT.   Recollections, 1828-1911 (by) Edwin A. Merritt.   Albany, J. B. Lyon company, printers, 1911.   1 p. 1., 188 p. front., ports., facsims.   23½ cm.   11-30417.
F124.M57

11786   MERRITT.   New Merritt records.   (Rhinebeck, N.Y., 1913)   cover-title. (66) p. 24 cm.   Comp. by Douglas Merritt.   Contents. - Early English Merritts. - Henry Merritt of Scituate. - Nicholas Merritt of Salem. - Philip Merritt of Boston. - William Merritt of New York. - Thomas Merritt of Rye. - John Merritt of Rye. - Westchester County Merritts. - Isaac Merriott of Burlington, N.J. - William Merritt of Cecil Co., Md. - Samuel Merritt of St. Pauls, Md. - Early American Merritts. - Various Merritts, 1700-1800.   13-16624.
CS71.M572   1913

11787   MERRITT.   Revised Merritt records, compiled by Douglas Merritt ... New York, T.A. Wright, 1916.   195 p. 24 cm.   17-8385.
CS71.M572   1916

11788   MERRITT.   Merritt family records: Guilford and Killingworth, Connecticut; Fair Haven, Benson, and Georgia, Vermont; St. Lawrence and Allegany counties, New York; Fort Dodge, Webster county, Iowa.   Compiled by Halsey Stevens ... Peoria, Ill. (1942)   cover-title, 6 1. 35½ x 21½ cm.   Reproduced from type-written copy.   44-1905.
CS71.M572   1942

MERRITT.   See also: BARTLETT, 1951
                      CRAWFORD, 1939

11789   MERROW.   Henry Merrow of Reading, Massachusetts, and his descendants named Merrow, Marrow, and Merry.   By Oscar Earl Merrow.   Winchester, Mass., 1954.   vii, 659 p. illus., port., facsims. 26 cm.   55-36307.
CS71.M5724   1954

11790   MERRY.   The Merry family of the town of Florida, Montgomery county, New York, what is at present (1937) known of their ancestry and a record of some of their descendants, by Herman Churchill.   Kingston, R. I., 1935 (i. e. 1937)   1 p. l., 19, 20 a - 20 b, 21-31 numb. l. 28 cm. Type-written. Includes "References." 41-38334.   CS71.M5727   1937

MERRYFIELD.   See MERRIFIELD.

MERRYMAN.   See MERRIMAN.

11791   MERRYWEATHER.   The Meriwethers and their connections.   A family record, giving the genealogy of the Meriweathers in America together with biographical notes and sketches ... By Louisa H. A. Minor.   Albany, N. Y., J. Munsell's sons, 1892.   180 p. front. (coat of arms) pl., ports. 24 cm. 9-12518.
                                                                                                    CS71.M573   1892

11792   MERRYWEATHER.   1631 to 1899.   The record of Nicholas Meriwether of Wales, and descendants in Virginia and Maryland.   By William Ridgely Griffith ... St. Louis, Nixon-Jones printing co., 1899.   vi p., 1 l., 172 p. coats of arms. 23½ cm. Blank leaves at end for additions. Additions in manuscript throughout text, and at end. Contains also the Griffith, Vaughan and Kean families. 24-12328.   CS71.M573   1899

11793   MARRYWEATHER.   Some notes on the family of Merryweather of England and America.   By E. A. Merryweather.   London, Research Pub. Co. (195-)   79 p. illus. 23 cm. 58-29253.
                                                                                                    CS71.M573

MERRYWEATHER.   See also: JONES, 1891
                                    LEWIS, 1938
                                    TAYLOR, 1898

11794   MERSHON.   Mershon news bulletin, the Association of the descendants of Henry Mershon, inc.   Philadelphia, Pa.,   v. 29 cm. Caption title. Editor: W. W. Fritz. 40-37504.   CS71.M575

11795   MERSHON.   My folks; story of the forefathers of Oliver Francis Mershon, M. D., as told by himself, in the words of Grace Lucile Olmstead Mershon.   (Rahway, N. J.) Priv. print. (Quinn & Boden company, inc., 1946)   vi p., 1 l., 227 p. front. (port.) maps. 24 cm. 46-4329.
                                                                                                    CS71.M575   1946

MERTZ.   In vertical file under PRANKE family.   Ask reference librarian for this material.

11796   MERVYN.   Fasciculus mervinensis; being notes historical, genealogical, and heraldic of the family of Mervyn.   By Sir William Richard Drake ... London, (Printed by Metchim & son) 1873.   (184) p. illus. (coats of arms) fold. geneal. tables. 31 cm. Various paging. Privately printed. 7-12662.
                                                                                                    CS439.M45   1873

11797   MERVYN.   Tabular pedigree of the Durford abbey branch of the Mervyn family.   (London, 1873)   6 p. illus. (coats of arms) 29½ cm. Reprinted from Fasciculus Mervinensis ... By Sir William Richard Drake. London, 1873. 31 cm. app. 2. (p. i-iv) Issued also in Miscellanea genealogica et heraldica. n. s. 1874, v. 1 p. 423-426.
                                                                                                    CS439.M45   1873a

11798   MERVYN.   Notes of the family of Mervyn of Pertwood.   By Sir William Richard Drake, F. S. A.   Privately printed.   London 1873.   1 p. l., 21, (2), x, (1), 8 p. illus. (coats of arms) fold. geneal. tab. 30 cm. Reprinted from the author's "Fasciculus Mervinensis ... London, 1873. p. 39-59 and Appendix I. 17-29960.
                                                                                                    CS439.M45   1873b

11799   MERVYN.   Devonshire notes and notelets, principally genealogical and heraldic.   By Sir William Richard Drake, F. S. A.   London, Priv. print. (1888)   iv, (2), 230 p., 1 l., 231-417 p. incl. illus., geneal. tables (part fold.) facsims. front., plates, ports. 29½ cm. "Fifty copies only." Contents. - Mervyn of Marwood. - Armorial bearings of Boteler and Drake. - Cutcliffe of Damage. - Richard Drake of Esher. - Whitfield and Garland of Marwood. - Heath of Exeter. - Pedigree of royal descents of some Devonshire families. - Hatch of Wollegh, Aller and Satterleigh. - Hamlyn and Hammett of Woolfardisworthy and Clovelly. - Chichester of Youlston, Hall and Arlington. 5-143.
                                                                                                    CS437.D4D8

MERVYN.   See also: BRAMSHOTT, DA670.H2C2
                                    MARVIN.

11800   MERWIN.   Miles Merwin, 1623-1697, and one branch of his descendants, by Carolin Gaylord Newton.   (Durham, Conn.) 1909.   1 p. l., 105, 87 p. front., plates, ports. 23 cm. "Miles Merwin, 1772-1859. His ancestors and descendants, pub. in memory of Mrs. Phebe Camp Merwin White" (87 p.) was comp. mainly by Elizabeth Maddock Noble and Sarah Baldwin Noble, and pub. in 1903 in a History of Middlesex County. 13-13695.   CS71.M578   1909

11801   MERWIN.   Genealogical outline of Charles L. Merwin family of East Palestine, Ohio.
(Washington? 1959)   geneal. table. 28 cm. 59-51446.   CS71.M578
        —— Notes to Genealogical outline of the Charles L. Merwin family.   (Washington? 1959)
10 l. 28 cm. Bound with the main work. 59-51446.   CS71.M578   1959

11802   MERWIN.   Miles Merwin (1628-1697) Association.   (Milford? Conn.) 1960.   16 p. illus. 23 cm.
60-39198.   CS71.M576   1960

11803   MERWIN.   Merwin family in vertical file.   Ask reference librarian for this material.

11804   MERWIN.   Milestones.   Miles Merwin Association.   In vertical file.   Ask reference librarian for this.

        MERWIN.   See also: ARCHDALE, CS439. A597A7
                             HAVEN, 1927

        MERWYN.   See MERWIN.

        MERZ.   In vertical file under PRANKE family.   Ask reference librarian for this material.

        MESHEK.   See MISHEK.

11805   MESIER.   History and reminiscences of the Mesier family, of Wappingers Creek.   Together with a short history of Zion church ... by Henry Suydam.   (New York) Priv. print., 1882.   42 numb. l. incl. front., illus., pl. 24½ cm. The illustrations are mounted photos. 13-33797.   CS71.M58   1882

        MESQUITA.   See PEREIRA FORJAZ DE SAMPAIO, 1889

11806   MESSAM.   Genealogical material of Catherine (Messam) Smith; Messam and Godsby families of Lincolnshire, England.   (Mrs.) Monroe Iverson (compiler)   1 reel positive.   Microfilm 6801
                                                                         Microfilm reading room

        MESSEIN.   See BAILLY DE MESSEIN.

        MESSELIERE.   See FROTIER DE LA MESSELIERE.

11807   MESSENGER.   The paternal lineage and some of the descendants of Isaac Messenger of Connecticut.   (n. p.) 1962.   210, 30 l. 28 cm. 63-6296.   CS71.M584   1962

11808   MESSENGER.   The Messenger family in the Colony of Connecticut; genealogy and narrative of the Messenger family, concentrating on descendants of Edward Messenger, Bloomfield, Connecticut, and allied families.   Compiled by Nettie Post Wright and Nettie Wright Adams.   Narrated & arranged by Nettie Wright Adams (Mrs. James P. Adams)   West Hartford, Conn., Printed by T. B. Simonds, 1963.   viii, 176 p. illus., ports. 29 cm. 64-2486.   CS71.M583   1963

11809   MESSENGER.   The paternal lineage and some of the descendants of Isaac Messenger of Connecticut.   2d ed. (n. p., 1964-   v. 28 cm. 65-694.   CS71.M584   1964

        MESSENGER.   See also MESSINGER.

        MESSER.   See CORLISS, 1875

        MESSICK.   See HOWARD, 1961

        MESSERVY.   See ADAMS, 1963a

MESSIMER. See CRAIG, 1960a

11810   MESSINGER.   Genealogy of the Messinger family.   Compiled by Hon. George W. Messinger.
Albany, J. Munsell, 1863.   14 p. 23½ cm. Title vignette. "Reprinted from the N. E. historical and genealogical register for
October, 1862." 9-12533.   CS71.M584   1863

11811   MESSINGER.   The Messinger family in Europe and America.   By George Washington
Messinger ... With a memoir of Hon. Daniel Messinger of Boston, by John Ward Dean, A.M.   Re-
printed from the N. E. historical and genealogical register for October, 1862.   Lowell, Mass., G.M.
Elliott, 1882.   12 p. 24½ cm. 9-12532.   CS71.M584   1882

11812   MESSINGER.   Notes on the Messenger and Hendrickson families and descendants of John S.
Messenger and Ruth Rhodes and of Abraham H. Hendrickson and Elizabeth Ludlam.   Compiled by
Morris P. Ferris, of counsel to executors of Sarah A. Messenger, deceased, .. New York (1916)
cover-title, 1 p. 1., 61, (17) p. 23 cm. 17-3894.   CS71.M584   1916

11813   MESSINGER.   A history of the Messenger family; genealogy of the ancestry and descendants
of John Messenger and his wife, Anne Lyon Messenger, and allied families of Col. Matthew Lyon and
Capt. James Piggott.   St. Louis, Mound City Press, 1934-48.   2 v. ports., coat of arms. 20 cm. Bibliography:
v. 1, p. 9-10.   36-14659 rev. *   CS71.M584   1934

11814   MESSINGER.   Ida Amelia; a true story connected with the Messenger family of Illinois (St.
Clair county) by Estelle Messenger (Mrs. Frederick C. Harrington) ... (St. Louis, Mimeographed by
West end letter shop, 1940)   2 p. 1., 79 (i. e. 85) p., 2 1. front. (2 port.) 21 cm. "References": p. (81) 41-3514.
                                                                                            CS71.M584   1940

11815   MESSINGER.   The Messinger family of Pennsylvania and the western states; Michael
Messinger of Forks township, Northampton county, Pennsylvania, and some of his descendants, compiled by Mrs. May (Tibbetts) Jarvis ... (San Diego, Calif., 1942)   2 p. 1., vi, 129 (i. e. 138) numb. 1., 3 1. plates
(part mounted) ports., facsims. (1 fold.) coat of arms. 29 x 22½ cm. Typewritten. 43-18597.
                                                                                            CS71.M584   1942

11816   MESSINGER.   Meisinger family tree.   By Eldon Meisinger.   (1st ed.)   Plattemouth, Neb.,
c. 1962.   176 p. 29 cm. 62-38544.   CS71.M514   1962

         MESSINGER.   See also MESSENGER.

11817   MESSLER.   A history or genealogical record of the Messler (Metselaer) family, compiled,
arranged and edited by Remsen Varick Messler; together with a prefatory note and biographical
sketches of the editor's father, grandfather, and great-grandfather ... Chicago, The Lakeside press,
1903.   106 p., 1 1. front., port. 24 cm. !'Printed for private distribution. " "The edition of this work is limited to two hundred copies, of
which this volume is numbered 87. " p. 99-106 blank, for family record. 3-15153.   CS71.M585

11818   METCALF.   Genealogy of a branch of the Metcalf family, who originated in West Wrenthm,
Mass.; with their connections by marriage.   Prepared by E. W. Metcalf for distribution at the cele-
bration of the niniteth birthday of Caleb Metcalf, 23 July, 1867. (n. p., 1867?)   cover-title, 12 p. 23½ cm.
Two commemorative poems inserted at end. 13-25482.   CS71.M588   1867

11820   METCALF.   Metcalf genealogy.   Prepared by Isaac Stevens Metcalf, of Elyria, Ohio, for
the children and descendants of Isaac Metcalf, who was born at Royalston, Massachusetts, February
3, 1783, and died in Boston, April 17, 1830.   Cleveland, the Imperial press, 1898. 62 p. 23½ cm.
"Printed for private circulation. " 2-22147.   CS71.M588   1898

11821   METCALF.   Genealogy and family history of the Metcalf family, for five generations, from
1700 to 1910.   Compiled by James T. Metcalf.   Washington, D. C. (1911?)   2 p. 1., (3)-24 p., 1 1. 22½ cm.
"Printed for distribution among relatives. " 15-6235.   CS71.M588   1911

11822   METCALF.   Barnabas Metcalf of Franklin, Mass., and his descendants, by Frank Johnson Metcalf.   ("Reprinted from the Dedham historical register for October, 1893, and January, 1894") Dedham, Mass., 1894.   16 p.   front.   24½ cm.   Contains additions and corrections in ms. in the text and 3 typewritten pages of additions, inserted as pages 14 a, 15 a and 17.   15-19127.   CS71.M588   1894

11823   METCALF.   William Henry Metcalf; a biography by his daughter, Julia Metcalf Cary; to-gether with sundry interesting facts and some genealogical records of the Metcalf family.   New York, The Press of the Woolly whale, 1937.   3 p. l., 71 p., 1 l. incl. illus. (mounted facsim.) mounted ports.   20½ cm.   "Printed on Tracy mould made paper by George W. Van Vechten, jr., fifty copies of this book for members of the family have been completed in the month of June, 1937."   37-22059.   CT275.M512C3

11824   METCALF.   (Bible records of the descendants of Michael Metcalf.   n. p., 194-?)   (3) l.   28 cm.
50-32397.   CS71.M588

11825   METCALF.   Metcalfe & related families; history, records.   Washington, L. K. McGhee (1965?)   1 v. (various pagings) ports. 28 cm.   "The allied famil(i)es are Hathaway, 2 different Lane families, Barker, Summers, Pickett, Farrar, Payne, and Barnes.   65-68425.   CS71.M588   1965

METCALF.   See also :   ALLEN, 1921
                          DEMING, 1941
                          DRIVER, 1889
                          GAMBLE, 1906
                          HARRIS, 1861
                          SNYDER, 1958

METCALFE.   See METCALF.

11826   METHAM.   Some Howdenshire villages.   By Col. P. Saltmarshe ... Metham.   (In East Riding antiquarian society.   Transactions ... Hull, 1909.   21½ cm.   v. 15, p. 71-84; v. 16, p. 1-49.   pl., coat of arms, fold. geneal. tab.) 21-9499.
                                                                        DA670.Y59E2 vol. 15-16

11827   METHENY.   Metheny family: origin of the seigneures de Methenay.   By William Blake Metheny ... Philadelphia, Pa., 1937.   4 p. l., 1 - 1A, 2-5, 34 numb. l.   29 cm.   Type-written.   Newspaper clippings mounted at end.   Contains bibliographical references.   37-31881.   CS599.M47   1937

METHERD.   See FOX, 1924

11828   METHOLD.   Pedigree of the Methwold family, now called Methold. from 1180 to 1870.   Com-piled by some of the members of the family.   London, Printed by T. Moring (1869)   2 p. l., 5-34 numb. l.
28½ cm.   19-3639.   CS439.M46

METHOT.   See GUOIN, CS90.G7

METHWOLD.   See METHOLD.

METSELAER.   See MESSLER.

11829   METZ.   Metz family; genealogy of Jacob Metz of Rosenthal, Germany, and Boonville, Ind-iana, compiled by Edmund Joseph Longyear.   Altadena, Calif., Priv. print. for the author (The Arthur H. Clark company, Glendale, Calif.) 1932.   3 p. l., (11) - 64 p. front. (port.) 24½ cm.   "Two hundred copies ... printed ... May, 1932."   32-13995.   CS71.M596   1932

11830   METZGER.   Christian Metzger, founder of an American family, 1682-1942, with his an-cestors back to 1542 and a who's who of living descendants, fifth, sixth, seventh and eighth gener-ations; a history, by Ella Metsker Milligan ... Denver, Col. (Ann Arbor, Mich., Edwards brothers, inc.) 1942.   xv, (1), 477, (21) p. incl. front., illus., diagr. ports., facsims. (1 fold.) fold. tab. 26 cm.   Lithoprinted.   Map on lining papers.   42-11473 rev.   CS71.M6   1942

MEURDAC.   See MURDAC.

11831   MEYER.   Caspar Meier and his successors: C. & H. H. Meier, Caspar Meier & co., L. N. von Post & Oelrichs, Oelrichs & Kruger, Oelrichs & co.   October 12, 1798 - October 12, 1898. (New York, Priv. print., 1898)   1 p. l., (7)-116, (1) p.   illus., port. 26 cm.   7-37058.
CT275.M465605

11832   MEYER.   The Henry Meyer family of the town of Mequon, Ozaukee County, Wisconsin.   (By Balthasar Henry Meyer.   Washington, 1922)   cover-title, 8 l. plates, ports., facsims. 23½ cm.   "Private print."   The plates, on verso of each leaf, are mounted photographs within ornamental border.   Author's name, place of publication and date, in ms. on cover. 22-7833.
CS71.M995   1922

11833   MEYER.   Meyer and Sturbaum.   By Eva Oma Firestone.   Upton, Wyo. (1946)   33 p. port. 22 cm.   47-5806 *.
CS71.M613   1946

11834   MEYER.   The Meyer family tree, seven generations 1774-1960; with some records dating back to 1550.   Compiled by Jimmie & Adolph Meyer.   St. Paul (1961?)   unpaged. illus. 30 cm.   62-35623.
CS71.M613   1961

11835   MEYER.   Genealogy of the Meyers (Moyer) family (by I. Austin Meyers.   Wilmington, Del., 1968)   ii, 26 l. 30 cm.   Caption title.   Cover title: The Meyers (Moyer) family history, 1708-1968. 70-3064.   CS71.M613   1968

MEYERS.   See: BLAUVELT, 1957
                MEYER.

MEYNDERTS.   See SNYDER, 1958

MEYSINGER.   See MEISINGER. (MESSINGER, 1962)

MICHAEL.   See HARRISON, 1910a

MICHAELIS.   See GOODLOCK, 1951

MICHAUX.   See: BLACK, 1954
                WATKINS, 1957

MICHEK.   See MISHEK.

MICHELET.   See MICKLEY, 1893

11836   MICHENER.   The Micheners in America.   By Anna E. Shaddinger.   Rutland, Vt., C.E. Tuttle Co. (1958)   627 p. illus. 22 cm.   58-9312.   CS71.M622   1958

11837   MICHIE.   The Michies (by Thomas Michie)... (Pittsburgh, Pa., 1942?)   76 (i.e. 78), 3, 11 numb. l. 28 cm.   Caption title.   Reproduced from type-written copy.   Extra numbered leaves 45 a - 45 b inserted.   Includes the Watson and Johnson families.   42-16474.   CS71.M623   1942

11838   MICKEL.   The Mickels of South Jersey.   By Samuel L. Mickel.   Bridgeton, N.J., 1955.   53 p. 24 cm.   56-18654.   CS71.M624   1955

MICKLE.   See JARRATT, 1957

11839   MICKLEY.   The genealogy of the Mickley family of America.   Together with a brief genea-logical record of the Michelet family of Metz, and some interesting and valuable correspondence, bio-graphical sketches, obituaries and historical memorabilia.   Compiled by Minnie F. Mickley. Mickleys, Pa. (Newark, N.J., Printed by Advertser printing house) 1893.   182 p., 1 l. ports., coat of arms. 22 cm.   9-12531.   CS71.M625   1893

11840   MICO.   The Mico college, Jamaica; some account of the Mico family, the story of the Mico fund, its diversion to the West Indies, and its latest developments in Jamaica, with a brief history of the college, by Frank Cundall ... Kingston, Jamaica, Printed for the directors of the Mico college by the Gleaner company, ltd., 1914.   5 p. l., 98 p. front., plates, ports. 18½ cm. 15-6634.

LC2862 K5M5

MIDDAGH.   See CRALL, 1903

11841   MIDDLEBROOK.   Register of the Middlebrook family, descendants of Joseph Middlebrook of Fairfield, Conn., by Louis F. Middlebrook ... Hartford, Conn.   (C. L. & B. co.) 1909.   2 p. l., (7)-411, (1) p. incl. pl. 27½ cm. "This edition is limited to two hundred and fifty-two copies. no. 2." 9-18929.

CS71.M627   1909

MIDDLECOFF.   See MIDDLEKAUFF.

11842   MIDDLEKAUFF.   A brief history of the Mittlekauff-Middlekauff, Middlecalf-Middlecoff families, beginning August 24, 1728.   By Jehu Baker Middlecoff ... Duluth, Minn. (1910)   4 geneal. tab. 62 x 45½ cm. 20-5530.

CS71.M629   1910

11843   MIDDLEMORE.   Some account of the family of Middlemore, of Warwickshire and Worcestershire, by W. P. W. Phillimore ... assisted by W. F. Carter ... London, Printed for private circulation, and issued by Phillimore and co., 1901.   xvi, 327, (1) p. front. (port.) illus. (coats of arms) plates, map, geneal. tables (part fold.) 29 cm. Blank pages at end for additional record. "Pedigree of Middlemore": p. 1-7; "Middlemore of Lusby, co. Lincoln": p. 8-10, proof with ms. corrections inserted at p. 243. "The present volume is the outcome of searches instituted nearly twenty years ago by Mr. Thomas Middlemore, now of Melsetter ..... 15-22621 rev.

CS439.M47

——— The family of Middlemore.   Supplement.   (London, Printed for private circulation and issued by Phillimore and co.) 1904.   (329)-360 p. 29 cm.
——— The family of Middlemore.   2d supplement.   (London, Printed for private circulation and issued by Phillimore and co.) 1908.   (361)-370 p. 29 cm. 15-22621 rev.

CS439.M47
Suppl.

11844   MIDDLETON.   The earls of Middleton, lords of Clermont and of Fettercairn, and the Middleton family.   By A. C. Biscoe.   London, H. S. King & co., 1876 (1875)   x p., 1 l., 398 p. 19½ cm. 4-2251.

DA758.3.M6B6

11845   MIDDLETON.   Notes on the Middleton family of Denbighshire & London, &c., with special reference to (1) Middleton of Cadwgan hall, Wrexham; (2) Middleton of Chirk castle (baronets); (3) Middleton of Ruthin & London (baronets) &c., &c., &c., by William Duncombe Pink.   Reprinted, with additions, from "The Cheshire sheaf" (new series) in the "Chester courant," 1891. (Chester, Eng.)   62 p. 24½ cm. "One hundred copies only printed for private circulation." 16-25573.

CS459.M5

11846   MIDDLETON.   Pedigree of Middleton or Myddelton of Chirk castle, Denbigh, Stanstead Mountfichet, Essex, etc.   By Gery Milner-Gibson-Cullum ... London, Mitchell and Hughes, 1897.   44 p. 26 cm. Published also in Miscellanea genealogica et heraldica, London, 1897. 26½ cm. 3d ser., vol. II, p. 213-235, 261-279. 23-14536.

CS459.M5   1897

11847   MIDDLETON.   The Middleton and Bathurst families.   By Edmund Burrus Middleton.   (n. p., 19 -)   15 l. illus. 30 cm. 56-45731.

CS71.M632

11848   MIDDLETON.   Pedigree of the family of Myddelton of Gwaynynog, Garthgynan and Llansannan, all in the county of Denbigh.   Attempted by W. M. Myddelton ... Privately printed.   Horncastle, W. K. Morton & sons, ltd., 1910.   4 p. l., 99 p. col. front., illus., plates, ports., facsims., coats of arms. 30 cm. 18-11233.

CS459.M8

11849   MIDDLETON.   Life in Carolina and New England during the nineteenth century, as illustrated by reminiscences and letters of the Middleton family of Charleston, South Carolina, and of the De Wolf family of Charleston, South Carolina, and of the De Wolf family of Bristol, Rhode Island. (By Alicia Hopton Middleton) Bristol, R. I., Priv. print., 1929.   xii p., 2 l., (3)-233, (1) p. front., plates, ports., facsim., coats of arms. 25 cm. "500 copies... printed by D. B. Updike ... Boston, August, 1929." Contents. - A family record by Alicia H. Middleton. - Record by Nathaniel R. Middleton, jr. - Reminiscences by Nathaniel R. Middleton. - Record of the Marston family from the reminiscences of Annie E. Marston De Wolf - Appendices ... 29-24632.

F273.M62

11850   MIDDLETON.   Robert Middleton (ca. 1651 - ca. 1707) of Charles and Prince Georges County Maryland, and numerous descendants of his.   By John Goodwin Herndon.   (Lancaster? Pa.) 1954 (i.e. 1955)   72 p. 26 cm.   "Limited to 100 copies." A revision and enlargement of an "article ... which appeared in the Pennsylvania genealogical magazine in its 1952 and 1953 issues." Bibliographical footnotes. 55-18420.

CS71.M632   1955

11851   MIDDLETON.   Family record, collected & compiled by Callie George Middleton, 1941-42. Revisions & additions by Tredgar O. Middleton, 1955-56.   (n.p., 1957?)   74 l. illus. 29 cm. 58-40719.

CS71.M632   1957

MIDDLETON.   See also: SEMMES, 1918
SEMMES, 1956

MIETZNER.   In vertical file under PRANKE family.   Asl reference librarian for this material.

11852   MIFFLIN.   Charles Mifflin, M.D., with an account of his ancestors and ancestral connections, by Benjamin C. Mifflin.   Cambridge, Printed at the Riverside press, 1876.   3 p. l., 63 p. front. (port.) 25 cm.   Printed for private distribution. Two copies only on Japanese paper. The photographs of Samuel Mifflin, wife and grandchild, from the originals by Copley, mentioned in the note, are not inserted in this copy. 19-2010.   CS71.M633   1876

11853   MIFFLIN.   Memoranda relating to the Mifflin family.   By John Houston Merrill.   (Philadelphi) Printed for private distribution (1890)   91 p. pl. 24½ cm. 9-15618.

CS71.M633   1890

11854   MIFFLIN.   Life and ancestry of Warner Mifflin, Friend - philanthropist - patriot; compiled by Hilda Justice.   Philadelphia, Ferris & Leach, 1905.   240 p. front. (coat of arms) fold. map, 2 facsim. 22 cm. 5-14821.   CS71.M633   1905

MIFFLIN.   See also: BISHOP, CS439.B553
WHITNEY, 1925
WILSON, 1961

11855   MIKESELL.   William Jackson Mikesell and the Mikesell family by Jerome B. Mikesell. (Chicago? 1966)   68 l., 69-101 p. illus., facsims., ports. 28 cm. "Pioneers of Marion County ... by W. M. Donnell. Des Moines, Iowa, Republican Steam Printing House, 1872." (p. 187-211) inserted. 67-9229.   CS71.M64   1966

MIKSCH.   See CLEWELL, 1907

MILBOURNE.   See: BISHOP, 1877
WHITNEY, 1925

MILBY.   See PUCKETT, 1960

11856   MILDMAY.   Genealogical memoranda relating to the family of Mildmay.   Privately printed. London, Taylor & co., printers, 1871.   1 p. l., 19 p. illus. (coats of arms) 28½ cm. Mildmay pedigrees, communicated by E. J. Sage. Issued also in Miscellanea genealogica et heraldica, v.2. p.192-200. 261-269. 9118128.

CS439.M5

11857   MILDMAY.   A brief memoir of the Mildmay family, compiled by Lieut.-colonel Herbert A. St. John Mildmay.   London and New York, Priv. print. by John Lane, 1913.   4 p. l., (3)-262 p., 1 l. plates, ports. 23 cm. "One hundred and fifty copies of this book have been printed." 23-18868.   CS439.M5   1913

11858   MILES.   Genealogy of the Miles family.   (Lowell, Mass., Norton, printer, 1840) 12 p. 20 cm. Half-title. Preface signed: Henry A. Miles. 14-11884.   CS71.M642   1840

11859   MILES.   Annals of Miles ancestry in Pennsylvania and story of a forged will, by Charles H. Banes ... Philadelphia, G. H. Buchanan & company, 1895.   182 p. front., illus., plates (part fold.) ports., facsims. 20½ cm. 10-5271.   CS71.M642   1895

11860   MILES.   ... The Miles family of Concord, Mass.   By Henry A. Miles.   Lowell, Mass., 1840.   Boston, Mass., Privately reprinted by F. J. Wilder, 1915.   2 p. l., (3) - 12 p.   20½ cm.   (Wilder's genealogical reprints.   Series M. no. 1)   "Limited edition of ten copies of which this is no. 6."   28-29663.   CS71.M642   1915

11861   MILES.   Miles genealogy; John Miles of Concord, Massachusetts, and his descendants, by Jonas M. Miles.   Boston, C. E. Goodspeed & company, 1920.   2 p. l., 48 p.   22½ cm.   20-7237.
                 CS71.M642   1920

             MILES.   See also: DAY, 1923
                                 NOURSE, 195-

11862   MILHOUS.   History of the Milhous family in South Carolina, by Evelyn Perry Milhous (Mrs. A. P. Ferguson) ... Miami, Fla., Printed through co-operation of the Miami herald, 1944.   12 l.   28 x 22 cm.   "Historical sources and references": 9th - 12th leaves.   "References for further research": 12th leaf.   45-13961.
                 CS71.M644   1944

11863   MILHOUS.   West with the Milhous and Nixon families; a story of the forebears of Richard Milhous Nixon.   By Raymond Martin Bell.   Washington, Pa., 1954.   4 l.   map.   28 cm.   54-18582.
                 CS71.N74   1954a

             MILHOUSE.   See MILHOUS.

11864   MILK.   History and genealogy of the Milk-Milks family, by Grace Croft, and by assisting authors: Lee Milk (and others) Provo, Utah, 1952.   308 p.   illus.   28 cm.   53-18470.
                 CS71.M647   1952

11865   MILK.   History and genealogy of the Milk-Milks family, by Grace Croft, and by assisting authors: Lee Milk (and others) 2d ed., rev.   Provo, Utah, 1956.   354 p.   illus.   28 cm.   57-43903.
                 CS71.M647   1956

11866   MILLAIS.   The lineage and pedigree of the family of Millais;   recording its history from 1331 to 1865.   Being an extract from an "Armorial of Jersey," by J. Bertrand Payne ... With illustrations from designs by the author.   London, Priv. print., 1865.   8 p.   front., illus., pl., coats of arms.   39 cm.   Title vignette.   15-21491.   CS439.M52

             MILLANGES.   See MILLIKEN.

             MILLAR.   See MILLER.

             MILLEDGE.   See HABERSHAM, 1901

11867   MILLER.   Memoirs of an old disciple and his descendants: Christian Miller, Sarah S. Miller, Isaac L. K. Miller, Rev. John E. Miller ... By Francis M. Kip ... With an introductory chapter, by Thomas De Witt ... New York, R. Carter, 1848.   xii, (13)-309 p.   19 cm.   14-791.
                 CS71.M65   1848

11868   MILLER.   A short historical account of the Miller & Morris families, collated partly from tradition; but mostly from authentic records.   By Morris Miller.   Knoxville, O., Stokes bro's, printers, 1876.   296, (5) p.   16 cm.   22-13261.   CS71.M65   1876

11869   MILLER.   Memorials of Hope park, comprising some particulars in the life of our dear father, William Miller, and notices of his more immediate ancestors; together with a list of his engravings.   London, Printed for the compiler by Simmons and Botten, 1886.   viii p., 1 l., 352 p., 2 l., vii-xxxv p.   front. (port.) illus., pl.   28½ cm.   The plates are mounted photographs.   "Fifty copies only printed for private circulation."   no. 41.   24-12192.   CS479.M55A5

11870   MILLER.   Ancestry of the children and grandchildren of Warwick P. and Mary M. Miller.   (Spencerville? Md., 1896)   20 p.   23½ cm.   Printed on one side of leaf only.   Preface signed: Warwick P. Miller.   Spencerville, Md.   9-12530.   CS71.M65   1896

11871   MILLER.   Historical sketch of the Miller family.   By Laura H. Young.   (n.p., 1897)
14 p., 1 l. 22 cm.   Caption title.   "Read at the reunion picnic of the Miller families, held in C. C. Bartholomew's grove in Clinton, July 5, 1897 by the writer Miss Laura H. Young of Deansboro."   25-7738.   CS71.M65   1897

11872   MILLER.   History and genealogies of the families of Miller, Woods, Harris, Wallace, Maupin, Oldham, Kavanaugh, and Brown (illustrated) with interspersions of notes of the families of Dabney, Reid, Martin, Broaddus, Gentry, Jarman, Jameson, Ballard, Mullins, Michie, Moberley, Covington, Browning, Duncan, Yancey and others, by W. H. Miller ... (Lexington, Ky., Press of Transylvania co.) 1907.   2 p. l., (3)-728, 127 p. illus., ports. 24½ cm. 8-6966.   CS71.M65   1907

11873   MILLER.   Descendants of Captain Joseph Miller of West Springfield, Mass., 1698-1908, by C. S. Williams.   New York (Press of T. A. Wright) 1908.   3 p. l., 3-39 l. 2 port. (incl. front.) 23 cm.   "Privately printed edition of twenty copies, no. 13."   12-30971.   CS71.M65   1908

11874   MILLER.   The Miller family; an address delivered before the Miller family re-union associ-ation of North Waldoboro, Maine, September 7, 1904.   By Frank Burton Miller ... Rockland, Me., The Caslon press print, 1909.   2 p. l., (9)-47 p. front., plates. 22 cm. 13-9470.
                                                                                                       CS71.M65   1909

11875   MILLER.   A family of Millers and Stewarts, by Dr. Robert F. Miller.   St. Louis, Mo., 1909
64 p. col. plates (incl. coats of arms) ports., facsims. 28 cm.   Pages 51-52 and 61-62 are repeated.   Notes in ms. throughout the text.
Contains genealogies of the Gass, Galbraith, Cummins and Weston families.   17-19218.   CS71.M65   1909a

11876   MILLER.   The Reverend Alexander Miller of Virginia and some of his descendants.   By Milo Custer.   (Bloomington, Ill., 1910)   36 p. illus., ports. 23 cm. 11-1402.
                                                                                                       CS71.M65   1910

11877   MILLER.   William Miller chart, about sixteen hundred seventy (1670) in Scotland, and about seventeen hundred twenty (1720) of Bucks County, Penna.; genealogical chart from Miller to Brownfield famalies (sic) Made for R. L. Brownfield, Jr. and Rex Newlon Brownfield.   (n.p.) 1910.   geneal table.
71 x 44 cm. fold. to 31 x 44 cm.   Manuscript. 55-55832.   CS71.M65   1910a

11878   MILLER.   The genealogy of the descendants of Frederick and Mary Elizabeth Peery Miller, comp. by John Peery Miller ... Xenia, O., Smith advertising co., 1913.   103 p. incl. front., illus., plates, ports., plan. 23 cm. 20-9240.   CS71.M65   1913

11879   MILLER.   The Millers of Haddington, Dunbar and Dunfermline; a record of Scottish book-selling, by W. J. Couper ... London (etc.) T. F. Unwin (1914)   318, (1) p. front., illus., plates, ports., facsims.
21½ cm.   "Bibliography: I. Books, etc., written or edited by the Millers of Dunbar and Haddington. II. The East Lothian press. III. The Dun-fermline press": p. 263-312. 15-1910.   Z325.M6C7

11880   MILLER.   The Miller family magazine; genealogical, historical and biographical.   v. 1-2, no. 2; Jan. 1916 - Apr. 1917.   New York city, N. Y., W. M. Clemens, 1916-17.   2 v. in 1. 23 cm.
quarterly.   Edited by W. M. Clemens.   No more published.   16-2766 rev.   CS71.M65   1916

11881   MILLER.   Genealogical notes of the Miller, Quarrier, Shrewsbury, Dickinson, Dickenson families, and the Lewis, Ruffner, and other kindred branches, with historical incidents, etc., by D. C. Gallaher ... (Charleston, W. Va., Tribune ptg. co.) 1917.   104 p. 23½ cm. 34-32117.
                                                                                                       CS71.M65   1917b

11882   MILLER.   The Millers of Millersburg and their descendants, with kindred families of Miller, McGee, Jameston, Read, Scott, Wyatt, Donnelly, White, Washington, Blackwell, Smith, Mayfield, Johnson, Kuykendall, Beene, Sadler, Clark, Woodfin, Whiteside and Myers.   Compiled for Gustavus Hindman Miller, of Chattanooga, by John Bailey Nicklin, jr. ... (Nashville, Brandon printing company) 1923.   xix, 485 p. plates, ports., facsim. 24 cm. 23-7278 rev.   CS71.M65   1923

11883   MILLER.   Ten generations of Millers, by Francis P. Lamphear of the ninth generation.   In-scribed to Milton Miller and Irene Johnson of the tenth.   New York (Yankee press) 1923.   1 p. l., 33
(1) p. illus. (incl. ports.) 25½ cm. 24-6785.   CS71.M65   1923a

11884   MILLER.   History of George Miller, sr., and Catherine, his wife, and their descendants. (Dayton, O., Press of the Groneweg printing co.) 1926.   4 p. l., (11)-172 p., 1 l., (5) p. 20½ cm. Compiled by A.B. Miller, John A. Miller, and F.M. Petry. 27-11946.   CS71.M65   1926

11885   MILLER.   Sketch of Miller (English) and Calhoun-Miller (Scotch-Irish) families, with their genealogy, by Mrs. Florence McWhorter Miller ... (Atlanta, Ruralist press, inc., c.1927) 180, xvi p. plates, ports. 18 cm. 27-8163.   CS71.M65   1927

11886   MILLER.   The Millar-du Bois family; its history and genealogy, written and compiled by Eva Miller Nourse.   (n. p.) 1928.   3 p. l., 411 p. front., plates, ports., facsim., coats of arms. 26½ cm. Blank pages for Memorandum (408-411) 39-12245.   CS71.M65   1928

11887   MILLER.   The Millers of Millersburg, Kentucky, by Harry Middleton Hyatt.   Vienna, A. Holzhausen's successors, 1929.   x, 200 p. pl. 24½ cm. 29-19878.   CS71.M65   1929

11888   MILLER.   ... The lineage of the Miller family and allied families of Fayette County, Pennsylvania, and Frederick County, Maryland, by Milton M. Darby and Clarence A. Miller, LL.M. (n. p., 1930)   123 l. 28½ cm. Type-written. Allied families: Getzendanner, Davis, Britt, Greenlee, Curstead, Smith. CA30-536 unrev.   CS71.M65   1930

11889   MILLER.   A history and genealogy of the Miller family, 1725-1933, published by Milo H. Miller ... Pittsburgh, 1933.   7 p. l., 3-146 p. illus. 23 cm. 33-22548.   CS71.M65   1933

11890   MILLER.   The Miller family, descendants of Frank Miller, who settled in Waldoborough, Mass., now Maine, in 1753.   By Frank Burton Miller ... Rockland, Me., Courier-gazette press, 1934.   174 p. front., plates, ports. 22½ cm. 35-13983.   CS71.M65   1935

11891   MILLER.   Jacob Miller of 1748, his descendants and connections ... collected and compiled by J. Carson Miller.   Moores Store, Va., J. C. Miller, 1936 -   v. front. (geneal. tab.) pl., ports. 23 cm. 37-424.   CS71.M65   1936

11892   MILLER.   The 101 ranch, by Ellsworth Collings, in collaboration with Alma Miller England, daughter of the founder of the 101 ranch.   Norman, University of Oklahoma press.   1937.   xiv, 249, (1) p. front., plates, ports. 23½ cm. Illustrated lining-papers. "First edition May 10, 1937." 37-13798.   F694.C66

11893   MILLER.   The Isaac Miller family (by) Emory Norris ... (Columbus, O., c.1938) cover-title, 31 p. 23 cm. Reproduced from type-written copy. 41-31425.   CS71.M65   1938

11894   MILLER.   The ancestry of Sarah Miller, 1755-1840, wife of Lieut. Amos Towne of Arundel (Kennebunkport) Maine, by Walter Goodwin Davis.   Portland, Me., The Southworth-Anthoensen press, 1939.   4 p. l., (3)-94 p. illus. (coat of arms) 23 cm. Includes also Emery, Gates, Lassell, Brown, Allanson, Dixon and Watts families. 39-32325.   CS71.M65   1939

11895   MILLER.   Millersville and the Miller family (by) Helen Miller Penzel Ritgerod (and) Henry A. Ritgerod.   Fayetteville, Ark., The authors (1939)   3 p. l., 93 p. pl. (ports.) map, geneal. tables. 27½ cm. Reproduced from type-written copy. 40-34272 rev.   CS71.M65   1939a

11896   MILLER.   Genealogy of the Miller and Pursel families, compiled and edited by Vida Miller Pursel ... Published by Miller and Pursel families. (Bloomsburg, Pa., Smith printing shop) 1939.   166 p. 23½ cm. 40-33921.   CS71.M65   1939b

11897   MILLER.   Genealogy of the descendants of Andrew (Müller) Miller of Millers Mills, N.Y. came from Germany, 1760, lived in Rensselaer county, N.Y., moved to Herkimer county, 1790 ... prepared by Doris Miller Schneider and John H. Schneider ... (Winnetka? Ill., 1940)   1 p. l., 41 p. 23½ cm. Bibliographical references in Introduction. 41-372.   CS71.M65   1940

11898   MILLER.   Miller outline chart, with some collateral lineages.   (By Edward Miller Jefferys) (Philadelphia? 1941?)   23 p. 23 cm. Portrait of Elizabeth Miller I, on cover. Errata slip mounted on p. (3) of cover. 42-8629.   CS71.M65   1941

11899   MILLER.   Joseph Miller of Newton, Massachusetts, his descendants in America and his ancestry in England, by Spencer Miller ... New York, Priv. print., 1942.   xv p., 1 l., 62 p., 1 l. front., illus.
(incl. facsim.) map, geneal. tables.   27 cm.   "Two hundred and fifty copies ... have been privately printed."   "Reprinted from the Record of
the New York genealogical and biographical society for April, 1939 through July, 1940."   42-8630.   CS71.M65   1942

11900   MILLER.   Family history of the descendants of John F. Miller and Magdalena Miller, by
Emanuel J. Miller ... Wilmot, O., E. J. Miller, 1943.   1 p. 1., 105 p. 23 cm.   Cover-title: John F. Miller family
history.   Imprint from label mounted on t.-p.   45-8047.   CS71.M65   1943

11901   MILLER.   The descendants of Samuel S. Miller, 1812-1892, of Frederick county, Maryland,
Seneca county, Ohio, and Steuben county, Indiana, by Willis Harry Miller, B.A.   Hudson, Wis.,
Star-observer print, 1944.   1 p. 1., 28 p. illus. (ports.) 20 cm. 44-8692.   CS71.M65   1944

11902   MILLER.   Fabulous empire; Colonel Zack Miller's story.   By Frederick Benjamin Gipson.
With an introd. by Donald Day.   Boston, Houghton Mifflin Co., 1946.   ix, 411 p. 21 cm. 46-6960 rev.*
                                                                             F694.M6G5

11903   MILLER.   The Miller and Davis families.   (Record of the descendants of Peter Miller and
Catherine Sheeler and Thomas Davis and Rebecca Tribby.   By Fenton Gall.   Fleetwood, Pa.) 1948.
iv, 83 l. plates. 28 cm. Cover title.   49-22661*   CS71.M65   1948

11904   MILLER.   William Miller of Bucks County, Pennsylvania, by Robert L. Brownfield, Jr. (and)
Rex Newlon Brownfield.   (n.p., 1951)   7 l. geneal. table. 29 cm.   Typesript.   Holograph and typewritten material inserted.
52-35759.   CS71.M65   1951

11905   MILLER.   Grace Gilbert Robertson and Henry Hollis Miller (Americanized from "Melchers")
more generally known as Hollis Henry Miller; with their forebears, including families of Hollis,
English, (Ingles), Choate, Green, Ferris, Piper, Farish, Rogers, Tunstall, Turner, Christmas,
Cotton, Ashby, Combs, Temple, Hill, Arnal, Savage.   By Ben Robertson Miller.   Rev. Baton Rouge,
La., c.1962.   75 p. illus. 28 cm.   62-53336.   CS71.M65   1962

11906   MILLER.   Genealogy and family history of Daniel T. Miller, Jr.   Written by Daniel T. Miller,
Jr.   Research by Mrs. Daniel T. Miller, Sr., and Grace Farrell.   (Hartford?) 1952.   22 l. 22 cm.
54-32490.   CS71.M65   1952

11907   MILLER.   Miller genealogy; Griffey Garten Miller and his descendants.   By Wilmot Polk
Rogers.   Santa Rosa, Calif., 1958.   14 l. 28 cm. 59-132.   CS71.M65   1958

11908   MILLER.   Family record of Eli J. Miller and Veronica Weaver, and their descendants.   By
Glenn Alva Miller.   Plain City, Ohio, 1961.   unpaged. illus. 22 cm.   63-37030.   CS71.M65   1961

11909   MILLER.   A Miller family tree grows into a forest.   By Josie Baird.   Rotan, Tex. (1965)
1 v. (various pagings) illus., ports. 28 cm.   "Compiled at the request of the Billy Miller family at its annual reunion held   the first Saturday and
Sunday in June, 1965, Stephenville, Texas." 66-749.   CS71.M65   1965

11910   MILLER.   The family of John Miller, 1858-1934 and wife, Kate Schecke Miller, 1862-1935,
by Schuyler C. Brossman.   (Rehrersburg? Pa., 1966)   (4) l. ports. 30 cm. Cover title.   67-2302.
                                                                CS71.M65   1966

11911   MILLER.   Genealogy of Miller-Haromon-Powell-Moore and allied families, by Guy M. Sone and
Ruth Wells Sone.   1968.   245 l. illus., facsims., geneal. tables, maps, port. 29 cm.   Bibliographical footnotes.   78-4417 MARC.
                                                                CS71.M65   1968

11912   MILLER.   History of the Miller family of Appleton, Me. (by) Royce W. Miller.   Gloucester,
Mass., 1968.   64 p. 22 cm. 75-12285 MARC.   CS71.M65   1968b

11913   MILLER.   Miller family cemetery inscriptions from the original records of Apple's Church,
Frederick Co., Md.   5 p. In vertical file.   Ask reference librarian for this material.

MILLER.   See also:

ABEL, 1928	DENSLOW, 1940	PEDEN, 1961
ATKINSON, 1933	DULIN, 1961	ROSE, 1922
BACON, 1958	DUNHAM, 1956	ROTHWELL, 1964
BARNARD, 1954	ENDERS, 1960	SAENGER, n. d. Microfilm 4065 CS
BATTEY, 1940a	EVERHART, 1931	SMITH, 1942
BEARDSLEY, 1958	FULTON, 1925	STEVENS, 1948
BEYER, 1955	GOLSON, 1959	TODD, 1960
BROWN, 1935	HOLE, 1904	TRUEBLOOD, 1964
BRUMBACH, 1961	HOLSINGER, 1959	WALTMAN, 1928
CHURCHILL, 1935	KURTZ, 1925	WEISER, 1960
CONRAD, 1957	McNAIR, 1935	WOOD, 1905
COOPER, 1906	MAUPIN, 1962	ZERBE, F157.S3E9
CORN, 1959	MULFORD, 1920	No. 553 - Goodhue county.
DAVIDSON, CS71.D252	PAGE, 1953	No. 1547 - Cabell county.
DENNIS, 1959	PECK, 1955	

MILLES.   See MILLS.

11914   MILLET.   Ancestors and descendants of Thomas Millett, from Chertsey, Surreyshire, England to Dorchester, Massachusetts, and his wife, Mary Greenoway.   By George Francis Millett. (Mesa? Ariz.) 1959 -   v. illus., ports. 24 cm.   60-32525.   CS71.M652   1959

MILLET.   See also: ELLIS, 1941
                             RICHARDSON, 1960

MILLETT.   See MILLET.

MILLHOUSE.   See MILHOUS.

MILLICAN.   See MILLIKEN.

MILLIGAN.   See CAMPBELL, 1960

MILLIKAN.   See MILLIKEN.

11915   MILLIKEN.   Notes of the Millikan family.   By Millard F. Hudson.   (San Francisco, 1902)
p. 55-60. 24 cm.   Caption title.   Detached from California historic-genealogical society, Publication no. III, 1902.   38M1264T.
                                                                                                                CS71.M654   1902

11916   MILLIKEN.   History of the families Millingas and Millanges of Saxony and Normandy, comprising genealogies and biographies of their posterity surnamed Milliken, Millikin, Millikan, Millican, Milligan, Mulliken and Mullikin, A.D.800 - A.D.1907; containing names of thirty thousand persons, with copious notes on intermarried and collateral families, and abstracts of early land grants, wills, and other documents ... Compiled by Rev. Gideon Tibbetts Ridlon, sr. ... Lewiston, Me., Pub. by the author, 1907.   xxxvi, 846 p. front., plates, ports., coats of arms. 25 cm.   Folded leaf containing addenda to p.490-492 inserted after p.510. 7-41060.   CS71.M654   1907

11917   MILLIKEN.   The Millken and Milligan family of Pennsylvania and Ohio; comp. by Mrs. C. E. Smith.   Columbus, O., 1920.   48 l. illus. (incl. ports.) 20½ x 27 cm.   A collection of data relating to the Milliken ancestry of Sarah Augusta (Prior) Smith, consisting of printed and ms. leaves with mounted photos, fastened together in binder.   CA20-307 unrev.
                                                                                                                CS71.M654   1920

11918   MILLIKEN.   Milliken and Milligan (family of Pennsylvania and Ohio) By Sarah Augusta Smith.   Columbus, 1921.   1 v. (unpaged) ports., map, facsims., photos. 28 cm.   Caption title.   Most of the text in ms; the illustrative material is mounted. 22-2704 rev. •   CS71.M654   1921
              —— Milligan (Millikan) family.   1949 addenda (to 1920 record) comp. by Rae (White) Evans and Sarah A. (Prior) Smith.   (n. p., 1949)   12 l. group port. 28 cm.   CS71.M654   1921 Add.
                                                                                                                Rare book coll.

11919   MILLIKEN.   Milliken war data and lineage of world war soldiers.   Columbus, O., 1934.
(62) p.   mounted ports.   29 cm.   Introduction signed: (Mrs. Chas. E.) Sarah Augusta Prior Smith.   A scrap book containing manuscript type-written and printed matter relating to the war records of descendants of Abraham Stiles and John Milliken, to aid them to obtain membership in Daughters and Sons of American revolution societies.   34-35357.   CS71.M654   1934

11920   MILLIKEN.   Genealogical, historical and biographical sketches of descendants from families of the four James Millikens ... By Clarence Greene Hildreth.   (Pittsburgh, G. H. Alexander & co., inc. printers) 1936.   38 p.   ports.   coats of arms.   22½ cm.   S. L. 7/16/60   CS71.M959   1936

MILLIKEN.   See also: BERNARD, 1922
                              STILES, 1920
                              MULLIKEN.

MILLIKIN.   See MILLIKEN.

MILLINGAS.   See MILLIKEN.

MILLINGTON.   See SYNGE,

11921   MILLIS.   The Millis, Clark, Bruner, Stuart, Holstine, Neal, Wilson and Faucett families of William Alfred Millis and Laura Martha Millis as of 1944.   Rev., enl. and published by Fred Millis.   Indianapolis, 1944.   64 p.   illus., coat of arms, forms, ports.   24 cm.   "Originally compiled 1920-1934."   65-8737.
                                                                                        CS71.M655   1944

11922   MILLS.   A genealogy of the descendants of Thomas Mills, one of the first settlers in Dumbarton, N. H.   Prepared by Ella Mills.   Marlboro, Mass., Times book and job print., 1893.
32 p.   20 x 16 cm.   Errata slip inserted.   9-12529.   CS71.M657   1893

11923   MILLS.   Genealogy of the Mills family.   (New York, The De Vinne press) 1896.
36 p., 1 l.   17 cm.   Preface signed: S. L. M., i. e. Susan Lawrence Mills.   17-15779.
                                                                                        CS71.M657   1896

11924   MILLS.   George Mills, a soldier of the revolution with a genealogy of his descendants, by Borden H. Mills.   Albany, N. Y., 1911.   2 p. l., 42, (4) p.   23 cm.   12-11749.
                                                                                        CS71.M657   1911

11925   MILLS.   Something about the Mills family and its collateral branches, with autobiographical reminiscences, compiled and prepared by Frank Moody Mills (April 4, 1911)   Sioux Falls, S. D., 1911.
219, (2) p.   front., pl., ports.   24 cm.   Illustrated lining-papers.   27-19583.   CS71.M657   1911a

11926   MILLS.   ... Early marriage records of the Mills family in the United States; official and authoritative records of Mills marriages in the original states and colonies from 1628 to 1865, ed. by William Montgomery Clemens.   1st ed. (limited)   New York, W. M. Clemens, 1916.   55 p.   23 cm.
(The Clemens American marriage records, v. 6)   16-11122.   CS71.M657   1916

11927   MILLES.   York co., Penn.   Milles wills.   (In Genealogy; a monthly magazine of American ancestry, edited by William Montgomery Clemens ... Hackensack, N. J., 1918.   23 cm.   vol. viii, p. 17-20)   39M2433T.
                                                                                        CS42.G7 vol. 8

11928   MILLS.   Genealogical and historical records of the Mills and Gage families, 1776-1926, 150 years, compiled by Stanley Mills.   Hamilton, Canada, The Reid press limited, 1926.
101 p.   illus. (incl. ports., map, coat of arms)   26 cm.   Ruled pages for "Births", "Deaths" and "Marriages" (96-99)   Part one: "The United empire loyalists ... "   32-30543.   CS71.M657   1926

11929   MILLS.   Peter Mills and Mary Shirtcliffe Mills of St. Mary's county, Maryland; an historical sketch of their origin, lives and some of their descendants and collateral kinsfolk, 1635-1935, by James Abell Mills ... (Elizabeth, N. J., Press of Colby & McGowan, inc., c. 1936)   64 p.   front., ports.
22½ cm.   "Edition limited to one hundred copies."   36-34112.   CS71.M657   1936

11930   MILLS.   The Mills family of Screven County, Ga.   By Clyde Dixon Hollingsworth.   (n. p., 194 -)   (16) l.   28 cm.   54-46388.   CS71.M657

11931   MILLS.   The family of Captain John Mills of Medway and Sherborn, Mass., and Amherst, N.H., by William Carroll Hill ... Milford, N.H., Printed at the Cabinet press (1942)   2 p. l., 3-136 p. front., illus. (facsims.) plates, ports. 22½ cm.   42-25331.   CS71.M657   1942

11932   MILLS.   Andrew Mills and his descendants, with genealogies of related families, by Eva Mills Lee Taylor.   Bethesda, Md.   (Strassburg, Va., Printed by the Shenandoah publishing house, inc) 1944.   v, 150 p.   23½ cm.   Bibliographical foot-notes.   45-9089.   CS71.M657   1944

11933   MILLS.   A South Carolina family: Mills-Smith, and related lines, by Laurens Tenney Mills, with addenda by Lilla Mills Hawes and Sarh Mills Norton.   (n. p., 1960)   158 p.   illus.   24 cm.   60-43302.   CS71.M657   1960

11934   MILLS.   The Mills, Cope, and related families of Georgia.   Compiled and written by Thomas H. Goddard (and) John H. Goddard, Jr.   Philadelphia, Dunlap Print. Co. (1962)   300 p.   illus.   23 cm.   62-52175.   CS71.M657   1962

11935   MILLS.   The Mills, Payton, Mott, and Butler families; my grandparents and their ancestors, showing the lines of connection with the families who married into them.   By Mabelle (Mills) Kirkbride.   Bridgeport, Pa., Priv. print. (by) Chancellor Press, 1963.   xvii, 302 p.   ports.   24 cm.   Includes bibliographies.   64-1358.   CS71.M657   1963

11936   MILLS.   The Mills family; twelve generations descended from pilgrim Simon Mills I from Yorkshire, England, 1630, including English background to A.D. 1080 (by Vera Elizabeth Mills (Mrs. Edmund Haeger) n.p., 1963)   313 p.   illus., ports.   29 cm.   66-47887.   CS71.M657   1963a

11937   MILLS.   Ancestors and descendants of Henry and Mary Folger Mills, compiled by Paul Mills. (1st ed.)   Portland, Or., Metropolitan Press, 1966.   138 p.   illus., ports.   23 cm.   67-4132.   CS71.M657   1966

11938   MILLS.   The John-Simon Mills line of Windsor and Simsbury, Connecticut and some descend-ants of John and Damaris Phelps Mills of Canton, Connecticut, by Eunice M. Lamb.   Burlington, Vt., Chadwato Service, 1968.   1 v. (various pagings) illus., maps, ports. 28 cm.   Includes bibliographies.   Contents. - Section I: A study relative to Simon Mills, early settler of Windsor, Connecticut. - Section II: An illustrated preview of the John-Simon Mills line of Windsor and Simsbury, Conn. - Sction III: A genealogy of the John-Simon Mills line of Windsor and Simsbury, Connecticut.   70-3442 MARC.   CS71.M657   1968

MILLS.   See also:

CLENDINEN, 1923	HALSEY, 1927	MAULSBY, 1902
DICKERSON, 1919	HAY, 1923	ROSENBERGER, 1958
DOUBLEDAY, 1924	HIGBIE, 1914	TYSSEN, CS439.T93
ESPENET, CS439.E82	IRONMONGER, 1956	VINTON, 1858a
GOODLOCK, 1951	McKEE, 1900	WILCOX, 1911a

11939   MILLSPAUGH.   Millspaugh-Milspaw.   By Francis Corwin Millspaugh.   (Swampscott, Mass., 1949)   312 p.   31 cm.   61-33971.   CS71.M6573   1959

11940   MILNE.   Milne family.   By Alexander Du Bin.   Philadelphia, Historical Publ. Society, 1948. (11) p.   26 cm.   49-18838*.   CS71.M6575   1948

MILSPAW.   See MILLSPAUGH.

11941   MILTON.   Papers connected with the affairs of Milton and his family.   Ed. by John Fitchett Marsh, from the original documents in his possession.   (Manchester) Printed for the Chetham society, 1851.   1 p. l., 46 p. 1 illus., fold. pl. (facsims.)   23 x 18 cm.   (Chetham miscellanies. v. 1 (no. 1) In Remains, historical & literay, connected with the palatine counties of Lancaster and Chester, pub. by the Chetham society.   vol. XXIV.   18-5241.   DA670.L19C5 v. 24

11942   MILTON.   The Milton genealogy, 1636-1960.   By Hugh Meglone Milton.   (Washington? 1960)
(vi), 98, 13 l. illus., map, col. coat of arms. 29 cm. Cover title. Bibliography: leaf (vi) 61-31859.
CS71.M6577   1960

MILTON.   See also KINNEY, 1903

11943   MILWARD.   Pedigree of Milward, of Tullogher and Ballynelinagh, co. Kilkenney, & of Alice
Holt, Hants, with branches and notes ... Compiled by C. Milward ... (London, Printed by Phipps &
Connor) 1880.   1 p. 1., 8 p. illus., 5 fold. geneal. tab. 26½ x 33 cm. Title vignette: coat of arms. Contains pedigrees of the
Pearson, Archer, Dawson and Fell families. 16-2833.
CS439.M53

11944   MINEAR.   The Minear family (Minear, Menear, Myneer, Manear, Mineer) (By Charles
Joseph Maxwell) (Dalls? Tex., Ginn & co., 1926)   127 p. 25½ cm. Introduction signed: Charles Joseph Maxwell.
Caption title. 26-17560.
CS71.M658   1926

11945   MINEAR.   Descendants of John Minear, 1732-1781.   By Charles Joseph Maxwell.   Dallas,
1948.   232 p. 28 cm. 49-2376*.
CS71.M658   1948

11946   MINER.   Life of Alonzo Ames Miner. . . By George H. Emerson. . . Boston, Universialist publishing
house, 1896.   xvi, 555 p. front., plates, ports., coat of arms. 24 cm. 15-12371.
BX9969.M5E6

11947   MINER.   Our ancestors; Miners - Averys - Strongs - Morgans, comp. by Phebe Elizabeth
Miner Gardner ... North Adams, Mass., Advance press, 1901.   169 p. front., illus. (ports.) plates, fold. geneal.
tab. 20½ cm. Author's descent from Charlemagne: fold. geneal. tab. 20-2601.
CS71.M659   1901

11948   MINER.   Centennial of Miner family.   (In Ohio archaeological and historical quarterly. Columbus, 1906. 23½ cm.
v. 15, p. 407-418. illus.) 18-7073.
F486.O51 vol.15

11949   MINER.   One branch of the Miner family with extensive notes on the Wood, Lounsberry,
Rogers and fifty other allied families of Connecticut and Long Island, by Lillian Lounsberry (Miner)
Selleck.   New Haven, Conn., D. L. Jacobus, 1928.   xiv, 260 p., 1 l. front. (col. coat of arms) plates, ports., fold.
geneal. tables. 24 cm. 29-15227.
CS71.M659   1928

11950   MINER.   Genealogy of branches of families of Miner (Minor), Waters, O'Hare, and Thies in
England, Ireland, Germany, and America, 1327 to 1963.   By Lulu Irene (Waters) Hare.   (Washington?
1964)   97 p. illus., ports. 30 cm. 65-9228.
CS71.M6645   1964

11951   MINER.   Mainer family in vertical file.   Ask reference librarian for this material.

MINER.   See also: BABCOCK, 1909
DOW, 1939
MINOR.
OLIVER, 1956
TUTTLE, 1871

11952   MINET.   Some account of the Huguenot family of Minet, from their coming out of France at
the revocation of the edict of Nantes MDCLXXXVI, founded on Isaac Minet's 'Relation of our family,'
by William Minet ... (London, Priv. print. for the author by Spottiswoode & co., 1892)   vii p., 2 l.,
240 p. front., plates, ports., facsim., fold. geneal. chart. 31 cm. An edition of 250 copies printed. 9-18127.
CS439.M54

11953   MINIER.   The Minier family, especially descendants of George W. Minier, of Minier, Illinois.
By Sarah Minier (Sanborne) Weaver.   Donna, Tex., 1926.   18 numb. l. illus. 35 x 23 cm. Type-written. Signed:
Sarah Minier Sanborne Weaver.   The illustrations are mounted. 27-3240.
CS71.M662   1926

MINNICH.   See WALTMAN, 1928

11954   MINNIS.   Minnis family of Ireland and America, comp. by Elizabeth Austin ... Carrolton,
Mo., Press of the Republican-record, 1913.   31 p. plates, ports. 23½ cm. 14-16977.
CS71.M664   1913

MINNITT.   See CROSSLEY, CS439.C835

11955   MINNS.   Genealogical histories of Minns and allied families, in the line of descent of Miss Susan Minns.   Issued under the editorial supervision of Ruth Lawrence ... New York, National Americana society, 1925.   2 p. l., 65 p. plates, ports., facsims., col. coats of arms. 34½ cm.   Printed on one side of leaf.   Bound in blue levant with leather doublures; inlaid, gold tooled. Allied families: Ball, King, Cunningham, Wheeler, Boylston, Gardner, Parker, Blood, Sawtell, Lakin, Bacon, Hancock, Prentice, Russell, Torrey, Wilson, Woodhall, Grindall, Mansfield, Hooker.   26-4217.

CS71.M6643   1925

11956   MINOR.   Volunteer service in Army of Cumberland.   Pt. first.   History of the volunteers from Clarksfield, Huron Co., Ohio, in the 101st O. V. I. ... Pt. second.   List of the volunteers from Wakeman, O., the whole war.   And their history since ... Pt. third, Sergeant Benj. T. Strong's biography, and history of the Chickamauga campaign ... Pt. fourth.   Descendants of Justus Minor, who moved from Conn. in 1821 to Wakeman, O.   All these several pieces written up and published by C. R. Green ... 1913-14.   Ed. 200.   (Olathe? Kan., 1914)   (48) p. illus., pl., ports. 21 cm.   Various paging.   Pt. 3-4 have special title-pages.   Cover-title: The part we took in the great rebellion.   Or, some history 50 years after, by a Buckeye.   1914.   15-23143.

E525.5.101stG

11957   MINOR.   A historical pamphlet.   Wakeman, Ohio.   Lives of the volunteers in the civil war.   The "Minor" family as pioneers in Wakeman.   Justus & Cyrus M., 1821.   Charles E. Minor, 1866.   By Charles R. Green ... (Olathe, Kan.) 1914.   cover-title, (22) p. 2 port. 20½ cm. 15-4459.

F499.W14G7

11958   MINOR.   The Minor family of Virginia, by John B. Minor ... (Lynchburg, Va., J.P.Bell company (inc.) c.1923)   2 p. l., (3)-125 p. 23½ cm. 23-7842.   CS71.M6645   1923

11959   MINOR.   The Minor family of Virginia, by John B. Minor ... (Lynchburg, Va., J.P.Bell company (inc.) c.1923)   2 p. l., (3)-125 p. 23½ cm. 23-7842.   CS71.M6645   1923

11960   MINOR.   Ter-centenary anniversary of the Minor-Miner family in America, 1630-1930.   By W. R. Mack.   (Chicago, 1930)   cover-title, 1 p. l., 20 p. 20½ cm.   Signed: W.R.Mack.   Typewritten additions mounted on two of the pages, and also inserted at end.   33-34833.   CS71.M6645   1930

MINOR.   See also MINER.

11961   MINOT.   A genealogical record of the Minot family in America and England.   Boston, Priv. print., 1897.   1 p. l., 55 p., front. (coat of arms) plates, facsims. 26 cm.   "Two hundred copies printed.   no. 49."   Note signed: Joseph Grafton Minot.   9-12528.   CS71.M665   1897

11962   MINOT.   The Minot family; record of births, marriages and deaths, 1754-1934, copied from family Bibles.   (By James Jackson Minot) (Boston? 1934)   (20) p. 21½ cm.   Additions in manuscript.   Blank pages for additions (14-20) 34-29291.   CS71.M665   1934

11963   MINOT.   Ancestors and descendants of George Richards Minot, 1758-1802, with especial reference to the descendants of George Richards Minot, 1813-1883, and reference to the descendants of William Minot, 1817-1894 and reference to the descendants of Francis Minot, M.D. 1821-1899.   Compiled by James Jackson Minot, M.D.   (n. p.) 1936.   66 p. incl, mounted illus. (coat of arms) 23½ cm.   Blank pages for additions (61-66) Bibliography: p. 58-60.   37-16850.   CS71.M665   1936

MINOT.   See also ANDERSON, 1916

MINOTT.   See ANDERSON, 1916

11964   MINSHALL.   Thomas and Margaret Minshall who came from England to Pennsylvania in 1682, and their early descendants: to which are added some accounts of Griffith Owen and descendants for a like period.   By one of the sixth generation. (Jacob Painter. Lima? Pa.) 1867.   2 p. l., 8 p. 19½ cm.   9-12527.   CS71.M666   1867

MINSHALL.   See also MINSHULL.

11965   MINSHULL.   Minshull pedigrees, from the heraldic visitations of Cheshire, 1613 and 1663, in the College of arms.   London, Priv. print., 1869.   1 p. l., 9 p. illus. (coats of arms) 29 x 22 cm.   Title vignette: coat of arms.   Communicated by J. Bellamy Minshull, esq.   Issued also in Miscellanea genealogica et heraldica, v.2, p.182-190.   9-18125.

CS439.M6

11966   MINSHULL.   Lineage of Miss Minerva Gertrude Culton, 1869-1942 ... By Mary (Turpin) Layton.   Washington, D.C. (1943)   cover-title, 35 l. 29 x 23 cm.   Partly type-written, partly handwritten.   44-29926.

CS71.M666   1943

MINTNER.   See COVINGTON, 1956

MINTO, Earls of.   See ELIOT, CS479.E5

MINTURN.   See WANTON, F76.R52 no.3

MIRICK.   See MERRICK.

MIRIHIL.   See MURIEL.

MISCAMPBELL.   See BLAKENEY, 1928

11967   MISCHLER.   History of the Mishler families and their descendants ... John Milton Mishler, historian.   (Reading, Pa., Press of E. Pengelly & bro., 1921)   cover-title, 30 p. incl. illus., ports. 23 cm.   32-1222.

CS71.M667   1921

MISCK.   See MISHEK.

11968   MISENER.   The Misener family in New Jersey and Canada.   By Ray Sells Morrish.   Flint, Mich., 1951.   8 p. 23 cm. 52-18600.

CS71.M6675

MISER.   See MEISSER.

MISHECK.   See MISHEK.

MISHEK.   See INECK, 1965

MISTER.   See REED, 1963

11969   MISTROT.   The Mistrot-Segura story in Louisiana and Texas, by Mistrot Cartier.   (Houston, 1965)   82, xii l. illus., ports. 29 cm.   Bibliography: leaf xii. 65-51590.

CS71.M66716 1965

MISTZNER.   In vertical file under PRANKE family.   Ask reference librarian for this material.

11970   MITCHELL.   Consanguinity of the families of the Gibbses and Mitchells, in London, Ireland, Scotland, Germany and Wales, with some remarks on the settling of the island of Bermuda, New England, Virginia, &c.   By Bejamin Gibbs Mitchell, born in the parish of Warwick, island of Bermuda, August 5th, 1793.   Baltimore, Printed by Sherwood & co., 1864.   32 p. 22½ cm.   An effort to establish the claim to the estate of John Gibbs, deceased, of London.   "More of Jennens' estate": p. 29 - 32. 19-19893.

CS439.M63   1864

11971   MITCHELL.   The Mitchell family of North Yarmouth, Maine (by) William Mitchell Sargent.   Yarmouth, Me., "Old times" office, 1878.   1 p. l., 9 p. incl. coat of arms. 23 cm.   Author's autographed copy.   34-17823.

CS71.M668   1878

11972   MITCHELL.   Genealogical memoranda relating to the Mitchell and Sykes families.   Privately printed.   London, Mitchell and Hughes, printers, 1878.   7 p. coats of arms. 28 cm.   Communicated by J.W. Mitchell.   Published also in Miscellanea genealogica et heraldica.   London, 1880, n.s., v.3, p.101-104, 143. 17-27679.

CS439.M63   1878

11973   MITCHELL.   The Mitchell, Bryant and Orr families, and sketches of the last two hundred and seventy-four years; by Seth Bryant.   Boston, 1894.   32 p. front. (port.) 18½ cm.   "A chapter of events, taken from Edward H. Savage's valuable book, 'Boston events' ": p. 26-32.   3-17340.   F74.E18B9

11974   MITCHELL.   David and Margaret Mitchell, emigrants from Ulster, Ireland, to the American colonies in 1763; an account of their lives, with a genealogy of their descendants.   By James Mitchell ... Boston, Mass.   (Press of Blanchard printing company, 1907)   2 p. l., (7)-241 p. front., illus. (incl. ports.) 24 cm.   20-22884.   CS71.M668   1907

11975   MITCHELL.   The Mitchell family magazine, genealogical, historical and biographical.   Ed. by William Montgomery Clemens.   v.1, v.2 no. 1-2; January, 1916-Apr. 1917.   New York city, N.Y., W. M. Clemens, 1916-17.   2 v. in 1. 23 cm. quarterly. No more published. 16-2765 rev.
                                    CS71.M668   1916-17

11976   MITCHELL.   Pennsylvania Mitchell marriages.   (By William Montgomery Clemens.)
(In Genealogy; a monthly magazine of American ancestry, edited by William Montgomery Clemens ... Hackensack, N.J., 1918.   23 cm.
vol. viii, p.1-5   39M2432T.   CS42.G7 v.8
          —— Separate   CS71.M668   1918

11977   MITCHELL.   Mitchell record compiled by Clarence Blair Mitchell.   (Princeton, N.J., Printed at the Princeton university press) 1926.   3 p. l., 183 p. front. (fold. geneal. tab.) ports. 24½ cm.   "Privately printed for the use of the family."   Relates mainly to the descendants of Moses Mitchell, 1698? - 1775.   Blank pages for "Notes" and "Index" (167 - 170, (2))   26-10711.   CS71.M668   1926

11978   MITCHELL.   The Mitchell line, 1811-1929.   The Walsh line.   (By Joseph Charles Fegan) (Washington? D.C., 1929)   2 l. 25 cm. 29-12027.   CS71.M668   1929

11979   MITCHELL.   ... Mitchell family records, by J. Montgomery Seaver.   Philadelphia, American historical-genealogical society (1929)   41 p. front. (4 port.) coat of arms. 29 cm.   Coat of arms of the Mitchell family on recto of frontispiece.   Pages 40-41 blank for "Family record."   "References": p. 39.   40-18915.
                                    CS71.M668   1929a

11980   MITCHELL.   History of the Mitchell family, George Mitchell of Perry Valley branch;   I. Mitchell Dreese, PH.D., historian.   (n.p., 1934)   cover-title, (2), 8, (2) p. 22 cm.   Blank page for "Autographs" at end.   Coat of arms on cover.   38-14739.   CS71.M668   1934

11981   MITCHELL.   A brief outline of descendency from Matthew Mitchell, 1590-1645.   By Donald Iowa Mitchell.   Washington, 1963.   1 v. (unpaged) 30 cm.   64-3489.   CS71.M668   1963

11982   MITCHELL.   Mitchell genealogy, also Billingslea, Blound, Garland, Ryan, Slatter, Stone. (By William Augustus Mitchell.   (West Point, N.Y., 1936)   119 l. 2 maps, 12 geneal. tab. 22½ cm.   Type-written. The maps and genealogical tables are blue-prints.   Title from cover.   Introduction signed: W. A. Mitchell.   38-14713.
                                    CS71.M668   1936

11983   MITCHELL.   Mitchell family record.   By Bessie (Hanchett) Mitchell.   Nora Springs, Iowa, 1938.   5 l. 36 cm. 62-56136.   CS71.M668   1938

11984   MITCHELL.   Mitchell family bulletin.   v. 1 -   no. 1 -   April 1940 - White Plains, N.Y., 1940 -   v. 28 cm. quarterly.   Caption title.   "Issued by Natalie M. Seth."   Paged continuously. Reproduced from type-written copy.   41-373.   CS71.M668   1940

11985   MITCHELL.   Mitchell-McGlocklin and allied families, a genealogy ... by Austin Wheeler Smith.   Cookville, Tenn., 1940.   1 p. l., 85 numb. l. 29½ cm.   Reproduced from type-written copy.   "Sources of information": leaf 4.   42-452.   CS71.M668   1940a

11986   MITCHELL.   The descendants of George and Ann Hodge Mitchell of Devonshire, England. By Rollin Edwards Drake.   (Ann Arbor, Mich.) 1949.   66 p. illus., ports. 24 cm. 50-25480.
                                    CS71.M668   1949

11987   MITCHELL.   A Mitchell group: Adam, Jane, and Robert, and some of their descendants.
(Long Beach? Calif.)   1963.   177 p. illus., ports., maps, facsims. 23 cm. Bibliography: p. 177. 64-1265.

CS71.M6672   1963

11988   MITCHELL.   The Mitchell-Doak group: history, biography, genealogy (by) Harry E. Mitchell.
(Long Beach? Calif.)   1966.   249 p. illus., maps, ports. 23 cm. Bibliography: p. 249. 66-7387.   CS71.M6672   1966

11989   MITCHELL.   Ancestry of William Spingler Mitchell, Cornelius von Erden Mitchell, John
Van Beuren Mitchell.   Edited by H. Minot Pitman.   (n. p.) 1967.   viii, 499 p. illus., coats of arms (incl. 1 col.),
geneal. tables, ports. 24 cm.   Includes bibliographies.   68-2251.   CS71.M6672   1967

11990   MITCHELL.   Mitchell-Pearman families, by B. S. Mitchell.   Honea Path, S.C., 1967.
1 v. (various pagings) 28 cm.   Cover title: Mitchell-Pearman families of South Carolina.   75-9206 MARC.

CS71.M6672   1967b

MITCHELL.   In Perry county, Pa. families.   In vertical file.   Ask reference librarian for this material.

MITCHELL.   See also:

ACKLEY, 1960
ALLARDICE, 1841   GILL, CS479.G5   ROBERTS, 1953
ANDERSON, 1916   HITE, 1960   SALISBURY, 1892
BRAYTON, 1922   KIMBROUGH, 1960   SHIPLEY, 1964
BRAYTON, HV5232, W7H5   McCURDY, 1892   SMALL, 1910 & 1934
DEPEW, 1918   MATTHEW, 1940   YOUNG, 1937
DICKERSON, 1919   OLIVER, 1956
GALLOWAY, 1939   PARISH, 1925

MITFORD-BARBERTON.   See BARBER, 1934

11992   MITSUI.   The house of Mitsui (by) Oland D. Russell ... Boston, Little, Brown and company,
1939.   xi p., 3 l., (3)-328 p. col. front., plates, ports. 24½ cm. "First edition. Published August 1939." 39-27690.

DS834.5.M5R8

11993   MITTONG.   Genealogy of the Mittong family and connection, by Benjamin Franklin Wilson.
(Wheeling, W. Va., c.1926)   187 p. ports. 23½ cm. Cover-title: Mittong family history and connections. 26-24127.

CS71.M669   1926

MITZNER.   In vertical file under PRANKE family.   See reference librarian for this material.

MITZNERA.   In vertical file under PRANKE family.   Ask reference librarian for this material.

11994   MIX.   A brief account of the life and patirotic services of Jonathan Mix of New Haven, being
an autobiographical memoir.   Ed. from the original manuscript, with notes and additions, together
with copies of the United States patents for carriage springs; an account of the Mix family in New
Haven and of the descendants of Jonathan Mix, by William Phipps Blake.   New Haven, Printed by Tuttle,
Morehouse & Taylor, 1886.   xii, 98 p. 24 cm. 12-18982.   CS71.M67   1886

11995   MIX.   The family tree of Mrs. Irene Howe Mix Root ... George Fuller Green, delineator.
Kansas City, Mo., 1935.   geneal. tab. illus. (coats of arms) 79 x 47 cm. In manuscript. "References." 38-32665.

CS71.M67   1935

MIX.   See also: DILLON, 1927
No. 553 - Goodhue county.

MIXEL.   See MIKESELL.

MIXER.   See REMINGTON, 1960

MIZE.   See TELFORD, 1956

MIZELL. See SMITH, 1960

MIZER. See MEISSER.

11996   MOAK. The Moak and related families of South Carolina and Mississippi, 1740-1960; with notes as to members of the family in Tennessee and Illinois and also notes as to other Moak families in New York, Pennsylvania, Maryland, and Virginia. By Lennox Lee Moak. Fort Washington, Pa. (1960)   310 l. illus. 28 cm. 61-34230.   CS71.M68   1960

11997   MOAK. Descendants of Jacob Moak of New Scotland. By Elizabeth Janet McCormick. (New York?) 1942.   118 p. 28 cm. Bibliography: p. 117-118.   52-49963.   CS71.M68   1942

11998   MOATS. Tevalt Moats; copyright ... by Howard B. Grant ... Philippi, W. Va., H. B. Grant, 1936.   1 l. 28½ x 23 cm. Caption title. Text runs parallel with back of cover. Mimeographed. 38M832T.   CS71.M69   1936

11999   MOBBS. The Mobbs' claim to the Wenlock estates ... London, 1866.   23 p. 21 cm. Contents - Outline of the case. - Pedigree of the Mobbs family. - The will of John Mobbs of Islington, 10th May 1790. - The case. 16-17288.
CS439.M65

MOBERLY. See HILL, 1961

12000   MOBLEY. The Mobleys and their connections. By William Woodward Dixon. (n. p., 1915) Microfilm copy made in 1942 by the Library of Congress. Negative. Collation of the original, as determined from the film: 146 p. ports., coat of arms. Mic 50-152.   Microfilm CS-1
—— Copy 2   Microfilm 101
Microfilm reading room

MOEN. See NELSON, 1938a

MOFFAT. See MOFFATT.

12001   MOFFATT. The clan Moffat in America, a family genealogy, by George West Maffett, historian-in-chief, assisted by the clan historians. (n. p., n. d.)   3 reels. Microfilm copy of the ms., made in 1951 by the Genealogical Society of Utah. Positive. Collation of the original, as determined from the film: 3 v. illus., ports. Mic. 53-1077.   Microfilm CS-13
Microfilm reading room.

12002   MOFFATT. Ballybay Moffetts; a brief history of the Crievagh house, Ballybay, county Monagahan, Ireland, branch of the Moffett family, by George and Adam Moffett, assisted by others of the name. (n. p.) 1908.   105 p., 1 l., (6) p. incl. fold. geneal. tables. front. 21½ cm. Pages 23-105 printed on rectos only. Blank pages for Births, Deaths, and Marriages (6 at end) "The data of the families living in England and Ireland was furnished by Rev. Joseph Moffett and Frank J. Moffett, esq." 35-28840.   CS71.M695   1908

12003   MOFFATT. Moffat genealogies: descent from Rev. John Moffat of Ulster County, New York, by R. Burnham Moffat. (New York Press of L. Middleditch co.) Priv. print., 1909.   4 p. l., 13-158 p. incl. pl., map. 25 cm. 10-2626.   CS71.M695   1909

12004   MOFFATT. William and Barbara Moffatt. (By James Robert Moffatt. Memphis, Printed by Clark Johnston, 1939?)   cover-title, 43 p. plates, ports. 22½ cm. Introductory remarks signed: James R. Moffatt. 41-14297.
CS71.M695   1939

12005   MOFFATT. Moffatana bulletin. (An occasional publication) v. 1, no. 1-5; Apr. 1907 - Feb. 1915. Lawrence, Kan., G. W. Maffet, 1907-15.   5 nos. in 1 v. illus. 28 cm. G. W. Maffet, editor. 12-24987.
CS71.M695   1907

MOFFATT. See also: BEAL, 1956
EUBANK, 194-

MOFFET. See MOFFATT.

MOGRIDGE. See HUDSON, DA690.W6H8

12006 MOHLER. Genealogy of the Ludwig Mohler family in America, covering a period from April 4, 1696, to June 15, 1921 ... Compiled and edited by Cora Garber Dunning ... (Lincoln, Neb., The editor, 1921) 63 p. illus. (incl. ports.) 23½ cm. "Published ... under auspices of the Nebraska state historical society." Cover-title: Mohler-Garber family history. 21-11583 rev.   CS71.M698   1921

12007 MOHLER. Mohler-Moler genealogy, particularly from George Adam and Eve Moler, compiled by Charles Clyde and Lydia (Stouffer) Moler, with the assistance of others. Edition one. Hagerstown, Md., 1954.   101 l. 29 cm. "Supplement one": leaves 80 -82.   CS71.M698   1954
        —— Supplement two: corrections and additions. Hagerstown, Md., 1955.   13 l. 29 cm. Bound with the main work. 57-43904.   CS71.M698   1954

12008 MOHLER. The Mohler family of Ohio, descendants of Jacob Mohler, grandson of Ludwig Mohler of Lancaster County, Pennsylvania. Beaver Falls, Pa., 1958.   92 p. illus. 23 cm. 59-21525.   CS71.M698   1958

MOHN. See No. 553 - Goodhue county.

12009 MOHUN. Dunster and its lords, 1066-1881. By H. C. Maxwell Lyte ... With a descriptive sketch of Dunster castle by G. T. Clark, F.S.A., and a chapter on the siege and surrender of Dunster castle by E. Green. Printed for private circulation. (Exeter, Printed by W. Pollard) 1882. vi, (4), (vii)-xv, 145, (1) p. illus., plates, plans, coats of arms. 26 cm. An edition of 200 copies printed. "Most of the following pages have already appeared in different numbers of the following journals for the years 1880 and 1881, having had their origin in a paper read before the Royal archaeological institute at Dunster, in August, 1879." cf. Pref. 19-2309.   DA690.D85L75

12010 MOHUN. A history of Dunster and of the families of Mohun & Luttrell, by Sir H. C. Maxwell Lyte ... London, The St. Catherine press ltd., 1909.   2 v. illus., plates, ports., map, plans. 25½ cm. Paged continuously. 9-22284.   DA690.D85L8

MOIR. See MOORE.

12011 MOISE. The Moise family of South Carolina; and account of the life and descendants of Abraham and Sarah Moise who settled in Charleston, South Carolina, in the year 1791 A.D. Columbia, S.C., Printed by R.L.Bryan Co., 1961.   304 p. illus. 24 cm. 61-42046.   CS71.M6985   1961

12012 MOLENAAR. Genealogy; Molenaar and Geijsbeck Molenaar. (Chula Vista, Calif.) 1913. geneal. tab. 25½ x 36½ cm. 43-22091.   CS71.M699   1913

12013 MOLER. From the records of the American ancestry of John Mason Moler ... (By William Heidgerd) Washington, 1942.   1 p. l., 12 numb. l., 2 l. 29 cm. Type-written (carbon copy) "This is copy #2." 43-685.   CS71.M7   1942

12014 MOLER. See MOHLER.

12015 MOLESWORTH. Pedigree of Molesworth. Copied from the original roll on vellum in the possession of Major Molesworth. (London, 1877?)   (4) p. 28½ cm. Caption title. Issued also in Miscellanea genealogica et heraldica, n.s., v.2, p.280-283. 9-18123.   CS439.M7

MOLETTE. See MORANGE.

12016 MOLINEAUX. An account of the family and descendants of Sir Thomas Molyneux, kt., chancellor of the exchequer in Ireland, to Queen Elizabeth. Evesham (Eng.) Printed by J. Agg, 1820. vi, 103 (i.e.105), (1) p. port. 24½ cm. Number 63-64 repeated in paging. Preface signed: Capel Molyneux. Additions in manuscript throughout text. "Memorial of the life of Wm. Molyneux, esq.", an autobiography: p. (51)-78. Includes bibliography. 40-16314.   CS499.M6   1820

12017 MOLINEAUX. Memoir of the Molineux family; by Gisborne Molineux ... For private circulation only. (London, Printed by J.S.Virtue and co., limited) 1882.   4 p. l., 155, (1) p. 3 fold. geneal. tables. 30 cm. Title vignette. 3-29159.   CS439.M74

12018   MOLINEAUX. Genealogy of William Molyneux and descendants down to A. D. 1890.   Also an historical sketch of the Molyneux, Bird and Warren families, the first settlers in what is now Sullivan County, Pennsylvania.   By George Molyneux Pardoe ... Sioux City, Ia., Goldie bros. book and job printers, 1894.   23, (1) p. fold. chart. 23 cm.   The Edward Molyneux branch of the family is subject to "hematophilia" and "a chart is appended showing the occurrence of the bleeding trait through six generations." 13-9630.   CS71.M722   1894

12019   MOLINEAUX. History, genealogical and biographical, of the Molyneux families, by Nellie Zada Rice Molyneux.   Syracuse, N. Y., C. W. Bardeen, 1904.   370 p. front., illus. (incl. ports.) 24 cm.   "Authorities for Molyneux genealogy": p. 7-8. 5-4280.   CS71.M722   1904

MOLINEAUX.   See also: BRABAZON, 1825
CROSSLEY, CS439.C835
ROYD, CS439.R75
STANLEY, DA28.35.S8R6

MOLINEUX.   See MOLINEAUX.

MOLMER.   In vertical file under PRANKE family.   Ask reference librarin for this material.

12020   MOLTER. The Molter family, a biographical history and genealogy of the descendants of Dr. Philip Ludwig Mölter, who migrated from Germany to New York state about 1786, compiled by Ella Daily Fox.   (n. p.) 1932.   368 p. front., plates, ports., fold. map (in pocket) facsim. 23½ cm.   Some numbered pages left blank for notes.   Allied families: Becker, Hagadorn, Vrooman and Mitchell. 33-29124.   CS71.M73   1932

MOLTER.   See also L. C. additions and corrections, no. 9

MOLTON.   See MOULTON, 1922

MOLYNEUX.   See MOLINEAUX.

12021   MONCKTON. A genealogical history of the family of Monckton, comprising a full account of Yorkshire and Kentish branches, with some particulars of the principal members of the Nottinghamshire, Staffordshire, and Northamptonshire branches ... By David Henry Monckton ... Printed for private circulation only.   London, Mitchell and Hughes, 1887.   xii, 199, (1), cxiiv p. front., illus., 49 pl. (incl. ports., facsims., col. coat of arms) 5 geneal. tab. (4 fold.) 32 cm.   "One hundred and five copies ... printed and issued of which this is no. 68. D. Henry Monckton." 14-19509.   CS439.M76

MONCREIFF.   See MONCRIEFF.

MONCRIEF.   See MONCRIEFF.

12022   MONCRIEFF. The house of Moncrieff, by George Seton ... Edinburgh, Printed for private circulation, 1890.   vi, (2), 186 p. front. (col. coats of arms) col. illus., 6 double geneal. tab. 29 cm.   "One hundred and fifty copies printed for private distribution by Sir Alexander Moncreiff, K. C. B., representative of the family of Culfargie, of which this is no. 17." 22-641.   DA758.3.M65S4

12023   MONCRIEFF. The Moncreiffs and the Moncreiffes; a history of the family of Moncreiff of that ilk, and its collateral branches, by Frederick Moncreiff and William Moncreiffe.   Edinburgh, Priv, print. by T. and A. Constable, ltd., 1929.   2 v. fronts., illus., plates, ports., geneal. tables (part fold.) facsims. 30 cm.   Paged continuously.   Some of the plates are accompanied by guard sheets with descriptive letterpress. 30-29.   CS479.M65

MONCRIEFF.   See also VAWTER, 1905

12024   MONCURE. House of Moncure genealogy ... including European & colonial ancestral background, compiled by Marion Moncure Duncan, Adrian Cather Miller (and) Peyton Sagendorf Moncure.   (Alexandria? Va.) 1967.   1 v. (various pagings) illus., coats of arms, facsims., geneal. tables (1 fold. in pocket) 29 cm.   "A supplement to Hayden's Virginia genealogies." Includes bibliography. 67-28800.   CS71.M735   1967

12024 cont.   —— First supplement, including the colonial library of Reverend John Moncure, together with corrections and additions to original volume (by) Marion Moncure Duncan, Adrian Cather Miller (and) Peyton Sagendorf Moncure.   (Alexandria? Va.) 1968.   39 p. facsims. 28 cm.

CS71.M735   1967
Suppl.

MONCURE.   See also: GLASSELL, F225.H41
No. 430 - Adventurers of purse and person.

12025   MONELL.   A genealogy of the Monell family; an account of James Monell who settled in Wallkill Precint, part of present Orange County, New York, in 1723 and of his known descendants in all Monell branches down to the present time.   By Wesley Logan Baker.   Rutland, Vt., Tuttle Pub. Co., 1946.   266 p. illus. 24 cm. 50-32104.

CS71.M737   1946

MONET.   See MONNET.

MONEY.   See MONNET.

MONFODE.   See KERR, 1880

MONIZ.   See PERESTRELLO, 1892

12026   MONNET.   Monnet family genealogy, an emphasis of a noble Huguenot heritage, somewhat of the first immigrants Isaac and Pierre Monnet; being a presentation of those in America bearing the name as variously spelled, Monet, Monete, Monett, Monette, Monnet, Monnett, Monnete, Monnette, Monay, Maunay, Money, Monie, Monnie, Monat, Monatt, Manett, Mannett, Munnitt, Munnett, Manee, Maney, Amonnet, Amonet, etc., with complete genealogies of the main lines; including the history of la noble maison de Monet de la Marck, seigneurs et barons, from the year 1632; the genealogy of siegneurs de Monnet, la maison de Salins, from the year 1184; and containing short accounts of certain of the Pillot, Nuthall, Sprigg, Hillary, Mariarte, Crabb, Williams, Osborn, Burrell, Hellen, Lake and Bird, Caldwell, Slagle, Reichelsdörfer, Hagenbuch, Schissler, Braucher, Wayland Wilhoit, Kinnear, Hull, Ludwig, Lutz, et al., families connecting with the ancestral lines. With coats of arms, facsimiles of original documents and records, maps and charts, color plates and cuts of distinguished members of the family, in illustration.   Written and comp. by Orra Eugene Monnette ... (Los Angeles, Cal., C. F. Bireley company, 1911)   9 p. l., 5-1151, 16, lxxviii p. incl. illus., plates, ports., maps, facsims., coats of arms. col. front., col. pl. 26 cm. "This edition of the Monnet family genealogy, consisting of approximately twelve hundred pages, bound in buckram, stamped in gold and with color plate frontispiece and dedicatorial page, is limited to three hundred and fifty copies ..... no. 28." 16 blank pages for additional records precede index. 11-8960.

CS71.M74   1911

MONNETTE.   See MONNET.

12027   MONROE.   Some remarkable passages in the life of the Honourable Col. James Gardiner, who was slain at the battle of Preston-Pans, September 21, 1745.   With an appendix relating to the antient family of the Munro's of Fowlis.   By P. Doddridge ... Edinburgh, Printed by A. M'Caslan, 1772.   vi, 173 p. 16 cm. 5-1101.

DA67.1G2D6   1772

12028   MONROE.   Another edition of the above.   London, Printed for J. Buckland (etc.) 1785.
xii, (13)-280 p. 17½ cm. 4-688.

DA67.1.G2D6   1785

12029   MONROE.   Another edition of the above.   Edinburgh, Printed for W. Anderson, Stirling; (etc., etc.,) 1791.   287 p. 16½ cm. 36-5862.

DA67.1.G2D6   1791

12030   MONROE.   Another edition of the above.   London, Printed for the booksellers, 1794.
287 p. 16½ cm. 33-30466.

DA67.1.G2D6   1794

12031   MONROE.   Another edition of the above.   Boston: Printed & published by Lincoln & Edmands, no. 53, Cornhill. 1811.   263, (1) p. 18 cm. "The Christian warrior animated and crowned. A sermon, occasionaed by the heroic death of the Hon. Col. James Gardiner. By P. Doddridge": p. (233)-263. 5-1103.

DA67.1.G2D6   1811

12032   MONROE.   The Munroe genealogy   By John G. Locke.   Boston and Cambridge, J. Munroe and company, 1853.   15 p. 25½ cm. Reprinted from his "Book of the Lockes.." 1853, p. 302-313. 9-12324.   CS71.M753   1853

12033   MONROE.   History of the Munros of Fowlis, with genealogies of the principal families of the name: to which are added those of Lexington and New England.   By the late Alexander Mackenzie ... Inverness (Scot.) A. & W. Mackenzie, 1898.   xv, 632 p. 23 cm. 9-19338.

CS479.M8   1898

12034   MONROE.   A sketch of the Munro clan, also of William Munro who, deported from Scotland, settled in Lexington, Massachusetts, and some of his posterity, together with a letter from Sarah Munroe to Mary Mason descriptive of the visit of President Washington to Lexington in 1789.   By James Phinney Munroe.   Boston, G. B. Ellis, 1900.   80 p. 25 cm. 1-22485.   CS71.M753   1900

12035   MONROE.   John Munroe and Old Barnstable.   1784-1879.   Sketch of a good life; an anniversary tribute, by Elizabeth Munroe.   (Yarmouthport) C. W. Swift, printer (1909)   3 p. l., 135 p. ports. 22½ cm. 12-27324.   CS71.M753   1909

12036   MONROE.   The Monros of Auchinbowie and cognate families, by John Alexander Inglis.   Edinburgh, Privately printed by T. and A. Constable, 1911.   viii p., 2 l., 219, (1) p. illus., plates, ports. 26 cm. Includes genealogies of the Binning family, the Scotts of Bavelaw and the Boyds of Kipps. 12-7893.

CS479.M8   1911

12037   MONROE.   Genealogy of Josiah Munroe, revolutionary soldier, who died in the service of the continental army at Valley Forge, February 19, 1778 ... By G. S. Northrup.   St. Johns, Mich., G. S. Northrup, 1912.   xv, 422 p. 21½ cm. 13-392.   CS71.M753   1912

12038   MONROE.   Foulis castle and the Monroes of lower Iveagh.   By Horace Monroe ... London, Mitchell, Hughes and Clarke, 1929.   4 p. l., 83 p. fold. front., plates (1 col.) map, geneal. tables (part fold.) 22½ cm. 46-34162.   CS499.M66   1929

12039   MONROE.   ... Calendar of writs of Munro of Foulis, 1299-1823, edited by C. T. McInnes ... Edinburgh, Printed for the Society by J. Skinner & company, ltd., 1940.   2 p. l., 136 p. 26 cm. (Scottish record society.   Publications. v. 71, pts. 136-137) 41-26084 rev.   CS460.S4 vol. 71

12040   MONROE.   Monroe family, Fowler family, Perrie family, Stevens family.   By Francis Truman Monroe.   (Jamaica? N. Y.) 1952.   1 v. (various pagings) ports., map. 29 cm.   Bibliography: leaf (24) 53-30284.

CS71.M753   1952

12041   MONROE.   The ancestors and descendants of Albert Nelson Monroe of Swansea and Brighton, Mass., 1819-1902.   By Estelle (Wellwood) Wait.   (Newton Centre? Mass.) 1958.   29 p. illus. 23 cm. 58-33885.   CS71.M753   1958

12042   MONROE.   History and genealogy of the Lexington, Massachusetts Munroes, compiled by Richard S. Munroe.   (Holyoke? Mass.) 1966.   ix, 468 p. 24 cm. 66-31278.   CS71.M9678   1966

MONROE.   See also: MUNRO clan.
SAUNDERS, 1939
No. 553 - Goodhue county.

MONSELL.   See MUNSELL.

12043   MONSON.   ... Proceedings of the first (& 2d) Munson family runion, held in the city of New Haven, Wednesday, August 17, 1887, & Aug., 19, 1896.   New Haven, Tuttle, Morehouse & Taylor, printers, 1887, 1896.   2 v. 23 cm.   Cover-title: A Hartford & New Haven pioneer ... 3-31340.

CS71.M755

12044   MONSON.   ... Historical address of the first Munson family reunion held in the city of New Haven, Wednesday, August 17, 1887.   New Haven, Tuttle, Morhouse & Taylor, printers, 1887.
1 p. l., p. (13)-56. 23½ cm.   By Myron A. Munson.   At head of title: 1637-1887.   Cover-title: A Hartford and New Haven pioneer (Thomas Munson)   Also published in Proceedings of the first Munson family reunion ... New Haven, 1887. 17-19083.   F97.M96

12045   MONSON.   1637-1887.   The Munson record.   A genealogical and biographical account of Captain Thomas Munson (a pioneer of Hartford and New Haven) and his descendants.   By Myron A. Munson ... New Haven, Conn., Printed for the Munson Association, 1895.   2 v. fronts., illus., plates, ports., maps, facsims., fold. geneal. tables, diagrs. 27½ cm. Paged continuously. 9-12323.   CS71.M755   1895

12046   MONSON.   Traditions concerning the origin of the American Munsons, gathered and digested by Myron A. Munson.   New Haven, The Tuttle, Morehouse & Taylor press, 1897.   1 p. l., 6 p. 23½ cm. 12-20291.   CS71.M755   1897

12047   MONSON.   The Portsmouth race of Monsons - Munsons - Mansons, comprising Richard Monson (at Portsmouth, N. H., 1663) and his descendants; being a contribution to the genealogy and history of five generations ... by Myron Andrews Munson ... New Haven, Conn. (The Tuttle, Morehouse & Taylor press) 1910.   xii, 89 p. incl. front., illus. fold. geneal. tab. 21 cm. 11-557.
                                                                                                  CS71.M755   1910

12048   MONSON.   Ten million acres; the life of William Benjamin Munson, by Donald Joseph in collaboration with Mary Tonkin Smith-Denison, Tex., Priv. print. (New York, William E. Rudge's sons) 1946.   6 p. l., (3)-257, (1) p. front., illus. (incl. ports., facsims.) fold. geneal. tab. 24½ cm. "Published to commemorate the one hundredth anniversary of the birth of William Benjamin Munson ... Limited to one hundred copies ... Number 24." 47-16760.
                                                                                                  CT275.M768J6

        MONSON.   See also: JOHNSON, 1961a
                             STRONG, 1912
                             No. 553 - Goodhue county.

        MONTAGNE.   See EARLE, 1924

12049   MONTAGUE.   (Montague family genealogical tree)   New York, American college of heraldry,
18 -   geneal. tab. 46 x 32 cm. fold. to 23 x 16 cm. Lithographed. 2-9837.   CS71.M759   18 -

12050   MONTAGUE.   Letters addressed to Mrs. Basil Montagu and B. W. Procter by Mr. Thomas Carlyle.   (London) Printed for private circulation (Chiswick press, 1881)   2 p. l., 33 p. 19 cm. First edition. Published by the daughter of Mrs. Basil Montagu in answer to Carlyle's description of the "Montagu menagerie" in his "Reminiscences," published London, 1881. cf. Pref., signed: Anne Benson Procter, March 1881. 18-23849 rev.   PR4433.A5M6 1881

12051   MONTAGUE.   Meeting of the Montague family at Hadley, Mass., Aug. 2, 1882.   Boston, Franklin press: Rand, Avery and company, 1882.   107 p., 1 l. front. (port.) pl. 24½ cm. Editor's note signed: Richard Montague. 9-12322.   CS71.M759   1882

12052   MONTAGUE.   History and genealogy of the Montague family of America, descended from Richard Montague of Hadley, Mass., and Peter Montague of Lancaster Co., Va., with genealogical notes of other families by name of Montague.   Compiled by George Wm. Montague.   Rev. and ed. by William L. Montague ... Amherst, Mass., Press of J. E. Williams, 1886.   vii, (8)-785 p. front., plates, ports., col. coats of arms. 23½ cm. 2 ms. leaves inserted between p. 712-713. 9-12321.
                                                                                                  CS71.M759   1886

12053   MONTAGUE.   The Montagues of Boughton and their Northamptonshire homes, by C. Wise ... Kettering, W. E. & J. Goss, 1888.   101, vi p. front., pl., fold. plans. 19 cm. 12-24992.
                                                                                                  CS439.M77   1888

12054   MONTAGUE.   History and genealogy of Peter Montague, of Nansemond and Lancaster counties, Virginia, and his descendants, 1621-1894.   Compiled and published by George William Montague ... Amherst, Mass., Press of Carpenter & Morehouse, 1894.   1 p. l., 494 p. front., ports., fold. geneal. tab., coats of arms (part col.) 23 cm. 9-12319.   CS71.M759   1894

12055   MONTAGUE.   Hinchingbrooke.   By Edward George Henry Montagu ... London, A. L. Humphreys, 1910.   2 p. l., 50, (1) p. 25½ cm. Coat of arms, in gold, on cover. 10-25077.   CS439.M77   1910

12056   MONTAGUE.   The way of the Montagues, a gallery of family portraits.   By Bernard Falk. London, New York, Hutchinson (1947)   319 p. plate, ports. 23 cm. 48-12730*.   DA28.35.M6F3

12057   MONTAGUE.   Genealogy of John V. Montague, Middlebury, Connecticut; born: April 5, 1878, Bandera, Texas; died: Aug. 15, 1960, Middlebury, Connecticut.   This history and genealogy was compiled, designed and drafted by John V. Montague, himself.   (Middlebury, Conn.) c. 1961.
geneal. table.   coats of arms.   205 x 106 cm.   61-26605.   CS71.M759   1961

MONTAGUE.   See also: BROWN, DA664.C6R6
WARFIELD, 1937
No. 430 - Adventurers of purse and person.

MONTCHANIN.   See DU PONT, 1923

MONTCHENSI.   See addenda.

MONTEITH.   See MENTEITH.

12058   MONTFORT.   The life of Simon de Montfort, earl of Leicester, with special reference to the parliamentary history of his time, by George Walter Prothero ... London, Longmans, Green, and co., 1877.   xii, 409 p.   2 fold. maps.   19 cm.   5-970.   DA228.M7P9

12059   MONTFORT.   A genealogical history of Montfort-sur-Risle and Deeley of Halesowen, by R. Mountford Deeley ... With frontispiece and 14 illustrations.   London, C. Griffin and company limited, 1941.   xiii, 96 p. incl. front., illus. (incl. ports., maps, coat of arms) geneal. tables, diagr. 20 cm.   A45-1065. CS439.M773   1941

12060   MONTFORT.   Monfort (i.e. Montfort) family; (also) Ray and McChesney families.   (By Ray Roberts Knight.   (Minneapolis, 195-?)   10 l.   28 cm.   54-19888.   CS71.M78   1951

MONTFORT.   See also: LUMPKIN, 1940
RAND, 1936
RAND, 1940

MONTGOMERIE.   See MONTGOMERY.

12061   MONTGOMERY.   Memorials of the Montgomeries, earls of Eglinton, by William Fraser. Edinburgh, 1859.   2 v. illus. (incl. coats of arms, 1 col.) plates, ports., facsims. (part double) 28 x 22 cm.   8-22937.
DA758.3.M7F8

12062   MONTGOMERY.   A genealogical history of the family of Montgomery, including the Montgomery pedigree.   Comp. by Thomas Harrison Montgomery ... Philadelphia, Printed for private circulation (H. B. Ashmead, printer) 1863.   xii p., 2 l., (9)-158 p. fold. geneal. tab.   25 cm.   9-12320.
CS71.M788   1863

12063   MONTGOMERY.   Memorables of the Montgomeries, a narrative in rhyme, composed before the present century, printed from the only copy known to remain, which has been preserved above sixty years by the care of Hugh Montgomerie, senior at Eaglesham, long one of the factors of the family of Eglintoun.   Glasgow, Printed by R. and A. Foulis, 1770.   2 p. l., iii p., 1 l., 7 p.   30 cm.   Added t.-p. has imprint: "New York, Printed for the King of clubs, 1866."   Edition of 100 copies.   Edited by David Williams Patterson.   16-5672.
CS479.M74   1866

12064   MONTGOMERY.   A sketch of the life of the Rev. Joseph Montgomery, by John Montgomery Forster.   Harrisburg, Pa., Printed for private distribution, 1879.   47 p.   24½ cm.   17-9742.
CS71.M788   1879

12065   MONTGOMERY.   History of the descendants and connections of William Montgomery and James Somerville, who emigrated to America from Ireland, in the opening years of the 19th century. (Albany, J. Munsell's sons, 1897)   112 p. illus. (ports.) 19 cm.   Compiled by Frank Montgomery.   Blank pages at end for memoranda.   1-5881.   CS71.M788   1897

12066   MONTGOMERY.   A genealogical history of the Montgomerys and their descendants, by D. B. Montgomery ... Owensville, Ind., J. P. Cox, 1903.   436 p. illus. (plan) ports. 23½ cm.   "Previous histories": p. 6-10.
40-18335.   L.C. COPY REPLACED BY MICROFILM.   CS71.M788   1903
Microfilm 17440 CS

12067   MONTGOMERY.   Memoir of Thomas H. Montgomery ... together with extracts from his personal notes on his parents.   By Thomas H. Montgomery ... Philadelphia, Harris & Partridge, 1905. 51 p. 23½ cm.   Bibliography of published works of Thomas Harrison Montgomery, 1830-1905; p. 30-31.   6-4958.

CT275. M584M5

12068   MONTGOMERY.   The Montgomery family magazine, genealogical, historical and biographical ... v. 1-2 (no. 1-8); July 1915-Apr. 1917.   New York city, N. Y. (1915-17)   2 v. in 1.   22 cm.   quarterly. W. M. Clemens, editor and publisher.   No more published?   15-25691 rev.   CS71. M788   1915-17

12069   MONTGOMERY.   The history and genealogy of Montgomery, McTaggart, Hunter and Carswell families ... Compiled by Nettie McTaggart, Mrs. Bessie Shandley (and) Frances Colean.   (Springfield, Ill., Hartman printing co.)   1925.   11 l.   23½ cm.   Additions in manuscript.   35-21374.   CS71. M788   1925

12070   MONTGOMERY.   Montgomery genealogy (by) C. G. Hurlburt ... San Diego, Calif., 1926. 2 p. l., (3)-66 p.   port.   23 cm.   Blank pages at end for "Family record. "   27-11119.   CS71. M788   1926

12071   MONTGOMERY.   The descendants of James and Lydia Montgomery, compiled by John F. Montgomery.   (Manchester, Vt., Journal press) 1933.   40 p.   15 cm.   33-31501.   CS71. M788   1933

12072   MONTGOMERY.   The Montgomery family of Paradise, by T. Montgomery Lightfoot ... and Elizabeth B. Montgomery ... (n. p.) 1934.   29 p. incl. illus., pl.   23 cm.   Address presented before the Northumberland county historical society, Sunbury, Pa.   36-14642.   CS71. M788   1934

12073   MONTGOMERY.   The ancestors of James Montgomery and the descendants of James and Lydia Montgomery, compiled by Jean Montgomery Riddell.   (n. p., 1938)   46 p.   22½ cm.   39-9246.

CS71. M788   1938

12074   MONTGOMERY.   The family of Montgomery, edited by Alexander Du Bin.   Philadelphia, The Historical publication society (1943)   3 p. l., 132 p.   front. (coat of arms) illus.   25½ cm.   "Based on the 'genealogical history of the family of Montgomery', by Thomas Harrison Montgomery and printed for private circulation at Philadelphia in 1863. " - Foreword. 44-1001.   CS71. M788   1943

12075   MONTGOMERY.   Origin and history of the Montgomerys, Comtes de Montgomery, Ponthieu, Alençon and La Marche, Earls of Arundel, Chichester, Shrewsbury, Montgomery, Pembroke, Lancaster, Mercia, Eglinton and Mountalexander, Princes de Bellême, Marquis de Montgomery de Lorges.   Edinburgh, W. Blackwood, 1948.   xvi, 303 p.   plates, ports.   30 cm.   48-24804*.   CS439. M774   1948

12076   MONTGOMERY.   Pioneer families of Franklin County, Virginia.   By Marshall Wingfield. Berryville, Va., Chesapeake Book Co., 1964.   373 p.   23 cm.   65-2628.   F232. F7W52

12077   MONTGOMERY.   A genealogical history of the families of Montgomerie of Garboldisham, Hunter of Knap and Montgomerie of Fittleworth, by Charles A. H. Franklyn.   Ditchling, Ditchling P., 1967.   xvi, 124 p.   12 plates, illus., coats of arms, facsims., ports.   26 cm.   Limited ed. of 126 signed and numbered copies.   No. 7. 68-98895.   CS439. M774   1967

MONTGOMERY.   See also:

ARCHDALE, 1925	BILLINGS, 1931	DANN, 1943
ARMSTRONG, CS61. A6 vol. 2	BROWN, 1903	GREELEY, CS439. G75
ARUNDEL, CS439. A7	CAIRNS, CS479. C16	KAUFMAN, 1892
BATEMAN, 1960	CROMWELL, 1967	SMITH, 1921a
BILLINGS, 1927	CROW, 1961	No. 516 - Notable southern families.

12078   MONTMORENCY.   Genealogical memoir of the family of Montmorency, styled De Marisco or Morres; ancient lords De Marisco and De Montemarisco, in the peerage of England and Ireland. Most respectfully addressed to His Majesty Louis XVIII, king of France and Navarre. . By Hervey de Montmorency-Morres ... Paris, Printed by J. R. Plassan, 1817.   3 p. l., 75 p., 1 l., (2), xxxvi p., 1 l., ccclxiii p., 1 l.   front., illus. (coats of arms) plates.   28 cm.   26-22629.   CS439. M775   1817

MONTRAS.   See MONTROSS.

12079   MONTRESOR.   The Montrasor journals; edited and annotated by G. D. Scull ... (New York, Printed for the Society, 1882)   xiv, 578 p. 2 port. (incl. front.) maps (1 fold.) plans. 25 cm. (Added t. - p.: Collections of the New York historical society ... 1881.   Publication fund series (v. 14))   From the original mss. in the possession of the Montrésor family. 1-13392.

F116. N63 vol. 14

12080   MONTRESOR.   Memoirs of the Montrésors.   Wilton (Eng.) 1941-43.   2 v. 26 cm. Typewritten. Vol. 2 has imprint: Alverstoke, Hants.   Contents. - v.1. James Gabriel Le Trésor to John Montrésor.   With an Appendix dealing with the genealogy of the Le Trésor family and a general index. - v.2. James Montrésor to the present time.   50-44931.   CS439. M777   1941

MONTRESS.   See MONTROSS.

MONTROSE.   See MONTROSS.

MONTROSE, Marquises of.   See GRAHAM.

12081   MONTROSS.   Montross: family history; Pierre Montras and his descendants, a record of 300 years of the Montras, Montross, Montrose, Montress family in the United States and Canada, by John Wilson Taylor and Eva Mills (Lee) Taylor.   (Staunton? Va., 1958)   861 p. illus. 28 cm. 59-2850.

CS71. M7885   1958

MOOAR.   See MOORE.

12082   MOOD.   Family album, an account of the Moods of Charleston, South Carolina, and connected families ... By Thomas McAlpin Stubbs.   (Atlanta, Curtiss printing company, inc., 1943) 2 p. l., vii-ix, 246 p. ports. 23½ cm.   Bibliography: p. 225-227.   43-14315.   CS71. M8   1943

MOODIE.   See MOODY.

12083   MOODY.   Biographical sketches of the Moody family: embracing notices of ten ministers and several laymen, from 1633 to 1842 ... By Charles C. P. Moody.   Boston, S. G. Drake, 1847. 168 p. 16½ cm.   9-12317.   CS71. M816   1847

12084   MOODY.   The Moodie book; being an account of the families of Melsetter, Muir, Cocklaw, Blairhill, Bryanton, Gilchorn, Pitmuies, Arbekie, Masterton, etc., etc.   By the Marquis of Ruvigny and Raineval ... (London?) Priv. print., 1906.   2 p. l., (iii)-iv, (2), 132 p. front., illus., plates, ports., facsim., fold. geneal. tab. 28½ x 22½ cm. "One hundred and fifty copies ... printed ... No. 111." 16-18073.

CS479. M76

12085   MOODY.   Descendants of William Moody.   (By Herbert Albion Moody) (Turners Falls, Mass., 1916)   cover-title, 6 l. fold. geneal. tab. 28 cm. Type-written. The genealogical table is a blue print. Coat of arms on cover. 25-2345.   CS71. M816   1916

12086   MOODY.   Genealogy of the Moody family, collected and arranged by Sarah Moody Alvord. Winsted, Conn., 1916.   17 p. 20 cm. 34-2725.   CS71. M816   1916a

12087   MOODY.   Moody family record; the ancestry and descendants of Dr. Thomas Moody, a Revolutionary soldier, born in Cumberland County, Virginia, 1759; also notes on related families. Helen Foster Snow (and others) compilers.   Ed. Edward Grant Moody.   Delta, Utah, Dr. Thomas Moody Family Organization, 1957.   327 p. illus. 28 cm. 57-40148   CS71. M816   1957

12088   MOODY.   The old home.   By Mabel H. Huse.   Boston, Meador Pub. Co. (1957) 69 p. illus.   21 cm.   57-45931.   CS71. M816   1957a

MOODY.   See also: DUMMER, LD7501. S72D6
FOGG, 1851
HOLTON, 1887
KILBORN, 1957
LEDLIE, 1961
MUNN, 1881

12089   MOOMAW.   Moomaw; an account of some of the descendants of Lenhart Mumma, b. circa 1690, d. 1770, who arrived in Philadelphia Sept. 19, 1732.   With a detailed account of the descendants of Benjamin Franklin Moomaw, 1814-1900.   Compiled (by) Mildred Moomaw Coleman.   (Richmond? 1964?)   31 1.   28 cm.   65-51595.   CS71.M817   1964

12090   MOON.   The Moons and kindred families, by J. W. Moon.   Atlanta, Ga., Stein printing company (c. 1930)   3 p. 1., 99 p.   coat of arms.   23½ cm.   30-16593.   CS71.M818   1930

12091   MOON.   Sketches of the Moon and Barclay families, including the Harris, Moorman, Johnson, Appling families, compiled by Anna Mary Moon.   (Chattanooga, c. 1939)   108 p.   23½ cm.   Bibliography: p. 96-98.   39-2083.   CS71.M818   1939

            MOON.   See also: MOORE, 1918
                     No. 430 - Adventurers of purse and person.

12092   MOORE.   Memoirs of Captain Roch (pseud. of Thomas Moore) the celebrated Irish chieftain. With some account of his ancestors.   Written by himself.   Paris, A. & W. Galignani, 1824. xv, 311 p.   19 cm.   "Precaced by the editor" signed: S. E.   4-1769.   DA912.M82

12093   MOORE.   The Moore rental.   Ed. by Thomas Heywood ... (Manchester) Printed for the Chetham society, 1847.   4 p. 1., iii - lii, 158 p.   front. (plan) 23 cm.   (Added t.-p.: Remains historical and literary connected with the palatine counties of Lancaster and Chester.   vol. XII) Contains a historical introduction and many biographical notes concerning tenants and landholders.   Notes on the Stanley family: p. 135-142.   15-25118.   DA670.L19C5 v. 12

12094   MOORE.   Proceedings of the centennial reunion of the Moore family, held at Belleville, Ill., May 31 and June 1, 1882.   Arranged and pub. by Dr. D. N. Moore & McCabe Moore ... St. Louis, Mo., A. R. Fleming, printer, 1882.   82 p.   21½ cm.   9-12328.   CS71.M82   1882

12095   MOORE.   The families of Moir and Byres, by Andrew J. Mitchell Gill of Savock.   Edinburgh, Scott & Ferguson; (etc., etc.,) 1885.   2 p. 1., viii, 232 p., 1 1.   2 pl. (coats of arms) incl. front. 29½ cm.   "This impression consists of two hundred and fifty copies."   15-3545.   CS479.M6   1885

12096   MOORE.   A history of the descendants of Shildes Moore, in America.   Covering a period of one hundred and fifty-nine years, from 1732 to 1891.   By George L. Moore.   (Belleville, Ill., R. A. Moore, 189-)   156, 4, (3) p.   22½ cm.   9-21009.   CS71.M82   189-

12097   MOORE.   The Historical journal of the More family.   no. 1-22.   v. 1, 1-18.   v. 2, no. 1-6, 9-12.   Apr. 1892 - 1926.   Newark, N. J. 1892-1926.   32 nos.   illus. (incl. ports.) 25½ cm.   annual (irregular) Pub. in Newark, N. J., 1892-93; Bangor, Pa., 1896-1902; Seattle, 1904; New York, 1905; Seattle, 1906-Apr. 1915; Roxbury, N. Y., Aug. 1915 - Descendants of John More (1745-1840) of Rosbury, N. Y. Issued by the John More Association.   11-14789.   CS71.M82   1892

12098   MOORE.   History of the More family, and an account of their reunion in 1890, by David Fellows More, under the direction of the Historical committee, with a genealogical record, by Charles Church More.   Binghamton, S. P. More, 1893.   6 p. 1., (iii)-xxxi, 400 p.   front., plates, ports., facsims., map, geneal. tables.   25½ cm.   9-12316.   CS71.M82   1893

12099   MOORE.   A history of Col. James Moore of the revolutionary army, together with an account of his ancestors and descendants and the distribution of his estate, eighty-seven years fater his death, in the case of Hopkins vs. Moore, Supreme court of Pennsylvania, March term, 1814, no. 82, and under the order of the Orphans' court of Philadelphia, April term, 1891, no. 177.   Compiled and edited by G. Heide Norris ... (Philadelphia, Times printing house) 1893.   cover-title, 57 p. fold. geneal. tab. 23 cm.   3-484.   E263.P4M3

12100   MOORE.   Ancestors and descendants of Andrew Moore.   1612-1897.   By John Andrew Moore Passmore ... Philadelphia (Lancaster, Pa., Wickersham printing company) 1897.   2 v.   fronts., plates, ports., coats of arms.   24½ cm.   Paged continuously.   9-12315.   CS71.M82   1897

12101   MOORE.   American ancestral chart, including dates of leading events of a branch of the family of Rev. John Moore of Newtown, L. I., which settled in Pennsylvania.   Compiled from wills, deeds, family records and other authentic sources, by J. W. Moore ... (Easton? Pa.) c. 1897. geneal. tab.   108 x 71½ cm.   fold. to 25½ x 18½ cm.   No. 217.   9-12314.   CS71.M82   1897a

12102   MOORE.   Memorial of the loyalist families of William Moore, Josiah Hitchings and Robert Livingstone, who settled in Saint David, New Brunswick, about the year 1785, and incidentally of other families; comp. by John Elliott Moore.   Lewiston, Printed at the Journal office, 1898.
100 p. front., plates, ports., facsim. 22 cm. 3-22485.   CS71.M82   1898

12103   MOORE.   Descendants of Andrew Moore of Poquonock and Windsor, Conn.   By Hon. Horace L. Moore ... Lawrence, Kan., Journal publishing company, 1900.   11 p. 27 cm. 1-9344.
                                                                                 CS71.M82   1900

12104   MOORE.   Genealogy of a branch of the Moore family, descendants of Deacon John Moore, of Windsor, Conn.   (New York, 1900)   19, (1) p. front. 19½ cm. On cover: The Moore family, 1900. Dedication signed:
Edward Joseph Moore. 40-2262.   CS71.M82   1900a

12105   MOORE.   Mooar (Moors) genealogy.   Abraham Mooar of Andover and his descendants. Boston, Mass., C. H. Pope, 1901.   4 p., 2 l., (7)-97 p. 24½ cm. "Introductory" signed: George Mooar. 4-27137.
                                                                                 CS71.M82   1901

12106   MOORE.   Origin and history of the name of Moore, with biographies of all the most noted persons of that name.   And an account of the origin of surnames and forenames.   Together with over five hundred Christian names of men and women and their significance.   The Crescent family record. Chicago, Ill., American publishers' association, 1902.   5 p. l., iv, 35-112, 14 p., 1 l. illus. 23 cm. Forms for
"Crescent family records": 14 p. at end. 22-17215.   CS71.M82   1902

12107   MOORE.   Andrew Moore of Poquonock and Windsor, Conn., and his descendants, by Hon. Horace L. Moore ... Lawrence, Kan., Journal publishing company, 1903.   308 p. front., ports. 23½ cm.
4-17863.   CS71.M82   1903

12108   MOORE.   Rev. John Moore of Newtown, Long Island, and some of his descendants.   Compiled by James W. Moore ... Easton, Pa., Printed for the publisher by the Chemical publishing company, 1903.   541 p. front., plates, ports., maps, plans, facsims. 33 x 26 cm. 4-6744.

                                                                                 CS71.M82   1903a

12109   MOORE.   Some descendants of John Moore of Sudbury, Mass., by Ethel Stanwood Bolton. Boston, Press of D. Clapp & son, 1904.   22 p. 24½ cm. "Reprinted from New-England historical and genealogical register,
vols. 57 and 58." 4-24948.   CS71.M82   1904

12110   MOORE.   Richard Mower of Lynn and some of his descendants.   Comp. and arranged by Edward L. Smith from material gathered by Nahum W. Mower of Jaffrey, N. H., and Mrs. Earl A. Mower of Lynn, Mass.   East Jaffrey, N. H., The Monadnock press, 1904.   16 p. 23 cm. 5-33950.
                                                                                 CS71.M82   1904a

12111   MOORE. Six centuries of the Moores of Fawley, Berkshire, England, and their descendants amid the titled and untitled aristocracy of Great Britain and America, by David Moore Hall.   Richmond, Va., Printed for the committee by O. E. Flanhart printing co., 1904.   v, (1), 96, (vii)-xi p.
incl. illus. (coats of arms) plates, ports. 22½ cm. 11-27769.   CS71.M82   1904b

12112   MOORE.   Moir genealogy and collateral lines, with historical notes, by Alexander L. Moir .. (Lowell, Mass., The author, c. 1913)   1 p. l., 492 p. front. (coats of arms) illus., plates, ports. 24 cm. p. (402)-411,
blank for "Family record." "Five hundred copies printed. Number 40." 13-21750.   CS71.M82   1913

12113   MOORE.   Chronological history of William and Harriett Moore.   And their relatives and decendents (!) Together with an account of their travels from the time they left England, with their parents ... by U. S. Moore.   Lomas, Ill., 1904.   3 p. l., 2-140 p. incl. illus., pl., ports. 15½ cm. 30-22507.
                                                                                 CS71.M82   1904c

12114   MOORE.   Genealogy and recollections (by) A. A. Moore.   San Francisco, Priv. print. by The Blair-Murdock company, 1915.   viii p., 1 l., 3-170 p. front., plates, ports., facsims. 24½ cm. The plates are all mounted.
15-24480 rev.   CS71.M82   1915

12115   MOORE.   Erminois; a book of family records, compiled by Rev. C. Moor, D. D. ... Kendal, T. Wilson and son, 1918.   xii, 144 p. front., plates, ports., coat of arms. 30 cm. Illustrated t.-p. Contains also the Nicholson, Knight, Hoare and Sale, Frewen, Scott, Congherst, and Laton, Stevens, Grimston, Moon, Cameron and Maitland families. 25-12940.

CS439.M78   1918

12116   MOORE.   The descendants of Ensign John Moor of Canterbury, N. H.   Born 1696 - died, 1786, by Howard P. Moore.   (Rutland, Vt., The Tuttle company) 1918.   370 p. plates, ports., facsims., geneal. tab. 23½ cm. "250 copies printed." Pages 113-124 left blank for "Family record." 21-16577.

CS71.M82   1918

12117   MOORE.   A century of persecution under Tudor and Stuart sovereigns from contemporary records, by the Rev. St. George Kieran Hyland ... With a frontispiece of Loseley hall.   London, K. Paul, T. Trubner & co., ltd.; New York, E. P. Dutton & co., 1920.   xvi, 494 p. front., fold. geneal. tab. 22½ cm. "Loseley manuscripts published in this volume": p. 453-462. "Other documents quoted in this volume": p. 463-465. 20-15464.

BX1492.H8

12118   MOORE.   Mower family history; a genealogical record of the Maine branch of this family, together with other branches of the family tree.   Walter L. Mower, compiler.   Portland, Me., The Southworth press, 1923.   xvii, 233 p. incl. front., ports. coat of arms. 22 cm. 24-340.

CS71.M82   1923

12119   MOORE.   Genealogy of the Moore family of Londonderry, New Hampshire, and Peterboroguh, New Hampshire, 1648-1924.   (Peterborough, N.H., Transcript printing company, 1925)   109, (4) p. front., pl., ports. 23 cm. Foreword signed by Geo. W. Moore, who began the work, and by William Moore and Harriet L. Moore, who completed it. Four pages at end for "Family record". 28-1721.

CS71.M82   1925

12120   MOORE.   ... Moore family records, by J. Montgomery Seaver.   Philadelphia, Pa., American historical-genealogical society (1929)   90, (3) p. front. (incl. 3 port.) coat of arms. 29 cm. Coat of arms of the Moore family on recto of frontispiece and, in colors, on leaf inserted at end. Three blank pages at end for "Family record". "References": p. 89-90. 40-9662.

CS71.M82   1929

12121   MOORE.   Abstract of Moore records of South Carolina, 1694-1865, by Janie Revill.   Columbia, S. C., The State company (c. 1931)   46 p. 23 cm. 31-34608.   CS71.M82   1931

12122   MOORE.   Moore line: paternal lineage of Anna Maria Moore Allen, by Mary Louise Moore and Anna Allen Wright.   (n. p.) 1933.   geneal. tab. 92 x 49 cm. fold. to 38 x 49 cm. Blue-print. 35-28830.

CS71.M82   1933

12123   MOORE.   Edgecombe county records - Moore.   Arranged by Sybil Hyatt.   Kinston, N. C., 1933.   1 l. 28 x 21½ cm. Caption title. Type-written. 44-27974.   CS71.M82   1933a

12124   MOORE.   William Henry Moore and his ancestry, with accounts of the Moore families in the American colonies, 1620-1730 (by) L. Effingham de Forest ... and Anne Lawrence de Forest.   New York, N. Y., The De Forest publishing company, 1934.   2 p. l., ix-xv, 564 p. incl. illus., plates, ports., maps (1 fold.) plans, facsims. front. 26 cm. "This is number 48 of an edition limited to one hundred and fifty copies, designed and privately printed for Edward Small Moore, and Paul Moore." Includes bibliographies. 35-6419.

CS71.M82   1934

12125   MOORE.   The Moore-More-Mure family ... (By Mrs. Edith Tunnell.   Yonkers, N. Y. c. 1935)   2 l. 28 cm. and map 47 x 66 cm. "Other references": leaf 2. 38M5286T.   CS439.M78   1935

12126   MOORE.   Ancestry of Sharpless Moore and Rachel (Roberts) Moore, with their direct ancestors to and including thirty-six first or immigrant ancestors with some old world pedigrees and origins and direct descendants, compiled by their granddaughter Blanche (Moore) Haines.   (Three Rivers? Mich.) 1937.   214 p. front., pl., ports., maps, coats of arms, fold. geneal. tab. 24 cm. Includes bibliography. 38-12410.

CS71.M82   1937

12127   MOORE.   Moore and allied families: the ancestry of William Henry Moore (by) L. Effingham de Forest ... and Anne Lawrence de Forest.   New York, N. Y., The De Forest publishing company, 1938.   xxii, 744 p. incl. front., plates, map, facsims. 25½ cm. Title vignette. "An edition limited to one hundred and fifty copies,' designed and privately printed for Edward Small Moore and Paul Moore, at the Argus press, Albany, New York." Includes bibliographies. 39-9507.

CS71.M82   1938

251

12128   MOORE.   The Moores of Moore hall, by Joseph Hone.   London, J. Cape (1939)
287 p. front., pl., ports. 20½ cm. "First published 1939." 40-13310.   DA916.3.M6H6

12129   MOORE.   Ancestry of Clarence Bloomfield Moore of Philadelphia, by the late Clara Jessup Moore, edited by Baron Harold de Bildt ... and Milton Rubincam. (Washington, D.C., 1940)
8 p. 26½ cm. "Reprinted from National genealogical society quarterly ... March 1940." 40-37505.   CS71.M82   1940

12130   MOORE.   The captives of Abb's valley, a legend of frontier life, by the Rev. James Moore Brown ... New ed., with introduction, notes and appendices, maps and illustrations, by Robert Bell Woodworth, D.S.C.   Staunton, Va., Printed for the author by the McClure co., inc., 1942.
xviii, (2), 94, 254 p. front., illus. (incl. ports., maps) 23½ cm. "The text ... has been printed verbatim from the edition of 1854 issued at Philadelphia, Pa. by the Presbyterian board of publication and Sunday school work, with the four original illustrations." - Foreword. "The house of Moore; genealogical appendix ... by Robert Bell Woodworth": p. 1-254. Includes bibliographies. 43-5510.   E85.B88

12131   MOORE.   Pioneers; a record of the Moore-Downey-Cowger families: who were pioneers of White County, Indiana, and their ancestors (by A. Judson Arrick, Thomas S, Cowger, and John C. Downey) v.1. (Monticello, Ind., 1942?)   187 p. 23 cm. No more published. 72-7108 MARC.   CS71.M82   1942

12132   MOORE.   History of the Moore family. (By Gladys Harper) (Shelbyville, Ill., Shelby county leader, 1946)   cover-title, 3 p. l., 79 p., 1 l. illus., plates, ports., col. coat of arms. 25 cm. Foreword signed: Gladys Harper.
47-15322.   CS71.M82   1946

12133   MOORE.   Chronicles of the More family.   Ed. Grace Van Dyke More.   Published upon the occasion of the sixty-fifth anniversary of the organization of the John More Association. (Greensboro? N.C., 1955)   xvi, 424 p. illus., ports., map. 24 cm. 55-3452.   CS71.M82   1955

12134   MOORE.   Moore genealogy, compiled by Mrs. Herman Moore. (South Plymouth? N.Y., 1962)   17 l. coat of arms. 30 cm. 63-5339.   CS71.M82   1962

12135   MOORE.   The ancestors of Richard Allan Moore and Calvin Cooper Moore, by Robert Allan Moore and Ruth Miller Moore.   Brooklyn, 1964.   iii, 209 p. facsims., geneal. tables, maps. 28 cm. 64-5602.   CS71.M82   1964

12136   MOORE.   The ancestors of Richard Allan Moore and Calvin Cooper Moore, by Robert Allan Moore and Ruth Miller Moore.   Brooklyn, 1964.   iii, 209 p. facsims., geneal. tables, maps. 28 cm. 64-5602.   CS71.M82   1964

12137   MOORE.   The Moore's of Mecklenburg County.   By James Ballagh Moore.   Kochi, Japan (1967?)   96 l. 26 cm. 78-11093 MARC.   CS71.M82   1967

MOORE.   See also:

ALDERMAN, 1957
ATWOOD, CS439.A8
BACKHOUSE, DA690.M74C3
BAKER, 1961
BASSETT, 1926
BROWN, 1931
BROWN, 1939a
CAIRNS, CS479.C16
CLEEK, 1957
CORN, 1959
HAYNES, 1902
HOOD, 1960

HUTCHINS, 1938
JAMES, 1913a
JAMES, 1961
JUNKINS, 1908
KATHAN 1902
LAWRENCE, F127.L8N5
LEWIS, 1901
LUXMOORE, CS439.L89
McCLARY, E171.A53 v.13
MAXWELL, 1916
MILLER, 1968

O'MORE.
PRICE, 1944
REICHNER, 1918
ROBERTS, F159.R48R6
SELDEN, 1911
SIAS, 1953
TODD, 1909
TRUESDELL, 1960
No. 579 - Monroe, N.H.
No. 1547 - Cabell county.
No. 3509 - Orange county.

MOORE.   See also L.C. additions and corrections page 15.

12138   MOORHEAD.   History of the Moorhead family, from the latter part of the sixteenth century to the present time.   Compiled and published by A. T. Moorhead.   Indiana, Pa., 1901.   79, 7 p. ports. 20 cm. 4-27257.   CS71.M825   1901

12139   MOORHEAD.   Whirling spindle; the story of a Pittsburgh family, by Elizabeth Moorhead ...
(Pittsburgh) University of Pittsburgh press, 1942.   xix p., 1 l., 317 p., 1 l. incl. front. plates, ports., facsims. 22 cm.
43-9655.   CS71.M825   1942

        MOORHEAD.   See also: BARNETT, 1882
                                 MOREHEAD.

12140   MOORHOUSE.   Will of Thomas Moorhouse.   Re: Moorhouse genealogy.   Moorhouse letters.
(London? Ont., 1942)   1 p. l., 2, 15, 13 numb. l. 29 cm.   Type-written copy (carbon) made by Edwin Seaborn from original manuscripts. 43-3682.   CT310.M58W5

12141   MOORHOUSE.   The Moorhouses of Bear Creek, Bathurst, and Brockville.   By Eric Gelling
Moorhouse.   Kingston, Can., Jackson Press, c.1962.   411 p. illus. 24 cm. 63-5338.
                                                                                                    CS71.M839   1962

        MOORHOUSE.   See also RHODES-MOORHOUSE.

12142   MOORMAN.   History of the Moorman family.   (By Leila Venable (Mason) Eldridge) (Atlanta,
1942)   cover-title, 27 p. 16½ cm.   Reprint, with additions on the Jones family by Harrison Jones, of a series of articles by Mrs. Thomas
Moorman Eldridge issued in the Sunday American, Atlanta. cf. Foreword. 43-2863.   CS71.M83   1942

12143   MOORMAN.   An extensible genealogy of the Moorman family from Zachariah (English) and
Mary Chandler (Irish) A.D.1620.   With compendium of name-finder, biographical (cento) notes, and
bibliography, by Virginia T. Neuberger (and others.   Norman? Okla., 1956 -   1 v. (loose-leaf) geneal.
tables. 58 cm. Cover title: Moorman - an American genealogy. Holograph and typescript copy. Errata slips inserted. 57-29526.
                                                                                                    CS71.M83   1956

12144   MOORMAN.   The descendants of Zachariah Moorman, in the male line.   By Ambrose Carroll
Moorman.   (St. Benedict? Or.) 1966.   (18) l. coat of arms. 28 cm. Bibliography: leaf (18) 68-1798.
                                                                                                    CS71.M83   1966

        MOORMAN.   See also: CLARK, 1934
                                 MOON, 1939
                                 REYNOLDS, 1950

        MOORS.   See MOORE, M.82

        MORAN.   See: GARDNER, 1959
                       WHITAKER, 1935

        MORARTY.   See VANDERPYL, 1933

12145   MORDAUNT.   Massingham Parva, past and present.   By the Rev. Ronald F. McLeod.
London, Waterlow & sons, limited, 1882.   xiv, 163 p. 27 cm. "Pedigree of the Mordaunts of Massingham Parva": p. xiv.
"Births, marriages and deaths extracted from the parish registers"; p. (139)-163. 16-20940.
                                                                                                    DA690.M475M3

        MORDAUNT.   See also: ALNO, CS419.(3
                                 BOLEYNE, CS438.R4

        MORDECAI.   See MYERS, 1913

        MORE.   See MOORE.

        MOREAU.   See LOWE, 1940

12146   MOREHEAD.   Family records of the "Morehead", Turner, Elliott, Warder, Morris, Hooe,
Shotwell, Nebecker, Russell families.   Los Angeles, Cal., Press of the Neuner co. (19 -)   40 numb. l.
37 x 23 cm. Preface signed: Charles R. Morehead. Mimeographed. Text runs parallel with back of cover. 34-14611.
                                                                                                    CS71.M835   19 -

12147   MOREHEAD.   The Morehead family of North Carolina and Virginia (by) John Motley Morehead (III) New York, Priv. print. (by the De Vinne press) 1921.   x p., 2 l., 3-147, (1) p. front., illus., plates, ports., col. coat of arms. 31 cm. Plates are accompanied by guard sheet with descriptive letterpress. "Edition of fity copies." This copy not numbered. 21-6431.   CS71.M835   1921

MOREHEAD.   See also MOORHEAD.

12148   MOREHOUSE.   Ancestry and descendants of Gershom Morehouse, jr. of Redding, Connecticut, a captain in the American revolution.   (New Haven, Conn., Press of Tuttle, Morehouse & Taylor, 1894)   40 p., 1 l. 22 cm. "Compiled from information furnished by Mr. Nelson D. Adams ... Mr. A. W. Morehouse ... Mr. Augustus C. Golding ... and from town, state and family records." "Printed for private circulation by a descendants of Captain Gershom Morehouse." Cornelius Starr Morehouse. 8-19268.   CS71.M838   1894

MOREHOUSE.   See also MALTBY, 1895

MOREL.   See: DU BOISBAUDRY, 1958
                      LAFITTE, 1927

12149   MORELAND.   Thanks for yesterday; the Moreland family history (1796-1956)   By Edna (Robertson) Moreland.   (Greenville? Pa., 1956)   53 p. illus. 19 cm. 58-49105.   CS71.M84   1956

MOREY.   See MOWRY.

MORFORD.   See ROOSEVELT, 1902

12150   MORGAN.   Our family genealogy.   Printed for the family, but not published.   Morgan. Avery ... William Avery Morgan ... Hartford, Press of Case, Tiffany and company, 1851. 16 p. 23½ cm. Preface signed: N.H. Morgan. 1-28288.   CS71.M848   1851

12151   MORGAN.   Morgan genealogy.   A history of James Morgan, of New London, Conn., and his descendants; from 1607 to 1869 ... With an appendix, containing the history of his brother, Miles Morgan, of Springfield, Mass.; and some of his descendants ... By Nathaniel H. Morgan.   Hartford, Press of Case, Lockwood & Brainard, 1869.   280 p., 1 l. front., illus., ports. 23½ cm. "A history of the family of Miles Morgan, who emigrated from England, and settled at Springfield, Mass., A.D. 1636, compiled by Titus Morgan, jun., one of his descendants. Middletown, Oct. 1809": p. (227)-246. 9-13820.   CS71.M848   1869

12152   MORGAN.   Limbus patrum Morganiae et Glamorganiae.   Being the genealogies of the older families of the lordships of Morgan and Glamorgan.   Now, for the first time, collected, collated and printed by George T. Clark ... With indexes of names and places.   London, Wyman & sons, 1886. 2 p. l., 620 p. fold. geneal. tables. 26 cm. 16-10156.   CS458.G6C6

12153   MORGAN.   Collections towards historical and gnealogical memoirs of the Morgan family as represented in the Peerage of England by the Right Hon. the Lord Tredegar.   Comp. and ed. by G. Blacker Morgan.   Memorials of John ap Morgan of Caerleon, obiit 1524; and of Edward Morgan of Llantarnam abbey, Monmouthshire, 1549-1633.   With autotype of portrait and fac-similes of documents and of the old heraldic stained glass at Llantarnam abbey, etc.   London, Priv. print., 1890.   42 p. front. (port.) fold. facsims., col. coats of arms. 27 cm. At head of title: coat of arms. 20-18037.   CS439.M783

12154   MORGAN.   A history of the family of Morgan, from the year 1089 to present times.   By Appleton Morgan, of the twenty-seventh generation of Cadivor-fawr.   New York, For subscribers only (1902?)   297 p. incl. plates, ports. front., pl., ports. 21½ cm. Five hundred copies printed, of which this is no. 461. 3-11084.   CS71.M848   1902

12155   MORGAN.   The Miles Morgan family of Springfield, Massachusetts, in the line of Joseph Morgan of Hartford, Connecticut, 1780-1847.   By Frank Farnsworth Starr.   Hartford, Conn., 1904.   72 p. front. (fold. geneal. tab.) 25½ cm. Compiled and enlarged by Frank Farnsworth Starr, from a sketch by Dr. Titus Morgan of his branch of the Morgan family. 40-37506.   CS71.M848   1904

12156   MORGAN.   History of the descendants of David Morgan in America, geanology (!) traced through the Morgan and Howard families, written and published by William Allen Daily.   Indianapolis, Ind., 1909.   cover-title, 11 p. 25 cm. 37-5918.   CS71.M848   1909

12157   MORGAN.   Historical reference to Pricketts' fort and its defenders, with incidents of border warfare in the Monongahela Valley and ceremonies at unveiling of monument marking site of Prickett's fort, erected in 1774; including brief sketches of Major William Haymond and the ancestors of the Morgan and Prickett families, by Henry Haymond ... (Clarksburg? W. Va., 191-?)   16 p. illus. 23 cm.
"Roll of Captain William Haymond's company of Monongalia County militia while stationed at Prickett's fort ... April, May, and June ... 1777": p. 10. "Pay roll ...": p. 12. 21-13615.   E83.77.H4

12158   MORGAN.   Descendants of Thomas Morgan, b.1756, and his wife Jane Jenner, b.1767, d. 1835 ... (n.p., 1913?)   geneal. tab. 43 x 28 cm. fold. to 21½ x 10 cm. Signed in ms.: Reginald B. Henry. 19-4282.   CS71.M848   1913

12159   MORGAN.   Ancestry and descendants of Catherine Weas of West Virginia.   Compiled from sources in the Historical department of Iowa by Lizzie E. Boice Jones and Martha Armstrong Watson. Des Moines, Ia., 1920.   geneal. tab., illus. (coats of arms) 111½ x 235 cm. fold. to 36 cm. Cover-title: Genealogy. Family of Zedekiah Morgan, revolutionary sodier from Connecticut. Blue print. 24-20331.   CS71.M848   1920

12161   MORGAN.   Francis Morgan, an early Virginia burgess, and some of his descendants. Comp. by Annie Noble Sims, from the notes of Mr. Willim Owen Nixon Scott, and from original sources. Savannah, Ga., Braid & Hutton, inc., printers, 1920.   1 p. l., 194, xi p. 23 cm. 20-23921.
                                                                                         VS71.M848   1920a

12162   MORGAN.   ... Report of the Col. Morgan Morgan monument commission ... Charleston, W. Va. (Jarrett printing co.) 1924.   99 p. incl. front., illus., ports., facsims., geneal. tab. 23 cm. At head of title:
State of West Virginia. Haze Morgan, chairman of the working committee. Edition limited to nine hundred copies, of which this is number 861.
"A brief history of the family of Colonel Morgan Morgan (by French Morgan)": p. (64)-97. 25-27118.   F241.M84

12163   MORGAN.   The families of John Rittenhouse Morgan, John Orsemus Stanley and Daniel Woolsey Blatchley, compiled by Anna Stanley Blatchley. (Fort Scott? Kan., 1929)   cover-title, (45) p.
23½ cm. "References": p. (4) Author's autographed presentation copy. 31-18496.   CS71.M848   1929

12164   MORGAN.   Morgan and allied families, compiled for Mrs. Walter Samuel Carpenter, Jr. by George Valentine Massey. (n.p.) 1941.   117 p. 30 cm. "Bibliography of sources covered": p. 113-117. 50-43163
                                                                                         CS71.M848   1941

12165   MORGAN.   A history & genealogy of the family of Col. Morgan Morgan, the first white settler of the State of West Virginia. By French Morgan. Washington, 1950.   476 l., 200 p. maps,
28 cm. Typescript. "Four copies typed of which this is no. 4." Bibliography: leaf 476. 52-28100.
                                                                                         CS71.M848   1950

12166   MORGAN.   Ancestry of Richard Dorsey Morgan. By George Valentine Massey. (Dover? Del., 1953)   x, 160 p. illus., ports., geneal. tables. 25 cm. Bibliographical footnotes. 54-2111.
                                                                                         CS71.M848   1953

12166a   MORGAN.   Ancestors of William Morgan, 1769-1825, Pembroke, N.H.; Richard Morgan, progenitor.   By Helen (Richardson) Kluegel. Honolulu, 1962.   1 v. 29 cm. 63-30223.
                                                                                         CS71.M848   1962

12167   MORGAN.   Morgan-Holdridge family.   By LaDoris (Morgan) Whitney.   Dallas, SMU Print. Dept., 1965.   1 v. (unpaged) 30 cm. 65-8489.   CS71.M848   1965

12168   MORGAN.   A history and genealogy of the family of Col. Morgan Morgan, the first white settler of the State of West Virginia. By French Morgan. Washington, 1950 (i.e.1966)   442, 217, 11 p.
illus., maps, ports. 21 cm. Cover title: Descendants of Colonel Morgan Morgan. Originally issued in four typescript copies; reissued with additions. Supplement, 1966, by Virginia Chaplin Tuttle (11 p., 3d group) also issued separately. Bibliography: p. 441. 66-17770 rev.
                                                                                         CS71.M848   1966

12169   MORGAN.   A family history of David Morgan, James W. Ross, Charles Thomas Birch, and following generations, by Bernhard Martin Mehl and John Emory Birch.   Writings compiled by Marjory Mehl Goodenough.   (1st ed. Anaheim, Calif., Printed by United Reprographics, 1967)   42 l.   28 cm.
Bibliography: leaf 38.   67-19858.   CS71.M848   1967

12170   MORGAN.   George Morgan, pioneer importer and breeder of American herefords, by B. W. Allred.   With appendixes prepared by W. R. Pagel.   Oldtown, Md., 1967.   22, 4, 6, 6 l.   ports.   30 cm.
77-7609 MARC.   CS71.M848   1967b

12171   MORGAN.   (Supplement to CS71.M848 1962 - Helen Richardson Kluegel, Ancestors of William Morgan, 1769-1825)   In vertical file.   Ask reference librarian for this material.

MORGAN.   See also:

AVERY, 1926	FISH, 1941	POOL, 1958
BOONE, 1922	FORBES, CS479.F6	REICHNER, 1918
CARPENTER, 1950	GOODWIN, 1915	RITTENHOUSE, 1897
CORN, 1959	JOHNSON, 1961	STRANGE, 1915
CROSSLEY, CS439.C835	LONG, 1925	STUART, 1938
DE RAPELJE, 1948	MINER, 1901	WALWORTH, E171.A53 v.20
DUNHAM, 1956	PLUMB, E171.A53 v.15	YATES, 1906

MORGELL.   See BRERWOOD, DA690.C5E2

MORIN.   See CHOQUETT, F1054.R5D3

MORISON.   See MORRISON.

MORLEY.   See: CASS, DA690.B23C3
                 COOK, HV250.D6J3

12172   MORNAY.   ... A huguenot family in the XVI century.   The memoirs of Philippe De Mornay, sieur du Plessis Marly, written by his wife.   (Charlotte Arbaleste de Mornay)   Translated by Lucy Crump, with an introduction.   London, G. Routledge & sons, ltd.; New York, E. P. Dutton & co. 1926?)   2 p. l., iii-vii, 300 p.   front., plates, ports.   23 cm.   (Half-title: Broadway translations)   This translation is from the edition edited by Mme. de Witt, for the Société de l'histoire de France, 1868.   26-5753.   DC112.M95

12173   MORR.   Genealogy of the Morr family.   By Calvin F. Moyer.   Assisted by Miss Mary E.
Morr.   Ashland, O., Printed by The Sun publishing company, 1896.   295 p. incl. pl.   23½ cm.   9-12310.
                                                                                                  CS71.M872   1896

MORRELL.   See MORRILL, M874

MORRES.   See MONTMORENCY.

12174   MORRILL.   The Morrills of the seventeenth century, and the first generation of the eighteenth, in America.   Camden, Ala., Printed by E. D. Morrill, 1886.   geneal. tab.   43½ x 30 cm.   23-18590.
                                                                                                  CS71.M874   1886

12175   MORRILL.   American ancestry of Benjamin Morrill and his wife, Miriam Pecker Morrill, of Salisbury, Mass., and their descendants of 1901;   compiled by Horace Edwin Morrill.   Dayton, O., 1903.   5-21 p.   23½ cm.   2 blank leaves between p. 12 and (17) included in paging.   4-29760.
                                                                                                  CS71.M874   1903

12176   MORRILL.   Hibbard Morrill and his descendants 1640-1910.   Written and comp. by Mrs. Betsey Morrill Spencer ... (Middlebury, Vt., Press of Seymour brothers, 1910)   47 p.   22½ cm.   Blank pages for births, marriages, etc. at end.   11-7228.   CS71.M874   1910

12177   MORRILL.   Morrill kindred in America ... by Annie Morrill Smith ... New York, The Lyons genealogical company, 1914-31.   2 v. fronts., illus., plates, ports., maps, facsims., coats of arms, 2 fold. geneal. tab. 23½ cm.   Vol. 2 published by the Grafton press.   The genealogical tables are at the end of v.1 with blank pages for additional records.   Bibliography: v.1, p.133-135.   Vol. 1. Ann account of the descendants of Abraham Morrill of Salisbury, Massachusetts 1632-1662 through his eldest son Isaac Morrill 1640-1713. - v.2. An account of the descendants of Abraham Morrill of Salisbury, Massachusetts 1632-1662, through his three sons, Mr. Isaac, Capt. Jacob and Lieut. Moses Morrill, to 1931.   14-19997 rev.   CS71.M874   1914

12178   MORRILL.   The ancestry of Daniel Morrell of Hartford, with his descendants and some contemporary families, compiled by Francis V. Morrell ... (Hartford) J.W.Morrell, 1916.   2 p. l., 126 p. front., illus. (coat of arms) ports. facsim. 23 cm.   "Printed for private distribution, no. 219."   16-14585.   CS71.M874   1916

12179   MORRILL.   The Morrills and reminiscences, by Charles Henry Morrill.   Chicago, and Lincoln, University publishing co. (c.1918)   2 p. l., 160 p. front., plates, ports., fold. geneal. tab. 20 cm.   Autobiography.   18-11150.   CS71.M874   1918

12180   MORRILL.   Morrill lineage, by Lois Fooshee Williamson.   Topeka, Kan., M. and M. Print. Co., 1964.   27 p. coat of arms, facsim., ports. 22 cm.   65-2429.   CS71.M874   1964

12181   MORRILL.   Three generations; the fortunes of a Yorkshire family.   By Anne Vernon. London, Jarrolds, 1966.   191 p. front. (diagr.) 16 plates (incl. ports., facsims.) map, 23½ cm.   Bibliography: p. 185.   66-76784.   CS439.M4   1966

MORRILL.   See also: LOGAN, 1923
                            LOVELL, 1940
                            TUCKER, 1957

12182   MORRIS.   (A lithographed tree chart of the descendants of Anthony Morris, 2d born at St. Dunstans Stepney of London, Aug. 23, 1654 and his wife Mary Jones)   Compiled by Anthony Saunders Morris.   Philadelphia, Printed by F. Bourquin & co., 1861.   geneal. tab. 180 x 150 cm. (6 x 5 ft.) fold. to 46 x 47 cm.   38M2921T.   CS71.M876   1861   Office.

12183   MORRIS.   The lineal ancestors of Edward Morris and Mercy Flynt, of Wilbraham, Mass. Comp. by Jonathan Flynt Morris ... Hartford, Press of Wiley, Waterman & Eaton, 1882.   74, (1) p. 23 cm.   For private circulation.   Only 60 copies printed.   3-3837.   CS71.M876   1882

12184   MORRIS.   A genealogical and historical register of the descendants of Edward Morris of Roxbury, Mass., and Woodstock, Conn.   Comp. by Jonathan Flynt Morris ... Hartford, Conn., Pub. by the compiler (Case, Lockwood & Brainard co., printers) 1887.   xvii, 406 p. front., plates, ports. facsim. 24 cm.   9-12312.   CS71.M876   1887

12185   MORRIS.   A sketch of the life of Sylvester Morris, by his grand-daughter Kate Morris Cone. Boston, Printed by A. Mudge & son, 1887.   44 p. 2 port. (incl. front.) 22½ cm.   Contains genealogical notes of the Morris, Converse, Washburn and Weston families.   16-17952.   CS71.M876   1887a

12186   MORRIS.   Ephraim and Pamela (Converse) Morris, their ancestors and descendants.   By Tyler Seymour Morris.   Chicago, 1894.   207 p. front., pl., ports., maps (part fold.) 24½ cm.   9-12311.   CS71.M876   1894

12187   MORRIS.   The Morris family of Philadelphia; descendants of Anthony Morris, born 1654 - 1721 died.   By Robert C. Moon ... Philadelphia, R. C. Moon, 1898-1909.   5 v. fronts., plates, ports., maps, facsims. 26 cm.   Vols. 1-3 paged continuously; v.4-5, supplement, paged continuously.   Vols. 1-3 published in 1898; v.4 in 1908; v.5 in 1909.   CS71.M876   1898

——— Descendants of Samuel Morris, 1734-1812.   Supplement.   Philadelphia, 1959. vii, 163 p. port. 27 cm.   Prepared and brought up to date by the Morris Family Publication Committee.   98-1344 rev. 3.   CS71.M876   1898   Suppl.

12188   MORRIS.   Among ourselves: to a mother's memory; being a life story of principally seven generations, especially of the Morris-Trueblood branch, including not only descendants of Benoni and Rebecca (Trueblood) Morris, but their relatives and connections ... by Sarah P. Morrison,   v. 1- ... Plainfield, Ind., Publishing association of Friends, 1901 -   v. fronts., plates, ports. 19½ cm. Contents. - v.1. Out of North Carolina. - v.2. Catherine and her surroundings. - v.3. Catherine and her household. 2-3285 rev.   CS71.M876 1901-04

12189   MORRIS.   The ancestry of Rosalie Morris Johnson, duaghter of George Calvert Morris and Elizabeth Kuhn, his wife, comp. by R. Winder Johnson.   (Philadelphia) Printed for private circulation only by Ferris & Leach, 1905-08.   2 v. front., facsim., geneal. tables. 27½ cm. Vol. 1 not numbered. Vol. 2 contains mainly a record of the Flemish ancestry of the Stier family. 5-42413.   CS71.M876   1905

12190   MORRIS.   The Morris family of Morrisania.   By W. W. Spooner.   (In American historical magazine. New York, 1906. 24½ cm. v. 1, no. 1, p.25-44. illus. (ports.) 9-3907.

                     E171.A53 vol.1
—— Copy 2, detached.   CS71.M876   1906

12191   MORRIS.   Descendants of Lewis Morris of Morrisania, b.1671, d.1746, first governor of New Jersey as a separate province, 1738-1746.   Compiled by Elizabeth Morris Lefferts.   New York, Arranged and printed by T. A. Wright (1907?)   106 1. 50 x 31 cm. Printed on one side of leaf only. 8-2768.
                      CS71.M876   1907

12192   MORRIS.   A transcript of the register of the parish church, Bretforten, in the county and diocese of Worcester, from A. D.1538 to A. D.1837; transcribed and ed. with XXIII appendices, by the Rev. W. H. Shawcross ... The indexes by Miss Muriel Wilson.   Evesham (Eng.) H. W. Mayer, 1908. 5 p. l., 4, (1), 4-83, 107 numb. l. pl., 3 port. 30 x 23½ cm. Includes three half-titles: Volume I. The Bretforten register ... Volume II. The 23 appendices ... Index to the appendices ... "Eighty copies only of this work have been printed, ... 10-9484.

                  CS436.B73

12193   MORRIS.   The Morris family of South Molton, Devon, by R. Burnet Morris ... For private circulation.   Guildford, Printed by Billing & sons, limited, 1908.   50 numb. l. fold. geneal. tab. 27½ cm. 20-15218.   CS439.M785

12194   MORRIS.   Genealogy of the Morris family; descendants of Thomas Morris of Connecticut, comp. by Mrs. Lucy Ann (Morris) Carhart; ed. by Charles Alexander Nelson, A.M.   New York, The A. S. Barnes company, 1911.   ix, 478 p. front. (port.) 23 cm. 11-8581.   CS71.M876   1911

12195   MORRIS.   The Morris manor; address delivered at the fifth annual meeting of the New York branch of the Order or colonial lords of manors in America, December 9, 1916, by Lucy D. Akerly ... (Baltimore? 1916?)   29 p. incl. col. front. illus. (ports.) 23½ cm. (Order of colonial lords of manors in America. New York branch. Publications. 20-16020.   E186.99.O6N5
—— Copy 2.   F128.68.B8A3

12196   MORRIS.   The records of the Morris family, by S. L. Morris ... Atlanta, Ga., Hubbard bros, (1922)   104 p. incl. front., illus., ports. 20½ cm. 22-25792.   CS71.M876   1922

12197   MORRIS.   Descendants of the Rev. Isaac Morris ... by Scotland G. Highland ... An historical and genealogical narrative ... (Clarksburg, W. Va., 1928)   1 p. l., 9 p. 30 cm. Reprinted from the Clarksburg exponent-telegram, Clarksburg, W. Va., Sunday, July 1, 1928. 28-25720.   CS71.M876   1928

12198   MORRIS.   ... Morris family records, by J. Montgomery Seaver.   Philadelphia, American historical-genealogical society (1929?)   51 p. illus. (ports.) 23½ cm. Pages 50-51 blank for "Family record". Coat of arms of Morris family on cover. "References": p. 49. 40-18916.   CS71.M876   1929

12199   MORRIS.   ... A genealogy of a tribe of noble patriots; uncovering the hidden past for a period of 200 years 1734-1934; a brief historical sketch of the Morris-Beck-Dean-Chipley families and coordinate families, Sanders-Turner-Patton-Highland, compiled by Charles E. Dean ... (New Orleans, c,1935)   cover-title, (3)-74 p. illus. (part col.; incl. ports.) 31 cm. "Edition limited." Duplicates of pages 5-6, 71-72 laid in. "Descendants of Rev. Isaac Morris." Text on pages (2) - (3) of cover. 35-32763.
                  CS71.M876   1935

12200   MORRIS.   Handbook of the James Morris museum and the Aline Brothier Morris reading room, compiled by the trustees of the Aline Brothier Morris fund; edited by C. Murray Keefer ... Morris, Conn. (c. 1935)   1 p. l., 60 p. plates, ports. 19 cm.   Contents. - The James Morris library building. - Views of James Morris museum and Aline Brothier Morris reading room. - The Morris family. - Deacon James Morris. - Major James Morris. - Colonel Dwight Morris. - Aline Brothier Morris. - Gift in trust to the town of Morris.   35-8736.   Z733.M87

12201   MORRIS.   The east side of New Haven harbor; Morris cove (Solitary cover), the Annex (the Indian reservation), South end & Waterside, 1644 to 1868, by Marjorie F. Hayward; text and maps based on researches by Marjorie F. Hayward and Donald V. Chidsey, frontispiece & maps drawn by Don Forrer.   New Haven, New Haven colony historical society, 1938.   viii, 86 p. front., illus. (maps) 24 cm.   "Published by the Pardee-Morris house committee on the Pardee genealogical fund."   Bibliography: p. 82.   38-38247.

F104.N6H37

12202   MORRIS.   The Morris family tree; a genealogy with history and biographies, compiled and published by Oliver M. Morris.   Long Beach, Calif., 1940.   168 p. incl. plates, ports. 28 cm.   On cover: The Jonathan II and Abigail Morris family tree, 1789-1940.   41-11040.   CS71.M876   1940

12203   MORRIS.   The Isaac Morris family, with the connecting families, by Franklin Morris.   Editor, Maude Ladell Fletcher.   Amarillo, Tex., 1941.   18 p. l., 100 numb. l. 28½ cm.   Reproduced from type- written copy.   42-15622.   CS71.M876   1941

12204   MORRIS.   Morris family; (also) Arnold, Barrett, Clark, Hill, Keaton, Nicholson, Page, Pool, Pritchard, Prather, Shattuck, Symons (and) White (families.   Minneapolis, 1952?)   7 l. 28 cm.   54-19889.   CS71.M876   1952

12205   MORRIS.   Roster, 1953, Morris family.   (n. p., 1953)   unpaged. 28 cm.   53-40250.
CS71.M876   1953

12206   MORRIS.   A Morris family of Mecklenburg County, North Carolina.   By Whitmore Morris. (San Antonio? 1956)   128 p. 24 cm.   56-29466.   CS71.M876   1956

12207   MORRIS.   Morris genealogy, 1605 to 1959.   By Nelle (Morris) Jenkins.   Tuscaloosa, Ala., Willo Pub. Co. (1959)   172 p. illus. 23 cm.   59-51285.   CS71.M876   1959

12208   MORRIS.   Some descendants of Richard Morris and Sarah Pole of Morrisania, with many collateral lineages.   By Kathryn (Morris) Wilkinson.   Milwaukee, 1966.   xi, 292 p. illus., ports. 29 cm.   Cover title: A Morris lineage.   Includes bibliographies.   67-3389.   CS71.M876   1966

MORRIS.   See also:

12209   MORRISON.   The history of the Morison or Morrison family with most of the "Traditions of the Morrisons" (clan Mac Gillemhuire), hereditary judges of Lewis, by Capt. F. W. L. Thomas, of Scotland, and a record of the descendants of the hereditary judges to 1880.   A complete history of the Morison settlers of Londonderry, N.H., of 1719, and their descendants, with genealogical sketches. Also, of the Brentwood, Nottingham, and Sanbornton, N. H. Morisons, and branches of the Morisons who settled in Delaware, Pennsylvania, Virginia, and Nova Scotia, and descendants of the Morisons of Preston Grange, Scotland, and other families.   By Leonard A. Morison ... Boston, Mass., A. Williams & co., 1880.   468 p. front., illus., plates, ports, fold. map. 24 cm.   9-12309.   CS71.M88   1880

12210   MORRISON.   John Hopkins Morison, a memoir.   (By George Shattuck Morison.)   Boston and New York, Houghton, Mifflin and company, 1897.   v p., 1 l., 298 p. 2 ports. (incl. front.) 20½ cm.   "Prepared by Dr. Morison's children." - Pref.   "List of published writings of John H. Morison": p. (291)-293.   13-2730.   F74. M66M78

12211   MORRISON.   Genealogy of the descendants of John Morrison and Prudence Gwyn ... Presented by George H. Morrison, Montgomery, N.Y.   (Newburgh?) Newburgh journal print, 1907.
2 p. l., 31 numb. geneal. tab. (part double) 33½ cm.   17-30089.   CS71.M88   1907

12212   MORRISON.   The Morrison family ...   (New York, Printed by Manger, Hughes & Manger)
1923.   (16) p. incl. coat of arms. 16½ cm.   24-8613.   CS71.M88   1923

12213   MORRISON.   The centenary of James Morison, the "hygeist," by John Malcolm Bulloch.
(Aberdeen) Aberdeen university press, 1925.   cover-title, 24 p. incl. geneal. tab.   pl.   22 cm.   25-15878.
R489. M6B8

12214   MORRISON.   History of a branch of the Morrison family whose progenitor emigrated to America, and located in Virginia in colonial days ... Also a sketch of the New Hampshire and Pennsylvania Morrisons settling in those states at an earlier date.   By Granville Price Morrison ... (Charleston, W. Va., Jarrett printing co., 1928?)   103 p.   illus. (incl. ports., coat of arms) 23½ cm.   29-13047.
CS71.M88   1928

12215   MORRISON.   Samuel Morrison of Bucks and Lycoming counties, Pennsylvania and some of his descendants, with a brief sketch of John Owen, 1741-1843, of Carroll township, Chautauqua county, New York and his descendants, compiled and edited by E. J. P. Sage.   (n. p.) 1934.   3 p. l., 90 numb. l.,
7 l. 17 cm.   "Privately printed. no. 3."   Photostat reproduction (positive)   Collation of original: 2 p. l., 90, (4) p.   Type-written and manuscript additions reproduced from original copy.   "Reference authorities" and foot-notes.   35-13997.
CS71.M88   1934

12216   MORRISON.   The Morrison family of the Rocky River settlement of North Carolina; history and genealogy by Adelaide and Eugenia Lore and Robert Hall Morrison.   By Adelaide McKinnon Lore.
(Charlotte? N. C., 1950)   543 p.   illus., maps. 24 cm.   Bibliography: p. 506.   50-37568.   CS71.M88   1950

12217   MORRISON.   Nathaniel Morison and his descendants.   By George Abbot Morison.   Peterborough, N. H., Peterborough Historical Soceity, 1951.   220 p.   illus., ports., geneal. table. 24 cm.   52-29341.
CS71.M88   1951

12218   MORRISON.   The Clan Morrison; heritage of the Isles.   By Alick Morrison.   Edinburgh,
W. & A. K. Johnston (1956)   31 p.   illus. 19 cm.   (W. & A.K. Johnston's Clan histories) 58-38693.
CS479.M77   1956

12219   MORRISON.   Tombstone inscriptions of Cherry Fork Cemetery, Adams County, Ohio, and genealogical gleanings, compiled by Lillian Colletta and Leslie E. Puckett.   Denville, N.J., 1964.
viii, 91 p.   illus., map. 28 cm.   65-3529.   F499.C38C6

12220   MORRISON.   The Morrison family of Arkansas and other places and their relatives by marriage.   Compiled by D. A. Morrison.   San Jose, Calif. (1968)   221 p.   coats of arms, facsims. ports.
30 cm.   68-5719.   CS71.M88   1968

        MORRISON.   See also: ADAMS, CS71.A2
                           BENJAMIN, CS71.B468
                           BLACKHALL, CS479.B6
                           BLACKHALL, DA750.N5 no. 29
                           EARHART, 1935
                           STROWBRIDGE, 1891

        MORRON.   See FLAGG, 1903

        MORROW.   See: COCHRAN, CT275.C656C6
                        PEDEN, 1961
                        STAIRS, 1906

12221　MORSE.　Memorial of the Morses; containing the history of seven persons of the name, who settled in America in the seventeenth century.　With a catalogue of ten thousand of their descendants. ... Boston, W. Veazie, 1850.　viii, 225, (156) p.　coats of arms (part col.) plates, ports., map.　24 cm.　By Abner Morse. 1-13573.　　　　CS71.M885　1850

12222　MORSE.　Life, letters, and wayside gleanings, for the folks at home.　By Mrs. B. H. Crane ... Boston, J. H. Crane ... Boston, J. H. Earle (1880)　480 p. incl. front. (port.) 22½ cm.　The experiences of a minister's wife in various parishes.　Contents. - 1st book.　The Morses and Vermont. - 2d book.　Northampton.　To friends at home. - 3d book. Boston. - 4th book.　Dorchester. - 5th book.　Woonsocket, R.I., in 1867. - 6th book.　Greenfield, Mass. - 7th book.　North Springfield, Vt. - 8th book, Retiring from the field.　12-31662.　　　　F8.C89

12223　MORSE.　The Morse record.　A history of the proceedings of the Morse society in annual meetings, December 4, 1895, and a souvenir of the dinner at the Windsor hotel, New York city, on the same evening.　Hartford, Plimpton print (1895)　44 p.　front. (port.) 24 cm.　2 leaves following p. 7 inserted. Edited by J. H. Morse.　9-12307.　　　　CS71.M885　1895

12224　MORSE.　Memorial of the family of Morse.　Compiled from the original records for the Hon. Asa Porter Morse, by Henry Dutch Lord.　For private distirbution only.　Cambridgeport, Mass., Harvard printing company, 1896.　(556) p.　front., pl., ports., facsim., coats of arms.　22½ cm.　Various pagings. 　　　　CS71.M885　1896

———— Index, family of Morse, compiled by Mrs. G. M. Brumbaugh.　(n. p., n. d.) (61) p.　26½ cm.　9-12308 rev.　　　　CS71.M885　1896

12225　MORSE.　Morse genealogy, comprising the descendants of Samuel, Anthony, William, and Joseph Morse and John Moss: being a revision of the Memorial of the Morses, pub. by Rev. Abner Morse in 1850.　Comp, by J. Howard Morse and Miss Emily W. Leavitt under the auspices of the Morse society.　New York (Springfield, Mass., Springfield printing and binding company) 1903 - v. in　23 cm.　Title vignette (seal of the society)　6-1314.　　　　CS71.M885　1903 　　　　Microfilm 8745 CS

12226　MORSE.　Descendants of Captain George Barbour of Medfield, including allied families of Adams, Babcock, Battle, Beals, Blake, Bullard, Clark, Dana, Daniels, Farr, Fisher, Fiske, Greenwood, Haven, Hawes, Hooker, Hunting, Johnson, Littlefield, Loker, Lovell, Marsh, Metcalf, Morse, Partridge, Perry, Pierce, Rice, Richardson, Sawin, Smith, White, and Wight.　(1643-1900) Comp. by Edmund Dana Barbour.　Boston, 1907.　7 v. 29 cm.　Type-written; only three copies made.　Mounted portrait of author in vol. I.　Descendants of Mary Barbour and Jonathan Morse: v. 5.　Descendants of Elizabeth Barbour and Daniel Morse: v. 6-7. Consolidated index of vol. I-VII ... Comp. by Edmund Dana Barbour.　Boston, 1907.　725 l. 20 cm.　　CS71.B24　1907 L. C. COPY REPLACED BY MICROFILM.　　　　Microfilm 8634 CS

12227　MORSE.　Descendants of Samuel Morse of Worthington, Massachusetts, by Harriet Morse Weeks ... Pittsfield, Mass., Press of the Eagle printing and binding co., 1907.　2 p. l., (3)-56, (20) p. 23½ cm.　11-3364.　　　　CS71.M885　1907

12228　MORSE.　Genealogiae; or, Data concerning the families of Morse, Chipman, Phinney, Ensign and Whiting (including new and unpublished material) edited by Wm. Inglis Morse ... Boston, Mass., N. Sawyer & son, inc., 1925.　xvi, 189 p.　front., plates, ports., facsims., 2 geneal. tab. (1 fold.) 24½ cm. "Edition limited to 200 copies."　Morse, Chipman and Phinney families, compiled by Mary Lovering Holman;　Ensign and Whiting families, compiled by Nellie Goodrich Eno;　English notes compiled by Juliet M. Morse.　25-15956.　　　　CS71.M885　1925

12229　MORSE.　One branch of family of John Morse (Moss) of New Haven and Wallingford, Ct., 1639-1708.　From Memorial of Morses, by Rev. Abner Morse.　(New York, J. C. Wait, 1930) fold. geneal. tab. 20½ cm.　Caption title.　Cover-title: Some descendants of John Morse (1634-1708) of New Haven, Conn.　31-20888. 　　　　CS71.M885　1930

12230　MORSE.　The ancestors and descendants of George Milton Morse of Putnam, Connecticut, compiled and edited by his granddaughter, Lelia Morse Wilson.　(Putnam, Conn., Patriot press, inc., 1930)　49 p. incl. illus., fold. geneal. tab., coat of arms. pl., port., 21 cm.　Blank pages at end for additions.　Additions in manuscript. 37-38460.　　　　CS71.M885　1930a

12231   MORSE.   A chapter in the genealogy of the Morse family, tracing some of the ancestors and descendants of Enoch Gerrish Morse, of Tremont, Ill.   Compiled by Lucy Smith (Morse) Caldwell ... (New York? 1931?)   4 p. l., (5) - 15 p. 25½ cm.   "Fifty numbered and signed copies are printed on hand made paper for private circulation ..." This copy not numbered.   "Printed souces of information about the Morses": 4th prelim. leaf. 32-5813.

CS71.M885   1931

12232   MORSE.   Ancestry and descendants of Sarah Morse Haynsworth; a South Carolina supplement to the histories of the Morse, (Moss), Tomlinson, Welles, Curtis, and Shelton families of Connecticut, by Hugh Charles Haynsworth ... Sumter, S. C., Osteen pub. co., 1939.   1 p. l., 52 p. 23½ cm.   "Privately printed for distribution among the members of the family."   Includes bibliographical references. 40-367.   CS71.M885   1939

12233   MORSE.   Blood of an Englishman ... by Edward C. Morse.   Abilene, Tex., Jones of Texas, 1943.   4 p. l., 301 numb. l. 29 x 22½ cm.   Reproduced from type-written copy.   History of the Morse family. 44-26064.

CS71.M885   1943

12234   MORSE.   A record of the Morse family through one line of Samuel Morse of Medfield, Massachusetts, 1587-1654.   By Ruth Evelyn (Morse) Parkhurst.   (Washington? 1963)   41 l. 31 cm.
Bibliography: p. 37-38, 65-74986.   CS71.M885   1963

12235   MORSE.   Your ancestors.   By Philip McCord Morse.   (Winchester? Mass., 1967)
vii, 120 p. illus., map, ports. 28 cm. 68-3895.   CS71.M885   1967

MORSE.   See also:

BARBER, 1907	HAYNSWORTH, CS71.M885	PARKER, 1915
CHUTE, 1894	JENNINGS, 1923	TODD, 1909
DAWSON, 1874a	McHARG, 1905	TONGUE, 1949
DOWSE, 1890	MOSS.	VAN METER, F450.V26
HALL, 1902		

12236   MORSMAN.   Mary, Edgar and Truman Morsman and their ancestors in the United States of America.   (By Edgar Martin Morsman) (Omahan, Neb., 1932)   cover-title, 39 numb. l., 41-50 p. 27½ cm.
32-30549.   CS71.M886   1932

12237   MORSMAN.   Edgar Martin Morsman, and His four sons.   (Omaha? Neb., 1963)   70 p. illus.
25 cm. His four sons, by the author's son Edgar M. Morsman. 63-51246.   CS71.M886   1963

12238   MORTEYN.   The Morteyns of Marston and Tillsworth, by G. Andrews Moriarty ... Exeter, W. Pollard & co., ltd. (1922)   12 p. 24 cm. Reprinted from the Genealogist, n.s., vol. XXXVIII, 1922. 38-4590.

CS439.M786M6

12239   MORTIMER.   ... Cadwalader, Arthur and Brutus in the Wigmore manuscript ... by Mary E. Giffin ... (Cambridge, Mass., 1941) 1 p. l., p. 109-120. 24 cm. Part of thesis (PH.D.) - University of Chicago, 1939. "The manuscript ... contains a ... genealogy of the Mortimer family, and was apparently prepared by the Mortimers to advance their claim to the throne in the fourteenth century." - p.111.   "Private edition, distributed by the University of Chicago libraries, Chicago, Illinois." "Reprinted from Speculum, vol. XVI, January, 1941." Bibliographical foot-notes. 42-18133.

CS439.M7865 1941

MORTIMER.   See also: AMES, 1889
COOK, 1941
DE NORTHWOOD.   (addenda)
LINDLEY, 1950
WASHINGTON.

12240   MORTON.   Memoranda relating to the ancestry and family of Hon. Levi Parsons Morton, vice-president of the United States (1889-1893).   By Josiah Granville Leach ... Cambridge, Printed at the Riverside press, 1894.   4 p. l., 191 p. front., plates, fold. geneal. tab. 24½ cm. 9-12524.
CS71.M89   1894

12241   MORTON. Morton data. (St. Joseph? Mo., 1901) cover-title, 22 p. 17½ cm. Signed: Daniel Morton, M.D.
1-3984.   CS71.M89   1901

12242   MORTON.   The ancestry of David Morton, prepared by his son, Daniel Morton ... St. Joseph, Mo., 1901.   geneal. tab.   16 x 45½ cm. fold. to 23 x 11 cm.   CA 10-688.   CS71.M89   1901b
—— Copy 2.   Inserted in his "Mortons and their kin."

12243   MORTON.   George Morton of Plymouth Colony and some of his descendants, by John K. Allen. Chicago, Printed for private circulation, by J. K. Allen, 1908.   1 p. l., 43, (3) p. 25 cm. 8-13738.   CS71.M89   1908a

12244   MORTON.   David Morton, a biography, by Bishop Elijah Embree Hoss ... Nashville, Tenn., Publishing house of the Methodist Episcopal church, South, Smith & Lamar, agents, 1916.   x, 214 p.   front., plates, ports., fold. map, fold. geneal. tab., facsims. 21 cm. 16-11218.   BX8495.M7H6

12245   MORTON.   The Mortons and their kin.   A genealogy and a source book.   By Daniel Morton ... Comp. between the years 1880 and 1920 and assembled in two typewritten volumes, volume one being the Mortons, and volume two being the Morton kin. ... St. Joseph, Mo., 1920.   2 v. fold. geneal. tables. 28 cm.   Relates to the Morton family of Virginia and especially to John Morton and his descendants.   Type-written; only 3 copies of the work have been made.   Paged continuously.   21-8404.   CS71.M89   1920

12246   MORTON.   A genealogy of the Morton family, with related genealogies, compiled and edited by Wm. Markham Morton.   (Ellsworth, Wis., Hall's printing co.) c.1930.   47 p. 22½ cm. 30-15230.   CS71.M89   1930

12247   MORTON.   Reminiscences, by Daniel Morton ... A medical, social and civic history of St. Joseph, Missouri, covering nearly fifty years, written at various times.   Assembled and bound for preservation by the author in the year 1937.   St. Joseph, Mo. (1937 -   v. 28 x 22 cm. Mimeographed.   "This is the first volume of a series of Reminiscences that are intended for my family primarily." - Foreword, v.1.   "Family tree of Daniel Morton.": fold. geneal. tab. inserted in v.1. 37-18050.   F474.S1M7

11248   MORTON.   The Morton family tree; Chauncey Morton and Betsey Pike, their ancestry and descent.   By John Nece Morton.   Springfield, Mo., c.1947.   125 p. illus., ports. 23 cm. 48-573*.   CS71.M89   1947

11249   MORTON.   William Morton of Windsor, Conn., and some of his descendants who are also descendants of Thomas Burnham; by Ulysses Grant Morton and Addie Le Duc Morton.   Fenton, Mich., 1950.   xi, 412 p. ports. 23 cm. 51-15509.   CS71.M89   1950

12250   MORTON.   The American ancestors and descendants of Doctor Charles Silas (Bigelow) Morton and Mary Lavalette Gilliam Morton, by Virginia Martin Brown, their grand-daughter. (Laurel? Md., 1964)   120 l. illus., geneal. tables, ports. 28 cm. Bibliography: leaf 116. 64-5543.   CS71.M89   1964

12251   MORTON.   In vertical file.   Ask reference librarian for this material.

MORTON.   See also:
LINDLEY, 1950
BARD, F128.25.V27
CHAMBERS, 1957
CROCKER, 1923
DOUGLAS, DA750.B2 vol.94
DUNHAM, 1956
PLUMMER, 1885
PLUMMER, 1894
SANDERS, 1939
STRANGEWAYES, 1878
WATKINS, 1957
WYMAN, 1927
YOUNG, 1937
No. 3509 - Orange county.

12252   MOSELEY.   Family memoirs.   By Sir Oswald Mosley, baronet.   (n.p.) Printed for private circulation, 1849.   2 p. l., iv, 78 p., 1 l., xxviii p. front. (port.) illus., plates (1 col.) fold. facsim. 28 x 23 cm. Colored coat of arms on facsimile. 18-20836.   CS439.M788   1849

12253   MOSELEY.   Mosley family.   Memoranda of Oswald and Nicholas Mosley of Ancoats, from the Manchester sessions ms. in the Free reference library, Manchester. Edited, with a genealogical introduction, by Ernest Axon.   (Manchester, Eng.) The Chetham society, 1902.   vi, 63 p. 22½ cm.   (In Chetham miscellanies. New series, v. 1 no. 4) 2-27323.   DA670.L19C5 n.s. vol. 47, no. 4

12254   MOSELEY.   Genealogy of Moseley family of Bedford County, Va.   By George Carrington Moseley, M.A. (Richmond, 1912?)   9 p. 22½ cm. 12-24997.   CS71.M898   1912

12255   MOSELEY.   (Photostat reproduction of a genealogical chart of the Moseley family, compiled by Eugene F. McPike) (n. p.) 1930.   geneal. tab. 48½ x 36 cm.   "Compiled from data in manuscript collections of Mrs. J. Melville Brown ... Mrs. Henry Seely Thomas and Mr. E. J. Frost."   31-30055.   CS71.M898   1930

12256   MOSELEY.   Moseley-Mousley index to genealogy, by Franklin Mousely.   (Philadelphia) The Historical society of Pennsylvania, 1942.   2 p. l., 27 p. 29 x 23½ cm. Type-written (carbon copy) 46-41564.
CS71.M898   1942

   MOSELEY.   See also: JONES, F74.D5C6
                        PERRY, 1911

12257   MOSER.   The descendants of Dunham Martin Moser, 1803-1895.   With notes on related families of Srodes and Krider.   Compiled by Roy Radford Moser, Joseph A. Berfanger, Catherine M. Hanchett, and others.   (n. p.) Printed for the family, 1968.   68 p. 29 cm. 74-8466 MARC.
CS71.M899   1968

12258   MOSER.   The descendants of Johann Moser, 1839-1886 and Katharina Barbara Kammerer, 1839-1912 of the Grand Duchy of Baden, Germany and Muscatine, Iowa.   By Gerald Wilson Cook.   (n. p. , 1969)   vii, 177 p. illus., maps, ports. 29 cm. "Copy 23 of 200 copies." Bibliography: p. 167-168. 78-88333 MARC.
CS71.M899   1969

   MOSER.   See also WILSON, 1890

12259   MOSES.   Historical sketches of John Moses, of Plymouth, a settler of 1632 to 1640; John Moses, of Windsor and Simbury, a settler prior to 1647; and John Moses, of Portsmouth, a settler prior to 1647; and John Moses, of Portsmouth, a settler prior to 1640.   Also a genealogical record of some of their descendants.   By Zebina Moses.   Hartford, Conn., Press of the Case, Lockwood & Brainard company, 1890-1907.   2 v. in 1,/ illus., maps (part cold.) 23½ cm. Paged continuously. 8-2377.
CS71.M91   1890-1907

12260   MOSES.   Moses; a record of the Moses tribe (Kentucky)   By Richard Asberry Moses.   (Emlyn? Ky., 1965)   171 p. illus., coat of arms, ports. 23 x 29 cm. Cover title. The Moses tribe - Ky. Nancy Ann Davis Birkey, editor. 65-6808.   CS71.M91   1965

   MOSES.   See also: DRIVER, 1889
                        WATERHOUSE, 1949

12261   MOSHER.   Origin and history of the Mosher family and genealogy of one branch of that family from the year 1600 to the present time.   Compiled by William C. Mosher ... (Los Angeles, The Times-mirror print) 1898.   48 p. incl. front. (port.) 23 ½ cm. Authorities: p. 48. 18-22796.
CS71.M915   1898

12262   MOSHER.   One branch of the Mosher family in America ... (By William Leaton Porter) (n. p., 1941)   11 numb. l. 28 x 21½ cm. Caption title. Type-written. "Compiled ... from data gathered by Mr. Harry A. Phelps, of Gloversville, N. Y." - Author's letter. 41-25189.   CS71.M915   1941

   MOSHER.   See also No. 553 - Goodhue county.

   MOSLEY.   See MOSELEY.

12263   MOSS.   Family sketch, Moss, Hall, Jennings, etc., by Alice Jennings.   (Los Angeles? Calif.) 1923.   3 p. l., 60 numb. l. 18½ cm. Type-written. Additions in manuscript throughout text. Caption title: Moss and Hall lines of ancestry, including Lathrop, Judd , Stanley, Steele, Gaylord and others. 23-14467.   CS71.J545   1923

12264   MOSS.   Chronicles of the Moss family; being a series of historical events and narratives in which the members of this family have played an important part ... Compiled and written by Rose Moss Scott.   (n. p.) 1926.   36 p. illus. (ports.) 23 cm. 27-18334.   CS71.M918   1926

12265   MOSS.   Moss-Harris pedigree chart.   Ancestors and descendants of Samuel Lyons Moss and his wife Isabelle (Harris) Moss.   From notes of Sanford A. Moss.   (Somerville, Mass.) 1934. cover-title, 4 numb. 1. group port., gold. geneal. tab. 24½ cm. (Wilder's genealogical brochures. Ser. N, no.1) Reproduced from typewritten copy. "Only 30 copies made for family and library distribution." 35-28826.   CS71.M918   1934

12266   MOSS.   The Staffordshire family of Moss, together with other genealogies.   (By Arthur William Moss)   Walsall (Eng.) Press of T. Richmond, 1937.   2 p. 1., 3-39 p. front., pl. (ports.) geneal. tables (part fold.) 24½ cm. Introduction signed: Arthur W. Moss. Includes pedigrees of the Howell, Cotton, Jones and Warington families. 38-32349.
                                                                        CS439.M7883 1937

12267   MOSS.   Genealogy of John Moss and his wife, Rebecca (Lyons) Moss, by Sanford A. Moss ... Rutland, Vt., The Tuttle publishing company, inc., 1937.   24 p. 22½ cm. "References": p. (5)-6. 37-38451.
                                                                        CS71.M918   1937

12268   MOSS.   ... Moss-Harris pedigree chart.   3d ed., rev. to July, 1939.   Ancestors and descendants of Samuel Lyons Moss and his wife Isabelle (Harris) Moss.   Compiled by Sanford A. Moss, Lynn, Mass., 1934.   (Lynn, 1939)   fold. geneal. tab. 26½ x 101 cm. fold. to 26½ x 21 cm. Reproduced from type-written copy. 40-2263.   CS71.M918   1939

12269   MOSS.   Genealogy of Samuel Moss and his wife, Eleanor Tittermary (Mercer) Moss, by Sanford A. Moss ... Lynn, Mass., The Lynn mailing company, 1940.   1 p. 1., 20 numb. 1. 28 cm. Reproduced from type-written copy. Bibliography: leaves 7 a and 7 b, mounted on leaves 6 and 7. 41-6096.
                                                                        CS71.M918   1940

12270   MOSS.   Moss-Harris pedigree chart; ancestors and descendants of Samuel Lyons Moss and his wife Isabelle (Harris) Moss, by Sanford A. Moss ... Lynn, Mass., The Lynn mailing company, 1943.   1 p. 1., 25 numb. 1. group port., fold. geneal. tab. 28 x 22 cm. Reproduced from type-written copy. In manuscript on t.-p.: Fourth edition Oct. 1943. 44-28181.   CS71.M918   1943

12271   MOSS.   Biographical sketches of the Mosses: Paul Moss, Thaddeus A. Moss, Howell Moss, Howell C. Moss, Henry Moss, Amanda Holden Moss.   By William Paul Moss.   (Odessa? Tex.) c.1960.   1 v. (unpaged) ports. (part col.) col. coat of arms. 37 cm. 61-20890.   CS71.M918   1960

12272   MOSS.   The Moss family: William Paul Moss, Thaddeus Augustus Moss, Amanda Holden Moss, Howell Moss, Crestus Howell Moss, Henry Moss, their families and progenitors.   (Compiled and written by Paul Moss.   Odessa? Tex., 1964)   26 p. port. 23 cm. 64-55046.
                                                                        CS71.M918   1964

12273   MOSS.   A genealogical record of the Moss family in America; John Moss, Sr.'s line.   By Columbus Joseph Moss.   Lake Charles, La. (1964 -   1 v. (loose leaf) ports. 30 cm. Includes bibliography. 64-54831.   CS71.M918   1964a

12274   MOSS.   The David Moss family: Warren and Granville Co., N.C. Green, Adair, Mercer, Boyle, Barren, Hart, and Warren Co., Ky. Williamson and Maury Co., Tenn. Mississippi. By T.C. Moss. (Memphis) Printed by C. Johnson and Associates, 1968.   79 p. 28 cm. 70-6590 MARC.   CS71.M918   1968

          MOSS.   See also: LEWIS, 1901
                             McHARG, 1905

          MOSSER.   See MERCER.

12275   MOSTYNE.   History of the family of Mostyn of Mostyn, by the Right Hon. Lord Mostyn ... and T. A. Glenn.   London, Harrison and sons, limited, 1925.   xiv p., 1 1., 208 p. front., plates, ports. 27 cm. "154 copies of this book privately printed and the type distributed; this copy being no. 22." Signed: Mostyn. The portraits, including frontispiece, are mounted. 26-13600.   CS439.M7885M6

12276   MOTT.   The descendants of Adam Mott, of Hempstead, Long Island, N.Y.   A genealogical study.   By Edw. Doubleday Harris ... (New York, 189-?)   8 p. 24 cm. 4-26192,
                                                                        CS71.M92   189-

12277   MOTT.   Adam and Anne Mott: their ancestors and their descendants.   By Thomas C. Cornell, their grandson ... Printed for the family.   Poughkeepsie, N.Y., A. V. Haight, printer, 1890.
1 p. l., viii, (9)-418 p., 1 l. fronts., illus., plates, ports., maps, facsims. (part fold.) geneal. tables. 26 cm. 9-12302.
CS71.M92   1890

12278   MOTT.   Mott, Hopper, Striker,   New York, The Historical company, 1898. 18 p. geneal. tab.
23½ cm.   Signed: Hopper Striker Mott.   9-12303.
CS71.M92   1898

12279   MOTT.   The descendants of Adam Mott of Hempstead, Long Island, N.Y.   A genealogical study.   Rev. Ed.   By Edw. Doubleday Harris ... Lancaster, Pa., The New era printing co., 1906.
cover-title, 8 p. 23½ cm.   Text on inner side of front and back cover.   9- 22857.
CS71.M92   1906

12280   MOTT.   James Mott of Dutchess County, N.Y., and his descendants.   By Edward Doubleday Harris ... New York, Press of T. A. Wright (1912)   iv, 58 p. 23½ cm. 12-8147.
CS71.M92   1912

12281   MOTT.   The Mott family in France, by Donald Moffatt, with illustrations by Hildegard Woodward.   Boston, Little, Brown and company, 1937.   x, 284 p. illus. 20 cm. "First edition." 37-14690.
DC33.7.M6   1937

MOTT.   See also: MILLS, 1963
GAGE, 1910

12282   MOTTIER.   Mottier family, Gentle family, Trailor (Trailer) (Traylor) family, Butts (Butt) family (by Charles H. Mottier.   n.p., 1966)   1 v. (various pagings) illus., geneal. table, ports. 28 cm. 67-9211.
CS71.M922   1966

12283   MOULDER.   Moulder's record of the Moulder family of America, listing three thousand descendants and inlaws of the Moulder family, covering a period of the last two hundred years, and representing ten years work on the part of the author.   Written and published by George Chester Moulder ... Lebanon, Mo., 1933.   171 (i.e.186) p. incl. port., geneal. tab. 26½ cm. Autographica reproduction to manuscript copy. Paging irregular. 39-12242.
CS71.M923   1933

12284   MOULDER.   The Moulder family tree and early family history in the United States.   By George B. Moulder.   (Nashville? 195 -)   (19) l. group port., facsims., fold. geneal. tables. 38 cm. Cover title. Mounted photocopy of ms.   59-24166.
CS71.M923

12285   MOULE.   Elmley Lovett and the Moules of Sneads Green.   By Horace Monroe ... London, Mitchell, Hughes and Clarke, 1927.   26 p. plates, ports., 3 fold. geneal. tab. 22½ cm. Includes bibliography. 40-16292.
DA690.E32M6

12286   MOULTHROP.   Genealogical charts, the Brown-Moulthrop families (by) Nelson O. Rhoades.   (Mexico, Mex.) 1918.   cover-title, 9 geneal. tab. (part fold.) 35 cm. 19-2006.
CS71.M925   1918

12287   MOULTHROP.   The Moulthrop family of Connecticut, direct line of descent of Colonel Samuel Parker Moulthrop and family, of Rochester, New York.   (Rochester? 1925?)   (10) p. illus.
19 cm. 29-10278.
CS71.M925   1925

MOULTHROP.   See also RHODES, 1920

12288   MOULTON.   A genealogical register of some of the descendants of John Moulton, of Hampton, and of Joseph Moulton, of Portsmouth.   Comp. by Thomas Moulton.   Portland (Me.) Printed by B. Thurston & company, 1873.   viii, (9)-44 p. 19 cm. Blank leaves at end for memoranda. 2-6359.
CS71.M927   1873

12289   MOULTON.   A history of the Moulton family; a record of the descendants of James Moulton of Salem and Wenham, Massachusetts, from 1629-1905.   Stuart, Ia., W. P. Moulton and children, 1905.   2 p. l., 56 p. coat of arms. 23 cm. Compiled by Eben Hobson Moulton and Henry A. Moulton. The general history of the Moulton family, by Augustus F. Moulton, and the coat of arms, reprinted from the Maine historical and genealogical record, 1888. 17-6148.
CS71.M927   1905

12290   MOULTON.   Moulton annals, by Henry W. Moulton, ed. by his daughter Claribel Moulton. Chicago, Ill., E. A. Claypool, 1906.   454 p. front., plates, ports., fold. geneal. tab., col. coats of arms. 23½ cm. 7-36945.

CS71.M927   1906

12291   MOULTON.   Molton family and kinsmen; Hooks, Hunter, Whitfield, Linn, Tuttle, Henley, Harris, Summerlin, Ware, Glover, Smith, Williams, Upmann and others.   Reminiscences to the year 1857, by Thomas Hunter Molton, 1922.   (Birmingham, Ala., Press of Birmingham publishing company, 1922)   4 p. l., (7)-145 p. plates, ports., coat of arms. 23½ cm. The plates are printed on both sides. 25-9573.

CS71.M927   1922

MOULTON.   See also: KING, 1897
LIVINGS, 1927
MARSTON, 1898

12292   MOUNSEY.   Paterson, Mounsey, Latimer (Lotimer) Rogerson and allied families; a genea-logical compilation.   By James Latimer Bothwell.   (n. p.) 1947.   (70) p. 28 cm. With additions and corrections in ms. 49-21026*.

CS71.M9275   1947

12293   MOUNT.   History and genealogical record of the Mount and Flippin families.   By Julius Allen Mount.   (n. p.) 1954.   120 p. illus. 24 cm. 54-44774.

CS71.M9277   1954

12294   MOUNTAIN.   ... Notes on the Mountain, Drake and MacPike families.   By Eugene Fairfield MacPike of Chicago.   (Philadelphia, 1928)   7 p. 25 cm. At head of title: Notes, queries and corrections. "Reprinted from the Publications of the Genealogical society of Pennsylvania, March, 1928." CA29-29 unrev.

CS71.M928   1928

12295   MOUNTBATTEN.   Manifest destiny; a study in five profiles of the rise and influence of the Mountbatten family.   London, Cassell (1953)   226 p. illus. 23 cm. 54-1187.

CS439.M79   1953

12296   MOUNTBATTEN.   The Mountbatten lineage; the direct descent of the family of Mountbatten from the House of Brabant and the rulers of Hesse.   Prepared for private circulation.   (n. p.) 1958.   458 p. illus., ports., maps (1 fold. col. in pocket) coats of arms. 23 cm. Bibliography: p. 452-456. 59-40473.

CS439.M79   1958

12297   MOUNTBATTEN.   The Mountbattens; the last royal success story.   By Alden Hatch.   New York, Random House, (1965)   viii, 472 p. illus., geneal. table, ports. 25 cm. Bibliography: p. 459-461. 65-11283.

CS439.M79   1965

12298   MOUNTBATTEN.   The Mountbattens.   By Alden Hatch.   London, W. H. Allen, 1966.   viii, 469 p. 17 plates (incl. ports., diagr.) 22½ cm. Bibliography: p. 457-458. 66-71014.

CS439.M79   1966

12299   MOUNTBATTEN.   From Battenberg to Mountbatten (by) E. H. Cookridge.   London, Barker (1966)   x, 313 p. 16 plates (ports.) diagrs. 22½ cm. Bibliography: p. (298)-302. 66-74598.   CS439.M79   1966a

12300   MOUNTCASTLE.   A family heritage, the house of Mountcastle, a brochure.   By Indi Anna Leona Richards.   (1st ed.) Middletown, Conn., 1959.   14 l. illus. 28 cm. 59-3566.

CS71.M929   1959

12301   MOURNING.   Roger Mourning and his descendants.   By Kenneth William Mourning.   Toledo (1948)   8, 8, 17 l. mounted photos., map. 29 cm. Title from label mounted on cover. Three papers delivered at annual meetings of the family. 49-13704*.

CS71.M93   1948

12302   MOURNING.   Roger Mourning; his book.   By Kenneth Mourning Waddell.   Washington, 1969.   1 v. (various pagings) illus., maps, photos. (part col.), ports. 30 cm. 79-4180 MARC.   CS71.M93   1969

MOUSLEY.   See MOSELEY.

MOWAT.   See SINCLAIR, 1884

MOWBRAY. See: STOURTON, 1899
VAN NOSTRAND, E171.A53 vol.19

MOWER. See MOORE.

12303   MOWRY. The descendants of Nathaniel Mowry, of Rhode Island. By William A. Mowry ...
Providence, S. S. Rider, 1878.   343 p. plates, facsims. 23½ cm.   CS71.M936   1878
—— Supplement ... Boston, The Everett press, 1900.   95 p. front. 23½ cm.   (With his The Mowry
family monument ... Boston, 1898) 9-11925 rev.   CS71.M936   1898

12304   MOWRY. A family history. Richard Mowry, of Uxbridge, Mass., his ancestors and his
descendants. By William A. Mowry ... Providence, S.S. Rider, 1878.   239 p. plates, ports., facsims. 24 cm.
9-12523.   CS71.M936   1878a

12305   MOWRY. A genealogy of one branch of the Morey family 1631-1890. Ed. for Moses Conant
Warren by Emily Wilder Leavitt. (Boston) Printed for private circulation (by A. Mudge & son) 1890.
vi, 30 p. 26 cm. (with Warren, Mary Parker. A genealogy of one branch of the Warren family ... Boston, 1890. 9-17839.
CS71.W29   1890

12306   MOWRY. The Mowry family monument, near Woonsocket, R.I. Erected by Hon. Arlon
Mowry. (By William Augustus Mowry) Boston, Printed by D. Clapp & son, 1898.   14 p. front., plates,
ports. 23½ cm. Caption title: A unique family monument. By William A. Mowry ... "Reprinted from the New-Eng. historical and genealogical
register for April, 1898, with additions." With this are bound the author;s Supplement to The descendants of Nathaniel Mowry of Rhode Island.
Boston, 1900 and The Mowry family monument, near Woonsocket, R.I. ... Boston, 1901. 9-12522 rev.   CS71.M936   1898

12307   MOWRY. The Mowry family monument, near Woonsocket, R.I. Erected by Hon. Arlon
Mowry. (By William Augustus Mowry) Boston, The Everett press, 1901.   16 p. front., plates, ports.
23½ cm. (With his The Mowry family monument. Boston, 1898) "Reprinted from the New England historical and genealogical register for April,
1898 with additions." 2-13016 rev.   CS71.M936   1898

12308   MOWRY. Supplement to the Descendants of Nathaniel Mowry of Rhode Island, by William A.
Mowry. Boston, The Everett press, 1900.   95 p. front. 23½ cm. 2-13015.   CS71.M936   1900

12309   MOWRY. The descendants of John Mowry of Rhode Island. By William A. Mowry ...
Providence, R. I., Preston & Rounds co., 1909.   292 p. front., plates. 22 cm. 10-15832.
CS71.M936   1909

12310   MOWRY. A history of the Mowry family of Pittsburgh, Penna., 1740-1940, by William B.
Mowry, M.D., and Robert B. Mowry, D.D.S. 1st ed., 1940. (Pittsburgh, Printed by Curry-Thompson
co., 1941)   61 p. 23½ cm. Bibliography: p. 47. 42-18895.   CS71.M936   1941

12311   MOWRY. Genealogy, the descendants of Augustus Mowry, 1784-1941. (By Robert D. Mowry)
Chicago, Ill., Schmidt printing company, 1942.   94, (6) p. incl. front. (ports.) illus. (incl. coat of arms) 23½ cm.
Preface signed: Robert D. Mowry. Six blank pages at end for "Memorandun.'' 42-9866.   CS71.M936   1942

MOWRY. See also: TUCKER, 1957
WATERBURY, 1930

12312   MOYER. Genealogy of the Moyer family, by Rev. A. J. Fretz ... (Netcong, N.J., Union
Times print) 1909.   144 p., 2 l. front., plates, ports. 22 cm. Blank pages for "Additional records": at end. 10-10180.
CS71.M938   1909

MOYER. See also: GRIM, 1934
MEYER.
MYERS, 1890
STAUFFER, 1897
WEISER, 1960

MOYLE. See MOULE.

MOZIER.   See BANKS, 1938

12313   MUCKLESTON. Muckleston of Merrington.   7 l. 33 x 21½ cm.   Manuscript (written on side of leaf) containing genealogical notices concerning the Muckleston family.   2-8918.
CS439.M8

12314   MUDGE. Memorials: being a genealogical, biographical and historical account of the name of Mudge in America, from 1638 to 1868.   By Alfred Mudge ... Boston, Printed by A. Mudge & son, for the family, 1868.   xiv p., 1 l., 443 p. front., ports., fold. facsim. 24½ cm. Blank leaves at end for "Family record." 9-12520.
CS71.M944   1868

12315   MUDD. The Mudd family of the United States.   By Richard Dyer Mudd.   (Saginaw? Mich., 1951)   xi, 1461 p. illus., ports., maps, coat of arms, facsims. 29 cm. Bibliography: p. 1379-1388.
CS71.M942   1951

—— List of corrections, by Richard D. Mudd.   (Saginaw, Mich., 1968)   50 p. 26 cm. 51-7181.
CS71.M942   1951
Corrections.

12316   MUDD. Descendants of Dr. Samuel Alexander Mudd.   By Richard Dyer Mudd.   Saginaw, Mich. (1961)   11 p. 23 cm. 63-26447.
CS71.M942   1961

12317   MUDD. Descendants of Dr. Samuel Alexander Mudd.   By Richard Dyer Mudd.   3d ed. (Saginaw, Mich., 1968)   17 p. map. 23 cm. Cover title. 73-2171.
CS71.M942   1968

MUDD.   See also SEMMES, 1956

12318   MUDGE. Mudge memoirs: being a record of Zachariah Mudge, and some members of his family; together with a genealogical list of the same.   Compiled from family papers & other sources. Illustrated with portraits.   Edited and arranged by Stamford Raffles Flint ... Truro, Printed by Netherton & Worth, 1883.   xix, (1), 258 p. ports., 2 fold. tab. (1 geneal.) 22 cm. "Only one hundred copies printed." Contains also memoirs of Thomas, Richard, John, William, Zachariah (1770-1852) and Richard Zachariah Mudge.   A list of the portraits, with names of the artists, owners, and history of the original paintings: folded table inserted at end. 18-20834.
CS439.M83

12319   MUDGE. John Mudge and Hannah Hutchinson, first settlers of Plymouth, Ct.   Compiled by Florence A. Mudge. (Danvers, Mass., 1930)   13 p. 23½ cm. Caption title. Cover-title: First settlers of Plymouth, Vermont. "The Putnam ancestry of Hon, Calvin Coolidge": p. 11-13. "Deprint from vol. 18, Danvers hist, collections", in manuscript on cover. 31-19483.
CS71.M944   1930

12320   MUDGETT. Thomas Mudgett of Salisbury, Massachusetts and his descendants, by Mildred D. and Bruce D. Mudgett. Bennington, Vt., 1961.   169 p. illus. 28 cm. 61-65200.
CS71.M945   1961

12321   MUELLER. The story of Joseph Mueller of Council Bluffs, Iowa, and of his German forebears and American descendants.   By his son, Ralph S. Mueller ... (Cleveland, 1936)   1 p. l., IV numb. l., 1 l., 139 numb. l. port., 3 fold. geneal. tab. 28½ cm. Mimeographed. 36-11408.
CS71.M946   1936

12322   MUELLER. Our Müller clan; a volume of authentic, historical and genealogical material concerning the family, that has been distributed to the relatives each Christmas from 1941 to 1957. By Charles Miller. (Ames? Iowa, 1958?-   v. maps, geneal. table, mounted photos. 29 cm. Most of the text is typescript (carbon copy) Part of the material also appears in the author's The Beyer-Miller family. 25 copies. No. 22. 59-24892.
CS71.M946   1958

12323   MUHLENBERG. In memoriam. Henry Melchior Mühlenger, 1711, 1742, 1787. Commemorative exercises held by the Susquehanna synod of the Evangelical Lutheran church, at Selinsgrove, Penna., October 18 and 19, 1887. Published for the synod's committee. Philadelphia, Lutheran publication society, 1888.   61 p. front. (port.) 22 cm. Contents. - Lutheranism in America prior to the coming of Mühlenberg, by Rev. S. E. Ochsenford. - Pietism and Halle, by Rev. John B. Focht. - Henry Melchior Mühlenberg, by Rev. Prof, E. J. Wolf. - The Mühlenberg family, by Rev. J. G. Morris. - Lutheranism in America since the death of Mühlenberg, by Rev. M. S. Cressman. 23-3539 Rev.
BX8080.M9S85

12324   MUHLENBERG.   Descendants of Henry Melchoir Muhlenberg.   By Henry Melchior Muhlenberg Richards.   (Lancaster, Pa.) Pennsylvania-German Society, 1900.   89 p. ports. 25 cm. (Pennsylvania-German genealogies) "Prepared by authority of the Pennsylvania-German Society." 68-42682.

CS71.M95   1900

12325   MUHLENBERG.   Muhlenberg album.   (New Haven, Tuttle, Morehouse & Taylor press, 1910)   6 l. 30 pl. 28½ x 36 cm. Cover-title. The text is signed Henrietta Meier Oakley, John Christopher Schwab. "The album aims to commemorate the 200th anniversary of the landing in America, on June 17, 1710 of John Conrad Weiser." It is a collection mainly of the portraits and heirlooms of Anna Maria Weiser and Rev. Dr. Henry Melchior Muhlenberg, their children and grandchildren, as far as they could be found. 10-26400.

CS71.M95   1910

12326   MUHLENBERG.   The descendants of Henry Melchior Muhlenberg.   Corrections & additions requested by J. C. Schwab.   (Washington, 1912)   geneal. tab. 99 x 99 cm. fold. to 34 x 50 cm. 13-2605.

CS71.M95   1912

12327   MUHLENBERG.   A brief monograph with reference to the mother of the leading family in the American life of the epoch which inaugurated freedom and independence for the American people and government, and for the church and word of the Lord Jesus in government, and for the church and word of Lord Jesus in America.   By W. C. Heyer ... Shamokin, Pa., The Leader publishing company (c. 1916)   38 p. 22½ cm. On cover: Anna Weiser Muhlenberg (Mrs. Patriarch H. H. M.) a morning star in the destiny of a continent. 17-4332.

CS71.M95   1916

12328   MUHLENBERG.   The fighting parson of the American revolution; a biography of General Peter Muhlenberg, Luthern clergyman, military chieftan, and political leader, by Edward W. Hocker ... Philadelphia, Pa., Pub. by the author, 1936.   191 p. front. (port.) plates. 20 cm. "Authorities": p. (184)-186. 36-31557.

E207.M95H6

12329   MUHLENBERG.   The Muhlenberg family, a bibliography compiled from the subject union catalog (of) Americana-Germanica of the Carl Schurz memorial foundation, by Felix Reichmann. Philadelphia, Carl Schurz memorial foundation, inc., 1943.   43 p. 21 cm. (Bibliogrphies on German American history) No. 1) "Lithoprinted." 44-411.

Z860.85R4

12330   MUHLENBERG.   The Muhlenbergs of Pennsylvania.   By Paul A. W. Wallace.   Philadelphia, University of Pennsylvnia Press, 1950.   ix, 358 p. illus., ports. 25 cm. Bibliographical references included in "Notes" (p. 321-342) 50-5892.

CS71.M95   1950

MUHLENBERG.   See also WEISER, 1960

MUIR.   See MOODY, 1906

12331   MULFORD.   A genealogy of the family of Mulford.   By William Remsen Mulford ... Reprinted from the New England historical and genealogical register for April, 1880.   Boston, Printed by D. Clapp & son, 1880.   12 p. 25½ cm. 9-12519.

CS71.M955   1880

12332   MULFORD.   Colonial ancestors and descendants, Gardiner, Conkling, Lindsley, Mulford, Pierson, Miller, Lillibridge, Hazard, Stephens, Wallace, Horn, Davis, Bentley, Rosenberry, Boyd. By Uri Mulford.   Corning, N.Y., U. Mulford, c. 1920.   2 p. l., 3-26 p. 1 col. illus. 17½ cm. 20-13996.

CS71.M955   1920

12333   MULFORD.   Mulford family.   By Thelma Antrim (Beck) Ellis.   Trenton, N.J., 1965. 148 l. mounted col. illus., mounted ports. 30 cm. 66-47776.

CS71.M955   1965

MULFORD.   See also: CORY, 1937
PESHINE, 1916
SUTLIFF, 1897

12334   MULHOLLAND.   The Mulhollands; history, genealogy, letters. Index.   By Virginia Carter Stumbough.   Peoria, Ill., 1941.   1 v. 33 cm. Loose-leaf. Reproduced from type-written copy. 41-14723.

CS71.M956   1941

MULL.   See BERRY, 1933

12335   MULLANPHY.   The descendants of John Mullanphy, Saint Louis philanthropist, compiled by Harriet Lane Cates Hardaway.   (n. p.) 1940.   3 p. l., 76, (6) p., 1 l. front. (fold. geneal. tab.) 29½ cm.   Reproduced from type-written copy.   40-34623.   CS71.M957   1940

MULLEN.   See No. 2070 - Memories ... of ... North Carolina.

MULLENIX.   See HAMLETT, 1958

MULLER.   See: BEATTY, 1886
                          MAGINET, 1961

12336   MULLET.   We would remember; a near complete genealogical compilation of the Mollat immigrants of 1833 and 1851.   By Nadine (Mullet) Getz.   Dayton, Ohio, Printed by the Otterbein Press, 1950.   264 p. ports., facsims. 23 cm.   51-4571.   CS71.M9574   1950

12337   MULLICA.   Eric Mullica and his descendants: a Swedish pioneer in New Jersey; together with a description of the Mullica River region in Burlington and Atlantic counties, N. H., and an account of the early generations of the family in the vicinity of Mullica Hill and Swedesboro, Gloucester County, N. J.   By Charles J. Werner ... New Gretna, N. J., C. J. Werner, 1930.   117 p. incl. geneal. tables. 23½ cm.   "One hundred copies printed of which this is no. 65." "Political divisions of the Mullica River region (1676-1891)": p. 10-21.   "Genealogy of the Mullica family": p. 41-117.   30-12590.   CS71.M958   1930

12338   MULLIGAN.   Hercules Mulligan, confidential correspondent of General Washington, by Michael J. O'Brien, LL. D.   New York, P. J. Kenedy & sons (c. 1937)   3 p. l., 13-190 p. front., facsims. 20½ cm.   38-797.   E302.6.M8803

12339   MULLIKEN.   Mullikins of Maryland; an account of the descendants of James Mullikin of the western shore of Maryland, by Elizabeth Hopkins Baker.   State College, Pa., Elizabeth H. Baker, 1932.   3 p. l., 204 p. plates, ports., coats of arms. 23½ cm.   "Sources": p. (183) 32-15346.   CS71.M959   1932

12340   MULLIKEN.   Genealogical, historical, and biographical sketches of descendents (sic) from families of the four James Mullikins and Captain Thomas Mullikin 1650 (1387 through the Belt family) to January 1936 ... an autographed limited ed.   By Clarence Greene Hildreth.   (n. p.) c. 1936.   1 v. (unpaged) ports., coats of arms. 23 x 37 cm.   Typescript (carbon copy) 62-55440.   CS71.M959   1936

MULLIKEN.   Mulliken family by Thomas J. Hall.   page 209.   CS71.H177   1941

12341   MULLIKEN.   Mullikins and Mullicans of North Carolina; a history of Lewis Mullikin and his descendants, covering the period since his arrival in Rowan County, North Carolina, in 1781 from the western shore of Maryland.   By N. Spencer Mullican.   Winston-Salem (1953?)   218 p. illus., ports., mounted coat of arms. 20 cm.   55-44915.   CS71.M9587   1953

MULLIKEN.   See also MILLIKEN.

MULLIKIN.   See MULLIKEN.

MULLINEUX.   See WOOD, 1937

MULLINS.   See: MILLER, 1907
                           QUISENBERRY, 1897
                           VAN NOSTRAND, E171.A53 vol.19

MULLOY.   See THOMPSON, 1907

MULLOCK.   See KETCHAM, 1954

12342   MULOCK.   The family of Mulock, by Sir Edmund Bewley ... Dublin, The author, 1905.
xv, 32 p. front., plates, ports., fold. geneal. tab. 26½ cm.   17-19247.   CS499.M8

MULOCK.　See also:　MELLARD, CS439.M387
　　　　　　　　　　　READ, CS439.R28

12343　MUMFORD.　Mumford memoirs; being the story of the New England Mumfords from the year 1655 to the present time.　By James Gregory Mumford, M.D.　Boston, Priv. print. by D.B. Updike, the Merrymount press, 1900.　xxx p., 1 l., 248 p. fold. geneal. tab.　25 cm.　0-3722 rev.

CS71.M961　　1900

MUMFORD.　See also CHESEBROUGH, 1900.

MUMMA.　See MOOMAW.

12344　MUMSEN.　Chronicle of American members of the Broder Mumsen family, published by the Society of American members of the family, edited by Knud Melf Hansen ... Detroit (Chesterfield press) 1927.　xvi, 64 p. front., illus. (coat of arms) maps. 22 cm.　A summary in English of v.1 of the family records, the "Chronik-blatter", giving the line of descent from the ancestor Broder Mumsen of each member of the family that came to America, and a full record from the time of his or her arrival in this country.　28-28401.

CS71.M963　　1927

MUNCASTER, Barons of.　See PENNINGTON.

12345　MUNDAY.　Nicholas Mundy and descendants who settled in New Jersey in 1665.　Compiled by Rev. Ezra F. Mundy ... Lawrence, Kan., Press of Bullock printing company, 1907.　144, (16) p. front., plates, ports. fold. map.　20½ cm.　7-33615.

CS71.M965　　1907

MUNDY.　See MUNDAY.

12346　MUNGER.　The Munger book; something of the Mungers, 1639-1914, including some who mistakenly write the name Monger, and Mungor, compiled by J. B. Munger, 1894-1914, with the valued assistance of the late Jno. E. Munger ,... and Francis E. Munger ... (New Haven) The Tuttle, More-house & Taylor company, 1915.　xviii p., 1 l., 614 p. front., ports., fold. geneal. chart, col. coat of arms.　25½ cm.　15-3987.

CS71.M967　　1915

12347　MUNGER.　See also:　EDGE, DA690.B44H3
　　　　　　　　　　　　WARD, CS71.W26, 1926

12348　MUNN.　Chart XXI. - Munn, Holton, Foote, Beecher, Moody, Lyman, Parsons, Seward, Farwell and Forward.　New York, 1881.　geneal. tab. 22 x 28 cm.　"Initial to large radial charts of the Foote, Beecher and Seward families, as pages of the grand folio in preparation for the bicentennial, 1976."　CA7-1506 unrev.

CS71.H758　　1881

MUNN.　See also:　BROWN, 1931
　　　　　　　　　EDGE, 1889
　　　　　　　　　HOLTON, 1881

MUNNINGS.　See MANNING, 1902

12349　MUNRO.　The ancient clan Munro of Foulis; tracing some cadet families of Munro, Monro, Munroe, and Monroe.　By Malcolm Monroe.　(n. p.) c.1959.　(2) l. (geneal. table) 18 cm.　59-3565.

CS479.M8　　1959

MUNRO.　See also MONROE.

MUNROE.　See MONROE.

12350　MUNS.　Muns Doolittle genealogy, compiled by Gertrude Fisher Harding.　(n. p.) 1940.　53 p., 1 l. incl. ports. 23 cm.　40-14632.

CS71.M968　　1940

12351　MUNSELL.　Genealogy of the Windsor family of Munsell.　From Stile's History of ancient Windsor.　(New York, 1859)　8 p. 24½ cm.　Caption title.　Compiled by Joel Munsell.　"Reprinted without material change in the New England genealogical register for July 1880 and also in the Loomis genealogy in 1880."　cf. F. Munsell, Genealogy of the Munsell family, 1884.　9-12298.

CS71.M969　　1859

12352   MUNSELL.   Biographical sketch of Joel Munsell.   By George R. Howell.   To which is appended a genealogy of the Munsell family, by Frank Munsell.   Boston, Printed for the New England historic, genealogical society, 1880.   16 p. front. (port.) 25½ cm.   "Reprinted from the New England historical and gene-alogical register for July, 1880." 9-12300.
CS71.M969   1880

12353   MUNSELL.   A genealogy of the Munsell family (Munsill, Monsell, Maunsell) in America, by Frank Munsell.   Albany, N. Y., J. Munsell's sons, 1884.   164 1. plates, coat of arms. 23½ cm.   Printed on one side of leaf only.   Title vignette.   9-12299.
CS71.M969   1884

12354   MUNSELL.   A genealogy of the Munsell family, with lineages of related families: Bissell, Bogardus, Bronck, Cooke, Coonley, Drake, Houghtaling, Loomis, Paine, Stiles, and Taylor; and a line of descent from Rolfe, duke of Normandy, A. D. 860.   By Claude Garfield Munsell.   South Nor-walk, Conn., J. Munsell's Sons, 1950.   52 p. port., coat of arms. 24 cm.   Cover title: Munsell genealogy. 52-23861.
CS71.M969   1950

MUNSELL.   See also MAUNSELL.

12355   MUNSEY.   A Munsey-Hopkins genealogy, being the ancestry of/Andrew Chauncey Munsey and Mary Jane Merritt Hopkins,   the parents of Frank A. Munsey ... by D. O. S. Lowell ... Boston, Priv. print., 1920.   1 p. l., v-xvii, 216 p. fold. geneal. tab.   24 cm.   Contents. - pt. I. The Munsey line. - pt. II. The Hopkins line. - pt. III. Who's who in some allied families.   20-13607.
CS71.M972   1920

MUNSILL.   See MUNSELL.

MUNSON.   See MONSON.

MURDAC.   See MURDOCK.

12356   MURDOCK.   Murdock genealogy, Robert Murdock, of Roxbury, Massachusetts, and some of his descendants, with notes on the descendants of John Murdo of Plymouth, Massachusetts, George Murdock of Plainfield, Connecticut, Peter Murdock of Saybrook, Connecticut, William Murdoch of Philadelphia, Pennsylvania, and others, compiled by Joseph B. Murdock ... Boston, C. E. Goodspeed & co., 1925.   274 p. front. (coat of arms) 25 cm.   26-5988.
CS71.M974   1925

MURDOCK.   See also: BOCLAND (DE), 1924
                                     CROSS, 1913
                                     TILSON, 1911

12357   MURE.   The historie and descent of the house of Rowallane.   By Sir William Mure, knight, of Rowallan.   Written in, or prior to 1657.   Glasgow, Printed for Chalmers and Collins, 1825.   viii, (9)-141 p. 22½ cm.   Preface signed: William Muir.   Published also in the Scottish text society, Edinburgh, 1898. 22 cm.   v. 2, p. (235) - 256. 20-16680.
CS479.M85

12358   MURE.   Selections from the family papers preserved at Caldwell ... Glasgow. (Ed. William Mure) (Reprinted by W. Eadie and company) 1854.   2 pt. in 3 v. fronts. (pt. II, port.) plates, facsims., col. coat of arms. 27 x 22 cm.   (The Maitland club. Publications. no. 71) Title vignette. Part I imperfect: p. 289-296 wanting. Edited and presented to the club by William Mure.   Published 1883 as no. 7 of the New club series.   Contents. - pt. I. Introductory memoir. Miscellaneous papers (1496-1741) Factory accounts of the estate of Caldwell during the minorities of James and William Mure, by Hew Mure ... and Thos. Robison ... 1644 - 1654.   Series of tacks or leases, and other contracts relative to land in the west of Scotland - from 1586 to 1853. - pt. II. vol. I: Correspondence and miscellaneous papers of Baron Muro (1733-1764) vol. II: Correspondence and miscellaneous papers of Baron Mure (1765-1775) Papers of uncertain date.   Correspondence of Prof Jardine, etc.   Correspondence, etc. of William Mure, esq., 1777-1821.   18-14286.
DA750.M3 no. 71

12359   MURE.   Selections from the family papers preserved at Caldwell ... Paisley, A. Gardner, 1883.   2 pt. in 3 vol. fronts. (pt. II, port.) plates, facsims., col. coat of arms. 28 x 21½ cm. (Half title: The new club series. (no. 7)) "This edition ... is limited to eighty-six copies, of which this is number 83."   Published in 1854 as no. 71 of the Maitland club publications. 18-10509.
DA758.3.C2M8

MURE.   See also: CARSTAIRES, 1843
                             MOORE.

273

MURET. See RIX, 1957

MURFF, 1955

12360   MURIEL. A Fenland family: some notes on the history of a family surnamed Muriel; edited and printed as a basis for further research by J. H. L. Muriel. Ipswich (Suffolk), East Anglian Magazine Ltd. (1968)   (1), 95 p. coat of arms, facsim., geneal. tables. 22 cm. 78-376700.
CS439.M87   1968

12361   MURPHY. The Murphy family; genealogical, historical and biographical, with offical statistics of the part played by members of this numerous family in the making and maintenance of this great American republic, by Michael Walter Downes. Hartford, Conn., The Case, Lockwood & Brainard company, 1909.   iv p., 1 l., 7-363 p. front. (col. coat of arms) ports. 19½ cm. 25-4512.
CS71.M978   1909

12362   MURPHY. Our own people, the lives and achievements of the Murphys in Ireland and America, by Timothy C. Murphy, collaborated by Eugene L. Murphy. (Norwood, Mass., Norwood press) Published privately, 1935.   2 p. l., 31 p. front. (coat of arms) 22 cm.   36-12559.
CS71.M978   1935

12363   MURPHY. John Murphy and some of his descendants: a report to the family. By Deacon Murphy. (Brooklyn? 1958)   63 p. 28 cm. 58-36404.
CS71.M978   1958

12364   MURPHY. Tennessee Murphys-Murpheys and allied families. By Marion Emerson Murphy. 1st ed. (n. p.) 1968 -   v. 28 cm. Contents. - v.1. Braceys, Gossetts, Heads, Justices, Mitchells, Morgans, Murpheys, Murphys, Parkers, Winters, and others. 68-6371.
CS71.M978   1968

MURPHY. See also: ALDERMAN, 1957
ALEXANDER, 1924
BEATTY, 1886
WALLACE, 1958
WILLIAMS, 1949b
VAN NESS, 1960

12365   MURRAY. Letters of James Murray, loyalist; edited by Nina Moore Tiffany, assisted by Susan I. Lesley. Boston, printed: not published, 1901.   ix p., 2 l., 324 p., 1 l., 3 pl., 7 port. (incl. front.) 3 double facsim. 22½ cm. Genealogy of Murrays: Appendix, p.291-315. 2-458.
E278.M98M9

12366   MURRAY. The heraldry of the Murrays, with notes on all the males of the family, descript- ions of the arms, plates and pedigrees, by G. Harvey Johnston ... Edinburgh and London, W. & A. K. Johnston, limited, 1910. x p., 1 l., 111 p. VIII col. coats of arms (incl. front.) 26½ cm. "125 copies of this work have been printed, of which only 100 will be offered to the public." 22-9022.
CR1669.M8J6

12367   MURRAY. ... Murray family records, by J. Montgomery Seaver. Philadelphia, Pa., American historical-genealogical society (1930)   63, (1) p. front. (ports.) coat of arms, 2 fold. geneal. tab. 28½ cm. "References": p. 63. 32-34834.
CS71.M9785   1930

12368   MURRAY. The five sons of "Bare Betty", by her descendants Colonel Hon. Arthur C. Murray ... with a preface by Lord Tweedsmuir ... (John Buchan) ... London, J. Murray (1936)   211 p. front., illus. (incl. facsims.) ports. 22 cm. Contents. - Their ancestry. - Patrick, fifth lord Elibank. - George, sixth lord. - The Hon. Rev. Dr. Gideon Murray. - The Hon. Alexander Murray. - General Hon. James Murray. 36-17629.
DA810.E4M8

12369   MURRAY. The Murray-Conwell genealogy and allied families ... compiled by Maude Levering Lawrence and Geraldine Lawrence Lombard. (St. Paul, Minn., 1938)   115 p. front. (port.) 24 cm. Blank pages for additions (108-110) Includes bibliography. Data collected and preface signed by Winifred Conwell (Murray) Milne. 40-2179.
CS71.M9785   1938

12370   MURRAY. The descendants of Jonathan Murray of East Guilford, Connecticut. By William Breed Murray. Peoria, Ill., Lithographed by Illinois Valley Pub. Co. (195-)   ix, 376 p. illus., ports. 24 cm. 58-36399.
CS71.M9785

274

12371   MURRAY.   Murray genealogy and family history;   notebook.   By James Ellis Murray.
Kansas City, Mo., c. 1959.   1 v.(loose leaf)   2 maps (fold. in pocket) coat of arms, diagrs. 30 cm.   "No. 57."   Includes bibliographical references.   59-51284.   CS71.M9785   1959

12372   MURRAY.   Descendants of James Murray and Jemima Morgan of Baltimore County, 1704-
1964 (by) Robert Barnes.   Baltimore, 1964.   24 l. geneal. tables. 29 cm. 64-57912.   CS71.M9785   1964

   MURRAY.   See also: BASKERVILLE, 1917
                         BEATTY, 1886
                         CRITTENDEN, 1936
                         HOLLIDAY, 1962
                         POCAHONTAS, 1887
                         SKEET, CS438.S5

12373   MURROW.   The Murrow family of Virginia, Kentucky, Indiana, Iowa, and Kansas.   Descendants of James Murrow ... A partial genealogy, compiled from 1910 to 1940, by Charles Harland
Mirrow (!) ... (Des Moines? 1940?)   22 l. 28½ cm.   30½ cm.   Type-written.   Includes the Blue family.   44-16349.
                                                                              CS71.M9786   1940

   MURYHULL.   See MURIEL.

   MUSCHITZ.   In vertical file under PRANKE family.   Ask reference librarian for this material.

12374   MUSGRAVE.   The story of the luck of Edenhall, by Amanda B. Harris, together with Longfellow's poem "The luck of Edenhall" and "Edenhall", by Susan Coolidge (pseud.);   illustrated by
Edmund H. Garrett.   Boston, D. Lothrop company (1888)   (15) p. illus. 30 cm.   Illustrated cover.   Longfellow's
poem translated from Uhland.   28-15786.   PS2271.L8   1888

12375   MUSGRAVE.   The Musgroves of Longdale, a family record in story form with an addendum
concerning the author and his immediate family.   By Lewis Stansbury Musgrove.   (New York, 1946)
5 p. 1. 91 (i.e.107), (3), 20 p., 4 l. col. front. (coat of arms) ports., map, facsim. 28½ x 22½ cm. 46-19645.
                                                                              CS71.M97865   1946

12376   MUSGRAVE.   A history of a Quaker branch of the Musgrave family of the north of Ireland,
Pennsylvania, North Carolina, Illinois, and elsewhere, with selected papers relating to the ancient and
landed Musgraves of England.   1st ed.   By Stanley Musgrave Shartle.   Indianapolis, 1961.
200 p. illus., ports., coat of arms. 28 cm. 61-11931.   CS71.M97865   1961

   MUSGRAVE.   See also YATES, 1887

   MUSGROVE.   See MUSGRAVE.

12377   MUSICK.   Genealogy of the Musick family and some kindred lines, by G. C. Musick.   (1st ed.)
Meadow Bridge, W. Va., 1964.   vi, 160, 24 p. illus., ports. 23 cm. 65-1200.
                                                                              CS71.M97868   1964

12378   MUSICK.   Marriage records of Cole County, Missouri, 1821-1900, compiled from original
certificates & licenses, with notes on genealogy, by Guy M. Sone & Ruth Wells Sone.   Jefferson City,
Mo., 1964.   414 l. facsims. 28 cm. 65-3528.   F472.C65S6

   MUSITS.   In vertical file under PRANKE family.   Ask reference librarian for this material.

   MUSS.   In vertical file under PRANKE family.   Ask reference librarian for this material.

   MUSSCHITZ.   In vertical file under PRANKE family.   Ask reference librarian for this material.

12379   MUSSER.   Musser and allied families, a genealogical study with biographical notes, compiled
and privately printed for Dorothy Musser by the American historical company, inc.   New York, 1941.
163 p. plates, ports., facsim., col. coats of arms, col. geneal. tables. 32 cm.   Title-page and "dedication" ornamented in colors; colored
initials.   Some of the plates accompanied by guard sheets with descriptive letterpress.   Bound in blue levant, gold tooled, with coats of arms of the
Moser (Musser) and Shipley families on covers.   Includes bibliographical notes.   41-15608.
                                                                              CS71.M9787   1941

MUSSER.   See also: DODDRIDGE, 1961
                     MERCER.

MUSSITS.   In vertical file under PRANKE family.   Ask reference librarian for this material.

MUSTERS.   See WANDESFORD, CS439.W288

12380   MUSTOE.   Chambers Mustoe; copyright ... by Howard B. Grant ... Philippi, W. Va., H.B. Grant, c.1936.   1 l. 28½ x 23 cm.   Caption title.   Text runs parallel with back of cover.   Mimeographed.   38M822T.
CS71.M9788   1936

12381   MUSTOE.   James Mustoe; copyright ... by Howard B. Grant ... Philippi, W. Va., H.B. Grant, c.1936.   1 l. 28½ x 23 cm.   Caption title.   Text runs parallel with back of cover.   Mimeographed.   38M825T.
CS71.M9788   1936a

12382   MUTCH.   Genealogy of the Mutch family, by James Robert Mutch.   Charlottetown (Can.) Printed by the Patriot job print, 1929.   94 p. incl. front. 2 pl. (incl. ports.) 29 cm.   Blank pages at end for additions.   35-30098.
CS71.M98   1929

MYDDLETON.   See MIDDLETON.

12383   MYERS.   Genealogy of the Meyer family.   By Henry Meyer.   Cleveland, O., Printed by Lauer & Mattill, 1890.   131 p. 20½ cm.   9-12301.
CS71.M995   1890

12384   MYERS.   The poems of J. F. Myers, together with biography.   (n.p., 1906)   1 p. l., iv, 200 p. 2 port. 19½ cm.   Imperfect: t.-p. wanting.   Half-title.   Genealogy of the Myers family: p. 169-186.   Genealogy of the John Lindley, sr., family: p. 187-196.   Genealogy of the William W. Birdsell family: p. 197-200.   11-20978 rev.
PS2459.M5   1906

12385   MYERS.   Biographical sketches of the Bailey-Myers-Mason families, 1776 to 1905; key to a cabinet of heirlooms in the National museum, Washington.   (Washington? D.C.) Priv. print., 1908.   142 p. front., plates, ports., facsim. 29 cm.   By Mrs. Cassie Mason (Myers) James.   9-12407.
CS71.M995   1908

12386   MYERS.   Records of the Myers, Hays, and Mordecai families from 1707 to 1913.   By Caroline (Myers) Cohen.   Published for the family (1913?)   57 p. 24 cm.   50-49166.   CS71.M995   1913

12387   MYERS.   Myers and Eatherton families of Hancock and Wyandotte counties, Ohio, allied families with these in Ohio, Koh(e(r, Brown, Pratt, Treece, Clark, Kanouse, Rex, Keenan, Corbin, Lockwood, by Lester T. Wilson.   St. Petersburg, Fla. (1946)   12 p. 23 cm.   46-23128.
CS71.M995   1946

12388   MYERS.   The Martin Myers family, 1793-1964, by Lloyd E. Kelly.   (n.p., 1964)   72 l. 30 cm.   Cover title.   66-98560.   CS71.M995   1964

12389   MYERS.   Home folks book of the Darius Myers family; a collection of letters, genealogical records, stories, accounts, (and) histories.   Compiled by Violet M. Beck.   San Diego, Calif., Arts & Crafts Press (1969)   416, 23 p.   illus., facsims., ports. 29 cm.   Part of the illustrative matter is colored.   "Second Homefolks book of the Darius Myers Family, 1710-1968.   The first was published in 1926."   Includes bibliographies.   72-8732 MARC.
CS71.M995   1969

MYERS.   See also: CAMPBELL. 1921   HOLSINGER, 1959
                    CASS, DA690.B23C3   MEYER, 1922
                    CLENDINEN, 1923   MILLER, 1923
                    HASSELBACH, 1910   MOYER, 1896
                    HILTON, E171.A53 vol.16

12390   MYGATE.   A historical notice of Joseph Mygatt, one of the early colonists of Cambridge, Mass., and afterward one of the first settlers of Hartford, Conn.; with a record of his descendants.   By Frederick T. Mygatt ... Brooklyn, Printed by the Harmonial association, 1853.   116 p. 25½ cm.   3-7929
CS71.M996   1853

MYGATT.   See MYGATE.

12391   MYLNE.   The Mylne family.   Master masons, architects, engineers, their professional career, 1481-1876.   Printed for private circulation by Robert W. Mylne ... London, 1877.   3 p. l., 31 p. 1 l.   illus. (incl. coat of arms, facsim.) 26 cm.   Title vignette: coat of arms.   Portrait of Robert Mylne inserted at page 17.   Contents. - The Mylne family ... comp. by Wyatt Papworth ... for the Dictionary of architecture, of the Architectural publication society, published for the Society.   London, 1876.   p. 1-14. - Register of arms. - Lyon office - Scotland - 1672.   p. 15. - The Mylne family.   From the History of the Lodge of Edinburgh (Mary's Chappel, no. 1) by D. Murray Lyon (Blackwood, Edinburgh, 1873) p. 17-24. - Contract by the master masons and fellow-craftsmen of the ancient Lodge of Scone and Perth, on the decease of John Mylne, master mason and master of the said lodge, p. 25-31.   22-633.

CS479. M88

12392   MYLNE.   Master masons to the crown of Scotland and their works.   By Rev. Robert Scott Mylne ... Edinburgh, Scott & Ferguson (etc.) 1893.   xviii p., 1 l., 307, (1) p. col. front. (coat of arms) illus., plates, ports., plans, facsims.   39 cm.   Contents. - book I.   Royal architecture prior to the reformation. - book II.   Result of the union of Great Britain under one crown. - book III.   The restoration of the house of Stuart. - book IV.   The descendants of the master mason to Queen Anne. - Pedigrees. 2-5404.

NA972. M9

12393   MYNDERSE.   McClellan, Mynderse and allied families, genealogical and biographical, prepared and privately printed for Helen Livingston McClellan by the American historical society, inc.   New York, 1928.   151 p. plates, ports., col. coats of arms. 23 cm.   Alternate pages blank.   Published also under title "McClellan, Mynderse and allied families, by E. D. Clements" in Americana, v. 23, 1929, p. 26-85.   "A hunting log, by Edwin McClellan": p. (31)-151. 30-24869 rev. 3.

CS71. M997   1928
Office.

──── Copy 2.   Title-page in colors. Printed on Japanese vellum. Lacks Livingston coat of arms. Bound in blue levant, gold tooled and inlaid, with leather doublures.

Rare book room.

12394   MYNDERSE.   McClellan, Mynderse and allied families, genealogical and biographical, prepared and privately printed for Helen Livingston McClellan by the American historical society, inc.   New York, 1930.   163 p. plates, ports., col. coats of arms. 23 cm.   Alternate pages blank. Published also under title: McClellan, Mynderse and allied families, by E. D. Clements" in Americana, v. 23, 1929, p. 26-85.   Title page in colors.   "A hunting log, by Edwin McClellan": p. (43)-163.   Bound in blue levant, gold tooled and inlaid, with leather doublures. 33-15350 rev.

CS71. M997   1930

MYNDERSE.   See also McCLELLAN, 1928

MYRICK.   See MERRICK.

MYSER.   See MEISSER.

MYTINGER.   See JENNINGS, 1899

MYTTON.   See WESTON, 1899

N

NÄF.   See NEFF.

12395   NAESETH.   The Naeseth-Fehn family history; the history and genealogy of two large inter-related families, including the cognate lines of Stuverud, Neset, Bonhus, Gunderson, Haraldsen, Stephens, Ullevig, and Stenstadvold.   By Gerhard Brandt Naeseth.   Madison, Wis., 1956.
346 p. illus. 24 cm. 59-53266.   CS71.N14   1956

12396   NAFZGER.   History of the Nafzger family in America (various spellings of name, Naftzger, Naffziger, Nofziger, Noftsinger, Noffsinger, Nofsinger.)   Also genealogy of various branches; collected and compiled by Glea Brown Richer.   (South Whitley, Ind., Stump printing company, c. 1939)
176 p. illus. 23½ cm. Errata slip mounted on p. 88. Blank pages for "Memoranda" (172-176) 39-16996.   CS71.N16   1939

   NAGEL.   See: BLAUVELT, 1957
               GÜNTHER, CS629.G8

   NAGEREL.   See DU PONT, 1923

   NAGLEE.   See No. 1547 - Cabell county.

12397   NAIRNE.   John Nairne (1711-1795) minister of Anstruther Easter, and his descendants.
By Charles Sylvester Nairne.   (London) Printed for private circulation by McCorquodale (1931)
47 p. illus. 26 cm. 57-55992.   CS71.N17   1931

12398   NANCE.   The Nance memorial; a history of the Nance family in general, but more particularly of Clement Nance, of Pittsylvania County, Virginia, and descendants, containing historical and biographical records with family lineage, by Geo. W. Nance ... Bloomington, Ill., J.E. Burke & co., printers, 1904.   xvi, 354 p. front., illus. (incl. ports.) 23½ cm. 4-30105.   CS71.N176   1904

12399   NANCE.   Nance register; a book of genealogy.   Compiled by Martin L. "Pete" Nance.
(Editor: Elizabeth Ann "Nance" Casto) Shreveport, La. (1966)   523 p. illus., coat of arms, ports. 28 cm.
67-437.   CS71.N176   1966

   NANGLE.   See FRENCH, 1847

12400   NANSIGLOS.   The Nansiglos family.   By G. Andrews Moriarty ... (Reprinted from "Misc. gen. et her.", June, 1923.)   London, Mitchell Hughes and Clarke, 1923.   11 p. 25½ cm. 24-30587.
                                                                                                 CS439.N25

12401   NAPIER.   Memoirs of John Napier of Merchiston, his lineage, life, and times, with a history of the invention of logarithms.   By Mark Napier, esq.   Edinburgh, W. Blackwood; (etc., etc.) 1834.
xvi, 534 p. illus., plates, 4 port. (incl. front.) facsims. (1 fold.) 28 ½ x 22½ cm. 5-12354.
                                                                                                 QA29.N2N2

12402   NAPIER.   Notes on the pedigree of Her Most Serene Highness Ann Groom, duchess of Mantua and Montferrat in Italy ... and of her son, His Highness Charles Ottley Groom Napier, prince of Mantua and Montferrat;   master of Lennox...Comp. from public and private documents.   By the late John Riddell ... assisted by M. Berryer, jun., and J. Montgomery.   To which is added the descent of the duchess from 300 emperors, kings, and princes ... and an introductory essay by an advocate of the Scottish bar.   London, For private circulation, 1879. 40p. 22 cm. Introduction signed: W.F. 10-5832.
                                                                                                 CS439.N3

12403   NAPIER.   The pedigree of Her Most Serene Highness, the Duchess of Mantua, Montferrat, and Ferrara; Nevers, Réthel and Alençon; Countess of Lennox, Fife, and Menteth; Baroness of Tabago; in which is traced her descent from King David, the houses of Gonzaga, Paleologus, Este, Bourbon, Lennox, Napier, etc.   With the roll of Mantuan medallists.   Compiled from public and private documents, by the late John Riddell ... assisted by His Royal Highness the late Comte de Chambord, M. Berryer, junior, and J. Montgomery, esq. ... with a preface containing the opinion of Her Majestys attorney general on the proof of this pedigree.   A new ed., rev. and enl.   With portraits of the family.   London, For private circulation, 1885.   2 p. l., xxxi, (1), 69, (1) p. front., illus. (coats of arms) xli pl. (incl. ports., facsims., fold. geneal. tab.) 29½ x 23 cm.   Title vignette (arms of the Gonzaga family) 24-19239.

CS439.N3   1885

12404   NAPIER.   A history of the Napiers of Merchiston shewing their descent from the earls of Lennox of Auld and their marriage into the family of the Scotts of Thirlestane, comp, from old records. (London) Priv. print. J. & E. Bumpus ltd., 1921.   xi, (1), 234 p. front., illus. (coats of arms) plates, ports. 27 cm. "This edition is limited to 100 copies, of which this volume is no, 19." 22-19648.   DA758.3.N4H5

12405   NAPIER.   Tha hast na peer: notes on his family history, by John Hawkins Napier, III. (Alexandria? Va., 1967)   25 l. 30 cm. 67-7756.   CS71.N1785

        NAPIER.   See also: LENNOX, DA758.3.L6N2
                             STEVENS, 1957

12406   NASH.   Fifty Puritan ancestors, 1628-1660; genealogical notes, 1560-1900, by their lineal descendants, Elizabeth Todd Nash.   New Haven, The Tuttle, Morehouse & Taylor company, 1902. xii, 182, (8) p. plates, ports., facsims., fold. geneal. tables. 27 cm.   Blank pages for "Descendants record" (8 at end) 2-8223.

CS71.N25   1902

12407   NASH.   The Nash family; or, Records of the descendants of Thomas Nash, of New Haven, Connecticut.   Collected and compiled by the Rev. Sylvester Nash, A.M. ... 1640.   Hartford, Press of Case, Tiffany & company, 1853.   iv, (5)-304 p. front., ports. 23½ cm.   Blank leaves at end for "Family record." 9-12552.

CS71.N25   1853

12408   NASH.   A genealogical record of the descendants of William Nash of Bucks County, Pennsylvania.   Together with historical and biographical sketches, and illustrated with portraits and other illustrations.   By Rev. A. J. Fretz ... Butler, N.J., Press of Pequannock, Valley Argus, 1903. 88, 6 p. front., pl., ports. 23 cm. 4-29758.   CS71.N25   1903

12409   NASH.   Francis Nash of Braintree, Mass., and 480 of his descendants.   (By Vernon Sirvillian Phillips) (Columbus, O., 1932)   cover-title, 45 numb. l. 29 cm. Type-written. "The Puritan manuscripts, Vernon S. Phillips": leaf 1. 32-24486.   CS71.N25   1932

12410   NASH.   Francis Nash of Braintree, Mass. and 1550 of his descendants ... Akron, O., 1933. 1 p. l., 4, ii, iv-xii, 5-112 p. illus. (plan) 2 port. on 1 pl. 28½ cm. Typewritten. "The Puritan manuscripts, Vernon S. Phillips." "References": p. 3. 34-8475.   CS71.N25   1933

12411   NASH.   Nashes of Ireland: Richard & Alexander Nash of Eatern Shore and their allied families, 1200-1956.   By Anna Catherine (Smith) Pabst.   (Delaware? Ohio) c. 1963.   441, lxxi, 44 p. maps, facsim. 29 cm. Bibliographical footnotes. 64-2152.   CS71.N25   1963

12412   NASH.   Amasa Nash family, 1794-1968.   Researched and compiled by Ruth E. (Nash) Summerlott.   (Middleville, Mich., 1968?)   1 sheet. 122 x 93 cm. fold. to 31 x 24 cm. Reproduction of MS. Includes bibliography. 70-2722 MARC.   CS71.N25   1968

        NASH.   See also: CLARK, 1877
                           PAGE, 1911
                           SHAKESPEARE, RR2901.B3
                           SHAKESPEARE, PR2901.F7

        NASON.   See: HAWLEY, 1929
                       LAYTON, 1877

12413   NATHAN.   Nathan family chart with intermarriages.   By Sanford A. Moss.   Lynn, Mass.,
1939.   geneal. tab.   38 x 51 cm.   Photostat of manuscript copy (positive)   39-16925.   CS71.N275   1939

12414   NATION.   Descendants of Mattison Nations and Cynthia Garrett.   By Loye Eugene Nations.
Columbia, S.C. (1969)   173 p.   ports.   28 cm.   74-8072 MARC.   CS71.N277   1969

NATIONS.   See JOHNSON, 1956a

12415   NAUDAIN.   Excerpts from the de Rapelje, Remsen (van der Beeck) Swain, Clark, Clayton,
Morgan, Boyce, Naudain, Steel and Stockton genealogies.   By George Valentine Massey.   (n. p.) 1948.
Microfilm copy of typescript.   Positive.   Collation of the original, as determined from the film: 77 l.   plates, ports., facsim.   Includes biblio-
graphical references.   Mic 52-435.   Microfilm CS-8

12416   NAVARRE.   Navarre: or, Researches after the descendants of Robert Navarre ... And some
historical notes on families who intermarried with Navarres ... Compiled by Christian Denissen ...
(Detroit, Mich., J. F. Eby & co., 1897)   418 p.   front. (port.)   24 cm.   9-12554.
CS71.N321   1897

NAVARRE.   See also HALL, 1892

12417   NAVARRO.   From legend to reality: the De Berry-Navarro story.   By Susan Daugherty
Navarro.   (Pecos, Tex., 1964)   35 p.   illus., facsims., map.   28 cm.   65-51582.
CS71.N322   1964

12418   NAY.   Genealogy of the Nay family, a record of the descendants of Jacob Nay of Virginia from
1723 to 1949, with supplement.   By Ernest Omar Nay.   (Terre Haute? Ind., 1949)   512 p.   illus., ports.
24 cm.   49-28142.   CS71.N33   1949

NEAL.   See NEALE.

12419   NEALE.   Photograph of silver cup brought to America by the immigrant ancestor of the Neale
family, showing the arms.   (n. p., n. d.)   plate.   17½ cm.   41-38335.   CS71.N345

12420   NEALE.   The Neal record: being a list of the descendants of John Neale, one of the early
settlers of Salem, Mass.   Compiled by Theodore Augustus Neal ... Boston, H. W. Dutton & son,
printers, 1856.   80 p.   front. (fold. geneal. tab.)   24 cm.   Title vignette.   2-5566.
CS71.N345   1856

12421   NEALE.   Genealogy of the Neal family.   (Boston, H. W. Dutton & son, 1856)   geneal. table.
21½ x 55½ cm.   Reprinted from The Neal record.   By Theodore Augustus Neal ... Boston, 1856.   2-8910.
CS71.N345   1856a

12422   NEALE.   John Neill, of Lewes, Delaware, 1739, and his descendants.   (Compiled by Edward
Duffield Neill)   Philadelphia, Priv. print. for the family (Collins, printer) 1875.   3 p. l., 127 p.   facsim.,
geneal. tables.   24 cm.   9-15619.   CS71.N345   1875

12423   NEILL.   Historical notes on the ancestry and descendants of Henry Neill, M. D.   (By Edward
Duffield Neill) Privately printed.   (n. p.) 1886.   33 p.   22½ cm.   1-16051.
CS71.N345   1886

12424   NEALE.   Charters and records of Neales of Berkeley, Yate and Corsham, by John Alexander
Neale.   (London and Warrington, Printed for private circulation (by Mackie and co., limited) 1906.
3 p. l., 263 p. illus. (incl. coat of arms)   27 cm.   46-41444.   CS439.N32   1906

———— Supplement ... London and Warrington, Mackie and co., limited, 1927.   3 p. l., 84 p. pl.,
port.   27½ cm.   Title vignette (coat of arms)   CS439.N32   1906
Supplement.

———— Further addenda to supplement ... London and Warrington, Mackie and co., limited,
1929.   1 p. l., 85-104 p.   27½ cm.   46-41444.   CS439.N32   1906
Suppl. a

12425   NEALE.   The Neil family, Sweden-America, 1718-1908, by Rosa Neil Crandall ... Albion, N.Y., A.M.Eddy press, 1908.   73 p. illus. (incl. ports.) 23 cm. 9-13947.   CS71.N345   1908

12426   NEALE.   A son of the American revolution; being the life and reminiscences of Basil Llewellin Neal ... (Washington, Ga., The Washington reporter print, 1914)   135, (1) p. incl. illus., ports. pl. 20 cm. "Genealogy": p. 119-130. 17-20878.   CT275.N4A3

12427   NEALE.   From generation to generation.   The genealogies of Henry Moore Neil, Abby Grosvenor Tillinghaste, Guy Mallon, Albert Neilson Slayton, Byron Lakin Bargar, Alfred Hastings Chapin.   Compiled by Julia Evans (Stone) Neil.   (Columbus, O., The Champlin press, 1915) 131 p. front., ports. 25½ cm. 16-23003.   CS71.N345   1915

12428   NEALE.   Neal family compiled by Emma E. (Neal) Brigham ... Springfield, Mass., 1938 1 p. l., vii-xvi, 378 p. illus. (incl. coats of arms) port., facsim. 23½ cm. 39-8744.   CS71.N345   1938

12429   NEALE.   The ancestry of Joseph Neal, 1769-c.1835, of Litchfield, Maine, by Walter Goodwin Davis.   Portland, Me., The Southworth-Anthoensen press, 1945.   6 p. l., (3)-145 p. illus. (facsims.) 23 cm. 45-10199.   CS71.N345   1945

        NEALE.   See also: DRIVER, 1889   NEIL.
                                HALEY, 1900   SEMMES, 1918
                                JOLLIFFE, 1893   SEMMES, 1956
                                LA RUE, 1921   ZIMMERMAN, 19 -
                                LESNETT, 1931

        NEALE.   See also Colonial families of the Southern States by Stella P. Hardy.   Page 394
                                                                        CS61.H3   1911

        NEAVE.   See ATKINSON, 1933

        NEDE.   See NEED.

        NEDELS.   See NEEDLES.

12430   NEED.   A history of the family of Need of Arnold, Nottinghamshire, by Michael L. Walker. London, Research Pub. Co. (c.1963)   28 p. geneal. table. 23 cm. "Limited edition of 100 copies of which this is copy no. 65." Bibliographical references included in "Notes" (p.19-22) 64-56304.   CS439.N324   1963

        NEEDE.   See NEED.

12431   NEEDHAM.   Tables of descendants of Francis Jack Needham, twelfth viscount, first earl of Kilmorey (whose eldest child was born in 1787), who were alive on Christmas day, 1900.   Arranged according to their relationship to the undersigned: Robert Needham Cust ... Prepared with the kind assistance of his niece, Beatrice Frances Cust ... (Hertford, Printed by S. Austin and sons, 190-?) 16 p. 24 cm. Contents. - table I. Male branch: issue of Francis Jack, second earl of Kilmorey. - tables II-V. Female branches. Cust, Higginson, Bridgeman, Knox. - Four daughters of Francis Jack, first earl of Kilmorey. 18-4080.   CS439.N325

        NEEDLES.   See MANN, 1876

12432   NEEL.   The Neel-Dickson genealogy.   By William Trent Neel.   (2d ed.)   Rev. to Jan. 1, 1949.   Bryn Mawr, Pa. (1953?)   726 l. 29 cm. 54-36919.   CS71.N345   1953

12433   NEELY.   Neely family chart of West Virginia, compiled by Mrs. E. Camden Jones.   (Smithton? W. Va.) 1910.   6 p. 43 cm. Manuscript; typed title page supplied. 54-50860.   CS71.N37   1910

        NEELY.   See also: ADAMS, 1950
                                STEEN, 1959

12434   NEELY.   Material in vertical file.   Ask reference librarian for this material.

        NEESON.   See WOOD, 1939

NEET. See REASOR, 1941

12435   NEFF. A chronicle, together with a little romance regarding Rudolf and Jacob Näf, of Frankford, Pennsylvania, and their descendants, including an account of the Neffs in Switzerland and
America. By Elizabeth Clifford Neff ... Cincinnati, O., Press of R. Clarke & company, 1886.
352 p. illus., plates, facsim. 22½ cm. 9-12553.   CS71.N383   1886

12436   NEFF. Addenda. Näf-Neff history, regarding the origin and meaning of the name of Neff.
Together with the revolutionary records of Captain Rudolf Neff, Ensign Aaron Scout, Major Thomas
Smyth, jr. Cleveland, O., The author, 1899.   35 p. 21½ cm. 9-12536.   CS71.N383   1899

12437   NEFF. A memorial of the Neff family, with special reference to Francis Neff and some of
his descendants, compiled by Elmer Ellsworth Neff ... Altoona, Penna., Mirror printing company,
1931.   xiv, 24, 24a-b, 25-34, 34a-b, 35-132, (8) p. front. (port.) coat of arms. 23½ cm. Lettered on cover: Neff history. Blank pages
for "Memorandum" (8 at end) 32-25141.   CS71.N383   1931

12438   NEFF. The descendants of William Neff who married Mary Corliss, January 23, 1665,
Haverhill, Massachusetts. By Dorothy (Neff) Curry. (n.p., 1958?)   unpaged. illus. 24 cm. 60-30134.
                                                                                 CS71.N383   1958

12439   NEFF. From the Alps to the Appalachians; a brief history including some of the Neff families of Switzerland, Germany, Pennsylvania, Virginia, and statistics on the descendants of Michael H.
Neff, 1833-1922, of the Shenandoah Valley of Virginia. Arlington, Va., Beatty, 1967.   xii, 148 p. illus.,
coat of arms, ports. 24 cm. Bibliography: p. 131-133. 67-31539.   CS71.N383   1967

          NEFF. See also: BURNETT, 1953
                            CORLISS, 1875
                            STRICKLER, 1925

12440   NEGUS. Negus family ancestry through Terrell, Wing, Coppock lines; complete ancestral
lines back to King Egbert of England, 802 A.D.; direct descent from kings of England and families of
English nobility, inclduing such names as Plantagenet, deClare, Fitz Alan, Marney, Muscegros,
Beauchamp, Bassett, Bohun, Quincy, and many others. By Ira Elwood Nolte. Anoka, Minn. (1962?)
36 p. 22 cm. 62-41382.   CS71.N388   1962

          NEIFF. See NEFF.

12441   NEIGHBOR. Descendants of Leonard Neighbour, immigrant to America, 1738. By L. B.
Neighbour ... Dixon, Ill., Star job rooms, 1906.   viii, 48 p. incl. front. plates, ports., map, facsim. 20 cm. 6-10673.
                                                                                 CS71.N397   1906

          NEIGHBOUR. See: NEIGHBOR.
                            No. 9847 Hackettstown.

12442   NEIKIRK. Ohio descendants of seventeenth century ancestors in Plymouth and Providence
Plantations, Massachusetts Bay and Connecticut Colonies, New York, Pennsylvania, Virginia, Mary-
land, New Jersey, 1620-1960. By Floyd Edwin Neikirk. (Clyde? Ohio, 1960?)   109 (i.e. 112), (35) l.
geneal. tables. 29 cm. Sequel to Genealogy of Clark Rathbun Cleveland. Contains Genealogy of Edna Marea Neikirk Greiner; and, The story of
Jonathan Rathbone Jr., a kinsman of Sandusky County, Ohio, by the questing yankee, Floyd E. Neikirk, serially published in the Clyde (O.) Enterprise,
October 8, 1959 to June 23, 1960. Includes bibliographies. 62-38838.
                                                                                 CS71.N398   1960

          NEIL. See NEALE.

          NEILL. See: JOHNSON, 1961
                        NEALE. N.345

          NEILSON. See NELSON.

          NEISH. See MacNISH. (addenda)

12443   NELL.   The Nell family in the United States, by Rev. Raymond Boyd Nell ... Minneapolis,
Minn., Colwell press, 1929.   66, (38) p. 20 cm. 31-31258.   CS71.N4   1929

12444   NELLIS.   Following "the old Mohawk turnpike" ... Saint Johnsville, N.Y., Press of the Enter-
prise and news, 1927.   27 p. incl. illus., map. 23½ cm. Title vignette. Illustration on cover. Prepared and published by Lou D.
MacWethy. cf. p.(2) Contents. - The old Palatine church. - The Nellis family in colonial days (by Milo Nellis) - The Cochran house, by S.L.
Frey. - Klock and Nellis families. CA 31-22 unrev.   F129.P15M17

         NELLIS.   See also: KLOCK, 1960
                              NOLTE, 1960

12445   NELMS.   Families of Reverend John A. Nelms, Methodist minister, and wife, Mary Bell
Crain Nelms; C. C. Nelms and wife, Delilah Damron Nelms; George Damron and wife, Delilah Fisher
Damron; Moses Allen and wife, Malvina Owens Allen; A. Ford and wife, Lucy Ford; Dr. Wm.
Hunter and wife, Minerva Hunter, all of whom were among the first settlers at Ector, Fannin County,
Texas, in the days of the Republic of Texas, by Vivian and Brenda Newingham.   Bonham, Tex. (1966)
51 l. 28 cm. Cover title. 67-9231.   CS71.N415   1966

12446   NELMS.   Ancestors and their descendants of our great, great, great, grandparents: Rever-
end John A. Nelms, Methodist minster, and his wife, Mary Belle Crain Nelms, who settled in Fannin
County, Texas, in the days of the Republic of Texas.   Compiled and edited by Vivian Newingham
Herriage and Brenda Newingham.   Bonham, Tex., 1968.   20 l. 28 cm. Cover title: Reverend John A. Nelms,
Methodist minister, and wife, Mary Bell Crain Nelms. 78-3235.   CS71.N415   1968

         NELMS.   See also HOLLAND, 1959

12447   NELSON.   The royal descent of Nelson and Wellington from Edward the First, king of England,
with tables of pedigree and genealogical memoirs, comp. by George Russell French ... London, W.
Pickering, 1853.   xiv, 207, (1) p. incl. geneal. tables. ports. 19½ cm. 21-19027.
                                                                   CS418.F83

12448   NELSON.   A family record of the descendants of Thomas Nelson and Joan, his wife.   By one
of them.   Haverhill, E. G. Frothingham, printer, 1868.   32 p. 19½ cm. 9-12551.
                                                                   CS71.N43   1868

12449   NELSON.   Descent of John Nelson and of his children; with notes on the families of Tailer
and Stoughton.   New York (The De Vinne press) 1886.   50 p., (1) l. port., 2 coats of arms. 24½ cm. By Temple
Prime. 13-17825.   CS71.N43   1886

12450   NELSON.   Descent of John Nelson and of his children with notes on the families of Tailer and
Stoughton, by Temple Prime ... 2d ed. New York (The De Vinne press) 1894.   61 p. illus., port. 24½ cm.
9-12548.   CS71.N43   1894

12451   NELSON.   Lieutenant David Nelson and his descendants, by Harriet McIntyre Foster.   (n. p.
190-)   cover-title, 18 p. front., plates, ports. 23 cm. 8-22337.   CS71.N43   190-

12452   NELSON.   Contributions towards a Nelson genealogy ... pt. 1.   By William Nelson.   Paterson, N.J., The Paterson history club, 1904 -   1 v. 28 cm. "One hundred copies printed." Contents. - pt. I.
Some Neilsons of Scotland. 4-35306.   CS71.N43   1904

12453   NELSON.   The Nelson family.   A compilation from many sources of the Nelson family, in
both England and America, temporarily arranged for the use of inquirers who may be interested, and
who may desire to further the perfection of the work by any corrections or additions to the same.
(By Cortez Nelson) (New York, 1906)   4 p. l., 210 (i.e. 215) numb. l. 28 x 22 cm. Type-written. Additions and
corrections in manuscript; slips with additions and newspaper clippings inserted. Bibliography: 3d - 4th prelim. leaves. 44-17891.
                                                                   CS71.N43   1906

12454   NELSON.   A genealogical history of the Nelson family, by Thomas Nelson, with an introduction by the right honourable the Earl Nelson.   (King's Lynn, Thew & son, printers and stationers

to His Majesty the King, 1908) 67, (1), xxvii, (2), 11 p. incl. pl. (coat of arms) illus., facsim., geneal. tables (part fold.) 28 cm. Contains pedigrees of the Smyth, Donne, Halcott, Holley, Pretyman, Bland, Rolfe, Suckling, Bolton, Thurlow, Turnour and Eyre families. Inserted at end are four leaves containing reviews of the work reprinted from various periodicals. 12-19127. CS439.N33

12455 NELSON. Family record of Joseph and Margaret M. Nelson. (n. p., 1908) 6 numb. l., 1 l. 31 x 21½ cm. Caption title. Type-written. Signed: T. W. Sheriffs. 44-17654. CS71.N43 1908

12456 NELSON. The Nelsons of Burnham Thorpe; a record of a Norfolk family compiled from un- published letters and notebooks, 1787-1842, by M. Eyre Matcham, with a photogravure frontispiece and fourteen other illustrations. London, John Lane; New York, John Lane compnay, 1911 306 p. incl. front. plates, ports. 23 cm. 11-16771. DA87.1.N3M2

12457 NELSON. Genealogy and history of the Nelson family. 1378-1928. By Andrew G. Nelson. (Kasson, Minn., Press of Nottage bros., 1928) 1 p. l., 46 p. illus. (incl. ports.) 2 fold. geneal. tab. 21 cm. Blank pages for additions (41-46) Foreword signed: A. G. Nelson. 38-14708. CS71.N43 1928

12458 NELSON. ... Nelson family records, by J. Montgomery Seaver ... Philadelphia, Pa., American historical-genealogical society, 1929. 34 p. illus. (ports.) 23 cm. Coats of arms on cover. "References": p. 29-30. 30-8669. CS71.N43 1929a

12459 NELSON. Wilderness home, 1854. By Joseph Sophornius Nelson. (Sioux Falls? S. D., c. 1958) 323 p. illus. 20 cm. 59-30583. CS71.N43 1958

12460 NELSON. ... Our family genealogy, including the Nelson, Johnson, Roach, Smith, Little, Cox, Dawson-Wooten, and Chapman families, each related to the other by descent or marriage, or both. Compiled by Rev. Wm. E. Cox, and Mrs. Olivia Cox McCormac, with the help of other members of the family, also research work of Miss Marybelle Delamar and other genealogists. (Southern Pines, N. C.) The Mary Nelson Smith family, 1938. 5 p. l., 109, (8) p. 2 port. (incl. front.) 23½ cm. Blank ruled pages for memoranda (8 at end) "This book is one of 300 numbered copies, printed for distribution in the several related families listed herein. No. 85." 30-15107. CS71.N43 1938

12461 NELSON. The Nelson-Moen family of the town of Tumuli, Otter Tail county, Minnesota. Fergus Falls, Minn., Ukeblad publishing company (1938) 24 p. illus. (incl. ports.) 22 cm. "Author's preface" signed: Bersvend J. Blikstad. 39-16902. CS71.N43 1938a

12462 NELSON. Geneology (sic) of the Daniel Nelson family of Nelsonville, Ohio, 1638 - Thomas Nelson, Rowley, England, 1958, by John F. Nelson. (Bowling Green? 1958) 1 v. (various pagings) 28 cm. Cover title. "Supplement 1960" (9 leaves) inserted. To be kept up to date through news letters. Includes bibliography. 68-1266. CS71.N43 1958b

12463 NELSON. Descendants of John Nelson, Sr. - Mary Toby, Stafford County, Virginia, 1740- 1959, with related families. By Olive (Nelson) Gibson. (Redlands? Calif., 1961) 349 p. illus. 23 cm. 62-2315. CS71.N43 1961

12464 NELSON. Anthony Nelson: seventeenth century Pennsylvania and New Jersey, and some of his descendants. By Elmer Garfield Van Name. Haddonfield, N. J., 1962. 53 p. illus. 23 cm. 63-38810. CS71.N43 1962

12465 NELSON. The Nelson family of Plymouth, Middleboro, and Lakeville, Massachusetts; a genealogical and biographical record and family history story. By William Ripley Nelson. (Nantucket, Mass.) 1963. 228 l. fold. map, facsims., geneal. tables, photos. 29 cm. 64-1085. CS71.N43 1963

12466 NELSON. Our family genealogy, revised: including the Nelson, Johnson, Roach, Smith, Little, Cox, Dawson, and Chapman families, each related to the other by descent or marriage, or both. Compiled by Wm. E. Cox and Olivia Cox McCormac. 2d ed. compiled by Jeannette Cox St. Amand. (n. p.) Mary Nelson Smith Family, 1967. ix, 279 p. illus., map, ports. 24 cm. 67-9512. CS71.N43 1967

12467 NELSON. John Nelson, his family and descendants. By Everetta Heisner. (Chicago? 1967) 88, 13 p. illus., ports. 28 cm. 67-31866. CS71.N43 1967b

12468   NELSON.   Nelson family in vertical file.   Ask reference librarian for this material.

NELSON.   See also: FUNSTEN, 1926   PEDEN, 1961
                        GIRDLESTONE, CS439.G53   REICHNER, 1918
                        HYDORN, 1934   No. 553 - Goodhue county.
                        PAGE, 1883   No. 579 - Monroe, N. H.

NEPHEW.   See HABERSHAM, 1901

12469   NESBIT.   History of the family of Nisbet or Nesbitt in Scotland and Ireland. From memoranda written by Alexander Nesbitt ... and completed by his widow, Cecilia Nesbitt, June, 1898.   Torquay, Printed for private circulation by A. Iredale (1891)   1 p. 1., 61, (1) p., 1 l. 23½ cm. 22-2781.
CS479.N4

12470   NESBIT.   A genealogy of the Nesbit, Ross, Porter, Taggart families of Pennsylvania, by Blanche T. Hartman.   Pittsburgh, Pa., Priv. print., 1929.   xi p., 1 l., 229, (1) p. front., plates, ports., facsims., 21 geneal. tab. (part fold.) 24 cm. "Including the allied families of Hamilton and Kneeland of Cleland." 29-29960.   CS71.N48   1929

12471   NESBIT.   An American family; the Nesbits of St. Clair, by Charles Francis Nesbit.   Washington, D. C., 1932.   228 p. 22 cm. 32-17489.   CS71.N48   1932

12472   NESBIT.   Nisbet of that ilk (by) Robert Chancellor Nesbitt ... London, J. Murray, 1941.   7 p. 1., 322 p. illus., plates (part col.) ports., maps, 2 col. coats of arms (incl. front.) geneal. tables (2 fold., 1 in pocket) 26½ cm. Bibliography: p. 312-315. A 42-4068 rev.   CS479.N4   1941

12473   NESBIT.   Cairnhill, by Hamilton More Nisbett and Stair Carnegie Agnew.   Edinburgh, Moray Press, 1949.   215 p. illus., coats of arms. 23 cm. 49-29623*.   CS479.N4   1949

12474   NESBIT.   Nisbet narrations.   By Newton Alexander Nisbet. (1st ed.)   Charlotte, N. C., Printed by Crayton Print. Co., 1961.   439 p. coat of arms. 28 cm. Bibliography: p. 437. 61-45495.
CS71.N48   1961

NESBIT.   See also: ALEXANDER, 1960
                        HARVEY, 1899
                        McNAIR, 1935
                        NISBET. (addenda)

NESBITT.   See NESBIT.

NESHAM.   See JAMES, 1913a

12475   NESOM.   Nesom family record and history (by) C. S. Nesom.   Dallas, 1967.   1 v. (various pagings) 30 cm. 78-3708 MARC.   CS71.N485   1967

12476   NESTER.   Descendants of Jacob Nester, 1761-1844 (by Carl K. Nestor.   Kingwood, W. Va., 1963?)   viii, 142 p. 30 cm. Half title. 65-3324.   CS71.N49   1963

NESTOR.   See NESTER.

NETHERCLIFT.   See ROWLAND, CS439.R7

12477   NETTERVILLE.   ... Case of James Netterville, claiming the title of Viscount Netterville of Ireland.   (London, Robins and sons, printers, 1829?)   30 p., 1 l. fold. geneal. tab. 43 cm. Caption title. On verso of last leaf, as filing title: Netterville peerage. Case of James Netterville, esq. 31-6529.   LAW

12478   NETTERVILLE.   Minutes of evidence taken before the Committee for privileges, to whom the petition of James Metterville esquire, of Frahane, to His Majesty, claiming the title, dignity and honour of Viscount Netterville of the kingdom of Ireland, stands referred ... (London) 1830.   62 p. 33 cm. (Parliament, 1830. H. of L. Papers and bills) (206) 31-6528.   LAW

12479   NETTERVILLE.   Minutes of evidence taken before the Committee for privileges to whom was referred the petition of Arthur James Netterville of Cruicerath in the county of Meath esquire, to Her Majesty, praying Her Majesty to be graciously pleased to admit his claim to the dignity of Viscount Netterville, and to declare that he is entitled to the said dignity and all the rights and privileges appertaining thereunto, together with Her Majesty's reference thereof to this house, and the report of the attorney general thereon thereunto annexed ... (London, 1861-67)   102 p. 24 cm. (Sessional papers, 273 of 1861; E of 1862; D of 1864; B of 1867) 24-20420 rev.   CS496.N4G6   1861

12480   NETTERVILLE.   Netterville peerage.   In the House of lords.   Case on behalf of Arthur James Netterville of Cruicerath in the county of Meath esquire, claiming to be Viscount Netterville of Douth in the peerage of Ireland.   (London, Printed by C. F. Hodgson, 1834?)   11 p. fold, geneal. tab. 32 cm. 24-20419.   CS496.N4G6   1834

NETTERVILLE.   See also JOHNSON, 1961

12481   NEUKIRK.   Ohio descendants of seventeenth century ancestors in Plymouth and Providence Plantations, Massachusetts Bay and Connecticut Colonies, New York, Pennsylvania, Virginia, Maryland, New Jersey, 1620-1960.   By Floyd Edwin Neikirk.   (Clyde? Ohio, 1960?)   109 (i.e.112), (35) l. geneal. tables. 29 cm.   Sequel to Genealogy of Clark Rathbun Cleveland.   Contains Genealogy of Edna Marea Neikirk Greiner; and, The story of Jonathan Rathbone Jr., a kinsman of Sandusky County, Ohio, by the questing Yankee, Floyd E. Neikirk, serially published in the Clyde (O.) Enterprise, Oct. 8, 1959 to June 23, 1960.   Includes bibliographies.   62-38838.   CS71.N398   1960

NEVE.   See LE NEVE.

12482   NEVERS.   Memoir of Col. Samuel Nevers, late of Sweden ... by William Nevers 3d ... Norway (Me.) Press of G. W. Millett, 1858.   iv, (5)-80 p. 13½ x 11 cm. 13-2640.   F29.S94N5

12483   NEVEU.   Les Neveu de Montreuil-Bellay.   By Charlotte Neveu.   (n. p., 1962?)   209 l. 28 cm. Bibliography: leaves 208-209. 63-48011.   CS599.N45   1962

12484   NEVILLE.   The armorial windows erected, in the reign of Henry VI.   By John, viscount Beaumont, and Katharine, duchess of Norfolk, in Woodhouse chapel, by the park of Beaumanor, in Charnwood forest, Leicestershire, including an investigation of the differences of the coat of Neville. By John Gough Nichols, F.S.A.   (Westminster, J. B. Nichols and sons) 1860.   2 p. l., 50 p., 1 l. illus. (incl. coats of arms) 2 geneal. tab. (incl. front.) 25 cm.   "Read at the Annual meeting of the Leicestershire architectural and archaeological society of Loughborough, July 27th, 1859."   Printed at the expense of William Perry Herrick. 21-3222.   CR1627.L4N5

12485   NEVILLE.   An historical and genealogical account of the noble family of Nevill, particularly of the house of Abergavenny, and also a history of the old land barony of Abergavenny.   With some account of the illustrious family of the Beauchamps, and others, through whom it descended to the present Earl of Abergavenny.   Accompanied with notices of the castles, seats and estates belonging to the family, and their heraldic honours.   By Daniel Rowland, esq.   London, Printed by S. Bentley, 1830.   2 p. l., 227, xxiv (i.e.xxvi) p. front., illus., (coats of arms) plates, ports. v. double geneal. tab. 44½ cm Page xxvi incorrectly numbered xxiv. 19-14745.   CS439.N35   1830

12486   NEVILLE.   De Nova Villa: or, The house of Nevill in sunshine and shade, by Henry J. Swallow ... Newcastle-on-Tyne, A. Reid; (etc., etc.) 1885.   xix, 334 p. front., illus., 8 pl., 3 port., geneal. tables. 22½ cm.   The House of Abergavenny: p. 225-243. 9-11269.   CS439.N35   1885

12487   NEVILLE.   ... The Nevilles of Warwick, by Frederick E. Melton.   London, New York (etc.) T. Nelson and sons (1913)   128 p. 8 col. pl. (incl. front.) 20 cm. (Famous families in British history) 15-15080.   DA28.35.N5M5

12488   NEVILLE.   A genealogical record of one branch of the Neville family.   By William Neville Collier.   (Long Beach? Calif.) c.1953.   21 l. 29 cm. 54-20078.   CS71.N5   1953

12489   NEVILLE.   The descendants of Thomas M. Neville and Theresa Nevin.   Compiled by Ruth D. Neville Jones.   Neville, Ohio (1970)   (14) l. 30 cm. 70-11912 MARC.   CS71.N5   1970

NEVILLE. See also: BRASFIELD, 1959
         BRENT, 1936
         DRUMMOND, CS419.D7
         ROLFE, CS439.R65

NEVINS. See: JOWITT, CS439.J76
       RICHARDSON, 1929

12490 NEVIUS. Joannes Nevius, schepen and third secretary of New Amsterdam under the Dutch, first secretary of New York city under the English; and his descendants. A.D. 1627-1900 ... By A. Van Doren Honeyman. Plainfield, N.J., Honeyman & co., 1900. 732 p. col. front. (coat of arms) plates, ports., facsims. 25½ cm. Mar. 22, 1900-71.   CS71.N529 1900

NEW. See WYATT, 1949

12491 NEWBAKER. A genealogical record of the descendants of Andrew Newbaker of Hardwick township, Warren County, N.J. ... By Rev. A.J. Fretz ... Netcong, N.J., Union Times print, 1908. iv, (5)-40 p., 1 l. front., pl., ports. 22 cm. 8-27372.   CS71.N533 1908

12492 NEWBERY. The Newberys; an account of some notable members of this old Berkshire family. By Edmund Newbery. Rusper, Sussex (1960) 16 p. illus. 23 cm. 60-38622. CS439.N37 1960

NEWBERY. See also NEWBURY.

12493 NEWBOLD. Bloomsdale, sketches of the old-time home of the John Newbold family, with genealogical notes, compiled by Helen Van Uxem Cubberley. (Stanford University, Printed by Stanford university press) 1930. xi, 61 p. front., illus., ports. 25 cm. "Privately printed." 31-22370.

                              CS71.N534 1930

12494 NEWBOLD. Newbold family notes, compiled by Helen Van Uxem Cubberley. (Stanford University, Printed by Stanford university press) 1937. ix, 46 p. front., illus. (incl. facsims., coat of arms) plates, ports. 24½ cm. "Privately printed." "The Newbolds of Bloomsdale, by Francis Van Uxem": p. 35-46. Selections from the "Newbold family and connections ... collected between 1888 and 1926 by William Romaine Newbold, and presented by his estate to the Genealogical society of Pennsylvania." cf. Foreword. 39-8743.   CS71.N534 1937

12495 NEWBOLD. Family of Charles and Frances Lowe Newbold, ancestors and descendants. Made by Fleming Newbold. Washington, D.C., 1939. geneal. tab. 28 x 68 cm. 40-6186.

                              CS71.N534 1939

12496 NEWBOLD. Newbold genealogy in America; the line of Michael Newbold, who arrived in Burlington County, New Jersey, about 1680 and other Newbold lines, including that of Thomas Newbold, who arrived in Somerset County, Maryland, about 1665. By Charles Platt. New Hope, Pa., 1964. ix, 198 p. illus., facsims., geneal. tables, ports. 26 cm. 64-8627.   CS71.N534 1964

NEWBOLD. See: COMLY, 1939
         DAVIS, 1939

12497 NEWBOLT. Pedigree of the old Winton family the Newbolts, and their descendants. Eastbourne, Priv. print, by H. Brewster, 1895. v, 36 p. 21 cm. Preface signed: Edward Dorrien Newbolt. Contains also the Digby, Dorrien and Rice families. 20-19565.   CS439.N38

12498 NEWBURY. The Newberry family of Windsor, Connecticut, in the line of Clarinda (Newberry) Goodwin, of Hartford, Connecticut, 1634-1866; comp. by Frank Farnsworth Starr for James J. Goodwin. Hartford, Conn. (Cambridge, University press, J. Wilson and son) 1898. 70 p. fold. geneal. tab. 24½ cm. 98-105 rev.   CS71.N535 1898

12499 NEWBURY. Newberry genealogy; the ancestors and descendants of Thomas Newberry, of Dorchester, Mass., 1634. 920-1914. By J. Gardner Bartlett ... Boston, Mass., Pub. by the author for J.S. Newberry, 1914. v, 156 p. front. (col. coat of arms) plates, ports. 25 cm. "Published for limited circulation." 15-15680.   CS71.N535 1914

NEWBURY. See NEWBERY.

12500 NEWCOMB. Genealogical memoir of the Newcomb family, containing records of nearly every person of the name in America from 1635 to 1874. Also the first generation of children descended from females who have lost the name Newcomb by marriages. With notices of the family in England during the past seven hundred years. By John Bearse Newcomb ... Elgin, Ill., Printed for the author by Knight & Leonard, Chicago, 1874. 2 p. l., 600 p. front., ports., facsims. 23½ cm. 9-12540 rev. CS71.N54 1874

12501 NEWCOMB. Newcombe genealogy, by Grace Fielding Hall. Yarmouthport, Mass., C. W. Swift, 1914. cover-title, (4) p. 25 cm. (Library of Cape Cod history & genealogy, no. 42) 14-21774. CS71.N54 1914

12502 NEWCOMB. Andrew Newcomb, 1618-1686, and his descendants; a revised edition of "Genealogical memoir" of the Newcomb family, published 1874 by John Bearse Newcomb ... compiled and revised by Bethuel Merritt Newcomb ... New Haven, Conn., Priv. print. for the author by the Tuttle, Morehouse & Taylor co., 1923. 4 p. l., 1021 p. front., illus. (plan) ports., facsims. 26½ cm. "Contains all of the records of the 1874 edition ... so far as the branch of Andrew Newcomb is concerned." - Introd. 23-15605. CS71.N54 1923

NEWCOMB. See also: ABELL, 1928
DAY, 1916

12503 NEWCOME. The diary of the Rev. Henry Newcome, from September 30, 1661, to September 29, 1663. Edited by Thomas Heywood ... (Manchester) Printed for the Chetham society, 1849. 3 p. l., xl, 242 p. 25 cm. (Added t.-p.: Remains, historical and literary, connected with the palatine counties of Lancaster and Chester. v. 18) 17-15251. DA670.L19C5 v. 18

12504 NEWCOME. The autobiography of Henry Newcome, M. A. Ed. by Richard Parkinson ... (Manchester) Printed for the Chetham society, 1852. 2 v. 22½ cm. (Added t.-p.: Remains, historical and literary, connected with the palatine counties of Lancaster and Chester, pub. by the Chetham society. vol. XXVI-XXVII) Paged continuously; each volume has also special t.-p. The introduction includes a memoir of the Newcome family by the Rev. Thomas Newcome (p. iv-xxii) 18-5247. DA670.L19C5 v. 26-7

12505 NEWCOMEN. The family of Newcomen, of Saltfleetby. By the Rev. W. G. D. Fletcher ... (In reports and papers read at the meetings of the architectural societies ... Lincoln, Eng., 1897. vol. XXIV, p. 145-161) 25-17983. NA12.A2 vol. 24

NEWCOMEN. See also: CRALL, 1908
CROSSLEY, CS439.C835

12506 NEWCOMER. Genealogical chart of Newcomer, Baer and McIlhenny famalies (sic) The Baer connection, the latter part of McIlhenny connection, and the latter part of Newcomer connection is according to the best memory of Mrs. Sophie Newlon Brownfield, July, 1909. Made by R. L. Brownfield, Jr. and by Rex Newlon Brownfield. (n. p.) 1910. geneal. table. 98 x 43 cm. fold. to 29 x 43 cm. Manuscript. "Newcomer family chart no. 1, of Lancaster County, Penna., about seventeen hundred twenty (1720)" "Baer family chart about seventeen hundred twenty (1720) of Leacock Township, Lancaster County, Penna." "McIlhenny chart. Number two (2)" 55-55830. CS71.N542 1910

12507 NEWCOMER. Newcomer family of Lancaster County, Pennsylvania, by Robert L. Brownfield, Jr. (and) Rex Newlon Brownfield. (n. p., 1951) 7 l. geneal. table. 36 cm. Typescript. Two letters inserted. 52-35761. CS71.N542 1951

12508 NEWCOMER. Newcomer genealogy. By Jerome Keahr Huddle. (n. p.) 1955. 7 l. 37 cm. Caption title. Typescript. 56-630 rev. CS71.N542 1955

NEWDEGATE. See NEWGATE.

NEWDIGATE. See NEWGATE.

12509 NEWELL. Thomas Newell, who settled in Farmington, Conn., A. D., 1632. And his descendants. A genealogical table, comp. by Mrs. Mary A. (Newell) Hall. Southington, Conn., Cochrane bros., book and job printers, 1878. 268 p. incl. front. (port.) 19 cm. 9-12539. CS71.N545 1878

12510   NEWELL.   Newell.   By C. C. Baldwin ... (Cleveland, Leader printing compnay, 1882)
1 p. l., p. (167)-171. 23½ cm. From the author's Candee genealogy, Cleveland, 1882. 14-11913.

CS71.N545   1882

12511   NEWELL.   Newell ancestry; the story of the antecedents of William Stark Newell, by
William M. Emery.   (Boston) Priv. print. (Thomas Todd company) 1944.   xi, 226 p. col. front. (coat of arms)
plates, ports. 24½ cm. 44-47574.

CS71.N545   1944

NEWELL.   See also: BASSETT, 1926   LEWIS, 1900
                      CANDEE, 1882   NEWHALL.
                      HABERSHAM, 1901   WHITING, 1889
                      LANE, 1899

NEWEY.   See WOOD, 1937

12512   NEWGATE.   Notes on the parish of Harefield, county of Middlesex, collected and arranged
by William Frederick Vernon, of Harefield park.   For private circulation only.   London, Dalton and
Lucy, 1872.   vii, 62 p. 3 fold. geneal. tab. 21½ cm. Contains pedigrees of the Newdegate family, and the families of Ashby of
Breakspear and Cooke of Harefield. 19-6530.

DA690.H25V4

12513   NEWGATE.   The Cheverels of Cheverel manor.   (Being the correspondence of Sir Roger and
Lady Newdigate, ed.) by Lady Newdigate-Newdegate ... London, New York (etc.) Longmans, Green,
and co., 1898.   xv, 231 p. 6 port. (incl. front.) 23½ cm. Correspondence of Sir Roger and Lady Newdigate, the Sir Christopher and
Lady Cheverel of George Eliot's "Scenes of clerical life." 5-649.

DA506.N5N5

12514   NEWGATE.   Gossip from a muniment-room; being passages in the lives of Anne and Mary
Fitton, 1574 to 1618; transcribed and edited by Lady Newdigate-Newdegate.   (2d ed.) London, D. Nutt,
1898.   1 p. l., xvii, 186, (1) p. 3 port. (incl. front.) tab. 22½ x 18½ cm. Consisting chiefly of the correspondence of Anne Fitton (Lady
Newdigate) Printed, September 1897. Reprinted, February 1898. 5-886.

DA358.F5

NEWGATE.   See also: BOWDOIN, 1887
                        BOWDOIN, 1894
                        McCURDY, 1892
                        SALISBURY, 1892

12515   NEWHALL.   The Newhall family of Lynn, Massachusetts.   By Henry F. Waters.   Pt. I.
(From Historical collections of Essex institute, vols. XVIII and XIX)   Salem, Printed for Essex
institute, 1882.   1 p. l., 109 p. 24½ cm. No more published? 20-9251.

CS71.N548   1882

12516   NEWHALL.   The record of my ancestry, by Charles L. Newhall ... Southbridge, Herald
power print, 1899.   222 p. front., illus., plates, ports., fold. geneal. tab., facsims. 23½ cm. 1-2126.

CS71.N548   1899

         —— Copy 2
         —— Addenda et corrigenda.   (Southbridge? 1905?)   16 p. 23 cm. (With his The record of my ancestry,
Southridge, 1899)

CS71.N548   1905

12517   NEWHALL.   Edwin White Newhall, born 7 May 1856, died 28 October 1915 ... (San Fran-
cisco? 1917?)   3 p. l., 18 p., 1 l., 20-111 p., 1 l. mounted front., mounted plates, mounted ports., double facsim. 22½ cm. "Newhall
genealogy": 3d prelim. leaf, p. 1-11. 46-29393.

CT275.N483N4

         NEWHALL.   See also NEWELL.

12518   NEWHARD.   Descendants of Michael Newhard, 1737-1968.   Compiled by Charles F. Holman.
Sharon, Vt. (1969)   16 p. 29 cm. Cover title. 75-7086 MARC.

CS71.N549   1969

12519   NEWKIRK.   ... Geneology (!) and history of the Newkirk, Hamilton and Bayliss families, by
Thomas J. Newkirk.   Evanston, Ill. (1916)   88 p. incl. 2 port. port. 22½ cm. 16-14832.

CS71.N55   1916

12520   NEWKIRK.   ... The van Nieuwkirk, Nieukirk, Newkirk family.   (By Adamson Bentley Newkirk) Philadelphia, Hall of the Historical society of Pennsylvania, 1934.   vii, 105 p. front., plates. 27 cm. "Publications of the Genealogical society of Pennsylvania ... March 2934.   Special number." Caption title: Some descendants of Gerret Cornelisse and Mattheus Cornelisse van Nieuwkirk. From the manuscript of the late Adamson Bentley Newkirk ... in the collections of the Genealogical society of Pennsylvanie.   "Foreword" signed: P. F. N. (i. e. Philip Ford Nieukirk) Errata slips inserted.   34-32587 rev.

F146.G325   1934

NEWKIRK.   See also NEIKIRK, 1960

12521   NEWLAND.   Newland and Newlon family charts, about seventeen hundred twenty (1720) of Chester County and York County, Penna.; genealogical chart of the Newlon family, compiled and made by Robert Long Brownfield, Jr. and Rex Newlon Brownfield.   (n. p.) 1909.   geneal. table. 771 x 43 cm. fold. to 31 x 43 cm. Manuscript. 55-55823.

CS71.N558   1909

12522   NEWLAND.   The Newland (Newlon) family, a brief genealogy and history of the family whose various branches may use either of these spellings and of other families, related, or unrelated, who may spell or pronounce their name similarly.   By Robert E. Newland and Leon L. Newland ... (Gerard, Kan., E. Haldeman-Julius co., 1946)   47-17681.

CS71.N558   1946

12523   NEWLAND.   Newland and Newlon parents, by Robert L. Brownfield, Jr. (and) Rex Newlon Brownfield.   (n. p., 1951)   12 l. geneal. table. 36 cm. Typescript. Holograph and typewritten material inserted. 52-35760.

CS71.N558   1951

NEWLANDS.   See NEWLAND.

12524   NEWLIN.   Newlin family and collateral lines, edited by Alexander Du Bin.   Philadelphia, The Historical publication society (1942)   2 p. l., 56 p. 24½ cm. Reproduced from type-written copy. Pages 55-56 blank for "Family record." Includes the Marshall, Hadley, Walter, Johnson, Sproul, Kitt and Speakman families. 42-12578.

CS71.N56   1942

12525   NEWLIN.   The Newlin family; ancestors and descendants of John and Mary Pyle Newlin, by Algie I. Newlin.   With the collaboration of Harvey Newlin.   Greensboro, N. C., 1965.   x, 578 p. illus., ports. 28 cm. 66-1370.

CS71.N56   1965

NEWLON.   See NEWLAND.

12526   NEWMAN.   Rehoboth in the past.   An historical oration delivered on the fourth of July, 1860, by Sylvanus Chace Newman ... Pawtucket, Printed by R. Sherman, 1860.   112 p. 23 cm. Descendants of Rev. Samuel Newman, p. 62-68. 1-12392.

F74. R3N5

12527   NEWMAN.   The Newman story, 1618-1958.   By Howard Fleming Newman.   San Francisco, McDougall Press, 1959.   85 p. 22 cm. 59-3575.

CS71.N565   1959

12528   NEWMAN.   Newman family letters.   Ed. Dorothea Mozley.   London, S. P. C. K., 1962. xx, 219 p. illus., ports. 22 cm. 64-4284.

CS439.N395   1962

NEWMAN.   See also: DOWSE, 1890
                                  LLOYD, 1912
                                  McELWEE, 1959

12529   NEWMARCH.   The Newmarch pedigree, verified by public records, authentic manuscripts, and general and local histories.   Printed for private circulation only.   Cirencester, E. Baily (1868) vii, 36, (3) p. incl. geneal. tab. 21 cm. Preface dated 1868 and signed, "Geo. Fred. Newmarch ... Chas. H. Newmarch." 4-12434.

CS439.N4

12530   NEWPORT.   Genealogical account of the family of Newport, of High Ercall, in the county of Salop, afterwards earls of Bradford.   Bridgnorth, Printed by W. J. Rowley (1851?)   37 p. 29 cm. Dedication signed: George Thomas Orlando Bridgeman. 24-7996.

CS439.N415

NEWPORT.   See also: HATTIE, 1936
WESTON, 1899

12531   NEWSOM.   Memorials of the families of Newsom and Brigg.   Edited by Rev. J. E. Brigg, formerly vicar of Hepworth.   Printed for private circulation.   Huddersfield, A. Jubb and son, ltd., printers (1898)   98 p.   21½ cm.   Contains also accounts of the Shrapnell, Bowden and Dickinson families.   17-19246.
CS439. N42

12532   NEWSOM.   John Edward Newsom and his ancestors.   By Edwin Earl Newsom.   (Salisbury, Conn., 1967 -   v.   29 cm.   Includes bibliographical references.   68-836.   CS71. N567   1967

12533   NEWTON.   Genealogical memoranda relating to the family of Newton.   Privately printed. London, Taylor & co., printers, 1871.   1 p. l., 12 p.   illus. (coats of arms) 28½ cm.   Pedigree, copied from an entry made by Sir Isaac Newton, with additions by the Rev. John Mirehouse, rector of Colsterworth.   Issued also in Miscellanea genealogica et heraldica, n. s. v. 1, p. 169-176, 191-194.   9-18126.
CS439. N43

12534   NEWTON.   The Colchester, Conn., Newton family.   Descendants of Thomas Newton of Fairfield, Conn., 1639, compiled by Clair Alonzo Newton ... Naperville, Ill., 1911-49.   2 v.   fronts., illus., plates, ports., facsims.   20 cm.   Vol. 2 has title: Newton families of colonial Connecticut.   11-29857 rev.
CS71. N57   1911

12535   NEWTON.   Richard Newton of Sudbury, Massachusetts, 1638-9; also an account of the Indian raid in Barnard, Vermont, August 9, 1780.   Compiled for private distribution by Rev. William Monroe Newton.   (Woonsocket, R. I. , W. M. Newton & son) 1912.   (9), 52 p.   23½ cm.   "One hundred copies of this book are printed."   This copy not numbered.   12-21738.   CS71. N57   1912

12536   NEWTON.   Newton genealogy, genealogical, biographical, historical; being a record of the descendants of Richard Newton of Sudbury and Marlborough, Massachusetts 1638, with genealogies of families descended from the immigrants, Rev. Roger Newton of Milford, Connecticut, Thomas Newton of Fairfield, Connecticut, Matthew Newton of Stonington, Connecticut, Newtons of Virginia, Newtons near Boston.   Compiled by Ermina Newton Leonard.   De Pere, Wis., B. A. Leonard, 1915. viii, 872 p.   29 cm.   15-14391.   CS71. N57   1915

12537   NEWTON.   Newton (the descendants of Thomas Newton 1660-1721) by E. J. Bullard.   Detroit, Mich.   (1926?)   16 l.   24 x 21½ cm.   Type-written.   27-8370.   CS71. N57   1926

12538   NEWTON.   History of the Newton families of colonial America, with American history of family interest not obtainable elsewhere, compiled by Clair Alonzo Newton ... Naperville, Ill., 1927 -   v.   front., illus. (incl. ports., facsims.) 20½ cm.   Contents. - I. Thomas Newton. Louisbourg letter, 1745. Connecticut at Louisbourg, 1745.   20-4768.   CS71. N57   1927

12539   NEWTON.   Pioneer Newtons of southwest Texas, and genealogies.   By Jemmie (Newton) Clark.   (Redlands? Calif., c. 1959)   118 p.   illus. 23 cm.   60-34869.   CS71. N57   1959

NEWTON.   See also:

ALDERMAN, 1957	HAYWARD, 1922	PATE, 1958
BITTON, DA690. B62E4	HEMENWAY, 1912	SELDEN, 1911
BLITHFIELD, 1919	LEE, 1954	TALIAFERRO, 1926
BRENT, 1936	LONG, 1956	TORRENCE, 1931
BULLARD, 1920	OTIS, 1851	WALTMAN, 1928
CUTLER, 1897a	PARKER, 1940	WOOLSEY, 1900
FLAGG, 1903	PATE, 19 -	WOOLSEY, CS71. W916

12540   NICCUM.   The Niccum-Nickum family in America: data.   By H. Norman-Niccum.   Tecumseh, Kan., c. 1960.   18 l.   34 cm.   60-22682.   CS71. N586   1960

NICCUM.   See also NYCUM.

12541   NICE.   The Nice family history; descendants of Henry Clemmer Nice, 1822-1892.   Compiled by Hazel Nice Hassan.   Normal, Ill., 1965.   ix, 217 p. illus., facsims., ports. 23 cm. Bibliography: p. 201-202. 66-679.   CS71.N59   1965

12542   NICE.   The biography of Mary Catherine, eleventh child of Philip and Rebecca (Meek) Nice. Rockford, Ill., 1969.   xii, 115 p. illus., fold. facsims., fold. geneal. table, maps, ports. 21 cm. Includes bibliographical references. 74-10899 MARC.   CS71.N59   1969

12542a   NICHOLAS.   The Nicholases of Pennsylvania in the Civil War 1861-1865, by Jerry F. Peter. (Wilmington? Del., 1968)   iv, 160 p. 29 cm. Bibliography: p. 100. 68-5477.   CS71.N5992   1968

                NICHOLAS.   See: DIXON, 1932
                                              LEWIS, 1901

                NICHOLK.   See NICHOLS.

                NICHOLLS.   See DERR, 1960

12543   NICHOLS.   The Nicholl family of Orange County, New York.   (New York, D. Taylor, printer, 1886)   1 p. l., iv, (3)-62 p. front., illus. 22½ cm. By William Leonard Nicoll. Privately printed. 9-12538.   CS71.N6   1886

12544   NICHOLS.   A paper written for the Bucks archaeological & architectural society.   By the Rev. John Benthall ... Newport Pagnell, Printed by J. Line, 1888.   2 p. l., (3)-10 p. col. coat of arms, fold. geneal. tables. 25½ cm. An account of the parish of Willen and the Nicolls family. 18-5036.   DA690.W612B4

12545   NICHOLS.   Sergeant Francis Nicholls of Stratford, Connecticut, 1639, and the descendants of his son, Caleb Nicholls, by Walter Nicholls ... New York, The Grafton press, 1909.   101 p. col. front. 24½ cm. L.C. COPY REPLACED BY MICROFILM.   10-1444.   CS71.N6   1909
                                                                                                                                  Microfilm 8650 CS

12546   NICHOLS.   Ancestors of Willard Atherton Nichols, who participated in the civil and military affairs of the American colonies, and those who were soldiers in the continental armies during the war of the revolution, and those who served in the war of 1812.   (Redlands, Cal., 1911)   64 p. incl. front., illus., plates. 16½ cm. Cover-title: Nichols genealogy. Introduction signed: William Atherton Nichols. With this is bound his Major-General Nathaniel Folsom, Colonel Nicholas Gilman, Governor John Taylor Gilman, soldiers of the revolution. (Redlands, Cal., 1902) 12-24492.
                                                                                                                                  CS71.N6   1911

12547   NICHOLS.   The Nichols families in America.   (By Leon Nelson Nichols)   (New York, 1919) cover-title, 16 p. 22½ cm. Foreword signed: Leon Nelson Nichols. 41-31426.   CS71.N6   1919

12548   NICHOLS.   Nichols genealogy; ancestry and descendants of Thomas Nichols of East Greenwich, Rhode Island and Danby, Vermont.   Edited by Nathan Round Nichols.   (Congress Park? Ill., 1923)   162 p. illus. (incl. ports., coat of arms) 24 cm. 24-13795.   CS71.N6   1923a

12549   NICHOLS.   Richard Nichols, the immigrant, collected and compiled by George E. Nichols ... 1928.   Sydney, N.Y., Printed by Sidney favorite printing co., 1929.   1 p. l., 9-46 p. 1 illus., plates, col. coat of arms. 24 cm. 31-20872 rev.   CS71.N6   1929

12550   NICHOLS.   Ancestors and descendants of Joseph F. and Lydia W. Nichols.   (By Sarah Hayden (Powell) Tozer)   (n.p., 1930)   (11) p. 14 cm. On cover: Forget-me-nots gathered by Aunt Sarah. Sarah H. Tozer, Christmas 1930. 35-28837.   CS71.N6   1930

12551   NICHOLS.   Some ancestors and the descendants of George W. Nichols, compiled by Nellie O. Nicholas, assisted by Belle N. French.   (n.p., 1932?)   (32) p. 15 cm. 36-3764.   CS71.N6   1932a

12552   NICHOLS.   Nichols marriages in New England before 1750 identified (by) Frederic C. Torrey, A.M.   Washington, D.C., 1934.   cover-title, 1 p. l., 7 numb. l. 28 cm. Type-written. Additions and corrections in manuscript. 34-42444.   CS71.N6   1934

12553   NICHOLS.   Eaton-Nichols genealogy to accompany Richard Nichols, the emigrant. (By George Emery Nichols) (Horseheads, N.Y., 1935?)   1 p. l., 1, 1½-32, 32½-45 numb. l. 28 cm. Type-written with additions in manuscript. Title from type-written label mounted on cover. "Material furnished by C. W. Eaton, Newton Center, Mass., to George E. Nichols, Bainbridge, N. Y. Typed by Harriet and Bessie Nichols, Horseheads, N. Y." 36-24713.   CS71.N6   1929a

12554   NICHOLS.   A history of Greene and vicinity, 1845-1929, by Squire G. Wood.   Providence, R. I., Priv. print., 1936.   101 p. front. (port.) illus. (map) geneal. tables. 23½ cm. "History of the 'South farm' now part of the 'Arnold farms'; the Nichols family, the Wood family, 1929": p. (71)-101. 37-13805.   F89.G7W6

12555   NICHOLS.   The Nicols family of Maryland (by) Katharine Nicols Grove.   (n. p., 1939?)   17 p. coat of arms. 22½ cm. "Reference": p. 15. 40-18324.   CS71.N6   1939

12556   NICHOLS.   The Nicoll family and Islip grange, address before the Order of colonial lords of manors in America, April 21, 1938, with additions, by Rosalie Fellows Bailey ... (New York, 1940)   94 p., 1 l. illus. (incl. port., facsim.) 23½ cm. (Publications of the Order of colonial lords of manors in America, no. 29) "Printed for the Order of colonial lords of manors in America, by the John B. Watkins company, New York, May, ninteen forty. The edition is limited to seven hundred copies." 40-29604.   CS71.N6   1940

12557   NICHOLS.   James Nichols (Nickels) of Searsport and his descendants, 1733-1943, compiled by Charles J. Nichols ... (Portland, Me.)   Priv. print. (The Southworth-Anthoensen press) 1944.   xx, 104 p. plates, ports., plan, facsim. 23½ cm. 44-12313.   CS71.N6   1944

12558   NICHOLS.   The Nichols family of north Georgia and the related Cansler, Black, Puett, Coffey, and Boone families: outline for a family history, by Thelma K. Bevan, Owen N. Meredith (and) Robert M. McBride.   Nashville, 1960.   139 p. 28 cm. 60-13711.   CS71.N6   1960

12559   NICHOLS.   Nichol and Osborn family tree, printed and collected by Jack Ryan Nichol.   1st ed.   San Jose, 1963 (c. 1962)   1 v. (various pagings) illus., ports., fold. geneal. tables. 27 cm. 62-17743.
                     CS71.N599   1963

12560   NICHOLS.   The descendants of Ezra Nichols, 1763-1827, by Helen M. Bruce and Dorothy E. Bruce.   Newtown, Conn., Mimeographed by B & W Services, 1964.   1 v. (unpaged) 30 cm. "Copy 2B of 300." 64-2854.   CS71.N6   1964

12561   NICHOLS.   Witch's breed: the Peirce-Nichols family of Salem, by Susan Nichols Pulsifer.   Cambridge, Mass., Dresser, Chapman & Grimes (1967)   448 p. illus., ports. 24 cm. Bibliography: p. 439-441.
                     CS71.N6   1967

————— Supplement, by Susan Nichols Pulsifer.   Cambridge, Mass., Dresser, Chapman & Grimes (1967)   179 l. illus., geneal. tables. 28 cm. Bibliography: leaf 6. 67-18351.   CS71.N6   1967
                                                                                                          Supp.

NICHOLS.   See also:

BROWN, 1939a	DIXON, 1922	LEWIS, 1960
BRUMBACH, 1961	DODGE, 1925	NICHOLL, 1894 (addenda)
CHAMBERLAIN, 1880	GAMBLE, 1906	PLUMB, E171.A53 vol. 15
CHICKERING, 1919	GRANT, CS479.G7	WALTMAN, 1928
DILLON, 1927		

12562   NICHOLSON.   Pedigree of the Nicolson family.   (n. p., 1929?)   geneal. tab. 57½ x 27 cm. Reproduced from manuscript copy. 46-35303.   CS71.N63   1929

12563   NICHOLSON.   A summary of the genealogy of the Nicholson and Stowers families of the South, with their principal branches, by John Bradford Nicholson.   Brooklyn, N. Y. (1936)   1 p. l., 22 numb. l. 28 cm. Mimeographed. 38-32649.   CS71.N63   1936

12564   NICHOLSON.   The Clan Nicolson.   By James Gordon Nicholson.   Edinburgh, Printed by T. and A. Constable (195-?)   104 p. illus. 21 cm. 57-46283.   CS479.N5

NICHOLSON.　See also:　BATTEY, 1940b　　LIVINGSTON, 1939
　　　　　　　　　　　　　DOBELL, 1929　　　MOORE, 1918
　　　　　　　　　　　　　DOUBLEDAY, 1924　STEVENS, 1911
　　　　　　　　　　　　　GALLATIN, 1916　　TEETOR.
　　　　　　　　　　　　　LARKIN, 1964

NICKELS.　See NICHOLS.

12565　NICKERSON.　... Genealogies by James W. Hawes.　William Nickerson.　Yarmouthport, Mass., C. W. Swift, 1911.　cover-title, 17 p. 25½ cm.　(Library of Cape Cod history & genealogy, no. 102)　12-25001.
　　　　　　　　　　　　　　　　　　　　　　　　　　　CS71. N66　　1911

12566　NICKERSON.　... Nickerson.　Children of William (1) Nickerson, by James W. Hawes.　Yarmouthport, Mass., C. W. Swift, 1912.　cover-title, 16 p. 25½ cm.　(Library of Cape Cod history & genealogy, no. 91)　12-25002.　　　　　　　　　　　　　　　　CS71. N66　　1912

12567　NICKEY.　A history of the Nickey family in America, 1700 A. D - 1940 A. D.; with genealogical tables for eight generations, developed from the researches of thirty years, by Ella Metsker Milligan ... Denver, Col., 1940.　1 p. l., v, 236 (i. e. 303), (14) p.　front., illus., plates, ports., facsim., geneal. tab. 26½ cm.　Photoprinted.　Includes 21 extra numbered pages and 46 unnumbered pages.　40-9805 rev.
　　　　　　　　　　　　　　　　　　　　　　　　　　　CS71. N67　　1940

NICKOLS.　See NICHOLS.

NICKUM.　See NICCUM.

NICOLL.　See NICHOLS and addenda.

NICOM.　See NICCUM.

NIEMITZ.　See NIMITZ.

12568　NIEPCE.　Notes sur la famille Niépce.　By Louis Armand-Calliat.　Chalon-sur-Saône; Mâcon, impr. Buguet, 1966.　48 p. plates. 24 cm.　Illustrated cover.　Bibliographical footnotes.　67-82966.
　　　　　　　　　　　　　　　　　　　　　　　　　　　CS599. N53　　1966

NIEUKIRK.　See NEWKIRK.

NIGH.　See NYE.

12569　NIKĽOS.　In vertical file under PRANKE family.　Ask reference librarian for this material.

NILES.　See VINTON, 1858a

12570　NIMITZ.　My name is Nimitz.　By Sister Joan of Arc.　San Antonio, Standard Print. Co., 1948.　115, (4) p. illus., ports., coats of arms., geneal. table. 21 cm.　Bibliography: p. (116-119)　48-2644*.
　　　　　　　　　　　　　　　　　　　　　　　　　　　CS71. N685　　1948

NIMMONS.　See BOWEN, 1960

12571　NIMS.　... Dedication of the Godfrey Nims memorial, the eleventh reunion of the Nims family association, and field day of the Pocumtuck Valley memorial association; Deerfield, Massachusetts.　Thursday, August thirteenth, nineteen hundred fourteen. (Greenfield, Mass., Press of E. A. Hall & co., 1914?)　55 p. front. 23½ cm.　Cover-title: "Nims memorial, Deerfield, 1914."　"Stray leaves from the ancestral tree. By Madella S. Nims:" p. (11)-27.　"Echoes from Canada.　By Frederick Candee Nims" p. (28)-35.　"The story of Godfrey Nims.　By Francis Nims Thompson": p. (36)-44.　17-29463.　　　　　　　　　　CS71. N69　　1914

12572　NIMS.　"The story of Godfrey Nims, " as read to the Nims family association, at Deerfield, Massachusetts, on August 13, 1914, by Francis Nims Thompson. (Greenfield, Mass., Printed by E. A. Hall & company, c.1914)　7 p., 8-19 numb. l. 23 cm.　14-14311.　　　　　　F74. D4T4

12573   NIMS.   Nims family.   CS90. R3   1917

12574   NINDE.   Genealogic snapshots of the family of James Ninde, of Tewkesbury, and his wife, Sarah Ward, 1740 to 1929 (by) Henry S. Ninde.   Rome, N.Y., Briggs, printer, 1929.   24 p. 19 cm.
30-1662.   CS71. N716   1929

NIPPS.   See DUNAWAY, 1959a

NISBET.   See NESBIT and addenda.

NISBETT.   See NESBIT.

12575   NISCHELSKI.   Nischelski family.   CS629. D4   1910

12576   NISWONGER.   The Niswongers; "these are my people," by Leonard Roy and Estella L. Niswonger.   (n.p.) 1960.   16 l. illus., coat of arms. 28 cm. 60-42639.   CS71. N718   1960

NITZEL.   See HAMMOND, 1941

NIVIN.   See: EVANS, 1922
                      EVANS, 1930

12577   NIXON.   The Washington County, Pennsylvania, ancestors of Vice-President Richard M. Nixon, by Raymond M. Bell and Jessica C. Ferguson.   Washington, Pa., 1953.   unpaged. illus. 28 cm.
53-26787.   CS71. N74   1953

12578   NIXON.   The Nixon chart.   By Raymond Martin Bell.   Washington, Pa., 1954.   (1) l. 28 cm.
and geneal. table. 35 x 49 cm. fold. to 35 x 24 cm. Caption title. Table, reproduced from manuscript copy, has caption title: Ancestry of Richard Milhous Nixon, b. Jan. 9-1913, Yorba Linda, Cal. 54-18581.   CS71. N74   1954

12579   NIXON.   The early Nixons of Texas; with genealogies by Dr. and Mrs. Pat Ireland Nixon, Jr. El Paso, Tex., C. Hertzog, 1956.   172 p. illus. 24 cm. 56-57454.   CS71. N74   1956

12580   NIXON.   From James to Richard; the Nixon line.   By Raymond Martin Bell.   Washington, Pa., 1957.   (4) l. 29 cm. 57-23991.   CS71. N74   1957

12581   NIXON.   The story of the Robert P. Nixon family of Boothsville, West Virginia.   By Justin Wroe Nixon (n.p., 1961?)   59 p. illus. 23 cm. 63-2737. See L.C. Additions and corrections No. 246.   CS71. N74   1961

12582   NIXON.   From James to Richard; the Nixon line.   By Raymond Martin Bell.   2d ed.   Washington, Pa., 1969.   17 l. maps. 29 cm. Cover title. 79-8896 MARC.   CS71. N74   1969

12583   NIXON.   Senator Richard M. Nixon.   In vertical file.   Ask reference librarian for this material.

12584   NIXON.   The Washington Reporter paper Jan. 19th, 1953.   In vertical file.   Ask reference librarian for this material.

NIXON.   See also: FRENCH, CS499. F7
                            JENNINGS, 1899
                            MILLHOUS, 1954a
                            ROBINSON, 1952

12585   NOAKES.   Noakes pioneers of Utah; a biographical, genealogical, and historical record of the Thomas and Emma (Inkpen) Noakes family of Udimore, England, Litchfield, Ohio, Salt Lake City, Charleston, and Springville, Utah.   They were among the earliest of the Mormon migration to Zion and the Provisional State of Deseret in the Great Salt Lake Basin of North America.   Compiled by Arthur D. Coleman.   Provo, Utah, J. G. Stevenson, (1965)   xvi, 4, 280 p. map, ports. 25 cm. 65-18342.
                                                                           CS71. N745   1965

NOBLAT.   See NOBLET.

12586   NOBLE.   History and genealogy of the family of Thomas Noble, of Westfield, Massachusetts. With genealogical notes of other families by the name of Noble.   Comp. by Lucius M. Boltwood ... Privately printed.   Hartford, Conn., Press of the Case, Lockwood & Brainard company, 1878.
viii, (13)-869, (1) p. pl., ports. 23½ cm.   L.C. COPY REPLACED BY MICROFILM. 9-12537.   CS71.N75   1878

12587   NOBLE.   A soldier of three wars; Nathan Noble of New Boston (now Gray, Maine) the story of an ancestor, by Nathan Goold ... Portland, Me., The Thurston print, 1898. 1 p. l., 25 p. 23 cm. 2-20210.
E275.N75

12588   NOBLE.   The Indian's administration of justice.   The sequel to the Wiscasset tragedy ... Read before the ... society, February 24, 1898.   (In Collections and proceedings of the Maine historical society. Portland, 1899. 23½ cm. 2d ser., v.10, p.185-211 incl. plan) A15-1266.   F16M33 2d ser. vol.10

12589   NOBLE.   Christopher Noble of Portsmouth, N.H., and some of his descendants, compiled by the late Frank Albert Davis ... (n. p., 1941?)   cover-title, 351-364, 27-40, 183-190, 245-252, 373-384 p. 24½ cm.
"Printed pages from the New England historical and genealogical register, vol. 94, October 1940, and vol. 95, January, April, July, October, 1941."
43-47914.   CS71.N75   1941

12590   NOBLE.   The descendants and antecedents of Milton Bird & Leonora Dougherty Noble.   By M. Birdie (Noble) Feiner.   (Ann Arbor? Mich., 1961)   398 p. illus. 22 cm. 61-30491.
CS71.N75   1961

12591   NOBLE.   The Nobles and the Raders; being a compilation of members and descendents (sic) of the Noble and Rader families who were amongst the earliest pioneer settlers of Mercer County, Illinois.   By Robert Melville Danford.   (Limited private ed.)   New York, 1967.   212 p. illus. 29 cm.
Cover title: The Noble-Rader families; pioneer settlers of Mercer County, Illinois. 76-7953 MARC.
CS71.N75   1967

12592   NOBLE.   Noble.   Compiled and drawn by Charles M. Noble.   1935.   Additions and corrections by Charles M. Noble.   1955.   sheet. Photocropy of MS. (Princeton? N.J., 1955) 34 x 77 cm. 72-229845 MARC.
CS71.N75   1955

NOBLE.   See also: CALHOUN, 1957
                     CAMPBELL, 1927
                     FELL.
                     GENTRY, 1909
                     THOMAS, 1908
                     WALTMAN, 1928

12593   NOBLES.   Some of the descendants of Luther Nobles, son of —— & Harsha Nobles (by) Roy V. Sherman.   (Akron, Ohio, 1969)   33 p. illus., ports. 23 cm. 75-8075 MARC.
CS71.N7512   1969

12594   NOBLET.   Genealogical collections relating to the families of Noblet, Noblat, Noblot and Noblets, of France; Noblet and Noblett, of Great Britain; Noblet, Noblett, Noblit and Noblitt, of America; with some particular account of William Noblit of Middletown township, Chester county (now Delaware county), Pennsylvania, U.S.A.   Comp. by John Hyndman Noblit ... (Philadelphia) Printed for private circulation by Ferris & Leach, 1906.   401 p. col. front., illus., pl., 9 facsim. in colors. 24½ cm.   "A limited edition of this book has been printed for private circulation, of which this is no. 84." "Blank pages at the end ... for addition of notes and family records." - Pref. 7-5087.   CS71.N752   1906

12595   NOBLET.   Down the centuries with the Noblitts, 1180-1955; genealogy, biography, history of the families Noblet, Noblett, Noblette, De Noblette, Noblit, Noblitt, compiled by Loren Scott Noblitt and Minnie Walls Noblitt.   Greenfield, Ind., Mitchell-Fleming Print., 1956.   211 p. illus. 24 cm.
Bibliography: p. (206)-211. 57-16759.   CS71.N752   1956

NOBLIT.   See NOBLET.

NOBLOT.   See NOBLET.

NOCK. See KNOX.

12596 NOEL. Some letters and records of the Noel family, comp. by Emilia F. Noel. London, The St. Catherine press, ltd. (etc.) 1910. x p., 1 l., 110, (3) p. front. (coat of arms) illus., plates, ports., facsims., 7 fold. geneal. tab. 24½ cm. 12-22026. CS439.N5

12597 NOEL. My wanderings and memories, by Lady Norah Bentinck ... London, T. F. Unwin ltd. (1924) 272 p. front., illus. (facsim.) plates, ports. 23 cm. 24-13689. DA566.9.B4A3

12598 NOEL. Eighty years in America, by Frank Leland Noel & Mary Eliza Roberts Noel. Compiled by Jennie Noel Weeks. Edited by Bessie N. Scroggins & Robert P. Cooper. (Salt Lake City, c.1962) 170 p. illus. 29 cm. 63-40461. CS71.N76 1962

12599 NOEL. The Noels and the Milbankes: their letters for twenty-five years, 1767-1792; presented as a narrative by Malcolm Elwin. London, Macdonald & Co., 1967. 471 p. front., 10 plates (incl. ports., facsims.), diagrs. 24½ cm. Bibliographical references included in "Notes on Sources" (p.429-450) 67-112245. CS439.N5 1967

NOFTSGER. See CLARK, 1962

NOLAN. See BOWMAN, 1940

NOLAND. See JOHNSON, 1961

NOLCKEN. See HUDSON, DA690.W6H8

12600 NOLTE. The Nolte family, ancestry and descendents of Herman and Sarah Nolte; geneological (sic) charts of other Nolte families. By Ira Elwood Nolte. Anoka, Minn. (1960?) 244 p. illus., ports., maps, coat of arms, facsims. 28 cm. 62-41771. CS71.N78 1960

NOOTS. See NUTS.

12601 NORBECK. The Norbecks of South Dakota, by Peter Norbeck (1936) and George Norbeck (1938) (Redfield? S.D., 1938) 104 p. ports., fold. geneal. tab. 20½ cm. Information supplied by Laura Norbeck. cf. "Acknowledgment and appreciation." 40-2264. CS71.N82 1938

12602 NORCROSS. The English Norcross family and some of the descendants of William (3) Norcross, 1699 to America. By Elsie M. Cameron. (Detroit? 1954) 88 p. 23 cm. 55-18666. CS71.N83 1954

NORD. See No. 553 - Goodhue county.

NORDFJORD. See NORFIOR.

12603 NORDSTROM. Nordstrom and related families; a genealogical and biographical study. By Hilma (Johnson) Pearson. Long Prairie, Minn., Printed by the Hart Press, 1960. 205 p. illus. 26 cm. 61-20691. CS71.N84 1960

12604 NORFIOR. Opplysninger om en slekt Norfior (Nordfjord) ved Røros kobberverk. Med en kort, innledning om verkets opprinnelse, Bergstadens tidlige befolkning og arbeidsforhold. By Aage Henrick Irgens. Røros, I kommisjon hos Amnéus' boghandel (1961) 192 p. 23 cm. On spine: Norfiorslekten. 74-212112. CS919.N6 1961

NORFLEET. See: RAND, 1936
RAND, 1940

12605 NORLIE. Norlie-Bonhus family tree. By Olaf Morgan Norlie. Northfield, Minn., Eilron Mimeopress, 1949. 4 v. (1650 l.) maps. 29 cm. Includes bibliographies. 49-29890 *. CS71.N85 1949

12606 NORMAN. Crean Brush, loyalist, and his descendants, by Jane Norman Smith. (n.p.)
1938. 30 p. incl. geneal. tables. 24 cm. 42-30845. E278.B863S5

NORMAN. See also ACKLEY, 1960

NORMAN MEVERELL. See BLITHFIELD, 1919

12607 NORMANDIE. Annals of de Normandie as preserved in documents, notes, private papers, public records, genealogies, the writings of old authors, and the registers of the city of Geneva; collated, translated and explained by Arthur Sandys. Cambridge (Mass.) Printed at the Riverside press, 1901. 4 p. l., 308 p. front. (coat of arms) 24 cm. "Fifty copies only, printed for the family." 17-20720.
CS599.N6
Office.

12608 NORRES. Miscellanea Palatina: consisting of genealogical essays illustrative of Cheshire and Lancashire families, and of a Memoir on the Cheshire Domesday roll, compiled from original authorities. By George Ormerod ... Not published. (London, T. Richards, printer) 1851.
3 pt. in 1 v. front., illus., 3 pl., geneal. tab. (part fold., part double) 24½ cm. Each part has special t.-p.: pt. 1-2 paged continuously. Part 1, "A memoir on the Lancashire home of Le Noreis or Norres", is "a private re-impression ... of a memoir read on April 4, 1850, at the meeting of the Historic society of Lancashire and Cheshire, and printed in the second vol. of their Proceedings." CS437.C408

——— Additions and index to Miscellanea Palatina ... (London, T. Richards, 1856) 8 p. 23 cm.
4-25002-3. CS437.C408

NORREYS. See: HAYES, DA690.B74K3
PETTY, BX5195.T5B6

12609 NORRIS. The Norris papers. Edited by Thomas Heywood ... (Manchester) Printed for the Chetham society, 1846. 3 p. l., (iii)-xxxiii, (1), 190 p. 22½ cm. (Added t.-p.: Remains, historical and literary, connected with the palatine counties of Lancaster and Chester. vol. IX) 17-15252. DA670.L19C5 vol.9

12610 NORRIS. Lineage and biographies of the Norris family in America from 1640 to 1892. With references to the Norrises of England as early as 1311 ... By Hon. Leonard Allison Morrison ... Boston, Mass., Damrell & Upham, 1892. 207 p. front., ports. 23 cm. 9-12556.
CS71.N858 1892

12611 NORRIS. (Ancestry of Nixon Grosvenor Norris. n.p., 19 -) geneal. tab. 67 x 60 cm. fold. to
31 cm. Blue-print. 22-22874. CS71.N858 19 -

12612 NORRIS. Ancestry and descendants of Lieutenant Jonathan and Tamesin (Barker) Norris of Maine, in which are given the names, and more or less complete records, from 1550 to 1905, of about twelve hundred persons ... by their great-grandson Henry McCoy Norris ... New York, The Grafton press, 1906. (64) p. incl. 2 charts. front. (port.) 24½ cm. "Two hundred copies of this book has been printed from type ....." This copy not numbered. 6-9616. CS71.N858 1906

12613 NORRIS. The Norris family of Maryland, by Thomas M. Myers. Limited edition. New York, W. M. Clemens, 1916. 119 p. 23 cm. 16-2037. CS71.N858 1916

12614 NORRIS. The Norris family of Maryland and Virginia; genealogy of Thomas Norris, 1361-1930, by Harry Alexander Davis ... Washington, D.C., 1941. 4 v. port. 29 x 22½ cm. Type-written. 44-23448.
CS71.N858 1941

12615 NORRIS. The John Hanson Norris family. By Edwin Warfield Beitzell. Washington, 1947.
20 l. coat of arms. 29 cm. Caption title. 50-21691. CS71.N858 1947

12616 NORRIS. Kentucky descendants of Thomas Norris of Maryland, 1630-1953, and allied families. By Gertrude (Cleghorn) Josserand. (Dodge City? Kan., 1953?) 134 p. ports., coat of arms. 29 cm.
Bibliography: p. 122. 57-43891. CS71.N858 1953

NORRIS. See also: AVINGER, 1961
ROBINSON, 1952
SINCLAIR, 1896

NORSVING.   See NORSWING.

12617   NORSWING.   Outline chart of the ancestries of Knut Gudmundson Norsving and his wife Ingeborg Boyesdatter Bø, compiled by A. A. Veblen from data in Tore Ey: "Vang og Slire" and other available sources, 1931.   Northfield, Minn., Mohn printing company, 1933.   geneal. tab. 81 x 27 cm.   "Part of the data in generation V and all in generation W has been added by the publishers from information supplied by members of the Norswing family." Includes "Sources".   39-14789.
CS71.N859   1933

12618   NORTH.   ... An account of the celebration of the diamond wedding of Dea. Frederick and Harriet North, including poems, programme of exercises, letters of congratulation from relatives and friends, addresses, etc., with a sketch of their golden wedding in 1880; also a short genealogical record of that branch of the family.   By F. A. North.   Hartford, Conn., Press of the Case, Lockwood & Brainard company, 1890.   64 p. 21½ cm.   At head of title: 1830 - June 14-1890.   5-27470.
CS71.N86   1890

12619   NORTH.   John North of Farmington, Connecticut, and his descendants; with a short account of other early North families, by Dexter North.   Washington, D. C., 1921.   xi, 322 p. 24 cm. 22-22879.
CS71.N86   1921

12620   NORTH.   The Caleb North genealogy, descendants of Caleb North who came from Ireland to Philadelphia in 1729 (by) Dexter North.   Washington, D. C., 1930.   cover-title, 90 numb. l. 27 cm. Autographed from type-written copy.   30-9798.
CS71.N86   1930

NORTH.   See also: KEYES, 1914
No. 3939 - Colebrook.

12621   NORTHCOTE.   The life of the late Right Honourable the Earl of Iddesleigh ... and a complete history of the Northcoate family.   By Charles Worthy ... London, Hamilton, Adams & co.; (etc., etc.,) 1887.   56 p. front. (port.) 19 cm. 5-642.
DA565.I2W9

NORTHCOTE.   See also NORTHCUTT.

NORTHCOTT.   See NORTHCUTT.

12622   NORTHCUTT.   Northcutt and allied families, by Dolly Northcutt and Amelia Sparkman Castleberry.   Longview, Tex., Morris publishing company, 1938.   (432) p. 21½ x 17 cm. Various pagings.   38-37535.
CS71.N87   1938

12623   NORTHCUTT.   The Northcutt families of Kentucky.   By Dolly Northcutt.   (n. p.) c. 1960   1 v. (loose leaf) 34 cm. 60-33216
CS71.N87   1960

12624   NORTHCUTT.   Florence May Nicholls, Jesse Griffin Northcutt and their ancestors, by Florence Northcutt Hagler.   (n. p.) 1965.   64 p. illus., ports. 22 cm. Bibliography: p. 62. 66-57124.
CS71.N87   1965

NORTHEY.   See DE CLARE, 1921

NORTHROP.   See NORTHRUP.

12625   NORTHRUP.   The Northrup-Northrop genealogy; a record of the known descendants of Joseph Northrup, who came from England in 1637, and was one of the original settlers of Milford, Conn., in 1639.   With lists of Northrups and Northrops in the revolution, by A. Judd Northrup ... New York, The Grafton press (c. 1908)   x p., 1 l., 461 p. ports. 24 cm. 8-3092.
CS71.N877   1908

12626   NORTHRUP.   Northrup genealogy, 1637-1914; a history of the ancestors and descendants of William Northrup, an early settler in the town of Masonville, N. Y. ... Comp. and fifty copies printed for private circulation, by George Clark Northrup ... (Elizabeth, N. J., The Northrup press, 1914)   16 p. 23½ cm. "Family record blanks": p. (13)-16. 14-20606.
CS71.N877   1914

12627   NORTHRUP.   The Northrup family.   By Jack Clifford Northrup.   (Hillsdale? Mich., 1960?)
5 l. 29 cm.   Caption title.   63-53823.   CS71.N877   1960

NORTHRUP.   See also: INGHAM, 1933
                                    INGHAM, 1948

NORTHUMBERLAND, Earls of.   See PERCY.

12628   NORTHUP.   Some records of the Northup and Tucker families of Rhode Island, with notes on
intermarrying families.   (By Mrs. Carrie Eastman (Secombe) Chatfield) Minneapolis (Boston, Press of
D. Clapp & son) 1914.   31 p. 25 cm.   Comp. by Mrs. Edward C. Chatfield (i.e. Mrs. Carrie Eastman (Secombe) Chatfield) cf. Pref.
14-19567.   CS71.N878   1914

NORTHUP.   See also DIXON, 1952

12629   NORTON.   Descendants and ancestors of Charles Norton of Guilford, Connecticut.   (By
Albert B. Norton) Washington, W. H. Moore, printer, 1856.   cover-title, 26 p. 22½ cm.   Contents. - pt. 1. Descendants of Charles Norton. - pt. 2. Ancestors of Charles Norton.   9-12535. L. C. Copy replaced by microfilm.   CS71.N886   1856
                                                                                        Microfilm, 9233 CS

12630   NORTON.   A genealogy of the Norton family, with miscellaneous notes.   (Compiled by
William Henry Whitmore)   Reprinted from the New England historical and genealogical register for
July, 1859.   Boston, H. W. Dutton and son, printers, 1859.   10 p. 24 cm.   9-12550.
                                                                                        CS71.N886   1859

12631   NORTON.   Norton family.   CS71.I65   1880

12632   NORTON.   Norton, By C. C. Baldwin ... (Cleveland, Leader printing company, 1882)
1 p. l., p. (173)-181. 23½ cm.   From the author's Candee genealogy. Cleveland, 1882.   14-11914.   CS71.N886   1882

12633   NORTON.   Some descendants of John Norton of Branford, 1622-1709, with notes and dates of
other emigrant Nortons, etc.   (By) Walter Whittlesey Norton.   Lakesville, Conn., The Journal press,
1909.   67 p. incl. pl. (ports.) 24½ cm.   10-2786.   CS71.N886   1909

12634   NORTON.   The Norton-Lathrop-Tolles-Doty American ancestry of Ralph Tolles Norton,
James Edward Norton, Arden Lathrop Norton, Frank Porter Norton; their children; and the Wright-
Briggs-Cogswell-Dudley American ancestry of Ellen Cogswell-Wright-Norton and Frances Cogswell-
Wright-Norton; and some family and local history.   Compiled by James E. Norton, 1916, with some
added data of subsequent events.   (n. p.) 1935.   1 p. l., (5)-187 p. plates, coats of arms. 24½ cm.   Blank pages for
"Addenda" (44-47) On cover: Some Norton and Wright pedigrees and family and local history.   36-3771.
                                                                                        CS71.N886   1935

NORTON.   See also: BROCKWAY, E171.A53 vol.13   IRELAND, 1880
                                    BUNNELL, 1937   LEWIS, 1960
                                    CANDEE, 1882   POSTON, 1942
                                    HAMMACK, 1955   ROBINSON.

12635   NORWOOD.   Notes on the Norwood family, by William Otis Sawtelle.   (n. p., 192-?)
23 p. 23 cm.   28-15962.   CS71.N889   192-

12636   NORWOOD.   Genealogy of the Norwood, Hogg, Lovick, Benners and Howell, Garrett,
Harrison lines, compiled by Alves Norwood Apperson, 1944.   Portland, Or., Binfords and Mort (1944)
5 p. l., (7)-160 p. front., plates, ports., coats of arms. 25½ x 18½ cm.   46-3815.   CS71.N889   1944

12637   NORWOOD.   The Norwoods (by) G. Marion Norwood Callam.   Bushey Heath, Hertfordshire,
A. E. Callam, 1963 -   v. illus., map, geneal. table. 22 cm. 500 copies. No.149. 65-6548.   CS71.N889   1963

12638   NORWOOD.   "General" John Norwood and related lines, compiled by William Howard Norwood
in co-operation with James Harvey Norwood, Sr., and Henry Offie Norwood.   (Dallas, Trumpet Press)
1964.   x, 424 p. col. coat of arms, ports. 24 cm.   67-4249.   CS71.N889   1964

NORWOOD. See also: DOBYNS, 1908
                                       HALLOWELL, 1893
                                       HORNE, 1936
                                       KINNISON, 1956

12639   NOTT. Nott family memorials. Privately printed. London, Mitchell and Hughes, printers,
1879.   cover-title, 4 p. coat of arms. 28 x 22½ cm. Genealogical table. 3-3035 rev.   CS439.N65

        NOTT. See also ALNO, CS439.A59

12640   NOURSE. A genealogy of the Nurse family for five generations. By John D. Ames ...
(In Putnam's monthly historical magazine ... Salem, 1893. 28 cm. v.1, p.96-102. pl.) 20-23925.   F1.P98
        —— Copy 2, detached.   Nurse ancestry of General Philip Reade: 1 leaf inserted.   CS71.N933   1893

12641   NOURSE. James Nourse and his descendants ... Compiled by Maria Catharine Nourse Lyle.
Lexington, Ky., Transylvania printing co., 1897.   iv p., 1 l., 163 p. front., plates, ports., facsim., tab. 25½ cm.
Printed by request. Elizabeth Nourse Chapline and her descendants: p. 77-92. 1-10273.   CS71.N933   1897

12642   NOURSE. Unpublished letters of Dolly Madison to Anthony Morris relating to the Nourse
family of the Highlands, by Grace Dunlop Peter.   (In Columbia historical society, Washington, D.C. Records. Washington, 1944. 23 cm. v. 44-45, p.215-239) A45-2241.   F191.C72 vol.44-5

12643   NOURSE. Records of Nourse and Boyd descendants based on the family and connections of
Alfred T. Nourse. By Hugh Campbell Boyd Nourse. (Montreal, 195-)   43 p. 28 cm. "The Edmund Miles
family, compiled by Jean M. Ray as a supplement ... 1959" (6 p.) inserted. 59-41351.   CS71.N933

12644   NOWELL. Nowell family. Being a brief account of Captain Peter Nowell of York, Maine,
and some of his descendants. Compiled by Herbert C. Varney ... 1901, assisted by Joshua T. Nowell
... 1903. (n.p., 1903?)   2 p. l., 7 numb. l. 28 cm. Type-written (carbon copy) 37-38428.   CS71.N934   1903

12645   NOWELL. Nowell and allied families, a genealogical study with biographical notes. Compiled and privately printed for Mrs. James A. Nowell by the American historical company, inc. New
York, 1941.   229 p. pl., port., col. coats of arms, col. geneal. tab. 33 cm. Alternate pages blank. Title-page ornamented in
colors; colored initials. Plate accompanied by guard sheet with descriptive letterpress. Bound in blue levant, gold tooled, with coat of arms of
the Noel (Nowell) family on covers. Includes the Hammond, Kennard Small and Frost families. Includes bibliographical notes. 41-17606.
                                              CS71.N934   1941

12646   NOWLIN. The Nowlin-Stone genealogy; a record of the descendants of James Nowlin, who
came to Pittsylvania County, Virginia, from Ireland about 1700; of Bryan Word Nowlin, grandson of
James Nowlin, who was born in Pittsylvania County, Virginia, about 1740; of Michael Nowlin; and of
the earlier Nowlins (Nowlans) of Ireland; and also a record of the descendants of George Stone; and
of James Hoskin Stone, who was born in Pittsylvania County, Virginia, in 1778; and also a record of
the descendants of Edmund Fitzgerald. By James Edmund Nowlin ... edited by Mary Nowlin ... Salt
Lake City, Utah (c.1916)   548 p. plates, ports., coats of arms (part col.) 24 cm. "Authorities": p. (19) 17-12852.
                                              CS71.N94   1916

12647   NOYES. A genealogical account of the Noyes family, together with the Dike family, and
Fuller and Edson families. Compiled by Jacob Noyes ... East Abington, Abington standard press,
1869.   12 p. front. 22½ cm. 40-37507.   CS71.N955   1869

12648   NOYES. Noyes' genealogy. Record of a branch of the descendants of Rev. James Noyes,
Newbury, 1634-1656. Compiled by Horatio N. Noyes. Cleveland, O., 1889.   32 p. illus. 23 cm. 9-12555.
                                              CS71.N955   1889

12649   NOYES. Noyes pedigree. By James Atkins Noyes ... (Re-printed from the New England
historical and genealogical reigster for Jan. 1899) Boston, Printed by D. Clapp & son, 1899.
11 p. 24½ cm. 17-6154.   CS71.N955   1899

12650   NOYES. Descendants of Reverend William Noyes, born, England, 1568, in direct line to La
Verne W. Noyes and Frances Adelia Noyes-Giffen. Allied families of Stanton. Lord. Sanford..

12650 continued: Coddington. Thompson. Fellows. Holdredge. Berry. Saunders. Clarke. Jessup. Studwell. Rundle. Ferris. Lockwood. ... Compiled by Horace True Currier. Chicago, Ill., L.W. Noyes, 1900. 115 p. front., plates, ports. 24 cm. "The publisher of this book has gathered and caused to be gathered the statistics herein contained." cf. "Introductory," signed: La Verne W. Noyes. 16-7850.

CS71. N955   1900

12651   NOYES.   Genealogical record of some of the Noyes descendants of James Nicholas and Peter Noyes... Collected and compiled by Col. Henry E. Noyes, U. S. A., and Miss Harriette E. Noyes ... Boston, Mass., 1904.   2 v. fronts., (ports.) illus., plates. 24½ cm.   Contents. - v.1. Descendants of Nicholas Noyes. - v.2. Descendants of James and Peter Noyes.   4-6903.

CS71. N955   1904

12652   NOYES.   Noyes-Gilman ancestry; being a series of sketches, with a chart of the ancestors of Charles Phelps Noyes and Emily H. (Gilman) Noyes, his wife ... St. Paul, Minn., Printed for the author by the Gilliss press, New York, 1907.   xii, 467, (1) p. front., plates, ports., facsims., fold. chart. 29½ cm. "This book is one of an edition of two hundred copies. Privately printed." This copy not numbered. Bibliography: p. (423)-436. 7-30857.

CS71. N955   1907

NOYES.   See also: CHESTER, 1886
                        CHUTE, 1894
                        GRIMALDI, CS439. G78

NUDD.   See DOW, 1929

NUGENT.   See FRENCH, 1847

NULL.   See GREENLEE, 1956

NUNEMACHER.   See CLAUSER, 1959

12653   NUNN.   The Nunn family, a short sketch of John Milton Nunn + Sallie Heiston Nunn, their ancestors and descendants.   (By Charles Greenwood Nunn) (Milwaukee? 1939)   64 p. incl. illus. (coats of arms) mounted plates, fold. geneal. tab. 20½ cm. "Compiled by Chas. G. and Henry L. Nunn." 43-49415.

CS71. N97   1939

12654   NUNN.   Nunn (family) Lenoir County, North Carolina.   By Sybil Hyatt.   Kinston, N. C., 1945.   24 l. 30 cm.   Typewritten (carbon copy)   Additions in ms.   50-22616.

CS71. N97   1945

NUNN.   See also No. 9846 - Hackettstown.

NUNNALLY.   See FRANKLIN, F232. C52T5

NURSE.   See NOURSE.

NUSSBAUMER.   See NUSSBAUM.

NUSTT.   See NUTS.

NUSZ.   See NUTS.

NUTHALL.   See: MONNET, CS71. M74, 1911
                        MULLIKIN, 1936

NUTS.   See BOOHER, 1956

NUTT.   See BRENT, 1936

NUTTER.   See COX, 1939

12655   NUTTING.   Nutting genealogy.   A record of some of the descendants of John Nutting, of Groton, Mass.   By Rev. John Keep Nutting.   Syracuse, N. Y., C. W. Bardeen, 1908.   277, (1) p. incl. front. (map) illus., ports. 24 cm. 9-9530.

CS71. N987   1908

12656   NUTTING.   Genealogy of first four generations and names of fifth generation of male descend-
ants of John Nutting of Groton, Mass., 1620-1650-1676, compile and published as a supplement to the
Nutting genealogy of the descendants of John Nutting of Groton, Mass., as published by Rev. John Keep
Nutting ... in 1908.   Compiled by Homer W. Brainard ... Collaborated and privately printed by Walter
M. Nutting ... (Faribault, Minn.) 1927.   1 p. 1., 5-8, (4), 9-52 p. illus. 23½ cm.   30-9803.

CS71.N987   1927

12657   NUTTING.   Genealogy of descendants of John Nutting of South Amherst, Mass., by Walter M.
Nutting.   Faribault, Minn., 1929.   340 p. plates, ports. 24½ cm.   Blank pages for "Family records" (335-340) 30-9801.

CS71.N987   1929

12658   NUZUM.   The Nuzum family; showing some branches in Ireland, Australia, and America.
By Harry Ward Williams. (n. p., 1952)   318 p. illus. 24 cm. 53-23280.   CS499.N8   1952

12659   NYCUM.   Some Nycum descendants, also some Nickum, Nicom, Niccum.   Data compiled by
Norman Niccum and Homer C. Nycum.   Outline arr, by Homer C. Nycum.   Kalamazoo, Mich., (1963)
303 p. illus., ports., maps. 29 cm. 63-24029.   CS71.N989   1963

   NYCUM.   See NICCUM.

12660   NYDEGGER.   Nydegger family chronicles, being a brief history of the origin of the Nydegger
family, with special reference to the Nydeggers of Switzerland, and America, by James Archibald
Nydegger ... Baltimore, Md., Press of Meyer & Thalheimer, 1930)   5 p. 1., (9)-123 p. plate, ports., coat of
arms. 20 cm. 31-3307.   CS71.N992   1930

12661   NYE.   (Genealogical chart of Benjamin Nye family, Sandwich, 1636)   Boston, Boston bank
note & lith'g. co. (19-?)   geneal. tab. illus. (coat of arms) 58½ x 79½ cm. fold. to 29½ x 20 cm. 4-30106.

CS71.N994   19 -

12662   NYE.   A genealogy of the Nye family.   Compiled by George Hyatt Nye ... and Frank E. Best
... Ed. by David Fisher Nye ... (Cleveland) The Nye family of America association, 1907.
3 p. 1., (11)-704, (8) p. plates (part col.) ports. 23½ cm. (Half-title: Benjamin Nye of Sandwich, Massachusetts, his ancestors and descendants)
"This edition is limited to five hundred copies.   This copy is number 355. "   Eight blank pages at end for record of births, marriages and deaths.
8-30518.

CS71.N994   1907

12663   NYE.   A genealogy of the Nye family.   By George Hyatt Nye.   (Cleveland) Nye Family of
America Association, 1907-67.   4 v. illus., coats of arms (part col.), ports. 24 cm.   Vol. 1 has half title: Benjamin Nye of
Sandwich, Massachusetts, his ancestors and descendants; v. 3 has subtitle: Nyes of German origin; v. 4 has subtitle: A supplement to volumes I, II
& III.   Vol. 1 compiled by G. H. Nye and F. E. Best; v. 2 compiled by R. G. Nye and L. B. Nye; v. 3-4 compiled by R. G. Bye.   Supplementary
record of the descendants of Hannah S. Nye inserted in v. 1 at p. 222.   Copy 2 of v. 1, a photo-offset reprint made in 1967?, has Second edition
lettered on cover. 8-30518.

CS71.N994   1907

12664   NYE.   Genealogy of George Nye (Nigh) family, 1755-1965, by Willis and Wanda Nye. (Galion?
Ohio, 1965-   1 v. (loose-leaf) illus., coat of arms, port. 29 cm.   Cover title. 65-4852.   CS71.N994   1965

   NYE.   See also: ENDERS, 1960
                  OLIN, 1892

12665   NYMAN.   John Nyman, Emma J. Nyman and their known ancestors, kinsmen (and) descendants.   Svea, Minn., Family Pub. Co., c. 1960.   179 1. illus. 30 cm. 62-46551.   CS71.N995   1960

O

12666　OAK.　Oak - Oaks - Oakes.　Family register, Nathaniel Oak of Marlborough, Mass., and three generations of his descendants in both male and female lines,　by Henry Lebbeus Oak;　with sketch of life of Henry Lebbeus Oak ...　Printed for subscribers with permission of the New England historic genealogical society of Boston, Mass., to whom the author bequeathed the original manuscripts by Ora Oak ... Los Angeles, Out West co.print, 1906.　84, vi p. front. (port.) 24 cm.　7-3677.

CS71.O1　1906

OAK.　See also:　OAKES.
WALTON, 1898

12667　OAKELEY.　The Oakeley pedigree, by Edward Francis Oakeley.　London, Printed for private circulation by Mitchell, Hughes and Clarke, 1934.　2 p. l., 142 p. illus. (facsims., coats of arms) 29 cm. Interleaved.　40-284.　CS439.O2　1934

12668　OAKLEY.　Early Westchester families.　By Howard Linden Jones.　(Orlando? Fla., 1953?) 316 l. maps (1 fold.) coat of arms. 29 cm.　Typescript (carbon copy) Errata slip inserted.　55-59183.　CS69.J6

12669　OAKES.　The turn of the century;　the record of the house of Thomas Oakes and company as their centennial anniversary is celebrated, 1830-1930.　Prepared and privately printed for Thomas Oakes and company, by the American historical society, inc.　(New York) 1930.　40 p. front., plates, ports., facsim., coat of arms.　27½ cm.　Coat of arms accompanied by leaf with descriptive letterpress.　44-14707.

TS1425.O3A5

OAKES.　See also OAK.

OAKS.　See:　OAK.
PRICHARD, 1960

OATES.　See:　McELWEE, 1959
SPEER, 1956

12670　OATMAN.　Captivity of the Oatman girls:　being an interesting narrative of life among the Apache and Mohave Indians:　containing also an interesting account of the massacre of the Oatman family, by the Apache Indians, in 1851;　the narrow escape of Lorenzo D. Oatman;　the capture of Olive A. and Mary A. Oatman ... as given by Lorenzo D. and Olive A. Oatman ... to the author, R. B. Stratton.　(2d ed.)　San Francisco, Whitton, Towne & co's Excelsior steam power presses, 1857. xiii, (15)-231 p. incl. illus., port., map. 18 cm.　2-16688 rev.　E87.O11

12671　OATMAN.　Another edition of the above.　14th thousand.　New-York, Pub. for the author, by Carlton & Porter, 1858.　290 p. incl. front. (port.) illus., 2 pl. pl., port. 19 cm.　20-7027.

E87.O12

12672　OATMAN.　Oatman;　some of the descendants of Johannes Outman, 1654-1716, and his wife Femmetje Kock, 1654-1732, compiled by W. E. Osborn and Ralph I. Oatman.　(n. p., 194-?) 1 v. (unpaged) 29 cm.　At head of title: Othman, Van Otman, Otman, Outman.　56-45185.　CS71.O12

O'BANNON.　See JENNINGS, 1961

OBEAR.　See MILLS, 1962

OBENOUR.   See WILSON, 1959

12673   OBER.   The Maryland Obers' ancestry, 1559-1962.   Notes of Frank B. Ober.   (Baltimore, 1963)   83 p. illus., geneal. tables, ports. 29 cm.   76-10618 MARC.   CS71.O122   1963

12674   OBERHOLTZER.   A genealogical record of the descendants of Martin Oberholzer together with historical and biographical sketches and illustrated with portraits and other illustrations.   By Rev. A. J. Fretz ... Milton, N.J., Press of the Evergreen news, 1903   v, (1), 254 p. front., plates, ports. 22 cm.   11-14239.   CS71.O123   1903

12675   OBERHOLTZER.   Some account of Jacob Oberholtzer, who settled, about 1719, in Franconia township, Montgomery county, Pennsylvania, and of some of his descendants in America, by Elisha S. Loomis ... Cleveland, O., 1931.   412 p., 1 l. front., plates, ports. 23½ cm.   Lettered on cover: Jacob Oberholtzer genealogy.   Each plate accompanied by guard sheet with descriptive letterpress.   "This edition is limited to 300 numbered copies, of which this book is no. 1." 32-7468.   CS71.O123   1931

OBERMAYER.   See OVERMYER.

12676   OBERTEUFFER.   The genealogy of the Oberteuffer family, prepared in 1936 by Delbert Oberteuffer.   (Columbus, O., 1936)   geneal. tab. 27½ x 41½ cm.   A chart prepared to accompany the author's manuscript history of the Oberteuffer family, now on file in the Pennsylvania historical society and the New York public library, cf. verso of chart. 41-38336.   CS71.O124   1936

OBIER.   See CANON, 1948

12677   O'BRIEN.   Historical memoir of the O'Briens.   With notes, appendix, and a genealogical table of their several branches.   Compiled from the Irish annalists.   By John O'Donoghue ... Dublin, Hodges, Smith, & co., 1860.   xxxii, 551 p. incl. geneal. tables. 22½ cm. 4-34864.   DA916.3.O202

12678   O'BRIEN.   The O'Briens of Machias, Me., patriots of the American revolution: their services to the cause of liberty.   A paper read before the American-Irish historical society at its annual gathering in New York city, January 12, 1904.   By Rev. Andrew M. Sherman ... Together with a sketch of the clan O'Brien, by Thomas Hamilton Murray.   Boston, For the Society, 1904.   87 p. front. (port.) plates. 23 cm. 5-4396.   CS71.O13   1904

12679   O'BRIEN.   Noel and the genealogy of the O'Briens; being a history of the town of Noel, Nova Scotia, its inhabitants and descendants.   (By Royal G. O'Brien)   (New Bedford, Mass., R. G. O'Brien & E. R. O'Brien, c.1925)   (50) p. front. (coat of arms) plates, port. 17 cm.   "We are indebted to Charles Brown, B.A., and Rebecca O'Brien for the history (Noel a century ago and since)   And also to Albert O'Brien, who is mainly responsible for the gathering of the genealogy." - Pref. 25-21503.   F1039.5.N702

12680   O'BRIEN.   Pedigree of the family of O'Brien from the Irish annals, with copious notes and references.   By Réamonn Moulton Seán O'Brien.   (London, 1947)   geneal. table on sheet 133 x 75 cm. fold. to 45 x 75 cm. 52-20675.   CS499.O2   1947
Folio.

12681   O'BRIEN.   History of the O'Briens from Brian Boroimhe, A.D.1000 to A.D.1945.   By Donough O'Brien.   London, New York, Batsford (1949)   302 p. plates, ports. 24 cm.   Corrigenda slip inserted.   50-1485.   CS499.O2   1949

12682   O'BRIEN.   The descendants of Henry Martin O'Brien and his wife, Lydia Houghton.   With sketches of the families of O'Brien, Houghton, Evelyn, Hely, and Day.   By Willis Harry Miller.   Hudson, Wis., Star-Observer Print, 1956.   52 p. illus. 21 cm. 59-33173.   CS71.O13   1956

12683   O'BRIEN.   In vertical file.   Ask reference librarian for this material.

12684   O'BYRNE.   Historical reminiscences of O'Byrnes, O'Tooles, O'Kavanaghs.   And other Irish chieftains.   By O'Byrne.   (Printed for private circulation.)   London, Printed by M'Gowan and co., 1843.   x, 96 p. 20½ cm. CA20-36 unrev.   DA916.3.A103

O'BYRNE. See also O'TOOLE, 1890

OCHELTREE. See OCHILTREE.

12685 OCHILTREE. History of the house of Ochiltree of Ayrshire, Scotland, with the genealogy of the families of those who came to America and of some of the allied families 1124-1916, by Clementine (Brown) Railey ... Sterling, Kan., Bulletin printing company, 1916. 3 p. l., (v)-xxiv, 25-380 p. plates, ports. 27 cm. 17-28899. CS71.O16 1916

OCHILTREE. See also WILSON, 1898a

OCHS. See BOEHM, 1902

12686 OCHTERLONEY. The Ochterloney family of Scotland, and Boston, in New England. By Walter Kendall Watkins. Boston, U.S.A., Priv. print. (The Bartlett press) 1902. 16 p. plates, port. 24½ cm. 20-2612. CS71.O17 1902

12687 OCHTERLONEY. The Ochterloney family of Scotland, and Boston, in New England. By Walter Kendall Watkins. Boston, U.S.A., Printed for the author, 1902. 11 p. 24½ cm. Caption title: The Scotch ancestry of Maj.-Gen. Sir David Ochterloney, bart., a native of Boston, in New England. "Reprinted from New-Eng. historical and genealogical register for April, 1902." 20-2611. CS71.O17 1902a

OCHTERLONEY. See also COCHRAN, 1904

12688 O'CONNELL. O'Connell family history, (By Curran De Bruler) (San Jose? Calif., 1964?) 18 l. 28 cm. Caption title. By Curran DeBruler, Sr., and June Joyce Larson. - Letter from Mrs. Larson. Typescript. Bibliography: leaf 1. 71-200639. CS71.O178 1964

O'CONNER. See O'CONOR.

O'CONNOR. See O'CONOR.

12689 O'CONOR. ... The O'Connor-Conner-Simmons families, compiled by Lula Price O'Conner (Mrs. Wm. Edward Cox), with the help of other members of the family and research work of several genealogists. Southern Pines, N.C., W. E. Cox., jr., 1941. vi p., 1 l., 81, (7) p. incl. front. (coat of arms) plates, ports. 22½ cm. "150 numbered copies ... No. 11." Includes the Kavanaugh, Harrison and Poindexter families. 41-10113. CS71.O18 1841

12690 O'CONOR. The anonymous claim of Mr. Arthur O'Conor, as "a member of the Belanagare family," of descent from the O'Connors of Ballintubber, considered in relation to public records. By Roderic O'Conor ... Dublin, McGlashan & Gill, 1859. viii, 90 p., 1 l. 17 cm. 45-34173. CS499.O32 1859

12691 O'CONOR. A historical and genealogical memoir of the O'Connors, kings of Connaught, and their descendants: collected from the annals of Ireland, and authentic public records. By Roderic O'Conor ... Dublin, McGlashan & Gill; London, Simpkin, Marshall, & co., 1861. vi, 105, (1), xii, 23 p. port., maps (1 double) fold. geneal. tan. 16½ cm. "An argumentative dialogue on the assumption of the modern epithet or title of Don": 23 p. at end. Bibliographical foot-notes. 45-34172. CS499.O32 1861

12692 O'CONOR. The O'Conors of Connaught: an historical memoir. Comp. from a ms. of the late John O'Donovan, LL.D., with additions from the state papers and public records. By the Rt. Hon. Charles Owen O'Conor Don. Dublin, Hodges, Figgis, and co., 1891. xxiv, 395 p. front., illus., 9 pl. geneal. tables (part fold.) 26 cm. 6-20520. DA916.3.O303

12693 O'CONNOR. Genealogical tree of the O'Connor family. n.p., 19-? 17, 1 p. 41 cm. CS499.O3

12694 O'CONNOR. The O'Connor family; families of Daniel and Mathias O'Connor of Corsallagh house, Achonry county, Sligo, Ireland, A.D. 1750, with notes on the Hagadorn, Furman, Williams and Eaton families, of New York. By Watson Burdette O'Connor ... Brooklyn, N.Y., Printed by the Connell press, 1914. 1 p. l., 21, (1) p. front. (coat of arms) pl., geneal. tab. 21 cm. 16-2753. CS71.O18 1914

12695   O'CONNOR. The broken clans, the Connors and O'Connors, by John M. MacNulty ... San Diego, Calif., Press of Frye & Smith, 1929.   1 p. l., 5-64 p. 19 cm. "List of authorities": p. 6. 29-23743.
CS499.O32M3

12696   O'CONNOR. ... The O'Connor-Conner-Simmons families, compiled by Lula Price O'Conner (Mrs. Wm. Edward Cox), with the help of other members of the family and research work of several genealogists.   Southern Pines, N.C., W.E.Cox, jr., 1941.   vi p., 1 l., 81, (7) p. incl. front. (coat of arms) plates, ports. 22½ cm. "150 numbered copies ... No. 11." Includes the Kavanaugh, Harrison and Poindexter families. 41-10113.
CS71.O18   1941

12697   O'DALY. The tribes of Ireland: a satire, by Aenghus O'Daly; with poetical translation by the late James Clarence Mangan; together with an historical account of the family of O'Daly; and an introduction to the history of satire in Ireland.   By John O'Donovan ... Dublin, J. O'Daly, 1852.   112 p. 23 cm. Irish and English on opposite pages. 2-6324.
PB1398.O4

12698   O'DALY. History of the O'Dalys; the story of the ancient Irish sept; the race of Dalach of Corca Adaimh; compiled by Edmund Emmet O'Daly ... New Haven, Conn., Printed by the Tuttle, Morehouse and Taylor company, 1937.   2 p. l., (vii)-xix, 546 p. front., illus. (coat of arms) plates, fold. geneal. tables, 24 cm. "Authentic works comprising the main reference sources of the history of the O'Dalaigh": p. 534-537; "Government publications": p. 537-538. 38-31.
CS71.O2   1937

12699   O'DALY. Dailey, Jenkins, Gardiner and allied families: a genealogical study with biographical notes.   Compiled and priv. print. for Ethelyn Wells Dailey Smith, by the American Historical company, inc.   New York, 1956.   171 p. col. illus., col. coats of arms, geneal. table. 33 cm. Issued in a case. 56-56139.
CS71.O2   1956

12700   O'DANIEL. Snatches of O'Daniel, Hamilton, and allied ancestry and history in Maryland and Kentucky, by a native of Kentucky. (Victor Francis O'Daniel) Somerset, O., The Rosary press, 1933.   101 p. illus., ports. 22½ cm. Pages left blank at end for additional record. 33-31498.
CS71.O21   1933

12701   O'DAVOREN. The O'Davorens of Cahermacnaughton, Burren, co. Clare ... by Dr. George U. Macnamara.   Limerick, Printed by Guy and co., ltd., 1912-13.   2 v. illus. (plans) pl. 21½ cm. Contents. - pt. I. (Historical) - pt. II. Genealogical. 20-4303.
CS499.O33

ODDIE.   See SMITH, 1878a

ÖDEGAARDEN.   See SKAVLEM, 1915

12702   ODELL. Pedigree of Odell of United States and Canada.   1639-1894 ... Six lines of descent traced by Rufus King ... (New York, Press of De Vinne & co., 1894)   geneal. tab. 58½ x 88 cm. fold. to 23½ cm. 9-12826.
CS71.O23   1894

12703   ODELL. Odell genealogy, United States and Canada (1635-1935); ten generations in America in direct line.   Compiled by a descendant - Minnie A. Lewis Pool, (Mrs. Sherman Ira Pool) ... Monroe, Wis., E. A. Odell, 1935.   123 p. front., illus. (incl. coats of arms) 20 cm. 36-2363.
CS71.O23   1935

12704   ODELL. List of Odell family members interred in churchyard of St. Paul's Church, Eastchester, Mount Vernon, New York. (n. p., 194-?)   3 l. 28 cm. Typewritten (carbon copy) 50-21258.
CS71.O23

12705   ODELL. Odell bulletin ... no. 1 -   New York city, F. C. Haacker, 1944 -   nos. plates, maps. 28 cm. Reproduced from type-written copy. 44-52698.
CS71.O23   1944

12706   ODELL. Abel and Polly Manning Cooper, Fielding and Sarah Hunt Meek, their ancestors and descendants. By May (Cooper) Burnham. (Tulsa? Okla., 1960)   75, 48 p. illus. 26 cm. 61-34405.
CS71.O23   1960

12707   ODELL.   Abel and Polly Manning Cooper, Fielding and Sarah Hunt Meek, Frances Holbert and Lewis Westerman: their ancestors and descendants.   By May (Cooper) Burnham.   (Tulsa, Okla., 1960)   1 v. illus. 26 cm. 62-454.   CS71.O23   1960a

12708   ODELL.   In vertical file.   Ask reference librarian for this material.

ODELL.   See also ELIOT, 1961

12709   O'DEMPSEY.   An account of the O'Dempseys, chiefs of clan Maliere, by Thomas Mathews. Dublin, Hodges, Figgis & co., ltd.; (etc., etc.,) 1903.   4 p. l., 203 p. 20 cm. 17-2882.   CS499.O35

12710   O'DEVELIN.   The O'Develins of Tyrone, the story of an Irish sept now represented by the families of Devlin, Develin, Develyn, Develon and Devellen, by Joseph Chubb Develin ... Rutland, Vt., The Tuttle publishing co., inc. (c.1938)   137 p. col. front. (coat of arms) 24 cm. Map on lining-papers. Bibliography: p. (121)-125. 38-23724.   CS499.O36D4

12711   O'DEVELIN.   The story of an Irish sept, the O'Devlins of Tyrone, now represented by the families of Devlin, Develin, Develyn, D'Evelyn, Develen, Develan, Develon, Devellen, Devellin, etc., by Joseph Chubb Develin ... 2d ed.   (Philadelphia, College offset press, 1947)   xi, 179 p. 23 cm. First edition, 1938, has title: The O'Develins of Tyrone, the story of an Irish sept. Bibliography: p. 162-173. 47-19007.   CS499.O36   1947

12712   O'DEVELIN.   The story of an Irish sept, the O'Devlins of Tyrone, now represented by the surnames of Devlin, Develin, Develyn ... etc.   With accompanying information about the septs of MacCabe, MacCaffrey, MacCawell ... and others.   By Joseph Chubb Develin.   3d ed.   Philadelphia, (1951)   xii, 200 p. 24 cm. First ed. published in 1938 under title: The O'Develins of Tyrone, the story of an Irish sept.   Bibliography: p. (177)-189. 51-11566.   CS499.O36   1951

12713   ODIORNE.   Genealogy of the Odiorne family.   With notices of other families connected therewith.   By James Creighton Odiorne ... Boston, Printed by Rand, Avery, and company, 1875.   222 p. incl. front. (coat of arms) 23½ cm. 9-12827.   CS71.O24   1875

12714   ODIORNE.   Genealogy of the Odiorne family in America.   By James Creighton Odiorne.   Rev. in 1966 by David Walter Odiorne.   Published by a family committee: Harold and Julia Odiorne, Norman and Daisy Odiorne, Milo and Betty Odiorne.   Ann Arbor, Mich., Arbortown Book Co., 1967 (c.1966)   293 p. illus., coat of arms, map. 22 cm. Bibliography: p. 245-248. 66-28204 MARC.   CS71.O24   1967

ODIORNE.   See also: BRACKETT, 1917
                        WILCOX, 1911 b

O'DOCHARTY.   See DOHERTY.

O'DOGHERTY.   See DAUGHHETEE.

12715   O'DONNELL . ... The life of Hugh Roe O'Donnell, prince of Tirconnell (1586-1602), by Lughaidh O'Clery.   Now first published from Cucogry O'Clery's Irish manuscript in the R. I. Academy with historical introduction, translation, notes, and illustration, by the Rev. Denis Murphy ... Dublin, Fallon and co., 1895.   clviii, 338 p. front., plates, facsims. 24½ x 20½ cm. Title and text in Irish and English. 5-1421.   DA937.5.O303

12716   O'DONNELL.   A short history of a notable Irish family, by P. C. Gallagher ... Written by request of Ernest A. Chapman in further explanation of the booklet entitled "The mystery pearl shells". London, 1927.   10 p. pl., col. coat of arms. 24 cm. 28-17759.   DA937.5.O3G3

12717   O'DONNELL.   The Irish future and the lordship of the world, by C. J. O'Donnell ... (London) C. Palmer (1929)   265, (1) p. front., ports., II diagr. (1 fold.) 22 cm. "The last princely family of Ireland (the O'Donnells)": p. 245-(266) 30-16144.   DA960.O385

12718   O'DONNELL.   John O'Donnell of Baltimore, his forbears & descendants, collated & compiled by E. Thornton Cook.   London, The Favil press ltd., 1934.   6 p. l., 64 p., 1 l. XII pl. (incl. ports., maps, music) 2 col. coats of arms (incl. front.) 27 cm.   "This edition privately printed for Columbus O'Donnell Iselin, esquire, of New York is limited to three hundred copies of which this copy is no. 40."   The coats of arms are accompanied by guard sheets with descriptive letter-press.   One leaf containing poetry facing plate IV.   Folded genealogical tables in pocket at end.   Bibliography: p. 59.   34-35358.

CS71.O26   1934

12719   O'DONOGHUE.   ... An Leabhar muimhneach maraon le suim aguisini.   Tadhug O'Donnchadha ... do chuir i n-eagar.   Baile Atha Claith, Arna chur amach d'Oifig diolta foillseachain rialtais (1940)   xxxix, 535 p. fold. tab., diagr. 25 cm.   At head of title: Coimisiun laimhscribhinni na hEireann.   Biography and genealogy of leading families of Munster and Ireland, compiled from ancient sources and continued in some cases to the beginning of the eighteenth century, when the manuscripts were made.   cf. Reamhradh.   Includes pedigrees of the O'Donoghues of Desmond to Teige the Generous, A. D. 1320. from Cathan O Duinnin's poem on the families of UfEachach (fold. geneal. tab. between p. 532 and p. 533) 42-30102.

CS497.M8B6

O'DONOGHUE.   See also LEDLIE, 1961

12720   O'DONOVAN.   Pedigree of the ancient family of Donovan or O'Donovan, with additions by John O'Hart ... Asbury Park, N.J., Martin & Allardyce (190-?)   cover-title, (8) p. 24 cm.   Coat of arms on cover. 19-19892.   CS499.O38

O'DOWD.   See FIACHRACH, 1844a

12721   ODWYER.   The O'Dwyers of Kilnamanagh; the history of an Irish sept, by Sir Michael O'Dwyer ... London, J. Murray (1933)   vii, 358 p. fold. map, fold. geneal. tab. 22 cm. 33-30137.

DA916.3.O35O4

O'DWYER.   See O'KENNEDY, 1938

OELMICKER.   See ELLMAKER.

12722   OEN.   Family tree of Henry Oen, 1825-1902.   Compiled by Mary M. Einhart and corrected to July 1, 1966 for distribution.   (Toledo? Ohio, 1966)   22 l. illus., ports. 36 cm. 67-55070.

CS71.O3   1966

OERTLEY.   See ORTLEY.

12723   OESAU.   Claus Oesau and his descendants.   Francis W. Laurent: compiler and editor. (Madison, Wis., College Print. & typing Co.) 1968.   viii, 136 p. illus., geneal. tables, ports. 22 cm. Bibliography: p. 131-135.   77-11800 MARC.   CS71.O315   1968

OETEL.   In vertical file under PRANKE family.   Ask reference librarian for this material.

OFFENSEND.   See HOLCOMB, 1961

OFFICER.   See POT, 1935

12724   OFFLEY.   An account of the Offley family, written in the days of James I. by an unknown author: to which is added A pedigree comp. by G. C. Bower, and H. W. F. Harwood.   (Thirty copies privately reprinted from the Genealogist, n. s., vols. XIX and XX).   Exeter, Printed by W. Pollard & co. ltd., 1904.   2 p. l., 65 p. front. 24½ cm.   "A manuscript relating to the family of Offley": p. 3-21. 23-18864.

CS439.O45

OFFLEY.   See also: HARRISON, 1910a
                      No. 430 - Adventurers of purse and person.

OFFUTT.   See LUCKETT, 1938

OFSTEDAHL.   See No. 553 - Goodhue county.

12725   OGBURN.   As I was told about the Ogburn & Wynne families.   By Rubyn (Reynolds) Ogburn.
Richmond, Dietz Press (1958)   158 p. 22 cm. 58-40282.   CS71.O32   1958

12726   OGDEN.   Proceedings of the centennial anniversary of the Presbyterian church at Sparta, N.J.,
November 23, 1886, together with a history of the village, by the Rev. Theodore F. Chambers.   New
York, The Williams printing company, 1887.   106 p. plan. 23½ cm. Lettered on cover: Sparta centennial, 1786-1886.
"Ogden genealogy, by Rev. A. A. Haines": p. (69)-71. 9-28858.   F144.S7C4

12727   OGDEN.   The Ogdens of South Jersey.   The descendants of John Ogden of Fairfield, Conn.,
and New Fairfield, N.J.   Born, 1673, died 1745.   (Philadelphia, 1894)   35, (1) p. 24½ cm. By William O.
Wheeler and Edmund D. Halsey. 2-6780.   CS71.O34   1894

12728   OGDEN.   Descendants of Robert Ogden, 2d, 1716-1787.   By Edmund Drake Halsey.   Amenia,
N.Y., Walsh & Griffen, printers, 1896.   82 p. 23½ cm. 1-18706.   CS71.O34   1896

12729   OGDEN.   The Quaker Ogdens in America;   David Ogden of ye goode ship "Welcome" and his
descendants 1682-1897;   their history, biography, and genealogy, by Charles Burr Ogden, based upon
original researches by Charles Smith Ogden ... Philadelphia, Printed by J. B. Lippincott company, 1898.
2 p. l., (3)-245 p. front., illus., plates, ports., map. 25½ cm. "A limited edition, and for private distribution." 9-12825.
                                                                        CS71.O34   1898

12730   OGDEN.   Ogden family history in the line of Lieutenant Benjamin Ogden, of New York (born
June 22, 1735 - died August 16, 1780) of the Prince of Wales' American regiment, and his wife Rachel
Westervelt, with some account of his ancestry and descendants.   Orange, N.J., The Orange chronicle
co., printers, 1906.   1 p. l., iii, (3), 6-116 p. 22½ cm. "Privately printed." Introduction signed: Anna S. Vermilye. 31-9480.
                                                                        CS71.O34   1906

12731   OGDEN.   The Ogden family in America, Elizabethtown branch, and their English ancestry;
John Ogden, the Pilgrim, and his descendants, 1640-1906, their history, biography & genealogy; comp.
by William Ogden Wheeler; ed. by Lawrence Van Alstyne and Rev. Charles Burr Ogden, PH. D.
Philadelphia, Printed for private circulation by J. B. Lippincott company, 1907.   xii, (2), 531 (1) p. col. front.,
illus., plates, ports., map, facsims. 27½ cm. Title within ornamental border.   8-1763.   CS71.O34   1907
         —— (Charts compiled by) Lawrence Van Alstyne.   New Haven, Conn., The Tuttle, Morehouse
& Taylor press (1907)   38 fold. geneal. tab. 27 cm. 8-1763.   CS71.O34   1907a

12732   OGDEN.   Ogden-Preston genealogy.   The ancestors and descendants of Captain Benjamin
Stratton Ogden and his wife Nancy (Preston) Ogden, compiled by Josie Powell Stone and William Ogden
Powell.   (St. Peter, Minn., Press of the St. Peter herald, 1914)   31, (1) p. 23½ cm. p. 27-31 blank for additional
records. 14-14946.   CS71.O34   1914

12733   OGDEN.   Rachel Ogden, a loyalist ancestress (by) Sophie Radford de Meissner.   (n. p.,
1928?)   (21) p. 21½ cm. Bibliographical foot-notes. 29-1788.   E277.W54

               OGDEN.   See also: LINDLEY, 1950
                                    McCURDY, 1892
                                    SALISBURY, 1892
                                    WEST, 1939

12734   OGILVIE.   The Ogilvies of Montreal, with a genealogical account of the descendants of their
grandfather, Archibald Ogilvie ... Montreal, Printed for private circulation by the Gazette printing
company, 1904.   5 p. l., (3)-98 p. illus., plates, ports., facsims. 25 cm. "Prefatory remarks" signed: J. A. G. (i. e. John Alexander
Gemmill) Title vignette: coat of arms. 37-16831.   CS90.O45G4

12735   OGILVIE.   In defence of the regalia, 1651-2: being selections from the family papers of the
Ogilvies of Barras; edited, with introduction, by Rev. Douglas Gordon Barron ... With photogravure
frontispiece and nine illustrations.   London, New York (etc.) Longmans, Green and co., 1910.
xvi, 371 p. front., illus., plates, map, facsim. 24½ cm. Contents. - Prefatory note. - Introduction. - Regalia papers. - Miscellaneous papers. -
Genealogy of the family of Ogilvy of Barras. - Index. CA 12-603D.   DA112.B2

12736   OGILVIE.   Seafield correspondence from 1685 to 1708, edited, with introduction and annotations, by James Grant ... Edinburgh, printed at the University press by R. and A. Constable for the Scottish history society, 1912.   xxvi, 497, (1) p., 1 l. front. (port.) 23 cm. (Half-title: Publications of the Scottish history society.   New series, vol. III)   "A contribution to the numerous published letters written by, to, or concerning the Chancellor Earl of Seafield." - Introd.   12-16576.   DA750. S25 n. s. v. 3

OGILVIE.   See also AIRLIE, 1924

12737   OGILVIE-GRANT.   The rulers of Strathspey, a history of the lairds of Grant and earls of Seafield, by the Earl of Cassillis ... Inverness, The Northern counties newspaper and printing and publishing company, limited, 1911.   xii, 211 p. 10 pl. (2 col.) 5 port. (incl. front.) 23 cm. 11-14590.   CS479. O5

12738   OGLANDER.   Nunwell symphony, by Cecil Aspinall-Oglander.   With photographs by Hans Wild.   2d impression.   London, The Hogarth press, 1945 (i. e. 1946)   x, 11-233 p. front., plates, ports., facsims., fold. geneal. tab. 22 cm. "Second impression - February, 1946." A 46-5618.   CS439. O48   1946

12739   OGLE.   Ogle and Bothal: or, A history of the baronies of Ogle, Bothal, and Hepple, and of the families of Ogle and Bertram ... To which is added, accounts of several branches of families bearing the name of Ogle settled in other counties and countries; with appendices and illustrations compiled from ancient records and other sources, by Sir Henry A. Ogle, baronet.   (Printed privately) Newcastle-upon-Tyne, A. Reid & company, limited, 1902.   1 p. l., 426, lxx p. 14 pl. incl. front. (part coats of arms) geneal. tables (part fold.) 29 cm.   Works consulted: p. ii-iii.   15-19676.   CS439. O5

12740   OGLE.   ... A short history of the Ogle family, compiled by Anna Ogle Kirkpatrick.   Morrison, Ill., The Shawver publishing co., 1927.   (21) p. 17½ cm. (American families series) A 32-2439.   CS71. O36   1927

OGLE.   See also: BLACK, 1954
                        CARR, 1893
                        CAVENDISH, 1752

12741   OGLETHORPE.   Oglethorpe of Oglethorpe.   Oglethorpe of Rawdon.   (In Miscellanea genealogica et heraldica.   London, 1914, 27 cm. ser. 4, vol. 5, p. 224-226. illus. coats of arms.)

CS410. M5 ser. 4 v. 5

12742   OGSTON.   Supplement to the Genealogical history of the family of Ogston.   Edinburgh, Priv. print., 1897.   xi p., 2 l., 174 p. plates, maps (1 fold.) double facsim., double geneal. tables. 22½ cm. 20-16684.   CS479. O6

12743   O'HARA.   History, antiquities, and present state of the parishes of Ballysadare and Kilvarnet, in the county of Sligo; with notices of the O'Haras, the Coopers, the Percevals, and other local families.   By T. O'Rorke ... Dublin (etc.) J. Duffy and sons (1878)   xiv p., 1 l., 544 p. illus. 19 cm. 2-29205.   DA995. B1806

O'HARE.   See JELKE, E171. A53v. 19

12744   O'HEGARTY.   The O'Hegarty family, by John Hagerty.   Cohasset, Mass., 1941.   60 l. pl., port., facsim., col. coat of arms. 28½ cm.   Type-written; leaves variously numbered; the illustrative matter is mounted.   Includes bibliographies.   42-49733.   CS71. O38   1942

12745   O'HEGARTY.   Pedigree of the O'Hegerty family, by Henri Eltz and John Hagerty.   Cohasset, Mass., 1948.   folder. 46 x 60 cm.   Consists of a mounted leaf with caption title and bibliography, and a mounted geneal. table, with col. coats of arms.   48-10224*.   CS499. O4   1948

12746   O'HIGGINS.   Contribution toward a bibliography of the O'Higgins family in America, by Robert A. Lord ... (Durham, N. C., 1932)   cover-title, p. 107-138. 26½ cm.   "Compiled under the auspices of the Inter-American bibliographical association."   "Reprinted from the Hispanic American historical review.   vol. XII, no. 1, February, 1932." 32-24775.   Z8642. 4. L86

12747   OHL.   Ohl genealogy and history, 1710-1951.   Warren, Ohio, Cox Lithographing Corp.
(1951)   viii, 187 p. illus., ports., coat of arms. 22 cm. 51-34687.   CS71.O39   1951

OHLER.   See also PAINE, 1913

12748   OHM.   Georg Simon Ohm; ein forscher wächst aus seiner väter art, von ritter con Füchtbauer
... Berlin, VDI-verlag gmbh, 1939.   vii, 246 p. front., illus., plates, ports., plans, facsims., fold. geneal. tab. 21 cm.
"Georg Simon Ohm als glied seiner sippe" (fold. geneal. tab.) and "Ahnentafel fur Georg Simon Ohm und siene geschwister, bearbeitet von dr. phil.
Ernst Deuerlein" (p.200-214) "Die bedeutesten wissenschaftlichen leistungen von Georg Simon Ohm, dargestellt von prof. dr. Chr. Fuchtbauer":
p. 216-224. "Verzeichnis der schriften G. S. Ohms in zeitlicher reihenfolge": p. 226-228. "Nachweis der quellen": p. 232-236. 39-21649.

QC16.O45F8

OHRUDORF.   See ORNDORFF.

O'KAVANAGH.   See O'BYRNE, 1843

12749   O'KELLY.   Secret history of the war of the revolution in Ireland, 1688-1691, written under
the title of "Destruction of Cyprus," by Charles O'Kelly ... Edited from four English copies and a
Latin ms. in the Royal Irish academy, with notes, illustrations, and a memoir of the author and his
descendants, by John Cornelius O'Callaghan, M. R. I. A.   Dublin, For the Irish archaeological society,
1850.   3 p. l., xix, 546, 29 p. 24 x 20 cm. (Irish archaeological society. Publications) Half-title: Macariae excidium; or, The destruction
of Cyprus; containing the last warr and conquest of that kingdom. Written originally in Syriac by Philotas Phylocypres. Translated into Latin by
Gratianus Ragallus, P. R. And now made into English by Colonel Charles O'Kelly. A. D. 1692. 3-6223.   DA900.I5   1850

12750   O'KELLY.   The Jacobite war in Ireland (1688-1691) ... By Charles O'Kelly ... Ed. by
George Noble, count Plunkett ... and the Rev. Edm. Hogan ... 3d ed.   Dublin, Sealy, Bryers and
Walker, 1894.   1 p. l., xii, 115 p. front. (port.) 18 cm. (The Irish home library) 3-6685.

DA945.O41

12751   OKELY.   Okely. A pedigree and family history of the lineal descendants of John Okely, of
Bedford, England, which dates from about 1650 to the present time. To which is added the collateral
branches of de Guylpyn, West and Wade. ... Isaac E. Wade, editor. Pittsburg, Pa., 1899.
91 p. front., port., geneal. tables. 25 cm. Blank pages at end for "Family record" (4) Contains also Townsend, Hoopes and Wilson families.
35-21392.   CS71.O4   1899

12752   O'KENNEDY.   Records of four Tipperary septs, the O'Kennedys, O'Dwyers, O'Mulryans,
O'Meaghers, by Martin Callanan ... Galway, O'Gorman, ltd., printinghouse, 1938.
2 p. l., 7-180 (i.e.186) p., 1 l. 22 cm. Errata slip inserted. 45-33765.   CS499.O43   1938

12753   OKEOVER.   A history of the family of Okeover of Okeover, co. Stafford, by Major-general
the Hon. Geo. Wrottesley ... London, Harrison and sons, printers, 1904.   3 p. l., (3)-187, xviii p. illus.,
plates, facsim. 26 cm. "Reprinted from vol. VII, new series, of Staffordshire collections." "Pedigree of Okeover of Okeover, co. Stafford":
p. 180-187. 19-3360.   CS439.O56

OKEY.   See LUCAS, 1964

OKILL.   See STUART, 1920

O'KILLIA.   See KELLEY.

12754   OKLESHEN.   Geneology (sic) Okleshen, Gregory, Stih, Steh, Babich families. By John A.
Stih. (LaSalle? Ill.) 1965.   84 p. illus., ports. 22 cm. Cover title. Pages 75-84, blank for "Notes." 68-5212.

CS71.O42   1965

O'LAUGHLIN.   See COX, 1948

12755   OLCOTT.   Descendants of Thomas Olcott, one of the first settlers of Hartford, Connecticut.
By Nathaniel Goodwin ... Hartford, Press of Case, Tiffany & Burnham, 1845.   xii, (13)-63, (1) p. 22½ cm.
9-12979.   CS71.O43   1845

12756   OLCOTT.   The descendants of Thomas Olcott, one of the first settlers of Hartford, Ct., by Nathaniel Goodwin ... Revised edition, with an explanatory preface and important additions.   By Henry S. Olcott ... Albany, N.Y., J. Munsell, 1874.   xxxi, (33)-124 p. front. (coats of arms) 23½ cm. 9-12549.

CS71.O43   1874

12757   OLCOTT.   The Olcott family of Hartford, Connecticut, in the line of Eunice (Olcott) Goodwin, 1639-1807; compiled by Frank Farnsworth Starr for James J. Goodwin.   Hartford, Conn. (Cambridge, University press, J. Wilson and son) 1899.   84 p. front. (fold. geneal. tab.) 24½ cm. 99-4019 rev. L. C. COPY REPLACED BY MICROFILM.

CS71.O43   1899
Microfilm 8651 CS

12758   OLCOTT.   Josiah Olcott and Deborah Worth, his wife.   A record of their descendants and notes regarding their ancestors.   (By Albert Rathbone)   (New York, N.Y., Press of B. H. Tyrrel) 1937.   2 p. l., 85 p. 25 cm. Includes nine blank pages for "Memoranda". 38-36153.

CS71.O43   1937

12759   OLCOTT.   The Olcotts and their kindred from Anglo-Saxon times, through Roncesvalles to Gettysburg and after.   By Mary Louisa Beatrice Olcott.   (1st ed.) New York, National Americana Publications, 1954.   315 p. illus., ports., maps, col. coats of arms. 35 cm. Bibliography: p. 274-275. 55-1402.

CS71.O43   1954

12760   OLCOTT.   The Olcotts and their kindred, from Anglo-Saxon times through Roncesvalles to Gettysburg and after.   By Mary Louisa Beatrice Olcot.   (2d ed.) New York, National Americana Publications, 1956.   315 p. illus., ports., maps, col. coats of arms, geneal. tables. 28 cm. "100 copies." No. 7. Bibliography: p. 274-275. 56-4303.

CS71.O43   1956

OLCOTT.   See also BURR, E171.A53 v.16

OLDAKER.   See HUDSON, DA690.W6H8

OLDEN.   See WRIGHT, 1960

12761   OLDENBOURG.   Das Geschlecht Oldenburg zur Oldenburg und die Munchener Verlegerfamilie Oldenbourg; eine Familienchroniküber 4 Jahrhunderte.   By Johannes Hohlfeld.   (München, R. Oldenbourg, 1940)   305 p. illus. (part col.) ports., maps, geneal. tables. 26 cm. "Bibliographie": p. 283-289. AF 48-2058*.

CS629.O4   1940

OLDENBURG.   See OLDENBOURG.

12762   OLDFATHER.   The genealogy of the Oldfather family, compiled by Rufus A. Longman ...   Cincinnati, O., R. A. Longman (1911)   220 p. incl. plates, ports. 24 cm. 11-25335.

CS71.O44   1911

12763   OLDFATHER.   A post office directory of the Oldfather family relationship, being a supplement to the family genealogy, published by R. A. Longman.   Cincinnait, O., 1912.   39 p. 23 cm. 35-9805.

CS71.O44   1912

OLDFIELD.   See HERIOT, 1939

OLDHAM.   See: KIRKPATRICK, 1911
                MILLER, 1907
                PHELPS, 1960

12764   OLDKNOW.   History of the Oldknow family, with a genealogical chart of the descendants of Thomas Oldknow and Phoebe Mathers, his wife, sketches of individuals, and notices of families connected with them from 1708 to 1928, comp, by William Henry Oldknow ... (Atlanta? 1928) 2 p. l., 7-111 p., 1 l. front., ports., fold. geneal. tab. 23 cm. Blank pages for "Record of recent family events" (104-111) 29-1597.

CS71.O446   1928

12765   OLDOFREDI.   Cenno genealogico sulla famiglia degli Isei, ora Oldofredi, per Damiano Muoni ... Milano, Tipografia letteraria, 1870.   15 p. 23½ cm. 13-21612.   CS769.O5

OLDRID.   See CLARK, CS438.C5

12766   OLDS.   The Olds (Old, Ould) family in England and America; American genealogy, by Edson B. Olds; English pedigree, by Miss Susan S. Gascoyne Old ... Compiled and published by Edson B. Olds.   Washington, D.C., 1915.   359 p. front. (coat of arms) fold. geneal. tab.   23½ cm.   15-20948.
CS71.O435   1915

12767   O'LEARY.   The family of Ethel Rita Landau Voorhis.   By Harold Van Buren Voorhis. (Brooklyn, 1960)   (7) l. 29 cm. 60-50828.   CS71.O45   1960

OLEY.   See No. 1547 - Cabell county.

12768   OLGERD.   Political & diplomatic history of Russia, by George Vernadsky.   Students' ed. Boston, Little, Brown and company, 1936.   ix p., 2 l., (3)-499 p. incl. geneal. tables. maps (part fold.) 22½ cm.   Maps on lining-papers.   "General bibliography": p. (467)-470.   Bibliography at end of each chapter.   36-11172.   DK61.V4

12769   OLIN.   Biographical sketches and records of the Ezra Olin family; by Geo. S. Nye ... Chicago, W. B. Conkey co., printers, 1892.   441 p. front., ports., fold. geneal. tab. 24 cm. 3-17339.
CS71.O46   1892

12770   OLIN.   A complete record of the John Olin family, the first of that name who came to America in the year A.D.1678.   Containing an account of their settlement and genealogy up to the present time - 1893.   By C. C. Olin ... Indianapolis, Baker-Randolph co., printers, 1893.   2 p. l., (3)-228, xcvi p. front., ports. 22 ½ cm.   Four blank leaves inserted after p. 228 for "Family record."   "Reminiscences of the busy life of Chauncey C. Olin": p. i-lxxv. 9-12824.   CS71.O46   1893

12771   OLIN.   Biographical sketches of the Samuel Olin family, by Oran Baber.   (Madison, Wis., Tracy and Kilgore, printers) c.1921.   130 p. incl. ports. 23½ cm. 23-6503.   CS71.O46   1921

12772   OLIN.   The William Olin family of West Greenwich, R. I., and Laurens, N.Y., and some of his ancestors and descendants.   By William Gideon Closson.   Flushing, N.Y., 1956.   60 l. illus. 29 cm. 59-33216.   CS71.O46   1956

12773   OLIPHANT.   The Jacobite lairds of Gask, by T. L. Kington Oliphant ... London, Grampian club, C. Griffin and co., 1870.   xxiv, 504 p. port., facsims. (1 fold.) 23 cm. 20-18082 rev. 2.
DA758.3.O5K5

12774   OLIPHANT.   The Oliphants of Gask; records of a Jacobite family by E. Maxtone Graham (E. Blair Oliphant).   London, J. Nisbet & co., ltd., 1910.   xix, 513 p., 1 l. incl. front. pl., ports. 26 cm.   Appendix III: Letter from Professor Samuel Grant Oliphant of Olivet College, Michigan, on the subject of members of the Oliphant family in America.   Appendix IV: Genealogical sketch of the Kington family.   11-2507.   CS439.O6

12775   OLIPHANT.   Samuel Duncan Oliphant, the indomitable campaigner; his Scottish, colonial and American family history with emphasis on his heroic Civil War record.   By Fred Smith.   (1st ed.) New York, Exposition Press (1967)   203 p. illus., facsims., map (on lining-paper), ports. 21 cm.   Includes music.   Bibliography: p. (201)-203. 67-24269.   CS71.O468   1967

12776   OLIPHANT.   Oliphant family.   Additional material in vertical file.   Ask reference librarian for this.

12777   OLIVE.   James Olive family, Wake County, N.C.   (Norfolk? Va., Olive Family Association, 1965)   ix, 281 p. illus., coats of arms, ports. 23 cm.   79-10431 MARC.   CS71.O469   1965

OLIVE.   See also: BOYD, 1948
RIX, 1957

12778   OLIVER.   Ancestry of Mary Oliver, who lived 1640-1698, and was wife of Samuel Appleton, of Ipswich.   By William S. Appleton.   Cambridge, Press of J. Wilson and son, 1867.   1 p. l., 29 p., 1 l. geneal. table. 24 ½ cm. 9-12546.   CS71.O48   1867

12779   OLIVER.   Genealogy of descendants of Thomas Oliver, of Bristol, England, and of Boston, New England, in the direct line of Rev. Daniel Oliver, late of Boston.   Prepared by Henry K. Oliver. Salem, Mass., 1868.   7 p. 23½ cm. Caption title. 3-7923.   CS71.O48   1868

12780   OLIVER.   Sepulchral memorials of Bobbingworth, Essex.   With genealogical notes and pedigrees.   (London) Priv. print. for F. A. Crisp, 1888.   4 p. l., 61 p. illus., 2 pl. (coats of arms) fold. geneal. tab. 29½ cm. Interleaved. "One hundred copies only of this vol. ... have been printed. This copy is no. 27." Edited by Fred. A. Crisp. Genealogical table: Oliver pedigree. Contents. - Monumental inscriptions, etc. - Rectors of Bobbingworth. - Wills, pedigrees, etc., Bourne, Cowper and Cure pedigrees. 11-34066.   CS436.B65

12781   OLIVER.   Oliver genealogy; a record of the descendants of Joseph, Reuben, and Levi Oliver of New York, Pennsylvania, and Delaware 1727-1888, and of Pierre Elisee Gallaudet, M. D. of New Rochelle, New York 1711-1888.   By Rev. Horace Edwin Hayden ... New York (Press of J. J. Little & co.) 1888.   23, 4 p. front. 25½ cm. Reprinted from the New York Genealogical and biographical record, July and October, 1888, and January, 1889. 13-14110.   CS71.O48   1888

12782   OLIVER.   The Olivers of Cloghanodfoy, and their descendants.   Compiled by Major-General J. R. Oliver ... 3d ed. ... London, Printed by the Army and Navy co-operative society, limited, 1904. 48 p. 18 cm. 15-19652.   CS499.O47

12783   OLIVER.   History of the Oliver, Vassall and Royall houses in Dorchester, Cambridge and Medford, by Robert Tracy Jackson ... Boston, 1907.   17 p. 3 pl. 25 cm. Reprinted from the Genealogical magazine, January, 1907, vol. II, no. 1. "References": p. 16-17. 7-22901.   CS71.O48   1907

12784   OLIVER.   Ancestry, early life and war record of James Oliver, M. D., practicing physician fifty years.   Athol, Mass., The Athol transcript company, 1916.   4 p. l., 151 p. front. (port.) 23 cm. "Report of Committee on education of the Massachusetts state grange ... December ... 1899" (p. 119-129) has special t.-p. 37-16950.   CS71.O48   1916

12785   OLIVER.   Descendants of the Honorable Andrew Oliver of Boston (1706-1774) and his first wife (Mary (Fitch) Oliver and his children by his second wife Mary (Sanford) Oliver, also certain inter-marriages of Olivers and Hutchinsons.   Compiled by William H. P. Oliver.   (n. p.) Printed for private distribution, 1937.   1 p. l., 19 p. 25 cm. 39-12246.   CS71.O48   1937

12786   OLIVER.   Oliver-Miner ancestors and descendants.   By Frederick Lansing Oliver.   Myrtle M. Jillson, co-compiler-editor.   (Newton, Mass.) 1956.   126 p. 22 cm. 60-22308.   CS71.O545   1956

12787   OLIVER.   Henry (William) Oliver, 1807-1888; ancestry and descendants.   By Henry Oliver Rea.   Dungannon, Northern Ireland, Printed by the Tyrone Print, Co., 1959.   55 p. illus., ports., facsims., 2 geneal. tables. 29 cm. In portfolio. "For private circulation only." 400 copies printed. No. 238. 61-44768.   CS71.O47   1959

12788   OLIVER.   Faces of a family; an illustrated catalogue of portraits and silhouettes of Daniel Oliver, 1664-1732, and Elizabeth Belcher, his wife, their Oliver descendants and their wives, made between 1727 and 1850.   By Andrew Oliver.   (Portland, Me.) 1960.   xvii, 42 p. ports., geneal. tables. 25 cm. 61-35194.   CS71.O47   1960

12789   OLIVER.   Oliver-Sistrunk families, Orangeburg area, South Carolina, by Georgie I. Adams Lefvendahl.   (Orangeburg? S. C.) 1964.   73 l. illus., ports. 28 cm. 64-7239.   CS71.O47   1964

OLIVER.   See also: BLACK, 1903   GUÉRIN, 1890
                      DE MOSS, 1950   HUTCHINSON, 1865
                      ELIOT, 1907   LINCOLN, 1930
                      FANEUIL, 1851   WATKINS, 1957

12790   OLIVIER.   The Olivier de Vezin, Peloquan, Chauffe familys (sic.   Lake Charles? La.) 1967. 1 v. (various pagings) illus. 30 cm. 68-1081.   CS71.O49   1967

OLIVIER.   See also: FANEUIL, 1851
                       SEBOR, 1923

OLM.   See OHM, 1939

12791   OLMSTEAD.   An abridged genealogy of the Olmstead family of New England.   By Elijah L. Thomas ... Albany, J. Munsell, 1869.   1 p. l., 30 p. 17 cm. 9-12543.   CS71.O5   1869

12792   OLMSTEAD.   Genealogy of the Olmstead family in America, embracing the descendants of James and Richard Olmstead and covering a period of nearly three centuries, 1632-1912, comp. by Henry King Olmstead, M.D.; rev. and completed by Rev. Geo. K. Ward, A.M.; advisory committee: John Bartow Olmsted, Right Rev. Charles T. Olmsted, Mrs. Henry S. Stearns, Prof. Everett Ward Olmstead, ex-off.   New York, A. T. De La Mare printing and publishing company, td., 1912.   xx, 518 p., 1 l. front., plates, ports., facsims. (1 double) col. coat of arms. 27 cm. 12-27609.   CS71.O5   1912

12793   OLMSTEAD.   Another edition of the above.   1912 (-14)   xx, 589 p. front., plates, ports., facsim., col. coat of arms. 27 cm. "Supplement containing additional data, correction of errors, allied families, biographical notes, late accessions to roll of Olmsted family association, New York, 1914": p. 521-589. 21-6657.   CS71.O5   1912a

12794   OLMSTEAD.   Arthur George Olmstead, son of a Pennsylvania pioneer; boy orator of Ulysses; for the freedom of the slave; defense of the Union; development of the northern tier; citizen, jurist, statesman.   By Rufus Barrett Stone.   Philadelphia, The John C. Winston company, 1919.   268 p. front., illus. (incl. maps, facsims.) ports. 21½ cm. 19-10311.   F154.O5

12795   OLMSTEAD.   Some brief notes on the Olmstead family, arr. & published by Edward Coolbaugh Hoagland.   Wysox, Pa., 1955.   (3) l. 30 cm. 56-23400.   CS71.O5   1955

OLMSTEAD.   See also: BASSETT, 1926
BROWN, 1937
FOY, 1932
PARSONS, 1867

OLMSTED.   See OLMSTEAD.

12796   OLNEY.   A genealogy of the descendants of Thomas Olney, an original proprietor of Providence, R. I., who came from England in 1635.   By James H. Olney ... (Providence, Press of E. L. Freeman & son) 1889.   4 p. l., 293 p. front. (facsim.) port. 23½ cm. Binder's title: Olney memorial. 1-6142.   CS71.O51   1889

12797   OLOFSSON.   The known descendants of Carl Olofsson born in 1685 in Sweden, 1685-1953, in fourteen States, Canada, and Scandinavia.   By Clarence Stewart Peterson.   (Baltimore? c, 1953)   69 l. illus. 28 cm. 54-31923.   CS71.O515   1953

OLSEN.   See No. 553 - Goodhue county.

12798   OLSON.   Family tree of Hans and Karen Olson, November 3, 1839 to November 11, 1948.   By Henry T. Henryson.   St. Paul (1948?)   1A - 92A, 1 B - 92 B p. 15 x 23 cm. 49-26961.   CS71.O52   1948

OLSON.   See also: TONGUE, 1949
WANGENSTEEN, 1964

12799   OLYPHANT.   Olyphant genealogy, compiled & executed - 1937-38 for J. K. Olyphant, jr ...   New York city (1938)   2-21 numb. l. 30 cm. Photostat reproduction (positive) Title and text within ornamental border. Bibliographical foot-notes. 41-374.   CS71.O54   1938

12800   O'MADDEN.   Genealogical, historical, and family records of the O'Madden's of Hy-Many, and their descendants.   Dublin, W. Powell, printer, 1894.   72 p. 22 cm. Preface signed Thomas More Madden. 9-19106.   CS499.O5

O'MADDEN.   See also MADDEN.

12801   O'MAHONY.   History of the O'Mahony septs of Kinelmeky and Ivagha ... By Rev. Canon O'Mahony.   Cork, Guy and company, limited, 1913.   2 p. l., (2)-169 p. illus. (incl. plan, facsim.) plates, coat of arms. 25½ cm.   Reprinted from Journal of the Cork historical and archaeological society, 2d ser., v. 12-16, 1906-1910. 20-15237.
CS499.O55

12802   O'MEAGHER.   Some historical notices of the O'Meaghers of Ikerrin ... By Joseph Casimir O'Meagher ... American ed.   New York, 1890.   216 p. front., illus., plates (part col.) ports., 2 maps, facsim. 25½ cm. Title vignette.   Date on title-page and copyright date changed to 1893.   "American notes": p. 157-185. 9-8418.
CS499.O6

—— Copy 2.
CS71.O55   1890

O'MEAGHER.   See also O'EKNNEDY, 1938

O'MELVENY.   See MOORE, 1915

12803   OMOHUNDRO.   The Omohundro genealogical record; the Omohundros and allied families in America: blood lines traced from the first Omohundro in Westmoreland County, Virginia, 1670, through his descendants in three great branches and allied families down to 1950.   Staunton, Va., Manufactured for the author by McClure Print. Co., 1950-51 (c. 1951)   xvi, 1287 p. illus., ports., geneal. tables, 26 cm. 51-8723.
CS71.O56   1951

12804   O'MORE.   Notes on an old pedigree of the O'More family of Leix.   By Sir Edmund T. Bewley ... (Read January 31, 1905)   (In Royal society of antiquaries of Ireland, Dublin.   The journal ... 1905.   Dublin, 1906. 25½ cm. vol. XXXV, p. 53-59) 19-3376.
DA900.R88

12805   O'MULLALLY.   History of O'Mullally and Lally clann; or, The history of an Irish family through the ages entertwined with that of the Irish nation ... By (Dennis Patrick O'Mullally) ... Chicago, 1942)   11 p. l., 536 p. incl. illus. (incl. ports., map, coat of arms) geneal. tables. front. (port.) 23½ cm. 42-18919.
CS499.O64   1942

O'MULRYAN.   See O'KENNEDY, 1938

12806   OMWAKE.   The Omwakes of Indian Spring farm; pictorial, descriptive, biographical. Cincinnati, O., 1926.   96 p. illus. (incl. ports.) 28 cm.   "Material prepared by George L. Omwake and made into a book by John Omwake." 27-8478.
CS71.O57   1926

12807   ONDERDONK.   Genealogy of the Onderdonk family in America, compiled by Elmer Onderdonk ... With revisions, addenda and appendix, by the publisher, Andrew J. Onderdonk ... New York, Priv. print., 1910.   374 p. front., 3 pl. 24 cm. Edited by Florence E. Youngs. 10-9116.   CS71.O58   1910

ONDERDONK.   See also: BLAUVELT, 1957
                           JOHNSON, 1957

O'NEAL.   See: JARRATT, 1957
                  O'NEILL.

O'NEIL.   See O'NEILL.

O'NEIL-ROBINS.   See No. 430 - Adventurers of purse and person.

12808   O'NEILL.   The O'Neills of Ulster; their history and genealogy by Thomas Mathews ... With illustrations, some notices of the northern septs; and an introduction by Francis Joseph Bigger ... Dublin, Sealy, Bryers & Walker, 1907.   3 v. fronts. (part col.) plates, ports., fold. map, fold. geneal. tables. 19 cm. 9-15745.
CS499.O65

12809   O'NEILL.   O'Neals and Lodges of Rockville, Maryland.   (By) Florence W. Layton. (Washington, 1944)   2 l. 28 x 21½ cm. Caption title, in manuscript. Type-written. 45-21835.   CS71.O583   1944

12810   O'NEILL.   Irish chiefs and leaders.   By Paul Walsh. Edited by Colm O Lochlainn.   Dublin, Sign of the three Candles (1960)   334 p. 23 cm. 61-66526.   DA916.4.W3

12811   O'NEILL.   The John and Nannie O'Neil family: pioneers of Midway, Utah; emigrants from Dalry, Scotland; had ancestral ties in Ulster, Ireland; a biographical, genealogical, and historical record, compiled and published to commemorate the 100th anniversary of their arrival in Utah on October 3, 1864.   Provo, Utah, J. G. Stevenson, c.1963.   xvi, 4, xvii-xviii, 251 p. illus., ports., map. 24 cm. 63-17620.   CS71.O584   1963

O'NEILL.   See also JOLLIFFEE, 1893

12812   ONG.   The Ong family of America.   By Albert R. Ong ... Martins Ferry, O., 1906. 171 p., 1 l. front., pl., ports. 20 cm. Blank leaves for "Family record" (12 at end) 35-28841.   CS71.O585   1906

12813   ONSLOW.   Some west Surrey villages, by E. A. Judges ... With an introduction by the Right Hon. Viscount Midleton... With numerous illustrations by Laurence Davis and others, and many reproductions of old prints.   Guildford (Eng.) 'Surrey times' printing and publishing co., ltd., 1901. xiv (i.e.xvi), 142, (1) p. front., illus., plates, ports., facsims. 28½ cm. Page xvi incorrectly numbered xiv.   Contents. - Gomshall and Shere - Reginald Bray and William Bray. - Henry Drummond and Albury. - Albury park and village. - From Chilworth to Shalford. - Peaslake, Holmbury St. Mary, and Ewhurst. - Cranleigh and Hascombe. - Knowle and the Onslows. - In the Fold country (Alfold, Dunsfold. and Chiddingfold) - Amid the pines and heather. - On the banks of the Wey: Eashing (Shackleford), Peper Harow, and Elstead. - Tilford and the White monks. - Seale, Puttenham, and Compton. 2-21045.
                                                                                                                         DA670. S96J9

12814   ONSLOW.   The Onslow family, 1528-1874, with some account of their times.   By Colwyn Edward Vulliamy.   London, Chapman & Hall, 1953.   x, 277 p. illus., ports. 23 cm. A 54-364.
                                                                                                                         CS439.O62   1953

12815   ONTHANK.   The Onthank family, its history and genealogy.   By Arthur Heath Onthank. Martinsville, Ind., Martinsville Reporter Press, 1959.   211 p. 24 cm. 59-28587.   CS71.O587   1959

12816   OOTHOUT (family)   (In "Genealogical notes of New York and New England families." Comp. by S. V. Talcott ... Albany, 1883. 24 cm. p. 183-192, 417-420, 441-444) 13-9622.   F118. T14
           —— Copy 3, detached.   CS71.O59   1883

OPDYCK.   See OPDYKE.

12817   OPDYKE.   The Op Dyck genealogy, containing the Opdyck - Opdycke - Opdyke - Updike American descendants of the Wesel and Holland families, by Charles Wilson Opdyke, with an investigation into their Op Den Dyck ancestors in Europe, by Leonard Eckstein Opdycke ... Albany, N.Y., Printed for Charles W. Opdyke, Leonard E. Opdycke and William S. Opdyke, by Weed, Parsons & co., 1889.   ix, (33), 499 p. incl. plan. plates, ports., facsims., plan. 25½ cm. 9-12541.   CS71.O61   1889

OPDYKE.   See also UPDIKE.

12818   OPIE.   William Oppie of Somerset County, New Jersey, and some of his descendants, with other Opie families mentioned; compiled by Esther Opie Van Ness, with John E. Eldridge as collaborator on the early history.   (Ann Arbor? Mich., 1958)   xv, 299 p. illus., ports., maps (2 on lining papers) coats of arms (1 mounted col.) 23 cm. "Limited eiditon of 400 copies." No. 330. Bibliography: p.7.   CS71.O64   1958
           —— Supplement and corrections to the Oppie-Opie genealogy.   Compiled by Esther Opie Van Ness.   (Phoenix? 1966)   xii, 132 p. illus.,ports. 21 cm. Addendum slip inserted. 58-11847 rev.   CS71.O64   1958
                                                                                                                         Suppl.

OPPIE.   See OPIE.

12819   ORANGE-NASSAU.   Tableau de l'histoire des princes et principauté d'Orange.   Divisé en quatre parties selon les quatre races qui y ont regné souverainement depuis l'an 793.   Commencant a Guillaume au Cornet, premier prince d'Orange.   Jusques a Frederich Henry de Nassay, a present regnant.   Illustré de ses genealogies & enrichi de plusieurs belles antiquités avec leurs tailles douces. La Haye, Impr. de T. Maire, 1639.   10 p. l., 903 (11) p. plates (part double) ports., fold. geneal. tables. 40 cm. By Joseph de La Pise. Added t.-p. engr. 1-9695.   DJ150. L3

12820   ORANGE.   The history of the most illustrious William, prince of Orange: deduced from the first founders of the antient house of Nassau, together with the most considerable actions of this present prince.   (London) 1688.   3 p. 1., 190, (8) p. 19 cm. 5-6744.

DJ186.H67

12821   ORANGE.   Histoire du stadhouderat dpuis son origine jusqu'a present.   Par M. l'abbe Raynal. 6. ed. ... (Paris?) 1750.   2 v. 16½ cm. 5-6733.   DJ146.R2   1750b

12822   ORANGE.   The history of the house of Orange; or, A brief relation of the glories and mag-nanimous achievements of His Majesty's renowned predecessors, and likewise of his own heroic actions till the late wonderful revolution; together with the history of William and Mary, king and queen of England, Scotland, France and Ireland, &c. being an impartial account of the most remark-able passages and transactions in these kingdoms, from Their Majesty's happy accession to the throne to this time.   By Richard Burton (pseud.)   A new edition.   Westminster, M. Stace, 1814.   iv, 144 p. front. 21½ cm. Title in red and black within line border. 1st edition; London, 1693. 4-29581.   DJ150.C95

12823   ORANGE.   Juliana von Stolberg, ahnfrau des hauses Nassau-Oranien.   Nach ihrem leben und ihrer geschichtlichen bedeutung quellenmassig dargestellt von dr.   Ed. Jacobs ... Wernigerode, O.   Hendel in Halle, a. d. s. 1889.   xii, 515, (1) p. illus., fold. facsim., fold. geneal. tab. 26 cm. "Die vorliegende schrift wurde zuerst in kürzerer gestalt im jahre 1884 bei familienfeier des hauses Stolberg-Wernigerode überreicht." - p. (v) 9-18510.

DD491.H62J7

12824   ORANGE-NASSAU.   Nassau-Saarbrücken and Mörs.   Ein beitrag zur geschichte des oranis-chen successionsstreites ... Von Wilhelm Martin Dienstbach.   Frankfurt a. M., Druck von Voigt & Gleiber, 1905.   265, (1) p. 3 facsim. on fold. pl. 24 cm. Inaug, diss. - Zürich. Vita. Plate printed on both sides. "Quellen": p. 4-6. 9-21041.   DD491.M6D5

12825   ORANGE.   Guillaume d'Orange et les origines des Antilles françaises, étude historique d'après les chroniques de l'époque et de nombreux documents inédits, accompagnée d'un exposé de la descendance de Guillaume d'Orange et de pièces justificatives, par le vicomte du Motey ... Paris, A. Picard et fils, 1908.   xi, 471 p. 25 cm. p. 329-414, La descendance de Guillaume d'Orange. 10-11762.

F2151.D93

12826   ORBEC.   Études sur la généalogie des seigneurs d'Orbec et de Bienfaite.   Chartes inédites des XIIe et XIIIe siècles relatives à des donations au couvent de Saint-Saëns-en-Caux.   (Bernay, Impr. Claudin) 1940.   42 p. facsim., geneal. tables. 23 cm. "Extrait du Bulletin de la Société d'études historiques d'Orbec (Calvados), tome II, no. 7, années 1937-1938." Latin text of manuscripts belonging to Saint-Saens abbey; French translation and commentary by Marcel Orbec. 48-43465*.   CS599.O7   1940

12827   ORBELL.   Sturdy sons; a flashback into the cheerful yesterday of a New Zealand family. Dust cover jacket drawn by Syd Scales; line blocks for chapter headings, etc. drawn by Elizabeth H. Miller.   By Charles Homes Miller.   Dunedin, N. Z., Printed by Otago daily times (1958) 206 p. illus. 23 cm. 59-33605.   CS2049.O7   1958

ORCHARD, Ona.   See book of Additions and corrections no. 116

12828   ORD.   Ord family.   Article in Washington Post, Tues, Oct. 11, 1960.   In vertical file. Ask reference librarian for this material.

ORDRONAUX.   See KINGMAN, 1911

12829   O'REILLY.   Irish chiefs and leaders.   By Paul Walsh.   Edited by Colm O Lochlainn. Dublin, Sign of the Three Candles (1960)   334 p. 23 cm. 61-66526.   DA916.4.W3

OREN.   See PRAY, 1957

12830   ORENDORFF.   Orendorff genealogy, by Milo Custer.   Bloomington, Ill., 1919. 1 p. 1., 6 p. ports. 24½ cm. 19-8778.   CS71.O67   1919

ORFEUR.   See YATES, 1887

12831   ORLAND.   A survey of the Orland family; William Powers Orland branch, by Frank A. Orland.   (Centerbury? Ohio, 196-)   1 v. (various pagings)   mounted coat of arms, geneal. table, mounted ports.   30 cm.   Title from label mounted on cover.   65-3527.   CS71.O72

12832   ORLEBAR.   The Orlebar chronicles in Bedfordshire and Northamptonshire, 1553-1733; or, The children of the Manorhouse and their posterity, by Frederica St. John Orlebar.   London, Mitchell Hughes and Clarke, 1930 -   v. plates, ports.   25½ cm.   Edited by R. R. B. Orlebar.   "Supplement.   Orlebar pedigree" compiled by Gerald Orlebar: p. (307)-321.   40-285.   CS439.O63   1930

12833   ORMISTON.   The Ormistons of that ilk, by W. J. Ormston.   (London) 1933.   26, (6) p.   front. (col. coat of arms) 18 cm.   Blank pages for "Memoranda" (6 at end)   35-13684.   CS479.O7   1933

12834   ORMISTON.   The Ormistons of Teviotdale.   By Thomas Lane Ormiston.   Exeter, (Eng.) W. Pollard, 1951.   ix, 377 p.   geneal. tables.   29 cm.   Bibliography: p. (369)-371.   Errata slip inserted.   52-34423.   CS479.O7   1951

ORMOND.   See: BUTLER, DA940.5.O7C2
FITZGERALD, DA916.3.D4H3

12835   ORMSBY.   Pedigree of the family of Ormsby, Formerly of Ormsby in Lincolnshire, now of Ireland.   Comp. by J. F. Fuller ... London, Mitchell and Hughes, 1886.   20 p.   18½ cm.   20-23954. Published also in "Misc. gen. et herald", London, 1888. 2nd series. vol. II, p. 173-179, 205-208, 219-224, 234-235.   CS439.O65

12836   ORMSBY.   A short account of the family of Ormsby of Pittsburgh.   By Oliver Ormsby Page ... Albany, N. Y., J. Munsell's sons, 1892.   46, (2) p.   29 cm.   9-12542.   CS71.O73   1892

12837   ORMSBY.   Ormsby families of Connecticut prior to 1800, compiled by Claude W. Barlow for Francis Gratacap Ormsby.   (Worcester? Mass.) 1965.   35 p.   30 cm.   66-47782.   CS71.O73   1965

ORMSBY.   See also: BREED, 1958
PULFORD, CS439.P85

ORNDORF.   See ORNDORFF.

12838   ORNDORFF.   From mill sheel to plowshare; the story of the contribution of the Christian Orndorff family to the social and industrial history of the United States, by Julia Angeline Drake ... and James Ridgely Orndorff.   Cedar Rapids, Ia., The Torch press (c. 1938)   xii, 271 p.   illus., plates, 2 port. (incl. front.) maps (2 fold.) facsims.   23½ cm.   Map on lining-papers.   39-1028.   CS71.O74   1938

12839   ORNDORFF.   John Orndorff, Pennsylvania pioneer, and his ancestors: Johannes Peter Orndorff, John Orndorff, Junior, William Orndorff (and) John Orndorff.   Compiled by John Barclay Orndorff, assisted by his daughter, Nora Lee Orndorff.   (Waynesburg? Pa., 1953)   50 p.   illus. 23 cm. 54-19778.   CS71.O74   1953

ORNDORFF.   See also: REID, 1960
RUDOLPH, 1962

ORNE.   See PAINE, 1904

12840   ORR.   Brief sketch of the genealogy of Captain Thomas Orr, late of Franklin County, Pennsylvania and his descendants, compiled by John G. Orr ... and James P. Orr ... (n. p.) 1923. 23 p. 24 cm.   24-29281.   CS71.O75   1923

12841   ORR.   Nine generations of Orrs in America, 1700-1954, with information concerning their marriages into the families of Scott, Jones, Hull, Watson, and Wallace.   By Warren Henry Orr. (Chicago? 195-)   185 p.   illus. 24 cm.   56-45184.   CS71.O75

ORR.   See also: BUZZELL, 1964   McCALL, CS478.M15
HALL, 1892   MITCHELL, F74.E18B9

ORREBY. See OLDFORD, CS437.C408 vol.2

12842   ORRELL.   Notes on the genealogy and history of the Cheshire branch of the Orrells ...
Negative.   2316
                                                                        Microfilm reading room.

12843   ORTEGA.   A California pioneer.   By Zoeth S. Eldredge.   (San Francisco, Publication com-
mittee of the Society, 1902)   p. 39-49. 22½ cm. Caption title. Excerpt from Publication no. 3 of California historic-genealogical
society, 2902, p. 39-49.   F864.O78

ORTH.   See BEATTY, 1886

ORTLEY.   See WILBUR, 1961

12844   ORTON.   An account of the descendants of Thomas Orton, of Windsor, Connecticut, 1641
(principally in the male line) By Edward Orton ... Columbus, O., Press of Nitschke brothers, 1896.
220 p. illus., ports., VIII geneal. tab. (part fold.) 23 cm.   9-12544.   CS71.O78   1896

12846   ORTON.   Dr. Myron and Mary Hoit Orton, their ancestors and descendants, by R. W. G. Vail
and Marie Rogers Vail.   (Concord? N.H., 1966)   205 p. illus., facsim., ports. 24 cm.   Includes bibliographies.
67-26.   CS71.O78   1966

ORTON.   See also BULLARD, 1935

12847   ORVIS.   The Orvis family. (By Edwin Waitstill Orvis) (New York, F. W. Orvis, printer,
189-?   cover title, 15 p. 15 x 15 cm.   5-452.   CS71.O79

12848   ORVIS.   The Orvis family. (New York, F. W. Orvis, printer, 1895)   cover-title, 13 p., 1 1.
15 x 15 cm.   Edited from the papers of Edward Everett Orvis by Francis W. Orvis. cf. Pref. note. 5-1246.   CS71.O79   1895

12849   ORVIS.   Outlines of the Orvis family ... (By Francis Wayland Orvis) (n.p.) 1913.   cover-title,
54 (2) p. 25 cm. Introduction signed: Francis W. Orvis. First published in 1911. Two pages at end left blank for "The Orvis family record."
20-9245.   CS71.O79   1913

12850   ORVIS.   A history of the Orvis family in America, by Francis Wayland Orvis.   Hackensack,
N.J., The Orvis company, inc., 1922.   2 p. l., (9)-203 p. front., illus. (incl. ports., facsims.) 28 cm.   An outgrowth of
the two pamphlets published by the author in 1911 and 1913, under title: Outline of the Orvis family. 23-14862.   CS71.O79   1922

12851   ORWIG.   The descendants of Gottfried Orwig, 1719-1898 ... Edited and compiled by Geo. W.
Wagenseller ... Middleburgh, Pa., Wagenseller publishing company, 1898.   cover-title, 181-208 p. 18½ cm.
Taken from the author's "History of the Wagenseller family in America." 9-12545.
                                                                        CS71.O8   1898

ORWIG.   See also HARSH, 1947

12852   ORZELSKI.   Annales domus Orzelsciae, per Joannem Orzelski ... Anno Domini MDCXI.
(Posnaniae, typis Ludovici Merzbachianis, 1854)   (36) p. 3 pl. (2 col.) 32 cm. Preface signed: T. com: Dzialynski.
16-24165.   CS879.O7

12853   OSBORN.   The pastor of the old stone church.   Mr. Hotchkin's memorial, Judge Elmer's
eulogy, and Mr. Burt's address, commemorative of Rev. Ethan Osborn ... Philadelphia, W. S. and A.
Martien, 1858.   143, (1) p. front. (port.) pl. 19½ cm. 33-24793.   BX9225.O7H6

12854   OSBORN.   The Osborne and Leeds families.   (In Ancestral stories and traditions of great families illustrative of
English history. By John Timbs ... London, 1869. 18½ cm. p. 76-79) 5-5847.
                                                                        DA28.35.A1T5

12855   OSBORN.   Genealogy of the Osborn family from 1755 to 1891.   (Princeton, N.J., W. C. C. Zapf, printer, 1891)   11 p. 22½ cm.   Caption title.   Comp. by Henry Runyan.   "The name was originally spelled Osberne: also, Orsborne, Osbourne, Osborne, and Osborn are found to have been derived from the same source." - p. (1) 2-28226.

CS71.O81   1891

12856   OSBORN.   Flower-Allen-Osborn; the lineal ancestors and descendants of Ransom and Amanda Allen Osborn of Oak Hill, Greene County, New York, compiled by Albert Osborn.   (St. Augustine, Fla., Standard printing co.) 1930.   1 p. l., 24 p. 23½ cm.   "Privately printed."   30-13837.   CS71.O81   1930

12857   OSBORN.   The Osborn family of Peabody.   (By) John O. Buxton.   (Salem? Mass.) 1938.
1 p. l., xxx numb. l. geneal. tab.   29 cm.   42-7164.   CS71.O81   1938

12858   OSBORN.   Genealogy of Edward and Sarah (Burchett) Osborn of Floyd County, Kentucky.   By Donald Lewis Osborn.   Lee's Summit, Mo. (1970)   12 p.   22 cm.   Bibliographical footnotes.   74-11163 MARC.

CS71.O814   1970

OSBORN.   See also: HARRISON, 1910a   PECK, 1955
                       HATHAWAY, 1961   PHIPPS, 1894
                       HOWARD, 1929   SMITH, 1964
                       MONNET, 1911   THOMPSON, 1930
                       NICHOL, 1963

OSBORNE.   See OSBORN.

OSBOURNE.   See OSBORN.

O'SCANLON.   See SCANLON.

12859   OSER.   Chronik der Basler Familie Oser, von Max Oser und Paul Roth.   (Basel, 1948)
224 p. plates, ports., col. coat of arms, geneal. tables, facsims.   25 cm.   50-19416.   CS999.O8   1948

12860   OSGOOD.   A genealogy of the descendants of John, Christopher and William Osgood, who came from England and settled in New England early in the seventeenth century.   Compiled by the late Ira Osgood.   Edited by Eben Putnam.   Salem, Mass., Printed at the Salem press, 1894.
xiii, 478 p. front. (coat of arms) 23½ cm.   9-12547.   CS71.O82   1894

12861   OSGOOD.   A family memento by Wilbur D. Osgood, the Osgood home.   Elizabethtown, N.Y., 1913.   95 p. incl. illus., pl., ports. 18½ cm.   31-33660.   CS71.O81   1913

12862   OSGOOD.   Descendants of William Osgood.   By Everett W. Osgood.   Holland, Mich., 1914.
1 card.   7½ x 12½ cm.   Microprint copy.   Collation of the original: 12 p.   23 cm.   Micp. 58-65.   Microcard CS71

12863   OSGOOD.   Osgood and Silsby families.   (By Mrs. May (Tibbetts) Jarvis.   San Diego, Calif., 1941)   45 l. 28½ cm.   Title from cover.   Type-written.   "Osgood and Silsby families, compiled by Mrs. May (Tibbetts) Jarvis, of San Diego, Calif., from records contributed by the late George Selden Silsby of Coldwater, Kans., formerly of Bango, Maine, 1926." - Author's letter.
41-17607.   CS71.O82   1941

12864   OSGOOD.   The history of John, Christopher, and William Osgood; additions to, and corrections of, the history published in 1894.   (By) Frank Storey Osgood ... Newburyport, Mass., 1942.
        1 v. front., plates, ports., facsims., coat of arms. 28½ cm.   Variously paged.   Part of the illustrative material is mounted.   A special copy of "A genealogy of the descendants of John, Christopher and William Osgood ... compiled by the late Ira Osgood.   Edited by Eben Putnam.   Salem, 1894," with type-written additions and extra illustrations.   43-1469.   CS71.O82   1942

12865   OSGOOD.   Osgood family in vertical file.   Ask reference librarian for this material.

OSGOOD.   See also: REPALJE, CS69.H7
                       RHODES, 1920
                       TAPLEY, 1900

OSIAS.   See OZIAS.

OSIO.   See OZIAS.

OSIUS.   See OZIAS.

OSLER.   See TOY, 1909

12866   OSORIO.   A memoir of the Lady Ann de Osorio, countess of Chinchon and vice-queen of Peru (A. D. 1629-39) with a plea for the correct spelling of the Chinchona genus, by Clements R. Markham ... London, Trubner & co., 1874.   xi, (1), 99 p. illus., col. plates, map. 26 cm.   Genealogical tables in text: "Osorio, marquises of Astorga: created 1465 A.D.": "Cabrera y Bobadilla, marquises of Moya and counts of Chinchon": "Seize quartiers of Ana de Osorio, countess of Chinchon, vice-queen of Peru."   Contents. - Preface. - The Osorios. - Lady Ana de Osorio. - Counts of Chinchon. - The fourth count of Chinchon. - Chinchon. - The Chincona genus. - Appendix: List of Chinchona species.   16-20175.   F3444.C53

12867   OSTRANDER.   A genealogical history of the Stephen Ostrander branch of the Ostrander family in America, 1660-1902.   (Danville, Pa., 1902)   geneal. tab.   40½ x 30½ cm.   Signed: Ogden H. Ostrander. 4-17861.   CS71.O85   1902

12868   OSTRANDER.   Ostrander and allied families, a genealogical study with biographical notes, compiled and privately printed for Lenore McGrath Ostrander, by the American historical society, inc., New York, 1936.   99 p. plates, ports., map, col. coats of arms. 32 cm.   Title-page and "Dedication" ornamented in colors; colored initials.   Coats of arms accompanied by guard sheet with descriptive letterpress.   Allied families: McGrath, Skeels, Fargo, Rogers, Wells, and Hyde.   Includes bibliographical references.   Bound in blue levant, gold tooled.   36-30642 rev.

CS71.O85   1936

12869   OSTRANDER.   The house of Ostrander, compiled by Manly Ostrander.   (Deseronto, Ont., 1942)   cover-title, 32 p. illus. (ports.) 23½ x 12½ cm.   43-4195.   CS71.O85   1942

12870   O'SULLIVAN.   Genealogical notes relative to the family of O'Sullivan.   (London) Printed by Warde and Betham (1805)   14 p. 28 cm.   Reprint from "The baronetage of England.   By Wm. Betham.   London, 1805." v. 5, p. 556-567.   16-17283.   CS499.O68

O'SULLIVAN.   See also SULLIVAN.

12871   OSWELL.   Pedigrees and genealogical memoranda relating to the family of Oswell of Shrewsbury, etc.   By the Rev. W. H. Oswell ... London, Mitchell, Hughes and Clarke, 1906.   16 p. 28 cm.   Reprinted from Miscellanea genealogica et heraldica.   4th ser., vol. II, 1906.   "Royal descent of Oswell": p. 8-9.   "Pedigree of Lloyd of Leaton, co. Salop": p. 10-11.   23-14539.   CS439.O67

OSY.   See COGEL, 1959

OTEY.   See HAIRSTON, 1940

12872   OTIS.   A genealogical memoir of the family of Richard Otis, and collaterally of the families of Baker, Varney, Waldron, Watson, Bean, Smith, Stackpole, Wentworth, Carr, Purington, Beede, Newton, Heard, Ham, Tuttle, Pinkham, Chesley, Cogswell, Wallingford, &c.; etc.   Prepared and arranged for publication by Horatio N. Otis, of New York.   Boston, N. E. Historical & genealogical register office, 1851.   1 p. l., 48 p. 23¾ cm.   Reprinted from New England historical and genealogical register, v. 5, 1851, p. 177-223.   22-6302.   CS71.O88   1851

12873   OTIS.   A discourse on the life and character of Dea. Joseph Otis, delivered in the Second Congregational church, Norwich, Conn., March 19, 1854.   With an appendix by the pastor, Alvan Bond ... Norwich, A. Stark, printer, 1855.   75 p. 17 cm. 23-70.   CT275.O75B6

12874   OTIS.   Otis; the story of an old house.   (Washington, 1892)   cover-title, 22 p. illus., ports. 24 cm.   Signed: Caroline Healey Dall.   Printed for private circulation.   The house was built at 34 Chambers streets, Boston, in 1800 by George Washington Otis, of Scituate.   15-19118.   CS71.O88   1892

12875   OTIS.   Birthplace of the patriot James Otis, by Francis W. Sprague ... (Boston, T. R. Marvin & son, printers) 1917.   1 p. l., 3-9 numb. l. front. (port.) map. 23 cm.   17-7044.

E302.6.O8S76

12876   OTIS. Généalogie de la famille Otis, branche canadienne, par Gérard Malchelosse ... Préface de Benjamin Sulte. Montréal, G. Ducharme, 1921.   86 p. incl. front. (port.) 22 cm. 22-631.
CS90.O7

12877   OTIS. A genealogical and historical memoir of the Otis family in America, compiled and arranged from various sources by William A. Otis ... Chicago (Schulkins, inc.) 1924.   4 p. l., 698, 28 p., 1 l. front., plates, ports., maps, facsims., fold. geneal. tab., col. coat of arms. 27½ cm. Blank pages for "Records" (687-698) 25-10187.
CS71.O88   1924

12878   OTIS. My father and mother (Newton Otis - Eunice Collins Otis) and their forefathers, by Merrill E. Otis ... Kansas City, Mo., 1927.   1 p. l., (9)-72 p. front., illus. (incl. facsims.) ports. 24 cm. 28-1175.
CS71.O88   1927

12879   OTIS. Notes on the Otis family and related families. By David Sanders Clark. Washington, 1965.   1 v. (various pagings) 29 cm. 66-47773.
CS71.O88   1965

12880   OTIS. The Otis family, in Provincial and Revolutionary Massachusetts (by) John J. Waters, Jr. Chapel Hill, Published for the Institute of Early American History and Culture at Williamsburg, Va., by the University of North Carolina Press (1968)   xi, 221 p. illus., maps, ports. 24 cm. "Notes on sources": p. (209)-212. 68-54951.
CS71.O88   1968

OTIS.   See also: LEONARD, 1928
ROBINSON, 1894
SMITH, 1923a

OTIS-RICHIE.   See SEBOR, 1923

OTIS-LEROY.   See SEBOR, 1923

12881   O'TOOLE. Les O'Toole; notice sur le clan our la tribu des O'Toole, princes d'I'Muréday et d'I'Mailey dans la Province de Leinster en Irlande, dans les derniers temps lords ou chefs de Féra-Coulan, Fertry et Castle-Kévan, au comté moderne de Wicklow, issus de Catir-Mor, roi suprème d'Irlande, et de plusieurs de ses successeurs, rois provinciaux de Leinster; avec blasons de la race, carte chorographique de l'ancien pays des O'Toole, et tableau de filiation jusqu'au jour actuel. Extrait des Collections nationales irlandaises de Charles-Denis comte O'Kelly-Farrell. La Réole, Imprimerie Vigouroux, 1864.   2 p. l., 10 l. col. coat of arms, 2 fold. geneal. tab. 37½ cm. Title vignette. 24-20.
CS499.O7   1864

12882   O'TOOLE. History of the clan O'Toole ... and other Leinster scpts. By the Rev. P. L. O'Toole ... Dublin, M. H. Gill and son; New York, Benziger brothers; (etc., etc.,) 1890.   xv, (1), 603, (2), 52, 7 p. col. front. (coat of arms) plates, ports., fold. maps, plan, fold. geneal. tables. 27½ cm. "The history of the clan O'Byrne (Ui Faelan)": 52 p. 2-8379 rev.
CS499.O7   1890

O'TOOLE.   See also O'BYRNE, 1843

O'TOOMEY.   See TOOMEY.

OTT.   See JAMES, CS439.J3

12883   OTTER. Pedigree of the family of Otter of Welham, in the county of Nottingham, and elsewhere, with notes. Compiled by Captain A. E. Lawson Lowe, F.S.A. Privately printed. London (Printed by Mitchell and Hughes) 1880.   15 p. incl. geneal. tab. coat of arms. 28½ cm. 2-30582.
CS439.O7

OTTOLENGUI.   See MOISE, 1961

OUDEWATER.   See OUTWATER.

OULD.   See OLD.

OULDFIELD. See OLDFIELD.

12884 OUSELEY. Genealogy of the Ouseley family. Compiled by Richard Kelly. Rev. and brought up to the present date by his surviving relative. (Dunmor co. Galway.) A few copies only printed for private reference. (n.p., 1899?) 15, (1) p. 19 cm. Last page left blank for "Memoranda." 17-15265.
CS439.O75

12885 OUTLAW. Outlaw genealogy, including English records, coat of arms, will of Edward Outlaw dated 1713, brief biographical sketches and an account of the first Grady-Outlaw reunion. By Albert Timothy Outlaw. Wilson, N.C., P.D.Gold publishing co., c.1930. 71, (1) p. incl. coat of arms. 22½ cm. 31-2764.
CS71.O92   1930

OUTLAW. See ANDERSON, 1940a

OUTLAWE. See OUTLAW.

12886 OUTWATER. Some genealogical data of the Outwater, Breasted, Bertholf, Lozier, Van Bussum, Cudeback and Provoost families. (New York) 1924. cover-title, 20 p. fold. geneal. tab. 27 cm. Reprinted from the New York genealogical and biographical record, October, 1924. The direct American lineage of Samuel Outwater. "Authorities": p. 20. 25-12676.
CS71.O94   1924

12887 OVENSHINE. The family of Richard Powell and Emma Tipton Ovenshine. (n.p., 1963) 48 l. fold. geneal. table (in pocket) 29 cm. Cover title. 64-1060.
CS71.O95   1963

12888 OVERBECK. The Sippe (clan) Overback-Averbeck, by Alvin H. Overbeck. (Mason City, Iowa, Klipto Printing Co., 1966) 77, x p. illus., geneal. table, map. 24 cm. 63-9566.
CS71.O955   1966

OVERMAN. See TRUEBLOOD, 1964

12889 OVERMYER. Overmyer history and genealogy from 1680 to 1905, collated by Barnhart B. and John C. Overmyer ... Fremont, O., C.S. Beelman, printer, 1905. 4 p. l., 297, 39 p. plates, ports., 23 cm. 5-35769.
CS71.O96   1905

OVERSTREET. See HORINE, 1966

12890 OVERTON. The early descendants of Wm. Overton & Elizabeth Waters of Virginia, and allied families ... by W. P. Anderson. (Cincinnati? O., 1938) cover-title, 160 p. 22½ cm. References: p. 2-4. 39-9248.
CS71.O962   1938

12891 OVERTON. The Overton genealogy; the Overton family of Long Island, New York, especially the descendants of David Overton of Southold and Coram, 1640-1965, by Alvin R. L. Smith. (Centereach, N.Y.) 1965 (c.1966) 121 p. illus., coat of arms. 23 cm. 67-283. CS71.)962   1966

12892 OVERTON. Some ancestry of and the descendants of Ernest C. Overton: as of July 17, 1967. Compiled by Ernest C. Overton. Mechanicville, N.Y. (1967) (13), 155, 50 l. (chiefly forms, geneal. tables) 23 x 36 cm. Typescript. 68-2614.
CS71.O962   1967

OVERTON. See also: ANDERSON, 1945
MEAD, 1921

12893 OVERTURF. History of the Overturfs. (By Jesse Ray Overturf) (Palo Alto, Calif., 1941) cover-title, 33 p. illus. (incl. ports.) fold. facsim. 23 cm. "Collected, organized and ordered printed by Jesse R. Overturf." Part II (p. 19-33) written by N. F. Overturf. 42-5164.
CS71.O9624   1941

12894 OVIATT. Oviatt family. from extracts of Tring, Hertfordshire, England, church registers and other sources. Compiled by Rev. G. Bell of Eastercroft, Langdon street, Tring, Herts, England, and edited by Evelyn Briggs Baldwin. Washington, D.C., 1925. 4 l. 33 cm. Type-written. 25-28131.
CS439.O77

12895   OVIATT.   Oviatt, Hendrick and allied families, compiled by Mary Elizabeth (Oviatt) Brown-ing.   (n. p.) 1930.   4 p. l., 119 numb. l., 3 l. 28 cm.   Type-written.   A leaf (not included in the collation) containing "Generations" precedes each family.   "References."   CA 31-350 unrev.   CS71.O963   1930

OVIATT.   See also CAMP, 1961

OWDEN.   See GREER, 1897

12896   OWEN.   (A family tree of John Owen, a Colonial settler in North Carolina) Original drawn by Miss M. C. Bagley.   Jackson, N. C. (18 -   geneal. tab. 60 x 45½ cm. 39M1088T.   CS71.O97   18 -

12897   OWEN.   Memoirs of the ancient family of Owen of Orielton, co. Pembroke.   Comp. by J. Roland Phillips, esq. ... London, Printed at the Chiswick press, 1886.   2 p. l., 92, (4) p. 22½ cm. 14-16645.
CS459.O8

12898   OWEN.   Pedigree of Owen of Llunllo and Bettws, co. Montgomery; Tedsmore, Woodhouse, Condover, and Whiteley (now Kynaston of Hardwick) co. Salop.   With grant of a canton and crest to the arms of Edward Owen of Shrewsbury.   Compiled by Geo. Grazebrook ... Privately printed.   London, Mitchell and Hughes, 1887.   20 p. col. front. (coat of arms) pl., illus. 26 cm. 10-11539.   CS439.O8

12899   OWEN.   ... Genealogical record of the Owens family, with sketches of the Byrnes kindred, by Edward W. Owens ... Sioux City, Ia. (1929)   197 p. illus. (ports.) 20 cm.   Cover-title: Genealogy: Owens and Byrnes.   "Religion and other subjects by the author, and selected articles from various authors," with special t.-p: p. 141-192. 29-25247.
CS71.O97   1929

12900   OWEN.   ... Owen family records, by J. Montgomery Seaver ... Philadelphia, Pa., American historical-genealogical society, 1929.   2 p. l., 7-34 p. illus. (ports.) 23 cm.   Coat of arms on cover.   "References": p. 30-31.   30-8668.   CS71.O97   1929a

12901   OWEN.   Owen family association. Annual reunion (announcement) (n. p.)   no. 28 cm.   53-53561 and 57-54513.   CS71.O97   1938

12902   OWEN.   Owen family association.   Annual reunion (Minutes)   (n. p.)   v. 28 cm.   Title varies slightly.   57-55127.   CS71.O97   1938a

12903   OWEN.   Owen family association.   Annual newsletter.   (n. p.)   no. 28 cm.   Title varies slightly.   53-30333 rev.   CS71.O97   1939

12904   OWEN.   Owen family history, with an incomplete genealogy of the Daniel family, by T. M. Cunningham ... (Denton, Tex.) 1940.   42 p. 20 cm. 40-34273.   CS71.O97   1940a

12905   OWEN.   Owens-Grubbs and allied families of Virginia and Kentucky, compiled by Lockwood Barr ... (New York?) 1940.   52 l. fold. geneal. tab. 29 cm.   Type-written with genealogical table in manuscript.   Introductory note signed: Berenice Owens Barr (Mrs. Lockwood Barr)   Includes bibliographical notes.   41-375.
CS71.O97   1940b

12906   OWEN.   Descendants of John Owen of Windsor, Connecticut (1622-1699); a genealogy, edited by Ralph Dornfeld Owen.   Philadelphia, 1941.   5 p. l., 13-532 p. pl., ports. 23½ cm. 42-23980.
CS71.O97   1941

12907   OWEN.   ... Owens-Grubbs, families of Virginia and Kentucky,   compiled by Lockwood Barr ... (New York? 1942)   41 l. fold. geneal. tab. 29½ x 23 cm.   Type-written, with genealogical table in manuscript. 43-10570.
CS71.O97   1942

12908   OWEN.   Genealogy of the descendants of Daniel Owen, Jr., of McHenry, Illinois, with especial attention given to the descendants of his son Edwin Mortimer Owen and the allied families of Norton, Warner, Stanton & Patterson; also brief notices of the following families allied by marriage with the Owens: Beach, Birdsey, Bronson, Brown, Carrington, Chesebrough, Denison, Gallup, Gardner, Gay, Holmes, Hunn. Lupton and Magoffin.   By Charles Starr Owen.   Chicago, Printed by Fawley-Brost Co., 1947.   76 p. illus. 24 cm. 52-34239.   CS71.O97   1947

12909   OWEN.   History of the family of Judge David Allen Owen, son of Samuel Tine and Sarah Ward (Knight) Owen.   By Bonner Frizzell.   Palestine, Tex., 1962. 93 l. illus. 28 cm. 63-4366.

CS71.O97   1962

12910   OWEN.   Daniel Grant Owen: his ancestors, descendants, and their kin.   By Frances Benson Chandler.   Albany, Ga.   (1968)   168 p. coats of arms. 19 cm. 68-3133.   CS71.O97   1968

OWEN.   See also:

ANDERSON, 1909	GUSTIN, 1900	MORRISON, 1934
BESSELLIEU, 1959	HABERSHAM, 1901	ROGERS, 1958
CAMPBELL, 1911	HANMER, CS439.H283	TWEEDIE, 1956
CRERAR, 1942	JOHNSON, 1961	WEST, 1930
CROSSLEY, 1835	MAURICE, CS459.M3	WOOD, 1937
CUNLIFFE, CS439.C87	MINSHALL, 1867	

OWINGS.   See: RANDOLPH, 1961
STODDARD, 1959

12911   OXENBRIDGE.   The Oxendbridges of Brede place, Sussex, and Boston, Massachusetts.   By William Durrant Cooper ... London, J. R. Smith, 1860.   20 p. front., pl. 22 cm.   Reprinted from the Sussex archaeological collections, vol. XII.   Supplementing the account of the Oxenbridge family contained in the author's "Notices of Winchelsea," in Sussex archaeological collections, v. 8, p. 213-233.   5-25489.   CS71.O98   1860

12912   OXENREIDER.   Oxenreider's family tree, by Clayton D. Oxenreider, 1911 & 1912.   (Reading? Pa., 1955?)   geneal. table.   139 x 186 cm. fold. to 35 x 38 cm.   Blueprint containing dates through 1953, with a 1955 date added in ink. In portfolio.   62-1119.   CS71.O982   1955

12913   OXNARD.   Martha Prebel Oxnard, eldest child of Brig. -General Jedidiah Preble and Mehitable Bangs, 1754-1824, and her descendants to 1869.   (Prepared for the genealogy of the Preble family in America, by Geo. Henry Preble) (Boston, 1868)   8 p. 15½ cm. Caption title. Reprinted from the author's "Genealogical sketch of the first three generations of Prebles in America," Boston, 1868.   16-11126.

CS71.O985   1868

OXSHEER.   See BEAL, 1956

12914   OZIAS.   History of the Osio, Osius, Ozias families, including the genealogy of the Vaudois family of Antoine Ozias and his wife, Isabeau Lormeiasse, also the Maneval family; also included is history of the allied families of Reverend Jacob Christman and Casper Potterf, compiled by a descendant of the Ozias, Maneval, Christman, Potterf families, Albert Lawrence Rohrer.   (Ann Arbor, Mich., Lithoprinted by Edwards brothers, inc.) 1943.   ix, 255, (5) p. illus. (incl. ports., maps, facsims., coats of arms) fold. geneal. tab.   28 x 22½ cm.   Cover-title: History and genealogy of the Ozias family.   Bibliography: p. 180.   44-3662.

CS71.O988   1943

P

PABODY.   See PEABODY.

12915   PACA.   Paca, signer, friend of Washington and Lafayette: the Paca family.   By Wanda R. Paca.   (Santa Monica, Calif., 1963)   unpaged. illus. 30 cm. 63-5379.   CS71.P115   1963

PACE.   See No. 430 - Adventurers of purse and person.

12916   PACK.   Wilhelm Gustav Pack family record (dating from 1840 through 1962.)   By Gustav Carl Pack. (Trenton? 1963)   1 v. (unpaged) ports., facsims. 30 cm. Cover title. 64-203.   CS71.P118   1963

12917   PACK.   A bit of Pack history or biography.   Compiled and written by Wehrli D. Pack.   Provo, Utah, J. G. Stevenson, 1969.   vii, 283 p. illus., facsims., ports. 25 cm. 74-7773 MARC.   CS71.P118   1969

PACK.   See also HATCH, 1930

12918   PACKARD.   The genealogies of Samuel Packard, of Bridgwater, Mass., and of Abel Packard, of Cummington, Mass.   By Rev. Theophilus Packard ... New York, G. W. Wheat & co., printers, 1871.   85 p. front. 22½ cm. 31-33665.   CS71.P12   1871

12919   PACKARD.   Celebration of the two hundred and fiftieth anniversary of the landing of Samuel Packard in this country, August 10, 1638.   At Brockton, Massachusetts, August 10, 1888.   (Brockton) Packard memorial association, 1888.   72 p. front. 23½ cm. Cover-title: Proceedings of the Packard memorial association, August 10, 1888. Edited by Bradford Kingman. 17-30085.   CS71.P12   1888

12920   PACKARD.   Packard ancestry.   2d ed.   By Isabel (Sewall) Hunter.   (Arlington, Va.) 1946.   geneal. table. 30 x 44 cm. Photocopy (negative) 48-14050*.   CS71.P12   1946

PACKARD.   See also: BOWEN, 1931a
                        LEONARD, 1928

PACKER.   See: ELDRIDGE, 1925
                  FISH, 1867

PADDOCK.   See: GRAY, E171.A53 vol.18
                   GRISWOLD, 1898
                   WALKER, 1964

12921   PADDLEFORD.   Our Paddleford descendants; William and Hannah (Hoit) Paddleford and their children: Hannah Paddleford-Gove (David Poland) ... By Frank Stewart Kinsey.   (Chula Vista? Calif.) 1960.   33 p. illus. 29 cm. 61-25336.   CS71.P123   1960

PADDLEFORD.   See also No. 579 - Monroe, N.H.

12922   PADELFORD.   1628.   Descendants of Jonathan Padelford.   1858.   Prepared and compiled by S. C. Newman ... Providence, A.C. Greene and brother, printers, 1859.   geneal. tab. 54 x 68 cm. 3-8711.   CS71.P123   1859   Folio.

PADEN.   See PEDEN, 1961

PADLEFORD.   See DEAN, E398. D28

PADGETT.   See BROWNLEE, 1937

PAGAN.   See PATTERSON, 1865

PAGANELL.   See PAYNELL.

12923   PAGE.   Family chart (of the Page family of Virginia)   Richmond, Lith. of L. F. Citti (n. d.)
geneal. table.   55 x 129 cm. fold. to 55 x 52 cm.   Reproduced from manuscript copy.   51-25325.   CS71. P133

12924   PAGE.   Genealogy of the Page family in Virginia.   Also a condensed account of the Nelson,
Walker, Pendleton and Randolph families, with references to the Byrd, Carter, Cary, Duke, Gilmer,
Harrison, Rives, Thornton, Wellford, Washington, and other distinguished families in Virginia.   By
one of the family.   New York, Jenkins & Thomas, printers, 1883.   250 p. incl. illus., plates, ports. 25½ cm.
24-3047.   CS71. P133   1883

12925   PAGE.   Genealogical registers of the ancestors and descendants of the following persons:
Lemuel Page and Polly Paige, Peter Joslin and Sarah Kidder, with brief accounts of them and their ancestors.   (By Luke Joslin Page)   Boston, 1887.   155 p.   21½ x 21½ cm.   "Note" signed: L. J. P. (i. e. Luke Joslin Page)
34-32588.   CS71. P133   1887

12926   PAGE.   Genealogy of the Page family in Virginia.   Also a condensed account of the Nelson,
Walker, Pendleton, and Randolph families, with references to the Bland, Burwell, Byrd, Carter, Cary,
Duke, Gilmer, Harrison, Rives, Thornton, Welford, Washington, and other distinguished families in
Virginia.   By Richard Channing Moore Page ... 2d ed.   New York, Publishers' printing co., 1893.
x, 275 p. incl. illus., ports.   25 cm.   9-17828.   CS71. P133   1893

12927   PAGE.   Table showing ancestors and descendants of Nathaniel Page (1742-1819) of Bedford,
Mass., and of his wife ... Boston, Published by the compiler, Charles E. Lauriat company, 1899.
geneal. table.   58 x 96½ cm. fold. to 11 x 13½ cm.   An edition of two hundred and fifty copies printed.   11-20777.
CS71. P133   1899

12928   PAGE.   History and genealogy of the Page family from the year 1257 to the present; with
brief history and genealogy of the allied families Nash and Peck, by Chas. N. Page.   Des Moines, Ia.,
The author (c. 1911)   141 p., 1 l. incl. illus., ports.   col. front.   (coat of arms) 20 cm.   12-299.
CS71. P133   1911

12929   PAGE.   In memoriam.   Susan M. (Page) Currier, 1838-1910 ... Newburyport, Mass., 1912.
39 p.   front.   (port.) 24 cm.   "Genealogical records": p. (33)-39.   37-16957.   CS71. P133   1912

12930   PAGE.   Page descent; line of descent from Nicholas Page of England to Charles Lawrence
Peirson of Boston.   Salem, Mass., The Salem press co., 1915.   (18) p.   illus. (coats of arms) 20 cm.   2d edition,
corrected and enlarged.   16-14831.   CS71. P133   1915

12931   PAGE.   Genealogical chart of the Page family, tracing the descendants of Hugo Page from the
year 1257 ... chart I -   Point Loma, Calif., C. N. Page, 1917 -   fold. geneal. tab.   illus.   (coats of
arms) 30 cm.   Each genealogical table has the Page coat of arms, and "References and authorities cited."   24-6777.   CS71. P133   1917

12932   PAGE.   History and description of the great Page estate ... said to be the largest unsettled
estate in England, if not in the entire world, includes the best residence section of London.   (By) Chas.
N. Page ... Point Loma, Cal., c. 1917.   cover-title, 31 p. illus. (incl. coat of arms) 18½ cm.   18-2321.
CS439. P2

12933   PAGE.   Connecticut Pages who settled in Broome County, New York, during the latter part of
the eighteenth century.   By Fred E. Page.   Binghamton, N. Y., 1948.   7 l. 28 cm.   Caption title.   Typewritten.
50-38243.   CS71. P133   1948

12934   PAGE.   Wisonsin Page pioneers and kinsfolk , by Ethel McLaughlin Turner, Paul Boynton Turner (and) Lucia Kate Page Sayre.   Waterloo, Wis., Artcraft Press, 1953.   487 p. illus. 24 cm.   56-45182.
CS71.P133   1953

12935   PAGE.   Livre généalogique de la famille Pagé.   By Lucien Pagé.   (Coteau-du-Lac? Qué., 1955)   94 l. illus., ports., map, geneal. table. 29 cm. Title from cover. Bibliography: leaves 91-94. 58-15477.
CS90.P2   1955

PAGE.   See also: BYRD, E159.G55   POCAHONTAS, 1887
                    DRAKE, 1962   VITTUM, 1922
                    HASKELL, 1926   WASHINGTON, CS69.W5
                    HAYES, DA690.B74K3   WELCH, 1961
                    LIGON, 1947   No. 1547 - Cabell county.

PAGENELL.   See PAYNELL.

12936   PAGET.   Memoir of the Hon. Sir Charles Paget, G.C.H., 1778-1839, with a short history of the Paget family, by the Very Rev. Edward Clarence Paget ... With 13 illustrations.   London, New York (etc.) Longmans, Green and co., 1913.   ix, 130 p., 1 l. front., plates, ports., facsim. 24½ cm. 19-17175.
DA88.1.P13P4

12937   PAGET.   The Paget brothers, 1790-1840, edited by Lord Hylton ... London, J. Murray, 1918.   xvii, 364 p. front., ports. 22½ cm. A selection from the private correspondence of Sir Arthur Paget. 19-7072.   DA522.F19A3

12938   PAGET.   The Paget family of Virginia, Kentucky, and Indiana ... By Stratton O. Hammon.   Louisville, Ky., 1941.   geneal. tab. 54 x 86½ cm. fold. to 27½ x 22 cm. 41-14797.   CS71.P137   1941

PAGET.   See also BACKHOUSE, DA690.M74C3

PAGITT.   See PAGET.

12939   PAINE.   The family of Paine.   (By Elisha Thayer) (Hingham, F. Farmer, printer, 1835)   p. (115)-118. 25½ cm. Detached from the author's Family memorial ... Hingham, F. Farmer, Printer, 1835. 38M5133T
CS71.P146   1835

12940   PAINE.   The Paynes of Suffolk.   Extracted from "The visitation of Suffolke." (By William Harvey.   Edited by Joseph Jackson Howard ... Lowestoft (Eng.) Printed by S. Tymms, 1867.   21 p. coats of arms. 26 x 20½ cm. Interleaved. 2-26607.   CS439.P215   1867

12941   PAINE.   The genealogy of the families of Payne and Gore.   Comp. by W. H. Whitmore.   Boston, Press of J. Wilson & son, 1875.   1 p. l., 30 p. front. (port.) 22½ cm. Added t.-p.: The publications of the Prince society for distribution. Revised from the Mass. hist. soc. Proceedings, 1875, p. 405-425. 9-14800. L.C. COPY REPLACED BY MICROFILM.
CS71.P146   1875
Microfilm 19730 CS

12942   PAINE.   Genealogical notes on the Paine family of Worcester, Mass., by Nathaniel Paine ...   Albany, Priv. print., 1878.   27 p. plates, facsim., fold. geneal. tab. 25½ cm. "Originally prepared for the 'Paine genealogy,' ed. and pub. by H. D. Paine of New York." Edition of 50 copies. 20-11358.   CS71.P146   1878

12943   PAINE.   Paine family records: a journal of genealogical and biographical information respecting the American families of Payne, Paine, Payn &c.   Ed. by H. D. Paine ... New York (Albany, J. Munsell, printer) 1880-83.   2 v. in 1. map, geneal. charts, facsims. 24½ cm. 9-12857. L.C. COPY REPLACED BY MICROFILM.
CS71.P146   1880-83
Microfilm 8653 CS

12944   PAINE.   Paine genealogy. Ipswich branch.   Including a brief history of the Norman race (to which all families of "Paine" belong) from its origin until the conquest and the crusade in which Hugo de Payen served.   By Albert W. Paine ... Bangor, Me., Printed by O. F. Knowles & co., 1881.   184 p. front. (coat of arms) illus. 23½ cm. 9-12858.   CS71.P146   1881
Microfilm 8653

12945 PAINE. Chart no. 3, showing ancestry and descendants of Gen. Edward Paine, founder of Painesville, Ohio; compiled by Rev. Jason L. Paine ... Fayette, Ia., 1902. geneal. tab. 66 x 38 cm. fold. to 22½ cm. 11-32001. CS71.P146 1902

12946 PAINE. Barnabas Payne and his son John C. Payne, some data of biography and genealogy that concern their many descendants, compiled by W. O. Payne. Nevada, Ia. (1903) 13 p. illus. (facsim.) 23½ cm. Caption title. 37-21312. CS71.P146 1903

12947 PAINE. A sketch of the children of Dr. William Paine, 1774-1869. By Mrs. E. O. P. Sturgis. (Worcester, Mass., Priv. print., the Hamilton press, 1904) cover-title (2)-16 numb. 1. 25½ cm. Printed on one side of leaf only. 11-14240. CS71.P146 1904

12948 PAINE. The Paynes of Hamilton, a genealogical and biographical record, by Augusta Francelia Payne White. Illustrated. New York, T. A. Wright, 1912. 3 p. l., 245 p. front., illus., plates. 24½ cm. Assisted by Linda May Clatworthy. "The Paynes of England and Normandy," by Mary Lovering Holman: p. 1-11. 12-16845. CS71.P146 1912

12949 PAINE. Paine ancestry. The family of Robert Treat Paine, signer of the Declaration of Independence, including maternal lines. Compiled by Sarah Cushing Paine. Edited by Charles Henry Pope. Boston, Mass., Printed for the family (Press of D. Clapp & son) 1912. 1 p. l., 334 p. 2 fold. geneal. tab. 30 cm. 13-248. CS71.P146 1912a

12950 PAINE. Ancestors and descendants of David Paine and Abigail Shepard, of Ludlow, Massachusetts, 1463-1913. Compiled by Clara Paine Ohler ... Lima, O., 1913. 252 p. front., plates, ports., coats of arms. 23½ cm. Cover-title: The Paine-Shepard genealogy, 1463-1913. Eight blank leaves at end for additional records. Contents. - Paine. - Ohler. - Compton. - Roby. - Shepard. - Spur. - Leonard. - Tileston. - Bridgman, - Adams. - Webb. - Pierce. - Bass families. 13-26673. CS71.P146 1913

12951 PAINE. ... Payne or Paine - Truro, by Shebnah Rich. Yarmouthport, Mass., C. W. Swift, 1913. cover-title, 5 p. 25½ cm. (Library of Cape Cod history & genealogy, no. 70) 17-6132. CS71.P146 1913a

12952 PAINE. My ancestors; a memorial of John Paine and Mary Ann May of East Woodstock, Conn. Lovingly compiled by their son Lyman May Paine, of Chicago, Ill. (Chicago, Ill.) Printed for private circulation, 1914. 1 p. l., 240 p. illus. (incl. ports., facsims., coats of arms) 27½ cm. p. 237-240 left blank for "Memoranda." 15-28184. CS71.P146 1914

12953 PAINE. The discovery of a grandmother; glimpses into the homes and lives of eight generations of an Ipswich-Paine family gathered together by one of the ninth for the tenth, eleventh and twelfth generations. Newtonville, Mass., H. H. Carter, 1920. 341 p., 1 l. front., plates, ports., facsims., coat of arms. 23 cm. "Limited edition." Signed: Lydia Augusta Carter. 20-6433. CS71.P146 1920

12954 PAINE. Ancestors and descendants of Stephen Paine, born April 30, 1708. By Mrs. Dora (Pope) Worden) Ithaca, N.Y. (1921) geneal. tab. 35½ x 38 cm. 21-19738. CS71.P146 1921

12955 PAINE. History of Samuel Paine, jr., A. D. 1778-1861, and his wife Pamela (Chase) Paine, 1780-1856, of Randolph, Vt., and their ancestors and descendants. Compiled and edited by their grandson, Albert Prescott Paine. (Randolph Center, Vt., 1923) 217, (1) p. incl. front. illus. (ports.) 23½ cm. 25-2073. CS71.P146 1923

12956 PAINE. Thomas Payne of Salem and his descendants; the Salem branch of the Paine family, by Nathaniel Emmons Paine, an enlargement of the Southold branch of the Paine family, by Horace Marshfield Paine. (Haverhill, Mass., Record publishing company) 1928. 4 p. l., 3-178 p. front., plates, ports., facsims. (part double) 24½ cm. 29-11907. CS71.P146 1928

12957 PAINE. Ancestors and descendants of James Payne of Pomfret, Conn., and Hauppauge, L. I. (by) Sarah C. P. Smith (and) Margretta C. Payne ... (Northport, N. Y., Printed by Northport observer, 1932) 80 p. illus. (incl. port.) 23½ cm. 35-14012. CS71.P146 1932

12958   PAINE.   Paine genealogy and allied lines, ancestors of William Alfred Paine, compiled by his wife, Ruth F. W. Paine.   Rutland, Vt., The Tuttle publishing compnay, inc., 1936.   80 p. 2 port. (incl. front.) 2 fold. geneal. tab. 23½ cm.   "Rectitude before expediency, a discourse preached ... Dec. 30, 1860. by ... Rev. Albert Paine": p. 14-21. 38-14735.
                                                                                                                                      CS71. P146   1936

12959   PAINE.   Ancestors and descendants of Joseph Payne the sixth of West Turin, N.Y.   Compiled by Edward Payne Scheidleman.   (Rome, N.Y., Rome sentinel company, 1937)   (34) p. illus. 20½ cm.   On cover: The Paynes of Turin. 37-21328.
                                                                                                                                      CS71. P146   1937

12960   PAINE.   The Paynes of Virginia, by Brooke Payne ... Richmond, Va., The William Byrd press, inc., 1937.   ix p., 3 l., 3-543, (5) p. fold. diagr. 23½ cm.   Blank pages for "Additions and corrections" (5 at end) "Authorities consulted": p. 38-39. 37-37566.
                                                                                                                                      CS71. P146   1937a

12961   PAINE.   Mayflower ancestries; Walker, Cobb, Paine, Swift (and) Higgins ... (By) Gustavus Swift Paine.   Southbury, Conn., and New York, 1946.   8 l. 28 x 21½ cm.   Typewritten.   46-21210.
                                                                                                                                      CS71. P146   1946

         PAINE.   See also: BAX, CS439. B3575   LEONARD, 1928
                              BROMWELL, 1900   PAGE, 1953
                              BROWN, 1931   SMITH, 1878a
                              BUCK, 1917   THAYER, 1835
                              GLASS, 1946   WAY, CS439. W375
                              HAMMACK, 1955   No. 1547 - Cabell county.

12962   PAINTER.   Our ancestors ... (Descendants and relatives of Samuel Painter of Phila., Pa., 1707, with allied families, being the ancestors of the author, J. Painter ... Lima? Pa.) 1869.   2 p. l., 20, (4) p. geneal. tab.   20 x 15½ cm.   Genealogical table: Ancestry of Enos Painter and Hannah Minshall. 9-12844.
                                                                                                                                      CS71. P148   1869

12963   PAINTER.   Genealogy and biographical sketches of the family of Samuel Painter, who came from England and settled in Chester County, Pennsylvania, about the year 1699.   By Orrin Chalfant Painter ... Baltimore, Press of J. S. Bridges & co., 1903.   54 p. illus. (incl. map, facsims., coat of arms) ports. 35½ cm. 17-9732.
                                                                                                                                      CS71. P148   1903

12964   PAINTER.   Autobiography of Thomas Painter, relating his experiences during the war of the revolution.   Printed for private circulation. (Washington? D.C., 1910)   106 p. pl., port., double geneal. tab. 24 cm. 10-18016.
                                                                                                                                      E275. P14

12965   PAINTER.   Painter (Bender) family.   By Ray C. Thomas.   In vertical file.   Ask reference librarian for this material.

         PAINTER.   See also: HUNT, 1906
                                PARISH, 1925

         PAISER.   In vertical file under PRANKE family.   Ask reference librarian for this material.

         PAIZER.   In vertical file under PRANKE family.   Ask reference librarian for this material.

         PAJARI.   See BAJARI.

12966   PALEN.   Family tree for female descendants of 3 Leopold Palen.   By Vern W. Palen.   Data correct to approximately Jan. 1, 1965.   Yonkers, N.Y. (1965)   geneal. table. 43 x 56 cm. fold. to 28 x 22 cm. 66-38219 rev.
                                                                                                                                      CS71. P155   1965

12967   PALEN.   Chart, coat-of-arms, photos, etc.   In vertical file.   Ask reference librarian for this material.

         PALEOLOGUS.   See WILLOUGHBY, DA250. R72

12968   PALGRAVE.   A pedigree of the Palgrave family.   Yarmouth branch, from the registers and inscriptions in the church, etc.   (n. p., n. d.)   geneal. table.   28 x 37 cm.   40M3852T.

CS439. P22

12969   PALGRAVE.   Palgrave family memorials.   Edited by Charles John Palmer and Stephen Tucker (Rouge Croix).   Norwich, Printed by Miller and Leavins (for private distribution only) 1878.   4 p. l., 208 p. illus., plates (1 col.) ports. 25½ cm. Edited with the assistance of Charles Bridger. 4-21363.

CS439. P22

PALGRAVE.   See also SANDYS, 1897

PALK.   See PITMAN, CS439. P62

PALLEN.   See No. 2070 - Memories ... of ... N. C.

12970   PALLISSARD.   The generations.   By Julia (Lecour) Bowe.   (Chicago? 1959)   177 p. illus.   28 cm. 59-65304.

CS71. P16   1959

12971   PALMER.   The pedigree of the ancient family of the Palmers of Sussex, 1672.   Copied from the original ms. in the possession of Charles James Palmer, esq., of Dorney court.   Together with extracts from registers, inscriptions on coffin-plates, etc. illustrating the Palmer genealogy.   (London) Priv. print. 1867.   34 p. illus. (coats of arms) 28½ cm. By Roger Jenyns. 9-19126.

CS439. P26

12972   PALMER.   A genealogical and historical account of the family of Palmer, of Kenmare, co. Kerry, Ireland.   Comp. from old family documents, etc., in possession of Edward Orpen Palmer, Killowen, Kenmare, co. Kerry, esquire, the present head of the family, by his son, the Rev. A. Henry Herbert Palmer, of Monkstown, co. Dublin.   London, Priv. print., 1872.   14 p. 27 cm. Armorial bookplate of Robert Hovenden as frontispiece. 15-23252.

CS499. P3

12973   PALMER.   A genealogical record of the descendants of John and Mary Palmer, of Concord, Chester (now Delaware) co., Pa.; especially through their son, John Palmer, jr., and sons-in-law, William and James Trimble.   With notes of ancestry, or information, of many of the families with whom they intermarried.   By Lewis Palmer ... Philadelphia, J. B. Lippincott & co., 1875.   2 p. l., 9-474 p. front., illus. (incl. ports.) 20½ cm. 1-21320.

CS71. P175   1875

12974   PALMER.   Volume no. 1 of Palmer records.   Proceedings, or memorial volume of the first Palmer family re-union held at Stonington, Conn., August 10 & 11, 1881, the ancestral home/of /Walter Palmer, the pilgrim of 1629.   Being also a part of the genealogical, biographical, and historical records of the family, as contained in the several addresses, etc. delivered on the occasion of the reunion.   (Artotype illustrations)   Edited by Noyes F. Palmer.   (Brooklyn) Brooklyn union-argus, 1881.   295, (1) p. front., ports., fold. facsim. 24 cm. 5-25478.   CS71. P175   1881

12975   PALMER.   Supplement to Volume no.1 of Palmer records.   Addresses, poems, proceedings of the second Palmer family re-union, held at Stonington, Conn., August 10. 11 & 12, 1882 ... Under the auspices of the Palmer re-union association.   Edited by Noyes F. Palmer.   Jamaica, L. I., N. Y. (1882)   119 p. 23 cm. 5-25479.   CS71. P175   1882

12976   PALMER.   Constitution and by-laws, and officers of the Palmer reunion association, organized November 28, 1881.   New York, Association, 1882.   22 p. 17½ cm. 16-11503.

CS71. P175   1882a

12977   PALMER.   A brief genealogical history of the ancestors and descendants of Deacon Stephen Palmer, of Candia, Rockingham county, N. H., with some account of the other lines of descent from his original American ancestor, Thomas Palmer, one of the founders of Rowley, Mass., in 1639.   Brooklyn, N. Y., (J. E. & G. H. Rowe, typographers) 1886.   xi, 95 p. front. (fold. geneal. tab.) 24 cm. Compiled by Frank Palmer from material collected by Josiah Palmer, and supplemented by the compiler's own memoranda. 9-12856 rev.

CS71. P175   1886

12978   PALMER.   Genealogy of that branch of the Palmers emanating from the marriage of Gershom Palmer, son of Walter Palmer, of Nottinghamshire, England, and Ann Denison, A. D. 1667.   By Walter Palmer and Mrs. Lydia C. Dorrance ... Plainfield, Conn., Printed by A. J. Ladd, 1887.   83 p., 1 l. 20½ cm.   19-14395.   CS71. P175   1887

12979   PALMER.   Some account of the Palmer family of Rahan, county Kildare, Ireland; with notes on the families of Colley, Loftus, Peyton, Brooke, La Pole, Cobham, Courtenay, Bohun, Braybrooke (by) Temple Prime ... New York (The De Vinne press) 1890.   50 p. 22½ cm. Bibliography: p. 50. 18-23439.
                                                                                                        CS71. P175   1890

12980   PALMER.   Pedigree of the Palmer family, formerly of Southmolton and Great Torrington, Devon.   Rev. by F. T. Colby ... Exeter, W. Pollard & co., printers, 1892.   1 p. l., 13 p. 28½ cm. 50 copies printed for private circulation.   16-8305.   CS439. P26   1892

12981   PALMER.   Some account of the Palmer family of Rahan, county Kildare, Ireland, by Temple Prime ... 4th ed.   New York (The De Vinne press) 1903.   53 p. incl. ports. 24½ cm. 28-12386.
                                                                                                        CS71. P175   1903

12982   PALMER.   Palmer groups.   John Melvin of Charlestown and Concord, Mass., and his descendants.   Gathered and arranged for Mr. Lowell Mason Palmer of New York.   By Miss Emily Wilder Leavitt.   Privately printed.   Boston, Press of D. Clapp & son, 1901-5.   1 p. l., x, (5)-450, xl p., 2 l. fold. geneal. tables. 27 cm. 5-28030.   CS71. P175 1901-05

12983   PALMER.   A genealogical record of the descendants of John and Mary Palmer of Concord, Chester (now Delaware) co., Pa. in two divisions - Palmer-Trimble.   Palmer division, embracing also, largely, the surnames: Almond, Arment, Baker ... and others.   New ed., compiled by Lewis Palmer, 1910.   (Chester) Press of Chester times, 1910.   xi, 1120, (2) p. front., illus. (coat of arms) plates, ports., map, facsims. 27½ cm. Part 2 has title: A genealogical record of the descendants of William and Ann (Palmer) Trimble, of Concord, Delaware county, Pa., and James and Mary (Palmer) Trimble of West Bradford, Chester county, Pa.   Trimble division, embracing also, largely the surnames Baily, Baldwin, Benington ... and others.   39-12249.   CS71. P175   1910

12984   PALMER.   Ancestral chart of William Lincoln Palmer.   (Boston, 1913)   geneal. tab., 41½ x 37 cm. fold. to 21½ x 19½ cm.   14-1951.   CS71. P175   1913

12985   PALMER.   Palmer pedigree of William Lincoln Palmer.   (Boston, 1916)   cover-title, (2) p. 30 cm. Blank leaf at end for "Notes."   16-11410.   CS71. P175   1916

12986   PALMER.   The early history of the Palmer family.   (By Greville Horsley Palmer)   (n. p., 1918)   10 p. 2 fold. geneal. tab. 22½ cm. Signed: Greville H. Palmer. Author's autograph in manuscript, on cover. Abstract of the will of Ralph Palmer, of Marston: 2 p. inserted at end. 25-11759.   CS439. P26   1918

12987   PALMER.   Ancestral chart.   The revised chart of the American ancestors of William Lincoln Palmer of Boston, Mass., January 1st, 1921, with all official offices held by his ancestors whether ecclesiastical, civil or military;   also all Mayflower passengers who are ancestors, officially marked in chart.   Boston, Mass., 1921.   geneal. tab. 23½ x 42½ cm. fold. to 25 x 22½ cm. 20-22883.
                                                                                                        CS71. P175   1921

12988   PALMER.   Genealogical records taken from the family Bible of James Monroe Palmer, born 1822, died 1897, and Caroline Frances Bacon, his wife, born 1830, died 1899, of Boston, Massachusetts. (Boston, Mass., Printed by W. L. Palmer, 1924)   (8) p. 15½ cm. Caption title. 24-20335.
                                                                                                        CS71. P175   1924

12989   PALMER.   The Palmer family, Leroy Griffin Palmer branch.   (n. p., 1944)   2 numb. l. 35½ x 21½ cm.   "Typed & mimeographed September, 1944." 45-8048.   CS71. P175   1944

12990   PALMER.   A genealogy of the family of Henry Palmer of County Somerset, England and allied lines in the United States, 1635-1957; with biographical sketches.   By Edwin Obadiah Palmer.   Hollywood, Calif. (1959)   xii, 135 p. ports., coats of arms. 24 cm. 59-43021.   CS71. P175   1959

12991   PALMER.   The descendants of George Palmer & Phebe Draper.   By Sarah (Palmer) Collin-wood.   Provo, Utah, J. G. Stevenson (1962 or 3)   1210 p. illus. 25 cm. 63-37714.

CS71.P175   1963

12992   PALMER.   Genealogy of the Palmer family of New York State, and allied families of Hansen, Devereux, Eichelberger, Johnson, Elliott (and) Crissy; also genealogy of the Eaton family descended from John of Dedham and allied families of Gale, Bancroft, Eaton, Hall (and) Hicks.   Sioux City, Iowa (1964?)   1 v. (various pagings) illus., geneal. table, ports. 30 cm. 66-54957.   CS71.P175   1964

12993   PALMER.   Palmer families in America, compiled and arr. by Horace Wilbur Palmer.   Edited by Nellie Morse Palmer.   Neshanic, N.J., Neshanic Print. Co., 1966.   v. port. 24 cm. Contents. - v. 1. Lt. William Palmer of Yarmouth, Mass. and his descendants of Greenwich, Conn. 67-6549.

CS71.P175   1966

12994   PALMER.   The Ancestral lines of Truman Dixon Palmer and Emma Calista Barrett with descendants.   (n. p., 1967?)   ii, 196 p. coats of arms, ports. 24 cm. Cover title: Palmer-Barrett genealogy. "Much of the research and work on this genealogy has been done ... by Ethel Duffy Turner." 67-9529.

CS71.P175   1967

12995   PALMER.   The descendants of John Palmer of Detroit.   By Sabria Ann (Palmer) Lamb.   (Detroit? 1950)   (32) p. 30 cm. Caption title. Additions and corrections in ms. 51-17435.   CS71.P175   1950

PALMER.   See also:

BACKHOUSE, DA690.M74.C3	COLBY, 1880	JOHNSON, 1961
BASSETT, 1926	COLBY, 1884	KINNISON, 1956
CATESBY, 1914	DE LODBROKE, DA690.L17.H4	LINDLEY, 1950
CHUTE, 1894	DRIVER, 1889	POUND, 1949
CLARK, 1904	JOHNSON, 1930a	TYLER, 1925

12996   PALMERLEE.   The Palmerlee family; a genealogy of the descendants of Heman Palmerlee (1786-1859) & Stephen Asa Palmerlee (1803-1869) with lines of descent from the XVI century, by Albert E. Palmerlee.   Lawrence, Kan., 1967.   v, 111 p. illus., coats of arms, facsims., geneal. tables, map, ports., 28 cm. Bibliography: p. 87. 67-31015.   CS71.P18   1967

12997   PALMES.   Pedigree of Palmes, of Naburn.   (n.p., 18 -) geneal. tab. illus. (coat of arms) 75 x 37 cm. fold. to 37 x 28½ cm. 40M3851T   CS439.P263

12998   PALOMARES.   Windows in an old adobe (by) Bess Adams Garner; foreword by J. Gregg Layne.   Pomona, Calif., Printed by Progress-bulletin in collaboration with Saunders press, Claremont, Calif., 1939.   7 p. 1., 245, (1) p. 24 pl. (incl. ports., facsim.) on 12 1., 39 geneal. tab. on 17 1. 20½ cm. Map on lining papers. "First edition limited to 2000 copies." Includes genealogical tables of the families of Jose Cristobal Palomares and Ricardo Vejar, material collected by Maria Lugarda Palomares. Bibliography: p. 235-236. 40-4682.   F864.G23

12999   PAMA.   Het geslacht Pama; geschiedenis van een Humsterlandse familie gedurende vyf eeuwen.   By C. Pama.   Kaapstad, 1956.   159 p. 20 cm. 58-45930.   CS1619.P3   1956

PANCAKE.   See No. 1547 - Cabell county.

13000   PANCOAST.   Pancoast family, with Potts line.   By Alexander Du Bin.   Philadelphia, Historical Publ. Society, 1948.   6 p. 26 cm. 49-19804.   CS71.P2   1948

13001   PANCOAST.   Pancoast family; some descendants of John Pancoast, Quaker emigrant to Burlington County, West Jersey, in America, from Northampton Shire, England, October 1680, on the ship Paradise.   Compiled by Thelma Beck Ellis.   Trenton, N.J., 1965.   135 1. mounted col. illus., mounted ports. (1 col.) 28 cm. 65-71315.   CS71.P2   1965

13002   PANCOAST.   Pancoats family.   Additional material in vertical file.   Ask reference librarian for this material.

13003   PANET.   La famille Panet, par Pierre-George Roy ... Lévis Québec, J.-A.-K. Laflamme, imprimeur) 1906.   212 p. plate, ports. 23½ cm. Tiré à 150 exemplaires. 7-24302.   CS90. P3

13004   PANMURE.   Liber cartarum prioratus Sancti Andree in Scotia e registro ipso in archivis baronum de Panmure hodie asservato.   Edinburgi, 1841.   lxiv p., 1 l., 432, lvii p. facsims. 27½ x 21½ cm. (Bannatyne club. Publications. v. 69) Edited by Thomas Thomson, president of the Bannatyne club. cf. p. x-xi. 24-6044.

DA750. B2

PANNEBECKER.   See PENNYPACKER.

PANNILL.   See: FITZHUGH, 1961
                        LIGON, 1947
                        No. 3509 - Orange county, Va.

PAPIN.   See CHOUTEAU, 1893

13005   PAQUET.   La paroisse de Saint-Nicolas.   La famille Pâquet et les familles alliées, par Hormisdas Magnan... Québec, Impr. Laflamme, 1918.   3 p. l., 334 p. plates, ports. 23 cm. 20-22505.
CS90. P4

13006   PAQUET.   ... Zéphirin Paquet, sa famille, sa vie, son oevre.   (frère Marie Alcas) Québec, 1927.   2 p. l., vi, 374, (2) p. front., illus. (incl. plans) ports. 19 cm. At head of title" Essai monographie familiale. 34-39636.   CT310. P3A7

13007   PARDEE.   Genealogy of one line of the Pardee family and some memoirs, by Aaron Pardee. Wadsworth, O., 1896.   1 p. l., 69 p., 1 l. ports. 21½ cm. 38-32663.   CS71. P224   1896

13008   PARDEE.   Pardee's old Morris house, public museum and civic center at Morris Cove, New Haven, Conn.   Gift of William Scranton, Pardee; plans and notes by Walter Stone Pardee ... (Chicago, Ill., 1923)   ii, 15 umb. 1. plates, plans, maps. 29½ cm. Photostat of type-written copy. Text parallel with back of cover. On cover: George Pardee, the first (1623-1700) New Haven, Conn., and others. Includes "A Pardee genealogy." 24-1232.

F104. N6P2

13009   PARDEE.   ... The Pardee genealogy, edited by Donald Lines Jacobus, M. A.   New Haven, Printed for the Society, 1927.   viii, 693 p. front., illus. (incl. ports., facsims.) fold. maps, fold. facsim. 24½ cm. At head of title: New Haven colony historical society. The William Scranton Pardee fund. Title vignette: New Haven Colony historical society. 27-18004.   CS71. P224   1927

13010   PARDEE.   The Pardee family in America.   (By William Henry Adams)   Highland Park, Mich., 1936.   2 p. l., 5 numb. 1. 32 cm. Typewritten. Caption-title. Signed: William H. Adams. 37M40T.
CS71. P224   1936

13011   PARDEE.   Pardee and Ives families.   Edited by Alexander Du Bin and Grace Ives Maluge. Philadelphia, Historical publication Society, 1950.   34 p. 26 cm. 51-27507.   CS71. P224   1950

PARDEE.   See also MORRIS, 1938

PARIS.   See PARRIS.

13012   PARISH.   John Parish of Groton, Mass., and some of his descendants, by Roswell Parish, jr. Boston, New England historic and genealogical society, 1909.   12 p. 22½ cm. (Register reprints, series A. no. 35) "Reprinted from the New England historical and genealogical register for October, 1909." 17-31805.   CS71. P225   1909

13013   PARISH.   The Parrish family (Philadelphia, Pennsylvania) including the related families of Cox, Dillwyn, Roberts, Chandler, Mitchell, Painter, Pusey, by Dillwyn Parrish, 1809-1886.   With special reference to Joseph Parrish, M. D., 1779-1840, with sketches of his children, by members of the family and others; compiled by his granddaughter, Susanna Parrish Wharton.   Philadelphia, George H. Buchanan company, 1925.   336 p. incl. front., illus., plates, ports., facsims. (1 fold.) 25 x 20½ cm. 25-18272.   CS71. P225   1925

13014   PARISH.   Early reminiscences, by Samuel L. Parrish ... (New York, Printed by B. H. Tyrrel, inc., c.1927)   2 p. l., 3-92 p.   front., illus. (incl. ports.) 23½ cm.   "Early reminiscences associated with the life and family of - Sarah Redwood Parrish."   28-3218.   CS71.P225   1927

13015   PARISH.   The Parrish family including the allied families of Belt, Boyd, Cole and Malone, Clokey, Garrett, Merryman, Parsons, Price, Tipton, with special reference to Mercelia Louise Boyd ... Genealogist Katherine Cox Gottschalk.   Compiled and published by Scott Lee Boyd.   Santa Barbara, Calif., 1935.   3 p. l., v-vii, 9-413 p. ports., facsims. 27 cm. 36-14655.   CS71.P225   1935

13016   PARISH.   New England Parish families; descendants of John Parish of Groton, Mass., and Preston, Conn., by Roswell Parish.   Rutland, Vt., The Tuttle publishing company, inc. (1938) xiv p., 1 l., 502 p. front., ports. 23½ cm.   "Compiled by Roswell Parish, jr., from notes gathered by his father, Roswell Parish."   Bibliography: p. (x)-xiv, 1 l.; also "References: throughout text.   39-10120.   CS71.P225   1938

13017   PARISH.   Parrish, Dack families.   By John Ford Parrish.   (Salt Lake City? 195-) 159 l. 29 cm. 56-44761.   CS71.P225

PARISH.   See also HILDRETH, 1950

13018   PARK.   Ruper-Park (families. n.p., 19 -)   4 l. 28 cm. 53-33632.   CS71.P235

13019   PARK.   The Park record; containing an account of the ancestry and descendants of Thomas Kinnie Park and Robert Park, of Groton, Conn., and Grafton, Vt. ... Comp. by Edwin H. Park ... (Denver, Col., Bartow & Ray print, 1902)   88 p., plates (1 col.) ports., geneal. tab. 23 cm. 3-26843.
                                                                                                      CS71.P235   1902

13020   PARK.   Genealogy of the Parke families of Connecticut; including Robert Parke, of New London, Edward Parks, of Guilford, and others.   Also a list of Parke, Park, Parks, etc., who fought in the Revolutionary War.   By Frank Sylvester Parks.   Washington, 1906.   333 p. coats of arms, ports. 21 cm. "No. 165." 8-29597 rev.   CS71.P235   1906
————— Additions and corrections to the Parke families of Connecticut.   (Washington, 1922?) 25-32 p. 23 cm.   Detached from Parks records, compiled and pub. by Frank S. Parks, v. 3, pt. 4,   CS71.P235   1906
                                                                                                      Suppl.

13021   PARK.   Kinfolks of William Parke and Synah Perry & Josiah Wilson and Margaret Crow, including the related families of Hammonds, Lewis, Stephens, Wheeler, Estes, Lynn, Hopper, Ficklin, Ellis, and others.   By Margie Ellis Howell.   Kansas City, 1967.   1 v. (various pagings) illus., maps, ports. 28 cm. Bibliography: p. F-1. 70-3931.   CS71.P235   1967

13022   PARK.   Genealogy of the Parke families of Massachusetts; including Richard Parke, of Cambridge, William Park, of Groton, and others.   Compiled by Frank Sylvester Parks ... Washington, D. C. (Presswork by the Columbia polytechnic institute printing office) 1909.   262 p. col. front. (coat of arms) illus., ports. 21 cm. "No. 11." "Privately printed." 9-7532.   CS71.P235   1909

13023   PARK.   Some account of the Park family and especially of the Rev. Joseph Park, M. A., 1705-1777, and Benjamin Parke, LL. D., 1801-1882.   Westerly, R. I., The Westerly historical society, 1917.   ix, 36 p., 1 l. front., plates, port., coat of arms. 20½ cm. "Of this book two hundred copies have been printed for private distribution." "Authorities cited": p. 4. 18-3893.   CS71.P235   1917

13024   PARK.   Genealogy of the Parke family, nine generations from Arthur and Mary Parke, 1720-1920.   (n.p., 1920?)   116 p. 23½ cm. Preface signed: John P. Wallace. 28-23902.   CS71.P235   1920

13025   PARK.   Ancestry of Cyrenius Parks of Canada, and some of his descendants. (By Frank Sylvester Parks)   Washington, D. C., 1922.   cover-title, 8 p. 23 cm. (Parks records. v. 3, pt. 3) "Compiled and published by Frank S. Parks." 25-6686.   CS71.P235   1922
                                                                                                      vol. 3, pt. 3

13026   PARK.   Ancestry of Halsey Park of Walpole, Can., and some of his descendants.   Washington, D. C., 1922.   cover-title, 8 p. 23 cm. (Parks records. v. 3, pt. 5) "Compiled and published by Frank Sylvester Parks, from information contained in letters received through the efforts of Dr. Philip P. Park of Hamilton, Ont., and forwarded by him to the compiler." 25-6685.
                                                                                                      CS71.P235   1922
                                                                                                      vol. 3 pt. 5

13027   PARK.   Genealogy of Arthur Parke of Pennsylvania and some of his descendants.   Comp. by Frank Sylvester Parks ... Washington, D. C., 1922.   19, (1) p. 22 cm.   Compiled partly from personal research and partly from information collected by Dr. Charles Ross Parke.   Printed as part of the "Park records, " v. 3.   22-22876.

CS71. P235   1922

13028   PARK.   Park family of Washington Co., Pennsylvania.   Washington, D. C. (1922?)
8 p. 23 cm. (Parks records. v. 3, pt. 14) Caption title. Compiled by F. S. Parks, almost entirely from "Biographical sketch of the Park family of Washington County, Pa., by W. J. Park". 25-6681.

CS71. P235   1922
vol. 3 pt. 14

13029   PARK.   Parke coats-of-arms.   Washington, D. C. (1922)   8 p. front. (col. coat of arms) illus. 23 cm.
(Parks records. v. 3, pt. 8) Caption title. "Compiled and published by Frank S. Parks." 25-6683.

CS71. P235   1922
vol. 3 pt. 8

13030   PARK.   Parks and Park in the census of 1790.   (First census of the United States)   Compiled by Frank Sylvester Parks.   Washington, D. C., 1922.   cover-title, 8 p. 23 cm. (Parks records, v. 3, pt. 2) 25-6682.

CS71. P235   1922
vol. 3, pt. 2

13031   PARK.   Simon Parke of Franklin, Pa., and descendants.   Washington, D. C. (1922?)
8 p. 23 cm. (Parks records. v. 3, pt. 9) Caption title. "The facts in regard to Simon Park and his descendants were collected and written out by Mrs. Anna E. Park Warner" ... Rewritten by Frank Sylvester Parks. 25-6680.

CS71. P235   1922
vol. 3, pt. 9

13032   PARK.   Park family of Westchester Co., New York.   Washington, D. C. (1922?)   8 p. 23 cm.
(Parks records. v. 3, pt. 10) Caption title. "Compiled by Frank Sylvester Parks, from information contained in 'The history of Rye, N. Y. ', by Charles W. Baird, N. Y., 1871; from a search of some of the county records; the census of 1790, and personal letters. 25-6684.

CS71. P235
vol. 3, pt. 10

13033   PARK.   Ancestors and descendants of Joel Parke of East Troy, Pa., compiled by John M Stanton.   (Elmira, N. Y., 1923)   24 p. 24 cm. (Parks records. v. 3, pts. 11, 12, 13) Caption title. Cover-title: Joel Parke and descendants. A supplement to "The Parke families of Connecticut" (by Frank S. Parks) "The facts in regard to Joel Parke and his descendants were compiled from information collected by Albert T. Parke. " 25-6679.

CS71. P235   1922
vol. 3 pts. 11, 12, 13

13034   PARK.   John Parks and his family, by Charlotte Ellen Heilbronn.   (Manila, P. I., Press of Kriedt printing co., 1925)   2 p. l., (9)-27 p. 19 cm.   Additions and corrections in manuscript throughout text. 31-20889.

CS71. P235   1925

13035   PARK.   Park of Kentucky, 1747-1929; biographical sketches and genealogy of the descendants of Ebenezer Park, pioneer, of Madison County, Kentucky; with brief notices of the allied families: Benton, Boian, Campbell, Chenault, Clark, Cobb, Covington, Dillingham, Duncan, Elliott, Gum, Henderson, Hume, Jacobs, Keller, Kidwell, Rayburn, Scrivner, Wagers, Wilson, and others.   Compiled and published by Nell Park Gum.   Frankfort, Ky., 1929.   x, 148, xv p. front. (port.) 23½ cm. 29-24857.

CS71. P235   1929

13036   PARK.   The ancestry of Rev. Nathan Grier Parke & his wife Ann Elizabeth Gildersleeve.   Edited by Donald Lines Jacobus.   Woodstock, Vt., 1959.   146 p. ports., facsim. 24 cm. Includes bibliographies.
61-34221.

CS71. P235   1959

13037   PARK.   A genealogy of the Park family, 1860-1960.   By Thomas John Claggett.   (Wayne? Pa., 1960?)   19 p. 22 cm. 61-42044.

CS71. P235   1960

13038   PARK.   The Park family in America, compiled by Sarah Hoyt Brown Park and Hazel Park Potter.   Mount Morris, Ill., 1964.   73 l. 30 cm. On cover: The Park family in America, 1635-1964. 64-55035.

CS71. P235   1964

13039   PARK.   The Parke scrapbook, collected and compiled by Ruby Parke Anderson.   Edited by Elizabeth Hunter Ruppert.   Baltimore, Port City Press, 1965.   v. illus., ports. 24 cm.   Facsim. of the "Records of the Separate Church (Preston, Conn.) by Rev. Paul Park, from 1747 to 1800": v. 1, p. (29) - (191)   Includes bibliographies.   65-26058.

CS71.P235   1965

13040   PARK.   William and Elizabeth Park, by Elizabeth B. Bedell.   (Tottenville? N.Y., 1968) 22 p.   illus., geneal. table (fold. in pocket), ports. 22 cm.   68-6667.

CS71.P235   1968

PARK.   See also:

ARMSTRONG, CS61.A6 v.3	CHAMPNEY, 1855	HUME, 1926 v.2
AVERY, 1919	CLARK, 1906a	LLOYD, 1898
AVERY, 1925	COMBERFORD, DA690.W39B1	SNYDER, 1958
AVERY, F116.N28 v.52	CROCKER, 1923	WASHINGTON, 1879
BIDDLE, E207.B5B5	FULHAM, 1910	WOOD, 1909

PARKE.   See PARK.

13042   PARKER.   The life and acts of Matthew Parker, the first archbishop of Canterbury in the reign of Queen Elizabeth. ... Compiled faithfully from records, registers ... authentic letters, and sundry other original mss.   In four books.   To which is added, an appendix, containing various transcripts of records, letters ... and other secret papers ... By John Strype, M.A.   London, J. Wyat, 1711. 3 p. l., xxvi, 448, (441) - (452), 449-544, 208 (i.e. 204) p. front. (port.) 2 illus., fold. tab. 31½ cm.   Frontispiece is portrait of Parker by George Vertue.   Appendix has special t.-p. and paging.   Pages 172-175 of the appendix are omitted in numbering.   "Pedigree of Sir John Parker, knight": Appendix, p.3.   12-18340.

BX5199.P3S9

13043   PARKER.   A brief history of the ancestors and descendants of Scarborough Parker, one of the pioneers of Jay, Franklin County, Maine.   By Millard M. Parker ... Boston, W. F. Brown & co., printers (1879)   33 p. 21½ cm.   "Read before the Parker cousins association, at East Livermore, Me., August 13th, 1879." 17-15777.

CS71.P24   1879

13044   PARKER.   Some Rhode Island Parkers, by Prescott A. Parker.   Montrose, Ala. (188-?) 11 l. illus. (mounted ports.) 14½ x 21 cm.   Text runs parallel with back of cover, within folded t.-p.   31.33657.

CS71.P24   188-

13045   PARKER.   The genealogy of Wm. Thornton Parker, A.M., M.D. of Boston, Mass.   Born January 8th, 1818.   Died March 12th, 1855.   Contributed by his son, Wm. Thornton Parker ... Newport, R.I., J.P.Sanborn, printer, 1888.   10 p. 23 cm.   9-12854.

CS71.P24   1886

13046   PARKER.   The Parker family.   A short record of the Roxbury branch of the Parker family, of Reading, Massachusetts, and some of their descendants.   By George H. Parker ... Cullman, Ala., Alabama tribune print, 1890.   2 p. l., 11 p. 22 cm.   Interleaved. 37-21318.   CS71.P24   1890

13047   PARKER.   (Descendants of Jacob Parker, born Woburn, Mass., died Chelmsford, Mass., 1699)   (n.p. 1891?) geneal. table. 33 x 55 cm.   Photostat reproduction (positive) of manuscript genealogical chart. 37M1684T.

CS71.P24   1891

13048   PARKER.   Family records.   Parker - Pond - Peck.   By Rev. Edwin Pond Parker ... 1636-1892.   Hartford, Conn., Press of the Case, Lockwood & Brainard co., 1892.   51 p., 7 l. 24½ cm.   A brief sketch of the Pond family showing our derivation through Wealthy Ann (Parker) Pond.   Taken from the "Pond genealogy": p. 45-51.   p. 32-43 partly blank for additions and corrections.   Seven leaves of additions interspersed.   Mc. corrections and additions. 9-12855.

CS71.P24   1892

13049   PARKER.   Genealogy and biographical notes of John Parker of Lexington and his descendants. Showing his earlier ancestry in America from Dea. Thomas Parker of Reading, Mass., from 1635 to 1893.   By Theodore Parker.   Worcester, Mass., Press of C. Hamilton, 1893.   4 p. l., 528 p. front., illus., plates, ports. 24 cm.   9-12853.   CS71.P24   1893

13050   PARKER.   Gleanings from Parker records, A. D. 1271 to 1893, by William Thornton Parker ..
Haverhill, Mass., Press of Chase brothers, 1894.   51 p.   plates, ports., coat of arms.   24½ cm.   8-11880.
CS71. P24   1894

13051   PARKER.   Glances at the ancestors of John Parker.   (Born 1807, died 1891.)   (Columbus?
Ohio, 1895)   16 p.   22 cm.   Note on verso of title signed: Harvey Parker Ward.   Intended as an addition to the author's memorial sketch of
his grandparents, John Parker and Peris Follett Parker, published in 1893.   cf. Note.   The first Jewetts in America: p. 12-16.   6-15864.
CS71. P24   1895

13052   PARKER.   ... History and genealogy of the family of Deacon Lovel Parker, who emigrated
from Barkhamsted, Conn., to Kinsman, Ohio, in the year 1816, compiled by Rufus H. and L. N. Parker.
(Syracuse, N. Y., The Mason press) 1898.   3 p. l., (5)-80 p.   plates, ports.   27 cm.   At head of title: 1643-1898.
38-32662.   CS71. P24   1898

13053   PARKER.   Genealogical memoranda relating to the family of Parker of Upton house, Upton
Cheyney manor, Bitton, Gloucestershire; and Welford house, Keynsham, Somerset; of Henbury,
Clifton, Bristol, London, and elsewhere.   From 1543 to 1898.   Compiled by Edward Milward Seede
Parker, gent., of Welford house, Keynsham, Somersetshire, 1898.   Bristol, Lavars & co., 1899.
42 p., 1 l.   34 cm.   With this is bound the author's "Comprehensive pedigree, no. 2.   The Perrott family ... 1909. "   19-2313.
CS439. P27

13054   PARKER.   (A family tree of John Parker, a colonial settler in North Carolina) Original drawn
by Miss M. C. Bagley ... from data furnished by B. F. Bullard of Savannah Ga.,   (Jackson, N. C.) 1906.
geneal. tab.   60 x 45½ cm.   39M1089T.   CS71. P24   1906

13055   PARKER.   Parker in America 1630-1910.   What the historians say of them; what a large
number say of themselves; genealogical and biographical; interesting historical incidents.   Compiled
and edited by Augustus G. Parker ... Buffalo, N. Y., Niagara frontier publishing company (1911)
9 p. l., (3) - 592 p.   front. (port.)   23 cm.   11-28748.   CS71. P24   1911

13056   PARKER.   Archelaus R. Parker and his descendants by Milo Custer.   Bloomington, Ill., 1912.
cover-title, (24) p. incl. ports.   23 cm.   12-7171.   CS71. P24   1912

13057   PARKER.   The history of Peter Parker and Sarah Ruggles of Roxbury, Mass. and their an-
cestors and descendants, with the best wishes of the author, John William Linzee, jr. ... Boston,
Mass., Priv. print. (S. Usher) 1913.   xii, 609 p.   front., ports.   25 cm.   Blank pages interspersed.   13-23049.
CS71. P24   1913

13058   PARKER.   Great grandfather's clock at the old Parker homestead, Bradford, Massachusetts.
A. D. 1760, by W. Thornton Parker ... Northampton, Mass., 1913.   10, (1) p.   front. (coat of arms) plates, ports.,
25 cm.   15-7575.   CS71. P24   1913a

13059   PARKER.   Gleanings from colonial and American records of Parker and Morse families,
A. D. 1585-1915, by William Thornton Parker ... Northampton, Mass. , 1915.   (68) p.   plates, ports., coats
of arms.   25 cm.   Each article has special t. -p. and separate paging.   Contents. - Lieut. Colonel Moses Parker ... 1914. 20 p. - Great grandfather's clock at the old Parker homestead, Bradford, Massachusetts. A. D. 1760 ... 1913. 12 p. - Major Abner Morse, esqr. ... 1915. 32 p.
17-9756.   CS71. P24   1915

13060   PARKER.   New England Indian war veterans, A. D. 1675 - A. D. 1885, of Abraham Parker's
family, comp. by his great, great, great grandson, William Thornton Parker ... Northampton, Mass.,
1921.   12, (1) p.   front. (port.)   23 cm.   Cover-title: Parker Indian war veterams of New England ...   26-23743.
E82P24
—— Copy 2.   CS71. P24   1921

13061   PARKER.   The genealogy of Wm. Thornton Parker ... Dartmouth and Harvard, of Boston,
Mass.   Born January 8, 1818, died March 12, 1855.   Contributed by his son Wm. Thornton Parker,
M. D., Munich, 1873 ... (n. p., 1922?)   cover-title, 9 p. ports. 23½ cm.   "Extract from a letter written by Dr. Benjamin
Parker of 'Richlands' ... to his daughter Marie", inserted between pages 6 and 7.   22-12438.   CS71.P24   1922

13062   PARKER.   New England war veterans of the American revolution and of later wars of Abraham Parker's family and of his brothers James, Joseph, John and Jacob, compiled by his great, great, great grandson, William Thornton Parker ... Northampton, Mass., 1923.   (15) p. 24 cm. 23-14441.
CS71. P24   1923

13063   PARKER.   The Parker and Kearny families of New Jersey (by) Captain James Parker ... a paper read before the New Brunswick historical society, February 18, 1897.   Perth Amboy, N.J., 1925.   40 p. 23 cm.   "No. 158.   One hundred and sixty-nine copies ... were printed." 41-41201.
CS71. P24   1925

13064   PARKER.   Descendants of Samuel Parker, revolutionary soldier of Coventry, Conn., and Byron, N.Y.   Compiled by Mary A. Moulthrop.   Rochester, N.Y., 1927.   29 p. 19 cm. 29-10279.
CS71. P24   1927

13065   PARKER.   Grand Mountain typewriting school, conducted through correspondence, by Jim Parker, Tecumseh, Oklahoma in the interest of his nieces and nephews.   Family histories and a record of home study in the Parker family.   (n. p. 1929?)   98 p. illus. (incl. ports.) 24 cm. 40-37508.
CS71. P24   1929

13066   PARKER.   Record of the Parker family of the parish of St. James Goose Creek and of Charleston, South Carolina, compiled and edited by Ellen Parker ... (Charleston, S. C.) 1930.   2 p. 1., 8 numb. 1.   28 x 21½ cm.   Corrections in manuscript. 44-26058,
CS71. P24   1930

13067   PARKER.   Some descendants of six pioneers from Great Britain to America.   (By Horatio Newton Parker) (n. p., 1940)   cover-title, (2), 25 p. 23 cm. Compiled by Horatio Newton Parker.   An account of the Parker, Hall, Newton, De Wolf, Evans and Irwin families.   "Sources": p. 23-25. 40-34624.
CS71. P24   1940

13068   PARKER.   Histories of the families of Archibald Parker, Lettie Parker and of Joseph Thomas.   Compiled originally in 1932 and revised in 1940 by Ray C. Thomas ... Gary, Ind. (1940)   3 p. 1.,   3-24 numb. 1. 35 cm.   Reproduced from type-written copy. 41-6097.
CS71. P24   1940a

13069   PARKER.   Timothy Parker, 1696-1737, of Reading and Roxbury, Massachusetts, and his family.   By Alice Lucinda Priest.   Brookline, 1942.   91 p. 25 cm.   Manuscript. 49-36525*.
CS71. P24   1942

13070   PARKER.   Background of Iowa territorial pioneers as exemplified by the ancestry of Francis Parker and his wife, Rhoda Chaplin.   Compiled by Gurney Chaplin Gue ... (n. p.) 1945.   92 p. incl.   geneal. tables. 23½ cm.   "Incomplete list of source books": p. 91-92. A 45-4679.
CS71. P24   1945

13071   PARKER.   Parker genealogy, a genealogy of the Chelmsford and Peabody branch of the Parker family.   Rev. ed.   By Lena Parker Goodwin.   Meredith, N.H., Pub. by Meredith News Press, 1947.   19 p. 23 cm. 48-14879*.
CS71. P24   1947

13072   PARKER.   The Parker family history.   By Donald Dean Parker.   (Brooklings, S. D., 1947)   102 p. illus., ports., maps. 28 cm.   (With his as issued: The Graham-Patterson family history.   (Brookings, S. D.) 1947) 48-2146*.
CS71. G74   1947a

13073   PARKER.   Lamb-Parker-Richardson families.   A collection of MSS, genealogical notes, deeds, etc.   In vertical file.   Ask reference librarian for this material.

13074   PARKER.   The Lewis Parker family.   By Lois (White) Patton.   Hartwell (Ga.) Sokol Printers, 1958.   27 p. 22 cm. 59-33585.
CS71. P24   1958

13075   PARKER.   Ancestors and descendants of Cader Atkins Parker, 1810-1886, by his great grandson, Robert Samuel Roddenbery.   Adel, Ga., Press of the Patten Publishers (1959)   140 p. illus. 24 cm.   59-10861.
CS71. P24   1959

PARKER.   Parker family in vertical file.   Ask reference assistant for this material.

13076   PARKER.   Nathaniel Parker (2), 1651-1737, Reading, Massachusetts and his descendants, showing their ancestry in America from Thomas Parker (1), 1609-1683, Puritan emigrant from England to Massachusetts in 1635; a biographical and historical genealogy.   (Kershaw? S.C., 1966)   xvi, 146 p. illus., ports. 24 cm. On cover: Nathaniel Parker (2) and his descendants. Bibliography: p. 129. 67-2164.

CS71.P24   1966

PARKER.   See also:

ALDERMAN, 1957	DAINGERFIELD, 1928	JOHNSON, 1961
BROWN, 1938a	DAVIS, 1939	MINNS, 1925
BUTTERFIELD, 1944	FARMER, 1897	POWELL, 1891a
CALHOUN, 1957	GAMBLE, 1906	THIGPEN, 1961
CURTIS, 1912	HUMPHREY, 1938a	

PARKES.   See PARK

13077   PARKHILL.   Gift of heritage.   By Genevieve Parkhill Lykes.   (n. p., 1969)   295, (2) p. illus. 25 cm. Bibliography: p. (297) 76-7649 MARC.

CS71.P244   1969

PARKHILL.   See also ALEXANDER, 1960

13078   PARKHURST.   A fragment of the Parkhurst genealogy prepared from the records by Charles H. Parkhurst.   Providence, R. I., Printed for private distribution, 1883.   19 p. 23½ cm. 8-22338.

CS71.P246   1883

13079   PARKHURST.   The Parkhurst family.   Descendants of Ephraim Parkhurst, of Framingham, Mass.   (By Wellington Evarts Parkhurst) (n. p., 1897)   21 p. incl. illus., 2 pl. (port., coat of arms) on 1 l. 19½ cm. 4-22378 rev.

CS71.P246   1897

13080   PARKHURST.   John Parkhurst, born May 2, 1760, at Weston, Massachusetts, his ancestors and descendants.   Prepared by Gabriel H. Parkhurst ... Bath, N. Y., Press of the Courier company limited, 1897.   51 p. pl., ports., col. coat of arms. 25 cm. Printed for private distribution. 20-9256.

CS71.P246   1897a

13081   PARKHURST.   Historical facts relating to the Cutler Mills school district of Ashland, nos. 6 and 5, formerly no. 13 of Framingham.   Including references to the Parks Corner (no. 3) district of Framingham, of which no. 13 was formerly a part.   By Wellington Evarts Parkhurst.   Clinton (Mass.) Press of W. J. Coulter, 1897.   35 p. illus. (incl. port.) 23 cm. "The Parkhurst family": p. (29)-35. Other biographical and genealogical notices included. 22-10763.

F74.A86P2

13082   PARKHURST.   The Parkhurst historical and genealogical association of America.   Baltimore, Md., 1900.   cover-title, (8) p. 22 cm. Contains constitution, by laws and list of members. 1-19500 rev.

CS71.P246   1900

13083   PARKINSON.   The Old-Church clock.   By Richard Parkinson... 5th ed.   Edited, with a biographical sketch of the author, by John Evans.   Manchester, A. Heywood & son; (etc., etc.) 1880. 5 p. l., (ix)-xcvii p., 2 l., 255, 12 p. plates, 2 ports. (incl. front.) facsim. 26½ cm. Title vignette. 1st edition, 1843; this edition is reprinted from the 4th edition published by the author in 1852. Commemorative of the Rev. Robert Walker, of Seathwaite. A memoir of Robert Walker from Mr. Wordsworth's notes to his series of sonnets on the River Duddon: p. 9-32. Contains pedigree and history of the Parkinson and Walker families. 15-22588.

PR5126.P5705 1880

13084   PARKINSON.   The Parkinson family of Lancashire, historical sketch, by Richard Ainsworth ... Accrington, Wardleworth ltd., printers, 1932.   19 (5) p. coat of arms. 21 cm. Blank pages for "Notes" (3 at end) 32-33849.

CS439.P275A5

13085   PARKINSON.   Major James Parkinson, 1791-1872.   (By Bell Winning Pendergast) (London? Ont., 1942)   2 p. l., 23 numb. l., 14 l., 19 numb. l. 29 cm. Foreword signed: Winning Pendergast. Type-written copy (carbon) made by Edwin Seaborn from the original. Includes genealogy of the Parkinson family and documents relating to the same. 43-32940.

CT310.P32P4

PARKS.   See PARK.

PARKYNS.   See PERKINS.

13086   PARLIN.   The Parlin genealogy.   The descendants of Nicholas Parlin of Cambridge, Mass. Compiled by Frank Edson Parlin ... Cambridge, Mass.   (T. R. Marvin & son, printers) 1913.
289 p. front. (col. coat of arms) plates (part col.) ports. 24½ cm. 14-5213.   CS71.P252   1913

13087   PARMAN.   The saga of the Parman family.   By Opal Miller Soetaert.   Edited by Jane McClanahan.   (Kansas City, Mo.) 1967.   56 l. 28 cm. "Supplement to The saga of the Parman family: Lineal descendants of James Wesley Parman and Martha Catherine Gibbs, by Rhoda Catherine (Parman) Gentry. 1967": leaves (28)-47. 68-2257.
CS71.P2524   1967

13088   PARMELEE.   Biography of Rev. Ashbel Parmelee, D. D.   Philadelphia, J. W. Lewis & co., 1880.   27 p. front. (port.) 22½ cm. The family of Parmalee: one leaf inserted at end. 24-18832.   BX9225.P3B5

13089   PARMELEE.   Parmelee data.   v. 1 - Jan. 1, 1940-   (Washington)   v. 26 cm. Frequency varies. Editor: v. 1-5, no. 2, D. H. Smallwood. Vols. 1-8 accompanied by indexes (subject, author, daughters, and all other persons) 8 v. 40-9806 rev.   CS71.P2527   1940

PARMELEE.   See also: SALISBURY, 1892
VAN NESS, 1960

13090   PARMENTER.   Parmenter portals.   Issued in Long Beach, Calif.   At head of title: Pioneer Parmenters of America.   v. 2, no. 1.   Feb. 1963.   In vertical file.

13091   PARMENTIER.   Model lay activity; the Brooklyn Parmentier family, by Sister Mary James Lowery ... Brookly, 1940.   1 p. l., ii, 89 p. plates, plan. 21 cm. Thesis (M.A.) - St. John's university, 1940. "Source material": p. 84-89. 42-9340.   CS71.M2528   1940

PARMLEE.   See PARMLY.

13092   PARMLY.   The greatest dental family.   By Lawrence Parmly Brown ... (Philadelphia, 1923?)
cover-title, 30 p. ports., facsims. 24½ cm. "Reprinted from the Denatl cosmos for March, April and May 1923." A history of the Parmly family. 29-7820.   CS71.P253   1923

PARMLY.   See also PARMLEE.

13093   PARNELL.   The life of Charles Stewart Parnell, with an account of his ancestry.   By Thomas Sherlock.   With an appendix, containing most interesting details of C. S. Parnell's early life, and of the Parnell, Stewart, and Tudor families.   Boston, Providence, Murphy & McCarthy, 1881.
202 p. front. (port.) 19 cm. 5-1214.   DA958.P2S5

13094   PARRACK.   The Parrack family.   By Juanita Mae Parrack Collins.   Marceline, Mo., Priv. print. for the author by Pischel Yearbooks (1969)   31 p. facsim., ports. 29 cm. "Limited to 50 copies." 76-218619 MARC.   CS71.P26   1969

PARREY.   See PERRY.

PARRIS.   See TILSON, 1911

PARRISH.   See PARISH.

13095   PARROTT.   History of the Parrott, Bateman, Brown families in America, by Gertrude Brown Henderson.   Sioux City, Ia., Goldie publishing co., 1933.   3 p. l., 5-27, (6) p. 2 port. 22 cm. "Collected by Oswell Chase Brown, over a period of thirty years, through correspondence, and from personal interviews and search of records." - Foreword. Blank pages for memoranda (3 at end) 33-21379.   CS71.P262   1933

PARROTT.   See also: COOPER, 1967
WOOD, 1966

13096 PARRY. Parry family records. Private ed. Philadelphia, D. C. Ryan, printer, 1877.
34 p. incl. front., plates. 20½ cm. Compiled by Richard Randolph Parry. Front. and 2 plates from S. F. Hotchkins' "York Road old and new"
inserted. 9-13000.

CS71. P264   1877

13097 PARRY. Genealogical abstracts of Parry wills, proved in the Prerogative court of Canterbury
down to 1810 with the administrations for the smae period, by Lieut-Colonel G. S. Parry. London,
G. Sherwood, 1911.   2 p. l., 150, (2) p. 29 cm. 12-24346.   CS439. P28

13098 PARRY. The family of Henry Parry of Pittsburgh, Pennsylvania. By Milton Rubincam.
In vertical file.   Ask reference librarian for this material.

13099 PARRY. Parry family in vertical file.   Ask reference librarian for this material.

PARRY. See also: ACKLEY, 1960   HALLEY, 1910
                   FITZ RANDOLPH, 1946a   JOLLIFFE, 1893
                   FULLWOOD, 1912   PARK, 1959
                   GAMBLE, CS71.G191   STUART, 1911
                   GARNIER, CS439.G37   WILSON, 1961

13100 PARSHALL. (James Parshall and his descendants ... By James C. Parshall. Syracuse, N. Y..
Priv. print., 1900)   iv, 38 p. 24½ cm. Title-page wanting. 1-5671.   CS71. P266   1900

13101 PARSHALL. The history of the Parshall family, from the conquest of England by William of
Normandy, A. D. 1066, to the close of the 19th century. By James Clark Parshall ... Syracuse (Press
of Crist, Scott & Parshall, Cooperstown, N. Y.) 1903.   4 p. l., 280, (12), xxi p. front., col. pl. (coat of arms) ports.
27 cm. Following p. 280 are 12 pages left blank for "Marriages, births and deaths". This edition is limited to 300 copies, of which this is no. 8.
3-22118.   CS71. P266   1903

13102 PARSHALL. The Parshall family, A. D. 870-1913; a collection of historical records and notes
to accompany the Parshall pedigree, by Horace Field Parshall, D. Sc. London, F. Edwards, 1915.
viii, 186 p. front., plates, fold. map. fold. geneal. tables, col. coats of arms. 26 cm. Title vignette. "One hundred copies of this book have
been printed for private circulation." American branch, "James Pershall and his descendants": p. 151-186. Pedigree of the Windsor family:
p. 176. 16-5054.   CS439. P29

13103 PARSHALL. To and from James and Catharine Parshall, by Frank Nellis Parshall and Homer
Leroy Parshall. (Manhattan? Kan., 1968)   x, 388 p. illus., col. coat of arms, geneal. table, ports. 28 cm. 400 copies.
No. 48. Pages 383-388, blank for "Marraiges," "Births," and "Deaths," Includes bibliographical references. 68-6256.

CS71. P266   1968

PARSHALL. See also DAVIS, 1927a

PARSLEY. See WALTMAN, 1928

13104 PARSONS. Genealogical record of the family of Parsons and Leonard, of West Springfield,
Massachusetts, Prepared by Samuel L. Parsons, Brooklyn, N. Y. New York, J. W. Amerman, printer,
1867.   40 p. front. (port.) illus. (coat of arms) 20 cm. Compiled partly from the work of Samuel Holden Parsons, "The Parsons family,"
first published in the New England historical and genealogical register in 1847. Contains also Sutherland and Olmstead families. Additions and
corrections in manuscript. 21-12485.   CS71. P269   1867

13105 PARSONS. Radial charts. Cornet Joseph Parsons (of Springfield, Mass., 1635, through Hon.
Francis Parsons of Hartford, Ct., born 1795. By David Parsons Holton and Frances K. (Forward)
Holton. New York, 1877)   geneal. tab. 44 x 67 cm. fold. to 13½ x 24 cm. 9-18731.

CS71. P269   1877

13106 PARSONS. (Radial chart of descendants of Cornet Joseph Parsons of Springfield, Mass., 1635,
through Thomas Parsons of New London, Conn., born 1791. By David Parsons Holton and Frances K.
(Forward)   Holton. New York, 1877)   geneal. tab. 43½ x 67½ cm. fold. to 13½ x 23½ cm. 9-18732.

CS71. P269   1877a

13107   PARSONS.   Descendants of Thomas and Katherine (Hester) Parsons, of England, through their grandson Dea. Benjamin of Springfield, Massachusetts.   New York, 1878.   geneal. tab. coat of arms. 77½ x 71 cm. fold. to 30 x 24½ cm.   Signed David Parsons Holton and Frances K. (Forward) Holton.   9-15008.

CS71. P269   1878

13108   PARSONS.   A partial genealogy of the descendants of Samuel Parsons, of East Hampton, L. I., 1650.   Constructed mainly from town and church records, by George R. Howell ... Albany, 1879. 20 p. 23 cm. 13-6112.

CS71. P269   1879

13109   PARSONS.   Genealogy of the family of Lewis B. Parsons (second.) Parsons-Hoar ... St. Louis, Perrin & Smith printing co. (1900)   109 p. ports. 23 cm.   Parsons - Springfield, Mass., 1636; Hoard - Gloucester, England, 1632.   Contents. - English family of Parsons. - American family. - Genealogy in the maternal line of Hoar. - Recollections of Lewis B. Parsons by (members of his family and Rev. Joseph R. Page) - Tribute by Joseph L. Daniels to Philo Parsons. - The Hoar family in America and its English ancestry. Extracts from a recent publication by George Frisbie Hoar, of Mass. - Rail and river army transportation in the civil war, by Gen. Lewis B. Parsons. 1-5674.

CS71. P269   1900

13110   PARSONS.   Cornet Joseph Parsons one of the founders of Springfield and Northampton, Massachusetts; Springfield, 1636; Northampton, 1655.   An historical sketch from original sources ... by Henry M. Burt, with supplementary chapters ... by Albert Ross Parsons.   Garden City, Long Island, N. Y., A. R. Parsons (1901)   187 p. front., illus. (coat of arms) pl., ports. 23 cm.   On verso of t. - p.: "Copyright 1898"; published 1901. 1-11004 rev.

CS71. P269   1901

13111   PARSONS.   Parsons family; descendants of Cornet Joseph Parsons, Springfield, 1636 - Northampton, 1655, by Henry Parsons ... New York, Frank Allaben genealogical company (c. 1912-20) 2 v. col. front., plates, ports., coats of arms. 25 cm. 13-21459 rev.

CS71. P269   1912

13112   PARSONS.   Eli Parsons of Enfield, Connecticut and Columbia Township, Bradford County, Pennsylvania, and his brother Thomas Parsons of Enfield, Connecticut and town of Franklin, Delaware County, New York, by John A. Parsons ... (New York) Priv. print., 1924.   2 p. l., xi-xxi, 128, (40) p. front. (port.) 24 cm.   Ruled pages "For additional family records" (3-40 at end)   "The Wilber fam.": p. 113-5, 25-511.

CS71. P269   1924

13113   PARSONS.   Charles Parsons, his life and work, by Rollo Appleyard.   London, Constable & co., litd., 1933.   xiii, 334 p. front., illus. (incl. facsim., coat of arms) plates, ports., fold. geneal. tab., diagr. 22½ cm.   "Books of reference": p. 316-317.   34-1409.

TA140. P3A6

13114   PARSONS.   The house of Cornet Joseph Parsons, together with the houses of a line of his descendants and their allied families, 1655-1941.   (By Henry Parsons.   Kennebunk? Me., 1941) (25) p. 27 (i. e. 28) pl., coat of arms. 26½ cm. 41-16669.

CS71. P269   1941

PARSONS.   See also:

BASSETT, 1926	GREEN, 1878	LAYTON, 1885
BRADFORD, 1900a	HENRY, 1905	MASON, 1964
CHANDLER, 1911	HOGG, 1959	PARISH, 1935
ELLERY. 1956	HOLTON, 1881	WISWALL, 1961
GILES, 1864		

13115   PARTHEMORE.   Genealogy of the Parthemore family.   1744-1885.   By E. W. S. Parthemore. Harrisburg, Pa., L. S. Hart, printer, 1885.   viii, 242 p. 23 cm. 9-12852.

CS71. P273   1885

13116   PARTRIDGE.   (Ancestors and descendants of Joseph Lyman Partridge and Zibiah Nelson Willson.   n. p. 19 -)   geneal. tab. 50½ x 84 cm. 39M581T.

CS71. P275   19 -

13117   PARTRIDGE.   Partridge genealogy.   Descendants of John Partridge of Medfield, Mass.   By George Homer Partridge, B. S.   Boston, Press of D. Clapp & son, 1904.   v, (3)-46 p. front., facsim. 23½ cm. "Reprinted in part from New England historical and genealogical register." 4-24960.

CS71. P275   1904

13118   PARTRIDGE.   Partridge genealogy, descendants of George Partridge of Duxbury, Massachusetts, by George Henry Partridge.   Priv. print. (Norwood, Mass., The Plimpton press) 1915.   ix, 41 (1) p. front., plates, fold. geneal. tab. 24 cm.   "These records were collected, verified and compiled by Mrs. Edward C. Chatfield of Minneapolis." - Pref. 15-16917.

CS71. P275   1915

13119   PARTRIDGE.   Partridge genealogy; descendants of George Partridge of Duxbury, Massachusetts, compiled by Myrtle Dennis Lundberg and Marie Ray Davis.   (Portland? Ore., 1965)
91 l. 29 cm. Bibliography: leaf 91. 65-3341.   CS71.P275   1965

          PARTRIDGE.   See also: CROSSETT, 1937
                                  LYMAN, 1865
                                  ROBINSON, 1894
                                  SMITH, 189 -

13120   PASCHAL.   Some Paschal ancestors, descendants, and allied families.   Compiled by Rosa Lee Price Paschal (Mrs. John Jones Paschal).   (Wolfe City, Tex., Southern Baptist Press, 1969)
445 p. illus., col. coat of arms, ports. 23 cm. 73-82474 MARC.   CS71.P28   1969

          PASCHALL.   See: BYRD, E159.G55
                            LLOYD, 1912

          PASLEY.   See ROBERTSON, 1959

13121   PASSE, van de.   L'Oeuvre gravé des van de Passe, décrit par D. Franken Dz. ... Amsterdam. F. Muller & co.; (etc., etc.) 1881.   xxxviii, (2), 318 p., 1 l. 27½ cm. 21-17812 rev.
                                                               NE670.P2F7

13122   PASSAVANT.   Some account of Dettmar Basse and the Passavant family and their arrival in America.   By Zelie Jennings, their grand-daughter.   (Pittsburgh, 1903)   1 p. l., 23 p. 14½ cm. 13-9631.
                                                               CS71.P29   1903

          PASTEAU.   See PATHAULT.

13124   PASTON.   Sketch of the history of Caister castle, near Yarmouth; including biographical notices of Sir John Fastolfe and of different individuals of the Paston family ... ed. by Dawson Turner ... London, Whittaker and co. (etc.) 1842.   2 p. l., 144 p. front., plates, plan, fold. geneal. tab. 23½ cm. 20-20254.
                                                               DA690.C13T8

13125   PASTON.   Account of a manuscript genealogy of the Paston family, in the possession of His Grace, the Duke of Newcastle, communicated to the Norfolk and Norwich archaeological society, by Francis Worship, esq.   Norwich, Printed by C. Muskett, 1852.   1 p. l., 55 p. front. (coat of arms) geneal. tab.
32 cm. Published also in Norfolk archaeology ... Norwich, 1855, vol. IV, p. 1-55. 20-15240.
                                                               CS439.P295

          PASTON.   See also CALL, 1920

          PASTON-COOPER.   See GUERIN, 1890.

13126   PASTORIUS.   The life of Francis Daniel Pastorius, the founder of Germantown, illustrated with ninety photographic reproductions, by Marion Dexter Learned ... with an appreciation of Pastorius by Samuel Whitaker Pennypacker ... Philadelphia, W. J. Campbell, 1908.   x, 324 p. front., plates, fold. map,
facsims. 25½ cm. "Only 1000 copies of this work have been printed." This copy not numbered. Ancestors: p. 1-49. 8-30517.
                                                               F152.L43

13127   PASTORIUS.   One line of the Pastorius family of Germantown, Pennsylvania, and its intermarriages, including notes on the families of Antes, Levering, Lincoln, Lucken, Shoemaker, Stark, Tyson, Wilson, Wolf and Wunder, by S. Foster Damon.   Cambridge, Mass., 1926.   2 p. l., 22 numb. 1.
28 cm. Autographed from type-written copy. 26-9531.   CS71.P292   1926

13128   PASTOUR DE COSTEBELLE.   Un colonial sous Louis XIV, Philippe de Pastour de Costebelle, gouverneur de Terr-neuve puis de l'île Royale, 1661-1717, par Robert Le Blant.   Dax, P. Bradeu,
1935.   256 p., 1 l. 25 cm. Imprint on cover: Paris, A. Margraff; Dax, P. Pradeu. 36-11402.   F1123.C67

13129   PATE.   Pate, Adams, Newton, and allied families principally in Richmond, Scotland and Robeson Counties in North Carolina and Marlboro County, South Carolina.   By Julia Claire Pate.   Red Springs, N. C., 1958.   153 l. illus. 29 cm. 58-47837.   CS71.P3   1958

13130   PATE.   The American geneology (sic) of the Pate family from their landing in Virginia, 1650, to the present time in our line of descent; including a sketch of their origin and history in England, back to the fifteenth century, with a description of the Pate coat of arms.   By John Ben Pate. Amboy, Ga. (19 -)   21 p. 17 cm. 61-42481.   CS71. P3

PATERSON.   See PATTERSON.

13130a PATMORE.   Portrait of my family, 1783-1896, by Derek Patmore.   New York and London, Harper & brothers, 1935.   x p., 2 l., 270 p., 1 l. front., pl., ports. 22½ cm. "A ... portrait of Coventry Patmore, set against the background of his family." - p. 4.   "First edition."   35-22363.   PR5143. P35

PATRICKSON.   See STORY, 1920

13131   PATRIZI.   The Patrizi memoirs; a Roman family under Napoleon, 1796-1815;   By Maddalena (Gondi) marchesa Patrizi-Naro-Montoro.   Tr. by Mrs. Hugh Crawford Fraser. New York, Brentano's, 1915.   xv, 327 p. plates, ports. 23 cm. 48-39393*.

DG812.7.P3   1915a

PATTEE.   See CORLISS, 1875

13132   PATTEN.   Patten genealogy.   William Patten of Cambridge, 1635, and his descendants, by Thomas W. Baldwin ... Boston, T. W. Baldwin, 1908.   5 p. l., 290 p. map, fold. facsim. 24½ cm. 8-30519.
CS71. P316   1908

13133   PATTEN.   Patten, Buchanan and allied families, a genealogical study with biographical notes, compiled and privately printed for Mrs. James A. Patten, by the American historical society, inc. New York, 1934.   216 p. plates, ports., col. coats of arms, geneal. tables (part col.) 33 cm. Title-page and dedication in colors. Includes bibliographical references.   35-14011 rev.   CS71. P316   1934
Office.

13134   PATTEN.   The Patten families; genealogies of the Pattens from the north of Ireland, usually called "Scotch-Irish", with some branches of English ancestry settling in Maine and New Hampshire, by Howard Parker Moore ... Ann Arbor, Mich., Edwards brothers, inc., 1939.   ix, 194 p. incl. illus. (incl. ports., maps, facsims., coat of arms) geneal. tables. 28 cm. Lithoprinted. "Of this book there have been printed 150 copies only." 39-32996.   CS71. P316   1939

13135   PATTEN.   The ancestry of James Patten, 1747? - 1817, of Arundel (Kennebunkport) Maine, by Walter Goodwin Davis.   Portland, Me., The Southworth-Anthoensen press, 1941.   xii, 113 p. 23 cm. Includes the Johnston family.   41-14798.   CS71. P316   1941

PATTEN.   See also: MANLEY, 1938
                              PETTY, BX5195. T5B6
                              STANTON, 1922
                              STONE, 1930

13136   PATTERSON.   A record of the families of Robert Patterson (the elder), emigrant from Ireland to America, 1774; Thomas Ewing, from Ireland, 1718; and Louis Du Bois, from France, 1660; connected by the marriage of Uriah Du Bois with Martha Patterson, 1798.   Part first containing the Patterson lineage ... (Philadelphia) Press of J. C. Clark, 1847.   iv, 5-103 p. 24½ cm. Edition of one hundred and fifty copies; printed for the use of the family conexion only.   Introduction signed: William Ewing Du Bois.   25-2337.
CS71. P317   1847

13137   PATTERSON.   The birthplace and parentage of William Paterson, founder of the Bank of England, and projector of the Darien scheme: with suggestions for improvements on the Scottish registers.   By William Pagan ... Edinburgh, W. P. Nimmo, 1865.   3 p. l., 146 p. 18½ cm. 10-10269.
HG2994. P2

13138   PATTERSON.   The life of John Paterson, major general in the Revolutionary army; by his great-grandson, Thomas Egleston ... New York, London, G. P. Putnam's sons, 1894.   xi, 293 p. front. (port.) plates, 9 maps. VI geneal. tab. 25 cm.   Appendix: The Paterson families.   "List of books and manuscripts from which information has been obtained": p. 274-276.   12-20366.   E207. P3E3

13139   PATTERSON.   Concerning the forefathers; being a memoir, with personal narrative and letters of two pioneers, Col. Robert Patterson and Col. John Johnston, the paternal and maternal grand fathers of John Henry Patterson of Dayton, Ohio, for whose children this book is written by Charlotte Reeve Conover.   (1st ed.)   (New York, The Winthrop press, c. 1902)   xviii, 432, (20) p. col. front., illus., plates, ports., maps, facsims. (1 col.) 28½ x 18½ cm. Ornamental t. - p. Limited edition of 1, 000 numbered and registered copies. This copy not numbered.   3-18202.
CS71. P317   1902

13140   PATTERSON.   The Patterson family, a geneological (!) history, compiled by Robert A. Patterson.   (Carrollton, O., Press of The Chronicle, 1909)   1 p. 1., 18 p. 15½ cm. 25-19243.
CS71. P317   1909

13141   PATTERSON.   Patterson genealogy; descendants of John Patterson of Argylshire, Scotland, comp. by Guy S. Rix.   Concord, N. H., 1914.   9. (1) p. 23 cm. 16-14525.   CS71. P317   1914

13142   PATTERSON.   Ancestry and descendants of William Patterson of Vershire, Vermont.   By Lewis C. Patterson.   n. p. 1917.   603 p. Typewritten.   CS71. P317   1917

13143   PATTERSON.   James Patterson of Conestoga manor and his descendants, compiled and edited by Edmund Hayes Bell and Mary Hall Colwell.   Lancaster, Pa., Wickersham printing company, 1925.   x p., 2 1., (3)-314 p. front., plates. ports., maps. facsims. (1 fold.) 25½ cm. 25-7307.   CS71. P317   1925

13144   PATTERSON.   Genealogy of the Patterson, Wheat and Hearn families, by Rowena Emmeline Hearn Randle ... Richmond, Ind., G. O. Ballinger co., 1926.   259 (2) p. front., ports. 23½ cm. Contains blank pages for "Record". 26-5985.
CS71. P317   1926

13145   PATTERSON.   Pattison, Frink and allied families, genealogical and biographical; prepared and privately printed for Grace E. Pattison, by the American historical society, inc.   New York, 1929.   177 p. ports., col. coats of arms. 30 cm. Versos blank. Coats of arms accompanied by guard sheets with descriptive letter-press. Allied families: Thayer. Mather. Lay and Brewster   Dedication signed: Grace E. Pattison.   30-11220 rev. 2.
CS71. P317   1929

13146   PATTERSON.   Patterson-Piggott family of St. Louis County, Missouri.   By Carl William Veale.   Los Angeles, 1947.   5 1. 27 cm. Includes also the Veale family. "Lists the descendants of William & Asenath (Piggott) Patterson."   48-19707 rev. *
CS71. P317   1947

13147   PATTERSON.   An informal history of Virginia-Kentucky Pattesons in Illinois, their forbears and their kin including the Lewises of Llangollen.   By Ethel Marion Smith.   (Washington, 1948)   vi, 208 1. plates. ports. 29 cm. 48-25908*.
CS71. P317   1948

13148   PATTERSON.   The Zacheus Patterson descendants, together with those of the following related families of George Gundry, Selden Bennett, Platt Johnson, Martin Van Sickle, Ezekiel Solomon (and) Benson Hunt.   By Eldon P. Gundry.   Flint, Mich., Artcraft Press, 1957.   270 p. ports., geneal. tables. 22 cm.   57-42221.
CS71. P317   1957

13149   PATTERSON.   Permelia Richardson Patterson.   This is your life.   By Mrs. Alfred R. Boyd.   Excerpt from The Leader. Roanoke. Alabama (newspaper). August 13. 1959. In vertical file. Ask reference librarian for this material.

13150   PATTERSON.   Graham Patterson of Portage, New York; his ancestry and descendants.   By Norman George Patterson.   (Minneapolis?) 1961.   53 1. 29 cm. 61-40564.
CS71. P317   1961

13151   PATTERSON.   The Patterson clan.   By Melvin Patterson.   Leon R. Patterson, supporter of the project.   (n. p., 1961)   43 p. illus. 34 cm. 63-39428.   CS71. P317   1961a

13152   PATTERSON.   The Patterson & Pattison Family Association; a contribution of various Patterson and Pattison family records compiled to aid others in their genealogical research on these families as well as for those who spell the name in other ways.   (Minneapolis?) 1963 -
v. (loose-leaf) geneal. tables, map. 29 cm. Title on label on cover: Record book. Corr. in ms. 65-4350.   CS71. P317   1963

PATTERSON. See also:

AGNEW, 1926
CAMPBELL, 1935
DRIVER, 1889
ESPENSCHIED, 1949

GORDON, PR4433.A65
GRAHAM, 1947a
HARRISON, F497.H5H5
McDILL, PN4899.C4T83

MAJOR, 1915
MOUNSEY, 1947
STANTON, 1922
WOOD, 1909

PATTESON. See PATTERSON.

PATTISON. See PATTERSON.

13153   PATTON. Tombstone inscriptions of Cherry Fork Cemetery, Adams County, Ohio, and genealogical gleanings, compiled by Lillian Colletta and Leslie E. Puckett. Denville, N.J., 1964. viii, 91 p. illus., map. 28 cm. 65-3529.   F499.C38C6

13154   PATTON. Patton and allied families. By Rose Owen (McDavid) Munger. (n.p., c.1958) 85 p. illus., ports. 24 cm. 64-3491.   CS71.P319   1958

13155   PATTON. A chronicle of the American lineage of the Pattons. By Charles Lanphier Patton. (Springfield? Ill.) c.1954.   198 p. illus. 28 cm. 54-31957.   CS71.P319   1954

13156   PATTON. Patton family.   E207.M5G6

PATTON. See also: DINWIDDIE, 1957
ECHOLS, 1956
HIGHLAND, 1926
HIGHLAND, 1936
HOWE, 1961

13157   PAUGH. Garrett county history of the Paugh family, by Charles E. Hoye. (Oakland? Md.,
1936)   mounted l. 48 cm. Probably reprinted from the Mountain democrat. 41M3030T.
CS71.P323   1936

13158   PAUL. ... Family register of Richard Paul, born in England and emigated to America during the early part of 1635. Also of his descendants as far as ascertained. Traced by Dea. Luther Paul of Newton, Mass., the sixth generation, Fulton Paul, Hudson, New York, and Martha C. Crane of Dedham, Mass., of the eighth generation. (n.p., 1896)   7 geneal. tables. 24 x 33 cm. Caption title. At head of title: This sheet corrected to August, 1895. Manuscript corrections to February, 1907. 9-30704.
CS71.P324   1896

13159   PAUL. The ancestry of Katharine Choate Paul, now Mrs. William J. Young, jr.   Compiled by Edward Joy Paul ... Milwaukee, Burdick & Allen, 1914.   10 p. l., (15)-386 p. 2 port. (incl. front.) 27 cm. This volume is number 46. "References to the sources of information": p. (317)-346. Bibliography: p. (347)-373. 15-13192.
CS71.P324   1914

13160   PAUL. ... Paull-Irwin; a family sketch, by Elisabeth Maxwell Paull. (Boston, T. R. Marvin & son, printers) Priv. print., 1915.   viii, 198 p. front., plates, ports. 24 cm. "One hundred copies printed." "Admiral John Paul Jones": p. 1-21. 15-18260.   CS71.P324   1915

13161   PAUL. The descendants of Henry and Susannah Paul. (Huntington, Ind., 1917)   1 p. l., 68 p.
30 cm. Caption title. Text parallel with back of cover, and in form of genealogical table. Introductory remarks signed: Herman Taylor.
19-14510.   CS71.P324   1917

13162   PAUL. Joseph Paull of Ilminster, Somerset, England and some of his descendants who have resided in Philadelphia, Penn., by Henry N. Paul. (Philadelphia) 1933.   157 p. front., illus. (plan) 23½ cm.
39-16927.   CS71.P324   1933

13163   PAUL. ... Paull-Irwin, a family sketch by Elisabeth Maxwell Paull. Enl. ed., indexed. (Baltimore, Md., Printed by N. T. A. Munder) 1936.   268 p. incl. front. plates, ports. 25½ cm. "Privately printed, 1915, 1936." Coat of arms on cover. "Admiral John Paul 'Jones' ": p. (11)-37. Includes bibliography. 37-5912.
CS71.P324   1936

13164   PAUL.   Remembranzas de familia (bosquejos biográficos) por Guillermo Vargas Paúl. (Bogotá, Editorial Minerva limitada) 1945.   4 p. l., (7)-237 p., 1 l. plates, ports., coat of arms. 19 cm. Cover-title: Los Paul en America (remembranzas de familia) Includes bibliographies. 47-18709.   CS329.P3   1945

13165   PAUL.   Paul family record, 1763-1963.   Compiled and edited by Lawrence W. Shultz with the aid of many members of the Paul family.   Including the 1917 record of the descendents of Henry and Susannah Brumbaugh Paul of Martinsburg, Pennsylvania; and one earlier generation of Daniel Paulus; and the data of generations since 1917, edited by Herman Taylor.   Winona Lake, Ind., Printed by the Light and Life Press, 1963.   307 p. illus. 29 cm. 63-5253.   CS71.P324   1963

PAUL.   See also: HALLOWELL, 1924
KINSOLVING, 1935
LLOYD, 1912
TORRENCE, 1894

PAULDING.   See: GRINNELL, 1913
TREMAN, 1901

13166   PAULET.   An architectural memoir of Old Basing church, Hants, by the Rev. Reginald A. Cayley, M.A., the armorials and monuments of the Paulet family, dukes of Bolton, and marquesses of Winchester, by S. James A. Salter ... Basingstoke, Printed by C. J. Jacob, 1891.   24 p. 21½ cm. 18-12300.   NA5471.B25C3

13167   PAULETT.   The father of representative government in America.   (By William Robertson Garrett) (Nashville? Tenn., 189-?)   31 p. pl., port. 21 cm. Caption title. Cover-title: History of the first legislative assembly ever convened in America. Signed: W. R. Garrett ... Nashville, Tenn. An account of the Virginia assembly of 1619. Also published with cover-title: The Paulett family. Includes mention of a few members of the Paulett family. 22-24429.   F229.G233

13168   PAULLIN.   The Paullin family of southern New Jersey, by Charles O. Paullin.   Washington, D.C., Mimeoform press, 1933.   cover-title, 4 p. 28 cm. 33-14350.   CS71.P33   1933

13169   PAULLIN.   The Paullin family of southern New Jersey.   By Elmer Garfield Van Name. (Haddonfield? N.J.) 1958.   31 p. 23 cm. 78-225538 MARC.   CS71.P33   1958

13170   PAVEY.   The Pavey family of Ohio, history and genealogy, by Charles C. Pavey ... (New York, 1940)   2 v. 29 cm. Type-written. "Preliminary statement" signed: Mary S. Pavey, Frank D. Pavey. Includes also the Stafford, Adams, Calloway, Wallace, Weir and Brooks families.   Contents. - 1. The Isaac Pavey family. - II. The Jesse Pavey family. 41-4996.   CS71.P335   1940

PAWAR.   See PUAR.

13171   PAWLING.   Henry Pawling and some of his descendants.   By Mrs. Katherine (Wallace) Kitts. Sharon Hill, Delaware County, Pa., 1903.   46 p. 23 cm. 19-20219.   CS71.P34   1903

13172   PAWLING.   Pawling genealogy, by Albert Schoch Pawling.   Lewisburg, Pa., 1905. 84 p. front. (port.) 22 cm. 6-20.   CS71.P34   1905

13173   PAWLING.   ... Some account of the Pawling family of New York and Pennsylvania.   Contributed by Josiah Granville Leach.   (In Genealogical society of Pennsylvania. Publications. Philadelphia, 1920. 25 cm. v.7, p. 1-25) 21-8411.   F146.G32   vol.7

PAWLING.   See also: BURHANS, 1894
VAN DEUSEN, 1947

13174   PAXSON.   Genealogical data of the Paxson, Harding, and allied families, copied by Henry W. Scarborough, from a notebook kept by Hugh P. Paxson.   (Philadelphia, 1923)   8 l. 34 cm. Type-written. 23-2855.   CS71.P3418   1923

13175   PAXTON.   The Paxtons: their origin in Scotland, and their migrations through England and Ireland, to the colony of Pennsylvania, whence they moved South and West, and found homes in many states and territories ... By W. M. Paxton ... Platte City, Mo., Landmark print, 1903.   3 p. 1., 420, 65 p. plates (1 col.) ports. 23½ cm. 3-17939.   CS71.P342   1903

13176   PAY.   Pay-Goble pioneers of Nephi, Juab County, Utah.   This is a historical, biographical and genealogical account of Richard Pay, 1821-1893, and Mary Goble, 1843-1913 ... Compiled in 1968 by Arthur D. Coleman.   Salt Lake City, Utah, 1968.   xlviii, 150 1. 22 cm. 68-55592.
                                                                                                 CS71.P343   1968

13177   PAYNE.   Ancestors and descendants of James Payne of Pomfret, Conn., and Hauppauge, L. I. (by) Sarah C. P. Smith (and) Margretta C. Payne ... (Northport, N. Y., Printed by Northport observer, 1932)   80 p. illus. (incl. port.) 23½ cm.   Blank pages throughout text for "Memoranda". 35-14012.
                                                                                                 CS71.P146   1932

13178   PAYNE.   The Paynes of Virginia, by Brooke Payne ... Richmond, Va., The William Byrd press, inc., 1937.   ix p., 3 1., 3-543, (5) p. fold. diagr. 23 ½ cm.   Blank pages for "Additions and corrections" (5 at end) "Authorities consulted": p. 38-39. 37-37566.   CS71.P146   1937a

13179   PAYNE.   Family tree of George Payne (1778-1856) of Porter, Gallia County, Ohio.   By J. Barton Payne.   Wheaton College, Ill., 1960.   geneal. tables. In vertical file. Ask reference librarian for this material.

          PAYNE.   See also: BAX, 1936   LINDLEY, 1950
                                 BEAL, 1956   SMITH, 1878a
                                 GALCERÁN DE PINÓS, 1915   WAY, 1914
                                 LEWIS, 1901

13180   PAYNELL.   Historical details of the ancient religious community of secular canons in York prior to the conquest of England ... with biographical notices of the founder, Ralph Paynell, and of his descendants, of whom William Paynell, his eldest son, founded the priory of Drax.   By Thomas Stapleton.   (London, 1847)   231 p. 2 plates. 23 cm.   (Royal archaeological institute of Gt. Brit. and Ire.   Memoirs illustrative of the hist. and antiq. of York. v.1)   DA20. R382 vol. 1

13181   PAYSON.   Payson (genealogy) By Frank Barrows Freyer.   Denver, 1939.   geneal. table. 41 x 30 cm. fold. to 30 x 20 cm.   Photocopy (positive) 50-44079.   CS71.P344   1939

          PAYSON.   See also USHER, 1923

          PAYTON.   See PEYTON.

13182   PAYZANT.   In vertical file.   Ask reference librarian for this material.

13183   PEABODY.   A genealogy of the Peabody family, as compiled by the late C. M. Endicott, of Salem.   Revised and corrected by William S. Peabody, of Boston.   With a partial record of the Rhode Island branch by B. Frank Pabodie, of Providence ... Boston, D. Clapp & son, 1867.   2 p. 1., 60, (1) p. illus., col. pl. (coat of arms) 24 cm. 1-22228.   CS71.P35   1867

13184   PEABODY.   Elizabeth (Alden) Pabodie and descendants.   By Mrs. Charles L. Alden ... Salem, E. Putnam, 1897.   125 p. 23½ cm. 24-8611.   CS71.P35   1897

13185   PEABODY.   A genealogy of the descendants of Moses and Hannah (Foster) Peabody; giving the line of descent from the first settler and following the descent through both men and women to the eleventh generation; comp. by Mary Ellen Perley.   Salem, Mass., Newcomb & Gauss, printers, 1904.   47 p. 23½ cm. 5-13011.   CS71.P35   1904

13186   PEABODY.   Peabody (Paybody, Pabody Pabodie) genealogy.   Comp. by Selim Hobart Peabody ... Ed. by Charles Henry Pope.   Boston, Mass., Charles H. Pope, 1909.   (iii)-xvii, 396 p. front., plates, ports., facsims. 24 cm. 10-18019.   CS71.P35   1909

13187   PEABODY.   The ancestry of Franklin Merriam Peabody, collected and made into this book as a mark of the affection of his grandfather Franklin Asbury Merriam, compiled by Sidney Augustus Merriam ... Sickels ancestry by William Jones ... (Salem, Mass., Newcomb & Gauss co., printers) 1929.   136 p., 1 l. front., ports. 24 cm.   30-9802.   CS71.P35   1929

13188   PEABODY.   The Peabody sisters of Salem.   By Louise (Hall) Tharp.   (1st ed.)   Boston, Little, Brown, 1950.   x, 372 p. illus., ports. 23 cm.   "Sources and acknowledgments": p. 357-358.   49-49265*.
CS71.P35   1949

13189   PEABODY.   Captain Joseph Peabody; East India merchant of Salem (1757-1844) A record of his ships and of this family, compiled by William Crowninshield Endicott.   Edited and completed, with a sketch of Joseph Peabody's life, by Walter Muir Whitehill.   Salem (Mass.) Peabody Museum, 1962.   xv, 358 p. illus., ports. 26 cm.   Bibliographical footnotes.   63-5009.   CS71.P35   1962

13190   PEABODY.   The Peabody influence; how a great New England family helped to build America, by Edwin P. Hoyt.   New York, Dodd, Mead (1968)   xvi, 302 p. illus., ports. 24 cm. Bibliography: p. 293-294.   68-57197.   CS71.P35   1968

       PEABODY.   See also: GENTRY, 1909
                              VAN NOSTRAND, E171.A53 v.19
                              WILLARD, 1915a

       PEACH.   See CLEAVER, CS439.C655

13191   PEACHY.   A memorial history of Peter Bitsche, and a complete family register of his lineal descendants and those related to him by intermarriage, from 1767 to 1892.   Chronologically arranged.   With an appendix of those not received in time for their proper place.   By Samuel M. Peachey ... Lancaster, Pa., J. Baer's sons, printers, 1892.   205 p. 17½ cm.   9-7290.   CS71.B634   1892

13192   PEACOCK.   The family history and the lineage of Peacock from England to America, 1835 (by) Gertrude W. Lundberg.   (Glenview? Ill., 1966)   34 l. illus., ports. 31 cm.   66-59147.
CS71.P357   1966

       PEARCE.   See PIERCE.
                 RIX, 1957

13193   PEARL.   Some of John Pearl's descendants, by Alice Heath (Fairbanks) Dow.   Detroit, Printed by W. C. Heath (1901?)   1 p. l., 33 p. 2 front. (port.) pl. 23½ cm.   3-4174.   CS71.P36   1901

       PEARL.   See also: GILMORE, 1925
                            LEONARD, 1928

       PEARMAN.   See MITCHELL, 1967 b

13194   PEARSALL.   History and genealogy of the Pearsall family in England and America.   Clarence E. Pearsall, editor; Hettie May Pearsall, assistant editor;   Harry L. Neall, associate genealogist and historian ... (San Francisco, Printed by H. S. Crocker company, inc.) 1928.   3 v. illus., plates (part fold., incl. music) ports., maps (part fold.) facsims. (part fold.) coats of arms (1 mounted col.) 26 cm.   Paged continuously.   30-10228.
CS71.P3615   1928

13195   PEARSON.   Genealogical records of the pioneer families of Avon, N.Y. Pierson, Waterous, Hosmer, Martin, etc., and their descendants.   Committee: Judge John Pierson ... W. H. C. Hosmer ... S. Amanda Whitbeck ... Rochester, N.Y., Express printing house, 1871.   cover-title, 32 p. 22½ cm. Includes reports of annual meetings of descendants of early settlers, 1864-1870.   7-22428.   F129.A96G3

13196   PEARSON.   Pierson genealogical records, collected and compiled by Lizzie B. Pierson ... Albany, J. Munsell, 1878.   vii, (8)-104 p. front. 24 cm.   9-12849.
CS71.P362   1878

13197   PEARSON.   The descendants of Stephen Pierson of Suffolk county, England, and New Haven and Derby, Conn.   1645-1739.   By Frederick Lockwood Pierson ... Amenia, N.Y., Walsh & Griffen, 1895.
1 p. l., 33 p. front. (port.) 25 cm. 1-13552.   CS71.P362   1895

13198   PEARSON.   A tribute, by Cora Pierson Hopkins.   Topeka, Kan., Crane & company, 1913.
4 p. l., 11-71 p. front., illus. 19½ cm.   A history of the settlement, in this county, of Abraham Pierson the first and second, with some genealogical data.   16-2756.   CS71.P362   1913

13199   PEARSON.   The Peirson family in Wayne County, New York.   With early history of the family pre-dating the Wayne County arrival.   1638-1916.   Compiled and written by S. S. Peirson, of the eighth generation, Newark, New York.   Newark, N.Y., Printed by Arcadia advertising co., 1917.
2 p. l., 7-115 p. front. (col. coat of arms) illus. (incl. ports.) fold. geneal. tab. 23 cm. 17-19213.   CS71.P362   1917

13200   PEARSON.   Crispin Pearson of Bucks county, Pennsylvania, 1748-1806; a genealogy compiled and published by Annie Pearson Darrow, edited by William C. Armstrong.   New Brunswick, N.J., J. Heidingsfeld company, 1932.   166 p. front., plates, ports., fold. map. 24 cm. Bibliography: p. 158-159. 32-34836.
                                                                                                                  CS71.P362   1932

13201   PEARSON.   Chronicles of the Pearson, Roscoe and Raiford families, compiled by Josephine A. Pearson.   (n.p.) 1938.   26 l. 3 col. coats of arms. 30 cm. "Type-written (carbon copy) "Sketch of Rev. Philip A. Pearson":
4th - 11th leaves. 40-37509.   CS71.P362   1938

13202   PEARSON.   Benjamin and Esther (Furnas) Pearson, their ancestors and descendants, compiled and edited by Geo. M. Pearson ... Los Angeles, Calif., Times-mirror printing & binding house, 1941.
3 p. l., 538 p. front., illus. (maps) pl., ports. 24 cm. 41-25785.   CS71.P362   1941

13203   PEARSON.   Genealogy (of) the Pierson family, the Marsh family, the Clark family (and) the Baker family. By Arthur Newton Pierson.   (n.p.) 1945.   (33) l. plates, map, geneal. tables. 28 cm. 49-38077*.
                                                                                                                  CS71.P362   1945

         PEARSON.   See also:

             BACKHOUSE, CS439.B18   LLOYD, 1912   POUND, 1904
             BEWLEY, 1946a   MILWARD, CS439.M53   SAGE, 1908
             HEATH, 1914   MULFORD, 1920   SCRIPPS, CS439.S25
             HUNTER, 1934   PEDEN, 1961   STOUT, 1960

13204   PEASE.   An account of the descendants of John Pease, who landed at Martha's Vineyard in the year 1632.   By Frederick S. Pease ... Albany, Printed by J. Munsell, 1847.   vi, (7)-52 p. illus. (coat of arms) 21 cm. 9-12851.   CS71.P363   1847

13205   PEASE.   The early history of the Pease families in America.   By Austin Spencer Pease. Springfield, Mass., S. Bowles & co., printers, 1869.   v, (2), 102 p. front., illus. (coat of arms) ports. 24 cm. 9-12850.   CS71.P363   1869

13206   PEASE.   The early history of the Pease families in America.   By Austin Spencer Pease. Springfield, Mass., S. Bowles & co., printers, 1869.   v, (2), 102 p. front., illus. (coat of arms) ports. 24 cm. 9-12850 rev.   CS71.P363   1869
         —— Copy 2.   (With Pease, David. A genealogical and historical record of the descendants of John Pease ... 1869 pt. 11)
                                                                                                                  CS71.P363   1869a

13207   PEASE.   A genealogical and historical record of the descendants of John Pease, sen., last of Enfield, Conn., compiled by Rev. David Pease and Austin S. Pease ... Springfield, Mass., S. Bowles & company, printers, 1869.   xxiv, 401, (1) p. front., ports. 24 cm. With this is bound, as part II, Pease, Austin Spencer. The early history of the Pease families in America ... Springfield, Mass., 1869. 24-16090.   CS71.P363   1869a

13208   PEASE.   The Pease family, Essex-York-Durham, 10 Henry VII to 35 Victoria (by) Joseph Foster, 1871, Charles Pease, 1872.   Darlington, Printed for private circulation by J. H. Bell, 1872

13208 continued. (8) l. 14 geneal. tab. 24 x 31 cm. Title vignette (coat of arms) Interspersed with blank leaves. Printed on one side of leaf only. The Peases of Essex and of Sikehouse and Fishlake, comp. by Joseph Foster, 1871; The Peases of Darlington, comp. by Charles Pease, 1872. 20-23950.

CS439. P33

13209 PEASE. Albert S. Pease, selections from his poems, with an autobiography and a genealogy of his descendants. New York, J. T. White & co., 1915. (117) p. front., ports. 20½ cm. 16-4597.

PS2539. P237 1915

PEASE. See also: ROBSON, 1892
SMITH, 1878a
WILSON, 1890
WOOD, 1937

13210 PEASLEE. History of the Peaslee, Balch, Stonebraker family. Who, as pioneers, settled in the great woods of New York in 1838; the treeless prairies of Iowa Territory in 1844, and on the Sac and Fox reserve, Kansas, in 1870. Taken from a book on Osage County history, entitled, "Annals of Lyndon," by Charles R. Green ... Lyndon, Kan., 1897. 12, (1) p. 13 cm. Edition limited to 50 copies. 11-30211.

CS71. P364 1897

13211 PEASLEE. The Peaslees and others of Haverhill and vicinity. By E. A. Kimball. Haverhill, Mass., Chase bros., 1899. 72 p. front., plates 25 cm. Aug. 17, 99-53. CS71. P364 1899

13212 PEASLEY. The Paslay genealogy. By Robert Buckingham Paslay. (Spartanburg? S. C., 1956) 21 l. 36 cm. 56-34664. CS71. P365 1956

13213 PEASLEY. Peasley family in vertical file. Ask reference librarian for this material.

13214 PACHENIK. The Pechenik family; a genealogy of Dovid Hennoch Pechenik and his descendants and remembrances of life in Eastern Europe. By Ralph Selitzer. (1st ed.) Passaic, N.J., Cameo Print. Co. (1969) 62 p. illus., geneal. tables, col. maps (on lining paper), ports. 27 x 32 cm. "Limited to 250 numbered copies of which this is number 93." Bibliography: p.5. 73-98500 MARC. CS71. P366 1969

13215 PECK. A genealogical history of the descendants of Joseph Peck, who emigrated with his family to this country in 1638; and records of his father's and grandfather's families in England; with the pedigree extending back from son to father for twenty generations; with their coat of arms, and copies of wills. Also, an appendix, giving an account of the Boston and Hingham Pecks ... By Ira B. Peck. Boston, Printed by A. Mudge & son, 1868. 1 p. l., 442 p. front., 2 pl. (incl. col. coat of arms) ports., fold. geneal. tab. 24 cm. 14-20033. CS71. P367 1868

13216 PECK. A genealogical account of the descendants in the male line of William Peck, one of the founders in 1638 of the colony of New Haven, Conn. By Darius Peck. Hudson, Bryan & Goeltz, printers, 1877. 253 p. front. (port.) 23½ cm. 2-22146 rev. CS71. P367 1877
——— Appendix by John Hudson Peck, (2628), to genealogy of the descendants of William Peck of New Haven, Conn., by Hon. Darius Peck. (1363). (Troy? N.Y., 1896?) xv p. 24 cm. (With Peck, Darius. A genealogical account of the descendants in the male line of William Peck. Hudson, 1877) "Books cited": p. ii. 2-22146 rev.

CS71. P367 1877

13217 PECK. Appendix by John Hudson Peck, (2628), to genealogy of the descendants of William Peck of New Haven, Conn., by Hon. Darius Peck, (1363). (Troy? N.Y., 1896?) xv p. 24 cm. 6-22694.

CS71. P367 1877

13218 PECK. Luther Peck and his five sons, by Rev. J. K. Peck ... New York, Eaton & Mains; Cincinnati, Cuts & Jennings, 1897. 246 p. front., ports. 18½ cm. 12-37590.

BX8495. P44P4

13219 PECK. Peck family record, male and female lines. v. 1 - no. 1 -
Rome, N.Y., 1914 - v. 27 cm. 34-35346. CS71. P367 1914

13220   PECK.   Peck, Adams and allied families; genealogical and biographical.   Prepared and privately printed for Rebecca P. Dusenbery and Belle P. Bryant.   New York, The American historical society, inc., 1925.   3 p. l., 163 p. plates (1 col.) ports., facsims., geneal. tables, col. coats of arms. 32 cm.   Title within colored ornamental border.   Colored initials and tail-pieces.   Contains allied families of Walter Schuyler, Barclay, Loomis, Skinner, Washington, Cornell, Van Rensselaer and Schenck.   26-16558 rev. 2.
CS71.P367   1925

13221   PECK.   History of a distinctive family of Scranton and Lackawanna County, Pennsylvania, by S. Fletcher Weyburn ... Scranton, Pa.   (c.1929)   31 p. illus. (incl. ports.) 23 cm. (Lackawanna historical society. (Publication) Series no. 12)   "This history is not a genealogy of the Peck family, as such, but, rather, an historical record of a single branch of that large and influential family, particularly that of Rev. George Peck." - p.2 of cover.   Bibliography: p. 30.   29-22309.
F157.L15L24

—— Copy 2.   No. 12.
CS71.P367   1929

13222   PECK.   The book of Pecks.   By Herbert Watson Peck.   (Liverpool?) 1954.   viii, 232 p. illus., ports., coats of arms, facsims., geneal. tables.   29 cm.   500 copies printed.   57-38706.   CS439.P3356   1954

13223   PECK.   Genealogy of Joseph Peck and some related families, including the Bordens, the Fowles, the Winters, the Grovers, the Carpers, the Clays, the Chapmans, the Staffords, the McClures, the Meeks, the Molletts (and) the Osbornes.   By George Braden Roberts.   (States College, Pa.) c.1955.   344 p. illus. 29 cm. 55-4413.   CS71.P367   1955

13224   PECK.   Peck family in vertical file.   Ask reference librarian for this material.

PECK.   See also:

BASSETT, 1926	KENT, 1961	PAGE, 1911
HASKINS, 1911	KITCHEL, 1913	PARKER, 1892
HUMFREVILLE, 1903	LEWIS, 1900	SELLECK, 1912
JARRATT, 1957	LINDLEY, 1950	

PECKER.   See MORRILL, 1903

13225   PECKHAM.   Peckham genealogy: the English ancestors and American descendants of John Peckham of Newport, Rhode Island, 1630, by Stephen Farnum Peckham; assisted as to the English ancestry by Reverend Harry John Peckham and his son Arthur Nyton Peckham; assisted as to the American descendants by Byron J. Peckham.   New York, The National historical company (1922)   596 p. incl. front. (coat of arms) plates, ports., facsim. 24 cm.   Title-page illustrated in colors; most of plates printed on both sides.   22-19694.
CS71.P368   1922

13226   PECKHAM.   The Peckham tree grows, by Grace A. Sherman.   (Perry, N.Y., Comfort crafts-men) 1944.   44 p. illus. (incl. ports., coats of arms) 25 cm. 45-7078.   CS71.P368   1944

13227   PECKHAM.   Genealogy of one branch of the Peckham family of Newport and Westerly, R. I. and its allied families, compiled by William Perry and John Earle Bentley.   Documentary evidence by Emilie Sarter.   (Dallas? 1957?)   197 p. illus. 22 cm. 58-25429.   CS71.P3358   1957

13228   PECKHAM.   See also: KING, CS439.K7
KURTZ, 1925

13229   PEDDICORD.   Kelion Franklin Peddicord of Quirk's scouts, Morgan's Kentucky cavalry, C.S.A.; biographical and autobiographical, together with a general biographical outline of the Peddicord family, by Mrs. India W. P. Logan.   New York and Washington, The Neale publishing company, 1908.   170 p. 4 port. (incl. front.) 21 cm. 8-19229.   E605.P37

13230   PEDEN.   The Pedens of America; being a summary of the Peden, Alexander, Morton, Morrow reunion 1899, and an outline history of the ancestry and descendants of John Peden and Margaret McDill, Scotland, Ireland, America, 1768-1900 (by) Eleanor M. Hewell ... (n. p., 1900)   303 p. front., plates ports. 23½ cm. 15-5257.   CS71.P37   1900

13231   PEDEN.   The Pedens of America; an outline history of the ancestry and descendants of John Peden and Margaret McDill Peden: Scotland, Ireland, America (by) Eleanor M. Hewell (and others. Greenville? S.C., 1961)   654 p., illus.   24 cm.   60-13366.   CS71.P37   1961

PEDEN.   See also FOWLER, 1940

13232   PEDERSEN.   Descendants of John Oluf Pedersen.   By Edwin Volberg Johnson.   (Sarasota? Fla., 1954)   unpaged. 28 cm. 54-44776.   CS71.P3713   1954

13233   PEDERSEN.   The fruition of a Danish dream.   By Henry L. Peterson.   Wichita, Kan., Garman Print. & Lithograph, c.1960.   260 p. illus. 23 cm.   60-46104.   CS71.P3713   1960

13234   PEDERSEN.   Slaegten Pedersen fra Them Sogn.   Om Peder Andersen i Over Langkaer, født 1807, og hustru, deres forfaedre og efterkommere.   Nordisk slaegtsforskning.   Skals, Bredegaard, 1968.   (132) l. illus., facsim., ports. 30 cm. Four geneal. tables in plastic cover inserted. 75-421541.
                                                                                      CS919.P35   1968

PEDLER.   See PEDLAR.

13235   PEDRICK.   A genealogical and biographical record of the Pedrick family of New Jersey, 1675-1938, traced and assembled by Hubert B. Shoemaker ... (Philadelphia, Pa., Printed by Temple type-crafters, 1938)   xix, 314 p., 1 l., 315-341 p. incl. col. front. (coat of arms) 23½ cm. Pages (321) - (322) blank. 41-376.
                                                                                      CS71.P372   1938

PEDRICK.   See also BAVIS, 1880

13236   PEEBLES.   Peebles, ante 1600-1962, gathered and compiled by Anne Bradbury Peebles. (Fort Lauderdale? Fla.) J.H. Peebles (1962)   191 p. illus. 29 cm. 63-30266.   CS71.P3726   1962

13237   PEEBLES.   Robert Peebles from Ulster, 1718, Patrick of Pelham, Mass., 1738; some of their descendants, with some other Peebles.   Compiled by Leslie A. Peebles in collaboration with Mrs. E. G. (Thelma) Peebles.   (Marathon, N.Y.,   1964)   242, a-c p. illus. (part col.) coat of arms, facsims., maps, ports. 29 cm. Bibliography: p. 8-9. 66-34995.   CS71.P3726   1964

PEEBLES.   See also: COVINGTON, 1956
                      DAVIS, 1939

13238   PEEL.   The descendants of ... Robert Peel (1723-95), founder of the Lancashire cotton manu-facture.   Compiled by Joseph Foster.   London, Strangeways, printers (1893?)   2 fold. geneal. tab. illus. (coats of arms) 94 x 96 cm. fold. to 24 x 16 cm.   Contents. - chart I. The descendants of William and Edmund, sons of Robert Peel and The descendants of Sir Robert Peel, bart., 3rd son of Robert Peel. chart II. Descendants of Jonathan, 4th son of Robert Peel, and The descendants of Laurence, Joseph and John, sons of Robert Peel, together with the family of Joseph Peel of Fzeley, co. Staff. 24-2117.   CS439.P34

PEEL.   See also: FARMER, 1897
                   SAUNDERS, 1897

PEELE.   See PATE, 19 -

13239   PEEPLES.   Our Peeples family ("Just among ourselves") ... a genealogy of the descendants of William Peeples and wife Rebecca Johnson.   By Rachel Emmeline (Peeples) Rogers.   Atlanta, 1953. 154 l. 29 cm. 54-44844.   CS71.P373   1953

PEERSON.   See No. 5536 - Sloopers.

13240   PEFFLEY.   The Peffley - Peffly - Pefley families in American and allied families, 1729-1938; being a historical and genealogical record ... compiled, edited and published by Mary M. Frost and Earl C. Frost.   Los Angeles, Calif., 1938.   2 p. l., 7-245, xxx p. ports., map, facsim. 23½ cm. "Four hundred copies printed and numbered. This copy is number 86." 38-20788.   CS71.P375   1938

PEFFLY.   See PEFFLEY.

PEFLEY.   See PEFFLEY.

13241   PEIRCE.   The Peirce family of the old colony: or, The lineal descendants of Abraham Peirce ... By Ebenezer W. Peirce ... Boston, Printed for the author, D. Clapp & son, 1870.   xx, 490 p. pl. 24 cm.   3-3807.   CS71.P616   1870

13242   PEIRCE.   Contributions biographical, genealogical and historical.   By Ebenezer Weaver Peirce ... Boston, Printed for the author, by D. Clapp & son, 1874.   1 p. l., ix, 443 p. front., illus., pl. 24 cm. "List of families included in the 'Contributions': Barnaby, Bartlett, Booth, Brownell, Caswell, Gardiner, Godfrey, Harlow, Howland, Haskins, Macomber, Pearce, Richmond, Rogers, Rounsevill, Sheffield, Shelley, Warren, Weaver, Williams." 3-3804.   CS71.P616   1874

13243   PEIRCE.   Solomon Peirce family genealogy; containing a record of his descendants, also an Appendix containing the ancestry of Solomon Peirce and his wife Amity Fessenden.   Comp. and arranged by Marietta Peirce Bailey.   Arlington, Mass. (Boston, Press of G. H. Ellis co.) 1912. viii p., 1 l., 181 p. front. (port.) plates. 24½ cm. 13-5629.   CS71.P616   1912

13244   PEIRCE.   Genealogy of the family of Major Samuel Peirce, by George M. Buck.   Atlanta, Ga., Hubbard & Bolton company, 1916.   1 p. l., 5-74. (1) p. 21½ cm. 16-10694.   CS71.P616   1916

PEIRCE.   See also: PIERCE.
NICHOLS, 1967
No. 430 - Adventurers of purse and person.

PEIRET.   See SEBOR, 1923

13245   PEIRPOINT.   Lucy & Oliver, some West Virginia genealogy: Peirpoint, Smell, Jones, Fetty. By Alpheus Beede Stickney.   Pittsburgh, c. 1953.   86 l. geneal. table. 28 cm. Includes bibliographical references. 53-25012.   CS69.S8

PEIRSEY.   See No. 430 - Adventurers of purse and person.

13246   PELHAM.   Memoirs of the administration of the Right Honourable Henry Pelham, collected from the family papers, and other authentic documents.   By William Coxe ... London, Longman, Rees, Orme, Brown, and Green, 1829.   2 v. front. (ports.) geneal. tables. 28 cm. 4-34869.
DA501.P3C8

13247   PELHAM.   The house of Brocklesby, and other poems.   Dedicated to the Earl of Yarborough. By Robert Franklin ... Hull, Printed by S. Dibb & co., 1844.   vii, (1), 79, (1) p. 20½ cm. Contents. - The house of Brocklesby. - Lines on visiting Thornton Abbey. - The justice of the peace. - The village churchyard. - The village clerk. - Coronation ode. 20-11053.   PR4705.F72H7

13248   PELHAM.   Historical and genealogical notices of the Pelham family.   By Mark Antony Lower ... (n. p.) Priv. print., 1873.   2 p. l., 58 p. illus. 36 x 25 cm. 45-42265.   CS439.P347   1873

13249   PELHAM.   Herbert Pelham, his ancestors and descendants.   By Joseph Lemuel Chester, LL. D.   (Boston, 1879)   11 p. 25½ cm. Caption title. "Reprinted from the New England historical and genealogical register for July, 1879." 5-14692.   CS71.P382   1879

13250   PELL.   Pedigree of Pell of Walter Wellingsley Lincolnshire, Norfolk, and Pelham, Westchester County, N. Y. ... (n. p., 18 -)   geneal. tab. 61½ x 97 cm. fold. to 24½ x 15½ cm. Coat of arms. Autographed. 10-4375.   CS71.P385

13251   PELL.   The Pell manor; address prepared for the New York branch of the Order of colonial lords of manors in America, by Captain Howland Pell ... Baltimore, 1917.   20 p. incl. illus., pl. 23½ cm. (Order of colonial lords of manors in America.   New York branch.   Publications.   20-16022.   E186.99.O6N5
——— Copy 2.   F128.68.B8P38

13252   PELL.   Fort Ticonderoga in history, by Helen Ives Gilchrist ... (Ticonderoga? Printed for the Fort Ticonderoga museum (192-?)   101 p. incl. illus., plates, ports., maps, plan, facsim. front. 23 cm. "The Pell family and the restoration of Fort Ticonderoga": p. 98-99. Bibliography: p. 100-101. 24-17722.   E199.G46

13253   PELL.   Pelliana.   Pell of Pelham.   v. 1, no. 1-6?; n.s., v. 1 -   (n. p.) 1934.   v. illus.
facsims., ports. 23 cm.   Privately printed.   Vol. 1, no. 1 limited to 225 copies.   34-18222 rev.   CS71.P3845

13254   PELL.   A brief, but most complete & true account of the settlement of the ancient town of
Pelham, Westchester county, state of New York, known one time well & favourably as the Lordshipp
& mannour of Pelham, also the story of the three modern villages called the Pelhams, compiled by
Lockwood Barr ... Richmond, Va., The Dietz press, inc., 1946 (i.e. 1947)   4 p. 1., (vii)-xv, 28 p., 1 1.,
(29)-190 p. front., illus. (incl. coats of arms) plates, ports., maps (part fold.)   facsim., geneal. tables (1 fold.) 23½ cm.   Bibliography:
p. (166)-169.   47-3441.   F129.P38B3

PELL.   See also WHIPPLE, 1917

13255   PELLY.   The Pelly family in England, with a table of descent.   Ed. by Douglas Raymond
Pelly.   Printed for private circulation.   (n. p., 1912)   121 p.   front., ports., fold. geneal. tab.   25 cm.   Title
vignette: coat of arms.   "The greater part of this book is practically a transcript of mss. compiled by the late Miss Katherine Fry." - Pref.
17-21452.   CS439.P35

PELOT.   See BEVILLE, 1917

13256   PELOUBET.   Family records of Joseph Alexander de Chabrier de Peloubet, the first of the
name in the United States, with the funeral address of his eldest son L. M. F. Chabrier Peloubet, who
died Nov. 28, 1885.   (Rahway, N.J., The Mershon co. press) printed for the family, 1892.
37 p.   front., plates, facsims., coat of arms (col.) 24 cm.   Compiled by Joseph Peloubet.   9-18733.   CS71.P392   1892

13257   PELOUBET.   History of the Chabrier de Peloubet family.   Granslated by Alice Peloubet
Norton (and) Mrs. G. G. Phipps.   (n. p., 19 -)   43 1.   28 cm.   53-34072.   CS599.P4

13258   PELTON.   Genealogy of the Pelton family in America.   Being a record of the descendants of
John Pelton who settled in Boston, Mass., about 1630-1632, and died in Dorchester, Mass., January
23rd, 1681.   By J. M. Pelton.   Albany, N.Y., J. Munsell's sons, 1892.   1 p. 1., 722 p. front., pl. (coats of
arms) ports. 21½ cm.   9-12848.   CS71.P393   1892

PELTON.   See also THOMPSON, 1915

13259   PELTZ.   Peltz record, Rev. Philip Peltz, D.D., Reformed Protestant Dutch Church.   New
York, American Historical Co., 1948.   vii, 315, iii p.   illus., ports., maps, facsims. 24 cm.   On spine: Peltz, De Witt,
certain of their companies.   "De Witt record, Rev. John De Witt, D.D., Reformed Protestant Dutch Church": p. 221-315.   49-410 rev.*
                                                                        CS71.P3933   1948
———— De Witt-Peltz, a supplement ,.. New York, American Historical Co., 1950.
317-363, v p.   illus., ports. 24 cm.   CS71.P3933   1948
                                                                        Suppl.

13260   PEMBER.   John Pember, the history of the Pember family in America.   (By Mrs. Celeste
(Pember) Hazen)   (Springfield, Vt., c. 1939)   2 p. 1., 7-324 p., 1 1. 23 cm.   39-5238.   CS71.P3936   1939

13261   PEMBERTON.   The diary of John Pemberton, for the years 1777 and 1778.   Ed. from the
mss. in the possession of the society, by Eli K. Price.   A paper read before "The Numismatic and
antiquarian society of Philadelphia" ... July 5, 1866.   Philadelphia, H. B. Ashmead, printer, 1867.
14 p. 25 cm.   The "Diary" (p.(3)-5) is taken from ms. notes, made in "Poor Will's pocket almanack" in 1777 and 1778.   The remainder of the work
treats of Pemberton's ancestry, and of the banishment of Friends from Pennsylvania during the revolution.   3-15627.   E275.P39

13262   PEMBERTON.   The records of the Pemberton family.   Principally from "Memorials of the
city of Boston".   (Westerly, R. I.) 1890.   26 p. 20 cm.   Privately printed.   34-19795.
                                                                        CS71.P394   1890

13263   PEMBERTON.   The Pemberton family.   By Walter K. Watkins.   Boston, D. Clapp & son,
printers, 1892.   9 p. 24 cm.   "Reprinted from the N. E. historical and genealogical register for October, 1892, with additions and
corrections."   Imperfect: lacks portrait of Rev. Ebenezer Pemberton.   17-31803.   CS71.P394   1892

13264   PEMBERTON.   Notes on the Pemberton family, ancestors of Emilius Oviatt Randall.   By Miss Evelyn Rich ... (Columbus, O., 1898)   p. 113-118. 24½ cm. (With Ward, Harry Parker. Notes on the family of Ward ... (Columbus, O., 1898) Caption title.   Detached from The "Old northwest" genealogical quarterly, July 1898.   38M4087T
CS71.W26   1898

13265   PEMBERTON.   Pembertons of Nevis and St. Christopher.   (London, 1911)   32 p. 27 cm. Communicated by Major-General R. C. B. Pemberton.   Reprinted from Carribbeana, London, 1910-11. 27 cm.   v. 1, p. 266-272, 305-312, 337-344; v. 2, p. 33-40.   Coat of arms.   23-14001.
CS209.P4

PEMBERTON.   See also: ELLIS, F3.T61
                                          LLOYD, 1898
                                          MAXWELL, 1916

PEMBLETON.   See PENDLETON.

PEMBRUGGE.   See VERNON, 1924

13266   PENCE.   The history of Judge John Pence and descendants, born in Shenandoah County, Virginia, January 15, 1775.   Resided in Champaign County, Ohio, Bartholomew County, Indiana, and Henderson County, Illinois.   Compiled and published by Kingsley Adolphus Pence, his grandson ... Denver, Col., 1912.   126 p. incl. front. plates, ports., fold. geneal. tab. (in pocket) 23½ cm.   13-390.
CS71.P395   1912

13267   PENCE.   A history of Pence place names and early Pences in America, with genealogies. By Monroe Conger Pence.   Mountain View, Calif., c. 1961.   31 p. coat of arms. 23 cm. Cover title. Includes bibliographical references.   61-59722.
CS71.P395   1961

PENCE.   See also CRONE, 1916

13268   PENDARVIS.   The genealogy of the Pendarvis-Bedon families of South Carolina, 1670-1900, together with lineal ancestry of husbands and wives, who intermarried with them;   also references to many associated southern families.   Compiled by James Barnwell Heyward.   Atlanta, Ga., Foote & Davies company, 1905.   221 p. illus. (part col.) 26½ cm. 8-10317.   CS71.P397   1905

13269   PENDEREL.   The Boscobel tracts, relating to the escape of Charles the Second after the battle of Worcester and his subsequent adventures;   ed. by John Hughes ... 2d ed.   Edinburgh and London, W. Blackwood and sons, 1857.   5 p. l., 399 (1) p. incl. geneal. tables. 6 pl. (incl. front.) map, plan. 22 cm. Contents. - Introduction. - Diary, compiled by the editor - Extracts from Lord Clarendon. - Letter from a prisoner at Chester. - the king's narrative, ed. by Pepys. - Boscobel, pt. I-II (by Thomas Blount) - Mr. Whitgreave's narrative. - Mr. Ellesdon's letter. - Mrs. Anne Wyndham's "Claustrum regale reseratum." - (Genealogical) appendix: The Penderel and Yates families.   The Whitgreaves.   The family of Wyndham.   The family of Lane.   Col. Wm. Carlos pedigree.   3-26230.
DA446.H89

13270   PENDERGAST.   The story of a pioneer family, by A. W. Anderson ... Sponsored and published by Jamestown historical society.   (Jamestown, N. Y.) 1936.   1 p. l., 13 p. Nov. 8, 1938.
CS71.P398   1936

13271   PENDLETON.   Brian Pendleton and his descendants, 1590-1910, with some account of the Pembleton families of Orange County, N. Y., Otsego County, N. Y., and Luzerne County, Pa., and notices of other Pendletons of later origin in the United States, comp. by Everett Hall Pendleton. (East Orange? N. J.) Priv. print., 1910 (c. 1911)   3 p. l., v-x p., 1 l., 860 p. front., ports., map, facsims. 24 cm. Appendix XI: 8 blank pages inserted for the family records of later generations. 11-21183.   CS71.P399   1910

13272   PENDLETON.   Early New England Pendletons; with some account of the three groups who took the name Pembleton, and notices of other Pendletons of later origin in the United States.   By Everett Hall Pendleton.   (South Orange? N. J., 1956)   viii, 354 p. port., map, facsims. 25 cm. Bibliographical references included in "Appendix XI" (p. 294-337)   56-34876.   CS71.P399   1956

PENDLETON.   See also: CARD, E171.A53 v. 20   PAGE, 1893
                     DILLON, 1927   SCHOONMAKER, 1930
                     DU VAL, 1931   TUTT, 1925
                     JOHNSON, 1930b   WINSTON, 1927
                     PAGE, 1883

13273   PENFIELD.   The genealogy of the descendants of Samuel Penfield, with a supplement of Dr. Levi Buckingham line, and the Gridley, Dwight, Burlingham, Dewey, and Pyncheon collateral lines, compiled and edited by Florence Bentz Penfield.   (Reading, Pa., Printed at Harris Press, 1963)
ii, 321 p. 23 cm. 68-5321.
                                                     CS71.P3993   1963

PENFOLD.   See LINDSAY, 1917

PENGRY.   See PINGRY.

13274   PENHALLOW.   Memoir of the Penhallow family: with copies of letters and papers of an early date.   Compiled by Pearce W. Penhallow ... Boston, D. Clapp & son, printers, 1878.   22 p. 24 cm.
"From the New-England historical and genealogical register for Jan. 1878." 18-379.
                                                     CS71.P3995   1878

13275   PENHALLOW.   Penhallow family.   With copies of letters and papers of an early date.   As published in the New-England hist. and gen. register for January, 1878, and now with additions and brief notices of some contemporary families.   Compiled by Pearce W. Penhallow.   Boston, Press of D. Clapp & son, 1885.   2 p. l., 47 p. fold. geneal. tab. 23½ cm. 25-19273.   CS71.P3995   1885

13276   PENLAND.   Lists of descendants and short sketches of George Penland, 1778-1877 (and) Harvey Monroe Penland, 1812-1889.   By Blanche (Penland) Browder.   (Laurel? Md., 1958)
17 l. illus. 29 cm. 58-40069.
                                                    CS71.P3998   1958

13277   PENLAND.   The Penland family of North Carolina.   By Blanche (Penland) Browder.   Laurel, Md., 1959.   27 l. 30 cm. 63-5523.   CS71.P3998   1959

13278   PENLEY.   Penley family in England and America; being principally an account of the ancestry and descendants of Joseph Penly of Danville, Maine, 1756-1844.   By Robert Irving Penley.   Alexandria, Ont., 1958.   85 l. 30 cm. 58-39455.   CS71.P4   1958

PENLY.   See PENLEY.

13279   PENN.   A calm appeal to the people of the state of Delaware ... Philadelphia: Printed by Zachariah Poulson, junr., no. 80, Chestnut-street. (1793)   22 p. 21 cm. Signed: Tho. McKean, Edmund Physick; dated: Philadelphia, September 3d 1793.   A statement of the claim of the heirs of William Penn to the ownership of land in the state of Delaware.
1-23422.
                                                     F168.M15
                                                     Rare book room.

13280   PENN.   William Penn, proprietary of Pennsylvania, his ancestry and descendants.   Philadelphia, 1852.   geneal. tab. 19 x 45½ cm. "To Granville John Penn, esquire, on his visit to Pennsylvania, Philadelphia, June 1st, 1852." Signed: Thomas Gilpin.   Table has mounted engraved portrait of William Penn. 12-25497.
                                                     CS71.P411   1852

13281   PENN.   The Penns & Peningtons of the seventeenth century, in their domestic and religious life: illustrated by original family letters; also incidental notices of Thomas Ellwood, with some of his unpublished verses.   By Maria Webb ... London, F. B. Kitto, 1867.   xiv p., 1 l., 430 p. front. (port.) 3 pl., 3 facsim. 19½ cm. 8-16830.   F152.2W36

13282   PENN.   The Penns & Peningtons of the seventeenth century in their domestic and religious life, illustrated by original family letters, also incidental notices of their friend Thomas Ellwood, with some of his unpublished verses.   By Maria Webb.   Philadelphia, H. Longstreth, 1868.   446 p. 20 cm. 50-42915.   F152.2.W36   1868

13283   PENN.   The Penn family.   By John Jay Smith.   (Philadelphia, 1870)   cover-title, p. xv-xl. 25½ cm.
From Memoirs of the Historical society of Pennsylvania, v.9, 1870. 9-13010.   CS71. P411   1870

13284   PENN.   The Penn family (from Lippincott's magazine) by John Jay Smith.   (Philadelphia, J.B.
Lippincott & co., 1870)   cover-title, p. (149-162) 23½ cm. 9-18734.
CS71. P411   1870a

13285   PENN.   Articles, wills and deeds creating the entail of Pennsylvania and three lower counties
upon Delaware in the Penn family.   Philadelphia, 1870.   2 p. l., 177 (i.e. 178) p. 23 cm. 10-21783.
F152. 2. A79

13286   PENN.   A pedigree & genealogical notes, from wills, registers, and deeds, of the highly
distinguished family of Penn, of England and America, designed as a tribute to the memory of the great
and good William Penn.   Compiled and published by James Coleman.   London, J. Coleman, 1871.
24 p. front. (port.) illus., 2 fold. geneal. tab. 22 cm. 11-17115.   CS439. P4   1871

13287   PENN.   The proprietary title of the Penns ... (Philadelphia? 1871)   cover-title, 8 p. 21½ cm.
Signed: Eli K. Price. "Reprinted from the American law register for August, 1871." 12-11591.   F152. 2. P94

13288   PENN.   Sir William Penn, knight, admiral, and general-at-sea; great-captain-commander in
the fleet.   A memoir: by P. S. P. Conner ... Philadelphia, Press of J. B. Lippincott & co., 1876.
70 p. 27½ cm. "Authorities": p.9. 8-28772.   DA86. 1. P4C7

13289   PENN.   Genealogical gleanings, contributory to a history of the family of Penn.   By J. Henry
Lea ... (Philadelphia, Printed by J. B. Lippincott company, 1890)   51 p. 25 cm. Caption title. Reprinted from
the Pennsylvania magazine of history and biography. April-October, 1890. 8-16755.
F152. 2. L43

13290   PENN.   A short account of Penn of Pennsylvania and his family.   Philadelphia, The Historical
register publishing co., 1895.   cover-title, 8 p. 25½ cm. "A paper read January 16, 1895, by Eliza Penn-Gaskell Hancock, before the National society of colonial dames of America ... in New York city." 10-31416.   F152. 2. H23

13291   PENN.   The family of William Penn, founder of Pennsylvania, ancestry and descendants.   By
Howard M. Jenkins ... Philadelphia and London, The author, 1899.   x, 260 p. front., plates, ports., facsim.
25 cm. June 15, 99-84.   F152. 2. J52

13292   PENN.   The Penn titles to Northampton County lands.   By Calvin G. Beitel ... (n.p., 1900)
34 p. fold. front. (facsim.) 2 fold. maps. 23½ cm. Printed slip attached to t.-p. The maps are blue-prints. 19-17560.
F157. N7B4

13293   PENN.   The general title of the Penn family to Pennsylvania, an abstract prepared by the honorable John Cadwalader ... deceased, continued to the present time by William Brooke Rawle.   Philadelphia, 1900.   iv, 5-75 p. pl. 25 cm. Reprint from the Pennsylvania magazine of history and biography. 1-18191.
F152. 2. C12

13294   PENN.   The Penn family of Virginia; a chronological record.   Limited ed.   New York, W.
M. Clemens, 1915.   12 p. 23 cm. 15-19465.   CS71. P411   1915

13295   PENN.   The making of William Penn, by Mable Richmond Brailsford; with woodcut frontispiece by Clare Leighton and other illustrations.   London, New York (etc.) Longmans, Green and co.,
1930.   xxiv, 367, (1) p. incl. mounted front. plates, ports. 22 ½ cm. Bibliography: p. 361-363. 30-25086.
F152. 2. B81

13296   PENN.   The Penns of Pennsylvania and England, by Arthur Pound ... New York, The Mac-
millan company, 1932.   xx, 349 p. front., plates, ports., maps, geneal. tables (1 fold.) facsim. 24½ cm. "A partial list of the
published works of William Penn": p. 319-320; Bibliography: p. 337-339. 32-23126.   F152. 2. P88

13297   PENN.   The Penn patents in the forks of the Delaware, by A. D. Chidsey, jr. ... Easton, Pa.
(Printed by the John S. Correll co., inc.) 1937.   91 p. 2 port. (incl. front.) double maps, tables (1 double) 28½ cm.
(Northampton county historical and genealogical society. Publications. vol. II) "Edition limited to two hundred copies." Centents. - The Penn

13297 continued: patents in the forks of the Delaware. - John and Thomas Penn visit the site of Easton. - Descendants of William Penn. - The Penn title. - Maps. - Map index. 37-23649.

F157.N7N85 vol. 2

13298 PENN. Further light on the ancestry of William Penn, by O. F. G. Hogg. (London, Society of Genealogist) 1964. 43 p. illus., geneal. tables. 22 cm. Bibliographical references included in "Notes" (p. 42-43) 68-33260 rev.

CS439.P4 1964

13299 PENN. Penn family in vertical file. Ask reference librarian for this material.

PENN. See also: CRISPIN, 1901
HAIRSTON, 1940
HANNIS, 1911
McCANN, 1955
WASHINGTON, E187.5.S88

PENNEBAKER. See ELIOT, 1961

PENNELL. See LLOYD, 1912

13300 PENNEY. A genealogical record of the descendants of Thomas Penney of New Gloucester, Maine, compiled by J. W. Penney ... Portland, The Thurston print, 1897. 3 p. l., 162 p. front., illus., ports. 24 cm. 9-12847.

CS71.P412 1897

13301 PENNEY. My ancestors, by Norman Penney ... Bishopsgate, E.C., and Ashford, Kent., Printed for private circulation by Headley brothers, 1920. xvi, 234, (2) p. front., plates, ports., col. coat of arms. 22 cm. "This ed, is limited to two hundred and fifty numbered copies, of which this is no. 79." Part II: The Ianson family, p. 149-218. Contains also genealogies of the Grover, Rickman, Horne, Raylton, and Dixon families. 20-23956.

CS439.P42

PENNEY. See also: BELL, 1893
FOSTER, 1895
KETCHAM, 1954

13302 PENNIMAN. Ancestral lineage of Josiah Harmar Penniman, and James Hosmer Penniman, whose immigrant ancestor was James Penniman, of Massachusetts. Reprint from Colonial families of the United States of America, volume VII ... (New York, Boston, The Grafton press, 1920) 1 p. l., p. 377-382. illus. (coat of arms) 25 cm. 21-13572.

CS71.P413 1920

PENNIMAN. See also VINTON, 1857a

13303 PENNINGTON. The Pennington family. By Capt. A. C. M. Pennington ... Boston, Printed by D. Clapp & son, 1871. 18 p. 24½ cm. "Reprinted, with additions, from vol. XXV of the N. E. historical and genealogical register." 34-32129 rev.

CS71.P4133 1871

13304 PENNINGTON. Pedigree of Sir Josslyn Pennington, fifth baron Muncaster of Muncaster and ninth baronet. Compiled chiefly from deeds and charters in H. M. record office, by Joseph Foster ... London, Priv. print., at the Chiswick press, 1878. v, (3)-73 numb. 1. illus. (coats of arms) 33 cm. Lettered on cover: Penningtoniana. 19-3368.

CS439.P43

13305 PENNINGTON. The Penningtons, pioneers of early Arizona; a historical sketch by Robert H. Forbes. Published by the Arizona arrchaeological and historical society. Lancaster, Pa., The New Era printing company) 1919. iii, (1), 42 p. front. (port.) illus. (incl. ports., maps) 21 cm. "References": p. 41-42. 38-20403.

F811.F67

PENNINGTON. See also: ASKEW, 1911
FELL, DA690.P35F4
LITZENBURG, 1948
PENN, F152.2.W36

13306   PENNOCK.   Christopher Pennock married prior to 1675 Mary Collet, daughter of George Collet of Clonmell, Ireland ... died in Philadelphia in 1701 ... Caroline Pennock, delineator.   Philadelphia, Lith. of J. T. Bowen (19 -?)   5 geneal. charts. 60 x 90 cm. 14-10159.

CS71.P415   19 -

PENNY.   See PENNEY.

13307   PENNYPACKER.   The Pennypacker reunion, October 4, 1877.   (Philadelphia, Bavis & Pennypacker, printers, 1878)   iv, 50, (1) p. front. (facsim.) plates, ports., map. 27 cm. Compiled by Samuel Whitaker Pennypacker. 9-12845.

CS71.P416   1878

13308   PENNYPACKER.   The pedigree of Samuel Whitaker Pennypacker, Henry Clay Pennypacker, Isaac Rusling Pennypacker, James Lane Pennypacker, of Philadelphia, sons of Isaac Anderson Pennypacker and Anna Maria Whitaker.   (By Samuel W. Pennypacker)   Philadelphia (Globe printing house) 1892.   3 l., 2 fold. geneal. tab. 39½ cm. Col. coat of arms mounted on verso of front cover. "Fifty copies privately printed. no. 48." 9-15010.

CS71.P416   1892

13309   PENNYPACKER.   Hendrick Pannebecker, surveyor of lands for the Penns, 1674-1754, Flomborn, Germantown and Shippack; by Hon. Samuel W. Pennypacker, LL.D.   Philadelphia, Priv. print, 1894.   164 p. incl. front. (coat of arms) plates, ports., facsims. 26½ cm. "150 copies on paper hand-made for the edition. no. 139." "The Pennypacker family in the war of the rebellion": p. 135-149.   "Origin of the family": p. 9-18. 10-10917.

F152.P42
Office.

13310   PENNYPACKER.   The descent of Samuel Whitaker Pennypacker ... from the ancient counts of Holland.   With authorities in proof, Philadelphia, 1898.   25 p. front. 23½ cm. "Forty copies printed." Comp. by Samuel W. Pennypacker. 9-12846.

CS71.P416   1898

13311   PENROSE.   The Penrose family, by George Hoffman Penrose.   (n.p., 18 -?)   6 l. 26½ cm. Photostat copy (negative) 38M3593T.

CS71.P417   18 -

13312   PENROSE.   History of the Penrose family of Philadelphia, by Josiah Granville Leach ... Philadelphia, Pub. for private circulation by D. Biddle, 1903.   5 p. l., 163 p. col. front. (coat of arms) illus., plates, ports., facsims. 24½ cm. Title in red and black within ornamental border. "Two hundred and fifty copies printed." 4-6904.

CS71.P417   1903

13313   PENROSE.   The Penroses of Fledborough parsonage, lives, letters and diary, edited by Rev. A. B. Baldwin ... Hull (Eng., etc.) A. Brown & sons, limited (1933)   xii, 134 p. front., illus. XI pl. (incl. ports.) 22 cm. 40-16299.

CS439.P44   1933

13314   PENROSE.   Biography of the late Boies Penrose and family, copyright ... (by) J. Wesley Waters.   (Philadelphia, The Sumner printing press) c.1939.   (8) p. 22 cm. 39-17556.

CT275.P564W3

13315   PENROSE.   The Penrose family of Wheldrake, Yorkshire, England, and of Ballykean, County Wicklow, Ireland, together with an account of their known descendants in the British Isles and the United States of America to the year 1961.   By George Englert McCracken.   Des Moines, 1961. 49 l. 36 cm. 62-27115.

CS71.P417   1961

PNROSE.   See also: HALLOWELL, 1893
                                ROBERTS, F159.R48R6

PENTZ.   See CRONE, 1924

PEPER.   See PEPPER.

PEPLOE.   See BROWN, 1888

13316   PEPOON.   Captain Daniel Pepoon and Levina Phelps, his first wife; Elizabeth James, his second wife.   A partial record of their descendants and notes regarding their ancestors.   (New York,

13316 continued: N.Y., Press of B. H. Tyrrel) 1940.   2 p. l., 124 p., 1 l. 24 cm. Blank pages for "Memoranda" interspersed.   Bibliographical references included in foreword.   41-7030.   CS71.P42   1940

PEPPARD.   See No. 9847 - Hackettstown.

13317   PEPPER.   Pepper genealogy; ancestors and descendants of Robert Pepper of Roxbury, Mass., compiled by Emily Clark Landon.   Angola, N.Y., 1932.   2 p. l., (7)-80, (14) p. illus. (coat of arms) 23 cm. "Additions and corrections" on slip attached to back fly-leaf.   32-30548.   CS71.P422   1932

13318   PEPPER.   Genealogy of the Pepper family in America.   By Carlton D. Pepper.   Richmond, 1960.   119 l. illus. 30 cm. 60-37209.   CS71.P422   1960

PEPPER.   See also LAWSON, 1903

13319   PEPPERELL.   The life of Sir William Pepperrell, bart,, the native of New England who was created a baronet during our connection with the mother country.   By Usher Parsons.   2d ed.   Boston, Little, Brown and company; London, S. Low, son and company, 1856.   xii, 356 p. fold. map. 21 cm. 12-26340.   E198.P424

13320   PEPPERRELL. Pepperrell genealogy ... by Usher Parsons.   (Boston, 1866)   6 p. 24 cm. Reprinted from the New England historical and genealogical register for January, 1866.   38M3534T.   CS71.P424   1866

13321   PEPPERRELL.   Field day, 1893 (Sept. 8 and 9 at Kittery Point and Portsmouth)   (In its Collections and proceedings.   Portland, 1893.   23½ cm.   2d ser., v. 4, p. 424-434)   Paper by J. P. Baxter, "Piscataqua and the Pepperrells," p. 426-430.   A 15-1150.   F16.M33 vol. 4

13322   PEPPERRELL.   The Pepperrell portraits.   By Cecil Hampden Cutts Howard ... (Salem? Mass., 1894?)   cover-title, 12 p. 24½ cm. "From the Historical collections of the Essex Institute, v. 31," 2-25715.   CS71.P424   1894

13323   PEPPERRELL.   The Pepperrells in America, by Cecil Hampden Cutts Howard ... Salem, Mass., Printed for the Essex institute, 1906.   2 p. l., 106 p. front., plates, ports. 25 cm. "From the historical collections of the Essex institute, volumes XXXVII-XLII." 9-21012.   CS71.P424   1906

PEPPERRELL.   See also: ELLIS, F3.T61
                                         JARVIS, CT275.J4C6
                                         LAYTON, 1885
                                         QUIMBY, 1906
                                         SALTER, 1900

13324   PEPYS.   Genealogy of the Pepys family, 1273-1887; compiled by Walter Courtenay Pepys ... London, G. Bell and sons, 1887.   73 p. geneal. tables (part fold.) 21 cm. Title vignette; head and tail pieces; initials. 2-30576.   CS439.P45

13325   PEPYS.   More Pepysiana; being notes on the Diary of Samuel Pepys and on the genealogy of the family with corrected pedigrees, by Walter H. Whitear ... London, Simpkin, Marshall, Hamilton, Kent & co. ltd., 1927.   2 p. l., iv p., 2 l., 177 p. 1 illus., 2 port., geneal. tables (2 fold.) 23 cm. 28-9953.   DA447.P4W6

13326   PEPYS.   Eight generations of the Pepys family, 1500-1800, by Edwin Chappell ... London, The author, 1936.   110 p. fold. geneal. tab. 23 cm. "Only 500 copies printed." "List of works consulted": p. 109-110.   37-18880.   CS439.P45   1936

PERCEVAL.   See: DRUMMOND, CS419.D7
                                 O'HARA, 1806
                                 YVERY, 1742

PERCIE.   See PERCY.

13327　PERCY.　An extract of the History and genealogy of the noble families of the earl and countess of Northumberland ... Dublin, Printed by S. Powell, in Dame-street, opposite Fownes's street, for the author, 1764.　6 p. l., 60 p. 20½ cm. Dedication signed: Richard Griffith. 23-2552.

DA28.35.P5G7

13328　PERCY.　Illustrations of Alnwick, Prudhoe and Warkworth.　For private distribution. (London? 1857?)　1 p. l., 40, (7) p. incl. geneal. tables. 92 (i.e. 95) pl. incl. front., plans, facsim.) 32½ cm. Engr. t.-p. The plates are chiefly from drawings by Orlando Jewitt. Contents. - Description of the plates, by C. H. Hartshorne. - Surnames of the families whose arms compose a shield of quarterings of alliances appertaining to the ... Duke of Northumberland. - Descent of the most noble race of Percy, earls and dukes ot Northumberland ... 3-16674.

DA690.A4I2

13329　PERCY.　Family record of the Connecticut branch of the Percy family.　Compiled by Truman Percy ... Norfolk, Va., H. C. Percy, 1873 (Boston, Mass., Reprinted by Goodspeed's book shop, inc., 1941)　11 p. 13½ cm. Text on p. (2) of cover. "Only 40 copies printed." 41-7031.

CS71.P428　1873

13330　PERCY.　Annals of the house of Percy, from the conquest to the opening of the nineteenth century.　By Edward Barrington de Fonblanque ... London, Printed by R. Clay & sons, for private circulation only, 1887.　2 v. col. fronts., plates, ports., facsims. (1 fold.) fold. geneal. tab. col. coat of arms. 26½ cm. Folded genealogical table in pocket, at end of vol. I. 22-9020.

DA28.35.P5D4

13331　PERCY.　A history of the house of Percy from the earliest times down to the present century, by Gerald Brenan; edited by W. A. Lindsay ... London, Freemantle & co., 1902.　2 v. front., pl. (part col.) port., fold. facsim. (part fold.) geneal. tab. (part fold.) 23 cm. Title in red and black. 2-28385.

DA28.35.P5B8

13332　PERCY.　The Percy Chartulary.　Durham, Pub. for the Society by Andrews & co.; (etc., etc.) 1911.　xv, (1), 548 p. 23 cm. (Half-title: The publications of the Surtees society ... vol. CXVII for the year 1909) "Apparently compiled in the time of Henry, fourth Lord Percy of Alnwick, upon his creation as Earl of Northumberland. It contains no later handwriting, and no document of later date than ... July, 1377. The volume consists of over eleven hundred conveyances of property which directly or eventually came to the Percy inheritance. About half ... is copied with lands in Yorkshire, and a quarter in Northumberland." - Introd. Edited by Miss M. T. Martin. 12-11785.

DA20.S9 vol. 117

13333　PERCY.　Percy bailiff's rolls of the fifteenth century.　Durham, Pub. for the Society by Andrews & co.; London, B. Quaritch, ltd., 1921.　xiv, 133 p. 22½ cm. (Added t.-p.: The publications of the Surtees society ... vol. CXXXIV for the year 1921) Edited by J. C. Hodgson. Contents. - Historical introduction: - Bailiff's rolls of the fourth Earl of Northumberland. - Household roll of the seventh Earl of Northumberland - Observations and notes on the Bailiff's rolls. 21-22307.

DA20.S9　vol. CXXXIV

13334　PERCY.　The estates of the Percy family, 1416-1537.　By John Malcom William Bean. (London) Oxford University Press, 1958.　x, 176 p. geneal. tables. 22 cm. (Oxford historical series. British series) Based on thesis, Oxford University. Bibliography: p. (163)-167. 58-4214.

HD594.B4

13335　PERCY.　Household papers.　Henry Percy, 9th earl of Northumberland.　Edited for the Royal Historical Society by G. R. Batho.　London, Royal Historical Society, 1962.　lvii, 190 p. facsims. 22 cm. (Camden third series, v. 93) Bibliography: p. xi-xvi. 63-1938.

DA20.R91 vol. 93

PERCY.　See also: MAJOR, 1915
PIERCE, 1947

13336　PERDUE.　Descendants of Dr. William Perdue, who settled in Chester county, Pennsylvania, in 1737-38, and his wife, Susanna (Pim) Perdue.　Part II. Ancestors of Lucinda Maria (Smith) Perdue giving Smith, Potter and Hamilton lines.　John Purdue, founder of Purdue university.　Compiled by Robert Hartley Perdue.　Cleveland, O., 1934.　3 p. l., iv numb. l., 1 l., v-xi, 168 numb. l. map. 28½ cm. Three half-titles not included in pagination. "Original typewritten manuscript." "John Purdue, founder of Purdue university": p. 154-166. "Records searched and examined": 1 l., numb. l. v-xi. 35-23561.

CS71.P43　1934

——— Copy 2.　"Reproduced by the hectograph process." "This ... edition consists of 52 copies so reproduced."

13337　PEREIRA FORJAZ DE SAMPAIO ... Noticias biographica, 1888. Jayme Pereira de Sampaio Forjaz de Serpa Pimentel. Lisbon, Typographia Castro irmão, 1889. 342 p., 1 l. port. 20 cm. "Reformed as Noticias biographicas publicadas em 1866 pelo conselheiro Adrião Pereira Forjaz de Sampaio." - p. (5) 35-20730.

CS969.P35P4

13338   PERES.   The Peres family, by Sam Shankman.   Kingsport, Tenn., Southern publishers, inc.
(1938)   xiv p., 1 l., 241 p. front., plates, ports., facsims. (1 double) 21 cm.   Speeches and essays of Hardwig Peres: p. (79)-241.
39-10121.
CS71.P434   1938

13339   PERESTRELLO.   ... A mulher de Colombo (Notas extraidas d'um estudo inedito)   (By
Antonio Maria de Freitas) Lisbon, Pap. e typ. Guedes, 1892.   59 p., 4 l. incl. geneal. tab. 22½ cm.   Author's
pseud., "Nicolau Florentino," at head of title.   "Arvores genealogicas: Quadro genealogico das familias Moniz e Perestrello (Palestrello); Arvore
genealogica de Colombo; Materiaes consul ados": 4 l. at end.   3-31199.
E113.C3

13340   PERIGAL.   Some account of the Perigal family ... London, Harrison and sons, 1887.
44 p. fold. geneal. tab., coat of arms. 21½ cm.   "Printed for private circulation." Preface signed: Frederick Perigal. 40-286.
CS439.P47   1887

        PERINE.   See PERRIN.

13341   PERKINS.   A private proof printed in order to preserve certain matters connected with the
Boston branch of the Perkins family ... Boston, T. R. Marvin & son, printers, 1885.   29 p. 23 cm.
Signed: A. T. P. (i.e. Augusts Thorndike Perkins) 21-12483.
CS71.P45   1885

13342   PERKINS.   Letters ocncerning the Perkins family ... Salem, Printed at the Salem press, 1887.
24 p. front., illus. 23 cm.   Contents. - Notice of the Perkins arms in England. From Essex institute Historical collections. - Two historical
letters from Augustus T. Perkins pedigree, by Wm. H. Whitmore. Copied from N. E. Hist. geneal. register. 5-27447.
CS71.P45   1887

13343   PERKINS.   Genealogy of the Newman Perkins family, beginning with Newman Perkins 1st, who
came to America with Roger Williams on his second boyage in 1631, to March 1, 1888.   (n. p.) Post
Steam Print., 1888.   48, 3 p. 22 cm. Photocopy (postive): (27) l. 22 x 28 cm.   Each leaf represents two pages of the original.
"Commentary on the Genealogy of the Newman Perkins family (by) John B. Perkins" (typescript: 4 l.) inserted. 64-58145.
CS71.P45   1888a

13344   PERKINS.   ... Constitution and by-laws of the Harford historical society; with sketch of its
history, list of members, contributors, etc., etc. ... 1889.   Baltimore, Guggenheimer, Weil & co.,
1889.   37, (8) p. 23 cm.   Eight blank leaves at end with caption: Memoranda.   Record of the Perkins family, by Albert P. Silver: p. 33-34.
17-15491.
F187.H2H55

13345   PERKINS.   The family of John Perkins of Ipswich, Mass. Complete in threee parts.   By
Geo. A. Perkins ... Salem, Printed for the author by the Salem press publishing & printing co., 1889.
3 pt. in 1 v. facsims., coat of arms. Pt. I. Quartermaster John Perkins; pt. OO. Deacon Thomas Perkins; pt. III, Sergeant Jacob Perkins.
9-12842.
CS71.P45   1889

13346   PERKINS.   A private proof printed in order to preserve certain matters connected with the
Boston branch of the Perkins family ... Boston, T. R. Marvin & son, printers, 1890.   112 p. 24 cm.   By
Augustus Thorndike Perkins. 3-7934.
CS71.P45   1890

13347   PERKINS.   Memoir of Augustus Thorndike Perkins, A. M.   By William H. Whitmore.   (Re-
printed from the Proceedings of the Massachusetts historical society, June, 1892)   Cambridge, J.
Wilson and son, 1892.   14 p. front. (port.) 24½ cm. 3-20238.
CT275.P57W4

13348   PERKINS.   The history of Ufton Court, of the parish of Ufton, in the county of Berks, and of
the Perkins family: compiled from ancient records, by A. Mary Sharp ... London, E. Stock; (etc.,
etc,) 1892.   xvii, 276 p. incl. front., illus., plans, fold. geneal. tables.   26 cm.   "A roll of the pioneers of New England of the name of
Perkins" (supplied by D. W. Perkins, of Utica, New York): p. 247-261. 10-34033.
CS439.P48   1892

13349   PERKINS.   Notes on the Perkins families in England: chiefly extracts from probate registries:
with several pcdigrees appended.   By D. W. Perkins. Salem, 1894.   2 p. 1., 61 p. geneal. tables (1 fold.)
24½ cm. 3-29174 rev.
CS439.P48   1894

13350   PERKINS.   Owls nest, a tribute to Sarah Elliott Perkins, by her grand-daughter Edith Perkins
Cunningham.   (Cambridge, Mass.)   Printed at the Riverside press for private distribution, 1907.
viii p., 2 l., 322, (1) p. front., plates, ports., fold. geneal. tables.   23 cm.   "Family of Samuel Gardner Perkins" and "Family of Andrew
Elliott": 2 genealogical tabkes.   35-16212.   CT275. P574C8

13351   PERKINS.   Perkins families in the United States in 1790 ... Compiled by D. W. Perkins.
Utica, N. Y., 1911.   1 p. 1., 46 p. 23 cm. 12-16319.   CS71. P45   1911

13352   PERKINS.   Genealogical notes concerning the Perkins, Taylor, and allied families, by
William Titcomb Perkins.   Saco, Me., The Streeter press, 1914.   35 p. incl. plates, ports. 22 cm.   Contains
the Perkins, Taylor, Hill, Titcomb, Walker, and Whitten families.   20-7230.   CS71. P45   1914

13353   PERKINS.   The descendants of Edward Perkins of New Haven, Conn. (by) Caroline Erickson
Perkins.   Rochester, N. Y., 1914.   135 p. front. (port.) 23 cm.   On cover: The descendants of Edward Perkins of New
Haven, Conn.   By Caroline E. Perkins and Perley Derby.   31-19469.   CS71. P45   1914a

13354   PERKINS.   New edition of the records of the family of Rufus Perkins of Rockingham and
Chester, Vt., 1781-1803 ... and his children, Moses, Rufus, Amasa, Betsey, and Silas, who settled
in Addison, Rutland, and Windsor counties, Vermont, especially his son Rufus Perkins, who settled in
East Middlebury, Vermont, and grandson Rufus Lyman Perkins of East Middlebury and Rutland, Vermont ... By Henry E. Perkins ... Troy, N. Y., H. Stowell & son, printers, 1916.   69, viii p. front. (port.)
23 cm. 16-17374.   CS71. P45   1916

13355   PERKINS.   The Perkins family in ye olden times.   The contents of a series of letters by the
late Mansfield Parkyns ... Edited and privately printed by D. W. Perkins.   Utica, N. Y., 1916.
88 p. illus. (incl. coats of arms) map. 23 cm. 16-14973.   CS439. P48   1916

13356   PERKINS.   The Perkins family, a sketch of intercolonial migration.   By Emily Ritchie
Perkins.   Contributed by the late Miss Emily Ritchie Perkins.   (In Genealogical society of Pennsylvania. Publications. Philadelphia, 1920. v. 7, p. 163-178) 21-8413.   F146. G32 vol. 7

13357   PERKINS.   "Gentleman" John Perkins, by W. W. Scott.   Lenoir, N. C., The Lenoir news-
topic (1920)   3 p. 1., 84, (4) p. 23 cm. 21-2413.   CS71. P45   1920

13358   PERKINS.   ... Perkins family records, by J. Montgomery Seaver.   Philadelphia, American
historical-genealogical society (1929)   52 p. front. (4 port.) coat of arms. 29 cm.   Coat of arms of the Perkins family on
recto of frontispiece.   Page 52 blank for "Family record".   "References": p. 50-51.   40-18917.
                                                                            CS71. P45   1929

13359   PERKINS.   Family record.   (n. p., 193-?)   1 v. 31 cm.   Binder's title.   A collection of genealogical
material in ms., holograph letters, photographs, etc. relating to the family of Edward T. Perkins.   49-58280 *.
                                                                            CS71. P45

13360   PERKINS.   The Perkins family ... by A. E. Perkins ... New Orleans, La., 1944.
32 p. illus. 22 cm.   Reproduced from type-written copy.   44-24460.   E185. 97. P47

13361   PERKINS.   A genealogy of the Perkins family ... by A. E. Perkins ... New Orleans, La.,
1944.   31 p. illus. (port.) 21½ cm.   Reproduced from type-written copy.   45-379.   E185. 97. P465

13362   PERKINS.   What I know about my ancestors, and their families.   Also: some account of my
wife's ancestors, and their families.   By Edward Perkins.   Weymouth, O., 1888.   (Chicago? 1947)
3 p. 1., 33 numb. 1. 29 x 23 cm.   Half-title: The Perkins family.   Copied by Victor J. Andrew from the original manuscript which is in the
possession of Morton O. Perkins.   47-24802.   CS71. P45   1947

13363   PERKINS.   Jacob Perkins, of Wells, Maine and his descendants, 1583-1936.   By Thomas
Allen Perkins.   Edited and arr. for publication by Harold Clarke Durrell.   Haverhill, Mass., Record Pub.
Co., 1947 (c. 1948)   239 p. illus. 25 cm. 56-39544.   CS71. P45   1948

13364   PERKINS.   Kinsfolk of the Perkins family.   By Clarence Alexander Perkins.   (n. p.) 1953.
83 p. 24 cm. 54-31066.   CS71. P45   1953

13365   PERKINS.   The Perkins family of Virginia; descendants of Nicholas Perkins who died ca. 1654 in Charles City County.   (Compiled by William K. Hall.   Edited, arr., typed by George F. Browning, Jr.   Bridgeport? Ala., 1953)   7 1.   29 x 40 cm.   77-12658 MARC.   CS71.P45   1953b

13366   PERKINS.   Descendants of Nicholas Perkins of Virginia.   By William Kearney Hall.   (Ann Arbor? 1958, c.1957)   700 p.   coat of arms.   29 cm.   58-26547.   CS71.P45   1958

13367   PERKINS.   Perkins family in vertical file.   Ask reference librarian for this material.

PERKINS.   See also:

CURD, 1927	HAIRSTON, 1940	WILD, 1959
DE CLARE, 1921	LA VEILLE, 1933	WOOLSEY, 1900
GILLETT, 1928	LUTER, 1959	No. 553 - Goodhue county.
GILPIN, 1927	WHITE, 1900	

13368   PERLEY.   A genealogical chart of the male descendants of Allen Perley, comp. and pub. by Geo. Augustus Perley ... Fredericton, New Brunswick, The author, 1877.   13 p.   25 cm.   Title vignette: coat of arms (col.)   9-15605.   CS71.P451   1877

13368a   PERLEY.   History and genealogy of the Perley family, compiled by M. V. B. Perley ... Salem, Mass., The compiler, 1906.   xxii, 748 p.   front., illus., plates, ports., fold. geneal. tab.   24½ cm.   6-32120.   CS71.P451   1906

PERLEY.   See also PORTER, 1907

PERRAULT.   See: CASGRAIN, CS90.C3
                      TÊTU.   Microfilm 8861, CS90.T45

PERRIE.   See MONROE, 1952

13369   PERRIN.   Genealogy of the Perrin family, compiled by Glover Perin ... St. Paul, Pioneer press co., 1885.   224 p.   20 cm.   Alternate leaves blank for "Family record."   9-12841.   CS71.P458   1885

13370   PERRIN.   Daniel Perrin, "The Huguenot," and his descendants in America, of the surnames, Perrine, Perine, and Prine, 1665-1910.   Compiled by Howland Delano Perrine ... South Orange, N.J., Priv. print. (Press of T. A. Wright) 1910.   4 p. l., 547 p.   front., illus., plates, ports., col. coat of arms, maps (part fold.) facsims.   26½ cm.   "Edition of numbered and signed copies limited to two hundred and fifty, of which this is no. 108."   10-25098.   CS71.P458   1910

13371   PERRIN.   The story and documentary history of the Perine house, Dongan Hills, Staten Island, headquarters of the Staten Island antiquarian society, by Charles Gilbert Hine.   (New York?) Staten Island antiquarian society, inc., 1915.   1 p. l., 7-88, (3) p.   front., plates (part col.) 26½ cm.   Contents. - pt. I. Story of the locality known as Dongan Hills, formerly Garretsons. - pt. II. The story of the old Perine house. - pt. III. The several ownerships of the Perine homestead, as shown by state and county records ... arranged and annotated by Howland Delano Perrine.   17-12073.   F127.S7H68

13372   PERRIN.   The generations of the Perrin family and relations from 1620 to 1920; illustrated by many steel engravings of homes, groups of families and individuals.   With some original songs and poems.   By the Rev. D. A. Perrin ... Normal, Ill., D. A. Perrin & co., c.1921.   35, (13) p.   illus. (incl. ports.)   23 cm.   Music: p. (6) - (13) at end.   21-9396.   CS71.P458   1921

13373   PERRIN.   Geneology (!) and records of the Perrines (by) William Davison Perrine.   1665-1935.   (n. p.) 1935.   (4) p.   illus. (coat of arms) 22½ cm.   35-28838.   CS71.P458   1935

13374   PERRIN.   Daniel Perrin "the Huguenot," and his descendants in America.   Compiled by C. E. Perrine, James A. Perrine and Ollie Negley Kern.   (Raritan? Ill.) Review atlas printing co., 1942.   44 p.   illus. (coat of arms) plates, ports.   25½ cm.   "Copies limited to one hundred and fifty ... No. 1."   44-1904.   CS71.P458   1942

PERRIN. See also: ADAMS, 1958
ANDERSON, 1902
PURDY, 1911
SNYDER, 1958
STEVENS, 1957

PERRINE. See PERRIN.

PERROT. See PERROTT.

13375 PERROTT. The history of that most eminent statesman, Sir John Perrott, knight of the Bath, and lord lieutenant of Ireland ... Now first published from the original manuscript, written about the latter end of the reign of Queen Elizabeth ... London, 1728. 3 p. l., xi, (12)-315, (5) p. 19 cm. 4-34338.
DA937.R25

13376 PERROTT. An appeal to His Royal Highness, the Prince regent, on a system of oppression and injustice, evinced towards a family distinguished by their sufferings in the cause of royalty. By Sir Edward Perrott, bart ... London, Printed for the author, by J. G. Barnard, 1812. 2 p. l., 84 p. 21½ cm. 15-12536.
CS439.P49 1812

13377 PERROTT. Perrot notes; or, Some account of the various branches of the Perrot family. By Edward Lowry Barnwell, M.A. Printed for the Cambrian archaeological association. London, J. R. Smith (etc.) 1867. iv, 216 p. front., illus. (coats of arms) plates. 25½ cm. An edition of 100 copies, reprinted from the "Archeologia cambrensis," 1866. 20-23947.
CS459.P4

13378 PERROTT. Comprehensive pedigree, no. 2. The Perrott family. Worcestershire branch. William Perrott to Robert Jason Perrott, Humphrey Parker Perrott, 1550-1907. Tables one to five. By Edward Milward Seede Parker, gent. ... 1909. Weston-super-Mare, Hyssett & Pope, 1909. 16 p. 34 cm. Bound with the author's Genealogical memoranda relating to the family of Parker ... Bristol, 1899. 19-2312.
CS439.P27

PERROTT. See also BASKERVILLE, 1930

13379 PERRY. Memoranda concerning descendants of John Perry, John Strong, John Fyfe, Robert Gray. Cincinnati, G. E. Stevens & co., 1878. 1 p. l., iii, 28 p. 22½ cm. "Explanatory" signed: Aaron Fyfe Perry. 20-20507.
CS71.P462 1878

13380 PERRY. Amos Perry of Providence and his paternal ancestors in America. (n. p. 1889) 7 p. 24 cm. An edition of 100 copies. "Perry of Bitham house", and "Perry of Woodrooff": 3 clippings from "Landed gentry" inserted. 24-11485.
CS71.P462 1889

13381 PERRY. Descendants of Jonathan Perry, of Topsham, Maine, to the fifth generation; comp. by Arthur L. Perry ... Augusta, Press of C. E. Nash, 1890. 13 p. 24 cm. Four blank leaves at end for "Family record of." 9-12840.
CS71.P462 1890

13382 PERRY. The Perry family of Hertford County, North Carolina, by ex-Judge Benj. B. Winborne ... (Raleigh, Edwards-Broughton printing co., 1909) 64 p. incl. front. (port.) 20 cm. 13-19966.
CS71.P462 1909

13383 PERRY. Our Perry family in Maine; its ancestors and descendants, by Rev. Charles Nelson Sinnett ... Lewiston, Me., The Journal printshop, 1911. 127 p. plates, ports. 24 cm. 11-23364.
CS71.P462 1911

13384 PERRY. Some of the ancestors of Oliver Hazard Perry of Lowell, Mass. ... compiled by Mrs. F. W. Brown. Edited and published by Charles H. Pope. Boston, 1911. 2 v. 24 cm. 18-15858.
—— Pt. I. Perry ancestry. CS71.P462 1911a
—— Pt. II. Moseley ancestry. CS71.M898 1911

13385   PERRY. The Perrys of Rhode Island, and tales of Silver Creek; the Bosworth-Bourn-Perry homestead, revised and enlarged from a lecture ... at the Public library, Cambridge, N.Y., April 13, 1909, by Rev. Calbraith Bourn Perry ... (vol. 1.) New York, T. A. Wright, 1913.   1 v. front., plates, ports., 25 cm. 13-24821.   CS71. P462   1913

13386   PERRY. Arthur Cecil Perry and his ancestry. Compiled by Arthur C. Perry, jr., and Eugene R. Perry. New York, Priv. print., 1925.   15 p. 27 cm. 25-13344.   CS71. P462   1925

13387   PERRY. A branch of the Peery family tree; ancestors and descendants of James Peery who came to Delaware about 1730, by Lynn Perry.   Strasburg, Va., Printed by Shenandoah publishing house, inc., 1931.   125 p. incl. front. (coat of arms) illus. (ports.) 19½ cm. 31-21759.
CS71. P462   1931

13388   PERRY. An incomplete history of the descendants of John Perry of London, 1604-1954; compiled by Bertram Adams, assisted by numerous members of the family. Salt Lake City, Printed by Utah Print. Co., 1955.   xv, 738 p. illus., ports. 24 cm. Bibliography: p. 656. 56-18670.   CS71. P462   1955

13389   PERRY Ezra Perry of Sandwich, Massachusetts, and some of his descendants in Saratoga County, New York. By Ruth Vesta Pope Werner. Rosengarten. Washington, 1955 (i.e. 1960) unpaged. 28 cm. 61-21315.   CS71. P462   1960

13390   PERRY. Perry family history, consisting of biographical sketches of Stephen Chadwick Perry and his four wives: Susannah Colista Hidden, Anna Maria Hulet, Margaret Eleanor Stewart, and Marry Boggs, with their posterity. Also sketches of his ancestors back to 1615. Compiler: Ivan Perry. Provo, Utah, J. G. Stevenson, (1966 -   v. ports. 25 cm. Bibliography: p. 401. 67-5886.
CS71. P462   1966

13391   PERRY. A history of the John Wesley Perry, Jr., family. By Charles Wesley Perry. Provo, Utah, J. G. Stevenson, 1967.   viii, 96 p. illus., coat of arms, facsim., geneal. table, ports. 25 cm. 68-1858.
CS71. P462   1967

PERRY. See also: BLAUVELT, 1957   JONES, 1961
                   CORN, 1959   SMITH, 1915
                   DOBYNS, 1908   SNYDER, F545. S67
                   HERRING, 1916   No. 430 - Adventurers of purse and
                                              person.

PERSHALL. See PARSHALL.

13392   PERSHING. The Pershing family in America; a collection of historical and genealogical data, family portraits, traditions, legends and military records. Philadelphia, Pa., Printed by George S. Ferguson co. (c. 1924)   xi, 13-434 p. col. front., illus. (incl. ports., facsims.) 23½ cm. Foreword signed: Edgar Jamison Pershing. 24-32144.   CS71. P466   1924

PERSINGER. See GLASSBURN, 1964

13393   PERSON. Amos Person(s): his forebears and descendants. With supplemental Hodge genealogy. By Barbara Roach Knox. (Fort Worth, Tex., Higgins Print. Co., 1967)   156 p. illus., ports., 27 cm. Bibliography: p. 145. 67-66408.   CS71. P468   1967

13394   PERSONS. Persons lineage. By George Fuller Walker. (Atlanta? 1951)   xi, 192 p. mounted illus., mounted ports., coat-of-arms, geneal. tables. 34 cm. "Three hundred copies." Errata slip inserted. Bibliographical footnotes. 52-18605.   CS71. P468   1951

PERSSE. See MAUNSELL, CS439. M37

PERTH. See DRUMMOND, DA758. 3. D8M2

13395   PERTON. Connected annals of the manor and family of Perton of Perton co., Stafford, from the earliest recorded times; by Edward A. Hardwicke ... Calcutta, Printed by Cones & co., 1897. 2 p. 1., 50 p. 26 cm. 3-1422.   CS439. P5

371

PESCOD.   See PESCUD.

13396   PESCUD.   Three courageous women and their kin; a Pescud family genealogy.   By Elizabeth (Hogg) Ironmonger.   (Berryville, Va., Chesapeake Book Co., 1965)   iv, 278 p. 24 cm. Bibliographical footnotes.   65-5363.
CS71. P469   1965

PESHALE.   See: PARSHALL.
WESTON, 1899

13397   PESHINE.   The Peshine family in Europe and in America; notes and suggestions for a genealogical tree, from the beginning of the fourteenth century to the present day, with some biographical sketches and much data relating to the Ball, Mulford and Pye families; comprising all information at hand, whether based on tradition or on existing records, the whole collected, arranged and commented upon by John Henry Henry Hobart Peshine ... Santa Barbara, Cal. (F. Morley, printer) 1916.   viii p., 1 l., 109 p. 24½ cm. 16-18627.
CS71. P622   1916

13398   PESTALOZZI.   Geschichte der Familie Pestalozzi.   By Hans Anton Pestalozzi.   (Zürich, Buchverlag NZZ, 1958)   408 p. illus., 44 plates. 29 cm. 60-17614.   CS999. P4   1958

PETER.   See PETERS.

13399   PETERS.   A history of the Rev. Hugh Peters ... With an appendix.   By the Rev. Samuel Peters ... New-York, Printed for the author, 1807.   vi, 155 p. 22 cm. Contains a genealogical account of William Peters of Boston, and of his descendants: p. (109)-155. 4-33491.   DA407. P4P4

13400   PETERS.   Life and time.   A birth-day memorial of seventy years.   With memories and reflections for the aged and the young.   By Absalom Peters, D. D. ... New York, Sheldon & company; Boston, Gould & Lincoln, 1866.   80 p. 17½ cm. Poems. Appendix: Notes, explanatory and biographical (etc.) 24-17864.
PS2554. P33

13401   PETERS.   A Peters lineage, five generations of the descendants of Dr. Charles Peters, of Hempstead.   Compiled by Martha Bockée Flint.   (Poughkeepsie, N. Y. ? 1896?)   1 p. l., 164, xi p. front. 25 cm. 1-18169.   CS71. P48   1896

13402   PETERS.   Peters of New England: a genealogy, and family history; compiled by Edmund Frank Peters and Eleanor Bradley Peters (Mrs. Edward McClure Peters) ... New York, The Knickerbocker press, 1903.   2 p. l., xxi p., 1 l., 444 p. front., plates, ports., fold. facsims. 22½ cm. 3-31014.
CS71. P48   1903

13403   PETERS.   Richard Peters, his ancestors and descendants.   1810.   1889.   Ed. and comp. by Nellie Peters Black.   Atlanta, Foote & Davies company, 1904.   145 p. front., pl., ports., fold. geneal. tab., coats of arms. 22½ cm. 11-22360.   CS71. P48   1904

13404   PETERS.   The Peters family genealogical record and history.   Negative. 1 reel.
4515
Microfilm reading room.

PETERS.   See also: ENDERS, 1960
LANE, 1941
MacDONALD, 1880

PETERSEN.   See BLACK, 1956

13405   PETERSON.   The Peterson family of Duxbury, Mass.   By William Bradford Browne.   (Reprinted from the New England historical and genealogical register for April, July and October, 1916)   Boston, 1916.   1 p. l., 26 p. 23 cm. 17-6129.   CS71. P485   1916

13406   PETERSON.   Historical and genealogical account of the Peterson family.   (By William Henry Peterson) Barnard, Mo., Rush printing co., 1926.   (367) p. plates, ports., facsims., fold. geneal. tables. 24 cm.

13406 continued: Blank pages for Memorandum (294-341) Half-title: Genealogical records and sketches of the descendants of Lawrens Peterson and Nancy Jones-Peterson, who planted the family tree in America before the revolutionary war, compiled by William Henry Peterson, Samuel Jackson Peterson, Charles Everett Peterson, edited by Ruth Gould-Peterson, Samuel Jackson Peterson, jr. 30-11219.

CS71.P485   1926

13407   PETERSON.   The story of an American family, 1706-1957; the Peterson family history (by J. Maynard Peterson and Nelle Grace McKay.   n.p., 1957)   57 p. illus. 23 cm. 58-34607. CS71.P485   1957

13408   PETERSON.   Finding our forefathers (by) Eunice Anderson Koller (and) Pearl Peterson Nordstrom.   (n.p., c.1962)   v. illus., ports., fold. map, genealogical tables. 29 cm. Includes bibliographical references. 63-1765.   CS71.P485   1962

PETERSON.   See also: BARROW, 1941
BLAUVELT, 1957
KURTZ, 1925
POTTS, 1895
No. 553 - Goodhue county.

PETRE.   See: FERMOR, 1887-92

PETRIE.   See KLOCK, 1960

13410   PETRUSHEVYCH.   (Narys istorii rodu Petrushevychiv)   By Ivan Oleksander Maksymchuk. 1967.   288 p. illus., facsims., ports. 21 cm. 77-39142. (title romanized)   CS543.P4   1967

PETRY.   See MILLER, 1926

PETTENGILL.   See BARTLETT, 1915

13411   PETTIBONE.   Genealogy of the Pettibone family.   Compiled by I. Fayette Pettibone.   Chicago, Brown, Pettibone & Kelly, 1885.   48 p. 25½ cm. A revision of an edition compiled in 1855, from material collected by John Owen Pettibone. 24-20310.   CS71.P489   1885

13412   PETTIJOHN.   Something of the Pettijohn (Pettyjohn) family, with particular reference to the descendants of James Pettyjohn of Hungar's Parish, Northampton County, Virginia, comp. by Era Jane Pettijohn Chamberlain and Clive Abraham Pettijohn.   (n.p.) Priv. print., 1948.   iii, 201 p. illus., ports. 23 cm. 48-23450 *.   CS71.P495   1948

PETTINGELL.   See PETTINGILL.

13413   PETTINGILL.   A Pettingell genealogy; notes concerning those of the name, comp. by the late John Mason Pettingell; arranged for publication by Charles Henry Pope ... edited and compared with the compiler's notes by Charles I. Pettingell.   Boston, Mass. (The Fort Hill Press) 1906. xiv, (3)-582 p. front., ports. 25½ cm. 6-20196.   CS71.P511   1906

13414   PETTINGILL.   (Ancestry of Frank Hervey Pettingell.   Los Angeles, California genealogical society, 1915?)   geneal. tab. 42½ x 48½ cm. (fold. to 22 cm.) Autugraphed. 17-15783.   CS71.P511   1915

13515   PETTINGILL.   The ancestry of Andrew Haskell Pettingell, 1827-1898, of Newburyport, Massachusetts, by Laura K. Pettingell (and) John M. Pettingell, Jr.   (n.p.) 1964.   36, (10) l. geneal. tables, maps. 28 cm. Bibliography: leaves 32-35. 65-29128.   CS71.P511   1964

13516   PETTIS.   Pettis family chart, as comp. by J. H. Clements, with the assistance of Mrs. Emergene A. Roberts.   (Kansas City, Mo., Gallup map & supply company) c.1921.   geneal. tab. 72 x 115 cm. Blue-print. 21-22175.   CS71.P518   1921

PETTIT.   See LEWIS, 1901

13517   PETTITT.   Genealogy of Pettit families in America, descendants of John Pettit, 1630-1632, first of that name in America.   Compiled and edited by Katherine Louise Van Wyck ... South Pasadena,

13517 continued: Calif., 1936. 3 p. 1., 80 numb. 1. pl. (ports.) facsims., 2 fold. geneal. tab. 27½ cm. Mimeographed. Ten additional unnumbered leaves interspersed. Bibliography: numb. 1. 74-75. 38-32648. CS71.P5185 1936

13518 PETTUS. Genealogy of the Pettus family, compiled ... by Mrs. Pocahontas (Hutchinson) Stacy ... Washington, D.C., 1942. 1 p. 1., 38 numb. 1., 10 1. plates, coat of arms. 28 cm. Type-written, with additions in manuscript. 43-1298. CS71.P5187 1942

13519 PETTUS. The Pettus family (by) Pocahontas (Hutchinson) Stacy (Mrs. L. Clarence) Compiled and edited by A. Böhmer Rudd. Washington, 1957. 67 p. illus. 28 cm. 57-14517 rev. CS71.P5187 1957

PETTUS. See also: LANE, 1941
MEAD, 1921

13520 PETTY. The Albert Petty family; a genealogical and historical story of a sturdy pioneer family of the West, based on records of the past and knowledge of the present. By Charles Brown Petty. Salt Lake City, Deseret News Press (1953?) vi, 322p. illus. (part col.) ports., map. coats of amrs (part col.) 28 cm. "A chart of the church established by Jesus Christ": (2) p. inserted. 54-31922. CS71.P5188 1953

13521 PETTY. The Petty and Francis families and allied lines. By Zora Petty Billingsley. Amarillo, Tex., 1967. 175 p. ports. 27 cm. 67-8876. CS71.P5188 1967

PETTY. See also BAVIS, 1880

13522 PETTY FITZMAURICE. Glanerought and the Petty-Fitzmaurices, by the Marquis of Lans-downe. London, New York (etc.) Oxford university press, 1937. xxviii, 226 p., 1 1. incl. geneal. tables. front., plates, ports., maps. facsim. 22½ cm. Bibliography: p. xxvii-xxviii. 38-11843. DA990.K4L35

13523 PEVEREL. Sompting: reprinted from Dallaway and Cartwright's history of the Rape of Bramber, Sussex. (London?) Priv. print. for F. J. Comber, 1886. 12 p. 28 cm. Pedigree of Peverel: p. 3-6. 19-10621. DA690.S64D3

PEVEREL. See also BROWN, 1903

PEVERIL. See PEVEREL.

13524 PEVERLY. Peverly family, Thomas Peverly of Portsmouth, N.H., 1623-1670, and some of his descendants, by Henry Winthrop Hardon. Boston, Priv. print. (Wright and Potter printing company) 1927. 58 p.,1 1., (4) p. front. (port.) 23½ cm. "Of this book there have been printed one hundred copies only. This copy is no. 12." Blank pages for "Memoranda" (4 ate end) 27-22845. CS71.P519 1927

13525 PEYTON. The adventures of my grandfather. With extracts from his letters, and other family documents, prepared for the press with notes and biographical sketches of himself and his son John Howe Peyton, esq., by John Lewis Peyton ... London, J. Wilson, 1867. x, 249 p. 22 cm. Narrative of the circumstances connected with the settlement of M. Jean Louis or John Lewis and his family in Virginia, p. 215-224; Correspondence relating to Braddock's campaign, p. 225-249. 3-471. F229.P51

13526 PEYTON. Memoir of William Madison Peyton, of Roanoke, together with some of his speech-es in the House of delegates of Virginia, and his letters in reference to secession and the threatened civil war in the United States, etc. etc. By John Lewis Peyton ... London, J. Wilson, 1873. vii, 392 p. 22 cm. Appendixes: A. Abridged genealogy, or pedigree of the ancient noble family of Peyton: p. (311)-336; Isleham Hall, the priory and church, co Cambridge, England: p. 337-354. - B. Memoranda of the Preston family by O. Brown: p. (335)-374. - C. Abridged pedigree of the Lewis family: p. 375-379. - D. Extract from the Washington pedigree ... by John Washington: p. (380)-383. 12-16467. F230.P51

13527 PEYTON. Biographical sketch of Anne Montgomery Peyton, by her son J. L. Peyton. "A contribution to the Lewis memorial volume originated by the trustees and faculty of Roanoke college, Salem, Virginia, and to be publihsed during the first centennial year of the republic of the United States of America." Guernsey, F. Clarke, 1876. 32 p. 20½ cm. "Reprinted from the Guernsey magazine." "Descendants of Anne Montgomery Peyton": p. (30)-31. 5-27468. F230.P47

13528   PEYTON.   Genealogy of the Peyton family embracing the lineage of certain 2 immigrant children of that Henry Peyton of "Lincoln's Inn, " Amiger, England, middle 1600 immigrants to Virginia; 4 (1) Col. Valentine Peyton, 7 (1) Henry Peyton, adult, and including the lineage of the immigrant Robert Peyton, son of Thomas Peyton, son of Sir Edward Peyton of "Isselham, " in England.   With appendix of connecting Farish family.   By Avery Henry Reed.   (Charlottesville? Va.) c. 1963
107 p.   illus. , ports.   29 cm.   64-454.   CS71. P5195

13529   PEYTON.   Peyton-Quirk families, by M. T. Peyton.   (Midland, Tex., 1968)   vi, 286 p. illus. ,
facsims. , ports.   24 cm.   68-6372.   CS71. P5195   1968

PEYTON.   See also: BARKSDALE, 1922   PALMER, 1890
                                 BEAL, 1956   ROGERS, 1958
                                 CROSSLEY, CS439. C835   STRONG, 1912
                                 GLASSELL, 1891   WOOLSEY, 1940

13530   PFANDER.   Charles Pfander family; Iowa pioneers from Ohio.   By Homer Garrison Pfander.
Clarinda, Iowa, 1949.   109 p. illus. , ports. 29 cm. 49-6312. *   CS71. P52   1949

13531   PFAUTZ.   A family record of John Michael Pfautz, a native of Switzerland, Europe, who emigrated from the Palatinate to America, about the year 1707, and his posterity down to the year 1880. Compiled by John Eby Pfautz ... Lancaster, Pa., J. Baer's sons, printers, 1881.   iv, 5-70 p. 16 cm.
2-3996.   CS71. P522   1881

13532   PFEIFFER.   Genealogy of Dr. Francis Joseph Pfeiffer of Philadelphia, Pennsylvania, and his descendants.   1734-1899.   By Edwin Jacquett Sellers.   Philadelphia (Press of J. B. Lippincott co.)
1899.   67 p. front. (port.) 25 cm.   Edition limited to two hundred copies, of which this is no. 20.   9-12839.
                                                                                      CS71. P526   1899

13533   PFEIFFER.   A genealogy list for Peter Pfeiffer (Pifer) George Pfeiffer, Anna Barbara (Pfeiffer) Bietsch (Beach) (and) Margaretha Anna (Pfeiffer) Nicklas, by Margaret Pfeiffer Brown ... Peoria, Ill.,
M. P. Brown, 1934.   (23) p. front. , illus. , ports. 23 cm.   Blank pages for "Memorandum" (22-23) 39-16907.
                                                                                      CS71. P526   1934

13534   PFEIFFER.   "Frederick and his followers" on the Pyfer family tree.   As started by Jacob S. Pyfer in 1906 and continued by his brother, Amos M. Pyfer, his son, George A. Pyfer, and brought up to date by Gladys Pyfer Hammer in 1963.   (Polo, Ill.) 1963.   79 l. illus. 28 cm.   63-5411.
                                                                                      CS71. P526   1963

PFERSCHING.   See PERSHING.

13535   PFINGSTEN.   Dear cousin; (a history of Heinrich Pfingsten and Sophia, nee Schutte, their ancestors from 1604 to 1812, their descendants from 1812 to the present, 1965.   By Colleen Mary (Wilken) Knake.   Urbana, Ill., 1965)   276 p. illus. , facsims. , geneal. tables, map, ports. 29 cm.   Cover title.   500 copies
printed, no. 290.   Prepared by Mrs. Ellery Knake and Elmer Pfingsten.   66-57757 rev.
                                                                                      CS71. P528   1965

PFIRSCHING.   See PERSHING.

13536   PFOST.   The slaughter of the Pfost-Greene family of Jackson county, W. Va.   A history of the tragedy, with a notice of the early settlers of Jackson county, a sketch of the family and John F. Morgan ... By Okey J. Morrison ... (Cincinnati, The Gibson and Sorin co., printers, 1868)   96 p. illus. (incl.
ports.) 23½ cm.   12-26591.   F247. J2M8

PFRENCH.   See FRENCH.

PHANEUF.   See FARNSWORTH, CS90. F3

PHELIPS.   See PHILLIPS.

13537   PHELPS.   Genealogy of Othniel Phelps, esq., of Aylmer, Canada West, Prepared expressly for him, by request, by his esteemed friend, and distant relative, Oliver Seymour Phelps ... St. Catharines, H. F. Leavenworth's "Herald" power press, 1862.   44 p., 1 l. 23 cm. 9-12838.

CS71.P54   1862

13538   PHELPS.   The Phelps family.   An interesting letter touching the genealogical record of one branch of the Phelps family.   By Oliver Seymour Phelps.   Big Rapids (Mich.) Pioneer-magnet print, 1878.   13 p. 18½ cm. 9-12837.   CS71.P54   1878

13539   PHELPS.   A genealogical record of the descendants of Joseph and Jemima (Post) Phelps, of Hebron, Connecticut.   Showing also, in brief, the several links in the genealogical chain which connects them with the old Puritan, William Phelps, who came to America in 1630; with some historical notes and data relating to the common family name.   By Dudley Post Phelps ... (Syracuse, N.Y., C.W. Bardeen) 1885.   3 p. 1., 5-96 (i.e.104) p. front. (phot.) illus. 23½ cm. (School bulletin publications) Edited by Anna Redfield Phelps.   Pages 77 a-h and alternated pages from 80 - 96 left blank for "A genealogical record." 9-29649.

CS71.P54   1885

13540   PHELPS.   Genealogy and a short historical narrative of one branch of the family of George Phelps, since the founding of the family in America, by William and George Phelps in 1630.   Ed. by Alanson Hosmer Phelps.   San Francisco, Cal., 1897.   2 p. 1., 9-192 p., 1 l. front., plates, ports., coat of arms. 23½ cm.   Four blank pages at end for "Family record." "Of this book two hundred copies only exist, which are for private circulation."

CS71.P54   1897

13541   PHELPS.   The Phelps family of America and their English ancestors, with copies of wills, deeds, letters, and other interesting papers, coats of arms and valuable records.   Comp. by Judge Oliver Seymour Phelps, of Portland, Oregon, and Andrew T. Servin, of Lenox, Mass ... Pittsfield, Mass., Eagle publishing co., 1899.   2 v. front., illus., plates, ports., maps, plans, facsims., coats of arms. 24½ cm. Paged continuously. 1-21628.   CS71.P54   1899

13542   PHELPS.   ... Our ancestors ... James Andrew Phelps, genealogist.   Brooklyn, N.Y., Bureau for genealogical research, 1913.   20 l. illus. (coats of arms) 22½ cm. 14-3069.

CS71.P54   1913

13543   PHELPS.   The family of Phelps.   1520-1900.   (Caro, Mich., Fred Slocum's printing works, 1900.   cover-title, 7 l. 24½ cm. Compiled by Mrs. Alice M. Phelps Thomas. 13-6113.   CS71.P54   1900

13544   PHELPS.   The Phelps family.   A history of the ancestors and the descendants of Josiah Phelps of Stafford Springs, Conn., and Pittsford, N.Y.   Comp. by Louise (Copeland) Phelps ... Oak Park, Ill. (1918)   2 p. 1., 21 l. 18 cm. Type-written. Edited by Mrs. Anson Marston (i.e. Mrs. Mary Alice (Day) Marston) Additions and corrections in ms. throughout text. 23-6175.   CS71.P54   1918

13545   PHELPS.   Phelps family in Fulton co., N.Y., by W.L. Porter, Chicago.   (Chicago? 1940?) 2 p. 1., 10 numb. l., 2 l. map. 28 cm. Type-written. 41-6098.   CS71.P54   1940

13546   PHELPS.   The Phelps family of Virginia and Kentucky and allied families.   By Nancy Reba Roy.   La Mesa, Calif. (1960?)   166 l. 28 cm. 62-3814.   CS71.P54   1960

PHELPS.   See also:

CARTER, 1958b	MERRILL, 1899	SEHFFIELD, 1936
DAY, 1916	NASH, 1902	THOMPSON, 1915
FLAGG, 1903	POLLOCK, 1932	WYMAN, 1941
FOSTER, 1897	SHEFFIELD, 1922	No. 3939 - Colebrook.
GOODWIN, E171.A53 vol.13		

13547   PHIFER.   Genealogy and history of the Phifer family. (Charlotte, N.C., Presbyterian standard publishing company, 1910)   53, (1) p. 21 cm. Written in 1883 by Charles H. Phifer but never published. cf. Pref., signed George E. Wilson. 1910. Manuscript notes throughout the text. "The Phifer family of North Carolina, a genealogical abstract, comp. by Robert S. Phifer ... Jackson, Mississippi, 1922": 75 numbered leaves consisting of manuscript notes, mounted newspaper clippings, and mounted photographs, inserted in front of the book. 23-1897.   CS71.P543   1910

13548   PHILBRICK.   A genealogy of the Philbrick and Philbrook families, descended from the emigrant, Thomas Philbrick, 1583-1667.   By Rev. Jacob Chapman ... Exeter, N.H., Exeter gazette steam printing house, 1886.   202 p. front., ports. 23 cm. 9-12836.   CS71.P545   1886

PHILBRICK.   See also: BLAKE, 1948
                                 DRAKE, 1962

PHILBROOK.   See PHILBRICK.

PHILIBERT.   See HAYES, DA690.B74K3

PHILIPOT.   See PHILPOT.

PHILIPS.   See PHILLIPS.

PHILIPSE.   See PHILLIPS.

PHILLIMORE.   See FILMER.

13549   PHILLIPS.   The Phillips family and Phillips Exeter academy.   (From the North American review for July, 1858) Boston, Crosby, Nichols and company, 1858.   26 p. 22 cm. By Joseph Gibson Hoyt. Cover-title.   A review of Taylor's Memoir of His Honor Samuel Phillips, and of the Catalogue of the Phillips Exeter academy for 1857-8. 14-19469.   LD7501.E9P4 1858

13550   PHILLIPS.   Philips family.   Re-union and names of descendants.   1877.   Philadelphia, W. Syckelmoore, printer, 1880.   62 p. 17½ cm. "Descendants of Joseph amd Mary Philips, from 1755 to 1880": p. 24-58. 26-19565.   CS71.P555   1880

13551   PHILLIPS.   Phillips genealogies; including the family of George Phillips, first minister of Watertown, Mass. ... also the families of Ebenezer Phillips, of Southboro, Mass., Thomas Phillips, of Duxbury, Mass., Thomas Phillips, of Marshfield, Mass., John Phillips, of Easton, Mass., James Phillips, of Ipswich, Mass.   With brief genealogies of Walter Phillips, of Damariscotta, Me., Andrew Phillips, of Kittery, Me., Michael, Richard, Jeremy and Jeremiah Phillips, of Rhode Island; and fragmentary records, of early American families of this name ... Comp. by Albert M. Phillips.   Auburn, Mass. (Press of C. Hamilton, Worcester, Mass.) 1885.   xii p., 2 l., (9)-233 p. front., ports. 24 cm. 9-12835.   CS71.P555   1885
                                 Microfilm 8654

13552   PHILLIPS.   Outline of the Phillips genealogy for 300 years, 1587-1887, and of the Coventry, N.Y. branch of the Phillips family for 100 years ... (Newtown? Conn., 1886)   geneal. tab. 58½ x 41 fold. to 30½ cm. Compiled by James Phillips Hoyt. 9-15012.   CS71.P555   1887

13553   PHILLIPS.   The family and vicissitudes of John Phillips, senior, of Duxbury and Marshfield. A vexatious snarl in the genealogy of an old colony progenitor disentangled.   By Azel Ames ... Malden, Mass., Press of G. E. Dunbar, 1903.   33, vi p., 3 l. plates, facsims. 24 cm. 5-24237.   CS71.P555   1903

13554   PHILLIPS.   The history of the family of Philipps of Picton ... London, Darling & son, ltd., 1906.   2 p. l., 271 p. geneal. tables. 26 cm. "Note" signed: Mary Margaret Philipps. 40-287.   CS439.P52   1906

13555   PHILLIPS.   ... Philipse manor hall, Yonkers, N.Y.   The site, the building and its occupants. By the secretary of the American scenic and historic preservation society.   (In American scenic and historic preservation society. Thirteenth annual report, 1908. Albany, 1908. 23 cm. p. (161)-247. pl., fold. plan) Bibliography: p. 246-247. 14-4410.   E151.A51 vol. 13

13556   PHILLIPS.   Philipse manor hall at Yonkers, N.Y.; the site, the building and its occupants, by Edward Hagaman Hall, L.H.D.   New York, N.Y., The American scenic and historic preservation society, c.1912.   255 p. xiv pl. (2 fold.; incl. ports., plan) 19 cm. Coat of arms on cover. Enlarged from an article published as an appendix to the 13th annual report of the American scenic and historic preservation society, 1908. 12-11737.   F129.Y5H17

13557   PHILLIPS.   Family record of Jeremiah Phillips, D.D., missionary to Orissa, India. 1812 - 1912.   Compiled by his daughter, Harriet Phillips Stone.   (n.p., 1913)   46 p. plates, ports. 20½ cm.   Pages 43-46 left blank for additional record.   Limited edition.   16-2752.
CS71.P555   1913

13558   PHILLIPS.   The manor of Philipsborough; address written for the New York branch of the Order of colonial lords of manors in America, by Edward Hagaman Hall, L.H.D.   Baltimore, 1920.
35 p. incl. front., illus., (incl. ports., coat of arms) fold. pl.   23½ cm.   (Order of colonial lords of manors in America. Publications)
20-16025.
E186.99.O6 no.7
—— Copy 2
F127.W5H17

13559   PHILLIPS.   Short history of the Philips-Yarbrough families.   Some material first gathered by the late Jere C. Philips, Birmingham, Alabama.   Added to, compiled, edited and published by Reuben Littleton Philips and wife, May Siddons Philips.   Pauls Valley, Okl., 1928.   cover-title, 1 l., 48 p.
18½ cm.   29-2575.
CS71.P555   1928

13560   PHILLIPS.   John Phillips of Grafton, Rensselaer county, New York, and 120 of his descendants, The Puritan manuscripts.   (By) Vernon S. Phillips ... Akron, O.   (1933)   1 p. l., 19 numb. l. 29 cm.
Typewritten.   "References": leaf 1.   33-25763.
CS71.P555   1933

13561   PHILLIPS.   James Phillips, jr., by Walter De Blois Briggs, his grandson.   San Francisco, 1935.   5 p. l., 145 p., 1 l. front., illus., plates, ports., map, facsims. (1 fold.) 24½ cm.   "This edition is limited to one hundred and fifty copies printed at the Grabhorn press ... in October, 1935."   36-5.
CT275.P5928B7

13562   PHILLIPS.   Phillips family history; a brief history of the Phillips family, beginning with the emigration from Wales, and a detailed genealogy of the descendants of John and Benjamin Philips, pioneer citizens of Wilson county, Tenn., by Harry Phillips ... Lebanon, Tenn., The Lebanon democrat, inc., 1935.   3 p. l., 242, xix p. front., pl., ports. 23½ cm. 35-9128 rev.
CS71.P555   1935

13563   PHILLIPS.   John I. Phillips; copyright ... by Howard B. Grant ... Philippi, W. Va., H.B. Grant, c. 1936.   1 l. 28½ x 23 cm.   Caption title.   Text runs parallel with back of cover.   Mimeographed. 38M828T.
CS71.P555   1936

13564   PHILLIPS.   The Phillips family of Brighton, by Desmond Hannon.   (London, Harrison & sons, ltd.) 1938.   30 p., 1 l. pl., ports. 23½ cm. 45-33966.
CS439.P52   1938

13565   PHILLIPS.   Ancestry of Frederick Philipse, first lord and founder of Philipse manor at Yonkers, N.Y., by Thomas Capek ... New York, The Parbar company, 1939.   28 p. incl. front., plates, port., coats of arms. 23½ cm. 39-20663.
CS71.P555   1939

13566   PHILLIPS.   Genealogy of Rev. Reuel Phillips, sr., and his 14 children and descendants.   Compiled by Myrtle H. Phillips ... (Los Angeles, New method printing co., c. 1941)   154, (3) p. incl. illus., ports. front. 30 cm. 41-28035.
CS71.P555   1941

13567   PHILLIPS.   ... Phillips family tree, by Sanford A. Moss ... Lynn, Mass., 1942.   geneal. tab. 29½ x 58 cm.   Photostat (positive) of manuscript copy. 42-20959.
CS71.P555   1942

13568   PHILLIPS.   Wesley Reuel Phillips' diary, adjunct to the Phillips genealogy and the Butel genealogy, by Dr. Phillips, (Myrtle Hannah Phillips) (Los Angeles, 1947)   1 p. l., 44 p. illus. (incl. ports., facsim.) 29½ x 23 cm. 47-21844.
CS71.P555   1947

13569   PHILLIPS.   Phillips family.   Ginther ancestors contributed by Jennie E. Stewart.   By Eva Oma Firestone.   (n.p., 1947?)   44 p. 22 cm.   Cover-title: Descendants of Hiram and Mary Phillips, with ancestors of John Solomon Ginther. 48-19708*.
CS71.P555   1947a

13570   PHILLIPS.   My ancestry. By Frank McGinley Phillips.   Rev. De Land, Fla., 1959.
(4) p. 24 cm. 59-36855.
CS71.P555   1959

PHILLIPS.　See also:

BATTEY, 1940b	JARRATT, 1957	SALISBURY, 1885
BRUMBACK, 1961	LEONARD, 1928	SMITH, 1964a
BYRD, E159.G56	LEWIS, 1901	THRUSTON, 1909
DEAN, 1940	MAY, 1929	TUCKER, 1957
FERMOR, 1887-92	PETTY, BX5195.T5B6	VAN METER, F450.V26
HALL, 1959	PHOENIX, 1875	WASHINGTON, E159.G56
HUNTER, 1959		YANCEY, 1958

PHILLPOT.　See PHILPOT.

13571　PHILPOT.　The Philpott family of Maryland and Virginia, preliminary genealogical notes (also Philpot, Phillpot, Phillpott, Philipot, Philpotts, etc.)　By Walter Burges Smith.　Washington, 1960. 30 l.　34 cm.　62-48085.
CS71.P559　1960

13572　PHINIZY.　The Phinizy family in America, by Ferdinand Phinizy Calhoun.　Atlanta, Ga., Johnson-Dallis co., printers (1925?)　3 p. l., (3)-176 p. front., plates, ports., map, facsims., fold. geneal. tab. 25½ cm. Blank leaves interspersed for additions.　25-9901.
CS71.P572　1925

PHINIZY.　See also no. 516 - Notable southern families vol. 1

13573　PHINNEY.　Phinney genealogy; a brief history of Ebenezer Phinney, of Cape Cod, and his descendants, from 1637 to 1947.　Rutland, Vt., Tuttle Pub. Co. (1948?)　146 p. plates, ports. 24 cm. "Two hundred copies printed.　No. 91."　50-34908.
CS71.P5723　1948

13574　PHINNEY.　Finney-Phinney families in America: descendants of John Finney of Plymouth and Barnstable, Mass., and Bristol, R. I., of Samuel Finney of Philadelphia, Pa., and of Robert Finney of New London, Pa.　From the notebooks of Howard Finney, Sr.　(Richmond?) 1957.　viii, 298 p. 24 cm. Helen B. Hartman edited the original manuscript and prepared it for publication.　57-36819.
CS71.P5723　1957

PHINNEY.　See also:　BROWN, 1929
HAYFORD, 1901
MORSE, 1925

13575　PHIPPS.　The life of Colonel Pownoll Phipps ... with family records, by Pownoll W. Phipps ... Printed for private circulation.　London, R. Bentley and son, 1894.　vii, 228 p. 12 geneal. tab. 21 cm. "A list of books referred to, and containing interesting matter bearing on our family": p. 227-228.　Contains also pedigrees of the Tierney, Ramsay, Osborne and Riall families.　21-2247.
CT788.P58P5

13576　PHIPPS.　Notes on Phipps and Phip families of England, Ireland, the West Indies, and of New England.　Part I-II ... Preliminary sketch.　By Major H. R. Phipps ... Lahore, Printed at the "Civil and military gazette" press, by S. T. Weston, 1911.　2 v. fold. geneal. tab. 21 cm.　Contents. - Pt. I. Phipps of Nottingham & Reading, 1570-1700. - Pt. II. (1) Phipps of St. Christopher's, West Indies, 1670-1800.　(2) Descendants of Sir Constantine Phipps, (barons & earls of Mulgrave, viscounts & marquises of Wormanby) 1685 to 1863.　13-9852.
CS439.P53　1911

13577　PHIPPS.　The ancestors and descendants of John Phipps, of Sherborn, 1757-1847, abridged from the Phipps genealogy ... by Frederick Lewis Weis.　Lincoln, R. I., 1924.　1 p. l., 24 p. 23 cm. Title vignette (coat of arms of Sir William Phips, royal governor of Massachusetts) 25-19276.
CS71.P573　1924

PHIPPS.　See also STUART, 1961

13578　PHOENIX.　The descendants of John Phoenix, an early settler in Kittery, Maine.　By Stephen Whitney Phoenix ... New York, Priv. print. (Bradstreet press) 1867.　5 p. l., 51 numb. l., (2) l. 27 cm. "Edition 100 copies, octavo; 5 copies, quarto.　All for presentation."　9-12834.
CS71.P574　1867

13579　PHOENIX.　(Ancestry of Jonas Phillips Phoenix.　New York, 1875)　geneal. tab. 25½ x 35½ cm. fold. to 17½ x 25½ cm.　Compiled by Stephen Whitney Phoenix.　Reprinted in the compiler's Whitney family.　N. Y., 1878.　v. 1 no. 1589 1-8123.
CS71.P574　1875

13580   PHOENIX.   The Phoenix family of New York.   Compiled by S. Whitney Phoenix.   (New York? 1880)   geneal. tab. 23½ x 23 cm. fold. to 23 x 17½ cm.   9-12833.   CS71.P574   1880

13581   PIATT.   Don Piatt: his work and his ways.   By Charles Grant Miller ... Cincinnati, R. Clarke & co., 1893.   vi, (11)-381 p. front. (port.) plates (incl. facsim.) 20 cm.   "Ancestry": p. (11)-31.   9-23201.
                    F496.P587

13582   PIATT.   The tribe of Jacob (Piatt) by N. Louise Lodge ... 3d ed.   (Springfield, Mo., Young-Stone printing co., c.1934)   2 p. l., 170 p., 2 l. 26 cm. 41-38338.   CS71.P577   1934

        PIATT.   See also McKINNEY, 1905

13583   PICARD.   The Picards or Pychards of Stradewy (now Tretower) castle, and Scethrog, Breck-nockshire; Ocle Pichard, Almaly, Staunton-on-Wye, Over Letton, Merston, Bredwardine, Hopton Hagurnel in Great Cowarne, Bishop's Stanford, Cradley, Pengethley, etc., Herefordshire; Sapey Pichard, and Suckley, Worcestershire.   With some account of the family of Sapy, of Upper Sapey, Herefordshire.   London, Golding and Lawrence, 1878.   4 p. l., 183 p. front., plates, fold. geneal. tables, 2 col. coats of arms. 27 cm. The plates are mounted photographs. Contains genealogical tables: "Pedigree of Bernard Newmarch" and "Pedigree of Pichard of Suckley, and Cooke of co. Worcester." 17-29946.   CS459.P5

        PICHARD.   See PICARD.

13584   PICHER.   Genealogy of Oliver Stanton Picher and Marion Lewis Picher.   By Oliver Stanton Picher.   (Honolulu, Star-Bulletin Print. Co., 1967)   196 p. ports. 25 cm.   Imprint in ms. on t.p.   30 copies. 73-47.   CS71.P579   1967

13585   PICKENS.   Cousin Monroe's history of the Pickens family.   By Monroe Pickens.   Revised and published by Kate Pickens Day.   (Easley, S.C., 1951)   279 p. ports., coat of arms. 24 cm. 51-48263.
                    CS71.P58   1951

13586   PICKENS.   Pickens family chart.   By Raymond M. Bell.   1 p. in vertical file.   Ask reference librarian for this material.

13587   PICKENS.   Pickens family. (Male descendants)   In vertical file.   Ask reference librarian for this.

13588   PICKERING.   Genealogical data respecting John Pickering of Portsmouth, N.H., and his de-scendants.   Boston, 1884.   III p., 1 l., 5-32 p., 1 l. 23½ cm.   Explanation signed: R.H.E. i.e. Robert Henry Eddy. 1-546.   CS71.P6   1884

        —— Supplement to Genealogical data ... By Robert Henry Eddy.   Boston, 1884.   28 p. 23½ cm. 1-547.   CS71.P6   1884a

13589   PICKERING.   The Pickering genealogy, comprising the descendants of John and Sarah (Burrill) Pickering of Salem, by Charles Pickering Bowditch.   (n.p.) 1887.   1 p. l., 73 (i.e. 79) numb. l. 53½ x 72½ cm. In portfolio.   "One hundred copies privately printed." 8-18405.   CS71.P6   1887

13590   PICKERING.   The Pickering genealogy: being an account of the first three generations of the Pickering family of Salem, Mass., and of the descendants of John and Sarah (Burrill) Pickering, of the third generation.   By Harrison Ellery and Charles Pickering Bowditch ... Privately printed (Cambridge, University press, J. Wilson and son) 1897.   3 v. front., plates, ports., facsims., geneal. tables (part fold.) 29 cm. Paged continuously.   "One hundred copies printed." 9-14809.   CS71.P6   1897

        PICKERING.   See also: CHALCROFT, 1939
                                COX, 1939
                                FOX, CS439.F7
                                ROBINSON, 1894
                                UMFREVILLE, CS439.U4

13591   PICKET.   The Picket family.   (Richmond, Va., 1909)   (2) p. 43½ cm.   From the Richmond, Virginia, Times-Dispatch of Sunday, April 11, 1909.   By Thomas Lee Broun. CA12-1174.   CS71.P612   1909

13592   PICKETT.   Bibliography of Doctor Thomas Edward Pickett of Maysville, Kentucky.   Kentucky historical society.   Frankfort, 1914.   16 p. port. 24 cm. (Kentucky historical series. 8th ser.) Biographical sketches containing references to Dr. Pickett's scientific and professional activities.   No titles of books or articles written by him are mentioned. 14-31338 rev. *

CT275. P63K4

13593   PICKMAN.   The diary and letters of Benjamin Pickman (1740-1819) of Salem, Massachusetts, with a biographical sketch and genealogy of the Pickman family by George Francis Dow.   Newport, R. I., 1928.   x, 230 p., 1 l. front., plates, ports. 24½ cm. "One hundred and twenty-five copies printed at the Wayside press, Topsfield, Massachusetts." Title vignette: coat of arms. "Biographical sketch of Mrs. Mary (Toppan) Pickman, 1744-1817, written by her son Hon. Benjamin Pickman": p. (75)-86.   28-24820 rev.

CS71. P613   1928

PICKMAN.   See also SAUNDERS, 1897

PICOLET.   See: SHYROCK, 1877
SHYROCK, 1929a

13594   PIDCOCK.   History of the Pidcock family and association.   By Gladys Gray Pidcock.   (White House? N. J., 1959?)   131 p. illus. 23 cm. 61-24097.

CS71. P614   1959

PIDCOCK.   See also HENZEY, CS439. H4

13595   PIER.   Thomas Pier.   By Clara J. McCabe.   (Clarence? N. Y.) 1958.   207 p. 28 cm. 59-27017.

CS71. P615   1958

13596   PIERCE.   My ancestors in America.   Comp., printed and pub. for gratuitous distribution among near relatives, by Wm. Blake Pierce.   Chicago, 1864.   iv, 5-48 p. 22½ cm. Contains also the Blake, Tappan and Holmes families.   19-10587.

CS71. P616   1864

13597   PIERCE.   Peirce genealogy, being the record of the posterity of John Pers, an early inhabitant of Watertown, in New England ... with notes on the history of other families of Peirce, Pierce, Pearce, etc.   By Frederick Clifton Peirce ... Worcester, Press of C. Hamilton, 1880.   xviii p., 1 l., (17)-278 p. 3 l. front., ports. 24 cm.   Genealogy of the family of Daniel Pierce of Watertown and Newbury, 1634: p. (231)-266.   9-12832 rev.

CS71. P616   1880

13598   PIERCE.   Pierce genealogy, being the record of the posterity of Thomas Pierce, an early inhabitant of Charlestown, and afterwards Charlestown village (Woburn), in New England, with wills, inventories, biographical sketches, etc.   By Frederic Beech Pierce ... Assisted and edited by Frederick Clifton Peirce ... Worcester, Press of C. Hamilton, 1882.   xx p., 2 l., (17)-367 p., 1 l. front., ports., facsims., coat of arms. 24 cm. 9-12831.

CS71. P616   1882

13599   PIERCE.   Pearce genealogy, being the record of the posterity of Richard Pearce, an early inhabitant of Portsmouth, in Rhode Island, who came from England, and whose genealogy is traced back 972.   With an introduction of the male descendants of Josceline de Louvaine ... By Col. Frederick C. Pierce ... Rockford, Ill. (Press of J. Munsell's sons, Albany) 1888.   150 p. 23½ cm. 9-12830.

CS71. P616   1888

13600   PIERCE.   Pierce genealogy, no. IV.   Being the record of the posterity of Capt. Michael, John and Capt. William Pierce, who came to this country from England.   By Frederick Clifton Pierce ... Albany, N. Y., Pub. for the author by J. Munsell's sons, 1889.   441 p. 24 cm. 9-12829.

CS71. P616   1889

13601   PIERCE.   The Pierce family record 1687-1893.   A new ed., rev. and augm. with an appendix containing notices of related families, Hardy, Grafton, Gardener, Dawes, Lathrop, Cordis, Russell, Haswell, Gray, Chipman, Blanchard, Holland, May, West, Wyman, Cobia, etc.   By E. W. West ... New York, Bradstreet press, 1894.   2 p. l., 97, (1) p. 23 cm. 9-12828.   CS71. P616   1894

13602   PIERCE.   Family records relating to the families of Pearce of Holsworthy; Edgcumbe of Laneast; Eliot of Lostwithiel; Livingstone of Calendar; Reynolds of Exeter; Gayer of Liskeard; and others.   Comp. and illustrated by Sir Edward Robert Pearce Edgcumbe ... Exeter, W. Pollard & co., printers, 1895.   5 p. l., (17)-111 p. front., illus., ports., coat of arms, geneal. tab. 31 cm. "Edition of 120 numbered copies of which this is no. 3", signed by the author. 24-6052.

CS438. E4

13603 PIERCE. Pierce genealogy. being a partial record of the posterity of Richard Pearse, an early inhabitant of Portsmouth in Rhode Island, who came from England, and whose genealogy is traced back to 972. By Clifford George Hurlburt ... San Diego, Cal., G. E. White, 1927.
2 p. l., (3)-220 p. plates, port. 22½ cm. Blank pages at end for "Family record". 28-11916. CS71.P616 1927

13604 PIERCE. Seven Pierce families; a record of births, deaths and marriages of the first seven generations of Pierces in America, including a record of the descendants of Abial Peirce to the present, collected by Harvey Cushman Pierce. Washington, D.C., 1936. xlviii, 324 p. 2 port. 24 cm. Bibliography: p. xi. 36-17960. CS71.P616 1936

13605 PIERCE. Genealogy and history of Peirce and Darby families with collateral lineages of Warren, Fiske, Conant, Bemis and others, from Rognwald, 931 A.D. to the thirty-sixth generation in America. Author and compiler by Lucy Bender. (Langley Field, Va., 1936) 78 numb. l. col. coat of arms. 28 cm. Type-written. Includes bibliographical references. 36-30625. CS71.P616 1936a

13606 PIERCE. Thirty-one generations; a thousand years of Percies and Pierces, 972 to 1948. Limited ed. By Barnard Ledward Colby. (New London, Conn., 1947) 31 p. 22 cm. 48-422*. CS71.P616 1947

13607 PIERCE. Our heritage, an historical narrative, by Jette Pierce Lawrence for her family. Climax, Mich. (1958) 131 l. illus. 28 cm. 59-507. CS71.P616 1958

13608 PIERCE. Pearce pioneers in Kentucky. With notes on related families: Akin, Anderson, Arras, Benedict, Burden, Carroll, Gilbertz, Hoepfinger, Jordan, Ligon, Majors, Moss, Redmond, Stanhope, Stapleton, Swafford, Tipton, Torr. Compiled and published by Marvin J. Pearce, Sr. El Cerrito, Calif. (1969) 180 p. illus., coats of arms, ports. 28 cm. 70-10619 MARC. CS71.P616 1969

PIERCE. See also:

BEVILLE, 1917	EDGCUMBE, CS438.E4	PERCY.
BLACK, 1966	GREENLEE, 1956	ROBERTS, 1946
BOSE, E171.A53 vol.18	LINCOLN, 1930	SCHWARTZ, 1961
BROWN, 1929	PAINE, 1913	STEEL, 1905
CARTER, 1958	PEIRCE.	WHITCOMB, 1888
DOBYNS, 1908		

PIERCEALL. See ABEL, 1928

13609 PIERPONT. Hurstpierpoint; its lords and families, ancient and modern. By William Smith Ellis ... London, J. R. Smith; (etc., etc., 1859?) 1 p. l., 39 p. incl. geneal. tables. front., illus., plates. 22 cm. (Hazlitt tracts, v.4, no.1) Pedigrees of Bowett, Warren and Pierpoint. "Reprinted from vol. XI of the Sussex archaeological collections", 1859, p. (50)-88. 23-679. AC911.H3 v.4 no.1

13610 PIERPONT. A genealogical abstract of descent of the family of Pierrepont, from Sir Hugh de Pierrepont, of Picardy, France, A.D.980. Compiled by Edward J. Marks. New Haven, Conn., Hoggson & Robinson, printers, 1881. 41 p. front. (coat of arms) 22½ cm. On cover: The Pierrepont family from 980 - 1881. 40-18332. CS71.P625 1881

13611 PIERPONT. Pierrepont genealogies from Norman times to 1913, with particular attention paid to the line of descent from Hezekiah Pierpont, youngest son of Rev. James Pierpont of New Haven, by R. Burnham Moffat. (New York) Priv. print. (L. Middleditch co.) 1913. 211 p. incl. plates, group of ports., coat of arms. front. 25 cm. 13-6556. CS71.P625 1913

13612 PIERPONT. Pierpont genealogy and connecting lines, particularly Rev. John Pierpont of Hollis street church, Boston, Massachusetts. Compiled from authentic sources by his granddaughter Mary Pierpont Barnum. Edited by his grandson Arthur Edwin Boardman. Printed by his great grandson James Allen Crosby. Boston, 1928. 42 p. plates, ports., coats of arms. 24½ cm. Contains Barnum, Boardman and Powell genealogies. 28-9889. CS71.P625 1928

13612a PIERPONT.   Francis H. Pierpont, Union war governor of Virginia and father of West Virginia, by Charles H. Ambler ... Chapel Hill, The University of North Carolina press, 1937.   xiii, 483 p. front., illus. (incl. facsims.) plates, ports., maps (1 fold.) 24 cm.   "This edition is limited to twelve hundred copies ... "Notes on Pierpont (Peirpoint) genealogy": p. (391)-398.   "Selected bibliography": p. (455) - 467.   37-17670.

E534. P65

13613   PIERPONT.   The Pierpoint-Pierpont family of Maryland, Virginia, West Virginia.   By Kathryn (Pierpoint) Hedman.   (Alexandria? Va.) c.1953.   162 p. illus., coat of arms.   23 cm.   Includes genealogical information compiled by Hattie Malone Pierpoint, printed in 1969.   53-37768.

CS71. P623   1953

13614   PIERPONT.   The Pierreponts, 1802-1962; the American forebears and the descendants of Hezekiah Beers Pierpont and Anna Maria Constable.   By Abbot Low Moffat.   (Washington) 1962. 81 p. illus. 24 cm.   At head of title: Pierrepont genealogy.   Correction leaf, dated Mar. 12, 1963 inserted.   63-47605.

CS71. P625   1962

PIERPONT.   See also HILL, E171. A53 v. 13

13615   PIERROT.   Pierrot-Liengme-Fleming-Gatewood lineage.   By Richard Stephen Uhrbrock. (n. p., 1966)   32 l. 29 cm.   Photocopy.   Bibliographical references included in "Notes" (leaves 31-32) 67-87.

CS71. P627   1966

PIERSEY.   See PERCY.

PIERSON.   See PEARSON.

13616   PIETY.   An early history of the Piety family and kinsmen, 1654-1956.   By Charles Robert Piety.   (n. p., introd. 1956)   182 p. illus. 22 cm.   62-66166.   CS71. P628   1956

PIFER.   See PFEIFFER.

PIGGE.   See TURNIDGE, 1935

PIGGOT.   See PIGOT.

PIGGOTT.   See PIGOT.

13617   PIGOT.   The rare quarto edition of Lord Byron's "Fugitive pieces" described by Herbert C. Roe; with a note on the Pigot family.   Nottingham, Printed for private circulation, Derry & sons, ltd., 1919.   30 p. front. (port.) 3 facsim. 23½ cm.   20-16120.   PR4363. R6

13618   PIGOT.   Papers from an iron chest at Doddershall, Bucks, selected and edited by G. Eland ... Aylesbury, G. T. De Fraine & co., ltd., 1937.   2 p. l., iii, 104 p. front., pl., port., plan, facsim. 25½ cm.   The documents reproduced here are, in the main, concerned with county administration in Buckinghamshire, 1553-1696.   cf. Introd.   39-25068.

DA670. B9E4

PIGOT.   See also: ANDREWS, CS439. A59
                    LEE, DA670. L19C5 vol. 97
                    MESSINGER, 1934

PIGOTT.   See PIGOT.

13619   PIKE.   Records of the Pike family association of America, 1900/1901 -   Saco, Me., Press of W. L. Streeter, 1902-   v. illus., plates, ports., fold. plan. 21-22½ cm.   Vol. for 1904 has imprint: Lynn, Mass., Press of G. H. & A. L. Nichols, 1905.   7-23343.

CS71. P636   1902

13620   PIKE.   Pike and Pyke families in Great Britain, with incidental references to those of Peicke and Piek in Germany and Holland.   Arranged and edited by Eugene Fairfield MacPike ... Chicago, 1931. 86 l. coat of arms, facsims. 36 cm. Photostat reproductions.   "Abbreviations of sources": 3d leaf.   Contents. - Pike and Pyke families in Great Britain. - Appendices: I. Extracts from parish register of St. Leonard's, Shoreditch, London. - II. List of Pike and Pyke wills and administrations in

13620 continued: P.C.C., London. - III. "Pyke or Pike families of London and Greenwich". - IV. "Isaac Pyke governor of St. Helena" (from Notes and queries, 1930, v.158-159) - V. Jeanssen, Johnson, Wilkieson families (Notes & queries, 1929, v.157; 1930, v.158) - VI. India office records. - VII. Selected pages from "Das geschlecht Peicke" (with reproduction of t. -p., Magdeburg, 1915) - VIII. Selected pages from "Het geslacht Piek" (with reproduction of t. -p., Rotterdam, 1916) - IX. Extracts from city archives of Amsterdam, etc. - X. Pieks and Pikes in Holland and Germany . - XI Miscellaneous notes. 31-20701.

CS439. P54   1931

13621   PIKE.   Genealogical notes on the Pike and Pyke families ... (By Eugene Fairfield McPike) (London, Printed by A. W. Sampson & co., 1934)   14, (2) p. 25 cm.   Caption title.   Signed: E. F. M. (i. e. Eugene Fairfield McPike)   Bibliographical foot-notes.   34-6228.

CS439. P54   1933

13622   PIKE.   The Pike family in southeastern Pennsylvania.   By Alfred John Pike.   (n. p., 1950)
10, 9 l.   28 cm.   52-20626.

CS71. P636   1950

PIKE.   See also: ALDEN, 1923   McPIKE, 1927
                       FULLWOOD, 1912   McPIKE, 1930
                       HALLEY, 1906   McPIKE, 1938
                       HALLEY, 1909   STUART, 1911
                       HALLEY, 1910   STUART, 1912
                       McPIKE, 1912

13623   PILCHARD.   Pilchards of Delmarva.   By Richard Stephen Uhrbrock.   (Athens, Ohio, 1967)
49 l.   29 cm.   Bibliography: leaves 17-19.   68-308.

CS71. P64   1967

PILCHER.   See: CAMPBELL, 1911
                    DU VAL, 1931
                    PILCHARD.

13624   PILKINGTON.   Genealogy of the Pilkingtons of Lancashire, (Pilkington, Rivington, Durham, Sharples, Preston, St. Helens, and Sutton.)   Compiled by the late John Harland... Edited by William E. A. Axon ... (Manchester, Printed by C. Simms) for private circulation, 1875.   lxv p., 1 l., 31, 37-63, (1) p. front.   22½ cm.   Eight blank pages inserted between p. 31 and 37.   "Pedigrees": 1 l., 31 p.   "Remarks on the pedigree of the Pilkington of Pilkington ... By William Langton": p. 37-41.   24-14209.

CS439. P55   1875

13625   PILKINGTON.   The history of the Lancashire family of Pilkington and its branches from 1066 to 1600.   Compiled from deeds, charters, wills, inquisitions post mortem, public records, and antient manuscripts, by Lieut-Colonel John Pilkington ... 2d and rev. ed., greatly enlarged, with numerous appendices and illustrations.   Liverpool, T. Bracknell, limited, 1894.   xv, 128 p. col. front. (coat of arms) illus., pl., port., geneal. tab.   (part fold.)   24½ cm.   3-7430.

CS439. P55

13626   PILKINGTON.   Harland's history and pedigrees of the Pilkingtons, from the Saxon and Norman times to the present century, collected from the ancient records, deeds, charters, &c., with engravings.   With twelve sheet pedigrees containing the descent from the lords of Pilkington, and Rivington, to branches of the Pilkingtons of Staunton, Yorkshire baronets, Halliwell, Sharples, and Queen's co., Bolton, Preston, St. Helens, Westmeath, Kildare, Cape Town, and United States.   Kirwan family, of the Galway tribes, from the kings of Ireland ... Appendix of Irish deeds registered.   4th ed. (limited to 125 copies) by R. G. Pilkington ... Dublin, Printed by A. Thom & co. (limited) 1906.   xix, 176 p. front., 12 fold. geneal. tab., coats of arms.   25½ cm.   First published in 1875 under title "Genealogy of the Pilkington family of Lancashire," edited by William E. A. Axon.   19-1537.

CS439. P55   1906

13627   PILKINGTON.   History of the Pilkington family of Lancashire and its branches, from 1066 to 1600.   Comp. from ancient deeds, charters, pipe rolls, de banco rolls, final concords, wills, and other authentic sources, by Lieut-Colonel John Pilkington ... 3d ed.   Rewritten and considerably extended, with revised pedigrees and additional illustrations.   Liverpool, Priv. print. for the author by C. Tinling & co., ltd., 1912.   3 p. l., ix-xvi, 309, (1) p.   col. front., illus., plates, maps, facsims., fold. geneal. tab.   31 cm. Folded table in pocket at end of book.   12-24281.

CS439. P55   1912

PILLER.   In vertical file under PRANKE family.   Ask reference librarian for this material.

PILLOT.   See MONNET, 1911

13629   PILLSBURY.   Account of the proceedings at the reunion of the Pillsbury family at Newbury-port, Mass., September, 1891.   With an illustration showing the ancient Phillsbury mansion at New-buryport ... Salem, Mass., The Salem press publishing and printing co., 1891.   16 p. front. 24 cm.
"Fifty copies printed." 4-27607 rev.   CS71. P643   1891

13630   PILLSBURY.   Notes on the Pillsburys of Leek, county Stafford, England.   By Miss Emily A. Getchell and Eben Putnam.   (From the Historical collections of the Essex institute, vol. XXXI. 1895) (Salem, Mass., 1895)   1 p. l., 24 p. fold. geneal. tab. 24½ cm. 4-24938.   CS439. P6

13631   PILLSBURY.   ... The Pillsbury family: being a history of William and Dorothy Pillsbury (or Pilsbery) of Newbury in New England, and their descendants to the eleventh generation.   Compiled by David B. Pilsbury and Emily A. Getchell.   Everett, Mass., Mass. pub. co., 1898.   xxix, 307 p. front., plates, ports. 22 ½ cm. 9-12999.   CS71. P643   1898

13632   PILSBURY.   Ancestry of Charles Stinson Pillsbury and John Sargent Pillsbury, compiled for Helen Pendleton (Winston) Pillsbury by Mary Lovering Holman ...(Concord, N. H., Priv. print. at the Rumford press) 1938.   2 v. front., pl., ports. 24½ cm. Paged continuously. "Only 100 copies printed of which this is no. 100."
39-9242.   CS71. P643   1938

PILSBURY.   See also PILLSBURY.

PILSON.   See McCLURE, 1914

PINARD-LAUZIÈRE.   See GOUIN, CS90. G7

PINCH.   See FRY, 1938

13633   PINCHART.   Étude sur la famille noble de Pinchart du XV au XVIII siècle.   Bruxelles, 1955.
28 l. coat of arms, geneal. tables. 27 cm. Bibliography: leaf 26. 64-48615.   CS809. P5   1955

13634   PINCHBECK.   Notes on the Pinchbeck family of the United States.   By Raymond Bennett Pinchbeck.   (Richmond? 1954)   73 p. 36 cm. 55-29223.   CS71. P644   1954

13635   PINCKARD.   (Pinckard family data.)   (42 p.) in vertical file.   Ask reference librarian for this material.

13636   PINCKNEY.   ... The Pinckney family.   (By George Stayley Brown.   Yarmouth, N. S., 1909)
1 p. l., 11 p. 21 cm. (Yarmouth genealogies, no. 110) "Reproduced from the Yarmouth herald, June 22, 1909." 15-19126.
                                                                 CS71. P645   1909

PINCKNEY.   See also: DRURY, 1952
                       HILL, 1907

PINE.   See No. 1547 - Cabell county.

13637   PINEO.   Pineo.   By Harold Pineo Jackson.   (Montclair, N. J., 1968)   9 l. 28 cm. Bibliography:
leaf 9. 68-5768.   CS71. P646   1968

PINEO.   See also GESNER, 1912

13638   PINGRY.   A genealogical record of the descendants of Moses Pengry, of Ipswich, Mass., so far as ascertained; collected and arranged by William M. Pingry.   Ludlow, Vt., Warner & Hyde, printers, 1881.   186 p., 1 l. front., ports. 23½ cm. 9-12998.   CS71. P648   1881

13639   PINKHAM.   Richard Pinkham of old Dover, New Hampshire and his descendants East and West, by Rev. Charles Nelson Sinnett.   Concord, N. H., Rumford printing company, 1908.
308 p. front., plates, ports. 23 cm. 8-18060.   CS71. P65   1908

PINKHAM.   See also OTIS, 1851

13640   PINNEY.   Genealogy of the Pinney family in America, by Laura Young Pinney.   San Francisco, Harr Wagner publishing company, 1924.   61 p. 20 cm. 25-2072.   CS71.P656   1924

PINNEY.   See also: BACKHOUSE, DA690.M74C3
EDSON, 1901

PINS, De.   See GALCERAN DE PINÓS, 1915

PINTO DE MESQUITA.   See MESQUITA.

13641   PIPER.   Genealogy of the family of Solomon Piper, of Dublin, N.H.   Boston, Dutton and
Wentworth, printers, 1849.   20 p. 23 cm. Dedication signed: Solomon Piper. 2-1520.   CS71.P665   1849

13642   PIPER.   Genealogy of Elisha Piper, of Parsonsfield, Me., and his descendants, including
portions of other related families.   With an appendix, containing genealogies of Asa Piper, of Wakefield, N.H., Solomon Piper, of Boston, Mass., Stephen Piper, of Newfield, Me., and their immediate
descendants.   From 1630 to 1889.   By Horace Piper ... Washington, D.C., 1889.   121 p. 22 cm.
9-12997.   CS71.P665   1889

13643   PIPER.   Nathaniel Piper of Ipswich, Massachusetts, and some of his descendants, 1653-1934,
compiled by Fred Smith Piper.   Lexington, Mass., Priv. print., 1935.   1 p. 1., 18, (3) p. front. (port.)
23½ cm.   Additional leaf inserted before p. 17.   35-9813.   CS71.P665   1935

PIPER.   See also: ROBERTSON, 1964
YOUL, 1914

PIPES.   See: GRAY, 1960a
HALEY, 1900

13644   PIRCKHEIMER.   ... Die älteren Pirckheimer; geschichte eines Nürnberger patriziergesch-
lectes im zeitalter des frühhumanismus (bis 1501)   Aus dem nachlass herausgegeben von Hans Rupprich.
Mit diner einführung von Gerhard Ritter.   Leipzig, Koehler & Amelang, 1944.   258 p., 1 l. fold. geneal.
table. 23 cm. At head of title: Arnold Reimann. Bibliographical foot-notes. AF 47-2010.   CS649.P5   1944

13645   PIRKLE.   ... The Pirkles and their descendants in the U.S.A., by Prof. John A. Cagle.
Greenville, Tex. (c.1933)   2 p. 1., (1), 165, (27) p. port. 22½ cm. "A compilation of years of work on part of the author in
gathering information on the Pirkle family from the American revolution, including the many branches of this family up to 1923." 34-2244.
                                                                                       CS71.P669   1933

13646   PIRTLE.   The family of John and Amelia Fitzpatrick Pirtle, another family of distinction from
the Lincoln country of Kentucky, showing the paternal heirs as of January, nineteen thirty-five of Major
John B. Pirtle tracing from his grandparents Rev. John Pirtle and Amelia Fitzpatrick Pirtle of Kentucky,
written and compiled by Henry M. Johnson (and) Henry J. Tilford ... (Louisville, Ky., Designed and
printed by Gibbs-Inman company incorporated) 1936.   80 p. incl. front., illus., ports. 25 cm. Blank pages for
"Family record" (74-80 at end) 37-10366.   CS71.P673   1936

13647   PITCAIRN.   The history of the Fife Pitcairns, with transcripts from old charters, by
Constance Pitcairn.   Edinburgh and London, W. Blackwood and sons, 1905.   xviii, 533 p. front. (col. coat
of arms) illus., plates, ports., facsim., fold. geneal. tables. 23 cm. 15-6733.   CS479.P5   1905

13648   PITKIN.   Pitkin family of America.   A genealogy of the descendants of William Pitkin, the
progenitor of the family in this country, from his arrival from England in 1659 to 1886 ... Also,
additional notes of the descendants of Martha Pitkin, who married Simon Wolcott ... By A. P. Pitkin.
Hartford, Conn.   (Press of the Case, Lockwood & Brainard co.) 1887.   xciii p., 1 l., 325 p. front., plates,
ports., facsims., fold. maps., coats of arms. 27½ cm. 9-14804.   CS71.P684   1887

PITKIN.   See also: McCURDY, 1892
SALISBURY, 1892

13649   PITMAN.   Descendants of John Pitman, the first of the name in the colony of Rhode Island. Collected by Charles Myrick Thurston ... New York, The Trow & Smith book manufacturing co., 1868. 48 p. 23½ cm. (With his Descendants of Edward Thurston ... New York, 1868) "250 copies printed." p. 49-55 at end contain ms. notes. 9-14776.   CS71.T544   1868

13650   PITMAN.   Descendants of Benjamin Pitman, fifth generation from Henry Pitman of Nassau, with his ancestry to John Pitman, first of the family in the colony of Rhode Island, as compiled by Charles Myrick Thurston, in 1868, continued to January 1, 1915, by Theophilus T. Pitman.   (Newport, R.I.) 1915.   40 p. incl. front.   23 cm.   18-2201.   CS71.P686   1915

13651   PITMAN.   History and pedigree of the family of Pitman of Dunchideock, Exeter, and their collaterals and of the Pitmans of Alphington, Norfolk and Edinbugh, with part pedigrees and account of families connected by marriage - Andrew, Sanders, Barnes, Kitson, Astley, Keats, Northcote, Gordon, Walrond, Bulteel, Stappleton, Harris, Senhouse, Coker, Manley, Palk and Williams, with biographies of individuals and memoirs of - Admiral Sir R. G. Keats, G.C.B. - Sir John Kennaway, 1st bart. - Sir Robert Palk, bart. - Dr. Keats of Blundells - Stringer Laurence - Clive - Christopher Harris and Sir Francis Drake, etc. and with extracts from wills and parish registers, and list of Dunchideock title deeds and other family papers.   By Charles E. Pitman ... (London) Mitchell, Hughes and Clarke, 1920.   x, 181 p. map, fold. geneal. tab.   26½ cm.   "Authorities consulted": p. vii-ix.   23-14007.   CS439.P62

13652   PITMAN.   Frederick Cobbe Pitman and his family, by Harry Anderson Pitman.   (London) Adlard & son, limited, 1930.   1 p. l., 67, (1) p. front. (coat of arms) pl., ports.   22 cm.   Printed for private circulation. 32-33109.   CS439.P62   1930

13653   PITMAN.   History and pedigree of the family of Pitman of Dunchideock, Exeter, and their collaterals and of the Pitmans of Alphington, Norfolk and Edinburgh, with part pedigrees and account of families connected by marriage ... By Charles E. Pitman ... (London) Mitchell, Hughes and Clarke, 1920.   x, 181 p. map, fold. geneal. tab.   26½ cm.   "Authorities consulted": p. vii-ix.   23-14007.   CS439.P62

PITMAN.   See: PITTMAN.
          THURSTON, 1868

PITNER.   See FISHER, 1890

13654   PITT.   The house of Pitt, a family chronicle.   By Sir Tresham Lever.   (1st ed.) London, J. Murray (1947)   xii, 378 p. ports., facsim., geneal. table.   22 cm.   48-14126*.   DA28.4.P5L4

PITT.   See also PITTS.

PITTENDREIGH.   See THOMPSON, CS479.T5

13655   PITTENGER.   A history of the Pittenger family in America, by F. Hiner Dale ... (Ann Arbor, Mich., Edwards brothers, inc., 1942)   3 p. l., 34 p. 21 cm.   "Lithoprinted."   Cover-title: The Pittenger family in America ... 1665-1942.   43-14997.   CS71.P689   1942

13656   PITTIS.   Pittis genealogy; the Pittis family in England and America, four hundred and sixty-four years, sixteen generations, 1480 to 1944.   Allied families with extra records: Arnold, Birney, Brooke, Dore, Godfrey, Hout, Isham, Legg or Legge, McCullough (and) Stephens.   By Margaret Birney Pittis.   Cleveland, O., The author, 1945.   xv, (2), 315 p. incl. illus. (incl. maps, facsim., coat of arms) ports. 24 cm. "References": p. 31, 305.   45-9201.   CS71.P6895   1945

13657   PITTMAN.   Pittman family record (by) Lona McRee Elrod (secretary, Publications Committee) Pittman Family Society.   2d ed.   Athens, Ga., 1958.   97 l. 30 cm.   60-35498.
                                                                          CS71.P6897   1958

PITTMAN.   See also PITMAN.

13658   PITTS.   Proceedings of the Bostonian society at its regular meeting, May 11, 1886: p. (3)-4. Sketches of various members of the Pitts and Bowdoin families and of their connection with the colonial history of Boston and Massachusetts.   5-6276.
                                                                          F73.4.G65

PITTS.   See also: BACKHOUSE, DA690.S97R9
STOUT, 1960

13660   PIXLEY.   William Pixley of Hadley, Northampton, and Westfield, Mass., and some of his descendants.   Data collected by Edward Evans Pixley and Franklin Hanford, arranged for publication by Edward Dinwoodie Strickland ... Buffalo, N.Y. (Printed by P. Paul and company) 1900.   95 p. front., 23 cm. 6-872.
CS71.P694   1900

13661   PIZARRO.   The Harkness collection in the Library of Congress.   Documents from early Peru, the Pizarros and the Almagros, 1531-1578.   Washington, U. S. Govt, print. off., 1936.
xi, 253 p. 26 cm. "Second in the series of publications made by the Library of Congress from the great collection of early Spanish manuscripts concerning the new world, presented to it in 1929 by Mr. Edward S. Harkness." - Pref.   Spanish and English.   The documents have been transcribed, translated and annotated by Stella R. Clemence. cf. Introd. pref. signed: J. F. Jameson, chief of the Division of manuscripts.   36-26004.
F3442.U58

13662   PLACE.   Genealogy of the Place family. (By Guy Scoby Rix.   n.p., 1916?) 76 l. 28 cm.
type-written.
CS71.P697   1916

PLACE.   See also BOOTES, 1961

13662a   PLAISTED.   Lieut. Roger Plaisted of Quamphegon (Kittery) and some of his descendants.   Comp. and printed by M. F. King.   Portland, Me., 1904.   3 p. l., 66 numb. l. front. 24½ cm. The frontispiece is a mounted photograph. "Number 24.   29 copies only." 22-25800.
CS71.P698   1904

13663   PLAISTED.   The Plaisted family of North Wilts, with some account of the branches of Berks, Bucks, Somerset, and Sussex, by Arthur H. Plaisted.   Westminster, The Westminster publishing co., 1939.   xvii, 273, (5) p. front. (coat of arms) 1 illus., plates, ports., maps, geneal. tables (part fold.) 22 cm. Maps on lining-papers. Fifteen genealogical tables on thirteen folded leaves in pocket. Four ruled pages at end for "Notes." "List of authorities": p. 257-259. 42-1340.
CS439.P63   1939

PLANE.   See KING, CS439.K7

PLANER.   See GÜNTHER, CS629.G8

13664   PLANT.   The life of Henry Bradley Plant, founder and president of the Plant system of railroads and steamships and also of the Southern express company.   By G. Hutchinson Smyth, D. D.   New York and London, G. P. Putnam's sons, 1898.   xi, 344 p. 2 port. (incl. front.) pl. 14 cm. Plant genealogy prepared by G. S. Dickerman: p. 307-337. 10-23006.
CT275.P663S6

13665   PLANT.   The house of Plant of Macon, Georgia; with genealogies and historical notes.   By G. S. Dickerman.   New Haven, The Tuttle, Morehouse & Taylor co., 1900.   259 p. front., plates, ports., geneal. tables. 24½ cm. Oct. 18, 1900-77.
CS71.P699   1900

13666   PLANT.   Genealogical supplement to The house of Plant.   By Martha (Plant) Ellis Ross.   Macon, Ga., Southern Press, 1963.   80 l. illus., ports., coats of arms, geneal. tables (part fold.) 25 cm. 64-3914.
CS71.P699   1963

13667   PLANTAGENET.   The blood royal of Britain; being a roll of the living descendants of Edward IV. and Henry VII, kings of England, and James III., king of Scotland, by the Marquis of Ruvigny and Raineval.   With a series of portraits.   London and Edinburgh, T. C. & E. C. Jack, 1903.   xi, 620, (1) p. front. (facsim. in colors) 19 port., geneal. tables. 29 cm. Title in red and black. p. 1-80 contain CXXXIV genealogical tables. 4-31170.
CS418.R7

13668   PLANTAGENET.   The Plantagenet roll of the blood royal; being a complete table of all the descendants now living of Edward III., king of England, by the Marquis of Ruvigny and Raineval ...   The Isabel of Essex volume, containing the descendants of Isabel (Plantagenet) countess of Essex and Eu; with a supplement to the three previous volumes.   London and at Edinburgh, T. C. & E. C. Jack, 1908.   2 p. l., vii-xiii, 684 p., 1 l. incl. geneal. tables. 29 cm. Title in red and black. "This edition is limited to five hundred and twenty copies." 9-7088.
CS418.R945

13669 PLANTAGENET. Some royal descents, by the Marquis of Ruvigny ... (London?) Priv. print., 1909. 1 p. 1., 86 geneal. tab. 28½ cm. "Special tables for Ruvigny's 'Plantagent roll of the blood royal.'" 9-24285.

CS418.R88

PLANTAGENET. See also CRALL, 1908

PLANTIN. See WHITNEY, 1866

PLASKITT. See WORTHINGTON, 1886

13670 PLATT. The Platt lineage; a genealogical research and record, by G. Lewis Platt ... New York, T. Whittaker, 1891. iv, (5)-398 p. incl. illus. (coat of arms) 21 cm. Interleaved. 5-16542.

CS71.P719 1891

13671 PLATT. Notes upon the ancestry of John Platt, born in Burlington Coutny, N.J., Aug. 13, 1749; died near Wilmington, Del., Dec. 1823, and also, a list of his descendants. (Philadelphia., 1896) 30 p., 1 1. 26 cm. Printed for private distribution. Preface signed Franklin Platt. 9-12996.

CS71.P719 1896

13672 PLATT. George Wood Platt and his descendants ... by Emilie L. Platt. (Brooklyn) 1943. cover-title, 24 p. 23 cm. Additions and corrections in manuscript. 44-20544.   CS71.P719 1943

13673 PLATT. Platt genealogy in America, from the arrival of Richard Platt in New Haven, Connecticut, in 1638. By Charles Platt. New Hope, Pa., 1963. 453 p. illus. 26 cm. 63-11569. CS71.P719 1963

13674 PLATT. Thomas Platt of Burlington, New Jersey, and his descendants. By Charles Platt. Peterborough, N.H., R.R. Smith Co., 1967. xvi, 364 p. illus., facsims., map, ports. 27 cm. On spine: Thomas Platt genealogy. Bibliography: p. 357-358. 67-14502.   CS71.P719 1967

PLATT. See also: AVERY, 1925
                   MARKS, 1902
                   PRIME, 1887
                   PRIME, 1897
                   TODD, 1867
                   TREADWELL, 1883

PLAXACO. See PLAXCO.

13675 PLAXCO. Plaxco-Robinson; being an account of two of the ancient Presbyterian families of upper South Carolina (particularly situated in York and Chester Counties) by Samuel Brooks Mendenhall and William Boyce White, Jr. Foreword by Mary C. Simms Oliphant. (1st ed. Rock Hill? S.C.) 1958. xviii, 160 p. group port. 21 cm. "Limited to three hundred numbered copies." L.C. copy not numbered. 58-12369.

CS71.P72 1958

PLAXCO. See McELWEE, 1959

PLAXICO. See: McELWEE, 1959
                PLAXCO.

13676 PLAYFAIR. Notes on the Scottish family of Playfair. Compiled by Rev. A.G. Playfair. (Tunbridge Wells, Printed by C. Baldwin) 1913. xv, 62 p. 12 port., xv fold. geneal. tab. 23 cm. A 3d edition, enlarged and corrected, with additional tables and 12 portraits inserted. 19-1536.   CS479.P7

PLAYFAIR. See also: ROGERS, CS479.R7
                      ROGERS, CS477.P5R7

PLAYSTEAD. See PLAISTED.

PLAYTERS.   See CLOPTON, 1939

PLEAS.   See LANCASTER, 1902

13677   PLEASANTS.   (Genealogical chart of the Pleasants family compiled by Joseph R. Hunneycutt)
(n. p.) 1938.   geneal. tab.   100 x 57½ cm.   38-32671.   CS71.P722   1938

PLESINGTON.   See RIGMAYDEN, DA670.L19C5 vol. 104-105

13678   PLESSEN.   Die Plessen, Stammfolge vom XIII. bis XX.   Johrhundert.   By Max Naumann.
Görlitz, C. A. Starke, 1940.   183 p.   plates, ports. , coats of arms (part col.) geneal. tables.   26 cm.   "Gedrucktes Schrifttum":
p. 156-160.   49-43055*.   CS629.P57   1940

PLEXACO.   See PLAXCO.

PLEXICO.   See PLAXCO.

PLIMALE.   See PLYMALE.

PLEXCO.   See PLAXCO.

13679   PLIMPTON.   A genealogy and historical notices of the family of Plimpton or Plympton in
America, and of Plumpton in England.   By Levi B. Chase.   Hartford, Conn., Plimpton mfg. co. print
(1884)   240 p.   front. (coat of arms) ports.   23½ cm.   9-12995.   CS71.P728   1884

13680   PLOWDEN.   Records of the Plowden family, by B. M. P.   (n. p.) Printed for private circula-
tion, 1887.   iv, 177, (1) p. , 1 l. front. (mounted phot.) pl. , geneal. tables (part fold. , 2 in pockets) 25 cm.   Preface signed: B. M. P.
(i. e. Barbara Mary Plowden)   Contains also the Cholmeley and the Dundas pedigrees.   24-8353.
CS439.P65   1887

13681   PLOWDEN.   Records of the Chicheley Plowdens A. D. 1590-1913, with four alphabetical
indices, four pedigree sheets, and a portrait of Edmund, the great Elizabethan lawyer, by Walter F. C.
Chicheley Plowden ... Printed for private circulation.   London, Heath, Cranton & Ouseley, ltd., 1914.
vii, (2), 191, (1) p.   front. (port.) geneal. tables.   25 cm.   Two folded genealogical tables in pockets.   The American Plowdens: p. 43-47.
14-7740.   CS439.P65

13682   PLOWMAN.   A register of Plowmans in America, as far as obtained with tracings of families,
and extracts from English and American records.   Collected and printed for private circulation by
Benjamin H. F. Plowman.   New York, 1901.   3 p. l., 90 p. illus. (coat of arms) 21 cm.   24-5662.
CS71.P732   1901

PLUM.   See PLUMB.

13683   PLUMB.   The Plumbs.   1635-1800.   By H. B. Plumb ... 2d ed.   (Wilkes-Barre? Pa.) 1893.
1 p. l., 102 p. front. (ports.) map, coats of arms.   22 x 36 cm.   First edition published in 1890.   Two pages of additional information concerning Samuel Plumb and Lydia Ann Seelye, 1026, inserted after p. 78.   9-14802.   CS71.P734   1893

13684   PLUMB.   Genealogical memoranda relating to the families of Plumbe & Tempest.   (n. p.)
Priv. print., 1898.   3 p. l., 45 p. plates, coats of arms, facsims.   30 cm.   Compiled by Mrs. Tempest of Broughton hall, Skipton-in-
Craven.   "Pedigree of Plumbe" compiled by Sir Robert Tempest Tempest, bart.   21-21731.   CS439.P68

13685   PLUMB.   Plumb.   (Compiled by George T. Plumb and Maurice W. Plumb.   n. p., 1954)
10 p. illus. 19 cm.   55-22760.   CS71.P734   1954

PLUMB.   See also: BLACKMAN, 1894
BUNNELL, 1937

PLUMBE.　See PLUMB.

PLUME.　See PLUMB.

PLUMER.　See PLUMMER.

PLUMME.　See PLUMB.

13687　PLUMMER.　Proceedings upon the dedication of Plummer hall, at Salem, October 6, 1857: including Rev. Mr. Hoppin's address and Judge White's memoir of the Plummer family.　Salem, W. Ives & G. W. Pease, 1858.　97 p. front. 24 cm. 1-11602.　　　　　　　F74.S1S146

13688　PLUMMER.　Genealogy of the Plummer family.　By Robert Plummer.　(n. p.) 1880. geneal. table. 24 cm. Photocopy (negative) 50-44072.　　　　　　CS71.P735　　1880

13689　PLUMMER.　Genealogical record of the compiler's branch of the Plummer family, by Jane Plummer Thurston ... (Portland) Printed by B. Thurston & co., 1885.　22 p. 22 cm. Cover-title: 1635-1885. History of the ancient Plummers and Mortons and their descendants in America, from 1635-1885 ...　9-12859.
　　　　　　　　　　　　　　　　　　　　　　　　CS71.P735　　1885

13690　PLUMMER.　The Plummer system of genealogical enumeration.　Lineage of Mr. Francis Plumer, Newbury, Massachusetts, 1635.　San Francisco, A. Plummer, 1904.　cover-title, 64 p. 17 cm. p. 17, 29, 34, 36, 64 left blank.　Comp. by Alvin Plummer.　9-12860.　　　　CS71.P735　　1904

13691　PLUMER.　The Plumer genealogy.　Francis Plumer, who settled at Newbury, Massachusetts, & some of his descendants, by Sidney Perley.　Salem, Mass., The Essex institute, 1917. 1 p. l., 259 p. illus. 24 cm. 18-15861.　　　　　　　　　　CS71.P735　　1917

13692　PLUMMER.　Out of the depths; or, The triumph of the cross, by Nellie Arnold Plummer ... Hyattsville, Md., 1927.　412 p. illus. (incl. ports.) 22 cm. "The story of a colored American ... Adam Francis Plummer." 28-3324.　　　　　　　　　　　　　　　　　BX6455.P6P6

　　　　PLUMMER.　See also:　HANAFORD, 1915
　　　　　　　　　　　　　　HITE, 1960
　　　　　　　　　　　　　　KIMBROUGH, 1960

13693　PLUMPTON.　Plumpton correspondence; a series of letters, chiefly domestick, written in the reigns of Edward IV, Richard III, Henry VII, and Henry VIII.　Edited by Thomas Stapleton from Sir Edward Plumpton's book of letters: with notices historical and biographical of the family of Plumpton, of Plumpton, Com. Ebor.　London, Printed for the Camden Society by J. B. Nichols, 1839.　cxxxviii (i. e. 146), 312 p. geneal. table. 22 cm. (Camden society (London) Publications, no. 4) A17-1186*.　　DA20.C17 vol. 4

　　　　PLUMPTRE.　See COOTE, CS499.C75

13694　PLUMSTED.　Chronicles of the Plumsted family with some family letters, compiled and arranged with notes.　By Eugene Devereux.　Philadelphia, 1887.　168 p. 25 cm. "One hundred numbered copies privately printed.　no. 58."　16-5352.　　　　　　　　CS71.P738　　1887

　　　　PLUNKETT.　See LONG, 1956

13695　PLYLER.　The Plyler genealogy, 1688-1965.　By Herman Starnes.　(Monroe, N. C., 1966) xi, 196 p. col. coat of arms, maps. 24 cm.　Pages 191-196 blank for "Notes."　66-15996.　　CS71.P739　　1966

13696　PLYMALE.　The Plymale family in America.　By John Fred Plymale.　Huntington, W. Va., Printed by Commercial Print. & Lithographing Co., 1967.　ii, 196 p. illus., facsims., ports. 28 cm. 68-1760.
　　　　　　　　　　　　　　　　　　　　　　　　　　　CS71.P7392

13697　POAGE.　The descendants of Robert and John Poage, pioneer settlers in Augusta County, Va.; a genealogy based on the manuscript collection of Prof. Andrew Woods Williamson, Henry Martyn

13697 continued: Williamson, and John Guy Bishop, supplemented and arr. by Robert Bell Woodworth.
Complete ed.   Staunton, Va., Priv. print. by the McClure Print. Co., 1954.   xiii, 1372, 5 p. illus., ports.
24 cm.   On cover: Bishop (and) Woodworth.   55-15418.   CS71.P74   1954

     POAGE.   See also: SAMPSON, 1922
                 No. 1547 - Cabell county.

13698   POCAHONTAS.   Pocahontas, alias Matoaka, and her descendants through her marriage at
Jamestown, Virginia, in April, 1614, with John Rolfe, gentleman; including the names of Alfriend,
Archer, Bentley, Bernard, Bland, Bolling, Branch, Cabell, Carlett, Cary, Dandridge, Dixon, Douglas,
Duval, Eldridge, Ellett, Ferguson, Field, Fleming, Gay, Gordon, Griffin, Grayson, Harrison,
Hubard, Lewis, Logan, Markham, Meade, McRae, Murray, Page, Poythress, Randolph, Robertson,
Skipwith, Stanard, Tazewell, Walke, West, Whittle, and others.   With biographical sketches by
Wyndham Robertson, and illustrative historical notes by R. A. Brock.   Richmond, J. W. Randolph &
English, 1887.   vii, (1), 84 p. front. (port.) 25 cm. 9-15610.   CS71.R747   1887

     POCHMAN.   See ROQUEMORE, 1942

     PÖCKEL.   See BÖCKEL.

13699   POCOCK.   (Pedigree of Pocock connected with Innes, from the year 1160.   n.p., 1840?)
14 l. 1 pl. (coat of arms) 36½ cm.   No. t.-p.   Lithographed facsim.   Text and blank pages alternate in pairs. 2-27580.
                                            CS439.P7

13700   POCOCK.   Notes on the Pocock family, compiled by Edward Kinsey Voorhees.   Atlanta, Ga.,
1930.   1 p. l., 18 numb. l. 18 cm. Type-written. 30-23736.   CS71.P75   1930

13701   POE.   The origin and early history of the family of Pöe or Poe, with full pedigrees of the Irish
branch of the family and a discussion of the true ancestry of Edgar Allen Poe, the American poet; by
Sir Edmund Thomas Bewley ... Dublin, Printed for the author by Ponsonby & Gibbs, 1906.   xiv, 88 p.
fold. geneal. tables. 26½ cm.   "Two hundred copies of this work have been printed, of which this is no. 79." 9-23742.
                                            CS499.P7B5

     POE.   See also: CARPENTER, 1959
                    DAY, 1963

     POEDERLÉ.   See OLMEN DE POEDERLÉ.

13702   POELLNITZ.   Baron Poellnitz, born in Germany.   (By Frank Mandeville Rogers) (Florence,
S.C. 1933)   5 numb. l. 34 cm. Type-written. Caption title. Signed: Frank M. Rogers. 34-14609.   CS71.P753   1933

13703   POELLNITZ.   ... Geliebte schatten, eine chronik der heimat; mit 20 bildern in tiefdruck.
By Gret (Jehly) Gulbransson.   Berlin, G. Grote, 1934.   4 p. l., 3-283 p. front., illus., plates, ports. 20 cm.
(Half-title: Grote'-sche sammlung von werken zeitgenössischer schriftsteller, bd. 210.)   History and reminiscences of the family of Vanda von
Poellnitz, the author's mother. 36-17227.   CS629.P6G8

13704   POELLNITZ.   Little acorns from the mighty oak.   By Henry Poellnitz Johnston.   (Birmingham, Ala., Featon Press, 1962)   xvii, 357 p. (p. 356-357, blank for "My own notes") col. coats of arms. 24 cm. 62-12568.
                                        CS71.P753   1962

     POHL.   See WOOD, 1937

     POHLY.   See GOODLOCK, 1951

     POINDEXTER.   See JUNKINS, 1908

     POISER.   In vertical file under PRANKE family.   Ask reference librarian for this material.

13705   POLE.   The history of the life of Reginald Pole ... (By Thomas Phillips)   2d ed. ... London,
Printed for T. Payne at the Mews-gate (etc.) 1767.   2 v. front. (fold. port.) fold. geneal. chart. 22 cm. 22-2798.
                                      DA317.8.P6P4   1767

13706   POLE.   Pedigree of the Pole-Carew family of Devon.   Reprinted from the Visitations of the county of Devon, with additions and corrections.   By Lieutenant-Colonel J. L. Vivian.   Exeter, W. Pollard & co., printers, 1892.   1 p. l., 4 p. 29 cm. 16-8321.   CS439.P75

13707   POLE.   The reign of Elizabeth, 1558-1603, by J. B. Black ... Oxford, The Clarendon press, 1936.   vii, (1), 448 p. fold. maps, fold. plan, fold. geneal. tables. 22½ cm. (Half-title: The Oxford history of England, ed. by G. N. Clark) Bibliography: p. (412)-430.   36-19574.   DA355.B65

13708   POLE.   And in the New World.   By Constance Pole Bayer.   (Miami, Fla.) 1968.   x, 87 p. illus., geneal. tables, map, ports. 23 cm. Limited ed. of 500 copies. Bibliography: p. 86-87. 68-58195.   CS71.P755   1968

POLE.   See also: BOLEBEC, 1925
                                 BONVILLE, 1955

POLE-CAREW.   See POLE, 1892

POLEGREEN.   See SMITH, 1942

13709   POLEY.   The Poleys of Suffolk.   Extracted from "The visitation of Suffolke."   (By William Harvey) Ed. by Joseph Hackson Howard ... Lowestoft, Printed by S. Tymms, 1866.   1 p. l., 24, (12) p., 1 l. illus., coats of arms. 28 cm. 20-18090.   CS439.P76

13710   POLHEMUS.   History and geneaology (sic): Polhemus, Woolley, Totten, Clayton, Bedell.   Material collected (and) organized by J. Wilbur Clayton, Mrs. I. Lester Bedell, and John H. Overturf.   West Orange, N.J., 1954.   35 p. coat of arms. 24 cm. On cover: 1284-1954. 55-24195.   CS71.P756   1954

13711   POLK.   Memoirs of a southern woman "within the lines," and a genealogical record, by Mary Polk Branch.   Chicago, The Joseph G. Branch publishing co. (c.1912)   107 p. incl. front., illus., ports. 19½ cm. 12-20143.   F214.B81

13712   POLK.   Polk family and kinsmen.   By William Harrison Polk.   (Louisville, Ky., Press of the Bradley & Gilbert co., 1912)   1 p. l., (vii-xxvii, 742 p. incl. plates, ports. front. 23½ cm. Title vignette. Pollock crest. Introductory signed: William Harrison Polk. 13-24653.   CS71.P76   1912

13713   POLK.   The North and South American review, by J. M. Polk ... Austin, Tex., Press of Von Boeckmann-Jones co., printers, 1912.   61 p. incl. front. (port.) illus. 22½ cm. "A genealogical tree of the Polk family," folded chart 43½ x 56½ cm. inserted at end. 12-8426.   E605.P775

13714   POLK.   Ezekiel Polk and his descendants, by Wilmot Polk Rogers.   (San Francisco, 1939)   114, 32 numb. l. 28 cm. Caption title. Type-written; additions and corrections in manuscript. "Some of this material was included in a series of articles "The Polks of North Carolina and Tennessee," which appeared in the New England historical and genealogical register beginning with the issue of April 1923 and concluding in the issue of July 1924." - Foreword. "Vindication of the revolutionary character and services of the late Colonel Ezrkiel Polk of Mecklenburg, N. C. Prepared and published by order of the Tennessee state central committee": p. 7-29 (2d group) Includes also the Alexander, Campbell, McNeal and Rogers families. 40-2267.   CS71.P76   1939

13715   POLK.   Some descendents (!) from Cap't William Polk of Accomac, Va., by W. L. Porter, Chicago.   (Chicago, 1941)   3 p. l., 2-15 numb. l. 28 cm. Type-written. "References": leaf 14. 41-6099.   CS71.P76   1941

13716   POLK.   Polk family in vertical file.   Ask reference librarian for this material.

POLK.   See also: ALLEN, 1960   WILSON, 1961
                                 ARMSTRONG, CS61.A6 vol.1   WOODRUFF, 1934a
                                 FOY, 1933   No. 516 - Notable southern families.
                                 POLLOCK, 1939   Vol. 1

13717   POLLARD.   The ancestry and descendants of Jonathan Pollard (1759-1821).   With records of allied families.   Compiled by Lucien M. Underwood.   Syracuse, N.Y., Priv. print., 1891.   cover-title, 20 p. 26 cm. 200 copies printed. 9-12994.   CS71.P771   1891

13718   POLLARD.   Pollard genealogy; being a record of one line of the Pollard family descended from Thomas Pollard of Billerica, Mass.   Compiled by Stephen Pollard.   East Orange, N.J., Printed by F. L. Pollard, 1902.   cover-title, 8 p. 25 cm. 2-27741.   CS71.P771   1902

13719   POLLARD.   The history of the Pollard family of America.   By Maurice J. Pollard.   Dover, N.H., 1960 (c. 1961)-1964 (c. 1965)   2 v. illus., facsims., ports. 29 cm. 61-34264 rev.

CS71.P771   1961

13720   POLLARD.   Note on the descendants of Joseph Pollard (1 p.)   Photographs of family record page from personal Bible of Martha Elizabeth Hutchinson Pollard (3 p.)   Photograph of commission of Joseph L. Pollard (in the Virginia militia, 1864) (2 p.)   Photographs of family record paper from Hutchinson Bible from the homeplace of Martha Elizabeth Hutchinson Pollard (3 p.)   In vertical file. Ask reference assistant for this material.

POLLARD.   See also MAY, 1929

13721   POLLEY.   See SNYDER, 1958

13722   POLLOCK.   Pollock genealogy.   A biographical sketch of Oliver Pollock, esq., of Carlisle, Pennsylvania, United States commercial agent at New Orleans and Havana, 1776-1784.   With genealogical notes of his descendants.   Also genealogical sketches of other Pollock families settled in Pennsylvania.   By Rev. Horace Edwin Hayden.   Harrisburg, Pa., L. S. Hart, printer, 1883. 2 p. l., 59 p. 25 cm. 9-12993.   CS71.P777   1883

13723   POLLOCK.   Pollock: a record of the descendants of John, James, Charles, and Samuel Pollock, who emigrated from Ireland to Pennsylvania about 1750 ... (Harrisburg, Pa.) 1884. cover-title, 26 p. 24½ cm.   Edition of twenty-five copies reprinted by the author from a larger work entitled, "A biographical sketch of Oliver Pollock ... with genealogical notes of his descendants ... By Rev. Horace Edwin Hayden." Harrisburg, Pa. 1883, p. 26-51. 9-12861.

CS71.P777   1884

13724   POLLOCK.   Beatrice Hale Pollock.   Ancestors to five and ten generations.   Comprising the following families: Adams, Arms, Ball, Barden, Belden, Burt, Chandler, Chapin, Cooke, Crossman, Graves, Hale, Hitchcock, Hopkins, Hubbard, Longley, Merrick, Phelps, Pollock, Simpson, Smead, Stanley, Smith, Taylor, Walker, Warner, Webster, Wells, Winslow, etc., etc.   CS71.P777   1932

13725   POLLOCK.   David Pollock of Westmoreland county, Penna., and his descendants.   Compiled by Helen Coloa (Pollock) Griffith and Captain Edwin T. Pollock ... (The latter's work mostly between 1902 and 1907) (n.p., 1936?)   83 l. 27 cm.   Consists of type-written manuscript and mounted printed material. 38M937T.

CS71.P777   1936

13726   POLLOCK.   An American farmer's family correspondence with Scotland, 1802-1834; edited with notes by David Buchan Morris ... Stirling (Scot.) A. Learmonth & son, "Journal" office, 1937. 35 p. 18½ cm.   "Submitted to the Stirling natural history and archaeological society, 16th February, 1937." "Published for gratuitous private circulation."   Correspondence of George Pollock with his family in Stirling, Scotland. "Pollock family": p. 5-11. 38-36152.

CS71.P777   1937

13727   POLLOCK.   Descendants of David Pollock, 1755-1841, by Doyle M. Craytor.   (Cincinnati, 1941)   1 v. 28½ cm. Loose-leaf. Blue print. "Other Polk genealogies": leaf 3. "Authorities": leaf 25. 42-7165.

CS71.P777   1941

POLLOCK.   See also POLK.

POLLOK.   See POLLOCK.

POLLOK-MAXWELL.   See MAXWELL.

POLNITZ.   See LONG, 1925

POLYTHRESS.   See POCAHONTAS, 1887

POMERAY.　See POMEROY.

POMEREY.　See POMEROY.

13728　POMEROY.　A study in heredity: - the Pomeroys in America.　By Wm. W. Rodman.　(New Haven, 1889)　cover-title. p. 161-174. 23½ cm.　From the New Englander and Yale review for Sept. 1889. 9-12992.

CS71. P785　　1889

13729　POMEROY.　Eltweed Pomeroy of Dorchester, Mass., and Windsor, Conn., and four generations of his descendants.　By William Woodbridge Rodman ... Boston, D. Clapp and son, 1903. 15 p. 25½ cm.　"Communicated by Mrs. Henry Thorp Bulkley of Southport, Conn." "Reprinted from New-England historical and genealogical register, for July, 1903, with some additions." 4-33868.

CS71. P785　　1903

13730　POMEROY.　Romance and history of Eltweed Pomeroy's ancestors in Normandy and England. (Toledo, O., Press of the Franklin printing co., 1909)　vii, (9)-81 p. front., plates, facsim. 25 cm. Introduction signed: Albert A. Pomeroy. 9-21825.

CS71. P785　　1909

13731　POMEROY.　History and genealogy of the Pomeroy family, collateral lines in family groups, Normandy, Great Britain and America; comprising the ancestors and descendants of Eltweed Pomeroy from Beaminster, County Dorset, England, 1630 (1631) ... (by) Albert A. Pomeroy.　(Toledo, O., The Franklin printing and engraving company, 1912-22)　3 pt. in 2 v. illus., plates, ports., map, facsims., 3 col. coats of arms (incl. fronts.) 27 cm. Blank pages at end for "Births," "Marriages", and "Deaths". Illustrated t. - p. "This edition is limited to 400 numbered copies." This copy not numbered. Part 3 printed at Detroit by Geo. A. Drake & co. 12-27783.

CS71. P785　　1912

13732　POMEROY.　Pomeroy; interesting English records supplemental to the History and genealogy of the Pomeroy family.　(By Charles Arthur Hoppin) (Toledo, O., 1915)　29 p. illus. (facsims.) 26½ cm. Title vignette: coat of arms. A letter from C. A. Hoppin, of London, to A. A. Pomeroy. 15-24543.

CS71. P785　　1915

13733　POMEROY.　The house of de la Pomerai; the annals of the family, which was, from the conquest to 1548, seated at Beri (Berry Pomeroy), in Devonshire, and, from c. 1620 to 1719, resident at Sandridge in Stoke Gabriel, in that county: the status of the lords of Beri: their castle home.　Together with many notices of scions of the house and of other bearers of the de la Pomerai (Pomeroy) name.　With appendix: 1720 onwards.　By Edward B. Powley ... (Liverpool) University press of Liverpool; (etc., etc.) 1944.　xxiii p., 1 l., 134, (1) p. front., illus. (incl. map, plan) plates, geneal. tables (2 fold.) 29½ x 22½ cm. "Only 250 copies ... printed ... No. 17." Bibliography: p. viii-xxi. 44-52640.　CS439. P762　　1944

13734　POMEROY.　History and genealogy of the Pomeroy family and collateral lines, England, Ireland, America; comprising the ancestors and descendants of George Pomeroy of Pennsylvania. By Edwin Moore Pomeroy.　(Philadelphia?) W. McL. and J. N. Pomeroy, 1958.　xxxii, 1454 p. illus., ports., coats of arms (1 col.) geneal. tables. 25 cm. Bibliography: p. ix-xix. 59-31260.　CS71. P785　　1958

POMEROY.　See also:　COOPER, 1930
　　　　　　　　　　　　　KING, 1956
　　　　　　　　　　　　　LAWRENCE, 1881

POMROY.　See POMEROY.

POMPILIE.　See PUMPELLY.

13735　POND.　A genealogical record of Daniel Pond, and his descendants, by Edward Doubleday Harris ... Boston, W. P. Lunt, 1873.　210 p. 23½ cm. 9-12991.　CS71. P796　　1873

13736　POND.　A genealogical record of Samuel Pond, and his descendants.　By Daniel Streator Pond ... (New London, O., Printed for the compiler by G. W. Runyan) 1875.　1 p. 1., (5)-126 p. 23½ cm. 9-12990.

CS71. P796　　1875

13737   POND.   John Pond of North Carolina; his ancestry from the pioneer, Samuel Pond, and his descendants including Dailey, Stitt, and Frazee lines, compiled by Rachel Adams Cloud Pond and Clifton Ray Pond.   New York, 1965.   283 p. maps. 29 cm.   "Revised edition of the Pond, Dailey, Stitt and Franzee lines to be found in the Pond-Adams families, produced by the compilers in 1959." 65-5530.   CS71. P796   1965

POND.   See also PARKER, 1892

13738   PONROY.   Descendence de Lorian Ponroy (1600?-1645?) (par Guy Ponroy et Jean Marc Monin) Paris, 1961 -   1 v. (loose-leaf) map. 27 cm.   L. C. copy imperfect: map mutilated.   64-6301.
CS599. P67

13739   PONSONBY.   The Ponsonby family, by Major-General Sir John Ponsonby ... London, The Medici society, 1929.   2 p. l., vii-xi p., 1 l., xiii-xvi p., 2 l., 3-263, (1) p. incl. geneal. tables. mounted front., plates, ports. 24½ cm. 35-19611.   CS439. P763   1929

13740   POOL.   The history of Edward Poole of Weymouth, Mass. (1635) and his descendants, by Murray Edward Poole ... (Ithaca, N. Y.) Press of the Ithaca democrat, 1893.   164 p. 23½ cm. 9-13226.
CS71. P821   1893

13741   POOL.   Pedigree of the family of Poole of Gloucester and Wilts.   Compiled by J. Renton Dunlop, F. S. A.   (Reprinted from "Miscellanea genealogica et heraldica")   London, Mitchell, Hughes and Clarke, 1919.   1 p. l., 13 p. plates. 26 cm. 23-14532.   CS439. P765

13742   POOL.   A branch of the Poole family in America descended from John Pool of Rockport, Massachusetts, including the allied families of Haskell, Norwood, Storey, Butman, Rand, Kendall, compiled and arranged from various sources by Frederick Arthur Poole, jr.   Chicago, Priv. print., 1927.   159, (1) p. front. (map) ports. 29½ cm.   Printed on one side of leaf only.   Each plate accompanied by guard sheet with descriptive letterpress.   "An edition limited to fifty copies printed on Italian hand-made paper, five copies printed on Japanese vellum, and two copies for copyright purposes."   Bibliography: p. (141)-145.   27-18002.   CS71. P821   1927

13743   POOL.   A genealogical history of the Poole, Langston, Mason families and kindred lines of upper South Carolina as chronicled by Bessie Poole Lamb ... assisted by Mary-Mack Poole Ezell ... (Enoree? S. C.) 1931.   9 p. l., 251 p. front., illus. (incl. ports., coat of arms) 23 cm. 39-12234.
CS71. P821   1931

13744   POOL.   American cavalcade; a memoir on the life and family of De Witt Clinton Poole, by John Hudson Poole ... Pasadena, 1939.   xiii, 350 p., 1 l. front., plates, ports. (part col.) double maps, geneal. tables, facsims. 24½ cm.   "150 copies ... were privately printed by the Ward Ritchie press."   39-20047.   CT275. P6813P6

13745   POOL.   Descendants of Stephen Decatur Pool.   (n. p., 196-)   geneal. table (117 x 158 cm. fold. to 28 x 29 cm.) in portfolio. 31 cm. 67-51341.   CS71. P821   1960z

POOL.   See also: COLEMAN, 1937
EVANS, 1956
GAMBLE, 1906
GILES, 1864

POOLE.   See POOL.

13746   POOR.   The Poor-Poore family gathering ... Poor-Poore-Littel family association.   (1st -
1881-   Salem, Mass. (etc., 1881?) -   v. plates, ports. 22-30 cm.   triennial. (1900 catalog lists 1st-3d., 6th-7th, Sept. 14, 1881-1887, 1896-1899. Salem, ... 1881-1900. 5 v. 23½ cm. 9-1387) 4-8400 rev.
CS71. P823   1881a

13747   POOR.   Triennial reunion of the Poor-Poore-Little family association.   (n. p.) 18   nos. in   v. 22 cm. Title varies: Programme of the ... triennial gathering of the Poor-Poore family association.   Triennial reunion of the Poor-Poore-Little family association. 45-52299.   CS71. P823   1881b

13748   POOR.   My four great grandmothers.   (By Agnes Blake Poor) (n. p., 1919?)
1 p. l., 19 p. 19 cm. "References": p. 19. 39-16928.   CS71. P823   1919

POOR.   See also: BRAYTON, 1922
                   VAN HOOK, 1957

POORE.   See POOR.

13749   POPE.   Pope: his descent and family connections.   Fact and conjectures.   By Joseph Hunter
... London, J. R. Smith, 1857.   46 p. 20 cm.   (On cover: Mr. Hunter's critical and historical tracts.   no. v)   Contents. -
I. The Popes. - II. The Turners.   10-8230.   PR3633.H8

13750   POPE.   Genealogy of a portion of the Pope family together with biographical notices of Col.
William Pope, of Boston, and some of his descendants.   Boston, D. Clapp, printer, 1862.   68 p.
23½ cm.   By William Pope.   3-3827.   CS71.P826   1862

13751   POPE.   Notice of some of the descendants of Joseph Pope, of Salem.   By Henry Wheatland.
(In Essex institute.   Historical collections.   Salem, 1868.   23½ cm.   v. 8, p. 104-118)   3-7932.   F72.E7E81

——— (n. p. 1869?)   14 p. 25½ cm.   Reprint, with omission of 1st 2 pararaphs. 3-7933.   CS71.P826   1868
13752   POPE.   Genealogy of Major General John Pope, U. S. Army.   (Omaha, 1875?)   geneal. tab.
50½ x 40½ cm.   A leaf of typewritten corrections taken from "Colonel Nathaniel Pope and his descendants," by G. W. Beale, added. 13-9626.
                                                                CS71.P826   1875

13753   POPE.   A genealogy of the Pope family of Kentucky.   By Dr. Nathaniel Field, of Jeffersonville,
Ind., November 7th, 1879.   Jeffersonville, Ind., Evening news print, 1879.   cover-title, 15 p. 15 cm.
25-14352.   CS71.P826   1879

13754   POPE.   Ancestry of Capt. Ebenezer Pope.   Genealogical notes.   Elizabeth, N. J., Cook &
Hall, printers, 1882.   7 p. 23½ cm.   Signed: Frank L. Pope. 2-4441.   CS71.P826   1882

13755   POPE.   A genealogy of the Pope family of Kentucky.   By Dr. Nathaniel Field, of Jeffersonville,
Ind., November 7th, 1879.   Jeffersonville, Ind., Evening news print, 1879.   cover-title, 15 p. 15 cm.
25-14352.   CS71.P826   1879
                                                                Office.

13756   POPE.   A history of the Dorchester Pope family.   1634-1888.   With sketches of other Popes
in England and America, and notes upon several intermarrying families.   (By) Charles Henry Pope ...
Boston, The author, 1888.   vi, (7)-339, (1), 6 p. front., illus., fold. geneal. tab., coats of arms. 24½ cm. 9-12989.
                                                                CS71.P826   1888

13757   POPE.   Genealogy of Thomas Pope (1608-1683) and some of his descendants.   By Franklin
Leonard Pope.   Boston, Press of David Clapp & son, 1888.   22 p. 25 cm.   Reprinted from the New Eng. historical
and genealogical register for Jan., 1888. 14-4710.   CS71.P826   1888a

13758   POPE.   Genealogy of Thomas Pope (1608-1683) and his descendants, by Mrs. Dora Pope
Worden, Prof. Wm. F. Langworthy, Mrs. Blanche Page Burch, with a preliminary history by the late
Franklin Leonard Pope.   Hamilton, N. Y., The Republican press, 1917.   143 p. incl. front., plates, ports.
24 cm.   17-18813.   CS71.P826   1917

13759   POPE.   ... A book of remembrance; being a short summary of the service and sacrifice
rendered to the empire during the great war by one of the many patriotic families of Wessex: the Popes
of Wrackleford, co, Dorset.   With a foreword by Thomas Hardy, O. M.   London, Priv. print., The
Chiswick press, 1919.   151, (1) p. front., pl., ports. 26½ cm.   Leaf numbered 128* inserted between 128 and 129. Plates accompanied by guard sheets with descriptive letterpress.   Coat of arms on cover.   Intoduction signed: R. G. B., H. P.   (i. e. Richard Grosvenor Bartlett and
Hilda Pope) 40-267.   CS439.P766   1919

13760   POPE.   Old Hemlock; the letters and poems of Elnathan (6) Pope, together with those of his
mother, Ruth Hammond Pope, his wife, Mary Huntoon Pope, and those of his uncle, Thomas Faunce
Hammond, copied and arranged by Emelia Pope Sutherland ... (n. p., 193-)   1 p. 1., (5)-73 p. illus. (map)
23 cm.   39-32321.   CS71.P826   193-

13761   POPE.   Georgia descendants of Nathaniel Pope of Virginia, John Humphries of South Carolina, and Allen Gay of North Carolina, by John D. Humphries.   (Atlanta? 1934)   40 p. 18½ cm. 34-32121.
CS71.P826   1934

13762   POPE.   Pioneer Popes.   A history of the Plymouth Popes who descended from one Thomas Pope of Plymouth and Dartmouth, Massachusetts; became pioneers in Vermont, New York, Pennsylvania, Wisconsin and Nebraska, 1627 to 1937, by Amelia Pope Sutherland ... (n.p., 1938)   1 p. l., 5-170 p. illus. (maps) mounted ports., fold. geneal. tables. 23 cm. Blank page for additional record (p. 158) 39-12254.
CS71.P826   1938

POPE.   See also: BULLITT, 1920
                   HUMPHREY, 1938a
                   McADAMS, 1936
                   MEIGS, 1906
                   TURNER, CS439.T9

13763   POPE.   Pope family in vertical file.   Ask reference librarian for this material.

13764   POPHAM.   The Sagadohoc colony, comprising The relation of a voyage into New England; (Lambeth ms.) with an introduction and notes.   By the Rev. Henry O. Thayer, A.M.   Portland, Me., Printed for the Gorges society, 1892.   xi, 276 p. front. (port.) 4 pl., 2 maps, fold. plan, facsim. 22 x 19 cm. (The Gorges society. (Publications) IV) Title vignette. No. 134 of a limited edition of 200 copies. "The relation of a voyage into New England, which is ascribed to Capt. James Davies of the expedition, is reproduced from a transcription of the original manuscript in the library of Lambeth palace, London." cf. Pref. "The literature": p. (87)-156. "The Popham family": p. 240-255. List of members of the Gorges society, 1892: p. (271)-276. 3-493.
F16.G66

POPHAM.   See also: BARBER, DA690.L982C6
                     CALSTON, 1900

13764a   POPPLE.   Popple of Hulle (Eng.) and the Board of trade.   (By Fairfax Harrison.)   (Pedigree chart compiled by F.H.)   (n.p., 1926)   geneal. tab. 40 x 55 cm. Photostat from type-written copy. "Authorities cited." 26-19813.
CS439.P767

PORDAGE.   See also: BOWDOIN, 1887
                      BOWDOIN, 1894

PORTAGE.   See PORDAGE.

13765   PORTER.   The descendants of John Porter, of Windsor, Conn., in the line of his great, great grandson, Col. Joshua Porter, M.D., of Salisbury, Litchfield County, Conn., with some account of the families into which they married ... Saratoga Springs, N.Y., Printed for the compilers by G.W. Ball, 1882.   3 p. l., 125 p. 25½ cm. Preface signed: Henry P. Andrews. P. Porter Wiggins. 17-30088.
CS71.P839   1882

13766   PORTER.   The descendants of John Porter of Windsor, Conn.   1635-9.   Compiled by Henry Porter Andrews.   Saratoga Springs, G.W. Ball, printer, 1893.   2 v. phot. 25½ cm. Paged continuously. 9-12987.
CS71.P839   1893
Microfilm 8683

13767   PORTER.   Porter family record.   Buffalo, Peter Paul book co., printers (1896)   cover-title (20) p. 26 cm. 2 p. at end left blank for family record. Preface signed: Cyrus Kinne Porter. 9-12986.
CS71.P839   1896

13768   PORTER.   Genealogies and reminiscences.   Compiled by Henrietta Hamilton McCormick.   Rev. Ed.   Chicago, The author, 1897.   3 p. l., 5-213 p. front., illus. (coats of arms) pl., ports. 24 cm. Additions in manuscript.   Contains the Porter, Grigsby, McNutt, McChesney, Hamilton and McCormick families. 32-5812.
CS71.P839   1897

13769   PORTER.   A Porter pedigree; being an account of the ancestry and descendants of Samuel and Martha (Perley) Porter of Chester, N.H., who were descendants of John Porter, of Salem, Mass. and of Allan Perley, of Ipswich, Mass.   Compiled by Miss Juliet Porter.   Worcester, Mass., 1907.   161 p. 23½ cm. Blank leaves at end for memoranda. 8-17714.
CS71.P839   1907

13770   PORTER.   The descendants of Moses and Sarah Kilham Porter of Pawlet, Vermont, with some notice of their ancestors and those of Timothy Hatch, Amy and Lucy Seymour Hatch, Mary Lawrence Porter and Lucretia Bushnell Porter.   Compiled by John S. Lawrence.   Grand Rapids, Mich., F. A. Onderdonk, printer, 1910.   xiii, 190 p.   front. (facsim.) 24 cm.   "300 copies of the book have been printed."   Blank pages at end.   11-6467.   CS71.P839   1910

13771   PORTER.   John Porter and his descendants, comp. by Arthur Amasa Porter.   Portage, Wis., 1917.   (44) p.   illus. (incl. ports.) 26 cm.   20-22878.   CS71.P839   1917

13772   PORTER.   Sixty-odd, a personal history, by Ruth Huntington Sessions.   Brattleboro, Vt., Stephen Daye press (c.1936)   xiv p., 1 l., 429 p. incl. geneal. tab.   23½ cm.   36-29241.   CT275.S433A3

13773   PORTER.   Genealogy of the Porter, Merrick-Sherwin and allied families, by W. L. Porter.   Chicago, Ill., 1937.   2 p. l., 20 numb. l., 2 l.   map. 28½ cm.   Mimeographed.   37-10354.   CS71.P839   1937

13774   PORTER.   The descendants of Peter Porter, an emigrant of 1621, compiled by William Arthur Porter, M.A.   Minneapolis, Minn., Argus publishing co., 1937.   177 p. front., illus., plates, ports. 22½ cm.   38-19578.   CS71.P839   1937a

13775   PORTER.   The ancestors of Jermain and Louise Porter; being an account of one of the lines of descendents (!) of Daniel Porter, 1644, together with data on some of the female branches of the family.   Compiled, chiefly from family records, by John Jermain Porter ...   Hagerstown, Md., 1940.   2 v.   illus. (part mounted; incl. ports., coats of arms) facsims., geneal. tables (1 fold.) 29 cm.   Paged continuously.   Part II: Female branches of the Porter family.   "25 copies made."   Reproduced from type-written and handwritten copy, and printed matter, including newspaper clippings, etc.   "Historical sketch of the Cincinnati observatory, 1843-1918, by Jermain G. Porter," published by the University (pt. 1., leaves E3-E8) has special t.-p.   "Partial list of papers published by John Jermain Porter, 2nd": pt. 1, leaves F14-F16.   "References to Porter family in America": pt. 1, leaf A9.   Includes the Jermain, Hall, Whitaker, Starrett, Snowden, Frazer, Doty and Faxon families.   41-6100.   CS71.P839   1940

13776   PORTER.   John Porter of Windsor, Conn., and his parents: further notes, by John Insley Coddington ... (New Haven, 1941)   cover-title, 5 p. 23½ cm.   "Reprinted from 'The American genealogist' July, 1941."   42-4027.   CS71.P839   1941

13777   PORTER.   Corridors by candlelight; a family album with words.   By Anna Clyde Plunkett.   San Antonio, Naylor Co. (1949)   xi, 189 p. illus., ports., coats of arms. 22 cm.   49-3938*.   CS71.P839   1949

13778   PORTER.   The Porter family history, consisting of biographical sketches of Sanford Porter of Brimfield, Mass., his posterity, and ancestry to John Porter of Westerly, R. I., 1799-1885.   1st ed.   Delta, Utah, c.1957.   v. illus., ports., maps. 24 cm.   58-17279.   CS71.P839   1957

13779   PORTER.   The descendants and ancestors of Samuel Porter and Elnora Eliza Rudolph.   By Samuel Doak Porter.   (Ann Arbor? Mich.)   1959.   44 p. illus. 22 cm.   59-35706.   CS71.P839   1959

13780   PORTER.   Genealogy of George and Elizabeth Porter.   By Wade Thompson Porter.   Rev.   Denver, 1962.   59 l. coat of arms. 30 cm.   62-68149.   CS71.P839   1962

13781   PORTER.   A genealogy of the descendants of Richard Porter, who settled at Weymouth, Mass., 1635, and allied families: also, some account of the descendants of John Porter, who settled at Hingham, Mass. 1635, and Salem (Danvers) Mass., 1644.   By Joseph W. Porter ... Bangor, Burr & Robinson, printers, 1878.   343, (1) p. 23¾ cm.   L. C. COPY REPLACED BY MICROFILM.   9-12988.   CS71.P839   1878

13782   PORTER.   The descendants of John Porter of Windsor, Conn. 1635-9.   Comp. by Henry Porter Adnrews.   Saratoga Springs, G. W. Ball, printer, 1893.   2 v. phot. 25½ cm.   Paged continuously.   L. C. COPY REPLACED BY MICROFILM.   9-12987.   CS71.P839   1893
Microfilm 8683 CS.

13784   PORTER.   Porter family of Kentucky.   By Emma Rouse Lloyd.   (Available for consultation at Lloyd library.   309 West Court Street, Cincinnati 2, Ohio.

13785   PORTER.   The family of Lemuel T. Porter of Alabama.   In vertical file.   Ask reference librarian for this material.

PORTER.   See also: ANDERSON, 1902   GRIGSBY, 1905
                      ARCHDALE, 1925   LINCOLN, 1930
                      BLACK, 1954   NESBIT, 1929
                      BRAYTON, 1922   ROUSE, 1932
                      BREED, 1958   WILD, 1959
                      FRISBIE, E171.A53 vol.19   No. 3939 - Colebrook.

13786   PORTERFIELD. The Porterfields.   By Frank Burke Porterfield.   Roanoke, Va., Southeastern Press (1948, c.1947)   344 p. 24 cm. 48-15447*.   CS71.P84   1948

PORTERFIELD.   See LUCAS, 1964

PORTEUS.   See TOWLES, 1957

13787   PORTWOOD.   Notes on the family of Page and Ann Portwood.   By Louis Ansel Duermyer.
Wilmington, Del., 1949.   22 1. 30 cm. 49-24791*.   CS71.P845   1949

13788   POSEY.   Posey-Wade-Harrison (Emison) and other families of Maryland and Virginia, with supplement to The Emison Family.   Microfilm, positive.   6048
                                                                     Microfilm reading room.

13789   POSNER.   The Posner family tree, by Stanley I. Posner, Helen Posner Fried (and) Milton Posner.   New York, Posner Family Circle, inc., c.1953.   60 p. illus. 28 cm. 54-20796.
                                                                     CS71.P85   1953

13790   POST.   The Post family, by Marie Caroline De Trobriand Post (Mrs. Charles Alfred Post)
New York, S. Potter, 1905.   xii, 314 (i.e.318) p., 1 l., xxv p., 1 l. col. front., ports., coats of arms (part col.) 24 x 18½ cm.
"Sources of information": p. (x)-xii. 5-16612 rev.   CS71.P857   1905

13791   POST.   American lineage of Hoyt Post, of Detroit, Michigan.   (Detroit?) 1908.
cover-title, 24 p. front. (port.) 23 cm. 16-11127.   CS71.P857   1908

POST.   See also: BLAUVELT, 1957
                    VAN NOSTRAND, E171.A53 v.19

13792   POSTLETHWAITE ... Report of the Committee having charge of the marking of the site of the Postlethwaite tavern where the first courts of justice in Lancaster County were held... Lancaster, Pa.,
1915.   2 p. 1., p. 219-305. illus., 4 pl. (incl. front.) map. 24½ cm. (Papers read before the Lancaster County historical society ... Oct. 1,
1915 ... vol. xix, no.8) "Postlethwaite family, 1750": p. 293-299. "Minutes of October meeting": p. 302-305. 16-6839.
                                                                     F157.L2L5 v.19

13793   POSTON.   Elias B. Poston and his ancestors, with a record of his descendants.   Compiled and written by Elias Olan James and Glenna Lucile James ... Oakland, Calif., E. O. James, c.1942.
3 p. 1., iii, 201, (4) p. maps, facsim. 27½ cm. Reproduced from type-written copy. Includes the Norton, Spencer and Farra families.
"Footnotes to authorities cited in Chapter I": p. 14. 42-22758.   CS71.P86   1942

13794   POSTON.   John Hamill Poston, 1786-1848; his ancestors and descendants; a Poston family genealogy.   By Colin James.   Denver, 1959.   73 p. illus. 30 cm. 60-22688.   CS71.P86   1959

13795   POSTWICK.   Postwick and relatives: written in the early part of the eighteenth century, by Thomas Harrison, of Great Plumstead, co. Norfolk; illustrated with notes, and ed. by his grandson's grandson, James Hargrave Harrison, and now first printed from the original manuscript.   (For private circulation only.)   Great Yarmouth, 1858.   27, (1) p. 1 illus. (coat of arms) 24 cm.   "One hundred copies."   16-19764.

CS439. P77

POT.   See POTTS.

POTE.   See HOLSINGER, 1959

POTT.   See POTTS.

POTTENGER.   See GLASSBURN, 1964

13796   POTTER.   Genealogies of the Potter families and their descendants in America to the present generation, with historical and biographical sketches.   Edited by Charles Edward Potter.   Boston, A. Mudge & son, printers, 1888.   4 p. l., (289) p. front., ports. 35 cm. Various paging. 9-15011.

CS71. P868   1888

13797   POTTER.   The New Haven (Conn.) Potters, 1639.   By James Shepard ... Boston, Press of D. Clapp & son (1902)   9 p. 25 cm.   "Reprinted from New-England historical and genealogical register for Jan. 1900.   Republished by the author, New Britain, Conn. 1902."   2-24596.

CS71. P868   1902

13798   POTTER.   1765-1906.   The descendants of John Potter.   (Compiled by Mrs. Wayland Manning.   Dedham, Mass.)   1906.   cover-title, 1 l., 28 p. 23 cm. 8-33002.

CS71. P868   1906

13799   POTTER.   The Potter record (by Frank Hunter Potter and Robert Potter.   n. p., 1921?)
30 p. ports. 23 cm. 50-50480.   CS71. P868   1921

13800   POTTER.   More memories, Orlando Bronson Potter and Frederick Potter.   New York (Press of J. J. Little & Ives company) 1923.   6 p. l., 3-359 p. plates, ports. 21½ cm.   Dedication signed: Blanche Potter.   "Only fifty copies of this book have been printed, of which this is no. 37."   The plates are mounted photographs.   26-10947.

CT275. P72P6

13801   POTTER.   Genealogies of the Eseck Potter, Lawrence Barber, Henry Zimmer and related families and their descendants in the United States to the present generation.   A compendium of family pictures, ancient history and vital statistics of 1000 people, with photographic blue prints of nearly 300 persons and two dozen places, including a full page coat of arms in colors.   1st ed. ... Collected, arranged and sold by Ezra Cornelius Potter.   Ames, Ia., 1933.   1 p. l., 70 p., 1 l., (6) p. incl. pl., geneal. tab. pl., ports. (incl. front.) facsim., col. coat of arms. 18 cm.   Multigraphed (blue-printed) Blank pages for "Family records" (4 at end) 36-14656.

CS71. P868   1933

13802   POTTER.   Some Potters and some Eddys, a memorandum, by David Potter ... San Francisco, W. Kibbee & son, 1946.   3 p. l., 37 p. 22½ cm. 47-18457.   CS71. P868   1946

13803   POTTER.   A Potter-Richardson memorial, the ancestral lines of William W. Potter of Michigan and his wife, Margaret (Richardson) Potter.   Compiled by Doreen Potter Hanna and Louise Potter. (n. p., 1957)   335 p. illus. 29 cm. 58-39457.   CS71. P868   1957

POTTER.   See also: BAILEY, 1892   COLBY, 1880
                        BARRETT, F74. C8P8   DILLON, 1927
                        BRUCE, 1914   GLEN, 1923
                        CHUTE, 1894   HOBHOUSE, 1934a
                        CHAMBERS, F142. M7M38

POTTERF.   See OZIAS, 1943

POTTINGER.   See: JAMES, 1913a
                   SINCLAIR, 1960

POTTORF.   See OZIAS, 1943

13804   POTTS.   Memorial of Thomas Potts, junior, who settled in Pennsylvania; with an historic-genealogical account of his descendants to the eighth generation.   By Mrs. Thomas Potts James.   Cambridge (Mass.) Priv. print. (University press) 1874.   x, (2), 416, (2) p. front., plates, ports., facsims. 22½ cm. Title vignette: coat of arms. 9-12984.   CS71.P871   1874

13805   POTTS.   Our family ancestors.   By Thomas Maxwell Potts ... Canonsburg, Pa., The author, 1895.   xiii, (1) p., 1 l., 428 (i.e. 434) p. front., plates, ports., facsims., fold. geneal. tab., coats of arms. 23 cm. 9-12985.   CS71.P871   1895

13806   POTTS.   Historical collections relating to the Potts family in Great Britain and America, with a historic-genealogy of the descendants of David Potts, and early Anglo-Welsh settler of Pennsylvania, including contributions by the late William John Potts.   Compiled by Thomas Maxwell Potts ... Canonsburg, Pa., The compiler, 1901.   xxxv, 619, 620a-h, (621)-736 p. front., illus. (incl. facsims.) plates (1 col.) ports., geneal. tables (part fold.) coats of arms. 24 cm. Extra leaf, p. 570½ - 570¾ inserted before p. 571. Contents. - pt. 1. The Potts family in Great Britain. By William John Potts. - pt. 2. The Potts family in America. - pt. 3. David Potts and his descendants. 5-16558.   CS71.P871   1901

13807   POTTS.   The Potts line, 1670-1929.   (By Joseph Charles Fegan) (Washington? D.C., 1929) geneal. tab. 31 x 34 cm. fold. to 24½ x 16 cm. 29-12026.   CS71.P871   1929

13808   POTTS.   Philippe Pot, grand sénéchal of Burgundy, with genealogy of the Pot family in France and other additions to "Early records of Simpson and allied families," including Frézel or Fraser, Hart, Haudt or Hout, Officer, Potts, Souillé or Souville, Stringer, by Helen A. Simpson ... Somerville, N.J., Press of the C.P. Hoagland company, 1935.   vii, 304 p. plates, port., facsims. 24½ cm. On spine: Simpson and allied families, vol. II. Bibliography: p. iii-v. 35-6660.   CS599.P73   1935

13809   POTTS.   Potts family.   By Alexander Du Bin.   Philadelphia, Historical Publ. Society, 1948.   4 p. 26 cm. 49-2930*.   CS71.P871   1948

13810   POTTS.   Sir James Earle, Kt., and Dr. Percival Pott.   By W.H. Challen.   The genealogists' magazine, vol. 12, September, 1955, No. 3   CS410.S61

POTTS.   See also: HOGG, 1921   LLOYD, 1912
                    HOLSTEIN, 1892   SIMPSON, 1927
                    JAMES, 1921   TERRILL, DA664.M3T6
                    LEE, 1954   TYREL, 1916

POU (PEW)   See GOLSAN, 1959

13811   POULLAIN.   Poullain family in vertical file.   Ask reference librarian for this material.

13812   POULIN.   Les trois souches Poulin au Canada, 1639-1968.   By Joseph Philippe Poulin.   Québec, 1968.   314 p. 28 cm. Cover title. 70-439268.   CS90.P6   1968

13813   POUND.   The Pound and Kester families, containing an account of the ancestry of John Pound (born in 1735) and William Kester (born in 1733) and a genealogical record of all their descendants and other family historical matter.   Compiled by John E. Hunt.   1st ed.   Chicago, Regan printing house, 1904.   628 p. 23½ cm. 4-5928.   CS71.P876   1904

13814   POUND.   Memoirs.   With histories of Pound-Murphy-Willingham-Palmer-Pitts families ... By Jerome Balaam Pound.   (Miami Beach? Fla., 1949)   xvii, 340 p. illus., ports., coats of arms. 25 cm. 50-586.   CT275.P752.A3

13815   POUNTNEY.   The Pountney family, an account of the descendants of William Pountney of Birmingham, by Edwin Pountney Davis.   Annapolis, Md., The Capital-gazette press, 1933.   2 p. l., 20, (3) p. 23½ cm. Blank pages for "Additional records" (17-20) 35-15332.   CS71.P882   1933

13816   POWE.   The line of descent of Thomas Powe, compiled by Wm. Godfrey, 1931.   Rev. 1936 by J. R. T.   (Cheraw? S. C., 1936)   geneal. tab.   illus. (col. coat of arms) 54 x 47½ cm. 41-38339.
CS71.P8827   1936

13817   POWELL.   A tribute to the memory of James A. Powell: by A. Gerald Hull.   Delivered by request of the Delphian institute, at Union college, July 23d, 1829.   (New York, 1829?)   128 p. front. (port.) 2 pl., geneal. tables. 22 cm. Genealogy: p. 79-128. 12-18976.
CS71.P883   1829

13818   POWELL.   Memorial of Thomas Powell, esq., who died at his residence in Newburgh, on Monday, May 12, 1856, in the eighty-eighth year of his age, by Rev. R. B. Van Kleeck, D. D.   New York, Printed for private circulation, 1857.   2 p. l., 107 p., 2 l. front. (port.) 3 pl. 26 cm. Contents. - Introductory notice. - Memorial, by Rev. R. B. Van Kleeck, D. D. - Sermon, by Rev. J. H. Hobart Brown. - Obituary, from Newburgh telegraph. - Resolutions of the Board of trustees. - Funeral services. - Proceedings of public meetings. - Family register. 20-18023.
CT275.P76V3

13819   POWELL.   Family records of the Powells and Griffiths, with extracts from the writings of John Powell, by his grand-daughter, Rachel Powell.   Philadelphia, J. A. Wagenseller, 1866.   110 p. 19 cm. 10-5268.
CS71.P883   1866

13820   POWELL.   A biographical sketch of Col. Leven Powell, including his correspondence during the revolutionary war.   Edited by Robert C. Powell, M. D.   Alexandria, Va., G. H. Ramey & son, 1877.   3 p. l., 104 p. 22½ cm. 100 copies printed for private circulation. Includes brief notices of the Powell family. "Letters from Col. George Johnston, jr.": p. (35)-62.   "Letters from Rev. David Griffith, M. D.": p. (63)-80. 13-2607.
E263.V8P8

13821   POWELL.   Authentic genealogical memorial history of Philip Powell, of Mifflin County, Pa., and his descendants and others, with miscellaneous items and incidents of interest.   By Rev. John Powell.   Vol. 1 ... Dayton, O., Pub. for the author, 1880.   xxi, (23)-447 p. 19 cm. 9-12983.
CS71.P883   1880
Microfilm 8671

13822   POWELL.   The pedigree of the family of Powell of Horsley in the county of Denbigh.   With a slight sketch of the village of Horsley, the parish and church of Gresford, and the castle and town of Holt.   Also pedigree of the descendants of Powell, settled in Liverpool, Chester, St. Albans and London.   (London) 1891.   2 p. l., 185p. front., illus., plates, plans, coats of arms (part col.) 51½ cm. "Only 25 copies printed, of which this is no. 20." "Appendix, consisting of wills, letters, collateral pedigrees, and other documents relating to the Powell family": p. (98)-185. Preface signed: Ellison Powell. 21-14028.
CS439.P79   1891

13823   POWELL.   The pedigree of the family of Powell, sometime resident at Mildenhall, Barton Mills, and Hawsted, in co. Suffolk, and afterwards at Homerton and Clapton, co. Middlesex, and elsewhere, from Henry VII to Victoria.   To which are added pedigrees of the families of Baden and Thistlethwayte, of co. Wilts.   Comp. and ed. by Edgar Powell.   London, Printed for the editor, 1891.   vii, 139, (1) p. front. (facsim.) pl., coat of arms, fold. geneal. tab. (in pocket) 28½ cm. Blank pages for genealogical memoranda (42-52) "Parker, Kipling, and Clark pedigree": p. 92-93. 22-644.
CS439.P79   1891a

13824   POWELL.   Long Island genealogies.   Families of Albertson, Andrews, Bedell, Birdsall ... Willets, Williams, Willis, Wright, and other families.   Being kindred descendants of Thomas Powell, of Bethpage, L. I., 1688.   Compiled by Mary Powell Bunker.   Albany, J. Munsell's sons, 1895.   350 p. fold. map. 22½ cm. x 18½ cm. (Half title: Munsell's historical series, no. 24) 3-13311.
F127.L8B9

13825   POWELL.   The diary of Walter Powell of Llantilio Crossenny in the county of Monmouth, gentleman.   1603-1654.   Transcribed, and notes added by Joseph Alfred Bradney, F.S.A.   From the original mss. in the possession of Sir Henry Mather Jackson, bart., to which is added a pedigree and portrait of the diarist.   Bristol, J. Wright & co., 1907.   x p., 1 l., 48 p. front., (port.) fold. geneal. tables. 26 cm. 16-25577.
CS439.P79

13826   POWELL.   The life of William Dummer Powell, first judge at Detroit and fifth chief justice of Upper Canada.   By the Honourable William Renwick Riddell... Lansing, Michigan Historical commission, 1924.   305 p. pl., ports. 23½ cm. 25-27044.
F1032.P88

13827   POWELL.   Powell, family of Va., Conrad, family of Winchester, Va., Fauntleroy, family of Va., Magill, family of Winchester, Va., Holmes, family of Va. (Washington, D.C., 1928) cover-title, 17 fold. geneal. tab., 3 fold. maps.   59 cm.   Compiled by Col. P. C. Fauntleroy.   Blue-print charts.   28-15346.

CS71.P883   1928

Office.

13828   POWELL.   Some descendants of the Connecticut and Massachusetts branch of the Powell family, by William P. Powell.   Springfield, Mass.   (The Pond-Ekberg company, printers) 1931. 16 p. incl. front., diagr. 23 cm.   32-33197.   CS71.P883   1931

13829   POWELL.   History and genealogies of the Powells in America, compiled by Charles S. Powell ... (St. Petersburg, Fla.; St. Petersburg printing co.) c. 1935.   297, 54 p., 1 l.   illus. (incl. map) 23½ cm. 36-7750.   CS71.P883   1935

13830   POWELL.   The family tree of Col. Leven Powell's line of the Powells of Virginia, compiled by Rosalie Noland Ball ... (n. p.) 1938.   1 v.   illus., plates (1 mounted) ports., facsims., coats of arms, fold. geneal. tables. 29½ cm.   Loose-leaf.   Autographica reproduction of manuscript copy.   Bibliography: p. 12.   40-8603.

CS71.P883   1938

13831   POWELL.   Benjamin and Ambrose Powell of Culpeper county, Virginia; with many descendants of Benjamin.   Compiled by Katharine Lee de Veau.   (n. p.) 1941.   3 p. l., 259 numb. l., 9 l. 28½ cm. Reproduced from type-written copy.   Blank leaf for "Future records" at end.   41-11041.   CS71.P883   1941

13832   POWELL.   The Powell family of Norfolk and Elizabeth City Counties, Virginia, and their descendants, with notes and data on the collateral families of Bush, Beckwith, Bowles, Cargill, Carter, Clemens, Conner, Creed, Daines, Dendy, Lucas, Maddux, Middleton, Osborn, Smith, Watkins, and Williams.   By Silas Emmett Lucas.   (Birmingham? Ala., 1961)   305 p.   23 cm.   61-11040.

CS71.P883   1961

POWELL.   See also: CAMPBELL, 1911
DUNHAM, 1956
HUTCHINS, 1938
MEAD, 1933
MILLER, 1968
PIERPONT, 1928

POWER.   See POWERS.

13833   POWERS.   The Powers family: a genealogical and historical record of Walter Power and some of his descendants to the ninth generaion.   Compiled by Amos H. Powers ... Chicago, Fergus printing co., 1884.   199 p. front., ports. 23½ cm.   9-12982.   CS71.P888   1884

13834   POWERS.   How Neshobe came up into the Green Mountains; also the discovery of Lake Bombazon by Samuel de Champlain; compiled by John MacNab Currier, M. D.   Newport, Vt., 1914. 34 p. front., plates. 23½ cm.   "On Oct. 20, 1761 the town of Brandon was chartered by Capt. Josiah Powers ... by the name of Neshobe." - p. 7.   24-162.   F57.R9C9

13835   POWERS.   A genealogical record of the Powers, Harris and allied families.   More particularly of the descendants of Nathaniel Powers and Esther Johnson, John Hough Harris and Lucy May.   Compiled by William P. Powers ... Los Angeles, Calif., 1915.   geneal. tab. illus. (ports.) 47 x 72½ cm.   Autographed from manuscript copy.   23-18598.   CS71.P888   1915

13836   POWERS.   Powers-Banks ancestry, traced in all ines to the remotest date obtainable, Charles Powers, 1819-1871, and his wife Lydia Ann Banks, 1829-1919, prepared by their son, Wm. H. Powers. Ames, Ia., J. L. Powers, 1921.   325 p. front., illus. (incl. maps, facsims.) plates, ports. 24½ cm.   21-12155.

CS71.P888   1921

13837   POWERS.   Some annals of the Powers family.   Compiled by W. P. Powers.   Los Angeles, Cal., 1924.   304 p., 1 l. incl. front., illus. (incl. ports.) fold. port. 21 cm.   25-11204.   CS71.P888   1924

13838   POWERS.   Captain Enoch Powers and his wife Sophia Teresa Collins, with notes on their descendants.   A grandson's tribute.   (By Albert Carlos Bates) Hartford, 1945.   28 p. 22½ cm. 46-15702.   CS71.P888   1945

13839   POWERS.   The Powers family of Dutchess County.   By Benjamin Mather Powers.   Kansas City, Mo., Lowell Press, 1968.   167 p. facsims., ports. 22 cm. 74-5606.

                                                                                                            CS71.P888   1968

13840   POWERS.   A record of my paternal ancestors, compiled by Robert B. Powers.   Delaware, Ohio, 1967 (c. 1969)   361 p. illus., coat of arms, maps, ports. 29 cm. Cover-title: My paternal ancestors: Avery, Benjamin, Powers, Scott, Treat. Includes bibliographical references. 78-8999 MARC.   CS71.P888   1969

POWERS.   See also: DUNHAM, 1956
                                  HYNES, 1957
                                  McKINNEY, 1967
                                  MATTHEW, 1940
                                  SALMANS, 1936
                                  STODDARD, 1959

13841   POWNALL.   Thomas Pownall, M.P., F.R.S., governor of Massachusetts Bay, author of The letters of Junius; with a supplement comparing the colonies of Kings George III and Edward VII, by Charles A. W. Pownall ... London, H. Stevens, son & Stiles (c. 1908)   ix, 470, 56, 25 p. front., illus., plates, ports., maps, facsims. (partly fold.) fold. diagr. 25½ cm. "The works published by Thomas Pownall," Appendix, p. 3-6. Genealogy - Appendix, p, 19-25 and fold. diagr. 9-9266.   F67.P89

13842   POWNALL.   The descendants of George and Eleanor Pownall, Quakers, by Sterling Wallace Edwards.   Washington, D.C., 1945.   8 p. 1., 7-167 (i.e. 169) numb. 1. 28½ x 22½ cm. Includes extra numbered leaves 68a-68b. Reproduced from type-written copy. Includes the Wallace family. Bibliography: leaves 152-154. 46-15279.

                                                                                                            CS71.P8883   1945

POWNEY.   See HAYES, DA690.B74K3

13843   POWYS.   Welsh ambassadors (Powys lives and letters) by Louis Marlow (pseud. for Louis Umfreville Wilkinson) London, Chapman and Hall ltd. (1936)   xi, 284 p. front., ports. facsim. 22½ cm. Contents. - The one Powys and the many. - Sadism and masochism. - More about John Cowper. - Early letters. - Llewelyn. - John Cowper (1906-1911) - Theodore (1908-1935) - Llewelyn itinerant. - A check list of the books of Llewelyn Powys, by L. E. Siberell (p. 265-268) - A check list of the books of John Cowper Powys, by L. E. Siberell and P. H. Muir (p. 269-273) - Introductions and contributions by John Cowper Powys to books other than his own (p. 274-275) - A check list of the books of T. F. Powys, by B. van Thal and P. H. Muir (p. 276-281) - List of paintings by Gertrude Powys. - Books of Philippa Powys (and) A. R. Powys (p. 284)   36-7283.   PR6031.O867Z96

POYNTER.   See MACDONALD, 1960

13844   POYNTZ.   Historical and genealogical memoir of the family of Poyntz, or, Eight centuries of an English house.   By Sir John Maclean ... (Only 75 copies printed.) Exeter, Priv. print. for the subscribers by W. Pollard & co., 1886.   viii, 310 p. front., illus., plates, ports., coats of arms, facsims. 29 cm. In two parts. 21-14030.   CS439.P792   1886

PRAA.   See VAN NESS, 1960

PRAHNKE.   In vertical file under PRANKE family.   Ask reference librarian for this material.

PRANCKE.   In vertical file under PRANKE family.   Ask reference librarian for this mateiral.

PRANCKEN.   In vertical file under PRANKE family.   Ask reference librarian for this material.

PRANCKH.   In vertical file under PRANKE family.   Ask reference librarian for this material.

PRANDKE.   In vertical file under PRANKE family.   Ask reference librarian for this material.

PRANDKE.   See PRANKE.

PRANDTKE. In vertical file under PRANKE family. Ask reference librarian for this material.

PRANGHE. In vertical file under PRANKE family. Ask reference librarian for this mateiral.

PRANKA. In vertifal file under PRANKE family. Ask reference librarian for this material.

13845 PRANKE. Pranke family history and genealogy. Prepared by Richard Nicholas Pranke and Mrs. Richard Nicholas Pranke (nee Marie Elizabeth Tschida) (St. Paul? Minn.) 1968. 176 l. ports. (part col.) 29 cm. Typescript (carbon copy) 68-1213.   CS71.P89   1968

13845a PRANKE. Pranke family in vertical file. Ask reference librarian for this material.

PRANKEN. In vertical file under PRANKE family. Ask reference librarian for this material.

PRANKIE. In vertial file under PRANKE family. Ask reference librarian for this material.

PRANSCHKE. In vertical file under PRANKE family. Ask reference librarian for this material.

PRANSKE. In vertical file under PRANKE family. Ask reference librarian for this material.

PRANTCKE. In vertical file under PRANKE family. Ask reference librarian for this material.

PRANTKA. In vertical file under PRANKE family. Ask reference librarian for this material.

PRANTKE. In vertical file under PRANKE family. Ask reference librarian for this material.

13846 PRATHER. Louisville's first families; a series of genealogical sketches by Kathleen Jennings, with drawings by Eugenia Johnson. Louisville, Ky., The Standard printing co. (c.1920) 176 p. incl. front., plates, ports. 20½ cm. Contains the Bullitt, Prather, Clark, Churchill, Pope, Speed, Joyes, Veech, Thruston, Taylor, Bate and Floyd families. 20-11014.   F459.L8J5

13847 PRATHER. Prather family. (By Thomas John Hall, 3rd.) page 216.   CS71.H177   1941

13848 PRATHER. A Prather family record, chiefly of the John Smith Prathers. Kept by Eva Hampton Prather ... 1658-1945. Brookhaven, Ga. (1945) 146 p. 25½ x 20 cm. In manuscript. Includes "References" 45-10065.   CS71.P9   1945

13849 PRATHER. (Genealogical chart of the Prather family. By Wayne Collier. Newark, Ohio, 1954) geneal. table. 60 x 45 cm. fold. to 30 x 23 cm. Reproduced from ms. copy. 63-39427.   CS71.P9   1954

PRATHER. See also ADAMS, 1939

13850 PRATT. Pratt memorial. By Rev. Stillman Pratt. Middleboro', Mass. (Printed at the Gazette office, 1860) 8 p. 23½ cm. Caption title. 12-25496.   CS71.P914   1860

13851 PRATT. The Pratt family: or, The descendants of Lieut. William Pratt, one of the first settlers of Hartford and Say-Brook, with genealogical notes of John Pratt, of Hartford; Peter Pratt, of Lyme; John Pratt (Taylor) of Say-Brook. By Rev. F. W. Chapman ... Hartford, Printed by Case, Lockwood and company, 1864. 420 p., 1 l. front. (coat of arms) ports. 23½ cm. 4-22951.   CS71.P914   1864

13852 PRATT. Sketch of the life of Samuel F. Pratt with some account of the early history of the Pratt family. A paper read before the Buffalo historical society, March 10th, 1873. By William P. Letchworth. Buffalo, Press of Warren, Johnson & co., 1874. 1 p. l., (7)-211 p. front., pl., ports., facsims. 21½ cm. 9-12862.   CS71.P914   1874

13853 PRATT. The ancestry and posterity of Deacon Seth Pratt of Bridgewater. (By Simeon Pratt) (n. p., 1874?) 3 p. l., 22, xxiii-xxxix p. 32 cm. In manuscript. "The compilation of Simeon Pratt at the age of 82 years 1874." Genealogical table inserted. Accompanied by collection of family letters. 38M3810T.   CS71.P914   1874a
Office.

13854   PRATT.   The Pratt family.   A genealogical record of Mathew Pratt of Weymouth, Mass., and his American descendants.   1623-1888.   Boston (Printed by C. H. Heintzemann) 1889.   (3)-226 p. facsims. 24 cm. Ed. by Francis Greenleaf Pratt.   The Pratts of Weymouth.   By Hon. Gilbert Nash. - Genealogical researches by Judge E. Granville Pratt: p. 11-16. 9-13009   CS71. P914   1889

13855   PRATT.   Phinehas Pratt and some of his descendants.   A monograph prepared by Eleazer Franklin Pratt.   Boston, Printed for private distribution (by T. Marvin & son) 1897.   164 p. front. (port.) pl. 24½ cm. 9-12981.   CS71. P914   1897

13856   PRATT.   ... The ancestry and the descendants of John Pratt of Hartford, Conn.   Compiled .. by Charles B. Whittelsey ... By authority of Walter W. Pratt ... Hartford, Conn., The Case, Lockwood & Brainard company, 1900.   204 p. 24 cm. At head of title: 1538-1900. 0-3145 rev.
                                                                                                           CS71. P914   1900

13857   PRATT.   Supplement to a history entitled "The Pratt family; or, The descendants of Lieut. William Pratt, one of the first settlers of Hartford and Say-Brook"; being a continuation of the record in the line of Zadock and Hannah Pratt of Stephentown and Jewett, New York.   Printed by the co-opera- tion of many of the descendants, for private distribution among subscribing members of the family. (New York, A. F. Southcombe) 1916.   3 p. 1., 58 p. front. (coat of arms) 22½ cm. "The information contained in this book was gathered and compiled by Frank E. Pratt." 17-19205.   CS71. P914   1916

13858   PRATT.   The American ancestors and descendants of Simon Newcombe Pratt, and his wife Deborah Isabel Nelson ... compiled by their granddaughter Jennie M. Patten.   Yuma, Col., 1917. 2 p. 1., 3-38 p. 20½ cm. 33-29118.   CS71. P914   1917

13859   PRATT.   Seven generations; a story of Prattville and Chelsea, by Walter Merriam Pratt. (Norwood, Mass.) Priv. print., 1930.   xiii p., 1 1., 419 p. front., illus. (incl. facsims.) plates, ports. 23½ cm. Maps on lining papers. 30-15232.   F74. C5P96

13860   PRATT.   A Pratt book; the American ancestors and descendants of Simon Newcomb (7) Pratt and his wife Deborah Isabel (3) Nelson and ancestral records, by Jennie M. Patten, Anna Pratt Armstrong (and) John Pratt Nesbit, 1623-1938.   (n. p., 1938?)   145 (i. e. 150) numb. 1., 146-161 p. front. (coat of arms) ports. 28 cm. Includes extra numbered leaves 10 a, 104 a, 129a-129 c. Reproduced from type-written copy. Cover-title: Ancestors and descendants of Simon Newcomb Pratt. 41-1461.   CS71. P914   1938

13861   PRATT.   Genealogy of Richard Henry Pratt and his wife, Anna Laura Mason Pratt.   (By Mason Delano Pratt) (San Francisco, Priv. print., 1943)   cover-title, 41, (5) p. illus. (ports.) 28 x 22 cm. "Edition 250 copies." 44-8690.   CS71. P914   1943

13862   PRATT.   The ancestors and descendants of Elisha Pratt of Turner, Maine.   By Francis Henry Russell.   (Kensington, Md.) 1948.   24, (16) p. 27 cm. "References": p. (25) 50-22855.
                                                                                                           CS71. P914   1948

13863   PRATT.   The ancestors and descendants of Elisha Pratt of Turner, Maine.   By Francis Henry Russell.   (Turner? Me.) 1963.   43 p. 28 cm. Bibliography: p. 22. 64-54996.
                                                                                                           CS71. P914   1963

13864   PRATT.   Pratt pioneers of Utah; a biographical, genealogical and historical account of the Obadiah and Jemima (Tolls) Pratt eighteenth century family of the Hudson River Valley area, compiled by Arthur D. Coleman.   Provo, Utah, J. G. Stevenson (c. 1967)   xxxii, 427, 196, 26 p. illus., geneal table, maps, ports. 25 cm. 67-26231.   CS71. P914   1967

13865   PRATT.   Abraham ... the father of us all; a Pratt family history, three hundred fifty years of the history and ancestry of the Pratts of Marion, N. Y.   By Kenneth Charles Pratt.   Oxford, Conn., 1968.   215 p. illus., ports. 29 cm. Bibliography: p. (201)-204. 68-58101 MARC.   CS71. P914   1968

13866   PRATT.   Wives and daughters of the Pratt pioneers of Utah, compiled by Arthur D. Coleman. Salt Lake City, 1969.   xi, 276 1. illus. 22 cm. Title on spine: Pratt wives & daughters of Utah. 70-89852 MARC.
                                                                                                           CS71. P914   1969

PRATT.   See also: BARTLETT, 1951   SMITH, 1946a
                           GREEN, CS499.G78   SOUTHWORTH, 1903
                           HABERSHAM, 1901   TIERS, 1942
                           SMALL, 1910   YOUNG, 1913
                           SMALL, 1934

PRAUNCHKE.   In vertical file under PRANKE family.   Ask reference librarian for this material.

13867   PRAY.   The Pray family of Heckholzhausen, Germany, and descendants in America.   By Kenneth Duane Miller.   (Chicago? 1957)   175 p. illus., ports., map, coat of arms. 24 cm. 57-36820.
                                      CS71.P916   1957

13868   PREBLE.   Brigadier General Jedidiah Preble and his descendants.   (n.p., 18 -)
p. (41)-59. Foot notes. 37M790T.   CS71.P222   18 -

13869   PREBLE.   A genealogical sketch of the Preble families, resident in Portland, Me., A.D.1850 ... Printed, but not published.   Portland (Me.) Harmon and Williams, printers, 1850.
28 p. 23½ cm. Dedication signed: Wm. P. Preble. 41-41203.   CS71.P922   1850

13870   PREBLE.   The last tragedy of the Indian wars: the Preble massacre at the Kennebec ... By Henry Otis Thayer ... Read before the ... society, April 30, 1903.   (In Collections of the Maine historical society. Portland, 1904. 23½ cm. 3d ser., v. 1, p. 406-422) A 15-1303.   F16.M33 3d ser.v.1

13871   PREBLE.   John Preble of Machias (1771-1841) and his descendants, by William Preble Jones.   Somerville, Mass., 1929.   32 p. 23 cm. 29-12016.   CS71.P922   1929

13872   PREBLE.   Four Boston grandparents, Jones and Hill, Preble and Eveleth and their ancestry, by William Preble Jones.   Somerville, Mass., 1930.   91 p. pl., ports. 24 cm. 31-2233.
                                      CS71.J76   1930

13873   PREBLE.   Genealogical sketch of the first three generations of Prebles in America: with an account of Abraham Preble the emigrant, their common ancestor, and of his grandson Brigadier General Jedediah Preble, and his descendants.   By Geo. Henry Preble ... Boston, Printed for family circulation, D. Clapp & son, 1868.   3 p. l., iv, (5)-336 p. front., illus. (coat of arms) plates, port., photos., facsims. 25½ cm. One hundred and twenty five copies printed. no. 67. 9-12863.   L.C. COPY REPLACED BY MICROFILM.   CS71.P922   1868
                                      Microfilm 8684 CS

PRECKENDORF.   See PRACKENDORF.

PREE.   See PRAY, 1957

13874   PRÉFONTAINE.   Généalogie de la famille Préfontaine, par l'abbé G. A. Dejordy ... St. - Hyacinthe, Impr. "La Tribune," 1909.   2 p. l., (7)-20 p. 16½ cm. 11-30423.
                                      CS90.P8

13875   PREFONTAINE.   Prefontaine family.   F1054.R5.D3

PREHEIM.   See GRABER, 1948

13876   PREHN.   The ancestry of Nicholas Davis, 1753-1832, of Limington, Maine.   By Walter Goodwin Davis.   Portland, Me., Anthoensen Press, 1956.   239 p. illus. 24 cm. 57-22949.
                                      CS71.D26   1956b

PRENCE.   See CROCKER, 1923

13877   PRENTICE.   The history and genealogy of the Prentice or Prentiss family, in New England, from 1631 to 1852.   Collected by C. J. F. Binney.   Boston, The author, 1852.   iv, 272, 8 p. front., plates, ports. 22½ cm. 9-13233.
                                      CS71.P927   1852

13878 PRENTICE. The history and genealogy of the Prentice, or Prentiss family, in New England, etc., from 1631 to 1883. By C. J. F. Binney ... 2d ed. Boston, The editor, 1883. iv, 2 l., 446 p. front., illus. (coat of arms) pl., ports. 24 cm. Title vignette: col. coats of arms. 9-13232.

CS71.P927   1883

13879 PRENTICE. The life and times of Seargent Smith Prentiss. By Joseph D. Shields. Philadelphia, J. B. Lippincott & co., 1884. 442 p. front. (port.) 23 cm. "Appendix. Genealogy of the Prentiss family. Furnished by Seargent Prentiss Nutt, of Mississippi": p. 441-442. 16-23634.

E340.P9S55

13880 PRENTICE. Descendants of Rev. Amos Prentice (1804-1849) subsequent to conclusion of Charles James Fox Binney's Prentice-Prentiss family, second edition, published 1883. Compiled by John K. Prentice ... (Barrington, Ill.) 1942. 1 p. l., 54 (i. e. 57) numb. l. 2 coats of arms (incl. col. front.) 29 x 23 cm. Reproduced from type-written copy. Bibliography: leaf 5. 43-48619.

CS71.P927   1942

13881 PRENTICE. Joshua Prentice, his ancestors and descendants. 1st ed. By Willard Jenison Prentice. (Baltimore) 1946. 66 l. illus., ports., maps (1 fold.) col. coat of arms. fold. geneal. table. 29 cm. Bibliography: leaf 58. 47-2514 rev. *

CS71.P927   1946

————Supplement no. 1 -   Baltimore, c.1948. v. fold. geneal. table. 27 cm. "Whitman National Monument, Washington" (15 p.) inserted in no. 1.

CS71.P927   1946
Suppl.

13882 PRENTICE. Eight generations, the ancestry, education and life of William Packer Prentice, by his son William Kelly Prentice. Princeton, N.J., 1947. 303 p. front., plates, ports. 23 cm. Bibliography: p. (293)-294. 47-22111.

CS71.P927   1947

13883 PRENTICE. Prentiss Hubbard and allied families: genealogical and biographical. Compiled for "Colonial and revolutionary lineages of America." New York, Priv. print. for Mrs. Frederick S. Webber by the American Historical Co., 1962. vii, 193 p. plates, ports., col. coats of arms. 32 cm. 62-51889.

CS69.A57

PRENTICE.   See also: BALDWIN, 1881
GLEASON, 1960
MINNS, 1925

PRENTISS.   See PRENTICE.

13884 PRESBREY. William Presbrey, of London, England, and Taunton, Mass., and his descendants, 1690-1918. Research made and records compiled by Rev. Joseph Waite Presby ... (Rutland, Vt., The Tuttle company, 1918) 151 p. port. 23½ cm. 19-3963.

CS71.P929   1918

PRESBREY.   See also FLAGG, 1903

PRESBRY.   See PRESBREY.

13885 PRESCOTT. Life of William Hickling Prescott, by George Ticknor. Boston, Ticknor & Fields, 1864. 1 p. l., x, 491 p. front. (port.) illus., pl., double facsim. 25½ cm. Appendix A: The Prescott family, p.449-460; appendix E: Translations of Mr. Prescott's histories, p. 469-471. 4-17200/3.

PS2657.T5

13886 PRESCOTT. The Prescott memorial: or, A genealogical memoir of the Prescott families in America. In two parts. By William Prescott ... Boston, Printed by H. W. Dutton & son, 1870. (iii)-xiv p., 1 l., 653 p. front., port. coat of arms. 23½ cm. In two parts, each pt. having separate title-page. Title vignettes (coats of arms) Contents. - pt. 1 ... John Prescott, of 1640, and his descendants. - pt. 2. ... James Prescott, of 1665. and his descendants. 9-13004.

CS71.P93   1870

13887 PRESCOTT. Life of William Hickling Prescott, by George Ticknor. Philadelphia, J. B. Lippincott company (1903) xii, 458 p. front., ports. 19½ cm. Appendix A: The Prescott family. 4-24931.

PS2657.T5   1903

13888 PRESCOTT. A history of the White family, by Rev. William Prescott White, D. D. Brook, Pa., The Edwards press, 1925. 20 p. 1 l. Nov. 8, 1938.

CS71.W585   1925

PRESCOTT.   See also: BARRETT, F74.C8P8   HANAFORD, 1915
                       BREREWOOD, DA690.C5.E2   LAWRENCE, 1856
                       DRAKE, 1962   WOLCOTT, 1939
                       ELLIS, F3.T61

13889   PRESGRAVE.   Presgraves in Rutlandshire, England, 1540-1668.   By James Cawood Presgraves.   Potomac, Md., 1965.   iii, 24, (1) p. map (part col.) 23 cm.   Bibliography: p. (25) 66-87793.
CS439.P794   1965

PRESGRAVES.   See PRESGRAVE.

PRESSLY.   See FLENNIKEN, 1926

13890   PREST.   The Prest family, being a record of the descendants of Edward Prest.   Compiled by
his great-grandson John Bottomly Prest.   (New York, T. A. Wright, inc.) 1930.   27 p. front., ports. 23 cm.
"The Bottomly family, being a record of the descendants of Nathaniel Bottomly, compiled by ... John Bottomly Prest. 1930. This record shows
the inter-marriage of the Bottomly and Livermore families, the latter dating from John Livermore (1606), the ancestor of all the Livermores in the
United States", with special t.-p.: p. (17)-27. 31-20874.   CS71.P938   1930

13891   PRESTON.   Memoranda of the Preston family.   By Orlando Brown.   Albany, J. Munsell, 1864.
26 p. 24 cm. First printed for private distribution in 1842. 25 copies reprinted in Albany, 1864. 9-13002.
CS71.P94   1864

13892   PRESTON.   (In Peytoun, John L.   Memoir of William Madison Peyton, of Roanoke.   London,
1873.   22 cm.   app. B)   9-13003.   F230.P51

13893   PRESTON.   Historical sketches and reminiscences of an octogenarian.   By Thomas L. Preston.
Richmond, Va., Pub. for the author by B. F. Johnson publishing co., 1900.   1 p. l., 7-170 p. front. (port.)
24 cm. Sketches of Washington County, Virginia, including an account of the Preston family. 0-4775.
F232.W3P8

13894   PRESTON.   The Preston genealogy; tracing the history of the family from about 1040, A.D.,
in Great Britain, in the New England states, and in Virginia, to the present time.   Edited by L. A.
Wilson, at the instance and under the direction of William Bowker Preston.   Salt Lake City, Utah, The
Deseret news, 1900.   2 p. l., viii p., 1 l., 368 p. front., plates, ports., fold. geneal. tables.   23½ cm. Edition of 300 copies.
Feb. 21, 1901-156.   CS71.P94   1900

13895   PRESTON.   The Preston genealogy, Orange County branch, and sketch of the life of the author,
David C. Preston.   Middletown, N.Y., Stivers printing company, 1909.   5 galley proofs. 15½ cm.
CS71.P94   1909

13896   PRESTON.   The Preston genealogy, Orange County branch and life sketch of the compiler,
David C. Preston.   Middletown, N.Y., For D. C. Preston by Stivers printing company, 1913.
25 p. front., illus., ports. 24½ cm. 13-8952.   CS71.P94   1913

13897   PRESTON.   Calendar of the Gormanston register, from the original in the possession of the
right honourable the viscount of Gormanston.   Prepared and edited by James Mills ... and M. J.
McEnery ... Dublin, Printed at the University press, for the Royal society of antiquaries of Ireland,
1916.   2 p. l., (iii)-xix, 252 p. 26 cm. (Half-title: Royal society of antiquaries of Ireland. Extra volume. 1916) Half-title: Calendar
of the Gormanston register, circa 1175-1397. The ancient register book of the Lords of Gormanston is primarily an entry book of the title-deeds of
their estates at the end of the fourteenth century, and seems to have been prepared or begun in 1397-8 for the purpose of registering the title-deeds of
the property inherited or acquired by Sir Christopher Preston. 16-23828.   DA995.G7G6

13898   PRESTON.   Descendants of Roger Preston of Ipswich and Salem village, by Charles Henry
Preston.   Salem, Mass., The Essex institute, 1931.   1 p. l., ii p., 1 l., 355 p. front. (facsim.) plates. 23½ cm.
"Reprinted from the Historical collections of the Essex institute, volumes LXI-LXVII." 31-17169.
CS71.P94   1931

13899   PRESTON.   William Preston of Newcastle-upon-Tyne, England, and Philadelphia, Pennsylvania, and allied families, by Charles Starne Belsterling ... Philadelphia, Pa., The Dolphin press, 1934.

13899 continued: 172 p. front., illus., plates, ports., facsims. (1 double) col. coats of arms, fold. geneal. tables. 26 cm. "Only 150 copies ... printed, of which this is no. 38." Bibliography: p. 9-11. 34-29269.

CS71.P94   1934

13900   PRESTON.   Descendants of Thomas Preston, of London, England.   1748-1825.   Compiled by Enid Dickinson Collins.   Jamaica, N.Y., 1940.   1 p. l., 7 numb. l. 28 cm. Type-written (carbon copy) Leaf 7 blank for "Additional information." 41-14799.

CS71.P94   1940

13901   PRESTON.   The Preston genealogical story.   By John Frederick Preston.   Washington, 1963. ix, (i.e. xii) l., 67 (i.e. 83) p. mounted col. illus., maps (on cover) 28 cm. Text mounted on p. (2) of cover. Bibliography: leaf v (i.e. viii) 64-565.

CS71.P94   1963

PRESTON.   See also:

BASSETT, 1930	HOWE, 1961	PEYTON, F230.P51
BRUNNELL, 1937	HUMFREVILLE, 1903	WASHINGTON, E159.C56
BYRD, E159.G58	JOHNSTON, 1897	WELLWOOD, DA890.D9C4
DRAPER, 1871	OGDEN, 1914	WHITE, E171.A53 v. 20
FERRIN, 1915		

PREUT.   See PREWITT.

PREVOST.   See MALLET, 1930

13902   PREWITT.   Notes on the Prewitt-Light; Ringler-Hollowell and allied families.   (By Lester Dee Prewitt) (Forest City, Ia., Summit printing company, 1939)   2 p. l., 30, (14) p. 22 cm. Pages (5)-(6) blank for "Addenda". 40-8610.

CS71.P943   1939

13903   PREWITT.   Pruitt-Prewitt ancestors.   By Charles Raymond Dillon.   (Los Angeles? 1960) 242 p. 29 cm. 60-36355.

CS71.P943   1960

PREWITT.   See also LEWIS, 1901

13904   PRICE.   Centennial meeting of the descendants of Philip and Rachel Price.   Philadelphia, Caxton press of C. Sherman, son & co., 1864.   86 p. 20 cm. (With his Discourse on the family as an element of govern-ment. Philadelphia, 1864) Signed: Eli K. Price. 9-5336.

HQ734.P9

—— Copy 2.   CS71.P946   1864

13905   PRICE.   The golden wedding of Benjamin and Jane Price.   With brief family record ... Philadelphia, J. B. Lippincott & co. (1870)   48 p. 19½ cm. 9-13231.

CS71.P946   1870

13906   PRICE.   The Price family of "Cool Water," Hanover County, Va.   Maternal ancestry, and descendants in two lines to the year 1906, comp. by Theodore H. Price and Charlotte P. Price.   New York, Arranged and printed by T. A. Wright (1906)   broadside. 72 x 99½ cm. fold. to 37 cm. 17-6159.

CS71.P946   1906

13907   PRICE.   John Price the emigrant, Jamestown colony 1620, with some of his descendants, by the Rev. Benjamin Luther Price ... Alexandria, La.   (1910)   3 p. l., 62 p. 25 cm. 11-5631.

CS71.P946   1910

13908   PRICE.   (Rev. Jacob Price chart) (Pottstown, Pa., 1910)   geneal. tab. 69½ x 69 cm. Signed: Geo. F. P. Wanger. 11-28589.

CS71.P946   1910a

13909   PRICE.   Thomas Price (a pioneer in Posey County, Indiana) and his descendants; a history and genealogy, by Rev. John E. Cox ... Owensville, Ind., Printed in the Messenger office, 1926. 129, (1) p. pl., ports. 23 cm. 26-11271.

CS71.P946   1926

13910   PRICE.   A genealogy of the descendants of Rev. Jacob Price, evangelist, pioneer, compiled for the Price family association by Geo. F. P. Wanger. Harrisburg, Pa., The Evangelical press, 1926. x, 832 p. incl. front., illus., ports. fold. pl., fold. facsim. 24 cm. 26-14565.

CS71.P946   1926

13911   PRICE.   ... Price family history, by J. Montgomery Seaver.   Philadelphia, Pa., American historical-genealogical society (1927?)   39, (2) p. illus. (ports.) 23½ cm.   Two blank pages at end for "Family records".   Coat of arms of the Price family on cover.   "References": p. 38-39.   40-18918.
CS71.P946

13912   PRICE.   The annals of our kin, compiled by Mary Pearl Brown Price (Mrs. Eugene Miller Price) ... (Atlanta) The author, 1940.   vi, 95 p. ports. 21 cm. Includes the Price and Brown families. 40-29605.
CS71.P946   1940

13913   PRICE.   The Prices and the Moores; James Valentine Price and Pattie Moore Price of Rockingham county, North Carolina: their antecendents and their children, by Harold Coy.   Sponsored by Thomas Moore Price, Oakland, California.   (New York, International press, 1944)   xiii, 330, (12) p.   ports., facsims. 27 cm. Map on lining papers. 45-12458.
CS71.P946   1944

13914   PRICE.   The Price family of Barrett Township, Monroe County, Pennsylvania.   By Violet (Hallett) Price.   Boston, Christopher Pub. House (1948)   86 p. front. 21 cm. 48-10208*.
CS71.P946   1948

13915   PRICE.   The Price family tree; a keepsake for the descendants of Thomas Davis Price, 1826-1900, and his wife Sarah Jane Jones, 1831-1917, of the Welsh Hills, near Newark and Granville, Ohio.   By John Marshall Price.   New York, N.Y., 1957.   32 p. 22 cm. 58-36418.   CS71.P946   1957

13916   PRICE.   The Nunnery-Wolf-Price family, 1808-1963, some of the ancestors and all of the known-to-us descendants of James Price and his wife Clarky Nunnery Price.   By Rosa Lee Paschel.   Jackson, Miss. (1963?)   44 p. 22 cm. 64-3357.   CS71.P946   1963

13917   PRICE.   Price-Goldsmith-Lowenstein, and related families, 1700-1967.   By Katherine Goldsmith Lowenstein.   Harriet Stryker-Rodder, editor.   New York, 1967.   1, 49 p. illus., facsims., geneal. tables, ports. 28 cm. Cover title. 70-5699 MARC.   CS71.P946   1967

PRICE.   See also:

ARCHDALE, 1925   LEWIS, 1960   STEEN, 1959
BOND, 1872   MARTIN, 1943   WHEELER, 1920
CURD, 1938   MOAK, 1960   YOUNG, 1937
GUÉRIN, 1890   PARRISH, 1935   No. 430 - Adventurers of purse
GUSTIN, 1900   SCRUGGS, 1912   and person.
LEONARD, 1928   SMITH, 1927b   No. 9847 - Hackettstown.

13918   PRICHARD.   Prichard of Preston.   (In Records of the parish church of Preston in Amounderness, by Tom C. Smith ... Preston, London, 1892.   29 x 22½ cm. app. B.)   2-22238.
DA690.P93S6

13919   PRICHARD.   Early days in Cadiz.   Genesis of Cadiz and Harrison county, Ohio, with genealogical notes of the Pritchard-Dewey and other families ... (Cadiz) Cadiz Republican print, 1898.   cover-title, 14 p. pl., ports., fold. plan. 23 cm. By Orville C. Dewey and Mrs. Clara Hyde (Dewey) Hogg. 4-37292.
F499.C1D5

13920   PRICHARD.   Memorials of the Prichards of Almeley and their descendants.   Compiled by Isabel Southall ... 2d ed., cor. and enl. ... Birmingham (Printed at the Midland counties herald office) 1901.   4 p. l., 131, (1) p. front. 23 cm. "Privately printed." Includes also the Southall, Smith, and Young families. 40-16319.
CS439.P795   1901

13921   PRICHARD.   Descendants of William Prichard, by A. M. Prichard ... Charleston, W. Va., Tribune ptg. co., 1912.   1 p. l., 59 p. port. 22 cm. 12-18165.   CS71.P947   1912

13922   PRICHARD.   The Prichard family; history and genealogy of the descendants of James and Elizabeth Hughes Prichard of New Castle, Kentucky, by Martha Coleman Johnson ... (n. p.) 1915.   3 p. l., (5)-230 p. front., illus. (ports.) 24 cm. Lettered on cover: Prichard-Pritchard, 1745-1915. 15-16623.
CS71.P947   1915

412

13923   PRICHARD.   The Prichard-Pritchard genealogy of the New England, or northern family branch, from the first known settler of that name, Roger Prichard, 1600-1671, to 1960.   (Takoma Park, Md., 1960)   22 1. 28 cm. 61-35643.   CS71.P947   1960

13924   PRICHARD.   Pedigree of the noble family of Pritchard or Prichard ... London, 1919.
cover-title, 5 p. 25½ cm.   Title vignette: coat of arms. 20-7106.   CS439.P795

13925   PRICHARD.   A compilation of some of the descendants of Roger Prichard, c.1600-1671; a Welshman who brought his family to Massachusetts Bay Colony in 1636; a pioneer of Springfield, Massachusetts, and of Wethersfield, Milford, and New Haven, Connecticut.   By Jacob Le Roy Pritchard.   (San Jose? Calif., 1953)   51 p. coat of arms. 19 cm. Bibliography: p. 50-51. 54-24346.
                                                                                          CS71.P947   1953

          PRICHARD.   See also: BAX, 1936
                                 DAVIS, 1959
                                 FOSTER, 1941
                                 JAMES, 1913a
                                 No. 1459 - Early families of ... Kentucky.

13926   PRICKETT.   The Pricketts of Allerthorpe, by F. Fenton Prickett, with an Introduction by Colonel Prickett.   London, Elson & sons, printers, 1918.   3 p. 1., (5)-44 p. plates, fold. geneal. tab. 18½ cm.
25-11761.   CS439.P797

          PRICKETT.   See also : HAYNES, 1902
                                  MORGAN, 191-

          PRICKITT.   See PRICKETT.

13927   PRIDEAUX.   Pedigree of the family of Prideaux of Luson in Ermington, Devon.   Compiled by T. Engledue P. Prideaux ... Exeter, W. Pollard & co., 1889.   1 p. 1., 16 p. illus. (coat of arms) 28½ cm. 2-30600.
                                                                                          CS439.P8

13928   PRIDEUX.   Sutcombe church and its builders, by Edith K. Prideux.   Exeter, J. C. Commin, 1913.   46, (2) fold. front. (plan) illus., plates, fold. geneal. tables (in pocket) 22½ cm. (With Devon & Cornwall notes & queries. Exeter, J. G. Commin, 1915. v. 8) Genealogical tables have colored coats of arms. Issued as appendix to Devon & Cornwall notes and queries v. 8, pt. 1-2 (Jan.-Apr. 1914) 25-14809.   DA670.D49D4   v. 8

13929   PRIDEUX.   Prideaux families.   By Clifford Prideaux Feathers.   Menlo Park, Calif., 1953 -
1 v. (loose-leaf) coats of arms. 28 cm. 54-32697.   CS71.P948   1953

          PRIDEAUX.   See also FOX, CS439.F7

13930   PRIEST.   The Priest family; a collection of data, original, contributed and selected, concerning various branches of the Priest family.   Compiled by Geo. E. Foster ... Ithaca, N.Y., West Hill press, 1900.   (549) p. front., pl., port. 19 cm. Various paging. 2-7560.
                                                                                          CS71.P949   1900

13931   PRIEST.   Priest genealogies and allied lineages, compiled by Grace Dunlap.   Huntsville, Ark., Century Enterprises, Genealogical Services, 1969.   (3), 82 p. ports. 28 cm. Bibliography: 3d prelim. page.
77-6723 MARC.   CS71.P949   1969

13932   PRILLAMAN.   The Prillaman family; an account of the descendants of Jacob Prillaman, Sr. (1721-1796) of Franklin County, Virginia.   By Ellen Stanley Rogers.   (Hyattsville? Md.) c.1959.
107 1. 30 cm. 59-43496.   CS71.P95   1959

13933   PRIME.   The autobiography of an octogenarian, containing the genealogy of his ancestors, sketches of their history, and of various events that have occurred during his protracted life ... By D. N. Prime ... Newburyport, W. H. Huse & co., printers, 1873.   xi, (11)-293 p. front. (port.) 18½ cm.
9-20753.   F74.R88P9

13934   PRIME.   Some account of the family of Prime of Rowley, Mass.   With notes on the families of Platts, Jewetts, and Hammond.   (Temple Prime, Huntington, Suffolk Co., N. Y., U. S. A.)   New York, 1887.   40 p.   24½ cm.   9-13005.   CS71.P952   1887

13935   PRIME.   Notes genealogical, biographical and bibliographical, of the Prime family.   By E. D. G. Prime ... (Cambridge, Mass.)   Printed for private use (University press) 1888.
1 p. 1.   118 p.   23 cm.   9-13229.   CS71.P952   1888

13936   PRIME.   Prime.   The descendants of James Prime, who was at Milford, Conn., in 1644, with some names in allied families.   Comp. for private use only by Ralph E. Prime ... Yonkers, N. Y., Printed by G. B. Mottram, 1895.   1 p. 1., 31, (13) p.   24 cm.   9-13228.   CS71.F952   1895

13937   PRIME.   Some account of the family of Prime, of Rowley, Mass.   With notes on the families of Platts and Jewett by Temple Prime ... 2d ed.   New York (The De Vinne press) 1897.   79 p. incl.
ports.   24½ cm.   9-13230.   CS71.P952   1897

13938   PRINCE.   Some memoirs of the life and writings of the Rev. Thomas Prince, together with a pedigree of his family.   By Samuel G. Drake ... Boston, Office of the New England historic-genea-logical register, 1851.   12 p.   2 port.   (incl. front.)   24 cm.   9-13012.   CS71.P955   1851

13939   PRINCE.   Memoirs of the Rev. Thomas Prince.   By Samuel G. Drake.   (In Prince, T. A.   A chrono-logical history of New England, in the form of annals ... 3d ed.   Boston, 1852.   23 cm.   p. (3) - 12)   Includes pedigree of the Prince family.
9-13013.   F7.P96

13940   PRINCE.   A chronological history of New-England, in the form of annals ... from the dis-covery of Capt. Gosnold in 1602 to the arrival of Governor Belcher in 1730.   With an introduction con-taining a brief epitome of ... events abroad, from the creation ... By Thomas Prince ... 3d ed.: To which is added, a memoir of the author, an attempt towards a perfect catalogue of his writings, a genealogy of his family, and the names of the subscribers to the original edition.,   By Samuel G. Drake.   Boston, N. E.   Printed by Kneeland & Green for S. Gerrish.   MDCCXXXVI.   Boston: (Nathan Hale) published by Cummings, Hilliard & co., 1826.   Boston, Antiquarian bookstore, 1852.   13, (1), (3)-12, (iii)-xxi, (2), 25-439 p.   front., illus., plates, ports., coat of arms.   23 cm.   "This edition consists of but thirty copies."   Includes the "Annals of New England", Sept. 28, 1630 to Aug 5, 1633.   "We have completed the (last) sentence from Winthrop's Journal." p. 433.   1-14468.
          F7.P96

13941   PRINCE.   Elder John Prince of Hull, Mass., a memorial, biographical & genealogical, by George Prince, of the 6th generation.   (Boston, Mass., S. W. Symonds, printer, 1888)   31, (1) p.
19½ cm.   Caption title.   35-28842.   CS71.P955   1888

13942   PRINCE.   Princes.   Records of our ancestors: containing a complete list of all persons by the name of Prince, who served in Lexington alarm, April, 1775, revolutionary war, war of 1812, and the civil war 1861-65 ... Edited and published by Frank A. Prince ... Franklin, Mass., Sentinel pub-lishing co., 1898.   2 p. 1., 88 p.   23 cm.   (With his The genealogy of the Prince family ... 1899)   Pages 79-86 left blank for "Remarks".   99-3200 rev.   CS71.P955   1899
——— Copy 2.   CS71.P955   1898

13943   PRINCE.   Descendants of Daniel Prince, born May 1st, 1775.   By Frank A. Prince ... Danielson, Conn., J. H. Briggs (1898)   11 p.   front.   23¾ cm.   9-13224.   CS71.P955   1898a

13944   PRINCE.   (In his Genealogy of the Prince family from 1660 to 1899.   Danielson, Conn., 1899.
23 cm.   p. 5-11)   9-13225.   CS71.P955   1899

13945   PRINCE.   The genealogy of the Prince family.   From 1660 to 1899.   Compiled, arranged, and published by Frank A. Prince ... Danielson, Conn., J. H. Briggs, printer, 1899.   3 p. 1., 5-153 p.
front., plates, ports.   23 cm.   With this is bound: ... Records of our ancestors: containing a complete list of all persons by the name of Prince, who served in Lexington alarm,   April, 1775, revolutionary war, war of 1812, and civil war, 1861-65 ... Edited and published by Frank A. Prince. Franklin, Mass., 1898.   99-3199 rev.   CS71.P955   1899

13946   PRINCE.   Ancestors of Thomas Prince, 1749/50-1840; John Prince of Hull, Mass., progenitor By Helen (Richardson) Kluegel.   Kaneohe, Hawaii, 1964.   1 v.   (various pagings)   geneal. table.   29 cm.   "Book 6, family group 7 ... in a series found on (the author's) sixteen great-great-grandparents."   74-3932.   CS71.P955   1964

13947   PRINCE.   Letters to Christopher Prince, 1855-1865.   Journals of Eliza Prince, 1859-1860. Middletown, N.Y., Whitlock Press (1969)   ix, 215 p. illus. 23 cm.   Edited by Arthur Spear. 77-84402 MARC.
CS71.P955   1969

PRINCE.   See also MACKEY, 1957

PRINDLE.   See PRINGLE, P.957

PRINE.   See PERRIN.

13948   PRINGLE.   The memoirs of Walter Pringle, of Greenknow; or, some of the free mercies of God to him, and his will to his children, left to them under his own hand.   Ed. by the Rev. Walter Wood, A.M.   With notes and an appendix, containing an account of the families of Gordon and Seton, the most ancient possessors of Greenknow; and also of the Pringles of Galashiels, of Whytebank, of Stitchel, of Greenknow, of Torwoodlee, and the homes of Bassendean.   Edinburgh, W.P. Kennedy; (etc., etc.) 1847.   xii, 132 p. 17½ cm.   1st edition, 1723.   This edition is reprinted from the 3d edition of 1751, and has been carefully corrected from a manuscript copy placed at the disposal of the editor, by Sir John Pringle. cf. Pref. 15-19002.
BX9225.P75A3 1847

13949   PRINGLE.   The Prindle genealogy, embracing the descendants of William Pringle the first settler, in part for six, seven and eight generations, and also the ancestors and descendants of Zalmon Prindle for ten generations,   covering a period of two hundred and fifty-two years, 1654 to 1906. Compiled by Franklin C. Prindle ... New York, The Grafton press, 1906.   xvii p., 1 l., 335 p. pl., 3 port. (incl. front.) 24 cm.   "Three hundred copies of this book have been printed from type ..."   This copy not numbered. 6-36884.
CS71.P957   1906

13950   PRINGLE.   The records of the Pringles or Hoppringills of the Scottish border, by Alex. Pringle ... Edinburgh, London, Oliver and Boyd, 1933.   xii, 349, (1) p. 23½ cm. "References": p. xi-xii. 33-22287.
CS479.P8

13951   PRIOLEAU.   The family of Priuli, also called Prioli, Priolo, Prioleau.   (Paper read before the Huguenot society, April 13, 1894) by Edward M. Gallaudet ... (New York, 1894)   23 p. 25½ cm. Caption title.   Reprinted from the Proceedings of the Huguenot society of America, vol. II, 1894, p. 299-321. 9-13223.
CS71.P958   1894

13952   PRIOR.   Records of Timothy Prior, and Nathan Prior, Feb. 10, 1922.   Comp. by Smith, Sarah Augusta (Prior) - "Mrs. C.E. Smith".   (Columbus, O., 1922)   56, (2) p. incl. illus., 2 fold. geneal. tab. 31 cm.   Illustrations include portraits and facsimiles.   A collection of data relating to the Prior ancestry of Sarah Augusta (Prior) Smith, consisting of printed and manuscript material with mounted photographs, fastened together in binder. 22-6307.   CS71.P96   1922

13953   PRIOR.   Descendants of Marvin Sylvestor and Alonzo Bailey Prior.   By Dorotha Perkins Furman.   (Shrewsbury, Mass.) 1967.   57 l. 30 cm. Cover title: Prior lineage: Shust and Furman families. "A supplement to the Tabor genealogy written by Ann and Albert Wright, 1846-1966." 67-9219.   CS71.P96   1967

PRIOR.   See also: CHALFANT, 1959
                     MILLIKEN, 1921
                     ROSE, 1922
                     STILES, 1920

PRITCHARD.   See PRICHARD.

13954   PRITCHETT.   Pedigree of Pritchett from De la Bere of Kynnersley, Hereford; Perks of Drayton in Brimfield, Hereford; and Pritchett of Bilbury in Richard's castle.   Compiled by G. Milner Gibson Cullum ... and James Pigott Pritchett ... (London, Mitchell and Hughes, 1892)   2 p. front. (coats of arms) 44 cm. Caption title. 19-3364.   CS439.P83

13955   PRITZKER.   The Pritzker book; honoring the past, bringing togetherness to the present, lighting a path for the future.   By Lee Pritzker.   (Baltimore, c.1962)   304 p. illus. 24 cm. 63-2237.
CS71.P962   1962

PRIULI. See PRIOLEAU.

PROBST. See BROBST.

13956   PROBY.   A catalogue of the pictures at Elton hall in Huntingdonshire, in the possession of Colonel Douglas James Proby, by Tancred Borenius ... and the Rev. J. V. Hodgson ... with a preface by Granville Proby.   London and Boston, The Medici society, limited, 1924.   3 p. 1., v-xlvi, 124 p., 1 l. front., plates, ports., fold. geneal. tab.   32 x 26 cm.   "Of this edition 350 copies have been printed. ... number 53.   37-6906.

N5245. P75

PROBYN. See HOPKINS, OS439.H7

13957   PROCHAZKA.   The Prochazkas from Kutna Hora, Bohemia, by George A. Prochazka, Jr. (Springfield? N.J.) 1965.   iv, 297 p. illus., maps, ports. 28 cm.   "A limited edition, privately distributed. Copy no. 36." 66-33434.

CS71. P963   1965

PROCTER. See PROCTOR.

13958   PROCTOR.   The Procter gathering, in commemoration of the one hundredth anniversary of the wedding day of their progenitors, Mr. Joseph Proctor and Miss Elizabeth Epes, together with the genealogy of the family.   (By George H. Proctor) Gloucester, Mass., Procter brothers, printers, 1868.   46 p. 23 cm.   George H. Proctor, secretary.   "Genealogy of the Procter family, by Joseph O. Procter": p. (33)-44. 20-22882.

CS71. P964   1868

13959   PROCTOR.   A genealogy of descendants of Robert Proctor of Concord and Chelmsford, Mass. With notes of some connected families, by William Lawrence Proctor and Mrs. W. L. Proctor. Ogdensburg, N.Y., Republican & journal print, 1898.   vi p., 1 l., 307 p. front., plates, ports., coat of arms. 24½ cm. 9-13227.

CS71. P964   1898

13960   PROCTOR.   Tucson, Tubac, Tumacacori, Tohell. A 1st limited ed. By Gil Procter. Tucson, Arizona Silhouettes, 1956.   110 p. illus. 24 cm.   56-42535.

F811. P76

13961   PROCTOR.   The Proctor family and related lines, 1635-1958.   By Chester Lincoln Somers. (Hamilton? Mass., 1958)   unpaged. 28 cm. 58-38373.

CS71. P964   1958

PROCTOR.   See also: DINWIDDIE, 1957
                                   MANNING, 1897a
                                   SAUNDERS, 1897
                                   WALTON, 1898

PRONG.   See ALEXANDER, 1960

PROPST.   See SHELTON, 1962

13961a   PROSSER.   Prosser family in vertical file.   Ask reference librarian for this material.

PROUD.   See PROUT.

PROUDE.   See PROUT.

13962   PROUDFIT.   Historical sketch of the Proudfit family of York County, Pennsylvania, with a complete record of the descendants of Alexander Proudfit and Martha McCleary; compiled by Margaret Compton. Meadville, Pa., 1911.   100 p. front., plates, ports. 23½ cm.   Blank leaves interspersed for memoranda. 12-7591.

CS71. P966   1911

PROUDFOOT.   See PROUDFIT.

13963   PROUT.   Ancestry of Capt. Timothy Prout, of Boston, Mass. By J. Henry Lea. Boston, D. Clapp & son, 1901.   14 p. fold. geneal. tab. 24 cm.   Reprinted from the New Eng.. hist. and geneal. register for Jan., 1901. 1-23272.

CS71. P968   1901

PROUT.   See also PROUTY.

PROUTE.   See PROUT.

PROUTEE.   See PROUT.

PROUTEY.   See PROUTY.

13964   PROUTY.   Prouty (Proute) genealoyg, compiled by Charles Henry Pope ... Boston, Mass.,
C. H. Pope, 1910.   vii, 239 p. plates.   13½ cm.   "This edition is limited to three hundred copies, of which this is number 112."
11-14779.   CS71.P9683   1910

PROUTY.   See also: ALEXANDER, 1960
                                  PROUT.

PROVOOST.   See PROVOST.

13965   PROVOST.   Genealogical notes of the Provoost family of New York.   By Edwin R. Purple ...
New York, Priv. print., 1875.   32 p. front. (port.) 26½ cm.   "Edition - one hundred copies.   From the New York genealogical and
biographical record.   With additions."   3-17363.   CS71.P969   1875

13966   PROVOST.   Biographical and genealogical notes of the Provost family from 1545 to 1895.   By
Andrew J. Provost.   New York.   1895.   4 p. l., 11-131, xvi p., 1 l. pl., port.   27 cm.   3-483.
                                                                                                   CS71.P969   1895

13967   PROVOST.   A record of the descendants of Nicholas Provost.   By Kennell Philip Brown.
(Jeanerette? La., 1957?)   56 p. 22 cm. 58-4011.   CS71.P969   1957

PROVOST.   See also OUTWATER, 1924

PROWDE.   See PROUT.

13968   PROWSE.   Notes on the family of Prowse, of Compton Bishop, co. Somerset, with notes and
inscriptions from Axbridge church, Somerset, by Edward Fry Wade.   Privately printed.   London,
Mitchell and Hughes, 1879.   18 p.   28 cm.   Published also in Miscellanea genealogica et heraldica, London, 1880.   27 cm.
n.s., vol. III.   20-15250.   CS439.P84

PROUTE.   See PROUT.

13969   PRUDDEN.   Peter Prudden; a story of his life at New Haven and Milford, Conn., with the
genealogy of some of his descendants and an appendix containing copies of old wills, records, letters,
and papers.   By Lillian E. Prudden.   (New Haven, Conn., The Tuttle, Morehouse & Taylor co.) 1901.
169 p. front., pl., plan, facsim.   19½ cm.   May 23, 1901-86.   CS71.P971   1901

PRUDDEN.   See also: BOYSE, 1943
                                    SEBOR, 1923

13970   PRUDE.   An historical and genealogical record of the Prude and McAdory families, by James
Oscar Prude, sr., and Mary Eloise Prude.   (Tuscaloosa, Ala., Weatherford printing co., c. 1939)
5 p. l., (3)-328 p. port. 23½ cm. 39-17557.   CS71.P972   1939

PRUDEN.   See: CARMAN, 1935
                          PRUDDEN.

PRUETT.   See PREWITT.

PRUITT.   See PREWITT.

PRUNTY.   See BOWMAN, 1940

13971   PRYER.   Pryer genealogy.   By Alvin Seaward Van Benthuysen.   Brooklyn, 1948.
42 l. 32 cm. Typescript (carbon copy) 72-2258.   CS71.P9725   1948

PRYLIMAN.   See PRILLAMAN.

13972   PRYNNE.   The annals of the Parish of Swainswick (near the city of Bath) with abstracts of the register, the church accounts and the overseers' books.   By R. E. M. Peach ... London, S. Low, Marston, Searle & Rivington, limited; (etc., etc., pref. 1890)   xi, 183 p. fold. front. (map) 1 p., geneal. tab. (part fold.) 29½ x 22½ cm. "One hundred copies only of this edition have been printed." No. 100. "William Prynne": p. 32-61. 2-29051.
DA690.S968P3

PUCHOT.   See DU PONT, 1923

13973   PUCKETT.   Puckett points; some facts concerning the family of Richard Puckett of Lunenburg county, Virginia, together with data relating to the allied families of McConnico and Daugherty, compiled from personal accounts, old letters, histories, county records, etc. by Irene D. Gallaway.   (Little Rock, Ark., Democrat p. & l. co.) 1931.   39 p. 23 cm. On cover: The Puckett family. 31-31263.
CS71.P973   1931

13974   PUCKETT.   Some Pucketts and their kin.   By Hester Elizabeth Garrett.   (Lansing? Mich., 1960)   285 p. illus. 28 cm. 60-38917.   CS71.P973   1960

13975   PUCKETT.   The roots and some of the branches of the Puckett family tree.   By Christine (South) Gee.   (Greenwood, S.C., 1958)   vi, 136 p. illus., coat of arms, geneal. table. 24 cm. 63-52206.
CS71.P973   1958

PUCKETT.   See also: ARNOLD, 1930
                       HIGHBAUGH, 1961

PUDERBAUGH.   See PUTERBAUGH.

PUETT.   See NICHOLS, 1960

13976   PUFFER.   The family of Puffer of Massachusetts.   By W. S. Appleton.   Boston, D. Clapp & son, 1882.   1 p. l., 9 p. 26 cm. Corrected and enlarged from the New Eng. hist. and geneal. register for July, 1868. 9-13222.
CS71.P977   1882

13977   PUFFER.   Descendants of George Puffer of Braintree, Massachusetts, 1639-1915; by Charles Nutt ... Worcester, Mass., 1915.   376 p. front., ports. 24 cm. 16-6069.
CS71.P977   1915

13978   PUGH.   Reading backward, by Luella Knott.   Macon, Ga., The J. W. Burke company, 1941.
8 p. l., 222 p. incl. front., illus., pl., ports., coats of arms. 23½ cm. "Letters ... written primarily for the Knott grandchildren." - Pref. "Leaves from the family album": p.(163)-219. Bibliography: 6th prelim. leaf. 46-36859.   CS71.P979   1941

PUGH.   See also JAMES, 1913a

PUGSLEY.   See DE LA VERGNE, 1925

13979   PUKEY.   See CONRAD, 1957

PULESTON.   See COOK, 1857

13980   PULFORD.   The barons of Pulford in the eleventh and twelfth centuries and their descendants, the Reresbys of Thrybergh and Ashover, the Ormesbys of South Ormesby, and the Pulfords of Pulford castle; being an historical account of the lost baronies of Pulford and Dodleston in Cheshire, of seven knights' fees in Lincolnshire attached to them, and of many manors, townships and families in both counties, by Sir George R. Sitwell ... Scarborough, Printed and sold by Sir George Sitwell, 1889.
3 p. l., xlvi, 104, (17) p. front. (facsim.) 23 cm. "Two hundred and fifty copies printed, each of which is numbered and signed." no. 18. 15-21497.   CS439.P85

13981   PULITZER.   The World, the flesh and Messrs, Pulitzer, by James W. Barrett ... New York, The Vanguard press (c. 1931)   6 p. 1., 3-117 p. 19½ cm. 31-8393.   PN4899. N42W63

PULLAM.   See PULLIAM.

PULLEINE.   See PULLIAM.

PULLEN.   See PULLIAM.

13982   PULLEYN.   The Pulleyns of Yorkshire, by Catharine Pullein ... with map and illustrations. Leeds, J. Whitehead & son, printers, 1915.   xii, 798, (2) p. front. (fold. map) illus. (incl. plans, facsims., coats of arms) plates, ports. 22 cm. 19-15835.   CS439. P9

PULLIAM.   See DEAKINS, 1957

PULLUM.   See PULLIAM.

PULMAN.   See COLBY, 1880

13983   PULSIFER.   Ancestry and descendants of Jonathan Pulsifer and his wife Nancy Ryerson Pulsifer of Poland and Sumner, Maine; compiled by William E. Pulsifer ... (New York) Priv. print. by the author, 1928.   71 p. incl. front., pl., ports., coat of arms. 23½ cm. 28-23775.

CS71. P981   1928

13984   PUMPELLY.   Short history of the ancestors and founders of the Pumpelly family, taken from the oldest traditions, by Major Harmon Pumpelly Read ... Also two letters by Captain Samuel Pumpelly, one to Solon Pumpelly the other to Geo. James Pumpelly esq. Albany, September 20th, 1893.   Albany, N. Y., C. Munsell, 1893.   25 p. front. (coat of arms) 24 x 18½ cm. "Twenty-five copies printed." 44-23655.

CS71. P9815   1893

PUMPELLY.   See also ROSS, 1908

PUMPELY.   See PUMPELLY.

PUMPILLY.   See PUMPELLY.

13985   PUNCHARD.   A tribute to the memory of John Punchard: a sermon preached at his funeral, February 16, 1857, by Samuel M. Worcester ... With an appendix containing obituary notices of Mr. Punchard, his revolutionary recollections, his last days, and the genealogy of the Punchard family. Boston, Printed for private circulation (by Cowles & co.) 1857.   1 p. 1., 69 p. front. (port.) 23½ cm. 9-13221.
CS71. P982   1857

13986   PUNCHARD.   Punchard of Heanton-Punchardon.   Records of an unfortunate family.   By E. G. Punchard ... A few copies only for private circulation.   (Plymouth?) 1894.   44, 17, 17 p. incl. fold. geneal. tables. 30 cm.   Reprinted from the Transactions of the Devonshire association for the advancement of science, literature, and art, Plymouth, 1893. In 3 parts, separately paged.   Additions in manuscript.   Part II. Punchard wills and administrations (Devonshire) Cir. 1500 to 1850.   Pt. III. Punchard wills and administrations.   (Norfolk and Suffolk Cir. 1500 to 1800. 21-17145.   CS439. P95

PURCELL.   See: McLEAN, 1942
                          MILLER, 1939
                          ROBERTSON, 1926

PURDON.   See COOTE, CS499. C75

13987   PURDUM.   Genealogical workbook re Purdum.   (By) Ernest Alton Ewers (Mrs. Ernest Alton Ewers) Crete, Ill., 1965.   1 v. (various pagings) 29 cm. Caption title. 65-66442.   CS71. P9835   1965

13988   PURDY.   Allied families of Purdy, Fauconnier, Archer, Perrin, by Anna Falconer Perrin and Mary Falconer Perrin Meeker.   New York, Frank Allaben genealogical company (c. 1911)   9 p. 1.,

13988 continued: 15-114 p. front., plates, ports., maps, fold. geneal. tables, coats of arms. 24½ cm. "Only seventy-five copies of this book have been printed .... This copy is no. 40." "Public research references": p. 95-98. 11-5625.

CS71.P984   1911

13989   PURDY.   Genealogy record of Purdy, Coffin, Noble, and Spencer families: Ross C. Purdy, compiler. (Columbus, O., 1944)   46 numb. 1. incl. 2 port. on 1 1., 2 coats of arms, geneal. tables. 28 x 22 cm. Reproduced from type-written copy. Bibliography: leaves 10-11. 45-726.

CS71.P984   1944

PURDY.   See also: DOBELL, 1929
REYNOLDS, 1959
STRANGE, 1915

PUREFOY.   See No. 430 - Adventurers of purse and person.

13990   PURIFOY.   ... Descendants of John Purifoy who were Confederate soldiers, by Francis Marion Purifoy ... Montgomery, 1904.   cover-title, p. 441-444. 24½ cm. (The Alabama historical society. Montgomery. Reprint no. 20) 9-13007.

CS71.P985   1904

13991   PURINGTON.   ... Lieutenant John Purington: his English and American ancestry. His descendants bearing the name, Purington, Purrington, Purinton, and with other forms of spelling.   Compiled by Rev. Charles N. Sinnett.   Brainerd, Minn.   (19 -)   1 p. 1., 234 numb. 1. 23 cm. Caption title. Typewritten (carbon copy) Additions and corrections in manuscript. 21-18367.

CS71.P9855   19 -

13992   PURINGTON.   ... Puddington-Purrington-Purinton. By Evelyn Rich.   Yarmouthport, Mass., C. W. Swift, 1917.   cover-title, (4) p. 24½ cm. (Library of Cape Cod history & genealogy, no. 30) 40-37510.

CS71.P974   1917

13993   PURINGTON.   Purinton family record of David and Harry (by Florence A. Fletcher.   Long Beach, Calif., 1964?)   23 1. 32 cm. Caption title. 64-56579.

CS71.P974   1964

PURINGTON.   See also OTIS, 1851

PURINTON.   See PURINGTON.

13994   PURMORT.   Purmort genealogy; consisting of nineteen generations, nine in England, ten in America, by Rev. Charles H. Purmont ... Des Moines, Ia., The Homestead company, 1907.   1 p. 1., (5)-148, (13) p. col. front. (coat of arms) illus., plates, ports. 23½ cm. 10-2632.

CS71.P986   1907

13995   PURPLE.   In memoriam. Edwin R. Purple. Born, 1831. Died, 1879. New York, Priv. print., 1881.   12 p. front. (port.) 27 cm. "In part condensed from memorial sketches read before the New York genealogical and biographical society, by Charles B. Moore ... and the New York academy of Medicine, by Lawrence Johnson." "Edition one hundred and twenty copies ... 15 Whatman's drawing paper, no. five." Signed: Samuel S. Purple. 3-20250.

CT275.P884P8

13996   PURPLE.   Contribution to the history of ancient families of New Amsterdam and New York. By Edwin R. Purple.

F128.25 R97

PURRINGTON.   See PURINGTON.

PURSEL.   See PURCELL.

PURSELL.   See PURCELL.

13997   PURVES.   Purves family, compiled from existing records and from the material furnished by living descendants of Sir William Purves.   Historical Publication Society.   Philadelphia (c. 1939)   20 p. coat of arms. 26 cm. L. C. copy imperfect: p. 11-14 wanting. 48-35389*.

CS71.P9865   1939

13998   PURVIS.   The Purvis family in Virginia and their kin.   By Alice Lee Simpson Oliver. (Shipman? Va., 1969)   148 1. coats of arms. 29 cm. Title from label on cover. Reproduction of MS. 77-2724.

CS71.P9867   1969

13998a   PUSEY.   The Pusey family.   A brief historical sketch of its origin in England and America.
Compiled from traditional and authentic sources by Pennock Pusey ... Wilmington, Del., Wood &
Bancroft, 1883.   14 p. illus. 19½ cm. 9-13220.   CS71.P987   1883

    PUSEY.   See also: MEEDS, 1936
                        PARISH, 1925

13999   PUTERBAUGH.   Puterbaugh; Butterbaugh; Puderbaugh.   By Marie (Galbreath) Good.   (n. p.,
195-)   unpaged. illus. 30 cm. 61-39256.   CS71.P988

    PUTMAN.   See PUTNAM.

14000   PUTNAM.   A history of the Putnam family in England and America.   Recording the ancestry
and descendants of John Putnam of Danvers, Mass., Jan Poutman of Albany, N. Y., Thomas Putnam of
Hartford, Conn.   By Eben Putnam ... Salem, Mass., The Salem press publishing and printing co.,
1891-1908.   2 v. fronts., plates, ports., geneal. tables (part fold.) fold. map, col. coats of arms. 23½ cm. No publisher or place of
publication given on t.-p. of vol. II. Issued in 9 parts. Putnam leaflets, v. 1, p. 71-72, inserted at end of v. 1, containing index to heads of families. 9-13234.   CS71P99   1891

14001   PUTNAM.   The Putnam lineage; historical-genealogical notes concerning the Puttenham
family in England, together with lines of royal descent, and showing the ancestors of John Putnam of
Salem and his descendants through five generations, together with some account of other families of the
name and of the Putnams of the Mohawk valley.   By Eben Putnam ... Salem, Mass., The Salem press
company, 1907.   clii, 341, xxvii p. front., illus., plates, ports. (1 mounted) fold. map, coats of arms (part col.) geneal. tables
(part fold.) 24 cm. "Edition, 125 copies." 8-5254 rev.   CS71.P99   1907

14002   PUTNAM.   A brief history of the Andrew Putnam (Buttman, Putnam) Christian Wyandt, (Weyandt,
Weygandt, Voint, Wyand) and Adam Snyder families (Schneider) of Washington County, Maryland, by E.
Clayton Wyand, A.M.   (Hagerstown, Md., Hagerstown bookbinding and printing co., c. 1909)
103 p. front., plates, ports. 21½ cm. 9-26651.   CS71.P99   1909

14003   PUTNAM.   Genealogical sketch of the Andrew Putnam family, comp. by Judge Job Barnard ...
for the Chautauqua County historical society, 1916.   (Partly revised.   1918) Conneaut, O., The
Conneaut printing co., 1919.   29, (2) p. 22½ cm. Two pages at end left blank for additional "Family genealogy." 19-7390.
                                                                                                     CS71.P99   1919

14004   PUTNAM.   The Hon. Samuel Putnam and Sarah (Gooll) Putnam, with a genealogical record of
their descendants.   Comp. by Elizabeth Cabot Putnam and Harriet Silvester Tapley.   (Reprinted from
the Danvers historical collections, volume x)   Danvers, Mass., 1922.   1 p. l., 42 p. front., ports. 23½ cm.
22-25794.   CS71.P99   1922

14005   PUTNAM.   Report of (1st) -   meeting. ... Putnam association of America.   New
York & London, G. P. Putnam's sons, 1923 -   v. front. (port.) plates. 23½ cm. 31-22375.
                                                                                                     CS71.P99   1923-

14006   PUTNAM.   Israel Putnam, major-general in the Continental army, Rufus Putnam, brigadier-
general in the Continental army, and their service in the French and Indian war, and in the American
revolution; an address by George Haven Putnam ...   (In Putnam association of America.   Report of (1st) meeting ...
New York & London, 1923. 23½ cm. p. (5-45) 31-22376.   CS71.P99   1923-

14007   PUTNAM.   Some Danvers acres and associations connected therewith, by Ezra D. Hines.
1897.   Salem, Mass., Newcomb & Gauss co., printers, 1930.   2 p. l., (3)-22 p. front., plates. 25 cm.
30-15225.   F74.D2H65

14008   PUTNAM.   Putnam genealogical chart from 16th century until 20th century, tracing the descendants of the early Virginia, Kentucky, Carolina Putnams, who are descended from Thomas Putnam,
who landed in Virginia 1647 from England ... Compiled by Thomas Russell Putnam.   (n. p.) 1938.
gemeal. tab. 37 x 54 cm. Photostat (negative) 38-14726.   CS71.P99   1938

14009   PUTNAM.   Putnam genealogy (Recording the descendants of Thomas Putnam, the immigrant to Virginia 1647 - Also contains an enumeration of the living descendants of the "Virginia-Carolina-Kentucky" Putnams; Also contains brief genealogies of the Harper, Grover, and McGlasson families, compiled by Thomas Russell Putnam ... Okmulgee, Okla., 1938.   (107) p. 29½ cm. Type-writtem. 38M3912T.
CS71.P99   1938a

14010   PUTNAM.   House of Putman.   By Corinne (Putman) Mehringer.   (n. p., 1951?)   (8) l.   illus.
29 cm.   52-22224.
CS71.P99   1951

14011   PUTNAM.   Putnam family in vertical file.   Ask reference librarian for this material.

        PUTNAM.   See also: BROWN, 1931
                             CROWNINSHIELD, 1922
                             JENKINS, 1904
                             MUDGE, 1930
                             UPTON, 1874
                             No. 553 - Goodhue county.

        PUTTENHAM.   See PUTNAM.

        PYCHARD.   See PICARD.

        PYE.   See PESHINE, 1916

        PYKE.   See PIKE.

        PYFER.   See PFEIFFER.

14012   PYLE.   Pyle family history, 1594-1954, by Lela Livingston (and others.   n. p.) H. Pyle
(1954 or 5)   76 p. 22 cm. 56-46835.
CS71.P995   1955

        PLYE.   See also LLOYD, 1912

        PYLES.   See DODSON, 1959

14014   PYNCHON.   Pynchon.   By C. C. Baldwin ... (Cleveland, Leader printing company, 1882)
1 p. l., p. (183)-204 incl. illus., geneal. tables. 23½ cm. From the author's Candee genealogy, Cleveland, 1882. 14-11915.
CS71.P997   1882

14015   PYNCHON.   Record of the Pynchon family in England and America.   Comp. by Dr. J.C.
Pynchon ... Springfield, Mass., Weaver, Shipman and company, printers, 1885.   23, (1) p. front. (port.)
23½ cm. 6-28548.
CS71.P997   1885

14016   PYNCHON.   Wills of the English Pynchons, 1528-1654, and of William Pynchon, 1662, founder
of Springfield, Massachusetts.   Boston, D. Clapp & son, printers, 1894.   1 p. l., 23 p. 25 cm. Reprinted
from "Genealogical gleanings in England," By H. F. Waters. In N. E. historical and genealogical register for April 1894. 17-6147.
CS71.P997   1894

14017   PYNCHON.   Record of the Pynchon family in England and America.   Originally comp. by
Dr. Joseph Charles Pynchon ... (Rev. by W. F. Adams) Springfield, Mass., "Old Corner book store,"
1898.   23, (1) p. front. (port.) pl. 23 cm. 11-22490.
CS71.P997   1898

14018   PYNCHON.   Facsimiles of some English deeds, leases and other documents, about 1525 to
1686, relating to William Pynchon and his son John, who settled Springfield, Massachusetts in 1636.
28 pl. in portfolio. 44 x 58 cm. Photostat copies (positive and negative) of 11 documents, made from the originals for the Connecticut Valley
historical society, Springfield, Mass., 1924. 26-3080.
CS71.P997   1924

        PYNCHON.   See also: CANDEE, 1882
                              CLARK, 1896
                              WHITING, 1912

PYNDAR.　See LYGON, 1929

PYNE.　See GALCERÁN DE PINÓS, 1915

14019　PYOTT.　Notes to genealogical chart or pedigree of the descendants of James Pyott. merchant, Montrose, by Horatius Bonar ... (n. p.) 1914.　10 numb. 1. 11 fold. geneal. tab. 27½ cm. Lettered on cover: Pyott or Maitland pedigree. "The family of James Pyott (junior) changed their name to Maitland before 1774. " 17-29944.　CS479.P9

14020　PYRTLE.　Early Virginia families: Pyrtle, Davis, Turner, Martin, by E. Ruth Pyrtle ... (Lincoln, Neb., Chaflin printing co., 1930)　47 p. front. (port.) 22½ cm. 31-18254.
F225.P98

Q

QUACKENBOS.   See QUACKENBUSH.

QUACKENBOSCH.   See QUACKENBUSH.

14021   QUACKENBUSH.   The Quackenbush family in Holland and America, comp. by Adriana Suydam Quackenbush ... Paterson, N.J., Quackenbush & co., 1909.   221 p. incl. illus. (coat of arms) plan. 25½ cm. Title vignette (coat of arms) 11-23367.   CS71.Q1   1909

14022   QUACKENBUSH.   Quackenbush genealogy.   Published for Peter Quackenbush in 1915, rev. and supplemented by Helen Russell (Quackenbush) Winans.   Paterson, N.J., 1937.   (22) p. coat of arms (on cover) 23 cm. 51-50044.   CS71.Q1   1937

14023   QUACKENBUSH.   Quackenbush family in vertical file.   Ask reference librarian for this material.

QUACKENBUSH.   See also BLAUVELT.

QUACKINBUSH.   See QUACKENBUSH.

QUADRING.   See CRALL, 1908

14024   QUARLES.   Stamboom van het geslacht Quarles van omstreeks 1420 tot 1 Mei, 1909.   Den Hoag (1909?)   geneal. table. 87 x 166 cm. fold. to 46 x 63 cm. Additions and corrections in manuscript by Daisy M. Quarles. 53-50271.   CS71.Q17   1909

14025   QUARLES.   Records of William Quarles of Ipswich, Mass.   Compiled by Mrs. D. M. Quarles with the assistance of Hattie B. Wyatt, and material furnished by Clara M. McGuigan.   (n.p., 1952?)   35 l. 28 cm. 52-42143.   CS71.Q17   1952

14026   QUARLES.   Quarles of England.   By Daisey (Middleton) Quarles.   (n.p.,) 1952?)   1 v. (various pagings) fold. geneal. table. 28 cm. Typescript; additions and corrections in ms. 53-22975.   CS71.Q17   1952a

14027   QUARLES.   Quarles of Holland, compiled from research work in various libraries and from records sent by William Quarles von Ufford of Stockholm, Sweden.   (n.p., 1952?)   1 v. (various pagings) coats of arms (part col.) fold. geneal. table. 28 cm. "English ancestry of the Holland Quarles fams." Typescript. 53-22976   CS71.Q17   1952b

QUARLES.   See also: BLAKENEY, 1928
                     WINSTON, 1927

14028   QUARRIER.   A genealogical table and history of the Quarrier family, in America.   By a descendant (Alexander Thomas Laidley) Charleston (W. Va.) Moore's printing office, 1890.   43, (1) p. 28 x 35 cm. Interleaved. 9-14801.   CS71.Q2   1890

QUARRIER.   See MILLER, 1917

QUARTERMAIN.   See PETTY, BX5195.T5B6

QUARTIER.   See GAGNON, 1914

14029   QUATTLEBAUM.   Quattlebaum family history.   By Manning Marcus Quattlebaum. Savannah, 1950.   280 p. 28 cm. 51-24082.   CS71.Q22   1950

14030   QUATTLEBAUM.   Quattlebaum, a Palatine family in South Carolina.   By Paul Quattlebaum.
(Conway? 1950)   1 v. 23 cm.   Reprinted from the South Carolina historical and genealogical magazine, v. 48, no.1-4, Jan.-Oct., 1947
and v. 49, no. 1-4, Jan.-Oct., 1948.   52-41625.   CS71.Q22   1950a

QUAYLE.   See TERRELL, 1921

QUEAL.   See FRENCH, 1912

14031   QUEEN.   Some of the Queen family of Maryland.   (n. p.) 1933.   1 p. l., 21, 21a-66 numb. l.
22½ cm.   Type-written.   Blank leaves (22-24, 65-66) for additions.   By Mrs. Mary Susan (Oakley) Hawley and John Church Hawley.
34-14606.   CS71.Q3   1933

14032   QUEEN.   The Queen family; early history and family tree.   (2d ed.) Reedsville, O., S. P.
Queeb (1942)   3 p. l., 210 p. port. 23 cm.   Compiled by Stephen Post Queen, Charles A. Queen, and Stewart L. Queen. cf. Pref.
44-19825.   CS71.Q3   1942

14033   QUEEN.   My Maryland heritage; the ancestry of William Queen.   By Judith Simms.   Fred-
erick, Md., 1963.   1 v. (unpaged) illus., col. coats of arms, geneal. tables, maps, ports. 30 cm. Thesis - College of Notre Dame
of Maryland.   Bibliography: 5 leaves at end.   64-56160.   CS71.Q3   1963

14034   QUEIROZ.   Antiga familia do sertão. By Esperidião de Queiroz Lima.   (Rio de Janeiro)
AGIR, 1946.   331 p. illus., ports., map. 24 cm. 49-53529 *.   CS309.Q4   1946

QUELL.   See WADDELL, 1959

QUERANGAL.   See KERANGAL.

QUEREAU.   See CAROW.

QUESENBERRY.   See QUISENBERRY.

14035   QUICK.   A genealogy of the Quick family in America (1625-1942) 317 years, by Arthur Craig
Quick ... South Haven and Palisades Park, Mich., Priv. pub. by A. C. Quick (1942)   xxv, 483 p. illus.
(incl. ports., maps) 20½ cm.   43-4197.   CS71.Q4   1942

QUIENCHANT.   See KINCHANT.

QUIGLEY.   See McKINNEY, 1905

QUILLAN.   See MACQUILLIN.

QUILLEN.   See MACQUILLIN.

QUILLIAN.   See MACQUILLIN.

QUILLIN.   See MACQUILLIN.

14036   QUIMBY.   Quinby chart: ancestors of Thomas Quinby, of Stroudwater, Maine, and his wife,
Jane Elizabeth Brewer, compiled by Henry Cole Quinby.   N(ew) Y(ork, 1906?)   geneal. tab. 31½ x 68 cm.
Ancestors: Haskell, Freeman, Pearson, Titcomb, Dole, Brewer, Frost and Pepperell.   11-14237.   CS71.Q5   1906

14037   QUIMBY.   A record of the line of descent from Robert Quinby of Amesbury, Mass., who in
1659 received land by allotment in Massachusetts colony, to Benjamin Quinby (Quimby) 1768, of Unity,
N.H., and a complete record of Benjamin's descendants, collected and comp. by Rev. S. E. Quimby.
Bristol, N.H., R.W. Musgrove, printer, 1910.   29 p. 19½ cm. 11-4150.   CS71.Q5   1910

14038   QUIMBY.   Genealogical history of the Quinby (Quimby) family in England and America, by
Henry Cole Quimby ... New York city (Rutland, Vt., The Tuttle company) 1915-23.   2 v. front., illus.
(incl. coats of arms) plates (1 fold.) ports., facsims. 26½ cm. Vol. (2) has title: The Quimby-Quinby family of Sandwich, N.H., and is
lettered on cover: Quinby-Quimby family history. vol.II. 16-8612 rev.   CS71.Q5   1915-23

QUIMBY.   See also FIELD.   E171. A53 v. 20

14039   QUIN.   The family history of Peter Quin, compiled by Madge Quin Fugler, 1922.   Rev. and edited by Jerome C. Hafter, 1963-64.   (Greenville? Miss., 1964)   1 v. (various pagings) coat of arms. 28 cm.
65-431.   CS71. Q48   1964

QUINBY.   See   QUIMBY.

14040   QUINCY.   Memoranda respecting the families of Quincy and Adams ... (Havana, 1841)
1 p. l., 9 p.   col. coat of arms.   21½ cm.   Cushing's "Anonyms" give J. Grace as possible author of this work.   10-30157.

                                                                                                        CS439. Q7

14041   QUINCY.   A pride of Quincys.   Massachusetts Historical Society.   Boston, 1969.
(52) p. illus., ports.   28 cm.   (A Massachusetts Historical Society picture book)   77-6104 MARC.   CS71. Q52   1969

QUINCY.   See also SALISBURY, 1885

QUINEY.   See SHAKESPEARE, PR2910. F7

QUINTARD.   See LINDLEY, 1950

14041a   QUINTON.   Quinton family in vertical file.   Ask reference librarian for this material.

QUINTON.   See also REICHNER, 1918

QUIRK.   See: PEYTON, 1968
                   No. 1547 - Cabell county.

14042   QUIRÓS.   Los Quirós en Costa Rica (estudio genealógico)   By Ernesto Quirós Aguilar.
San José, C. R., Imp. Trejos Hermanos, 1948.   48 p. ports. 23 cm.   "Fuentes consultadas": p. 48.   48-26605*.
                                                                                                        CS149. Q5   1948

14043   QUISENBERRY.   Genealogical memoranda of the Quisenberry family and other families, including the names of Chenault, Cameron, Mullins, Burris, Tandy, Bush, Broomhall, Finkle, Rigg, and others.   By Anderson Chenault Quisenberry ... Washington, D. C., Hartman & Cadick, printers, 1897.
204 p. pl., ports. 24 cm.   9-13252.   CS71. Q9   1897

14044   QUISENBERRY.   Memorials of the Quisenberry family in Germany, England and America.
Compiled and edited by Anderson C. Quisenberry ... Washington, D. C., Gibson bros., printers, 1900.
137 p. col. front., plates, port., facsims.   24½ cm.   No. 51 of an edition of 150 numbered copies.   1-19505.

                                                                                        CS71. Q9   1900

QUISENBERRY.   See also MILLER, 1907

R

RABB.   See JOHNSON, 1961

RABOLD.   See WEISER, 1960

RACE.   See WALWORTH, E171.A53 v.20

RADCLIFF.   See RADCLIFFE.

14045   RADCLIFFE.   The history of the township of Meltham, near Huddersfield; in the West-Riding of the county of York; from the earliest time to the present.   By the late Rev. Joseph Hughes .. ed. with additions by C. H. Huddersfield, J. Crossley & co., 1866.   xi, (1), 303, (1) p. front. 20½ cm. "C.H." i.e. Catharine Hughes.   2-24108.   DA690.M56H9

14046   RADCLIFFE.   Pedigree of Radclyffe.   London, Priv. print., 1876.   cover-title, (3) p. illus. (coat of arms) 29 x 22½ cm.   From Register of pedigrees, "Norfolk 2," in the College of arms.   Published also in Miscellanea genealogica et heraldica, n.s., v.2, p. 297-299.   9-18124.   CS439.R2   1876

14047   RADCLIFFE.   Letters of Richard Radcliffe and John James of Queen's college, Oxford, 1755-83; with additions, notes, and appendices.   Ed. by Margaret Evans.   Oxford, Printed for the Oxford historical society at the Clarendon press, 1888.   xxxiv, (2), 306 p. fold. geneal. tab.   23 cm. (On cover: Oxford historical socieyt. (Publications, vol. IX)   The prefatory note, the appendices, and the greater part of the notes are due to J. R. Magrath. cf. Preface.   Contains also letters by John James, jun., and Jonathan Boucher.   3-17069.   DA690.O97O8

14048   RADCLIFFE.   A short history of Todmorden, with some account of the geology and natural history of the neighbourhood; by Joshua Holden, M.A.   With 25 illustrations.   Manchester, The University press, 1912.   xiv, 242 p. incl. front., illus. fold. map. 19½ cm. (Half-title: Publications of the University of Manchester.   Historical ser. no. xv) On verso of t.-p.: University of Manchester publications, no. LXVII. "The genealogies of the Radcliffe and Fielden families": p. 231-233.   13-8491.   DA690.T63H6

14049   RADCLIFFE.   Joseph Radcliff and his descendants, 1802-1924, by Grace Radcliff Evans. Decatur, Ill., 1924.   1 p. l., 30 numb. l. 28½ x 22 cm.   Reproduced from type-written copy, with additions and corrections in manuscript.   25-12669.   CS71.R125   1924

14050   RADCLIFFE.   The book of the Radclyffes; being an account of the main descents of this illustrious family from its origin to the present day, compiled from a variety of sources, including public records and private evidences, by Charles P. Hampson ... Edinburgh, Priv. print. by T. amd A. Constable ltd. at the University press, 1940.   xxv, (1), 317, (1) p. incl. geneal. tables. front. (coat of arms) plates, ports.   27½ cm.   "This work is limited to 250 copies."   Bibliography: p. 305.   A 41-2982.   CS439.R2H25

14051   RADCLIFFE.   Memoirs of Stephen E. Radcliff, written by himself.   (London? Ont., 1942) 209 l.   mounted photos., coat of arms.   26 cm.   Leaves variously numbered.   Type-written (carbon copy) "An account of settlement in Middlesex county, western Ontario." - Ms. note on t.-p.   42-20789.   F1059.M6R2

14052   RADCLIFFE.   John Ratcliffe genealogy, Chatham County, N.C. descendants, by Clarence E. Ratcliff, 1963.   (Spring Arbor, Mich., 1963)   41 l. 30 cm.   Bibliography: leaves 36-37.   64-55841.
                                                                                CS71.R125   1963

14053   RADCLIFFE.   American Radcliffes: Carolina, Kentucky, Pennsylvania branch.   (n.p.. 1963?) 2 fold. geneal. tables.   46 cm.   Photocopy (negative)   65-572.   CS71.R125   1963a

RADCLIFFE.   See also: BEAUMONT, DA690.M56H9
                                          LEWEN, 1919

RADCLIFF.   See RADCLIFFE.

RADCLYFFE.   See RADCLIFFE.

RADER.   See: BARROW, 1941
                        NOBLE, 1967

RADFORD.   See WHARTON, 1960

14054   RADTKE.   The story of the Wilhelm Friedrich Radtke family, written for the family.   By
Lorraine Marian Radtke.   Milwaukee, Radtke Reports, 1957.   150 p. illus. 23 cm. 57-45362.
                                                                                                                CS71. R13   1957

RADWAY.   See ALEXANDER, 1960 (Addenda)

RAFFENSPERGER.   See MARKEY, 1961

14055   RAGATZ.   Memoirs of a Sauk Swiss; being an account of the Ragatz family's journey to
North America and pioneer days in Wisconsin territory by the Reverend Oswald Ragatz.   Translated
and edited by Lowell Joseph Ragatz ... (Menasha? Wis.) 1935.   cover-title, p. (183) - 228. pl., port. 23 cm.
Reprinted from the Wisconsin magazine of history, December, 1935." 36-11410.   CS71. R14   1935

RAGER.   See RIEGER.

14056   RAGLAND.   Genealogy of the Ragland families, and numerous other families of prominence
in America with whom they have intermarried, by Margaret Miriam Strong (Mrs. Philip H. Hale) ...
St. Louis, Mo., 1928.   5 p. l., 121 p front. (port.) pl. 24 cm. Blank pages (16 at end) inserted. 28-21382.
                                                                                                                CS71. R143   1928

RAGLAND.   See also RAND, 1936

14057   RAGSDALE.   Godfrey Ragsdale from England to Henrico County, Virginia; one documented
line of descent covering three hundred twenty-seven years in America.   By Caroline Nabors Skelton.
Franklin Springs, Ga., Advocate Press, 1969.   48 l. illus., 5 geneal. tables. 28 cm. 70-218655 MARC.
                                                                                                                CS71. R145   1969

14058   RAHN.   Genealogical information regarding the families of Hornberger and Yingling and related families of Eckert, Lenhart, Steffy, Gerwig, and Rahn.   By Claude Jerome Rahn.   Vero Beach,
Fla., 1951.   164 p. 23 cm. 52-22297.   CS61. R3

RAIFORD.   See also PEARSON, 1938

14059   RAIGECOURT.   Maison de Raigecourt.   (By Jean Joseph Lionnois) Nancy, Chez la veuve
Leclerc, imprimeur de l'intendance, 1777.   cxxiv, 239 p., 1 l., c p. illus. (coats of arms) geneal. tables (part fold.)
29 cm. 46-45134.   CS599. R29L5

14060   RAIKES.   Robert Raikes and Northamptonshire Sunday schools.   Historical & biographical
account of the Raikes family, and notices of the formation of the earliest Sunday schools in Northamptonshire.   With appendix: a list of publications by Northamptonshire authors ... relating to Sunday
schools; books printed by the Raikes family at Northampton and Gloucester; a brief account of the
originators of Sunday schools; historical notes, etc., etc.   London, E. Stock; Northampton, Taylor
& son; (etc., etc.) 1880.   iv, 56 p. 21½ cm. (Hazlitt tracts, v. 30, no. 8) Compiled from the author's contributions to Northampton newspapers, with additional information.   cf. Preface signed John Taylor.   Edited by the Rev. P. M. Eastman. 23-4332.
                                                                                                                AC911. H3
                                                                                                                vol. 30, no. 8

14061 RAIKES. Pedigree of the family of Raikes, formerly of Kingston-upon-Hull (originally of Kelfield and Cawood, near Selby, Yorkshire). Compiled from the wills, parish registers, and other documents collected by Lieut-Colonel G. A. Raikes, F.S.A., by Joseph Foster, M.A. (London, Printed by Wyman & sons, ltd., 1897) geneal. tab. illus. (coat of arms) 98 x 64 cm. fold. to 26 cm. Contains also the descendants of Thomas Raikes, governor of the bank of England, 1797-99. 24-39. CS439.R23

RAILEY. See: RANDOLPH, 1929
RANDOLPH, 1933

RAILTON. See MALLOCH, 1857

RAINBOROWE. See RAINSBOROUGH.

RAINEY. See HARPER, 1939

14063 RAINSBOROUGH. ... The Rainborowe family. Gleanings by Henry F. Waters ... With annotations by Isaac J. Greenwood ... (Reprinted from the N. E. historical and genealogical register for April, 1886.) New York, Priv. print. (Boston, Press of D. Clapp & son) 1886. 16 p. 25½ cm. Fifty copies printed, of which this is no. 43. 9-13251. CS71.R159 1886

14064 RAINSFORD. ... Table of descent of the family of Rainford of Rainford, (or Ranford, or Ransford,) co. Lancs., and probably prior to that the sea-coast district of Randers fiord, Denmark, the family being variously spelled as Ransford, Ragensford, Rayensfords, Ravensford, Rainforth, Ranford, Randford, Rainsford, and upwards of twenty other ways ... Compiled and collated by Alfred Ransford ... (Wisbech?) 1907. sheet. illus. (coats of arms) 105 x 63½ cm. fold. to 32 x 26 cm. "Authorities consulted." 19-3640. CS439.R24

14065 RAINSFORD. The Rainsford family, with sidelights on Shakespeare, Southampton, Hall and Hart, embracing 1000 years of the Rainsford family and their successive partakings in the main lines of national life, by Emily A. Buckland ... Worcester (Eng.) Phillips & Probert, ltd., The Caxton press (1932) 3 p. l., 9-337 p. illus. (incl. ports., facsims.) 22½ cm. Title vignette; coat of arms. "Authorities": p. 10. Includes bibliography. 40-16298. CS439.R24 1932

RAINTON. See TAYLOR, 1875

14066 RAIZENNE. Notes généalogiques sur la famille Raizenne. (Ottawa, 1917) 80 p. incl. illus., pl. 17½ cm. Signed: Soeur St. Jean l'Évangéliste. (Secular name: Guillelmine Raizenne) Cover-title: Genealogical notes: Josiah Rising and Abigail Nims, and their descendants. 18-11226. CS90.R3

RAKESTRAW. See BELL, 1959

14067 RALEIGH. The life of Sir Walter Ralegh. Based on contemporary documents ... Together with his letters; now first collected. By Edward Edwards ... (London) Macmillan & co., 1868. 2 v. port. (front., v.1) 3 facsims. (incl. front., v.2) geneal. tables. 22½ cm. 4-34695. DA86.22.R2E2

14068 RALEIGH. Raleigh pedigree. Extracted from the records of the College of arms. (By Rogers Coxwell Rogers) London, Priv. print. (Taylor and co., printers) 1869. 1 p. l., 3 p. facsim., coats of arms. 29 cm. Title vignette, coat of arms. Communicated by R. R. Coxwell-Rogers. Reprinted from Miscellanea genealogica et heraldica, v.2, p. 155-157. L.C. COPY REPLACED BY MICROFILM. 3-1423 rev. CS439.R25 1869
Microfilm 10311 CS

14069 RALLI. A pedigree of the Rallis of Scio. 1700 to 1892. (London, 1896) 1 p. l., 8, 2-16 numb. l. 30 cm. "The pedigree was commenced many years ago, by Alexander Pandia Ralli and Alexander Antonio Ralli." - Pref. 21-19036. CS739.R3P4

14070 RALLO. The Rallo family; a great American saga, by Joseph S. Rallo and Mary Hulbert. New York, F. Fell (1966) 248 p. illus., ports. 22 cm. 66-20405. CS71.R17 1966

RALTON. See MALLOCK, 1857

RAMAGE.　See LONG, 1956

RAMBO.　See KEYES, 1914

RAMEY.　See:　CHALFONT, 1959
　　　　　　　　　CLOUD, 1965
　　　　　　　　　REMEY.

14071　RAMEZEY.　La famille de Ramezay, par Pierre Georges Roy.　Lévis, 1910.　54 p.　23 cm.
"Tiré à 100 exemplaires."　24-8343.　　　　　　　　　　　　　　　　CS90. R35

14072　RAMIREZ DE ARELLANO.　Orígenes portorriqueños, por Enrique Ramírez Brau.　Del año
1653 al 1853.　San Juan, P. R., Imprenta Baldrich (1942　　　v. ports., facsims. (1 fold.) geneal. tables.
24 cm.　Vol. 2 has subtitle:　Don Antonio Ramírez de Arellano y sus descendientes ... Prólogo por Manuel Rodríguez Serra.　43-2857 rev.
　　　　　　　　　　　　　　　　　　　　　　　　CS259. R3　　　1942

14073　RAMIREZ DE PRADO.　... Una familia de ingenios:　los Ramírez de Prado, por Joaquín de
Entrambasaguas.　Madrid, 1943.　　2 p. l., (7)-244 p. ports., facsims., coat of arms.　25½ cm.　(Revista de filologia española.
- Anejo XXVI)　At head of title: Consejo superior de investigaciones cientificas ... On cover: Consejo superior de investigaciones cientificas.
Patronato "Menéndez y Pelayo."　Instituto "Antonio de Nebrija."　Bibliographical foot-notes.　A44-1711.
　　　　　　　　　　　　　　　　　　　　　　CT1358. R3E5

RAMSAY.　See:　DOUGLAS, DA758. 381T2
　　　　　　　　　　RAMSEY.

RAMSBERG.　See THOMAS, 1905

RAMSBURG.　See THOMAS, 1905

RAMSDEN.　See JAMES, 1913a

14074　RAMSEY.　Bamff charters, A. D. 1232-1703, with introduction, biographical summary and
notes; edited by Sir James H. Ramsay, bart. ... London, New York (etc.)　Oxford university press,
H. Milford, 1915.　　viii, (2), 392 p.　2 pl., fold. facsim.　24 ½ cm.　16-24207.
　　　　　　　　　　　　　　　　　　　　CS479. R3

14075　RAMSEY.　The Ramsays of New Scotland.　By Elizabeth Janet MacCormick.　(Jamaica, N. Y.,
1950?)　　6 l.　28 cm.　52-21272.　　　　　　　　　CS71. R18　　　1950

14076　RAMSEY.　Genealogy of the Ramsey family in the Southern United States, 1740-1962.　By
James Thomas Ramsey.　(Houston, Tex., 1962)　　75 l.　illus.　30 cm.　62-66112.　　CS71. R18　　　1962

RAMSEY.　See also:　DOUGLAS, DA758. 3A1T2
　　　　　　　　　　　　FULTON, 1900
　　　　　　　　　　　　HARRISON, 1893
　　　　　　　　　　　　PHIPPS, 1894

RAMY.　See REMEY.

RANALD.　See CLANRONALD.

14077　RAND.　A genealogy of the Rand family in the United States;　compiled by Florence Osgood
Rand.　New York, The Republic press, 1898.　　269 p., 1 l.　front., port.　24½ cm.　"A partial list of books consulted":
p. (5-6)　3-1676.　　　　　　　　　　　　　　　　CS71. R187　　　1898

14078　RAND.　Rand-Hale and allied families, a genealogical study, compiled and privately printed
for Nettie Hale Rand, by the American historical society, inc.　New York, 1936.　159 p.　ports., col.
coats of arms, col. geneal. tables.　32 cm.　Some of the plates are accompanied by guard sheets with descriptive letterpress.　Allied families:
Norfleet, Strong, Lumpkin, Stokes, Montfort, Hopson, Womack and Le Despenser.　Includes bibliographical notes.　37-9446.
　　　　　　　　　　　　　　　　　　　　　　CS71. R187　　　1936

14079   RAND.   Rand - Hale - Strong and allied families; a genealogical study with the autobiography of Nettie Hale Rand.   Compiled and privately printed for Nettie Hale Rand by the American historical company, inc.   New York, 1940.   191 p. pl., ports., col. coats of arms, geneal. tables.   32 cm.   Some of the plates are accompanied by guard sheets with descriptive letterpress.   Genealogical tables decorated in colors.   Allied families: Norfleet, Parker, Lumpkin, Hopson, Ragland, Womack, Stokes, Montfort, and LeDespenser.   Includes bibliographical notes.   41-10114.   CS71. R187   1940

RAND.   See also RANDS.

14080   RANDALL.   Genealogy of a branch of the Randall family.   1666 to 1879.   Collected and arranged by a member of the family.   (Norwich, Chenango union, 1879)   289 p. 24 cm. Title vignette: coat of arms.   Leaf inserted between p. 28-29, and 44-45.   Introduction signed: Paul K. Randall.   3-5050.   CS71. R19   1879

14081   RANDALL.   Poems of nature and life, by John Witt Randall; edited by Francis Ellingwood Abbot, with an introduction on the Randall family ... Boston, G. H. Ellis, 1899.   566 p. 2 port. (incl. front.) 24 cm. 5-16217.   PS2675. R2   1899

14082   RANDALL.   Genealogy of the descendants of Stephen Randall and Elizabeth Swezey ... 1624 - 1668, Clarkenwell, St. James' parish, London, England; 1668-1738, Rhode Island and Connecticut, 1738-1906, Long Island, New York.   (New York, J. S. Ogilvie publishing co., 1906?)   64 p. front. (port.) 21 cm.   Comp. by Stephen Morehouse Randall.   7-39275.   CS71. R19   1906

14083   RANDALL.   A biographical history of Robert Randall and his descendants 1608-1909.   By William L. Chaffin.   New York, The Grafton press, 1909.   xx, 247 p. 24 cm. 9-26006.   CS71. R19   1909

14084   RANDALL.   The Randall-Mayor pedigree ... compiled by Col. Herbert A. Walters, V. D. Printed for private circulation only.   (n. p.) 1910.   2 geneal. tab. accompanied by "References and proofs in confirmation of the pedigree."   Contents.   Table I. Descendants of Professor John Randall, Mus. doc., of Cambridge.   illus. (coats of arms) 60 x 157 cm. Table II. Pedigree of Mrs. William Randall and Mrs. Edward Randall (formerly the Misses Sarah and Ann Mayor) illus. (coats of arms) 72 x 61½ cm.   References and proofs ... of the pedigree.   28 p. 20 ½ cm. 17-23933.   CS439. R26

14085   RANDALL.   Reminiscences, by U. S. Randle.   (Washington, D. C., Judd & Detweiler, c. 1924)   47 p. incl. facsims. ports.   23½ cm.   "Edition limited to four hundred copies."   Lettered on cover: The future of Washington, and Reminiscences by U. S. Randle.   A compilation of information concerning Colonel Arthur E. Randle, including facsimiles of letters addressed to him, his speech on the city of Washington, genealogy, etc.   24-16308.   F199. R196

14086   RANDALL.   Randall and allied families; William Randall (1609-1693) of Scituate and his descendants, with ancestral families, by Frank Alfred Randall, C. E.   Chicago, Raveret-Weber print-ing company, 1943.   xiv, 582 p. incl. front. (map) illus. (incl. facsims.) ports. 23½ cm. 43-15925.   CS71. R19   1943

14087   RANDALL.   Genealogy of Randall-Bristow & allied families, compiled by Joyce Randall Sone, Ruth Wells Sone (and) Guy M. Sone.   (n. p.) 1965.   193 l. illus., facsims., ports. 28 cm.   Bibliography: leaves 191-193. 66-37690.   CS71. R19   1965

RANDALL.   See also: CHUTE, 1894
                                       COX, 1939
                                       DAVIDSON, BX5199. D25P5
                                       EMISON, 1947
                                       PAGE, 1953

14088   RANDERSON.   Genealogy of J. Howard Randerson and allied families, with letters.   By John Jeffry Howard Randerson.   (n. p., 19 -)   (8) p. illus., incl. ports., facsims. 23 cm.   Title vignette: coat of arms. "Privately printed."   33-17584.   CS71. R192   19 -

RANDLE.   See RANDALL.

14089   RANDOLPH.   Family history written by C. C. Randolph ... A history of the ancestors and relatives of C. C. Randolph.   Alliance, O., The Review publishing co., 1908.   32 p. 23 cm. 25-19244.   CS71. R193   1908

14090   RANDOLPH.   (Family tree of the Randolphs of Virginia.   By Mrs. Kate Estess (Du Val) Harrison.   n. p., 19 ?)   geneal. tab.   56 x 33 cm.   Photostat copy (positive) 38M1053T.   CS71.R193   1920

14091   RANDOLPH.   Randolphs of Virginia, by Kate Du Val Harrison.   (n. p.) 1928.   geneal. tab. illus. (coat of arms)   125 x 83 cm.   fold. to 34 x 21½ cm.   Planographed.   36-30617 rev.   CS71.R193   1928

14092   RANDOLPH.   Selections from the family history of Randolph, Dandridge, Armistead, Langbourne, Carter and Williams clans in Virginia, 1650 to 1930 A. D.   (n. p., 1930?)   53 p.   fold. geneal. tab. 22½ cm.   34-32604.   CS71.R193   1930

14093   RANDOLPH.   Descent of the Randolph and Carter families (of New York and Philadelphia) (By Edmund Randolph) New York, T. A. Wright, inc. (1932)   geneal. tab. illus. (coats of arms) 59 x 63 cm. "Only 53 copies printed. " 33-3890.   CS71.R193   1932

14094   RANDOLPH.   Brief sketches of the Randolphs, the Woodsons, the Keiths, the Strothers, the Pleasants, the Raileys, the Mayos, the Owsleys and the Whitleys, by William Edward Railey ... (Frankfort, 1933)   3 p. l., (5)-113 p.   front., plates, ports., coats of arms.   23 cm.   On cover: The Raileys and kindred families. Running title: The Randolphs and their connections.   "These sketches were first printed in the 'Register', a magazine published by the Kentucky historical society. " 34-35348.   CS71.R193   1933

14095   RANDOLPH.   The Randolphs of Virginia, a compilation of the descendants of William Randolph of Turkey island, and his wife Mary Isham of Bermuda hundred, by Robert Isham Randolph ... (Chicago? 1936?)   1 p. l., 5-404 p.   26 cm.   Coat of arms on cover.   Bibliography: p. 9.   37-9442.   CS71.R193   1936

14096   RANDOLPH.   The Randolphs; the story of a Virginia family, by H. J. Eckenrode.   Indianapolis, New York, The Bobbs-Merrill company (1946)   310 p.   front., plates, ports.   22 cm.   "First edition." 46-6799.   CS71.R193   1946

14097   RANDOLPH.   William Randolph I of Turkey Island, Henrico County, Virginia, and his immediate descendants.   By Wassell Randolph.   Memphis, Seebode Mimeo Service;   distributed by Cossitt Library, 1949.   115 p. 27 cm.   Bibliography: p. 1-3.   50-1593.   CS71.R193   1949

14098   RANDOLPH.   Henry Randolph I, 1623-1773 (sic) of Henrico County, Virginia, and his descendants.   Preceded by short review of the Randolph family in early England and elsewhere.   By Wassell Randolph.   Memphis, Distributed by Cossitt Library, 1952.   105 p. 27 cm.   53-2197.   CS71.R193   1952

14099   RANDOLPH.   Pedigree of the descendants of Henry Randolph I (1623-1673) of Henrico County, Virginia.   By Wassell Randolph.   Memphis, Distributed by Memphis Public Library, 1957. 227 p.   28 cm.   Sequel to Henry Randolph I, 1623-1773 (sic) of Henrico County, Virginia, and his descendants.   58-33887.   CS71.R193   1957

14100   RANDOLPH.   Daniel Fitz Randolph, his ancestry and descendants; an American branch of the Fitz Randolph family.   By Oris Hugh Fitz Randolph.   (Anamosa? Iowa) 1959.   55, (9) p. group port., coat of arms.   22 cm.   Bibliography: p. 54-55.   "Fitz Randolph generations from Rolf the Norseman to Edward the pilgrim": 1 fold. sheet inserted.   62-35885.   CS71.R193   1959

14101   RANDOLPH.   The first Randolphs of Virginia.   By Roberta Lee Randolph.   Washington, Public Affairs Press (1961)   66 p.   port.   23 cm.   Includes bibliographical references.   61-8448.   CS71.R193   1961

RANDOLPH.   See also:

14102   RANDS.   Genealogy of the Rands family and records on allied families Winn, Turner, Connelly, McCollum, Parsons, Baylor, Boone, and Bryan, by Robert D. Rands, Sr.   Lake Wales, Fla. (1967, c. 1968)   vi, 78 p. illus., geneal. tables, ports. 29 cm. Pages 55-78, blank for "Additional family records." 68-2709.

CS71. R196   1968

RANDS.   See also RAND.

RANFORD.   See RAINSFORD, 1907

RANKEN.   See RANKIN.

14103   RANKIN.   Marking the old "abolition holes."   By Felix J. Koch ...   (In Ohio archaeological and historical quarterly.   Columbus, 1913.   23 cm. v. 22, p. 308-318. illus.) An account of the Rankin family and their homestead at Ripley, Ohio, where slaves were aided to escape after crossing the Ohio River. 18-13523.   F486. O51 vol. 22

14104   RANKIN.   The Rankin and Wharton families and their genealogy, by Rev. S. M. Rankin ... (Greensboro, N. C., J. J. Stone & co., printers and binders, 1931)   viii, 9-295 p. front., plates, port. 22½ cm. Blank pages for additional record (259-278) "Limited edition." 32-6810.   CS71. R211   1931

14105   RANKIN.   Peter Rankin's descendants; the descendants of Peter (1753/4-1842) and Margaret Rankin from Kilsyth, Scotland.   By Paul Tory Rankin.   Ann Arbor, Mich., University Microfilms, 1961.   110 p. illus. 23 cm. 62-36811.   CS71. R211   1961

RANKIN.   See also: McAMIS, 1948
MASSIE, 1942

RANNEL.   See REYNOLDS.

14106   RANNEY.   Middletown Upper Houses; a history of the north society of Middletown, Connect-icut, from 1650 to 1800, with genealogical and biographical chapters on early families and a full genealogy of the Ranney family, by Charles Collard Adams ... New York, The Grafton press, 1908. xxv, 847 p. front., illus., plates, ports., facsims. 24 cm. Most of the plates printed on both sides. "This edition, published under the auspices of the Soceity of Middletown Upper Houses, incorporated, is limited to six hundred copies, of which this is number 76." 8-16493.

F104. C8A2

RANSBARGER.   See BRUMBACH, 1961

RANSIER.   See ROBINSON, 1952

14107   RANSOM.   A genealogical record of the descendants of Captain Samuel Ransom, of the Con-tinental army, killed at the massacre of Wyoming, Pa., July 3d, 1778.   Compiled by his great-great-grandson, Captain Clinton B. Sears ... St. Louis, Nixon-Jones printing co., 1882.   234 p. front. (port.) 22½ cm. 9-13250.   CS71. R212   1882

14108   RANSOM.   Genealogical sketch of Pelatiah Ransom and his children.   (Litchfield, Conn., 1898)   cover-title, 12 p. 23 cm. Compiled by William L. Ransom. 10-2785.   CS71. R212   1898

14109   RANSOM.   Historical outline of the Ransom family of America, and genealogical record of the Colchester, Conn., branch, by Wyllys C. Ransom, A. M.   Ann Arbor, Mich., Press of Ann Arbor plant, The Richmond & Backus company, 1903   4 p., 1 l., iv, (7)-408 p. front., ports. 23½ cm. 4-1602.

CS71. R212   1903

14110   RANSOM.   Ransom genealogy, by Harry B. Ransom.   Photographed by George L. Schlaepfer. Grosse Pointe Farms, Mich., 1958.   Microfilm copy (positive) of typescript. Collation of the original, as determined from the film: 1 v. (various pagings) Mic. 58-6873.   Microfilm 5730 CS

RANSOM.   See L. C. Additions and corrections, no. 16

RANSOM.   See also: ATKINSON, 1933
TAFT, 1908

14111   RANTOUL.   Some material for a history of the name and family of Rentoul, Rintoul, Rantoul, compiled by Robert S. Rantoul ... Salem, The Salem press, 1885.   1 p. l., 28 p. front. (port.) 24½ cm. "Reprinted from Historical collections of the Essex institute, vol. XXI, nos. 10, 11, 12." 37-21320.   CS71. R215   1885

14112   RAOUL.   The family of Raoul, a memoir by Mary Raoul Millis.   (Asheville, N. C.) Priv. print. (The Miller printing company) 1943.   xi, 224 p. incl. front. plates, port. 24 cm. 43-7806.
CS71. R22   1943

14113   RAPALJE.   American genealogy, being a history of some of the early settlers of North America and their descendants, from their first emigration to the present time ... By Jerome B. Holgate ... Albany, Printed by J. Munsell, 1848.   1 p. l., 244 p., 1 l. 30 cm. Contents. - Rapalje. - Johnson. - Manoers and patroons in New Netherlands. - Van Rensselaer. - Gardiner. - Beekman. - Bleecker. - De Graaf. - Hoffman. - Kip. - De Lancey. - Barclay - Roosevelt. - Van Schaick. - Livingston. - Lawrence. - Osgood. - Jay.   9-25093 rev.   CS69. H7

RAPALJE.   See also: ALMY, 1897
VAN NORDEN, 1923

14114   RAPELJE.   Excerpts from the de Rapelje, Remsen (van der Beeck) Swain, Clark, Clayton, Morgan, Boyce, Naudain, Steel and Stockton genealogies.   By George Valentine Massey.   (n. p.) 1948.   Microfilm copy of typescript. Positive. Collation of the original, as determined from the film: 77 l. plates, ports., facsim. Includes bibliographical references.   Mic 52-435.   Microfilm CS-8
Microfilm reading room.

RAPPOPORT.   See RAPOPORT.

14115   RARIG.   Genealogy of the Rarig family showing the descendants of John Rarig and his wife, Mary Ann Kisner, together with a short biography of these pioneers, their children and grand children (by) Willard R. Rhoads.   Numidia, Pa., 1935.   1 p. l., 2-181 p. 23 cm. 36-1633.
CS71. R223   1935

14116   RASCO.   The family of Edward Hampton Rasco and connexions.   By Sarah Ada Rasco Crumpton.   Birmingham, Ala., Banner Press (1967)   75 p. col. coat of arms. 26 cm. 67-23706.
CS71. R224   1967

14117   RASKOB.   Raskob-Green record book.   (By John Jakob Raskob)   Claymont, Del., 1921.   6 p. l., 3-144 p. illus., plates, ports., fold. maps, facsim., geneal. tables (part fold.) 28 cm. "Archmere" signed: Helena Springer Green Raskob: p. 129-144. "Chart of Maryland families, A. D. 1634; Green-Thomas-Wheeler. Comp. from court records and family Bible records, Varina J. Corbaley, 1918." "Drawings by Horace T. Carpenter." 21-21360.   CS71. R225   1921

14118   RASMUSSEN.   Rasmussen-Jensen family genealogy (by John A. Lundberg.   Portland, Or.)   1968.   18 l. 29 cm. Cover title. 70-5401 MARC.   CS71. R228   1968

RASNAKE.   See MUSICK, 1964

RASNICK.   See RASNAKE.

RATCLIFF.   See JARRATT, 1957

RATCLIFF.   See RADCLIFFE.

RATCLIFFE.   See RADCLIFFE.

RATEW.   See RETTEW.

14119   RATHBONE.   The Rathbone family historian ... F. P. Rathbone, editor.   v. 1 - Jan. 1892 -   Oberlin, Kans., 1892 -   v.   24 cm. (v.1-2: 31 cm) monthly. Vol. 1 no. 1 autographed from type-written copy. 24-20314.   CS71. R234   1892-

14120   RATHBONE.   Rathbone genealogy, by John C. Cooley.   A complete history of the Rathbone family, dating from 1574 to date.   Syracuse, N. Y., Press of the Courier Job Print, 1898.

14120 continued: 824, xiii p. illus., port., plates 24 cm. 3-3813 rev.   CS71.R234   1898

—— Index. Compiled by Margaret Stewart Dale. Arcadia, Calif., M.C.Brown & M.S.Dale, 1966.   253 p. 28 cm. 3-3813 rev.   CS71.R234   1898
Index.

14121   RATHBONE. Richard Rathbone (by) Douglas Merritt (Rhinebeck, N.Y., 19 -?)   (6) p. 24 cm.
Caption title. Genealogical table in ms. at end. Allied families: Brown, Collins of Lynn, Newhall of Lynn, Wightman of Kingston, R.I., Updike of Wesel, Germany, Smith of Narragansett, Holmes of Kingston and Dodge of Block Island. CA17-1624.   CS71.R234   19 -

14122   RATHBONE. Samuel Rathbone and Lydia Sparhawk, his wife. A record of their descendants and notes regarding their ancestors. (By Albert Rathbone) (n.p.) 1937.   2 p. l., 74 p. 25 cm. Includes ten blank pages for "Memoranda". Slip with additions mounted on p. (72) 38-36154.   CS71.R234   1937

14123   RATHBONE. Rathbun-Rich and allied families; a manuscript covering the ancestry of Dyer Dana and Susan Rathbun who settled at Howard, Steuben County, New York, in the year 1816. (Harrisburg, Pa., 1947)   33 l. 28 cm. Caption title. Typewritten (carbon copy) 50-22619.   CS71.R234   1947

RATHBONE. See also: JOHNSON, 1961
NEIKIRK, 1960
REYNOLDS, CS439.R47
WILSON, 1890

RATHBUN. See RATHBONE.

RATKEY. See RADTKE.

RATZLAFF. See DECKER, 1959

RAU. See SNYDER, 1958

14124   RAUB. Introduction, Raub family history, by Edward B. Raub. (Indianapolis, 1943)
9 numb. l. 29 x 22½ cm. Caption title. Reproduced from type-written copy. 43-15924.   CS71.R234   1943

14125   RAUCH. A family chronicle, with comments on the passing show. By John George Rauch. Indianapolis, 1954 (i.e. 1958)   375 p. illus. 26 cm. 58-10232.   CS71.R244   1958

RAUCH. See also LONG, 1956

RAUSCH. See ROUSH.

14126   RAUSS. Memorabilia concerning the Rev. Lucas Rauss, one of the early ministers of the Evangelical Lutheran church in America: including an account of his ancestors and descendants ... By the Rev. Luther A. Gotwald ... York, Pa., O. Stuck, printer, 1878.   68 p. 23 cm. 10-1489.
CS71.R248   1878

14127   RAVENEL. Ravenel records. A history and genealogy of the Huguenot family of Ravenel, of South Carolina; with some incidental account of the parish of St. Johns Berkeley, which was their principal location. The book is intended for private distirbution. By Henry Edmund Ravenel. Atlanta, Franklin Print. and Pub. Co., 1898.   v, 279 p. plates, ports. 22 cm. 1-27667 rev.   CS71.R253   1898

—— A supplement (by) William Jervey Ravenel. (Charleston? S.C., 1964)   ii, 10 p. geneal. table (mounted on cover) 24 cm. cover title. 1-27667 rev.   CS71.R253   1898
Suppl.

RAVENELLE. See CASAVANT, CS90.C25

RAVENELLE LALIME. See CHOQUETTE, F1054.R5D3

14128   RAVENSCROFT. The family of Ravenscroft. By W. Ravenscroft, F.S.A., and the Rev. R. Bathurst Ravenscroft. (Reprinted from "Miscellanea genealogica et heraldica") London, Mitchell, Hughes and Clarke, 1915.   4 p. l., 54 p., 1 l. front., illus. (coat of arms) pl., ports. 29 cm. Blank pages at end for "Addenda." 19-1533.   CS439.R27

RAVOT.   See HUGUENIN, F268.D372

RAWDON.   See: Addenda.
VANREIN, E171.A53 v.16

14129   RAWLE.   Records of the Rawle family, collected from national archives, parish registers, wills, and other sources.   By Edwin John Rawle.   Taunton (Eng.) Printed for private circulation by Barnicott and Pearce, Athenaeum Press, 1898.   xii, 324 p. illus., ports., fold. col. map, geneal. table.   26 cm. "Edition of seventy-five copies only, of which this is no. 46." 58-53815.   CS439.R272   1898

RAWLE.   See also: BYRD, E159.G55
WASHINGTON, E159.G56

RAWLINGS.   See: COOCH, 1962
ROLLINS.
TREES, 1960
No. 3509 - Orange county.

14130   RAWLINSON.   A history of the Rawlinson family, by Harry H. Rawlinson.   (Montgomery, Ala., 1966)   iv, 136 l. illus., coat of arms, map.   30 cm.   Title from label mounted on binder.   "The Rawlinsons and their collections, by W. Y. Fletcher": leaves 119-136.   67-9206.   CS71.R258   1966

14131   RAWSON.   The Rawson family.   Memoir of Edward Rawson, secretary of the colony of Massachusetts Bay, from 1651 to 1686; with genealogical notices of his descendants.   By Sullivan S. Rawson ...   Boston, Pub. by the family, 1849.   iv, (5)-146, 2 p. front., port.   24½ cm.   9-13248.   CS71.R262   1849

14132   RAWSON.   The Rawson family.   A revised memoir of Edward Rawson, secretary of the colony of Massachusetts Bay, from 1650 to 1686; with genealogical notices of his descendants, including nine generations.   By E. B. Crane ...   Worcester (Mass.) Pub. by the family, 1875.   xv, 334 p., 1 l. front., plates, ports.   24 cm.   Blank pages at end for "Family record."   The memorial published by Sullivan S. Rawson in 1849, has been made the groundwork for this work. cf. Preface.   9-13249.   CS71.R262   1875

14133   RAWSON.   The ancestry of Edward Rawson, secretary of the colony of Massachusetts Bay.   With some account of his life in old and New England.   By Ellery Bicknell Crane ...   Worcester, Mass., Private press of F. P. Price, 1887.   2 p., 1., (3)-54 p. front. (port.) coat of arms.   25 cm.   An edition of one hundred copies printed.   Reprinted from the Proceedings of the Worcester society of antiquity for 1887.   "Stanhopes connected with the Rawsons": p. 39-49. 17-19206.   CS71.R262   1887

RAWSON.   See also: DOW, 1939
TAFT, 1908
YAWLEY, 1939

14134   RAY.   Sketch of the life and times of Dr. David Ray.   Boston, Printed for private circulation, 1881.   24 p. incl. front., illus.   18½ cm.   Dedication signed: G.B.H. i.e. Grinfill Blake Holden.   Contains an account of the meeting of the descendants of Dr. Ray on the 125th anniversary of his birth, Sept. 7, 1876.   2-26038.   F29.O88H7

14135   RAY.   The journal of Dr. Caleb Rea.   Written during the expedition against Ticonderoga in 1758.   Ed. by his great grandson, F. M. Ray.   Salem, Mass., 1881.   71 p.   23½ cm.   Reprinted from Essex institute.   Historical collections.   Salem, Mass., 1881. vol. 18.   20-6166.   E199.R25

14136   RAY.   The Ray genealogy showing the line of descent from Daniel Ray, who settled at Plymouth colony about 1630.   Grinnell, Ia., Ray & Frisbie, printers (1919)   28 p.   17½ cm.   Foreword signed: W. G. Ray.   Cover-title: A brief history of the descendants of Gilbert Ray, a soldier of the revolution.   "This booklet ... consists chiefly of 'Recollections' written by Orin Linden Ray in the years from 1885 to 1888, mostly published in the Poultney, Vt. journal." - Foreword.   32-3315.   CS71.R268   1919

RAY.   See also: ROYD, CS439.R75
SANDYS, 1897

14137   RAYBURN.   The descendants of Henry Rayburn of Virginia (by) Parke Jones (and) John T. Roberts.   (St. Paul?) 1947.   19 p.   20 cm.   Caption title.   48-16123*.   CS71. R269   1947

14138   RAYBURN.   The descendents (sic) of Edward Rayburn.   (Editor, Earle H. Morris.   Associ-- ate editor, John T. Roberts.   (Charleston? W. Va., 1950)   85, 11 p.   29 cm.   Cover title.   51-24210.
CS71. R269   1950

RAYLTON.   See PENNEY, 1920

14139   RAYMOND.   Genealogical memoranda relating to the family of Raymond of Kintbury, Berk- shire.   (n. p., 188-?)   8 p.   28 cm.   Signed: Reginald Stewart Boddington.   21-11824.
CS439. R275

14140   RAYMOND.   Genealogies of the Raymond families of New England, 1630-1 to 1886.   With a historical sketch of some of the Raymonds of early times, their origin, etc.   Compiled by Samuel Ray- mond ... New York, Press of J. J. Little & co., 1886.   v, 298 p., 1 l.   front., ports.   22 cm.   "List of authors": p. iv-v.   3-18044.   CS71. R27   1886

14141   RAYMOND.   Raymond arms and allied lines (Thatcher.   Barker.   Thomas.)   An heraldic interpretation of the original crests and coats-of-arms granted to the several families.   For private circulation.   London, J. A. Ringrose, 1913.   (13) p.   coats of arms.   24½ cm.   By Jerome Arthur Ringrose.   17-9741.
CS71. R27   1913

14142   RAYMOND.   Notes on the Raymond, Abbot, Jackson, and allied families ... By John Marshall Raymond.   (Palo Alto? Calif., 1962)   181 p.   illus.   23 cm.   62-59778.
CS71. R27   1962

14143   RAYMOND.   Raymond genealogy; descendants of Richard Raymond.   By Samuel Edward Raymond.   Assisted by Louvern Horn Raymond.   Seattle (1969 -   v.   22 cm.   Bibliographical footnotes. 77-10811 MARC.   CS71. R27   1969

RAYMOND.   See also BAILEY, 1892

14144   RAYNARD.   Descendants of Philip Raynard, ca. 1805-1884, and Frances Holland Raynard, ca. 1821-1906.   Lewes, Del., 1962.   71 p.   illus.   23 cm.   63-39423.   CS71. R274   1962

14145   RAYNER.   Rayner family history.   (By William Henry Rayner)   (n. p., 1916?)   72 p.   illus. (incl. ports.)   29 cm.   Caption title.   Blank pages throughout text for "Additional record".   "Foreword" signed: Wm. H. and John A. Raynor. 37-16959.   CS71. R276   1916

RAYNER.   See RAYNOR.

14146   RAYNOR.   The Raynor family, a record of some of the descendants of Edward Raynor, 1624- 1686.   By William Frederick Cornell.   Freeport, N. Y., 1946.   41, 4 l.   28 cm.   Type-written.   49-21030*.
CS71. R277   1946

14147   RAYNOR.   The Raynor (Rayner)-Burnham families; a history of these families and many of their related lines, their intermarriages, and their marriages with the Colwell family.   By Emma Julia (English) Machacek.   Schuyler, Neb., 1965 -   1 v.   (loose-leaf) illus., facsims., map, ports.   28 cm. 66-30542.   CS71. R277   1965

RAYNOR.   See also DICKERSON, 1919

14148   REA.   Samuel Rea, 1725-1811; heritage and descendants.   By Henry Oliver Rea. Dungannon, Northern Ireland, Printed by the Tyrone Print. Co., 1960.   70 p.   illus., ports., facsims., 2 geneal. tables.   29 cm. In portfolio.   "For private circulation only."   300 copies printed.   No. 154.   61-39254.
CS71. R282   1960

REA.   See also RAY, 1881

14149   READ. 1598. Descendants of John Read. 1859. Published by Orin A. Read ... Providence, R. I., A. C. Greene, printer, 1859.   geneal. tab. 136 x 90 cm. fold. to 58 x 41 cm. 35-21358.
CS71. R284   1859

14150   READ. History of the Reed family in Europe and America. By Jacob Whittemore Reed ... Boston, Printed by J. Wilson and son, 1861.   viii, 588 p. front., ports. 23 cm. 9-13245.
CS71. R284   1861

14151   READ. Seth Read, lieut-col. continental army; pioneer at Geneva, New York, 1787, and at Erie, Penn., June, 1795. His ancestors and descendants. By his great granddaughter, Mary Hunter Buford. Boston, 1895.   4 p. l., 7-166 p. front., pl., port. 22½ x 17 cm. 9-13247.
CS71. R284   1895

14152   READ. Souvenir programme of the semi-centennial meeting of the Reed family in the Reed locust grove, August 28, 1895, Taunton, Mass. (Taunton, Mass., J. S. Sampson, printer, 1895)
8 p. front., pl. 23½ cm.   9-13246.   CS71. R284   1895a

14153   READ. A record of the Redes of Barton Court, Berks; with a short précis of other lines of the name. By Compton Reade. (To which is added an account of the Reades of Rossenarra by R. Reade Macmullen, esq.) ... Hereford, Jakeman and Carver, 1899.   3 p. l., 148 p. front., ports. 26½ cm.
"The American line": p. 104-118. 15-13923.   CS439. R3

14154   READ. A royal lineage: Alfred the Great. 901-1901. By Annah Robinson Watson. Richmond, Va., Whittet & Shepperson, printers, 1901.   100 p., 1 l. front., pl., coats of arms. 25 cm. Printed in purple.
Some American descendants of Alfred the Great and other sovereigns: p. 91-100. 1-23286 rev.
CS71. R284   1901a

14155   READ. The Reed genealogy; descendants of William Reade of Weymouth, Massachusetts, from 1635 to 1902 ... by John Ludovicus Reed ... (Baltimore, Md., Printed by the Friedenwald company, 1901)   xxxix, 746 p. front., plates, ports., double geneal. tab. 23½ cm. 2-4710.
CS71. R284   1901

14156   READ. The Reades of Blackwood hill, in the parish of Horton, Staffordshire; a record of their descendants: with a full account of Dr. Johnson's ancestry, his kinsfolk and family connexions, by Aleyn Lyell Reade ... Privately printed for the author. London, Spottiswoode & co. ltd., 1906.
xx, 283 p., 1 l., xlii p. front., illus. (facsims.) XVII pl. (incl. ports.) XXIX double geneal. tab. 33½ cm x 28 cm.
CS439. R28

14157   READ. Proceedings of the Reade historical and genealogical association, with papers on the family history read at its first three annual meetings. Boston, Printed for the Association, 1907.
52 p. front., ports. 23½ cm. 10-1488.   CS71. R284   1907

14158   READ. Chart showing the descent of the family of General John Meredith Read from the Mayflower families of Cushman, Allerton, Warren, Bradford and Cook, and from the early New England families of Waterman, Freeman and Marshall. (Prepared by Major Harmon Pumpelly Read, 1907)
(n. p., 1907)   geneal. tab. 35 x 28 cm. 45-45519.   CS71. R284   1907a

14159   READ. Reed-Read lineage. Captain John Reed of Providence, R. I., and Norwalk, Conn., and his descendants through his sons, John and Thomas, 1660-1909. By Ella Reed-Wright. (Waterbury, Conn., The Mattatuck press, inc., 1909)   xvi p., 1 l., 717, lxiii p. front., plates, ports. 25 cm. 9-29144.
CS71. R284   1909

14160   READ. Ezra Reed and Esther Edgerton. Their life and ancestry, by Charles E. Benton ... Poughkeepsie, N. Y., Press of the A. V. Haight co., 1912.   94 p. front., fold. geneal. tab. 25½ cm. "Some of the sources of information": p. (83)-84. 12-11748.   CS71. R284   1912

14161   READ. The Reed family, by S. V. Talcott. Rearranged and published by Martin & Allardyce. Frankford, Phila., 1912.   cover-title, 17 p. 19½ cm. 12-25487.   CS71. R284   1912a

14162   READ.   Read genealogies, of the brothers and sisters and families and descendants of Israel Read, Abner Read, John Read, Polly Read (Hetherington) William Read, Wolcott Read, Lewis Read, Nathaniel Read, comp. by Rev. Henry Martyn Dodd ... Edition 1st.   (Utica, N.Y., Printed by L. C. Childs & son co., c.1912)   277, (2), ii-xxii p., 1 l. 23½ cm. 13-8629.

CS71. R284   1912b

14163   READ.   Genealogical record of the Reads, Reeds, the Bisbees, the Bradfords of the United States of America in the line of Esdras Read of Boston and England, 1635-1915.   Thomas Besbedge or Bisbee of Scituate, Mass., and England, 1634 to 1915.   Governor William Bradford of Plymouth, Mass., and England, 1620 to 1915.   And their connections, with biographical sketches, illustrations, military services, &c. &c.   By Axel Hayford Reed ... (Glencoe, Minn., 1915)   5 p. l., 7-163, (1) p. incl. front., illus., plates, ports. 24 cm. 16-17485.

CS71. R284   1915

14164   READ.   The Reed family of Topsham and Brunswick, Maine.   Comp. by Rev. Charles N. Sinnett.   Brainerd, Minn. (1920)   1 p. l., 34 l. 32 cm. Type-written. 21-3728.   CS71. R284   1920

14165   READ.   Some of the descendants of John Read, senior, of Newport, Rhode Island, and Free-town, Massachusetts.   1646-1924.   Compiled by Commander George H. Reed ... edited by George Holmes Read ... (n. p.) 1924.   60, (5) p. front., pl., ports. 23 cm. "Privately printed, 150 copies only. This copy is number 100." 25-11280.

CS71. R284   1924

14166   READ.   Genealogy of the Reid family of North Carolina and Georgia, by Rosa Talbot Knight. (n. p., 1924?)   2 p. l., 57 numb. l. 29 cm. (With her Genealogy of the Talbot and Wingfield families. n.p., 1924?) Type-written. 25-24233.

CS71. T14   1924

14167   READ.   The Read family.   (By Fred R. Parnell)   (In Niagara historical society. (Publications) Niagara (Ont.) 1925. 22 cm. no. 37, p. 19-31) Signed: Fred R. Parnell. CA 33-733 unrev.   F1059. N5N52 no. 37

14168   READ.   History and genealogy of the Reed family; Johann Philib Ried, Rieth, Riedt, Ritt, Rit, Rüdt, etc., in Europe and America, an early settler of Salford Township, (New Goshenhoppen region) Philadelphia County, Pennsylvania.   Including Reeds other than our family of this locality, an addenda, etc.   By W. H. Reed ... Norristown, Pa. (The Norristown press) 1929.   3 p. l., v-xviii, 529 p. front., illus., plates, ports., maps(1 fold.) facsims. 27½ cm. Plate preceding p. 189 accompanied by leaf with descriptive text. "The edition is limited to three hundred copies." - p. xiii. 29-27668.

CS71. R284   1929

14169   READ.   ... Reed family records, by J. Montgomery Seaver ... Philadelphia, American hist-orical-genealogical society (1929)   65 p. front. (incl. 3 port.) coat of arms. 29 cm. Coat of arms of the Reed family on recto of frontispiece. Pages 63-64 blank for "Family record". "References": p. 61-62. 40-18919.

CS71. R284   1929b

14170   READ.   The Reads and their relatives; being an account of Colonel Clement and Madam Read of Bushy Forest, Lunenburg County, Virginia, their eight children, their descendants, and allied fam-ilies, by Alice Read (Mrs. Shelley Rouse) Cincinnati, Johnson & Hardin press, 1930.   xi, 688 p. front., plates, ports. 24 cm. 30-21078.

CS71. R284   1930

14171   READ.   Allied families of Read, Corbin, Luttrell, Bywaters.   Starting from Culpeper county, Virginia, their descendants are now planted in every state westward to the Pacific.   My wife's kin. Compiled by A. M. Prichard.   Staunton, Va. (The McClure co., inc., printers) 1930.   292 p. port. 24 cm. 31-18269.

CS71. R284   1930a

14172   READ.   (Genealogy of the Valentine-Reed families.   By Lillian Reed.   193-?) 4 v. 25 cm. Manuscript. 56-53693.

CS71. R284

14173   READ.   Ancestors of the descendants of Arthur Lathrop Reed and Beulah Douglas Reed, copy-righted ... by Arthur L. Reed.   Anoka, Minn., c.1931.   2 geneal. tab. 79 x 77½ cm. fold. to 27 x 23 cm. Blue-prints. Includes "Reference books". 31-24454.

CS71. R284   1931

14174   READ.   Distinguished descendants of Colonel Clement Read, and Bushy Forest and other Charlotte county homes of the early Reads.   Two addresses delivered at "Greenfield" by Dr. J. D. Eggleston, president of Hampden-Sydney college, and Judge Robert F. Hutcheson, of the circuit court

14174 continued: of Virginia, at the annual meeting of the Association for the preservation of Virginia antiquities - October 22, 1932. (n. p., 1932) 44, (1) p. plates. 20 cm. 33-15348.

CS71. R284   1932

14175   READ.   Two Baptist pioneer preachers of Texas and their genealogy, by Della Tyler Key ...
(n. p., 1939?)   9, (1). 10-36 p. illus. (incl. ports.) 18½ cm. Bibliography: p. 36. 41-78.

BX6495. R4K4

14176   READ.   "The brotherhood of man" in some of the families of: IV. - Reid; V. Gaston and VI. -
Simonton, - in America.   By Lewin Dwinell McPherson ... (Washington, D. C., 1939)   1 p. l., 50 p.
illus. (port.) 32½ cm. Caption title.   Autographic reproduction of type-written copy.   "VII. Harvey, VIII. Tomlinson.   By Mrs. Lewin D.
(Hannah Elizabeth Weir) McPherson": p. 31-36.   "Sources of information": p. 37-40.   40-6185.   CS71. R284   1939

14177   READ.   Descent of Colonel George Reade, from medieval and modern kings, Knights of the
garter, and from thirteen sureties and seven other barons for the Magna charta of A. D. 1215.   Copyright ... by John S. Wurts.   Philadelphia, Pa., Brookfield publishing co., c. 1941.   geneal. tab.
36 x 76 cm. fold. to 36 x 25½ cm. 41-17608.   CS71. R284   1941

14178   READ.   A genealogical record concerning Captain Samuel Reed and Mary Winship Reed and
all their descendants of January 1, 1953.   Captain Samuel Reed and Mary Winship were married,
November 30, 1783, Woolwich, Maine.   (New York?) 1953.   154 p. illus. 29 cm. 53-26137.

CS71. R284   1953

14179   READ.   Reed descendants: thirteen generations, including the ancestors and descendants of
Paul Reed, 1605-1955; also other line descendants of his immigrant ancestor William Reade, b. 1605,
England.   By Bertha (Bortle) Adlridge.   Victor, N. Y., 1955.   139 p. illus. 23 cm. 57-44851.

CS71. R284   1955

14180   READ.   Stories about some of my New England ancestors in history and family life.   By Anna
(Reed) Parsons.   (n. p.) 1957.   60 p. illus., ports., facsims., geneal. table. 23 cm.   Title on spine: My New England ancestors.
Bibliography: p. 60.   58-20903 rev.   CS71. R284   1957

14181   REED.   A genealogical and biographical record concerning Amos Reed and Annie (Webb)
Reed and all of their descendants to January 1, 1955.   By Worrall Dumont Prescott.   (New York?)
1956.   265 p. illus. 29 cm.   "Amos Reed and Annie Webb were married, January 18, 1776, Woolwich, Maine.   Amos was a son of Jonathan
Reed and Keziah Converse Reed." 56-4946.   CS71. R284   1956

14182   READ.   A Reed family in America, with special reference to the family and descendants of
William Reed, 1818-1895, whose ancestral home was in Itawamba County, Mississippi.   By Forrest
Francis Reed.   Nashville, Tennessee Book Co., 1962.   83 p. illus. 23 cm. 62-41767.

CS71. R284   1962

14183   READ.   Reid family; Jeremiah Reid of Timber Ridge, Hampshire County, Virginia, and some
descendants and affiliations.   By Robert E. Reid.   (n. p., 1960?)   278 p. illus. 29 cm. 61-21314.

CS71. R284   1960

READ.   See also:

BAKER, 1870	KERR, CS479.K5	SAMPSON, 1922
BEAL, 1956	LITTLE, 1940	SMITH, 1928
BENSON, 1932	LLOYD, 1912	TALBOT, 1924
ENDERS, 1960	McNARY, 1914	TALBOT, 194-
GUERIN, 1890	MELLARD, CS439.M387	TAYLOR, 1898
HAMILTON, 1933a	MILLER, 1923	THAYER, E171.A53 vol. 20
HAMILTON, 1934	POUND, 1904	WATSON, 1801
HARRIS, 1934	REED.	WATSON, 1910
HITE, 1960	ROSS, 1908	WILLIS, 1898
JAMES, 1913a	RUCKER, 1927	No. 7422 - E. Barnet.

READE. See READ.

READER. See FISHER, 1890

14184   READING. Genealogical and biographical memorials of the Reading, Howell, Yerkes, Watts, Latham, and Elkins families, by Josiah Granville Leach. Philadelphia, Printed for private circulation by J. B. Lippincott co., 1898.   7 p. l., 3-285, (1) p. col. front., illus. (part col.) plates, ports., facsim., 2 geneal. charts. 28 cm. Two hundred copies printed on paper hand-made for this edition. no. 113. 9-13001.   CS71. R287   1898

14185   READING. (Chart showing the ancestry of Eleanor Lee Reading Templeman) compiled by Eleanor Lee Templeman. (Arlington, Va., 1944)   geneal. tab. 43 x 43½ cm. Photostat (positive)   45-14190.
CS71. R287   1944

────── Supplemental sheets ... Arlington, Va. (1944)   62 l. 28 x 21½ cm. Type-written (carbon copy); additions in manuscript. Includes the Reading, Guild, Washington, Lee, Clarkson, Heriot, Sayre and Roberts families. Bibliographical foot-notes. 45-14190.
CS71. R287   1944
Suppl.

REAGOR. See FROST, 1962

REAM. See STUKEY, 1939

14186   REAMS. The Reams, Reames family and allied families. By Harry Clyde Smith. (n. p., 1954)   186, 82 p. 22 cm. 54-44775.   CS71. R289   1954

REAMY. See REMEY.

14187   REARDEN. History and genealogy of Rearden family in America, 1700 to 1936, with collateral families and war records, compiled by Lucy Bender. (n. p., 1936)   (213) p. mounted pl., facsim., col coat of arms. 28 cm. Mimeographed. Title from cover. 38-14711.   CS71. R29   1936

14187a   REASONER.   17 notebooks concerning the Reasoner family.   In Manuscript Division.

14188   REASOR. A history of the Michael Reasor and allied families. Copyright ... by F. Hiner Dale ... Guymon, Okla., 1941.   3 p. l., 5-233, (7) p. pl., ports. 24 cm. Seven blank pages at end for additional records. Includes the Dale, Neet and Gilkeson families. 41-18207.   CS71. R2905   1941

14189   REASOR. Michael Reasor and Anna Herbert descendants, and related families of Brown, Pectol, Galloway, Scott, Razor, and McCutcheon. By Eunice Ann Cox Herbert. (Burbank, Calif., Malan Industries, (1969, c.1968)   xix, 700 p. illus., facsims., ports. 24 cm. Revision of A history of the Michael Reasor and allied families, by F. H. Dale. 77-11799 MARC.   CS71. R2905   1969

14190   REAU. Famille Alexis Reau, petites notices biographiques et généalogiques. Les Trois-Rivières, Imp. Le bien public, 1923.   69 p., 1 l. front. (fold. geneal. tab.) 22 cm. 35-16245.
CS90. R38F3

14191   REBER. Genealogy of the Reber family descended from Johan Bernhard Reber, 1738. Compiled by Morris B. Reber ... Reading, 1901.   40 p. plates, facsim. 23 cm. Published for the family. 5-448.
CS71. R291   1901

RECKARD. See RICKARD.

14192   RECORDS. Records family records (Laban Records branch of the Josiah Records family) by Francis A. Records. (Seattle? Wash., 1965)   vi, 116 l. mounted group port. 30 cm. Additions and corrections in MS. 65-74985.   CS71. R297   1965

14193   RECORDS. Spencer Records, 1762-1850, and his descendants, by Naomi M. Hougham. (Franklin? Ind.) 1965.   1 v. (various pagings) 30 cm. 66-49832.
CS71. R297   1965a

14194 RECTOR. History of the descendants of John Jacob Rector ... by Levi Brimner Salmans ... Guanajuato, Mex., The editor, 1936. 374 (i.e. 384) p. incl. plates, ports., facsims. ports. 35 cm. Edition limited to 200 copies. Includes extra numbered pages. 41-11224. CS71.R3 1936

RECTOR. See also: BRUMBACH, 1961
HOWARD, 1929

14195 REDDEN. The Stephen J. Redden family of Worcester County, Maryland. By Richard Stephen Uhrbrock. (Athens? Ohio) c.1960. 20 1. 28 cm. 61-25344. CS71.R312 1960

14196 REDDEN. John & Nehemiah Redden of Worcester County, Maryland (by) Richard S. Uhrbrock. (Athens? Ohio, 1966) 10 1. 29 cm. Caption title. 66-7905. CS71.R312 1966

14197 REDDINGTON. John Redington of Topsfield, Massachusetts, and some of his descendants, with notes on the Wales family. By Cornelia M. Redington Carter. Edited by Josiah Granville Leach, LL.B. Boston, Press of D. Clapp & son, 1909. 4 p. l., (3)-86 p. front., plates, ports. 24½ cm. "Reprinted with additions from the New England historical and genealogical register for July, 1907." Appendix: The counsels and directions of Ebenezer Wales, esq. to his children. Published from the author's manuscript found among his papers after his death. To which is prefixed, a short account of the character of the author. Boston, Printed and sold at N. Coverly, jun., 1813: p. (61)-79. 9-6115. CS71.R313 1909

14198 REDDITT. Family record of the Redditt families, researched and compiled by W. M. Redditt, Jr., with the help of Don M. Creveling. (Shreveport, La., 1965) vi, 215 p. illus., ports. 23 cm. "No. 196 of 500 copies." 65-4704. CS71.R3134 1965

REDE. See READ.

REDEL. Redel family in vertical file under PRANKE. Ask reference librarian for this material.

14199 REDFEARN. History of the Redfearn family, compiled by Daniel Huntley Redfearn. Miami, Fla., 1942. 3 p. l., 160 p. 23 cm. 43-1838. CS71.R314 1942

14200 REDFEARN. History of the Redfearn family. By Daniel Huntley Redfearn. Rev. ed. Miami, Fla., 1954. viii, 327 p. ports. 23 cm. "Books written by members of this family": p. (317)-318. 55-17618.
CS71.R314 1954

14201 REDFIELD. Genealogical history of the Redfield family in the United States. By John Howard Redfield ... Albany, Munsell & Rowland; New York, C. B. Richardson, 1860. viii, 337 p. ports. 23½ cm. "A revision and extension of the genealogical tables compiled in 1839, by William C. Redfield." 9-13244.
CS71.R315 1860

REDFIN. See REDFIELD.

REDINGTON. See REDDINGTON.

14202 REDMAN. History of the Redman farm, so called, and of the title thereto, situate in Canton, Norfolk county, Massachusetts. Now mostly owned by Henry L. Pierce, esq., of Boston. Compiled by Ellis Ames ... Boston, Printed by W. Bense, 1870. 32 p. fold. plan. 24 cm. Contains some Redman family history. 1-11286. F74.C2A5

14203 REDMAN. The Redmans of Levens and Harewood. A contribution to the history of the Levens family of Redman and Redmayne in many of its branches. By W. Greenwood ... Kendal, T. Wilson, 1905. xv, 283, (1) p. front., plates (part fold.) fold. plan, fold. facsims., fold. geneal. tables, coats of arms. 23½ cm. 15-20213. CS439.R35

14204 REDMAN. The Redman genealogy to January 1, 1966. By Lorena (Redman) Histed. (Fillmore? N.Y., 1966) 26 1. (chiefly geneal. tables) 30 cm. Caption title. On cover: The Redman genealogy, 1770-1966. 67-1827. CS71.R318 1966

REDMAN. See also LINGARD, 1930

14205   REDVERS.   Records of the corporation of the borough of New-Lymington, in the county of Southampton.   Extracted from the muniments in the possession of the mayor and town council, and other authorities, in the year 1848.   By Charles St. Barbe ... (London) Printed for private circulation by Nichols & son (1849?)   3 p. l., (iii)-iv, 47 p. 1 illus., 2 fold. plans, 2 fold. geneal. tab. 31½ x 24½ cm. Lettered on cover: Borough of Lymington. Edited by John St. Barbe. Folded tables: "Pedigree of De Redvers & Courtenay, earls of Devon, who held the lordship of Lymington" and "Pedigree of Burrard from Berry's Hampshire genealogies." 18-22147.   DA690. L89S3

REDWAY.   See ARNOLD, 1948

REDWOOD.   See PARRISH, 1927

REECE.   See REES.

14206   REED.   History of the Reed family in Europe and America.   By Jacob Whittemore Reed ... Boston, Printed by J. Wilson and son, 1861.   viii, 588 p. front., ports. 23 cm. 9-13245.
                                                                            CS71. R284   1861

14207   REED.   Reed-Read lineage.   Captin John Reed of Providence, R. I., and Norwalk, Conn. and his descendants through his sons, John and Thomas, 1660-1909.   By Ella Reed-Wright.   (Waterbury, Conn., The Mattatuck press, inc., 1909)   xvi p., 1 l., 717, lxiii p. front., plates, ports. 25 cm. 9-29144.
                                                                            CS71. R284   1909

14208   REED.   The Reed family, by S. V. Talcott.   Rearranged and published by Martin & Allardyce.   Frankford, Phila., 1912.   17 p. 19½ cm. cover-title. 12-25487.   CS71. R284   1912a

14209   REED.   History and genealogy of the Reed family; Johann Philib Ried, Rieth, Riedt, Ritt, Rit, Rüdt, etc., in Europe and America, an early settler of Salford Township, (New Goshenhoppen region) Philadelphia County, Pennsylvania.   Including Reeds other than our family of this locality, an addenda, etc.   By W. H. Reed ... Norristown, Pa.   (The Norristown press) 1929.   3p. l., v-xviii, 529 p. front., illus., plates, ports., maps (1 fold.) facsims. 27½ cm. Plate preceding p. 189 accompanied by leaf with descriptive text. "The edition is limited to three hundred copies." - p. xiii. 29-27668.   CS71. R284   1929

14210   REED.   ... Reed family records, by J. Montgomery Seaver ... Philadelphia, American historical-genealogical society (1929)   65 p. front. (incl. 3 port.) coat of arms. 29 cm. Coat of arms of the Reed family on recto of frontispiece. Pages 63-64 blank for "Family record." "References": p. 61-62. 40-18919.   CS71. R284   1929b

14211   REED.   The Reed family in central Texas; a memorial on the marking of the graves of Michael and Martha Burnett Reed, July 13, 1947.   (Austin? 1947)   22 p. illus. 19 cm. Contributions by Malcolm D. McLean, Stella McKay Mewhinney, and Lina Rogers Kemp. 75-12628 MARC.   CS71. R284   1947

14212   REED.   Stories about some of my New England ancestors in history and family life.   By Anna (Reed) Parsons.   (n. p.) 1957.   60 p. illus., ports., facsims., geneal. table. 23 cm. Title on spine: My New England ancestors. Bibliography: p. 60. 58-20903 rev.   CS71. R284   1957

14213   REED.   A genealogy of the Reed (Reid) family, embracing the lineage of 5 Reed children, descendants of (I) John Reed and Mary Drake (Reed) including pedigree of some close affiliated families: Brewer, Mister, Davis, Martin, and Lovelace.   By Avery Henry Reed.   (Charlottesville? Va.) c. 1963.   2 v. illus., ports., maps. 29 cm. 64-622.   CS71. R284   1963

14214   REED.   A Reed family story.   By Vera Colton Halstead.   (New Fairfield, Conn., 1965)   41, (6) l. geneal. tables. 29 cm. Cover title. Bibliography: leaf (47) 72-3097.   CS71. R284   1965

14215   REED.   The Reed family; a history and genealogy of William S. and Elizabeth Berlin Reed with William Reed's lineage to John Reed, the immigrant.   By Judith Etzel King.   (Nixon? N.J., 1966)   iv, 113 l. 30 cm. "Footnotes": leaf 113. 67-5812.   CS71. R284   1966

14216   REED.   The ancestry and descendants of Mitchell Reed and his wife, Sarah Foster, with notes on some related families: Shannon, Wortman, Armstrong, and Moore.   By Arthur Reed Armstrong.   Littleton, Colo., 1967.   122, xviii p. maps, ports. 29 cm. "Two hundred copies." Bibliography: p. 121-122.   68-3498.   CS71. R284   1967

REED. See also READ.

REEDER. See LA VELLE, 1957

REEDER. See READER.

14217   REES. Genealogy of the Reese family in Wales and America, from their arrival in America
to the present time. By Miss Mary E. Reese. Richmond, Va., Whittet & Shepperson, 1903.
322 p. front. 19½ cm. 5-7998.   CS71. R328   1903

14218   REES. David Rees of Little Creek Hundred; and the descendants of John Rees, his son.
Compiled and published by Thomas Hale Streets ... Philadelphia, Pa., 1904. 80 p. 21 cm. On cover: Number
one. Some allied families of Kent County, Delaware. 7-36558.   CS71. R328   1904

14219   REES. Rees history, by Gladys Wilkinson Lawrence ... (n. p., 1932?) cover-title, 20 p. incl.
illus., ports. 22 cm. 33-25765.   CS71. R328   1932

14220   REES. The house of Rees with allied families, 1800-1938, by Edwin Starkey. Oklahoma
City, 1938.   84 p. illus. (ports.) 28 cm. Includes blank pages for memoranda. 38-25887.   CS71. R328   1938

14221   REES. Genealogy of Winston Reece's family, compiled by Viola Estella Reece. (n. p.)
1938.   cover-title, (7) p. 21 cm. 38-36183.   CS71. R328   1938a

14222   REES. Genealogy of Winston Reece's family, compiled by Viola Estella Reece. 2d ed.(n. p.)1949.
13 p. 21 cm. Cover title. 50-21819.   CS71. R328   1949

14223   REES. Jane Harris of Rocky River; she linked the Carolinas. By Jenness (Reese) Reyes.
(Oakland? Calif., 1964)   273 p. 28 cm. Bibliographical footnotes. 64-39409.   CS71. H315   1964

        REES.   See also: DAVIS, 1927a
                            FLETCHER, 1909
                            PUGH, 1941

        REESE.   See REES.

        REEVE.   See REEVES.

14224   REEVES. Reeves family in America. (n. p., 192-?)   geneal. table. 122 x 82 cm. 47-42474 *.
                                                                                   CS71. R331

14225   REEVES. The Reeves family; Walter Reeve of Burlington County, New Jersey, and a number
of his descendants through ten generations, 1650-1930, compiled (from notes left by Samuel V. Reeves)
by Clara Swain Stevens, a neice(!) and Clara B. Birch (nee Reeves) a daughter. Merchantville, N.J.,
H. S. Craig, printer (c. 1930)   102 p. front. (port.) illus. (facsims.) fold. geneal. tabl 21½ cm. 30-23567.
                                                                                   CS71. R331   1930

14226   REEVES. Ancestral sketches. (A chronicle of the pioneer East Tennessee families:
Reeves, Miller, De Vault, and Range of Washington County; Robeson of Sullivan and McMinn Counties;
and Easley, Hamilton, Acuff, and Vincent of Sullivan County; and certain of their antecedents in New
Jersey, Pennsylvania, Maryland, Virginia, and North Carolina) Lynchburg, Va., J. P. Bell Co., 1951.
ix, 113 p. illus., ports. 25 cm. 52-18602.   CS71. R331   1951a

14227   REEVES. 1700-1900: ancestry and posterity of Johnson Reeves, born October 16, 1799,
died July 19, 1860, and a memorial sermon by Samuel Beach Jones. By Francis Brewster Reeves.
Philadelphia, Printed by Allen, Lane & Scott (pref. 1900)   65 p. illus. 26 cm. 62-56137.
                                                                                   CS71. R331   1900

        REEVES. See also: DAVIS, 1927a   REICHNER, 1918
                             MOAK, 1960   SINNOTT, 1905

REGISTER.　See McAMIS, 1948

REHDER.　See No. 553 - Goodhue county.

REIBER.　See GOODLOCK, 1951

REICH.　See HAYNES, 1922

14228　REICHEL.　(In Miscellanea genealogica et heraldica.　London, 1874.　27 cm.　(n. s., v. 1, p. 276 -279)　2-26604.　　　　　　　　　　　CS410. M5 n. s. vol. 1

REICHELSDÖRFER.　See MONNET, 1911

REICHERT.　See No. 553 - Goodhue county.

14229　REICHNER.　Reichner and Aiken genealogies, compiled and edited by L. Irving Reichner of Philadelphia, Pa.　(Philadelphia? 1918?)　5 p. l., 226 p. 23 cm.　"Twenty-five copies printed, of which this is no. 4." Contents. - pt. I. The ancestors of Louis Reichner, jr., and Christiana Stephens, his wife. - pt. II. The ancestors of William D. Aiken and Alice H. Slawson, his wife.　18-23440.　　　　　　　　CS71. R34　　1918

REID.　See:　READ.
　　　　　　　REED.

14230　REIFF.　John George Reiff and descendants.　By John Merle Rife.　New Concord, Ohio, Reiff Press (1960)　73 p. 23 cm.　60-44622.　　　CS71. R347　　1960

REIFF.　See also RIFE.

14231　REIFSNYDER.　Reifsnyder-Gillam ancestry.　Edited by Thomas Allen Glenn ... at the request of Howard Reifsnyder ... Philadelphia, Priv. print., 1902.　2 p. l., 90 p., 1 l. plates, fold. facsim., geneal. tab., 2 coats of arms (incl. front.) 26½ cm.　"Additions and corrections": slip inserted at end.　Includes also the families of Longacre, Ellis, Evans, Humphreys, Plantagenet, Hallowell, Roberts, and Lloyd.　40-2250.
　　　　　　　　　　　　　　　　　　CS71. R35　　1902

REIGART.　See KEENER, 1923

REINACKER.　See EICHELBERGER, 1901

14232　REINBOLD.　The Ludwig Reinbold family.　By William Henry Rinkenbach.　(n. p.) 1960. 31, (24) l.　coat of arms.　28 cm.　Typescript (carbon copy) Bibliography: leaf (32) 62-48864.　CS71. R357　　1960

REINDAHL.　See FELLAND, 1940

14233　REISING.　Genealogy of the family of Antony and Ella M. (Baatz) (Derby) Reising, of Florence, Florence Twp., Erie County, Ohio.　By Claude Charles Hamel.　Amherst, 1951.　3 l. 27 cm. 52-20693.
　　　　　　　　　　　　　　　　　　CS71. R36　　1951

14234　REIST.　Peter Reist of Lancaster county, Pennsylvania, and some of his descendants by Henry G. Reist ... Schenectady, N. Y., 1933.　118 p. front., double facsims. 25 cm. 34-10435.
　　　　　　　　　　　　　　　　　　CS71. R37　　1933

REIST.　See KALBFLEISCH, 1956

REMALY.　See REMELY.

REMBERT.　See POELINITZ, 1962

14235　REMELY.　Genealogical records of one branch of the Remely-Remaly family in America: descendants of Ambrose and Anna Barbara Remely, originally De Remley, Huguenots.　Compiled by Evelyn Martz Guldner.　(Cedar Grove? N. J.) 1966.　41 l. 29 cm.　Cover title: Remely-Remaly family, 1749-1966. 66-59142.　　　　　　　　　　　　CS71. R38　　1966

14236   REMEY.   Records of the families Remey and Mason, of Burlington, Iowa, and the city of Washington.   (Washington, 1923?)   1 v. 28 cm. Cover-title. "Prepared by B. F. Johnson." Type-written; various pagings. Book-plate (portrait of George Collier Remey and Mary Josephine Mason Remey) mounted on p. (2) of cover.   Contents. - A brief historical sketch of the Remey family tracing the descent of George Collier Remey. - Descent of George Collier Remey. - A brief historical sketch of the Howland family from which descended Eliza Smith Howland, the mother of George Collier Remey. - From the records of the Howland family. - A brief historical sketch of the Mason family tracing the descent of Mary Josephine Mason Remey, wife of George Collier Remey. - Letter from Mrs. Blanche Mason Chapman to Mrs. Gertrude Gear Stubbs. - Letter from Mrs. Gertrude Gear Stubbs to Mrs. Mary J. Remey. - Letter from George W. Mason to Mrs. Gertrude Gear Stubbs. - The Mason family records taken from the history of the First church of Hartford, Connecticut. - From records of the Gear family. - Record of the Whitmore or Wetmore family.   26-4222 rev.

CS71. R386   1923

14237   REMEY.   Reminiscences of his childhood, 1874-1884 (by) Charles Mason Remey.   (n. p., 1943?)   4 v. (314 l.) illus. (part mounted) ports., plans. 28 cm. (His Remey family records.) 58-3236.

CS71. R386   1943

14238   REMEY.   The Remi family in America, by B. W. Rhamy, M. D. (Bonnelle William Rhamy) Fort Wayne, Ind., 1937.   443 l. 29½ cm. Type-written (carbon copy) 37-38445.   CS71. R386   1937

14239   REMEY.   The Remy family in America, 1650-1942, compiled by Bonnelle William Rhamy ... Fort Wayne, Ind., 1942.   3 p. l., 492 p. front., illus. (incl. maps, coats of arms) ports., facsims. 28½ cm. Reproduced from type-written copy. 42-23917.   CS71. R386   1942

14240   REMEY.   Reminiscences of the summer school Green-Acre, Eliot, Maine; of seasons there, of happenings there, and some of the people who went there and the things they did.   By Charles Mason Remey.   (n. p.) 1949.   2 v. mounted illus., ports. 28 cm. (His Remey family records.) 58-3335.

CS71. R386   1949

14241   REMEY.   A series of twelve of the preliminary architectural designs for a mausoleum for the Remey family.   By Charles Mason Remey.   (n. p., 1954?)   21 l. ports., facsim., plans. 28 cm. (His Remey family records) 58-3336.   CS71. R386   1954

14242   REMEY.   Houses in which the Remey family, their forebears, and their children have lived. By Charles Mason Remey.   (n. p.) 1957.   2 v. mounted illus., port., facsims., plans. 28 cm. (His Remey family records) 58-3331.   CS71. R386   1957

14243   REMEY.   The Remey family of the United States of America, 1654-1957.   By Charles Mason Remey.   (n. p.) 1957.   81 l. plates, ports., coat of arms, facsims. 28 cm. (His Remey family records) 58-3333.

CS71. R386   1957a

14244   REMEY.   Reminiscences of his boyhood; life at the United States Navy Yard, Washington, D. C., 1884-1886 (by) Charles Mason Remey.   (n. p.) 1958 -   v. ports. 28 cm. (His Remey family records) 58-3337.   CS71. R386   1958

14245   REMEY.   The Remēum; place of commemoration and sepulture of the family of Rear Admiral George Collier Remey, United States Navy, and his wife Mary Josephine Mason, their descendants, forbears & friends.   (n. p., 1958)   28 l. plates, ports., coat of arms, facsims., geneal. table, photos., plan. 28 cm. (His Remey family records) 58-3332.   CS71. R386   1958a

REMEY.   See also JOHNSON, 1956.

REMI.   See REMEY.

REMICH.   See REMICK.

14246   REMICK.   Genealogy of the Remick family.   By Oliver Philbrick Remick.   Boston, Press of D. Clapp & son, 1893.   7 p. 25 cm. 3-20240.   CS71. R387   1893

14247   REMICK.   Remick genealogy, compiled from the manuscript of Lieutenant Oliver Philbrick Remick for the Maine historical society, by Winifred Lovering Holman ... (Concord, H. N., Rumford press) 1933.   2 p. l., 211, (2) p. illus. (map) port. 24½ cm. "One hundred copies of this book were printed." 34-12547.

CS71. R387   1933

REMICK.   See also WARREN, 1949

14248   REMINGTON.   Thomas Remington of Suffield, Conn., and some of his descendants, by Louis Marinus Dewey.   Boston, New England historic genealogical society, 1909.   9 p. 24½ cm. 10-4263.
CS71. R388   1909

—— Supplement.   Boston, New England historic genealogical society, 1910.   2 p. 24 cm.
Caption title.   Reprinted from Register for January, 1910.   10-4264.   CS71. R388   1910

14249   REMINGTON.   Remingtons of Utah with their ancestors and descendants.   By Ward Jay Roylance.   Salt Lake City, 1960.   455 p. illus. 29 cm. 61-42031.   CS71. R388   1960

REMINGTON.   See also: STRONG, 1871
                         WOOD, E171. A53 v. 14

REMLEY.   See AULD, 1933

14250   REMSBERG.   Genealogy of the Remsberg family in America, by Rev. W. L. Remsberg ... (Middletown, Md., 1912)   cover-title, 48 p. 16 cm. 27-15874.   CS71. R389   1912

REMSEN.   See: DE RAPELJE, 1948
                  JOHNSON, CT275. J675A3

REMY.   See REMEY.

14251   RENAUD.   La famille Renaud d'Avène des Méloizes, par Pierre-Georges Roy.   Levis, 1907.
50 p. illus. (incl. ports.) 23½ cm.   "Tiré à 100 exemplaires numérotés."   This copy not numbered. 9-29902.
CS90. R4

RENDLEMAN.   See RANDLEMAN.

RENEAU.   See PALLISSARD, 1959

RENFRO, RENFROW.   See PUCKETT, 1960

14252   RENICK.   Renick-Morris ancestral chart, compiled for Gertrude Trimble (Renick) Bell, wife of James Duncan Bell.   By Julia Hoge (Spencer) Ardery.   Drawn by Bayless Hardin.   (Frankfort? Ky.) 1944.   geneal. table. coats of arms. 27 cm. Photocopy (positive) 50-50337.   CS71. R394   1944

14253   RENICK.   The Renicks of Greenbrier, by B. F. Harlow, Jr., and other assistants.   (Bridgewater, Va.) 1951.   110, 22 p. illus. 25 cm. 58-25482.   C571. R394   1951

14254   RENFREW.   Several ancestral lines of James P. Renfrew and his wife, Ella Black, married at Mirabile, Mo., Aug. 31, 1871, with a full genealogical history of their descendants to 1925, by James P. Renfrew ... Alva, Okla., Alva record print (1926)   5 p. l., 117 p. front., pl., ports., coat of arms. 24 cm.
26-16373.   CS71. R393   1926

RENNOLDS.   See REYNOLDS.

14255   RENOLL.   Daniel Renoll, Huguenot and some of his descendants, by Katharine E. S. Morris. (St. Petersburg, Fla.   Printed by the St. Petersburg Print. Co., 1969)   x, 41 p. illus., facsims., ports. 28 cm.
68-59321. MARC.   CS71. R3945   1969

RENOUARD.   See JAMES, CS439. J3

14256   RENTON.   Renton (family) (n. p., 188-?)   12 l. 20 cm. 48-31962*.   CS479. R45

RENTOUL.   See RANTOUL.

14257   RENWICK.   Genealogy of the Renwick family ... Compiled by Helen H. McIver.   (n. p.) 1924.
23 p. 23 cm. 24-12327.   CS71. R395   1924

RENWICK.   See also: BARD, F128.25.V27
TODD, 1867

14258   REQUA.   The family of Requa; 1678-1898.   Compiled by Rev. Amos C. Requa ... Peekskill, N.Y., 1898.   xxxviii p., 1 l., 63 p. front., plates, ports. 24½ cm. 9-13243.   CS71.R427   1898

14259   RERESBY.   The memoirs and travels of Sir John Reresby, bart.   The former containing anecdotes, and secret history, of the courts of Charles II. and James II.   The latter (now first published) exhibiting a view of the governments and society in the principal states and courts of Europe during the time of Cromwell's usurpation.   London.   Printed for E. Jeffery and J. Rodwell, 1813.   xii, 414 (i.e. 416), (31) p. 23½ cm.   Some copies of this edition contain plates and portraits.   2-30591.   DA447.R4A2

RERESBY.   See also PULFORD, CS439.P85

RESSEGUIE.   See RESSIGUIE.

14260   RESSIGUIE.   The Resseguie family.   A historical and genealogical record of Alexander Resseguie of Norwalk, Conn., and four generations of his descendants.   Compiled by John E. Morris.   Hartford, Conn., Press of the Case, Lockwood & Brainard company, 1888.   99 p. 23 cm. 9-13242.
CS71.R435   1888

14261   RESZKE.   Jean de Reszke and the great days of opera, by Clara Leiser; with a foreword by Amherst Webber.   New York, Minton, Balch & company, 1934.   xiv, 337 p. front., illus. (facsims., music) plates, ports. 24 cm. Bibliography: p. 323-324. 34-4696.   ML420.R36L41

RETAN.   See WILBUR, 1936

14262   RETTEW.   The descendants of Aaron Rettew.   (By Annie Elizabeth (Rettew) Hunter)   (Reading, Pa., 1938?)   cover-title, 78, (24) l. 29 cm.   Typewritten (carbon copy) "One of five copies." 47-41484*.
CS71.R438   1938

14263   RETTEW.   Genealogy of John Michael Bohner.   By Dorothy Rettew Lewis.   (Alexandria, Va., 1967)   36 l. illus., ports. 30 cm. "A continuation of one branch of the family mentioned in ... Descendants of Aaron Rettew, by Annie Rettew Hunter." 68-2227.   CS71.R44   1967

14264   REUMERT.   Slaegten Reumert, dens historie og stamtavle.   By Emmerik Reumert.   Kobenhavn, E. Munksgaard, 1948.   68 p. ports. 25 cm. 49-26252*.   CS909.R48   1948

REVERCOMB.   See RUBINCAM.

REVELL.   See ELY, 1910

REVETT.   See FAUCONBERGE, CS439.F3

REW.   See AREW.

14265   REX.   Jonas Rex and wife Rhoda (Milliken) Rex family and family military data.   Comp. by Mrs. Sarah Augusta Prior Smith (Mrs. C. E. Smith) ... Columbus, O., 1922.   1 p. l., (2) p., 1 l. illus. (incl. ports.) 121 x 50 cm. fold. to 31 x 25 cm.   A collection of data relating to the Rex ancestry of Sarah Augusta (Prior) Smith, consisting of printed and manuscript material with mounted photographs, fastened together in binder. 22-6308.   CS71.R445   1922

14266   REX.   George Rex genealogy, ancestry and descendants of George Rex first of England to Pennsylvania in 1771, by Leda Ferrell Rex.   Wichita, Kan., Priv. pub., 1933.   iv, (3), 192 p. plates, ports., facsims. 24 cm.   Originally undertaken by Charles Swan Rex, and after his death, carried on for a time by his son, George B. Rex. cf. Pref. 33-8511.   CS71.R445   1933

14267   REXFORD.   Genealogical history showing the paternal line of descent from Arthur Rexford, a native of England, who married Elizabeth Stevens, of New Haven, Conn., in 1702.   Compiled by John De Witt Rexford.   Janesville, Wis., Gazette printing company, printers, 1891.   74, (4) p. 22½ cm. 9-13241.
CS71.R455   1891

REYERSE.　See VAN NORDEN, 1923

REYNER.　See LANE, 1857

REYNES.　See DEACON, 1898

14268　REYNOLDS.　Reynolds and his candidate for district judge.　To the people of Atchison county, Kansas.　(Comp. by C. W. Benning)　(Atchison? Kan., 1887)　61 p. fold. form.　20½ cm.　Cover-title. Signed: C. W. Benning ... (and) H. C. Solomon.　46-44340.　CT275. R49B4

14269　REYNOLDS.　"99 years" among the family archives.　The readin', 'ritin' and religion; rites, customs and doings of our forefathers.　By Chas. H. B. Field ... (Montrose, O.)　Printed at home, 1893.　1 p. l., 8 p., 1 l.　11½ x 10½ cm.　CA9-2577.　CS71. R464　1893

14270　REYNOLDS.　Reynolds family genealogy.　(By Marcus Tullius Reynolds)　(Albany, 1898) 1 p. l., 60 (i. e. 63) numb. l.　35 cm.　Type-written.　Additional numbered leaves after 3 and 29.　Additions and corrections in manuscript. The author has "collected and compiled the earlier and collateral data ... supplementing the work begun by his father Dexter Reynolds. "　35-21383.　CS71. R464　1898

14271　REYNOLDS.　A history of the works of Sir Joshua Reynolds, P. R. A., by Algernon Graves, F. S. A., and William Vine Cronin ... London, Pub. by subscription for the proprietors by H. Graves and co., limited, 1899-1901.　4 v. fronts., 154 pl. (incl. ports., facsims.) 28½ cm.　Paged continuously.　"Pedigree of the Reynolds family": v. 4, p. 1675-1677.　"Concerning the parentage and kinsfolk of Sir Joshua Reynolds and certain other matters.　By Sir Robert Edgcumbe": v. 4, p. 1679-1703.　14-3547.　ND497. R4G75

14272　REYNOLDS.　The parentage and kinsfolk of Sir Joshua Reynolds, P. R. A., by Sir Robert Edgcumbe.　Reprinted privately by kind permission from "A history of the works of Sir Joshua Reynolds" by Algernon Graves, F. S. A., and William Vine Cronin.　London, Printed at the Chiswick press, 1901.　31, (1) p. 28½ cm.　Seventy-five copies printed.　"Pedigree of the Reynolds family": p. 3-5. 15-14361. ND497. R4E4

14273　REYNOLDS.　... Annual reunion, the Reynolds family association ... Middletown, Conn., Pelton & King, printers and bookbinders,　v. pl. 24½ cm.　Editors:　Mrs. Mary Fosdick. 1913-20, Miss Fannie D. Holmes. - 1921 -　Mrs. Anna C. Rippier.　10-4377.　CS71. R464　1902

14274　REYNOLDS.　Ancestors and descendants of William and Elizabeth Reynolds of North Kings-town, R. I.　By Thomas A. Reynolds ... and William A. Reynolds ... Edited and arranged by Alfred C. Willits ... (Philadelphia, Printed by J. B. Lippincott company) 1903.　42 p.　24 cm.　5-12573. CS71. R464　1903

14275　REYNOLDS.　A partial record of the ancestors and a complete record of the descendants of Christopher and Charissa (Huntington) Reynolds of Mansfield, Connecticut.　Compiled by Mrs. Jane Adaline (Eaton) Wight, Springfield, Mass.　(Springfield? Mass., 1905)　38 p., 9 l. 23 cm.　Blank pages for additions.　5-42577.　CS71. R464　1905

14276　REYNOLDS.　Reynolds-Rathbone diaries and letters, 1753-1839, ed. by Mrs. Eustace Greg. (Edinburgh) Printed for private circulation (University press) 1905.　x, 203, (3) p. front., plates, ports. 23 cm. 16-14968.　CS439. R47

14277　REYNOLDS.　Partial genealogy of John Reynolds, born in England in 1612 (supposedly), sailed from Ipswich county, Suffolk.　A part of his lineage to 1916, as comp. and pub. by Alvah Reynolds, Altona, Illinois, September, 1916.　With a chapter of heraldry extending back to 1327. Galesburg, Ill., Wagoner printing company, 1916.　1 p. l., (5)-160 p. illus., port., coat of arms.　23½ cm.　Alternate pages from 8 to 140 left blank for "Records. "　16-25273.　CS71. R464　1916

14278　REYNOLDS.　Genealogical sketches of Reynolds, Fewells, Walls and kindred families. Winston-Salem, N. C., The Commercial printers, inc. (1923)　56 p. illus. (port.)　23 cm.　"Introductory" signed John Fewell Reynolds.　23-14466.　CS71. R464　1923

14279   REYNOLDS.   The history and descendants of John and Sarah Reynolds (1630?-1923) of Water-town, Mass., and Wethersfield, Stamford and Greenwich, Conn.   Edited and compiled by Marion H. Reynolds ... Data on living generations collected by Mrs. Anna C. Rippier ... Brooklyn, N.Y., The Reynolds family association, 1924.   505 p., 2 l. incl. front. illus. (facsims., coats of arms) ports. 24 cm. On cover: Family of Westchester, Greenwich, Dutchess, etc. 24-14138.   CS71.R464   1924

14280   REYNOLDS.   The history and one line of descendants of Robert and Mary Reynolds (1630?-1928) of Boston, Mass.   Compiled by Marion H. Reynolds ... Brooklyn, N.Y., The Reynolds family association, 1928.   92 p. front., plates, ports. 23½ cm. On cover: Robert and Mary Reynolds of Boston and the Hyatt family of Princeton, N.J. The material for this book has been extracted from genealogical notes of the compiler, and from data collected over many years by Mrs. Alpheus Hyatt. 28-12383.   CS71.R464   1928

14281   REYNOLDS.   The history and descendants of John and Sarah (Backus) Reynolds of Saybrook, Lyme and Norwich, Conn., 1655-1928; edited and compiled by Marion H. Reynolds ... data on living generations collected by Mrs. Anna C. Rippier ... Brooklyn, N.Y., The Reynolds family association, 1928.   4 p. l., 5-71 p. front., plates, ports., facsims. 23½ cm. 29-5422.   CS71.R464   1928a

14282   REYNOLDS.   ... Reynolds family records, by J. Montgomery Seaver.   Philadelphia, Pa., American historical-genealogical society (1929)   37, (3) p. front. (incl. 3 port.) coat of arms. 29 cm. Coat of arms of Reynolds family on recto of frontispiece. Two pages at end blank for "Family records". "References": p. 36-37. 40-18920.   CS71.R464   1929

14283   REYNOLDS.   The history and some of the descendants of Robert and Mary Reynolds (1630? -1931) of Boston, Mass.   Compiled by Marion H. Reynolds ... Brooklyn, N.Y., The Reynolds family association, 1931.   3 p. l., (5)-236 p. front., illus. (incl. facsims., geneal. tables) plates, ports., fold. plan. 23½ cm. Second edition. On cover: The Reynolds family, Boston, 1630. The Hyatt family included in the first is omitted in the present edition. 31-18234.   CS71.R464   1931

14284   REYNOLDS.   Reynolds family history & genealogy, 1630-1933, by Carolyn B. Ellis ... (Findlay, O.) c.1934.   2 p. l., 2-49 numb. l. port. 26½ cm. Photolithographed. The photostat portrait has on verso a sworn statement regarding the history of the print, signed by the author. CA34-530 unrev.   CS71.R464   1934

14285   REYNOLDS.   The Peter Reynolds family of Lawrence county, Pennsylvania, by Joseph B. Reynolds.   Ann Arbor, Mich., Planographed by Edwards brothers, inc., 1940.   2 p. l., 46 p. illus. (map, col. coat of arms) 21 cm. 40-11986.   CS71.R464   1940

14286   REYNOLDS.   The Rennolds - Reynolds family of England and Virginia, 1530-1948.   By Stephen Frederick Tillman.   Washington, 1948.   vii, 255 p. ports., coat of arms. 28 cm. 57-58313.
                                                                                                 CS71.R464   1948

14287   REYNOLDS.   The Reynolds family of Dayton.   By Robert Davis Hughes.   Dayton, Reynolds & Reynolds Co., 1949.   87 p. illus., ports., geneal. tables. 26 cm. Includes bibliographies. 50-11729.
                                                                                                 CS71.R464   1949

14288   REYNOLDS.   Christopher Reynolds and his descendants.   By Stephen Frederick Tillman.   Chevy Chase, Md., 1959.   464 p. ports., col. coat of arms. 28 cm. Cover title: Reynolds family, 1530-1959. 61-37635.   CS71.R464   1959

14289   REYNOLDS.   Reynolds Family Association.   Annual.   New York (etc.) Press of the De-Vinne-Brown Corp. (etc.)   v. in   illus., ports. 23-25 cm. First reunion held in 1892; no reports were published for 1st-7th reunion (1892-97) Many vols. are combined issues. Title varies: -1915, 1919-20, Annual reunion. - 1916-18, 1921-22, Annual report. 10-4377 rev.   CS71.R4633

REYNOLDS.   See also: CHESTER, 1955   PETTY, BX5195.T5B6
                          COLBY, 1880   PIERCE, 1895
                          CONKLING, 1909   RUNNELLS, 1873
                          EATON, 1900a   SCISM, 1942
                          EDGCUMBE, CS438.E4   No. 430 - Adventurers of purse, etc.
                          EPPERSON, 1931   No. 3509 - Orange county.

REZIN.   See HOLCOMB, 1961

RHAMY.   See REMEY.

14290   RHEA.   Ray-Rhea: a family book of history and genealogy for Rhea and related families, by Joseph C. Rhea, Jr. (Naperville? Ill.) 1969.   ix, 360, xlvi p. illus., facsims., ports. 23 cm. Pages 350-360 blank for notes. 76-6345 MARC.
CS71. R468   1969

RHEA.   See also No. 516 - Notable southern families vol. 2

14291   RHEES.   Rev. Morgan John Rhys, "The Welsh Baptist hero of civil and religious liberty of the 18th century."   By John T. Griffith ... Lansford, Pa., Leader job print, 1899.   4 p. l., (7)-126 p. 19 x 15 cm. "Family records: Rhees family, Loxley family, Lowry family": p. 74-80. 99-2414 rev.
BX6495. R53G7

RHEINBOLDT.   See REINBOLD.

RHEM.   See PERRY, 1946

RHEMY.   See REMEY.

RHINELANDER.   See LISPENARD, E171. A53 v. 14

RHOADS.   See: MAGINET, 1961
                         RHODES.

14292   RHODES.   History of the Rhodes family. (n. p., n. d.)   1 l. 27½ cm. 40M3358T.
CS71. R475

14293   RHODES.   Pedigree of the family of Rhodes, of New Zealand, recorded in the Heralds' college, in the register marked Norfolk XI., folio 222.   Compiled and edited by Fretwell W. Hoyle ... Sheffield, Pawson and Brailsford, printers, 1865.   6 p. 27 cm. Title vignette; interleaved. 2-26593.
CS439. R5

14294   RHODES.   Genealogy, history and traditions of Thomas Rhodes (1695? - 1761?) and his descendants, collected and edited by Thomas Willett Rhodes ... Syracuse, N. Y., Mason press, 1898.   56 p. illus. (ports.) 23½ cm. 40-2266.
CS71. R475   1898

14295   RHODES.   The Rhodes family in America.   Pub. by Nelson Osgood Rhoades.   v. 1, no. 1 -   June 1919 -   Los Angeles, Cal., 1919 -   no. fold. geneal. tab. 23 cm. triennially. 20-2614.
CS71. R475   1919-

14296   RHODES.   Ancestral lineages of Nelson Osgood Rhoades and Frances James (Brown) Rhoades ... Reprint from the Colonial families of the United States of America, volume VII. (New York, Boston, The Grafton press) 1920.   cover-title, 21 p. illus. (coat of arms) 25½ cm. Copyright 1920 by Nelson Osgood Rhoades. Contains also the Richmond, Osgood and Moulthrop families.   21-2416.
CS71. R475   1920

14297   RHODES.   My ancestry, by Thomas L. Rhoads ... Reading, Pa., Reading eagle press, 1938.   122 p. 21 cm. 38-20792.
CS71. R475   1938

14298   RHODES.   Genealogy of the Rhodes family.   By Charles Dudley Rhodes. (n. p., 194-)   1 v. 29 cm. Title from label mounted on cover. A collection of genealogical material, photographs, newspaper clippings, holograph letters, etc. 49-58281 *.
CS71. R475

14299   RHODES.   Genealogy of Zachariah Rhodes and his wife, Joanna Arnold.   By Sarelia Arthur Rhodes.   Cromwell, Conn., 1953.   1 card. 7½ x 12½ cm. Microprint copy of typescript. Collation of the original" 21 p. illus., facsim., geneal. table. 28 cm. Micp 58-64.
Microcard CS71

14300   RHODES.   The Rhodes family in America; a genealogy and history, including Rhodes coats of arms, sketch of the English family, immigrants to America, charts, and other illustrations, from 1497 to the present day. (1st ed.) By Howard Jacklin Rhodes. New York, Greenwich Book Publishers,

14300 continued: (1959)   525 p. illus., ports., maps, coats of arms, facsims.   24 cm.   "Five hundred copies ... printed."
Bibliographical foot-notes.   59-8018.

CS71.R475   1959

RHODES.   See also: HAYNES, 1893
                       HILL, 1907
                       MAULSBY, 1909
                       TREES, 1960
                       WENTWORTH, DA690.B24W6
                       No. 3509 - Orange county.

RHORER,   See HOUSER, 1910

RHUE.   See AREW.

RHYNE.   See HOFFMAN, 1915

RIALL.   See PHIPPS, 1894

14301   RIBAS.   ... Biografía del general José Félix Ribas, primer teniente de Bolívar en 1813 y
1814 (época de la guerra á muerte) Madrid, Editorial-América (1918?)   302 p. 22½ cm. (Biblioteca
Ayacucho ... (xxiv) "Genealogía de los Ribas": p. 296-298. "Bolívar en Casacoima": p. (299)-302. 19-4288.

F2324.R48

RIBBLE.   See BUCHANAN, 1929

14302   RIBLET.   Descendants of Christian Riblet, and his son Bartholomew Riblet, and genealogical
family history, collected and compiled 1925, by David Franklin Shull and Laura H. S. Shull.   Philadelphia, Pa. (1925)   37 p. 23 cm. 28-23910.   CS71.R486   1925

14303   RICARD.   ... La vie d'un avocat jurisconsulte au XVII siècle, J. - M. Ricard, 1622-1678,
Par Pierre Leborgne ... (et) René Largillière ... Paris, Champion; Beauvais, Imprimerie départe-
mentale, 1920.   xv, 123 p., 1 l. 25½ cm. (Publications de la Société académique de l'Oise. Documents. t. v) "Les Ricard à
Beauvais": p. (1)-8. "Bibliographie des oeuvres de Ricard": p. xv. Bibliographical foot-notes. 23-13996.   DC130.R5L4

RICAUD.   See CROSLAND, 1958

14304   RICE.   A genealogical history of the Rice family: descendants of Deacon Edmund Rice, who
came from Berkhamstead, England, and settled at Sudbury, Massachusetts, in 1638 or 9; with an
index ... By Andrew Henshaw Ward ... Boston, C. B. Richardson, 1858.   viii, 379 p. 24 cm. 9-13641.

CS71.R496   1858

14305   RICE.   Charlemont as a plantation.   An historical discourse at the centennial anniversary of
the death of Moses Rice, the first settler of the town, delivered at Charlemont, Mass., June 11, 1855.
By Joseph White.   Boston, Press of T. R. Marvin & son, 1858.   48 p. 23 cm. Descendants of Moses Rice: p. 45-46.
1-11289.   F74.C3W5

14306   RICE.   The fourth annual meeting of the Hench, Dromgold, Hartman, Rice and Ickes re-union.
Groff's park, Perry County, Pennsylvania.   On Thursday, August 9th, 1900.   (New Bloomfield, 1900?)
16 p. 18½ cm. Signed Rev. Vernon Rice. Cover-title: History of the Rice or Reiss family. 1-3405.

CS71.R496   1900

14307   RICE.   Exercises held at the dedication of a memorial to Major Jonas Rice, the first perm-
anent settler of Worcester, Mass., on Wednesday, Oct. 7, 1903, and at the reunion of the descendants
of Edmund Rice, who settled in Sudbury, Mass., in 1639, held in Salisbury hall, Worcester, Mass., on
the afternoon of the same day.   Worcester, Mass. (Press of C. Hamilton) 1903.   iv, (5)-72 p. front., pl.,
ports. 26½ cm. Reprinted from the Proceedings of the Worcester society of antiquity. 15-20666.   CS71.R496   1903

14308   RICE.   (The ancestry and descendants of John Rice, 1646-1781) compiled from town records
by Henry Byron Phillips. (n. p.) 1903.   geneal. tab. illus. (coat of arms) 41½ x 55 cm. Blue print. 25-21369.

CS71.R496   1903a

14309   RICE.   Descendants of Joseph Rice of Conway, Massachusetts ... Prepared by Rev. Edwin B. Rice, M. A.   New York City, 1904.   28 p. pl., ports. 23 cm. 5-447.   CS71. R496   1904

14310   RICE.   The story of the Rice boys, captured by the Indians, August 8, 1704, as written by Rev. Ebenezer Parkman, May, 1769.   (Westborough, Mass.) Westborough historical society, 1906.   6 p., 1 l. front. 20½ cm. 19-20104.   E87. R49

14311   RICE.   Conway, Mass., and the Rice family.   By the Rev. Edwin B. Rice ... New York, 1909.   49 p. plates, ports. 23 cm. 11-21015.   CS71. R496   1909

14312   RICE.   Descendants of Benjamin Rice, of Conway, Mass.   By the Rev. Edwin B. Rice ... New York, 1909.   35 p. pl. 23 cm. Title vignette (coat of arms) 11-21732.   CS71. R496   1909a

14313   RICE.   By the name of Rice; an historical sketch of Deacon Edmund Rice, the pilgrim (1594-1663) founder of the English family of Rice in the United States; and of his descendants to the fourth generation.   Done briefly by omitting some 15000 names that can be had upon application to the author. By Charles Elmer Rice ... Alliance, O., Press of The Williams printing co., 1911.   96, (2) p., 1 l. 19½ cm. "Limited edition." Coat of arms of William Rice, 1555, on loose leaf. 11-1896.
    CS71. R496   1911

14314   RICE.   ... Descendants of Mary Ann Rice and Mordica Ladd to 1915.   Valhalla, N. Y. (1915) geneal. tab. illus. (coat of arms) 76 x 53½ cm. Compiled by Earl C. L. Van Wert. At head of chart: "XXXVIII generations." 17-24550.
    CS71. R496   1915

14315   RICE.   Koamalu; a story of pioneers on Kauai, and of what they built in that island garden, by Ethel M. Damon ... Honolulu, Priv. print. (Honolulu star-bulletin press) 1931.   2 v. fronts., illus. (incl. facsims.) plates, ports., maps. 23½ cm. Paged continuously. Preface signed: Ethel Moseley Damon (and) Mary Dorothea Rice Isenberg. Contents. - v. 1. Hannah Maria Rice.   Early settlers on Kauai. - v. 2. Paul Isenberg. 32-7355.   DU629. K3D3

14316   RICE.   Short biographical history of Leonard G. Rice and family, by John S. White and Ethellynn R. White.   (Santa Monica, Calif., Press of D. C. Freeman, c. 1938)   32 p. 23 cm. 38-17343.
    CS71. R496   1938

14317   RICE.   Edmund Rice and his family, by Elsie Hawes Smith.   Written for the Edmund Rice (1638) association, inc.   (Boston, The Meador press) 1938.   100 p. 21 cm. Bibliographical references in fore- word. 38-24162.   CS71. R496   1938a

14318   RICE.   Colonel William Rice and Wealthy Cottrell, his wife.   A record of their descendants and notes regarding their ancestors.   (By Albert Rathbone) (New York, N. Y., Press of B. H. Tyrrel) 1938.   3 p. l., 3-118 p., 1 l. 25 cm. Blank pages for "Memoranda" interspersed. "Foreword" gives sources. 39-12248.
    CS71. R496   1938b

14319   RICE.   We sought the wilderness.   By Claton Silas Rice.   (Seattle? 1949)   257 p. coat of arms. 15 cm. 51-22664.   CS71. R496   1949

14320   RICE.   Rice family.   By Mary Olive Eddy.   (n. p., 195-?)   41 l. illus. 29 cm. Compiled by Mary O. Eddy, based largely on material prepared by Nancy L. Coulter Eddy. 63-5343.   CS71. R496   1950z

14321   RICE.   More about those Rices.   By Elsie Hawes Smith.   Boston, Meador Pub. Co. (1954) 109 p. 21 cm. 54-41974.   CS71. R496   1954

14322   RICE.   A genealogical history of the Rice family: descendants of Deacon Edmund Rice, who came from Berkhamstead, England, and settled at Sudbury, Massachusetts, in 1638 or 9; with an index ... By Andrew Henshaw Ward.   Boston, C. B. Richardson, 1858. (n. p., Edmund Rice (1638) Associa- tion, 1958)   viii, 379 p. 24 cm. 59-31109.   CS71. R496   1958

14323   RICE.   William Rice of Frederick County, Maryland, and some of his descendants.   Some historical notes on Jefferson, Maryland, incorporated in 1832 from the towns of New Town (Trap) and New Freedom.   By Millard Milburn Rice.   Walkersville, Md., 1962.   19, 15, 2 l. map, plans. 28 cm. Cover title. 63-30236.   CS71. R496   1962

14324   RICE.   The story of Marcellus Moss Rice and his Big Valley kinsmen.   By John Rice Irwin. Montevallo, Ala., Printed by the Times Print. Co., c. 1963.   161 p. illus., ports., geneal. table. 24 cm. Bibliographical references included in "Footnotes" (p.159-161) 64-1703.   CS71. R496   1963

RICE.   See also: BENT, 1903   HENCH, 1913
                      BROMWELL, 1910   KING, 1956
                      CALHOUN, 1957   NEWBOLT, 1895
                      CLARK, 1906   REMINGTON, 1960
                      CROCKER, 1923   RYLE, 1961
                      DAVIS, 1959

14325   RICH.   Genealogy;   Descendants of Jonathan Rich ...   Prepared by George Rich.   Columbus, O., Press of Nitschke brothers, 1892.   1 p. l., (5)-39 p. 20½ cm. 9-13642.
                                                                        CS71. R5   1892

14326   RICH.   ... Richard Rich of Dover Neck, by Shebnah Rich.   Yarmouthport, Mass., C. W. Swift, 1913.   cover-title, 7 p. 25½ cm. (Library of Cape Cod history & genealogy, no. 56) 17-6140.
                                                                        CS71. R5   1913

14327   RICH.   Early Rich history and ancestry of Jonathan Rich, jr., Ft. Covington, N. Y., prepared by George Rich.   Cleveland, O., 1922.   46 p. 21 cm. Title vignette: coat of arms. 23-5453.
                                                                        CS71. R5   1922

14328   RICH.   Pioneer life in Ashtabula county, by Joseph A. Howells.   (In Ohio archaeological and historical quarterly. Columbus, O., 1927. 23½ cm. vol. XXXVI, p. 551-562) Includes an account of the Rich family. 31-17615.
                                                                        F486. O51 vol. 36

14329   RICH.   History of the first 100 years in Woolrich, by M. B. Rich.   (Williamsport, Pa., The Grit publishing co.) 1930.   6 p. l., (11)-233, (3) p. front., illus., plates, ports. 24 cm. An account of the Woolrich woolen mills and the Rich family. 30-21656.   TS1615. U6 R5

14330   RICH.   Rathbun-Rich and allied families; a manuscript covering the ancestry of Dyer Dana and Susan Rathbun who settled at Howard, Steuben County, New York, in the year 1816.   By Frederick Rathbun Townroe.   (Harrisburg, Pa., 1947)   33 l. 28 cm. Caption title. Typewritten (carbon copy) 50-22619.
                                                                        CS71. R234   1947

14331   RICH.   The Riches of Reading.   By Paul Rich.   (n. p., 195-?)   (4) l. 28 cm. 59-33193.
                                                                        CS71. R5   1950z

14332   RICH.   Eri Rich family tree: Ancestors and descendants to and from Chester County, Pennsylvania; Guilford and Randolph Counties, N. C.; Wayne County, Indiana; Hamilton County, Indiana; Grant County, Indiana.   Prefaced with an account of Rich family in England.   By Everett Eri Thomas. Indianapolis, John Woolman Press, 1963.   63 l. group port., facsims. 30 cm. 63-24439.
                                                                        CS71. R5   1963

RICH.   See also AUSTIN, 1968

14333   RICHARD.   The Richard genealogy; being a record of Charles and Jacob Richard, and all their known descendants, by Charles J. Berry.   Minneapolis, Minn., The author, 1926.   iv, 176 p. front., pl., port. 23½ cm. Autographed from type-written copy. "Authorities cited": p. 157. 26-12185.   CS71. R512   1926

RICHARD.   See also: DUNHAM, 1956
                         SCHMIDT, 1899

14334   RICHARDS.   The life and time of Giles Richards (1820-1860) by Ophia D. Smith.   Columbus, O., The Ohio state archaeological and historical society, 1936.   xii, 130 p. front. (port.) 23½ cm. (Half-title: (Ohio state archaeological and historical society) Ohio historical collections. vol. VI) "Based upon a manuscript collection found in the old Richards home ... now in the Library of Miami university at Oxford, Ohio." - Editorial introd. 37-27720 rev.   F486. O526 no. 6

14335   RICHARDS.   Genealogy; the James Francis Richards branch of a Richards family of New England, that of Edward Richards, Dedham, Massachusetts, 1635-1684.   By Arthur Wescate Richards. (Sarasota, Fla., Star printing company, 1942)   100 (i. e. 106) p. incl. illus. (incl. coat of arms) plates, ports. (part mounted) maps (part fold.) 23½ cm. Compiled by Arthur Wescate Richards ... and Benjamin Richards. "150 copies." Includes four mounted errata slips. "Bibliography and sources": p. 5.   43-6118.
CS71. R5122   1942

14336   RICHARDS.   The descendants of the Richards families of Jackson County, Indiana.   By Aute Richards.   Tucson, Ariz., 1961.   58 l. col. coat of arms. 28 cm. Bibliography: leaves 53-54. 62-36487.
CS71. R5122   1961

14337   RICHARDS.   Family empire in Jersey iron; the Richards enterprises in the pine barrens (by) Arthur D. Pierce.   New Brunswick, N. J., Rutgers University Press (1964)   xvii, 286 p. illus., facsims., maps, ports. 22 cm. Bibliography: p. (275)-278.   64-24737.
CS71. R5122   1964

RICHARDS.   See also: BASSETT, 1926   HOGG, 1959
                        BATEMAN, 1952   JONES, 1934
                        DUPUY, 1910   SMITH, 1946a
                        GARDINER, 1960 STOUT, 1960
                        HARRISON, 1910a

14338   RICHARDSON.   The annals of the Cleveland Richardsons and their descendants, compiled from family manuscripts, etc.   By George Richardson ... New Castle-upon-Tyne, 1850.   iv, 92 p. 19½ cm. Not published. 10-15894.
CS439. R53

14339   RICHARDSON.   History of a branch of the Richardson family, from 1682 to 1860, in the United States.   New York, Dexter & co., 1860.   17 p. front. (port.) pl. 24 cm. Edited with additions by Samuel Richardson from material gathered by David Thomas, 1855. 18-374.
CS71. R52   1860

14340   RICHARDSON.   Collectanea Bradfordiana: a collection of papers on the history of Bradford, and the neighborhood.   Collated, and edited with notes, by Abraham Holroyd.   Saltaire, A. Holroyd, 1873.   4 p. l., 184 p. front. 22 cm. Title vignette: plan of Bradford. Contains the pedigrees of the Sharps of Little Horton and the Richardsons of Bierley. 15-8490.
DA690. B7H6

14341   RICHARDSON.   The Richardson memorial, comprising a full history and genealogy of the posterity of the three brothers, Ezekiel, Samuel, and Thomas Richardson, who came from England, and united with others in the foundation of Woburn, Massachusetts, in the year 1641, of John Richardson, of Medfield, 1679, of Amos Richardson, of Boston, 1640, of Edward and William Richardson, of Newbury, 1643, with notices of Richardsons in England and elsewhere ... By John Adams Vinton ... Portland, Me., Printed for subscribers by B. Thurston & co., 1876.   xv, 944 p. front., ports. 24 cm. 9-13643.
CS71. R52   1876
Microfilm 11455

14342   RICHARDSON.   Notes on the Richardson and Russell families.   By James Kimball ... From the Essex institute historical collections, vol. XVI.   Salem, Printed at the Salem press, 1880.   39 p. 24 cm. Issued as a continuation to the "Richardson memorial" in the line of Moses Richardson, 1722-1775. 9-13639.
CS71. R52   1880

14343   RICHARDSON.   Chronicles of St. Mark's Parish, Santee circuit, and Williamsburg township, South Carolina.   1731-1885.   By James M. Burgess, M. D.   Columbia, S. C., C. A. Calvo, jr., printer, 1888.   108 p. 21 cm. 2-25794.
F277. S2B9
—— (Index) ... (n. p., 19 -)   1 p. l., 16 numb. l. 25½ x 20½ cm. Type-written copy.   F277. S2B9   Index.

14344   RICHARDSON.   Records of a Quaker family: the Richardsons of Cleveland.   With portraits of Isabel Casson, Jonathan Priestman, and John Richardson Procter.   By Anne Ogden Boyce.   London, S. Harris & co., 1889.   xii, 298 p. front., port. 25½ cm. 2-11419.
CS439. B53   1889

14345   RICHARDSON.   ... A genealogical record of families in the descending line of Samuel Richardson born in England about 1610, through ten generations to the present date.   Comp. by Joseph Hammond.   Keene, N. H., Darling & company, 1896.   22 p. 18½ cm. At head of title: 1610. 1896. 9-13640.
CS71. R52   1896

14346   RICHARDSON.   Genealogy of Harry Alden Richardson of Dover, Delaware.   Compiled by J. Granville Leach, president of the American genealogical company.   (Dover, Printed by J. Kirk & son) 1897.   3 p. l., 222, (4) p.   18½ cm.   26-16555.   CS71.R52   1897

14346a   RICHARDSON.   Supplement to the Richardson memorial; prepared by Isaac Richardson and Franklin Richardson ... Portland, Me., The Thurston print, 1898.   34 p. 25½ cm. 3-22487.
CS71.R52   1898

14347   RICHARDSON.   The Richardsons of West Mill, Herts, England, and Woburn in New England.   (By) Walter Kendall Watkins.   Boston (Press of D. Clapp & son) 1903.   6 p. front. 24½ cm. Cover-title: Supplement.   Richardson ancestry.   Reprinted from the New-England historical and genealogical register for July 1903, p. 297-300, with title: Some early emigrants from Herts, England.   17-9735.   CS71.R52   1903

14348   RICHARDSON.   Richardson-De Priest family, by the Rev. Robt. Douglas Roller, D. D.   (Charleston, W. Va., The Tribune printing co., 1905)   50 p. 21½ cm. 5-36488.   CS71.R52   1905

14349   RICHARDSON.   Amos Richardson of Boston and Stonington, with a contribution to the history of his descendants and the allied families of Gilbert, Edwards, Yarrington, and Rust ... By Rosell L. Richardson ... 2d ed.   New York, The author, 1906.   147 p. 24 cm. 7-11.   CS71.R52   1906

14350   RICHARDSON.   Captain Edward Richardson; a memorial, with genealogical records of some of his ancestors and descendants, by Elizabeth Wills Vernon Radcliffe.   Privately printed.   (Salem, Mass., Newcomb & Gauss, printers) 1923.   2 p. l., 81 p. front., plates, ports. 25 cm. 24-1757.
CS71.R52   1923

14351   RICHARDSON.   The book of Richardson, by Mrs. Pattie Stone ... Rome, Ga., 1926.   (Washington, 1941)   12 l.   28 cm.   Caption title.   A type-written copy with introduction and explanatory foot-notes by George Magruder Battey.   With this is bound: Battey, George Magruder.   A clue in the solution of the 150-year-old Ga. - S.C. Mayo-Terrell mystery.   Washington, D.C., 1941.   42-20960.   CS71.R52   1926

14352   RICHARDSON.   The story of the Richardson family, by Mary E. Colby.   Dallas, Or., Printed by Itemizer-observer, 1929.   2 p. l., 7-22 p. illus. (ports.) 23 cm. "Personal recollections, by Earle Richardson": p. 15-22.   34-32109 rev.   CS71.R52   1929a

14353   RICHARDSON.   Thomas Richardson of South Shields, Durham County, England, and his descendants in the United States of America.   Compiled by Mary Thomas Seaman ... New York (T. A. Wright, inc.) 1929.   241 p. plates, ports., map, facsims., fold. geneal. tables, 2 coats of arms (incl. front.) 24½ cm. "No. 39." Contains "References".   Contains also the Allen, Cooper, Elliott, Fitzwater, Gibbons, Growdon, Hoskins, Howell, Husband, Nevins, Parry, Randolph, Worrell and Yarnall families.   30-126.   CS71.R52   1929

14354   RICHARDSON.   The Richardson family, pioneers of Oregon and Utah; an account of the lives of the descendants of Shadrach and Betsy Richardson of Kentucky compiled from the family traditions and records covering the migration of its members from Kentucky to Illinois, Iowa, Oregon, and Utah.   (Dallas, Polk co., Or., Printed by the Itemizer-observer, 1940)   39 p. incl. front., illus. (ports.) 23 cm.   First published in 1929 under title, "The story of the Richardson family, by Mary E. Colby."   The present edition includes "Personal recollections, by Earle Richardson,"   "The Richardson family in Utah, by Mrs. Sarah E. R. Burgin," and other accounts of the family.   41-1647.
CS71.R52   1940

14355   RICHARDSON.   (Genealogical data on the Richardson family.   By George Magruder Battey. Washington?, D.C., 1941?)   2 l. 28½ cm.   Type-written.   41M3437T.   CS71.R52   1941

14356   RICHARDSON.   The book of Richardson, by Mrs. Pattie Stone ... Rome, Ga., 1926 (Washington, 1941)   12 l. 28 cm.   Caption title.   A type-written copy with introduction and explanatory foot-notes by George Magruder Battey.   With this is bound: Battey, George Magruder.   A clue in the solution of the 150-year old Ga.-S.C. Mayo-Terrell mystery.   Washington, D.C., 1941.   42-20960.   CS71.R52   1926

14357   RICHARDSON.   Foster-Richardson genealogical lines.   (By George Richardson Foster. Boston, 1944)   1 v. 25 cm.   Cover-title.   Consists of 1 leaf (foreword) and the Dec. 1944 issue of the New England historical and genealogical register, the article by G. R. Foster on the Foster-Richardson genealogical lines being p. 361-366.   "Additional Richardson data," dated Dec. 1944: leaf inserted.   Includes "References."   45-16769.   CS71.F756   1944

14358   RICHARDSON.   Descendants of William Richardson (1620-1657) immigrant ancestor of Newbury, Massachusetts and his wife, Elizabeth Wiseman.   By Helen (Richardson) Kluegel.   Honolulu, 1959.   unpaged.   30 cm.   61-40566.   CS71. R52   1959

14359   RICHARDSON.   Collateral lines of descendants of William Richardson of Newbury, Mass. By Helen (Richardson) Kluegel.   (n. p.) 1960.   unpaged.   29 cm.   61-37624.   CS71. R52   1960

14360   RICHARDSON.   The Richardson family; a Richardson family genealogy.   By Fontella Catherine (Richardson) Abbott.   (Boise, Idaho, 1964)   1304, (54) p. illus., coats of arms, ports. 29 cm.   On spine: 1774-1964.   65-2722.   CS71. R52   1964

14361   RICHARDSON.   Richardson-Hartley-Arender and related families; a list of the known descendants of Elijah Richardson of Tennessee and Frank Hartley of South Carolina, both of whom moved to Mississippi about 1815.   Compiled by Thomas F. Richardson.   (n. p., 1969)   399 p. illus., ports. 24 cm. 71-7933 MARC.   CS71. R52   1969

14362   RICHARDSON.   Lamb-Parker-Richardson families.   A collection of MSS, genealogical notes, deeds, etc.   In vertical file.   Ask reference librarian for this material.

14363   RICHARDSON.   (Supplement to Helen Richardson Kluegel's Collateral Lines of Descendants of William Richardson of Newbury, Mass., 1960.)   In vertical file.   Ask reference librarian for this material.

RICHARDSON.   See also:

BOWMAN, 1940	HILDRETH, 1950	SMALL, 1905
BROWN, 1929	HORTON, CS439. H754	SMITH, 1878a
CARD, E171. A53 vol. 20	IRONMONGER, 1956	VINTON, 1858a
CLIFTON, 1935	LAWSON, 1903	WATKINS, 1957
DARROW, 1933	POTTER, 1957	WILSON, BX7791. R5
DUPUY, 1910	SEAMAN, 1927	YAWKEY, 1939
FOSTER, 1944		

14364   RICHCREEK.   The family and descendants of David and Mary Penn, Richcreek.   By Bernard Richcreek.   (Jackson Heights? N. Y.) 1954.   149, 6 l. 29 cm.   "The family and descendants of Henry George and Anna Ufur Stark (by) Bernard Richcreek, 1954": 6 leaves at end.   55-38569.   CS71. R525   1954

RICHENDERFER.   See KLINE, 1960

RICHER-LAFLÈCHE.   See GOUIN, CS90. G7

14365   RICHMAN.   The Richman family, variously spelled Riechmann, Riechman, Richmann and Richman ... compiled by Carl L. Richman.   Tipton, Ind., 1927.   1 p. l., (46) p., 2 l. 29 cm.   Autographed from type-written copy.   Two leaves at end left blank for additional record.   27-11106.   CS71. R53   1927

RICHMANN.   See RICHMAN.

14366   RICHMOND.   The Richmond family 1594-1896, and pre-American ancestors, 1040-1594; by Joshua Bailey Richmond ... with facsimiles of signatures, commissions, and other documents ... Boston, The compiler, 1897.   xxiii p., 1 l., 614 p. front., plates (part col.) port., facsims. 28½ cm.   9-13638.   CS71. R533   1897

14367   RICHMOND.   Richmond family records, by Henry I. Richmond ... London, Adlard & son, limited, 1933 -   2 v. plates, map, plan. 22 cm.   34-35351.   CS71. R533   1933

14368   RICHMOND.   Genealogy of a branch of the Richmond family which came from Rhode Island to Ohio and settled in Amherst Township, Lorain Co., Ohio.   By Claude Charles Hamel.   Amherst, 1949. 9 l. 27 cm. Typewritten.   "References": leaf 9.   50-25465.   CS71. R533   1949

14369   RICHMOND.   Richmond family in vertical file.   Ask reference librarian for this material.

RICHMOND. See also: BAYLISS, 1875
PIERCE, 1874
RHODES, 1920
YERBURGH, 1912
No. 1547 - Cabell county.

RICKARD. See ELDRIDGE, 1925

14370   RICKARDS.   Rickards of Evenjobb and his descendants.   A family history.   For private circulation.   Cardiff, W. Lewis, printer, 1905.   45 p.   22½ cm.   Title vignette (coat of arms)   Signed: Robert Rickards.
19-3375.
CS459. R5

RICKARDS. See also JENNINGS, 1899

14371   RICKENBACKER.   The inspiration and lives of Elizabeth Basler Rickenback and William Rickenbacker.   By Marian Pflaum Darby.   (Columbus?) 1963.   24 p.   illus., ports., map, facsim., geneal.
tables.   26 cm.   64-1166.
CS71. R536   1963

14372   RICKER.   A brief history of the Riker family, from their first emigration to this county in the year 1638, to the present time.   By James Riker, jun. ...   New York, D. Fanshaw, printer, 1851.
19 p.   illus. (coat of arms)   22½ cm.   6-20513.
CS71. R54   1851

14373   RICKER.   The Riker family.   By James Riker.   (In his The annals of Newtown, in Queens county, New-York
...   New-York, 1852.   23 cm.   p. 299-315.   illus. (coat of arms)   31-575.
F129. N75R5

14374   RICKER.   Records of some of the descendants of George and Maturin Ricker, who were early at Dover, N.H.: and who were killed by the Indians, June 4, 1706.   Compiled by William B. Lapham
...   Augusta, Me., Sprague, Owen & Nash, printers, 1877.   1 p. l., 20 p.   front. (port.)   23½ cm.   9-13637.
CS71. R54   1877

RICKER. See also: LOVELL, 1940
RIKER.

14375   RICKETSON.   William Ricketson, William Ricketson, jr., and their descendants, by Grace Williamson Edes.   Boston, Priv. print., 1917-32.   2 v.   24 cm.   "Edition 100 copies." - (v.1), p. (ii)   "Edition 50
copies." - v.2, p. (ii)   Vol. II has title: William Ricketson and his descendants.   18-14384.
CS71. R542 1917-32

RICKETTS. See: LONG, 1956
No. 1520 - Cabell county.

RICKEY. See DUPUY, 1910

RICKMAN. See PENNEY, 1920

RICKS. See: HENDRICKS, 1963
RIX.

RICKSECKER. See CLEWELL, 1907

RIDDELL. See RIDDLE.

RIDDICK. See DINKINS, 1908

14376   RIDDLE.   A genealogical sketch of the Riddell family, including a list of the descendants of the three brothers, Hugh, Gawn and Robert, who came to America in 1737.   By W. P. Riddell ... New
Orleans, 1852.   44 p., 1 l.   23 cm.   35-21363.
CS71. R543   1852

14377   RIDDLE.   History of the ancient Ryedales, and their descendants in Normandy, Great Britain, Ireland, and America, from 860 to 1884.   Comprising the genealogy and biography for about one thousand years of the families of Riddell, Riddle, Ridlon, Ridley, etc. ... By G. T. Ridlon ... Manchester, N.H., The author, 1884.   x, 786 p. front., plates (part col.) ports. 25 cm. 9-13823.

CS71. R543   1884

14378   RIDDLE.   Old Newbury and the pioneers.   By the author of "The hunter of the Shagreen" (Albert Gallatin Riddle) ... (For a few friends) (Cleveland, O., W. W. Williams, 1885)   72 p. 14 cm. "Inscription", containing information about Riddle family, signed: A.G.R.   In verse.   30-14653.

PS2699. R605

14379   RIDDELL.   Robert Burns and the Riddell family.   By J. Maxwell Wood ... Dumfries, Scot., R. Dinwiddie, 1922.   4 p. 1., 172 p., 1 1., vii p., 1 1. front., 9 pl., 2 port. 20½ cm. 24-2861.

PR4333. W6

14380   RIDDLE.   Riddle family of Maryland.   In vertical file.   Ask reference librarian for this material.

RIDDLE.   See also: AKERS, 1957
BRENDLINGER, 1941
SELDEN, 1911
THOMAS, 1914

RIDENBAUGH.   See HALL, 9143a

14381   RIDENOUR.   Autobiography of Peter D. Ridenour with genealogies of the Ridenour and Beatty families.   By Peter Darcuss Ridenour.   Kansas City, Hudson press, 1908.   323 p. front., plates, ports. 24 cm. 35-16391.

CS71. R55   1908

14382   RIDEOUT.   Ancestors of Nathaniel Rideout, 1762-1795, Cumberland Co., Maine.   By Helen (Richardson) Kluegel.   Honolulu, 1963.   1 v. (various pagings) 28 cm.   "Book 5 (of a series founded on the author's 16 great-great-grandparents) family group V, Abraham (1) Rideout, progenitor, arrival date uncertain."   65-66469.

CS71. R555   1963

14383   RIDEOUT.   Rideout family record.   The first ancestor was Abraham Rideout, who came from England to America at a date unascertained.   In vertical file.   Ask reference librarian for this material.

14384   RIDER.   ... Descendants of William Rider, of Cambridge, Watertown, and Sherborn, Mass. (by) Henry F. Ryther.   Newport, Vt., 1903.   geneal. tab. 60 x 23 cm. 31-20882.

CS71. R56   1903

14385   RIDER.   ... Genealogies by James W. Hawes.   Ryder.   Yarmouthport, Mass., C. W. Swift, 1911.   cover-title, 19 p. 25½ cm. (Library of Cape Cod history & genealogy, no. 98) 12-24999.   CS71. R56   1911

14386   RIDER.   Ryder family of Putnam County, N.Y.   (By Clayton Ryder)   Poughkeepsie, N.Y., Oxford Pub. Co., 1911.   39 p. coat of arms. 23 cm. 50-46409.   CS71. R56   1911a

14387   RIDER.   ... The Rider family of Yarmouth.   Yarmouthport, Mass., C. W. Swift, 1913. cover-title, 6 p. 25 cm. (Library of Cape Cod history & genealogy, no. 66) 17-6134.

CS71. R538   1913

14388   RIDER.   The Rider or Ryder family; notes on the different branches of the family, compiled by E. B. Baldwin.   (n.p., 1925)   1 p. 1., 28 1. 33 cm. Type-written. 26-3103.   CS71. R56   1925

14389   RIDER.   Preliminary materials for a genealogy of the Rider (Ryder) families in the United Sates.   Arranged according to the "Rider trace" system of presentation.   By Fremont Rider.   Middletown, Conn., Godfrey Memorial Library, 1959.   3 v. 26 cm. 59-43174.

CS71. R56   1959

14390   RIDER.   Genealogy of the Rider-White families.   By Minnie Emma (White) Rider.   (n. p., 196-)   1 v. (various pagings) 29 cm. Cover title. 64-5540.   CS71. R56   1960z

14391　RIDER.　The genealogy of Harold M. Ryder and Frances B. Ryder.　By Robert Freese. (Lincoln Park, N.J.)　Oldstyle Press (1967)　1 v. (unpaged) coat of arms, geneal. tables.　23 cm.　125 copies printed. Copy 15.　67-27174.　　　　　　　　　　　　　　　　　　　　　　　　　　　CS71. R56　　　1967

14392　RIDGELY.　Founders of the colonial families of Ridgely, Dorsey, and Greenberry, of Maryland, by Henry Ridgely Evans ... Washington, D.C., Sold by W. H. Lowdermilk & co., 1935. 45 p.　front. (port.) plates, facsim.　24 cm.　35-24882.　　　　　　　　　　CS71. R564　　　1935

14393　RIDGELY.　Garrett county history of pioneer families ... The Ridgely family, by Charles E. Hoye.　(Oakland, Md., 1936)　mounted l.　48 cm.　No. LXVI of a series of articles contibuted to the Mountain democrat.　Reprinted from the issues of Jan. 2 and 9, 1936.　41M3025T.　　　　　　　CS71. R564　　　1936

14394　RIDGELY.　A calendar of Ridgely family letters, 1742-1899, in the Delaware State archives; ed. and comp. by Leon de Valinger, Jr., state archivist, and Virginia E. Shaw, classifier.　Family data supplied by Mrs. Henry Ridgely.　Dover, Del., Pub. priv. by some descendants of the Ridgely family for the Public Archives Commission, 1948 -　　v. illus., ports., facsims.　27 cm.　"Three hundred copies printed."　49-637*.　　　　　　　　　　　　　　　　　　　　　　　CD3159.5. R5A5

14395　RIDGELY.　What them befell; the Ridgelys of Delaware & their circle in colonial & Federal times; letters, 1751-1890.　By Mable Loyd Ridgely.　Portland, Me., Anthoensen Press, 1949. xxi, 427 p.　illus., ports., facsims., geneal. tables.　26 cm.　49-49585*.　　CS71. R565　　　1949

　　　　RIDGELY.　See also DORSEY, 1898

　　　　RIDGEWAY.　See RIDGWAY.

14396　RIDGWAY.　Descent of the Ridgway-Ridgeway family in England and America, by George C. Ridgway.　2d ed.　Evansville, Ind., 1926.　129, (7) p.　illus. (incl. coats of arms)　plates.　20½ cm.　Blank pages for additions (6 at end)　First edition published in 1875.　cf. Pref.　36-12560.　　　　CS71. R565　　　1926

14397　RIDGEWAY.　Family trails across America: Higday, Ridgeway, Gannaway, Benefield, Van Slyck, Warren, Robertson and allied lines.　Hamilton Higday, compiler.　Seattle, Wash., Pigott-Washington press, 1933.　87 p.　illus.　23 cm.　34-17815.　　　　　　CS71. H6365　　　1933

14397a　RIDGEWAY.　Ridgeway Reunion - 1950.　In vertical file.　Ask reference librarian for this material.

　　　　RIDGWAY.　See also:　FIRNSTEN, 1926
　　　　　　　　　　　　　　　HIGDAY, 1933
　　　　　　　　　　　　　　　ROACH, 1951

　　　　RIDLEY.　See RIDDLE, 1884

　　　　RIDLON.　See RIDDLE, 1884

　　　　RIDLOWNA.　In vertical file under PRANKE family.　Ask reference librarian for this material.

14398　RIEGEL.　Partial genealogy and history of the Riegel family in America.　By Benjamin Franklin Fackenthall.　(n.p., 1963)　210 l.　illus., port., geneal. tables.　28 cm.　63-37720.
　　　　　　　　　　　　　　　　　　　　　　　　　　　　　　　　　　　　CS71. R566　　　1963

14399　RIEGER.　John Bartholomew Rieger, pioneer minister and physician; biographical sketch with genealogical data, by Ora Merle Hawk Pease ... (Salem, Or., Statesman publishing co., 1946) (23) p.　23½ cm.　"References and authorities": p. (23)　47-22264.　　CT275. R566P4

　　　　RIEHM.　See REAM.

　　　　RIEM.　See REAM.

　　　　RIESE.　See RIES.

RIESEN.   See FRIESEN.

14400   RIESER.   A charted record of the Jacob, Ulrich, and Philip Rieser families in America.   By Nellie Wallace Reeser.   (Indianapolis, 1969)   1100 p.   23 x 37 cm.   Title page, foreword, and index in typescript; records in MS. on printed geneal. forms entitled: One family group records.   74-10620 MARC.   CS71. R5665   1969

14401   RIFE.   John and Mary J. Rife of Greene county, Ohio, their ancestors and descendants, by Geo. W. Rife.   3d ed. rev. by J. Merle Rife.   Richmond, Ind., J. M. Rife, 1935.   5 p. 1., 42 (3) p. illus. (ports.) 23 cm.   Ruled pages for "Addenda" (3 at end)   35-32270.   CS71. R567   1935

RIFE.   See REIFF.

RIFFLE.   See GREENLEE, 1956

RIG.   See RIGGS.

RIGAULD.   See RIGGALL.

14402   RIGBY.   Colonel Alexander Rigby: a sketch of his career and connection with Maine as pro-prietor of the Plough patent and president of the province of Lygonia.   By Charles Edward Banks ... (Portland, Me.) Priv. print., 1885.   57 p.   front. (port.) illus. (map, coats of arms)   23½ x 18 cm.   Title vignette.   "The owners of this patent ... were members of the strange sect ... called the Family of love or Familists ..." - p. 30.   Reprinted from the Maine historical and genealogical recorder.   Fifty copies printed, of which this is no. 37.   Pedigree of Rigby: on slip attached.   21-4365.
F23. R56

RIGBY.   See VENN, 1904

RIGG.   See RIGGS.

14403   RIGGALL.   The family Riggall-Rigauld.   By Robert Marmaduke Riggall.   (London, 1963) (8) p.   geneal. table, ports.   19 cm.   68-52316.   CS439. R54   1963

RIGGIN.   See PEPPER, 1960

RIGGLESWORTH.   See JOLLIFFE, 1893

14404   RIGGS.   Genealogy of the Riggs family, with a number of cognate branches descended from the original Edward through female lines and many biographical outlines, by John H. Wallace.   vol. 1. New York, The author, 1901 -   vii, 147 p.   front. (port.) 24½ cm.   9-13636.   CS71. R57   1901

14405   RIGGS.   The Riggs family of Maryland; a genealogical and historical record, including a study of the several families in England, by John Beverley Riggs.   Baltimore, Md.   (The Lord Balti-more press) 1939.   xx, 534 p., 1 l.   front. (col. coat of arms) plates, ports.   24 cm.   "This edition is limited to 250 copies, book number 85."   Includes bibliography.   39-32212.   CS71. R57   1939

14406   RIGGS.   Our El Dorado, by John Casey Riggs and Jeanette Riggs Roll.   Dos Cabezas, Ariz., c. 1957.   95 p.   ports., coat of arms.   23 cm.   58-27749.   CS71. R57   1957

RIGGS.   See also: ACKLEY, 1960
GOODMAN, 1916
HYNES, 1941
MAY, 1928
MILLET, 1959
QUISENBERRY, 1897

14407   RIGMAYDEN.   The history of the parish of Garstang in the county of Lancaster.   By Lt. -colonel Henry Fishwick ... (Manchester) Printed for the Chetham society, 1878-79.   2 v.   illus. (coat of arms) fold. geneal. tables.   23 cm.   (Added t. -p.: Remains, historical and literary, connected with the palatine counties of Lancaster and Chester.   v. 104-105)   Contains genealogical tables of the Rigmayden, Plesington, Catterall, Brockholes and Whitehead families.   18-3651.
DA670. L19C5

RIKER. See: LAWRENCE, 1923
RICKER.

14408   RILAND. Three hundred years of a family living, being a history of the Rilands of Sutton Coldfield. By the Rev. W. K. Riland Bedford, M. A. Birmingham, Cornish brothers, 1889.
1 p. 1.. ix. (1). 175. (3) p. incl. geneal. tab. front. (fold. map) 3 port. 26½ cm. "Only fifty copies of this edition have been printed ... No. 28." 2-29111.   CS439. R55

RILEY. See: EMISON, 1947
HUNTER, 1959
RANNEY, F104. C8A2

14409   RINEHART. Garrett county history Rinehart family. By Charles E. Hoye. (Oakland, Md., 1934)   1 1. 54 cm. Detached from the Mountain democrat, January 31st, 1935. 38M1242T.   CS71. R574   1934

14410   RINEHART. Rinehart descendants of Johann Georg and Eliza Margretha Reinhard, 1752-1954. Allied families of Anspach, Cox, Dimm, James, Pfoutz, Tibbens, Ulsh. By Glenna (James) Mosgrove. Mansfield, Ill., Mrs. C. A. Mosgrove, c. 1954.   286 p. illus. 28 cm. 55-27375.
CS71. R574   1954

14411   RING. A history of the Ring family, A. D. 1631 to A. D. 1928. (By Clark Lombard Ring) (n. p., 1928?)   (8) p. 23 cm. Author's name on cover. 32-30552.   CS71. R58   1928

14412   RING. The genealogy of the descendants of Jere Foster Ring, and Phebe Ellis of Weld, Maine, published by Harry P. Ring. Wilton, N.H., 1931.   cover-title, (43) p. ports. 15 cm. 33-6866.
CS71. R58   1931

14413   RING. Ancestors of Welding Ring and his wife Ida Malvina Mailler, compiled for Julia Frances Ring as her gift to Welding Ring Ward, Katharine Ring Ward, Giovanni Welding Luzzatto, by Josephine C. Frost. (Brooklyn?) 1935.   356 p. front., plates, ports., facsims. (1 double) 25 cm. "References" at the end of each family group. 36-3775.   CS71. R58   1935

14414   RING. Our family tree. By Beryl Ring. (Tacoma, 1967?)   120, (98) p. illus., facsims., geneal. tables, map, ports. 29 cm. Includes bibliographies. 67-6135.   CS71. R58   1967

RING. See also HOPKINS, 1936

14415   RINGO. Genealogy of the Ringo-Morgan-Bryan family. Comp. by Nat U. Ringo. Revised by Ottis Orr Bongo. Muncie, Ind., 1933.   127 p. Typewritten.   CS71. R584   1934

14416   RINGO. Ringo reunion in print. Society of Ringo descendants in America. v. 1 - Oct. 1934 -   Covington, Ky., 1934 -   v. 31 cm. "This paper is published annually by the Society of Ringo descendants in America." 35-14585.   CS71. R584   1934a

14417   RINKENBACH. The Rinkenbach family in Germany, Lorraine, and the United States. By William Henry Rinkenbach. (n. p.) 1955.   18 1. 29 cm. 61-36178.   CS71. R586   1955

RINTELMANN. See RANDLEMAN.

RINTOUL. See RANTOUL.

14418   RIPLEY. Genealogy of a part of the Ripley family, compiled by H. W. Ripley ... Newark, N.J., A. S. Holbrook, printer, 1867.   iv, 5-48 p. 20 ½ cm. 9-13635.   CS71. R59   1867

14419   RIPLEY. Record of some of the ancestors and descendants of Willis Johnson Ripley (1822-1869) and his wife Delite (Post) Ripley (1829-1900) ... (By) Willis Johnson Ripley, II ... (Grand Rapids, Mich., 1941)   1 p. 1., 26 numb. 1. 28½ cm. Caption title. Reproduced from type-written copy. Bibliography: prelim. leaf. 41-3515.   CS71. R59   1941

RIPLEY. See also GOULD, 1897

14420   RIPPLE.   The Ripple families, 1750-1938.   (By Ned Burton Smith)   (Youngstown, O., 1938)
5 l. 28 cm. Caption title. Mimeographed; additions in manuscript. Signed: Ned Smith. 41-38340.   CS71.R592   1938

14421   RISELING.   A survey of the Riseling family; Anderson Jackson Riseling branch.   By Frank
Addison Orland.   (Centerburg? Ohio, 1961?)   iii, 35, 8, 6 l. mounted illus., geneal. tables, mounted ports. 30 cm.
Title from label mounted on cover. 65-574.   CS71.R593   1961

14421a   RISER.   Riser family in vertical file.   Ask reference librarian for this material.

14422   RISING.   James Rising of Suffield, Conn., and some of his descendants, by Louis Marinus
Dewey.   Boston, New England historic genealogical society, 1909.   11 p. 24½ cm. 10-5043.
                                                               CS71.R594   1909
——— Copy 2.   (In New England historical and genealogical register. Boston, 1909. 24½ cm. v. 63, p. 333-341)
                                                               F1.N56 vol. 63

14423   RISLEY.   The Risley family history, including records of some of the early English Risleys;
a genealogy of the descendants of Richard Risley, of Newtown (Cambridge), Massachusetts (1633), and
of Hartford, Connecticut (1636); an account of the family reunion at Hartford, August 3, 1904, and a
list of the founders of the commonwealth of Connecticut; by Edwin H. Risley ... New York, The
Grafton press, 1909.   7 p. l., (3)-306 p. front., illus., plates, map. 24½ cm. 10-649.
                                                               CS71.R595   1909

       RISLEY.   See also CULEHETH, CS439.C85

       RITCH.   See HOOD, 1960

14424   RITCHIE.   Thomas Ritchie; a study in Virginia politics, by Charles Henry Ambler ...
Richmond, Va., Bell book & stationery co., 1913.   5 p. l., (9)-303, xvi p. plates, 2 port. (incl. front.) 22 cm.
"Genealogy of William Roane and Mary Upshur": p. 301-303. 13-21487.   E340.R6A4

14425   RITCHIE.   The Ritchies in India; extracts from the correspondence of William Ritchie,
1817-1862; and personal reminiscences of Gerald Ritchie, comp. and ed. by Gerald Ritchie ... London, J. Murray, 1920.   xvi, 398 p. front., pl., ports., maps, fold. geneal. tab. 22½ cm. 21-5846.
                                                               CS439.R555

       RITCHIE.   See also: KINSOLVING, 1935
                             SEBOR, 1923
                             TELFORD, 1956

       RITTERHAUSEN.   See RITTENHOUSE.

14426   RITTENHOUSE.   (Ancestors and descendants of William Rittenhouse, 1644-1708, and allied
families. n.p., 189-?)   36 geneal. tables (in portfolio) 63 cm. In manuscript, intended to comprise v. 2 of D.K. Cassel's A genea-
biographical history of the Rittenhouse family. 53-47030.   CS71.R613

14427   RITTENHOUSE.   A genea-biographical history of the Rittenhouse family and all its branches
in America, with sketches of their descendants, from the earliest available records to the present
time, including the birth of Wilhelm in 1644 ... By Daniel K. Cassel ... With an introduction by Alvah
Rittenhouse, M.D.   Vol. 1.   Philadelphia, The Rittenhouse memorial association, 1893.   xlix, 272 p.,
10 l. front., illus., plates (part col.) ports., maps. facsims. 23 cm. "Memoranda for marriages, births, deaths, etc.": 10 l. at end. Bibliography: p. xix. Binder's title: Origin and history of the Rittenhouse family. Vol. 1. Three generations in Europe, 1591 to 1644. Four generations in America, 1644-1825. The author published a supplementary volume under title: The family record of David Rittenhouse, recording his
sisters Esther, Anne and Eleanor ... Norristown, Pa., 1897. 3-24629.   CS71.R613   1893

14428   RITTENHOUSE.   The family record of David Rittenhouse; including his sisters Esther,
Anne and Eleanor.   Also, Benjamin Rittenhouse and Margaret Rittenhouse Morgan.   By Daniel K.
Cassel ... Norristown, Pa., Herald printing and binding rooms, 1897.   139 p. ports. 23 cm. Cover-title:
Family of Matthias Rittenhouse. Supplements the author's Genea-biographical history of the Rittenhouse family, v. 1, Philadelphia, 1893. 3-22496.
                                                               CS71.R613   1897

14429   RITTENHOUSE.   Rittenhouse genealogy debunked (by) Calvin Kephart.   (Washington, c.1939)
8 p. 26 cm.   "Reprinted from National genealogical society quarterly, December, 1938."   42-20519.   CS71.R613   1939

RITTENHOUSE.   See also: HITE, 1960
                                             HOLSTEIN, 1892
                                             LAWSON, 1903
                                             SUTTON, 1935

14430   RITTER.   Family register of George Christian Ritter of Leiningen, Rheinpfalz, Baiern,
Germany, and his descendants from the year of our Lord 1735 to the year 1905, comp. by Philip John
Ritter ... Philadelphia, Walther printing house (1905)   316, (20) p., 1 l. incl. plates, ports. 26 cm.   Blank pages
at end for "Family register continued."   Additions in ms. to 1916.   Added t.-p. and p. (1)-(88) in German.   21-12156.
                                                                                                              CS71.R616   1905

14431   RITTER.   Ritter genealogy.   A record of five generations of the descendants of Daniel Ritter
of Lunenburg, Mass.   By Ezra S. Stearns.   Fitchburg, The Sentinel printing company, 1911.
10 p. 23½ cm.   12-60.   CS71.R616   1911

14432   RITTER.   The Ritter families, 1705-1938.   (By Ned Burton Smith)   Youngstown, O., 1938.
1 l. 28 cm.   Caption title.   Mimeographed.   Signed: Ned Smith.   41-38341.   CS71.R616   1938

14433   RITTER.   Die Verwandtschaft Johann Peter Ritters (1722-1784) und seiner beiden Frauen;
ein Beitrag zur Geschichte des Oldenburger Honoratiorentums.   By Walter Schaub.   (Oldenburg, 1955)
22 l. 30 cm.   (His Familienkundliche Beiträge, Heft 1)   57-21463.   CT1098.R5S3

14434   RIVES.   A memento of ancestors and ancestral homes, written for her nieces and nephews
by Margaret Rives King ... Cincinnati, R. Clarke & co., 1890.   139 p. front. 23 cm.   "Printed for private distribution only."   Contents. - Ancestral homes in Virginia. - Old Virginia life. - Ancestors. - Cincinnati fifty years ago. - Memoirs of Rookwood.
8-19754.   F230.K53

14435   RIVES.   Reliques of the Rives (Ryves) by James Rives Childs ... being historical and genealogical notes of the ancient family of Ryves of County Dorset and of the Rives of Virginia.   An essay:
sociological and historical, of a family's contribution to the making of a nation.   Lynchburg, Va.,
J. P. Bell company, inc., 1929.   xxx, 750 p. front. (col. coats of arms) plates, ports., facsim., 2 fold. geneal. tab. (in pocket)
24 cm. 29-30535. rev.   Microfilm 8672.   CS71.R623   1929
           The descendants of William Christopher Rives and Mary Rives; a supplement to Reliques
of the Rives, no. 2654, p. 483.   Compiled during 1933 and 1934 by Whitmore Morris.   San Antonio,
1954.   32 l. 29 cm.   Caption title.   29-30535 rev.   CS71.R623   1929
                                                                                              Suppl.

14436   RIVES.   Green Rives of Dinwiddie County, Virginia, and Lincoln County, Tennessee, and his
descendants.   By John Robert Thomas Rives.   Birmingham, Ala., Printed by A. H. Cather Pub. Co.,
1958.   103 p. illus. 23 cm.   58-36405.   CS71.R623   1958

RIVES.   See also: PAGE, 1883
                                  RYVES.
                                  WATKINS, 1957

14437   RIVINGTON.   The publishing family of Rivington, by Septimus Rivington, M.A.   London,
Rivingtons, 1919.   xxii p., 1 l., 182 p. incl. geneal. tab. illus., ports. (incl. front.) fold. tab., facsims. (1 fold.) 23 cm.
20-7856.   Z325.R47

14438   RIVINUS.   Riviniana; records and memoirs of the Rivinus family collected on both sides of
the Atlantic by Emilie Markoe Rivinus, assisted by Cecilia Florentina Rivinus.   Philadelphia, Priv.
print., 1945.   80 p. incl. front., illus. (incl. coat of arms) geneal. tables. 24 cm.   "Sources of information": p. 80.   46-7377.
                                                                                              CS71.R624   1945

14439   RIX.   History and genealogy of the Rix family of America, containing biographical sketches
and genealogies of both males and females, compiled by Guy S. Rix ... New York, The Grafton press,
1906.   2p l. iii-xiii, 240 p. front., col. pl., ports. 24 cm.   6-16285.   CS71.R626   1906

14440   RIX.   History and genealogy of the Ricks family of America; containing biographical sketches and genealogies of both males and females.   Compiled by Guy S. Rix ... Published and for sale by Joel Ricks, Logan, Utah for the Ricks family.   Salt Lake City, Press and bindery of Skelton publishing co., 1908.   184 p. front., 2 pl. (1 col.) ports. 24½ cm. 8-27170.   CS71. R626   1908

14441   RIX.   Descendants of the Ricks family in the Tennessee valley, with excursus on many allied families, 1820-1936. (Tuscumbia, Ala., 1936)   5 p. 1., 71 numb. 1. 23 cm. Type-written. Dedication signed: Annibel Stine. "The data has been supplied mostly by Miss Ethal Ricks Clark": Intro. 39-12253.

CS71. R626   1936

14442   RIX.   History and genealogy of the Ricks family of America; containing biographical sketches and genealogies of both males and females.   Compiled and published by family representatives: Howard Ricks, chairman.   For descendants of Isaac Ricks and his wife, Kathren, born in England in 1638 and allied families.   Rev. ed. (Salt Lake City, Ricks Family Association) 1957.   767 p. illus. 24 cm.   The first part is a copy of History and genealogy of the Ricks family of America, compiled by Guy S. Rix. 61-37633.

CS71. R626   1957

RIX.   See also SHELLEY, 1909

14443   RIXEY.   The Rixey genealogy, with references to the Morehead, Hunton, Gibbs, Hall, Thomas, Jones, Lewis, Chancellor, Pendleton, Smith, and other allied families, by Randolph Picton Rixey. Lynchburg, Va., Printed by J. P. Bell company, 1933.   ix, 427 p. incl. geneal. tables. front., plates, ports., facsims., coats of arms (part col.) 23½ cm. Includes blank pages for "Family record"' (396-408) 33-20417.   CS71. R627   1933

14444   RIXFORD.   Rixford Miscellanea.   In vertical file.   Ask reference librarian for this material.

14445   ROACH.   Roach, Roberts, Ridgeway, and allied families.   By Marielou (Roach) Fair.   (Mansfield? La., 1951?)   258 p. illus. 24 cm. 55-19918.   CS69. F34

ROACH.   See also: LEE, 1954
                                   NELSON, 1938
                                   NELSON, 1967

ROADES.   See RHODES.

14446   ROANE.   Thomas Ritchie; a study in Virginia politics, by Charles Henry Ambler ... Richmond, Va., Bell book & stationery co., 1913.   5 p. 1., (9)-303, xvi p. plates, 2 port. (incl. front.) 22 cm. "Genealogy of William Roane and Mary Upshur": p. 301-303. 13-21487.   E340. R6A4

14447   ROBARDS.   A history of the Robards family.   By Bessie (Robards) Farrior.   Oxford, N. C. (1959?)   1 v. 28 cm. 59-43501.   CS71. R6285   1959

14448   ROBB.   Life and times of Robert Robb, esq. Muncy Township, Lycoming County, Pa.   By John F. Meginness (John of Lancaster) Muncy, Luminary press, 1899.   53 p. 20 cm. Cover-title: History of a remarkable character of revolutionary times. Robert Robb and his trouble with the Committee of safety. 1778. 8-34514.

E263. P4M4

14449   ROBB.   Robb-Lanterman family record, by Henrietta Robb ... Springfield, Ill., Illinois state register, 1902.   170 p. illus., geneal. tables. / 16 cm. Descendants of John Robb and Peter Lanterman, 1700 to 1902. Interspersed with blank leaves; marginal notes and "addenda" in manuscript to 1913. L. C. COPY REPLACED BY MICROFILM. 13-25487.

CS71. R629   1902
Microfilm 8672 CS

14450   ROBB.   Charles Spittal Robb.   In vertical file.   Ask reference librarian for this material.

ROBB.   See also McDONNELL, 1959

ROBBENS.   See ROBBINS.

14451   ROBBIA, DELLA.   Della Robbia papers; suggestions for their use, together with a short treatise on the work of the Della Robbia.   Springfield, Mass., The P. P. Kellogg division, United States envelope company, c.1926.   20 l. incl. front., 1 mounted col. illus., 8 pl. (1 mounted; part col.) 49 cm.   Illustration and plates consist of samples of paper.   Seven of the plates and accompanying letterpress, printed on outside of double leaves on opposite pages.   Ornamental borders in blue.   Plate (28 x 21½ cm.) laid in.   "This book designed by O. W. Jaquish and produced under his supervision by William Edwin Rudge." 42-42741.
                                                                                                                                    TS1220.U5

ROBBIN.   See ROBBINS.

14452   ROBBINS.   Chart of the descendants of John Robbins, of Wethersfield, Ct., through his great grandson, Capt. Elisha Robbins ... (New York?) c.1881.   geneal. tab.   52 x 84 cm.   Compiled by David Parsons Holton.   10-5269.   CS71.R632   1881

14453   ROBBINS.   Memoir of Hon. James Murray Robbins.   (Cambridge, J. Wilson and son, 19 -?) 17 p. 23½ cm.   By Estes Howe.   Privately printed for the family.   A sketch of his ancestry, p. (3)-11.   10-4767.   CS71.R632   19 -

14454   ROBBINS.   Gleanings of the Robins or Robbins family of England.   With lithograph of armorial window and other engravings.   By the Rev. Mills Robbins ... Devizes, C. H. Woodward, printer, 1908.   112 p. front., plates, 5 fold. geneal. tab. 21 cm.   For private circulation only.   First edition published in 1880.   17-30475.
                                                                                                                                    CS439.R556

14455   ROBBINS.   ... The Robbins family of cape Cod.   Compiled by H. N. Latey.   Yarmouthport, Mass., C. W. Swift, 1917.   cover-title, 23 p.   24 cm.   (Library of cape Cod history & genealogy, no. 28)   40-37511.
                                                                                                                                    CS71.R632   1917

14456   ROBBINS.   The facts of a family; Robyn 1377 to Robins 1939.   (New York, 1939) 1 v. facsims. 29 x 25 cm.   Title from cover.   Loose-leaf.   Reproduced from type-written copy.   41-5825.
                                                                                                                                    CS71.R632   1939

          —— Appendix to "Facts of a family," wills, portraits, etc.   (New York?) 1940.   1 v. pl., ports., facsims. 28 x 22 cm.   Title from label mounted on cover.   Loose-leaf.   Reproduced from type-written copy.   41-5825.
                                                                                                                                    CS71.R632   1939
                                                                                                                                    Appendix.

14457   ROBBINS.   History of the Robbins family of Walpole, Massachusetts, descendants of William and Priscilla Robbins.   By Dana Watkins Robbins.   Loveland, Colo., O. B. Robbins, 1949.   (A)- Y, 221 p. illus., ports., facsims., maps.   29 cm.   52-17511.   CS71.R632   1949

14458   ROBBINS.   Ancestry of Dr. Burtis France Robbins and his descendants.   Maud Bliss Allen, (compiler)   1 reel. Pos.   6799
                                                                                                                         Microfilm reading room.

14459   ROBBINS.   The saga of "Auntie" Stone and her cabin: Elizabeth Hickok Robbins Stone (1801- 1895) a pioneer woman who built and owned the first dwelling, operated the first hotel, built the first flour mill, and erected the first brick kiln in the city of Fort Collins, Colorado.   With the overland diary of Elizabeth Parke Keays.   Centenary ed.   By Nolie Mumey.   Boulder, Colo., Johnson Pub. Co., 1964.   xix, 128 p. illus. (part col.) facsim., geneal. table, ports.   31 cm.   "No. 174 of a limited edition of five hundred signed and numbered copies." Bibliographical footnotes.   64-54971.   F784.F56M8

14460   ROBBINS.   John Robins of Branford and Lyme, Connecticut and related families in descent from William, compiled by Janis H. Miller.   Washington, 1966.   128 p. 29 cm.   Includes bibliographies. 66-7232.   CS71.R632   1966

          ROBBINS.   See also: CHAMBERLAIN, 1880   PEPPER, 1960
                                 GRIM, 1934   TODD, 18 -
                                 HOLLIDAY, 1962   No. 3939- Colebrook.
                                 NOYES, 1907

          ROBEN.   See ROBBINS.

          ROBENS.   See ALEXANDER, 1960

14461   ROBERDEAU. Genealogy of the Roberdeau family, including a biography of General Daniel Roberdeau, of the revolutionary army, and the Continental congress; and signer of the Articles of confederation.   By Roberdeau Buchanan.   Printed for private distribution.   Washington, J. L. Pearson, printer, 1876.   vii, (9)-196 p. front., pl., geneal. tab. 21½ cm. 9-13634.   CS71. R639   1876

ROBERSON.   See WILFORD, 1959

ROBERT.   See ROBERTS.

14462   ROBERTS.   Some memorials of the family of Roberts, of Queen's Tower, Sheffield, as exemplified by kindred, affinity and marriage.   By Samuel Roberts . . . Sheffield, Parkin and Bacon, printers, 1862.   64 p. 22 cm. "For family distribution." "References": p. 62-64. 15-19653.   CS439. R56   1862

14463   ROBERTS.   The annals of Cranbrook church; its monuments.   (Cranbrook, Printed by G. Waters, 1873)   cover-title, 90 p. illus., geneal. tab. 21½ cm. By William Tarbutt. "Second lecture, read before the Cranbrook literary association on the 13th of January, 1870." Pedigree of the descendants of Walter Roberts, fl. 1442-1522: geneal. tab. 15-21495.
CS439. R56   1873

14464   ROBERTS.   The Roberts family of Simsbury, Connecticut, in the line of Captain Lemuel Roberts, 1742-1789.   Compiled by Frank Farnsworth Starr for James J. Goodwin.   Hartford, Conn. (Cambridge, J. Wilson & son) 1896.   54 p. fold. geneal. tab. 25 cm. 9-13633.
CS71. R64   1896

14465   ROBERTS.   A Quaker of the olden time, being a memoir of John Roberts, by his son, Daniel Roberts, with particulars of the Roberts family collected from original documents and other sources. Edited by Edmund T. Lawrence, with prefatory letter by Oliver Wendell Holmes . . . London, Headley brothers, 1898.   507 p. incl. illus. (incl. port., facsims.) 18½ cm. "The bibliography of the memoir of John Roberts": p. 477-487. 2-26551.   BX7795. R6R6 1898

14466   ROBERTS.   Old Richland families; including descendants of Edward Roberts, Thomas Roberts, Thomas Lancaster, Peter Lester, Casper Johnson, Hugh Foulke, Jacob Strawn, Richard Moore, William Jamison, Robert Penrose, Joseph Ball, Morris Morris, the Greens, Shaws, Edwardses, Heacocks, Thomsons, Hallowells, and Spencers.   Historical and genealogical data being derived largely from the records of Friends and other original sources.   By Ellwood Roberts . . . Norristown (Pa.) M. R. Wills, 1898.   xii, (13)-246 p. front., plates (1 fold.) ports., map, plans, facsim. 25 cm. Records of Richland meeting: p. (37)-76. 1-19518.   F159. R48R6

14467   ROBERTS.   The Roberts family; a genealogy of Joseph Roberts of Windham, Maine,   18th century.   By Mrs. Amorena Grant . . . Chicago, West Chicago press association (1902)   143 p. illus. (incl. ports.) 23 cm. 3-17711.   CS71. R64   1902

14468   ROBERTS.   The coat of arms of the Roberts family, by George C. Martin.   Asbury Park, N.J., Martin & Allardyce, 1915.   cover-title, 13 p. 6 pl. (coats of arms) 20 cm. 15-13926.
CR1629. R6

14469   ROBERTS.   . . . The Roberts genealogy, by J. Montgomery Seaver.   Philadelphia, American historical-genealogical society (1928?)   45 p. illus. (ports.) 23½ cm. Pages 44-45 blank for "Family record".   Coat of arms of the Roberts family on cover. "References": p. 43   40-18921.   CS71. R64   1928

14470   ROBERTS.   Ancestral study of four families: Roberts, Griffith, Cartwright (and) Simpson . . . (Terrell? Tex.) 1939-48.   2 v. (1073 p.) illus., ports., facsims., coats of arms. 27 cm. "Published for private distribution." Includes bibliographies. 40-6563 rev. *   CS71. R64   1939

14471   ROBERTS.   Ancestry of Clarence V. Roberts & Frances A. (Walton) Roberts; comprising a chart and sketches of some fifty-six ancestral families who settled mostly in or near Philadelphia, Pennsylvania.   Published by the compiler, Clarence V. Roberts.   (Philadelphia, Pa., Wm. F. Fell co., printers) 1940.   4 p. l., vii-x, 326 p. col. front. (incl. 4 coats of arms) illus. (incl. map) pl., facsims. 27½ cm. "Ancestral chart compiled, 1930-40, by Charles R. Barker, Warren S. Ely and Clarence V. Roberts" (fold. geneal. tab.) in pocket. Includes the Foulke, Brooke, Green, Lukens, Ambler and Conrad families. Includes bibliographies. 41-4326.   CS71. R64   1940

14472   ROBERTS.   Three pioneer Rapides families, a genealogy by George Mason Graham Stafford ... New Orleans, Pelican publishing company (1946)   2 p. l., 470 p. 24 cm. Bibliography at end of each part. 46-3749.   CS71.R64   1946

14473   ROBERTS.   Roberts and Mitchell families.   (By Ray Roberts Knight) (Minneapolis, 1953)
6, 2 l. 28 cm. 54-19890.   CS71.R64   1953

14474   ROBERTS.   The first of the Roberts and Crane families who settled in western North Carolina and some of their descendants.   By Lloyd Bascombe Craine.   (St. Paul) 1955.   148 p. illus. 24 cm.
58-44311.   CS71.R64   1955

14475   ROBERTS.   Roberts and allied families.   By Tolva (Roberts) Whitehead.   Atlanta (1960)
653 p. illus., ports., maps, coats of arms. 24 cm. Bibliography: p. 590-604. 61-20701.   CS71.R64   1960

14476   ROBERTS.   Pencoyd and the Roberts family.   By David Goldsmith Loth.   New York (1961?)
62 p. illus. 24 cm. 61-36033.   CS71.R64   1961

14477   ROBERTS.   Roberts family, Connecticut to California, by Daphne R. Hartle, Jennie N. Weeks (and) Margaret Watkins.   (Salt Lake City?) 1965.   432, xix p. illus., geneal. tables, fold, map, ports. 29 cm. Bibliography: p. 431-432. 66-753.   CS71.R64   1965

14478   ROBERTS.   Roberts family genealogy.   By Sesta Tuttle Matheison.   (Adrian? Mich., 1867?)
ii, 14 p. coat of arms, geneal. tables. 22 cm. Cover title. 68-7712.   CS71.R64   1967

ROBERTS.   See also:

CLEWELL, 1907	LINDLEY, 1950	ROACH, 1951
HAYES, 1952	MOORE, 1937	SMALL, 1910
HITE, 1960	PARISH, 1925	SMALL, 1934
JOHNSON, 1961	REIFSNYDER, 1902	SMITH, 1957a
LANCASTER, 1902		TALIAFERO, 1960

14479   ROBERTSON.   The history and martial atchievements of the Robertson's of Strowan.   As it is selected from the works of the best historians, that have writen of the origin and valiant atchievements of this honourable family, and their decendants.   And the poems.   On various subjects and occasions by the Honourable Alexander Robertson of Strowan ... Edinburgh, A. Robertson (1785)
6, ii, iii, 63, (2) 167 p. 17½ cm. 10-20201.   PR3669.R18   1785

14480   ROBERTSON.   The barons Reid-Robertson of Straloch, by the Rev. James Robertson, with appendix from other sources ... Blairgowrie, Printed at the Advertiser office, 1887.   2 p. l., (5)-64 p.
19 cm. "Substantially a print of a ms. written in the year 1728." Appendix: Gen. John Reid, p. 55-61. 21-17141.
CS479.R6   1887

14481   ROBERTSON.   The genealogy of the families of Douglas of Mulderg and Robertson of Kindeace with their descendants.   Dingwall, A. M. Ross, 1895.   84 p.   CS479.D6   1895

14482   ROBERTSON.   Stemmata Robertson et Durdin.   Being tables comprising the known ancestors of the children of Herbert Robertson and his wife Helen Alexandrina Melian née Durdin, and (except in some foreign families) brothers and sisters of these ancestors.   Compiled chiefly from printed authorities by Herbert Robertson.   48 copies printed as a private family record.   London, Mitchell and Hughes, 1893-95.   xi, 464 p. 28½ cm. Coat of arms on t.-p. "This copy is no. 48." 16-20943.   CS479.R6   1893

14483   ROBERTSON.   Donald Robertson and his wife, Rachel Rogers, of King and Queen County, Virginia, their ancestry and posterity; also, a brief account of the ancestry of Commodore Richard Taylor of Orange County, Virginia, and his naval history during the war of the American revolution. By William Kyle Anderson.   (Detroit, Mich., Winn and Hammond, printers, introd. 1900)
263, xxvi p., 1 l. front., pl., port. 23 cm. 3-6082.   CS71.R645   1900

14484   ROBERTSON.   Donald Robertson and his wife, Rachel Rogers, of King and Queen County, Virginia, their ancestry and posterity; also, a brief account of the ancestry of Commodore Richard Taylor of Orange County, Virginia, and his naval history during the war of the American revolution. By William Kyle Anderson.   (Detroit, Mich., Winn and Hammond, printers, introd. 1900) 263, xxvi p., 1 1. front., pl., port. 23 cm. 3-6082.   CS71. R645   1900

14485   ROBERTSON.   Genealogy of the Robertson, Small and related families: Hamilton, Livingston, McNaughton, McDonald, McDougall, Beveridge, Lourie, Stewart.   By Archibald Robertson Small ... Indianapolis, A. G. Small, 1907.   5 p. 1., (9)-249, (9) p. front. (port.) 24 cm. Edited by A. G. Small. 9-7061 rev.
CS71. R645   1907

14487   ROBERTSON.   The Robertson, Purcell and related families, by Laura Purcell Robertson of Kansas City, Missouri.   (n. p.) 1926.   1 p. 1., vii-xi, 242 p. front., illus. (incl. ports., coats of arms) 24½ cm. Contains also the Thompson, Ford and Jennings families. 26-20217.   CS71. R645   1926

14488   ROBERTSON.   ... Robertson family records, by J. Montgomery Seaver.   Philadelphia, Pa., American historical-genealogical society, 1928.   (7), 7-123, (3) p. front. (col. coat of arms) 2 pl. (incl. ports.) 28 cm. Autographed from type-written copy. References: p. (124) 29-18826.   CS71. R645   1928

14489   ROBERTSON.   Descendants of John Robertson, 1796-1860 and John Lee, 1786-1865, both of Johnstown, Fulton co., N. Y. ... (by) Leon R. Brown.   Rochester, N. Y., 1936.   1 p. 1., 14, 14a, 15-19 numb. 1. 28 cm. Mimeographed. 36-11409.   CS71. R645   1936

14490   ROBERTSON.   A genealogy of the Robertson family, compiled by Edna Robertson Vacher. (Washington, D. C., 1942)   4 p. 1., 44 numb. 1. 5 port. on 1 1., coat of arms. 27½ cm. Preface signed: Edna Robertson Vacher. Bibliographical references in preface. 42-3728.   CS71. R645   1942

14491   ROBERTSON.   The Robertson girls: Elmira Webber and Ann Eliza; a partial record of their antecedents and descendants.   Material assembled by Inez Rice De Busk and Katherine Bradley Robertson. (n. p.) 1947.   81 1. 28 cm. Typewritten. Includes bibliographies. 49-22749*.   CS71. R645   1947

14492   ROBERTSON.   Blaze and Hetty Robertson of South Branch, Virginia, and their descendants; other Robertson's and Robinson's.   By Robert Abner Love.   Arlington, Va. (1950)   71 p. map. 29 cm.
50-12454.   CS71. R645   1950

14493   ROBERTSON.   The Robertsons, Clan Donnachaidh of Atholl, by Iain Moncreiffe of Easter Moncreiffe.   Edinburgh, W. & A. K. Johnston & G. W. Bacon (1954)   32 p. illus. 19 cm. (W. & A. K. Johnston's clan histories) 55-42332.   CS479. R6   1954

14494   ROBERTSON.   The Reverend George Robertson (1662-1739) rector of Bristol Parish, Virginia (1693-1739) and his descendants.   By Wassell Randolph.   Memphis, Distributed by Cossitt Library, 1955.   93 p. 27 cm. "Complementary to the author's prior publication 'The Reverend George Robertson and Bristol Parish, Virginia.' " 55-3018.   CS71. R645   1955

14495   ROBERTSON.   The ancestry of Benjamin Otis Robertson, Sr.   By Amanda (Blalock) Robertson. (Arlington? Va.) c. 1959.   1 v. (various pagings) ports., facsims. 29 cm. "Only three copies have been reproduced ... by Mr. Al. Clarke." Includes bibliographical references. 60-19217.   CS71. R645   1959

14496   ROBERTSON.   The Robertson family of Culpeper County, Virginia.   By John Frederick Dorman.   Richmond, 1964.   187 p. illus., col. coat of arms. 24 cm. Limited to 250 copies. Bibliographical references included in "Notes" (p. 128-173) 64-66216.   CS71. R645   1964

14497   ROBERTSON.   A history of the Robertson-Carter and allied families.   By Clarence and Lillie Robertson Carter.   Negative.   Microfilm 4779
Microfilm reading room.

14498   ROBERTSON.   Robertson family genealogical chart.   In vertical file.   Ask reference librarian for
this material.

ROBERTSON.   See also: ATHOLL, CS479. R6   LANGFORD, 1936
                        BLAKENEY, 1928   RANDOLPH, 1961
                        CALHOUN, 1957   ROBINSON.
                        DOUGLAS, 1895   STEVENS, 1956
                        HARLLEE, 1934

14499   ROBESON.   An historical and genealogical account of Andrew Robson, of Scotland, New Jersey
and Pennsylvania, and of his descendants from 1653 to 1916, begun by Susan Stroud Robeson, assisted
by Caroline Franciscus Stroud, compiled, edited and published by Kate Hamilton Osborne.   Philadelphia, Press of J. B. Lippincott company, 1916.   xvi, 760 p. incl. col. front. (coat of arms) plates, ports. 24½ cm.
16-22763.   CS71. R65   1916

ROBESON.   See ROBINSON.

14500   ROBIDOUX.   Memorial to the Robidoux brothers; a history of the Robidouxs in America;
manuscripts, titles, quotations and illustrations, by Orral Messmore Robidoux.   Kansas City, Mo.,
Printed by Smith-Grieves company, 1924.   7 p. l., 17-311 p. front., illus. (incl. facsims.) plates, ports., map. 24 cm.
Includes sketches of early Missouri history.   24-11168.   CS71. R655   1924

ROBIE.   See ROBY.

ROBIN.   See ROBBINS.

ROBINS.   See ROBBINS.

14501   ROBINSON.   Genealogical history of the families of Robinson, Saffords, Harwoods, and Clarks.
By Sarah Robinson.   Bennington, Vt., 1837.   iv, (5)-96 p. 20 cm. 12-21701.   CS71. R66   1837
                                                                                 Office.

14502   ROBINSON.   Memoir of the Rev. William Robinson, formerly pastor of the Congregational
church in Southington, Conn.   With some account of his ancestors in this country.   By his son, Edward
Robinson ... Printed as manuscript, for private distribution.   New York, J. F. Trow, printer, 1859.
xii, 214 p. 23 cm. Part I: Ancestors of the Rev. William Robinson, p. 1-63. 10-10179.
                                                                         CS71. R66   1859

14503   ROBINSON.   A discourse of the warr in Lancashire.   Edited by William Beamont, esq.
(Manchester) Printed for the Chetham society, 1864.   3 p. l., (iii)-xxxiv p., 2 l., (3)-164 p. front. (port.) illus.,
pl. 23 cm. (Added t. - p: Chetham society. Remains historical & literary connected with the palatine counties of Lancaster and Chester.
vol. LXII) Frontispiece is a mounted photograph. Pedigree of Robinson family: p. xxxii. 16-10648.   DA670. L1905 v. 62

14504   ROBINSON.   Fragments of family and contemporary history.   Gathered by T. H. R. (i.e.
Thomas H. Robinson) Pittsburgh, Printed by Bakewell & Marthens, 1867.   v, (7)-142 p. 19½ cm. "Family
register": p. (99)-142. 4-8408.   CS71. R66   1867

14505   ROBINSON.   Recollections of olden times: Rowland Robinson of Narragansett and his unfortu-
nate daughter.   With genealogies of the Robinson, Hazard, and Sweet families of Rhode Island.   By
Thomas R. Hazard ... Also, genealogical sketch of the Hazards of the middle states, by Willis P.
Hazard ... Newport, R. I., J. P. Sanborn, 1879.   288 p. pl. 22½ cm. 9-13630.
                                                                         CS71. R66   1879

14506   ROBINSON.   Descendants of Alexander Robinson and Angelica Peale.   (Washington, D. C.,
1896)   89 l. port. 26½ x 20½ cm. By William Carvel Hall. Autographed from typewritten copy. 0-13632.
                                                                         CS71. R66   1896

14507   ROBINSON.   William and Anne Robinson of Dorchester, Mass.; their ancestors and their descendants.   By Edward Doubleday Harris ... Boston, Press of D. Clapp & son, 1890.   60 p. fold. geneal.
tab. 25½ cm. "Two hundred and fifty copies." 9-13631.   CS71. R66   1890

14508   ROBINSON.   Items of ancestry, by a descendant, I. M. R. (Mrs. Ida May (Frost) Robinson.
Privately printed.   Boston, D. Clapp & son, 1894.   93 p. illus. 24½ cm. 10-11178.   CS71. R66   1894

14509   ROBINSON.   Descendants of Timothy Robinson. (By Samuel Burnham Shackford.)   (n. p.,
19 -)   76 1. 28 cm.   Type-written.   Includes bibliography.   37-38425.   CS71. R66   19 -

14510   ROBINSON.   Ancestor hunting.   Some account of a week spent in Windham county, Vermont,
during the month of June, 1901 ... By Hamline E. Robinson ... Maryville, Mo., Priv. print. by the
author, 1901.   12 p. illus. (port.) 18 cm.   "Only fifty copies ... were printed privately by the author .... July, 1901.   This is
number 10.   H. E. Robinson. "   3-33148.   CS71. R66   1901

14511   ROBINSON.   The Robinson family.   By James Polk Sherman.   Compliments of James P.
Sherman.   Waterloo, Ia., 1901.   28 1. 20½ x 27½ cm.   "To whom it may concern": leaf affixed to cover.   1-27668.
                                                                                            CS71. R66   1901a

14512   ROBINSON.   Thomas Robinson and his descendants, by Thomas Hastings Robinson.   Rev. ed.,
1902.   Harrisburg, Pa., Harrisburg publishing company, 1902.   233 p. front., plates, ports. 22½ cm. 5-37638.
                                                                                            CS71. R66   1902

14513   ROBINSON.   The Robinsons and their kin folk (1st) -   series.   Robinson family genealogical and historical association.   (190-) -   ... New York, Pub. by the association, 1902 -
v. front. (v. 3) illus. (incl. facsims.) plates (part col.) ports.   23 cm.   The above title appears in v. 1 and 4, only on cover.   It appears on
t. - p. and cover of v. 2 and 3.   Contains list of officers, constitution and by-laws, historical sketches, members of Association, etc.   7-23697.
                                                                                            CS71. R66   1902-

14514   ROBINSON.   A historical sketch of the Robinson family of the line of Ebenezer Robinson, a
soldier of the revolution.   Born at Lexington, Mass., Feb. 14th, 1765.   Died at South Reading, Vt.,
Oct. 31, 1857.   By Jane Bancroft Robinson ... Detroit, Mich.   (Speaker printing company) 1903.
viii, 5-68 p., 1 l. incl. front., illus., map.   col. pl. 23 cm.   Introduction signed: George O. Robinson, Jane B. Robinson.   6-858.
                                                                                            CS71. R66   1903

14515   ROBINSON.   Colonial and revolutionary ancestry: some account of the New England descent of
Hamline Elijah Robinson ... Maryville, Mo., Priv. print., 1903.   28 p. incl. facsims. 24 cm.   Forewords signed
Hamline Elijah Robinson.   "Only 100 copies of this pamphlet were privately printed by the compiler in January, 1903, of which this is number 9."
3-26269.   CS71. R66   1903a

14516   ROBINSON.   The Adin Robinson family and collaterals.   By John Bunyan Robinson ... (Liberty-
ville, Ill., 1904)   62 p. front., ports., fold. geneal. tables. 20 cm. 23-14454.   CS71. R66   1904

14517   ROBINSON.   ... John Robinson of Leyden, and his descendants to the sixth generation.   Yarmouthport, Mass., C. W. Swift, 1913.   cover-title, (4) p. 25½ cm.   (Library of Cape Cod history & genealogy, no. 57)   The
substance of this article copied from a ms. of Freeman Robinson of East Falmouth, is said to have been compiled by John Jenkins of Falmouth.
17-6162.   CS71. R66   1913

14518   ROBINSON.   Ancestry and posterity of George McCook Robinson.   Pierre, S. D., 1914.
geneal. tab. 29½ x 55½ cm.   Compiled by Doane Robinson.   15-229.   CS71. R66   1914

14519   ROBINSON.   Midshipman to Congress, by the Hon. John B. Robinson.   Media, Pa., Published
privately, 1916.   323 p. front., pl., ports. 21 cm. 24-11009.   F154. R66

14520   ROBINSON.   Wallace Fulham Robinson: his ancestry - personal history - business enterprises.   His public benefactions: Jennie M. Robinson maternity hospital; Robinson hall, at Dartmouth
college, Hanover, N. H.; Town hall, Reading, Vt.; Union church, South Reading.   Ed. by Harry E.
Robinson.   Cambridge, Mass., The University press 1917.   3 p. l., 109, (1) p. front., plates, ports. 24½ cm.
Running title: Robinson memorial.   22-18815.   CS71. R66   1917

14521   ROBINSON.   Genealogy and family register of George Robinson, late of Attleborough, Mass.,
with some account of his ancestors, comp. by one of his sons, in 1829.   Hallowell, Glazier, Masters
& co., printers, 1831.   Boston, Mass., Reprinted by C. E. Goodspeed & company, 1919.   36 p. 16½ cm.
"This edition is limited to fifty copies."   20-9246.   CS71. R66   1919

14522 ROBINSON. ... The Robinson family and their correspondence with the Vicomte and Vicomtesse de Noailles; a paper read before the society, August 21, 1922, by Anna Wharton Wood. Newport, R. I., 1922. 39 p. 23½ cm. (Bulletin of the Newport historical society, no. 42) "Society notes, officers, etc.": p. 36-39. 23-788.
F89.N5N615 no. 42

14523 ROBINSON. Robinson genealogy; descendants of the Rev. John Robinson, pastor of the Pilgrims ... (Boston) The Robinson genealogical society (1926 -   v. front., plates, ports., map. 23½ cm. Ruled pages (16 at end of v. 1) Preface to v. 1 signed: Charles Edson Robinson, historiographer. 26-6371.   CS71.R66   1926

14524 ROBINSON. Annals of a happy family, by Mary C. Robinson. (Concord, N. H.) Priv. print. (The Rumford press, c. 1933)   3 p. l., 163 p., 1 l. 24 cm. "The edition of this book is limited to 50 numbered copies." This copy is not numbered. An account of the author's family. 35-20094.   CS71.R66   1933

14525 ROBINSON. A Virginia gentleman and his family, by Nathalie Robinson Boyer. Philadelphia, The author, 1939.   7 p. l., (13)-200 p. front., ports. 24½ cm. "This limited edition consists of 300 numbered copies." 39-33445.
CS71.R66   1939

14526 ROBINSON. Robinson, Baldwin, and affiliated families; genealogies of the following families: Robinson, Baldwin, Clark, Clason, Haymond, Keen, Roderick, Nixon, Norris, Ransier, and Stratton. (n. p., c. 1952)   194 p. illus. 29 cm. 58-46323.   CS71.R66   1952

14527 ROBINSON. Genealogical and ancestral notes. By William Hopple Edwards. (Meriden, Conn., 1953-62)   4 v. geneal. tables. 29 cm. Includes bibliographical references. Contents. - (1) ser. 1, v. 1. Ancestors of John Edwin Robinson and Stella Adolphus Robinson. - (2) ser. 1, v. 2. 47 families of Robinson ancestors. ser. 1A. The descendants of Isaac and Mary Robinson of Falmouth, Mass.; married 1760. - (3) ser. 2. Ancestors of Mary Elizabeth Billard. - (4) ser. 3. Ancestors of William Lemly Edwards and Stella Lee Edwards. 54-31342.   CS71.R66   1953
—— Another issue.   CS71.R66   1953a

14528 ROBINSON. A short pedigree of the late Senator from Arkansas, Joseph Taylor Robinson, a descendant of English families, descenant of Edward I. By Charles M. Robinson Skarda. Little Rock, 1956 -   v. 30 cm. 57-12020 rev. 2.   CS71.R66   1956

14529 ROBINSON. The Robinson family register (Robinson clan) By Charles M. Robinson Skarda. (Little Rock, Ark., 1958)   19 p. 28 cm. 59-27013.   CS71.R66   1958

14530 ROBINSON. Robinson family memories. By James Lowry Robinson. (n. p., 1962?) iii, 108 l. ports. 29 cm. Cover title. 63-50737.   CS71.R66   1962

14531 ROBINSON. Pioneers of Pittsburgh, The Robinsons. By Dorothy Smith Coleman. 55-77. Western Pa. Hist. Mag. v. 2:1 4 p. Index of names. Typed. In vertical file.   Ask reference librarian for this material.

14532 ROBINSON. Jennie M Robinson, her ancestors & her descendants. By Floyd Mallory Shumway. New York, 1964.   iii, 75 l. 30 cm. Bibliography: leaves 63-75. 64-7170 rev.   CS71.R66   1964

ROBINSON. See also:

ATHOLL, CS479.R6	GILES, 1864	McCLESKEY, 1968
BARLOW, 1891	GLASSBURN, 1964	McKINNEY, 1905
BATES, 1962	GLASSELL, 1891	MALCOLM, 1950
BUFORD, 1903	GOLSAN, 1959	PATTERSON, 1917
BURTON, 1906	GOODNER, 1960	PLAXCO, 1958
COE, 1961	HARRISON, 1910a	POCAHONTAS, 1887
DULIN, 1961	HOGG, 1921	ROBERTSON.
EVANS, 1940	JENNINGS, 1961	SHORTHOUSE, 1902
FLAGG, 1903	KELLEY, 1892	SILL, 1942
FOLLETT, 1896	LIGON, 1947	WANTON, F76.R52 vol. 3
GENTRY, 1909	MACKEY, 1957	WATSON, CS71.W34
		No. 1459 - Early families of Ky.

14533   ROBISON.   A genealogy of the Robison family of Juniata county, Pennsylvania, 1732-1938. Compiled and copyrighted by Robert P. Thompson.   San Diego, Calif., 1938.   4 p. l., 30 numb. l., 1 l., 31-69 numb. l.   2 mounted col. pl., mounted port., 2 fold. maps, facsim. fold. geneal. tab.   29 cm.   Mimeographed.   39-1900.

CS71. R662   1938

14534   ROBSON.   ... Pedigrees of families from which Elizabeth, daughter of Thomas and Elizabeth Robson (of Darlington, Sunderland & Liverpool) and late wife of Joshua Green of Stansted Montfitchet Essex, was descended ... Comp. from private papers and public sources, both printed and manuscript by Joseph J. Green ... 1888-1892.   Hampstead, 1892.   31 l.   37 cm.   Consists of 17 cyclostyle pedigrees mounted on cardboard.   Contents. - Billany of Skeffling and Ross in Holderness, co. York. - Cleaving, of Owstwick, co. York. - Clyff of Fishlake, co. York. - Coates of Lynesack, Smelt house and Caselee, co. Durham. - Coldwell of Cudworth, co. York, Darlington, &c. - Fox of Standingholme, co. York. - Hedley of Hedley-on-the-Hill, co, Northumberland. - Hunter, of co. Durham. - Kitching of Owstwick, co. York. - Lister of Tunstall, in Holderness, co. York. - Maire, of Rennish, Hilston, and Belford, co. York. - Pease of Yorkshire, Darlington, &c. - Robson, of Darlington, Sunderland, Liverpool, Huddersfield, Saffron Walden, &c., &c. - Stather, or Stadder, of North Cave, co, York. - Stephenson of Carnaby, Bridlington, &c., co. York. - Thorp of Aldborough, co. York. - Ward of co. Durham.   21-8066.

CS439. R563

14535   ROBSON.   The oldest London bookshop, a history of two hundred years, by George Smith and Frank Benger, to which is appended a family correspondence of the eighteenth century.   London, Ellis, 1928.   1 p. l., v-viii, 141 p.   front., illus., plates (incl. ports., facsims.)   29 x 23 cm.   "A list of the more important books and manuscripts quoted or consulted": p. viii.   Contents. - The building of New Bond street and of this bookshop. - John Brindley, 1728-1758. - James Robson, 1759-1806. - John Nornaville and William Fell, 1806-1830. - Thomas and William Boone, 1830-1872. - Frederick Startridge Ellis, 1872-1885. - Gilbert Ifold Ellis, 1885-1902. - J. J. Holdsworth and George Smith, 1902 -   - The Robson family correspondence.   29-8923.

Z325. E47S6

ROBSON.   See also: DUNHAM, 1956
                        SMITH, 1878a

14536   ROBY.   Pedigree of Roby of castle Donington, co. Leicester.   Manchester, The author, 1889.   51 p.   front. (fold. geneal. tab.)   22 cm.   Introduction signed: Henry J. Roby.   16-17289.   CS439. R565

14537   ROBY.   A genealogical history of the Robie family in England and America (compiled by Eva Barbara (Robie) Schwarting and Margaret Dorothy (Robie) Ninteman)   New York, c. 1956.   244 l.   illus.   30 cm.   56-25027.   CS71. R656   1956

14538   ROBY.   A genealogical history of the Robie family in England and America (compiled by Eva Barbara (Robie) Schwarting and Margaret Dorothy (Robie) Ninteman)   New York, c. 1956.   244 l.   illus.   30 cm.   56-25027 rev.   CS71. R656   1956
        —— Supplement.   (Compiled by Margaret Dorothy (Robie) Ninteman and Eva Barbara (Robie) Schwarting, assisted by George Randolph Robie)   New York, 1964.   v, 117, 23 l.   illus.   30 cm.   Bibliography: leaf i-ii.   56-25027 rev.   CS71. R656   1956
                                                                                                                                       Suppl.

ROBY.   See also: CORLISS, 1875
                     PAINE, 1913

ROBYN.   See ROBBINS.

ROBYNS.   See ROBBINS.

14539   ROCHAT.   Mrs. Louise E. Bettens.   New York, 1916.   7 p. l., 27, (14) p.   front., plates, ports. 23½ cm.   Compiled by her son: Edward Detraz Bettens.   The plates are accompanied by descriptive letterpress.   "Of this book one hundred and fifty copies have been printed for private distribution."   "Printed on Japan paper, bound in levant, with doublure and silk flyleaf."   "This copy one of twenty-six containing additional pages."   On cover: 1917.   The portraits are reproductions from miniatures by Alyn Williams. 18-1482.

CT275. B567B4
Office.

14540   ROCHAT.   The family of Mrs. Louise E. Bettens, born Rochat and of Alexander Bettens. (New York, 1918)   15 p.   25 cm.   Compiled by her son: Edward Detraz Bettens.   A correspondence concerning the Rochat and Bettens family.   18-6016.   CS71. R663   1918

14541   ROCHAT.   The family of Mrs. Louise E. Bettens, born Rochat.   New York, 1918.
4p., 1 l., 5-71 (i.e. 73) p. incl. front., pl. ports. 25 cm.   Compiled by her son: Edward Detraz Bettens.   "Three hundred and fifty copies of this book, printed for private distribution, are reprints, with some additional matter, of what was recently published in the less durable form of pamphlets."   The portraits are reproductions from miniatures by Alyn Williams.   A correspondence concerning the Rochat and Bettens families.
18-20897.   CS71. R663   1918a

ROCHE.   See FITZGERALD, DA937. 5D4S3

14542   ROCHESTER.   Early history of the Rochester family in America, with charts of the family and its connections from 1640 to 1882.   Collected and compiled by Nathaniel Rochester ...   Buffalo, N. Y., Printing house of Matthews, Northrup & co., 1882.   15 p., 10 l. incl. XI geneal. charts. front. (col. coat of arms) port. 28 cm.   "The Beatty family" (in ms.): p. 15.   Newspaper clipping concerning William Beatty Rochester is inserted.   Additions and corrections in ms. throughout the book.   15-6395.   CS71. R665   1882

14543   ROCHESTER.   Pedigree of Rochester of Terling, Essex, by Charles Shepard.   Troy, N. Y., 1921.   geneal. tab. 36 x 44½ cm. Blu-print. 21-19032.   CS439. R567

14544   ROCHESTER.   Backward glances at old Rochester, by Katharine Rochester Montgomery Osgood.   Buffalo, N. Y., Foster & Stewart publishing corporation, 1937.   3 p. l., 56 p. front. (facsim.) 20 cm.   "Records and recollections (of the Rochester family") - Foreword. 38-2884.   F129. R7O84

14545   ROCHESTER.   Centennial and bicentennial: Nathaniel Rochester, 1752 (and) Thomas Rochester Shepard, 1852.   Rochester, N. Y., 1952.   16 p. 24 cm. 53-18473.   CS71. R665   1952

ROCHESTER.   See also: DODSON, 1959
                                      SHEPARD, 1905

14546   ROCHFORT.   Notes on the history of the family of Rochfort or Rochefort, with genealogies of the principal Irish branches of the house ...   1st ed.   Oxford, 1890.   x, 200 p. 18 cm. Preface signed: R. Rochfort Forlong. 17-23938.   CS499. R6

14547   ROCK.   Rock family history, 1807-1969; from Ireland to the United States of America. Compiled and edited by Margaret M. Wagner.   Cedar Rapids, Iowa (1969)   299 p. illus., ports. 28 cm. Bibliography: p. 270-272. 73-9444 MARC.   CS71. R668   1969

14548   ROCKEFELLER.   The transactions of the Rockefeller family association for ...   1905-1909. (v. 1 - with genealogy ...   New York, The Knickerbocker press, 1910 -   1 v. front., illus. (incl. map, facsims.) plates (1 col.) 24½ cm. Editors: 1905 -   H. O. Rockefeller, B. F. Rockefeller, C. Rockefeller. Genealogy compiled by Henry Oscar Rockefeller: p. 148-329. 10-28361.   CS71. R67   1910

14549   ROCKEFELLER.   (Family tree of the descendants of John Peter Rockefeller) Drawn and arranged by Henry O. Rockefeller ...   Brooklyn, N. Y., 1914.   geneal. tab. 28 x 35½ cm. 14-20951.
                                                                                                                   CS71. R67   1914

14550   ROCKEFELLER.   Rockefeller family association news. v. 1,   Brooklyn, N. Y., 19 - v. 23 cm. Editor: H. O. Rockefeller. 38M3938T.   CS71. R67   1927

14551   ROCKEFELLER.   John D. Rockefeller, 1839-1937, industrial pioneer and man.   By Wallace Trevor Holliday.   New York, Newcomen Society of England, American Branch, 1948.   32 p. illus., port. 23 cm.   "Address... delivered at a national Newcomen dinner ...   held ...   at New York ...   on March 4, 1948." 48-4326*.
                                                                                                                   CT275. R75H6

14552   ROCKEFELLER.   The fabulous Rockefellers; a compelling, personalized account of one of America's first families.   By Robert Silverberg.   Derby, Conn., Monarch Books (1963)   157 p. 19 cm. (Monarch select books) 63-1101.   CS71. R67   1963

14553   ROCKEFELLER.   Pocantico; fifty years on the Rockefeller domain.   Observed by Tom Pyle and told to Beth Day.   (1st ed.) New York, Duell, Sloan, and Pearce (1964)   240 p. illus., geneal. table, col. map (on lining papers) ports. 24 cm. 64-24480.   CS71. R67   1964

ROCKEFELLER.   See also: FREAD, 1969
HALL, 1943a

ROCKHOLD.   See DODDRIDGE, 1961

ROCKNE.   See No. 553 - Goodhue county.

14554   ROCKWELL.   The Rockwell family in America.   A genealogical record, from 1630 to 1873.
By Henry Ensign Rockwell.   Boston, Rockwell & Churchill, 1873.   v, 7-224 p. col. front. (coat of arms) 24 cm.
9-13019.   CS71.R683   1873

14555   ROCKWELL.   A genealogy of the families of John Rockwell, of Stamford, Conn., 1641, and
Ralph Keeler, of Hartford, Conn., 1639.   Comp, by James Boughton ... New York, W. F. Jones, 1903.
xc, 525 p. front., ports. 24 cm. 9-30476.   CS71.R683   1903

14556   ROCKWELL.   Eleven centuries of the remote ancestry of the Rockwell family, by Donald
Shumway Rockwell ... Berkeley, Cal., The Gillick publishing co., 1914.   17 l. front. (port.) 17 cm.
Edited from the manuscripts of Ada Bell Trowbridge Peterson. 15-2075.   CS71.R683   1914

14557   ROCKWELL.   The Rockwell family in one line of descent, by Francis Williams Rockwell ...
Pittsfield, Mass., 1924.   3 p. 1., 233 p. illus. (incl. facsims., plan) fold. geneal. tab. 24 cm. Edited with additions by Samuel
Forbes Rockwell. cf. Preface. 24-10201.   CS71.R683   1924

14558   ROCKWELL.   Fifty-seven generations of the ancestry of the Rockwell family, by Harold F.
Bayles.   (Akron, O., 1930)   7 p. 15½ cm. 31-16348.   CS71.R683   1930

14559   ROCKWELL.   Three centuries of the Rockwell family in America, 1630-1930.   Prepared for
Françoise Jeanne Anne Loula Rockwell and Kiffin Yates Rockwell II by their father Paul Ayres Rockwell.
Paris, Priv. print., 1930.   1 p. 1., (4)-83 p. ports., double geneal. tab. 19½ cm. Author's ms. note: 50 copies printed of which
this is no. 16. Paul Ayres Rockwell. 31-19474.   CS71.R683   1930a

ROCKWELL.   See also: BENEDICT, F129.S697 v.33
CROCKER, 1923
SANBORN, 1928
No. 3939 - Colebrook.

14560   ROCKWOOD.   A historical and genealogical record of the descendants of Timothy Rockwood
... Compiled from authentic sources.   By E. L. Rockwood ... Boston, Mass., The compiler, 1856.
146, v, (1) p. front. 20 cm. 9-13629.   CS71.R684   1856

14561   ROCKWOOD.   The descendants of Benjamin Rockwood, sr., of Grafton, Mass., with some
account of his ancestry and the early Rockwoods in Massachusetts.   By Charles A. Flagg.   Washington,
D. C. (Press of Gibson bros.) 1905.   36 p. 23½ cm. 5-27472.   CS71.R684   1905

ROCKWOOD.   See also: ADAMS, F63.M88 vol. I
FLAGG, 1903

14562   RODD.   The Rodd family of Devonshire and Prince Edward island.   (By John Smith Kendall)
(Berkeley, Calif., 1945)   1 p. 1., 5-22, 15 numb. 1. 28 x 21 ½ cm. Caption title. Type-written (carbon copy)   46-23131.
CS90.R6   1945

14563   RODEFFER.   The Rodeffer family of Rockingham County, Virginia, a record of the descendants of Conrad and Nancy Showalter Rodeffer, 1805-1948.   By Carrie Effie (Rodeffer) Power. (Phoebus,
Va., 1948)   vii, 267 p. port., facsim. 24 cm. 48-10485*.   CS71.R686   1948

14564   RODEHEAVER.   Garrett county history of pioneer families, by Charles E. Hoye ... The
Rodeheaver family.   (Oakland, Md., 1936?)   mounted 1. 48 cm. Reprint of no. LXXXVI of a series of articles contributed
to the Mountain democrat. 41M3026T.   CS71.R687   1936

RODENBOUGH.   See KAUFMAN, 1892

RODENHAUSER. See HARTMAN, 1952

14565   RODERICK. Our kin, the Rodericks, Slifers, Arnolds, Millers, and allied family lines. By Ella Maude (Brooks) Dulany. Kingfisher, Okla. (1964)   75, (1), 14 l. illus., maps. 28 cm. Caption title. Bibliographical references included in "Acknowledgments & thanks": leaf (76) 64-25765.   CS71.R6877   1964

RODERICK. See also ROBINSON, 1952

14566   RODES. A short history and genealogy of the English family Rodes, who reached America in the 17th century and first settled in New Kent County, Virginia, by Shelley Rodes Patterson. (New York, The Ferris printing co.) 1929.   3 p. l., 3-48 p. front. (coat of arms) pl., ports. 24½ cm. "This edition is limited to fifty copies of which this is no. 25." "Books consulted": p. 31. 29-18038.   CS71.R688   1929

RODES. See also: LEWIS, 1901
                 RHODES.

RODES-THOMSON. See WITHERSPOON, 1922

RODGER. See RODGERS.

14567   RODGERS. The family of Samuel Rodgers, 1838-1911. Compiled by Robert H. Rodgers. (Cambridge? Mass.) 1965.   viii, 55 p. 22 cm. 50 copies printed. No. 32. Includes bibliographies. 66-47381.   CS71.R69   1965

RODLON. See RIDLON.

14568   RODMAN. Genealogy of the Rodman family, 1620 to 1886. By Charles Henry Jones. Philadelphia (Printed by Allen, Lane & Scott) 1886.   287 p., 2 l. ports., facsim. 26 cm. 9-13259.   CS71.R693   1886

14569   RODMAN. Notes on Rodman genealogy. By William Woodbridge Rodman ... (New Haven, Conn.) Printed for the author (Tuttle, Morehouse & Taylor, printers) 1887.   27 p. 24½ cm. 9-13258.   CS71.R693   1887

RODMAN. See also ROTCH, 1947

14570   RODNEY. Pay-day at Babel, and odes. By Robert Burton Rodney ... New York, D. Van Nostrand, 1872.   64, (1) p. 16 cm. Prefatory note about Rodney family: p. (5) Dramatic poem. 30-992.   PS2724.R5

14571   ROE. Historic records of an old family. (Ancestry of Francis Asbury Roe) (n.p., 1890) 19 p. 23½ cm. Signed: Francis Asbury Roe. Addendum, September 1890: p. 17-19. 23-1893.   CS71.R698   1890

14572   ROE. The diary of Captain Daniel Roe, an officer of the French and Indian war and of the revolution: Brookhaven, Long Island, during portions of 1806-7-8; with introduction and notes by Alfred Seelye Roe ... Privately printed by the annotator, Worcester, Massachusetts, 1904. Worcester, The Blanchard press, 1904.   1 p. l., (5)-64 p. incl. illus., ports., facsims. front. 26 cm. Genealogy: p. 5-14. 4-30123.   F129.B6R6

14573   ROE. David Roe of Flushing, Long Island, and some of his descendants; a record of six generations, by Clarence Almon Torrey. Tarrytown, N.Y., Roe printing company, 1926. 3 p. l., 46 p. front. (port.) 24½ cm. 27-15871.   CS71.R698   1926

14574   ROE. John Roe of Brookhaven, Long island, and some of his descendants, a record of six generations, by Clarence Almon Torrey, PH.B. Boston, 1941.   4 p. l., 66 numb. l. 28 cm. Type-written. 41-14800.   CS71.R698   1941

14575   ROE. Eli Roe of Portage Prairie, St. Joseph County, Indiana, and some of his descendants. By Lutie Calista (Roe) Glover. Ed. by Charles Harvey Roe. (Tarrytown? N.Y.) 1947.   38 l. 29 cm. 48-14873*.   CS71.R698   1947

14576 ROE. Frederick Roe and some of his descendants, 1802-1955. Associate families: Brakefield, Coblentz, Gebhart, Lindley, Paine, Spitler. By Harrison Norman Roe. Hartford City, Ind. (1963?) 20, (21) l. 31 cm. 64-5541.
CS71. R698 1963

14577 ROE. Brief record of certain descendants of David Roe of Flushing, Long Island, New York, including John Martindale of Philadelphia, Pennsylvania and Martin Tichenor of New Haven, Connecticut and Newark, New Jersey, including Theophilus Blake of Greenbrier County, Virginia. (New York? 1965?) 1 v. (various pagings) illus., geneal. tables, ports. 29 cm. Half title: History of certain Roe and Tichenor families in the U. S. A. 67-6123.
CS71. R698 1965

ROE. See also: CONKLING, 1909
ELIOT, 1936

14578 ROEBLING. The Roeblings; a century of engineers, bridge-builders and industrialists; the story of three generations of an illustrious family, 1831-1931, by Hamilton Schuyler. Princeton, Princeton university press, 1931. xx, 424, (1) p. front., illus., plates, ports., facsims. 24 cm. Includes bibliographies. 31-31716.
TA140. R7S4

14579 ROEBUCK. The Roebuck family in America; a preliminary report. By Bette Dickson Casteel. (1st ed. Alameda, N.M., 1969) viii, 173 p. facsims., geneal. tables. 28 cm. 73-8526 MARC.
CS71. R7 1969

ROED. See KRUSE, 1924

14580 ROESLER. The house of Roesler, 1535-1932, compiled by Frank Emil Roesler. Kansas City, Mo. (1932) 1 p. l., 31 numb. l., 3 l., 14 numb. l. illus. (incl. coats of arms) plates. 29 cm. Mimeographed. "The ancient and honorable order of redheads": 14 numb. leaves at end. 32-30557.
CS71. R72 1932

14581 ROESVIK. Gards- og aettebok for Ola-garden, Røsvik, Vigra. (Av Martinus El. Røsvik Vigra, 1968) 31 (i. e. 62) p. illus., ports. 31 cm. 77-454029.
CS919. R68 1968

ROGER. See ROGERS.

14582 ROGERS. A collection from the miscellaneous writings of Nathaniel Peabody Rogers. 2d ed. Manchester, N.H., W. H. Fisk; (etc., etc.) 1849. xxiv, 380 p. front. (port.) 19½ cm. The first edition appeared under title: A collection from the newspaper writings of Nathaniel Peabody Rogers. Concord, 1847. 9-11014.
F8. R72

14583 ROGERS. Genealogical memoir of the family of Rev. Nathaniel Rogers of Ipswich, Essex co., Mass. ... son of Rev. John Rogers, of Dedham, Essex, old England ... (By a descendant.) (n. p., 1851) 48 (i. e. 50) p. incl. port. 22½ cm. Caption title. Errata slip inserted and newspaper clipping mounted on fly-leaf. Reprinted from New England historical and genealogical register, April, 1851. 3-6542 rev.
CS71. R73 1851

14584 ROGERS. John Rogers: the compiler of the first authorised English Bible; the pioneer of the English reformation; and its first martyr. Embracing a genealogical account of his family, biographical sketches of some of his principal descendants, his own writings, etc. etc. By Joseph Lemuel Chester. London, Longman, Green, Longman, and Roberts, 1861. xii, 452 p. front. (port.) plates. 22 cm. 10-10228 rev.
BX5199. R73C5

14585 ROGERS. Genealogy of Rogers of Dowdeswell, in the county of Gloucester. Copied from a pedigree certified by George Harrison, Windsor herald, in the possession of R. R. Coxwell-Rogers, esq., of Dowdeswell court. (London?) Priv. print., 1869. 1 p. l., 10 p. illus. (coat of arms) 28½ cm. 2-27568.
CS439. R6

14586 ROGERS. The Scottish house of Roger, with notes respecting the families of Playfair and Haldane of Bermony. By the Rev. Charles Rogers ... 2d ed. Edinburgh, Printed for private circulation (McFarlane & Erskine, printers) 1875. 44 p. 22½ cm. 6-11673.
CS479. R7

14587 ROGERS. An historical summary of the Roger tenants of Coupar. By James Cruikshank Roger ... London, Printed by Henderson, Rait & Fenton, 1879. ix, 34 p. 22 cm. 18-20367.
CS479. R7 1879

14588   ROGERS.   Descendants of the Rev. Daniel Rogers, of Littleton, Mass. (By John Ward Dean. Boston, 1885)   8 p. 25½ cm.   "Reprinted from the N. E. historical and genealogical register for July, 1885." 5-14267.   .

CS71. R73   1885

14589   ROGERS.   The Rogers family, of the county of Essex, England, and Essex County, Massachusetts. By Henry F. Waters ... (Boston, 1887)   geneal. tab. 29 x 26 cm.   "Reprinted from the New England historical and genealogical register for April, 1887." 9-13257.

CS71. R73   1887

14590   ROGERS.   Four Perthsire families: Roger, Playfair, Constable and Haldane of Barmony, by the Rev. Charles Rogers ... Edinburgh, Priv. print. (by T. A. Constable at the Edinburgh University press) 1887.   vi p., 1 l., 137 p. 24 x 19 cm.   "One hundred and twenty-five copies." 11-4469.

CS477. P5R7

14591   ROGERS.   The John Rogers families in Plymouth (Mass.) and vicinity.   By Josiah H. Drummond. (Read before the Maine historical society, Dec. 19, 1895) (Portland, Me., 1895)   26 p. 24 cm. 1-18328.

CS71. R73   1895

14592   ROGERS.   James Rogers of Londonderry and James Rogers of Dunbarton.   (By Hon. Josiah H. Drummond... Manchester, N.H., S.C. & L. M. Gould) 1897.   1 p. l., 12 p. 22 cm.   A new ed. published in 1902 under title: The two James Rogers. 4-36354.

CS71. R73   1897

14593   ROGERS.   The Rogers family of Georgetown (Me.) By Josiah H. Drummond. (Portland, 1897?)   cover-title, 37 p. 24 cm. 9-13255.

CS71. R73   1897a

14594   ROGERS.   The John Rogers families in Plymouth (Mass.) and vicinity.   2d and rev. ed.   By Josiah H. Drummond. (Portland, Me., 1898)   cover-title, 27 p. 24½ cm.   "Read before the Maine historical society, December 19, 1895." 1-18329.

CS71. R73   1898

14595   ROGERS.   John Rogers of Marshfield and some of his descendants.   By Josiah H. Drummond ... West Hanover, Mass., R. B. Ellis, 1898.   iv, 5-194 p. 24 cm. 9-13256.

CS71. R73   1898a

14596   ROGERS.   Hope Rogers and his descendants.   Comp. by James S. Rogers ... Boston, Printed by D. Clapp & son, 1901.   7 p. 24 cm.   "Reprinted from New-Eng. historical and genealogical register for Jan., 1901." 5-444.

CS71. R73   1901

14597   ROGERS.   The two James Rogers: James Rogers of Londonderry and James Rogers of Dunbarton.   A genealogical research, by Hon. Josiah H. Drummond.   Manchester, N.H., 1902.   15 p. illus. (port.) 23½ cm.   First published in 1897, under title "James Rogers of Londonderry and James Rogers of Dunbarton."   Biographical sketch of the author, by G. W. Browne: p. 13-15. 4-36356.

CS71. R73   1902

14598   ROGERS.   James Rogers of New London, Ct., and his descendants.   By James Swift Rogers ... Boston, The compiler, 1902.   514 p. front., pl., port., facsim. 24 cm. 2-24344.

CS71. R73   1902a

14599   ROGERS.   A history of our family, (Rogers of Westmeon) 1451-1902.   Compiled from authoritative documents. By Julian C. Rogers.   London, Printed by Phipps & Connor, limited, Westminster, 1902.   ix, 102 p. front., plates, ports., II fold. geneal. tab. 25 cm.   "The Heron pedigree, 1451-1902": geneal. tab. no. II. 16-18071.

CS439. R6   1902

14600   ROGERS.   The Rogerenes; some hitherto unpublished annals belonging to the colonial history of Connecticut, pt. I. A vindication, by John R. Bolles, pt. II. History of the Rogerenes, by Anna B. Williams, appendix of Rogerene writings ... Boston, Stanhope press, F. H. Gilson company (1904)   396 p. 25½ cm.   The Rogerenes were a religious sect founded by John Rogers. 4-22000.

F97. B69

14601   ROGERS.   Biographical notes and genealogical tables giving line of descent of Jonathan J. Rogers and other descendants of Ezra Earll and Mary Sabin from the Mayflower pilgrims Francis Cooke and Richard Warren. By C. H. Weygant.   Newburgh, N. Y., Newburgh journal print, 1905.   45 p. 23½ cm.   Blank pages at end for "Additional records."   "Jonathan J. Rogers" ... in ms. on t.-p. 9-28471.   CS71. R73   1905

14602   ROGERS.   The ancestors and descendants of Luke Rogers and Sarah Wright Brown.   By Ethel Brigham Leatherbee.   Boston, Privately printed by T. R. Marvin & son, printers, 1907.   71 p. front. ports. 2 geneal. tab. 24½ cm.   The two genealogical tables, "Pedigree of Luke Rogers" and "Pedigree of Sarah Wright Brown," precede the frontispiece. 14-5652.   CS71. R73   1907

14603   ROGERS.   Lineage of the Rogers family - England, embracing John Rogers the martyr; emigrant descendants to America and issue, by John Cox Underwood ... (New York, Press of W. E. Rudge, c.1911)   36 p. front., pl., port., map, coats of arms. 32 cm. 11-29737.   CS71. R73   1911

14604   ROGERS.   History of the Rogers families in Maine.   Compiled by Rev. Charles Nelson Sinnett.   Brainerd, Minn. (1920)   1 p. l., 42 l. 36 cm. Type-written. 21-3729.   CS71. R73   1920

14605   ROGERS.   The ancestors and descendants of Dr. David Rogers, by Edward Francis Frémaux de Beixedon, jr.   (n.p., 1921)   123 p. ports., coats of arms. 30 cm. Contains also the Austin family. 23-14868.   CS71. R73   1921

14606   ROGERS.   ... Rogers family records, by J. Montgomery Seaver.   Philadelphia, Pa., American historical-genealogical society (1929?)   67, (3) p. illus. (ports.) 23½ cm. Three blank pages at end for "Family records". Coat of arms of the Rogers family on cover. "References": p. 66-67. 40-18922.   CS71. R73   1929

14607   ROGERS.   Rogers groups, thought and wrought by John Rogers, by Mr. and Mrs. Chetwood Smith; with introduction by Clarence S. Brigham ... Boston, C. E. Goodspeed & co., 1934.   6 p. l., 145 p. incl. illus., plates, facsims. front., plates, ports. 26½ cm. Issued in case. "Of this book five hundred and sixty-five copies have been printed by the Davis press, of Worcester, Massachusetts. Regular edition four hundred and ten copies - special edition one hundred and fifty-five copies, of which only one hundred copies are for sale. This is ... the special edition. Unnumbered copy for the Copyright office." Genealogies": p. (137) - 140. 35-932.   NB237. R65S6

14608   ROGERS.   Some recent finds regarding the ancestry of General George Rogers Clark, by R. C. Ballard Thruston ... Louisville, Ky., 1935.   1 p. l., 34 p. incl. pl., map, facsims. 25 cm. "Reprinted from the Filson club history quarterly, Louisville, Kentucky, January, 1935." 35-13982.   CS71. R73   1935

14609   ROGERS.   Rogers; some of the descendants of Giles Rogers, an immigrant to Virginia in 1664 ... including the family names of Barksdale, Croghan, Gatewood, George, Gwathmey, O'Fallon, Temple, Thruston, Tyler, Underwood, etc., compiled as the first step towards a chart by Hopewell L. Rogers ... Louisville, Ky., 1940.   1 p. l., 5-10, (114) p. 27½ cm. Reproduced from type-written copy. Bibliographical references included in introduction. 41-7032.   CS71. R73   1940

14610   ROGERS.   (Descendants of James Rogers of New London, Conn.) By Homer P. Rogers. (194-?)   11 v. (loose leaf) ports., geneal. tables. 30 cm. Typewritten manuscript; with holograph matter, clippings, and other source material. 51-23773.   CS71. R73

14611   ROGERS.   The Rogers family, by Corinne Rogers Guyton ... Blue Mountain, Miss., 1942. 49 (i.e. 53), (2) p. plates, ports. 22 cm. Two blank pages at end for "Addition data," Cover-title: My family. 43-1067.

                                                                                                      CS71. R73   1942

14612   ROGERS.   The Rogers-Turfler family, a search for ancestors (by) I. Newton Williams ... Bradley Beach, N. J., C. W. Smith press, 1946.   120 p. incl. front., illus. (facsim.) ports. 23½ cm. 47-21361.
                                                                                                      CS71. R73   1946

14613   ROGERS.   Rogers, Ward, Shipman, and allied families, by Harold I. Meyer, Mrs. Sylvan L. Mouser (and) Mrs. Voris R. Norton.   Chicago (1949?)   1 v. (various pagings) illus. 26 cm. "Reproduced from... the Indiana magazine of history, beginning with vol. XLIV, no. 4, Dec. 1948, continuing through vol. XLV, no. 3, Sept. 1949." 52-26992.
                                                                                                      CS71. R73   1949

14614   ROGERS.   Genealogy of Rogers, Peyton, Owens, Sone, Marrs, Jennings, Jouett, and allied families.   By Guy McClure Sone.   (Jefferson City? Mo.) 1958.   189 l. illus. 29 cm. 58-31474.
                                                                                                      CS71. R73   1958

14615   ROGERS.   Descendants of John Rogers of Boxford, Massachusetts, through his son, Nathaniel. By Edwinna (Dodson) Bierman.   San Gabriel, Calif., 1964.   33 p. 22 cm.   Consists of a copy of the text of Genealogy of John Rogers of Boxford, Mass. (Winchester, Ind., 1882) followed by the same material grouped into families by the compiler.   65-29671.

CS71. R73   1964

14616   ROGERS.   Rogers genealogy; Charles Thomas Rogers and descendants.   Compiled by Lewis G. Rogers, Sr. and Wilmot Polk Rogers.   Santa Rosa, Calif., 1965.   10, 3 p. 29 cm.   65-51593.

CS71. R73   1965

14617   ROGERS.   Dr. John Rogers, 1794-1832.   By Ellen Stanley Rogers.   (Hyattsville? Md.) 1966. 49 p. 28 cm.   Bibliographical footnotes.   68-545.   CS71. R73   1966

14618   ROGERS.   History and genealogy of the Jonathan Rogers family.   (Norristown? Pa.) 54, vi p.   map, 22 x 36 cm.   Cover title.   Prepared under the direction of a committee of the Rogers Family Association.   Edited by Jean Rogers Holt; Robert T. Holt, associate.   68-829.   CS71. R73   1967

   ROGERS.   See also:

ALDERMAN, 1957	KINNEY, 1903	PITTMAN, 1958
BARLOW, 1891	LEE, 1954	POCAHONTAS, 1887
BENJAMIN, 1911	LEWIS, 1960	POELINITZ, 1933
CODY, 1915	MACKEY, 1957	POELINITZ, 1962
COOPER, 1939	McKINNEY, 1905	POLK, 1939
CROCKER, 1923	MEAD, 1917	RYLE, 1961
CUNLIFFE, CS439. C87	MINER, 1928	SAMPSON, 1922
FARISH, 1967	NOYES, 1907	SINNOTT, 1905
HAYNES, 1922	OSTRANDER, 1936	SMITH, 1913
HOPKINS, 1936	PIERCE, 1874	TORRENCE, 1938

   ROGERSON.   See MOUNSEY, 1947

14619   ROGGE.   Het geslacht Rogge te Zaandam; drie eeuwen familiegeschiedenis tegen den achter- grond van nering en bedrijf.   Koog aan de Zaan, P. Out, 1948.   200 p. facsim. 24 cm.   Errata slip inserted. 49-27010 *.   CS829. R56   1948

14620   ROHRBACH.   John R. Rohrbach (Rohrabaugh) 1728-1821: descendants and marriage connect- ions, by James D. Rorabaugh.   Parsons, W. Va., McClain Print. Co., 1966.   476 p. illus., coat of arms, ports. 23 cm.   66-30409.   CS71. R736   1966

14621   ROHRBOUGH.   The Rohrbough family.   By Fred Ware Rohrbough.   (Baton Rouge? La., 1962) 130 l. illus.   30 cm.   62-44261.   CS71. R75   1962

14622   ROHRER.   The saga of a people; a history of Johanne Rohrer, with a genealogy of his de- scendants, by Lister O. Weiss and Noah R. Getz.   (Mount Joy, Pa., Bulletin, 1939)   41 p. map. 20 cm. Blank pages at end for additions.   40-2276 rev.   CS71. R74   1939
   —— Supplement of the Johannes Rohrer family history, 1939-1967 (by) Lister O. and Edna M. Weiss.   (Orville? Ohio, 1967)   51 l. 30 cm.   CS71. R74   1939
                                                                                                            Suppl.

14623   ROHRER.   John Rohrer of Lancaster county, Pennsylvania; a paper outlining some of the results of a research in the records of Alsace; Switzerland; Lancaster, Pennsylvania; and Hagers- town, Maryland, made by Albert L. Rohrer.   Maplewood, N. J. (Ann Arbor, Mich., Edwards brothers, inc., lithoprinters) 1941.   1 p. l., 15 p. front. (coats of arms) 2 maps on 1 l. 27½ cm.   41-8757.

CS71. R74   1941

14624   ROKEBY.   Œconomia Rokebiorum; an account of the family of Rokeby written by Ralph Rokeby, one of the Council of the north in the reign of Queen Elizabeth, edited by A. W. Cornelius Hallen ... (Presented with the first volume of Northern notes and queries.)   Edinburgh, D. Douglas, 1887.   41 p. 25 cm.   Written in 1565 "and afterwards found and renewed by the same Ralph Rokeby, Jan. 30, 1593." "The transcript from

14624 continued: which this version of Œconomia is printed, was made in 1712 for Richard Boyleston by his wife Rhoda, daughter of George Rokeby, who possessed a copy of the book." cf. Dedication.   Additional Rokeby pedigree: p. 33-35.   18-20370.

CS439. R63

14625   ROKSVAG.   Roksvåg-slekta i Bremsnes; utarb. og samlet ved Hans Nilsen og Jakob Grønvik. By Hans Peter Nilsen.   Kristiansund N. , O. B. Sverdrups trykkeri, 1947.   37 l. 26 cm. 49-54805*.

CS919. R7   1947

ROLAND.   See ROWLAND.

ROLATER.   See HOWE, 1960

14626   ROLFE.   Pocahontas, alias Matoaka, and her descendants through her marriage at James-town, Virginia, in April, 1614, with John Rolfe, gentleman; including the names of Alfriend, Archer, Bentley, Bernard, Bland, Bolling, Branch, Cabell, Catlett, Cary, Dandridge, Dixon, Douglas, Duval, Eldridge, Ellett, Ferguson, Field, Fleming, Gay, Gordon, Griffin, Grayson, Harrison, Hubard, Lewis, Logan, Markham, Meade, McRae, Murray, Page, Polythress, Randolph, Robertson, Skipwith, Stanard, Tazewell, Walke, West, Whittle and others.   With biographical sketches by Wyndham Robertson, and illustrative historical notes by R. A. Brock.   Richmond, J. W. Randolph & English, 1887.   vii, (1), 84 p. front. (port.) 25 cm. 9-15610.   CS71. R747   1887

14627   ROLFE.   Rolfe family records, volume II, by R. T. and A. Günther ... London (etc.) Printed for the authors by Hazell, Watson & Viney, ld., 1914.   xii, 386, 29 p. illus., plates, ports. 20 cm.   Appendix, 29 p., has separate t.-p.: "Family chronicles (section 1 a The Temple family) by Lilian Clarke.   Wellingborough, Perkins and co. 1912." The original plan was to publish as v. 1 the reminiscences of the present head of the family and his life at Heacham hall in his youth.   cf. Pref. date June, 1914. 15-19681.

CS439. R65

14628   ROLFE.   Pocahontas ... etc.   Reprint of No. 14627.   Baltimore, Southern Book Co., 1956. 84 p. 22 cm. 61-49177.   CS71. R747   1956

14629   ROLFE.   Pocahontas ... etc.   Reprint of No. 14627.   Baltimore, Genealogical Pub. Co.. 1968.   vii, 84 p. 23 cm. Reprint of the 1887 ed. 76-3327 MARC.   CS71. R747   1968

ROLFE.   See also: CHAMBERS, 1957   WHITTIER, 1912
                          ECHOLS, 1956   No. 430 -Adventurers of purse...
                          NELSON, CS439. N33   No. 1547 - Cabell county.
                          POCAHONTAS, 1887

ROLLE.   See BARBER, DA690. L982C6

14630   ROLLINS.   Notes relating to Rawlins, or Rollins with notices of early settlers of the name in America, and family records of Thomas, of Boston, Nicholas, of Newbury, William, of Gloucester. By John R. Rollins ... Lawrence, Mass., G. S. Merrill & co., printers, 1870.   3 p. l., (5)-84 p. 23 cm. 11-6017.   CS71. R754   1870

14631   ROLLINS.   Records of families of the name Rawlins or Rollins, in the United States.   In two parts ... Compiled by John R. Rollins.   Lawrence, Mass., G. S. Merrill & Crocker, printers, 1874. xiv p., 2 l., 348 p. front. (port.) illus. (coat of arms) 23 cm.   Contents. - pt. 1. Family records of James Rawlins, of Dover, and his descend-ants. - pt. 2. Partial records of the families of Nicholas Rawlins, of Newbury, William Rawlins, of Gloucester, Thomas Rawlins, of Scituate, Thomas Rawlins of Boston, Henry Rollins, of Pennsylvania, Charles Rawlins, of Delaware, and notices of other families who settled in Virginia and Maryland, and in other parts of the country. 9-13235 rev.

CS71. R754   1874
—— Copy 2.   17-31798.   CS71. R754   1874a

14632   ROLLINS.   Rollins family in vertical file.   Ask reference librarian for this material.

ROLLINS.   See also RAWLINGS.

14633   ROLLO.   A genealogical record of the descendants of Alexander Rollo, of East Haddam, Conn., 1685-1895, with biographical notes.   By John Hollenbeck Rollo.   Wilmington, Del. , Priv. print. for the author, 1896.   56 p. 24½ cm. "Edition of 75 copies." no. 1 of 9 extra copies. 9-13254.   CS71. R755   1896

ROLPH.   See WHEELER, 1920

ROMAINE.   See: DAVIS, 1956
                         ROMEYN.

ROMANES.   See CALL, 1920

14634   ROMANOV.   Political & diplomatic history of Russia, by George Vernadsky.   Students' ed.
Boston, Little, Brown, and company, 1936.   ix p., 2 l., (3)-499 p. incl. geneal. tables.   maps (part fold.) 22½ cm.   Maps
on lining-papers.   "General bibliography": p. (467)-470.   Bibliography at end of each chapter.   36-11172.
                                                                                                            DK61.V4

ROMARA.   See LONGESPÉE

14635   ROMER.   Historical sketches of the Romer, Van Tassel and allied families, and tales of the
neutral ground.   (Buffalo, N.Y., W. C. Gay printing co., inc., c.1917)   viii, 151 p. incl. front., illus. (map)
plates, coats of arms, ports.   23½ cm.   Reprinted in part from various sources.   Ed. by John Lockwood Romer.   17-12394.
                                                                                                            CS71.R765   1917

ROMER.   See also JAMES, 1913a

14636   ROMEYN.   The Romine family (Romeyn, Romaine, Romyn, etc.) compiled by Mildred A.
McDonnell.   (Takoma Park, Md., 1966-68)   2 v. (397 l.) 28 cm.   CS71.R767   1966
            —— Index.   (Takoma Park, Md., 1966-68)   2 v. (154 l.) 28 cm.   Includes bibliography.   66-31538.
                                                                                                            CS71.R767   1966
                                                                                                            Index.

14637   ROMINE.   The Romine family.   By William Bethel Romine.   Pulaski, Tenn., Pulaski citizen,
1930.   (13) p. 23 cm.   61-57911.   CS71.R767   1930

ROMINE.   See ROMEYN.

ROMYN.   See ROMEYN.

RONAN.   See RONAYNE, 1917

14638   RONAYNE.   Notes on the family of Ronayne or Ronan of counties Cork and Waterford (as they
appeared in the "Journal" of the Cork historical and archaeological society for April-June, July-September, October-December, 1916: and April-June, July-September, 1917.) By Frederick W. Knight.   To
which are appended Notes on the families of Desmond and Ronayne by E. C. R. (Edward Camillus
Ronayne), from the April-June, 1916, no. of the same "Journal."   Cork, Printed by Guy and co. ltd.,
1917.   47, (1) p. front. (coat of arms) 24½ cm.   20-16683.   CS499.R7

14639   RONEY.   Roney genealogy (!) the story of Captain John Otto Roney and Harriet Burnham
Robinson, of Thomaston, Maine, & their descendants.   1st ed. ... (By) John Roney Grindell.   Providence, R. I., Eastern magazine agency, c.1947.   14 p. 28 cm.   47-24696.   CS71.R77   1947

14640   RONEY.   The John Roney family of Philadelphia, Pennsylvania, including references to the
allied families Cresson, Jones, Eckel, Morris, Cox, and Keith.   By Laurence Prescott Keith. Chicago,
1948.   geneal. table.   56 x 64 cm. fold. to 28 x 22 cm.   "One hundred copies ... No. 33."   50-21404.   CS71.R77   1948

14641   RONSHEIM.   The Ronsheim family from Abterode (by) Edw. J. Ronsheim, Sr.   Anderson, Ind.
(1954?)   16 l. 32 cm.   Caption title.   71-6680 MARC.   CS71.R773   1954

RONSPIESS.   In vertical file under PRANKE family.   Ask reference librarian for this material.

14642   ROOD.   The Rood-Rude record.   v. 1 -   Nov. 1953 -   Prairie du Sac,
Wis.   v. 28 cm.   irregular.   Editor: 1953 -   R. R. Buell.   57-58661.   CS71.R775   1953

ROOD.   See also THORNGATE, 1906

ROOF.   See No. 3888 - Twigs from family trees.

ROOKES.   See: ATKINSON, 1923
SHARP, QB36.S5C9

14643   ROOKS.   The Gerrit Hendrik Rooks family history, compiled by Russell Rooks, assisted by Gerritt J. Rooks.   (Arlington? Va., 1959?)   61 l.   29 cm.   62-27262.   CS71.R777   1959

14644   ROOME.   (Peter Willemse and Hester Van Gelder Roome)   In vertical file.   Ask reference librarian for this material.

14645   ROOP.   Genealogy of the Roop family; the descendants of Christian Roop, 1733-1810, traced down for five generations from 1733.   By Herbert G. Englar.   Westminster, Md., Press of the Times Print. Co. (19 -)   87 p.   23 cm.   58-52192.   CS71.R779

14646   ROOP (RUPP).   Isaac Roop (Rupp) goes West.   Compiled from family papers, public and published records.   By Wendell Roop.   73-82 p.   Reprint.   In vertical file.   Ask reference assistant for this material.

ROOS.   See: JUSTIN, 1900
WHITMORE, 1875

ROOSENBOOM.   See ROSEBOOM.

14647   ROOSEVELT.   The Roosevelt genealogy, 1649-1902; comp. and pub. by Charles Barney Whittelsey ... Hartford, Conn., Press of J. B. Burr & co., 1902.   121 p.   24 cm.   "Addenda": 6 leaves inserted after p. 106.   2-15636.   CS71.R781   1902

14648   ROOSEVELT.   The ancestry of Theodore Roosevelt; a genealogical record from 1649, with notes on the families of Baillee, Bulloch, Douglas, Elliott, Irvine, Stewart, Van Schaack; with complete name index.   New York, W. M. Clemens, 1914.   20 p.   23 cm.   Compiled by William M. Clemens.   14-10216.   CS71.R781   1914

14649   ROOSEVELT.   All in the family, by Theodore Roosevelt; with 16 illustrations.   New York, London, G. P. Putnam's sons, 1929.   vi, 189 p.   front., pl., ports.   22½ cm.   29-18407.   F757.3.R78

14650   ROOSEVELT.   Franklin D. Roosevelt's colonial ancestors; their part in the making of American history, by Alvin Page Johnson ... with portrait frontispiece and charts.   Boston, Lothrop, Lee & Shepard co. (c.1933)   222 p. incl. geneal. tables.   front. (port.)   20½ cm.   Maps on lining-papers.   Contents. - The Roosevelts. - The Waltons. - The Aspinwalls. - The Howlands. - The Delanos. - The Church family. - The Lymans. - The Robbins family. - General review.   33-5082.   CS71.R781   1933

14651   ROOSEVELT.   ... The house of Roosevelt.   By Paul Haber.   New York, The Author's publishing company, 1936.   3 p. l., 89 p.   21½ cm.   36-13161.   E810.H23

14652   ROOSEVELT.   The house of Roosevelt (by) Paul Haber.   Rev. ed.   Brooklyn, N.Y., The Author's publishing company (c.1936)   123 p.   illus. (incl. port., facsims., coats of arms)   19 cm.   36-25759.   E810.H232

14653   ROOSEVELT.   An imperial saga; the Roosevelt family in America, by Bellamy Partridge.   New York, Hillman-Curl, inc., 1936.   xvi p., 1 l., 19-325 p. incl. front. (port.) geneal. tables.   ports.   24½ cm.   Illustrated lining-papers.   "Books consulted and quoted": p. 315-316.   36-20860.   E757.3.P36

14654   ROOSEVELT.   Odyssey of an American family; an account of the Roosevelts and their kin as travelers, from 1613 to 1938, by Hall Roosevelt in collaboration with Samuel Duff McCoy ... New York and London, Harper & brothers, 1939.   xv p., 2 l., 339, (1) p.   front., illus., plates, map, ports., facsims.   24½ cm.   Map on lining-papers.   "First edition."   39-9014.   E757.3.R76
—— Copy 2   CS71.R781   1939

485

14655   ROOSEVELT.   Sind die Roosevelts Juden?   Von Adolf Schmalix.   Weimar, Weimarer druck- und verlagsanstalt gebr. Knabe, kg., 1939.   46 p. map, geneal. tables. 21 cm. "Quellenangabe": p. 46. 40-25541.

CS71.R781   1939a

14656   ROOSEVELT.   The Theodore Roosevelt family in Egypt, from the book Strolls along the Nile, the river of life; being the reminiscences of a world traveller, by Albert Charles Cosman.   (Denver, 194-)   20 p. l., 45 (i.e.46) numb. l., 1 l. mounted port. 20½ x 25½ cm. Photocopy (negative) of the type-written original in the possession of Mrs. Ethel Roosevelt Derby.   The preliminary leaves include reproductions of letters to and from the author.   46-42286.

E757.C84

14657   ROOSEVELT.   The Roosevelts and America, by M. Fortescue Pickard.   London, H. Joseph limited (1941)   11, 17-288 p. front., plates, ports., fold. geneal. tab. 22 cm. "First published in October, 1941." 42-12693.

E757.3.P5

14658   ROOSEVELT.   The amazing Roosevelt family, 1613-1942 (by) Karl Schriftgiesser.   New York, W. Funk, inc. (1942)   xii, 367 p. 24½ cm. Bibliography: p. 355-358. 42-11995.   E757.3.S4

14659   ROOSEVELT.   The strenuous life; the "Oyster Bay" Roosevelts in business and finance, by Wm. T. Cobb.   New York, William E. Rudge's sons (1946)   5 p. l., 99, (1) p. illus. (incl. ports., map, facsims.) coat of arms. 28½ x 21 cm. Genealogical table on lining-paper. Bibliography: p. 99. 47-1373.

CS71.R781   1946
Rare book coll.

14660   ROOSEVELT.   White House diary, by Henrietta Nesbitt, F.D.R.'s housekeeper.   (1st ed.) Garden City, N.Y., Doubleday, 1948.   314 p. 21 cm. 48-7746*.   F204.W5N4

14661   ROOSEVELT.   The strange death of Franklin D. Roosevelt; history of the Roosevelt-Delano dynasty, America's royal family.   By Emanuel Mann Josephson.   (1st ed.) New York, Chedney Press (1948)   333 p. ports., facsims., geneal. tables. 21 cm. 48-3458 rev. *.   E807.J65

14662   ROOSEVELT.   Theodore Roosevelt.   In vertical file.   Ask reference librarian for this material.

ROOSEVELT.   See also: LIVINGSTON, 1939
RAPALJE, CS69.H7
TODD, 1867

14663   ROOT.   Root genealogical records.   1600-1870.   Comprising the general history of the Root and Roots families in America.   By James Pierce Root ... New York, R. C. Root, Anthony & co., 1870.   2 p. l., 9-533 p. geneal. tab. 21½ x 18½ 9-13021.   CS71.R782   1870

14664   ROOT.   A branch of the Root family.   By Hazel Esther Drake.   (Rippey? Iowa) 1948.   112 p. illus., ports., coat of arms. 22 cm. Cover title. 49-18010*.   CS71.R782   1948

ROOT.   See also: DUNHAM, 1956
HALE, 1948
MESSENGER, E171.A53 vol. 20

ROOTE.   See ROOT.

ROOTES.   See ROOT.

14665   ROPER.   The Ropers of Sterling and Rutland, by Ella E. Roper ... East Orange, N.J., Pub. under the auspices of the Roper association by F. H. Colvin, 1904.   2 p. l., 7-472, (1) p. incl. plates. 21 cm. 6-24869.   CS71.R784   1904

14666   ROPER.   The Roper family.   Reproduced from an old book.   London, Research Pub. Co., 1960.   16 p. coat of arms. 23 cm. "Limited edition of 100 copies ... no. 33." Bibliographical footnotes. 61-25486.

CS439.R66   1960

ROPER.   See also WILLIAMS, 1940a

14667   ROQUEMORE.   Some early Texas families: Roquemore, Lacey, Fouts, Pochmann, Burrows, and one hundred and fifty related families; a genealogy, by Virginia Ruth Fouts Pochman.   (Madison, Wis., 1942)   cover-title, 40 p. illus. (ports.) 21½ cm. Text on p. (3) and (4) of cover. Reproduced from type-written copy. 43-1068.   CS71. R79   1942

14668   ROQUEMORE.   The Roquemore report of 1967.   By Josephine Costello Huffaker.   (Dallas, 1967)   vi, 278 p. illus., ports. 24 cm. Bibliography: p. 278. 68-2538.   CS71. R79   1967

          RORABAUGH.   See: ROHRBACH.
                                       ROHRBOUGH.

          ROREBOUGH.   See ROHRBOUGH.

          RORISON.   See SKINNER, 1935

14669   RORY.   Irish family history ... By Richard F. Cronnelly.   Dublin, Printed by Goodwin, son, and Nethercott, 1864.   2 v. in 1. 22½ cm. Contents. - pt. I. A history of the Clanna-Rory, or Rudricians, descendants of Roderick the Great, monarch of Ireland ... to which is added a paper on the authorship of the "Exile of Erin" by a septuagenarian. - pt. II. A history of the Clan Eoghan, or Eoghanachts, descenants of Eoghan More, or Eugene the Great. 3-4650.   CS498. C8

14670   ROSAS.   ... Cartas privadas de la familia de Rosas.   By A. Taullard.   Buenos Aires, Imp. López, 1924.   71 p. incl. illus., ports. 24 cm. 32-24477.   F2846. T28

14671   ROSBRUGH.   Rosbrugh, a tale of the revolution; or, Life, labors and death of Rev. John Rosbrugh ... chaplain in the Continental army; clerical martyr of the revolution, killed by Hessians, in the battle of Assumpink, at Trenton, New Jersey, Jan. 2d, 1777.   Founded upon a paper read before the New Jersey historical society at its meeting in Trenton, January 15th, 1880; to which is appended genealogical data of all the Rosbrughs of the connection in America: by Rev. John C. Clyde ... Easton (Pa.) 1880.   4 p. l., 101 p. maps, facsim., diagrs. 23 x 19 cm. "Thatcher family": p. (89)-91. Leaf of "Addenda" inserted between p. 92 and (93) Supplementary matter dated 1882: p. (93)-101. 2-516.   E263. P4R72

14672   ROSBRUGH.   The Roseborough family.   By Wilson F. Rosebraugh.   (Newark? Ohio, 1955)   11 l. map. geneal. tables. 29 cm. 56-23141.   CS71. R795   1955

14673   ROSBRUGH.   The Rosebrugh family story, also spelled Rosbrugh, Rosebrough, Roseborough, Rossborough, Rosebrook, etc.   By Harold Rosebrugh.   Galt, Ont., Printed by Galt Printers, 1965.   xiv, 168 p. illus., coat of arms, ports. 23 cm. 66-88108.   CS71. R795   1965

          ROSCOE.   See: PEARSON, 1938
                                     SEYMOUR, 1917

14674   ROSE.   A genealogical deduction of the family of Rose of Kilravock, with illustrative documents from the family papers, and notes.   Edinburgh (T. Constable) 1848.   1 p. l., viii, 531, (1) p. double front., illus., pl., facsim. 25½ cm. (On cover: The Spalding club, Aberdeen. (Publications. 17)   Title vignette in colors. By Hugh Rose. Continued to 1753 by Lachlan Shaw. Ed. by Cosmo Innes. 4-24737.   DA750. S8 vol. 17

14675   ROSE.   A chart of the ancestors and descendants of Rev. Robert Rose, born at Wester Alves, Scotland, February 12, 1704, came to Virginia in 1725, died June 30, 1751; prepared by W. G. Stanard, for Miss Annie Fitzhugh Rose Walker.   Richmond, W. E. Jones, printer, 1895.   1 p. l., fold. geneal. tab. 19 cm. 9-13018.   CS71. R796   1895

14676   ROSE.   Rose, Miller, Pryor (Prior) Ekelberry.   Charts & records ... Comp. by Sarah Augusta Prior Smith - (Mrs. Charles Ellsworth Smith) ... Columbus, O., 1922.   2 p. l., 86 (i. e. 93) p. incl. illus., 2 fold. geneal. tab. 31 cm. Illustrations include portraits and facsimiles. A collection of data, consisting of printed and manuscript material, with mounted photographs fastened together in binder.   CA22-520 unrev.   CS71. R796   1922

14677   ROSE.   The domestic papers of the Rose family, edited by Alistair & Henrietta Taylor ... Aberdeen, Milne & Hutchison, 1926.   vi, (4), 188 p. front., ports. 22 cm. A selection from the papers of William Rose of Montcoffer. 27-267.   CS479. R82

14678   ROSE.   Genealogy of the family of Rose of Holme Rose, Nairnshire, as compiled by the late Henry Rose, esq., of Ruallan, Nairn, and brought down to date with introductory sketch by H. T. Donaldson, late county clerk, Nairn ... Aberdeen, Printers Milne and Hutchison, 1929.   31 p. 24 cm. 45-25694.   CS479. R818

14679   ROSE.   Colonel William Rose of Tennessee, his ancestors and descendants, 1034-1938. Also the history of other families, not of the Rose name, who have married into the family: Cockrill, Abernathy, Washburn, Sloan, Norwood, Patton, Teasdale, McLaurine.   By Virginia Rose.   (Jonesboro? Ark., 1939)   283 p. illus., port., coat of arms. 24 cm. 56-53694.
                                                                                                 CS71. R796   1939

14680   ROSE.   The Rose family of colonial Virginia and medieval Scotland, compiled by W. H. T. Squires ... Norfolk, Va., 1942.   146 numb. 1. 29½ x 23 ½ cm.   Type-written, with additions and corrections in manuscript. Bibliographical foot-notes. 44-1133.   CS71. R796   1942

14681   ROSE.   A partial genealogy of the Rose families of Granville, Ohio.   By Mary Belle Linnell. (n. p., 1968?)   58 1. 29 cm. Includes bibliographies. 68-1875.   CS71. R796   1968

          ROSE.   See also: BENDALL, 1945
                               COMBERFORD, DA690. W39B1
                               LAMB, 1904
                               PETTY. BX5195. T5B6
                               WOOD, F159. P6K9
                               WRIGHT, 1960

14682   ROSEBOOM.   1630-1897.   A brief history of the ancestors and descendants of John Roseboom (1739-1805) and of Jesse Johnson (1745-1832).   Comp. by Catharine Roseboom, Dr. J. Livingston Roseboom, Rev. Henry U. Swinnerton and Joseph H. White, Cherry Valley, N. Y.   (Printed at the Co-operative press, Cambridge, Mass., 1897?)   140 p. incl. front. 24½ cm. 9-13253.
                                                                                                 CS71. R798   1897

14683   ROSEBUSH.   The Rosier-Rosebush family with allied families: Burdick-Hubbard, Peckham, Sheldon, Perkins, Richmond, Finkle, and others.   By Waldo Emerson Rosebush.   (Appleton, Wis., Published by Badger Print. Co., 1954)   183 p. illus., ports., maps (part fold.) facsims. 28 cm. On spine: C. C. Nelson Pub. Co. Bibliography: p. 30-47. 55-22498.   CS71. R7985   1954

14684   ROSECRANS.   The Rosenkrans family in Europe and America.   Compiled by Allen Rosenkrans ... Newton, N. J., New Jersey herald press, 1900.   332 p., 1 1. front., illus., plates, ports. 27 cm. 4-30111.
                                                                                                 CS71. R799   1900

14685   ROSECRANS .   Glimpses through portals of the past, by Warren Rosecrans Hedden (and others.   New Haven? 192-)   67 1. 28 cm. Caption title. "Additions and corrections": leaf inserted. An account of the Heddon and Earle families, comp. by A. W. Earle. 49-35028*.   CS71. R799

          ROSÉE.   See JACQUIER DE ROSÉE.

14686   ROSEL.   Stemmata Rosellana; compiled from inquisitiones post mortem, parliamentary records, rotuli hundredorum, chancery recports, etc., etc.   By Clifford Stanley Sims ... Philadelphia, W. F. Geddes, 1859.   8 p. 19½ cm. 3-7930.   CS71. R811   1859

14687   ROSEL.   Stemmata Rossellana; the lineage and history of the family of Rossell, comp. and arranged from A. D. 760 to A. D. 1859, by Prof. Clifford/S. Sims ... 2d ed., extending the history to A. D. 1912, rev. and ed. by Prof. Hugh B. Rossell ... Washington D. C., J. H. Polkinhorn, printer, 1912. 18 p., 1 1. front. (port.) illus. (coat of arms) 22 cm. Supplement: October 15, 1912 to May 4, 1921, 1 leaf at end. 21-9393.
                                                                                                 CS71. R811   1912a

          ROSEL.   See also ROSSELL.

14688   ROSENBERG.   The Milesian origin of "Rosenberg of Bath".   (n. p., 18 -)   geneal. tab. 45 x 71½ cm. fold. to 22½ x 12½ cm. Blue print. 24-29129.   CS439. R67

14689   ROSENBERGER.   The Rosenberger family of Montgomery County.   Historical and genealogical sketches.   By Edward Mathews.   Harleysville, Pa., I. R. Haldeman, 1892.   4 p. l., 60 p. front., ports. 22½ cm. 9-13020.
CS71. R813   1892

14690   ROSENBERGER.   A genealogical record of the descendants of Henry Rosenberger of Franconia, Montgomery Co., Pa.   Together with historical and biographical sketches, and illustrated with portraits and other illustrations.   By Rev. A. J. Fretz ... With an introduction by Prof. Seward M. Rosenberger, of Quakertown, Pa.   (Milton, N. J.) 1906.   336, (1) p. incl. front. pl., ports. 21½ cm. 8-30310.
CS71. R813   1906

14691   ROSENBERGER.   A record of the descendants of James Henry Rosenberger (1821-1867) of Boone County, Indiana, by his first wife, Elizabeth Mills (1821-1864) and his second wife, Almyrah (Greist) Hadley (-1922) Compiled by William B. Lindley and Mrs. Homer G. Rosenberger, Jr. (n. p.) 1958.   73 l. illus. 30 cm. 60-43196.
CS71. R813   1958

14692   ROSENBERGER.   The Pennsylvania Germans; a sketch of their history and life, of the Mennonites, and of side lights from the Rosenberger family, by Jesse Leonard Rosenberger ... Chicago, Ill., The University of Chicago press (c. 1923)   x, 173 p. front. (port.) plates. 19½ cm. 23-18101.
F160. G3R66

14693   ROSENBERGER.   Some notes on the Rosenberger family in Pennsylvania & Virginia, 1729-1950.   Richmond, Printed for private circulation (by) the William Byrd Press, 1950.   vii, 39 p. 26 cm. Bibliographical footnotes. 51-407.
CS71. R813   1950

14694   ROSENBERGER.   A partial list of the descendants of Erasmus Rosenberger who lived in Hanover Township, Lancaster County, Pennsylvania, in the 1750's and settled in Berkeley County, Virginia, now West Virginia, in 1776.   By Francis Coleman Rosenberger.   Washington, 1951.   27 l. 28 cm. Typescript. 52-23554.
CS71. R813   1951

14695   ROSENBERGER.   Genealogy of the Baker family; descendants of John Nicholas Baker, 1701-63 (a native of Germany, he came to the United States in 1754 (with some connecting lines. Assembled in 1952-1953; rev. in 1954. Strasburg, Va., c. 1955.   233 l. illus. 29 cm. 55-21264 rev.   CS71. B17   1955
———— The Rosenberger family; an addition to the Baker genealogy. Strasburg, Va., c. 1956   234-255 l.   29 cm.
CS71. B17   1955
Suppl.

ROSENBERGER.   See also: COLVER, 1922
MULFORD, 1920

ROSENBERRY.   See ROSENBERGER.

ROSENCRANS.   See ROSECRANS.

ROSENKRANS.   See ROSECRANS.

ROSENMÜLLER.   See MAXWELL, 1916

ROSER.   See WOOD, 1937

14696   ROSEWELL.   Sir Henry Rosewell: a Devon worthy.   His ancestry and history ... By Frances B. James.   (Read at Exeter, July, 1888) ... (London, 1888)   cover-title, 10 p. 23 cm. (Reprinted from the Transactions of the Devonshire association for the advancement of science, literature, and art. 1888. - xx. pp.113-122)   22-6210.
DA378. R6J3

ROSKELLEY.   See HENDRICKS, 1963

14697   ROSS.   A genealogical account of the Rosses of Dalton, in the county of Dumfries, from their first settlement in Scotland, in the twelfth century, to the year of Our Lord 1854.   By George Parker Knowles ... London, Printed for private circulation only, by Harrison and sons, 1855.   8 p. illus. (coat

14697 continued: of arms) fold. geneal. tab. 25 cm. "Only seventy-five copies printed." "Coulthart, of Coulthart, Collyn, and Ashton-under-Lyne. Derived from the family muniments, and brought down to A.D. 1853, by Alexander Cheyne ... of Ashton-under-Lyne, co. Lancaster ... and George Parker Knowles, of Machester": geneal. tab. 15-23251.

CS479. R83

14698 ROSS. Rossiana; papers and documents relating to the history and genealogy of the ancient and noble house of Ross, of Ross-shire, Scotland, and its descent from the ancient earls of Ross, together with the descent of the ancient and historic family of Read, from Rede of Trough-end, Reade of Barton Court, Berks, and Read of Delaware. Also some account of the related families ... By Major Harmon Pumpelly Read ... Being a compilation of original documents found in the archives of the late General John Meredith Read, original articles by the author and compiler, and articles already published, including the descent of the earls of Ross, by the late Francis Nevile Reid, esq. Albany, N.Y. (Press of the Argus co.) 1908. xiii p., 1 l., (xv)-xix p., 1 l., 431 p. incl. col. front., illus. plates, ports., geneal. charts (part fold.) 24 cm. "The Argus company certifies that there have been three hundred copies ot this book rpinted from type in the year ninetten hundred and eight, of which this is no. 2." 9-5692.

CS71. R825 1908

14699 ROSS. A record of the descendants of Isaac Ross and Jean Brown, and the allied families of Alexander, Conger, Harris, Hill, King, Killingsworth, Mackey, Moores, Sims, Wade, etc. Comp. by Anne Mims Wright (Mrs. William R.) ... Jackson, Miss., Consumers stationery and printing co., 1911. 2 p. l., (9)-233, (10) p. front., plates, ports. 28 cm. 13-731.

CS71. R825 1911

14700 ROSS. Clan Ross in America. (Annual) (n.p.) v. illus., ports. 24 cm. 58-15916.

CS71. R825 1914

14701 ROSS. History of the Ross family. (Extracts from the historical address at the annual reunion of the Ross family at Pleasant Garden, N.C., on August 9th, 1928) By Dr. William Thornton Whitsett ... Greensboro, N.C., 1928. 1 p. 54 x 37 cm. fold. to 28 x 22 cm. From Greensboro patriot, Greensboro, N.C., August 9, 1928. 33-29127.

CS71. R825 1928

14702 ROSS. ... Ross family records, by J. Montgomery Seaver. Philadelphia, American historical-genealogical society (1929) 36 p. front. (incl. 3 port.) coat of arms. 29 cm. Coat of arms of the Ross family on recto of frontispiece. Pages 35-36 blank for "Family record". "References": p. 34. 40-18923.

CS71. R825 1929

14703 ROSS. Dr. Samuel Ross of Colerain, Massachusetts, ancestors and descendants, by David Caldwell MacBryde. (n.p., 1933?) 1 p. l., 12 numb. l. 28 cm. Typewritten; additions and corrections in manuscript. 33-34828.

CS71. R825 1933

14704 ROSS. Dr. Samuel Ross of Coleraine, Massachusetts; ancestors and descendants, by David Caldwell MacBryde. (Washington, D.C., c. 1934) 1 p. l., 20 p. front. (col. coat of arms) 18 cm. 34-32176.

CS71. R825 1934

14705 ROSS. Hosea Ballou Ross I, August 7, 1844 - August 30, 1928, Mary Elizabeth Johnson, August 29, 1848 - March 23, 1934. (By Winn Johnson Ross) (n.p., 1935) (43) p. illus. (incl. ports.) 17½ cm. 37-5915.

CS71. R825 1935

14706 ROSS. The Ross family, a short account of its history and traditions, by Douglas H. Ross. (New York? 1946?) 1 p. l., 3 numb. l. mounted coat of arms. 29½ x 23 cm. 46-15282.

CS71. R825 1946

14707 ROSS. The clan Ross. By Donald MacKinnon. Edinburgh, W. & A. K. Johnston & G. W. Bacon (1957) 32 p. illus. (part col.) map, col. coat of arms. 19 cm. (W. & A. K. Johnston's clan histories) 58-26271.

CS479. R83 1957

14708 ROSS. Concerning my ancestors, relatives, and descendants. By Ruth (Ross) Curray. (Cedar Rapids, Iowa, 1959?) 57 l. illus. 30 cm. 60-35388. CS71. R825 1959

14709 ROSS. The general history of the Ross family of Tain, Ross-shire, Scotland, a genealogical record from 1830 to 1962. By Mrs. William Ross Dickinson. Britton, S. D., 1962. 48 l. 29 cm. 63-34857.

CS71. R825 1962

14710   ROSS.   The Ross tribe of Dan, compiled by Velma L. Van Housen, 1921.   Re-edited by Lula Root.   (Utica? N. Y.) 1963.   1v .   (unpaged) geneal. table, ports.   22 cm.   65-34676.

CS71. R825   1963

14711   ROSS.   The great clan Ross, with highland notes and genealogies of the cadet branches in Scotland and the new world (by) John Robert Ross in collaboration with Charles Campbell Ross and A. C. Gordon Ross.   (Lindsay, Ont., J. Deyell, c.1968)   xvi, 197 p.   illus.   (part col.) coat of arms, facsim., geneal. tables, maps (on lining papers), ports.   24 cm.   Bibliography: p. xv-xvi.   77-443019 MARC.   CS479. R83   1968

ROSS.   See also: COULTHART,   CS479. C85   RUGGLES, 1901
                    NESBIT, 1929   SELDEN, 1911
                    PLANT, 1900   WHITNEY, 1925
                    ROBSON, CS439. R563   WOOD, 1925
                    ROSE, DA750. S8 vol. 17

ROSSEDAL.   See No. 5536 - The sloopers.

14712   ROSSELL.   Stemmata Rosellana; compiled from inquisitiones post mortem, parliamentary records, rotuli hundredorum, chancery reports, etc., etc.   By Clifford Stanley Sims ... Philadelphia, W. F. Geddes, printer, 1859.   8 p.   19½ cm.   3-7930.   CS71. R827   1859

14713   ROSSELL.   Stemmata Rossellana; the lineage and history of the family of Rossell, compiled and arranged from A. D. 760 to A. D. 1859, by Prof. Clifford S. Sims ... 2d ed., extending the history to A. D. 1912, revised and edited by Prof. Hugh B. Rossell ... Washington, D. C., J. H. Polkinhorn, printer, 1912.   18 p.   front.   (port.) illus.   (coat of arms) 22 cm.   13-388.   CS71. R827   1912
         ——— Another copy.   With supplement: Oct. 15, 1912 to May 4, 1921: leaf at end.   21-9393.   CS71. R827   1912a

14714   ROSSELL.   Stemmata Rossellana; history, traditions, biography, genealogy and heraldry of the Rossell family ... By Clifford Stanley Sims.   3d ed., edited by Hugh B. Rossell ... Washington, D. C., The editor, 1939.   viii, 118 p. incl. front., illus.   (incl. ports., coats of arms) 24½ cm.   44-32309.

CS71. R827   1939

14715   ROSSETTI.   Dante Gabriel Rossetti; his family-letters, with a memoir by William Michael Rossetti ... Boston, Roberts brothers, 1895.   2 v.   fronts., ports., double facsim. 23 cm.   Contents. - v.1. Dedication. Preface.   Memoir. - v.2. Family letters.   28-8891.   PR5246. A51

14716   ROSSETTI.   The Rossetti family, 1824-1854, by R. D. Waller ... (Manchester) Manchester university press, 1932.   xii, 324 p.   front., plates, ports., facsims.   24 cm.   (Half-title: Publications of the University of Manchester ... English series no. 21) Publications of the University of Manchester no. 217.   Bibliography: p. 298-302.   32-29351.

PR5236. R9W3

14717   ROTCH.   The Rotches.   By John Morgan Bullard.   New Bedford, 1947.   583 p.   plates, ports. 24 cm.   Includes the Bullard and Rodman families.   48-10484 *.   CS71. R829   1947

ROTCH.   See also LAWRENCE, 1904

14718   ROTE.   Genealogy chart of the George Rote family.   Compiled by Robert G. Rote from material collected & documented by Alvin F. Rote & Robert Lewis Rote.   Monroe, Wis., 1961.   geneal. table   138 x 57 cm.   Fold. to 49 x 37 cm.   68-7044.   CS71. R8292   1961

14719   ROTH.   A genealogical study of the Nicolaus and Veronica (Zimmerman) Roth family, 1834-1954, by Ruth C. Roth in collaboration with Roy D. Roth.   Elkhart, Ind., 1955.   331 p.   illus.   28 cm. 55-43959.   CS71. R8293   1955

ROTHENHEFFER.   See RODEFFER, 1948

14720   ROTHGEB.   Papa's diary.   By Rita Rothgeb White.   Luray, Va.   (Printed by Lauck & Co.) 1961.   80 p.   illus.   23 cm.   300 copies.   70-207428.   CS71. R8295   1961

ROTHGEBS.   See STRICKLER, 1925

14721   ROTHROCK.   Rothrock families.   Bulletin.   v. 1 -   Jan. 1938 -
(n. p.) 1938 -   v. monthly. 27½ cm. Editor: 1938 - Mrs. Mae Rothrock Gage, Newton, Ia. 38-14727.
CS71. R83   1938

14722   ROTHROCK.   Some descendants of Johann Georg Rothrock, 1721-1806.   By Edgar Paul
Rothrock.   Vermilion, S. D., 1960.   49 l. illus.   30 cm.   62-35624.   CS71. R83   1960

14723   ROTHROCK.   Forbears, family, and descendants of Henry Rothrock (son of Joseph Rothrock)
By Charles C. Turner.   (Bradenton? Fla., 1967?)   25 l. geneal. table, ports. 27 cm. Cover title. 74-5673 MARC.
CS71. R83   1967

ROTHROCK.   See also RODERICK, 1964

14724   ROTHSCHILD.   The romance of the Rothschilds, by Ignatius Balla.   London, E. Nash, 1913.
295, (1) p. front., plates, ports.   23 cm.   13-7352 rev.   HG1552. R8B3 1913
———— Another copy.   39-25604.   HG1552. R8B3 1913a

14725   ROTHSCHILD.   Meyer Amschel Rothschild, der gründer des Rothschildschen bankhauses,
von Christian Wilhelm Berghoeffer.   3. aufl. wohlfeile volksausgabe.   Frankfurt am Main, Englert &
Schlosser, 1924.   3 p. l., 176 p., 1 l. illus. (incl. facsim.) pl. 25 cm. 38-29326.   HG1552. R8B4 1924

14726   ROTHSCHILD.   The reign of the house of Rothschild (by) County Egon Caesar Corti, translated from the German by Brian and Beatrix Lunn; 1830-1871.   New York, Cosmopolitan book cor-
poration, 1928.   x, 457 p. front., plates, ports., double geneal. tab. 24½ cm. "Notes": p. 435-450; Bibliography: p. 451-457.
28-25668 rev.   HG1552. R8C58

14727   ROTHSCHILD. ... The rise of the house of Rothschild, By Egan Caesar Corti.   Translated
from the German by Brian & Beatrix Lunn.   London, V. Gollancz ltd., 1928.   463 p. front., plates, ports.,
coats of arms, facsims. 24 cm. At head of title: Count Corti. This work appraises the important influence of the Rothschild family on the
politics of the period, 1770-1830, in Europe and throughout the world. cf. Foreword. "Notes": p. 443-456; Bibliography: p. 461-463. 28-16369.
HG1552. R8C6   1928a

14728   ROTHSCHILD.   Five men of Frankfort; the story of the Rothschilds, by Marcus Eli Ravage
... with five portraits by Karl S. Woerner. New York, L. MacVeagh, The Dial press; Toronto,
Longmans, Green & company, 1928.   5 p. l., 3-341 p. front., ports. 23½ cm. 29-9114.
HG1552. R8R2

14729   ROTHSCHILD.   A century between, by Robert Henrey.   New York, Longmans, Green and
co., 1937.   4 p. l., 325 p. front., plates, ports., facsim. 22 cm. Printed in Great Britain. The story of the descendants of Nathan
Rothschild. 38-5476.   CS439. R68

14730   ROTHSCHILD.   The magnificent Rothschilds, by Cecil Roth.   London, R. Hale, limited,
1939.   4 p. l., 13-291 p. front., plates, ports., fold. geneal. tab. 22½ cm. "First impression January 1939 ... Third impression February
1939." 39-20628.   CS439. R68   1939b

14731   ROTHSCHILD.   The Rothschild money trust, by Andrew Fabius ... San Antonio, Tex., (1940)
4 p. l., 7-229 p. illus. (port.) 22 cm. 42-7096.   HG1552. R8F3

14732   ROTHWELL.   A Rothwell book, comprising the descendants of Claiborne Rothwell of Albemarle County, Virginia, through nine generations, and interesting sketches about some of his descendants, arr. and compiled by Myra Smith Fischer.   (Memphis? 1964)   xviii, 434 p. illus., facsims., map, ports.
28 cm.   64-55510.   CS71. R84   1964

ROTISLAV.   See No. 14634 - Romanov.

ROUBIDOUT.   See ROBIDOUX.

14733   ROULHAC.   Genealogical memoir of the Roulhac family in America.   By Helen M. Prescott.
Atlanta, Ga., American publishing and engraving co., 1894.   109 p. col. front. (coat of arms) 20½ cm.   "The
greater part ... copied from the memoirs of Francis L. G. Roulhac." 9-13239.   CS71. R86   1894

14734   ROUILLARD.   Notes historiques et les descendants d'Antoine Rouillard au Canada, 1649-1959.   By Brother Colomban.   (n.p., 1959?)   289 p. illus., ports., maps, facsim., geneal. tables. 26 cm. 63-28919.
CS90. R63   1959

14735   ROUND, Round, Rounds genealogy, descendants of John Round of Swansea, Massachusetts, who died 1716 and Rounds families of undetermined relationship, edited by Nathan Round Nichols. (Congress Park? Ill., 1928)   259 p. illus. (ports.) 21½ cm. 29-10242.   CS71. R862   1928

14736   ROUNTREE.   Rountree chronicles, 1827-1840; documentary primer of a Tar Heel faith.   By Charles Crossfield Ware.   Wilson, N.C., North Carolina Christian Missionary Convention, 1947.
64 p. plate, ports., facsims. 24 cm. 47-31191*.   BX7331. P5R68

14737   ROUNDY.   The Roundy family in America, from the sixteen-hundreds, compiled by Everett Ellsworth Roundy ... (Dedham, Mass., c.1942)   7 p. l., 561 p. front., illus., plates, ports., coat of arms. 24½ cm.
46-35003.   CS71. R8624   1942

ROUNSEVELL.   See ROUNSEVILLE.

ROUNSEVILL.   See ROUNSEVILLE.

14738   ROUNSEVILLE.   The Rounsevell family, by Ebenezer Weaver Peirce.   (Somerville, Mass., The Craigie press, 1932)   (31) p. 23½ cm. Reprinted from the author's "Contributions biographical, genealogical and historical ... Boston, 1874", and edited with notes by Philip Winslow Rounsevell. cf. Foreword. 33-15349.   CS71. R863   1932

ROUNSEVILLE.   See also PIERCE, 1874

14738a   ROUNTREE.   Rountree chronicles, 1827-1840; documentary primer of a Tar Heel faith.   By Charles Crossfield Ware.   Wilson, N.C., North Carolina Christain Missionary Convention, 1947.
64 p. plate, ports., facsims. 24 cm. 47-31191*.   BX7331. P5R68

14739   ROUNTREE.   Rowntree and Rountree family history, 1521-1953.   By Joseph Gustave Rountree.   (Beeville? Tex., 1959)   94, xlvi p. 28 cm. 59-33192.   CS71. R8636   1959

ROUS.   See ROUSE.

14740   ROUSE.   Diary of John Rous, incumbent of Santon Downham, Suffolk, from 1625 to 1642. Edited by Mary Anne Everett Green ... (London) Printed for the Camden society, 1856.   xii, 143 p.
22½ x 17 cm. (Camden society. Publications, no. LXVI) A 17-1238.   DA20. C17 vol. 66

14741   ROUSE.   Clasping hands with generations past, by Emma Rouse Lloyd.   (Cincinnati) Priv. print. (Wiesen-Hart press) 1932.   6 p. l., 3-228, (7) p. front., illus. (incl. ports., facsims.) 23½ cm. "Five hundred copies printed for Emma Rouse Lloyd." Blank pages for "Notes" (230-235) Bibliography: p. 207-210. Contents. - Rouse family. - Zimmerman family. - Tanner family. - Henderson family. - McClure family. - Porter family, - Alliied families. - Our colored folk. - Appendix. 32-25410.
CS71. R864   1932

14742   ROUSE.   Rouse family of Virginia and Kentucky.   By Emma Rouse Lloyd.   (Available for consultation at Lloyd Library, 309 West Court Street, Cincinnati 2, Ohio.

14743   ROUSH.   The Roush family in America (their contribution to the "new country") by Rev. L. L. Roush.   (In Ohio archaeological and historical quarterly. Columbus, O., 1927. 23½ cm. vol. XXXVI, p. 116-144. illus. (port.)
31-17347.   F486. O51 vol. 36

14744   ROUSH.   History of the Roush family in America, from its founding by John Adam Rausch in 1736 to the present time.   By Lester Le Roy Roush.   Strasburg, Va., Printed by Shenandoah Pub. House, 1928 - (63)   3 v. illus., col. coats of arms, ports. 24 cm. Imprint varies: v.2, Parkersburg, W. Va., Printed by M. C. Roush, Banner Print. Co.; v.3, Athens, Ohio, Printed by Lawhead Press. Vol. 3 has title: History of the Roush (Rausch) and allied families in America, with reference to European background. Vol. 2 "Compiled by Mrs. Julia Roush O'Melia and her staff of research workers, edited by Lester Le Roy Roush." Includes bibliographies. 29-6439 rev. 2.   CS71. R865   1928

14745   ROUSH.   The Roush family in the making of America.   By Lester Le Roy Roush.   (In Ohio state archaeological and historical quarterly. Columbus, O., 1936. 23 cm. vol. XLV, p. 197-239) 41-4847.   F486. O51 vol. 45

14746   ROUSH.   The forebears and the descendants of Michael and Eve Breon Roush; pioneers of the days of the covered wagon.   Compiled by their grand-daughters: Mary Etta Bordner Coons, Jessie Elizabeth Roush, Lucy Margaret Roush.   (n.p.) 1938.   2 p. l., 7-46 p. 2 pl. (incl. port.) on 1 l. 23½ cm. 39-12220.   CS71.R865   1938

        ROUSH.   See also MORR, 1896

14747   ROUSMANIERE.   New England heritage of Rousmaniere, Ayer, Farwell, and Bourne families. By Rosalie Fellows Bailey.   New York, 1960 -   v. illus. 23 cm. 62-41030.   CS71.R866   1960

14748   ROUSSEAU.   Rousseau biographies.   By Inez Jane Dennis.   (Cornwall Bridge? Conn.) 1965. 52 p. ports. 23 cm. 66-430.   CS71.R867   1965

        ROUTH.   See STAFFORD, 1962

        ROUTT.   See HIGHBAUGH, 1961

        ROUTTEN.   See IRONMONGER, 1956

14749   ROUX.   A catalogue of a loan exhibition of ship portraits by the Roux family of Marseilles, showing the work of Antoine Roux, Antoine Roux fils, Frederic Roux, Francois Roux, and Louis Roux, with a brief account of the family.   To be held at the Penobscot marine museum ... from July 1st to September 15th, 1939.   (Searsport, Me., Penobscot marine museum, c.1939)   32 p. incl. VIII pl. on 4 l. 26½ cm. "Limited edition." 40-8879.   VM307.P4

14750   ROUZE.   Genealogy of the Joseph Rouze family, collected by his granddaughter, Mrs. Ellan A. (Nellie) Hunter Sherman.   (Lincoln, Neb., Claflin printing co.) 1928.   64 p. illus. (incl. ports.) 23½ cm. Pages left blank throughout text for additions.   37-38421.   CS71.R868   1928

14751   ROW.   Memorials of the family of Row.   (By James Maidment)   Edinburgh, 1828.   1 p. l., v, (2), 10 p., 1 l., (6) p., 1 l., (5) p. 21 cm.   "Impression is limited to forty copies." - Introd. note.   The two sermons have separate title-pages and paging.   Contents. - Introductory notice. - Commendatory verses prefixed to Mr. John Rowe's Hebrew grammar. - Memorials of the family of Row (taken from a ms. account written of his maternal ancestry by Robert Mylne, jun.) - The Red-Shankes sermon: preached at Saint Giles church in Edenburgh, the last Sunday in April, by a Highland minister. Ierem. 30 (a reprint of the London edition in 1642 of the sermon called Pockmanty sermon, by James Row) - A cupp of bon-accord, or Preaching. By Mr. James Row, sometyme minister at Strowan. Preacht by him at Edenburgh, in Saint Geiles church, the text, i.e. Jeremiah 30 v.17 ... From an original ms. in the Library of David Laing, esq., 1828. 22-2779,   CS479.R835

14752   ROWAN.   The old Kentucky home immortalized by Stephen C. Foster; its song and the story, by Young E. Allison.   Federal Hill, Bardstown, Ky., 1923.   40 p. incl. front., illus. (incl. ports.) 20½ cm. "Published under the auspices of My old Kentucky home commission. (Publication director: C.I.Hitchcock, Louisville)" "A rapid sketch of the Rowan family and Federal Hill and an account of the times and circumstances under which "My old Kentucky home' was written." "Cartulary of Foster's songs": p. 39-40. 24-28846.   ML3561.O5A5

14753   ROWE.   The descendants of Franklin and Mary Notes Rowe of Humboldt County, Iowa, with some notes on their ancestors.   By Velma (Rowe) Coffin. (Storm Lake? Iowa) c.1955.   87 p. illus. 24 cm. 56-17866.   CS71.R878   1955

14754   ROWELL.   Biographical sketch of Samuel Rowell and notices of some of his descendants; with a genealogy for seven generations, 1754-1898.   By Roland Rowell ... Manchester, N.H., W.E.Moore, 1898.   216 p. front., illus., pl., ports. 23 cm. Dec.21, 98-78.   CS71.R881   1898

14755   ROWELL.   The register of Rowells; a brief record of male Rowells with years of birth, death, and marriage, with maiden name of wife, of children, of places lived and of principal ativities. 2d ed.   Concord, N.H., Printed by the Concord Press, 1957.   37 p. 23 cm. 59-4424.   CS71.R881   1957
        —— Supplement.   Concord, N.H., Printed by the Concord Press, 1959.   23 p. 23 cm. 59-4424.   CS71.R881   1957   Suppl.

14756   ROWLAND.   Notes about the Rowland, Mallet, and Netherclift families and some relations and friends.   London, Printed for private circulation by Spottiswoode and company limited, 1909.
18 p. 18½ cm. "One hundred copies only printed." Compiled by Ralph Thomas cf. Pref. Bibliography of Serjeant Ralph Thomas, 1803-1862, and family: p. 15-17.   11-3645.   CS439. R7

14757   ROWLAND.   A genealogical sketch of the posterity of John Rowland of Rhosybayvil, parish of Bayvil, Pembroke, Wales, and afterwards of East Whiteland, Chester co., Pa.   By Henry J. Rowland and Edward K. Rowland ... (Philadelphia, Printed by J. B. Lippincott company) 1893.   2 p. l., 3-32, (1) p.
20 cm.   Blank pages at end for "Line of descent." 9-13236.   CS71. R883   1893

14758   ROWLAND.   History of the Rowland family, with names of the descendants of Aaron and Levi Rowland, Mrs. Esther King and Mrs. Nancy Wood, by Dr. F. E. Weeks.   (Kipton, O.) 1910.
12 p. illus. (ports.) 23 cm. 16-11502.   CS71. R883   1910

ROWLAND.   See also HORNE, 1936

ROWLEE.   See ROWLEY.

14759   ROWLEY.   Lieut. Heman Rowlee (1746-1818) and his descendants, by Willard Winfield Rowles ... Ithaca, N. Y. (Press of Andrus & Church) 1907.   138 p. front., ports. 24½ cm. "Edition of 150 copies."
7-29603.   CS71. R884   1907

14760   ROWLEY.   Descendants of Moses Rowley, Cape Cod, Mass., about 1715, also descendants of George Warner, Wittenberg, Germany, born 1720.   By H. S. Russell ... Pittsfield, Mass., Eagle printing and binding company, 1908.   54 p. 18½ cm. Printed for private circulation. 10-9115.
CS71. R884   1908

14761   ROWLEY.   Some descendants of Thomas Rowley of Windsor, Connecticut, with lineage of families allied by marriage.   By Mildred Gertrude Crankshaw.   (n. p., 1961)   69, (19) l. coat of arms.
28 cm.   Cover title: Thomas Rowley of Windsor and descendants, 1669-1961. 61-46821.   CS71. R884   1961

ROWLEY.   See also: BASSETT, 1926
                                      LESNETT, 1931
                                      LEE, 1954

ROWNTREE.   See ROUNTREE.

ROWBERRY.   See SALISBURY, 1961

14762   ROY.   Honor thy father.   Memorial of the one hundredth birthday of John Roy 1798 July 31st 1898.   Died October 1st, 1878 ... Compiled by Joseph Edwin Roy.   (n. p., 1898)   47 p. incl. illus., 2 port.
(incl. front.) 21½ cm. "Printed for private circulation." 33-37704.   CT275. R798R6

14763   ROY.   The Roy family of Virginia and Kentucky, compiled by Nancy Reba Roy.   Fellows, Calif., 1935.   190 p. 23½ cm. 37-38440.   CS71. R8842   1935

ROY.   See also: KIRKPATRICK, 1927
                              PALLISSARD, 1959

ROYAL.   See STEVENS, 1957

14764   ROYALL.   The New-England Royalls.   By Edward Doubleday Harris.   A reprint from the N. E. historical and genealogical register, with additions.   Boston, D. Clapp & son, printers, 1885.
27 p. front. (fold. geneal. tab.) 25½ cm. 19-10588.   CS71. R8844   1885

14765   ROYALL.   The old Royall house, by Helen Tilden Wild ... Salem, Mass., The Salem press company, 1908.   1 p. l., 8 p. front. 25½ cm. Reprinted from the Massachusetts magazine, vol. 1, no. 3. 9-27669.
F74. M66W6

ROYALL.   See also: OLIVER, 1907
                                  No. 430 - Adventurers of purse and person.

14766   ROYCE.   Roys family records, compiled by Miss Julia M. Roys ... Oxford, N. Y., branch of the Roys family, compiled by L. I. Dodge ... (Oxford, N.Y., The Review press, 1909)
19 p.   front. (group port.)   20½ cm.   37-21324.   CS71. R8846   1909

14767   ROYDON.   Three Roydon families.   (By Ernest Bland Royden)   Edinburgh, Printed by R. & R. Clark, ltd., 1924.   xix, 244 p.   front. (port.)   illus. (coats of arms)   plates, double geneal. tables.   32 cm.   Preface signed: E. B. Royden.   25-1099.   CS439. R75

14768   ROYDON.   A manor through four centuries, by A. R. Cook.   London, New York (etc.) Oxford university press, 1938.   ix, (1) p., 1 l., 194 p., 1 l.   front., 1 illus., plates, ports., fold. plans, facsim., fold. geneal. tables.   22½ cm.   39-5684.   DA664. R6C6

14769   ROYDS.   The pedigree of the family of Royds.   By Sir Clement Molyneux Royds, C. B. London, Mitchell, Hughes and Clarke, 1910.   viii, 110 p., 1 l.   plates, ports., col. coats of arms, map.   30 cm.   Contains also pedigrees of the Beswicke, Calverley, Clegg, Gilbert, Hudson, Littledale, Meadowcroft, Molyneux, Rawson, Smith and Twemlow families.   15-19677.   CS439. R76

        ROYE.   See ROY.

14770   ROYER.   Genealogical records of the Royer family in America, or more especially those of Sebastian Royer's family, based on original records of Michael Zug.   By Rev. J. G. Francis ... Lebanon, Pa., J. G. Francis (c. 1928)   3 p. l., (v)-xlv, (2), 654 p.   front., plates, ports., facsims., col. coats of arms. 25½ cm.   Blank leaves for "Additional records" (4 inserted between pages (640) and 641)   31-496.   CS71. R885   1928

14771   ROYER.   Jacob Royer family.   (By John Fleck Royer)   (Harrisburg, Pa., 1945)   cover-title, 1 p. l., 50 numb. l.   29½ x 23 cm.   Reproduced from type-written copy.   Compiled by John F. Royer.   cf. Pref.   46-15281.
                                    CS71. R885   1945

        ROYER.   See also GIFT, 1909

        ROYS.   See ROYCE.

14772   RÜBEL.   Nachfahrentafeln Rübel, von Eduard Rübel und Wilhelm Heinrich Ruoff.   Hrsg. von der Helene und Cécil Rübel Familienstiftung.   Zürich, In Kommission bei Schulthess, 1943 -
v.   maps, diagrs.   30 cm.   Contents. - (1.) Bd. Berg-Jülich.   48-41787*.   CS999. R8   1943

        RUBEY.   See TODD, 1960

        RUBIDOUX.   See ROBIDOUX.

14773   RUBINCAM.   ... Memorial of the Rev. John Philip Rubenkam; with an analytical study of the origin of the Rubincam-Revercomb family of Pennsylvania and Virginia.   By Milton Rubincam.   Washington, D. C., 1937.   1 p. l., 33 numb. l.   29 cm.   Type-written.   "Principal authorities": leaf 33.   37-16838.
                                    CS71. R886   1937

14774   RUBINCAM.   The German background of the Rubincam-Revercomb family of Pennsylvania and Virginia, by Milton Rubincam ... (Washington, D. C., 1938)   7 p.   23 cm.   Caption title.   39-12251.
                                    CS71. R886   1938a

14775   RUBINCAM.   Report on the genealogy of the Rubincam-Revercomb family.   By Milton Rubincam.   (Hyattsville, Md., 1947)   40 l.   30 cm.   Caption title.   50-21407.   CS71. R886   1947

14776   RUBINCAM.   Ahnentafel; or, Table of ancestors of the Rubincam family of Green Meadows, Maryland.   By Milton Rubincam.   (Hyattsville?) 1954.   38 l.   28 cm.   55-19908.   CS71. R886   1954

14777   RUBINCAM.   Studies in ancestral biography.   By Milton Rubincam.   (n. p.) 1955 -
        no.   27 cm.   Contents. - no. 1. Johann Philipp Rübenkam (1670-1725)   56-33577.   CS71. R886   1955

14777a   RUBINCAM.   The family of Jacob Revercomb, the first of the race in Virginia, by Milton Rubincam ... (Richmond, Va., 1938)   7. (1) p.   23 cm.   caption title.   "Reprinted from Tyler's quarterly historical and genealogical magazine. October. 1938.   40M641T.   CS71. R886   1938

14778   RUBY.   Preliminary checklist of the descendants of Joseph and Ann Hunter Rubey.   By Edward Ernest Rubey.   (n.p., 1947)   4, 60, 10 l.   30 cm.   Typewritten (carbon copy) 48-16125*.
CS71. R8865   1947

14779   RUCH.   Sarah Verena Ruch and Charles Orin Ruch, Jr.; ancestral and family record, showing lineage through following families: Ruch, Fuller, Ross, Stalder, Bonham (and) Johnson; also partial family records giving Kampf, Bryan, Phillips connections.   (Chattanooga, 1952)
1 v. 29 cm. 52-32272.
CS71. R8867   1952

14780   RUCKER.   History of the Rucker family and their descendants.   Sketches of Carter, Barton, Early, Johns, Lee, Martin, Pendleton, Reade, Seldon, Taliaferro, Witt and Wyatt families.   (By Mrs. Edythe Johns (Rucker) Whitley.) (Nashville, Hermitage printing co.) 1927.   2 p. l., iii-ix, 308 p. 24 cm.
Coat of arms on cover. Ruled pages for "Record of births, marriages and deaths" (189-196) Half-title: Ruckers and connections, by Edythe Johns Rucker Whitley. 27-13340.
CS71. R887   1927

14781   RUCKER.   The Rucker family genealogy, with their ancestors, descendants and connections, compiled by Sudie Rucker Wood from original records, letters and other material collected over a period of thirty years.   Richmond, Va., Old dominion press, inc., 1932.   7 p. l., 585 p. front. (ports.)
coats of arms (1 col.) 23½ cm. 32-19020.
CS71. R887   1932

14782   RUCKER.   The genealogy of the Rucker family.   By LauraLee (Bush) Rucker.   (1st ed.   New York? c, 1963)   148 p. 21 cm. 64-4973.
CS71. R887   1963

RUCKLE.   See WALTMAN, 1928

14783   RUDD.   Records of the Rudd family, collected and arranged by Mary Amelia Rudd.   Bristol, J. W. Arrowsmith, 1920.   xii, 280 p. front., illus. (coats of arms) plates, ports., 10 fold. geneal. tab.   26 cm. 21-3209.
CS439. R78

14784   RUDDACH.   Ruddach family.   By Mildred (Ruddach) Bobinger.   (Arlington? Va.) 1956.
16 l. 29 cm. 56-44907.
CS71. R8875   1956

14785   RUDDIMAN.   Notes on the Ruddimans, by George Harvey Johnston.   (Edinburgh?) 1887.
(5) p. l.,   xix, (3) p. 4 port., 3 fold. geneal. tab. (incl. front.) 32 cm. "Only 25 copies printed of which this is no. 9." Works of Thomas Ruddiman: p. (1) following p. xix. 14-3809.
CS479. R84   1887

RUDE.   See ROOD.

14787   RUDKIN.   The Rudkins of the county Carlow.   By Sir Edmund T. Bewley ... (Reprinted from the Genealogist, new series, vol. XXI, p. 145)   Exeter, W. Pollard & co., ltd., printers, 1905.
20 p. 24 cm. 17-23922.
CS499. R8

RUDISILL.   See HOFFMAN, 1915

14788   RUDOLPH.   (Genealogy of the Rudolph family)   By Frances Lee (Wilson) Rudolph.   Prepared by Mrs. C. F. Rudolph ... Washington, D.C., 1945.   3 p. l., 45, 10 numb. l. 28 x 22 cm. Type-written. "Source of information": 3d prelim. leaf. 45-21717.
CS71. R888   1945

14789   RUDOLPH.   Descendants of Jacob and Rachel Rudolph.   Robert Reuben Rudolph, John and Elizabeth Chism, Thomas F. Woods, Isaac Hust (and) Alexander Black, sr.   Compiled by Mrs. C. F. Rudolph ... Washingtdon, D.C., 1945-1946.   3 p. l., 41, 10 numb. l. 28½ x 22 cm. Type-written. "Source of information": 3d prelim. leaf. 46-21030.
CS71. R888   1945a

RUDRICIANS.   See RORY.

14790   RUDSTON.   Hayton notes.   By Lord Hawkesbury.   (In East Riding antiquarian society.   Transactions ... Hull, 1904.   22 cm.   v. 11, p. 123-125.   fold. geneal. table.)   Pedigree of Rudston of Hayton: geneal. table.   21-9497.   DA670. Y59E2 vol. 11

RUDOLPH.   See BRUMBACH, 1961

RUDULPH.   See MANLY, 1930

RUDY.   See WESTHAFER, 1912

RUE.   See: AREW.
                    LA RUE.
                    REICHNER, 1918

14791   RUF.   Ruf, Haight, Eddy, Sumner, Hatch and allied families, genealogical and biographical. A private publication compiled and printed for Alpha H. Ruf, by the American historical society, inc. New York, 1932.   3 p. l., 175 p. plates, ports., col. coats of arms, col. geneal. tables.   32½ cm.   Title-page and dedication in colors; initials.   The coats of arms and one plate are accompanied by guard sheets with descriptive letterpress.   Bound in blue levant, gold tooled and inlaid, with leather doublures.   33-22551 rev.   CS71. R8886   1932

14792   RUFFIN.   Ruffin, and other genealogies.   compiled by R. B. Henry.   (n. p., 1918) broadside.   30 x 31½ cm.   Contains Beverley, Bland, Bolling, Burke, Byrd, Carter, De Jarnette, Meade, Randolph, Ruffin, Shippen, Skipwith, Tayloe, Willing and Wormeley families.   19-4283.   CS71. R889   1918

14793   RUFFIN.   Ruffin genealogy (by) L. B. Hatke, Genealogical research.   Richmond, Va., 1932. geneal. tab.   155 x 103 cm.   40M3322T.   CS71. R889   1932

RUFFIN.   See also HENRY, 1922

RUFFNER.   See STRICKLER, 1925

14794   RUGELEY.   Twenty-one sons for Texas.   By Arda (Talbot) Allen.   (Limited ed.)   San Antonio, Naylor Co.   (1959)   x, 233 p. illus., ports., coat of arms.   22 cm.   59-14818.
CS71. R92   1959

14795   RUGG.   The descendants of John Rugg, by Ellen R. Rugg ... New York, F. H. Hitchcock (c. 1911)   4 p. l., 580 p.   24 cm.   11-13211.   CS71. R93   1911

14796   RUGGLES.   Evidences of the derivation of the Ruggles families of England and America from that of Ruggeley of Staffordshire.   By Henry Stoddard Ruggles ... (New York, 1894)   4, (1) p.   24½ cm. Reprinted from the New York genealogical and biographical record for October 1894.   "De Ruggele, Ruggles.   From the Boston Transcript": (1) p. at end.   18-23438.   CS71. R932   1894

14797   RUGGLES.   The genealogy of Thomas Ruggles of Roxbury, 1637, to Thomas Ruggles of Pomfret, Conn., and Rutland, Vt.   The genealogy of Alitheah Smith, of Hampton, Conn., the wife of Thomas Ruggles, and the genealogy of the descendants - in part - of Samuel Ladd of Haverhill, Mass. By Franklin Ladd Bailey.   (Boston) 1896.   (3)-44 p.   23½ cm.   3-3836.   CS71. R932   1896

14798   RUGGLES.   The Ruggles lineage.   Five generations.   By Henry Stoddard Ruggles ... (n. p.) Priv. print., 1896.   14 p. col. front. (coat of arms)   24½ cm.   9-13238.   CS71. R932   1896a

14799   RUGGLES.   General Timothy Ruggles, 1711-1795.   By Henry Stoddard Ruggles ... (Wakefield? Mass.)   Priv. print., 1897.   40 p. front. (coat of arms)   24½ cm.   "Some papers bearing the signature of General Ruggles": p. (25)-30.   "Letter from General Peck": p. (31)-40.   12-30961.   F67. R93

14800   RUGGLES.   Ancestors of Benjamin Ruggles, senator from Ohio, 1815-1833, John Ruggles, s senator from Maine, 1834-1840, Nathaniel Ruggles, M. C. from Massachusetts, 1813-1819, Charles Herman Ruggles, M. C. from New York, 1821-1823, by Henry Stoddard Ruggles.   (n. p., 19 -?) 3 p. l., 6-61 numb. l.   front., illus. (coat of arms) ports.   29½ cm.   In manuscript.   21-17508.   CS71. R932   19 -

14801   RUGGLES.   The Ruggles, Kingsley, Ross and Goodwin revolutionary ancestry of Henry Stoddard Ruggles, with the Ruggles, Ryan, Kingsley, Ross and Goodwin arms, from family book-plates and silver.   (n. p., 1901?)   2 p. 1., 36 p. incl. 4 coats of arms.   front.   22 cm.   Three extra plates inserted.   1-4125.

CS71. R932   1901

14802   RUGGLES.   Ruggles homesteads, by Henry Stoddard Ruggles ... (Wakefield, Mass., 1912)
12 numb. 1.   front., plates.   26 cm.   Privately printed.   12-13049.

CS71. R932   1912

14803   RUGGLES.   The family of Ruggles, by Frances Cowles.   New York (McClure syndicate) 1912.
11 p. incl. front. (coat of arms)   17½ cm.   "Reprinted from a series of American family history by Frances Cowles, published by the McClure syndicate, New York."   Facsimile of a manuscript list of the portraits owned by the Roxbury historical society: 1 leaf at end.   25-2335.

CS71. R932   1912a

14804   RUGGLES.   The Ruggles family, England and America (by) Henry Stoddard Ruggles.   (Wakefield, Mass., 1917)   2 v. fronts., plates, ports., coats of arms, facsim.   29½ cm.   "One of an edition of twenty-five copies.   No. 20." "Special copy containing extra illustrations and fac-similes of autographs, and to which is appended an account of the allied families of Kingsley, Ross and Goodwin."   Eleven extra plates added in 1923.   22-25801.

CS71. R932   1917

        RUGGLES.   See also: CHUTE, 1894
                                 PARKER, 1913
                                 STROUSE, 1966
                                 TUCKER, 1901

14805   RULON.   The Rulon family and their descendants.   Philadelphia, Lineaweaver & Wallace, printers, 1870.   43 p., 1 1.   22½ cm.   Comp. by John C. Rulon.   9-13237.

CS71. R935   1870

        RUMP.   See BROWNLEE.   F268. H65

14806   RUMPH.   Genealogy of the Rumph family of South Carolina.   By A. S. Salley, jr.   Birmingham, Ala., Leslie printing and publishing co., 1903.   cover-title, 10 p.   23½ cm.   3-14590.

CS71. R938   1903

14807   RUMPH.   The Rumph and Frederick families, genealogical, and biographical;   with allied families of Datwyler, Harrisperger, Hesse, Kaigler. Rickenbacker, Murph, Wolfe, Jamison, Carmichael, Cooner, Gholson, Pooser, Wannamaker, Glover, Walter, Farrior, Shuler, Funches, Feaster, Cart, Cain, Robinson, Felder, Slappey, Plant, Jones, Davenport, Walker Everett, Haslam, Walker, Norris, Rowe, and other families.   By Louise Frederick Hays.   (Atlanta, J. T. Hancock, 1942)
242 p. incl. illus.   (incl. ports., map) pl., coats of arms (part col.)   27½ cm.   Privately published - limited edition.   Volume no. 118.
42-51114.

CS71. R938   1942

        RUMPH.   See also: BROWNLEE-HOLMAN, 1937
                              GOLSAN, 1959

        RUNDLE.   See NOYES, 1900

        RUNKEL.   See RUNKLE.

14808   RUNKLE.   The Runkle family;   being an account of the Runkels in Europe, and their descendants in America, by Ben Van. D. Fisher ... New York, T. A. Wright, 1899.   366 p. incl. col. pl. (coat of arms) pl.   24½ cm.   3-3831.

CS71. R942   1899

        RUNNELL.   See RUNNELLS.

14809   RUNNELLS.   A genealogy of Runnels and Reynolds families in America;   with records and brief memorials of the earliest ancestors, as far as known and of many of their descendants, bearing the same and other names.   In three parts, with an appendix.   By Rev. M. T. Runnels, A. M. ...
Boston, A. Mudge & son, printers, 1873.   xvi, 354 p., 1 1.   24 cm.   Blank pages at end for "Family record."   Contents. -
pt. 1. A genealogical memoir of Samuel Runels, of Bradford, Mass., 1703-1745. - pt. 2. A genealogical memoir of Job Runels, or Runals, of Durham, N.H., 1713-1762. - pt. 3. A genealogical memoir of John Runels, or Runals, of Durham, N.H., 1718-1756.   9-13240.

CS71. R943   1873

RUNNELLS.   See also REYNOLDS.

RUNNELS.   See RUNNELLS.

RUNYAN.   See RUNYON.

14810   RUNYON.   Genealogy of the Runyan family.   (By Henry Runyan)   (Princeton, N.J., 1891)
cover-title, 1 p. l., 8 p., 1 l.   22½ cm.   "Savidge family record" on verso of prelim. leaf.   "Record of the Runyan family":   folded leaf inserted.
L. C. copy imperfect: preliminary leaf wanting.   2-837 rev.   CS71. R944   1891

14811   RUNYON.   Runyon genealogy; a genealogy of the Runyon families who settled early in Kentucky, North Carolina, Virginia, and West Virginia, by Robert and Amos Runyon.   Brownsville, Tex.,
1955.   194 p.   22 cm.   56-17707 rev.   CS71. R944   1955
——— Supplement.   By Robert Runyon.   Brownsville, Tex., c. 1962.   195-234 p.   illus.   22 cm.
56-17707 rev.   CS71. R944   1955
                                                                              Suppl.

RUNYON.   See also FITZGERALD, 1942

RUPERT-PARK.   See PARK, 19 -

RUPLEY.   See BOGLE, 1937

14812   RUPP.   A brief biographic memorial of Joh. Jonas Rupp, and complete genealogical family
register of his lineal descendants, from 1756 to 1875.   With an appendix.   By I. Daniel Rupp.   W.
Philadelphia, Pa., L. W. Robinson (1875)   xi p., 2 l., (13)-292 p. incl. front. (port.) 19 cm.   Blank pages at end for
"Family record."   9-13017.   CS71. R946   1875

14813   RUPPERT.   Some German, English, Irish, French, Dutch, Scottish, and American ancestors
of Raymond Robert Ruppert, Jr. and William Hunter Ruppert.   By Elizabeth Miller (Hunter) Ruppert.
(Washington? 1959)   46 l.   36 cm.   59-43500.   CS71. R947   1959

14814   RURIK.   ... Chronique dite de Nestor ... Traduite sur le texte slavon-russe, avec introduction et commentaire critique, par Louis Leger ... Paris E. Leroux, 1884.   xxviii, 399 p.   fold. geneal. tab.
28 cm.   (Publications de l'École des langues orientales vivants.   (II ser. - vol. XIII)   36-2482.   DK70. N45

RUSCOE.   See BENEDICT, F129. S697 v. 33

14815   RUSH.   Rush of Byberry; Captain John Rush, formerly of Cromwell's Horse, settled in
Byberry, Pa. in year 1683 (and his descendants) (n. p., 187-)   geneal. table.   25 cm.   38M4205T.
                                                                              CS71. R952   187-

14816   RUSH.   Descendants of John Rush.   (Philadelphia, 1893)   p. 325-335.   25 cm.   Caption-title.
37M1685T.   CS71. R952   1893

14817   RUSH.   A history of the Rush family, by Matthias Rush.   Pittsburg, Pa., Press W. M. Dick
& co., 1899.   (Fargo, N. D., 1934)   4 p. l., 9-63 (i. e. 59) numb. l., 35 p. mounted photos. (incl. port.)   17 x 13 cm.
"Photographically copied by Harry S. Rush ... from an original loaned to him by Charles C. Rush ... 1934."   "Notes by Harry S. Rush": 35 p. at
end.   44-22940.   CS71. R952   1934

14818   RUSH.   A memorial containing travels through life or sundry incidents in the life of Dr.
Benjamin Rush, born Dec. 24, 1745 (old style) died April 19, 1813; written by himself; also extracts
from his commonplace book as well as a short history of the Rush family in Pennsylvania.   Published
privately for the benefit of his descendants by Louis Alexander Biddle ... (Philadelphia, Made at the
Sign of the ivy leaf) 1905.   4 p. l., 130, 130 a-130 b (131)-262 p.   ports. (incl. front.) fold. geneal. tab.   25 cm.   "A brief
account of the ancestors and descendants of Benjamin Rush ... Compiled ... by ... Henry J. Williams": p. (237)-262.   6-20342.
                                                                              E302. 6. R85R9

14819   RUSH.   Historical and genealogical account of the Rush family, by Sylvester R. Rush.
Omaha, Festner printing company, 1925.   167 p.   plate, ports., col. coat of arms.   24 cm.   Contains also the Babbit and
Leonard families.   26-2177.   CS71. R952   1925

14820   RUSH.   Rush & Skinner families of Lower Turkeyfoot.   (By Harry Speer Rush)   (Fargo, N. D., 1943)   205 l. incl. fold. maps.   28½ x 22½ cm.   Binder's title.   Leaves variously numbered.   Addenda slip inserted.   Reproduced from type-written copy.   44-3254.   CS71. R952   1943

14821   RUSH.   David Rush and his descendants, and stories of the community.   By Mary Jane (Rush) Broadwater.   (Bradley? S. C., 1963)   238 p.   illus.   24 cm.   54-44843.   CS71. R952   1953

14822   RUSH.   Rush genealogy; (Captain Peter Rush of Pa., and his descendants, with notes on Dr. Benjamin Rush.   By Jason Adamson.   Turlock, Calif. ? 1965?)   96 p.   (p. 95-96 blank) illus.   22 cm.   Bibliography: p. 81-82.   66-37298.   CS71. R952   1965

14823   RUSHBROOK.   Rushbrook parish registers, 1567-1850, with Jermyn and Davers annals.   Woodbridge, G. Booth, 1903.   viii, 486 p.   front., illus., plates, ports., fold. plan.   22 cm.   Preface signed: "S. H. A. H. " i. e. Sydenham Henry Augustus Hervey.   Contents. - Preface. - Registers. - Church briefs and memoranda. - Monumental inscriptions. - List of Christian names. - Lay subsidies. - Rectors and curates. - Wills. - Jermyn annals. - Davers annals. - Rushbrook family. - Rushbrook hall. - Catalogue of portraits. - Folkes family. - Tom Martin's notes. - Short notes. - Corrections. - Index to registers. - Index to Jermyns. - General index.   11-5063.

CS436. R85

14824   RUSHMORE.   The Rushmore family in America.   By Herbert Armstrong Poole.   Palm Beach, Fla., 1958.   90 l.   29 cm.   58-41133.   CS71. R953   1958

RUSHMORE.   See also DICKERSON, 1919

RUSK.   See POUND, 1904

14825   RUSLING.   The Rusling family, by James F. Rusling ... Philadelphia, Printed for private circulation by J. B. Lippincott company, 1907.   5 p. l., 159, (1) p.   front., plates, ports., fold. geneal. tab.   25 cm.   7-42335.   CS71. R956   1907

14826   RUSSELL.   An impartial and full account of the life & death of the late unhappy William lord Russel, eldest son and heir of the present Earl of Bedford, who was executed for high treason, July 21, 1683, in Lincolns-Inn-fields.   Together with the original and rise of the Earls of Bedford: giving a brief account of each of them.   London, G. Swinock, 1684.   2 p. l., 96 p.   front. (port.)   15 cm.   "To the reader" signed: A. L.   44-38856.   LAW

14827   RUSSELL.   The duty of resignation under afflictions, illustrated and enforced from the example of Christ, in a sermon preached at Charlestown, April 17, 1796.   Occasioned by the death of the Honourable Thomas Russell, esquire, who died in Boston, April 8, 1796, aged fifty-six.   By Jedidiah Morse, D. D., minister of the congregation in Charlestown.   Published at the request of the mourners.   Boston, Printed by Samuel Hall, in Cornhill, 1796.   31 p.   19½ cm.   13-6008.   F69. R97   Office

14828   RUSSELL.   Anecdotes of the house of Bedford, from the Norman conquest to the present period ... London, J. S. Barr (1797)   1 p. l., (v)-vii, 284 p.   21 cm.   Written in answer to "A letter to a noble lord" by Edmund Burke.   cf. Lowndes.   5-14523.   DA28. 35. R8A6

14829   RUSSELL.   An historical and topographical account of the town of Woburn, its abbey, and vicinity; containing also a concise genealogy of the house of Russell, and memoirs of the late Francis duke of Bedford ... Woburn, S. Dodd, 1818.   xvi, (17)-140 p.   front.   18 cm.   Dedication signed: Stephen Dodd.   2-22233.   DA690. W84D6

14830   RUSSELL.   History and description of Woburn and its abbey, etc., etc.   By J. D. Parry ... London, Longman, Rees, Orme, Brown, and Green; (etc., etc., pref, 1831)   xii p., 2 l., 320 p.   front. pl. (part fold.)   19 ½ cm.   Contents. - pt. 1. History of the town.   The ancient abbey.   Biography of the Russell family.   Sketch of the Gordon family.   Description of the town.   Vicinity of Woburn. - pt. 2. Woburn abbey.   Portraits and paintings. │ Sculpture gallery.   Gardens and park.   2-29217.   DA690. W84P2

14831   RUSSELL.   Historical memoirs of the first race of ancestry, whence the house of Russell had its origin: from the subjugation of Norway to the Norman conquest.   By J. H. Wiffen ... London, Longman, Rees, Orme, Brown, Green, and Longman (etc.) 1833.   2 p. l., 78 p.   fold. geneal. tab.   24½ cm.   4-33694.   DA28. 35. R8W5

14832   RUSSELL.   Historical memoirs of the house of Russell; from the time of the Norman conquest.   By J. H. Wiffen ... London, Longman, Rees, Orme, Brown, Green, and Longman (etc.) 1833.
2 v. illus., 6 pl., 2 port. (incl. front.) fold. geneal. tab.   25 cm.   4-33695.   DA28.35.R8W52

14833   RUSSELL.   Sketch of the history of the house of Russell.   By David Ross ... London, W. S.
Orr & co.; (etc., etc.) 1848.   3 p. l., 84, viii p. 17½ cm. (Notes on the nobility, no. 1) 2-20540.
                                                                           DA28.35.R8R6

14834   RUSSELL.   Stemmata Rosellana; compiled from inquisitiones post mortem, parliamentary
records, rotuli hundredorum, chancery reports, etc., etc.   By Clifford Stanley Sims ... Philadelphia,
W. F. Geddes, printer, 1859.   8 p. 19½ cm. 3-7930.   CS71.R827   1859

14835   RUSSELL.   Russell-Phillips.   A note upon title "Phillips" in Appendix to "Bond's genealogies
of Watertown." (Boston, 1873)   3 p. 25½ cm. Caption title. Signed: M. W. R. "Reprinted from the New-England historical
and genealogical register for July, 1873." 38M4335T.   CS71.R965   1873

14836   RUSSELL.   Genealogy of that branch of the Russell family which comprises the descendants
of John Russell of Woburn, Massachusetts, 1640-1878.   By John Russell Bartlett.   Providence, Priv.
print. (by the Providence press company) 1879.   212 p. front., pl., ports. 26 cm. List of the author's works: p.131-
133. 3-31330.   CS71.R965   1879

14837   RUSSELL.   William Russell and his descendants, by Anna Russell Des Cognets ... Lexington,
Ky., Printed for the family, by S. F. Wilson, 1884.   4 p. l., 124 p. 23½ cm. 39-16913.
                                                                          CS71.R965   1884

14838   RUSSELL.   A genealogy.   Comprising some of the ancestors and all the descendants of John
and Hannah (Fincher) Russell.   By Isaac S. Russell.   (New Market, Md., 1887)   2 p. l., 29, (1) p.
15 x 28½ cm. 9-13016.   CS71.R965   1887
                                                                          Microfilm 9709 CS

14839   RUSSELL.   Biographical catalogue of the pictures at Woburn abbey, compiled by Adeline
Marie Tavistock and Ela M. S. Russell ... London, E. Stock, 1890-92.   2 v. ports. 23½ cm. Vol. 2 compiled by Adeline Marie Bedford and Ela M. S. Russell. L. C. copy imperfect: v. 2, p. 219-401 wanting. 45-50908.   N7622.B4

14840   RUSSELL.   A descriptive and historical account of the Russell monuments in the Bedford
chapel at Chenies, with notices of other family monuments of Swyre, Watford, Thornhaugh, Bisham
and Westminister abbey, by George Scharf ... F. M. O'Donaghue ... and Everard Green ... London,
Printed by Spottiswoode & co., 1892.   vi, 124 p. 29½ cm. "Limited to one hundred copies." 22-638.
                                                                          DA690.C485S3

14841   RUSSELL.   Russell (family) (By Thomas Bellows Wyman.   Boston, D. Clapp and son, 1879)
8 p. 25½ cm. 39M422T.
                                                                          CS71.R965   1897a

14842   RUSSELL.   Descendants of William Russell, Cambridge, Mass., about 1640, by Hezekiah
Stone Russell, of Pittsfield, Mass.   March 1, 1900.   Printed for private circulation.   Pittsfield,
Mass., Eagle publishing company, 1900.   52 p. 18 cm. 1-20890.   CS71.R965   1900

14843   RUSSELL.   The descendants of John Russell of Dartmouth, Mass.   By Barrett Beard Russell.
Boston, New England historic genealogical society, 1904.   20 p. 24½ cm. (Register reprints, series A. no. 9) "Reprinted from New-England historical and genealogical register, vols. 57 and 58." 17-31806.   CS71.R965   1904

14844   RUSSELL.   An Account of the Russell family of Charlestown, from a book in the handwriting
of Miss Mary Russell, who died in 1806, and from other family records in possession of Richard
Sullivan, of Boston.   (n. p.) 1904.   42 l. 28 cm. 65-88866.   CS71.R965   1904a

14845   RUSSELL.   An account of some of the descendants of John Russell, the emigrant from Ipswich,
England, who came to Boston, New England, October 3, 1635.   Together with some sketches of the
allied families of Wadsworth, Tuttle, and Beresford.   By the late Gurdon Wadsworth Russell ... Ed.

14845 continued: by Edwin Stanley Welles. Hartford, Conn. (The Case, Lockwood & Brainard co.) 1910.
318 p. fronts. (port.) illus., plates, facsim., geneal. tab., coats of arms. 24 cm. Gurdon Wadsworth Russell, M.D., LL.D., 1815-1909, by Samuel Hart, p. 17-22. English abstracts by J. R. Hutchinson, p. 23-103. "Two hundred copies printed, number 66." 10-24498.

CS71. R965   1910

14846   RUSSELL.   The Russells of Birmingham in the French revolution and in America, 1791-1814, by S. H. Jeyes ... London, G. Allen & company, ltd., 1911.   xvi, 309 p. col. front., plates, ports., facsims. 22 cm. Edited after the author's death by David Hannay. cf. Pref. note. 12-857.   DA522. R8J5

14847   RUSSELL.   An historical and topographical account of the town of Woburn, its abbey, and vicinity; containing also a concise genealogy of the house of Russell, and memoirs of the late Francis duke of Bedford ... Woburn, S. Dodd, 1918.   xvi, (17)-140 p. front. 18 cm. Dedication signed: Stephen Dodd. 2-22233.

DA690. W84D6

14848   RUSSELL.   The ancestors and descendants of Abel Russell, revolutionary soldier from Westford, Massachusetts, and Fayette, (Starling Plantation) Maine.   Comprising one of the lines of descent from William and Martha Russell, of Cambridge in Massachusetts, who came to America from England about the year 1640.   Comp. by Arthur J. Russell and Mrs. S. R. Child.   Minneapolis, Press of Augsburg publishing house, 1922.   42 p. 1 l. front., pl., ports. 18½ cm. Blank pages at end for "Family records". 23-878.   CS71. R965   1922

14849   RUSSELL.   A genealogical register of the descendants of Robert and Agnes (Leitch) Russell, emigrants from Glasgow, Scotland, to Benton County, Minnesota, and pioneer experiences ... Compiled by their grandchildren, and published by Nelson and Robert F. Flint ... North St. Paul, Minn. (Printed by the North St. Paul courier, 1923)   44 p. plates, ports. 22 cm. 27-11122.

CS71. R965   1923

14850   RUSSELL.   Ancestors of Joseph Russell, compiled by Mrs. Louise Stowell, daughter of Seth Reed and Harriet Russell and descendants of Josiah Russell and Betsy Hastings, compiled by Merl A. Russell, son of George F. Russell.   (n. p., 1928?)   cover-title, (40) p. 23 cm. 40-37512.

CS71. R965   1928

14851   RUSSELL.   Two centuries of family history, a study in social development, by Gladys Scott Thomson ... London, New York (etc.) Longmans, Green and co., 1930.   x, 369 p. col. front., ports., map, facsims., fold. geneal. tab. (in pocket) 22½ cm. The genealogical table is illustrated with coats of arms. 30-31153. DA28. 35. R8T6

14852   RUSSELL.   The narrative of George Russell of Golf hill, with Russellania and selected papers. Edited by P. L. Brown; line drawings by Stirling Paterson.   London, Oxford university press, H. Milford, 1935.   8 p. l., (3)-469, (1) p. col. front., illus., plates (part col.) ports., maps (part double) fold. geneal. tab. 25½ cm. Maps on lining papers. "A story of beginnings in Port Phillip ... It consists mainly of two parts. The chief of these is the Narrative of George Russell of Golf hill, manager of the Clyde company from the year 1836. Subsidiary to the Narrative there is the Russellania or History of the Russells (by George Russell, esq., of Pitbladdo, collected and arranged by John Russell, Beanston, June 1841)" - Introd. Appendixes: I. Old Van Diemen's land: Manifold papers. - II. Essays by Janet Laing: 1. Boglily. 2. Balwearie. 3. "Two South street", Elie. Bibliography: p. (437)-445. 35-37316.

DU222. R8A5

14853   RUSSELL.   Life in a noble household, 1641-1700 (by) Gladys Scott Thomson ... London, J. Cape (1937)   406, (1) p. front., pl., ports. 23 cm. "First published January 1937 ... Third impression February 1937." "Based upon the household papers - account books, bills and letters - handled by the officials and servants of William Russell, fifth earl and first duke of Bedford." - Pref. 37-17986.   DA377. 2. R8T45   1937b

14854   RUSSELL.   The Russells in Bloomsbury, 1669-1771 (by) Gladys Scott Thomson ... London, J. Cape (1940)   384 p. incl. tables. front., plates, ports., 2 plans (1 fold.) 2 facsim. 23 cm. "First published 1940." Continues the author's "Life in a noble household, 1641-1700." A41-2793.   DA377. 2. R8T46

14855   RUSSELL.   The ancestors and descendants of Col. James Russell of Temple, Maine, born at Townsend, Massachusetts, December 30, 1795, son of Ephraim Russell and Mary Porter; died April 4, 1856.   By Francis Henry Russell. (Kensington, Md., 194-)   14 l. 28 cm. 50-44967.

CS71. R965

14856   RUSSELL.   Russell families of seventeenth century New England.   By George Ely Russell. (Chesterland, Ohio) 1955.   25 p. 28 cm. 56-36297.   CS71.R96   1955

14857   RUSSELL.   Genealogy of the Russell family.   By Lyman Brightman Russell.   San Antonio, Printed by the Naylor Co. (1959)   68 p. 20 cm. 59-4665.   CS71.R96   1959

14858   RUSSELL.   The ancestors and descendants of James Russell of Temple, Maine.   By Francis Henry Russell.   (Turner? Me.) 1963.   32 p. 28 cm. Bibliography: p. 11-13. 64-54995.
                                                                                                               CS71.R965   1963

14859   RUSSELL.   The ancestors and descendants of James Russell of Temple, Maine (by) Francis H. Russell.   (Turner, Me.) 1968.   33 p. 27 cm. Bibliography: p. 12-14. 79-6118 MARC.
                                                                                                               CS71.R965   1968

14860   RUSSELL.   Richard Russell, M.D. (1687-1759)   By W.H. Challen.   Sussex Notes and Queries, vol. XIV, May, 1955, p. 16-19.   In vertical file.   Ask reference librarian for this material.

          RUSSELL.   See also:

                    AIKEN, 1939   GRINNELL, 1913   STUART, CS421.R8
                    ANDERSON, 1966   GRISWOLD, 1898   TRACY, 1895a
                    BEAMAN, 1931   MINNS, 1925   WARREN, 1884
                    CAMPBELL, 1911   RICHARDSON, 1880   WHITNEY, 1925
                    FLETCHER, CS439.F53   SCARBOROUGH, 1951   No. 1547 - Cabell county.
                    GIBBON, 1918   STEEN, 1959

14861   RUSSEY.   The Russey family in America; a genealogy of James Russey, 1755-1962.   By George Sirrine Russey.   Edited and published by John Wesley Russey, Jr.   San Antonio, 1963
iii, 129 p. 29 cm. Bibliography: p. 116-118.   CS71.R97   1963
          —— A supplement of additions and corrections to a genealogy of James Russey.   (Edited and) published by John Wesley Russey, Jr.   San Antonio, 1967.   13 p. 28 cm. On cover: Supplement to the 1963 edition.
Bibliography: p. 12. 64-7526.   CS71.R97   1963

          RUSSY.   See RUSSEY.

14862   RUST.   Record of the Rust family: embracing the descendants of Henry Rust, who came from England and settled in Hingham, Mass.   1634-1635.   By Albert D. Rust ... Waco, Tex., The author, 1891.   xvi, 527, (1) p. front., plates, ports., facsims. 22½ cm. 9-13015.   CS71.R97   1891

14863   RUST.   ... The Rust family.   (Yarmouth, N.S., 1909)   1 p. l., 9 p. 21 cm. (Yarmouth genealogies, no. 108) "Reproduced from the Yarmouth herald, May 25, 1909." Compiled by George Stayley Brown. 15-19125.
                                                                                                               CS71.R97   1909

14864   RUST.   Rust and allied families; genealogical and biographical.   Prepared and privately published for Eunice Plunkett Mesmer, by the Lynchburg engraving company.   Lynchburg, Va., 1939.
5 p. l., (13)-37 p., 1 l. illus. (mounted port., coat of arms) 28½ cm. "This edition is limited to fifty copies." Bibliography" p. 37.
40-5548.   CS71.R97   1939

14865   RUST.   Rust of Virginia; genealogical and biographical sketches of the descendants of William Rust, 1654-1940.   Prepared under the direction and published by Ellsworth Marshall Rust.   Washington, 1940.   2 p. l., xlii, 463 p. front. (col. coat of arms) plates, ports. 24 cm. 40-33922.
                                                                                                               CS71.R97   1940

          RUST.   See also: CARPENTER, 1930
                               LA RUE, 1921
                               RICHARDSON, 1906
                               ROST.
                               STRONG, 1912

          RUTGERS.   See SHEAFE, 1923

14866   RUTHERFORD.   The Rutherfurds of that ilk, and their cadets.   Comp. from the public records and other authentic sources.   (By Thomas H. Cockburn-Hood)   Edinburgh (Scott and Ferguson, and Burness and company, printers to Her Majesty) 1884.   3 p. l., 2, (iii)-xciv p., 4 l., 36, 8, (8,5)-56, (4,3)-62, xl p. front., illus. (part col.) facsims. (part fold.) fold. map, fold. geneal. tab. in pocket. 29 cm. Half-title, "Pedigree of Rutherford, Lord Rutherford, " has col. coat of arms. Edited by Rev. Walter Macleod. Pedigree of Rutheroord, Lord Rutheroord, as set forth by Sir Robert Douglas, baronet of Glenbervie, ed. 1764: p. iii-xciv. The Rutherfords of that ilk. By Thomas Hood. Additions and corrections. By C. H. E. Carmichael, esq. 4 l., 36 p., has prefatory note dated 1899. Supplementary additions, mostly by the late Mr. James Tait: 56 p. Miscellaneous contributions: 62 p. Appendix: List of Rutherfurd entries in the old registers on Jedburgh and surrounding parishes: xl p. 13-10234.

CS479. R85
Microfilm 12107 CS

14867   RUTHERFORD.   Family records and events.   Compiled principally from the original manuscripts in the Rutherford collection.   By Livingston Rutherfurd.   New York, Printed at the De Vinne press, 1894.   xvi p., 1 l., 355 p. front., plates, ports., facsims., fold. geneal. tables. 25 cm. Title vignette: coat of arms. 9-13014.

CS71. R975   1894

14868   RUTHERFORD.   Genealogical history of the Rutherford family, by William Kenneth Rutherford and Anna Clay (Zimmerman) Rutherford.   Shawnee Mission, Kan., Intercollegiate Press, 1969 -   v. illus., ports. 24 cm. (Bibliography: v. 1, p. 340-350. 77-6715 MARC.

CS71. R975   1969

14869   RUTHERFORD.   General Griffith Rutherford and allied families, Harsh, Graham, Cathey, Locke, Holeman, Johnson (and) Chambers.   Compiled and written by Minnie R. H. Long ... Milwaukee, Printed at the Wisconsin Cuneo press, 1942.   xi, 194 p. front., plates, ports., facsims., coats of arms. 23½ cm. Bibliography: p. 187-188. 43-3675.

CS71. R975   1942

14870   RUTHERFORD.   The family Rutherford and kin, by Lizzie Finch Rutherford and Hobart Key, Jr.   Marshall, Tex., Port Caddo Trading Co. (1963?)   102 p. illus., geneal. table, ports. 23 cm. 65-404.

CS71. R975   1963

RUTHERFORD.   See also: BARD, F128. 25. V27   LEWEN, 1919
BINGHAM, 1898 and 1920   LONG, 1956
CLARKSON, 1876   THOMAS, 1878
HARKNESS, 1958   No. 1547 - Cabell county.

RUTHERFURD.   See RUTHERFORD.

14871   RUTHRAUFF.   History of the Ruthrauffs, 1560-1925, by Mary Ruthrauff Hoover.   (Kansas City, Mo., Smith-Grieves company, c. 1925)   (iii)-xvi, 380 p. pl., ports., facsims., fold. geneal. tab., col. coat of arms. 24½ cm. Leaf of errata inserted at p. 366. "Quellen zur geschichte der familie Rudrauff ... zusammengestellt Darmstadt im sommer 1924, von regierungsrat Rudolf Schafer" (p. 9-32) with English translation by Johanna Lorey (p. 33-56) 39-12229.

CS71. R978   1925

14872   RUTHVEN.   Papers relating to William, first earl of Gowrie, and Patrick Ruthven, his fifth and last surviving son.   Private impression.   London, Printed by J. E. Taylor & co., 1867.   xii, 115 p. 23 cm. By John Bruce, 1802-1869. Reprinted from the Transactions of the Society of antiquaries 1849 and 1851; vol. 33, p. 143-173; vol. 34, p. 190-224. Contents. - Observations on the trial and death of William, earl of Gowrie, A. D. 1584, and on their connection with the Gowrie conspiracy, A. D. 1600. - Observations upon certain documents relating to William, first earl of Gowrie, and Patrick Ruthven, his fith and last surviving son. 9-11827.

DA789. B8

14873   RUTHVEN.   Ruthven correspondence.   Letters and papers of Patrick Ruthven, earl of Forth and Brentford, and of his family: A. D. 1615 - A. D. 1662.   With an appendix of papers relating to Sir John Urry.   Ed., from the original mss., by the Rev. William Dunn Macray, M. A.   London, J. B. Nichols and sons, 1868.   4 p. l., lxviii, 182 p., 1 l. 27½ cm. "The principal portion of the book is printed from a ms. volume preserved among Dr. Rawlinson's collections in the Bodleian library, marked with the reference A. 148 ... previously in the possession of John Urry, student of Christ Church. " To the members of the Roxburghe club ... dedicated and presented by ... Buccleuch and Queensberry." 11-17422.

PR1105. R7   1868
Office.

14874   RUTHVEN.   The Ruthven of Freeland peerage and its critics, by J. H. Stevenson.   Glasgow, J. MacLehose and sons, 1905.   vi, 84 p. 22½ x 18 cm. 6-15829.   CS479. R9

14875   RUTHVEN.   The Ruthven family papers; the Ruthven version of the conspiracy and assasination at Gowrie House, Perth, 5th August, 1600, critically rev. and ed. by Samuel Cowan... London, Simpkin, Marshall, Hamilton, Kent & co., ltd., 1912.   207, (1) p. front., illus., ports. 19 cm. 13-54.   DA789.C88

RUTHVEN.   See also DOUGLAS, DA758.3A1T2

14876   RUTLEDGE.   Memories of the Rutledge family of New Salem, Illinois, after their removal to Iowa, with personal letters from Mrs. Sarah Rutledge Saunders, youngest sister of Ann Rutledge, sweetheart of Abraham Lincoln, and documents from other living descendents (!)   Compiled by Jane Hamand, for the Decatur Lincoln memorial collection.   (n. p.) 1921.   40 l. 28½ cm.   Photostat (negative) of type-written copy.   Title-page type-written.   32-29590.   CS71.R982   1921

RUTSON.   See JAMES, 1913a

14877   RUTTER.   Le Roter, or Rutter, of Kingsley, co. pal. Chester.   By T. Helsby ... (London, 1872)   22 p. illus., double pl., fold. map, 5 fold. geneal. tab.   22 cm.   Two of the genealogical tables are in pocket.   Reprinted from the "Reliquary, quarterly archaeological journals and review," vol. XII, p. (129)-138 (January, 1872) and p. 229-238 (April, 1872) 8-17015.
CS439.R8

RUTTER.   See also YERKES, 1904

14878   RYAN.   An Australian story, 1837-1907.   By Maie Casey.   London, M. Joseph (1962)   194 p. illus.   23 cm.   63-59252.   CS2009.R9   1962

14879   RYAN.   Journey's end; genealogy of John Jacob Ryan and Mary Anne Hargrave family.   By Flavia (Vincent) Reeds.   (Lake Charles, La., 1966)   xx, 224 p. 29 cm. Bibliography: p. (180) 66-5208.
CS71.R98   1966

RYAN.   See also: MITCHELL, 1931
                   MITCHELL, 1936

14880   RYE.   An account of the family of Rye.   By Walter Rye.   (London) Priv. print. (Mitchell and Hughes, printers) 1876.   2 p. l., 100, iv p., 1 l., (v)-xxiv, (v)-viii, (101)-108 p. fold. geneal. tables, 28½ cm.   Pages 1-40 first published in "Herald and genealogist," vols. VI, VII, VIII, and p. 41-60 in "The Genealogist," vol. I.   "Note as to Edward Rye of Whitwell," by Charles Jackson, 1869; iv p.   "Fief of De Beaufoe or Rye.   From the History of the hundred of Launditch in Norfolk.   By G. A. Carthew": 1 l., p. v-xxiv inserted after p. iv.   19-2307.   CS439.R85

RYEDALE.   See RIDDLE.

14881   RYERSON.   The genealogy of the Ryerson family in America.   1646-1902.   By Louis Johnes Ryerson, A.M.   New York, Press of Jenkins & McCowan, 1902.   89 p. front. 21 cm. 2-24852.
CS71.R993   1902

14882   RYERSON.   The Ryerson genealogy; genealogy and history of the Knickerbocker families of Ryerson, Ryerse, Ryerss; also Adriance and Martense families; all descendants of Martin and Adriaen Reyersz (Reyerszen), of Amsterdam, Holland, by Albert Winslow Ryerson ... ed. by Alfred L. Holman.   Chicago, Priv. print. for E. L. Ryerson, 1916.   xv, 433 p., 1 l. col. coat of arms. 27½ cm. 17-5421.
CS71.R993   1916

14883   RYMES.   Rymes genealogy.   Samuel Rymes, of Portsmouth, N. H., and his descendants.   Compiled for Christopher E. Rymes.   Somerville, Mass., 1897.   13 numb. l. 25½ x 20½ cm. 9-13006.
CS71.R995   1897

14884   RYLE.   History of the Ryle family, compiled by Mrs. Mamie Williamson, copied by William and Anne Fitzgerald.   (Florence? Ky.) 1955.   69, 22 l. illus. 28 cm. 56-23138.
CS71.R994   1955

14885   RYLE.   Some descendants of John Ryle of Anson County, North Carolina, and the Ryle family of Boone County, Kentucky.   Compiled by Herbert E. Ryle and Elbert Stephens Ryle.   Stevensville, Md., 1961.   107 l. 29 cm. 62-654 rev.   CS71.R994   1961

14886   RYMER.   A family chronicle of S. Bradford Rymer.   By Zola (Rymer) Graf.   (Edited by Catherine R. Kane, assisted by Catherine A. Morrissey.   Dunkirk, N. Y., 1960)   139 p. illus. 26 cm.
60-3501.
                                                                                                                    CS71. R9948   1960

14887   RYON.   The Ryon-Billings colonial ancestry; a compilation of the forebears of the author and his wife Priscilla Alden Billings Ryon, by William E. Ryon, Jr.   Winter Haven, Fla., Star Press, 1969.
viii, 63 p. illus., geneal. table, ports.   24 cm.   Bibliography:. p. 59.   79-10588 MARC.
                                                                                                                    CS71. R996   1969

RYON.   See also COVINGTON, 1956

RYTHER.   See RIDER.

RYVES.   See RIVES.

S

14888   SABIN.   The Sabin family of America.   The four earliest generations.   By the Rev. Anson Titus, jr. ... Weymouth, Mass., 1882.   cover-title, 1 p. 1., 7, (4) p. 24½ cm.   "Reprinted from the New Eng. historical and genealogical register for January, 1882." 9-13720.   CS71.S116   1882

14889   SABIN.   A genealogical record of the ancestors of the present generation of the Sabin family, compiled by Mrs. Lucy Whitman Sabin Andriance.   (n. p.) 1895.   12 p. 19 cm.   Mounted photograph at end. Blank leaves interspersed.   Type-written matter and newspaper clippings in pocket.   Author's autograph, and notes opposite p. 7, in manuscript. 32-4298.   CS71.S116   1895

14890   SABIN.   The family and descendants of Rev. James Sabine, by his grandson, John Dickinson Sabine ... Washington, D. C., Printed for private circulation, 1904.   15 p. 2 port. 23 cm. 5-436 rev.
                                                        CS71.S116   1904

14891   SABIN.   The Sabin family of America.   (By Joel Sabin Griswold)   (Pasadena? Calif., 1930?) cover-title, 12 p. 21 cm.   Introduction signed: Joel Sabin Griswold. 31-18516.   CS71.S116   1930

14892   SABIN.   Sabin(e): the history of an ancient English surname, illustrated by a chronological list of instances from Saxon times to the nineteenth century; together with numerous pedigrees, etc. London (W. H. W. Sabine): New York (Colburn & Tegg) 1953.   105 l. illus. 29 cm. 53-36240.
                                                        CS439.S13

         SABIN.   See also: BLAKENEY, 1926
                             CUMMINS, 1958
                             EARLE, 1901
                             GREER, 1940

         SABINE.   See SABIN.

14893   SACKETT.   The Family record.   Devoted for 1897 to the Sackett, the Weygant and the Mapes families, and to ancestors of their intersecting lines.   no. 1-12; Jan. -Dec. 1897.   Newburgh, N. Y., C. H. Weygant, 1897.   1 v. 30 cm. Edited by Charles H. Weygant.   No more published. 1-27653.
                                                        CS71.S121   1897

         SABO.   See SAEBU.

14894   SACKETT.   Family record: consisting of genealogical table and biographical notes relating to ancestors of Adam Tredwell Sackett, their children and children's children.   By Charles H. Weygant. Newburgh, N. Y. (Journal printing house and book bindery) 1899.   31 p. 24½ cm. 22-13255.
                                                        CS71.S121   1899

14895   SACKETT.   The Sacketts of America, their ancestors and descendants, 1630-1907; by Charles H. Weygant ... Newburgh, N. Y. (Journal print) 1907.   553 p. illus. (coat of arms) 26 cm. 7-31429.
                                                        CS71.S121   1907

         SACKETT.   See also: DE MOSS, 1950
                               STANTON, 1960

14896   SACKVILLE.   Memoirs of the antient and noble family of Sackville.   Collected from old records, wills, manuscripts, our most approv'd historians, and other authorities.   Humby inscrib'd to His Grace Lionel, duke of Dorset ... by Arthur Collins, esq.   London, Printed in the year 1741.
1 p. l., p. (501)-595. plates (1 fold.) 22½ cm.   A separate from the author's Peerage of England ... 2d ed.   London, 1741, v. 1, p. 501-595, with special t. -p. and two engravings inserted.   20-15878.   CS439.S15

14897   SACKVILLE.   An historical and topographical sketch of Knole in Kent; with a brief genealogy of the Sackville family.   By John Bridgman.   2d ed.   London, W. Lindsell, 1821.   viii, 164 p.   9 pl.
22½ cm.   3-15902.   DA690.K7B8

14898   SACKVILLE.   The visitor's guide to Knole, in the county of Kent, with catalogues of the pictures contained in the mansion, and biographical notices of the principal persons whose portraits form part of the collection.   By John H. Brady, F. R. A. S.   Sevenoaks, Printed by and for J. Payne, 1839.
xx, 258 p. front., illus., pl., fold. geneal. tab.   23½ cm.   The family of Sackville, p. 19-67.   2-21788.
                          DA690.K7B7

14899   SACKVILLE.   Knole and the Sackvilles, by V. Sackville-West.   London, W. Heinemann,
1923.   xvi, 230, (2) p. incl. geneal. tab.   plates, ports., facsim.   26 cm.   First published, November 1922; new impression, January
1923.   23-7666.   DA690.K7S3

14900   SACKVILLE.   History of the Sackville family (earls and dukes of Dorset) together with a description of Knole, early owners of Knole and a catalogue raisonné of the pictures and drawings at Knole, by Charles J. Phillips ... London (etc.) Cassell and company limited (1930)   2 v. fronts., illus.
(incl. map, plans) plates, ports., facsims., geneal. tables (1 fold.) coats of arms.   33 cm.   30-14405.   CS439.S157

SACKVILLE.   See also STRANGE, 1915

14901   SADLEIR.   "Great trees from little saplings grow"; a genealogical narrative touching the life of Sir Ralph Sadleir and his descendants, with comments on the locale of family activities, ancient and modern, by Cora Smith Gould, tenth lineal descendant from Edward and Anne Leigh Sadleir.   Illustrations from paintings, drawings, photographs and original documents.   New York, Priv. print. by Bartlett Orr press, 1931.   2 v. fronts., illus., plates, ports., facsims., coats of arms.   32 cm.   Vol. II has sub-title: A genealogical narrative touching the lives of the Jellett families, from William Jellett, born 1632, and Katharine Morgan, his wife, down through the centuries to the present era, 1931, with comments on the locale of family activities, ancient and modern, by Cora Smith Gould, sixth lineal descendant from William and Katharine.   31-7095 rev.   CS439.S16G6

SADLER.   See MILLER, 1923

SADLEYER.   See SADLEIR.

SADLIER.   See SADLEIR.

14902   SADOWSKI.   ... Polish pioneers of Virginia and Kentucky, by Miecislaus Haiman, with notes on genealogy of the Sadowski family, by A. Clay Sandusky.   Chicago, Ill., Polish R. C. union of America, 1937.   84 p. incl. front., illus. (facsims.) 22 cm.   (Annals of the Polish Rom. Cath. union archives and museum.   vol. II)
Bibliography: p. 80-84.   37-23338.   F235.P7H3

14903   SAENGER.   The house of Sanger; a record of the descendants of Conrad Sänger I, died 1822, and his wives, Nancy Miller and Ann Brillinger.   By Nettie Mabelle Senger.   (Fort Wayne? n. d.)
3 reels.   Microfilm copy of typescript, made in 1953 by the Historical Society of York County, Pa.   Positive.   Collation of the original, as determined from the film: 3 v. illus., ports., coat of arms, facsims.   Mic 56-4277.   Microfilm 4065 CS

14904   SÁENZ.   ... Los Sáenz, Valiente, y Aguirre.   By Ricardo de Lafuente Machain.   (Buenos Aires, "La Baskonia", 1931)   2 p. l., 9-215 p., 1 l. illus., plates, ports., facsims. (part fold.) geneal. tables (1 fold.) coats of arms.   32 cm.   Folded facsimiles have guard sheets with descriptive letterpress.   "De esta obra se ha hecho un tiraje especial de 100 ejemplares numerados."   This copy not numbered.   "El presente trabajo fué presentado al primer Congreso de genealogía y heráldica, celebrado en Barcelona en 1929 y retenido por la Real academia de la historia, para su publicación." - p. 209.   33-16510 rev.
                          F2805.L24

14905   SAFFIN.   The Saffin family.   By Isaac J. Greenwood ... (Boston, 1891)   4 p. 23½ cm.   Reprinted from the New England historical and genealogical register for January, 1891.   20-9239.
CS71.S125   1891

14906   SAFFORD.   The Saffords in America, June, 1923.   Edward S. Safford, compiler.   (n. p.) 1923.   cover-title, (405) p. 28½ cm.   Type-written in two parts with indexes.   23-14456.
CS71.S127   1923

14907   SAFFORD.   The Ohio valley Saffords, originally compiled in 1895 by Reginald Heber Smith and Sidney Methiot Culbertson, from the notes and researches of Judge William Harrison Safford, and his son William Edwin Safford, revised, enlarged and continued to 1932, by Sidney Methiot Culbertson. Denver, Col., The Kistler press, 1932.   2 p. l., vi, (2), 240 p. 25 cm.   Blank pages for "Births", Marriages, "Deaths" (231-240) 33-6868.
CS71.S127   1932

SAFFORD.   See also: FOLLETT, 1896
HUNTER, 1934
ROBINSON, 1837

14908   SAGE.   Genealogical record of the descendants of David Sage, a native of Wales; born 1639, and one of the first settlers of Middletown, Connecticut. - 1652.   Carefully prepared and rev. by the author from authentic records.   Middletown, Conn., Pelton & King, printers, 1878.   82 p. incl. pl. (coat of arms) front., photos. 23 cm. Interleaved. Compiled by Elisha L. Sage. 9-13719.
CS71.S129   1878

14909   SAGE.   A sketch of Dr. John Smith Sage, of Sag-Harbor, N. Y., by Anna Mulford, with an Appendix, containing some interesting letters of his father, Dr. Ebenezer Sage, written in the early part of the century, and other matters relating to Sag-Harbor.   Sag-Harbor, J. H. Hunt, printer, 1897.   3 p. l., 83 p. 23 cm.   Appendix (p. (27)-60):   Cooper the novelist and Dr. Ebenezer Sage. 24-15399.   R154.S2M8

14910   SAGE.   History of the Sage and Slocum families of England and America, including the allied families of Montague, Wanton, Brown, Josselyn, Standish, Doty, Carver, Jermain or Germain, Pierson, Howell.   Hon. Russell Sage and Margaret Olivia (Slocum) Sage.   The Slocum families showing three lines of descent from the signers of the Mayflower compact.   By Henry Whittemore ... New York, 1908.   27, xix, (30)-44 p., 2 l., (3)-50 p. illus., plates, ports. 31 cm. 9-29215.
CS71.S129   1908

14911   SAGE.   Genealogical record of the descendants of David Sage, a native of Wales; born 1639, and one of the first settlers of Middletown, Connecticut - 1652.   Carefully prepared and revised by 1515 Elisha L. Sage, in 1878, from authentic records.   Brought to date (1919) by 232 Charles H. Sage. Batavia, N. Y., C. H. Sage, 1919.   128 p. incl. front. (coat of arms) 23½ cm. Interspersed with blank pages. 23-999.
CS71.S129   1919

14912   SAGE.   The Jonathan Sage family; descendants of David Sage of Middletown, Connecticut, second branch.   (Normal? Ill.) Priv. print., 1951.   vii, 94 p. illus., facsims. 24 cm. 52-16775.
CS71.S129   1951

14913   SAGE.   Sage family: autobiography of Parthena (Smith) Sage, 1824-1909, wife of Horatio Sage.   With descendants and notes on Smith - Chaffee - Foster.   Prepared by Helen Foster Snow. (Madison, Conn., 1953?)   13 l. 29 cm. 62-59759.
CS71.S129   1953

14914   SAGE.   The march of the Sages.   Research: John Edward (Pat) Gwin-Sage, Marguerite (Sage) Parker (Mrs. Sterling Parker).   Editor: Bonnie (Sage) Ball.   Associate editor: Sybil Dawson Scofield. (Radford, Va., Commonwealth Press, c. 1967)   575 p. illus. 24 cm. Includes bibliographical references. 68-2537.
CS71.S129   1967

14915   SAGE.   Sage-Cowan-Stone-Saunders families in North Carolina.   7765
Microfilm reading room.

SAGE.   See also No. 3939 - Colebrook.

14916   SAGER.   The valiant seven, by Netta Sheldon Phelps, illustrated by Helen Hughes Wilson. Caldwell, Id., The Caxton printers, ltd., 1941.   221 p. col. front., illus., plates. 23½ cm. Illustrated lining-papers in color. 41-4139.
PZ9.P55Va

SAGERS.   See STOUT, 1960

14917   SAHLER.   The genealogy of the Sahlers, of the United States, of America, and of their kinsmen, the Gross family.   By Louis Hasbrouck Sahler.   Utica, N. Y., L. C. Childs & son, printers (1895)   37, (1) p. front. (port.) 30 x 24 cm. 1-27979.   CS71.S13   1895

ST. ANGE.   See CHARLY SAINT-ANGE.

ST. AUBURN.   See HALE, 1892

14918   SAINT-CASTIN.   ... Le baron de Saint-Castin, chef abénaquis.   Montréal, Éditions de l'A. C.-F.   (1939)   219 p., 2 l. illus. (map) 20½ cm. (Documents historiques) "Bibliographie": p. (213)-215. A43-1420.
F1038.S125

14919   SAINT CLAIR.   Genealogie of the Sainteclaires of Rosslyn, by Father Richard Augustin Hay, prior of St. Pieremont, including the chartulary of Rosslyn.   Edinburgh, T. G. Stevenson, 1835.
3 p. l., xxii, 176 p. fold. plates (incl. front.) 22½ cm.   "One hundred and eight copies on small paper.   Twelve copies on large thick paper." Edited by James Maidment.   17-23082 rev.   CS479.S25   1835

14920   SAINT CLAIR.   Histoire généalogique de Saint Clair et ses alliances (France - Écosse) par L.-A. de Saint Clair.   Paris, Impr. Hardy & Bernard, 1905.   112 p. front. 25½ cm. Frontispiece: Saint Clair 1005-1905, followed by col. coat of arms.   15-3551.   CS599.S3

SAINT CLAIR.   See also SINCLAIR.

14921   SAINTHILL.   An olla podrida; or, Scraps, numismatic, antiquarian, and literary.   By Richard Sainthill ...   London, Printed (for private distribution only) by Nichols and son, 1844-53.
2 v. illus., plates (incl. ports.) tables (part fold.) facsims. (part fold.) 25½ cm.   Pedigrees of Sainthill and Yarde: v. 1, p. 308, 317-321. coat of arms.   10-21193.   CJ35.S2 vol. 1

14922   SAINTHILL.   The history of the Sainthill family, by Ammabel St. Hill.   London, Mitchell, Hughes and Clarke (1938)   x, 79 p. incl. col. front. plates, ports., facsim., coat of arms.   28½ cm.   40-289.
CS439.S17   1938

14923   ST. JOHN.   The will of Samuel St. John ... 1844.   (New Haven? 1852?)   1 p. l., 23 p. front. (port.)   22 cm.   Title vignette.   A new edition, with a likeness of Mr. St. John.   On the t.-p. is a view of his tomb in the New Haven cemetery. cf. p. (14)   Genealogical history of the St. John family, by S. D. Pardee: p. 15-23.   19-20217.   CS71.S143   1852

14924   ST. JOHN.   The St. John genealogy; descendants of Matthias St. John of Dorchester, Massachusetts, 1634, of Windsor, Connecticut, 1640, of Wethersfield, Connecticut, 1643-1645, and Norwalk, Connecticut, 1650, by Orline St. John Alexander.   New York, The Grafton press, 1907.   xv, 624 p. front., plates, ports. 25½ cm.   "Five hundred copies ... No. 29."   7-20517 rev.   CS71.S143   1907
—— Revised edition of the index ... New York, The Grafton press, 1909.   cover-title, 1 p. l., 551-628 p. 25½ cm.   7-20517 rev.   CS71.D143   1907
Index

ST. JOHN.   See also: DOWNEY, 1931
SHEFFIELD, 1929
SHEFFIELD, 1932
SWAIN, 1896
WHITING, 1873

14925   ST. LEGER.   The history and description of Leeds castle, Kent.   By Charles Wykeham Martin ...   Westminster, Nichols and sons, 1869.   x, 210 p., 1 l., xxxvi p. illus., 8 phot. incl. front., plan, tab. (partly fold.) facsim. 38½ cm.   Contains pedigree of the St. Leger, Colepeper, Fairfax, Martin, and Wickham families.   3-3479.
DA690.L39M3

SAINT-LEGERS.   See BACKHOUSE, DA690.S97R9

ST. LEGOR.   See No. 430 - Adventurers of purse and person.

ST. MAUR.   See SEYMOUR.

512

14926 SAINT-OURS. Histoire de la seigneurie de St. Ours ... 1. ptie. Montréal, Impr. de l'Institution des sourds-muets, 1915. 1 v. front. (ports.) illus., plates. 27 cm. By Azarie Couillard Després. 16-7061.

F1054.S34C8

ST. VRAIN. See DE LASSUS.

14927 SALAZAR. ... Linaje de Hortún de Salazar, señor de la torre de Allende, 1400-1943. (Santiago del Nuevo Extremo, Chile, Las prensas de "El Esfuerzo," 1944) vii, 204 p., 1 l. plates, ports., facsims., coat of arms. 27 cm. At head of title: Jorge de Allende-Salazar Arrau. 46-15113. CS319.S3 1944

SALE. See MOORE, 1918

SALESBURY. See SALISBURY.

14928 SALIS. I Salis di Valtellina e il loro palazzo in Tirano, memoria presentata alla Societa storica valtellinese. By Renzo Sertoli Salis. Sondrio, Tip. Bettini e Ramponi, 1953. 28 p. illus. 25 cm. 60-25134. CS769.S3 1953

14928a SALIS. The De Salis family in the British Commonwealth; genealogical tables and short historical notes on past and present members. (Thornbury, Bristol, 1959) 35 p. fold. geneal. tables. 25 cm. Cover title. 61-34890. CS439.S174 1959

SALIS. See also CASTELBERG, 1959

14929 SALISBURY. Family memorials. A series of genealogical and biographical monographs on the families of Salisbury, Aldworth-Elbridge, Sewall, Pyldren-Dummer, Walley, Quincy, Gookin, Wendell, Breese, Chevalier-Anderson, and Phillips. With fifteen pedigrees and an appendix. By Edward Elbridge Salisbury. Privately printed. (New Haven, Press of Tuttle, Morehouse & Taylor) 1885. 2 v. fold. geneal. tables. 37 cm. Paged continuously. 9-14120. CS71.S167 1885

14930 SALISBURY. Seventeen pedigrees from "Family-memorials," by Edward Elbridge Salisbury. Priv. print. (New Haven, Conn., Press of Tuttle, Morehouse & Taylor) 1885. (3) p. fold. geneal. tables. 37 cm. Contents. - Pedigrees of the families of Salisbury, Aldworth-Elbridge, Sewall, Pyldren-Dummer, Walley, Quincy, Gookin, Wendell, Breese, Chevalier-Anderson, and Phillips. 9-14119. CS71.S167 1885a

14931 SALISBURY. The Salisburian; historical, biographical and genealogical records of the house of Salisbury, originally of Massachusetts, later of Phelps, New York, by Elon Galusha Salisbury. v. 1 - Jan. 1917 - Phelps, N.Y., The Flintside press, 1921 - v. ports. 21 cm. irregular. 31-4349. CS71.S167 1917-

14932 SALISBURY. Genealogy of the Richard Salisbury family. (Salisbury reunion association) (n. p., 1924) 2 p. l., 7-56 p. 21 cm. Publication committee; C. E. Morey, W. A. DeVolt, C. L. Spencer, O. C. West. Contains also a brief history of the Association. "Authorities consulted": p. 10. 37-16979.

CS71.S167 1924

14933 SALISBURY. The Joshua Salisbury family book of remembrance; a genealogical-historical and biographical dictionary of Joshua Salisbury, his ancestry, his descendants, and allied families. By Louis Salisbury Leatham. Ann Arbor, Mich., Edwards Bros., 1961. 851 p. illus. 29 cm. 61-9626. CS71.S167 1961

SALISBURY. See also BARBER, DA690.L982C6

14934 SALKELD. The Salkeld family of Pennsylvania, from John who emigrated in 1705, to the fourth generation so far as known. By a descendant. (Jacob Painter. n. p.) 1867. cover-title, 1 p. l., 8 p. illus. 21½ cm. 9-13718. CS71.S168 1867

SALLEE. See PARKER, 1959 (addenda)

SALLEY. See WANNAMAKER, 1937

SALLIS.　See SALIS.

14935　SALMANS.　History of the Salmans family, by Levi Brimner Salmans ... Guanajuato, Mex., The editor, 1936.　2 p. l., 3-205 (i. e. 211) p. incl. plates, ports.　35 cm.　Includes extra numbered pages.　The Power family included. 41-38342.　　　　CS71. S17　　1936

SALSBURY.　See SALISBURY.

14936　SALTER.　First families of old Monmouth: Salter family.　By J. E. Stillwell ... (New York, 1882)　11 p.　23 cm.　(With Salter, Edwin.　Memorial services and notices of George William Salter ... Washington, 1882)　Caption title. 9-13821.　　　　CS71. S177　　1882

14937　SALTER.　Memorial services and notices of George William Salter, of Washington, D. C. ... Washington, R. Beresford, printer, 1882.　46 p., 1 l.　front. (port.)　illus.　23 cm.　Ed. by Edwin Salter.　9-13822.　　　　CS71. S177　　1882

14938　SALTER.　John Salter, mariner, by William Tibbits Salter ... Philadelphia, J. Highlands, 1900.　58 p.　front., ports.　19½ cm.　3-27030.　　　　CS71. S177　　1900

14939　SALTER.　Rev. William Salter, D. D., 1821-1910, minister of the Congregational church and society of Burlington, Iowa, 1846-1910.　(Des Moines, 1911)　2 p. l., p. (560)-644, 63-66.　front., pl., ports., geneal. tab.　23 cm.　A memorial tribute by the Rev. James L. Hill, reprinted from the Annals of Iowa, vol. IX, no. 8, 3d ser., and an editorial, "William Salter," reprinted from vol. x, no. 1, 3d ser., p. 63-64.　"Published works by Dr. Salter": p. 64-66 at end.　16-14524.
　　　　BX7260. S2H5

14940　SALTER.　The Salters of Portsmouth, New Hampshire, by William M. Emery ... New Bedford, Mass.　(New Bedford printing co.) 1936.　2 p. l., (3)-60 p.　front., pl., ports.　23 cm.　37-7882.　　　　CS71. S177　　1936

14941　SALTER.　Gawin Lane Corbin Salter, a gentleman and a scholar, 1814-1890.　By Oscar Lane Shewmake.　Richmond (1960)　106 p.　illus.　24 cm.　61-36021.　　　　CS71. S177　　1960

SALTER-WELD.　See No. 430 - Adventurers of purse and person.

14942　SALTONSTALL.　Pedigree of Saltonstall.　Collated and arranged by Geo. D. Phippen. (Boston, S. G. Drake, 185-?)　geneal. tab.　53½ x 71½ cm.　"Prepared for Mr. Drake's folio edition of the History of Boston." With coat of arms (mounted)　3-11077.　　　　CS71. S179　　185-

14943　SALTONSTALL.　Ancestry and descendants of Sir Richard Saltonstall, first associate of the Massachusetts Bay colony and patentee of Connecticut.　(Cambridge) Printed at the Riverside press, 1897 .　xii, 265 p.　front., plates, ports., facsims. (part fold.)　fold. geneal. tables, col. coats of arms.　26 cm.　Compiled by Leverett Saltonstall.　Title vignette: coat of arms.　For private distribution.　9-13717.　　　　CS71. S179　　1897

SALTONSTALL.　See also: COOCH, 1962
　　　　　　　　　　　　　MUMFORD, 1900
　　　　　　　　　　　　　WANTON, F76. R52 vol. 3

SALTUS.　See LUDINGTON, 1925

SALUSBURY.　See SALISBURY.

SAMBORNE.　See SANBORN.

14944　SAMES.　Sames.　(Compiled by James W. Sames, III.　Midway? Ky., 1965?)　13 l. of geneal. tables, 32 p.　col. coat of arms (on cover)　36 cm.　Cover title.　65-71322.　　　　CS71. S182　　1965

SAMMONS.　See: DUNHAM, 1933
　　　　　　　　　　PECK, 1955

SAMPLE.　See CARTER, 1958b

14945   SAMPSON.   The Sampson family, by Lilla Briggs Sampson ... Baltimore, Williams & Wilkins co. (c.1914)   vii, 238 p. front. (coat of arms) plates, ports., geneal. tables (1 fold.) 21½ cm. 15-2660 rev.
CS71.S189   1914

14946   SAMPSON.   Kith and kin, written, at their urgent request, for the children of Mr. and Mrs. John Russell Sampson, by their mother.   It includes records of their ancestors bearing the names Baker, Baldwin, Breckinridge, Brown, Bryson, Byrd, Curd, Dudley, Goodman, Horsley, Kennedy, Le Bruen, McClanahan, McDowell, McKesson, Poage, Reed, Rogers, Thornton, Trice, Sampson, and Woods.   By Anne Eliza (Woods) Sampson.   Richmond, William Byrd Press, 1922,   247 p. geneal. tables. 26 cm. Blank leaves interspersed. "Authorities": p. (3)-4. 23-17610 rev.*   CS71.S189   1922
——— Supplement, 1929. (n.p.1929?)   (11) p. geneal. tables. 26 cm. Caption title.
CS71.S189   1922
Suppl.

14947   SAMPSON.   New light on the history of the Sampson family; with special reference to the line of descent through Jane Sampson to her granddaughter, Marietta Wood Todd (by) Edwin S. Todd. Springfield, O., 1939.   10 numb. 1. 29½ cm. Caption title. Typewritten (carbon copy) Text runs parallel with back of cover. Foreword includes bibliographical references. 40-18935.   CS71.S189   1939

14948   SAMPSON.   Our New England Sampsons, and some related families: Bradford, Barton, Banks, Batchelder, Walker, Marsh, Appleyard, Loane, Buzzell, Dunham, and others.   With historical sketch of early family roots in Europe from A.D.1066. (New York? Priv. published, 1953)   192 p. illus., ports., fold. map, coats of arms. 23 cm. "One of the original edition of one hundred volumes." - Ms. note on p. (2) of cover. 54-37785.
CS71.S189   1953

SAMPSON.   See also: FOSTER, 1930
GILES, 1864

SAMS.   See LEE, 1957

14949   SAMUEL.   Records of the Samuel family, collected from essays, mss., and other sources by J. Bunford Samuel ... Philadelphia, Printed for private circulation by J. B. Lippincott company, 1912. 4 p. 1., 55, (1) p. front., plates, ports., fold. geneal. tab., col. coat of arms. 25 cm. "Of this volume one hundred copies have been printed and the type distributed." 12-26390.   CS71.S194   1912

14950   SAMUEL.   Records of the Samuel family, by J. Bunford Samuel ... 2d ed., compiled by Sanford A. Moss ... Lynn, Mass., 1939.   2 geneal. tab.   30 x 44½ cm. fold. to 30 x 23 cm. Blue-print. "A new edition of the Family tree in the original volume, from Mr. Samuel's notes of additional research ... " 41-38343.
CS71.S194   1939

14951   SAMUEL.   The Samuel family of Liverpool and London, from 1755 onwards; a biographical and genealogical dictionary of the descendants of Emanuel Samuel.   By Ronald James D'Arcy Hart. With a foreword by Viscount Samuel.   London, Routledge and Paul (1958)   xv, 118 p. ports., geneal. tables. 26 cm. 58-3981.   CS439.S177   1958

SAMUEL.   See also GRAY, 1938

SAMWORTH.   See No. 1547 - Cabell county.

14952   SANBORN.   Genealogy of the Sanborn family.   By Nathan Sanborn ... Boston, Printed by H. W. Dutton, 1856.   21 p. illus. (coat of arms) 23½ cm. "From the N. England hist. & gen. register, July and October, 1856." 34-32136.   CS71.S198   1856

14953   SANBORN.   The Sambornes of England and America.   By Victor Channing Sanborn.   (Concord? Mass., n.d.)   11 p. 25 cm. Two holograph letters by the author inserted. "Reprinted from the New England historical and genealogical register for July, 1885." 58-54597.   CS71.S198

14954   SANBORN.   Sanborn family in the United States and brief sketch of life of John B. Sanborn, with speeches and addresses. (By John Benjamin Sanborn) St. Paul, H.M. Smyth printing co., 1887.

14954 continued: (321) p. 2 port. (incl. front.) 23½ cm. "The Sambornes of England and America. By V. C. Sanborn": p. 1-14. "The Sanborn family, by Nathan Sanborn": p. 15-40. With this are bound his Reminiscences of the campaigns against Vicksburg ... 1887. and his Oration delivered before the Society of the Army of the Tennessee ... 1887. 24-4258. CS71.S198 1887

14955 SANBORNE. Notes on the English ancestry of the following American families: Samborne or Sanborn ... Bachiler or Batcheller ... Blake ... Levet, Lovet, Leavitt ... Kirtland or Kirkland ... by V. C. Sanborn. Boston, D. Clapp & son, printers, 1894. 16 p. 23½ cm. 40-37513.
CS71.D198 1894

14956 SANBORN. The American and English Sambornes. (With a notice of Rev. Stephen Bachiler) By V. C. Sanborn. Concord, N. H., Printed by the Republican press association, 1895. 25 p. front., illus. (incl. port.) 25½ cm. Title vignette: coat of arms. "Reprinted from the Granite monthly." 9-13716.
CS71.S198 1895

14957 SANBORN. Genealogy of the family of Samborne or Sanborn in England and America. 1194-1898. By V. C. Sanborn ... (Concord, N. H., Rumford press) 1899. xiii p., 1 l., 692 p. col. front. (coat of arms) illus. plates, ports., fold. map, facsim., geneal. tables. 25 cm. Privately printed for the author. "The author attributes much of the completeness of his volume to the collections made by the late Dr. N. Sanborn, and Prof. Dyer H. Sanborn." - N. E. hist. and geneal. register, April, 1899. The New Hampshire way of life (1800-1860). By F. B. Sanborn of Concord, Mass.: p. 613-628. 3-6521.
CS71.S198 1899

14958 SANBORN. The English ancestry of the American Sanborns. A supplement to the Samborne-Sanborn genealogy. By V. C. Sanborn. (n. p.) Priv. print. for the author, 1916. 24 p. front. (coat of arms) 25½ cm. 17-11812. CS71.S198 1916

14959 SANBORN. The ancestry of Frederic Rockwell Gladstone Sanborn ... by Frederic Rockwell Sanborn. (Brooklyn?) Priv. print., 1928 - v. fold. geneal. tab. 22½ cm. Chart of the royal ancestry of Frederic Rockwell Gladstone Sanborn at end of v. 1. 29-462. CS71.S198 1928

SANBORN. See also: DRAKE, 1962
TUCKER, 1957

14960 SANCHEZ. The Sanchez family of St. Augustine, Florida, collected for Ruth Waldren Hill. By Ianthe (Bond) Hebel. Daytona Beach, Fla., 1957. 55 l. 30 cm. 67-31820. CS71.S199 1957

SANDELL. See: HARRIS, 1934
STUART, 1938

14961 SANDEMAN. The Sandeman genealogy, comp. by John Glas Sandeman from family notes, memoranda, and the original manuscript by David Peat. Printed for circulation among members of the family. Edinburgh, G. Waterston & sons, 1895. 3 p. l., viii, 36 p., 1 l. front. (coat of arms) illus. 27½ cm. Interleaved. 19-3377. CS479.S28

SANDEMAN. See also GLAS, 1917

14962 SANDERS. Genealogy, ancestors and descendants of John Sanders, Fort Covington, N. Y., prepared by George Rich. Cleveland, O., 1922. 1 p. l., 5-42, (6) p. 20 cm. 22-6535.
CS71.S256 1922

14963 SANDERS. The Sanders family of Grass Hills; the life of Lewis Sanders, 1781-1861, with interesting historical events of that period; also the genealogy of the Sanders family and all families closely allied. By Anna Virginia Parker. Madison, Ind., Coleman Print. Co. (1966) v, 172 p. illus. 23 cm. 66-5151. CS71.S213 1966

SANDERS. See also SAUNDERS.

14964 SANDERSON. The Saunderson family of Little Addington. Reprinted from Northamptonshire notes & queries, parts IV and VI, 1884-85. Northampton, The Dryden press, Taylor & son, 1887. 10 p. front. (coats of arms) 22½ cm. Slip mounted on t. -p.: "Ed. by the Rev. W. D. Sweeting, M. A., vicar of Maxey, Market Deeping." Additions and corrections in ms. 20-15231. CS439.S18

14965   SANDERSON.   The Sanderson homes at Piety Corner, Waltham.   (Waltham?) Priv. print.,
1899.   30, (1) p. front., illus. 20½ cm. Prefatory note signed: Benj. Worcester. 17-24553.

CS71. S218   1899

14966   SANDERSON.   Six North country diaries ... Durham (Eng.) Published for the Society by
Andrews & co. ; (etc., etc.) 1910.   ix, 360 p. geneal. tables. 22½ cm. (Added t. -p. : The publications of the Surtees society
... vol. CXVIII) Preface signed: J. C. Hodgson.   The Diary of John Aston "is a journal written during the first Bishops' war by an eye-witness to the
events therein related. " - Introduction, p. 1.   Contents. - Preface. - Diary of John Aston. - Diary of Christopher Sanderson. - Pedigree of Sanderson
of Eggleston. - Diary of Nicholas (i. e. Jacob) Bee. - Pedigree of Bee of Durham. - Diary of John Thomlinson. - Pedigree of Thomlinson of Blencogo. -
Pedigree of Gyll of Barton. - Diary of Thomas Gyll. - Pedigree of Brown of Alnwick. - Diary of Nihcolas Brown. - Index to place names. - Index of
personal names. 10-24307.

DA20. S9 vol. 118

14967   SANDERSON.   The house of John Sanderson and his wife, Elizabeth Teasdale; married at
Morland, died at Skeels, Westmorland Co., England.   Compiled and printed by their great great great
grandson, John R. C. Sanderson.   (Topeka? Kan., 1964)   50 1. 29 cm. Additions and corrections in MS. 64-56380.

CS71. S218   1964

SANDERSON.   See also WHITAKER, CS439. W485

14968   SANDFORD.   Robert Sandford and his wife Ann Adams Sandford, with some of their descend-
ants, 1615-1930, also brief notes on several allied families including Alden, Brewster, Chilton, Stinson,
Topping, Standish, White, Sumner, Rogers, and others, by Josephine Sandford Ware.   Rutland, Vt.,
Printed for private circulation by the Tuttle company (1930?)   3 p. 1., (9)-85 p. 25 cm. 31-9479.

CS71. S219   1930

SANDON.   See CRALL, 1908

14969   SANDS.   The direct forefathers and all the descendants of Richardson Sands; together with
the genealogies of my direct maternal ancestors, by Benjamin Aymar Sands.   New York, 1916.
99 p. 25 cm. Pages 28-52, 82-92 blank for "Notes. " 50 copies printed. 62-55441.   CS71. S22   1916

SANDS.   See also SANDYS.

14970   SANDWITH.   The Sandwiths of Helmsley, co. York.   A short preliminary pedigree, by L. S.
(Lincoln Sandwith) London, Phillimore & co., 1897.   24 p. 28½ cm. 21-10455.   CS439. S19

14971   SANDYS.   Descent of Comfort Sands and of his children, with notes on the families of Ray,
Thomas, Guthrie, Alcock, Palgrave, Cornell, Dodge, Hunt, Jessup.   (By Temple Prime) New York
(The De Vinne press) 1886.   91. (1) p. geneal. tables. 25½ cm. (With his Descent of Comfort Sands ... 2d ed.   New York,
1897) "General bibliography": p. 91. 9-13645.   CS71. S22   1897

14972   SANDYS.   Descent of Comfort Sands and of his children, with notes on the families of Ray,
Thomas, Guthrie, Alcock, Palgrave, Cornell, Dodge, Hunt, Jessup.   By Temple Prime ... 2d ed.
New York (The De Vinne press) 1897.   32 p. geneal. tables. 25½ cm. Bibliography: p. 31-32. 9-13715.

CS71. S22   1897

14973   SANDYS.   History of the family of Sandys of Cumberland, afterwards of Furness in North
Lancashire, and its branches in other parts of England and in Ireland, by E. S. Sandys ... Barrow-in-
Furness, Barrow printing co., ltd., 1930.   2 v. front., illus. (incl. coats of arms) plates, ports., plans, facsims., fold.
geneal. tables. 26 cm. "For private circulation only. " "Part 2 - Pedigrees. " "List of records and authorities": pt. 1, p. 280-286. 32-19775.

CS439. S195

14974   SANDYS.   Descendants of James Sands of Block Island.   With notes on the Walker, Hutchinson, Ray, Guthrie, Palgrave, Cornell, Ayscough, Middagh, Holt, and Henshaw families.   By Malcolm
Sands Wilson.   New York, Priv. print., 1949.   109 p. coat of arms. 25 cm. 49-29542 *.

CS71. S22   1949

14975   SANDYS.   Dawn to twilight in American colonization; the story of the Sandys and others who
settled Virginia and the other colonies.   By Charles Herbert Sandy.   With an appendix on the Sandy
genealogy from 1379 to 1960.   (1st ed.) New York, Exposition Press (1962)   224 p. illus. 21 cm.
62-4145.   CS71. S22   1962

SANDYS. See also: BRADHURST, 1910
DILLON, 1927
SANDS.

14976 SANFORD. Sanford genealogy; the branch of William of Madison, N.Y., of the sixth American generation. By Heman Howes Sanford. Syracuse, N.Y., 1894. 70 p. front., ports. 24 cm. 9-13714.
CS71.S223 1894

14977 SANFORD. The Sanford family of Newton, Conn., in old and new England. Genealogical. By William Atwater Sanford of New York, N.Y. (New York, Wynkoop, Hallenbeck, Crawford co., 1905?) 160 p. illus. 15½ x 19½ cm. Cover-title: The Sanford family of England, Milford, Conn., and Newton, Conn. Pages 95-160 are forms for additional data. A39-147.
CS71.S223S2

14978 SANFORD. Thomas Sanford, the emigrant to New England; ancestry life and descendants, 1632-4. Sketches of four other pioneer Sanfords and some of their descendants, in appendix, with many illustrations, by Carlton E. Sanford ... Rutland, Vt., The Tuttle company, printers (c.1911) 2 v. fronts., plates, ports., map, facsims., coats of arms. 26 cm. Paged continuously. "The medieval origins of the Sanfords and the origin of Thomas Sanford who came to America in 1632-4, by Charles A. Hoppin", v.1, p.13-52. L.C.COPY REPLACED BY MICROFILM. 11-11088.
CS71.S223 1911
Microfilm 8860 CS

14979 SANFORD. The Sanford association of America. 4th-5th reunion, 1910-1911. Milford, Conn., 1912. 2 v. plates, ports. 25½ cm. 12-30781. CS71.S223 1912

14980 SANFORD. Ancestors and descendants of Gilbert and Esther Ann (Low) Sanford of New Jersey and New York city; families of Sanford, Shreve, Low, Prentice and Smith, by Sanford A. Moss ... Lynn, Mass., The Lynn mailing company, 1944. 2 p. l., 45 numb. l. 28 cm. Reproduced from type-written copy. 45-2646. CS71.S223 1944

14981 SANFORD. The Sanford genealogy from 1795 to 1959, with marriages to Swannell, McMinn, Lane, Ivins. By Theodore W. Roth. (New York? 1959) geneal. tables. 44 x 61 cm. fold. to 23 x 11 cm. "Exhibit 51." Photocopy (negative) of typescript. 63-48178. CS71.S223 1959a

14982 SANFORD. President John Sanford of Boston, Massachusetts and Portsmouth, Rhode Island, and descendants with many allied families, 1605-1965. Also adding the male members given in the "William Sanford of Madison, New York" genealogy by Heman Howes Sanford, 1890, with many families brought up to date. Rutland, Vt., Printed by Sharp Printing (1966) xv, 399 p. geneal. table. 24 cm. 66-8695. CS71.S223 1966

14983 SANFORD. The Sanfords of Amsterdam; the biography of a family in Americana, by Alex M. Robb. New York, William-Frederick Press, 1969. 217 p. illus., ports. (part col.) 23 cm. 68-20175 MARC.
CS71.S223 1969

SANFORD. See also: BASSETT, 1926
BEACH, 1898
CHUTE, 1894
NOYES, 1900

SANGER. See ADAMS, F63.M88 vol.1

SANGWIN. See CHAPPELL, 1929

14984 SANKEY. Sankey pedigrees. (Printed for private circulation only) (Swansea, Printed at "The Cambrian" office) 1880. 3 p. l., 2 pl. (coats of arms) 23 geneal. tab. (1 fold.) 25 cm. Blank leaves interspersed. Caption title: Memorials of the family of Sankey. A.D.1207-1880, printed from the genealogical collection of Clement Sankey Best-Gardner, of Eaglebush, Neath. 15-25141. CS439.S2

14985 SANNER. One hundred years later: autobiographies of five children (Hattie Frisby Sanner Johnston, Laura Belle Sanner Finnegan, James Harris Sanner, George Roberts Sanner, Jr., Wilmer Mackey Sanner) Baltimore, W. M. Sanner Co., c.1962) viii, 45 p. illus., ports., fold. map, facsims. 28 cm. "Two hundred and fifty copies were printed ... number 16." A sequel to This trail of life, the autobiography of George R. Sanner, the father of the five children. 63-25436. CS71.S23 1962

14986   SANNER.   The Sanner family in the United States: John Sanner and his descendants; George Ludwig Sanner and his descendants; Jacob Sanner and his descendants.   (Baltimore, W. M. Sanner Co., 1968)   1 v. (various pagings) illus., facsims., ports. 29 cm. Includes bibliography. 68-3897.

CS71.S23   1968

14987   SANSON.   Memoirs of the Sansons, from private notes and documents.   (1688-1847)   Edited by Henry Sanson ... London, Chatto & Windus, 1876.   2 v. in 1. 20½ cm. Abridged translation of the author's "Sept générations d'exécuteurs."   First published in 6 vols., Paris, 1862-63. 3-3028.

HV8553.S43

14988   SANSON.   Memoirs of the Sansons; or, Seven generations of executioners (1688-1847)   Edited by Henry Sanson, late executioner of the Court of justice, of Paris.   New York, G. Munro, 1882.   69 p. 42 cm. (Seaside library. v. 58, no. 1187) An abridged translation of "Sept générations d'exécuteurs," Paris, 1862-1863. 2-28709.

PZ1.S44 vol. 58

14989   SANSON.   The guillotine and its servants, by G. Lenôtre (pseud.) (Louis Léon Théodore Gosselin) Translated by Mrs. Rodolph Stawell.   London, Hutchinson & co. (1929)   2 p. l., 7-282 p. front. (port.) 24 cm. 29-19015.

HV8555.G6

14990   SANSOM.   In vertical file.   Ask reference librarian for this material.

14991   SANTANDER.   ... La familia de Santander.   By Luis Eduardo Pacheco.   3. ed.   Cucuta, Imp. departamental, 1940.   3 p. l., (v)-xix, 84 p., 2 l. incl. geneal. tab. port. 24½ cm. Bibliographical references included in "Notas" (p. (77)-84) 43-8873.

F2273.S2487   1940

14992   SANTEE.   Genealogy of the Santee family in America.   Comp. and pub. by Ellis M. Santee ... Cortland, N.Y., Standard printing co., 1899.   127 p. incl. front., ports. 26 cm. 9-13713 rev.

CS71.S234   1899

14993   SANTEE.   Genealogy of the Santee family in America.   By Ellis Monroe Santee.   Hunlock Creek, Pa., 1927.   211 p. illus. 27 cm. 61-58058.   CS71.S234   1927

SANTO.   See SELDEN, 1931

14994   SANXAY.   The Sanxay family, and descendants of Rev. Jacques Sanxay, Huguenot refugee to England in sixteen hundred and eighty-five.   Preface and compilation by Theodore F. Sanxay ... New York, Printed for private use, 1907.   217 p. incl. pl. facsim. 23½ cm. "The Sanxay family. Errata et corrigenda." 1 l. pasted on verso of p. 217. "The Sanxay family. Notes - Addenda et corrigenda." 4 p. inserted after p. 210. 8-20204.

CS71.S238   1907

14995   SAPP.   A history of the Sapp family; compiled and published by J. Gooden Sapp and H. W. Stanley, 1910.   1 p. l., 102 p. 24½ cm. 4 leaves inserted at end for "Continuation of the line of." 10-28803.   CS71.S24   1910

SAPY.   See PICARD, CS459.P5

14996   SARCHET.   The genealogy of the Sarchet family, from the island of Guernsey to Cambridge, Ohio, in 1806.   (By Cyrus Parkinson Beatty Sarchet) (Cambridge, O., Herald print, 1902)   1 p. l., (11) p. illus. 23½ cm. 3-22475 rev.   CS71.S242   1902

SARES.   See SEARS, S44

SARGEANT.   See SARGENT.

14997   SARGENT.   Genealogical chart of the Sargent family.   Designed and comp. by Samuel Andrews ... Boston, C. Cook's lithography, 1851.   geneal. tab. 65 x 422 fold. to 65 x 38 cm. 9-18730.

CS71.S245   1851

14998   SARGENT.   Genealogy of the Sarge(a)nt family.   Descendants of William of Malden, Mass.   By Aaron Sargent ... Boston, S.G. Drake, 1858.   108 p. 19½ cm. L.C. COPY REPLACED BY MICROFILM. 9-13712.

CS71.S245   1858
Microfilm 17945 CS

14999   SARGENT.   Reminiscences of Lucius Manlius Sargent: with an appendix containing a gene-alogy of his family, and other matters.   By John H. Sheppard.   Boston, D. Clapp & son, 1871.
3 p. l., (5)-51 p. front. (port.) 24 cm. 1-26882-M2.   CS71.S245   1871

15000   SARGENT.   ... Colonel Paul Dudley Sargent of Sullivan, Maine, and family.   Contributed by Ignatius Sargent, esq., of Machias, Me.   (In Bangor historical magazine ... Bangor, Me., 1887. 24 cm. vol. II. no. VII, p. (125)-132) "With some additions by the editor of the Historical magazine." 18-22768.   F16.M21 vol. 2
        —— Separate, with cover-title: Col. Paul Dudley Sargent, of Sullivan, Maine.   Reprinted from the Bangor historical magazine.   Bangor, Press of B. A. Burr, 1887.   CS71.S245   1887

15001   SARGENT.   Sargent genealogy.   Hugh Sargent, of Courteenhall, Northamptonshire, and his descendants in England.   By John S. Sargent ... William Sargent, of Malden, New England, and his descendants in America.   By Aaron Sargent ... Somerville, Mass., A. Sargent, 1895.   218 p. plates, ports., maps, geneal. tables, coats of arms. 23½ cm. "Compiled and published by Aaron Sargent." 9-29051.
                                                                        CS71.S245   1895

15002   SARGENT.   Sargent record.   William Sargent, of Ipswich, Newbury, Hampton, Salisbury and Amesbury, New England, U.S., with his descendants and their intermarriages, and other Sargent branches.   Compiled by Edwin Everett Sargent, St. Johnsbury, Vt.   St. Johnsbury, Vt., The Caledonian company, 1899.   331 p. incl. front., illus. ports., coats of arms. 24 cm. 99-2839.   CS71.S245   1899

15003   SARGENT.   Some descendants of Digory Sargent.   By Henry Ernest Woods, A.M.   Boston, New-England historic genealogical society, 1904.   12 p. 24 cm. "Reprinted from New-England historical and gene-alogical register for October, 1904." 4-21129.   CS71.S245   1904

15004   SARGENT.   ... The Sargent family and the old Sargent homes.   By Charles Edward Mann.   Lynn, F. S. Whitten, 1919.   64 p. 23½ cm. At head of title: "Cape Ann in story, legend and song. Section five." "Cape Ann in story, legend and song," in five sections, originally printed in the Gloucester times. 19-11624.
                                                                        CS71.S245   1919

15005   SARGENT.   Portraits of Epes and Ann Sargent, children of William Sargent, second, and their descendants, in the Sargent-Murray-Gilman house, Gloucester, Massachusetts, 1921. (n.p., 1921)
11 p. 22½ cm. Caption title. 21-14450.   CS71.S245   1921

15006   SARGENT.   Early Sargents of New England, by Winthrop Sargent ... (Philadelphia, Ad-service printing co., 1922)   53 p., 1 l. incl. front. (ports.) plates, coats of arms. 23 cm. Privately printed. The plates are mounted photographs.   Author's autographed presentation copy. 22-13260.   CS71.S245   1922

15007   SARGENT.   Epes Sargent of Gloucester and his descendants, arranged by Emma Worcester Sargent; with biographical notes by Charles Sprague Sargent.   Boston and New York, Houghton Mifflin company, 1923.   xxi, 323, 68, xxv p. front., ports. 28½ cm. Title vignette (coat of arms, reproduced from the book-plate of Epes Sargent, jr., engraved by Paul Revere) "This edition is limited to five hundred copies ... This is number 146." "The descendants of Epes Sargent ... are indebted to ... Winthrop Sargent, of Haverford, Pa., for this volume. At his request Dr. Samuel Worcester ... began in 1912 to gather information which is the basis of this genealogy. He ... died in 1918 before his work was completed ... Mrs. Paul Dana ... took up the work in 1920 and occupied herself in gathering and arranging additional information. Mrs. Dana died in 1922 ... Mr. Winthrop Sargent at once assumed the ... work of gathering the additional information needed for the book, and his wife ... arranged the different family groups and prepared the manu-script in its final form for the printer." - Pref.   "A list of the publications of the descendants of Epes Sargent, compiled by Julia Mehitable Johnson": p. (1)-68, at end.   23-18935.
                                                                        CS71.S245   1923

15008   SARGENT.   The English ancestors of Epes Sargent, by Lieut-Colonel H. G. Le Mesurier, C.I.E. (a descendant) (Exmouth? Eng.) Priv. print. (1928)   40 p. 28 cm. Printed in Great Britain. 28-30651.
                                                                        CS71.S245   1928

        SARGENT.   See L.C. additions and corrections, no. 1

        SARGENT.   See also: PAINE, 1936   VAN HOOK, 1957
                               SAUNDERS, 1930   WARDWELL, 1897
                               TUCKER, 1957   No. 553 - Goodhue county.

SARRAN. See MALHIOT, 1965

15009   SARTAIN.   Annals of the Sartain tribe, 1557-1886.   (Philadelphia? 1886?)   73 p. plates (part col.) ports.   23½ cm.   By John Sartain.   "Printed, not published."   Printed on one side of leaf only.   1-27957.   CS71.S249   1886

15010   SARVIS.   The Sarvis-Ickes genealogy, with historical notes, 1943; the record of the descendants of Johnson Sarvis and Sarah Ickes and earlier notices, compiled by Roscoe Johnson Sarvis ... Aberdeen, S. D., 1943.   cover-title, (3)-30 p.   23 x 18 cm.   Reproduced from type-written copy.   43-14330.
CS71.S25   1943

15011   SAS.   Stamboom der familie t'Sas.   By Maurits Sacré.   Merchtem, Drukkerij Sacré, 1951. geneal. table.   44 x 63 cm. fold. to 22 x 16 cm.   (His Uitgaven over de nalatenschap van J.J.t'Kint, H)   Cover title.   54-37255.
CS829.S23   1951

15012   SASSOON.   The Sassoon dynasty, by Cecil Roth.   London, R. Hale limited, 1941.   280 p. front., plates, ports., geneal. tables (1 fold.) 22 cm.   A41-3726.   CS439.S22   1941

15013   SASSOON.   The Sassoons (by) Stanley Jackson.   (1st ed.)   New York, Dutton, 1968. xiii, 304 p. illus., ports. 24 cm.   Bibliography: p. (292)-295.   67-11386.   CS439.S22   1968

15014   SASSOON.   The Sassoons (by) Stanley Jackson.   London, Heinemann, 1968.   (15), 304 p. 22 pl., illus., facsims., geneal. tables, ports.   26 cm.   Bibliography: p. (292)-295.   68-103254.
CS439.S22   1968b

15015   SATER.   Henry Sater, 1690-1754, the recital of the life and character of an early adventurer to Virginia, and subsequently a settler of the province of Maryland under Lord Baltimore.   A representative colonist ... whose strong religious convictions led to the organization of the parent Baptist society of the province ... By Isaac Walker Maclay ... (New York, P. Barnes) 1897.   1 p. l., 75, (1), lxl p. front., plates. 23 cm.   The Sater genealogy: p. (1)-lxl, at end.   11-23156.   F184.S25

15016   SATER.   Sater, Hadges, Johnson, Wakefield, McClure, and Hathaway families, Hamilton County, Ohio.   By Stanley William McClure.   Harrison, Ohio (194-?)   14 l. 37 cm.   Caption title, in manuscript.   L.C. copy imperfect: McClure and Hathaway families? wanting.   56-57050.   CS71.S254

SATHRUM.   See No.   553 - Goodhue county.

15017   SATTELMEIER.   Man in action; the happy life of a clergyman and his family, with a short sketch on the origin of religion, God's unfolding purpose, American missions.   By Frederick Albert Sattelmeier.   (Palm Springs, Calif., Distributed by F. A. Sattelmeier) 1966.   xvi, 211 p. illus., facsims., geneal. table, maps, ports. 22 cm.   Bibliography: p. 211.   67-13359.   CS71.S26   1966

SATTERLEE.   See: CHESEBROUGH, 1903
DAVIS, 1927a
DICKERSON, F127.L8W48
MERVYN, CS437.D4D8

SATTERLEIGH.   See SATTERLEE.

SATTERLY.   See SATTERLEE.

SATTERTHWAITE.   See: SHEAFE, 1923
WILSON, CS439.W55

15018   SAUMEREZ.   Annals of some of the British Norman isles, constituting the bailiwick of Guernsey, as collected from private manuscripts, public documents and former historians ... by John Jacob ... Part I.   Comprising the Casket lighthouses, Alderney, Sark, Herm, and Jethou, with part of Guernsey ... Paris, Printed for the author, 1830.   xv, (5), 489, (1), xx p., 1 l., 287 p. front., illus., plates, fold. geneal. tab. 26½ cm.   The second part was never published; but some of the materials collected for it were preserved and are herewith added at the end with half-title: Annals. Second part. 287 p.   Contains an account of the Somery, de Sausmarez, or Saumarez family of Guernsey, with folded genealogical table.   21-17135.   DA670.G9J3

15019   SAUNDERS.   Mr. William Saunders and Mrs. Sarah Flagg Saunders, late of Cambridge, with their family record and genealogy.   (n. p.) Printed for private distribution, 1872.   39 p. 19½ cm.
23-14460.   CS71.S256   1872

15020   SAUNDERS.   The founders of Massachusetts Bay colony.   A careful research of the earliest records of many of the foremost settlers of the New England colony: comp. from the earliest church and state records, and valuable private papers ... by Sarah Saunders Smith ... Pittsfield, Mass., Press of the Sun printing company, 1897.   372 p. front., illus., plates, ports., plan, facsims., coats of arms. 23½ cm.
An account of the author's various lines of ancestry.   4-15544.   CS71.S256   1897

15021   SAUNDERS.   Genealogy of the Cortland county, N. Y., branch of the Sanders family.   (By Charles Walton Sanders)   (New York, Printed by Meyer bros., 1908)   111 p. (3 l.) incl. coat of arms. ports., fold. geneal. tab. 26 x 20½ cm.   "Two hundred copies only ... No. 87. "   The genealogy was begun by Joshua C. Sanders and completed by Charles Walton Sanders.   8-31819.   CS71.S256   1908

15022   SAUNDERS.   Sanders family history, by Robert Wilson Sanders.   Greenville, S. C., 1920.
40 p. 21 cm.   29-1781.   CS71.S256   1920

15023   SAUNDERS.   Colonel Paul Dudley Sargent.   1745-1827 ... (Philadelphia? 1920)   cover-title, 46 p.
illus. (incl. ports., facsims.) 21 cm.   Printed for private circulation.   Note, p. (4) signed: Winthrop Sargent.   Contents. - Colonel Paul Dudley Sargent of Sullivan, Maine. - Concerning Col. Paul Dudley Sargent and his daughter, Mrs. Julia Sargent Johnson. - Sanders' ancestry (from notes by Dr. Samuel Worcester) - The Sargent family of Gloucester, by Charles Sprague Sargent.   21-2810.

E207.S24S242

15024   SAUNDERS.   Genealogy, ancestors and descendants of John Saunders, Fort Covington, N. Y., prepared by George Rich.   Cleveland, O., 1922.   1 p. 1., 5-42, (6) p. 20 cm.   22-6535.
CS71.S256   1922

15025   SAUNDERS.   Newell Sanders; a biography, by Rufus Terral.   (Kingsport, Tenn.) Priv. print. (Kingsport press, inc.) 1935.   xvii, 310 p. front., plates, ports. 24½ cm.   "The family": p. 283-284. 36-16185.
F436.S23

15026   SAUNDERS.   Saunders and allied families; genealogical and biographical, compiled and privately printed for Bolena S. Munn, by the American historical company, inc.   New York, 1939.
215 p. plates, ports., 6 col. coats of arms on 1 l. 32½ cm.   Alternate pages blank.   Coats of arms accompanied by guard sheet with descriptive letterpress.   Allied families: Creason, Munro, Hix, Woodson, Morton, Anderson, Aston, Davis.   Includes bibliography. 40-8334.
CS71.S256   1939

15027   SAUNDERS.   The Sanders of Kentucky, a family history (by) Walter Ray Sanders.   Litchfield, Ill., 1946.   1 p. 1., 22 numb. 1. 28 x 21½ cm.   Genealogical table inserted. 46-21033.   CS71.S256   1946

15028   SAUNDERS.   Notes on the Sanders family and related families.   By David Sanders Clark. Washington, 1956.   1 v. 30 cm.   59-25184.   CS71.S256   1956

15029   SAUNDERS.   Sage-Cowan-Stone-Saunders families in North Carolina.   Microfilm reading room.   7765

SAUNDERS.   See also:

DRIVER, 1889	PITMAN, 1920	SEMMES, 1956
HALE, 1948	SANDERS.	STOTT, 1944
HALL, 1959	SARGENT, E207.S24S242	TODD, 1909
NOYES, 1900	SEMMES, 1918	No. 4646- Franklin county.

SAUNDERSON.   See SANDERSON.

15030   SAVAGE.   Savidge family record.   (n. p., 18 -)   1 p. 23 cm.   Descendants of John Middleton Savidge,
CA 9-6031.   CS71.S264

15031 SAVAGE. The ancient and noble family of the Savages of the Ards, with sketches of English and American branches of the house of Savage, comp. from historical documents and family papers, and edited by G. F. A. (i.e. George Francis Savage-Armstrong) ... London, New York (etc.) M. Ward & co., limited, 1888. xiv p., 1 l., 388 p. incl. front., illus. (incl. coats of arms) plans. 29 cm. 15-23249.
CS439.S23

15032 SAVAGE. Family of John Savage of Middletown, Conn., 1652. By James Francis Savage. Boston, D. Clapp & Son, printers, 1894. 41 p. fold. geneal. table. 23 cm. "A reprint of an article in the New-England historical and genealogical register for July, 1894, with additions." Pref. to Supplement, p. (29)-38, dated 1898. Bibliography: p. (3) 15-1354 rev. *.
CS71.S264   1894

15033 SAVAGE. A genealogical history of the Savage family in Ulster; being a revision and enlargement of certain chapters of "The Savages of the Ards," comp. by members of the family from historical documents and family papers, and ed. by G. F. S. A. ... (George Francis Savage-Armstrong) London, Printed at the Chiswick press, 1906. xix, 381, (1) p. front., illus. (incl. coats of arms) plates, plans. 30 cm. 20-15856.
CS499.S3

15034 SAVAGE. Major Thomas Savage of Boston, and his descendants, by Lawrence Park. Boston, Press of D. Clapp & son, 1914. 3 p. l., (3)-78 p. front., ports. 25 cm. Reprinted from the New England historical and genealogical register, vol. LXVII and LXVIII. 15-4633.
CS71.S264   1914

15035 SAVAGE. Savage, Tisdale and allied families, genealogical and biographical. Prepared and privately printed for Mary (Tisdale) Savage ... New York, The American historical society, inc., 1926. 101 p., 1 l. plates, ports., col. coats of arms. 31½ cm. Title within ornamental border. Bound in blue levant with leather doublure; inlaid, gold tooled. Allied families: Barnum, Burt, Graham, Drummond, Ruthven, Carnegie, Morris. Dedication signed: Mary (Tisdale) Savage. Published also under title "Savage and allied families, by W. S. Finley" in Americana, vol. XIX, 1925, p. 387-409. "References": 1 leaf at end. 27-15867 rev. 2.
CS71.S264   1926
Office.

15036 SAVAGE. Garrett county history of Savage family, by Charles E. Hoye ... (Oakland, Md.) 1934. 1 l. 33 cm. "From Mountain democrat, issue of December 20th, 1934." 38M1244T.
CS71.S264   1934

15037 SAVAGE. The family of Savage of co. Wilts., with a passing note on the dormant earldom of Rivers, by L. Graham H. Horton-Smith ... Devizes, C. H. Woodward, 1944. cover-title, (309)-332 p. 22½ cm. "A reprint from volume 50, number 158, of 'The Wiltshire magazine'." A45-2819.
CS439.S23   1944

15038 SAVAGE. Savage-Springer family histories. By Howard Mayo Savage. (Washington? 1953) 146 p. illus. 29 cm. 53-22583.
CS71.S264   1953

SAVAGE. See also: BRENT, 1936
RANNEY, F104.C8A2
RUNYON, 1891
WHITE, E171.A53 vol. 20
No. 430 - Adventurers of purse and person.

SAVARY. See SAVERY.

15039 SAVERY. The Savery families of America (Savory and Savary). By A. W. Savary ... Boston, Press of D. Clapp & son, 1887. 1 p. l., 20 p. 25 cm. "Reprinted from the N. E. historical and genealogical register for Oct., 1887." 17-9734.
CS71.S266   1887

15040 SAVERY. A genealogical and biographical record of the Savery family (Savory and Savary) and of the Severy family (Severit, Savery, Savory and Savary) descended from early immigrants to New England and Philadelphia, with introductory articles on the origin and history of William Savery, minister of the Gospel in the Society of Friends and appendixes containing an account of Savery's invention of the steam engine ... By A. W. Savary ... Assisted in the genealogy by Miss Lydia A. Savary ... Boston, The Collins press, 1893. xx p., 1 l., 266 p. incl. 2 facsim. 2 pl. (incl. front.) 18 port. 24 cm. 6-1096.
CS71.S266   1893

15041   SAVERY.   Genealogical sketch of some of the descendants of Robert Savory of Newbury, 1656, compiled by Fred W. Lamb, a descendants.   2d ed., rev. and enl.   Manchester, N.H., Printed by the John B. Clarke company, 1904.   cover-title, 16 p.   port.   24 cm.   4-18958.   CS71.S266   1904

15042   SAVERY.   Savery and Severy genealogy (Savory and Savary)   A supplement to the Genealogical and biographical record published in 1893, comprising families omitted in that work, and other notes, additions, and corrections; being a continuation of the notes, additions, and corrections in the original work from page xx, by the author, A. W. Savary ... Boston, The Fort Hill press, 1905.
58 p.   4 port.   (incl. front.)   24 cm.   6-1097.   CS71.S266   1905

15043   SAVERY.   Memorial volume, selections from the prose and poetical writings of the late John Savary, ed. by his friend John Albee, to which is added a genealogical record of the Savary-Hall families by Miss Marion H. Shumway.   Chicago, Privately printed, 1912.   v, 270 p.   ports.   22 cm.   Contents. -
pt. I. Life of John Savary. - pt. II. Poems of John Savary. - pt. III. Essays of John Savary.   12-29960.   PS2779.S6   1912

SAVERY.   See also: ANDERSON, 1902
                              LAMB, 1900
                              LAMB, 1904

SAVIDGE.   See SAVAGE.

SAVIGE.   See SAVAGE.

15044   SAVILE.   Antiquarian notices of Lupset, the Heath, Sharlston and Ackton, in the county of York.   By the author of the Topography of Hallamshire and of South Yorkshire.   (London, Printed by J. B. Nichols and son) 1851.   5 p. l., (3)-107, (1) p.   front.   28½ cm.   Preface signed: J.H.   (i.e. Joseph Hunter)   Lupset under the Saviles: p. 11-32.   Lupset under the Wittons: p. 33-39.   15-22363.   DA690.L86H8

15045   SAVILE.   Savile correspondence.   Letters to and from Henry Savile, esq., envoy at Paris, and vice-chamberlain to Charles II and James II, including letters from his brothers George, marquess of Halifax ... Ed. by William Durrant Cooper ...(London) Camden society, 1858.   2 p. l., xxiv.   316 p.
21 cm.   (Camden society.   (Publications) no. 71)   Contains genealogical matter and pedigree of the Savile family.   17-3795.
DA20.C17 no.71

15046   SAVOIE.   La généalogie de la famille Savoie (origine Acadienne).   Accompagné de quelques courtes notions sur la dispersion des Acadiens en 1758 et d'une très gracieuse lettre du Rév. C.-A.-O. Savoie, ptre. Chanoine et curé de Ste.-Ursule, Qué.   Ce travail lui est respectueusement dédié, ainsi qu'à mon cousin, le capitaine C.-O.   Savoie, de Kankakee, Ills., en souvenir reconnaissant de sa constante affection, par Caroline Hamelin (née Martin)   (Montréal, Impr. "Le Devoir") 1912.
64 p.   ports.   22½ cm.   14-2868.   CS90.S3

SAVORY.   See SAVERY.

15047   SAWHILL.   Ancestors and descendants of James Alexander Sawhill, by Jesse W. and Grace Dague Shields.   Grosse Pointe, Mich., 1958.   54 l.   28 cm.   59-29170.   CS71.S268   1958

15048   SAWHILL.   The Sawhill family.   By Benjamin Wesley Sawhill.   (Sharon, Pa., D. B. Sawhill, 1964)   x, 193 l.   29 cm.   65-89161.   CS71.S268   1964

15049   SAWIN.   Sawin; summary notes concerning John Sawin, and his posterity.   By Thomas E. Sawin.   Wendell (Mass.) The author, 1866.   48 p.   21 cm.   9-13711.   CS71.S27   1866

SAWTELL.   See: GAMBLE, 1906
                           MINNS, 1925

15050   SAWYER.   Centennial celebration of the town of Orford, N.H., containing the oration, poems and speeches, delivered on Thursday, September 7, 1865, with some additional matters relating to the history of the place.   (Manchester, N.H., H.A. Gage, printer, 1865)   145 p.   21½ cm.   "Biographical sketches":
p. (103)-142.   "Soldiers from Orford who served in the late war": p. 143-144.   Bound at end: Strong (family): (2) p.;   Sawyer (family): 1 l.
1-10780.   F44.0606

15051   SAWYER.   Sawyers in America; or, A history of the immigrant Sawyers, who settled in New England; showing their connection with colonial history ... etc., also, wonderful increase of the descendants of Thomas Sawyer, one of the nine first settlers who organized the town of Lancaster and gave it its name.   By Amory Carter ... (who, by a sad accident, has become blind).   Worcester, Press of E. R. Fiske, 1883.   2 p. l., (9)-120 p. 25½ cm.   "Incomplete (p. 33-64 wanting) Comprising all of the work that could be found after the death of the author." - Cover title.   4-22332 rev.
CS71.S272   1883

15052   SAWYER.   A genealogy of some of the descendants of William Sawyer, of Newbury, Mass., embracing ten generations and one hundred and seven families.   By Nathaniel Sawyier,.. and Joseph Burbeen Walker... Manchester, N.H., Printed by W. E. Moore, 1889.   47, xii p. front., plan. 27 cm.   At head of title: 1640 ... 1889.   The first six generations and a portion of the seventh prepared by Nathaniel Sawyier, the remainder compiled by J. B. Walker. 9-13710.
CS71.S272   1889

15053   SAWYER.   Some descendants of William Sawyer, of Newbury, Mass.   By W. S. Appleton.   Boston, Press of D. Clapp & son, 1891.   1 p. l., 11 p. 23½ cm.   "Corrected and enlarged from the New-England historical and genealogical register for April, 1874." 9-13709.
CS71.S272   1891

15054   SAWYER.   Family history of Col. John Sawyers and Simon Harris, and their descendants, comp. by Dr. Madison Monroe Harris, a great grandson of Col. John Sawyers and a grandson of Simon Harris.   Knoxville, Tenn., Press of the Knoxville lithographing company, 1913.   195 p. illus. (incl. ports.) coats of arms. 26 cm.   "Colonel John Sawyers - Simon Harris; their relatives and descendants in the various wars from 1774 to 1898.   By W. R. Carter": p. 139-161. 19-3962.
CS71.S272   1913

15055   SAWYER.   The Sawyer family of Hill, New Hamsphire.   Betfield and Thomas Sawyer, their ancestry and posterity, by Rev. Roland D. Sawyer.   Ware, Mass. (1928)   cover-title, 16 p. 19 cm.   31-22373.
CS71.S272   1928

15056   SAWYER.   The genealogy of a Sawyer family of Moravia, N.Y., by Leslie L. Luther.   Moravia, 1964.   23 p. 23 cm. 65-2795.
CS71.S272   1964

SAWYER.   See also: CHASE, 1930   SMALL, 1910
                      HUTCHINS, 1961   SMALL, 1934
                      REMINGTON, 1960   WALKER, 1895
                      SEARS.   WALKER, 1909

SAWYIER.   See SAWYER.

SAX.   See CASTELBERG, 1959

15057   SAXE.   Genealogy of the Saxe family.   (New York? 1930)   1 p. l., vi, 3-88 p. 27 cm.   Foreword signed: J. G. S. (i. e. John Godfrey Saxe) Interleaved.   Based in part on manuscript compiled by Hannah Saxe Drury. cf. Foreword. 30-5644.
CS71.S2725   1930

SAXE-COBURG.   See HANOVER, House of, 1960

SAXON.   See MARTIN, 1946

SAXTON.   See FAXON, 1880

15058   SAYE.   The Saye family.   By Eugene Herschel Saye.   Birmingham, Ala., c. 1955.   108 p. illus. 23 cm. 55-30286.
CS71.S2727   1955

SAYER.   See SEARS.

15059   SAYLER.   A history of the Sayler family; being a collection of genealogical notes relative to Daniel Sayler of Frederick County, Maryland, who came to America about 1725-1730, and his descendants.   By James Lanning Sayler.   Albany, N.Y., J. Munsell's sons, 1898.   164 p. pl., ports., facsim. 30½ cm. 9-14807.
CS71.S273   1898

SAYLER.   See also STAUFFER, 1897

15060 SAYLES. Sayles (genealogical chart) (n. p., 18 -) geneal. tab. 35½ x 56 cm. fold. to 23 x 9½ cm.
6-38503. CS71.S274 18 -

15061 SAYLES. Sayles and allied families, genealogical and biographical. Prepared and privately printed for Mary Dorr (Ames) Sayles ... New York, The American historical society, inc., 1925. 117 p. plates, ports., facsim., col. coats of arms. 35 cm. Title within colored border. Printed on one side of leaf only. Coats of arms accompanied by guard sheets with descriptive letterpress. Bound in green levant with leather doublure; inlaid, gold tooled. Allied families: Ames and Dorr. Dedication signed: Mary Dorr (Ames) Sayles. Published in part under title "Sayles family by Mrs. Herold R. Finley" in Americana, vol. XVIII, 1924, p. 328-343. 26-4221 rev. 2. CS71.S274 1925

SAYLES. See also BRAYTON, 1922

SAYRE. See: GREENLEE, 1956
SEARS, S44

15062 SAYWARD. The Sayward family. Being the history and genealogy of Henry Sayward of York, Maine, and his descendants. With a brief account of other Saywards who settled in America. By Charles A. Sayward. Ipswich, Mass., Independent press, E. G. Hull, 1890. vi, 168, (2), (173)-177 p. coats of arms. 22 cm. p. (173)-176 duplicated. 9-13668. CS71.S276 1890

SCAGEL. See HUNKINS, 1961

15063 SCALES. A history of the Scales of northeast Mississippi. By Charles Maurice Scales. Macon, Miss. (1966) 142 p. illus., ports. 30 cm. 66-3355. CS71.S28 1966

SCALES. See also No. 1547 - Cabell county.

15064 SCAMMON. Material for a genealogy of the Scammon family in Maine. Salem, Printed by Salem press publishing and printing co., 1892. 2 p. l., 21 p. 25 cm. Introduction signed: Benj. N. Goodale. 9-13667. CS71.S283 1892

SCANLAN. See SCANLON.

15065 SCANLON. Genealogy of the O'Scanlon (Scanlan, Scanlon) family. (Durham, N. C., 1938) 23 p. 23½ cm. Foreword signed: David Howard Scanlon. On cover: I am of Ireland. Blank page for "Memo." (p. 23) 39-9247. CS71.S285 1938

15066 SCARBOROUGH. (Genealogical chart of the Scarborough-Butler family) By George Valentine Massey. Raymond L. Sutcliffe, artist. (n. p., n. d.) geneal. table. coats of arms. 46 x 59 cm. fold. to 32 x 26 cm. Photocopy (positive) 50-21251. CS71.S3

15067 SCARBOROUGH. Photostat facsimiles of manuscripts relating to the ancestry of Henry W. Scarborough of Philadelphia (July 24, 1870 - October 10, 1935) and of his wife Clara Hagerty Scarborough (1870-1932) Bequeathed by him to the Library of Congress. (Washington, D. C.) 1936. 23 1. 44 cm. The photostats are mounted. 38M4295T. CS71.S3 1936
Office.

15068 SCARBOROUGH. Southern kith and kin; a record of my children's ancestors. By Jewel (Davis) Scarborough. Abilene, Tex., Printed by Abilene Print. Co. (1951-57) 4 v. illus. 24 cm. 58-26543. CS71.S3 1951

SCARBOROUGH. See also: DAVIS, F159.B8D3   RUDER, F159.S63R3
    HAWORTH, 1902   SNYDER, 1958
    KIRK, 1912   WAPLES, 1910a
    PEARSON, 1932   WISE, F221.V82

SCARBURGH. See: HARRISON, 1910a
WISE, 1918
No. 430 - Adventurers of purse and person.

15069   SCARRITT.   The history of the Scarritt clan in America.   By Ralph Emerson Pearson.   (Falls Church? Va.) c.1938-48.   2 v. illus., ports. 23 cm. Includes bibliographies. 38-17342 rev.*   CS71.S315   1938

15070   SCACHERD.   Memoir of the late Thomas Scatcherd, barrister-at-law, Queen's counsel and member of Parliament for the North Riding of Middlesex, Canada.   A family record.   By William Horton ... London, Ontario, 1878.   vi p., 1 l., (9)-212 p., 1 l., (4) p. front. (port.) 21 cm. 3-17348.
F1058.S28

SCATTERGOOD.   See WETHERILL, 1882

SCAWEN.   See BLUNT, 1911

SCEARSTAN.   See SEARS.

SCHAAR.   See SZOLD, 1960

SCHABING.   See SCHABINGER.

SCHACHT.   See No. 553 - Goodhue county.

SCHAEFFER.   In vertical file under PRANKE family.   Ask reference librarian for this material.

SCHAEFFER.   See also: LINDLEY, 1950
                                    SHAFER.

15071   SCHAFF.   Schaff.   (New York city, 1935)   cover-title, 17, (1) p. incl. pl. 21 cm. "Compiler, Schuyler R. Schaff." - p.2. 35-9131.   CS71.S32   1935

SCHAFFER.   In vertical file under PRANKE family.   Ask reference librarian for this material.

15072   SCHAFFNER.   History and descendants of Martin Shaffner.   By Mina (Good) Pinkerton. (n.p.) c.1959.   256 p. illus. 21 cm. Cover title: Shaffner family history. 59-31689.   CS71.S3203   1959

15073   SCHALL.   The Schall family in America; a history of the descendants of Michael Schall, born 1739 - died 1830, by Margaret Schall Hotham ... Indiana, Pa., H. Hall, inc. (c.1938)   166 p. illus. (incl. ports.) 22 cm. 38-39411.   CS71.S3205   1938

15074   SCHALLER.   The history of Benedict II and Rosina Haeni Schaller family, 1759-1957.   By Grover L. Schaller.   Daytona Beach, Fla., College Pub. Co. (1958)   xii, 229 p. plates, ports., coat of arms. 24 cm. 58-38375.   CS71.S3206   1958

SCHALLER.   In vertical file under PRANKE family.   Ask reference librarian for this material.

15075   SCHARNAGEL.   Descendants of John and Mary Scharnagel in the families of Willenborg, Eischeid, and Testroet.   By Deloris (Pitkin) Bennett.   (West Covina? Calif.) 1960.   1 v. illus. 24 cm. 61-59769.   CS71.S3207   1960

SCHARTEL.   See GRIM, 1934

15076   SCHAUB.   The Schaubs and Vests of North Carolina.   By Annie Mary (Vest) Russell.   (Washington? 1965)   1 v. (various pagings) illus., coats of arms, ports. 30 cm. 66-47384.   CS71.S32075   1965

SCHAWINGEN.   See SCHABINGER.

SCHEER.   See SLEAR, 1929

SCHEIBLY.   See SHEIBLEY.

15077   SCHEIDELMANN.   Genealogy, history of the Scheidelmann family, descendants of Christina Loucks and John Scheidelmann.   (By Anna Mary Sophia Kathrine (Genning) Rutz) (Rome, N.Y., 1947)   28 l. 28 cm. Cover title. Addenda slip inserted. 48-16646*.   CS71.S3208   1947

15078 SCHELL. Schell; or, Researches after the descendants of John Christian Schell and John Schell. Compiled by Christian Denissen ... (Detroit, J. F. Eby & company, c. 1896) 94 p. front., ports. 24 cm. 9-13666. CS71.S321 1896

15079 SCHELL. The ancestry of Ellen Schell Garber, by Hon. William P. Schell. Madison, Ind. (1898) 25 p. 23½ cm. 25-14354. CS71.S321 1898

15080 SCHELLHOUSE. Genealogy of the Schellhouse family of Vermilion Township, Erie County, Ohio, which married into the Koppenhafer and Leidheiser families. By Claude Charles Hamel. Amherst, 1948. 6 l. 27 cm. Typewritten. 50-25467. CS71.S322 1948

15081 SCHENCK. Memoir of Johannes Schenk, the progenitor of the Bushwick, L. I., family of Schenck. By P. L. Schenck, M. D. Flatbush, L. I., 1876. xii, 83, (9) p., 2 l. front., plates, coats of arms. 22 cm. The (9) p. at end left blank for "Descendants of Johannes Schenck." The plates are mounted photographs. "Statement of John J. Schenck": p. 31 - 37. Sketch of the Schenck family": p. 46-83. 17-21246. L. C. COPY REPLACED BY MICRFOFILM. CS71.S324 1876
Microfilm 13971 CS

15082 SCHENCK. The Rev. William Schenck, his ancestry and his descendants ... compiled by A. D. Schenck, U. S. army. Washington, R. H. Darby, 1883. 163 p. incl. col. front. (coat of arms) geneal. tables (part fold.) 23 cm. 9-13665. CS71.S324 1883

15083 SCHENCK. The Blyenbeck and Afferden branch of the family of Schenck van Nydeck. From the Family of Schenck van Nydeggen. Cologne, 1860. Hampton, Va., Normal school press print, 1885. cover-title, 26 p. 23 cm. Compiled by Alexander Du Bois Schenck. "26 pages, intended to take the place of pages 20 to 23 of the author's Schenck genealogy, published in 1883, and gives the ancestry of Roelof, who came to Long Island, N. Y., 1650." 9-13664. CS71.S324 1885

15084 SCHENCK. The ancestors and descendants of Rulef Schenck; a genealogy of the Onondaga County, New York, branch of the Schenck family. By Benjamin Robinson Schenck, M. D. from records and notes compiled by Adrian Adelbert Schenck. Detroit, Mich. (The Wilson printing company) 1911. 160 p. front. (col. coat of arms) plates, ports. 21 cm. 12-24707. CS71.S324 1911

15085 SCHENCK. Joseph and Mary Schenck, their ancestors and descendants, compiled by Lt. Col. Casper Schenk ... (Des Moines? Ia.) 1938. 1 p. l., 80 p. incl. illus., ports., 20 geneal. tab. front. (col. coat of arms) 23½ cm. "Printed as manuscript, planograph process." Genealogical tables 2-20 reproduced in facsimile from manuscript. 38-36173. CS71.S324 1938

15086 SCHENCK. Andeck American colonial ancestry; an outline of the places in history of colonial fathers of our children, compiled by Lt. Col. Casper Schenk. Des Moines, Ia., 1942. 6 p. l., (3)- 267 numb. l. col. front. (port.) pl. 25½ cm. Type-written. Bibliographical foot-notes. 42-50342. CS71.S324 1942

15087 SCHENCK. Johannes Schenk of Bushwick, Long Island, and his descendants, a genealogy. Comp. by Marguerite Schenck Maires and Gladys Marie Muller. Brooklyn, 1948. xii, 87 p. illus., geneal. tables. 24 cm. On spine: Schen(c)k genealogy. "100 copies ... printed ... of which this is copy 2." Bibliography: p. 79. 48-10339*. CS71.S324 1948

SCHENCK. See also: CONOVER, 1912
CRAWFORD, E171. A53 vol. 16
GUSTIN, 1900
PECK, 1925

SCHERDEL. See SCHARTEL.

SCHERER. See SHERER.

15088 SCHERMERHORN. Genealogy of a part of the third branch of the Schermerhorn family in the United States, compiled by Louis Y. Schermerhorn ... Philadelphia, Printed for private circulation by J. B. Lippincott company, 1903. 3 p. l., (7)-19 numb. l., 1 l. 29½ cm. 4-8405 rev. CS71.S326 1903

15089   SCHERMERHORN.   Schermerhorn genealogy and family chronicles, by Richard Schermerhorn, jr.   New York, T. A. Wright, 1914.   3 p. l., 419 p. front. (col. coat of arms) illus., plates, ports. 24½ cm.
Illustrated t.-p.   14-12120.   CS71.S326   1914

SCHERR.   See no. 1547 - Cabell county.

SCHERRER.   See: GOODNER, 1960
                        SHERER.

SCHERTEL.   See CLAUSER, 1959   (addenda)

15090   SCHETKY.   The Schetky family, a compilation of letters, memoirs and historical data, by Laurence Oliphant Schetky.   Portland, Or., Priv. print. by Portland printing house, inc., 1942.
213 p. incl. front., ports., coats of arms.   21 cm.   "Letters of the John George Christoffer Schetky family (literatim copies)": p. 149-213.
42-50004.   CS71.S328   1942

SCHIEFER.   See WHITFIELD, 1965

15091   SCHIEFFELIN.   ... One hundred years of business life. 1794-1894.   New York, W. H. Schieffelin & co. (1894)   56 p. plates, ports., facsims.   24 cm.   21-14603 rev.   CT275.S344O6

15092   SCHIEFFELIN.   Jacob and Hannah (Lawrence) Schieffelin of New York.   By Isaac J. Greenwood, A.M. ... Boston, D. Clapp & son, printers, 1897.   7 p. 24½ cm.   Reprinted from New-Eng. hist. and geneal.
register for October, 1897.   9-13663.   CS71.S331   1897

15093   SCHIEFFELIN.   Schieffelin genealogy ... Compiled by Maud Schuyler Clark; del. H.S. Clark, jr.   (n.p.) 1934.   geneal. tab.   64 x 113 cm. fold. to 34½ x 27 cm.   "Sources."   35-20350.
                                                                                                 CS71.S331   1934

15094   SCHIEFFELIN.   Schieffelin genealogy, chart no. 2: for the descendants of Jacob Schieffelin, 4th.   By Maud Schuyler Clark.   (New York? 1949?)   geneal. table on 2 sheets.   46 x 68 cm. fold. to 18 x 23 cm.
Accompanied by a geneal. table (27 x 41 cm.) showing ancestry of Hannah Lawrence who married Jacob Schieffelin, 3d.   63-28083.
                                                                                                 CS71.S331   1949

SCHIEFFELIN.   See also THOMAS, 1878

15095   SCHILLING.   Schillingische Familienchronik.   By Heinrich Schilling.   Ulm/Donau, Verband des Hauses Schilling, 1917 -   v. (loose-leaf) geneal. table.   30 cm.   "Quellen zur Geschichte der Familie Schilling."
                                                                                                 CS629.S275   1917

15096   SCHIMPF.   Biographical sketches of the Schimpf family.   By Charles James Shimp.   1st ed. (Springfield? Ill.) 1965.   194 p. 29 cm.   Bibliography: p. 133-135.   65-69573.
                                                                                                 CS71.S333   1965

SCHINTZE.   See SCHUSTER, 1951

SCHISSLER.   See MONNET, 1911

15097   SCHLABACH.   Daniel Schlabach family history; descendants of Daniel Schlabach and Sally Kaufman, by Emanuel J. Miller ... Sugarcreek, O., Royal printing co. (1942?)   1 p. l., 32 p. 21 cm.
Label mounted over imprint: Wilmot O., E. J. Miller.   45-27298.   CS71.S336   1942

15098   SCHLABACH.   The Schlabach family of Northampton County, Pennsylvania.   By George Pendleton Slayback.   (Allentown, Pa., Schlechter's, 1969)   132 p. illus., geneal. tables, map, ports. 29 cm.
100 copies printed of which this is no. 51.   70-3111 MARC.   CS71.S336   1969

15099   SCHLAPPICH.   The Schlappich family in the United States of America.   By Samuel Jonas Schlappich.   (Lake Worth? Fla., 1958?)   93 p. illus. 20 cm.   59-21564.   CS71.S338   1958

15100   SCHLATTER.   Anna Schlatter und ihre kinder, von Johannes Ninck; mit 28 abbildungen.
4. -5. tausend.   Leipzig und Hamburg, G. Schloessmann (c. 1934)   207, (1) p.   front., illus. (facsim.) plates, ports.   20 cm.   "Quellenangaben und erläuterungen": p. 206-(208)   35-7069.   CT1398.S43N5   1934a

SCHLEAR.   See SLEAR.

SCHLEER.   See SLEAR.

SCHLEGEL.   See SLAGLE.

SCHLEIFER.   See SLIFER.

15101   SCHLEY.   Among the ancestors of Sturges Belsterling Schley, compiled by Charles Starne
Belsterling.   New York, N. Y., 1943.   5 p. l., 142 p. plates, ports., 3 col. coats of arms on 1 l.   23½ cm.   "100 copies ...
printed ... No. 17."   Bibliography: p. 60, (127)-142.   44-25541.   CS71.S34   1943

SCHLIER.   See SLEAR.

SCHLOSSBERGER.   See GÜNTHER, CS629.G8

SCHLOSSTEIN.   See FOSTER, E171.A53 v. 18

SCHMEISSER.   See HAY, 1923

SCHMELTZER.   See SMELSER, 1961

SCHMETTON.   See SCHMETTAU.

15102   SCHMIDT.   Smaller New York and family reminiscences.   De Rham, Schmidt, Bache, Barclay,
Paul Richard.   (By Oscar Egerton Schmidt)   (New York, 1899)   77, (1) p. incl. ports.   front.   23½ cm.   Dedication signed: O. E. S.   (i. e. Oscar Egerton Schmidt)   25-2340.   CS71.S353   1899

15103   SCHMIDT.   The August Schmidt, Martin Boese, Peter Schroeder, Andrew Unruh family records.   By Mary (Schmidt) Kliever.   (n. p.) 1962.   1 v. (various pagings) 29 cm.   65-89133.
CS71.S353   1962

SCHMIDT.   See also: BARNITZ, 1961
                                    DECKER, 1959
                                    WITTENBERGER, 1958

15104   SCHMIERER.   The Schmierer and Meisenholder family history.   By Thomas Jules Schmierer.
(n. p.) c. 1961.   191 l.   illus.   28 cm.   61-37613.   CS71.S354   1961

SCHMIERER.   See MEISENHOLDER, 1959

SCHMITTIN.   In vertical file under PRANKE family.   Ask reference librarian for this material.

SCHMOYER.   See WALTMAN, 1928

15105   SCHMUCKER.   Life and times of Rev. S. S. Schmucker ... By Peter Anstadt ... York, Pa.,
P. Anstadt & sons, 1896.   vii, (9)-392 p. front. (port.) plates.   21½ cm.   "Family record of S. S. Schmucker ...": p. 24-27.
"A complete list of his publications": p. 262-265.   BX8080.S3A6

15106   SCHMUCKER.   The Schmucker family and the Lutheran church in America, by Rev. Luke
Schmucker.   (n. p.) 1937.   2 p. l., 7-76 p.   21½ cm.   37-10360.   CS71.S355   1937

15107   SCHMUTZ.   Robert Allen Smutz, his ancestors and kinfolk.   Being some account of certain
families, among others, listed in the table of contents, and including an appendix which relates an
account of some ancestors of his wife, Joycelynn (Mason) Smutz and their sons, Bill and Mark.   By
Harold Turk Smutz.   Webster Groves, Mo., 1963.   vi, 165, x, iv-xxiii, xiii-xxiv l.   coat of arms.   29 cm. Bibliography:
leaves xiii-xxiv (5th group)   64-3603.   CS71.S356   1963

15108   SCHMUTZ.   The ancestors and descendants of Isaac Smutz, 1810-1867, and his wife, Sarah Stauffer, 1816-1891.   Hyattesville, Md., 1958.   44 p. illus. 22 cm. 59-25912.

CS71.S356   1958

SCHMUTZ.   See also SMOOT.

15109   SCHNEBELE.   Genealogical register of the male and female descendants of John Jacob Schnebele, now Snively, and also of the male and female descendants of Samuel Bachtel, and the relationship existing between the said two families.   Chambersburg, Pa., Printed by M. Kieffer, 1858.
31 p. 17 cm. 57-54542.   CS71.S358   1858

15110   SCHNEBELE.   Genealogical memoranda.   Snively, A.D.1659 - A.D.1882.   Compiled and arranged by (Rev.) William Andrew Snively ... (Brooklyn? 1883)   77 p. 22 x 18 cm. Printed for private circulation. Pages partly blank. 2-9835.   CS71.S358   1883

Microfilm 10614

15111   SCHNEIDER.   Ancestors of Vera Louise Schneider, compiled by Donald G. Gilbert. Frederic, Mich., 1969.   1 v.(various pagings) geneal. tables. 30 cm. Includes bibliographical references. 73-3436 MARC.

CS71.S678   1969

SCHNEIDER.   See also SNYDER.

15112   SCHNITLER.   Stamtavle over de adgangsberettigede til R. B. Schnitler og fru Normandine Thesen legat, paa foranstaltning af legatets sekretær udarbeidet ved ingeniør Ch. Delgobe.   Kristiania, H. Sogns bogtrykkeri, 1902.   1 p. l., VIII fold. tab. 33½ x 30 cm. Contents. - tab. I-III. Sogneprest Balthasar Schnitlers linje - tab. IV-V. Premiermajor Hans Hagerup Krags linje. - tab. VI-VII. Holtsfyrste Hans Peter Schnitlers linje. - tab. VIII. Traelasthandler Christen Brochmanns linje. 13-22723.   CS919.S4

15113   SCHÖLLEIN.   In vertical file under PRANKE family.   Ask reference librarian for this material.

15114   SCHOENBERG.   Castles to cabins; the record of three pioneer families: the Schoenbergs, the Heitstumans and the Haupts.   Compiled and published by the Jacob A. Schoenberg family.   Spokane, 1966.   163 p. illus., geneal. tables, maps (on lining papers) ports. 24 cm. 66-3115.   CS71.S3554   1966

SCHOENIKE.   See SCHWEFEL, 1953

15115   SCHONBERG.   Chronicles of the Schönberg-Cotta family; a tale of the reformation, by Mrs. Andrew Charles ... (New York) A.L.Burt company (1896)   1 p. l., v, 430 p. front. 19 cm. (On cover: The Home library) 4-21344.   PZ3.C38C6

15116   SCHOFER.   Johan Georg Schofer family history; containing records of antecedents in Europe, an account of the migration of the family to America in eighteen hundred and thirty-two, biographical sketches of members of the family in this country, together with data of related persons, places and events; material gathered and arranged by Henry Morris Schofer. (Aristes, Pa.) 1934.   2 p. l., 9-167, (1), xii p. front., illus. (incl. ports., facsims.) fold. geneal. tab., diagr. 27½ cm. On cover: Centennial edition, 1832-1932. "The former edition of this history ... was published in 1897." - Foreword. 34-24855.   CS71.S359   1934

15117   SCHOFF.   The descendants of Jacob Schoff, who came to Boston in 1752 and settled in Ashburnham in 1757; with an account of the German immigration into colonial New England, by Wilfred H. Schoff.   Philadelphia (Printed by J. McGarrigle) 1910.   163 p. plates. 24 cm. 10-28508.

CS71.S36   1910

15118   SCHOFF.   A memorial of the one hundredth anniversary of the marriage of Philip Schoff and Elizabeth Ramsay, April 10, 1794, by their grandaughter (!) Eloise (Walker) Wilder, April 10, 1894. Greenfield, Ind., Wm. Mitchell printing co., 1922.   311 p. illus. (incl. ports., coats of arms) 20 cm. Edited by Mrs. Fanny Ramsay (Wilder) Winchester. "Philip Schoff, a boy soldier of the American revolution, 1778; a member of Washington's army during the Whiskey insurrection 1794, and a soldier in the war of 1812, with an account of his ancestors and descendants by his great granddaughter, Fanny Ramsay (Wilder) Winchester": p. (45)-311. 25-11794.   CS71.S36   1922

SCHOFIELD. See STOUT, 1960

15119 SCHOLES. American descendants of George Scholes of Accrington, Lancashire, England, compiled by George Scholes. Lake Forest, Ill., Heitman printing company, 1944. 62 p. illus., (incl. ports., maps, facsim.) 23½ cm. 45-13962.   CS71.S375   1944

15120 SCHOLL. Descendants of John Peter Scholl and his wife Anna. Susanna Dorothea Scholl, and genealogical family history, with short sketch of Philip Scholl and descendants. Illustrated. By A. G. Scholl ... Mifflintown, Pa., The Juniata herald publishing co., 1903. 87 p. ports., facsims. 22 cm. Partially compiled by George Scholl. cf. Introd. 18-16011.   CS71.S38   1903

15121 SCHOLL. Scholl, Sholl, Shull genealogy, the colonial branches, by John William Scholl. New York, The Grafton press (c.1930) xxxi, 879 p. front., plates, ports., facsims., col. coats of arms. 27 cm. 30-11176.
                                                                          CS71.S38   1930

15122 SCHOLL. Shull, Burdsall, Stockton, and allied families; a genealogical study with biographical notes, compiled and privately published for Rena Shull McCahan by the American historical company, inc. New York, 1940. 4 p. l., 538 p. plates, ports., facsims. (1 col.; part double) col. coats of arms, col. geneal. tables (1 double) 32 cm. Most of the plates are accompanied by guard sheets with descriptive letterpress. Includes bibliographical notes. 41-10331.   CS71.S38   1940
                                                                          Rare book coll.

15123 SCHOLL. Genealogical record and family history of that branch of the Scholl family who were among the pioneers of Fayette County, Indiana. By Jonas Edgar Scholl. (Connersville? Ind.) 1959. 63 l. illus. 28 cm. 63-1391.   CS71.S38   1959

        SCHOLL. See also: BOONE, 1922
                            THOMAS, 1955

15124 SCHOOLEY. A pioneer Schooley family, by May Schooley Ivey ... Miami, Fla., The Franklin press, inc. (c.1941) 6 p. l., 58 p. incl. front. (coat of arms) illus. (incl. ports.) maps. 25½ cm. 41-8756.
                                                                          CS71.S381   1941

        SCHOOLEY. See also: LUNDY, 1903
                              SYRON, 1925
                              WILSON, 1959

15125 SCHOONMAKER. Relative to the biography, ancestry and descendants of David Alyea Schoonmaker and his wife Anna Louise Pendleton, compiled by William Heidgerd ... (n. p.) 1939. 1 p. l., 3, 5 numb. l. 28 cm. 39-12227.   CS71.S382   1939

15126 SCHOONMAKER. Schoonmakers in the Hudson Valley, compiled by Ruth & William Heidgerd. New Paltz, N. Y., 1951. 160 p. 30 cm. Addenda slips inserted. 52-16780 rev.   CS71.S382   1951

        SCHOONMAKER. See also: ELDRIDGE, 1925
                                 MANY, 1961

15127 SCHOONOVER. The Schoonover & allied families; or, Jacob Schoonover of Standing Stone, Pa., and his descendants, from records gathered largely by Neva Schoonover Robinson, arr. & published by Edward Coolbaugh Hoagland. Wysox, Pa., 1954. 23 l. 30 cm. 56-23390.   CS71.S383   1954

        SCHNOOVER. See also No. 3888 - Twigs from family trees.

15128 SCHOPPE. The Schoppe family genealogy, 1782-1932, by Mary Coffin Schoppe... (n. p., 1932) 201, (7) p. illus. 19 cm. Six blank pages at end for "Births", "Marriages" and "Deaths". 40-32886.   CS71.S384   1932

15129 SCHOTT. Frederick Schott of Derry township, Lancaster county, Pennsylvania, and descendants, by Kate S. Curry. Washington, D. C., 1933. vii, 89 (2) p., 1 l. front. (mounted coat of arms) 23 cm. Hectographed. Frontispiece is a photograph. "Done for Kate Singer Curry by the National genealogical society, Washington, D. C." 33-34827.
                                                                          CS71.S385   1933

15130   SCHOU.   The Skow family; descendants of Hans Christian Schou and Kjersten Jorgensen of Klakring, Denmark, by Frances Hansen Ehrig.   (Richland, Wash.) 1966.   xxvi, 85 p. illus., maps, ports. 28 cm. 68-3892.   CS71.S386   1966

SCHOULER.   See WARREN, 1884

SCHOWINGEN.   See SCHABINGER.

SCHRADER.   See KROUPA, 1957

SCHRAG.   See GRABER, 1948

SCHRAGEN.   See SCHABINGER.

SCHRANTZ.   See HOLL, 1891

SCHRIMER.   See GRIM, 1934

SCHROEDER.   In vertical file under PRANKE family.   Ask reference librarian for this material.

SCHROEDER.   See also: KALBFLEISCH, 1956
                                     SCHMIDT, 1962

SCHROEDERN.   In vertical file under PRANKE family.   Ask reference librarian for this material.

SCHRUM.   See SHRUM.

SCHULZE.   See SHULTZ.

SCHUMACHER.   See SHOEMAKER.

15131   SCHUMM.   History of the John George Schumm family.   (n. p.) 1928.   cover-title, 52 p. illus. (incl. port.) 23 cm.   Appreciation signed: Wm. J. Schumm, Paul T. Schumm, Hugo J. Schumm, committee. 28-23911.
CS71.S39   1928

15132   SCHUMM.   History of the John George Schumm family.   (By Wm. J. Schumm, Paul T. Schumm, and Hugo J. Schumm) 2d ed.   (n. p.) 1951.   78 p. illus. 23 cm. Cover title. 52-22220.
CS71.S39   1951

15133   SCHUREMAN.   Schureman genealogy.   Prepared by Richard Wynkoop ... New York, M.F. Schureman, 1889.   cover title, 55 p. 23½ cm. 9-13744.   CS71.S552   1889

SCHUREMAN.   See also: SHERMAN, S552
                                      WRIGHT, 1960

SCHUST.   See PRIOR, 1967

15134   SCHUSTER.   In the stream of time, a historical family sketch, by O. J. Schuster.   (Washington, D.C., 1934)   cover-title, (2), 25 p. 18½ cm. 34-42440.   CS71.S395   1934

15135   SCHUSTER.   The Schuster, Schintze, Walz, and Vervenne families.   By William Carl Kiessel.   (Tenafly? N.J., 1951)   1 v. (unpaged) 29 cm. Title on label mounted on cover. Typescript. Bibliography: leaf at end. 52-24604.   CS71.S395   1951

15136   SCHUYLER.   Schuyler family.   By Joel Munsell.   (Albany?) Priv. print., 1874.   11 p. illus. 24 cm. Edition of thirty copies printed. Reprinted from the N. Y. genealogical and biographical record. vol. 5, 1874, p. 60-68. 9-13662.
CS71.S397   1874

15137   SCHUYLER.   Colonial New York; Philip Schuyler and his family, by George W. Schuyler ...
New York, C. Scribner's sons, 1885.   2 v. 22 cm. 3-5265.   F122.S39

15138   SCHUYLER.   A godchild of Washington, a picture of the past.   By Katharine Schuyler Baxter.
London and New York, F. T. Neely (c. 1897)   651 p. incl. front., illus., plates. 30 cm. Published by subscription for
private circulation only.   Includes sketches of many notable New Yorkers of the latter part of the 18th and of the 19th centuries. 10-31666.
                                                                              F123.B35

15139   SCHUYLER.   The Schuyler family, an address read before the New York branch of the Order
of colonial lords of manors in America, April, 1925, by Montgomery Schuyler ... (Baltimore?) 1926.
55 p. col. front. (coat of arms) illus. (incl. ports., facsims.) 23½ cm.   Order of colonial lords of manors in America.   Publications, no. 16)
38-20400.   E186.99.O6 No. 16

          SCHUYLER.   See also: BARD, F128.25V27   LIVINGSTON, 1939
                                 BYRD, E159.G55   PECK, 1925
                                 GARDNER, 1929   WASHINGTON, E159.G56
                                 HERKIMER, 1903

15140   SCHWAB.   Fort number eight, the home of Gustav and Eliza Schwab, compiled by their
daughter Lucy Schwab White for their grandchildren and great-grandchildren, that they may know something of the rock whence they are hewn.   (New Haven) 1925.   2 p. l., 45, (1) p. front., ports. 22½ cm. "Five
hundred copies privately printed by the Yale university press in December, 1925."   26-153.   CS71.S398   1925

          SCHWAB.   See SWOPE.

          SCHWALM.   See ZERBE, F157.S3E39

          SCHWARTAN.   See No. 553 - Goodhue county.

15141   SCHWARTZ.   (Simpson-Trow and Pierce-Swartz family history.   Pierre? S. D., 1961?)
24 l.   36 cm.   64-6105.   CS71.S3985   1961

          SCHWARTZ.   In vertical file under PRANKE family.   Ask reference librarian for this material.

          SCHWARTZ.   See also SCHLATHER, E171.A53 v.17

15142   SCHWEDLER.   Stammbaum der Freiherren von Schwedler mit anverwandten Linien. Family
tree of the Freiherren von Schwedler with related lines.   By Ferdinand Alfred Bruno Julius von
Schwedler.   Erforscht 1917-1947.   Karlsruhe, Brooklyn, c.1947.   geneal. table. 54 x 50 cm. fold. to 31 x
21 cm.   50-22615.   CS629.S37   1947

15143   SCHWEFEL.   Schwefel, Dornfeld, Schoenike genealogy. By Ralph Albert Dornfeld Owen.
Philadelphia, 1953.   399 p. illus. 23 cm. 54-44841.   CS71.S399   1953

15144   SCHWEITZER.   Christentum und kultur bei Albert Schweitzer; eine einführung in sein denken
als weg zu einer christlichen weltanschauung, von dr. Fritz Buri ... Bern, Leipzig, P. Haupt, 1941.
3 p. l., 9-145 p. 21 cm.   A43-763.   CT1098.S45B8

15145   SCHWEITZER.   Albert Schweitzer.   By Rudolf Grabs.   Berlin, Steuben-Verlag P. G. Esser
(c.1949)   428 p. port. 21 cm. "Die Werke Albert Schweitzers": p. 422-423. 50-33302.
                                                                      CT1098.S45G7

15146   SCHWEITZER.   Albert Schweitzer: Christian revolutionary, by George Seaver.   London,
J. Clarke & co., ltd. (1944)   111, (1) p. 20½ cm. "First published 1944." Bibliography: p. (5)-6. 45-4882.
                                                                      CT1098.S45S3

          SCHWENK.   See STRASSBURGER, 1922

          SCHWIEKENDICK.   See SCHWECKENDIEK.

SCHWING. See SWING.

SCHWINGLE. See SWINGLEY, 1926

SCIDMORE. See SKIDMORE.

15147   SCISM. The Scism and allied families; a history of the Scism and allied families containing genealogical and historical information. By DeLos Mac Scism. (Oklahoma City?) Scism Family Association, 1942.   271 p. illus. 24 cm. 62-55147.   CS71.S3995   1942

15148   SCLATER. Sterne's Eliza; some account of her life in India: with her letters written tween 1757 and 1774, by Arnold Wright and William Lutley Sclater. London, W. Heinemann, 1922. vi, (2), 199 p. incl. geneal. tab. 4 port. (incl. front.) 23½ cm. "Descent of Elizabeth Draper": p. (191) 23-6994.
                                                                                                   DS470.D7W7

15149   SCLATER. The Sclater family in Virginia, compiled by George Selden Wallace. Huntington, W. Va., 1938.   19, 7a numb. l. 25½ cm. Mimeographed, with printed t.-p. 39-14786.   CS71.S4   1938

15150   SCOFIELD. Scofield (family, 1610-1950. n.p., 1950)   geneal. table. 28 x 57 cm. fold. to 28 x 20 cm. 52-64162.   CS71.S42   1950

        SCOFIELD. See also No. 553 - Goodhue county.

        SCOGEN. Southside Virginia families. By John Bennett Boddie. See additions and corrections, no. 240.

15151   SCOGGIN. Genealogical serendipity. Compiled by J. Sharon Johnson Doliante. Alexandria, Va., 1965 -   v. illus., geneal. table (on lining paper) fold. map (on lining paper) ports. 29 cm. 65-22375.
                                                                                                   CS71.S423   1965

        SCOGGIN. See also: LONG, 1937
                             LONG, 1965

        SCOINGEN. See SCHABINGER.

        SCORAH. See COOKE, HU250.D6J3

15152   SCOTHORN. The Scothorn family. By Ralph Hoover Lane. Washington, 1955. 149 p. 28 cm. 56-36298.   CS71.S426   1955

        SCOTHORN. See also EILER, 1929

        SCOTHOWE. See SKOTTOWE.

15153   SCOTT. A true history of several honourable families of the right honourable name of Scot, in the shires of Roxburgh and Selkirk, and others adjacent. Gathered out of ancient chronicles, histories and traditions of our fathers, by Captain Walter Scot ... Edinburgh, 1688; reprinted by Balfour & Smellie, 1776.   1 p. l., iii, 3-60 p., 2 l., 97, (2) p. 23 cm. 2 parts in 1 volume. Part 2 has special t.-p.: Satchels's post'ral, humbly presented to his noble and worthy friends of the names of Scot and Elliot, and others ... In verse. 14-15115.
                                                                                                   CS479.S4   1776

15154   SCOTT. Pedigree of the family of Scott of Stokoe. Reprinted from the original edition 1783, with introduction, continuation, &c. London, J. G. Bell, 1852.   47, (1) p. 28½ cm. Title vignette. "Only 75 copies printed." Introduction signed: William Robson Scott. Reproduction of original t.-p.: Pedigree of Scott, of Stokoe, in the parish of Symondburn, and county of Northumberland; and late of Toderick, Selkirkshire, North Britain. Compiled by William Scott, M.D. ... Newcastle. Printed by T. Angus, 1783. 17-2877.   CS439.S24   1852

15155   SCOTT. An early New England marriage dower, with notes on the lineage of Richard Scott of Providence. By Martin B. Scott ... Reprinted from the New England historical and genealogical register. Boston, D. Clapp & son, printers, 1868.   9 p. 24½ cm. 20-17034.   CS71.S43   1868

15156   SCOTT.   Antiquity of the name of Scott, with brief historical notes.   A paper read before the Western reserve historical society, by Martin B. Scott ... Boston, D. Clapp & son, 1869.
15 p. 25½ cm.   Reprinted from the New England historical and genealogical register for April 1869.   20-17033.

CS71.S43   1869

15157   SCOTT.   ... Memorials of the family of Scott, of Scot's hall, in the county of Kent.   With an appendix of illustrative documents.   By James Renat Scott ... London, J. R. Scott, 1876.   viii, (2), 266 p., 1 l., lxxxii p.   illus. (incl. ports., coats of arms, facsims.) 31½ cm.   Coats of arms are part colored.   Initials and head-pieces. At head of title: "Printed for private circulation and for subscribers only." 16-12982.   CS439.S24   1878

15158   SCOTT.   Genealogical memoirs of the family of Sir Walter Scott, bart., of Abbotsford, with a reprint of his Memorials of the Haliburtons, by the Rev. Charles Rogers ... London, The Grampian club, 1877.   lxxii, 78 p.   front., illus. (coat of arms) 22½ cm.   2-4055.   CS479.S4

15159   SCOTT.   The Scots of Buccleuch.   By Sir William Fraser.   Edinburgh, 1878.   2 v. illus., plates (part col.) incl. ports., facsims., coats of arms. 25½ cm.   Title-page illus.: Doorway of Branxholme hall. Impression - one hundred and fifty copies.   no. 111.   Contents. - v.1. Memoirs, etc. - v.2. Muniments, etc.   12-38112.   DA758.3.S4F7

15160   SCOTT.   Dorothea Scott, otherwise Gotherson and Hogben, of Egerton house, Kent, 1611-1680.   A new and enl. ed.   By G. D. Scull ... Oxford, Printed for private circulation by Parker and co., 1883.   vi, (3), 222 p. front., 4 fold. geneal. tab., facsim. 21½ cm.   Contains a reprint with reproduction of original t.-p. of "To all that are unregenerated: a call to repentance from dead works, to newness of life, by turning to the light in the conscience, which will give the knowledge of God in the face of Jesus Christ.   By Dorothea Gotherson ... London, Printed in the year, 1661" (p. (77)-125) A discourse of polletique and civill honor by Thomas Scott: p. (145)-198.   18-3655,   CT788.S38S4

15161   SCOTT.   Sir Walter Scott.   By Richard Holt Hutton.   New York, Harper & brothers (1887) viii, 177 p. 17½ cm. (Half-title: English men of letters; ed. by John Morley) On cover; Harper's handy series. no. 121. "Ancestry, parentage and childhood": p. 1-17.   13-33729.   PR5332.H8   1887

15162   SCOTT.   Upper Teviotdale and the Scotts of Buccleuch, a local and family history, by J. Rutherford Oliver.   With illustrations of border scenery, by T. H. Laidlaw.   Hawick, W. & J. Kennedy, 1887.   xii, 470 p. front. (port.) illus., 2 fold. maps. 26 cm.   13-2261.   DA880.R805

15163   SCOTT.   A genealogical history of the family of Scott of Thirlestane; extracted from "Some old families," by H. B. McCall, F.S.A.   (n. p.) Priv. print., 1890.   1 p. l., (171)-236 p. incl. illus., geneal. tables. 2 pl., facsims. 29 x 23 cm.   4-9682.   CS479.S3

15164   SCOTT.   Metrical history of the honourable families of the name of Scot and Elliot, in the shires of Roxburgh and Selkirk.   In two parts, gathered out of ancient chronicles, histories, and traditions of our fathers.   Compiled by Captain Walter Scot of Satchells, Roxburghshire, with prefatory notices.   Edinburgh: Printed M.DC.LXXXVIII. - M.DCC.LXXVI.   Edinburgh, Reprinted for private circulation, 1892.   x p., reprint: 1 p. l., iii, 60 p., 2 l., 97 p. 25½ cm. (Half-title: Scottish literary club. (Publications) no. II) Each part has special t.-p.   Part 1 retains the original title (1688): A true history of several honourable families of the right honourable name of Scot, in the shires of Roxburgh and Selkirk ... By Captain Walter Scot, an old souldier and no scholler, and one that can write nane, but just the letters of his name ... Part 2 has t.-p.: Satchels's post'ral, humbly presented to his noble and worthy friends of the names of Scot and Elliot, and others ... Dictated, not written.   cf. Pref.   "Impression limited to fifty copies solely for the subscribers." "Prefatory notice" signed: T.G.S. (i. e. Thomas George Stevenson) 26-8919.   CS479.S4   1892

15165   SCOTT.   Hugh Scott, an immigrant of 1670, and his descendants ... By John Scott.   (Nevada, Ia., J.M. Scott, printer, 1895)   1 p. l., viii, 322 p., 1 l., iv p. front., illus., plates, ports. 22½ cm. 1-10212.   CS71.S43   1895

15166   SCOTT.   Memoirs of the life of Sir Walter Scott, bart., by John Gibson Lockhart ... (Large paper ed.) Boston and New York, Houghton, Mifflin and company, 1901.   10 v. fronts., plates, ports. 23 cm. Added title-page engraved, with coat of arms in gilt and colors.   "Six hundred copies printed." This copy not numbered. Edited by Susan M. Francis.   "Biographical sketch of John Gibson Lockhart": v. 1, p. (xiii)-xxxvi.   Appendix (v.10) includes additional genealogical data and a bibliography of Scott's works (p. 208-214) 2-202.   PR5332.L6   1901

15167   SCOTT.   Genealogical record of the descendants of Thomas Scott, born 1744, the record covering the entire period of the history of the family in America.   Edited by Clinton S. Scott ... (Phoenix? Ariz.) 1902.   53 p. ports. 23½ cm. 34-35353.   CS71.S43   1902

15168   SCOTT.   Letters, hitherto unpublished, written by members of Sir Walter Scott's family to their old governess; ed., with an introduction and notes, by the warden of Wadham college, Oxford. London, E. G. Richards, 1905.   2 p. l., 164 p. front. (fold. facsim.) 20 cm.   "Of the forty-seven letters (to Miss Millar) twenty-eight were written by Charlotte Sophia Scott ... twelve by Anne Scott." - p. 16-17. 6-24914.

PR5332.L5

15169   SCOTT.   Descendants of William Scott of Hatfield, Mass., 1668-1906.   And of John Scott of Springfield, Mass., 1659-1906.   By Orrin Peer Allen ... Palmer, Mass., Pub. by the author, 1906.   220 p. front., plates, ports. 23½ cm. 6-33647.   CS71.S43   1906

15170   SCOTT.   The Scott family of Shrewsbury, N.J.   Being the descendants of William Scott and Abigail Tilton Warner.   With sketches of related families.   By Arthur Stanley Cole.   Red Bank, N.J., the Register press, 1908.   72, (1) p. pl., ports., facsims., geneal. tab. 27½ cm. 8-30312.

CS71.S43   1908

15171   SCOTT.   The Scotch-Irish and Charles Scott's descendants and related families, by Orion C. Scott ... (Berwyn, Ill., Printed by J. H. Watson, c.1917)   111, (4) p. front., illus. (map) ports. 22½ cm. 18-555.

CS71.S43   1917

15172   SCOTT.   The Scott genealogy, by Mary Lovering Holman ... Comp. by the author for Harriett Grace Scott.   Boston, Mass., 1919.   5 p. l., (3)-402 p. front., plates, ports. 24 cm.   Contents. - pt. 1. Descendants of John Scott of Roxbury, Massachusetts. - pt. 2. Ancestral lines of Harriett Grace Scott. - Appendix: Benjamin Scott of Braintree, Massachusetts. Benjamin Scott of Rowley, Massachusetts. Joseph Scott of Rowley, Massachusetts. 20-17038.   CS71.S43   1919

15173   SCOTT.   ... History of the Scott family, by Henry Lee.   New York, R. L. Polk and company, inc. (c.1919)   117 p. 20 cm. (The Maxwell series. Famous old families) 23-14461.   CS71.S43   1919a

15174   SCOTT.   Our clan; a biological and genealogical account of the family of Rev. Andrew Scott, its ancestry and posterity, ed. by Thomas Jefferson Scott, D.D., assisted by Wilfred W. Scott; with contributions by members of the clan.   (Lancaster, Pa.)   Priv, print., 1920.   xiv, 124 p. front., plates, ports. fold. geneal. tab. 24 cm. 21-6950.   CS71.S43   1920

15175   SCOTT.   Scott, 1118-1923; being a collection of "Scott" pedigrees containing all known male descendants from Buccleuch, Sinton, Harden, Balweary, etc., compiled and arranged by Keith S. M. Scott ... with an introduction by ... Captain the Hon, W. T. Hepburne-Scott, younger, of Harden. Illustrated by Mr. A. G. Law Samson ... London, The Burke publishing company, ltd.; (etc., etc.) 1923.   xxiii, 312 p. incl. front., illus. (coats of arms) 24 cm.   No. 76 of an edition of 170 copies.   Pages 308-312 left blank for "Corrections and additions". 25-23603.   CS479.S4   1923

15176   SCOTT.   ... Scott family records, by J. Montgomery Seaver ... Philadelphia, Pa., American historical-genealogical society, 1929.   1 p. l., 5-46 p. illus. 23 cm.   Coat of arms on cover.   "References": p. 41-42. 30-8677.   CS71.S43   1929

15177   SCOTT.   Scott family letters; the letters of John Morin Scott and his wife, Mary Emlen Scott; with notes relating to them, their ancestors and their descendants.   Compiled and edited by their great-grand-daughters, Maria Scott Beale Chance and Mary Allen Evans Smith ... (Philadelphia) Priv. print. (The Biddle press) 1930.   392 p., 4 l. front. (col. coat of arms) plates, ports., facsims., fold. geneal. tables. 24½ cm.   Plate following page 344 accompanied by leaf with descriptive text.   Blank leaves for "Additional family records" (3 at end) 31-989.   CT275.S3485A3

15178   SCOTT.   A genealogical history of the Scott family, descendants of Alexander Scott who came to Augusta county, Virginia, ca. 1750, with a history of the families with which they intermarried, compiled by Josephine McCord Vercoe.   (n. p.) 1939 - (40)   9 p. l. 177 (i. e.183) numb. l., 3 l. 28½ cm.   Type-written (carbon copy), with additions in manuscript. Includes 4 extra numbered and 2 unnumbered leaves. Leaves 27-28 incorrectly inserted after leaf 29.   "Additional records. 1940": leaves 160-(180) 41-38344.   CS71.S43   1940

15179   SCOTT.   A genealogical history of the Scott family; descendants of Alexander Scott who came to Augusta county, Virginia, ca. 1750; with a history of the families with which they intermarried, compiled by Josephine McCord Vercoe.   (Columbus, O., 1940)   8 p. l., 182 numb. l. 28½ cm.   Reproduced from type-written copy. "Revised copy, November 1940." - Manuscript note on fly-leaf. 41-1215.   CS71.S43   1940a

15180   SCOTT.   The arms of Richard Scott, by Richard LeBaron Bowen ... (Boston, 1942)
29 p. plates, col. coat of arms.   24 cm.   "Reprinted with additions from the New England historical and genealogical register, vol. XCVI, no. 1, January, 1942."   42-17874.   CS71.S43   1942

15181   SCOTT.   Our family.   By Malvina May Sykes.   (Limited ed.   Washington, Priv. print.,
1949)   164 p. 23 cm.   49-27657 *.   CS71.S43   1949

15182   SCOTT.   The Scott family.   By Wesley Merritt Tryon.   (Wheaton? Md., 195-)
11 p. 23 cm.   59-35700.   CS71.S43

15183   SCOTT.   Arthur Martin Scott, 1777-1858, his ancestors and his descendants.   By Elisha
Harrison Scott.   Dayton, Otterbein Press, 1951.   131 p. ports., col. coat of arms. 23 cm. 53-39538.
                                                                                                                          CS71.S43   1951

15184   SCOTT.   Descendants of Thomas Scott.   By Lewis Scott Dayton.   LaMoille, Ill., 1956.
22 1. 30 cm. 56-28895.   CS71.S43   1956

15185   SCOTT.   The family of Thomas Scott and Martha Swan Scott, a century in America, 1856-
1956; a sketch by a grandson, George Tressler Scott.   Montclair, N.J., Priv. print. by Montclair
Print. Co. (1956)   70 p. illus. 24 cm. Includes bibliography. 57-392.   CS71.S43   1956a

15186   SCOTT.   History of the Silas H. Scott family, 1839-1956, compiled by Olin S. Hockaday &
Mrs. Pierce Johnson.   (Commerce? Tex.) 1956.   unpaged. illus. 29 cm. 56-12957.
                                                                                                                          CS71.S43   1956b

15187   SCOTT.   The Scotts.   Edinburgh, W. & A. K. Johnston & G. W. Bacon (1957)   31 p. illus.
(part col.) map, col. coat of arms. 19 cm. (W. & A. K. Johnston's clan histories) 58-26277.   CS479.S4   1957

15188   SCOTT.   The genealogy of the Scott and Galloway families: Scotland, Mifflin County, Pennsylvania (and) Bourbon County, Kentucky.   By Ruth (Hendricks) DeVerter.   (Baytown, Texas, 1959)
xiii, 379 1. illus., ports., maps, coat of arms. 29 cm. (Her Our pioneer ancestors. v.2) 59-25991.   CS71.S43   1959

15189   SCOTT.   Collected papers: armorial, genealogical, and historical.   By Richard Le Baron
Bowen.   Rehoboth, Mass., 1959.   1 v. (various pagings) illus., port., coats of arms (part col.) facsims., geneal. tables.
24 cm.   "Limited to eighty copies ... No. 11." Bibliographical footnotes. 58-59748.   CS71.S43   1959a

15190   SCOTT.   Scott family (Adam Calhoun)   By Genevieve L. Carter.   (Sedalia? Mo.) 1959.
46 1. 29 cm. 61-35188.   CS71.S43   1959b

15191   SCOTT.   The descendants of John Scott from 1777.   (Compiler: Walter T. Scott.   1st ed.
Warner Robins? Ga., 1965)   84 1. ports. 28 cm. 300 copies printed. 65-89150.
                                                                                                                          CS71.S43   1965

15192   SCOTT.   Material in vertical file.   Ask reference librarian for this.

SCOTT.   See also:

ADIE, CS477.S5G7
AGNEW, 1926
ALLARDYCE, 1839
BALLIOL, 1914
BASSETT, 1926
BAVIS, 1880
BEAL, 1956
BISHOP, 1951
BOLEBEC, DA690.M51.P5
BOWSER, 1962
CALHOUN, 1957
CARTER, 1958
CHIPP, 1933

CLARK, CS438.C5
DAY, 1916
DOUGLAS, DA758.3.A1T2
ELIOT, 1907
GILMORE, 1932
GLASSELL, 1891
HASKELL, 1926
HERRON, 1935
JOHNSON, 1956
McCALL, 1917
MACGINNIS, 1892
MILLER, 1923

MONROE, CS479.M8
MOORE, 1918
NAPIER, 1921
RANDLEMAN, 1965
RANDOLPH, 1961
RYLE, 1961
STUART, 1961
TELFORD, 1956
WALBRIDGE, 1898
WHITE, 1920
No. 1547 - Cabell county.
No. 3509 - Orange county.

SCOTT-MURRAY.   See No. 1834 - Medmenham.

SCOVEL.   See SCOVILLE.

SCOVILL.   See SCOVILLE.

15193   SCOVILLE.   Scoville family records.   By Charles Rochester Eastman.   (Cambridge? Mass.)
1910-11.   3 pts. port., coat of arms. 23 cm. No more published? Contents. - (pt. 1) A preliminary brochure. - pt. 2. Descendants of
Arthur Scovil of Boston, Middletown and Lyme, Conn. - pt. 3. Harwinton (Conn.) branch. 11-2695 rev. *
CS71.S432   1910

15194   SCOVILLE.   A survey of the Scovils or Scovills in England and America; seven hundred
years of history and genealogy, by Homer Worthington Brainard.   Hartford, Priv. print., 1915.
586 p. plates, ports., maps., facsim., fold. geneal. tab. 25 cm. Ed. mainly from the material collected by Frederick John Kingsbury and
Barclay Allaire Scovil.   Two hundred and fifty copies printed.   "The Scovilles of Wessex, 1194 to 1660, by Charles Arthur Hoppin": p. 9-94.
16-6216.
CS71.S432   1915

15195   SCOVILLE.   Arthur Scovell and his descendants in America, 1660-1900, compiled by Jennie
M. (Scoville) Holley and Homer Worthington Brainard ...   Rutland, Vt., The Tuttle publishing compnay,
inc. (1941)   xvi p., 1 l., 285, (5) p. pl. 24 cm. "Five blank pages at end for "Family records."   "Scoville publications": p. xvi.
42-7574.
CS71.S432   1941

SCOVILLE.   See also: BULLARD, 1935
                        KINGSBURY, 1934
                        KINGSBURY, 1937

SCOWINGE.   See SCHABINGER.

15196   SCRANTON.   A genealogical register of the descendants of John Scranton of Guilford, Conn.,
who died in the year 1671.   Compiled by Rev. Erastus Scranton, A.M. ... Hartford, Press of Case,
Tiffany and company, 1855.   104 p. 23½ cm.   9-13661. CS71.S433   1855

15197   SCRASE.   Genealogical memoir of the family of Scrase.   By Mark Antony Lower ... London,
J. R. Smith, 1856.   1 p. l., 18 p. incl. illus., geneal. tables. 22 cm. (Hazlitt tracts, v. 4, no. 3) "Reprinted from the Sussex
archaeological collections, vol. VIII." 23-1835. AC911.H3 vol. 4 no. 3

15198   SCRIPPS.   History of the Scripps family.   By James E. Scripps.   Detroit.   Printed for private circulation (J. F. Eby & co.) 1882.   27 p. front. (port.) illus., pl., diagr. 21½ cm. 3-7925.
CS71.S434   1882

15199   SCRIPPS.   Memorials of the Scripps family.   A centennial tribute.   By James E. Scripps.
Detroit, Printed for private circulation (J. F. Eby & co.) 1891.   vii, (1), 187 p. front., illus., plates, ports., fold.
geneal. tables, diagr. 24½ cm. "Only one hundred copies printed, for private circulation, all of which are numbered and signed. This copy is
no. 57 (signed) James E. Scripps." 9-13660. CS71.S434   1891

15200   SCRIPPS.   An attempt to establish the descent of the Scripps family from Anthony Pearson.
By James E. Scripps.   Detroit, 1900.   10 p. 21½ cm. Cover-title. 40 copies printed for private circulation. 1-19230.
CS439.S25

15201   SCRIPPS.   A genealogical history of the Scripps family and its various alliances.   By James
E. Scripps.   Detroit, Printed for private circulation (R. L. Polk printing co., ltd.) 1903.   iv, (5)-87 p.
front. (port.) 3 fold. geneal. tab. 24½ cm. "One hundred and twenty copies printed, of which this is no. 65 (signed) James E. Scripps." 4-6826.
CS71.S434   1903

15202   SCRIPPS.   The descendants of William Armiger Scripps, 1798-1927.   (Rushville, Ill., The
Rushville times co., 1927.   (8) p. incl. 1 illus., ports. 6 fold. geneal. tab. 20 cm. Foreword signed: May Deacon. 37-21310.
CS439.S25   1927

15203   SCROGGINS.   Scrogin, Scroggin, Scroggins (by A. E. Scroggins.   Dodge City? Kan. 1964)
77 p. illus., geneal. tables, col. map. 28 cm. Cover title. 66-37691. CS71.S4345   1964

15204   SCROGGS.   Pedigree of the Scroggs family.   By J. Renton Dunlop, F.S.A.   (Reprinted from "Miscellanea genealogica et heraldica") London, Mitchell, Hughes and Clarke, 1918.   1 p. 1., 18 p.   illus. (coats of arms) plates.   25½ cm.   23-14541.
CS439.S27

15205   SCROGGS.   The family of Scroggs, by J. Renton Dunlop ... London, Priv. print. by Mitchell, Hughes and Clarke, 1929.   4 p. 1., 116 p.   plates, port., fold. geneal. tab., coats of arms.   22½ cm.   Contents. - The family of Scroggs and the descent of the manor of Patmore hall, Hertfordshire. - The Lord Chief Justice, Sir William Scroggs.   His origin and career. - Albury church, Hertfordshire. - The Bedfordshire branch of the Scroggs family.   40-273.
CS439.S27   1929

SCROGGS.   See also: CARSON, 1935
HARRIS, 1934

SCROGIN.   See SCROGGINS.

15206   SCROPE.   Wensleydale; or, Rural contemplations: a poem.   By T. Maude, esq. ... 4th ed. Richmond (Yorkshire, Eng.) T. Bowman; (etc., etc.) 1816.   xx, (21)-122 p.   front., fold. tab.   22½ cm.   Contains Pedigree and genealogical notes of the Scrope family.   2-22327.
DA670.W47M1

15207   SCROPE.   De controversia in curia militari inter Ricardum Le Scrope et Robertum Grosvenor milites: rege Ricardo Secundo, MCCCLXXXV - MCCCXC e recordis in turre Londinensi asservatis. (London, Printed by Samuel Bentley, 1832)   2 v. illus.   30½ cm.   Vol. 2 has title: The controversy between Sir Richard Scrope and Sir Robert Grosvenor, in the Court of chivalry ... containing A history of the family of Scrope and biographical notices of the deponents. By Sir N. Harris Nicolas, K.H.   1832.   Half-title: The Scrope and Grosvenor controversy.   Only 100 copies printed for private circulation.   The first volume contains the official record of the trial and the depositions of the witnesses printed from the original documents in the Record office.   A third volume treating of Grosvenor and his witnesses was projected, but never published.   cf. Dict. nat. biog.   24-20904.
DA28.35.S3A3

15208   SCROPE.   A dissertation on the history of hereditary dignities, particularly as their course of descent, and their forfeiture by attainder.   With special reference to the case of the earldom of Wiltes.   By W. F. Finlason ... London, Butterworths, 1869.   vi, (3)-110 p.   22½ cm.   19-13596.
LAW.

15209   SCROPE.   A great historic peerage: the earldom of Wiltes, by John Henry Metcalfe.   London, Printed for the author at the Chiswick press, 1899.   5 p. 1., 58, 7, (1) p.   iv pl. (incl. front., port., fold. geneal. tab.)   26½ cm.   Geneal. table: Pedigree of Simon Conyers Scrope of Danby-on-Yore, esquire, claiming the honour and dignity of Earl of Wiltes.   Title in red and black.   "Only five hundred copies printed, six of which are for presentation" ... 4-12427.
CS439.W56

15210   SCROPE.   William Throope and Adrian Scrope.   The family tradition; history of the Scrope family and the barony of Bolton; Bolton castle; proceedings at the trial of Adrian Scrope; the regicides and the ancestral chart of Adrian Scrope ... Research and narrative by Evelyn Fish Knudson.   East St. Louis, Ill., Priv. print. by A. J. Throop and D. A. Throop, 1943.   3 p. 1., 74 p., 1 l.   pl.   23 cm.   Colored coat of arms of the Scrope family on cover.   Bibliography: p. 73-74.   45-13061.
CS71.S435   1943

SCROPE.   See also DUNSTANVILLE, DA690.C42S4

15211   SCRUGGS.   Scruggs genealogy; with a brief history of the allied families Briscoe, Dial, Dunklin, Leake and Price, comp. by Ethel Hastings Scruggs Dunklin.   New York, Laplante & Dunklin printing company, 1912.   223, xiii p. incl. front. (coat of arms)   20 cm.   Nine blank pages for "Additional notes," following p. 223. 19-20220.
CS71.S436   1912

SCRUGGS.   See also BEVILLE, 1917

15212   SCRYMGEOUR ... Inventory of documents relating to the Scrymgeour family estates, 1611. Edited by J. Maitland Thomson, LL.D.   Edinburgh, Printed for the Society by J. Skinner & company, ltd., 1912.   v, 70 p.   26 cm.   (Scottish record society.   Publications.   42)   13-11780.
CS460.S4 vol. 42

15213   SCUDAMORE.   A view of the ancient and present state of the churches of Door, Home-Lacy, and Hempsted; endow'd by the Right Honourable John, lord viscount Scudamore.   With some memoirs of that ancient family; and An appendix of records and letters relating to the same subject ... By — Matthew Gibson ... London, Printed by W. Bowyer, for R. Williamson, 1727.   4 p. l., 238 p. fold. pl. 25 cm.   20-22109.   DA660.G4

SCUDAMORE.   See also SKIDMORE.

SCUDDER.   See: BUTLER, 1919
                            DAVIS, 1927a

15214   SCULL.   Genealogical notes relating to the family of Scull.   Compiled by G. D. Scull.   Private impression.   (London) 1876.   12 p. 28 cm.   Title vignette: coat of arms.   Issued also in Miscellanea genealogica et heraldica, n. s. v. 2, p. 230-234, 265-268, 277-279.   9-18122.   CS439.S3

15215   SCULL.   The family of Scull ... Philadelphia, The John C. Winston company (1930)
1 p. l., 27, 25 p. front., illus. (incl. maps, facsims.) plates (1 col.) ports. (1 col.) 25 cm.   Limited to 300 copies.   Title vignette: coat of arms.   One plate accompanied by guard sheet, with descriptive letterpress.   Foreword signed: William Ellis Scull.   Contents. - Early history of the family of Scull of Wales, England and Holland.   By William Le Hardy ... - Notes on the Scull family of New York, New Jersey and Pennsylvania.   By William Ellis Scull.   (Reprinted ... from Publications of the Genealogical society of Pennsylvania, vol. x, no. 3)   32-24488.

                                                                                CS71.S437   1930

SCULL.   See also: HALLOWELL, 1924
                                  THOMAS, 1896

SEABORN.   See: DETLOR, 1942
                              SIEBERN.
                              WHITEHOUSE, 1946

SEABURY.   See GOULD, 1897

SEAFIELD, Earls of.   See: GRANT.
                                            OGILVIE.

15216   SEAGER.   Descendants of Joseph Seager and Mehitable Parsons of Connecticut.   By Dorothy J. Raymoure.   Grand Rapids, 1957.   7 l. 28 cm.   62-41013.   CS71.S4373   1957

15217   SEAGRAVE.   Genealogy, biography, and history.   Genealogy of the Seagrave family, from 1725-1881, as descended from John and Sarah Seagrave, who came from England.   With several appendices ... relating to the families mentioned in the record.   By Daniel Seagrave.   Worcester, Printed by Tyler & Seagrave, 1881.   55, 38 p., 1 l. front. (coat of arms) 25 cm.   Blank pages at end for additional records. 9-13659.   CS71.S4375   1881

SEAGRAVE.   See also STOURTON, DA28.35S85M7

SEAL.   See ENDERS, 1960

15218   SEALE.   Seale (and allied families.   3d ed., rev. Lynn Haven? Fla., 1954)   211 l. illus. 29 cm.   57-43890.   CS71.S4378   1954

15219   SEAMAN.   A copy of an account written by Jordan Seaman of Jericho, tracing the family of Seamans descended from Capt. John Seaman of Hempstead.   (New York, 1860)   6 l. 43½ cm. 9-13818.
                                                                                CS71.S438   1860

15220   SEAMAN.   Links in genealogy; memorial of Samuel Hicks Seaman and his wife, Hannah Richardson Husband, compiled by their daughter, Mary Thomas Seaman ... (New York, T. A. Wright, inc.) 1927.   247 p. fold. geneal. tables, fold. facsims. 24½ cm.   Contains also the Hicks, Jewett, Richardson and other families. 28-18402.   CS71.S438   1927

15221   SEAMAN.   The Seaman family in America as descended from Captain John Seaman ... compiled by Mary Thomas Seaman ... assisted by James Haviland Seaman, jr.   (New York, T. A. Wright, inc.) 1928.   5 p. l., 3-338 p. front. (coat of arms) plates, fold, facsims. 24½ cm. 30-13140.   CS71.S438   1928

15222   SEAMAN.   The Seamans family in America as descended from Thomas Seamans of Swansea, Massachusetts, 1687, compiled by John Julian Lawton with the financial assistance of Charles Seamans Brown.   Syracuse, N.Y., Priv. print., 1933.   xv, 299 p. , 1 l. plates, ports. 24½ cm. "References": p. (279) 34-51.   CS71.S438   1933

15223   SEAMAN.   The Seaman family of the Middle West; an account of the descendants of William Seaman, who died in Washington County, Pennsylvania, in 1814.   By William Millard Seaman.   East Lansing, Mich., 1952.   26 l. 29 cm. 53-36206.   CS71.S438   1952

15224   SEAMAN.   Seaman, Hunt, Wright genealogy; compiled by William M. Seaman in collaboration with Irene Macy Strieby, Helen Vogt, and others.   (Indianapolis?) 1957.   70 p. 23 cm. 57-45932.   CS71.S438   1957

SEAMAN.   See also: DOWNEY, 1931
                               THOMAS, 1850

SEAMANS.   See SEAMAN.

SEAMER.   See SEYMOUR.

SEAMONDS.   No. No. 1547 - Cabell county.

15225   SEARIGHT.   A record of the Searight family (also written Seawright.)   Established in America by William Seawright, who came from near Londonderry ... to Lancaster County, Pennsylvania, about 1740; with an account of his descendants as far as can be ascertained ... By James Allison Searight.   Uniontown, Pa. (Richmond, Ind., Press of M. Cullaton & co.) 1893.   228 p. incl. illus., plates, ports., front., ports. 23 cm. 9-13658.   CS71.S439   1893

15226   SEARIGHT.   In loving memory of a revered father and a sainted mother. (By James Allison Searight) (Richmond, Ind., M. Cullaton & co., printers, 1893)   66 p. incl. illus., ports., facsim. front. 19 cm. Biographical sketches of William Searight and Rachel (Brownfield) Searight-Stidger and their children.   Also in author's a Record of the Searight family ... Uniontown, Penn., 1893: p. 84-154. 14-11910.   CS71.S439   1893a

15227   SEARIGHT.   Genealogical chart of Searight family from James A. Searight's book, "In memoriam."   Compiled by R. L. Brownfield, Jr. and Rex Newlon Brownfield. (n. p.) 1910.   geneal. table. 71 x 43 cm. fold. to 31 x 43 cm. Manuscript. "Searight family chart, about eighteen hundred and twelve (1812) in Fayette Co., Penna." 55-55827.   CS71.S439   1910

15228   SEARS.   Searstan family, of Colchester, England.   Landed at Plymouth, May 8th, 1630 ... (n. p., 18 -)   1 p. l., 18, (2) p. illus., pl. 23½ cm. Engraved t.-p., with vignette (coat of arms) "Genealogical notices. - Morant's History of Essex - Halsted's History of Kent - Herald's visitations - Sir Bernard Burke's Works and Somerby's Collections in England." 37-16849.   CS71.S44   18 -

15229   SEARS.   Genealogies and biographical sketches of the ancestry and descendants of Richard Sears, the Pilgrim ... (By Edmund Hamilton Sears) Boston, Crosby, Nichols, and company, 1857.   1 p. l., 96 p. front. (port.) plates. 20½ cm. Preface signed: E. H. S. Issued as an appendix to his Pictures of the olden time ... Boston, 1857. 9-15612.   CS71.S44   1857

15230   SEARS.   (Sears genealogy. Family tree of) Richard Sears, born 1590, married Dorothy Thatcher, at Plymouth in 1632.   Comp. by Olive H. (Sears) Kelley.   Drawn by George E. Jones, Boston.   New York, Am. photo-lithographic co., c.1874.   geneal. tab. 71 x 61 cm. fold. to 36½ x 31 cm. Mounted on linen with rollers. 3-17342.   CS71.S44   1874

15231   SEARS.   Some doubts concerning the Sears pedigree.   By Samuel Pearce May, Newton, Mass.   Reprinted from the New England historical and genealogical register for July, 1886.   Boston, Printed by D. Clapp & son, 1886.   10 p. 28 cm. Refers to the Sears pedigree as printed in the Appendix to "Pictures of the olden time," by Edmund Hamilton Sears. Boston, 1857. 17-6149.   CS71.S44   1886

15232   SEARS.   The descendants of Richard Sares (Sears) of Yarmouth, Mass., 1638-1888.   With an appendix, containing some notices of other families by the name of Sears.   By Samuel P. May ... Albany, N.Y., J. Munsell's sons, 1890.   x p., 1 l., 665 p. front. (port.) 24 cm. Title vignette. 9-13657.

CS71.S44   1890

15233   SEARS.   Sayre family; lineage of Thomas Sayre, a founder of Southampton, by Theodore M. Banta ... New York, (The De Vinne press) 1901.   xv, 759 p. front., plates, port., facsim., fld. geneal. tab. 25½ cm. Title vignette. 2-981   See additions and corrections no. 244. 2-981.   CS71.S44   1901

15234   SEARS.   Descendants of Deacon Ephraim Sayre, by Harrison Monell Sayre.   Columbus, O. (Ann Arbor, Mich., Edwards brothers, inc., lithoprinters) 1942.   viii, (2), 75 p. incl. front., illus. pl., ports. 24 cm.   Coat of arms on recto of frontispiece. 42-15367.   CS71.S44   1942

SEARS.   See also: SAWYER.   STANTON, 1922
                                 SAYRE.

SEARSTON.   See SEARS.

15235   SEATON.   The Seaton family, with genealogy and biographies, by Oren Andrew Seaton, editor. Topeka, Kan., Crane & company, 1906.   441 p. incl. front., illus. 2 pl., 4 port. 23½ cm. Bibliography: p. 14-15. 7-1948.   CS71.S441   1906

15236   SEATON.   The Seatons of western Pennsylvania, by Jane Snowden Crosby.   New York, N.Y., The Hobson book press, 1945.   2 p. l., vii-viii, 63 p. 21½ cm. Reproduced from type-written copy. Bibliography: p. (61)- 63. 46-2170.   CS71.S441   1945

15237   SEATON.   A Seaton-Zenor family history; the descendants of Col. Howson Kenner Bonam Seaton and Sarah Kenner Prichard Seaton, by Howard C. Nelson and Esther C. Nelson.   (Urbana? Ill.) c. 1963.   110 l. 28 cm. 64-72.   CS71.S441   1963

SEATON.   See also: SETON.
                     WALWORTH, E171.A53 vol. 20

15238   SEAVER.   The Seaver family.   A genealogy of Robert Seaver of Roxbury, Massachusetts, and some of his descendants.   By William Blake Trask.   Boston, D. Clapp & son, printers, 1872. 2 p. l., 52 p. illus. (facsim., coat of arms) 24 cm. "Edition of one hundred and fifty copies." "Reprinted from the New-England historical and genealogical register for July, 1872, with an appendix." 37-21340.   CS71.S442   1872

15239   SEAVER.   The Seaver genealogy; a genealogy, history and directory ... of the Seaver (Seavers, Sever, etc.) families of Europe and America including descendants of the immigrant Robert Seaver, who came from England to Massachusetts in 1633; early English branch, dating back to A.D.1287; the Irish branch, dating back to A.D.1471, the Scottish branch, including descendants of King David of Scotland; the German branch, and the French branch, by Jesse Seaver ... Philadelphia, 1924.   1 p. l., ii, 114, ix, (1) p. 28 cm. Autographed from type-written copy.   Coat of arms on cover. "First edition - 200 copies." —— General index.   Additional names of children, grandchildren, towns, occupations and intermarriages of the Seaver genealogy, by Jesse Seaver.   Addenda by Henry Gardner Seaver ... Westfield, N.J., 1924.   cover-title, 24 p. 28 cm. Bound with: Seaver, Jesse. The Seaver genealogy ... Philadelphia, 1924. 25-2343.
CS71.S442   1924

SEAVERNS.   See SEVERNS.

SEAVERS.   See SEAVER.

15240   SEAVEY.   The ancestry of Elisha Porter Seavey, 1838-1913.   By James Thomas Matthews Seavey.   (Ann Arbor, Mich., 1958)   36 p. 22 cm. 59-21426.   CS71.S4423   1958

SEAVEY.   See also CROCKER, 1923

SEAVIE.   See SEAVEY.

SEAVY. See SEAVEY.

SEAWARD. See SEWARD.

SEAWELL. See SEWALL.

SEAWRIGHT. See: SEARIGHT.
TELFORD, 1956

SEBO. See SAEBU.

15241 SEBOR. The descendants of Jacob Sebor, 1709-1793, of Middletown, Connecticut. Compiled by Helen Beach. (n. p.) 1923. 108 p., 1 l. 23 cm. Pages 52-57 left blank. Contains also the ancestry of the De Koven, Winthrop, Shirreff, Isaacs, Peiret, Prudden, Webber-Jans, Kiersted-Smedes, Bryan, Beach, Wadsworth, Otis-Ritchie, Otis-Leroy, Alsop, Olivier, Ingersoll, Shepard, Sherwood, Eaton-Jones, Blount and Watts families. 24-6792. CS71.S4425   1923

15242 SEBREE. 1892. History of the Sebree family. By W. E. Sebree ... 1749. (New York, 1892) 75 p. 19½ x 16 cm. 9-13654. CS71.S443   1892

15243 SECKFORD. The statutes, and ordinances, for the government of the almshouses, in Woodbridge, in the county of Suffolk, founded by Thomas Seckford, esquire ... in the twenty-ninth year of the reign of Queen Elizabeth, 1587. Together with others subsequent, made by Sir John Fynch, knight, and Henry Seckford, esquire, 1635. Sir Joseph Jekyle, knight, and Sir Peter King, knight, 1718., Sir Thomas Sewell, knight, and Sir John Eardley Wilmot, knight, 1767. (governors for the time being) To which are annexed, a translation of the queen's letters patent for the foundation of the alsm-house; - an abstract of Mr. Seckford's will; - a concise account of the founder; - and a genealogical table of his ancient family ... At the end is prefixed, notes relating to Woodbridge priory; together with the ancient monumental inscriptions in the parochial church, and those of late date. Collected and published by Robert Loder. Woodbridge, Printed and sold by the editor; (etc., etc.) 1792. 2 p. l., x, 24, (2), 7, (1) p. front. (port.) 2 col. pl., plan, fold. geneal. tab. 28 cm. 15-22369. DA690.W87L7

SECREST. See SPAID, 1922

15244 SEDDON. The correspondence of Nathan Walworth and Peter Seddon of Outwood, and other documents chiefly relating to the building of Ringley chapel. Ed., with notes, by John Samuel Fletcher ... (Manchester) Printed for the Chetham society, 1880. 3 p. l., (iii)-xxvii p., 1 l., 110 p., 1 l. front., plates, fold. geneal. tab. 23 cm. (Added t. -p.: Chetham society. Remains, historical & literary, connected with the palatine counties of Lancaster and Chester. vol. CIX) "Family of Nathan Walworth": p. ix. "The family of Peter Seddon of Prestolee": geneal. tab. 17-3794. DA670.L19C5 v. 109

SEDDON. See also WALWORTH, DA670.L19C5 v. 109

SEDGELEY. See SEDGLEY.

SEDGLEY. See BURBANK, 1928

15245 SEDGWICK. A Sedgwick genealogy; descendants of Deacon Benjamin Sedgwick. By Hubert Merrill Sedgwick. New Haven, New Haven Colony Historical Society, 1961. 360 p. illus. 23 cm. 62-4861. CS71.S446   1961

SEDGWICK. See also: KING, 1897
TODD, 1867

SEE. See: JARRATT, 1957
PECK, 1955

SEEBACH. See No. 553 - Goodhue county.

15246 SEEDE. Genealogical memoranda relating to the family of Seede, of Gloucestershire and Wiltshire. Compiled by Edward Milward Seede-Parker, esq. (Reprinted from "Miscellanea genealogica et heraldica," vol. IV, 1890) London, Mitchell and Hughes, 1890. 16 p. front. (port.) 28 cm. 16-20942. CS439.S32

544

15247   SEELEY.   Sketches and notes on the life and times of Robert Seeley, by Rev. Raymond Hoyt Seeley, D. D., as read before the Massachusetts historical society.   (Haverhill, Mass., Stiles' printery, 1901?)   31 p. front. (port.) 23 cm. Privately printed. Edited by Mary Wayne Seeley La Monte. cf. manuscript note in book. Edited by Mary Wayne Seeley La Monte. cf. manuscript note in book. Authorities quoted: p. 5. 25-2334.   CS71.S452   1901

15248   SEELEY.   Ancestry of Daniel James Seely, St. George, N.B., 1826, and of Charlotte Louisa Vail, Sussex, N.B., 1837 - St. John, N.B., 1912; with a list of their descendants.   Compiled by Colonel William Plumb Bacon ... (New York, Press of T. A. Wright, 1914?)   185 p. 2 fold. geneal. tab. 24 cm. On cover: Seely-Vail ancestry. 14-12258.   CS71.S452   1914

15249   SEELEY.   The Seelye centennial.   Paper read by Hon. Alfred Seelye Roe at the celebration of the one-hundredth anniversary of the Seelye family in this county.   Saturday, August 28, 1915. (n. p.) 1915.   9 p. 23 cm. Caption title. To celebrate the migration of Joseph Seelye and family into the Genesee country. 17-19202.   CS71.S452   1915

SEELEY.   See also: CHASE, 1963
                                    CILLEY.

SEELY.   See SEELEY.

SEGAR.   See MEADE, 1921

15250   SEGRAVE.   The Segrave family 1066 to 1935, by Charles W. Segrave, assisted by Thomas U. Sadleir ... London, Novello & company, ltd. (1936)   xv, 237 p. double front., plates, ports., maps, facsims., geneal. tables (part double, part fold.) 27 cm. Title vignette: coat of arms. 38-16675.   CS439.S325   1936

SEGRAVE.   See also STOURTON, 1899

SEGURA.   See MISTROT, 1965

15251   SEHNER.   The Sehner ancestry.   Compiled from authentic records ... Dedicated to John Fick Sehner by Samuel Miller Sener ... Lancaster, Pa., 1896.   6 l. illus., coat of arms. 24½ x 20 cm. Cover-title. Fifty copies on plain paper; twenty-five copies on paper made at the Ivy Mill, Delaware County, Pa., prior to the revolution. no. 20 - Ivy Mill paper. 9-13655.   CS71.S456   1896

15252   SEIDNER.   The story of a dozen generations.   By Orrin Wade Sidener.   (Tulare? Calif., 1961?)   1641 p. port. 30 cm. 64-55920.   CS71.S4563   1961

SEITNER.   See SEIDNER.

SEISS.   See SHEIBLEY, 1924

15253   SEITER.   The Seiter family record; specifically the Philip Theodore Seiter family tree, 1634-1962.   By Mary Helen (Seiter) Whaley.   Valley Stream, N.Y., 1962.   12, 4 p. 24 cm. 63-30219.   CS71.S4565   1962

SEIXAS.   See MOISE, 1961

15254   SELBY.   Selbyana: an attempt to elucidate the origin and history of a once considerable family, in the county of Buckingham, Selby of Wavendon.   Carlisle, Printed by F. Jollie, 1825.   iv, 40 p. 29½ cm. Title vignette: engr. coat of arms. 20-18078.   ,   CS439.S33

15255   SELBY.   Selby family notes; some materials for the 1929 reunion of families having members descended from Martha Damarias Selby Brooks and from Josias Wright Brooks.   Edited by Charles L. Stewart ... Bement, Ill., Distributed by S. A. Clark, 1929.   1 p. l., 14 numb. l. 28 cm. Type-written. "The body of this publication, the ... Genealogy of the Selbys and historical data, is a legacy of the Hon, Thomas Henry Selby ..." CA 29-690 unrev.   CS71.S457   1929

15256 SELBY. A short sketch of some of the descendants of William Selby, who was born June 15, 1717, and his second wife, Dorothy Booge ... (Brookfield, O., 1939) 1 v. mounted illus., pl. (ports.) 27½ cm. Loose-leaf. Reproduced from type-written copy. Introduction signed: Fred Erwin Fowler. 40-18322.

CS71.S457   1939

15257 SELBY. Short sketches of some of the descendants of William Selby, born June 15, 1717, and Dorothy Booge, his second wife. 2d ed., enl. (Brookfield, Ohio, 1950) 1 v. (various pagings) 28 cm. Addenda slip inserted. 51-30098.

CS71.S457   1950

15258 SELBY. The house of Selby (by Forest T. Selby. Charlotte? N.C.) 1962. 1, 44 p. illus., port. 29 cm. Cover title. Bibliography: p. 37. 67-57354.

CS71.S457   1962

15259 SELDEN. Calvin Selden, of Lyme, and his children. An address delivered at a meeting of the Selden family at Fenwick Grove, Saybrook, Conn., August 22, 1877, by Daniel C. Eaton. New Haven, 1877. 15 p. 25½ cm. "Printed not published." 16-17950.

CS71.S458   1877

15260 SELDEN. Seldens of Virginia and allied families, by Mary Selden Kennedy. New York, Frank Allaben genealogical company (c. 1911) 2 v. ports. coats of arms. 20½ cm. 12-17468.

CS71.S458   1911

15261 SELDEN. Selden ancestry; a family history, giving the ancestors and descendants of George Shattuck Selden and his wife, Elizabeth Wright Clark (by) Sophie Selden Rogers, Elizabeth Selden Lane (and) Edwin van Deusen Selden ... Oil City, Pa., E. van D. Selden (c. 1931) 523 p. front., plates, ports., facsim., fold. geneal. tables (2 in pocket) coats of arms. 25 cm. With genealogical tables of the Selden, de Santo Domingo and de Chappotin families. 32-12020.

CS71.S458   1931

15262 SELDEN. Selden chart, compiled by Albert Augustus Selden. (n. p.) Executed by Milton H. Kroeger, 1937. geneal. tab. illus. (coats of arms) 41½ x 59½ cm. Reproduced from manuscript copy. "References." 38-32676.

CS71.S458   1937

15263 SELDEN. Selden and kindred of Virginia, by Edna Mae Selden ... Richmond, Va., Virginia stationery company (1941) 224 p. incl. geneal. tables, coat of arms. 24 cm. Pages 157-180 blank for "Notes." "Historical and genealogical authorities consulted and quoted": p. 153. 42-10566.

CS71.S458   1941

15264 SELDEN. Some descendants of Thomas Selden, and a facsimile of an ancient Selden family tree. By Pauline (Pearce) Warner. Illus. by Sidney E. King. Tappahannock, Va., c. 1967. 40, (2) p. illus. 28 cm. Photocopy of MS. 68-2903.

CS71.S458   1967

15265 SELDEN. See also: FITZHUGH, 1932
                               RUCKER, 1927

15266 SELDOMRIDGE. A history of the Zeltenreich Church and a list of the descendants of Andreas Seltenreich. By Amos Leon Seldomridge. New Bloomfield, Pa., 1949. 11, 26 p. 28 cm. 50-16933.

BX9581.NS3

SELDON. See SELDEN.

15267 SELECMAN. The Selecman family news letter; by Redmond S. Cole. v. 1 June 1938 -   Tulsa, Okl., 1938 - v. 25½ cm. Caption title. 38M4551T.

CS71.S4584   1938

15268 SELECMAN. The Selecman family, a history of Henry Selecman and his wife, Margaret Harmon, of Occoquan, Virginia, and their descendants, and items dealing with families related to them. By Redmond Selecman Cole. Tulsa, Okl., R. S. Cole, 1942. 151 p. pl., ports., facsim. 27½ cm. Reproduced from type-written copy. 43-3384.

CS71.S4584   1942

15269 SELIGMAN. ... The family register of the descendants of David Seligman. (Baltimore, N. T. A. Munder and company) 1913. 2 p. l., 3-93 p., 1 l. incl. ports. 30 cm. The portraits are mounted photographs. "This book was designed by William Aspenwall Bradley ... The title page decorations and the frames for the portraits were drawn by Thomas Maitland

15269 continued: Cleland. One hundred copies have been printed and numbered. " cf. Notes at end of book. 20-23922.

CS71.S459 ·1913

15270 SELL. Sell genealogy. By Anna May Sell. Hanover, Pa., 1958. 27 l. 31 cm. 59-48035.

CS71.S4597 1958

SELL. See also: SELLERS.
SELLS.
SILL.

15271 SELLARDS. The Sellards through two centuries. By Elias Howard Sellards. Austin, Tex., 1949. 132 p. illus., ports. 25 cm. "Privately printed edition, 130 copies ... No. 130." "References cited": p. 125-127. 50-16812.

CS71.S46 1949

15272 SELLECK. Selleck and Peck genealogy, comp. by William Edwin Selleck. Chicago, Priv. print., 1912. 2 p. l., 74 p. front., plates, ports., facsims., coats of arms. 24½ cm. 12-24791. CS71.S462 1912

15273 SELLECK. Selleck memorial, with collateral connections, by William Edwin Selleck ... Chicago, Priv. print. (R. R. Donnelley and sons company) 1916. 85 p., 1 l. front., pl., ports., facsim., fold. geneal. tables, coats of arms. 24 cm. 17-19709. CS71.S462 1916

15274 SELLERS. S(ellers) July, 1886. (n. p.) Siddall brothers, printers, 1886. 1 p. l., 101 p. 23 cm. Versos blank. Descendants of Philip Henry Sellers; includes also the Wampole, Jaquett, Foote and Cox families. 17-24549.

CS71.S467 1886

15275 SELLERS. Partial genealogy of the Sellers and Wampole families of Pennsylvania; by Edwin Jaquett Sellers. Philadelphia, Printed for private circulation by J. B. Lippincott company, 1903. 139 p. incl. front. (port.) 25 cm. "Edition of one hundred and fifty copies. " 4-4287. CS71.S467 1903

15276 SELLERS. Sellers family of Pennsylvania, and allied families, by Edwin Jaquett Sellers. Philadelphia (Press of Allen, Lane & Scott) 1925. 2 p. l., 58 p. 24 cm. "Edition limited to one hundred and fifty copies. " "The present work is a revision of Partial genealogy of the Sellers and Wampole families, by the writer, in 1903. " 25-11482.

CS71.S467 1925

15277 SELLERS. David Sellers, Mary Pennock Sellers, by their daughter, Sarah Pennock Sellers; written in 1916, published in 1928 ... (Philadelphia, Press of Innes & sons, 1928) 4 p. l., 7-155 p., 1 l. illus. (map) plates, 2 port. (incl. front.) facsim. 24½ cm. 28-21234. CS71.S467 1928

15278 SELLERS. Partial genealogy of the Sellers and Wampole families of Pennsylvania; by Edwin Jaquett Sellers. Philadelphia, Printed for private circulation by J. B. Lippincott company, 1903. 139 p. incl. front. (port.) 25 cm. "Edition of one hundred and fifty copies. " Genealogy of "David Wampole Sellers": p. 20-111. 4-4287. CS71.S467 1903

SELLERS. See also: JONES, 1936
LLOYD, 1912
SELL.
SELLS.
SILL.

15279 SELLS. The first four generations of the Sells family in America. By Ray Sells Morrish. Flint, Mich., 1956. (7) p. illus. 22 cm. 56-46912. CS71.S468 1956

15280 SELLS. Sells chronology; a chronological index to early records of the Sells, Sills, Zell & Von Zellen family of Pennsylvania, (by) Louis Duermyer. Staten Island, N.Y., 1962. 21 l. facsim. 30 cm. 68-5223. CS71.S4683 1963

SELLS. See also: SELL.
SELLERS.
SILL.

SELOOVER. See COLES, 1926

15281   SELOVER.   Selover-Slover family, 1682-1941.   (Egeland, N.D., Mabel J. Hadler, 1941)
cover-title, 2 p. l., 269 numb. l., 2 l. 28 cm. Reproduced from type-written copy. Foreword signed: Mabel Jacques Hadler. 42-25751.
CS71.S469   1941

15282   SELVIG.   The Selvig story, by Mina Selvig Johnson, as told to Carol Johnson.   (Angwin?
Calif., 1952)   72 p. illus. 21 cm. 52-25617.   CS71.S4697   1952

SEMER.   See SEYMOUR.

15283   SEMMES.   The Semmes and allied families.   By Ralph Thomas Semmes.   Baltimore, The
Sun book and job printing office, inc., 1918.   381 p. front., plates, ports. 24½ cm. Arranged for publication by Lydia
B. Brown. 18-22969.   CS71.S47   1918

15284   SEMMES.   The Maryland Semmes and kindred families; a genealogical history of Marmaduke
Semme(s), gent., and his descendants, including the allied families of Greene, Simpson, Boarman,
Matthews, Thompson, Middleton, and Neale.   Baltimore, Maryland Historical Society, 1956.
341 p. illus. 24 cm. 56-14671.   CS71.S47   1956

15285   SEMPHILL.   The poems of the Sempills of Beltrees, now first collected, with notes and biographical notices of their lives, by James Paterson ... Edinburgh, T. G. Stevenson, 1849.   civ, 142 p.
20 cm. "Impression strictly limited to two hundred and fifty copies." The Packman's paternoster, by Sir James Sempill, has reproduction of the
original t.-p.: "A pick-tooth for the pope: or, The packmans paternoster. Set down in a dialogue betwixt a packman and a priest. Tr. out of
Dutch by S.I.S. and newly augm. and enl. by his son R.S. ... Edinburgh, Printed for Andrew Anderson, anno 1669." Contents. - The preface. -
Genealogical account of the Sempills of Beltrees. - Epitaphs on Sir James and Robert Sempill. - The pack-mans paternoster, poem by Sir James
Sempill. - Poems by Robert Sempill. - Poems by Francis Sempill. - Notes. - Appendix. 2-13202 rev.   PR2339.S5A16

15286   SEMPILL.   Archaeological and historical collections relating to the county of Renfrew ...
Parish of Lochwinnoch.   Paisley, A. Gardner, 1885-90.   2 v. col. front. (v.1) 28 pl. (part col. and fold.) 30 cm.
The Latin documents are followed by English translations and abstracts. "290 copies printed, of which this is no. 33." The frontispiece is the
Sempill arms. By Sir Eustace Herbert Maxwell, bart. Contents. - I. Crawfurd's description of the county, 1710. Account of the Sempill family,
comp. by the late Dr. Crawfurd of Johnshill. Charters and other documents relating to the parish of Lochwinnoch and the house of Sempill. -
II. (Continuation of charters, &c.) Rental of Lord Semple, 1644. Poll tax roll of the parish of Lochwinnoch, 1695.   DA880.R4A6
22-18042.

SEMPILL.   See also SEMPLE.

15287   SEMPLE.   Genealogical history of the family Semple from 1214 to 1888.   Compiled and
arranged by William Alexander Semple ... Hartford, Conn., Press of the Case, Lockwood & Brainard
company, 1888.   59, (1) p. col. front. (coat of arms) 23 cm. Blank pages at end for memoranda. 9-13656.
CS71.S473   1888

SEMPLE.   See also: ROBINSON, 1900
                      SEMPILL.

15288   SENÉCAL.   Généalogie de la famille Senécal par l'abbé G. A. Dejordy.   St. Hyacinthe,
L'Impr. "Du Courrier," 1909.   cover-title, 22 p. 17 cm. 11-30424.   CS90.S5

SENÉCAL.   See also CHOQUETTE, F1054.R5D3

SENASAC.   See SENESAC.

SENER.   See SEHNER.

15289   SENGLAUB.   Descendants and families of the Senglaub genealogy.   Compiled, edited (and)
rev. by Mrs. O. W. Senglaub.   Milwaukee, 1962.   38, 8 l. 28 cm. 65-51581.   CS71.S477   1962

15290   SENESAC.   Genealogy: Napoleon Senésac family.   By Arthur Thomas Senasac.   (San Francisco, 1968)   28 l. ports. (part col.) 29 cm. Title from label on cover. 73-5977 MARC.
CS71.S475   1968

SENHOUSE. See PITMAN, 1920

SENN. See LONG, 1956

15291 SENSEMAN. (Senseman family tree) Drawn by C. M. Senseman. New York city (1915)
geneal. tab. 16 x 22 cm. 16-6850.   CS71.S48   1915

SENSENEY. See SENSENIG.

SENSENICH. See SENSENIG.

15292 SENSENIG. The "Sensineys" of America: Senseny, Sensenig, Sensenich, Senseney, compiled by Barton Sensenig, collaborating with R. Eugene (Sensenig) Montgomery, Dr. Roscoe Lloyd
Sensenich, Jeannette Senseney, and others. Philadelphia, Pa. (Printed by Lyon & Armor, inc.) 1943.
vi, 7-159 p. plates, ports. 23½ cm. 43-7283.   CS71.S482   1943

15293 SENTER. ... The journal of Isaac Senter, physician and surgeon to the troops detached from
the American army encamped at Cambridge, Mass., on a secret expedition against Quebec, under the
command of Col. Benedict Arnold, in September, 1775. Philadelphia, The Historical society of
Pennsylvania, 1846. Tarrytown, N.Y., Reprinted, W. Abbatt, 1915. 1 p. l., ii, 60 p. front. (port.)
facsim. 26½ cm. (The Magazine of history with notes and queries. Extra number. 42 (pt. 1) At head of title: As near a fac-simile as
possible. 15-26804.   E173.M24 no. 42

15294 SERAPHIM. Baltische Schicksale, im Spiegel der Geschichte einer kurländischen Familie,
1756 bis 1919. By Ernst Seraphim. Berlin, Verlag Grenze und Ausland, 1935. 256 p. illus. (part col.)
facsim. 25cm. 49-34286*   CS887.S47   1935

SERGEANT. See SARGENT.

SERGEANT. See WARDWELL.

SERING. See SYRON.

15295 SERJEANTSON. The Serjeantsons of Hanlith, by Rev. R. M. Serjeantson ... illustrated by
R. J. Serjeantson and T. Shepard. (Northampton, Eng., Mark, printer, 1908?) cover-title, 34 p., 1 l.,
(35)-95 p. illus. (incl. coats of arms) plates, ports., fold. geneal. tab. 26 cm. In 2 parts. Contents. - pt. I. Early references to the
Serjeantsons of Hanlith and Malham. - pt. II. The Serjeantsons of Hanlith, Wakefield and Camphill. 16-23500.   CS439.S34

15296 SERRELL. (Ancestors and descendants of William Serrell and Ann Boorn, compiled by
Lemuel W. Serrell. n. p., 1888) geneal. tab. 42 x 37 cm. 18-8387.
                                                                     CS71.S485   1888

15297 SERRELL. Serrell family history. By Alice Dorothy Serrell. Rochester, Mich., 1933.
geneal. table. 40 x 59 cm. Manuscript. 53-51309.   CS71.S485   1933

15298 SERVEN. The Serven family in America, compiled by A. R. Serven. (Washington, D. C.)
1933. 39 p. front. (port.) 26½ cm. 33-15351.   CS71.S49   1933

SERVEN. See also COLE, 1876

15299 SERVOS. The United empire loyalists of Canada, illustrated by memorials of the Servos
family. By William Kirby ... Toronto, W. Briggs, 1884. 20 p. 22½ cm. Reprinted from "The Canadian Methodist
magazine." 25-5902.   F1058.K57

15300 SERVOS. ... Family history ...(Niagara, Ont.) 1901. 1 p. l., 46 p. 2 port. 21 cm. (Niagara
historical society. (Publications) no. 8) Contents. - The Servos family, by Wm. Kirby. - The Whitmore family, by Wm. Kirby. - The Jarvis
letters, by Miss M. A. Fitz Gibbon. - Robert Land, U. E. loyalist, by J. H. Land. 14-20019. F1059.N5N52 no. 8

SERVEN. See BLAUVELT, 1957

SESENY.   See SENSENIG.

15301   SESSIONS.   Materials for a history of the Sessions family in America, the descendants of Alexander Sessions of Andover, Mass., 1669.   Gathered by Francis C. Sessions.   Albany, N.Y., Munsell's sons, 1890.   1 p. l., 252 p. front., plates, ports., geneal. tables. 21 x 17½ cm. 9-13653.

CS71.S493   1890

15302   SESSIONS.   The settlement of Ionia, Mich., by Samuel Dexter, with a history of the Sessions family of the branch of Alonzo Sessions and Celia Dexter Sessions.   (Sioux Falls, S.D., Sessions-Mannix printing co., 1914)   (41) p. illus. (ports.) 22 cm. On cover: Sessions-Dexter family history. 1914. Blank leaves at end for additions. 37-21337.

CS71.S493   1914

SESSIONS.   See also ATKINSON, 1933

SESSOMS.   See BRYANT, 1968

15303   SETÄLÄ.   E. N. Setälän suku; Heikki Sonnista E. N. Setälän lasten-lasten lapsiin asti, 1455-1962.   Matrikkelin toimittanut Salme Setälä.   (Helsingissä) Kokemäen Setälät (1964)   63 p. geneal. tables. 21 cm. Cover title. 76-382392.

CS885.S4   1964

15304   SETON.   The history of the house of Seytoun to the year M.D.LIX.   By Richard Maitland. With the continuation, by Alexander viscount Kingston, to M.DC.LXXXVII.   Glasgow, 1829. xi, 132 p. illus., ports. 27 cm. (Maitland Club (Glasgow. Publications) 1) "75 copies printed for the Maitland Club. Printed also for the Bannantyne Club." - Lowndes. Bibl. man. (App.) "Printed from two manuscripts in the Library of the Faculty of Advocates." - Pref. "Collections upon the life of Alexander Seaton, Dominican freir, confessor to King James the Fifth," by R. Wodrow: p. (113)-128. 4-11238 rev*

DA750.M3 no.1

15305   SETON.   The genealogy of the house and surname of Setoun, by Sir Richard Maitland of Ledington, knight.   With the chronicle of the house of Setoun, compiled in metre by John Kamington, alias Peter Manye. &c. &c.   Edinburgh (W. Aitken, printer) 1830.   xiii, 64 p. front. (port.) pl., facsim., geneal. tab. 27 cm. "The text of this volume is printed from a manuscript in the possession of Mr. Hay of Drummelzier ... It seems to have been written (i.e. copied) by George, third earl of Wintoun ... In numberless instances it differs from the pedigree lately printed, (History of the house of Seytoun ... by Sir Richard Maitland, published 1829, by the Maitland club) and contains various notices, which Sir Richard Maitland, or Lord Kingston, thought proper afterwards to omit." - Pref. 4-11237.

CS479.S5

15306   SETON.   Memoir of Alexander Seton, earl of Dunfermline, president of the Court of session, and chancellor of Scotland, with an appendix containing a list of the various presidents of the Court and genealogical tables of the legal families of Erskine, Hope, Dalrymple, and Dundas; by George Seton ... Edinburgh and London, W. Blackwood and sons, 1882.   xiv, 217 p. front., plates, port. group, facsim., fold. geneal. tables. 23½ cm. 14-21072.

DA803.2.D8S4

15307   SETON.   Seton of Parbroath, in Scotland and America, printed for private circulation ... New York (Jersey City, Press of Wm. Pairson) 1890.   28 p. 20 cm. Preface signed "R.S." i.e. Robert Seton. 3-2818.

CS71.S495   1890

15308   SETON.   A history of the family of Seton during eight centuries, by George Seton, advocate ... Edinburgh, Priv. print. by T. and A. Constable, 1896.   2 v. fronts., illus., plates, ports., col. coats of arms, geneal. tables. 29 cm. Title vignette: coat of arms. "Impression 212 copies all numbered, and of which nos. 1 to 12 are on large paper." This copy no. 76. 14-9009.

CS479.S45

15309   SETON.   An old family, or The Setons of Scotland and America, by Monsignor Seton ... New York, Brentano's, 1899.   xxiii, 438 p. front., illus., plates, col. pl. (coat of arms) ports., facsim. 23½ cm. 5-19073.

CS71.S495   1899

15310   SETON.   The life story of Mother Seton, by Louise Malloy.   (Baltimore, Carroll publishing co., c.1924)   29 p. illus. (port.) 19½ cm. 24-23076.

BX4705.S57M3

15311   SETON.   Fyvie castle, its lairds and their times, by A.M.W. Stirling ... London, J. Murray (1928)   xvi, 426 p. front., 1 illus., plates, ports. 22½ cm. 36-11473.

DA890.F9S7

SETON.   See also: PRINGLE, 1847
                      SEATON.

SEVER.   See SEAVER.

15312   SEVERANCE.   The Severans genealogical history, comp. by Rev. John F. Severance ...
Chicago, R. R. Donnelley & sons company, 1893.   xix, 78 p. 1 l., 2-58 p. incl. front. (port.) 24 cm.   "The Seaverns
genealogical history ... Huntington, Ind., Printed for the author, 1893": 58 p.   3-17747.   CS71.S498   1893

15313   SEVERANCE.   The Severance genealogy; the Benjamin, Charles, and Lewis lines of the
seventh generation, compiled by Henry Ormal Severance ... Columbia, Mo., Lucas brothers, 1927.
29 p. 22½ cm.   "This edition is limited to 100 copies of which this is number 41." 27-19110.   CS71.S498   1927

SEVERANS.   See SEVERANCE.

SEVERIT.   See SAVERY.

SEVERNS.   See: COLLORD, 18 -
                   SEVERANCE, 1893

15314   SEVERSMITH.   Colonial families of Long island, New York and Connecticut, being the ancestry & kindred of Herbert Furman Seversmith ... By Herbert Furman Seversmith ... (Los Angeles,
1944 -   v. 28½ x 23 cm.   "Twenty-five mimeographed copies, of which this is number 9." 46-21031.
                                                          CS71.S499   1944

SEVERSMITH.   See also COLLIER, 1947

SEVERY.   See SAVERY.

15315   SEVIER.   Sevier family history, with the collected letters of Gen. John Sevier, first Governor
of Tennessee, and 28 collateral family lineages, by Cora Bales Sevier and Nancy S. Madden.   Washington, 1961.   xvi, 558 p. illus., ports., maps, col. coats of arms, facsims. 29 cm. Bibliography: p. 540-544. 61-36667.
                                                          CS71.S492   1961

15316   SEVIER.   The Sevier family.   By Zella Armstrong.   Chattanooga, Lookout Pub. Co., 1926.
(16), 325 p. port. 24 cm. (Her Notable southern families, v. 4) Bibliography: 13th prelim. page. 26-5305 rev.*   See also vol. 1
                                                          CS61.A6 vol. 4

SÉVIGNÉ.   See DU BOISBAUDRY, 1958

15317   SEWALL.   Pedigree of Sewall.   (Principally compiled from materials furnished by the Rev.
Samuel Sewall of Burlington, Mass.) (n. p., 185-)   geneal. tab. 32 x 48 cm. 2-8911.
                                                          CS71.S513   185-

15318   SEWALL.   Diary of Samuel Sewall.   1674-1729.   v. 1 (-3) (In Collections of the Massachusetts historical society.   Boston, 1878-82.   24½ cm.   Ser. 5, v. 5-7)   "Genealogy of the Sewall family.
and those allied to it": v. 1 (v. 5 of ser.), p. xi)-xl. 10-12994.   F61.M41 ser. 5, vols. 5-7
       —— Copy 2.   Separate   F67.S45

15319   SEWALL.   Thomas Sewall; some of his ancestors and all of his descenants: a genealogy (by)
Henry Sewall Webster.   Gardiner, Me., 1904.   20 p. 23 cm. 5-3002.   CS71.S513   1904

15320   SEWALL.   The Sewells of the isle of Wight, with an account of some of the families connected
with them by marriage, by Mountague Charles Owen.   (Manchester, Eng., Machester Courier ltd.,
printers, 1906)   xvi, 188, (1) p. front., plates, ports., fold. geneal. tab. 23½ cm. "Printed for private circulation." 12-29769.
                                                          CS439.S36

15321   SEWALL.   The Sewells in the new world.   By Sir Hector L. Duff ... Exeter, W. Pollard &
co., ltd., 1924.   x, 122 p. front., illus. (coats of arms) ports., fold. geneal. tab. 23 cm. "The house of Livingston": p. 106-122.
25-1231 rev.   CS90.S55

15322   SEWALL.   The genealogy, with historical and personal comments, of the known descendants of Col. Benjamin Seawell, sr., and Lucy Hicks, compiled and arranged by a great grandson, Ben Lee Seawell.   South Pasadena, Calif.   (Printed by L. C. Mock) 1935.   1 p. 1., 139, (1) p. front. (coat of arms) illus., (incl. ports.)   23 cm.   36-761.   CS71.S513   1935

15323   SEWALL.   History of the Sewell families in America; narrative and statistics compiled after many years of careful research.   By Worley Levi Sewell.   (Palm Beach? Fla.) 1955.   198 p. illus., map, facsims.   24 cm.   55-12690.   CS71.S513   1955

15324   SEWALL.   One Sewell family.   By Roy Brown Sewell.   (Atlanta, 1960)   xiv, 94 p. illus., ports., coat of arms.   24 cm.   61-22907.   CS71.S513   1960

SEWALL.   See also: DUMMER, LD7501.S72D6   KAUFMAN, 1892
                      ELLIS, F3.T61   MAJOR, 1915
                      HUNTER, 1942   SALISBURY, 1885
                      HUNTER, 1944

15325   SEWARD.   The Seaward and Seward families of the United States.   By Alvin Seaward Van Benthuysen.   Brooklyn (1947)   x, 304 1.   29 cm.   Typewritten (carbon copy)   49-22657*.
                                                                      CS71.S515   1947

15326   SEWARD.   Obadiah Seward of Long Island, New York, and his descendants.   By Frederick Whittlesey Seward; arr. and ed. by Marjorie Seward Cleveland.   (Goshen, N.Y., 1949, c.1948)   vi, 288 p. illus., ports., coat of arms.   24 cm.   49-22975*.   CS71.S515   1949

15327   SEWARD.   (Genealogical data relating to descendants of Ebenezer Seward, copied from family records written in a copy of the 4th ed. of I. D. Williamson's An argument for the truth of Christianity, in a series of discourses, 1844, known as "Ebenezer Seaward, his book."   With photocopies of affidavits, records, etc., and the Mayflower ancestry of the Goss and Seward (Seward) families, by Paul Henry Goss.   n.p., 195-)   1 v.   29 cm.   55-58671.   CS71.S515

SEWARD.   See also: FRENCH, 1812
                      GOSS, 1950
                      HOLTON, 1881
                      VAN BENTHUYSEN, 1926

SEWELL.   See SEWALL.

SEWI.   See SEAVEY.

SEWY.   See SEAVEY.

SEX.   See KING, CS439.K7

SEXTON.   See: ARCHDALE, 1925
                 BASSETT, 1926

SEYBOLT.   See KETCHAM, 1954

SEYDENER.   See SEIDNER.

SEYDNER.   See SEIDNER.

SEYDNOR.   See SEIDNER.

SEYMOR.   See SEYMOUR.

15328   SEYMOUR.   Genealogy of the descendants of Richard Seymour from the first settlement of Hartford, Ct., in 1635. Brockport, N.Y., Democrat steam print, 1880.   15 1.   16 cm.   Part of leaves printed on both sides.   Interspersed with blank leaves.   Title from Springfield Pub. Libr.   A33-1307.

15329   SEYMOUR.   The Seymour family.   By Tyler Seymour Morris.   A reprint from the Morris genealogy.   Chicago, 1900.   1 p. l., 147-181 p. 23½ cm. 2-22613.   CS71.S52   1900

15330   SEYMOUR.   Annals of the Seymours, by H. St. Maur, being a history of the Seymour family, from early times to within a few years of the present.   London, K. Paul, Trench, Trübner & co., ltd., 1902.   xii, 534 p. front., pl., port., fold. geneal. tab. 25½ cm. Title in red and black; title vign. (port.) Appendix D: The honourable entertainment given to the Queen's Majesty in progress, at Elvetham, Hampshire, by the Right Honourable the Earl of Hertford. 1591: p. 462-476.   2-28512.   DA306.S4S3

15331   SEYMOUR.   Richard Seymour, Hartford, 1640; a paper read before the Connecticut chapter, Daughters of founders and patriots of America, at Norwalk, Conn., February 13th, 1903, by Mrs. Maria Watson Pinney ... (New Haven, The Tuttle, Morehouse & Taylor press, 1903?)   34 p. front., plates. 23½ cm. 4-13409.   CS71.S52   1903

15332   SEYMOUR.   Arms and pedigree of Seymour of Payson, Illinois, showing descent from Edward, duke of Somerset, lord protector of England (1547), and Sir William de St. Maur, of Woundy and Penhow, Monmouthshire (1240)   Compiled with proofs and references to authorities from the results of re-searches made by the Genealogical department of the Grafton press and published in the year 1906.   N. Y., Grafton press, 1906.   31 p. col. pl. (coat of arms) 30 cm. "Authorities": p. (25)-31. 6-42440.   CS71.S52   1906

15333   SEYMOUR.   The Seymour family, history and romance, by A. Audrey Locke ... London, Constable and company, ltd., 1911.   viii, 386 p. front., ports. 21½ cm. 11-29854.
DA28.35.S5L7

15334   SEYMOUR.   A record of the Seymour family in the revolution.   (Litchfield? Conn., 1912)   40 p. 2 port. (incl. front.) 30½ cm. Preface signed: Morris Woodruff Seymour.   "This is no. 65 of a limited edition of two hundred and fifty copies." 12-8148.   CS71.S52   1912

15335   SEYMOUR.   Extract from "Collin's Peerage of England, " (edition of 1762) written by then head of the family, Edward Seymour, ninth duke of Somerset, and printed in London.   (New York, Printed by D. Seymour, press of R. T. Voss, 1913)   1 p. l., 139-182 p. 23½ cm. Half-title. Caption and running title: Seymour, duke of Somerset. The descendants of Richard who came to America in 1639 and settled at Hartford, Conn.: p. 182. 13-8478.
CS439.S38

15336   SEYMOUR.   The English home and ancestry of Richard Seamer or Semer of Hartford, Conn., progenitor of the Seymours of Connecticut and New York.   Communicated to the New England historical and genealogical register by George D. Seymour from researches by J. Gardner Bartlett.   Boston (Stanhope press, F. H. Gilson company) 1917.   12 p. 27 cm. "Reprinted from the New England historical and genealogical register, for April, 1917." 17-30091.   CS71.S52   1917

15337   SEYMOUR.   Richard Seymour of Hartford and Norwalk, Conn., and some of his descendants, communicated by Seymour Morris ... (Boston, 1918)   15 p. 25 cm. Caption title. Reprint from the New England historical and genealogical register for July 1918. 19-2007.   CS71.S52   1918

15338   SEYMOUR.   Seymour family, Seamer, Seamor, Seemer, Seemor, Semor, Semer, Seymore, Seamore.   (Compiled by Jennie E. Seymour Hammond and J. Boyd) (West Hartford? Conn., 1931)   v. fold. geneal. tables. 29 cm. Type-written, and photostat reproductions of manuscript genealogical charts. The charts A, B, C, D, and accompanying genealogies, partially outline the families of Richard Seymour and his four sons, Thomas, John, Zachariah and Richard to the ninth generation. Preliminary matter including "Authorities" (7 l.) repeated in each volume. The L. C. has a separately issued set of the charts under title "Partial outline of the Seymour family". 31-19481.   CS71.S52   1931

15339   SEYMOUR.   A history of the Seymour family; descendants of Richard Seymour of Hartford, Connecticut, for six generations; with extensive amplification of the lines deriving from his son John Seymour of Hartford, compiled and arranged for publication under the direction of George Dudley Seymour, by Donald Lines Jacobus, based primarily on the manuscript collections of Mary Kingsbury Talcott and of Seymour Morris, which the author has augmented with an introduction, various memora-bilia and appendices, and a picture gallery of Seymour family portraits, houses, seals, chests and family memorials.   New Haven, Conn. (Printed by the Tuttle, Morehouse & Taylor company) 1939.   xiv p., 1 l., 662, (8) p. front., illus. (incl. ports., facsim., coat of arms) 25 cm. Blank pages for "Family notes" (8 at end) "Bibliography, Seymour family": p. (547)-548. "Bibliography of George Dudley Seymour": p. (578)-582. 39-20810.   CS71.S52   1939

15340   SEYMOUR.   The naughty Seymours: companions in folly and caprice, by Bernard Falk ... with a special note on Sir Richard Wallace, who inherited the fortune of Richard Seymour-Conway, 4th marquis of Hertford.   London and Melbourne, Hutchinson & co., ltd.   (1940)   278 p. front., plates, ports., facsim. 24 cm.   "Erratum" slip inserted.   " 'The naughty Seymours' may fittingly be described as a companion volume to 'Old Q's daughter,' published in 1937." - Foreword, p. 19.   41-12941.   DA28.35.S5F25

SEYMOUR.   See also: FLAGG, 1903   MORRIS, 1894
                         GRISWOLD, 1898   STAWELL, 1910
                         HALL, 1943a   TUCKER, 1901
                         HIGHBAUGH, 1961   TYLER, 1912b
                         KING, 1956

SEYTOUN.   See SETON.

15341   SFORZA.   The story of the Sforzas, by L. Collison-Morley ... London, G. Routledge & sons, limited, 1933.   xii, 312 p. front., plates, ports., map. 22½ cm. Bibliography: p. 305-308. 34-1540.   DG463.8.S4C6

15342   SHACKELFORD.   The Shackelford family, its English and American origins, and some of its branches, by Robert B. Shackelford ... Charlottesville, Va., Jarman's incorporated, printers, 1940. 84 p. incl. front., illus. (incl. ports.) 23½ cm. 40-7957.   CS71.S523   1940

15343   SHACKELFORD.   George Shackelford and Annette Jeter and their descendants; editor-in-chief, Edward Madison Shackelford ... and assistant editor, Franklin Shackelford Moseley ... Montgomery, Ala., The Paragon press, 1941.   3 p. 1., 11-132, (4) p. front., illus. (incl. ports.) 21 cm. "The Shackelford family association": p. 107-120. 41-12300.   CS71.S523   1941

SHACKELFORD.   See also BATEMAN, 1952

SHADDOCK.   See GRAY, 1938

SCHAEFFER.   See GRIM, 1934

15344   SHAFER.   ... A rebel of '61.   By Jos, R. Stonebraker ... New York and Albany, Wynkoop, Hallenbeck, Crawford co., printers, 1899.   116 p. front., illus. (facsims.) plates, ports., fold. geneal. tab. 23½ cm. 99-3416.   E605.S88

15345   SHAFER.   Memoirs and reminiscences, together with sketches of the early history of Sussex county, New Jersey, by Rev. Casper Schaeffer, M. D.   With notes and genealogical record of the Schaeffer, Shaver or Shafer family, compiled by William M. Johnson.   Hackensack, N. J., Priv. print., 1907.   187 p. front. (port.) plates. 25 cm. "Two hundred and fifty copies printed." 8-10855.   F149.S8S2

15346   SHAFER.   Ancestors of Jacob Shaffer and his wife Cordelia Hunt, showing descent from Leete, Ketcham, Benton, Brewer, Conkling, Brush, Platt, Whitehead, Wood and other pioneer families, and through the Chaunceys, from many of the royal families of Europe, compiled by Josephine C. Frost (Mrs. Samuel Knapp Frost) ... (New York?) 1927.   83 p. fold. geneal. tab. 23½ cm. Half-title: Shaffer-Hunt genealogy. "Only fifty copies of this book have been printed." 28-1173.   CS71.S525   1927

15347   SHAFER.   The genealogical history of Jacob Shafer, memorial album, comp. by Agnes Hodgins Tolbert, Edith Shaffer Hodgins and Ruth Myers Goppert.   Arr. and rev. by Agnes Hodgins Tolbert.   Belleville, Kan., Telescope Pub. Co. (1947)   43 p. illus., ports., geneal. tables. 26 x 45 cm. 48-13523*
CS71.S525   1947

15348   SHAFER.   Shafer-Huston family history.   By Francis Merton Marvin.   (Bartonsville? Pa.) 1951 (i.e. 1952)   471 p. illus. 23 cm. 52-36937.   CS71.S525   1952

15349   SHAFER.   Genealogical data concerning the ancestors and descendants of John Jacob Shaffer, 1763-1816, of Mercersburg, Franklin County, Pennsylvania.   With supplementary data on the Lesch, Kopp, Reiss, and Krafft families of Heidelberg and Tulpehocken townships, Berks County, Pennsylvania. By Mr. and Mrs. A. Nello Shaffer and Frederick S. Weiser.   Gettysburg, Pa., Priv. print., 1958. 39 p. ports., map. 23 cm. 59-508.   CS71.S525   1958

SHAFER.   See also: CHAMBERS, F142.M7M38
GERNHARDT, 1904
GRIM, 1934

SHAFFER.   See: NESTER, 1963
SHAFER.
WALTMAN, 1928

15350   SHAFFNER.   Notes on the Shaffner family.   (n. p., 18 -)   p. 5-7   24 cm.   40M61T.

CS71.S526   18 -

SHAFFNER.   See also SCHAFFNER.

SHAIKH.   See Maulana Azad Abul Kalam.   (In main catalog)

15351   SHAKESPEARE.   Shakespeare's home at New Place, Stratford-upon-Avon.   Being a history of the "Great house" built in the reign of King Henry VII., by Sir Hugh Clopton, knight, and subsequently the property of William Shakespere, gent., wherein he lived and died.   By J. C. M. Bellew.   London, Virtue brothers and co., 1863.   xv, (1), 380 (i.e. 382) p.   front., plates, 7 geneal. tab. (6 fold.)   19½ cm.   Genealogical tables of the Shakespeare, Arden, Clopton, Combe, Underhill, Hales, Nash, Forster, and Hathaway families.   17-21215.   PR2916.B3

15352   SHAKESPEARE.   History of William Shakespeare, player and poet; with new facts and traditions.   By S. W. Fullom ... 2d ed.   London, Saunders, Otley and co., 1864.   vii, 372 p.   21 cm.
16-20860.   PR2894.F8   1864

15353   SHAKESPEARE.   Original memoirs and historical accounts of the families of Shakespeare and Hart, deduced from an early period, and continued down to this present year 1790.   By John Jordan ... With drawings of their dwelling houses, and coats of arms.   Now first printed, A. D. 1865.   London, Printed by T. Richards 1865.   vii, 84 p.   20½ x 17 cm.   Preface signed: J. O. Halliwell.   Ms. note (signed: J. O. H.) :   Ten copies only.   Number three.   Without drawings.   17-17946,   PR2901.J7

15354   SHAKESPEARE.   Shakespeareana genealogica.   Part I. Identification of the dramatis personae in Shakspeare's historical plays: from K. John to K. Henry VIII.   Notes on characters in Macbeth and Hamlet.   Persons and places belonging to Warwickshire, alluded to in several plays.   Part II. The Shakspeare and Arden families, and their connections: with tables of descent.   Comp. by George Russell French ... London and Cambridge, Macmillan and co., 1869.   xiii, (1), 590 p.   illus., geneal. tables (part fold.)   22½ cm.   10-4339.   PR2901.F7

15355   SHAKESPEARE.   The gentle Shakspere: a vindication.   By John Pym Yeatman ... London, The Roxburghe press; (etc., etc., 1896)   1 p. 1., xi, 317, (12) p., 1 1.   27 cm.   Title in green.   Contains chapters on the Arden family; the Blunts of Kiddermeister; the Griffin family, with pedigree.   3-7770.   PR2894.Y4

15356   SHAKESPEARE.   Shakespeare's family; being a record of the ancestors and descendants of William Shakespeare, with some account of the Ardens, by Mrs. C. C. Stopes ... London, E. Stock; New York, J. Pott & company, 1901.   vii p., 2 1., 257 p.   front. (port.) illus., pl., fold. map.   23½ cm.   2-14913.   PR2901.S7

15357   SHAKESPEARE.   Shakespeare's "American Descendants".   By Milton Rubincam.   In vertical file.   Ask reference librarian for this material.

SHAKESPEARE.   See also HALLEN, CS439.H26

SHALER.   See KIRKPATRICK, 1911

15358   SHALLCROSS.   A brief lineage of the very ancient family and surname of Shallcross, or Shawcross, of that manor, in the High Peak, co. Derby; illustrating to the memory of posterity, the connection of that house with equestrian, noble, and royal families; attempted, MDCCCXCVI., incompletely, by a scion of the family.   Evesham, Knapton and Mayer, 1896.   43 numb. 1. incl. illus., pl., coats of arms, facsims. front.   23 cm.   Printed on one side of leaf only.   Half-title: A brief of a lineage, etc., by William Henry Shawcross, vicar of Bretforton.   "A descent from Edward I, king of England": p. 17.   16-2832.   CS439.S39

15359   SHALLCROSS.   Shallcross pedigrees.   Ed. by the Rev. W. H. Shawcross, alias Shalcrosse ... Assisted by William Gilbert ... The index by Miss Muriel Wilson ... Hemsworth, C. E. Turner, 1908.   18, xii-ccvi numb. 1. plates, ports. 33½ cm. Printed on one side of leaf only. "200 copies only of this work have been printed and the type ... distributed." - Pref. 20-19564.   CS439.S39   1908

SHALLY.   See SHELLEY.

15360   SHAMBACH.   My ancestors and genealogical history of the Shambach family, by LeRoy F. Shambach. (Middleburg, Pa., 1968)   xxi, 282 p. illus., ports. 24 cm. 68-6675.   CS71.S527   1968

SHANDY.   See RANDLEMAN, 1965

15361   SHANK.   Genealogical diagram, dedicatory to the lineal descendants of Adam Shank, through his son Henry to the fourth generation, compiled by John Longenecker.   Wilmot, O., 1908.   geneal. tab. 28 x 35 cm. 25-7736.   CS71.S5275   1908

15362   SHANK.   Genealogy of John Shank, Ariaen Degoede, Elijah Teague, and Thomas Swann.   By Henry Mercer Shank. (Denver, 1960)   82, (12) p. illus. 28 cm. 60-16334.   CS71.S5275   1960

15363   SHANKS.   Ancestry of James Shanks of Huron County, Ohio.   By Harry Stanley Blaine.   Toledo, Mimeographed by G. A. Blaine, 1951.   60, xi p. ports., map, geneal. table. 29 cm. 52-34237.   CS71.S5277   1951

15364   SHANNON.   Shannon genealogy; genealogical record and memorials of one branch of the Shannon family in America; compiled by George E. Hodgdon.   Rochester, N. Y. (The Genesee press) 1905.   2 p. 1., (ix)-xxxi, 578 p. front. (port.) illus. (incl. ports., facsims.) fold. geneal. tables, double facsim. 28½ cm. Prefatory note by R. C. Shannon. "Number 150 of an edition of three hundred copies printed for private distribution only." 5-27412.   CS71.S528   1905

SHANNON.   See also: BOYLE, 1734
DODDRIDGE, 1961
SILL, 1942
SMITH, 1889a

15365   SHAPLEIGH.   The descendants of Alexander Shapleigh the immigrant; a series of historical papers and records.   By Hannah Chandler Shapleigh Tibbetts.   With introd. and supplementary material by Frederick E. Shapleigh.   Kittery, Me., Shapleigh Family Association, 1968.   xvi, 96 p. illus., col. coat of arms, maps, ports. 23 cm. "Presented at the annual meetings of the (Shapleigh Family) Association during the years 1910-1925." 68-57221.   CS71.S529   1968

15366   SHARP.   Records of the Sharpe family in England and America from 1580 to 1870.   By W. C. Sharpe.   Seymour, Ct., W. C. Sharpe, 1874.   27 p. 17 cm. 9-13652.   CS71.S53   1874

15367   SHARP.   A royal descent; with other pedigrees and memorials.   Compiled by Thomasin Elizabeth Sharpe.   London, Mitchell and Hughes, printers, 1875.   x p., 1 l., 135 p. 33 x 26 cm. One hundred copies ... printed." Includes the direct descents of every member and branch of the author's family. cf. Pref. 16-8329.   CS439.S395   1875

15368   SHARP.   Sharpe genealogy and miscellany.   By W. C. Sharpe ... Seymour, Conn., Record print, 1880.   178 p. front. (coat of arms) ports., facsim. 17 cm. 9-13651.   CS71.S53   1880

15369   SHARP.   Life and correspondence of Abraham Sharp, the Yorkshire mathematician and astronomer, and assistant of Flamsteed; with memorials of his family, and associated families.   By William Cudworth ... London, S. Low, Marston, Searle & Rivington, ltd.; (etc., etc.) 1889.   xvi, 342 p. front., illus. (incl. diagrs.) 2 pl., 2 ports., facsims., tables (part fold.) 25½ x 19½ cm. "Memorials of the Sharp family and associated families": p. (217)-311. 4-2794.   QB36.S5C9

15370   SHARP.   The Sharpes.   no. 1-32. (By William Carvosso Sharpe.   Seymour, Conn., Printed by the author) 1893-96.   212 p. illus. (ports. and coat of arms) ports. 22½ cm. Caption title. Pub. monthly as a supplement to his Sharpe genealogy and miscellany ... Seymour, Ct., 1880. No more published. 9-13647.   CS71.S53   1893

15371   SHARP.   ... The Sharp papers in the Brookline public library.   (Brookline, Mass., 1895)
(7)-14 p.   21 cm.   (Brookline historical publication society.   Publications.   (1st ser.) no. 2)   Caption title.   6-9036.
F74. B9B8 vol. 1

15372   SHARP.   The Sharpe family.   With royal and other descents.   Compiled by Thomasin
Elizabeth Sharpe.   (London) Priv. print., E. Stock, 1901.   iv p., 1 l., 58 p.   front.   (coat of arms) geneal. tab.
26 cm.   40-16318.   CS439. S395   1901

15373   SHARP.   The Sharps of Chester County, Pennsylvania, and abstracts of records in Great
Britain.   By William Carvosso Sharpe.   Seymour, Conn., W. C. Sharpe, 1903.   36 p.   22½ cm.   5-4107.
CS71. S53   1903

15374   SHARP.   A royal descent; with other pedigrees and memorials, by Thomasin Elizabeth
Sharpe.   Reprinted and corrected.   London, Mitchell, Hughes and Clarke, 1904.   x p., 1 l., 129 p. incl.
double geneal. tab.   31½ cm.   Includes the direct descents of every member and branch of the author's family.   cf. Pref. of 1st ed.   40-16317.
CS439. S395   1904

15375   SHARP.   James Sharp and his descendents.   Compiled by M. E. Barnes, M. D., the Rev. J. A.
Barnes, D. D.   Greenville, O., 1927.   1 p. 1., 13 numb. 1.   30 cm.   Autographed from type-written copy.   With this is bound
the authors' James Hutchison and his descendants ... Greenville, O., 1927.   L. C. COPY REPLACED BY MICROFILM.   28-8058.
CS71. S53   1927
Microfilm 8746 CS

15376   SHARP.   A contribution towards the early history of the Sharp family of Burlington county,
New Jersey, by Milton Rubincam ... (Newark? N. J., 1940?)   cover-title, p. (8)-14.   23 cm.   "Reprinted from the
Genealogical magazine of New Jersey, issue of January, 1940."   Bibliographical foot-notes.   41-10332.   CS71. S53   1940

15377   SHARP.   The Sharp family of New Jersey, with Mather and Mattison connections.   By Benjamin
Mather Powers.   Kansas City, Mo., Pub. for the author by Brown-White-Lowell Press, 1948.
47 p.   21 cm.   48-21602 *.   CS71. S53   1948

15378   SHARP.   Know your relatives: the Sharps, Gibbs, Graves, Efland, Albright, Loy, Miller,
Snodderly, Tillman, and other related families.   By Genevieve Elizabeth (Cummings) Peters.   (Arlington? Va.) 1953.   169 p.   28 cm.   58-49595.   CS71. S53   1953

15379   SHARP.   Robert and Grizella (McCormick) Sharp and their descendants.   John and Margaret
(Finley) Hutchison and their descendants, compiled by Milford E. Barnes and Andrew Wallace Barnes.
Iowa City, Iowa, 1965.   60 p.   28 cm.   Includes bibliographies.   66-48762.   CS71. S53   1965

SHARP.   See also: BELL, 1951   GENTRY, 1909
                        BELL, 1959   HAYNES, 1902
                        BELL, 1967   RICHARDSON, DA90. B7H6
                        CALHOUN, 1957   WETHERELL, 1902
                        CARTER, 1940   No. 430 - Adventurers of purse and person.
                        DAVIS, 1939

SHARPE.   See SHARP.

SHARPLES.   See SHARPLESS.

15380   SHARPLESS.   Family record; containing the settlement, and genealogy to the present time,
of the Sharples family, in North America.   Wtih an appendix, containing memorials of the dying
sayings, &c., of several deceased members of the family; not before published.   By Joseph Sharpless.
Philadelphia: Published and sold by the author, no. 30, Arch street.   1816.   2 p. 1., (3)-88, (4), (89)-132 p.
17½ cm.   "Appendix: containing memorials of several deceased members of the family", with separate t. -p.: p. (89)-132.
CS71. S532   1816

15381   SHARPLESS.   Genealogy of the Sharpless family, descended from John and Jane Sharples,
settlers near Chester, Pennsylvania, 1682: together with some account of the English ancestry of the
family, including the results of researches by Henry Fishwick, F. H. S., and the late Joseph Lemuel

GENEALOGIES IN THE LIBRARY OF CONGRESS

15381 continued: Chester, LL.D.; and a full report of the bi-centennial reunion of 1882.   Compiled by Gilbert Cope ... Philadelphia, For the family, under the auspices of the Bi-centennial committee, 1887.   xvi, (3)-1333 p. front., illus., plates, ports., map, facsims., geneal. tables. 28 cm. Contains reprint of title-page and preface of Family record ... by Joseph Sharpless, Philadelphia, 1816, which this work supersedes. 9-13650.   CS71.S532   1887

15382   SHARPLES.   The Sharples, their portraits of George Washington and his contemporaries; a diary and an account of the life and work of James Sharples and his family in England and America, by Katharine McCook Knox.   New Haven, Yale university press;   London, H. Milford, Oxford university press, 1930.   xvi, 133 p. incl. front., illus., ports., facsims. 28½ cm. "The diary and letters of Ellen Sharples ... are freely quoted in these pages." - p. (3) 31-621.   ND497.S445K6

15383   SHARPLESS.   Sharples family, with collateral lines of Hunn and Jackson.   By Alexander Du Bin.   Philadelphia, Historical Publ. Society, 1948.   11 p. 26 cm. 49-18839*.   CS71.S532   1948

   SHARPLESS.   See also MOORE, 1937

15384   SHARRARD.   The descendants of William Sharrard, who emigrated to U.S.A. from England in 1760, U.E.L., came to Canada after the American war of independence.   Died in 1823.   Compiled by his great great grandson, Edward H. Phillips, at Saskatoon, 1939 ... Revised to Feb. 13/1944.   (Saskatoon, Can. 1944)   1 p. l., 9 (i.e.11) numb. l. 34½ x 26 cm. Includes extra numbered leaves 5a - 5b. Blue-print. Includes in manuscript, brief outlines of the Giffin and Clow families, by L.M.Giffin. "References": leaf 3. 44-35603.   CS90.S56   1944

15385   SHARTLE.   Shartle genealogy; an historical account of the American ancestry, life, and descendants of Philip Shartle I.   1st ed.   By Stanley Musgrave Shartle.   Indianapolis, 1955.   68 l. illus. 28 cm. 56-19043.   CS71.S5324   1955

15386   SHATTUCK.   Memorials of the descendants of William Shattuck, the progenitor of the families of America that have borne his name; including an introduction, and an appendix containing collateral information.   By Lemuel Shattuck ... Boston, Printed by Dutton and Wentworth for the family, 1855.   3 p. l., 414 p. front. (port.) 23½ cm. 9-13649.   CS71.S533   1855

15387   SHATTUCK.   Genealogy of a branch of the Shattuck family, early settlers in Brownhelm, Lorain County, Ohio, about 1850.   By Claude Charles Hamel.   Amherst, 1948.   12 l. 27 cm. Typewritten. "References": leaf 12. 50-25032.   CS71.S533   1948

   SHATTUCK.   See also: BLOOD, 1960
                               CLARK, 1898

15388   SHAVER.   Frederick Shaver, 1747 Germany - Sussex County, New Jersey, 1823, and his descendants.   By Frederick Howell Shaver.   Mount Vernon, Iowa, D. S. Herring (1943?)   111 l. 28 cm. 52-49966.   CS71.S534   1943

   SHAVER.   See also: SHAFER.
                            STRICKLER, 1925

15389   SHAW.   Memorials of the clan Shaw ... (Dundee) Printed for private circulation, 1868.   2 p. l., xii p., 1 l., (4) p., 1 l., (3)-24, (2) p. 21½ cm. Dedication signed: W.G.S. (i.e. William George Shaw) 14-1667-8.,   ——— Appendix to Memorials of clan Shaw.   (n.p., 1869?)   12 p. 21½ cm. (With his Memorials of the clan Shaw)   CS479.S55

15390   SHAW.   A genealogical account of the Highland families of Shaw, by Alexander Mackintosh Shaw.   (London, Printed by W. P. Griffith & son) 1877.   2 p. l., 115 p. 22 cm. Title vignette; coat of arms. "One hundred copies privately printed. No. 94." 17-23940.   CS479.S55   1877

15391   SHAW.   Families of Shaw, Clark, Gow (by) Charles Fraser Mackintosh, LL.D. (Glasgow, J. Mackay, 1898)   cover-title, p. (83)-122. illus. (incl. coats of arms) 27½ cm. Running title: Minor septs of Clan Chattan. Separates from the author's "An account of the confederation of Clan Chattan." Glasgow, 1898. Contents. - no. v. The Shaws of Rothiemurchus. - no. VI. The Clarks. - no. VII. The Gows-Sliochd Gow Crom. 15-6721.   CS479.S55   1898

558

15392   SHAW.   Shaw records; a memorial of Roger Shaw, 1594-1661, by Harriette F. Farwell. Bethel, Me., E.C.Bowler, 1904.   435 p. front., pl., ports., facsim. 23½ cm. 4-33881.

CS71.S535   1904

15393   SHAW.   George Bernard Shaw, his life and works, a critical biography (authorized) by Archibald Henderson ... with 33 illustrations, including two plates in colour (one from an autochrome by Alvin Langdon Coburn, the other from a water-colour by Bernard Partridge), two photogravures (Coburn and Steichen), and numerous facsimiles in the text.   Cincinnati, Stewart & Kidd company, 1911.   xxii, 528 p. illus. (incl. facsims.) plates (1 col.) ports. (incl. col. front.) fold. facsim., fold. geneal. tab. 23 cm. Appendix: Genealogical chart of the Shaw family of counties Tipperary, Kilkenny and Dublin, together with other lineal ancestors of George Bernard Shaw. 11-31884 rev.

PR5366.H42

15394   SHAW.   Shaw, the name, the coats of arms and records of various families of the name in Great Britain and the United States;   compiled by George Castor Martin.   Asbury Park, N.J.Martin & Allardyce, 1913.   cover-title, 27 p. fold. pl. (coats of arms) 20 cm. 14-3725.

CS71.S535   1913

15395   SHAW.   Lemuel Shaw, chief justice of the Supreme judicial court of Massachusetts, 1830 - 1860, by Frederic Hathaway Chase.   Boston and New York, Houghton Mifflin company, 1918. vi p., 1 l., 330 p., 1 l. front. (port.) 21 cm. 18-8313.   LAW

15396   SHAW.   Ancestors of Amyntas Shaw and his wife Lucy Tufts Williams, showing Mayflower lines never before published from Myles Standish, John Alden, William Mullines and Thomas Rogers, comp. for their daughter Isabella M. Knowlton by Josephine C. Frost (Mrs. Samuel Knapp Frost) ... (New York?) 1920.   1 p. l., 5-84 p. plates, ports. 29 cm. 21-6316 rev.   CS71.S535   1920

15397   SHAW.   Bernard's brethren (by) Charles Macmahon Shaw; with comments by Bernard Shaw. London, Constable & company, ltd. (1939)   5 p. l., 161 (i.e. 217) p. front. (2 port.) 22½ cm. "Passages on the pages printed in red (56 p.) are comments and interpolations made by Bernard Shaw while reading the ms." - Publisher's note.   "First published 1939." 39-20845.

PR5366.S54   1939

15398   SHAW.   History of the Shaw family and descendants of Anthony Shaw, the first American ancestor who arrived before 1653.   (By Frederick Benjamin Shaw) (Arlington? Va., 1942?) cover-title, 19 (i.e. 23) p. 21 cm. 42-16149.   CS71.S535   1942

15399   SHAW.   They took the high road: The Lady Gurtha and the Catamount o' the North, The princess Yleria and the Mac-in-Sagart, The Puritan woman and the Scots cavalier, The Virginia girl and Washington's rifleman; romances of the Shaws of Scotland and America.   A novel by Gurthie Shaw Patch.   Richmond, Va., The Dietz press, incorporated (1946)   3 p. l., ix-xiii p., 1 l., 374 p. 23½ cm. 47-957.

PZ3.P2694 Th

15400   SHAW.   Record of some of the descendants of Abraham Shaw and Bridget Best, with special emphasis on the line of John (6)   Compiled by Edith Whitney Shaw, assisted by Elizabeth J. MacCormick. (n. p., 1953)   14 l. 28 cm. 53-40249.   CS71.S535   1953

15401   SHAW.   Shaw family history; a bulletin recording genealogical information about descendants of Josephine (Davis) Shaw and James Edward Shaw.   By James Marvin Varner.   (1st ed.) Atlanta, Creative Pub. Co. (1968)   23 p. geneal. table, group port. 30 cm. "A centennial edition commemorating the 100th anniversary of the marriage of James Edward Shaw and Josephine Meire Davis, December 13, 1968." 74-1954.

CS71.S535   1968

15402   SHAW.   Descent and Descendants of John L. Shaw (1809-1890) of Morrow County, Ohio.   By Ivyl W. Shaw.   In vertical file.   Ask reference librarian for this material.

SHAW.   See also: AGNEW, 1926   KING, 1897
                     BISBEE, 1936   ROBERTS, F159.R48 R6
                     BROWN, 1884   TUCKER, 1901
                     DAVIS, 1959

SHAWCROSS.   See SHALLCROSS, 1908

15403   SHAWVER.   ... The George Shawver family tree compiled by Rev. L. D. Shawver, James C. Shawver, Iva Lou Shawver-Osborn and A. E. Shawver.   Morrison, Ill., The Shawver publishing co. (19 -)   (24) p. 17½ cm. (American families series) With Shawver, J. L. ... The Daniel Shawver family tree ... 1927.   40-996.
CS71.S5357   1927

15404   SHAWVER.   ... The Daniel Shawver family tree compiled by John L. Shawver ... and other members of the family.   Morrison, Ill., The Shawver publishing co., 1927.   (69) p. 17½ cm. (American families series) With this is bound: Shawver. L. D. ... The George Shawver family tree ... Morrison, Ill. (19 -) 39-12250.
CS71.S5357   1927

SHEAD.   See also WADSWORTH, E171.A53 v. 14

15405   SHEAFE.   The Sheafe family of old and New England.   By Walter Kendall Watkins, Malden, Mass.   Boston, Printed for the author, 1901.   14 p. 24½ cm. "Reprinted from New-Eng. historical and genealogical register for April, 1901." 18-376.
CS71.S536   1901

15406   SHEAFE.   Biographical and historical sketches of the Sheafe, Wentworth, Fisher, Bache, Satterthwaite and Rutgers families of America ... (n. p.) 1923.   3 p. l., 9-123 p. plates, ports. 26½ cm. 23-16825.
CS71.S536   1923

SHEAFE.   See also BASSETT, 1926

SHEAKLEY.   See LARIMER, 1903

15407   SHEARER.   The Shearer-Akers family, combined with "The Bryan line" through the seventh generation; arranged to be continuable indefinitely, both as a genealogy and a picture gallery in each of the three lines, by blank pages inserted in the last four generations and index on which new names and pictures may be inserted at their proper places, by Rev. James William Shearer, D. D.   (Somerville, N. J., Press of the Somerset messenger) 1915.   171 p. incl. ports. 22 cm. 16-6217.
CS71.S538   1915

15408   SHEARER.   Florence Elizabeth Shearer; genealogy of Florence Elizabeth Shearer (Honeybun) daughter of Charles Raymond Shearer and Florence Carrie Harder ... Collected and systematized by her father, Charles Raymond Shearer ... Columbus Junction, Ia., B. H. Shearer, 1939.   1 p. l., 125 p. 22½ cm. On cover: Genealogical record of the Shearer and Wise family relationship. 40-2268.
CS71.S538   1939

SHEARER.   See also McCLARY, E171.A53 v. 13

15409   SHEARTS.   Genealogy of Jacob Shearts family.   By James Hervey Sherts.   (Pittsburgh?) 1963.   1 v. illus. (part col.) col. coats of arms, facsims., geneal. tables (1 on 4 fold. sheets in pocket) 30 cm. Caption title. Title on label mounted on cover: Jacob Shearts family genealogy. Typescript. 66-57011.
CS71.S539   1963

15410   SHEDD.   Register of the Shedd family association ... (v. 1) - 7 1911-1918.   Boston, Mass., 1911-1918.   7 v. fronts., plates, ports. 25 cm. Secretary: 1911-1915 Frank Edson Shedd. 1916 - Sherwin L. Cook. 14-6297.
CS71.S541   1911-

15411   SHEDD.   Daniel Shed genealogy; ancestry and descendants of Daniel Shed of Braintree, Massachusetts, 1327-1920, by Frank E. Shedd; with English ancestry by J. Gardner Bartlett.   Boston, The Shedd family association, 1921.   xv, (1), 796 p. front., illus. (maps) plates, ports., facsims. 24½ cm. Edited for the Shedd family association, from Mr. Shedd's manuscript, by J. Gardner Bartlett. 22-6008.
CS71.S541   1921

SHED.   See also DIXON, 1922

SHEE.   See EVELYN, CS439.E9

SHEETE.   See CRAIG, 1960

15412   SHEETS.   History and genealogy of the John Sheets family.   (Convoy? O.) 1940.
cover-title, 36 p. illus. (incl. ports.) 23 cm. "An appreciation ... of ... Myrtle O. Sheets, who compiled the Sheets family history": leaf
inserted before p. 1. "Some facts about our reunions": 4 p. inserted at end. 43-31761.   CS71.S5413   1940

15413   SHEFFER.   The Sheffer family, Staunton, Virginia ... By Charles Loeber.   Staunton, Wright
printing co., 1942 -   geneal. tables. 43 x 24 cm. 44-22703.   CS71.S5414   1942

15414   SHEFFER.   The Sheffer family of Shenandoah County, Virginia.   (By Charles Loeber)   December 30, 1728 - December 30, 1944.   (n. p.) 1944.   16 p. 21 cm. "Proof printed November 30, 1944." 47-29916*.
    CS71.S5414   1944

SHEFFER.   See also SNYDER, 1958

15415   SHEFFIELD.   A character of John Sheffield, late duke of Buckinghamshire; with an account of
the pedigree of the Sheffield family: to which is annex'd His Grace's last will and testament, written
with his own hand.   London, Printed by J. Stagg, 1729.   1 p. l., 48 p. 20 cm. Head and tail pieces. 20-15243.
    DA437.B75C5

15416   SHEFFIELD.   Sheffield, St. John and allied families, genealogical and biographical, prepared
and privately printed for Mrs. George St. John Sheffield, by the American historical society, inc.   New
York, 1929.   137 p. ports., col. coats of arms (1 mounted) 23 cm. Title-page in colors. Bound in blue levant, gold tooled and inlaid,
with leather doublures.   Allied families: St. John, Stockton, Thorpe and King.   Published in part, under title "Sheffield, St. John and allied
families, by E. C. Finley", in Americana, v. 26, 1932, p. 40-84.   29-14717 rev. 2.   CS71.S5415   1929
    Office

15417   SHEFFIELD.   Sheffield, Daggett and allied families, a genealogical study with biographical
notes, prepared and privately printed for Mrs. George St. John Sheffield, by the American historical
society, inc.   New York, 1932.   273 p. plates, ports., facsims., col. coats of arms, col. geneal. tables. 33 cm. Some of
the coats of arms are accompanied by guard sheets with descriptive letterpress.   Published also in Americana, by E. C. Finley, under titles
"Sheffield, St. John and allied families" (v. 26, 1932, p. 40-84) and "Daggett and allied families" (v. 26, 1932, p. 85-172) Includes bibliographical
notes.   Bound in blue levant, gold tooled and inlaid, with leather doublures. 34-17811.   CS71.S5415   1932

15418   SHEFFIELD.   Notes on Penn'a, Ohio, Ill., Mo., Kan., and Neb. families of Sheffield, Wagner,
Phelps and others.   Being a copy of a hand-constructed book by Vernon R. Sheffield, Indianola, Ia.,
1922.   Copied by Dr. G. W. Brugler, for his own use, and this copy deposited to ensure preservation
of the data.   (n. p., 1936?)   23 l. 23 cm. Type-written (carbon copy) 38M4499T.
    CS71.S5415   1936

SHEFFIELD.   See also PIERCE.

SHEFFNER.   See SCHAFFNER.

SHEHY.   See WILSON, E171.A53 v. 16

15419   SHEIBLEY.   Descendants of my great-grandparents,   by (Mrs. A. R.) Laura Willhide
Johnston, assisted by Frank A. Johnston; being a record of the descendants of my great-grandfather,
Peter Scheibly ... my great-grandfather Wertz ... my grandfather, Conrod Willhide ... and my great-
grandfather, John George Seiss, jr. ...   (Harrisburg, Pa., Evangelical press, c. 1924)   474 p. incl.
front., illus., ports. 22½ cm. 24-5586.   CS71.S542   1924

15420   SHELBURNE.   The Shelburne family of Montgomery coutny, Virginia, by Robert Craig
Shelburne.   (n. p., 1935?)   7 l. 28 cm. Mimeographed. 38M4503T.   CS71.S5426   1935

15421   SHELBURNE.   Rev. Samuel Shelburne and his descendants, by Robert Craig Shelburne, also
Susan Anne Shelburne and her descendants.   (n. p., 1935?)   3 l. 28 cm. Mimeographed. 38M4501T.
    CS71.S5426   1935a

15422   SHELBURNE.   The Shelburne family, by Robert Craig Shelburne.   (n. p., 1936?)   55 l.
28½ cm. 38M4502T.   CS71.S5426   1936

15423   SHELBURNE.   The Shelburne family; origin of the name.   (By Robert C. Shelburne)
8 l.   CS71.S5426   1939

15424   SHELBURNE.   The monuments erected to the memory of our dead.   (The tombstone inscriptions pertaining to the Shelburne and related families, Montgomery county, Virginia).   By: Robert
Craig Shelburne ... (n. p., 1939?)   41 l. 28 cm. Type-written. The wills of Thomas Pettus and James Shelburne: 4 fold.
leaves inserted at end. 40-2269.   CS71.S5426   1939a

15425   SHELBURNE.   The Shelburne family ... by Robert Craig Shelburne ... Richmond, Va. (1943)
1 p. l., 12 numb. l., 1 l. 29½ x 23½ cm. Type-written. "The Shelburne genealogical series is a release in manuscript form to historic societies
and libraries of a book - The Shelburne family - to be published in the future." 44-28182.   CS71.S5426   1943

15426   SHELBURNE.   The Shelburne family, by Robert Craig Shelburne ... (Christiansburg, Va.,
1944 -   v. 29½ x 23½ cm. Loose-leaf; type-written (carbon copy) 44-30855.   CS71.S5426   1944

15427   SHELBURNE.   The Shelburne family; the maternal genealogy.   By Robert Craig Shelburne.
(New Orleans? 1951?)   4, 3 l. 35 cm. 53-34069.   CS71.S5426   1951

15428   SHELBURNE.   The Shelburne family.   By Robert Craig Shelburne.   (New Orleans? 1951?)
4 l. 35 cm. 53-34070.   CS71.S5426   1951a

15429   SHELBURNE.   The Shelburne family.   By Robert Craig Shelburne.   (n. p., 1952)
5 l. 36 cm. 52-29657.   CS71.S5426   1952

15430   SHELBURNE.   The Shelburne family.   By Robert Craig Shelburne.   (n. p., 1952)
(1) l. 36 cm. Caption title. 54-20792.   CS71.S5426   1952a

15431   SHELBURNE.   The Shelburne family; the colonial family at Jamestown and Brisland (i. e.
Bisland) Parish, James City County, Virginia.   (n. p., 1952)   (1) l. 36 cm. Caption title. 54-20793.
                                                                        CS71.S5426   1952b

15432   SHELBURNE.   The Shelburne family.   By Robert Craig Shelburne.   (Roanoke? Va., 1953)
unpaged. 28 cm. 54-27656.   CS71.S5426   1953

15433   SHELBURNE.   The Shelburne family.   By Robert Craig Shelburne.   (n. p. 1953)   (4) l. 36 cm.
Descendants of Thomas Shelburne, a young Welshman, who settled at Jamestown in 1607. 54-32606.   CS71.S5426   1953a

15434   SHELBURNE.   The Shelburne family bible record.   In vertical file.   Ask reference librarian for
this material.

15435   SHELBURNE.   Shelburne family.   By Robert Craig Shelburne.   In vertical file.   Ask reference
librarian for this material.

15436   SHELBY.   A report on the first three generations of the Shelby family in the United States of
America.   (n. p., 1927)   cover-title, 18 p. fold. map, geneal. tab. 23 cm. Signed: Cass K. Shelby. Foot-notes. 28-10812.
                                                                        CS71.S5428   1927

15437   SHELBY.   Sketches of the Shelby, McDowell, Deaderick, Anderson families, compiled by
Anna Mary Moon.   (Chattanooga, c. 1933)   150 p. ports. 23½ cm. "Bibliographies": p. 143-146. 33-6913.
                                                                        CS71.S5428   1933

15438   SHELBY.   Garrett county history Shelby family, by Charles E. Hoye.   (Oakland, Md.) 1935.
1 l. 39 cm. Detached from the Mountain democrat, February 14, 1935. 38M1245T.   CS71.S5428   1935

15439   SHELBY.   The Shelby family; ancestry and descendants of John Shelby and his son David
Shelby, pioneers of Tennessee, by Howard S. Galloway.   Mobile, Ala., Printed for the author by Gill
Print. Co. (1964)   xxxi, 352 p. illus., ports. (1 col.) 24 cm. Pages 346-352 blank for "Family record." Bibliography: p. 343-345.
64-5099.   CS71.S5428   1964

15439a   SHELBY.   Shelby family in vertical file.   Ask reference librarian for this material

SHELBY. See also: HART, 1923
No. 516 - Notable southern families vol. 2

15440   SHELDON. The Sheldon magazine; or, A genealogical list of the Sheldons in America, with biographical and historical notes, and notices of other families with which this intermarried ... By Rev. Henry Olcott Sheldon ... Loudonville, O., 1855-57.   xi, (1), 113 (i.e. 231) p.   facsims.   21½ cm.   p. 1-112 numbered in duplicate.   Issued in 4 no.: no. 1, 1855; no. 2-4, Jan., Apr., Oct., 1857.   No. 2-3 have imprint: Sidney, O., S.H. Mathers & co., 1857; no. 4, Sidney, O., Printed at the Journal office, 1857.   9-13648.   CS71.S543   1855

15441   SHELDON. Historical sketch of the Sheldon family, prepared and read by Harry W. Sheldon of Yonkers, New York, at the second annual reunion of the Sheldon family, held at Rupert, Vermont, August 8, 1912. Schenectady, N.Y., R.F. Sheldon, 1913.   20 p.   16½ cm.   25-12828.
CS71.S543   1913

15442   SHELDON. Elizabethan Sheldon tapestries, by John Humphreys ... London, Oxford university press, H. Milford, 1929.   27, (1) p.   XIII pl. on 9 l. (incl. front., port.)   2 fold. geneal. tab.   29 x 22½ cm.   "Read April 3rd 1924.   Reprinted (with additions) from 'Archaeologia', vol. LXXIV, by permission of the Council of the Society of antiquaries."   29-21273.
NK3043.H8

15443   SHELDON. The Sheldons; being some account of the Sheldon family of Worcestershire and Warwickshire, by E. A. B. Barnard ... Cambridge (Eng.) The University press, 1936.   xi, 138, (2) p.   front., IX pl. (incl. ports., facsim.)   19 cm.   Title vignette: "Arms of Sheldon".   37-19036.   CS439.S397B3

15444   SHELDON. The Sheldon magazine, with index; a genealogical list of the Sheldons in America, with notices of other families with which this intermarried. By Henry Olcott Sheldon. Sidney, Ohio, S. H. Mathers, 1857. Reprinted with corrections and additions. Edited and transcribed by Leland Locke Sheldon. New York, Genealogical Committee, Sheldon Family Association, 1961.
1 v. (various pagings) port. 23 cm. Cover title. At head of title: Vol. no. IV, October 1857. 61-34742 rev.   CS71.S543   1961

SHELDON. See also: BARNES, 1958
CORLISS, 1924
DILLON, 1927
HOTTON, 1877
WHITE, E171.A53 vol. 20

15445   SHELFER. Shelfer family in vertical file.   Ask reference librarian for this material.

15446   SHELLENBERGER. Contribution to the genealogy of the family of John Shellenberger, watch-maker in Geneva, Switzerland, who arrived in America in 1754 from Switzerland, organized down to the 5th generation, by Edward Lawver Burchard ... as compiled from original sources, interviews and publications with collaterial (!) families interpolated, with introductory historical background of the Shellenberger families. Chicago, Ill., 1939.   1 p. l., 41, 41a-41b, 42-57, 57a-57e, 58-77 numb. l. 27½ cm.   Mimeo-graphed.   Cover-title: Shellenberger (Shellabarger) family and genealogy of John Shellenberger, by Edward Lawver Burchard.   Provisional edition. 40-8604.   CS71.S5435   1939

15447   SHELLEY. The pedigree of Percy Bysshe Shelley, now first given from the records of the College of arms. (By Stephen Isaacson Tucker) London, Printed for private distribution, 1880.
19 p. front. (port.) illus. (incl. coats of arms) fold. geneal. tab.   28 cm.   "This private issue of the Shelley pedigree is limited to one hundred copies, fifty for England and fifty for America.   This copy is no. 3.   English issue."   "Advertisement" signed: H. Buxton Forman.   An extra copy of the genealogical table is inserted.   21-14027.   CS439.S398   1880

15448   SHELLEY. Memorials of the family of Shelly of Great Yarmouth, their ancestors and de-scendants. Compiled by John Shelly ... London, Printed for private circulation and issued by Phillimore and co., 1909.   4 p. l., 47, (1) p.   front., plates, ports., geneal. tab.   29 cm.   One hundred copies printed.   Blank leaves inserted at end.   11-13021.   CS439.S4

SHELLEY. See also PIERCE, 1874.

SHELLY. See SHELLEY.

15449   SHELLHOUSE.   Genealogy of the Schellhouse family of Vermilion Township, Erie County, Ohio, which married into the Koppenhafer and Leidheiser families.   By Claude Charles Hamel.   Amherst, 1948.   6 1.   27 cm.   Typewritten.   50-25467.   CS71.S322   1948

SHELLYE.   See SHELLEY.

15450   SHELMERDINE.   Extracts from church registers relating to the family of Shelmerdine ... London, Mitchell and Hughes, printers, 1879.   1 p. l., 6 p.   illus.   28 cm.   Privately printed.   23-14531.
CS439.S42

15451   SHELOR.   Pioneers and their coat of arms of Floyd county ... (Floyd, Va.) c. 1938. (160) p.   front. (port.)   coats of arms.   23½ cm.   "Genealogies of prominent early settlers of the Blue ridge plateau of Virginia, by Susan Jefferson Shelor."   Includes Shelor, Howard, Jefferson, Banks, Goodson, Barnard, Dodd, Cannaday, Gardner, Dillon, Gravely and Ross families.   39-469.
CS71.S544   1938

15452   SHELOR.   Pioneers and their coat of arms of Floyd County; genealogies of prominent early settlers of the Blue Ridge Plateau of Virginia.   By Susan (Jefferson) Shelor.   Winston-Salem, N.C., Printed by Hunter Pub. Co., c. 1961.   216 p.   port., coats of arms.   24 cm.   63-34856.
CS71.S544   1961

15453   SHELTON.   Reunion of the descendants of Daniel Shelton, at Birmingham, Conn., June 14th, 1877.   Newburgh, N.Y., E.N. Ruttenber & son, printers, 1877.   104 p.   front.   26 cm.   "Genealogy of the Shelton family, comp. by J. de F. S." (i.e. Jane de Forest Shelton: p. (41)-93.   Ed. by Edward Nelson Shelton.   9-13746.
CS71.S545   1877

15454   SHELTON.   Brief memoir of the family of Shelton of Connecticut.   Boston, 1857.   5 p.   24 cm.   "Reprinted from the New England historical and genealogical register," v. 11, 1857, p. 271-272.   Signed: B.H.D. i.e. Benjamin Homer Dixon.   9-13747.   CS71.S545   1857

15455   SHELTON.   A history of the Shelton family of England and America ... by Mildred Campbell Whitaker (Mrs. Alexander Edward Whitaker) ... (St. Louis, The Mound City press, 1941)   6 p. l., 275 p.   front.   plates, ports., facsims. (part fold.) geneal. tables (part fold.) coats of arms (1 fold.)   25 cm.   "A supplement to the 'Genealogy of the Campbell, Noble, Gorton, Shelton, Byrd, Gilmore and allied families' by the same author, published in 1927."   41-11222.
CS71.S545   1941

15456   SHELTON.   Descendants of Henry Shelton's daughter, Ann.   Compiled by Genevieve (Logan) Prather and Elizabeth Prather Ellsberry.   Chillicothe, Mo., E.P. Ellsberry, 1960.   115 1.   illus.   28 cm. 61-35644.   CS71.S545   1960

15457   SHELTON.   The Sheltons, inclduing a brief outline of allied families: the Lowe, Sherrill, and Propst families and their ancestry, by Z. F. Shelton.   Montgomery, Ala., 1962.   189, ix p.   coat of arms, facsim., port.   29 cm.   65-3094.   CS71.S545   1962

SHELTON.   See also: CAMPBELL, 1927
PUCKETT, 1960

15458   SHENSTONE.   Family of Shenstone the poet.   (n.p., 1890?)   cover-title, 4 p.   28 cm.   Signed: "H. Sydney Grazebrook."   "Extracts from the parish registers of Halesowen, co. Worcester": p. 1-3.   "From the parish registers of Rowley-Regis, co. Stafford": p. 3-4.   16-23842.   CS439.S43

15459   SHEPARD.   Descendants of Edward Shepard, Cambridge, Mass. (1639).   By James Shepard, Naman Sheppard, A. E. B. Shepherd.   Reprinted from the New England historical and genealogical register for July, 1878.   Boston, D. Clapp & son, printers, 1878.   18 p.   26 cm.   9-13745 rev.
CS71.S547   1878

15460   SHEPARD.   A genealogical history of William Shepard of Fossecut, Northamptonshire, England, and some of his descendants, by George L. Shepard, Boston, Mass.   Salem, Mass., Observer book and job print, 1886.   63 p.   front.   25 cm.   9-13644.   CS71.S547   1886

15461   SHEPARD.   Some family and friendly recollections of 70 years, of Mary Elizabeth Brandreth, widow of Henry Rowland Brandreth ... and daughter of Henry John Sheperd, Q.C., and Lady Mary Shepherd ... For private circulation only.   (Westerham, Eng., Printed by C. Hooker, 1886?)
1 p. 1., 188 p., 1 1., xxxii p., 1 1.   17 cm.   15-22613.   CT788.B772A3

15462   SHEPARD.   Ralph Shepard, Puritan, by Ralph Hamilton Shepard.   Printed for private circula-tion.   Dedham, Mass., 1893.   1 p. 1., ix, 50 p.   front. (map) 27 cm.   "Limited to fifty numbered copies. no. 19."   Appendix D: Descendants of Ralph Shepard and Thanklord, his wife, to the second generation.   Comp. by E. N. Sheppard (p. 48-50) 15-5261.
                                                                                                         CS71.S547   1893

15463   SHEPARD.   History of the Shepard family.   By Chester Brown.   Published by the author, East Hardwick, Vt.   Montpelier, Press of the Argus and patriot co., 1894.   16 p. 23 cm. 2-4437.
                                                                                                         CS71.S547   1894

15464   SHEPARD.   Isaac A. Sheppard: a brief account of his ancestors and some collateral relatives, together with an autobiographical sketch.   Philadelphia, Priv. print. for the use of his family, 1897.
37 p. front. (port.) 31½ cm.   "Genealogy of the Westcott family": p. 11-15.   Preface signed: Isaac A. Sheppard.   10-5270.
                                                                                                         CS71.S547   1897

15465   SHEPARD.   Ralph Shepard and some of his descendants.   By Alice T. (Pickford) Brockway ... (Dedham, Mass., 1903)   4 p. 24 cm.   Caption title.   "Reprinted from the Dedham historical register (XIV, 27-31) for Jan., 1903."
4-35820.   CS71.S547   1903

15466   SHEPARD.   Golden lives; a memoir of Charles and Katherine Rochester Shepard.   Cam-bridge, Mass.) Priv. print. at the Riverside press, 1905.   2 p. 1., 36 p., 1 1. front., ports. 23½ cm.   "By Mary Shepard, Thomas Rochester Shepard and Charles Edward Shepard." - Ms. note on half-title.   Autograph presentation copy to the Library of Congress by Charles Shepard II; with two pages of "Family notes" and a note concerning "Golden lives" mounted on fly leaves; and a clipping, also mounted, from the Dansville express, Nov. 18, 1920, containing a description of the Charles Shepard homestead offered as a home for the Dansville library.
20-15 rev.
                                                                                                         CS71.S547   1905

15467   SHEPARD.   Genealogical record.   Shepard family.   (Albany, 1920)   geneal. tab. 29 x 37½ cm.
Photostat reproduction made at Albany, N.Y., March 1920, cf. chart prepared by Walter Joy Shepard, printed about 1885; with manuscript marginal notes and additions by Charles Shepard.   Troy, N.Y., April 4, 1920.   20-7231.   CS71.S548   1920

15468   SHEPARD.   Pedigree of Shepard of Dansville, New York, formerly of Plainfield, Connecticut, by Charles Shepard.   Troy, N.Y., 1921.   geneal. tab. 80 x 56 cm. fold. to 20½ x 29 cm.   Blue-print.   Edition of 50 copies.   22-6305.   CS71.S547   1921

15469   SHEPARD.   The descendants to the fourth generation of Thomas Shepard of Malden, Massa-chusetts, by Charles Shepard ... Troy, N.Y., and Washington, D.C., C. Shepard, 1922.
geneal. tab. 83 x 55½ cm. fold. to 22 x 31½ cm.   22-12436.   CS71.S547   1922

15470   SHEPARD.   Pedigree of the Sheppard family of Bedfordshire, England, by Charles Shepard.   Troy, N.Y., C. Shepard, 1922.   geneal. tab. 21½ x 54 cm. fold. to 18 x 31 cm.   Blue-print.   Edition limited to 25 copies.
22-6212.   CS439.S44

15471   SHEPARD.   Family tree of Perry Melville Shepard, his sister and brothers, showing lineages of both their mother and father ... prepared by Perry M. Shepard ... Geneva, N.Y., 1939.
geneal. tab. 30 x 54 cm.   Reproduced from type-written copy.   41-31427.   CS71.S547   1939

15472   SHEPARD.   Intermarriages of ancestors of Frederick West Shepard & Deborah Stuart Shepard ... (Geneva, N.Y., 1939)   geneal. tab. 37½ x 32 cm.   Compiled by Perry Melville Shepard.   Reproduced from type-written copy.   41-31428.   CS71.S547   1939a

15473   SHEPARD.   History, genealogies, biographies of the Shepherd and related families since their coming to America more than 280 years ago, by Frank C. Shepherd.   (Wewoka? Okl., 1943?)
1 p. 1., 400, 22 (i. e. 24) p.   plates, ports.   22 x 18½ cm.   Cover-title: Genealogy, the Shepherd line.   The illustrative material consists of blue-prints.   Reproduced from type-written copy.   44-29922.   CS71.S547   1943
          —— Another issue.   With differences in the illustrative matter.   CS71.S547   1943a

15474 SHEPARD. Ancestors and descendants of Albro Dexter Shepard and his wife Alice Zeviah Sill. By Winifred C. Shepard. (Allison? Iowa) 1949. 119 p. ports. 23 cm. Cover title: Shepard-Sill families, 1603-1949. 51-27737. CS71.S547 1949

15475 SHEPARD. The Shepard genealogy; being a record of the descendants of Ralph Shepard, 1606-1693, and the associated families of Crossman, Culver, Fuller, Johnson, Kidder, Rowley, and Wild. Edited and published by Lowell Shepard Blaisdell and Hanaford Eugene Shepard. (Phoenix? Ariz.) 1952 (i.e. 1953) 133 1. 30 cm. 54-19237. CS71.S547 1953

15476 SHEPPARD. The Benjamin Kirk Sheppard family, with brief data about allied families of John Kennedy, James Dunkle, James Pilcher, Robert Sage, Robert Aikin, Barnett Vandervort and John Henry. By Carl Dunkle Sheppard. Akron, Ohio, 1964. 64 1. geneal. table. 29 cm. 64-3458. CS71.S547 1964

SHEPARD. See also:

BOOHER, 1954   FOXWELL, 1941   PAINE, 1913
CLARK, 1948   JAQUETTE, 1922   SEBOR, 1923
DODGE, 1896a   LONG, 1956   THRALL, 1968
DUKE, 1909   MACKEY, 1957   No. 1547 - Cabell county.

15477 SHEPARDSON. Shepardson - a family story. By Francis W. Shepardson, PH.D. (Chicago, 1906?) 6 p. 24½ cm. Caption title. 15-1785. CS71.S548 1906

15478 SHEPARDSON. The Shepardson family. A record of the early generations in America. By Francis Wayland Shepardson. (Chicago, Ill., 1907) 7 p. 24½ cm. Caption title. "Record of the first five generations of American Shepardsons." "John Eaton Shepardson ... and Albert R. Shepardson ... are working with me in this study": p. 7. 7-12501. CS71.S548 1907

15479 SHEPARDSON. The Shepardson family. A record of the line of Daniel Shepardson, Granville, Ohio. By Francis Wayland Shepardson. (Chicago, 1907) 8 p. 24½ cm. (Shepardson leaflets. no. 2) Caption title. 15-1786. CS71.S548 1907a

15480 SHEPARDSON. The Shepardson family. Beginning with the sixth generation in America. By Francis Wayland Shepardson. (Chicago, 1907) 8 p. 25 cm. (Shepardson leaflets. no. 3) caption title. 15-1787. CS71.S548 1907b

15481 SHEPARDSON. The Shepardson family. A record of the line of Samuel Shepardson, Guilford, Vermont. By Francis Wayland Shepardson ... August 1, 1907. (Chicago? Ill., 1907) 16 p. 24½ cm. Caption title. No. 4 of the Shepardson leaflets, cf. Shepardson, The Shepardson family. A record of the line of Zephaniah Shepardson, 1907 (p. 19) 7-31023. CS71.S548 1907c

15482 SHEPARDSON. The Shepardson family. Branches of the family in the United States when the first census was taken in 1790, by Francis Wayland Shepardson. (Chicago) 1912. 14 p. 24 cm. (Shepardson leaflets no. 6) Caption title. 12-25492. CS71.S548 1912

15483 SHEPARDSON. The Shepardson family. Some miscellaneous records of several generations. By Francis Wayland Shepardson. (Chicago) 1912. 8 p. 24½ cm. (Shepardson leaflets. no. 7) Caption title. 12-31005. CS71.S548 1912a

15484 SHEPARDSON. The Shepardson family history; a record of the line of Newell Alonzo Shepardson, Hastings, Nebraska. By Walter Kenneth Shepardson. Warsaw, Mo., 1957. 11 p. 24 cm. 57-41123. CS71.S548 1957

SHEPARDSON. See also ABELL, 1936

SHEPHERD. See: LUCAS, 1964
                    SHEPARD.

SHEPHERDSON. See SHEPARDSON.

SHEPPARD.   See SHEPARD.

SHEPPEY.   See No. 430 - Adventurers of purse and person.

SHERBORN.   See SHERBURNE.

SHERBROOK.   See TAYLOR, 1875

15485   SHERBURNE.   A history of the family of Sherborn.   By Charles Davies Sherborn.   London,
Mitchell and Hughes, 1901.   viii, 212 p. front. (coat of arms) 22 ½ cm. "Only 250 copies printed." "Sherborn arms and 'Ex
libris' ": p. 152-157. "Literature, etc. referred to": p. 160-164. 2-7435.

CS439.S45

15486   SHERBURNE.   Some descendants of Henry and John Sherburne of Portsmouth, N.H., by
Edward Raymond Sherburne.   Boston, New-England historic genealogical society, 1904.   22 p. 25 cm.
"Reprinted from the New England historical and genealogical register, vol. 58 and 59." "Register re-prints, series A, no. 8." 20-9263.

CS71.S55   1904

SHERBURNE.   See also: ROBINSON, 1894
                                        Addenda.

15487   SHEREMETEV.   In Russian.   Title transliterated: Rodoslovie Sheremetevykh.   By
Aleksandr Platonovich Barsukov.   ... 1899.   2 p. l., (3)-36 p. 32½ x 25½ cm. 48-40366.

CS859.S45   1899

15488   SHERER.   A genealogy of the Scherer-Sherer family, by Floyd Haight ... (Dearborn? Mich.)
1937.   27 numb. l., 4 l. 28½ cm. Reproduced from type-written copy. Appendix: leaf mounted on inside of cover. 43-39539.

CS71.S5515   1937

15489   SHERER.   The Scherer family of Montgomery county, Illinois (by) Walter R. Sanders ...
Litchfield, Ill., 1945.   57 p. illus. (ports.) 23 cm. Military record and genealogical table of the Scherer family inserted.
46-20860.

CS71.S5515   1945

SHERER.   See also COLER, 1900

15490   SHERFEY.   The Sherfey family in the United States, 1751-1948 (Scherffig in Germany); an
historical and genealogical record.   Original record compiled by William Emory Sherfey.   Present
record edited & published by H. E. Sherfey.   (Greensburg? Ind., 1948?)   303 p. illus., ports. 29 cm.
Cover title: Sherfey genealogy. 51-24076.

CS71.S5516   1948

SHERFREY.   See PEFFLEY, 1938

15491   SHERIDAN.   Memoirs of the public and private life of the Right Hon, R. B. Sheridan, with a
particular account of his family and connections.   By John Watkins ... 2d ed. ... London, Printed for
H. Colburn, 1817.   2 v. fronts., ports. 22 cm. 10-8306.

PR3683.W3

15492   SHERIDAN.   Genealogical table of the families of Sheridan, Lefanu and Knowles, comp. by
Francis Harvey, privately printed for James McHenry.   London, 1875.   1 p. l., (2) p., 2 geneal. tab. 33 cm.
"Only forty copies printed." The genealogical table with a key, showing those members of the families who were authors, and giving a list of their
works, was compiled to illustrate the life of James Sheridan Knowles. 22-18189.

CS439.S46

15493   SHERIDAN.   The lives of the Sheridans.   By Percy Fitzgerald ... With engravings on steel
by Stodart and Every.   London, R. Bentley and son, 1886.   2 v. 6 port. (incl. fronts.) fold. facsims. 23 cm. 10-11933.

PR3683.F5

15494   SHERIDAN.   ... The Sheridans ... written by Percy Fitzgerald.   London, Printed by the
Grolier society (190-)   2 v. col. front., plates, ports., fold. facsims., fold. geneal. tab. 23 cm. (Beaux & belles of England)
"Imperial edition." Published, 1886, under title: The lives of the Sheridans. 44-50095.

PR3683.F5

15495   SHERIDAN.   The Andrew Sheridan family; an account of him and his descendants as far as is known at present.   By Charline Elizabeth Gadde.   (n. p., 1952)   36 l.   28 cm.   53-30285.

CS71.S5517   1952

SHERIDAN.   See also LE FANU, 1924

15496   SHERIN.   The Sherin family; a brief history, prepared from facts and records submitted by members of the family in the U. S. and Canada, written and published in January, 1936, by Gilbert W. Sherin.   Wilmington, Del., c.1936.   1 p. 1., 28 p.   illus. (ports., facsims.) 23 cm.   36-16179.

CS71.S5518   1936

SHERLEY.   See SHIRLEY.

15497   SHERMAN.   (Pedigree of Sherman of Dedham.   n. p., n. d.)   geneal. tab.   21½ x 28 cm.   fold. to 21½ x 15 cm.   Title from label mounted on cover.   38-32656.   CS71.S552

15498   SHERMAN.   Records of the Sherman family, as relating to the ancestors and descendants of Benj. Sherman, from Henry Sherman, county of Suffolk, England, down to the thirteenth generation. By David H. Sherman.   (n. p.) 1887.   94 p.   illus.   23½ cm.   Blank pages at end for "Births, marriages, deaths."   A complete record of the descendants of Henry Sherman down to the 7th generation, by the Rev. David Sherman of Wilbraham, Mass., was first pub. in the New England hist. & geneal. register and is here reproduced entire in the appendix.   16-23281.   CS71.S552   1887

15499   SHERMAN.   Sherman, Charles, Gass, Phipps, and allied families (including Lainson)   Genealogical records   compiled by Dorothy Alice (Sherman) Lainson (Mrs. Clarence R.)   (Rockford? Ill., 1963?)   1 v. (various pagings) coats of arms.   30 cm.   Includes bibliographies.   67-3975.   CS71.L188   1963

15500   SHERMAN.   The Sherman family.   By Albert James Fisher.   (West Long Branch? N. J., 1967)   80, (7) p.   ports.   18 cm.   Bibliography: p. (87)   68-21.   CS71.S552   1967

15501   SHERMAN.   Some of the descendants of Philip Sherman the first secretary of Rhode Island, by Roy V. Sherman.   (Akron? Ohio, 1968)   662 p.   illus., coat of arms, facsims., ports.   24 cm.   68-4556.

CS71.S552   1968

15502   SHERMAN.   Schureman genealogy.   Prepared by Richard Wynkoop... New York, M. F. Schureman, 1889.   cover-title, 55 p. 23½ cm.   9-13744.   CS71.S552   1889

15503   SHERMAN.   Ancestry of Rev. John Sherman and Capt. John Sherman.   (Boston) 1897.   cover-title, 9 p.   fold. geneal. tab.   22 cm.   Reprinted from the New England hist. and geneal. register for 1897.   Compiled by Charles Atwood White.   13-33798.   CS71.S552   1897

15504   SHERMAN.   Genealogy of one branch of the Sherman family from Samuel Sherman of Stratford, Conn., the first American ancestor, in 1640, down to Jotham Sherman of Newtown, Conn., of the fifth generation, and most of his descendants down to the eighth and ninth generation.   Compiled by Walter S. Booth ... and Mrs. Hosea B. Northrop ... (Milwaukee, Wis., Press of the Evening Wisconsin co.)   1900.   11 p.   20 cm.   1-3286.   CS71.S552   1900

15505   SHERMAN.   Schuremans, of New Jersey, by Richard Wynkoop ... 2d ed.   New York, Printed by the Knickerbocker press, 1902.
——— Supplement, January, 1906 ... Additions and correction.   (New York?) c.1906.
26 p.   illus. (incl. ports.) 23 cm.   Caption title.   2-15180.   CS71.S552   1902

15506   SHERMAN.   Schuremans of New York, comp. by Richard Wynkoop ... New York, Printed by The Knickerbocker press, 1903.   1 p. 1., 41 p.   illus., port. 23 cm.   3-9359.   CS71.S552   1903

15507   SHERMAN.   A branch of the Sherman family descended from Philip Sherman, first secretary of the colony of Rhode Island, by Frank Dempster Sherman.   (Boston? 1907)   cover-title, 4 p. 24½ cm. "Reprinted from the New England historical and genealogical register for July, 1907."   7-39276.

CS71.S552   1907

15508   SHERMAN.   Autobiography of Samuel Sterling Sherman, 1815-1910.   Chicago, M. A. Donohue & co., 1910.   117 p. incl. front. (port.) 21½ cm. 22-2805.   CT275.S4853A3

15509   SHERMAN.   Armorial bearings of Sherman of Watertown, Mass.   For private circulation. London, J. A. Ringrose, 1913.   (10) p. front., illus., coats of arms. 19½ cm. Comp. by Jerome Arthur Ringrose. 17-9738.
CS71.S552   1913

15510   SHERMAN.   The ancestry of James Morgan Sherman and his descendants, by Frank Dempster Sherman.   New York, Priv, print., 1915.   55, (2) p. front. (coat of arms) 21½ cm. Additions: 1 leaf inserted after p. 36. 16-5069.   CS71.S552   1915

15511   SHERMAN.   The ancestry of John Taylor Sherman and his descendants, by Frank Dempster Sherman.   New York, Priv. print., 1915.   57, (2) p. front. (coat of arms) 21½ cm. Additions: 1 leaf inserted after p. 36. 16-5989.   CS71.S552   1915a

15512   SHERMAN.   Genealogy of the Sherman family, by Bradford Sherman.   Chicago, 1916.   cover-title, (6) p. 21 cm. 17-33.   CS71.S552   1916

15513   SHERMAN.   Sherman genealogy including families of Essex, Suffolk and Norfolk, England, some descendants of the immigrants, Captain John Sherman, Reverend John Sherman, Edmund Sherman and Samuel Sherman, and the descendents of Honorable Roger Sherman and Honorable Charles R. Sherman, by Thomas Townsend Sherman ... New York, T. A. Wright, 1920.   xvi, 473, 1 p. plates, ports., facsims., coats of arms. 24½ cm. 20-16006.   CS71.S552   1920

15514   SHERMAN.   Sherman genealogy in the direct line from Thomas Sherman, I (c 1443-1493) through Rev. John Sherman, VII (1913-1685) to John Sherman, XII (1796-1869) and all his descendants: also all children of the direct line who came to or were born in New England, and many of their descendants: also mention of other Sherman lines, by Charles Pomeroy Sherman.   Atlantic City, Brooks & Idler, 1922.   2 p. l., 68 p. 17 cm. 22-13532.   CS71.S552   1922

15515   SHERMAN.   Descendants of William Sherman of Marshfield, Massachusetts, by Mary Lovering Holman ... Compiled by the author for Harriett Grace Scott ... (Concord, N. H., The Rumford press) 1936.   3 p. l., 529 p. front. (port.) 24½ cm. 37-523.   CS71.S552   1936

15516   SHERMAN.   Sherman family, a partial chart.   Compiled and drawn by: Charles M. Noble ... Trenton, N. J., 1946.   geneal. tab. coat of arms. 77 x 117½ cm. Reproduced from manuscript copy. 46-14820.   CS71.S552   1946

15517   SHERMAN.   Sherman and allied families.   By Bertha Mary (Ludwig) Stratton.   Staten Island, N. Y. (1951)   310 p. illus., ports., map, coats of arms. 23 cm. 56-23139.   CS71.S552   1951

15518   SHERMAN.   Some of the descendants of Philip Sherman, first secretary of Rhode Island. By Roy Vivian Sherman.   (Akron? Ohio) c. 1953.   unpaged. 28 cm. 54-19894.   CS71.S552   1953

15519   SHERMAN.   New light on Henry Sherman of Dedham, Essex, England, and some notes on his descendants, also Wm. Freeborn's English home and wife.   By Bertha Mary (Ludwig) Stratton.   Staten Island, N. Y. (c. 1954)   66 p. illus., ports., maps, coats of arms, facsim. 23 cm. 55-18994.
CS71.S552   1954

SHERMAN.   See also: ALLEN, 1938   O'DALY, 1956
                        ALLEN, 1939   RICHARDS, F74.D7J7
                        ANDERSON, 1916   STORY, 1920
                        BELFRY, 1888   TALCOTT, 1937
                        GLEASON, 1960   TUCKER, 1901

15520   SHERRARD.   The Sherrard family of Steubenville.   By Robert Andrew Sherrard.   Together with letters, records and genealogies of related families.   Edited by Thomas Johnson Sherrard. Philadelphia, The J. B. Rodgers printing company, 1890.   xi, 409 p. 24 cm. 9-13743.
CS71.S553   1890

SHERREN.   See STORY, 1920

15521   SHERRILL.   The descendants of Samuel Sherrill, of Easthampton, Long Island, New York, by Charles H. Sherrill, jr.   New York, 1894.   4 p. l., 132 p. fold. geneal. tables.   24 cm.   9-13742.
CS71.S554   1894

15522   SHERRILL.   The Sherrill genealogy; the descendants of Samuel Sherrill of East Hampton, Long island, New York, by Charles Hitchcock Sherrill.   2d and rev. ed., compiled and edited by Louis Effingham de Forest.   (New Haven, Printed by the Tuttle, Morehouse & Taylor company) 1932.
vii, 281, (3) p. front. (coat of arms) 24 cm.   Blank pages for "Addenda" (3 at end) First published in 1894 under title: The descendants of Samuel Sherrill, of Easthampton, Long island, New York. Bibliography: p. (237)-239. 32-16520.
CS71.S554   1932

15523   SHERRILL.   The Sherrill family: 1531 members - 12 generations, 300 years in America.   By Walter Lee Kitchens.   Texarkana (Tex., 1962)   29 p. 33 cm.   62-6358.
CS71.S554   1962

SHERRILL.   See also SHELTON, 1962

SHERTEL.   See SCHARTEL.

SHERTS.   See John Buchman family tree.   In vertical file.   Ask reference librarian for this material.

SHERWIN.   See PORTER, 1937

15524   SHERWOOD.   Daniel L. Sherwood and his paternal ancestors, including Sherwood evidences both in England and America from the first mention of the name in history, about seven hundred and fifty years ago, down to and including Thomas Sherwood, the American pioneer, and Francis Sherwood, the Maryland pioneer, and some of their many descendants.   In ten chapters, genealogical and bio-graphical.   By Andrew Sherwood ... Portland, Or., Ryder printing co., 1929.   390 p. plates, ports.
23½ cm. 29-23222.
CS71.S5542   1929

SHERWOOD.   See also: BLAUVELT, 1957
                                            BROMWELL, F180.B86
                                            HERIOT, 1931
                                            SEBOR, 1923

15525   SHETHAR.   Genealogy of the Shethar family ... New York, C. S. Williams, 1904.
56 l. 23 cm. Compiled by C. S. Williams.   "Edition of 35 copies."   This copy is no. 19.   12-30968.
CS71.S5543   1904

15526   SHETLEY.   Shetley genealogy.   (Compiled by Darius Harrison Shetley.   1st ed.   Greenville? S. C., 1965)   40 p. ports. 22 cm.   65-6805.
CS71.S55435   1965

SHETLEY.   See also HOFFMAN, 1915

SHEW.   See DUNHAM, 1933

SHEWELL.   See SEWALL.

SHEWFELT.   See SHUFELT, S5613

SHEWMAKE.   See SHUMATE.

SHIBUYA.   See IRIKIIN.

SHIELD.   See LIGON, 1947

15527   SHIELDS.   Daniel Shields, of county Antrim, Ireland, and his descendants in America, by Robert J. Shields ... New York, T. A. Wright, 1903.   18 p. front., plates, ports. 19 cm. 12-1822.   CS71.S5545   1903

15528   SHIELDS.   The Shields family.   (Chattanooga, 1916)   (3) p. ports.   30 cm.   (Notable southern families)
Detached from the Lookout of Dec. 16, 1916.   55-49905.   CS71.S5545   1916

15529   SHIELDS.   Daniel Shields of County Antrim Ireland and his descendants in America, by
Robert J. Shields ... (New York? 1930?)   41 p. plates, ports. 23½ cm. 31-19472.   CS71.S5545   1930

15530   SHIELDS.   A history of the Shields family; a selective genealogy of the descent of William
Shields, born, County Armagh, Ireland, 1728, died, Frederick County, Maryland, 1797.   By John
Edgar Shields.   Harrisburg, Pa., Printed by Triangle Press (1968)   116, (9) p. illus., facsims., ports. 23 cm.
Bibliography: p. 116-(117) 68-5503.   CS71.S5545   1968

SHIELDS.   See also: LAMBING, 1896
                       JOHNSON, 1962
                       STOUT, 1960
                       No. 516 - Notable southern families.

SHIFLETT.   See GLICK, 1959

15531   SHILLABER.   Record of proceedings at the first gathering of descendants of John Shillaber, at
the old homestead, Peabody, Mass., October 4, 1877 ... Boston, C. W. Calkins & co., printers, 1877.
48 p. 18 x 14 cm. At head of title: 1880. A family souvenir. 1877. Cover-title: Shillaber.   8-22385 rev.
                                                                        CS71.S555   1877

SHILLABER.   See also SAUNDERS, 1897

SHILLEA.   See SHELLEY.

SHILLEY.   See SHELLEY,

SHILLY.   See SHELLEY.

SHILTS.   See ALEXANDER, 1960

SHIMADZU.   See SHIMAZU.   (In main catalog)

15532   SHIMER.   History and genealogy of the Shimer family in America, by Allen R. Shimer ...
Allentown, Pa., Press of Berkemeyer, Keck & co., 1908 - 1931.   5 v. fronts., plates, ports. 24 cm. 16-7102.
                                                                        CS71.S5554   1908

15533   SHIMER.   Notes on the Shimer, Dreisbach, and Boyer families, by Charles S. Boyer.
Camden, N.J., 1936.   13, (1) p. 24½ cm. 36-30612.   CS71.S5554   1936

SHIMP.   See SCHIMPF.   (In main catalog)

SHIN.   See SHINN.

15534   SHINE.   History of the Shine family in Europe and America, by John W. Shine.   (Sault Ste.
Marie? Mich., 1917?)   2 p. l., 104, xvi p. ports. 24 cm. 23-18586.   CS71.S5558   1917

15535   SHINN.   The history of the Shinn family in Europe and America, by Josiah H. Shinn ...
(Chicago) The Genealogical and historical publishing company (1903)   434 p. incl. front., illus., ports. 26 cm.
p. 427-434 blank for Family record.   "Numbered copy 1."   Abner Shinn": 1 l. and portrait inserted at p. 364.   3-17940.
                                                                        CS71.S556   1903

15536   SHINN.   Ancestors and descendants of Samuel and Olive Carroll Shinn, prepared by Charles
W. Shinn.   (South Haven, Mich.) 1946.   16 p. 24 cm. Colored coat of arms of the Shinn family on cover.
47-24730.   CS71.S556   1946

SHINN.   See also: ARNY, 1961
                     FARR, 1927

15537   SHIPLEY.   The Shipleys of Maryland; a genealogical study, prepared by committees appointed at the Shipley reunion, College Park, Maryland, August 29, 1937.   (Baltimore, Printed by Reese press, c. 1938)   281, (7) p. incl. illus. (incl. facsims.) ports. col. coat of arms. 24½ cm.   "Copyright ... by the Shipley clan of Maryland."   Blank ruled pages for memoranda (7 at end)   Bibliography: p. 281,   38-23722.

CS71.S5567   1937

15538   SHIPLEY.   Shipley, Mitchell, and Thompson families; notes based in part on researches of Kate A. Thompson.   By Stith Thompson.   Bloomington (Ind.) 1964.   1 v. (various pagings) geneal. tables. 29 cm.   65-2486.

CS71.S5567   1964

SHIPLEY.   See also MUSSER, 1941

15539   SHIPMAN.   Genealogy of the Shipman family.   By Edward Perrine Cody.   (Wethersfield? Conn., 1949?)   geneal. table. 94 x 97 cm. fold. to 47 x 37 cm. Reproduction of original ms. compiled in 1948.   CS71.S55675   1949
—— Additions to the Genealogy of the family of Edward Shifton (Shipman) and his first wife Elizabeth Comstock of Wethersfield, Connecticut.   (Wethersfield? 1951)   geneal. table. 82 x 43 cm. Reproduction of original ms. compiled in 1951.   Add.   CS71.S55675   1949
—— Addition to the Genealogy of the family of Edward Shipton (Shipman) and his first wife Elizabeth Comstock.   (Wethersfield? 1951)   geneal. table. 42 x 47 cm. fold. to 42 x 32 cm. Reproduction of original ms. compiled in 1951.   CS71.S55675   1949   Add. 2

15540   SHIPMAN.   History of the Shipmans.   (Authors: Rita Shipman Carl and Angela Shipman Crispin.   Ann Arbor, Shipman Historical Association, 1954.   unpaged. 29 cm. 54-1968.

CS71.S55675   1954

15541   SHIPMAN.   History of the Shipmans, descended from Edward Shipman ... born in Nottinghamshire, England ... moved to Saybrook, Conn., about 1635 ... died at Saybrook Sept. 15, 1697. (Authors: Rita Shipman Carl and Angela Shipman Crispin.   Ann Arbor, Shipman Historical Association, 1954)   unpaged. port. 29 cm. "An expanded and revised edition." - Copyright application. 54-35803.

CS71.S55675   1954a

15542   SHIPMAN.   History of the Shipmans, descended from Edward Shipman ... born in Nottinghamshire, England ... moved to Saybrook, Conn., about 1635 ... died at Saybrook, Sept. 15, 1697. (Compiled by Rita Shipman Carl, Angela Shipman Crispin, and William Henry Shipman.   Ann Arbor? Mich., Shipman Historical Association, 1955)   2 vol. illus. 29 cm. 55-56943.   CS71.S55675   1955

15543   SHIPMAN.   The Shipman family in America.   Compiled by Mrs. Wayne A. Carl (Rita Shipman) (and others.   n. p., 1962)   688 p. illus. 29 cm. 62-20150.   CS71.S55675   1962

SHIPMAN.   See also: FISHER, 1890
SOUTHWORTH, 1903

15544   SHIPP.   The Shipp genealogy from Essex, Caroline, Faquier (!) Counties, Virginia, to Green, Taylor, Woodford, Jefferson, Fayette, Christian, Bourbon, Scott, Christian (sic), Owen Counties, Kentucky, and Johnson County, Indiana.   Litchfield, Ill., 1946.   50 l. geneal. table. 28 cm. 49-22656*.

CS71.S5568   1946

SHIPP.   See also DULIN, 1961

15545   SHIPPEN.   Letters and papers relating chiefly to the provincial history of Pennsylvania, with some notices of the writers.   (By Thomas Balch) Privately printed.   Philadelphia, Crissy & Markley, printers, 1855.   cxxxviii, 312 p. 20½ cm. A selection from the "Shippen Mss." in possession of the Historical society of Pennsylvania; with other letters, papers, etc. 1-10398.   F152.B17

15546   SHIPPEN.   Genealogy of the descendants of Dr. Wm. Shippen, the elder, of Philadelphia; member of the Continental congress.   By Roberdeau Buchanan ... Privately printed.   Washington, J. L. Pearson, printer, 1877.   16 p. 23½ cm. The first three generations are taken, aided by a few dates or facts from other sources, from the genealogy published in 1855 by Thomas Balch entitled: Letters and papers relating chiefly to the provincial history of Pennsylvania. 9-13741.   CS71.S557   1877

15547   SHIPPEN.   The English ancestors of the Shippen family and Edward Shippen of Philadelphia; by Thomas Willing Balch ... Philadelphia, 1904.   20 p. front. (port.) pl. 25½ cm.   Reprinted from the Pennsylvania magazine of history and biography.   Oct., 1904.   5-4111.

CS71.S557   1904

15548   SHIPPEN.   The passing of an old landmark ... Lancaster, Pa., 1914.   2 p. l., p. 251-276. plates. 24½ cm.   (Papers read before the Lancaster County historical society ... December 4, 1914 ... vol. XVIII, no. 10)   By William Uhler Hensel.   An account of the Shippen house, Lancaster, Pa.   "Minutes of December meeting": p. 275-276.   17-23120.

F157.L2L5 vol.18

15549   SHIPPEN.   Seven generations of physicians.   By George Shuyler Bangert ... (New York, A. R. Elliott publishing company, 1920)   cover-title, 8, (1) p. 20½ cm.   "Reprinted from the New York medical journal for August 28, 1920."   An account of the Shippen family.   CA 31-348 unrev.

R154.S46B3

15550   SHIPPEN.   Nancy Shippen, her journal book; the international romance of a young lady of fashion of colonial Philadelphia, with letters to her and about her.   Compiled and edited by Ethel Armes ... Philadelphia, London, J. B. Lippincott company, 1935.   3 p. l., 5-348, (1) p. col. front., 1 illus., plates, ports., facsims. (incl. music) fold. geneal. tab., coat of arms. 23 cm.   Plans on lining-papers.   "First edition."   Bibliography: p. 317-(321) 35-32239.

E302.6.L67L6

SHIPPEN.   See also: HUIDEKOPER, 1931a
                        WILLING, 1941

15551   SHIPWAY.   The "Principal genealogical specialist;" or, Regina v. Davies and the Shipway genealogy, being the story of a remarkable pedigree fraud.   By W. P. W. Phillimore ... London, Phillimore & co., 1899.   64 p. fold. front., fold. pl., fold. facsim. 21½ cm.   3-3190.

CS439.S48

SHIRBURNE.   See SHERBURNE.

15552   SHIRK.   John Shirk, veteran of the war of 1812; his ancestors and his descendants, by Nannie Hammer Betts.   (n.p.) 1934.   3 p. l., 104 p. plates, ports., facsims. 24 cm.   37-21326.

CS71.S5576   1934

15553   SHIRLEY.   Stemmata Shirleiana; or, The annals of the Shirley family, lords of Nether Etindon, in the county of Warwick, and of Shirley, in the county of Derby ... Westminster, Priv. print. by J. B. Nichols and son, 1841.   vi p., 1 l., 271, (1), 80 p. illus. (incl. coats of arms) pl., fold. geneal. tab. 18½ cm.   Title vignette (coat of arms)   The 2d edition, 1873, has dedication signed: Evelyn Philip Shirley.   "Appendix of deeds and other evidences illustrating the early descents of the Shirley family": 80 p. at end.   Contains also pedigrees of the Braose, Staunton, Lovett, Devereux and Ferrers, Washington and Ireton families.   21-1475.

CS439.S485   1841

15554   SHIRLEY.   The Sherley brothers, an historical memoir of the lives of Sir Thomas Sherley, Sir Anthony Sherley, and Sir Robert Sherley, knights.   By one of the same house.   Chiswick, Press of C. Whittingham, 1848.   viii, 110 p. 25 x 20 cm.   "To the president and members of the Roxburghe club this memoir compiled from materials hitherto inedited, is dedicated and presented by ... Evelyn Philip Shirley."   Rev. William Edward Buckley's copy (name in red in list of members)   12-16230.

PR1105.R7   1848

15555   SHIRLEY.   ... Lough Fea ... London, Priv. print. (Chiswick press, C. Whittingham, printer) 1859.   23, (1) p. 21½ cm.   "An account of Lough Fea house by E. P. Shirley." - Brit. mus. Catalogue.   16-23495.

CS499.S5   1859

15556   SHIRLEY.   ... Lough Fea ... 2d ed.   London, Priv. print., 1869.   26 p. 22 cm.   Two autograph letters of author mounted in front of this copy.   16-23497.

CS499.S5   1869

15557   SHIRLEY.   Lower Eatington: its manor house and church.   London, Priv. print. at the Chiswick press, 1869.   73, (3) p. illus. 22½ cm.   Title vignette; line borders.   Dedicatory lines signed "E.P.S." i.e. Evelyn Philip Shirley.   2-30181.

DA690.E18S5

15558   SHIRLEY.   Stemmata Shirleiana; or, The annals of the Shirley family, lords of Nether Etindon in the county of Warwick, and of Shirley in the county of Derby ... 2d ed. cor. and enl.   Westminster, Nichols and sons, 1873.   vi p., 3 l., 435, (1) p. illus., geneal. tables (1 fold.) 29 cm.   Dedication signed: Evelyn Philip Shirley.   14-19508.

CS439.S485   1873

15559   SHIRLEY.   A genealogical table of the noble family of Shirley, earl Ferrers &c.   London,
H. W. Reach (1903?)   geneal. tab.   60 x 74 cm.   Blue-print.   36-5859.   CS439.S485   1903

15560   SHIRLEY.   A brief history and genealogy of the Shirley family, by Mrs. Augusta Letitia
Shirley Moore.   (Oklahoma City, 1911)   cover-title, 1 p. 1., (5)-55, (2) p.   ports.   22½ cm.   Two pages at end left blank
for "Births."   21-13628.   CS71.S5575   1911

15561   SHIRLEY.   From England to North Carolina: two special gifts.   By Ethel Stephenson Arnett.
(1st ed.)   New Bern, N. C., Tryon Palace Restoration, 1964.   93 p.   illus.   26 cm.   Bibliographical references included in "Notes" (p. 87-93)   64-8371.   CS71.S5575   1964

SHIRLEY.   See also No. 4639 - Smithfield.

SHIRREFF.   See SEBOR, 1923

15562   SHIVELY.   (Descendants of Christian Shively of Warwick Township, Lancaster County, Pa.
(By Arthur Geiger Black)   Kansas City, Mo., 1942?)   2 v.   illus.   maps (part fold.)   facsims.   31 cm.   Photocopy
(negative)   47-40806*.   CS71.S5576   1942

15563   SHLUGER.   The Good life: Alexander L. Shluger.   (New York? 1945?)   cover-title, 32 p.   illus.
(mounted port.)   26 cm.   "Save for the sketch of Alex Shluger's life, most of the tributes published here were given at a memorial meeting at the
HIAS ... in New York city ... February 18th, 1945 ... Included are the resolutions adopted at the annual re-union of the Thomas Davidson society,
April 15th, 1945, and the tributes given at that meeting." - p. 2.   47-15320.   CT275.S4883G6

15564   SHOBE.   A genealogy of the Shobe, Kirkpatrick and Dilling families, compiled and published
by F. D. Shobe.   Chicago, Ill., 1919.   2 p. 1., (1), 184 p. incl. illus. (ports.) geneal. tables.   26½ cm.   37-16853.
                CS71.S5577   1919

15565   SHOBE.   A genealogy of the Shobe, Kirkpatrick, and Dilling families.   By Franklin Dilling
Shobe.   (Chicago, 1950)   xix p., reprint (184 p. illus., ports.)   27 cm.   Cover title.   Additions in ms.   Includes reproduction of
original ed. published in 1919.   50-55425.   CS71.S5577   1950

SHOCKLEE.   See WORLAND, 1968

SHOCKLESS.   See WORLAND, 1968

15566   SHOEMAKER.   Some account of the life and family of George Shoemaker, for half a century
flour inspector of Georgetown, D. C.   By Edward Shoemaker.   West Washington, D. C., Priv. print.
(by) L. E. Mankin (1882)   cover-title, 18 p.   21 cm.   7-1507.   CS71.S558   1882

15567   SHOEMAKER.   The Shoemaker family.   By Thomas H. Shoemaker.   Philadelphia, Printed by
J. B. Lippincott company, 1893.   112 p.   pl., ports.   26 cm.   9-13740.
                CS71.S558   1893

15568   SHOEMAKER.   The Indian and the pioneer, an historical study, by Rose N. Yawger ...
Syracuse, N. Y., C. W. Bardeen, 1893.   2 v. in 1.   fronts., plates, maps.   23 cm.   (On cover: School bulletin publications)
Contains genealogies of the Shoemaker, Van Sickle and Yawger families.   4-32407.   E99.I7Y3

15569   SHOEMAKER.   Genealogy of the Shoemaker family of Cheltenham, Pennsylvania, comp. by
Benjamin H. Shoemaker.   Philadelphia, Printed for private circulation by J. B. Lippincott company,
1903.   x, 524 p. 10 pl., 20 port. (incl. front.) plan, 2 facsim.   27½ cm.   "Edition limited to four hundred copies of which this is no. 135."
3-31207.   CS71.S558   1903

15570   SHOEMAKER.   The Shoemaker family of Shoemakersville, Pennsylvania, 1682-1909.   Reading, Pa.   (Printed by L. S. Mohr) 1909.   2 p. 1., 42 p.   front., illus., plates, ports.   21 cm.   20-7227.
                CS71.S558   1909

15571   SHOEMAKER.   The Michael Shoemaker book (Schumacher) (by) Williams T. Blair.   Printed
for J. I. Shoemaker, Wyoming, Pa.   Scranton, Pa., International text book press, 1924.   xii, 995 p.
front., plates, ports. (1 fold.)   24½ cm.   Bibliography: p. 971-977.   27-25026.   CS71.S558   1924

15572   SHOEMAKER.   A genealogical and biographical record of the Shoemaker family of Gloucester and Salem counties, N.J., 1765-1935.   Traced and assembled by Hubert Bastian Shoemaker ... (Philadelphia, Pa., Printed by Temple type-crafters, 1935)   xiii; 236 p. col. front. (coat of arms) plates. 24 cm. "This edition is limited to 300 copies." 41-38345.   CS71.S558   1935

SHOEMAKER.   See also: PASTORIUS, 1926
                                           STRASSBURGER, 1922

15573   SHOFFNER.   The history of one branch of the Shoffner family; or, John Shofner and his descendants, including also Records of the Shoffner reunions.   By C. L. Shoffner ... Nashville, Tenn., McQuiddy printing company, 1905.   1 p. l., (7)-131 p. front. (port.) 19½ cm. 22-1705.   CS71.S5583   1905

SHOFFSTALL.   See No. 1547 - Cabell county.

SHOLL.   See SCHOLL.

15574   SHONKWILER.   Daniel Shonkwiler, Senior, and some of his descendants, 1781-1954.   By William Forrest Shonkwiler.   (n.p., 195-)   33 p. illus. 28 cm. 58-37843.   CS71.S55835

15575   SHONKWILER.   The Napoleon Bonaparte Shonkwiler family, by William F. Shonkwiler, Helen I. Shepherd & Nadine Woolridge.   St. Louis, 1966.   iii, 41 p. facsims., ports. 28 cm. Cover title. 67-9391.
                                                                                              CS71.S3814   1966

SHOOK.   See FROST, 1962

SHOOP.   See ENDERS, 1960

15576   SHOPP.   Shopp's Station.   By Nora Belle Thompson.   (Lancaster? Pa., 1958)   28 p. illus. 23 cm. 58-36407.   CS71.S55837   1958

SHORES.   See EVERHART, 1883

15577   SHORT.   Ohio Valley culture as reflected in the Short family, 1790-1860. By Irving Frederick Ahlquist.   Urbana, 1947.   14 p. 23 cm. Abstract of thesis - Univ. of Illinois. Vita. Illinois Univ. Lib. for Library of Congress. A48-3245*.   CS71.S5584   1947

SHORT.   See also: BOONE, 1902
                                  HASSARD, 1858
                                  WILFORD, 1959

SHORTALL.   See GARVEY, 1883

15578   SHORTER.   Old Shorter houses and gardens, by Annie Kendrick Walker ... New York, T. A. Wright, 1911.   3 p. l., 5-66 p. plates, ports. 19½ cm. "Edition of one hundred copies of which this is no. -." 12-949.
                                                                                              CS71.S5585   1911

SHORTER.   See also: HURT, 1948
                                   HURT, 1952

15579   SHORTHOUSE.   Memorials of the families of Shorthouse and Robinson and others connected with them.   Printed in commemoration of the one hundredth birthday of Sarah Southall, 12th September, 1901 ... Birmingham, Morland & Henson, 1902.   4 p. l., 90 p. front., plates, ports., fold. geneal. tab., facsims. 27 cm. "For private circulation."   "Prefatory note" signed: William Ransom, Margaret Evans, Isabel Southall. 40-283.   CS439.S488   1902

15580   SHOTWELL.   Annals of our colonial ancestors and their descendants; or, Our Quaker forefathers and their posterity ... Embracing a genealogical and biographical register of nine generations ... of the Shotwell family in America ... together with the pedigree and near kindred of the author's parents, Nathan and Phebe B. (Gardner) Shotwell ... Comp. by Ambrose M. Shotwell ... Lansing, Mich., Printed for the author by R. Smith & co. (1897)   viii, 299, (1) p. incl. ports. front., illus., plates, ports. 27½ cm. Blank leaves inserted. 9-13739.   CS71.S559   1897

SHOTWELL.   See also WILSON, 1959

15580a   SHOUSE.   The Shouse family (prepared by Thomas R. Shouse)   (Liberty, Mo., 1928)
cover-title, (63) p. 18 cm. 31-22377.   CS71.S5595   1928

15581   SHOUSE.   Johan Adam Schaus (Shouse) of Easton, Pennsylvania and some of his descendants,
prepared by H. T. Cory.   Washington, D. C., 1931.   1 p. l., 11 numb. l. 29 cm. Type-written. 31-22378.
CS71.S5595   1931

15582   SHOUSE.   Henry Shouse, his forebears and some of his descendants.   By Mary Armstrong
Shouse.   (n. p.) 1957.   48 l. 28 cm. 58-23814.   CS71.S5595   1957

15583   SHOUSE.   Shouse families; a partial listing of the descendants of some colonial families.
By Eugene Earl Trimble.   Kensington? Md., 1963.   iv, 126 p. 28 cm. Includes bibliographical references.
78-5674 MARC.   CS71.S5595   1963

SHOUSE.   See also ALLEN, 1921

15584   SHOWALTER.   History of the Showalter family.   By Portia (Showalter) Everett.   (Brookville?
Ind., 1964)   84 p. illus. 23 cm. 64-55042.   CS71.S5598   1964

SHOWALTER.   See also BAKER, 1964

SHRAPNELL.   See NEWSOM, 1898

15585   SHREVE.   The genealogy and history of the descendants of Mercy Shreve and James White,
by L. P. Allen ... Greenfield, Ill., Priv. print., 1897.   viii, 135, 110 p. front. (coat of arms) pl., ports. 23½ cm.
"Sketches of Thomas White, of Ohio (son of Mercy Shreve and James White) His children and grandchildren" has special title-page and separate
paging. 9-13738.   CS71.S56   1897

15586   SHREVE.   The genealogy and history of the Shreve family from 1641.   By L. P. Allen.
Greenfield, Ill., Priv. print., 1901.   viii, 664 p. front., pl., ports., coats of arms. 24½ cm. 1-7151.
CS71.S56   1901

15587   SHREWSBURY.   Shrewsbury and Warth families of early Virginia.   Research and compilation
by Mrs. E. James Gambaro (nee, Harriet Guild Shrewsbury) New York, 1968.   15 l. geneal. tables. 30 cm.
Cover title. 71-6751 MARC.   CS71.S5602   1968

SHREWSBURY.   See MILLER, 1917

SHRIMPLIN.   See WHITE, 1940

15588   SHRIVER.   History of the Shriver family.   Dedicated to the rising generation of the Shriver
family in loving memory of our ancestors ... (By Pearl J. Shriver) (n. p., 1925?)   (52) p. incl. illus., ports.,
front. 23 cm. Blank pages for "Births, marriages, deaths" (46-48) Preface signed: P.J. Schriver. Additions inserted at end (4 p.) 31-18267.
CS71.S5603   1925

15589   SHRIVER.   A history of the Shriver family, with particular reference to Jacob Shriver (1714-
1792) his son Lewis Shriver (1750-1815) and their descendants.   By Harry Clair Shriver.   (n. p.,
1962)   45 l. 29 cm. 62-6537.   CS71.S5603   1962

15590   SHRIVER.   History of the Shriver family and their connections, 1684-1888.   By Samuel S.
Shriver.   Published for members of the family.   Baltimore, Press of Guggenheimer, Weil, 1888.
(n. p., 1962)   160, (8) p. front., geneal. tables. 29 cm. Includes 4 geneal. tables added in 1962 at end of the first part by R. J. Shriver
and A. Elizabeth Shriver Ritterhoff.   "Supplement, 1766-1892": p. (161) - (168) 63-35722.
CS71.S5603   1962a

15591   SHRODE.   America's greatest pioneer family; history of the Shrode family in America, by
I. T. Taylor ... (Nashville, McQuiddy pty. co., 1945)   9 p. l., 345 p. incl. front., ports., coats of arms. 23½ cm.
Includes the Taylor, Duffey and Jamison families. 45-11297.   CS71.S5604   1945

15592   SHROPSHIRE.   The Shropshires and allied families.   By Lennoe Lee (Schermerhorn) Drew.
Birmingham, Ala., Birmingham Print. Co. (1948)   xvii, 180 p. illus., ports. 24 cm. 48-11658*.
CS71.S56045

15593   SHRUM.   The history of the Schrum-Shrum family, compiled by Vernon J. Schrum.   Raleigh,
N. C. (1968)   83 l. col. coat of arms. 28 cm. 72-8148 MARC.   CS71.S56048

15594   SHRYOCK.   (Genealogical chart of the Shryock family.   By Joseph Grundy Shryock.   n. p.,
1929)   geneal. tab. illus. (coat of arms) 91 x 93 cm. Blue-print. Contains "References". 29-25266.
CS71.S5605   1929

15595   SHRYOCK.   (Ancestral chart of Joseph Grundy Shryock and Aimée Caroline Picolet) Compiled
by Joseph Grundy Shryock.   (n. p.) 1929.   geneal. tab. illus. (coat of arms) 61 x 91 cm. Blue print. "References."
31-22374.
CS71.S5605   1929a

15596   SHRYOCK.   ... Genealogical fan chart showing many "Shryock" collateral lines ... Washing-
ton, D. C., 1930.   geneal. tab. illus. (coats of arms) 92 x 122 cm. (With his Shryock genealogy; descendants of the emigrant ancestor
John Schryock ... Philadelphia, Penna., 1930) Title in manuscript on verso of chart. "Revised (4-16-1930) blue print ... To replace the old print
now void in the Library of Congress." 30-30494.
CS71.S5605   1930

15597   SHRYOCK.   Shryock genealogy; descendants of the emigrant ancestor John Schryock, born in
Germany in 1705, emigrated to America in 1733.   By Joseph Grundy Shryock ... Philadelphia, Penna.,
1930.   1 p. l., 15 numb. l. front., ports., col. coat of arms. 29½ cm. Blue-print. 30-13820.   CS71.S5605   1930a

15598   SHRYOCK.   Shryock.   (Ancestors of Joseph Grundy Shryock)   (n. p., 1930)   2 p., 1 l. port.
27 cm. "Authorities": p. (2) 31-19490.   CS71.S5605   1930b

15599   SHRYOCK.   The Shryock line, descendants of Hans Jarick (or Hans Jerg) Schreyack (Johannes
George Schreyack) (By Rhea Edna (Duryea) Johnson.) (Philadelphia, 1945) (i.e.91)   3 p. l., 90
(i.e.91) numb. l. illus. (coats of arms) 29½ cm. Includes extra numbered leaf 79 a. Compiled by Rhea Duryea Johnson. cf. Foreword.
46-1546.
CS71.S5605   1945

15600   SHUBRICK.   ... Report of the Special committee of the Chamber of commerce on relief of
the family of the late Lieutenant Edmond Templer Shubrick, U.S.N., submitted to the chamber at the
regular monthly meeting, held February 1, 1866, and unanimously adopted.   (New York, 1866)
4 p. 23½ cm. 18-20435.   E182.S558

SHUCK.   See McCHORD, 1941

15601   SHUEY.   History of the Shuey family in America, from 1732 to 1876.   By D. B. Shuey, A. M.
Lancaster, Pa., Pub. for the members of the family, by the author, 1876.   viii, 9-279 p. 19 cm. Leaf con-
taining Revised data received Dec. 18, 1877, inserted. 9-13737.
CS71.S561   1876

15602   SHUEY.   History of the Shuey family in America from 1732 to 1919.   2d ed.   By Dennis
Boeshore Shuey.   Galion, O., The author, 1919.   381 p. 24 cm. 20-1910.   CS71.S561   1919

15603   SHUFELT.   Our folks: a history of the Shufelt family (Shufelt, Shufeldt, Shewfelt and Zufelt)
compiled by Henry B. Shufelt, principally from material collected by Allen E. and Mrs. Clapper.
(Monteal? Canada) Shufelt Family Association (1935)   269 p. 25 cm. 38-32644 rev.   CS71.S5613   1935

15604   SHUFORD.   The genealogy of my family.   By Thomas Rhyne Shuford.   Shreveport, La., 1948.
7 l. 29 cm. Tyepwritten. 50-28696.   CS71.S5615   1948

SHULER.   See AVINGER, 1961

SHULL.   See: GLICK, 1959
                       SCHOLL, 1940

15605   SHULTZ.   ... The George Shultz family, by Wilbur L. Shultz.   Morrison, Ill., The Shawver publishing co. (1926?)   22 p. 27½ cm. (American families series) 31-19485.   CS71.S562   1926

15606   SHULTZ.   A genealogy of the Shultz, Cupp, Weyand and Pisel families which have descended from Michael Shultz, a pioneer settler in Somerset county, Pennsylvania, many of whose descendants have also been pioneers throughout the United States and Canada ... Collected and assembled , .. by Charles Ross Shultz ... (Pittsburgh? 1945)   2 p. l., 205, (4) p. pl., ports. 22½ cm. Reproduced from type-written copy. "Second edition." - 2d prelim. leaf.   45-9544.   CS71.S562   1945

15607   SHULTZ.   Shultz family record, 1716-1966; from Hesse-Darmstadt to Huntingdon and Hagerstown, compiled and edited by Lawrence W. Shultz.   North Manchester, Ind., 1966.   528 p. illus., geneal. table, maps, ports. 29 cm. 67-7584.   CS71.S562   1966

15608   SHUMAN.   The George Shuman family; genealogy and history from the time of arrival in America, in 1760, to the year 1913, by William C. Shuman ... Evanston, Ill., W. C. Shuman, 1913.   341 p. incl. front., illus. (incl. ports.) 26½ cm. 36-12589.   CS71.S5627   1913

15609   SHUMATE.   The Shumate family; a genealogy.   By Theodor Friedrich Von Stauffenberg.   Washington, P. E. Hendrick, 1964.   x, 271 p. facsims., geneal. tables. 28 cm. Bibliography: p. 242-246.   65-757.   CS71.S5628   1964

15610   SHUMWAY.   Genealogy of the Shumway family in the United States of America, comp. by Asabel Adams Shumway ... New York, T. A. Wright, 1909.   478 p. front., plates, ports. 24 cm. Edition limited to 200 copies.   12-1811.   CS71.S563   1909

15611   SHUMWAY.   Sands Shumway, his ancestors & his descendants.   By Floyd Mallory Shumway.   New York (1963)   20 l. 30 cm. Bibliography: leaves 18-20.   65-75056.   CS71.S563   1963

15612   SHUPE.   Genealogy of the Shupe family, early settlers of Amherst, Lorain County, Ohio.   By Claude Charles Hamel.   Amherst, 1948.   7 l. 27 cm. Typewritten. "References": leaf 7.   50-25468.   CS71.S565   1948

15613   SHURTLEFF.   Brief notice of William Shurtleff, of Marshfield.   By Nathaniel Bradstreet Shurtleff.   Boston, Priv. print., 1850.   19 p. 18 cm. 3-7920.   CS71.S566   1850

15614   SHURTLEFF.   Shirecliffe.   (Descendants of William Shurtleff of Marshfield, Mass.) By Dr. Henry C. Shurtleff.   Philadelphia, 1895.   geneal. tab. 28 x 56 cm. fold. to 23½ x 14 cm. 2-12085.   CS71.S566   1895

15615   SHURTLEFF.   Descendants of William Shurtleff of Plymouth and Marshfield, Massachusetts, compiled by Benjamin Shurtleff (6th) ... Revere, Mass., 1912.   2 v. front., plates, ports., plan, facsims., col. coat of arms.   24 cm.   "The earlier portions of this work were compiled by Dr. Nathaniel B. Shurtleff." 13-1818.   CS71.S566   1912

15616   SHUSTER.   Daniel Shuster (1752-1818) geneological (!) and historical records of his descendants to 1943 ... (Columbus, O., Hollenback press) c. 1944.   (3)-112 p. 24 cm. Most of the laves printed on one side only. 44-35602.   CS71.S567   1944

SHUTE.   See: KELLEY, 1892
                       VENABLE, 1961

15617   SHUTTLEWORTH.   The house and farm accounts of the Shuttleworths of Gawthorpe hall, in the county of Lancaster, at Smithils and Gawthorpe, from September 1582 to October 1621.   Ed. by John Harland ... (Manchester) Printed for the Chetham society (1856)-58.   4 v. fronts. (v. 1-2; v. 2, port.) 23 x 18 cm. (Added t. -p.: Remains, historical & literary, connected with the palatine counties of Lancaster and Chester, pub. by the Chetham society. vol. XXXV, XLI, XLIII, XLVI) Paged continuously. Each volume has special t. p.; v. 4 has also general t. - p.   Appendix. I. The Shuttleworths and their residences. II. Prices, wages, &c: v. 2, p. (259)-393. 18-5252.   DA670. L19C5 vol. 35, 41, 43, 46

15618   SIAS.   The Sias family in America, 1677 to 1952; the first 275 years.   From materials gathered through long and painstaking efforts by many members of the family.   By Azariah Boody Sias. Orlando, Fla., Printed by Florida Press, 1952 (i.e. 1953)-57.   2 v. illus., ports., maps (on lining papers) geneal. table. 24 cm. Vol. 2: Supplement. Bibliography: v.1, p. (703); v.2, p.439-440. 53-32942 rev.

CS71.S569   1953

15619   SIBBET.   Genealogy of the Sibbet and the Witherspoon families.   By Jesse (Laing) Sibbet. (Pasadena? Calif., 1954)   14, 20 l., 2 geneal. tables (in envelope) 24 cm. 55-25884.

CS71.S5697   1954

15620   SIBBET.   History of the Sibbet family.   By Jessie (Laing) Sibbet.   (Pasadena, Calif., Sibbet Publications, 1969)   126 p. illus., 2 fold. geneal. tables (1 in pocket), ports. 28 cm. Bibliographical footnotes. 76-5399 MARC.

CS71.S5697   1969

15621   SIBERT.   The Sibert family of South Carolina and Alabama.   Compiled by J. Luther Beeson. (Mobile, Ala., Press of Acme printing company, 1928)   17 p., 1 l. 24 cm. 28-9891.

CS71.S563   1928

15622   SIBLEY.   The ancestry, life and times of Hon. Henry Hastings Sibley.   By Nathaniel West. Saint Paul, Minn., Pioneer press publishing co., 1889.   x, 596 p., 1 l. front. (port.) 23 cm. "Official military reports and dispatches ... Henry Hastings Sibley, first (and second Sioux campaigns) 1862-(1863)" p. 458-549. 11-30219.

F606.S565

15623   SIBLEY.   Ancestry and life of Josiah Sibley, born April 1st, 1808, at Uxbridge, Mass., died December 7th, 1888, at Augusta, Ga.; compiled by Robert Pendleton Sibley, John Adams Sibley (and) James Longstreet Sibley ... Augusta, Ga., Williams press, 1908.   120, iii p. incl. illus., plates (1 col.) ports., facsims., col. coat of arms. port. 24 cm. One leaf of "Errata" inserted before t.-p. 39-16930.

CS71.S571   1908

SIBLEY.   See also TURNER, 1936

15624   SICARD.   Histoire d'une famille de Languedoc; (cinq cents ans d'histoire familiale, les Sicard au diocèse de Saint-Pons.   Par Roger Sicard.   Paris, 1962)   305 p. illus. 28 cm. 63-37572.

CS599.S56

15625   SICKELS.   The Frank E. Sickels family; in memory of Frank Edward Sickels (1860-1920) and Annie Lawrence Sickels (1861-1916), by their daughter Eleanor M. Sickels.   (n.p.) 1966. 119 l. 28 cm. Bibliographical footnotes. 67-6150.   CS71.S5712   1966

SICKELS.   See also PEABODY, 1929

15626   SIDDALL.   Siddalls in America (the Phineas line)   By Teckla Anne (Fisher) Siddall.   (Sherman Oaks? Calif.) c.1962.   172 p. illus. 24 cm. 62-36814.   CS71.S5713

SIDENER.   See SEIDNER.

SIDENOR.   See SEIDNER.

15627   SIDERFIN.   History of the Siderfin family of West Somerset.   By James Sanders ... Exeter, W. J. Southwood and co., 1912.   47 p. illus. (coats of arms) fold. geneal. tab. 21 cm. 16-15064.

CS439.S492

SIDGWICH.   See BENSON, 1895

SIDNER.   See SEIDNER.

15628   SIDNEY.   Sydney papers, consisting of a journal of the Earl of Leicester, and original letters of Algernon Sydney.   Ed. with notes, &c., by R. W. Blencowe ... London, J. Murray, 1825. xxxvi, 284 p. 2 facsim. 23 cm. 4-24420.   DA306.S6L4

15629   SIDNEY.   The pedigree of Sir Philip Sidney,   Comp. by Robert Cooke ... Copied from the original roll, in the possession of Alexander Nesbitt, esq., F. S. A., of Hatchford.   London, Priv. print. (Taylor and co., printers) 1869.   1 p. l., 7 p. illus., pl. 29 cm. Title vignette. The restorations made by T. W. King. Issued also in Miscellanea genealogica et heraldica. v. 2, p. 160-167. 9-18121.   CS439.S5

15630   SIDNEY.   Memoirs of the Sidney family, by Philip Sidney ... London, T. F. Unwin, 1899.   xv p., 1 l., 232 p. 7 port. (incl. front.) 2 facsim. 21 cm. 1-6164.   DA306.S6S5

15631   SIDNEY.   The Sidneys of Penshurst, by Philip Sidney ... with six photogravures ... London, S. H. Bousfield & co., ld., 1901.   vii (i. e. viii), 277, (2) p. incl. geneal. tab. front., 5 port. 22½ cm. Page viii erroniously numbered vii.   "An extended and ... revised edition of the author's Memoirs of the Sidney family." - Pref. 2-12141.   DA306.S6S52

15632   SIDNEY.   ... Report on the manuscripts of Lord de l'Isle & Dudley preserved at Penshurst place ... London, H. M. Stationery off., 1925 -   v. 25 cm. At head of title, v. 1 -   : Historical manuscripts commision. Prepared and edited by Mr. C. L. Kingsford. cf. v. 1, p. (2) 27-1796.   DA25.M2D35

SIDNEY.   See also BROWN, CD1069.B2

SIDNOR.   See SEIDNER.

15633   SIDWELL.   A genealogy of the Pennsylvania, Maryland and Ohio branches of the Sidwell family, compiled from various published and unpublished sources, by a member of the family.   Washington, D. C., 1930.   1 p. l., 58 numb. l. 27 cm. Type-written. 32-5814.   CS71.S5714   1930

15634   SIEBERN.   Some Siebern (Seaborn) records.   By William Heller Dyar.   (n. p.) 1963.   v, 65, xv l. illus., ports., maps, coats of arms. 29 cm. 63-23645.   CS71.S5716   1963

15635   SIEBERT.   The Abraham J. Siebert family record.   By Lydia Eck Cooper.   North Newton, Kan., Bethel College Historical Library, 1959.   93 p. 30 cm. 65-4966.   CS71.S5718   1959

SIEBERT.   See also DECKER, 1959

SIEGFRIED.   See CLEWELL, 1907

SIFAKAS.   See SĒPHAKAS.

15636   SIGGINS.   Genealogical gleanings of Siggins and other Pennsylvania families; a volume of history, biography and colonial, revolutionary, civil and other war records including names of many other Warren County pioneers, comp. by Emma Siggins White, assisted by Martha Humphreys Maltby.   Kansas City, Mo., Tiernan-Dart printing co., 1918.   xii p., 1 l., (5)-714 p. front., illus., plates (1 col.) ports., coats of arms (part col.) 24 cm. "References consulted": p. vii-viii. 18-18121.   CS71.S572   1918

15637   SIGLER.   Our Sigler ancestors: early settlers in Mifflin county, Pennsylvania, by Raymond Martin Bell ... Carlisle, Pa., 1934.   1 p. l., 17 p. 23 cm. 34-5043.   CS71.S578   1934

15638   SIGLER.   The Sigler family of Mifflin County, Penna.   By Raymond Martin Bell.   Washington, Pa., 1958.   20 l. 28 cm. Published in 1934 under title: Our Sigler ancestors. 58-45418.   CS71.S578   1958

SIGLER.   See also BACON, 1958

15639   SIGOURNEY.   Genealogy of the Sigourney family.   By Henry H. W. Sigourney.   Boston and Cambridge, J. Munroe and company, 1857.   31 p. 25 cm. 9-13734.   CS71.S579   1857

SIGOURNEY.   See also FANEUIL, 1851

SIKES.   See: HUNTER, 1959
               SYKES.

15640   SILER.   The Siler family, a compilation of biographical and historical sketches relating to the descendants of Plikard Dederic and Elizabeth Siler, with genealogical chart; compiled by A. O. Siler. (Charleston, W. Va., Tribune printing co.) 1922.   242 p. 19 cm.   37-38454.   CS71.S58   1922

15641   SILER.   The family of Weimar Siler, 1755-1831.   By Leona Cornelia (Bryson) Porter.   Published by the committee appointed at the 100th meeting.   Franklin, N. C., 1951 (i. e. 1952)
178 p. illus. 24 cm. 52-41629.   CS71.S58   1952

15642   SILL.   Genealogy of the descendants of John Sill, who settled in Cambridge, Mass., 1637. Albany, Munsell & Rowland, 1859.   vi, (7)-108 p. 18½ cm.   Preface signed: George G. Sill.   Edited by Louisa P. Sill and Henry A. Sill.   9-13736.   CS71.S583   1859

15643   SILL.   My mother's family, Shannon-Sill, Pennsylvania and Ohio, Hamilton-Robinson, Virginia and Indiana (by) Edith Attkison Rudder.   (Salem? Ind., 1942?)   38 p. 23 cm.   Pages 35-38 blank for "Record." 42-16002.   CS71.S583   1942

SILL.   See also: BELDEN, E171.A53 vol. 13
                            SELL.
                            SELLERS.
                            SELLS.
                            SHEPARD, 1949

SILLEY.   See CILLEY.

15644   SILLIMAN.   The Silliman family; Pennsylvania and South Carolina lines, by Robert B. Silliman.   Dumaguete City, Philippines, Silliman University Press, 1966.   xiii, 206 p. geneal. tables. 22 cm. 66-5856.   CS71.S5834   1966

SILLIMAN.   See also ANDERSON, 1916

15645   SILLS.   A historical and genealogical record of Fanny Sills and related families of Nash County, North Carolina (by) Lawrence C. Bryant.   Orangeburg, South Carolina State College, c. 1968. v, 84 p. 29 cm. Cover title. 78-2463.   CS71.S5836   1968

SILSBEE.   See SILSBY.

15646   SILSBY.   A genealogical account of Henry Silsbee, and some of his descendants.   By James A. Emmerton, M. D. ... Salem, Essex institute, 1880.   71 p. 24½ cm.   From Historical collections of Essex institute, v. 17, 1880, p. 257-323. 9-13735.   CS71.S584   1880

15647   SILSBY.   Three generations of Silsbees and their vessels.   By Martha Williamson Forsyth Duren.   (Salem, Mass., Newcomb & Gauss, printers) 1924.   1 p. l., 57 p. front., plates, ports. 25 cm.   "Privately printed for John Silsbee Lawrence." 25-1778.   CS71.S584   1924

SILSBY.   See also: DRIVER, 1889
                            OSGOOD, 1941

SILVA.   See CAPADOSE, 1936

15648   SILVER.   The Silver family in America, from 1637 to 1925; a genealogy by Z. S. Fink. (Holdrege, Neb., 1925)   1 p. l., 18 p. 24 cm.   Autographed from type-written copy.   Bibliography: p. 18. 26-390.
                                                                                                 CS71.S585   1925

SILVERSON.   See TANEY, 1935

SILVERTOOTH.   See FROST, 1962

SILVESTER.   See ARCHER, 1937

SIMCOCK.   See SIMCOX.

15649   SIMCOX.   Some records of an old house.   (By John Walford Simcox)   Birmingham, Cornish brothers, 1896.   3 p. l., 21 numb. l. incl. front., illus., pl. 21 x 24 cm. Signed J. W. Simcox.   24-2116.
DA690. B6S5

SIMCOCK.   See SYRON, 1925

15650   SIMKINS.   Garrett county history of the Simkins family, by Charles E. Hoye.   (Oakland? Md., 19 -?)   1 l. 45 cm. 38M1256T.   CS71. 85858   19 -

SIMMONDS.   See SIMMONS.

15651   SIMMONS.   Genealogy of the Simmons family of Maine and Massachusetts, by Frederick Johnson Simmons.   (Limited ed. of 100 copies.)   Reprint from Sprague's Journal of Maine history. Dover, Me., 1920.   47 p. 23 cm. 22-4166.   CS71.S586   1920

15652   SIMMONS.   History of the Simmons family, from Moses Simmons 1st. (Moyses Symonson) ship Fortune, 1621, to and including the eleventh generation in some lines, and very nearly complete to the third and fourth generations from Moses 1st.   By Lorenzo Albert Simmons.   Lincoln, Neb., 1930.   xxvi p., 1 l., 288, (16) p. front., plates, ports. 23 cm. Title vignette. "Only 300 copies have been printed. " This copy not numbered. Blank pages for "Memorandum" (16 at end) 32-15813.   CS71.S586   1930

15653   SIMMONS.   The Simmons family at Harvard university, and other data; Esther Minerva Simmons and Baxendale memorial foundation at Harvard; John Simmons, founder of Simmons college; compiled by Frederick J. Simmons.   Keene, N.H., 1931.   16 p. front., pl., ports. 23 cm. 31-19475.
CS71.S586   1931

15654   SIMMONS.   The ancestry of John Simmons, founder of Simmons college, compiled by Henry S. Rowe ... Cambridge, Priv. print. at the Riverside press, 1933.   4 p. l., 88 p. front. (port.) pl. 23 cm. "One hundred and fifty copies of this book were printed. " 33-14696 rev.   CS71.S586   1933

15655   SIMMONS.   John & Susan Simmonds and some of their descendants, with related ancestral lines, compiled by Frank William Simmonds ... Rutland, Vt., The Tuttle publishing company, inc. (1940)   222 p. front., illus. (coat of arms) plates, ports., maps, facsims. 23½ cm. 40-6188.
CS71.S586   1940

15656   SIMMONS.   History of the Simmons and Hamilton families, compiled 1930-1949.   By Green-berry Simmons.   Based on information obtained from Kate Simmons Fultz and other reliable sources. (Louisville, 1949)   21 l. 35 cm. 50-19622.   CS71.S586   1949

15657   SIMMONS.   The Simmons family at Boston University and at Tufts College.   Descendants of Thomas Simmons, of Scituate, Mass., and of Moses Simmons, of Duxbury, Mass.   By Frederick Johnson Simmons.   Ship Fortune 1621.   Biographical and genealogical sketches.   Lisbon, N.H., Ammonoosuc Press, 1953.   51 p. illus. 23 cm. 53-36205.   CS71.S586   1953

15658   SIMMONS.   The Silver Creek Simmons family, descendants of Willis and Jane Goslin Simmons, by Edna Simmons Campbell and Hansford L. Simmons.   (Tallahassee? Fla., 1955?)   343 l. illus. 28 cm. 57-36844.   CS71.S586   1955

15659   SIMMONS.   Our Simmons family at the University of Maine.   By Frederick Johnson Simmons. (Montclair? N.J., 1957?)   unpaged. illus. 24 cm. 59-21429.   CS71.S586   1957

15660   SIMMONS.   Name Jeremiah in the Simmons family.   By Daisie Dean Winifred (Simmons) Howe.   (n.p., 1963)   23 l. 30 cm. Cover title. Bibliography: l. 2. 64-494.   CS71.S586   1963a

15661   SIMMONS.   Notes from a Simmons scrapbook (kept by James Burke Simmons.   By Daisie D. W. Howe.   n.p., 1963)   63 l. 28 cm. 63-47608.   CS71.S586   1963

15662   SIMMONS.   Bala Chitto Simmons family; descendants of Richard and Ann Tyler Simmons, by Hansford L. Simmons.   McComb, Miss. (1965?)   (11), 428 p. illus., ports. 29 cm. With additions and corrections in Ms. by the author. Bibliography: 7th prelim. page. 68-3849.   CS71.S586   1965

SIMMONS.　See also:　BAKER, 1870　　　WINTERTON, 1964
　　　　　　　　　　　　　HARRIS, 1941　　　No. 1547 - Cabell county.
　　　　　　　　　　　　　O'CONNOR, 1941

15663　SIMMS.　Sims family, 1926.　(By Clifford Stanley Sims) (n. p., 1926)　5 p. l., 1 l., 12-32, (6) p. illus. (coat of arms) 6 pl. 28½ cm.　Pages 12-31 are copied from what is known as the Sims family Bible.　The 6 plates are photgraphic reproductions from the Bible which was in 1752 the property of the Rev. John Brainard, missionary to the Indians and now belongs to his great, great, great, great, great grandson, Clifford Stanley Lewis.　28-5764.　　　CS71. S614　　1926

15664　SIMONDS.　Autobiography.　James Beart Simonds, late principal of the Royal veterinary college, professor of cattle pathology, &c. (with portrait)　(In the Veterinarian.　London, 1894.　22 cm.　v. 67, nos. 797-804)　Bound as a separate volume with cover-title: History of the Simonds family.　20-23302.　　　SF601. V5

15665　SIMONS.　From the landing of the Pilgrims in 1620; a brief but accurate genealogy concerning the families of Jennie Bessie Gowdy and her husband Adolphus Ezra Simons with allied families of their descendants ... (n. p., 1951?)　132 p.　ports.　24 cm.　52-20628.　　　CS71. S588　　1951

15666　SIMONS.　Thomas Grange Simons III, his forebears and relations.　By Robert Bentham Simons.　Charleston, 1954.　211 p. illus.　24 cm.　56-3193.　　　CS71. S588　　1954

　　　　　SIMONS.　See also:　COGEL, 1959
　　　　　　　　　　　　　　　HARRIS, 1941

15666a　SIMONSON.　The Morton Lincoln Simonson family.　By John Carl Simonson.　(Oklahoma City?) 1961.　1 v.　illus.　28 cm.　61-43180.　　　CS71. S589　　1961

15667　SIMONSON.　The Housman (Huysman) - Simonson family of Staten Island, N. Y.　By Elmer C. Van Name.　(1955).　10 p.　In vertical file.　Ask reference librarian for this material.

　　　　　SIMONSON.　See BILLOU family in vertical file.　　Ask reference librarian for this material.

　　　　　SIMONSON.　See HOUSMAN folder in vertical file.　　Ask reference librarian for this material.

　　　　　SIMONTON.　See READ, 1939

15668　SIMPKINS.　Samuel Grant Simpkins; a memorial, prepared by Peter Thacher.　Boston, Printed by G. H. Ellis, 1890.　41 p.　24½ cm.　26-5935.　　　CT275. S5216T5

15669　SIMPSON.　Genealogy of the original Simpson family, of York and Hancock counties, Me., by John S. Emery of Boston, Mass. ... Bangor, Me. (1891)　cover-title, 51 p.　24½ cm.　"Reprinted from the Bangor historical magazine."　Henry Simson, Sympson, Simpson of York.　Comp. by J. W. Porter: p. 50-51.　18-377.
　　　　　　　　　　　　　　　　　　　　　　　　　　　　　　　　　　　　CS71. S59　　1891

15670　SIMPSON.　The Simson and Gillespie genealogy.　(Philadelphia, 1902?)　geneal. tab.　54 x 40 cm. (fold. to 20½ cm.)　Compiled by Samuel Richards Shipley.　Descendants of the Rev. Andrew Simson and John Gillespie of Scotland in the line of George Gillespie.　17-19212.　　　CS71. S59　　1896

15671　SIMPSON.　The Simpsons of Rye Top, Cumberland Valley, Pennsylvania, by Elizabeth Simpson Bladen ... Philadelphia, Press of Allen, Lane & Scott, 1905.　34 p.　22 cm.　11-1135.　CS71. S59　　1905

15672　SIMPSON.　Early records of Simpson families in Scotland, North Ireland, and easter United States, with a history of the family of the compiler, Helen A. Simpson, and including genealogies of allied families Hout, Stringer, Potts and Dawson.　Philadelphia, J. B. Lippincott company, 1927.　x, 382 p.　illus., ports.　24½ cm.　Bibliography: p. v-vi.　29-16347.　　　CS71. S59　　1927

15673　SIMPSON.　Additions and corrections to early records of Simpson families and allied families of Hout, Stringer, Potts and Dawson, by the compiler Helen A. Simpson ... Philadelphia, J. B. Lippincott company. 1929.　1 p. l., 82 p.　24½ cm.　　　CS71. S59　　1927
　　　　　　　　　　　　　　　　　　　　　　　　　　　　　　　　　　　　Suppl.

15674   SIMPSON.   Lineage from Thomas Simpson of Paxtang for Thomas Hambly Beck, Esq.   By George Valentine Massey.   (Wilton, Conn.) 1948.   102 p. map, facsims., photos. 29 cm. Cover title: The Simpson genealogy. "Twelve copies ... 9th copy." "Fort Augusta Sunbury, Northumberland County": folder (7 p.) inserted. Includes bibliographical references. 49-20924*.   CS71.S59   1948

15675   SIMPSON.   The Simpsons of Paxtang and Sunbury, Pennsylvania.   By George Valentine Massey.   (n. p., 1949)   59-68 p. 25 cm. "Reprinted from the Pennsylvania genealogical magazine, volume XVII, December, 1949." 50-39919.   CS71.S59   1949

SIMPSON.   See also: CALHOUN, 1957   SCHWARTZ, 1961
                       KELLEY, 1889   SEMMES, 1918
                       POLLOCK, 1932   SEMMES, 1956
                       ROBERTS, 1939

15676   SIMS.   The Symmes memorial.   A biographical sketch of Rev. Zechariah Symmes, minister of Charlestown, 1634-1671, with a genealogy and brief memoirs of some of his descendants ... And an autobiography.   By John Adams Vinton ... Boston, The author, 1873.   1 p. l., xvi, 184 p. front. (port.) 24 cm. 9-13824.   CS71.S99   1873

15677   SIMS.   Sims family, 1926.   (By Clifford Stanley Sims) (n. p., 1926)   5 p. l., 1 l., 12-32, (6) p. illus. (coat of arms) 6 pl. 28½ cm. Pages 12-31 are copied from what is known as the Sims family Bible. The 6 plates are photographic reproductions from the Bible which was in 1752 the property of the Rev. John Brainard, missionary to the Indians and now belongs to this great, great, great, great, great grandson, Clifford Stanley Lewis. 28-5764.   CS71.S614   1926

15678   SIMS.   Sims family records, compiled by Christine O. Atwell ... from old family letters; local church and newspaper items.   (Cazenovia, N.Y., 1933)   10 l., 2-107 numb. l. 28 cm. Type-written. "Quoted authorities": 3d prelim. leaf. 34-17810.   CS71.S614   1933

15679   SIMS.   Contribution to the history and story of the family of Stephen Sims and descendants, by his grandson, Frederick A. Sims.   (n. p.) 1937. 2 p. l., (3)-55 p. ports. 19 cm. 38-14734.   CS71.S614   1937

15680   SIMS.   Adam Symes and his descendants, by Jane Morris.   Philadelphia, Dorrance and company (1938)   403 p. 22½ cm. 38-19807.   CS71.S614   1938

15681   SIMS.   The genealogy of the Sims family of Virginia, the Carolinas and the gulf states, by Henry Upson Sims ... Kansas City, Mo., Print. priv. for the author by E. L. Mendenhall, inc. (1940) 1 p. l., iv, (2), 238 p. 24 cm. Bibliographical foot-notes. 41-12301.   CS71.S614   1940

15682   SIMS.   The Paris (Pariss-Parish) Henry Sims branch of the Sims family of Scotland, England, Ireland, and America.   By Almon James Sims.   (Knoxville, Tenn., 1948)   38 l. col. coat of arms. 28 cm. Caption title. 50-25472.   CS71.S614   1948

15683   SIMS.   The Pariss Sims family and related families, 1765-1965, by Almon J. Sims.   Knox-- ville, Tenn., 1965.   114 p. illus., coat of arms, ports. 24 cm. 67-1560.   CS71.S614   1965

SIMS.   See also: DUKE, 1940
                    MACKEY, 1957
                    SCARBORO, 1951

SIMSON.   See SIMPSON.

15684   SINCLAIR.   Memoirs of the life and works of the late Right Honourable Sir John Sinclair, bart., by his son, the Rev. John Sinclair ... Edinburgh, W. Blackwood and sons; (etc., etc.) 1837. 2 v. 19½ cm. Genealogy: v. 1, p.1-8. 4-34665.   DA522.S6S6

15685   SINCLAIR.   An historical account of the Macleans of Duart castle, and the genealogy of the children and grand-children of Rev. John Campbell Sinclair, together with an obituary of the latter, by Brevard D. Sinclair ... (Columbus, O.) Columbus steam printing works print, 1879.   1 p. l., 38 p. incl. geneal. tab. 30 cm. "A short sketch of the Davidson and Brevard families of Mecklenburg County, North Carolina": p.35. Ms corrections in text. 1-6388.   CS71.S615   1879

15686   SINCLAIR.   Caithness family history, by John Henderson ... Edinburgh, D. Douglas, 1884.
xxxi, 341, (1) p. 25½ cm.   Title vignette (coat of arms) Edited by A. B. H.   11-14208.

CS479.S6   1884

15687   SINCLAIR.   The Sinclairs of England.   London, Trübner & co., 1887.   viii, 414 p. 19 cm. By
Thomas Sinclair. Pub. anonymously. 8-22943.

DA28.35.S6S6

15688   SINCLAIR.   The history of the Sinclair family in Europe and America ... Giving a genealogical and biographical history of the family in Normandy, France; a general record of it in Scotland,
England, Ireland, and a full biographical and genealogical record of many branches in Canada and the
United States ... Forty-seven pages relating to the Cilley, Clark, Hodgdon, Jones, Merrill, and Norris
families.   By Leonard Allison Morrison ... Boston, Mass., Damrell & Upham, 1896.   453 p. illus.,
plates, ports., map, facsims. 24 cm. 9-13733.

CS71.S615   1896

15689   SINCLAIR.   The Saint-Clairs of the Isles; being a history of the sea-kings of Orkney and their
Scottish successors of the sirname of Sinclair.   Arranged and annotated by Roland William Saint-Claire
... Auckland, N. Z., H. Brett, 1898.   5 p. l., iii, (1), 558 p. illus., map. 26 cm. 9-24157.

CS479.S25   1898

15690   SINCLAIR.   The Sinclairs of Roslin, Caithness, and Goshen; by the Rev. A. Maclean
Sinclair.   Charlottetown, P. E. Island, The Examiner publishing company, 1901.   45 p. 19 cm. "Only
one hundred copies have been printed." 3-30944.

CS479.S6   1901

15691   SINCLAIR.   Caithness in the 18th century, by John E. Donaldson.   Edinburgh & London, The
Moray press (1938)   199 p. 21½ cm.   "First published 1938."   "Largely based on the family papers and letters of the Sinclairs of
Mey in Caithness." - Foreword.   Bibliographical foot-notes.   39-14251.

DA890.C14D6

15692   SINCLAIR.   The Sinclaire family of Belfast, N. Ireland and their descendants, 1660-1960.
By St. Claire (Lappe) Daub.   (Springfield, Pa., 1960)   55 l. 29 cm. 61-37638.

CS71.S615   1960

15693   SINCLAIR.   The Sinclaire family of Belfast, N. Ireland and their descendents (sic) 1660-1964.
By St. Claire (Lappe) Daub.   (Springfield, Pa., 1964?)   91 l. 29 cm. Cover title. Additions and corrections in
manuscript. 65-2882.

CS71.S615   1964a

15694   SINCLAIR.   The Sinclair family of Virginia; descendants of Henry Sinclair, born in Aberdeen,
Scotland, the second son of the Earl of Caithness, and his son John Sinclair, 1755-1820, and allied
families.   Compiled by Jefferson Sinclair Selden, Jr.   (Hampton? Virginia, c.1964)
387 p. illus. 24 cm. 65-3212.

CS71.S615   1964

SINCLAIR.   See also: ADIE, CS477.S5G7
ATKINSON, 1933
CHISHOLM, 1948
EMISON, 1947

SINCLAIRE.   See SINCLAIR.

15695   SINE.   The book of the Sines.   By Columbus B. Sines.   Oakland, Md., c.1958.
96 p. illus. 27 cm. 58-33886.

CS71.S616   1958

SINE.   See also MACK, 195 -

15696   SINES.   Garrett county history of the Sines family ... By Charles E. Hoye.   (Oakland, Md.)
1934.   1 l. 30 cm.   "Reprint from Mountain democrat, Sept. 20, 1934." 38M1255T.   CS71.S616   1934

15697   SINES.   Sines family in vertical file.   Ask reference librarian for this material.

SINES.   See also SINE.

SING. See SYNG.

SINGE. See SYNG.

15698   SINGLETARY. Singletary family in vertical file.   Ask reference librarian for this material.

15699   SINNETT. Annals of the Sinnott, Rogers, Coffin, Corlies, Reeves, Bodine and allied families, by Mary Elizabeth Sinnott, edited by Josiah Granville Leach, LL.B. Philadelphia, Printed for private circulation by J. B. Lippincott company, 1905.   5 p. l., (vii)-viii, 277, (1) p. col. front., (coat of arms) illus., plates, port., facsims., geneal. tables (part fold.) 26½ cm.   "Two hundred and fifty copies ... printed." 5-41001.   CS71.S617   1905

15700   SINNETT. Sinnett genealogy. Michael Sinnett of Harpswell, Maine, his ancestry and descendants, also records of other Sinnetts, Sinnotts, etc., in Ireland and America. By Rev. Charles Nelson Sinnett ... Concord, N.H., The Rumford press, 1910.   137 p. front. 22½ cm. 10-16179.
CS71.S617   1910

15701   SINNETT. James Sinnett, pioneer of the Granville, Ohio, colony: ancestry and descendants. Comp. by Rev. Chas. N. Sinnett. Brainerd, Minn. (1920)   1 p. l., 19 numb. l. 33 cm. Type-written. 21-9024.
CS71.S617   1920

SINNOT.   See SINNETT.

SINNOTT.   See SINNETT.

15702   SINSABAUGH. History of the family of Sinsabaugh, Sincebaugh, Sincerbeaux, Sincerbox, 1700-1900. By Frank H. Rathbun. (n.p., 1955?)   25 p. 28 cm. 56-53108.   CS71.S618   1955

SINTON. See SCOTT, 1923

SIPHAKAS. See SĒPHAKAS.

SIRK. See CRONE, 1924

SIRRINE. See SYRON.

SISK. See PEDEN, 1961

15703   SISSON. Luther Sisson of Easton, Mass. His ancestry & descendants. Compiled ... by Arthur A. Wood. Slocum, R. I., Printed by A. A. Wood, 1909.   1 p. l., 13 p. 18½ cm. 10-15831.
CS71.S619   1909

15704   SISSON. Genealogy of the Sisson kindred in America; photostats of Bible records and will, copies of photostats of Bible records. Presented to Congressional library by Illinois state conference of the Daughters of the American revolution, General Henry Dearborn chapter, Chicago, Illinois ... Compiled by (Mrs. Burt T.) Gertrude S. Wheeler ... 1843-1945. Chicago, (1945)   3 p. l., 77 (i.e. 79) numb. l. 28½ x 22½ cm. Type-written (carbon copy) "General bibliography": p. 43-48. 45-19616.
CS71.S619   1945

SISSON. See also: BENZ, 1931
KING, 1956
MERRILL, 1949

SISTRUNK. See OLIVER, 1964

15705   SITGREAVES. Pedigree of a nitwit. By Marguerite (Sitgreaves) Aimi. (1st ed.) New York, Vantage Press (1955)   232 p. illus. 21 cm. 55-10852.   CS71.S6195   1955

15706   SITWELL. Left hand, right hand! (By) Sir Osbert Sitwell ... Boston, Little, Brown and company, 1944.   xvi, 327, (1) p. 22½ cm. "An Atlantic monthly press book." Autobiography. "First edition." 44-4450.
PR6037.I.83Z5

15707   SITWELL.   Left hand, right hand! An autobiography by Osbert Sitwell ... London, Macmillan & co. ltd., 1945 -   v. front., plates, ports., fold. geneal. tab. 22½ cm.   45-5448.

PR6037.I.83Z512

15708   SIZER.   Sizer genealogy; a history of Antonio de Zocieur, who changed his name to Anthony Sizer, and Abel Sizer, Daniel Sizer, Lemuel Sizer, Sarah Sizer Bill, Samuel Sizer, William Sizer, the six of his twelve children who left descendants, including many other Sizer families.   Compiled and edited by Lillian Hubbard Holch (Mrs. Henry George Holch) ... Brooklyn, N. Y., Bowles-printer, 1941. 4 p. l., 489 p. front. (port.) 23½ cm.   43-1837.

CS71.S62   1941

SKAGGS.   See HIGHBAUGH, 1961

15709   SKARDA.   The Skarda family reunion, John Cain Park, Stuttgart, Arkansas, Sunday, August 3, 1958;   "Iowa" Skardas in Arkansas.   By Charles M. Robinson Skarda.   Little Rock, Ark., 1958. 9 l. 29 cm.   59-7718.

CS71.S6205   1958

15710   SKAVLEM.   The Skavlem and Odegaarden families; being a genealogical record and pioneer history of the Skavlem and Odegaarden families from their emigration from Norway down to the present. With ninety-nine portraits and other illustrations.   Written and compiled by Halvor L. Skavlem. (Madison, Wis., Tracy & Kilgore printers) 1915.   xiii, 245, (10) p. illus. (incl. ports.) 24 cm.   "Only 200 copies printed."   Nine pages at end for "Amended records and corrections" and "Continued family records." 42-31365.

CS71.S621   1915

SKEELS.   See OSTRANDER, 1936

15711   SKEET.   History of the families of Skeet, Somerscales, Widdrington, Wilby, Murray, Blake, Grimshaw, and others.   By a connection of the same.   London, Mitchell Hughes and Clarke, 1906. 2 p. l., 179 p. illus. (coats of arms) pl., ports. 29½ cm.   Compiled by Francis John Angus Skeet.   "Seventy-five copies only of this work were printed"; this copy not numbered. 17-19258.

CS438.S5

15712   SKELTON.   The Skeltons of Paxton, Powhatan County, Virginia, and their connections, including sketches of the families of Skelton, Gifford and Crane ... By P. Hamilton Baskerville ... Richmond, Va., Old dominion press, inc., printers, 1922.   xiv, 119 p. front., illus., plates, ports., facsim., v fold. geneal. tab. 24 cm.   Title vignette (coat of arms) Printed for private distribution.   "Authorities": p. (xi)-xii. 22-19489.

CS71.S622   1922

SKELTON.   See also JONES, 1891

15713   SKENE.   Memorials of the family of Skene of Skene, from the family papers, with other illustrative documents, edited by William Forbes Skene ... Aberdeen, Printed for the New Spalding club.   1887.   xiv p., 1 l., 269, (1) p., 1 l. front., illus., 5 pl. (2 col.) 26½ cm.   (On cover: New Spalding club. Publications, no. 1) "525 copies printed. no. 45."   Appended: "New Spalding club. Reports of committees. 1887." (38 p.) 15-2453.

DA750.N5 vol. 1

15714   SKENE.   Descent of the family of Skene. (By Henry John Trotter) (Aberdeen, 1888) geneal. tab. 51 x 69 cm. fold. to 26 x 19½ cm.   Compiled by Henry John Trotter, from the Memorials of the family of Skene, by William Forbes Skene.   Additions and corrections in manuscript. 21-2248.

CS479.S62

SKEY.   See RUSSELL, DA522.R8J5

15715   SKIDMORE.   A genealogical and biographical record of the pioneer Thomas Skidmore (Scudmore) of the Massachusetts and Connecticut colonies in New England and of Huntington, Long Island, and of his descendants through the branches herein set forth; including other related branches of the Skidmore family, with historical sketches of places where the several branches settled and of events in which representative members participated.   Compiled ... by Emily C. Hawley.   (Brookfield Center, Conn.) E. C. Hawley, 1911.   xx, 359 p., 1 l. col. front. (coat of arms) plates (1 col.) ports. 24½ cm. 11-22400.

CS71.S624   1911

15716   SKIDMORE.   Skidmore family of central New Jersey. By James Wilbur Clayton.   West Orange, N.J. (1961)   1 v. 38 cm. 62-35592.

CS71.S624   1961

SKIDMORE.   See also: BANNING, E171.A53 vol. 19
SCUDAMORE, 1727

15717   SKIFF.   The descendants of James Skiff of London, England, and Sandwich, Mass., who died after 1688.   By Frederick Lockwood Pierson ... Amenia, N.Y., Walsh & Griffen, 1895.
24 p. 24½ cm. 9-13732.   CS71.S626   1895

15718   SKILES.   Notes on the Skiles family genealogy.   By Robert Cutten Read.   (Wilton? Conn., 1955?)   11, 5, 15 p. illus. 28 cm.   "Genealogy of the Cutten family of Nova Scotia; (excerpts) by George Barton Cutten": 15 p. at end.
56-23396.   CS71.S6268   1955

SKILES.   See also McAfee, 1929

15719   SKILLINGS.   The Skillings family, by William M. Sargent, esq. ... Portland, Me., S.M.
Watson, 1885.   22 p. 23 cm.   Republished from Maine historical and genealogical recorder, vol. 2, no. 2, 1885. 1-10197 rev.
CS71.S627   1885

15720   SKILLINGS.   Memoir of Robert F. Skillings, with genealogy and poems, by Franklin Skillings.
Portland (Me.) Smith & Sale, printers, 1911.   75 p. front., illus., plate, ports.   20½ cm.   Poems, chiefly by Robert F.
Skillings: p. (31)-75. 11-27528.   CS71.S627   1911

15721   SKILLMAN.   The Skillmans of New York.   Compiled by Francis Skillman ... (New York,
Press of Jones & co.) 1892.   90 p. 23½ cm. 9-13731.   CS71.S628   1892

15722   SKILLMAN.   The Skillman genealogy.   (By William E. Skillman) (195-?)   (1) l. 28 cm.
Caption title. Typescript. 77-809.   CS71.S628

15723   SKILLMAN.   To the water's edge; Skillman, Galley, Atkinson and allied families, by
Margaret A. S. Atkinson.   Philadelphia (c.1967)   238 p. illus., ports.   24 cm.   "Limited to two hundred copies."
Bibliography: p. 237-238. 68-3677,   CS71.S628   1967

SKILLMAN.   See also: FITZGERALD, 1942
WALLIN, 1934

15724   SKILTON.   Doctor Henry Skilton, and his descendants; ed. by John Davis Skilton ... New
Haven, Conn., Press of S. Z. Field, 1921.   1 p. l., (5)-421 p. front., illus. (incl. ports.) pl. facsims. 24½ cm.   Full-
page illustrations.   Compiled for the association by the Publication committee, John Davis Skilton, chairman.   Bibliography: p. (7)-8.   "Roll of
honor, those who served in the world war": p. 361-375.   CS71.S6285   1921
——— Supplement I ... by The Doctor Henry Skilton association; editors, George Warner
Skilton, B.S., secretary of the ... association, and Henry Irving Skilton, B.S., registrar.   (New
Haven, Conn.) 1927.   p. 413-492 incl. plates, ports.   23 ½ cm.   Some of the plates are printed on both sides. 22-6009.
CS71.S6285   1921
Suppl.

15725   SKILTON.   ... The Doctor Henry Skilton house, Southington, Hartford county, Connecticut
... (By John Davis Skilton) (Hartford? 1930?)   3 p. l., 6-10 numb. l., 3 l., a-p leaves. illus., plates, plans, facsims.,
28 x 21½ cm.   (Old houses of Connecticut, historical and technical information ... collected and compiled by the Connecticut society of colonial
dames of America) Illustration on t. - p.   "Compiled by John Davis Skilton ... and Henry Alstone Skilton."   This is one of fifty reproductions,
mimeographed and photostated from the original copy of the book in the Connecticut state library at Hartford.   "The information in this booklet regarding Doctor Skilton is taken from: Doctor Henry Skilton and his descendants ... New Haven, Conn. ... 1921, and Supplement I to Doctor Henry
Skilton and his descendants ... 1927." 30-29408.   F104.S73S62

15726   SKILTON.   The Skilton family reunion.   Skilton family association (n. p.)   v. in   ports.
23-28 cm.   annual.   Isses for 19   pub. under an earlier name of the assn: Skilton Reunion Association.   Issues for 19   include reports of the
Doctor Henry Skilton Association.   50-30782.   CS71.S6285   1931

15727   SKILTON.   Skilton family in vertical file.   Ask reference librarian for this material.

15728   SKINKER.   Samuel Skinker and his descendants; an account of the Skinker family and all their
kindred who have the blood of Samuel Skinker in their veins, by Thomas Keith Skinker ... (n. p.) The

15728 continued: author, 1923.   6 p. l., 298 p. front., illus. (coat of arms) ports. 24½ cm. Leaf of corrections inserted between 2d and 3d preliminary leaves.   Blank pages for notes (16 at end)   33-6853.   CS71.S6287   1923

15729   SKINNER.   Skinner of Bolingbroke, and Thornton college, Lincolnshire.   Privately printed. London, Printed by Taylor and co., 1870.   4 p. illus. (coat of arms) 29 cm. Title vignette: coat of arms.   Communicated by Charles Jackson, esq., of Doncaster.   Issued also in Miscellanea genealogica et heraldica.   n.s. v.1, p. 80-82.   9-18119.
CS439.S55

15730   SKINNER.   The Skinner kinsmen.   (Prospectus)   (Washington, D.C., 19 - 2 l. 28 cm.
38M4586T.   CS71.S629   19 -

15731   SKINNER.   Richard Skinner of Marblehead and his Bible.   Some materials for a Skinner genealogy.   By Miss Elizabeth Ellery Dana ... (Boston?) 1900.   1 p. l., 10 p. 23½ cm.   Caption title.   Cover-title: The Skinner family of Marblehead.   Reprinted from the New England historical and genealogical register, Oct., 1900.   1-367.
CS71.S629   1900

15732   SKINNER.   The Skinner kinsmen, 1915-1929.   (List of members)   (n.p., 1929)   (6) p. 11 x 13 cm.   38M4587T.   CS71.S629   1929

15733   SKINNER.   Skinner and allied families, a genealogical study with biographical notes, compiled and privately printed for Jeannette C. Whittemore Skinner, by the American historical society, inc. New York, 1935.   95 p. plates, ports., col. coats of arms. 32½ cm.   Alternate pages blank.   Title-page, dedication and initials decorated in colors.   Bound in blue crushed levant, gold tooled.   Allied families: Whittemore, Rorison, Gilbert, Stow, Easton.   Bibliographical notes throughout text.   36-14661 rev.   CS71.S629   1935

15734   SKINNER.   A sporting family of the old South, by Harry Worcester Smith, with which is included Reminiscences of an old sportsman, by Frederick Gustavus Skinner.   Albany, N.Y., J.B.Lyon company, 1936.   xvii, 477 p. front., plates, ports., facsims. 24 cm.   Illustrated lining-papers; descriptive text on verso of front lining-paper and two plates; one plate accompanied by leaf with descriptive text.   Added t.-p.: A sporting family of the old South; the story of five generations of sportsmen, starting with John Stuart Skinner, 1788, and ending with his great-great grandson, 1936: John Stuart Skinner ... Frederick Gustavus Skinner ... Frederick Stuart Greene ... Francis Thornton Greene ... by Harry Worcester Smith ... Included in this volume are the Reminiscences of an old sportsman and other articles by Frederick Gustavus Skinner: published for private subscription.   "Acknowledgments": p. xvii.   37-1076
SK33.S63
Office.
—— Copy 2   Shelf.

15735   SKINNER.   The ancestry of Carolyn Gail Skinner.   By Eugene Elam Skinner.   (Dallas, 1950) 1 v. (unpaged) 29 cm.   50-38419.   CS71.S629   1950

15736   SKINNER.   Meet the family.   By Eugene Elam Skinner.   (A new, expanded ed. of The ancestry of Carolyn Gail Skinner.   Dallas, 1957)   1 v. (various pagings) illus. 29 cm.   58-24628.
CS71.S629   1957

SKINNER.   See also: BROWN, 1931
COLBY, 1880
PECK, 1925
RUSH, 1943

15737   SKIPWITH.   A brief account of the Skipwiths of Newbold, Metheringham and Prestwould, comp. by Fulwar Skipwith ... (For private circulation only)   Tunbridge Wells, W. Brackett, printer, 1867. 2 p. l., 46 p. fold. geneal. tables.   22 cm.   Title vignette (coat of arms) 23-18867.   CS439.S58

SKIPWITH.   See also: CRALL, 1908
HENRY, 1922
MASSINGBERD, DA690.O6M3
POCAHONTAS, 1887

SKIPWORTH.   See HENRY, 1922

SKITES.   See McAFEE, 1929

15738   SKOTTOWE.   The leaf and the tree, the story of an English family, by Philip F. Skottowe.
London, Research Pub. Co. (1963)   85 p. illus., ports. 25 cm. 65-83758.   CS439.S582   1963

15739   SKOUSEN.   Skousen family news.   (Family association bulletin)   In vertical file.   Ask
reference librarian for this material.

        SKOW.   See SCHOU.

        SKRIMSHER.   See LODBROKE.

15740   SKRINE.   Skrine of Warleigh in the county of Somerset, with pedigrees, being some materials for a genealogical history of the family of Skrine, by E. W. Ainley Walker ... Taunton (Eng.)
Priv. print. at the Wessex press, 1936.   xii, 269 p. front. (coat of arms) pl., double geneal. tab. 29 cm.   "Of this book
two hundred copies only were printed of which this is no. 171."   "For much of the history of the family of Skrine, and for the main pedigree of the
Warleigh branch the writer is indebted to the researches of the late Henry Duncan Skrine ... On his scattered notes and papers ... together with
additions ... by his eldest son, the late Colonel Henry Mills Skrine ... the present sketch has drawn extensively ... A special debt of thanks must be
gratefully acknowledged to ... A. W. Vivian-Neal." - Foreword.   36-20767.   CS439.S583

15741   SLACK.   Records of the Slacke family in Ireland.   By Helen A. Crofton.   (London? 1922?)
60 p. illus. (coat of arms) 26½ x 21 cm.   Cover-title: The Slacke family in Ireland.   Errata slip inserted.   46-36961.
                                                                                            CS499.S55   1922

15742   SLACK.   The Slack family, more particularly an account of the family of Eliphalet Slack and
his wife Abigail Cutter, their ascendants, descendants and relations as compiled by Rev. William
Samuel Slack ... Alexandria, La., The Standard printing co., 1930.   7 p. l., (20)-252 p., 1 l. illus. (plan)
ports. 24 cm.   "Edition limited to 100 copies. This is no. 46."   "The Slack family in America, by Charles Wesley Slack of Boston, Mass., in
the year 1882, and with additions by Rev. William Samuel Slack, Alexandria, La., in the year 1930": p. 151-215.   Contains also the Cutter and
Woolfolk families.   31-31260.   CS71.S6296   1930

15743   SLACKE.   An account of the family of Slacke or Slack of Brownside, co. Derby, by F. A.
Slacke ... (n. p., 1930?)   2 p. l., 447 (i. e. 453) numb. l. incl. geneal. tables (part fold.) fold. geneal. chart. 23½ cm.   Type-
written.   Notes and additions on verso of many leaves.   Coat of arms on cover.   32-9415.   CS439.S585A3

        SLACKE.   See SLACK.

15744   SLADE.   William Slade of Windsor, Conn., and his descendants, by Thomas Bellows Peck.
Keene, N. H., Sentinel printing company, 1910.   vii, 197 p. front., plates, ports. 24 cm. 10-16405.
                                                                                            CS71.S63   1910

15745   SLADE.   North Swansea cemetery records; a reprint with some additions from three small
yards, i. e. "Slade burying ground", "Col. Peleg Slade private cemetery" and "the Bleachery grave
yard" in the town of Swansea and locality in Massachusetts ... compiled and privately published by
Marion Pearce Carter ... Attleboro, Mass., 1927.   Reprint, 1930.   1 p. l., 19 numb. l. 28 cm.   Autographic reproduction of type-written copy.   CA31-406 unrev.   F74.S993C32

15746   SLADE.   The Slade-Babcock genealogical newsletter.   Newhall, Calif.   v. 28 cm. 74-102.
                                                                                            CS71.S6298

        SLADE.   See also: BRAYTON, 1922
                             STOUT, 1960

        SLADER.   See BOOTH, 1923

15747   SLAFTER.   Memorial of John Slafter, with a genealogical account of his descendants, including eight generations.   By the Rev. Edmund F. Slater, A. M.   Privately printed for the family.
Boston, Press of H. W. Dutton & son, 1869.   x, 155 p. front., plates, ports. 24 cm. 9-13730.
                                                                                            CS71.S631   1869

        SLAGLE.   See MONNET, 1911

15748   SLATER.   The historic Boston tea party of December 16, 1773.   Its men and objects: incidents leading to, accompanying, and following the throwing overboard of the tea.   Including a short account of the Boston massacre of March 5, 1770.   With patriotic lessons therefrom adapted to the present time.   By Caleb A. Wall ... Worcester, Mass., Press of F. S. Blanchard & co., 1896.
87 p. front. (port.) 4 pl. 23 cm. Peter Slater's descendants: p. 31-35. 7-22437.   E215.7.W18

SLATTER.   See MITCHELL, 1936

15749   SLAUGH.   Legacy; the story of George Alfred Slaugh and Rachel Maria Goodrich, their children, and their children's children.   By Gladys Slaugh Jacobson.   (Salt Lake City, Utah) 1964.
287 p. illus., geneal. tables, ports. 29 cm. 79-8522 MARC.   CS71.S6313   1964

15750   SLAUGHTER.   Genealogy of the Slaughter family since 1720.   (Charlottesville, Printed by J. Alexander, 1870)   16 p. 22½ cm. Caption title. Photostat reproduction (positive) Signed: Slaughter W. Ficklin. Based upon the data collected by William Slaughter. cf. p. (1) 40-2246.   CS71.S6314   1870

15751   SLAUGHTER.   The name Slaughter in England; a research report.   By Helen (Slaughter) Gilbert.   (Boulder, Colo., 1966)   iv, 34 p. illus., geneal. table. maps, port. 29 cm. "120 copies" ... Copy no. 72."
Bibliography: p. 33-34. 66-30720.   CS439.S586   1966

SLAUGHTER.   See also: No. 430 - Adventurers of purse and person.
                                     No. 3509 - Orange county, Va.

15752   SLAWSON.   The Slason, Slauson, Slawson, Slosson family, compiled by George C. Slawson.
(Waverly, N.Y., Printed by the Waverly sun, inc., 1946)   1 p. l., xiii, 453 p. 24 cm. 46-5478.
                                     CS71.S63145   1946

SLAWSON.   See also REICHNER, 1918

SLAYBACK.   See SCHLABACH.

15753   SLAYMAKER.   History of the descendants of Mathias Slaymaker, who emigrated from Germany and settled in the eastern part of Lancaster County, Pennsylvania, about 1710.   Compiled by Henry Cochran Slaymaker.   Lancaster, Pa., 1909.   344 p. front., plates, ports. 24 cm. 13-4157.
                                     CS71.S6315   1909

15754   SLAYTON.   Genealogical and biographical sketch of the Slayton family.   (Manchester, N.H.)
1879.   12 p. 10½ cm. Compiled by Hiram King Slayton. 14-12747.   CS71.S632   1879

15755   SLAYTON.   History of the Slayton family.   Biographical and genealogical.   Compiled by Asa W. Slayton ... Grand Rapids, Mich., Printed by Dean printing company, 1898.   5 p. l., 5-330 p. incl. front., illus., ports., facsims. 24 cm. 5-34124.   CS71.S632   1898

SLAYTON.   See also NEALE, 1915

15756   SLEAR.   ... Slear genealogy, a history of the Slear family, compiled by A. D. Miller ... with data furnished by Miss Mary C. Slear ... (Rev. ed.) Norristown, Pa., Eureka printing press, inc., 1929.   68 p. 27 cm. On cover: 2d ed. 45-47760.   CS71.S6325   1929

SLECHT.   See SLEIGHT.

SLEEPER.   See AUSTIN, 1911

SLEER.   See SLEAR.

SLEGHT.   See SLEIGHT.

SLEGT.   See SLEIGHT.

15757   SLEIGHT.   Sleights of Sag Harbor; a biographical, genealogical and historical record of 17th, 18th and 19th century settlers of eastern Long island and the Hudson valley in the state of New York ... By Harry D. Sleight.   Sag Harbor, N. Y., 1929.   1 p. l., (7)-306 p., 1 l., xii p.   24 cm.   "One hundred copies printed by the Hampton press, of Bridgehampton, N. Y., and the type then destroyed."   32-34117.   F129. S12S6

15758   SLEMONS.   A short account of the Slemons family (Slemon, Slemmons, Slemon, Slamon, Sleeman, Slemen, Slammon, Slimmon, Slewman, Sluman, Sleuman, Sleuthman, etc.)   By John A. Slemons.   (London, 1932)   3 p. 23 cm.   Caption title.   "Reprinted from The Genealogical quarterly, autumn (September) 1932."   32-33201.   CS71. S633   1932

SLIFER.   See RODERICK, 1964

SLINGSBY.   See COGHILL, 1879

SLOAN.   See CARPENTER, 1959

15759   SLOAT.   History of the Sloat family of the nobility of Holland and numerous descendants who settled in America; data gathered in Holland and America by Mrs. Geo. Washington Holland and preserved for future generations ... (n. p., 1931?)   2 p. l., (9)-74 p. incl. ports.   port., col. coats of arms.   26 cm. 33-6837. (Full name Emma Florence (Sloat) Holland)   CS71. S6335   1931

15760   SLOAT.   The Sloat family.   From charts made by John Drake Sloat, assembled by May Hart Smith.   Ontario, Calif. (1943?)   98, 18 l. 28 cm.   L. C. copy imperfect: leaf 64 wanting.   Photocopy (negative) 48-33840*.   CS71. S6335   1943

SLOCOMB.   See SLOCUM.

15761   SLOCUM.   A short history of the Slocums, Slocumbs and Slocombs of America, genealogical and biographical; embracing eleven generations of the first-named family from 1637 to 1881; with their alliances and the descendants in the female lines so far as ascertained ... By Charles Elihu Slocum ...   Syracuse, N. Y., The author, 1882.   643, (1) p. col. front. (coat of arms) ports. 23½ cm.   "No. 300." 9-13805.   CS71. S634   1882

15762   SLOCUM.   History of the Slocums, Slocumbs and Slocombs of America, genealogical and biographical, embracing twelve generations of the first-named family from A. D. 1637 to 1908, with their marriages and descendants in the female lines as far as ascertained ... By Charles Elihu Slocum ...   Defiance, O., The author, 1908.   xv, (1), 543 p. plates, ports.   24 cm.   Supplement to and issued as vol. 2 of the 1882 edition.   Phonetic spelling.   9-25799.   CS71. S634   1908

SLOCUM.   See also: AIKEN, 1939
CRAPO, 1912
JOHNSON, 1961
SAGE, 1908

SLOCUMB.   See SLOCUM.

SLOET.   See SLOAT.

15763   SLONAKER.   A history and genealogy of the Sonaker descendants in America since early 1700, compiled and edited by James Rollin Slonaker ... Los Angeles, Calif., Lyday printing company, C. S. Lyday (1941)   732 p. 24 cm.   "Five hundred copies printed."   "References": p. 611-617.   "General literature": p. 618-623. 42-451.   CS71. S6345   1941

15764   SLOSSON.   Slosson genealogy.   By D. Williams Patterson.   (New York? 1872?)   20 p. 23½ cm. Caption title.   Reprinted from the New York genealogical and biographical record.   New York, 1872.   24½ cm.   v. 3, p. 107-116, 165-175. 20-7224.   CS71. S635   1872

SLOT.   See: SLOAT.
VAN NORDEN, 1923

SLOTE.   See SLOAT.

SLOVER.   See SALOVER.

15765   SLOUGH.   Record of descendants of George and Eliza C. Slough.   By Elsie (Welker) Thomas (Nashville) Benson Print. Co., 1963.   v, 15 l.   28 cm.   64-32459.   CS71.S6354   1963

SLUYTER.   See BOUCHELLE, F161.D34 vol. 1 No.7

15766   SLYFIELD.   Slyfield Manor and family of Great Bookham, Surrey, compiled by John H. Harvey and Gordon N. Slyfield,   (n. p., 1953)   unpaged.   illus.   23 cm.   54-37075.
CS439.S587H3

SMACK.   See JAYNE, 1926

15767   SMALL.   Genealogical records of George Small, Philip Albright, Johann Daniel Dünckel, William Geddes Latimer, Thomas Bartow, John Reid, Daniel Benezet, Jean Crommelin, Joel Richardson.   Compiled by Samuel Small, jr.   Philadelphia, Printed for private circulation by J. B. Lippincott company, 1905.   5 p. l., 362, (1) p.   front., ports., coats of arms.   27½ cm.   "This edition is limited to one hundred copies."   "Revised and edited by Anne H. Cresson.   17-31794.   CS71.S636   1905

15768   SMALL.   Descendants of Edward Small of New England, and the allied families, with tracings of English ancestry, by Lora Altine Woodbury Underhill.   Cambridge, Priv. print. at the Riverside press, 1910.   3 v.   fronts. (v. 3, col. coat of arms) plates, ports., maps, facsims.   23½ cm.   Allied families: Heard. - Hatch. - Sawyer. - McKenney. - Mitchells from Plymouth. - Cooke. - Jenney. - Cushman. - Allerton. - Andrews. - Stetson. - Pratt. - Chandler. - Roberts. - Mariner. - Dyer. - Mitchells from Kittery. - Talbot.   11-977.   CS71.S636   1910

15769   SMALL.   Descendants of Edward Small of New England and the allied families, with tracings of English ancestry, by Lora Altine Woodbury Underhill.   Rev. ed.   Boston and New York, Houghton Mifflin company, 1934.   3 v.   fronts., plates (1 double) ports., maps (part double) facsims. (part double) 2 coats of arms (inc. front., v.3) 23 cm.   Paged continuously.   Allied families: Heard, Hatch, Sawyer, McKenney, Mitchells from Plymouth, Cooke, Jenney, Cushman, Allerton, Andrews, Stetson, Pratt, Chandler, Roberts, Mariner, Dyer, Mitchells from Kittery, Talbot.   35-637.
CS71.S636   1934

15770   SMALL.   Small family genealogy, showing the descendants of Christian Small and his wife Louise Bohnhardt, by Warren G. Klees.   Bloomsburg, Pa., 1964.   21 p.   19 cm.   Cover title.   65-451.
CS71.S636   1964

SMALL.   See also: BARNES, 1958
NOWELL, 1941
ROBERTSON, 1907
THAYER, 1948

SMALLWOOD.   See CROOKE, 1942

15771   SMART.   The Smartt and descendant families, by J. Findley Smartt ... St. Louis, Mo., Mound city press, inc., 1943.   216 p.   20 cm.   44-853.   CS71.S6362   1943

SMART.   See also: HARRISON, 1910a
LUTER, 1959

15772   SMATHERS.   Smathers from Yadkin Valley to Pigeon River; Smathers and Agner families. By Sadie (Smathers) Patton.   Hendersonville, N.C., 1954.   56 p.   illus.   24 cm.   54-31924.
CS71.S63623   1954

15773   SMEAD.   Our footprints and footprints of our parents; a Smead genealogy, compiled by Edwin Billings Smead.   Greenfield, Mass. (Press of E. A. Hall & company) 1928.   1 p. l., (5)-132. 133A-133B, 133-152 p.   plates, port.   21 cm.   Blank pages for "Record" (115-118) 31-2254.   CS71.S6363   1928

15774   SMEAD.   Smead, a list of Smead sons born before 1850, with an index of their wives.   (Compiled by) Marshall S. Walker jr.   (Glen Ridge, N.J.) 1945.   19 l.   28 x 22 cm.   Reproduced from type-written copy. "Sources": leaf 17-19.   46-14649.   CS71.S6363   1945

SMEAD.   See also POLLOCK, 1932

15775   SMEDAL.   The Smedal family history and genealogy, by Erling A. Smedal.   (Decorah, Iowa, Anundsen Pub. Co., 1966)   140, 52 p. illus., geneal. tables, map, ports.   24 cm.   66-6168.

CS71.S6364   1966

15776   SMEDBERG.   Genealogy of the Smedberg family, compiled by Helen H. McIver.   (n.p.) 1923.
16 p. 23 cm.   24-7456 rev.   CS71.S6365   1923

SMEDES.   See SEBOR, 1923

15776a   SMEDLEY.   Genealogy of the Smedley family, descended from George and Sarah Smedley, settlers in Chester County, Penna.; with brief notices of other families of the name, and abstracts of early English wills.   Published pursuant to the will of Samuel Lightfoot Smedley, of Philadelphia, Pa. Compiled by Gilbert Cope ... Lancaster, Pa., Wickersham printing company, 1901.   xi, 1000 p. front.,
illus., plates, ports., maps (part fold.) facsims. 29 cm. 2-17584.   CS71.S637   1901

SMEDLEY.   See also KING, 1933

SMELL.   See PEIRPOINT, 1953

15777   SMELSER.   Asters at dusk, the Smelser family in America, by Polly Pollock.   Dayton, Ohio, c. 1961.   278 p. illus. 28 cm. 61-45115.   CS71.S639   1961

SMELSER.   See also SMELTZER.

15778   SMELTZER.   Smeltzer history and genealogy.   Compiled by Jesse A. Smeltzer and Ralph E. Smeltzer.   (Privately printed.   Elgin, Ill., Brethren Press) 1968.   91 p. 28 cm. 79-7880 MARC.

CS71.S6392   1968

SMELTZER.   See also SMELSER.

SMELZER.   See SMELTZER.

SMILEY.   See DARBY, 1930

15779   SMITH.   Collections relating to Henry Smith, esq., some time alderman of London; the estates by him given to charitable uses; and the trustees appointed by him.   London, Printed by J. Nichols, 1800.   182 p. front., pl. 25 cm. Dedication signed: William Bray.   Descendants of Sarah, niece of Henry Smith: 12 geneal. tables, p. 153-175.   With this is bound: The decree, deed of uses, and will of Henry Smith ... Printed by order of the trustees.   1781. 22-2784.   DA676.8.S6B7

15780   SMITH.   The lives of William Smyth, bishop of Lincoln, and Sir Richard Sutton, knight, founders of Brasen Nose college; chiefly compiled from registers and other authentic evidences: with an appendix of letters and papers never before printed.   By Ralph Churton ... Oxford, University press, for the author, 1800.   xxviii, 553 (20) p. front., plates (part fold.) ports. (part fold.) geneal. tables (part fold.) 22 cm. 2-19951.   LF554.A3C4   1800

15781   SMITH.   Notices relating to Thomas Smith of Campden, and to Henry Smith, sometime alderman of London.   By the late Charles Perkins Gwilt ... London, Printed by G. Woodfall, 1836.
vi p., 1 l., 80 p. incl. illus., geneal. tables. front., plates. 28 cm. "Not printed for sale."   Preface signed: Joseph Gwilt.   14-12053.   CS439.S6   1836

15782   SMITH.   The life of Captain John Smith.   The founder of Virginia.   By W. Gilmore Simms ... 6th ed.   Boston, Sanborn, Carter, Bazin & co. (c. 1846)   3 p. l., vii, (9)-379 p. front. (port.) 7 pl. 19½ cm.
Added t.-p., engr., has imprint: Boston, J. Philbrick.   17-18120.   F229.S745

15783   SMITH.   Family register of the descendants of Nathaniel Smith, jr., to which is prefixed some notices of his ancestors.   Utica, D. Bennett, 1849.   44 p. 20 cm. Author's name in ms., on t-p. 20-7225.

CS71.S643   1849

15784   SMITH.   Genealogy of the family of William Smith of Peterborough. N.H. Keene, Printed by H. Kimball, 1852.   24 p. 23½ cm. Explanation signed: L. W. Leonard, Samuel Abbot Smith. 9-13729.

CS71.S643   1852

15785   SMITH.   The olden time of Carolina.   By the octogenarian lady, of Charleston, S.C. (Mrs. Elizabeth Anne Poyas) Charleston, S.C., Courtenay & co., 1855.   iv, 202 p. 12 o. Contains the genealogy of the Thomas Smith family. 1-10807.

F269.P88

15786   SMITH.   Capt. John Smith; a biography.   By George Canning Hill.   Boston, Hill & Libby, 1858.   viii, (9)-286 p. plates. 17½ cm. (Added t.-p.: American biography) 5-34060.

F229.S72

15787   SMITH.   The heraldry of Smith.   Being a collection of the arms borne by, or attributed to, most families of that surname in Great Britain, Ireland and Germany.   Comp. from the Harleian mss. and other authentic sources, by H. Sydney Grazebrook, esq. ... London, J. R. Smith, 1870.   2 p. l., xix, 119, (1) p. 32 pl. (coats of arms) 22 cm. Added t.-p., illustrated: A booke of ye armes of most houses of ye Smithes in England and Germanie. 10-8192.

CR1629.S6

15788   SMITH.   Family records and recollection.   By Melania (Boughton) Smith.   New York, J.W. Amerman, printer, 1870.   53 p. 22 cm. 57-55148.

CS71.S643   1870

15789   SMITH.   Smith centennial memorial.   Rutland, Tuttle & co., printers, 1872.   56 p. 22½ cm. A celebration by the descendants of Samuel and Hannah Smith, who settled at Bridport, Vt., September 8, 1770. 19-6639.

CS71.S642   1872

15790   SMITH.   The heraldry of Smith in Scotland with genealogical annotations, being a supplement to Grazebrook's "Heraldry of Smith." (By Francis Montagu Smith) London, J. R. Smith, 1873.
32 p. 21½ cm. Preface signed: F.M.S. 9-9155.

CS1669.S6

15791   SMITH.   Mementos of the golden wedding (of Mr. and Mrs. William Sidney Smith) at Long-wood, with genealogies.   1873.   N(ew) Y(ork) E. S. Dodge & co., printers (1874?)   3 p. l., 77, (7) p. ports., coats of arms. 21½ cm. "Devised, compiled, designed and written by Eleanor Jones Smith." 17-21247.

CS71.S643   1874

15792   SMITH.   A genealogical record of the Smiths of Oyster River from the first settler in 1630 to 1874; with some account of the immediate ancestors of Hon. Valentine Smith and his descendents (!) Comp. and arranged by Ballard Smith, jr. (Louisville) Courier-journal print (1875)   28 p. 22 cm. Title vignette: coat of arms. 9-13728.

CS71.S643   1875

15793   SMITH.   The Burlington Smiths.   A family history.   By Richard Morris Smith.   Philadelphia, Printed for the author, by E. Stanley Hart, 1877.   2 p. l., (7)-296 p. front., phot. 27½ cm. Accompanied by an addendum of 1880, 9 p. 23½ cm. 2-18432.

CS71.S643   1877

15794   SMITH.   Lives of the Lords Strangford, with their ancestors and contemporaries through ten generations.   By Edward Barrington De Fonblanque ... London, Paris & New York, Cassell, Petter & Galpin (1877)   viii, 298 p. 23 cm. Customer Smythe and his descendants. 4-34664.

DA306.S8D3

15795   SMITH.   The pedigree of Smith (sometime Smyth, Smythe, and Smithe), now Smith-Marriott, of Sydling and the Down house, Dorset, baronet, (formerly of Exeter, Madford and Larkbeare, Devon); also of Suttons, Essex, baronet ... Edited by the Rev. Edward Floyer Noel Smith ... Printed for private circulation.   London, Harrison and sons, 1878.   iv, (5)-14 p. fold. geneal. tab. 22 cm. Title vignette: coat of arms. 16-9135.

CS439.S6   1878

15796   SMITH.   Annals of Smith of Cantley, Balby, and Doncaster, county York; embracing elabor-ate pedigrees of the connected families and biographical notices of their more eminent members. Comp. by Henry Ecroyd Smith ... Printed for subscribers only. (Sunderland, Hills and co.) 1878.
2 p. l., 277, 24 p. front., illus., pl., ports., facsim. 26½ cm. Contains genealogies of the Kilholm or Killam, Aldam, Stacye or Stacie, Payne, Stepney, Gulston or Gulson, Akroyd or Ecroyd, Oddie, Robson, Hedley, Pease, Dixon, Coates, Richardson, Mayson, Dearman, Waterhouse, Barton, Clough, Hagen, Tyson, Whalley, Harrison and Darby families. 16-17295.

CS439.S6   1878a

15797 SMITH. Genealogy of William Smith, of Wrightstown, Bucks County, Pa. 1684. By Josiah B. Smith ... Newton, Pa. (Philadelphia, Pa., Collins printing house) 1883. vi p., 1 l., 113 p. 27½ cm. 9-13727. CS71.S643 1883

15798 SMITH. Genealogy of Robert Smith, of Buckingham, Bucks county, Pa. 1719. By Josiah B. Smith ... Newtown, Pa., 1885. ix p., 1 l., 52 p. 27½ cm. 35-21376. CS71.S643 1885

15799 SMITH. In memoriam Hon. Elizur Smith. Born January 5, 1812. Died at Lee, April 3, 1889. Funeral services, resolutions, extracts from the press, genealogical, 1889. Lee, Mass., E. S. Rogers, printer, 1889. 1 p. l., (40) p. 20½ cm. Genealogy: p. (37)-40. 18-3652. CT275.S52815

15800 SMITH. A genealogical history of the descendants of the Rev. Nehemiah Smith of New London County, Conn., with mention of his brother John and nephew Edward. 1638-1888. By H. Allen Smith ... Albany, N.Y., J. Munsell's sons, 1889. 318 p. front., plates, ports. 23½ cm. 9-13726. CS71.S643 1889

15801 SMITH. Genealogical records of Wellington Smith and family. Collected and arranged by Wellington Smith. (n. p.) 1889. 28 l. front. (port.) 28 cm. "Families represented ... Canfield, Yale, Ingersoll, Edwards, Shannon, Clark, Bullard, Bulkley." Additions and corrections in manuscript. "Authorities consulted": 2d leaf. "A copy of the will of Stephen Hopkins, of Plymouth. Dated June 6, 1644": 26th-28th leaves. 40-18931. CS71.S643 1889a

15802 SMITH. Ancestral and revolutionary history of the Smith, Partridge, Treat, Woodruff and Lowry families. Compiled by Henry Whittemore. New York, Heroes of the revolution publishing co., 189-. 15 p. illus. (ports.) pl. 27 cm. 17-24546. CS71.S643 189-

15803 SMITH. A complete genealogy of the descendants of Matthew Smith of East Haddam, Conn., with mention of his ancestors. 1637-1890. By Mrs. Sophia (Smith) Martin ... Rutland, The Tuttle company, printers, 1890. 269 p. 24 cm. Blank leaves inserted. 9-13725. CS71.S643 1890

15804 SMITH. John Smith of Milford, New Haven colony, 1640; and his descendants to the fifth generation. Compiled by Robert Atwater (Bassett, Clark) Smith ... (Boston? 1891) 7 p. 24½ cm. Caption title. Reprinted from New Eng. hist. and geneal. register for July, 1891. 9-13724. CS71.S643 1891

15805 SMITH. Pedigree of Smyth of Hill hall, Essex. Comp. by H. Farnham Burke ... and J. Jackson Howard ... London, Mitchell and Hughes, 1891. 8 p. 25½ cm. Published also in "Miscellanea genealogica et heraldica." London, 1892, 2d ser., vol. IV, p. 241-247. 20-16682. CS439.S6 1891

15806 SMITH. Ebenezer and Ruth Smith and their descendants. By Albert Dickerman. Muskegon? Mich., 1891. 85 p. 23 cm. 62-56131. CS71.S643 1891a

15807 SMITH. Theydon Mount: its lords and rectors. With a complete transcript of the parish registers and monumental inscriptions. Edited by J. J. Howard and H. Farnham Burke with the assistance of Rev. L. N. Prance, rector. (n. p.) Priv. print. (1894) xiii, 66, 6 p. front. (coat of arms) 25½ x 19½ cm. "Sixty copies only." "Pedigree of Smith of Hill Hall, Essex": 6 p. at end. 4-23527 rev. CS436.T5

15808 SMITH. A memorial of Rev. Thomas Smith (second minister of Pembroke, Mass.,) and his descendants ... A full genealogical record. 1707-1895. Compiled by Susan Augusta Smith. Plymouth, Avery & Doten, printers, 1895. 146 p., 1 l. front., plates, ports., map. 22 cm. 9-13723. CS71.S643 1895

15809 SMITH. Some account of the Smiths of Exeter and their descendants. By one of them (Arthur M. Smith). Printed for private circulation. Exeter, W. Pollard & co., printers, 1896. 59 p. fold. geneal. tables. 22½ cm. 4-1233. CS439.S6 1896

15810 SMITH. Wills of the Smith families of New York and Long Island, 1664-1794: careful abstracts of all the wills of the name of Smith recorded in New York, Jamaica, and Hempstead prior to 1794, with genealogical and historical notes: by William S. Pelletreau ... New York, F. P. Harper, 1898. xiii, 151 p. front. (port.) 24 cm. "Edition limited to 340 copies, no. 2." 3-17353. CS71.S643 1898

15811   SMITH.   A family history and fity-two years of preacher life in Mississippi and Texas ...
By Rev. Wesley Smith, of the Texas conference, Methodist Episcopal church, South. Nashville, Tenn.,
University press company, 1898.   167 p., 19 l. ports. 23 cm.   Appendix, "Family record," 19 l. left blank. 15-6392.

CS71.S643   1898a

15812   SMITH.   The Smiths and Walkers of Peterborough, Exeter, and Springfield. By F. B. Sanborn.
(Concord, N.H., 1899)   28 p. incl. front. illus. (incl. ports.) 26 cm. Caption title. Cover-title: The Walkers of Peterborough
in New Hampshire. Concord, October, 1899. 25-6697.

CS71.S643   1899

15813   SMITH.   A complete list of the descendants of Joseph Smith and Deliverance Lane ... published by John K. Simpson.   Arlington Heights, Mass. (19 -)   (4) p. illus. 41½ cm. 37-16847.

CS71.S643   19 -

15814   SMITH.   Genealogical pamphlets (proof sheets) Ipswich, Mass. no. 2-6.   Providence, R. I.,
A. Caldwell, 1900.   (49) p. 24½ cm.   Contents. - no. 2. John and Elisabeth Smith, 1664. - no. 3. Richard and Hannah (Cheney) Smith,
1660. - no. 4. -George and Mary Smith, 1648. - no. 5. Thomas Smith, inn-holder, 1680. - no. 6. Scattering Smith families, and unarranged Smith
names. 1-16049.

CS71.S643   1900a

15815   SMITH.   Some account of the family of Smith, anciently of Shute in Devonshire.   Edited by
W. P. W. Phillimore ... London, Printed for private circulation and issued by Phillimore & co., 1900.
viii, 32 p. front. (coat of arms) plates, port. 28½ cm.   Tabular pedigrees of Smith: p. 2, 8. 15-22366.

CS439.S6   1900

15816   SMITH.   The home of the Smith family in Peterborough, New Hamsphire.   1749-1842.   By
Jonathan Smith ... Clinton (Mass.) Press of W. J. Coulter, 1900.   x, 202 p. incl. 2 facsim. front., 8 pl., port.,
fold. plan. 20 cm.   "To preserve, first, the known facts and traditions ... of the old family home in Peterborough; and, second, all that can now
be learned of its first two proprietors, William Smith and Jonathan Smith." - Pref. 5-16557.

CS71.S643   1900

15817   SMITH.   Origin and history of the name of Smith, with biographies of all the most noted
persons of that name.   And an account of the origin of surnames and forenames.   Together with over
five hundred Christian names of men and women and their significance.   The crescent family record
... Chicago, Ill., American publishers' association, 1902.   4 p. l., iv p., 1 l., 9-112, (14) p., 1 l. front., illus.,
23½ cm. Forms for "Crescent family records": (14) p. at end. 11-32000.

CS71.S643   1902

15818   SMITH.   The Smith family, being a popular account of most branches of the name - however
spelt - from the fourteenth century downwards, with numerous pedigrees now published for the first
time, by Compton Reade ... London, E. Stock, 1902.   xxiv, 280 p. 23 cm. 3-1339.

CS439.S6   1902

15819   SMITH.   Asahel Smith of Topsfield, with some account of the Smith family.   By Joseph F.
Smith, jr ... (Topsfield Mass., 1902)   p. 87-101. front. (ports.) facsim. 22½ cm. 38M4612T

CS71.S643   1902a

15820   SMITH.   The history of a banking house, (Smith, Payne and Smiths.)   By Harry Tucker
Easton ... London, Blades, East & Blades, 1903.   xvi, 127 p. incl. fold. geneal. tab. plates, ports., facsim. 27 cm.
15-24600.

HG3000.L84S5

15821   SMITH.   The Smith family; being a popular account of most branches of the name - however
spelt - from the fourteenth century downwards, with numerous pedigrees now published for the first
time, by Compton Reade ... Popular ed.   London, E. Stock, 1904.   xxiv, 280 p. incl. front., illus., geneal.
tables. 22 cm. L. C. COPY REPLACED BY MICROFILM. 22-3938.

CS439.S6   1904
Microfilm 10312 CS

15822   SMITH.   Record of the Smith family descended from John Smith, born 1655 in County Monaghan, Ireland.   Philadelphia (Press of G. F. Lasher) 1906.   272 p. 27 cm. Preface signed: Joseph S. Harris. Blank
leaves inserted for notes. "The history of the descendants of John Smith, born in Ireland in 1686, died in Uwchlan, Chester Co., Pa. ... 1765; and
his wife Susanna, born in Ireland in 1691, died in Uwchlan ... 1767." 6-18332.

CS71.S643   1906

15823   SMITH.   Reunion of the descendants of William Smith held in Peterboroguh, N.H., August 10th, 1904.   (Ed. by Jonathan Smith)   Clinton (Mass.)   Press of W. H. Benson, 1906.   4 p. 1., (5)-176 p. front., plates. 20½ cm.   10-15830.   CS71.S643   1906b

15824   SMITH.   History and records of the Smith-Carington family from the conquest to the present time, with full account of the various seats and places with which its members have been connected, including Carrington in Cheshire, Ashby Folville in Leicestershire, Wootten Wawen in Warwickshire, and Blackmore and other places in Essex ... Ed. by Walter Arthur Copinger ... London, H. Sotheran and company, 1907.   3 p. 1., v-xii, (4), 697, (1) p. front. (coat of arms) illus., plates, fold. map, plan, geneal. tables (part fold.) 29 cm.   Ed. from notes by Richard Smith-Carington.   cf. Dedication.   14-17782-3.   CS439.S65

———— Pedigree of Smith-Carington of Covington, co. Chester, and Ashby Folville, co. Leicester &c.   (London, 1907)   geneal. chart. 113 x 325 cm fold. to 27½ x 37½ cm.   In box.   To accompany the History and records of the Smith-Carington family.   14-17782-3.   CS439.S652

15825   SMITH.   Biographical sketches of Joseph Smith the prophet and his progenitors for many generations, by Lucy Smith ... Lamoni, Ia., The Reorganized church of Jesus Christ of latter day saints, 1908.   1 p. 1., iv, 371 p. 20 cm.   22-14659.   BX8695.S6S6

15826   SMITH.   Jesse Smith, his ancestors and descendants, by L. Bertrand Smith.   New York, F. Allaben genealogical company, 1909.   187 p. front. 24½ cm.   (On verso of half-title: Allaben genealogical series) Title within ornamental border.   9-14468.   CS71.S643   1909

15827   SMITH.   A New Hampshire farm and its owner ... Clinton, Press of W. H. Benson, 1909. 4 p. 1., 213 p. front., ports. 20½ cm.   Preface signed: "J.S., C.S." i.e. Jonathan Smith, Caroline Smith.   "This little volume is a continuation of the 'Home of the Smith family.'"   9-25406.   CS71.S643   1909a

15828   SMITH.   Smith, with collateral lines: Chipman, Divine, Huckins, Jones, Lewis (Barnstable branch) and Mayflower connection; ancestral record of Frances Amelia (Smith) Lewis, comp. and prepared by Harriet Southworth (Lewis) Barnes.   Philadelphia, 1910.   51 p. 19½ cm. 10-13760.   CS71.S643   1910

15829   SMITH.   Facts and fancies of family history, by Elizabeth Eunice Smith Marcy.   Drawings by the author.   Evanston, Ill., Bowman publishing company, 1911.   3 p. 1., 11-160 p. plates, 2 port. (incl. front.) coat of arms.   21 cm.   On cover: Facts and fancies. Memorial. Poems. Contains Smith, Clark, Sparrow and Cooke families.   "In memoriam, Elizabeth Eunice Smith Marcy, 1821-1911: p. 137-150.   "A few selections from Mrs. Marcy's hymns and poems": p. 151-160. 34-29289.   CS71.S643   1911

15830   SMITH.   Smith-Bonham, 1631-1908.   Chicago, E. L. Smith, priv. print (1911?)   42 1. incl. illus., ports.   20 cm.   Preface signed: Emmet L. Smith.   With the exception of 2 1. printed on one side of leaf only.   11- 22129.   CS71.B712   1911?

15831   SMITH.   Notes and illustrations concerning the family history of James Smith of Coventry (b. 1731 - d. 1794) and his descendants, with tables of pedigrees; comp. by Lady Durning-Lawrence. West Norwood, S.E., Priv. print. by Truslove & Bray, ltd., 1912.   xii, 131, (1) p. incl. plates, ports.   17 double geneal. tab. 21½ cm.   14-7738.   CS439.S6   1912

15832   SMITH.   Memorial tribute to John Smith and Martha Pickens, by Grace Smith Pettijohn. Indianapolis, Ind., 1912.   (58) p. illus. (incl. ports.) pl., fold. geneal. tab. 23½ cm.   37-16947.   CS71.S643   1912

15833   SMITH.   Report, Asscoiation descendants of Ralph Smith of Hingham and Eastham, Massachusetts (inc.)   Yarmouth Port, Cape Cod, Mass., The Register press, 1913.   v. 16-20 cm. Title varies slightly.   41-38346.   CS71.S643

15834   SMITH.   Genealogies of an Aberdeen family, 1540-1913, by the Rev. James Smith, B.D. Aberdeen, Printed for the University, 1913.   x, 148 p. front., illus., plates, ports., fold. plan. 25 cm. (Half-title: Aberdeen university studies.   no. 63) "The wreck of the Oscar, 1st April 1813": p. 121-124.   "The Indian mutiny": p. 125-134.   "India office record of Lieut. John Chalmers, M.A.": p. 135.   15-4653.   CS479.S64

15834a SMITH. Ralph Smyth of Hingham and Eastham, Mass., and his descendants, by Dr. Dwight Smith ... New York, T. A. Wright, 1913. 4 p. l., 174 p. front. (port.) 24½ cm. Blank leaves at end for "Additional records." Edition limited to 100 numbered copies; this copy not numbered. Contains also "a line of descent from Thomas Rogers and of Stephen Hopkins." 13-19965.

CS71.S643   1913

15835 SMITH. Autobiographical notes, letters and reflections, by Thomas Smyth, D. D. Edited by his granddaughter Louisa Cheves Stoney. Charleston, S. C., Walker, Evans & Cogswell company, 1914. 4 p. l., (3)-784 p. front., illus. (ports., coat of arms) 24½ cm. "Appendix: Smyth genealogy": p. 743-751. 14-16976.

BX9225. S56A3

15836 SMITH. The family of Hugh Smith. Page 97.

CS71.G657   1915

15837 SMITH. Genealogy of Consider Smith of New Bedford, Mass.; with notes on allied families of Mason and Thwing, by Llewellyn Tarbox Smith ... Boston, T. R. Marvin & son, printers, 1915. 26 p. 2 port. (incl. front.) 23½ cm. Two poems, by the author, inserted. 15-16626.

CS71.S643   1915

15838 SMITH. A sketch of the Cotton Smith family of Sharon, Connecticut; with genealogical notes, by Bayard Tuckerman. Boston, Priv. print. (Plimpton press, Norwood, Mass.) 1915. 4 p. l., 3-73 (1) p. front., ports. 21 cm. 15-25101.

CS71.S643   1915a

15839 SMITH. Genealogy of the Smith, Walkup, Bell, Perry and allied families. Data collected and compiled by John Fraser Smith. Chicago, Ill., 1915. 1 p. l., 37, v p. front. (coat of arms) 23 cm. 16-9799.

CS71.S643   1915b

15840 SMITH. A record of the family of Roswell Smith, son of Steel Smith of Farmington, Conn., Windsor, Vermont, and other localities, with residence of descendants, so far as is known to date. (Washington, D. C.) 1919. 47 p. front. (port.) fold. geneal. tab. 23½ cm. Prefatory remarks signed: Henry E. Perkins. "Genealogical tree compiled through the kindness of Lawrence Brainard ... Boston, Mass., January, 1918; to whom we are indebted for some of our early data of the Smith family": fold. geneal. tab. 19-14394 rev.

CS71.S643   1919

15841 SMITH. A new edition of the record of the family of Roswell Smith and Roswell Smith, second of the family of Steel Smith of Farmington, Conn., Windsor, Vermont, and other localities, with residence of descendants so far as is known to date. (Rutland, Vt., The Tuttle co.) 1921. 80 p. front. (port.) fold. geneal. tab. 23½ cm. Prefatory remarks signed: Henry E. Perkins. "Genealogical tree, comp. through the kindness of Lawrence Brainard ... Boston, Mass., January, 1918; to whom we are indebted for some of our early data of the Smith family": fold. geneal. tab. 21-17506.

CS71.S643   1921

15842 SMITH. Ancestors of Henry Montgomery Smith and Catherine Forshee, and their descendants to the present time, besides the four main lines Smith-Montgomery, Forshee-Weaver, are the inter-related families Van Giesen, Hoskins, Baird, Sanders, Wheeler, Morse, Hiscock, Cole, Ives, Mullen, Bouck, Zogbaum, Fairchild, Pitkin, Stupp, Dennis, Clark, Lewis, Siter, Hunt, Crofoot, Storms, Crane, Hamlin, Reed, Howard, Howe, Pittman, Critcherson, Dunning, and a Smith collateral line, by Annie Morrill Smith ... Brooklyn, N. Y., A. M. Smith, 1921. 139 p. 2 port., map. 23½ cm. Bibliography: p. 115. 21-21208.

CS71.S643   1921a

15843 SMITH. Family tree book, genealogical and biographical, listing the relatives of General William Alexander Smith and of W. Thomas Smith, comp. by them. Data for the Flake tables gathered by Mrs. Julia Flake Burns and by Osmer D. Flake. (Evansville? Ind.) W. R. Smith (1922) 304 p. illus. (incl. ports.) 3 col. coats of arms. 28 cm. An edition of 1,000. 22-22878.

CS71.S643   1922

15844 SMITH. Ancestry of Henry Boynton Smith, Frederick Southgate Smith, Horatio Southgate Smith, comp. by Henry Smith Munroe, with aid from Alice Durant Smith. Litchfield, Conn., Printed for private distribution, Enquirer press, 1922. 2 v. front. (port.) fold. maps, fold. geneal. tab. 26 cm. 22-17211.

CS71.S643   1922a

15845 SMITH. Ancestry of Samuel Smith, jr. and Moses Fay Smith and descendants of Samuel Smith, jr. and Molly Clark and Moses Fay Smith and Candace Allen, all of Barre, Massachusetts, as compiled by Arthur Henry Bassett, Tacoma, Washington ... Tacoma, Wash., Smith-Kinney co., printers, 1922. geneal. tab. 96 x 61 cm. 23-2856.

CS71.S643   1922c

15846   SMITH.   The genealogy of the descendants of Samuel Smith, sr., and Elizabeth (McCleave) Smith, by John Peery Miller ... (Xenia, O., The Aldine publishing house) 1922.   118 p. incl. illus. (ports., map) pl. 23 cm.   Errata slip inserted.   37-16970.   CS71.S643   1922g

15847   SMITH.   The chronicles of a Puritan family in Ireland (Smith (formerly) of Glasshouse) by G. N. Nuttall-Smith ... from notes collected by R. Wm. Smith, junr. ... and from other sources. (London) Printed by F. Hall at the Oxford university press, 1923.   2 p. l., 139 p. front., pl., ports., fold. map, fold. geneal. tab., coat of arms.   24 cm.   24-25661.   CS499.S6

15848   SMITH.   Genealogy of the descendants of Robert Smith, who settled near Castle Shannon, Washington Co.   Now in Allegheny Co., Pennsylvania.   1772.   (Williamsport, Williamsport printing & binding co., 1923)   311, (1) p. illus. (ports., facsims.) 23 cm.   "Foreword", signed: Edward U. Smith.   23-13405.   CS71.S643   1923

15849   SMITH.   Abiel Smith and Lydia Otis.   (Lincoln, R. I., 1923)   11, (1) p. pl., ports. 22½ cm.   Introduction signed: Robert Lewis Weis.   25-21368.   CS71.S643   1923a

15850   SMITH.   The genealogy and history of the John Keysar Smith family of Valley Rest, Florence, Nebraska, by Angeline Smith Pickering Crane and Cora Phebe Smith Mullin.   (Omaha, Citizen printing co., 1924)   4 p. l., 243 p., 2 l. 21½ cm.   "Genealogy of Smith, Douglas, Crane, Baxter, Denison, Stanton, Gardiner, Griswold, Tracy, Nehemiah Smith, Bourne, Lord, Lee, Browne, Hyde, Wolcott, Hough, Brewster Mayflower line, etc." 24-30876.   CS71.S643   1924

15851   SMITH.   Some descendants of Henry Smith and Thomas Birchard, who came to America about 1635.   Compiled and arranged by Howard B. Smith ... Omaha, Neb., 1924.   111 p.   22½ cm.   27-1288.   CS71.S643   1924a

15852   SMITH.   The descendants of Joel Jones; a revolutionary soldier, born in Charlton, Mass., in 1764, and died in Crawford County, Pa., in 1845.   Together with an account of his ancestors, back to Lewis and Ann Jones, of Watertown, Mass., who came to America about 1635, also the descendants of Lemuel Smith, born in Ware, Mass., in 1770, came to Crawford County, Pa., in 1817, and died in 1855. With an account of such of his ancestors as can now be located, by Elbert Smith, one of the descendants. Rutland, Vt., The Tuttle company, 1925.   414 p. ports., fold. geneal. tables. 24½ cm.   "Some of the authorities consulted": p. 10.   Contains also accounts of the Sprague, Southgate and Jenkins families.   25-8057.   CS71.J76   1925

15853   SMITH.   Fourth annual Christmas plea, by Scotland G. Highland ... Dedicated by the author to his maternal ancestor John Smith, born 1655, great grandfather of Robert Fulton, born at Fulton house, Fulton (then Little Britain) Township, Lancaster County, Pennsylvania, November 14, 1765; died in New York, February 24, 1815.   An historical and genealogical narrative ... (Clarksburg, W. Va., 1926)   (18) p. illus. 30 cm.   "Reprinted from the Clarksburg exponent, Clarksburg, West Virginia, Saturday morning, December 25, 1926." 27-3866.   CS71.S643   1926

15854   SMITH.   The Smiths of Smithtown, an address read before the New York branch of the Order of colonial lords of manors in America, April, 1926, by Mrs. Charles Hilton Brown.   Baltimore, 1927. 28 p. front. (coat of arms) illus. 23½ cm.   (Order of colonial lords of manors in America.   Publications, no. 17) 38-20412.   E186.99.O6 no.17

15855   SMITH.   A history of the descendants of Peter Smith, compiled by Marhsall M. Smith. (Marion Center, Pa.)   1927.   21 numb. l. 29 cm.   Autographed from type-written copy. 27-11117.   CS71.S643   1927

15856   SMITH.   Ancestors of Hiram Smith, and his wife Sarah Jane Bull, compiled for their granddaughter May (Smith) Pfeiffer, by Josephine C. Frost ... (n. p.) 1927.   30 p. 23½ cm.   Half-title: Smith-Bull genealogy. 28-7306.   CS71.S643   1927a

15857   SMITH.   The Sydney-Smith and Clagett-Price genealogy, with the Lewis, Montgomery, Harrison, Hawley, Moorhead, Rixey, Doniphan, Waugh, Anderson, Randolph, Mott, Drake, Butcher, Triplett, Humphrey, Ball, Porter, Brown, Dorsey, Cooper, Stuart, Strother, families with whom they intermarried, and some of their descendants, by Lucy Montgomery Smith Price ... Strasburg, Va.,

15857 continued: Printed by Shenandoah publishing house, 1927.   324 p. front., plates, ports., facsims., geneal. tables, coats of arms. 26 cm. 28-8620.   CS71.S643   1927b

15858   SMITH.   Records and charts of the James, Didenhover, Dowling, Brown, Christian Smith, Reed, Huston, Prutzman and Elder families.   Compiled by Mrs. Charles E. Smith.   (Columbus, O., 1928)   21 l. illus. (incl. ports., facsims.) 6 fold. geneal. tab. 31 cm. Several leaves left blank for additions. A collection of data relating to the ancestry of Charles Adelbert Smith, consisting of printed and manuscript material, with mounted photographs, fastened together in binder. 28-5863.   CS71.S643   1928

15859   SMITH.   Family gatherings relating to the Smith and Blanchard families, with a memoir of the Rev. Elias Smith, pastor of Middleton, Mass.; by his grandson George Peabody, edited by William Crowninshield Endicott, the younger, grandson of George Peabody, and great-great-grandson of the Rev. Elias Smith.   Danvers, Mass., 1929.   6 p. l., 3-170 p., 1 l. front., plates, ports. 25 cm. "Two hundred and fifty copies printed on Glaslan handmade paper at the Wayside press, Topsfield, Massachusetts." 29-18101.   CS71.S643   1929

15860   SMITH.   The Smiths of Virginia; a history and genealogy of the Smiths of "Big Spring plantation", Frederick County, Virginia, together with a chronicle of the Drugan and the Carnahan families of Pennsylvania and Ohio.   By Blanche T. Hartman.   Pittsburgh, Pa., Priv. print., 1929.   5 p. l., 99 p. front. (port.) 2 fold. geneal. tab. 24 cm. "Fifty copies of this work have been printed." Includes also "Thompson-McCreary descendants." 30-3075.   CS71.S643   1929a

15861   SMITH.   Ancestry and posterity of Joseph Smith and Emma Hale, with little sketches of their immigrant ancestors, all of whom came to America between the years 1620 and 1685, and settled in the states of Massachusetts and Connecticut, compiled and written by Mary Audentia Smith Anderson.   Independence, Mo.   (Herald publishing house) 1929.   720 p. incl. front., illus., ports. fold. geneal. tables. 24 cm. "Limited edition." 30-12282.   CS71.S643   1929b

15862   SMITH.   Report, Association descendants of Ralph Smith of Hingham and Eastham, Massachusetts (inc.)   Yarmouth Port, Cape Cod, Mass., The Register press, 193   v. 16-20 cm. Title varies slightly. 41-38346.   CS71.S643

15863   SMITH.   Genealogical record of Ephraim Smith and his lineal descendants.   Begun by George M. Austin; completed by Florence Austin and Marshie Austin.   (n.p.) 1931.   27 p. 33 cm. 61-57912.   CS71.S643   1931b

15864   SMITH.   Our family circle, compiled by Annie Elizabeth Miller ... Macon, Ga., Press of the J. W. Burke company, 1931.   550 p. front. (coats of arms) illus. (incl. ports.) 23½ cm. Contents. - House of Landgrave Smith. - The "twenty children." - Second Landgrave Smith and Mary Hyrne. - House of Robert. - House of Bostick. - House of Lawton. - House of Grimball. - House of Erwin. - House of Daniel. - House of Stafford. - House of Maner. 31-18577.   CS71.S643   1931

15865   SMITH.   The Smith family of Pennsylvania, Johann Friederich Schmidt, 1756-1812 by J. Bennett Nolan ...   (Reading, Pa.)   The family, 1932.   203 p. front., plates, ports., facsim. 25½ cm. 32-33200.   CS71.S643   1932

15866   SMITH.   From then until now, by Pauline Smith Crenshaw ... Montgomery, Ala., The author (1932)   1 p. l., ii, (3)-170 p., 1 l., iii-xiv p. front. (ports.) 23½ cm. A genealogy of the Smith and allied families. 34-17816.   CS71.S643   1932a

15867   SMITH.   The Smiths of Haverstraw, some notes on a Highland family (by) LeRoy Elwood Kimball.   (New York? 1935)   cover-title, p. 392-404. pl. 23 cm. "Reprinted from New York history, vol. XVI, no. 4, October, 1935." 36-30616.   CS71.S643   1935

15968   SMITH.   Smith-Hooker genealogy, by Della S. Bishop.   Ithaca, N.Y. (Printed by Stuart & son) 1936.   ix, 342 p. plates, ports., col. coats of arms. 23½ cm. 39-16900.   CS71.S643   1936

15869   SMITH.   The Rock Smith family to the tenth generation, by Valentine W. Smith; an historical sketch and genealogical record of the family, based upon the collection of old, original family papers left by William Smith in the old homestead at Merrick, Long Island, in 1884.   Jamaica, N.Y., The Queens borough public library, 1937.   ix, 112 p. plates, ports., fold. map, fold. geneal. tab. 26½ cm. 37-2780.   CS71.S643   1937

15870   SMITH.   The Smith family of Pennsylvania; a genealogy of the descendants of the Smith family ... together with an account of the origin of the name.   Compiled by Mary J. M. (Griggs) Heyward.   Pasadena, Calif. (1937)   10 p. l., 46 numb. l. incl. illus. (mounted ports.) geneal. tab.   20 cm.   Introduction signed: Richard Heyward.   Mimeographed.   30-12228.   CS71.S643   1937a

15871   SMITH.   Garrett county history of pioneer families ... The Smith family, by Charles E. Hoye.   (Oakland, Md., 1937)   mounted l.   33 x 27 cm.   Newpaper clipping.   No. xcviii of a series of articles contributed to the Mountain democrat.   41M3027T.   CS71.S643   1937c

15872   SMITH.   Descendants of Amos Smith and Sarah Beers.   Compiled by Ella Smith Moon.   Niles, Mich., 1938.   1 p. l., 27 numb. l., 4 l.   34 cm.   Type-written.   Text runs parallel with back of cover.   39-12241.   CS71.S643   1938

15872a   SMITH.   The ancestry of Leroy Smith, compiled by Leroy Smith ... Brooklyn, N. Y. (1938) -45.   2 v.   mounted pl.   20, 22 cm.   Type-written (carbon copy)   40-18930 rev.   CS71.S643   1938a

15873   SMITH.   Charles Smith and Rachel Amy Bryant; their ancestors and descendants, by Tenney Smith.   Brattleboro, Vt., The Vermont printing company, 1938.   404 p.   front., plates, ports., facsims., col. coats of arms.   24 cm.   41-377.   CS71.S643   1938b

15874   SMITH.   Reuben Smith of Pittsford, Vermont.   A record of more than 450 of his descendants. With will, inventory, war records, census reports, deeds, contracts, signatures, etc.   Allied families: Ezra Mead.   Burton.   Herrick.   Dean.   Barker.   Clifford.   Manley.   Whedon.   Harrison.   Holden. Hendee.   Spurling.   Compiled and distributed by Fannie Smith Spurling.   Delavan, Wis. (1939)   1 p. l., iii p., 1 l., 75 (i.e. 77) p.   29 cm.   Two unnumbered pages inserted between p. 58 and 59.   Autographic reproduction of type-written copy.   40-8612.   CS71.S643   1939

15875   SMITH.   Mayos of Virginia and kinsmen, Smiths of Virginia and others of the connection. By their relative, George Magruder Battey III ... (Washington, D. C., 1940)   1 p. l., 4 l.   28 cm.   Type-written (carbon copy)   41M182T.   CS71.M47   1940

15876   SMITH.   Journal of Jesse N. Smith, compiled and edited by Nephi Jensen.   (Salt Lake City, Stevens & Wallis, inc., 1940)   136 p. incl. front., ports. (1 double)   19½ cm.   40-33662.   BX8695.S55A35

15877   SMITH.   James Smith, Berwick, 1668, some of his descendants, by Edwin E. Smith ... (Kennebunk, Me., Printed by the Star print, inc., 1940)   54 p.   24½ cm.   41-5560.   CS71.S643   1940b

15878   SMITH.   The Smith-Jarratt genealogy, by Austin Wheeler Smith.   Cookeville, Tenn., 1941.   vii, 204 numb. l.   pl. (coats of arms)   27½ cm.   Reproduced from type-written copy.   "Sources of information": leaves v-vii.   42-453.   CS71.S643   1941

15879   SMITH.   A colonial history and genealogy of the Bickleys, Gardners, Polegreens, Millers, Dottins, Husbands, ancestors of Mrs. Elizabeth Smith Deavenport, Rochester, New York ... by Marion Gertrude Deavenport.   Rochester, N. Y. (Printed by Verwey printing company) 1942.   5 p. l., 170 p.   front., illus., plates, ports.   23½ cm.   42-51495.   CS71.S643   1942

15880   SMITH.   The chronicles of the descendants of Ephraim Smith.   By Hugh Howard Hays.   (Cleveland? pref. 1942)   unpaged.   illus.   22 cm.   61-57916 rev.   CS71.S643   1942a
—— Extension.   (Patton? Calif., 1961?)   85 p.   illus.   22 cm.   CS71.S643   1942a Suppl.

15881   SMITH.   ... Smythe-Thorpe family of St. Mary's, Georgia, compiled by Lockwood Barr ... Pelham Manor, N. Y., 1944.   19 l.   29 x 23½ cm.   Type-written (carbon copy)   44-3251.   CS71.S643   1944

15882   SMITH.   Genealogy of the noble Smith family, by George Magruder Battey, III.   (Washington) 1944.   cover-title, 1 p. l., 8 numb. l.   28½ x 23 cm.   Type-written (carbon copy)   44-30854.   CS71.S643   1944a

15883   SMITH.   Notes on the genealogy of one Smith family, by Edward D. Smith.   Atlanta, Ga., 1944.   110 1. incl. mounted photos. (ports.) geneal. tables.   27½ x 21½ cm.   One of the genealogical tables is a photocopy (negative) 46-14713 rev.
CS71.S643   1944b

—— Supplemental pamphlet containing correction of errors and certain additions.   (n. p.) 1946.   12 numb. 1.   27½ x 21½ cm.   46-14713 rev.
CS71.S643   1944b
Suppl.

15884   SMITH.   The Smith family of Withcote, and Wethersfield, Conn.   (By John Smith Kendall) (Berkeley, Calif., 1945)   10, 33 numb. 1.   28 x 21½ cm.   Caption title.   Type-written (carbon copy) 46-23123.
CS71.S643   1945

15885   SMITH.   Smith family, descendants of George and Barbara (Bash) Smith of Westmoreland county, Pennsylvania, and Coshocton county, Ohio, whose children migrated westward through Hancock county, Indiana, and Madison county, Iowa, with allied lines of Bash, Waters, Ruby, Hogle, and Murphy, by Margaret R. Waters and Donald D. Murphy.   (Indianapolis) 1946.   3 p. 1., 280 p. 28 x 22 cm. 47-18165.
CS71.S643   1946

15886   SMITH.   Mormon genealogies; the Smith, Pratt, Young, Richards and allied families. (Salt Lake City, 1946)   2 p. 1., ii, 2-127 (i. e.133) p.   geneal. tables.   28 x 21½ cm.   Compiled by Stanford J. Robinson.   cf. Pref. 47-19556.
CS71.S643   1946a

15887   SMITH.   John Smith, Esquire: his ancestors and his descendants; a story of the pioneers. (n. p., c. 1948)   180 p. illus., ports. 24 cm. 49-15034. *
CS71.S643   1948

15888   SMITH.   Kin of Mellcene Thurman Smith (Mrs. Edward T.) (n. p., 195-)   1027 p. 24 cm. 57-37611 rev.
CS71.S643

15889   SMITH.   Geneology (sic) of the Smiths, 1756-1951, for the Smiths, of the Smiths, and by a Smith.   (Ridgefield? Wash., 1951)   23 p. ports. 22 cm. 52-41634.
CS71.S643   1951

15890   SMITH.   The Smith and McWilliam family of Manhattan.   By Jennie Dwight Wylie.   (n. p., 1952?)   18 p. illus. 23 cm. 54-16676.
CS71.S643   1952

15891   SMITH.   Lieut. Samuel Smith, his children and one line of descendants and related families. By James William Hook.   (New Haven, 1953)   377 p. 23 cm. 53-38381.
CS71.S643   1953

15892   SMITH.   A family named Smith; a story of the Smith, Tittle, Adams, Coffee, Hicks, Brown, and related families.   1st ed.   By Lola Gene (Howard) Chaudoin.   (Norman? Okla., 1954)   67 p. illus., ports., maps, facsims. 25 cm.   "200 copies." Bibliographical footnotes. 54-36918.
CS71.S643   1954

15893   SMITH.   A family biography; the story of Edward Willis & Jonnie Robertson Smith and their ten children.   (n. p., c. 1954)   354 p. illus. 27 cm. 55-25883.
CS71.S643   1954a

15894   SMITH.   The Smith family record, made by Clayton D. Oxenreider in 1912, with some additions in 1953.   (Reading? Pa., 1955?)   geneal. table. 248 x 97 cm. fold. to 42 x 33 cm. Blueprint with a 1955 date added in ink. In portfolio. 62-1166.
CS71.S643   1955a

15895   SMITH.   The book of John Smith and his descendants.   By Marvin Eugene Harris.   (1st ed.) Columbus, Ohio (1955)   141 p. illus. 18 cm. 56-25340.
CS71.S643   1955

15896   SMITH.   The descendants of Edward Greenlee of West Virginia.   Winter Park, Fla., Printed by the Winter Park Herald, 1956.   436 p. illus. 29 cm. 60-24140.
CS71.G8142   1956

15897   SMITH.   Burr Smith family ancestry; European and American ancestry of Mary Anne Lee Wooster and Millie Burr Smith.   With appendices on the ancestry of the Banker family of Kingsboro, New York, and the Smith family of Somerset, Michigan.   By Francis Medhurst.   Detroit, Harlo Print. and Pub. Co., 1956.   123 p. col. coats of arms, geneal. tables. 29 cm. 56-12817.
CS71.S643   1956

15898   SMITH.   Record of the posterity of Samuel Harrison Smith and Caroline Mooney Smith and Mary Ellen Batman Smith.   By Alta (Alldredge) Dayton.   (n. p.) 1957.   182 p. illus. 24 cm. 58-1299.
CS71.S643   1957

15899   SMITH.   Ancestry and descendants of Henry Perkins Smith and Christiana (Long) Smith.   With added data of Henry's brothers and sisters and their families and of Henry's father's and mother's brothers and sisters and their families.   By Georgiana (Hathaway) Randall.   (Keedysville? Md.) 1958.   273 p. illus. 23 cm. 58-46328.   CS71.S643   1958

15900   SMITH.   The transatlantic Smiths.   By Robert Allerton Parker.   New York, Random House, (1959)   237 p. 22 cm. Includes bibliography. 59-5710.   CS71.S643   1959

15901   SMITH.   The genealogy of one Smith family, including Smiths, Coxes, Mizells, Loves, Bryans, Crittendens, Mahones, Flournoys, Marshalls.   By Edwin Virginius Smith.   (Auburn, Ala., 1960)   40 1. 28 cm. 61-34222.   CS71.S643   1960

15902   SMITH.   Descendants of Appleby Smith, compiled by Marshall Morgan.   (n. p. 196?)   1 v. (unpaged) 28 cm. 68-39208.   CS71.S643

15903   SMITH.   Ancestry, biography, and family of George A. Smith, compiled by his granddaughter, Zora (Smith) Jarvis.   (Provo? Utha, 1962.   1 v. illus. 28 cm. 62-41018.   CS71.S643   1962

15904   SMITH.   Absalom Wamsley Smith, his ancestry and his descendants; nine generations of the Smith family.   By Maud (Bliss) Allen.   (Salt Lake City? 1962?)   iv, 391 p. illus., coats of arms, facsims., geneal. tables, ports. 28 cm. 65-73822.   CS71.S643   1962a

15905   SMITH.   Whence come, whither go.   By Stanley Phillips Smith.   Oakland, Md., 1963.   iii, 24 p. geneal. table. 28 cm. Bibliography: p. 10-11. 64-2560.   CS71.S643   1963

15906   SMITH.   Jeremiah Smith, Missouri pioneer: his kin and descendants.   By R. Ewing Stiffler.   (Denver? 1963?)   412 p. mounted illus., facsims., geneal. tables, col. maps, mounted ports. 29 cm. "Limited to 75 copies ... Copy no. 32." Some pages have typewritten annotations added. 64-3831.   CS71.S643   1963a

15907   SMITH.   Smith genealogy (Absalom Smith) Sept. 1933.   By Jesse Lowe Smith.   (Newark? Ohio, 1964)   12 1. 28 cm. Caption title. 65-81838.   CS71.S643   1964c

15908   SMITH.   Some Smiths, Osborns, and allied families of New England and Ohio, compiled by Estelle Clark Watson.   Skokie, Ill., Guild Press, 1964.   69, (27) p. geneal. table, port. 28 cm. 65-405.
CS71.S643   1964

15909   SMITH.   Smith and Phillips history; a genealogical history of the families of James and Mary Smith, Samuel and Lydia Smith, and Francis and Mary Phillips.   By Yolande (Templeton) Newman.   (Ann Arbor, Mich.) 1964.   270 p. maps, ports. 24 cm. 64-66307.   CS71.S643   1964a

15910   SMITH.   Treasured trails; Utah pioneer Jorgen Smtih.   By Adelia (Mott) Pierce.   (Salt Lake City) 1964.   xviii, 265 p. illus., facsims., geneal. tables, maps, ports. 24 cm. 65-71307.   CS71.S643   1964b

15911   SMITH.   The Joseph Smith family of Gloucester and Salem Counties, N. J.   The James Dye family of Gloucester County, N. J.   By Elmer Garfield Van Name.   Haddonfield, N. J., 1964.   32, (1) p. ports. 23 cm. Cover title. Bibliography: p. (33) 71-6471 MARC.   CS71.S643   1964d

15912   SMITH.   The Smith-Spilman lineage, by Malcolm L. Melville.   Forestville, Calif. (1966)   ii, 43 p. illus., ports. 22 cm. 68-127432.   CS71.S643   1966

15913   SMITH.   My ancestors and descendents, by Carl B. Smith.   Tampa, Fla., 1967.   vi, 56, (68) p. illus., geneal. tables, ports. 24 cm. Bibliography: p. v. 67-7067.   CS71.S643   1967

15914   SMITH.   The John Richey Smith and Sarah B. Martin Smith family history.   Compiled by Anna C. Smith Pabst.   Delaware, Ohio, 1967.   177, xviii 1. illus., maps, ports. 27 cm. Cover title. 67-9208.
CS71.S643   1967b

15915   SMITH.   A letter to my grandchildren, with pictures of some recent forebears, researched and written by C. Aubrey Smith.   Austin, Tex., Printed by Von Boeckmann-Jones (1967)   47 p. illus., facsims., fold. geneal. tables, ports.   24 cm.   70-4262.   CS71.S643   1967c

15916   SMITH.   Smith - Maxson genealogy, compiled for descendents and other relatives of Irving William Smith and Eva Maxson Smith, by Jane Smith Greene and William B. Greene.   Wheaton, Ill., Available at Du Page County Historical Society, 1968.   Geneal. table.   56 x 84 cm. fold. to 23 x 15 cm.   Includes bibliography.   76-881.   CS71.S643   1968

15917   SMITH.   Nicholas Smith, 1629; genealogy, by Richard J. Smith.   (Everett, Mass., 1968)   125 p. 22 cm.   Cover title.   68-59607 MARC.   CS71.S643   1968b

15918   SMITH.   Genealogies: Smith, Bussell, Wood, Bryant (by Mable Smith Saunders assisted by Marjory Smith Faeth.   Kansas City? Mo., 1968?)   80 l.   illus., coats of arms, facsims., geneal. tables, ports. (part col.) 29 cm.   79-4243.   CS71.S643   1968c

15919   SMITH.   Something about some Smiths; an account of part of the Samuel Smith family dating from 1730 and ending in 1969, by David A. Harris.   Tallahassee, Fla. (1969)   xv, 358 p. ports.   37 cm.   78-7017 MARC.   CS71.S643   1969

15920   SMITH.   Smith genealogy.   Ancestry and descendants of Absalom Wamsley Smith.   Maud Bliss Allen compiler.   1 reel positive.   6800   Microfilm reading room.

15921   SMITH.   Smith family (Michael Smith, Revolutionary soldier).   In vertical file.   Ask reference librarian for this material.

SMITH.   See also:

ACKLEY, 1960	GRIM, 1934	MILLS, 1960
AKERS, 1957	GRINDELL, 1957	MOULTON, 1922
ALDERMAN, 1957	GRISWOLD, 1898	NELSON, 1938
ANDERSON, 1902	HACKETT, 1937	NELSON, 1967
BEACH, 1960	HANAFORD, 1915	OTIS, 1851
BEAL, 1956	HARRIS, 1908	PARK, 1965
BENSON, 1895	HIGHLAND, 1936	PATE, 19 -
BERKELEY, DA28.35.B5S6	HIGHLAND, 1936a	POLLOCK, 1932
BLAUVELT, 1957	HOLLAND, 1959	POMEROY, 1958
BONHAM, 1911	HOLSINGER, 1950	RANDOLPH, 1961
BRASFIELD, 1959	HUDSON, DA690.W6H8	RANNEY, F104.C8A2
BRUMBACH, 1961	HUNTER, 1934	REICHNER, 1918
CALHOUN, 1957	JAGGER, 1942	ROTHWELL, 1964
CLARK, 1898	JONES, 1925	ROYD, CS439.R75
COVINGTON, 1956	JOHNSON, 1961	RUGGLES, 1896
CRAPO. 1912	LEWIS, 1901	SAUNDERS, 1897
CROCKER, 1923	LEWIS, 1960	SEMMES, 1956
DAVIDSON, 188-	LINDLEY, 1950	SLOAT, 1943
DICKERSON, 1919	LLOYD, 1912	STARKWEATHER, 1925
DRAKE, 1962	LUTER, 1959	STEWART, 1960
ENDERS, 1960	McALLISTER, 1900	STOUT, 1960
EVELYN, 1920	MACKEY, 1957	THIGPEN, 1961
EWBANK, 1963	McCLARY, 1896a	TOPHAM, 1911
FIELD, 1877	MANLEY, 1938	TORRENCE, 1894
FOSTER, 1897	MARSH, 1896a	TORRENCE, 1938
GENTRY, 1909	MARSH, 1935	TOWNE, 1927
GILBERT, 1959	MASSENGILL, 1931	TUCKER, 1957
GILES, 1965	MAXWELL, 1916	VANDERPYL, 1933
GOLSAN, 1959	MILLER, 1923	WARD, CS439.W295
GOULD, 1897	MILLER, 1951	WARNER, 1956
GREENLEE, 1956	MILLET, 1959	WAY, 1914

SMITH continued:

WEARY, 1921	WILLIS, 1898	No. 430 - Adventurers of purse
WEBB, 1940	WITHERSPOON, 1922	and person.
WEISER, 1960	WOOD, E171.A53 v.14	3939 - Colebrook.
WETHERILL, 1882	WRIGHT, 1924	4639 - Smithfield.
WILDER, 1960	YANCEY, 1958	

SMITH-CARRINGTON. See: SMITH, 1907
BERTIE, CR3899.R7

15923 SMOCK. Genealogical notes on the Smock family in the United States, from genealogical registers, local histories, church records, family records, state archives, and mss. in the possession of the compiler. Comp. by John C. Smock, PH.D. Albany, N.Y., F.S.Hills, 1922. vi, 47 p. front. (port.) 24½ cm. 23-7446. CS71.S653 1922

SMOCK. See also JUSTIN, 1900

15924 SMOOT. The Mississippi, and other songs, by George P. Smoote. 2d ed. Chicago, F.J. Schulte & company (c.1891) xvii, 5-115 p. incl. front. (port.) 19 cm. "Memoir": p. vii-xvii. 34-36869. PS2878.S5M5 1891

15925 SMOOT. The Smoots of Maryland and Virginia; a genealogical history of William Smute, boatright, of Hampton, Virginia, and Pickawaxon, Maryland, with a history of his descendants to the present generation, by Harry Wright Newman. Washington, D.C. (Lynchburg, Va., J.P.Bell, co.) 1936. xv, 218 p. incl. front., coat of arms. plates, ports., map, coat of arms. 24½ cm. "This edition is limited to 250 copies, your book is numbered 88." CS71.S6536 1936

SMOOT. See SCHMUTZ.

SMOOTS. See SCHMUTZ.

SMOTHERMON. See BROWN, 1967b

15926 SMOUSE. The history of the Smouse family of America. By J. Warren Smouse, Martins-burg, Pa. Martinsburg, Pa., Herald print, 1908. 112 p. incl. front. ports. 24 cm. 21-21529. CS71.S654 1908

15927 SMULL. Memorial of John Augustus Smull. Ed. by William H. Egle ... Harrisburg, Pa., L. S. Hart, printer, 1881. 50 p. front. (port.) 30½ x 24 cm. Ancestry: p. 6-8. Proceedings of the House of representatives of Pennsylvania: p. 33-50. 19-1000. F154.S63

SMUT. See SCHMUTZ.

SMUTZ. See SCHMUTZ.

15928 SMYSER. Minutes of the centennial celebration, held by the descendants of the elder Matthias Smyser, May 3rd, 1845, on the farm of Samuel Smyser, in West Manchester township, York co., Pa. Carlisle, Pa., Printed by A. Rudisill, 1852. 34 (i.e.28) p. 15½ cm. Pages 27 and 28 incorrectly numbered 29 and 34. Manuscript note on cover: Written, printed & published by Abraham Rudisill, a tailor, in York, Pa. 1-19549 rev. CS71.S667 1852

15929 SMYSER. History of the Smyser family in America, September 1731 - September 1931, by Amanda Lydia Laucks-Xanders. (York, Pa., York printing company, c.1931) 260 p. incl. col. coats of arms, plates, ports. 28½ cm. Title vignette (coat of arms) "Minutes of the centennial celebration, held by the descendants of the elder Matthias Smyser, May 3rd, 1845, on the farm of Samuel Smyser, in West Manchester township, York co., Pa." first published in 1852: p. (203)-212. 32-562. CS71.S667 1931

15930   SMYSER.   Bicentennial meeting of the Smyser family in America, York fair grounds, June twenty-second, nineteen hundred and forty-six, York, Pennsylvania.   York, Pa., Printed for the association (by) the Maple Press Company, 1947.   107 p. illus., ports.   21 cm.   Cover title: The Smyser family in America.   52-31765.
CS71.S667   1947

SMYSER.   See also: SCHMEISSER.
KURTZ, 1925

SMYTH.   See SMITH.

SMYTHE.   See SMITH.

15931   SMYTHIES.   Records of the Smythies family.   Compiled by Major R. H. Raymond Smythies. London, Priv. print., Mitchell Hughes and Clarke, 1912.   xii, 101 p., 26 l.   2 pl., 38 port. (incl. front.)   29½ cm. Each plate accompanied by guard sheet with descriptive letterpress.   First pub. in the "Miscellanea genealogica et heraldica," London, 1910, 4th ser., v.4, and here republished with additions and corrections.   "Addenda": 26 leaves left blank for additional records.   17-2889.
CS439.S67

SNAPP.   See RUDOLPH, 1962

15932   SNEAD.   The Sneads of Fluvanna, by Mrs. William E. Hatcher (Virginia Snead Hatcher) ... Historical and biographical ... Roanoke, Va., The Stone printing & mfg. co., 1910.   117, (1) p.   front., plates, ports., coat of arms.   23 cm.   20-23924.
CS71.S668   1910

15933   SNEAD.   An American saga; the story of the Snead family of Accomac County, Virginia, and of Kentucky.   Edited by William E. Stokes, Jr., from materials collected by William Scott Snead. (North Garden? Va., 1952)   54 p. illus., ports., coat of arms, fold. geneal. table.   23 cm.   52-30913.
CS71.S668   1952

15934   SNEDDEN.   Mountain cattle and frontier people, by Genevra Sisson Snedden, assisted by many of the family group; stories of the Snedden family, 1867 to 1947.   (Palo Alto, Calif., 1947) xiii, 158 p.   illus., ports., map (on lining-papers) 23 cm.   47-6529*.
F596.S67

SNEDEKER.   See WRIGHT, 1960

15935   SNELL.   (A collection of newspaper clippings and other miscellaneous material relating principally to the Snell family, selected from the Enterprise and News, St. Johnsville, N.Y., 1928, and written in part by Edward S. Smith.   St. Johnsville, 1928?)   1 v.   24 cm.   48-35058*.
CS71.S6685   1928

15936   SNELL.   The Snell family, by Edward S. Smith ... St. Johnsville, N.Y., 1934.   1 p. l., (7)- 35 p.   24 cm.   "Reprinted from the Enterprise and news, St. Johnsville, N.Y."   36-6010.
CS71.S6685   1934

SNELL.   See also: ALDEN, 1925
STOKES, CS439.S897

SNELLGROVE.   See SNELGROVE.

SNEWLI.   See SNEWLIN.

15937   SNEWLIN.   Die Freiburger Familie Snewlin.   Rechts- und sozialgeschichtliche Studien zur Entwicklung des mittelalterlichen Bürgertums.   Freiburg i. Br., Wagnersche Universitätsbuchhandlung, 1967.   xxx, 240 p., 3 l.   23 cm.   (Veröffentlichungen aus dem Archiv der Stadt Freiburg 1. Breisgau, 9)   Cover title: Die Freiburg atrizier-Familie Snewlin.   Issued also as Diss, Freiburg 1. Br., 1964.   Bibliography: p. xv-xxx.   76-434603.
CS719.S6   1967

SNEYD.   See SNEAD.

SNICKERS.   See: KINNEY, 1903
WASHINGTON, 1897

SNIVELY.   See: FALL, 1961
                  SCHNEBELE.

SNODDERLY.   See SHARP, 1953

15938   SNODGRASS.   Snodgrass records, Owen County, Indiana, 1831-to-1927.   By John S. Snod-
grass ... (n. p., 1927)   2 p. l., (11) p. ports. 16½ cm.   Cover-title: Family record of the J. S. Snodgrass family.   Additions and
corrections in ms.   28-5832.   CS71. S669   1927

SNODGRASS.   See also KENDALL, 1942

15939   SNOW.   Biography and family record of Lorenzo Snow, one of the twelve apostles of the Church
of Jesus Christ of latter-day saints.   Written and compiled by his sister, Eliza R. Snow Smith ... Salt
Lake City, Utah, Deseret news company, printers, 1884.   xvi, 581 p. 2 port. (incl. front.) 23½ cm.   "Genealogies":
p. 488-495.   BX8695. S75S6

15940   SNOW.   History of the family of Benjamin Snow, who is a descendant of Richard Snow of
Woburn, Massachusetts.   Compiled and published by Owen N. Wilcox ... Cleveland, Press of the
Gates legal publishing company, 1907.   5 p. l., 386, (7) p. front. (fold. facsim.) plates, ports. 26 cm.   Blank pages in-
serted at end "For family additions."   10-15834.   CS71. S67   1907

15941   SNOW.   The William Snow family.   Descendants of William Snow, who landed at Plymouth,
Mass., in 1635.   Pub. by Edwin H. Snow.   Providence, Snow & Farnham co., printers, 1908.
65 p. 24 cm. 21-8417.   CS71. S67   1908

15942   SNOW.   ... Nicholas Snow of Eastham and some of his descendants, together with Samuel
Storrs, Thomas Huckins, Elder John Chipman, and Isaac Wells, allied to the Snows by marriage.   By
James W. Hawes.   Yarmouthport, Mass., C. W. Swift, 1916.   cover-title, 24 p. 24½ cm. (Library of Cape Cod
history & genealogy, no. 34) 16-4761.   CS71. S67   1916

15943   SNOW.   The history of the Snow families of Maine.   Compiled by Rev. Charles N. Sinnett.
Brainerd, Minn. (1920)   1 p. l., 55 l. 32 cm. Type-written. 21-3727.   CS71. S67   1920

15944   SNOW.   The Snow-Estes ancestry ... Nora E. Snow, author and publisher; compiled by
Myrtle M. Hillson.   Hillburn, N. Y., 1939.   2 v. fronts., plates, ports., facsims. 25 cm.   Blank pages for "Family register",
and folded genealogical charts in pocket, at end of each volume.   Includes "References".   39-23658.
                                                                                   CS71. S67   1939

SNOW.   See also: BROWN, 1929
                    CROCKER, 1923
                    HOPKINS, 1936
                    TAYLOR, 1935
                    VAN NOSTRAND, E171. A53 v. 19
                    WASHINGTON, CS69. W5

15945   SNOWBERGER.   Family records of Snowberger and Kegarise, by Hilda Snowberger Chance.
(Chester? Pa., 1964)   (10), 27 p. illus., geneal. table, ports. 28 cm.   Cover title.   Bibliography: 1st prelim. page.   "Additions
and corrections": (6) p. inserted.   64-55585 rev.   CS71. S672   1964

SNOWDEN.   See: PORTER, 1940
                  THOMAS, 1878

15946   SNYDER.   Familien geschichte von F. Schneider.   Washington, D. C., 1882.   52 l. col. illus.,
mounted ports., col. coat of arms. 39 cm.   Half-title: Familien verzeichniss von Friedrich Schneider aus Lauffen.   The t. - p. and half-title are
in colors.   The text is in manuscript, with colored ornamental borders, initials, cpaitals, head and tail pieces.   Blank leaves, some with ornamental
borders, interspersed.   Newspaper clippings and manuscript notes inserted.   Bound in leather, gold-tooled, mounted with silver coat of arms and
corners.   31-20891.   CS71. S678   1882

15947   SNYDER.   Adam W. Snyder and his period in Illinois history, 1817-1842.   By John Francis Snyder ... Springfield, Ill., The H. W. Rocker co., printers, 1903.   392, (2) p. front., port. 20 cm.
Appendix: The Snyder genealogy. - John Francis Perry and his family. - Speech delivered in the state Senate on the bill to reform the judiciary (by A. W. Snyder) - Muster roll of Capt. Snyder's company in the Black Hawk war.   3-29527.   F545. S67

15948   SNYDER.   History of the family of Snyder (Schneider) (Snider) more particularly of the branch headed by Frederick and son William of Whitley county, Kentucky, by Joseph B. Snyder ... (St. Louis) St. Louis law printing co. (c. 1940)   cover-title, iv, 72, viii p. illus. (coat of arms) port. 21 cm.   Bibliography: p. 61. 40-6189.   CS71. S678   1940

15949   SNYDER.   Snyder-Brown ancestry.   By Harold Minot Pitman.   (Bronxville? N. Y.) 1958. 264 p. illus. 28 cm.   59-30582.   CS71. S678   1958

15950   SNYDER.   Genealogy of the family of Maria Elizabeth and George Michael Schneider.   By Stella (Morava) Snyder.   (Washington, 1960)   10 l. 28 cm. 61-34223.   CS71. S678   1960

15951   SNYDER.   Record of descendants of George Schneider.   By Elsie (Welker) Thomas. (Dresden? N. Y.) c. 1962.   13 l. 28 cm. 63-1055.   CS71. S678

15952   SNYDER.   The pedigree of Oliver Snyder (2 Feb 1878 - 10 Feb 1925) and his wife Emmaline (Kline) Snyder (13 Nov 1881-28 Oct 1964) and a list of their descendants of Berks County, Pennsylvania, United States of America (by) Schuyler Calvin Brossman.   (Behrersburg? Pa., 1964)   sheet. 2 mounted ports. 28 x 77 cm. folded to 28 x 22 cm.   Typescript. 66-7258.   CS71. S678   1964

SNYDER.   See also: ENDERS, 1960
HARBAUGH, CS71. H255
HOLSINGER, 1959
PUTNAM, 1909
WEISER, 1960

SOBANSKY.   See KOZIK family folder in vertical file.   Ask reference librarian for this material.

15953   SODEN.   Descendants of William Soden and George King.   By Neta (Kellogg) Melton.   (Palo? Iowa) 1959.   96 l. 29 cm. 60-24287.   CS71. S679   1959

SOFER.   See SCHREIBER.

15954   SOHIER.   La veritable origine de la tres-illustre maison de Sohier, avec une table genea-logique de la ligne principale & directe, embellie d'un court recit des branches qui en sont sorties, depuis six cens ans, ou environ jusques à present.   Le tout verifié par titres, chartres, monumens, & histoires authentiques.   (Leyden, François Hacke, 1661)   7 p. l., 275, (7) p. illus. (engr. coats of arms, seals, facsims.) port. 52 cm.   Half-title.   The engraved title, with arms of the Sohier and other families, and the portrait of Constantin Sohier are en-graved bt Petrus Holsteyn.   Dedication signed: J. C. D. D. (Jean Carpentier) 24-8348.   CS439. S69

SOLBÉ.   See GUÉRIN, 1890

SOLE.   See SOULE.

SOLLERS.   See TANEY, 1935

15955   SOLLEY.   Thomas Solley and his descendants; the story of a hunt for an ancestor, by George Willis Solley; published by Edward Jucket Morgan.   (Fitchburg, Mass., Sentinel printing company) 1911.   6 p. l., 205 p. front., plates, ports., facsims., geneal. tables, coat of arms. 21½ cm.   "Solley bibliography": p. 180. 31-18247.   CS71. S68   1911

SOLLY.   See SOULE.

SOLOMON.   See PATTERSON, 1957

SOULIS.   See SOULE.

GENEALOGIES IN THE LIBRARY OF CONGRESS

SOMERFORD. See ATKINSON, 1933

15955 a SOMERS. Essay on the life and character of John lord Somers, baron of Evesham ... By Richard Cooksey ... Worcester, Printed by J. Holl for the author, and sold by J. Bew (etc.) London, 1791.   4 p. l., 167 p., 1 l. fold. geneal. tab. 27½ x 22 cm. 5-5141.   DA462.S6C7

15956 SOMERS. A history of the Somers mansion, by Herbert N. Moffett ... and Lewis D. Cook ... Somers Point, N.J., Atlantic county historical society (1942)   cover-title, 24 p. incl. 1 illus., facsim. 23½ cm. 44-28729.   F144.S57M6

SOMERSALL. See ZIMMERMAN, CS71.Z73 19 -

SOMERSCALES. See SKEET, CS438.S5

15957 SOMERSET. The Somerset sequence; with an introd. by Sir Osbert Sitwell. By Horatia (Somerset) Durant. London, Newman Neame, 1951.   223 p. illus., ports., facsim. 23 cm. Bibliography: p. 206-212. 52-18717.   CS439.S695   1951

15958 SOMERVILLE. Memoirs of the family of Somerville, from the year 1066 to the year 1677, copied from the original manuscript in the possession of Lord Somerville. (n.p.) 1800.   1 p. l., (4) p. 1 l., 674 p. 40 cm. In manuscript; copied from the original in the possession of Lord Somerville, 1800. The text is preceded by an "Epistle direct to my sones, 1679", signed: James Somervill. 23-15536.   DA758.3.S7S6

15959 SOMERVILLE. Memorie of the Somervilles; being a history of the baronial house of Somerville ... By James, eleventh lord Somerville ... Edinburgh, A. Constable; (etc., etc.) 1815. 2 v. fronts. (ports.) plates, fold. geneal. tab. 24 cm. Ed. by Sir Walter Scott. 15-25126.   DA758.3.S7S7

15960 SOMERVILLE. The Somerville family and descendants, 1789-1963, compiled by Violette Somerville Machir. (n.p., 1963)   208 p. illus., ports. 21 cm. Cover title. 64-4239.   CS71.S683   1963

SOMERVILLE. See also: HEAD, 1917
MONTGOMERY, 1897
TIERNAN, 1898
TOWNSEND, DA419.T7T7

15961 SON. The Son family. By Harold William Hein. Milwaukee, 1957.   geneal. table. 35 x 122 cm. fold. to 35 x 28 cm. Reproduced from ms. copy. 63-3623.   CS71.S685   1957

15962 SONDLEY. My ancestry, by F. A. Sondley ... Families; Sondley, Crawford, Alexander, Davidson, Cunningham, Forster, Heath, Young, Sams, Somerville, Ware, Stuart ... Privately published by some descendants of the families mentioned. Asheville, N.C., 1930.   289 p. incl. front. (port.) mounted col. plates, coats of arms. 25 cm. Ruled pages (110 at end) 31-4628.   CS71.S687   1930

SONE. See ROGERS, 1958

SONN. See SON.

SONNIN. See KRUSE, 1924

15963 SOPER. Soper, Gildersleeve, Smith (and) Rogers families of Northport, L.I. By Willard Harvey Gildersleeve. Hackensack, N.J., 1952.   2 cards. 7½ x 12½ cm. Microprint copy of Typescript. Collation of the original: 46, 12 l. 28 cm. Micp 58-67.   Microcard CS71

15964 SORENSEN. Ancestry of Carma Erika Jacobsen compiled by Anna E. M. S. Jacobsen; edited and published by T. Harold A. Jacobsen. Salt Lake City, Utah, Beacon press, 1943 -   v. front., phot., ports. 24½ cm. "Printed for private distribution." pt. 2 edited by Erika Jacobsen. Contents. - pt. 1. Father's mothers line. - pt. 2. Mother's mother's line. 44-1735   CS71.J183   1943

15965 SORLEY. Sorley pedigree; a compilation of the ancestry and descendants of Colonel Lewis Stone Sorley and Nan Merrow Sorley. (n.p., 1965)   88 l. geneal. tables. 30 x 44 cm. Bibliography: leaves 3-5. 74-207410.   CS71.S688   1965

610

15966   SORREL.   Genealogie de la famille Sorrel ... par R. Gabriel Heymann.   Grenoble, France, 1928.   geneal. tab.   142 x 165 cm.   In manuscript.   Compiled for Frederic Louis Huidekoper, to accompany his "Genealogy of the Sorrel family of Dauphiné, France, since A.D. 1403 ... 1930".   30-9201.   CS71.S69   1930

15967   SORREL.   The genealogy of the Sorrel family of Dauphiné, France, since A.D. 1403.   Together with data in respect to the American branch, and the descent from that branch of Stuart Elliott Huidekoper ... and Frederick Fitz-James Christie Huidekoper ... compiled by Frederic Louis Huidekoper.   Gstaad, Canton of Bern, Switzerland, 1930.   343 p.   mounted coats of arms (1 col.)   28 cm.   In manuscript; with mounted copies of documents and correspondence, part in manuscript and part type-written.   "Genealogie de la famille Sorrel" (1 p. l., 10 numb. l.) and "Tables des références" (4 numb. l.) both by Gabriel Heymann are inserted: also a copy of "A short sketch of the life of Francis Sorrel ... and his family tree down to ... 1892 ... by Aminta Sorrel Mackall" (1 p. l., 8 numb. l.) and a copy of the author's pamphlet "Huidekoper. American branch".   Accompanied by a genealogical chart by Gabriel Heymann.   30-9200.   CS71.S69   1930

15968   SOTHERON.   Genealogical memoranda relating to the family of Sotheron, of counties Durham, Northumberland, York, etc., and to the sept of MacManus ... (By Charles Sotheran) London, Taylor and co., 1871.   1 p. l., 91 p.   illus.   28½ cm.   Privately printed.   2-9853.   CS439.S7

   SOUILLÉ.   See POTTS, 1935

15969   SOULE.   The Soule family, of North Yarmouth and Freeport, Maine.   (By Dr. Charles E. Banks and Enos Chandler Soule.)   Yarmouth, Me., "Old times" office, 1882.   1 p. l., 31 numb. l.   24 cm.   3-3805.   CS71.S72   1882

15970   SOULE.   A contribution to the history, biography and genealogy of the families named Sole, Solly, Soule, Sowle, Soulis, with other forms of spelling, from the eighth century to the present, with notes on collateral families both foreign and American, illustrated with portraits, residential views, monuments and heraldic insignia.   Comp. and published by Rev. G. T. Ridlon, sr. ... Lewiston, Me., Journal press, 1926.   2 v.   plates, ports., col. coats of arms.   25 cm.   "Only five hundred copies printed."   27-1875.   CS71.S72   1926

15971   SOULE.   Soule newsletter.   v. 1 -   Jan. 1967 -   S. Duxbury, Mass., Soule Kindred.   v.   28 cm.   quarterly.   77-203365.   CS71.S717

   SOULLIE.   See SOUILLÉ.

15972   SOUPIRAN.   La famille Soupiran.   By Pierre Geoges Roy.   Lévis, 1935.   36 p.   26 cm.   56-57057.   CS90.S63   1935

15973   SOUSA.   Sousa family in vertical file.   Ask reference librarian for this material.

15974   SOUTH.   Genealogical notes on the South family from the States of New Jersey, Pennsylvania, Maryland, Virginia, South Carolina, Kentucky, and Texas.   By Christine (South) Gee.   (Greenville? S.C., 1963)   v, 163 p.   illus., geneal. tables, port.   24 cm.   64-4059.   CS71.S723   1963

   SOUTHALL.   See: BAX, 1936
                       PRICHARD, 1901
                       SOUTHWORTH.

15975   SOUTHCOTE.   The Southcote family: memoirs of Sir Edward Southcote, knight.   (Roehampton, Eng., St. Joseph's printing office, 1872)   50 p.   21½ cm.   Half-title.   Sir Edward Southcote to his son John: p. 23-26.   Sir Edward Southcote to his son Philip: p. 27-50.   14-3802.   CS439.S72

15976   SOUTHCOTE.   The Southcote family: memoirs of Sir Edward Southcote, knight.   (In Morris, John, ed.   The troubles of our Catholic forefathers related by themselves.   London, Burns and Oates, 1872.   22 cm.   1st series, p. (361)-410)   14-3803.   BX1492.M6 vol. 1

15977   SOUTHER.   Souther and Vandiver lineage chart.   By John H. Vandiver.   Yakima, Wash., 1960.   geneal. table.   56 x 83 cm.   fold. to 29 x 21 cm.   60-40189.   CS71.S725   1960

   SOUTHERLAND.   See SUTHERLAND.

SOUTHESK, Earl of.   See CARNEGIE, CS476.S7A4

SOUTHEY.   See No. 430 - Adventurers of purse and person.

15978   SOUTHGATE.   Monograph on the Southgate family of Scarborough, Maine, their ancestors and descendants.   By Leonard B. Chapman ... Portland, Me., H. W. Bryant, 1907.   viii, 60 p. pl., 2 port. 24½ cm.   7-37725 rev.   CS71.S726   1907

SOUTHGATE.   See also: DU VAL, 1931
                                       JONES, 1925

15979   SOUTHWELL.   The book of Robert Southwell, priest, poet, prisoner, by Christobel M. Hood, F. R. HIST. S.   (Mrs. Ivo Hood)   Oxford, B. Blackwell, 1926.   vii, 157 p. front., pl., port., fold. geneal. tab.   20 cm.   A selection of Southwell's shorter poems, with a biographical and critical introduction: p. 1-77.   27-18652.
                          PR2349.S5A6   1926

15980   SOUTHWICK.   Genealogy of the descendants of Lawrence and Cassandra Southwick of Salem, Mass.   The original emigrants, and the ancestors of the families who have since borne his name.   By James M. Caller ... (and) Mrs. M. Ober ... Salem, Mass., J. H. Choate & co., printers, 1881.   2 p. l., iii-v, 609 (i. e. 611) p.   front., fold. pl., ports.   21 cm.   "Errata 64 a-b": 2 p. at end.   Contents. - Introduction. - Preamble: Setting forth reasons and causes for separating and dissenting from the Established church of the old colony of Massachusetts Bay by the Quakers in 1656. - Historical extracts. - Genealogy.   6-44366.   CS71.S727   1881

15981   SOUTHWICK.   Early history of the Puritans, Quakers and Indians, with a biography of the Quaker martyr Lawrence Southwick, emigrant founder of the Southwick family in America;   the powerful influence which these factors exercised in the drawing of the Declaration of independence and Constitution of the United States ... (Lynn, 1931)   cover-title, 20 p. illus. 23 cm.   Signed: Walter H. Southwick. 31-22364.   F75.F9S7

15982   SOUTHWICK.   The line of Orin Southwick (1789-1881) a descendant of Lawrence and Cassandra Southwick of Salem, Massachusetts, compiled by Orin Edward Southwick.   Champlain (N. Y.) Priv. print. at the Moorsfield press, 1932.   49, (4) p.   24½ cm.   "Eighty-three copies of this genealogy were printed ... in December, 1932 ... number 82."   "I have extracted from the Genealogy of the descendants of Lawrence and Cassandra Southwick, compiled by James M. Caller ... and Mrs. Maria A. Ober ... material relating to ... (the line of Orin Southwick) including the record of each descendant.   To this I have added information on members of the family in the eighth, ninth, tenth and eleventh generations of my own line." - Foreword.   Blank pages for "Genealogical notes" (8, 50-52)   33-1539.   CS71.S727   1932

SOUTHWICK.   See also: LANDEFELD, 1954
                                      THAYER, E171.A53 v. 20

SOUTHWOOD.   See LAWSON, 1903

15983   SOUTHWORTH.   Descendants of Constant Southworth.   2d ed.   By George C. S. Southworth. Salem, O., Press of Harris & co,, 1897.   32 p. 22½ cm.   9-13722.   CS71.S728   1897

15984   SOUTHWORTH.   Southworth, with collateral lines: Buckingham, Collier, Kirtland, Pratt, Shipman;   ancestral record of Henry Martyn Lewis, comp. and prepared by Harriet Southworth (Lewis) Barnes.   Philadelphia, 1903.   50 p. 19½ cm.   10-14168.   CS71.S728   1903

15985   SOUTHWORTH.   A genealogy of the Southworths (Southards) descendants of Constant Southworth, with a sketch of the family in England, by Samuel G. Webber ... Boston, Mass., The Fort Hill press, S. Usher, 1905.   v, 487 p. front., plates, col. coat of arms, fold. geneal. tab. 24½ cm.   Plates accompanied by guard sheets with descriptive letterpress.   37-38447.   CS71.S728   1905

15986   SOUTHWORTH.   Essays and poems, by George Champlin Shepard Southworth ... Ed. and pub. by his son, George Shepard Southworth ... (Indianapolis? G. S. Southworth, 1929?)   7 p. l., 288 p. front., plates (incl. coat of arms) ports.   22½ cm.   Includes the author's Recollections (p. 222-288) and genealogical extracts from his The descendants of Constant Southworth (p. 216-218)   30-27910.   PS2894.S13   1929

15987   SOUTHWORTH.   Hiram Southworth, his ancestors and descendants (by) G. C. Southworth. A history of the Southworths of northwestern Pennsylvania. (Ann Arbor, Mich., Edwards brothers, inc.) 1943.   vi, 150 p. incl. front.   (coat of arms) illus. (incl. facsim.) pl., ports., maps, plans, fold. map, fold. geneal. tables. 28½ x 22 cm.   "Lithoprinted."   44-1902.   CS71.S728   1943

15988   SOUTHWORTH.   Southworth genealogy; the antecedents, contemporaries, and descendants of the Rev. Joseph S. Southworth.   By Jay La Drew Southworth.   (Mountain Home? Ark., 1957. 36 l. 28 cm.   59-20374.   CS71.S728   1957

15989   SOUTHWORTH.   The ancestry of Ensign Constant and Captain Thomas Southworth of Plymouth and Duxbury, Massachusetts.   By Frederick Lewis Weis.   Dublin, N.H., 1958.   47 p. illus. 23 cm. 61-24095.   CS71.S728   1958

SOUTHWORTH.   See also: BROWN, 1929
                          HOLLAND, DA690.S19C9
                          KIMBROUGH, 1960
                          WILBUR, 1936
                          WOOLSEY, 1900

SOUTTER.   See KNOX, 1895

SOUVILLE.   See SOUILLÉ.

SOUVILLY.   SOUILLÉ.

15990   SOWER.   Genealogical chart of the descendants of Christopher Sower, printer, of Germantown, Philadelphia, Pa.   Comp. by Charles G. Sower.   Philadelphia, C. G. Sower, 1887.   geneal. tab. illus.   315½ x 111½ fold. to 26½ x 19½ cm.   "For private distribution among members of the family. 9-14805.
                                                                                            CS71.S73   1887

15991   SOWERBY.   The Sowerby saga, being a brief account of the origin and genealogy of the Sowerby family and of its history from earliest times down to the present; based upon recent research into available extant literature.   By Arthur De Carle Sowerby in collaboration with Alice Muriel Sowerby and Joan Evelyn Stone.   Washington, 1952 -   v. in   28 cm.   52-28096 rev.
                                                                                            CS71.S7314   1952

SOWLE.   See SOULE.

15992   SPACH.   Descendants of Adam Spach, compiled by Henry Wesley Foltz.   Autobiography and memoirs of Adam Spach and his wife, translated from the German records and prepared for this volume by Miss Adelaide L. Fries ... Winston-Salem, N. C., Wachovia historical society, 1924. xxvi, 170, 170 a, 171-202 p. front., plates, ports. 33½ cm.   Ruled pages for additional records (171-202) 25-510.
                                                                                            CS71.S732   1924

SPAFARD.   See SPOFFORD.

SPAFFORD.   See SPOFFORD.

SPAFORD.   See SPOFFORD.

SPAHR.   See: DODDRIDGE, 1961
                SPARR.

SPAHT.   See SPAID.

15993   SPAID.   Spaid genealogy from the first of the name in this country to the present time, with a number of allied families and many historical facts.   Compiled by Abraham Thompson Secrest ... Columbus, O., Privately printed for the compiler by Nitschke bros., 1922.   viii, 395 p. incl. front. illus. (incl. ports.) 24 cm.   "Of this edition of 500 copies of the Spaid genealogy, this is no. 441." Contains also the Secrest, Hellyer, Anderson and Frye families. 24-32145.   CS71.S733   1922

SPAIN.   See: HARRIS, 1962
JAMESON, 1960

SPALDING.   See SPAULDING.

15994   SPANGLER.   The autobiography of Mary R. Luster, Springfield, Missouri, written in her eighty-first and eighty-second years.   Springfield, Mo., Printed by Cain printing co. (c.1935)
196, (1) p. front. (port.) 21 cm. 35-19401.   CT275.L845A3

15995   SPANGLER.   Spangler and allied families, prefaced by a biographical memorial to Col. Tileston Fracker Spangler, compiler of the genealogical records.   New York, Priv. print. for Mary H. B. G. Spangler, by the American historical society, inc., 1937.   237 p. 2 port., col. coat of arms. 32 cm.
Coat of arms accompanied by guard sheet with descriptive letterpress.   Allied families: Tarrance, Trego, Wyatt, Blake, Tillinghast and Fuller.
38-36150.   CS71.S734   1937

15996   SPANGLER.   Eight centuries of Spanglers; twenty-two generations from 1150 A.D. to 1939 A.D.; descendants of George Spangler (1150-1190) ... with special reference to those sons of Rudolph Spangler of Adams county, Pennsylvania, who emigrated to Ohio between 1800 and 1825.   Compiled by Belmont Farley ... Washington, D.C., 1939.   1 p. l., 60 p. port. 28½ cm. Reproduced from type-written
copy. Leaf of additions inserted between p. 50 and 51. 41-7469.   CS71.S734   1939

SPANGLER.   See also SPENGLER.

15997   SPANN.   A history of the Spann family.   By Joseph Earle Steadman.   With attached Hammond connections, compiled by Edward Spann Hammond from notes of James H. Hammond.   (Batesburg? S.C., 1968?)   90 p. illus., coats of arms, ports. 24 cm. Bibliography: p. 61-62. 70-5365 MARC.
CS71.S7345   1968

15998   SPANTON.   The Spanton family with a short account of Spaunton.   By A. T. Spanton, B.A. (Printed for private circulation only) Hanley, Allbut and Daniel, 1897.   25 p. 28½ cm. 20-15251.
CS439.S725

15999   SPARE.   Descendants of Samuel Spare.   Compiled by John Spare ... New Bedford, Mass., P. Howland, jr., printer and engraver, 1884.   68 p. incl. plates. pl. 23½ cm. 9-13721.
CS71.S735   1884

16000   SPARE.   The Spare family; Leonard Spare and his descendants.   Norristown, Pa., Spare family association, 1931.   xiv, 309 p. front., illus. (facsim.) plates, ports. 23½ cm. "The committee, in 1930 engaged Mr. Edward W. Hocker to assist in compiling the history." - Pref. Bibliography: p. vi-vii. 32-4300.
CS71.S735   1931

16001   SPARGO.   Notes on the name and the family of Spargo of Mabe parish in Cornwall, by John Spargo.   (Old Bennington? Vt.) 1945.   50 p. illus. (port., map) 24 cm. Bibliography: p. 49-50. 46-1020.
CS71.S7355   1945

SPARGUR.   See LUCAS, 1964

16002   SPARHAWK.   Family of Nathaniel Sparhawk of Cambridge.   (By William Sumner Appleton. Boston, 1865)   2, (1) p. 25½ cm. Caption title. "From the N. E. historical and genealogical register for April, 1865." 6-2653.
CS71.S736   1865

16003   SPARHAWK.   Materials for a genealogy of the Sparhawk family in New England.   Compiled by Cecil Hampden Cutts Howard ... Salem, Salem press, 1892.   1 p. l., 113 p. 24½ cm. 2-8719.
CS71.S736   1892

SPARHAWK.   See also: JARVIS, CT275.J4C6
RATHBONE, 1937

16003a SPARKMAN.   Sparkman family in vertical file.   Ask reference librarian for this material.

16004   SPARKS.   Genealogical memoranda relating to the Sparks and Tickell families.   Compiled by Reginald Stewart Boddington.   London, Priv. print. (by Mitchell and Hughes) 1877.   10 p. 28 cm. Reprinted from "Miscellanea genealogica et heraldica." n.s.v.2, 1877, p.469-474. 9-18120.   CS439.S73

16005   SPARKS.   The Sparks quarterly.   v.1 -   (no. 1 -   ) Mar. 1953 -
(Ann Arbor)   v. in   illus., facsim., maps, ports. 29 cm.   Official publication of the Sparks Family Association.   Indexes:
Vols. 1-5, 1953-57, with v.1-5.   70-12632.   CS71.S7364

16005a   SPARR.   Sparr-Spahr family; descendents of Johann Georg Sparr, 1699-1777; 150 years, 1699-1849.   Descendents of Hanns Michael Sparr, 1703-1778; 150 years, 1703 to 1853.   Pocatello, Idaho, 1963.   24, iv, 49 1. 30 cm. 66-99115.   CS71.S737   1963

        SPARR.   See also ALEXANDER, 1892

16006   SPARROW.   Genealogy of the Sparrow family, 1623-1871, by Miss Sarah Sparrow.   Norton, Mass., Printed by Lane brothers, 1888.   (Boston, Mass., Reprinted by Goodspeed's book shop, inc., 1938)   14 p. 21½ cm. "Only 50 copies printed." Preface signed: J.H.D. (i.e. Joshua Harvey Doane) 39-9245.   CS71.S738   1888

        SPARROW.   See also: BANNING, 1924
                              SMITH, 1911

16007   SPAULDING.   Record of the descendants of Samuel Spalding, of Merrimack, N.H., down to 1857.   By Edward Henry Spalding.   Nashua, Printed by A. Beard, 1857.   24 p. 19 cm. Additions in manuscript at end. 25-25196.   CS71.S739   1857

16008   SPAULDING.   Spalding memorial: a genealogical history of Edward Spalding, of Massachusetts Bay, and his descendants.   By Samuel J. Spalding ... Boston, A. Mudge & son, printers, 1872.
xi, 619 p. col. front., col. plates (coats of arms) ports. 24 cm. 1-6089.   CS71.S739   1872

16009   SPALDING.   Spalding memorial and personal reminiscences, by Phineas Spalding, M.D., and Life and selected poems of Caroline A. Spalding.   (Haverhill, N.H., Printed at Cohos steam press) for private distribution, 1887.   3 p. l., (5)-323, (1) p. front. (port.) 22 cm. "Life and character of Caroline Anastasia Spalding, by Rev. George B. Spalding, D.D.": p. (181)-192. Autograph letter of author inserted. 22-22855.   CS71.S739   1887

16010   SPAULDING.   Autobiographical sketch of Rev. Royal Crafts Spaulding, and extracts from letters of himself, and of his wife, Jerusha Bryant Spaulding.   With notes and explanatory text, arranged and ed. by Francis Barnes.   Houlton, Me., Press of W.H. Smith, 1891.   53 p. front. (port.) plates. 23 cm. Cover-title: Spauldingiana 1800-1884. 4-27575.   CS71.S739   1891

16011   SPAULDING.   The Spalding memorial: a genealogical history of Edward Spalding of Virginia and Massachusetts bay and his descendants; with a record of their military services in the colonial, revolutionary and civil wars: together with information concerning ... other branches of the ... family. By Charles Warren Spalding ... Rev. and enl. (from the original publication by Rev. S.J. Spalding) ... Chicago, American publishers' association, 1897.   2 p. l., ii p., 1 l., vi, (15)-1276 p. col. front., plates, ports., plan, facsim., col. coats of arms. 23½ cm. 1-6090.   L.C. COPY REPLACED BY MICROFILM.   CS71.S739   1897
                                                                                              Microfilm 10904 CS

16012   SPAULDING.   A Kentucky pioneer, by Most Rev. John Lancaster Spalding... introduction by Hon. Patrick H. Callahan ... (Champaign, Ill., The Twin city printing company, c.1932)   xix p., 1 l., 23-111, (1) p. pl., port. 20 cm. A narrative poem. Introduction includes a short genealogy of the Spalding family. 33-5432.   PS2894.S2K4   1932

16013   SPAULDING.   The American ancestry of Rev. Jacob Franklin Spalding, M.D., minister and doctor.   By Henry Alanson Tredwell.   Cambridge, Mass., 1955.   (10) l. 28 cm. 56-15928.   CS71.S739   1955

16014   SPAULDING.   The Spalding family of Maryland, Kentucky, and Georgia.   A history of how the pioneer Catholic Spalding family in America originated in Maryland and spread to Kentucky, Georgia, and other States.   By Hughes Spalding.   (Atlanta? 1963-65)   2 v. ports. 24 cm. Contents. - v.1. From 1658 to 1963. - v.2. From 1658 to 1965. 63-24315 rev.   CS71.S739   1963

SPAULDING.   See also: CLEMENTS, 1928
STICKNEY, 1910

16015   SPEAKMAN.   The Speakman family in America, including descendants of Thomas and Ann (Harry) Speakman of Chester county, Pennsylvania, married in 1714, and of William and Mary (Townsend) Speakman of Berkshire in England, married in 1738, compiled by Emma Speakman Webster. Philadelphia, H. Ferris, 1930.   3 p. l., 19-122 p. front., 22 pl. on 11 l. incl. ports., map, facsims.   22½ cm.   Two pages of additions and corrections inserted at p. 25; additions in manuscript on p. 118.   36-24712.   CS71.S7395   1930

SPEAKMAN.   See also NEWLIN, 1942

16016   SPEAR.   Spear family records, 1644-1921.   M. Caroline Eastman Leach.   (Tufts College, Mass.) The Tufts college press, 1922.   70 p. 25 cm. 23-9056.   CS71.S74   1922

16017   SPEAR.   The Speare family from 1642, genealogical record of certain branches by Charles Leon Speare.   Rutland, Vt., The Tuttle publishing company, inc., 1938.   5 p. l., 294 p. front., ports., col. coat of arms.   "Through the courtesy of Mr. Sceva Speare of Nashua, New Hampshire, The Speare family by Mr. C. L. Speare ... is being issued." Mr. Speare, because of illness, was unable to complete his work.   Bibliography: 4th prelim. leaf. 39-9243.   CS71.S74   1938

16018   SPEAR.   The ancestry of Annis Spear, 1775-1858, of Litchfield, Maine, by Walter Goodwin Davis.   Portland, Me., The Southworth-Anthoensen press, 1945.   5 p. l., (3)-172 p. front. (port.) geneal. tab. 23 cm.   Bibliographical foot-notes. 46-18271.   CS71.S74   1945

16019   SPEAR.   Our family heritage.   By Minnie (Speer) Boone.   New York, American Historical Co., 1956.   xii, 198 p. illus., col. coats of arms, facsim. 24 cm. 56-44154.   CS71.S743   1956

16020   SPEAR.   Spear family in vertical file.   Ask reference librarian for this material.

16021   SPEDDING.   The Spedding family.   With short accounts of a few other families allied by marriage.   By Captain John Carlisle D. Spedding ... (Printed for private circulation.)   Dublin, Printed by A. Thom and co. (limited) 1909.   iv p., 2 l., 128 p. front., plates, ports., coats of arms, 2 fold. geneal. tab. 26 cm. Contains also accounts of the Carlisle, Benn, Brownrigg, Deey and Froude families. 15-21511.   CS439.S74

16022   SPEECE.   (Genealogical chart of descendants of Conrad Speece, 1775-1820, immigrant from Mannheim)   Folded chart.   In vertical file.   Ask reference librarian for this material.

16023   SPEED.   Records and memorials of the Speed family.   Collected and prepared for publication by Thomas Speed, and published by the Louisville and Memphis families, for distribution among all the branches.   Louisville, Ky., Courier-journal job printing company, 1892.   206 p. plates, ports. 22 cm. 9-13817.   CS71.S742   1892

16024   SPEED.   Judge John Speed and his family.   A paper prepared for the Filson club, and read at its meeting, June 4, 1894, by the Rev. John H. Heywood ... Louisville, J. P. Morton & company, 1894. 35 p. 22 cm. L. C. COPY REPLACED BY MICROFILM.   CS71.S742   1894
Microfilm 8674 CS

SPEED.   See also BULLITT, 1920

SPEER.   See SPEAR, 1956

SPEIRS.   See WALLACE, CS479.W37

16025   SPELMAN.   Spelman genealogy; the English ancestry and American descendants of Richard Spelman of Middletown, Connecticut, 1700, by Fannie Cooley Williams Barbour.   New York, Frank Allaben genealogical company (c. 1910)   559 p. col. front. (coat of arms) plates, ports., map, plans, facsims. 25 cm. CS71.S744   1910

16026   SPENCER.   Spencer family history and genealogy.   (Milwaukee, Wis., 1889)   1 p. l., 26 p. illus. (incl. ports.) coats of arms. 21½ x 28 cm.   Preface signed: Robert C. Spencer. 9-13816.   CS71.S745   1889

16027   SPENCER.   The Thomas Spencer family in Hartford, Connecticut, in the line of Samuel Spencer, of Cromwell, Connecticut, 1744-1818.   Compiled by Frank Farnsworth Starr for James J. Goodwin.   Hartford, Conn. (Cambridge, J. Wilson and son) 1896.   44 p. fold. geneal. tab. 25½ cm. 9-13814.

CS71.S745   1896

16028   SPENCER.   The Maine Spencers.   A history and genealogy, with mention of many associated families.   By W. D. Spencer.   1596-1898.   Concord, N.H., The Rumford press, 1898.   247 p. incl. front., illus., ports., col. coat of arms. 2 fold. maps. 19½ cm. 9-13815.   CS71.S745   1898

16029   SPENCER.   Genealogical sketch of the descendants of Samuel Spencer of Pennsylvania, by Howard M. Jenkins ... Philadelphia, Ferris & Leach, 1904.   vii, 250 p. 24 cm. 7-38429.

CS71.S745   1904

16030   SPENCER.   Spencer family record of the Springfield, Vt. and Evansville, Wis, Spencers. Descendants of Garrard Spencer of Haddam, Conn.   Emigrant of 1630.   By William Henry Spencer ... New York, T. A. Wright, 1907.   57 p. pl., coat of arms. 24½ cm. On cover: Spencer family record. 10-15241.

CS71.S745   1907

16031   SPENCER.   Genealogy of the Spencer family.   By Albert H. Spencer.   (River Edge? N.J.) 1956.   39 p. facsims., geneal. table. 23 cm. Cover title: Spencer genealogy. Additions dated Feb. 5, 1962 (1 fold. 1.) inserted at end. 62-2391.   CS71.S745   1956

16032   SPENCER.   Spencer descendants of Gerard Spencer the emigrant, by Rachel Davis Spencer and Herbert Reynolds Spencer.   Erie, Pa., 1941.   geneal. tab. 117 x 105 cm. fold. to 35 x 24 cm. Blueprint. 41M3328T.   CS71.S745   1941

16033   SPENCER.   Herbert E. Spencer, his ancestors & his descendants.   By Floyd Mallory Shumway.   New York, 1964.   35 1. 30 cm. Bibliography: leaves 30 - 35. 64-4399.   CS71.S745   1964

16034   SPENCER.   Spencer Records, 1762-1850, and his descendants, by Naomi M. Hougham. (Franklin? Ind.) 1965.   1 v. (various pagings) 30 cm. 66-49832.   CS71.S745   1965

16035   SPENCER.   Revolutionary ancestors of Julia Spencer Ardery (Mrs. William Breckenridge) "Rocclicgan," Paris, Bourbon Co., Kentucky.   Drawn by Bayless Hardin.   Frankfort, Ky. (193-) geneal. table. coats of arms. 25 cm. Photocopy (positive) 50-50338.   CS71.S745

SPENCER.   See also: DINWIDDIE, 1957   STANHOPE, 1911
                         GRESLEY, CS49.G75   STEEL, 1905
                         McDONELL, 1959   STUART, CS421.R8
                         POSTON, 1942   No. 430 - Adventurers of purse
                         ROBERTS, F159.R48R6   and person.

16036   SPENCER-STANHOPE.   Annals of a Yorkshire house from the papers of a macaroni & his kindred, by A. M. W. Stirling ... London, John Lane; New York, John Lane company, 1911. 2 v. col. fronts., plates, ports., facsims., fold. geneal. tables. 23 cm. "Although the life of Walter Spencer-Stanhope occupies a large proportion of the present volumes, it is not the object of these pages to present one particular biography. They aim rather to be a record of certain facts and anecdotes gleaned from the papers of that old Yorkshire house of which he became owner." - Pref. 11-5002 rev. DA483.S7S7

16037   SPENGLER.   The annals of the families of Caspar, Henry, Baltzer and George Spengler, who settled in York county, respectively, in 1729, 1732, 1732 and 1751.   With biographical and historical sketches, and memorabilia of contemporaneous local events, by Edward W. Spangler ... York, Pa. (Printed by the York daily publishing co.) 1896.   xii, 605 p. front., illus., plates, ports., facsims., geneal. tables, col. coat of arsm. 25½ cm. 9-13813.   CS71.S734   1896

SPENGLER.   See also SPANGLER.

SPENSER.   See SPENCER.

SPERRY.   See: BASSETT, 1926
                 CURTIS, 1912
                 HUMFREVILLE, 1903
                 SWEET, 1940

16038   SPESSARD.   A brief history of the Spessard family, and a complete genealogical family register, with a few brief biographical sketches from early records and other available sources, by H. L. Spessard ... Hagerstown, Md., Hagerstown bookbinding & printing company, 1930.
2 p. l., 7-116 p. front. (coat of arms) ports. 28 cm.   31-9481.   CS71.S748   1930

16039   SPICER.   History of the descendants of Peter Spicer, a landholder in New London, Connecticut, as early as 1666, and others of the name.   With appendix containing short accounts of allied families.   Compiled by Mrs. Susan Spicer Meech and Miss Susan Billings Meech ... (Boston, F. H. Gilson company) c. 1911.   xiv, 610 p. illus., plates, ports., facsims., fold. geneal. tab., 2 col. coats of arms (incl. front.)
24 cm.   "Addenda 2, containing additions and corrections": 10 p. inserted at p. 570.   11-26224.   CS71.S75   1911

    SPICER.   See also GILL, CS439.G46

    SPICHER.   See SPEICHER.

16040   SPIEGELBERG.   The Spiegelbergs of New Mexico, merchants and bankers, 1844-1893.   By Floyd S. Fierman.   (El Paso, Texas Western College Press) 1964.   48 p. illus., ports. 23 cm. (Southwestern studies v. 1, no. 4) Cover title. Biblio. refs. p. 45-48. 64-4018.   F805.J4F52

    SPIERS.   See WALLACE, CS479.W37

16041   SPILLMAN.   Spilman papers, compiled by Malcolm L. Melville, Forestville, Calif., 1965.
viii, 477 l. 29 cm. Cover title: Spillman papers. 65-89160.   CS71.S754   1965

    SPILLMAN.   See also DIXON, 1932

    SPILMAN.   See SPILLMAN.

    SPINCE.   See: ADIE, CS477.G7
                     FOSTER, 1871

    SPITTAL.   See FORRESTER, 1905

    SPIVEY.   See DRAPER, 1964

16042   SPODE.   Old Spode, by T. G. Cannon; with fifty-seven plates.   London, T. W. Laurie, ltd.
(1924)   x p., 1 l., 82 p., 57 l. col. front., 56 pl. 22 x 17½ cm. Frontispiece accompanied by guard sheet with descriptive letterpress.
24-30750.   NK4087.S6C3

16043   SPODE.   Spode & his successors; a history of the pottery Stoke-on-Trent, 1765-1865, by Arthur Hayden ... with 24 colour plates & 64 pages of illustrations in black and white.   London, New York (etc.) Cassell & company, ltd. (1925)   xxiii, 204 p. col. mounted front., plates (part col. mounted) ports., facsims.
25 cm. Each colored plate accompanied by guard sheet with descriptive letterpress. Bibliography: p. xix. 25-11552.   NK4087.S6H3

16044   SPODE.   Antique blue and white Spode, by Sydney B. Williams, with a foreword by H. Granville Fell ... With 123 illustrations.   London & Malvern Wells, B. T. Batsford ltd. (1943)   xviii, 242 p.
incl. plates (part col.) col. front. 25 x 19½ cm. "First edition published winter, 1943." 44-6908.   NK4087.S6W5

16045   SPOFFORD.   A family record, of the descendants of John Spofford, and Elizabeth, his wife, who came from England to America, and settled at Rowley, in 1638.   By Jeremiah Spofford ... Haverhill, E. G. Frothingham, printer, 1851.   64 p. 22½ cm. 9-13812.   CS71.S762   1851

16046   SPOFFORD.   A family record of the descendants of John Spofford, who emigrated from England, and settled at Rowley, Essex County, Mass., in 1638.   By Jeremiah Spofford, M. D. (2d ed.) Haverhill, E. G. Frothingham, printer, 1869.   127, (1) p. 19 cm. 9-13790.   CS71.S762   1869

16047   SPOFFORD.   A genealogical record, including two generations in female lines of families, spelling their names Spofford, Spafford, Spafard, and Spaford, descendants of John Spofford and Elizabeth Scott who emigrated, in 1638, from Yorkshire, England, and settled at Rowley, Essex County, Mass.   By Dr. Jeremiah Spofford ... Memorial ed. by his daughter, Alphia T. Spofford.   Boston, Printed by A. Mudge & son, 1888.   1 p. 1., 502 p. front., plates, ports., col. coat of arms. 24 cm. 9-13811.

CS71.S762   1888

16048   SPOFFORD.   ... A genealogical account of the Spofforth or Spofford family.   By Ashworth P. Burke ... London, Harrison and sons, printers, 1897.   2 p. 1., (3)-19, (1) p. 27 cm. At head fof title: Reprinted from "Burke's family records." 8-30522.

CS71.S762   1897

16049   SPOFFORD.   Souvenir of Old home week, Georgetown, Massachusetts, July 25-28, 1909. Boston, Mass., Press of J. G. Allen, 1909.   31 p. illus. 21 cm. "The Spofford family": p. (5)-10. 17-24562.

F74.G3S7

16050   SPOFFORD.   Genealogy, Thompson-Spafford, 1630 to 1930; Chase-Gordon, 1788 to 1930. Osborn-Gadsby, Gadsby-Woodcock ... Compiled by John H. Thompson.   Thorold, Ont. (1930?)
120 p. front., pl., ports. (1 double) facsims., col. coats of arms. 24½ cm. 32-21343.   CS71.T47   1930

SPOFFORD.   See also GILMORE, 1925

16051   SPOKESFIELD.   The Spokesfield families in America, and kindred families, by Walter Earnest Spokesfield.   Jamestown, N. D., 1926.   44 1. illus. (incl. port., map) 30 cm. Type-written. The illustrations are mounted photographs. 26-3111.   CS71.S7625   1926

16052   SPOONER.   Genealogical memoranda relating to the family of Spooner.   Communicated by Colonel J. L. Chester.   (n. p., 187-)   1 1. 27 cm. Caption title. 9-18117.

CS439.S76   1870

16053   SPOONER.   Notes relating to the Spooner family, contributed by the Rev. T. P. Wadley ... (London, Mitchell & Hughes, printers, 187-)   3 p. 28½ cm. Caption title. 9-18118.

CS439.S76   1870a

16054   SPOONER.   Memorial of William Spooner, 1637, and of his descendants to the third generation; of his great-grandson, Elnathan Spooner, and of his descendants, to 1871.   By Thomas Spooner. Private ed.   Cincinnati, R. Clarke & co., 1871.   vii, (9)-242 p. 24 cm. "Edition, 150 copies, no. 109." 9-13810.

CS71.S763   1871

16055   SPOONER.   Records of William Spooner, of Plymouth, Mass., and his descendants.   v. 1. By Thomas Spooner.   Cincinnati (Press of F. W. Freeman) 1883.   694 p. 24 cm. This work is intended to supplement and complete the author's "Memorial of William Spooner, 1637", issued in 1871. L. C. COPY REPLACED BY MICROFILM. 9-13809.

CS71.S763   1883

16056   SPOONER.   A brief sketch of the ancestry of Alden Spooner, late of Brooklyn, L. I.   With a record of his descendants to August, 1909.   Compiled by Alden S. Huling.   Topeka, Kan. (Hall lithograph company) 1909.   26, (1) p. front. (port.) 24 cm. Printed on one side of leaf only. Corrections and additions in manuscript. 11-1060.   CS71.S763   1909

SPOONER.   See also BAILEY, 1892

16057   SPOOR.   The Spoor family in America; a record of the known descendants of Jan Wybesse Spoor who migrated from Holland, and settled in the Hudson River Valley in the middle of the seventeenth century; compiled by Marie A. Underwood.   New York (Lancaster, Pa., Press of The New era printing company) 1901.   viii, 165 p. pl., map, facsims. (part fold.) 24 cm. "Four hundred copies of this book have been privately printed of which this copy is number 110." 3-3834.   CS71.S764   1901

16058   SPOTSWOOD.   Genealogy of the family of Spottiswoode, from the ms. collection of Father Augustine Hay, canon-regular of Saint Genevieve of Paris, prior of Saint Pieremonte, etc.
(In Spottiswoode miscellany ... (ed. by J. Maidment) Edinburgh, 1844-45. 2 v. 22½ cm. no. 1, p. 1-16) 21-11821.   DA750.S9 vol.3
——— Separate.   CS439.S765

16059   SPOTSWOOD.   Genealogy of the Spotswood family in Scotland and Virginia.   By Charles Campbell ... Albany, J. Munsell, 1868.   2 p. l., (3)-44 p. 24½ cm. 9-13808.

CS71.S765   1868

16060   SPOTSWOOD.   The descent of General Robert E. Lee, from King Robert the Bruce, of Scotland.   A paper read before the Southern historical association, of Louisville, Ky., March 29, 1881, by Wm. Winston Fontaine, A.M., principal of Holyoke academy.   (n.p., 1881?)   cover-title, 6 p., 1 l. 25½ cm. "Descendants of Gov. Spotswood and his wife": 1 leaf at end. 26-19564.

CS71.S765   1881

16061   SPOTSWOOD.   Chart of the Spotswood family, particularly the descendants of General Alexander Spotswood who married Elizabeth Washington ... Prepared by C. Aubrey Nicklas.   New York, N.Y., 1932.   geneal. tab. illus. (coat of arms) 41½ x 61 cm. 33-311.

CS71.S765   1932

SPOTSWOOD.   See also: BLACK, 1954   SPRUANCE, 1933
                          GURLEY, 1968   STRAHAN, Z325.S7A9
                          JUNKINS, 1908   No. 3509 - Orange county.
                          SELDEN, 1911

SPOTTISWOOD.   See SPOTSWOOD.

SPOTTSWOOD.   See SPOTSWOOD.

SPOTTS.   See WASSELL, 1962

SPRAGGINS.   See LONG, 1956

SPRAGINS.   See ECHOLS, 1956

16062   SPRAGUE.   The genealogy of the Sprague's in Hingham, arranged in chronolgical order, to the fourth generation, counting from William Sprague, one of the first planters in Massachusetts, who arrived at Naumkeag from England in the year 1628.   To which is prefixed a short account of the first settlement of this country before the arrival of the Old charter in 1630.   Hingham, H. Sprague, 1828. 60, (8) p. 18½ cm. Compiled by Hosea Sprague. Appendix: p. 49-60 has date May 1, 1829. Additions: Ralph Sprague, in Charlestown in 1628, and his four sons, John, Richard, Phinehas, and Samuel, and his daughter Mary (1883) (8) p. at end. 9-13807.

CS71.S766   1828

16063   SPRAGUE.   Memorials of the Sprague family; a poem recited at a meeting in Duxbury of the descendants and connections of Hon. Seth Sprague, on the occasion of his eighty-sixth birthday, July 4th, 1846.   With the family genealogy and biographical sketches in notes.   By Richard Soule, jr. ... Boston, J. J. Munroe and company, 1847.   xii, 191 p. front., plates, ports., facsims. (part fold.) 20 cm. 9-13806.

CS71.S766   1847

16064   SPRAGUE.   History of the Sprague families, Rhode Island cotton manufacturers and calico printers from William I. to William IV., with an account of the murder of the late Amasa Sprague, father of Hon. Wm. Sprague, ex-U.S. senator from Rhode Island.   By Benjamin Knight, sr.   Santa Cruz, H. Coffin, book and job printer, 1881.   2 p. l., (3)-74 p. 23½ cm. 9-13804.

CS71.S766   1881

16065   SPRAGUE.   Sprague family items.   By Dwight H. Kelton ... (Montpelier, Vt., 1894) 6 p. 24 cm. Caption title. One hundred copies printed. 9-13803.

CS71.S766   1894

16066   SPRAGUE.   Genealogy (in part) of the Spragues families in America descended from Edward Sprague of England, from 1614 to 1902.   With the wills of Edward Sprague and that of his son William who settled in Hingham, Mass., in 1636.   Compiled by Augustus B. R. Sprague ... Worcester, Mass., The compiler, 1902.   32 p. 23½ cm. 2 blank leaves at end for "Additional records." 15-12370.

CS71.S766   1902

16067   SPRAGUE.   Genealogy (in part) of the Sprague families in America.... Rev. ed. (of No. 16066) with corrections and additions.   Compiled by Augusts B. R. Sprague ... Worcester, Mass., Pub. by the compiler, 1905.   49 p. 23 cm. 7-31304.

CS71.S766   1905

16068   SPRAGUE.   The brothers Ralph and William Sprague and some of their descendants, by Frank William Sprague.   Boston, New England historic genealogical society, 1909.   14 p. 25 cm. "Reprinted from the New England historical and genealogical register for April, 1909." 9-20544.   CS71.S766   1909

16069   SPRAGUE.   The founding of Charlestown by the Spragues, a glimpse of the beginning of the Massachusetts Bay settlement, by Henry H. Sprague.   Boston, W. B. Clarke co., 1910.   39 p. fold. facsim. 24½ cm. 11-4218.   F74.C4S7

16070   SPRAGUE.   Sprague families in America, compiled and published by Warren Vincent Sprague, M. D.   Rutland, Vt., The Tuttle company, printers, 1913.   578 p. col. front. (coat of arms) plates, ports. 23½ cm. "Additions and corrections 1928"; 8 pages inserted at end. 13-9560 rev.   CS71.S766   1913
———— Supplement to Sprague families in America.   (Chauncey, O., 1940-41)   1 v. 29 cm.   Caption title. Loose-leaf. Reproduced from type-written copy. 13-9560 Rev.   CS71.S766   1913
Suppl.

16071   SPRAGUE.   The Ralph Sprague genealogy, compiled and published by E. G. Sprague ... Montpelier, Vt., The Capital city press (1913)   322 p. plates, ports., col. coat of arms. 24 cm. 13-25655.   CS71.S766   1913a

16072   SPRAGUE.   Hon. Seth Sprague of Duxbury, Plymouth County, Massachusetts; his descendants down to the sixth generation and his Reminiscences of the old colony town ... (n. p.) 1915.   8 p. 1., 134 p., 1 1., 12 p., 3 1., 14 p. illus., pl. 27½ cm. Preface signed: W. B. W. (i. e. William Bradford Weston) "Reminiscences of the olden times in the old colony town of Duxbury, Plymouth County, Massachusetts, by Hon. Seth Sprague. Jotted down by him when past his 84th years. 1845, " has separate t. -p. and pagination: 3 1., 14 p. at end. 15-22255.   CS71.S766   1915

16073   SPRAGUE.   Supplement to the Sprague families in America, comp. and pub. by Frank H. Sprague, Grafton, N. D.   Grand Forks, N. D., Times-Herald pub. co., 1915.   48 p. ports. 23½ cm. 16-6344.   CS71.S766   1915a

16074   SPRAGUE.   The Spragues of Malden, Massachusetts, by George Walter Chamberlain ... Boston, Mass., Printed for private circulation only, 1923.   viii, 317 p. front., plates, ports., double facsims. 26 cm. "500 copies printed from type." 23-18102.   CS71.S766   1923

SPRAGUE.   See also: BASS, 1896
DILLON, 1927
EPPERSON, 1931
JONES, 1925

16075   SPRATT.   Thomas Dryden Spratt's recollections of his family.   By Zach Spratt.   (Washington? 1962)   74, (5), 29, 27 1. illus. 29 cm. Contents. - Recollections of his family, by T. D. Spratt. - Addenda, by Z. Spratt. - Descendants of Thomas "Kanawha" Spratt, by A. W. Cockrell, Jr. - History of the Old Indian Fort at Fort Mill, S. C., by Z. Spratt. 63-6485.   CS71.C7663   1962

16076   SPRATT.   The Moses Spratt family of Platte County, Missouri, with allied families of Angell, Giraud, Pompey, Vornberg and Zucco.   By Sherman Lee Pompey.   (Pasadena? Calif., 1965)   100, a-g 1. illus., map. ports. 28 cm. 66-7362.   CS71.S7663   1965

16077   SPRIGG.   Genealogy of the Spriggs and other families connected therewith.   By George Trimnell Spriggs.   Lachute, Quebec, Printed by Giles Pub. House, 1949.   48 p. coats of arms. 22 cm. Cover title: Spriggs genealogy. 49-20828*.   CS71.S767   1949

SPRIGG.   See also: MONNET, 1911
MULLIKIN, 1936

16078   SPRING.   Lineage and tradition of the family of John Springs III, edited by and cover and title designed by Maud Craig Mathews.   Atlanta, Press of Foote & Davies co., 1921.   418, (12) p. front., illus., plates, ports., facsims., coat of arms. 24 cm. Page of "Errata" inserted between p. (10) and (11) Twelve blank pages at end for "Family record". Compiled by Mrs. Julia Amanda Gibson. cf. Pref. 40-2249.   CS71.S768   1921

16079   SPRING.   The Springs of Lavenham, and the Suffolk cloth trade in the XV and XVI centuries, by Barbara McClenaghan ... Ipswich (Eng.) W. E. Harrison (1924)   xii p., 1 l., 90 p. illus., 4 fold. maps, 19 cm. "Pedigree of the Springs of Lavenham": p. (85) "Authorities": p. ix-xiii. 24-18350.   HD9901.7.S8M3

SPRING.   See also: BARNES, 1939
BARNES, 1941
DINKINS, 1908
MANLEY, 1938

SPRINGALL.   See also CLARK, CS438.C5

16080   SPRINGER.   A genealogical table and history of the Springer family, in Europe and North America, for eight centuries, from the earliest German princes; origin of the name, etc.   By M. C. Springer.   Philadelphia, Press of Dickson & Gilling (c. 1881)   114 p. front. (port.) plates, fold. geneal. tables, coat of arms. 23½ cm. 9-13802.   CS71.S769   1881

16081   SPRINGER.   Chart no. I. Showing the derivation of Louis II (the Springer) (By Moses C. Springer) Printed especially for the Newberry library, and given with the compliments of Mrs. Warren Springer, 1897. (Philadelphia? 1897)   geneal. tab. 64 x 54 cm. fold. to 17 cm. Reprint of charts no. 1 and 2 from the author's Genealogical table and history of the Springer family ... Philadelphia, 1881. combined on one sheet with coat of arms and explanation added. 3-5054.   CS71.S769   1897

16082   SPRINGER.   A genealogical table and history of the Springer family in Europe and North America ... by M. C. Springer.   Revisions and additions by E. L. Scribner.   Amesbury, Mass., Guild & Cameron, printers (1917)   1 v. plates, ports., fold. geneal. tables, coat of arms 23½ cm. First edition: Philadelphia, 1881. Contents. - vol. 1. From the earliest German princes and origin of the name to Charles Christopher Springer, sr., 1658-1738, inclusive. 17-31793.   CS71.S769   1917

16083   SPRINGER.   A Springer genealogy, especially the New England descendants of Lorentz Springer, as delineated by Elestus Martin Springer on a "family tree," 1880. (n. p., 195-?)   42 l. 31 cm. Typescript. 64-7280.   CS71.S769

16084   SPRINGER.   Genealogy of Lorenze Springer family, Sweden, Delaware, Maine.   By Edward Perrine Cody. (Wethersfield? Conn., 1952)   geneal. table. 79 x 92 cm. fold. to 43 x 33 cm. Reproduction of original ms. dated March 1952.   CS71.S769   1952

——— Springer family.   Additions to chart compiled March 1952. (Wethersfield? Conn., 1952)   geneal. table. 71 x 89 cm. Reproduction of original ms. dated July 1952. 52-64164.   CS71.S769   1952   Suppl.

16085   SPRINGER.   Charles Springer of Cranehook-on-the-Delaware, his descendants and allied families.   By Jessie Evelyn Springer. (Springfield? Ill., 1965?)   ii, 344 p. illus., facsims., ports. 25 cm. Bibliographical footnotes. 65-5484.   CS71.S769   1965

16086   SPRINGER.   Springer family in vertical file.   Ask reference librarian for this material.

SPRINGER.   See also: CLINGAN, 1962
SAVAGE, 1953
TODD, 1909

16087   SPRINGS.   The squires of Springfield.   By Katherine (Wooten) Springs.   Charlotte, N. C., W. Loftin (1965)   viii, 350 p. illus., geneal. table, ports. 25 cm. 65-14774.   CS71.S768   1965

SPRINGS.   See also SPRING.

SPRINGTEN.   See BLAUVELT, 1957

SPROUL.   See: NEWLIN, 1942
SPROULE.

16088   SPROULE.   Robert Sproule of Miami County, Ohio, formerly of County Tyrone, Ireland, and some of his descendants with lineage of families allied by marriage 1775-1966.   By Hazel Sproul Wright.   (Lincoln, R. I., 1966-68)   2 v. illus. geneal. tables, map. 30 cm.   Contents. - pt. 1. Lineage of Robert Sproule of Miami County, Ohio; 1775-1966. - pt. 2. Robert Sproule; lineage charts of the Spreuls of Cowdon and Robert Spreul, original settler, 1650 A. D. of Goland, County Tyrone, Ireland.   78-3105 MARC.   CS71.S7695   1966

        SPROULE.   See also BASKERVILLE, 1930

16089   SPROUSE.   Tales thrice told; or, Family folklore.   By Gertrude (Sprouse) Shannon.   Nashville, Parthenon Press (1961)   130 p. 20 cm.   61-59826.   CS71.S77   1961

        SPROWL.   See SPROULE.

16090   SPRUANCE.   The Spruance family in Delaware, 1733-1933 with collateral relations and ancestral lines including the Spotswood family in Virginia and the Willing family in Pennsylvania ... (by) W. C. Spruance.   Wilmington, Del., 1933.   49 p. illus. (incl. ports., map, plan, facsims., coats of arms) 28½ cm. Photostat reproduction (positive)   "William Corbit Spruance family tree ... was drawn ... by William Corbit Spruance, based on an original tree prepared by his brother, Arthur Willing Spruance."   33-25766.   CS71.S771   1933

16091   SPRUILL.   Memories and records of eastern North Carolina.   By Mary (Weeks) Lambeth. (Nashville? 1957)   252 p. illus. 24 cm.   57-59414.   F253.L3

        SPUR.   See PAINE, 1913

16092   SPURGEON.   The Spurgeon family; being an account of the descent and family of Charles Haddon Spurgeon, with notes on the family in general, particularly the Essex branch, from 1465 (5 Edward IV) to 1905 (4 Edward VII) by W. Miller Higgs.   London, E. Stock, 1906.   ix, 54 p. front., ports., facsims., fold. geneal. tab.   26½ cm.   18-16057.   CS439.S77

        SPURGEON.   See also BOONE, 1922

16093   SPURR.   Spurr genealogy, being 10 generations of the descendants of Robert Spurr, who was in Dorchester, Massachusetts in 1654, excluding the branch that settled in Nova Scotia in 1760 which is being done separately.   Burlington, Vt., Chedwato Service, 1966.   ii, 108 p. 28 cm.   66-6395.
                                                                          CS71.S772   1966

        SPYKER.   See SPEICHER.

16094   SQUIER.   Ancestry of Ellis Squier and his descendants.   (n. p., 19 -)   14 p. plates, ports., col. coat of arms.   29½ cm.   39-16898.   CS71.S773   19 -

16095   SQUIER.   Genealogy of a branch of the Squire family that settled in Erie Co., Ohio, and married into the Baatz family of that county.   By Claude Charles Hamel.   Amherst, 1948.   8 l. 27 cm. Typewritten.   "References": leaves 7-8.   50-25031.   CS71.S7732   1948

16096   SQUIER.   Genealogy of a branch of the Squire family that settled in Erie County, Ohio, and married into the Baatz family of that county.   By Claude Charles Hamel.   Rev. Elyria, Ohio, 1960. 7 l. 27 cm.   61-37620.   CS71.S7732   1960

        SQUIRE.   See also: FOSTER, 1895
                              FOY, 1933
                              KENYON, 1935

        SQUIERS.   See SQUIER.

        SRUM.   See SHRUM.

        STAATS.   See STATES.

16097 STACKHOUSE. The book of the descendants of John Stackhouse and Elizabeth Buckingham, his wife. The which also containeth a historie of the forefathers of ye said John, and likewise somewhat concerning those of ye said Elizabeth: now first brought together by Powell Stackhouse and William R. Stackhouse, Moorestown, N.J., The Settle, press, 1906. 45 l. col. front. 25½ cm. No. 43 of 55 copies printed. 8-14341. CS71.S775   1906

16098 STACKHOUSE. Stackhouse, an old English family, sometime of Yorkshire. Edition limited. Moorestown, N.J., The Settle press (1906) 1 p. l., 107 p. front. 21 cm. By William Romig Stackhouse. 6-36082. CS439.S8

16099 STACKHOUSE. A historical sketch of the first ancestors of the Stackhouse family in America, by William R. Stackhouse & Powell Stackhouse, jr. With an introduction by A. M. Stackhouse, M. D. (Moorestown, N.J., The Settle press, 1907) 60 p. 19½ cm. 7-27760. CS71.S775   1907

16100 STACKHOUSE. The Stackhouse family: pt. I. History of Stackhouse from 1086 to 1935, by William R. Stackhouse; pt. II. Descendants of William and Mary (Bethea) Stackhouse from 1760 to 1930, by Walter F. Stackhouse. Marion, S.C. (Dillon, S.C., Herald publishing company) 1935. 241 p. incl. front. (col. coat of arms) port. pl., ports. 23½ cm. 37-16971. CS71.S775   1935

16101 STACKPOLE. History and genealogy of the Stackpole family, by Everett S. Stackpole. (Lewiston, Me., Press of Journal company, 1899) 245 p. front., plates, ports. 24 cm. 9-14470. CS71.S776   1899

16102 STACKPOLE. History and genealogy of the Stackpole family, by Everett Stackpole. 2d ed. (Lewiston, Me., Journal print-shop and bindery) 1920. 352 p. front., plates, ports., coat of arms. 23½ cm. 21-18365. CS71.S776   1920

STACKPOLE. See also: OTIS, 1851
WELCH, 1902

STACY. See: ELY, 1910
SMITH, 1878a
STUART, 1895
WILSON, 1890

STACYE. See STACY.

STAFFERTON. See HAYES, DA690.B74K3

16103 STAFFORD. A contribution to the genealogy of the Stafford family in America; containing an account of Col. Joab Stafford, and a complete record of his descendants in the male lines. By Henry Marvin Benedict. Albany, J. Munsell, 1870. 27 p. front. (port.) illus., fold. diagr. 25 cm. An edition of 150 copies only. 9-13800. CS71.S779   1870

16104 STAFFORD. The Stafford lineage book, tracing the male line of descent from Jarvis Stafford to the seventh generation, with allied families. By Mable K. Stafford. Duluth, Minn. (Press of Mattocks McDonald company) 1932. (122) p. illus. (incl. ports., coat of arms) pl. 23½ cm. Blank pages for "future records of births, marriages, deaths ... etc." (93-122) Allied families: Insley, McMillin, Gibson, Boyd, and others. 32-35513. CS71.S779   1932

16105 STAFFORD. General Leroy Augustus Stafford, his forebears and descendants; a genealogy compiled by his grandson, Dr. G.M.G. Stafford ... New Orleans, Pelican publishing company (1943) 4 p. l., 474 p., 1 l., (35) p. front., ports., facsims., diagr. 23 cm. Bibliography at end of each chapter. 43-4194. CS71.S779   1943

16106 STAFFORD. The West Ulster Staffords and their descendants. By Thomas Albert Stafford. (1st ed.) Chicago, 1952. 41 l. illus. 29 cm. 52-40175. CS71.S779   1952

16107   STAFFORD.   The descendants of James Stafford.   By Cornelia (Wearn) Henderson.   (n. p.,
1957)   43 p. illus. 23 cm. 58-16962.   CS71.S779   1957

16108   STAFFORD.   Laban Stafford, his ancestors and descendants; a genealogy.   By Ernest Nean
Stafford.   With a chapter on Thomas Stafford of Plymouth and his descendants and other Stafford
families.   (Escondido? Calif., 1962)   286 p. ports., map, col. coat of arms, facsims. 28 cm. 62-14614.
                                                                                                CS71.S779   1962

          STAFFORD.   See also:

               BONVILLE, DA250.R72   JARRATT, 1957   WALBRIDGE, 1898
               DEAL, 1939   PAVEY, 1940   WILLOUGHBY, DA250.R72
               DRAKE, 1878   PECK, 1955
               GRESLEY, CS439.G75   SMITH, 1931

          STAGEBERG.   See No. 553 - Goodhue county.

          STAGG.   See DUMONT, 1960

          STÄHELIN.   See STEHELIN.

16109   STAHL.   The Stahl family history, Jacob Peter Stahl, historian.   Dayton, O., 1924.
2 p. l., (9)-140 p., 1 l. front., illus. (incl. ports.) 24 cm. 26-4223.   CS71.S781   1924

16110   STAHL.   Genealogy of the family of William Stahl and his wife Elizabeth Boyer Stahl.   By
Lillian Eleanor (Elder) Hull.   Mansfield, Ohio, Printed by the Richland Print, Co., 1945.   184 p. port.
23 cm. Cover title: The origin of the Stahl family in America. 50-19134.
                                                                                                CS71.S781   1945

          STAIR, Earl of.   See DALRYMPLE.

16111   STAIRS.   Family history, Stairs, Morrow; including letters, diaries, essays, poems, etc.
(By William James Stairs)   Halifax, N.S., McAlpine publishing company ltd., 1906.   4 p. l., 264 p. 23 cm.
Includes "The Stairs family", "Diary", "Letters", "Writings", etc. of W.J. Stairs, and "The Morrow family" by Mrs. Susan Stairs; edited by their
children. 32-19200.   CS71.S782   1906

          STALCUP.   See STALLCOP.

16112   STALEY.   Staley family record: William Staley (1773-1850) Elizabeth Faust Staley (1778-
1854)   By Sara A. Staley.   (Plymouth Meeting? Pa., 1960 or 61)   89 l. 30 cm. 61-38326.
                                                                                                CS71.S7825   1960z

          STALEY.   See also No. 1547 - Cabell county.

16113   STALINS.   Histoire, généalogie et alliances des Stalins de Flandre, depuis le XVIe siècle,
et quelques considérations sur le briquet héraldique dit Briquet de Bourgogne ou Fusil de la Toison
d'or.   Illustrations documentaires de J. A. van Hemelryck et André Pichon.   Gand, G. de Tavernier
(1945)   292 p. illus., ports., maps, coats of arms. 33 cm. "Archives et ouvrages consulté": p. (257)-263. AF 48-672* Harvard
Univ. Library for Library of Congress.   CS809.S8   1945

          STALKER.   See ROBSON, 1892

16114   STALLARD.   Stallard families.   (London, Mitchell, Hughes and Clarke, 190-?)   15, (1) p.
26½ cm. Caption title. Compiled by Arthur Dudley Stallard. 16-17287.   CS439.S82

16115   STALLCOP.   An outline of the lineage and migrations of the Stallcop (Stalcup - Stallcup -
Staulcup) families.   Showing their relationship to each other.   Copyright ... by L. D. Stallcup.
Tampa, Fla., c.1937.   8 l. 32½ x 23 cm. Text runs parallel with back of cover. Mimeographed. 37-3000.
                                                                                                CS71.S783   1937

STALLCUP.   See STALLCOP.

16116   STALLWORTH.   Stallworths and related families with their descendants and connections. Compiled from original records, letters and other material.   By Hugh Wagner Stallworth.   (n.p.) 1966.   xvii, 207 p. ports. 29 cm. 66-7329.   CS71.S7832   1966

16117   STALNAKER.   Captain Samuel Stalnaker, colonial soldier and early pioneer and some of his descendants; an illustrated history of the early Stalnaker pioneers, compiled by Leo Stalnaker. (Tampa, Fla.) 1938.   1 p. 1., 49, (3) p. illus. (incl. map, facsim.) 29 x 21 cm. The illustrations are mounted photographs. Bibliography: p. (2) at end.   47-35553.   CS71.S7833   1938

STAMFORD.   See BACKHOUSE, DA690.M74C3

16118   STAMM.   The Stamm family of Ohio and Kentucky (by) Edw. J. Ronsheim, Sr.   Anderson, Ind. (1954?)   24 1. 32 cm. Caption title. 75-6681 MARC.   CS71.S7835   1954

STAMPER.   See COBB, 1961

STANARD.   See POCAHONTAS, 1887

STANBERY.   See STANSBURY.

STANBURY.   See STANSBURY.

STANCHFIELD.   See STINCHFIELD, 1963

16119   STANDISH.   The Standishes of America.   By Myles Standish ... Boston, Mass., Priv. print. for the author by S. Usher, 1895.   x, (5)-151 p. incl. coat of arms. front., plates, ports. 24½ cm. "This edition consists of one hundred copies, of which this is no. 100." 9-13801.   CS71.S784   1895

16120   STANDISH.   Charters and deeds relative to the Standish family, of Standish and Duxbury, Co. Lancaster.   Edited by J. P. Earwaker ... Manchester, A. Sutton (1898)   1 p. 1., 90 p. 25½ cm. Manuscript note: No. 102. Only 110 copies printed. 2-20295.   CS439.S83

16121   STANDISH.   Captain Myles Standish: his lost lands and Lancashire connections.   A new investigation.   By the Rev. Thomas Cruddas Porteus ... Manchester, The University press; London, New York (etc.) Longmans, Green & co., 1920.   5 p. 1., 115 p. front. (port.) illus. (incl. map) 5 pl. 19 cm. (Half-title: Publications of the University of Manchester. Historical series. No. XXXVIII) On verso of t.-p.: University of Manchester publications. No. CXXXV. Bibliography: 4th preliminary leaf. 20-23000.   F68.S87

16122   STANDISH.   ... Calendar of the Standish deeds, 1230-1575, preserved in the Wigan public library together with abstracts made by the Rev. Thomas West in 1770 of 228 deeds not now in the collection, by the Rev. Thomas Cruddas Porteus ... with a foreword by the Rt. Hon. the Earl of Crawford and Balcarres ... Wigan, The Public libraries committee, 1933.   xiv, 156 p. 22 cm. At head of title: Wigan public libraries. "Errata" slip inserted. "Addenda and corrigenda": 2 leaves inserted. "Reprinted from the Wigan observer." 33-15415 rev.   CS439.S83   1933
            —— Index to the Calendar of the Standish deeds 1230-1575, by the Rev. T. C. Porteus ... compiled by Arthur John Hawkes ... Wigan, Printed for the Public library committee, by T. Wall and sons, ltd., 1937.   xxxii p. 21½ cm. (With Calendar of the Standish deeds, 1230-1575. Wigan, 1933)
                                                                              CS439.S83   1933

16123   STANDISH.   Ada Ball Cass, a descendant of Captain Myles Standish.   By Earle Millard Cass. (New Castle, Pa.) Published privately, 1949.   17 p. 21 cm. Includes bibliographies. 50-28698.
                                                                              CS71.S784   1949

16124   STANDISH.   Myles Standish; notes, comments, and genealogy.   By Harry Humphrey Read. Edited, annotated, and published by Thomas Carpenter Read.   Charleston, S.C., 1961. 29 p. illus., port. 22 cm. Cover title. 61-37886.   F68.S88

STANDISH. See also: SAGE, 1908
WASHINGTON, DA660.S85

16125 STANFORD. Stanford genealogy, comprising the descendants of Abner Stanford, the revolutionary soldier; by Arthur Willis Stanford. Yokohama, Printed by the Fukuin printing co., ltd., 1906. 149 p. front. (port.) 22½ cm. 8-4336. CS71.S785 1906

16126 STANFORD. The Stanfords of Dublin, by Rev. Arthur Willis Stanford ... Kobe (Japan) The Fukuin printing co., ltd., 1919. 1 p. l., 16 p. 22½ cm. Bibliographical foot-notes. 36-3766. CS71.S785 1919

16127 STANFORD. The Stanfords and their name. By Laura Stanford Gorsuch. (Lebanon? Pa., c.1961) 21 p. illus. 24 cm. 62-656. CS71.S785 1961

STANFORD. See also: CRAPO, 1912
TODD, 1909

STANGEY. See KALBFLEISCH, 1956

16128 STANHOPE. Notices of the Stanhopes as esquires and knights, and until their first peerages in 1605 and 1616. Unpublished. London, Printed by A. and G. A. Spottiswoode, 1855. 41, (1) p. 24 cm. Compiled by Philip Henry Stanhope. Interleaved with ms. additions. Preface signed: Mahon. 15-22640.
CS439.S84

16129 STANHOPE. Annals of a Yorkshire house from the papers of a macaroni & his kindred, by A.M.W. Stirling ... London, John Lane; New York, John Lane, company, 1911. 2 v. col. fronts., plates, ports., facsims., fold. geneal. tables. 23 cm. "Although the life of Walter Spencer-Stanhope occupies a large proportion of the present volumes, it is not the object of these pages to present one particular biography. They aim rather to be a record of certain facts and anecdotes gleaned from the papers of that old Yorkshire house of which he became owner." - Pref. 11-5002 rev. DA483.S7S7

16130 STANHOPE. Lord Chesterfield, by Samuel Shellabarger ... London, Macmillan and co., limited, 1935. xiv, 422 p. front. (port.) 23 cm. Bibliography: p. 395-403. 36-9624. DA501.C5S5

STANHOPE. See also: CROSSLEY, CS439.C835
RAWSON, 1887

16131 STANHOUSE. The Stanhouse family. By Edwin Warfield Beitzell. Washington, 1948. 9 p. 28 cm. Caption title. 50-25476. CS71.S786 1948

16132 STANLEY. Memoirs, containing a genealogical and historical account of the antient and honourable house of Stanley, from the conquest to the death of James late earl of Derby, in the year 1735; as also a full descritpion of the Isle of Man, &c. ... Manchester, Printed by J. Harrop. 1767. 1 p. l., 238 p. illus. 26 cm. By John Seacome. The description of the Isle of Man has special t.-p.: A complete history of the Isle of Man. 2-2171. DA28.35.S8S5

16133 STANLEY. The history of the house of Stanley, from the conquest, to the death of the Right Honorable Edward, late earl of Derby, in 1776. Containing a genealogical and historical account of that illustrious house. To which is added, a description of the Isle of Man. Preston, Printed by E. Sergent, 1795. 2 p. l., 616 p. front. (port.) 21 cm. By John Seacome. 2-22792. DA28.35.S8S52

16134 STANLEY. The earls of Derby and the verse writers and poets of the sixteenth and seventeenth centuries, by Thomas Heywood ... Manchester, Printed by Robinson and Bent, 1825. ii, 44 p. 25½ cm. "Only fifty copies printed for private distribution ... " - Ms. note on fly-leaf. According to Lowndes 64 copies were printed. Author's presentation copy to William Ford, interleaved, with manuscript additions (some of them lithographed) letters, and portraits (7) inserted. Republished in a much revised form in the Chetham society's Remains ... v.29, 1853. 16-23856. DA358.D4H4

16135 STANLEY. Sketch of the history of the house of Stanley, and the house of Sefton. By David Ross ... London, W. S. Orr and co., 1848. 1 p. l., 61, xviii, 12, vi p. 17½ cm. inlaid to 26 cm. Extra illustrated by the insertion of portraits, engravings, autographs, coats of arms, newspaper cuttings, etc. Between p. 34 and 35 are inserted two extracts from Edmund Lodge's Portraits of illustrious personages of Great Britain: James Stanley, earl of Derby (8 p. ports.) and Charlotte de La Tremoüille (7 p. ports.) Book plate of Sir Rowland & Stanley, bart. 14-15133. DA28.35.S8R6

16136   STANLEY.   The earls of Derby and the verse writers and poets of the sixteenth and seventeenth century, by Thomas Heywood ... (Manchester) Printed for the Chetham society, 1853.   3 p. l., 63, 5 p. 23 cm. (Added t.-p. The Stanley papers, pt.I.)   Chetham society. Remains historical & literary ... of Lancaster and Chester. vol. XXIX. Much revised edition; first printed privately in 1825. 16-4136.   DA670.L19C5 vol. 29

16137   STANLEY.   The house of Stanley; including the sieges of Lathom house, with notices of relative and co-temporary incidents, &c.   By Peter Draper ... Ormskirk, T. Hutton, 1864.   1 p. l., 342 p. pl. port., plan. 21½ cm. First published in part in the Ormskirk advertised. 2-19046.   DA28.35.S8D8

16138   STANLEY.   The great Stanley: or, James, VIIth earl of Derby, and his noble countess, Charlotte de La Tremouille, in their land of Man.   A narrative of the XVIIth century.   Interspersed with notices of Manx manners, customs, laws, legends, and fairy tales.   Copiously illustrated, from Manx scenery and antiquities, by Alfred D. Lemon and J. T. Blight.   By the Rev. J. G. Cumming ... London, W. Macintosh, 1867.   viii, 279, (1) p. front., illus. 19 cm. 3-8421.   DA670.M2C9

16139   STANLEY.   The Stanleys of Knowsley; a history of that noble family, including a sketch of the political and public lives of the Right Hon, the earl of Derby, K.G. and the Right Hon. Lord Stanley, M.P.   By William Pollard.   Liverpool, E. Howell, 1868.   viii, 239, (1) p. front. (port.) 20 cm. 2-3641.   DA28.35.S8P7

16140   STANLEY.   Historical sketches of the house of Stanley and biography of Edward Geoffrey, 14th earl of Derby ... By Thomas Aspden.   2d (cabinet) ed. ... Preston, The author; (etc., etc., pref. 1877)   x, (5)-112, (2), lii p. 2 front. (port.) 25 cm. 2-19038.   DA28.35.S8A8

16141   STANLEY.   The Stanley families of America as descended from John, Timothy, and Thomas Stanley of Hartford, Ct. 1636.   Compiled by Israel P. Warren, D.D.   Portland, Me., Printed by B. Thurston & co., 1887.   viii, 9-352 p. front., ports. 23 cm. 9-13799 rev.   CS71.S787   1887
—— First supplement ... Compiled by Comdr. Emory Day Stanley, U.S.N.   (n. p., 1924)   1 p. l., 31 p. ports. 23 cm.   CS71.S787   1887   Suppl. 1
—— Revision to 1946 of the First supplement to the Thomas Stanley section of the Stanley families of America ... Compiled by E. D. Stanley.   Minneapolis, Minn., Stanley iron works, inc. (1946)   1 p. l., 61 p. illus. (ports.) 21½ cm.   CS71.S787   1887   Suppl. 2

16142   STANLEY.   The girlhood of Maria Josepha Holroyd (Lady Stanley of Alderley).   Recorded in letters of a hundred years ago: from 1776 to 1796.   Edited by J. H. Adeane ... London, New York etc.) Longmans, Green and co., 1896.   xviii, 420 p. front., ports. 23½ cm. Illustrations on t.-p. 38-38144.   CT788.S7A3

16143   STANLEY.   The early married life of Maria Josepha, lady Stanley, with extracts from Sir John Stanley's 'Praeterita'.   Edited by one of their grandchildren, Jane H. Adeane ... London, New York (etc.) Longmans, Green, and co., 1899.   xvi p., 1 l., 461 p. incl. geneal. tab. front., ports., facsim. 23½ cm. Illustration on t.-p. "Extracts from Sir J.T. Stanley's mss. up to the time of his marriage, and afterwards of selections from the correspondence of his wife, Maria Josepha." - Pref. 38-38145.   CT788.S7A4

16144   STANLEY.   First supplement to the Stanley families of America, as descended from John, Timothy and Thomas Stanley of Hartford, Conn., 1636.   Compiled by Israel O. Warren, D.D., 1887.   Supplement compiled by Comdr. Emory Day Stanley ... (n. p., 1924)   1 p. l., 31 p. ports. 22 cm. 25-21350.   CS71.S787   1924

16145   STANLEY.   Virginia Quaker Stanleys and descendants, compiled by Celeste Terrell Barnhill, a descendant.   Assisted by George Tatum Stanley ... and Clayton V. Stanley. (Miami Beach? Fla.) 1931.   1 p. l., 48 numb. l. 29 cm. Reproduced from type-written copy. Includes the Crew family. 31-31267.   CS71.S787   1931

16146   STANLEY.   The ladies of Alderley: being the letters between Maria Josepha, lady Stanley of Alderley, and her daughter-in-law, Henrietta Maria Stanley, during the years 1841-1850; edited by

16146 continued: Nancy Mitford, with a foreword by Lord Stanley of Alderley.   London, Chapman & Hall, ltd. (1938)   xxxii, 315 p. front., plates, ports. 22½ cm. "First published 1938." 38-38777.   CT788.S7A43

16147   STANLEY.   The Stanleys of Alderley; their letters between the years 1851-1865, edited by Nancy Mitford.   London, Chapman & Hall, ltd. (1939)   xxiv, 383 p. front., ports. 22 cm. "First published 1939." A companion volume to the editor's The ladies of Alderley.   "Appendix: The two hundred and sixty-four descendants of Edward, 2nd lord Stanley of Alderley, and of the Hon. Henrietta Maria Dillon, his wife.   (Tabulated by Sir Gerald Grove, bt., of Ferne)": p. 365-373.   40-3994.

CT788.S7A44

16148   STANLEY.   History and genealogy of the Stanley family.   By Edna (Stanley) Pickett.   (Plainfield, Ind., 1949)   144 p. coat of arms. 24 cm. 49-5914*.   CS71.S787   1949

STANLEY.   See also:

ATKINSON, 1933   LEWIS, 1910   POLLOCK, 1932
BARBER, 1879   MORGAN, 1929   RAWSON, 1887
BASSETT, 1926   MOORE, DA670.L19.C5 v.12 SHAKESPEARE, 1918
GRESLEY, CS439.G75   NORRES, 1851   SNYDER, 1958
JENNINGS, 1923

16149   STANSALL.   A genealogy of the Stansel family, by Thomas McAdory Owen.   Carrollton, Ala., West Alabamian print, 1900.   7 p. front. (port.) 23½ cm. 2-13283.   CS71.S7878   1900

16150   STANBURY.   The descendants of John Stansbury of Leominster.   Compiled by Frederick Howard Wines for the information of the family.   Springfield, Ill., The H. W. Rokker printing house, 1895.   vii, 55 p. 23½ cm. 12-24994.   CS71.S788   1895

16151   STANSBURY.   The history and connection of the Stansbury-Tyler-Adee families, compiled from the records by Frederick S. Tyler.   Washington, D.C., 1933.   17 p. 22 cm. 33-36200.
CS71.S788   1933

16152   STANSBURY.   Genealogy of the Stansbury family.   This genealogy carries down the family line from Detmar Sternberg, from the time he came to America, in 1658, to John and Doras (Sater) Stansbury.   From there on the names of their descendants are recorded.   1658-1938.   (Mountain View, Calif., Printed by J. L. Stansbury, 1938)   80 p. 19½ cm. Preface signed: Iva Scheffel. "Recollections" by J.L. Stansbury: p. 7-14. Includes the Sater genealogy. 40-8611.   CS71.S788   1938

16153   STANSBURY.   Genealogy of the Stansbury family ... 1658-1938.   (Mountain View, Calif., Printed by J. L. Stansbury, 1942)   119 (i.e.123) p. 19½ cm. Includes extra numbered pages 34A, 34B, 36A and 36B. Preface signed: Iva Scheffel. Supplement (p. (81)-103) includes data to 1942. "This genealogy carries down the family line from Detmar Sternberg, from the time he came to America, in 1658, to John and Doras (Sater) Stansbury. From there on the names of their descendants are recorded." "Recollections" by J.L. Stansbury: p. 7-14. 42-50346.   CS71.S788   1942

STANSBURY.   See also ROBINSON, 1894

STANSEL.   See STANSALL.

STANSFELD.   See SHARP, QB36.S5C9 and addenda.

16155   STANTON.   Thomas Stanton of Stonington, Conn.   An incomplete record of his descendants. Prepared by John D. Baldwin of Worcester, Mass.   Worcester, Printed by Tyler & Seagrave, 1882.
52 p. 24 cm. 12-31017.   CS71.S791   1882

16156   STANTON.   A record, genealogical, biographical, statistical, of Thomas Stanton, of Connecticut, and his descendants.   1635-1891.   By William A. Stanton, PH. D., D. D.   Albany, N. Y., J. Munsell's sons, 1891.   613 p. port. 24 cm. 9-13798.   CS71.S791   1891

16157   STANTON.   A book called Our ancestors the Stantons, by William Henry Stanton ... Philadelphia, Priv. print. for W. H. Stanton, 1922.   649 p. front., illus., plates (part fold.) ports., maps (part fold.) fold. facsims., geneal. tables (1 fold.) 25 cm. Two pl. contain mounted samples. Blank p. for Records (606-637) Contains geneal. tabs. also of the Bailey, Bundy, Clendenon, Davis, Dawson, Doudna, Hodgin, Patten, Patterson, Sears and Vernon families. 23-579.   CS71.S791   1922

16158   STANTON.   Garrett county history of Stanton family, by Charles E. Hoye ... (Oakland, Md.) 1934.   1 l. 33 cm.   "From Mountain democrat. Issue of December 27th, 1934."   38M1246T.

CS71.S791   1934

16159   STANTON.   The history of my grandmother Sacket-Stanton.   Compiled for Roland Mather Hooker.   By Winifred Lovering Holman.   (Lexington? Mass.) Mimeographed by A. Darling Secretarial Service, 1960.   107 l. 28 cm.   60-27730.   CS71.S791   1960

STANTON.   See also: CONVERSE, 1905
HOLBROW, 1901
NOYES, 1900
SMITH, 1924
STARKWEATHER, 1925
STAUNTON, CS439.S886

16160   STANWOOD.   A history of the Stanwood family in America, by Ethel Stanwood Bolton.   Boston, Mass., Rockwell and Churchill press.   1899.   317 p. plates, ports., facsims., geneal. tables.   23 cm.   9-13797.

CS71.S792   1899

STANWOOD.   See also SHANNON, 1905

16161   STAPELTON.   The Stapeltons of Yorkshire, being the history of an English family from very early times; by H. E. Chetwynd-Stapylton ... With illustrations by the author.   London, New York, and Bombay, Longmans, Green, and co., 1897.   xii, 333 p. incl. front., illus., geneal. tables, pl., ports. 23½ cm.
Different branches of the family spell the name: Stapelton, Stapilton, and Stapylton.   4-2252.

CS439.S86

16162   STAPELTON.   The early history of Bedale in the North riding of Yorkshire ... London, E. Stock, 1907.   xix, 134 p., 1 l. front., illus., 4 pl., col. plan, 3 geneal. tab.   28 cm.   By Hardy Bertram McCall.   "Practically a history of the parish ..." "chiefly concerned with events ... before the sixteenth century." cf. Preface.   Contents. - The town. - The manor before the fourteenth century. - The Stapletons of Bedale. - The successors of Katherine Fitz Alan. - The church. - The ecclesiastical history.
11-10105.   DA690.B35M2

STAPELTON.   See also: CLOPTON, 1939
FARNHAM, CS439.F25
PITMAN, CS439.P62

STAPILTON.   See STAPELTON.

16163   STAPLES.   Proceedings at the dedication of a monument to Sergeant Abraham Staples of Mendon, Massachusetts, October 31, 1877.   Providence, S. S. Rider, 1880.   55 p.   24½ cm.   10-9968.
CS71.S793   1880

16164   STAPLES.   Staples, Wealtha Staples; with records relating to some of the Berkley-Taunton, Massachusetts families ... Springfield, Mass., Priv. print., 1911.   70 p. incl. front., pl. map, plates, ports., double map.   24 cm.   Compiled by William Frederick Adams.   11-16549.   CS71.S793   1911

16165   STAPLES.   Some of the descendants of Peter Staple(s) of Kittery, Maine.   By Edward Staples Cousens Smith.   Schenectady, 1950.   5 l. 28 cm.   52-20627.   CS71.S793   1950

STAPLES.   See also: BEACH, 1960
STARKWEATHER, 1925
STARKWEATHER, 1926

STAPLETON.   See: BARNEY, 1912a
PITMAN, 1920
STAPELTON.
STARKWEATHER, 1925
STARKWEATHER, 1926

16166   STAPLEY.   The baronetcy of Stapley.   By H. W. Forsyth Harwood ... Exeter, (Eng.)
W. Pollard & co., ltd. (1902)   25 p. 25 cm. "Reprinted from the Genealogist, n. s., vol. XVIII, January, 1902." 40-16305.
CS439.S87   1902

16167   STAPLEY.   The Stapley papers.   Compiled by Harry Stapley, F.S.A. (Irel.) London, Printed for private circulation, and issued by Phillimore & co., 1905.   2 p. 1., 37 p. 28½ cm. 15-20217.
CS439.S87

STARBARD.   See STARBIRD.

16168   STARBIRD.   Ancestors and descendants of Winfield Scott Starbird and Emeline Hardy (Roberts)
Starbird, by Alfred Andrews Starbird.   (Burlington? Vt.) 1941.   1 p. 1., 61 p. 23½ cm. 42-4028.
CS71.S7935   1941

16169   STARBIRD.   Genealogy of the Starbird-Starbard-family, by Alfred A. Starbird.   (Burlington,
Vt., The Lane press, inc., 1942?)   2 p. 1., 179 p. 24 cm. Errata slips inserted. 44-5048.
CS71.S7935   1942

STARBOARD.   See STARBIRD.

16170   STARBUCK.   Our family's Starbuck ancestry, 1604-1963, by George Edward McConnell and
David Ross McConnell.   (Mount Vernon? Ohio, 1963)   106 p. coat of arms, geneal. tables, maps. 29 cm. 500
copies printed.   No. 166. Bibliography: p. 95. 64-56206.   CS71.S79354   1963

16171   STARBUCK.   Starbuck family in vertical file.   Ask reference librarian for this material.

STARBUCK.   See also: HUNT, 1946
TEETOR, CS71T

16172   STARE.   A record of what little I know about the ancestors of the Stare family, by F. A. Stare
... Columbus, Wis. (Madison, Wis., Democrat printing company) 1938.   cover-title, 15, (1) p. illus.
(ports.) 21 cm. 40-37515.   CS71.S7936   1938

16173   STARIN.   The Starin family in America.   Descendants of Nicholas Ster (Starin), one of the
early settlers of Fort Orange (Albany, N. Y.).   By William L. Stone ... Albany, N. Y., J. Munsell's
sons, 1892.   233 p. 27 cm. 9-13796.   CS71.S794   1892

STARIN.   See also WASHINGTON, CS69.W5

16174   STARK.   Origin of the Stark family of New Hampshire and a list of living descendants of
General John Stark, comp. by George Stark of Nashua, N. H.   (Nashua, N. H., pref. 1887)
(3)-13 p. front. 23 cm. A13-2138.   CS71.S795   1887

16175   STARK.   ... Gen. John Stark's home farm.   A paper read before the Manchester historic
association October 7, 1903.   By Roland Rowell.   Manchester, Printed by the J. B. Clarke co., 1904.
22 p. 23 cm. At head of title: Manchester historic association. 5-21476.   CS71.S795   1904

16176   STARK.   The Aaron Stark family; seven generations of the descendants of Aaron Stark of
Groton, Connecticut, by Charles R. Stark ... (Boston, Wright and Potter) 1927.   4 p. 1., 141 p. front. (port.)
illus. (coat of arms) 25 cm. 27-21414.   CS71.S795   1927

16177   STARK.   A Stark genealogy; some descendants of John Stark from Scotland to the United
States abt. 1710 and his son James Stark born in Scotland in 1695 ... By Jane Harter Abbott.   Santa
Barbara, Calif. 1928-1931.   Type-written manuscript accompanied by source material including letters, printed matter, plates,
coats of arms, etc. in tin box located in Rare book room.   Inventory of contents in vertical file under STARK family.   Ask reference librarian for
this material. 39-M427T.   Office.   CS71.S795 1928-31

16178   STARK.   Oliver Starks, b. isle of Man, imigrated (!) to the United States.   Genealogical
notes.   Compiled by Jane H. Abbott.   (n. p., 1928)   7 l. 30 cm. Typewritten. Includes "Authorities". 34-8472.
CS71.S795   1928

16179   STARK.   John Stark, wife Janet Morton, from Linlithgow, Scotland to Allegheny county, Pennsylvania ... Genealogical notes and records.   Compiled by Jane H. Abbott, 1928-1929.   (n. p., 1929)   14 1. 30 cm. Typewritten. Includes "Authorities". 34-8469.   CS71. S795   1929a

16180   STARK.   Thomas Stark, of Virginia, to South Carolina, South Carolina to Tennessee and returned to South Carolina.   Genealogical notes and records.   Compiled by Jane H. Abbott, 1928-1929. (n. p., 1929)   35 1. 30 cm. Typewritten. Includes "Authorities". 34-8470.   CS71. S795   1929b

16181   STARK.   Jeremiah Stark of Culpeper county, Va., later of Allen county, Ky. and some descendants.   Genealogical notes and records.   Compiled by Jane H. Abbott.   1928-1930.   (n. p., 1930) 64 1. 30 cm. Typewritten. Includes "Authorities". 34-8471.   CS71. S795   1930

16182   STARK.   Stark - of German lineage in the United States.   Notes. Compiled by Jane H. Abbott, 1928-1933.   (n. p., 1933)   9 1. 30 cm. Typewritten. "Authority": 3d leaf. 34-8473.   CS71. S795   1933

16183   STARK.   The genealogy of Joshua Stark, an early settler of Granville, Ohio.   By Mary Belle Linnell.   (n. p., 1966?)   38 1. 29 cm. 66-57726.   CS71. S795   1966

                STARK.   See also: JELKE, E171. A53 v. 19
                                      NEWELL, 1944
                                      PASTORIUS, 1926
                                      RICHCREEK, 1954
                                      WINSLOW, 1935

16184   STARKEY.   The Starkeys of New England, and the descendants of George Lawrence.   By Miss Emily Wilder Leavitt.   Boston, D. Clapp & son, printers, 1892.   10 p. 24½ cm. 29-7566.
                                                                                                      CS71. S7955   1892

16185   STARKEY.   The Starkeys of New England and allied families, comp. for Albert Crane, esq., by Emily Wilder Leavitt.   (Springfield, Mass.) Press of Springfield printing and binding company, 1910.   xiv p. 1 1., 149 p. front. (port.) pl. 24½ cm. Allied families: Lawrence, Waite, Balcom. Graves, Capron and Blackington. 11-8929.   CS71. S7955   1910

                STARKEY.   See also: CRANE, 1931
                                       STARKIE.

16186   STARKIE.   The Starkie family of Pennington and Bedford, in the parish of Leigh, co. Lancaster.   Two papers contributed to the Leigh Chronicle "Historical and genealogical notes."   By J. Paul Rylands, F. S. A.   Leigh, Lancashire (Eng.) 1880.   17 p. front. 21½ cm. "Not published." 3-6489.
                                                                                                      CS439. S88

                STARKIE.   See also: CRANE, 1931
                                       STARKEY.

16187   STARKWEATHER.   A brief genealogical history of Robert Starkweather of Roxbury and Ipswich, Massachusetts, who was the original American ancestor of all those bearing the name of Starkweather, and of his son John Starkweather of Ipswich, Mass., and Preston, Conn., and of his descendants in various lines, 1640-1898.   By Carlton Lee Starkweather ... (Auburn, N. Y., Press of Knapp, Peck & Thomson) 1904.   356 p. front., plates, ports. 24 cm.   "Three hundred copies. no. 29." 7-31021.
                                                                                                      CS71. S796   1904

16188   STARKWEATHER.   The Starkweather-Staples genealogy of the Hamilton, Madison County, New York, branches, and their California connections, including the Allen, Billings, Bostwick, Crandall, Kehoe, Meier, Smith and Stanton families ... Compiled and published by R. P. Starkweather ... San Francisco, 1925.   2 p. 1., 9-127 p. 23 cm. 25-11203.   CS71. S796   1925

16189   STARKWEATHER.   The Starkweather-Staples genealogy of the Hamilton, Madison County, New York branches, and their California connections.   2d ed. ... Compiled and published by R. P. Starkweather ... San Francisco and Oakland, Calif., 1926.   4 p. 1., 11-159 p. 23 cm. 26-8476.
                                                                                                      CS71. S796   1926

STARKWEATHER.   See also L. C. additions and corrections, no. 18

STARLING.   See SULLIVANT, 1874

16190   STARR.   A history of the Starr family of New England, from the ancestor, Dr. Comfort Starr of Ashford, county of Kent, England, who emigrated to Boston, Mass., in 1635; ... by Burgis Pratt Starr ... Hartford, Conn., The Case, Lockwood & Brainard co., print., 1879.   3 p. l., x, 588, (2) p. front., pl., ports., coats of arms.   24 cm.   "Supplemental to the Starr family. Hartford, Dec. 1, 1880": 579-588. (2) p. Printed circulars concerning the Starr family inserted.   20-9253.   CS71.S7965   1879

16191   STARR.   Letter of Frederick Starr, Rochester, N. Y., May 21, 1866 to his nephew.   In vertical file.   Ask reference librarian for this material.

16192   STARR.   Starr family in vertical file.   Ask reference librarian for this material.

STARR.   See also: AVERY, 1926
DICKERMANN, 1897
EATON, 1895
HYNES, 1957
SMEDLEY, 1901
STRONG, 1871

STARRETT.   See: ALEXANDER, 1960
PORTER, 1940

16193   START.   A genealogical record of the Start family in America, by William A. Start, A. M. Boston, Mass., W. Spooner, printer, 1894.   29, (1) p. 24 cm. 9-13795.   CS71.S797   1894

16194   STATES.   Genealogy of the States family.   Compiled by James Noyes States ... New Haven, Conn., 1913.   1 p. l., 187 p. front. (port.) plates. 23 cm. 15-8034.   CS71.S7975   1913

STATEN.   See STATON.

16195   STATES.   Genealogy of the Staats family, by Harold Staats.   Approved by National Staats reunion association.   (Ripley, W. Va., H. Staats, etc.) c. 1921.   2 p. l., (7)-255, (1) p. front., illus. (incl. ports.) fold. plates, fold. geneal. tables, col. coat of arms, diagrs.   26 cm. 21-14635.   CS71.S7975   1921

STATHER.   See ROBSON, CS439. R563

16196   STATON.   Staton history; every Staton we could find in the world.   By John Samuel Staton. Charlotte, N. C., Print. priv. for Staton families by Brooks Litho, 1960.   406 p. illus. 24 cm. 60-1173.   CS71.S7976   1960

16197   STAUDT.   The Staudt-Stoudt-Stout family of Pennsylvania and their ancestors in the Palatinate. A preliminary study (by) Richard W. Staudt, Buenos Aires, S. A., and Rev. John Baer Stoudt, D. D., Allentown, Pa., U. S. A. (n. p., 1925)   1 p. l., (5)-149 p. 23 cm. On cover: Staudt, Stoudt, Stout, 1535-1925. Contents. - The Staudt ancestors in the Palatinate, presented to his American kinsfolk at their thirteenth family reunion, by Richard W. Staudt, Buenos Aires, S. A. - The descendants of the Staudt immigrants to Pennsylvania, by Rev. John Baer Stoudt, D. D.   25-18691.   CS71.S7978   1925

16198   STAUDT.   The Staudt-Stoudt-Stout family of Ohio and their ancestors at home and abroad. Preliminary edition.   Collected and printed by Herald F. Stout ... (n. p., 1934)   1 p. l., vi, 177, 20 p. 21½ cm. "Additions and corrections": 20 p. at end. 34-32607.   CS71.S7978   1934

16199   STAUDT.   The Staudt-Stoudt-Stout family of Ohio and their ancestors at home and abroad. Preliminary edition.   Collected and printed by Herald F. Stout ... (n. p., 1935)   7 p. l., vi, 276, 79, (9) p. front. (ports.) illus. (incl. map, coats of arms) pl.   21 cm. "A limited edition of two hundred copies." "Additions and corrections": 79 p. at end. 35-28832.   CS71.S7978   1935

STAUDT. See also: STOUT, 194-
ZERBE, F157.S3E39

16200 STAUFFER. A genealogical record of the descendants of Daniel Stauffer and Hans Bauer and other pioneers, together with historical and biographical sketches, and a short history of the Mennonites ... By Rev. Henry S. Bower ... With a history of the house of Hohenstaufen, by Fred. Raumer, of Germany. Harleysville, Pa., News printing house, 1897. 203 p. front., ports. 21½ cm. "History of the house of Hohenstaufen," tr. from the German: p. 7-13. 2-29720.   CS71.S798   1897

16201 STAUFFER. Genealogical memoranda. Stouffer, A.D.1630 - A.D.1903. Comp. and arranged by (Miss) Kate S. Snively ... (Hagerstown, Md., 1903.) 104 p. 21½ cm. 12-30963.
                                                                                CS71.S798   1903

16202 STAUFFER. Records of the proceedings of the John Stauffer memorial association ... Ringtown, Pa., 1911 -   v. 23½ cm. 21-8409.   CS71.S798   1911-

16203 STAUFFER. Stauffer genealogy of America and history of the descendants of Jacob Stauffer, from the earliest available records to the present time. With a few illustrations. Compiled by Ezra N. Stauffer ... (Scottdale, Pa., Printed by Mennonite pub. house, c.1917) 179, (1) p. illus. (incl. ports.) 20 cm. 18-1898.   CS71.S798   1917

16204 STAUFFER. Genealogical memoranda: Stouffer, 1579-1943, compiled and arranged, 1903 (by) Kate S. Snively. Revised, 1943 (Descendants of Jacob Stouffer, 1773-1843) (by) C.S. Stouffer. (Pottstown, Pa., The Feroe press, 1943) 4 p. l., (7)-130 p. incl. plates, ports., coat of arms. 23½ cm. Cover-title: Stouffer genealogy. 44-9249.   CS71.S798   1943

16205 STAUFFER. A Stouffer line of descent that originated in Lancaster County, Pennsylvania. (n.p.) For private distribution among families of the line, 1951. 61 p. illus. 24 cm. 52-43026.
                                                                                CS71.S8874   1951

STAUFFER. See also: SCHMUTZ, 1958
STOVER.

STAULCUP. See STALLCOP.

16206 STAUNTON. The family of Staunton, of Staunton, Nottinghamshire. An essay by G.W. Staunton and F.M. Stenton, M.A. Newark, S. Whiles, 1911. 72 p. incl. illus., 2 pl. plates, fold. geneal. tab. 22½ cm. 15-13925.   CS439.S886

STAUNTON. See also SHIRLEY, CS439.S485

16207 STAVELY. The Stavely family of Frederick W. Stavely; the early Staveleys, the Staveleys of Ireland (and) the Stavelys of America. (Akron, Ohio) 1969. 175 p. illus., coats of arms, facsims., geneal. tables, ports. 23 cm. 71-7846 MARC.   CS71.S7983   1969

STAVER. See STOEVER.

16208 STAWELL. A Quantock family. The Stawells of Cothelstone and their descendants, the barons of Stawell of Somerton, and the Stawells of Devonshire and the county Cork. Compiled and edited by Colonel George Dodsworth Stawell ... Taunton, Barnicott and Pearce, the Wessex press, 1910. xxix p., 1 l., 566 p. front., illus., plates, ports., facsim., 14 fold. geneal. tab., coats of arms. 29 cm. "Addenda and errata": (2) p. inserted. Includes also genealogies of the Lovel and St. Mauer, of Castle Cary, Holbrooke, Towgood, and Cooper families. 10-27635.
                                                                                CS439.S89

STAWELL. See also STOWELL.

STAWSON. See SLAWSON, 1946

STAYTON. See STATON.

16209   STEARNS.   Stearns family record.   (Santa Barbara, Cal., 1894)   1 p. l., 8 p. 20 cm. Caption
title. Foreword signed: John P. Stearns.   11-14788.   CS71.S799   1894

16210   STEARNS.   Genealogies of the Stearns, Lane, Holbrook and Warren families.   (n. p., 1898)
59 p. illus. (coats of arms) pl., port. 24½ cm.   "Compiled by Mary Stearns Brooke." 39-16906.   CS71.S799   1898

16211   STEARNS.   Genealogy and memoirs of Isaac Stearns and his descendants.   By Mrs. Avis
Stearns Van Wagenen.   (Syracuse, N. Y., Courier printing co., 1901)   2 p. l., 744 p. pl. (part col.) port.
25½ cm. Binder's title: Stearns genealogy and memoirs, v.1.   Vol. 2 appeared the same year under title: Genealogy and memoirs of Charles
and Nathaniel Stearns ... 2-16609.   CS71.S799   1901
                                                                      vol. 1

16212   STEARNS.   Genealogy and memoirs of Charles and Nathaniel Stearns, and their descendants.
By Mrs. Avis Stearns Van Wagenen.   (Syracuse, N. Y., Courier printing co., 1901)   2 p. l., (7)-531 p.
pl. (part col.) port. 25 cm. Binder's title: Stearns genealogy and memoirs, v.2.   Vol. 1 appeared the same year under title: Genealogy and
memoirs of Isaac Stearns ... 2-16610.   CS71.S799   1901
                                                                      vol. 2

16213   STEARNS.   Memoranda of the Stearns family, including records of many of the descendants,
by Willard E. Stearns.   Fitchburg (Mass.) Printed by the Sentinel printing company, 1901.
2 p. l., (3)-173 p. 24 cm. 6-16209.   CS71.S799   1901a

              STEARNS.   See also: BLACKMAN, 1894
                                     KNAPP, 1909
                                     McFARLAND, 1885
                                     STERNE.
                                     WYMAN, 1927

16214   STEBBINS.   A genealogy of the family of Mr. Samuel Stebbins and Mrs. Hannah Stebbins, his
wife, from the year 1707 to the year 1771.   With their names, time of their births, marriages and
deaths of those that are deceased.   (By Luke Stebbins) Hartford, Printed by Ebenezer Watson, for
the use of the descendants now living.   1771.   xi, (12)-24 p. 20 cm. Half-title: A genealogical catalogue. "This is
probably the first genealogical work published in this country." - Sabin, Bibl. Amer. 39-12252.
                                                                      CS71.S81   1771
                                                                      Office.

16215   STEBBINS.   Memoir of the Stebbins family.   Collected and compiled by Daniel Stebbins ...
(n. p., 1873)   38 p. 22 cm. Caption title. Pages 30-35 printed on one side of leaf only. Blank leaves interspersed. 40-2273.
                                                                      CS71.S81   1873

16216   STEBBINS.   A genealogy of the family of Mr. Samuel Stebbins, and Mrs. Hannah Stebbins, his
wife, from the year 1707, to the year 1771.   With their names, time of their births, marriages and
deaths of those that are deceased.   Hartford, Printed by E. Watson, for the use of the descendants now
living, 1771.   (By Luke Stebbins. Reprinted with additions. Boston, 1879)   xi, (12)-31 p. geneal. tab.
24 cm.   "The preceding is an exact copy of a work believed to be the first American genealogy, and so rare that only two perfect copies exist. We
have added a name index and a tabular pedigree, and have printed only one hundred copies. No. 70. Library committee of the New England
historical and genealogical society." 9-13794.
                                                                      CS71.S81   1879

16217   STEBBINS.   An inquiry as to the heirs at law of Maria Stebbins, who died intestate, in New
York, April 8th, 1875 ... Which is necessarily a genealogical table of the descendants of her two
grandfathers Theophilus Stebbins and Robert Whitlock, both of Ridgefield, Fairfield County, Connecticut.   Being a list of their descendants down to and including a living representative of each branch.
Compiled by A. S. Wheeler ... New York, P. Eckler, printer, 1880.   20 p. 23 cm. 3-17717.
                                                                      CS71.S81   1880

16218   STEBBINS.   The Stebbins genealogy, by Ralph Stebbins Greenlee and Robert Lemuel Greenlee
... Chicago, Ill., Priv. print. (M. A. Donohue & company) 1904.   2 v. fronts., plates, ports., fold. map, facsims.
30½ cm. Paged continuously. 4-33879.   CS71.S81   1904

16219   STEBBINS.   The Rowland Stebbins family.   Page 21.   CS71.G657   1915

16220   STEBBINS.   Genealogy of the Stebbins family including kindred lines of Swetland, Wilcox and Cheney families, by Willis Merrill Stebbins.   Lincoln, Nebr., Brown printing service (c. 1940)
123, (7) p. incl. illus., plates, ports., geneal. tab.   23 cm.   Seven blank pages at end for "Family records".   Bibliographical references in "Conclusion" (p. 111-112) 40-14633.   CS71.S81   1940

16221   STEBBINS.   A genealogy and history of some Stebbins lines; data to 1953.   By John Alfred Stebbins.   (Hi Vista? Calif., 1953?)   x, 190 p. illus., ports. 24 cm.   "The individual ... and generation numbers are the same as in the Greenlee Stebbins genealogy."   Author's corrections in ms.   Errata slip mounted on p. 60.   59-33187.
CS71.S81   1953

STEBBINS.   See also: DUNHAM, 1956
                                    GRAY, E171.A53 v. 18
                                    WHITE, E171.A53 v. 20

16222   STECHER.   Cord Stecker and his descendants in Europe and America; a brief family history and genealogy.   In collaboration with Willy Stecker and Kurt Vorwerk.   By Robert M. Stecher.   Cleveland, 1961.   1 v. illus.   30 cm.   62-36504.   CS71.S8115   1961

STECKER.   See STECHER.

STEDMAN.   See: BARTON, 1908
                               JOHNSON, 1962

STEDWELL.   See STUDWELL.

STEEDALE.   See STUDWELL.

STEEDALE.   See STUDWELL.

STEEDWELL.   See STUDWELL.

STEEL.   See STEELE.

16223   STEELE.   Steele family.   A genealogical history of John and George Steele, (settlers of Hartford, Conn.,) 1635-6, and their descendants.   With an appendix, containing genealogical information respecting other families of the name who settled in different parts of the United States.   By Daniel Steele Durrie ... Albany, N.Y., Munsell & Rowland, 1859.   x, 145 p. illus., facsim. 25½ cm. 9-13789.
CS71.S812   1859

16224   STEELE.   The Holy Bible. ... Philadelphia: Printed and published by M. Carey & son, no. 126, Chestnut street, 1818.   p. 678 contains, in manuscript, the family record of the William Steele and Daniel Hoopes families. 35-24723.   BS185.1818.P5

16225   STEELE.   The descendants of George Steele of Barthomley, Cheshire, England, and Chester county, Pennsylvania, compiled by Frederick D. Stone, jr.   Philadelphia, For private distribution, 1896.   40 p. plates, III geneal. tab. (part fold.) 25 cm.   "Limited to fifty copies.   No. 46." Prepared for publication by Witmer Stone. cf. p. 3-4.   45-33714.   CS71.S812   1896

16226   STEELE.   Archibald Steele and his descendants; a short historical narrative of Archibald Steele the first ... and his descendants, with genealogical tables showing the proper place in the family of every member of it whose name could be learned.   By Newton Chambers Steele, M.D.   Chattanooga, Tenn., The MacGowan & Cooke co., 1900.   143 p. front., ports. 23½ cm. 1-5422.
CS71.S812   1900

16227   STEELE.   Captain Ninian Steele and his descendants.   A short historical narrative of Ninian Steele and his descendants, with genealogical tables showing the proper place in the family of every member of it whose name could be learned.   By Newton Chambers Steele, M.D.   Chattanooga, Tenn., The Macgowan & Cooke co., 1901.   100 p. plates, ports. 23 cm. 2-5511 rev.   CS71.S812   1901

16228   STEELE.   Thomas Steel of Boston and some of his descendants, 1664-1905; also including the family and American ancestry of Samuel and Olive (Pierce) Steele, pioneers of Koshkonong, Wis., 1842. Also the families of Laura J. and Louisa L. (Pierce) Arkins, of Denver, Colorado.   Prepared and published by George W. Steele.   Los Angeles, Calif., Times-mirror printing and binding house, 1905. xx, 54 p. front., illus. (coat of arms) 20 cm.   Contains also Pierce, Tibbetts and Spencer families. 17-31789.

CS71.S812   1905

16229   STEELE.   (The Steele family.   By John Nolley McCue.   Mexico, Mo. 1912)   p. 174-232, illus. (coat of arms) pl. 23 cm.   Caption title.   Detached from the McCues of the Old Dominion ... Compiled by John N. McCue, Mexico, Mo. 1912.   Typewritten and manuscript additions in pocket at end.   38M2388T.   CS71.S812   1912

16230   STEELE.   A genealogy of the descendants of James Steele and his wife Mary, late of Clinton district, Monongalia county, Virginia (now West Virginia) for the entertainment and instruction of the family and for handy reference, compiled by Donley M. Steele, a great-great-grandson.   (n. p.) 1919. (336) p. front., illus. (incl. ports.) 27½ cm. 32-1225.   CS71.S812   1919

16231   STEELE.   The Steele family in America, a genealogical history of John and George Steele, settlers of Connecticut in 1635, and their descendants, with an appendix containing genealogical information respecting other families of the name in America ... Copyright ... by Steele Barnett ... Tulsa, Okl., c. 1935.   cover-title, (74) p. 37 cm. Mimeographed. CA25-824 unrev.   CS71.S812   1935

16232   STEELE.   The Steel family; descendants of James Steel of Kent Co., Del., and Philadelphia, compiled by Joy Steel Williams (Mrs. S. Miller Williams, Jr.) Robinson, Ill., 1958)   65 l. 30 cm. 58-36508.   CS71.S812   1958

16233   STEELE.   A Yankee pedigree, by Robert G. Steele.   (Whittier, Calif., Stockton-Doty Trade Press) 1969.   147 p. illus., ports. 24 cm. 70-10429 MARC.   CS71.S812   1969

STEELE.   See also: BASSETT, 1926   JENNINGS, 1923
CAMPBELL, 1960   LIVINGSTON, 1939
CRONE, 1916   McCLURE, 1914
CRONE, 1924   McCUE, 1912
DE RAPELJE, 1948   ROBINSON, 1894

16234   STEELMAN.   Jonathan and Hannah Steelman; a family tree or record of the decendents (!) of their four children.   Pub. by the author, Thomas Hess, Millville, N. J.   Camden, N. J., L. F. Bonaker & son, printers, 1910.   176 p. illus. (incl. ports.) 23½ cm. 10-9638.

CS71.S813   1910

16235   STEELMAN.   The Jonathan and Hannah Steelman family.   By Sarah (Raynor) Lawyer. (Elkton? Md., c.1952)   106 p. illus. 24 cm. 58-27069.   CS71.S813   1952

16236   STEEN.   The Steen family in Europe and America.   A genealogical historical and biographical record of nearly three hundred years, extending from the seventeenth to the twentieth century.   By the Rev. Moses D. A. Steen ... Cincinnati, O., Monfort & company, 1900.   562 p. incl. illus. ports. 23½ cm. 0-6712 rev.   CS71.S814   1900

16237   STEEN.   The Steen family in Europe and America; a genealogical, historical and biographical record of nearly three hundred years, extending from the seventeenth to the twentieth century.   2d ed., rev. and enl. By the Rev. Moses D. A. Steen ... Cincinnati, O., Montfort & company, 1917. 740 p. incl. illus., ports. 23½ cm. 17-8899.   CS71.S814   1917

16238   STEEN.   Who's who in the Steen-Neely family, over two hundred years in America, 1738-1959; some of the ancestors and all of the known to us descendants of Carroll Jeffries Steen and Margaret Ann Neely Steen.   Booneville, Miss., Milwick Print. Co., 1959.   76 p. 24 cm.   "A supplement to The Steen family in Europe and America, by Moses D. A. Steen, D. D., published 1900-1917." 60-37435.

CS71.S814   1959

STEEN,   See also: ARTHUR, 1942
GREGORY, 1937

STEENBERGEN.   See BEAL, 1956

16239   STEENROD.   A genealogical study of the Steenrod family.   By Robert L. Steenrod.   Belvidere, Ill., 1960.   21 p. 28 cm. 60-39979.   CS71.S815   1960

16240   STEER.   Steere genealogy; a record of the descendants of John Steere, who settled in Providence, Rhode Island, about the year 1660, with some account of the Steeres of England, by James Pierce Root.   Cambridge (Mass.) Printed at the Riverside press, 1890.   vi, (2), 216 p. front., illus. (coats of arms) plates, ports., fold. map, double plan, facsims., double geneal. tab. 32½ cm. 22-17218.   CS71.S818   1890

16241   STEER.   A genealogy of a Steer family.   Comprising some of the ancestors and nearly all the descendants of Joseph and Grace (Edgerton) Steer.   By Isaac S. Russell.   (New Market, Md., 1891?)   1 p. l., 113, (10) p. 19½ x 30½ cm. Cover-title: Steer genealogy. 45-50275.   CS71.S817   1891

16242   STEER.   ... The Steer family.   (Philadelphia, 1943)   24 l. mounted illus. (incl. ports.) 28½ x 22½ cm. Leaves variously numbered; reproduced from type-written copy. Compiled by Rhea Duryea Johnson. cf. leaf 8. 46-15315.   CS71.S817   1943

16243   STEER.   Abstracts of wills and administration papers: the Steer family ... (by) Rhea Duryea Johnson.   Philadelphia, Pa. (1946?)   15 numb l. 28½ x 22 cm. 46-19248.   CS71.S817   1946

STEERE.   See: STEER.
               TUCKER, 1957

STEES.   See MORR, 1896

STEEVENS.   See STEVENS.

STEEVES.   See STIEF.

16244   STEFFEY.   The Steffeys in America, from colonial days to the space age, by Marguerite Steffey Snyder.   (Washington? 1964)   v, 120 p. illus. 23 cm. Bibliography: p. 111. 65-542.   CS71.S819   1964

STEFFY.   See: HORNBERGER, 1951
               STEFFEY.

STEH.   See STIH.

16245   STEIGERWALT.   The Steigerwalt family, 1767-1967.   By Mabel Steigerwalt.   Mifflintown, Pa., Printed by Stutzman Print., 1967.   1 v. (unpaged) 22 cm. 67-66371.   CS71.S82   1967

STEIGERWALT.   See also LEIBY, 1956

STEIN.   See SCHNEIDER, 1969

16246   STEINBACH.   The Steinbach or Steinbaugh family, province of lower Rhine, Alsace-Lorraine, and Ohio and Indiana, U.S.A.   By Paul Logan DeVerter.   (Baytown, Tex., 1958)   13 l. illus. 29 cm. 58-3996.   CS71.S821   1958

STEINBAUGH.   See STEINBACH.

16247   STEINER.   The genealogy of the Steiner family, especially of the descendants of Jacob Steiner, by Lewis H. Steiner, M.D. and Bernard C. Steiner, PH.D.   Baltimore, Press of the Friedenwald co., 1896.   103 p. 24½ cm. 9-13793.   CS71.S822   1896

STEINERT.   See STINARD.

16248   STEINES.   Briefe der nach Amerika ausgewanderten familie Steines.   Fur die verwandten, freunde und bekannten der ausgewanderten; fur alle diejenigen, welche sich fur auswanderungen interessiren; besonders aber fur diejenigen, welche selbst nach den Vereinigten Staaten Nordamerika's auszuwandern gedenken.   Herausgegeben von Friedrich Dellman... Briefe aus Bremen, Baltimore und St. Louis, nebst anhang.   Wesel, Beckersche buchhandlung, 1835.   1 p. 1., viii, 142 p. 20 cm. 24-6790.
E165. D35

16249   STEINHAUER.   Some genealogical notes on the Steinhauer family, of Saint Louis and Denver, originally from the Pfalz, or Palatinate, of Germany ... Karl Frederick Steinhauer, the compiler. (St. Louis, Mo., 1930)   cover-title, (4) p., 1 1. 30 cm. Hektographed. Contains also a genealogical table of the Chobard family. CA32-634 unrev.   CS71.S828   1930

16250   STEINHAUER.   A chart of the genealogical connections of the Steinhauer family of the United States, originally from Lohnweiler (formerly Lohweyler) and other villages near Lauterecken in the Pfalz of Germany, compiled largely from sixteenth, seventeenth, and eighteenth century registers of the Lutheran church of Lauterecken (now preserved in the Protestant archives at Speyer am Rhein), by Lt. Karl F. Steinhauer.   Issue 6.   Jacksonville, Fla., c. 1938.   geneal. tab. illus. (incl. maps, coat of arms) 76½ x 118 cm. fold. to 27½ x 21 cm. Title also in German. Blue-print. Includes the Grossarth family. 38-31190.
CS71. S828   1938

16251   STEINHAUER.   Steinhauer (Steinhawer) lineage of Karl Frederick Steinhauer from 1586. (Jacksonville, Fla., c. 1938)   1 1. 35 cm. Mimeographed. "An extract from A chart of the genealogical connections of the Steinhauer family of the United States, originally from Lohnweiler (formerly "Lohweyler") and other villages near Lauterecken. in the Pfalz of Germany." Issue 6. 1938." 40M878T.   CS71. S828   1038a

16252   STEINHAUER.   Steinhaurer genealogy source documents, compiled by Karl F. Steinhauer. 8th ed. of a Steinhauer genealogy ... Chicago, 1943 -   v. illus. (incl. ports., maps) 28 cm. Reproduced from type-written copy. Contents. - pt. 1. Steinhauer lineage of the author-compiler. 43-1840.
CS71. S828   1943

STEINHAWER.   See STEINHAUER.

16253   STEINMETZ.   Genealogy and family history of Johann Herman Steinmetz, born in Etzel, Germany, 9 November 1848, resident at Edwardsville, Illinois 1870-1940 ... By Ferdinand Henry Steinmetz.   (Union Springs? N. Y.) 1960.   55 p. illus. 28 cm. 61-22318.   CS71. S83   1960

16254   STELL.   A tree is planted; the family tree and a bit of history of the Stells.   By Susie (Brunson) Stell.   (Plainview? Tex., 1960?)   224 p. illus. 22 cm. 62-30194.
CS71. S833   1960

STELL.   See also JOHNSON, 1893

STELLE.   See STELL.

16255   STEMPLE.   History of the Stemple family, 1660-1960.   By Jay Stemple.   Art work (by) Eugene Stemple.   (Salem? Va.) 1960-66.   2 v. (chiefly geneal. tables) 45 cm. (v.2: 22 x 27 cm.) Vol. 1 consists of 7 fold. geneal. tables in portfolio. Vol. 2, published by Whittet and Shepperson, Richmond, Va., has title: A genealogy of the Stemple family (Godfrey Stemple branch) 61-47591 rev.   CS71. S835   1960

STENNIS.   See PEDEN, 1961

STEPHENS.   See: STEVENS.
            BLACK, 1954
            RYLE, 1961

16256   STEPHENSON.   At home and on the battlefield; letters from the Crimea, China and Egypt, 1854-1888, by Sir Frederick Charles Arthur Stephenson ... together with a short memoir of himself, of his brother, Sir William Henry Stephenson, K. C. B. and of their father, Sir Benjamin Charles Stephenson, G. C. H.   Collected and arranged by Mrs. Frank Pownall, with an introduction to the

16256 continued: Egyptian letters by Field-Marshall Lord Grenfell ... London, J. Murray, 1915.
xvi, 383, (1) p. pl., 3 port. (incl. front.) 23 cm. Appendices: I. Some account of Mary and Charlotte Stephenson (1771-1850; 1772-1853), sisters of Sir Benjamin Stephenson, written by their niece, Charlotte Augusta Stephenson (p. 363-370) - II. The romantic story of Mrs. George Coxe (1753-1843), told by her great-niece, Charlotte Augusta Stephenson (p. 371-377) 15-16615.   D400. S7 A3

STEPHENSON.   See: JOHNSON, 1961
                     STEVENSON.

16257   STEPNEY.   Some notices of the Stepney family.   Private impression.   London, Printed by Taylor and co., 1870.   87 p. 22 cm. Comp. by Robert Harrison. 17-23929.   CS439. S893

STEPNEY.   See also SMITH, 1878

16258   STERLING.   Historical and genealogical sketch of James Sterling.   By Edward Boker Sterling. Flemington, N.J., H. E. Deats, 1893.   (29) p. incl. ports. 12 cm. (On cover: Hunterdon historical series, no.3) 5-34085.   CS71. S838   1893

16259   STERLING.   The Sterling genealogy, comp. and illustrated by Albert Mack Sterling.   New York, The Grafton press (c. 1909)   2 v. fronts. (1 col.) illus., plates, ports. 23½ cm. Paged continuously. Illustrated t.-p. Each plate accompanied by guard sheet with descriptive letterpress.   "This edition is limited to fifty copies printed from type on Strathmore Japan paper, and contains fifty special photogravure illustrations.   Each copy is numbered and signed by the author.   The number of this copy is one of two extra."   "Major James Sterling of Burlington, New Jersey, and his descendants, compiled and contributed by Edward Boker Sterling, of Trenton, New Jersey": v. 2, p. (1104)-1148.   9-31825.   CS71. S838   1909

STERLING.   See also STIRLING.

STERN.   See STEARNS.

16260   STERNE.   The life of Laurence Sterne.   By Percy Fitzgerald ... With illustrations from drawings by the author and others ... London, Chapman & Hall, 1864.   2 v. fronts. (v.1, port.) plates, fold. geneal. tab. 19½ cm. 12-39890.   PR3716. F5

16261   STERNE.   The life of Laurence Sterne, by Percy Fitzgerald, with an introduction by Wilbur L. Cross ... New York, J. F. Taylor & company (c. 1904)   2 v. 5 pl., 5 port. (incl. fronts.) 24 cm. (Half-title: The works and life of Laurence Sterne (York ed.)) 5-9701.   PR3711. C7 vol. 11-12

STERNE.   See also STEARNS.

16262   STERRETT.   The Sterrett genealogy; families of Pennsylvania, Virginia, Canada & others, compiled by T. Woods Sterrett ... New Haven, Conn., The Tuttle, Morehouse & Taylor company, 1930. vii, 284 p. front. (port.) fold. plans. 23½ cm. 37-21341.   CS71. S839   1930

16263   STETSON.   A genealogical and biographical sketch of the name and family of Stetson; from the year 1634, to the year 1847.   By John Stetson Barry ... Boston, Printed for the author, by W. A. Hall & co., 1847.   116 p. 22½ cm. Title vignette: coat of arms. 9-13792.   CS71. S84   1847

16264   STETSON.   Stetson kindred of America (inc.) ... Comp. by the secretary.   Medford, Mass., Press of J. C. Miller, jr., 1907 -   v. fronts., plates, ports., fold. chart. 23½ cm. George W. Stetson, secretary, 1906-1911; Nelson M. Stetson, 1914 -   25-19271.   CS71. S84   1907-

16265   STETSON.   Stetson kindred of America incorporated.   (New Haven) Priv. print. (Yale university press) 1932.   cover-title, 13, (1) p. 23½ cm. Coat of arms on cover. Description of the organization, and purposes of the association. 33-6862.   CS71. S84   1932

16266   STETSON.   Stetson kindred of America incorporated. (New Haven) Priv. print. (Yale university press) 1932.   cover-title, 10 p., 1 l. 23½ cm. Coat of arms on cover. Contains agreement of the association, act of incorporation, and by-laws. 33-6863.   CS71. S84   1932a

16267   STETSON.   The descendants of Cornet Robert Stetson of Scituate, Massachusetts, sixteen hundred and thirty-four, edited by Oscar Frank Stetson.   (Providence) Stetson kindred of America, inc., 1933 -   v. col. coat of arms. 25 cm. Incorporates material collected by Nelson Mitchell Stetson, supplementing "A genealogical and biographical sketch of the name and family of Stetson ... (Boston, 1847) by John Stetson Barry". 33-14360.   CS71.S84   1933

STETSON.   See also: BARRY, 1909
                      BENSON, 1920
                      SMALL, 1910
                      SMALL, 1934

STEUART.   See STUART.

16268   STEVENS.   Record of Josiah Stevens' family.   (n. p., 18 -)   geneal. tab. 24½ x 31 cm. fold. to 24½ x 16 cm. Photostat reproduction (positive) 38M3982T.   CS71.S844   18 -

16269   STEVENS.   Pedigree of the family of Stevens of Vielstone, Cross and Winscott ... Exeter, W. Pollard & co., printers, 1891.   cover-title, 4 p. 30 cm. 21-18019.   CS439.S894

16270   STEVENS.   Genealogy of the Stevens family, from 1635 to 1891, tracing the various branches from the early settlers in America.   Compiled by Frederick S. Stevens ... Bridgeport, J. H. Cogges-well, printer (c. 1891)   3 p. l., (v)-vi, (7)-52 (i. e. 58) p., 4 l. ports., facsims. 24½ cm. 9-13791.   CS71.S844   1891

16271   STEVENS.   ... The Stephens family, with collateral branches.   By Edward Stephens Clark, M. D.   San Francisco, J. Winterburn company, printers and electrotypers, 1892.   v, (3), 185 p. front., ports. 23½ cm. (The American genealogical record. v. 1) Descendants of Peter Stephens of Virginia. 9-13748.   CS71.S844   1892

16272   STEVENS.   Record of the Stevens family presented to Charles Tracy Stevens and Emeline N. Upson, by Oliver Stevens. 1844.   Meriden, Conn., Reprinted, H.W.Lines, 1893.   11 p. 23 cm. (With Stevens, Elisha. Elisha Stevens, fragments of memoranda ... (Meriden, Conn., 1922) 24-6087.   E275.S84

16273   STEVENS.   Ancestral genealogical record and history of the Stevens family, of Norfolk, Conn., by Nathaniel B. Stevens.   Winsted, Conn., 1896.   52 p. illus. (incl. ports., facsim.) 22½ cm. 25-12672.   CS71.S844   1896

16274   STEVENS.   Stevens genealogy.   Some descendants of the Fitz Stephen family in England and New England.   By C. Ellis Stevens ... New York, Priv. print., 1905.   92 p., 1 l. illus., plates, facsims., coats of arms. 26 cm. Imprint date corrected from 1904 to 1905. 5-12242.   CS71.S844   1905

16275   STEVENS.   Genealogy of the Stevens and Tripp and allied families from 1520 to 1906.   (Chicago? c. 1906)   48 p. ports. 20½ cm. Compiled by Mrs. Mary E. (Stevens) Ghastin. 6-41531.   CS71.S844   1906

16276   STEVENS.   A genealogy of the lineal descendants of John Steevens, who settled in Guilford, Conn. in 1645.   Compiled by Charlotte Steevens Holmes, 1906.   Edited by Clay W. Holmes, A.M., Elmira, N.Y. (Elmira, Advertiser press, 1906)   162 p. 24 cm. 6-29103.   CS71.S844   1906a

16277   STEVENS.   The Stevens genealogy, embracing branches of the family descended from Puritan ancestry, New England families not traceable to Puritan ancestry, and miscellaneous branches wherever found, together with an extended account of the line of descent from 1650 to the present time of the author, Dr. Elvira Stevens Barney.   Salt Lake City, Utah, Skelton publishing co., 1907.   xii p., 1 l., 17-319 p. incl. front., plates, port., coat of arms. 24 cm. 17-30087.   CS71.S844   1907

16278   STEVENS.   Stephens-Stevens genealogy, lineage from Henry Stephens, or Stevens of Stoning-ton, Connecticut, 1668, by Plowdon Stevens.   New York, Frank Allaben genealogical company, 1909.   358 p. pl., ports., facsims. 20 cm. (Allaben genealogical series) 9-22996.   CS71.S844   1909

16279   STEVENS.   Genealogical-biographical histories of the families of Stevens, Gallatin and Nicholson; compiled by Mr. Byam Kerby Stevens.   New York, National Americana society, 1911.
1 p. 1., 36 p.   4 port. (incl. front.) 35 cm. 14-10220.   CS71.S844   1911

16280   STEVENS.   Erasmus Stevens, Boston, Mass., 1674-1690, and his descendants, from material collected by Eugene R. Stevens, New York, 1837-1905.   Rev. by Colonel William Plumb Bacon ... (New York, Press of Tobias A. Wright) 1914.   4 p. 1., 7-116 p. 2 port. 24½ cm. 15-8148.
                                                                                                     CS71.S844   1914

16281   STEVENS.   Peter Stephens and some of his descendants, 1690-1935, edited by Dan V. Stephens ... cover design and pen drawings by Clarence Ellsworth.   Fremont, Nebr., Hammond & Stephens co., 1936.   7 p. 1., 72 (185) p. illus. (map) plates, ports., facsim. 24 cm. Ruled pages for "Family record" (177-185) Illustrated lining-papers. 37-717.   CS71.S844   1936

16282   STEVENS.   Calendars of manuscript collections in New Jersey.   Preliminary volume.   Calendar of the Stevens family papers, Lieb memorial library, Stevens institute of technolgoy, Hoboken, New Jersey.   Prepared by the New Jersey Historical records survey project, Research and records section, Division of professional and service projects, Work projects administration.   Sponsored by New Jersey State planning board and the National archives.   Newark, N.J., The Historical records survey, 1940.   4 p. 1., 112 numb. 1. 27½ cm.   Reproduced from type-written copy. Bibliography: leaves 110-111. 40-26873.
                                                                                          CD3389.5.S8H5   1940

16283   STEVENS.   Stephens family genealogies; Peter- Joshua - William - Alexander, 1690-1938.   Rev. ed.   Edited by Dan V. Stephens ... Pen drawings by Clarence Ellsworth.   Fremont, Nebr., Hammond & Stephens co., 1940.   150, (429) p., facsim. (1, 19 p.), (151) p. incl. illus., ports., facsim. 24½ cm.   Map and illustration on lining-papers. Four ruled pages for "Family record" at end. Originally published under title: Peter Stephens and some of his descendants, 1690-1935. Includes facsimile of chapter I of Thomas Stephens' "The castle-builder; or, The history of William Stephens, of the Isle of Wight ... London, 1759." 41-4997.   CS71.S844   1940

16284   STEVENS.   ... Descendants of John Stevens of Andover ... by Horace N. Stevens ... Plain-field, N.J., 19   geneal. tab. 53½ x 43 cm. Contents. - no.2. Descendants of Nathaniel Stevens, 1786-1865, of the sixth generation from John Stevens, 1605-1662, who came to America in 1638. 44-19067.   CS71.S844   1941

16285   STEVENS.   Stevens-Washburn, with related lines, particularly the antecedents, relatives, and descendants of Captain James Holmes Stevens and of Dr. Abner Standish Washburn (by) Annie Stevens Jones.   Lonsdale, Ark., The Ozark guide press (1946)   195, (4) p. 21 cm. 47-16534.
                                                                                                     CS71.S844   1946

16286   STEVENS.   Ancestry of Colonel John Harrington Stevens and his wife Frances Helen Miller, compiled for Helen Pendleton (Winston) Pillsbury.   By Mary (Lovering) Holman.   (Concord, N.H., Priv. print, at the Rumford Press) 1948-52 (i.e.53)   2 v. illus., ports. 25 cm. On spine: The Stevens Miller ancestry. "110 copies printed." W.L.Holman, editor of v.1, author of v.2. 48-11657 rev.*   CS71.S844   1948

16288   STEVENS.   The Stevens genealogy and family history: Richard of Taunton, Mass., Henry of Stonington, Conn., and their descendants in N.C., Ind., and N.Y., including some named Stephens.   By Clarence Perry Stephens.   Escalon, Calif., c.1950.   93 p. geneal. table. 29 cm. Bibliography: p.36. 50-39682.
                                                                                                     CS71.S844   1950

16289   STEVENS.   Ancestry and descendants of Carlos and Belinda Eldredge Stevens.   By Ruth (Brown) McAllister.   Denver, 1960.   109 p. coats of arms. 29 cm. "100 copies ... no. 41." 62-2663.
                                                                                                     CS71.S844   1960

16290   STEVENS.   Stevens families of Wilkinson County, Georgia.   Compiled by Mable McDaniel and Elizabeth Wright.   (Dallas? Tex.) c.1956.   72 p. illus. 28 cm. 57-17607.   CS71.S844   1956

16291   STEVENS.   Stevens-Davis and allied families; a memorial volume of history, biography, and genealogy.   By Marie (Stevens) Walker Wood.   Macon, Ga., 1957.   xi, 474 p. illus., maps, coats of arms, geneal. tables.   25 cm.   "150 copies ... printed for private circulation."   Bibliography: p. 459-460.   57-12341.

CS71.S844   1957

16292   STEVENS.   Footprints down the centuries; a Vermont heritage.   By Ethel (Mayhew) Stevens. Boston, Chapman & Grimes (1961)   169 p. illus. 22 cm. 61-7943.   CS71.S844   1961

16293   STEVENS.   Genealogy of Thomas White Stephens and his wife Mary Elizabeth Tyler and of their collateral relatives.   By Frank Fletcher Stephens.   Columbia, Mo., Printed by Journal Press, 1962.   39 p. illus. 21 cm.   62-66117.   CS71.S844   1962

16294   STEVENS.   A history of the Stevens and Townsend families, by Harold W. Hein.   Brookfield, Wis., 1966.   214 l. illus., col. coat of arms, facsims., geneal. tables, maps (part fold. part col.) ports.   29 cm.   Typescript (carbon copy)   68-5239.   CS71.S844   1966

16295   STEVENS.   The descendants of Samuel Stevens, with histories of allied families; a biographical and genealogical record.   Baltimore, 1968.   xiii, 576 p. illus., facsims., maps, ports. 29 cm. Bibliography: p. 529-536.   68-31795.   CS71.S844   1968

16296   STEVENS.   Stevens, Clough and Willey families.   In vertical file.   Ask reference librarian for this material.

STEVENS.   See also:

BISBEE, 1936	KEENER, 1923	REICHNER, 1918
BUCK, 1917	MAJOR, 1915	SELDEN, 1911
BULLARD, 1935	MONROE, 1952	TOWNLEY, 1888
DICKEY, 1935	MOORE, 1918	WOODRUFF, 1925
FOSTER, 1953	MULFORD, 1920	

16297   STEVENSON.   A genealogical table of the Stevenson family, from 1735 to 1880.   With memoranda of a few names found in the table.   Compiled by J. M. S.   (i. e. John McMillan Stevenson.) ... (n. p.) Printed for the descendants, 1880.   20 p. fold. geneal. tab. 17 cm. Not published. 3-29500.

CS71.S847   1880

16298   STEVENSON.   Thomas Stevenson of London, England and his descendants, by John R. Stevenson, A.M., M. D.   Flemington, N. J., H. E. Deats (1902)   1 p. l., ii, 3-180 p., 1 l. col. front., port. 24 cm. 2-27218.   CS71.S847   1902

16299   STEVENSON.   A genealogical sketch of the family of Arthur Stevenson.   Born 1751, died 1821.   By Dr. John R. Stevenson.   Flemington, N. J., H. E. Deats, 1903.   12 p. 24 cm. "Two hundred copies reprinted from volume nine of the Jerseyman by Anthony Kilgore."   3-31342.   CS71.S847   1903

16300   STEVENSON.   Genealogical and biographical records of William Stephenson and his descendants ... Compiled and published by Mrs. Elizabeth Mitchell Stephenson Fite ... New York, The compiler (1905)   32 numb l. fold. geneal. tab. 23½ cm. Author's autographed presentation copy to the Library of Congress. 6-3626.   CS71.S847   1905

16301   STEVENSON.   The Stephenson family; a genealogical sketch of the Stephenson family from Henry Stephenson of Scotland, to the present time, by J. C. Stephenson ... Nashville, Tenn., The author, 1906.   126 p. 19½ cm. 15-5258.   CS71.S847   1906

16302   STEVENSON.   Records of a family of engineers, by Robert Louis Stevenson, London, Chatto & Windus, 1912.   3 p. l., 229 p., 1 l. 19½ cm. Contents. - Introduction: The surname of Stevenson. - I. Domestic annals. - II. The service of the northern lights. - III. The building of the Bell Rock.   13-6046.   TA140.S78S7

16303   STEVENSON.   At home and on the battlefield; letters from the Crimea, China and Egypt, 1854-1888, by Sir Frederick Charles Arthur Stephenson ... together with a short memoir of himself, of his brother, Sir William Henry Stephenson, K. C. B. and of their father, Sir Benjamin Charles

16303 continued: Stephenson, G.C.H.   Collected and arranged by Mrs. Frank Pownall, with an introduction to the Egyptian letters by Field-Marshal Lord Grenfell ... London, J. Murray, 1915.
xvi, 383, (1) p. pl., 3 port. (incl. front.) 23 cm. Appendices: I. Some account of Mary and Charlotte Stephenson (1771-1850; 1772-1853),
sisters of Sir Benjamin Stephenson, written by their niece, Charlotte Augusta Stephenson (p. 363-370) - II. The romantic story of Mrs. George Coxe
(1753-1843), told by her great-niece, Charlotte Augusta Stephenson (p. 371-377)   15-16615.   DA400.S7A3

16304   STEVENSON.   A history and genealogical record of the Stevenson family, from 1748 to 1926.
By Rev. Samuel Harris Stevenson, Rev. T. A. Harris and Hon. W. F. Stevenson.   (n. p., 1926)
238 p. 21 cm. Compiled from the data collected by Samuel Harris Stevenson, for the Stevenson book, published about 1898, and the additional
material gathered by John Abner Harris and brought up to date by William F. Stevenson.   26-14843.   CS71.S847   1926

16305   STEVENSON.   The manuscripts of Robert Louis Stevenson's Records of a family of engineers;
the unfinished chapters, edited with an introduction by J. Christain Bay ... Chicago, W.M.Hill, 1929.
92 p., 1 l. front. (geneal. tab.) facsims. 28 ½ cm. "Three hundred copies." "Set in Garamond type and printed on Rives hand made paper at
the Torch press, Cedar Rapids, Iowa. "   30-3185.   TA140.S78S65

16306   STEVENSON.   The Stevenson family tree; genealogy extended to 1940 ... compiled by Adda
Westcott Stevenson ... Minneapolis, Minn., 1940.   cover-title, 11 p. 18 cm. 41-31429.
                                                    CS71.S847   1940

16307   STEVENSON.   The Stevenson family history; consisting of biographical sketches of the
Joseph Stevenson family which came to America in 1828, including sketches of the lives of their wives
and husbands.   2d ed.   Provo, Utah, 1955 -   v. illus., ports. 28 cm. An enlargement of The life of Edward
Stevenson, compiled and edited from his journals, autobiography, letters, and papers by J. G. Stevenson as a thesis (M. A.) Brigham Young University.
Bibliographical footnotes.   56-45692.   CS71.S847   1955

16308   STEVENSON.   Pioneers on the Bullskin; the Stephenson story.   By Mignon Larche.   Eureka
Springs, Ark., Times-Echo Pub. Co., 1960.   272 p. illus. 23 cm. 60-9673.   CS71.S847   1960

16309   STEVENSON.   The Stevenson family, a record of the descendants of James Stevenson, Burgess
of Paisley in 1753.   Bolton-on-Swale, Richmond (Yorks.), Hew S. Stevenson, 1965.   (1), ix, 146 p. col.
front., plates (incl. ports.) diagrs. 25½ cm. 66-74386.   CS439.S8944   1965

16310   STEVENSON.   Stevenson family history; from the Eastern Shore of Maryland (Old Somerset,
renamed Worcester County) to Woodford County, Kentucky, to Putnam County, Indiana, with allied families.   By Margaretta Stevenson.   New York, 1966.   162 p. 22 cm. Includes bibliographical references. 68-1392.
                                                    CS71.S847   1966

16311   STEVENSON.   Descendants of Edward and Mary Stevenson of Baltimore County, Maryland,
by Robert Barnes.   (Baltimore?) 1966.   iii, 82 l. 30 cm. "Based on notes compiled ... by Mrs. F.C.Rogers." 100 copies.
No. 60.   68-2712.   CS71.S847   1966b

16312   STEVENSON.   Adlai Stevenson family.   In vertical file.   Ask reference librarian for this material.

          STEVENSON.   See also: GALLOWAY, 1939
                                  JENNINGS, 1899
                                  McCORMICK, E184.S4M2
                                  ROBSON, 1892
                                  STIMSON.
                                  THURBURN, 1864

          STEVINTON.   See BLITHFIELD, 1919

16313   STEWART.   A narrative genealogy of the Stewarts of Sequatchie Valley, Tennessee, and
allied families.   By Mary (Stewart) Blakemore.   Richmond, Dietz Press, 1960.   xvi, 227 p. illus., ports.,
fold. map. coats of arms, facsims., geneal. table. 26 cm. Cover title: Stewarts of the Sequatchie Valley, Tennessee. 60-1074.
                                                    CS71.S93   1960

16314   STEWART.   The family of Thomas Stewart of Madison County, Alabama.   By Mary Bivin
Geron Countess.   (Huntsville? Ala., 196-)   11 l. 28 cm. Bibliographical footnotes. 68-1766.   CS71.S93

16315   STEWART.   Some record of the Stewarts of Ashbourne and Hambrooke Point, Dorchester County, Maryland.   By Robert G. Stewart.   Washington (1963)   88 p. 28 cm. Cover title. Includes bibliographies. 64-1137.   CS71.S9295   1963

16316   STEWART.   The James Stewart family of early Augusta County, Virginia, and descendants, 1740-1960, by Florence S. Dickerson.   (Parsons? W. Va., 1966)   318 p. illus., col. coat of arms, ports. 22 cm. 66-27493.   CS71.S93   1966

16317   STEWART.   Genealogy; John Stewart, Rosherry, Ireland descendants through his son, James. Compiled by Ludwig A. Beckman, Jr.   (Starkville, Miss., Printed by Johnson, 1968)   104 p. illus., ports. 28 cm. 68-59277.   CS71.S93   1968

16318   STEWART.   Stewart descendants.   v. 1 -   1945 -   (Olathe? Kan.) Stewart Society of America.   v. in   22 cm. annual. Publication suspended 1956-59. 63-50733.   CS71.S9295

STEWART.   See also: BATEMAN, 1960
CALHOUN, 1957
DAWKINS, 1968
PEDEN, 1961
STUART.
Addenda

STEYNMETS.   See VAN WINKLE, F116.N36 vol. 56

STIBOLT.   See DAVIS, 1939

STICKLAND.   See STRICKLAND, 1964

16319   STICKNEY.   The Stickney family: a genealogical memoir of the descendants of William and Elizabeth Stickney, from 1637 to 1869.   By Matthew Adams Stickney ... Salem, Mass., Printed for the author, Essex institute press, 1869.   viii, 526 p. front., illus., plates, ports. 23½ cm. "Edition of 500 copies" 9-14117.   CS71.S854   1869

16320   STICKNEY.   Stickney.   Spaulding.   Lawrence.   (West Townsend? Mass.) 1910.   (1), 11 p. 18 cm. Explanations signed: Alvah Franklin Stickney.   Alternate pages left blank for "Additions and corrections."   Ms. corrections. 12-59.   CS71.S854   1910

16321   STICKNEY.   Stickney genealogy, by C. P. Stickney.   (n. p., 1920)   cover-title, 30 p. incl. ports. 18 cm. 23-14465.   CS71.S854   1920

16322   STICKNEY.   Alpheus Beede Stickney, his descendants and some of their ancestors, 1558-1965: Beede, Berkey, Burley, Boulter, Prescott, Shaw, Swaine, Wiggin, Sleeper, Stickney.   Cleveland (1965) 38 l. illus., geneal. tables, ports. 28 cm. 100 copies printed. No. 57. 66-5331.   CS71.S854   1965

STICKNEY.   See also EVANS, 1946

STIDHAM.   See STRETCHER, F163.S46

STIDOLFE.   See STUDWELL.

STIDULFE.   See STUDWELL.

16323   STIEF.   Samphire greens; the story of the Steeves.   By Esther (Clark) Wright.   Kingsport, N. S. (1961)   94 p. map. 23 cm. 78-217310 MARC.   CS71.S855   1961

STIER.   See: CALVERT, 1905-8
COGEL, 1959
MORRIS, 1905

16324   STIFF.   Collections relating to the family of Stiff.   By W. P. W. Phillimore ... Part I. The origin of the surname.   The medieval Stiffs of Hawkesbury.   Stroud, Printed for private circulation by J. White, 1892.   cover-title, 42 p. front., illus. 23 cm. Issued also in Gloucestershire notes and queries. London, 1891-93, v. 5. "Hawkesbury church": p. 41-42. 15-21493.   CS439.S895

STIH.   See OKLESHEN, 1965

16325   STILES.   The Connecticut family of Stiles.   (By Henry Reed Stiles.   New York, C. B. Norton, 1859)   31 p. illus. 24½ cm. Caption title. Cover-title: Genealogy of the Stiles family. From Stiles's History of anceient Windsor (N. Y., 1859) p. 777-807. 3-15288.   CS71.S856   1859

16326   STILES.   Contributions towards a genealogy of the (Massachusetts) family of Stiles, descended from Robert, of Rowley, Mass., 1659-1860.   By Henry R. Stiles, M. D.   Albany, J. Munsell, 1863. 48 p. 21½ cm x 18½ cm. 100 copies printed. 9-14116.   CS71.S856   1863

16327   STILES.   The Stiles family in America.   Genealogies of the Massachusetts family, descendants of Robert Stiles of Rowley, Mass. 1659-1891.   And the Dover, N. H., family, descendants of William Stiles of Dover, N. H., 1702-1891.   By Mrs. Mary Stiles (Paul) Guild ... With a prefatory chapter on the origin of the family name; and an appendix on the family in England.   By Henry R. Stiles ... Albany, N. Y., J. Munsell's sons, 1892.   vi, 683 p. front., illus., ports. 24 cm. 9-14114.   CS71.S856   1892

16328   STILES.   The Stiles family in America.   Genealogies of the Connecticut family.   Descendants of John Stiles, of Windsor, Conn., and of Mr. Francis Stiles, of Windsor and Stratford, Conn., 1635-1894; also the Connecticut New Jersey families, 1720-1894; and the southern (or Bermuda-Georgia) family, 1635-1894.   With contributions to the genealogies of some New York and Pennsylvania families ... By Henry Reed Stiles ... Jersey City, Doan & Pilson, printers, 1895.   xii, 782 p. front., illus., ports., coats of arms. 26 cm. 9-14115.   CS71.S856   1895

16329   STILES.   A history of the Kentucky and Missouri Stiles, with a sketch of New Jersey and other kindred.   By La Fayette Stiles Pence.   Albany, N. Y., J. Munsell's sons, 1896.   45 (1) p., 1 l. front., ports., coat of arms. 22½ cm. Original imprint "Lebanon, Ky., W. T. Hawkins " corrected to " Albany, J. Munsell's sons. " 1-10281.   CS71.S856   1896

16330   STILES.   Abram Stiles (Styls and Styles); John Milliken (Milligan and Milligin).   Comp. by Mrs. Sarah Augusta Prior Smith.   Columbus, O., 1920.   cover-title, 35 l. illus. (incl. ports.) 20½ x 27 cm. A collection of revolution societies, for the descendants of Abram Stiles and John Milliken, especially for descendants of John Prior and wife Patience Milliken, consisting of manuscript leaves with mounted photographs fastened together in binder. 21-2007.   CS71.S856   1920

16331   STILES.   Stiles genealogy; Dan Stiles of Shoreham, Vermont, great-great-great grandson of Robert Stiles who lived in Rowley, Mass., in 1659, by John M. Stanton ... Rutland, Vt., The Tuttle company, 1933.   3 p. l., (5)-30 p. port. 23 cm. Blank pages for "Family notes" (28-30) 35-8176.   CS71.S856   1933

16332   STILES.   James Styles of Kingston, New York, and George Stuart of Schoolcraft, Michigan; their descendants and allied families with an historical narrative, by Jeannette Paddock Nichols ... Swarthmore, Pa., The author, 1936.   4 p. l., 7-214 p. front., ports. 23½ cm. Bibliography: p. 171-173. 36-16902.   CS71.S856   1936

16333   STILES.   The family of David Stiles; or, The ten tribes of the house of David.   The ancestry and posterity of David Stiles, a native of New Jersey, an immigrant to Kentucky, by Lewis Ogden Stiles. Louisville, Ky., Mayes printing company, 1939.   310 p. illus. (maps, coat of arms) plates, ports., facsim. 20½ cm. Part VI. The history of the Stiles family in Kentucky and Missouri by La Fayette Stiles Pence (with reproduction of title-page of original edition. Lebanon, Ky., 1896)": p. 105-150. 39-24955.   CS71.S856   1939

16334   STILES.   The family of Jonathan Stiles of Guernsey County, Ohio; his ancestors and descendants, and allied families.   By Jessie Vernan Stiles.   (Greenfield? Ind., 1957.   398 p. illus. 24 cm. 57-42219.   CS71.S856   1957

STILES.   See also: HABERSHAM, 1901
                       HUMFREVILLE, 1903
                       MILLIKEN, 1934
                       O'DALY, 1956
                       THOMPSON, 1915

16335   STILLMAN.   Miscellaneous compositions in poetry and prose, by William Stillman.   New London, Printed by F. H. Bacon, 1852.   iv, 188 p. front. (port.) 16½ cm.   The genealogy of the Stillman family: p. 1-6.
17-21565.   PS2919.S785   1852

16336   STILLMAN.   ... History and genealogy of George Stillman, 1st, and his descendants through the line of Deacon William Stillman, by Edgar Stillman.   Westerly, R. I. (E. A. Stillman, printer, 1903)
1 p. l., (xiii)-xxxi p., 1 l., 42 p. pl.   21½ x 28 cm.   At head of title: 1654-1903.   4-22359 rev.   CS71.S857   1903

STILLMAN.   See also No. 3939 - Colebrook.

STILLSON.   See STILSON.

16337   STILLWELL.   Early memoirs of the Stilwell family, comprising the life and times of Nicholas Stilwell, the common ancestor of the numerous families bearing that surname, with some account of his brothers John and Jasper and incidentally a sketch of the history of Manhattan Island and its vicinity, under the Dutch, with some contributions to a genealogy of the family.   By Benjamin Marshall Stilwell. New York, The National printing company, 1878.   xii p., 1 l., (25)-289 p. 25 cm.   9-14113.
                                                                                                          CS71.S858   1878

16338   STILLWELL.   Notes on the descendants of Nicholas Stillwell, the ancestors of the Stillwell family in America.   By William H. Stillwell.   New York, E. W. Nash, 1883.   2 p. l., (3)-62 p. 23½ cm.
9-14122.   CS71.S858   1883

16339   STILLWELL.   History and genealogical record of one branch of the Stilwell family, September 1, 1914, by Dewitt Stilwell, with introduction and contributions by Lamont Stilwell ... Solvay, N. Y., The Martin press, 1914.   94 p. front., plates, ports. 23 cm.   14-21195.
                                                                                                          CS71.S858   1914

16340   STILLWELL.   Stillwell genealogy ... By John Edwin Stillwell.   (New York, 1929-31)
4 v. col. front. (coat of arms) plates, ports., maps (part double, 1 fold.) 31 cm.   Binder's title.   "M^{ris} Cooke's meditations, being an humble thanks giving to her heavenly Father for granting her a new life, having concluded her selfe dead, and her grave made in the bottome of the sea, in that great storme rivall at Corcke. Corke, Printed, and reprinted at London by C. S. ..." (with reproductions of original t.-p.): vol. I, p. (105)-112. Vol. III in 3 parts, paged continuously, each with special t.-p. Vols. III-IV edited by Harrison McNear. The double facsimile in vol. IV. is a photostat reproduction of a poem "supposed to have been written by Elizabeth Gillies, mother of Dr. John E. Stillwell". Contents. - I. The history of Lieutenant Nicholas Stillwell, progenitor of the Stillwell family in America ... - II. The history of Captain Richard Stillwell and his descendants. - III. The history of Captain Nicholas Stillwell ... and his descendants. The history of William Stillwell ... The history of Captain Thomas Stillwell ... - IV. History of Captain Jeremiah Stillwell, Anne Stillwell Britton, Alice Stillwell Holmes, Mary Stillwell Mott, Daniel Stillwell, John Stillwell ... and appendix of allied families ... 33-315.
                                                                                                          CS71.S858   1929-31

STILLWELL.   See also: BRADHURST, 1910
                         PERRIN.
                         WILSON, 1929

16341   STILSON.   Notes on the genealogy of the Stilson family, compiled by William Charles Stillson ... Ann Arbor, Mich., Edwards brothers, inc., 1939.   ix, 126 p. illus. (incl. ports.) 2 fold. geneal.
tables, fold. map. 21 cm.   "There are one hundred copies." "Lithoprinted." 39-32326.   CS71.S8587   1939

STILSON.   See also LITTLE, 1958

STILWELL.   See STILLWELL.

STIMPSON.   See: STIMSON.
                   WILSON, 1929

16342   STIMSON.   Genealogy of the Stimpson family of Charlestown, Mass., and allied lines.   By Charles Collyer Whittier.   Boston, Press of D. Clapp & son, 1907.   2 p. l., (3)-206 p. front., plates, ports. 23½ cm. 7-21726.   CS71.S859   1907

STIMSON.   See also JONES, 1941a

16343   STINARD.   Descendants of Frederick Stinard (Friedrich Steinert) by Jesse Floyd Stinard and Paul Johnson Slate.   East Orange, N.J., Printed by Essex Mailings (1966)   130 p. 90 cm. 66-7840.   CS71.S8592   1966

16344   STINCHFIELD.   The Stinchfield-Stanchfield family.   By Roger Adams Stinchfield.   (Boston? 1963)   238 p. 24 cm. 63-49852.   CS71.S8593   1963

STINSON.   See STEVENSON, 1926

STIPPS.   See also McKEE, 1900

16345   STIRLING.   The Stirlings of Keir, and their family papers.   By William Fraser.   Edinburgh, Priv. print., 1858.   lxx, 622 p. incl. illus., plates, ports., facsims. 22 cm. Plates, ports., etc. printed on both sides. Illus. part colored.   One hundred and fifty copies ... no. 23. 8-22922.   DA758.3. S75F8

16346   STIRLING.   Comments in refutation of pretensions advanced for the first time, and statements in a recent work "The Stirlings of Keir and their family papers," with an exposition of the right of the Stirlings of Drumpellier to the representation of the ancient Stirlings of Cadder; by John Riddell ... Edinburgh, Printed for private circulation by W. Blackwood and sons, 1860.   2 p. l., xx, 260 p., 1 l. incl. geneal. tables. 27½ x 21½ cm. 4-10982.   DA758.3.S75F83

16347   STIRLING.   The armorial bearings of the Stirlings of Keir and others of the name; a series of designs for dessert-plates.   Glasgow, 1860.   2 p. l., 3-15, (1) p. illus., 50 numb. pl. 35½ cm.   "The impression is limited to twenty-six copies, one of which is on vellum." Full description of each plate given in the contents. 19-8255.   CR1669.S85A7

16348   STIRLING.   The Stirlings of Craigbernard and Glorat, representatives of the house of Cadder and the earls of Bothwell, and notices of their cadets; some leaves of Lennox history, with appendix of charters and other documents.   By Joseph Bain, F.S.A.SCOT.   Edinburgh, Priv. print., 1883.   xxxiv, 127 p. pl. 22½ x 17½ cm.   Title vignette (col. coat of arms) ; plate of seals and arms.   "The book has been prepared and printed at Sir Charles Stirling's cost." 14-15111.   CS479.S7   1883

16349   STIRLING.   Ancient castles and mansions of Stirling nobility.   Described & illustrated by J.S. Fleming ... With pen and ink sketches by the author.   Paisley and London, A. Gardner, 1902.   xiii, (17)-475 p. incl. illus., plates. front., 2 pl. 27½ x 22 cm. Illustrated t.-p. 2-17566.   NA7336.S8F6

STIRLING.   See also STERLING.

STIRLING, Earls of.   See ALEXANDER.

16350   STITES.   The James-Stites genealogy, including mention, among others, of the following family names: Alward, Casad (Cosad, Cossart), Coon, Cox, Duling, Gerlach, Lange, Martin, Schäfer, Tingley, by Edmund J. James ... (New York, 1898)   cover-title, 6 p. 27½ cm. Caption title: The Stites and James genealogy.   By Edmund J. James.   Continued from the New York genealogical and biographical record for July, Oct., 1897, p.165-166, 237-239. Reprinted from the New York genealogical and biographical record for April, 1898, p.93-98. 9-14111.   CS71.S861   1898

STITES.   See also CLARK, 1948

STITH.   See BUCKNER, 1907

STITT.   See HOGG, 1921

STOBO.   See BULLOCH, 1911

16351   STOCKER.   Michael Stucker of 1759 and his kinsmen.   By Essie Stucker.   (n. p., 1957)
218 p. illus. 29 cm.   "Sequel to book II (vol. I) George Stucker, which was compiled and edited by Jennie E. Stewart. "

—— Supplement.   (n. p.) 1958.   111 p. illus. 28 cm. 57-32288 rev.

CS71.S8617   1957
CS71.S8617   1957
Suppl.

16352   STOCKETT.   Genealogy of the family of Stockett, 1558-1892.   By Frank H. Stockett.
(Baltimore, Printed by W. R. Boyle & son, 1892)   33 numb. 1. 25½ cm. Photostat copy. 24-18943.

CS71.S862   1892

16353   STOCKING.   The Stocking ancestry; comprising the descendants of George Stocking, founder
of the American family, edited and published by Rev. Charles Henry Wright Stocking ... (Chicago) The
Lakeside press, 1903.   v, 205 p., 1 1. port. 25 cm. 3-11296.   CS71.S864   1903

STOCKING.   See also: BASSETT, 1926
                        RANNEY, F104.C8A2

STOCKLEY.   See CUSTIS, 1925

16354   STOCKTON.   Poems: with autobiographic and other notes.   (Illustrated by Darley, Hoppin,
and others)   By T. H. Stockton ... Philadelphia, W.S. & A.Martien, 1862.   ix p., 1 1., 321 p. front., plates.
19 cm. Plates engraved by Frank R. Stockton. 34-11860.   PS2929.S4   1862

16355   STOCKTON.   A history of the Stockton family.   By J. W. Stockton.   Philadelphia, Press of
Patterson & White, 1881.   70 p., 1 1. incl. front. (coat of arms) 20 cm. Blank pages at end for "Genealogy of the Stockton family."
9-14094.   CS71.S866   1881

16356   STOCKTON.   The Stockton family in England and the United States.   Compiled by William
Francis Cregar.   Philadelphia, Patterson and White, 1888.   cover-title, p. 21-31, 91-118. front. (coat of arms)
28½ cm.   A reprint of the author's "Ancestry of Samuel Stockton White." 1888. 16-2749.   CS71.S866   1888

16357   STOCKTON.   The Stockton genealogy.   By Rev. Elias Boudinot Stockton.   Plate 1 -
generations 1 -   New York, The Genealogical compiling and publishing co., c.1909 -
28½ cm. 10-2130.   CS71.S866   1909

16358   STOCKTON.   The Stockton family of New Jersey, and other Stocktons, by Thomas Coates Stockton ... Washington, D.C., The Carnahan press, 1911.   xxviii p., 1 1., 350 p. front. (coat of arms) plates, ports.,
map. 23½ cm. 11-9936.   CS71.S866   1911

16359   STOCKTON.   Home of Richard Stockton, signer of the Declaration of independence, Princeton,
New Jersey (by) Mable Lorenz Ives ... (Upper Montclair, N.J., Lucy Fortune, c.1932)   3 p. 1., 10 p.
incl. front. (port.) illus. 23 cm. "Pre-print series" of Washington's headquarters series. 33-11649.

E302.6.S85 I9

16360   STOCKTON.   Stockton family.   By Thomas John Hall.   Page 283.   CS71.H177   1941

16361   STOCKTON.   A house called Morven, its role in American history, 1701-1954, by Alfred
Hoyt Bill, in collaboration with Walter E. Edge, with an essay on the architecture by George B. Tatum.
Princton, N.J., Princeton University Press, 1954.   206 p. illus. 23 cm. Includes bibliography. 54-6074.
F144.P9B5

16362   STOCKTON.   The Stockton family of Georgia.   By Charles Sullivan Broward.   (Coral Gables?
Fla., 1962)   27 1. ports., coat of arms, facsims. 28 cm. Caption title. 63-39430.   CS71.S866   1962

16363   STOCKTON.   Life sketches and reminiscences of T. J. Stockton, Sr., written by himself,
Maryville, Mo., 1878.   (Maryville? Leah Hill Moore, 1969)   33, 8, (3) p. 28 cm. Cover title. 79-6607 MARC.
CS71.S866   1969

STOCKTON.   See also: BYRD, E159.G55   SCHOLL, 1940
                          CHASTAIN, DC111.C47   SHEFFIELD, 1929
                          DE RAPELJE, 1948   SHEFFIELD, 1932
                          LARZELERE, 1950   WHITE, 1888
                          MERSHON, 1946

16364   STOCKWELL.   The Stockwell family; adventures into the past: being an account of our research into the history of the Stockwell family.   By Irene Dixon Stockwell.   (Janesville? Wis., 1968)
111 1. 29 cm. Bibliography: leaves 109-111. 79-1225.   CS71.S867   1968

16365   STODDARD.   A genealogy of the family of Anthony Stoddard, of Boston ... Boston, Printed by Coolidge and Wiley, 1849.   23 p. illus. (coat of arms) 24 cm. Compiled by Charles Stoddard and Elijah W. Stoddard. "Rev. and enl. by Elijah W. Stoddard and republished in 1865." 9-14109.   CS71.S869   1849

16366   STODDARD.   Anthony Stoddard, of Boston, Mass., and his descendants: a genealogy.   Originally compiled by Charles Stoddard and Elijah W. Stoddard, and published in 1849.   Rev. and enl. by Elijah W. Stoddard, and republished in 1865 ... New York, Press of J. M. Bradstreet & son, 1865.
2 p. 1., 95 p. illus. (coat of arms) 31 cm. Two portraits inserted between p. 52 - 53 and p. 54-55. 9-14110.   CS71.S869   1865

16367   STODDARD.   Ralph Stoddard, of New London and Groton, Ct., and his descendants: a genealogy.   Compiled by Rev. E. W. Stoddard ... New York, Press of Poole & Maclauchlan, 1872.
2 p. 1., 36, (2) p. illus. (coat of arms) 24 cm. 3-2819.   CS71.S869   1872

16368   STODDARD.   John Stoddard of Wethersfield, Conn., and his descendants. 1642-1872. A genealogy: by D. Williams Patterson ... Author's ed.   (Newark Valley? N.Y.) 1873.
96 p. incl. front. (coat of arms) 24½ cm. Printed for private circulation. 1-13641 rev.   CS71.S869   1873

16369   STODDARD.   Anthony Stoddard, of Boston, Mass., and his descendants: 1639-1873. A genealogy.   Appendix, by E. W. Stoddard ... New York, Press of Poole & Maclauchlan, 1873.
vii, (100)-273, xvi p. front. (coat of arms) port. 25½ cm. Cover-title: Genealogy of the Stoddard family. Appendix. 1639-1873. Appendix to "Anthony Stoddard, of Boston, Mass., and his descendants" originally compiled by Charles Stoddard and Elijah W. Stoddard and pub. in 1849. Rev. and enl. by Elijah W. Stoddard and republished in 1865. Paging continuous with 1865 ed. 14-11907.   CS71.S869   1865
                                                                                                 App.

16370   STODDARD.   Some of the ancestors of Rodman Stoddard, of Woodbury, Conn., and Detroit, Mich.   A compilation by Edward Deacon ... Bridgeport, Conn., Press of Stiles & Tucker, 1893.
86 p. illus., pl., plans, geneal. tables (part fold.) col. coat of arms. 23½ cm. 9-14108.
                                                                                        CS71.S869   1893

16371   STODDARD.   The Stoddard family; being an account of some of the descendants of John Stodder of Hingham, Massachusetts Colony.   Compiled by Francis Russell Stoddard, jr.   New York, The Trow press, 1912.   148 p. 24½ cm. 13-12342.   CS71.S869   1912

16372   STODDARD.   Stoddard-Sudduth papers.   By Mary (Sudduth) Stoddard.   (n. p., 1959 or 60)
281 p. illus. 24 cm. 61-23417.   CS71.S9315

        STODDARD.   See also: BASSETT, 1926
                                  BROWN, E171.A53 vol. 15
                                  FRANCIS, 1933
                                  FRANCIS, 1933a

        STODDER.   See STODDARD.

        STODOLFE.   See STUDWELL.

16373   STOEVER.   A genealogical and biographical sketch of a branch of a family tree; the Stoever family, compiled by Addie Johnston Staver ,,, and Nora Bartholomew King ... from biographies, histories of counties, church records ... with a great many dates transcribed from tombstones in a number of Pennsylvania cemeteries.   (Elmira, N. Y., The Commercial press, 1931)   1 p. 1., 5-64 p.
illus. incl. ports. 23½ cm. Blank pages for additional record (56-64) On cover: 1685-1931. 32-6812.   CS71.S872   1931

STOFFELSEN.   See VAN WINKLE, F116.N36 vol.56

STODGHILL.   See STURGILL, 1960

STOKEPORT.   See NORRES, 1851

16374   STOKES.   American family antqiuity, being an account of the origin and progress of American families, traced from their progenitors in this country, connected with their history abroad ... By Albert Welles ... New York, Society library, 1880-81.   3 v. pl., ports., photos., col. coats of arms.   34½ cm.   "In memoriam: a biographical sketch of Thomas Stokes, by James S. Dickerson, D.D. ": v.1, p. (205)-212.   Contents. - v.1. Washington, Barron, Buell, Cary, Page, Frost, Stokes, Dunbar, Grace. - v.2. Kip, Cooke, Lyon, Kendall, Flower, Starin, Connor, Mortimer. - v.3. Snow, Wheeler, Martin, Conover, Fish. Waterbury, Babcock.   9-25091.   CS69.W5

16375   STOKES.   The pedigree of John Stokes of Seend, co. Wilts.   Edited by Arthur Schomberg, London, Mitchell and Hughes, 1886.   10 p. illus. (coat of arms) 28 cm.   "Reprinted from Miscellanea genealogica et heraldica, vol. II., second series."   17-21451.   CS439.S897

16376   STOKES.   The Ohio branch of the Stokes family.   (Dayton, O., 1899?)   cover-title, 1 p. l., (5)-17, (1) p. 22 cm.   Compiled by William J. Worth Stokes, and distributed in printed form through the generosity of Benjamin A. Stokes, deceased. cf. Pref.   24-6787.   CS71.S874   1899

16377   STOKES.   Genealogy of the Stokes family, descended from Thomas and Mary Stokes who settled in Burlington County, N.J.   Compiled from notes of the late George Haines ... Hon. Charles Stokes ... and other members of the family.   With some additions by the compiler, Richard Haines ... Camden, N.J., S. Chew & sons company, printers, 1903.   2 p. l., 339 (i.e. 381) p. plates, ports., map.   27 cm. With many extra numbered pages.   4-17862.   CS71.S874   1903

16378   STOKES.   Some notes on the Stokes family (counties Wilts and Gloucester).   Reprinted ... from "Wiltshire notes and queries", ed. by Arthur Schomberg.   Devizes, "Gazette" printing works, 1909.   cover-title, 94 p. illus., plates, ports., coats of arms.   29 cm.   Additions and corrections in manuscript.   21-10451.   CS439.S897   1909

16379   STOKES.   Stokes records; notes regarding the ancestry and lives of Anson Phelps Stokes and Helen Louisa (Phelps) Stokes.   In 4 vols.   New York, 1910-15.   3 v. illus., ports., maps, facsims., geneal. tables.   28 cm.   Vol. 2 was never published.   52-54736.   CS71.S874   1910

16380   STOKES.   A little-known adventure of Thomas Stokes - 1665. by Milton Rubincam ... (Newark, N.J., 1938)   p. 73-82.   23 cm.   Caption title.   Detached from the Genealogical magazine of New Jersey.   October 1937.   40M642T.   CS71.S874   1938

16381   STOKES.   A critical analysis of the Stokes pedigree, by Milton Rubincam ... (Newark? N.J., 1941)   cover-title, 20 p.   23 cm.   "Reprinted from Proceedings of the New Jersey historical society, issue of April, 1941."   Bibliographical foot-notes.   41-10333.   CS71.S874   1941

16382   STOKES.   Stokes families (1201-1930)   (By J. Lemacks)   Copied by Mrs. C. F. Rudolph ... from a mimeographed copy in the possession of Mrs. Nora E. Stokes ... (n.p., 1946)   1 p. l., 10, 3 numb. l.   29 x 22½ cm.   Type-written (carbon copy)   Author's name from caption title.   "Page 8, paragraph 4, the marriage, death and children of Thomas Graham Stokes, is an addition to the original copy.   Page 9 and 10, the family of James M. Stokes was added ... in 1930 ... by Mr. James M. Stokes." - p.1.   48-14061.   CS71.S874   1946

        STOKES.   See also: BELL, F232.L9B4   LUMPKIN, 1940
                              DOWLING, 1959   RAND, 1936
                              HALLOWELL, 1924   RAND, 1940
                              LANCASTER, 1902   WASHINGTON, CS69.W5

16383   STOLLENWERCK.   The Stollenwerck, Chaudron & Billon families in America, a narrative with lineage listing 1740 (circa) - 1947, by Frank and Dixie Orum Stollenwerck.   (Baltimore? 1948)   148 p. ports., map (on lining-papers) facsims.   27 cm.   48-4465*.   CS71.S875   1948

        STOLLERY.   See GRINDELL, 1957

STOLP. See LAWSON, 1903

STOMBAUGH. See FISHER, 1950

16383 a STONE. Genealogy of the Stone family originating in Rhode Island. By Richard C. Stone. Providence, Knowles, Anthony and co., 1866.   viii, 193, 12 p. front., port. 23½ cm. 3-3830.
CS71.S88   1866

16384 STONE. The family of John Stone, one of the first settlers of Guilford, Conn. By William L. Stone ... Albany, J. Munsell's sons, 1888.   viii, 184 p. front. (coat of arms) pl., port. 23½ cm. 9-14106.
CS71.S88   1888

16385 STONE. Souvenir of a part of the descendants of Gregory and Lydia Cooper Stone. 1634-1892. By Mrs. John Livingston Stone. (Marlborough? Mass., 1892)   78 p. 18½ x 15½ cm. Blank leaves inserted. 9-14107.
CS71.S88   1892

16386 STONE. The English ancestry of Simon and Gregory Stone. By William E. Stone ... Boston, D. Clapp & son, printers, 1897.   2 p. l., (3)-12 p. 24 cm. A photographic copy of the will of Symond Stone, 1506, is inserted; also, genealogical notes in ms. 17-9745.
CS71.S88   1897

16387 STONE. Records in manuscript of the Stone family in England, copied from wills, registers, etc., accompanied by two registers, etc., accompanied by two volumes of genealogical tables in manuscript) (n. p., n. d.)   5 v. 31 cm. 40M897T.
CS439.S8972
Office.

16388 STONE. Book II. of the family of John Stone, one of the first settlers of Guilford, Conn.; also, names of all the descendants of Russell, Bille, Timothy and Eber Stone. By Truman Lewis Stone. 1639 ... 1897. Buffalo, N. Y., C. W. Moulton, 1898.   x, (2), 339, (9) p. front., plates, ports., coat of arms. 21½ cm. Printed on one side of leaf only. A continuation of W. L. Stone's Genealogy of the Stone family. 1-24381.
CS71.S88   1898

16389 STONE. Simon and Joan (Clarke) Stone of Watertown, Mass., and three generations of their descendants. By David H. Brown ... Boston, Stone family association, 1899.   8 p. 24½ cm. Reprinted from the New-Eng. hist. and geneal. register for July, 1899.   9-14103.
CS71.S88   1899

16390 STONE. Dea. Simon Stone of Watertown, Mass., and some of his descendants. By David H. Brown ... (Boston, 1899)   6, (1) p. 25 cm. Caption title. Specimen of the Register plan for arranging genealogies. Reprinted from the New-Eng. hist. and geneal. register for July, 1899. 10-1493.
CS71.S88   1899a

16391 STONE. Stone family association, 1897-1901. Catalogue of members, with lines of descent. Edited from the membership blanks, by Agnes Wyman Lincoln. Boston, 1901.   92 p. 23½ cm. 17-6155.
CS71.S88   1901

16392 STONE. The Oxford descendants of Gregory Stone of Cambridge, Massachusetts, by George E. Stone. Amherst, Mass., Press of Carpenter & Morehouse, 1904.   iv, 50 p., 1 l. 23½ cm. 5-26774.
CS71.S88   1904

16393 STONE. From generation to generation. The genealogies of Dwight Stone and Olive Evans, compiled by Julia Evans (Stone) Neil. Columbus, O. (The Champlin press) 1907.   169 p. 25 cm. 23-18592.
CS71.S88   1907

16394 STONE. Notes about the family of Stone living some time in the parish of Ardleigh, Essex. Published by the Stone family association. (By Reginal Hall Grubbe) Boston, Press of D. Clapp & son, 1907.   22 p. 23½ cm. The notes gathered by the Rev. R. H. Grubbe and edited by Agnes W. Lincoln. 24-6507.
CS439.S8972

16395 STONE. A stone genealogy, by Daniel C. Stone ... (n. p., 1910)   1 p. l., 7-53 p. front., illus. (coat of arms) port. 24 cm. 20-9255.
CS71.S88   1910

16396   STONE.   Stone family, by Josiah Paine.   Yarmouthport, Mass., C. W. Swift, 1911.
cover-title, 4 l. 25½ cm.   (Library of Cape Cod history & genealogy. no. 93)   12-30948.   CS71.S88   1911

16397   STONE.   Gregory Stone genealogy; ancestry and descendants of Dea. Gregory Stone of
Cambridge, Mass., 1320-1917, by J. Gardner Bartlett ... Boston, The Stone family association, 1918.
vi p., 2 l., 905 p. front., plates. 25 cm. 18-18523.   CS71.S88   1918

16398   STONE.   Simon Stone genealogy: ancestry and descendants of Deacon Simon Stone of Watertown, Mass., 1320-1926.   By J. Gardner Bartlett ... Boston, Stone family association, 1926.
vi p., 2 l., 802 p. front., plates, ports. 24 cm. 27-19490.   CS71.S88   1926

16399   STONE.   ... Stone family records, by J. Montgomery Seaver.   Philadelphia, American historical-genealogical society (1929)   59 p. front. (4 port.) coat of arms. 29 cm. Coat of arms of the Stone family on recto
of frontispiece. Pages 58-59 blank for "Family record". "References": p. 56-57. 40-18925.
CS71.S88   1929

16400   STONE.   The ancestry of Sarah Stone, wife of James Patten of Arundel (Kennebunkport)
Maine, by Walter Goodwin Davis.   Portland, Me., The Southworth press, 1930.   5 p. l., 3-152 p. incl.
geneal. tab. 23 cm. Contains also the Dixey, Hart, Norman, Neale, Lawes, Curtis, Kilborne, Bracy, Bisby, Pearce, Marston, Estow and Brown
families. 31-9482.   CS71.S88   1930

16401   STONE.   The Stones of Poynton manor. A genealogical history of Captain William Stone, gent.
and merchant, third proprietary governor of Maryland, with sketches of his English background and a
record of some of his descendants in the United States, by Harry Wright Newman.   (Washington, D. C.)
The author, 1937.   1 p. l., (vi)-vii, 47 p. coat of arms. 24 cm. "This edition is limited to 200 copies. Your book is numbered 35."
39-9238.   CS71.S88   1937

16402   STONE.   The Stones of Surry.   By Charles Haywood Stone.   Charlotte, N. C., Observer
Print. House (1951)   272 p. illus. 21 cm. 51-35821.   CS71.S88   1951

16403   STONE.   Samuel Stone and his wife, Mary Ann Chunn; a story of their lives, including early
residence in Virginia, Tennessee, and Alabama, their migration to Missouri and later to the Republic
of Texas, with data concerning their family and descendants, and also including some genealogical
history proving the ancestry of Mary Ann Chunn.   By Dolly Mary Stone.   San Antonio, Naylor Co.
(1955)   87 p. 22 cm. 55-13826.   CS71.S88   1955

16404   STONE.   The Stones of Surry.   By Charles Haywood Stone.   Rev. ed.   Charlotte, N. C.,
Observer Print. House, 1955.   499 p. illus., ports., col. coat of arms, geneal. tables. 21 cm. 61-48082.
CS71.S88   1955a

16405   STONE.   Such as I have, give I thee; a history of the east Texas Stones.   By Leila Stone
LaGrone.   Carthage, Tex. (c. 1967)   vii, 175 p. illus., map, ports. 24 cm. Bibliography: p. 145-162. 68-1135.
CS71.S88   1967

16406   STONE.   Sage-Cowan-Stone-Saunders families in North Carolina.   7765
Microfilm reading room.

16407   STONE.   Stone family in vertical file.   Ask reference librarian for this material.

STONE.   See also: BENDALL, 1945   PETTY, BX5195.T5B6
                     BLAKE, 1948   UPTON, 1874
                     McCLARY, E171.S53 vol. 13   WARD, 1930
                     MITCHELL, 1931   WEITZEL, 1883
                     MITCHELL, 1936   No. 516 - Notable southern families.
                     NOWLIN, 1916   vol. 1

16408   STONEBRAKER.   ... A rebel of '61.   By Jos. R. Stonebraker ... New York and Albany,
Wynkoop, Hallenbeck, Crawford co., printers, 1899.   116 p. front., illus. (facsims.) plates, ports., fold. geneal. tab.
23½ cm. 99-3416.   E605.S88

STONEBRAKER.   See also PEASLEE, 1897

STONEHAM.   See: ESPENET, CS439.E82
MANNING, 1956

STONER.   See BOONE, 1922

STONESTREET.   See LEWIS, 1901

16409   STONEY.   Genealogical record of Joseph Stoney of Huddersfield, England, and his descendants.   Comp. by H. T. Cory.   Dec. 1915.   (n. p., 1915)   1 p. l., 13 numb. l.   28½ cm.   Type-written.   21-9019.
CS71.S883   1915

16410   STONEY.   (Genealogy of the Stoney family by William Shannon Stoney.   n. p., 1932)
18 numb. l. incl. mounted port.   28 cm.   Type-written.   32-12877.   CS71.S883   1932

16411   STONG.   The Stong genealogy of Canada and United States (1800-1958.   Toronto, 1958)
79 p. ports.   20 cm.   64-54994.   CS90.S66   1958

16412   STONOR.   Minutes of evidence given before the committee of privileges, to whom the petition of Thomas Stonor, of Stonor, in the county of Oxford, esquire, claiming to be senior co-heir to the barony of Camoys, was referred ... (London, 1839?)   497 (i. e. 499) p.   coats of arms (part fold.)   33½ cm.   (Sessional papers 118.1 - 118.8 of 1838; 167 of 1839) Pages 485-486 repeated in numbering.   Interspersed with blank pages, with addition pedigrees added in ms.   17-23089-90 rev.   CS423.C3G7

—— Camoys peerage.   Supplemental case on behalf of Thomas Stonor of Stonor, in the county of Oxford, esquire, claiming to be senior coheir to the barony of Camoys.   (London, 1839?)
36 p.   33½ cm.   (With Minutes of evidence ... (London, 1839?))   CS423.C3G7

16413   STONOR.   Camoys peerage.   Supplemental case on behalf of Thomas Stonor of Stonor, in the county of Oxford, esquire, claiming to be senior coheir to the barony of Camoys.   (London, 1839?)
36 p.   33½ cm.   17-23089-90   CS423.G3G7

16414   STONOR.   The Stonor letters and papers, 1290-1483; ed. for the Royal historical society, from the original documents in the Public record office, by Charles Lethbridge Kingsford ... London, Offices of the Society, 1919.   2 v.   fronts. (v. 1, map) facsim., fold. geneal. tables.   22 cm.   (Royal historical society. Publications. Camden third series, vol. XXIX-XXX) 21-13590.   DA20.R91 3rd ser.
vol. XXIX-XXX

STOOKEY.   See GOODNER, 1960

16415   STOOPS.   Genealogy of Phillip Stoops, prepared for Wheeler and Stoops reunion.   (n. p., 19 -)
1 p. l., 5-87 p. 22 cm.   "Apology to readers" signed: Frank S. Campbell, Ella Wheller Campbell, Elden A. Robb, committee appointed at the eleventh annual reunion.   37-16973.   CS71.S8835   19 -

STOOTHOOF.   See BERGEN, 1866

16416   STOPPEL.   The Stoppel family in the United States, 1845-1968, by Gerald C. Stoppel (and) Beverly A. Stoppel.   (Rochester? Minn., 1968)   (47) l.   29 cm.   70-3513.   CS71.S8837   1968

16417   STORER.   Annals of the Storer family, together with notes on the Ayrault family, by Malcolm Storer.   Boston, (Wright and Potter) 1927.   107 p. illus. (coats of arms) fold. geneal. tables.   25 cm.   On cover: Storer and Ayrault families.   28-12381.   CS71.S884   1927

16418   STORER.   The Storer family, 1725-1962.   By Mahlon A. Storer.   (Mundelein? Ill., 1963?)
98 l. ports., coat of arms.   29 cm.   Cover title.   64-2150.   CS71.S884   1963

STORER.   See also GOUGH, 1850

STOREY.   See STORY.

16419   STORK.   The Stork family in the Lutheran church: or, Biographical sketches of Rev. Charles Augustus Gottlieb Stork, Rev. Theophilus Stork, D. D., and Rev. Charles A. Stork, D. D., by John·G. Morris ... Philadelphia, Lutheran publication society (c. 1886)   263 p. front. (2 port.) 19½ cm. 12-36862.
BX8080. S75M6

16420   STORK.   The genealogy of the descendants of Moses Stork, Scarborough, Yorkshire, old England, compiled by C. A. Storke.   Santa Barbara, Calif., 1925.   cover-title, 21 p. 19 cm. 37-38432.
CS71. S885   1925

16421   STORK.   The English Storkes in America, compiled by C. A. Storke ... (Santa Barbara, Calif., Printed by the News-press publishing company, c. 1936)   2 p. l., iii, (238) p. front., plates, ports., plan, 2 facsim. 26 cm. Various pagings. Includes blank pages for family records. "References": p. (234) - (237) 36-7387.
CS71. S885   1936

STORKE.   See STORK.

16422   STORM.   Old Dirck's book; a brief account of the life and times of Dirck Storm of Holland, his antecedents, and the family he founded in America in 1662.   By Ravmond William Storm.   (New York?) 1949.   402 p. illus., ports., maps (part col.) 25 cm. Bibliography: p. 402. 49-17661*.   CS71. S8855   1949

STORMS.   See BLAUVELT, 1957

16423   STORR.   Notes on the families of Storr of Hilston and Owstwick in Holderness, in the East Riding of Yorkshire, with pedigrees and fasimile original signatures, compiled by A. B. Wilson-Barkworth ... Cambridge, Macmillan and Bowes, 1890.   2 p. l., 13 p. illus. (incl. coats of arms) fold. facsims., fold. geneal. tab. 30 cm. 24-1601.   CS439. S8973

STORR.   See also STORRS.

16424   STORROW.   Washington Irving and the Storrows; letters from England and the continent, 1821-1828, edited by Stanley T. Williams.   Cambridge, Mass., Harvard university press, 1933.   ix, 136 p. 2 port. (incl. front.) facsim. 21 cm. 33-16815.   PS2081. A47

16425   STORRS.   The Storrs family.   Genealogical and other memoranda collected and compiled by Charles Storrs.   New York, Priv. print., 1886.   xviii p., 1 l., (11)-552 p. front. (port.) geneal. tables, coats of arms. 27½ cm. "Limited edition of five hundred numbered copies. no. 88." 9-14105.
CS71. S886   1886

STORRS.   See also STORR.

16426   STORY.   The family of Story, of Lockington, co. Leicester.   By the Rev. W. G. D. Fletcher ...(Reprinted from the Leicestershire architectural and archaeological society's Transactions.) Leicester, Clarke and Hogson, 1893.   1 p. l., 20 p. 24½ cm. 21-8062.   CS439. S8975   1893

16427   STORY.   Elisha Story of Boston and some of his descendants, comp. by Perley Derby, with additions by Frank A. Gardner, M. D. ... Salem, Mass., Essex institute, 1915.   1 p. l., 28 p. front., ports. 24½ cm. "One hundred copies reprinted from the Historical collections of the Essex institute, volumes L and LI. " 20-9243.
CS71. S887   1915

16428   STORY.   Storeys of old; historical, biographical, and genealogical observations on the Storey and Story family.   Prominent members of the same of the four northern counties - Northumberland, Cumberland, Durham and Westmorland, including the branches settled in Lancaster and Furness. Preston, Exors. of C. W. Whitehead, printers, 1920.   359, xxxvii p. plates, ports., fold. geneal. tables, coats of arms. 31 cm. Lettered on cover: R. E. K. Rigbye (Cross Fleury) The plates are mounted photographs. Books, pamphlets, manuscripts &c consulted and quoted: p. 354-359. Storys of the United States: P. 161-167. Contains also the Patrickson, Sherren and Lushington families. 25-9349.
CS439. S8975   1920

16429   STORY.   The family Storey; George Storey & his descendants, 1725-1955.   Editors: William Millard and Peggy Storey (and others.   Mississippi City, Miss., 1955)   124 p. illus. 29 cm. 55-42370.
CS71. S887   1955

STORY.   See also JELKE, E171. A53 v. 19

16430   STOTESBERY.   Partial genealogy of the Stotesbery family; contains a complete listing of all the descendants of the eight great-grandparents of the author, listed by families, and a partial search of the ancestors of the author as far as records and time permitted prior to date of publication.   By Russell Lorlys Stotesbery.   Minneapolis (1950?)   (a) - c, 35 l. port., geneal. table.   23 cm.   "Corrections": 3 leaves inserted.   52-31764.   CS71. S8872   1950

16431   STOTESBERY.   Genealogy of the Stotesbery family and associated female lines, 1359-1952 AD. By Russell Lorlys Stotesbery.   Rev. (Minneapolis? 1951)   25 l. illus.   29 cm.   52-34241.   CS71. S8872   1951

16432   STOTT.   Stott, Saunders, Converse and allied families; a genealogical record compiled and privately published for Cornelia Saunders Stott by the American historical company, inc.   New York, 1944.   225 p. plates, ports., facsims., col. coats of arms, col. geneal. tables.   32 x 26 cm.   Some of the plates accompanied by guard sheets with descriptive letterpress.   Includes bibliographical references.   45-381.   CS71. S8873   1944

STOTTERNHEIM.   See STUTTERHEIM.

STOUFFER.   See STAUFFER.

STOUGH.   See HESTER, 1905

16433   STOUGHTON.   Descendants of Thomas Stoughton (1600-1661) of Dorchester, Mass.   By George W. Fuller.   Potsdam, N. Y., Herald-recorder press, 1929.   2 p. l., (3)-34 p. 13½ cm. 29-11906.   CS71. S8875   1929

16434   STOUGHTON.   The English ancestry of Thomas Stoughton, 1588-1661, and his son Thomas Stoughton, 1624-1684, of Windsor, Conn.; his brother Israel Stoughton, 1603-1645, and his nephew William Stoughton, 1631-1701, of Dorchester, Mass.   (Supplemented and organized by Ethel Mc-Laughlin Turner and Paul Boynton Turner.   Waterloo? Wis., 1958)   159 p. illus. 24 cm.   58-3992.   CS71. S8875   1958

STOUGHTON.   See also: BARRETT, 1906
                                         JONES, F74. D5C6
                                         NELSON, 1894
                                         PAGE, 1953

16435   STOUT.   The history of the Stout family.   First settling in Middletown, Monmouth County, New Jersey.   (Glenarm, Ill., 1901?)   48 p. 18 cm.   Originally compiled and published, 1823, by Capt. Nathan Stout.   Reprinted in 1878, with additions by Mrs. Sarah Weart and other descendants, and by Joab P. Stout of Glenarkm, Ill., 1901.   cf. ms. note on t. -p.   15-12367.   CS71. S888   1901

16436   STOUT.   The Stout family of Delaware: with the story of Penelope Stout.   Compiled and published by Thomas Hale Streets.   Philadelphia, Pa., 1915.   107 p. 20½ cm.   On cover: Number five.   Some allied families of Kent county, Delaware.   16-2177.   CS71. S888   1915

16437   STOUT.   The history of the Stout family, first settling in Middletown, Monmouth county, New Jersey, in 1666 ... Originally compiled and published in 1823 by Capt. Nathan Stout.   Reprinted in 1878 with additions by Mrs. Sarah Weart and other descendants, and by Joab B. Stout ... in May 1906.   Bethlehem, Pa., G. A. Chandler, 1929.   1 p. l., 32 p. 23 cm.   30-13839.   CS71. S888   1929

16438   STOUT.   The Stout family of New York city and in the state of Kentucky; pedigree, by Ephraim Stout Lillard ... (Washington, D. C., c. 1939)   2 p. l., 2 geneal. tab.   27½ cm.   40-3761.   CS71. S888   1939

16439   STOUT.   Stout and allied families.   By Herald Franklin Stout.   (Dover? Ohio, 194-)   1 v. (various pagings)   maps.   19 cm.   Includes bibliography.   53-50279.   CS71. S888

16440   STOUT.   Richard Stout of New Jersey, a history of patronymic descendants (by) H. F. Stout. (Dover? O.) 1941.   2 p. l., iii, 256 numb. l., 40 l. 27 cm. Type-written. "Source bibliography": leaf ii. 42-7166.
CS71.S888   1941

16441   STOUT.   Stout and allied families.   By Herald Franklin Stout.   (Dover? Ohio, foreword 1943)
75, 343 l. 26 cm. Bibliographical references in foreword. 48-32621*.
CS71.S888   1943

16442   STOUT.   The Stout, Disney, Clinton, Morrison, Grey of Ruthyn Magna carta & royal descent. By Ephraim Stout Lillard ... (Washington, Court of Neptune press, 1945)   cover-title, fold. geneal. tab.
21½ cm. Includes bibliography. 46-23253.
CS71.S888   1945

16443   STOUT.   Genealogy of the Sagers, Fisk, and Stout families.   By Wayne Dunham Stout.   Salt Lake City, 1960.   583 p. illus. 24 cm. 60-39189.
CS71.S888   1960

STOUT.   See also: COX, 1944
CRONE, 1916
CRONE, 1924
EGE, 1911
STAUDT.
STRASSBURGER, 1922

16444   STOUTENBOROUGH.   Stoutenborough history.   By Marie Rybolt.   Kenney, Ill., 1968.
94 p. illus., ports. 29 cm. Cover title: Stoutenborough family history. Bibliography: p. 92-94. 68-7905.
CS71.S889   1968

STOUTENBOROUGH.   See also CRAWFORD, E171.A53 v. 16

STOUVER.   See STOVER.

STOVALL.   See: HEAD, 1963
SCARBOROUGH, 1951

16445   STOVER.   A genealogical record of the descendants of Henry Stauffer and other Stauffer pioneers, together with historical and biographical sketches.   By Rev. A. J. Fretz ... Harleysville, Pa., Press of the Harleysville news, 1899.   371 p. front., plates, ports. 22 cm. Binder's title: The Stauffer-Stover family history. Descendants of Henry Stauffer changed name to Stover, about 1793. Some members of other branches of the family have also made the change. 1-709.
CS71.S89   1899

16446   STOVER.   Stover genealogy, biography and history; a genealogical record of the descendants of William Stover, pioneer, and other Stovers, by Bertha E. Hughey.   Portland, Or., Bertha E. Hughey (c. 1936)   246 p., 2 l. front. (port.) plates, 19¾ cm. "Books of reference": leaf 1 at end. 36-9685.
CS71.S89   1936

STOVER.   See also: GREENLEE, 1956
LINK, 1951
MOHLER, 1958
STAUFFER.
STRICKLER, 1925
VEACH, 1913

STOW.   See STOWE.

16447   STOWE.   Ancestry and some of the descendants of Capt. Stephen Stowe of Milford, Conn. Collected by Nathan Stowe. (Milford, The Lyon quality printer) 1924.   24 p. 22½ cm. 24-12329.
CS71.S892   1924

STOWE.   See also: ADAMS, F104.R3T6   RANNEY, F104.C8A2
CHAFFEE, 1911   SKINNER, 1935
CHAFFEE, 1952   SULLENS, 1942

657

16448   STOWELL.   Condensed genealogy Stowell family with allied families ... Comp. and ed. by Charles Henry Stowell, M.D.   Lowell, Mass., 1912.   18 l. front. (port.) plates, fold. geneal. tab.   24 x 27½ cm. "Outline chart of 'The Stowell family,' 1913": folded genealogical table inserted at end.   "This book is not for sale.   It is printed for private distribution and the edition is limited to 30 copies."   Allied families: Farrow, Cheney, Wiswall, Jackson, Page, Dunster, Lawrence, Washington, Boynton.   14-21196.   CS71.S893   1912

16449   STOWELL.   Stowell genealogy; a record of the descendants of Samuel Stowell of Hingham, Mass., by William Henry Harrison Stowell ... Rutland, Vt., The Tuttle company, 1922. 980 p. front., plates, ports. 24½ cm. 22-14733.   CS71.S893   1922

16450   STOWELL.   Stowell Family Association.   Bulletin, 1925 -   (n. p.)   v. in   illus. 23 cm. Title varies: 1925, Programme. - 1926, Proceedings (of the) annual meeting, - 1927   Annual meeting. (Proceedings) - 19   History (and proceedings)   Bound with various miscellaneous publications of the society.   33-31486 rev.   CS71.S893   1925

16451   STOWELL.   1066 - Stowells in Quantock, England, 1635 - Stowells in Hingham, Mass. 1927 - Stowells in every state of the union, prepared for the third annual meeting of the Stowell family association at the "Old ship" meeting house, Hingham, Mass., Saturday, September 10, 1927 ... by Charles Henry Stowell, M.D.   Lowell, Mass., 1927.   (8) p. illus. 23 cn.   On cover: The Stowell family, 1066 to 1927. 41-31430.   CS71.S893   1927

        STOWELL.   See also STAWELL.

        STOWER.   See NICHOLSON, 1936

        STOWERS.   See STOWER.

16452   STOWITS.   Stowits and Gibson families of the Mohawk valley, by Roderick J. Cant.   St. Johnsville, N.Y., Enterprise & news, 1931.   cover-title, 13 p. illus. 25½ cm. 31-11331.   CS71.S895   1931

        STOY.   See JOHNSON, 1961

16453   STRACHAN.   Memorials of the Scottish families of Strachan and Wise, by the Rev. Charles Rogers ... Printed for private circulation.   (Edinburgh, Printed by M'Farlane and Erskine) 1877. 2 p. l., 123 p. 21½ cm. 1st edition, 1873. 15-23250.   CS479.S73

        STRACHAN.   See also STUART, 1920

16454   STRACHEY.   The Strachey family, 1588-1932; their writings and literary associations.   By Charles Richard Sanders.   (Durham, N.C.) Duke University Press, 1953.   x, 337 p. illus., ports., coat of arms. 24 cm. Bibliographical footnotes. 53-8266.   CS439.S8978   1953

16455   STRACHEY.   Uncommon people; a study of England's élite.   By Paul Bloomfield.   London, H. Hamilton (1955)   xi, 219 p. ports., geneal. tables. 22 cm. 56-18674.   HT647.B55   1955

16456   STRACHEY.   The Strachey family, 1588-1932; their writings and literary associations.   By Charles Richard Sanders.   New York, Greenwood Press, 1968 (c.1953)   x, 337 p. illus., coat of arms, geneal. tables, ports. 24 cm. Bibliographical footnotes. 68-29748.   CS439.S8978   1968

        STRACHEY.   See also No. 430 - Adventurers of purse and person.

        STRAFFORD, earls of.   See WENTWORTH.

16457   STRAHAN.   The story of a printing house; being a short account of the Strahans and Spottiswoodes.   2d ed.   London, Spottiswoode & co., ltd., 1912.   5 p. l., 61, (1) p., 1 l. front., illus., pl., ports., facsims. (part fold.) geneal. tables. 23½ cm. Pref. signed: R. A. A. -L.   i. e. Richard Arthur Austen-Leigh.   13-12897.
                                                                                                         Z325.S76A9

16458   STRANAHAN.   Genealogies of the Stranahan, Josselyn, Fitch and Dow families in North America.   Brooklyn, N.Y., Priv. print. H.M.Gardner, jr., printer) 1868.   126, (2) p. facsims., coats of arms, geneal. tables. 21½ cm. Interleaved.   Two photographs inserted.   200 copies printed.   9-15621.
                                                                                                         CS71.S896   1868

STRANG.   See STRANGE.

16459   STRANGE.   Memoirs of Sir Robert Strange, knt., engraver ... and of his brother-in-law
Andrew Lumisden ... By James Dennistoun ... London, Longman, Brown, Green, and Longmans, 1855.
2 v. gronts., plates. 19½ cm. 11-7899.   NE642.S8D4

16460   STRANGE.   History of the Strang family, by Richard Wynkoop.   (n.p., 1908?)   (60) p. 21½ cm.
Consists of manuscript notes on the Strang family made in a blank book.   L.C. COPY REPLACED BY MICROFILM.   25-19245.
                                                                        CS71.S898   1908
                                                                        Microfilm 8751 CS

16461   STRANGE.   Strange; biographical and historical sketches of the Stranges of America and
across the seas, comp. by Alexander Taylor Strange.   (Hillsboro? Ill.) 1911.   1 p. l., (5)-137. viii p.
illus. (ports.) 23 cm. 15-14795.   CS71.S898   1911

16462   STRANGE.   The Strang genealogy, descendants of Daniel Streing, of New Rochelle, New York,
with special records of the Purdy, Ganung, Kissam, Sackett, Bloomfield, Keeler, Belcher, Morgan,
Whitney and Thorne families, by Josephine C. Frost ... Brooklyn, N.Y., Bowles - printer, 1915.
5 p. l., 190 p.   front. (col. coat of arms) pl. 24½ cm. 15-7828.   CS71.S898   1915

16463   STRANGE.   Jacobean tapestry.   By Nora Kathleen Strange.   London, New York, S. Paul
(1947)   147 p.. ports. 22 cm. 47-29860*.   NE642.S8S8

16464   STRANGEWAYES.   Pedigree of Strangewayes and Morton.   Comp. by George Harrison
Rogers-Harrison ... (London) Priv. print., 1878.   1 p. l., (2) p. front., fold. geneal. tab., coats of arms. 33 cm.
Published also in Miscellanea genealogica et heraldica, 1880, n.s. III, p. 22-24. 20-15252.   CS439.S898

STRANGFORD, Viscounts.   See SMITH.

16465   STRASSBURGER.   The Strassburger family and allied families of Pennsylvania; being the
ancestry of Jacob Andrew Strassburger, esquire, of Montgomery County, Pennsylvania, by his son
Ralph Beaver Strassburger.   Gwynedd Valley, Pa., Printed for private circulation, 1922.   520 p. front.,
illus., plates (1 fold.) ports., fold. geneal. tab., facsims. 27½ cm. 23-17794.   CS71.S899   1922

16466   STRATFORD.   Long forgotten days (leading to Waterloo) by Ethel M. Richardson ... London,
Heath, Cranton limited, 1928.   403 p. front., plates, ports. 22½ cm. Record, based upon letters and seven short diaries written
between 1738 and 1815, of the Irish family of Stratford and its descendants in a female line.   The account closes with a description of the battle of
Waterloo by Sir William Verner, great-grandson-in-law of John Stratford, 1st earl of Aldborough.   30-12239.   CS499.S75

16467   STRATHEARN, Earls of.   Three Celtic earldom, Atholl, Strathearn, Menteith (critical and
historical recital so far as known) by Samuel Cowan ... Edinburgh, N. Macleod, 1909.   109 (1) p. front.
(fold. facsim.) 23 cm. Title vignette. 11-1553.   DA775.C75

STRATHEARN.   See also ALLARDICE, CS478.N5

16468   STRATTON.   Stratton genealogy of Long Island, N.Y.   (n.p., 1901)   2 p. l., (93) p. plates.
22 cm. Preface dated Natchez, Miss., 1901.   Compiled by Sidney Vanuxem Stratton.   Ms. notes by H.P. Gerald.   1-20900.
                                                                        CS71.S9   1901

16469   STRATTON.   A book of Strattons; being a collection of Stratton records from England and
Scotland, and a genealogical history of the early colonial Strattons in America, with five generations of
their descendants; compiled by Harriet Russell Stratton ... New York, The Grafton press, 1908-18.
2 v. fronts.. illus., plates, facsims., geneal. tables (1 fold.) 25 cm. Volume II has imprint: New York, F.H. Hitchcock. 8-22251 rev.
                                                                        CS71.S9   1908

STRATTON.   See also ROBINSON, 1952

16470   STRAUB.   Life and civil war services of Edward A. Straub ... Written by himself.   Milwaukee, Wis., Press of J.H. Yewdale & sons co., 1909.   246 p. front. (port.) 22 cm. Ancestry: p. (7)-18. 18-1485.
                                                                        CT275.S6665

STRAUGHAN.   See STRAWN.

STRAW.   See BLACKMAN, 1894

STRAWBRIDGE.   See STROWBRIDGE.

STRAWN.   See ROBERTS, F159. R48 R6

STRAYHORN.   See CRAIG, 1891

16471   STRECKER.   The Strecker genealogy; history of the descendants of Johann Konrad Strecker of Alsfeld, Germany.   (1st ed.)   By Esther (Ashley) Spousta.   Rogers, Ark., 1955.   91 p.   illus.   21 cm.   56-26181.   CS71.S912   1955

16472   STRECKER.   Strecker genealogy, by Helen L. Hall.   (Hutchinson, Kan. ?) 1966.   xiii, 666 p. illus., col. coats-of-arms, geneal. tables (7 fold. in pocket) fold. map, ports.   29 cm.   "Genealogy of the Strecker family, from a manuscript by Doctor Charles Strecker ... (translated from the) original German version published ... 1896-1897": p. i-xiii, 1-256.   66-29374.   CS71.S912   1966

16472 a   STREET.   Ancestry of Mrs. Levi Parsons Morton (Anna Livingston Reade Street)   By Charlotte L. Livingston.   (n. d.)   92 p. illus., col. coats of arms.   35 cm.   Manuscript.   50-56250.   CS71.S914

16473   STREET.   The Street genealogy.   Compilation begun by Henry A. Street ... Completed, edited and published by Mrs. Mary A. Street ... Exeter, N.H., Printed by J. Templeton, 1895.   viii, 542 p., 1 l. plates (part fold.) ports., coats of arms.   23½ cm.   9-14104.   CS71.S914   1895

STREET.   See also HALE, 1913

16474   STREETER.   Some account of the early Streeters of Massachusetts.   By Edward Doubleday Harris, esq., of Brooklyn, N.Y.   (Boston, 1882)   4 p. 24½ cm.   "Reprinted from the New-England historical and genealogical register for April, 1882."   18-371.   CS71.S915   1882

16475   STREETER.   A genealogical history of the descendants of Stephen and Ursula Streeter of Gloucester, Mass., 1642, afterwards of Charlestown, Mass., 1644-1652.   With an account of the Streeters of Goudherst, Kent, England.   By Milford B. Streeter ... Salem, Mass., E. Putnam, 1896.   xxxvii, 323 p. illus., fold. geneal. tab.   24½ cm.   9-14102.   CS71.S915   1896

16476   STREETER.   Streeter-Adams records from a Streeter family Bible, contributed by Milford B. Streeter ... (Boston, 1931)   4 p. 24½ cm.   "Reprinted from the New England historical and genealogical register for October, 1931."   31-35122.   CS71.S915   1931

16477   STRETCHER.   Allied families of Delaware: Stretcher, Fenwick, Davis, Draper, Kipshaven, Stidham.   By E. J. Sellers.   Philadelphia (Press of J. B. Lippincott co.) 1901.   171 p. illus. 25½ cm.   Edition limited to 200 copies.   1-26937.   F163.S46

16478   STRETLEY.   ... The Stretley family of Bucks, and Oxon, by G. Andrews Moriarty ... (Aylesbury and Tring, G.T. De Fraine & co., ltd., printers, 1939)   p. 379-397. fold. geneal. tab.   25 cm.   Caption title.   "Reprinted from the 'Records of Bucks', vol. XIII, part 6, 1939."   41-31721.   CS439.S8985   1939

16479   STRETTON.   The Stretton manuscripts: being notes on the history of Nottinghamshire, by William Stretton, (of Lenton Priory), died 1828.   Nottingham: Priv. print., 1910.   3 p. l., xiii p., 2 l., 241 p. col. front., illus., 11 pl.   29½ cm.   Edited by G. C. Robertson.   "Stretton of Lenton", a genealogical sketch by John T. Godfrey: p. (i) - xiii.   11-2029.   DA670.N9S7

16480   STREYNSHAM.   Notes relating to the family of Streynsham, of Feversham, Kent.   Originally brought together and comp. by the Rev. G. Streynsham Master, M. A., 1874.   With additional information collected by General Sir Anthony B. Stransham, K. C. B., a descendant of that family, between 1874 and 1879 ... (London) Mitchell & Hughes, 1879.   59 p. illus. (coats of arms, facsims.) 28½ cm.   "18 copies printed for private circulation only."   Contains also ... Towneley, Bugge, Vah'n, Wightman and Bayfield families.   20-19567.   CS439.S899

STREYNSHAM.   See also MASTER, CS439.M36

16481   STRIBLING.   Stribling and related families.   By Mary Frances Stribling Moursund.   (Austin,
Texas, Printed by Von Boeckmann-Jones Co., 1967)   144 p. illus., coats of arms (on lining papers), ports. 24 cm.
68-1355.   CS71.S9155   1967

STRIBLING.   See also: CARPENTER, 1959
                        KINNEY, 1903
                        VAWTER, 1905

16482   STRICKLAND.   Sizergh castle, Westmorland, and notes on twenty-five generations of the
Strickland family.   Compiled by the Lady Edeline Strickland.   Kendal, T. Wilson, 1898.
1 p. l., 12, (24) p. illus. 30½ cm. 24-2118.   CS439.S8995

16483   STRICKLAND.   The Strickland family of Georgia and Wilson Strickland of Gwinnett co., Ga.,
genealogy, copyrighted ... by Fitzhugh Lee.   Covington, Ga., c.1939.   cover-title, 11 p. 23 cm. 39-16995.
                                                                          CS71.S916   1939

16484   STRICKLAND.   The early history of the Stricklands of Sizergh, together with some account
of the allied families of d'Eyncourt, Fleming, Greystoke, and Dunbar, by S. H. Lee Washington ...
Boston, Mass., The Rumford press (1942)   5 p. l., 9-100 p. front. (facsim.) pl., port., geneal. tables. 23½ cm.
"First published 1942." "Reprinted with additions, from the New England historical and genealogical register." Bibliographical foot-notes.
43-46265 rev.   CS71.S916   1942

16485   STRICKLAND.   Strickland; more particularly the descendants of William George Strickland.
By Esther (Birch) Kelso.   (Rehoboth Beach? Del., 1964)   ix, 249 p. illus., coat of arms, ports. 24 cm. Includes
music. 65-3069.   CS71.S916   1964

16486   STRICKLAND.   Strickland and allied families query and answer exchange.   This is a family
association bulletin.   In vertical file.   Ask reference librarian for this material.

STRICKLAND.   See also EAVENSON, 1933

16487   STRICKLER.   Forerunners; a history or genealogy of the Strickler families, their kith and
kin, including Kauffmans, Stovers, Burners, Ruffners, Beavers, Shavers, Brumbachs, Zirkles,
Blossers, Groves, Brubakers, Neffs, Rothgebs and many other early families of Shenandoah, Rockingham, Augusta, Frederick and Page counties of the Shenandoah Valley; a memorial to those who have
gone before, by Harry M. Strickler.   From about 1700 to the present time, 1924 ... (Harrisonburg,
Va., H.M. Strickler, c.1925)   2 p. l., xv, (2)-425, (3) p. front. (coat of arms) plates, ports., facsim. 22 cm. Blank pages
for "Memorandum" (3 at end) 25-19754.   CS71.S917   1925

16488   STRICKLER.   Stricklers of Pennsylvania; a history of the Strickler families who emigrated
from Switzerland and settled principally in Bucks, Lancaster, York and Lebanon counties in Pennsylvania, by Abigail H. Strickler, Jacob S. Strickler, Alice N. Strickler (and) Mame E. Strickler.   (Scottdale, Penna.) The Strickler reunion association of Pennsylvania (Printed by the Mennonite publishing
house) 1942.   5 p. l., 420 p. front., illus. (facsim., coat of arms) plates, ports. 23½ cm. Begun by Mrs. Abigail M. Strickler, completed by Alice N. Strickler and Mame E. Strickler; the data of Henry Strickler, son of the immigrant, gathered by Jacob S. Strickler. 42-17214.
                                                                          CS71.S917   1942

16489   STRICKLER.   Daniel and Mary Strickler, pioneers; a family record for Daniel and Mary
Hammaker Strickler, Pennsylvania Dutch pioneers of 1839, Wayne County, Indiana, with illustrations,
history of the Strickler family and other background information.   By Kenneth J. Nicholson and Frances
Fouts Wilson.   (Flagstaff, Ariz.) 1964.   1 v. (various pagings) illus., maps, ports. 28 cm. Includes bibliography.
65-2747.   CS71.S917   1964

16490   STRIEBY.   Strieby genealogy and history 1726-1967.   Compiled by Byard B. Strieby, B.
Beatrice Strieby (and) Irene M. Strieby.   Des Moines (1967)   xii, 252 p. coat of arms, facsims., maps. 28 cm.
68-5478.   CS71.S9173   1967

STRIKER.   See STRYKER.

STRINGER. See: POT, 1935
SCARBOROUGH, 1951
SIMPSON, 1927

16491   STRITE.   The history and genealogical records of the Strite and allied families of Lancaster, Dauphin, and Franklin Counties, Pa. and Washington County, Md.   Compiled by Carl E. Robinson and Amos W. Strite.   (Hagerstown, Md., A Strite) 1963.   815 p. illus. 22 cm. 64-5328.

CS71.S9176   1963

16492   STRITTMATTER.   A Strittmatter family tree, compiled by Rev. Blase Strittmatter ... (Latrobe, Pa., c.1936)   45, 45a, 45a, 46-76, 46-76, 77-91 p. ports. 28½ cm. Mimeographed. CA36-164 unrev.

CS71.S92   1936

STROBRIDGE.   See STROWBRIDGE.

STRODE.   See: DRAPER, 1964
STROUD.

16493   STRONG.   Centennial celebration of the town of Orford, N.H., containing the oration, poems and speeches, delivered on Thursday, September 7, 1865, with some additional matters relating to the history of the place.   (Manchester, N.H., H.A.Gage, printer, 1865)   145 p. 21½ cm. "Biographical sketches": p. (103)-142. "Soldiers from Orford who served in the late war": p. 143-144. Bound at end: Strong (family): (2) p.; Sawyer (family): 1 l. 1-10780.

F44.O606

16494   STRONG.   The history of the descendants of Elder John Strong, of Northampton, Mass.   By Benjamin W. Dwight ... Albany, N.Y., J. Munsell, 1871.   2 v. ports. 23½ cm. Paged continuously. 9-14101.

CS71.S923   1871

16495   STRONG.   Stemmata Strongeania; or, The heraldic annals of the Strong family.   Together with heraldic and genealogical notes on Burley, Mayhew, Peyton, Manson, Echlin, Clinton, Maxwell, Barrett, Jenks, Rust, and other families with whom they are matrimonially allied ... London, E. T. Sutton, 1912.   (4) p., 7 l., (6), 12 p. illus. (coats of arms) pl. 20½ cm. 25-25324.   CR1629.S8S8

16496   STRONG.   The Strongs of Strongsville, descendants of John Stoughton Strong and Eliphalet Strong.   Supplementary to the History of the Strong family, by Benjamin W. Dwight.   By Albert Strong.   Fort Dodge, Ia., 1931.   91 p. incl. front. (port.) plates. 24 cm. 32-24483.   CS71.S923   1931

16497   STRONG.   The Strongs of Loudonville, Ohio, descendants of Elder John Strong, compiled by Earl Poe Strong.   (Mansfield, O., The author) 1936.   73 numb. l. incl. 1 illus., ports., coats of arms. 28 cm. Mimeographed. Includes bibliographies. 37-423.   CS71.S923   1936

16498   STRONG.   Capt. John Strong of Thetford, Vermont, and some of his descendants... Compiled by Mrs. May (Tibbetts) Jarvis ... (San Diego, Calif., 1940?)   45 l. mounted port., coat of arms. 28 cm. Caption title. On cover: The Strong family, 1630 to 1940. Type-written. 41-16670.

CS71.S923   1940

STRONG.   See also: BISSELL, 1927   MINER, 1901
CALVERT, DA536.C2R5   PERRY, 1878
CARPENTER, 1930   RAND, 1936
GRANNIS, 1929   RAND, 1940
HERKIMER, 1903   STEVENS, 1956
LANE, 1941

STROOP.   See BELL, 1960

16499   STROTHER.   The Strothers of Alnwick, Bilton, and Newton on the Moor, Northumberland.   Compiled by A. Strother ... London, Mitchell and Hughes, 1891.   19 p. incl. geneal. tab. 28 cm. 2-30578.

CS439.S9

16500   STROTHER.   William Strother, of Virginia, and his descendants.   By Thomas McAdory Owen ... Harrisburg, Pa., Harrisburg publishing co., 1898.   cover-title, (27)-51 p. 25½ cm.   From Publications of the Southern history association, April, 1898.   9-14100.   CS71.S925   1898

16501   STROTHER.   William Strother, of Virginia, and his descendants.   By Thomas McAdory Owen.   (In Southern history association. Publications. Washington, D.C., 1898.   24 cm.   v.2, p. (149)-173)   15-21036.
                                                                                                                        F206.S73 vol. 2

16502   STROTHER.   Strother's journal, written by a tradesman of York and Hull, 1784-1785.   Ed. by Caesar Caine ... London, A. Brown & sons, ltd. (1912)   xi, 138 p. front., illus., plates, port., maps. 19 cm.   Contents - pt. I. Notes by the editor on the word and family "Strother." - pt. II. The journal (with notes) - pt. III. The Strother pedigree.   12-24692   DA690.H9S8

16503   STROTHER.   The Strother family and their Campbell-Cummings connections, compiled by Adeline Strother Hutchinson ... (Saint Louis, Armet publishing & printing co., 1939)   56 p. 23 cm.   "Prepared for publication by Anita Calvert Bourgeoise."   40-2254.   CS71.S925   1939

            STROTHER.   See also: BUCKNER, 1907
                                       CARR, 1893
                                       JOHNSTON, 1897
                                       TAYLOR, 1898

16504   STROUD.   The Strouds; a colonial family of English descent, by A. B. Stroud.   Lakeland, Fla., The Child printery, 1919.   263 p. plates, ports., coats of arms. 23½ cm.   Pages 239-246 left blank for "Family history," "Births," "Marriages," and "Deaths."   20-7233.   CS71.S9255   1919

16505   STROUD.   The Stroud family history, descendants of Captain Richard Stroud of New London, Connecticut, by Harriet D. Lowell.   Rutland, Vt., The Tuttle company, 1934.   40 p. front., ports. 23 cm.   35-9804.   CS71.S9255   1934

16506   STROUD.   Strode and Stroud families in England and America.   By James Strode Elston. Rutland, Vt., Tuttle Pub. Co. (1949)   123 p. geneal. table. 24 cm.   Bibliography: p. (102)-110.   50-344.
                                                                                                                        CS71.S9255   1949

16507   STROUD.   A saga of Strouds & Strodes.   By Octavia (Jordan) Perry.   (Baltimore, 1966) v, 159 p. illus., coats of arms, ports. 24 cm.   66-30462.   CS71.S9255   1966

16508   STROUSE.   Genealogical material concerning the families of Valentine Strouse and Charles Ruggles and Valentine's father, Joseph (Strauss) Strouse of Dry Run Road, Pine City, near Elmira, New York (by Walter and Leah Strouse.   Elmira? N.Y.) 1966.   1 v. (various pagings) 28 cm.   Cover title. 66-8130.
                                                                                                                        CS71.S9257   1966

16509   STROWBRIDGE.   Genealogy.   Strobridge Morrsion or Morison Strawbridge.   By Mrs. Mary Stiles (Paul) Guild ... Lowell, Mass., Vox populi press, S.W.Huse & co., 1891.   xviii p., 1 l., 299 p. front., pl., ports., coat of arms. 24 cm.   "Edition limited to 500 copies. no. 44." "Part two. Genealogy of the descendants of William and Sarah (Montgomery) Morrison ...: p. (157)-226.   "A partial genealogy of the Strawbridge family in America": p. (227)-280.   9-14098.
                                                                                                                        CS71.S926   1891

16510   STRUTHERS.   Descendants of James Struthers and Mary Watson, compiled by J. Dean Bacon. Chicago, Ill. (1935)   18 p. 24 cm.   On cover: Struthers genealogy. 36-3769.   CS71.S927   1935

16511   STRUTHERS.   The Struthers family.   (Minneapolis, Minn., University printing co., 1938) cover-title, 47, (1) p. port., fold. geneal. tab. 19½ cm.   Foreword signed: Frank Struthers. 40-2274.   CS71.S927   1938

            STRUTHERS.   See also BACON, 1958

16512   STRUTT.   The Strutt family of Terling, 1650-1873, by Charles R. Strutt.   (London, Printed by Mitchell, Hughes & Clarke) 1939.   vii, 113 p. illus., fold. geneal. table, ports. 28 cm.   Bibliographical footnotes.   76-217295 MARC.   CS439.S913   1939

STRÝCKER.   See STRYKER.

16513   STRYKER.   Genealogical record of the Strÿcker family.   Compiled by William S. Stryker ...
Printed for private distribution.   Camden, N.J., S. Chew, printer, 1887.   112 p. 23½ cm.   An edition of 300
copies printed.   no. 206.   L. C. COPY REPLACED BY MICROFILM.   9-15617.   CS71.S928   1887
                                                                                                                Microfilm 13555 CS

STRYKER.   See also: BUTLER, 1919
                        MOTT, 1898
                        No. 9847 - Hackettstown.

STUARD.   See STUART.

16515   STUART.   The Stewarts.   Edinburgh.   v. 22 cm.   Published for the Stewart society.   55-35398.
                                                                                                                CS479.S748

16516   STUART.   A chronological, genealogical and historical dissertaion of the royal family of the
Stuarts, beginning with Milesius, the stock of those they call the Milesian Irish, and of the old
Scottish race; and ending with His present Majesty K. James the 3d of England and Ireland, and of
Scotland the 8th.   By Mathew Kennedy ... Paris, L. Coignard, 1705.   249, (3) p. 19 cm.   A10-2534.
                                                                                                                CS479.S75   1705

16517   STUART.   A genealogical history of the royal and illustrious family of the Stewarts, from the
year 1034 to the year 1710.   Giving an account of the lives, marriages, and issue of the most remarkable persons and families of that name, to which are prefixed, fisrt(!) a general description of the shire
of Renfrew, the peculiar residence and ancient patrimony of the Stewarts; and, secondly, a deduction
of the noble and ancient families, proprietors there for upwards of 400 years, down to the present
times ... Edinburgh, Printed by J. Watson, 1710.   4 p. l., 95, 90, (2) p. 30 cm.   Dedication signed: George Crawfurd.
14-15113.   CS479.S75   1710

16518   STUART.   A genealogical and historical account of the illustrious name of Stuart.   From the
first original to the accession to the imperial crown of Scotland.   Being the long-expected work of that
great antiquary, David Symson, M. A., historiographer royal for Scotland.   Edinburgh, D. Freebairn
and H. Knox, 1712.   2 p. l., (8), 155 p. 18½ cm.   16-9136.   CS479.S75   1712

16519   STUART.   The divine catastrophe of the kingly family of the house of Stuarts: or, A short
history of the rise, reigne, and ruine thereof.   Wherein the most secret and chamber abominations of
the two last kings are discovered, divine justice in King Charles his overthrow vindicated, and the
Parliaments proceedings against him clearly justified.   By Sir Edward Peyton ... London, T. Warner,
1731.   2 p. l., 68 p. 19½ cm.   4-35283.   DA375.P5

16520   STUART.   An historical genealogy of the royal house of Stuarts, from the reign of K. Robert
II, to that of K. James VI.   Taken from the most authentic authors, both Scotch and English.   By the
Rev. Mark Noble ... London, Printed for R. Faulder, 1795.   8 p. l., 312 p. front., plates, fold. geneal. tab.
28½ cm.   Clipping inserted: The royal family and clan of Stewart with col. coat of arms.   10-11654.
                                                                                                                CS479.S75   1795

16521   STUART.   Genealogical history of the Stewarts, from the earliest period of their authentic
history to the present times.   Containing a particular account of the origin and successive generations
of the Stuarts of Darnley, Lennox, and Aubigny, and of the Stuarts of Castelmilk; with proofs and references; an appendix of relative papers; and a supplement ... By Andrew Stuart ... London, Printed
for A. Strahan (etc.) 1798.   xxiii, 468 p. fold. geneal. tab. 29 x 22½ cm.   8-17000.
                                                                                                                DA758.3.S8S8

16522   STUART.   Supplement to the Genealogical history of the Stewarts, with corrections and
additions: and containing answers to an anonymous attack on that history, published at Edinburgh in
February 1799, under the title of "The genealogical history of the Stewarts refuted."   By Andrew
Stuart ... London, Printed for T. Cadell jun. and W. Davies, 1799.   iv, 106 p., 1 l. incl. geneal. tables.
29 x 22½ cm.   8-17001.   DA758.3.S8S8a

16523   STUART.   The genealogy of the Stewarts refuted: in a letter to Andrew Stuart ... (By Sir Henry Steuart)   Edinburgh, Printed for Bell & Bradfute; (etc., etc.) 1799.   viii, (3)-169 p., 1 l. fold. geneal. tab.   23 cm.   Bibliographical foot-notes.   28-5249.

CS479.S75   1799

16524   STUART.   A genealogical account of the royal house of Stuart, kings of Scotland, from the year 1043, to its union with the English crown, in the reign of James the Sixth, king of Scotland: also from that time to the commencement of the illustrious house of Brunswick, and down to the present period.   By Thomas Waterhouse ... Grantham, Printed for the author by R. Storr, 1816.   xi, (13)-120 p., 1 l. fold. geneal. tab.   23½ cm.   10-11537.

CS479.S75   1816

16525   STUART.   A general description of the shire of Renfrew, including an account of the noble and ancient families ... To which is added, a genealogical history of the royal house of Stewart, and of the several noble and illustrious families of that name, from the year 1034 to the year 1710 ... Published in 1710, by George Crawfurd ... and continued to the present period, by George Robertson ... Paisley, Printed by J. Neilson, sold by H. Crichton; (etc., etc.) 1818.   16, (9)-522 p., 1 l. front., 3 pl., 2 fold. maps, fold. facsim.   29 cm.   Includes reprint of original t. - p.: A genealogical history of the royal and illustrious family of the Stewarts ... Edinburgh, 1710.   3-29092.

DA880.R4C83

16526   STUART.   The Salt foot controversy, as it appeared in Blackwoods' magazine; to which is added A reply to the article published in no. XVIII of that work; with other extracts, and an appendix, containing some remarks on the present state of the Lyon office ... (By John Riddell)   (n. p., 1819?)   iv, 125, (1) p.   23 cm.   "Only 100 copies printed."   Preface signed: J. R.   Contains the letter by Candidus (pseud.) concerning the descent of the Stewarts of Allanton and reply, also Letter to Sir Henry Stewart, bart., with Remarks on the letter by George Robertson.   20-15233.

CS479.S75   1819

16527   STUART.   The Coltness collections, M. DC. VIII. - M. DCCC. XL. ... (Edinburgh) Printed for the Maitland club, 1842.   xxii p., 2 l., 438 p. facsims., fold. geneal. tables.   27 x 22 cm.   (The Maitland club. (Publications. no. 58))   Preface signed: James Dennistoun.   Presented to the club by James Bogle.   Contents. - Preface. - 1. Memorials of the Stewarts of Allanton, Coltness, and Goodtrees, by Sir Archibald Stewart Denham, 1608-1698. - 2. A journey in England, Holland and the Low Countries, by Mrs. Calderwood of Polton, 1756. - 3. Memoir of Sir James Steuart Denham, bart of Coltness and Westshield, compiled for the Lady Frances Steuart (by Dr. Kippis), 1713-1780. - 4. Notices of the family of Coltness and its descendants, collected from original sources by the editor, 1630-1840. - Appendix.   17-4.

DA750.M3 no. 58

16528   STUART.   The descendants of the Stuarts.   An unchronicled page in England's history.   By William Townend.   2d edition with additions.   London, Longman, Brown, Green, Longmans, & Roberts, 1858.   2 p. l., iii, (iii)-xxx, 346 p. 2 port. (incl. front.) fold. geneal. tables.   22 cm.   3-32651.

DA814.A1T7

16529   STUART.   The red book of Grandtully, by William Fraser ... Edinburgh, 1868.   2 v. plates, ports., facsims., col. coat of arms.   25½ cm.   Title in red within ornamental border.   "Impression: One hundred copies ... Printed for Sir William Drummond Steuart, baronet of Grandtully.   no. 51."   Contents. - I. Introduction.   Memoirs.   Charters.   Pedigrees. - II. Letters.   11-21779.

DA758.3.S8F7

16530   STUART.   Lives of the last four princesses of the royal house of Stuart.   By Agnes Strickland ... London, Bell and Daldy, 1872.   xxviii p., 1 l., 377 p. front. (port.) 20½ cm.   Contents. - Mary, princess-royal of Great Britain, eldest daughter of Charles I. - Princess Elizabeth, second daughter of Charles I. - Princess Henrietta Anne, youngest daughter of Charles I. - Louisa Maria, youngest daughter of James II.   5-948.

DA377.1.S9

16531   STUART.   Historic memorials of the Stewarts of Forthergill, Perthshire and their male descendants; with an appendix containing title-deeds and various documents of interest in the history of the family; edited by Charles Poyntz Stewart ... Edinburgh (etc.) Printed for private circulation by W. & A. K. Johnston, 1879.   iv, (4), 161 p. front., plates, fold. facsims., geneal. tables (part fold.) col. coats of arms.   28 cm.   14-15112.

CS479.S75   1879

16532   STUART.   The Stewarts of Appin.   By John H. J. Stewart, F. S. A. Scot., and Lieut-Col. Duncan Stewart ... Edinburgh, Printed for private circulation by Maclachlan and Stewart, 1880.   1 p. l., 214 p. col. front., illus., pl., col. coats of arms.   27½ x 22½ cm.   3-12069 rev.

CS479.S75   1880

16533   STUART.   Pedigree of the house of Stewart.   N.B. - This pedigree, founded upon the accounts printed in Wood's edition of Douglas' peerage and other printed books (with some corrections and additions), was compiled for the Stewart exhibition, by W.A.Lindsay ... London and Bungay, R. Clay and sons, limited (1889?)   geneal. tab. col. coat of arms.   66 x 130 fold. to 24 x 19½ cm.   6-45683.

CS479.S75   1889

16534   STUART.   The royal house of Stuart; illustrated by a series of forty plates in colours drawn from relics of the Stuarts by William Gibb.   London, 1890.   3 p. l., 40 col. pl. 44½ x 31½ cm.   The introductions to the plates by Sir John Skelton.   In portfolio.   3-30578.

DA958.3.S8G5

16535   STUART.   The Stuart dynasty: short studies of its rise, course and early exile.   The latter drawn from papers in Her Majesty's possession at Windsor castle.   By Percy M. Thornton ... London, W. Ridgway, 1890.   xxv p., 1 l., 491, (1) p. front., ports., fold. geneal. tab. 23½ cm. 1-19156.

DA958.3S8T5

16536   STUART.   Some account of the Stuarts of Aubigny, in France, (1422 - 1672.)   By Lady Elizabeth Cust.   London, Priv. print. at the Chiswick press, 1891.   4 p. l., 130 p., 1 l. front., 2 fold. geneal. tab. 22 cm. "250 copies only printed." 14-21093.

CS479.S75   1891

16537   STUART.   The Isle of Bute in the olden time; with illustrations, maps, and plans, by James King Hewison ... Edinburgh and London, W. Blackwood and sons, 1893-95.   2 v. illus., 25 pl. (incl. col. front., v.2) 2 maps (incl. front., v.1) plans, 2 facsim., 3 geneal. tab. 25 cm. 4-8045.

DA880.B9H6

16538   STUART.   Genealogical history of the Duncan Stuart family in America.   Our branch and its connections.   Together with a tracing of the ancestry and origin of the various branches.   By Joseph A. Stuart.   (n.p.) Caxton press, 1894.   1 p. l., 183 p. front., illus. (incl. coat of arms, facsim.) port. 19 cm.   The coat of arms, and 2 illus. of Stuart plaid are colored.   Text includes genealogical tables.   15-8351.

CS71.S93   1894

16539   STUART.   History and geanology (!) of the Stewart, Elliott and Dunwody families.   By Joseph Gaston Bulloch ... Savannah, Ga., Print of Robinson printing house, 1895.   1 p. l., 23 p. 22½ cm.   "Stacy family": p. (22)-23. 3-26847.

CS71.S93   1895

16540   STUART.   An old Stuart genealogy.   A paper read before ye Sette of odd volumes, February 5th, 1897 ... By Marcus B. Huish ... arts-man ... London, Imprynted at ye Bedford press, 1898.   48 p. front. (fold. facsim.) 3 pl. 14½ x 11½ cm.   (Half-title: Privately printed opuscula of ye Sette of odd volumes, no. XLIV)   Plates accompanied by guard sheets with descriptive letterpress.   "This edition is limited to 249 copies, and is imprynted for private circulation only. no. 31."   "The document ... purports to be 'the genealogy of Robert Steward, late Lord Prior but first Dean of Ely, taken from the Heralds office anno one thousand five hundred and twenty-five.' " 17-17598.

AC1.S5 no. 44

——— Copy 2.

CS479.S75   1898

16541   STUART.   The Stewarts of Coitsville, a history of Robert and Sarah Stewart of Adams county, Pa., and their descendants, with a part of their ancestors.   Youngstown, O., T. Kerr & son, printers, 1899.   190, (8) p. plates, ports., plan. 28 cm.   Published by a committee consisting of Mrs. Sallie Giesy Stewart, Miss Alice Caroline Stewart. Rev. J.A.Bailey and Hugh T. Stewart. - cf. Note. 37-21330.

CS71.S93   1899

16542   STUART.   Studies in peerage and family history.   By J. Horace Round ... Westminster, A. Constable and company, ltd., 1901.   xxxi, 496 p. front. 23 cm.   Contents. - The peerage. - The origin of the Stewarts. - The counts of Boulogne as English lords. - The family of Ballon and the conquest of South Wales. - Our English Hapsburgs. - The origin of the Russells. - The rise of the Spencers. - Henry VIII. and the peers. - Charles I. and Lord Glamorgan: pt. 1. Glamorgan's dukedom. pt. 2. Glamorgan's treaty. - The abeyance of the barony of Mowbray. - The succession to the crown. 2-25354.

CS421.R8

16543   STUART.   The story of the Stewarts ... Printed for the Stewart society.   Edinburgh, G. Stewart & co., 1901.   3 p. l., 194 p., 1 l. front., 4 geneal. tab. 26 x 20½ cm.   By James King Stewart.   Title vignette.   "Authorities for the story," p. (3) 4-849.

DA758.3.S8S7

16544   STUART.   The Stuarts, being illustrations of the personal history of the family (especially Mary queen of Scots) in XVIth, XVIIth and XVIIIth century art; portraits, miniatures, relics, &c. from the most celebrated collections.   By J. J. Foster ... London, Dickinson's; New York, E. P. Dutton & Co., 1902.   2 v. cxxix pl. (incl. fronts., illus., ports., maps, facsims.) 39½ cm.   "The author's edition of this work consists of five

16544 continued: hundred and fifty copies of which this is no. 61." "A short biographical summary of the sovereign Stuarts. Genealogical table": v.1, p. (xii) - (xiv) "Portraits of Mary Stuart": v.2, p. (139)-150. 3-15102.

DA758.3.S8F5

16545   STUART.   Genealogy of the Stuard family in America, comp. by Edward H. Young.   (Washington? D.C.) 1903.   cover-title, 1 p.l., 13, (1) p. 23½ cm. 3-32789 rev.

CS71.S93   1903

—— Supplement.   Copyrighted ... by Edward H. Young.   Washington, D.C. c.1922.
6 l. 28 cm. Autographed from type-written copy.

CS71.S93
Suppl.

16546   STUART.   The Jacobite peerage, baronetage, knightage and grants of honour; extracted, by permission from the Stuart papers now in possession of His Majesty the king at Windsor castle, and supplemented by biographical and genealogical notes, by the Marquis of Ruvigny and Raineval ... Edinburgh and London, T.C. & E.C. Jack, 1904.   xvii, (1) p., 1 l., 266, (1) p. 28½ cm. 4-17247.

CS474.R8

16547   STUART.   Genealogy and biography of the descendants of Walter Stewart of Scotland, and of John Stewart, who came to America in 1718, and settled in Londonderry, N.H., by Frank Severance ... Greenfield, Mass. (Printed by T. Morey & son) 1905.   xi, 215 p. ports., facsims. 19½ cm. "Edition limited to 100." This copy not numbered. 5-5433.

CS71.S93   1905

16548   STUART.   The heraldry of the Stewarts, with notes on all the males of the family, descriptions of the arms, plates and pedigrees, by G. Harvey Johnston ... Edinburgh and London, W. & A. K. Johnston, limited, 1906.   3 p. l., iii-viii, (3), 12-92 p. illus., VIII col. pl. 26½ cm. "220 copies of this work have been printed, of which only 200 will be offered to the public." "Some Stewart books": p. 86. 10-25804.

CR1669.S8J7

16549   STUART.   The Stuarts, being outlines of the personal history of the family, illustrated from portraits, miniatures, &c., in the most celebrated collections, by J. J. Foster ... London, Dickinsons, 1907.   6 p. l., 250 p. front., illus., ports. facsims. 30 cm. "A short biographical summary of the sovereign Stuarts": leaves (6) - (7) Carefully revised, with some omissions from the two volume folio edition, published in 1902. 19-1534.

DA758.3.S8F6

16550   STUART.   Colonel George Stewart and his wife Margaret Harris, their ancestors and descendants with appendixes of related families ... a genealogical history, by Robert Stewart ... Lahore, India, Printed at the "Civil and military gazette" press, 1907.   5 p. l., (3)-522 p. front., plates, ports. 27 cm. 9-5231.

CS71.S93   1907

16551   STUART.   ... Exhibition of Stuart and Cromwellian relics and articles of interest connected with the Stuart period, at the Guildhall, Cambridge, May 15-20, 1911. (Cambridge, Deighton, Bell & co.; (etc., etc.) 1911.   21, (3), 102 p. incl. geneal. tables. front., pl., 2 port. 21½ cm. 11-32339.

DA380.C3

16552   STUART.   Reminiscences, by James Stuart.   London, Printed for private circulation at the Chiswick press, 1911.   xv, (1), 302 p., 1 l. front., plates, ports. 22½ cm. "Preface by the compiler" signed: Helen Caroline Colman. Pedigree tables of James Stuart and Laura Elizabeth Colman: p. 283-285. 19-3351.

DA565.S87A3

16553   STUART.   Stuart: Freeman: Parry: Pyke families. (London, Athenaeum press, 1911)
cover-title, 6 p. 16 cm. Signed: Eugene F. McPike. "Reprinted from Notes and queries, August 26, 1911. (II S. IV 164)" 25-21024.

CS439.S915   1911

16554   STUART.   Stuart: Freeman: Day: Pyke families. (By Eugene Fairfield McPike) (London, Athenaeum press, 1912)   cover-title, 6 p. 16 cm. "Reprinted from Notes and queries, July 13, 1912. (II S. VI. 25)" 25-20784.

CS439.S915   1912

16555   STUART.   Genealogy of Hugh Stewart and descendants, compiled by Francenia Stewart White, Esther Stewart Hunt, Emma Stewart Lyman, 1892-1895; 1912.   Columbus, O., The F. J. Heer printing company, 1914.   xv p. 2 l., 181, 12 p. front., plates, ports., coat of arms. 23 cm. Record of the family of Joseph S. Gillespie (incomplete): 12 p. at end. 28-25736.

CS71.S93   1914

16556   STUART.   ... History of the Stewart or Stuart family, by Henry Lee.   New York, R. L. Polk and company, inc. (1920)   125 p. 20 cm. (The Maxwell series.   Famous old families) 35-21365.

CS71. S93   1920

16557   STUART.   ... Miss Jane Stuart, 1812-1888, her grandparents and parents; a paper read before the Society, November 17th, 1919, by Miss Mary E. Powel ... Newport, R. I., 1920.
19 p. 23½ cm. (Bulletin of the Newport historical society, no. 31)   "The account of the first two generations is taken largely from three articles written by Miss Jane Stuart and printed in Scribner's magazine, 1876-7." 20-12619.   F89. N5N615 no. 31

16558   STUART.   The house of Stuart and the Cary family, James II. and Torre abbey, by Hugh R. Watkin.   Exeter, J. G. Commin, 1920.   1 p. l., 46 p. pl. (ports.) 22½ cm. (With Clarke, Kate M.   The misericords of Exeter cathedral.   Exeter, J. G. Commin, 1920) Running title: Cary of Cockington.   Issued as appendix to Devon & Cornwall notes & queries, v. 11, pt. 3-4 (July-Oct. 1920) 25-14807.   DA670. D49 D42

16559   STUART.   The Revd. John Stuart, D. D., U. E. L., of Kingston, U. C., and his family; a genealogical study, by A. H. Young.   Kingston, Whig press (1920?)   2 p. l., 64 p. ports. 23½ cm. "Extract from Dr. Strachan's funeral sermon on Dr. John Stuart": p. 47-53. 21-22273.   CS90. S7

16560   STUART.   Stewart clan magazine. v. 1 -   July 1922 -   Filley, Neb., G. T. Edson, 1922 -   v. illus. 24 cm. monthly. Caption title. 26-4228.   CS71. S93   1922

16561   STUART.   ... Stewart family records, by J. Montgomery Seaver.   Philadelphia, Pa., American historical-genealogical society (1929?)   62, (3) p. illus. (ports.) 23½ cm. Three blank pages at end for "Family records" Coat of arms of the Stewart family on cover.   "References": p. 61-62.   40-18924.
CS71. S93   1929

16562   STUART.   The reign of Elizabeth, 1558-1603, by J. B. Black ... Oxford, The Clarendon press, 1936.   vii, (1), 448 p. fold. maps, fold. plan, fold. geneal. tables. 22½ cm. (Half-title: The Oxford history of England, ed. by G. N. Clark.   Bibliography: p. (412) - 430. 36-19574.   DA355. B65

16563   STUART.   Stuart and allied families, a genealogical record with biographical notes, compiled and privately printed for Elbridge Amos Stuart by the American historical company, inc. ... New York, 1938.   149 p. plates, ports., facsim., col. coats of arms. 33 cm. Includes the Horner, Morgan, Duncklee, Sanborn, Hadley, Gandy and Bailey families.   Includes bibliographical notes. 42-4309.

CS71. S93   1938

16564   STUART.   Days gone by, by Ellinor Stewart Heiser... Baltimore, Md.   (Waverly press inc.) 1940.   5 p. l., 117 p. front., plates, ports. 23½ cm. 41-10570.   CT275. H52A3

16565   STUART.   The history of the Stuarts, earls of Traquair, barons Linton & Cabarston, and Charles Edward Traquair Stuart-Linton, by L. G. Pine ... (London) 1940.   cover-title, 27 p. 25½ cm. "Addendum slip" mounted on p. 18.   41-7367.   CS479. S75   1940

16566   STUART.   ... A few of the Stewart clan in America, as collected and arranged by Harry Augustus Phelps ... (Gloversville, N. Y., 1943)   2 p. l., 10 numb. l. 28 x 21½ cm. At head of title: 1746-1943. Reproduced from type-written copy. 44-18442 rev.   CS71. S93   1943

16567   STUART.   A stewart family and some others.   By William B. Stewart.   (1st ed.) Cleveland, Gates Press, 1947.   199 p. ports., fold. geneal. table (in pocket) 26 cm. 47-5866*.   CS71. S93   1947

16568   STUART.   Genealogy of John Stewart, brother of Walter Stewart, of Londonderry, N. H., Boxford, Hopkinton, and Blandford, Mass., and Suffield, Conn.   By Claude Charles Hamel.   Amherst, Ohio, 1951.   5 l. 27 cm. 52-20694.   CS71. S93   1951

16569   STUART.   Genealogy of the family of Walter Stewart of Londonderry, N. H., Boxford, Hopkinton and Blandford, Mass.   By Claude Charles Hamel.   (Amherst? Ohio) 1951.   50 l. 27 cm. Typescript. Bibliography: leaves 44-47. 52-21867.   CS71. S93   1951a

16570   STUART.   Days gone by.   By Ellinor (Stewart) Heiser.   Baltimore, 1953.   98 p. illus. 24 cm. 54-16672.   CT275. H52A3   1953

16571   STUART.   The Stewarts, the Highland branches of a royal name.   By John Stewart.   Edinburgh, W. & A. K. Johnston, (1954)   32 p. illus. (part col.) col. map, coats of arms (part col.) 19 cm. (W. & A. K. Johnston's clan histories) 56-27749.   CS479.S75   1954

16572   STUART.   Stewarts, Dressers, Tafts, Cones.   By Frank Stewart Kinsey.   Los Angeles, Calif.. American Offset Printers, 1956.   386 p. illus. 28 cm. 58-25394.
                                                                                          CS71.S93   1956

16573   STUART.   Sampson Stewart, his royal ancestors and some of his descendants; a genealogical and biographical reference book.   By Sidney (Wright) Blount.   (1st ed, Altus, Okla., 1961)
xxxiv, 500 p. illus., ports., coat of arms. 21 cm. 61-16970.   CS71.S93   1961

16574   STUART.   Stuart letters of Robert and Elizabeth Sullivan Stuart and their children, 1819-1864, with an undated letter prior to July 21, 1813.   Introd. by Helen Stuart Mackay-Smith Marlatt.   (Washington?) 1961.   2 v. (xii, 1058 p.) illus., ports., geneal. table. 26 cm. "500 copies." 61-17426.   CS71.S93   1961a

16575   STUART.   Stewart genealogy.   (Researched by M. Stewart DeWitt.   Washington, 1967)
(23) l. 30 cm. Caption title. 67-7771.   CS71.S93   1967

              STUART.   See also:

                  AGNEW, 1926   FLEWELLEN, 1958   RUDDIMAN, 1901
                  ARCHDALE, 1925   LISPENARD, E171.A53 vol.14   STEWART.
                  BOWERS, 1872   McKee, 1900   STILES, 1936
                  BRUCE, DA758.3.C26C3   MILLER, 1909   TRAILL, 1902
                  DIXON, 1922   PARNELL, DA958.P2S5   VANREIN, E171.A53 vol.16
                  DOUGLAS, DA758.3.A1T2   ROBINSON, 1907   WALKER, 1902
                  ERSKINE, CS479.E7   ROBERTS, 1960   WILSON, 1890

16576   STUART-WORTLEY.   The first Lady Wharncliffe and her family (1779-1856) by her grandchildren, Caroline Grosvenor and the late Charles Beilby, lord Stuart of Wortley ... London, W. Heinemann, ltd., 1927.   2 v. fronts., plates, ports., fold. geneal. tables. 23 cm. Family letters, woven into a connected narrative. "Charles Beilby Stuart Wortley", by Joan Buchan: v.1, p. ix-xx. 28-21814.   DA536.W55G7

16577   STUBBS.   The descendants of John Stubbs of Cappahosic, Gloucester County, Virginia 1652.   By William Carter Stubbs ... New Orleans, American printing co., 1902.   116, iv p. incl. illus., port. 22½ cm.
9-20751.   CS71.S932   1902

16578   STUBBS.   ... Genealogical history of the family of the late Bishop William Stubbs, compiled by himself.   Edited by Francis Collins ... (Leeds and London) Printed for the Society (by J. Whitehead and son) 1915.   xii, 386 p. incl. front. (coat of arms) geneal. tables, 23 cm. (The Yorkshire archaeological society ... Record series. vol. LV) 17-9510.   DA670.Y59Y6 vol.55

16579   STUBBS.   Abstracts of divisions of estates of Stubbs and allied families of Marlboro County, South Carolina, by Leonardo Andrea and Joseph Edward Hill.   Columbia? S.C., 1964.   323 l. 29 cm.
"Number 41 of 100 copies." - MS note on flyleaf. 64-56205.   CS71.S932   1964

16580   STUBBS.   The descendants of John Stubbs of Cappahosic, Gloucester County, Birginia, 1652.   By William Carter Stubbs. Name index added, compiled by Hattie Stubbs Dickson.   Corpus Christi (Tex.) Professional Print. Co., 1966.   116, xi p. coat of arms, ports. 22 cm. 68-7423.
                                                                                          CS71.S932   1966

              STUBBS.   See also: FAIRFAX, 1882
                                      HARDING, 1904
                                      PATE, 19 -
                                      SHARP, 1875
                                      SHARP, 1904

STUCKY.   See: CRONE, 1924
                   GRABER, 1948

16581   STUDEBAKER.   A pioneer family (1736-1966) by E. Irene Miller.   Tipp City, Ohio (1966)
7 p. 30 cm.   66-3074.   CS71.S9325   1966

16582   STUDEBAKER.   Additional meterial in vertical file.   Ask reference librarian for this material.

16583   STUDWELL.   Studwell family of Fairfield County, Connecticut.   (Stamford? Conn.) 1899.
45 p.   20 cm.   Compiled by James Willette Studwell.   11-19469.
                                                                         CS71.S933   1899

16583 a STUDWELL.   Studwell family of Fairfield County, Connecticut, 1640.   Andrews family of
Bartholomew County, Indiana, 1834.   By Julia Idabelle Studwell Andrews.   (Fort Wayne, 1967)
26 p. col. coats of arms. 22 cm.   Cover title.   Page 36 blank for "Notes."   68-5187.
                                                                         CS71.S933   1967

16584   STUDWELL.   The Studwell family: outline of 1000 years of history.   By William Emmett
Studwell.   Washington, 1967.   24 p. 18 cm. Cover title. Bibliography: p. 23-24. 70-1665.
                                                                         CS71.S9332   1967

        STUDWELL.   See also NOYES, 1900

        STUDY.   See BENNER, 1931

16585   STUENKEL.   History and geneology (sic) of the family of Johann Heinrich Stuenkel and
Margareta Stuenkel, by Francelia and Selma Stuenkel.   Chicago, Priv. print., 1954.   104 p. illus.
28 cm.   54-35801.   CS71.S9334   1954

16586   STUKELEY.   The family memoirs of the Rev. William Stukeley, M. D., and the antiquarian
and other correspondence of William Stukeley, Roger & Samuel Gale, etc.   Durham,(Eng.)   Pub. for
the society by Andrews & co.; (etc., etc.,) 1882-87.   3 v. front. (port.) illus., plates. 23 cm. (Added t.-p.: Publications of the Surtees society ... vol. LXXIII, LXXVI, LXXX) Preface signed: W. C. Lukis.   Portrait engraved from painting by Sir G. Kneller.
24-22174.   DA20.S9 vols.73,76,80

16587   STUKEY.   Genealogy of the Stukey, Ream, Grove, Clem, and Denniston families, by Elmer
Leonidas Denniston, D. O.   Harrisburg, Pa., The author, 1939.   2 p. l., vii-xvii, (1), 591 p. fronts., plates,
ports., plan. 24 cm.   39-29866 rev.   CS71.S9335   1939

        STULL.   See BELL, 1960

16588   STUMP.   Stump of Maryland; substantial copy of genealogical record of the Stump family of
Maryland, compiled by Albert P. Silver and Henry W. Archer, 1891.   With the lines of Reuben Stump
and Alexander Hamilton Stump rev. to 1955; including a chart of the male members of the family
bearing the Stump name, prepared by H. Arthur Stump in 1923.   New York, 1955.   ii, 64 p. coat of
arms, geneal. table. 25 cm. 56-19042.   CS71.S9337   1955

        STUMP.   See also HERMAN, 1929

        STURBAUM.   See MEYER, 1946

        STURDIVANT.   See MALLARD, 1960

16589   STURGEON.   A genealogical history of the Sturgeons of North America.   (By Claudius T.
McCoy)   Cincinnati, O., 1926.   239, (12) p. front. (col. coat of arms) ports. 24 cm. Blank pages for "Births", "Marriages",
"Deaths", and "Memoranda" (12 at end) "Au revoir" signed: C. T. McCoy. 27-4724.
                                                                         CS71.S934   1926

        STURGEON.   See also: HIGHBAUGH, 1961
                                 HOGG, 1921

STURGES. See STURGIS.

16590   STURGILL.   The Sturgill family in America, a preliminary history.   By David Andrew
Sturgill.   College Park, Md., c. 1960.   1 v. 28 cm. 60-37883.   CS71.S9345   1960

16591   STURGIS.   A few stray leaves from the genealogies of the Sturges and Colman families.
Compiled by Alonzo W. Sturges.   Lewiston, Me., 1898.   1 p. 1., 16 p. illus. 19½ cm. 9-14099.
                                                            CS71.C935   1898

16592   STURGIS.   ... From books and papers of Russell Sturgis, by his son Julian Sturgis.   Oxford,
Printed at the University press (1893?)   2 p. 1., 272 p. front., ports. 24 cm. "For private circulation only." 21-11426.
                                                            CT275.S897S8

16593   STURGIS.   From 1530 to 1900.   Complete lineage of the Sturges families of Maine, from De
Turges, England, and cape Cod, Massachusetts, to Vassalboro and Gorham.   With other Sturges
genealogy.   Compiled by Alonzo Walton Sturges.   Lewiston, Me., 1900.   40 p. illus., 2 port. (incl. front.)
23½ cm. 1-2124.   CS71.S935   1900

16594   STURGIS.   Solomon Sturges and his descendants; a memoir and a genealogy, compiled by
Ebenezer Buckingham.   New York, The Grafton press, 1907.   84 p., 1 1. front., plates, ports., 2 fold. geneal.
tab. 24½ cm. Blank leaves at end of volume for "Memoranda." 8-302.   CS71.S935   1907

16595   STURGIS.   ... The Sturgis family of Yarmouth.   Yarmouthport, Mass., C. W. Swift, 1912.
cover-title, 4 p. 25½ cm. (Library of Cape Cod history & genealogy, no. 82) 17-6146.   CS71.S935   1912

16596   STURGIS.   Edward Sturgis of Yarmouth, Massachusetts, 1613-1695, and his descendants.
Roger Faxton Sturgis, editor.   Boston, Mass., Printed for private circulation at the Stanhope press,
1914.   1 p. 1., 88 p. 24½ cm. 15-3638.   CS71.S935   1914

16597   STURGIS.   The descendants of Robert Shaw Sturgis & Susan Brimmer Inches, compiled by
Charles Inches Sturgis.   Philadelphia, Priv. print., by Wm. F. Fell co., 1943.   1 p. 1., 2 numb. 1., 3-40,
(10) p. 31½ x 25 cm. "100 copies." 44-1003.   CS71.S935   1943

16598   STURGIS.   The descendants of Nath'l Russell Sturgis, with a brief introductory sketch of his
ancestors in England and the Massachusetts colony.   Boston (Printed by G. H. Ellis) 1900.
iv, (2), 75 p. 32 cm. Edition of 100 copies. Pages 64-75 left blank for additional data. 23-14468.   CS71.S935   1900a

16599   STURGIS.   The descendants of Nath'l Russell Sturgis, with a brief introductory sketch of his
ancestors in England and in the Massachusetts colony, compiled by Francis Shaw Sturgis and printed in
1900.   Revised to date by Esther Mary Sturgis and John Hubbard Sturgis, January 1, 1925.   Boston
(Geo. H. Ellis co. (inc.)) 1925.   3 p. 1., 88 p. 31 cm. "Second edition of 125 copies." Blank pages for additions (85-88)
37-16945.   CS71.S935   1925

16600   STURM.   Genealogy of the Sturm family; a record of the decendants of Jacob Sturm of
Sharpsburg, Maryland, from 1750 to 1936, compiled by Lloyd Elmer Sturm, edited by Margaret H.
Sturm.   (Clarksburg, W. Va.. Clarksburg publishing company, c. 1938)   296 p. plates, ports. 23½ cm.
39-468.   CS71.S936   1938

16601   STURTEVANT.   The Sturtevant family of Wisconsin, compiled by John Loomis Sturtevant.
Wausau, Wis., 1934.   39 p. incl. coat of arms. 23 cm. 34-10433.   CS71.S937   1934

          STURTEVANT.   See also: BARD, F128.25V27
                                    HASKELL, 1926
                                    LINDLEY, 1950
                                    TILSON, 1915
                                    VAN RENSSELAER, CS69.S7
                                    WOODRUFF, 1925

     STÜSSE.   See STOSS.

STUTSMAN.   See: HOCHSTETLER, 1938
HOWELL, 1922

16602   STUTTERHEIM.   Die Herren und Freiherren von Stutterheim/Alt-Stutterheim.   Lebensbilder von Kurt von Stutterheim.   Eckart von Stutterheim.   Neustadt a. d. Aisch, Degener, 1965.   289 p.
several leaves of illus., geneal. table.   24 cm.   (Bibliothek familiengeschichtlicher Arbeiten.   Bd. 33.)   Bibliography: p. 264-269.   67-96393.
CS629.S88

STUTTERNHEIM.   See STUTTERHEIM.

STUVERUD.   See NAESETH, 1956

16603   STUYVESANT.   Peter Stuyvesant, an address delivered at the annual meeting of the Order of colonial lords of manors in America.   April 21st, 1930 (by) Stuyvesant Fish.   Baltimore, 1930.
39 p.   front., illus., (incl. ports., facsims.)   23½ cm.   (On cover: (Order of colonial lords of manors in America.   New York branch.   Publications) no. 22)   34-8736.
E186.99.O6N5 no. 22
—— Copy 2.
F122.1.S924

STUYVESANT.   See also: BARD, F128.25Y27
VAN RENSSELAER, 1907

STYLES.   See STILES.

16604   STYRING.   The royal heirs of Canute in South Yorkshire.   By Harold Knight Styring.   Sheffield, c. 1961.   (8) p.   21 cm.   63-1099.
CS439.S917   1961

16605   STYRING.   Earls without coronets; the Styr dynasty (by) Harold K. Styring.   Sheffield, Printed by Hartley, 1965.   xvii, 89 p.   geneal. tables (part folded) port.   23 cm.   "References": p. 86.   65-88870.
CS439.S916   1965

16606   STYRING.   The Styron (Styring) family in America.   By Dora Adele Padgett.   (Washington?)
1966.   87 p.   fold. facsims., geneal. tables, maps.   28 cm.   Bibliography: p. 80-81.   67-89.   CS71.S939   1966

STYRON.   See STYRING.

16607   SUAREZ.   ... Biografía de don Joaquín Suárez.   Su descendencia en el Uruguay, Brasil y Argentina (por) Celia S. de Pérez Gomar.   (Buenos Aires, Talleres gráficos de J. Castagnola) 1941.
148 p.   pl., ports., facsims., geneal. tables.   20 cm.   43-11920.   F2726.S94   1941

SUCKLING.   See NELSON, CS439.N33

SUDDARTH.   See SUDDERTH.

SUDDUTH.   See STODDARD, 1959

16608   SÜRGEN.   Die Sürgen.   Geschichte der Freiherren von Syrgenstein.   Bearb.   nach den von dem verstorbenen Ludwig Freiherrn Zu Rhein gesammelten Quellen und ergänzt.   Ludwig Zenetti.
(Augsburg; Seitz in Kommission 1965)   159 p., 21 l. of illus.   24 cm.   (Schwäbische Genealogie, Bd. 1)   Bibliography:
p. 145 - (146)   73-389431.   CS648.S95S38 Bd. 1

16609   SUGDEN.   Sugden family of South Norwalk, Conn., Bridgewater, Conn., and Flushing, N. Y.
By Willard Harvey Gildersleeve.   Hackensack, N. J.   (1953)   2 cards.   7½ x 12½ cm.   Microprint copy of typescript.   Collation of the original: 36, 3 l.   28 cm.   Micp. 58-61.   Microcard CS71

16610   SUGG.   Sketches of the Sugg family (of Orange county, North Carolina) by Eugene Sugg.
(n. p., 1940?)   cover-title, 11 numb. l.   30 cm.   Bibliography: leaves 9-11.   40-18933.   CS71.S94   1940

SUGG.   See also TYSON, 1941

16611   SUHR.   Slektshistorie for slekten Suhr i Alta.   Utgitt av Kåre Suhr.   (Elvebakken, 1966)
34 p.   ports.   21 cm.   68-135967.   CS919.S77   1966

SUILLEE. See SOUILLÉ.

16612   SULLENS.   Among my pioneer ancestors.   A sketch on group of pioneer Missouri families, from whom writer is descended ... by Anna B. Sartori ... (St. Louis, Mo.) 1942.   1 p. l., iii, 115 numb. 1. fold. geneal. tab. 29 cm. Loose-leaf: reproduced from type-written copy. "Suggested references": p. 52. Includes the Sullens, Hildebrand, Williams, Stow, Bromelsick and Longworth families. 42-7575.   CS71.S946   1942

16613   SULLIVAN.   The Sullivan family of Sullivan, Maine.   With some account of the town.   By John S. Emery. (Bangor, Me., 1891)   cover-title, 22 p. 23½ cm. Caption title: The Sullivan family. Descendants of Capt. Daniel Sullivan of Sullivan, Maine. Reprinted from the Bangor historical magazine, 1891. 11-20390.   CS71.S95   1891

16614   SULLIVAN.   Materials for a history of the family of John Sullivan of Berwick, New England, and of the O'Sullivans of Ardea, Ireland.   Chiefly collected by the late Thomas Coffin Amory.   With a pedigree of O'Sullivan Beare, by Sir J. Bernard Burke ... Printed for private distribution.   Cambridge, J. Wilson and son, 1893.   x p., 1 l., 170 p. incl. geneal. tables (partly fold.) front. (coat of arms) pl., map. 25½ cm. p. 155-170 blank. Compiled by Gertrude E. Meredith. 9-14093.   CS71.S95   1893

16615   SULLIVAN.   A family chronicle, derived from notes and letters selected by Barbarina, the Hon. Lady Grey; edited by Gertrude Lyster.   London, J. Murray, 1908.   xi, 344 p. 8 pl. (incl. front., ports.) 22½ cm. 8-18702.   DA536.S95L8

16616   SULLIVAN.   Jeremiah Sullivan of Summit county, Ohio, his descendants, and collateral lines ... (St. Paul, Minn., 1942)   17, 6 numb. 1. 28 cm. Caption title. Type-written. "Sources": 1.16. 42-21287.   CS71.S95   1942

16617   SULLIVAN.   Parker Sullivan of New Jersey and allied families, a genealogical enumeration. By James Latimer Bothwell.   Boise, Idaho, 1946.   (27) 1. 28 cm. Type-written. 48-16122*.   CS71.S95   1946

SULLIVAN.   See also: O'SULLIVAN.
                                      SULLIVANT.

16618   SULLIVANT.   A genealogy and family memorial, by Joseph Sullivant ... Columbus, O., Printed at Ohio state journal book and job rooms, 1874.   1 p. l., 372, (3) p. front. (col. coat of arms) geneal. tables. 28 cm. "350 copies printed for private distribution." Allied families: Starling, Archer, Holloway, Reamey, Price, Smith, Neil, McDowell, O'Hara, Marshall, Sands, Underhill. 4-36681.   CS71.S952   1874

SULLIVANT.   See also SULLIVAN.

16619   SUMMERBELL.   Public activites of Rev. J. J. Summerbell, D. D., compiled by his son, Rev. Carlyle Summerbell ... Dayton, O., The Christian publishing association (c. 1916)   169 p. front. (port.) 19½ cm. 17-555.   BX6793.S887

16620   SUMMERHAYS.   The Joseph William-Hilda Johnson Summerhays Family Society news.   v. 1 -
            June 1942 -   (Beverly Hills, Calif.)   v. in   illus., ports. 24 cm. monthly.
57-32283.   CS71.S9547   1942

SUMMERLIN.   See MOULTON, 1922

16621   SUMMERS.   A history of George Summers of Douglass and Lower Dublin townships, Montgomery County, Pennsylvania. (n. p., 1918?)   34 p. 22½ cm. Preface signed: G. Byron Summers. 26-17562.   CS71.S955   1918

16622   SUMNER.   Memoir of Increase Sumner, governor of Massachusetts.   By his son William H. Sumner.   Together with a genealogy of the Sumner family.   Prepared for the New England historical and genealogical register.   Boston, S. G. Drake, 1854.   70 p. front. (port.) illus., facsims. 23½ cm. Reprinted from the New Eng. hist. and geneal. register for April, 1854, p. (105)-128. "Genealogy of the Sumner family. By William B. Trask": p. (39) -70. 9-14095.   CS71.S956   1854

16623   SUMNER.   Pedigree of the direct line of Gov. Sumner.   (Boston, 1856)   geneal. tab.
27½ x 28½ cm. fold. to 20 cm.   By William Blake Trask.   1-19652.   CS71.S956   1856

16624   SUMNER.   Record of the descendants of William Sumner, of Dorchester, Mass., 1636, by
William Sumner Appleton.   Boston, D. Clapp & son, printers, 1879.   v, 204 p. port. 26½ cm. Inserted:
Additions and corrections to Sumner genealogy to January 1881, 1882, 1883, 1895, 1900, 1902.   2-6080.   CS71.S956   1879

16625   SUMNER.   Additions and corrections to Sumner genealogy.   To January, 1900.   (n. p., 1900)
3 p. 26 cm.   37M41T.   CS71.S956   1900

16626   SUMNER.   History of Sumner family, by William S. Sumner.   Nashville, Tenn., Parthenon
press (1932)   79 p. 23½ cm. 32-33199.   CS71.S956   1932

SUMNER.   See also: BENSON, 1920
BIRD, 1905
KINGSBURY, 1904
RUF, 1932
RYAN, 1962

16627   SUNDERLAND.   Biographical sketch and recollections of the lives of Thomas Sunderland (2d)
and Sarah Broadhead Sunderland (Lovell) and Genealogical notes on their ancestry and posterity.   Biography by Rev. James Sunderland, D. D. and Rev. Jabez Thomas Sunderland ... Genealogical notes
collected, arranged and published by Lester Thomas Sunderland.   Kansas City, Mo., 1914.
113 p. xxxvi pl. (incl. front) fold. geneal. tables. 24 cm. Most of the plates are portraits. Pages 85 - 100 left blank for "Other family records".
Presentation copy no. 112. 24-4254.   CS71.S958   1914

SUNDERLAND.   See also McCANN, 1955

SUPPES.   See HAY, 1923

16628   SUPPLEE.   History of the Supplee-De Haven family.   Compiled by Mrs. Irene D. S. Conard.
Norristown, Pa. (1935?)   16 numb. l. 28 cm. Photostat (positive) of type-written copy. 36-1637.   CS71.S96   1935

SURBAUGH.   See BRUMBACH, 1961

SURDAM.   See SUYDAM.

SURREY, Earls of.   See WARREN.

SURRATT.   See PATTERSON, 1961

SURTEES.   See JAMES, 1913a

SUTCLIFFE.   See SUTLIFF.

16629   SUTER.   Memories of yesteryear; a history of the Suter family.   By Mary Eugenia Suter.
Drawings by Sallie Wenger Weaver.   Waynesboro, Va., Printed by C. F. McClung (1959)
x, 187 p. illus., ports., col. coat of arms. 24 cm. 59-46108.   CS71.S963   1959

16630   SUTHERLAND.   Sutherland records.   Compiled by Douglas Merritt ... New York, T. A.
Wright, 1918.   76 p. 24 cm. 18-18563.   CS71.S965   1918

16631   SUTHERLAND.   Notes on the Southerland, Latham and allied families; register of the ancestors of Imogen Southerland Voorhees, compiled by Edward Kinsey Voorhees.   Atlanta, Ga., 1931.
2 p. l., v, 137 (i. e. 138) numb. l. 27½ cm. Reproduced from type-written copy. Includes extra numbered leaf 89a. "For private distribution."
31-9475.   CS71.S965   1931

16632   SUTHERLAND.   Clan Southerland association.   Annual bulletin ... (of the) 7th -
annual gathering(s) 1939 -   (Rosehill? N. C., 1939 -   v. 24-28 cm. No bulletins issued for the 1st-6th gatherings.
Issues for 1939-40 reproduced from type-written copy. 40-37514 rev.   CS71.S965   1939

16633   SUTHERLAND.   Sutherlands of Ngaipu.   By Alexander Sutherland of New Zealand.   Wellington, A. H. & A. W. Reed (1947)   141 p. plates, ports., coat of arms, geneal. table. 22 cm. 47-8325*.

CS2049.S85   1947

16634   SUTHERLAND.   "We cousins" (Virginia to Texas) A genealogy of several of the families comprising the Alabama settlement of Austin's Colony, 1830 and 1831, now Texas, and including the other Virginia lines of the Sutherland family.   By Florence (Sutherland) Hudson.   San Benito, Tex., c. 1957. -   v. 29 cm. 57-35647.

CS71.S965   1957

16635   SUTHERLAND.   Sutherland records, found in Georgia, Illinois, Indiana, Kentucky, Maryland, North Carolina, South Carolina and Virginia (by Henry C. Sutherland.   Crown Point? Ind., 1968)   245 p. 22 cm. 68-5562.

CS71.S965   1968

SUTHERLAND.   See also: EATON, CS90.E2
GORDON, DA758.3.S95G6
HITE, 1960
HUTCHINS, 1938
PARSONS, 1867
SINCLAIR, 1884

16636   SUTLIFF.   A record of the ancestors and the descendants of Betsy Mulford Sutliff, compiled by her granddaughter Mary Louisa Sutliff.   Albany, N. Y., For Orange press, Brandow printing co., 1897.   50 p. front., ports. 23 cm. "150 copies printed for private distribution only." "Reminiscences of Betsey Mulford Sutliffe by her grandson, Frank Barnard Sutliff": p. 7-14. 17-21245.

CS71.S966   1897

16637   SUTLIFF.   A genealogy of the Sutcliffe-Sutliffe family in America from before 1661 to 1903. The descendants of Nathaniel Sutcliffe, with a brief account of their English ancestry back to 1500 - also the ancestry of families related by intermarriage, by Bennett Hurd Sutliffe ... Hartford, Conn., R. S. Peck & co., printers and engravers (1903?)   242 p. front., plates, ports. 23½ cm. 12-22681.

CS71.S966   1903

16638   SUTLIFF.   A history of the American and puritanical family of Sutliff or Sutliffe, spelled Sutcliffe in England.   The first American family (A. D. 1614) connected with New England, and amongst the first to be connected with the settlement of the original English possessions in the New World, and a genealogy of all the descendants through Nathaniel Sutliff, jr.   By Samuel Milton Sutliffe, jr., esq. Downers Grove, Ill., The Kelmscott press, 1909.   199 p. front., ports., coats of arms. 23 cm. 10-1714.

CS71.S966   1909

SUTLIFF.   See also: CLEVELAND, 1949
CLOPTON, 1939

SUTLIFFE.   See SUTLIFF.

16639   SUTPHEN.   The Sutphen family; genealogical and biographical notes on nine American generations, together with pre-American data and many notes on allied families.   (By William Gilbert Van Tassel Sutphen)   New York, 1926.   xix, 110 p., 2 l. front. (coat of arms) pl., plan. 24½ cm. "The material upon which this genealogical record ... is founded, was originally collected by Mr. A. V. D. Honeyman." - Foreword, signed: Van Tassel Sutphen. 28-30439.

CS71.S9665   1926

SUTPHIN.   See BUTTERWORTH, 1960

16640   SUTTON.   History of Dudley castle and priory, including a genealogical account of the families of Sutton and Ward.   By Charles Twamley.   London, J. R. Smith, 1867.   1 p. l., iv p., 1 l., 132 p. 2 geneal. tab. 19½ cm. 2-28924.

DA690.D81T9

16641   SUTTON.   Junior branches of the family of Sutton, alias Dudley, by H. Sydney Grazebrook. (London, Harrison and sons, 1889)   178, xiv p. front. (fold. geneal. tab.) 23½ cm. (In William Salt archaeological society. Collections for a history of Staffordshire. v. 8 (pt. II))   14-11655.

DA670.S69S69 vol. 10

—— Copy 2, separate.   CS439.D85

16642   SUTTON.   Genealogical notes of the Sutton family of New Jersey, by Edward F.H. Sutton ... New York, T.A.Wright, 1900.   2 p. l., (5)-46 numb. l., 1 l. 23 cm. "Printed for private circulation." "Authorities": leaves 45-46. 12-1819.   CS71.S967   1900

16643   SUTTON.   An ancestral chart and handbook; genealogical notes of the Sutton and Rittenhouse families of Hunterdon county, New Jersey; with Mattison, Bonham, Fuller, and Fox connections and some record of the Barrick and Shepherd families, by Olive Barrick Rowland.   Richmond, Garrett & Massie, 1935.   xiii p., 1 l., 199 p. front., plates, ports., XIII geneal. tab., coat of arms., 23½ cm. Frontispiece accompanied by guard sheet with descriptive letterpress. Includes bibliographies. 35-29161.   CS71.S967   1935

16644   SUTTON.   The Suttons of Caroline county, Virginia, by T. Dix Sutton.   Richmond, Va., Richmond press, inc., 1941.   99 p. 23½ cm. A41-4767. Univ. of Va. Lib. for L. of C.   CS71.S967   1941

16645   SUTTON.   Descendants of John Sutton and his wife, Temperance Lane, compiled by Carrie Tarleton Goldsborough and Anna Goldsborough Fisher.   Lexington, Ky., Clay printing company, 1941.   ix, 179 p. 23½ cm. 43-7281.   CS71.S967   1941a

SUTTON.   See also: DUDLEY, 1882
                                    FIELD, E171.A57 vol. 20
                                    SMITH, LF554.A3C4

SUVILLY.   See SOUILLÉ.

16646   SUYDAM. ... Hendrick Rycken, the progenitor of the Suydam family in America.   A monograph by Rev. J. Howard Suydam ... New York, The Knickerbocker press, 1898.   41 p., 1 l. front. (port.) 2 pl., coats of arms. 27 cm. At head of title: 1663. Published by request. 9-14097.   CS71.S968   1898

16647   SUYDAM.   Genealogy of the Surdam family (by) Charles Edward Surdam.   (Morristown, N.J., The Jerseyman press, Pierson & Surdam, 1909)   3 p. l., 260 p. front., plates, ports. 18½ cm. Blank pages for "Memoranda": p. 258-260. 11-5632.   CS71.S968   1909

SUYDAM.   See also DUER, E171.A53 v. 13
                                    RICKER, 1851

16648   SVIATOSLAV.   Political & diplomatic history of Russia, by George Vernadsky.   Students' ed. Boston, Little, Brown, and company, 1936.   ix p., 2 l., (3)-499 p. incl. geneal. tables. maps (part fold.) 22½ cm. Maps on lining-papers. "General bibliography": p. (467)-470. Bibliography at end of each chapter. 36-11172.   DK61.V4

16649   SWADNER.   John Swadner and his descendants, by Grace Radcliff Evans ... Decatur, Ill., 1919.   (32) l. 28 cm. Autographed from type-written copy. 20-3365.   CS71.S9745   1919

16650   SWAIN.   (Pedigree of the Swain family.   (Milwaukee (1895)   geneal. tab., 27 x 43 cm. fold. to 21 cm. Ancestry of William Chester Swain. 1-8450-M1.   CS71.S97   1895

16651   SWAIN.   Swain and allied families, including Tilley, Howland, Chipman, Hale, Barrett, Gilbert, Fox, Brayton, Egerton, Huntington, St. John, Keyes.   Compiled by William C. Swain ... Milwaukee, Wis., Press of Swain & Tate company, 1896.   137 p. front., fold. pl., ports., fold. facsims., col. coat of arms. 23 cm. 9-14096.   CS71.S97   1896

16652   SWAIN.   The descendants of Francis Swayne and others, comp. by Norman Walton Swayne ... Philadelphia, Printed for private circulation by J. B. Lippincott company, 1921.   154 p. 24½ cm. "One hundred and fifty copies of this book have been printed ..." 22-1047.   CS71.S97   1921

SWAIN.   See also: CASTLE, 1922
                                   DE RAPELJE, 1948
                                   SALISBURY, 1892

16653   SWALLOW.   Genealogy of the Swallow family, 1666-1910.   White Hall, Ill., Pearce bros., 1910.   1 p. l., 206, (11) p. plates, ports. 22½ cm. Compiled by Mrs. Alice Baker, Ed. and Marcus North and Lena Ellis, cf. Pref. Corrections and additions in manuscript throughout the book. 27-19581.   CS71.S971   1910

16654   SWALLOW.   The Swallows and Gastons; a family history from the earliest records in American colonies to the present generation.   Compiled and edited by I. F. Swallow ... Kansas City, Mo. (1941)   60 p. illus. (ports., map, facsims.) 23½ cm.   41-22948.   CS71.S971   1941

16655   SWAN.   Ancestors of Alden Smith Swan and his wife Mary Althea Farwell, compiled for their daughter Florence Althea Gibb, by Josephine C. Frost ... New York, The Hills press, 1923.
v, 258 p. plates, ports. 24 cm.   "Only fifty copies of this book have been printed, ..."   Royal ancestry of John Prescott of Lancaster, Mass.: p. 167-184. 24-5966.   CS71.S972   1923

16656   SWAN.   John Swan, c. 1695 - c. 1780, of Stow, and Lunenburg, Massachusetts, and Peterborough, New Hampshire, and descendants, by Alice L. Priest ... Brookline, Mass., 1934.   2 p. l., 43 numb. 1.   ports. 27½ cm. Type-written. 34-32133.   CS71.S972   1934

16657   SWAN.   John Swan, c. 1695 - c. 1780, of Stow and Lunenburg, Massachusetts and Peterborough, New Hampshire, and descendants, by Alice L. Priest ... Brookline, Mass., 1936.   2 p. l., 52, 60-181, 183-212 numb. 1. pl., ports., map, facsims. (2 fold.) 28½ cm.   Type-written; notes in manuscript.   Numbers 53-59, 182 omitted in paging. Typewritten "Additions made October 28, 1936": leaf inserted at end. 36-24711.   CS71.S972   1936

SWAN.   See also: BRONSDON, 1902
                              CHESEBROUGH, 1903
                              DAVIS, 1934
                              DE KARAJAN, DG735.6.H3
                              LUCAS, 1964
                              SHANK, 1960
                              No. 430 - Adventurers of purse and person.

SWANGO.   See HOLLON, 1958

SWANN.   See: SHANK, 1960
                         SWAN.

SWANSON.   See No. 553 - Goodhue county.

SWANWICK.   See HENRY, 1890

SWANZY.   See FRENCH, CS499.F7

16658   SWARR.   A biographical history of the Swarr family of Lancaster county, Pennsylvania, by Jacob Mellinger Swarr ... (Lancaster) The author, 1909.   32 p. front., plates. 18½ cm. 37-21347.   CS71.S972   1909

16659   SWART.   The Swart family (by) Myrtle C. Nanninga-Myers.   (Abilene, Kan.) 1969.
44, 7 1. 29 cm. On cover: 1750-1960.   The Swart family arrived in United States in 1872 from Germany. 78-3113 MARC.   CS71.S9727   1969

SWART.   See also BRAY, 1941

SWARTHOUT.   See SWARTWOUT.

16660   SWARTLEY.   A genealogical record of the descendants of the Swartley family of Bucks and Montomgery counties, Pa.   Together with brief historical and biographical sketches and illustrated with several portraits and other illustrations.   By Rev. A. J. Fretz ... Netcong, Printed at the Eagle office, 1906.   2 p. l., (3)-81 p. pl., ports. 21½ cm. 8-30142.   CS71.S973   1906

SWARTOUT.   See SWARTWOUT.

SWARTWOLD.   See SWARTWOUT.

SWARTWOOD.   See SWARTWOUT.

16661   SWARTWOUT. The Swartwout chronicles 1338-1899, and the Ketelhuyn chronicles 1451-1899 by Arthur James Weiss ... New York, Trow directory printing and bookbinding co., 1899.   x, 754 p. col. front., illus. (incl. facsims.) ports., maps (part fold.) col. coats of arms.   28 x 23 cm.   L. C. COPY REPLACED BY MICROFILM.   0-989 rev.

CS71.S974   1899
Microfilm 10930 CS

SWARTWOUT. See also: DODDRIDGE, 1961
                       KETCHAM, 1954

SWARTZ. See SCHWARTZ.

16662   SWARTZENDRUBER. The Fred and Sarah (Yoder) Swarzendruber history; a story of their faith and life, with historical, genealogical and religious records of their ascendants and descendants, gathered from the earliest available data to the present time, 1958 A. D.   By Amos Gingerich. (Parnell, Iowa, 1958)   180 p. illus. 25 cm. 59-37838.   CS71.S9743   1958

16663   SWARTZENDRUBER. Information before we enter into the Joseph J. and Barbara Brenneman Swartzendruber genealogy; let us take a review of the progenitorial families historical record, 1743-1961.   By P. Swartzentruber. (n. p., 1961?)   51 p. 22 cm. 63-23571.

CS71.S9743   1961

16664   SWASEY. Genealogy of the Swasey family which includes the descendants of the Swezey families of Southold, Long island, New York, and the descendants of the Swayze families of Roxbury, now Chester, New Jersey, by Benjamin Franklin Swasey, Exeter, N. H.   Cleveland, O., Privately printed for Ambrose Swasey, 1910.   3 p. l., 5-525 p. front., plates, ports., fold. geneal. tables. 23½ cm. Errata slip inserted between p. 478 and 479.   Title from Kansas Hist. Soc. for L. of C.   A33-2021.   CS71.S9745   1910

SWASEY. See also: BROWN, 1959
                    WELLS, 1900

SWAYNE. See SWAIN.

SWAYZE. See JOHNSON, 1961

16665   SWEADNER. John Swadner and his descendants, by Grace Radcliff Evans ... Decatur, Ill., 1919   (32) l. 28 cm. Autographed from type-written copy. 20-3365.   CS71.S9749   1919

16666   SWEARINGEN.   Family historical register, comp. by a member of the family. Washington, C. W. Brown, 1884.   iv, (2), 117 p. 22 cm. Preface signed: H. H. S. i. e. Henry Hartwell Swearingen. 9-13828.   CS71.S975   1884

16667   SWEARINGEN. Family register of Gerret van Sweringen and descendants.   Compiled by a member of the family.   2d ed.   Washington, Printed for the compiler, 1894.   3 p. l., 80 p. 23½ cm. Preface signed: H. H. S. i. e. Henry Hartwell Swearingen. 9-14090.   CS71.S975   1894
        —— Reprint. Cleveland, ... the House of service ... 1914.   24-20309.   CS71.S975   1894a

16668   SWEARINGEN. Some Brysons & Swearingens. Original compilers: Sarah Ellen (Smith) Campbell & Homer C. Nycum.   Outline arr. by Homer C. Nycum (Kalamazoo, Mich.,) H. C. Nycum (1965)   294 p. illus., coats of arms, facsims., geneal. tables, maps, ports. 29 cm. 65-3190.   CS71.B9165   1965

16669   SWEET. Genealogy of the Sweet family. (n. p., 183-)   1 l. 35 cm. 38M627T.   CS71.S976   183-

16670   SWEET. Silas Sweet of New Bedford, Mass., and Bradford, Vermont, and his descendants. By Charles Sweet Johnson, LL. B.   Private ed. Washington, D. C., 1898.   19, (2) p. 24½ cm. 9-14092.   CS71.S976   1898

16671   SWEET. The John C. Sweets of Minneapolis.   A little story of the family life and history of John Cochrane Sweet and his wife, Mary Lougee Sweet, written as a souvenir for their descendants on the occasion of Mr. Sweet's seventieth birthday.   April 24th, 1940. Minneapolis, Minn., Hayward

16671 continued: brief company, printers (1940)   67 p. illus. (plan) pl., ports., 9 coats of arms on 1 l., 2 fold.
geneal. tab. 26½ cm.   Includes also the Sperry and Leavenworth families.   41-20663.   CS71.S976   1940

SWEET.   See also: ROBINSON, 1879
SANBORN, 1928
STOUT, 1960
SWETT.

16672   SWEETING.   Sweeting family.   (By Walter Debenham Sweeting)   (For private circulation)
Peterborough (Eng.) 1880.   (20) p. 21½ cm.   Caption title.   Notes in manuscript throughout text.   Signed: W. D. Sweeting.
22-2790.   CS439.S92

SWEETING.   See also LANGFORD, 1936

16673   SWEETLAND.   The descendants of Aaron and Patience Sweetland, of Hebron, Conn.   (Denver,
Col., 1890)   30 p. 15½ x 14½ cm.   Preface signed: Lucy W. S. Jerome, Denver, Colo., January 30, 1890.   9-14091.   CS71.S977   1890

SWEETLAND.   See also: BASSETT, 1926
STEBBINS, 1940

16674   SWEETSER.   The Sweetser family of Maryland, by Lester Durand Gardner.   (Baltimore,
1932)   cover-title, p. (139)-147.   25½ cm.   Genealogical table attached to cover.   "Reprinted from the Maryland historical magazine
XXVII, no. 2, June, 1932."   32-19216.   CS71.S9774   1932

16675   SWEETSER.   Seth Sweetser and his descendants, by Philip Starr Sweetser.   Philadelphia,
Integrity press (1938)   2 p. l., 427 p.   front., plates, map, facsims.   23½ cm.   "Sweetser authors": p. 371-373.   Bibliography:
p. 374-379.   39-12569.   CS71.S9774   1938

SWEETSER.   See also: DUMONT, 1960
WELLS, 1903

SWEEZY.   See DAVIS, 1927a

SWEIGARD.   See ENDERS, 1960

SWEKENDIK.   See SCHWECKENDIEK.

SWETLAND.   See EATON, 1900

16676   SWETT.   Mementos of the Swett family.   By John Wingate Thornton.   In memoriam.   Rox-
bury, Priv. print., 1851.   26 p. facsims. 24½ cm.   Title vignette: coat of arms.   One hundred copies.   Reprinted in the New
Eng. hist. and geneal. register, vol. 6, 1852, p. 49-62.   9-13827.   CS71.S978   1851

16677   SWETT.   Swett genealogy; descendants of John Swett of Newbury, Mass.   By Everett S.
Stackpole ... Lewiston, Me., The Journal printshop (1913?)   2 p. l., (7)-123 p.   plates.   23½ cm.   13-9471.   CS71.S978   1913

SWETT.   See also: REMINGTON, 1960
SWEET.

SWICKARD.   See BOWERS, 1935

16679   SWIFT.   The memoirs of Gen. Joseph Gardner Swift, LL. D., U. S. A., first graduate of the
United States Military academy, West Point, chief engineer U. S. A. from 1812 to 1818.   1800-1865.
To which is added a genealogy of the family of Thomas Swift, of Dorchester, Mass., 1634, by Harrison
Ellery ... Priv. print. (Worcester, Mass., Press of F. S. Blanchard & co.) 1890.   1 p. l., (5)-292, 58 p.,
1 l., vii, xi p. illus., pl., ports. 30 cm. 9-14806.   CS71.S98   1890

16680   SWIFT.   William Swyft of Sandwich and some of his descendants.   1637-1899.   Compiled by George H. Swift ... Millbrook, N. Y., Round table press, 1900.   3 p. l., 165 p., 1 l. plates. 24 cm. Interleaved. 9-29648.   CS71.S98   1900

16681   SWIFT.   The Swift family of Philadelphia, by Thomas Willing Balch ... Philadelphia, 1906. 32 p. front. (port.) 25½ cm. Reprinted from the Pennsylvania magazine of history and biography, April, 1906. 6-20349.   CS71.S98   1906

16682   SWIFT.   ... William Swift and descendants to the sixth generation, by Eben Swift. Yarmouth-port, Mass., C. W. Swift, 1923.   cover-title, 70 p. 25½ cm. (Library of Cape Cod history & genealogy, no. 15) 40-18934.   CS71.S98   1923

16683   SWIFT.   My father and my mother, by Helen Swift.   Chicago, Priv. print. (The Lakeside press, R. R. Donnelley & sons company) 1937.   xii p., 1 l., 167, (1) p. col. front., illus. (coat of arms) plates, ports. 24 cm.   Frontispiece accompanied by guard sheet with descriptive letterpress.   "Genealogies": Swift. Higgins. Descent from Elder William Brewster.   Robert Swyft of Rotherham (p. (157) - 167) 37-5533.   CT275.S9868S9

16684   SWIFT.   The Swift family; historical notes, compiled by the late Katharine Whitin Swift and published by her husband Elijah Kent Swift.   Whitinsville, Mass., 1955.   170 p. 25 cm. 56-1674.   CS71.S98   1955

            SWIFT.   See also: DOUBLEDAY, 1924
                                 HANAFORD, 1915
                                 MANLEY, 1938
                                 NOYES, 1907

16685   SWIGER.   A genealogical and biographical history of the Swiger family in the United States of America, by Ira L. Swiger.   (Fairmont, W. Va., Fairmont printing & pub. co., c. 1916)   361, xvi, (2) p. front., illus. (ports., facsims.) pl. 24 cm. Blank pages for "Family record" (356-361) "Numbered copy 48. Author's autograph." 24-16958.   CS71.S982   1916

16686   SWINDELL.   Swindell-Hoover.   Some ancestors of Edwin Wallace Swindell and his wife, Joy Lorraine Hoover, of Berkeley, California, compiled by Ella Foy O'Gorman (Mrs. Michael Martin O'Gorman) (n. p.) 1936.   4 p. l., 60 numb. l., 2 l., 61-133 numb. l., 1 l. front., plates, ports., geneal. tab. 28 cm.   Typewritten. "References." 36-24710.   CS71.S983   1936

16687   SWINDELL.   Swindell-Hoover.   Ella Foy O'Gorman, compiler.   (n. p.) 1936.   geneal. tab. 39 x 65 cm. 36-24709.   CS71.S983   1936a

            SWINDELL.   See also: FOY, 1932
                                    FOY, 1933

16688   SWING.   ... Events in the life and history of the Swing family.   Examples of indomitable energy and perseverance ... Written by Gilbert S. Swing.   Camden, N. J., Graw, Garrigues & Graw, printers, 1889.   398 p. incl. front., illus., plates, ports. 20 cm. At head of t. - p.: Biographical sketches of eminent men. 9-13826.   CS71.S981   1889

16689   SWING.   The first five generations of the Swing family in America.   Compiled by Albert H. Swing and Harry P. Swing.   (Bryn Mawr? Pa.) 1961.   235 p. illus. 24 cm. 63-24030.   CS71.S984   1961

16690   SWINGLE.   History of the Swingle family, compiled by Mrs. C. F. Martzolff.   Columbus, O., The Southard novelty co., 1925.   212 p. illus. (incl. ports., facsim.) 23½ cm. 39-12239.   CS71.S985   1925

            SWINGLE.   See also SWINGLEY, 1926

16691   SWINGLEY.   Family record of the ancestors and lineage various branches of the Zwingli family of Switzerland, also the Zwingle, Zwingly, Schwingle, Swingle and Swingley family in Switzerland, Germany and United States, 1380-1926, compiled by J. A. Swingley, with a brief history of the author and his own family record.   (n. p.) 1926.   88 p. front. (col. coat of arms) 1illus. (incl. ports.) 23 cm. "Authorities consulted": p. 4. 26-16559.   CS71.S986   1926

16692   SWINK.   Genealogy; the Swink family of Missouri, by Robert A. Swink.   Pasadena, Calif., Press of the Star-News publishing co., 1940.   3 p. 1., (5)-77 (i. e. 79) p. illus. (ports.) 16½ cm. Blank verso and recto omitted in numbering.   Includes also the Lewis and Hickman families.   41-9422.   CS71.S9873   1940

16693   SWINNEY.   Swinney family in vertical file.   Ask reference librarian for this material.

16694   SWINTON.   The Swintons of that ilk and their cadets.   Edinburgh (T. & A. Constable) 1883.   xx, 114 p., 1 1., cclii p. illus., plates, fold. facsim.   24½ cm.   One hundred and fifty copies printed.   Prefatory note signed: A. C. S.   i. e. Archibald Campbell Swinton.   "Appendix of charters and other documents": p. (i) - ccxxv.   12-31628.   CS479.S8

16695   SWINTON.   The family of Swinton.   By Captain George S. C. Swinton ... Exeter, W. Pollard & co., printers, 1899.   1 p. 1., 8 p. 23 cm.   Reprinted from "The Genealogist", n.s., vol. xv.   38-38115.   CS439.S93   1899

16696   SWINTON.   Concerning Swinton family records and portraits at Kimmerghame.   Privately printed.   Edinburgh, K. Lindsay, 1908.   vi p., 1 1., 245 p. geneal. tab. 22 cm.   Dedication signed: A.C. and J. L. Campbell Swinton.   15-19685.   CS479.S8   1908

16697   SWINTON.   Autobiographical and other writings, by Alan A. Campbell Swinton ... London, New York (etc.) Longmans, Green and co., 1930.   ix, 181 p. front., ports. 22½ cm.   Contents. - Biography. - Verses. - Addresses: I. Science and early civilisation. - II. Molecular physics and wireless communication.   III. Early days of electricity supply in Great Britain.   VI. Progress and promise.   V. Discovery and invention. - Addendum: Obituary notice.   30-18855.   Q171.S98

          SWIRE.   See HOLBROW, 1901

          SWISHER.   See MACGINNIS, 1891

16698   SWITZER.   (The Swtizer, Bull, Beurmann and Griffith ancestry of Helen Beurmann Switzer. n. p., 1926)   14 1. 28 cm.   Typewritten.   27-11107.   CS71.S987   1926

16699   The descendants of John Andrew Switzer, Harrisonburg, Virginia.   By George Frederick Switzer.   Harrisonburg, 1951.   32 p. illus. 29 cm.   52-34238.   CS71.S987   1951

          SWITZER.   See also: CRONE, 1916
                                 CRONE, 1924
                                 RUDOLPH, 1962
                                 No. 1547 - Cabell county.

16700   SWOFFORD.   One man and his family; John Franklin Swofford, 1853-1921.   By Minnie Ray Bachman Swofford.   (Lubbock? Tex,, 1968)   147 1. illus., facsim., ports. 23 cm.   68-6016.   CS71.S9874   1968

          SWOFFORD.   See also HOLLAND, 1959

          SWOOPE.   See LEWIS, 1901 (in addenda)

16701   SWOPE.   History of the Swope family and their connections.   1678-1896.   Comp. and ed. by Gilbert Ernest Swope.   Lancaster, Pa., T.B. & H.B. Cochran, printers, 1896.   390 p. incl. front., plates, ports., facsims., geneal. tables.   pl., ports., col. coat of arms. 26 cm.   9-13825.   CS71.S988   1896

          SWOPE.   See also KEENER, 1923

          SWORD.   See SWORDS.

16702   SWORDS.   Sword and Swords genealogy; a comprehensive genealogy of the descendants of Henry Swords, edited by Elmer Bernard Sword, and researched by Dolores Jean (Sword) Williams.   Tokyo, 1958.   140 p. 21 cm.   59-21240.   CS71.S989   1958

16703   SWYNNERTON.   A history of the family of Swynnerton of Swynnerton, and of the younger branches of the same family settled at Eccleshall, Hilton, and Butterton.   By the Hon. and Rev. Canon Bridgeman.   (In William Salt archaeological society.   Collections for a history of Staffordshire.   London, 1886.   24½ cm.   vol. VII, pt. 2. pl., 2 fold. geneal. tab.)   Contains four genealogical tables of the Vernon family of Hilton.   24-25171-2.   DA670. S69S6 vol. 7

———— Additions to the History of the Swynnertons, printed in vol. VII "Staffordshire collections" by the Rev. Charles Swynnerton, F.S. A.   (In William Salt archaeological society.   Collections for a history of Staffordshire. London, 1900.   24½ cm.   vol. III, new ser., p. (71)-120.   2 pl.)   24-25171-2.   DA670. S69S6   n. s. vol. 3

SYDDALL.   See SIDDALL.

16704   SYDENHAM.   Sydenham of Brympton.   Compiled by Hugh Stanley Head.   (London, 1889?) cover-title, 8 p.   3 pl.   27 cm.   Interleaved.   2-27582.   CS439. S95

16705   SYDENHAM.   The history of the Sydenham family, collected from family documents, pedigrees, deeds, and copious memoranda, by the late Dr. G. F. Sydenham of Dulverton.   Edited by A. T. Cameron ... With ... a chart pedigree of the senior (Dulverton) branch of the family.   East Molesey, Surrey, Priv. print. by E. Dwelly, 1928.   xi, 803 p.   front., plates, ports., facsims., fold. geneal. tab., coats of arms. 26 cm.   "Three hundred copies printed of which this is no. 163."   Bibliography: p. (767)-774.   28-22787.   CS439. S95   1928

SYDNER.   See SEIDNER.

SYDNEY.   See SIDNEY.

SYDNOR.   See SEIDNER.

16706   SYKES.   Genealogical memoranda relating to the family of Sikes, of Hackney, etc., compiled by Henry Wagner ... London, Priv. print. (Mitchell and Hughes, printers) 1877.   8 p.   fold. geneal. tab. 32 x 24 cm.   44-34848.   CS439. S96   1877

SYKES.   See also: MITCHELL, CS439. M63
                        SCOTT, 1949
                        VENN, 1904
                        No. 1547 - Cabell county.

SYMES.   See SIMS.

16707   SYMINGTON.   Genealogy of the Symington family.   By Henry Paton.   Edinburgh, 1908. 55 p.   col. coat of arms.   26 cm.   56-53583.   CS479. S9   1908

SYMMES.   See SIMS.

SYMONS.   See No. 2070 - Memories... of ... North Carolina.

SYMONDS.   See BAKER, 1870

16708   SYNG.   Syng of Philadelphia.   (Philadelphia, Printed by Sherman & co., for P. S. P. Conner, 1891)   1 p. 1., 8 numb. 1., 1 1.   30 cm.   Caption title.   Edition, 100 copies.   Signed: Philip Syng Physick Conner.   15-8346.   CS71. S995   1891
                                                                                                Microfilm 8675

16709   SYNG.   The family of Synge or Sing.   Pedigree tables of families bearing the above name, and notes intended to be read in conjunction with the tables, dealing chiefly with the family of Synge or Sing, of Bridgnorth, in Shropshire, and its branches in Ireland, America, Australia, New Zealand, etc., but also including families of the name settled in London, America, Canada, Devonshire, etc. ... (By Katharine Charlotte (Swan) Synge)   3 p. 1., (iii)-xix, 71, xxi-xxxvi, (3) p.   illus. (port.)   45 cm.   Coat of arms on t.-p. Foreword signed: K. C. Synge.   38-32346.   CS439. S97   1937

SYNG.   See also MANLY, 1930

SYNGE.   See SYNG.

SYNNOT.   See SINNETT.

16710   SYRON.   Syron-Searing, wills, deeds and ways; together with copious American and old country notes on the allied families of: Bonnell, Simcock, Schooley, Van Buskirk.   By Carolyn Syron Valentine (who is akin to them all)   Washington, D. C.   June 1925.   (Washington, D. C., 1925)
1 p. 1., iv, 202 (i. e. 211), 14, 31 numb. 1.   28 cm.   Type-written.   Maps and genealogical tables in pen and ink.   25-12627.

CS71. S996   1925

16711   SYRON.   Daughters of the Drumlin farms ... by Dr. Caro Syron Valentine ... (Washington, 1931)   2 p. 1., 4, 4a, 5, 5a-b, 6-332 (i. e. 333) numb. 1.   28½ cm.   Type-written.   Number 88 duplicated in paging.   Contains references to 61 families of Wayne and adjacent counties.   31-23230.

CS71. S996   1931

T

16712   TAAFFE.   Memoirs of the family of Taaffe.   Not published.   Vienna (Printing-office of M. Auer) 1856.   372 p. 9 pl., 6 port. (incl. front.) fold. geneal. tab.   23 cm.   Contents. - Pedigree. - Correspondence of Theobald Taaffe, earl Carlingford. 1665 - 1667. - Correspondence of Francis Taaffe, earl of Carlingford, 1670-1704. - Observations on affairs in Ireland from the settlement in 1691 to the present time, by Nicholas lord viscount Taaffe, pub. London, 1766. - John Taaffe's correspondence during his sojourn at Lisbon. - Count Francis Taaffe to Lady Clementina Taaffe-Bellew, July 5, 1788. - Extracte aus den feld - und hofkriegsräthlichen acten des K.K. Kriegsarchivs ... - Posessions.   Edited by Karl Taaffe.   Contains the rare suppressed leaf: p. 195-196.   9-14901.
CS439. T15

TAANUM.   See THAANUM.

16713   TABER.   The genealogy of the Taber family.   By Russel Taber.   Wheeling, W. Va., West Virginia printing co., printers, 1893.   45 p. 23 cm. 37-16951.
CS71. T113   1893

16714   TABER.   Taber genealogy; descendants of Thomas, son of Philip Taber; compiled by George L. Randall.   (New Bedford, Mass., Vining press, 1924)   469, xlix p. incl. front. (coat of arms) plates, ports. 23½ cm. Plates are printed on both sides. 25-1479.
CS71. T113   1924

16715   TABER.   Taber genealogy; descendants of Joseph and Philip, sons of Philip Taber, by Anna Allen Wright (and) Albert Hazen Wright.   Ithaca, N.Y., 1952 -   v. maps. 27 cm. Cover title. Contents. - pt. 1. First four generations. 53-15949.
CS71. T113   1952

TABER.   See also GRIFFIN, F129. S74G8

16716   TABOR.   Silver Dollar; the story of the Tabors, by David Karsner.   New York, Covici, Friede (c. 1932)   viii p., 2 l., 354 p. front., plates (incl. music) ports. 21½ cm. "Acknowledgments": p. 349-350. 32-5360.
CT275. T15K3

16717   TACHE.   La famille Taché, par Pierre-Georges Roy.   Levis (Québec, J. -A. -K. -Laflamme, imprimeur) 1904.   200 p. ports. 22½ cm. "Tiré à 200 exemplaires." 5-442.   CS90. T2

16718   TACKETT.   The American Pioneer.   Magazine of the Tackett-Tacket-Tackitt families of America.   No. 1 (January, 1964)--   In vertical file.   Ask reference librarian for this material.

TACKET.   See TACKETT.

TACKITT.   See TACKETT.

TADES.   See VAN WINKLE, F116. N36 vol. 56

TAELMAN.   See TALLMAN.

16719   TAFT.   Robert Taft; (family tree) Cincinnati, Ehrgott, Forbriger, lith. (18 -)   col. geneal. table. 64 x 51 cm. fold. to 33 x 27 cm.   CS71. T124

—— Another isse.   (2 copies)   Photocopy (one negative) (Washington, Library of Congress Photoduplication Service, 1951) 60 x 45 cm. fold. to 41 x 34 cm. 3-17334 rev. *.   CS71. T124

16720   TAFT.   Taft family gathering.   Proceedings at the meeting of the Taft family, at Uxbridge, Mass., August 12, 1874.   Uxbridge, Printed by Spencer brothers, 1874.   103 p. 22½ cm. 1-20887.
CS71. T124   1874

16721   TAFT.   A meeting of the descendants of Ebenezer and Mary (Howard) Taft, at the Chestnut Hill meeting-house in Blackstone, Mass. ... August 11, 1891, with the address of Rev. Carlton A. Staples, and other proceedings on that occasion.   (Boston, G. H. Ellis, 1891?)   27, (1) p. 23½ cm. 2-24815.

CS71.T124   1891

16722   TAFT.   Ancestry of William Howard Taft, by Mabel Thacher Rosemany Washburn.   New York, Frank Allaben genealogical company (c. 1908)   52 p. incl. front., illus., 2 pl., port. 22½ cm. (On cover: Genealogical miniatures, ed. by Mable T. R. Washburn) 8-29861.

CS71.T124   1908

16723   TAFT.   The Taft kin.   (By Anson Titus) (Boston? 1909?)   cover-title, 8 p. 18½ cm. "The Taft kin appeared as a signed article on the editorial page of the Boston evening transcript of March 4th, 1909." 31-18518.

CS71.T124   1909

16724   TAFT.   Life of Alphonso Taft, by Lewis Alexander Leonard ... New York, Hawke publishing company (incorporated) (1920)   3 p. l., (11)-307 p. incl. illus., plates, facsims. front. (port.) plates. 23½ cm. "Sources": p. (15) 20-11649.

E415.9.T121.5

TAFT.   See also: FLAGG, 1903
GUILD, 1891
RAWSON, 1875
TYLER, 1882

TAGGART.   See NESBIT, 1929

16725   TAI.   Tai shih tsu p'u.   Tai shih tsu p'u pien chi hui.   57, 31, 75 p. ports. 27 cm. 74-835828.

CS1169.T3   1969
Orien. China.

TAILER.   See TAYLOR.

TAILLEFER.   See BORLASE.

16726   TAINTER.   The genealogy and history of the Taintor family, from the period of their emigration from Wales, to the present time.   By Charles M. Taintor.   Greenfield, Printed by Merriam and Mirick, 1847.   iv, (5) - 82 p., 1 l. 17 cm. 9-14563.   CS71.T133   1847

16727   TAINTER.   A history and genealogy of the descendants of Joseph Taynter, who sailed from England April, A. D. 1638, and settled in Watertown, Mass.   Prepared by Dean W. Tainter ... For private distribution.   Boston, Printed by D. Clapp, 1859.   vii, (1), (7)-100 p. illus. 24 cm. Four pages at end for Family record. 9-14564.   CS71.T133   1859

TAINTER.   See also LOOMIS, 1880

TAINTOR.   See TAINTER.

TAI-YEN.   See DAYAN-QAN.

16728   TALBOT.   Descendants of Peter Talbot.   (n. p., n. d.)   1 p. l., (7)-40 p. 25 cm. Running title.   45-25180.   CS71.T14

16729   TALBOT.   An history of the manor and manor-house of South Winfield, in Derbyshire ... By Tho. Blore ... London, Printed by D. Brewman, 1793.   1 p. l., 100 p. 5 pl., 2 fold. tab. 30 x 24 cm. 3-6108.

DA690.W764B6

16730   TALBOT.   The House of Talbot.   (In Ancestral stories and traditions of great families illustrative of English history. By John Timbs ... London, Griffith and Farran, 1869. 18½ cm. p. 135-142) 5-5847.

DA28.35.A1T5

16731   TALBOT.   Talbot (family)   (Honey Brook, Pa., Printed at the Herald, 19 -)   cover-title, 4 p. 23½ cm. 38-36170.   CS71.T14   19 -

16732   TALBOT.   A descriptive catalogue of the Penrice and Margam abbey manuscripts in the possession of Miss Talbot of Margam; by Walter de Grey Birch ... 4th series.   London, Priv. print., 1903-05.   3 v. 25½ cm. 8-2483.   DA740.G5T3

16733   TALBOT.   Peter Talbot of Dorchester, Mass., and some of his descendants.   Comp. by Solomon Talbot of Sharon, Mass. ... Chicago, E. S. Talbot, 1909.   cover-title, 1 p. 1., p. 65-74. 23½ cm.
Edited by Edward A. Claypool.   CS71.T14   1909
          —— Copy 2 .   (In Old Northwest genealogical quarterly. Columbus, O., 1909. 24½ cm. vol. XII, p. 65-74) 17-21248-9.
                                                                  F476.O42 vol. 12

16734   TALBOT.   Lineage of the Talbot family from Le Sire Talebot A.D. 1066 to and including Peter Talbot of Dorchester, and Roger Talbot of Boston, Massachusetts.   Also the lineage of the Talbots of Bashall, and earls of Shrewsbury.   By Archie Lee Talbot ... Wilton, Me., J.W.Nelson, printer, 1914.   66 p., 1 l. 23½ cm. 14-2001.   CS71.T14   1914

16735   TALBOT.   The English ancestry of Peter Talbot of Dorchester, Mass.   Comp. for Emily Talbot Walker, a descendant of Peter Talbot, by J. Gardner Bartlett.   Boston, Mass., Priv. print., 1917.   2 p. 1., 116 p. front. (col. coat of arms) plates, facsim. 24 cm. "One hundred and fifty copies of this book have been printed, of which this is number 36." 17-22078.   CS439.T18

16737   TALBOT.   Genealogy of the Talbot and Wingfield families of Virginia and Georgia, by Rosa Talbot Knight. (n.p., 1924?)   2 p. 1., 102 numb. 1. 29 cm. Type-written. With this is bound the author's Genealogy of the Reid family of North Carolina and Georgia. (n.p., 1924?) 25-24232.   CS71.T14   1924

16738   TALBOT.   Descendants of Richard and Elizabeth (Ewen) Talbott of Poplar Knowle, West River, Anne Arundel County, Maryland, compiled by Ida Morrison (Murphy) Shirk.   Baltimore (Day printing co.) 1927.   4 p. 1., (5) - 569 p. front., plates, ports. 25 cm. "Edition of 350 copies." 27-20830.
                                                                  CS71.T14   1927

16739   TALBOT.   Genealogy of the Talbot-Reid and allied families.   By Rosa Viola (Talbot) Knight. Safety Harbor, Fla. (194-?)   290 (i.e.291) 1. 30 cm. 55-19922.   CS71.T14

16740   TALBOT.   A family history. By Loren Clifford Talbot.   (Indianola, Iowa, Record and Tribune Co., 1950)   200 p. ports., coat of arms (on cover) 32 cm. Cover title. 50-1817.   CS71.T14   1950

16741   TALBOT.   History of the Talbots and their kinsmen.   By Loren Clifford Talbot.   (Des Moines, Law Brief Co., 1951)   vi, 338 p. illus., ports., coat of arms (on cover) 31 cm. Cover title. "This supplement ... is to a more or less extent a rewrite of some chapters in (the author's A family history)" 52-39908.
                                                                  CS71.T14   1951

16742   TALBOT.   Genealogical sketch of certain of the American descendants of Mathew Talbot, gentleman. By Robert Howe Sletcher. (Leesburg, Va.) 1956.   70 p. geneal. tables. 26 cm. Bibliography: p. (57) - 60. 56-11767.   CS71.T14   1956

          TALBOT.   See also: HAMLETT, 1958   SMALL, 1934
                               HOWARD, 1961   TOWLES, 1957
                               PETTY, BX5195.T5B6   TUCKER, 1901
                               SMALL, 1910

          TALBOTT.   See TALBOT.

16743   TALCOTT.   Talcott pedigree in England and America from 1558 to 1876.   Compiled by S.V. Talcott.   Albany, Weed, Parsons and company, 1876.   316 p. col. front. (coat of arms) plates, ports., fold. geneal. tables. 23½ cm. Blank leaves inserted for Memoranda. 9-14565.   CS71.T142   1876

16744   TALCOTT.   General George Talcott and Angelica Bogart, his wife.   Robert Shearman and Anna Maria Sherman, his wife.   A record of their descendants and notes regarding their ancestors. (New York, N. Y., Press of B. H. Tyrrel) 1937.   2 p. l., 60 p. 24½ cm.   Blank pages for "Memoranda" (57-58) Typewritten slip of additions mounted on p. (57)   38-32672.   CS71.T142   1937

TALCOTT.   See also BASSETT, 1926

TALEMAN.   See TALLMAN.

16745   TALIAFERRO.   The Taliaferro family.   (Chattanooga, 1916?)   (2) p. 30 cm.   (Notable southern families) Detached from the Lookout.   55-49902.   CS71.T146   1916

16746   TALIAFERRO.   Ancestry and posterity of Dr. John Taliaferro and Mary (Hardin) Taliaferro, with notes on Berryman, Newton, Beheathland, Franklin, Lingo and other southern families.   Compiled by Willie Catherine Ivey and dedicated to the memory of Dr. John Taliaferro ... Tennille, Ga., 1926.   p. 92-164 incl. illus. (coat of arms) ports. 28 cm. Caption title. 37-16980.   CS71.T146   1926

16747   TALIAFERRO.   (Genealogical chart of the Taliaferro family, by) W.B.McGroarty, Falls Church, Fairfax Co., Va.   (n. p.) 1927.   geneal. tab. 92 x 72 cm. 27-19106.   CS71.T146   1927

16748   TALIAFERRO.   (Genealogical chart of the Taliaferro family. By William Buckner McGroarty. 2d ed., corr. to date, Dec. 1, 1934. Falls Church, Va., 1934)   geneal. table. 76 x 85 cm. fold. to 39 x 44 cm. 47-43217*.   CS71.T146   1934

16749   TALIAFERRO.   Listen, my children.   By Julia (Sessions) Young.   (Washington? 1953) ii, 58 p. illus., ports., coat of arms, facsims. 22 cm. 54-16338.   CS71.T146   1953

16750   TALIAFERRO.   Taliaferro-Toliver family records.   By Nellie Cadle (Watson) Sherman. (Peoria, Ill.) 1960, c.1961.   203, 39 p. port., coats of arms. 22 cm. 61-24296.   CS71.T146   1960

16751   TALIAFERRO.   See also: CAMPBELL, 1911   WHITAKER, 1930
                                    DUMONT, 1960   WILLIS, 1898
                                    MARSHALL, 1885   ZIMMERMAN, 19 -
                                    RUCKER, 1927

TĀLIB.   See ABŪ TĀLIB.

16752   TALLEY.   A history of the Talley family on the Delaware, and their descendants; including a genealogical register, modern biography and miscellany.   Early history and genealogy from 1686. By George A. Talley.   Philadelphia, Moyer & Lesher, printers, 1899.   1 p. l., 252 p. plates, port., plan. 24 cm. 21-19735.   CS71.T148   1899

TALLMADGE.   See TALMADGE.

16753   TALLMAN.   (The descendants of Mary Townley Lawrence and Timothy Talman) (n.p., 190-) geneal. tab. 43 x 71 cm. fold. to 21½ x 16½ cm. Reproduced from manuscript copy. 5-16536 rev.   CS71.T15   190-

16754   TALLMAN.   Honorable Peleg Tallman, 1764-1841, his ancestors and descendants, by William M. Emery.   (Boston, Mass., Thomas Todd company, printers) 1935.   6 p. l., 260 p., 1 l. front., illus., plates, ports., facsims. 24 cm. "Privately printed: This edition is limited to four hundred copies of which this copy is no. 144." "This volume had its inception in the work of ... Walter H. Sturtevant ... who over a long period of years took much enjoyment in collecting material relating to the life of his great-grandfather, Honorable Peleg Tallman, and in compiling genealogies of the ancestors and descendants of that progenitor." - Introductory. "Authorities": p. 84-85, 107. 36-14657.   CS71.T15   1935

16755   TALLMAN.   Toul-main, Tallman, Talman, Taleman, Taelman (by) Stephen G. Talman. (n. p.) 1936.   geneal. tab. 30½ x 45 cm. Photostat copy (pos.) 37-5914.   CS71.T15   1936

TALLMAN.   See also: BLAUVELT, 1957
                        BOONE, 1922
                        WELLS, 1892

16756 TALMADGE. The Talmage genealogy. Compiled and believed to be correct, by Sineus C. M. Talmage. East Hampton, N.Y., The Star press, 1901. 50 p. incl. front. (coat of arms) ports., fold. plan. 22 cm. 24-3046.
CS71.T151 1901

16757 TALMADGE. The Talmadge, Tallmadge and Talmage genealogy; being the descendants of Thomas Talmadge of Lynn, Massachusetts, with an appendix including other families, by Arthur White Talmadge. New York, The Grafton press, 1909. xi, 373 p. front., plates, ports., fold. maps. 24 cm. "Only two hundred and fifty copies of this book printed ..." 9-31826.
CS71.T151 1909

TALMADGE. See also VAN RENSSELAER, CS69.S7

TALMAGE. See TALMADGE.

TALMAN. See TALLMAN.

TANCRED. See TANKARD.

TANDY. See also: KAY, 1931
LEWIS, 1906
QUISENBERRY, 1897

16759 TANEY. Taney and allied families, a genealogical study with biographical notes, compiled and privately printed for Katharine T. Silverson by the American historical society, inc. New York, 1935. 279 p. pl., ports., col. coats of arms. 31 cm. Some of the plates are accompanied by guard sheets with descriptive letterpress. Allied families: Silverson, Grubb, Funk, Cheney, Sollers and Brooke. Includes bibliographical notes. 35-17578 rev.
CS71.T16 1935

16760 TANGER. The Tanger-Metzger genealogy, with a record of the descendants of John and Catharine (Metzger) Tanger, 1773-1950, and data on the Lottman, Rudisil, Snavely, Hess, Harnish, Zercher, and Gall families of Lancaster County, Pennsylvania. Gettysburg, Pa., 1955. 90 p. illus. 24 cm. 56-781 rev.
CS71.T162 1955
—— Some notes on the ancestors of Esther Snavely, 1803-1832, widow of Michael Bergtold and wife of Jacob Tanger. Gettysburg, Pa., 1957. 12 l. 28 cm.
CS71.T162 1955 Suppl.

16761 TANKARD. The life of Dr. John Tankard, by Georgianna Fitzhugh. Onancock, Va., Eastern Shore of Virginia Historical Society, 1965. 130 p. illus., fold. geneal. tables, ports. 23 cm. 200 copies. First published in 1907. 66-57742.
CS71.T165 1965

16762 TANKERSLEY. Genealogy of the Tankerlsey family in the United States. Printed about 1895. By Charles Wesley Tankersley. Atlanta, Ga., Re-issued by R.P. Rogers, 1950. 30 l. 28 cm. 51-4628.
CS71.T166 1950

16763 TANNEHILL. Tannehill. By Letitia (Tannehill) Coe. (n.p., 196-) 19 l. 29 cm. 63-5337.
CS71.T1667

16764 TANNER. The genealogy of the descendants of Thomas Tanner, sr. of Cornwall, Connecticut, with brief notes of several allied families; also short sketches of several towns of their early residence. A Columbian memorial, by Rev. Elias F. Tanner ... Lansing, Mich., D.D.Thorp, printer, 1893. xviii p., 1 l., 110 p. front. (port.) 19½ cm. 9-14566.
CS71.T167 1893

16765 TANNER. William Tanner of North Kingstown, Rhode Island and his descendants. By Rev. George C. Tanner, D.D. ... (Minneapolis) Pub, by the author, 1905. 216 p. front., ports., facsim. 23 cm. 8-30309.
CS71.T167 1905

16766 TANNER. William Tanner, sr., of South Kingstown, Rhode Island, and his descendants, in four parts, by Rev. George C. Tanner ... Pub. by the author. (Northfield, Minn., Press of the Northfield news, inc.) 1910. 470, xlvi p. front., plates, ports. 23 cm. 11-25121.
CS71.T167 1910

16767   TANNER.   Descendants of John Tanner; born August 15, 1778, at Hopkintown, R.I., died April 15, 1850 at South Cottonwood, Salt Lake County, Utah; comp. by Maurice Tanner (his great grandson) (n. p.) The Tanner family association, 1923.   264 p. illus. (ports.) 23½ cm.   The first part of the genealogy is taken from records prepared by George C. Tanner.   23-18602.   CS71. T167   1923

16768   TANNER.   Tanner family of Virginia and Kentucky.   By Emma Rouse Lloyd.   (Available for consultation at Lloyd Library, 309 West Court Street, Cincinnati 2, Ohio.

             TANNER.   See also: ROBERTS, 1946
                                   ROUSE, 1932
                                   TRACY, 1904
                                   No. 553 - Goodhue county.

16769   TAPLEY.   Genealogy of the Tapley family.   Compiled by Harriet Silvester Tapley.   Danvers, Mass.   (Printed by the Endecott press) 1900.   1 p. l., xix, 256 p. front., plates, ports., maps. 24 cm. "Gilbert Tapley, of Salem, Massachusetts, 1634-1714, and his descendants": p. (77)-225. 1-16041.   CS71. T173   1900

             TAPP.   See CLOYD, 1912

16770   TAPPAN.   Memoir of Mrs. Sarah Tappan: taken in part from the Home missionary magazine, of November, 1828, and printed for distribution among her descendants ... New-York, West & Trow, printers, 1834.   150 p. front. (port.) 19½ cm. Preface signed: L. T. (i. e. Lewis Tappan) "Family record": p. 119-150. 10-12537 rev.   BR1725. T25A4

16771   TAPPAN.   The Toppans of Toppan's lane, with their descendants and relations.   Collected and arranged by Joshua Coffin.   Newburyport, W. H. Huse & co., printers, 1862.   30 p. incl. mounted phot. 22 cm. 3-7936.   CS71. T175   1862

16772   TAPPAN.   The family records of James and Nancy Dunham Tappan, of the fourth generation, formerly of Woodbridge, Middlesex County, N. J., and their children of the fifth generation ... by Peter P. Good ... Liberty, Union County, Ind., 1884.   10, (3)-126 p. 27 cm. 25-3686.   CS71. T175   1884

16773   TAPPAN.   A sketch of the life of Rev. Daniel Dana Tappan with an account of the Tappan family, prepared by his children.   Boston, Press of S. Usher, 1890.   28 p. 23½ cm. 8-25311.   CS71. T175   1890

16774   TAPPAN.   Tappan-Toppan genealogy; ancestors and descendants of Abraham Toppan of Newbury, Massachusetts, 1606-1672, by Daniel Langdon Tappan.   Arlington, Mass., Priv. print. by the compiler, 1915.   4 p. l., 164 p. front. (coat of arms) 2 pl., port. 24½ cm. "Two hundred copies printed." 15-18653.   CS71. T175   1915

16775   TAPPAN.   Abraham Tappan (Toppan, Tappen), Edward Babbitt (Bobet), William Makepeace, John Tisdale, John Dunham, Thomas Rogers, James M. Irish, Joseph Bennett.   From genealogies and personal notes of Mildred Tappen.   Compiled by Lois Wilson Cronbaugh.   (n. p.) 1959.   64 l. 30 cm. 62-1791.   CS71. T175   1959

             TAPPAN.   See also: ANTILL, 1899
                                   CRAPO, 1912
                                   PIERCE, 1864
                                   TODD, 1909

             TAPPEN.   See TAPPAN.

             TARAZONA.   See CARBAJO.

16776   TARBELL.   Genealogical and biographical notes on the Tarbell-Tarble family, also associated families.   By Betty Lee (Tarble) Turner.   (Marshall, Ill., 1962)   1 v. (various pagings) illus. 29 cm. 63-30237.   CS71. T182   1962

16777   TARBELL.   Thomas Tarbell and some of his descendants.   By Charles Henry Wight. Boston, New England historic genealogical society, 1907.   18 p.   25 cm.   (Register re-prints, series A, no. 19) Reprinted from the New England historical and genealogical register, v. 61.   18-375.   CS71. T182   1907

TARBET.   See SALISBURY, 1961.

TARBLE.   See TARBELL.

16778   TARIEU de LANAUDIÈRE.   La famille Tarieu de Lanaudière par Pierre-Georges Roy ... Lévis, 1922.   230 p. 24½ cm. 26-2978.   CS90. T26

TARIEU de LANAUDIÈRE.   See also JARRET de VERCHÈRES, 1913

16779   TARLETON.   The Tarleton family.   Compiled by C. W. Tarleton ... 1900.   Concord, N. H., I. C. Evans, printer, 1900.   244 p. illus., plates, ports., geneal. tables. 23½ cm. 3-3817.   CS71. T188   1900

16780   TARLETON.   California letters of William Gill, written in 1850 to his wife, Harriet Tarleton in Kentucky; edited by Eva Turner Clark ... New York, Downs printing company, 1922.   43 p. front. (fold. map) port., facsims. 29½ cm. "One hundred copies privately printed." "Ancestral notes": p. 42-43. 23-14835.   F865. G47

16781   TARLETON.   Tarleton records, containing the descendants of the three brothers, John, Jeremiah, and Caleb Tarleton of Maryland and Kentucky and of Caleb Tarleton of West Virginia.   Compiled by Carrie Tarleton Goldsborough and Anna Goldsborough Fisher.   Atlanta, Williams Print. Co., 1950.   214 p. coat of arms. 24 cm. 50-38829 rev.   CS71. T188   1950

TARLETON.   See also GILL, F865. G47

TARR.   See GILES, 1864

TARRANCE.   See SPANGLER, 1937

TARRANT.   See TUGGLE, 1936

TARTER.   See DARTER.

16782   TASCHEREAU.   Branche aînée de la famille Taschereau en Canada.   (Ottawa, 1896)   33 p. 22 cm. Comp. by Sir Henri Elzeár Taschereau. 8-8731.   CS90. T3

16783   TASCHEREAU.   La famille Taschereau, par Pierre-Georges Roy ... Lévis (Québec, Imprimerie mercantile) 1901.   199, (1) p. illus., plates, ports., coat of arms. 22½ cm. "Tiré à 200 exemplaires. no. 65." 20-22508.   CS90. T3   1901

TASKER.   See SELDEN, 1911

TATAM.   See TATUM.

16784   TATE.   The name and family of Tate, compiled by Homer R. Tate.   Effingham, Ill., 1945.   22 l. incl. coat of arms. 29 x 23 cm. 47-21982.   CS71. T196   1945

16785   TATE.   Elizabeth De La Mare Tate, her ancestry and descendants.   By Nicholas Groesbeck Morgan.   (n. p.) c. 1949.   37 p. ports. 28 cm. 49-27539*.   CS71. D335   1949

16786   TATE.   The Tate family of Fayette County, Indiana.   By Ruby (Tate) Rynearson.   (Connersville, Ind., 1949)   48 p. illus., ports. 24 cm. 50-22852.   CS71. T196   1949

16787   TATE.   Van Buren Tate; diary, ancestors, descendants.   By Rachel Tate Smith.   (Albany? Tex.) 1968.   4, 16, (46) p. illus., ports. 28 cm. "Van Buren Tate's diary": p. (1) - 16 (2d group) 72-1226.   CS71. T196   1968

TATE.   See also: BOONE, 1902
KINNEY, F225.M15
McCLURE, 1914

TATEM.   See TATUM.

TATHAM.   See TATUM.

TATMAN.   See TOTMAN.

TATLOCK.   See TRUEBLOOD, 1964

16788   TATMAN.   Old families and tales of old Chicot; or, Miss Emma's memoirs.   Compiled by C. T. Thompson.   Baton Rouge, Printed by Harrell-Hannaman Letter Shop, c. 1959.   45 1. illus. 28 cm. 60-26371.
F379.C5T5   1959

TATOM.   See SCARBOROUGH, 1951

16789   TATTERSALL.   Memories of Hurstwood, Burnley, Lancashire.   With tales and traditions of the neighbourhood.   By Tattersall Wilkinson and J. F. Tattersall ... Burnley, J. & A. Lupton; London, J. S. Virtue & co., limited, 1889.   5 p. 1., 166 p. front., illus., pl., port., facsim., fold. geneal. tab. 26 cm. 2-21678.
DA690.H95W6

TATTERSHALL.   See FOX, CS410.G5 vol.30

16790   TATTNALL.   ... An account of the Tattnall and Fenwick families in South Carolina.   By D. E. Huges Smith.   (Charleston, S. C., 1913)   (3)-19 p. 25 cm. 38M4600T.   CS71.T2   1913

16791   TATUM.   Tatum narrative, 1626-1925, by Richard P. Tatum.   Philadelphia, Penna., 1925.   110 p. front., plates, ports., fold. geneal. tab. 24½ cm. The author died April 8, 1925, and his wife published the work in October, 1926. 26-21720.
CS71.T22   1926

16792   TATUM.   Family record: Edward Tatum; the forgotten Revolutionary soldier of Jefferson County, Alabama (by) Edward S. Smith.   Baltimore, Logical Products, inc. (1968)   ii, 22 p. 29 cm.   Bibliographical references included in "Notes" (p. 15-17) 68-5247.
CS71.T22   1968

16793   TAUNTON.   The Tauntons of Oxford, by one of them.   London, E. Stock, 1902.   viii, 66 p. front., plates, ports., facsim. 26 cm.   Compiled by William Garnett Taunton.   Contains also genealogies of various families with which the Tauntons have intermarried. 3-17708.
CS439.T3

16794   TAVENNER.   Descendants of George Tavenner.   By Lois Esther (Hammond) Rose.   (Canoga Park? Calif.) 1962.   21 1. 30 cm. 63-34848.   CS71.T23   1962

TAYER.   See THAYER.

TAYLARD.   See TAYLOR.

16795   TAYLOR.   (Ancestry and descendants of Rev. John Taylor of Deerfield, Mass., 1787-1806, grandson of Rev. Edward Taylor of Westfield, Mass., 1671)   New York, Lith. by Hatch & co., 1859.   geneal. tab. 41 x 53½ fold. to 23 x 13½ cm. 9-14567.   CS71.T24   1859

16796   TAYLOR.   Re-union of the family of Joseph Taylor, at Middletown, New Jersey, in 1861 ...   Printed for private circulation.   N(ew) Y(ork) W. Everdell's sons, printers, 1861.   1 p. 1... 9 numb. 1.   24 cm. Compiled by Asher Taylor. 18-15860.   CS71.T24   1861

16797   TAYLOR.   Genealogy of the Taylors.   Compiled, designed and written by Asher Taylor, 1854.   Rev. and corr.   (New York?) 1866.   mounted geneal. tab. (facsim.) 32 x 26 cm. 9-15611 rev.
CS71.T24   1866

16798   TAYLOR.   The family pen.   Memorials biographical and literary, of the Taylor family of Ongar.   Edited by the Rev. Isaac Taylor, M.A. ... London, Jackson, Walford and Hodder, 1867.
2 v.   18½ cm.   14-20091.   PR5549.T2   1867

16799   TAYLOR.   Some account of the Taylor family (originally Taylard).   Comp. and ed. by Peter Alfred Taylor ... London, Printed for private circulation, 1875.   ix, 2, 699 p.   front., plates, ports., facsims., col. coats of arms.   32 cm.   "100 copies.   no. 5."   "A historic-genealogical memoir of the family of Taylor of Aubrey house, showing its connection with the ancient family of the Taylards of Huntingdonshire.   By Joseph Lemuel Chester ... December 1863": p. 1-87.   Contains also genealogical tables of the Juxon, Fox, Sherbrooke, Clarke, Rainton Crispe, Mayo, Gage, Courtauld families. 16-8307.   CS439.T34   1875

16800   TAYLOR.   Genealogy of Judge John Taylor and his descendants.   Detroit, Mich., The Richmond & Backus co., printers, 1886.   88 p.   front. (coat of arms)   18½ cm.   "Note" (p. 87) signed: E. T.   (i. e. Elisha Taylor)
43-35970.   CS71.T24   1886
        —— Copy 2.   "Errors and additions," 1894 (11 p.) inserted between pages 86 and 87.   Ms. and type-written notes on the Leonard family inserted at end.   9-14568.   CS71.T24   1886a

16801   TAYLOR.   A memoir of the family of Taylor of Norwich, by Philip Meadows Taylor ... (London) Priv. print. (by Spottiswoode and co.) 1886.   2 p. l., 91 p.   18½ cm.   16-17285 rev.
                                                                                            CS439.T34   1886

16802   TAYLOR.   Descendants of Joseph Taylor, of Kennet, Chester Co., Pa.   By Gilbert Cope.   West Chester, Pa., 1891.   geneal. tab.   56 x 43½ fold. to 22 x 14½ cm.   9-14569.
                                                                                            CS71.T24   1891

16803   TAYLOR.   Some account of the ancestors, relatives and family of Henry Boardman Taylor, with a memoir written by himself, and a supplement by Rev. B. S. Taylor, brought down to October 1892.   (n. p., 1892)   72 p.   front., (port.)   19½ cm.   16-4783.   CS71.T24   1892

16804   TAYLOR.   Rev. Edward Taylor, 1642-1729.   New-York, Priv. print. (The De Vinne press) 1892.   80 p.   18 cm.   "A part has been published in the 'New-York Evangelist.'   I have added a written sketch by Miss Emma C. Nason, which was published in a series of articles in the 'Advocate and guardian' in 1880 and 1881." - Introd. note signed: John Taylor Terry.   Contents. - Rev. Edward Taylor. - Ruth Taylor and her five daughters, by Emma C. Nason. - More about Ruth Taylor, her ancestors and descendants.   10-31151.
                                                                                            BX7260.T28T4

16805   TAYLOR.   Poems and writings of Henry Wyllys Taylor of Hartford.   Compiled and arranged by Alice J. Meins ... Hartford, Conn., Press of the Case, Lockwood & Brainard company, 1895.
4 p. l., 9-461 p.   front. (port.)   pl.   20½ cm.   Taylor genealogy: p. 9-14; Biography: 15-18.   31-14102.
                                                                                            PS2999.T47

16806   TAYLOR.   Some notable families of America; by Annah Robinson Watson.   New York, 1898.
xiv, 110 p.   front., illus., pl., ports., coats of arms.   22½ cm.   Contents. - Dedication. - Family mottoes. - Proem. - Taylor family, biographical sketch and record of. - Allerton. - Willoughby. - Brewster. - Thompson. - Madison. - Lee. - Strother. - Warner. - Reade. - Lewis. - Meriwether. - Walker. - Maury. - Thornton. - Hornsby.   4-8403.   CS71.T24   1898

16807   TAYLOR.   (History of the Taylor family by Jane Taylor Joy)   (Northampton Mass., 1898)
1 p. l., 25 numb. l., 2 l., 2-7 numb. l.   33 cm.   Type-written.   Text runs parallel with back of cover.   Copied from the original manuscript by Grace Taylor Locke, Feb. 28, 1934.   38M1742T.   CS71.T24   1898a

16808   TAYLOR.   Origin and history of the name of Taylor, with biographies of all the most noted persons of that name.   And an account of the origin of surnames and forenames.   Together with over five hundred Christian names of men and women and their significance.   The Crescent family record.   Chicago, Ill., American publishers' association, 1902.   5 p. l., iv, 33-112, (14) p., 1 l.   illus.   23 cm.   Forms for "Crescent family records": 14 p. at end.   22-17214.   CS71.T24   1902

16809   TAYLOR.   History of John Taylor of Hadley, including account of the organization and meetings of the Taylor reunion association of Hadley, Massachusetts, and the genealogy of the descendants of the ancestor.   (By) Rev. Elbert O. Taylor, historian and compiler ... Boston, Pub. by the Association, 1903.   111 p. incl. plans.   front., plates, ports.   24½ cm.   5-469.   CS71.T24   1903

16810   TAYLOR.   Family record of the descendants of Dr. Edward Taylor.   By William Shipley
Taylor.   Philadelphia, Printed by G.W.Jacobs (1903-54)   2 v. illus. 24-28 cm.   Vol. 2, without imprint, by
J.G.Taylor.   Contents. - (1) To December 1903. - (2) To December 1953.   57-45361.   CS71.T24   1903a

16811   TAYLOR.   The Taylor-Livingston centenary in Franklin County.   (In Ohio archaeological and
historical quarterly.   Columbus, 1904.   23½ cm.   v.13, p. 486-503. illus.)   18-8571.   F486.O51 vol.13

16812   TAYLOR.   John Taylor and his Taylor descendants.   By Benjamin Franklin Taylor.   (n.p.,
1907)   25 p. front. (facsim.) ports.   23 cm.   Cover-title.   7-23344.   CS71.T24   1907
—— Copy 2.   (In The South Carolina historical and genealogical magazine.   Charleston, S.C., 1907.   23½ cm.   Vol. VIII,
no.2, p.95-119.   ports., facsim.)   Caption title.   44-16761.   F266.S55 vol. 8 no. 2
—— Detached.   CS71.T24   1907a

16813   TAYLOR.   A life of John Taylor ... prebendary of Westminster, & friend of Dr. Samuel
Johnson.   Together with an account of the Taylors & Websters of Ashburne, with pedigrees and copious
genealogical notes, by Thomas Taylor ... London, The St. Catherine press, ltd. & J. Nisbet & co.
(1910)   xviii, 150 p. front. (coat of arms) pl., ports., 2 fold. geneal. tab. (In pocket)   23 cm.   34-21381.
BX5199.T32T3

16814   TAYLOR.   ... The Taylor family of Yarmouth.   Yarmouthport, Mass., C.W.Swift, 1912.
cover-title, 13 p.   25 cm.   (Library of Cape Cod history & genealogy, no. 75)   17-6145.   CS71.T24   1912

16815   TAYLOR.   ... Richard Taylor, tailor, and some of his descendants, by James W. Hawes.
Yarmouthport, Mass., C.W.Swift, 1914.   cover-title, 36 p.   25½ cm.   (Library of Cape Cod history & genealogy.   no. 48)
14-17828.   CS71.T24   1914

16816   TAYLOR.   Taylor record, Lenoir county, N. C.   Copied about 1916 by Sybil Hyatt.
Kinston, N. C. (1916)   2 l.   28 x 21½ cm.   Caption title.   Type-written.   44-27973.
CS71.T24   1916

16817   TAYLOR.   Taylor family record, 1770-1916.   Compiled by Arthur Taylor Carr., Isadore
Austin, Mary E. Price, Ralph Hisey, committee.   (n.p., 1916)   cover-title, 17 p.   20½ cm.   25-13338.
CS71.T24   1916a

16818   TAYLOR.   Taylor family association, incorporated.   Year book ... v.1-2.   1924-29.
Louisville, Ky. (1926?) -   2 v. plates, ports.   23 cm.   30-1648.   CS71.T24   1924

16819   TAYLOR.   Descendants of Robert Taylor, one of the colonizers and early settlers of
Pennsylvania under William Penn, with special reference to the descendants of his son Isaac, and his
daughters, Rachel Livesey and Mary Lewis, by Alfred Rudulph Justice ... Philadelphia, A.R.Justice
and J.W.Taylor, 1925.   113 p. front., fold. facsims.   24 cm.   "Edition limited to seventy copies."   27-7387.
CS71.T24   1925

16820   TAYLOR.   History of the Taylor family, the descendants of William and Ann (Wilson) Taylor
of Lawrence County, Pennsylvania.   Records gathered by Thomas M. Taylor, 1895, revised and added
to by Thomas M.Stewart, 1925.   Filley, Neb., Printed for the Taylor family association, 1925.
2 p. l., 64 p. pl. (ports.) 23½ cm.   Six leaves at end left blank for additions.   28-18065.   CS71.T24   1925a

16821   TAYLOR.   ... Taylor family records, by J. Montgomery Seaver, assisted by Mildred E.
Shumaker.   Philadelphia, Pa., American historical-genealogical society (1929)   79 p. front. (4 port.)
coat of arms.   29 cm.   Coat of arms of the Taylor family on recto of frontispiece.   Pages 77-78 blank for "Family records".   "References":
p. 75-76.   40-18926.   CS71.T24   1929

16822   TAYLOR.   Genealogical history of the Taylor, Farwell, Washburn, and other families, being
the maternal ancestry of Robert Fremont Herron of Los Angeles, California ... Compiled by Ella Foy
O'Gorman.   (Washington, D. C.) 1930 (i.e.1932)   4 p. l., 1, 1-16, 16a-66, 66a-95 numb. l., 2 l., 96-282 numb. l.,
1 l. front., ports., 2 geneal. tab.   29 cm.   Typewritten.   Contents. - pt. I. Taylor, Farwell and allied families. - pt. II. Washburn and allied
families.   34-5045.   CS71.T24   1930
Office.

16823   TAYLOR.   Descendants of John Taylor of Windsor by William Othniel Taylor ... with additions by Edwin T. Pollock ... (n. p.) 1931.   4 v. 32 cm. Type-written. Volume 4: Index. 33-18729.

CS71. T24   1931

16824   TAYLOR.   Taylor of Tennessee.   By Zella Armstrong.   Pemphlet edition.   Chattanooga,
Lookout Pub. Co. (1933?)   36 p. 24 cm. (Notable southern families) "Limited to 150 copies." 33-6864 rev. *

CS71. T24   1933

16825   TAYLOR.   Genealogy Taylor-Snow, in memory of Oscar Taylor and Malvina Snow Taylor, by
Charissa Taylor Bass and Frank Nelson Bass.   Freeport, Ill., C. T. Bass, 1935. 2 v. in 1. front. (double
geneal. tab.) illus. (incl. ports.) 34 x 44 cm. "Two hundred copies of this book were printed." The genealogical table is a phtostat reproduction. Index at end has separate paging. 35-14612.

CS71. T24   1935

16826   TAYLOR.   The Taylor family ... (By Mrs. Edith Tunnell.) (Yonkers, N. Y., c. 1935)
2 l. 28 cm. and map 47 x 66 cm. 38M5287T.

CS439. T34   1935

16827   TAYLOR.   Family history.   Anthony Taylor of Hampton, New Hampshire, founder, pioneer,
town father, and some of his descendant, 1635-1935, compiled, edited and published by Harold
Murdock Taylor ... (Rutland, Vt., The Tuttle publishing company, inc., 1935)   530 p., 1 l. front., plates,
ports., maps, facsims. (1 double) 23½ cm. Cover-title: Anthony Taylor family history, 1635-1935. Tercentenary edition. 37 10868 rev.

CS71. T24   1935a

———— Additions.   (Rutland, Vt., The Tuttle publishing company, inc., 1945)   134 p. front.,
plates, ports., map. 23½ cm. "Supplementary edition, December, 1945."

CS71. T25   1935a
Additions.

16828   TAYLOR.   William Harrison Taylor and four generations of the Taylor family (by) Alan
McLean Taylor.   (Adrian? Mich., 1936)   81 p. 23 cm. 37-16834.

CS71. T24   1936

16829   TAYLOR.   The Taylors of Ongar; portrait of an English family of the eighteenth and nineteenth centuries.   Drawn from family records by the great-great niece of Ann and Jane Taylor.   Doris
Mary Armitage.   Cambridge (Eng.) W. Heffer & sons, ltd.   (1939)   xviii, 252 p. incl. illus., plates, ports.
front. 22½ cm. "Some works by the Taylor family": p. xvii-xviii. "A Taylor miscellany": p. 179-235. 39-20740.

PR4712. G6Z55

16830   TAYLOR.   Genealogical history of the Taylor family.   By Burnice Elizabeth (Taylor)
Buchanan.   (Atlanta) 1939.   35 p. 23 cm. 50-47925.

CS71. T24   1939

16831   TAYLOR.   Annals of a Bucks county family of Old Taylorsville, Pennsylvania, by Mary Snyder
Taylor.   (Bogota, N. J., Dancey printing co., c. 1940)   xiii, 300 p. incl. front. plates, ports., maps (part fold.)
facsim., 3 fold. geneal. tab. (in pocket) 23½ cm. An account of the Taylor family. 40-6564.

CS71. T24   1940

16832   TAYLOR.   The Taylor family of dentists.   By Edward C. Mills.   (In The Ohio state archaeological and
historical quarterly. Columbus, Ohio, 1947. 23 cm. v. 56, p. 392-398. illus., port.) Bibliographical footnotes. A48-2027 *.

F486. O51 vol. 56

16833   TAYLOR.   Jasper Taylor and his descendants; with genealogies of related families.   By
Eva Mills (Lee) Taylor.   Bethesda, Md., 1950.   vii, 233 p. 24 cm. 50-3066.   CS71. T24   1950

16834   TAYLOR.   The Taylors of Tabernacle; the history of a family, including the genealogy of its
descendants with biographical sketches and family journals with daily accounts of life in Haywood
County, Tennessee, for over a century ... Taylor Kinsfolk Association at Tabernacle Church.
Brownsville, Tenn., 1957.   628 p. illus. 24 cm. 57-12869.   CS71. T24   1957

16835   TAYLOR.   Descendants of James (I) Taylor, great-great-grandfather of Zachary (III) Taylor,
twelfth President of the United States.   By John Taylor. (Kansas City? Mo.) 1958.   15 l. 29 cm.
58-33132.   CS71. T24   1958

16836   TAYLOR.   Taylor family genealogy.   By John Taylor.   (Kansas City? Mo.) c. 1958.
10, 41 l. 29 cm. 58-33261.   CS71. T24   1958a

16837   TAYLOR.   Southern Taylor families, 1607-1830. By Albert Eugene Casey. With the assistance of Donna Smith Gordon, G.H.L. Dunagin, and Martha B. Thorn. Birmingham, Ala., Published privately for the Amite County Historical Fund, 1958.   319 p. 29 cm. 59-19544.   CS71.T24   1958b

16838   TAYLOR.   Taylor; John Taylor (3-24-1771/9-19-1839) and his wife Elizabeth Lafler and their descendants comprising 8 generations.   Gathered, compiled, indexed, and mimeographed by great-granddaughter Fannie Belle Taylor Richardson (Greenwood, Ind.) 1959.   64 p.   illus. 29 cm. 59-43209.
CS71.T24   1959

16839   TAYLOR.   The Lineage and the descendants of Tarpley Early Taylor.   Prepared by his children and grandchildren.   (n.p., 1959?)   15 p. 19 cm. 60-41073.   CS71.T24   1959a

16840   TAYLOR.   Historic genealogy sketch; the Taylors of western Pennsylvania (by) Zera Gibson Taylor.   (St. Petersburg, Fla.) 1965.   73 p.   coat of arms. 28 cm. On cover: Taylors of western Pennsylvania. 66-8469.
CS71.T24   1965

16841   TAYLOR.   The family of James Francis Taylor, with related families of Wooten, Vernon, Harrington and Pool, by M. Blair Autry (and) Mamie Taylor Autry.   Corsicana, Tex., 1967.
219 p. illus., ports. 29 cm. Bibliography: p. 219. 67-6967.   CS71.A935   1967

TAYLOR.   See also:

BACKHOUSE, DA690.M74C3	HAYNES, 1922	POLLOCK, 1932
BACKHOUSE, CS439.B18	HERNDON, 1930	ROBERTSON, 1900
BELL, F232.L9B4	HYNES, 1941	SELDEN, 1911
BULLITT, 1920	JOHNSON, 1930b	SHRODE, 1945
CAREW, 1954	JONES, 1941	WALLACE, 1930
CARPENTER, 1959	KAY, DA690.T93S3	WATSON, 1910
CARTER, 1927	KINNEY, F225.M15	WEEKS, 1933
CASTLE, 1923	KINNISON, 1956	WILBUR, 1936
CRANMER, 1965	LANDOR, 1912	WILDER, 1960
CROCKER, 1923	LINDLEY, 1950	WILFORD, 1959
DOBYNS, 1908	LOMAX, 1913	WILLIS, 1898
DRAKE, 1962	MACLIN, 1928	WINSTON, 1927
DWIGHT, 1874	MAY, 1969	No. 553 - Goodhue county.
FOY, 1931	NELSON, 1886	No. 1547 - Cabell county.
GLASSELL, 1891	NELSON, 1894	No. 3509 - Orange county.
	PERKINS, 1914	No. 3939 - Colebrook

TAYLOR-CARY.   See No. 430 - Adventurers of purse and person.

TAYNTER.   See TAINTER.

TAZEWELL.   See POCAHONTAS, 1887

TEACHOUT.   See COATES, 1901a

TEAGARDEN.   See TEGARDEN.

TEAGLE.   See IRONMONGER, 1956

TEAGUE.   See SHANK, 1960

TEAL.   See TEALL.

16843   TEALL.   Genealogical and historical notes of the Teall family. (Chicago, 1889)
cover-title, 7 p. 22½ cm. Introduction signed: Edward M. Teall. 5-16527.   CS71.T253   1889

16844   TEALL.   Descendants of Oliver Teall, and allied families, by Dora Pope Worden. Ithaca, N.Y., 1922.   cover-title, 13 p. illus. 23 cm. Mounted portrait of Oliver Teall on cover. 24-3043.   CS71.T253   1922

16845 TEALL. Teall genealogical records in England and America, compiled by Mrs. Emma Elisabeth (Teall) Dunn ... Los Angeles, Cal., Gem publishing company, 1926. 59 p. incl. front., illus., coat of arms. 22½ cm. Three blank pages at end for more "Genealogical records." 27-11114. CS71.T253 1926

16846 TEASDALE. ... Treatise on the origin and early history of the Teesdale-Teasdale family; with especial reference to the Reverend Thomas Teasdale, of Sussex county, New Jersey, who died in 1827. By Milton Rubincam. Washington, D.C., 1937. 1 p. l., 21 numb. l., 2 l. 29 cm. Type-written. "Authorities consulted": 2 leaves at end. 37-16837. CS71.T255 1937

16847 TEASDALE. Historical outline of the Teasdale-Teesdale families, by Milton Rubincam ... Washington, D.C. (1939) (7) p. 26 cm. "Reprinted from the National genealogical society quarterly, September, 1939." Bibliographical foot-notes. 40-18337. CS71.T255 1939

TEBBS. See BROWN, 1930

16848 TEDFORD. A Tedford family history. By Victor Charles Detty. Carlisle, Pa., 1956. 185 p. illus. 23 cm. 56-13386. CS71.T256 1956

TEEGARDEN. See TEGARDEN.

TEEGUARDEN. See TEGARDEN.

16849 TEEL. Genealogies of the Teel family of New England and of the family of David Thomas of Middleboro, Massachusetts, together with the ancestry of Frank Herbert Teel and of his wife Grace Carroll Thomas and a register of descendants of Gershom Teel, Benjamin Swan, Horatio Nelson Thomas and Prentice Howes. (Menlo Park? Calif., 1964) ix, 196 p. geneal. table. 23 cm. Cover title: Teel and Thomas genealogies. Bibliography: p. 174-181. 65-406. CS71.T253 1964

TEESDALE. See TEASDALE.

16850 TEETOR. Teetor, Nicholson and allied families, a genealogical study with biographical notes, privately printed for Leora E. (Nicholson) Teetor, compiler of the genealogy herein ... New York, The American historical company, inc., 1943. 263 p. plates, ports., col. geneal. tab., col. coat of arms. 32½ x 25 cm. Bound in blue crushed levant, gold tooled. Printed on one side of leaf only. Some of the plates accompanied by guard sheets with descriptive letterpress. Allied families: Macy, Barnard, Folger, Starbuck, Gardner and Coffin. Includes bibliographical references. 44-2227. CS71.T257 1943

16851 TEETOR. A history of the Teetor family, 1730-1966. By Paul Teetor. West Islip, N.Y., 1967. 73 l. 29 cm. 79-10616 MARC. CS71.T257 1967

TEFFE. See TEFFT.

16852 TEFFT. A partial record of the descendants of John Tefft, of Portsmouth, Rhode Island, and the nearly complete record of the descendants of John Tifft, of Nassau, New York ... Together with other miscellaneous records. Compiled by Maria E. (Maxon) Tifft ... Buffalo, N.Y., The Peter Paul book company, 1896. 4 p. l., 9-159 numb. l. 24½ cm. Index in pocket on back cover. 9-14556. CS71.T259 1896

16853 TEFFT. The Tefft ancestry, comprising many hitherto unpublished records of descendants of John Tefft of Portsmouth, Rhode Island; compiled and edited by Rev. Charles H. W. Stocking ... (Chicago) The Lakeside press, 1904. 2 p. l., 102 numb. l., 1 l. 23½ cm. Printed on one side of leaf only. 12-1820. CS71.T259 1904

TEFFT. See also DILLON, 1927

16854 TEGARDEN. Genealogy and biographical sketches of descendants of Abraham Tegarden, from arrival in America, including European background. By Helen Elizabeth Vogt. Berkeley, Calif. (Printed by Consolidated Printers) 1967. 696 p. illus., facsims., ports. 23 cm. Cover title: Descendants of Abraham Tegarden. 67-26911. CS71.T262 1967

16855 TEGGE. The Tegge-Allen family. By Clara Stearns Scarbrough. Georgetown, Tex., Sun Publishers, 1967. vii, 24 p. facsim., ports. 26 cm. Bibliography: p. 20-21. 68-5598.
CS71.T263 1967

TEISEN. See TYSON.

16856 TELFORD. Threads of ancestors: Telford, Ritchie, Mize, by Leila Ritchie Mize (and) Jessie Julia Mize. (Athens? Ga., 1956) 273 p. illus. 24 cm. 58-24992.
CS71.T265 1956

16857 TELL. Släktregister och minnesteckning över stamfäderna förre dragon Per Andersson Tell och hans hustru Karna Tell, född Jönsdotter. Släktforskningen omfattar tiden 1763-1965. By August Munthell. (Malmö, 1966) (19) p. illus. 29 cm. "Omskrivning och rättelse av släktregister över Per Andersson Tell - Karna Jönsdotter Tell" (4) leaves inserted. 72-424624.
CT1328.T44M8

16858 TELLER. Teller and related families ... (by) Lillis Teller Van Antwerp ... and ... Katherine V. A. Venable ... (n. p., 1936?) 131 numb. l. 29½ x 24 cm. Type-written (carbon copy) 45-40093.
CS71.T27 1936

16859 TELLER. Teller family in America, record of a hundred years. By Chester Jacob Teller. (Philadelphia) Cousins' Publ. Committee, 1944. 221 p. 26 cm. "One hundred numbered copies ... No. 83." 45-16771 rev. *
CS71.T27 1944

  —— Supplement. no. 1 - (n. p.) 1948 - v. 24 cm.
CS71.T27 1944 Suppl.

16860 TELLER. New Teller generations; sequel to Teller family in America. By Chester Jacob Teller. (Library ed. Philadelphia) Cousins' Publication Committee, 1953. 64 p. 26 cm. 53-37308.
CS71.T27 1953

TELLER. See also REICHNER, 1910

16861 TEMPEST. Pedigree of the Tempests ... designed and executed by Frederick T. E. Rusby. Leeds, 1934. geneal. table, illus. (col. coat of arms) 70 x 104½ cm. fold. to 36½ x 31½ cm. 39-23111.
CS439.T345 1934

TEMPEST. See also PLUMB, 1898

16862 TEMPLE. An account of the Temple family, with notes and pedigree of the family of Bowdoin. Reprinted from the New England historical and genealogical register, with corrections and additions, by W. H. Whitmore. Boston, Printed for private circulation only, by Dutton and Wentworth, 1856. 15 p. 23 cm. 16-4785.
CS71.T258 1856

16863 TEMPLE. Some account of the Temple family. (By Temple Prime) New York, 1887. 100 p. fold. geneal. tab. 25 cm. (With his Some account of the Temple family. 3d ed. New-York, 1896. Copy 2) 3-479.
CS71.T285 1896

16864 TEMPLE. Some account of the Temple family; by Temple Prime ... 2d ed. New-York (De Vinne press) 1894. 111 p. incl. illus., geneal. tables (partly fold.) 25 cm. 3-477.
CS71.T285 1894

16865 TEMPLE. Some account of the Temple family; by Temple Prime ... 3d ed. New-York (De Vinne press) 1896. 146 p. incl. illus., geneal. tab., port., fold. geneal. tab. 25 cm. 3-2404.
CS71.T285 1896

16866 TEMPLE. Some account of the Temple family, by Temple Prime. 4th ed. New York (The De Vinne press) 1899. 77 p. incl. illus. (coats of arms) geneal. tables. ports., fold. geneal. tab. 24 cm. Bibliography: p. 62-65. 3-478.
CS71.T285 1899

16867   TEMPLE.   Some account of the Temple family: appendix; by Temple Prime ... New York
(De Vinne press) 1899.   1 p. l., 162 p. illus., port. 25 cm. 3-476.   CS71. T285   1899a

16868   TEMPLE.   Some Temple pedigrees.   A genealogy of the known descendants of Abraham
Temple, who settled at Salem, Mass., in 1636 ... Added genealogies of Temple families settling ...
elsewhere.   Also brief genealogies of families connected ... By Levi Daniel Temple.   Boston, D.
Clapp & son, 1900.   316 p. front., ports. 23½ cm. 1-19543.   CS71. T285   1900

16869   TEMPLE.   The Temple memoirs; an account of this historic family and its demesnes; with
biographical sketches, anecdotes & legends from Saxon times to the present day; including a frontispiece in colours, thirty-four plates & two sheet pedigrees.   By Colonel John Alexander Temple ...
assisted by Harald Markham Temple.   London, H. F. & G. Witherby, 1925.   206 p. col. front., plates, ports.,
fold. geneal. tables, coats of arms. 26½ cm. "Only 250 copies of this edition have been printed. ...No. 107" 25-19179.
                                                    CS439. T35

16870   TEMPLE.   The descendants of Roswell Temple and Elizabeth Case who lived in Washington
County, New York, from 1801 to 1893.   Also the genealogy of all their offspring to and through the
year 1946, being a supplement to "Some Temple pedigrees" by Levi Daniel Temple.   Los Angeles,
1947.   53 p. ports., map, facsim. 22 cm. 48-14256*.   CS71. T285   1947

          TEMPLE.   See also: CLARK, CS438. C5
                                 GURNEY, DC11. N845G7
                                 HAWES, 1932
                                 LAKE, 1956
                                 ROLFE, CS439. R65

16871   TEMPLEMAN.   (Chart showing the ancestry of Robert Morris Templeman) compiled by
Eleanor Lee Templeman.   Arlington, Va. (1943)   geneal. tab. 20½ x 40 cm. Photostat (positive) 45-14189.
                                                    CS71. T286   1943

          —— Supplement to chart.   Templeman family.   History & heraldry.   (Arlington, 1943)
4 l. 28½ x 22 cm. Caption title. Type-written (carbon copy) 45-14189.   CS71. T286   1943
                                                    Suppl.

16872   TEMPLETON.   Templeton family tree, data by L. B. Templeton, jr; S. D. Trowbridge, delineator.   (Indianapolis, Print. by Indianapolis blue print & supply co.) c. 1933.   geneal. tab. 83 x 41 cm.
fold. to 22 cm. 33-36891 rev.   CS71. T287   1933

16873   TEMPLETON.   The Templeton and allied families; a genealogical history and family record,
compiled by YoLande Templeton Clague.   South Bend, Ind., The author (c. 1936)   7 p. l., (13)-169 p.
front., ports. 23½ cm. 37-525.   CS71. T287   1936

16874   TEMPLETON.   Templeton family history; records and descendants of the Templetons who
first settled in what is now Laurens County, South Carolina, together with brief sketches of other
Templetons who settled in other parts of South Carolina and other States.   (Union? S. C.) c. 1953.
viii, 155 p. ports., col. coat of arms, facsims. 24 cm. Errata slip inserted. 53-31331. CS71. T287   1953

16875   TEMPLETON.   Templeton family record, a genealogical record of the family of James and
Sarah (Hutchason) Templeton as of July 1, 1953.   (Ann Arbor? 1953)   65 p. illus. 23 cm. 53-36244,
                                                    CS71. T287   1953a

          TEMPLETON.   See also CURTIS, 1912

16876   TEMPLIN.   The Templin family.   By Loruma Templin Buchanan.   1957.   In vertical file.
Ask reference librarian for this material.

          TEN BROCK.   See TEN BROECK.

16877   TEN BROECK.   General Abraham Ten Broeck.   (By George Edwin Bartol Jackson.)   (Portland, Me., S. Berry, printer, 1886.   12 p. front. (port.) 21½ x 17½ cm. "Genealogy of the Ten Broeck family," p. 7-12.
9-17835.   CS71. T289   1886

16878   TENER.   Tener; a history of the family in France, Ireland, and America.   (n.p.) Priv. print., 1949.   83 p. illus., ports., coat of arms.   22 cm.   Prepared, printed and distributed at the request of Hampden E. Tener. 49-54935*.   CS71.T29   1949

TENISON.   See TENNYSON.

16879   TENNANT.   Genealogy of the Tennant family; their ancestors and descendants through many generations, by Rev. Albert Milton Tennant, with contributions from other members of the family. Dunkirk, N.Y., Dunkirk printing company, 1915.   356 p. plates, ports. 24 cm.   "Daniel Tennant of Waterville, N.Y.; his family, descendants, and ancestors, by Willis H. Tennant": p. 305-314. 16-23276.   CS71.T297   1915

16880   TENNANT.   ... Genealogical notes on the family of Rev. William Tennent.   Compiled by Rev. Frank R. Symmes.   Freehold, N.J., 1926.   1 l. 37 x 26 cm. fold. to 27 x 19 cm.   Caption title.   Photostat copy (positive) "From the Monmouth democrat, Freehold, N.J., Oct. 14, 1926." "Sources of information." 36-12563.   CS71.T297   1926

16881   TENNANT.   Genealogy of the Tennant family; a record of kinship with Thomas Tennant (1755-1821) and his wife Ann Hill (1764-1840) by Robert D. Tennant.   (North Bay, Ont., 1963?) 1 v. (various pagings) illus., facsims., maps, ports. 29 cm.   Includes bibliography. 65-52808.   CS71.T296   1963

16882   TENNANT.   The Tennant history (1803-1964) by Louise Tornquist, Bette Tornquist Smith (and) Coral Willoughby.   (n.p., 1964)   80 p. illus., ports. 24 cm. 65-4227.   CS71.T297   1964

TENNANT.   See also: McCLURE, 1934
                         ROGERS, 1921

TENNENT.   See TENNANT.

16883   TENNEY.   Genealogy of the Tenney family.   no. 2.   Prepared by Samuel Tenney.   Boston, 1851.   broadside. 26 x 35½ cm.   CS71.T299   1851

16884   TENNEY.   Genealogy of the Tenney family, more particularly of the family of Daniel Tenney, and Sylvia Kent, his wife, late of Laporte, Lorain County, Ohio.   From 1634 and 1638 to 1875.   Compiled by Horace A. Tenney.   Madison, Wis., M.J. Cantwell, printer, 1875.   76 (i.e. 80) p. 23½ cm. 9-14562.   CS71.T299   1875

16885   TENNEY.   The Tenney family; or, The descendants of Thomas Tenney, of Rowley, Mass. 1638-1890.   By M.J. Tenney.   Boston, Mass., American printing and engraving company, 1891. 369 p., 1 l. incl. col. front. (coat of arms) ports. 23 cm. 9-14561.   CS71.T299   1891

16886   TENNEY.   The Tenney family; or, The descendants of Thomas Tenney, of Rowley, Massachusetts, 1638-1904, revised with partial records of Prof. Jonathan Tenney.   By M.J. Tenney.   Concord, N.H., The Rumford press, 1904.   691 p. col. front. (coat of arms) plates, ports. 23½ cm. 5-1162.   CS71.T299   1904

16887   TENNEY.   Tenney.   (A genealogical chart of the maternal ancestry of George Parmelee Castle, for whom it was) compiled by Lawrence Brainerd.   Boston, Mass., 1922.   geneal. tab. 60 x 95 cm.   Contains a few manuscript and type-written additions.   Accompanying this chart are: The Ancestry of Hannah Griswold, wife of Jesse Tenney, geneal. tab. 68½ x 23½ cm.   Griswold family. Geneal. tab. 35 cm. 25-12675.   CS71.T299   1922

16888   TENNEY.   The royal ancestry of Deacon Levi Tenney, compiled by Sarah Louise Kimball, together with A short sketch of the origin and development of the science and art of heraldry, by Maude Stevens Ingelow, A.M.   Prepared for George Parmelee Castle ... Palo Alto, 1928.   2 p. l., 7-95, (1) p. illus. 22 cm.   A leaf numbered 76a inserted.   "A short sketch ... of herladry" (p. 81-95) has special t.-p.   Bibliography: p. 77 and 95. 36-5186.   CS71.T299   1928

TENNEY.   See also ATWOOD, 1888

TENNYSON.   See CROSSLEY, CS439.C835

16889   TENNYSON-D'EYNCOURT.   Genealogical history of the family of Tennyson D'Eyncourt, of Bayons manor, in the county of Lincoln.   By John Bernard Burke, esq.   London, 1846.   1 p. l., 15p. front. (coat of arms) port., geneal. tab.   23 cm.   (With his Bayons manor, in the county of Lincoln.   London, 1852)   Reprinted from the Landed gentry.   The portrait of John, the Good, king of France. is from a facsimile, printed in 1858 by Mr. Edward Poynter from the contemporary portrait preserved amongst the royal relics in the Louvre.   21-3217.   DA 690. B33B8

16890   TENZER.   Jubilee volume of the Michael Tenzer family circle.   Tenth anniversary (5687 - 5697) (1927-1937);   a record of the activities and achievements of the Michael Tenzer family circle, including articles on the Jewish family by outstanding rabbis and scholars.   Compiled and edited by Solomon Kerstein.   New York (Printed by Ginsberg linotyping co.) 1937.   4 p. l., ii, 205, (1) p.   illus. (facsims.)   23½ cm.   37-16826.   CS71. T2995   1937

16891   TERBORCH.   ... Gérard Terburg (Ter Borch) et sa famille, par Émile Michel.   Paris, J. Rouam;   (etc., etc., 1887)   71, (1) p.   illus. (incl. ports.) fold. pl.   26½ cm.   (Les artistes célèbres)   "Bibliographie et catalogue": p. (68)-69.   F3680 rev.   ND653. T4M6

16892   BLAUVELT.   The Blauvelt family genealogy;   a comprehensive compilation of the descendants of Gerrit Hendricksen (Blauvelt) 1620-1687, who came to America in 1638.   By Louis Leon Blauvelt. East Orange? N. J. Association of Blauvelt Descendants, 1957.   1064 p.   illus., maps, col. coat of arms, facsims. 29 cm.   56-10931.   CS71. B6476   1957

16893   TERRELL.   A genealogical history of the Tyrrells sometime of the French Vexin, Poix in Picardy, Guernanville in Normandy, Laingaham in Essex, Kingsworthy and Avon Tyrrell in Hampshire; Castleknock in co. Dublin ... With pedigrees from B. C. 443 to the present day.   An appendix containing the descents of some families (and their connections) with whom alliances have been contracted, and a roll of arms.   Compiled by Joseph Henry Tyrrell.   (n. p., 1904?)   1 p. l., 202, 29 p. front., (coats of arms) 29½ x 23 cm.   "100 copies privately printed.   No. 33. "   "Corrigenda" and "Addenda" slip inserted.   "Authorities": p. 11, 1st group. 10-5861.   CS439. T92
                                                                  Microfilm 10314 CS

16894   TERRELL.   Further genealogical notes on the Tyrrell-Terrell family of Virginia and its English and Norman-French progenitors, by Edwin H. Terrell.   2d ed., with addenda and corrigenda. San Antonio, Tex., 1909.   41 p. incl. coat of arms.   23 cm.   9-9948.   CS71. T3   1909

16895   TERRELL.   The genealogy of Richmond and William Tyrrell or Terrell (descended from the family of Tyrrell of Thornton Hall, Buckinghamshire, England), who settled in Virginia in the seventeenth century.   Compiled (and issued as a Supplement to his "Genealogical history of the Tyrrells") by Joseph Henry Tyrrell.   (n. p., 1910?)   (1), 29 p. incl. geneal. tables (part fold.) front. (coat of arms) 30 x 23 cm. Cover-title: The Tyrrells or Terrells of America.   "150 copies privately printed.   No. 62. "   14-309.   CS71. T3   1910

16896   TERRELL.   Mannington hall and its owners.   By Charles S. Tomes ... Norwich, Goose & son, ltd., 1916.   2 p. l., 66 p. illus. (incl. coats of arms) plates, fold. maps, fold. geneal. tab. 22½ cm.   "The history of the manor of Mannington extends back to the period of the Norman conquest, whilst during the 850 years which have since elapsed it has passed through the hands of only four families, the Tyrels, the Lumnors, the Potts and the Walpoles. " - p. 2.   "Arms of some of the families mentioned": p. 64-66.   28-19376.   DA664. M3T6

16897   TERRELL.   Ancestral lineage of the mother of Alexandros J. Quayle, and his sisters, Papie Lee Quayle, and Maud C. Quayle, and brother, James Quayle.   (By Alexandros Jack Quayle)   (Los Angeles, The McBride printing co., 1921)   6 p.   21½ cm.   Caption title.   Cover-title: A genealogy line of the Terrills. Type-written and manuscript corrections.   21-13993.   CS71. T3   1921

16898   TERRELL.   Richmond, William and Timothy Terrell, colonial Virginians ... compiled by Celeste Jane Terrell Barnhill ... Greenfield, Ind., The Mitchell company, 1934.   1 p. l., v-xv, 339 p. 24½ cm.   Title vignette (coat of arms) 35-13991.   CS71. T3   1934

16899   TERRELL.   A genealogy line of the Tyrrell, Terrell and Terrill family of Virginia and Texas, and its English and Norman progenitors, by Roy Lee Terrell. Grass Valley, Calif. (Grass Valley herald) 1934.   (12) p.   illus. (coat of arms) 21 cm.   38-14740.   CS71. T3   1934a

16900   TERRELL.   Following the trail; a genealogical study of the Terrell and related families, by Georgia Wharton Lamb.   Manassas, Va. (Manassas journal press, 1939)   1 p. l., 48 p., 1 l. fronts., plates, ports. 25 cm. 39-20805.   CS71.T3   1939

16901   TERRELL.   Following the trail; a genealogical study of the Terrell and related families, by Georgia Wharton Lamb.   Manassas, Va. (Manassas journal press, 1940)   1 p. l., 84, (6) p. fronts., illus. (map, coat of arms) plates, ports. 26 cm. "Revised edition." 40-13579.   CS71.T3   1940

16902   TERRELL.   Terrell notes (on the English Terrells who settled in Virginia, the Carolinas and Georgia, compiled by George Magruder Battey) (Washington, 1943)   2 p. l., 5 numb. l., 1 l. 28 x 21½ cm. Type-written (carbon copy) 44-19033.   CS71.T3   1943

16903   TERRELL.   Genealogy of the Tirrell family of Weymouth, Mass.   Published by the author, 1851.   (Boston,) Reprinted by Goodspeed's book shop, inc., 1943.   2 p. l., (3)-33 p. 18½ cm. Cover-title: Tirrell family. Dedication signed: Benj. Tirrell. "50 copies printed." 43-14314.   CS71.T3   1943a

16904   TERRELL.   Who was James (or Timothy) Terrell, killed by Indians in Georgia? ... By George Magruder Battey III ... Washington, D.C., 1945.   7 l. 28 x 22 cm. Type-written (carbon copy); leaves variously numbered. 48-14033.   CS71.T3   1945

16905   TERRELL.   The Tirrell, Tirrill, Terrill, Tyrrell book; descendants of William Therrell. By Robert Wilson Tirrell.   Englewood, N.J., 1967.   iv, 564 p. illus., coat of arms, facsims., maps, ports. 26 cm. "References and sources": p. 511-515. 67-17812.   CS71.T3   1967

16906   TERRELL.   Terrell and Carruth genealogy, by John H. Parker. (Liberty? Miss.) c. 1967. 88, (16) p. geneal. table. 28 cm. Bibliography: p. (89) 68-1717.   CS71.T3   1967b

        TERRELL.   See also: KEY, 1931
                                LEWIS, 1893
                                WATKINS, 1964
                                No. 3509 - Orange county.

        TERRILL.   See TERRELL.

16907   TERRY.   The English founders of the Terry family.   Edited by Henry K. Terry.   "For private circulation."   London, H.K.Terry & co. (18 -)   viii, 43, (1) p. front., illus. (facsims., coat of arms) 18 cm. 24-1348.   CS439.T38

16908   TERRY.   Notes of Terry families, in the United States of America, mainly descended from Samuel, of Springfield, Mass., byt including also some descended from Stephen, of Windsor, Conn., Thomas, of Freetown, Mass., and others.   By Stephen Terry ... Hartford, Conn., The compiler, 1887. viii, 343 p. 23½ cm. 9-14557.   CS71.T329   1887

16909   TERRY.   Terry clock chronology, comp. by (June) Barrows Mussey and Ruth Mary Canedy, for Charles Terry Treadway.   Bristol, Conn., C. T. Treadway, c. 1948. 30 l. map. 22 x 28 cm. "Sources": p. iv-v. 48-4762*.   CS71.T329   1948

16910   TERRY.   Notes on the Terry family and related families.   By David Sanders Clark.   Washington, 1957.   1 v. 30 cm. 58-21177.   CS71.T329   1957

16911   TERRY.   Sarah Harper and her descendants, the Terrys; their royal and colonial ancestry. By Micajah Boland. (Richmond?) 1958.   35 p. geneal. table. 23 cm. 58-44147.   CS71.T329   1958

16912   TERRY.   Genealogy of the James Terry 1701 branch of the Virginia-North Carolina Terry family tree, compiled by Maude Terry Moon and Gifford Clark Terry. With special emphasis on the descendants of William H. and Jemima Norwood Terry, 19th cent. residents of Chatham County ... N.C.   Sandwich, Ill., Printed by J.W. Terry, 1964.   39 l. illus., map, ports. 27 cm. On cover: Colonial Terrys. 65-3477.   CS71.T329   1964

TERRY.   See also: DAVIS, 1888   KELLOGG, 1898a
                                 DOUBLEDAY, 1924   PEDEN, 1961
                                 DOUBLEDAY, 1936   STOUT, 1960
                                 DOWNS, 1959   THROOP, 1936
                                 GRIFFIN, F129.S74G8   YATES, 1926

TERWILLIGER.   See No. 553 - Goodhue county.

16913   TESDALE.   The church and parish of St. Nicholas, Abingdon; The early grammar school, to the end of the sixteenth century; Fitzharris, an old Abingdon manor, the Tesdales and the Bostocks, by Arthur E. Preston ... Oxford, The Clarendon press for the Oxford historical society, 1935. xiv p., 2 l., (3) - 7, 507 p. front., plates, ports., plans (part fold.) facsim., fold. geneal. tables. 22½ cm. (Half-title: Oxford historical society. (Publications) v. 99) "References": p. (xiii) - xiv. 36-9834.   DA690.O97O8 v. 99

TESTROET.   See SCHARNAGEL, 1960

TETER.   See: DODDRIDGE, 1961
                      MAXWELL, 1918

16914   TETER-TEETER.   In vertical file.   Ask reference librarian for this material.

16914a   TETU.   Histoire des familles Tetu, Bonenfant, Dionne et Perrault, par Mgr. Henri Tetu ... Quebec, Dussault & Proulx, 1898.   638 p. 23 cm. 9-19123.   CS90. T45
                                                                                                              Microfilm 8861

TEW.   See CALVERT, DA536. C2R5

16915   THAANUM.   The Thaanum genealogy; some descendants of Christen Taanum of Ørsted, Denmark, and related families of Graver, Langberg, Due, Schou, Urth and Quistgaard, of Denmark, and Faber of Luxembourg, including biographical and genealogical sketches and pictures, and the six Thaanum brothers: Anders, Wilhelm, Christian, Ditlev, Hans and Jens, who emigrated to America between 1886 and 1903.   (n. p.) 1962.   39 l. illus. 29 cm. 63-37723.   CS71. T34   1962

THACKER.   See WINTERTON, 1964

THACHER.   See THATCHER.

16916   THACKERAY.   The Thackerays in Indian and some Calcutta graves, by Sir William Wilson Hunter ... London, H. Frowde, 1897.   191, (1) p. 19 x 15 cm. Corrigenda slip inserted. "First edition, January 1897." 21-18041.   CS439. T4

THACKERAY.   See also: BACKHOUSE, DA690. M74C3
                                          RITCHIE, 1920

16917   THATCHER.   Genealogy, and biographical sketches, of the descendants of Thomas and Anthony Thacher, from their settlement in New England, June 4th, 1635.   Vineland, N. J., Independent printing house, 1872.   2 p. l., 92 p. coat of arms. 21 cm. Preface signed: D. W. Allen. 3-7922.   CS71. T367   1872

16918   THATCHER.   An old family.   (By Mrs. Sarah Elizabeth (Washburn) Heald.)   Orange, N.J., 1882.   48 p. ports. 20½ cm. Ms. notes inserted. Poems by Mrs. Hannah B. Washburn: p. (19)-48. 20-5525.   CS71. T367   1882

16919   THATCHER.   Memoir of the Hon. Peter Thatcher of Cleveland, Ohio.   By Samuel Briggs ... Cleveland, Printed for the family, 1883.   8 p. front. (port.) illus. (coat of arms) 25½ cm. "Reprinted from the N. E. Historical and genealogical register for January, 1883. " 18-370.   CS71. T367   1883

16920   THATCHER.   The Thacher family.   Facts which have been ascertained within eighteen months past, touching the early history of the Thacher family in England, chiefly through the indefatigable labors of Miss Julia W. Redfield of Pittsfield, Mass., with certain comments thereupon.   (Boston, Mass., 1885)   6 p. 20½ cm. Caption title. Signed Peter Thacher. 10-4265.   CS71. T367   1885

16921   THATCHER.   Thacher-Thatcher genealogy ... By John R. Totten ... (New York) New York genealogical and biographical society, 1910-1918.   34 pts. in 1 v.   plates, ports., 2 coats of arms (incl. col. front: v.1) 26½ cm.   Paged continuously.   "Edition of one hundred copies."   Includes "Authorities."   No more published.   44-53095.

                                            CS71.T367   1918

        —— Index. ... Copied and compiled by Gertrude A. Barber.   (New York, 1943)   1 p. l., 173 numb. l.   28 x 21½ cm.   Type-written (carbon copy)   44-53095.   CS71.T367   1918 Index.

16922   THATCHER.   Thacher-Thatcher: a record of the descendants of Rev. Peter Thacher, 1545-1624.   Compiled & published by Marion H. Thatcher.   Grand Rapids (1967)   53 l.   30 cm.   "From material gathered by Fent Edwin N. Thatcher."   67-8471.   CS71.T367   1967

        THATCHER.   See also: CROCKER, 1923
                                CULBERTSON, 1961
                                GUITERAS, 1926
                                RAYMOND, 1913

        THAXTER.   See WHEELER, 1898

16923   THAYER.   Family memorial.   Part 1. Genealogy of fourteen families of the early settlers of New-England, of the names of Alden, Adams, Arnold, Bass, Billings, Capen, Copeland, French, Hobart, Jackson, Paine, Thayer, Wales and White ... All these families are more or lesss connected by marriage, and most of them of late generations, the descendants of John Alden.   Part II. Genealogy of Ephraim and Sarah Thayer, with fourteen children ... By Elisha Thayer ... Hingham, J. Farmer, printer, 1835.   viii, (9)-180, 100 p.   24 cm.   A large portion of the 2d part was collected and arranged by Dr. Samuel W. Thayer, with additions by Stephen W. Jackson.   9-14558.   CS71.T37   1835

16924   THAYER.   Memorial of the Thayer name, from the Massachusetts colonony of Weymouth and Braintree, embracing geneological (!) and biographical sketches of Richard & Thomas Thayer, and their descendants, from 1636 to 1874.   By Bezaleel Thayer ... Oswego, R.J.Oliphant, 1874.   vi, (7)-708 p. front. (port.)   23½ cm.   9-14559.   CS71.T37   1874

16925   THAYER.   Thayer ancestry.   Supplement to the "Family memorial of the early settlers of New England" in the line of Col. Abraham Thayer, his ancestors and descendants.   By Mrs. Albert Hastings Pitkin ... Hartford, Conn., 1890.   1 p. l., 58 p.   front., ports.   24½ cm.   "Edition limited to fifty copies. no. 20."   Contents. - pt. I. Historical notes on the ancestry of Lydia Thayer. - pt. II. Historical notes on the ancestry of Abraham Thayer.   9-14555.   CS71.T37   1890

16926   THAYER.   Ancestors of Adelbert P. Thayer, Florine Thayer McCray and Geo. Burton Thayer, children of John W. Thayer and Adaline Burton.   Compiled by Geo. Burton Thayer.   Also, reminiscences of a Christmas eve at Windermere and some early events in the life of the writer ... Hartford, Conn., Press of the Plimpton mfg. co., 1894.   180 p.   fronts. (ports.)   24 cm.   "Edition limited to 50 copies.   no. 36." On cover: Thayer and Burton ancestry.   14-10167.   CS71.T37   1894

16927   THAYER.   Descendants of Rufus and Pamela (Throop) Thayer, with some little account of their ancestry.   Compiled and arranged for George Thayer, by Clarence E. Peirce ... Pawtucket, R.I., The A. Sutcliffe co., printers, 1896.   69 p.   front. (port.)   23 cm.   Pages (3) - (45), odd pages blank.   One leaf inserted after p. 44.   "Limited edition of 100 numbered copies.   no. 18."   9-14554.   CS71.T37   1896

16928   THAYER.   Catálogo biográfico de la casa de Thayer de Braintree, por Luis Thayer Ojeda ... Snatiago de Chile, 1904.   63 p.   28½ cm.   "Edicion reservada para la familia Thayer.   Ejemplar num. 37."   4-35804.   CS71.T37   1904

16929   THAYER.   Tayer (Thayer) family entries in the parish register of Thornbury, Gloucestershire, England.   Communicated by Walter Faxon, esq. and Edward Henry Whorf, esq.   With introduction and notes by Henry Ernest Woods, A.M.   (Boston, 1906)   Caption title.   Reprinted from the New England historical and genealogical register for July, 1906.   "Abstracts of wills relating to the Tayer (Thayer) family of Thornbury, Gloucestershire, England, Communicated by Henry Ernest Woods, A.M.": p. 9-11.   6-28553.   CS71.T37   1906

16930   THAYER.   The Thayer family of Brockworth according to the researches of Rev. Canon William Bazcley (i.e. Bazeley) by Luis Thayer Ojeda ... Santiago de Chile, Imprenta moderna, 1907. 36 p. pl. 28 cm. 7-31040.   CS439. T45

16931   THAYER.   The Thayer family of Thornbury; a study trying its reconstitution, by Tomas Thayer Ojeda.   (Santiago de Chile?) Imprenta moderna, 1907.   31 p. 28½ cm. 7-23347.
                                                                                                   CS71. T37   1907

16932   THAYER.   Genealogy of the descendants of William Turpin Thayer of Bellingham, by Luis Thayer Ojeda.   Valp(araiso) Ipp. (!) Roma (1933?)   43 p. facsim. 19 cm. "Thayer's bibliography": p. 41-43. 35-15333.   CS71. T37   1933

16933   THAYER.   Garrett county history Thayer family.   By Charles E. Hoye ... (Oakland, Md.) 1935   1 l. 43 cm. "Mt. democrat issue March 21, 1935." 38M1259T.   CS71. T37   1935

16934   THAYER.   The A, B, C's of the law; the legal trials, troubles and vicissitudes of the Thayer family, by Bessie N. Page ... (Boston) c. 1937.   2 p. l., vii, 155 numb. l. diagr. 29½ cm. Reproduced from type-written copy. 38-3935.   LAW.

16935   THAYER.   Some notes and corrections referring to Thayer genealogy according to the re-searches of Walter E. Thayer, esq., by Luis Thayer-Ojeda ... Valparaiso, Imprenta y encuadernac-ión Roma, 1937.   28 p. 18½ cm. 38-36156.   CS71. T37   1937

16936   THAYER.   Martin Clinton Thayer, his ancestors and descendants.   By Ruth (Thayer) Ravenscroft.   (Colorado Springs, 1943-48)   4 v. in 6. plates, map, facsims. 28 cm. Typescript. Includes vols. of various editions. 44-10786 rev. 2*.   CS71. T37   1943

16937   THAYER.   Martin Clinton Thayer, his ancestors and descendants.   By Ruth (Thayer) Ravens-croft.   Rev. Ed.   (Colorado Springs, 1947 -   v. plates, map, facsims. 28 cm. Typewritten. 44-10786 rev.   CS71. T37   1947

16938   THAYER.   Three hundred ancestors of Brackett Marston Thayer.   By Louis Clark Mathewson. (n. p.) c. 1948.   37 l. 30 cm. "Sources": leaves 35-37. 49-13707*.   CS71. T37   1948

              THAYER.   See also: BASSETT, 1926
                                      LINDLEY, 1950
                                      PATTERSON, 1929
                                      VINTON, 1858a

       THEBAUDEAU.   See D'AMOURS, 1961

16939   THIGPEN.   The Thigpen tribe.   By Alice (Whitley) Smith.   Edited by Casey Thigpen.   (n. p., 1961)   312 p. illus. 29 cm. 61-33962.   See also L. C. Additions and Corrections no. 245.   CS71. T4   1961

16940   THIGPEN.   The Thigpen tribe.   By Alice (Whitley) Smith.   Edited by Casey Thigpen.   (Rev. Yanceyville? N. C., 1963, c. 1961)   434 p. illus., ports., map, coat of arms. 29 cm. 63-54827.
                                                                                                   CS71. T4   1963

16941   THISTLETHWAITE.   The Thistlethwaite family.   A study in genealogy.   By Bernard Thistle-thwaite.   Vol. I. London, Printed for private circulation by Headley brothers, 1910.   xxxii, 326 p. front., fold. geneal. tables. 22 cm. "No more published." 16-12999.   CS439. T47

       THISTLETHWAYTE   See POWELL, 1891 a

16942   THOM.   The Thom family, the descendants of Joseph Thom and Elizabeth Craig Thom of Westmoreland county, Pennsylvania.   By Jay Webb Thom ... and Nelle Bigham Robinson.   Franklin, Ind., J. W. Thom, 1931.   2 p. l., 66 numb. l. 22 cm. Type-written. 32-29586.   CS71. T44   1931

16943   THOM.   The American ancestors of Margaret Esther Bouton Thom and William John Thom ... (Ann Arbor, Mich., Lithoprinted by Edwards brothers inc., 1944)   xvi, 253 p. incl. front., illus. (incl. map, coats of arms) ports., facsims. 6 fold. geneal. tab.   28½ x 22½ cm.   Preface signed: Henry Earle Riggs.   Includes the Thom, Bouton, Craig, Culbertson, Bracken, Cushman, Woodsum and Farwell families.   "Sources": p. 251-253.   45-2647.   CS71.T44   1944

16944   THOM.   Genealogy of the Thom and the Laing families.   By Jessie (Laing) Sibbet.   (Pasadena, Calif., 1957)   24 l. geneal. table.   28 cm.   57-46791.   CS71.T44   1957

16945   THOMAS.   Descendants of John Thomas, commencing with John Thomas Seaman, of Sackville, New Brunswick, grand-son of John Thomas, 4th.   (By Leonard J. Thomas)   Eden, Me., N. Thomas & son, printed at the office of the Boston post (1850)   geneal. tab.   61 x 49 cm. fold. to 25 x 16 cm.   L. C. COPY REPLACED BY MICROFILM.   4-27761.   CS71.T46   1850
Microfilm 18262 CS

16946   THOMAS.   Descendants of John Thomas, who removed from Wales, G. B., to America, and married in Boston, Massachusetts, to Elizabeth, March 30th, A. D. 1667.   (n.p., 1869)   geneal. tab. illus. (coat of arms) 60½ x 49 cm. fold. to 30 x 24½ cm.   4-27762 rev.   CS71.T46   1869

16947   THOMAS.   Genealogical record of the family of Thomas, compiled from papers in possession of Dr. J. Hanson Thomas.   By Douglas H. Thomas ... Baltimore, C. Harvey & co., printers, 1875.   78 p., 1 l. 19½ cm.   9-14553.   CS71.T46   1875

16048   THOMAS.   Genealogical notes: containing the pedigree of the Thomas family, of Maryland, and of the following connected families: Snowden - Buckley - Lawrence - Chew - Ellicott - Hopkins - Johnson - Rutherford - Fairfax - Schieffelin - Tyson and others ... By Lawrence Buckley Thomas. Baltimore, L. B. Thomas, 1877.   197 p. illus., facsim., coats of arms.   27½ cm.   9-14769-70.   CS71.T46   1877

——— Part second ... Baltimore, L. B. Thomas, 1878.   54, (2) p. front., coats of arms.   30½ cm. Seventeen autographed leaves at end.   Contains additions and corrections to first part.   9-14769-70.   CS71.T46   1878

16949   THOMAS.   The early history of Merion.   And An old Welsh pedigree.   By James J. Levick ... Philadelphia, Collins printing house (1880)   cover-title, (41) p. 25½ cm.   "Extracted from the Pennsylvania magazine of history and biography. vol. IV, 1880."   Caption title: John ap Thomas and his friends.   A contribution to the early history of Merion ... 18-16817.   F159.M5L6

16950   THOMAS.   Pedigrees of Thomas, Chew, and Lawrance, a West River register and genealogical notes, by Rev. Lawrence Buckley Thomas ... New York, T. Whittaker, 1883.   136 p. 1 l.   xix (1), 137-139, (1) p. front., illus., (coats of arms) plates, ports., geneal. tables. facsims. 25 cm.   "Relates to descendants of Philip Thomas of Md., John Chew of Jamestown, Va., and Thomas Lawrence of N. J. and Pa." - Munsell.   3-6541.   CS71.T46   1883

16951   THOMAS.   The Thomas family of Hilltown, Bucks County, Penn'a.   By Edward Mathews. Landsdale, Pa., A. K. Thomas, 1884.   3 p. l., 68 p., 1 l. 23½ cm.   9-14552.   CS71.T46   1884

16952   THOMAS.   Genealogical records and sketches of the descendants of William Thomas of Hardwick, Mass. ... By A. R. Thomas ... Philadelphia and London, F. A. Davis, 1891.   xi, 221 p. front., plates, port. 24 cm.   "Sources of information": p. ix.   3-3818.   CS71.T46   1891

16953   THOMAS.   The Thomas book, giving the genealogies of Sir Rhys ap Thomas, K. G., the Thomas family descended from him, and of some allied families.   By Lawrence Buckley Thomas, D. D. New York city, The H. T. Thomas company, 1896.   xxi, 627 p. front., illus., plates, ports., maps, coats of arms. 27 cm.   "The large paper edition of The Thomas book is limited to two hundred and fifty copies of which this is number 79."   9-14575.   CS71.T46   1896

16954   THOMAS.   Genealogy.   Descendants of Gabriel Thomas, John Thomas, Vaentine Thomas, Christian Thomas and George Ramsburg.   Compiled by Professor Cyrus Thomas ... (Washington?) 1905.   cover-title, 19 p. 23½ cm.   5-34133.   CS71.T46   1905

16955   THOMAS.   The Thomas family, as descended from David and Anna Noble Thomas, by William Thomas Lyle ... Philadelphia, 1907.   Union Springs, N. Y., J. B. Hoff, Advertiser print, 1908.
75, (9) p. 23½ cm. 10-6535.   CS71. T46   1908

16956   THOMAS.   Thomas family of Talbot County, Maryland, and allied families, by Richard Henry Spencer ... Baltimore, Williams & Wilkins company, 1914.   2 p. l., iv p., 2 l., 180 p. front., ports., coats of arms. 23½ cm.   "A limited edition of one hundred and fifty copies of this book has been printed, of which this is no. 125."   Allied families: The De Courcys, Riddells, Lowes, Leeds's, Leighs, Goldsboroughs, Dickinsons, Dalls, Bringiers, Martins, Spencers, Francis's, Kerrs, Markoes, Trippes, Hemsleys, Ridgelys. 15-7827.   CS71. T46   1914

16957   THOMAS.   Maternal ancestry of Frank Trumbull and of his brothers Robert Morris Wilton and Charles Julius Trumbull and of his sister Mary Trumbull Vaughn, also the ancestry of John Lilburn Thomas of Washington, D. C., and of all other descendants of James Wilton Thomas.   New York, Priv. print., 1917.   30 p., 1 l. incl. front. (mounted port.) 23½ cm.   "One hundred numbered copies of this book have been printed ... The number of this copy is 79." 18-7486.   CS71. T46   1917

16958   THOMAS.   Descendants of James Wilton Thomas and Eliza Ann Johnson, also the biography of John Lilburn Thomas, also containing an account of the migration of the Thomas and Johnson families and others to Missouri.   (New York, L. Middleditch company, 1917)   15 p. incl. port. 26½ cm. An edition of 100 copies.   CS71. T46   1917a
——— Revision of February 18, 1918.   (New York, L. Middleditch, 1918)   13 p. port. 26½ cm.
Imperfect: portrait wanting. 18-8388-9.   CS71. T46   1918

16959   THOMAS.   ... The portraits of Isaiah Thomas, with a genealogy of his descendants by Charles Lemuel Nichols.   Reprinted from the Proceedings of the American antiquarian society for October, 1920.   Worcester, Mass., The Society, 1921.   32 p. front., ports. 25 cm. 21-19144.
                                                                                                                CS71. T46   1921

16960   THOMAS.   Family history and reminiscences by Jessie Thomas Knapp.   (n. p., 1926)
57 l. 28 cm. Type-written. Includes the author's Thomas, Macy and Hollenbeck ancestry.   CS71. T46   1926
——— Additions.   "Saga notes, after or golden glow .." (n. p. 1930) CA29-554 unrev. CS71. T46   1926a

16961   THOMAS.   ... Thomas family records, by J. Montgomery Seaver.   Philadelphia, American historical-genealogical society (1929)   52 p. front. (incl. 3 port.) coat of arms. 29 cm. Coat of arms of the Thomas family on recto of frontispiece.   Pages 50 - 51 blank for "Family record".   "References": p. 48-49. 40-18927.
                                                                                                                CS71. T46   1929

16962   THOMAS.   ... Genealogical records of the families of Thomas, Emory, Coursey, Hodgson, and Meredith of Maryland.   Presented to the publisher by Mrs. Joseph Baldridge (Katherine) national vice chairman of the D. A. R. Museum committee ... Annapolis, Md., Published by Annie Walker Burns, 1936.   1 p. l., 23, 1a - 11a, 1b - 6b, 1c - 4c numb. l. 28 cm. At head of title: Vol. 1, Genealogical section. Mimeographed.
A40-3403.   CS71. T46   1936

16963   THOMAS.   Our kinsmen, a record of the ancestry and descendants of Griffith Thomas, a pioneer resident of Orange county, North Carolina, by Grace Harper Wingert.   (Springfield, O., 1938)
135 p. illus. (ports.) 22 cm. 39-12258.   CS71. T46   1938

16964   THOMAS.   Thomas family. (By Thomas John Hall, 3rd)   p. 227 and 230.   CS71. H177   1941

16965   THOMAS.   Genealogy of Thomas family, bt George Leicester Thomas ... Washington, D. C., Judd & Detweiler, c. 1942.   3 p. l., 197 p. front., illus. (incl. maps) ports. 23 cm. 42-50292.
                                                                                                                CS71. T46   1942

16966   THOMAS.   Notes on the Thomas family portraits.   By Clarence Saunders Brigham.
(In American Antiquarian Society, Worcester, Mass. Proceedings. Worcester, 1947. 25 cm.   v. 56, p. (49)-54) A48-986*.
                                                                                                                E172. A35 vol. 56

16967   THOMAS.   Peter and Mary Thomas, their ancestors and descendants.   A brief review of the Friends movement in America, by Helena May Hargrave.   Mary T. Hall's book: genealogy of the Babb, Thomas and Thomas families, by Mary T. Hall, with notes by Tacy E. Thompson.   1st ed.

16967 continued: Honolulu, 1950. 1 v. (unpaged) geneal. tables, map. 28 cm. 66-81704.

CS71.T46   1950

—— Supplement to the 1950 edition of the Peter and Mary Thomas genealogy, compiled by George M. Hargrave. The westward movement; a brief story of the migration of Friends to the "Northwest Territory," by Helena May Hargrave. Mountain View, Calif., 1963 (i.e. 1964?) xii, 224 p. illus., coat of arms, geneal. tables, maps. 28 cm. Title page bound in following preliminary pages. 66-81704.

CS71.T46   1950
Suppl.

16968   THOMAS.   Genealogy of Thomas family.   By George Leicester Thomas.   (Adamstown? Md.) c.1954.   xi, 472 p. illus., ports., maps, coat of arms. facsims. 24 cm. 54-19892.   CS71.T46   1954

16969   THOMAS.   Thomas, Scholl, Clements, etc.   By Frances Halbert Atkinson.   (Greenup, Ky., 1955)   3 l. 34 cm. 56-39545.   CS71.T46   1955

16970   THOMAS.   A record of the George Thomas family and allied families.   By Mary Leah (Kime) Pratz.   (n.p.) 1963.   53 l. 30 cm. Typescript (carbon copy) 66-57112.   CS71.T46   1963a

16971   THOMAS.   The Thomas brothers of Mattapany: their ancestry, the manor house, their descendants.   By Thomas Armstrong.   (Washington) c.1963.   viii, 264 p. illus., ports., maps, facsims. 29 cm. Limited to 50 copies, no. 2. Bibliographical footnotes. 64-2149.   CS71.T46   1963

16972   THOMAS.   Amos Thomas family tree; ancestors and descendants to and from Wales, England, Island of Barbados ... Prefaced with an account of Thomas family in England and Wales.   By Thomas Everett Eri.   Indianapolis, J. Woolman Press, 1965.   ii, 139 l. illus., map. 30 cm. 68-5224.   CS71.T46   1965

16973   THOMAS.   The Thomas family, 1655-1967.   By Helen Glasbrenner.   (Denver) Printed by E. Glasbrenner (1967)   217 p. illus., ports. 28 cm. 67-9703.   CS71.T46   1967

16974   THOMAS.   Chronological outline of the life of Elder David Thomas.   3 p.   In vertical file. Also additional Thomas material in vertifal file.   Ask reference librarian for this material.

THOMAS.   See also:

BASSETT, 1926	JONES, 1936	PURDY, F116.N28 v,51
BEATTY, 1886	LLOYD, 1912	RAYMOND, 1913
BOARMAN, 1934	McCOMBIE, CS479.M18S6	SANDYS, 1897
COMSTOCK, 1964	NICHOLS, 1909a	TEEL, 1964
HUMPHREY, 1938	PARKER, 1940	WILFORD, 1959

16975   THOMASON.   A brief history of the family Thomason in England and the United States, by Robert Stewart Thomason, with some account of his branch.   New York city (The Scribner press) 1938-40. 2 p. l., 78 p. front. (col. coats of arms) plates, ports., maps (part fold.) geneal. tab. 24 cm. "One of twenty five copies printed, and the type distributed." 41-1462.   CS71.T465 1938-40

16976   THOMASON.   A brief history of the family Thomason in England and the United States, by Robert Stewart Thomason, with some account of his branch.   Rev. ed.   New York city, 1945. 2 p. l., 96 p. front. (col. coats of arms) plates, ports. maps, (part double) facsims., geneal. tab. 24½ cm. "One of fifty copies printed, and the tupe distributed." Bibliography: p. 91. 46-21035.   CS71.T465   1945

16977   THOMASON.   Our kith and kin.   By Aimee Young (Roberts) Thomason.   Tuscaloosa, Ala., Willo Pub. Co. (1962?)   191 p. illus., ports., geneal. tables (1 fold.) 23 cm. Errata sheet mounted on p.5. Genealogical table with corrections in manuscript mounted as p.44. 64-304.   CS71.T465   1962

THOMASON.   See also PEDEN, 1961

THOMLINSON.   See TOMLINSON.

THOMOND.   See O'BRIEN, 1947

16978   THOMPSON.   Thompson wills; a list of Thompson wills in the Archdeacontry of Richmond, 1750-1817, York Prerogative court, 1760-1840, Canterbury Prerogative court, 1750-1841, and Abstracts of Thompson wills and administrations.   (n. p., n. d.)   1 p. l., 136, (1), 52 l. 35 cm. In manuscript. Twelve type-written leaves of Abstracts of wills, 1751-1778, are inserted at end.   The Abstracts of wills, 52 numb. l., have on verso of the leaf preceding each will a genealogical table of the line covered by the will.   25-19804.   CS439. T49

16979   THOMPSON.   A genealogy of John Thomson, who landed at Plymouth, in the month of May, 1622.   By Ignatius Thomson.   Taunton, Printed by E. Anthony, 1841.   84 p. 14½ cm. 3-7926.
                                                                            CS71. T47   1941

16980   THOMPSON.   Thomson pedigree.   Extracted from the records of the College of arms. (n. p., 185-)   4 p. incl. geneal. tab., coat of arms. 28½ cm. Caption title. Interleaved. Communicated by Richard Edward Thomson, of Kenfield. 2-26609.   CS439. T5

16981   THOMPSON.   Memorials of the families of Mr, James Thompson and of Dea. Augustus Thompson, of Goshen, Connecticut.   Hartford, Press of Case, Tiffany and company, 1854.   iv, (5) - 106 p. 23½ cm. "Dedicatory letter" signed: Edward W. Hooker.   "The following sketches have been prepared and printed for circulation among the relatives of the indiciduals whose names stand on the title-page, and are in no sense published." 9-14574.   CS71. T47   1854

16982   THOMPSON.   A memoir of Judge Ebenezer Thompson of Durham, New Hampshire, with some account of his parentage and offspring.   By his great-granddaughter, Mary P. Thompson ... Concord, N. H., Printed by the Republican press association, 1886.   86 p. facsims. 22½ cm. Printed for private circulation only. 9-14576.   CS71. T47   1886

16983   THOMPSON.   Memorial of James Thompson, of Charlestown, Mass., 1630-1642, and Woburn, 1642-1682; and of eight generations of his descendants.   By Rev. Leander Thompson ... For the Thompson memorial association.   Boston, Press of L. Barts & co., 1887.   246 p. front., plates, ports. 23½ cm. 9-14573.   CS71. T47   1887

16984   THOMPSON.   The Thompson family ...(Pottsville, Pa., 1887)   cover-title, 20 p. 23 cm. Interleaved: additions in manuscript. Prepared by Heber S. Thompson with the co-operation of Theodore Samuel Thompson. 25-7739.
                                                                            CS71. T47   1887a

16985   THOMPSON.   John Thomson and family.   By John Bodine Thompson ... Williamsport, Pa., Gazette and bulletin printing house, 1889.   29 p. fold. map, facsims. 24½ cm. 9-14570.
                                                                            CS71. T47   1889

16986   THOMPSON.   John Thomson and family.   (In Meginness, John F.   Otzinachson; a history of the West Branch Valley of the Susquehanna... Williamsport, Pa., 1889. 26½ cm. v.1, p. 513-537) 9-14571.
                                                                            F157. S9M4

16987   THOMPSON.   A genealogy of the descendants of John Thomson of Plymouth, Mass.   Also sketches of families of Allen, Cooke and Hutchinson.   By Charles Hutchinson Thompson ... Lansing, D. D. Thorp, printer, 1890.   272 p. front., ports. 23½ cm. "The basis of this work is a 'Genealogy of John Thomson' by Ignatius Thomson, published in 1841." 9-14572.   CS71. T47   1890

16988   THOMPSON.   The Thomson family; or, The pedigree, descendants, and other kindred of Alexander Thomson, Greens, Monquhitter, Abderdeenshire; and of Elizabeth Clark, his wife.   Compiled by Henry Morton Thomson, M. A., and Andrew Sherran Thomson.   Norwich, Printed for the authors by Jarrold and sons (1896)   4 p. l., 61 p. incl. VI geneal. tab. ports. 35 cm. 17-21447.
                                                                            CS479. T5

16989   THOMPSON.   Thompson and Given families, with their ancestral lines and present branches: Rev. Samuel F. Thompson; Ellen Kerr Given.   Hamilton, Ohio, Brown & Whitaker, 1898.
Microfilm copy (positive) made by the Library of Congress Photoduplication Service.   Collation of the original, as determined from the film: 238 p. ports. Mic. 62-7462.   Microfilm 7400 CS

16990   THOMPSON.   Our Thompson family in Maine, New Hampshire and the West, by Rev. Charles N. Sinnett.   Concord, N. H., Rumford printing co., 1907.   293 p. plates, ports. 23 cm. 7-15933.
                                                                            CS71. T47   1907

16991   THOMPSON.   Lord Kelvin's early home: being the recollections of his sister the late Mrs. Elizabeth King; together with some family letters and a supplementary chapter by the editor, Elizabeth Thomson King.   With illustrations from Mrs. King's own drawings and those of her daughters. London, Macmillan and co., limited, 1909.   xii, 245 p. front., plates, ports., facsim. 23½ cm. 10-8725.

QC16.K3K5

16992   THOMPSON.   Andrew Thompson, the emigrant of Elsinborough, Salem County, New Jersey and one line of his descendants; comp. by David Allen Thompson.   Albany, N.Y., Weed-Parsons printing company, 1910.   47 p. 18½ cm. 11-704.   CS71.T47   1910

16993   THOMPSON.   Thompson lineage, with mention of allied families, by William Baker Thompson, compiler.   Harrisburg, Pa., Press of the Telegraph printing company (c. 1911)   131 p. illus. (incl. plan) 23½ cm. 11-20520.   CS71.T47   1911

16994   THOMPSON.   Edward Ridgely Thompson and Eliza Enlow, his wife.   Printed for their grandchildren.   (Portland, Me.) 1913.   7 p. 23 cm. Preface signed: Florence Whittlesey Thompson. 13-11876.

CS71.T47   1913

16995   THOMPSON.   The Thompson family, by Adrian Scott ... and Henry A. Whitney.   (Mendon) Mendon historical society, 1913.   38 p. 24 cm. 15-22258.   CS71.T47   1913a

16996   THOMPSON.   Thompson genealogy, the descendants of William and Margaret Thomson, first settled in that part of Windsor, Connecticut, now East Windsor and Ellington. 1720-1915, including many of the names of Chandler, Trumbull, Marsh, Pelton, Allen, Harper, Osborn, Hooker, Ellsworth, Stiles, Phelps, Bartlett, etc.   Compiled by Mary A. Elliott.   (New Haven, Conn.) The Thompson family association (1915?)   xi, 518 p. front., plates, ports. 25 cm. 16-23632.

CS71.T47   1915

16997   THOMPSON.   An account of some of the ancestors of Harry Thompson and Myra Hull, comp. by Clarence Willis Eastman.   Amherst, Mass., Priv. print., 1916.   cover-title, 27, (1) p. 23 cm. Contains also the Clark, Curtiss, Gunn, Peck, Stiles, Wells (Welles) and Judson families. 17-24552.

CS71.T47   1916

16998   THOMPSON.   The descendants of John Thomson, pioneer Scotch covenanter; genealogical notes on all known descendants of John Thomson, covenanter, of Scotland, Ireland and Pennsylvania, with such biographical sketches as could be obtained from available published records, or were supplied by the friends of those individuals who were too modest to tell of their own accomplishments, comp. for the cousins by Addams S. McAllister ... Easton, Pa., The Chemical publishing company, printers, 1917.   vi p., 1 l., 357 p. front., plates, ports. 23½ cm. 20-2051.   CS71.T47   1917

16999   THOMPSON.   Autobiography of Deacon John Thompson, of Mercer, Maine, with genealogical notes of his descendants.   Comp. by his grandson Josiah H. Thompson, in the year 1920.   Farmington, Me., Printed by the Franklin journal company (1920)   152 p. plates, ports. 23½ cm. Lettered on cover: Journal of John Thompson. 23-14869.   CS71.T417   1920

17000   THOMPSON.   A history of the family of Thomson of Corstorphine, by T. R. Thomson ... Edinburgh, 1926.   96, (2) p. front., illus. (incl. map, facsim.) mounted pl., ports., 3 fold. geneal. tab. 25½ cm. "Sixty copies only ... No. 24." Bibliographical foot-notes. 40-294.   CS479.T5   1926

17001   THOMPSON.   History of the Thompson family, from 1637 to 1860.   For my nephew, J. Thompson, esq.   Poughkeepsie telegraph steam press, 1865.   Boston, Edition of 50 copies reprinted by Goodspeed's bookshop, 1927.   1 p. l., (5) - 12 p. coat of arms. 17 cm. Signed: Asa A. Thompson. 27-25084.

CS71.T47   1927

17002   THOMPSON.   Genealogy, Thompson-Spafford, 1630 to 1930; Chase-Gordon, 1788 to 1930. Osborn-Gadsby, Gadsby-Woodcock ... Compiled by John H. Thompson.   Thorold, Ont. (1930?) 120 p. front., pl., ports. (1 double) facsims., col. coats of arms. 24½ cm. 32-21343.   CS71.T47   1930

17003   THOMPSON.   James Thompson of Holden, Mass., and his descendants, by Rev. Alven Martyn Smith and Benjamin Franklin Thompson.   Also James Thompson of Charlestown and Woburn, Mass.,

17003 contnued: and his descendants, as published by Rev. Leander Thompson, M. A., 1887.   Compiled, edited and controlled by Rev. Alven Martyn Smith.   So. Pasadena, Calif., A. M. Smith, 1932.
1 p. l., xi, 194 p. 27½ cm.   Mimeographed.   CA 32-905 unrev.   CS71. T47   1932

17004   THOMPSON.   Garrett county history of pioneer families ... The Lewis Thompson family, by Charles E. Hoye.   (Oakland, Md., 1937)   mounted l. 25½ cm.   Newspaper clipping.   No. XCIV of a series of articles contributed to the Mountain democrat.   41M3022T.   CS71. T47   1937

17005   THOMPSON.   Family of David Thompson, a revolutionary war soldier, collected and compiled by Joseph Wesley Thompson.   (Washington, D. C., Printing by Georgetown press, c. 1938)
2 p. l., 147, (6) p. incl. 1 illus., ports. 23½ cm.   Blank pages for memoranda (6) at end.   38-9612.
CS71. T47   1938

17006   THOMPSON.   Our William Thompson of Ireland and Pennsylvania and some descendants, by "May" Thompson Williamson.   Youngstown, O., The author, Mrs. W. P. Williamson, 1941.
xi, (3), 161 p. incl. coat of arms. 20 cm.   Blank pages for additions interspersed.   41-12594.
CS71. T47   1941

17007   THOMPSON.   The Thompson family of West Virginia and of California.   With notices of the families allied to it through marriage.   Compiled by John Smith Kendall.   Corrected to 1942.   (Berkeley? Calif., 1942)   38 l. 28½ cm.   Leaves variously numbered.   Type-written (carbon copy)   "Authorities": leaf 17.   43-2195.
CS71. T47   1942

17008   THOMPSON.   North Guilford pioneers, by Ida Palen.   New York, N. Y., The Hobson book press, 1946.   2 p. l., vii-viii p., 1 l., 165 p. plates, ports., facsims. 22 cm.   Reproduced from type-written copy. 46-15824.
F129. N813P3

17009   THOMPSON.   The ancestors of Rev. W. O. Thompson.   By Radiant B. (Word) Thompson. (n. p., 1946?)   5 l. 28 cm.   48-14040*.   CS71. T47   1946

17010   THOMPSON.   Thomson pedigree.   Extracted from the records of the College of arms ... By Richard Edward Thomson.   Communicated by R. E. Thomson, esq. ... (n. p. 18 -)
4 p. illus. (coat of arms) 28½ x 22 cm.   Caption title.   2-26609 rev.   CS439. T5

17011   THOMPSON.   Thompson genealogy, in memory of Lemuel Rawson Thompson.   By Effie (Thompson) Biggs.   (Weleetka, Okla., American Pub. Co., 1954, cover) 1955.   116 p. illus., ports.
24 cm.   Cover title.   With additions and corrections.   56-39426.   CS71. T47   1955

17012   THOMPSON.   Old families and tales of Old Chicot; or, Miss Emma's memoirs.   Compiled by C. T. Thompson.   Baton Rouge, Printed by Harrell-Hannaman Letter Shop, c. 1959.
45 l. illus. 28 cm.   60-26371.   F379. C5T5   1959

17013   THOMPSON.   Thompsons, mainly of Hanover & Louisa Counties, Virginia.   By Henry Lockhart.   (Oxford, Md., 1960?)   77 l.   30 cm.   60-43201.   CS71. T47   1960

17014   THOMPSON.   Beloved pioneers.   By Carrie (Thompson) Northey.   (n. p., c. 1961)
143 p. illus. 29 cm. 62-954.   CS71. T47   1961

17015   THOMPSON.   Life histories of George Thompson and Eliza Jane (Jennie) Sells and their descendants.   Compiled by descendants, with notes of important events from 1957 to August 1962. (Provo, Utah, Dept. of Extension Publications, Brigham Young University, 1962)   165 p. 28 cm.   63-5047.
CS71. T47   1962

17016   THOMPSON.   1800 census of Pennsylvania for the surname Thompson.   Copied for the Thompson family magazine by Beverly Margaret Stercula.   With appendix of 1820 census records of Tioga Co., Pa.; Union Co., Pa.; Warren Co., Pa; Washington Co., Pa.; Venango Co., Pa. (and) York Co., Pa.   By John Dorrance Morrell.   Fullerton, Calif., Thompson Family Association, 1963.
20 p. 31 cm. 64-5635.   CS71. T47   1963

17017   THOMPSON.   1820 and 1830 census of the State of Indiana for the surname Thompson. Copied for the Thompson family magazine, by Margaret R. Waters.   Fullerton, Calif., Thompson family magazine, 1963.   (18) l. 31 cm. 64-5634.   CS71.T47   1963a

17018   THOMPSON.   Thompson family history, 1741-1965 (by) Harry O. Thompson, Merle R. Thompson (and) Roy A. Thompson, (Hubbard? Iowa, 1965)   128 p. illus., ports. 22 cm. Cover title. 66-37692.
                                                                                    CS71.T47   1965

17019   THOMPSON.   Notes on A. Atwood Thompson and on some of his ancestors and descendants, and on related families Eltonhead and Thompson (by) Nora B. Thompson.   (Lancaster? Pa., c. 1966) 47 p. ports. 24 cm. "100 copies printed." 67-7068.   CS71.T47   1966

17020   THOMPSON.   Georgiana Schultz Thompson, her ancestors and descendants.   By Dorothy Wilcox.   Washington, Estate Book Sales, 1966 (c. 1967)   461 l. ports. 29 cm. Bibliography: leaf 12. 67-31899.
                                                                                    CS71.T47   1967

17021   THOMPSON.   Thompson and Given families.   By Rev. Samuel Findley Thompson. 238 p. illus.   Microfilm 7400

          THOMPSON.   See also:

          BANNING, 1924   HOLSINGER, 1959   SELDEN, 1911
          BANNING, E171. A53 v. 19   HUBBARD, 1914   SEMMES, 1918
          BASSETT, 1926   JAMES, 1913a   SEMMES, 1956
          CAMPBELL, 1960 (addenda)   LAURIE, 1901   SHIPLEY, 1964
          CLEMENS, 1940   LEONARD, 1928   SMITH, 1929a
          DINWIDDIE, 1957   LEONARD, 1930   TAYLOR, 1898
          GUTHRIE, 1953   MACKEY, 1957   VENABLE, 1961
          HANAFORD, 1915   NOYES, 1900   WILLIAMS, 1931a
          HARGETT, 1948   ROBERTS, F159. R48R6   WILSON, 1916
          HART, 1923   ROBERTSON, 1926

17022   THOMSEN.   Descendants of Hans Jørgen Thomsen and Ane Kjerstine Ditlevsen of Klejs, Denmark, by Frances Hansen Ehrig.   Richland? Wash.) 1962.   xiii, 58 p. illus., maps, ports. 28 cm. 65-89157.
                                                                                    CS71.T475   1962

          THOMSON.   See: ALLARDYCE.
                            THOMPSON.

          THOORSELL.   See LUNDEBERG, 1967

          THOREAU.   See ALCOTT, 1920

          THORESON.   See No. 553 - Goodhue county.

          THORFINNSON.   See No. 553 - Goodhue county.

17023   THORGERSEN.   Tilbageblik, erindringer og oplevelser; udg. af Ejler Thøgersen.   By Niels Thøgersen.   Grindsted, Grindsted bogtr., 1947.   159 p. illus., ports., 22 cm. 50-18802.
                                                                                    CT1278.T48A3

17024   THORN.   Genealogical record of John Thorne, also the direct descendants of James Thorne and Hannah Brown of Salisbury, Mass., and Kingston, N.H., also the families connected by marriage. Compiled by Edmund Dana Barbour ... 1900, for John Calvin Thorne ... Prepared, enlarged and published by Mr. Thorne ... (Concord, N.H., Ira C. Evans co., printers) 1913.   62 p. front. (coat of arms) pl., ports. 26 cm. Cover-title: Thorne genealogy, 1200-1900. L. C. copy imperfect: front. wanting. 15-3430.   CS71.T48   1913

17025   THORN.   Eight generations from William Thorne of Dorsetshire, England, and Lynn, Mass. Compiled by Joseph Middleton ... and Alan McLean Taylor ... (Boston) Priv. print. (T. R. Marvin & son, printers) 1913.   10 p. 25 cm. 16-23280.   CS71.T48   1913a

17026   THORN. A contribution to the history of the Thorns from the emigration of William Thorn from Dorsetshire, England, to Lynn, Mass., in the year 1638, and so, thru his family down to the fourth generation, and from two branches of the fourth generation down to the present time: with a genealogical table showing as far as many be their relationships and connections, by Anthony T. Thorn. (Ramah, Col.) 1915.   48 (i. e. 50) p. illus. (geneal. tree) 5 port. (incl. front.) 24 cm. Pages 46-48 left blank for "genealogical table." Added t. -p., illus., has title: History and genealogy of two branches from the fourth generation of the Thorne family from William Thorn, 1638-1914 ... "This is a private edition of fifty copies." 19-2013.   CS71.T48   1915

17027   THORN. Ancestors of Dr. Samuel Thorne (1767-1838) of Halifax County, N.C. By William Alexander Graham Clark. Washington, 1942.   geneal. table. 28 cm. Photocopy (positive) 52-47040.
CS71.T48   1942a

17028   THORN. Descendants of Dr. Samuel Thorne (1767-1838) of Halifax County, N.C.; a chart. By William Alexander Graham Clark. Washington, 1942.   geneal. table. illus. 74 x 31 cm. fold. to 23 x 31 cm. 52-47798.   CS71.T48   1942b

THORN.   See also: STRANGE, 1915
TOMPKINS, 1893
VAN DOREN, 1967

17029   THORNBURG. The Thornburg family in Randolph County, Indiana; (jointly compiled by Harold Thornburg and Willard Heiss. Indianapolis? 1959)   unpaged. 28 cm. 61-20700.
CS71.T4815   1959

THORNBURG.   See also No. 1520 - Cabell county.

17030   THORNBURY. Original source records relating to the Thornbury family, compiled by Delmar Leon Thornbury. Washington, D.C., 1931.   51 (i. e. 49) p. illus. (incl. maps, mounted coats of arms, mounted phot.) 24 cm. Nos. 46 and 47 omitted in paging. Type-written (carbon copy) Book-plate of D. L. Thornbury mounted on t. - p. 31-31257.
CS71.T482   1931

17031   THORNDIKE. Descendants of John Thorndike of Essex County, Massachusetts. By Morgan Hewitt Stafford. (Ann Arbor? Mich.) 1960.   349 p. 24 cm. 61-47629.   CS71.T4825   1960

THORNDIKE.   See also: CROCKER, 1923
SAUNDERS, 1897
WARREN, 1903

THORNE.   See THORN.

17032   THORNGATE. A historical sketch of the Thorngate-Rood family, descendants of George Thorngate, senior, and Matilda Blanchard, 1798-1906. Written by Hosea W. Rood ... Ord, Neb., H.M. Davis; North Loup, Neb., W.G. Rood (1910?)   3 p. l., (9)-196, (16) p. front., plates, ports., fold. tab. 19½ cm. 30-17860.   CS71.T483   1906

17033   THORNHILL. Gresham L. Thornhill geneology (sic) By Virginia (Goree) Hanby. Gadsden, Ala., 1954.   (31) l. 22 x 28 cm. 55-19906.   CS71.T484   1954

17034   THORNHILL. Thornhill genealogy, as compiled and published by T. J. Thornhill ... (Dallas, Tex.) 1940.   (149) p. front. (port.) illus. (port.) 24 cm. Various pagings. 41-23728.   CS71.T484   1940

THORNS.   See THORN.

17035   THORNTON. Thornton family. (By John Wingate Thornton. Boston, 1850)   geneal. tab. 19½ x 25 cm. 10-689.   CS71.T49   1850

17036   THORNTON. The family of James Thornton, father of Hon. Matthew Thornton. By Charles Thornton Adams. New York city, 1905.   34 p. 24 cm. 20-7235.   CS71.T49   1905

17036 a THORNTON. Some things we have remembered: Samuel Thornton, admiral, 1797-1859, Percy Melville Thornton, 1841-1911, by Percy Melville Thornton ... with portraits and other illustrations. London, New York (etc.) Longmans, Green and co., 1912.   xi, (1), 337, (1) p. front., 1 illus., plates, ports., facsims. 23cm. 12-18723.   CS439.T6

17037 THORNTON. Thornton family; a partial history (by W. N. Thornton) 2d ed. (Atlanta? 1967?)   1 v. (unpaged) illus. 29 cm. Cover title. 67-31933.   CS71.T49   1967

THORNTON. See also: BUCKNER, 1907   PAGE, 1883
                        EAVENSON, 1933   SAMPSON, 1922
                        KING, CS439.K7   TAYLOR, 1898
                        LOMAX, 1913   WILLIS, 1898

THOROGOOD. See HARRISON, 1910a

THOROWGOOD. See ELLIS, 1926

THOROUGHGOOD. See No. 430 - Adventurers of purse and person.

17038   THORPE. Genealogy of some early families in Grant and Pleasant districts, Preston county, West Virginia, also the Thorpe family of Fayette county, Pennsylvania, and the Cunningham family of Somerset county, Pennsylvania, by Edward Thorp King ... (Marshalltown? Ia.) 1933.   233 p. fold. front. 23½ cm. "It is hoped that it may, in part, supplement the genealogical work already done in 1914 by Cole and Morton." - Introd. The frontispiece is a roster of company H, 3d regt., P.H.B., Md. infantry. 33-33152.   F247.P9K6

THORPE. See also: LANDEFELD, 1954
                     ROBSON, CS439.R563
                     SHEFFIELD, 1929
                     SMITH, 1944

17039   THORSON. Thorson - Aase genealogy from 1492-1964, written and compiled by Mrs. Edgar Field (Ella Thorson) (Springdale? Wis., 1964 -   v. 28 cm. 65-575.   CS71.T4915   1964

17040   THRAILKILL.   Ancestral chart of Joseph C. Thrailkill, compiled by his daughter, Fanny Ferne Thrailkill. Minneapolis, Minn., 1934.   (12) p. double geneal. tab. 21½ cm. On cover: Thrailkill 1711-1934. 34-42442.   CS71.T492   1934

THRAILKILL. See also FRICK, 1934

17041   THRALL.   A Thrall genealogy. By Gordon Thrall. (Washington? 1958?)   24 l. 23 cm. 60-35499.   CS71.T4925   1958

17042   THRALL.   Notes on genealogy: branches of Thrall, Shepard, and related families, by George M. Shepard. St. Paul (Printed by St. Paul Associated Letter Co.) 1968.   284 p. illus., ports. 29 cm. 68-54546.   CS71.S547   1968

17043   THRELKELD.   Threlkeld genealogy, by Hansford Lee Threlkeld ... Morganfield, Ky., c.1932.   336 p. front., plates, ports., maps. 23½ cm. "Reference books on Threlkelds": p.(10) 32-34643.   CS71.T493   1932

17044   THRELKELD.   Threlkeld family data, compiled by Mamie Williamson, copied by William and Anne Fitzgerald. (Florence? Ky.) 1954.   3 l. 28 cm. 55-19911.   CS71.T493   1954

17045   THRESHER.   The de(s)cendants of Edmund Henry and Louisa Sabin Thresher. This is an account of the origin, migrations, and generations of the de(s)cendants of Edmund Henry and Lousia Sabin Thresher. By Paul Edwin Kaup. (Pittsburgh, 1966) c.1965.   vi, 38 l. port. 30 cm. 67-4840.   CS71.T494   1966

THRIFT. See COVINGTON, 1956

17046   THROCKMORTON.   The descendants of the Honorable Thomas Throckmorton, born 1739 in Virginia, and died at "Rich Hill", Kentucky, 1826, compiled by Charles Wickliffe Throckmorton. (New York, 1898)   geneal. tab.   37 x 47 cm.   A photostat of a manuscript copy.   26-16565.   CS71.T495   1898

17047   THROCKMORTON.   (Throckmorton pedigrees ... Extracted from the Visitations of the county of Huntingdon, Eng., made in 1613 and 1684, and from the ms collections of the late Ralph Bigland, sometime Somerset herald, marked R. B. G. vol. 7 fo: 341.   Examined by Charles H. Athill, Richmond herald, College of arms, London, for Col. Charles Wickliffe Throckmorton, New York.   n. p., 1896, 1902)   3 geneal. tab.   illus. (coat of arms)   38 x 46 cm.   Photostats of manuscript copies.   26-18868.   CS439.T65   1902

17048   THROCKMORTON.   (Throckmorton pedigree, compiled by C. Wickliffe Throckmorton.   New York, 1916)   geneal. tab.   illus. (coats of arms)   85 x 53 cm.   At head of table: Royal genealogical chart of George V, king of England ... compiled by Charles Marshall.   23-18597.   CS71.T495   1916

17049   THROCKMORTON.   Throckmorton pedigree, by Joseph Gardner Bartlett.   Troy, N.Y., C. Shepard, 1922.   geneal. tab.   72 x 53 cm. fold. to 30 x 26½ cm.   Compiled in 1915 by Mr. Bartlett for George Andrews Moriarty.   Blueprint.   22-6211.   CS439.T65

17050   THROCKMORTON.   The sieze (!) quarterings of Colonel John Aris Throckmorton.   C. Wickliffe Throckmorton, compiler.   New York, Keuffel & Esser co., 1925.   geneal. tab.   45 x 57½ cm.   Photostat copy.   26-21707.   CR1219.T6T6

17051   THROCKMORTON.   Throckmorton family history, being the record of the Throckmortons in the United States of America with cognate branches, emigrant ancestors located at Salem, Massachusetts, 1630, and in Gloucester county, Virginia, 1660, by Frances Grimes Sitherwood ... Bloomington, Ill., Pantagraph printing & stationery co., 1929.   416 p.   col. front., illus. (facsims.) plates, ports., map, coats of arms.   26 cm.   32-20379.   CS71.T495   1929

17052   THROCKMORTON.   A genealogical and historical account of the Throckmorton family in England and the United States, with brief notes on some of the allied families, by C. Wickliffe Throckmorton.   Richmond, Va., Old Dominion press, inc., 1930.   7 p. 1., 503, (1) p. illus., plates, ports., facsims., fold. map, fold. geneal. tables, coats of arms.   27 cm.   "This is a limited edition of three hundred copies of which this is number 97."   31-2246.   CS71.T495   1930

17053   THROCKMORTON.   Throckmorton, Barbour, Jones; a genealogy of these three families, and the associated Sherman, Garth and Vreeland families; with some early records of the Leftwich, Pendleton, Hopkins, Taylor, Ward, Hall and Dashiel families, by Otey Sherman Jones ... St. Louis, Mo. (1939)   3 p. 1., 79 (i. e. 84) numb. 1.   29½ cm.   Includes extra numbered leaves: 24 a - 24 d, 49 a.   Mimeographed.   "References" at the end of each chapter.   40-6198.   CS71.T495   1939

THROCKMORTON.   See also: CALVERT, BS185. 1802P5
DE LODBROKE, DA690. L17H4

17054   THROOP.   Throop genealogy, with special reference to the Throops of Grenville county, Ontario, Canada.   Compiled by Herbert D. Throop.   Ottawa, Can. (1931)   33 p.   23 cm.   32-20377.   CS71.T498   1931

17055   THROOP.   Some account of family stocks involved in life at Willowbrook, and of neighbors, residents and visitors, especially in the latter part of the nineteenth century.   (By Edward Sandford Martin) (New York) 1933.   viii, 120 p.   front., plates, ports.   20 cm.   "Copyright   ... by E. S. Martin."   "First edition."   34-304.   CS71.T498   1933

17056   THROOP.   Ancestral charts of George Addison Throop, Deborah Goldsmith.   Many historically interesting letters from the old traveling bag, saved throughout the years by James Addison Throop; compiled by Olive Cole Smith, edited by Addison James Throop.   East St. Louis, Ill., Printed by A. J. Throop and son, D. A. Throop, 1934.   266, (2) p., 2 1., (269)-331 p., 1 1. incl. front., illus., ports., facsims., fold. geneal. tab.   2 fold. forms.   25 cm.   Two blank pages for "Family record" following p. 266.   Includes also an account of William Coddington and of the Mason family.   40-32888.   CS71.T498   1934

THROOP.　See also:　CROSLAND, 1958
　　　　　　　　　　　　DOUBLEDAY, 1924
　　　　　　　　　　　　DOUBLEDAY, 1936
　　　　　　　　　　　　HYDE, 1864

THROPP.　See WORKIZER, 1905

17057　THRUSTON.　A sketch of the ancestry of the Thruston-Phillips families; with some records of the Dickinson, Houston, January ancestry, and allied family connections.　By Gen. Gates Phillips Thruston ... Nashville, Press Brandon printing company (pref. 1909)　viii, 64 p. front., xvi pl. (incl. ports., facsims.) 20 cm. 13-15795.　CS71.T53　1909

17058　THRUSTON.　A tribute to General Gates Phillips Thruston.　(Dayton, O., United brethren publishing house, 1914)　1 p. l., 129 p. front., illus. (incl. ports.) 23½ cm. Illustrations are mounted. Foreword signed: Eliza P. T. Houk. 14-12651.　CS71.T53　1914

17058a　THRUSTON.　Louisville's first families; a series of genealogical sketches by Kathleen Jennings, with drawings by Eugenia Johnson.　Louisville, Ky., The Standard printing co. (c.1920)　176 p. incl. front., plates, ports. 20½ cm. Contains the Bullitt, Prather, Clark, Churchill, Pope, Speed, Joyes, Veech, Thruston, Taylor, Bate and Floyd families. 20-11014.　F459.L8J5

17059　THURBER.　A heart-offering to the memory of the loved and the lost.　Boston, Press of G. C. Rand, 1853.　(By Charles Thurber)　Boston, Press of G. C. Rand, 1853.　259 p. front. (port.) 18½ cm. Poems in memory of his wife, child, and other relatives and friends. "Not published." cf. Pref., signed: Charles Thurber. 31-17969.　PS3062.T3

17060　THURBER.　The Thurber genealogy; descendants of John Thurber.　By Adolph Edward Thurber.　(New York?) 1954.　39 p. illus. 23 cm. 55-34561.　CS71.T535　1954

17061　THURBURN.　The Thurburns.　By Lieut. Col. F. A. V. Thurburn ... London, Printed by R. K. Burt, 1864.　40 p. front., fold. geneal. tables, facsim. 22½ cm. The plate and facsimile are mounted photographs. Contains also the Anderson, Stevenson, Boyd and Cumming families. 19-3631.　CS479.T55

THÜRLINGER.　See addenda.

THURLOW.　See:　COLLIER, 1951a
　　　　　　　　　NELSON, 1908

17062　THURMAN.　Descendants of John Thurman of Virginia, William Graves of Virginia and James Jones of South Carolina, by John D. Humphries.　(Atlanta, 1938)　81 p. 18½ cm. 39-3175.　CS71.T54　1938

17063　THURMAN.　The descendants of Edward Moroni Thurman.　By Merna Besella (Thurman) Madden.　Provo, Utah, J. G. Stevenson (1964)　iv, 222 p. illus., facsims., geneal. tables, map, ports. 25 cm. 64-5263.　CS71.T54　1964

17064　THURMOND.　The Thurmonds; a study in the genealogy and history of Philip Thurmond of Amherst county, Virginia and his descendants, by Shirley Donnelly ... (Oak Hill, W. Va., 1939)　2 p. l., (4)-47 p. illus. 23½ cm. "Edition limited to 125 copies and type destroyed. This is volume 45." Blank pages for "Notes" interspersed throughout text. 41-379 rev.　CS71.T542　1939

17065　THURSTON.　Descendants of Edward Thurston, the first of the name in the colony of Rhode Island.　Collected by Charles Myrick Thurston ... New York, The Trow & Smith book manufacturing co., 1868.　70 p. coat of arms. 23½ cm. Coat of arms mounted on p. (4) "250 copies printed." Pages 71-96 at end contain ms. notes. 9-14775.　CS71.T544　1868

17066　THURSTON.　Genealogy of Charles Myrick Thurston and of his wife, Rachel Hall Pitman, formerly of Newport, R. I. After December, 1840, of New York. Collected for the family by their son, Charles Myrick Thurston ... With an appendix, containing the names of many descendants of Edward Thurston and Henry Pitman.　New York, Printed by J. F. Trow & co., 1865.　80 p. 23½ cm. (With his Descendants of Edward Thurston ... New York, 1868) "Edition 250 copies." 9-14777.　CS71.T544　1868

17067   THURSTON.   The doings at the first national gathering of Thurstons at Newburyport, Mass., June 24, 25, 1885.   Portland, Me., B. Thurston, 1885.   3 p. l., (3)-75 p. 23 cm. Cover-title: 1635, first settlement, Thurstons at Newburyport; 1885 first national gathering. 45-45725.   CS71.T544   1885

17068   THURSTON.   Thurston genealogies.   Compiled by Brown Thurston.   ... Portland, Me., B. Thurston, and Hoyt, Fogg & Donham, 1880.   1 p. l., 7-598 p. illus., ports. 23½ cm. At head of title: 1635-1880. 9-14774.   CS71.T544   1880

17069   THURSTON.   ... Thurston genealogies.   Comp. by Brown Thurston ...   2d ed.   Portland, Me., B. Thurston, 1892. xvi, 9-744 p. illus., ports. 23½ cm. At head of title: 1635-1892. 9-14773. CS71.T544   1892

17070   THURSTON.   The ancestry of Walter M. Thurston.   Giving some account of the families of Carroll, De Beaufort, Merrill, Moore, Mosbaugh, Pearson, Pine, Poore, Reynolds, Van Kruyne and Von Bauer.   By John H. and Walter M. Thurston.   Saint Paul, Minn., Thurston & son, printers, 1894.   95 p. front. (coats of arms) ports. 20 cm. Some of the plates are mounted photographs. 23-14863.   CS71.T544   1894

       THURSTON.   See also: BUCKNER, 1907
                      CHUTE, 1894
                      HUNTER, 1944

17071   THWEATT.   Nine hundred years of Thweatt bloodline, family history.   By Silas Allen Thweatt.   Alhambra, Calif., Alhambra Review Print. Co. (1959)   172 p. 24 cm. 59-14860.   CS71.T546   1959

       THWEATT.   See also HUTCHINS, 1938

17072   THWING.   Thwing: a genealogical, biographical and historical account of the family.   By Walter Eliot Thwing.   Boston, D. Clapp & son, printers, 1883.   216 p. front. (coat of arms) pl., ports. 23½ cm. 9-11914.   CS71.T548   1883

       THWING.   See also SMITH, 1915

17073   THYNNE.   A history of Longleat, comp. from the best authorities, by A. Farquharson ... Frome, W. C. & J. Penny, 1882.   viii, 75, (1) p. 18 cm. 21-14026.   DA664.L7F3

       THYNNE.   See also BOTFIELD, CS439.B78

17074   TIBBETTS.   Gilbert Tippett, of Ballston, and his descendants.   (By William Solyman Coons) (Albany, 1919)   (8) p. 25½ cm. Caption title. Signed: W. S. Coons. Corrections in manuscript. 22-25793.   CS71.T552   1919

17075   TIBBETTS.   The Tibbetts family; Henry Tibbetts of Dover, New Hampshire, and some of his descendants ... compiled by Mrs. May (Tibbetts) Jarvis ... from records largely collected by the late Charles Wesley Tibbetts of Ogunquit beach, Moody, Wells, Maine.   (San Diego, Calif,) 1937-39.   2 v. plates, ports., facsims., coat of arms, fold. geneal. tab. 28½ cm. Cancel title. Original title: Henry Tibbetts of Dover, New Hampshire, and some of his descendants, contributed by Mrs. May (Tibbetts) Jarvis ...   Volume 2 has title: Henry Tibbetts of Dover, New Hampshire, and some of his descendants ... compiled by Mrs. May (Tibbetts) Jarvis ... from records obtained ... from original sources and from data found in published books. On spine, v.1: Tibbetts genealogy, 1635-1937; v.2: Tibbetts genealogy, 1635-1939. Contains type-written, photostat and manuscript material. 41-18208.   CS71.T552   1937-9

17076   TIBBETTS.   The Tibbetts family, a compilation of notes by John Minot Tibbetts.   (Lexington, Mass., 1942)   483 l. 28½ cm. Type-written. 42-9867.   CS71.T552   1942

       TIBBETTS.   See also: BLIN, 1914
                    SALTER, 1900
                    STEEL, 1905

17077   TICE.   The Tice families in America: Theis, Thyssen, Tyssen, Deis.   By James Strode Elston.   Rutland, Vt., Tuttle Pub. Co. (1947)   320 p. 24 cm. Bibliography: p. (275)-282. 49-15644*.   CS71.T553   1947

17078   TICHBORNE.   The Tichborne romance: a full and accurate report of the proceedings in the extraordinary and interesting trial of Tichborne v. Lushington, in the Court of common pleas, Westminster, for forty days, from Wednesday, May 10, to Friday, July 7, 1871; including the whole of the examination, cross-examination, and re-examination of the claimant.   2d ed., with addendum.   Manchester, J. Heywood; London, Simpkin, Marshall, & co.; (etc., etc., 1871)   440 p. 21½ cm. Portrait of plaintiff on cover.   "An action of ejectment brought by the plaintiff to recover possession of the Tichborne estates, in Hampshire.   The action is entered against Franklin Lushington, a tenant ... The plaintiff ... claims to be Sir Roger Charles Doughty Tichborne." - p. (3) 32-7198.

LAW

17079   TICHBORNE.   The Tichborne case, by Lord Maugham ... London, Hodder & Stoughton, 1936.   384 p. front., pl., ports., facsims. 22½ cm.   An account of the two Tichborne trials concerning Thomas Castro, otherwise called Arthur Orton, claiming to be Sir Roger Charles Doughty-Tichborne.   The first trial was held in the Court of common pleas.   In the second, the criminal trial, the defendant was tried for perjury before the Court of Queen's bench, April 23, 1873 - February 28, 1874.   Contents. - pt. I. Before the case began.   A Victorian love affair.   The travels of Roger Richborne.   The results of an advertisement.   The early life of Arthur Orton.   First steps in England. - pt. II. The claimant is recognized.   Preparations for the trial.   The Chile commission.   The Australian commission. - pt. III. Tichborne v. Lushington.   The claimant in the box.   The claimant's case continues.   The speech for the defence.   Evidence for the defendant. - pt. IV. The Queen v. Thomas Castro, otherwise Arthur Orton.   Evidence for the defendant.   The last act.   Appendices (Genealogical data on the Tichborne and Orton families, included) 37-2860.

LAW

17080   TICHELEN (VAN)   Genealogie der familie van Tichelen, 1200-1940, door B. W. van Schijndel, met medewerking van Henrij van Tichelen-Ide.   (Antwerpen, J. de Velder, 1942)   131, (1) p. incl. illus., plates, facsims., coats of arms (1 col.) fold. geneal. tables. 24½ x 19 cm.   Errata slip inserted.   Wisconsin university library for Library of Congress.   AF 47-2392.

CS809.T5S3

TICHENOR.   See: ROE, 1965
                        TICKNOR.

17081   TICKELL.   Thomas Tickell and the eighteenth century poets (1685-1740) containing numerous letters and poems hitherto unpublished, compiled from his family papers by Richard Eustace Tickell.   London, Constable & co. ltd., 1931.   xv, 256 p. incl. coat of arms. front. (port.) facsims., fold. geneal. tab., diagr.   22½ cm.   Bibliography of Thomas Tickell's writings: p. 187-197; "Authorities cited": p. 246-248.   32-1009.   PR3735.T5T5

TICKELL.   See also SPARKS, CS439.S73

17082   TICKNOR.   A partial history of the Tichenor family in America, descendants of Martin Tichenor of Connecticut and New Jersey, and a complete genealogy of the branch of the family descending from Isaac Tichenor, of Ohio, spelling the name Teachenor, with some references to the probable collateral lineage descended from William Ticknor of Massachusetts.   Kansas City, Mo., 1918-20.   39 p. front. (mounted phot.) illus. (incl. ports.) col. coat of arms. 25 cm.   "No. 9. 350 copies printed for private circulation."   Edited by Richard Bennington Teachenor from information compiled by James Tichenor and his son, Rev. Isaac Taylor Tichenor. cf. Introd.   "Addenda. May 1920": p. 33-39.   "Maternal ancestry; the Givauden family": p. 38-39.   18-15856 rev.   CS71.T554   1918

17083   TICKNOR.   The Ticknor family in America, being an account of the descendants of William Ticknor of Scituate and of other immigrants named Ticknor or Tickner.   Compiled by James Melville Hunnewell.   Boston, 1919.   vi, 246 numb. l. 29 cm. Type-written. 22-22877.   CS71.T554   1919

17084   TIDD.   A history of the Tidds of Ohio.   By Howard Harmon Tidd.   (n.p., 1958?)   175 p. illus. 22 cm. 58-24622.   CS71.T556   1958

17085   TIDWELL.   Census and other records of the Tidwell family.   By Charles Owen Johnson.   (Monroe? La., 1958?)   2 v. 30 cm. 59-21430.   CS71.T557   1958

TIDWELL.   See also: JOHNSON, 1961
                            McCALL, 1931

17086   TIEBOUT.   The ancestry and posterity of Cornelius Henry Tiebout of Brooklyn ...(n.p.)   Printed for private distribution, 1910.   80 p. front., illus. (coat of arms) 24 cm. Copy no. 41. Compiled and edited by Francis V. Morrell. cf. Preface, signed C. H. T. Manuscript notes and newspaper clippings inserted. 20-2610.   CS71.T558   1910

TIEBOUT.   See also TODD, 1867

718

TIERCENT.   See DU BOISBAUDRY, 1958

17087   TIERNAN.   The Tiernan family in Maryland.   As illustrated by extracts from works in the public libraries, and original letters and memoranda in the possession of C. B. Tiernan.   Baltimore, Gallery & McGann, 1898.   222 p. incl. plates, ports., facsims.   front. 22½ cm. 1-13588.

CS71. T564   1898

17088   TIERNAN.   The Tiernan and other families.   As illustrated by extracts from works in the public libraries, and original letters and memoranda in the possession of Charles B. Tiernan ... Baltimore, W. J. Gallery & co., 1901.   406 p. incl. plates, ports., facsims.   front. 22½ cm. 1-13589.

CS71. T564   1901

17089   TIERNEY.   The life of Colonel Pownoll Phipps ... with family records, by Pownoll W. Phipps ... Printed for private circulation.   London, R. Bentley and son, 1894.   vii, 228 p. 12 geneal. tab. 21 cm. "A list of books referred to, and containing interesting matter bearing on our family": p. 227-228.   Contains also pedigrees of the Tierney, Ramsay, Osborne and Riall families. 21-2247.   CT788. P58P5

17090   TIERS.   Some branches from the Tiers' family tree ... from records of Clarence Van Dyke Tiers ... Oakmont, Pa., 1941.   (10) p. 20½ cm. Includes four blank pages at end for "Additional records." 43-1841.

CS71. T565   1941

17091   TIERS.   Branches from the Matthew Pratt-Arundius Tiers family tree, 1734-1942.   (By Clarence Van Dyke Tiers) (Daytona Beach, Fla.) 1942.   8 p. 22 cm. Caption title. Author's name in manuscript on t.-p. Four blank pages at end for "Additional records." 43-4193.   CS71. P914   1942

17092   TIESZEN.   History and record of the Tieszen family.   By David D. Tieszen.   Marion, S. D., 1954.   123 p. illus. 24 cm. 57-15942.   CS71. T5654   1954

17093   TIFFANY.   The Tiffanys of America.   History and genealogy.   Pub. ... for and in the interest of Charles Lewis Tiffany of New York city, and of the Tiffany family.   By Nelson Otis Tiffany. (Buffalo, The Matthews-Northrup co., 1901?)   x, 254 p. front. (coat of arms) pl., ports. 26 cm. 15-232.

CS71. T566   1901

TIFFT.   See TEFFE.

17094   TIFFANY.   Genealogical sketch of the Tiffany family, as collected and arranged by Ella F. Wright.   Waterbury, Conn., Mattatuck press, The Waterbury blank book mfg. co., 1904.   92 p. front. (coat of arms) plates, ports. 23 cm. On cover: "My ancestry." 10-15242.   CS71. T566   1904

TIGNOR.   See DAMERON, 1953

17095   TILDEN.   Notes on the origin of the Tilden name and family, researches and compilation by Hon. Samuel Jones Tilden ... n. p., 1894)   1 p. l., 15, 59 (i.e.58) numb. l. 28 cm. 38M5175T.

CS71. T568   1894

17096   TILDEN.   The life of Samuel J. Tilden, by John Bigelow ... New York, Harper & brothers, 1895.   2 v. front., plates (1 double) ports., fold. geneal. tables. 23 cm. "Notes on the origin of the Tilden name and family, by Samuel J. Tilden": v. 1, p. 315-363. 4-16990.   E415. 9. T5B5

TILDEN.   See also AVERY, 1899

17097   TILDESLEY.   An historical and descriptive account of Blackpool and its neighbourhood.   Viz: Layton, Carlton, Poulton, Mains hall, Singleton, Thornton, Burn hall, Rossal, Bispham, Marton, Lytham, Southshore, &c. ... By William Thornber ... Poulton, Printed and pub. for the author by Smith, 1837.   2 p. l., v p., 1 l., (5)-345, (3), 4 p. illus., fold. geneal. tab. 17½ cm. 2-22382.   DA690. B633T4

TILESTON.   See PAINE, 1913

17098   TILFORD.   Tilford family in vertical file.   Ask reference librarian for this material.

TILFORD.　See also MAXWELL, 1916

17099　TILGHMAN.　Tilghman, Lloyd, Byrd lineage, compiled by Elmer Eugene Barker.　(n.p.)
1937.　geneal. tab.　illus. (coats of arms) 56 x 62 cm.　"Authorities."　Photostat (positive) 37-16972.

CS71.T573　1937

17100　TILGHMAN.　Tilghman-Tillman family, 1225-1945, by Colonel Stephen F. Tillman ... (Ann
Arbor, Mich., Lithoprinted by Edwards brothers, inc.) 1946.　vii, 473 p. incl. front. (col. coat of arms) illus.
(incl. ports.)　28 x 22½ cm.　46-23126.　CS71.T573　1946

17101　TILGHMAN.　Spes alis agricolam (Hope sustains the farmer)　Covering the years 1225 to
1961 of the Tilghman (Tillman) and allied families.　By Stephen Frederick Tillman.　(Chevy Chase?
Md., 1962)　320 p.　illus., ports., col. coats of arms.　29 cm.　Cover title.　62-66163.

CS71.T573　1962

　　　TILGHMAN.　See also: HOLLIDAY, 1962
　　　　　　　　　　　　　TILLMAN.

　　　TILL.　See LLOYD, 1912

　　　TILLER.　See BATES, 1911

　　　TILLETT.　See ALLISON, 1955

17102　TILLEY.　Genealogy of the Tilley family.　Compiled by R. Hammett Tilley ... Newport,
R.I., J.P. Sanborn, steam book and job printer, 1878.　79, (1) p.　coat of arms.　22½ cm.　9-13011.

CS71.T576　1878

17103　TILLEY.　Progeny and ancestry of Milton Popple Tilley of New Canaan, Connecticut.　By
Milton Popple Tilley.　(New Canaan? 1955)　30 p.　ports., coat of arms, facsim.　24 cm.　Cover title: Ancestral lines of
Milton Popple Tilley.　56-29470.　CS71.T576　1955

　　　TILLEY.　See also: HOWLAND, E171.A53 vol.12
　　　　　　　　　　　　SWAIN, 1896

17104　TILLINGHAST.　A little journey to the home of Elder Pardon Tillinghast, by John Avery
Tillinghast and Frederick Wheaton Tillinghast.　Read at the third reunion of the descendants of Deacon
Pardon and Mary (Sweet) Tillinghast in Providence, Rhode Island, September 4, 1908.　(Providence,
R.I., Standard printing company, 1908)　27, (1) p.　21½ cm.　9-1997.　CS71.T577　1908

　　　TILLINGHAST.　See also: NEALE, 1915
　　　　　　　　　　　　　　SPANGLER, 1937
　　　　　　　　　　　　　　WANTON, F76.R52 vol.3

　　　TILLIS.　See GREENLEE. 1956

17105　TILLMAN.　The Tillman family, by Stephen Frederick Tillman.　Richmond, Va., The
William Byrd press, inc., 1930.　6 p. l., 3-134 p. ports.　23½ cm.　31-9474.

CS71.T579　1930

17106　TILLMAN.　Family biography of Lewis Tillman, 2nd.　(Washington, D.C., c.1931)
117 p. pl., ports.　23½ cm.　Part of pages blank.　Half-title: Biography of a family.　"Prepared and published by Lewis Tillman, 3d,
Samuel E. Tillman, Edwin H. Tillman and Abram M. Tillman."　31-11190.　CS71.T579　1931

17107　TILLMAN.　... The Tilgham-Tillman families, 1638-1934, by Stephen Frederick Tillman,
Washington, D.C., 1935.　1 p. l., 635 p.　27 cm.　Type-written: corrections in ms.　38-M5179T
CS71.T579　1935

　　　TILLMAN.　See also: SHARP, 1953
　　　　　　　　　　　　TILGHMAN.

720

17108   TILLOTSON.   Genealogies of Miller and Tillotson, by Elbert H. T. Miller.   Fraser, Christie, Smith (and) Wheeler, by Laura Miller.   Scottsville, N.Y., 1951.   39 p. 22 cm. 52-244.
CS69.M5

17109   TILSON.   The Tilson genealogy, from Edmond Tilson at Plymouth, N.E., 1638 to 1911; with brief sketches of the family in England back to 1066, by Mercer V. Tilson.   Also brief account of Waterman, Murdock, Bartlett, Turner, Winslow, Sturtevant, Keith and Parris families, allied with the parents of the author.   (Plymouth, The Memorial press, 1911)   609 (1) p. ports. 24 cm. Title vignette: coat of arms. 11-32404.
CS71.T58   1911

17110   TILSON.   Tilson family in vertical file.   Please ask reference librarian for this material.

TILSON.   See also: DUNHAM, 1956
                        WYMAN, 1927

TILT.   See CHANCE, 1892

17111   TILTON.   History of the Tilton family in America, by Francis Theodore Tilton. v.I, no. 1 -
            (Clifton, N.J., 1927) -   v. 23 cm. 28-1174.
CS71.T582   1927

17112   TILTON.   The ancestry of Phoebe Tilton, 1775-1847, wife of Capt. Abel Lunt of Newburyport, Massachusetts.   By Walter Goodwin Davis.   Portland, Me., Anthoensen Press, 1947.   6 l., (3)-257 p. coats of arms, geneal. tab. 23 cm. 47-27248*.
CS71.T582   1947

TILTON.   See also DE MOSS, 1950

17113   TIMANUS.   Timanus family notes.   By Richard Wilson Cook.   South Orange, N.J., 1954. 25 l. illus. 29 cm. 60-38920.
CS71.T583   1954

17114   TIMBRELL.   A transcript of the register of the parish church, Bretforten, in the county and diocese of Worcester, from A.D. 1538 to A.D. 1837; transcribed and ed. with XXIII appendices, by the Rev. W. H. Shawcross ... The indexes by Miss Muriel Wilson.   Evesham (Eng.) H.W. Mayer, 1908. 5 p. l., 4, (1), 4-83, 107 numb. l. pl., 3 port. 30 x 23½ cm. Includes three half-titles: Volume I. The Bretforten register ... Volume II. The 23 appendices ... Index to the appendices ... "Eighty copies only of this work have been printed ... 10-9484.
CS436.B73

17115   TIMPERLEY.   Timperley of Hintlesham; a study of a Suffolk family, by Sir Gerald H. Ryan, bart., and Lilian J. Redstone; with 12 illustrations, 3 maps and 2 genealogical tables.   London, Methuen & co. ltd. (1931)   xiv p., 1 l., 160 p. front., illus. (coat of arms) plates, ports., maps (part double) fold. geneal. tables. 23 cm. 31-30751.
CS439.T67R8

17116   TIMS.   Some antecedents and descendants of Nathan Tims of Chester County, South Carolina.   By Eugene Chapel Tims.   Wolfe City, Tex., Printed by Henington Pub. Co., 1967.   42 p. ports. 23 cm. Cover title: Descendants of Nathan Tims. 73-10573 MARC.
CS71.T5835   1967

17117   TINDAL.   The descendants of Daniel Tindall c. (1770-1835) and his wife Mary E. Taggart (1769-1857) Robert Ferguson (17 - 18) Robert Bingham (1767-1824) and his wife Sarah Donnan (1770-1832) (by) Benjamin N. Meeds, jr. ... and William P. Meeds, jr.   Silver Spring, Md. 1936. 4 p. l., 41 p. 27 cm. Reproduced from type-written copy. "References": 2d prelim. leaf. 37-21344 rev.
CS71.T584   1936

TINDAL.   See also GENTRY, 1909

TINGLE.   See TINGLEY.

17118   TINGLEY.   The Tingley family, being a record of the descendants of Samuel Tingley of Malden, Mass., in both the male and female lines.   (— - 1666).   Compiled by Raymon Meyers Tingley ... (Rutland, Vt., Tuttle company) 1910.   894 p. 23½ cm. 12-2979.
CS71.T585   1910

17119   TINGLEY.   Some ancestral lines; being a record of some of the ancestors of Guilford Solon Tingley and his wife, Martha Pamelia Meyers, collected by their son, Raymon Meyers Tingley ... Rutland, Vt., The Tuttle publishing company, inc., 1935.   465 p. front., plates, ports. 28 cm. 36-30606.
CS71.T585   1935

17120   TINKER.   The ancestors of Silas Tinker in America.   From 1637.   A partial record, prepared by A. B. Tinker, of Akron, and read at the annual reunion of the descendants of Silas Tinker, at Ashtabula, O., August 15, 1889.   Akron, O., The Werner printing & litho. co. (1889?)   11 p. illus. (coat of arms) 22½ cm. 3-17714.
CS71.T589   1889

17121   TINKER.   A Tinker family.   The ancestors and descendants of Joseph Wescot Tinker, Ellsworth, Me., 1791-1868.   A descendant of John Tinker of Boston, 1638.   Compiled by Frederick James Libbie.   Boston, Priv. print.   (Press of the Libbie show print) 1900.   2 p. l., 36 p. front., ports. 23½ cm. "100 copies privately printed." 1-2620 rev.
CS71.T589   1900

17122   TINKEY.   The Tinkey family; some of the unions and reunions, compiled by the book committee, J. C. Tinkey, chairman.   (n. p.) 1922.   28 p. illus. (incl. ports.) 25 cm. Caption title. 33-29128.
CS71.T5895   1922

17123   TINKEY.   The Tinkey family; some of the unions and reunions, compiled by the Book committee, J. C. Tinkey, chairman.   (2d ed.) (n. p.) 1922 (i. e. 1944)   28 p. illus. (incl. ports.) 25 cm. Caption title.   "The Tinkey family ... Revised from 1922 to 1944, by J. Calvin Tinkey" (23 p. illus. (ports.)) inserted. 45-21896.
CS71.T5895   1944

17124   TINTLE.   The Tintle family, 1765-1968, by Frederick E. Traflet.   Butler, N.J., 1968.
v, 49 l. map. 28 cm. 68-58704.   CS71.T5897   1968

TIPPETT.   See TIBBETTS, 1919

17124a   TIPPIN.   Ancestry of Sanford Lathadeus Tippin family of Henderson county, Kentucky, by James Jackson Tippin ... (Shreveport, La., M. L. Bath company, limited, 1940)   2 p. l., (3)-38 p. 23½ cm.   Pages 34-38 blank for "Additional data".   "Includes a record of the ... Mayfield, Kinsey and Whitaker-Mann ancestries." - Introd. 40-9663.
CS71.T59   1940

17125   TIPPIN.   A brief history of George Manton Tippin, Sr., of Ireland, York County, South Carolina, and Washington County, Indiana, and his descendants.   By Ernest Elwood Tippin.   Wichita, Kan., Printed by Preston Print. Co., 1952.   94 p. 24 cm. 53-34774.   CS71.T59   1952

17126   TIPPING.   English Tipping ancestry of Sanford Lathadeus Tippin family of Henderson co., Kentucky (U.S.A.) by James Jackson Tippin ... Shreveport, La., Printed by Castle printing company, inc., 1942.   (4) p. 23 cm. Caption title.   "Reference books used": p. (4) 42-50343.   CS71.T59   1942

TIPTOFT.   See: DUNSTANVILLE, DA690.C42S4
                         GREY, 1868

17127   TIPTON.   Tipton family of Maryland, Virginia, Tennessee, Kentucky, Ohio, Indiana, Illinois, Missouri (By) Charles Brunk Heinemann.   Washington, D.C., 1934.   1 p. l., 29, 1, 2, 10 numb. l. 29 cm. Type-written (carbon copy)   Author's autographed presentation copy to the Library of Congress. 38M1096T.
CS71.T592   1934

17128   TIPTON.   Tipton family of Maryland, Virginia, Tennessee, Kentucky, Ohio, Indiana, Illinois, Missouri (by) Charles Brunk Heinemann ... Chicago, Ill. (1937)   1 p. l., 40, 11 numb. l. 28½ cm. Typewritten. 37-38453.   CS71.T592   1937

17129   TIPTON.   Tipton family of Maryland, Virginia, Tennessee, Kentucky, Ohio, Indiana, Illinois, Missouri (by) Charles Brunk Heinemann.   Washington, D.C., 1941.   1 p. l., 48 numb. l. 28½ cm. Type-written (carbon copy) 43-2194.   CS71.T592   1941

17130   TIPTON.   The Tipton family history.   By Whitney Hord Tipton.   Mr. Sterling, Ky., c.1948.
1 v. (unpaged) illus., ports., coats of arms. 26 cm. 50-39477.   CS71.T592   1948

17131   TIPTON.   Tipton family records in the present boundaries of the United States from colonial times to 1950.   By Charles Brunk Heinemann.   Washington (1950)   332, 49 l. coat of arms. 27 cm.   Typewritten (carbon copy) 51-24073.   CS71.T592   1950

17132   TISDALE.   Genealogy of Col. Israel Tisdale and his descendants, compiled in part and arranged by Edith Francena Tisdale.   Boston, Mass. (The Metcalf press) 1909.   3 p. l., 13-82 p. incl. pl., coat of arms. 2 port. (incl. front.) 23 cm.   Blank pages interspersed for "Births, marriages, deaths".   The plates are mounted.   On cover: A family register.   "A supplement to 'A family register'.   Genealogy of Col. Israel Tisdale and his descendants ... 1920": 15 leaves inserted at end. 34-14610.   CS71.T598   1909

         TIPTON.   See also: MASSENGILL, 1931
                               PARISH, 1935

17133   TISDALE.   Genealogy of a branch of the Tisdale family of Vermilion, Erie County, Ohio, and Lorain County, Ohio.   By Claude Charles Hamel.   Amherst, 1951.   5 l. 27 cm. 52-21274.
                                                                                              CS71.T598   1951

         TISDALE.   See also: SAVAGE, 1926
                               SAVAGE, E171.A53 v.19

         TISON.   See BINGHAM, 1920

         TITCOMB.   See: ELLIS, F3.T61
                          PERKINS, 1914
                          QUIMBY, 1906

17134   TITLER.   Titler and related families.   By Elmer Hale Snyder.   Chicago, Ill., 1938. 3 l. 28 cm.   Caption title.   Blue print.   40-2270.   CS71.T5987   1938

         TITMAN.   See No. 9846 - Hackettstown.

17135   TITSWORTH.   The Titsworth family.   By Will Bloss Titsworth.   (Hopkins, Minn., 1964?) 194 p. illus., ports. 22 cm. 65-9756.   CS71.T595   1964

17136   TITUS.   The Titus family in America.   Three generations, by the Rev. Anson Titus ... (New York, The New York genealogical and biographical society, 1881)   8 p. 25 cm.   Caption title.   Reprint from The New York genealogical and biographical society.   April, 1881. 11-8432.   CS71.T599   1881

17137   TITUS.   Titus family.   Of Long island and Dutchess county, N.Y.   Compiled by Andrew J. Provost, jr., C.E.   Darien, Conn., 1941.   2 p. l., 51 numb. l. coat of arms. 29 x 23½ cm.   Reproduced from typewritten copy. 44-18100.   CS71.T599   1941

17138   TITUS.   Titus family in America; eleven generations of the direct line from Robert Titus I to Dorothy Madalene Titus and Bursley Howland Titus XI and an appendix ... Compiled by Dorothy M. Titus, edited by Percy Hobart Titus ... Boston, Mass., The editor, 1943.   3 p. l., iii-iv, 9 numb. l., 1 l., xxvi, 8 numb. l., 1 l. front., ports., coat of arms. 28½ x 22 cm.   Reproduced from type-written copy.   "References": leaf 9. 44-1005.
                                                                                              CS71.T599   1943

17139   TITUS.   Titus family.   Of Long Island and Dutchess County, N.Y.   By Andrew Jackson Provost.   Rev. and enl.   Darien, Conn., 1945.   78 l. 29 cm. 51-29689.   CS71.T599   1945

17140   TITUS.   A Titus family: from Robert Titus, emigrant to Massachusetts, 1635, to Col. Henry Theodore Titus, founder of Titusville, Florida.   By Ianthe (Bond) Hebel.   Daytona Beach, Fla., 1968. 1 v. (various pagings) illus., facsims., 1 col. map, port. 30 cm.   On cover: The Titus family in America, 1635-1960. 72-10432 MARC.
                                                                                              CS71.T599   1968

17141   TOBEY.   Tobey (Tobie, Toby) genealogy: Thomas, of Sandwich, and James, of Kittery, and their descendants, by Rufus Babcock Tobey and Charles Henry Pope.   Boston, Mass., C.H. Pope, 1905. 334, 15, (1) p. pl., ports. 24 cm. 6-26011.   CS71.T628   1905

         TOBIE.   See TOBEY.

TOBIN.　See:　HAGOOD, 1946
　　　　　　　　　HALE, 1948

17142　TOCORNAL.　Tocornal family in vertical file.　Ask reference librarian for this material.

TOD.　See TODD.

TOBY.　See TOBEY.

17143　TODD.　The Todd genealogy; or, Register of the descendants of Adam Todd, of the names of Todd, Whetten, Brevoort, Coolidge, Bristed, Sedgwick, Kane, Renwick, Bull, Huntington, Dean, Astor, Bentzen, Langdon, Boreel, Wilks, De Nottbeck, Ward, Chanler, Cary, Tiebout, Bruce, Robbins, Waldo, Woodhull, Odell, Greene and Foster, with notices and genealogies of many persons and families con- nected with the beforementioned descendants.　By Richard Henry Greene, A.M.　New York, Wilbur & Hastings, 1867.　viii, (9)-143, xvii p.　23½ cm.　Blank leaves interspersed.　9-14778.　　CS71.T634　1867

17144　TODD.　The Todds, the Wheelers et id genus omne.　Boston, Printed by T. Todd, 1909.
63, (1) p. illus.　23½ cm.　Compiled by Thomas Todd.　11-32.　　CS71.T634　1909

17145　TODD.　Todds of the Eastern Shore, Maryland, comp. by J. R. Witcraft ... Frankford, Phila., Dispatch publishing house, 1912.　2 p. l., 80 p.　coat of arms.　22½ cm.　12-28453.
　　CS71.T634　1912b

17146　TODD.　The Virginia Todds, compiled by J. R. Witcraft ... Frankford, Phila., Dispatch pub- lishing house, 1913.　1 p. l., 34 p.　2 pl. (1 coat of arms)　22½ cm.　14-11765.
　　CS71.T634　1913

17147　TODD.　The Todd family in America; or, The descendants of Christopher Todd, 1637-1919, being an effort to give an account, as fully as possible of his descendants.　Comp. by John Edwards Todd, D.D., ed. by George Iru Todd.　Northampton, Mass., Press of Gazette printing co., 1920.
721 p. front. (col. coat of arms) plates, ports.　24 cm.　22-14288.　　CS71.T634　1920

17148　TODD.　God's infinite variety, an American, by Georgia Brake Todd.　(New York) National Americana publications, inc., 1939.　8 p. l., 15-498 p. front. (port.)　27½ cm.　An account of the Todd, Dodge, Brake, Guthridge and allied families.　Bibliography: p. 453-466.　39-33446.　　CS71.T634　1939

17149　TODD.　Todds of the St. Croix valley, by William Todd.　Mount Carmel, Conn., Priv. print., 1943.　24 p. pl., ports., fold. geneal. tab.　23½ cm.　"200 copies printed."　44-51425.　　CS71.T634　1943

17150　TODD.　A short history of the Todds and Friersons.　Other related families: Warnock, McAlister, James, Kolb, Pouncey (and) Crosland.　By Joseph Newton Todd.　Washington, 1951.
30 p. illus. geneal. tables.　23 cm.　76-220299 MARC.　　CS71.T634　1951

17151　TODD.　Speaking of families: the Tod(d)s of Caroline County, Virginia, and their kin (by) Ann Todd Rubey, Florence Isabelle Stacy (and) Herbert Ridgeway Collins.　Columbia, Mo., Artcraft Press, 1960.　628 p. illus.　24 cm.　61-489.　　CS71.T634　1960

17152　TODD.　Todd family in vertical tile.　Ask reference librarian for this material.

TODD.　See also:　DAVIS, 1939
　　　　　　　　　　EDWARDS, 1894
　　　　　　　　　　JAMES, 1913a
　　　　　　　　　　NASH, 1902
　　　　　　　　　　WINSTON, 1927

TODENI.　See BURRARD, CS439.B937

17153　TOERS.　The Toers-Tuers family, by Howard S. F. Randolph.　(n.p.) 1926.　cover-title, 36 p.
23 cm.　Reprinted from the Genealogical magazine of New Jersey.　Authorities: p. 1.　26-16573.
　　CS71.T641　1926

TOGWOOD.   See POMEROY, 1958

TOHRER.   See THORER.

17154   TOKE.   The account book of a Kentish estate, 1616-1704, edited by Eleanor C. Lodge ...
London, Pub. for the British academy by H. Milford, Oxford university press, 1927.   xlviii, 532 p. 2 fold.
maps, fold. geneal. tab. 26 cm. (British academy. Records of the social and economic history of England and Wales, vol. VI) "Internal evidence
goes to prove that from 1616 to 1680 the book must have been the work of Nicholas Toke of Godinton ... who died on the 29th November 1680; only
a few days before his death was the work taken up by his nephew and heir, Nicholas, afterwards Sir Nicholas Toke, who continued the book up to its
final entry." - Introd. 28-28217.   HC251. B7 vol. VI

       TOLER.   See MAUNSELL, CS439. M37

       TOLIVER.   See TALIAFERRO, 1960

17155   TOLL.   A narrative, embracing the history of two or three of the first settlers and their
families, of Schenectady.   Interspersed with a few anecdotal eccentricities and antiquities.   Together
with a description of the winter evening visits, recreations, and supper, and of the tea-parties of olden
times, with a few strictures on the change of times.   By Dan'l J. Toll ... (Schenectady) 1847.
57 p. 21½ cm. 20-20186.   F129. S5T65

17156   TOLL.   Genealogy of the Toll family (of Daniel and Simon) Branches, with allied families of
the former, together with a brief history of the founder, Karel Hansen Toll, by Dudley Toll Hill.
(Schenectady, N. Y., Gazette press) 1941.   1 p. l., 7-47 p. mounted illus., mounted port., fold. geneal. tab. 23 cm.
41-25786.   CS71. T65   1941

17157   TOLL.   Toll-Wolcott ancestors in America; (an index) By Charles Hansen Toll.   Northampton, Mass., 1961.   63 l. 24 cm. 62-41766.   CS71. T65   1961

17158   TOLLEMACHE.   The Tollemaches of Helmingham and Ham.   By Edward Devereux Hamilton
Tollemache.   Ipswich (Eng.) W. S. Cowell (1949)   208 p. plates, ports., coat of arms, geneal. table. 26 cm. Errata
slip inserted. Bibliography: p. 196. 50-35745.   CS439. T68   1949

       TOLLES.   See NORTON, 1935

       TOLLOVICS.   In vertical file under PRANKE family.   Ask reference librarian for this material.

       TOLLOVITS.   In vertifal file under PRANKE family.   Ask reference librarian for this material.

17159   TOLMAN.   The Needham branch of the Tolman family.   By Anna Maria (Tolman) Pickford
... Dedham, Mass., 1894.   1 p. l., 29 p. front. (port.) 24½ cm. Reprinted from the Dedham historical register, volumes v and
vi. for 1894, 95. 4-13413.   CS71. T652   1894

       TOLQUHON.   See FORBES.

17160   TOLTON.   "That their children may know": a record of the descendants of Edward Tolton.
By Lula (Tolton) Tanner.   (n. p., 1962?)   162 p. illus. 24 cm. 62-49399.   CS71. T653   1962

17161   TOMB.   Matthew Tomb and his descendants, some of them spelling the name Thom, 1758-1861.
Series A.   Data collected by Homer Thom ... edited by his brother, Charles Thom ... (Port Jefferson? N. Y., 1945?)   49 p. 24 cm. 45-21836.   CS71. T655   1945

17162   TOMBAUGH.   Tombaugh history, 1728-1930, compiled by Reno G. Tombaugh.   (n. p., 1930?)
85, (1) p. front., plates, ports. 23½ cm. "Authorities consulted": p. 3. 40-18937.   CS71. T656   1930

       TOMKINS.   See TOMPKINS.

17162 a TOMKINSON.   Genealogical memoirs of various families of Tomkinson.   (1620-1904)   By
Newton Powers Tomkinson.   (Philadelphia? c. 1904)   132 p. 27 cm. "This edition is limited to 164 copies. No. 1."
5-3482.   CS71. T658   1904

17163   TOMLIN.   Tomlin genealogy; Greenwich township branch and Heislerville branch, compiled by Charles Tomlin.   Cape May Court House, N.J., 1932.   19 p. 23½ cm. 32-6652.

CS71. T659   1932

17164   TOMLIN.   Tomlin genealogy ... compiled by Charles Tomlin.   Cape May Court House, N.J., 1932.   91 (2) p. incl. front., illus., ports. 23½ cm. Also issued in parts. Contents. - Mullica Hill line. - Blue Ball line. - Goshen line. - Greenwich township line. - Heislerville line. 32-19801.   CS71. T659   1032a

17165   TOMLINSON.   Henry Tomlinson, and his descendants in America, with a few additional branches of Tomlinsons, later from England.   By Rev. Samuel Orcutt ... New Haven, Conn., Press of Price, Lee and Adkins co., 1891.   xvi p., 1 l., (3)-228 p. col. front. (coat of arms) ports. 25½ cm. L. C. COPY REPLACED BY MICROFILM. 9-17830.   CS71. T66   1891
Microfilm 10009 CS

17166   TOMLINSON.   The Tomlinson book.   By Robert Rood Buell.   (Prairie du Sac? Wis.) 1956.   32, 17 p. 29 cm. Excerpt from the "Diary of John Tomlinson": 17 p. at end. 58-16145.

TOMLINSON.   See also: DAYTON, 1902
HARVEY, 1939
MORSE, 1939
READ, 1939
SANDERSON, DA20. S9 vol. 118

17167   TOMPKINS.   Cursory family sketches (of the Tompkins family) By S. Ann Garnett.   Privately printed.   (Albany, J. Munsell, printer) 1870.   140 p. 24 cm. "Autobiographical sketch": p. (53)-140. 9-14779.
CS71. T662   1870

17168   TOMPKINS.   A record of the ancestry and kindred of the children of Edward Tompkins, sr. late of Oakland, California (deceased) With an appendix.   Preliminary ed.   (Oakland, Cal.) Printed for the compiler, 1893.   2 p. l., 65 p. geneal. tables (part fold.) 26½ cm. Compiled by Edward Tompkins, jr. 1-22229.
CS71. T662   1893

17169   TOMPKINS.   The Tomkins - Tompkins geneology (!) compiled, printed and published by Robert A. Tompkins and Clare F. Tompkins ... (Los Angeles, Calif.) 1942.   1 p. l., 720 p. col. front. (coat of arms) 20½ cm. 42-8631.   CS71. T662   1942

17170   TOMPKINS.   Our folks; a genealogy of the ancestors and descendants of Reuben Tompkins. By Bess (Tompkins) Miller.   Corvallis, Ore. (c.1953)   20 p. illus. 23 cm. 56-22746.
CS71. T662   1953

TOMPKINS.   See also: MONROE, E171. A53 v. 14

17171   TONE.   History of the Tone family, beginning with Jean Tone of Tartas of province of Gascony, France, 1409, and genealogical records of his descendants in Normandy, France, England, Ireland and America.   Compiled by Dr. Frank Jerome Tone.   Niagara Falls, N.Y., c.1944.   185, (7) p. front., illus. (map, facsim., col. coat of arms) plates, ports. 23½ cm. 44-39334.   CS71. T663   1944

17172   TONER.   Genealogy of Thorsten Toner family, Odalen, Norway, in America, 1870-1968. (Co-compilers: Christine (Braaten) Quisley and Doris (Libby) Sellman.   Slayton, Minn., 1968 -   1 v. (loose-leaf) 30 cm. Title from label on cover. 73-12882 MARC.   CS71. T6635   1968

TONG.   See TONGUE.

TONGE.   See TONGUE.

17173   TONGUE.   A record of the descendants of Levi Nelson Tongue and Adeline Sutton Morse, with information concerning their ancestors, and four appendices concerning the families Lancaster, Bliesner, Hauger-Hauer (and) Olson, related by marriage.   Washington, 1949.   1 v. (various pagings) 28 cm. Cover title. 51-24212.   CS71. T664   1949

TONGUE.   See also STOUT, 1943

TOOKE.   See No. 430 - Adventurers of purse and person.

17174   TOOLE.   Our old man; a biographical portrait of Joseph Toole by his daughter, Millie Toole.
London, J. M. Dent (1948)   208 p. port.   22 cm.   49-18432*.   CT788.T67T65

17175   TOOMEY.   The O'Toomeys of Croom, and their descendants, by Thomas Noxon Toomey ...
Saint Louis, Mo., Printed for private distribution, 1920.   1 p. l., 17 p. front., ports. 23 cm. Title vignette: coat
of arms. 21-8528.   CS71.T665   1920

17176   TOPE.   History of the Tope family; setting forth a full account of the trials, successes,
peculiar characteristics, occupations, &c., of this race of people in this country down to date.   By M.
Tope ... Bowerston, O., The Patriot office, 1896.   78 p. 21 cm. 27-11116.   CS71.T671   1896

17177   TOPHAM.   The Topham family and their kindred (by) Washington Topham.   (Washington,
D. C., 1911)   35 l. 28 cm. Autographed from type-written copy. Contains also the Smith, Barron, and White families. 22-729.
                                                                          CS71.T672   1911

17178   TOPLIFF.   A sermon, preached at Dorchester, on the Lord's day after the interment of Mr.
Nathaniel Topliff, who deceased 4th December, 1819.   By Thaddeus Mason Harris ... Boston, Printed
by S. Phelps, 1820.   27 p. 22 cm. "Family record": p. 21-27. 16-17948.   CS71.T675   1820

17179   TOPLIFF.   Clement Topliff and his descendants in Boston, by Ethel Stanwood Bolton.   Boston,
Privately printed (The University press, Cambridge, Mass.) 1906.   3 p. l., 56 p. incl. geneal. tables. front.
(2 port.) facsim. 23½ cm. 7-2088.   CS71.T675   1906

17180   TOPLIFF.   Topliff's travels.   Letters from abroad in the years 1828 and 1829, by Samuel
Topliff ... From the original manuscript owned by the Boston athenaeum.   Edited with a memoir and
notes, by Ethel Stanwood Bolton.   Printed from the income of the Robert Charles Billings fund.
(Boston) The Boston athenaeum, 1906.   4 p. l., 245. (1) p. incl. geneal. tab. front. (port.) 4 pl., 2 maps (1 fold.)
3 facsim. (1 fold.) 23½ cm. (On verso of t. -p.: Robert Charles Billings fund. Publications, no. 2) 7-6782.   D919.T67

TOPPAN.   See TAPPAN.

17181   TOPPING.   Topping.   By Charles E. Topping.   Brooklyn (1958)   50 l. illus. 30 cm. 58-33884.
                                                                          CS439.T69   1958

TOPPING.   See also JAMES, 1961

TORBERT.   See PEPPER, 1960

TORRANCE.   See HART, 1923

17182   TORRENCE.   Chart of the Torrence, Findlay, Brownson, Paull, Irwin, McDowell and Smith
families of Pennsylvania.   Pub. as a memorial to Hon. John Findlay Torrence of Cincinnati by his
sister Harriet Rebecca Torrence Stewart.   Commenced in 1859 by John Findlay Torrence, rev. and
finished from data collected by him, by his nephew, William Torrence Handy in 1894.   Cincinnati, The
Henderson-Achert-Krebs lith. co. (1894)   geneal. tab. 92 x 131½ cm. 12-20293.
                                                                          CS71.T69   1894

17183   TORRENCE.   Torrence and allied families, by Robert M. Torrence ... under the auspices of
the Genealogical society of Pennsylvania.   Philadelphia, The Wickersham press, 1938.   8 p. l., 140 p.,
1 l., 141-559 p. plates, ports., maps (1 fold.) facsims. (part fold.) coats of arms. 25 cm. "Printed for private distribution." "References":
p. 295. 38-39412.   CS71.T69   1938

TORRENCE.   See also HART, 1923

17184   TORREY.   Memoir of Major Jason Torrey, of Bethany, Wayne County, Pa., by Rev. David
Torrey, D. D.   Scranton, Pa., J. S. Horton, 1885.   131 p. 23 cm. 9-29060.   F157.W35T6

17185   TORREY.   Genealogical notes, showing the paternal line of descent from William Torrey, of Combe St. Nicholas, Somerset County, England, A.D.1557, to Jason Torrey, of Bethany, Penn'a, with the descendants of Jason Torrey, and of his brothers and sister, to A.D.1884.   Compiled by John Torrey.   Scranton, Pa., J.S.Horton, 1885.   2 p. 1., (3)-50 p. 23½ cm.   9-14122 rev.   CS71.T694   1885

———— Supplement ... relating to the ancestry of the descendants of Jason Torrey, of Bethany, Pennsylvania; collected by Francis R. T. Thompson ... 1911.   Honesdale, Pa., Spencer bros., printers, 1911.   30 p. 23 cm. 9-14122.   CS71.T694   1885a

17186   TORREY.   A contribution toward a genealogy of all Torreys in America; being genealogical notes showing the paternal line of descent from William Torrey, of Combe St. Nicholas, Somerset County, England, A.D.1557, to Abner Torrey, of Weymouth, Massachusetts, with all descendants of Abner Torrey.   With an appendix.   Compiled by D. Torrey.   Detroit, J. F.Eby & co., printers, 1890.   2 p. 1., 145, lxi p. 23 cm. 9-14123.   CS71.T694   1890

17187   TORREY.   The Torrey families and their children in America.   v. 1-2 (by) Frederic C. Torrey ... Lakehurst, N.J., 1924-29.   2 v. front., illus. (incl. ports., maps, facsims., coat of arms) 23½ cm. 25-2006.   CS71.T694   1924-9

TORREY.   See also: BLAKE, 1916
HAVILAND, 1914
McLEAN, 1942
MINNS, 1925
TAFT, 1908

17188   TORSEY.   The Torsey family.   By Henry Torsey Fernald ...   (In The New England historical and genealogical register. Boston, 1907. 24½ cm. v. 61, p. 375-378)   F1.N56 vol.61

17189   TOSTRUP.   Familien Tostrup fra Lister (med 6 autotypier) samt foged Tostrups beskrivelse af Lister og Mandals amt of 1743 ved S. H. Finne-Grønn.   Christiania, Thronsen & co.s bogtrykkeri, 1897.   24, 40, (2) p. ports. 23½ cm.   "Efter et materiale, paa forhaand indsamlet af hr. godseier Christopher Paus ... der ... ogsaa har bekostet naervaerende arbeide udgivet." - Pref. note. 15-28036.   CS919.T7

TOTENHAM.   See TOTMAN.

17190   TOTMAN.   John and Thomas Totman (or Tatman) and their descendants.   By Rufus N.Meriam, A.M.   Worcester, Mass., F. P. Rice, 1895.   1 p. 1., 31 p. 24½ cm. 9-14121.   CS71.T717   1895

TOTMAN.   See also GALE, 1866

TOTTINGHAM.   See TOTMAN.

17191   TOTTY.   Letters of interest to the Totty family; facts pertaining to early Cooke County and Wheeler County, Texas.   By Alma Totty Seitz.   (Miami, Tex.) 1968.   13 1. 38 cm. Photocopies of 4 letters. 68-6255.   CS71.T718   1968

TOUCHETT.   See WHITNEY, 1925

TOUL-MAN.   See TALLMAN.

17192   TOUPS.   The Toups clan and how it all began; a detailed four hundred year genealogy of the Toups (Dubs) family.   Written and compiled by Neil J. Toups.   Lafayette, La., Neilson Pub. Co. (1969)   316 p. facsims., maps. 28 cm. 70-6235 MARC.   CS71.T7187   1969

17193   TOURISON.   Tourison and allied families; a genealogical study with biographical notes. Compiled under the direction of Thomas H. Bateman.   New York, Priv. print. for H. T. Biddle by the American Historical Co., 1952.   189 1. illus., ports., coats of arms, facsims., geneal. tables. 32 cm. Part of illustrative matter is colored. Errata (leaf) inserted. Bibliographical footnotes. 58-49593.   CS71.T719   1952

TOURNEUR.   See SNYDER, 1958

17194   TOURO.   ... The Touro family in Newport, by Morris A. Gutstein ... Newport, R.I., 1935.
44 p.   23 cm.   (Bulletin of the Newport historical society, no. 94)   "Gifts to the museum.   Books and pamphlets.   Report on the Wanton-Lyman-Hazard house.   Officers and committees of the society": p. 40-44.   37-1343.
CS71.T72   1935

17195   TOURTELLOT.   Genealogy of the Tourtellot family.   (By Jesse Steere Tourtellot)   (Pawtucket, R.I., 1854)   2 l.   28 cm.   Type-written.   Signed: Jesse Steere Tourtellot.   38M5225T.
CS71.T722   1854

17196   TOUSEY.   The Tousey family in America.   (Elmira, N.Y., The Osborne press, 1916)
124, (13) p.   illus. (coat of arms)   23 cm.   On verso of t.-p.: "Compilation by Theodore Cuyler Rose."   16-23616.
CS71.T725   1916

TOUSTAIN.   See DU PONT, 1923

17197   TOWER.   Tower genealogy.   An account of the descendants of John Tower, of Hingham, Mass.
Compiled under the direction of Charlemagne Tower ... Cambridge, J. Wilson and son, 1891.
xii, 689 p.   25 cm.   9-14124.
CS71.T738   1891

17198   TOWER.   The annual reports ... Tower genealogical society.   (Boston, Mass., The Society,
1909 -   v.   illus., plates, ports.   23 cm.   The reports for 1910-1915/16 are numbered 2d - 7th/8th, after which the numbering was discontinued; in the later numbers several years are combined in one issue.   The issues are grouped in volumes as follows: (v. 1, no. 1-5) annual reports 1909-1913/14; v. 2, no. 1-5. annual reports 1915/16 -   Title varies.   First report comprises: Report of the John Tower ter-centenary celebration and Tower reunion at Hingham, Massacusetts, May 29, 30 and 31, 1909.   13-8112 rev. 2.
CS71.T738   1909-

17199   TOWER.   The Tower and Converse families, ancestors of Rosa Georgiana (Tower) Read.   By
Thomas Carpenter Read.   (Charleston? S.C.) 1962.   12 p.   illus.   22 cm.   62-2264.
CS71.T738   1962

TOWER.   See also FORD, 1910

TOWERY.   See BEAN, 1961

TOWGOOD.   See STAWELL, CS439.S89

17200   TOWLE.   Descendants of Jonathan Towle, 1747-1822, of Hampton and Pittsfield, N.H., by
Alvin F. Towle, assisted by his son Herbert C. Towle, J. M. Moses, A.M., and G. C. Selden ...
Boston, Mass., C. W. Calkins & co., 1903.   312 p. incl. front., plates, ports., maps.   20 cm.   "Authorities quoted": p. 287.
4-3722.
CS71.T742   1903

TOWLE.   See also: CHAFFEE, 1911
DRAKE, 1962
RIVES, F230.K53

17201   TOWLER.   Genealogy; From the fruit of the garden.   Written and published by Juby E.
Towler.   (1st ed.)   Danville, Va. (1968)   2, iii, 262 p.   illus., coat of arms (on lining papers), map, ports.   22 cm.
76-1286.
CS71.T7429   1968

17202   TOWLES.   The Towles story from Henry, the emigrant of Accomac County, Virginia, to
Hester Towles and Jean Bryan Johnson.   Compiled by them (Hester Towles Purcell and Jean Bryon
Johnson)   Kansas City, Mo., 1957.   97 l.   29 cm.   60-22311.   CS71.T743   1957

17203   TOWNE.   Historical and biographical notes of the family of Towne.   Genealogical memoranda
of the ancestry and descendants of the late John Town, esq., of Georgia, Vermont.   Chicago, Printed
for private distribution, by H. Town, 1878.   16 p.   23 cm.   Compiled by Edwin Hubbard.   Genealogical memoranda of the
Towne family.   From the New Eng. hist. and geneal. register, vol. XX, p. 367.   By William B. Towers.   9-14536.   CS71.T744   1878

17204   TOWNE.   The Towne family memorial: comp. from the New England historical and genealogical register, Towne manuscripts, public and family records; for A. N. Towne, esq., San Francisco,
Cal., by Edwin Hubbard ... Chicago, Fergus printing company, 1880.   114, (ix)-xvi p.   illus.   24 cm.   In three
parts.   Pt. 1 and 2 "Compiled, largely, from mss of the late Wm. B. Towne of Milford, N.H."   9-14537.   CS71.T744   1880

17205   TOWNE.   The descendants of William Towne, who came to America on or about 1630 and settled in Salem, Mass.   Compiled by Edwin Eugene Towne ... Newtonville, Mass., The author, 1901. 6 p. l., 372 p. front., illus., ports. 24½ cm. 1-18718.   CS71.T744   1901

17206   TOWNE.   The descendants of William Towne, who came to America on or about 1630 and settled in Salem, Mass.   By Edwin Eugene Towne.   Newtonville, Mass., 1901.   372 p. illus., ports. 25 cm. Supplements, Dec. 1, 1951 (2 leaves) and Aug. 24, 1963 (2 leaves) inserted, and fold. leaf in pocket. 1-18718 rev. *
                                                                                 CS71.T744   1901

17207   TOWNE.   The ancestry of Lieut. Amos Towne, 1737-1793, of Arundel (Kennebunkport), Maine, by Walter Goodwin Davis.   Portland, Me., The Southworth press, 1927.   3 p. l., 3-81 p. front. (port.) illus. (map) 23½ cm. Contains also the Browning, Smith, French, Curtis and Looke families. 27-5357.
                                                                                 CS71.T744   1927

17208   TOWNE.   The story of an American achievement.   National blank book co.   Holyoke, Mass., c. 1943.   2 p. l., 7-89, (3) p. illus. (incl. ports., map, facsims.) 24 x 31½ cm. Diagrams on lining-papers. Cover-title: Through one hundred years, 1843-1943. 43-17419.   HD9839.B52N3

17209   TOWNE.   Some of the Towne family and the Salem witchcraft delusion, by Joseph L. Wheeler. Benson, Vt., 1969.   15 l. illus., map. 28 cm. 77-10629 MARC.   CS71.T744   1969

          TOWNE.   See also: DAVIS, 1959
                               WILD, 1959

          TOWNELEY.   See TOWNLEY.

17210   TOWNER.   A genealogy of the Towner family, the descendants of Richard Towner, who came from Sussex county, Eng., to Guilford, Conn., before 1685 ... by James W. Towner ... Los Angeles, Cal., Times-mirror printing and binding house (1910?)   269 p. front. (port.) 20 cm. 14-16770.
                                                                                 CS71.T745   1910

17211   TOWNER.   Extracts from A genealogy of the Towner family.   By James William Towner. (Santa Ana, Calif., 1910)   27 l. 29 cm. Cover title. 50-43164.   CS71.T745   1910a

          TOWNESEND.   See TOWNSEND.

17212   TOWNLEY.   History of the Lawrence-Townley, and Chase-Townley estates in England.   With copious historical and genealogical notes of the Lawrence, Chase, and Townley families ... By James Usher ... (New York?) 1883.   110 p. 24½ cm. Blank pages for "Notes". 9-14125.   CS71.T746   1883
          ——— Copy 2.   "A genealogy of the descendants of Thomas and Aquila Chase, containing the whole of the first three generations": broadside 30 x 22 cm. fold. and inserted at end.

17213   TOWNLEY.   The mystery solved.   Facts relating to the "Lawrence-Townley," "Chase-Townley," marriage and estate question.   With genealogical information concerning the families of Townley, Chase, Lawrence, Stephens, Stevens, and other families of America.   By Frank Alden Hill. Boston, Rand Avery company, 1888.   94 p. illus., facsim., fold. geneal. tables. 23 cm. Title vignette: coat of arms. 9-14126.   CS71.T746   1888

17214   TOWNLEY.   A genealogical chart, showing the main line of the Towneley family of Great Britain, together with some of the branches thereof.   Also showing the pedigree of those of the family who in the seventeenth and eighteenth centuries, emigrated to the United States of America, and settled in Elizabethtown, New Jersey, and Annapolis, Maryland ... By Frank Alden Hill.   Boston, Press of Rand Avery co., 1888.   geneal. tab. 97 x 61 cm. fold. to 25½ cm. Detached from his "The mystery solved." 1888. 1-26565.   CS71.T746   1888a

17215   TOWNLEY.   Other days, copyright ... by Charles V. Townley.   Olathe, Kan., Press of the Johnson County democrat, c. 1930.   152 p. plates, ports. 20½ cm. 30-20658.   CS71.T746   1930

          TOWNLEY.   See also STREYNSHAM, 1879

17216   TOWNSEND.   A memorial of John, Henry, and Richard Townsend, and their descendants.
New York, W. A. Townsend, 1865.   1 p. l., ix, (11)-233, (1) p. 21 cm. 3-3816.   CS71. T75   1865

17217   TOWNSEND.   A short history of the English Townsends.   By Martin I. Townsend of Troy,
New York ... Troy, N. Y., T. J. Hurley, printer, 1871.   8 p. 22½ cm. 18-7487.   CS71. T75   1871

17218   TOWNSEND.   The Townshend family.   By Charles Hervey Townsend ... Reprinted from the
New-England historic, genealogical register for Jan. 1875.   Boston, D. Clapp & son, printers, 1875.
15 p. illus. (coat of arms) 24½ cm. 21-6320.   CS71. T75   1875

17219   TOWNSEND.   Pedigree of the family of Townsend, with wills and notes relating to the family.
Edited by Reginald Stewart Boddington.   Privately printed.   London, Mitchell and Hughes, printers,
1881.   9 p. incl. geneal. tab. 27½ cm. Title vignette; interleaved. 2-27573.   CS439. T7

17220   TOWNSEND.   The Townshend family of Lynn, in old and New England, genealogical and biographical.   By Charles Hervey Townshend ... Rev. 3d ed.   New Haven, Conn. (Tuttle, Morehouse
& Taylor, printers, 1882)   138 p. 23½ cm. Title vignette: coat of arms. Reprinted with additions from the New England
historical and genealogical register, vol. 29, January, 1875. cf. Pref. 9-14550.   CS71. T75   1882

17221   TOWNSEND.   Notes on the Townsend family.   Compiled by Henry F. Waters.   Salem, Printed for the Essex institute, 1883.   1 p. l., 43 p. 24½ cm. 9-14127.   CS71. T75   1883

17222   TOWNSEND.   The Townshend family of Lynn, in old and New England, genealogical and biographical by Charles Hervey Townshend, of New Haven, Conn. ... Rev. 4th ed.   New Haven, Conn.
(Tuttle, Morehouse & Taylor, printers) 1884.   138 p. 23½ cm. Title vignette (coat of arms) Reprinted with additions
from the New England historical and genealogical register, vol. 29, January, 1875. 24-5661.   CS71. T75   1884

17223   TOWNSEND.   An officer of the Long Parliament and his descendants; being some account of
the life and times of Colonel Richard Townesend of Castletown (Castletownshead) & a chronicle of his
family.   With illustrations.   Ed. by Richard & Dorothea Townshend.   London, H. Frowde, 1892.
xv, (1), 295, (1) p. front. (fold. facsim.) pl., ports., fold. geneal. tables. 23 cm. Title vignette. Authorities consulted: p. xiv-xv.
"Double descent of the late Reverend Maurice Fitzgerald-Townshend - Stephens-Townshend of Castletown, otherwise castle Townshend, county Cork
... from Edward Stafford, third duke of Buckingham ..." A folded broadside with two illustrations, pasted on verso of title-page. 15-23254.
                                                         DA418. T7T7

17224   TOWNSEND.   The Townsend's.   Compiled by Malcolm Townsend ... (New York, Mooney &
co., 1895)   (110) p. illus., pl. 18 cm. 2-30134.   CS71. T75   1895

17225   TOWNSEND.   ... The direct ancestry and posterity of Judge Charles Townsend, a pioneer of
Buffalo, N. Y., with biographies of the individuals of the nineteen successive generations thus included,
and other matters of interest to the Townsend family, by Rev. Charles Townsend.   Orange, N. J.
(1897)   62 p. illus. (coats of arms) fold. geneal. tab. 23½ cm. At head of title: 1375-1897. Authorities: p. 6-7. 18-363.
                                                         CS71. T75   1897

17226   TOWNSEND.   Autobiography of Francis Torrey Townsend, and genealogy of the Townsends.
By Francis Torrey Townsend.   White River Junction, Vt., Cummings the printer, 1905.   102 p., 1 l.
front. (port.) 23½ cm. 25-20254.   CS71. T75   1905

17227   TOWNSEND.   Townsend genealogy; a record of the descendants of John Townsend, 1743-1821,
and of his wife, Jemima Travis, 1746-1832, by Cleveland Abbe assisted by Josephine Genung Nichols.
New York, F. Allaben genealogical company, 1909.   106 p. 20 cm. (On verso of half-title: Allaben genealogical
series) 9-7323.   CS71. T75   1909

17228   TOWNSEND.   Townsend-Townshend, 1066-1909; the history, genealogy and alliances of the English and American house of Townsend, comp. by James C. Townsend, 1865; Hon. Martin I. Townsend, 1871;
Charles Hervey Townsend, 1875; a pamphlet of Hon. Isaac Townsend Smith, 1904, now newly comp.,
rev. and illustrated by Margaret Townsend (Mdme. Giovanni Tagliapietra) New York (Press of the
Broadway publishing company) 1909.   3 p. l., 3-125 p. front., plates, ports. 26 cm. 9-29537.
                                                         CS71. T75   1909a

17229   TOWNSEND.   Some lines of the Townshend-Townsend families of old England, New England and Minnesota, compiled for Loretta Townsend Talbot, by Homer Worthington Brainard ... (Concord, N.H.) Priv. print. (Rumford press) 1931.   viii, 123 p. col. front. (coat of arms) plates, ports., fold. geneal. tab. 25 cm. "One hundred copies printed." 32-9748.   CS71.T75   1931

17230   TOWNSEND.   William Townsend of Tyringham, Massachusetts, his ancestors and descendants, with allied lines: Tolman, Sill, Skinner, Hitchcock, Bennett and Hiller, compiled by Marian Sill Cummings.   East Cleveland, O.   (The Waterbury press) 1932.   4 p. l., 3-42, (8) p., 1 l.   illus. (coat of arms) 15½ cm. 33-17588.   CS71.T75   1932

17231   TOWNSEND.   Lavenia Townsend, wife of William Buckley; with additional references and records of early Townsend families of Long island and New York city, N.Y., by Lucius Buckley Andrus ... and Julia C. Loving ... (n.p.) 1937.   ii, 104, 104½-105, 105½-141, 141½-142, 142½-143, 143½-170 numb. l. incl. pl., facsims. 28½ cm.   Autographic reproduction of type-written copy.   Title vignette: coat of arms of the Townsend family.   Blank leaves for additions (163-170) 38-14729.   CS71.T75   1937

17232   TOWNSEND.   Lavenia Townsend, wife of William Buckley (a narrative) ... (by) Lucius Buckley Andrus ... San Diego, Calif., 1939.   1 p. l., 79 numb. l. incl. facsims., geneal. tab. front. (port.) fold. map, coat of arms. 29 cm.   Autographic reproduction of type-written copy.   Leaves 59-71 blank for "Memoranda".   An account of the Townsend and allied families. 40-6181.   CS71.T75   1939

17233   TOWNSEND.   The genealogy and history of the Solomon Townsend family, 1754-1962 ... by Hollis L. Townsend and Lloyd R. Townsend.   (Cleveland?) 1962.   202 p. illus. 24 cm. 63-46818.   CS71.T75   1962

17234   TOWNSEND.   My lovely world, by Lulu Townsend Armstrong Geissinger (Mrs. Anthony Wayne Geissinger) (Columbus? Ohio, 1969?)   174 p. 23 cm. 71-4103 MARC.   CS71.T75   1969

TOWNSEND.   See also: ADAMS, 1950   STEVENS, 1966
                        ANDREWS, 1938   UNDERHILL, 1904
                        LEWKENOR, CS436.D25 UNDERHILL, CS436.D25
                        OKELY, 1899   No. 430 - Adventurers of purse
                        POOL, 1958   and person.

TOWNSHEND.   See TOWNSEND.

17235   TOY.   The story of the Toys, by Mary H. Dodge.   Cambridge, Printed at the Riverside press, 1909.   vi, (1), 106 p. front., plates, ports. 22½ cm. Foreword signed: S.W.D. (i.e. Susan Webster Dodge) 19-7642.   CS71.T754   1909

17236   TRABUE.   Colonial men and times; containing the journal of Col. Daniel Trabue, some account of his ancestry, life and travels in Virginia and the present state of Kentucky during the revolutionary period; the Huguenots, genealogy, with brief sketches of the allied families, ed. by Lilli Du Puy Van Culin Harper ... Philadelphia, Penna., Innes & sons, 1916.   6 p. l., 3-624 p. front., plates, ports., col. coats of arms. 27 cm.   The family of Trabue: p. (205)-275.   The family of Du Puy: p. (367)-417.   "List of works consulted": p. 592-595. 15-13853.   CS71.T756   1916

TRABUE.   See also FONTAINE, 1886

17237   TRACHT.   The Tracht family tree, compiled by Minnie C. Miller and Elizabeth Schaefer ... Galion, O. (Wilson printing co.) 1935.   33 p. illus. (incl. ports., map) 21½ cm. Errata slip inserted at p. 19. 35-28839.   CS71.T758   1935

17238   TRACY.   Genealogy of the family of Lt. Thomas Tracy, of Norwich, Connecticut.   Compiled from the genealogical works of the Hydes and Tracy's by Chancellor Reuben H. Walworth and other reliable sources.   By Mrs. Matilda O. Abbey ... Milwaukee, D.S. Harkness & co., printers, 1889.   141 p. illus. (incl. map) coats of arms. 22½ cm. On cover: The arms of Baron Sudeley (Charles Douglas-Richard-Hanbury-Tracy) Toddington, county Gloucester, England. 11-707.   CS71.T76   1889

17239   TRACY.   The ancestors of Lieutenant Thomas Tracy of Norwich, Connecticut.   By Lieutenant Charles Stedman Ripley ... Boston, A. Mudge & son, printers, 1895.   100 p. incl. geneal. tables.   front.
(coat of arms) 24 cm.   9-14128.   CS71.T76   1895

17240   TRACY.   Lineage of the Tracy family, with notes of the Lord, Garrett, Russell, and other
intermarrying families.   Compiled by Puella F. (Hull) Mason ... (n. p., 1895?)   32 p. 22½ cm.   Printed
on one side of leaf only.   9-14551.   CS71.T76   1895a

17241   TRACY.   Tracy genealogy.   Ancestors and descendants of Lieutenant Thomas Tracy of
Norwich, Conn.   1660.   Compiled by Everet E. Tracy ... Albany, N. Y., J. Munsell's sons, 1898.
294 p. front. (coat of arms) 30 cm. 9-14772.   CS71.T76   1898

17242   TRACY.   Tracy genealogy; ancestors and descendants of Thomas Tracy of Lenox, Massachusetts.   Compiled by Mattie Liston-Griswold.   Kalamazoo, Mich., Printed by Doubleday bros. &
company, 1900.   230 p. front., plates, ports., geneal. tables, coats of arms. 24 cm. 2-5565.
                                                                                                                          CS71.T76   1900

17243   TRACY.   Historical address before the fourth annual reunion of the Tracy family, at Goulds-
boro, Maine.   August 19, 1899, by N. B. Tracy.   Auburn, Me., Palmer print & stamp works, 1900.
32 p. front. (coat of arms) ports. 23 cm. 15-5259.   CS71.T76   1900a

17244   TRACY.   Leiutenant Thomas Tracy and "The widow Mason" of Wethersfield, Connecticut, and
Edward Mason's Wethersfield record, by Dwight Tracy ... Boston, 1907.   1 p. l., (4) p. 24½ cm.   "Reprint,
Boston Transcript, March, 1907."   "The lands of Edward Mason in Wethersfield, Ct.": p. (2-4) 18-372.   CS71.T76   1907

17245   TRACY.   Recently discovered English ancestry of Governor William Tracy of Virginia, 1620,
and of his only son, Lieutenant Thomas Tracy of Salem, Massachusetts, and Norwich, Connecticut, by
Dwight Tracy ... New Haven, Conn., The Journal of American history, 1908.   2 p. l., 3-31 p., 2 l. col.
front. (coat of arms) illus. (incl. facsims.) port. 27½ cm.   Originally published simultaneously in the Journal of American history and the
Connecticut magazine. 10-13757.   CS71.T76   1908

17246   TRACY.   The Tracy family ... The Winslow family ... Compiled by Scott Lee Boyd.   Santa
Barbara, Calif., 1933.   4 p. l., 247 p. incl. ports., coats of arms. 27½ cm.   "This edition is limited to two hundred copies; this
copy is number 76."   Bibliography: p. 1-2.   Contents. - pt. 1. Tracy lineage from Woden (Odin) through Princess Goda (who married Dreux) Sir
William de Traci, Louise Massa Tracy (who married Dr. Charles Edward Winslow) to Mercelia Louise Boyd. - The descent of Barbara Lucy, who
married Richard Tracy of Stanway. - The intermarrying families of Farnham, Russell, Garrett, Lord. - pt. 2. Winslow lineage from William
Wyncelowe to Mercelia Anna Winslow (who married Scott Lee Boyd) to Mercelia Louise Boyd. - The intermarrying families of Hatch, Peirce (or
Pierce), Boyd. 33-29116.
                                                                                                                          CS71.T76   1933

17247   TRACY.   The Tracy genealogy; being some of the descendants of Stephen Tracy of Plymouth
colony, 1623; also ancestral sketches and chart, compiled by Sherman Weld Tracy.   Rutland, Vt.,
The Tuttle publishing company, inc. (c. 1936)   242 p. front., plates, ports., map, facsims. (1 double) 2 geneal. tab.
(1 double) 23½ cm. 36-11534.   CS71.T76   1936

17248   TRACY.   Some of the descendants of Lieutenant Thomas Tracy of Norwich, Connecticut, compiled by Tracy Campbell Dickson ... (Philadelphia, Printed by the John C. Winston company, c. 1936)
195 p. 20½ cm. 37-1337.   CS71.T76   1936a

17249   TRACY.   ... The famous Tracys of Newburyport, Massachusetts.   The records of commissions issued were carefully gathered and assembled from official sources in the state archives and
other sources by Thomas P. Cahill.   Somerville, Mass., The Captain Jeremiah O'Brien's memorial
associates, c. 1942   12 p. 22½ cm.   Illustration (ensign of Massachusetts) on t.-p.   Caption title: The famous Tracys, ship
merchantmen and privateer captains of Newburyport, Mass., in the American revolution, 1775-1783.   "Read at the meeting of the Essex county
board, A.O.H., in Haverhill, Mass., September 28, 1941.   Published in the Irish echo, of New York city, October 18-25, 1941." 42-13276.

                                                                                                                          E271.C2

17250   TRACY.   Charles C. Tracy genealogy (by Harold W. and Helen R.) Mullenax.   (Tulsa? Okla.,
1967)   1 v. (various pagings) illus. 28 cm. 68-3494.   CS71.T76   1967

TRACY. See also: AVERY, 1926   HYDE, 1864
BRADHURST, 1910   ROBINSON, 1894
CHESTER, 1893   SMITH, 1924

17251   TRAFFORD. A history of the ancient chapel of Stretford in Manchester parish. Including sketches of the township of Stretford. Together with notices of local families and persons. By H. T. Crofton. (Manchester) Printed for the Chetham society, 1899-1903.   3 v. fronts., 21 pl., 14 port., 13 maps. 22½ cm. x 18 cm. (Added t.-p.: Remains historical and literary connected with the palatine counties of Lancaster and Chester. New series, v. 42, 45, 51) Vol. 3 contains biographical notices of the Trafford family. 4-2653.   DA670.L19C5

TRAIL. See TRAILL.

TRAILER. See TRAILOR.

17252   TRAILL. A genealogical account of the Traills of Orkney, with a pedigree table tracing their descent from the Traills of Blebo, in Fifeshire. By William Traill of Woodwick, M.D. Kirkwall, J. Calder, 1883.   2 p. l., xxi, (23)-80 p., 1 l. 3 numb. pl. 19 cm. Fifteen pages left blank for additions. 17-23939.   CS479.T7

17253   TRAILL. Genealogical sketches. The Frotoft branch of the Orkney Traills, their relations and connections. With copious notes, genealogical and otherwise. By Thomas W. Traill ... Written for private use only. (n. p.) The author, 1902.   x, 156 p. geneal. tables (1 fold.) 24 cm. "Only 40 copies ... printed ... No. 8." Contains also the Balfour, Baikie, Douglas, Mackenzie, Graham, Liddell, Watt and Honeyman families. "A few Irish Traills and others from Blebo, shewing the connection, etc., with the Orkney Traills": p. (89)-96. "Pedigree of the Steuarts": fold. geneal. tab. 20-15239.   CS479.T7   1902

TRAILL. See also GUTHRIE, 1902

TRAILOR. See MOTTIER, 1966

17254   TRAIN. Puritan's progress; an informal account: of certain Puritans & their descendants from the American revolution to the present time, their manners & customs, their virtues & vices. Together, with some possibly forgotten episodes in the development of American social & economic life during the last one hundred & fifty years. By Arthur Train ... New York, C. Scribner's sons, 1931.   3 p. l., ix-x p., 2 l., 3-477 p. 23½ cm. Bibliography: p. ix-x. 31-26548.   E161.T73

17255   TRAIN. John Trayne and some of his descendants, especially Charles Jackson Train, U.S.N., 1845-1906. By Susan Train Hand. New York, Priv. print., 1933.   x p., 1 l., 198 p., 1 l. front., plates, ports. 23½ cm. Title-vignette: U.S.S. Constellation. 34-1553.   CS71.T768   1933

17256   TRAIN. The Train family, 1635 to 1941, by May Philipps Train ... (Long Beach? Calif.) Priv. print. (1941?)   1 p. l., 51 (i.e. 69), viii p. 23 cm. 42-16151.   CS71.T768   1941

17257   TRAIN. Tracing backward; a gift to the children of Amos and Marian Train Hathaway, Harry De Pue II and Catharine Kinnear Train, John and Jane Train Flynn, grandchildren of Harold Cecil and May Philipps Train. (Washington?) 1963.   46 p. 22 cm. 63-5278.   CS71.T768   1963

17258   TRASK. Eliphalet Trask, born January 8, 1806, died December 9, 1890. Ruby Squier Trask, born August 22, 1811, died November 26, 1890. Married March 3, 1829. (Springfield, Mass., C. W. Bryan & co., printers, 1891?)   1 p. l., 125 p. front. (ports.) 23 cm. Caption title: "Trask memorial." Lettered on cover: "In memoriam." 16-25574.   CT275.T86E4

17259   TRASK. The Traske family in England. By William Blake Trask ... Boston, Printed by D. Clapp & son, 1900.   8 p. 24 cm. "Reprinted from New-Eng. historical and genealogical register for July, 1900." 3-27041.   CS71.T775   1900

17260   TRASK. Capt. William Traske and some of his descendants, by William Blake Trask ... assisted by Miss M. B. Fairbanks. Boston, Press of D. Clapp & son, 1904.   2 p. l., (3)-33 p. front. (port.) pl. 24½ cm. Cover-title: Trask. "Reprinted from New-England historical and genealogical register, vols. 55, 56 and 57." 12-17720.   CS71.T775   1904

TRASKE.   See TRASK.

TRATT.   See TROTT.

TRAUTMAN.   See TRAUTMANN.

17261   TRAUTMANN.   Trautman-Troutman family of Tulpehocken Township, Berks County, Pennsylvania, reunion leaflets of 1966 and 1967.   1966 compiled by Mrs. DeForest Trautman;   1967 compiled by Schuyler C. Brossman.   Rehrersburg, Pa., Trautman-Troutman Family Association (1967?)   7 l. illus. 28 cm. 72-392207 MARC.   CS71. T778   1967

17262   TRAVERS.   A collection of pedigrees of the family of Travers: or abstracts of certain documents collected toward a history of that family, by S. Smith Travers, esq.   Arranged by Henry J. Sides ... Oxford, Printed by J. H. and J. Parker, 1864.   2 p. l., 44 p. 3 double geneal. tab. 30 cm. L. C. COPY REPLACED BY MICROFILM. 17-21450.   CS439. T73   1864
Microfilm 10313 CS

17263   TRAVERS.   A pedigree with biographical sketches, of the Devonshire family of Travers, descended from Walter Travers of Nottingham, goldsmith.   By S. Smith Travers.   Now reprinted by Richard J. Hone, with a supplement from materials collected by him, and arranged by Frederick B. Falkiner ... (Dublin, Printed at the University press) 1898.   84 p. 3 fold. geneal. tab. 18½ cm. "Printed for private circulation, 100 copies." 17-21449.   CS439. T73   1898

17264   TRAVERS.   Descendants of Henry Travers of London, England and Newbury, Massachusetts, U. S. A.   Boston, Mass., N. H. Daniels, 1903.   147 p. front. (port.) coat of arms. 24 cm. 3-18490.   CS71. T78   1903

17265   TRAVERS.   The Travis (Travers) family and its allies: Darracott, Lewis, Livingston, Nicholson, McLaughlin, Pharr, Smith, and Terrell; including royal lines of descent.   By Robert Jesse Travis.   Savannah (c. 1954)   viii, 194 p. illus., ports. 24 cm. 55-24596.   CS71. T78   1954

TRAVERS.   See also HUNTER, 1934

TRAVIS.   See: TRAVERS.
No. 430 - Adventurers of purse and person.

17266   TRAYLOR.   The Traylor family.   By Edith Tunnell.   (New York? c. 1951)   geneal. table.
47 x 58 cm.   Includes colored coats of arms and maps.   56-41925.   CS71. T7815   1951

17267   TRAYLOR.   The Joel C. Traylor family.   Genealogical table in vertical file.   Ask reference librarian for this material.

TRAYLOR.   See also TRAILOR.

17268   TREADWAY.   History of the Tredway family;   William T. Tredway, editor and compiler. Pittsburgh, Pa., W. T. Tredway, c. 1930.   4 p. l., (xi)-xiv, 403, 18 p., 1 l., (4) p. incl. ports., coat of arms. 23½ cm.
Most of the data was gathered by Rev. Silas Baldwin Tredway.   cf. Dedication.   30-29367.   CS71. T781   1930

17269   TREADWAY.   ... Edward Treadway and his descendants, compiled by Oswell Garland Treadway.   Chicago, Ill.   (Champlin-Shealy company) 1931.   1 p. l., 125, xxxvii p. 23½ cm. At head of title: 1784-1859. 31-30057.   CS71. T781   1931

17270   TREADWAY.   Edward Treadway and his descendants.   News letter number 1 -
Chicago, Ill., O. G. Treadway (1933 -   v. 24 cm. Signed: Oswell G. Treadway. A supplement to the author's "Edward Treadway and his descendants". 35-14611.   CS71. T781   1931a

17271   TREADWAY.   Some descendants of Nathaniel Treadway ... (by) Horace Avery Abell. Rochester, N. Y., 1934.   22 numb. l. 27½ cm. Mimeographed. "References": leaf 17. 34-23206.   CS71. T781   1934

17272   TREADWAY.   Treadway and Burket families; a merger of the genealogical histories of the Treadway and Burket families in America, through the documented ancestry of Jonas Robert Treadway. By William Eugene Treadway.   (Topeka? Kan., 1951)   xi, 148 p. 24 cm. 51-6902.

CS71.T781   1951

17273   TREADWELL.   Down seven generations.   A rescript of Treadwell and Platt genealogy ... Prepared by Mrs. A. C. Maltbie.   (Syracuse, N.Y., School bulletin printing office, 1883)
35, (1) p. illus. (coats of arms) 26 cm. (School bulletin publications) 20-11353.   CS71.T782   1883

17274   TREADWELL.   Thomas Treadwell of Ipswich, Mass., and some of his descendants.   By William A. Robbins, LL.B.   Boston, Press of D. Clapp & son, 1906.   26 p. 25 cm. "Reprinted from the N.E. hist. and gen. register, vol. 60." 17-6158.   CS71.T782   1906

17275   TREADWELL.   Descendants of Edward Tre(a)dwell through his son John, by William A. Robbins ... New York (T. A. Wright press) 1911.   119 p. 27 cm. Edition of one hundred copies. Compiled mainly from data collected by Mrs. Elizabeth Ellen Schnebly Treadwell. "Reprinted from the New York genealogical and biographical record, April, 1911." 15-230.   CS71.T782   1911

17276   TREAT.   Memoir of Joshua Treat, the pioneer settler on Penobscot river.   (By Joseph Whitcomb Porter) Bangor, B. A. Burr, printer, 1889.   cover-title, 8 p. 25½ cm. "Reprinted from the Bangor historical magazine." "I am indebted to Mr. J. H. Treat, of Lawrence, Mass., for assistance in the preparation of this article." Signed: Editor (i. e. Joseph Whitcomb Porter) 35-21381.   CS71.T783   1889

17277   TREAT.   The Treat family: a genealogy of Trott, Tratt, and Treat for fifteen generations, and four hundred and fifty years in England and America, containing more than fifteen hundred families in America ... By John Harvey Treat, A.M.   Salem, Mass., The Salem press publishing & printing company, 1893.   xii, 637 p. front., illus., plates, ports., maps. 27½ cm. 9-14771.   CS71.T783   1893

TREAT.   See also: ANTHON, 1930   RANNEY, F104.C8A2
                        BASSETT, 1926   SMITH, 189-
                        HALL, 1902   TROTT.
                        O'DALY, 1956

TREDWAY.   See TREADWAY.

TREDWELL.   See TREADWELL.

17278   TREE.   Some account of the Tree family and its connections in England and America, edited by Josiah Granville Leach ... Philadelphia, Printed for private circulation by J. B. Lippincott company, 1908.   5 p. l., 3-107, (1) p., 1 l. front., plates, ports. 25 cm. "Two hundred copies of this book have been printed from the type." One leaf at end for Memoranda. 8-11767.   CS71.T785   1908

17279   TREES.   Trees, Rhodes, Van Meter, Du Bois, and allied families; genealogy.   By Marjorie Olive (Trees) Rhodes.   Washington, 1960.   115 l. 29 cm. Typescript. 60-50659.

CS71.T7853   1960

17280   TREFETHEN.   Trefethen, the family and the landing.   By Jessie B. Trefethen.   Portland, Me., House of Falmouth (1960)   61 p. illus. 23 cm. 61-22893.   CS71.T7855   1960

17281   TREGO.   A historical account of the Trego family.   By A. Trego Shertzer ... Baltimore, Press of I. Friedenwald, 1884.   vi, 138 p. front. (port.) 19½ cm. 9-14549.   CS71.T786   1884

TREGO.   See also SPANGLER, 1937

17282   TREGONNING.   Some stalwart Cornish emigrants: Henry and Susan Davies Tregonning, Daniel and Lavinia Paull Beckerleg; a sketch by their granddaughter, Ealeanor M. Tregoning. (Evanston? Ill.) 1963.   xiii, 113 p. illus., ports., 3 fold. maps, 4 fold. geneal. tables. 24 cm. Bibliography: p. 107. 63-22547.   CS71.T787   1963

17283   TRELOAR.   Treloar genealogy; tree of Treloar.   By Orson Lee Treloar.   Salt Lake City, Paragon Press (1962?)   309 p. illus. 24 cm. 62-14080.   CS71.T788   1962

TREMAINE.   See TREMAN.

17284   TREMAN.   The history of the Treman, Tremaine, Truman family in America; with the related families of Mack, Dey, Board and Ayers; being a history of Joseph Truman of New London, Conn.
(1666); John Mack of Lyme, Conn. (1680); Richard Dey of New York city (1641); Cornelius Board of
Boardville, N. J. (1730); John Ayer of Newbury, Mass. (1635); and their descendants.   By Ebenezer
Mack Treman and Murray E. Poole ... (Ithaca, N. Y.) Press of the Ithaca democrat, 1901.
2 v. col. front., plates (1 col.) ports., facsim. 23½ cm. 3-17517.   CS71.T789   1901

17285   TREMAN.   A family genealogy.   New York, Priv. print. for the descendants of Levi Tremain,
1908.   1 p. l., 6 p. incl. fold. geneal. tab. 23½ cm. Compiled by Henry Edwin Tremain. 12-11228.   CS71.T789   1908

17286   TREMENHEERE.   The Tremenheeres, by Seymour Greig Tremenheere.   (London, H. J.
Ryman ltd.) 1925.   2 p. l., iii-vii, 9-118 p., 1 l. front. (coat of arms) illus. (facsims.) plates, ports. 22 cm. 40-296.
CS439.T735   1925

17287   TRENCH.   Trench pedigree.   (Dublin? Priv. print., 1878)   18 numb. l. 33½ cm. Signed: Henry
Trench, January 1st, 1878. 19-3632.   CS499.T7   1878

17288   TRENCH.   A memoir of the Trench family, comp. by Thomas Richard Frederick Cooke-
Trench ... Privately printed.   (London, Spottiswoode & co., printers) 1897.   188 p. illus. (coats of arms)
plates, 2 fold. geneal. tab. 26 cm. 13-20066.   CS499.T7   1897

17289   TRENCHARD.   Harriett Trenchard's family, by Harold W. Hein.   (Brookfield? Wis.) 1963.
279 l. illus., facsims., geneal. tables, fold. map, photos, ports. 30 cm. Part of illustrative matter mounted. Typescript (carbon copy)
65-693.   CS71.T79   1963

17290   TRENHOLM.   (A genealogical chart of the descendants of William Trenholm) prepared by W.
de Saussure Trenholm.   New York, N. Y., 1930.   geneal. tab. 90 x 166 cm. Blue-print. 40-2275.
CS71.T8   1930

17291   TRENHOLME.   Trenholme in Yorkshire, with some notes on the Trenholme family, by the
Rev. Edward Craig Trenholme.   Oxford, A. T. Broome & son (1938)   vii, 96 p. incl. illus., plates, port., plan.
19½ cm. "References and notes": p. 79-81. 40-489.   DA690.T75T7

17292   TRENT.   The trail of the Trents.   By Logan D. Trent.   Boston, Christopher Pub. House
(1954)   289 p. 21 cm. 54-37072.   CS71.T812   1954

17293   TRESHAM.   The ruins of Liveden; with historical notices of the family of Tresham, and its
connexion with the Gunpowder plot, etc., etc., etc.   To which is added a legendary poem.   By T. Bell.
London, Whitaker and co., 1847.   1 p. l., 27 p. front. plates, geneal. tab. 27 cm. Title vignette: coat of arms. 9-11822.
DA392.1.T8B5

17294   TRESHAM.   Rushton: historical, biographical, archaeological.   Including sketches of the
Tresham and Cokayne families, a description of the triangular lodge, and notes of the hall, grounds,
and parish church.   By Sam. S. Campion.   Northampton, Taylor & son, 1878.   1 p. l., 16 p. 22 cm.
2-22926.   DA690.R88C1

17295   TRESHAM.   A complete account, illustrated by measured drawings, of the buildings erected
in Northamptonshire, by Sir Thomas Tresham, between the years 1575 and 1605.   Together with many
particulars concerning the Tresham family and their home at Rushton.   By J. Alfred Gotch ... Northampton, Taylor & son; (etc., etc.) 1883.   xvii, 44 p., 7 l. 34 pl. 39 cm. 15-21296.
NA997.T8G7

17296   TRESSEL.   Forbears, family, and descendants of John Tressel; genealogical, historical,
(compiled by Charles C. Turner.   Bradenton? Fla., 1969)   35 l. ports. 28 cm. Cover title. 74-12798 MARC.
CS71.T813   1969

TRESSEL.   See also SHUSTER, 1944

17297   TRESSLER.   Jonathan and Joseph Tressler and their descendants; a sketch made in 1948.
By Albert Willis Tressler.   Jacksonport, Wis., 1948.   v, 66 p.   28 cm.   48-26144*.
CS71.T814   1948

17298   TRESSLER.   The family of John Tressler and Elizabeth Loy Tressler; a sketch.   By George
Tressler Scott.   Loysville, Pa., Priv. print. for complimentary distribution to members of Tressler
and Loy families by the Tressler Orphans' Home (1949)   73 p.   illus., ports.   24 cm.   50-19139.
CS71.T814   1949

TREUTLEN.   See FLEWELLEN, 1958

17299   TREVELYAN.   Uncommon people; a study of England's élite.   By Paul Bloomfield.   London,
H. Hamilton (1955)   xi, 219 p.   ports., geneal. tables.   22 cm.   56-18674.
HT647.B55   1955

TREVETHAN.   See TREFETHEN.

TREVETHIN.   See TREFETHEN.

TREVOR.   See CARR, DA690.B23C3

TREWETT.   See TRUITT.

TREWITT.   See TRUITT.

TREWORGYE.   See BLAKE, 1948

17300   TREZEVANT.   The Trezevant family in the United States, from the date of the arrival of
Daniel Trezevant, Huguenot, at Charles Town, South Carolina, in 1685, to the present date, by John
Timothée Trezevant.   Columbia, S. C., Printed by the State company, 1914.   122 p.   2 facsim.   23½ cm.
16-671.
CS71.T824   1914

17301   TRICE.   Trice family tree.   By Phil Trice.   (Freeman, S. D., Pine Hill Press, 1968 -
v.   illus., col. coat of arms, facsims., ports.   29 cm.   "Limited edition of 500 copies."   78-4007 MARC.   CS71.T826   1968

TRICE.   See also SAMPSON, 1922

17302   TRICHEL.   J.B. Trichel, 1st sgt. & lt. at Natchitoches, La.   1774.   In Bolton, H. E.
Athanose de Mezieres.   Vol. 2 p. 107 & 110.
F373.B69 vol. 2

17303   TRIMBLE.   Autobiography and correspondence of Allen Trimble, governor of Ohio, with
genealogy of the family ... (Columbus? O.) 1909.   cover-title, 240 p.   illus., pl., ports.   25 cm.   Prepared and
edited by Mary McA. T. Tuttle and Henry B. Thompson.   cf. p. (1)   Reprinted from the "Old northwest"   genealogical society.   "Genealogy of
Trimble": p. 237-240.   9-20758.
F495.T83

17304   TRIMBLE.   Trimble families; a partial listing of the descendants of some colonial families.
By Eugene Earl Trimble.   (Kensington? Md.) 1958.   257 p.   29 cm.   60-35387.
CS71.T827   1958

TRIMBLE.   See also: PALMER, 1875
PALMER, 1910

17305   TRIMMER.   The family of Anthony Trimmer, Sr., who died 1754 in Roxbury Township,
Morris County, New Jersey.   By Raymond Martin Bell.   Washington, Pa., 1954.   (3) l.   28 cm.   54-18580.
CS71.T83   1954

17306   TRIMMER.   Trimmer family outline, by Raymond Martin Bell and Ira A. Brown.   Washington,
Pa., 1959.   unpaged.   28 cm.   63-24984.
CS71.T83   1959

17307   TRIMMER.   The Trimmer family: New Jersey, Pennsylvania, by Raymond Martin Bell and
Ira A. Brown.   Washington, Pa., 1962.   (6) l.   28 cm.   63-2390.
CS71.T83   1962

17308   TRIMMER.   Trimmer family.   By Raymond M. Bell.   Washington, Pa., Washington and Jefferson College, 1 Aug. 1958.   In vertical file.   1 p. mimeographed.   Ask reference librarian for this material.

TRIMMER.   See also WILSON, 1959

17309   TRIPLETT.   The descendants of Joseph Triplett of Hardy County, West Virginia, and Summit and Licking Counties, Ohio.   By Leonard Lytle.   Ballycastle, N. I.,   J. S. Scarlett & Son, printers, 1955.   12 p. 22 cm. 58-44313.   CS71.T834   1955

17310   TRIPP.   ... John Tripp of Portsmouth, R. I., and some of his descendants.   (Newport, 1883)
8 p. 22 cm.   Caption title.   Signed: Col. Thos. L. Casey.   "Reprinted from the Newport historical magazine, July, 1883."   35-21379.
CS71.T836   1883

17311   TRIPP.   Genealogy of the Tripp family descended from Isaac Tripp, of Warwick, R. I., and Wilkes-Barre, Pa.   By Arthur D. Dean ... Scranton, Pa., Printed for the author by F. H. Gerlock & co., 1903.   v, 128 p. ports. 24 cm. 3-24615.   CS71.T836   1903

17312   TRIPP.   Tripp genealogy; descendants of James son of John Tripp.   Compiled by George L. Randall.   (New Bedford, Mass., Vining press, printers, 1924)   236, xxviii p. incl. front. (coat of arms) 2 pl. (incl. ports.)   23½ cm.   The plates are printed on both sides.   24-24424.   CS71.T836   1924

17313   TRIPP.   Tripp wills, deeds and ways, with key to Tripp descents, via New England, and also New York, based largely on scores of wills and deeds, which we have ourselves abstracted from the original records.   We give a 60-page French-English story, we discuss several errors heretofore in print: two extensive, one touching founder John, himself ...   By Carolyne Syron Valentine)   Washington, D. C., Valentine research studio, 1932.   1 p. l., 59 numb. l., 4 l., 60-189 numb. l., 7 l. 28 cm.   Author's name lettered on cover.   Mimeographed.   32-6813.   CS71.T836   1932

17314   TRIPP.   Tripp, John Tripp, Joseph Tripp, Peleg Tripp, Benoni Tripp, Acus Tripp, William Tripp, Coggeshall Rathbone Tripp, Charles R. Tripp; also some other descendents (!) of William Tripp; also Coggeshall and Rathbone ancestors of Coggeshall Rathbone Tripp.   (n. p., 1935)
19 p. 29 cm.   Mimeographed.   On cover: Some descendents (!) of John Tripp of Rhode Island.   Blank pages for "Further notes by families concerned" (6 at end)   "Forward (!) signed: Charles D. Tripp.   37-21329.   CS71.T836   1935

17315   TRIPP.   (Genealogy of the Trippe family from Nicholis Trippe, fl. 1234, of Kent county, Eng., through the Maryland branch of the family, 1663-1935)   (New York, 1944)   82 numb. l. 2 geneal. tab. (incl. coats of arms) 29½ x 22½ cm.   Reproduced from type-written copy.   44-10787 rev.   CS71.T836   1944

17316   TRIPP.   Tripp family with collaterals; Mary Dobbs and descendants.   By Ethel Viola Lawrence.   (East Northfield? Mass.) 1948.   73 l. 29 cm. 52-21865.   CS71.T836   1948

TRIPP.   See also: STEVENS, 1906
THOMAS, 1914

TRIPPE.   See TRIPP.

17317   TRISTRAM.   Pedigree of the family of Tristram, of Belbroughton, Worcestershire.   (n. p.)
Priv. print., 1904.   1 p. l., 9 fold. geneal. tab. 29½ cm. 20-15256.   CS439.T74

17318   TRISTRAM.   Pedigree of the family of Tristram (alias Trystram and Trustram).   Compiled from a pedigree, from 1432 to 1909, registered at the Heralds' college, 1909, by Edward Tristram, F. S. A., with additional and supplemental matter, by E. J. Trustram, M. A. ... London, Mitchell, Hughes and Clarke, 1915.   14 p. illus. (coat of arms) 28 cm.   Reprinted from "Miscellanea genealogica et heraldica".   3d ser., v. 1, 1896.   23-14530.   CS439.T74   1915

17319   TRITSCH.   American descendants of Johann Henrich Tritsch (1678-1748), Hessian master-weaver.   By Ralph Hoover Lane.   Washington, 1954.   98 p. 28 cm. 55-19910.
CS71.T84   1954

17320   TRITTON.   Tritton; the place and family, by J. Herbert Tritton.   London, A. L. Humphreys, 1907.   xiv, 330, (1) p. front., plates, ports., fold. geneal. tab. 26 cm. Genealogical table in pocket. "Only 150 copies printed. no. 19." Bibliography: p. 314-317. 16-19790.   CS439.T75

17321   TROLAND.   The Troland chart ... New York, 1916.   broadside. 120 x 82 fold. to 33 cm. Compiled by James Robert Troland. Autographed. 17-6160-1.
———— Supplement.   New York, 1916.   broadside. 120 x 82 fold. to 33 cm. Autographed. Facsimile of letter of 1702 inserted to illustrate traits of family handwriting. 17-6160-1.   CS71.T85   1916

17321a TROLLOPE.   The family of Trollope.   By the Venerable Edward Trollope ... Lincoln, J. Williamson, printer, 1875.   1 p. l., 65 p. front., 2 pl. (coat of arms) 27½ cm. Title in red and black; red line borders. 2-27567.   CS439.T8
                                                                                                Microfilm 13936 CS

17322   TROLLOPE.   A memoir of the family of Trollope, comp, by the Rev. Mark Napier Trollope ... London, Printed by Spottiswoode & co., 1897.   vii p., 1 l., 125, (1) p. illus. (coats of arms) fold. map. 25 cm. 16-18072.   CS439.T8   1897

17323   TROLLOPE.   The Trollopes; the chronicle of a writing family, by Lucy Poate Stebbins and Richard Poate Stebbins.   New York, Columbia university press, 1945.   6 p. l., 394 p. front., ports., fold. geneal. tab. 22½ cm. "Notes" (bibliographical): p. (343) - 375. A45-4909.   PR5686.S8

17324   TROMPER.   The Tromper family of Rotterdam in the Netherlands; an outline of the history of the family from Pieter Tromper, 1460, to Jacob Tromper, 1626, the founder of the family in America, by Louis P. De Boer ... Edition of one hundred copies, privately printed.   New York (T. A. Wright press) 1914.   12 p. incl. front. (col. coat of arms) 36 cm. "Reprinted from the New York genealogical and biographical record, July, 1914." "Authorities": p. 12. 22-10226.   CS71.T855   1914

17325   TROTH.   Henry Troth, Sept. 4, 1794, May 22, 1842 ... Philadelphia, Priv. print., 1903.   44 p. front., plates, ports., facsims. 26½ cm. Preface signed: Samuel Troth. 11-1137.   CS71.T862   1903

17326   TROTH.   Genealogy of the Troth family of Burlington County, New Jersey, 1700-1800.   By Amos Haines Troth.   To which are added notes by Milton Rubincam. (Audubon? N.J.) Rubincam-Troth Archives of Family History, 1949.   20 l. 28 cm. 60-30137.   CS71.T862   1949

         TROTH.   See also HAYNES, 1902

17327   TROTMAN.   Collections relating to the family of Trotman.   Ed. by W. P. W. Phillimore ... Stroud, Printed for private circulation by J. White, 1892.   cover-title, 76 p. incl. illus., ports. pl., coat of arms. 22½ cm. 21-17146.   CS439.T82

17328   TROTMAN.   The Trotman family, 1086 to 1963.   By F. H. Trotman.   Mapperley Park, Nottingham, F. H. Trotman, 1965.   (3), 99 p. illus., tables, diagres. 30½ cm. 66-70532.   CS439.T82   1965

17329   TROTT.   The Trotts of Dorchester and Boston.   By Edward Doubleday Harris.   Boston, Press of D. Clapp & son, 1889.   4 p. fold. geneal. tab. 25½ cm. "Reprinted from the New England historical and genealogical register for January, 1889." 15-1357.   CS71.T8624   1889

17330   TROTT.   A genealogical and biographical record concerning Phebe (Reed) Trott and John Trott and all of their descendants to January 1, 1954.   Phebe Reed and John Trott were married, February 5, 1784, at Woolwich, Maine.   Phebe Reed was a daughter of Jonathan Reed and Keziah Converse Reed.   By Worrall Drumont Prescott. (New York?) 1954.   235 p. illus., port., geneal. table. 29 cm. 55-18993.   CS71.T8624   1954

         TROTT.   See also TREAT.

17331   TROTTER.   The pedigree of Henry John Trotter, esquire, who is descended from, and quarters the arms of, co-heiresses of the peerages (which are now in abeyance) of Aton, barons Aton of Aton; Umfraville, barons Umfraville of Prudhoe, earls of Angus, and reputed earls of Kyme. (Extracted from authenticated histories, Herald's visiations, and family deeds.) (n. p., 188-?)   geneal. tab. 61 x 77½ cm. fold. to 32 cm. 22-634.   CS439.T825

17332   TROTTER.   Trotter genealogy, the Virginia-Tennessee-Mississippi Trotter line, 1725-1948, comp. and ed. by Mrs. Isham Patten Trotter, Jr.   Louisville, Ky., Mayes Print Co.   (1948)
225 p. ports., coat of arms. 20 cm. Erratum slip mounted on p. 225. 49-20503 *.   CS71.T8623   1948

          TROUP.   George Michael Troup.   Governor of Georgia, 1823-1827.   In vertical file under
McIntosh.   Ask reference librarian for this material.

          TROUT.   See KINNEY, 1903

17333   TROUTBECK.   ... The humble petition of William Robson, Thomas Walton, and Robert Foggin, all of Newcastle-upon-Tyne, the heir-at-law and personal representatives of Catherine Robson, deceased; and of John Troutbeck Ainsley and William Ainsley, of the city of Durham, the heir-at-law, and personal representatives of Isabella Ainsley, deceased.   (London, Printed by W. Clowes and sons, 1852?)   17 p. 1 l. fold. geneal. tab. 33 cm. Caption title. Heirs at law of Samuel Troutbeck of Madras. 18-16651.
                                                         CS439.T83

17334   TROUTMAN.   Notes on Johann Philip Trautman (also known as Philip Troutman and Phil. Troutman) 9 Aug. 1758-23 Feb. 1830, of Tulpehocken Township, Berks County, Pennsylvania, compiled by Schuyler C. Brossman.   Rehrersburg, Pa., 1968.   (16) l. illus., facsims., ports. 29 cm. 70-3423 MARC.
                                                         CS71.T777   1968

          TROUTMAN.   See TRAUTMANN.

          TROW.   See SCHWARTZ, 1961

17335   TROWBRIDGE.   The Trowbridge family; or, The descendants of Thomas Trowbridge, one of the first settlers of New Haven, Conn.   Compiled at the request of Thomas Rutherford Trowbridge, of New Haven, Conn., by Rev. F. W. Chapman ... New Haven, Punderson, Chrisand & co., printers, 1872.   461 p. incl. front. port. 23 cm. 9-25089.   CS71.T863   1872

17336   TROWBRIDGE.   The Trowbridge genealogy.   History of the Trowbridge family in America, by Francis Bacon Trowbridge ... New Haven, Conn., Printed for the compiler (Press of the Tuttle, Morehouse & Taylor company) 1908.   848 p. col. front. (coat of arms) plates, ports., map, facsims. 28½ cm. "Edition, 550 copies." "Family register" (blank forms): p. (841)-848. 9-552.   CS71.T863   1908

          TROWBRIDGE.   See also WISWALL, 1961

17337   TROXLER.   Hundert Jahre Postdienst, durch vier sich folgende Generationen, sowie ein chronologisch-biographischer Stammbaum der Posthalterfamilie Troxler von Beromünster nebst Angaben über die luzernische und schweizerische Verkehrsentwicklung.   Beromünster, 1948.   36 p. plates, ports., geneal. table. 22 cm. 48-27493 *.   CS999.T7   1948

17338   TROYER.   Descendants of Jephtha A. Troyer, born in Holmes County, Ohio, A. D. 1825.   By Kate (Hershberger) Yoder.   Nappanee, Ind., Evangel Press (c. 1957)   175 p. illus. 21 cm. 58-28650.
                                                         CS71.T864   1957

17339   TRUBEE ... History of the Trubee family, by Harriet Trubee Garlick.   Bridgeport, Conn., The Marigold printing company, 1894.   150 p., 1 l. front., plates, ports., col. coat of arms. 23 cm. At head of title: 1275. 1894. Blank leaves at end for "Family record." 9-14546.   CS71.T865   1894

          TRUBEE.   See also TRUBY.

17340   TRUBSHAW.   Family records ... Stafford, Printed by R. & W. Wright, 1876.   58 p. front., plates. 19 cm. Dedication signed: Susanna Trubshaw. "Memoir of Mr. James Trubshaw, C.E., by the Rev. John Miller. From the obituary of the Gentleman's magazine, 1854": p. 51-58. 20-15236.   CS439.T835

17341   TRUBY.   Early history of Truby-Graff and affiliated families (by) Mary Truby Graff.   Kittanning, Pa. (c. 1941)   xiii, 367, (9) p. incl. front. (port.) illus. (incl. facsims., maps, coats of arms) 26½ cm. Nine pages at end blank for "Notes." 42-11474.   CS71.T866   1941

TRUBY.   See also TRUBEE.

17342   TRUDELLE.   ... Le premier Trudelle en Canada et ses descendants.   Québec, Imp. Brousseau & Desrochers, 1911.   158, iii p., 1 l.   plates, ports., coat of arms.   18 cm.   At head of title: 1645.   Preface signed: T. Alf Trudelle.   Blank leaves interspersed.   12-24993.   CS90. T7

17343   TRUE.   Genealogical tree: the True family, in America.   (Mason, Mich., 1924)
cover-title, 5 double numb. l. incl. illus., 4 geneal. tab.   45 x 75 cm.   Signed: Mrs. Statira True.   A history of Salisbury, New Hampshire: leaf 1.   The table of descendants of "Henry True of Salem" is signed: H. A. True, 1864.   37-16943.

CS71. T867   1924

TRUE.   See also SAUNDERS, 1897

17344   TRUEBLOOD.   The Trueblood family in America, 1682-1963; John Trueblood of Shoreditch, England, and his descendants, by Bula Trueblood Watson, with the editorial assistance of Felicity Trueblood.   (1st ed.   Worland? Wyo.)   Trueblood family in America, 1964.   xvi, 287 p.   coat of arms, facsims., geneal. table, ports.   29 cm.   Includes bibliographical references.   "Bibliography of related families": p. 227-228.   64-24920.

CS71. T8673   1964

TRUESDEL.   See JONES, 1961

17345   TRUESDELL.   Twelve generations from the colonial immigrant to the present time; a compilation by Wesley E. Truesdell;   three hundred years in America.   (n. p.) 1938.   (11) p.   20½ cm.   On cover: Massachusetts, Connecticut, New York, Vermont, Ohio Truesdell family record.   "The nucleus for this geneology (!) was obtained from 'Hillsdale history' by John Collin.   For the earlier records I am indebted to Mrs. Belle (Truesdell) Bradley, of Springfield, Mass."   40-9664.

CS71. T868   1939

17346   TRUESDELL.   Truesdell (genealogy) Trousdell, Truesdail, Truesdale, Truesdel, Trusdell; dealing principally with the descendants of Samuel Truesdell of Newton, Massachusetts.   By Karl Truesdell.   Chevy Chase, Md., 1955 (i. e. 1956)   5 v. (x, 881 l.) illus., coat of arms.   29 cm.   Typescript.   Bibliography: v. 1, leaves vii-viii.   56-36585.   CS71. T868   1956

17347   TRUESDELL.   The Trousdale genealogy;   descendants of John Trousdale of Orange County, North Carolina.   By Karl Truesdell.   Enlarged by Theodore McKee Trousdale, Jr.   Ruth (St. John) Trousdale, editor.   Ithaca, N. Y., J. B. Trousdale, 1960.   216 p.   illus.   29 cm.   60-37210.

CS71. T868   1960

17348   TRUESDELL.   Truesdell genealogy.   By Karl Truesdell.   Negative.   Microfilm 4511

17349   TRUELOCK.   Trulock and Truluck to 1948.   By Annie (Truluck) Knight.   (Tulsa, Okla., 1948)   82 p.   ports., col. coat of arms, facsims.   31 cm.   Cover title.   50-26009.   CS71. T8687   1948

17350   TRUMAN.   The Truman family, including President Harry S. Truman, compiled by: Rolland Truman ... Long Beach, Calif., 1945.   1 p. l., 28 numb. l.   front. (mounted coat of arms) 29½ x 23½ cm.   Type-written. 46-3273.   CS71. T869   1945

17351   TRUMAN.   Truman family in vertical file.   Ask reference librarian for this material.

TRUMAN.   See also: HOLLIDAY, 1962
                              TREMAN, 1901

17352   TRUMBULL.   A genealogy of the ancestors and descendants of George Augustus and Louisa (Clap) Trumbull, of Trumbull square, Worcester, Mass.   (Fairhaven? Mass.) 1886.   46 p.   pl., fold. geneal. tab.   26½ cm.   Preface signed: J. H. L. i. e. James Henry Lea.   "Printed for the family."   Only seventy-five impressions of this book have been printed, of which this copy is no. 28.   Trumbull and Clapp coats of arms on cover and geneal. tab.   Addenda and corrigenda, 1887: p. 43-46.   15-19117.   CS71. T87   1886a

17353   TRUMBULL.   Contributions to a Trumbull genealogy, from gleanings in English fields.   By J. Henry Lea.   Boston, D. Clapp & son, 1895.   27 p.   25½ cm.   "Reprinted from the New England historical and genealogical register, 1895."   9-14547.   CS71. T87   1895

17354   TRUMBULL.   A genealogical chart of some of the descendants of John Trumbull of Newcastle-on-Tyne, Northumberland, England, and Rowley, in the colony of Massachusetts Bay.   (n. p., 191-?)
geneal. chart. coat of arms.   53 x 71 cm.   18-8386.   CS71.T87   191-

TRUMBULL.   See also THOMPSON, 1915

17355   TRUSLOW.   Notes on the families of Truslow, Horler, and Horley from English records by James Truslow Adams ... Bridgehampton, L. I., Priv. print., 1920.   (19) p. 23 cm. "Forty copies only, printed." 20-13998.   CS439.T84

TRUSSELL.   See also No. 430 - Adventurers of purse and person.

17356   TRYE.   A sketch of the life and character of the late Charles Brandon Trye, esq. ... by the Rev. Daniel Lysons ... Gloucester, Printed by D. Walker, 1812.   2 p. l., (3)-30 p. front. (port.) 31 cm. The portrait is an engraving from the bust of Charles Brandon Tyre by Chas. Rofsi, R. A.   14-16433.   R489.T8L8

17357   TRYON.   The Tryon family.   By Wesley Merritt Tryon.   (Wheaton? Md., 1957)
12 p. 23 cm. 59-35701.   CS71.T874   1957

TRYWHITT.   See TYRWHITT, 1872

TSCHIDA.   In vertical file under PRANKE family.   Ask reference librarin for this material.

17358   TSCHUDI.   The history and genealogy of the Judy-Judah-Tschudy-Tschudin-Tschudi-Schudi family who have lived in America, Switzerland and other countries of the world ... (Los Angeles) c. 1954.   576 p. illus., ports., map, coats of arms. 27 cm. Bibliography: p. vii. 54-33301.   CS71.T885   1954

TSIDA.   Tsida family in vertical file under PRANKE family.   Ask reference librarian for this material.

17360   TUCK.   Tuck genealogy.   Robert Tuck, of Hampton, N. H., and his descendants.   1638-1877.   By Joseph Dow.   Boston, Printed for private distribution, press of D. Clapp & son, 1877.
viii, 138 p. 24½ cm. "Three hundred copies printed." 9-14548.   CS71.T889   1877

17361   TUCK.   John and Edward Tuck of Halifax County, Virginia, and some of their descendants.   By Alethea Jane Macon.   Macon, Ga., Printed by Southern Press (1964)   216 p. coat of arms. 24 cm. Bibliography: p. 188-189.   64-4058.   CS71.T889   1964

TUCK.   See also WALTMAN, 1928

17362   TUCKER.   Genealogy of the Tucker family, from various authentic sources ... By Ephraim Tucker ... (Worcester, Mass., Press of F. S. Blanchard & co.) 1895.   414 p. front., illus., ports., geneal. tables. 24 cm. 9-15019.   CS71.T89   1895

17363   TUCKER.   An account of the Tucker family of Bermuda.   From a history of the Emmet family, by Thos. Addis Emmet, M. D., LL. d.   New York, Bradstreet press, 1898.   13 p. ports., geneal. tables. 28 cm. No. 15 of a limited edition of 25 copies. 9-14545.   CS71.T89   1898

17364   TUCKER.   The Tucker genealogy; a record of Gilbert Ruggles and Evelina Christina (Snyder) Tucker, their ancestors and descendants; by Tyler Seymour Morris ... Chicago, 1901.
305 p. plates, ports., 3 fold. maps, facsims. 24½ cm. 3-30947.   CS71.T89   1901

17365   TUCKER.   Family memories, by Mary Ann Hubbard, November 2, 1820 - July 19, 1909.   By Mrs. Mary Ann (Hubbard) Hubbard.   (Chicago?) Printed for private circulation, 1912.
4 p. l., 146 p. 3 port. (incl. front.) 18 cm. Sketches of the Tucker and Hubbard family history, pioneer life in Illinois and Iowa, the Chicago fire of 1871, etc. 19-7863.   F484.3.H89

17366   TUCKER.   Durkee-Tucker, 1602-1927.   (By Mrs. Eliza Ann (Tucker) Bliefling) (Watertown, Mass., 1927)   cover-title, (26) p. 23 cm. 37-16944.   CS71.T89   1927

17367   TUCKER.   The story of a portrait, by Mrs. George P. Coleman.   Richmond, Va., The Dietz press, 1935.   4 p. l., 40 p. front. (port.) pl. 20 cm. Head-pieces. "The ... record of the life of Raeburn's beautiful Mrs. Lauzun." - 2d prelim. leaf. 36-13079.

CT338.L3C6

17368   TUCKER.   St. George Tucker, citizen of no mean city, by Mary Haldale Coleman (Mrs. George P. Coleman) ... Richmond, Va., The Dietz press, 1938.   3 p. l., 190 p. front., pl., ports. 23½ cm. 39-25462.

F230.T93

17369   TUCKER.   Tucker family of Bermuda and South Carolina, compiled by Caldwell Woodruff ... (from notes of George Haig Tucker) Linthicum Heights, Md., 1941.   2 p. l., 34 numb. l. 28 cm. Type-written. 41-28036.

CS71.T89   1941

17370   TUCKER.   Tales of the Tuckers; descendants of the male line of St. George Tucker of Bermuda and Virginia, by Beverley Randolph Tucker.   Richmond, Va., The Dietz printing company, 1942.   xxi, 170 p. front., ports., coat of arms. 23½ cm. 43-1842.

CS71.T89   1942

17371   TUCKER.   Morris Tucker and five generations of his descendants.   By Bertha W. Clark. Boston, 1957.   169 l. 30 cm. 57-40140.

CS71.T89   1957

17372   TUCKER.   Our families, Tucker-Scott; concerning the lineage of William Tucker, Jr., and his wife, Leila Sue Scott Tucker, their paternal and maternal ancestors and their descendants with allied families, by Virginia Tucker Oliver and Jane Young.   Proctor, Ark., Revilo Press (c.1965)   752 p. illus., facsims., ports. 26 cm. 65-26694.

CS71.T89   1965

TUCKER.   See also:

COCKERHAM, 1959	GREENLEE, 1956	SELDEN, 1911
COGHILL, 1956	HUBBARD, F484.3.H89	STEVENS, 1957
CRITTENDEN, 1960	McKAY, 1950	VAN HOOK, 1957
DICKERMAN, 1922	MILLET, 1959	WYMAN, 18 -
FLETCHER, 1909	NORTHRUP, 1914	

17373   TUCKERMAN.   Notes on the Tuckerman family of Massachusetts, and some allied families, by Bayard Tuckerman.   Boston, Priv. print., 1914.   4 p. l., 3-263 p. front., plates, ports. 24½ cm. "Sixty copies printed at the Riverside press." This copy not numbered. 15-8248.

CS71.T9   1914

TUCKWILLER.   See BRUMBACH, 1961

17374   TUDOR.   Lives of the Tudor princesses, including Lady Jane Grey and her sisters, by Agnes Strickland ... London, Longmans, Green, and co., 1868.   1p. l., (vii)-xxvii, (1), 392 p. front. (port.) pl. 19 cm. "Elizabeth Strickland ... wrote the lives of the Duchess of Suffolk, Lady Jane Grey, Lady Katharine Grey, and Lady Mary Grey." - Dict. nat. biog. Contents. - Princess Mary Tudor, queen of France and duchess of Suffolk. - Lady Jane Gray. - Lady Katharine Gray. - Lady Mary Gray. - Lady Eleanor Brandon. - Lady Margaret Clifford. - Lady Arbella Stuart. 5-947.

DA317.1.S9

17375   TUDOR.   Tudor queens and princesses by Sarah Tytler (pseud. of Henrietta Keddie)   London, J. Nisbet & co., 1896.   3 p. l., 418 p. front., ports. 20 cm. Contents. - Elizabeth Tudor. - Margaret Tudor, countess of Richmond. - Elizabeth of York. - Margaret Tudor. - Mary Tudor, queen dowager of France, and wife of Charles Brandon, duke of Suffolk. - Catherine of Arragon. - Anne Boleyn. - Jane Seymour. - Anne of Cleves. - Catherine Howard. - Catherine Parr. - Mary Tudor, queen of England. 1-1831.

DA317.1.K2

17376   TUDOR.   Deacon Tudor's diary; or, "Memorandoms from 1709, &c., by John Tudor, to 1775 & 1778, 1780 and to '93." A record of more or less important events in Boston, from 1732 to 1793, by an eye-witness.   Edited by William Tudor, A.B.   Boston, Press of W. Spooner, 1896.   1 p. l., vi, 110, (vii)-xxxvii, (7) p. front., ports. 25 cm. Tudor genealogy: p. xx-xxxvii. 9-14544.

CS71.T912   1896

17377   TUDOR.   The blood royal of Britain; being a roll of the living descendants of Edward IV. and Henry VI., kings of England, and James III., king of Scotland, by the Marquis of Ruvigny and Raineval. With a series of portraits.   London and Edinburgh, T. C. & E. C. Jack, 1903.   xi, 620, (1) p. front. (facsim. in colors) 19 port., geneal. tables. 29 cm. Title in red and black. p. 1-80 contain CXXXIV genealogical tables. 4-31170.

CS418.R7

17378   TUDOR.   The reign of Elizabeth, 1558-1603, by J. B. Black ... Oxford, The Clarendon press, 1936.   vii, (1), 448 p. fold. maps, fold. plan, fold. geneal. tables.   22½ cm.   (Half-title: The Oxford history of England, ed. by G. N. Clark)   Bibliography: p. (412)-430.   36-19574.   DA355. B65

　　　　TUDOR.   See also: GARDNER, F24. G25
　　　　　　　　　　　　　　　　PARNELL, DA958. P2S5

　　　　TUERS.   See TOERS.

17379   TUFNELL.   The family of Tufnell; being some account of the Elizabethan, Richard Tuffnayle, and his descendants; with a chapter on the properties of Langleys, Nun Monkton, and the manor of Barnsbury.   (By Mrs. Ellen Bertha (Gubbins) Tufnell)   Privately printed.   (Guildford and Esher, Printed by Billing and sons, ltd.)   1924.   vii, 74 p. front., ports. 26½ cm. Foreword signed: E. Bertha Tufnell.   Title vignette: coat of arms.   The plates are reproductions made by Emery Walker from the original paintings.   Bibliography: p. 67-68.   25-1257.   CS439. T845

　　　　TUFNELL.   See also BACKHOUSE, DA690. M74C3

17380   TUFTON.   Memorials of the family of Tufton, earls of Thanet; deduced from various sources of authentic information ... Gravesend, Printed by R. Pocock, 1800.   3 p. l., (v)-x, 156 p.   front., plates.   22½ cm.   Title vignette.   Dedication signed Robert Pocock.   9-18116.   CS439. T85

17381   TUFTS.   Tufts family history; a true account and history of our Tufts families, from and before 1638-1963.   By Jay Franklin Tufts.   Cleveland Heights, Ohio (1963)   280, xxxxx p. illus., ports., maps.   29 cm.   64-602.   CS71. T917   1963

　　　　TUFTS.   See also FLAGG, 1903

17382   TUGGLE.   Genealogy of the Tuggle family 1560-1936.   (By Henry Forbes Tuggle)   (n. p., 1936)   5 p. l., 157 (i. e. 159) p. pl., ports.   28 cm.   Mimeographed.   Title from cover.   Two blank pages not included in numbering.   Foreword signed: H. F. Tuggle, M. L. Tuggle.   "For the early part of the Tuggle, Turrant and Herndon histories, we are almost entirely indebted to Miss Susan Tuggle Herndon of Gradford, England, who made an exhaustive study of the early history of the three families. " - Foreword.   39-12256.   CS71. T92   1936

　　　　TUGGLE.   See also: BALLARD, 1947
　　　　　　　　　　　　　　　　PEDEN, 1961

　　　　TULBURT.   See HOWARD, 1961

17383   TULEY.   The Tuley family memoirs; an historical, biographical and genealogical story of the Tuleys and the Floyd family connection in Virginia, Kentucky, and Indiana, by William Floyd Tuley.   New Albany, Ind., W. J. Hedden, printer, 1906.   v, 6-75 p. incl. front., ports. port. 18½ cm.   22-22859.   CS71. T925   1906

17384   TULL.   John Porter Tull and his descendants.   By James Porter Tull.   Hartford, M. B. Hadlock (1942)   xvii, 170 p. ports., coat of arms.   23 cm.   With added t. p.: A biographical sketch of the life of John Porter Tull and his descendants, 1796-1942.   Edited by Maxine Tull-Boatner.   Includes bibliographies.   50-43165.   CS71. T926   1942

　　　　TULLER.   See HASKINS, 1911.

　　　　TUMLIN.   See BELL, 1959

17385   TUNNELL.   A genealogy of the Tunnell family of Delaware.   By James Miller Tunnell. (Georgetown? Del., 1954?)   100 l.   29 cm.   56-33578.   CS71. T927   1954

　　　　TUNNELL.   See also No. 527 - Notable southern families, vol. 3 page 129

17386   TUNSTALL.   The first Tunstalls in Virginia, and some of their descendants.   By Whitmore Morris.   (San Antonio, 1950)   xiii, 250 p. port.   24 cm.   Bibliography: p. 231-232.   50-54990.   CS71. T928   1950

17387   TUPPER.   Family records; containing memoirs of Major-General Sir Isaac Brock, K.B.,
Lieutenant E. W. Tupper, B.N., and Colonel William De Vic Tupper, with notices of Major-General
Tupper and Lieut. C. Tupper, R.N.; to which are added the Life of T-cum-seh, a memoir of Colonel
Haviland Le Mésurier, &c. &c. &c.   By Ferdinand Brock Tupper ... Guernsey, S. Barbet, 1835.
xii, 218 p. incl. front.   2 pl.   22 cm.   8-20226.   E353.1.B8T9

17388   TUPPER.   The tercentenary dedicatory volume of the Tupper family association of America,
incorporated, compiled by the executive committee.   (n. p., 1939?)   viii, 93 p. incl. front., illus. 20½ cm.
41-5561.   CS71.T93   1939

17389   TUPPER.   Thomas Tupper and his descendants.   By Franklin Whittlesey Tupper.   (2d ed.)
Boston, Tupper Family Association of America, 1945 (i.e. 1967)   71 p.   coat of arms.   23 cm.   74-11147 MARC.
                                                                               CS71.T93   1967

TUPPER.   See also: BROWN, 1959
                                GUÉRIN, 1890

TURFLER.   See ROGERS, 1946

17390   TURING.   The lay of the Turings: A sketch of thc family history, feebly conceived and im-
perfectly executed: Now dedicated to the chief with the sincerest respect and affection, by H. M'K.
(London, Savill and Edwards, printers, 1849?)   3 p. l., (3)-76, (2) p. front. (fold. geneal. tab.) 22 cm.   At head of title:
"A.D.1316-1849."   Compiled by Henry Mackenzie.   "Notes to the lay by R.F.T.," i.e. Sir Robert Frazer Turing. 18-23464.
                                                                               CS479.T8

17391   TURNAGE.   The Luter-Davis and allied families: Luter-Davis-Burkhalter-Smart-Perkins,
and others.   (Madison? Miss.) 1959.   141 p.   27 cm.   60-24618.   CS71.L972   1959

17392   TURNBULL.   William Turnbull, 1751-1822, with some account of those coming after, by
Archibald Douglas Turnbull ... (Binghamton, N.Y., Printed by the Vail Ballou press, inc., 1933)
vii, 175 p. front., pl., ports., plans (1 fold.) facsims., fold. geneal. tab.   24 cm. Privately printed.   Coat of arms on cover. 34-1554.
                                                                               F153.T86

TURNBULL.   See also: ELIOT, 1907
                                    TRIMBLE, 1958

17393   TURNER.   Genealogy of the descendants of Humphrey Turner, with family records.   In
two parts.   Compiled by Jacob Turner, esq.   Boston, D. Turner, jr., 1852.   iv (5)-63, (1) p. 23½ cm.
8 blank pages at end for "Family records." 9-14543.   CS71.T945   1852

17394   TURNER.   Pope: additional facts concerning his maternal ancestry.   By Robert Davies,
F.S.A., in a letter to Mr. Hunter, author of the tract entitled "Pope: his descent and family connections" ... London, J. R. Smith, 1858.   53, (1) p. 20 cm.   9-12693.   CS439.T9

17395   TURNER.   Pedigree of the Turner family, and its representatives in 1871.   Collected, from
authentic sources, by Hubert Smith ... Arranged and edited by ... Richard Woof ... Privately printed.
London, Taylor and co., printers, 1871.   8 p. 28½ cm.   Title vignette (coat of arms) Additions in manuscript; letter from
author inserted.   2-26600 rev.   CS439.T88

17396   TURNER.   Turner genealogy.   Privately printed.   (London, Mitchell & Hughes) 1884.
4 p. l., 88 p. incl. geneal. tables. front., plates, ports., facsims., coats of arms (part col.) 31½ cm.   (Half-title: The genealogy of the family
of Turner.   Compiled by the late Rev. Samuel Blois Turner) Title vignette: Colored coat of arms.   Preface signed: Marian Turner. 14-19510.
                                                                               CS439.T88   1884

17397   TURNER.   Asa Turner; a home missionary patriarch and his times, by George F. Magoun
... Introduction by A. H. Clapp, D. D.   Boston and Chicago, Congregational Sunday-school and publishing society (c.1889)   345 p.   front., plates, ports. 20½ cm.   Title vignette. 16-2758.   BX7260.T97M3

17398   TURNER.   The Turner family of Mulbarton and Great Yarmouth, in Norfolk: 1547-1894.
Collections & notes.   By Harward Turner.   For private circulation only.   London, Jarrold & sons
(1895)   4 p. l., 195 p. front., ports. 25½ cm.   15-19673.   CS439.T88   1895

17399   TURNER. In memoriam. Susan Wadden Turner. Professor William Wadden Turner, librarian of the Patent office, Washington, D.C.   Jane Wadden Turner, recorder of scientific collections and exchanges at the Smithsonian institution for thirty years, and for twenty years assistant librarian to the Library of Congress. (Washington, D.C., 1898)   19 p. 21½ cm. 160 copies printed. Signed: Caroline H. Dall. 14-11905.
CS71.T945   1898

17400   TURNER. The Turners of "Kinloch." By Elizabeth Turner Cox. The Plains, Va., (19 -) 1 v. (unpaged) 22 cm. "Compiled by Elizabeth Turner Cox and Llwyn Turner" in ms. on t.p.   52-52579.
CS71.T945

17401   TURNER. The Turner family magazine; genealogical, historical and biographical. Edited by William Montgomery Clemens.   v.1, v.2, no.1-2; Jan. 1916 - Apr. 1917. New York city, N.Y., W. M. Clemens, 1916-17.   2 v. in 1. 23 cm. quarterly. No more published. 16-2764 rev.
CS71.T945   1916

17402   TURNER. The Turner family of "Hebron" and Betterton, Maryland, by Henry Chandlee Forman ... (Baltimore, Waverly press, inc.) 1933.   ix, (1), 103 p. front., illus. (incl. ports., map, facsim., double geneal. tables, coat of arms) 19 cm. "List of references": p. 100-103. 36-12588.
CS71.T945   1933

17403   TURNER. The Turners of Grand Rapids, Michigan, and Clinton county, New York, also their Sibley connections, compiled by Ianthe Bond Hebel. Grand Rapids, Mich., 1936.   1 p. l., 21 numb. l., 1 l., 5 numb. l., 2 l. 28 cm. Type-written. Two leaves of photostat copies of articles, including illustrations, from the Grand Rapids herald, inserted after p. 21. "The Sibleys of Grand Rapids, Michigan" has special t.-p. Bibliography: 2 l. at end. 36-30615.
CS71.T954   1936

17404   TURNER. (Charts of the descendants of Thomas Turner, of England, who came to Virginia about 1650.) Thomas Turner Association. (n.p.) 1950 . (19) l. 22 x 28 cm. Additions and corrections in ms. 52-23550.
CS71.T945   1950

17405   TURNER. Forbears, family and descendants of Isaac Banning Turner (by Charles C. Turner. Bradenton? Fla., 196-)   45 l. facsim., ports. 28 cm. Cover title. 68-2624.   CS71.T945

17406   TURNER. Some Turners of Virginia. By Louise Patton Turner. (Tulsa? Okla., 1965) 54 l. 28 cm. Cover title. 66-47104.
CS71.T945   1965

17407   TURNER. How we lived, 1893-1918 (by) Ethel Turner Burnett. (Tampa? Fla., 1967, c.1966) 149 l. illus., facsims., geneal. tables, maps, ports. 28 cm. 67-7526.
CS71.T945   1967

17408   TURNER. Turner family of Virginia and Kentucky. By Emma Rouse Lloyd.   Available for consultation at Lloyd library, 309 West Court Street, Cincinnati 2, Ohio.

TURNER.   See also:

BASSETT, 1926	DURYEE, 1959	PYRTLE, 1930
CALHOUN, 1957	FELLOWS, 1940	SHARP (in vertical file)
COLE, 1927a	HOLLAND, 1959	TILSON, 1911
COOK, 1930	LEFTWICH, 1931	WRIGHT, 1929
DINWIDDIE, 1902	POPE, PR3633.H8	No. 579 - Monroe.
DORRANCE, 1937		

TURNEY.   See BURGESS, 1961

TURNLEY.   See ARMSTRONG, CS61.A6 vol.1

17409   TURNIDGE. The trail blazers, by Alice (Turnidge) Hamot; historical and genealogical record of early pioneer families of Oregon, Missouri and the South. Portland, Or., 1935.   5 p. l., 459 p. incl. front. (port.) illus. 22 cm. 35-2036.
CS71.T948   1935

17410   TURNLEY. Private biography of the Turnleys, by one of the family. (Parmenas Taylor Turnley. Chicago, Marsland & Tansey, printers, 1872?)   1 p. l., xiv, 152, (1), xxv p. port. 19 cm. 14-10157.
CS71.T954   1872

17411   TURNLEY.   Reminiscences of Parmenas Taylor Turnley, from the cradle to three-score and ten; by himself, from diaries kept from early boyhood.   With a brief glance backward three hundred and fifty years at progenitors and ancestral lineage.   Chicago, Donohue & Henneberry, printers (1892)
448 p. 2 pl., 2 port. (incl. front.) 20 cm. 3-31201.   E181.T95

TURNLEY.   See also No. 516 - Notable southern families vol. 1

TURNOVER.   See: NELSON, CS439.N33
                      TWINE.

17412   TURPIN.   The Turpin family.   An outline sketch, comp. and arranged by J. M. Bancroft ...
New York (1879)   fold. geneal. tab.   13 x 10½ cm.   18-367.   CS71.T958   1879

17413   TURPIN.   History and genealogy of the Jacob Turpin branch of the Turpin family, being a brief history and genealogy of the members of the first and second generations, and a genealogy of the members of all other generations down to the present time, prepared by P. T. Lambert ... 1907 to 1910.
(Greensburg, Ind., 1910)   134 p. front., 1 illus., ports. 19½ cm. 39-12235.   CS71.T958   1910

17414   TURPIN.   Antique Turpin dolls.   By Florrie Bell Holt.   Cincinnati (Talaria) 1961.
94 p. illus. 24 cm. (A Talaria book) 61-40070.   NK4892.C55   1961

17415   TURPIN.   Turpin family in vertical file.   Ask reference librarian for this material.

TURPIN.   See also ROBERTS, 1939

17416   TURRENTINE.   The Turrentine family.   By George Ruford Turrentine.   (n. p.) 1954.
128 l. illus. 28 cm. 55-32218.   CS71.T959   1954

17417   TURRENTINE.   The Turrentine family.   By George Ruford Turrentine.   (Rev. ed.)   Russell-
ville, Ark., 1954 (i.e. 1964)   133 p. illus., ports. 28 cm. 65-89144.   CS71.T959   1964

TURTON.   See BERNARD, 1922

TUTHILL.   See TUTTLE.

17418   TUTT.   (Descendants of Colonel Richard Tutt) compiled by C. Wickliffe Throckmorton ...
(n. p., n. d.)   geneal. tab. 25½ x 56 cm. 32-21628.   CS71.T96

17419   TUTT.   (The ancestry of Mrs. Mary Barnes Tutt Throckmorton)   By Charles Wickliffe
Throckmorton.   (New York, 1925)   geneal. tab. 25½ x 46 cm. Contains Tutt, Pendleton, Chichester and Mason families.
25-11810.   CS71.T96   1925

17420   TUTTLE.   A family meeting of the descendants of John Tuthill, one of the original settlers of the town of Southold, N. Y.   Held at New-Suffolk, L. I., August 28th, 1867.   Sag-Harbor, N. Y.,
Express print, 1867.   60 p. 22½ cm. Judge Tuthill's address, p. 6-34, reprinted in New England historical and genealogical register,
July 1868, p. 317-334. 9-14542.   CS71.T967   1867

17421   TUTTLE.   Address at the family meeting of the descendants of John Tuthill, one of the original settlers of Southold, N. Y., held at New Suffolk, L. I., August 28, 1867.   By Hon. William H.
Tuthill ... Boston, D. Clapp & son, printers, 1868.   23 p. 28 cm. Reprinted from the New Eng. hist. and geneal. register
for July, 1868. 9-14541.   CS71.T967   1868

17422   TUTTLE.   Family record of Calvin Tuttle and his wife Ruth Ann Miner, their ancestors and descendants.   Collected and compiled by Emmett George Tuttle, East Dorset, Vt.   1871.   Rutland,
Tuttle & co., printers, 1871.   26 p. 22½ cm. Blank pages at end for "Family record." 19-2009.   CS71.T967   1871

17423   TUTTLE.   1635.   William Tuttle of New Haven: an address delivered at the Tuttle gathering, New Haven, Conn., September 3d, 1873.   By Joseph F. Tuttle ... Newark, N. J., Printed at the office of
the Daily advertiser, 1873.   22 p. 25½ cm. 29-7569.   CS71.T967   1873

17424   TUTTLE.   The descendants of William and Elizabeth Tuttle, who came from old to New England in 1635, and settled in New Haven in 1639, with numerous biographical notes and sketches;   also, some account of the descendants of John Tuttle, of Dover, N.H.;   Richard Tuttle, of Boston;   John Tuttle of Ipswich;   and Henry Tuthill, of Hingham, Mass.   ... By George Frederick Tuttle ... Rutland, Vt., Tuttle & company, 1883.   viii, viii a - viii h, (ix) - lx, 754 p. col. front. (coat of arms) ports. 24½ cm. 9-14540.
                                                                                        CS71.T967   1883
                                                                                        Microfilm 9294 CS

17425   TUTTLE.   The Tuthill family of Tharston, Norfolk County, England and Southold, Suffolk County, New York, also written Totyl, Totehill, Tothill, Tuttle, etc., 1580-1757, by Lucy Dubois Akerly ... Edition of one hundred copies.   Privately printed.   (New York, Press of J. Little & co.) 1898.   12 p. illus. (coat of arms) 25½ cm. "Reprinted from the New York genealogical and biographical record for July and October, 1898." 24-12335.   CS71.T967   1898

17426   TUTTLE.   Descendants of William Tuthill (in America spelled Tuthill and Tuttle) alderman and mayor of Exeter ... Reprinted for the family.   London, 1918.   cover-title, (8) p. 23½ cm. Coat of arms on cover. 19-19899.   CS439.T912

17427   TUTTLE.   The Tuthill family tree on L. I., N. Y., starting at Daniel, known to be of the 4th generation from John Tuthill, Sr., a member of the 13 families who landed at Old Landing in Southold, L. I., in 1640.   Floral Park, N. Y. (1953) c. 1952.   geneal. table. 26 x 34 cm. 53-1706.
                                                                                        CS71.T967   1953

17428   TUTTLE.   Solomon Tuttle of old Mt. Comfort and his descendants ... By Julia Sevarine (Cannon) Reed.   Fayetteville, Ark., Washington County Historical Society, 1961.   87 p. illus. 28 cm. 61-3863.   CS71.T967   1961

          TUTTLE.   See also: FRENCH, 1940 a   HUGHES, 1879
                                FRISBIE, E171.A53 vol. 19   MOULTON, 1922
                                GRIFFIN, F129.S74G8   OTIS, 1851
                                HARRISON, 1893   ROBINSON, 1894
                                HILL, E171.A53 vol. 13   RUSSELL, 1910

17429   TWADDLE.   The Twaddles come to Wisconsin.   Prepared by the committee (appointed by the officers of the Twaddle Reunion.   Written by Bernard Smith and his wife, Jeanne.   Viola, Wis.,) Viola news, 1955.   unpaged. 23 cm. 56-32380.   CS71.T968   1955

17430   TWANBROOK.   Twenebrokes, or Twanbrook, of Appleton, Grappenhall, and Daresbury, in the county of Chester, A. D. 1170 to 1831.   A paper read before the Historic society of Lancashire and Cheshire, 26th November, 1885.   By John Paul Rylands, F. S. A.   Liverpool, T. Brakell, printer, 1887.   cover-title, 20 p., 1 l. pl., fold. geneal. tab. 21½ cm. Published also in the Transactions of the Lancashire and Cheshire society, Liverpool, 1888, v. 37, p. 1-20. 21-21738.   CS439.T9123

17431   TWEED.   Sketch of the James Tweed family, Wilmington, Mass.   By Benj. Walker.   Read at a family reunion, Foster's Pond, Andover, Mass., June 17, 1887.   Lowell, Mass., Courier press: Marden & Rowell, 1887.   30 p. 18½ cm. 9-14538.   CS71.T97   1887

17432   TWEEDIE.   The history of the Tweedie, or Tweedy, family; a record of Scottish lowland life & character.   By Michael Forbes Tweedie.   A. D. 1902.   London, W. P. Griffith & sons, ltd. (1902)   viii, 231 p. front., plates, facsims., coats of arms (part col.) 28½ cm. 20-15217.   CS479.T9

17433   TWEEDIE.   The annals of a Tweeddale parish; the history of the united parish of Broughton, Glenholm and Kilbucho (civil and ecclesiastical) by Rev. Andrew Baird ... Glasgow, J. Smith & son, ltd., 1924.   306, xix p. front., illus., plates, ports., plan. 22 cm. Contains histories of the Geddes, Tweedie, Fleming and Dickson families. 25-9057.   DA880.P3B3

17434   TWEEDIE.   The Dublin Tweedys; the story of an Irish family, 1650-1882.   By Owen Tweedy.   London, Vallentine, Mitchell (1956)   214 p. illus., ports., map, geneal. tables. 23 cm. 57-28036.
                                                                                        CS499.T8   1956

17435   TWEMLOW.   The Twemlows; their wives and their homes, from original records, by Francis Randle Twemlow ... Wolverhampton, Whitehead brothers, 1910.   2 p. 1., vii-xviii p., 1 l., 271, (4) p. illus. (incl. plans) plates, ports., maps, facsims., geneal. tables.   20 cm.   The maps, facsimiles and genealogical tables are folded.   20-15855.
CS439.T9125

TWEMLOW.   See also ROYD, CS439.R75

TWENTYMAN.   See GOODCHILD, CS439.G575

TWICHELL.   See TWITCHELL.

17436   TWILLEY.   Twilley record traced back to the Revolutionary War.   Data assembled by Wade T. Porter.   Denver, 1966.   27 (i.e. 41) l.   geneal. table.   30 cm.   Typescript (carbon copy)   The additional pages are numbered 3A, 10A-D etc.   66-5857 rev.
CS71.T972   1966
———— (Supplement.   Denver, 1967?)   geneal. table.   54 x 22 cm.   Photocopy of MS.   66-5857 rev.
CS71.T972   1966
Suppl.

17437   TWINING.   Genealogy of the Twining family, descendants of William Twining, sr.   Who came from Wales, or England, and died at Eastham, Massachusetts, 1659.   With information of other Twinings in Great Britain and America.   By Thos, J. Twining ... Chicago, Pub. for the author, 1890.   172 p., 1 l., xi p. incl. front., ports.   23 cm.   9-14539.
CS71.T973   1890

17438   TWINING.   Some facts in the history of the Twining family, from A.D. 577.   Compiled from private and public documents by the Rev. W. H. G. Twining ... London, Printed by T. Vickers-Wood, 1892.   vii, (9)-36 p. illus. (coats of arms) 21 cm.   "For private circulation."   Preface signed: "Louisa Twining."   16-20947.
CS439.T913

17439   TWINING.   The Twining family.   (Revised ed.)   Descendants of William Twining, sr., of Eastham, Massachusetts, where he died, 1659.   With notes of English, Welsh and Nova Scotia families of the name.   Fort Wayne, Ind., T. J. Twining, 1905.   xiii, 251 p. illus. (incl. ports., map) 23 cm. Compiled by T. J. Twining.   12-27323.
CS71.T973   1905

17440   TWINING.   Supplement to "Some facts in the history of the Twining family" ... Salisbury, Bennett brothers, printers, 1893.   34 p.   21 cm.   Signed: "Louisa Twining."   16-20943.
CS439.T913
Suppl.

17441   TWINING.   General N. F. Twining.   In vertical file.   Ask reference librarian for this material.

TWINING.   See also BRAYTON, 1922

17442   TWISDEN.   ... The Twysden lieutenancy papers, 1583-1668.   Edited with an introduction by Gladys Scott Thomson ... (Ashford, Printed for the Records branch by Headley brothers, 1926)   xi, 124, (2) p. incl. geneal. tab.   front. (fold. map) facsims.   22 cm.   (Added t.-p.: Kent archaeological society.   Records branch.   Kent records vol. x)   At head of title: Kent records.   Bibliographical foot-notes.   26-12207.
CS435.K6 vol. 10

17443   TWISDEN.   The family of Twysden and Twisden; their history and archives from an original by Sir John Ramskill Twisden, 12th baronet of Bradbourne, completed by C. H. Dudley Ward ... London, J. Murray (1939)   vii, 483 p. front., plates, ports., fold. geneal. tables.   23½ cm.   "First edition 1939."   Bibliographical foot-notes.   39-30929.
CS439.T914   1939

TWISDEN.   See also ROYDON, 1938

17444   TWITCHELL.   Genealogy of the Twitchell family; record of the descendants of the Puritan - Benjamin Twitchell, Dorchester, Lancaster, Medfield and Sherborn, Massachusetts, 1632-1927, compiled and edited by Ralph Emerson Twitchell ... New York, N.Y., Priv. print. for H. K. Twitchell, 1929.   5 p. 1., (ix)-lxi, 707 p. front., pl., ports.   26½ cm.   29-19077.
CS71.T976   1929

TWITCHELL.   See also: ADAMS, F63.M88 vol. 1
REMINGTON, 1960

TWYSDEN. See TWISDEN.

17445   TYLDESLEY.   The Tyldesleys of Lancashire: the rise and fall of a great patrician family.
By John Lunn.   Astley (Lancs.), John Lunn, 239 Church Road, 1966.   x, 195 p.   6 plates (incl. ports.) map, facsims., geneal. tables.   22½ cm.   67-108302.   CS439.T9148

17446   TYLER.   Brief genealogies of the Tyler, Taft, Wood, Bates & Hill families, ancestors of
Newell Tyler and wife.   Compiled by Newell Tyler ... Worcester, Mass., Printed by Tyler and
Seagrave, 1882.   17, (1) p. illus. 23½ cm. 8-6295.   CS71.T983   1882

17447   TYLER.   Daniel Tyler: a memorial volume containing his autobiography and war record,
some account of his later years, with various reminiscences and the tributes of friends.   New Haven,
Priv. print., 1883.   xvi, 186 p. incl. front. (port.) geneal. tab. port.   27 cm.   "Two hundred copies privately printed by Tuttle,
Morehouse & Taylor."   Prefatory note signed: Donald G. Mitchell.   Facsimile letter on p. (106-107)   "Abstract of the Tyler pedigree": p. (xiii)
13-23460.   E467.1.T9M6

17448   TYLER.   The letters and times of the Tylers.   By Lyon G. Tyler ... Richmond, Va., Whittet
& Shepperson; (etc., etc.) 1884-96.   3 v. fronts., pl. ports., facsims. (part fold.) 24½ cm.   Vol. 3 pub. Williamsburg, Va.,
1896, is a supplement to v.1-2.   Edition of v.3 limited to 250 copies.   10-7986.   E397.T98
                                                                                Office.

17449   TYLER.   (Tyler family association) Official report of the 1st-5th American Tyler family reunion ... 1896-1899.   Chicago, Ill.   (W.I.T. Brigham) 1897-1900.   5 v. fronts., illus., ports. 25 cm.   Edited
by W. I. T. Brigham.   Edition limited.   1-30848.   CS71.T983   1897

17450   TYLER.   Memorial of Hon, Samuel Tyler.   (Chicago, Ill.)   Priv. print for the family, May,
1900.   46 p., 1 l. front. (port.) 22½ cm.   Dedication signed: Caroline Tyler Clark and Sarah Ann (Tyler) Breslin.   Memorial service has
separate title-page with imprint, Lewiston, Printed at the Journal office, 1879.   Contents. - Autobiographical sketch. - A memorial service held at
the Congregation church, Brownfield, Maine, Febtuary 2d, 1879. - Genealogical record, p. 41-46.   10-26397.   CS71.T983   1900

17451   TYLER.   John W. Tyler, 1808-1888.   A memorial of the one hundredth anniversary of his
birth, September 27, 1908.   (Cedar Rapids, Iowa, Priv. print., The Torch press, 1908) 69 p. 1 l. front.
(port.) 4 pl. 22 cm.   Biographical and genealogical material collected by Joseph Z. Tyler and Mrs. Sue F. Odor, ed. by Alice S. Tyler.   8-37657.
                                                                                CS71.T983   1908

17452   TYLER.   The Tyler genealogy: the descendants of Job Tyler, of Andover, Massachusetts,
1619-1700, by Willard I. Tyler Brigham ... Plainfield, N.J., C.B. Tyler; Tylerville, Conn., R.U. Tyler,
1912.   2 v. 24 cm. 12-21584.   CS71.T983   1912

17453   TYLER.   Sir Charles Tyler, G.C.B., admiral of the White, by Colonel Wyndham-Quin ...
London, A. L. Humphreys, 1912.   vi, (2), 247, (1) p. front., plates, ports., fold. geneal. tab. 24 cm.   17-29936.
                                                                                DA88.1.T85W9

17454   TYLER.   William Tyler genealogy; the descendants of William Tyler, of Salem, New Jersey,
1925 (?)-1701, by Willard I. Tyler Brigham 1859-1904.   Albany, N.Y., D.A. Thompson, The Brandow
printing company, 1912.   55 p. 24 cm.   Introduction signed: David Allen Thompson.   13-24436.
                                                                                CS71.T983   1912a

17455   TYLER.   Autobiography of William Seymour Tyler ... and related papers; with a genealogy
of the ancestors of Prof. and Mrs. William S. Tyler, prepared by Cornelius B. Tyler.   (n.p.) Priv.
print., 1912.   3 p. l., (5)-324 p. front., pl., ports., fold. geneal. tables. 23½ cm.   "Genealogy" (p. (235)-324) contains Tyler,
Seymour, Whiting and Edwards ancestry.   Forbes Library for Library of Congress.   A16-1153.   CS71.T983   1912b

17456   TYLER.   Grandmother Tyler's book; the recollections of Mary Palmer Tyler (Mrs. Royall
Tyler) 1775-1866, edited by Frederick Tupper and Helen Tyler Brown ... New York & London, G.P.
Putnam's sons, 1925.   xxv, 366 p. front., plates, ports., fold. geneal. tables. 22 cm.   25-5464.
                                                                                E302.6.T93T9

17457   TYLER.   American backlogs; the story of Gertrude Tyler and her family, 1660-1860, compiled by her daughter and her grandson, Mrs. Theodore Roosevelt and Kermit Roosevelt ... New York, London, C. Scribner's sons, 1928.   7 p. l., 3-236 p.   front., plates, ports.   23½ cm.   Contents. - A number of Tylers. - Seafarers all; Benjamin Lee, Gertrude's maternal grandfather. - A schoolgirl's impressions of Paris under the second empire: correspondence between Gertrude Tyler and her family, 1852-1854. - The Quereaus (Carows)   28-25527.   CS71.T983   1928

17458   TYLER.   The Tyler, Elkins and allied families, a genealogical study, compiled and privately printed for George F. Tyler by Lewis historical publishing company inc.   New York, 1939.
5 p. l., 710 p.   col. coats of arms, col. geneal. tables.   33 cm.   The genealogical tables accompanied by guard sheets with descriptive letterpress. Includes bibliographical notes.   40-30390.   CS71.T983   1939
                                                                                                                          Office.

17459   TYLER.   The "Register" of Dr. William H. Tyler; a manuscript notebook belonging to Mrs. Perry A. Smedley, copied, annotated and somewhat rearranged by Elmer I. Shepard ... (Williamstown? Mass.) 1941.   1 p. l., 39 numb. l.   27½ cm.   (On cover: Berkshire geneological (!) notes, no. 2)   Reproduced from type-written copy. Includes also the Cook and Hamilton families.   41-25191.   CS71.T983   1941

17460   TYLER.   Tyler families of early Branford, Connecticut; lineage of Joel Ford Tyler (1802-1878) of North Haven, Conn., and Oswego, New York.   By Frederick Tyler Lawton.   Jamaica, N.Y., 1951.   77 l.   28 cm.   Typewritten (carbon copy)   Addenda slip inserted.   Includes references.   52-21266.   CS71.T983   1951

        TYLER.   See also: CASTLE, 1922   HUNTER, 1934
                              CROOKE, 1942   JAMES, 1912
                              HENSHAW, 1894   STANSBURY, 1933
                              HILDRETH, CT275.H597A5 UNGRICH, E171.A53 vol. 13

17461   TYNDALE.   Genealogy of the family of Tyndale, together with the pedigrees of several families with whom they have formed alliances, and shewing the connection with the line of Plantagenet. Comp. from public records and other authentic documents, with the authorities annexed, by B. W. Greenfield ... Westminster, Priv. print., by J. B. Nichols and son, 1843.   2 p. l., 6 fold. geneal. tab., 2 l. illus. (coats of arms)   50½ cm.   "References and authorities": 2 l. at end.   11-5263.   CS439.T915

        TYNDALE.   See also TINDALE.

        TYNES.   See No. 1547 - Cabell county.

17462   TYNG.   The Tyng family in America.   By Brother Anthony of Padua.   Poughkeepsie, N.Y., Marist Press (c. 1956)   107 p.   illus.   24 cm.   57-3181.   CS71.T985   1956

        TYREL.   See TERRELL.

        TYRRELL.   See TERRELL.

17463   TYRWHITT.   Notices and remains of the family of Tyrwhitt: originally seated in Northumberland, at Tyrwhitt (or Trewhitt); afterwards in Lincolnshire, at Kettleby, Stainfield, Scotter, and Cameringham; and more recently in Shropshire and Denbighshire.   (A.D. 1067-1857) ... (London, Bradbury and Evans, printers, 1857?)   vii, (1), 104 p.   25 cm.   Additions in ms. throughout text.   "Proeme" signed: R. P. T.   20-15881.   CS439.T925

17464   TYRWHITT.   Notices and remains of the family of Tyrwhitt: originally seated in Norhtumberland, at Tyrwhitt (or Trewhitt); afterwards in Lincolnshire, at Kettleby, Stainfield, Scotter, and Cameringham; and more recently in Shropshire and Denbighshire.   (A.D. 1067 to 1872) ... Originally printed 1858; reprinted 1862; re-printed 1872 with corrections.   Never published.   (London, Harrison and sons, printers, 1872)   viii p., 1 l., 140 p.   25½ cm.   Introduction signed: R. P. T.   i.e. Robert Philip Tyrwhitt.   24-6503.   CS439.T925   1872

17465   TWYSDEN.   ... The Twysden lieutenancy papers, 1583-1668.   Edited with an introduction by Gladys Scott Thomson ... (Ashford, Printed for the Records branch by Headley brothers, 1926)
xi, 124, (2) p.   front. (fold. map) facsims.   22 cm.   (Added t.-p.: Kent archaeological soc. Records branch. Kent records vol. x)   Genealogical tab. of the Twysden family, 1500-1672: p. xi.   Bibliographical foot-notes.   26-12207.   CS435.K6 vol. x

17466   TYSON.   A contribution to the history and genealogy of the Tyson and Fitzwater families. Comp. by Samuel Traquair Tyson.   (Los Angeles? Priv. pub.) 1922.   59 p. 23½ cm.   22-18305.

CS71.T985   1922

17467   TYSON.   Tyson and Sugg - Beaufort county, N.C. records, compiled by Sybil Hyatt. Kinston, N.C., 1941.   12 numb. 1. 28 cm.   Caption title.   Type-written.   42-6077.

CS71.T985   1941

17468   TYSON.   Tyson family and collateral lines.   By Alexander Du Bin.   Philadelphia, Historical Publ. Society, 1948.   10 p. 26 cm.   49-19150 *.

CS71.T985   1948

17469   TYSON.   Tyson-Kurtz and allied lines; a genealogical study with biographical notes.   New York, American Historical Company, inc., 1968.   2 v. (739p.) illus., col. coats of arms, facsims., col. geneal. tables, ports. 31 cm.   Contents. - v.1. American lines. - v.2. European lines.   73-8045 MARC.

CS71.T985   1968

TYSON.   See also: HEISEY, 1960
PASTORIUS, 1926
SMITH, 1878a
THOMAS, 1877

17470   TYSSEN.   A forgotten past; being notes of the families of Tyssen, Baker, Hougham, and Milles, of five centuries, by F. H. Suckling.   London, G. Bell & sons, 1898.   viii p., 1 l., 134 p. fold. geneal. tab. 24 cm.   "Books ... consulted": p. (vii)   "The Boddicotts and their kin": p. 52-65.   "The family of Yelloly": p. 78-81, 97-115. "The Yellolys of Cavendish Hall": p. 119-126.   3-7752.

CS439.T93

17471   TYSZKIEWICZ, Wladyslaw.   Z Rozwianej Przeszlosci. New York, 1963.   (Memoires, clippings, works, etc.) In vertical file.   Ask reference librarian for this material.

TYTTERY.   See HENZEY, CS439.H4

TYZACK.   See: HENZEY, CS439.H4
HENZEL, CS439.H4

U

17472   UBALDINI.   Istoria della casa de gli Vbaldini e de' fatti d'alcuni di quella famiglia ... Descritta da Giouambatista di Lorenzo Vbaldini.   E la vita di Niccola Acciaioli, gran siniscalco de' regni di Cicilia, e di Gierusalemme, descritta da Matteo Palmieri.   E l'origine della famiglia de gli Acciaioli; e i fatti de gli huomini famosi d'essa ... Firenze, Stamperia di B. Sermartelli, 1588.
10 p. l., 181 p. incl. illus., double pl., coat of arms. 23 cm. The double plate is numbered as two pages. "La vita di Niccola Acciaioli," translated by Donato Acciaioli, has special t.-p.   46-45132.   CS769.U2   1588

ÜBERCASTEL.   See CASTELBERG, 1959

17473   UHLER.   Genealogy of the Uhler family from the year 1735 to the younger generation.   Compiled by George H. Uhler ... Lebanon, Pa., The Report publishing co., 1901.   2 p. l., 35 p. incl. port.
15 cm. 1-3861.   CS71.U31   1901

17474   UHRBROCK.   The Uhrbrock family of Schleswig-Holstein, Hanover, New York and Maryland.   By Richard Stephen Uhrbrock.   (Athens? Ohio) 1966.   30, (1) l. 29 cm. Bibliographical references included in "Notes"
(leaf 31) 68-3902.   CS71.U34   1966

UJVARI.   In vertical file under PRANKE family.   Ask reference librarian for this material.

17475   ULATHORNE.   The chronicles of an ancient Yorkshire family: the Ullathornes or Ullithornes of Sleningford and some of their descendants, 1450-1960.   By Basil Leonard Kentish.   (Kelvedon, Eng., 1963)   viii, 113 p. illus., facsims., geneal. tables (2 fold.) map, ports. 24 cm. Issued in a folder with pockets for text and for the 2 fold. geneal. tables (Pedigrees I and II) "The main sources of information": p. 112-113. 66-82880.
                                                                                             CS71.U4   1963

ULLE.   See LINTON, 1963

ULLEVIG.   See NAESETH, 1956

ULLITHORNE.   See ULLATHORNE.

ULLRAM.   In vertical file under PRANKE family.   Ask reference librarian for this material.

ULRAM.   In vertical file under PRANKE family.   As reference librarian for this material.

17476   ULRICH.   The Von Reisenkampff-Ulrich family history, Europe and the United States (for use of family only) Compiled by Bartow A. Ulrich ... Chicago, The University printing co., c.1907.
(66) p. incl. illus., ports. 22½ cm. 8-320.   CS71.U45   1907

ULRICH.   See also HOLSINGER, 1959

UMFRAVILLE.   See UMFREVILLE.

17477   UMFREVILLE.   The Umfrevilles: their ancestors and descendants.   (London, Printed at Batten's office, 185-?)   45 p. illus. (coats of arms) 2 fold. geneal. tab. 31½ cm. Pickering pedigree: p. 43. 16-8319.
                                                                                             CS439.U4

UMFREVILLE.   See also HUMFREVILLE.

UMPHRAY.　See ADIE, CS477.S5G7

17478　UNCAPHER.　Ungerfehr, Uncapher, Unkefer, genealogica et biographica;　or, Genealogical notes concerning Martin Ungerfehr and his descendants, separated into two distinct branches, the larger branch being known by the name Uncapher while the smaller one is designated by the name Unkefer.　By Russell Harris Butler ... (n.p., 1925?)　　vi, 453 p. illus. (incl. ports.) 23½ cm. 27-3230.
　　　　　　　　　　　　　　　　　　　　　　　　　　　CS71.U48　　　1925

17479　UNDERHILL.　Underhill society of America.　Annual report.　(Brooklyn? 1894 -
　　v. illus., ports. 17 cm. Title of 2d report: Annual report of the secretary. Report year ends in May or June. CA7-2315 unrev.
　　　　　　　　　　　　　　　　　　　　　　　　　　　CS71.U55　　　1894

17480　UNDERHILL.　Constitution and by-laws of the Underhill society of America.　Organized in Brooklyn, N.Y., June 16, 1892.　Adopted October 7th, 1899.　(Brooklyn? 1899?)　　cover-title, 16 p.
13 cm. 7-30357.　　　　　　　　　　　　　　　　　CS71.U55　　　1899

17481　UNDERHILL.　... Ode to the memory of Captain John Underhill, by Fanny J. Crosby, the blind poet.　Brooklyn, N.Y. city, The Underhill society of America (1902)　　(4) p. 20½ cm. (Underhill society of America　Publication series no. I, October, 1902) 8-18429.　　　CS71.U55　　　1902
　　──　Copy 2　　　　　　　　　　　　　　　　　　E83.63.U58

17482　UNDERHILL.　... The Underhill and Townsend families;　a historical sketch by Hon. Isaac Townsend Smith.　Delivered at the 9th annual meeting of the Underhill society of America, held at Friends' meeting house ... Manhattan, N.Y. city ... May 18th, 1901, being the 271st anniversary of the arrival of Captain John Underhill in the ship "Mary & John," in Boston harbor.　Brooklyn, N.Y. city, Underhill society of America (1904)　　(8) p. 20½ cm. (Underhill society of America Publication series no. 2, October 1904)
Caption title. Additions in manuscript inserted. 5-5120.　　　CS71.U55　　　1904

17483　UNDERHILL.　The Underhill burying ground, an account of a parcel of land situate at Locust Valley, Long Island, New York, deeded by the Matinecock Indians, February twentieth, sixteen hundred and sixty seven, to Captain John Underhill for meritorious service and known as the Underhill burying ground;　compiled by David Harris Underhill and Francis Jay Underhill ... New York, Printed by the Hine publishing company, incorporated, 1826 (i.e. 1926)　　6 p. l., (3) - 79 p., 1 l. front. (map) plates, fold. map (in pocket) facsims. 29 cm. Coat of arms below title. "This edition privately printed ... is limited to five hundred copies. This is no. 32."
28-1550.　　　　　　　　　　　　　　　　　　　　F129.L78U5

17484　UNDERHILL.　Underhill genealogy, edited by Josephine C. Frost ... (New York?) Published privately by M. C. Taylor in the interests of the Underhill society of America, 1932.　4 v. fronts., plates, ports., plans (1 double) maps (1 double) facsims., coats of arms. 24½ cm. 32-11076.　　CS71.U55　　　1932

17485　UNDERHILL.　The Underhills of Warwickshire, their ancestry from the thirteenth century and their descendants in England;　with special reference to Captain John Underhill of the Kenilworth branch, afterwards of Massachusetts and Long island, New York;　an essay in family history, by J. H. Morrison ... Cambridge (Eng.) Priv. print. at the University press, 1932.　xiii, (1), 242 p., 1 l. front., illus. (maps) XXVII pl. (incl. facsims.) on 23 l., geneal. tables (part fold.) 31 cm. Coat of arms on cover. 33-22169.
　　　　　　　　　　　　　　　　　　　　　　　　　　　CS439.U45

17486　UNDERHILL.　John Underhill, captain of New England and New Netherland, by Henry C. Shelley ... New York, London, D. Appleton and company, 1932.　xii p., 1 l., 473 p. front., plates, ports., facsims., coat of arms. 24½ cm. "Only five hundred copies of this book have been printed from type and type distributed." This copy not numbered. 32-11428.　　　　　　　　　　　　　　　　F122.U68

17487　UNDERHILL.　To "Lawland's" ghost return; histories of the Clark, Underhill, Stites, Shepherd and Walker families.　By George Valentine Massey.　(n.p.) 1948.　Microfilm copy of typescript.　Positive. Collation of the original, as determined from the film: v. plates, ports., facsims. Includes bibliographical references. Mic 52-436.
　　　　　　　　　　　　　　　　　　　　　　　　Microfilm CS-8
　　　　　　　　　　　　　　　　　　　　　　Microfilm reading room.

UNDERHILL.　See also:　DUER, E171.A53 vol. 13　　HANMER, 1916
　　　　　　　　　　　　FROST, 1911　　　　　　SHAKESPEARE, PR2916.B3

17488   UNDERWOOD.   The Underwood families of Massachusetts.   (Boston, 1884)   8 p. 24 cm.   Compiled by Lucien Marcus Underwood.   "Reprinted from the N. E. historical and genealogical register for October, 1884." 9-14780.

CS71.U56   1884

17489   UNDERWOOD.   The Underwood families of America, compiled by Lucien Marcus Underwood, ed. by Howard J. Banker ... Lancaster, Pa., Press of The new era printing company, 1913.   2 v. fronts., plates, ports., col. coats of arms, geneal. tab.   23½ cm.   4 blank leaves for "Family records" inserted between p. 683 and 685 of v. 2.   14-4210.

CS71.U56   1913

17490   UNDERWOOD.   Notes regarding a branch of the Underwood family, by William Lawrence Underwood ... N(ew) Y(ork) R. T. Voss, 1917.   18, (2) p. front. (port.) col. coat of arms. 24 cm.   "Authorities regarding the families of Underwood": 1 p. at end. 17-10579.

CS71.U56   1917

17491   UNDERWOOD.   Antecedents and descendants of Levi Underwood, 1831-1885, and related families, by Dale C. Kellogg.   Elyria, Ohio, 1965.   105 p. illus., geneal. table, maps, ports. 23 cm. Bibliography: p. 83.   66-3072.

CS71.U56   1965

UNDERWOOD.   See also HILDRETH, 1950

UNGERFEHR.   See UNCAPHER.

UNKEFER.   See UNCAPHER.

17492   UNRAU.   The Rev. Peter Unrau genealogy, 1824-1969.   Compiled by Mr. and Mrs. Heary S. Goertzen and Katie Wedel.   (Newton? Kan., 1969)   iv, 159 p. illus., facsims., map, port. 30 cm. 76-7413 MARC.

CS71.U58   1969

17493   UNRUH.   The Peter Unruh genealogy beginning with Unrau born about 1675 ... (By Peter Unrau Schmidt) (Newton, Kan., Herold publishing co.) 1941.   128 p. 20 cm. Preface signed: P. U. Schmidt.   41-25190.

CS71.U6   1941

UNRUH.   See also: DECKER, 1959
SCHMIDT, 1962

UNTHANK.   See ONTHANK.

17494   UNTON.   The Unton inventories, relating to Wadley and Faringdon, co. Berks., in the years 1596 and 1620, from the originals in the possession of Earl Ferrers.   With a memoir of the family of Unton, by John Gough Nichols ... London, Printed for the Berkshire Ashmolean society, by J. B. Nichols and son, 1841.   lxxxviii, 56 p. 22½ x 17½ cm. 3-9288.

CS439.U5

17495   UNWIN.   Notes on the Unwin family, by J. D. Unwin.   London, G. Allen and Unwin ltd. (1934)   3 p. l., 9-45 p. 20 cm.   "The four of us, undersigned, are interested in the antiquities of the Unwin family, and have formed ourselves into a committee for the collection ... and private publication of the available data ... Joseph D. Unwin, Reginald Jennings, Philip L. Unwin, Stanley Unwin." - Foreword. 35-13715.

CS439.U55   1934

UPDIKE.   See OPDYKE, 1889

UPFOLD.   See PETTITT, 1936

17496   UPHAM.   Family history.   Notices of the life of John Upham, the first inhabitant of New England who bore that name: together with an account of such of his descendants as were the ancestors of Hon. Nathaniel Upham ... With a short sketch of the life of the latter.   By Albert G. Upham ... Concord, N. H., Printed by A. McFarland, 1845.   xi, (5)-92 p. 19 cm. 9-14783.

CS71.U67   1845

17497   UPHAM.   Genealogy and family history of a branch of the New England Upham family, settled in California, showing the ancestors of Isaac Upham, of San Francisco, and others.   (By) F. K. Upham.   (n. p.) Pub. for private circulation, 1884.   17 p., 1 l. 19½ cm. 9-14781.   CS71.U67   1884

17498   UPHAM.   Genealogy and family history of the Uphams, of Castine, Maine, and Dixon, Illinois, with genealogical notes of Brooks, Kidder, Perkins, Cutler, Ware, Avery, Curtis, Little, Warren, Southworth, and other families.   Compiled by F. K. Upham ... (Newark, N.J., Advertiser printing house) Printed for private circulation, 1887.   iv, (5)-68 p.   24 cm.   9-14782.
CS71.U67   1887

17499   UPHAM.   Upham genealogy.   The descendants of John Upham, of Massachusetts, who came from England in 1635, and lived in Weymouth and Malden.   Embracing over five hundred heads of families, extending into the tenth generation.   By F. K. Upham.   Albany, N.Y., J. Munsell's sons, 1892.   573 p. illus., plates, ports., facsim. 25½ cm. 9-14784.   CS71.U67   1892

17500   UPHAM.   Upham and Amherst, N.H., memories; the genealogy and history of a branch of the Upham family ... By Mrs. Mary Upham Kelley and Warren Upham.   (n.p.) Priv. print., 1897.
66 p. 23½ cm. 18-2448.   CS71.U67   1897

UPHAM.   See also DODGE, 1925

UPMANN.   See MOULTON, 1922

UPPLEBY.   See WILSON, 1890

17501   UPSALL.   Nicholas Upsall.   By Augustine Jones ... Reprinted from the New England historical and genealogical register for January, 1880.   Boston, Press of D. Clapp & son, 1880.   12 p. front.
26 cm. 19-13178.   F67U68

17502   UPSHER.   Upshur family in Virginia.   By John Andrews Upshur.   Richmond, Dietz Press, 1955.   xiii, 221 p. illus., ports., maps (on lining papers) geneal. table. 24 cm. Bibliographical footnotes. 56-283.
CS71.U68   1955

17503   UPSON.   The Upson family in America, compiled by the Upson family association of America.   New Haven, Conn., The Tuttle, Morehouse & Taylor company, 1940.   vi p., 1 l., 624 p. front., plates. 24 cm.
41-380.   CS71.U69   1940

17504   UPSON.   Directory of the Upson association of America.   (n.p., 1940)   19 p. 23 cm. 41-38347.
CS71.U69   1940a

UPSON.   See also WELTON, 1948

17505   UPTON.   The Upton memorial.   A genealogical record of the descendants of John Upton, of North Reading, Mass. ... together with short genealogies of the Putnam, Stone and Bruce families.   By John Adams Vinton ... Bath, Me., Printed for private use at the office of E. Upton & son, 1874.
viii p., 1 l., 547 p. illus., ports. 24 cm. 9-14785.   CS71.U71   1874

17506   UPTON.   Officers and constitution of the Upton family association.   (n.p., 1889?)
7 p. 22 cm. Caption title. 24-20326.   CS71.U71   1889

17507   UPTON.   Upton family records: being genealogical collections for an Upton family history.   By William Henry Upton ... Privately printed.   London, Mitchell and Hughes, 1893.   xiv p., 1 l., 518 p.
col. front., geneal. tables, coats of arms. 28½ cm. 9-15478.   CS71.U71   1893

17508   UPTON.   The Upton family, 1735-1964, of Upton, Kentucky.   By James Southerland Upton.   Conway, Ark., 1964.   44 l. coat of arms. 28 cm. 65-71310.   CS71.U71   1964

17509   UPWOOD.   Pedigree of the family of Upwood, of Lovell's hall, Terrington St. Clement's, co. Norfolk.   Comp. by Rev. C. R. Manning ... (London) Priv. print., 1891.   17 p. illus. (coat of arms) facsims.
29 cm. Published also in "Miscellanea genealogica et heraldica." London, 1892, 2d ser., vol. IV. 20-15238.   CS439.U6

17510   URAN.   The Urann family of New England including the descendants of Margaret (Urann) Gammell.   By Charles Collyer Whittier ... Boston, Press of D. Clapp & son, 1910.   59 p. 25 cm. Reprinted, with additions from the New Eng. hist. and geneal. register for Jan. and April, 1910. 10-16182.   CS71.U76   1910

URANN.   See URAN.

UREN.   See URAN.

URIN.   See URAN.

17511   URLIN.   Memorials of the Urlin family, comp. from original unpublished documents by Ethel L. H. Urlin, with pedigrees of all the well-known branches of the family, traced and prepared by Perceval Lucas.   Privately printed.   (n. p.) 1909.   94 p. 6 fold. geneal. tab. 26 cm. 15-13922.
CS439.U7

URLSPERGER.   See GÜNTHER, CS629.G8

17512   URNER.   Genealogy of the Urner family and sketch of the Coventry Brethren church in Chester county, Pennsylvania.   By Isaac N. Urner ... Philadelphia, Printed by J. B. Lippincott company, 1893. 179 p. front., plates, port. 25½ cm. The sketch of Coventry church was published separately in 1898. 9-14786.   CS71.U78   1893

17513   URQUART.   The works of Sir Thomas Urquhart of Cromarty, knight.   Reprinted from the original editions.   Edinburgh, 1834.   5 p. l., xxii, 419, (1) p. pl., 2 port. 26½ x 21½ cm. (Maitland club. Publications. no. 30) Title vignette. With reproductions of the original title-pages. 92 copies printed, some on large paper. Edited by Thomas Maitland; presented to the club by S. D. Stirling. Contents. -   ... A peculiar promptuary of time ... deducing the true pedigree and lineal descent of the ... Urquharts, in the house of Cromartie, since the creation of the world ... London, 1652. ...   18-14170.   DA750.M3 no. 30

17514   URQUHART.   Sir Thomas Urquhart of Cromartie, knight.   By John Willcock ... Edinburgh & London, Oliphant, Anderson & Ferrier, 1899.   xvi, 251 p. front., pl., port., facsim. 20½ cm. Title enclosed in ornamental border. Appendices: I. Primitve fathers and mothers of the name of Urquhart. - II. The admirable Crichton. 2-9166.
PR3736.U6W5

17515   URQUHART.   History of the family of Urquhart, by Henrietta Tayler.   Abderdeen, The University press, 1946.   vii, 304 p. illus., plates, ports., coat of arms. 25 cm. Bibliographical foot-notes. 47-15319.
CS479.U7   1946

17516   URSWICK.   Records of the family of Urswyk, Urswick, or Urwick, comp. by the late Thomas A. Urwick.   Edited by the Rev. William Urwick ... With illustrations by W. H. Urwick ... (St. Albans) Printed for private circulation by Gibbs & Banforth, the St. Albans press, 1893.   vi p., 1 l., 226 p. front., plates, coat of arms, IV geneal. tab. 22½ cm. 15-22637.   CS439.U75

17517   USHER.   A brief genealogy of the Usher family of New England.   By W. H. Whitmore.   Reprinted, with additions, from the New-England historical and genealogical register for Oct., 1869. Boston, D. Clapp & son, 1869.   1 p. l., 11 p. 24 cm. 9-14787.   CS71.U85   1869

17518   USHER.   The Ussher memoirs; or, Genealogical memoirs of the Ussher families in Ireland (with appendix, pedigree and index of names), comp. from public and private sources.   By Rev. Wm. Ball Wright ... Dublin, Sealy, Bryers & Walker; (etc., etc.) 1889.   3 p. l., xi, 306, (1) p. front., plates, coats of arms (part col.) 22 cm. Appendix XI, "Genealogy of the family of Ussher, as given by Sir William Betham, Ulster king of arms. With additions and corrections": p. 281-295. 15-6734.   CS499.U8W7

17519   USHER.   A memorial sketch of Roland Greene Usher, 1823-1895, by his son, Edward Preston Usher, to which is added a genealogy of the Usher family in New England from 1638 to 1895.   (Boston) Priv. print. for the family (Press of N. Sawyer & son)   160 p. front. (port.) 23½ cm. 8-811.
CS71.U85   1895

17520   USHER.   A short biographical sketch of Ellis Baker Usher of Hollis, Maine, by his grandson Ellis Baker Usher of La Crosse, Wis.   (n.p.) Priv. print., 1902.   14 p. front. (port.) 21½ cm. 2-15494.
CS71.U85   1902
Office.

17521   USHER.   In memoriam Adela Louise Usher, 1852-1922 ... Grafton, Mass., Priv. print., 1923. 39 p. incl. front., ports. 23½ cm. Compiled by her husband Edward P. Usher. "The ancestry and descendants of Mrs. Usher": p. 9-13. 27-726.
CS71.U85   1923

USHER.   See also: McKAY, 1955
                    PATE, 19 -

USILTON.   See USSELTON.

17522   USSELTON.   William Usilton of Kent county, Maryland (?-1729) and some of his descendants. (Chestertown, Md., c.1938)   cover-title, 31 p. 21 cm. "Compiled by Miss Sarah Elisabeth Stuart, of Chestertown, Maryland." - p. 31. 38-25121.   CS71.U87   1938

USSHER.   See USHER.

UTIE.   See No. 430 - Adventurers of purse and person.

UTTENHOVEN.   See UTTENHOFEN.

17523   UTTER.   Nicholas Utter of Westerly, Rhode Island, and a few of his descendants, by Katharine M. Utter Waterman ... and George B. and Wilfred B. Utter ... Westerly, R. I., The Utter company, printers, 1941.   4 p. l., (13)-176 p. front., pl., map, fold. geneal. tab. 24½ cm. 42-15372 rev.
                                                                        CS71.U89   1941

17524   UTTERBACK.   The history and genealogy of the Utterback family in America, 1622-1937, by William I. Utterback ... Huntington, W. Va., Gentry bros. printing company, 1937.   4 p. l., vii-ix, 470, (8) p. front., illus., plates, ports., facsims. 24 cm. Blank pages for "Family record" (8 at end) "Bibliography": p. 428-429. 38-36160.
                                                                        CS71.U9   1937

17525   UVEDALE.   Notices of the family of Uvedale of Titsey, Surrey, and Wickham, Hants.   By Granville Leveson Gower, M.P.   London, Cox & Wyman, printers, 1865.   132 p. incl. illus., geneal. tab. plates (part fold.) 21½ cm. Reprinted from the Surrey archaeological collections. 2-30571.
                                                                        CS439.U8

UZZELL.   See MAXWELL, 1916

V

17527   VAANDRAGER.   Genealogie van het geslacht Vaandrager.   By H. Barendregt.   (Rotterdam, 1955)   59 p. coat of arms, geneal. table. 19 cm. 56-21798.   CS829.V22   1955

17528   VACHELL.   A short account, or history of the family of Vachell.   By Ivor Vachell, B. A., and Arthur Cadogan Vachell.   Printed for private circulation among the members and connections of the family.   Cardiff, W. Lewis, printer, 1900.   1 p. l., 154 p. front., plates, facsim., coats of arms (part col.) 22½ cm. Vachell pedigree: p. 146-154. 16-2831.   CS439.V2

VADAKIN.   See TODD family in vertical file.   Ask reference librarian for this material.

VAH'N.   See STREYNSHAM, 1879

17529   VAIL.   Vail and Armstrong.   A short record of my ancestors beginning with John Vail, Southold, L. I. 1670-1760.   Francis Armstrong (from Ireland) 1727 - with a reference to the L'Hommedieu family, by Charles M. Vail.   Goshen, N. Y. (E. D. Croker & sons, printers) 1894. 57 p. front., facsim. 24 cm. 10-8905.   CS71.V129   1894

17530   VAIL.   Genealogy of some of the Vail family descended from Jermiah Vail at Salem, Mass., 1639 ... New York (The De Vinne press) 1902.   371, (1) p. incl. illus., facsim. 4 pl., map. 26 cm. Preface signed: Henry H. Vail. 3-17938.   CS71.V129   1902

17531   VAIL   A genealogy of the Vale and Garretson descendants; family records with biographical and historical records; by Lydia Anne Vale Leffler.   Ames, Ia., 1913.   2 p. l., (7)-194 p. 24½ cm. 16-5990.   CS71.V129   1913

17532   VAIL.   If a house could talk; being a history of a flood of released recollections, the resurrection of old letters and photographs pertaining to Litchfield and the Vaill homestead covering a past dating from 1867 to 1876 in which I was vitally interested, an unbridged past dating from 1876 to 1915, an interim of two years, when by some strange decreee of fate it was ordained that I should spend the summer months close by the spot on which Julia last tread the earth, and where her soul took flight, a fitting atmosphere in which to gather these stray leaves within the confines of these covers to the memory of Julia and for "auld lang syne," by Cora Smith Gould.   New York, Priv. print. by Rogers & company, inc., c. 1917.   93 p. front., plates, ports. 23 cm. 17-28463.   F104.L7G6

17533   VAIL.   Ancestors and descendants of Edwin Bishop Vail.   Privately published.   (Binghamton, N. Y.) 1918.   cover-title, 31 p. 25½ cm. Foreword signed: M. D. Vail. 19-7391.   CS71.V129   1918

17534   VAIL.   Genealogy of some of the Vail family descended from Thomas Vail at Salem, Massachusetts, 1640, together with collateral lines, by Wm. Penn Vail, M. D.   (Charleston, S. C., Presses of Walker, Evans & Cogswell company) 1937.   6 p. l., 3-592, 14 p. illus. (incl. ports., map, facsims., coats of arms) 22½ cm. Blank pages for "Addenda" (14 at end) Label mounted on lining-paper signed by the author. Copy no. 127. "Authorites": 4th-5th prelim. leaves. 38-794. (Copy 2 - No. 128)   CS71.V129   1937

17535   VAIL.   Moses Vail of Huntington, L. I., showing his descent from Joseph (2) Vail, son of Thomas Vail, at Salem, Massachusetts, 1640, together with collateral lines and with additions and corrections to both H. H. Vail's Jeremiah Vail family, pub. 1902, with his authorization, and to my compilation Thomas Vail - Salem 1640, pub. 1937. (Blairstown? N. J.) 1947.   524 p. illus., port., coat of arms. 23 cm. 49-19188*.   CS71.V129   1947

VAIL. See also: GRIFFIN, F129.S74G8
HOLBROOK, F1.N56 vol. 58
SEARS, 1901
SEELEY, 1914

VALE. See VAIL.

17536 VALENTINE. The Valentines in America 1644-1874. By T. W. Valentine ... New York, Clark & Maynard, 1874. iv p., 1 l., 248 p. front., plates, ports., map. 23 cm. 9-14788.

CS71.V158   1874

17537 VALENTINE. The Edward Pleasants Valentine papers, abstracts of records in the local and general archives of Virginia relating to the families of Allen, Bacon, Ballard, Batchelder, Blouet, Brassieur (Brashear) Cary, Crenshaw, Dabney, Exum, Ferris, Fontaine, Gray, Hardy, Isham (Henrico County) Jordan, Langston, Lyddall, Mann. Mosby, Palmer, Pasteur, Pleasants, Povall, Randolph, Satterwhite, Scott, Smith (the family of Francis Smith of Hanover County) Valentine, Waddy, Watts, Winston, Womack, Woodson ... Richmond, Va., The Valentine museum (1927) 4 v. illus. 23½ cm. Paged continuously. "The abstracts of wills, deeds and court orders ... now published ... are from the files of family papers bequeathed to the Valentine museum by the late Edward Pleasants Valentine ..." - Pref. Edited by Clayton Torrence. cf. Pref. Contents. - v.1. Allen-Gray. - v.2. Hardy-Pleasants. - v.3. Povall-Woodson. - v.4. Valentine and Smith, genealogical tables, bibliographical note, index. 29-15864.

F225.V17
Microfilm 19868

17538 VALENTINE. John Valentine, progenitor of the Valentine family in New England and a man of mark in Boston, by William Valentine Alexander. (Rutland, Vt., Priv. print. by the Tuttle publishing company, inc., c.1937) 65, (1) p. front., illus., plates, plan, facsim. 22½ cm. "Only one hundred copies of this book have been published, this one being number 64." 37-2556. F73.4.V29

17539 VALENTINE. Family records of John Jackson Valentine. (Memphis? Tenn., 1957) unpaged. 29 cm. 58-45116. CS71.V158   1957

17540 VALENTINE. Valentine military records. By Annie (Walker) Burns. Washington, L. H. Walker (1960?) 39 l. 28 cm. 60-35389. CS71.V158   1960

VALENTINE. See also: HARRIS, 1920
READ, 193-

17541 VALEUR. Chart, in vertical file. Ask reference librarian for this material.

VALIENTE. See SÁENZ.

17542 VALLÉ. Notes on the genealogy of the Vallé family. By Mary Louise Dalton. (In Missouri historical society. Collections. St. Louis, 1906. 24½ cm. vol. II, no. 7, p.54-82) 27-8371. F461.M66 vol. 2
——— Copy 2, separate. CS71.V181   1906

VALLE. See also PEOXOTO.

VALLEAU. See FAULKNER, 1911

17543 VALLEJO. The Vallejos of California. By Madie Brown Empáran. (San Francisco) Gleeson Library Associates, University of San Francisco, 1968. 464 p. ports. 27 cm. Bibliography: p. (449-451) 68-56147. CS71.V183   1968

17544 VALLETTE. See BRONSDON, 1902

17545 VALLGORNERA. Genealogías de la casa de Vallgornera. By José Gramunt y Subiela. Tarragona, 1942. 35 l. col. coat of arms, geneal. tables. 36 cm. "Bibliografía": leaf 34. 47-42473 *. CS959.V35G7

17546   VALLIANT.   Certain descendants of Robert Spencer Valliant and his wife Martha Hurlock through their eldest child, James Valliant (1795-1838) and his wife, Margaret Thompson.   By Elise Denison Brown Lane.   San Antonio, 1953.   unpaged.   28 cm.   54-31330.   CS71.V185   1953

17547   VALLON.   ... William Wordsworth and Annette Vallon.   London & Toronto, J. M. Dent & sons ltd. ;   New York, E. P. Dutton & co., 1922.   xiv, 146 p.   front., ports., facsims.   19 cm.   At head of title: Emile Legouis.   "Genealogy of the Vallons": p. 123.   23-9278.   PR5882.L55

17548   VALOIS.   Saint Joan of Arc; born January 6th 1412, burned as a heretic, May 30th, 1431, canonised as a saint, May 16th, 1920.   (By) V. Sackville-West.   London, Cobden-Sanderson (1936)
xiii, 436 p.   front., plates, ports., maps (1 fold.) facsims., geneal. tab.   22 cm.   "A short bibliography": p. 421-424.   36-18599.
DC103.S115   1936

17549   VAN ALEN.   Genealogical history of the Van Alen family, embracing a record of births, marriages and deaths, also biographical sketches ... (By Benjamin Taylor Van Alen)   Chicago, 1902.
42 p. incl. illus.   (incl. ports., facsims.)   coat of arms.   27 cm.   5-26501 rev.   CS71.V217   1902

17550   VAN ALSTINE.   Lambert Janse Van Alstyne and some of his descendants.   By one of them.   Amenia, N.Y., Walsh & Griffen, printers, 1897.   142 p.   24½ cm.   Introduction signed: Lawrence Van Alstyne.   9-14789.
CS71.V218   1897

VAN ALSTYNE.   See ROOSEVELT, 1902

17551   VAN ANDEN.   Van Anden family.   By Paul Wesley Prindle.   (Darien, Conn., 1951)
13, 7, (1) l.   36 cm.   Caption title.   "References": leaf (8) at end.   52-26999.   CS71.V2183   1951

VAN ARKEL.   See ARKEL.

VAN ARSDALE.   See CROW, 1961

VAN BAAL.   See REICHNER, 1918

17552   VAN BENSCHOTEN.   Concerning the Van Bunschoten or Van Benschoten family in America;   a genealogy and brief history ... The labors of William Henry Van Benschoten, West Park-on-Hudson, N.Y.   (Poughkeepsie, N.Y., The A. V. Haight co., printers) 1907.   lx, 813 p.   front., pl., ports.   26½ cm.
8-5840.   CS71.V219   1907

17553   VAN BENTHUYSEN.   The Van Benthuysen genealogy, also genealogies of the Seaward, Zwahlen, Weiss, Conklin, Obee and Dally families, and ancestry of Everett Seaward Van Benthuysen.   Brooklyn, 1926.   259 p.   31 cm.   Typewritten (carbon copy)   49-37038*.   CS71.V2194   1926

17554   VAN BENTHUYSEN.   The Van Benthuysen genealogy; descendants of Paulus Martense Van Benthuysen, of Bethuizen, Holland, who settled in Albany, N.Y., male and female lines; also, genealogies of certain branches of the Bleecker, Conde, DeForest, Lansing, Myer, Turk, Truex, Van Buren, Van Epps, Van Patten, Van Slyck, and other families of Dutch and Huguenot origin in New York, by Alvin Seaward Van Benthuysen and Edith M. McIntosh Hall.   Clay Center, Kan., Wilson Engraving and Print. Co., 1953.   592 p.   22 cm.   53-22742.   CS71.V2194   1953

VANBERG.   See No. 553 - Goodhue county.

VAN BIBBER.   See: BOONE, 1922
                           MEIGS, 1906

VAN BORSSELEN.   See VAN DER VEER, CS819.V3

17555   VAN BRUNT.   Genealogy of the Van Brunt family, 1653-1867.   By Teunis G. Bergen ...
Albany, J. Munsell, 1867.   vi p., 1 l., 79 p.   23½ cm.   9-14792.   CS71.V22   1867

VAN BRUNT.   See also: BERGEN, 1866
                               STONE, 1964

VAN BUNSCHOTEN.   See VAN BENSCHOTEN.

17556   VAN BUREN.   History of Cornelis Maessen Van Buren who came from Holland to the New Netherlands in 1631, and his descendants, including the genealogy of the family of Bloomingdale who are descended from Maas, a son of Cornelis Maessen.   By Harriett C. Waite Van Buren Peckham ... New York, T. A. Wright, 1913.   431 p. front. (col. coat of arms) plates, ports. 24½ cm. 14-12259.
CS71.V2214   1913

17557   VAN BUREN.   Cheney Garrett Van Buren and his family; a presentation of their lives and times as seen through the eyes and the heart of one great-granddaughter.   By Virginia (Christensen) Keeler.   Provo, Utah, J. G. Stevenson, c.1962.   459 p. illus. 25 cm. 63-30224.
CS71.V2214   1962

VAN BUREN.   See also DAWSON, 1874a

17558   VAN BUSKIRK.   The Van Buskirk family of Buskirk, Rensselaer County, New York, ed. by Milton Thomas.   Troy, N. Y., 1922.   3 p. l., 7 p. 28 cm. Type-written. "Eight numbered and signed copies ... This is copy no. 1."   First six generations (p. 1-3) taken from a manuscript, "The colonial ancestry of Miss Sarah Thurman of Troy, N. Y.", by Horace E. Mather. 23-13951.
CS71.V2217   1922

VAN BUSKIRK.   See also SYRON, 1925

VAN BUSSUM.   See OUTWATER, 1924

17559   VAN CATS.   The Van Cats family in the Netherlands and in New Netherland.   1060 - 1660. From a research made in Holland for Florence E. Youngs.   (n. p., 1936)   1 p. l., 30 numb. l. coat of arms. 29 cm. Type-written. 36-22550.
CS829.V24Y6

17560   VANCE.   An account, historical and genealogical, from the earliest days till the present time, of the family of Vance in Ireland, Vans in Scotland, anciently Vaux in Scotland and England, and originally de Vaux in France (Latin De Vallibus)   By William Balbirnie.   Printed solely for the use of the Vance family.   Cork, J. W. Noblett, 1860.   vii, (9)-70, 14 p. 22 cm. Photostat copy. (positive) "An historical and genealogical account of the family of Balbirnie, chiefly of the descendants of the Balbirnies of Inveryghty, in Forfarshire": 14 p. at end. 26-3112.
CS499.V3   1860
(and 1908)

17561   VANCE.   ... Vance family notes, also something of the allied lines of Waters, Harper, Demoss and others.   (By Mrs. Alice (Vance) Robinson.   (Seattle, Wash. 1940)   59 l. 28½ cm. Type-written and in manuscript.   Material collected by Mrs. Robinson for a history of the Vance family.   41M3598T.
CS71.V2218   1940

17562   VANCE.   The rich heritage; being the story of Harry and Annie Vance, their children, families, and ancestors.   By Joseph Harvey Vance.   (Lombard, Ill.) 1957.   74 p. illus., ports., coat of arms (on cover) geneal. tables. 28 cm. 57-36837.
CS71.V2218   1957

VANCE.   See also L. C. Additions and corrections no. 22

VANCE.   See also: GREGORY, 1937
                    HOGG, 1921
                    PUCKETT, 1960
                    No. 516 - Notable southern families, vol. 2.

17563   VAN CLEEF.   History of Jan Van Cleef of New Utrech, L. I., N. Y.   (1659) and some of his descendants, by Murray Edward Poole, D. C. L., LL. D.   (Ithaca) Press of the Ithaca journal, 1909.   (14) p. 23½ cm. 9-10023.
CS71.V222   1909

17563a   VAN CLEVE.   Van Cleve family by G. G. Wisda.   Page 258.   CS71.G6758   1940

VAN CLEVE.   See also BOONE, 1922

VAN CORTLAND.   See CONSTANT, 1903

17564   VAN CORTLANDT.   The Van Cortlandt manor; anonymous address read by the late Mrs. James Marsland Lawton, president-general of the Order of colonial lords of manors in America, at the sixth annual meeting of the New York branch held in the city of New York, January 26, 1918. Baltimore, 1920.   27 p. incl. front., illus., plates, ports.   23½ cm.   (Order of colonial lords of manors in America.   New York branch.   Publications.)
Plates and portraits printed on both sides.   20-16024.   E186.99.O6N5 No.6
—— Copy 2.   F127.W5V22

17565   VAN CORTLANDT.   The Van Cortlandt family, by L. Effingham De Forest ... New York, The Historical publication society (c. 1930)   (33) p. illus.   26 cm.   "Prepared as an example of the articles to be included in the series of volumes entitled The old New York families, which will be prepared under the editorial supervision of L. Effingham de Forest and published by the Historical publication society." Bibliography: p. (31-33) 31-4086.   CS71.V224   1930

VAN CORTLANDT.   See also: CONSTANT, 1903
WHITE, 1877

17566   VAN COTT.   Van Cott pioneers of Utah; an historical, biographical and genealogical account of the Losee and Lovina Pratt Van Cott family of Canaan, New York, and the westward migration of their progenitors and descendants.   Compiled by Arthur D. Cleman.   Provo, Utah, J. G. Stevenson (1967)
xii, 269 p. illus., coat of arms, maps, ports.   25 cm.   67-26230.   CS71.V226   1967

17567   VAN COUWENHOVEN.   The Van Couwenhoven family in the Netherlands and in New Netherland, 1440-1630, compiled by Florence E. Youngs and L. P. De Boer.   (n.p., 1935?)   1 p. l., 31 numb. l.
5 coats of arms on 1 pl.   29½ cm.   Type-written.   35-16216.   CS829.V26   1935

VAN CULEMBORG.   See: CULENBURG, CS829.C8
JAQUETT, 1922

VAN DAM.   See SMITH, 1962

17568   VANDENBARK.   History of the Vandenbark family, by Isa D. Reed and Helen Vandenbark. Chico, Calif., 1969.   xiii, 414 p. illus., maps, ports.   24 cm.   Pages 410-414 blank for "Notes."   Includes bibliographical references.
79-8076 MARC.   CS71.V227   1969

VAN DER BEECK.   See DE RAPELJE, 1948

17569   VANDERBILT.   The Vanderbilts and the story of their fortune.   By W. A. Croffut ... Chicago and New York, Belford, Clarke & company (1886)   xii, 310 p. front., plates, ports.   20 cm.   9-14793.
CS71.V228   1886

17570   VANDERBILT.   The Vanderbilt legend; the story of the Vanderbilt family, 1794-1940, by Wayne Andrews.   New York, Harcourt, Brace and company (c. 1941)   x, 454 p. front., 1 illus., plates, ports., fold. geneal. tab.   22 cm.   "First edition."   Bibliography: p. 413-422.   41-1648.   CS71.V228   1941

17571   VANDERBILT.   The Vanderbilts and their fortunes.   By Edwin Palmer Hoyt.   (1st ed.) Garden City, N.Y., Doubleday, 1962.   434 p.   25 cm.   62-7647.   CS71.V228   1962

VANDERBILT.   See also: BERGEN, 1866
BLAUVELT, 1957

17572   VANDERBURGH.   The family of Richard Vanderburgh of Richmond Hill (1797-1869)   Compiled by Wallace McLeod.   (London, Ont.) 1962.   ii, 32 l. 28 cm.   Supplement (8 p.) issued in Toronto, 1964, inserted at end.   65-48680.   CS71.V2282   1962

VANDERBURGH.   See also PALMER, 1959

17573   VANDERCOOK.   Vandercook-Jans, genealogical records in Holland and America, compiled by Mrs. Emma Elisabeth (Teall) Dunn ... (Los Angeles, Calif.) Gem publishing company, 1926.   15 p. front. (port.) 22½ cm.   Three blank pages at end for more "Genealogical records."   Printed slips of "Errata and additions" inserted and some corrections in manuscript.   27-11115.   CS71.V2283   1926

VANDERCOOK. See also: DWELLE, 1935
NEIKIRK, 1960

VAN DER HOVEN. See SNYDER, 1958

17574   VANDERLIP.   The Vanderlip, Van Derlip, Vander Lippe family in America; also including some account of the Von Der Lippe family of Lippe, Germany, from which the Norwegian, Dutch and American lines have their descent, comp. by Charles Edwin Booth ... New York, Pub. priv. (Press of L. Middleditch co.) 1914.   vi, 188 p. front. (port.) 23½ cm. 14-21773.

CS71.V2285   1914

17575   VAN DER MARK.   Van de Mark of Van der Mark ancestry. Part I. Europe, 700 A.D. to 1700 A.D. Part II. America, 1665 A.D. to 1942 A.D.   Compiled by John W. Van Demark, Walter B. Van Dermark, Kate Koon Bovey, Loretta M. Hauser (and) Clarence E. Hauser ... Minneapolis, K. K. Bovey, 1942.   4 p. 1., 7-394 p., 3 1. plates, ports., map, facsim., fold. geneal. tables. 24 cm. Three pages at end blank for "Births," "Marriages," "Deaths." Bibliography: p. 87-88, 335-336. 42-20201.   CS71.V229   1942

17576   VANDERPOEL.   Genealogy of the Vanderpoel family; with items of personal, plitical and social interest.   New York, Charles Francis press, 1912.   2 p. 1., (iii)-xix p., 1 1., (23)-731 p. illus., plates, ports., facsims. (part fold.) fold. plan, fold. geneal. tab., 2 col. coats of arms. 25 cm. 13-25974.   CS71.V23   1912

VANDERPOEL.   See also WALDRON, 1910

17577   VANDERPOOL.   Vanderpool family in vertical file.   Ask reference librarian for this material.

VANDERPOOL.   See also No. 3888 - Twigs from family trees.

17578   VANDERPYL.   Genealogical sketch of the families of Adrian and Lena (Morarty) Vanderpyl of Worcester, Massachusetts.   (With notes on the families of McIntosh, Case, Cooley, Leach, Bowman, Morarty and Smith) By Robert Adrian Vanderpyl.   Chicago, 1933.   cover-title, 2 p. 1., 20, (17) p., 6 fold. 1. ports. (incl. mounted photos.) VIII fold. geneal. tab. 20½ cm. Mimeographed. Additions and corrections in manuscript throughout text. Table IV is missing. 34-2753.   CS71.V233   1933

17579   VANDERPYL.   The family of van der Pyl in America (with notes on the antecedents of Casalena Morarty Van der Pyl, of Worcester, Massachusetts.) (By) Robert Adrian Van der Pyl.   Chicago (Lithoprinted by Edwards brothers, inc.) 1939 (i.e. 1946)   vii, 77 p. incl. front., illus. (coat of arms) ports., fold. geneal. tab. 23 cm. 47-2511.   CS71.V233   1946

VANDERSAAL.   See HEINECKE, 1881

17580   VANDERSLICE.   Van der Slice and allied families, compiled by Howard Vanderslice and Howard Norman Monnett.   (Los Angeles, Printed by the Neuner corporation, c.1931)   3 p. 1., 9-287, (16) p. illus. (maps) plates, ports., facsims. 20 cm. 31-30925.   CS71.C237   1931

17581   VANDERSLOOT.   History and genealogy of the Von der Sloot family; a comprehensive record of genealogical data and biographical and historical information, chronologically arranged, of members of the Vandersloot family; properly authenticated, and compiled with utmost care, by Lewis Vandersloot ... (Harrisburg? Pa., 1901)   68 (3) p. illus., tab. 31½ cm. 2-6242.   CS71.V24   1901

17582   VAN DER VEER.   The Van der Veer family in the Netherlands, 1150 to 1660, and 1280 to 1780, by Louis P. De Boer ... Brooklyn, N.Y., C.A. Ditmas (c. 1913)   4 p. 1., 62 p. front. (ports.) plates, map, geneal. tab., coat of arms. 24½ cm. "This edition, on fine paper, is limited to 125 copies. This is no. 25." Contents. - Introduction. - The Van Borsselen family. - The Van der Veer family. - Appendix I: Armoiries de la famille Van der Veer. - Appendix II: Direct male line of Pieter Corneliszen Van der Veer and of Cornelis Janszen Van der Veer, American progenitors. 14-310.   CS829.V3

17583   VAN DER VEER.   Vanderveer, by Lester Dunbar Mapes.   (Brooklyn? 1943?)   15 1. 35½ x 21½ cm. Caption title. Leaves variously numbered, reproduced from type-written copy. Additions and corrections in manuscript. Includes bibliographies. 44-2009.   CS71.V242   1943

VAN DER VEER.   See also BERGEN, 1866

VANDERVOORT.   See HALSEY, 1927

17584   VAN DER WERKEN.   The Van Derwerken - Van Derwerker family.   Compiled by Paul W. Prindle.   Johnstown, N.Y., Baronet Litho Co., 1966 (c.1967)   i, 370 p. illus., ports. (part col.) 24 cm. 67-2139.
CS71.V2218   1967

17585   VAN DERWERKER.   See VANDER WERKEN.

17586   VAN DEUSEN.   The history and genealogy of the Van Deusens of Van Deusen manor, Great Barrington, Berkshire County, Massachusetts.   By Louis Hasbrouck Sahler.   (Great Barrington, Berkshire courier company, 1893)   36 p. 22½ cm. 2-5328.
CS71.V243   1893

17587   VAN DEUSEN.   Abraham Van Deusen and many of his descendants, with biographical notes, 1635-1901.   By Charles B. Benson.   (New York, The De Vinne press, 1901)   xiv, 182 p. incl. front. (port.) plates, port. 24½ cm. 1-23736.
CS71.V243   1901

17588   VAN DEUSEN.   Van Deursen family.   (Washington, Gibson bros., printers, 1909)   (85)-89 p. 25 cm. Specimen sheets of a Van Deursen, Van Deusen, Van Dusen genealogy. By Albert H. Van Deusen. 9-3910.
CS71.V243   1909

17589   VAN DEUSEN.   Van Deursen family, by Captain Albert Harrison Van Deusen ... New York, Frank Allaben genealogical company (c.1912)   2 v. fronts. (v. 1: col. coat of arms) plates, ports., maps, facsims. 24 cm. 13-1347.
CS71.V243   1912

17590   VAN DEUSEN.   Ancestry and descendants of Cornelius and John T. Van Deusen, compiled by Elena T. Darling ... Vineland, N.J., Vineland historical and antiquarian society, 1927.   24 p. 25 cm. "One hundred copies of which this is number 31." 27-18504.
CS71.V243   1927

17591   VAN DEUSEN.   Van Deusen family and collateral lines of Pawling, Wallace, Kitts, Roach (and) Sproul.   By Alexander Du Bin.   Philadelphia, Historical Publ. Society, 1947.   18 l. 25 cm. 48-2631*.
CS71.V243   1947

17592   VAN DEUSEN.   A genealogy of the Van Duzee family, by Frederic P. Van Duzee.   (Reseda? Calif.)   Chedwato Service, 1964.   53 p. 28 cm. Errata slip inserted. 64-5604.
CS71.V243   1964

17593   VAN DEVENTER.   The Van Deventer family.   By Ida Christobelle Van Deventer.   Columbia, Mo., Press of E. W. Stevens Co., 1943.   257 p. plate, ports., fold. map. 24 cm. 43-18186 rev. *
CS71.V244   1943

VAN DEVENTER.   See also MATHEWS, 1925

17594   VAN DE WALL.   Some account of the ancient Dutch and Flemish family of Van De Walle, Vendewall, etc., etc., circa 1239-1902.   Compiled from many original and some printed sources, etc., by Joseph J. Green of Tunbridge Wells ... (Tunbridge Wells) 1902.   3 p. l., 160 numb. l., 1 l. 27 cm. 24-1357.
CS439.V25

VAN DE WALLE.   See VAN DE WALL.

VAN DIVER.   See SOUTHER, 1960

17595   VAN DOORN.   The Van Doorn family (Van Doorn, Van Dorn, Van Doren, etc.) in Holland and America, 1088-1908, by A. Van Doren Honeyman ... Plainfield, N.J., Honeyman's publishing house, 1909.   764, (2) p. col. front., illus., plates, ports. 25 cm. 9-13525.
CS71.V246   1909

17596   VAN DOREN.   That thy days may be long; history of the Van Doren, English and Thorne families and their descendants, by living members of the family.   Compiled by Elizabeth Virginia Fisher and Esther Thorne.   (n.p., c.1967)   309 p. illus., geneal. table, maps, ports. 28 cm. Bibliography: p. 294. 68-4412.
CS71.V247   1967

VAN DUZEE.   See VAN DEUSEN.

VAN DUSEN.   See VAN DEUSEN.

VANDYBOGURT.   See LUM, 1930

17597   VAN DYKE.   The Raritan; notes on a river and a family, by John C. Van Dyke ...   New Brunswick, N.J., Priv. print., 1915.   4 p. l., 5-89 p. double geneal. tab.   22 cm.   16-14833.
CS71.V248   1915

17598   VAN DYKE.   The Van Dyke family of Delaware and the intermarrying DuPonts.   Presented ... by George Magruder Battey III, a descendant of the original Jan Thomasse Van Dyke.   Washington, D.C., 1940.   1 p. l., 7, 3 numb. l. 28 cm. Type-written. Includes bibliographical reference. 41M187T.
CS71.V248   1940

17599   VAN DYKE.   Tennessee Van Duke genealogy by Judge Thomas Nixon Van Dyke of Athens, East Tennessee, 1872 ... Washington, D.C., 1940.   1 p. l., 8 numb. l. port. 28 cm. Type-written. "Copied by his grand-son George Magruder Battey III."   41-38348.
CS71.V248   1940a

17600   VAN DYKE.   The Van Dyke graveyard and its occupants at Athens in McMinn county, Tennessee.   By George Magruder Battey ... (Washington, D.C., 1940)   1 p. l., 3 numb. l. 28 cm.   Type-written (carbon copy) 41M188T.
CS71.V248   1940b

17601   VAN DYKE.   Van Dycks.   By Richard W. Cook.   South Orange, N.J., 1954.   41 l. 29 cm. 60-37085.
CS71.V248   1954

VAN DYKE.   See also: ARMSTRONG, CS61.A6 vol. 1
BATTEY, 1940
BARKSDALE, 1922
BEEKMAN, 1912
WALLIN, 1934

VANELTED.   See VAN ETTEN.

17602   VAN ETTEN.   Jacobus Jansen van Etten; some ten generations in America of Jacobus Jansen van Etten, immigrant, from Etten, North Brabant, Holland to Kingston, New York about 1663.   By Eva Alice Scott.   Youngstown, Ohio, 1950.   xx, 164 p. illus. 22 cm. "This edition is limited to 100 numbered copies." Bibliography: p. 141-142.   50-33990.
CS71.V25   1950

17603   VANETTEN.   Seven generations of John VanEtten from 1784 to 1968, with beginnings of Van-Etten family in America (by Leslie J. VanEtten.   Phoenix, 1968)   75 l. illus. 28 cm. Cover title. 68-5245.
CS71.V25   1968

17604   VANETTEN.   The Van Etten family of America, from 1658 to 1969, by Leslie J. VanEtten.   (Phoenix? Ariz., 1969)   212 p. illus., geneal. tables, map. ports. 28 cm. Bibliography: p. 187-188.   72-7778 MARC.
CS71.V25   1969

VAN EVERY.   See VAN IVEREN.

VAN FLEET.   See DAY, 1916

17605   VAN FOSSEN.   The Van Fossen family in America.   By Katherine (Hobson) Van Fossen.   Columbus, Ohio (1952)   192 p. 21 cm. 52-40173.
CS71.V252   1952

17606   VAN GELDER.   Early Van Gelder families in the United States of America, by Arthur P. Van Gelder.   Wilmington, Del., A. P. Van Gelder (1945)   2 p. l., 63 p. 3 port. on 1 l. 27½ cm. "An elaboration of the writer's genealogy of the three older Van Gelder families ... as it appeared in the New York genealogical and biographical record in 1944." - Pref. "Authorities": p. 54.   46-164.
CS71.V253   1945

VAN GILDER.   See VAN GELDER.

VAN GLAHN.   See DOMMERICH, 1930

VAN HATEN. See VAN ALEN.

VAN HAVRE. See COGEL, 1959

17607   VAN HECKE. Van Hecke allied ancestry; ancestry of Josina Van Hecke, wife of Roeland de Carpentier, pensionary of Ypres, grandparents of Maria de Carpentier, wife of Jean Paul Jaquet, vice-director and chief magistrate on the South river of New Netherland, 1655-1657, by Edwin Jaquett Sellers.   Philadelphia (Press of Allen, Lane & Scott) 1933.   2 p. l., 153, (1) p., 1 l. 24 cm. "Edition limited to one hundred copies." "This work is supplementary to 'De Carpentier allied ancestry', by the writer, and further elaborates the allied ancestry of Maria de Carpentier, wife of Jean Paul Jaquet, mentioned in the title." "Works of the author": 2d prelim. leaf. 33-33290.

CS809.V3S4

17608   VAN HEUSEN. The Van Heusen family.   Privately printed. (Asbury Park, N.J., Martin & Allardyce, 1910?)   cover-title, 8 p. 22 cm. 22-22875.   CS71.V254   1910

17609   VAN HOOK. The Van Hook and allied families.   By Bernice (Hubbard) Keister.   New York, American Historical Co., 1957.   387 p. 20 cm. 57-2354.   CS71.V255   1957

17610   VAN HOOSEAR.   A complete genealogy of the Van Hoosear family embracing all descendants of Rinear Van Hoosear, an officer in the revolutionary army, and a resident of Norwalk, Weston, Conn.; Ballston, N.Y.; and Wilton, Conn. by David Hermon Van Hoosear ... Norwalk, Conn., Printed for the author, 1902.   96 p. plates, ports. 23 cm. 6-10939.   CS71.V256   1902

17611   VAN HORN.   Our kindred, an historical record of the Van Horne family in America, from 1634 to 1888.   Fonda, N.Y., Mohawk Valley Democrat Print, 1888.   80 p. 22 cm. 12-24986 rev.*   CS71.V2565   1888

17612   VAN HORN.   Christian Barentsen Van Horn and his descendants, by C. S. Williams.   New York, C. S. Williams, 1911.   1 p. l., 136 numb. l. front. (coat of arms) plates, ports. 27 cm. Autographed from type-written copy. 11-2839.   CS71.V2565   1911

17613   VAN HORNE.   Joris Janzen Van Horne and his descendants, by C. S. Williams.   New York, C. S. Williams, 1911.   1 p. l., 75 numb. l. plates, ports., coat of arms. 27 cm. Autographed from typewritten copy. CA12-980   CS71.V2565   1911a

17614   VAN HEUSEN.   Chronicle of Van Hoosen centenary farm. By Sarah Van Hoosen Jones.   (Ann Arbor, Mich., Printed by Edwards Bros,, 1969)   235 p. illus., geneal. table, ports. 24 cm. 77-6218 MARC.   CS71.V254   1969

17615   VAN HORN.   Jan Cornelis van Horne, and his descendants, by C. S. Williams   New York, C. S. Williams, 1912.   1 p. l., 89 l. front. (coat of arms) pl. 27 cm. Edition of 25 copies, this copy not numbered. Autographed from typewritten copy. 13-11873.   CS71.V2565   1912

17616   VAN HORN.   The Van Horn family history.   By Francis Merton Marvin.   East Stroudsburg, Pa., Press Pub. Co. (1929)   464 p. plates, ports., coat of arms. 24 cm. 30-3959 rev.*   CS71.V2565   1929

17617   VAN HORN.   Our Van Horne kindred.   By Elsie (Overbaugh) Hallenbeck.   (Amsterdam? N.Y., 1959)   274 p. 23 cm. Revision of Our kindred, an historical record of the Van Horne family in America, by Abram Van Horne, published in 1888. 60-17161.   CS71.V2565

VAN HORNE.   See also: BLAUVELT, 1957
                        No. 9846 - Hackettstown.

17618   VAN HOUTEN.   Descendants of Roelof Van Houten of 1638.   By Herbert Stewart Ackerman. (Ridgewood, N.J., 1945)   iii, 236, (1) l. 29 cm. Binder's title. "Genealogical reference works": leaf at end. 45-14193 rev.*   CS71.V257   1945

—— Supplement.   Ridgewood (1946)   (33) l. 28 cm. Cover title. 45-14193 rev*

VAN HOUTEN.   See also BLAUVELT, 1957

VAN HOY. See BUTTERWORTH, 1960

VAN HUSEN. See VAN HEUSEN.

VAN KIRK. See WALLIN, 1934

17619   VAN KLEECK. The Van Kleeck family;   an account of its origin, and a record of that branch of it represented by the descendants of Tunis Van Kleeck of Poughkeepsie, N.Y.; with miscellaneous material. (Poughkeepsie) F. Van Kleeck, 1900.   50 p. front. 20 cm. By Frank Van Kleeck. "Historical notes on the first three generations of the ... family in America" comp. by Helen W. Reynolds: p. (5)-28. 2-25793.
CS71.V259   1900

17620   VAN KLEECK.   The Van Kleeck genealogy; descendants of all children, but Catherine, of Barent Baltus (Van Kleeck) of Haarlem, North Holland, who settled in Flatbush now part of Brooklyn, New York, before 1654 in both male and female lines; with additional descendants of his daughter Catherine who married Paulus Martense van Benthuysen of Benthuizen, South Holland who settled in Albany prior to 1654. By Alvin S. Van Benthuysen and Edwin Robert van Kleeck. Brooklyn, 1957. 417 l. 29 cm. 58-25407.
CS71.V259   1957

17621   VAN KOUGHNET. The Von Gochnats, by Lady Janc Van Koughnet. (London) Priv. print. by Messrs. Hatchard, 1910.   vii, 114, (1) p. front., illus., plates, ports. 26 cm. Title vignette (coat of arms) "Extracts from Lieut. Van Koughner's diary during Nile expedition, 1884-5": p. 17-96. 20-15255.
CS90.V3

VAN KORTRYK. See COURTRIGHT.

VAN KOUWENHOVEN. See CONOVER.

VAN LEEUWEN. See VAN LIEW.

17622   VAN LEUVENIGH. ... Hendrick van Leuvenigh of Newcastle County, Delaware, and some of his descendants. By Josiah Granville Leach.   (In Genealogical society of Pennsylvania, Publications. Philadelphia, 1920. 25 cm. v.7, p. 207-217) 21-8412.
F146.G32 vol.7

VAN LEUVENIGH. See also BARKSDALE, 1922

17623   VAN LIEW. Genealogy and annals of the Van Liew family in America from the year 1670 down to the present time. And a brief record of a few of the families with whom the Van Liew family intermarried. (St. Louis? c.1910)   18 p. front. (port.) 31 x 23 cm. By Thomas Lillian Van Liew. 11-556.
CS71.V262   1910

17624   VAN LIEW. Van Liew (Van L)ieu, (VanL)ew, genealogical & historical record (1670-1956) ... Rev. and augm. by Emerio R. Van Liew. (Upper Montclair? N.J.) 1956.   viii, 255 p. illus., ports., maps, coat of arms, facsims. 23 cm. 56-10373.
CS71.V262   1956

17625   VAN LOAN. Narrative giving a new historic fact never before published. Pietre van Loon, immigrant of 1581, hunted and fished on the upper waters of the Hudson River eleven years before its discovery by Hendrick Hudson ... A posthumous article, written by Benjamin Van Loan. Foot-notes from researches, by his cousin, Walton Van Loan. (Catskill, N.Y., W. Van Loan, 19 -?) (8) p. illus. (incl. port.) 23½ cm. 10-1498.
CS71.V266   19 -

17626   VAN METER. The origin and descent of an American Van Metre family collated from civil, church, military and family records. Compiled by Samuel Gordon Smyth ... (Lancaster, Pa., Lancaster press, inc., 1923)   2 p. l., 46 p. front. (col. coat of arms) plates, ports. 23½ cm. For private circulation. 24-21371.
CS71.V269   1923

17627   VAN METER. (The Van Meteren (Van Metre)/Dubois family chart. By Nellie Ray Van Metre Banfield. Fayetteville? Pa.) 1958.   sheet. 2 coats of arms. 357 x 59 cm. Photocopy of Ms. 73-229935 MARC.
CS71.V269   1958a

VAN METER.   See also: CORN, 1959   LEWIS, 1901
                          DUKE, 1900   LOPER, 1969
                          HITE, 1960   TREES, 1960
                          LA RUE, 1921

VAN METEREN   See VAN METER.

VAN METRE.   See VAN METER.

VAN NAARDEN.   See VAN NORDEN.

VAN NAERDEN.   See VAN NORDEN.

VAN NASSAU.   See NASSAU.

VANNEMAN.   See REICHNER, 1918

VAN NES.   See BURGHGRAEF.

17628   VAN NESS.   The Van Ness heritage and allied genealogies, 1546-1960.   By Lottye (Gray) Van Ness.   (Elizabeth? N.J., 1960)   88 l. coat of arms.   20 cm.   Errata slip inserted.   60-53098 .
                                                                                        CS71.V2693

17629   VAN NEYLEN.   De familie van Neylen (door) Jan Jacob Jordaens (pseud.) J van Noey.   (Antwerpen, Drukkerij De Vlijt (1957)   282 p. 22 cm. 58-45986.   CS809.V33   1957

VAN NIEUWKIRK.   See NEWKIRK.

17630   VAN NORDEN.   The Van Norden family, three hundred years in America, 1623-1923 (by) Theodore Langdon Van Norden.   South Salem, N.Y., The Horse and hound, 1923.   vi, 74 p. front., illus., ports. 21 cm. "Based upon data collected by ... Warner Van Norden." Allied families: Slot, Earle, Vreeland, Langton, Reyerse, Brinckerhoff. Rapalje, Warner, Hooghland, Bogardus, Mousnier de La Montagne, and Kip. 23-18846.   CS71.V2695   1923

17631   VAN NORDEN.   Van Norden family possessions, from the sixth and seventh generations in America (by) Theodore Langdon Van Norden.   South Salem, N.Y., The Horse and hound, 1926.
vi, 32 p. front. 21 cm. 26-9252.   CS71.V2695   1926

17632   VANNOY.   The Vannoy family history, compiled by Forest B. Vannoy Witte.   Edited by Jerry Wayne Ash.   (Bridgeport? W. Va.) Bridgeport News Print Shop, 1960.   vi, 23 l. 31 cm. 64-55190.
                                                                                        CS71.V2697   1960

VANNOY.   See also: HENDRICKS, 1963
                        HOOK, 1925

VAN NUYSE.   See BERGEN, 1866

VAN ORDEN.   See BLAUVELT, 1957

17633   VAN PELT.   A genealogy of the Van Pelt family, compiled by Effie M. Smith from records of family, church, state and nation.   (Chicago, The Rajput press, 1913)   251 p. incl. col. coat of arms. plates, ports. 23½ cm. "Authorities": p. 9. 15-14450.   CS71.V272   1913

17634   VAN PELT.   (History of the Van Pelt family by Ella E. Van Pelt Tilden.   Cleveland? 1930)
1 p. l., 32 (i. e. 33) numb. l. ports. (mounted photos.) facsims. 30 cm. One unnumbered leaf inserted between leaves 14 and 15. 31-31256.
                                                                                        CS71.V272   1930

17635   VAN RENSSELAER.   A legacy of historical gleanings, compiled and arranged by Mrs. Catherine V. R. Bonney.   With illustrations and autographs ... Albany, N.Y., J. Munsell, 1875.
2 v. fronts., illus., plates, ports. 23½ cm. 7-10452.   F119.B71

17636   VAN RENSSELAER.   A legacy of historical gleanings, compiled and arranged by Mrs. Catharina V. R. Bonney.   With illustrations and autographs ... 2d ed.   Albany, N. Y., J. Munsell, 1875.
2 v. fronts., illus., 2 pl., ports. 23½ cm. 14-20934.   F119. B72

17637   VAN RENSSELAER.   Ancestral sketches and records of olden times ... (By Sarah (Rogers) Van Rensselaer) For private circulation only.   New York, A. D. F. Randolph & company, 1882.
xiii, 375 p. 26 cm.   Monogram formed of letters S. V. R. on t.-p.   Contents. - The Huguenots. - The Bayards of New York. - Nicholas Bayard, and his times. - The "Tories" of the American revolution. - The growth of the city of New York from 1626. - Governor-General Samuel Vetch, of Nova Scotia. - Governor Fitch, of Connecticut, and his times. - Appendix. - The life and services of Stephen Van Rensselaer, by D. D. Barnard. - Historical sketch of the colony and manor of Rensselaerwyck, by D. D. Barnard. 6-9054 rev.   F120. V27

17638   VAN RENSSELAERS.   The Van Rensselaers of the manor of Rensselaerswyck.   (New York, E. Bierstadt, 1888)   21 p., 51 l. front. (coat of arms) 8 pl., 45 port. 28½ cm.   By May (King) Van Rensselaer.   Each plate is accompanied by a leaf with descriptive letterpress.   "Artotypes by E. Bierstadt, N. Y." 9-14791.   CS71. V274   1888

17639   VAN RENSSELAER.   Annals of the Van Rensselaers in the United States, especially as they relate to the family of Killian K. Van Rensselaer ... By the Rev. Maunsell Van Rensselaer ... Albany, C. Van Benthuysen & sons, 1888.   3 p. l., 241 p. front., pl., port., facsims. 25½ cm. 9-14790.
CS71. V274   1888a

17640   VAN RENSSELAER.   Fort Crailo, the Greenbush manor house.   By S. de L. Van Rensselaer Strong.   (n. p., 1898?)   31 p. 22½ cm. 41-36267.   F129. A3S8

17641   VAN RENSSELAER.   Historic families of America comprehending the genealogical records and representative biography of selected families of early American ancestry, recognized social standing, and special distinction; ed. by Walter W. Spooner.   New York, Historical families publishing association (1907)   3 p. l., 380 p. 8 col. pl. (coats of arms) 5 pl., 39 mounted port. (incl. front.) 36½ cm.   Contents. - Van Rensselaer. - Dana. - King. - Carroll of Maryland. - Dwight. - Stuyvesant. - Jay. - Frelinghuysen. - Chew. - Morris. - Langdon. - Hillhouse.   By Margaret P. Hillhouse. - Clarkson. - Talmage. - Willard. - Ewing. - Astor. - Lee of Virginia. 10-7843.   CS69. S7

17642   VAN RENSSELAER.   The Van Rensselaer manor; address delivered at the third annual meeting of the New York branch of the Order of colonial lords of manors in America, held in the city of New York, April 24, 1915, by Kiliaen Van Rensselaer.   Baltimore, 1917.   22 p. incl. illus., pl., 23½ cm.
(Order of colonial lords of manors in America.   New York branch.   Publications) 20-16021.   E186. 99. O6 No. 2
———— Copy 2.   F127. R32V27

17643   VAN RENSSELAER.   Inventory of the Rensselaerswyck manuscripts, edited from the original manuscript in the New York public library, by Victor Hugo Paltsits ... New York (Printed at the New York public library) 1924.   54 p. 25½ cm.   "Reprinted September 1924 from the Bulletin of the New York public library of May, June, July, 1924."   The inventory has caption: Inventory of patents, deeds, books, and papers relative to the estate of the late Stephen Van Rensselaer esquire deceased which came into the hands of Abraham Ten Broeck esquire, as executor of the said Stephen Van Rensselaer and now by him delivered to Stephen Van Rensselaer ... present proprietor of the manor of Rennelaerwyck. 25-16960.   CD3409. 5. V3N4   1924a

17644   VAN RENSSELAER.   The Van Rensselaer manor, address delivered at the third annual meeting of the New York branch of the Order of colonial lords of manors in America, held in the city of New York, April 24, 1915, by Kiliaen Van Rensselaer.   Reprinted in 1929, with some additions by Miss Florence Van Rensselaer and others.   Baltimore, 1929.   100 p. col. front., illus. (incl. ports.) 23½ cm.
(On cover: (Order of colonial lords of manors in America.   Publications) no. 21)   Blank pages (94-100)   Cover title: ... Rensselaerwyck patronship and manor; the pedigree of the Van Rensselaer family. 34-5928.   E186. 99. O6 No. 21
———— Copy 2.   F127. R32V27   1929

17645   VAN RENSSELAER.   Correspondence of Maria van Rensselaer, 1669-1689; translated and edited by A. J. F. van Laer ... Albnay, The University of the state of New York, 1935.   206 p. 23 cm.
35-28190.   F127. R32V29

17646   VAN RENSSELAER.   ... Chart of the Van Rensselaers, their patronship and family descent from Holland to Rensselaer Wyck, Rensselaer manor, Claverack & Greenbush, etc. in New York state, USA. ... Troy, N. Y., 1944.   3 geneal. tab. 28 x 34 cm.   Photostat reproduction (negative)   "Drafted under (the) auspices of the Public library, Troy ... and Albany, N. Y. Institute of history and art, A. K. Mosley, R. A." 44-35664.
CS71. V274   1944

17647   VAN RENSSELAER.   The Van Rensselaers in Holland and in America, by Florence Van Rensselaer, assisted by Ethel L. Fitz Randolph.   New York, 1956.   103 p. illus. 25 cm. 56-1675.

CS71.V274   1956

VAN RENSSELAER.   See also: BARD, F128.25.V27
BYRD, E159.G55
PECK, 1925
REPALJE, CS69.H7
SCHUYLER, F123.B35

VAN REYNEGOM DE BUZET.   See COGEL.

VAN RIESEN.   See FRIESEN.

VAN SCHAICK.   See: CLARKSON, 1876
REPALJE, CS69.H7

VAN SETTER.   See COGEL, 1959

17648   VAN SICKLE.   A history of the Van Sickle family, in the United States of America, embracing a full biographical sketch of the author; the early history of the world; the early history of the aborigines; the early history of America; the early history of the Netherlands; the derivation of names; the ancestral lineage; the genealogy; biographical sketches of its most distinguished members; and a family record ... By John W. Van Sickle ... Springfield, O., The author, 1880.   viii, 9-236 p. illus. 25½ cm. 9-14798.

CS71.V279   1880

VAN SICKLE.   See: PATTERSON, 1957
SHOEMAKER, E99.I7Y3

VAN SOLMS.   See SOLMS.

17649   VANSSAY.   ... Autour de l'expédition de Saint-Dominigue; les espoirs d'une famille d'anciens planteurs (1801-1804) Ed. Gabriel Debien.   (Port-au-Prince, Haiti) 1942.   2 p. l., 95 p. 24 cm. (Notes d'histoire coloniale.   III) At head of title: ... G. Deblen.   "Extrait de la Revue de la Société d'histoire et de géographie d'Haiti, vol. 13, no. 47 du mois d'octobre 1942, p. 1 à 95."   Chiefly correspondence between Achille and Armand de Vanssay and their mother during the years 1802-04.   45-3204.

F1923.D365

VAN STEENBERGH.   See CHIPP, 1933

VAN SWERINGEN.   See TIERNAN, 1901

VANSYOC.   See ELIOT, 1908

VAN TASSEL.   See ROMER, 1917

17650   VAN TUYL.   Notes on the Van Tuyl family.   By Alma H. Cramer.   Washington (1953)   92 l. 28 cm. 55-19913.

CS71.V2796   1953

17651   VAN TUYL.   Notes on the Van Tuyl family.   By Alma H. Cramer.   Washington, 1959.   41 l. 28 cm. 59-52120.

CS71.V2796   1959

17652   VAN UXEM.   Chappel-Van Uxem.   By Ella (Foy) O'Gorman.   1952.   sheet. A genealogical table consisting of a printed form filled out in MS.   Photocopy.   44 x 69 cm.   73-230295 MARC.

CS71.C467   1952a

VAN UXEM.   See CHAPPELL, 1953

17653   VAN VALKENBURGH.   Genealogy of the Van Valkenburgh family.   Further research compiled and printed by William Moore Van Valkenburgh II in 1953.   (n.p., 1953)   18 p. col. coat of arms. 23 cm. Cover title. 54-36429.

CS71.V2815   1953

17654   VAN VECHTEN.   The genealogical records of the Van Vechten's from 1638 to 1896.   By
Peter Van Vechten, jr. ... Milwaukee, Wis., Radtke bros. & Kortsch, printers, 1896.   117 p. illus., map,
facsim. 26 cm. 12-18977.   CS71.V282   1896

17655   VAN VLACK.   The Van Vlack family.   (n.p., 195-?)   6 l. 28 cm. 63-35492.
                                                                          CS71.V2825   1950z

VAN VLEET.   See DAY, 1916

17655a   VAN VOORHEES.   Notes on the ancestry of Major Wm. Roe Van Voorhis, of Fishkill, Duchess
County, New York.   By his grandson, Elias W. Van Voorhis ... (New York) For private distribution
only, 1881.   239 p. front., plates, ports., coat of arms, map. fold. facsim., fold. geneal. tab. 24 cm. 9-14796.
                                                                          CS71.V284   1881

17656   VAN VOORHEES.   Line of descent of Elias W. Van Voorhis, of 129 East 36th street, New
York city.   (New York? 1877?)   geneal. tab. 42½ x 45½ cm.   Compiled by Elias W. Van Voorhis. 2-8908.
                                                                          CS71.V284   1877

17657   VAN VOORHEES.   A genealogy of the Van Voorhees family in America; or, The descendants
of Steven Coerte Van Voorhees of Holland and Flatlands, L. I.   By Elias W. Van Voorhis ... New York
and London, G. P. Putnam's sons, 1888.   v, 725 p. front. (port.) pl., maps. 26½ cm. "Limited letter-press edition."
9-14795.   CS71.V284   1888

17658   VAN VOORHEES.   Ralph and Elizabeth Rodman Voorhees; a tribute by Oscar M. Voorhees ...
New York, The Tribute press, 1927.   viii, 267 p. front., illus. (incl. ports., coat of arms) fold. map, facsim. 23½ cm.
"(Traces) the four principal ancestral lines - Voorhees, Whitaker, Nevius and Rodman - with casual references to collateral lines." - p. 11. 27-23548.
                                                                          CS71.V957   1927

17659   VAN VOORHEES.   The Van Voorhees family.   (By Amos Earle Voorhies) (Grants Pass, Or.,
1932)   9 p. illus. (coats of arms) 22 cm.   Caption title. "By Amos Earle Voorhies." - p. (2) 33-9643.
                                                                          CS71.V284   1932

17660   VAN VOORHEES.   Historical handbook of the Van Voorhees family in the Netherlands and
America; with illustrations by Stephen J. Voorhies.   Van Voorhees association.   (New Brunswick,
N. J.) The Van Voorhees association, 1935.   3 p. l., 122 p. incl. illus., ports., maps, geneal. tab., coat of arms. 23 cm.
Selected papers which were presented at various meetings of the association.   cf. Foreword, signed: Oscar M. Voorhees, compiler and editor.
35-12599.   CS71.V284   1935

17661   VAN VOORHEES.   The Van Voorhees association at its tenth anniversary, 1932-1942, a review of activities and of the endeavor to compile a new Van Voorhees genealgoy, with accounts of some
members of the family whose careers should not be forgotten.   Published by direction of the tenth
annual meeting held at Hackensack, New Jersey, October 10, 1942.   (New Brunswick, N. J.) The Van
Voorhees association, 1942.   83 p. front., illus. (incl. ports.) 23 cm.   Coat of arms on cover.   Foreword signed: Oscar M.
Voorhees, compiler and editor. 43-49604.   CS71.V284   1942

VAN VOORHEES.   See also: CRAWFORD, E171.A53 vol. 16
                            ELDRIDGE, 1925
                            VOORHEES.

VAN VOORHIS.   See VAN VOORHEES.

VAN VRYLING.   See WILDER, CT275.W5586.A3

17662   VAN WAGENEN.   Genealogy of the Van Wagenen family from 1650 to 1884.   Part first, con-
taining the first three generations of the family complete, and then following down the descendants of
Aart Van Wagenen, the grandson of the first settler of the name in America.   By Gerrit Hubert Van
Wagenen ... (Brooklyn, N. Y.) Printed for private distribution, 1884.   2 p. l., x, 69 p. 24 cm. 9-15616.
                                                                          CS71.V285   1884
                                                                          Office.

17663   VAN WAGENEN.   The family of Garret Conrad Van Wagnen and his wife Mary Welton; being a
record of their children and of their descendants from the time of their marriage in 1811 to the present

17663 continued: time, 1942, by Frank L. Van Wagnen ... Buffalo, N.Y. (1942) 3 p. l., 67 (i.e. 74), xiv (i.e. xv) numb. l. 28 cm. Includes extra numbered leaves. Reproduced from type-written copy. Includes data from the Genealogy of the Van Wagenen family, by Gerrit Hubert Van Wagenen, 1884, with considerable additional material cf. Introd. 44-18348. CS71.V285 1942

17664 VAN WAGENEN. The ancestry of Garret Conrad Van Wagnen in the five collateral lines of Pels, Elting, Van Den Berg, Ten Eyck, and Bogart, and in the ten allied lines of Slecht, Lansing-Halenbeck, Rapalje, Van Arsdalen-Van Schouw, Bergen-Lubbertsen, Bodine-Crocheron. Buffalo, 1946. iii, 116, lxxii l. map, geneal. table. 28 cm. Includes data from the Genealogy of the Van Wagenen family, by Gerrit Hubert Van Wagenen, pub. in 1884. Includes bibliographies. 48-16828*. CS71.V285 1946

VAN WAGNEN. See VAN WAGENEN and WELTON, 1948

17665 VAN WINKLE. A genealogy of the Van Winkle family; account of its origin and settlement in this country with data 1630-1913. Description of the village of "Winkel," holland, with illustrations. By Daniel Van Winkle ... Jersey City, Datz press (c. 1913) 433 p. col. front. (coat of arms) 1 illus. pl. 22½ cm. 13-12501. CS71.V287 1913

VAN WINKLE. See also REICHNER, 1918

VAN WOERT. See SNYDER, 1958

17666 VAN WYCK. Descendants of Cornelius Barentse Van Wyck and Anna Polhemus, by Anne Van Wyck ... New York, T. A. Wright, 1912. 4 p. l., (7)-508 p. front., plates, ports., fold. map, plans. facsims., col. coat of arms. 25 cm. 6 blank leaves at end for "Additional records." 13-15258. CS71.V29 1913

VAN WYCK. See also BRUSH, 1904

VAN YESELSTEYN. See CRALL, 1908

VANZANTE. See BREED, 1958

17667 VARIAN. The book of the Varian family, with some speculations as to their origin, etc. By Sam Briggs ... Cleveland, O. (Printed by T. C. Schenck & co.) 1881. 4 p. l., 102 p. plates, ports. 24½ cm. "Edition 100 copies." 9-14797. CS71.V299 1881

17668 VARIAN. The Varian family. By Charles Arnold Varian. (n.p.) 1950. 112 l. illus. 29 cm. 59-40476. CS71.V299 1950

VARIAN. See also SNYDER, 1958

17669 VARICK. The Varick family, by Rev. B. F. Wheeler, D. D., with many family portraits. (Mobile? Ala., 1907) 3 p. l., 5-58 p., 1 l. front., ports., geneal. tab. 16 cm. Descendants of James Varick, founder of the African Methodist Episcopal Zion church. 7-21721. CS71.V3 1907

VARNALL. See MATLOCK, E262.P4M3

VARNUM. See WARD, 1926

17670 VARNEY. A discourse commemorative of John Riley Varney, preached at the First church, Dover, N.H., May 5, 1882, by his pastor, George Burley Spalding ... Dover, N.H., The Morning star steam job printing house, 1882. 19 p. 23½ cm. "Ancestral note": p. (18)-19. 16-7848. CS71.V318 1882

VARNEY. See also: HATHAWAY, 1961
OTIS, 1851

17671 VARNUM. The Varnums of Dracutt (in Massachusetts) a history of George Varnum, his son Samuel who came to Ipswich about 1635, and grandsons Thomas, John and Joseph, who settled in Dracutt, and their descendants. Compiled from family papers and official records by John Marshall Varnum ... Boston, D. Clapp & son, printers, 1907. vi p., 1 l., (5)-308 p. plates, ports., map, plans, facsims. 24 cm. 7-12874. CS71.V322 1907

VARRELL.   See VERRILL.

VASA.   See VASS.

VASCONCELLOS.   See PEREIRA, 1889

17672   VASEY.   Vasey family in vertical file.   Ask reference librarian for this material.

17673   VÁSQUEZ DE VELASCO.   ... Los Vásquez de Velasco, historia geneológica (!) de una noble e ilustre familia española del Perú ... By Ferdiand de Trazegnies.   Lima, Librería e imprenta Gil, s.a., 1945.   31 p. plates, coats of arms. 24½ cm. "De la Revista histórica, tomo XVI, entrega I y II." 47-17780.

CS379.V3   1945

17674   VASSALL.   The Vassalls of New England and their immediate descendants.   A genealogical and biographical sketch compiled from church and town records.   By Edward Doubleday Harris ... Albany, J. Munsell, 1862.   26 p. 24 cm. 3-26055.   CS71.V337   1862

17675   VASSALL.   A home of the olden time.   By Thomas C. Amory.   Boston, Printed by D. Clapp & son, 1872.   1 p. l., (5)-27 p. 25½ cm. Description of the house on Summer street, Boston, erected about 1730 by Leonard Vassall, with accounts of the families which occupiaed it. (Vassall and Gardner) "Reprinted from the New-England historical and genealogical register." 8-10577.

F73.8.V3A5

17676   VASSALL.   Vassal pedigree.   1500 to 1890.   (London? 1890)   9 numb. l. 34½ cm. Compiled by William Vassall.   Caption title.   Privately printed. 2-26592.

CS439.V3

17677   VASSALL.   Notes on Colonel Henry Vassall (1721-1769) his wife Penelope Royall, his house at Cambridge, and his slaves Tony & Darby ... By Samuel Francis Batchelder.   Cambridge, Mass., 1917.   1 p. l., (5)-85 p. 5 pl., 2 port. (incl. front.) plan, 2 facsim., fold. geneal. tab. 23½ cm. Six generations of the Vassall family shewing their connection with Christ church, Cambridge and its neighborhood.   Arranged from the work of Edward Doubleday Harris: geneal. tab. 18-3386.

F74.C1V3

17678   VASSALL.   John Vassall and his descendants, by one of them.   (Hertford, Eng., S. Austin and sons, ltd., printers, 1921)   40 p. 22 cm. Foreword signed: C.M.C. (i.e.Charles Maclear Calder) 22-22856.

CS71.V337   1921

VASSALL.   See also: OLIVER, 1907
                                No. 430 - Adventurers of purse and person.

VATER.   See VENABLE, 1961

17679   VAUCLAIN.   Steaming up! the autobiography of Samuel M. Vauclain, written in collaboration with Earl Chapin May.   New York, Brewer & Warren, inc., 1930.   7 p. l., 298 p. front., plates, ports. 23½ cm. "The Vauclain family": p. 291-293. 30-31146.   TJ140.V3A3

17680   VAUGHAN.   British antiquities revived, or A friendly contest touching the soveraignty of the three Princes of Wales, in ancient times, managed with certain arguments, whereunto answers are applyed.   To which is added, the pedigree of the Right Honourable the Earl of Carbery, lord president of Wales, with a short account of the five royal tribes of Cambria.   By Robert Vaughan ... Bala, Printed at the Cambrian press, by R. Saunderson, 1834.   9 p. l., (7)-80 p. 2 geneal. tab. (1 fold.) 28½ cm. First published in 1662. Pedigree of the Vaughan family, continued to 1834 by Joseph Morris of Shrewsbury: fold. geneal. tab. 19-3635.

CS454.V3

17681   VAUGHAN.   The history of Kington; with an appendix.   By a member of the Mechanics' institute of Kington.   Kington, C. Humphreys, 1845.   6 p. l., 303 p. 2 fold. geneal. tab. 23½ cm. Hergest court and the family of the Vaughans: p. 216-224. Pedigree of the family of Cheese: geneal. tab. 15-21502.

DA690.K575H4

17682   VAUGHAN.   Reminiscences of the Vaughan family, and more particularly of Benjamin Vaughan, LL. D.   Read before the New England historic-genealogical society, August 2, 1865.   By John H. Sheppard ... With a few additions, a genealogy and notes ... Boston, D. Clapp & son, printers, 1865. 40 p.   25½ cm.   5-17618.   CS71.V367   1865

17683   VAUGHAN.   Description of the armorial insignia of the Vaughans of Llwydiarth, which once surrounded their family pew in Llanfihangel church, but are now in Wynnstay chapel; with memorials of the Loyds of Dolobran and other cognate families.   By the Rev. W. V. Lloyd ...   (In Powys-land club, Welshpool, Wales.   Collections historical & archaeological relating to Montgomeryshire and its borders.   London, 1881.   22 cm.   vol. XIV, ii, 355-396 p.   illus., coats of arms)   16-25572.   DA740.M7P8 vol.14

17684   VAUGHAN.   The Vaughan family of Hertford County, N. C.   By ex-Judge Benj. B. Winborne .. (Raleigh, N. C., Edwards & Broughton printing company) 1909.   104 p.   front., ports.   20 cm.   Contains also the De Berry, Jenkins, and Dew families.   23-18595.   CS71.V367   1909

17685   VAUGHAN.   Reminiscences and genealogical record of the Vaughan family of New Hampshire, by George E. Hodgdon.   Supplemented by an account of the Vaughans of south Wales, together with copies of official papers relating to the Vaughan's of New Hampshire, taken out of the English colonial records in London.   By Thomas W. Hancock.   Rochester, N. Y., 1918.   2 p. l., iii-x, 169 p. front. (port.) pl. (coats of arms) double facsim., fold. geneal. tables.   27 cm.   Prefatory note signed: R. C. Shannon.   "Number 9 of an edition of three hundred copies printed for private distribution only."   18-7045.   CS71.V367   1918

17686   VAUGHAN.   Hallowell memories, by William Warren Vaughan.   Hallowell (Me.) Priv. print., 1931.   187, (8) p., 1 l.   20 cm.   Three photostat reproductions (2 fold., incl. map) inserted.   An account of the Vaughan family.   35-17577.   CS71.V367   1931

17687   VAUGHAN.   Vaughan family in vertical file.   Ask reference librarian for this material.

VAUGHAN.   See also: BEVILLE, 1917   JOHNSON, 1962
                               BRENT, CS71.B837   KIDD, E605.K5P5
                               DEPEW, 1959   MERRYWEATHER, 1899
                               GARDNER, F24.G28   SHANNON, 1905
                               JAMES, 1913a

17688   VAUX.   Vaux of Harrowden, a recusant family.   By Godfrey Anstruther.   Newport, Mon., R. H. Johns (1953)   xv, 552 p. illus., ports., map (on lining papers) facsims.   23 cm.   Bibliography: p. 521-546.   53-32771.   CS439.V35   1953

17689   VAWTER.   The Vawter family in America, with the allied families of Branham, Wise, Stribling, Crawford, Lewis, Glover, Moncrief, by Grace Vawter Bicknell.   Indianapolis, The Hollenbeck press, 1905.   viii p., 1 l., 442 p. front., illus. (plan) pl., ports., col. coat of arms.   24 cm.   6-1365.   CS71.V391   1905

VAWTER.   See also MAXWELL, 1916

17690   VEACH.   The American lineages of the Veach and Stover families.   Together with an appendix containing historical notes of Strasburg and vicinity; a list of the heads of families in Strasburg in 1785; a bibliograph of 98 books and references for students of history and genealogy; and blank spaces for family records.   Comp. and arranged by Robert Spangler Veach.   (n. p.) 1913. 1 p. l, (5)-115, (43) p.   23½ cm.   "Bibliograph of books and references for students of history and genealogy": p. (109)-115.   24 pages for "Family records" following p. 115.   14-12471.   CS71.V395   1913

17691   VEALE.   Veale family of Cornwall, parish of St. Columb Major.   By Carl William Veale. Los Angeles, 1947.   12. 4 l., 4 p.   28 cm.   Caption title.   Typewritten (carbon copy) 50-22853. CS71.V3953   1947

VEALE.   See also PATTERSON, 1947

17692   VEAZEY.   Pryor Gardner Veazey and some of his ancestors and descendants.   By John Veazey Chapman.   Tallahassee, 1965.   54 p.   illus., geneal. tables, ports.   28 cm.   77-3224 MARC. CS71.V3957   1965

17693   VEBLEN.   Veblen genealogy; an account of the Norwegian ancestry of the Veblen family in America, which was founded by Thomas Anderson Veblen and his wife Kari Bunde Veblen, compiled by Andrew A. Veblen.   San Diego, Calif., The author, 1925.   156 p. front. (ports.) fold. map. 22 cm. Autographed from type-written copy. 25-24207.   CS71.V396   1925

VEECH.   See BULLITT, 1920

17694   VEEDER.   The geneological (!) record of the Veeder family, compiled by Vreeland Y. Leonard ... (n. p.) 1937.   (352) p. 22 cm. Mimeographed. 38-14719.   CS71.V42   1937

17695   VEEN.   Een Friesch koopmansgeslacht; het geslacht Veen.   By Egbert Veen.   Amsterdam, L. J. Veen, 1947.   137 p. illus., ports., maps. geneal. tables. 26 cm. "Driehondered genummerde exemplaren ... No. 166." Harvard Univ. Library for Library of Congress. A49-5583 *.   CS829.V35   1947

VEEPOND.   See VIPONT.

17696   VEITCH.   In search of yesterday.   (By William Albert Veitch)   (Bowie, Md.? 1969?) 1 v. (various pagings) illus., maps. 29 cm. 77-10759 MARC.   CS71.V43   1969

VEJAR.   See PALOMARES, 1939

17697   VELDE.   The Tees Karsjen van der Velde family record.   By Winona Whittington Pfander. Peoria, Ill., 1950 (i.e. 1956)   viii, 103 p. ports., map, coat of arms. 28 cm. Imprint date, 1950, blotted out. 56-34880.   CS71.V44   1956

17698   VELDE.   Saape van der Velde-Wopkje Dykstra descendants.   By Conrad Vandervelde. Emporia, Kan. (1960)   33 l. 28 cm. 60-38921.   CS71.V44   1960

17699   VENABLE.   Venables of Virginia; an account of the ancestors and descendants of Samuel Woodson Venable of "Springfield" and of his brother William Lewis Venable of "Haymarket", both of Prince Edward County, Virginia, by Elizabeth Marshall Venable.   (New York) Printed exclusively for members of the family (c. 1925)   xvi p., 3 l., 5-208 p., 1 l. front., 1 illus., pl., ports. 23½ cm. "Sources": 1 page following p. xvi. 25-8684.   CS71.V447   1925

17700   VENABLE.   Historic Slate Hill plantation in Virginia, by Dr. J. D. Eggleston.   (Hampden-Sydney, Va., 1945)   24 p. incl. 2 pl. 23 cm. (Bulletin of Hampden-Sydney college. Vol. XXXIX, no. 2, October, 1945) 46-2755.   F234.S58E4

17701   VENABLE.   The ancestors and descendants of William Henry Venable.   By Henrietta (Brady) Brown.   Cincinnati, 1954.   198 p. 23 cm. 55-44910.   CS71.V447   1954

17702   VENABLE.   Some Venables of England and America; and brief accounts of families into which certain Venables married.   By Henrietta (Brady) Brown.   Cincinnati, Kinderton Press, 1961. 463 p. illus. 24 cm. 61-34224.   CS71.V447   1961

VENABLE.   See also WATKINS, 1957

VENESS.   See SMITH, 1942

17703   VENN.   Family memorials of the late Mr. & Mrs. R. Houghton, of Huddersfield; and of several of their children ... London, Printed for private circulation (Tyler & Reed, printers) 1846. 5 p. l., (3)-206, 15 p. 17 cm. Preface signed: H. H. (i. e. Miss H. Houghton) A letter from the Reverend Mr. Vann, A. M., late vicar of Huddersfield ... Halifax, Printed by E. Jacob, 1772 (15 p. at end) has reproduction of original t.-p. 21-3457.   CS439.H758

17704   VENN.   Annals of a clerical family, being some account of the family and descendants of William Venn. vicar of Otterton, Devon, 1600-1621, by John Venn ... London, New York, Macmillan and co., 1904.   xi, 296 p. illus., plates, ports., facsim., geneal. tables (part fold.) fold. map. 23 cm. Appendix contains pedigrees of the Fenn family, Bishop family of Lincoln, Gay, Ashton of Penketh, Rigby of Burgh and Layton, King family of Hull, Sykes family of Yorkshire. 11-14209.   CS439.V5

VENNER.   See BARBER, DA690.L982C6

VENTRIS.   See BASSETT, 1926

17705   VERDERY.   The Verderys of Georgia, 1794-1942, A. D.   A genealogical history of the American descendants of Jean Jacques de Verdery, counsellor to the King of France (Louis XVI) in the parliaments and courts of the province of Guienne, by his great great grand daughter, Emily Prather ... Atlanta, Williams printing company, 1942.   236 p. incl. illus. (incl. coat of arms) port. ports. 22½ cm. 42-18896.

CS71.V5   1942

VERDIER.   See: LAFITTE, 1926
                           LAFITTE, 1927

17706   VERDUN.   The abbey of St. Mary, Croxden, Staffordshire.   A monograph by Charles Lynam, F. S. A.   London, Sprague & co., limited, 1911.   vii, 19, ii, xx, xix p. front., 75 pl. (part fold., incl. plans) 2 facsim. (1 fold.) 32 cm.   The property of the Earl of Macclesfield.   "Sketch of the earlier Verduns": xix p. at end.   13-3654.

NA5471.C97L8

VERE.   See: ALNO, CS419.P3
                        CAVENDISH, 1752

VERMILYA.   See BENTON, 1906

17707   VERNA.   I Verna ... 1. edizione in copie numerate fuori commercio.   By Fernando Verna. Roma, 1968.   169 p. illus., plates, tables. 24 cm. "No. 38." 71-430434.   CS769.V43   1968

17708   VERNAL.   John Vernal, Sophia Spooner and their descendants.   (n. p., 1926)   cover title, 1 p. 1., 7, 2 numb. 1. 29½ cm.   Signed: Herbert Nelson Vernal.   Introductory note signed: Alvah Horton Sabin.   Type-written. 26-18313.

CS71.V529   1926

17709   VERNEY.   Inquiries into the origin and progress of the science of heraldry in England. With explanatory observations on armorial ensigns, by James Dallaway ... Gloucester, Printed by R. Raikes, for T. Cadell, London, 1793.   2 p. l., xiii, (1), 424 p., 2 l., cxii p. illus., plates (part col.) port., facsims., coats of arms (part col.) fold. geneal. tab. 31 cm.   Title vignette.   "Pedigree of Verney family": fold. geneal. tab. following p. 370.   "Observations on heraldick ensigns" has engraved half-title within ornamental border.   "The third part of The boke of St. Albans, printed from the original edition in 1486": p. lxv-cxii. 28-14089.

CR1612.D2

17710   VERNEY.   Letters and papers of the Verney family down to the end of the year 1639.   Printed from the original mss. in the possession if Sir Harry Verney, bart.   Edited by John Bruce, esq.   London, Printed for the Camden society, by J. B. Nichols and son, 1853.   xiv, (2), 308 p. double geneal. tab. 22½ x 17 cm. (Camden society, Publications, no. LVI) 17-1233.   DA20.C17 no. 56

17711   VERNEY.   Memoirs of the Verney family ... Compiled from the letters and illustrated by the portraits at Claydon house ... London and New York, Longmans, Green, and co., 1892-99.   4 v. fronts., illus., ports., facsim. 22 cm.   Title varies.   A later ed. appeared under title: Memoirs of the Verney family during the seventeenth century ... Contents. - v. 1-2. Memoirs of the Verney family during the civil war ... by Frances Parthenope Verney. - v. 3. Memoirs of the Verney family during the commonwealth, 1650 to 1660 ... by Margaret M. Verney. - v. 4. Memoirs of the Verney family from the restoration to the revolution, 1660 - 1696 ... by Margaret M. Verney. 8-23793.   DA377.2.V5A18

17712   VERNEY.   Memoirs of the Verney family during the seventeenth century; compiled from the papers and illustrated by the portraits at Claydon house, by Frances Parthenope Verney and Margaret M. Verney ... 2d ed., abridged and corrected by Margaret M. Verney ... London, New York and Bombay, Longmans, Green, and co., 1904.   2 v. fronts., illus., plates, ports., fold. geneal. tab. 20½ cm. Title vignettes. 6-1464 rev.   DA377.2.V5A2

17713   VERNEY.   Memoirs of the Verney family during the seventeenth century, compiled from the papers and illustrated by the portraits at Claydon house, by Frances Parthenope Verney and Margaret M. Verney ... 3d ed. ... London, New York (etc.) Longmans, Green and co., 1925.   2 v. fronts., illus., plates, ports., fold. geneal. tab. 20 cm. 26-6537.   DA377.2.V5A2   1925

17714   VERNON.   ... Memorial of Admiral Vernon from contemporary authorities, by William Frederick Vernon.   Printed for private circulation.   London, W. H. Dalton, 1861.   151 p. fold. geneal. tab. 17½ cm. At head of title: Vernon semper. viret. 21-11405.   DA87.1.V5V4

779

17715 VERNON. Haddon hall: an illustrated guide and companion to the tourist and visitor. With notices of Buxton, Bakewell, Rowsley, Matlock Bath ... By S. C. Hall ... and Llewellynn Jewitt ... Buxton, J. C. Bates, 1871. 2 p. l., 67 p. illus., plan. 21 cm. (Hazlitt tracts, v. 8, no. 2) 23-1160.

AC911.H3 vol. 8 no. 2

17716 VERNON. The Vernon family and arms. Communicated by Harrison Ellery ... (Boston, 1879) 8 p. illus. (coat of arms) 26 cm. 38M203T.

CS71.V53   1879

17717 VERNON. The diary of Thomas Vernon, a loyalist, banished from Newport by the Rhode Island general assembly in 1776. With notes by Sidney S. Rider. To which is added The Vernon family and arms (by Harrison Ellery) and the Genealogy of the family of Richard Greene, of Potowomut (by George Sears Greene) Providence, R. I., S. S. Rider, 1881. viii, 150 p. 21 cm. (Added t. -p.: Rhode Island historical tracts. no. 13) Rc - 2954.

E278.V54V5

17718 VERNON. Ayleston manor and church; being a history of the parish of Ayleston, Leicestershire, and its connections with the families of Pembrugge, Vernon and Manners, and an account of the parish church and its rectors, by M. Paul Dare ... with photographs by Mr. Lawrence A. Kellett and genealogies. Leicester, E. Backus, 1924. 6 p. l., 84 p. front., plates, fold geneal. tab. 20 cm. Bibliography: p. 77-78. 26-22551.

CS436.A9D3

VERNON. See also: CHANCE, CS439.C515
                      STANTON, 1922
                      SWYNNERTON, DA670.S69S6 v. 7 & n. s. vol. 3 & DA670.S68W7 vol. 20

17719 VERPLANCK. The history of Abraham Isaacse Ver Planck, and his male descendants in America. By William Edward Ver Planck. Fishkill Landing, N. Y., J. W. Spaight, 1892. vii, (1), (9)-306 p. incl. front., illus., facsim. pl. 21 cm. 9-15027.

CS71.V551   1892

17720 VERPLANCK. The site of the Assay office on Wall street, an illustrated historical sketch of the successive public buildings and men in public life connected with the site; interspersed with some family history, by William E. Verplanck. (Princeton, Princeton university press) 1921. 42 p., 1 l. incl. front., plates, ports. 23½ cm. 22-3085.

F128.67.W2V5

VERPLANCK. See also MAXWELL, 1916

17721 VERRILL. The ancestry, life and work of Addison E. Verrill of Yale University. By George Elliot Verrill. Santa Barbara, Calif., Pacific Coast Pub. Co. (1958) 99 p. illus. 24 cm. 58-37889.

CS71.V556   1958

17722 VERRILL. The history & genealogy of the Varrell-Verrill and associated families, by Harold F. Round. Bryn Mawr, Pa. (1968) iii, 446 p. maps, ports. 24 cm. 68-6325.

CS71.V52   1968

17723 VERSPECHT. Stamboom der familie Verspecht. By Maurits Sacré. Merchtem, Drukkerij Sacré, 1951-52. 2 geneal. tables. 65 x 63 cm. fold. to 22 x 17 cm; 62 x 69 cm. fold. to 25 x 16 cm. (His Uitgaven over de nalatenschap van J. J. t'Kint, D) Cover title; cover of table 1 dated 1952. 54-37254.

CS829.V56   1951

VERTREES. See LA RUE, 1921

VERVENNE. See SCHUSTER. 1951

VESCELIUS. See No. 9847 - Hackettstown.

17724 VESPUCCI. Vita e lettere de Amerigo Vespucci, gentiluomo fiorentino; raccolte e illustrate dall'abate Angelo Maria Bandini. Firenze, Stamperia all'insegna di Apollo, 1745. lxxvi, 125 p., 1 l. front., 1 illus., fold. geneal. tab. 23½ cm. The genealogical table is of the Vespueel family. Contents. - Vita di Amerigo Vespucci. - Lettera della isole nuovamente trovate in quattro suol viaggi. Data in Lisbona adi 4. di settembre 1584 (i. e. 1504) - Lettera indirzzata a Lorenzo di Pierframcesco de' Medici, 18. di luglio del 1500. - Relazione inedita intorno alla spedizione che fece il Re di Portogallo verso il Capo di Buona Speranza, de all citta di Clicut, mandata al magnifico Lorenzo di Pierfrancesco de' Medici da Amerigo Vespucci. - Lettera risguardante il suo terzo viaggio ... creduta indirizzata a Piero Soderini, ma ora ritrovata, mediante un' antica traduzione in latino della medesima, scritta a Lorenzo di Pierfrancesco de' Medici. 3-28376.

E125.V5V42

17725   VESPUCCI.   Americus Vespucci, eines florenzischen adelmannes, leben und nachgelassene briefe, worinnen dessen entdeckungen der neuen welt und die merkwurdigkeiten seiner reisen|historisch und geographisch beschrieben werden.   Aus dem italienischen des herrn abts.   Angelus Maria Bandini ubersetzet, und mit ammerkungen erlautert.   Hamburg, G. C. Grund; Leipzig, A. H. Holle, 1748.
5 p. 1., 299, (9) p. front., 1 illus. 19 cm. Translation of the first edition, Firenze, 1745. For contents see No. 17726. 35-16377.

E125. V5V494

17726   VESPUCCI.   The life and voyages of Americus Vespucius; with illustrations concerning the navigator, and the discovery of the New world ... By C. Edwards Lester and Andrew Foster.   New York, Baker & Scribner, 1846.   xviii p., 1 1., (21) - 431 p. incl. diagr. front. (port.) fold. geneal. tab. 24 cm. Contents.
pt. I. Biography (including Vespucci's letters of his four voyages) - pt. II. Illustrations. (i) Eulogium of Americus Vespucius (by S. Canovai)
II. A narrative addressed to Lorenzo di Pier-Francesco de' Medici; giving an account of the voyage and discoveries of Vasco da Gama beyond the cape of Good Hope, the authorship of which has been attributed to Americus Vespucius. III. Letters of Paolo Toscanelli to Columbus. IV. Macro Polo and his travels. V. Fellow-voyagers of Americus. Alonzo de Ojeda and Juan de la Cosa (abridged mainly from Irving's Lives of the companions of Columbus) VI. Documents relating to Americus Vespucius: Presented in the collection of Navarrete. VII. Letter of M. Ranke to M. de Humboldt, respecting the correspondence of Americus with Soderini and De' Medici.   VIII. The Vespucci family. 3-28377.

E125. V5L6

17727   VESPUCCI.   Vida y cartas de Américo Vespucio, recogidas y publicadas en el año 1745 por Angel María Bandini.   Versión moderna del italiano, arreglo y notas de José Miglia M.   Lima, Editorial P. T. C. M., 1948.   121 p. 21 cm. (Colección Mundo nuevo) 49-21916*.   E125. V5V497

VESSY.   See PORTER, 1941

VEST.   See SCHAUB, 1965

VETERIPONT.   See VIPONT.

VETTER.   See FEETER.

17728   VIALL.   Viall genealogy, 1618-1941.   By Harriet Nason Viall.   Berwyn, Ill., 1941.
geneal. table, coat of arms. 57 x 42 cm. fold. to 28 x 22 cm. 50-44073.   CS71. V632   1941

VIALL.   See also BUCK, 1917, suppl.

VICARS.   See BANNING, 1924

17729   VICK.   Vick of Vicksburg.   By Robert Arthur.   1953.   69 1. 32 cm. Typescript (carbon copy) On t. p.:
New Orleans, Louisiana, 5 June 1953. (Bibliography: leaves 68 - 69. 75-6673 MARC.   CS71. V635   1953

17730   VICKERS.   Vickers or Vickery family.   (Albany, N. Y., J. Munsell, printer, 1864)
5 p. 23 cm. By William Henry Whitmore. Caption title. Pages 4-5 "Lombard family." contain corrections on the Lombard genealogy printed in the New England historical and genealogical register, 1858. Reprinted from the New England hist. and geneal. register, 1864. p.186-188. 9-15022.

CS71. V637   1864

VICKERS.   See also VICKERY.

17731   VICKERY.   (The Vickery family) Compiled by Clara Audrea (Sibley) Paine.   (n. p.) 1923.
12 1. 24½ cm. Autographed from type-written copy. The ancestry and descendants of William Henry Vickery, b.1824. "Authority": 1. 3.
26-5596.   CS71. V637   1923

VICKERY.   See also VICKERS.

VICKEY.   See COLLIER, 1951a

17732   VICTORIA, queen of Great Britain, 1819-1901.   The ancestry of Her Majesty Queen Victoria, and of His Royal Highness Prince Albert.   Comprised in thirty-two tables, with biographical memoirs and heraldic notices.   By George Russell French ... London, W. Pickering, 1841.   xviii, (2), 411, (1) p.
incl. geneal. tables. 19 cm. 3-26012.   DA555. F87

17733 VICTORIA. Genealogy of Her Majesty Queen Victoria, through the Anglo-Saxon, Scottish, Norman, Welsh and Este-Guelphic lines, with illustrative historical notes. By an amateur. (Archibald N. Carmichael) Edinburgh (W. Macphail, printer) 1845. 1 p. l., 22 p. 23 cm. Signed: A.N.C. 10-19895.

DA558.C3

17734 VIDITO. Vidito, John Vidito of New York city and his descendants; a Huguenot founder of an American family. By Alice L. Priest. Brookline, Mass., 1932. 43 numb. l. 27 cm. Type-written. 32-14277.

CS71.V64 1932

17735 VIELE. Viele, 1659-1909. Two hundred and fifty years with a Dutch family of New York. Compiled by Kathlyne Knickerbocker Viele ... New York, T. A. Wright, 1909. 149 (i.e. 153) p. front., plates, ports. 24½ cm. Blank leaves at end for "Additional records." "Limited ed. of seventy-five copies of which this is no. 74." 11-705.

CS71.V65 1910

17736 VIELE. Viele records, 1613-1913; being a revised and enlarged edition of the Viele genealogy published in 1909, under the title, Two hundred and fifty years with a Dutch family of New York. Compiled and arranged by Kathlyne Knickerbacker Viele ... New York, T. A. Wright, 1913. 292 p. front., plates, ports. 24½ cm. Blank leaves at end for "Additional records." "Limited ed. of sixty copies of which this is no. 48." 13-20152.

CS71.V65 1913

VIELE. See also KNICKERBOCKER, 1916

17737 VIENNAY. La famille Viennay-Pachot, par Pierre George Roy. Lévis, 1915. 9 p. 24 cm. "Tiré à 100 exemplaires." 23-16890.

CS90.V5

17738 VIENS. The Viens family. By Norma Thornley Dare. (West Haven? Conn., 1968) iv, 55 l. 30 cm. 68-6574.

CS71.V66 1968

17739 VIETS. Viets family. Dr. John Viets of Simsbury, Connecticut (1710) and his descendants. By Francis H. Viets ... Providence, E. A. Johnson & co., printers, 1879. 31, (1) p. 22 cm. 9-15023.

CS71.V666 1879

17740 VIETZ. The genealogy of the Vietz family with biographical sketches; Dr. John Viets of Simsbury, Connecticut, 1710, and his descendants, written and compiled by Francis Hubbard Viets. (Hartford) The Case, Lockwood & Brainard co., 1902. 228 p. front., pl., port. 24½ cm. 2-8226.

CS71.V666 1902

17741 VILAS. A genealogy of the descendants of Peter Vilas. Compiled and edited by (467) C. H. Vilas ... Madison, Wis., The editor, 1875. 221 p. front., ports. 23½ cm. "Private edition." Blank leaves interspersed. 9-15024.

CS71.V698 1875

VILEY. See WITHERSPOON, 1922

17742 VILLAND. Villandane, ein etterrøknad i norsk aettesoge. By Lars Sigurdson Reinton. Oslo, I kommisjon hos J. Dybwad, 1939. xi, 258 p. plates, ports., fold. map. 24 cm. At head of title: Det Norske videnskaps-akademi i Oslo. Thesis - Oslo. Thesis note from label mounted on half-title. "Avstyttingar og kjelder": p. ix-xi. 46-30947 rev. *

CS919.V5 1939

17743 VILLIERS. A vanished Victorian, being the life of George Villiers, fourth earl of Clarendon, 1800-1870, by his grandson, George Villiers. London, Eyre & Spottiswoode, 1938. xiii p., 1 l., 17-377 p. 8 pl. (incl. front., ports.) 25½ cm. Bibliography: p. 365-366. 39-11777.

DA46.C6V5

17744 VILLIERS. Uncommon people; a study of England's élite. By Paul Bloomfield. London, H. Hamilton (1955) xi, 219 p. ports., geneal. tables. 22 cm. 56-18674.

HT647.B55 1955

17745 VINCENT. Memoir of Augustine Vincent, Windsor herald. By Nicholas Harris Nicolas ... London, W. Pickering, 1827. x, 125 p. illus. (coat of arms) 19 cm. Title vignette: coat of arms. 16-18059.

CS8.V5N5

17746   VINCENT.   Portions of Vincent and Boddington pedigrees.   Comp. by Reginald Stewart Boddington.   Private impression.   London, Mitchell and Hughes, 1876.   12 p.   illus. (coats of arms) 19 cm. Published also in "Miscellanea genealogica et heraldica".   London, 1877, n.s., vol. II, p. 239-247. 21-21741.   CS439.V55

17747   VINCENT.   Our family of Vincents; a history, genealogy, and biographical notices, compiled, edited, and prepared by Boyd Vincent.   Printed for private circulation.   Cincinnati, Stewart Kidd company (1924)   158 p. plates, ports. 19 cm. 24-8763.   CS71.V78   1924

17748   VINCENT.   Descendants of Pierre Vincent, Sr., & Catherine Galman, Acadians.   By Flavia (Vincent) Reeds.   (n. p., 1964)   106, 11, xiv p. 35 cm. 65-74984.   CS71.V78   1964

VINCENT.   See also: BESSELLIEU, 1959
                                  JOHNSON, 1961

VINES.   See WARD, 1900

VINING.   See ROGERS, 1902

VINSON.   See: JARRATT, 1957
                          No. 1547 - Cabell county.

17749   VINTON.   Genealogical sketches of the descendants of John Vinton of Lynn, 1648, and of several allied families ... with an appendix containing a history of the Braintree iron works, and other historical matter.   By John Adams Vinton.   Boston, S. K. Whipple and company, 1858.   xvi, 236 p. front., ports. 24 cm. 9-15025.   CS71.V79   1858

17750   VINTON.   The Vinton memorial, comprising a genealogy of the descendants of John Vinton of Lynn, 1648: also, genealogical sketches of several allied families ... With an appendix containing a history of the Braintree iron works, and other historical matter.   By John Adams Vinton.   Boston, S. K. Whipple and company, 1858.   xv, (1), 534, (4) p. front., ports. 23½ cm. 9-15026.
CS71.V79   1858a

VINTON.   See also FARWELL, 1934

17751   VIOLETT.   History of Sampson Violett, Revolutionary solder, 1776-1784, War of 1812-13. Life of Sampson Violett and Eve Hoover (Philips) Violett.   By Mary Catherine (Violett) Corbett. 1st ed.   (n. p.) Priv. print. (1947)   49 l. col. coat of arms. 28 cm. 49-38078*.
CS71.V8   1947

17752   VIPONT.   Family records, I. The Viponts.   II. The Ecroyds and Viponts.   III. The Biltons. Compiled by William Scruton ... Privately printed.   Bradford, G. F. Sewell, printer, 1904. 80 p. front., plates, ports., col. coat of arms. 19½ cm.   Compiled from material collected by the late Mrs. Hannah Dale and Mr. Thomas E. Scorah. cf. Pref. 24-29133.   CS439.V57S3

VISCONTI.   See ARCONATI-VISCONTI.

17753   VISSCHER.   Genealogy of the Visscher family.   This name is written in the old records Visscher, Visser, Visger, Visselaar. De Vysselaar and De Visser.   These names in English are Fisher ... (n.p., 1880)   (2) p. 34½ cm. Caption title. 9-15477.   CS71.V833   1880

17754   VISSCHER.   Visscher (family)   (In Talcott, Sebastian Visscher.   "Genealogical notes of New York and New England families."   Albany, 1883. 24 cm. p. 253-291) 13-9621.   F118.T14
          —— Copy 3, detached.   CS71.V833   1883

VISSCHER.   See also FISHER.

VITRÉ.   See LONGESPÉE, DA690.L15B6

17755   VITTUM.   The Vittum folks, by Edmund March Vittum and Linnie Bean Page ... (Muscatine, Ia.) Priv. print. for E. M. Vittum, 1922.   208 p. 18½ cm. 22-16242.   CS71.V85   1922

17756   VIVIAN.   Pedigree of the family of Vivian of Cornwall, reprinted, with additions, from the "Visitations of the county of Cornwall," ed. by Lieut.-Colonel John Lambrick Vivian.   (Exeter, W. Pollard, 1887)   cover-title, 22 p.   29 cm.   16-20945.   CS438.V6

17757   VIVIAN.   Vivians, by M. Vivian Hughes ... New York, Oxford university press, 1935.
4 p. l., 239, (1) p. plates, port.   21 cm.   "Printed in Great Britain."   The second volume of an autobiography, the first and third appeared under title "A London child of the seventies."   "A London girl of the eighties", respectively.   36-27012.   PR6015.U3V5 1935

VIVIAN.   See also: CARPENTER, 1961
DU PONT, 1923

17758   VIVION.   Vivion family of Virginia (by) Charles Brunk Heinemann.   Chicago, Ill., 1936.
2 p. l., 24, 24a-25, 5 numb. l.   29 cm.   Type-written.   37-5913.   CS71.V87   1936

17759   VLADIMIR.   Political & diplomatic history of Russia, by George Vernadsky.   Students' ed.
Boston, Little, Brown, and company, 1936.   ix p., 2 l., (3)-499 p. incl. geneal. tables.   maps (part fold.) 22½ cm.   Maps on lining-papers.   "General bibliography": p. (467)-470.   Bibliography at end of each chapter.   36-11172.   DK61.V4

VLIET.   See No. 9847 - Hackettstown.

17760   VOGEL.   Living a life; ed., with an introduction by William P. Vogel, Jr.   New York, 1947.
xxix, 165 p. port.   22 cm.   48-2688*.   CT275.T715A3

VOGENITZ.   See CLEWELL, 1907

17761   VOGT.   The Vogts von Berg in Düsseldorf and America, by Thomas Noxon Toomey.   Saint Louis, Mo., Printed for private distribution, 1921.   20 p. incl. front., illus. (ports.) 23 cm.   Title vignette: coat of arms.   "An edition limited to 200 copies of which this is copy no. 7."   21-20548.   CS71.V93   1921

17762   VOGT.   Vogt and allied families, genealogical and biographical.   Prepared and privately printed for Mary M. Vogt ... New York, The American historical society, inc., 1926.   57 p., 1 l. plates, ports., col. coats of arms.   32 cm.   Title within ornamental border.   Dedication signed: Mary M. Vogt.   Published in part under title "The Vogt family, by Ida A. Grover", in Americana, vol. XVIII, 1924, p. 75-78.   "References": 1 leaf at end.   Contains also the Zöeckler family.   26-18778 rev. 2.   CS71.V93   1926

VON BAUER.   See THURSTON, 1894

VON GOCHNAT.   See VAN KOUGHNET, 1910

VON HAYMERLE.   See BAILLIE, 1898

VON REISENKAMPFF.   See ULRICH, 1907

17763   VON ROSENBERG.   The von Rosenberg family of Texas.   A record with historical facts and legends of the ancient Prussian family.   This book contains the record of the first three generations in Texas, with their coats of arms brought to Texas by the pioneer father, Peter Carl Johann von Rosenberg.   Compiled by Alma von Rosenberg-Tomlinson, general chairman, and the branch chairmen. (n. p., 1949)   vii, 164 p. illus., group port., map, coats of arms, geneal. tables.   24 cm.   52-64413.   CS71.V94   1949

VON SCHNEIDAU.   See JEROME, 1957

VON WELSER.   See WELSER, 1666

17764   VOORHEES.   ... Voorhees.   Line of descent of Louis B. Voorhees.   (n. p., 1896)
6 l. illus. (coat of arms) 20½ cm.   Caption title.   Additions in manuscript.   9-14799.   CS71.V951   1896

17765   VOORHEES.   Ralph and Elizabeth Rodman Voorhees; a tribute by Oscar M. Voorhees ...
New York, The Tribute press, 1927.   viii, 267 p. front., illus. (incl. ports., coat of arms) fold. map, facsim.   23½ cm.
"(Traces) the four principal ancestral lines - Voorhees, Whitaker, Nevius and Rodman - with casual references to collateral lines." - p. 11.
27-23548.   CS71.V951   1927

17766   VOORHEES.   The John C. Voorheis branch of the Van Voorhees family in America.   Grants Pass, Or., Printed by the Daily courier (1939)   71 p., 1 l., (4) p. incl. front., illus. (incl. ports., coats of arms) 24 cm. "By Amos Earle Voorhies." - p. (2)   "Of this book one hundred and fifty copies were printed for private distribution only.   Number 123."   40-32889.
CS71.V951   1939

17767   VOORHEES.   Prominent families of Oklahoma; individual biographic studies.   Library ed. New York, Historical records, inc.   (1941? -   v. front. (coat of arms) 29½ cm.   Contents. - (v. 1) Voorhees family.   43-5743.
CS71.V951   1941

VOORHEES.   See also: BERGEN, 1866
VAN VOORHEES.

VOORHEIS.   See VOORHEES.

17768   VORAN.   The Voran story, 1805-1963, compiled by Hulda Kopper and P. P. Voran.   (Hutchinson, Kan.? 1963?)   46 l. geneal. table. 30 cm.   Cover title: The Voran family, 1805 - 1963. 65-71822.
CS71.V952   1963

VORCE.   See VORSE.

VORE.   See BASSETT, 1926

17769   VORPAGEL.   Bulletin.   Vorpagel Family Association.   v. 1-3, no. 1; Jan. 1961 - June, 1963. Burlington, Wis. (etc.)   3 v. in 2. illus. (part col.) ports., col. coats of arms. 30 cm.   Frequency varies.   No more published? 63-59200.
CS71.V95312

17770   VORSE.   A genealogical and historical record of rhe Vorce family in America, with notes on some allied families.   By Charles Marvin Vorce ... Cleveland, O., 1901.   1 p. 1., 111 p. ports., maps. 23½ cm.   One leaf of "Corrections and additions" inserted after p. 100. 1-26933.
CS71.V955   1901

VOSBURGH.   See HART, 1923

17771   VOSE.   Robert Vose and his descendants, compiled by Ellen F. Vose ... Boston, Mass., Priv. print. (S. Usher, The Fort Hill press) 1932.   3 p. 1., 724 p. front., pl. 24½ cm.   32-19021.
CS71.V96   1932

17772   VOSE.   Genealogical notes on the ancestry of some early settlers in the upper Wyoming valley including Lemuel Vose, 1753-1827, Thomas Vose, 1787-1821, Job Whitcomb, 1724-, John Skinner Whitcomb, 1766-1838, Azariah Winslow, 176- - 181-, together with several allied lines in New England of which it appears a few have not heretofore been traced.   By Archy Wright Barnes.   (n. p.) 1945.   75 l. fold. geneal. tab. 28 cm.   Type-written.   Bibliographical foot-notes.   45-15635.
F157.W9B3

VOSE.   See also: BARNES, 1939
BARNES, 1941

VOSS.   See GASCHEN, 1933

17773   VOUGHT.   The Vought family; being an account of the descendants of Simon and Christina Vought, by William Gordon Ver Planck ... New York, Press of T. A. Wright, 1907.   27 p. 28½ cm. "Edition of one hundred copies." 7-3678.
CS71.V972   1907-

17774   VREELAND.   History and genealogy of the Vreeland family, edited by Nicholas Garretson Vreeland.   Jersey City, N. J., Historical publishing co., 1909.   320 p., 2 l. incl. front., illus., plates (1 col.) ports., fold. map. 24½ cm.   Added t.-p. illus.: The Vreelands, their books ... title page and other drawings by Francis William Vreeland. 9-28956.
CS71.V979   1909

17775   VREELAND.   Annals of the Vreeland family.   By Louis Beach Vreeland.   Charlotte, N. C., c. 1950.   (78) l. 28 cm. 50-1484.
CS71.V979   1950

17776   VREELAND.   Annals of the Vreeland family.   By Louis Beach Vreeland.   Charlotte, N.C., c.1956.   119 p. 28 cm. 57-31371.   CS71.V979   1956

17777   VREELAND.   Last in line; a study of the ancestry of Robert Hydon Vreeland, by R. H. Vreeland.   (1st ed.   Hawthorne, Calif.) 1967.   vi, 99 l. illus., geneal. tables. 29 cm. 25 copies. Bibliography: leaves 92-97. 74-4152.   CS71.V979   1967

      VREELAND.   See also: HYNES, 1941-2
                                THROCKMORTON, 1939
                                VAN NORDEN, 1923

      VROMAN.   See VROOMAN.

      VROOM.   See: VAN NESS, 1960
                        No. 9847 - Hackettstown.

17778   VROOMAN.   Josiah B. Vrooman (Vroman) his ancestors and descendants, by Lora Vrooman Randall and Florence Vrooman Houghton.   El Paso, Tex., C. Hertzog, printer, 1946.   2 p. l., (ix) - xiii, (1), 217, (1) p. front., illus. (incl. port., map, facsim.) 24 cm. Bibliography: p. 197. 46-23268.
                                                          CS71.V9795   1946

17779   VROOMAN.   The Vrooman family in America, descendants of Hendrick Meese Vrooman who came from Holland to America in 1664, prepared by Grace Vrooman Wickersham and Ernest Bernard Comstock.   (Dallas) 1949.   341 p. illus., ports., maps, col. coat of arms. 22 cm. 49-26958*.
                                                          CS71.V9795   1949

      VROOMAN.   See also MOLTER, 1932

17780   VYNER.   Vyner.   The family history.   Revised and enlarged. ... (Leamington, D. Sarney, printer) 1887.   4 p. l., 250, xvi p. col. front. 22 cm. Compiled by Charles J. Vyner and his brother Col. Vtner; first printed in 1885. 13-13894.   CS439.V8

      VYVYAN.   See WILSON, 1890

W

WACKLEY. See WALKLEY.

WADDAMS. See GRAY, E171.A53 vol.18

17781   WADDEL. Memorials of academic life: being an historical sketch of the Waddel family, identified through three generations with the history of the higher education in the South and Southwest. By John N. Waddel ... Richmond, Va., Presbyterian committee of publication, 1891.   583 p. front. (port.) 20½ cm. 12-39757.   LA2317.W3A2

17782   WADDELL. The Waddell family. By Kenneth Mourning Waddell. (Washington, 1959 -   v. illus. 29 cm. 61-31768.   CS71.W116   1959

17783   WADDELL. Genealogy of the Waddell and the Halley families. By Jessie (Laing) Sibbet. (Pasadena, Calif., 1957)   20 l. geneal. table. 28 cm. 57-46792.   CS71.W116   1957

WADDEL, WADDELL. See also: BROWNLEE, 1937
CREWS, 1941
MAJOR, 1915

17784   WADDINGHAM. (Photostat reproduction of a chart of the Waddingham family) Compiled ... by Eugene F. McPike. (n.p.) 1930.   geneal. tab. 36 x 49 cm. 31-30053.   CS71.W117   1930

17785   WADDINGTON. Who's who in the family of Waddington, compiled by John Waddington ... from pedigrees collected by him and by Major-General Henry Ferrers Waddington. London, Wada limited, 1934.   xxii, 520 p. illus. (incl. port., coats of arms) 22 cm. 35-13703.   CS439.W2

17786   WADDINGTON. Genealogy of the Weddington family. By Andy Simmons Weddington. Pulaski, Tenn. (1960)   115 l. 28 cm. Caption title. 63-59231.   CS71.W118   1960

17787   WADE. The life of Benjamin F. Wade, by A. G. Riddle ... Cleveland, O., W. W. Williams, 1886.   310 p. front. (port.) 19 cm. Contains genealogy. 12-38015.   E415.9.W16R5

17788   WADE. The Wade genealogy, being some account of the origin of the name ... and genealogies of the families of Wade of Massachusetts and New Jersey ... (pt. 1-4) Comp. by Stuart Charles Wade ... New York, S. C. Wade, 1900-(03?)   4 v. in 1. front., illus. (coats of arms) plates, ports. 23½ cm. Pts. III-IV have imprint: Rutland, Vermont, The Tuttle company. Pt. I is an "Edition limited to 1000 copies, of which this is no. 3." Pts. II-IV "Privately printed - 500 copies." No more published. 9-15467 rev. 2   CS71.W119   1900

17790   WADE. The Wade family of southern Maryland. By Richard F. Scarborough. (n.p., 19-) 25 l. 31 cm. On cover, in ms.: Zachary Wade and descendants in Maryland. 59-35702.   CS71.W119

17791   WADE. The Wade family, Monongalia County, Virginia, now West Virginia. By Franklin Marion Brand ... (n.p., 1927)   486 p. incl. illus., coat of arms. 23½ cm. 28-6664.   CS71.W119   1927

17792   WADE.   My aunt Louisa and Woodrow Wilson (by) Margaret Axson Elliott.   Chapel Hill, The University of North Carolina press (1944)   vii, 302 p. 22 cm.   An account of the author's life spent in the homes of her aunt and brother-in-law.   44-40197.   E767.3.E4

17793   WADE.   The Wades; the history of a family, dealing with the kith and king of Zachary and Mary Hatton Wade, their descendants and related lines, male and female, in Maryland, Virginia, Tennessee, South Carolina, North Carolina, and other States.   Cairo, Ill. (1963)   247 p. illus., ports., facsims. 24 cm. 63-17254.   CS71.W119   1963

17794   WADE.   A pioneer southern family life, by Ronald E. Wade.   Gilmer, Tex. (1967)   vii, 56 p. illus., ports. 24 cm. 68-174.   CS71.W119   1967

17795   WADE.   Posey-Wade-Harrison (Emison) and other Families of Maryland and Virginia, with supplement to The Emison Family.   Positive.   6048
Microfilm reading room

17796   WADE.   Source material on the Wade genealogy gathered in various parts of the United States. Clippings, written material and photographs.   2 notebooks in vertical file.   Ask reference librarian for this material.

WADE.   See also: BEACH, 1960
OKELY, 1899
No. 9847 - Hackettstown.

WADDLE.   See McKEEVER, 1959

17797   WADHAM.   Wadham college, Oxford, its foundation, architecture and history, with an account of the family of Wadham and their seats in Somerset and Devon, by T. G. Jackson ... Oxford, Clarendon press, 1893.   xix, 228 p. incl. illus., geneal. tables. XVIII pl. (part fold. incl. front., plans, facsim.) 29½ cm. "175 copies only of this book are offered to the public. This is no. 90." 12-34627.   LF725.J2

17798   WADHAM.   Wadhams genealogy, preceded by a sketch of the Wadham family in England ... by Harriet Weeks Wadhams Stevens (Mrs. George Thomas Stevens) New York, Frank Allaben genealogical company (c. 1913)   v p., 3 l., 652 p. front., illus., plates, ports., geneal. tab., coat of arms. 25 cm. 14-2489.   CS71.W122   1913

WADLEIGH.   See BLAKE, 1948

17799   WADSWORTH.   Wadsworth. By C. C. Baldwin ... (Cleveland, Leader printing company, 1882)   1 p. l., p. (205)-215. 23½ cm. From the author's Candee genealogy, Cleveland, 1882. 14-11916.   CS71.W125   1882

17800   WADSWORTH.   ... Two hundred and fifty years of the Wadsworth family in America ... Containing an account of the family reunion, at Duxbury, Mass., September 13, 1882, and a genealogical register, prepared expressly for this work, by Horace Andrew Wadsworth ... Lawrence, Mass., Printed at the Eagle steam job printing rooms, 1883.   3 p. l., (8)-257 p. front., illus., ports., coat of arms. 24 cm. 9-15031.   CS71.W125   1883

17801   WADSWORTH.   Wadsworth; or, The charter oak, by W. H. Gocher ... Hartford, Conn., W. H. Gocher, 1904.   399 p. incl. front., plates, ports., facsims. 20 cm. Purporting to be based on papers found in an old chest in Hartford. 4-27367.   F97.G57

17802   WADSWORTH.   Wadsworths of Maryland. In vertical file.   Ask reference librarian for this material.

17803   WADSWORTH.   Thomas Wadsworth, Harford County, Maryland, 1800.   By Raymond Martin Bell.   Washington, Pa., 1963.   In vertical file.   Ask reference librarian for this material.

WADSWORTH.   See also: CANDEE, 1882
MARSHALL, 1913
RUSSELL, 1910
SEBOR, 1923

17804   WAEGER.   Waeger immigrants to colonial New York.   By Howard Carlyle Wagar.   (Highland Park? Ill.) 1955.   geneal. table.   125 x 82 cm. fold. to 30 x 23 cm.   55-37488.   CS71.W127   1955

17805   WAEGER.   Progenitors in the Wurttemberg Region, Germany, of the New York State Wagar-Wager-Weger families.   By Paul Wesley Prindle.   Darien, Conn., 1961.   21 l. 29 cm. 62-36491.
CS71.W127   1961

17806   WAGAMAN.   Miscellaneous papers on the Wagaman family.   Wagaman reunion association. Greensburg, Pa., 1940)   6 l. 28 cm.   Reproduced from type-written copy; imprint in manuscript.   41M3647T.
CS71.W13   1940

17807   WAGAMAN.   Historical notes and collections by the president, submitted to the twelfth annual reunion of the Wagaman reunion association, held at Bonneauville, Pennsylvania, June 21, 1941.   (n. p., 1941)   1 p. l., 18 numb. l. 28½ cm.   Reproduced from type-written copy.   Caption title: History of Wagaman family, by Philip Wagaman, 1924.   CS71.W13   1941

WAGAR.   See WAEGER.

17808   WAGENER.   From Wagner 1768 to Wagener 1968, by William Jon R. Wagener.   (Sturgeon Bay, Wis., Key Pub. Co., 1967)   42 p. illus., geneal. tables, maps (on covers), ports. 24 cm. Cover title. "200 copies." 67-66294.   CS71.W134   1967

WAGENER.   See also: EYERMAN, 1898 and 1902
                       MIXSELL, E171.A53 v. 15

17809   WAGENSELLER.   The history of the Wagenseller family in America, with kindred branches. Edited and compiled by George Washington Wagenseller.   Middleburgh, Penna., Wagenseller publishing co., 1898.   4 p. l., 69-225 p. incl. plates and ports. 19½ cm. Sept. 28, 98-120.   CS71.W132   1898

WAGER.   See WHIPPLE, 1917

WAGGONER.   See WAGNER.

17810   WAGGY.   The Waggy-Wagy family, compiled by Ollie Wagy and Goldie Hill.   (Afton, Okla.) 1968.   x, 89 l. 28 cm.   Includes bibliographical references.   75-590.   CS71.W1325   1968

17811   WAGLE.   The John Wagle genealogy, by Louis Ansel Duermyer.   Kansas City, Mo., 1947.
1 p. l., ii, 45 numb. l., 3 l. 28 x 22½ cm.   "200 copies ... This is copy number 002."   Includes the Cox family.   47-24689.
CS71.W133   1947

17812   WAGNER.   History of the Wagner family, by Nannie (Wagner) Kintner.   (Carrollton, O., Carroll chronicle press, 1917)   (12) p. illus. (ports.) 20½ cm. 25-19241.   CS71.W134   1917

17813   WAGNER.   Isaac Wagner family tree, with comments by E. R. Wagner, underwritten by Harry W. Wagner, Earl W. Wagner, Harold H. Wagner, Porter Metz, and Charles Metz.   San Francisco, Calif., Harr Wagner publishing company, 1928. vii. 56 p. front., plates, ports. 24 cm. 28-29664.   CS71.W134   1928

17814   WAGNER.   Johan Peter Wagner, born 1687 - died after 1750, Mohawk valley pioneer and his descendants ... Written by William P. Webster, Mrs. Hortense Wagner Green and others.   Reprinted from the Enterprise and news.   Saint Johnsville, N.Y., 1929.   cover-title, 3-31, (1) p. illus. 24 cm. (Wagner family of the Mohawk valley)   Wagner.   I)   34-17822.   CS71.W134   1929

17815   WAGNER.   History and genealogy of the Wagner-Waggoner-Wagoner family, 1941, by Clark R. Wagner ... Tiffin, O., Advertiser press (1941)   304 p. illus. (1 col.; incl. ports., map, facsim., coat of arms) 24½ cm.   Compiled by the Historical committee of the Wagner, Waggoner, Wagoner family, appointed at the 46th annual reunion, Clark R. Wagner, chairman.   42-20203.   CS71.W134   1941

17816   WAGNER.   Richard Wagner wie ihn heute sehen, von professor dr. Eugen Schmitz.   Dresden, Verlag Heimatwerk Sachsen v. Baensch stiftung (1937)   104 p. 18 cm. (Schriftenreihe: Grosse Sachsen, diener des reiches. bd. 2)   "Stammtafeln": p. 101-102.   "Literatur": p. 104.   38-35977.   ML410.W1S272

17817   WAGNER.   Richard Wagners sippe, vom urahn zum enkel, von Walter Lange.   Leipzig, M. Beck, 1938.   109 p. illus. (incl. ports., maps, facsims.) fold. geneal. tab. 27 cm. Genealogical table has caption: Richard Wagners sippe, vom urahn zum enkel, nach neuesten feststellungen unter benutzung der arbeiten von Carl Fr. Glasenapp, Werner Konstantin von Arnswaldt und Peter von Gebhardt, aufgestellt von Walter Lange. 39-295.   ML410.W1L18

17818   WAGNER.   Descendants of Sarah Drake (Wisner) Wagner.   1886 to 1943 incl.   Prepared by Mr. C. F. Rudolph ... Presented by Mrs. C. F. Rudolph, through Frances Scott chapter.   Washington, D. C., 1945.   3 p. l., 5, 3 numb. l. 28 cm. Type-written. 45-16767.   CS71.W134   1945

WAGNER.   See also: JOHNSON, 1956
SHEFFIELD, 1922
SHEFFIELD, 1936
WEISER, 1960
WITTENBERGER, 1958

WAGONER.   See WAGNER.

WAGY.   See WAGGY.

WAHAB.   See WAUCHOPE.

WAHULL.   See CHETWODE, CS439.C555

17819   WAILES.   From the mines to the sod: the story of the Wailes family since 1854.   By James Roy Wailes.   (Boulder, Colo.) 1968.   iii, 115 p. illus., ports. 29 cm. 78-7924 MARC.
CS71.W138   1968

17820   WAINWRIGHT.   Waintwrihht and related families, by Emerson B. Roberts.   (Wilkinsburg, Pa., 1942)   1 v. 8 geneal. tab. 28 cm. Loose-leaf. Reproduced from type-written copy. "Twenty copies ... this is the 9th copy." "July 22, 1935; revised ... March, 1942." 42-16003.   CS71.W14   1942

WAINWRIGHT.   See also GAMBLE, 1906

WAIT.   See WAITE.

17821   WAITE.   Fifty generations.   A. D. 420 to A. D. 1880.   Fifty lines of descent through the dark ages, or the intellectual night of a thousand years.   Boston, Rockwell & Churchill press (18 -) geneal. tab. 145 x 89 cm. fold. to 44 x 34 cm. "Compiled by a member of the New England historic-genealogical society." A chart of the Walte and allied families. 36-3763.   CS71.W144   18 -

17822   WAITE.   The Waite family of Boston, Mass.   By Henry E. Waite, esq., of West Newton, Mass.   Marshal Richard Waite, of Boston.   (Boston, D. Clapp & son, printers, 1877)   4 p. 24 cm. Caption title. "Reprinted from the N. E. hist. and gen. register for Oct. 1877." 17-9733.   CS71.W144   1877

17823   WAITE.   The Waite family of Malden.   By Deloraine P. Corey.   Malden (Mass.) Printed for private distribution (by D. Clapp & son) 1878.   11 p. 26 cm. Reprinted from the New Eng. hist. and geneal. register for April, 1878. 9-15033.   CS71.W144   1878

17824   WAITE.   A genealogical sketch of a branch of the Wait or Waite family of America.   By D. Byron Waite.   Canadice, N. Y., 1893.   3 p. l., 22 p. port., coat of arms. 15½ cm. 9-19762.
CS71.W144   1893

17825   WAITE.   Family records of the descendants of Thomas Wait, of Portsmouth, Rhode Island ... Collected, compiled and published by John Cassan Wait ... (New York? J. C. Wait) 1904.   2 p. l., 55 p. incl. illus., geneal. tab., coats of arms. front. (port.) 21½ cm. 4-1667.   CS71.W144   1904

17826   WAITE.   The Waite family of Malden, Mass.   By Deloraine P. Corey.   Malden, 1913.
129 p. front. (port.) 22 cm. Ed. by Walter Kendall Watkins. 13-23634.   CS71.W144   1913

17827   WAITE.   In memory of Horatio Loomis Wait.   1836-1916.   (Chicago, 1916)   23 (1) p. incl.
front., ports.   23 cm.   Portraits are mounted photographs.   Signed: James Joseph Wait, Henry Heileman Wait.   "Military order of the Loyal
legion of the United States.   In memoriam.   Companion Horatio Loomis Wait.... died at Chicago, Illinois, July 15, 1916": (4) p. inserted at
end.   19-6608.

E467.1.W14W2

17828   WAITE.   The Waites of Deanville, by Roy H. Waite.   College Park, Md., 1966.
xiv, 94 p.   illus., facsims., ports.   24 cm.   66-19090.

CS71.W144   1966

WAITE.   See also: HOYT, 1951
HYNES, 1957
REMINGTON, 1960
STARKEY, 1910

WAITHMAN.   See WILSON, 1890

WAITMAN.   See WIGHTMAN.

WAKE.   See HUNT, 1946

17829   WAKEFIELD.   Wakefield memorial, comprising an historical, genealogical and biographical
register of the name and family of Wakefield.   Compiled by Homer Wakefield, M.D. ... Bloomington,
Ill., Priv. print. for the compiler (Pantagraph printing and stationery co.)   1897.   xi p., 2 l., 352 p., 4 l.
incl. illus., ports., maps, facsims., coat of arms.   26 cm.   Of this edition of 500 copies of the Wakefield memorial, this is no. 319.   9-15032.

CS71.W147   1897

17830   WAKEFIELD.   The family of Henry Wakefield, North Carolina, 1805-1950.   (n.p., 1950?)
78 p.   group ports., coat of arms.   23 cm.   Foreword signed: Hazel Pugh, chairman (and others) publication committee.   62-3676.

CS71.W147   1950

WAKEFIELD.   See also: ADAMS, 1950
BACKHOUSE, CS439.B18
HUFFMAN, 1963
LLOYD, 1890
WILSON, 1890
NO. 3939 - Colebrook.

17831   WAKELEY.   Ebenezer Wakeley's leaflet.   Valuable colonial and revolutionary records.
(Chicago, 1911)   4 l.   illus. (ports.) facsims.   28½ cm.   Caption title.   Signed: Ebenezer Wakeley.   Contains also a copy of the
"Roster of Ninth company of the alarm list in the 4th Connecticut regiment.   1778."   11-30202.

CS71.W148   1911

WAKELEY.   See also WALKLEY.

17832   WAKEMAN.   Wakeman genealogy.   1630-1899.   Being a history of the descendants of Samuel
Wakeman, of Hartford, Conn., and of John Wakeman, treasurer of New Haven colony, with a few
collaterals included.   By Robert P. Wakeman,   Meriden, Conn., Journal publishing co., 1900.
3 p. l., (3) - 434 p. col. front., illus., plates, ports., facsims. (part fold.) coat of arms.   24 cm.   1-3988.

CS71.W15   1900

WAKEMAN.   See also: BATES, 1911
PETTY, BX5195.T5B6

WALBECK.   See BRENDLINGER, 1941.

17833   WALBRIDGE.   Descendants of Henry Wallbridge, who married Anna Amos, December 25th,
1688, at Preston, Conn., with some notes on the allied families of Brush, Fassett, Dewey, Fobes,
Gager, Lehman, Meech, Stafford, Scott.   Compiled by William Gedney Wallbridge ... (Philadelphia,
Press of Franklin printing company, 1898)   369 p. incl. front., (map) plates, ports., facsims.   28½ cm.   C-201.

CS71.W155   1898

WALCOTT. See WOLCOTT.

WALDBURGER. See BECHTEL, 1936

WALDEGRAVE. See CLOPTON, 1939

17834 WALDELAND. Stamtavle over Waldeland-slaegten og over endel af Grude-familien, af Mrs. Caia Waldeland. Minneapolis, Augsburg publishing house trykkeri, 1912. 25 p. 23 cm. On cover: Stamtavle 1911. 12-24988. CS71.W157 1912

WALDEN. See DICKERSON, 1961

17835 WALDO. Notes respecting the family of Waldo. (Edinburgh, Printed by Ballantyne and company, 1863) iv, 35 p. 22½ cm. Title vignette: coat of arms. Compiled by Morris Charles Jones. 9-18112. CS439.W25 1863

17836 WALDO. Waldo and Chase families. From the registers of the Church of All Hallows, Bread street, London; with additions from the Visitation of London, A.D. 1664. (By Coningsby Charles Sibthorp) (London) Priv. print. 1877?) cover-title, 4 p. illus. 28½ cm. Reprinted from Miscellanea genealogica et heraldica, London, 1877, new series. vol. II, p. 100-103. 9-12695. CS439.S26 1877

17837 WALDO. The genealogy and biography of the Waldos of America from 1650 to 1883. Compiled by Joseph D. Hall, jr., from town and private records, and from papers carefully collected by Judge Loren P. Waldo ... Charles E. Waldo ... Mrs. S. G. Waters ... Danielsonville, Conn., Press of Scofield & Hamilton, 1883. 134, xviii p. incl. pl., ports., coat of arms. 21 cm. 9-15034. CS71.W165 1883

17838 WALDO. Four generations of the Waldo family in America. By Waldo Lincoln. Boston, Printed by D. Clapp & son, 1898. 18, (3) p. front. 24½ cm. "Reprinted from New Eng. historical and genealogical register for April, 1898." 17-6153. CS71.W165 1898

17839 WALDO. Genealogy of the Waldo family; a record of the descendants of Cornelius Waldo, of Ipswich, Mass., from 1647 to 1900; compiled by Waldo Lincoln ... Worcester, Mass., Press of C. Hamilton, 1902. 2 v. plates, ports. 24½ cm. Paged continuously. 3-3722. CS71.W165 1902

17840 WALDO. Continuation of Waldo genealogy, 1900-1943, by Charles S. Waldo ... New York city, N.Y., Press of C. E. Fitchett (1943) 3 p. l., v-x, 295 p. plates, ports. 23½ cm. "Continues chronologically the Waldo genealogy ... by the late Waldo Lincoln ... and also supplements it as to events prior to the year 1900." - Pref. 45-378.

WALDO. See also TODD, 1867

17841 WALDRON. Pedigree of Waldron. Compiled from chancery records in the Tower of London, and from the parish register of Alcester, in Warwickshire, by H. G. Somerby, esq. (Boston, 1854) geneal. tab. 24 x 26½ cm. Reprinted from New England historical and genealogical register, v. 8, p. 78. 14-793. CS71.W167 1854

17842 WALDRON. Resolved Waldon's descendants. Vanderpoel branch. Descendants in the Vanderpoel branch of Resolved Waldron, who came from Holland to New Amsterdam in 1650. James Henry Slipper, M.A., compiler. (New York, Macgowan & Slipper, inc., general printers and stationers) 1910. 2 p. l., 69, (3) p. plates, ports. 28½ cm. 3 blank pages at end for "Memoranda." 13-3038. CS71.W167 1910

WALDRON. See also: GALE, 1866
OTIS, 1851
SNYDER, 1958

17843 WALES. Genealogy of the descendants of Timothy Wales, of Connecticut. Together with the counsels and directions of Ebenezar Wales, esq., to his children. (By Williams Howe Whittemore) Brooklyn, Press of H. M. Gardner, jr., 1875. 56 p. 21½ cm. "The cousels and directions of Ebenezer Wales," p. 29-56, has reproduction of original t.-p. with imprint: Boston, 1813. Preface signed: William Howe Whittemore. 20-7234. CS71.W173 1875

17844   WALES.   Genealogical and historical: (Wales family history) By Willard H. Cleland.   (Dallas, 1960)   16 l. 28 cm. Title from mounted label on cover.   Appendix A: Showing the genealogical record of the Richardson family in relation to the Wales family, by F. L. Richardson, Sr.   61-44634.   CS71.W173   1960

17845   WALES.   The ancestors and descendants of Peter Thatcher and Lucinda Stanton Wales.   By Adele Andrews.   (n. p.) 1965.   76 l. illus. 29 cm. Includes bibliographies. 68-40616.
CS71.W173   1965

WALES.   See also: BRENT, 1936
REDDINGTON, 1909
THAYER. 1835

17846   WALFORD.   In memoriam.   Bro. Cornelius Walford.   By his kinsman, Edward Walford . . . . rhymer to ye Sette of odd volumes.   London, Imprynted by Bro. C. W. H. Wyman, 1887.   48, (10) p., 1 l. front. (port.) illus. 14 x 11 cm. (Half-title: Privately printed opuscula issued to the members of the Sette of odd volumes. no. xv) "This edition is limited strictly to 255 copies, and is printed for private circulation only." Lists of club's publications and members: (11) p. at end. 17-17234,
AC1.S5 no. 15
Office.

17847   WALKE.   Walke family in Virginia.   Based upon data obtained from records in lower Norfolk and Princess Anne counties, family Bibles, &c. . . . (n. p., 1897)   geneal. tab.   43 x 70 cm. fold. to 25 x 15 cm. 6-38502 rev.   CS71.W178   1897

WALKE.   See also POCAHONTAS, 1887

WALKELY.   See WALKLEY.

17848   WALKER.   Memorial of the Walkers of the Old Plymouth colony; embracing genealogical and biographical sketches of James, of Taunton; Philip, of Rehobeth; William, of Eastham; John, of Marshfield; Thomas, of Bristol; and of their descendants from 1620 to 1860, by J. B. R. Walker, A. M. . . . Northampton (Mass.) Metcalf & co., printers, 1861.   460 p. ports. 25 cm.   p. 453-460 left blank for "Family record." 9-15045.   CS71.W18   1861

17849   WALKER.   Walker genealogy.   A record of the Walker families, of Shirley, Massachusetts, and their descendants.   By Seth Chandler.   Fitchburg, Mass., J. F. D. Garfield, 1887.   46 p. 24 cm. reprinted from Chandler's History of Shirley. 1-18162.   CS71.W18   1887

17850   WALKER.   The story of my ancestors in America, by Rev. Edwin Sawyer Walker . . . Chicago, D. Oliphant, printers, 1895.   72 p. front., pl., ports. 25 cm.   "Three hundred copies printed for private circulation ... No. 18." Bibliography: p. (69) 9-15044 rev.   CS71.W18   1895
—— Appendix ... Springfield, Ill., Illinois state journal co., printers, 1909.   3 p. l., 36 p., 2 l., 7 p. front. (port.) plates. 25 cm. "A sermon in course, upon the Thomas Strawbridge foundation, delivered by Rev. Edwin Sawyer Walker, A. M., in the Central Baptist church, Springfield, Illinois, on Sunday, October 11th, 1908": 2 l., 7 p. at end. 9-15044 rev. CS71.W18   1895
Appendix.

17851   WALKER.   Lewis Walker of Chester Valley and his descendants: with some of the families with whom they are connected by marriage.   1686-1896.   Collected, compiled and published by Priscilla Walker Streets.   Philadelphia, A. J. Ferris, printer, 1896.   2 p. l., 443 p. front., plates, 24½ cm. 9-15042.   CS71.W18   1896

17852   WALKER.   Genealogy of the descendants of John Walker of Wigton, Scotland, with records of a few allied families.   Also war records and some fragmentary notes pertaining to the history of Virginia.   1600-1902.   By Emma Siggins White ... Kansas City, Mo., Tiernan-Dart printing company, 1902.   xxx, 722 p. front., pl. (part col.) port., geneal. tab. 24 cm. 2-19111.
CS71.W18   1902

17853   WALKER.   Samuel Walker, of Woburn, Mass., and some of his descendants.   By Arthur G. Loring and William R. Cutter.   Boston, Press of D. Clapp & son, 1903.   9 p. 24 cm. "Reprinted from New-Eng. historical and genealogical register, for Oct., 1903." "Register reprint, series A, no. 3." 19-10586.
CS71.W18   1903

17854   WALKER.   Appendix to The story of my ancestors in America, by Rev. Edwin Sawyer Walker ... Springfield, Ill., Illinois state journal co., printers, 1909.   3 p. l., 36 p., 2 l., 7 p. 24½ cm. 9-28470.

CS71.W18   1909

17855   WALKER.   History of Walker family, 1775-1916, written by Minerva A. (Carr) Muir ... (Liberty, Ind., Express printing company, c.1916)   41 p. mounted illus. (port.) 20½ cm. 16-5604.

CS71.W18   1916

17856   WALKER.   Descendants of John Walker, of Gringley-on-the-Hill, Nottingham, England, by Mrs. Jane Jennings Eldredge. (n.p., 1919)   cover-title, 12 p. ports. 23 cm. 20-18295.   CS71.W18   1919

17857   WALKER.   Revolutionary service of Col. John Walker and family, and Memoirs of Hon, Felix Walker.   By Clarence Griffin ... Forest City, N.C., The Forest City courier, 1930.   23, (1) p. illus. (coat of arms) 22½ cm. 30-28492.   F258.W19

17858   WALKER.   Genealogy of John Walker from Ireland, 1720, and some of his ancestors in England and Ireland and some of his descendants in America.   Mrs. William W. (Malone) Neal ... colloborator.   Compiled by Robert Walton Walker ... 1900 to 1934. (Fort Worth, Tex., 1934?)   64 p. incl. front., illus., pl., ports., coats of arms.   23 cm.   Accompanied by 20 leaves of type-written material and two photographs (port., coat of arms) 37-38441.   CS71.W18   1934

17859   WALKER.   Walkers of yesterday; from Deputy Governor Richard Walker (1611-1687) of Lynn, Reading (Wakefield) and Boston to Captain Solomon Walker (1722-1789) of Woolwich, Maine, and on ... By Ernest George Walker ... (Washington, D.C., Ransdell inc., printers, c.1937)   xiii, 162 p. incl. front., illus. (incl. ports., maps, coat of arms) 24 cm.   "List of authorities consulted": p. (51) and 149. 37-12569.

CS71.W18   1937

17860   WALKER.   The family of George Walker of Philadelphia, by John Insley Coddington ... (New Haven, 1943)   cover-title, 11 p. 24½ cm.   "Reprinted from "The American genealogist," July, 1943."   Bibliographical foot-notes. 44-50046.   CS71.W18   1943

17861   WALKER.   Robert Walker of Boston, Massachusetts, by John Insley Coddington ... (New Haven, 1944)   cover-title, 12 p. 24½ cm.   Reprinted from 'The American genealogist,' July, 1944."   Bibliographical foot-notes. 44-50045.   CS71.W18   1944

17862   WALKER.   The Walker family, originally of the Yeocomico River section of Northumberland (subsequently Westmoreland) County, Virginia, stemming from William Walker, 1622/23-1657, and through one of his descendants, Joseph Rabley Walker, 1768-1816, who immigrated from Mecklenburg County in that state to South Carolina, circa 1806, and settled in Edgefield County near the town of that name; also a correction of certain errors in a chart of the Adams family, with which the Walkers are connected by marriage.   By Legaré Walker.   Summerville, S.C., 1945   vii, 60 p. 23 cm. 48-14978*.

CS71.W18   1945

17863   WALKER.   Walker wives.   By Gustavus Swift Paine.   Southbury, Conn., 1946.   29 l. 28 cm.   Typewritten (carbon copy) "Authorities": leaf 29. 48-16574 *   CS71.W18   1946

17864   WALKER.   Walker family tree; 410 years from 1540 to 1950 A.D.   By Arthur Howard Walker. New York, 1950.   geneal. table. 89 x 38 cm, fold. to 30 x 38 cm. 59-27019.   CS71.W18   1950

17865   WALKER.   George Walker (of Northumberland County, Pennsylvania and Tioga County, New York) and his descendants.   West Hartford, Conn., 1952.   33 l. 28 cm.   "Based principally on the account in 'History of Waverly, New York and vicinity' by Captain Charles L. Albertson." 54-37786.   CS71.W18   1952

17866   WALKER.   Ancestry and descendants of John Walker (1794-1869) of Vermont and Utah, descendant of Robert Walker, an emigrant of 1632 from England to Boston, Mass.   Published by the John Walker Family Organization.   Kaysville, Utah, Printed by the Inland Print. Co., 1953.   500 p. ports. 24 cm.   Contents. - Descendants of John Walker, compiled by R. W. Walker. - Ancestry of John Walker, compiled by N. C. Stevenson. 53-37769.   CS71.W18   1953

17867   WALKER.   The Walker heritage.   By Marie (Stevens) Walker Wood.   Macon, Ga., 1956.   xvi, 274 p. illus., ports., coats of arms, facsims., geneal. tables. 25 cm.   "200 copies ... printed for private circulation."   Bibliography: p. 264. 56-13024 rev.   CS71.W18   1956

17868   WALKER.   The story of the Maryland Walker family, including the descendants of George Brian Walker (and) Elizabeth Walker Beall.   (Allenwood, N.J.) 1957.   15 l. 31 cm. 58-46326.

CS71.W18   1957

17869   WALKER.   Descendants of Col. Eaton Walker: three of his children, Gabriel Benson Walker, Henrietta Walker, Elias Benson Walker.   By Claudia Louise Walker.   (n.p.) 1959.   69 l. 30 cm. 60-39208 rev.

CS71.W18   1959

17870   WALKER.   Ancestors of Francis Walker and Sarah Effie Vinton Kelley.   Compiled by James S. Elston.   Burlington, Vt., Chedwato Service, 1964.   130 p. facsims., geneal. tables, ports. 28 cm. 65-3070.

CS71.W18   1964

17871   WALKER.   Henson Walker family record.   (Floyd A. Walker, editor) Pleasant Grove, Utah (1965?)   xx, 1154 p. illus., facsims., geneal. tables, maps, ports. 23 x 38 cm. Corrections in MS. Bibliography: p. 1154. 65-5214.

CS71.W18   1965

17872   WALKER.   All that we inherit; being the family memorials of the Walkers and Mathers of Hobart, and the reminiscences and memories of James Backhouse Walker, solicitor, and Sarah Benson Walker, the wife of George Washington Walker, banker, both of early Hobart Town, Van Diemen's Land.   Compiled and narrated by Peter Benson Walker.   Hobart, J. Walch & Sons (1968)   xi, 158 p. illus., genealogical tables (part fold.) 19 cm.   Edition limited to 500 copies.   No. 273.   Bibliography: p. (157)-158.   79-439056 MARC.

CS2129.W3   1968

WALKER.   See also:

BAKER, 1961	HALL, 1952	PARKINSON, 1880
BEACH, 19 -	HUDSON, DA.690.W6H8	POLLOCK, 1932
BROUN, 1906	JONES, 1891	RICHARDS, F74.D7J7
CALHOUN, 1957	KANN, E171.A53 v.18	SELDEN, 1911
CLARK, 1948	LIGON, 1947	SMITH, 1899
COLBERT, 1956	MAXWELL, 1916	SNYDER, 1958
CRAM, 1934	PAGE, 1883	STEVENS, 1957
DIXON, 1922	PAGE, 1893	STOUT, 1960
DOUGHERTY, 19	PAINE, 1946	WILLIAMS, CS84.W6
GLAS, 1917		

17873   WALKLEY.   Genealogical index of some descendants of Richard Walkley of Haddam, compiled by Stephen Walkley.   Plantsville, Conn. (1911?)   1 p. l., 32 p. 22½ cm. p. 29-32 left blank for "Memoranda." 11-19424.

CS71.W20   1911?

WALKLEY.   See also WAKELEY.

WALKUP.   See SMITH, 1915b

17874   WALL.   Descendants of David Wall and Hannah Bailey; notes for a Wall genealogy.   (By Horace Holmes Wall) San Francisco, 1943.   42 p. 19½ cm. 44-30599.   CS71.W215   1943

17875   WALL.   A George Willard Wall memorial; the ancestral lines of George Willard Wall and his wife Celeste Augusta Nettleton.   By Juliette (Wall) Pope.   (Washington) 1959.   132 p. illus. 24 cm. 59-51442.

CS71.W215   1959

WALL.   See also: PARKHILL, 1969
REYNOLDS, 1923
VAN DE WALL.

17876   WALLACE.   Documents illustrative of Sir William Wallace, his life and times ... (Edinburgh) Printed for the Maitland club, 1841.   xlviii p., 1 l., 203 p. front. (facsim.) 27 x 22 cm. (The Maitland club. Publications. no. 54) Title vignette. "Introductroy notice" signed : Joseph Stevenson. Presented to the club by Robert Rodger. "Genealogie of the illustrious and ancient family of Craigie Wallace": p. (xliii) - xlviii. 18-14269.

DA750.M3 no.54

17877   WALLACE.   The Wallaces of Elderslie: reprinted from the transactions of the Archaeological society of Glasgow, 1884.   The two Elderslies: reprinted from the "Glasgow herald," of 13th September, 1884.   By J. O. Mitchell.   For private circulation only.   Glagow, Strathern & Freeman, 1884.
2 p. l., (3)-26 p.   23 cm.   20-15866.   CS479.W37

17878   WALLACE.   Life and times of Judge Caleb Wallace, some time a justice of the Court of appeals of the state of Kentucky.   By William H. Whitsitt.   Louisville, J. P. Morton & company, printers, 1888.   151 p.   32½ x 25 cm.   (On cover: Filson club publications, no. 4)   3-14624.   CS71.W22   1888
        —— Copy 2.   F446.F48

17879   WALLACE.   The book of Wallace, by the Rev. Charles Rogers ... Edinburgh, Printed for the Grampian club, 1889.   2 v. col. front. (coat of arms) 6 pl., 3 facsim.   26 x 21 cm.   "The impression of the work has been restricted to two hundred and fifty copies."   3-31631.   DA758.3.W3R7

17880   WALLACE.   Autobiography of Thomas Wilkinson Wallis, sculptor in wood, and extracts from his sixty years' journal, with twenty-four illustrations and four diagrams.   Louth, J. W. Goulding & son, printers, 1899.   xv, 244 p. front., plates, port. 22 cm.   "My ancestors": p. 1-6.   16-24500.
                                                                                                             NK9798.W3A3

17881   WALLACE.   Memoirs of the Staker Wallace, with genealogy of family, by Eunice Graham Brandt.   Chicago, J. S. Hyland & co., 1909.   1 p. l., 7-99 p. 20½ cm.   Coat of arms on cover.   20-15883.
                                                                                                             DA948.6.W3B7

17882   WALLACE.   The Wallace family in America; being an account of the founders and first col-onial families, and an official list of the heads of families of the name, resident in the United States in 1790.   By James A. Phelps.   New York, W. M. Clemens (1914)   27 p. 23 cm.   15-19463.
                                                                                                       CS71.W22   1914

17883   WALLACE.   Wallace; genealogical data pertaining to the descendants of Peter Wallace & Elizabeth Woods, his wife, compiled by George Selden Wallace ... Charlottesville, Va., The Michie company, 1927.   vi, 275 p. front. (port.) 23 cm.   27-24706.   CS71.W22   1927

17884   WALLACE.   Wallace genealogical data; suggestions for a Wallace family association, a national Wallace family reunion, and a complete Wallace genealogy, by J. Montgomery Seaver ... Philadelphia, Pa., Washington, D. C., American historical-genealogical society, 1927.   37, (1) p. 32½ cm.
Caption title.   Text runs parallel with back.   Autographed from type-written copy.   CA 29-180 unrev.
                                                                                                       CS71.W22   1927a

17885   WALLACE.   Wallis & Willcox, descendants of Martha (4) Davies; a supplement to The Davis family (Davis & David) compiled by Harry Alexander Davis.   Washington, D. C., 1928.   2 p. l., 24 p.
24 cm.   Autographed from type-written copy.   28-18066.   CS71.W22   1928

17886   WALLACE.   Wallace-Bruce and closely related families: Barefoots, Taylors, Wilsons, McKees, Douglasses, Liddells, Hendersons, Notestines and others; history and genealogy, written and compiled by James Wallace ... Northfield, Minn., Mohn printing company, incorporated, 1930.
3 p. l., 389 p. front., illus. (incl. ports., maps) 22 cm.   Includes blank pages.   30-33269.   CS71.W22   1930

17887   WALLACE.   Genealogy of the Wallace, Browne and allied families.   By Henry Agard Wallace.
Des Moines, 1933.   Microfilm copy.   Negative.   Collation of the original as determined from the film: 1 v. (unpaged) ports.
Mic 50-153.   Microfilm CS-2

17888   WALLACE.   The descendants and antecedents of Daniel and Abigail Howe Wallace, by Fred B. Wahr and Bessie C. Collins.   Ann Arbor, Edwards Letter Shop, 1948.   73 p. ports., geneal. table.
23 cm.   48-20455*.   CS71.W22   1948

17889   WALLACE.   Some history of the Wallace, Murphy, and Cooke families (1600-1957) compiled by Maggie Sallee prior to 1920.   Edited and completed by Mrs. H. Chris Wallace in 1957.   (Mon-mouth, Ill., 1958)   60 l. illus. 30 cm.   58-39452.   CS71.W22   1958

17890   WALLACE.   Genealogy of the Wallace family of Gransha, County Down, Northern Ireland, beginning with the Scottish soldier of the Battle of the Boyne, 1690, through 4 generations in Ireland and 6 generations in the United States of America (by Lawrence C. McClure and Dwight G. Wallace. Artesia, Calif.) 1964.   1 v. (chiefly fold. geneal. tables, fold. map) 30 cm. Cover title. 64-55036.   CS71.W22   1964

17891   WALLACE.   The clan Wallace, by Charles B. Wallace.   Dallas, Printed by Clan Wallace Society, 1967.   vi, 62 l. illus., coats of arms. 30 cm. Bibliography: p. 61-62. 67-8304.   CS479.W26   1967

17892   WALLACE.   Genealogy of the Wallace family reviewed and extended to 1967 in the United States.   By Lee Allen Wallace.   (Seal Beach, Calif., 1967)   25 l. 36 cm. Cover title. 74-9822 MARC.
CS71.W22   1967

17893   WALLACE.   The Wallace family in America, by James A. Phelps.   Dallas, Tex., Clan Wallace Society (1968)   ii, 27 l. 29 cm. Reprint of the 1914 ed. 75-5207 MARC.   CS71.W22   1968

17894   WALLACE.   Browne, Wallace, and allied families.   By Henry Agard Wallace.   neg. and pos.
Microfilm reading room
Microfilm 60

17895   WALLACE.   Addition material in vertical file.   Ask reference librarian for this material.

WALLACE.   See also:

CHAPMAN, 1919	PAVEY, 1940	VENABLE. 1961
GLASSELL, 1891	PERRY, 1913	WALTMAN, 1928
McCLENAHAN, 1912 and 1914	POWNALL, 1945	WILCOX, 1928
McCLURE, 1907	SELDEN, 1911	WILLIAMS, 1938a
MOAK, 1960	VAN DEUSEN, 1947	No. 1547 - Cabell county.
MULFORD, 1920		

WALLBRIDGE.   See: DIXON, 1922
WALBRIDGE.

WALLE, Van de.   See VAN DE WALL.

17896   WALLER.   A genealogy of the Waller family of Amots bruk, Sweden, and Kewanee, Illinois, by Dr. S. G. Youngert, assisted by Herman Ferdinand Södersteen ... and Archbishop Nathan Söder-blom ... Rock Island, Ill., Augustana book conern, 1931.   xvi, 99 p. plates, ports., facsim., col. coat of arms. 24½ cm. "This genealogy is printed in a bibliophile edition of one hundred numbered copies. This copy not numbered. 32-2322.
CS71.W225   1931

17897   WALLER.   Edgecombe county, N.C., records - Waller ... (n.p., 1942?)   3 numb. l. 28 x 22 cm. Type-written. 44-1936.   CS71.W225   1942

17898   WALLER.   The Waller family record, compiled by Anna Waller Sack, edited by Charles B. Aziere.   (Atchison, Kan., 1945)   74 p. 21½ cm. 46-14818.   CS71.W225   1945

17899   WALLER.   Some Waller family history.   By Joseph W. Waller.   (n.p., 1950)   124 l. illus., photos., coat of arms. 29 cm. Caption title. Typewritten. "Only two of these books have been made." Compiled by J. W. Waller and W. W. Waller. Bibliography: leaf 2. 51-21967.   CS71.W225   1950

WALLER.   See also: KEY, 1931
MAUNSELL, CS439.M37

WALLEY.   See SALISBURY, 1885

17900   WALLIN.   Wallin, Warren and allied families, a genealogical study with biographical notes, compiled and privately printed for Mr. and Mrs. Freeman F. Wallin, by the American historical society, inc.   New York, 1934.   4 p. l., 7-277 p. pl., ports., col. geneal. tab., col. coats of arms. 32½ cm. Alternate

17900 continued: pages blank.   Title page and Dedication ornamented in colors; initials and tailpieces in colors.   One of the plates accompanied by guard sheets with descriptive letterpress.   Bound in blue levant, gold tooled and inlaid, with leather doublures.   Allied families: Warren, Skillman, Van Kirk, Holcombe, Beekman and Van Dyck.   Bibliography throughout text.   36-12557 rev.

CS71.W23   1934

WALLING.   See SNYDER, 1958

WALLINGFORD.   See OTIS, 1851

WALLIS.   See WALLACE.

WALLS.   See PEPPER, 1960

17901   WALMESLEY.   Records of the Walmesley family copied from the parish registers of Blackburn, Broughton, Penwortham, etc., Lancashire, Eng., 1600-1843.   (Salt Lake City, Genealogical Society, Microfilm Division Custom Work, 1957)   Microfilm copy (positive) of manuscript.   Made for Maud Bliss Allen. Collation of the original, as determined from the film: 1 v. (various pagings)   Mic 58-6877.   Microfilm 5746 CS

WALMISLEY.   See WALMESLEY.

17902   WALMSLEY   Records from the Walmsley family copied from the Parish records of Blackburn Lancs.   1600-1843 and from Broughton Lancs. 1653-1804, from Perworthen 1608-1753. Positive.   (This appears to be the same as No. 17901)   Microfilm 5746
Microfilm reading room.

WALMSLEY.   See WALMESLEY.

WALN.   See HARRISON, 1932

17903   WALPOLE.   Walpole of Whaplode, co. Lincoln.   Being a genealogy of the Whaplode branch of the family of Walpole of Houghton, co. Norfolk.   Compiled by the Rev. Augustus Jessopp, D.D., and Everard Green ... (Norwich? 1874)   geneal. tab.   35 x 75½ fold. to 36 x 27 cm.   3-7449.
CS439.W28

17904   WALPOLE.   One generation of a Norfolk house: a contribution to Elizabethan history.   By Augustus Jessopp ... 2d ed.   London, Burns and Oates, 1879.   xxvi, 325 p. 22 cm.   Life of Henry Walpole, the Jesuit father, who was put to death in 1595, with some account of other members of the Walpole family.   8-23794.
DA353.A2W3

17905   WALPOLE.   Mannington and the Walpoles, earls of Orford.   By Lady Dorothy Neville.   With ten illustrations of Mannington hall, Norfolk.   London, The Fine art society, 1894.   42 p. 10 pl. (incl. front.) 22 x 28½ cm.   Plates are accompanied by descriptive letterpress.   24-7997.   CS439.W28   1894

17906   WALPOLE.   The later history of the family of Walpole of Norfolk, to which is prefixed some remarks as to the probable identity of the Houghton family with the early merchants of King's Lynn, by Walter Rye.   Norwich, Issued to subscribers only by H. W. Hunt, 1920.   52 p. fold. geneal. tab. 21½ cm.
21-8061.   CS439.w28   1920

WALPOLE.   See also TERRELL, 1916

WALROND.   See PITMAN, 1920

17907   WALSH.   Une famille royaliste irlandaise et française (1689-1789) ... (By Louis, duc de La Trémoille) Nantes, Impr. E. Grimaud et fils, 1901.   99 p. front., facsim. 30 x 23½ cm.   Cover-title: Une famille royaliste irlandaise et française et le prince Charles-Édouard.   Letters, for the most part by Antoine Walsh and Charles Edward, the Young Pretender; with an appendix of letters patent, issued by the French and English crowns to members of the Walsh family.   2-30580.
DA814.A5L29

17908   WALSH.   A royalist family Irish and French (1689-1789) and Prince Charles Edward; translated from the French by A. G. Murray Macgregor, with a map of the route of the 'Doutelle.'   Edinburgh, W. Brown, 1904.   viii, 118, (5) p. front., map, geneal. tab. 26 cm. "The edition is strictly limited to 320 copies." "Translated from Une famille royaliste ... (Nantes, 1901) a French publication unsigned but compiled from original mss. by the present Duc de la Trémoille ... The log-book of the Doutelle, which bore him (Prince Charles) to Scotland, appears on its pages for the first time." - Introd.   4-9493.

DA814. A5L3

17909   WALSH.   Walsh, the name and the arms.   Frankford, Phila(delphia) Pa., Martin and Allardyce, 1910.   cover-title, 8 p. fold. coat of arms. 16½ cm. 21-19828.   CR1629. W3

17910   WALSH.   The lament for John MacWalter Walsh, with notes on the history of the family of Walsh from 1170 to 1690, by J. C. Walsh, with a foreword by James J. Walsh ... New York, Kelmscott press (1925)   246 p. incl. maps. pl., col. coats of arms. 24½ cm. Cover-title: Walsh, 1170-1690. 26-129.

CS499. W35

17911   WALSH.   Walsh, Erwin, and allied families; a genealogical study with biographical notes. Prepared and privately printed for Winifred E. Walsh.   American Historical Company, inc., New York, 1954.   303 p. illus., ports., col. coats of arms., facsims., geneal. tables. 33 cm.   Includes bibliographical references. 55-26415.   CS71. W2317   1954

WALSH.   See also MITCHELL, 1929

WALSWORTH.   See: WALWORTH.
WILLIAMS, 1887

17912   WALTER.   Pedigree of Walter.   Compiled by C. Frederick Adams, jr.   Boston, 1854. geneal. tab.   22 x 35½ cm. fold. to 22½ cm.   Detached from the New Eng. hist. and geneal. register, 1854, v. 8, p.208a.   9-15043.

CS71. W232   1854

17913   WALTER.   The family of Walters of Dorset, Hants.   (London, London & county printing works, 1907)   3 p. l., 3-161, (1) p. 25 cm. Compiled by Fred Walters. cf. Pref.   Edited by Edmund Huth Walters. 23-18866.

CS439. W283

17914   WALTER.   The Walters family.   (By John Smith Kendall)   (Berkeley, Calif., 1945) (4) p. 28 x 21½ cm. Caption title.   Type-written (carbon copy) . 46-8645.   CS439. W283   1943

17915   WALTER.   Genealogical record of the descendants of John Walters and Mary de Vessaille. By James Stevenson Cushing.   (2d ed.   n. p., 1952)   62 l. illus. 28 cm. 54-19891.   CS71. W232   1952

WALTER.   See also: COLLINS, 1848
LA RUE, 1921
NEWLIN, 1942

WALTERS.   See WALTER.

17916   WALTHALL.   The Walthall family, a genealogical history of the descendants of William Walthall of Virginia, by Malcolm Elmore Walthall.   Richmond, Va., 1946.   1 p. l., v, 178 (i. e. 184) numb. l. incl. 1 illus., maps, diagrs. col. coat of arms. 28½ x 23 cm. Type-written (carbon copy) Includes extra numbered leaves. 46-21036.

CS71. W233   1946

17917   WALTHALL.   The Walthall family; a genealogical history of the descendants of William Walthall of Virginia.   By Malcolm Elmore Walthall.   Charlotte, N. C., C. D. Walthall, 1963. vii, 245, A64 l. illus., ports., maps, coat of arms, facsims., geneal. table. 28 cm. 64-991.   CS71. W233   1963

17918   WALTMAN.   The house of Waltman and its allied families, Alderson, Baker, Bowman, Bierly, Brittain, Caldwell, Campbell, Charleton, Craighead, Erwin, Fowler, Fox, Greene, Hamsphire, Harmon, Kuder, La Mance, Lutz, Lytle, McLane, Miller, Minnich, Newton, Nichols, Noble, Parsley, Ruckle, Schmoyer, Shaffer, Tuck, Wallace, Watkins, Wilson, Yonce, Zarfess and others; by Lora S. La Mance ... (St. Augustine, Fla., 1928)   3 p. l., 278 (i. e. 293), (8) p. front., illus. (incl. ports., facsims., coats of arms) col. coat of arms. 26½ cm. Fifteen full page illustrations are not included in paging. Blank pages for "Personal family record" (8 at end) "Bibliography to chapters I to V": p. 21-33. 30-15030.   CS71. W235   1928

17919   WALTON.   The compleat angler; or, The contemplative man's recreation, being a discourse of rivers, fish-ponds, fish and fishing.   Written by Isaak Walton, and instructions how to angel for a trout or grayling in a clear stream by Charles Cotton; with original memoirs and notes by Sir Harris Nicolas, K. C. M. G., and sixty illustrations from designs by Stothard and Inskipp.   London, Chatto and Windus, 1875.   3 p. 1., (v)-ccv p., 1 1., 320 p. front., illus., plates, ports., facsim. 20½ cm. Added t.-p., engraved. "Pedigrees of Walton, Hawkins, and Hawes": p. cxxxii - cxxxiii. "Pedigree of Cranmer": p. cxxxiv - cxxxv. "Pedigree of Cotton": p. ccii-cciii. "Pedigree of Ken": p. cciv. "Pedigree of Chalkhill": p. ccv. 10-5225.   SH433. A   1875

17920   WALTON.   Walton family records, 1598-1898, with intermarriages, the Oakes and Eatons, 1644-1898, and the Proctor family, 1634-1898.   Compiled by Josiah Proctor Walton.   Muscatine, Ia. (Printed by A. C. Hopkinson) 1898.   88, (10) p. incl. front. port. 19½ cm. Cover-title: Records of the Waltons', Proctor's Oakes' and Eaton's, 1598-1898. 99-2357.   CS71. W24   1898

17921   WALTON.   Genealogical chart showing a part of the American ancestry of Adelaide Bereman Walton.   (By Charles Strong Walton) Prepared ... by her father.   Los Angeles, Cal., 1905. geneal. tab. 55½ x 71 cm. fold. to 28½ x 18 cm. 6-28551.   CS71. W24   1905

17922   WALTON.   Notes on the family of Edward Walton, and some of its connections, by Chas. Cortlandt Walton, jr.   (Williamsburg, Va., 1925)   cover-title, 7 p. 23 cm. "Reprinted from William and Mary college quarterly." 27-728.   CS71. W24   1925

17923   WALTON.   The Walton family, by Joseph C. Martindale, M. D.   Frankford, Phila., Martin & Allardyce, 1911.   cover-title, 12 p. 19½ cm. 12-25490.   CS71. W24   1911

17924   WALTON.   ... Records of Richmond county, Georgia, formerly Saint Paul's parish, abstracted and compiled, 1927, by (Mrs. John Lee) Grace Gillam Davidson ... Athens, Ga., The McGregor co., 1929.   2 p. 1., 402 p. front. 24 cm. (Historical collections of the Georgia chapters, Daughters of the American revolution, vol. II) "The Walton family history ... compiled ... by Robert Walton Robertson ...": p. 329-340. 31-8020.

F281. D23 vol. 2

17925   WALTON. 1933 memoranda and 1934 supplement in re Walton families; (1) Robert Walton of St. Andrews, New Brunswick. (2) George Walton of Maine and New Hamsphire.   (3) George Walton of Virginia, signer of the Declaration of Independence.   Compliments Lucius Buckley Andrus.   Indianapolis, Ind.   (1934)   cover-title, 3 p. 1., 281-303 (i. e. 304) numb. 1., 1 1., 50 (i. e. 52) numb. 1. incl. illus., pl., ports., map, facsims. 27½ cm. Mimeographed text, with cover-title, and title of second part, multigraphed. Ruled leaves for "Memoranda" (39-50) Most of the illustrations are mounted. Leaves 281-303 are copied from "Supplement: a few facts about the Andrus family, its relatives and ancestors," with corresponding page numbers. 35-20362.   CS71. W24   1934

17926   WALTON.   Walton family of Hightstown and Dutch Neck, N. J.   Compiled 1933-1934 for A. V. Phillips ... Trenton, N. J., Traver's book store, 1935.   geneal. tab. 48 x 60 cm. fold. to 24 x 15 cm. "First edition, 1000." Title on envelope: Walton family chart; ancestors and descendents (!) of John Walton and Elizabeth Taylor ... 36-1636.

CS71. W24   1935

17927   WALTON.   The Walton family of New York, 1630-1940, by Annette Townsend (Mrs. Townsend Phillips) Philadelphia, Pa., The Historical publication society (1945)   52 (i. e. 54) p. incl. mounted geneal. tab. fronts. (incl. coats of arms) plates, ports., facsims. 24 cm. Includes also the Beekman family. Bibliography: p. 10. 45-9919.

CS71. W24   1945

17928   WALTON.   Walton family and collateral lines of Bonnell, Donnell, Dyre, Earle, England, Knight, Lamb, Nicholson, Potts, Root, Spittall, Trask, Wiedersheim. By Alexander Du Bin.   Philadelphia, Historical Publ. Society, 1947.   41 p. 26 cm. 48-16219*.   CS71. W24   1947

17929   WALTON.   Descendants of John Walton of Baltimore County, Maryland and Harrison County, Kentucky.   By Harry Middleton Hyatt.   New York, Alma Egan Hyatt Foundation, 1950.   73 p. 21 cm. 51-27710.   CS71. W24   1950

WALTON.   See also: ANDREWS, 1938
                    KNIGHT, 193-
                    ROBERTS, 1940
                    No. 1547 - Cabell county.

17930   WALTZ.   Waltz family history and genealogical record, in family classification, comprising upward of 3000 names of lineal decendants (!) of Frederick Reinhart Waltz.   Dayton, O., Reformed publishing company, printers, 1884.   xvi, (17)-128 p.   front. (port.) 23 cm.   Compiled by Levi Waltz. 4-33865.
CS71.W241   1884

17931   WALTZ.   The Waltz family ... compiled by Carl L. Richman.   Tipton, Ind., 1926.
1 p. l., (48) p., 2 l. 29½ cm.   Autographed from type-written copy. 27-727.
CS71.W241   1926

17932   WALWORTH.   The Walworths of America.   Comprising five chapters of family history, with additional chapters ... of genealogy.   By Clarence A. Walworth.   Albany, N.Y., The Weed-Parsons printing company, 1897.   vi, 196 p. plates, ports. 23 cm. 9-15041.
CS71.W242   1897

17933   WALWORTH.   Walworth-Walsworth genealogy, 1689-1962; descendants, male & female, of William Walworth & Mary Abigail Seaton.   By Reginald Wellington Walworth.   (Centreville? Md., c. 1962)   xvi, 949 p. illus., ports., col. coats of arms. 24 cm. 62-67518.
CS71.W242   1962

WALWORTH.   See also L.C. additions and corrections, no. 14

WALWORTH.   See also SEDDON, 1880

WALZ.   See SCHUSTER, 1951

WALZER.   In vertical file under PAIEN family.   Ask reference librarian for this material.

17934   WAMPLER.   The John Wampler family, by Dr. John S. Flory.   (Bridgewater? Va., 1929)
94 p. 3 pl. (incl. front.) 20 cm. 35-21384.
CS71.W245   1929

WAMPLER.   See also BAKER, 1964

WAMPOLE.   See: SELLERS, 1886
                      SELLERS, 1903

17935   WANDER.   The Wanderer-Wander family of Bohemia, Germany and America, 1450-1951. Being the partial story of Elias Wander or Crottendorf on the Zchopau River, Germany, the ancestor of a large glass-making family and his descendants in Europe and America.   It embraces the years 1450 to 1951.   This compilation is based on church records, family Bibles, journals and information supplied by living persons.   By Alwin Eugene John Wanderer.   (Ann Arbor? Mich., 1951)
175 p. illus., coats of arms (part col.) 29 cm. 52-34424.
CS71.W246   1951

WANDERER.   See WANDER.

17936   WANDESFORD.   Story of the family of Wandesforde of Kirklington & Castlecomer; compiled from original sources, with a calendar of historical manuscripts, ed. by Hardy Bertram M'Call ... London, Simpkin, Marshall, Hamilton, Kent & co., ltd., 1904.   xviii, 395, (1) p. front., illus., plates, ports., facsims., geneal. tables. coat of arms. 29 cm.   Contains also accounts of the Musters, Colvill and Fulthorpe families. 17-29940.
CS439.W288

WANDESFORD.   See also THORNTON, DA20.S9 vol. 62

17937   WANGER.   Genealogical chart of the descendants of Henry Wanger ... (Pottstown, Pa., 1910)
geneal. tab. 78 x 76½ cm.   Signed: Geo. F.P. Wanger. 11-28588.
CS71.W247   1910

17938   WANGER.   Genealogical chart of Helen Grubb Wanger ... Pottstown, Pa., 1910.
geneal. tab. 61 x 61½ cm.   By Geo. F.P. Wanger.   Blue-print. 11-30215.
CS71.W247   1910a

17939   WANGENSTEEN.   A record of the descendents of the Wangensteen-Olson families for eleven generations, corrected to January 21, 1964.   By Mable Oletta (Olsen) Connell.   (St. Aberdeen, S.D., 1964)   24 l. 28 cm.   Caption title. 64-3648.
CS71.W2467

17940   WANNAMAKER.   The Wannamaker, Salley, Mackay, and Bellinger families, genealogies and memoirs, compiled by J. Skottowe Wannamaker ... St. Matthews, S. C. (c.1937)   2 p. l., 7-485 p.
28 cm.   Includes blank pages for memoranda.   38-2250.   CS71.W2475   1937

WANNAMAKER.   See also: GOLSAN, 1959
                                        BROWNLEE, 1937

17941   WANTON.   History of the Wanton family of Newport, Rhode Island.   By John Russell Bartlett. Providence, S. S. Rider, 1878.   152 p. 21 x 16 cm.   (Added t.-p.: Rhode Island historical tracts. 1st ser. no. 3) "Originally appeared in the Providence Journal, in 1871." Four members of this family: William, John, Gideon and Joseph, served as governors of Rhode Island between 1732 and 1775.   Genealogical memoranda concerning families formed by marriage connections with the Wanton family: Arnold, Carey, Casey, Coddington, Coit, Dunnell, Ellery, Gould, Hazard, Hunter, Lyman, Minturn, Robinson, Saltonstall, Tillinghast: p. (115)-152. Rc-2965.

F76. R52 ser. 1, no. 3
—— Copy 2.   CS71.W248   1878

17942   WANTY.   Genealogical memoranda relating to the Huguenot family of de Vantier, anglais Wanty, collected and arranged, by Henry Peet ... Priv. print. (n.p.) 1902.   2 p. l., (3)-60 p. front., ports., map, fold. geneal. tab., coats of arms. 23 cm. 16-14967.   CS439.W29

17943   WANZER.   History of the Wanzer family in America, from the settlement in New Amsterdam, New York. 1642-1920 ... By William David Wanzer ... Medford, Mass., Medford mercury press, 1920.   121 p. front., plates, ports. 23½ cm. 21-6321.   CS71.W249   1920

WAPLES.   See HARRISON, 1910a

17944   WARBASSE.   Warbasse history; a study in the sociology of heredity.   By James Peter Warbasse.   Falmouth, Mass., Kendall Press, 1954.   226 p. illus. 24 cm. 54-29251.
CS71.W2497   1954

17945   WARBRICK.   Adventures in Geyserland; life in New Zealand's thermal regions, including the story of the Tarawera eruption and the destruction of the famous terraces of Rotomahana, told by Alfred Warbrick (Patiti) ... With a preface by James Cowan.   Dunedin and Wellington, New Zealand, A. H. and A. W. Reed (1934)   3 p. l., 11-157 p., 1 l. incl. geneal. tab. front., plates, ports., map. 19 cm. 36-10131.
DU411.W3

17946   WARBURTON.   Memoir of the family of Warburton, Garryhinch, in the King's County, Ireland, with proofs of the pedigree hereunto annexed; extracted from deeds and other documents in possession of the family, with other evidences from records of a public nature.   Comp. and arranged at the instance of Richard Warburton ... Dublin, Printed at the University press, by M. H. Gill, 1848.
v, 33 p. fold. geneal. tab. 21½ cm. 19-3362.   CS499.W3

17947   WARBURTON.   Arley charters.   A calendar of ancient family charters, preserved at Arley hall, Cheshire, the seat of R. E. Egerton-Warburton, esquire, with notes, and an explanatory introduction, by William Beamont, esquire ... London, McCorquodale and co., printers, 1866.
xlii, 75 p. pl. 32½ cm. 24-1368.   CS439.W293

17948   WARBURTON.   Genealogy of John Warburton and descendants, comp. by Ella Myrtle Pennington and Jennie Iola Warburton (n. p.) 1913.   21 p. 23½ cm. Title vignette: coat of arms. 15-19446.
CS71.W25   1913

17949   WARBURTON.   Warburtons of Sheffield, Yorkshire, England.   (Descendants of John Warburton of Sheffield, Yorkshire, and Katherine Taylor, in England and America.   Compiled for Kate Emma Warburton of Chicago) Chicago, 1921.   3 l. 29 cm. Caption title. Type-written. 27-19111.
CS71.W25   1921

17950   WARBURTON.   The Warburtons of Warburton and Arley, by Earl Cyrus Warburton (and) Geneva Warburton Dark.   Monterey, Calif., 1956.   101 p. illus., port., maps, coat of arms, facsims., geneal. tables, 26 cm. 56-44065.   CS439.W293   1956

WARBURTON.   See also: ADAMS, 1930
JAMES, 1913a

17951   WARD.   Ward family; descendants of William Ward, who settled in Sudbury, Mass., in 1639. With an appendix, alphabetically arranged, of the names of the families that have intermarried with them.   By Andrew Henshaw Ward ... Boston, S. G. Drake, 1851.   viii, (9)-265 p. front., ports. 23½ cm.
9-15040.
CS71.W26   1851

17952   WARD.   A memoir of the Rev. Nathaniel Ward, A.M., author of The simple cobbler of Agawam in America.   With notices of his family.   By John Ward Dean.   Albany, J. Munsell, 1868.
213 p. illus. 25 cm. Appendix I: Candler's pedigree of Ward. 10-12952.
PS858.W2Z6

17953   WARD.   A memoir of Lieut.-Colonel Samuel Ward, First Rhode Island regiment, army of the American revolution; with a genealogy of the Ward family.   By John Ward.   New York, 1875.
20 p. front. (port.) illus. (coat of arms) 27½ cm. Reprinted from the New York genealogical and biographical record, July 1875, vol. VI, p. (113)-128. 17-9743.
CS71.W26   1875

17954   WARD.   Notes on the family of Ward, of Columbus, Ohio, formerly of Great Yarmouth, England.   By Harry Parker Ward ... (Columbus, O., 1898)   p. (109)-113. col. coat of arms. 24½ cm. 39M68T.
CS71.W26   1898

17955   WARD.   A memorial of Hudson Champlin Ward (1830-1897) ... and a chapter memorial of his deceased eldest son, William Vines Ward.   By Harry Parker Ward ... Columbus, O., 1898.
163 p. incl. front., plates, ports., col. coat of arms. 24½ cm. "The edition of this memorial is limited to fifty copies. Each copy is signed and numbered and this book is number 24." "Notes on the family of Ward": p. 151-153. 15-6237.
CS71.W26   1898a

17956   WARD.   Notes on an old Baptist family: Ward of Nottingham.   Nottingham, Printed for private circulation, 1900.   4 p. l., 46 p., 1 l., (4) p., 1 l. front., illus. (incl. facsims.) ports., fold. geneal. tab. 26 cm. Preface signed: John T. Godfrey.   Edited from notes compiled by Mr. James Ward.   Smith family: p. (25)-31. 19-3358.
CS439.W295

17957   WARD.   The life of Dr. Isaac Blowers Ward (1800-1843) and of his wife Ann Vines (1803-1852); together with some accounts of their near relatives, particular mention being made of the late Caleb Vines, esq., of London; some brief genealogical notes on the Wards of Norfolk and Suffolk and the Vines family of Berkshire; also the complete genealogy of Dr. Ward's descendants to A.D. 1900.   By Harry Parker Ward ... Columbus, O., 1900.   6 p. l., 13-251 p. incl. front., illus. plates, ports., facsims., col. coat of arms. 24 cm. 6 blank leaves at end for "Additional record."   "The edition of this book is limited to thirty-five copies, each of which is numbered and signed, this being no. 27." 14-5654.
CS71.W26   1900

17958   WARD.   Association of descendants of Andrew Ward.   Report of the ... reunion 1st-2d.   New York (Colonial printing company) 1905-1908.   2 v. plates, ports. 23½ cm. Reunions held triennially. First reunion held May 10th, 1905. Second reunion held May 14th, 1908.   A 10-968.
CS71.W26   1905-

17959   WARD.   Genealogy and descendants of Rev. David Ward through Andrew Ward.   Compiled and arranged by Mrs. Frances B. Hamlin, wife of Rev. Teunis S. Hamlin, D.D., daughter of James H. Bacon and Amanda Ward, and granddaughter of Nathan Ward.   Washington, D.C., G.E. Howard, printer (1908?)   geneal. tab. col. illus. (coat of arms) 66½ x 51 cm. 8-18404.   CS71.W26   1908

17960   WARD.   Andrew Warde and his descendants, 1597-1910; being a compilation of facts relating to one of the oldest New England families and embracing many families of other names, descended from a worthy ancestor even unto the tenth and eleventh generaions, comp. under the direction of the Association of descendants of Andrew Ward, by George K. Ward, A.M., secretary; advisory committee: Frederick M. Ward, Emory McClintock, Abram Wakeman.   New York, A. T. De La Mare printing and publishing company, ltd., 1910.   604 p. front., plates, ports. facsims. 27 cm. 10-22834.   CS71.W26   1910

17961   WARD.   Another edition of the above.   4 p. l., (5)-604, 607-622 p. front. (coat of arms) plates, ports., facsim.
26½ cm. "Revised edition, supplement to first edition December, 1911." 20-7241.
CS71.W26   1910a

17962   WARD.   Genealogy of the family of Josiah Ward, sixth generation from William Ward.   (n. p.,
1914?)   cover-title, 15 p. 22 cm. Preface signed: Ebin Jennings Ward. 14-17283.   CS71.W26   1914

17963   WARD.   Battle hymns of the Wards from the Norman conquest to Julia Ward Howe; an address
delivered before the Phoebe Green Ward chapter, "D. A. R.", Westerly, April, 1920, by Gilbert
McClurg.   (Westerly, R. I.. The Utter company, printers, 1920)   16 p. 22½ cm. Caption title. On cover ...
Daughters of the American revolution, Rhode Island. 21-13637.   CS71.W26   1920

17964   WARD.   The William Ward genealogy; the history of the descendants of William Ward of
Sudbury, Mass., 1638-1925, by Charles Martyn ... New York, A. Ward, 1925.   xvii, 749, (1) p. front.,
plates, ports., maps, facsims. (1 double) 24½ cm. 25-11114.   CS71.W26   1925

17965   WARD.   Ward-Munger, Varnum-Martin genealogy.   Ancestors and descendants of James
Henderson Ward and Sarah Munger; Daniel Porter Varnum and Nancy Martin, collected and arranged
by Duren James Henderson Ward.   Denver, Up the Divide publishing co., 1926.   104 p., 1 l., (6) p. ports.,
plates. 20½ cm. "Autobiographical sketch": 4 p. at end. 26-21817.   CS71.W26   1926

17966   WARD.   Ward and allied families, a genealogical study with biographical notes, prepared and
privately printed for Marjorie Montgomery Ward, by the American historical society, inc.   New York,
1930.   183 p. plates, ports., col. coats of arms. 33 cm. Alternate pages blank. Allied families: Cobb, Bonnell, Bicknell and Stone.
36-6006 rev.   CS71.W26   1930

17967   WARD.   Springplace; Moravian mission and the Ward family of the Cherokee nation, by
Muriel H. Wright, from the genealogical notes of Miss Clara A. Ward and other sources.   (Guthrie,
Okla., Co-operative publishing co., c. 1940)   93 p. front., illus. (maps) plates, ports., facsim. 21 cm. 40-7515.
D99.C5W96

17968   WARD.   Descendants of Andrew Warde, with particular reference to those of William Ward
(1670-1775) who were pioneer settlers of the town of Coeymans (now Westerlo), N. Y., 1705-1797,
from Westchester county, N. Y. (by) Stephen H. Ward.   (Springfield? Ill.) 1942.   1 p. 1., 59 numb. 1.,
60-68 p. illus. (facsims.) 28 x 22 cm. Slip with additions inserted. Reproduced from type-written copy. "No. 35." "List of books and
references consulted": leaf 59. 44-1004.   CS71.W26   1942

17969   WARD.   Records of the Ward and Layton families, together with those of the O'Neal, Lodge,
and Lacey families.   (Washington, 1942)   cover-title, 1 p. 1., 22 numb. 1. 20 cm. Reproduced from type-written copy.
Foreword signed: Florence W. Layton. 45-33715.   CS71.W26   1942a

17970   WARD.   A memorial to Jane Elizabeth Parker Ward (Mrs. Hudson Champlin Ward) 1833 -
1914; plates only, text never completed.   By Annette Persis Ward.   (n. p., 1947)   (2) 1. plates, ports.,
maps. 26 cm. Additional family data: 6 leaves inserted. 47-27056*.   CS71.W26   1947

17971   WARD.   Ancestral families of the Wards; a genealogical study.   By Anna Daneker Ward.
Baltimore, 1950.   587 p. 29 cm. 51-24077.   CS71.W26   1950

17972   WARD.   Family history of Ward, Briggs, and allied lines, compiled 1962.   By Irene (Ward)
Kennedy.   Burbank, Calif., Malan Industries (c. 1962)   xxviii, 223 p. illus., ports., maps, col. coats of arms, geneal.
tables. 29 cm. 63-2738.   CS71.W26   1962

17973   WARD.   The Ward line of Rhoda Ann Ward McWhorter.   Compiled by Mabel Woods Hinricks.
(Beverly Hills? Calif., 1966)   76 p. illus., ports. 26 cm. 66-31541.   CS71.W26   1966

WARD.   See also:

ALDERMAN, 1957
ANDERSON, 1916
BRACKETT, 1917
CANON, 1948
COE, 1897
HUGHES, 1911

LOTHROP, 1901
PAINE, 1936
PECK, 1955
ROBSON, CS439.R563
ROSS, 1908

SUTTON, DA690.D81T9
TODD, 1867
WHIPPLE, 1917
WHITE, 1940
WILCOX, 1911b

WARDE.   See WARD.

WARDEDIEU.   See BODIAM.

WARDELL.   Wee WARDWELL.

17974   WARDEN.   Some records of persons by the name of Worden, particularly of over one thousand of the ancestors, kin, and descendants of John and Elizabeth Worden of Washington County, Rhode Island.   Covering three hundred years, and comprising twelve generations in America ... By O. N. Worden.   Lewisburg, Pa., Press of J. R. Cornelius, 1868.   164 p. 19 cm. 9-15047.

CS71.W263   1868

17975   WARDEN.   The ancestors, kin and descendants of John Warden and Narcissa (Davis) Warden, his wife.   Together with records of some other branches of Warden family in America.   By William A. Warden.   Worcester (Press of the Maynard-Gough co.) 1901.   iv p. 2 1., 248 p. front. (port.) illus. (ports.) 3 coats of arms on 1 pl. 24 cm. 1-26934.

CS71.W263   1901

17976   WARDEN.   Genealogy of Rev. Moses Warden, ordained in 1827 by Bishop Joshua Soule, D. D., of the Methodist Episcopal church.   Compiled by Charles D. Warden ... Los Angeles, 1924.   29 1. port. 22½ cm. 24-29284.

CS71.W263   1924

17977   WARDEN.   Some information about the name of Worden ... and descendants of Jonathan Worden of Westchester, New York and Westchester, Nova Scotia.   By Ernest Simeon Worden.   Cedar Rapids, Iowa, 1961.   28 p. 22 cm. 62-34133.

CS71.W263   1961

WARDEN.   See also: CURTIS, 1912
No. 579 - Monroe, N. H.

17978   WARDER.   The Warder family; a short history.   By Mary McGregor Miller.   (n. p.) 1957.   unpaged. illus. 22 cm. 60-38923.

CS71.W264   1957

17979   WARDLAW.   The Wardlaws in Scotland; a history of the Wardlaws of Wilton and Torrie and their cadets, by John C. Gibson ... With illustrations.   Edinburgh, W. Browne, 1912.   xxxv, 318 p. front., plates (part col.) 26½ cm. Impression, 200 copies. 12-24046.

CS479.W3

17980   WARDLAW.   Genealogy of the Wardlaw family, with some account of other families with which it is connected.   By Joseph G. Wardlaw.   (n. p., 1929)   3 p. 1., 215 p. ports., col. coat of arms. 23½ cm. 31-30058.

CS71.W265   1929

WARDLAW.   See also HAWES, E171.A53 vol.14

17981   WARDWELL.   Chart of the descendants of Thomas and Elizabeth Wardell of Boston, Mass. (n. p., 1897)   geneal. tab. 61 x 96 cm. fold. to 31½ x 21½ cm. Contains also list of "Descendants of Jonathan Sergeant." 3-30933.

CS71.W268   1897

17982   WARDWELL.   Wardwell.   A brief sketch of the antecedents of Solomon Wardwell, with the descendants of his two sons, Ezra and Amos, who died in Sullivan, N. H.   By Elizabeth Wardwell Stay.   Greenfield, Mass., Press of E. A. Hall & co., 1905.   22 p. 24½ cm. 10-2634.   CS71.W268   1905

17983   WARDWELL.   A brief history of the Wardell family, from 1734 to 1910, by Gertrude P. Smith.   Toronto, Jackson, Moss & company, printers, 1910.   5 p. 1., 15-104 p. front. (group port.) fold. geneal. tab. 18 cm. 31-35672.   CS90.W3   1910

17984   WARDWELL.   The Wardwells in a world of change.   Narrative by George R. Staley.   Genealogical data by Daniel W. Wardwell, Sr.   (Rome? N. Y., 1950)   51 p. coat of arms. 27 cm. 52-23551.

CS71.W268   1950

WARDWELL.   See also GUITERAS, 1926

17985   WARE.   The Weare family, of Hampton, New Hampshire, and North Yarmouth, Maine.   (By) (William M. Sargent)   Yarmouth, Me., "Old times" office, 1879.   1 p. 1., 8 p. fold. facsim. 23½ cm. 9-15168.

CS71.W27   1879

17986   WARE.   The descendants of Robert Ware of Dedham, Massachusetts ... Boston, Press of D.
Clapp & son, 1887.   47 p. facsims. 26 cm. "Reprinted from the New England historical and genealogical register for January, 1887."
9-15169.   CS71.W27   1887

17987   WARE.   Descendants of Henry Ware.   (Ancestors of Henry Ware and Ancestors of Mary
Clark and Elizabeth Bowes)   (n. p., 1893)   2 geneal. tab. 29½ x 120 cm. 24-20330.   CS71.W27   1893

17988   WARE.   Descendants of Elisha Ware, of Wrentham, Mass., to Jan. 1st, 1896.   (Milford,
Mass., 1896)   (8) p. illus. (incl. map. facsims.) fold. geneal. tab. 18 x 21½ cm. Caption title.   9-13008.
                                                                                                 CS71.W27   1896

17989   WARE.   Ware genealogy; Robert Ware, of Dedham, Massachusetts, 1642-1699, and his lineal
descendants.   Compiled by Miss Emma Forbes Ware ... Boston, C. H. Pope, 1901.   335 p. facsim.
25 cm. 2-17585.   CS71.W27   1901

17990   WARE.   Captain Jacob Ware, born, England, 1674, died Greenwich, N.J., 1775, and some of
his descendants, compiled by Sarah Frances Ware.   Vineland, N.J., Vineland historical and antiquarian society, 1935.   17 p. 25 cm. "One hundred and ten copies reprinted from the Vineland historical magazine." 35-13976.
                                                                                                 CS71.W27   1935

17991   WARE.   The family ... (By Henry Ware)   (Boston? 1944)   (4) p. 21½ cm. Caption title. An account
of the descendants of Rev. Henry Ware, junior. 44-10788.   CS71.W27   1944

17992   WARE.   Genealogy of the descendants of Joseph Ware of Fenwick Colony, England, 1675; his
successors in Florida.   Compiled by Franklin Ware, assisted by I. D. Ware.   Rev. by A. M. Ware
(and) John D. Ware.   (3d ed.   Tampa, Hillsboro Print. & Lithographing Co., 1969)   xi, 126 p. illus.,
facsim., ports. 21 cm. Cover title: Descendants of Joseph Ware, immigrant, 1675; his successors in Florida. 500 copies printed. No. 250.
76-80837 MARC.   CS71.W27   1969

          WARE.   See also: JOHNSON, 1961
                              MOULTON, 1922
                              WILDER, 1960
                              WILDER, 1969
                              No. 516 - Notable southern families, vol. 2

17993   WARFIELD.   The Warfields of Maryland.   By Professor Joshua Dorsey Warfield ... Baltimore, The Daily record company, 1898.   102 p. 23 cm. 9-15039.   CS71.W274   1898

17994   WARFIELD.   Bessie Wallis Warfield Simpson, her ancestral background, by Francis B. Culver
and William B. Marye.   (Baltimore?) 1937.   (10) p. incl. geneal. tables, col. coats of arms. 31 cm. 37M1579T.
                                                                                                 CS71.W274   1937

          WARIN.   See WARREN.

17995   WARING.   A short history of the Warings, by R. N. Waring ... Tyrone, Pa. (Printed by the
Herald) 1898.   60 p. maps, geneal. tables, coat of arms. 27½ cm. Maps and coat of arms printed on blue paper. Genealogical tables
inserted. Descendants of Richard of Boston, Mass., 1664, Benjamin of Charleston, S. C., 1691, and the Warings of Herefordshire, Eng. 9-15038.
                                                                                                 CS71.W277   1898

17996   WARING.   Genealogical table showing posterity of the Hereforshire, England, Edmund Waring
of 1724-1807.   Copyright ... by Robert Newton Waring.   (New York) c. 1943.   fold. geneal. tab. 59 cm.
The table is a blue-print, 231 x 58 cm. 43-5446.   CS71.W277   1943

          WARING.   See also: ATKINSON, 1933
                                JONES, 1891
                                WINSTON, 1927

          WARINGTON.   See MOSS, CS439M

17997   WARNE.   A genealogy of the Warne family in America; principally the descendants of Thomas Warne, born 1652, died 1722, one of the twenty-four proprietors of East New Jersey, by Rev. George Warne Labaw ... New York, Frank Allaben genealogical company (c. 1911)   701 p. front., illus., plates, ports., facsims., charts, col. coats of arms.   25 cm.   11-14529.   CS71.W279   1911

17998   WARNER.   The posterity of William Warner, one of the early settlers of Ipswich, Mass. With particulars of their estate, location, &c., from the town records, registries of probates and deeds, and old family records.   (Communicated for the N. E. hist. and gen. register, by Edward Warner ...) (Boston, 186-?)   11 p. 24 cm.   Caption title.   Reprinted with additions from the New England historical and genealogical register, 1866. 14-10170.   CS71.W28   186-

17999   WARNER.   Genealogical account of a branch of the descendants of Mark Warner, grandson of William Warner, who came from England to Ipswich, Mass. in the year 1637.   Prepared by Oliver Warner.   Boston, Wright & Potter, printers, 1872.   13 p. 23½ cm.   The genealogy was begun by Oliver Warner, 1780-1853, and brought down to date by his son, Oliver Warner.   17-15781.   CS71.W28   1872

18000   WARNER.   One of the Warner family in America.   Compiled by Andrew F. Warner.   Hartford, Conn., Printed for J. J. Warner by the Case Lockwood & Brainard co., 1892.   49 p. 23 cm.   Continued by J. J. Warner.   9-19761.   CS71.W28   1892

18001   WARNER.   Genealogy of the descendants of Omri Warner, and a more extended history of Milo Warner and his family, by C. O. Warner.   Los Angeles, Printed by the Wolfer printing co., 1916.   1 p. l., (7)-205 p. front., illus. (ports.)   20 cm.   18-18565.   CS71.W28   1916

18002   WARNER.   In memoriam Clement Edson Warner; edited by Fanny Warner and Lathrop Ezra Smith; genealogy by Ernest Noble Warner.   Madison, Wis., 1917.   71 p. front., illus. (incl. ports.)   19½ cm. 18-556.   CS71.W28   1917

18003   WARNER.   The descendants of Andrew Warner, compiled by Lucien C. Warner ... and Mrs. Josephine Genung Nichols.   New Haven, Conn., The Tuttle, Morehouse & Taylor co., 1919. viii, 804 p. illus. (incl. ports., coats of arms, facsims.) 24 cm.   19-12801.   CS71.W28   1919

18004   WARNER.   Letters and memories of Susan and Anna Bartlett Warner, by Olivia Egleston Phelps Stokes; with 22 illustrations ... New York & London, G. P. Putnam's sons, 1925.   x, 229 p. front., plates, ports., fold. facsims.   22 cm.   25-27795.   PS3156.S7

18005   WARNER.   Sir Thomas Warner, pioneer of the West Indies, a chronicle of his family by Aucher Warner ... with an introduction by the Rt. Hon. Viscount Elibank.   London, The West India committee (1933)   3 p. l., ix-xvii, 173, (1) p. front., plates, ports., facsims., coat of arms. fold. geneal. tables. 22½ cm.   "500 copies of this edition have been printed by Butler and Tanner limited, Frome and London." Colored coat of arms on cover.   Slip of "Errata" inserted at p. 1.   "Authorities": p. 164-165.   35-13688.   CS439.W297W3

18006   WARNER.   Warner history by Harold W. Osler.   (Salesville, O., 1935)   cover-title, 89, (5) p. pl. (ports.) fold. geneal. tab.   21½ cm.   "That particular branch of that family which settled in eastern Pennsylvania and were the descendants of Captain William Warner.   Special attention is given to the ancestors and descendants of John Lewis Warner."   Coats of arms of the Bye, Ellicott and Ely families on p. (2) - (4) of cover.   Blank pages for "Memorandum" (5) at end.   Corrections in manuscript.   35-20353.   CS71.W28   1935

18007   WARNER.   "Rhoda's chronicles" of the Warner family as written by Rhoda Warner Hinckley, 1829-1893, copied from her original manuscript by Doris Wolcott Strong in 1938.   (n. p., 1938)   1 p. l., 8 numb. l. 28 cm.   Type-written (carbon copy) 41-22227.   CS71.W28   1938

18008   WARNER.   Ancestry and descendants of Justus Warner, 1756-1856, one of the first group of settlers in 1811 to Liverpool (now Valley City) Medina county, Ohio, in the "Connecticut western reserve," edited and compiled by Doris Wolcott Strong ... Washington, D. C. (1941)   1 p. l., 18 numb. l. 28½ cm.   Type-written (carbon copy) 41-22228.   CS71.W28   1941

18009   WARNER.   A review of kinship, compiled by Howard Willard Warner, Ottawa, Canada, to commemorate the centennial anniversary of the arrival in Canada of the Samuel Warner branch of the lineage, village of Baconsthorpe, county of Norfolk, England ... By Howard Willard Warner. (Ottawa? 1943.   20 p. ports., coat of arms, geneal. tab. 23 cm. Cover-title: The genealogy of the Warner family. 44-14687.   CS90.W32   1943

18010   WARNER.   Descendants of William and Ann (Dyde) Warner, 1627-1954.   By Esther Mae (Winget) Warner.   (Xenia? Ohio) 1954.   119 p. illus. 22 cm. 54-31954.   CS71.W28   1954

18011   WARNER.   Register of the ancestors and descendants of Samuel Warner of Wilbraham, Mass., with descendants to the seventh generation of John (William) Warner of Ipswich, Mass. (by) Katharine Warner Radasch and Arthur Hitchcok Radasch.   2d ed.   (Springfield, Mass., Samuel Warner Association) 1956.   188 p. illus. 24 cm. 56-58493.   CS71.W28   1956

18012   WARNER.   Kinsmen all; descendants of Wettenhall Warner and related families, by E. Russ Williams, Jr.   (2d ed.   Bogalusa? La., 1968)   vi, 652 p. illus., facsims., ports. 29 cm. 76-6057 MARC.   CS71.W28   1968

WARNER.   See also:

DAINGERFIELD, 1949	HART, 1923	POLLOCK, 1932
DUNHAM, 1956	HOLCOMB, 1961	ROWLEY, 1908
FULTON, 1923	LEE-WARNER, 1937	VAN NORDEN, 1923
FUNSTEN, 1926	LEWIS, 1937	WILLIS, 1895
HABERSHAM, 1901	PETTY, BX5195.T5B6	

18013   WARREN.   Memoirs of the ancient earls of Warren and Surrey, and their descendants to the present time.   By the Rev. John Watson ... Warrington, Printed by W. Eyres, 1782.   2 v. front., illus., plates (part fold.) port. plans, facsims. (part fold.) geneal. tables (part fold.) 30 cm. Head and tail pieces; initials. Plates dated 1785. For complete analysis and collation see Moule, Thomas. Bibliotheca heraldica, p. 441-445. 3-6186.   CS439.W3

18014   WARREN.   Genealogy of Warren, with some historical sketches.   By John C. Warren ... Boston, Printed by J. Wilson and son, 1854.   5 p. l., (7)-113 p. front., plates, ports., facsim., geneal. tables (part fold.) 33 cm. Title vignette: coat of arms. 9-15479.   CS71.W29   1854

18015   WARREN.   The autobiography and genealogy of William Wilkins Warren.   Printed for family distribution.   Cambridge, J. Wilson and son, 1884.   59 p. front., plates, ports. 24½ cm. Contains also Bennett, Schouler, Russell, Cumings, Wilkins, Cheever and Hunt families. 20-19560.   CT275.W297A3

18016   WARREN.   Class memoir of George Washington Warren, with English and American ancestry, by his classmate Thomas C. Amory.   Together with letters, valedictory poem, odes, etc.   Boston, (Press of Rockwell & Churchill) 1886.   1 p. l., (5) - 122 p. illus. (coat of arms) 3 port. (incl. front.) 24 cm. 10-8979.   CT275.W294A7

18017   WARREN.   A genealogy of one branch of the Warren family with its intermarriages.   1637-1890 ... Comp. for Moses C. Warren by Mary P. Warren . Ed. by Emily W. Leavitt.   Printed for private circulation.   (Boston, A. Mudge & son) 1890.   iv, (1), 59 p. pl. 26 cm. Bd. with above: Emily W. Leavitt. A genealogy of one branch of the Conant family. 1890.   A genealogy of the Bogman family.   1890.   A genealogy of one branch of the Morey family. 1890. 1-16055.   CS71.W29   1890

18018   WARREN.   The Warren-Clarke genealogy.   A record of persons related within the sixth degree to the children of Samuel Dennis Warren and Susan Cornelia Clarke.   By Rev. Charles White Huntington.   Privately printed.   Cambridge, J. Wilson and son, 1894.   238 p. ports. 32½ cm. 9-25125.   CS71.W29   1894

18019   WARREN.   Richard Warren of the Mayflower and some of his descendants.   By Mrs. Washington A. Roebling ... Boston, Press of D. Clapp & son, 1901.   1 p. l., 39 p. 23 cm. "Edition fifty copies, of which this is no. 21."   One page of additions in ms. inserted after p. 8. 1-16040.   CS71.W29   1901

18020   WARREN.   Warren; a genealogy of the descendants of James Warren who was in Kittery, Maine, 1652-1656; compiled by Orin Warren ... Haverhill, Mass., The Chase press, 1902.   138 p. front., port. 23½ cm. 2-21264.   CS71.W29   1902

18021   WARREN.   The Warren, Jackson, and allied families; being the ancestry of Jesse Warren and Betsey Jackson, by Betsey Warren Davis.   Philadelphia, Printed for private circulation by J. B. Lippincott company, 1903.   6 p. l., 207 p. front., illus., pl., geneal. tab., facsims., coats of arms. 28 cm. 3-11297.   CS71.W29   1903

18022   WARREN. (A genealogical chart of the descendants of Christopher Warren and Alice Webb) (n. p., 1904?)   geneal. tab.   40 cm.   Autographic reproduction of type-written copy.   40M3163T.   CS71.W29   1904

18023   WARREN. Monument to Joseph Warren, its origin, history and dedication, 1898-1904. Boston, Municipal printing office, 1905.   110 p.   6 pl. (incl. front.) port.   25 cm.   The genealogy of Warren: p. 13 - 15. 5-36838.   F73.64.W28B7

18024   WARREN. Some descendants of Arthur Warren of Weymouth, Massachusetts Bay colony, by Warren Woden Foster ... With an introduction by Irving Lysander Foster ... Washington, D. C., Press of Judd & Detweiler, inc., 1911.   208 p.,1 l. front. (port.) 24 cm.   12-6111.   CS71.W29   1911

18025   WARREN. The journal of a British chaplain in Paris during the peace negotiations of 1801-2 from the unpublished ms. of the Revd. Dawson Warren, M.A., unofficially attached to the diplomatic mission of Mr. Francis James Jackson, ed. with notes, a preface, and historical introduction by A. M. Broadley ... With forty illustrations, chiefly from materials collected by Mr. Dawson Warren during his sojourn in France. London, Chapman and Hall, limited, 1913.   li, (1) 283 p. front., plates, ports., plans, facsims., fold. geneal. tab. 23 cm. Title in red and black. Running title: My Paris journal. A14-641. Title from Peabody Inst.
                                                                 DC194.W3

18026   WARREN. Eleven generations of descendants of James Warren who came from Scotland to South Berwick, Maine, about 1652. By Leon Hugh Warren ... (Washington, 1942)   1 p. l., 38 numb. l., 28 l. incl. geneal. tab. 27 cm. Type-written (carbon copy) ; table mimeographed. "Copy number 3." Bibliography: leaves 35-38. 43-757.
                                                                 CS71.W29   1942

18027   WARREN. Ada Ball Cass, a descendant of Warren of the Mayflower, by Earle Millard Cass ... (New Castle, Pa.) Pub priv., 1946.   2 p. l., 13 p. 20½ cm. Includes "References." 46-2649.
                                                                 CS71.W29   1946

18028   WARREN. Warren-Remick and allied families; a genealogical outline with biographical notes. Compiled and priv. print. for James G. Warren. American Historical Company, inc. New York, 1949.   175 p. plate, ports., col. coats of arms. 32 cm. Printed on one side of leaf only. 50-3649.
                                                                 CS71.W29   1949

18029   WARREN. The families of Warren and Johnson of Warrenstown, County Meath. By Franz V. Recum. New York, 1950.   9 p. illus. 22 cm. 50-33757.   CS499.W37   1950

18030   WARREN. The Warrens and you. By Elizabeth (Prather) Ellsberry. Kansas City, Mo., Brown-White-Lowell Press, 1958.   294 p. col. coat of arms. 24 cm. 58-19119.   CS71.W29   1958

18031   WARREN. Adriel Warren of Berwick, Maine; his forebears and descendants. By Vanetta (Hosford) Warren. Boston, 1964.   v, 189 p. illus., map, ports. 26 cm. 65-3072.   CS71.W29   1964

18031 a WARREN.   Warren family of Boston.   In vertical file.   Ask reference librarian for this material.

    WARREN. See also:

AVERY, 1919	GRINNELL, 1913	ROGERS, 1905
AVERY, 1925	MANLEY, 1938	STEARNS, 1898
BENZ, 1931	MAUNSELL, CS439.M37	VAN NOSTRAND, E171.A53 v.19
CONSTANT, F129.Y6C7	MOLINEUX, 1894	WALLIN, 1934
FLAGG, 1903	PIERCE, 1874	WHEELER, 1892

18032   WARRICK. Family of Samuel Warrick and Nancy Frazier Warrick, stories and genealogy ... by John A. Warrick ... (Chicago? 1923)   (16) p. illus. (incl. ports.) 20½ cm. 34-35361.   CS71.W292   1923

    WARRICK. See also McINTOSH, F129.C36M2

    WARRIN. See WARREN.

18033 WARRINER. The Warriner family of New England origin. Being a history and genealogy of William Warriner, pioneer settler of Springfield, Mass., and his descendants embracing nine genera- tions from 1638 to 1898. With an appendix containing genealogical notes of other persons and families in America bearing the same name. By Rev. Edwin Warriner ... Albany, N.Y., J. Munsell's sons, 1899. 287 p. incl. front. (port.) illus. 24 cm. 9-15037. CS71.W293 1899

WARRINER. See also WHITE, E171.A53 v.20

WARRINGTON. See PEPPER, 1960

WARTH. See SHREWSBURY, 1968

18034 WARTON. Biographical memoirs of the late Revd. Joseph Warton ... to which are added, A selection from his works; and a literary correspondence between eminent persons, reserved by him for publication. By the Rev. John Wooll ... London, Printed by L. Hansard, for T. Cadell and W. Davies, 1806. xix, (1), 407 p. incl. geneal. tab. front. (port.) pl., facsim. 28 x 22 cm. "Biographical memoirs": p. 1-103. A second volume promised by the editor was never published. 24-12942. PR3759.W3Z8

18035 WARWICK, Earls of. Thys rol was laburd & finished by Master John Rows of Warrewyk. London, W. Pickering, 1845 (1859) (102) p. col. front., 32 col. pl. 31 cm. A pictorial history of the earls of Warwick, printed from the Yorkist roll in possession of the Duke of Manchester. cf. Introduction (signed) William Courthope, March 30, 1859. "The date 1845 borne on the work refers to the plates and title page, which were prepared in that year." - Dict. of nat. biog. (under Courthope) "The publication of the roll was undertaken by the late Mr. William Pickering, in the year 1845, but ... left unfinished at his decease in 1854." - Pref. note. "Only 100 copies were printed." - Sonnenschein. Best books. 2-23580. DA690.W3R7

18036 WARWICK. Notes on some of the Warwicks of Virginia. (New Haven, Conn., 1937) 19 p. 22½ cm. Introduction signed: William A. Beardsley. 38-32674. CS71.W3 1937

WARWICK. See also CLEEK, 1957

WARWICK, Earls of. See also GREVILLE, CS439.G84 and No. 18035

18037 WASBROAD. ... La famille Wasbroad (tiré à 50 exemplaires) By Gérard Malchelosse. Montreal, 1937. His serie genealogique, fasc. no 2. CS90.W35 1937

18038 WASHBOURNE. The Washbourne family. Notes and records, historic and social of the ancient family of Washbourne of Washbourne, Wichenford and Pytchley from the 12th century to the present time ... Edited by R. E. M. Peach. Gloucester, Printed by J. Bellows, 1896. xviii, 141 p. incl. illus., geneal. tables. 21½ x 18½ cm. "For private circulation only." 9-11817. CS439.W33 1896

18039 WASHBOURNE. The Washbourne family of Little Washbourne and Wichenford in the county of Worcester, by James Davenport ... With fifteen illustrations. London, Methuen & co. (1907) xvii, 236 p. front., illus., plates, ports., map, fold. geneal. tab. 26 cm. 8-4340. CS439.W33 1907

18040 WASHBOURNE. Some notes on the Evesham branch of the Washbourne family, by E. A. B. Barnard, F.S.A. Evesham, England, W. & H. Smith limited, 1914. 2 p. l., 60 p. front., plates, facsim. 18 cm. "The second generation in America": p. 47-54. 25-126. CS439.W33 1914

WASHBOURNE. See also WASHBURN.

18041 WASHBURN. The Washburn family. Descendants of John of Plymouth, Mass., and William of Stratford, Conn., and Hempstead, L. I. Compiled by W. C. Sharpe ... Seymour, Conn., Record print, 1892. 16 p. illus. 21½ cm. 9-15036. CS71.W315 1892

18042 WASHBURN. Washburn family, 1591 to 1895. (Descendants of John Washburn who came to Duxbury, Mass. before 1632, n. p., 1895?) geneal. tab. 40 x 55 cm. Blue-print. 39M82T. CS71.W315 1895

18043 WASHBURN. Genealogical notes of the Washburn family, with a brief sketch of the family in England, containing a full record of the descendants of Israel Washburn of Raynham, 1755-1841. By Mrs. Julia Chase Washburn. (Lewiston, Me., Press of Journal co.) 1898.   104 p. front. (coat of arms) plates. 22½ cm. Ms. additions. 1-19531.

CS71.W315   1898

18044 WASHBURN. Washburn. A partial history of the family from the arrival of John Washburn about 1632 and a short sketch in England in reign of Edward III., 1327-1377. Mostly from data collected by Warren Azro Washburn. Felchville, Vt., Printed by D. E. Washburn, 1904.   1 p. l., (10) p. 19 cm. 17-9566.

CS71.W315   1904

18045 WASHBURN. Ebenezer Washburn; his ancestors and descendants, with some connected families. A family story of 700 years by Geo. T. Washburn. Pasumalai, South India, American mission Lenox press, 1913.   2 p. l., xv, 209 p. front., plates (incl. ports., coats of arms) 22 cm. 15-7826.

CS71.W315   1913

18046 WASHBURN. Abiel Washburn and his descendants, compiled by William Lewis Washburn. Patchogue, N.Y., 1914.   23 p. 25½ cm. 14-7318.   CS71.W315   1914

18047 WASHBURN. The American ancestry of Silence Washburn, wife of Jesse Washburn and mother of Daniel Washburn, who escaped the Wyoming massacre, by W. T. Stauffer. (Wilkes-Barre, Pa., 1928)   cover-title, 16 p. 23 cm. Reprint from Proceedings and collections of the Wyoming historical and genealogical society. vol. XXI. 29-10280.

CS71.W315   1928

18048 WASHBURN. The Richard Washburn family genealogy; a family history of 200 years; outlining the ancestors and decendants (!) of Richard Washburn (fifth generation in America) with some connected families; this volume also contains a short outline of some of the other descendants of William Washburn of Hempstead, Long island, New York, and John Washburn of Duxbury, Massachusetts, by Ada C. Haight (Mrs. H. Augustus Haight) assisted by Frank C. Lewis, M.D. Ossining, N.Y., 1937.   4 p. l., 1271, (1) p. front. (col. coat of arms) plates, facsim. 24½ cm. Blank page for "Memorandum" at end. "References": p. 1070-1074

CS71.W315   1937

18049 WASHBURN. My seven sons, by Lilian Washburn; the true and amazing story of the seven famous Washburn brothers, as told by the old grandsire, Israel, sr., and transcribed by his granddaughter, Lilian Washburn. Portland, Me., Falmouth publishing house, 1940.   5 p. l., 3-143 p., 1 l. 9 port. on 2 l. (incl. front.) 22 cm. "Of this special edition one hundred copies only have been printed. This is copy number 56 and is signed by Lilian Washburn. 40-32504.

CS71.W315   1940

18050 WASHBURN. William Washburn of Long Island, N.Y., ancestors and descendants, 1259-1935. (By Will Owens Washburn) (n.p., 1944?)   1 v. (unpaged) 29 cm. Cover title. Typescript (carbon) Includes bibliography. 54-47072.

CS71.W315   1944

18051 WASHBURN. Washburn family foundations in Normandy, England, and America. By Mabel Thacher Rosemary Washburn. Greenfield, Ind., W. Mitchell Print. Co., 1953 (i.e. 1954) 189 p. illus., ports., coats of arms. 25 cm. "Authorities for New York line": p. 171-175. 54-21302.   CS71.W315   1954

18052 WASHBURN. A genealogical history of the Washburns of Huron County, Ohio. By Mildred Jane (Smith) Parkinson. Milwaukee, 1954.   92 p. illus. 25 cm. 60-35502.   CS71.W315   1954a

18053 WASHBURN. The ancestors and descendants of Abraham Daniel Washburn and his wife, Flora Clarinda Gleason, Utah pioneers, 1805-1962. By Ella Almeda (Larson) Turner. (n.p.) c. 1963. 564 p. illus., ports., coats of arms. 24 cm. 63-25605.   CS71.W315   1963

18054 WASHBURN. Washburn-Latham. In vertical file.   Ask reference librarian for this material.

WASHBURN. See also: CHRYSLER, 1959   FOY, 1932
                      DUMONT, 1960   STEVENS, 1946
                      EASTMAN, 1928   TAYLOR, 1930
                      FAXON, 1880   WASHBOURNE.

18055   WASHINGTON.   A genealogical table of the Washington family of Whitfield, Lancaster ... by Thomas Gaillard ... New York, Engraved & printed by Ferd. Mayer & co., 1860.   geneal. tab. 59 x 74 cm.
38-32653.   CS71.W318   1860

18056   WASHINGTON.   The Washingtons; a tale of a country parish in the 17th century based on authentic documents, by John Nassau Simpkinson ... London, Longman, Green, Longman and Roberts, 1860.   xvi, 326, lxxxix, (1) p. front., illus. 20½ cm. Library of U.S. Dept. of State. SD 19-294.   PZ3.S52.W27

18057   WASHINGTON.   The home of Washington at Mount Vernon, embracing a full and accurate description, as well as of the birth-place, genealogy, character, marriage, and last illnesss of Washington, together with incidents pertaining to the burial ... By J. A. Wineberger.   Washington, T. McGill, printer, 1860.   iv, (5)-70 p. front. (port.) 5 pl. 21½ cm. Published, 1857, with title: A guide to the tomb of Washington, at Mount Vernon ... and 1858 with title: The tomb of Washington at Mount Vernon ... 19-19020.   E312.5.W765

18058   WASHINGTON.   ... The governor's message, and accompanying papers, in relation to certain memorials of the ancestors of Washington, with the report of the committee upon the same ... (Boston, 1861)   12 p. 25 cm. (General court, 1861. House (doc.) 199) Concerning the transmission to the state of Massachusetts of facsimiles of inscriptions in the parish church of Brington, England, of the father and the uncle of John Washington, the emigrant to Virginia, who was the great grandfather of George Washington. cf. p. 2. 15-28188.   CS71.W318   1861

18059   WASHINGTON.   Fac-similes of the memorial stones of the last English ancestors of George Washington in the parish church of Brington, Northamptonshire, England; permanently placed in the State house of Massachusetts.   Boston, W. White, printer to the state, 1862.   15 p. 29 cm. 1-2551.   CS71.W318   1862

18060   WASHINGTON.   A preliminary investigation of the alleged ancestry of George Washington; first president of the United States of America; exposing a serious error in the existing pedigree.   By Joseph Lemuel Chester ... (Reprinted from the Herald and genealogist, London, and the Heraldic journal, Boston.) Boston, H. W. Dutton & son, printers, 1866.   23 p. 25 cm. 10-10914.   CS71.W318   1866

18061   WASHINGTON.   The English ancestry of Washington, the genealogical portion of same furnished by Albert Welles ... collated by James Phillipse, esq., of London.   (n. p., 1876?)
p. 62 - 67. 23½ cm. Caption title. 25-19272.   CS71.W318   1876

18062   WASHINGTON.   The pedigree and history of the Washington family: derived from Odin, the founder of Scandinavia, B.C. 70, involving a period of eighteen centuries, and including fifty-five generations, down to General George Washington, first president of the United States.   By Albert Welles ... New-York, Society library, 1879.   vi, 7-12, xxxviii, (1), 370 p. front., plates, ports., col. coats of arms. 25½ cm. 9-15046.   CS71.W318   1879

18063   WASHINGTON.   Yorkshire as the home of the Washingtons.   (Newcastle-upon-Tyne, Printed by J. M. Carr, 1879)   1 p. l., (5)-48 p., 1 l. 24½ cm. By William Newsome. Privately printed. 2-17516.   CS71.W318   1879a

18064   WASHINGTON.   American family antiquity, being an account of the origin and progress of American families, traced from their progenitors in this country, connected with their history abroad ... By Albert Welles ... New York, Society library, 1880-81.   3 v. pl., ports., photos., col. coats of arms.
34½ cm. "In memoriam; a biographical sketch of Thomas Stokes, by James S. Dickerson, D. D.": v.1, p. (205)-212. Contents. - v.1. Washington, Barron, Buell, Cary, Page, Frost, Stokes, Dunbar, Grace. - v.2. Kip, Cooke, Lyon, Kendall, Flower, Starin, Connor, Mortimer. - v.3. Snow, Wheeler, Martin, Conover, Fish, Waterbury, Babcock. 9-25091.   CS69.W5

18065   WASHINGTON.   Origin of the stars and stripes, together with an accurate account of the Washington genealogy.   Prepared for the publishers by Edward W. Tuffley ... To accompany the Washington chart ... New York, Root & Tinker, 1883.   cover-title, 12 p. 18 cm. and chart. 66 x 51 cm. fold. to 24 x 26 cm.   The chart includes facsimiles of brasses in Great Brington church, Northamptonshire, and in Sulgrave church, Northamptonshire, and of the Washington shield and Washington arms and crest. "Compliments of the New York life insurance company." 14-5935.   CS71.W318   1883

18066   WASHINGTON.   The Castle Howell school record, comprising a list of pupils from the beginning, papers on the origin, name and changes, by principals, and miscellaneous articles, contributed
by old boys.   Lancaster, Printed for the subscribers by R. & G. Brash, 1888.   lxxvii p., 1 l., 261, (3) p.
front., plates (part fold. and col.) diagrs., map, fold. geneal. tab. 26½ cm. Preface signed: D. D. (i. e. David Davis) "The Washingtons and
their connection with Warton. By Henry Whitman": p. (192) - 204, with "Pedigree of the Washington family", and phototint of "The arms of
Washington on Warton church, and the "Washington house", Warton. 21-8270.   LF795. L45D3

18067   WASHINGTON.   George Washington and Mount Vernon.   A collection of Washington's unpublished agricultural and personal letters.   Ed. with historical and genealogical introduction by M. D.
Conway.   Brooklyn, N. Y., Pub. by the Society, 1889.   xcii, 352 p. front., illus., port. 24½ cm. (Long Island
historical society. Memoirs. v.4) 1-13381.   F116. L87 vol. 4

18068   WASHINGTON.   The writings of George Washington; collected and ed. by Worthington
Chauncey Ford ... New York & London, G. P. Putnam's sons, 1889 - (93)   14 v. 23½ cm. No. 666 of 750
copies printed. Letterpress edition. Appendix: "The Washington family," v.14, p. 317-431. 2-5665.

                                                    E312. 7   1889
                                                    vol. 14

18069   WASHINGTON.   An examination of the English ancestry of George Washington, setting forth
the evidence to connect him with the Washingtons of Sulgrave and Brington.   By Henry F. Waters ...
Boston, Printed for the New England historic genealogical society, 1889.   53 p. incl. pl. (coat of arms) front.
(map) fold. geneal. tab. 25 cm. Reprinted from the New Eng. hist and geneal. register for Oct., 1889. 10-10728.

                                                    CS71. W318   1889

18070   WASHINGTON.   The Washingtons and their connection with Warton.   By Henry Whitman.
With phototint of "The arms of Washington" on Warton church, and the "Washington House, Warton."
(Reprinted from the Castle Howell school record.)   Lancaster, Eng., E. & J. L. Milner; (etc., etc.,
1889)   18 p. front., fold. geneal. tab. 25½ cm. The pedigree is reprinted substantially from the one published by Albert Welles of New
York in 1879. 15-12368.   CS71. W318   1889a

18071   WASHINGTON.   George Washington's ancestors, the Washingtons of Sulgrave and Brington.
By William C. Wells ... London, Harrison and sons (189-?)   16 p. 21½ cm. Title vignette: Impression of the seal
of William de Wessyngton, on a deed dated 1360.   On verso of t. - p.: Pedigree of the "Washingtons of Northamptonshire and Virginia." 15-19146.

                                                    CS71. W318   189-

18072   WASHINGTON.   A genealogical history, beginning with Colonel John Washington, the emigrant,
and head of the Washington family in America.   Ed. and comp. by Thornton Augustin Washington.
Washington, D. C., Press of McGill & Wallace, 1891.   71 p. front. (coat of arms) fold. geneal. tab. 23½ cm. 10-5833.
                                                    CS71. W318   1891

18073   WASHINGTON.   The Irish Washingtons at home and abroad, together with some mention of
the ancestry of the American Pater patriae.   By George Washington ... and Thomas Hamilton Murray
... Boston, The Carrolton press, 1898.   43 p. 6 port. (incl. front.) 22 cm. 5-4395.
                                                    CS71. W318   1898

18074   WASHINGTON.   Experimental pedigree of the descendants of Lawrence Washington, 1635-
1677, of Virginia.   By Rev. Horace Edwin Hayden ... Reprinted from his volume of "Virginia genealogies," now in press. (Wilkes-Barre, Pa.) 1891.   cover-title, 6 p. 25 cm. 8-812.
                                                    CS71. W318   1891a

18075   WASHINGTON.   Wills of the American ancestors of General George Washington, in the line of
the original owner and the inheritors of Mount Vernon.   From the original documents and probate
records.   Edited by Joseph M. Toner, M. D.   Boston, New-England historic genealogical society, 1891.
19 p. facsim. 25 cm. Reprinted from the New Eng. hist. and geneal. register for July 1891. 10-10915.   CS71. W318   1891b

18076   WASHINGTON.   Wills of George Washington and his immediate ancestors.   Edited by
Worthington Chauncy Ford.   Brooklyn, N. Y., Historical printing club, 1891. 210 p. 23½ x 17½ cm.
250 copies printed. no. 61. 17-4545.   E312. 99   1891
          —— Copy 3.   No. 10   CS71. W318   1891c

18077   WASHINGTON.   The English ancestry of Washington.   By Moncure D. Conway.   (In Harper's
magazine.   New York, 1891.   25 cm.   v. 84, p. 877-889)   19-754.   AP2.H3
——— Copy 2, detached.   CS71.W318   1891d

18078   WASHINGTON.   ... The ancestry and earlier life of George Washington.   By Edward D.
Neill ... From Magazine of Pennsylvania historical society, October, 1892.   (In Macalester college, St. Paul,
Minn.   Dept. of history, literature, and political science.   Contributions.   St. Paul, 1890-92.   24 cm.   2d ser.   (1892) 1 p. 1., p.255-292.
(no. 11))   4-18857.   E173.M12

18079   WASHINGTON.   The Washington family.   (Reprinted from the "Writings of Washington,"
edited by Worthington Chauncey Ford) ... New York, 1893.   115 p.   fold. facsim., fold. geneal. tab.   23½ cm.
Fifty copies printed.   12-16570.   CS71.W318   1893

18080   WASHINGTON.   Notes and particulars regarding the ancestors of Gen. George Washington,
the first president of the United States of America.   With engravings of the old Washington homestead
in Little Brington, where his ancestors lived and the old Brington parish church where they were
buried.   Also sketch of the Washington coat of arms and crest with history of the origin of the stars
and stripes and spread eagle.   (n.p., c.1893)   (8) p.   illus.   13 cm.   Reproductions in color, of crest and coat of arms,
on verso of cover.   Cover-title: History of the ancestors of George Washington.   Dating back to the year 1532 ...   12-34881.
CS71.W318   1893a

18081   WASHINGTON.   Washington, Shakespeare and St. George, by Sarah M. and E. Colbert ...
Chicago, Western British American, 1893.   53 p.   illus.   20 cm.   The first paper on the Washington family in England was
written by Mrs. Sarah M. Colbert; the other two papers by Elias Colbert for the St. George society of Chicago.   16-20359.
CS71.W318   1893b

18082   WASHINGTON.   Descent of Doctor Bailey Washington of the U.S.N. as given by L.Q. Washing-
ton.   (n.p.) 1893.   1 p. 1., 10 numb. 1.   19 x 15½ cm.   In manuscript.   Title mounted on cover: Copies of Washington letters.   A
letter to Miss Maud Lee Davidge relative to her ancestry on the Washington side, from a manuscript on the Washington family by Lund Washington and
from other authentic sources.   CA 36-1701 unrev.   CS71.W318   1893c

18083   WASHINGTON.   The Washingtons and their colonial homes in West Virginia, by Mynna
Thruston.   (n.p., 19-)   cover-title, (29) p.   illus. (incl. map) fold. geneal. tab.   22½ cm.   37-10356.
CS71.W318   19 -

18084   WASHINGTON.   Genealogy of the Washington family ... (Los Angeles)   Sons of the revolution,
California, 1900.   cover-title, 13, (1) p.   geneal. tab.   26½ cm.   Caption title: The Washington family, compiled by Holdrdige Ozro
Collins.   1-1754.   CS71.W318   1900
——— Copy 2.   Portrait inserted.

18085   WASHINGTON.   Mount Vernon and the Washingtons.   (In Some colonial mansions and those who lived in them,
with genealogies of the various families mentioned; by Thomas Allen Glenn.   2d series.   Philadelphia, 1900.   24 cm.   p. 19-84)   Feb. 15,
1900-22.   E159.G56

18086   WASHINGTON.   The cradle of the Washingtons and the home of the Franklins, by Arthur
Branscombe.   Profusely illustrated by the author.   London and New York, The Anglo-American ex-
change (1901)   43, (1) p. incl. illus., 5 pl.   18 x 25 cm.   Illustrated t.-p. with vignettes (2 port.)   16-13004.
DA670.N7B7

18087   WASHINGTON.   In the shadow of the Lord; a romance of the Washingtons, by Mrs. Hugh
Fraser ... New York, H. Holt and company, 1906.   3 p. 1., 428 p.   19 cm.   6-32360.
PZ3.F864I

18088   WASHINGTON.   American shrines in England, by Alfred T. Story; with four illustrations in
colour and eighteen in monotone.   London, Methuen & co. (1908)   xi, 348 p.   illus., 16 pl. (4 col., incl. front.)
port.   20 cm.   Contents. - The Washingtons of Northamptonshire. - The cradle of the Washingtons. - Wormleighton - The Washingtons of Brington.
- The Spencer and Washington monuments at Brington. - Lawrence Washington, the rector of Purleigh. - The home of the Franklins. - Scrooby and
the Pilgrim fathers. - A Lancashire and a Suffolk hero (Miles Standish and John Winthrop) - Penn's homes and burial place. - The founder of Yale
college. - The founder of Harvard college. - Other memorials and shrines in and near London. - Some other heroes of American colonisation.
8-37390.   DA660.S85

18089   WASHINGTON.   Warton and George Washington's ancestors.   By T. Pape, B. A. (Morecambe, Visitor printing works, 1913)   46, (1) p. illus. (incl. ports.) fold. geneal. tab. 18½ cm. Title vignette: "The Washington arms & crest." 15-1499.   CS71. W318   1913

18090   WASHINGTON.   Sulgrave, the ancestral home of the Washingtons.   (Washington, D. C., Printed by J. F. McCarter, c. 1916)   cover-title, (6) p. 1 illus. 18 cm. Compiled by Fred James Woodward. 16-25271.
E312. 195. W89

18091   WASHINGTON.   The Washington manor house; England's gift to the world, by Ethel Armes ... New York, American branch of the Sulgrave institution (c. 1922)   39, (1) p. incl. front., illus. 22½ cm. Map on p. 3 of cover.   Genealogical table on verso of frontispiece.   "This book is issued under the auspices of the Women's committee, Sulgrave institution." 22-19486.
E312. 195. A7

18092   WASHINGTON.   The Kenmore mansion, built 1752, home of Colonel Fielding Lewis and his wife, Betty Washington, compiled by Mrs. Vivian Minor Fleming.   Fredericksburg, Va., The Kenmore association, c. 1924.   23, (1) p. illus. 23½ cm. 24-9255 rev.   F234. 19F8

18093   WASHINGTON.   Mount Vernon and the Washington family; a concise handbook on the ancestry, youth and family of George Washington, and history of his home ... prepared for the busy reader ... by Chester Hale Sipe ... (Butler, Pa., Ziegler printing co., inc.) c. 1924.   48 p. incl. front., illus., ports. 19 cm. 24-14603.   E312. 5. S62

18094   WASHINGTON.   Sulgrave manor ... Read at a meeting of Colonial dames in New Haven, Connecticut ... December 5, 1923, by Mrs. Wm. H. H. Smith.   Hartford, Conn., 1924.   15 p. illus. 20½ cm. Washington coat of arms on title page. Illustration on cover. Signed: Julia Welles Griswold Smith. 26-9529.
E312. 195. S64

18095   WASHINGTON.   Mount Vernon and the Washington family; a concise handbook on the ancestry, youth and family of George Washington, and history of his home.   3d and enl. ed. ... Prepared for the busy reader ... by Chester Hale Sipe ... (Butler, Pa., Ziegler printing co., inc., c. 1925)   3 p. l., 11-91 p. front., illus. (incl. ports.) 20 cm. 25-15953.   E312. 5. S62   1925

18096   WASHINGTON.   The family life of George Washington, by Charles Moore, with an introduction by Mrs. Theodore Roosevelt ... Boston and New York, Houghton Mifflin company, 1926.   xvi p., 1 l., 250 p. front., plates, ports., maps (1 double) facsims. 23½ cm. "This large-paper edition, printed at the Riverside press in Cambridge, Massachusetts, U. S. A., in February, 1926, is limited to three hundred and seventy-five numbered copies... No. 375." 26-9004.
E312. M75

18097   WASHINGTON.   The history of the Washington family, by H. Isham Longden ... Reprinted from "the Genealogists' magazine".   Northampton, W. Mark & co., ltd., 1927.   4 p. l., 55 (1) p. illus. (incl. facsim.) 18½ cm. 27-23970.   CS439. W335

18098   WASHINGTON.   Mount Vernon and the Washington family; a concise handbook on the ancestry, youth and family of George Washington, and history of his home.   4th ed., June, 1927, illustrated and indexed.   Prepared for the busy reader ... by C. Hale Sipe ... (Butler, Pa., C. H. Sipe, c. 1927)   3 p. l., 11-91 p. front., illus. (incl. ports.) 20 cm. 28-6519.   E312. 5. S62   1927

18099   WASHINGTON.   The history of Mount Vernon, America's patriotic shrine.   (Washington, D. C.) The National art service co., inc., c. 1928.   (18) p., 1 l. illus. 23 cm. On cover: By Alla Harman Rogers. "Drawings of interior views made by Francis K. Macnerhany from photographs furnished by Leet bros., inc." 30-1663.   E312. 5. R72

18100   WASHINGTON.   Mount Vernon; its children, its romances, its allied families and mansions, by Minnie Kendall Lowther ... Philadelphia, Chicago (etc.) The John C. Winston company (c. 1930)   2 p. l., ix-xvi p., 1 l., 282 p. incl. illus., pl., ports. front., pl. 20½ cm. 30-28202.   E312. 5. L925

18101   WASHINGTON.   The history of Mount Vernon, America's patriotic shrine.   Rev. ed.   (Washington, D. C.) The National art service co., inc., c. 1930.   (22) p., 3 l. illus. 23 cm. On cover: By Alla Harman Rogers. "Drawings of interior views made by Francis K. Macnerhany from photographs furnished by Leet bros., inc. 30-21279.
E312. 5. R72   1930

18102   WASHINGTON.   Washington's home and fraternal life, by Carl H. Claudy ... Washington, D.C., United States George Washington bicentennial commission, 1931.   2p. l., 68 p.   illus. (incl. ports.) 23 cm.   (On cover: Honor to George Washington ... Pamphlet no. 14)   "One of a series of 16 pamphlets authorized by the Congress of the United States."   "Selected authorities": p. 67-68.   Contents. - pt. I. Family life and friends. - pt. II. Fraternal life. - pt. III. Genealogical table. 31-28747.

E312.H77 no. 14

18103   WASHINGTON.   George Washington year by year, dates of important events relating to George Washington, 1183-1799, edited by Dr. Albert Bushnell Hart, issued by the United States George Washington bicentennial commission, Washington, D.C.   Washington, U.S.Govt. print. off., 1931. 16 p.   23½ cm.   "4th ed."   "Significant dates in Washington's ancestry, 1183-1730": p. 3-5.   31-28548.

E312.15.U5674

18104   WASHINGTON.   The writings of George Washington from the original manuscript sources, 1745-1799;   prepared under the direction of the United States George Washington bicentennial commission and published by authority of Congress;   John C. Fitzpatrick, editor ... Washington, U.S.Govt. print. off. (1931 -   v.   fronts. (ports.) illus. (plan) map, facsims. (part fold.) 24 cm.   "George Washington bicentennial edition." "One deviation has been made from the plan of including all of Washington's writings in this edition.   The Diary has been recently published by a skillful editor ... (and) has therefore been left out of the new set." - Foreword.   32-11075.

E312.7   1931

18105   WASHINGTON.   A chart of the Washington family, outlined with especial reference to the ancestors and descendants of Augustine Washington, the father of General George Washington ... Copyright ... (by) H. B. Castleman.   Phila(delphia) Pa., c. 1932.   geneal. tab.   145 x 78½ cm.   Mimeographed. CA 32-554 unrev.

CS71.W318   1932

18106   WASHINGTON.   The Washington ancestry, and records of the McClain, Johnson, and forty other colonial American families, prepared for Edward Lee McClain by Charles Arthur Hoppin ... Greenfield, O., Priv. print., 1932.   3 v.   fronts., illus., plates, ports., facsims., geneal. tables (part fold.) coats of arms. 29½ cm.   "This work, limited to three hundred copies, was printed for Edward Lee McClain, Greenfield, Ohio, by the Yale university press, in January 1932."   32-7698.

E312.19.H78

18107   WASHINGTON.   Mount Vernon; its children, its romances, its allied families and mansions, by Minnie Kendall Lowther ... Philadelphia, Chicago (etc.) The John C. Winston company (c. 1932) xiii (1), 302 p. incl. front., illus., plates, ports. plates.   20½ cm.   32-8634.   E312.L925   1932

18108   WASHINGTON.   Wakefield, birthplace of George Washington, by Charles Moore.   Washington, The Wakefield national memorial association, 1932.   vii, 33 p.   front., plates, port.   24½ cm.   32-13996.

E312.5.M65

18109   WASHINGTON.   The history of Mount Vernon, America's patriotic shrine.   Rev. ed. (Washington, D.C.) The Nationa Art service co., inc., c. 1932.   27 p., 2 l.   illus.   23 cm.   On cover: By Alla Harman Rogers.   "Drawings of interior views made by Francis K. Macnerhany from photographs furnished by Leet bros., inc."   32-11553.

E312.5.R72   1932

18110   WASHINGTON.   George Washington, year by year, dates of important events relating to George Washington, 1183-1799, edited by Dr. Albert Bushnell Hart, issued by the United States George Washington bicentennial commission, Washington, D.C.   (Washington, Govt. print. off., 1932) 16 p.   23 cm.   "6th ed."   "Significant dates in Washington's ancestry, 1183-1730": p. 3-5.   32-26420.   E312.15.U5676

18111   WASHINGTON.   History of the George Washington bicentennial celebration ... Literature series.   Washington, D.C., United States George Washington bicentennial commission, 1932. 3 v.   col. fronts., illus. (part col.; incl. ports., maps, plans, facsims.) col. fold. pl.   31½ x 24½ cm.   "Literature prepared and issued in connection with the celebration of the two hundredth anniversary of the birth of George Washington ... Restricted to re-publication of historical pamphlets that have had wide distribution." - Foreword.   Descriptive letter-press on versos facing the frontispieces, and on verso of plate.   Contains music.   Vols. 1-2 include bibliographies.   "Samples of Braille printing for the blind": v.2, p. (437) - (442)   "Living descendants of John Washington of Westmoreland county, Virginia, Lawrence Washington of Westmoreland county, Virginia, John Washington of Surry county, Virginia, compiled by Anne Madison Washington": v.3, p. 599-640 B.   33-26189 rev.

E312.6.U58

18112   WASHINGTON.   Some descendants of Colonel John Washington and of his brother Captain Lawrence Washington, founders of the Washington family of Westmorland county, Virginia, and records

18112 continued: of the allied families of Wheelwright, Hungerford, Pratt, Dodge, Conant, Chilton, Gwinn, Barton, Birkett, Warren, Wickliffe, Bailey, Massey, Pope, Townshend, and others, by Charles Arthur Hoppin.   New York, N. Y., 1932.   4 p. l., 150 - 150b numb. l., 1 l., 150c - 150 g, 151-229 numb. l., 12 l. front., pl., ports., coats of arms, fold. geneal. tab. 28 cm.   Mimeographed.   "The memorial service for Josephine Wheelwright Rust, at Wakefield, Westmoreland county, Virginia, February eleventh, 1932": 1 l. numb. l. 150c-150g. 32-30541.   CS71. W318   1932a

18113   WASHINGTON. Pedigree of George Washington, compiled by Katharine Beecher Stetson Chamberlin.   Pasadena, Calif., 1932.   sheet. illus. (coats of arms) 89 x 140 cm. 32-11353.
CS71. W318   1932b

18114   WASHINGTON. Sulgrave manor and the Washingtons; a history and guide to the Tudor home of George Washington's ancestors, by H. Clifford Smith ... With a foreword by Viscount Lee of Fareham ... London, J. Cape (1933)   259, (1) p. front., illus. (incl. map, plans, coats of arms, geneal. tab.) plates, port., facsim. 26½ x 20½ cm. Bibliography: p. 245-247. 34-821.   E312. 195. S62

18115   WASHINGTON. Direct line of living descendants of the Washington family ... Washington, D. C., United States George Washington bicentennial commission, 1933. 4 v. geneal. tables. 32 x 54 cm. Cover title. Contents. - I. John Washington, of Westmoreland county, Virginia. Lawrence Washington, of Westmoreland county, Virginia. John Washington, of Surry county, Virginia. - II. Betty Washington. - III. Augustine Washington. Charles Washington. Samuel Washington. - IV. John Augustine Washington. 47-33229.   CS71. W318   1933

18116   WASHINGTON. Edward Washington and his kin, by Cordelia Jackson ... Washington, D. C. (Mimeoform press) 1934.   3 p. l., 24, viii p. front. (port.) 23½ cm. 34-9648.   CS71. W318   1934

18116 a   WASHINGTON. "The Queen of England's American ancestry and cousinship to Washington and Lee".   in The New York Genealogical and Biographical Record v. 70 (July 1939), p. 201-205.   F116. N28 v. 70

18117   WASHINGTON. The Washingtons and their homes, by John W. Wayland ... Staunton, Va., McClure printing company, 1944.   xiii p., 2 l., 385 p. incl. front., illus. (incl. ports., maps, plans) 26 cm. "Three hundred copies printed ... No. 1." 45-2648.   CS71. W318   1944

18118   WASHINGTON. A genealogical historiography of General Washington. By Alphonse Joseph Carnevale. East Elmhurst, N. Y., Carnevale Publications, 1959.   geneal. table. illus., ports., coats of arms. 72 x 119 cm. fold. to 36 x 41 cm. 59-39666.   CS71. W318   1959

18119   WASHINGTON. The earliest Washingtons and their Anglo-Scottish connexions, by George S. H. L. Washington. Cambridge (Eng.) 1964.   x, 35 p. illus., geneal. table, ports. 23 cm. 66-38169.   CS439. W335   1964

18120   WASHINGTON. George Washington's family. In vertical file.   Ask reference librarian for this material.

18121   WASHINGTON. Washington family in Holland, Germany and Austria. In vertical file. Ask reference librarian for this material.

18122   WASHINGTON. Chart of the ancestry of General George Washington. Brookfield Pub. Co. Folded genealogical chart. 2 copies. In vertical file.   Ask reference librarian for this material.

18123   WASHINGTON. Additional material in vertical file.   Ask reference librarian for this material.

WASHINGTON.   See also:

BALL, 1885	LEOGE, 1926	SELDEN, 1911
BATHGATE (In vertical file)	MARTIAU, 1932	SHIRLEY, 1841
BLACKBURN, 1939	MILLER, 1923	WATSON, 1910
BUCKNER, 1907	PAGE, 1883	WHITAKER, 1930
FUNSTEN, 1926	PECK, 1925	WRIGHT, E312. 19. H79
HABERSHAM, 1901	PEYTON, F230. P51	

18124   WASS. The Wass family. By Walter Preston Wass. (n. p.) 1945.   56, (18), 57-84, 12 - S1. 29 cm. Bibliography: leaves (2) - (9) (2d group) 63-24316.   CS71. W3187   1945

18125   WASSELL.   The Wassell family, and its several branches in the United States.   Also a pedigree of one branch of the Spotts family.   By Wassell Randolph.   Memphis, Distributed by Memphis Public Library, 1962.   63 p. 28 cm. 63-26880.   CS71.W3195   1962

18126   WASSON.   Wassons of U. S. A., 1938-1939, copyright ... by W. A. Wasson.   (New York) c. 1943.   (31) p. illus. (map) 25½ cm.   Reproduced from manuscript copy. 43-8913.   CS71.W32   1943

WASSON.   See also BASSETT, 1930

18127   WASTENEYS, DE.   Some account of Colton and of the de Wasteney's family ... (Printed for private circulation) Birmingham, Houghton and Hammond, printers, 1879.   vi, (7) - 297, xv p. illus., plates, fold. plan, geneal. tables. 24 cm. By Frederick Perrott Parker. 18-3360.   CS439.W34

18128   WATERBURY.   Jonathan Waterbury genealogy; ancestry and some of the descendants of Jonathan Waterbury of Nassau, New York (1766-1825) with incidental matter concerning the origin of the Waterbury family and its early history in Europe and America and notes on the descendants of Joseph Waterbury (1778-1829) of Nassau, N. Y., and Roger Morey (1610-1669) of Providence, R. I.   By Grace A. Waterbury and Edwin M. Waterbury ... Oswego, N. Y., Published for the family for private distribution by Palladium-times, inc., 1930.   1 p. l., iii (1), 302 p. plates, ports., facsims., col. coat of arms. 24 cm. 33-29123.   CS71.W324   1930

WATERBURY.   See also: HALL, 1943a
WASHINGTON, CS69.W5

18129   WATERHOUSE.   (Waterhouse family tree, by Alice Waterhouse. n. p., 1898?)   geneal. tab. 58 x 45 cm. Photostat (positive) Author's name, and title in manuscript on back. 32-2624.   CS71.W326   1898

18130   WATERHOUSE.   The Waterhouse and other families of Stroudwater village, a suburb of Portland, Maine, by Leonard B. Chapman.   Portland, H. W. Bryant, 1906.   2 p. l., 27 p. 25 cm. 6-34286.   CS71.W326   1906

18131   WATERHOUSE.   Descendants of Richard Waterhouse of Portsmouth, N. H., with notes on the descendants of Jacob Waterhouse of New London, Conn., Joshua Waterhouse of New Jersey and others.   Also a sketch of the Waterhouse family in England.   Compiled by George Herbert Waterhouse ... (Wakefield, Mass., 1934)   3 v. plates (v. 1) 29 cm. Typewritten. Paged continuously. The plates are photographic reproductions. 34-8478.   CS71.W326   1934

18132   WATERHOUSE.   The ancestry of Joseph Waterhouse, 1754-1837, of Standish, Maine.   By Walter Goodwin Davis.   Portland, Anthoensen Press, 1949.   144 p. port., geneal. tables. 23 cm. 50-20333.   CS71.W326   1949

WATERHOUSE.   See also SMITH, 1878a

18133   WATERLOW.   Memoranda as to the Waterlow family.   (London, Waterlow brothers and Layton) 1883.   1 p. l., 35, (1) p. front., illus. (col. coats of arms) 26½ cm. Compiled by Alfred James Waterlow. Blank pages at end for additional record. Marginal notes, newspaper clippings, and letters inserted. 16-2835.   CS439.W35

18134   WATERMAN.   The Maine Watermans, with an account of their ancestors in Massachusetts, Rhode Island and Connecticut, by Charles E. Waterman ... Mechanic Falls, Me., Ledger publishing company, 1906.   100 p. incl. front. (port.) illus. 23½ cm. 6-43479.   CS71.W328   1906

18135   WATERMAN.   Genealogical line of paternal descent of Waterman family of Davenport, Iowa; compilation by Fred L. Waterman ... (Davenport) 1926.   geneal. tab. 28 x 49 cm. 26-20719.   CS71.W328   1926

18136   WATERMAN.   The Waterman family.   By Donald Lines Jacobus.   New Haven, E. F. Waterman, 1939-54.   3 v. fold. geneal. table. 26 cm. Vol. 3, by D. L. Jacobus and E. F. Waterman, has imprint: Hartford, Connecticut Historical Society.   Contents. - v. 1. Descendants of Robert Waterman of Marshfield, Massachusetts, through seven generations, based on the public records and several collections of family data, notably that of Edgar Francis Watermn. - v. 2. Descendants of Robert Waterman of Marshfield,

18136 continued: Massachusetts, from the seventh generation to date, based on the public records and several collections of family data, notably that of Edgar Francis Waterman. - v.3. Descendants of Richard Waterman of Providence, Rhode Island, together with records of many other family groups of the Waterman name. 40-9807 rev. *

CS71.W328 1939

18137 WATERMAN. Genealogical line of paternal descent of the Waterman family of Davenport, Iowa, compilation by Fred L. Waterman, May 20, 1926, and extended by him to Nov. 20, 1955. Davenport? 1955?) 16 p. 22 x 10 cm. 56-23452.

CS71.W328

WATERMAN. See also: ARNOLD, E171.A53 vol.12
BRIGGS, 1887
TILSON, 1911

WATEROUS. See PEARSON, F129.A96G3

18138 WATERS. The Holy Bible ... London, Printed by T. Baskett, M.DCC.LIX. Leaves inserted with manuscript notes on Waters family genealogy. 9-25719. RS185.1759.L6

18139 WATERS. Ancestry of the Waters family of Marietta. Ohio. (Marietta, O.) Priv. print., 1882. 2 p. l., 3-31, (1) p. col. front., illus. 23½ cm. By Wilson Waters. 9-15021. CS71.W33 1882

18140 WATERS. Reminiscences of the Bradford and Waters families. Marietta, O., Printed by J. Mueller & son, 1885. cover-title, 16 p. 25 cm. Edited by Mrs. Eliza Paddock (Waters) Sisson. 9-15172.

CS71.W33 1885

18141 WATERS. A genealogical history of the Waters, and kindred families, compiled by Philemon Berry Waters. Atlanta, Ga., Foote & Davies company, 1902. vii, 181 p. front. (coat of arms) ports., fold. geneal. tab. 19½ cm. 25-11778. CS71.W33 1902
Microfilm 8747

18142 WATERS. The Watters family; compiled by Dennis Alonzo Watters. Portland, Ore., 1915. 22 p. pl., ports., geneal. tab. 21 cm. 15-17579. CS71.W33 1915

18143 WATERS. Waters-Law and allied families. Mayflower ancestry of George Leland Waters. Richard Warren of the Mayflower, Richard Waters, Salem, Joseph Langrell, Plymouth, John Law, Concord, Thomas, Little, Plymouth, John Thomas, Marshfield, Nathaniel Tilden, Scituate, Rev. Michael Wigglesworth, Malden. Compiled by Philomene Jenkins (Mrs. Chas. H.) ... (Lincoln, Neb., The Keystone press, inc., 1928-29) 2 v. 24 cm. Each volume has also special t.-p. "References" at end of each family. Contents. - (1) Consider Law of Lebanon, Conn., and Oneida co., N.Y., his ancestors and descendants in the line of his daughter Caroline (Law) Waters. - (2) David Waters and Consider Law of Lebanon and Hebron, Connecticut, and Oneida co., N.Y. Their ancestors and some descendants in the line of their children, Aretus Waters and Caroline Law ... 31-20879. CS71.W33 1928

18144 WATERS. The Waters book; genealogy of Waters and allied families; posthumous papers. By Edith (Worley) Beatty. (n.p., 1950?) ix, 101 p. illus., ports., coat of arms. 24 cm. Caption title. "Addenda ... (Jan. 19, 1951)" (2) p. inserted. 52-20951. CS71.W33 1950

18145 WATERS. William Watters: his descendants and related families, compiled and edited by Juanita Watters, Nadine Lain (and) Ouida (Watters) Nelson. Cleburne, Tex., Hallman Print. & Office Supply, 1967. iv, 388 p. illus. 28 cm. Bibliography: p. 370-373. 67-31849. CS71.W33 1967

WATERS. See also: FLAGG, 1903   WINSTON, 1927
HALL, 1941   ZIMMERMAN, 19 -
HOGG, 1959   No. 430 - Adventurers of purse and person.
MANNING, 1897a

WATERWORTH. See VANDEVEER, 1960

WATHES. See WATTS.

18146   WATKINS.   A catalogue op (!) the descendants of Thomas Watkins, of Chickahomony, Va.; who was the common ancestor of many of the families of the name in Prince Edward, Charlotte, and Chesterfield counties, Virginia.   By Francis N. Watkins ... (Printed for private circulation.)   New-York, J. F. Trow, printer, 1852.   50 p.   18 cm.   7-40115.   CS71.W335   1852

18147   WATKINS.   The Watkins family of North Carolina, particularly enumerating those descendants of Levin Watkins of Duplin County, N.C., who emigrated to Alabama and Mississippi early in the nineteenth century.   By William B. Watkins ... Jackson, Tenn., McCowat-Mercer (1915?)   85 p.   illus., plates, ports.   22 cm.   23-18589.   CS71.W335   1915

18148   WATKINS.   Watkins family.   By Thomas John Hall, 3rd.   Page 202.   CS71.H177   1941

18149   WATKINS.   Tearin' through the wilderness; Missouri pioneer episodes, 1822-1885, and Genealogy of the Warkins family of Virginia and Missouri, by Marie Oliver Watkins and Helen Hamacher Watkins.   (Charleston? W. Va., 1957)   204 p.   illus.   24 cm.   58-3573.   CS71.W335   1957

18150   WATKINS.   The Watkins family, from the immigration of T. Malachi Watkins from Scotland down to 1964.   By Grace (Moran) Evans.   Tulia, Tex. (1964)   62 p.   ports.   28 cm.   65-3028.   CS71.W335   1964

WATKINS.   See also: BELL, 1927
                        CARTER, 1958
                        CURD, 1938
                        ROBARDS, 1959
                        WALTMAN, 1928

WATKINSON.   See HAVILAND, F127.W5P3

WATMOUGH.   See ELLIS, F3.T6

18151   WATSON.   A biographical sketch of Elkanah Watson, founder of agricultural societies in America, and the projector of canal communication in New York state, with a brief genealogy of the Watson family, early settled in Plymouth colony.   By Wm. R. Deane ... Albany (N.Y.) J. Munsell, 1864.   15 p.   front. (port.) illus.   24½ cm.   Reprinted from the New Eng. hist. and geneal. reg.: Biographical sketch, v.17, p.97; genealogy, v.18, p.363.   9-15171.   CS71.W34   1864

18152   WATSON.   John Watson, of Hartford, Conn., and his descendants.   A genealogy, by Thomas Watson.   New York, Printed for the U. Q. club, 1865.   47 p.   31½ cm.   Title vignette.   "Club copy. no. 12."   9-15480.   CS71.W34   1865

18153   WATSON.   Rockingham castle and the Watsons.   By C. Wise.   London, E. Stock; (etc., etc.,) 1891.   xvi, 256, (16) p.   illus., 5 pl. (incl. front.) 6 port., 2 plans (1 fold.) 7 geneal. tab. (part fold.)   26 cm.   Pref. signed "G. L. W."   (i.e. George Lewis Watson)   2-30195.   DA690.R68W8

18154   WATSON.   History and genealogy of the Watson family, descendants of Matthew Watson, who came to America in 1718.   Compiled by Mrs. Julia Draper (Watson) Bemis and Alonzo Amasa Bemis ... (Boston, Press of W. S. Best & co.) 1894.   vi p., 1 l., (9)-163, (1) p.   col. front. (coat of arms) port.   24 cm.   9-15170.   CS71.W34   1894

18155   WATSON.   A book in letter form prepared and written of the Watson genealogy, 1760-1909, by the author Martha Ziegler Watson ... Keyser, W. Va., Printed by The Mountain echo, 1909.   102 p.   incl. front., ports.   23 cm.   10-6528.   CS71.W34   1909

18156   WATSON.   "Of sceptred race," by Annah Robinson Watson ... Memphis Tenn., Early printing and publishing company, 1910.   6 p. l. (9)-379, (6) p.   plates, ports.   26 cm.   10-14238.   CS71.W34   1910

18157   WATSON.   History of the Watson family in America 1760-1914.   (Louisiana, Mo., 1914)   cover-title, (50) p.   illus. (incl. ports.)   22 cm.   Signed: Clayton Keith.   14-17282.   CS71.W34   1914

18158   WATSON.   Elihu Watson and Permelia Wright Niswanger Watson and descendants.   Compiled and published by Harry L. Watson ... Greenwood, S. C., Presses of the Index-journal co., 1933.
1 p. l., 54, (3) p. front. 28½ cm. 35-14599.   CS71.W34   1933

18159   WATSON.   ... Thomas and Rebecah (Moorman) Watson and their descendants, by Estelle Clark Watson (Mrs. Charles H.) (Evanston, Ill., 1940)   23 numb. l. 28½ cm. Caption title. Reproduced from type-written copy. 41-1216.   CS71.W34   1940

18160   WATSON.   Squires and dames of old Virginia.   By Evelyn (Kinder) Donaldson.   Los Angeles, Miller Print. Co., 1950.   xv, 309 p. illus., ports.   24 cm. Bibliography: p. 308-309. 50-12576.   CS71.W34   1950

18161   WATSON.   Jonas W. Watson (Lake Superior pioneer) ancestry and descendants.   By Jessie Elise Palmer Williams.   Marquette, Mich., Watson Family Book Committee, 1950.   104 p. illus., ports. 28 cm. 52-34742.   CS71.W34   1950a

18162   WATSON.   The Watson family of Barry County, Michigan.   Compiled by Lyle D. Holcomb, Jr. (Miami? Fla., 1966)   vii, 130 p. illus., map, ports. 28 cm.   "A Michigan heritage publication."   "Long ago in northwestern Barry County, Michigan (by) Claire Richard Watson": p. 17-126.   Bibliographical references included in "Introductory note" (p. ii-iv) 67-5693.
CS71.W34   1966

18163   WATSON.   A Quaker saga; the Watsons of Strawberryhowe, the Wildmans, and other allied families from England's north counties and Lower Bucks County in Pennsylvania, by Jane W. T. Brey. Philadelphia, Dorrance (1967)   xxvi, 646 p. illus., maps. 25 cm. Bibliographical footnotes. 66-11051.
CS71.W34   1967

     WATSON.   See also:

BASSETT, 1926	GRINDELL, 1957	OTIS, 1851
BROWN, 1930	LEWEN, 1919	VAN HOOK, 1957
COLE, 1927	MARSTON, 1873	No. 553 - Goodhue county.
DAY, 1916	MICHIE, 1942	

     WATT.   See WATTS.

     WATTENWEIL.   See: WATTENWYL
                                     WATTEVILLE.

     WATTENWYL.   See WATTEVILLE.

     WATTERS.   See WATERS.

     WATTERSON.   See LEDLIE, 1961

     WATTES.   See WATTS.

18164   WATTLES.   Autobiography of Gurdon Wallace Wattles.   Genealogy.   (New York, The Scribner press) 1922.   xii, 268 p. front., plates, ports., facsim. 25 cm. Privately printed. 22-13339.   CT275.W3294W3

18165   WATTS.   Wattes, Wattys, Wathes, de Wath, le Fleming.   Prepared by Albert Welles ... (n. p., n. d.)   16 p. 25½ cm. Caption title. 41M3392 T.   CS439.W36

18166   WATTS.   Letters respecting the Watt family, by George Williamson ... Greenock, Printed for the author by W. Johnston & son, 1840.   viii, 69 p. facsims. 23 cm. Letters concerning the ancestors of James Watt, the engineer. 20-16679.   CS479.W33

18167   WATTS.   ... A calendar of wills relating to the counties of Northampton and Rutland, proved in the court of the archdeacon of Northampton, 1510 to 1652.   Ed. by W. P. W. Phillimore ... London, C. J. Clark; Boston, Mass., Cupples & Hird (!); (etc., etc.) 1888.   xv, (1), 210 p. 25 cm. (Half-title: The Index library ... I) At head of title: The Index library. 1-4244.   CS434.B7 vol. 1

18168   WATTS.   Genealogy of the family of Watts, of Neen Savage.   By W. P. W. Phillimore ...
Shrewsbury, Printed for private circulation at the "Chronicle" office, 1894.   12 p. front. (coat of arms)
21½ cm.   21-19038.   CS439.W36

18169   WATTS.   Watts (Watt), (in New York and in Edinburgh, Scotland.)   Also Watts, Wattes,
Wattys, Wathes, de Wath, Le Fleming, (in England.)   All prepared by Albert Welles ... Compared
with the original manuscript ... by John Watts de Peyster ... New York, C. H. Ludwig, printer, 1898.
cover-title, 32 p. 13 cm.   Rose Hill Watt (Watts) Mansion in Edinburgh, Scotland.   Memorandum of George E. Bissell, sculptor, made during his
visit to Edinburgh, in 1893: p. 2-3 of cover.   Errata on page 4 ot cover.   11-706.   CS71.W35   1898

18170   WATTS.   Watts families of the southern states, by Charles Brunk Heinemann.   Washington,
D. C. (1934)   387 1. 28½ cm.   Type-written (carbon copy) Blank leaves interspersed. 34-17813.   CS71.W35   1934

18171   WATTS.   Watts families descended from early immigrants who settled in the Tidewater
counties of Virginia, compiled by Charles Brunk Heinemann ... Washington, D. C., 1940.
2, 174, 3-417 numb. 1. incl. facsim.   28½ x 22 cm.   Type-written (carbon copy) Newspaper clipping, with illustration of coat of arms, mounted
on leaf 11, 2d group.   43-47912.   CS71.W35   1940

18172   WATTS.   John Watt, pioneer; a genealogical collection (by) Frank H. Watt.   (Waco, Tex.,
Lithographed by Hill printing and stationery company, c. 1941)   4 p. 1., (5)-116 p. illus. (incl. ports., maps, coats
of arms) 23 cm.   Pages (109) - 110 blank for "Additional records." Includes the Simpson, Henderson, Pepper, Hedden, Tuttle, Doolittle and
Tower families.   41-22949.   CS71.W35   1941

18173   WATTS.   George Watt of Xenia.   The McClellans.   By Frank Hedden Watt.   (Waco? Tex.,
1947)   27 p. ports., coat of arms.   25 cm.   48-12969 *.   CS71.W35   1947

          WATTS.   See also: BRUMBACH, 1961   MILLER, 1939
                               DE PEYSTER, 1854   READING, 1898
                               DE PEYSTER, 1881   SEBOR, 1923
                               KING, 1948   TRAILL, 1902

          WATTSEE.   See WATTS.

          WATTYS.   See WATTS.

          WAUCHOP.   See WAUCHOPE.

18174   WAUCHOPE.   History and genealogy of the family of Wauchope of Niddrie-Merschell.   By
James Paterson ... Edinburgh (Printed for private circulation) 1858.   vi, (7) - 92 p. 29½ cm.   Coat of arms on
cover. 20-15857.   CS479.W35

18175   WAUCHOPE.   The Ulster branch of the family of Wauchope, Wauhope, Wahab, Waughop, etc.,
with notes on the main Scottish family and on branches in America and Australia.   Edited by Gladys
M. Wauchope ... from material collected by the late Robert Alexander Wauhope (Wahab) ... and the
late Edward Wauhope (Wahab) London, Simpkin, Marshall, ltd. (1929)   186 p. incl. front. plates, ports.,
maps, geneal. tables (part fold.) 22½ cm.   "First published in 1929." "References" at end of each chapter except one. 44-34283.
                                                                                   CS499.W38   1929

18176   WAUGH.   A pedigree of the descendants of John Waugh, D. D., bishop of Carlisle, shewing
their connection with the family of Tullie of Carlisle.   By Henry Wagner ... with an introduction by the
president.   (Reprinted from the Transactions of the Cumberland and Westmorland antiquarian and
archeological society) Kendal, Printed by T. Wilson, 1895.   cover-title, 440-448 p. fold. geneal. tab. 23 cm.
3-30924.   CS439.W37

18177   WAUGH.   One man's road; being a picture of life in a passing generation, by Arthur Waugh.
London, Chapman & Hall, ltd., 1931.   xv, 389, (1) p., 1 1. plates, ports., facsim. 23 cm. Autobiography. 31-34819.
                                                                                   PR6045.A96Z5 1931

          WAUGH.   See also No. 3509 - Orange county.

WAUHOPE.   See WAUCHOPE.

18178   WAY.   George Way and his descendants; historical and genealogical; their connection with the early Penobscot (Pejepscot) grants, and the famous lawsuits resulting therefrom 1628-1821. Boston, Printed by E. P. Whitcomb, 1887.   23 p. 23 cm. Signed: C. Granville Way. 10-12421.

CS71.W357   1887

18179   WAY.   History of the Way family; a record in chronological order of members of the Way family of Bridport, co. Dorset; Denham Place, co. Bucks; Spencer Grange and Spaynes hall, co. Essex.   From the earliest records to the present time, with full or partial pedigrees of Page of Wricklemarsh, Newnham of Maresfield, Hill of Poundsford, Payne, Lord Sheffield, Lord Stanley of Alderley, Cooke, Taylor of Ogwell, Ruggles Brise of Spains hall, Smyth of Ashton court, Kenrick of Woore, Ffarington of Worden, Cottrell Dormer of Rousham, Upton of Ingmire, Paxton of Durham, Norman of Claverham, etc.   By Herbert W. L. Way.   (London) Printed for private circulation by Harrison & sons, 1914.   viii, 133, (1) p. front., plates, ports. 26 cm. 21-21728.   CS439.W375   1914

18180   WAY.   The Ways of yesterday, being the chronicles of the Way family from 1307 to 1885, by A. M. W. Stirling ... London, T. Butterworth, limited (1930)   320 p. incl. illus., geneal. tables. front., plates, ports. 23 cm. 32-13990.   CS439.W375   1930

WAY.   See also PETTY, BX5195.T5B6

WAYCHOFF.   See WYCKOFF.

18181   WAYLAND.   The house of Wayland.   (By James Wayland)   London, Printed by Cooke & co., 1886.   1 p. l., 67 p. 2 port. (incl. front.) 18½ cm. 20-19561.   CS439.W38

WAYLAND.   See also MONNET, 1911

18182   WAYMAN.   Wayman wills and administrations preserved in the Prerogative court of Canterbury, 1383-1821.   By J. Harvey Bloom ... London, W. Gandy, 1922.   xii, 88 p. 21½ cm. 22-23311.   CS439.W39

WAYMAN.   See also MARTIN, 1965

18183   WAYMIRE.   John Rudolph Waymire and the first three generations of his descendants as known March 1, 1925.   Edited by William M. Reser ... Lafayette, Ind., 1925.   cover-title, 24 p. illus. (incl. ports.) 30 cm. 27-5358.   CS71.W358   1925

18184   WAYNE.   English ancestry of the Wayne family of Pennsylvania, by Edwin Jaquett Sellers. Philadelphia (Press of Allen Lane & Scott) 1927.   3 p. l., 51 p. front. (coat of arms) 24 cm.   "Edition limited to one hundred copies." Allied families: Bishop and Jackson. 27-7095.   CS71.W359   1927

18185   WAYNE.   Some of the Wayne families of Pennsylvania, Maryland, and the Mid-west States. By Arthur Alvin Wayne.   Evanston, Ill. (195-)   50 p. 25 cm. 57-30418.   CS71.W359   1950z

WAYNE.   See also: BYRD, E154.G56
WASHINGTON, E159.G56

18186   WEAR.   Descendants of east Tennessee pioneers, by Olga Jones Edwards and Ina Wear Roberts.   (Gatlinburg? Tenn., 1963)   315 p. illus., ports., map, coat of arms. 24 cm. 64-3706 rev.

CS71.W36   1936

WEARE.   See WARE.

18187   WEARY.   Chronological story of an old line patriotic pioneer, all American family with a historic published record extending back two full centuries.   Researched and comp. by Frank Orlando Weary of the fifth generation.   Akron, O. (1921)   45 p. illus., port. 23½ cm. Dedication signed: Earl De Loss Weary. Cover-title: Smith-Weary chronology. 21-19734.   CS71.W362   1921

WEATHERBY. See: CROSLAND, 1958
REICHNER, 1918

18188   WEAVER.   The Weaver family of New York city.   By Isaac J. Greenwood.   Boston, D. Clapp & sons, printers, 1893.   1 p. l., 13 p. front., pl. 17 cm.   Reprinted from the New-England historical and genealogical register for January, 1893.   L. C. COPY REPLACED BY MICROFILM.   12-27327.   CS71.W365   1893
Microfilm 8677 CS

18189   WEAVER.   ... Early marriage records of the Weaver family in the United States; official and authoritative records of Weaver marriages in the original states and colonies from 1628 to 1865, ed. by William Montgomery Clemens.   1st ed. (limited)   New York, W. M. Clemens, 1916.   32 p.   23 cm.   (The Clemens American marriage records, v. 1)   16-11123.   CS71.W365   1916

18190   WEAVER.   Record of William Weaver and his descendants, with a synopsis and history of his ancestors, collected and compiled by Ruth Irene Weaver ... Ellisville, Ill., 1925.   (111) p.   20 cm.   37-21336.   CS71.W365   1925

18191   WEAVER.   History and genealogy of a branch of the Weaver family, by Lucius E. Weaver.   Rochester, N.Y., 1928.   2 p. l., (7)-743 p. front. (col. coat of arms) pl., ports., geneal. tab.   23½ cm.   30-5235.   CS71.W365   1928

18192   WEAVER.   Weaver, Kiehl, Pool, Bierer-Müller families; genealogical data and charts.   By Samuel Pool Weaver.   (Spokane, 1953)   ix, 117, (42) p.   illus., ports., col. coat of arms, geneal. tables.   28 cm.   Last group of pages blank for "Individual family history."   53-26140.   CS71.W365   1953

18193   WEAVER.   The Weaver family.   (J. Clark Weaver, editor.   Gainesville, Fla., 1956)   55 p.   illus.   23 cm.   56-46909.   CS71.W365   1956

18194   WEAVER.   Genealogy of a branch of the Weaver family.   By William Otis Weaver.   (Wapello, Iowa) 1957.   unpaged.   37 cm.   58-20231.   CS71.W365   1957

18195   WEAVER.   The tribe of Jacob; the descendants of the revered Jacob Weaver of Reems Creek, North Carolina, 1786-1868 and Elizabeth Siler Weaver, by Pearl M. Weaver.   Weaverville, N.C., 1962.   viii, 141 p.   illus., map (on lining papers) ports.   24 cm.   65-9144.   CS71.W365   1962

WEAVER.   See also BACHMAN family tree in vertical file.   Ask reference librarian for this material.

WEAVER.   See also: ARNY, 1961   JENNINGS, 1899
                      BAILEY, 1892   JOHNSON, 1930 b
                      CRONE, 1916   PIERCE, 1874
                      CRONE, 1924   SMITH, 1921 a
                      EPPERSON, 1931   WEISER, 1960

18196   WEBB.   Webb (pedigree.   London, 1874)   1 l.   29 cm.   Communicated by Robert Edmond Chester Waters.   Reprinted from Miscellanea genealogica et heraldica, n. s. v. 1, 1874, p. 15.   9-18111   CS439.W4

18197   WEBB.   Reminiscences of Gen'l Samuel B. Webb, of the revolutionary army ... By his son, J. Watson Webb ... New York, Globe stationery and printing co., 1882.   402, x p. front. (port.) illus., pl.   27 cm.   p. 45-48 wanting.   A collection of some of the letters and correspondence of General Webb and of Silas Deane; published exclusively for family circulation.   Biographical sketch of General Webb, by J. A. Stevens, reprinted from the Historical magazine, June, 1880: p. 88-102.   "Genealogy of the Webb family": p. (i) - x.   13-22930.   E207.W36W3

18198   WEBB.   William Webb, September 19, 1746 - September 23, 1832; his war service from Long island and Connecticut, ancestry and descendants (by) Capt. R. H. Greene ... New York (Press of J. C. Hassel) 1914.   93 p. incl. front.   2 port., fold. geneal. tab.   24 cm.   "Two hundred copies ... Number 44."   "Two lines of descent from the Conqueror, through Henry I, two through Edela, four through Gundred, arranged by Richard Henry Greene": geneal. tab.   16-769.   CS71.W368   1914

18199   WEBB.   Ancestry and descendants of Nancy Allyn (Foote) Webb, Rev. Edward Webb, and Joseph Wilkins Cooch, by Mary Evarts (Webb) Cooch (Mrs. J. Wilkins Cooch)   Printed for private distribution.   Wilmington, Del., Star publishing co., 1919.   4 p. l., (3) - 157 p.   illus., plates, ports., coats of arms.   24½ cm.   Contents. - pt. I. Nancy Allyn (Foote) Webb. - pt. II. Rev. Edward Webb. - pt. III. The Cooch and Wilkins lineage.   19-15875.

CS71.W368   1919

18200   WEBB.   History of the Webb house, by Mrs. William H. H. Smith.   Read at the Webb house before the Society of Colonial dames, October 28th, 1919 ... (Hartford? Conn., 1919?)   16 p.   20½ cm. Illustration on cover.   Signed: Julia Welles Griswold Smith.   26-9525.

F104.W4S6

18201   WEBB.   Poems of Rebecca Couch ... Poems of Samuel Webb ... Poems of Rebecca Webb Artois ... Poems of Mary W. Artois ... Preceded by genealogical tables.   (n.p., 1921)   345 l.   ports. 23 cm.   Various pagings; type-written.   Compiled by Mary Webb Artois.   cf. Foreword.   Genealogies of the Webb, Hinchman and Couch families. The poems of Mary W. Artois are preceded by a bibliography of her original works and translations (3 l.)   37-12469.

PS591.F3A7

18202   WEBB.   Our Webb kin of Dixie; a family history, compiled from information gathered by William James Webb ... Mrs. Camilla Webb Davis ... Mrs. Anita Stewart Armstrong ... (and) Mrs. Lucy Webb Albert ... Oxford, N.C., W.J.Webb, 1940.   4 p. l., 176 p.   plates, ports., map, coats of arms, geneal. tables.   28 cm.   Contents. - pt. 1. The Webbs of Granville, by W.J.Webb. - pt. 2. Moore-Stanford-Dickins-Pullam families, by W.J.Webb. - pt. 3. The Smiths of Abram's plains, by Mrs. Camilla W. Davis. - pt. 4. The James Webb, jr. (B) family, by Mrs. Anita S. Armstrong.   40-7958.

CS71.W368   1940

18203   WEBB.   Genealogy of a branch of the Webb family which came to Amherst Township, Lorain County, Ohio in 1814 or 1815.   By Claude Charles Hamel.   Amherst, 1948.   4 l.   27 cm.   Typewritten. "References": leaf 4.   50-45222.

CS71.W368   1948

18204   WEBB.   Ancestors and family histories of Lucius Webb, Jr., and Emogene Fuller Webb.   By De Witt Clinton Webb.   (Washington? 1954?)   72 p.   illus.   29 cm.   55-26412.   CS71.W368   1954

WEBB.   See also: ARTOIS, PS591.F3A7   DRIVER, 1889
                      COVINGTON, 1956   GILES, 1864
                      CURTIS, 1919   PAINE, 1913
                      CRAWFORD, 1958   WILCOX, 1893
                      DANIEL, 1959   WILCOX, 1938

18205   WEBBER.   Genealogical sketch of the descendants of several branches of the Webber family. Who came to New York and New England in the early part of the seventeenth century.   Compiled from authentic sources by A. Button.   East Saginaw, Mich., L.S.Laing, printer, 1878.   42 p.   18 cm.   East Saginaw is crossed out in the imprint and Saranac written above.   9-15193.   CS71.W37   1878

18206   WEBBER.   Descendants of Andrew Webber, 1763-1845.   Compiled by Lorenzo Webber ... Portland, Mich., Doremus & Mauren, 1897.   1 p. l., 53 p., 1 l.   map.   21 cm.   9-15167.

CS71.W37   1897

18207   WEBBER.   Genealogy of the Webber family from its first settlement in America to the present date.   January 1900.   Collecteed (!) by Mrs. E. F. Oughtred ... Mrs. M. E. Franklin ... (Freeville, N.Y., George junior republic press) 1900.   cover-title, (11) p.   17½ cm.   16-23636.

CS71.W37   1900

18208   WEBBER.   The Richard Webber family, a genealogy from the first settlement in America ... Medina, O., The A. I. Root co., 1909.   2 p. l., 21 p.   23½ cm.   Compiled by Lucy Adelia Washburn.   9-25800.

CS71.W37   1909

18209   WEBBER.   Anneke Jans Bogardus and her New Amsterdam estate, past and present; romance of a Dutch maiden and its present day new world sequel; historical, legal, genealogical.   Compiled by Thomas Bentlye Wikoff.   Indianapolis, Ind., 1924.   276 p.   23½ cm.   24-23715.   CS71.J35   1924

18210   WEBBER.   Descendants of Michael Webber of Falmouth, Maine, and of Gloucester, Massachusetts, by George Walter Chamberlain, M.S.; with a preface by Winslow L. Webber.   Wellesley Hills, Mass., Webber foundation (c.1935)   5 p. l., (9) - 78 p. 24½ cm. On cover: The Webber genealogy, 1639-1934.   35-24883.   CS71.W37   1935

18211   WEBER.   Garrett county history of pioneer families ... The Henry Weber family.   (Oakland, Md., 1937)   mounted l. 23 cm. Newspaper clipping. No. xciii of a series of articles contributed to the Mountain democrat. 41M2955T.   CS71.W37   1937

18212   WEBBER.   Webber and allied family history records.   By Thomas Hoppel Webber.   Washington, A. W. Burns (195-)   172 l. 28 cm. 56-46028.   CS71.W37

18213   WEBER.   Genealogy of the Weber family of Elyria, Lorain County, Ohio, which married into the Hamel family of Amherst, Ohio.   By Claude Charles Hamel.   Amherst, 1948.   4 l. 27 cm. Typewritten. "References": leaf 4. 50-25030.   CS71.W37   1948

18214   WEBER.   Genealogy of the Weber family of Elyria, Lorain County, Ohio, which married into the Hamel family of Amherst, Ohio.   By Claude Charles Hamel.   Elyria, 1960.   6 l. 27 cm. 61-37621.   CS71.W37   1960

WEBBER.   See also: BOGARDUS, 1900
                       COURTRIGHT, 1925
                       GERHARDT, QD22.G4G8
                       JAMES, 1924
                       MANGOLD, 1937
                       MANGOLD, 1939

WEBBER-JANS.   See SEBOR, 1923

WEBER.   See WEBBER.

WEBLEY.   See CHAMBERS, F142.M7M38

18215   WEBSTER.   Genealogy.   The following account has been compiled by N. Webster.   Family of John Webster.   (New Haven, 1836)   8 p. 23½ cm. Caption title. 10-4372.   CS71.W38   1836

18216   WEBSTER.   Webster genealogy.   Comp. and printed for presentation only be Noah Webster.   New Haven, 1836.   With notes and corrections by his great-grandson, Paul Leicester Ford.   Brooklyn, N.Y., Priv. print., 1876.   3 p. l., 9 numb. l., (3) l. illus. 31 cm. Great-grandfather's books and pictures. By Horace E. Scudder: 2 leaves following leaf 9. Family of Gordon L. and Emily E. Ford: 1 leaf at end. 12-16571.   CS71.W38   1876
Microfilm 8748 CS

18217   WEBSTER.   Genealogy of some of the descendants of John Webster, of Ipswich, Mass. in 1635.   The earlier families compiled by Wm. B. Lapham, M.D., and the later by J. O. Webster, M.D.   Augusta, Me., C. E. Nash, 1884.   cover-title, 14 p. 24 cm. 9-15166.   CS71.W38   1884

18218   WEBSTER.   Genealogy of one branch of the Webster family, from Thomas Webster, of Ormesby, county Norfolk, England.   Compiled by Prentiss Webster ... Lowell, Mass., Printed by E. T. Rowell (1894)   45 p. 26 cm. Interleaved. 9-15165.   CS71.W38   1894

18219   WEBSTER.   Memorial poems and brief ancestral record of the Webster family and descendants, by J. C. Webster.   Hartford, Conn. (Press of the Hartford printing co.) 1904.   68 p. front. (port.) plates. 21 cm. 4-36961.   CS71.W38   1904

18220   WEBSTER.   Notes on the life of Noah Webster compiled by Emily Ellsworth Fowler Ford, edited by Emily Ellsworth Ford Skeel ... New York, Priv. print., 1912.   2 v. fronts., plates, ports., facsim. 20½ cm. "Check list of the writings of Noah Webster": v. 2, p. (523) - 540. "Authorities cited": p. (541) - 544. Memorials of some ancestors: v. 1, p. 1-11. Rebecca (Greenleaf) Webster's forbears: p. 249-267. 13-23041.   PE64.W5F7

18221 WEBSTER. Some of the descendants of John Webster of Ipswich, Massachusetts, 1634. Compiled by John C. Webster, M.D. Chicago, 1912. 92 p. 21 cm. 13-8300. CS71.W38 1912

18222 WEBSTER. History and genealogy of the Gov. John Webster family of Connecticut, with numerous portraits and illustrations. By the late William Holcomb Webster ... and Rev. Melville Reuben Webster ... final author, editor and publisher 1st ed. ... Rochester, N.Y., E.R. Andrews printing company, 1915. xvi, 1646 p. front., plates, ports. 26 cm. 15-21636. CS71.W38 1915

18223 WEBSTER. Birthplace of Daniel Webster, Franklin, New Hampshire; brief story of its restoration and presentation to the state. 2d ed. Franklin, N.H., Towne & Robie, printers, 1922. 20 p. front., illus., plates, ports. 15 cm. 38-17425. E340.W4W248

18224 WEBSTER. The descendants of Naylor Webster, 1749-1830 and Martha Fisher, 1749-1806, of Horsham township, Montgomery county, Penna., compiled by Webster Parry ... added to and rearranged in chart form for the Webster reunion of 1936 by Herman T. Lukens, in co-operation with many members of the family ... Chicago, Ill., H.T. Lukens (c.1936) cover-title, 1 p. l., 20 (i.e. 40) p., 1 l. 32 cm. 36-17336. CS71.W38 1936

18225 WEBSTER. Generations of Websters, compiled by Army L. Van Cott and Allen W. Leigh. Cedar City, Utah, Thomas Webster Family Organization, 1960. 282 p. illus. 23 cm. 62-38098. CS71.W38 1960

18226 WEBSTER. Webster family of New York. By Emma Rouse Lloyd. (Available for consultation at Lloyd library, 309 West Court Street, Cincinnati 2, Ohio.

WEBSTER. See also: BROWN, CD1069.B2 POLLOCK, 1932
FOSTER, 1897 TAYLOR, 1910
McHARG, 1905 WINDECKER, CS71.W
MADDOX, 1957

18227 WEDDERBURN. A genealogical account of the Wedderburn family, by James Wedderburn Webster, esq. ... Nantes, Printed at the author's private press, 1819. 2 p. l., 40 p. 20 cm. 16-20938. CS479.W4

18228 WEDDERBURN. The Wedderburn book, a history of the Wedderburns in the counties of Berwick, and Forfar, designed of Wedderburn, Kingennie, Ester Powrie, Blackness, Balindean, and Gosford; and their younger branches; together with some account of other families of the name. 1296 - 1896. By Alexander Wedderburn ... (n.p.) Printed for private circulation, 1898. 2 v. illus., plates, ports., facsims. (part double, part fold.) coats of arms. 29 cm. Contents. - I. The history. - II. The evidence. 22-2780. CS479.W4 1898

WEDDINGTON. See WADDINGTON.

WEDEL. See DECKER, 1959

18229 WEDGWOOD. A group of Englishmen (1795-1815) being records of the younger Wedgwoods and their friends, embracing the history of the discovery of photography and a facsimile of the first photograph, by Eliza Meteyard ... London, Longmans, Green, and co., 1871. xxii, 416 p. front. (facsim.) pl. 23 cm. 11-7923. NK4210.W42M5

18230 WEDGWOOD. A history of the Wedgwood family, by Josiah C. Wedgwood ... London, The St. Catherine press, ltd., 1908. xx p., 2 l., 325 p., 1 l. front., illus., plates, ports., map, geneal. tables. 30½ cm. 9-27941 rev. CS439.W42

18231 WEDGWOOD. Wedgwood pedigrees; being an account of the complete family reconstructed from contemporary records, by Rt. Hon. Josiah C. Wedgwood ... and Joshua G.E. Wedgwood ... Kendal, T. Wilson & son, printers, 1925. ix, 384 p. fold. geneal. tables. 23 cm. Colored coat of arms of the Wedgwood family on cover. 26-4720 rev. CS439.W42 1925

18232   WEDGWOOD.   The story of Wedgwood, 1730-1930; with a foreword by Sir Oliver Lodge, F. R. S.; illustrations and woodcuts.   2d ed.   (Wisbech, Eng.) Balding and Mansell (193-?)
48 p. illus. (incl. ports.)   23½ cm.   Genealogical table on p. (3) of cover.   41-41042.   NK4210.W4S8 1930

18233   WEDGWOOD.   Uncommon people; a study of England's élite.   By Paul Bloomfield.   London, H. Hamilton (1955)   xi, 219 p. ports., geneal. tables. 22 cm. 56-18674.   HT647.B55   1955

18234   WEEDON.   Weedon genealogy.   (Washington, D.C., 1908)   30 numb. l. 27½ cm. Autographed from typewritten copy.   Preface signed: John Horatio Nelson.   12-16321.   CS71.W392   1908

18235   WEEDON.   Weedon genealogy.   By Eleanor (Steltz) Kebler.   (Washington? 1960)   73 l. 29 cm.
"Based upon a previous thorough work on this subject by John Horatrio Nelson ... 1908 ... Adds to and corrects his findings." 62-35646.   CS71.W392   1960

WEEKES.   See WEEKS.

18236   WEEKS.   Geo. Weekes: genealogy of the family of George Weekes, of Dorchester, Mass., 1635-1650: with some information in regard to other families of the name: especially, Thomas, of Huntington, L. I., and Nathaniel, of Falmouth and Hardwick, Mass.   By Robert D. Weeks.   Newark, N. J., Press of L. J. Hardham, 1885.   viii, (9)-463, (1) p., 1 l., (2) p. front., illus. (coat of arms) ports. 25½ cm.
9-15163.   CS71.W395   1885

18237   WEEKS.   Leonard Weeks, of Portsmouth, and some of his descendants.   By the Rev. Jacob Chapman ... (Boston, 1885)   10 p. 24½ cm. Caption title. "Reprinted from the New Engalnd historical and genealogical register for July, 1885.   37-38437.   CS71.W395   1885a

18238   WEEKS.   Report of the Weeks family meeting for the centennial celebration of the settlement of Holland Weeks in Salisbury, Vt.   Held on August 23, 1888 at the residence of W. Harrison Bingham, in West Cornwall, Vt.   Middlebury, Vt., Register company, printers, 1888.   20 p. 22½ cm. Cover-title: Weeks family meeting.   3-14623 rev.   CS71.W395   1888

18239   WEEKS.   Leonard Weeks, of Greenland, N. H., and descendants, 1639-1888.   With early records of families connected, including the following names: - Bailey, Bartlett, Brackett. Burley. Chapman. Chesley. Clark. Eastman. Folsom. Fowler. French. Frost. Haines. Hilton. Home. Lane. March. Mead. Moody. Moore. Philbrook. Pickering. Perkins. Rollins. Sanborn. Scammon. Thompson. Wiggin and Wingate.   By Rev. Jacob Chapman ... Albany, N. Y., J. Munsell's sons, 1889.   xviii, 184 p. front., ports., fold. geneal. tab. 24 cm. 9-15164.   CS71.W395   1889

18240   WEEKS.   Geo. Weekes.   Genealogy of the family of George Weekes, of Dorchester, Mass. Part 2.   Comprising ancient history of this and other British families, with additional history of American families.   By Robt. D. Weekes.   Newark, N. J., Press of L. J. Hardham, 1892.   viii p., 1 l., 174 p. front. (coat of arms) plates. 25½ cm. 9-15162.   CS71.W395   1892

18241   WEEKS.   Descendants of Andrew Weeks.   New York, Angell's printing office, 1896.
63 numb. l. 23½ cm. Compiled by De Witt Clinton Weeks and Henry W. Clay Weeks.   3-20246 rev.   CS71.W395   1896

18242   WEEKS.   Samuel Weeks of Danville, Vermont, and descendants, with records of families connected, also David Preston Taylor of Lynchburg, Virginia, and some of his descendants, by Ernest A. Weeks.   Denver, Col., 1933.   60 p., 1 l. incl. pl. 2 port. (incl. front.) 22½ cm. 34-5044.   CS71.W395   1933

18243   WEEKS.   Genealogy of Francis Weekes ... and collateral lines, Bowne, Burrowes, Carpenter, Cooke, Cornell, Davenport, De Forest, Emery, Feake, Fones, Freeman, Goodwin, Fowler, Hoag, Ireland, Jansen, Kierstede, Kip, Montagne, Mosher, Paddy, Reddocke, Sands, Stevenson, Sutton, Taber, Thorn, Warren, Winthrop.   Compiled by Dr. Frank Edgar Weeks.   Kipton, O., 1938.   4 p. l., 183, 183½ - 411, 411½ - 497, 499-746 numb. l., 12 l. illus., pl., ports., maps, plans, facsims. 28 cm. Type-written.
Illustrations, plate, portraits, maps, plans and facsimiles are mounted.   No. 498 omitted in pagination.   38-14733.   CS71.W395   1938

18244   WEEKS.   Memories and records of eastern North Carolina.   By Mary (Weeks) Lambeth. (Nashville? 1957)   252 p. illus. 24 cm. 57-59414.   F253.L3

18245   WEEKS.   The Weeks family of southern New Jersey; including Ezekiel Weeks, 1750-1817, Zephaniah Weeks, 1758-1831, Weeks (Wicks) of Cape May County.   By Elmer Garfield Van Name. Haddonfield, N.J., 1967.   ii, 67 p. ports.   23 cm.   Cover title. Bibliography: p. 67.   68-5180.   CS71.W395   1967

18246   WEEKS.   Otis H. Weeks; his ancestors and allied families of Vermont and Utah.   Compiled by Louise W. Newby (and) Jennie N. Weeks.   Salt Lake City, N.E. and J. Weeks, 1968.   1 v. (various pagings) illus., facsims., ports. 22 x 37 cm.   68-5861.   CS71.W395   1968

WEEKS.   See also: BEVILLE, 1917
CRAM, 1934
POUND, 1901

18247   WEEMS.   History of the Weems family, by Douglas Andes Weems ... Annapolis, Md., Weems system of navigation, c. 1945.   42 p. ports., facsims., coats of arms, geneal. tables. 24 cm.   "First limited edition ... No. 100."   A reproduction of the t.-p. and p. 146-156 of v. 1 of "Travels in North America, in the years 1780, 1781 and 1782.   By the Marquis de Chastelleux ... Translated from the French by an English gentleman ..." London, 1787, mounted on p. (3) of cover. 45-7323.

CS71.W397   1945

WEESE.   See CHRYSLER.

18249   WEGELIN.   The Wegelin family and branches in the United States.   By Oscar Wegelin. Westfield, N.J., 1963.   8 p. 24 cm.   "40 copies printed."   64-31011.   CS71.W4   1963

18250   WEGMAN.   History of the Wegman families; or, The genealogy of the Wegmans ... The generations of Jacob Wegman, the first Wegman in America, 1715 to 1946, chronology of the Wegman reunions in Berks county, Pennsylvania.   By Charles S. Wegman ... (Reading, Pa., Printed by Wm. O. Flatt co., inc., 1946)   70 p. illus. (ports., coats of arms) 29 x 22 ½ cm.   46-7869.   CS71.W42   1946

18251   WEHLE.   Pilgrims of '48; one man's part in the Austrian revolution of 1848, and a family migration to America, by Josephine Goldmark; with a preface by Josef Redlich ... New Haven, Yale university press; London, H. Milford, Oxford university press, 1930.   xviii p., 2 1., (3)-311 p. front., plates, ports. 24 cm.   "Published on the Mary Cady Trew fund."   "Books and publications quoted": p. (297)-300. 30-31907. DB83.C6

18252   WEI.   Wei shih tsu p'u pien ts'uan wei yüan hui.   61, 2, 64 p. illus., ports.   26 cm.   78-835829.

CS1169.W4   1968
Orien. China

18253   WEIDENSALL.   Calendar of the Robert Weidensall correspondence, 1861-1865, at George Williams college, Chicago, Illinois.   Prepared by the Illinois Historical records survey project, Division of professional and service projects, Work projects administration.   Chicago, Ill., The Illinois Historical records survey project, 1940.   xiii p., 34 numb. 1. front. (port.) 27½ cm.   Reproduced from type-written copy.   Bibliography: leaf 28.   40-26389.   E601.W42

18254   WEIERSHEISER.   Genealogical and historical record of the ancestral descendants of Franz Weyershäuser of Erbsdorf, kreis Marburg i, Hesse, compiled and arranged by Nelson C. Weiersheiser. Buffalo, N.Y., 1923.   5 numb. 1., 3 1., 7-54 numb. 1., 55-59 p. 24½ cm.   "Of this edition ... there were printed 210 copies." 23-10556.   CS71.W425   1923

WEIGAND.   See DRESSER, 1913

WEIGHT.   See HALLEN, CS439.H26

WEIGHTMAN.   See WIGHTMAN.

18255   WEIKERT.   History of the Weikert family from 1735-1930 ... Harrisburg, Pa., The Tele-graph press (c. 1930)   5 p. 1., 9-357 p. incl. illus., plates, ports., music. front., col. coat of arms. 21½ cm.   Lettered on cover: By Edward L. Weikert, jr. 30-14518.   CS71.W4255   1930

18256   WEIL.   Strangers in the land; the story of Jacob Weil's tribe.   By Moses Rountree.   Philadelphia, Dorrance (1969)   177 p. illus., facsims., ports. 21 cm. 71-82026 MARC.   CS71.W4256   1969

18257   WEILL.   Weil-De Veil: a genealogy, 1360-1956.   Weil, Weill, Weyl, De Veil, DeVeille, De Weille.   Important figures among the descendants of Juda Weil, generations of rabbis, teachers, priests, ministers, writers, and a composer; a guide to German, Dutch, and English sources, with special emphasis on their interrelationship.   By Ernest B. Weill.   Scarsdale, N.Y., 1957.   44 p. illus., ports., fold. map, facsims., geneal. table. 28 cm. "Limited edition of 200 copies of which this is no. 121." Bibliography: p. 26-27. Bibliographical footnotes. 57-10313.   CS71.W4256   1957

18258   WEIMER.   Biographical sketches and family records of the Gabriel Weimer and David Weimer families, assembled by Louise Crise Potts.   (Rockvale, Tenn., 1936)   270 p. illus. (incl. ports., facsims.) 20½ cm. 41-23727.   CS71.W4258   1936

18259   WEINARD.   (Typewritten genealogical information concerning the Wells family.   Contained in letter from Mrs. F.F. Weinard, dated Urbana, Ill., June 12, 1938 to Miss Jessie F. Wheeler)   CS71.W455   1938

WEINGARTH.   See BUGH, 1943

WEIR.   See PAVEY, 1940

18260   WEIS.   The ancestry of the children of John Peter Carl Weis and Georgina Lewis, compiled by Frederick Lewis Weis ... (Meadville, Pa., 1922)   1 p. l., xxv (i.e. xxvii), (13) p. 21 x 41½ cm. Coat of arms of Weys mounted on p. (2) of cover. Allied families: Clap, Pierce, Dexter, Mears, Blake, White, Fessenden, Huchason, Merry, Knower, Curtis, Otis, Hersey, Richardson, Whitcomb, Burpee, Kendall, Phipps, Coolidge, Winch and Browne.   Additions and corrections in manuscript. Bibliography: p. (9) - (13) 25-19275 rev.   CS71.W426   1922

18261   WEIS.   The ancestors and descendants of Daniel Weis, "gentleman-at-arms" 1629, by the Reverend Frederick Lewis Weis.   Milton, Mass., 1927.   1 p. l., 45 p. illus. (coat of arms) plates. 23½ cm. 28-25722.   CS71.W426   1927

18262   WEIS.   A history and genealogy of Nicholas Weiss and his descendants, written and compiled by Lister O. (Bowers) Weiss and Edna M. (Fetzer) Weiss.   (Orrville? Ohio) 1962.   112 p. illus. 23 cm. 62-51606.   CS71.W426   1962

WEIS.   See also VAN BENTHUYSEN, 1926 and WEISSE.

18263   WEISBENDER.   Descendants of Adam Weisbender thru his son Peter Weisbender, 1822-1897, and his grandson Carl Joseph Weisbender, 1863-1932.   By Eugene Raymond Weisbender.   (n.p., 1960)   folder (7 p.) illus. 20 cm. 61-36480.   CS71.W427   1960

18264   WEISER.   The Weiser family, prepared by authority of the Pennsylvania-German society, by Henry Melchior Muhlenberg Richards ... (Lancaster, Pa.) The Society, 1924.   115 p. front., ports., 25½ cm. (Added t.-p: Pennsylvania-German genealogies) In Pennsylvania-German society. Proceedings and addresses ... Oct. 7, 1921. 1924. v.32. 24-24453.   F146.P23 v.32

18265   WEISER.   Old sherry; portrait of a Virginia family, by Frank J. Klingberg.   Richmond, Garrett and Massie, incorporated (c.1938)   xi p., 1 l., 218 p. front., pl., ports. 23½ cm. Includes letters (p. 36-199) written, with a few exceptions, by William Wirt Wysor from Spain, 1893-1897, to members of his family.   Contents. - Fugitive history. - The letters. - Conclusion. - Appendices. 38-30406 Rev.   CS71.W428   1938

18266   WEISER.   "A good Christian man"; the story of Jacob Weiser and his family.   Compiled for his descendants on the occasion of their reunion, June 29, 1952, at Pine Grove Furnace, Pennsylvania. By Frederick Sheely Weiser.   (n.p., 1952)   12 p. illus. 22 cm. 54-29253 rev.   CS71.W428   1952

18267   WEISER.   The Weiser family; a genealogy of the family of John Conrad Weiser, the elder (d.1746) Prepared on the two hundred fiftieth anniversary of his arrival in America, 1710-1960. Frederick S. Weiser, editor.   (Manheim, Pa.) 1960.   882 p. illus. 24 cm. 61-43177.   CS71.W428   1960

WEISER.   See also MUHLENBERG, 1910

WEISSE.   See: HUNT, 1866
                WEIS.

WEISSING.   See WIESINGER.

18268   WEITKAMP.   The genealogy of the Weitkamps, prepared by Arthur Robert Weitkamp. (Cincinnati? O.) 1941.   3 p. l., 51 numb. l.   28 cm.   Reproduced from type-written copy.   Leaves 38-41 blank for "Additional records."   41-12631.   CS71.W43   1941

18269   WEITZEL.   The Weitzel memorial.   Historical and genealogical record of the descendants of Paul Weitzel, of Lancaster, Pa.   1740.   Including brief sketches of the families of Allen, Byers, Bailey, Crawford, Davis, Hayden, M'Cormick, Stone, White, and others.   By Rev. Horace Edwin Hayden ... Wilkes-Barre, Pa.   (E. B. Yordy, printer) 1883.   81 p.   25 cm.   9-15161.   CS71.W434   1883

18270   WELBORN.   Welborn - Wilburn, history - genealogy; the families in Virginia, North Carolina, and South Carolina.   By Hiram Coleman Wilburn.   Waynesville, N. C., c. 1953.   104 p.   ports., coat of arms.   23 cm.   53-32941.   CS71.W44   1953

18271   WELBY.   Notices of the family of Welby, collected from ancient records, monumental inscriptions, early wills, registers, letters, and various other sources, by a member of the family.   For private circulation.   Grantham, Printed by S. Ridge, 1842.   2 p. l., (iii)-iv, (5)-97 p. fold. geneal. tab., coat of arms.   23 cm.   19-3359.   CS439.W43

18272   WELCH.   ... Ashbel Welch ... (New York, 1883)   1 p. l., 54 p. front. (port.) 26½ cm.   Preceded by "Welch notes" (9 l. in ms.) signed: Emma Finney Welch.   Memoir prepared by John Bogart is an extracts from the Proceedings of the American society of civil engineers, vol. ix, p. 137.   14-2698.   CS71.W442   1913

18273   WELCH.   Welch genealogy.   (n. p.,1902)   2 p. l., 69 numb. l. 19½ cm.   With this are bound: Kirk Boott and his experience in the British army, read by James B. Francis.   6 p.   Recollections of the old "Stackpole house", signed J. W. Ryan.   4 p. The Stackpole house.   13 p.   Edward St. Loe Livermore.   6 p.   Boston wharves.   2 p.   The Ripley school,   11 p.   The laying of the corner-stone of the new Boston post office.   October 16, 1871.   11 p.   Old south meeting house,   9 p.   23-16214.   CS71.W442   1902

18274   WELCH.   Ancestral colonial families; genealogy of the Welsh and Hyatt families of Maryland and their kin; giving the colonial generations of the Howard, Hammond, Maccubbin, Griffith, Greenberry, Dorsey, Van Sweringen, Baldwin, Gaither, Warfield and Duvall families.   By Luther W. Welsh ... Independence, Mo., Lambert Moon printing co., 1928.   4 p. l., (11) - 211, 4 p.   23½ cm.   Cover-title: Welsh-Hyatt and kindred.   28-29665.   CS71.W442   1928

18275   WELCH.   Welch and allied families, by Gustine Courson Weaver (Mrs. Clifford Weaver) Cincinnati, O., Powell & White (1932)   312 p. incl. illus., coats of arms.   front., ports.   21½ cm.   Bibliography: p. (13-14) 32-11056.   CS71.W442   1932

18276   WELCH.   Garrett county history of pioneer families, by Charles E. Hoye ... The Welch family.   (Oakland, Md., 1936)   mounted l.   27 x 21½ cm.   Newspaper clipping.   No. LXXVIII of a series of articles contributed to the Mountain democrat.   41M3028T.   CS71.W442   1936

18277   WELCH.   Descendants of James Welch, soldier in King Philip's war, 1675-76, by Charles B. Welch ... Tacoma, Wash., 1943.   2 p. l., 21 numb. l. 28 x 22 cm.   Reproduced from type-written copy.   44-36700.   CS71.W442   1943

18278   WELCH.   Descendants of James Welch, soldier in King Philip's war, 1675-76, by Charles B. Welch ... Tacoma, Wash., 1946.   48 p.   21 cm.   "First edition ... 1943, "   47-22265.   CS71.W442   1946

18279   WELCH.   Philip Welch of Ipswich, Massachusetts, 1654, and his descendants.   By Alexander McMillan Welch.   Richmond, W. Byrd Press, 1947.   354 p. 25 cm.   53-36208.   CS71.W442   1947

18280   WELCH.   Descendants of Edmund and Jonathan Welch, of Groton, Vermont.   By Lewis Scott Dayton.   In collaboration with Margaret Hooper Carter, Nora Belle Darling (and) Mary Tourtillot Aydelotte.   (La Moille? Ill., 1961?)   190 p.   30 cm.   61-36314.   CS71.W442   1961

18281   WELCH.   A family history: the ancestry of Ransom Frank Welch and Susan Curtis Welch.
By June Rayfield Welch.   (Dallas? Tex., 1966)   305 p. illus., geneal. tables, ports. 24 cm. 67-51.
CS71.W442   1966

18282   WELCH.   Official publication of the Welch-Welsh-Walsh Family Association.   Current
issues in vertical file.   Ask reference librarian for this material.   v.1, no. 1; Apr. 1959.

WELCH.   See also: BARBER, DA690.L982.C6   LONG, 1956
BURBANK, 1928   POUND, 1901
COWDEN, 1904   WELSH.
DAVIS, 1939

WELCKER.   See WELKER.

18283   WELD.   History of the Weld family, from 1632 to 1878, written by Mrs. Charlotte Weld
Fowler, at the advanced age of 86.   Middletown, Conn., Pelton & King, printers, 1879.
64 p. front. (port.) 23 cm. 20-16008.   CS71.W444   1879

18284   WELD.   A history of Leagram: the park and the manor, by John Weld ... (Manchester)
Printed for the Chetham society, 1913.   4 p. 1., (iii)-iv, 168 p. front. (map) 22½ x 17½ cm. (Added t.-p.: Remains,
historical and literary, connected with the palatine counties of Lancaster and Chester. New ser. v.72) 14-13718.   DA670.L19C5 v.72

18285   WELD.   Diaries and letters of Francis Minot Weld, M.D., with a sketch of his life, a brief
history and genealogy of the family of Weld, by Sarah Swan Weld Blake.   Boston, Priv. print., 1925.
XIX, (1), 245 p. front., illus., plates, ports., map, facsims. 24 cm. 25-11419.   R154.W33A3

18286   WELD.   Under the Black horse flag; annals of the Weld family and some of its branches, by
Isabel Anderson, LITT.D. (Mrs. Larz Anderson) ... Boston and New York, Houghton Mifflin company, 1926.   x, 291 p. front., plates, ports., diagrs. 21½ cm. 26-7553.   CS71.W444   1926

18288   WELD.   Weld collections, by Charles Frederick Robinson.   Ann Arbor, Mich., Priv. print.,
1938.   267 p. front. (col. coat of arms) illus. (port.) 27½ cm. "One hundred thirty-five copies printed. no. 110." Preface signed:
Lincoln H. Weld.   CS71.W444   1938
——— Supplement of additions and corrections, January, 1939.   New York, Priv. print., 1939
26 p. 23½ cm. 38-36146.   CS71.W444   1938
Suppl.

WELD.   See also: CROSSETT, 1937
No. 430 - Adventurers of purse and person.
No. 7472 - E. Barnet.

18289   WELDIN.   History and genealogy of the Weldin family in America, by Lewis Cass Weldin,
C.E., 1922.   (Pittsburgh, Pa.) 1939.   2 p. 1., 92, 18, 31 (i.e.32), 15, 7 numb. 1. 29 cm. Reproduced from type-written
copy. Edited by William Archie Weldin.   "Sources consulted": Appendix II, leaves 30-31. 42-4313.   CS71.W445   1939

WELDON.   See PUCKETT, 1960

WELEKER.   See WELKER.

18290   WELKER.   Record of descendants of Bernhardt Welker.   By Elsie (Welker) Thomas.
(Nashville?) Benson Print. Co., c.1962.   18 1. 28 cm. 62-41023.   CS71.W4457   1962

18291   WELLCOME. The Wellcome family of Freeman, Maine.   Israel Riggs Bray, 1808-1890.
Henry Solomon Wellcome, 1853-1936. (By George Burbank Sedgley) Phillips, Me., The Phillips
print shop, 1939.   26 p. pl., ports. 23½ cm. 40-18929.   CS71.W446   1939

WELLCOME.   See also BURBANK, 1928

18292   WELLER.   The Weller family; genealogy and sketch book, especially the ancestors and de-scendants of Joseph Weller (1793-1841)   Compiled and edited by Cassius M. Weller and Herbert C. Weller.   Toledo, O., H. C. Weller, c. 1946.   132 l. plates, ports. 28 x 22 cm.   Leaves variously numbered.   Errata slip inserted.   47-18164.   CS71. W4465 1946

WELLES.   See WELLS.

WELLESLEY.   See: NELSON, CS418. F83
            WESLEY.

WELLFORD.   See PAGE, 1883

18293   WELLINGTON.   A few facts concerning Roger Wellington and some of his descendants. Boston, A. Mudge & son, printers, 1892.   26 p. 20½ cm.   Dedication signed: A. W. Griswold.   16-23274.   CS71. W447   1892

WELLINGTON.   See also NELSON, 1853

18294   WELLMAN.   Descendants of Thomas Wellman of Lynn, Massachusetts, by Rev. Joshua Wyman Wellman, D. D.   Boston, Mass., A. H. Wellman, 1918.   xv, 581 p. pl., ports. (incl. front.) fold. facsim., col. coat of arms. 25 cm.   Edited by George Walter Chamberlain.   cf. Pref.   19-5763.   CS71. W452   1918

18295   WELLMAN.   ... Eleven generations of the Wellman-Allen line in America, prepared by Lucius E. Allen ... (Guntersville? Ala.) 1940.   2 p. l., 38 numb. l. plates, ports., facsims., coats of arms. 28 cm.   At head of title: 1640 - 1940.   "No. 37 of an edition of 100 copies."   41-12595.   CS71. W452   1940

18296   WELLMAN.   Some Wellman-Hackleman-Lines genealogy and family history.   By Clarence Perry Stevens.   Escalon, Calif., 1954.   108 p. illus. 27 cm.   61-45128.   CS71. W452   1954

WELLMAN.   See also: DRIVER, 1889
            JARRATT, 1957
            No. 1547 - Cabell county.

WELLNER.   See WOLCOTT, 1934

18297   WELLONS.   A historical sketch of the Wellons family, by Rev. James Willis Wellons ... Richmond, Va., The Central publishing company, 1910.   79 p. front., ports. 17½ cm.   Pages 77-79 blank for "Notes".   40-2277.   CS71. W453   1910

18298   WELLS.   A brief general history of the Welles, or Wells, family.   By Albert Welles.   New York, Narine & co., printers, 1848.   27 p. incl. geneal. tab. 22½ cm.   Relates chiefly to the English ancestors of Thomas Welles, of Hartford.   3-3192.   CS71. W455   1848

18299   WELLS.   History of the Welles family in England; with their derivation in this country from Governor Thomas Welles, of Connecticut.   By Albert Welles ... (Assisted by H. H. Clements, esq.) With an account of the Welles family in Massachusetts, by Henry Winthrop Sargent ... Boston, Press of J. Wilson and son, 1874.   1 p. l., 127 p. col. plates (coats of arms) diagrs. 25 cm.   3-6543.   CS71. W455   1874

18300   WELLS.   Genealogy of the Wells family, of Wells, Maine.   By Charles K. Wells.   Milwaukee, Press of Burdick & Armitage, 1874.   43, 38 p. 23½ cm.   Appendix: 38 p.   9-15160.   CS71. W455   1874a

18301   WELLS.   History of the Welles family in England and Normandy, with the derivation from their progenitors of some of the descendants in the United States ... By Albert Welles ... New York, A. Welles, 1876.   3 p. l., 312 p. front., plates (part col., coats of arms) ports. 23½ cm.   9-15158.   CS71. W455   1876

18302   WELLS.   Memoir of the life and character of Rev. E. M. P. Wells, D. D., of St. Stephens, Boston, Mass., by Dr. Samuel W. Francis ... Newport, R. I., C. E. Hammett, jr. (1878) 45 p. incl. geneal. tab. 17½ cm. 13-26807.   BX5995. W45F8

18303   WELLS.   William Wells of Southold and his descendants, A. D. 1638 to 1878.   By the Rev. Charles Wells Hayes ... Buffalo, N. Y., Baker, Jones & co., printers, 1878.   300 p. front., plates. 23 cm. 9-15035.   CS71. W455   1878

18304   WELLS.   Genealogy of Gen. James Wells and descendants ... Comp. 1883-1892.   (By Mary Josephine Roe) (Cincinnati, The Webb stationery & printing co., 1892)   142 p. fold. geneal. chart. 23 cm. Preface signed: Mary J. Roe.   9-15159.   CS71. W455   1892
                                                                                                        Microfilm 12366 CS

18305   WELLS.   List of ancestors and descendants of John Howell Welles, of Gilead parish, town of Hebron, county of Tolland, and state of Connecticut, grandson of Thomas Wells, the emigrant of Dudley, Worcestershire, England, who landed in Saybrook, Conn., in 1712.   (Washington, D. C., 1898)   geneal. tab. 44 x 71½ cm. fold. to 32 x 25 cm. 2 folded facsimiles inserted. Compiled by John Howell Welles. 9-15482.
                                                                                                        CS71. W455   1898

18306   WELLS.   The ancestry of Edward Wells of Quincy, Illinois; with a sketch of his life, by Lucy Elizabeth Woodwell.   Chicago, F. Wells, 1900.   x, 214 p. incl. geneal. tables. front., plates, ports., coats of arms. 21 cm. 19-14511.   CS71. W455   1900

18307   WELLS.   Genealogy of the Wells family, and families related (by) Gertrude W. Wells-Cushing (Mrs. William Tileston Cushing) Milwaukee, S. E. Tate & company, printers (1903?) 1 p. l., (5)-205 p. front., plates, ports. 23 cm. Contains also the Bigelow, Hitchings, Sweetser, and Wheelwright families. 20-22089.
                                                                                                        CS71. W455   1903

18308   WELLS.   William Wells and his descendants, 1755-1909; comp. by Frederick Howard Wells ... (Albany? N. Y., c. 1909)   117 p. pl. 23 cm. p. (101) - (108) blank for family records. No. 19 of an edition of 125 copies. 9-27024.   CS71. W455   1909

18309   WELLS.   Ancestry and descendants of Colonel Daniel Wells (1760-1815) of Greenfield, Massachusetts.   Prepared by Samuel Calvin Wells.   (Philadelphia? 1912)   65 p. front., ports., coat of arms. 24 cm. 12-27322.   CS71. W455   1912

18310   WELLS.   Genealogy: Wells, Sellew, Adams, Pratt, and Balch.   By Fred Harvey Benson. Arr. for the descendants of Russell and Patience Sophronia (Adams) Wells.   Syracuse, N. Y., 1925. 2 cards. 7½ x 12½ cm. Microprint copy of typescript. Collation of the original: 87 p. 22 cm. Micp. 58-68.   Microcard CS 71

18311   WELLS.   The English ancestry of Gov. Thomas Welles of Connecticut, by Lemuel A. Welles ... Boston, 1926.   30 p. 25 cm. "Reprinted from the New England historical and genealogical register for July and October, 1926. " 26-21818.   CS71. W455   1926

18312   WELLS.   Welles and allied families, genealogical and biographical, prepared and privately printed for Catherine J. Welles and Frances S. Welles by the American historical society inc.   New York, 1927.   232 p. plates, ports., col. coats of arms. 32½ cm. Title within colored border. Plates and coats of arms accompanied by guard sheets with descriptive letterpress. Bound in brown levant with leather doublure; inlaid, gold tooled. Allied families: Lord, Hyde, Saltonstall, Haynes, Gloves. "References": p. (228)-232. 28-4345 rev. 2.   CS71. W455   1927a
                                                                        also in office.   Rare book coll.

18313   WELLS.   Family notes by T. Tileston Wells, LITT, D,   New York, Priv. print., 1927. 35 p. illus. 23½ cm. Bibliography: p. 34-35. 27-18335.   CS71. W455   1927

18314   WELLS.   (A genealogical chart of the Wells family)   Compiled ... by Eugene Fairfield MacPike. (n. p.) 1934.   geneal. tab. 46 x 59 cm. Photostat (positive) of type-written copy. 34-17818.
                                                                                                        CS71. W455   1934

18315   WELLS.   Phineas Wells of New York and Virginia, by Howard B. Grant ... (Philippi, W. Va., H. B. Grant, c. 1935)   1 p. l., 8 numb. l. 28½ x 22 cm. 46-41563.   CS71. W55   1935

18316   WELLS.   (Genealogical information concerning the Wells family.   (Contained in letter from Mrs. F. F. Weinard, dated Urbana, Ill., June 12, 1938 to Miss Jessie F. Wheeler))   (Urbana, Ill., 1938)   3 l. 27½ cm. Type-written. 40M1233T.   CS71.W455   1938

18317   WELLS.   The Wells and allied families, by Guy Herbert Wells and Ruby Hammond Wells. Milledgeville, Ga., 1938.   4 p. l., 89 numb. l., 16 l. geneal. tab. 27½ cm. Mimeographed. One leaf mounted on inside of back cover. "Bibliography": numb. leaf 5. 39-32323.   CS71.W455   1938a

18318   WELLS.   The Wells family of Louisiana, and allied families, compiled by Dr. G. M. G. Stafford ... Baton Rouge, La.   (Alexandria, La., Printed by Standard printing company, inc.) 1941. 6 p. l., 385, (31) p. front., pl., ports., plan. 24 cm. "Copyright 1942." Bibliography at end of each chapter. 42-15624.
CS71.W455   1941

18319   WELLS.   The Wells family.   Compilers: Daniel Wells Norris and H. A. Feldmann.   Milwaukee, Wis., The Cramer-Krasselt co., 1942.   2 p. l., iii-xv, 437 p. ports., fold. geneal. tab. 23 cm. Bibliography: p. vi-xv. 42-25472.   CS71.W455   1942

18320   WELLS.   The life and public services of Thomas Welles, fourth governor of Connecticut, by Edwin Stanley Welles.   A paper read at the fourth annual meeting of the Welles family association, South Coventry, Connecticut, Saturday, June 8, 1940.   Wethersfield, Conn., The Welles family association, 1940.   18, (2) p. fold. facsim. 23½ cm. "500 copies printed." 41-19932.   F97.W47W4

18321   WELLS.   The Reverend William Wells, Bromsgrove, England and Brattleboro, Vermont; his family and descendants.   Quotations from family letters and records.   Compiled by James Hayden Wells and Anita Wells.   (San Diego? Calif.) 1951.   106 p. illus., ports., facsim. 24 cm. "One hundred copies printed."
CS71.W455   1951

——— Supplement to The Reverend William Wells, his family and descendants, compiled by James Hayden Wells and Helen Huggins Wells. (San Diego? Calif.) 1957.   21 p. 23 cm. "One hundred copies printed." 52-36936 rev.   CS71.W455   1951
Suppl.

WELLS.   See also:

BASSETT, 1926	HOUSTON, 1914	O'DALY, 1956
BLACKBURN, 1939	HUNNEWELL, 1906	OSTRANDER, 1936
BROWNING, 19 -	LINCOLN, 1961	PECK, 1955
DOWNS, 1959 a	LYON, 1934	PLUMB, E171.A53 v.15
HARRISON, 1932	MARMION, 1817	POLLOCK, 1932

18322   WELLWOOD.   Historical and statistical account of Dunfermline, by the Rev. Peter Chalmers ... Edinburgh and London, W. Blackwood and sons, 1844-59.   2 v. fronts., 25 pl. map, 2 plans, facsim., 2 fold. geneal. tab. 23 cm. Genealogical tables of the Wellwoods and of Preston of Valleyfield. 3-30699 rev.   DA890. D9C4

WELSAMER.   See WELSHEIMER.

18323   WELSER.   (Genealogical table of the family von Welser, beginning with Philip von Welser, d. 839 and Anna von Rappoltstein. n. p., 1666)   geneal. tab. illus. (incl. map, col. coats of arms) 96 x 266 cm. It was issued in 12 leaves, and these leaves have been mounted on one canvas 96 x 266 cm. At foot of table: J.J.L. inv. G. Strauch fec. 1666; additions to this chart have been made up to 1680. The table is in the form of a tree, at the base of which reclines the body of Philip von Welser in armor and the branches of the tree consist of about 540 colored coats of arms. At the right of the tree are 4 larger different arms of the Welser family; to the left a portrait of the canon of Basel, Emanuel Welser, d.1076, kneeling before the altar, bordered by his letter to his brother Octavianus about the origin of the family Welser. To the left of this is the map of Venezuela with the title: Venezuela, provincia in America occidentali. Quam olim Dni Velseri Patricii Augustani possidebant, a Carolo V. imperatore ipsis consignata. Em. Stenglin D. 21-21712.
CS629. W4

18324   WELSER.   ... Die Welser landen in Venezuela.   By Erich Reimers.   Leipzig, W. Goldmann (c. 1938)   199, (1) p., 1 l. 22½ cm. Maps on lining-papers. Contents. - Ambrosius Ehinger. - Nikolaus Federmann. - Philipp von Hutten. - Schluss. - Zeittafel. - Namenverzelchnis. - Literaturverzeichnis (p.200) 40-31739.   E135.G3R4

18325   WELSER.   ... Die schrecklichen pferde, der Welserzug nach Eldorado, roman.   By Bruno Brehm.   Mit zahlreichen zeichnungen von Hans Meid.   Berlin, P. Neff, 1943.   252, (1) p., 1 l. illus. 21½ cm. "30. - 50. tausend." 46-15031.   PT2603. R415S4

WELSER. See also FUGGER, 1928

18326   WELSH. The family of John Welsh, c.1704-1754, of Middletown, Dauphin County, Pennsylvania: being one of a series of genealogies on the Welch-Welsh-Walsh family in America. By Edwin Charles Welch. Santa Barbara, Calif., 1953. (54) p. 36 cm. 70-208066 MARC.   CS71.W46   1953

WELSH. See also WELCH.

WELSHAMER. See WELSHEIMER.

WELSHAMMER. See WELSHEIMER.

18327   WELSHEIMER. A history of the Welsheimer family, by Edith L. Welsheimer. Las Cruces, N. M., Bronson Print. Co., 1969.   126 p. illus., ports. 24 cm. 78-8144 MARC.   CS71.W464   1969

WELSHIMER. See WELSHEIMER.

WELSHMER. See WELSHEIMER.

WELSHYMER. See WELSHEIMER.

WELSIMER. See WELSHEIMER.

18328   WELTON. John Welton and his wife Mary Upson came from England about 1667 and settled in Waterbury, Ct. in 1679. (By John Welton) ... (n. p., 185-)   geneal. tab. 57 x 58½ cm. 9-19072.
CS71.W464   185-

18329   WELTON. The ancestry of Mary (Welton) Van Wagnen in the paternal line of Welton and in the three collateral lines of Upson, Buck, and Cossett, and the four allied lines of Andrews, Porter, Holcomb(e) (and) Sherwood. Buffalo, 1948.   60, xlii l. geneal. table. 28 cm. Bibliography: leaves xxxviii - xlii. 50-32034.   CS71.W464   1948

WELTON. See also FRISBIE, E171.A53 vol.19

WELTSIMER. See WELSHEIMER.

WELTZHEIMER. See WELSHEIMER.

WELTZYMER. See WELSHEIMER.

18330   WEMME. Goths and Vandals of the Wemme cases, by Robert Gordon Duncan (the Oregon Wildcat) Portland, Or., A. Wemme (c.1932)   374 p. plates. 20 cm. 45-32368.
CT275.W3865D8

18331   WEMYSS. Memorials of the family of Wemyss of Wemyss, by Sir William Fraser ... Edinburgh, 1888.   3 v. illus., coats of arms (part col.) facsims. (part double) 32 cm. Titles within ornamental borders. Privately printed. Contents. - I. Memoirs. - II. Charters. - III. Correspondence. 20-23935.   CS479.W5

18332   WENDELL. The direct ancestry of the late Jacob Wendell, of Portsmouth, New Hampshire, with a prefatory sketch of the early Dutch settlement of the province of New Netherland, 1614-1664. By James Rindge Stanwood ... Boston, D. Clapp & son, 1882.   49 p. front., illus., port., fold. geneal. tab. 26 cm. Special limited ed. Reprinted with additions, from the New Eng. hist, and geneal. register for July, 1882. 9-15157.
CS71.W47   1882

18333   WENDELL. Wendell family, edited by Alexander Du Bin. Philadelphia, The Historical publication society (c.1939)   15, (2) p. pl. (port., coat of arms) 25½ cm. Two blank pages for "Family record" at end. 41-6687.
CS71.W47   1939

WENDELL. See also: MAULE, 1925
SALISBURY, 1885

18334   WENDY.   Dr. Thomas Wendy.   By W. H. Challen.   Notes & Queries, vol. II, July and August, 1955, Nos. 7 & 8.   In vertical file.   Ask reference librarian for this material.

18335   WENGER.   History of the descendants of Christian Wenger who emigrated from Europe to Lancaster County, Pa., in 1727, and a complete genealogical family register ... With a few illustrations.   By Jonas G. Wenger ... Martin D. Wenger ... Joseph H. Wenger ... Elkhart, Ind., Mennonite publishing company, 1903.   259 p. front., plates, ports. 20 cm. 13-16016.   CS71.W473   1903

18336   WENHAM.   Hastings saga.   By Marion Alice Nona Marshall.   London, Saint Catherine Press, 1953-55.   2 pts. in 1 v. illus. 19 cm. 54-16655 rev.   CS439.W437   1953

WENIG.   See GOODLOCK, 1951

WENMAN.   See PETTY, BX5195.T5B6

18337   WENTWORTH.   A genealogical and biographical account of the descendants of Elder William Wentworth, one of the first settlers of Dover, in the state of New Hamsphire ... Boston, Printed by S. G. Drake, 1850.   20 p. illus. (coat of arms) 23 cm. By John Wentworth. Reprinted from the New Eng. hist. and geneal. register, October, 1850. 9-15156.   CS71.W478   1850

18338   WENTWORTH.   The Wentworth genealogy, comprising the origin of the name, the family in England, and a particular account of Elder William Wentworth, the emigrant, and of his descendants. By John Wentworth ... (Boston, Press of A. Mudge & son) 1870.   2 v. ports. (incl. front.) facsims. (1 fold.) geneal. tables. 24½ cm. Title vignette (coat of arms) "For private family distribution only." 3-5052.   CS71.W478   1870

18339   WENTWORTH.   The Wentworth genealogy: English and American.   By John Wentworth, LL.D. ... Boston, Little, Brown & co., 1878.   3 v. front., ports., facsim. 24 cm. 9-15155.   CS71.W478   1878

18340   WENTWORTH.   ... Wentworths at Bermuda.   By the Hon. John Wentworth.   (Boston, 1882) 4 p. 25½ cm. 39M157T.   CS71.W478   1882

18341   WENTWORTH.   Worthies, families, and celebrities of Barnsley and the district.   By Joseph Wilkinson.   London (etc.) Bemrose & sons (1883)   x p., 2 l., 512 p. front., pl., port. 19 cm. "The Earls of Strafford of Stainborough": p. 309-480. (From the Strafford mss.)   Contains the Wentworth, Wood, Becket, Wombwell, Armytage, Rodes, Hallifax and Brook families. 2-12510.   DA690.B24W6

18342   WENTWORTH.   The generations of a New-England family.   (By Alexander Ladd Hayes) Cambridge, Printed for private distribution at the University press (1885?)   22 p. 30½ cm. Introductroy notes signed: A. L. H. "Verses recited at the house of Mr. Charles E. Wentworth, in Cambridge, Mass., Christmas evening, 1885. Written by a descendant of all the ancestors named in the early generations and accompanied by scenes acted by other descendants. Includes the Ladd, Wentworth, Dudley, Glover and Haven families. 20-7228.   CS71.L154   1885

18343   WENTWORTH.   Three branches of the family of Wentworth.   I. Wentworth of Nettlestead, Suffolk.   II. Wentworth of Gosfield, Essex.   III. Wentworth of Lillingstone Lovell, Oxfordshire.   By William Loftie Rutton.   London (Mitchell and Hughes, printers) 1891.   xv, (1), 315 p. incl. geneal. tables. mounted front., plates, port., coats of arms, double geneal. tab. 26½ cm. "One hundred copies only printed, of which this is no. 93. (Signed) Wm. L. Rutton." Most of the plates are mounted. 4-10960.   CS439.W44

18344   WENTWORTH.   The loyal Wentworths, a companion volume to "King Monmouth", by Allan Fea; with 24 illustrations from original portraits, prints, sketches, etc., and genealogical tables. London, John Lane (1928)   xxvi p., 1 l., 267 p. front., plates, ports., facsim., fold. geneal. tables. 22½ cm. "The principal figure in ... (this volume is) Henrietta Maria, baroness Wentworth of Nettlestead." - Introd. 29-13966.   DA447.A3F4

18345   WENTWORTH.   The genealogy of Edward Norris Wentworth, junior; special project submitted in courses in community life and advanced biology at the University high school, University of Chicago, June 1928.   (Chicago, Printed by Hillison and Etten co.) 1928.   1 p. l., vi, 85 p. incl. front., illus., ports., coats of arms. fold. geneal. tables. 23 cm. 31-9471.   CS71.W478   1928

18346   WENTWORTH.   A Wentworth genealogy, compiled by Sterling B. Douglas.   Brookline, Mass.
(1966?)   52 p. port.   23 cm.   66-7484.   CS71.W478   1966

WENTWORTH.   See also: CLOPTON, 1939
                                          LADD, 1885
                                          LAYTON, 1885
                                          OTIS, 1851
                                          SHEAFE, 1923

18347   WENTZ.   Record of the descendants of Johann Jost Wentz, by Richard W. Wentz ... (Binghamton, N.Y.) Binghamton daily republican, 1884.   1 p. 1., 5-89 p. fold. geneal. tab. 22 cm. 44-52697.
                                                                                                         CS71.W48   1884

18348   WENTZ.   Wentz; a record of some descendants of Peter Wentz, the immigrant ... compiled
by Helen Wentz (and) Bertha Earnhart.   (Kennett Square, Pa., Kennett news and advertiser, c.1939)
214 p., 1 1. incl. front., illus., ports. facsims., fold. geneal. tab., col. coat of arms. 24 cm.   Addenda: A love story, by Dr. A. R. Wentz,
mounted on leaf at end. 39-17555.   CS71.W48   1939

WENZEL.   In vertical file under PRANKE family.   Ask reference librarian for this material.

18349   WERE.   The woollen manufacture at Wellington, Somerset, comp. from the records of an
old family business: by Joseph Hoyland Fox.   London, A. L. Humphreys, 1914.   viii, 120, (1) p. incl.
geneal. tables. front., pl., ports. 3 fold. facsim. 26 cm. 14-14503.   HD9901.8.W5F6

18350   WERGE.   The history of the family of Werge of Northumberland; with notices of the family
in Oxfordshire, and of the family of Worge in Sussex.   By Colonel Ralph Edward Carr ... and by
Cuthbert Ellison Carr (C.E.)   Newcastle-upon-Tyne and London, A. Reid sons & co., 1891. (1892)
xix p., 2 1., 86 p. front., plates, ports., coats of arms (1 col.) fold. geneal. tables. 38 cm.   "Special preface," p. ix-xv, is an obituary
of Ralph Edward Carr, who died April 9, 1892. 20-15249.   CS439.W45

WERLEY.   See BITTNER, 1930

WERSLER.   See ANDERSON, 1880

WERTS.   See No. 9847 - Hackettstown.

18351   WERTZ.   Stenographic report of proceedings had at the 2d reunion of the Wertz family ...
Oct. 25-27, 1912.   By William J. Snyder ... (Chicago, Printed by Regan printing company) 1912.
102 p. illus. (incl. ports.) fold. geneal. chart. 22½ cm. 13-1329.   CS71.W49   1912-

WERTZ.   See also SHEIBLEY, 1924

18352   WESCOTT.   An account of the English homes of three early "proprietors" of Providence,
William Arnold, Stukeley Westcott and William Carpenter, by Fred A. Arnold ... Providence (Press
of E. A. Johnson & co.) 1921.   43, (1) p. incl. illus., map. 25½ cm. 50 copies privately printed. no. 9. 21-14638.
                                                                                                        F89.P9A85

18353   WESER.   The Weser family.   By Edwin Warfield Beitzell.   Washington, 1948.   15 p. 28 cm.
Caption title. 50-22858.   CS71.W5   1948

18354   WESLAGER.   August Weslager and his family of Pittsburgh, Penna., by C. A. Weslager.
Wilmington, Del., 1964.   39 p. illus., maps, ports. 23 cm. "Limited edition of 100 copies." 65-89990.   CS71.W513   1964

18355   WESLEY.   Memoirs of the Wesley family; collected principally from original documents.
By Adam Clarke ... New York, Published by N. Bangs and T. Mason, for the Methodist Episcopal
church, 1824.   ix, (1), (11)-432 p. front., pl., fold. facsim. 22 cm. 36-23404.   BX8495.W35C6   1824

18356   WESLEY.   Memoirs of the Wesley family; collected principally from original documents.
By Adam Clarke ... 2d ed., rev. cor., and considerably enl. ... London, Printed for T. Tegg, 1843-44.
2 v. fronts. (ports.) fold. facsim. 18½ cm. 10-7502.   BX8495.W35C6

18357   WESLEY.   The life of the Rev. John Wesley ... Collected from his private papers and printed works; and written at the request of his executors.   To which is prefixed some account of his ancestors and relations; with the life of the Rev. Charles Wesley ... Collected from his private journal, and never before published.   By John Whitehead ... With an introduction by the Rev. Thomas H. Stockton.   2d American ed. ... Philadelphia, W. S. Stockton, 1845.   2 v. in 1. fronts. (ports.) 24 cm. 10-7576.   BX8495.W5W6   1845

18358   —— Another edition.   Boston, Hill & Brodhead, 1846.   2 v. in 1. fronts. (ports.) 23 cm.   10-7575.
                                                                                                 BX3495.W5W6   1846

18359   WESLEY.   Memoirs of the Wesley family; collected principally from original documents, by Adam Clarke ... 4th ed., rev., cor. and considerably enl. ... London, W. Tegg, 1860.   2 v. fronts. (ports.) fold. facsim.   19 ½ cm.   (Added t.-p.: The miscellaneous works of Adam Clarke ... vol. I-II)   Vol. 2: 3d edition (n.d.) 20-17865.
                                                                                                 BX8495.W35C6   1860

18360   WESLEY.   Anecdotes of the Wesleys: illustrative of their character and personal history. By Rev. J. B. Wakeley.   With an introduction by Rev. J. M'Clintock ... New York, Carlton & Lanahan; Cincinnati, Hitchcock & Walden, 1869.   391 p. 3 port. (incl. front.) 18 cm.   12-39764 rev.
                                                                                                 BX8495.W33W3

18361   WESLEY.   Memorials of the Wesley family: including biographical and historical sketches of all the members of the family for two hundred and fifty years; together with a genealogical table of the Wesleys, with historical notes, for more than nine hundred years.   By George J. Stevenson ... London, S. W. Partridge and co.; New York, Nelson and Phillips (1876)   XXIII, (1), 562 p. front. (ports.) fold. geneal. tab.   22 cm.   10-15131.   CS439.W46

18362   WESLEY.   The Wesley memorial volume; or, Wesley and the Methodist movement, judged by nearly one hundred and fifty writers, living or dead.   Edited by Rev. J. O. A. Clark ... New York, Phillips & Hunt; Cincinnati, Walden & Stowe; (etc.. etc.) 1881.   743, (1) p. incl. plates, ports., facsims. front. 23½ cm. "The Wesley family": p. (27)-50. Hymns, with music: p. 475-480.   37-12136.   BX8495.W5A15

        WESLEY.   See also L. C. additions and corrections, no. 7

18363   WESSELS.   Genealogical notes relating to Warnaer Wessels and his descendants, by Drs. J. G. B. Bulloch and Arthur Adams ... New York (T. A. Wright press) 1913.   15 p. 26½ cm. Edition of one hundred copies.   "Reprinted from the New York genealogical and biographical record, Oct. 1913."   14-12470.
                                                                                                 CS71.W515   1913

18364   WEST.   History of our West family, being a record of dates and events in connection there-with, compiled from family papers and public records.   By Arthur Anderson West.   For private circulation only.   (n. p.) 1893-1904.   2 v. illus., ports., maps (2 fold.) diagrs., geneal. tables. 28 cm. Cover-title: Our West family.   Additions and corrections in ms.   Includes mounted footnotes and "Supplement to Theydon Bois Parish magazine, May 1909" (4 p. inserted) signed. A. A. West.   57-55999.   CS439.W47   1893

18365   WEST.   The West family.   By George F. Bartlett.   New Bedford, 1898.   1 l. 28½ x 24 cm. Signed: George F. Bartlett.   24-11486.   CS71.W52   1898

18366   WEST.   Francis West of Duxbury, Mass., and some of his descendants, by Edward E. Corn-wall, M. D.   Boston, New England historic genealogical society, 1906.   14 p. 24½ cm. "Reprinted from the New England historical and genealogical register, April, 1906, with additions."   17-6152.   CS71.W52   1906

18367   WEST.   Benjamin West's family; the American president of the Royal academy of arts not a Quaker, by Charles Henry Hart.   With unpublished letters of West.   Philadelphia, 1908. 1 p. l., 33 p. 2 port. (incl. front.) 25½ cm. "Fifty copies reprinted from the Pennsylvania magazine of history and biography, for January, 1908." 8-29303.   CS71.W52   1908

18368   WEST.   Life and times of S. H. West; with an appendix on evolution, religion and spiritual phenomena.   By S. H. West ... (Bloomington, Ill., Pantagraph printing and stationery co., 1908) 298 p. front., plates, ports. 23½ cm.   8-18568.   CT275.W39A3

18369   WEST.   In remembrance of the West family reunion ... By Charles S. West.   Ionia, Mich.,
1912.   cover-title, (10) p. illus. (4 mounted phot.) 19½ cm.   13-1332.   CS71.W52   1912

18370   WEST.   William West of Scituate, R.I., farmer, soldier, statesman, by George M. West ...
St. Andrews, Fla., Panama city publishing co., 1919.   4 p. l., 32 numb. l. incl. 4 pl. 27 cm. "This edition is limited
to fifty numbered and signed copies ... no, 13." Signed: G.M.West. 20-2097.   F83.W51

18371   WEST.   The West family register; important lines traced 1326-1928, by Letta Brock
Stone ... Washington, D.C., W.F.Roberts company, inc., 1928.   xi, 493, (1) p. plates, ports., fold, maps, fold.
geneal. tables, 2 col. coats of arms (incl. front.) 24 cm.   "Limited edition of 300." 29-932.
                                                                              CS71.W52   1928

18372   WEST.   Genealogy of Isaac West, of Greenville County, South Carolina, by Broadus B. West.
(Spartanburg? S.C., 1929?)   53 p. 2 coats of arms (1 col.) 18½ cm. "References": p. 5. 30-9194.
                                                                              CS71.W52   1929

18373   WEST.   Joseph West and Jane Owen (by) Celeste Terrell Barnhill ... Greenfield, Ind., Press
Wm. Mitchell printing co. (1930)   3 p. l., 102 p. illus. (facsims., coat of arms) plates. 19½ cm. Type-written additions
mounted on fly-leaves. 31-2245 rev.   CS71.W52   1930

18374   WEST.   The West family with descendants of Eleazer West, 1752-1798? Goshen, N.Y.,
Prepared by E. B. Comstock.   Dallas, Tex., 1931.   1 p. l., 20 numb. l. 26½ cm. Typewritten. Additions and
corrections in manuscript throughout text. 34-8466.   CS71.W52   1931

18375   WEST.   Family tree of Eleanor Ogden West (Mrs. Perry M. Shepard) her sister and brother,
with lineages of their mother and father ... prepared by Perry M. Shepard ... Geneva, N.Y., 1939.
geneal. tab. 30 x 65 cm. Reproduced from type-written copy. 41-31431.   CS71.W52   1939

18376   WEST.   The royal lineage of Anne West who married Henry Fox of "Huntington," King
William county, Virginia.   Compiled by Ann W. Fox from sources named, and presented to the Society
of descendants of Henry Fox and wife Anne West ... (n.p., 1941?)   3 p. l., 39 p. coat of arms. 23 cm. Reproduced from type-written copy. "Sources": 2d prelim. leaf. 41-19785.   CS71.W52   1941

18377   WEST.   The noble lineage of the Delaware-West family of Virginia, through Col. John West,
his sons, and his daughter Anne West who married Henry Fox.   Edited by Margaret McNeill Ayres.
(Memphis?) 1958.   241 p. illus., ports., col. coat of arms, geneal. tables. 28 cm. 58-49594.   CS71.W52   1958

18378   WEST.   Genealogies of George West and James R. Kimble and their descendants through
Samuel and Elizabeth (Kimble) West, researched and prepared 1953-1963, by Austin L. Pino.   Ann
Arbor, Mich., Printed by University Microfilms, 1964.   64 p. map, group port. 23 cm. Includes mounted errata and
addenda slips. Bibliography: p. 6. 65-9641.   CS71.W52   1964

18379   WEST.   Claiborne Dandridge West of Buckingham County, Virginia; his ancestors and descendants, by Louetta West Wilson and John William Johnson.   With introd. by Floyd West.   Dallas,
Southern Methodist University Print, Dept., 1967.   xxxi, 312 p. illus., coats of arms, fold. geneal. table, map, ports.
28 cm. Bibliographical references included in "Notes" (p. xxi - xxiv) 67-16122.   CS71.W52   1967

WEST.   See also:

ATHERTON, 1952   GILPIN, 1870   PEDEN, 1961
ATHERTON, 1953   HARRISON, 1910a   POCAHONTAS, 1887
BURR, E171.A53   HUNTER, 1934   SELDEN, 1911
DUGAN, 1951   JUNKINS, 1908   WINSTON, 1927
FRASER, 1910   OKELY, 1899   No. 430 - Adventurers of purse
FULLER, n.d.   OKELY, 1929   and person.

18380   WESTBROOK.   Westbrook-Gage miscellany, a souvenir of the Westbrook-Gage reunion ...
Stoney Creek, Ontario, July 1, 1909. (Thamesville, Ont.) Thamesville herald, 1911.
2 p. l., (3) - 32 p. incl. illus. (port.) geneal. tab. pl. 23½cm.   "References in connection with the history of the Westbrook, Gage and allied
families": p. 9. 43-19197.   CS90.W45   1911

18381 WESTBROOK. Westbrook family history. By William John Coulter. (n. p.. 1951? -
v. 30 cm. Cover title. L. C. has only vol. 1. 51-27727. CS71.W522 1951

18382 WESTBROOK. The record and family of Nehemiah Westbrook. Prepared (by) William E.
Westbrooke. San Francisco, 1964. 45 l. 28 cm. 64-56519. CS71.W522 1964

18383 WESTBROOK. Westbrook and allied families: Foster, Barker, Fort, Sandeful, Lambert-h,
Hanson. By Blair Jones. Pell City, Ala. (pref. 1967) 167 p. 28 cm. 68-206. CS71.W522 1967

18384 WESTBY. The descendants of Gulbrand and Maria Westby, 1869-1969; the first six genera-
tions in America, by George Westby and Mildred Westby Gjerdrum. (Decorah, Iowa, Printed by the
Anundsen Pub. Co., 1969) ix, 194 p. illus., facsims., geneal. tables, ports. 23 cm. Bibliography: p. 183-184. 70-83115
MARC. CS71.W5225 1969

WESTCOTE. See WESTCOTT.

18385 WESTCOTT. Incidents in the life and times of Stukeley Westcote, with some of his descend-
ants. By J. Russell Bullock ... (n. p.) 1868. 7 p. l., (9)-34, (2). 161 p., 1 l., XX, XX a-c, xxi-xxvii p. illus. (facsims.)
plates, fold. map, col. coats of arms. 25 cm. Cover-title: Stokeley Westcote and some of his descendants. "Fifty copies only. Privately
printed. No. 38." "Authorities consulted": 6th prelim. leaf. 33-15352. CS71.W523 1886

18386 WESTCOTT. History and genealogy of the ancestors and some descendants of Stukely Westcott, one of the thirteen original proprietors of Providence Plantation and the colony of Rhode Island,
with especial mention of the Westcotts of Cheshire, Berkshire county, Massachusetts, and the Westcotts of Milford, Otsegon county, New York, and some of the allied families, incorporating, and extending, the research of the late Hon, J. Russell Bullock of Bristol, R. I. By Roscoe L. Whitman.
(Oneonta, N.Y., Otsego publishing company) 1932-39. 2 v. illus. (maps, coats of arms) plates, ports. (2 mounted)
mounted col. coats of arms. 26½ cm. Vol. 2 has title: Book of appendices to the History and genealogy of the ancestors and some descendants
of Stukely Westcott, 1592-1677. "Corrections and additions" (12 leaves) in pocket of v. 1. 33-17582 rev. CS71.W523 1932

18387 WESTCOTT. Westcott family in vertical file. Ask reference librarian for this material.

WESTCOTT. See also: BATTEY, 1940 b.
SHEPARD, 1897

18388 WESTERMAN. Frances Holbert Westerman, her ancestors and descendants. By May
(Cooper) Burnham. (Tulsa? Okla., 1953?) 148 p. illus. 26 cm. 58-25409. CS71.W524 1953

WESTERMAN. See also ODELL, 1960

18389 WESTERVELT. Genealogy of the Westervelt family. Comp. by the late Walter Tallman
Westervelt. Rev. and ed. by Wharton Dickinson. New York, Press of T. A. Wright, 1905.
vii, 175 p. front., plates, ports., coat of arms. 24½ cm. L. C. COPY REPLACED BY MICROFILM. 7-26434. CS71.W525 1905
Microfilm 12335 CS

WESTERVELT. See also BLAUVELT, 1957

WESTGATE. See JENNINGS, 1899

18390 WESTHAFER. The Westhafer genealogy, by Francis M. Westhafer. Greenwood, Ind.,
1912. 2 p. l., 7-62 p. illus. (incl. ports.) 24 cm. Pages at end left blank for "Additional family record". Portraits inserted. Contains
also the Rudy family. 23-14871. CS71.W528 1912

WESTHEIM. See JOHNSON, 1930

18391 WESTIN. The Westin lineage; a genealogy covering two hundred and seventeen years
(1722-1938), compiled and edited by Douglass Westin. Los Angeles, Calif. (c. 1939) vi, 64 p. 21½ cm.
"This edition limited to 50 copies." "Revised ... 1939." 39-7257. CS71.W529 1939

WESTLYE. See AASLAND, 1947

18392   WESTMORLAND.   Westmorland lineage and descendants of Thomas Westmoreland, the immigrant to Virginia.   Comp. by Edward A. Claypool ... Chicago, Ill., 1908.   37 l. 27 cm.   Type-written. Coat of arms (photograph) inserted.   21-2414.   CS71.W531   1907

WESTMORLAND. See also PEDEN, 1961

18393   WESTON.   The revolution.   Life of Hannah Weston; with a brief record of her ancestry. Also, a condensed history of the first settlement of Jonesborough, Machias and other neighboring towns.   By a citizen ... (George Washington Drisko)   Machias, Me., C. O. Furbush & co., 1857.   163 p., 1 l.   15½ cm.   Genealogy: p. 112-121.   "The liberty pole.   A tale of Machias." (From C. P. Ilsley's Forest and shore): p. (136) - 163.   7-13471 rev.   F29.J7D7

18394   WESTON.   The descendants of Edmund Weston of Duxbury, Mass., for five generations.   By Thomas Weston, jr. ... Boston, G. E. Littlefield, 1887.   23 p.   24 cm.   Reprinted from the New Eng. hist. and geneal. reg. for July, 1887.   9-15154.   CS71.W535   1887

18395   WESTON.   Annals of an old manor-house, Sutton Place, Guildford; by Frederic Harrison. Illustrated from original drawings by Wm. Luker, jun., W. Niven, and C. Forster Hayward (and A. Gladding) London and New York, Macmillan and co., 1893.   xvii, (1), 231 p. front., 66 pl. (part col.) 2 facsim., 9 double geneal. tab.   29 ½ x 23 cm.   Head and tail pieces.   "Pedigree of Weston in the British museum": p. 191-197 and geneal. tab.   2-22334.   DA690.S962H3

18396   WESTON.   History of the manor and parish of Weston-under-Lizard, in the county of Stafford.   Compiled from the mss. of the late Rev. the Hon. George T. O. Bridgeman, rector of Wigan, by the Rev. Ernest R. O. Bridgeman ... and Charles G. O. Bridgeman ... (London, Harrison and sons, 1899)   xviii, 345, xlv, (1) p. front., plates, ports., fold. map, fold. geneal. tables. 24 cm. (Added t.-p.: Collections for a history of Staffordshire, edited by the William Salt archaeological society.   Vol. XX, n.s. 2)   Contains pedigrees of Weston, Peshale, Mytton and Birmingham, Wilbraham, Ercall and Caverswall, Newport and Bridgeman families.   24-25173 rev.   DA670.S69S6 vol. 20 n.s. 2

18397   WESTON.   The revolution; life of Hannah Weston, with a brief history of her ancestry.   Also a condensed history of the first settlement of Jonesborough, Machias and other neighboring towns.   By George W. Drisko ... 2d ed.   Machias, Me., G. A. Parlin, 1903.   4 p. l., (3)-140 p. 18½ cm.   "First edition 1857."   "Descendants of Hannah and Josiah Weston": p. (105)-138.   37-14811.   F29.J7D72

18398   WESTON.   In memoriam, my father and my mother, Hon, Gershom Bradford Weston, Deborah Brownell Weston, of Duxbury, Massachusetts; memoirs of Capt. Ezra Weston (I), Ezra Weston (II), Gershom Bradford Weston, Alden Bradford Weston, Ezra Weston (IV) and Deborah Brownell Weston; Weston armorial bearings and descent.   By Edmund Brownell Weston.   Providence, R. I., 1916.   2 p. l., v p., 3 l., 3-93 p. plates, ports., coat of arms. 27½ cm. 16-24335.   CS71.W535   1916

WESTON.   See also: BALL, 1867   KIMBALL, 1902
                           BREREWOOD, DA690.C5E2   McFARLAND, 1948
                           ELIOT, 1895   MILLER, 1909

18399   WESTPHAL.   Westphal family in vertical file.   Ask reference librarian for this material.

18400   WETHERBEE.   Descendants of Israel Wetherbee (1756-1813) of Stow, Boxborough and Ashby, Massachusetts.   By David Kenneth Wetherbee.   (New Salem? Mass.) 1963.   iv, 213 l. 29 cm. 64-5051.   CS71.W538   1963

18401   WETHERED.   The Wethered book (by) Brandon Barringer (and) L. Wethered Barroll.   Peterborough, N.H., R. R. Smith (1967)   xv, 201 p. illus., geneal. table, ports. 23 cm.   Bibliography: p. 179-181. 66-26637.   CS71.W539   1967

WETHERED.   See also THOMAS, 1877

WETHERELL.   See WETHERILL.

18402   WETHERILL.   Tables which show, in part, the descendants of Christopher Wetherill.   Compiled by Charles Wetherill ... 1672-1882.   (n. p., 1882?)   3 p. l., 33 numb. geneal. tab.   illus. (coats of arms)   38 cm.   Privately printed.   Autographed from ms. copy.   Contains also Bavis, Lawrence, Scattergood, Smith and other genealogical tables.   24-8636.   CS71.W54   1882

18403   WETHERILL.   Records, English and colonial, of the Wetherill family.   The English records collected by George W. Marshall, 1897.   Arr. and the colonial records added by Charles Wetherill and W. Bleddyn Powell.   (Philadelphia? 1898?)   39 p.   illus.   26 cm.   59-55250.   CS71.W54   1898

18404   WETHERILL.   Genealogical sketch, tracing the descent of the children of Robert and Phoebe Ann (Delany) Wetherill through the Sharp, Keen, Sandelands, Taylor, Thomas, Henvis, Kite, Delany, West, Price and Wetherill families ... Chester, Pa., Printed for private circulation by J. Spencer, 1902.   98 (i. e. 100) p. incl. geneal. tab.   27 cm.   Photograph inserted.   "Only fifty copies printed, no. 44."   Introduction signed: H. G. Ashmead.   "Col. Sharp Delany": p. 69-98.   2-28231.   CS71.W54   1902

18405   WETHERILL.   Families from village Wetheral.   By Frank E. Wetherell.   (Des Moines)
1948.   118 p.   illus., map, coat of arms.   28 cm.   Cover title.   49-21027 rev. *   CS71.W54   1948
—— Supplement.   1949 -   pts. map (on cover) coat of arms (on cover) 29 cm.   Cover title.   CS71.W54   1948
Suppl.

WETHERILL.   See also LEWIS, 1901   (in addenda)

WETMORE.   See WHITMORE, W616

WETTLING.   See WHITLING.

WETZELL.   See BEAUMAN, E207.B37F2

WEYANDT.   See WYAND.

WEYBURN.   See WIBORNE.

WEYGANT.   See: ROGERS, 1895
SACKETT, 1897

18406   WEYERHAEUSER.   Timber concentration in the Pacific Northwest; with special reference to the timber holdings of the Southern Pacific railroad, the Northern Pacific railroad and the Weyerhaeuser timber company ... by Sarah Jenkins Salo.   Ann Arbor, Mich.   (Lithoprinted by Edwards brothers, inc.) 1945.   ix, 79 p., 1 l. incl. illus. (map) tables.   27½ cm.   Thesis (PH. D.) - Columbia university, 1945.   Vita.   Bibliography: p. 71-75.   Columbia univ, for Library of Congress.   A46-753.   HD9757.A5S3

18407   WEYERMAN.   History of the Wierman family.   By Maude (Wierman) Kennedy.   (York Springs? Pa.)   c. 1952.   40 p.   illus.   23 cm.   52-67547.   CS71.W548   1952

18408   WEYGANT.   The Weygant-Frase-Bechtel family record, 1523-1965.   By Esther Weygandt Powell.   Akron, Ohio, 1965.   ii, 104 p.   illus., facsims., maps, ports.   29 cm.   Paging irregular.   73-4988 MARC.   CS71.W5487 1965

18409   WEZENER.   Some account of the family of Wezener or Wiesener, of the town of Lauban, in the Margraviate of Upper Lusatia.   By Robert C. Jenkins ... (London) Priv. print. (Chiswick press) 1865.   30 p., 1 l.   21 cm.   10-25889.   CS679.W5

18410   WHALEY.   A limited genealogy study of descendants of Maj. Gen. Edward Whalley (the Regicide) Featuring Private Thomas Whaley, Lieut. Archibald Whaley of 1776 era descendants, Edward Charles Whaley, Joseph Whaley of Edisto Island, S. C. and descendants of Nathaniel Whaley in Delaware, Virginia, and Maryland with appropriate ancestral review, discussion and history 1067-1956, by W. Baynard Barton and Fannie May Dooley Barton.   (1st ed.) Stonega, Va., 1956.   143 l.   illus. (part col.), coat of arms, facsims., geneal. tables, ports., 3 plates.   24 cm.   Cover title: Whaleys, 1066; 1660-1956.   Half title: A volume on the family Whaleys.   "This first edition is limited to 31 completed volumes. "   72-3326 MARC.   CS71.W552 1956

18411 WHALEY. — (2d ed.) Stonega, Va., 1956 (i. e. 1967) 143 l. illus., facsims.. geneal. tables. 34 pl., ports. 24 cm. Cover title: Whaleys, 1066; 1660-1967. Half title: A volume on the family Whaleys. "This second edition is limited; 22 copies completed. 72-3298 MARC.

CS71. W552 1967

WHALEY. See also WHALLEY.

18412 WHALLEY. Pedigree of Whalley, from an ancient vellum roll late in the possession of the Rev. Cave Humfrey, rector of Laughton, Leicestershire (and now of Mrs. R. Hunt, of Boreatton) ed. by J. Fetherston, F. S. A. (n. p.) 1872. cover-title, 4 p. front. (coat of arms) 28½ cm. Title vignette. 2-26606.

CS439. W48

18413 WHALLEY. English record of the Whaley family and its branches in America, by Rev. Samuel Whaley. Ithaca, Andrus & Church. 1901. vi p., 1 l., 233, (1) p. incl. front. (port.) facsim. geneal. tables, coat of arms. 22 cm. 1-27960.

CS71. W552 1901

18414 WHALLEY. Preliminary notes on the Whaleys of Loudoun county, Virginia, and of their descendants who migrated to Kentucky, by Levi Kelsey Cramb ... (Fairbury, Neb.) 1943. 31 p. 29½ x 23 cm. Caption title. Cover-title: Whaleys of Loudoun county, Va. Reproduced from type-written copy. 44-3250.

CS71. W552 1943

18415 WHALLEY. Whaleys of Loudoun County, Virginia, and some of their descendants who migrated to Kentucky. By Levi Kelsey Cramb. Fairbury, Neb., 1947. 30 p. 29 cm. Caption title. 48-14048 *.

CS71. W552 1947

WHALLEY. See also: MASTER, 1874
SMITH, 1878 a
WHALEY.

18416 WHALLON. Some family records, by Rev. Edward Payson Whallon ... Partial histories of the Whallon, Hagaman, Bickle, Bridgeland, Kitchell, Pierson, Ball, Bruen, Crist, Hughes, Vincent, Bloodgood, Jans, Farrand and Tuttle families. By Edward Payson Whallon. Cincinnati, F. L. Rowe, 1934. 147 p. incl. front., illus. (incl. ports., coats of arms) 20 cm. "Kitchel family genealogy, compiled by Margaret Ellen Kitchel Whallon, supplementary to this book and to 'Robert Kitchel' and 'The Willis family' ": p. (129) - 147. 34-32140 rev. CS71. W553 1934

18417 WHARTON. Genealogy of the Wharton family of Philadelphia. 1664 to 1880. By Anne H. Wharton ... Philadelphia (Collins, printer) 1880. iv, (5) - 134 p., 1 l. front., pl. port. 25½ cm. "Edition: 150 copies octavo, 10 copies quarto. no. 119." 8-3838.

CS71. W554 1880

18418 WHARTON. Francis Wharton. A memoir. (By Mrs. Helen Elizabeth (Ashhurst) Wharton) Philadelphia, 1891. iv p., 1 l., 256 p. front., ports. 24½ cm. "Life at Cambridge", by A. V. G. Allen: p. 176-192. "Life at the Department of state", by John Bassett Moore: p. 211 - 229. E664. W55W4

18419 WHARTON. The Whartons of Wharton hall, by Edward Ross Wharton ... With portrait and illustrations. London, H. Frowde, 1898. viii, 67, (1) p. incl. front. (port.) plates. 18 cm. Note signed: Marie Wharton. Memoir of E. R. Wharton by J. S. Cotton. From the "Academy" of June 13, 1896: p. 1 - 10. Bibliography: p. (11) - 15. 12-31641.

CS439. W483

18420 WHARTON. Biographical memoranda concerning Joseph Wharton, 1826-1909, by his daughter Joanna Wharton Lippincott. (Philadelphia) Printed for private circulation by J. B. Lippincott company, 1909. 163 p. front., plates, ports. 21½ cm. 24-1347.

CT275. W45L5

18421 WHARTON. Notes on the Wharton family. Ed. Robert Wharton Moorhouse. Bryn Mawr, Pa:, 1958-60. (v. 1, 1960) 2 v. illus. 30 cm. Contents. - section 1. Descendants of George Wharton (1720? - 1770), arr. and edited by R. W. Moorhouse. - section 2. Descendants of Col. Samuel Wharton (1740-1824), based on data collected by M. T. Wharton and arr. by R. W. Moorhouse. 61-31374. CS71. W554 1958

18422 WHARTON. The Wharton sleeve, by Nathan Earl Wharton, 1949. Notes added by Robert Wharton Moorhouse, 1963. Bryn Mawr, Penn., (1963) 244 l. mounted illus., col. coats of arms, geneal. tables, map. 30 cm. Typed copy, carbon, no. 3. 65-2629.

CS71. W554 1963

WHARTON.   See also: ELLINWOOD, 1969
RANKIN, 1931

18423   WHATTON.   The family of Whatton; a record of nine centuries, being a reprint of articles by Henry Watkinson Whatton in the Gentleman's magazine of 1825, with additions, continuations, and illustrative documents, by J. S. Whatton ... assisted by the Rev. W.G.D.Fletcher ... Followed by a little autobiography by the former, and preceded by an introduction by O. F. Christie ... (London, The Sylvan press, 1930) xxx p., 1 1., 159 p. incl. front., illus. (facsim.) geneal. tables (part fold.) plates, ports., fold. geneal. tab. 23 cm. Each section is preceded by unnumbered leaf not included in the paging (5 leaves); one unnumbered page between p. 152-153.   40-300.

CS439.W4835 1930

18424   WHEAT.   Wheat genealogy; a history of the Wheat family in America, with a brief account of the name and family in England and Normandy.   v.1 ... Ed. by Silas C. Wheat.   Brooklyn, N.Y., S.C.Wheat, 1903.   1 v. front., ports., facsims. (1 fold.) 2 col. coats of arms. 23½ cm. 3-17525.   CS71.W556 1903

WHEAT.   See also PATTERSON, 1926

WHEATCRAFT.   See WITCRAFT.

WHEATLEIGH.   See WHEATLEY.

18425   WHEATLEY.   Genealogy of the Wheatley or Wheatleigh family.   A history of the family in England and America ... Compiled by Hannibal P. Wheatley ... (Farmington, N.H., E.H.Thomas, 1902)   1 p. 1., 154 p. illus., plates, ports. 23 cm. 3-25508.   CS71.W557 1902

WHEATON.   See: CONVERSE, 1887
LINCOLN, 1930

WHEDON.   See HUGHES, 1879

18426   WHEELER.   Extract from the Genealogical notes of the late General Joseph Wheeler of Alabama.   (n. p., n. d.)   1 1. 32½ cm. Type-written (carbon copy) 40M4067T.   CS71.W56

18427   WHEELER.   Wheeler and Warren families.   Descendants of George Wheeler, Concord, Mass., 1638, through Deacon Thomas Wheeler, Concord, 1696, and of John Warren, Boston, Mass., 1630, through Ebenezer Warren, Leicester, Mass., 1744.   Compiled by Henry Warren Wheeler. Albany, N.Y., J. Munsell's sons, 1892.   121 p. plates, ports. 22 cm. 9-25085.   CS71.W56 1892
Microfilm 8749 CS

18428   WHEELER.   American ancestors of the children of Joseph and Daniella Wheeler of whom we have records ... Compiled by Joseph and Daniella Wheeler ... Wheeler, Ala. (1896)   cover-title, 24 p. front., plates. 24 cm. 9-15020.   CS71.W56 1896

18429   WHEELER.   Genealogy of some of the descendants of Obadiah Wheeler of Concord, and Thomas Thaxter of Hingham.   By Henry M. Wheeler.   Worcester, Mass., F. P. Rice, 1898. 74 p. 2 geneal. tables. 26 cm. Additions and corrections: 4 p. inserted at end. 9-25086.   CS71.W56 1896

18430   WHEELER.   American ancestors of the children of Joseph and Daniella Wheeler, of whom we have records, and some account of English Hoo and Newdigate ancestors, compiled by Joseph and Daniella Wheeler.   (Wheeler? Ala., 1902?)   95 p. 24 cm. Addenda slip mounted on p. 79. 55-51359.
CS71.W56 1902

18431   WHEELER.   Genealogy of a branch of the Wheelers, comp. by Giles Wheeler of Concord, N.H., a descendant of Daniel Wheeler, of Hollis, N.H. ... Concord, N.H., Rumford printing company, 1908.   61 p. incl. front. (port.) 19 cm. 8-17713.   CS71.W56 1908

18432   WHEELER.   (Letter concerning the Wheeler family, from Rev. J. A. Frederick, to Miss Ellen May Howard (now Mrs. Ellen May Howard Bloedorn) (Bel Air, Md., 1908)   6 1. 21 cm. Photostat reproduction (positive) of manuscript copy. 41-38349.   CS71.W56 1908a

18433   WHEELER.   The genealogical and encyclopedic history of the Wheeler family in America, compiled by the American college of genealogy under the direction of Albert Gallatin Wheeler, jr. Boston, Mass., American college of genealogy, 1914.   xviii, 1257 p. front., ports. 24 cm. 14-10706.

CS71.W56   1914

18434   WHEELER.   A history of Hauppauge, Long Island, N.Y., together with genealogies of the following families: Wheeler, Smith, Bull Smith, Blydenburgh, Wood, Rolph, Hubbs, Price, McCrone, by Simeon Wood; ed. by Charles J. Werner.   New York, N.Y., C.J.Werner, 1920.   92 p. front. (port.) 20 cm. One hundred copies printed; this copy not numbered. 21-12140.   F129.H37W8

18435   WHEELER.   The Wheeler family of Rutland, Mass., and some of their ancestors, by Daniel M. Wheeler.   (Pittsfield, Mass., 1924)   2 p. l., 133 p. front., plates, ports. 23½ cm. The ancestors and descendants of Nathan Halladay, father of the author's mother: p. 99-133. 25-24217.   CS71.W56   1924

18436   WHEELER.   Genealogy of the descendants of Samuel H. and Sarah H. Wheeler of the Town of Berlin, Worcester County, Massachusetts, 1815-1932.   By Henry A. Wheeler.   (n. p., 1932?) 43 p. illus. 24 cm. 56-48945.   CS71.W56   1932

18437   WHEELER.   (Letter concerning the Wheeler family from Edward Jenkins to Mrs. Ellen May Howard Bloedorn)   (Villanova, Pa., 1941)   10 l. 18½ x 27 ½ cm. Photostat reproduction (negative) of manuscript copy. 44-13509.   CS71.W56   1941a

18438   WHEELER.   The genealogical history of the George Rose Wheeler family in America, compiled by American College of Genealogy under the direction of Albert Gallatin Wheeler and from family Bibles and from letters and other records.   (This material compiled by Herbert Newell Wheeler. n. p., 1947)   15 l. 28 cm. 53-32432.   CS71.W56   1947

18439   WHEELER.   Wheeler-Alden family; a contribution to a knowledge of the genealogy and family history of the families of William Archie Wheeler and Albert Martin Alden and certain other related families.   Compiled with the cooperation of other family members and the assistance of Elisabeth (Lines) Hagy.   Washington, 1962.   xi, 216 p. illus. 24 cm. (His The Albert Martin Alden family series, pt.1) 63-1216 rev.   CS71.W56   1962

18440   WHEELER.   Some de(s)cendants of Sergeant Thomas Wheeler of Concord, Mass., 1640-1969, by Joseph L. Wheeler.   Benson, Vt., 1969.   59 l. ports. 28 cm. Cover title. 73-10628 MARC.

CS71.W56   1969

WHEELER.   See also:

AVERY, 1925	MINNS, 1925	SISSON, 1945
BARRETT, F74.C8P8	NICHOLS, 1917	STOOPS, 19 -
BASSETT, 1926	PLUMB, E171.A3 vol.15	THOMPSON, 1911
EVANS, 1946	SEMMES, 1918	TODD, 1909
GARDNER, 1959	SEMMES, 1956	WASHINGTON, CS69.W5

18441   WHEELOCK.   The Wheelock family of Calais, Vermont; their American ancestry and descendants, by Marcus Warren Waite.   North Montpelier, Vt., The Driftwind press, 1940. 174 p., 1 l. incl. front., illus. ports. 21 cm. "Privately printed." 41-381.   CS71.W562   1940

18442   WHEELOCK.   Sketch of the life of Deacon Jonathan Wheelock of Cavendish, Vermont, by Gertrude Bernadette Wilgus.   Ascutney, Vt., 1942.   3 p. l., 74 (i.e. 75) numb. l. incl. 1 mounted illus., pl., maps (part fold.) geneal. tables (1 fold) 29 x 23 cm. Type-written. "No. 1 of 5 copies." Bibliographical foot-notes. 43-10360.

CT275.W528W5

WHEELOCK.   See also: CHUTE, 1894
                                    HARRIS, 1887
                                    LIVINGSTON, 1939
                                    WASHINGTON, 1932 a
                                    WELLS, 1903

18443   WHEELWRIGHT.   A frontier family, by Edmund March Wheelwright ... Cambridge, J. Wilson and son, 1894.   35 p. 27 cm.   "Reprinted from the Publications of the Colonial society of Massachusetts, vol. I."   "One hundred and ten copies printed on hand-made paper."   37-16958.

CS71. W563   1894

Microfilm 8750 CS

WHEELWRIGHT.   See also: AYER, F8. A97
                                                WASHINGTON, 1932 a
                                                WELLS, 1903

WHELDEN.   See WHELDON.

18444   WHELDON.   ... Early Wheldens of Yarmouth, by James W. Hawes.   Yarmouthport, Mass., C. W. Swift, 1914.   cover-title, 2 p. 25 cm.   (Library of Cape Cod history & genealogy. no. 43) 17-34.

CS71. W565   1914

WHELER.   See WHEELER.

18445   WHERRY.   History and genealogy of the family of David and Ann (Hall) Wherry and descendants, covering data from 1757 to 1904.   By John Hall Wherry.   (Denver, 1956?)   19 l. 36 cm.   "As copied ... (by) Mildred Edith (Young) Aday ... in June 1956."   66-57617.

CS71. W568   1956

WHETCOMBE.   See WHITCOMB.

18446   WHETHAM.   A history of the life of Colonel Nathaniel Whetham, a forgotten soldier of the civil wars, by Catherine Durning Whetham and William Cecil Dampier Whetham ...   London, New York (etc.) Longmans, Green and co., 1907.   xviii, 237 p. incl. front. (facsim.) illus., maps, geneal. tab. fold. plan. 24½ cm.   "List of the principal sources from which this book is compiled": p. ix-x.   8-22305 rev. 2.

DA407. W5D3

WHETSTONE.   See GOLSAN, 1959

WHETTEN.   See TODD, 1867

18447   WHIDDEN.   Genealogical record of the Antigonish Whiddens and a brief historical outline of the province of Nova Scotia and of the county and town of Antigonish, by D. G. Whidden.   Wolfville, Nova Scotia, 1930.   24 p. 22 cm.   Typewritten additions inserted throughout text.   "Corrected by the author, March 10, 1933." 33-14348.

CS90. W5

WHIDDON.   See HENDERSON, 1926

18448   WHINYATES.   Whinyates.   Family records.   By Major-General Frederick T. Whinyates ... (Cheltenham, Eng., Printed by G. F. Poole) 1894-96.   3 v. fronts. (v. 1, coat of arms) plates, ports., map, plan, facsims., geneal. tables. 34½ x 26½ cm.   Part of the illustrative material is folded.   "Only twenty-five copies ... printed." 44-29993.

CS439. W4838

WHIPKING.   See HARTMAN, 1954

18449   WHIPPLE.   A brief genealogy of the Whipple family; comp. for Oliver Mayhew Whipple, esq., of Lowell.   (Lowell (Mass.) Printed by E. D. Green & co.) 1857.   36 p. 22½ cm.   On verso of t.-p.: Compiled by John H. Boutelle of Woburn.   18-7489.

CS71. W574   1857

18450   WHIPPLE.   A brief genealogy of the Whipple families, who settled in Rhode Island ... By Henry E. Whipple ... Providence, A. C. Greene, printer, 1873.   1 p. l., 63 p. 22½ cm.   Mainly descendants pf Capt. John Whipple, 1616? - 85, of Providence, R.I.   1-5850.

CS71. W574   1873

18451   WHIPPLE.   Inquiries relating to the ancestors and descendants of Job Whipple, of Cumberland, Rhode Island, and Greenwich, Washington County, New York.   Comp. and pub. by Frank V. McDonald ... Cambridge, University press, J. Wilson & son, 1881.   46 p. 2 port. (incl. front.) 31 cm. 12-30783.

CS71. W574   1881

18452   WHIPPLE.   The presentation of flags to the schools of Portsmouth, N. H., October 9th, 1890, by Storer post, no. 1, Grand army of the republic, Department of New Hampshire, with an appendix

18452 continued: relating to the Whipple and Farragut schools. Portsmouth, N.H., 1890.
36 p. 23½ cm. (With Foster, Joseph. The soldiers' memorial. Portsmouth, N.H., 1893 - 1921 ... (Portsmouth, 1921)) Includes biographical notice of Gen. William Whipple and the Whipple family. 22-12445.　　　　F44.P8F68

18453　WHIPPLE.　The presentation of the portraits of General William Whipple, signer of the Declaration of independence, and of David Glasgow Farragut, admiral, United States navy, November 20th, 1891, by Storer post, no. 1, Grand army of the republic, Department of New Hampshire, to the city of Portsmouth, N.H., for the Whipple and Farragut schools. Portsmouth, N.H., 1891.
35, (1) p. 23½ cm. "Prepared for publication by Joseph Foster, secretary Entertainment committee, Storer post." Addenda relating to the Whipple and Farragut portraits, General Whipple's ancestors and James Russell Lowell: p. (23)-35. 19-3279.　　　　E302.6.W5G7

18454　WHIPPLE.　Genealogical notes of the Whiplle-Hill families, together with fragmentary records of other families ... Compiled by John Whipple Hill. Albany, N.Y., J. Munsell's sons, 1897.
3 p. l., 9 - 106 p. tab. 24 cm. Original imprint "Chicago, Fergus print. co." corrected to "Albany, J. Munsell's sons." 1-10280.
CS71.W574　1897

18455　WHIPPLE.　Genealogy of the Whipple-Wright, Wager, Ward-Pell, McLean-Burnet families, together with records of allied families, 1917. Comp. by Charles H. Whipple ... (Los Angeles, Press of Commercial printing house) 1917.　4 p. l., 11-117 p. illus., plates, ports., fold. geneal. tables, facsim., coats of arms (part col.) 24 cm. "Books referred to in compiling these records": prelim. leaf (3) An account of Bishop Whipple, including his autobiography: p. 28 - 41. 19-7388.　　　　CS71.W574　1917

18456　WHIPPLE.　Captain John Whipple. 1617-1685. And his descendants. (By Clair Alonzo Newton) Records furnished by Mrs. Minnie Newton Whipple. Mrs. May Sonnemann. Dr. Clara Maria H. McGuigan (and others) ... and Ralph Hemmenway records. Naperville, Ill., 1946.　1 p. l., (v) - xx, 69 p., 1 l., 275-268 p. 2 front. (ports., coat of arms) illus. 20½ cm. "Ralph Hemmenway. Roxbury, Mass. 1634. Supplementary records" has special t.-p. and separate paging. 46-23125.　　　　CS71.W574　1946

18457　WHIPPLE.　A partial list of the descendants of Matthew Whipple, the elder, of Bocking, Essex County, England. By Henry Burdette Whipple. High Point, N.C., 1965.　v, 197 l. geneal. tables.
28 cm. Cover title: Matthew Whipple of Bocking, England, & descendants. 66-582.　　　　CS71.W574　1965

WHIPPLE.　See also: DEERING, 1929
　　　　　　　　　　　　JOHNSON, 1963
　　　　　　　　　　　　LANE, 1857

18458　WHISHAW.　A history of the Whishaw family, by James Whishaw, edited by M.S. Leigh, with twelve plates and an endpaper map. London, Methuen & co. ltd. (1935)　ix, 228 p., 1 l. front., pl., ports., facsim. 22½ cm. 36-12015.　　　　CS439.W484

18459　WHISLER.　John Whisler, 1770, German immigrant to Cumberland County, Pennsylvania; a roster of descendants. By Ellen (Kirkpatrick) Korbitz. (Norman Korbitz, co-author. Burlington? Iowa, 1957)　29 p. illus. 22 cm. 57-31370.　　　　CS71.W576　1957

WHISLER.　See also WHISTLER.

18460　WHISTLER.　Abstracts of Whistler family probate records; originals found in Connecticut State Library. By Margaret Race Shaw. Hartford, 1946.　7 l. 28 cm. 48-23432*.
CS71.W577　1946

WHISTLER.　See also WHISLER.

WHISTON.　See DUNHAM, 1956

18461　WHITAKER.　Joseph Rusling Whitaker, 1824-1895, and his progenitors. A memoir by Samuel Whitaker Pennypacker. Philadelphia, 1896.　32, 42 p. front. (port.) 24½ cm. "150 copies privately printed." "Will and inventories of Joseph R. Whitaker": 42 p. at end. 12-12518.　　　　CS71.W578　1896

18462　WHITAKER.　Whitaker of Hesley hall, Grayshott hall, Pylewell park, and Palermo. Being some family records collected and arranged by Robert Sanderson Whitaker. London, Mitchell, Hughes

18462 continued. and Clarke, 1907. iv p., 2 l, 99, (1) p., 1 l., 48 p. incl. geneal. tables. front., plates, port., coats of arms (partly col.) 30 cm. 48 blank pages for "Addenda" at end. 10-15893. CS439.W485

18463 WHITAKER. Whitaker and allied families, genealogical and biographical, prepared and privately printed for Emma Whitaker Davis. New York, The American historical society, inc., 1930. 220 p. col. coats of arms. 22½ cm. Title-page decorated in colors. Some of the plates accompanied by guard sheets with descriptive letterpress. Bound in brown crushed levant, gold tooled and inlaid, with leather doublures. Allied families: Dunn, Edwards, Loving, Ernley, Green, Beall, Taliaferro, Willis, Washington. 30-31610 rev. 2. CS71.W578 1930
Office. Rare book coll.

18464 WHITAKER. Homestead Methodism (1830-1933) the history of Methodism in Mifflin township, Allegheny county, Pa., being the story of the first Methodist Episcopal church in that township, variously named the Whitaker church, the Franklin church, etc. ... By Wallace Guy Smeltzer ... (Pittsburgh, Printed by the D.K. Murdoch company, c. 1933) 167 p. front., plates, ports., map. 20 cm. "A bibliography of the more important records consulted": p. 167. BX8481.M8S5
—— Homestead Methodism supplement ... (by) Wallace Guy Smeltzer ... (Munhall? Pa.) The author (1934?) 32 p. incl. plan. 19 cm. Autographed from typewritten copy. 33-14156 rev. BX8481.M8S5
Suppl.

18465 WHITAKER. Our children's ancestry, by Sarah Cantey Whitaker Allen. (Milledgeville, Ga.) The author, 1935. 2 p. l., xi-xvii, 3-513 p. front., plates, ports., map, col. coats of arms, 2 fold. geneal. tab. 24 cm. "Family edition." Contents. - The Whitaker family. - The Cantey family. - The Gaines family. - The Harvie family . - The Cosby family. - The Leonard family. - The Moran family. - The Allen family. 35-8777. CS71.W578 1935

18466 WHITAKER. A família Aguiar Whitaker; estudo genealógico. Biografia dos seus fundadores e alguns descendentes, através da documentação escrita, tradição oral e recordacões pessoais do autor. Trabalho ilustrado com varios retratos e alguns desenhos do autor. São Paulo, 1950. 601 p. illus., ports. 29 cm. "Edição limitada de 300 exemplares, numerados de 1 a 300. Exemplar n.º 296." Bibliography: p. (539)-553. 51-31263 rev. CS309.W5 1950

18467 WHITAKER. My grandparents: their descendants and forebears. By Willie Kirby Whitaker. (Amory, Miss.) 1961. 26 l. illus. 28 cm. 63-1217. CS71.W578 1961

18468 WHITAKER. The Whittaker and allied families. By William Alexander Whitaker. (Altoona? Pa., 1962) 92 p. illus. 24 cm. 62-66162. CS71.W578 1962

WHITAKER. See also: AUSTIN, 18 -
HENDRIX, 1936
HOUSTON, 1914
PORTER, 1940
TIPPIN, 1939
WHITTIER, F22.E7E81 vol. 49

18469 WHITALL. John M. Whitall. The story of his life. Written for his grandchildren by his daughter, H.W.S. (Nrs, Hannah (Whitall) Smith) ... Philadelphia, Printed for the family, 1879. 1 p. l., 338 p. front. (port.) 20½ cm. Newspaper clipping inserted at end. 20-15235. CT275.W53S5

18470 WHITCHER. Descendants of Chase Whitcher of Warren, N.H., fourth in descent from Thomas Whittier of Salisbury (Haverhill) Mass. By William F. Whitcher. Woodsville, N.H., News book and job print., 1907. vii, 128 p. front., plates, ports. 23 cm. "100 copies printed. no. 55." 8-3801. CS71.W58 1907

WHITCHER. See also WHITTIER.

18471 WHITCOMB. Memorial of the Whitcomb and Pierce families ... Comp. by William Frederic Whitcomb. Boston, 1888. 23 p. 23½ cm. Interleaved. Title vignettes, coats of arms. 1-20753. CS71.W581 1888

18472 WHITCOMB. The Whitcomb family in America; a biographical genealogy with a chapter on our English forbears "by the name of Whetcombe." (By) Charlotte Whitcomb... Minneapolis, Minn., 1904. 621 p. col. front. (coat of arms) illus., plates, ports., map, facsims. 28 x 23½ cm. 5-27061. CS71.W581 1904

WHITCOMB.   See also CRAIG.

18473   WHITE.   Anderson Baker, esq.; Anna his wife, and others, appellants.   Stafford Lightburne, clerk, and others, respondents ... (London) 1762.   2 pamphlets. 45 x 28 cm. fold. to 28 x 11½ cm. Concerning title to Abraham White's estate known as lands of Aughavana in the county of Wicklow, Ireland. Contents. - I. The appellants case. - 2. The respondents case. 24-23916.   HD1186.G7B3

18474   WHITE.   Memorials of Elder John White, one of the first settlers of Hartford, Conn., and of his descendants.   By Allyn S. Kellogg.   Hartford, Printed for the family by Case, Lockwood and co., 1860.   xviii, (13) - 321, (1) p. 23 cm. 1-13599.   CS71.W585 1860

18475   WHITE.   The descendants of William White, of Haverhill, Mass.   Genealogical notices by Hon, Daniel Appleton White.   Boston, J. Wilson and son, 1863.   47 p. 27 cm. 10-4373.
                                                                                 CS71.W585   1863

18476   WHITE.   The descendants of Thomas White, of Marblehead and Mark Haskell of Beverly, Mass.   With a brief notice of the Coombs family.   Compiled by Perley Derby ... Boston, Press of D. Clapp & son, 1872.   iv p., 2 l., (9) - 81, (1) p. 24 cm. Interleaved. 1-10283.   CS71.W585   1872

18477   WHITE.   Henry White and his family ... (New York, 1877)   cover-title, 7 p. front. (port.) pl.
23½ cm. By John Austin Stevens. Reprinted from the Magazine of American history, Dec. 1877. 9-15494.   CS71.W585   1877

18478   WHITE.   A genealogical record of the family of White, by John Bartlett White, of East Killingly, Conn.   Danielsonville, Greenslitt & Hamilton, printers, 1878.   44 p. 18½ cm. 26-5621.
                                                                                 CS71.W585   1878

18479   WHITE.   Account of the meeting of the descendants of Colonel Thomas White, of Maryland, held at Sophia's dairy, on the Bush River, Maryland, June 7, 1877.   Including papers read on that occasion, together with others then referred to and since prepared.   Philadelphia, 1879.
211 p. fold. geneal. chart. 33 cm. Title vignette: coat of arms. Contents. - Preliminary statement by William White Bronson. - Colonel Thomas White of Maryland, by William White Wiltbank. - Bishop White and his descendants, by J. Brinton White. - Mary White. - Mrs. Robert Morris, by Charles Henry Hart. - The English ancestry of Col. Thos. White, by Joseph Lemuel Chester. - Pedigree of Colonel Thomas White of Harford County, Maryland, prepared by Joseph Lemuel Chester. - The descendants of Col. Thomas White, by Thomas Harrison Montgomery. 9-15481.

                                                                                 CS71.W585   1879

18480   WHITE.   The descendants of Col. Thomas White.   By Thomas Harrison Montgomery.
(In Bronson, William W.   Account of the meeting of the descendants of Colonel Thomas White of Maryland ... Philadelphia, 1879. 33 cm.
p. 125-194) 12-916.   CS71.W585 1879a

18481   WHITE.   In memory of Nathaniel White: born in Lancaster, N.H., Feb. 7, 1811; died in Concord, N.H., Oct. 2, 1880 ... Concord, N.H., Printed by the Republican press association, 1881.
123 p. front. (port.) 21 cm. Dedication signed: A. S. White. Genealogical sketch: p. 19-22. 10-13088.
                                                                                 F39.W58

18482   WHITE.   Memoir of Brig. Gen. Anthony Walton White of the Continental army.   Compiled by Anna M. W. Woodhull ... (n.p., 1882?)   11 p. front. (port.) 23½ cm. "Presented to the New Jersey historical society, at Newark, May 18th, 1882." Genealogical and biographical notes": p. 9-11. 1-24505.   E207.W58W8

18483   WHITE.   Genealogical memoranda relating to the family of White of Horsham, Steyning, Shipley, and Cowfold, co. Sussex, of Mitcham, Croydon, and Reigate, co. Surrey, and of London; with pedigree.   By R. Garraway Rice ... Lewes, H. Wolff "Sussex advertiser" office, 1886.   1 p. l., 127 - 159, (7) p. 22 cm. Reprinted from the "Sussex archaeological collections," vol. xxxiv, 1886. 17-9499.   CS439.W487

18484   WHITE.   Ancestry of Samuel Stockton White ... With accounts of the families of White, Newby, Rose, Cranmer, Stout, Smith, Stockton, Leeds, Fisher, Gardiner, Mathews, Elton, Revell, Stacye, Tonkin, Carey, and Johnson.   Compiled by William Francis Cregar ... Philadelphia (Press of Patterson and White) 1888.   viii, 161 p. plates (coats of arms) port., fold. facsim., fold. geneal. chart. 28 cm. 9-15493.
                                                                                 CS71.W585   1888

18485   WHITE.   Ancestry of the children of James William White, M. D., with accounts of the families of White, Newby, Rose, Cranmer, Stout, Smith, Stockton, Leeds, Fisher, Gardiner, Mathews,
Elton, Revell, Stacye, Tonkin, McLorinan, Dowse, Jewett, Hunt, Reddinge, Isbell, and Griswold.
Comp. by William Francis Cregar ... Philadelphia (Press of Patterson & White) 1888.   vii, 194 p.
plates (coats of arms) fold. facsim., fold. geneal. tab.   28 cm.   9-15492.

CS71.W585 1888a

18486   WHITE.   The descendants of William White of Haverhill, Mass.   Genealogical notices by
Hon, Daniel Appleton White.   1863.   Additional genealogical and biographical notices, by Annie
Frances Richards.   Together with portraits and illustrations ... Boston, Mass., American printing
and engraving company, 1889.   4 p. l., (7)-80 p. front., plates, ports., fold. facsims. 23 cm. 14-10175.

CS71.W585   1889

18487   WHITE.   The White family.   (By Henry Kirke White)   (Detroit, Mich., 1891)   44 p. 14½ x 20 cm.
Caption title.   Cover-title: The "Whites". Introduction signed: H. K. White.   22-13254.   CS71.W585   1891

18488   WHITE.   Rev. William S. White, D. D., and his times.   (1800-1873) An autobiography.   Ed.
by his son, Rev. H. M. White ... Richmond, Va., Presbyterian committee of publication, 1891.
284 p. front. (port.) 20 cm. 12-40232.   BX9225.W35A3

18489   WHITE.   ... Memorials of Roderick White and his wife, Lucy Blakeslee of Paris Hill, N.Y.,
with some account of their American ancestors and a complete record of their descendants.   By
Andrew C. White ... Ithaca, N.Y., Printed for the family, by Andrus & Church, 1892.   32 p. 26½ cm.
At head of title: 1632-1892.   p. 15-24 printed on one side of leaf only.   9-15491.   CS71.W585   1892

18490   WHITE.   Ancestral chronological record of the William White family, from 1607-8 to 1895.
Concord (N.H.) Printed by the Republican press association, 1895.   393 p. plates, ports. 23½ cm. Dedicatory preface signed by Thomas White and Samuel White.   9-15490.   CS71.W585   1895

18491   WHITE.   ... Papers of the White family of Brookline, 1650-1807.   (Brookline, Mass., 1895)
(35)-53 p. 21 cm. (Brookline historical publication society. Publications. (1st ser.) no. 4) Caption title.   6-9034.

F74.B9B8 no. 4

18492   WHITE.   The White family genealogy.   (n. p., 1897?)   4 p. 18½ cm. Caption title.   "From the
Narragansett sun of October 6, 1897."   8-22382 rev.   CS71.W585   1897

18493   WHITE.   Report of the reunion of John White's descendants at Salem Willows, Massachusetts,
on Sept. 1, 1897.   Arranged by the secretary (Almira Larkin White) Haverhill, Mass., Press of
Chase bros., 1898.   22 p. pl. 20 cm. 9-15488.   CS71.W585   1898

18494   WHITE.   John White of Watertown and Brookline, and some of his descendants.   By Thomas
J. Lothrop ... Boston, D. Clapp & son, printers, 1898.   8 p. 24½ cm. Reprinted from the New Eng. hist. and geneal.
register for Oct., 1898.   9-15489.   CS71.W585 1898a

18495   WHITE.   Genealogy of the White family, by Mrs. Jennett Nichols-Vanderpool.   Eaton, N.Y.
(1899)   95, ix p. incl. front. 23 cm. Frontispiece: residence of author, with her portrait on verso. 13-11874.   CS71.W585   1899

18496   WHITE.   Genealogy of the descendants of John White of Wenham and Lancaster, Massachusetts.   1638-(1909) ... By Almira Larkin White ... Haverhill, Mass., Chase brothers, printers,
1900-09.   4 v. fronts., plates, ports., maps, facsims. (2 double) geneal. tables (1 fold.) 23½ cm. Vol. 3: Haverhill, Mass., Press of
Nichols, "the printer"; v. 4: Press of the Nichols print.   Title varies: v. 1-2, Genealogy of the descendants of John White ... 1638-1900.   In two
volumes.   v. 3, Genealogy of the descendants of John White ... 1638-1905.   In three volumes.   v. 4. Genealogy of the ancestors and descendants
of John White ... 1574-1909.   In four volumes.   Oct. 11, 1900-128.

CS71.W585 1900-

18497   WHITE.   The children of Robert White of Messing, co, Essex, England, who settled in
Hartford and Windsor.   By a descendant ... Boston, Printed by D. Clapp & son, 1901.   1 p. l., 9 p.
24 cm. Reprinted from New-Eng. historical and genealogical register for January 1901, p. 22-31. 24-8635.

CS71.W585   1901

18498   WHITE.   The Nicholas White family, 1643-1900, compiled by Thomas J. Lothrop ... Taunton, Mass. (Printed by C. A. Hack & son)   1 p. l., 493 p. fold. geneal. tab. 24 cm. 3-16528.
CS71.W585   1902

18499   WHITE.   White family quarterly, an illustrated genealogical magazine devoted to the ancestry, history and genealogy of the descendants of John White of Wenham and Lancaster, Massachusetts.   v. 1-3; Jan., 1903 - Oct., 1905. Haverhill, Mass., A. L. White, 1903-05.   3 v. in 1. plates, ports., facsims. 24 cm. Almira L. White, editor. No more published. 9-3838.   CS71.W585   1903-1905

18500   WHITE.   ... John White of Muddy River and descendants of his youngest son, Benjamin.   A paper read before the society, April 22, 1903 and April 27, 1904, by Charles F. White ... Brookline, Mass., The Society, 1904.   38 p. (pl., port., map, geneal. tab. 24½ cm. (In Brookline historical society. Publications. no. 3 (pt. 1)) 5-33687.   F74.B9B85 no. 3

18501   WHITE.   Norman White, his ancestors and his descendants, compiled and edited by Erskine Norman White ... New York, 1905.   155 p. front., plates, ports., facsims. 21½ cm. Printed for private distribution. 5-41003.   CS71.W585   1905

18502   WHITE.   The White family. (2d ed., enl. and cor.) (Detroit, 1906)   35 p. 27 cm. Caption title. Cover-title: The Whites. Introduction signed H. K. White, Detroit, Mich., 1906. 8-2769.   CS71.W585   1906

18503   WHITE.   A genealogical history of the descendants of Peter White, of New Jersey, from 1670, and of William White and Deborah Tilton his wife, loyalists. By James E. White ... St. John, N. B., Barnes & co., 1906.   v, (1), 89, xv p. ports. 22½ cm. Supplementary matter, paged 89-92, inserted between p. 88-89. 10-11764.   CS71.W585 1906a

18504   WHITE.   Descendants of Thomas White of Weymouth, Mass., 1630-1907, by C. S. Williams. New York (Press of T. A. Wright) 1907.   88 numb. l. front., plates, ports. 23½ cm. "Privately printed edition of 25 copies. No. nineteen." Printed on one side of leaf only. 8-13737.   CS71.W585   1907

18505   WHITE.   A memorial to my grandmother, Sarah Thorne White, and her ancestry.   1908. Jessie Whitmore Patten Purdy.   (n. p., 1908)   23 p. 23½ cm. 8-18105.   CS71.W585   1908

18506   WHITE.   The homes and haunts of Henry Kirk White; with some account of the family of White, of Nottingham and Norfolk. By John T. Godfrey and James Ward. London, Simpkin, Marshall, Hamilton, Kent & co., ltd.; Nottingham, H. B. Saxton, 1908.   xii p., 1 l., (2) 284 p., 1 l. incl. front. (port.) illus. fold. geneal. tab. 22 cm. "The connecting notes of Southey ... have been freely adopted." - Pref. 26-11899.
PR5793.G6

18507   WHITE.   ... The White family of Yarmouth. Yarmouthport, Mass., C. W. Swift, 1912. cover-title, 9 p. 25 cm. (Library of Cape Cod history & genealogy, no. 88) Comp. by William P. Davis. 12-36958.   CS71.W585   1912

18508   WHITE.   Ancestry of John Barber White and of his descendants. Pub. by John Barber White, of Kansas City, Mo., comp. and ed. by Almira Larkin White ... Haverhill, Mass., Press of C. H. Webster, 1913.   355 p. front., plates, ports., double map, facsims. (1 double) coats of arms (part col.) 23½ cm. 13-23048.   CS71.W585   1913

18509   WHITE.   White family (males) (Boston, Printed by D. Clapp & son, 1914)   geneal. tab. 25 x 96 cm. By Edwin Russell Davol.   15-3554.   CS71.W585   1914

18510   WHITE.   A brief account of the families White and Clarke, prepared and privately printed by James Clarke White, Boston ... Salem, Mass., Printed by Newcomb & Gauss, 1915. 37 p. 15½ cm. 16-15603.   CS71.W585   1915

18511   WHITE.   Memorials of Elder John White, one of the first settlers of Hartford, Conn. and of his descendants, by Allyn S. Kellogg. Hartford, Printed for the family by Case, Lockwood and company, 1860. St. Paul, Minn., Reprinted by the North central publishing co., for Josephine A. Siems, 1917.   xviii, (13)-347 p. illus. (facsims.) 24 cm. "From ... (p. 324) the original Appendix has been carefully revised and brought up to date under the supervision of Josephine A. Siems." 39-16922.   CS71.W585   1917

18512   WHITE.   Genesis of the White family, a connected record of the White family beginning in 900 at the time of its Welsh origin when the name was Wynn, and tracing the family into Ireland and England.   Several of the name entered England with the Norman conqueror.   Representatives of the English branch emigrated to America in 1638.   The Scotts of Scot's hall in the county of Kent, England.   One of the oldest recorded families, their traditional history beginning in Ireland about 300 B. C.   The authenticated record herein given dates back to 400 A. D.   Emigration to America was in 1740.   Their descendants are to be found in every state of the Union.   Supplemental records, biographical sketches and coats of arms of nearly seventy allied families.   Comp. by Emma Siggins White, assisted by Martha Humphreys Maltby.   Kansas City, Mo., Tiernan-Dart printing co., 1920. xi, 346 p. col. front., illus., plates, ports., col. coats of arms.   27½ cm.   Contains the lineage of John Barber White.   20-11575.

CS71. W585   1920

18513   WHITE.   A history of the White family, by Rev. Wm. P. White, D. D.   (Honey Brook, Pa., The Edwards press) 1925.   20 p., 1 l.   22½ cm.   On cover: A study in ancestry.   38-36171.   CS71. W585   1925

18514   WHITE.   Ancestors and descendants of Thomas Howard White, compiled by Mrs. Horatio Ford.   South Euclid, O., 1928.   3 p. l., fold. geneal. tab.   24 cm.   29-25260 rev.   CS71. W585   1928

18515   WHITE.   John White, the patriarch of Dorchester (Dorset) and the founder of Massachusetts, 1575-1648, with an account of the early settlements in Massachusetts, 1620-1630, by Francis Rose-Troup ... New York, London, G. P. Putnam's sons, 1930.   xii, 483 p.   2 pl. (incl. front.) facsim.   24 cm. Bibliography: p. 467-469.   "John White's pedigree": p. 403-417.   "John White's works": p. 418-446.   Slip of "Errata" inserted.   31-3916.

F67. W595

18516   WHITE.   Descendants of Colonel Thomas White of Maryland.   Brought down from 1877 to about March 1, 1932 ... (Philadelphia, 1932)   11 p.   31 cm.   Caption title.   Signed: Wm. White.   41-22680.

CS71. W585   1932

18517   WHITE.   Garrett county history of White family.   By Chas. E. Hoye.   (Oakland, Md.)   1935. 1 l.   54 cm.   Detached from the Mountain democrat, September 19, 1935.   38M1257T.   CS71. W585   1935

18518   WHITE.   White family records; descendants of Peregrine White, son of William and Susanna (Fuller) White, 1620 to 1939, by Roscoe R. White ... (Clarksburg, W. Va.) c. 1939.   262 p. incl. front., illus., ports.   23½ cm.   Blank ruled pages for memoranda (248-250)   39-4719.   CS71. W585   1939

18519   WHITE.   Our ancestors, by Mildred White-Brann.   Dallas, Tex., c. 1940.   1 v.   plates, ports., facsims.   29½ cm.   Loose-leaf; portrait on cover.   Type-written (carbon copy)   Includes the White, Ward, Hull, Shrimplin and other allied families.   40-30391.   CS71. W585   1940

18520   WHITE.   Some records prior to 1700 of White of Bedfordshire, Buckinghamshire, Hertfordshire, Huntingdonshire and a few of other English shires, with incidental records of more than 80 other families, specially indexed, by William White ... Philadelphia, Printed by Allen, Lane & Scott (1945) cover-title, 1 l. l., 41 p.   23½ cm.   46-14254.   CS439. W487 1945

18521   WHITE.   Ephraim Godfrey White and his descendants, by Charles Sumner White.   (Des Moines, Printed by Register and Tribune, 1946)   2 p. l., 48 p.   24½ cm.   "Edition 150 copies."   47-15732.

CS71. W585   1946

18522   WHITE.   Some White family history.   By Arthur Kent White.   Denver, Pillar of Fire, 1948. 432 p.   illus., ports.   20 cm.   49-13232 *.   BX8795. P5W66

18523   WHITE.   White family papers, volume III.   By William White.   Haverford, Pa., 1950. 52 l., 1. 99.   28 cm.   Typescript from the author's larger work with same title.   Addenda to W. W. Bronson's "Account of the meeting of the descendants of Colonel Thomas White of Maryland, held ... June 7, 1877"   and W. White's "Descendants of Colonel Thomas White of Maryland, brought down from 1877 to about March 1, 1932. "   55-19925.   CS71. W585   1950

18524   WHITE.   The book of White ancestry.   By Carlyle Snow White.   (Guilford? Conn., 195-?) 1 v.   29 cm.   57-58312.   CS71. W585

18525   WHITE.   The White genealogy: a history of the descendants of Matthew and Elizabeth (Given) White of County Tyrone, Ireland, and Albany, New York.   Compiled to 1908 by William Durant and continued to 1951 by Alexander G. Rose, III.   Washington, Published privately for the editor, 1951. 233 l. mounted group ports.   27 cm.   51-8799.   CS71.W585   1951

18526   WHITE.   Genealogy of the White and Kersey families of the counties of Randolph and Guilford, North Carolina.   St. Petersburg, Fla. (1951?)   unpaged. illus. 22 cm. 53-37415.
CS71.W585   1951a

18527   WHITE.   One branch of the White family.   By Charles Henry White.   (Carmel, Calif., 1952)   ix, 52 p. illus., maps, coat of arms. 24 cm. Bibliography: p. 51. 54-22006.   CS71.W585   1952

18528   WHITE.   Descendants of Thomas White, Sudbury, Mass., 1638.   Cleveland, 1952. 93 p. illus. 29 cm. 59-46107.   CS71.W585   1952a

18529   WHITE.   James and Bessie (Black) White and their descendants, compiled by Milford E. Barnes and Mary E. (Robinson) Barnes.   Iowa City, Iowa, 1961.   34 p. 28 cm. 61-59719.
CS71.W585   1961

18530   WHITE.   Pioneers in their own rights.   By Henry Poelinitz Johnston.   (Birmingham, Ala., Featon Press, 1964)   xi, 638 p. coats of arms, maps. 24 cm. 63-15948.   CS71.W585   1964

18531   WHITE.   Ancestors and descendants of Jeremiah White (1772-1847) and Matilda Howell (1775-1863) of Southampton, Long Island, New York and East Durham, Greene County, New York, by Benjamin V. White.   (West Hartford? Conn., 1965)   iv, 137 p. illus., coats of arms, facsim., maps, ports. 24 cm. Includes bibliographies. 65-9533.   CS71.W585   1965

18532   WHITE.   A brief summary of the ancestors and descendants of Frances Ellen Sweetser White, 1851-1925, compiled by LeRoy T. Campbell.   La Jolla, Calif., 1965.   53 p. 30 cm. Alternate pages blank. Bibliography: p. 47. 66-3082.   CS71.W585   1965a

18533   WHITE.   The descendants of Nathaniel Smith White (by Walter H. McClenon.   Takoma Park, Md., 1966)   11 l. 28 cm. 66-8466.   CS71.W585   1966

18534   WHITE.   Barnard White.   This record prepared and edited by Ruth Johnson and Glen F. Harding.   (Provo, Utah) Brigham Young University Press (1967)   433 p. illus., ports. 29 cm. Cover title: Barnard White family book. Includes music. 67-6900.   CS71.W585   1967

18535   WHITE.   White-Cantrell and allied families.   By Hallie Cantrell White.   Huntsville, Ala., White Print Co., 1967.   169 p. illus., coats of arms, facsims., ports. 24 cm. Includes bibliographical references. 67-31100.
CS71.W585   1967

18536   WHITE.   We have identified thousands.   Enough! A compilation of White and allied families, by Adelaide M. and Eugenia W. Lore.   (Concord? N.C.) 1967.   192 p. 24 cm. 68-631.
CS71.W585   1967c

18537   WHITE.   White family in vertical file.   Ask reference librarian for this material.

WHITE.   See also:

ADAMS, 1894 a	GOLSAN, 1959	MARSHALL, 1913
BASSETT, 1937	GREENLEAF, 1929	MAUNSELL, CS439.M37
CHAMBERS, F142.M7M38	HARKNESS, 1958	MILLER, 1923
COOK, 1967	HARRISON, 1932	RANNEY, F104.C8A2
COVINGTON, 1956	HASKELL, 1887	RIDER, 196-
CUMMINGS, 1948	JOHNSON, 1961	ROTHWELL, 1964
DE MOSS, 1950	KEY, 1931	SHREVE, 1897
DICKEY, 1935	KINGSBURY, 1904	THAYER, 1835
EUBANK, 1938	KIRBY, 1898	TOPHAM, 1911

WHITE continued:

VAN HOOK. 1957   WEITZEL, 1883   WILDER, CT275.W546.D8
VINTON, 1858a   WIGHT.   WITHERSPOON, 1910

18538   WHITEBREAD.   Genealogy of the Whitebread family in America.   Compiled and published by
S. A. Whitebread ... Ottawa, Kan., N. Waring, printer, 1902.   52 p. 3 port. (incl. front.) 23½ cm.
40-2278.   CS71.W588   1902

18539   WHITEBREAD.   George Whitebread of Seven Oaks, County Kent, England, and some of his
descendants.   By Charles Whitebread.   (Washington, 1960)   unpaged. 23 cm. 61-20689.
                                                                          CS71.W588   1960

WHITECOTTON.   See SHUMATE, 1964

WHITECROFT.   See WITCRAFT.

18540   WHITEFOORD.   The Whitefoord papers; being the correspondence and other manuscripts
of Colonel Charles Whitefoord and Caleb Whitefoord, from 1739 to 1810; ed., with introduction and
notes, by W. A. S. Hewins ... Oxford, At the Clarendon press, 1898.   xxix, 292 p. 1 illus. 22½ cm. Contains
3 letters by Benjamin Franklin addressed to Caleb Whitefoord.   4-34673.   DA67.1.W5A2

18541   WHITEHEAD.   John Whitehead of New Haven and Branford, Conn.   By James Shepard.   (Reprinted from New-England historical and genealogical register for April, 1901.)   Republished by the
author, New Britain, Conn., 1902.   Boston, Press of D. Clapp & son (1902)   7 p. 25 cm. 3-474.
                                                                          CS71.W591   1902

WHITEHEAD.   See also: BEACH, 1960
                         IRWIN, n. d.
                         RIGMAYDEN, DA670.L19C5 vol. 104, 105 (Chetham series)

18542   WHITEHOUSE.   Extracts from 2 vols. of notes.   By George Whitehouse.   (n. p., 1946)
13, 5 l. group port.   27 cm.   Title from label mounted on cover.   "Prepared by Edwin Seaborn." - Ms. note on half-title. 48-22633*.
                                                                          CS90.W55   1946

WHITEHOUSE.   See also BRUEN, CS439.B86

18543   WHITELAW.   The house of Whitelaw, a short history from A. D. 1400 to A. D. 1900, by H.
Vincent Whitelaw ... Glasgow, Jackson, Wylie & co., 1928.   xii, 206 p. col. front., illus., plates, fold. genealogical tables, facsims., coats of arms. 22½ cm. 32-9142.   CS479.W55

18544   WHITELEATHER.   Andrew Whiteleather family geneology (sic).   Compiled by Martha
Whiteleather Monnette with the assistance of many others.   (n. p.) 1966.   115 p. 24 cm. 68-7765.
                                                                          CS71.W5915 1966

WHITEMAN.   See WIGHTMAN.

WHITEMORE.   See SKINNER, 1935

18545   WHITENER.   A brief family record of William Eli Whitener and Augusta Nicholas Whitener.
By Thomas Augustus Whitener.   Daytona Beach, Fla., 1962.   unpaged. illus. 22 cm. 62-51692.
                                                                          CS71.W5917 1962

18546   WHITENER.   A brief history of the family of the Rev. Pinkney Alexander Whitener and Dicey
Mariah Brendle Whitener: their ancestors and descendents (sic)   Arlington, Va. (cover 1962)
39 l. illus. 28 cm. 63-12952.   CS71.W5917 1962a

WHITENIGHT.   See KLINE, 1960

WHITESEDES.   See WHITESIDE.

18547   WHITESELL.   A brief history of Alamance County, North Carolina, with sketches of the Whitesell family and the Huffman family, by William Thornton Whitsett, PH. D.   Burlington, N. C., A. D. Pate & co., printers (c. 1926) 32 p. incl. front., illus. 23 cm. (On cover: Whitsett historical monographs, no. 4) 26-20778.   F262. A3W5

18548   WHITESIDE.   The Whitesides of Colerain: the revolutionary captain and the congressman. (By David Francis Magee)   (In Lancaster County historical society, Lancaster, Pa. Historical papers and addresses ... Lancaster, 1913. 24½ cm. v. 17, p. 227-241) 16-2308.   F157. L2L5 vol. 17

18549   WHITESIDE.   The Whiteside book.   By Clarence Cannon.   (Elsberry? Mo.) 1957. 203 p. 30 cm. 58-40728.   CS71. W592 1957

18549 a WHITESIDE.   Whiteside family in vertical file.   Ask reference librarian for this material.

WHITESIDE.   See also: JOHNSON, 1893 a
MILLER, 1923

WHITFELD.   See WHITFIELD.

18550   WHITFIELD.   Genealogical notes of the families of Whitfield and Garland, who were successively owners of the manor of Whitfield, in the parish of Marwood, co. Devon, from the reign of King John, down to 1710.   (In his Devonshire notes and notelets ... London, 1888. 29½ cm. p. 121-129 incl. fold. geneal. tab.) Paged also (71) - 79. L. C. COPY REPLACED BY MICROFILM. 27-20310.   SEPARATE. CS439. W488   CS437. D4D8

18551   WHITFIELD.   Whitfield, Bryan, Smith, and related families, compiled by Emma Morehead Whitfield, assisted by many members of these families.   Edited by Theodore Marhsall Whitfield. (Westminster, Md., 1948?-50)   2 v. plates, ports., fold. maps, col. coat of arms. geneal. tables. 25 cm. Errata slips inserted. Bibliography: v. 1, p. (327) - 340. 50-30812.   CS71. W594 1948

18552   WHITFIELD.   Whitfield history and genealogy of Tennessee, by Vallie Jo Whitfield.   (Walnut Creek? Calif.) 1964.   237 l. coat of arms, map, ports. 29 cm. 75 copies printed. No. 39. Includes bibliographies. 64-56301.   CS71. W594 1964

18553   WHITFIELD.   Whitfield, McKeel, Fox, Schiefer families, by Vallie Jo Whitfield.   (Pleasant Hill? Calif., 1965)   614 l. coat of arms, geneal. table, ports. (part mounted) 29 cm. Twenty-five copies. 65-71326.   CS71. W594 1965

WHITFIELD.   See also: MANNING, 1897a
MERWIN, CS437. D4D8
MOULTON, 1922

WHITGREAVES.   See PENDRELL, DA446. H89

18554   WHITIN.   The Whitin family; historical notes, compiled by the late Katharine Whitin Swift and published by her husband Elijah Kent Swift.   Whitinsville, Mass., 1955.   216 p. 25 cm. 56-25339.   CS71. W6   1955

18555   WHITING.   Memoir of Rev. Samuel Whiting, D. D., and of his wife, Elizabeth St. John, with references to some of their English ancestors and American descendants.   By William Whiting ... 2d ed. with notes and corrections. ... Boston, Press of Rand, Avery & company, 1873.   334 p. 21½ cm. Two hundred copies printed - not published. Geneal. tab.: "Pedigree of the Whiting family in America, who are descendants from Rev. Samuel Whiting and Elizabeth St. John" (56 x 43 cm. fold. to 21½ x 14 cm.) inserted. 10-15240.   CS71. W61   1873

18556   WHITING.   A sketch of the life of Col. Daniel Whiting of Dedham, Mass., 1732-1807, with genealogical and biographical notices of his descendants, and of the Haven and Newell families, with extracts from family letters, by Mehetable W. N. Davenport.   New York, Printed for private circulation, 1881.   122 p. 20½ cm. 30-16912.   CS71. W61   1881

18557   WHITING.   Whiting family, compiled by C. H. Pope.   (n. p.) 1900.   cover-title, 7 l. incl. illus., pl., facsim., col. coat of arms. 28½ cm. 18-12901.   CS71. W61   1900

18558   WHITING.   Whiting genealogy.   Nathaniel Whiting of Dedham, Mass., 1641, and five generations of his descendants.   Compiled by Theodore S. Lazell ... Boston, Mass.   (T. R. Marvin & son,
printers) 1902.   80 p.   24½ cm.   2-18462.   CS71. W61   1902

18559   WHITING.   Maternal ancestry of Charles Whiting MacNair, by Hannah Louise MacNair
Crawford.   Boston, Priv. print., 1912.   82 p.   front., plates, ports., facsims., fold. geneal. tables, coats of arms.   20½ cm.
"The ancestry of Margaret Wyatt, wife of Matthew Allyn of Braunton in Devon": geneal. tab.   16-1389.   CS71. W61   1912

18560   WHITING.   Ella Matteson Brown: her ancestors and some of her descendants.   By Elizabeth
(Thomson) Denison.   (n. p., 1952?)   53 l.   28 cm.   61-45117.   CS71. W61   1952

18561   WHITING.   The Whiting family in America;   descendants of Reverend Samuel Whiting and
Elizabeth St. John.   Prepared and distributed by Fanny W. Blanchard and Charles F. Whiting.   Wilton,
N. H., 1959.   2 geneal. tables.   56 x 65 cm.   fold. to 22 cm.   In portfolio (26 cm.)   Corrections in ms.   63-32601.
CS71. W61   1959

WHITING.   See also:

BINGHAM, 1898	EVANS, 1922	TYLER, 1912 b
BINGHAM, 1920	EVANS, 1930	WARNER, PS3156. S7
BLAIR, 1898	MORSE, 1925	No. 430 - Adventurers of purse and
BOARDMAN, 1849	STEVENS, 1957	person.

WHITINGTON.   See WHITTINGTON.

18562   WHITLING.   The Whitling genealogy, by William H. Whitling.   (Emlenton? Pa., 1965)
271 p.   illus., ports.   24 cm.   Cover-title: Whitling 1828-1965.   CS71. W613   1965

18563   WHITLOCK.   Liber famelicus of Sir James Whitelocke, a judge of the Court of King's bench
in the reigns of James I. and Charles I.   Now first pub. from the original manuscript.   Ed. by John
Bruce ... (Westminster) Printed for the Camden society, 1858.   (4), xx, 131, (1), 5, (3) p.   22½ x 17 cm.
(Camden society.   Publications, no. LXX)   Title from Univ. of Chicago.   A17-1242.   DA20. C17 vol. 70

WHITLOCK.   See also STEBBINS, 1880

18564   WHITMAN.   Memoir of John Whitman and his descendants.   By Ezekiel Whitman.   Portland,
Printed by C. Day & co., 1832.   44 p.   24½ cm.   20-9249.   CS71. W614   1832

18565   WHITMAN.   History of the descendants of John Whitman of Weymouth, Mass.   By Charles
H. Farnam ... New Haven, Tuttle, Morehouse & Taylor, 1889.   xv, 1246 p.   col. front. (coat of arms)   26 cm.
9-15487.   CS71. W614   1889

18566   WHITMAN.   Ancestors and descendants of Rev. Oramel Eleazer Wightman, late of Mohawk,
N. Y.   (n. p.) 1935.   17 l.   29 cm.   Hectographed.   Preface signed: Frederick Gates.   36-24708.   CS71. W659   1935

18567   WHITMAN.   Whitman and Rodgers families of New York and Greenbrier County, West
Virginia, by Homer C. Cooper.   (Athens? Ga.) 1968.   6 l.   28 cm.   76-3386 MARC.   CS71. W614   1968

WHITMAN.   See also: AVERY, 1925
                                         HOLBROOK, F1. N56 vol. 58   (N. E. Hist. & gen. register)

18568   WHITMARSH.   Genealogy of the Whitmarsh family.   Rev. ed.   West Bloomfield, N. Y.,
N. W. Bates, 1902.   (10) p.   16 cm.   Dedication signed: Newton Whitmarsh Bates.   2-24893.   (Book missing from L. of C.)

18569   WHITMARSH.   Genealogy of the descendants of John Whitmarsh of Wymouth, Mass.   By
Newton Whitmarsh Bates.   (Ashtabula, P. H. Fassett, printer) 1916.   85 p.   19½ cm.   16-11772.
CS71. W615   1916

WHITMARSH.   See also FAXON, 1880

WHITMER.   See MAGINET, 1961

18570   WHITMORE.   Record of the descendants of Francis Whitmore, of Cambridge, Mass.   Comp. by W. H. Whitmore.   Boston, Printed for private circulation only, by J. Wilson and son, 1855.
1 p. 1., 24 p. 23 cm.   "Reprinted with additions from Brook's History of Medford, Massachusetts."   cf. J. Munsell, American genealogy. 20-9250.
CS71.W616   1855

18571   WHITMORE.   Notes on the manor and family of Whitmore.   Compiled by W. H. Whitmore. Boston, Printed for private circulation only, by J. Wilson and son, 1856.   14 p. 23½ cm. 3-20776.
CS439.W5   1856

18572   WHITMORE.   The early days of Thomas Whittemore.   An autobiography: extending from A. D. 1800 to A. D. 1825.   Boston, J. M. Usher, 1859.   348 p. front. (port.) 20 cm. 17-14860.
BX9969.W6A3

18573   WHITMORE.   The Wetmore family of America, and its collateral branches: with genealogical, biographical, and historical notices.   By James Carnahan Wetmore.   Albany, Munsell & Rowland, 1861.   x, (2), 670 p. illus. (coat of arms) 25½ cm.   Descendants of Thomas Whitmore, 1615-1681. 9-15486.
CS71.W616   1861

18574   WHITMORE.   Whitmore tracts.   A collection of essays on matters of interest to persons bearing the name.   By William H. Whitmore.   Boston, D. Clapp & son, 1875.   (122) p. front. (port.) illus. (coat of arms) 23 cm.   Of this edition of forty-two copies, only twenty-five contain the sixth tract and the appendix.   Reprinted from the Herald and genealogist, and the N. E. hist. and geneal. register.   Contents. - no. 1. Whitmores of Whitmore, co, Stafford, Thurstanton, co. Chester, Claverley, co. Salop. - no.2. Whitmores of Caunton, co. Notts. - no.3. The Roos family of Laxton, co. Notts. - no.4. Whitmores of Madley, co. Stafford. - no.5. Wilcox family of Cambridge, Mass. - no.6. Abstracts of wills of Whitmores, from English records. - Appendix: Notes on the manor and family of Whitmore ... with special t. - p. Boston, 1856. 20-7229.
CS71.W616   1875

18575   WHITMORE.   Notes on the Whitmores of Madeley, Eng., and the Farrars and Brewers of Essex County, Massachusetts.   By William Henry Whitmore.   Boston, D. Clapp & son, 1875.
3 p. 1., (3) - 47 p. front. (port.) 23 cm. (His Tract no. 4) 2-19626.
CS439.W5   1875

18576   WHITMORE.   A genealogy of four branches of the Whittemore family; including the original Whittemore family of Hitchin, Hertfordshire, England; and a brief lineage of other branches. Nashua, N. H., B. B. & F. P. Whittemore, printers, 1880.   48 p. 23 cm.   The edition of 1890 published under author's name (i. e. B. B. Whittemore). 17-30086.
CS71.W616   1880

18577   WHITMORE.   The Whitmores of Ludson, co. Salop.   Communicated by William H. Whitmore. (n. p., 1885?)   9 p. 24 cm.   Based in part on records copied by J. L. Chester. 8-4651.
CS439.W5   1885

18578   WHITMORE.   A genealogy of several branches of the Whittemore family, including the original Whittemore family of Hitchin, Hertfordshire, England; and a brief lineage of other branches.   By B. B. Whittemore.   Nashua, N. H., F. P. Whittemore, printer, 1890.   106 p. 23 cm. 9-15485.
CS71.W616   1890

18579   WHITMORE.   A genealogy of several branches of the Whittemore family, including the original Whittemore family of Hitchin, Hertfordshire, England: and a brief lineage of other branches. (Rev. ed.)   By B. B. Whittemore ... Nashua, N. H., F. P. Whittemore, book and job printer, 1893.
1 p. 1., (3) - 132, (3) p. 24 cm.   "Obituary. Bernard Bemis Whittemore": 3 p. at end. 17-28710.
CS71.W616   1893

18580   WHITMORE.   The Whitmore family, by Wm. Kirby.   In Niagara historical society. (Publications) no. 8.
14-20019.
F1059.N5N52 no. 8

18581   WHITMORE.   The Whitmore genealogy, a record of the descendants of Francis Whitmore of Cambridge, Massachusetts (1625-1685) 1907.   Jessie Whitmore Patten Purdy.   (Reading, Pa., Pengelly & bro. printers, 1907)   ix p., 1 l., 13-158 p. 2 port. (incl. front.) 24 cm. 8-15501.
CS71.W616   1907

18582   WHITMORE.   Ancestors of Rev. Williams Howe Whittemore, Bolton, Ct., 1800 - Rye, N.Y., 1885, and of his wife Maria Clark, New York, 1803 - Brooklyn, 1886.   Compiled by William Plumb Bacon.   (New Britain, Conn., Adkins printing co., 1907)   5 p. l., 124 p.   plates, ports., double geneal. tables. 26½ x 20 cm.   "Edition 150 copies.   Printed for ... private distribution."   8-2767.   CS71.W616   1907a

18583   WHITMORE.   Whitmore families.   Francis Whitmore of Maine; ancestry and descendants. Abram Whittemore of Maine.   Whitmores in England.   (By Charles Nelson Sinnett)   Brainerd, Minn. (1922)   cover-title, 101 l. 34 cm.   Type-written.   "The Wetmore family.   Name of renown.   Variations of orthography.   By Eleanor Lexington (pseud.)":   3 l. at end.   22-4162.   CS71.W616   1922

WHITMORE.   See also: COLES, 1926
CROSSETT, 1937
GROUT, 1922
LOVELL, 1940
REMEY, 1923
SKINNER, 1935

18584   WHITNEY.   Incidents in the life of Samuel Whitney, born in Marlborough, Massachusetts, 1734.   Died at Castine, Maine, 1808.   Together with some account of his descendants, and other family memorials.   Collected by his great-grandson, Henry Austin Whitney.   Boston, Printed for private distribution (Cambridge, Riverside press) 1800.   x p., 1 l., 97 p., 1 l., xlii p.   plates.   35 cm.   One hundred copies printed.   24-4256.   CS71.S62   1860

18585   WHITNEY.   Whitney's "Choice of emblems."   A fac-simile reprint.   Ed. by Henry Green, M.A.   With an introductory dissertation, essays literary and bibliographical, and explanatory notes. London, Lovell Reeve & co.; (etc., etc.) 1866.   3 p. l., (v)-lxxxviii (i.e. xc) p.; facsim. (10 p. l., 230 p., illus.), (2), (231) - 440 p. illus., 63 (i.e. 72) pl. on 44 l., fold. tab.   26½ cm.   Reproduction of original t.p.: A choice of emblemes, and other devises for the moste parte gathered out of sundrie writers, Englished and moralized.   And divers newly devised, by Geffrey Whitney ... Imprinted at Leyden, In the house of Christopher Plantyn, by Francis Rephelengius.   M. D. LXXXVI.   The facsimile (photolithographed) is in two parts.   Most of the emblems are from earlier works published by Plantin, more than half being identical with those in the works of Alciati, Paradin, and Sambucus. cf. p. 252.   The 72 "illustrative plates" numbered 1-63) between pages 414 and (415) include facsimiles of many additional emblems, printers' devices, etc.   Genealogical tables of (1) Whitney, of Whitney, in Herefordshire." and (2) "Whitney of Chinnor and Islip, Oxfordshire."   18-23867.

PR2388.W4C5

18586   WHITNEY.   The Whitney family of Connecticut, and its affiliations; being an attempt to trace the descendants, as well in the female as the male lines, of Henry Whitney, from 1649 to 1878; to which is prefixed some account of the Whitneys of England.   By S. Whitney Phoenix ... New York, Priv, print. (Bradstreet press) 1878.   3 v. fold. geneal. tables.   28½ cm.   Paged continuously.   "Edition: 500 copies 4°. 10 copies folio.   All for presentation."   9-25087.   CS71.W62   1878

18587   WHITNEY.   Some of the descendants of John and Elinor Whitney, who settled in Watertown, Massachusetts, in 1635.   Compiled by William L. Whitney ... Pottsville, Pa., M.E.Miller, 1890. 101 p.   23½ cm.   Edition private - 100 copies.   9-15505.   CS71.W62   1890

18588   WHITNEY.   Whitney.   The descendants of John Whitney, who came from London, England, to Watertown, Massachusetts, in 1635.   By Frederick Clifton Pierce ... Chicago, The author, press of W. B. Conkey co., 1895.   692 p. incl. front., illus., plates. 26 cm.   9-18749.   CS71.W62   1895
L. C. COPY REPLACED BY MICROFILM.   Microfilm 8676 CS

18589   WHITNEY.   The ancestry of John Whitney who, with his wife Elinor, and sons John, Richard, Nathaniel, Thomas and Jonathan, emigrated from London, England, in the year 1635, and settled in Watertown, Massachusetts ... By Henry Melville ... New York, Printed at the De Vinne press, 1896. xviii, 295 p. col. front. (coat of arms) plates, fold. map, facsims., fold. geneal. tab.   26 cm.   600 copies printed.   9-18736. CS71.W62   1896

18590   WHITNEY.   William Whitney Rice.   A biographical sketch, by Rockwood Hoar.   Also The Whitney narrative, being an account of the Whitney family written by Mr. Rice.   Worcester, Press of C. Hamilton, 1897.   3 p. l., 5-83 p. front. (port.) 2 pl. 25½ cm.   10-12422.   E664.R49H6

18591 WHITNEY. A Watertown farm in eight generations. A memorial of the Whitney family.
By William H. Whitney ... Cambridge, Mass., 1898.   5 p. 1., 150 numb. 1., 8 1. maps. 24½ cm. Blue print
photographs. 9-15504.   CS71.W62   1898

18592 WHITNEY. The ancestry of Robert Whitney, traced in all lines possible to the sixth generation, and showing his descent from over twenty-five separate families, by Charles Shepard II, C.E.
Washington, D.C., C. Shepard, 1923.   geneal. tab. 37 x 56 cm. fold. to 30½ x 26 cm. (Shepard genealogical series,
no. 13) Blue-print. "Limited ed. of twenty five copies, of which this is no. 5." 23-26654.   CS439.W515

18593 WHITNEY. Whitney, Wyne and allied families, genealogical and biographical. Prepared for
Mrs. Mary C. Whitney ... New York, The American historical society, inc., 1925.   141 p., 3 1. pl.,
port., col. coats of arms. 31 cm. Versos blank. Bound in blue levant with leather doublure; inlaid gold tooled. Allied families: Wyne,
Clement, Russell, Touchett, Milbourne, Wye, Baskerville, Bray, Holland, Fitz-Alan. Devereux, Knowlton, Hastings, Ross and Goodenow.
"References": 1 leaf at end. 25-13342.   CS71.W62   1925

18594 WHITNEY. Genealogy of the Whitney family, compiled by Mrs. Robert Richardson Gum,
Frankfort, Ky. (n. p., 1926)   geneal. tab. 39 x 35½ cm. The ancestry of Mrs. Gum back to Adam. 27-19585.
CS71.W62   1926

18595 WHITNEY. Another edition of No. 18593. New York, The American Historical society,
inc., 1928.   28-13972.   CS71.W62   1928

18596 WHITNEY. Ancestors and descendants of Henry Austin Whitney, 1826 - 1889. Notes compiled by James Jackson Minot, M.D. (n.p.) 1934.   21 p. 23½ cm. Bibliography: p. 20-21. 34-32585.
CS71.W62   1934

18597 WHITNEY. Some more descendants of John and Elinor Whitney, by Edward Raymond Sandi-
ford. (Bloomfield? N.J., 1941)   1 p. 1., 8 numb. 1., 2 1. 28 cm. Reproduced from type-written copy. 41-6101.
CS71.W62   1941

>   WHITNEY. See also: BISBEE, 1936
                            CHASE, 1930
                            COLLIER, 1951 a
                            DAVIS, 1959
                            MARSH, 1888

        WHITON. See: LINDLEY, 1950
                      WHITTEN.

        WHITTAKER. See WHITAKER, 1962

        WHITTELSEY. See WHITTLESLEY.

        WHITTEMORE. See WHITMORE.

        WHITTEDS. See PADDLEFORD, 1960

18598 WHITTEN. Whitten and allied families. By Virginia (Wood) Alexander. (Columbia, Tenn.,
1966)   iii, 304 p. 22 cm. Bibliography: p. 269-272. 68-169.   CS71.W6225   1966

18599 WHITTEN. ... Commemoration of the ordination of John Milton Whiton to the ministry of
the Presbyterian church in Antrim, N.H. 1808. 1908. (Antrim? N.H.) Printed for the family,
1908.   42 p. plates, ports. 23½ cm. "Genealogical record": p. 39-42. 9-27479.   CS71.W622   1908

18600 WHITTEN. The Whiton family in America, the genealogy of the descendents (!) of Thomas
Whiton (1635) compiled by Augustus Sherrill Whiton ... (New London, Conn.) The Whiton family
association, inc., 1932.   2 p. 1., (7) - 8, (4), (9) - 258 p. incl. front., illus. plates, ports. 22 cm. "Edition of 400 copies,
printed for subscribers only." Blank pages at end for additions. 35-14597.   CS71.W622   1932

        WHITTEN. See also HOWARD, 1929

18601   WHITTET.   Whittet: a family record.   1657-1900.   Comp. by William Whittet ... (and) Robert Whittet ... Printed for family circulation only.   Richmond, Va., Whittet & Shepperson, printers, 1900.   6 p. l., (9)-153 p. front., plates, ports. 19 cm. 12-34879.   CS71.W623   1900

18602   WHITTIER.   Genealogy of two branches of the Whittier family, from 1620 to 1873.   By D. B. Whittier ... Boston, A. Mudge & son, printers, 1873.   22 p. fold. geneal. tab. 24 cm. Geneal. tab. lithographed in gold and colors. 9-15503.   CS71.W624   1873

18603   WHITTIER.   Genealogy of the Whittier family.   1622.   1822.   Compiled and arranged by Charles Collyer Whittier.   Boston, Heliotype printing co. (1882)   geneal. tab. 75 x 108 fold. to 24 x 17 cm. Printed for private distribution. Executed entirely with pen and ink by Burdett, and re-produced in heliotype. 9-15502. CS71.W624   1882

18604   WHITTIER.   Notes on the English ancestry of the Whittier and Rolfe families of New England, 1912.   (Boston, 1912)   cover-title, 14, (1) p. 15 cm. Signed: Charles Collyer Whittier. Reprinted from the New England historical and genealogical register for July 1912. 12-17270.   CS71.W624   1912

18605   WHITTIER.   The ancestry and descendants of Edmund Whittier, with a survey of the early Whittiers in America, and some notes on related ancestries, compiled by Bernard B. Whittier ... East Lansing, Mich., The College printery, 1917.   54 p. illus. (port.) fold. geneal. tab. 18 cm. 17-17322.   CS71.W624   1917

18606   WHITTIER.   The descendants of Thomas Whittier and Ruth Green, of Salisbury & Haverhill, Massachusetts, compiled by Charles Collyer Whittier.   Edited and supplemented by Earle O. Whittier. Rutland, Vt., The Tuttle publishing company, inc., 1937-39.   606 p. front., plates, port., map, facsim., col. coat of arms. 23 cm. On cover: Section I. 37-21319.   CS71.W624 1937-9

WHITTIER.   See also WHITCHER.

WHITTING.   See: EVANS, 1922
             WHITING.

18607   WHITTINGTON.   The model merchant of the middle ages, exemplified in the story of Whittington and his cat: being an attempt to rescue that interesting story from the region of fable, and to place it in its proper position in the legitimate history of this country.   By the Rev. Samuel Lysons ... London, Hamilton, Adams and co.; (etc., etc.) 1860.   vi, (7)-95 p. front. (port.) plates, fold. geneal. tab. 23 cm. "Pedigree of the family of Whittington ... ": fold. geneal. tab. (at end) 20-3128.   CT788.W65L8

WHITTINGTON.   See also: ALLEN, 19 -
                          GUNNING, DA690.S968P3
                          LIGON, 1947

WHITTLE.   See: LONG, 1956
                 POCAHONTAS, 1887

18608   WHITTLESEY.   Address of Elisha Whittlesey delivered at a meeting of the Whittlesey family, which convened at Saybrook, Connecticut, September 20, 1855.   Washington, 1855. 22 p. 22½ cm. 9-15500.   CS71.W627   1855

18609   WHITTLESEY.   Memorial of the Whittlesey family in the United States.   (Hartford, Conn.) The Whittlesey association, 1855.   vi, (60), (69) - 125 p. 23½ cm. And chart 185 x 25½ cm. fold. to 25 cm. Preface signed: John S. Whittlesey, Henry N. Whittlesey, Charles B. Whittlesey. 12-19014.   CS71.W627   1855a

18610   WHITTLESEY.   Military record of the descendants of John Whittlesey and Ruth Dudley, who were married at Saybrook, Conn., June 20, 1664.   Cleveland, O., Fairbanks, Benedict & co., printers, 1874.   14 p. 24 cm. 20-9248.   CS71.W627   1874

18611   WHITTLESEY.   Genealogy of the Whittelsey-Whittlesey family.   Compiled and published by Charles Barney Whittelsey ... Hartford, Conn., C. B. Whittelsey, Press of the Case, Lockwood & Brainard company, 1898.   414 p. front., plates, ports., map, coat of arms. 24 cm. Limited edition. 9-15501.   CS71.W627   1898

18612   WHITTLESEY.   Genealogy of the Whittlesey-Whittelsey family, by Charles Barney Whittel-sey ... 2d ed.   New York, London, Whittlesey house, McGraw-Hill book company, inc., 1941.
2 p. l., vii - xi. 650 p., 1 l. front., illus., (incl. ports., map, facsims.) col. coat of arms. 23½ cm. 41-19787.   CS71.W627   1941

WHITTLESEY.   See also DAWSON, 1874a

WHITWELL.   See WILSON, 1890

WHYTMAN.   See WIGHTMAN.

18613   WIARD.   Wiard family, by Captain George Knapp Collins for William Wolcott Wiard.
Syracuse, N.Y., 1912.   1 p. l., 5-61 p. front., pl., ports. 18½ cm. 30-4269.   CS71.W632   1912

WIATT.   See WYATT.

18614   WIBORNE.   Weyburn-Wyborn genealogy, being a history and pedigree of Thomas Wyborn of Boston and Scituate, Massachusetts, and Samuel Weyburn of Pennsylvania, with notes on the origin of the family in England and several branches in Kent County in particular, by S. Fletcher Weyburn ...
New York, Frank Allaben genealogical company (c. 1911)   218 p. front., plates, ports. msp. 24½ cm. 12-21737.
CS71.W633   1911

WICHEHALSE.   See BARBER, DA690.L982C6

WICHELHAUSEN.   See ACHELIS, 1938

18615   WICKENDEN.   Memoirs of the Thomas Rogers Wickenden family.   By Arthur Consaul Wickenden.   (Oxford? Ohio, 1962)   90 p. ports., col. coat of arms. 24 cm. 62-41763.
CS71.W635   1962

18616   WICKES.   Wickes family history.   By Forsythe Wickes.   (Newport? R.I., 1939?)
2 v. 23 cm. 60-57200.   CS71.W636   1939

18617   WICKHAM.   Wickham.   (Genealogical sketch by) C. A. Hoppin, jr.   Hartford, 1899.
12 p. 26 cm.   Caption title.   The ancestry and descendants of Thomas Wickham of Wethersfield, Conn. 1-23271.   CS71.W637   1899

18618   WICKHAM.   In memoriam.   Horace John Wickham, April 1, 1836 - May 11, 1914.
(London, 1914?)   21 numb. l., 1 l. front. (port.) 26 cm.   Signed at end: C. A. H. (i.e. Charles Arthur Hoppin)   Description
of the stamped envelope and stamped newspaper wrapper machines invented by Horace John Wickham: leaves 11 - 16.   Printed on vellum paper;
ornamented t.-p.; initials; first and last leaf of text within ornamental borders.   Bound in tree calf, old tooling.   22-5289.
T40.W5H6

18619   WICKHAM.   Ancestors of James Wickham and his wife Cora Prudence Billard, compiled by Josephine C. Frost (Mrs. Samuel Knopp Frost)   Brooklyn, N.Y., 1935.   207 p. 25 cm. 36-30626.
CS71.W637   1935

WICKHAM.   See also: DICKERSON, 1919
ST. LEGER, DA690.L39M3

WICKLIFFE.   See McCHORD, 1941

WICKOFF.   See WYCKOFF.

18620   WICKWARE.   Genealogy of the Wickware family;   containing an account of the origin and early history of the name and family in England, and the record of John Wickware, who emigrated to New London, Connecticut, in 1675, and of his descendants in America, by Arthur Manley Wickwire
... (New York and Meriden, Press of the Curtiss-Way company, c. 1909)   5 p. l., 13-283 p. front., plates,
ports., maps, facsims., fold. geneal. tab. 23½ cm. 9-29979.   CS71.W638   1909

WICKWIRE.   See WICKWARE.

WICOFF.   See WYCKOFF.

18621   WIDENER.   The Wideners in America, by Howard H. Widener ... Chili, N. Y., C. A. Nichols, jr. (1904)   330 p. front. (port.) 22 cm.   8-322.   CS71. W639   1904

18622   WIDENER.   Without drums, by P. A. B. Widener ... New York, G. P. Putnam's sons (c. 1940)   6 p. l., 3-279 p. front., plates, ports.   22 cm.   40-35778.   CT275. W5575. A3

18623   WIDENER.   Widener, Dunton, Elkins, Broomall and allied families: European and American descents.   Compiled and priv. print. for George Dunton Widener.   American Historical Company, inc.   New York, 1953.   viii, 800 p. plates, ports., col. coats of arms, facsims., geneal. tables. 33 cm.   In case.   Includes bibliographical references.   54-3536.   CS71. W639   1953

WIDDIFIELD.   See LUNDY, 1902

WIDDINGTON.   See SKEET, CS438. S5

WIDGER.   See WHITTIER, F72. E7E81 vol. 49

18624   WIEDE.   Ahnentafel Wiede, bearbeitet im auftrag von kommerzienrat Johannes Wiede ... von dr. Karl Steinmüller.   Leipzig, Zentralstelle für deutsche personen- und familiengeschichte, 1940.   8 p., 9-78 numb. l., 79-207 p. incl. geneal. tables (part double) front. (port.) col. coat of arms.   35 cm.   (Added t. - p: Stamm- und ahnentafelwerk der Zentralstelle für deutsche personen- imd familiengeschichte, schriftleitung: dr. Hohlfeld.   Bd. XXI)   47-39647.   CS629. W45   1940

18625   WIENS.   Wiens, 1803-1968 (by Mrs. John D. Goering)   (Burrton? Kan., 1968?)   1 v. (various pagings) 23 x 38 cm.   Cover title.   70-8525 MARC.   CS71. W642   1968

WIER.   See CARPENTER, 1959

WIESENER.   See WEZENER.

18626   WIGAN.   Chronik der familie Wigand.   Leipzig, W. Wigands buchdr., 1902.   4 p. l., 107 p. plates, ports.   23 cm.   Dedication signed: Ida Cichorius, Thekla Wigand, Rosi Wigand, Moriz Wigand, Otto Schaefer.   18-23472.   CS629. W5

18627   WIGGIN.   1813.   Charles E. Wiggin.   1888.   (Boston, G. F. Crook, printer, 1888?)   148 p. port.   15½ cm.   On cover: In memoriam C. E. W.   Compiled by J. H. Wiggin.   cf. p. 135.   "Genealogy and history": p. 71-148.   6-7074.   CS71. W655   1888

WIGGIN.   See also: GRIFFIN, F129. S74G8
             WHITE, 1906a

18628   WIGGINS.   Some descendants of Captain John Wiggins, with information on the families of Baker, Bostick, Buckner, Harris, Hunter, Kirby, Martin, Moffatt, Sloan, Stovall, Thomas, and Walker.   By Kathryn (Walker) Wiggins.   Paxton, Ill., Service Print, Co., 1955.   unpaged.   21 cm.   55-57455.   CS71. W656   1955

18629   WIGGINS.   Wiggins genealogy.   By Ruth Wiggins Shelton.   (Fayetteville, Ark., 1969.   (29) l. ports.   30 cm.   Cover title.   76-4107 MARC.   CS71. S656   1969

18630   WIGGINTON.   The Wigginton book.   By Clarence Cannon.   (Elsberry? Mo.) 1958.   unpaged.   29 cm.   58-40727.   CS71. W6564   1958

18631   WIGHT.   The Wight family.   Memoir of Thomas Wight, of Dedham, Mass., with genealogical notices of his descendants, from 1637 to 1840.   By Danforth Phipps Wight ... Boston, Press of T. R. Marvin, 1848.   119 p. 19½ cm.   9-15495.   CS71. W657   1848

18633   WIGHT.   The Wights.   A record of Thomas Wight of Dedham and Medfield and of his descendants 1635-1890.   By William Ward Wight ... Milwaukee, Swain & Tate, 1890.   xi, 357 p. 28½ cm.
"Of this edition of the Wights this is no. 612."   "List of authorities": p. 354-357.   Additional records for The Wights by William Ward Wight ...
Descendants of Joseph Wight compiled by Jennie Josephine Wight Howes (1657) North Andover, Mass., Dec. 1927.   1 pl. 7 l. 28½ cm.   Type-
written.   2-1652.
                                                                        CS71.W657   1890

WIGHT.   See also: CLEMENTS, 1928
                   WHITE.

18634   WIGHTMAN.   Records of the Wightman (Whiteman or Weightman) family.   By Bryan l'Anson
... London, Printed at the author's private press, 1917.   106 (i.e.110), (12) p.   front., illus., plates, port., coats of
arms.   30½ cm.   Four pages between p. 10 and 11   mor included in the pagination.   Each chapter preceded by its title within ornamental border.
25-5045.
                                                                        CS439.W518

18635   WIGHTMAN.   Ancestors and descendants of Rev. Oramel Eleazer Wightman, late of Mohawk,
N.Y.   (By Frederick Gates) (n.p.) 1935.   17 l. 29 cm.   Hectographed.   Preface signed: Frederick Gates.   36-24708.
                                                                        CS71.W659   1935

18636   WIGHTMAN.   George Wightman of Quidnessett, R. I. (1632-1721/2) and descendants:
Waitman, Weightman, Whiteman, Whitman, Whytman, Wightman, Wyghtman, compiled by Mary Ross
Whitman.   Chicago, Ill.   (Ann Arbor, Mich., Lithoprinted by Edwards brothers, inc.) 1939.
x, 476 p. incl. front. (facsim.) 1 illus. ports.   28 cm.   39-16997.   CS71.W659   1939

WIGHTMAN.   See also: MASTER, 1874
                       STREYNSHAM, 1879

18637   WIGRAM.   Biographical notes relating to certain members of the Wigram family, with such
information as is considered likely to be of use and interest, by Reginald S. Wigram ... (Aberdeen)
Priv. print. at the Aberdeen university press, 1912.   viii, 190 p. 23 cm.   20-15882.
                                                                        CS439,W52

18638   WIGSTON.   A calendar of charters and other documents belonging to the hospital of William
Wyggeston at Leicester, by A. Hamilton Thompson ... (Leicester) Pub. for the Corporation of the
city of Leicester by E. Backus, 1933.   2 p. l., (iii) - xlvi, 660 p. 23 cm.   34-9244.
                                                                        RA988.L4W8

18639   WIGTON.   Wigton.   By Mary Eliza (Wigton) Reeve.   (Clearfield, Pa., 1961)
169 l. 30 cm.   62-59970.   CS71.W662   1961

WIGTOWN, Earldom of.   See FLEMING.

WIKOFF.   See WYCKOFF.

WILBER.   See: PARSONS, 1924
                 WILBUR.

WILBERT.   See ENDERS, 1960

WILBOR.   See: ALEXANDER, 1960
                WILBUR.

WILBORE.   See WILBUR.

WILBOUR.   See WILBUR.

WILBRAHAM.   See WESTON, 1899

18640　WILBUR.　Genealogical record of the Wilbur family.　Compiled by Asa Wilbur ... Boston, Printed for the family (by Rand, Avery & Frye) 1871.　89 p.　19½ cm.　Part of the pages left blank for memoranda. 9-15499.　CS71.W666　1871

18641　WILBUR.　Life of Lafayette Wilbur, (autobiography) and family genealogy.　Jericho, Vt., Press of K. C. Butler, 1881.　75 p.　19 cm.　9-15498.　CS71.W666　1881

18642　WILBUR.　The Wildbores in America, a family tree, by John R. Wilbor.　Saint Paul, Minn., The author, 1907.　3 p. l., 4-145, 21 p.　25½ cm.　7-27164.　CS71.W666　1907

18643　WILBUR.　Ye Wildbore ... v. 1-5; Jan. 1929-Dec. 1933.　Baltimore, Md., The Wildbores in America, inc. (1929-33)　5 v. in 1.　23 cm.　monthly.　Caption title.　Edited by J. R. Wilbor.　No more published. 33-1932 rev.　CS71.W666　1929

18644　WILBUR.　The Wildbores in America, a family tree originally published in 1907, rev. and augm. in this 2d ed.　John Reid Wilbor, Benjamin Franklin Wilbour, compilers ... Baltimore, Md., G. W. King printing co., 1933 -　v. ports. coat of arms. 24 cm.　33-9647.　CS71.W666　1933

18645　WILBUR.　Genealogy of the Wilbour and allied families ... by Benjamin Franklin Wilbour. Little Compton, R. I., 1936.　409 l. incl. geneal. tables.　29 cm.　Type-written (carbon copy) Additions in manuscript. "Authorities for the ancestry of Ann (Marbury) Hutchinson": 46th - 47th leaves.　"Refferences (!)": 224th leaf.　Contents. - Ancestors and descendants of Benjamin F. Wilbour and his wife Abby Maria Taylor of Little Compton, R. I. - Ancestors and descendants of Thomas Northupp Browne and his wife Ann Knowles of South Kingstown, R. I.　38-32650.

CS71.W666　1936

18646　WILBUR.　Wilbur, McKelvey (and) Ortley family (i.e. families) of central New Jersey.　By James Wilbur Clayton.　West Orange, N.J. (1961)　1 v. 38 cm.　62-35628.

CS71.W666　1961

WILBUR.　See also:　CLAYTON, 1942
　　　　　　　　　　CREW, 1941
　　　　　　　　　　PARSONS, 1924

WILBURN.　See WELBORN.

WILBY.　See SKEET, CS438.S5

WILCOCKSON.　See WILCOX.

18647　WILCOX.　The Wilcox family.　By W. H. Whitmore.　(From the Hist. and gen. register for Jan. 1875).　Boston, Printed by D. Clapp & son, 1875.　cover-title, 8 p. 25½ cm.　9-15497.
CS71.W667　1875

18648　WILCOX.　The descendants of William Wilcoxson, Vincent Meigs, and Richard Webb.　Comp. by Professor Reynold Webb Wilcox ... New York, T. A. Wright, 1893.　75, vii, (1) p. 24½ cm.　12-1893.
CS71.W667　1893

18649　WILCOX.　A Wilcox-Brown-Medbery genealogy.　Comp. by William Alonzo Wilcox. Scranton, Pa., Printed for the author, 1902.　36 p.　22 cm.　"Elmhurst signal print.　No. 8, seventy-five copies printed." Includes only those lines represented in Pennsylvania or descended from Pennsylvanians.　2-24591.　CS71.W667　1902

18650　WILCOX.　Wilcox family history.　Being some account of the first five generations in direct line from William Wilcockson of Stratford, Connecticut, to Josiah Wilcox of Brecksville, Ohio.　Comp. by Owen N. Wilcox.　Cleveland, O., 1911.　63, (2) p. 25½ cm.　13-31.　CS71.W667　1911

18651　WILCOX.　Ivy Mills, 1729-1866.　Willcox and allied families, by Joseph Willcox.　Baltimore, Printed by Lucas brothers, inc., 1911.　130 p.　front., illus., plates, ports., facsims.　23 cm.　Printed for private circulation. "The contents of this book ... were, with few exceptions, printed at various thimes in the Records of the American Catholic historical society." - Pref. 13-244.　CS71.W667　1911a

18652   WILCOX.   Ivy Mills, 1729-1866, Willcox and allied families.   Supplement - Memoir of Mrs. Mary Brackett Willcox, by Joseph Willcox.   (Philadelphia, Press of G. H. Buchanan company) Priv. print., 1917.   80 p.   front., illus. (facsim.) plates, ports. 23½ cm.   Contains genealogies of the Brackett, Odiorne, Gibbons, Coffin, Woodbridge, Dudley, Ward and other allied families.   17-11813.   CS71.W667   1917

18653   WILCOX.   A preliminary report on the descendants of William Wilcoxson, "Father of Con-necticutt" ... Compiled and issued by Thomas Wilcox ... Los Angeles, Calif. (1937)   1 p. l., iv, 138 p. 28½ cm.   Mimeographed.   37-38426.   CS71.W667   1937

18654   WILCOX.   Wilcoxson-Wilcox, Webb and Meigs families, by Reynold Webb Wilcox ... New York, The National historical society, 1938.   2 p. l., 9-395 p. front., pl., ports., coats of arms. 24½ cm.   Compiled by Georgia Cooper Washburn from material collected by Dr. Reynold Webb Wilcox before his death in 1931.   cf. Pref.   Webb appendix, by Harrison Emmett Webb: p. (213) - 223.   39-15944.   CS71.W667   1938

18655   WILCOX.   A portion of the descendents (!) of Edward Wilcox of Rhode Island ... Compiled and issued by Janet Barrett Fee ... White Plains, N.Y. (1941)   49 l. 28 cm.   Type-written (carbon copy) 43-1484.   CS71.W667   1941

18656   WILCOX.   Daniel Wilcox of Puncatest and the genealogy of some of his descendants, com-piled by Herbert A. Wilcox.   South Pasadena, Calif., 1943.   4 p. l., 7-158 p. plates, 2 port. (incl. front.) 22 cm. 44-8691.   CS71.W667   1943

18657   WILCOX.   From the bend of the little river, a Wilcox book; immigrant ancestors and allied families; with a sketch and the descendants of George Wilcox.   By Irene (Wilcox) Lord.   (Los Angeles? 1954)   167 p. illus. 23 cm. 56-2197.   CS71.W667   1954

18658   WILCOX.   Wilcoxson and allied families: Willcockson, Wilcoxen, Wilcox.   Compiled and published by Dorothy Ford Wulfeck.   Waterbury, Conn., Printed (by) Commercial Service, 1958. 505 p. illus. 29 cm. 59-21555.   CS71.W667   1958

18659   WILCOX.   Descendants of William Wilcoxson of Derbyshire, England, and Stratford, Connecticut.   By Thomas Wilcox.   Pasadena, Calif., 1963.   xix, 335 p. 29 cm. 63-59225.   CS71.W667   1963

         WILCOX.   See also:

BARBER, 1911	HUGHES, 1917	STEBBINS, 1940
BROCKWAY, E171.A53 vol.13	MEAD, 1945	WALLACE, 1928
CARD, E171.A53 vol.20	MERRILL, 1888	WHITMORE, 1875
COATES, 1901 a	NASH, 1902	WILLCOX.
CURTIS, 1912	RANNEY, F104.C8A2	

         WILCOXEN.   See WILCOX.

         WILCOXSON.   See WILCOX.

18660   WILD.   The Wildes family of Burlington County, New Jersey, by Charles Shepard.   Albany, N.Y., 1920.   geneal. tab.   31 x 50½ cm.   Blue print.   20-20632.   CS71.W669   1920

18661   WILD.   The ancestry of Dudley Wildes, 1759-1820, of Topsfield, Massachusetts.   By Walter Goodwin Davis.   Portland, Me., Anthoensen Press, 1959.   193 p. illus. 23 cm. 60-22691.
                                                                                                    CS71.W669   1959

         WILD.   See also: FLETCHER, 1957
                            KING, CS439.K7

         WILDBORE.   See WILBUR.

18662   WILDER.   Genealogy (of Marshall Pinckney Wilder)   "This contains the lineage of Mr. Wilder's family, arranged from the 'Book of the Lockes': the History of Hingham, by Hon. Solomon

18662 continued: Lincoln; the History of Leominster, by Hon. David Wilder; and from other sources." (n. p., 1867)   4 p. 25½ cm. 38M626T.   CS71.W671   1867

18663   WILDER.   Memoir of Marshall P. Wilder.   By John H. Sheppard ... Boston, D. Clapp & son, printers, 1867.   1 p. 1., 54 p. port. 24 cm.   Genealogy: p. 51-54.   "From the New England historical and genealogical register for April, 1867."   1-25856.   S417.W6S5

18664   WILDER.   Records from the life of S. V. S. Wilder ... New York, American tract society (1867)   404 p. front. (port.) 19½ cm.   16-8326.   CT275.W5586A3

18665   WILDER.   Book of the Wilders.   A contribution to the history of the Wilders, from 1497, in England, to the emigration of Martha, a widow, and her family to Massachusetts Bay, in 1638, and so, through her family down to 1875; with a genealogical table ... By Rev. Moses H. Wilder.   New York, Printed by E. O. Jenkins for the compiler, 1878.   xvi, 394 p. front. (pl.) ports. 24 cm.   Title vignette: coat of arms. 9-15496.   CS71.W671   1878

18666   WILDER.   Joseph Wilder and his descendants.   2d ed.   Pembroke (Me.) Printed by the compilers, 1902.   10 p. 19 cm.   Preface signed: Sidney A. Wilder, Gerald G. Wilder.   3-27029.
                                                                                   CS71.W671   1902

18667   WILDER.   Memorials of Mary Wilder White, by Elizabeth Amelia Dwight, ed. by Mary Wilder Tileston; a century ago in New England.   Boston, Mass., The Everett press company, 1903. xx, 409 p. pl., 8 port. (incl. front.) facsim. 23½ cm.   Appendix contains the Wilder, Flagg and White genealogy.   3-31005.
                                                                                   CT275.W546D8

18668   WILDER.   ... A genealogy of the Wilder family of Hawaii.   Prepared at the request of the genealogical committee.   Honolulu, T. H., Paradise of the Pacific press, 1916.   7 p. 24 cm.   (Hawaiian historical society.   Genealogical series, no. 2)   "500 copies."   22-18366.   CS2209.W5

18669   WILDER.   Extracts from the Book of the Wilders by which the lineage of the Rhode Island Wilders is traced to Nicholas Wilder of England, 1485.   Also a sketch of the Wilkinson family.   Compiled by Mary Rose (Wilder) Turner.   Springfield, O., 1927.   1 p. 1., 19 numb. 1., 2 1. plates, coat of arms. 23 cm. 33-25764.   CS71.W671   1927

18670   WILDER.   Wilder family pedigree chart.   Clark W. Wilder, b. Wendal, Mass., Aug 2, 1783 and wife Pede Robbins, b. Keene, N.H., Nov. 15, 1794.   (Somerville, Mass., 1940) double geneal. tab. 21 x 35½ cm.   Photostat (positive) 40M4075T.   CS71.W671   1940

18671   WILDER.   Wilder genealogy (from Nicholas to Elmira (Wilder) Bryant, 1829-1907.   By James Elmer Manning.   Boston, 1948)   (17) 1. 29 cm.   Title from label mounted on cover.   50-21405.   CS71.W671   1948

18672   WILDER.   Wilder families in the southeastern United States; a belated 'though very imcomplete (sic) report of such part of them, of their origins, of their migrations and of their genealogies, as could be found in a cursory search.   By William Murtha Wilder.   (Albany, Ga., 1951) 334 p. illus., ports., maps, col. coat of arms. 22 cm. 51-4730.   CS71.W671   1951

18673   WILDER.   Descendants of James Wilder and Susan Wilmarth, compiled by Margaret McGregor, Hattie McGregor (and) Mary McGregor Miller.   Springfield, Ohio, 1959.   16 1. 28 cm. "Concerned only with the branch which settled in Ohio, near Cincinnati, and in Springfield, Ohio." 60-36354.
                                                                                   CS71.W671   1959

18674   WILDER.   Wilder and some connecting (especially some Ware) families in the Southeastern United States of America; a belated, 'though very incomplete, report of such part of them, of their origins, of their migrations, and of their genealogies, as could be found in a cursory search.   (2d ed.)   Albany, Ga. (1960)   574 p. illus. 22 cm.   First published in 1951 under title: Wilder families in the Southeastern United States.   60-43301.   CS71.W671   1960

18675   —— Wilder and some connecting ... families, etc.   (3d ed.   Columbus, Ga., Printed by Columbus Office Supply Co.) 1969.   1312 p. illus., col. coat of arms, geneal. tables, maps. 22 cm.   First published in 1951 under title: Wilder families in the Southeastern United States.   74-96900 MARC.   CS71.W671   1969

WILDER.   See also L. C. Additions and corrections no. 24.

WILDER.   See also WHITE, 1900

18676   WILDERMUTH.   Johann David Wildermuth and his descendants, 1752-1964.   Compiled and edited by Ruth Kline Lee.   (Milwaukee?) 1965.   102, (21) p. (p. (21) blank for "Notes") illus., ports. 28 cm. 66-37945.   CS71.W672   1965

WILDES.   See WILD.

18677   WILDMAN.   Genealogy of Rounsevelle Wildman, jr., born in Washington, D. C., Jan. 3, 1893, son of Rounsevelle Wildman and Letitia Aldrich.   (Hongkong? 189-)   2 l. 25 cm. Caption title. Compiled by Rounsevelle Wildman. 9-15476.   CS71.W673   189-

18678   WILDMAN.   A genealogy of the descendants of Thomas Wildman, 1613-1689, of Bedford, N.Y. (formerly a township under Connecticut jurisdiction) with an account of the ancient Wildman family in England, 1085-1634 A.D.   Compiled by Charles Elwood Nash.   Southington, Conn., C.E. Nash & co., 1946-   pts. geneal. tab. 23 cm. Bibliographical foot-notes. 46-6719.   CS71.W673   1946

WILDMAN.   See also WATSON, 1967

18679   WILDRICK.   John Wildrick of New Jersey, 1707-1793; a genealogy of the descendants of his son George Wildrick, by William Clinton Armstrong, Blairstown, New Jersey.   New Brunswick, N.J., J. Heidingsfeld company, 1933.   67 p. front., plates, ports. 23 cm. 34-14608.   CS71.W674   1933

18680   WILDY.   The Wildy family, 1500-1955, their ancestral tree.   (Compiled and edited by Mable Pearl Wildy and Alexander Clark Monroe Wildy.   1st ed.   Belleville? Ill., c. 1955)   xv, 832 p. illus., ports., col. coats of arms, facsims. 28 cm. Includes hymns with music. 57-34905.   CS71.W6744   1955

18681   WILEY.   Wylie genealogy.   Compiled by E. G. Wylie.   St. Louis, Mo., 1899.   geneal. tab. 56 x 43 fold. to 28 x 22 cm. Descendants of Samuel Wylie. 1-6039.   CS71.W675   1899

18682   WYLIE.   Wylie genealogy.   By E. G. Wylie ... Related families mentioned herein are: Bird, Bliss, Chapman, Fry, Gray, Griswold, Lovett, Taylor, Winn, Woods, etc.   St. Louis, Mo., A. Noble print. co., 1900.   30 p., 1 l. pl., ports. 21½ cm. Oct. 4, 1900-170.   CS71.W675   1900

18683   WILEY.   Historical data concerning the Wylie, and approximately one hundred related family names.   Assembled and charted by Ernest Gray Wylie.   Des Moines, Ia., 1915.   geneal. tab. 35 x 68. (fold. to 35 x 9 cm.) Text in eight columns on verso of chart. Allied families: Bird, Chapman, Fry, Gray, Lovett, Woods and others. 17-15780.   CS71.W675   1915

18684   WILEY.   Garrett county history of pioneer families ... The Wiley family.   By Chas. E. Hoye.   (Oakland, Md., 1937)   mounted l. 35½ cm. Newspaper clipping. No. XCV of a series of articles contributed to the Mountain democrat. 41M3029T.   CS71.W675   1937

WILEY.   See also: ABBOT, 1936
                    LOVELL, 1958 (in addenda)
                    MAXWELL, 1916

18685   WILFORD.   The Wilford-Williford family treks into America, by Eurie Pearl Wilford Neel; and a reprint of Counties of Christian and Trigg, Kentucky, historical and biographical, edited by William Henry Perrin, 1884.   (Nashville? 1959)   2 pts. in 1 v. illus., ports., maps. 24 cm. (Western Kentucky pioneer series, v. 2) Title from spine. Each part has special t.-p. Bibliography: pt. 1, p. xxiii-xxvi. 60-40186.   CS71.W676   1959

WILFORD.   See also BACKHOUSE, DA690.M74C3

18686   WILGUS.   A few of the descendants of John Wilgus.   By Edgar Hobart.   (San Francisco, 1902)   p. 61-65. 24 cm. Caption title. Detached from California historic-genealogical society. Publication no. III. 1902. 38M1174T.   CS71.W678   1902

18687   WILHELM.   A history of the Wilhelms and the Wilhelm charge, by the Historical committee (of St. Paul's church, Meyersdale, Pa.)   Meyersdale, Pa., The Wilhelm press, 1919.
3 p. l., (9) - 205 p. incl. front., plates, ports.   23½ cm.   20-632.   BX9569.S6M4

WILHOIT.   See: MONNET, 1911
No. 3509 - Orange county.

WILKERSON.   See TUCK, 1964

18688   WILKES.   By an Oregon pioneer fireside, compiled by L. E. Wilkes.   Hillsboro, Or.   (Hillsboro printing co.) 1941.   5 p. l., 13-134, (10) p.   illus. (incl. ports.)   23½ cm.   "The main part of the history of these poeple was ... written by Thomas S. Wilkes." - Introd.   42-23788.   F876.W5

18689   WILKES.   Wilkes family data, compiled by Mamie Williamson, copied by William and Anne Fitzgerald.   (Florence? Ky.) 1954.   7 l.   28 cm.   55-19909.   CS71.W69   1954

18690   WILKES.   The Wilkes chronology; an historical and genealogical document.   By Charles Denby Wilkes.   Vevey, Switzerland, Print, priv. by Société anonyme de l'impr. & lithographie Klausfelder, 1959.   67 p.   illus.   21 cm.   Cover title.   60-34429.   CS71.W679   1959

18691   WILKES.   Wilkes family history and genealogy; Thomas Wilkes (ca. 1735-1809) and his descendants.   By Ivan Ernest Bass.   Washington, 1965.   xvii, 621 p.   illus., facsims., ports.   24 cm.   66-756.
CS71.W679   1965

WILKES.   See also WILKS.

WILKEY.   See WILKIE.

18692   WILKIE.   A history of Louis Wilkey and Elizabeth (Glaeser) Wilkey and their descendants ... (by) Harry L. Wilkey.   (n. p., 1938?)   1 p. l., 9 numb. l.   35 cm.   Caption title.   Reproduced from type-written copy.
39-32312.   CS71.W68   1938

WILKIE.   See also: McCALL. CS478.M15
WOOD, DA690.C555H3

18693   WILKIN.   Robert Wilkin (1766-1835) and Mary (Hyde) Wilkin, their parents and descendants; a genealogy by Flora McIntyre and Lula M. Wilkin.   (Pasadena? Calif., 1962?)   xv, 802 p.   coat of arms.
22 cm.   63-26879.   CS71.W684   1962

18694   WILKIN.   The Wilkin family.   By Frances Bogue Salvino.   (1968?)   2 v. in l.   29 cm.   Binder's title: The Wilkin-Eylar families (by) Salvino.   Vol. 2 has title: The Eylar family, compiled by Frances Bogue Salvino (Mrs. Anthony William Salvino)   Typescript (carbon copy) 79-6039 MARC.   CS71.W684   1968

18695   WILKIN.   Wilkin family in vertical file.   Ask reference librarian for this material.

18696   WILKINS.   The family of Wilkins, compiled by Evalyn Park Selby Johnson (Mrs. Palmer W. Johnson) ... (Marion, S. C.) 1937.   3 p. l., (9) - 88 p.   24 cm.   39-32997.   CS71.W686   1937

18697   WILKINS.   The family of Bray Wilkins, "Patriarch of Will's hill," of Salem (Middleton) Mass., by William Carroll Hill ... Milford, N.H., The Cabinet press, 1943.   xi, 213 p.   front., plates, ports.   22½ cm.
44-1006.   CS71.W686   1943

18698   WILKINS.   The 16 children of Capt. William Wilkins and wife, Ann Elizabeth Terrell of Virginia and South Carolina.   By Celeste Jane (Terrell) Barnhill.   (Washington, 1943)   1 l.   28 cm.
Caption title; typewritten (carbon copy) Copied by George Magruder Battey.   48-39394 *.   CS71.W686   1943a

WILKINS.   See also: COOCH, 1962   WARREN, 1884
DAVIS, 1941   WEBB, 1919
HOUSTON, 1914   No. 430 - Adventurers of purse and person.

18699   WILKINSON.   Memoirs of the Wilkinson family in America.   Comprising genealogical and biographical sketches of Lawrance Wilkinson of Providence, R. I., Edward Wilkinson of New Milford, Conn., John Wilkinson of Attleborough, Mass., Daniel Wilkinson of Columbia Co., N.Y. ... and their descendants from 1645-1868.   By Rev. Israel Wilkinson, A.M. ... Jacksonville, Ill., Davis & Peniman, printers, 1869.   1 p. l., iv, 585 p. 22 cm. 9-17831.   CS71.W687   1869

18700   WILKINSON.   Wilkinson and Irvine (families) by Gladys Wilkinson Lawrence. (n.p., 1933?)
cover-title, 22, (10), 23-36, (6) p.   illus., plates, ports.   22 cm.   35-14586.   CS71.W687   1933

18701   WILKINSON.   A daughter of Maryland was the mother of Texas, Mrs. Jane Herbert (Wilkinson) Long, by Alexander H. Bell ... (Washington, D.C., The Law reporter printing company, 1937)
142 p.   23½ cm.   Running title: Genealogy of Jane Herbert (Wilkinson) Long.   37-16803.   CS71.W687   1937

18702   WILKINSON.   Genealogy of Wilkinson and kindred families.   By Marcellus McCowen Wilkinson.   Shelby, Shelby Book Store, 1949.   546 p. illus., ports., coats of arms. 24 cm. Errata slip inserted.
54-31055.   CS71.W687   1949

18703   WILKINSON.   The Wilkinson book.   By Clarence Cannon.   (Elsberry? Mo.) 1957.
94 p. 29 cm. 58-40729.   CS71.W687   1957

        WILKINSON.   See also: ALEXANDER, 1892
                                 BARLOW, 1891
                                 COLLOT D'ESCURY, 1896
                                 JAMES, 1913a
                                 WILDER, 1927

        WILKS.   See: DAVIS, 1927a
                      TODD, 1867

18704   WILLARD.   The Willard memoir; or, Life and times of Major Simon Willard; with notices of three generations of his descendants, and two collateral branches in the United States; also, some account of the name and family in Europe from an early day.   By Joseph Willard ... Boston, Phillips, Sampson & co., 1858.   xiii p., 1 l., 470 p., 1 l. front., plates, coat of arms. 23 cm. 9-18748.

                                                                                                     CS71.W695   1858

18705   WILLARD.   Willard genealogy, sequel to Willard memoir; materials gathered chiefly by Joseph Willard and Charles Wilkes Walker, ed. and completed by Charles Henry Pope.   Boston, Mass., Printed for the Willard family association, 1915.   viii, 768 p. front., pl., ports., fold. facsim. 24½ cm. 15-27575.
                                                                                                     CS71.W695   1915

18706   WILLARD.   Willard-Peabody genealogy, together with other interesting and historical data. Edited and compiled by Eugene Willard Montgomery.   Galena, Ill., 1915.   cover-title, 2 p. l., 21, 26 p.
illus. (mounted coat of arms) 21 cm. 24-25462.   CS71.W695   1915a

18707   WILLARD.   Heroic Willards of '76; life and times of Captain Reuben Willard of Fitchburg, Mass., and his lineal descendants, from 1775 to date; profusely embellished with authentic portraits not heretofore available; register of Willards in the revolution, and other wars, chonology of the George Willards, comp. by James Andrew Phelps.   New York, N.Y., Issued by the Genealogical bureau, 1917.   xi, 112 p., 1 l. plates, ports., coats of arms. 23½ cm. 17-15673.   CS71.W695   1917

18708   WILLARD.   A memorial to Henry Augustus Willard and Sarah Bradley Willard (by) Henry Kellogg Willard.   (Andover, Mas.) Priv. print., 1925.   xxvi, 376 p. incl. plates, ports., geneal. tables, coats of arms. fold. pl. 29½ cm.   Cover-title, half-title and running title: Willard-Bradley memoirs.   26-5448.   CS71.W695   1925

18709   WILLARD.   Twigs and branches; a Willard descendant tells of her family in America.   By Frances Cora (Ward) Wolfe.   (Chicago, 1953)   A - J, 100, K - Z p. illus., ports., geneal. table. 27 x 37 cm.
Additions and corrections in ms.   Most of the illustrative matter is mounted.   54-35813.   CS71.W695   1953

WILLARD.   See also: BARRETT, F74.C8P8   McINTOSH, F129.C36M2
                       CORK, Virginia C.   (In   MARSH, 1935
                          vertical file)   SAUNDERS, 1897
                       ELLIS, F3T61   VAN RENSSELAER, CS69.S7

18710   WILLAUER.   The Willauer family.   By Aaron L. Willouer.   (Philadelphia?) c.1960.
187 p.   illus.   24 cm.   61-20152.   CS71.W696   1960

18711   WILLCOMB.   Will cuma; or, Historical and genealogical notes on the Willcomb family.   By
Oliver Clifton Willcomb.   Lynn, Mass., L. C. Parker, 1892.   1 card.   7½ x 12½ cm.   Microprint copy.   Collation
of the original: 48 p.   illus.   19 cm.   Micp. 58-63.   Microcard CS 71

18712   WILLCOMB.   Genealogy of the Willcomb family of New England (1655-1902) Together with
a condensed history of the town of Ipswich, Mass. ... By Oliver Clifton Willcomb.   Lynn, Mass.,
1902.   viii (9), 302 p. incl. front., illus., plates, ports.   22 cm.   "Limited edition." p. 282 - 290 are blank.   3-20249.
                                                                          CS71.W697   1902

WILLCOCKSON.   See WILCOX.

WILLCOX.   See WILCOX.

WILLCOXEN.   See WILCOX.

WILLCOXON.   See HARROUN, 1964

WILLCOXSON.   See WILCOX.

WILLEMSEN.   See WILLIAMSON.

WILLENBORG.   See SCHARNAGEL, 1960

WILLET.   See WILLETT.

WILLETS.   See WILLETT.

18713   WILLETT.   Captain Thomas Willett, (the first mayor of New York.)   A paper read before
the New York genealogical and biographical society in New York, 13th June, 1890, by Thomas C.
Cornell.   With some notes of the Willitts.   (Being chapter XVII.) of Adam and Anne Mott, their ancestors and their descendants.   By Thomas C. Cornell ... Printed for the family.   Poughkeepsie,
N.Y., A. V. Haight, printer, 1890. 1 p. l.   (236)-251, 251 A -D p. illus. (facsims.)port. 27½cm. 7-7628.   CS71.W713   1890

18714   WILLETT.   Ancestors and descendants of James and Ann Willits of Little Egg Harbor, N.J.
By Alfred C. Willits ... (Philadelphia, J. B. Lippincott co.) 1898. 30 p. 24 cm. 1-20888.
                                                                          CS71.W713   1898

18715   WILLETT.   The Willet (Willets - Willett - Willits) genealogy, a compilation of all the
branches in England and America, by J. E. Bookstäver.   Binghamton, N.Y., Twentieth century publish-
ing company, 1906.   4 p. l., 142 numb. l., 4, ii-xvii, 13 l.   col. pl. (coat of arms) ports.   23½ cm.   Blue-print. 7-41058.
                                                                          CS71.W713   1906

18716   WILLETT.   Mary Browne; the true life and times of the daughter of Mr. John Browne, gent.,
commissioner of the United Colonies of New England; the wife of the Worshipful Thomas Willett,
merchant, captain and governor's assistant of New Plymouth, first English mayor of New York.   The
beginning of our United States of America and the important part played by the merchants.   Strung together from histories and records, by Elizabeth Nicholson White.   (Providence, R. I., Priv. print. for
the author by the Roger Williams press, E. A. Johnson company) 1935.   5 p. l., 3-266 p. incl. mounted front.
21½ cm.   "References": p. 245-248.   36-15246.   F7.W54

WILLETT.   See also: DAVOL, 1925   ODELL, 1960 a
                       HAVILAND, 1914   POWELL, F127.L8B9
                       LETTON, 1955

18717   WILLEY.   ... Family memorial of Darius Willey and wife, with their children.   August 15th, 1865 ... San Francisco, Bacon & company, printers, 1868.   141 p. 18 cm. "Printed for the use of the family." 39-12223.   CS71.W714   1868

18718   WILLEY.   A sketch of the destruction of the Willey family by the White Mountain slide, on the night of August 28, 1826, related by Edward Melcher, the only survivor of the party who discovered and removed the bodies of the unfortunate family from the ruins, on the 31st day of August, 1826. Lancaster, N.H., J. S. Peavey, printer, 1880.   1 p. l., 25 p. 17 cm. 19-8794.   F41.44 M51

18719   WILLEY.   Preliminary outline of the descendants of Isaac Willey, of New London, Conn. By Henry Willey ... New Bedford, Mass., E. Anthony & sons, 1886.   15 p. 22½ cm. 9-15468.   CS71.W714   1886

18720   WILLEY.   Isaac Willey of New London, Conn., and his descendants.   By Henry Willey ... New Bedford, Mass., Printed for the author (by E. Anthony & sons) 1888.   2 p. l., vi, 1 l., 166, 17 p. 24½ cm. No. 204. 9-15475.   CS71.W714   1888

18721   WILLEY.   The Willey slide; its history, legend, and romance ... A narrative giving briefly the history of Crawford Notch and the Willey slide, also the Soltaire legend and the Nancy romance. By Rev. Guy Roberts.   1st ed.   (Littletown, N. H., Courier printing co.) c. 1923.   42 p. 1 l. illus. 16 x 8 cm.   CA 23-201 unrev.   F41.6.C8R6

18722   —— The Willey slide ... 2nd ed. ... (Littleton, N. H., The Courier printing company) c. 1924.   43, (1) p. illus. 16 cm. 24-7735.   F41.6.C8R61

18723   WILLEY.   Stevens, Clough and Willey families.   In vertical file.   Ask reference librarian for this material.

WILLEY.   See also addenda.

WILLHIDE.   See SHEIBLEY, 1924

18724   WILLIAMS.   The genealogy and history of the family of Williams in America, more particularly of the descendants of Robert Williams, of Roxbury.   By Stephen W. Williams ... Greenfield (Mass.) Printed by Merriam & Mirick, 1847.   xxiv, (17) - 424 p. front., ports., coat of arms. 19 cm.   Index compiled by Mrs. J. M. Brumbaugh: 1 l. 48 p. inserted at end. 9-15474.   CS71.W72   1847

18725   WILLIAMS.   A sketch of the history of the family of Williams of Cowley Grove, in the parish of Hillingdon, Middx., and of Cote, near Bampton, Oxon.   Hillingdon, The Lodge, 1852. 22 p., 1 l. front. (coat of arms) port., fold. geneal. tab. 22½ cm. Dedication signed: Benjamin Williams. 20-15244.   CS439.W525

18726   WILLIAMS.   The Williams family, tracing the descendants of Thomas Williams of Roxbury, Mass.   Comp. by George Huntington Williams, with a preface by Prof. S. Wells Williams ... Boston, Printed for private distribution, 1880.   15 p. 26½ cm. "Reprinted from the New England historical and genealogical register for January, 1880." 16-4784.   CS71.W72   1880

18727   WILLIAMS.   The Williams family, tracing the descendants of Ezekiel Williams of Roxbury, Mass., compiled by Thomas W. Seward, Utica, N.Y.   Reprinted from the N. E. historical and genealogical register for July, 1882.   Boston, Printed for private distribution, 1882.   17 p. 25½ cm. 24-5156.   CS71.W72   1882

18728   WILLIAMS.   The Providence Plantations for two hundred and fifty years ... By Welcome Arnold Greene, and a large corps of writers.   Providence, R. I., J. A. & R. A. Reid, 1886. 3 p. l., (11) - 468, (2) p. incl. front., illus. 37 cm. Half-title on recto of frontispiece. "The reunion of the descendants of Roger Williams ... with the roll of those who attended": p. 466-468. Rc-3042.   F89.P9G8

18729   WILLIAMS.   The surnames and coats of arms of the Williamses, with an account of Robert Williams of Roxbury, and some of his descendants.   Comp. by A. D. Weld French.   (Boston) Priv. print. (by T. R. Marvin & son, 1886)   26 p., 1 l. 23 cm. 9-15473.   CS71.W72   1886

18730   WILLIAMS.   The descendants of Veach Williams, of Lebanon, Conn., who was of the fifth generation from Robert Williams, who came from England in 1637, and settled at Roxbury, Mass. Also, the ancestry of Lucy Walsworth, wife of Veach Williams.   By Alexander Hamilton Wright ... New Haven, Tuttle, Morehouse & Taylor, printers, 1887.   128, 35, 23, (1) p.   25 cm.   9-15472.

CS71.W72   1887

18731   WILLIAMS.   Ancestry of thirty-three Rhode Islanders (born in the eighteenth century); also twenty-seven charts of Roger Williams' descendants to the fifth generation, and an account of Lewis Latham, falconer to King Charles I; with a chart of his American descendants to the fourth generation, and a list of 180 existing portraits of Rhode Island governors, chief justices, senators, etc. ... By John Osborne Austin.   Albany, N.Y., J. Munsell's sons, 1889.   2 p. l., 139 (i.e. 141) p.   35 cm.   Verso of each leaf blank except page (128), which has recto blank.   Pages 128-141 erroneously numbered 126-139.   8-18608.

F78.A93

18732   WILLIAMS.   The Groves, and Lappan; (Monaghan County, Ireland).   An account of a pilgrimage thither, in search of the genealogy of the Williams family.   By John Fletcher Williams ... Saint Paul, Priv. print. for the family, 1889.   68 p.   illus., diagr.   24½ cm.   An edition of 150 copies printed.   9-15471.

CS71.W72   1889

18733   WILLIAMS.   Robert Williams of Roxbury, Mass., and his descendants.   Four generations. By Edward H. Williams, jr. ... Newport, R.I., 1891.   29 p., 1 l.   23 cm.   Reprinted from the Magazine of New England history, vol. 1, 1891.   p. 65-91.   Addenda, 1 l.   9-15470.

CS71.W72   1891

18734   WILLIAMS.   Richard Williams of Taunton, and his connection with the Cromwell family ... (Boston, 1897)   4 p.   24 cm.   Signed Josiah H. Drummond.   Caption title.   Reprinted from the New Eng. hist. and geneal. register for April, 1897.   9-15469.

CS71.W72   1897

18735   WILLIAMS.   Genealogical notes of the Williams and Gallup families, especially relating to the children of Caleb M. and Sabra Gallup Williams, descendants of Robert Williams of Roxbury, and Capt. John Gollop, sr. of Boston, Mass. ... (by) Charles Fish Williams ... Hartford, Conn., Press of the Case, Lockwood & Brainard company, 1897.   136 p.   front., illus. (incl. facsims.) ports., fold. geneal. tab., coats of arms.   23½ cm.   "The royal descent of Mrs. Hannah Lake Gallup, the wife of Captain John Gallup, jr.": geneal. tab. between p. 30 - 31. Blank pages at end for "Family record."   20-9257.

CS71.W72   1897a

18736   WILLIAMS.   Genealogy of Samuel Williams, of Grafton, N.H., fifth in descent from Richard Williams, of Taunton.   By Josiah H. Drummond.   Portland, Smith & Sale, printers, 1899. 20 p.   23½ cm.   9-17841.

CS71.W72   1899

18737   WILLIAMS.   The ancestors and descendants of Ezekiel Williams of Wethersfield, 1608-1907. Comp. by Mary Dyer (Williams) McLean.   (Hartford, The Case. Lockwood & Brainard company print) priv. print., 1907.   91, (1) p.   23 cm.   Edited by Charles M. Andrews.   13-2606.   CS71.W72   1907

18738   WILLIAMS.   Genealogy of the Williams family, descendants of George Williams, comp. by Richard J. Williams, jr.   Germantown, Penna., 1908.   3 p. l., (9) - 88 p.   28 cm.   15-6391.

CS71.W72   1908

18739   WILLIAMS.   The family of John Williams of Newbury and Haverhill, Mass.   By Cornelia Bartow Williams.   Boston, New England historic genealogical society, 1908.   10 p.   23 cm.   Reprinted from the New England historical and genealogical register for April, 1908.   17-6156.

CS71.W72   1908a

18740   WILLIAMS.   Williams genealogy, Wethersfield Cromwell branch.   Comp. by Murray Edward Poole.   (Ithaca, N.Y.), Press of the Ithaca Journal, 1910.   43 p.   23 cm.   Cover title: Ancestry and descendants of Josiah Williams, Cromwell, Conn. 1656 - 1910.   10-16181.

CS71.W72   1910

18741   WILLIAMS.   The Rev. Comfort Williams, first settled pastor in Rochester, N.Y., 1783-1825. With memoranda regarding family history; also an address. (Rochester, N.Y., 1910?)   34 p. incl. front. (port.) fold. geneal. tab.   23 cm.   Foreword signed: C. M. W. i.e. Charles Miller Williams.   11-31.

CS71.W72   1910a

18742   WILLIAMS.   Ancestry of General Sir William Fenwick Williams, of Kars, and incidentally a maternal line of the present marquis of Donegal.   Including genealogical sketches of the historic Annapolis royal families of Winniett, Dyson, Williams and Walker, and their connections, and a biographical sketch of the general.   By Judge A. W. Savary ... Exeter, W. Pollard & co., ltd., printers, 1911.   1 p. l., 15 p. port. 23½ cm. Reprinted from "The Genealogist, " n.s., vol. XXVII. 12-17271.   CS84.W6

18743   WILLIAMS.   History of the John and Lydia Rutan branch of the Williams family.   (Scranton, Prendergast press, 1914?)   42 p. 16 cm. Preface signed: Alvinza D. Williams. 19-4286.
CS71.W72   1914

18744   WILLIAMS.   Ancestry of Lawrence Williams: part I, Ancestry of his father, Simeon Breed Williams, descendant of John Williams of Newbury and Haverhill, Mass., 1600-1674; part II, Ancestry of his mother, Cornelia Johnston, descendant of Thomas Johnston of Boston, Mass., 1708-1767. Comp. by Cornelia Bartow Williams.   Chicago, Priv. print. (R. R. Donnelley and sons company) 1915.   291 p., 1 l. double front., illus. (coat of arms) plates, ports., facsims., fold. geneal. tables. 24½ cm. "This edition is limited to one hundred copies of which this is no. 100." 16-1387.   CS71.W72   1915

18745   WILLIAMS.   Early American families, the Williams, Moore, McKitrick, Fonda, Van Alen, Lanning, King, Justice, Cunningham, Longacre, Swanson and Cox families, with numerous related families, embracing the ancestors of perhaps 100,000 or more covering over 330 years, from 1580 to 1916 ... By Rev. W. A. Williams, D.D. ... Philadelphia (The author, 1916)   48 p. 8 pl. 21 cm. The plates, printed on both sides, consist of family portraits. 17-18480.   CS71.W72   1916

18746   WILLIAMS.   The Williams family of Virginia.   (Chattanooga, 1917?)   (3) p. 30 cm. (Notable southern families) Detached from the Lookout. 55-49904.   CS71.W72   1917

18747   WILLIAMS.   The Williams history, tracing the descendants in America of Robert Williams of Ruthin, North Wales, who settled in Carteret County, North Carolina, in 1763. Comp. by his great-grandson Milton Franklin Williams ... Ed. by H. M. Plaisted.   (St. Louis) M. F. Williams, 1921.   xxiv p., 1 l., 608 p. incl. front., illus., ports., facsims., coats of arms. plates (1 fold.) 31 cm. Blank pages for "Memoranda" (607 - 608) 21-20895.   CS71.W72   1921

18748   WILLIAMS.   Ancestry and posterity of Richard Williams of Taunton, Mass., by Charles C. Williams, M.D.   Los Angeles, Calif., 1924.   800 l. illus. (coat of arms) 28 cm. Type-written. 26-9530.   CS71.W72   1924

18749   WILLIAMS.   Descendants of John Williams of Newbury and Haverhill, Mass., 1600-1674. Compiled by Cornelia Bartow Williams ... and Anna Perkins Williams ... Chicago, Priv. print., 1925.   179, (1) p. double front., plates, ports., facsim., fold. geneal. tab., coat of arms. 24 cm. "This edition is limited to one hundred copies of which this is no. 18." 25-9457.   CS71.W72   1925

18750   WILLIAMS.   In memoriam, Harry L. Cole, Helen Elizabeth Cole.   (n. p.) Priv. print., 1926.   4 l. viii p. front., port. 23 cm. "Addendum. Williams line to Helen Elizabeth (Williams) Cole": p. i-viii. 32-32178.   CT275.C6775 I6

18751   WILLIAMS.   Ancestors and descendants of Joshua Williams, a Mayflower descendant and pioneer, by Gleason L. Archer ... Boston, Wright & Potter printing company, 1927.   63 p. 24 cm. 28-2223.   CS71.W72   1927

18752   WILLIAMS.   The families of Joshua Williams of Chester County, Pa., and John McKeehan of Cumberland County, Pa., with some allied families, compiled by Bessie P. Douglas.   Minneapolis, Minn., Augsburg press, 1928.   5 p. l., (13)-476 p., 1 l., (26) p. front., illus., plates, ports., facsims. 23½ cm. "Books and records quoted": 1 page after p. 476. 29-2117.   CS71.W72   1928

18753   WILLIAMS.   Genealogy, John Williams and Thankful Barlow, Benajah Tomson and Prudence Eldredge, compiled, 1931 by Charles Tomlin ... Clarence R. Brooks ... (n.p., 1931)   84 p. illus. (incl. ports.) 23½ cm. 31-35124.   CS71.W72   1931a

18754   WILLIAMS.   A partial historical and biographical genealogy of the descendants of John Williams, the English emigrant to America.   Compiled by Elisha M. Williams ... also Chronology of

18754 continued: the John H. Williams family, compiled by his daughter, Mrs. Laura Batdorf ...
Jackson, Tenn., McCowat-Mercer, 1931.   24 p. illus. (ports.) 18½ cm. "Henry Clay Williams, son of Elisha and Hanna
Williams": 1 fold. leaf inserted between p. 6 and 7. "Genealogy of the descendants of Elisha Williams; the Laura Ann Williams branch of the
family, compiled by E. M. Williams ... Jackson, Tenn., 1932": (4) p. inserted between p. 8 and 9. "Genealogy of the descendents (!) of Elisha
Williams; the Jeremiah McLene Williams branch of the family, compiled by E. M. Williams ... Jackson, Tenn., 1932": (4) p. inserted between
p. 12 and 13. "Genealogy of the descendants of John Williams; the Jeremiah Williams, jr. branch of Jeremiah Williams family, compiled by
D. O. Williams, Galion, O., 1932": (7) p. inserted at end. 33-6865.

CS71.W72   1931b

18755   WILLIAMS.   William J. Williams, portrait painter, and his descendants; family records, by
John F. Williams, jr. ... (Buffalo, Print. by C. C. Brock, c.1933)   4 p. l., 3-55, (2) p. col. front., plates,
ports., facsims., forms. 26½ cm. "Only 100 copies of this book were printed. This is number 82." "References": p. 55. Blank pages for
"Additions, clippings, etc." and "Autographs" (2 at end) 33-11233.

ND237.W718W5

—— Copy 2.

CS71.W72   1933

18756   WILLIAMS.   Old bayou Teche days, by one who lived and loved them, Lucy Williams Metcalf.
New Orleans, La., 1933.   1 p. l., 12 p. 5 port. on 1 pl. 22½ cm. "Genealogical data of the Williams family": p. 4-8.
34-23507.

CS71.W72   1933a

18757   WILLIAMS.   Old Bayou Teche days, by one who lived and loved them, Lucy Williams Metcalf.
(2. ed.) New Orleans, La. (1934)   cover-title, 12 p. 5 port. on 1 pl. 23 cm. "Genealogical data of the Williams family ..":
p. 4-8. 35-3355.

CS71.W72   1934a

18758   WILLIAMS.   The life, ancestors and descendants of Robert Williams of Roxbury in His
Majesty's province of Massachusetts bay in New England, 1607 - 1693; with biographical sketches of
the Rev. John Williams ... the Rev. Col. Elisha Williams ... Col. Ephraim Williams ... Col. William
Williams ... the Hon. Thomas Scott Williams ... the Rt. Rev. John Williams ... and of many other
descendants.   Together with a description and history of the coat-of-arms of the family by Harrison
Williams, LL.B.   Washington, D.C., W. F. Roberts company, 1934.   xi, 215, (1) p. front. (coat of arms)
1 illus. 23½ cm. "This edition limited to 300 copies of which this is no. 2." Bibliography: p. 207-209. 34-9036.

CS71.W72   1934

18759   WILLIAMS.   Emmanuel Williams of Taunton, Mass., a genealogy of some of his descendants
... by J. Oliver Williams. Brookline, Mass., 1935.   36 numb. l. 18 cm. 39M256T.

CS71.W72   1935

18760   WILLIAMS.   Old Bill Williams, mountain man, by Alpheus H. Favour.   Chapel Hill, The
University of North Carolina press (c.1936)   6 p. l., 229 p. incl. geneal. tab. col. front., plates, ports., fold. map,
facsims. 24 cm. Maps on lining-papers. Bibliography: p. (207) - 218. 36-10261.   F592.W672

18761   WILLIAMS.   Roger Williams descendants (five generations)   (Providence, R.I.) Roger
Williams family association, 1937.   (33) p. 23 cm. Title vignette (seal of the Association) 41-10334.

CS71.W72   1937

18762   WILLIAMS.   I remember; being the memoirs of Mrs. John Herndon (Maria Aurelia Williams)
James together with contemporary historical events and sketches of her own and her husand's families.
Edited and compiled by Charles Albert Sloane.   San Antonio, Tex., The Naylor company, 1938.
4 p. l., 301 p. front., ports., facsim. 21½ cm. Bibliography: p. 249. 39-142.   CT275.J295A3

18763   WILLIAMS.   A genealogy of Williams families, by J. Oliver Williams.   Brookline, Mass.,
1938.   5 p. l., 215 p. front., plates, ports., coats of arms. 24 cm. Research on the Emmanuel Williams line was started by Elisha C.
Leonard and Josiah H. Drummond. Part 2 published separately in 1935. - pt. 1. William Williams of New London county, Groton and
Ledyard, Connecticut, a genealogy of some of his descendants. - pt. 2. Emmanuel Williams of Taunton, Massachusetts, a genealogy of some of
his descendants. 38-5550.

CS71.W72   1938

18764   WILLIAMS.   James Tate Williams, his family and recollections, by Joseph Vincent Williams.
(Kingsport, Tenn., Kingsport press) 1938.   xiv, 250 p. front., pl., ports., facsim. 22 cm. Author's autographed presentation copy to the Library of Congress. 39-226,

CS71.W72   1938a

18765   WILLIAMS.   Genealogical table of the Williams family.   (n.p., 1939?)   9 l. 35 x 21½ cm.
Caption title. Type-written. 41M2958T.

CS71.W72   1939

18766   WILLIAMS.   The life and work of William Williams, M. P. for Coventry 1835-1847, M. P. for Lambeth 1850-1865, by Daniel Evans.   Llandyssul, South Wales, Gomerian press (1939) 3 p. l., (3) - 372 p., 1 l.   front., plates, ports., fold. geneal. tables.   23½ cm.   41-4397.   DA565. W56E85

18767   WILLIAMS.   Sidelights on Williams family history, by Carl Williams.   (Fort Pierce, Fla., 1940)   1 p. l., (5) - 89 p.   illus. (incl. port.) 20 cm.   Bibliography: p. 7.   40-8335.   CS71.W72   1940

18768   WILLIAMS.   Memoirs of a nonagenarian; some links with the Charleston of colonial days through the Williams-Roper families.   Compiled by John William Soady, 1940.   Richmond, Va., The Dietz press, 1940.   2 p. l., (3) - 36, (6) p.   front., plates, ports.   24½ cm.   Six blank pages at end ofr "Notes."   41-13410.
CS71.W72   1940a

18769   WILLIAMS.   Williams genealogy, by Mrs. Cora L. Williams Duvall.   (Hollywood, Calif., Melton printing co., c. 1941)   3 p. l., 58, (12) p.   ports., x fold. geneal. tab.   22 cm.   Eleven pages at end for additional "Family record," seven blank and four with facsimile reproductions from Williams family record.   41-20664.   CS71.W72   1941

18770   WILLIAMS.   Roger Williams of Providence, R. I.   (Compiled and published by Mrs. C. W. (Bertha Williams Anthony) and Mrs. C. H. (Harriett Wood Weeden)   Cranston, R. I., 1949) 220 p. illus.   27 cm.   Title from spine.   Coat of arms of the Roger Williams Family Association on cover.   "Contains the genealogical records of the Roger Williams Family Association."   50-1128.   CS71.W72   1949

18771   WILLIAMS.   Williams and Murphy records and related families.   By Robert Murphy Williams. Raleigh, N. C., Edwards & Broughton Co., 1949.   369 p.   illus.   23 cm.   53-34310.
CS71.W72   1949b

18772   WILLIAMS.   History of the Williams, Dressler families.   By William Morris Williams. (Tower Hill, Ill., 1949)   (52) p.   illus., ports.   30 cm.   Cover title.   50-26171.   CS71.W72   1949a

18773   WILLIAMS.   Williams-Enoch genealogy, with allied families; genealogy, history, biography, tradition, legends, anecdotes.   By Mabel C. Bean.   (Ann Arbor? 1953)   206 p.   illus., ports., coats of arms. 29 cm.   54-20077.   CS71.W72   1953

18774   WILLIAMS.   List of descendants of John Davis and Hannah Davis Williams.   Part I compiled by Louise Case, 1905; part II, additional information in-so-far as available, compiled by Eleanor H. D. Pearse, 1952-1954.   (Winnetka? Ill., 1954)   40 l.   22 cm.   54-35804.   CS71.W72   1954

18775   WILLIAMS.   American ancestry of Pryor Williams, an 1817 pioneer of Lawrence County, Indiana; the story of a Quaker heritage, by Ben F. Dixon and Alice L. (Dwelle) Dixon.   San Diego, Calif. (1959)   18 l.   facsims., geneal. table, ports.   30 cm.   65-70303.   CS71.W72   1959

18776   WILLIAMS.   Days before yesterday: a letter by Samuel Merrifield Bemiss (and) a few old letters.   (Richmond?) Privately printed, 1961.   44 p.   26 cm.   Fold. geneal. table mounted on lining paper.   61-9927.
CS71.W72   1961

18777   WILLIAMS.   The family history of John and Mary Williams, Quaker pioneers of Wayne County, Indiana, with four generations of their ancestors, and four (or more) generations of descendants, by Maude McCorkindale Bercich and Ethel McCorkindale.   San Diego, Calif., Family Historians, 1963.   vii, 79 l.   illus., ports.   29 cm.   (Benjamin Franklin junior historical series, no. 8)   Cover title: Your Quaker pioneers, John and Mary Williams, Wayne County, Indiana.   Bibliography: leaf 79.   65-1395.
CS71.W72   1963

18778   WILLIAMS.   Captain Isaac Williams and his grand children; the story of a fighting Quaker and three generations of Indiana pioneers, by Ben F. and Alice L. Dixon.   San Diego, Calif., Family Historians, 1963.   71 l.   illus., facsims., maps, ports.   30 cm.   (Benjamin Franklin junior historical series no. 7)   65-1394.
CS71.W72   1963a

18779   WILLIAMS.   Biographical record of Daniel and Mary (Jackson) Williams, early Kentucky pioneers.   Including portraits and biographies of their children: Thomas Williams, Daniel Jackson Williams, John Williams, Elijah Williams, Sarah Williams, Katharine (Williams) Orr, Mary (Williams)

18779 continued: Forsythe and their descendants, 1752-1898. Together with portrait and biography of Andrew Jackson, the seventh President of the United States; also photo-engraving of an old Williams' Homestead in Woodford County, Kentucky, where Daniel Williams, the pioneer and an officer in the Revolutionary War, died. Baltimore, 1898. (Lexington) University of Kentucky Library, 1964.
27 p. 29 cm. (Kentucky reprints, 2) Portrait and biography of Andrew Jackson and photo-engraving of the Williams' homestead lacking in the reprint. 64-64830.

F446.K59 no.2

18780 WILLIAMS. These are mine; one Williams family lineage. By Irene Williams. Washington, 1964. 149 p. illus., coat of arms, facsims., ports. 29 cm. Additions and corrections in MS. Bibliography: p. 139-141.
64-6288.

CS71.W72 1964

18781 WILLIAMS. Fifty-six generations; an ancestral journey through history, a genealogy compiled by John F. Williams II. San Diego, 1965. 108 p. illus., coats of arms (1 mounted col.) maps, ports. 29 cm.
100 copies. No. 52. Bibliography: p. 102 - (104) 65-5532.

CS71.W72 1965

18782 WILLIAMS. Early settlers of the Big Thicket: the Williams family, a brief history. By Lois Williams Parker. (n.p., 1966) 32 p. illus., ports. 24 cm. 66-5152.

CS71.W72 1966

18783 WILLIAMS. Williams family notes, by Robert W. Williams. Baltimore, 1967.
122 p. illus., facsim., fold. geneal. table (in pocket), ports. 29 cm. 68-5215.

CS71.W72 1967

18784 WILLIAMS. A Williams chronicle; descendants of Thomas Williams of Sullivan County, New York, and Jefferson County, Pennsylvania, including some families of Horton, Morris Hickox, Foster, Elwood, Rice, Zum Brunnen, Nolph, Crissman, Hastings, Edelblute, McKnight, and others, by Frances Hansen Ehrig. Richland, Wash. (Printed by J. W. Ehrig) 1969. 198 p. illus., facsims., group ports., maps. 28 cm. 76-97816 MARC.

CS71.W72 1969

WILLIAMS. See also:

ALDERMAN, 1957	HOLLAND, 1959	PECK, 1955
ALSTON, 1901	JAMES, 1913a	PETTY, BX5195.T5B6
ALLSTON, 1961	JOHNSON, 1961	PIERCE, 1874
ARMSTRONG, CS61.A6 vol.2	JONES, 1961	PITMAN, CS439.P62
AUSTIN, F28.A93	KENYON, 1935	POWELL, F127.L8B9
BARNES, 1935	KURTZ, 1925	PRINDLE, 1906
BRUMBACH, 1961	LAWSON, 1903	SHAW, 1920
CALLAWAY, 1929	LEWIS, 1901	SNYDER, 1958
CHESTER, 1955	LLOYD, 1912	TRUESDELL, 1960
COLBERT, 1956	MACKEY, 1957	WICKES, 1939
DIXON, 1927	MARSHALL, 1948	WILDER, 1960
DOUBLEDAY, 1924	MONNET, 1911	WYMAN, CS459.W9
FORMAN, 1966	MOODY, 1957	WYNN, 1876
GALL, 1953	MOULTEN, 1922	No. 553 - Goodhue county.
GERNHARDT, 1904	MULLIKIN, 1936	No. 3509 - Orange county.
GRAY, E171.A53 vol.18	O'CONOR, 1914	

18785 WILLIAMS-WYNN. Correspondence of Charlotte Grenville, lady Williams Wynn, and her three sons, Sir Watkin Williams Wynn, bart., Rt. Hon, Charles Williams Wynn, and Sir Henry Williams Wynn ... 1795-1832, ed. by Rachel Leighton ... London, J. Murray, 1920.
x, 414 p. front., ports. 22½ cm. 20-23210.

DA536.W65A3

18786 WILLIAMSON. The Williamson and Cobb families in the lines of Caleb and Mary (Cobb) Williamson of Barnstable, Mass., and Harford, Conn. 1896. Comp. by Frank Farnsworth Starr for James J. Goodwin. Hartford, Conn. (Cambridge, University press, J. Wilson & son) 1896.
66 p. fold. geneal. tables. 25 cm. 9-15466.

CS71.W729 1896

18787 WILLIAMSON. Genealogical records of the Williamson family in America. Tracing the wives back to the earliest settlers. Comp. by James A. Williamson, of the sixth generation. Wyoming, N.J., 1896. 2 p. l., 23 p. 24 cm. 11-28970.

CS71.W729 1896a

18788 WILLIAMSON. Memoir of Joseph Williamson, by William Cross Williamson. Boston, Press of D. Clapp & son, 1903. 9 p. front. (port.) facsim. 24½ cm. "Reprinted from the New-England historical and genealogical register." 26-2968. CT275.W5697W5

18789 WILLIAMSON. Historical and biographical sketch. One branch of the Williamson family from 1745 to 1906. Prepared and pub. by Rev. Robert Duncan Williamson. Troy, N.Y., R. D. Williamson (1906?) 71 p. front. (port.) 22½ cm. 10-2629. CS71.W729 1906

18790 WILLIAMSON. The story of my life (by) Frances Ann Strickland. (Memphis, Press of S.C. Toof & co., 1910) cover-title, 1 p. l., 21 p. ports. 18 cm. Notes on the Williamson family, in manuscript, at end of book. 24-14228. CT275.S8814A3

18791 WILLIAMSON. The Williamson family ... (Litchfield, Ill., 1945) 6 numb. l. 28½ x 22 cm. Caption title. Signed: Walter R. Sanders. 46-21032. CS71.W729 1945

18792 WILLIAMSON. South of the middle border, by Hugh P. Williamson, Dorrance & company (1946) x, 11-279 p. 19½ cm. Map on lining pages. 46-7075. F466.W75

WILLIAMSON. See also: BELL, F232.L9B4
BLACK, 1954
KING, 1933

WILLIE. See WILEY.

WILLIFORD. See WILFORD.

WILLIM. See MAYO, CS439.M38

18793 WILLING. Willing family and collateral lines of Carroll, Chew, Dundas, Gyles, Jackson, McCall, Moore, Parsons, Shippen, edited by Alexander Du Bin. Philadelphia, The Historical publication society (1941) 28 p. front., 7 port. on 1 l., 5 coats of arms on 1 l. 25½ cm. 41-23724. CS71.W7297 1941

WILLING. See also: FISHER, 1929
SPRUANCE, 1933

WILLINGHAM. Florida cousins, the descendants of William H. Willingham, by Kyle S. Van Landingham. (Fort Pierce, Fla., T.H. Field, 1967) 59 p. 21 cm. Includes bibliographical references. 67-9296. CS71.W7298 1967

WILLINGHAM. See also WILLIS, 1946

18794 WILLIS. The first wife of Governor Willys of Connecticut, and her family. By a descendant. (Charles Atwood White. Boston, 1899) 8 p. 24½ cm. Caption title. "Reprinted from the New-England historical and genealogical register. April, 1899." Ancestry of Mrs. Bridget (Young) Willys. 5-14261. CS71.W73 1899

18795 WILLIS. Willis records; or, Records of the Willis family of Haverhill, Portland, and Boston. By Pauline Willis ... London, Printed by St. Vincent's press (1906) 2 p. l., 115 p. 24½ cm. 7-17345 CS71.W73 1906

18796 WILLIS. A sketch of the Willis family of Virginia, and of their kindred in other states. With brief biographies of the Reades, Warners, Lewises, Byrds, Carters, Champes, Bassetts, Madisons, Daingerfields, Thorntons, Burrells, Taliaferros, Tayloes, Smiths, and Amblers. By Byrd Charles Willis and Richard Henry Willis ... Richmond, Va., Whittet & Shepperson, printers (1898) 1 p. l., 160 p. 19 cm. Added t.-p. with title vignette. Slip of "errata" inserted at end. 1-13601. CS71.W73 1898

18797 WILLIS. Willis records; or, Records of the Willis family of Haverhill, Portland, and Boston, By Pauline Willis ... 2d ed. Containing an index, corrections and additions. London, Printed by St. Vincent's press (1908) 2 p. l., 126 p. 24½ cm. 8-17991. CS71.W73 1908

18798 WILLIS. A sketch of the Willis family, Fredericksburg branch. By Byrd Charles Willis. Richmond, Printed by Whittet & Shepperson (1909) 116 p. front., ports. 21 cm. 48-32993* CS71.W73 1909

18799   WILLIS.   A history of the Willis family of New England and New Jersey and their ancestors, comprising the families of Farrand, Ball, Kitchell, Cook, Ward, Fairchild, Plume, Brune, Smith, Treat, Pierson, Crane, Cooper, Sanford, Sheafe and others; to which is added a history of the family of John Howard, esq., of Richmond, Virginia, and the Harris and Macleod families of Georgia, comp. in the year 1916 by Charles Ethelbert Willis and Frances Caroline Willis ... (Richmond, Va., Whit - more & Garrett, inc., printers, c. 1917)   5 p. l., (13) - 352 p. incl. front., illus., ports., coats of arms. 24 cm.   Eight blank pages for "Family record" inserted between p. 322 and (323) 17-12853.   CS71.W73   1917

18800   WILLIS.   A family history, compiled by Anne Willingham Willis ... Rome. Ga. (1946)
xiv, 207 p. incl. front. (port.) plates, col. coats of arms.   23½ cm.   Contents. - House of Willis. - House of Willingham. - House of Baynard. - House of Wright. - House of Harper. 47-16533.   CS71.W73   1946

18801   WILLIS.   The Willises of Virginia; a genealogical account of the descendants of Colonel Francis Willis of Gloucester County, Virginia.   Colonel Henry Willis of Fredericksburg and William Willis of Southside Crany Creek.   By Maud Potter.   Mars Hill, N. C., 1964.   160 p. coats of arms (1 col.) geneal. tables, ports.   24 cm.   Part of illustrative matter in pocket. 65-545.   CS71.W73   1964

18802   WILLIS.   The Willis family of Virginia and some of their descendants ... With brief biog - raphies of their ancestors: the Martiaus, Reades, Warners, Lewises, Washingtons, Byrds, Carters, Randolphs, Carys, Jacquelin-Amblers, and a few later kin: the Randolph-Hackleys, Garniers, Shippeys, Barkelys, Dorrs, Sawyers, Savages, Hogues, and Haywards.   With old records from Pensacola and Tallahassee, Florida.   (Mobile, Ala., Printed by Paper Work) 1967.   156 p. illus., geneal. table, ports.   27 cm. 68-7451.   CS71.W73   1967

       WILLIS.   See also: JOHN, 1959   SELDEN, 1911
                         LEWIS, 1901   STEVENS, 1957
                         PERRY, 1960   STODDARD, 1959
                         PHELPS, 1960   WHITAKER, 1930
                         POWELL, F127.L8B9   No. 3509 - Orange county.

       WILLISON.   See FORRESTER, 1905

18803   WILLISTON.   Williston genealogy.   Joseph Williston and Joseph Williston, jr., A. D. 1667 - A. D. 1747 and the descendants of Rev. Noah Williston.   With certain affiliated and allied branches, A. D. 1734 - A. D. 1912.   Comp. by A. Lyman Williston, M. A.   (Northampton, Mass., 1912)
28 p. 24½ cm. 13-7158.   CS71.W734   1912

       WILLITS.   See: CHRYSLER, 1959
                         WILLETT.

       WILLOUER.   See WILLAUER, 1960

18804   WILLOUGHBY.   The Willoughby family of New England.   By Isaac J. Greenwood.   Reprinted from the Historical and genealogical register for Jan. 1876.   New York, Priv. print., 1876.
15 p. 25 cm.   One hundred copies.   no. 95. 9-25084.   CS71.W739   1876

18805   WILLOUGHBY.   Suggestions and inquiries respecting the ancestry of Colonel William Willoughby.   (n. p., 1885)   11 p. illus. (coat of arms) 25½ cm.   "Privately printed." Signed: Mrs. Edward Elbridge Salisbury' (i.e. Mrs. Evelyn McCurdy Salisbury) 35-11240.   CS439.W527   1885

18806   WILLOUGHBY.   The strife of the Roses and days of the Tudors in the West.   By W. H. Hamilton Rogers ... illustrated by R. Gibbs ... Exeter, J. G. Commin; London, W. W. Gibbings, 1890.   6 p. l., 212, (1) p. front., plates, port.   23 cm.   Contents. - "Our steward of household." Robert, Lord Willoughby de Broke, K. G. - Extinct for the White rose. William, Lord Bouville, K. G. - Under the hoof of the white boar. Henry Stafford, 2d duke of Buckingham, K. G. - Unhorsed at Bosworth. - John, Lord Cheney, K. G. - "With the silver hand." Stafford of Suthwyke - archbishop and earl. - "They did cast him." Sir Thomas Arundell, K. B. - Of the imperial line. Theodoro Paleologus. 1-12444.   DA250.R72

18807   WILLOUGHBY.   Chronicles of the house of Willoughby de Eresby.   Comp. ... by the Hon. Elizabeth Heathcote Drummond Willoughby.   Illustrated with ancient coats of arms, and monuments, also with portraits from the originals in possession of the family.   London, Nichols & sons, 1896.
7 p. l., 231 p. front., illus. (incl. ports., coats of arms) 45 cm. 19-19894.   DA28.35.W5W6

18808   WILLOUGHBY.   The continuation of the history of the Willoughby family, by Cassandra, Duchess of Chandos; being vol. II of the manuscript.   Edited by A. C. Wood.   Eton, Windsor, Published for the University of Nottingham by the Shakespeare Head Press, 1958.   xix, 147 p. illus., ports. 23 cm.   Cover title: The Willoughby family.   "The first volume ... was printed, with a few omissions, in the report on the manuscripts of Lord Middleton at Wollaton Hall issued by the Historical Manuscripts Commission in 1911."   Bibliographical footnotes.   60-21744.

CS439. W527   1958

WILLOUGHBY.   See also: BERTIE, DA358. W7B5   SELDEN, 1911
BERTIE, DA358. B4A3   TAYLOR, 1898
McCURDY, 1892   No. 430 - Adventurers of purse
SALISBURY, 1892   and person.

18809   WILLS.   The Wills family.   (n. p., 18 -)   6 p.   23 cm.   Caption title.   Prefatory note signed: M. R. W., i. e. Allen Wood Wills.   12-30972.   CS71. W742   18 -

WILLS.   See also: HAMLETT, 1958
HAYNES, 1902
HOFFMAN, 1915
LONG, 1956
McKINLEY, 1905

WILLYS.   See WILLIS.

18810   WILMARTH.   The Wilmarth family descendants of Thomas of Massachusetts, by Elizabeth Wilmarth and Bessie Wilmarth Gahn.   Washington, 1953.   68 p. illus. 22 cm. 53-40555.

CS71. W743   1953

18811   WILMER.   History of the Wilmer family, together with some account of its descendants, by Charles Wilmer Foster ... and Joseph J. Green ... Leeds, Priv. print. by Goodall and Suddick, 1888. xvi, 423, (2) p., 1 l. front. (fold. map) 7 pl., 3 port., v fold. geneal. tab.   26 cm.   9-10087.

CS439. W53

WILMERDING.   See BRADHURST, 1910

18812   WILMOT.   The Wilmot family of New Haven, Conn.   By Donald Lines Jacobus.   Boston, New England historic genealogical society, 1904.   9 p. 25 cm.   "Reprinted from the New England historical and genealogical register for Jan. 1905."   17-6150.   CS71. W745   1904

18813   WILMOT.   Wilmot - Wilmoth - Wilmeth, compiled by James Lillard Wilmeth ... (Charlotte, N. C., Printed by Washburn printing compnay) 1940.   374 p., 1 l. illus. (port.) 24 cm. 41-904.

CS71. W745   1940

WILMOT.   See also: BASSETT, 1926
BUNNELL, 1937
COMSTOCK, 1964

18814   WILSON.   Memoir of the life and character of Thomas Wilson, esq., treasurer of Highbury college.   By his son.   (Joshua Wilson) 2d thousand.   London, J. Snow, 1849.   1 p. l., xii, 584 p. front. (port.) 23 cm. 2-29632.   CT788. W787W6

18815   WILSON.   Report to the Wilson association, U. S. A., made by H. O. Smith, A. D. 1866. Containing reports and information ... relative to the Wilson property in England, and several pedigrees of different branches of the Wilson family in America ... Middlebury, Register book and job printing establishment, 1866.   28 p. 23 cm.   Published by order of the Wilson association. 3-3832.

CS71. W75   1866

18816   WILSON.   The pedigree of Wilson of High Wray & Kendal and the families connected with them.   Comp. from private pedigrees and completed to the present time by Joseph Foster.   (London) Printed for private circulation (by Head, Hole & co.) 1871.   4 p. l., 146, (2) p. incl. front. (coat of arms) 29 cm. 11-5259.   CS439. W55

18817   WILSON.   The pedigree of Wilson of High Wray & Kendal, and the families connected with them.   2d ed.   By Sandys B. Foster.   Printed for private circulation ... (London, Printed by W. H. and L. Collingridge) 1890.   4 p. l., 238 p. 23 cm. Interleaved. Rev. and enl. with many additions from the 1st ed. by Joseph Foster, pub. in 1871. Contents. - Wilson of High Wray. - Wilson of Kendal. - Wilson of Leasegill. - Wilson of Helsington Hays. - Wilson of Rigmaden Park and Low Nook. - Argles of Eversley. - Beakbane of Lancaster. - Benson of Stang End. - Birkbeck of Mallerstang and Settle. - Bragg of Netherend. - Braithwaite of Kendal. - Braithwaite-Wilson of Plumtree hall. - Clapham of Newcastle-upon-Tyne. - Cotterell of Bath and Bristol. - Crewdson of Crook. - Darby of Coalbrookdale. - Darby of Stoke court. - Dickinson of Gildersome and Coalbrookdale. - Foster, late of le Court, Hants. - Fowler of Melksham. - Fox of Girsby and Statham. - Gibson of Whelprigg. - Hanbury of Holfield, Essex. - Harrison of Grassgarth. - Jowitt, formerly of Churwell, now of Leeds. - Lloyd of Dolobran. - Lloyd, royal descent. - Moser of Kendal. - Pease of Darlington. - Rathbone of Liverpool. - Uppleby of Barrow. - Waithman of Lindeth. - Wakefield of Sedgwick house. - Wakefield of New Zealand &c. - Wakefield, royal descent. - Whitwell of Kendal. - Wordsworth family. - Index of matches. 16-4346.

CS439. W55   1890

18818   WILSON.   Six generations of Friends in Ireland (1655 to 1890), by J. M. R. (Mrs. Jane Marion (Wakefield) Richardson) ... London, E. Hicks, jun., 1893.   4 p. l., 239, (4) p. 6 pl., 5 port. (incl. front.) 18 cm. Sketches of Thomas Wilson and some of his descendants, including the author's husband, John G. Richardson. 5-42737.

BX7791. R5

18819   WILSON.   The genealogy of the family of Nathaniel Wilson of Kittery, Me.   Born 1760. Died 1841.   By Fred A. Wilson.   (Nahant? Mass., 1894)   25 p. 24½ cm. 9-15192.

CS71. W75   1894

18820   WILSON.   The genealogy of the family of Elihu Parsons Wilson of Kittery, Me.   Born 1769. Died 1834.   By Fred A. Wilson.   (Nahant, Mas., 1894)   38 p. 24½ cm. 9-15191.

CS71. W75   1894a

18821   WILSON.   The early history of the Wilson family of Kittery, Maine.   By Fred A. Wilson ... Lynn, Mass., J. Macfarlane & co., 1898.   3 p. l., (9)-98 p. 24½ cm. Facsimile of signature of Gowen Wilson on title-page. 10-15191.

CS71. W75   1898

18822   WILSON.   A tribute to our ancestors.   Biographical and genealogical family history arranged and comp. by Hattie Wilson Shinn ... Fort Scott (Kan.) Monitor book and printing co., 1898.   106, (2) p. 4 pl. (photos.) 20½ x 25½ cm. The two pages at end numbered 50 A - B continue the Bruce line of Wilson, p. 50-51. Manuscript letter inserted between p. 54 and 55. A portrait and sketch of the life of Abner Shinn. 1907 (2 p.) laid in. 14-5447.   CS71. W75   1898a

18823   WILSON.   Some of the ancestors and the children of Nathaniel Wilson, esq., who was born October 10, 1808, at Pelham, N. H., and died March 15, 1864, at Lawrence, Mass.   Comp. by Henry Winthrop Hardon ... (n. p.) 1905.   geneal. tab. 65 x 47 cm. fold. to 11½ x 24 cm. 18-11606.

CS71. W75   1905

18824   WILSON.   Ancestry and descendants of Rev. John Wilson of Boston, Mass.   By Joseph Gardner Bartlett.   Boston, New England historic genealogical society, 1907.   16 p. front. (port.) 25½ cm. "Reprinted, with additions, from the New England historical and genealogical register, vol. 61. " "Register re-prints, series A, no. 18. " 7-17005.

CS71. W75   1907

18825   WILSON.   The Wilson family.   (Washington, 1911)   50 p. 18 cm. Foreword signed: Jno. H. Nelson. 11-30209.

CS71. W75   1911

18826   WILSON.   The Wilson family.   (Spartanburg, S. C., 1911)   1 p. l., 6 l. 5 geneal. tab. 22 cm. Interleaved; ms. additions.   This sketch was written by S. S. Wilson in 1871 and comp. with some additions by Benjamin F. Wilson. 13-9627.

CS71. W75   1911a

18827   WILSON.   The Wilsons, by James Francis Crocker.   Portsmouth, Va., Whitson & Shepherd, printers, 1914.   7 p. 22 cm. No. 4 in a volume of five genealogical tracts, to which is prefixed a general t. - p.: The Woodleys of the Isle of Wight County, Va. and other ancestors ... Portsmouth, Va., 1915. 15-10364.   CS71. W884   1915

18828   WILSON.   Genealogy of the Wilson-Thompson families; being an account of the descendants of John Wilson, of County Antrim, Ireland, whose two sons, John and William, founded homes in Bucks County, and of Elizabeth McGraudy Thompson, who with her four sons came from Ireland and settled

18828 continued: in Bucks County about 1740.   Comp. by the Wilson-Thomson family association. Ed. by Warren S. Ely ... Doylestown, Pa., Intelligencer print (1916)   v p., 1 l., 325, 58 p. plates.   23½ cm. 16-23637.   CS71.W75   1916

18829   WILSON.   Wilson family history.   By Edward Wilson.   Bloomington, Ill., Printed by M. Custer, 1918.   1 p. l., 28 p. pl., ports. 21½ cm. 18-7488.   CS71.W75   1918

18830   WILSON.   Isaac and Rachel Wilson, Quakers, of Kendal, 1714 - 1785, by John Somervell. London, The Swarthmore press ltd. (1924)   160 p. 21 cm. Title vignette. 25-20040.   BX7795.W57S6

18831   WILSON.   Sketch of lineal descendants of Samuel Wilson, sr.   By Mrs. J. B. Eaves.   (Rock Hill, S. C., The London printery, 1924?)   4 p. l., (3) - 117 p. port. 20 cm. 34-32113.
CS71.W75   1924

18832   WILSON.   Wilson genealogical data and suggestions for a Wilson family asscoiation, a national Wilson family reunion, and a complete Wilson genealogy, by J. Montgomery Seaver ... Philadelphia, Pa., Washington, D. C., American historical-genealogical society, 1927.   60, (1) p. 32½ cm. Caption title. Text runs parallel with back.   Autographed from type-written copy.   "References": p. (61) CA29-178 unrev.
CS71.W75   1927

18833   WILSON.   Wilson and allied families; Billew, Britton, Du Bois, Longshore, Polhemus, Stillwell, Suebering, compiled by Alfred Rudulph Justice ... Philadelphia, 1929.   179 p. front., ports., coat of arms. 24½ cm. 29-19512.   CS71.W75   1929

18834   WILSON.   John Wilson, 1740-1820, of Pittsylvania county, Va.   Data collected by Daniel Coleman of Norfolk, Va., member of "Virginia historical society", extending over a period of thirty years; revised and arranged by L. L. Cody of Macon, Georgia.   (n. p., 1929?)   1 p. l., 5-58 p. illus. (port.) 22 cm. On cover: Lumpkin-Wilson. 31-33655.   CS71.W75   1929a

18835   WILSON.   ... Edward Wilson of Nether Levens (1557-1653) and his kin.   By R. Percival Brown, M. A.   Kendal, T. Wilson & son, 1930.   2 p. l., 104 p. VII fold. geneal. tab. 22½ cm. (Cumberland & Westmorland antiquarian & archaeological society. Tract series, no. XII) 31-3923.   CS439.W55   1930

18836   WILSON.   Historical review of the Wilson family in America, by W. Willard Roberts. Bridgeport, Conn.   (Columbia printing co.) 1935.   (8) p. 25½ cm. 35-38357.   CS71.W75   1935

18837   WILSON.   Garrett county history, Wilson family, by Chas. E. Hoye ... (Oakland? Md., 1935?) 1 l. 38 cm. 38M1260T.   CS71.W75   1935a

18838   WILSON.   The Wilsons, a Banffshire family of factors, edited by Andrew Cassels Brown ... Edinburgh, Priv. print., A. Baxendine & sons, 1936.   ix p., 3 l., 277 p., 1 l. col. front., illus., plates, ports. (part col.) fold. geneal. tab. 27 cm. Sources: p. (vii) - viii. Pages (256) - (266) blank for "Supplementary information". 39-23085.
CS479.W58   1936

18839   WILSON.   The Woodrow Wilsons, by Eleanor Wilson McAdoo in collaboration with Margaret Y. Gaffey.   New York, The Macmillan company, 1937.   x p., 1 l., 301 p. front., plates, ports., facsim. 22 cm. "First printing."   37-27227.   E767.3.M22

18840   WILSON.   A tentative list of the descendants of William Wilson, born 1722 - died 1801. (By) C. J. Maxwell.   (Mesquite, Tex., Printed by the Texas Mesquiter, 1937)   12 numb. l. 55 cm. Assisted by R. E. Wilson. 37-21343.   CS71.W75   1937

18841   WILSON.   Hugh Wilson, a pioneer saint; missionary to the Chickasaw Indians and pioneer minister in Texas; with a genealogy of the Wilson family including 422 descendants of Rev. Lewis Feuilleteau Wilson, I., by T. M. Cunningham.   (Dallas, Tex., Printed by Wilkinson printing co., c. 1938)   xi, 150 p. illus. (incl. ports.) 19½ cm. Bibliography: p. 144-145. 39-20800.   BX9225.W463C8

18842   WILSON.   Wilson-DeLong, a study in the early Americanization of a typical American family (by) Laurence L. Wilson.   (n. p., 1938)   2 p. l., (3) - 15 p. 23½ cm. Title vignette. 38-36177.
CS71.W75   1938

882

18844   WILSON.   Captain Robert Wilson, patriot, soldier, citizen, 1754-1835.   (By Rose E. Thixton)
(Birmingham, Ala., 1942)   cover-title, 9 l. 28 cm. Type-written. 43-756.   CS71.W75   1942

18845   WILSON.   Descendants of William Wilson (1722-1801) and Elizabeth Blackburn, compiled by
C. J. Maxwell.   Dallas, Tex. (Ann Arbor, Mich., Edwards brothers, inc.) 1943.   1 p. l., 275 (i.e. 289)
p. 27½ x 21 cm. Includes extra numbered pages. "Lithoprinted." "Corrections and additions": leaf inserted. 43-14676 rev.
CS71.W75   1943

——— Supplement of additions and corrections ... Dallas, Tex. (Ann Arbor, Mich., Edwards
brothers, inc. 1944)   iii, 277-350 p. 27½ x 21½ cm. Lithoprinted. 43-14676 rev.   CS71.W75   1943
Suppl.

18846   WILSON.   The Wilson family of Beech island, South Carolina.   With notes on the allied
families of Jennings, O'Bannon, Bush, Miller, Boyd, Dunbar, Robison, Vince, Smith, Fickling,
Bender, Mills, Zubly, and Galphin.   Compiled by John S. Kendall.   Corrected and extended.   (Berkeley, Calif.) 1943.   42 l. 28½ x 22 cm. In manuscript, with type-written t.-p. 44-10621.   CS71.W75   1943d

18847   WILSON.   The "Wilson family of S. C. to Tennessee," compiled by Leona B. McQuiston.
(Washington, 1943?)   3 p. l., iii, 39 numb. l., 25 l. 28 x 21½ cm. Type-written, corrected in manuscript. Two slips with
additions inserted. 43-17724.   CS71.W75   1943a

18848   WILSON.   Wilson-Baird history, by Frank C. Shepherd.   (Wewoka? Okl., 1943)   3 p. l., 360
(i.e. 366), 15 p. illus., plates, ports. (part mounted) plan. 21½ x 18½ cm. Includes extra numbered leaves 170½, 237½ and 250½. The
illustrative material consists of blue-prints. Reproduced from type-written copy. 44-29924.
CS71.W75   1943b

——— Another issue.   Without extra numbered leaf 170$\frac{1}{2}$ and with differences in the illustrative
matter.   CS71.W75   1943c

18849   WILSON.   For the friends of Charles Crawford Wilson.   (Jersey City, 1945)   cover-title,
24 p. incl. group port. port. 23 cm. 47-15321.   CT275.W5812F6

18850   WILSON.   Notes on the genealogy of the Bethel, Vermont, Wilson family, compiled by
Harold F. Wilson.   (Pitman?, N.J., 1948)   20 l. 28 cm. Caption title. 68-34224.   CS71.W75   1948

18851   WILSON.   The Wilson family, Somerset and Barter Hill branch.   By Harry Herndon McLean.
Washington, N.C. (c.1950)   102 p. port. 24 cm. 51-18134.   CS71.W75   1950

18852   WILSON.   The Willson family tree.   By Martha Emma (Hutcheson) Wilson.   (Wapello? Iowa,
1956)   136 p. illus. 26 cm. 56-36671.   CS71.W75   1956

18853   WILSON.   A collection of genealogical and historical material on the Wilson family of Missouri, Colorado, and California; the Bowles family of Virginia, Missouri, and Colorado; the King
family of New York, New Jersey, and Colorado.   (n.p., 1957)   unpaged. 31 cm. 58-29026.
CS71.W75   1957

18854   WILSON.   The Willson family, 1672-1959.   By Richard Eugene Wilson.   Kent, Ohio, 1959.
324 l. illus. 29 cm.   CS71.W7425   1959

——— Supplement.   no. 1 -   1960 -   Kent, Ohio.   no. 28 cm. 61-37611.
CS71.W7425   1959
Suppl.

18855   WILSON.   Ancestry of Ralph Carmalt Wilson of Dover, Delaware.   By George Valentine
Massey.   (Dover? Del.) 1961.   82 l. 28 cm. 61-37626.   CS71.W75   1961

18856   WILSON.   A Carolina-Virginia genealogy.   By York Lowry Wilson.   Aldershot, Eng., Gale
& Polden, 1962.   ix, 349 p. col. coat of arms, geneal. tables. 24 cm. 62-66161.   CS71.W75   1962

18857   WILSON.   Descendants of William Wilson.   Compiled by Mrs. R. N. Syme (and) Mrs. D. E. McKenzie.   (Stockton? Calif., 1964)   62 l. 28 cm. 64-55840.   CS71.W75   1964

18858   WILSON.   The Wilson-Garner family of Darlington, S. C.   By Leola (Wilson) Konopa. (Columbia? S. C., 1964)   31 l. 29 cm. 65-1096.   CS71.W75   1964a

18859   WILSON.   Looking back through the years with the John and Mattie Wilson family, compiled by Ouida Day Bailey and Etkel Lindamood.   (Whittier, Calif., Printed by Funderburk, 1968)
111 p. illus., facsims., map, ports. 22 cm. 68-6018.   CS71.W75   1968

18860   WILSON.   The American heritage of our Wilson-Kellogg-Green-Staats families; from the Mayflower to clippers.   By Carol (Green) Wilson.   (San Francisco?, 1968)   56 l. illus., geneal. tables,
maps, ports. 34 cm. On cover: Our American heritage: Wilson-Kellogg-Staats families. 68-7422.   CS71.W75   1968a

18861   WILSON.   Col. Benjamin Wilson obituary.   See Virginia C. Cork in vertical file.   Ask reference
librarian for this material.

WILSON.   See also:

ATCHISON, 1878	HOUSTON, 1914	PASTORIUS, 1926
BEAL, 1956	JARRATT, 1957	PEDEN, 1961
BOWERS, 1872	KIRK, 1967	REYNOLDS, 1959
COCHRAN, CT275.C656C6	McCONNELL, 19 -	TAFT, 1908
DE MOSS, 1950	MAXWELL, 1916	WALLACE, 1930
EARLE, 1940	MILLS, 1960	WALTMAN, 1928
HAIRSTON, 1940	MINNS, 1925	No. 553 - Goodhue county.
HANAFORD, 1915	OKELY, 1899	No. 1547 - Cabell county.
HOUGEN, 1957	PARK, 1967	

WILTES, Earldom of.   See SCROPE.

18862   WILTSEE.   A genealogical and psychological memoir of Philippe Maton Wiltsee and his descendants, with a historical introduction referring to the Wiltsee nation and its colonies.   Pt. I. (Atchison? Kan.) 1908.   294 p. illus., ports. 25 cm. No more published. 8-18348 rev.*   CS71.W753   1908
———— Index compiled by Myrta Wilsey Burwash.   Washington, 1939.   55 l. 24 cm.
CS71.W753
Index a

———— Index to Memoir of Philippe Maton Wiltsee and his descendants, initially prepared by Myrta W. Burwash, modified and completed with the assistance of Theresa N. Swezey.   Brooklyn, A. Rogers, c.1950.   41 p. 23 cm.   CS71.W753   1908
Index b

WILTSIE.   See ELDRIDGE, 1925

18863   WIMBERLEY.   Memorials of the family of Wimberley of South Witham, Beechfield, and Ayscoughfee Hall, Lincolnshire, from original papers and documents collected by the late William Clarke Wimberley as arranged and comp. by his nephew, Colonel Reginald Justus Wimberley ... and also rev. by his nephew, Captain Douglas Wimberley ... Inverness, 1893.   iv, 36 p. 5 pl. (coats of arms)
geneal. tables (partly fold.) 29 cm. Title vignette: coat of arms. 10-1187.   CS439.W57

WIMBERLY.   See No. 9385 - Twiggs county.

WIMBLE.   See BASS, 1896

18864   WINANS.   The Winans family in America.   1939 minus 1664 equals 275 years ... (By Charles Augustus Winans)   Paterson, N. J., C. A. Winans, 1937 (i. e. 1939)   46 (i. e. 56) numb. l. fold. geneal. tab.
27½ cm. Reproduced from type-written copy. Includes extra numbered leaves 19 a, 21 a, 41 a - 41 h. "2d edition (revised 1939) 25 copies."
"This folio is made possible through the initiative and assistance furnished by Miss Mattie M. Bowman." Bibliography: leaf 43. 42-50540.
CS71.W755   1939

18865   WINBORNE.   The Winborne family, by Judge Benj. Brodie Winborne ... Raleigh, N.C., Presses of Edwards & Broughton (1905)   141, (12) p. ports. 27 cm. Blank pages for "Family record" (12 at end) 35-16386.   CS71.W756   1905

WINCH.   See HAYES, DA690.B74K3

18866   WINCHCOMBE.   Bucklebury.   A Berkshire parish, the home of Bolingbroke 1701-1715: by Arthur L. Humphreys, F.S.A.   Reading, Published by the author at York Lodge, 1932.   x, 614, (1) p. front., plates, ports., fold. map, fold. plan, facsims., fold. geneal. tables. 20 x 23 cm. "Authorities consulted" at end of some of the chapters. A33-2793.   Title from Newberry library.   DA690.B893H8

18867   WINCHELL.   Genealogy of the family of Winchell in America; embracing the etymology and history of the name, and the outlines of some collateral genealogies.   By Alexander Winchell, LL.D. ... Ann Arbor (Mich.) Dr. Chase's steam printing house, 1869.   271 p. 22½ cm. 9-15190.
                                                                        CS71.W758   1869

18868   WINCHELL.   The Winchell genealogy; the ancestry and children of those born to the Winchell name in America since 1635, with a discussion of the origin and history of the name and the family in England, and notes on the Wincoll family, by Newton H. Winchell ... and Alexander N. Winchell ... 2d ed. ... Minneapolis, Minn., H.V. Winchell, 1917.   xii, 554 p. front. (coat of arms) ports., fold. map. 24 cm. "The first edition ... was published in 1869 by Professor Alexander Winchell" under title: Genealogy of the family of Winchell in America. 18-12721.   CS71.W758   1917

18869   WINCHELL.   The Winchell family of Maine.   Comp. by Rev. Chas. N. Sinnett.   Brainerd, Minn. (1920)   1 p. l., 21 l. 28 cm. Type-written. 21-3725.   CS71.W758   1920

18870   WINCHESTER.   John Winchester 1616-1694, a settler of New England, and one line of his descendants.   By George R. Presson ... San Francisco & Oakland, Cal., Pacific press pub. co., 1897. 45 p. 25½ cm. Printed for private circulation. 9-15189.   CS71.W759   1897

18871   WINCHESTER.   Winchester notes, by Mrs. Fanny Winchester Hotchkiss.   New Haven, Conn., Printed by the Tuttle, Morehouse & Taylor co., 1912.   viii, 367 p. front., plates, ports. 26 cm. 12-12939.
                                                                        CS71.W759   1912

18872   WINCHESTER.   John Winchester of New England and some of his descendants, by Henry Winchester Cunningham ... (Boston, 1925)   139 p. 24 cm. "Reprinted from the New England historical and genealogical register, volumes 78 and 79, 1924-1925." 37-21325.   CS71.W759   1925

18873   WINCHESTER.   The Winchester family and related lines, 1792-1955.   By Chester Lincoln Somers.   Rev. (Hamilton? Mass.) 1955.   63 l. 29 cm. 56-19338.   CS71.W759   1955

18874   WINCHESTER.   The Winchester family of Gloucester.   By Chester Lincoln Somers.   (Hamilton? Mass.) 1956.   20 l. 29 cm. Supplements the author's The Winchester family and related lines, 1792-1955. 58-36400.
                                                                        CS71.W759   1956

WINCOLL.   See WINCHELL.

WINDEATH.   See BLATCHFORD, 1912

18875   WINDECKER.   Windecker, Gross and allied families, by Esther Gross Windecker, edited by Walter S. Finley.   New York, Priv. print. by the American historical company, inc., 1943. 229 p. plates, ports., col. coats of arms, col. geneal. tab. 32 x 25 cm. Most of the plates accompanied by guard sheets with descriptive letterpress. Allied families: Corey, Marsh, Hobert, Webster and Adams. Includes bibliographical references. Bound in blue crushed levant; gold tooled. 44-24409.   CS71.W76   1943

WINDEMOED.   See WINTERMUTE.

WINDEMUTH.   See WINTERMUTE.

18876   WINDER.   The Winders of Lorton.   By F. A. Winder, Southsea, Portsmouth.   (Reprinted from vol. XIV of the Transactions of the Cumberland and Westmorland antiquarian and archaeological society.)   Kendal, Printed by T. Wilson, 1896.   cover-title, p. 198-207.   double geneal. tab.   23 cm.   25-25798.

CS439.W573

18877   WINDER.   Winders of America: John Winder, of New York, 1674-1675, Thomas Winder, of New Jersey, 1703-1734, John Winder, of Maryland, 1665-1698;   comp. by R. Winder Johnson.   Philadelphia, J. B. Lippincott company, 1902.   1 p. l., 112 p.   pl., map, geneal. tab.   23 cm.   Printed for pirvate ciruclation.   Blank leaves inserted between p. 96 and 97.   3-3810.

CS71.W763   1902

WINDHAM.   See WYNDHAM.

18878   WINDSOR.   Historical collections of the noble family of Windsor; barons Windsor from the reign of King William the Conqueror, and earls of Plimouth from the reign of King Charles the Second; viscounts Windsor of the kingdom of Ireland from the reign of King William the Third; and barons Montjoy in England from the reign of Queen Anne.   Containing their births, marriages and issues: famous actions, both in war and peace: religious and charitable donations, deaths, places of burial, monuments, epitaphs, and valuable memoirs, never before printed.   Collected from records, old wills, authentic manuscripts, and our most approved historians.   By Arthur Collins, esq.   London, The author, MDCCLIV.   2 p. l., 87 p.   26½ cm.   39-23089.

CS439.W575   1754

18879   WINDSOR.   A genealogical account of the ancient Winsor family in the United States.   Collected principally from records in the several branches thereof, introduced by an account of their progenitors in the male line, for several generations previous to the emigrations to America.   By the late Olney Winsor.   Providence, L. W. Winsor, 1847.   12 p.   22½ cm.   Cover-title.   9-27353.

CS71.W766   1847

18880   WINDSOR.   A monograph of the Windsor family, with a full account of the rejoicings on the coming of age of Robert George Windsor-Clive, Lord Windsor, 27th August, 1878.   By W. P. Williams ... with portrait of Lord Windsor.   Cardiff, D. Owen & company, 1879.   viii p., 1 l., (6), 204 p.   front. (port.)   22 cm.   Frontispiece is a mounted photograph.   A brief memoir of Lord Windsor and a genealogical chart of the Windsor family: (6) p.   18-5941.

CS439.W575

18881   WINDSOR.   Our ambassador king; His Majesty King Edward VIII's life of devotion and service as Prince of Wales, by Basil Maine; with a foreword by Sir Harry Brittain ... with 32 illustrations.   London, Hutchinson & co., ltd. (1936)   2 p. l., 3-297, (1) p. incl. geneal. tab.   front., plates, ports.   22 cm.   "The first edition of this book appeared recently under the title of "The King's first ambassador".   It is now revised and brought entirely up to date."   36-20714.

DA580.M3   1936

18882   WINDSOR.   Andrew and Lydia Winsor genealogical chart, showing their descent from Joshua Winsor (originally Windsor)   By Kay Kirlin Moore.   Greenville, R. I., c.1950.   geneal. table.   22 x 36 cm.   50-39108.

CS71.W766   1950

WINDSOR.   See also: BRAMSHOTT, DA670.H2C2
DUCKETT, CS439.D815
McPHERSON, 1929
PARSHALL, CS439.P29

18883   WINE.   The Wine family in America.   By Jacob David Wine.   Forestville, Va., 1952 -   v.   illus.   24 cm.   53-4352.

CS71.W7665   1952

18884   WINEGAR.   Genealogy of the Winegar family as written by Ira Winegar, of Middlebury, Indiana, in ... letters addressed to Caleb Winegar, of Union Springs, N. Y.   Union Springs, J. B. Clarke, printer, 1859.   18 l.   28 cm.   Photocopy (positive) of typescript.   52-47039.

CS71.W767   1859a

18885   WINFIELD.   Legend of the Delaware: an historical sketch of Tom Quick.   To which is added the Winfield family; also, miscellaneous papers and articles.   By Wm. Bross ... Chicago, Knight & Leonard co., printers, 1887.   2 p. l., 195 p.   front. (port.) plates.   18½ cm.   Professes to be translation from a "Low Dutch" manuscript.   cf. Introd., signed Jacobus Van Wyck.   Contents. - Legend of the Delaware. - The Winfield family. - Immortality. - Punishment. - The thirteenth amendment. - Commercial crises. - Stanley's African explorations.   21-18298.

PS1124.B25L4   1887

WINFIELD.   See also TALBOT, 1924

18886   WING.   A historical and genealogical register of John Wing, of Sandwich, Mass., and his descendants, 1662-1881.   By Rev. Conway P. Wing ... (Carlisle? Pa.) 1881.   1 p. l., vi, 334 p. ports., fold. map, coat of arms.   20 cm.   33-14355.   CS71.W769   1881

18887   WING.   Wing family.   By W. H. Whitmore.   Reprinted from the N. E. hist. and gen. register for Oct. 1884.   Boston, D. Clapp & son, 1884.   4 p.   26½ cm.   9-15188.   CS71.W769   1884

18888   WING.   A historical and genealogical register of John Wing, of Sandwich, Mass. and his descendants, 1632-1888.   By Rev. Conway P. Wing ... 2d ed.   New York, The De Vinne press, 1888.   iv, 581 p. pl., ports., map, col. coat of arms.   32½ cm.   1-19529.   CS71.W769   1888

18889   WING.   The Owl.   v. 1 -   1899 -   Sandwich, Mass. (etc.)   Wing Family of America (etc.)   v. in   illus., ports.   25 cm.   Frequency varies.   Issues for Mar. 1936 - Mar. 1937 (v. 36-37) called v. 1, no. 1-2.   Title varies: 1936-37, Wing family annals. - 1938-54, Annals.   36-30608 rev. 2.
                                                                                                          CS71.W769   1899

18890   WING.   Some Wings of old Dartmouth and their homes, by William Arthur Wing.   (Sandwich? Mass., 1905)   cover-title, (8) p. illus.   26 cm.   11-1569.   CS71.W76   1905

18891   WING.   The ancient and honorable family of Wing; a family with a thousand years of history, by Albert E. Wing ... (Providence, R. I., Howard press, 1938.)   (16) p. incl. illus. (part mounted, incl. coat of arms) mounted ports.   25 cm.   Caption title.   Poem on p. (3) of cover.   "Of this brochure there were printed ... but two hundred copies." Bibliography: p. (16)   40-18939.   CS71.W769   1938

18892   WINGATE.   History of the Wingate family in England and in America, with genealogical tables.   Comp. by Charles E. L. Wingate.   Exeter, N.H.. J. D. P. Wingate, 1886.   292 p. col. front. (coat of arms) plates.   23 cm.   9-15187.   CS71.W77   1886

18893   WINGATE.   The Wingate-Winget family in America, by Esther Mae Winget Warner, compiler. Osborn, O., The Herald print shop (c. 1931)   4 p. l., 11-188 p. incl. col. front. (coat of arms) illus. pl., port. 23½ cm.   "References": p. 165-166.   32-4299.   CS71.W77   1931

18894   WINGATE.   The Wingate-Winget families in America.   By Esther Mae (Winget) Warner. Rev. (Xenia? Ohio, 1963)   279 p. illus., ports., col. coat of arms.   29 cm.   "References": p. 279.   64-301.
                                                                                                          CS71.W77   1963

WINGER.   See WENGER.

WINGET.   See WINGATE.

WINGFEILDE.   See WINGFIELD.

18895   WINGFIELD.   Muniments of the ancient Saxon family of Wingfield.   Comp. by Mervyn Edward, seventh viscount Powerscourt ... Privately printed.   London, Mitchell and Hughes, 1894. viii, 88 p. illus., plates (part col.) ports., facsims., col. diagr., coats of arms.   41½ cm.   Half-title: The family of Wingfield.   "The trial, execution, and death of Mary queen of Scots.   Comp. from the original documents by Charles Dack": p. (57)-63.   9-32042.
                                                                                                          CS439.W58

18896   WINGFIELD.   Some records of the Wingfield family, ed. by Lieut-Col. John M. Wingfield ... London, J. Murray, 1925.   ix, 263 p. front., plates, coats of arms, fold. geneal. tab.   23 cm.   "Sources from which information was chiefly obtained": p. 252.   26-13837.   CS439.W58   1926

18897   WINGFIELD.   The Wars of the Roses.   By Neal F. Mears.   Chicago, c. 1958.   geneal table. illus., map. coat of arms.   100 x 125 cm. fold. to 50 x 42 cm.   Caption title.   58-24627.   CS71.W773   1958

18898   WINGFIELD.   Pioneer families of Franklin County, Virginia.   By Marshall Wingfield. Berryville, Va., Chesapeake Book Co., 1964.   373 p.   23 cm.   65-2628.   F232.F7W52

18899   WINKLEY.   Documents relating to the Winkley family.   Compiled by William Winkley, jun. ... (Harrow) Printed at the Harrow press (1863)   10, (5) p., 15 l., (7) p. 8 double geneal. tab. 22½ cm. 16-19777.
CS439.W59

WINNE.   See EVANS, 1940

WINNIETT.   See WILLIAMS, CS84.W6

18900   WINSHIP.   The Winship family in America, giving the line of descent from Edward Winship, born in England in 1613, who came to Cambridge, Massachusetts, in 1635, to Jabez Lathrop Winship, born in Norwich, Conn., 1752, died in Brookville, Indiana, 1827, with the record of the families of his children and grandchildren, with their line of descent from William the Conqueror.   By Ernest B. Cole.   Indianapolis, Ind., 1905.   37 p. 19 cm. 6 blank leaves for records inserted between p. 34 and 35. 8-10316.
CS71.W777   1905

WINSHIP.   See also COLE, 1908

18901   WINSLOW.   Brief memoir of Dr. Winslow Lewis.   By John Hannibal Sheppard.... Albany, N.Y., J. Munsell, 1863.   33, (1) p. front. (port.) 22 cm. "From the New Eng. hist. and genealogical register." "Genealogy of the Winslow family," p. 20-23; "Genealogy of the Lewis family," p. 24-29; "Genealogy of the Greenough family," p. 30-33. 35M1187.
F1.N56   1863
—— Copy 2   Toner   R154.L43S5

18902   WINSLOW.   (Radial chart of descendants of Kenelm Winslow, through James Winslow of Falmouth, Me., 1728.   By David Parsons Holton.   New York) c.1877.   geneal. tab. 48 x 74½ cm. 2-12905.
CS71.W78   1877

18903   WINSLOW.   Job Winslow radial chart.   (New York, c.1877)   geneal. tab. 43 x 71 cm. By David Parsons Holton.   Descendants of Kenelm Winslow, through Job Winslow.   CA 16-697.
CS71.W78   1877a

18904   WINSLOW.   Winslow memorial.   Family records of the Winslows and their descendants in America, with the English ancestry as far as known.   Kenelm Winslow ... By David Parsons Holton ... and his wife, Mrs. Frances K. (Forward) Holton ... New York, D. P. Holton, 1877-88.   2 v. fronts., illus., ports., fold. geneal. tables, coat of arms. 24 cm. Paged continuously. 9-15186.
CS71.W78   1877-88

18905   WINSLOW.   Winslow papers, A.D. 1776-1826.   Printed under the auspices of the New Brunswick historical society.   Ed. by Rev. W. O. Raymond, M.A.   St. John, N.B., The Sun printing company, ltd., 1901.   3 p. l., (5) - 732 p. incl. illus., facsim. 9 pl., 6 port. 24½ cm. 5-12581.
F1043.R27

18906   WINSLOW.   Edward Winslow and his descendants.   1560-1911.   (Rutland? 1911?)   5 l. 23 cm. The ancestry of George Webb Benson. 20-2603.
CS71.W78   1911

18907   WINSLOW.   Genealogy of Edward Winslow of the Mayflower, and his descendants, from 1620 to 1865, by Maria Whitman Bryant, daughter of Elizabeth Winslow and (Judge) Kilborn Whitman, of Pembroke, Mass.   (New Bedford, Mass., E. Anthony & sons, inc., printers, c.1915)   x, 233 p. ports., coat of arms. 26½ x 21½ cm. Part of pages blank. Only 300 copies printed. "Explanatory" signed: Herbert Pelham Bryants. 15-25847.
CS71.W78   1915

18908   WINSLOW.   Mary Chilton's title to celebrity, investigated in behalf of a descendant of John Haward, minimus, by Charles Thornton Libby.   Boston, Printed for private distribution, The Fort Hill press, 1926.   27 p. front. (facsim.) 25½ cm. "... Mary Chilton ... is said to have been the first female who set foot on the Plymouth shore, 1620": p. (5) 27-25099.
F68.L7

18909   WINSLOW.   Autobiography of George W. Porter, reminiscences, observations and writings ... Punxsutawney, Pa., The Spirit publishing company, 1929.   xiv p. 1 l., 203 p. front., plates, ports., coat of arms. 23½ cm. "Genealogy of the Winslow family": p. 102-103. 31-7144.
CT275.P682A3

18910   WINSLOW.   Francis Winslow; his forebears and life, based upon family records and correspondence during XXX years, by Arthur Winslow ... Norwood, Mass., Priv. print. by the Plimpton press, 1935.   xiv p., 1 l., 352 p. front., plates, ports. 24 cm. "Limited ed. of 300 copies." 35-6842.
E182.W57

18911   WINSLOW.   Mayflower heritage; a family record of the growth of Anglo-American partner-
ship.   By Douglas Kenelm Winslow.   London, Harrap (1957)   200 p. illus.   21 cm.   Includes bibliography.
57-34910.   CS71.W78   1957

18912   WINSLOW.   Winslow family in vertical file.   Ask referenc librarian for this material.

         WINSLOW.   See also: CROCKER, 1923   TILSON, 1911
                                  FITZ RANDOLPH, 1946   TRACY, 1933
                                  FOSTER, 1889   TRUEBLOOD, 1964
                                  LEWIS, 1877   VAN NOSTRAND, E171.A53 vol. 19
                                  POLLOCK , 1932   VOSE, F157.W9B3

         WINSOR.   See WINDSOR.

         WINSTANLEY.   See CROPPER.

18913   WINSTON.   Genealogy of Isaac Winston and descendants.   By Elizabeth Winston (Campbell)
Hendrick.   (New York, Sackett & Wilhelms lithographing & printing co., 1899)   cover-title, 1 p. l.,
7 diagr.   36 x 44 cm.   0-1816 rev.   CS71.W782   1899
                                                                                  Microfilm 22467

18914   WINSTON.   The Winston family.   (Chattanooga, 1917?)   (2) p. 30 cm. (Notable southern families)
Detached from the Lookout.   55-49903.   CS71.W782   1917

18915   WINSTON.   Winston of Virginia, and allied families, compiled and edited by Clayton
Torrence.   Richmond, Va., Whittet & Shepperson, 1927.   xiv, 477, 10 p. front., illus. (coats of arms) plates,
ports., facsims., 5 fold. geneal. tab., map.   23 cm.   Some of the plates are printed on both sides.   Folded genealogical tables of "Ancestry of
Ann Lovelace, wife of John Gorsuch, Ancestry of Honorable John West, Descendants of Sir Thomas West, 2nd Lord De la Warr", and map are in
pocket.   Contains also the Waters, Bickerton, Todd, Bernard Robinson, Beverley, Waring, Pendleton, Taylor, Madison, Gregory, West, Claiborne,
Bassett, Cary, Burwell, Bacon, Littlepage, Quarles and Lovelace families.   27-20855.   See add. and corr. No. 240.   CS71.W782   1927

         WINSTON.   See also: BARTHOLOMEW, 1899
                                  BUTLER, 1945
                                  MASSIE, 1942
                                  PRICE, 1906
                                  4639 - Smithfield.

         WINTER.   See PECK, 1955

18916   WINTERMUTE.   The Wintermute family history; comp. by J. P. Wintermute ... Delaware,
O., 1900.   vii, (1), 9-335 p. front., pl., port.   24 cm.   2-8297.   CS71.W787   1900

18917   WINTERS.   A sketch of the Winters family.   Ed. by Jonathan H. Winters.   Dayton, O.,
United brethren publishing house, 1889.   3 p. l., (v) - (x), 11-186 p., 3 l. illus.   18 cm.   Two leaves at end left blank
for additional record. 20-22868.   CS71.W788   1889

18918   WINTERS.   Historical sketches of the Winters family, pioneer settlers of middle Tennessee,
by Ralph L. Winters.   Clarksville, Tenn., c. 1965 -   v. illus., map, ports. 29 cm. 66-3077.
                                                                                  CS71.W788   1965

18919   WINTERTON.   Winterton pioneers of Utah; a biographical, historical, and genealogical
record of the William Hubbard Winterton family who emigrated in 1863 from the textile factories of
Nottingham, England, to the farmlands of Charleston, Wasatch County, Utah, U. S. A.   Compiled in
1963 as a centennial memorial by Arthur D. Coleman.   Provo, Utah, J. G. Stevenson (1964)
xiv, 236 p. illus., maps, ports.   25 cm.   64-17734.   CS71.W789   1964

         WINTERSMITH.   See LA RUE, 1921

18920   WINTHROP.   Notes on the Winthrop family, and its English connections before its emigration to New England.   By William H. Whitmore ... Albany, J. Munsell, 1864.   6, (4) p. illus. (coat of
arms) 23 cm.   Reprinted with additions from the New Eng. hist. and geneal. register for April, 1864. 9-15185.   CS71.W79   1864

18921 WINTHROP. Life and letters of John Winthrop, governor of the Massachusetts-Bay company at their emigration to New England ... by Robert C. Winthrop. Boston, Ticknor and Fields, 1864 - 67. 2 v. fronts., 1 pl. 1 port., 4 facsim. 23½ cm. 4-17081/2   F67.W817

18922 WINTHROP. A pedigree of the family of Winthrop: lords of the manor of Groton, co. Suffolk, England; afterwards of Boston and New London, in New England ... Cambridge, J. Wilson and son, 1874. vi, 7-38 p. 24 cm. By Robert Charles Winthrop, jr. Printed for private reference only, with a view to correction and addition. 3-3815.   CS71.W79   1874

18923 WINTHROP. Some account of the early generations of the Wintrhop family in Ireland. (By Robert Charles Winthrop) Privately printed for correction and addition. Cambridge, J. Wilson and son, 1883. 24 p. 25 cm. Preface signed: R.C.Winthrop, jun. "Thirty three copies." 24-20305. CS71.W79   1883

18924 WINTHROP. A short account of the Winthrop family. Privately printed for convenient reference. Cambridge, J. Wilson and son, 1887. 16 p. 23½ cm. Prefatory note signed: Robert C. Winthrop, jr. 11-28974.   CS71.W79   1887

18925 WINTHROP. Evidences of the Winthops of Groton, co. Suffolk, England, and of families in and near that county, with whom they intermarried. (Boston) Priv. print., 1894-96. viii, 168 p. 31½ cm. Fifty copies printed, of which this is no. 46. This volume comprises the first four parts of an exhaustive work, entitled "Suffolk manorial families," and ed. by Joseph James Muskett, assisted by Robert C. Winthrop, jr. 9-18114.   CS439.W6

18926 WINTHROP. Ancestors of Henry Rogers Winthrop and his wife Alice Woodward Babcock, compiled for their daughter Alice Winthrop, by Josephine C. Frost (Mrs. Samuel Knapp Frost) ... New York? 1927. 595 p. 25 cm. 27-24035.   CS71.W79   1927

18927 WINTHROP. Winthrop hundred ... mirror of 100 British descendants of Col. John Winthrop, barrister at law, Inner Temple, London, leader of the Puritan migration to New England, 1630; copyrighted ... by Ellery Kirke Taylor ... Phila., Pa., c.1936. geneal. tab. illus. (port.) 45 cm. 40M3966T.   CS71.W79   1936

18928 WINTHROP. The lion and the hare; being the graphic pedigree of over one thousand descendants of John Winthrop, 1588-1649 ... (by) Ellery Kirke Taylor ... (Ann Arbor, Mich., Edwards brothers, inc., 1939) 3 p. 1., 77 p. incl. illus., 20 fold. geneal. tab. port. 28 cm. Portrait accompanied by guard sheet with descriptive letterpress. Lithoprinted. "One hundred and twenty-five copies printed, of which this is copy no. 3." "References": on each of the genealogical tables except the first. 40-3763.   CS71.W79   1939

18929 WINTHROP. The Winthrop family in America. By Lawrence Shaw Mayo. Boston, Massachusetts Historical Society, 1948. x, 507 p. ports., col. coat of arms, geneal. table. 29 cm. Correction slip inserted. Includes bibliographies. 48-11112*.   CS71.W79   1948

WINTHROP. See also: FROST, 1912
                      MAUNSELL, CS439.M37
                      SEBOR, 1923
                      WASHINGTON, E187.5.S88
                      WELLS, 1874

WIRE. See WYER.

18930 WIRZ. Wurts family; one of the series of sketches written for the Philadelphia North American, 1907-1913. Based on the manuscript of John S. Wurts, comp. 1902 and by him brought down to date. Philadelphia, Historical Publ. Society (c.1931) (24) p. ports. 26 cm. 48-35386*.   CS71.W965   1931

18931 WISDOM. Genealogy of the Wisdom family, 1675 to 1910. Compiled by George W. Wisdom ... (New York, C. H. Jones & co., printers, 1910) xv, (5) p., 1 1., 23 - 231 (i.e.240) p. front. (port.) illus. (incl. map) 19½ cm. Pages left blank throughout text for "Family record". "Crossing the plains in the early days": p. 176a - 176h. 28-6862.   CS71.W81   1910

18932   WISE.   ... Index to the act books of the archbishops of Canterbury, 1663-1859.   Compiled by the late E. H. W. Dunkin ... Extended and edited by Claude Jenkins ... and E. A. Fry ... London, The British record society, 1929 -   v. 26½ cm. (Half-title: The index library ... Issued by the British record society. 55.) Series title in part also at head of t. - p. Issued in parts, 1915 -   30-4603.   CS434.B7 vol. 55

18933   WISE.   Col. John Wise of England and Virginia (1617-1695); his ancestors and descendants, by Jennings Cropper Wise ... including many brief biographical notes.   (Richmond, The Bell book and stationery co., c. 1918)   352, (4) p. illus. (incl. ports.) fold. geneal. tables. 25 cm.   "Two hundred and seventy-five copies ... printed." Contains the Douglas, Beverley, Scarburgh and other families. "Authorities": p. (4) at end. 18-18127 rev.

CS71.W812   1918

18934   WISE.   History of the Wise and Wyse family of South Carolina; European, 1245-1750; American, 1750-1944, by Frederick Calhoun Wyse, jr. ... (Richmond, Printed by W. M. Brown & son) 1944.   4 p. l., 64, (3) p. illus. (facsim.) ports., fold. map, coat of arms, 2 geneal. tab. (1 fold.) 22½ cm.   "Sources of information": p. 64. 44-8693.   CS71.W812   1944

18935   WISE.   Legend of Louise; the life story of Mrs. Stephen S. Wise.   New York, Jewish Opinion Pub. Corp., 1949.   96 p. port. 21 cm. 49-9185*.   CT275.W58476W5

18936   WISE.   History of the descendants of Jacob Funck Wise.   By Vernon Laing Wise.   (Butler? Pa., 1962)   (48) p. ports. 22 cm. Cover title. 64-55033.   CS71.W812   1962

18937   WISE.   Wise-Tong pioneers of Clackamas, Oregon.   Compiled by Arthur D. Coleman. Provo, Utah, Printed by J. G. Stevenson, (1965)   xiv, 240 p. illus., maps, ports. 25 cm. 65-18343.

CS71.W812   1965

WISE.   See also: GLICK, 1959
                    HARRISON, 1910a
                    SHEARER, 1939
                    SNYDER, 1958
                    STRACHAN, CS479.S73
                    VAWTER, 1905

18938   WISEMAN.   The Wiseman family and the old church at New Salem: a brief sketch, written by the author, for his children and for gifts to a few personal friends, by C. M. L. Wiseman ... Columbus, O., Press of F. J. Heer, 1902.   38 p. front. (port.) illus. 20 cm. 4-27739 rev.

CS71.W814   1902

18939   WISEMAN.   Wiseman genealogy and biography, by B. W. S. Wiseman, M. D.   (Culver? Ind., 1910)   2 p. l., 7-134 p. front., illus. (incl. coat of arms) pl., port., facsims. 27½ cm. 15-8246.

CS71.W814   1910

18940   WISMER.   A brief history of Jacob Wismer and a complete genealogical family register with biographies of his descendants from the earliest available records to the present time.   With portraits and other illustrations.   By Rev. A. J. Fretz ... With an introduction by Eli Wismer.   Elkhart, Ind., Mennonite publishing co., 1893.   x p., 1 l., 372 p. front., plates, ports. 20 cm. 11-28971.   CS71.W815   1893

18941   WISNER.   The Wisners in America and their kindred; a genealogical and biographical history, by G. Franklin Wisner, B.S.   Baltimore, Md. (c. 1918)   6 p. l., (9)-270 p., 1 l., xviii p. illus. (incl. ports., plan, facsims.) geneal. tables (part fold.) 23½ cm. Title vignette: coat of arms. 18-18120.   CS71.W816   1918

WISNER.   See also WAGNER, 1945

WISSING.   See WIESINGER.

WISSINGER.   See WIESINGER.

18942   WISTAR.   A sketch of the life of Caspar Wister ... By W. S. W. Ruschenberger ... Reprinted from the Transactions of the College of physicians of Philadelphia, November 5, 1890.   Philadelphia, W. J. Dornan, 1891.   34 p. front. (port.) 23½ cm. 12-34877.   CS71.W8165   1890

18943   WISTAR.   The Wistar family.   A genealogy of the descendants of Caspar Wistar, emigrant in 1717.   Compiled by Richard Wistar Davids.   Philadelphia, 1896.   63 p.   front.   (fold. facsim.) 24 cm.
Inserted are three supplements containing "Corrections and additions" to Feb. 19, 1908. (19 p.) 12-30973.
CS71.W8165   1896

18944   WISTAR.   Observations in the European derivation of the American family of Wistars and Wisters.   (Philadelphia, 19 -?)   14 p.   mounted illus. (coat of arms) fold. geneal. tab.   22 cm.   By Isaac Jones Wistar.
12-30974.
CS71.W8165   190-

WISTAR.   See also HARRISON, 1932

WISTER.   See WISTAR.

18945   WISWALL.   The Wiswall family of America.   Four generations.   By the Rev. Anson Titus ... (Boston, 1886)   4 p.   24½ cm.   Caption title.   Reprinted from the New Eng. hist. and geneal. register for January, 1886.
9-18745.
CS71.W818   1886

18946   WISWALL.   A Wiswall line; ten generations in descent from Elder Thomas Wiswall of Dorchester, Massachusetts, 1635, to James Boit Wiswall, Wakefield, Massachusetts, 1925; compiled by Clarence Augustus Wiswall.   Boston, Mass., Priv. print., 1925.   59 p.   21 cm.   39-16934.
CS71.W818   1925

18947   WISWALL.   The Wiswall genealogy, 1450-1960.   By Joseph Michael Wiswall.   (Closter? N.J.) c. 1961.   viii, 109 p.   coat of arms, fold. geneal. table.   28 cm.   "Copy 18 of 25 copies."   61-39252. CS71.W818   1961

WISWALL.   See also JONES, F74.D5C6

18948   WITCRAFT.   Origin of the Witcraft family.   (By John R. Witcraft)   (pt. I - (Philadelphia, B. Hepworth & co., 1912?   v.   22½ cm.   12-24989.   CS71.W825   1912

WITH.   See WYTHE.

WITHER.   See WITHERS.

WITHERBEE.   See LISPENARD, E171.A53 v. 14 p. 262

18949   WITHEROW.   A history of David and Nancy Walker Witherow, Fairfield, Penna. and their descendants, with a brief sketch of the family of John Witherow, Revolutionary patriot, father of David.   By Mary (Witherow) Wantz.   (n. p., 1955)   79 p.   illus.   24 cm.   Based on an earlier work prepared by a publication committee, consisting of Flora W. Witherow and Belle Witherow Null.   This ed. prepared by a second publication committee, consisting of Belle Witherow Null and others; Mary Witherow Wantz, editor.   56-46910.   CS71.W8255   1955

18950   WITHERS.   Materials for a history of the Wither family.   By the Rev. Reginald F. Biggs-Wither ... Winchester (Eng.) Warren & son, 1907.   xviii, 271 p.   illus., plates, ports., col. coat of arms, fold. facsims., geneal. tables (part fold.) 26½ x 20½ cm.   10-24907.   CS439.W63

18951   WITHERS.   An unfinished history of the Withers family in Kansas City, Mo.   (By Webster Withers)   (Kansas City) Priv. print. at the Webb printing shop (1932)   3 p. l., 38 p.   23½ cm.   "This edition is limited to one hundred copies.   This is copy no. 89."   33-6849.   CS71.W8257   1932

18952   WITHERS.   Withers family of the County Lancaster, England, and of Stafford County, Virginia, establishing the ancestry of Robert Edwin Withers, III.   Presented by Robert Edwin Withers, sr.   Genealogists: Kathrine Cox Gottschalk and A. May Osler.   Richmond, Dietz Printing Co.   (1947)   xiv, 236 p.   plates, ports., maps (1 fold.) col. coat of arms, geneal. tables.   26 cm.   Cover title: Ancestry of Robert Edwin Withers, III.
47-5433 *.
CS71.W8257   1947

18953   WITHERS.   Withers - America; or, A collection of genealogical data concerning the history of the descendants in the male line of James Withers (1680/1 - 1746) of Stafford County, Virginia.   New York (1949?)   328 p.   ports., facsim.   23 cm.   50-31941 rev.   CS71.W8257   1949

18953 continued: —— Additional notes. (Washington, 1960?)   18, (2) l. 29 cm. Caption title. Typescript.
CS71.W8257   1949
Suppl.

WITHERS.   See also HOFFMAN, 1915

18954   WITHERSPOON.   Genealogy of the Witherspoon family, with some account of other families with which it is connected;   comp. by Joseph G. Wardlaw.   Yorkville, S. C., Printed at the Enquirer office, 1910.   3 p. l., 229 p. ports., coat of arms. 24 cm. Contains the Heathley, Donnom, Crawford, White, Dunlap and Jones families. 15-9686.
CS71.W826   1910

18955   WITHERSPOON.   My ancestors;   a brief account of the ancestry of Lister Witherspoon and his wife, Martinette Viley, of Woodford County, Kentucky.   (Washington, D. C., c. 1922)   303, (13) p. front., plates, ports., geneal. tables (2 fold.) facsims., coats of arms (1 col.) 27 cm. On verso of t. - p.: "Compiled by Martinette Viley Witherspoon, and privately printed for her children." Allied families: Martin, Rodes-Thomson, Douglas, Heale, Smith of "Purton", and others. 23-5216.
CS71.W826   1922

WITHERSPOON.   See also: ADAMS, 1939
SIBBET, 1954

WITHERSTINE.   See BENTLEY, 1905

18956   WITHEY.   The Withey-Grover-Geere-Bartlett families, compiled by Nellie Allen Bartlette, Mrs. James Ellwood Bartlett.   Winter Park, Fla., 1931.   3 p. l., 28 numb. l. 27½ cm. Type-written. 32-20375.
CS71.W827   1931

WITHEY.   See also WITHIE.

18957   WITHIE.   ... Pedigrees of the family of Withie, co. Devon, together with that of Fourdrinier in alliance with Grolleau.   Compiled by the Rev. F. G. Lee ... London, Mitchell and Hughes, printers, 1880.   cover-title, 11 p. illus. (coat of arms) 29 cm. "For private distribution." Reprinted from "Miscellanea genealogica et heraldica". London, 1880. 27 cm. (n. s., v. 3, p. 361-362, 373-379, 385-387) 2-26597.
CS439.W64

WITHIE.   See also WITHEY, 1931

WITHROW.   See BAREFOOT, 1966

18958   WITHYPOLL.   The family of Withypoll, with special reference to their manor of Christchurch, Ipswich, and some notes on the allied families of Thorne, Harper, Lucar, and Devereux, by G. C. Moore Smith ... Revised for the press, with additions, by P. H. Reaney ... (Letchworth, Hertfordshire, Printed by the Garden City press, limited) 1936.   100 p. front., illus. (incl. facsims., coat of arms) pl., ports., fold. geneal. tab. 30½ cm. (Walthamstow antiquarian society. Official publication no. 34) 37-38816.
CS439.W645S6

WITMER.   See WEISER, 1960

18959   WITSELL.   Some facts about the forebears and descendants of Dr. Charles and Emmeline Fishburne Witsell.   (Little Rock? Ark.) 1954.   17 l. 29 cm. 55-19912.   CS71.W8273

18960   WITT.   The Witt genealogy, compiled by Frank W. Balcomb ... Peabody, Mass., The Fraedy press (1943)   iv p., 1 l., 40 p. 21½ cm. "One hundred copies." 43-14671.   CS71.W8274   1943

WITT.   See also: FALL, 1961
HAMLETT, 1958
RUCKER, 1927

18961   WITTEN.   Dad and his folks, a history of the Witten and Graham families by James W. Witten.   (n. p.) 1932.   cover-title, 2 p. l., (2) - 85 p. plates, ports., coats of arms. 24 cm. "Edited by Letha and Frank Ledbetter." - Explanatory note. 32-23031.
CS71.W8277   1932

WITTEN. See also: EILER, 1929
No. 1459 - Early families of eastern ... Kentucky.

18962   WITTENBERGER.   Genealogy of the descendants of Josef Würtenberger and Anna Laüffer, who immigrated with four sons: Franz, August, Josef & Mathias from Gratz, Austria to United States of America, in April 1851 and Margaret, born in U.S.A.   By Ida Annette (Teeple) Wittenberger. Savanna, Ill., c.1958.   30 l. 30 cm. 59-20375.   CS71.W8278   1958

18963   WITTER.   A family record.   With a brief biographical sketch of William Clitus Witter. New York, J. Polhemus printing co., 1892.   21 l. plates, port. 30 cm. 13-11872.
CS71.W828   1892

18964   WITTER.   Witter genealogy; descendants of William Witter of Swampscott, Massachusetts, 1639-1659, compiled by Georgia Cooper Washburn from Witter family records and data gathered, and edited by Mabel Thacher Rosemary Washburn.   New York, The National historical company (c.1929) 394 p. col. front., pl., ports., facsim., coats of arms. 24½ cm. "Loveland ancestry (by Mabel T. R. Washburn) ... a reprint from the Journal of American history, volume XVI, number 4, 1918, subsequently reproduced in book-form": p. (219) - 261. "Extracts from the writings of Samuel Witter": p. (305) - 355. 32-2326.   CS71.W828   1929

WITTER.   See also ALLEN, 1872

18965   WITTEWRONGE.   Pedigree of Wittewronge of Ghent in Flanders, Stanton Barry (Bucks) and Rothamstead house (Herts), together with those of their descendants Lawes, Capper, Brooks, Gery, Le Heup, and Cullum.   By Gery Milner-Gibson-Cullum, F.S.A.   London, Mitchell, Hughes and Clarke, 1905.   42 p. pl., coats of arms. 27½ cm. Text runs parallel with back of cover. 10-3363.
CS439.W65

WITTON.   See SAVILE, DA690.L86.H8

18966   WITTRAM.   Drei Generationen.   Deutschland, Livland, Russland, 1830-1914.   Gesinnungen und Lebensformen baltisch-deutscher Familien.   Göttingen, Deuerlich (c.1949)   360 p. plates, ports. 24 cm. 50-31799.   CS887.W57   1949

18967   WITWER.   Witwer geneology (!) of America;   comp. by Reverend George Witwer ... (and) Ananias Clime Witwer ... (South Bend, Ind., Press of L. P. Hardy company, 1909)   256 p. illus. (incl. ports.) 22½ cm. 9-29349.   CS71.W833   1909

18968   WIXOM.   Wixom family history, compiled by J.H. Wixom and Ruth S. Widdison.   Salt Lake City (1963)   683 p. ports., col. coat of arms. 24 cm. 63-25357.   CS71.W835   1963

WIXOM.   See also RIX, 1957

18969   WODELL.   Genealogy of a part of the Wodell family from 1640 to 1880, with notices of some other families, copies of ancient interesting documents; and a condensed biograpny of the author as written by himself, Eli Wodell, 1880 ... (n.p., 1880?)   1 p. l., (11) - 98, (2) p. 25 cm. 6-28962.
CS71.W84   1880

18970   WODHULL.   ... Wodhull entries from the parish register of Thenford, Northamptonshire, England.   Communicated by Rufus King ... (New York, 1896)   p. (19) - 24. illus. (facsims.) 25 cm. Reprinted from the New York genealogical and biographical record for Jan. and April, 1896." 24-6509.   CS439.W66

18971   WOESTEMEYER.   Woestemeyer family genealogy.   By John A. Woestemeyer.   St. Paul, L. F. Knowles, 1940.   14 (i.e. 44) p. port. 29 cm. Includes extra numbered pages. Index on p. (3) of cover. Published as the September 1940 issue of the Knowles family. 57-54545.   CS71.K7296   1940

18972   WOESTMAN.   The Woestman family, genealogical and biographical, prepared and privately printed for Louise Woestman ... New York, The American historical society, inc., 1926. 43 numb. l., 1 l. ports., col. coat of arms. 32 cm. Dedication signed: Louise Woestman. Bound in blue crushed levant, gold tooled. 28-15341.   CS71.W843   1926
Office.

18973   WOGAMAN.   Wogaman, Burkett (and) Holdery (families)   By Ezra McFall Kuhns.   (Dayton, Ohio, 1948)   (11) p. 23 cm.   Cover title.   49-13269 *.
CS71.W845   1948

18974   WOGEN.   Lars and Mary Wogen.   By Joseph Glenn Wogen.   (Torrance? Calif., 1962)
85 p. illus. 28 cm. 62-43255.
CS71.W847   1962

WOHLERS.   See No. 553 - Goodhue county.

18975   WOLCOTT.   Society of Descendants of Henry Wolcott.   Report.   (n. p.)   v. 20 cm.
annual. 52-39041.
CS71.W8493

18976   WOLCOTT.   Memorial of Henry Wolcott, one of the first settlers of Windsor, Connecticut, and of some of his descendants.   By Samuel Wolcott ... New York, A. D. F. Randolph & co., 1881.
2 p. l., xviii, 439 p. front., plates, ports., facsims., coat of arms. 30½ cm.   Edition of 300 copies. Printed for private distribution. 9-15184.
CS71.W85   1881

18977   WOLCOTT.   A record of the descendants of James and Miriam Wolcott, by Chandler Wolcott.   Rochester, N. Y., C. Wolcott, 1907.   1 p. l., 35 p. pl. 18½ cm. 7-34807.
CS71.W85   1907

18978   WOLCOTT.   European and American family of Wolcott.   A record and chronicle containing origin, lineage and some history ... By Joseph Cooke Jackson ... New York, The author, 1912.
3 p. l., (5) - 96 p. 23½ cm.   Cover-title: British and American Wolcotts ... Half-title: British and American family of Wolcott; origin, lineage, service... "Designed expressly for those interested in the life and record of Henry Wolcott, the American colonial founder, and that of his ancestry and that of his direct descendants, whether living prior to, or subsequent to the date of the Wolcott memorial, published in New York, of which this is an immediate limited sequence. 12-25568.
CS71.W85   1912

18979   WOLCOTT.   Wolcott genealogy; the family of Henry Wolcott, one of the first settlers of Windsor, Connecticut, by Chandler Wolcott.   Printed for the Society of descendants of Henry Wolcott.   Rochester, N. Y., The Genesee press, 1912.   xxiv, 456 p. incl. front., 1 illus., pl. plates, ports., double facsim., coat of arms. 27½ cm. 12-26393.
CS71.W85   1912a

18980   WOLCOTT.   The Walcott book; history and genealogy of the American family of Walcott and notes of English Walcotts.   By Arthur Stuart Walcott.   Salem, Mass., S. Perley, 1925.   4 p. l., 279 p. front., plates, ports., plan. 24½ cm. Preface signed: Sidney Perley. 25-21783.
CS71.W85   1925

18981   WOLCOTT.   Wolcott vs. Walcott, etc.   Remarks by S. C. Evans ... descendant of Samuel Wolcott who m. Mercy Fosdick, May 27, 1725 (Chandler Wolcott book, pg. 364) (Who was the father of this Samuel Wolcott.) (n. p., 1928)   41 numb. l. 33 x 21½ cm. Type-written. CA29-553 unrev.
CS71.W85   1928

18982   WOLCOTT.   The two sister's poems and memoirs.   Composed by Eliza and Sarah G. Wolcott, of Connecticut.   New-Haven, Baldwin and Treadway, printers, 1930.   174 p. incl. front. 15 cm. 32-6982.
PS3348.W23

18983   WOLCOTT.   Genealogical table.   Showing the lineage of Margaret Wyatt, wife of Matthew Allyn, Devonshire, Eng., later of Windsor, Conn.   Also the descent of Henry Wolcott, Devonshire, Eng., later of Windsor, Conn., down to the compiler, Louis V. Wellner ... New York, N. Y., 1934.
fold. geneal. tab. illus. (coat of arms) 21 cm. Photostat reproduction (negative) "Blue ribon (!) series no. I. Issued May, 1934." 35-13995.
CS71.W85   1934

18984   WOLCOTT.   Family jottings (by) Roger Wolcott.   (Boston) Priv. print. (D. B. Updike, The Merrymount press) 1939.   ix, 120 p. 23½ cm. Includes bibliographies. An account of the Wolcott, Huntington, Prescott and allied families. 40-1205.
CS71.W85   1939

18985   WOLCOTT.   Wolcott genealogy; the family of Henry Wolcott, one of the first settlers of Windsor, Connecticut.   By Alice Böhmer Rudd.   Washington, Guild Pub. Co., 1950.   448 p. illus., ports., coat of arms. 29 cm. "Sponsored by the Society of Descendants of Henry Wolcott, incorporated." 50-14461.
CS71.W85   1950

WOLCOTT.   See also: BISHOP, 1877   SMITH, 1924
                       BLAKE, 1948   TOLL, 1961
                       GIBBS, 1933   TUCKERMAN, 1914
                       McCURDY, 1892   WALCOTT.
                       SALISBURY, 1892   Addenda.

WOLF.   See WOLFE.

18986   WOLFE.   A centennial memorial of Christian and Anna Maria Wolff, March twenty-fifth, 1863: with brief records of their children and relatives ... Philadelphia, 1863.   (iii) - viii, (9) - 113 p. ports. 27 cm.   Introductory note signed: George Wolff Fahnestock.   Partly interleaved.   One hundred copies privately printed, for the use of the descendants.   no. 57.   9-15183.   CS71.W855   1863

18987   WOLFE.   The Wolfes of Forenaghts, Blackhall, Baronrath, co. Kildare, Tipperary, Cape of Good Hope, &c.   Also the old Wolfes of co. Kildare, and the Wolfes of Dublin.   By Lieut-Colonel R. T. Wolfe.   2d ed.   Guildford, W. Matthews (1893)   xi, 107 p. fold. geneal. tab. 20½ cm. 1-14513.

CS499. W7

18988   WOLFE.   A genealogy of the descendants of John N. Wolff, (1729-1771) veteran (1746) of the third inter-colonial war, a resident of Lancaster County, Pennsylvania, and particularly of the descendants of his son John Wolff, (1764-1831) veteran of the war of the revolution, a resident of Lancaster, Pennsylvania and Byron, Ohio, by Frederick Lawrence Wolff ... assisted by Miss Jessica C. Ferguson ... Daniel Kaehel... and many others.   A bicentennial memorial of John Nicholas Wolff (born 1729) and Anna Maria Bower Wolff, his wife.   Omaha, Neb., 1729-1929.   3 p. l., 65 (i. e. 69) numb. l. front. (port.) 29 cm.   Type-written (carbon copy) Extra numbered leaves inserted. 29-27703.   CS71.W855   1929

18989   WOLFE.   Kith and kin of George Wolf, governor of Pennsylvania, 1829-1835, by Miss Clara A. Beck ... Easton, Pa., John S. Correll co., inc., 1930.   v, 65, (1) p. front., plates, ports. 23 cm. "Sources of information consulted": p. (66) 31-499.   CS71.W855   1930

18990   WOLFE.   Garrett county history of Wolf family.   By Charles E. Hoye.   (Oakland, Md.) 1934.   1 l. 37 cm.   Detached from the Mountain democrat, November 1, 1934.   38M1258T.   CS71.W855   1934

18991   WOLFE.   A brief history of the families of Andrew Jackson and Nancy Barton Wolfe in America, compiled by Preston Wolfe.   (n. p.) 1939.   2 p. l., 7-85 p. plates, ports., map, plan, facsims. 31 cm. 40-2181.   CS71.W855   1939

18992   WOLFE.   Some of the descendants of Henry Wolf who died in York County, Pennsylvania, in 1828.   (n. p.) 1947.   geneal. table. 58 x 89 cm. fold. to 30 x 25 cm. Blueprint. 50-25474.   CS71.W855   1947

18993   WOLFE.   The Wolfe, Hawkins, Sheets, Yates, Wheeler, and allied families.   By Lela (Wolfe) Prewitt.   (Fairfield? Iowa) 1964.   v, 126 p. geneal. table, port. 29 cm. 65-544.   CS71.W855   1964

18993a WOLFE.   Wolfe family in vertical file.   Ask reference librarian for this material.

        WOLFE.   See also: PASTORIUS, 1926
                             No. 553 - Goodhue county.

18994   WOLFENSBERGER.   Wolfensberger in America.   Compiled by Frances C. B. Francis (Mrs. Samuel K. Francis) Washington, 1967.   28 l. 30 cm. 70-4175.   CS71.W857   1967

        WOLFF.   See WOLFE.

18995   WOLLASTON.   Genealogical memoirs of the elder and extinct line of the Wollastons of Shenton and Finborough, their ancestors and connexions.   Illustrated with sheet pedigrees and shields of arms.   By Robert Edmond Chester Waters ... (A chapter from the unpublished memoirs of the Chesters of Chicheley.) London, The author, 1877.   vi, 66 p. front., illus. (coat of arms) 26 cm. "Only 35 copies printed for private circulation." 17-2885.   CS439. W67

        ——— (In his Genealogical memoirs of the extinct family of Chester of Chicheley ... London, 1878.   26½ cm. vol. II p. 541 - 603) 17-2886.   CS439. C55   1878

WOLLEN.　See WOOLLENS.

WOLLEY.　See CRALL, 1908

WOLLSCHLAEGER.　See WESLAGER.

WOLSEY.　See WOOLSEY.

WOLTERTON.　See also BASSETT, 1926

18997　WOLTZ.　The Woltz family.　Copyright ... by Flora Lee Woltz.　San Francisco, Calif.,
1939.　2 p. l., 125 numb. l., 13 l. 28½ cm.　Mimeographed.　40-512.　CS71.W86　1939

18998　WOLTZ.　The Woltz family, by Flora Lee Woltz.　2d ed.　(San Francisco, Calif., 1940)
3 p. l., 177 (i. e. 180), 20 numb. l. 28½ cm.　Includes extra numbered leaves 57 a and 144 a: number 172 repeated in foliation.　Mimeographed.
40-11988.　CS71.W86　1940

18999　WOLVERTON.　Wolverton family history (of Wolvertons of West Virginia) from the year of
1660 to 1960.　By Charles Evans Wolverton.　(Clarksburg? W. Va., 1960)　1 v. illus. 29 cm. 61-65255.
CS71.W863　1960

19000　WOMACK.　Womack genealogy.　This is a family association bulletin.　In vertical file.
Ask reference librarian for this material.

　　　WOMACK.　See also:　RAND, 1936
　　　　　　　　　　　　RAND, 1940

　　　WOMBWELL.　See WENTWORTH, DA690.B24W6

19001　WOOD.　A genealogy of one branch of the Wood family, from 1638 to 1870.　Brooklyn, N.Y.,
E. Darbee, printer, 1871.　26 p. 18 cm.　One page of errata inserted at end.　Dedication signed: T.W. Valentine. 23-14457.
CS71.W875　1871

19002　WOOD.　Pedigrees and memorials of the family of Woodd, formerly of Shynewood, Salop,
and Brize Norton, Oxfordshire; now of Conyngham hall, co. York, and Hampstead, Middlesex. And
of the family of Jupp, of London and Wandsworth.　Privately printed.　London, Mitchell and Hughes,
1875.　14 p., 1 l. front., illus. 28½ cm. 9-18115.　CS439.W7

19003　WOOD.　Parochial and family history of the parishes of Tintagel and Trevalga, in the county
of Cornwall.　By Sir John Maclean ...　Exeter, Printed for the subscribers by W. Pollard, 1877.
1 p. l., 118 p. front., illus., plates, plans. 29 cm.　"Fifteen copies only printed." A separate from the author's Parochial and family history
of the deanery of Trigg Minor in the county of Cornwall ... London, 1873-79, v. 3. p. (185) - 302.　Contains pedigrees of the Collow, alias Cullowe,
Lercedkne, Wood, Chilcott and Baron families. 15-7454.　DA690.T57M2

19004　WOOD.　A genealogical history.　Wood.　Read at the re-union of the Woods at East Smithfield, Pa., September 4th, 1882, by C. E. Wood, of Burlingame, Kansas.　Towanda, Pa., Alvord &
son, printers, 1882.　cover-title, 16 p. 20½ cm.　"The Wood reunion, September 4th, 1882, by Clay W. Holmes": p. (14) - 16.
18-373.　CS71.W875　1882

19005　WOOD.　A family history.　Composed and read by Ephraim Wood of Chicopee, Mass. ... at
the 50th anniversary of his parents' wedding.　(Seymour, Conn.) Printed at the Record office, 1883)
(3) p. 20½ cm.　No. t.-p. 1-15071.　CS71.W875　1883

19006　WOOD.　Brief history of the descendants of Thomas Wood and Ann, his wife.　Comp. by
Amasa Wood.　Worcester, Mass., Printed by D. Seagrave, 1884.　34 p. 23 cm. 6-7077.
CS71.W875　1884

19007　WOOD.　Descendants of the brothers Jeremiah and John Wood.　Comp. and pub. by William
S. Wood ... Worcester, Mass., C. Hamilton, 1885.　vii, (1) p., 1 l., (11) - 292 p. front., ports. 23½ cm. 9-15182.
CS71.W875　1885

19008   WOOD.   Genealogical, heraldic, and other records, with tables of founder's kin, of the family of Woodd, formerly of Shynewood and the White abbey, co. Salop (from co. York), and Brize Norton, Oxfordshire; now of Conyngham Hall, Knaresborough: Oughtershaw Hall, Skipton, co. York; Hampstead, Middlesex; Worlebury, Weston-super-Mare, and elsewhere.   Extracted from the records of the College of arms, London ... and from other sources, with proofs and evidences.   Privately printed. London, Mitchell and Hughes, 1886.   xii, 119 (i.e.127) p. incl. plates, geneal. tables (double and fold.) facsim., coats of arms (part col.) col. front.   29 cm.   Second edition.   Preface signed: Henry Woodd.   Pages 113 - 119 left blank for "Family register."   L. C. COPY REPLACED BY MICROFILM.   17-15266.   CS71.439.W7 1886
                                                                               Microfilm 8717 CS

19009   WOOD.   The parish of Chislet, Kent; its monuments, vicars and parish officers; with a digest of ancient documents now remaining in the parish chest.   By the Rev. Francis Haslewood ... Privately printed.   Ipswich, The author, 1887.   xiii, 193 p., 3 l. front. (port.) illus. (incl. facsims.) fold. geneal. tab.   27 cm.   "Two hundred and five copies privately printed."   "Pedigree of Wood and Wilkie": p. (172)   "Pedigree of Collard by Edward Maynard Collard": p. 192.   19-4764.   DA690.C555H3

19010   WOOD.   Wood family genealogy ... by F. I. Bishop.   Winthrop, Me.   (189-)   cover-title, 7 p. 18½ cm.   37-38429.   CS71.W875   189-

19011   WOOD.   ... A brief account of the Wood family in Virginia: containing a short memoir of James O. Wood and his ancestors from their earliest settlement in the colony of Virginia to his death. Written by M. B. Wood ... Philadelphia, Printed by J. B. Lippincott company, 1893.   89 p. 19 cm. 5-5119.   CS71.W875   1893

19012   WOOD.   The James Wood family record, 1771-1899.   (Cincinnati, O., 1899)   cover-title, 21, (1) p. illus. 20½ x 30½ cm.   Comp. by Merwin Sherman Turrill.   9-15483.   CS71.W875   1899

19013   WOOD.   A genealogy of the lineal descendants of William Wood who settled in Concord, Mass., in 1638.   Containing also revolutionary and other records.   Comp. by Clay W. Holmes.   (Elmira, N. Y., Advertiser print, 1901)   365 p. front. pl., ports. 24 cm. 1-13577.   CS71.W875   1901

19014   WOOD.   Descendants of the twin brothers John and Benjamin Wood.   Comp. and pub. by James A. Wood ... Concord, N. H., The Rumford press, 1902.   187 p. front. (port.) 19½ cm. 8-15275.
                                                                               CS71.W875   1902

19015   WOOD.   History and genealogy of the descendants of Abinah Wood and Susannah Humphreys. (By Percy Ashton Wood)   Andover, O., Press of the Citizen (1903)   (80) p. 23 cm.   Introduction signed: P. A. Wood, secretary.   On cover: Genealogy of Abinah Wood, Susannah Humphreys, and their descendants.   33-31488.
                                                                               CS71.W875   1903

19016   WOOD.   John Wood of Attercliffe, Yorkshire, England, and Falls, Bucks county, Pennsylvania and his descendants in the United States, by Arnold Wood.   New York, Priv. print., 1903. 2 p. l., (7) - 85 p. front. (fold. geneal. tab.) illus., plates, ports., fold. map, facsims. 24 cm.   "Of this book there have been printed but fifty copies for members of the family, of which this is number 4."   "References": p. 67.   40-2279.   CS71.W875 1903a

19017   WOOD.   The Wood family, Sackville, N. B. being a genealogy of the line from Thomas Wood, of Rowley, Mass., born about 1634, to Josiah Wood, of Sackville, N. B., born in 1843.   With many facts added concerning collateral lines ... Gathered and arranged by James Allen Kibbe ... (Sackville, N. B., J. Wood) 1904.   43, iii p. 24 cm. 5-13010.   CS71.W875   1904

19018   WOOD.   History of the Wood family, by James W. Wood ... Luray, Va., Zion's advocate print (1904?)   cover-title, 24 p. 19½ cm. 28-25724.   CS71.W875   1904a

19019   WOOD.   Genealogy of Peleg Wood and his wife, Rebecca Miller, and their descendants.   By James B. Bray.   Waverly, N. Y., 1905.   Microfilm copy, made in 1942 by the Library of Congress.   Negative.   Collation of the original, as determined from the film: 17 p.   Mic 51-40.   Microfilm CS-3

19020   WOOD.   The Woods-McAfee memorial, containing an account of John Woods and James McAfee of Ireland and their descendants in America, copiously illustrated with maps drawn expressly for this work, and embellished with one hundred and fifty handsomely engraved portraits, scenes, etc.

19020 continued: By Rev. Neander M. Woods ... With an introduction by Hon. Reuben T. Durrett ... In which, besides considerable new matter bearing on Virginia and Kentucky history, will be found mention of the families of Adams, Alexander, Behre, Bennett (etc., etc.,) ... Also some hitherto unpublished documents which constitute a valuable contribution to the pioneer history of Virginia and Kentucky. Louisville, Ky., Courier-journal job printing co., 1905.   xiii, (1), 503 p. incl. illus., plates, ports., facsims. front., 7 maps (6 fold.) fold. geneal. tab. 30 x 24 cm. Appendices: Journals of James and Robert McAfee kept in May-August, 1773 - Three ancient pioneer roads of interest to both Woodses and McAfees. - Some ancient documents of special interest to the Woodses. 6-3826.

CS71.W875   1905

19021   WOOD.   An account of the ancestry of Arba Thayer Wood, with a sketch of his life written for their children and grandchildren, by his widow, Ann Maria Wood ... Boston, Lincoln & Smith press, 1908.   65 p. 25½ cm. Blank pages inserted at end for additional records. 34-10429.

CS71.W875   1908

19022   WOOD.   A short history of descendants and allied families of Robert Woods of Ireland. (Versailles, Mo., W. W. Kinloch, printer, 1909)   2 p. l., 64 p. ports., coat of arms. 22 cm. p. 52-63 blank for "Family record." 15-16069.

CS71.W875   1909

19023   WOOD.   The Woods family of Groton, Massachusetts.   A record of six generation.   By Henry Ernest Woods ... (Boston, Press of D. Clapp & son) 1910.   39 p. 25 cm. "Privately reprinted from vol. 64, New Eng. hist. and geneal. register." 1-15498.

CS71.W875   1910

19024   WOOD.   The Wood family of Burslem, a brief biography of those of its members who were sculptors, modellers and potters.   By Frank Falkner.   With an introduction by William Burton, M.A. London, Chapman & Hall, limited, 1912.   xx, 118 p. col. front., illus., plates, ports., map, fold. geneal. chart. 29½ cm. "The edition of this work is limited to four hundred and fifty copies." Chapters 6 - 10 (p. 38-102) are based on diaries and private papers of Enoch Wood, and include extracts from them.   "Appendix A: List of mould or subject numbers of the Ralph Wood productions": p. 103-105.   "Appendix B: Index to collection of items of interest relating to Burslem, made by Enoch Wood, from which extracts have been taken": p. 106 - 110. "Appendix C: Alphabetical list of names appearing on Enoch Wood's map of Burslem in 1750 ... ": p. 111.   Title from Newberry Lib. A13-729.

NK4210.W6F3

19025   WOOD.   Descendants of Levi Wood, 1755-1833.   First of Middleboro, Massachusetts; sometime of Pelham, Massachusetts; last of Macedon, Wayne County, New York.   A family genealogy and directory with mention of some of the allied families.   Comp. by Verne Seth Pease; family data collected by Mrs. Mary (Wood) Church.   Richland Center, Wis., Democrat press, 1913. 3 p. l., 81 p. 25 cm. 13-16437.

CS71.W875   1913

19026   WOOD.   William Wood (born 1656) of Earlsferry, Scotland, and some of his descendants and their connections, by J. Walter Wood.   (New Haven) The Tuttle, Morehouse & Taylor company, 1916. 74 p. front. (coat of arms) pl., ports., fold. geneal. tables. 23½ cm. 16-16188.   CS71.W875   1916

19027   WOOD.   The compiler's lineage, beginning with John Wood living in Rehoboth in 1743.   Allen F. Wood, compiler.   New Bedford, Mass., 1916.   13 p. 18 cm. Author's portrait on cover. 17-9729.

CS71.W875   1916a

19028   WOOD.   History of the Alan Wood iron and steel company.   1792-1920.   (Philadelphia, 1920?) 2 p. l., 3-75, (1) p. incl. illus., plates, ports. 3 fold. pl. 23½ cm. "Prepared by Frank H. Taylor." - 2d prelim. leaf. "Published for private circulation." "Generations of some descendants of James Wood": p. 75. "Errata" slip mounted on 2d prelim. leaf. 28-396.

TN704.U5A5

19029   WOOD.   The Wood family of Shelf, Halifax Parish, Yorkshire, England, Massachusetts, Connecticut, Long Island, N.Y., and Canada.   Written by Colonel Casey A. Wood ... for his second cousin S. Casey Wood, the third, Toronto, Canada.   Chicago, Ill., 1920.   1 p. l., 39 l. 28 cm. Autographed from type-written copy. 20-17016.   CS71.W875   1920

19030   WOOD.   Biographical sketches of the Wood families, by J.S.F.Wood.   (Pierre, S.D., The Hipple printing company, 1923)   140 p., 1 l. illus. (ports.) 24 cm. "100 copies of this book were privately published for personal distribution only."   One type-written leaf with place and date of publication, inserted before t.-p. 40-37516.

CS71.W875   1923

19031   WOOD.   The early history of the Fifteenth ward of the city of Pittsburgh, by Mrs. S. Kussart. (Bellevue, Pa., Suburban printing co., c.1925)   90 p. plates, ports. 22½ cm. Contains genealogy of the Woods, Ross and Blair family. "References": p. 86 - 90.   25-7563.   F159.P6K9

19032   WOOD.   Genealogical record of Lieutenant Robert Winthrop Wood ... and Lieutenant Paul Douglas Wood ... compiled by their parents, Brigadier General Winthrop S. Wood ... and Pauline Culler Wood. (Washington? D. C.) 1934.   2 p. l., 82 numb. l., 3 l. 55 geneal. tab. 28½ cm. Type-written (carbon copy) with additions and corrections in manuscript. The genealogical tables are photostat copies (negative) 34-23199.

CS71.W875   1934

19033   WOOD.   The history of the Woods family, with a genealogy of Alexander Woods and his descendants ... by Roy Cleo Woods ... Ann Arbor, Mich., Edwards brothers, inc., 1936.   ix, 246 p. illus. (incl. ports., coats of arms) 22 cm. "Lithoprinted." 37-7109.

CS71.W875   1936

19034   WOOD.   Wood genealogy and other family sketches; genealogical memoranda of a branch of the Wood family in England and America.   Also sketches of related families including Daniels, Fraser, Pease, Newey, Mullineux, Owens, Harger, Pohl, Roser, Boyson and Gorton families.   Compiled by Leland N. Wood, assisted by his brother, George E. Wood ... Rutland, Vt., The Tuttle publishing co., inc., 1937.   130 p. pl., ports. 23½ cm. 37-38442.   CS71.W875   1937

19035   WOOD.   Samuel Woods and his family, by Ruth Woods Dayton (Charleston, W. Va., Hood-Hiserman-Brodhag company) 1939.   vii, 170 p. front., plates, ports. 24 cm. Consists largely of family letters, many (p. 23-110) written during the civil war. Contains also the Neeson family. 39-22918.   CS71.W875   1939

19036   WOOD.   The Wood family from Edmund Wood of Yorkshire to the Wood's of Clark county, Ohio ... (by) Edwin Smith Todd. Springfield, O., 1939.   13 numb. l. 29½ cm. Caption title. Type-written (carbon copy) Text runs parallel with back of cover. "Source material on the Wood family": leaf 13. 40-18936.

CS71.W875   1939a

19037   WOOD.   Ancestry of Thomas Jefferson Wood, 1843-1894; descendant from Edmund Wood of Yorkshire, England, immigrant to New England, 1635, by Charles Carroll Gardner.   Newark, N.J., E. L. Wood, 1940.   2 p. l., 14, 21-84 p. 8 geneal. tab. 28 cm. Autographic reproduction of type-written copy. 40-9808.

CS71.W875   1940

19038   WOOD.   The origin and genealogy of the Woods family, as can be traced from 1649-1895, compiled and published by Lucy Alexander Embrey. (Kingsport, Tenn., Kingsport press, inc., 1940)   3 p. l., xxxviii p. 19 cm. 41-31432.   CS71.W875   1940a

19039   WOOD.   Genealogy of the Wood family and allied lines, with references to French and Irish ancestry, by George E. Wood. (Schenectady? N. Y., Gazette press, 1942)   3 p. l., ix, 19 (i.e. 25) p., 1 l. 21½ cm. Cover-title: Wood genealogy. "Revised and edited by Wallace A. Wood, December 1, 1942." 44-24407.

CS71.W875   1942

19040   WOOD.   Descendants of Josiah Wood through his son David Wood, Albermarle County, Virginia. Hopkinsville, Ky., 1947.   6 p. 28 cm. Caption title. 50-22851.   CS71.W875   1947

19041   WOOD.   That yesterday was home. By Roy Bridges. Sydney, Australasian Pub. Co. (1948) ix, 243 p. plates, ports. 22 cm. Describes the lives of a family of colonists, the Woods of Sorell Valley in the south-east of Tasmania. 49-12757 *.   DU472.W6B7

19042   WOOD.   Yorkshire to Westchester; a chronicle of the Wood family.   By Herbert Barber Howe. Rutland, Vt., Tuttle Pub. Co., 1948.   290 p. illus., ports., map (on lining-papers) facsims. 24 cm. "250 copies ... No. 39." Bibliographical references included in "Notes." 49-2347 *.

CS71.W875   1948

19043   WOOD.   Wood-Woods exchange. (Washington)   v. 28 cm. quarterly. None published 1949, 1952, 1954. "Devoted to southern Wood and Woods families." 58-26909.

CS71.W875   1948a

19044   WOOD.   Descendants of Edmund Wood in America.   By Frank Douglas Halverson.   (n, p.)
1949.   (1), 12 1.   30 cm.   Caption title.   "List of reference books": prelim. leaf.   50-1566.   CS71.W875   1949

19045   WOOD.   One hundred ninety-six grandparents: some descendants of John Wood of Rhode
Island (1655) and some of their ancestors.   By Dorothy (Wood) Ewers.   (Crete, Ill., 1961?)
unpaged.   29 cm.   62-52659.   CS71.W875   1961

19046   WOOD.   An interim report on the Wood family genealogy.   By M. H. Wood.   (London?)
1963.   iv, 46 p.   map.   33 cm.   Cover title.   64-840.   CS439.W7   1963

19047   WOOD.   Genealogy of the descendants of Abraham Wood.   By Charles Fox Wood.   (Oklahoma
City? Okla., 1963?)   83 p.   ports.   24 cm.   64-2725.   CS71.W875   1963

19048   WOOD.   Workbook of families allied to Wood.   By Dorothy (Wood) Ewers.   (Crete, Ill., 19)63.
1 v. (unpaged)   29 cm.   "A first revision and extension of the second half of One hundred and ninety-six grandparents, some descendants of John
Wood of Rhode Island (-1655) and some of their ancestors. "   65-2180.   CS71.W875   1963a

19049   WOOD.   Drifting down Holston River way, 1756-1966.   By Mayme Parrott Wood.   (Maryville,
Tenn.,   1966)   240 p.   illus., coats of arms, geneal. tables,. map, ports.   26 cm.   67-1603.
CS71.W875   1966

19050   WOOD.   The history of the Wood and allied families, by Eleanor Duncan Wood and Eleanor
Wood Moose.   (Morrilton? Ark., 1969?)   28 p.   28 cm.   75-7114 MARC.   CS71.W875   1969

WOOD.   Wood family under ELLIOTT family in vertical file.   Ask reference librarian for this material.

WOOD.   See also L. C. Additions and corrections no. 11

WOOD.   See also:

ADAMS, F63.M88 v.1   FAIRFAX, 1882   PEDEN, 1961
AMES, 1900   GOODNER, 1960   ROBINSON, 1902
BACON, 1948   LAKE, 1956   SAMPSON, 1922
BARRETT, F74.C8P8   LLOYD, 1912   TYLER, 1882
BENEDICT, F129.S697V33   MILLER, 1907   VAN NESS, 1960
BLAUVELT, 1967   MINER, 1928   WENTWORTH, 1883
COLLOW. DA690.T57M2   NICHOLS, 1936   WHEELER, 1920
CRANMER, 1877   WOODS.

WOOD-JONES.   See No. 430 - Adventurers of purse and person.

WOODBERRY.   See THORNDIKE, 1960

19052   WOODBRIDGE.   Woodbridge family.   (By Mary K. Talcott.   Boston, 1878)   7 p.   24 cm.   Reprinted from the New England historical and genealogical register for July, 1878.   1-19669.   CS71.W878   1878

19053   WOODBRIDGE.   The Woodbridge record: being an account of the descendants of the Rev.
John Woodbridge, of Newbury, Mass.   Comp. from the papers left by the late Louis Mitchell ... New
Haven, Priv. print. (by Tuttle, Morehouse & Taylor) 1883.   3 p. l., 272 p.   front. (port.) fold. geneal. tables.
32½ cm.   Two hundred copies only of this book have been printed, of which this is no. 43.   Ed. by Donald Grant Mitchell and Alfred Mitchell.
9-15484.   CS71.W878   1883

WOODBRIDGE.   See also: BRACKETT, 1917
WALWORTH, E171.A53 vol. 20
WILCOX, 1911b

19054   WOODBURY.   A contribution to the history of the ancient family of Woodbury.   Communicated
by Robert S. Rantoul.   (From the Historical collections of the Essex institute, vol. XXIV, p.1)
(Salem, Mass., 1887)   cover-title.   42 p.   port.   25 cm.   17-19215.   CS71.W88   1887
——— Copy 2.   (In Essex institute, Salem, Mass. Historical colls. v.24 p. 1-42.   17-19216.   F72.E7E81 vol. 24

19055   WOODBURY.   John Woodbury and some of his descendants.   A paper found among the manuscripts of the late Perley Derby.   (Salem? Mass., 1900?)   cover-title, 24 p.   21 cm.   "From the Historical collections of the Essex institute, v. 35 and 36." 2-25018.   CS71.W88   1900

19056   WOODBURY.   Genealogical sketches of the Woodbury family, its inter-marriages and connections, by Charles Levi Woodbury; ed. by his sister, E. C. D. Q. Woodbury.   Manchester, N. H., Printed by the J. B. Clarke company, 1904.   251 p.   front.   26 cm.   4-32403.
                                                                                                                 CS71.W88   1904

19057   WOODBURY.   A sketch of John Page Woodbury with his genealogy from John Woodbury, by C. J. H. Woodbury ... From the Register of the Lynn historical society for the year 1910.   Lynn, Mass., F. S. Whitten printer, 1911.   10 numb. l.   front. (port.) 23½ cm.   Printed on one side of leaf only.   11-5707.
                                                                                                                 CS71.W88   1911

19058   WOODBURY.   Woodbury genealogy.   Woodbury Genealogical Society.   (Wakefield? Mass., 1957?)   3 v.   29 cm.   Cover title.   Introd. signed: Ruth A. Woodbury.   "Four copies... made." 58-33265.   CS71.W88   1957

        WOODBURY.   See also: KELLOGG, 1899
                                THORNDIKE, 1960
                                No. 553 - Goodhue county.

19059   WOODCOCK.   History of the Woodcock family from 1692 to Sept. 1, 1912, by William Lee Woodcock ... (Altoona, Pa., Printed by Altoona tribune, c. 1912)   62 p. incl. ports. 20½ cm.   13-17090.
                                                                                                                 CS71.W882   1912

19060   WOODCOCK.   John Woodcock of Rehoboth, Mass., 1647, and some of his descendants.   (By John Leighton Woodcock)   Chicago, Ill., W. B. Conkey company, 1913.   2 p. l., 7-145 p. front., pl., ports. 23½ cm.   Foreword signed: J. L. W. (i. e. John Leighton Woodcock) Additions and corrections in manuscript throughout the text. "Authorities and references": p. 9.   26-16556.   CS71.W882   1913

        WOODCOCK.   See also CUST, CS439. C9

        WOODD.   See WOOD.

        WOODLIN.   See MILLER, 1923

19061   WOODFIN.   Woodfin, Clark, 1722-1952.   By Fannie Maud (Woodfin) Ravan.   (South Pittsburgh, Tenn., R. M. Woodfin, 1952)   33 p. 16 cm.   Cover title.   61-20637.   CS71.W8825 1952

19062   WOODFORD.   Genealogy of the Woodford family.   (n. p., n. d.)   15 p. (on double leaves) 22 cm. In MS. on t. p.: By Dr. James S. Lane of Clark Co., Ky.   Photocopy.   65-89156.   CS71.W8826

        WOODFORD.   See also WOODFORDE.

19063   WOODFORDE.   Woodforde papers and diaries, edited with an introduction by Dorothy Heighes Woodforde ... London, P. Davies, 1932.   xvi, 259, (1) p. front., ports., fold. geneal. tab. 22 cm. 33-11249.
                                                                                                                 CS439.W72

        WOODFORDE.   See also JONES, 1891

19064   WOODGATE.   A history of the Woodgates of Stonewall Park and of Summerhill in Kent, and their connections, by the Rev. Gordon Woodgate, M. A., and Giles Musgrave Gordon Woodgate ... With 20 illustrations and index.   Wibech, Printed for private circulation by Balding & Mansell (1909) 1 p. l., 511 p. front., plates, ports., VII fold. geneal. tab. 26 cm. 19-1541.   CS439.W73

        WOODHALL.   See MINNS, 1925

        WOODHAMS.   See KING, CS439.K7

        WOODHOUSE.   See No. 430 - Adventurers of purse and person.

19065   WOODHULL.   Woodhull genealogy: the Woodhull family in England and America, comp. by Mary Gould Woodhull and Francis Bowes Stevens.   Philadelphia, H. T. Coates & co., 1904.   366, lvi, (6) p. col. front. (coat of arms) plates, ports., fold. facsims. 23½ cm. 4-36358.

CS71. W883   1904

WOODLAND.   See BASSETT, 1926

19066   WOODLEY.   The Woodleys of Isle of Wight County, Virginia.   A statement by James Francis Crocker.   Portsmouth, Va., W. A. Fiske's printery, 1914.   40 p. front. (port.) 22 cm.   No. 1 in a volume of five genealogical tracts, to which is prefixed a geneal. t.-p.:   The Woodleys of the Isle of Wight County, Va. and other ancestors. Portsmouth, Va., 1915. 15-10361.

CS71. W884   1915

WOODLIFFE.   See No. 430 - Adventurers of purse and person.

19067   WOODLING.   A biographical history and genealogy of the Woodling family, by Dr. Charles A. Fisher ... Selinsgrove, Pa., 1936.   cover-title, 43 p. 20 cm. 37-9438.   CS71. W8847   1936

19068   WOODMAN.   A list of some of the descendants of Mr. Edward Woodman, who settled at Newbury, Mass., 1635.   Comp. by Joshua Coffin.   Newburyport, Mass., Printed for Cyrus Woodman, at the Union job office, 1855.   16 p. 18 cm. 9-15181.   CS71. W885   1855

19069   WOODMAN.   A list of the descendants of Mr. Joshua Woodman, who settled at Kingston, N. H., about 1736 ... By J. H. Woodman.   Brunswick, Me., Press of J. Griffin, 1856.   54 p. 24 cm. 9-15180.   CS71. W885   1856

WOODMAN. See also: GAMBLE, 1906
LANE, 1912

19070   WOODMANS.   The Woodmans of Buxton, Maine.   A list of the children, and of the grandchildren and great-grandchildren bearing the Woodman name, of Joseph, Joshua, and Nathan Woodman, who settled in Narraganset no. 1, now Buxton, Me.:   preceded by a list and some account of the families of Benjamin, Joshua, and Edward from whom they were descended.   By Cyrus Woodman.   Boston, Printed for private use, by D. Clapp & son, 1874.   vi, 125 p. 26 cm.   8 blank leaves at back for records. 9-15179.

CS71. W885   1874

19071   WOODRING.   Descendants of Nicholas and Margaret (Frantz) Wotring.   By Mabel Armstrong (Ghering) Granquist.   Warren, Pa., 1948.   44 l. 28 cm.   48-18356*.   CS71. W886   1948

19072   WOODRING.   The Vautrin-Wotring-Woodring family, Lorraine-Alsace-Pennsylvania, 1640-1790, by Raymond M. Bell and Mabel G. Granquist.   Washington, Pa., 1953.   11 p. illus. 23 cm. 54-35799.

CS71. W886   1953

19073   WOODRING.   The Vautrin-Wotring-Woodring family; Lorraine-Alsace-Pennsylvania, by Raymond M. Bell and Mabel G. Granquist.   Rev. Washington, Pa., 1958.   12 p. illus. 28 cm. 58-31376.

CS71. W886   1958

WOODROFFE.   See WOODROOFFE.

19074   WOODROOFFE.   Pedigree of Woodroffe of Plusterwine, co. Gloucester ... London, Mitchell and Hughes, printers, 1876.   8 p. 28 cm.   Coat of arms inserted. Fifty copies privately printed.   Reprinted from Miscellanea genealogica et heraldica.   London, 1876. 26 cm. v. 2, p. 378-383. 20-15232.   CS439. W74   1876

WOODROOFFE.   See also CASE, DA690. B23C3

19075   WOODRUFF.   The Woodruffs of Westfield; the genealogy of the line beginning with the migration of John the elder from South Hampton, L. I., to Elizabeth Town, New Jersey, by Wilford B. Woodruff ... Westfield, N. J., The Standard publishing concern (19 -)   3 p. l., (11) - 47 p. incl. illus., plates, ports. front. (coat of arms) 23½ cm. Four leaves of type-written additions: two mounted on p. 11 and two, entitled Appendix, mounted on p. (3) of cover. 39-16935.   CS71. W887   19 -

19076   WOODRUFF.   A branch of the Woodruff stock; comp. by Francis E. Woodruff ... Morris-town N.J., Printed at "The Jerseyman" office, 1902-03.   2 v. map. 24 cm. Paged continuously. 9-15173.
CS71.W887   1902-

19077   WOODRUFF.   The Woodruffs of New Jersey who came from Fordwich, Kent, England, by way of Lynn, Massachusetts, and Southampton, Long Island, revised and enlarged from "A branch of the Woodruff stock," by Francis E. Woodruff ... New York, The Grafton press, 1909.   xii, 131 p. front., plates, ports., maps, diagr. 24½ cm. "Abbreviations and authorities": p. xi - xii. 9-9527.
CS71.W887   1909

19078   WOODRUFF.   Sketch of Col. Joseph Woodruff, revolutionary soldier, of Broro Neck, McIntosh County, Georgia, with list of his descendants.   Also "Narrative" of Jane Harris Woodruff, describing pioneer days in Florida, also notes on Capt. Ferdinand O'Neal of Lee's legion, also notes on Capt. Aaron Smith, of Ninety-six district, South Carolina, who was massacred by the Cherokee Indians, 1 July 1776, with his wife and five children, including some of his descendants.   Collected by Dr. Cald-well Woodruff.   Hyattsville, Md., 1917.   118 l. 25 cm. Autographed from type-written copy. 17-20877.
CS71.W887   1917

19079   WOODRUFF.   Woodruff genealogy; Matthew Woodruff of Farmington, Conn., 1640-1, and ten generations of his descendants, together with genealogies of families connected through marriage, Abbe genealogy, Sturtevant genealogy, Stevens genealogy, Burke genealogy, briefs from Kelly, Franklin and Folger genealogies.   Compiled by George N. Mackenzie ... George S. Stewart ... assist-ed by Frederick O. Woodruff ... Boston, Mass., The Everett print, 1925.   2 p. l., (3) - 29 p. 24 cm. A revised edition by George S. Stewart and Frederick O. Woodruff of the Woodruff genealogy prepared by Frederick O. Woodruff for volume III of Colonial families of the United States, edited by George N. Mackenzie. 25-9456.
CS71.W887   1925

19080   WOODRUFF.   Ancestries; Aphek Lorenzo Woodruff, Columbia Hill, Nevada county, Californ-ia, and his wife Nancy Polk Macy, Los Angeles, California ... compiled by Ella Foy O'Gorman (Mrs. Michael Martin O'Gorman) (n. p.) 1934.   5 p. l., 264 (i. e.) 270 numb. l., 1 l. front., plates, ports., geneal. tables. 28 cm. 38M3357T.
CS71.W887   1934a

19081   WOODRUFF.   Woodruff-Hart (families)   Ella Foy O'Gorman, compiler.   (n. p.) 1934.   geneal. tab. 33 x 70 cm. fold. to 24½ x 19 cm. Reproduction of manuscript genealogical chart. 35-14001.
CS71.W887   1934

19082   WOODRUFF.   A branch of the Woodruff family, from John Woodruffe, the younger John, Nathaniel Woodruff and Stephen Woodruff from Southampton, L. I., New York, 1640-1645.   (By Stephen Albert Woodruff) (Chicago, 1945)   cover-title, 14, (1) p. 18½ cm. Compilers name from caption title. 46-23127.
CS71.W887   1945

19083   WOODRUFF.   Woodruffs, from Matthew to Morgan and Franklin; a genealogy, by Franklin Kenneth Woodruff and Morgan Lewis Woodruff, Jr.   (n. p., 1960)   1 v. 30 cm. 60-39192.
CS71.W887   1960

19084   WOODRUFF.   Woodruffs; from Matthew, 1640, to Morgan and Franklin, 1961, a genealogy. From records of the church at Southington, Conn., with reference only to those records containing the name Woodruff, by Franklin Kenneth Woodruff and Morgan Lewis Woodruff, Jr.   (n. p., 1961 or 2)   1 v. 29 cm. 62-65918.
CS71.W887   1961

19085   WOODRUFF.   Woodruff genealogy; descendants of Mathew Woodruff of Farmington, Con-necticut.   By Susan Emma (Woodruff) Abbott.   Milford, Conn., 1963.   viii, 785 p. illus., ports., map. 24 cm. 63-23034.
CS71.W887   1963

19086   WOODRUFF.   Woodruff chronicles; a genealogy: the Long Island-New Jersey family of John Woodruffe, the immigrant ancestor to America.   Glendale, Calif., A. H. Clark Co., 1967 -   v. illus., geneal. table, ports. 25 cm. Includes bibliographical references. Contents. - v.1. Joseph Woodruff of Elizabethtown. Ben-jamin Woodruff of Elizabethtown. Selected source materials. 67-19471.
CS71.W887   1967

WOODRUFF. See also: EGGLESTON, 1935
HARRIS, 1941
SMITH, 189-
WOODROOFFE.

WOODRUFFE. See WOODRUFF.

19087 WOODS. Kith and kin, written, at their urgent request, for the children of Mr. and Mrs. John Russell Sampson, by their mother. It includes records of their ancestors bearing the names Baker, Baldwin, Breckinridge, Brown, Bryson, Byrd, Curd, Dudley, Goodman, Horsley, Kennedy, Le Bruen, McClanahan, McDowell, McKesson, Poage, Reed, Rogers, Thornton, Trice, Sampson, and Woods. By Anne Eliza (Woods) Sampson. Richmond, William Byrd Press, 1922. 247 p. geneal. tables. 26 cm. Blank leaves interspersed. "Authorities": p. (3) - 4. 23-17610 rev. *   CS71.S189   1922
—— Supplement, 1929. (n. p. 1929?)   (11) p. geneal. tables. 26 cm. Caption title.
CS71.S189   1922
Suppl.

19088 WOODS. The history of the Woods family, with a genealogy of Alexander Woods and his descendants ... by Roy Cleo Woods ... Ann Arbor, Mich., Edwards brothers, inc., 1936. ix, 246 p. illus. (incl. ports., coats of arms) 22 cm. "Lithoprinted." "An intimate picture of our family, by Alta Heiser": p. 133-185.
CS71.W875   1936

WOODS. See also: DINWIDDIE, 1957
WOOD, especially WOOD, 1905

WOODSIDE. See YEAGER, 1912

19089 WOODSON. Historical genealogy of the Woodsons and their connections, comp. by Henry Morton Woodson ... (Memphis) The author, 1915.   760 p. incl. front. plates, ports., 2 col. coats of arms. 31½ cm. 15-19543.   CS71.W889   1915

WOODSON. See Additions and Corrections No. 243

WOODSON. See also: BLACK, 1954   SAUNDERS, 1939
COOPER, 1930   STEVENS, 1957
DICKERSON, 1961   WATKINS, 1957
KNIGHT, 193-   YAWKEY, 1939
ROBARDS, 1959   No. 430 - Adventurers of purse and person.

WOODSUM. See THORN.

19090 WOODWARD. Genealogy of the Woodward family of Chester county, Pennsylvania, with an appendix giving a brief account of the Woodwards of some other portions of the United States. Compiled by Lewis Woodward, M. D. Wilmington, Del., Printed by Ferris bros., 1879.   114 p. 23½ cm. 2-4678.   CS71.W91   1879

19091 WOODWARD. Descendants of Samuel Woodward, of Bristol, Maine. Compiled by Frank E. Woodward ... Portland, Me., S. M. Watson, 1887.   14 p. 23 cm. "Reprint from the Maine historical and genealogical recorder." 37-16960.   CS71.W91   1887

19092 WOODWARD. John B. Woodward, a biographical memoir, by Elijah R. Kennedy. For private distribution. New York, Printed at the De Vinne press, 1897.   3 p. l., 222 p. front. (port.) 23 cm. Includes an account of Woodward's service as an officer of the 13th regiment of New York militia, 1861 - 1863. 13-33777.
E523.5.13th K

19093 WOODWARD. Dr. Henry Woodward, the first English settler in South Carolina, and some of his descendants, by Joseph W. Barnwell. (Charleston? 1907?)   cover-title, 13 p. illus. (coat of arms) 23 cm. 7-23346 rev.   CS71.W91.1907

19094   WOODWARD.   Biography of George Washington Woodward, by his son, George A. Woodward.
(N. p.) 1924.   66 p,   front.   (port.)   23 cm.   39-14769.   F153.W92

19095   WOODWARD.   Genealogy of the Woodward family, 1584-1926.   (By H. J. Spencer) (n. p.,
1926)   cover-title,   18 p.   28 cm.   Introduction signed: H. Jay Spencer.   28-13973.   CS71.W91   1926

19096   WOODWARD.   Some descendants of Nathaniel Woodward, mathematician, compiled by Percy
Emmons Woodward, edited for the author by Mary Lovering Holman.   Newtonville, Mass. (Concord,
N.H., Rumford press) 1940.   vii, 63 p. incl. front. (map) 24½ cm.   40-32944.   CS71.W91   1940

19097   WOODWARD.   The ancestors and descendants of Davis Woodward, 1806-1882, and his wife,
Mary Boyd, 1810-1890.   By Thompson Elwyn Woodward.   Hyattsville, Md., 1958.   68 p.   illus.   22 cm.
58-34736.   CS71.W91   1958

> WOODWARD.   See also: FLAGG, 1903
> MAYO, CS439. M38
> WOODWORTH.
> WRENN, 1922

19098   WOODWORTH.   Descendants of Walter Woodworth of Scituate, Mass.   Records compiled by
William Atwater Woodworth.   White Palins, N.Y., 1898.   viii, 134 p. 26½ cm.   9-15178.
CS71.W912   1898

19099   WOODWORTH.   Descendants of Walter Woodworth of Scituate, Mass.   Sketch of Samuel
Woodworth (3-4-6-6) and his descendants.   Samuel Woodworth and his poem, "The old oaken bucket."
Francis Chandler Woodworth, author of the bird song, "Chic-a-de-dee."   Poem by Nancy Adelia
Woodworth, "The old homestead."   Woodworths who were in the revolutionary army from Connecticut,
New York, etc.   Boston, E. B. Woodworth, 1901.   70 p. incl. illus. (coat of arms) facsim.   21 cm.   2-6096.
CS71.S912   1901

19100   WOODWORTH.   Life and descendants of Selah Woodworth, 1750-1823 ... Leon R. Brown
compiler.   (n. p.) 1940.   1 p. 1., 41 numb. 1.   front. (coat of arms) 27½ cm.   Reproduced from type-written copy.   41-905.
CS71.W912   1940

> WOODWORTH.   See also: ACKLEY, 1915
> BREWER, 1936
> CHUTE, 1894
> WOODWARD.

> WOODYEAR.   See also CROSSLEY, CS439. C835

> WOOLBRIGHT.   See JARRATT, 1957

> WOOLDRIDGE.   See: CHAPPELL, 1929
> LINDSAY, 1917

19101   WOOLF.   An index of the descendants of John Anthony Woolf and Sarah Ann DeVoe.   (Woolf
Family Organization.   (Salt Lake City? 1968)   viii, 323 p. illus., ports. 22 cm.   70-10572 MARC.
CS71.W914   1968

> WOOLFOLK.   See: SLACK, 1930
> No. 3509 - Orange county.

19102   WOOLLENS.   ... Woollens family records, by John Insley Coddington ... (Washington, 1930?)
91-94 p. 26 cm.   Caption title.   Detached from the National genealogical society quarterly.   Bibliographical foot-notes.   45-45724.
Sept. 1942, p. 91 ...   CS71.W915   1930

19103   WOOLLEY.   The Utah Woolley family, descendants of Thomas Woolley and Sarah Coppock of Pennsylvania.   By Preston Woolley Parkinson.   With brief notices of other families of the name.   Salt Lake City (1967)   xxxii, 1114 p. illus., col. coat of arms, facsims., geneal. tables, ports. 24 cm. 67-31470.

CS71.W9153   1967

19104   WOOLSEY.   The history of the life and times of Cardinal Wolsey, prime minister to King Henry VIII ... In which are interspersed the lives and memorable actions of the most eminent persons: and the whole illustrated with political and moral reflections.   Collected from antient records, manuscripts, and historians ... By Joseph Grove, gent.   London, Printed for J. Wood, 1748, 43-44.   4 v. 8 pl. (part fold.) 32 port. (incl. fronts.) 20 cm. Vol. 2-3 anon.; v.4 dedication signed J. Grove. Vol. 1: 2d ed., 1748, v.2-4: Printed by J. Pursey for the author, 1743-44. Vol. 2-4 contain, in the form of foot-notes: The secret history of the cardinal, by George Cavendish. This is a reprint of the 1641 ed. of his: Negotiations of Thomas Wolsey. cf. Dict. nat. biog. v.IX p.346. 4-25744.   DA334.W8G8

19105   WOOLSEY.   Letters of a family during the war for the union. 1861-1865. (New Haven, Conn., Tuttle, Morehouse & Taylor) 1899.   2 v. 20 cm. Ed. by Mrs. Georgeanna Muirson (Woolsey) Bacon and Mrs. Eliza Newton (Woolsey) Howland. "Printed for private distribution." Mar.30, 99-6.

E464.B13

19106   WOOLSEY.   Family records; being some account of the ancestry of my father and mother, Charles William Woolsey and Jane Eliza Newton.   (By Mrs. Eliza Newton (Woolsey) Howland) (New Haven, Conn., The Tuttle, Morehouse & Taylor press, 1900)   3 p. l., v-xii, 256 p. illus., plates, ports. 21 cm. On cover: Family records 1620-1840. 1-30095 rev.   CS71.W916   1900

19107   WOOLSEY.   Family of George Wood Woolsey and wife Sarah Nelson Woolsey, by Hester (Woolsey) Brewer.   Rutland, Vt., The Tuttle publishing co., inc. (c.1940)   134 p. illus. (coat of arms) 23 cm. Includes the Hedges, Biggs and Peyton families. Bibliography: p. 16. 40-30392.   CS71.W916   1940

19108   WOOLSEY.   Woolseys in America, the Richard Woolsey families.   By John Homer Woolsey. (Carmel, Calif.) 1959.   78 l. map, coat of arms, geneal. tables(1 fold. in pocket) 28 cm. "Book no. 24." Bibliography: leaves 75-78. 62-59758.   CS71.W916   1959

WOOLSEY.   See also CROPPER, CS439.C83

19109   WOOLSON.   The Woolson-Fenno ancestry and allied lines, with biographical sketches, by Lula May (Fenno) Woolson and Charles Amasa Woolson ... (Boston) Priv. print. (T. R. Marvin & son, printers) 1907.   2 p. l., iii, 7-143, (1) p. front., plates, ports., fold. geneal. tables. 24½ cm. 11-1571.

CS71.W9164   1907

WOOLSON.   See COOPER, 1930

19110   WOOLVERTON.   The Woolvertons; early legal records of the family in New Jersey, and the descendants of Charles Woolverton (2) to the seventh generation, by Emma Ten Broeck Runk.   Philadelphia, Press of Harris and Patridge, incorporated, 1932.   2 p. l., 3-91 p. 24½ cm. Lettered on cover: Wolverton records. 32-34496.   CS71.W9168   1932

19111   WOOLWORTH.   The descendants of Richard and Hannah Huggins Woolworth, who landed at Newbury, Mass., 1678; removed to Suffield, Conn., in 1685.   Comp. by Charlotte R. Woolworth, assisted by her daughter, Josephine L. Kimpton.   New Haven, Conn. (Press of C. H. Ryder) 1893.   209 p. ports. 25 cm. Interleaved. 9-15177.   CS71.W917   1893

WOOSTER.   See WORCESTER.

WOOTEN.   See: CARPENTER, 1950
PECK, 1955

WOOTTEN.   See WOOTEN.

19112   WORCESTER.   The Worcester family; or, The descendants of Rev. William Worcester, with a brief notice of the Connecticut Wooster family.   Collected by J. F. Worcester.   Lynn, W.W.Kellogg, printer, 1856.   iii, (1) p. illus. (coat of arms) ports. 23½ cm. 1-5427.   CS71.W92   1856

19113   WORCESTER.   Genealogy of the Woosters in America,   descended from Edward Wooster of Connecticut; also an appendix containing a sketch relating to the author, and a memoir of Rev. Hezekia Calvin Wooster, and public letters of General David Wooster.   By David Wooster ... San Francisco, M. Weiss, printer, 1885.   3 p. l., iii-v, 7-139, (1) p. mounted front., ports. (incl. mounted photos.) 24 cm.   "A brief memoir of the Rev. Hezekiah Calvin Wooster, by Rev. Elbert Osborn.   N. Y., 1837": p. 75-87.   33-15347.   CS71.W92   1885

19114   WORCESTER.   Captain Ira Beebe and Sergeant Walter Wooster, soldiers of the revolution. (Los Angeles, 1902)   cover-title, (11) p. pl., 2 port., facsim.   27 cm.   Comp. by Holdridge Ozro Collins.   5-3020.
                                                          E207.B4C7

19115   WORCESTER.   The descendants of Rev. William Worcester, with a brief notice of the Connecticut Wooster family.   First edition published by J. Fox Worcester, of Salem, Mass., in 1856. Rev. by Sarah Alice Worcester ... Boston, E. F. Worcester, 1914.   xxii, 270 p. front., plates, ports., col. coats of arms.   24½ cm.   1st edition has title: The Worcester family; or, The descendants of Rev. William Worcester.   15-5356.
                                                          CS71.W92   1914

19116   WORCESTER.   The Worcester family; or, The descendants of Rev. William Worcester, with a brief notice of the Connecticut Wooster family.   Collected by J. F. Worcester.   Lynn, W. W. Kellogg, printer, 1856.   iii, (1) p. illus. (coat of arms) ports.   23½ cm.   1-5427.   CS71.W92   1856
L. C. COPY REPLACED BY MICROFILM.   Microfilm 15578 CS

        WORCESTER.   See also CHUTE, 1894

19117   WORD.   Word family tree, compiled, delineated and copyrighted ... by Will F. Franke. (n. p.) c. 1933.   geneal. tab.   187 x 62 cm. fold. to 37½ x 62 cm.   Photocopy (negative) 47-36096.   CS71.W923   1933

19118   WORD.   The ancestors of Benjamin Franklin Word, compiled by his daughter, Mrs. Radiant B. (Word) Thompson.   (Fredericksburg, Va., 1946)   1 p. l., 4 numb. l. 28 x 21½ cm.   47-25231.
                                                          CS71.W923   1946

        WORDEN.   See WARDEN.

19119   WORDSWORTH.   Genealogical memoranda relating to the family of Wordsworth, collected by Edwin Jackson Bedford.   Privately printed. (Fifty copies only.) London, Mitchell and Hughes, printers, 1881.   27 p. incl. geneal. tab.   28 cm.   2-27572.   CS439.W78

19120   WORDSWORTH.   Letters of the Wordsworth family from 1787 to 1855, collected and ed. by William Knight ... Boston and London, Ginn and company, 1907.   3 v. fronts. (v.1: port.) illus. (plan) 18½ cm.   Mainly by William and Dorothy Wordsworth.   7-38248 rev.   PR5881.A3

19121   WORDSWORTH.   The correspondence of Henry Crabb Robinson with the Wordsworth circle (1808-1866) the greater part now for the first time printed from the originals in Dr. Williams's library, London.   Chronologically arranged and edited with introduction, notes and index by Edith J. Morley ... Oxford, The Clarendon press, 1927.   2 v. fronts., ports., facsims. (1 fold.) 23 cm.   Paged continuously.   "Contains all the letters of the Wordsworth family, and all the references to them and their affairs which are to be found in the letters of Crabb Robinson and in those of his friends ... in so far as these are preserved ... at Dr. Williams's library." - Foreword.   28-9583.
                                                          PR5881.A35

19122   WORDSWORTH.   Dorothy Wordsworth, the early years, by Catherine Macdonald Maclean ... London, Chatto & Windus, 1932.   xiii, 439, (1) p. front., plates, ports.   24 cm.   Bibliography: p. 393-429.   33-1996.
                                                          PR5883.M3   1932a

19123   WORDSWORTH.   Dorothy Wordsworth, the early years, by Catherine Macondald Maclean ... New York, The Viking press, 1932.   xiii, 439, (1) p. front., plates, ports.   23½ cm.   Printed in Great Britain.   Bibliography: p. 393-429.   32-26656.   PR5883.M3

        WORDSWORTH.   See also: LLOYD, 1890
                                  WILSON, 1890

        WORGE.   See WERGE, 1892

19124   WORKIZER.   The Workizer, Thropp & Cone families; biographical notes concerning their relations to historical events in the Schuylkill Valley and at Valley Forge, by Edward Payson Cone. New York, Priv. print., 1905.   2 p. l., 3-72 p. front., plates, ports., plan. 24 cm. 13-26806.

CS71.W925   1905

19125   WORKMAN.   Workman family history.   By Thelma (Chidester) Anderson.   Salt Lake City, 1962.   841 p. illus., ports., col. coat of arms. 24 cm. 62-58067.   CS71.W9254   1962

19126   WORLAND.   One man's family; the history and genealogy of the Worland family in America, 1662-1962, with supplements on the Clarkson family of Washington County, Kentucky and the Shocklees of Missouri, by Olive Lewis Kolb, Wilfrid V. Worland, and T. Vincent Worland.   Shelbyville, Ind., 1968.   xi, 1112 p. forms, genealotical tables, map (on lining papers) 29 cm. Bibliography: p. 1053-1056. 68-23786.

CS71.W9256

WORLEY.   See DODDRIDGE, 1961

WORMELEY.   See WORMLEY.

19127   WORMLEY.   Pedigree of the Wormeley family.   (n. p.) 1885 (i.e. 1888)   geneal. tab.   coat of arms. 58 x 27½ cm. Reproduced from manuscrkpt copy. 46-35302.   CS71.W926   1888

19128   WORRALL.   The Worrall family.   (San Diego, Calif., 1941?)   37 l. 2 mounted pl. on 1 l., maps (1 fold.) facsims., coat of arms, geneal. tables (1 fold.) 28 cm. Title from cover. "Records compiled by Mrs. May (Tibbets) Jarvis ... including data on the Worrall family, prepared for the compiler in the year 1918 by the late Gilbert Cope, esq. of West Chester, Pennsylvania." - Manuscript note on fly-leaf. One leaf of text and part of the plates are photostats. 41-17609.   CS71.W928   1941

WORRELL.   See RICHARDSON, 1929

19129   WORSHAM.   The Worsham family.   (n. p., 18 - ?)   5 l. 22½ cm. Photostat copy (positive) 39M403T.

CS71.W93   18--

19130   WORSLEY.   ... Pedigree of Worsley from Thomas Worsley of Stevenage.   (London, 1897) cover-title, fold. geneal. tab. 50 x 101½ cm. fold. to 26 cm. Compiled by Philip John Worsley, of Rodney Lodge, Clifton, Bristol, and by him entered at Heralds' college, 1897. 22-20776.   CS439.W8

WORSLEY.   See also BIRCH, DA670.L19C5 vol. 47

WORTH.   See HALLOWELL, 1924

19131   WOTHINGTON.   Proceedings at the celebration of the golden wedding of Mr. and Mrs. Orin S. Worthington, held at Spencer, Worcester County, Mass., October 19th, 1866.   Pawrucket, R. Sherman and company, printers, 1866.   24 p. 23½ cm. 21-8410.   CS71.W932   1866
Toner coll.

19132   WORTHINGTON.   A genealogical sketch of the Worthington and Plaskitt families with others (of Maryland) Baltimore, 1886.   20 p. 23½ cm. By Joshua Plaskitt. 9-15176.   CS71.W932   1886

19133   WORTHINGTON.   The genealogy of the Worthington family.   Comp. by George Worthington. (Cleveland, O.) 1894.   2 p. l., 9-489 p. front., (coat of arms) ports. 20½ cm. Descendants of Nicholas Worthington of Hatfield, Conn. 1-19525.   CS71.W932   1894

WORTHINGTON.   See also: ADAMS, CS439.A34
AMES, 1900
DORSEY, 1898
LA VELLE, 1957

WOTRING.   See WOODRING.

WRATHER.   See JAMES, 1913a

19134 WRAY. History of the Wrays of Glentworth 1523-1852. Including memoirs of the principal families with which they were connected. By Charles Dalton ... London, Chapman and Hall (limited); Aberdeen, Printed for the author by A. King & co., 1880-81. 2 v. fronts. (ports.) geneal. tables (part fold.) 22½ cm. Privately printed. 1-16378. CS439.W82
—— Appendix. London, Chapman and Hall, limited, 1880. cover-title, 48 p. 21 cm. 1-16378. CS439.W82a

19135 WREN. Patentalia: or, Memoirs of the family of the Wrens; viz., of Mathew bishop of Ely, Christopher dean of Windsor, &c. but chiefly of Sir Christopher Wren ... In which is contained, besides his works, a great number of original papers and records; on religion, politicks, anatomy, mathematicks, architecture, antiquities; and most branches of polite literature. Comp., by his son Christopher; now published by his grandson, Stephen Wren, esq; with the care of Joseph Ames ... London, Printed for T. Osborn (etc.) 1750. 2 p. l., xii, (4), 368 (i.e. 343), (4) p. 6 pl. (incl. diagrs.) 4 port. (incl. front.) fold. plan. 35½ cm. Nos. 121-124, 160-180 omitted in paging. Engraved dedication "To the Right Honourable Arthur Onslow." "Ex musaeo Huthii." 20-20243. CS439.W83

19135 a WREN. Memoirs of the life and works of Sir Christopher Wren, with a brief view of the progress of architecture in England, from the beginning of the reign of Charles the First to the end of the seventeenth century; and an appendix of authentic documents. By James Elmes ... London, Priestley and Weale, 1823. xxxvi, 532, 147, (1) p. front. (port.) 10 pl. (partly fold. incl. plans, diagrs.) 27½ cm. 11-7133. NA997.W8E4

19136 WREN. ... Sir Christopher Wren: his family and his times, with original letters and a discourse on architecture hitherto unpublished. 1858-1723. By Lucy Phillimore ... New York, Harper & brothers (1881) 1 p. l., 44 p. illus. 30 cm. (Harper's Franklin square library. no. 218) Caption title. 10-9084. NA997.W8P5

19137 —— Another edition. London, K. Paul, Trench & co., 1881. xvi, 362 p. front. (3 port.) pl. 22 cm. 11-7134. NA997.W8P52

19138 WREN. Parentalia, etc. (Reprint of No. 19135) London, Printed for T. Osborn, 1750. (Farnborough, Hants, Eng., Gregg Press, 1965) xii, 368 p. illus., facsims., maps, (part fold.) ports. 34 cm. 67-302. CS439.W83 1965

19139 WRENN. Wrenn-Woodward; genealogical notes collected and arranged by Mary Middleton Wrenn (née Woodward.) Washington, D.C., 1922. 160, (1) p. incl. coats of arms. fold. geneal. tab. 24 cm. Interspersed with blank leaves. One page of errata inserted at end. 24-3049. CS71.W94 1922

WRENN. See also WREN.

19140 WRIGHT. Wright family memorials gathered by Anna E. (Wright) Mathews, for the descendants of her grandfather Justus Wright, of South Hadley, Mass. Boston, Press of J. A. Crosby, 1886. 1 p. l., 42 p. 19½ cm. Six pages left blank for "Additional notes." 16-5355. CS71.W95 1886

19141 WRIGHT. Ancestral line of Stephen Mott Wright from Nicholas Wright, the colonial ancestor; comp. by Henry Whittemore. New York, The Lotus press (1899?) 23, (1) p. front. (port.) illus., geneal. tab. 25 cm. Originally published in the author's "Heroes of the revolution and their descendants;" reissued, with additions, for private circulation. 3-20267. CS71.W95 1899

19142 WRIGHT. Colonial families and their descendants, by one of the oldest graduates of St. Mary's hall, Burlington, N.J. "The first female church-school established in the United States, which has reached its sixty-first year ... Its noble founder being the great bishop of bishops," George Washington Doane ... Baltimore, Press of the Sun printing office, 1900. xvi, 239 p. incl. front. plates, ports. 19 cm. A history of the Wright family of Maryland and its branches. By Mrs. Mary Edwardine (Bourke) Emory. A-15-701. CS71.W95 1900

19143 WRIGHT. Genealogy of the Wright family from 1639 to 1901. Eight generations. Comp. and written by Rev. Henry W. Wright ... Middletown, Conn., Pelton & King, printers, 1901. 16 p. 24½ cm. 3-27045. CS71.W95 1901

19144   WRIGHT.   Some early Wright families of the Colony and State of Virginia.   By Arthur Alvin
Wayne.   Evantston, Ill. (19 -)   58 p. 25 cm. Typescript. 61-40554.   CS71.W95

19145   WRIGHT.   The Wright ancestry of Carolina, Dorchester, Somerset and Wicomico counties,
Maryland, by Capt. Charles W. Wright.   (Baltimore, Baltimore city printing and binding co.) 1907.
218 p. incl. front. 23½ cm. 10-9118.   CS71.W95   1907

19146   WRIGHT.   The Wright family, by S. V. Talcott.   Rearranged and pub. by Martin & Allardyce.
Frankford, Phila., Martin & Allardyce, 1912.   cover-title, 20 p. 19½ cm. 12-25486.
                                                                               CS71.W95   1912

19147   WRIGHT.   History of the Wright family who are descendants of Samuel Wright (1722-1789)
of Lenox, Mass., with lineage back to Thomas Wright (1610-1670) of Wethersfield, Conn. (emigrated
1640) and showing a direct line to John Wright, lord of Kelvedon hall, Essex, England, ed. by William
Henry Wright and Gertrude Wright Ketcham.   Denver, The Williamson-Haffner co. (c.1913)
2 p. l., 9-235 p. col. front. (coat of arms) illus., ports. 23½ cm. 13-6746.   CS71.W95   1913

19148   WRIGHT.   The Wright-Chamberlin genealogy from emigrant ancestors to present generations,
by Eunice Miena Barber.   (Binghamton, N.Y., The Vail-Ballou company) 1914.   6 p. l., 462 p. front., plates,
ports., facsims. 24½ cm. 14-14751.   CS71.W95   1914

19149   WRIGHT.   The Wright family; a genealogical record from 1740 to 1914, of the descendants
of Peter Wright, 1740-1821, with military histories of members of this family and a directory of descendants now living whose addresses are known, comp. by Fred Philo Wright.   Oswego, N.Y.
(1914?)   (34) p. 23 cm. 15-14796.   CS71.W95   1914a

19150   WRIGHT.   Genealogical and biographical notices of descendants of Sir John Wright of Kel-
vedon Hall, Essex, England; in America, Thomas Wright, of Wethersfield, Conn., Dea. Samuel
Wright, of Northampton, Mass., 1610-1670, 1614-1665.   Compilation and annotations by Curtis
Wright.   Carthage, Mo., 1915.   321 p. incl. front., plates, ports., fold. map, col. coats of arms. 24 cm. 21-19736.
                                                                               CS71.W95   1915

19151   WRIGHT.   Wright marriages in New York.   (By William Montgomery Clemens)   (In Genealogy;
a monthly magazine of American ancestry, edited by William Montgomery Clemens, New York city, N.Y., 1917. 23 cm. vol. VII, p. 49-60)
37-16965.   CS42.G7 vol.7
       —— Separate.   CS71.W95   1917

19152   WRIGHT.   ... The Washington-Wright connection and some descendants of Major Francis
and Anne (Washington) Wright.   By Charles Arthur Hoppin.   (In Tyler's quarterly historical and genealogical magazine. (Richmond) 1923. 24½ cm. vol. IV, no. 3, p. (153) - 314) The above article is followed by "The good name and fame of the Washingtons", by the same author (p. 315-356) CA 25-84 unrev.   E312.19.H79

19153   WRIGHT.   The Wright family of Oysterbay, L. I., with the ancestry of and descent from
Peter Wright and Nicholas Wright, 1423-1923 ... Compiled by Howland Delano Perrine ... New York,
1923.   3 p. l., 236 p. front., illus., plates, ports., maps (1 fold.) facsims., fold. geneal. tables, col. coat of arms. 26 cm. "Edition of
numbered and signed copies limited to two hundred and ten. no. 50." Some of the plates are printed on both sides. Contains also genealogical
table of Beaupre of Outwell, co. Norfolk. 24-2635.   CS71.W95   1923

19154   WRIGHT.   Four revolutionary soldiers and their descendants, Alexander Sleeth, Gabriel
Wright, David Smith, John Hacker ... by Eloise M. Roberts.   Avard, Okla., 1924.   1 p. l., 47, (8) p.
mounted port. 23½ cm. The Wright, Sleeth, Smith and Hacker ancestry of Mrs. Roberts. 25-7745.   CS71.W95   1924

19155   WRIGHT.   Anthony Wright, of Loudoun County, Virginia, and his descendants.   Compiled by
Howland Delano Perrine ... New York, 1925.   1 p. l., 86 numb. l. 27 cm. Type-written. Leaves 82 - 86 left blank for
"Addenda". 25-12671.   CS71.W95   1925

19156   WRIGHT.   The Wright family; descendants of the Wryta family of Bayeux, Normandy, to
England in 1066, with some of the descendants in America of the Kelvedon line of Sir John Wright, of
Kelvedon hall, county Essex, England, and of the Kilvestone line of Sir Thomas Wright, of Kelvestone

19156 continued: hall, county Norfolk, England, with additional genealogies of the Turner, Belsher, Riley, Lingo, and Blakely families.   Compiled by George William Wright ... Albany, Or., 1929.
102 p. incl. front., illus., ports., fold. map, col. coats of arms.   23 cm.   33-9646.   CS71.W95   1929

19157   WRIGHT.   The Wright family history and genealogy, 1633-1946, by James Long Wright, sr. (Santa Barbara, Calif., Printed for the author by the Schauer printing studio, inc., 1946)   xiv, 115 p. incl. illus. (port., coat of arms) port. fold. geneal. tab. 23½ cm. "Limited to one hundred copies, of which this copy is no. 41." 47-202.
                                                                                           CS71.W95   1946

19158   WRIGHT.   Ancestry and descendants of Jonathan Calkins Wright, 1760-1958.   (By Rachel (Nelson) Nutter) (Madison? Wis., 1958?)   xvii, 403 p. illus., geneal. table, map, ports. 28 cm. 65-88881.
                                                                                           CS71.W95   1958

19159   WRIGHT.   Our family ties; some ancestral lines of Marcus S. Wright, Jr. and Alice Olden Wright.   South River, N.J., 1960.   107 p. illus. 24 cm. 62-3066.   CS71.W95   1960

19160   WRIGHT.   Wright family history.   By Edman Wait Wright.   Elyria, Ohio, 1961.
58 p. illus., geneal. tables, maps. 29 cm. 65-571.   CS71.W95   1961

19161   WRIGHT.   Our parents, Delos C. and Emily A. (Hazen) Wright: their ancestry, by Albert Hazen Wright (and) Anna Allen Wright.   (Ithaca? N.Y.) 1964.   2 pts. (365, 34 l.) in 1 v. 28 cm. 65-42174.
                                                                                           CS71.W95   1964

19162   WRIGHT.   The valley of the God-almighty Joneses.   By Maginel (Wright) Barney.   (1st ed.) New York, Appleton-Century (1965)   156 p. illus., ports. 21 cm. Autobiographical. 64-24475.
                                                                                           CS71.W95   1965

19163   WRIGHT.   A family history: Wright-Lewis-Moore and connected families; early settlers, Greene County, Georgia. By John Wright Boyd.   Atlanta (1968)   xxv, 731 p. illus., col. coats of arms, facsims., maps, ports. 24 cm. 68-26729.   CS71.W95   1968

WRIGHT.   See also:

BALL, 1908	CALHOUN, 1957	PAINE, 1919
BARLOW, 1891	DUNHAM, 1916	POWELL, F127.L8B9
BARNES, 1939	FROST, 1962	STEVENS, 1957
BARNES, 1941	HANNA, 1905	STUART, 1961
BARTLETT, 1951	JOHNSON, 1961	TODD, 1960
BASSETT, 1926	LAWSON, 1903	WHIPPLE, 1917
BAVIS, 1880	LEWIS, 1901 (addenda)	WILDER, 1900
BLACK, 1956	LEWIS, 1910	WILLIS, 1946
BRAYTON, 1922	McCANN, 1955	WRIGHT, 1955 (addenda)
	NORTON, 1935	No. 3509 - Orange county.

19164   WRIGHTSON.   Pedigree of the family of Wrighton as constructed by the Rev. W. G. Wrightson ... London, Printed at the Chiswick press, for private presentation only, 1894.   21, (2) p. 22 cm. 16-17290.
                                                                                           CS439.W84

WRIGHTSON.   See also MALLOCH, 1857

WROTHAM.   See BASSETT, 1926

19165   WROTTESLEY.   History of the family of Wrottesley of Wrottesley, co. Stafford.   By Major-Gen. the Honble. George Wrottesley ... Exeter (Eng.) W. Pollard & co., 1903.   1 p. l., 433 p. illus., plates, facsim. 24 cm. Supplement to the Genealogist. 4-12415.   CS439.W86

WROTTESLEY.   See also GRESLEY, CS439.G75

WÜRTENBERGER.   See WITTENBERGER.

WUNDER. See PASTORIUS, 1926

19166   WUNDERLICH.   Genealogical record of the Wunderlich family in America.   Seventeen branches.   Compilied by Charles Albert Cornman ... Assisted by Danile Wunderlich Nead ... Carlisle, Pa., Cornman printing co., 1911.   x, 211, xviii p.   port.   23½ cm.   14-2031.

CS71.W96   1911

19167   WÜRMLI VON ESCHENBACH.   Die Würmli von Eschenbach.   Nebst nachträglichen zusätzlingen Ergänzungen vom Herausgeber.   Johann Paul Zwicky.   Zürich, 1949.   66 p.   21 cm.   50-16353.

CS999.W8   1949

19168   WURTS.   Wurts family; one of the series of sketches written for the Philadelphia North American, 1907-1913.   Based on the manuscript of John S. Wurts, comp. 1902 and by him brought down to date.   By Frank Willing Leach.   Philadelphia, Historical Publ. Society (c. 1931)   (24) p.   ports.   26 cm.   48-35386*.

CS71.W965   1931

WYAND.   See PUTNAM, 1909

WYANDT.   See WYAND.

19169   WYANT.   History of the Abram Wyant family.   By Charline Elizabeth (Appleby) Gadde.   (N. p., 1951?)   6 l.   28 cm.   53-32479.

CS71.W968   1951

19170   WYATT.   Genealogical memoranda relating to Richard Wyatt, of Hall Place, Shackleford, citizen and carpenter of London; with an account of the almshouses of his foundation at Godalming, under the care of the Worshipful company of carpenters, the governors.   Comp. by Edward Basil Jupp ... (London, 1870)   1 p. 1., 53 p.   front., facsims., coats of arms.   23 cm.   "Privately printed, 150 copies."   21-3441.

CS439.W83

19171   WYATT.   The history of Boxley parish; the abbey, rood of grace, and abbots; the clergy; the church, monuments and registers; including an account of the Wiat family, and of the trial on Penenden heath in 1076 ...   By J. Cave-Browne ... Maidstone, Printed for the author by E. J. Dickinson, 1892.   vi, (2), 225 p.   front., pl., port., plans, geneal. tab.   22½ cm.   1-18134.

DA690.B69C3

19172   WYATT.   The ancestry of Margaret Wyatt, wife of Matthew Allyn of Braunton in Devon, and later of Windsor in Connecticut ...   (By) Charles Knowles Bolton.   (Boston, 1898)   geneal. chart.   84 x 53½ cm. fold. to 30 x 17½ cm.   9-18746.

CS71.A43   1898a

19173   WYATT.   The Wyatt family of Baltimore (by) J. B. N. W. (James Bosley Noel Wyatt)   (n. p.)   1920.   19 p.   20 cm.   Title vignette (coat of arms)   21-8408.

CS71.W97   1920

19174   WYATT.   The genealogy of the Wyatt family, comp, by Alden H. Wyatt.   Knoxville, Ia., A. H. Wyatt (1921)   35 p.   illus. (mounted coat of arms)   23 cm.   22-12440.

CS71.W97   1921

19175   WYATT.   A history of the Wyatt, New and Gatewood lineage.   By Zona (Gatewood) Canterbury.   (n. p.) c. 1949.   85 p.   illus., ports., coat of arms, geneal. tables.   24 cm.   Copyright date stamped on t. p.   Bibliography: p. 16.   50-38233.

CS71.W97   1949

19176   WYATT.   Families of Joseph and Isaac Wyatt, brothers, who were sons of Zachariah ("Sacker") and Elizabeth (Ripley) Wyatt, of Durant's Neck, Perquimans County, North Carolina ...   Washington, c. 1950.   206 p.   illus., ports.   23 cm.   "Compiled for private distribution."   50-39476.

CS71.W97   1950

19177   WYATT.   The Wyatt family records; the descendants of E. J. Wyatt, of Pittsylvania County, Virginia, and his lineal descent from John Wyatt, early pioneer, of Halifax County, who is presumably the descendant of Adam Wyatt through the Rev. Haute (Hawte) Wyatt, who emigrated from England to Virginia, in 1621.   By Lucile Rebecca (Douglass) Wyatt.   Richmond, Dietz Press, 1957.   130 p.   illus.   24 cm.   58-3933.

CS71.W97   1957

19178   WYATT.   Wyatt family in vertical file.   Ask reference librarian for this material.

WYATT.   See also:

ATKINSON, 1959	GUNNING, 1907	SCOTT, CT788.S38S4
CHENEY, 1960	MILLER, 1923	SPANGLER, 1937
CORN, 1959	PUCKETT, 1960	WHITING, 1912
EVANS, 1940	RUCKER, 1927	No. 430 - Adventurers of purse and
GENTRY, 1909		person.

WYBORNE.   See WIBORNE.

19179   WYCHE.   James Wyche family history.   By Charles Walter Allison.   (Charlotte, N. C., 1955)
171 p. illus. 24 cm. 56-18659.   CS71.W973   1955

WYCHE.   See also ALLISON, 1955

WYCHOFF.   See WYCKOFF.

19180   WYCKOFF.   The Wyckoff family in America, a genealogy; prepared from the manuscript genealogical collections of the late William F. Wyckoff of Jamaica, New York, edited and published by Mr. and Mrs. M. B. Streeter.   Rutland, Vt., The Tuttle company (c.1934)   5 p. l., (9) - 536 p. front.,
plates, ports., fold. map, facsims. (part fold.) 24 cm. On cover: Pieter Wyckoff. "This edition is limited to two hundred copies. No. B."
34-15831.   CS71.W975   1934

19181   WYCKOFF.   The Wyckoff family bulletin.   (Summit, N. J., etc., Wyckoff Association in America)   v. 24 cm. Frequency varies. Began in 1937. Cf. Union list of serials. Some numbers lack title. Vols. for
include the Report of the   annual meeting of the Wyckoff Association in America. 68-42197.
                                                                                          CS71.W9748

19182   WYCKOFF.   A Directory of the Wyckoff family in America.   1st -   East Orange,
N. J. (etc.)   v. 23 cm. annual. Compiler: 1939 -   W. W. Wyckoff. Some directories issued with the Wyckoff family
bulletin. 68-2438.   CS71.W9747

19182a WYCKOFF.   Wyckoff family miscellaneous material in vertical file.   Ask reference librarian for
this material.

WYCKOFF.   See also: BERGEN, 1881
                       CHRYSLER, 1959

WYCOFF.   See WYCKOFF

WYE.   See WHITNEY, 1925

19183   WYER.   Some descendants of Edward Wyer of Charlestown, Massachusetts, 1658-1910.
(Albany, N. Y., The Gateway press) 1910.   2 p. l., 6 p. 22 cm. Fifty copies printed for members of the family, December,
1910. 11-26811.   CS71.W98   1910

19184   WYER.   The Nantucket Wyers, compiled by James I. Wyer, jr.   Albany, N. Y. (Printed at the
Marion press, Jamaica, N. Y.)   1911.   26 p., 1 l. 23 cm. "Two hundred copies privately printed." 11-22357.
                                                                                          CS71.W98   1911

19185   WYER.   Some descendants of Edward Wyer of Charlestown, Massachusetts, 1658-1935.   2d
ed.   Albany, 1935.   15 p. 23 cm. Foreword signed: J. I. W. (i.e.James Ingersoll Wyer) "One hundred copies printed December
1935. no. 59." Bibliography: p. 15. 39-22763.   CS71.W98   1935

19186   WYER.   Descendants of Edward Wyer, first generation, and James Ingersoll Wyer, II,
seventh generation.   By James Ingersoll Wyer.   Newark, N. J., The "Wyer weekly," 1942.
geneal. tab. 43½ x 47 cm. Reproduced from type-written copy. 44-1940.   CS71.W98   1942

WYER.   See also WARE.

WYETH.   See WYTHE.

WYGANT.   See CHIPP, 1933

WYGHTMAN.   See WIGHTMAN.

19187   WYKEHAM.   The life of William of Wykeham, bishop of Winchester. Collected from records, registers, manuscripts, and other authentic evidences, by Robert Lowth ... London, Printed by A. Millar in the Strand; and R. and J. Dodsley, in Pall-Mall, 1758.   xxviii, 404 p. front., pl., fold. geneal. tab. 21 cm.   Title vignette. Coat of arms on genealogical table. 22-22765.   DA237.W8L6

19188   WYKEHAM.   Life of William of Wykeham, sometime bishop of Winchester and lord high chancellor of England; with appendices, by George Herbert Moberly ... Winchester, Warren & son; (etc., etc.) 1887.   5 p. l., ix-xix, (1), 318 p. front. (fold. facsim.) fold. map, fold. geneal. tab. 23 cm. 22-22766.
DA237.W8M6

WYKEHAM.   See also: ATKINSON, 1933
PETTY, BX5195.T5B6

WYKOFF.   See WYCKOFF.

WYLEY.   See WILEY.

WYLIE.   See WILEY.

19189   WYLLYS.   Captain Nathan Hale, 1755-1776: Yale college 1773; Major John Palsgrave Wyllys, 1754-1790: Yale college 1773; friends and Yale classmates, who died in the country's service, one hanged as a spy by the British, the other killed in an Indian ambuscade on the far frontier. A digressive history now told with many antiquarian excursions, genealogical, architectural, social, and controversial: with an account of some members of a great patrician family, their manorial establishment in Hartford, their custody for generations of the Charter of King Charles the Second, and the story of the hiding thereof. By George Dudley Seymour. New-Haven, Priv. print. for the author (The Tuttle, Morehouse & Taylor company) 1933.   xxv p., 2 l., (3) - 296 p., 1 l. front., plates, ports., facsims. (1 double) 24½ cm.   "1000 copies printed of which 35 copies numbered and signed by the author have been reserved for the Walpole society." 33-36986.
E280.H2S512

19190   WYLLYS.   The Wyllys papers; correspondence and documents chiefly of descendants of Gov. George Wyllys of Connecticut, 1590-1796. Hartford, Connecticut historical society, 1924. xl, 567, (1) p. illus. (facsim.) 25 cm. (Added t.-p: Collections of the Connecticut historical society, vol. XXI) Edited by Albert C. Bates. "Sketch of Governor George Wyllys, by Lemuel A. Welles ...": p. (xix) - xl. "Roll of Col. William Whiting's regiment, 1709": p. 361 - 372. Includes list of freemen in Middletown and lists of families in Windsor, Hartford, and Wethersfield, 1669-1670, which constitute the only census of any towns in Connecticut before 1700. cf. p. 190. 25-27064.
F91.C7 vol. 21
——— Copy 2.
F97.W98

19191   WYMAN.   (Pedigree chart giving the ancestors of Harry H. Wyman, carrying the line back to Ezekiel Wyman, b. 1712) (n. p., 18-?)   geneal. tab. 24 x 31 cm. In manuscript. 38M3564T.
CS71.W984   18 -

19192   WYMAN.   The Wyman families in Great and Little Hormead, Herts county, Eng., by Horace Wyman. Worcester, Mass., 1895.   cover-title, 3 - 20 p. 18 x 24 cm. 37-31899.   CS439.W92   1895

19193   WYMAN.   Some account of the Wyman genealogy and Wyman families in Herts county, England.   By Horace Wyman. Worcester, F. S. Blanchard & co., 1897.   39 p. incl. front., illus., facsims., coat of arms. 21 cm. 16-23850.   CS439.W92

19194   WYMAN.   A brief record of the lives and writings of Dr. Rufus Wyman (1778-1842) and his son Dr. Morrill Wyman (1812-1903) by Morill Wyman, jr. Privately printed. Cambridge (Mass.,

19194 continued: The Riverside press) 1913.   4 p. l., 132 p., 1 l. front., plates, ports. 22 cm. "From the records of the trustees of the Massachusetts general hospital, 25th July, 1913" (an acknowledgment of the gift of a bronze bust of Dr. Wyman): 1 leaf inserted between p. 50 and (51) "Bibliography, list of publications, books and pamphlets written by Dr. Morrill Wyman": p. (129) - 132. 13-25457.

R154.W8W8

19195   WYMAN.   A history of the Wyman, Stearns, Morton, Tillson and Clifford families, arranged and published by Oliver Morton Clifford ... from notes and data left by Mrs. Susan Stearns Wyman Holmes ... (n. p., 1927)   (40) p. illus. incl. coats of arms. 24 cm. Some of the illustrations are mounted. 38-32657.

CS71.W984   1927

19196   WYMAN.   Wyman historic genealogy, ancestors and descendants (1595-1941) of Asa Wetherby Wyman.   Lowell genealogy supplement, ancestors and descendants (1220-1941) of Martin Luther Lowell. Phelps ancestral lines, Phelps (1520-1941) Foote (1593-1941) St. John-Whiting (1066-1941).   By Vincent D. Wyman ... Coral Gables, Private printing, Parker art printing association, 1941.   1 p. l., (v) - xi, 144 p., 1 l. 24 cm. Blank leaf at end for "Current family record." "Errata and Addenda" (3 leaves) inserted at end. 42-18888.

CS71.W984   1941

19197   WYNCOOP.   Wynkoop family; a preliminary genealogy, by Richard Wynkoop ... New York, Press of Wynkoop & Hallenbeck, 1866.   34 p. 23 cm. 9-15175.   CS71.W985   1866

19198   WYNCOOP.   Wynkoop genealogy in the United States of America.   Also a table of Dutch given names.   By Richard Wynkoop ... 2d ed.   New York, Press of Wynkoop & Hallenbeck, 1878.   2 p. l., 130, (127) - 130 p. pl. (coat of arms) 23½ cm. Supplement repeated with additions: p. (127) - 130. 9-15174.

CS71.W985   1878

19199   WYNCOOP.   Wynkoop genealogy in the United States of America, by Richard Wynkoop ... 3d ed.   New York, The Knickerbocker press, 1904.   xliv, 214 p. incl. front., illus. coats of arms. 24 cm. 4-8697.

CS71.W985   1904

19200   WYNDHAM.   A family history, 1410-1688; the Wyndhams of Norfolk and Somerset, by the Hon. H. A. Wyndham.   London, New York (etc.) Oxford university press, 1939.   vii, 323, (1) p. front. (port.) fold. plan, fold. geneal. tables. 22 cm. 40-14492.

DA28.35.W9W9

WYNDHAM. See also PENDEREL. DA446.H87

WYNKOOP. See WYNCOOP.

19201   WYNN.   Wynnstay & the Wynns.   A volume of varieties.   Put together by the author of "The gossiping guide to Wales." (Askew Roberts) Oswestry, (Eng.) Woodall and Venables, 1876.   3 p. l., (iii) - viii, 122, (2) p. front., plates, ports. 22 x 17 cm. Title vignette (coat of arms) 19-3355.   CS459.W9   1876

19202   WYNN.   Ancestry of Dr. Thomas Wynne, speaker of the first Assemby of Pennsylvania, etc. Who was born in the parish of Yskeiviog, near Caerwys, in Flintshire, North Wales, in the year 1627, and who removed to the province of Pennsylvania with William Penn, in the good ship "Welcome," in the year 1682. (From the authorities cited in proof) By Richard Y. Cook ... Printed for private distribution. Philadelphia, Pa., 1904.   21 p. front. (port.) 38½ cm. 12-25501.   CS71.W986   1904

19203   WYNN.   The Wynnes; a genealogical summary of the ancestry of the Welsh Wynnes, who emigrated to Pennsylvania with William Penn.   By T. B. Deem ... Indianapolis, Aetna printing co., 1907.   340 p. incl. fronts., (incl. coats of arms) illus., plates, ports., maps, facsims. 29 x 21½ cm. 24-4250 rev.

CS71.W986   1907

19204   WYNN.   Calendar of Wynn (of Gwydir) papers, 1515-1690, in the National library of Wales and elsewhere.   Aberystwyth, The National library of Wales; London, H. Milford; (etc., etc.) 1926.   3 p. l., ix - xx, 511, (1) p. 26½ cm. "1,000 copies of this work were printed for the National library of Wales by the Western mail limited, Cardiff, 1924-6." 27-9993.   CS459.W9   1926

19205   WYNN.   Ancestors and descendants of John Quarles Winn and his wife Mary Liscome Jarvis, including also the descendants of their parents, compiled and edited by the Reverend David Watson

19205 continued: Winn and Elizabeth Jarvis Winn.   Baltimore, Md.   (Lord Baltimore press) 1932.
xvii, 226 p. front., plates, ports., facsims., geneal. tab., col. coats of arms.   26 cm.   Genealogical tables on lining-papers.   "References" at
end of most of the chapters.   33-34829 rev.   CS71.W986   1932

19206   WYNN.   Winn memoirs; Jesse Durrett Winn, his family and descendants, collected, compiled and written by James French Winn.   Cynthiana, Ky., The Hobson press, 1942.   2 p. l., vii - ix, 49 p.
23 cm.   Reproduced from type-written copy.   "First printing."   42-50347.   CS71.W986   1942

          WYNN.   See also: BEAN, 1965   LINDLEY, 1950
                              CORN, 1959   OGBURN, 1958
                              EVANS, 1940   WHITNEY, E171.A53 vol. 16
                              GWYDIR, CS459.G8   WHITNEY, 1925

19207   WYNNE.   The Wynne diaries; edited by Anne Fremantle ... London, Oxford university press,
H. Milford, 1935 -   v. front., illus., pl., ports., fold. maps, geneal. tables. 22½ cm.   Diaries of Elizabeth and
Eugenia Wynne.   In editing their diaries the editor has used, "principally, Betsey's, but Eugenia's wherever hers was fuller or more vivacious".
Whenever they separated she has given both their entries.   cf. Pref., p. ix.   Bibliography: v. 1, p. 319.   36-3966.   D360.F7

          WYNNE.   See also WYNN.

19208   WYNYARD.   The family of Wynyard.   (London, 1877?)   (4) p. 28½ cm.   Communicated by Rev.
C. W. Bingham.   Reprinted from "Miscellanea genealogica et heraldica," n.s., 1877 v. 2, p. 269-272.   9-18113.
                                                                                         CS439.W94

          WYSONG.   See No. 4639 - The story of Smithfield.

          WYSE.   See WISE.

Y

19209   YALE.   The Yale family, or The descendants of David Yale, with genealogical notes of each family.   By Elihu Yale ... New Haven, Storer & Stone, printers, 1850.   201 p. 23 cm. 9-18747.

CS71.Y18   1850

19210   YALE.   Yale genealogy and history of Wales.   The British kings and princes.   Life of Owen Glyndwr.   Biographies of Governor Elihu Yale ... Linus Yale, sr., and Linus Yale, jr. ... Maurice Fitz Gerald ... Roger de Montgomery ... and other noted persons.   By Rodney Horace Yale.   Beatrice, Neb.   (Printed by Milburn and Scott company) 1908.   4 p. 1., (3) - 597, xxv p. incl. 1 col. illus., maps. front., plates, ports., facsims., fold. geneal. tab. 18 cm. 9-9945.

CS71.Y18   1908

YALE.   See also SMITH, 1889a

19211   YANCEY.   Genealogy of Yancey, Medearis, and related lines; compiled by William Howard Norwood in cooperation with James Harvey Norwood, Sr. and Olivia Yancey Lacy.   (Corsicana? Tex.) 1958.   261 p. illus., ports., mounted col. coat of arms, facsims. 29 cm. Bibliography: p. 3. 59-20367.

CS71.Y185   1958

——— Appendix "A."   (By) Douglas Mannon Willis.   (Corsicana? Tex.) 1959.   A46 p. illus., ports. 28 cm. 59-20367 rev.

CS71.Y185   1958
App.

19212   YANDES.   Daniel Yandes and his family, pioneers from Pennsylvania to Indiana, 1818; compiled, and presented to his descendants, by his granddaughters Annabelle Robinson, Mary Yandes Robinson, Josephine Robinson.   Crawfordsville, Ind., R. E. Banta, 1936.   6 p. 1., 205 p., 1 1. front., plates, ports., facsims. 24 cm. 36-11414.

CS71.Y2   1936

YARBOROUGH.   See LONG, 1956

YARBROUGH.   See PHILLIPS, 1928

YARDE.   See SAINTHILL, CJ35.S2 vol. 1

19213   YARDLEY.   Genealogy of the Yardley family, 1402-1881.   By Thomas W. Yardley.   Philadelphia, W. S. Schofield, 1881.   257 p. incl. front. (geneal. tab.) 25 cm. Every other page left blank. Title vignette: colored coat of arms. 24-4260.

CS71.Y27   1881

19214   YARDLEY.   Pedigree of the family of Yardley, of Chatham, co. Kent.   Comp. by William Brigg ... from the 'Visitation of Kent 1663-1668,' parish registers, wills, etc., and deeds in the possession of Edward Stone, esq.   Privately printed.   London, Mitchell and Hughes, 1891.   8 p. pl. 25½ cm. 2-26605.

CS439.Y3

19215   YARDLEY.   Sir George Yeardley, or Yardley, governor and captain general of Virginia, and Temperance (West) lady Yeardley, and some of their descendants.   (By) Thomas Teackle Upshur ...   (Nashville, 1896)   cover-title, 36 p. 30 cm. "Reprinted from American historical magazine, Nashville, Tenn., Oct. 1896."   9-15028.

CS71.Y27   1896

19216   YARKER.   Genealogy of the surname Yarker; with the Leyburn, and several allied families; resident in the counties of Yorkshire, Durham, Westmoreland, and Lancashire, including all of the name in Cumberland, Canada, America, and Middlesex.   (From the conquest to the present time) Collected by John Yarker ... (Privately printed) Manchester, A. M. Petty & co., printers, 1882.
1 p. l., 46 p. 2 pl. (coats of arms) 29 cm. Pedigree: p. 17-33. "Authorities": p. 46. 15-25120.

CS439.Y4

19217   YARNALL.   Yarnall family and collateral lines.   By Alexander Du Bin.   Philadelphia, Historical Publ. Society, 1948.   18 p. 26 cm. 49-18840 *.

CS71.Y285   1948

YARNALL.   See also: MATLACK, F263.P4M3
RICHARDSON, 1929

YARRINGTON.   See YERRINGTON.

19218   YATES.   Memorials of a family in England and Virginia.   A.D. 1771-1851.   Comp. and ed. by A. E. Terrill ... Printed for private circulation.   (London and Aylesbury, Printed by Hazell, Watson, & Viney, ltd.) 1887.   viii, 383 p. 23 cm. Composed mainly of letters to and from John Yates of Walnut Grove, Virginia. Contains genealogies of the Yates, Aglionby, Orfeur, Lamplugh, and Musgrave families. 17-19217.

CS71.Y33   1887

19219   YATES.   The Yates book.   William Yates and his descendants; the history and genealogy of William Yates (1772-1868) of Greenwood, Me., and his wife, who was Martha Morgan, together with the line of her descent from Robert Morgan of Beverly, by Edgar Yates ... Old Orchard, Me., Printed by E. M. Yates and E. Yates, 1906.   2 p. l., 46 p., 1 l. front., ports., facsims. 22 cm. 6-46223.

CS71.Y33   1906

19220   YATES.   Descendants of Michael Yates by his son, Abner and John.   (By) Richard Yates. Springfield, Ill. (1906?)   geneal. tab. 72 x 85 cm. fold. to 14½ x 24 cm. Printed on both sides. Cover-title: The Yates family. 10-15956.

CS71.Y33   1906a

19221   YATES.   Ancestors of James Wilson Yates and his wife Nancy Davis Terry, showing Mayflower descent ... compiled for their daughter Irene Yates Shaffer, by Josephine C. Frost (Mrs. Samuel Knapp Frost) ... New York, F.H. Hitchcock, 1926.   2 p. l., (3) - 94 p. fold. geneal. tab. 24 cm. "Only fifty copies of this book have been printed ... This copy is number 20." 27-3057.

CS71.Y33   1926

19222   YATES.   John Yates of England and Virginia.   His family and descendants, compiled by Elizabeth Daniel.   (Charles Town, W. Va.) 1936.   (16) p. 22½ cm. 37-5919.

CS71.Y33   1936

19223   YATES.   Yates family. (By Thomas John Hall.)   Page 244.

CS71.H177   1941

19224   YATES.   The Yates family in Virginia, descendants of George Yate(s) deputy provincial surveyor of Maryland (16— - 1691) ... Compiled by Mrs. J. Brent Clarke (Elizabeth Waters) ... Washington, 1942.   161 l. incl. fold. geneal. tab. 28 ½ cm. Type-written. Leaves variously numbered. Leaf (notes copied from an old book owned by J, S. Johnson, Lexington, Ky., mounted between cellophane covers) inserted between l. 106 and 107; additional notes mounted on versos of l. 107 and 108. Includes bibliography.   Contents. - pt. 1. Report of research in Maryland (Newman) - pt. 2. Report of research in Virginia (Newman) - pt. 3. Miscellaneous family records.   42-21465.

CS71.Y33   1942

19225   YATES.   Genealogy of Nancy Compton White's ancestors and descendants, 1664 to 1944 ... compiled by Mr. and Mrs. Perry S. White.   Hutchinson, Kan., 1944.   47 l. 29½ x 23 cm. Reproduced from type-written copy. Includes "Sources." 45-13060.

CS71.Y33   1944

YATES.   See also: COVINGTON, 1956
DUNHAM, 1956
EDGECOMBE, 1968
JAMES, 1913 a
PENDEREL, DA446.H89

19226   YAW.   The Yaw-Yeaw family in America.   By Clarence Arthur Phillips.   (n. p., Yaw-Yeaw Family Society) 1962.   211 p. 28 cm. 63-35721.

CS71.Y34   1962

19227   YAW.   Yaw-Yeaw family Society Bulletin.   No. 8, 1962 -   In vertical file.   Please ask reference librarian for this material.

YAWGER.   See SHOEMAKER, E99.I7Y3

19228   YAWKEY.   Yawkey, Richardson and allied families; a genealogical study with biographical notes, compiled and privately printed for Cyrus Carpenter Yawkey by the American historical company, inc.   New York, 1939.   277 p. plate, ports., facsim., col. coats of arms. 32 cm. Some of the coats of arms accompanied by guard sheets with descriptive letterpress. Includes bibliographical notes. Allied families: Carpenter, Gale, Cheney, Rawson and Woodson. 40-4940.
CS71.Y35   1939

19229   YEA.   The history of the family of Yea, formerly of Pyrland, in the parish of Taunton St. James ... with divers other considerable possessions, all situated within the several counties of Somerset, Devon & Dorset.   Taunton, G. Vincent, 1885.   4 p. l., 129, lxxi, (1), iv p. pl. (2 mounted phot.) double geneal. tab. (with col. coat of arms) 26 cm. Comp. by Alfred James Monday for Sir Francis Grant, to perpetuate the memory of his maternal ancestors, the ancient and honourable Somersetshire family of Yea. cf. Dedication. 16-23488.
CS439.Y5

19230   YEAGER.   A brief history of the Yeager, Buffington, Creighton, Jacobs, Lemon, Hoffman and Woodside families, and their collateral kindred of Pennsylvania.   Compiled by Hon, James Martin Yeager ... (Lewistown, Pa., 1912)   1 p. l., 7-277, (1) p. front., illus. (incl. ports., maps, facsims., coat of arms) fold. geneal. tab. 23½ cm. 25-345.
CS71.Y37   1912

YEAGER.   See also STRASSBURGER, 1922

YEAKLEY.   See DEPPEN, 1940

YEAMANS.   See YEOMANS.

YEARDLEY.   See: ELLIS, 1926
                          YARDLEY.
                          No. 430 - Adventurers of purse and person.

19231   YEATER.   Genealogies of John J. Yeater and Sarah Jeanette (Ellis) Yeater his wife.   Written in 1912 by Sarah J. Yeater for her grandson Lawrence K. Yeater.   Sedalia, Mo., Sedalia printing company, 1912.   cover-title, 36 p. 23½ cm. 13-12590.   CS71.Y38   1912

19232   YEATMAN.   The Yeatmans in America.   By Walter Clark Yeatman.   (Los Angeles, 1933)   24 l. geneal. table. 29 cm. Cover title. 54-54367.   CS71.Y39   1933

19233   YEATMAN.   The ancestry of Preston Yeatman of Huntsville, Alabama; from William Yeatman who came from England to American in 1651 to America Yeatman Geron who died in 1871.   Compiled from records of Walter C. Yeatman and other sources.   (Huntsville? Ala., 196-)   20 l. coat of arms. 28 cm. Pagination partly in manuscript. Bibliographical footnotes. 68-2620.
CS71.Y39

YEAW.   See YAW.

YELLOLY.   See TYSSEN, CS439.T93

YENDELL.   See HOLBROOK, F1N56 vol. 58

19234   YEOMANS.   The Yeamans-Yeomans-Youmans genealogy.   By Grant Samuel Youmans.   Rutland, Vt., Tuttle Pub. Co., 1946.   127 p. port., coats of arms. 24 cm. Includes bibliographies. 49-40798*.
CS71.Y43   1946

19235   YEOMANS.   Yeomans gena-map showing landing dates and movements of direct ancestors, drawn May 1948.   By Clifton Yeomans.   (n. p., 1948?)   map. 59 x 81 cm. fold. to 29 x 41 cm. Reproduction of original ms. 50-38882.
CS71.Y43   1948

19236   YERBURGH.   Some notes on our family history, by E. R. Yerburgh.   London, Constable and company ltd., 1912.   xiii, 324 p. fold. geneal. tables. 22½ cm. Contains genealogical notes on the Clifford, Lowther, Richmond, Gledhill, Blamire, Bayne, Armstrong, Higgin and Yerburgh families. 19-3354.   CS439.Y6

19237   YERKES.   Chronicle of the Yerkes family, with notes on the Leech and Rutter families, by Josiah Granville Leach ... Philadelphia, Printed for private circulation by J. B. Lippincott company, 1904.   xi, (1), 262 p. front., plates, ports., facsims., fold. geneal. tab. 27½ cm. "Two hundred and fifty copies printed on paper hand-made for this edition." 4-14170.   CS71.Y48   1904

YERKES.   See also: LEWIS, 1901 (addenda)
                                        READING, 1898

YERRINGTON.   See RICHARDSON, 1906

19238   YINGLING.   Genealogical information regarding the families of Hornberger and Yingling and related families of Eckert, Lenhart, Steffy, Gerwig, and Rahn.   By Claude Jerome Rahn.   Vero Beach, Fla., 1951.   164 p. 23 cm. 52-22297.   CS61.R3

19239   YINGLING.   The Yingling genealogy.   By Claude Jerome Rahn.   Vero Beach, Fla., 1958.   246 p. 28 cm. 59-19680.   CS71.Y5   1958

19240   YINGLING.   Om Ynglingatal og de norske Ynglingekonger i Danmark, af Gustave Storm.   Christiania, P. T. Mallings bogtrykkeri, 1873.   24 p. 20 cm. Running title: Ynglingeaetten i Danmark. Saerskilt aftryk af Historisk tidsskrift, III. 13-21184.   DL162.S8

19241   YNTEMA.   The family of Hessel O. Yntema, Frisian immigrant to Michigan, 1847.   By Mary Elizabeth (Loomis) Yntema.   Holland, Mich., Klaasen Print Co. (c.1958)   72 p. illus. 23 cm. 59-27025.   CS71.Y53   1958

YOAKUM.   See YOCUM.

YOCOM.   See YOCUM.

19242   YOCUM.   A history of the Yoakum, Yocom, Yocum families and others however the name is spelled ... by Harry Clyde Smith.   (Glendale, Calif., 1963)   xxxi, 741 p. port. 23 cm. Bibliography: p. iv. 63-47607.   CS71.Y534   1963

YOCUM.   See also ANDERSON, 1948

19243   YODER.   Descendants of Daniel Yoder, 1793-1849, and related families.   By John W. Ging-erich.   Kalona, Iowa, 1963.   94 p. illus. 23 cm. 63-6137.   CS71.Y535   1963

YOKUM.   See YOCUM.

YONCE.   See WALTMAN, 1928

19244   YOOLOW.   Report of the proceedings under a brieve of idiotry, Peter Duncan against David Yoolow, tried at Coupar-Angus, 28-30 Jan. 1837.   With an appendix of relative documents, and an introduction, by Ludovic Colquhoun ... Edinburgh, T. Clark, 1837.   xliv, 116, 19 p. 23 cm. Proceedings in a Sheriff court. 40-1286.   LAW
———— Copy 2.   "Extracts from the records of the Kirk-session of Kettins (relating to the Yoolow family) (Communicated by Mr. James Gibb ...)"   (7 p. facsim.) inserted after p. 116.   LAW

19245   YORK.   Memoirs of the rival houses of York and Lancaster, historical and biographical: embracing a period of English history from the accession of Richard II. to the death of Henry VII.   By Emma Roberts ... London, Harding and Lepard (etc.) 1827.   2 v. front. (port.) 22 cm. 2-18557.   DA245.E644

19246   YORK.   The York family, by William M. Sargent ... Portland, Me., S. M. Watson, 1885.   cover-title, 22 p. illus. (coat of arms) 23½ cm. Reprint from the Maine historical and genealogical recorder. 14-784.   CS71.Y54   1885

19247   YORK.   Chronicles of Erthig on the Dyke, by Albinia Lucy Cust (Mrs. Wherry) ... with thirty-three illustrations ... London, John Lane; New York, John Lane company; (etc., etc.) 1914. 2 v. fronts., plates, ports. 23½ cm. 14-17237.   DA745.E7W5

YORK.   See also: HYDORN, 1934
                             REICHNER, 1918

19248   YOUL.   A few memoirs of the family of Sir James Arndell Youl ... and his wife née Cox. Compiled from papers in the possession of his daughter, Miss Louisa Youl. (London, The Solicitors' law stationery society, ltd., 1914)   56, (8) p. incl. front., illus. (incl. facsims.) fold. geneal. tab. 23½ cm. Seven blank pages at end for "Notes".   Includes also the Piper and Cox families. 40-19734.   CS439.Y7   1914

19249   YOUNG.   A short memoir of James Young, merchant burgess of Aberdeen, and Rachel Cruickshank, his spouse, and of their descendants: With an appendix, containing notices as to the connections, by marriage and otherwise, of many of that family.   Comp. from authentic sources, and now printed for the information of the said descendants; in regard to whom the details have been brought down to the year 1860.   (Aberdeen, Printed by J. Craighead & co., 1861)   1 p. l., 42, lxxi p. 2 port. (incl. front.) facsim. 28½ cm. Preface signed: A.J. i.e. Alexander Johnston. 12-31712.   CS479.Y7

19250   YOUNG.   Fragmentary records of the Youngs, comprising, in addition to much general information respecting them, a particular and extended account of the posterity of Ninian Young, an early resident of East Fallowfield township, Chester County, Pa.; comp. from the best published and other sources.   By I. Gilbert Young, M.D. ... In two parts.   Philadelphia, W. S. Young, 1869. 2 p. l., vi, (7) - 113 p. 24 cm.   Contents. - pt. 1. General facts relative to the Youngs. - pt. 2. The descendants of Ninian Young. 9-15029.
                                                                                        CS71.Y7   1869

19251   YOUNG.   Abraham Young and Hannah Winne, his wife, of the Mohawk Valley, by J. A. Young. (Chilhowee? Mo.) 1886?   9 l. geneal. table. 31 cm. Typescript. 65-79394.   CS71.Y7   1886

19252   YOUNG.   Rev. Christopher Yonges and Pastor, John Youngs.   Thomas Youngs, of Oyster Bay, and his descendants.   (By Daniel Kelsey Youngs) The 250th anniversary of Pastor Youngs' settlement.   Oyster Bay (Jamaica, N.Y., C. Welling, printer) 1890.   142 p., 1 l. 23½ cm. Blank pages at end for "Additional record". 24-4251.   CS71.Y7   1890

19253   YOUNG.   Young family tree.   (Memorial and family tree of Michael Cadet Young of Brunswick County, Va., and of his descendants 16 — to 1895) Washington, D.C., 1895.   fold. geneal. chart 25 x 32½ cm.   Compiled by Calvin Duvall Cowles. 9-17840.   CS71.Y7   1895

19254   YOUNG.   The Brigham Young family,   This is an outline of the Brigham Young family, from 1721 to the fathers and mothers of the present generation ... Provo, Utah, Skelton, Maeser & co., printers (1897)   geneal. tab. 43 x 28 cm. fold. to 22½ cm.   Compiled for the Young family association. 5-13226 rev.
                                                                                        CS71.Y7   1897

19255   YOUNG.   Pedigree of the family of Young, Isle of Wight (by) Sidney Young.   London, Mitchell and Hughes, 1900 - 07.   2 geneal. tab. 35 x 50 cm. 25-14568.   CS439.Y8   1900

19256   YOUNG.   A brief history of Thomas Young and his descendants, by Laura Young Pinney.   San Francisco, Press of R. R. Patterson (1904)   77 p. 18 cm.   17-31800.   CS71.Y7   1904

19257   YOUNG.   ... Youngs family.   Vicar Christopher Yonges, his ancestors in England and his descendants in America; a history and genealogy, by Selah Youngs, jr. ... New York, 1907. vii, 377 p. 58 pl. (incl. front., ports., facsim.) 26½ cm. 7-20635.   CS71.Y7   1907

19258   YOUNG.   The mansion and family of Notley Young.   By George C. Henning.   (In Columbia historical society. Records ... Washington, 1913. 23½ cm. v. 16, p. 1-24 incl. 2 geneal. tab.) Read before the Society January 16, 1912. A 14-251.   F191.C72 vol. 16

19259   YOUNG.   A history of the families of Young and Goodall (Isle of Wight).   By Sidney Young ... London, Priv. print. by G. Barber, 1913.   1 p. l., 30 p. front. (port.) illus. (incl. plan, facsims.) 2 pl. (1 fold.) 2 fold. geneal. tab. 26 cm. 19-8256.   CS439.Y8

19260   YOUNG.   470 years of service of the Young, Gould, Sexton, and Phillips families, 1455-1925. By Stanley H. Fidler. (n.p., 1926?)   (6), 44 p. illus., facsim., ports. 23 cm. "Historical paper read at the annual meeting, August 14th, 1925, of the Descendants of the French Creek Pioneers, held in the French Creek Presbyterian Church, French Creek, W. Va." Bibliography: 3d - 5th prelim. pages. 67-7610.   CS71.Y7   1926

19261   YOUNG.   ... Young family records, by J. Montgomery Seaver.   Philadelphia, Pa., American historical-genealogical society (1929)   48 p. front. (incl. 3 port.) coat of arms. 29 cm. Coat of arms of the Young family on recto of frontispiece.   Page (46) - (47) blank for "Family records".   "References": p. 44-45.   40-18928.   CS71.Y5   1929

19262   YOUNG.   The Young family of Bristol, by Walter Jorgensen Young.   Fredericksburg, Va., C. A. Carmichael (c.1937)   4 p. l., 55 p. illus. (ports.) 23½ cm.   Cover-title: The Bristol Youngs in America, 1057-1937. Coat of arms on cover.   Includes "Collateral branches, Morton, Hieatt and others."   37-29107.   CS71.Y7   1937

19263   YOUNG.   Lineal ancestors of Rufus Rennington Young and Jane Vosburgh and of their descendants, genealogical, historical and biographical.   Compiled from various genealogies and histories for private distribution among interested parties and libraries ... (n.p.) 1937.   1 p. l., 50 p. illus., ports. 22½ cm. "Authorities consulted" at end of most of the sections. 38-36168 rev.   CS71.Y7   1937c

19264   YOUNG.   "(A missing branch of the Young family tree)" (n.p., 1937?)   geneal. tab. 43 x 55 cm. 40M1456T.   CS71.Y7   1937b

19265   YOUNG.   Brigham Young's wives, children and grand children.   (Salt Lake City, Utah, c.1940) cover-title, 4 l. illus. (ports.) 41 cm. "Compiled by Mabel Young Sanborn." 40-11987.   CS71.Y7   1940

19266   YOUNG.   ... Captain Peter Young (1738-1784) mariner of Philadelphia ... (by) Lockwood Barr.   Pelham Manor (New York) 1945.   34 l. fold. geneal. tab. 29 x 22½ cm. Caption title. Bibliography: 32d leaf. 47-18456.   CS71.Y7   1945

19267   YOUNG.   Our Young family in America.   By Edward Hudson Young.   Durham, N.C., 1947. xvii, 315 p. illus., ports., map, geneal. tables (part fold.) 24 cm. 48-698*.   CS71.Y7   1947

19268   YOUNG.   The Young (Jung) families of the Mohawk Valley, 1710-1946.   By Clifford Marvin Young.   Albany (1947)   xii, 354 p. illus., ports. 24 cm. In 2 pts., pt. 2 by Edwin H. Young. 47-11123*.   CS71.Y7   1947a

19269   YOUNG.   John Young of Eastham, Massachusetts, descent to Elkanah Young of Eastham and Mt. Desert, Maine, and his known descendants, by Elisabeth Ridgely Young and Kendall A. Young. Baltimore, 1950.   232 l. geneal. table. 24 cm. Typewritten. 51-28860.   CS71.Y7   1950

19270   YOUNG.   The Young family.   By Whitney Hord Tipton.   (Mt. Sterling, Ky., 1953?) 1 v. (unpaged) illus., ports., coats of arms. 26 cm. Cover title. 54-38536.   CS71.Y7   1953

19271   YOUNG.   The ancestry of Brian L. Young, showing lines to Revolutionary soldiers and European royalty.   Corr. to May 1, 1957.   By Brian Llewellyn Young.   Indexed.   Including the ancestry and descendants of Martin Dennis Young and Martha Malinda Shoop.   Seattle (1957) 22 p. 28 cm. 59-37500.   CS71.Y7   1957

19272   YOUNG.   Historical narrative and genealogy of the Parmiter, Young, Draper families.   By Frances (Draper) Thomsen.   Falls Church, Va., 1958.   1 v. illus. 29 cm. 58-34735.   CS71.Y7   1958

19273   YOUNG.   Our children's ancestors, including those named Young, Ullman, Asire, Conrad, Whitmer, Cross, Stratton, Whittlesey, McLain (by) Robert W. Young and Evelyn Cross Young.   San Diego, Calif. (1966)   1 v. (various pagings) illus. 24 cm. 400 copies printed. Includes bibliography. 66-7305.   CS71.Y7   1966

YOUNG.   See also:

BARRY, 1909
BROWN, 1937
CARSON, 1935
DAVIS, 1927a
DOWNS, 1959 a
DRAPER, 1964
ESPINET, CS439. E82
GALE, 1866

GODDARD, 1965
GRIFFIN, F129. S74G8
HAM, 1949
KLINE, 1941
McCALL, CS478. M15
MACGINNIS, 1892
MOODY, 1957

PEDEN, 1961
SHELLEY, 1909
SMITH, 1946a
STOUT, 1960
WILLIS, 1899
WILLIS, F1. N56 vol. 53
No. 553 - Goodhue county.

YOUNGBERG.   See No. 553 - Goodhue county.

19274   YOUNGBLOOD.   Youngblood-Armstrong and allied families, by Frances Youngblood and Floelle Youngblood Bonner.   (Pensacola? Fla., 1962)   327 p. illus.   24 cm.   62-16376.
CS71. Y73   1962

YOUNGBLOOD.   See also HEAD, 1963

YOUNGDAHL.   See No. 553 - Goodhue county.

19275   YOUNGER.   An account of the family of Younger, county Peebles, by A. W. Cornelius Hallen ... Edinburgh, Priv. print. at the University press, by T. & A. Constable, 1890.   1 p. l., 19 p. double geneal. tab.   29 cm.   22-11842.
CS479. Y8

YOUNGHUSBAND.   See JAMES, 1913a

19276   YOUNGLOVE.   The Younglovés in military service of the U.S.A., by (Mrs. W. A. Kelsey) (n. p., n. d.)   8 l. 27 cm.   Type-written.   CA 29-688 unrev.   CS71. Y78

YOUNGLOVE.   See also BENSON, 1920

19277   YOUNGMAN.   Genealogy and biographical sketches of the Youngman family.   By David Youngman, M. D. ... Boston, Press of G. H. Ellis, 1882.   26 p. 24½ cm.   9-15030.
CS71. Y79   1882

YOUNGMAN.   See also LITTLE, 1940

YOUNGS.   See: GEER, 1914
                          YOUNG.

19278   YOUNKER.   Descendants of Joel B. Younker (1809-1879) and Sarah (Stiffler) Younker (1813-1893)   A genealogy listing 325 descendants of a pioneer family of Pennsylvania "Dutch" ancestry, married in New Philadelphia, Ohio, migrated to Iowa, and back treked to Geneseo, Illinois.   By R. Ewing Stiffler.   Denver (1947)   (a) - j, 30 p. photos.   29 cm.   "First edition ... limited to 50 copies ... No. 1." 48-16082*.
CS71. Y793   1947

19279   YOUNT.   A brief sketch of the origin of the Young family in America, compiled by W. C. Yount ... addendum by Wm. M. Yount.   (n. p., 1936)   1 p. l., 16, (1) p. 15½ cm.   36-30623.
CS71. Y795   1936

YOURING.   See URAN.

19280   YOUSE.   A record of a family who — "carry on" ... by Fannie Johnson Landes.   (La Grange, Ill., 1942)   23 p. illus. (ports., facsims.) 19½ cm.   Cover-title: "Carry on."   Type-written additions inserted.   43-14994.
CS71. Y798   1942

925

19281   YOWELL.   Yowell; a genealogical collection, compiled and privately printed by Clark S. Yowell.   Somerville, N. J., 1931.   96 p. incl. coat of arms.   26 cm.   "Two hundred copies printed ... First impression. December, 1931."   CS71.Y83   1931

19282   YOWELL.   The Yowells of the Deep South, by Margaret Barclay.   (New York? 1965) 104 p. ports.   29 cm.   Supplement to Yowell; a genealogical collection, by C. S. Yowell.   65-9759.   CS71.Y83   1965

19283   YULE.   Genealogical sketches of James Yuill of Ramsay Township, Lanark County, Ontario, and descendants.   By John Herbert James Yule.   Washington, 1953.   134 p.   28 cm.   53-40553.   CS71.Y88   1953

YURAN.   See URAN.

19284   YURI.   Political & diplomatic history of Russia, by George Vernadsky.   Students' ed. Boston, Little, Brown, and company, 1936.   ix p., 2 l., (3) - 499 p. incl. geneal. tables.   maps (part fold.) 22½ cm. Maps on lining-papers.   "General bibliography": p. (467) - 470.   Bibliography at end of each chapter.   36-11172.

DK61.V4

19285   YUST.   Fred Yust, Kansas pioneer; a biographical sketch, by William Frederick Yust ... drawings by Georgianna Hill Stone.   Winter Park, Fla., The College press, 1937.   1 p. l., 75 p. front., illus., ports.   20½ cm.   "Short sketches of his children": p. (49) - 65.   37-21622.   CT275.Y8Y8

19286   YVERY.   A genealogical history of the house of Yvery; in its different branches of Yvery, Luvel, Perceval, and Gournay ... (By James Anderson)   London, H. Woodfall, jun., 1742.   2 v. illus. (coats of arms) plates, ports., mounted plans, geneal. tables (1 fold.) 24 cm.   Title vignettes: engraved coats of arms.   Material was collected by John Perceval, first earl of Egmont, and compiled under the superintendence by James Anderson and William Whiston.   Portraits by John Faber, the younger, and one portrait of Sir Philip Perceval by William Henry Toms.   Bibliographical foot-notes.   20-13039.

CS439.Y9   1742

Z

19286 a ZABRISKIE. Historical sketch of the Zabriskie homestead (removed 1877), Flatbush, L. I., with biographical accounts of some of those who have resided in it. By P. L. Schenck ... Brooklyn, N. Y., 1881. 100 (i. e.102) p. front., plates, ports., fold facsim., fold. geneal. tab. 23 cm. Appendix, p. 81-94. contains "The Zabriskie genealogy," by Chancellor A. O. Zabriskie, and "Sketch of the Lott family," by Jeremiah Lott. 9-29301. CS71.Z12 1881

19287 ZABRISKIE. "(Family records copied from pages 1 to 8 of Christian Zabriskie's family Bible, now in the possession of George Olin Zabriskie) (n. p.) 1937. 4 numb. 1. 26½ cm. Type-written. 40M1475T. CS71.Z12 1937

19288 ZABRISKIE. The Zabriskie family; a three hundred and one year history of the descendants of Albrecht Zaborowskij (ca. 1638-1711) of Bergen County, New Jersey. (Salt Lake City?) 1963. 2 v. (1950 p.) illus., port., map, facsims. 24 cm. 63-21602. CS71.Z12 1963

19289 ZAHNISER. The Zahnisers, a history of the family in America. By Kate M. Zahniser and Charles Reed Zahniser ... Mercer, Pa., K. M. Zahniser, 1906. 218 p. 12 pl. (incl. ports.) 23½ cm. All except one plate printed on both sides. 'Revolutionary war records of Mathias Zahniser I' 1 l. inserted after title page. 13-11884. CS71.Z20 1906

19290 ZANDER. Mecklenburg to Wisconsin; the Johann Zander family migration, 1854-1856. By Lucile Ottilie (Zander) Uspensky. (n. p., 1965) xii, 63, A - V leaves. illus., maps. 30 cm. Bibliography: leaves 54-59. 65-29753. CS71.Z25 1965

19291 ZANE. Zane's Trace, by Clement L. Martzolff ... Columbus, O., Press of F. J. Heer, 1904. 1 p. 1., 297 - 331 p. illus. 23 cm. "Reprinted from the Ohio archaeological and historical society publications." 5-16870. F495.M38

19292 ZANE. My Zane lineage, by Myra N. Martin. Waverly, Ill., 1964. 25 l. 30 cm. Typescript. 66-98686. CS71.Z28 1964

ZANE. See also BELL, 1960

ZARFESS. See WALTMAN, 1928

19293 ZARTMAN. The Zartman family, by Rev. Rufus Calvin Zartman ... Philadelphia, Lyon & Armor, 1909. xvi, 431 p. incl. front., illus. ports., facsim. 23 cm. 10-789. CS71.Z39 1909

19294 ZARTMAN. The Zartman family, 1692-1942. (Rev. and enl.) By Rev. Rufus Calvin Zartman ... Rutland, Vt., The Tuttle publishing company, inc. (1942) xix, (3), 432, (2) p. front., illus. (facsim.) plates, ports., col. coat of arms. 24 cm. 42-50295 rev. CS71.Z39 1942
—— Supplement. The family of Isaac and Rebecca Zartman, 1942-1957, by Josephine C. Diefenbach. (n. p.. 1957) 18 p. 23 cm. Bound with the main work. 42-50295 rev. CS71.Z39 1942

19295 ZAVITZ. Material re: Messrs, Doan, Zaxitz (!), Vail, Haight, Chase, & Sparta. (London? Ont., 1943?) 194 l. mounted photos. 28 x 23 cm. Title from label mounted on cover. Type-written (carbon) copy made by Edwin Seaborn from the originals. Contents. - Daniel Zavitz' diary. - Zavitz records and Samuel Vail's will. - Genealogy of the family of Haight. - Diary of Ida Hiaght. - A history of the society of Friends of Lobo township. - Autobiography of Amasa Chase. - Pioneers of Sparta district. - Paper on the Friends' settlement. - East Elgin pioneer homes. - Grave of Joshua Doan. - A few memories of Maria E. Haight. - Poetry of Joshua Gilliams Doan. - Memoirs of Mrs. Rundle. - Letters. - Genealogy of the Chase family. 43-22820. CS90.Z3 1943

ZEA BERMÚDEZ. See BERMÚDEZ.

19296   ZEARING.   The Zearings; a pioneer Illinois family, with an account of the life of James Roberts Zearing, M. D., by Luelja Zearing Gross.   (Springfield, Ill., Phillips bros. print., 1921) 76 p. plates, ports.   23 cm.   Reprinted from the Transactions of the Illinois state historical society for 1921.   23-6176.

CS71. Z54   1921

ZEARLEY.   See DARBY, 1930

ZECHIEL.   See STAHL, 1924

ZECHMAN.   See GRIM, 1934

19297   ZEHNER.   The first Zehner-Hoppes family history; Adam Zehner, John Michael (Habbas) Hoppes of Schuylkill county, Pennsylvania, and descendants, pioneer farmers and millers, by the Zehner Indiana branch of the Pennsylvania, Ohio, Indiana, Illinois, Wisconsin relative societies, 1939 A. D.   Mrs. Ellen Priscilla (Zehner) Carpenter, compiler.   (South Bend, Ind., Mirror press inc., c. 1939)   3 p. 1., (9) - 110 p., 1 1., 111 - 214, (16) p. IX pl. (incl. ports.) 24½ cm. Blank pages for "Memoranda" (16) at end.   39-22762.

CS71. Z6   1939

19298   ZERBE.   Blue book of Schuylkill County; who was who and why in interior eastern Pennsylvania, in colonial days.   The Huguenots and Palatines; their service in Queen Anne's French and Indian, and revolutionary wars.   History of the Zerbey, Schwalm, Miller, Merkle, Minnich, Staudt, and many other representative families.   By Mrs. Ella Zerbey Elliott ... (Pottsville) Pottsville, Pa., "Republican," 1916.   2 p. 1., vi p., 2 1., (9) - 456 p. illus., plates, maps (1 fold.) facsims. (1 double) 23½ cm. 16-1746.

F157. S3E39

ZERBEY.   See ZERBE.

ZEVE.   See SEAVEY.

ZEVIE.   See SEAVEY.

ZEVYE.   See SEAVEY.

19299   ZIEGLER.   The Ziegler family record.   A complete record of the Ziegler family from our ancestor, Philip Ziegler, born in Bern, Switzerland, in 1734, down to the seventh and eighth generations; including also those who are directly descended from the family as far as data could be obtained.   By Elder Jesse Ziegler, assisted by Rev. Daniel P. Zeigler.   Royersford, Pa., J. Ziegler, 1906.   118 p. 23 cm. 6-24868.

CS71. Z66   1906

19300   ZIEGLER.   Ziegler genealogy, Nicholas, Michael, Peter family tree, compiled by John A. M. Ziegler ... Sponsored by the Peter Ziegler association.   Published by the author.   Huntington Park, Calif., Glenn printing company (1935)   2 p. 1., 3-46 p. 23½ cm. 36-3762.

CS71. Z66   1935

ZIEGLER.   See also: BROWN, 1959
                                    CRONE, 1924
                                    DULIN, 1961
                                    STRASSBURGER, 1922

ZIEMER.   See MEISINGER, 1962

ZIERLEIN.   See ALBRECHT, 1952

19301   ZIMMER.   Genealogy of a branch of the Zimmer family from Robens Housa, Hesse-Cassel (now the Prussian Province of Hessen-Nassau) Germany.   By Claude Charles Hamel.   Amherst, Ohio, 1948.   7 1. 27 cm. Type-written. Bibliography: leaves 6-7. 50-25029.   CS71. Z72   1948

ZIMMER.   See also POTTER, 1933

19302   ZIMMERMAN.   Zimmerman, Waters and allied families, by Dorothy Edmonstone Zimmerman Allen ... (n. p., 19 — ?)   4 p. l., 162 p. front., plates, ports., geneal. tables, coats of arms. 23½ cm. 10-1449.
CS71. Z73   19 -

19303   ZIMMERMAN.   Zimmerman and allied families. (By Thomas John Hall.) Page 191.
CS71. H177   1941

19304   ZIMMERMAN.   Zimmerman family of Pennsylvania and Kentucky.   By Emma Rouse Lloyd.
(Available for consultation at Lloyd Library, 309 West Court Street, Cincinnati 2, Ohio)

ZIMMERMAN.   See also: ENDERS, 1960
KLOCK, 1960
ROUSE, 1932

ZIMMERMANN.   See ZIMMERMAN.

19305   ZIMPLEMAN.   Genealogy of Waldine Zimpleman Kopperl, by Della Archer.   (Galveston? Tex., 1932?)   2 p. l., 68 numb. l. 28 cm. Tyep-written (carbon copy) 32-30542.   CS71. Z75   1932

19306   ZINK.   The Zink families in America; including many of the Archer, Colglazier, Marshal, Martin, Perisho, Seaton and Zimmerly families, by Dora Zink Kellogg ... Omaha, Neb., Citizen printing co., c. 1933.   1 p. l., i - ii p., 3 l., (3) - 316, 69 p. fold. geneal. tab. 22½ cm. 34-1751.
CS71. Z8   1933

ZINK.   See also KEPHART, 1950

19307   ZINN.   The John Jacob Zinn family of Lancaster, Penna.   By Ralph E. K. Jones ... Data also by Mabel McCloskey, data partly by Miss Lottie Bausman ... (Warren? O., 1935)   2 p. 28 cm. Typewritten. 38M1707T.   CS71. Z83   1935

19308   ZINN.   History and genealogy of the Zinn family, compiled by Mabel McFatridge-McCloskey ... (n. p.) 1937.   (58) p. ports. 22 cm. 37-38448.   CS71. Z83   1937

ZINN.   See also BROWN, 1930

19309   ZIRKLE.   History of the ancestors of Claiborne Joseph Zirkle and Frances Anne Hite, the former formerly of New Market, Va., the latter formerly of Luray, Va.   By Frank McKay Bowie. Alexandria (1948?)   23 l. 27 cm. First three words of title crossed out. 49-22655*.   CS71. Z833   1948

19310   ZIRKLE.   Yesteryears and yesterdays.   By David Luther Zirkle.   (Oxford, Kan., Oxford register) c. 1956.   113 p. 19 cm. 57-20450.   CS71. Z833   1956

19311   ZIRKLE.   Zirkle family history, compiled by J. William Harpine.   (Harrisonburg? Va., 1963?)   150, v p. 28 cm. Cover title. 64-4972.   CS71. Z833   1963

ZIRKLE.   See also STRICKLER, 1925

ZITKA.   See KROUPA, 1957

ZOECKLER.   See VOGT, 1926

ZOELEN.   See GROENINX VAN ZOELEN.

ZOIKL.   In vertical file under PRANKE family.   Ask reference librarian for this material.

19312   ZOLLMAN.   Descendants of William and Mary Bousman Zollman, compiled by Wilbur B. Zollman.   Roanoke, Va., 1942.   17 l. 26 x 20½ cm. Reproduced from type-written copy. 43-46652.
CS71. Z836   1942

19313   ZORBAUGH.   Ancestal trails; history of the Zorbaugh family, the Evans family, the McClure family, the Harvey family, the Clapp family, compiled by Charles Louis Zorbaugh.   (Wooster, O., The Collier printing company) 1941.   267 p. front. (port.) 23½ cm.   "Limited edition of 100 copies.   Number 61." Errata slip mounted on p. (4) Pages 261-267 blank "to continue the record of births, deaths and marriages."   42-23920.

CS71. Z84   1941

ZOUCH.   See No. 430 - Adventurers of purse and person.

19314   ZOUCHE.   The dove;   or, Passages of cosmography; a poem: by Richard Zouche ... Reprinted from the original edition of 1613; with a memoir and notes, collected and arranged by Richard Walker ... Oxford, H. Slatter; London, T. Rodd, 1839.   2 p. l., xliii, 82 p. incl. geneal. tab.   front. (port.) 33½ cm.   With reproduction of original t. -p.   19-3328.

PR2405. Z6D8

19315   ZUBER.   Ancestry and kindred of W. P. Zuber, Texas veteran.   By William Physick Zuber. (Iola? Tex., 1905)   16 p. 23 cm.   21-9018.

CS71. Z85   1905

ZUFELT.   See: DAYTON, 1961
                        SHUFELT.
                        STOUT, 1960

ZUG.   See HERTZLER, 1885

19316   ZUMOFF.   Our family; a history of five generations in pictures & script, 1831-1956. Originated and designed by Abraham Zumoff.   Edited by Nathan Zumoff, assisted by Barnett Zumoff. Drawing by Leon Israel (Lola)   (New York) Printed by Academy Photo-Of(f)set (1956 or 7 - 1 v. (loose-leaf) illus.   43 cm.   57-58327.

CS71. Z88   1956

19317   ZUMWALT.   The Andrew Zumwalt family, by Paul L. Reed.   (1st anniversary ed.)   Baltimore, Deford, 1964 -   v. illus., ports. 24 cm.   "A publication of the Zumwalt Historical Committee."   Contents. - v. 1. The first four generations of Zumwalts in America.   64-66345.

CS71. Z9   1964

19318   ZUNZ.   Leopold Zunz und seine familie.   Ein gedenkblatt an sein erstes centennarium. (10. august 1894.) Von dr. M. Brann und prof. dr. D. Kaufman ... Breslau, S. Schottlaender, 1895. cover-title, 32 p. fold. geneal. tab. 24 cm.   "Sonder-abdruck aus: 'Monatsschrift für geschichte und wissenschaft des judenthums,' 38. jahrgang, heft 11."   39M3020.

BM755. Z8B7

ZWAHLEN.   See VAN BENTHUYSEN, 1926

ZWINGLE.   See ZWINGLI.

ZWINGLY.   See SWINGLI, 1926

ADDENDA

K - Z

A361 KANTAKOUZENOS. The Byzantine family of Kantakouzenos (Cantacuzenus) ca. 1100-1460; a genealogical and prosopographical study, by Donald M. Nicol. Washington, Dumbarton Oaks Center for Byzantine Studies, trustees for Harvard University; (distributed by J. J. Augustin, Locust Valley, N. Y.) 1968. xliii, 265 p. illus., facsims., fold. geneal. tables, ports. 24 cm. (Dumbarton Oaks studies, 11) Bibliography: p. xxvii-xliii. 70-12056 MARC. CS739.K3 1968

KANTAKUZEN. See KANTAKOUZENOS.

A362 KAUFMAN. Autumn leaves from family trees: historical, biographical, and genealogical materials relating to the Cauffman, Chidsey, Churchman, Foster, Montgomery, Rodenbough, Shewell and affiliated families. Gathered and pressed, for whom it may concern, by a kindman, Theo. Francis Rodenbaugh ... New York (Clark and Zugalla, 1892) 304 p. front., illus., plates, ports., fold. geneal. tables. 23½ cm. Added t.-p., engr. "One hundred and fifty copies printed." 9-13219. CS71.K21 1892

A363 KEAHEY. Keahey clansmen and their kin, Slay, Summerall, Smith. By Emma Barrett Reeves. (Waco, Tex., Printed by Texian Press, 1969) xi, 430 p. illus., coats of arms, geneal. tables, map, ports. 24 cm. Bibliographical footnotes. 73-94457 MARC. CS71.K223 1969

A364 KEITH. The castle of Dunnottar and its history, by Rev. Douglas Gordon Barron ... with a description of the building, by W. Mackay Mackenzie, M. A., and G. P. H. Watson. Edinburgh and London, W. Blackwood and sons, 1925. xxxiii, 148 p. front., illus. (incl. plans) plates, ports., facsims. 29 x 23½ cm. 26-14319. DA877.D8B3

A365 KEITH. The Family tree of George Keith and Elizabeth Seat (by Marvyn F. Keith and others. n. p., 1970) vii, 140, xii p. ports. 28 x 43 cm. Cover title. 75-21302 MARC. CS71.K28 1970

A366 KELLOGG. Family meeting of the descendants of Charles Kellogg, of Kelloggsville, N. Y., with some genealogical items of the Kellogg family. Reprinted from the New England historical and genealogical register for July, 1858. (By Day Otis Kellogg) Boston, H. W. Dutton and son, printers, 1858. cover-title, 8 p. 23 cm. "Family meeting ..." signed: D. K. L.; "Genealogical items ..." by D. O. Kellogg. L. C. COPY REPLACED BY MICROFILM. CS71.K291 1858
Microfilm 21995 CS

A367 KEMBLE. The Kembles of New York and New Jersey. (Reprint of the "Prefatory note" to the second volume of the "Kemble papers" in the "Collections" of the New York historical society for 1883 and 1884, printed in 1889). (New York, Printed for the Society, 1889?) cover-title, vii-xxiii p. front. (port.) 25 cm. Signed: Edward F. De Lancey. 9-11460. CS71.K49 1889

A368 KETELHODT. Urkunden und Geschichte des Geschlechtes der Freiherrn von Ketelhodt. (Hrsg. von Vredeber, Freiherr von Ketelhodt.) (Bindlach über Bayreuth, Blumenstr. 17, Selbstverlag, des Herausgebers) 1964. 136 l. with illus., front. 30 cm. N. T. "Ergänzungen zur Familiengeschichte 1964" (8 l.); "Der mecklenburgische Hotorden de la fidelité et constance (2 l.); "Auszüge aus Lebens- und Charakterzeüige Sr. Exellenz Herrn Carl Gerd von Ketelhodt ..." (4 l.) inserted. 71-474100. CS629.K52 1964

KEYES. See also SWAIN, 1896

A369 KILHAM. Notes on the descendants of Austin and Alice Kilham and related families. By Austin D. Kilham. Charlottesville, Va., Bailey Print., 1970. 1 v. (various pagings) illus., facsims., geneal. tables, ports. 29 cm. "Compiled by Austin D. Kilham with the help of Mrs. Fannie M. Clark." Includes the family groups: Betts, Bridge, Chadwick,

A369 continued: Chilton, Coffin, Gookin, Myrack (McMerrick), Winslow. Part 2, consisting chiefly of geneal. charts, issued separately also. 75-112738 MARC.   CS71.K483   1970

A370 KILLAM. Killam family in vertical file.   Ask reference librarian for this material.

A371 KING. The King family; a history and genealogy of Robert and Hannah Forker King, by Judith E. King. (Cincinnati, 1970)   v, 78 l. illus. (part col.), group port. 29 cm. 74-16072 MARC.   CS71.K53   1970

A372 KING. Our King family: their ancestors, in-laws, and descendants. By Oscar Benjamin King. (Fort Worth, Tex., Manney Co., 1970)   283 p. illus., facsim., ports. 23 cm. Bibliography: p. 281-283. 74-129548 MARC.   CS71.K53   1970b

A373 KINSEY. The U. S. according to us. By Margaret Riser Kinsey. (Lamesa, Tex., 1970) 42 p. geneal. table, map. 23 cm. No. 27 of 65 privately printed copies. Bibliography: p. 41. 77-21115 MARC.   CS71.K559   1970

A374 KLINGENBERG. Die Klingenbergs in Südafrika 1859-1968. Familienjubiläumsbuch. By Hedwig Schütte. (Vryheid/Natal, 198 Commission Str. H. Schütte, 1967)   400, 12 p. with illus. 25 cm. 76-522860.   CS1599.K57   1967

KNICKERBACKER. See KNICKERBOCKER.

A375 KNOLLMAN. A Knollman family history. Compiled by Leona E. Bodey. Cincinnati (1970) 54, x l. 22 x 28 cm. 76-20296 MARC.   CS71.K7286   1970

KNOWLES. See ALTMAN (addenda)

KNOYLE, KNOYLES. See KNOWLES.

A376 KOCH. The Johann Philipp Koch family. By Martha Lois Koch Long. (Chicago? 1971) xii, 291 p. illus., geneal. tables, ports. 23 cm. 78-278733 MARC.   CS71.K77   1971

A377 KROUPA. The Kroupa genealogy ... a history of the Kroupa, Lada, Zitka, Schrader (i.e. Schrader/Schroedter), Santovsky (i.e. Santovsky/Santowski), and Marcelbetts families. Los Angeles (1957?, c.1960)   276 l. illus., facsims., geneal. tables, ports. 29 cm. 60-145.   CS71.K953   1957

KUDER. See WALTMAN, 1928

KULP. See also KOLB.

A378 LACKEY. Lackey family history. By Richard S. Lackey. Forest, Miss. (1962) 27 l. 28 cm. 63-47606.   CS71.L14   1962a

A379 LACKOR. The Lackor family (Lackore-Lacore-La Core-Lucore) By Mary McCall Middleton. Strasburg, Va., Printed by Shenandoah Pub. House (c.1970)   x, 205 p. 24 cm. Includes bibliographical references. 75-24075 MARC.   CS71.L144   1970

LACORE. See LACKOR.

A380 LADD. The descent of George Edgar Ladd, 1864-1940, from Daniel Ladd of Haverhill, Massachusetts, together with an account of his descendants, 1890-1969, compiled by Dorothy D. (Ladd) Clapp & Verner W. Clapp. Chevy Chase, Md., 1970.   89 p. facsims., ports. 23 cm. Part I, The descent of George Edgar Ladd (p. 9-38) consists of excerpts from The Ladd family, by Warren Ladd. Includes bibliographical references. 75-117935.   CS71.L154   1970

A381 LA FOLLETTE. Three thousand years with the crusading La Follettes. By Robert Hoath La Follette. (Albuquerque, N. M., 1970)   197 p. 29 cm. 70-20368 MARC.   CS71.L18   1970

A382   LANE.   A Lane genealogy.   Compiled by Frank Nelson Hall.   Denton, Tex., 1965.
19 l. 29 cm. 70-275275.   CS71.L266   1965

A383   LANGSTON.   Descendants of Solomon Langston of Laurents County, South Carolina, through his son, Bennett.   By Carroll Spencer Langston.   Rev. and partly brought up to date.   (Williamsville, Ill.) 1969.   57 l. 28 cm. Includes bibliographical references. 76-262468 MARC.   CS71.L2747   1969

A384   LANPHEAR.   Geneology (sic) and history: Lanphear, Lamphier, Lanphere, and related families in America.   By Edward Everett Lanphere.   Rev. ed.   Chapel Hill, N.C., 1967.   264 p. 29 cm.
Cover title: Lanphere and related families; genealogy.   Additions, corrections and p. 93-264 in MS.   1958 ed. by Frances Lanphere Elder and Edward Everett Lanphere, published under title: History and genealogy of the Lanpheres and the Pierces.   74-11494 MARC.
                                                                                             CS71.L278   1967

A385   LANPHERE.   The Lanphere and related families genealogy.   By Edward Everett Lanphere.
Rev. ed.   Chapel Hill, N.C., 1970.   xi, 175 p. 28 cm. 1967 ed. published under title: Genealogy and history: Lanphear, Lamphier, Lanphere, and related families in America.   78-159542 MARC.   CS71.L278   1970

A386   LAWRENCE.   History of the Lawrence family in England, Virginia, and North Carolina, with historical sketches and genealogical outlines of the Lawrence family in Connecticut, Maryland, Massachusetts, New Jersey, New York, and South Carolina.   Also including genealogical records of other families converging with the Lawrence family of Virginia-North Carolina;   Vaughan with Lawrence 1805, Rea with Lawrence 1836, Jordan with Darden, 1825, Darden with Pruden 1844, Pruden with Lawrence 1870, Moorman with Lawrence 1901.   Bristol, Va., 1964-(65)   2 v. mounted col. coat of arms.
29 cm.   Vol. 2 has title: The related families of Jameson family of Virginia and Norfleet family of Virginia and North Carolina.   Addenda inserted.   65-41940.   CS71.L42   1964

A387   LAWTON.   The descendants of Thomas Lawton of Portsmouth, Rhode Island.   By Elva Lawton.
New York (1949)   xvi, 239 l. coats of arms. 29 cm. 79-268313 MARC.   CS71.L4254   1949

A388   LEE.   Related to Lee (by R. H. Melville Lee.   Oxford, 1963 -   pts. in   v.   illus., coats of arms (part col.), geneal. tables, maps (part col.), ports. 23 cm. Cover-title. Pt. 1: 100 copies; no. 54. 74-16360 MARC.
                                                                                             CS71.L48   1963

LEE.   See also SMITH, 1924

LEEKE.   See also LEAKE.

LEFFLER.   See also BROMWELL.

A389   LEIGH.   Leigh, Lee, Lea, Ley, Lay, Loy, Lees, Leas, Lease.   Index from the notebooks of Mrs. Edward B. Lee.   Long Beach, Calif., 1969 -   v. 28 cm. 70-14381 MARC.   CS71.L517   1969

A390   LEIPER.   Genealogical lineage of Priscilla Jones Macon Leiper;   Macon, Fitzhugh, Ashton, Washington families.   By Esther Agnes Leiper Shumaker.   (Houston, Tex., Harper Leiper Studios, 1969)   xxxiv, 72 p. illus., coats of arms, ports. 28 cm. 78-11941 MARC.   CS71.L519   1969

A391   LEWIS.   Lewisiana; or, The Lewis letter.   A monthly inter-family paper.   v.1-17; Jan./ Dec. 1887 - June 1907.   Lisle, N.Y. (etc.) 1887-1907.   17 v. in 6. illus. (incl. ports.) 23-24 cm. No numbers issued from Jan. 1890 to June 1893, inclusive.   Title varies: Jan. 1887-Dec.1889, Lewis letter.   Pub. monthly by the Lewis league.   July 1893-June, 1907, Lewisiana; or, The Lewis letter.   Vol. 1, no.1/12, 2d edition.   Published in Lisle, N.Y., 1887-89; Elliott, Conn., 18 - 1898; Guilford, Conn., 1898-1907.   No more published.   20-22279.   CS71.L675

A392   LEWIS.   Family record of Lawrence Lewis (Washington's nephew), and Nellie Park Custis (Washington's adopted daughter.)   Transcribed from Martha Washington's Bible, which was sold by order of H. L. D. Lewis, administrator to the estate of Mrs. Lorenzo Lewis, at the auction rooms of Thomas Birch's son, auctioneers ... Philadelphia, Pa., December 11th, 1890.   Mr. Stan. V. Henkels, auctioneer.   (Philadelphia? 1890)   8 p., 1 l. 32 x 25½ cm. Cover-title: Description of the Martha Washington Bible. Includes a description of the Bible, with reprint of its title-pages, and an extract from the Pennsylvania gazette of June 2, 1802, announcing the death of Martha Washington.   7-4198.   CS71.L675   1890

A393   LEWIS.   Book XVIII. of the genealogy of the Lewis family, by Simeon D. Lewis.   Buffalo, C. W. Moulton, 1891.   66 p. front. (port.) 17½ cm. First published as "Book xviii" in the Lewis letter edited by F. P. Lewis. Pages (55)-60 left blank for "Family record." 22-10221.   CS71. L675   1891

A394   LEWIS.   Genealogy of the Lewis family in America, from the middle of the seventeenth century down to the present time.   By Wm. Terrell Lewis ... Louisville, Ky., Pub. by the Courier-journal job printing co., 1893.   3 p. l., (3)-454 p. 23½ cm. 9-11615.   CS71. L675   1893

A395   LEWIS.   — 1694. Lewis congress. 1894. Celebration of the two hundredth anniversary of their residence in Virginia by the Lewis family, at Bel-air, Spotsylvania County, September 4th, 1894.   Frankfort, Ky., G. A. Lewis, printer, 1894.   129, 5, (1) p. front., illus., pl., ports. 24½ cm. "George A. Lewis, publisher." 8-12876.   CS71. L675   1894

A396   LEWIS.   Lewis genealogy, by Alfred A. Langworthy. (Hopkinton? R. I.) 1895.   cover-title. 31 numb. l. 30 cm. Type-written, with title in manuscript. Imperfect; leaf 4 wanting. 38M2006T.   CS71. L675   1895

A397   LEWIS.   Genealogies and sketches of some old families who have taken prominent part in the development of Virginia and Kentucky especially, and later of many other states of this Union.   By Benjamin F. Van Meter.   Louisville, J. P. Morton & company, 1901.   v, 3-183 p. fronts., ports. 25 cm. Contents. - Lewis family. Phillips family. - Moss family. - Van Meter family. - Cunningham family. - Harness family. - (J. H. McNeill and his company of rangers.) 1-26291.   F450. V26

A398   LEWIS.   Lewis.   By Rosalind Williamson Lewis. (New York? c. 1969)   279 p. illus., coats of arms (part col.), maps, ports. 23 cm. Bibliography: p. 277-279. 72-253530 MARC.   CS71. L675   1969

A399   LEWIS.   Lewis family in vertical file.   Ask reference librarian for this material.

A400   LEYENBERGER.   A family of five republics; a sketch of the origin of the Layenberger-Lineberger-Linebarger-Lionberger families.   By Paul Myron Linebarger ... and Walter Franklin Lineberger ... Hammond, Ind., W. B. Conkey company, 1925.   43 p. 19½ cm. "Published at the expense of the authors as a contribution to the monument fund of the 'family of five republics.' " 25-15879.   CS71. L683   1925

LIGON.   See also: HENRY, 1961
                   MOODY, 1957

A401   LINDSEY.   The Lindseys; a genealogy of Thomas and Mary Frost Lindsey and their descendants.   Compiled by Ferrell A. Brown.   Point Lookout, Mo., S of O Press, The School of the Ozarks (1970)   xiii, 182 p. coat of arms. 23 cm. Bibliography: p. 147. 73-20350 MARC.   CS71. L7533   1970

A402   LINVILLE.   The Linville family in America, compiled and written by Alice Eichholz.   (n. p., c. 1970)   366 p. geneal. tables. 29 cm. Includes bibliographical references. 75-278727 MARC.   CS71. L76   1970

A403   LISENBY.   Lisenby family in vertical file.   Ask reference librarian for this material.

A404   LITUNOV.   Litunovy. (Title romanized)   By Iosif Michaĭlovich I͡Udovich.   1969.   112 p. with illus. 17 cm. 76-556934.   CT1218. L49I8

A405   LOGAN.   The Logan story.   By John O'Brien.   Brisbane, Smith & Paterson, 1969.   107 p. 24 cm. Edition limited to 500 copies. 71-487848 MARC.   CS2089. L6   1969

A406   LONGBOTTOM.   The Bottum (Longbottom) family album; an historical and biographical genealogy of the descendants of Daniel (-1732) and Elizabeth (Lamb) Longbottom of Norwich, Connecticut.   By Rebekah (Deal) Oliver.   Denver, W. K. Oliver, 1970.   xiii, 340 p. illus., facsims., maps, ports. 28 cm. Includes bibliographical references. 77-122616 MARC.   CS71. L85   1970

A407   LORY.   Chronik des Geschlechts Lory von Stalden (Konolfingen). Jubiläumsschrift zum 200-jährigen Bestehen der Stiftung unserer Vorfahren.   By Martin Lory. (Allmendingen-Tun, Lontschenenweg 45, im Selbstverlag,) 1966.   30 p. 21 cm. 75-527115.   CS999. L65   1966

A408   LOVE.   Progenitors of the Love families.   Prepared by Tracy R. Love from the records made by William DeLoss Love II of Hartford and Mrs. Helen D. Love Scranton of New Haven and Madison. (Denver? 1952?)   sheet.   56 x 67 cm. fold. to 41 x 34 cm.   Additions and changes in MS.   70-252527 MARC.

CS71. L895   1952

A409   LOVE.   The Chickasaw Loves and allied families.   By Marie Garland.   Ardmore, Okla., Ardmore Photocopy Co. (1970)   x, 180 p.   illus., maps.   28 cm.   Includes bibliographies.   75-244716 MARC.

CS71. L895   1970

A410   LOVE.   Love family in vertical file.   Ask reference librarian for this material.

A411   LOVEJOY.   The Lovejoy genealogy, with biographies and history, 1460-1930, especially recording the American descendants and the English ancestry of John Lovejoy (1622-1690) of Andover, Mass., and of Joseph Lovejoy (1684-1748) of Prince George County, Md., but also embracing all known data on other persons bearing the Lovejoy name, whether or not identified with the emigrant ancestors. Compiled, written, edited, and published by Clarence Earle Lovejoy ... (New York, 1930)
466 p. 2 col. coats of arms on 1 plate, facsims., map, plates, ports.   24 cm.   "This is copy no. 93 of an edition of 300." Signed: C. E. Lovejoy.
30-18836.   CS71. L896   1930

———— Supplement, written by H. K. MacKechnie.   (n. p., 196-)   4 l. geneal. table. 31 cm.

CS71. L896   1930
Suppl.

A412   LOVELL.   A biographical genealogy of the Lovell family in England and America, by May Lovell Rhodes, and T. D. Rhodes.   (Asheville, N. C.) Biltmore Press, 1924.   6 p. l., 15-221, (3) p.
20½ cm.   Title vignette.   Blank pages for "Notes" (3 at end)   25-6160.   CS71. L899   1924

A413   LOVELL.   History of the town of Rockingham, Vermont: including the villages of Bellows Falls, Saxtons River, Rockingham, Cambridgeport, and Bartonsville, 1907-1957, with family genealogies, by Frances Stockwell Lovell and Leverett C. Lovell.   Bellows Falls, Vt., Published by the town, 1958.
553 p. illus. 24 cm.   59-21556.   F59. R7L6

A414   LOVELL.   The Wolf and Little Wolf; being a history of the Lovell's of England and America and the Lovewell's of America.   Compiled and edited by Sherman Lee Pompey.   (Kansas City, Mo., 1962? -   v. 29 cm.   Typescript (carbon copy)   72-244647 MARC.   CS71. L899   1962

LOVEWELL.   See LOVELL (addenda)

A415   LOWELL.   (Ancestry of Elizabeth Rebecca Lowell)   (n. p. 18 -)   geneal. tab. 35 x 50 cm.
37M276T   CS71. L915   18 -

LÖWENGUT.   See LEVEGOOD.

A416   LÖWENSTEIN.   De familie von Castelberg.   By Erwin Poeschel.   Aarau, H. R. Sauerländer, 1959.   567 p. 36 plates (incl. ports.) 3 fold. geneal. tables (in pocket) 23 cm.   Bibliographical references included in "Abkürzungen"
(p. 9-11) 61-24220.   CS999. C3   1959

LUCORE.   See LACKOR (addenda)

A417   LUNT.   A history of the Lunt family in America, comp. by Thomas S. Lunt.   Salem, Mass., The Salem Press company (1914)   7 p. l., 292 p. incl. front. (port.) illus., col. coat of arms. 23½ cm.   14-10108.
CS71. L964   1914

LYTLE.   See also HOGG, 1921

———————

A417a   McALPINE.   McAlpine, "Son of the Hills"; some of the ancestry of Robert Eugenius McAlpine and his wife Anna Hepburn Ballagh and their descendants.   By James Ballagh Moore.   Kochi, Japan (1970)   ii, 100 p. geneal. tables. 25 cm.   Pages 25-100 printed on double leaves, Chinese style.   74-15749 MARC.
CS71. M1144   1970

A418   MacBRYDE.   The clan McBryde; a brief history of John and Mary Wilkerson McBryde and their descendants (by A. M. Patterson. n. p.) 1967.   iv, 153 p.   coat of arms.   28 cm.   Includes bibliographical references.   71-630295 MARC.   CS71.M119   1967

A419   McCHESNEY.   The descendants of Robert McChesney of Monmouth Co., N.J.   (by Katherine E. Schultz.   Annville, Pa., 1966)   172 l.   map.   30 cm.   71-261980 MARC.   CS71.M125   1966

A420   McCHESNEY.   The McChesney family of Rensselaer County, New York, by Paul W. Prindle. With additions by Katherine E. Schultz.   (Annville? Pa., 1969?)   571 p.   maps.   29 cm.   Based on Prindle's work with the same title published in 1960.   74-247967 MARC.   CS71.M125   1969

A421   McCHESNEY.   The McChesneys of Caldwell Co., Ky.   (by Katherine E. Schultz.   Annville, Pa., 1969)   82 l.   map.   30 cm.   71-18994 MARC.   CS71.M125   1969b

A422   McCLELLAN.   Descendants of Michael McClellan and Jane Henry of Colrain, Mass.   By Lois McClellan Patrie.   (Troy? N. Y., c. 1970)   vii, 141 p.   ports.   22 cm.   73-21078 MARC.   CS71.M12786   1970

A423   McCLUNG.   The McClung genealogy.   A genealogical and biographical record of the McClung family from the time of their emigration to the year 1904.   By Rev. William McClung ... Pittsburgh, Pa., McClung printing company, 1904.   296 p.   front., plates, ports.   23½ cm.   4-31004.   CS71.M128   1904

A424   MACOUGALL.   McDougal genealogy; the known descendants in the United States of America of Robert McDougal of western Scotland (1748-1832)   (n. p., 1954)   55 l.   illus., coat of arms, maps.   30 cm.   Covers the period 1748-1954.   CS71.M137   1954
          ——— McDougal genealogy revision (to July 1, 1964) n. p., 1964)   1 v.   29 cm.   Title from label on cover.   Replacement pages for the main work.   55-19919.   CS71.M137   1954

A425   MacDUFFEE.   MacDuffee Clan of America.   Journal.   no. 1 -   Sept. 1969 -   (Hendersonville, N. C.?)   no.   22 cm.   75-19093.   CS71.M1383

        McDUFFIE.   See MACDUFFEE (addenda)

A426   McEACHERN.   The family of Daniel and Mary McEachern of Carroll County, Mississippi, compiled and edited by Sally Stone Trotter.   Greenville, Miss., Priv. print. by Burford Bros.   Print. Co., 1969.   57 p.   illus., ports.   29 cm.   71-11942 MARC.   CS71.M1389   1969

A427   McGIRT.   The descendants of Archibald McGirt, III and John McGirt, 1745-1969.   Compiled by Louise W. Love (Wilmington, N. C., 1969)   103 p.   coats of arms, facsims.   22 cm.   Cover title: The McGirt clan.   75-18778 MARC.   CS71.M146   1969

A428   McLAURIN.   G. G. McLaurin and some of his kin; sketches and genealogy, by G. G. McLaurin.   Dillon? S. C., 1970.   xiii, 175 p.   illus., ports.   24 cm.   73-21094 MARC.   CS71.M1618   1970

        McLOUGHLIN.   See also McLAUGHLIN.

A429   McMILLAN.   Daniel McMillan history and geneology (!)   (By) the McMillan family association, 1939-40 ... (Chicago, the Galewood press, 1940)   (119) p.   illus.   24½ cm.   "Manuscript ... assembled by Laura J. Lant." Includes the Marshall family.   43-35095.   CS71.M1675 1940a

A430   McNAIR.   McNair, McNear, & McNeier genealogies, compiled by James Birtley McNair.   Chicago, The author, 1923.   vii, 315 p.   ports., facsim., coats of arms.   22½ cm.   Bibliography: p. 17-18.   23-8159.   CS71.M168   1923

A431   MACNISH.   The history of the clan Neish or MacNish of Perthshire and Galloway, by David MacNish ... and William A. Tod ... With a foreword by W. C. Mackenzie.   Edinburgh and London, W. Blackwood and sons, 1925.   xiv, 198 p.   2 l.   22½ cm.   Numbered list of works cited as authorities: p. xi-xii. 26-18737.   CS479.N35

A432   McPHAIL.   Duncan Campbell McPhail and his descendants.   By Fannie Vann Simmons. (Raleigh, N. C., Printed by Litho Industries) 1968.   xv, 738 p. illus., col. coats of arms, geneal. tables. 25 cm. 71-12197 MARC.   CS71. M17156 1968c

   MACRAS.   See MACDONALD, DA750. S25.   2nd ser. vol. 5

   MAIER.   See MAYER (addenda)

A433   MAITLAND.   Maitland of Lethington, and the Scotland of Mary Stuart, a history.   By John Skelton ... Edinburgh and London, W. Blackwood and sons, 1887-88.   2 v. 23 cm. Closes with 1573. 3-28332.
                                                                                            DA787. M2S6

A434   MANNING.   Manning family, prominent members of Old Pinhook Church (by Carl H. Hawkins. Richmond, Ind., 1970)   14 p. illus., geneal. tables, ports. 30 cm. 70-24095 MARC.   CS71. M283   1970

   MANNING.   See also ODELL, 1960

A435   MARGITSON.   Too late for tears.   By Lilias Rider Haggard.   Bungay (Suffolk), Waveney Publications (1969)   156 p. 8 plates. illus., geneal. tables, ports. 23 cm. 73-474260 MARC.   CT788. M2167H3

A436   MARR.   Maar family records.   Compiled from various sources by Rev. Charles Maar ... Albany, N. Y., 1913.   cover title. 3-13 p. 24½ cm. 13-16996.   CS71. M35   1913

A437   MARSH.   Genealogy of the family of George Marsh, who came from England in 1635 and settled in Hingham, Mass.   By E. J. Marsh.   Leominster, Press of F. N. Boutwell, 1887.   vii, (9)-197, xxxii p. 23½ cm. L. C. COPY REPLACED BY MICROFILM. 9-8511   CS71. M365   1887
                                                                                            Microfilm 21923 CS

A438   MARTIN.   Some Martin, Jeffries, and Wayman families and connections of Virginia, Maryland, Kentucky, and Indiana, compiled by Estelle Clark Watson.   Skokie, Ill., Guild Press, 1965. vii, 273 p. geneal. tables, port. 28 cm. Bibliography: p. 193-194. 65-5591   CS71. M38   1965

A439   MARTIN.   The Flemington Martins.   By Arthur Morrison Martin.   Columbia, S. C., State Printing Co., 1970.   viii, 114 p. illus., facsim., map. 24 cm. 70-128479 MARC.   CS71. M38   1970

   MARTIN.   See also: DULIN, 1961
                      RATHLOFF (addenda)

   MARVYN.   See MARVIN.

A440   MASON.   Mason family data as of March 27, 1824   By George Graham.   (1968?)   (2) l. 34 cm. Typescript (carbon copy) Caption title. "Copied from the original court records ... U. S. District Court, Frankfort, Ky., by R. Carter Pittman." 77-12702 MARC.   CS71. M41   1968b

A441   MASON.   Ancestors and descendants of Eugene Waterman Mason, including the Stursberg ancestry of Mrs. Mason.   Edited and expanded by Harriet Stryker-Rodda.   (Bernardsville? N. J.) 1968.   77 p. illus., ports. 28 cm. Bibliography: p. 65-66. 79-11936 MARC.   CS71. M41   1968c

A442   MATHEWS.   The Mat(t)hews family; an anthology of Mathews lineages.   Compiled by John R. Boots, Jr.   Ocala, Fla., c. 1970.   vi, 808 p. illus., coats of arms, ports. 23 cm. Includes bibliographical references. 79-22449 MARC.   CS71. M44   1970

A443   MATTESON.   Memories of Mary Hulburt Matteson; with lineages of Mary Hulburt and Horace Matteson (Shanghai, China, Printed for private distribution by M. M. Wilbur, 1938)   6 p. l., 175 p. front., pl., ports. 24½ cm. Foreword signed: Mary Matteson Wilbur. 38-36148.   CS71. H964   1938

A444   MATTHEWS.   Walter Matthews (1845-1930) of May's Lick, Mason County, Kentucky, and his descendants.   By Mitchell Dudley Matthews.   Princeton, N. J., Four Bears Press, 1968. 66 p. port. 22 cm. 68-22089 MARC.   CS71. M44   1968c

A445   MAXWELL.   The ancestry of Lucy Florence Maxwell (1891-1964) compiled by James Thomas Ramsey, Jr.   (Easton, Md.) 1970.   v, 160 l. geneal. tables, maps. 30 cm. Includes bibliographical references.   76-278770 MARC.   CS71. M465   1970

A446   MAY.   The Mays family; a sequel to "The Mays family" by Samuel Edward Mays, by Ivan K. Mays.   (Austin, Tex.) 1970.   124 (i. e. 106) p. illus., facsims. 28 cm. Includes a portion of Genealogy of the Mays family and related families to 1929 inclusive, by S. E. Mays (54 p. on (29) p.), published with cover title "The Mays family." 74-19129.   CS71. M467   1970

A447   MAYER.   The Mayer family, by Harriet Hyatt Mayer.   (Annisquam, Mass., 1911)   (10) p. illus., geneal. tables. 31 cm. Caption title: The Mayer family, 1604-1911. "Edition of the 150 copies." "This pamphlet is designed to supplement the 'Memoirs and genealogy of the Maryland and Pennsylvania(n) family of Mayer.' by Brantz Mayer, Baltimore, 1878." 11-30061.   CS71. M468   1911

      MAYR.   See MAYER (addenda)

A448   MEGEE.   Ancestral trails; with genealogical notes on the following families: Megee, Ford, Futrell, Dunbar (and) Stover.   By Vernon Edgar Megee.   (Austin? Tex., 1969)   ii, 148 l. 29 cm.   76-253243 MARC.   CS71. M4926   1969

A449   MEHERRIN.   The living dream; a story of upper-South Carolina pioneers, by George R. Mayfield, III.   (Columbia, S. C., printed by R. L. Bryan Co., 1971)   239 p. geneal. tables. 24 cm.   72-153542 MARC.   CS71. M5   1971

A450   MELAS.   Mia oikogeneia, mia historia.   (Title romanized) By Leōn Iōannou Melas.   1967.   2 v. in 1 (1052 p.) illus., facsims., geneal. tables, plates (part col.), ports. (part col.) 25 cm. Bibliography: CS739. M27   1967   p. (1005)-1007. 70-511756.

A451   MERENS.   Les Merens, 1806-1920.   By Jean Lahille.   (Preface de Gustave Thibon.) Illustrations de Micheline Melmer-Ruph.   Paris (16e), l'auteur, 149, rue de la Pompe, (1969.)   ii, 128 p. plates (part col.) geneal. table. 19 cm. N. T. 76-475187.   CS599. M455   1969

A452   MERRILL.   Some descendants of Nathaniel Merrill, who was in Newbury, Massachusetts, 1635.   Researched and compiled by Winnifred M. Robinson.   Arranged and published by H. W. Merrill, Jr.   (Kingsport, Tenn., 1970)   33 p. 28 cm. Cover title. 70-11939 MARC.   CS71. M57   1970

A453   METCALF.   Genealogical table, shewing the descents of certain families from King Egbert, Charlemagne, Alfred the Great, Rollo, William the Conqueror, Saint Margaret, queen of Scotland, Saint Louis IX, king of France, Saint Ferdinand II, king of Castile and Leon and King Edward III.   Names of families whose royal descents are given: Ashby, Babington, Bethell, Bowstead, Crossland, Currie, Cust, Faber, Fisting, Hebblethwaite, Howard, Hutchinson, Lascelles, Mauleverer, Marwood, Metcalfe, Mitford, Mortimer, Neville, Ommanney, Orme, Percy, Pinkney, Robinson, Scongall, Slingsby, Talbot, Tugwell, Vanstraubensie, Vyner, Weston, Wilcox.   Compiled, written and emblazoned by John Henry Metcalfe.   London, Printed by J. B. Day (1871?)   geneal. tab. illus. 94 x 72 cm. fold. to 29 x 25 cm. Photostat (positive) of manuscript copy. 35-21382.   CS25. M4

      MEYER.   See also: MAYER.
               MYERS.   . M995

A454   MICHENER.   More Micheners in America.   Compiled by Anna E. Shaddinger.   Hatfield, Pa., Bonekemper Typesetting (1970)   1116 p. 24 cm. 72-141858 MARC.   CS71. M622   1970

A455   MICKELSON.   Mickelson and Peterson: family sketch, by Raymond A. Dieter, Jr., Bette Dieter, Andrew Mickelson, and family members.   1st ed.   (Chebanse? Ill.) 1970.   xix, 99 l. geneal. tables. 30 cm. 74-24099 MARC.   CS71. M6244   1970

A456   MILEY.   The Miley family history, 1495-1964, by Paul Newcomer Miley, David Ray Miley (and) Ray Leonard Miley.   (Ann Arbor, Mich., Priv. print, by Edwards Bros., 1965)   xi. 130 p. illus., map, ports. 24 cm. Cover title. Pages (109)-130 blank for "Future Miley history." 75-11647 MARC.   CS71. M643   1965

ADDENDA

A457   MILLS.   Historical origins of the Lucy Bingham and John D. Mills family of Stinking Creek (Knox County) Kentucky, by Glen D. Mills (Norman, Okla.) c. 1966.   11 p. ports. 23 cm. The ports are on (10) leaves stapled to p. (3) of cover.   67-6903.   CS71. M657   1966b

MILROY.   See WILSON, 1898a

A458   MILWARD.   The Milward family of Lexington, Kentucky, 1803-1969.   By Margaret Taylor Macdonald.   (1st ed.   Dallas? 1970)   vi, 177 p. illus., ports. 29 cm. Bibliography: p. 154-160. 70-122369 MARC.   CS71. M6578   1970

MITCHELL.   See also JOHNSON, 1967b

A459   MIXON.   The Mixon-Mixson family.   By John Leslie Mixon.   (Fort Worth, Tex., American Reference Publishers, c. 1969)   386 p. illus., port. 25 cm. 71-19033 MARC.   CS71. M673   1969

MIXSON.   See MIXON (addenda)

MOGAN.   See BREWSTER (addenda)

A460   MOLER.   From the records of John Mason Moler (Detroit? 1942)   1 p. l., 2-32 (i. e. 34), (5) p. 24 cm.   Includes extra numbered pages 12a - 12b.   44-30865.   CS71. M7   1942a

MOLLETT.   See PECK, 1955

A461   MONK.   The Monk family, by Charles H. Bowman, Jr.   Southern Pines, N. C., 1969.   40 l. 29 cm. 72-6588 MARC.   CS71. M738   1969

A462   MONROE.   Genealogy of the Monroes.   By A. B. Monroe.   1890.   sheet. 54 x 42 cm. Photocopy of MS. 75-239359.   CS71. M753   1890

A463   MONTCHENSI.   Historical memorials of the College of St. John Evangelist Rushworth or Rushford, co. Norfolk.   Founded by Edmund de Gonville A. D. 1342.   By the Rev. E. K. Bennett ... History of the college;   original statutes;   appendix and notes, calendar of charters, ... Norwich, A. H. Goose & Co., 1887.   2 p. l., 126 p. front. (col. plan) plates. 29 cm. "Reprinted from the Proceedings of the Norfolk and Norwich archaeological society." Ms note: "Twenty five copies printed." Rushworth and the Montchensi family: p. 52-56. Pedigree of the Gonville family: p. 63-73. 15-9768.   CS436. R87J6

A464   MONTEFELTRO.   I Montefeltro.   By Gino Franceschini.   (Milano), Dall'Oglio, 1970.   587 p. 16 plates. 23 cm. (Grandi famiglie) 7000 It 70-Mar Bibliography: p. (579)-587. 79-523779.   CS769. M63   1970

MONTMORET.   See MONTMOROT.

A465   MOODY.   The James F. Moody family history, by Marie Moody Foster and Erma Melton Smith.   (Chicago) Adams Press (1970)   455 p. illus., coat of arms, facsim., ports. 23 cm. 79-104057 MARC.   CS71. M812   1970

A466   MORGAN.   Morgan genealogy.   A history of James Morgan, of New London, Conn. and his descendants;   from 1607 to 1869 ... With an appendix, containing the history of his brother, Miles Morgan, of Springfield, Mass.:   and some of his descendants ... By Nathaniel H. Morgan.   Hartford, Press of Case Lockwood & Brainard, 1869.   280 p., 1 l. front., illus., ports. 23½ cm. "A history of the family of Miles Morgan, who emigrated from England, and settled at Springfield, Mass. A. D. 1636, compiled by Titus Morgan, jun., one of his descendants. Middletown, Oct. 1800": p. (227)-246. 9-13820.   CS71. M848   1869
Microfilm 22231 CS

MORGAN.   See also CARPENTER, 1970

A467   MORRIS.   Memoranda of the descendants of Amos Morris of East Haven, Conn.   New York, A. S. Barnes & Company, 1853.   103 p. front., coat of arms. 18½ cm. Introduction signed: E. L. Hart. O. Street. 9-12305.   CS71. M876   1853

A468   MORRIS.   The letters of Lewis, Richard, William, and John Morris, of Anglesey (Morrisiaid Mon), 1728-1765.   Transcribed from the originals and edited by John H. Davies.   Aberystwyth, Published privately by the editor and printed for him by Fox, Jones & Co., Oxford, 1907 (i. e. 1906)-09.
2 v. 23 cm. Issued in 8 pts. English or Welsh. "Three hundred copies ... No. 300." Bibliographical footnotes. 75-238327 MARC.
CS439. M785   1906

A469   MOWER.   Mower genealogy, 1690 to 1897.   By Ephraim Mower ... (n. p. 1897)
10 p. geneal. tab. 25½ cm. Caption title. 9-12313.   CS71. M82   1897b

A470   MOYER.   A genealogical record of the descendants of Christian and Hans Meyer and other pioneers, together with historical and biographical sketches ... By Rev. A. J. Fretz ... With an introduction by A. N. Moyer.... Harlysville, Pa., News printing house, 1896.   xiv p., 1 l., (17)-739 p. front.,
plates, ports. 20½ cm. Cover-title: Moyer family history. 9-12521.   CS71. M938   1896

A471   MUDD.   The Mudd family of the United States (by) Richard D. Mudd.   (2d ed.   Saginaw? Mich., 1970)   2 v. (xi, 1834 p.) illus., coat of arms, facsims., maps, ports. 29 cm. Bibliography: v.2, p.1379-1388. 73-108250 MARC.
CS71. M942   1970

A472   MUELLER.   Mogens, Hanne og Kirsten Müller's aner, af D. Müller.   København, 19
v. illus., ports. 26 cm. 76-492480.   CS909. M78   1969

A473   MUHLENBERG.   The Muhlenbergs of Pennsylvania, by Paul A. W. Wallace.   Freeport, N.Y., Books for Libraries Press (1970, c. 1950)   ix, 358 p. illus., ports. 24 cm. Includes bibliographical references.
75-124264 MARC.   CS71. M95   1970

A474   MULLENDORE.   The Mullendores, 1771-1962; data compiled 1953-1962.   By Naomi Mullendore Hougham.   (Franklin? Ind. 196-)   1 v. (various pagings) 30 cm. 73-265611 MARC.
CS71. M9572 1960z

A475   MULLINS.   The descendants of Gordon Lambert Mullins & Nancy Jane Courson; statistical data, compiled by James L. Mullins.   With an introd. by Ronald G. Mullins.   Dallas Center, Iowa, 1968.   (77) l. 30 cm. 74-17002 MARC.   CS71. M9594   1968

A476   MUNDEN.   From the House of Munden; 5 generations, 1829-1970.   Compiled and published by Thomas E. & Vivian A. Platt.   (Temple City? Calif., 1970)   xii, 63, 10, A-B l. 30 cm. 73-15912 MARC.
CS71. M966   1970

A477   MUNRO.   The Clan Munro, Clannan Rothaich; a beacon ablaze.   Edinburgh, W. & A. K. Johnston & G. W. Bacon.   32 p. col. illus., map, col. coat of arms. 19 cm. (W. & A. K. Johnston's clan histories) Bibliographical
footnotes. 61-39894.   CS479. M8   1954

A478   MUNSEY.   The Munsey ancestors of Rhoda Munsey Weems Carter (1814-1899) of Russell County, Virginia, and Newton County, Missouri.   By John Denton Carter.   (Biloxi, Miss., 1969)
5 l. 28 cm. 70-16335 MARC.   CS71. M972   1969

A479   MURRAY.   The descendants and progenitors of Thomas Henry Murray and Mary Jane Compton, by James H. L. Lawler.   (St. George, Utah, 1970)   17 p. geneal. table. 31 cm. Cover title. "Murray newsletter
#19, ... April 1970" (2 l.) inserted. 78-16361 MARC.   CS71. M9785   1970

A480   MYERS.   Caspar Meier and his successors; C. & H. H. Meier, Caspar Meier & co., L. N. von Post & Oelrichs, Oelrichs & Kruger, Oelrichs & co.   October 12, 1798 - October 12, 1898.   (New York, Priv. print., 1898)   2 p. l., (7)-116, (1) p. illus., port. 26 cm. 7-37058.   CT275. M4656. O5

A481   MYERS.   The Myers family history.   By Larry Kent Myers.   (South Bend, Ind., 1969)
72 l. illus., ports. 28 cm. Cover title. 79-13275 MARC.   CS71. M995   1969b

ADDENDA

A482   NELSON.   Pedigree of Mrs. Parley (Nelson) Bognan.   Compliments of Col. Albert A. Pope
(compiler)   Boston, 18 -?   geneal. tab.   54½ x 38 cm. fold. to 11 x 19 cm.   19-7389.   CS71.N43   18 -

A483   NELSON.   The Nelsons and Scotts of DeSoto Parish, Louisiana and related families.   Compiled and edited by Ouida Watters Nelson & Edward Kenneth Nelson.   Shreveport, La., Printed by
Professional Business Services, 1969.   vii, 225 p.   illus., coats of arms (part col.), maps, ports. 28 cm.   Bibliography:
p. 217.   70-15819 MARC.   CS71.N43   1969

      NELSON.   See also CONSTANT, F129.Y6C7

A484   NESTER.   Descendants of Jacob Nester, 1761-1844 (by Carl K. Nestor.   Kingwood, W. Va.,
1963?)   viii, 142 p. 30 cm. Half title. 65-3324.   CS71.N49   1963
   —— Addenda.   Smithfield, Pa., 1967.   (19) p. 28 cm. Caption title.   CS71.N49   1963
                                                                                Addenda

      NEWCOMER.   See also McILLHENY, n.d.

A485   NEWTON.   Rev. Roger Newton, deceased 1683, and one line of his descendants, by Caroline
Gaylord Newton, 1912.   (Durham? Conn., 1914?)   192, (3)-54. (3) p. plates, ports. 23 cm. Contains additions and
"errata" to 1914.   "Abner Newton, 1764-1852. His ancestors and descendants. Published in memory of Deacon Gaylord Newton 1903": 54 p. at
end.   Extracts from the New Haven register of March 21, 1914, and the Times-leader of March 23, 1914, on Henry Gleason Newton: p. 53-54.
15-4462.   CS71.N57   1914

A486   NICE.   The Nice family history; descendants of Henry Clemmer Nice, 1822-1892.   By Hazel
Nice Hassan.   Normal, Ill., 1965.   ix, 217 p. illus., facsims., ports. 23 cm. Bibliography: p. 201-202. 66-679.
                                                                                CS71.N59   1965

A488   NICHOLS.   Family record (incomplete) of James Nichols, born in Londonderry, N.H., or
vicinity, in the year 1733, by E. P. Nichols (170) of Searsport, Maine.   Belfast, Me., G. W. Burgess,
1882; Newburyport, Mass., 1923.   35 l. 28 cm. "Revised by Frank Storey Osgood." Autographed from typewritten copy.
24-12333.   CS71.N6   1923

A489   NICKERSON.   "From Pilgrims and Indians to kings and indentured servants"; an ancestry of the
brothers: Clinton Elwood Nickerson... and Vernon Roscoe Nickerson... and their cousins, the brothers:
James Elwin Nickerson... and Leighton Ainsworth Nickerson... By Vernon Roscoe Nickerson.   (Taunton,
Mass.) 1970.   243 l. ports. 29 cm. 80 copies printed. No. 33. Includes biblio. refs. 70-19128 MARC.   CS71.N66   1970

      NICKLOS.   In vertical file under PRANKE family.   Ask reference librarian for this material.

A490   NICOL.   CS479.G7   1904

A491   NICOLL.   The descendants of John Nicoll of Islip, England who died A. D. 1467.   (n. p., 1894?)
3 p. l., (3)-62 p. front. (coat of arms) 24 cm. Introduction signed: Edward Holland Nicoll. 31-33668.   CS71.N6   1894

A492   NISBET.   Alexander Nisbet's heraldic plates originally intended for his "System of Heraldry"
lately found in the library of William Eliott Lockhart, esq. of Cleghorn now reproduced with introduction and notes genealogical and heraldic by Andrew Ross, Marchmont herald, E. C. Francis J. Grant,
Carrick pursuivant ... Edinburgh, G. Waterston & sons, 1892.   lx, 192 p. incl. illus., coats of arms. 26 cm.
"Only two hundred copies printed for sale, of which this is no. 176." 25-1269.   CR1659.N5

A493   NIXON.   Nixon family memorials.   Published for the descendants of William Nixon and his
wife Yanacha Ayers of Sussex County, New Jersey, by Jean W. Cox, editor.   Compiled by: Melville
Campbell Harper (Mrs. Jesse C.), Elizabeth Nixon Hegele (Mrs. A. J.), Jean White Cox (Mrs. Ralph L.)
and many other interested members of the Nixon family.   (Connellsville, Pa., 1970)   xxi, 1202 p.
illus., facsims., geneal. tables, maps, ports. 29 cm. 75-13329 MARC.   CS71.N74   1970

A494   NIXON.   The ancestry of Richard Milhous Nixon.   By Raymond Martin Bell.   2d ed.   Washington, Pa., 1970.   64 l. illus. 29 cm. 76-16804 MARC.   CS71.N74   1970b

A495   NOLAND.   The Stephen-Daniel line of the Noland family (by) Edw. J. Ronsheim, Sr. Anderson, Ind., 1954.   76 l. coat-of-arms. 28 cm. Caption title. 77-13592 MARC.   CS71.N774   1954

NOORDSTRANDT.   See NOSTRANDT (addenda)

NORFLEET.   See LAWRENCE, 1964 (addenda)

NORTHCOTE.   See also PITMAN, CS439.P62 n.d.

A496   NOSTRAND.   Nostrand family in vertical file.   Ask reference librarian for this material.

A497   NOSTRANDT.   A genealogy of the Nostrandt family in America, with emphasis on the descendants who settled in central New York State, by Leslie L. Luther. (n.p.) 1969.   95 l. map, ports. 23 cm.   71-12714 MARC.   CS71.N92   1969

A498   OBLINGER.   History of the Oblinger - Oplinger - Uplinger family, by Wm. H. Rinkenbach. 1964.   59, (60-62) l. illus., col. coat of arms. 30 cm. Cover title. Typewcript (carbon copy) Bibliography: leaves (60-62)   76-13644 MARC.   CS71.O127   1964

A499   O'BYRNE.   The O'Byrne mill; digging for facts and fantasies. By Cecelia Christina O'Byrne. (Gladewater, Tex., Printed by Acme Duplicating Services, c. 1970.   184 p., (p. 183-184 blank for notes) illus., coat of arms, map, ports. 24 cm. 78-23991 MARC.   CS71.O15   1970

O'BYRNE.   See also O'TOOLE, 1890 (addenda)

A500   OCHS.   Up from the Volga; the story of the Ochs family. By Grace Lillian Ochs. Nashville, Southern Pub. Association (1969)   128 p. 21 cm. 75-98155 MARC.   CS71.O165   1969

A501   ODELL.   (O'Dell family tree chart, by Ludella Seabolt and Cleoris O'Dell. 1970?)   sheet. Photo-offset of MS. Parsons, W. Va., McClain Print. Co., 1970. 53 cm. Title, authorship, and imprint from copyright application. 70-262469 MARC.   CS71.O23   1970

A502   OEHLER.   Lebensbild von Karl Gottlieb Reinhard Oehler, 1797-1874, seinen Kindern und Enkeln, nebst ausgewählten Abschnitten aus den Erinnerungen von Robert Oehler sowie den Tagebüchern und Briefen Karl Reinhard Oehlers. Zusammengestellt im Auftrag von Alfred Oehler-Wassmer von Robert Oehler-Hartmann. Aarau, 1956.   222 p. geneal. tables, plates, ports. 23 cm. Cover title: Die Oehler von Aarau. 73-258477.   CS629.O34   1956

A503   OEN.   The Henry Oen family tree, by Mary (Heinl) Einhart. (n.p.) 1970.   18 l. 36 cm. "Original booklet compiled by Bernard W. Heinl, August, 1948. Updated by Mary (Heinl) Einhart July 1, 1966 (Family tree of Henry Oen, 1825-1902) Second updating, May 15, 1970." 72-19864 MARC.   CS71.O3   1970

O'FARRELL.   See FARRALL. (addenda)

A504   OGDEN.   The John Ogden family genealogy, 1807-1968. Compiled by Galen B. Ogden. Elgin, Ill., (1969)   104 p. 28 cm. 76-11938 MARC.   CS71.O34   1969

A505   O'KELLEY.   Four O'Kelly sons and some of their descendants, allied families. By Althea Jane Macon. (n.p., 1970)   205 p. coat of arms. 24 cm. Imprint added in manuscript on t.p.: Washington, Ga., Printed by Wilkes Pub. Co., 1970. Bibliography: p. 162-163. 77-18686 MARC.   CS71.O395   1970

A506   OLIVER.   The Olivers. By Oliver William Lienhard. (St. Louis, Mo., 1969?)   39 p. 29 cm. Cover title. 70-11651 MARC.   CS71.O47   1969

A507 O'NAN. Treasure up the memory; some genealogical notes relating to the O'Nan and allied families. By James Frederick O'Nan. (Cincinnati? 1969) vii, 149 p. geneal, table, plan. 24 cm. 70-20873 MARC.
CS71.O575 1969

O'NEILL. See also O'NEAL.

OPLINGER. See OBLINGER (addenda)

OSBERNE. See OSBORN.

A508 OTEY. John Otey of New Kent County, Virginia: descendants and related families. By Arthur Bledsoe Carpenter. (Richmond, Va., 1966?) xviii, 228 p. illus., facsims., maps, ports. 29 cm. 70-16060 MARC.
CS71.O87 1966

A509 O'TOOLE. History of the clan O'Toole ... and other Leinster septs. By the Rev. P. L. O'Toole ... Dublin, M. H. Gill and son; New York, Benziger brothers; (etc., etc.) 1890. xv, (1), 603, (2), 52, 7 p. col. front. (coat of arms) plates, ports., fold. maps, plan, fold. geneal. tables. 27½ cm. "The history of the clan O'Byrne (Ui Faelan)": 52 p. 2-8379 rev.
CS499.O7 1890
Microfilm 19902 CS

A510 OVERTON. Some ancestry of and the descendants of Ernest C. Overton: as of July 17, 1967. Compiled by Ernest C. Overton. Mechanicville, N.Y. (1967) (13), 155, 50 l. (chiefly forms, geneal. tables) 23 x 36 cm. Typescript. 68-2614 MARC.
CS71.O962 1967

A511 OVERTON. The American ancestry and descendants of Joel Overton, 1779-1844 and Naomi Wells, 1775-1865, his wife. By Ernest Clark Overton. (Albany, N.Y., Fort Orange Press, 1970) 1 v. (unpaged) geneal. tables. 24 cm. Cover title: Ancestry and descendants of Joel Overton and Naomi Wells. 77-19127 MARC.
CS71.O962 1970

A512 OVIATT. Oviatt-Hallam family tree. By Mary Oviatt Spieckermann. (Laramie, Wyo., 1970) 14 p. group port. 28 cm. 75-271079 MARC.
CS71.O963 1970

PADDOCK. See WHIPPLE, 1969 (addenda)

A513 PAGE. The Page family of Grand Rapids, Michigan, from Concord, Vermont. By Ianthe (Bond) Hebel. (Daytona Beach? Fla.) 1945. 2 v. 24-29 cm. Vol. 1 consists chiefly of genealogical lists and family history, v.2 of correspondence. 74-12030 MARC.
CS71.P133 1945

PAISANT. See PAYZANT (addenda)

A514 PALMER. A genealogy of the family of Henry Palmer of County Somerset, England and allied lines in the United States, 1635-1957; with biographical sketches. By Edwin Obadiah Palmer. Hollywood, Calif., (1959) xxxi, 135 p. ports., coat of arms. 24 cm. 59-43021.
CS71.P175 1959

A515 PANKEY. The Pankey family of Virginia, 1635-1968. By William Russell Pankey. Richmond, Va., 1968. vii, 67 p. illus., coat of arms, ports. 24 cm. 70-253318 MARC.
CS71.P22 1968

A516 PANKEY. John Pankey of Manakin Town, Virginia, and his descendants (and) descendants and connections of his son Stephen Pankey, Sr., of Lucy's Springs, Chesterfield County, Virginia. Ruston, La., 1969 - v. illus., ports. 27 cm. 68-58361 MARC.
CS71.P22 1969

A517 PARK. Allen Park, 1745-1805 of Rowan County, North Carolina and Madison County, Kentucky; including some of his descendants and allied families. By Evelyn Potter Park. Chandler, Okla,, W. R. Park, 1970. x, 300 p. illus., facsims., geneal. tables, maps, ports. 29 cm. Includes bibliographies. 71-20521 MARC.
CS71.P235 1970

A518   PARKER.   This is the story of Melissa Sallee Parker Van Sant.   By Mary Elizabeth Ireland.
Hill City, S. D., W. Parker, 1959,   53 l. illus. 30 cm. 60-22683.   CT275. V392 I7

A519   PARKER.   The story of the Parker family.   By Beulah McKaughan Bowling.   1966.
(5) l. 28 cm.   Caption title.   Typescript (carbon copy) with notes in manuscript.   Mounted col. photo.   Bibliography: leaf (5)   75-234056 MARC.
CS71. P24   1966b

A520   PARLI.   The Parli family record.   By Arnold Schuetz.   Humboldt, Neb., 1937.
47 p. illus., ports. 24 cm.   77-18339 MARC.   CS71. P2515   1937

A521   PARLI.   The Parli family record, 1970.   Based on The Parli family record as compiled by
Arnold Schuetz, 1937.   Compiled by Irene Parli (and) Sara Browder.   Sonora, Calif., 1970.
1 v. (unpaged) illus. 30 cm.   77-18312 MARC.   CS71. P2515   1970

A522   PARRISH.   One branch of the Parrish family of Bulloch County, Georgia.   By Alvaretta Kenan
Register.   (Norfolk? Va.) 1966.   iii, 78 l. coats of arms, geneal. table.   30 cm.   Includes bibliographical references.
73-13804 MARC.   CS71. P225   1966

A523   PARSONS.   Parson(s) family history; Southeast Alabama branch.   By Marie (Parsons) Whitaker.
(Washington?) 1970.   39 p. ports. 28 cm.   Includes bibliographical references.   77-13288 MARC.   CS71. P269   1970

PATAULT.   See PATHAULT.

PATEAU.   See PATHAULT.

PATHEAU.   See PATHAULT.

A524   PATTERSON.   John Patterson and his descendants (by) Charles Platt, Jr.   Glenside, Pa.,
W. L. Auch, Printer, 1970.   xvi, 152 p. illus., facsims., geneal. tables, map, ports. 27 cm.   76-134202 MARC.
CS71. P317   1970

A525   PAXTON.   Paxton family in vertical file.   Ask reference librarian for this material.

A526   PAYNE.   George Payne family tree in vertical file.   Ask reference librarian for this material.

A527   PAYZANT.   The Payzant and allied Jess and Juhan families in North America, compiled by
Marion M. Payzant.   Wollaston, Mass. (1970)   xxix, 452 p. illus., coat of arms, maps, ports. 24 cm.   72-16783 MARC.
CS71. P347   1970

A528   PEACOCK.   The Peacock, Rueff, Kittle, Van Duesen, Quackenbos, McCarn, Kayser, and related families in New Netherland, 1623-1759; a genealogical essay tracing the settlement of early
Walloon, Dutch, Danish, Norwegian, French, Palatine German, English, Scotch, and Irish families in
New Netherland, Novo Belgio, at Fort Orange, Rensselaerswyck, Beverwyck, Schenectady, New Amsterdam, and vicinity, in New York State, and showing their relationship in the ancestry of the compiler, with biographical descriptions of the first settlers and certain of their descendants.   Webster,
N. Y., 1970.   168 p. coats of arms, facsim., geneal. tables. 28 cm. Bibliography: p. 159-168. 77-278730 MARC. CS71. P357   1970

A529   PECHELL.   To commemorate the hundredth anniversary of the famous dinner, given at No. 6
Stratford place, to Sir Paul Pechell, (then Lieut-colonel Pechell) created a baronet in 1797, and to every
one of the then existing members of the Pechell family, by his sister Mary, and her husband, general
Caillaud, February the 11th, 1796.   (London, Hatchards, 1896)   19, (1) p. fold. geneal. tab. 15½ cm. Additions
in manuscript. "This exact copy of the account of that memorable occasion, written by Sir Paul Pechell, with his own hand, which he describes as
"'The ever-to-be-remembered eleventh of February, 1796, by those who bear the name of 'Pechell', is printed and presented to some of Sir Paul
Pechell's descendants by his great-grandson, Hervey Charles Pechell." 24-1595.   CS439. P335

PEIRSON.   See PEARSON.

PELLEKAAN.   See PELLECAEN.

PELLICAAN.   See PELLECAEN.

PELLIKAAN.   See PELLECAEN.

A530   PENN.   A pedigree & genealogical notes, from wills, registers, and deeds, of the highly distinguished family of Penn, of England and America, designed as a tribute to the memory of the great
and good William Penn ... London, J. Coleman, 1871.   24 p. front. (port.) illus., 2 fold. geneal. tables. 22 cm.
11-17115.   CS439. P4   1871

A531   PENNINGROTH.   Descendants of Friedrick Wilhelm Penningroth.   By Charles Penningroth.
(Cedar Rapids? 1967?)   iix (i. e. viii), 117, 53, 27 l. ports. 28 cm. 75-12120 MARC.   CS71. P4132   1967

A532   PERCY.   Thirty-one generations; a thousand years of Percys and Pierces 972-1969.   By
Barnard Ledward Colby.   (New London, Conn., 1969)   23 p. 22 cm. Cover title. Page 23 blank for "Notes."
77-82641 MARC.   CS71. P616   1969b

A533   PEREIRA.   Vida e morte de um capitão-mor.   São Paulo, Conselho Estadual de Cultura (1969)
376 p. illus., facsims., ports. 24 cm. 77-467041.   CS309. P47   1969

A534   PETERSON.   8 x 14 = 1; a partial inventory of the ancestry of Daniel Warren Peterson, edited
by James Ballagh Moore.   Kochi, Japan (1970)   101 p. 25 cm. 70-18282 MARC.   CS71. P485   1970

PETERSON.   See also MICKELSON, 1970 (addenda)

A535   PETTIBONE.   Pettibone register; descendants of John Pettibone, c. 1633-1713, an original
proprietor of Simsbury, Connecticut.   Compiled by Kathryn S. and James W. Pontius.   (n. p.) 1970.
iv, 64 p. 23 cm. 73-128923 MARC.   CS71. P489   1970

A536   PETTY.   The Petty and Francis families and allied lines.   By Zora Petty Billingsley. Amarillo,
Texas, 1967.   175 p. ports. 27 cm. 67-8876.   CS71. P5188   1967
—— Supplement no. 1 - Amarillo, Tex. (1969-   CS71. P5188   1967
                                                                       Suppl.

PEW.   See POU.

A537   PHELPS.   The Phelps family of America and their English ancestors, with copies of wills,
deeds, letters, and other interesting papers, coats of arms and valuable records.   Comp. by Judge
Oliver Seymour Phelps, of Portland, Oregon, and Andrew R. Servin, of Lenox, Mass ... Pittsfield,
Mass., Eagle publishing co., 1899.   2 v. front., illus., plates, ports., maps, plans, facsims., coats of arms. 24½ cm.
Paged continuously. 1-21628.   CS71. P54   1899
                                                                       Microfilm 21000 CS

A538   PHILPOT.   English and American backgrounds of a Philpott family line of Virginia and Maryland
U. S. A., a progress report in the form of an annotated bibliography, by Charles H. Philpott. (Durham?
N. C.) 1970.   iii, 31 l. 29 cm. Includes bibliographical references. 71-13711 MARC.   CS71. P559   1970

A539   PIERCE.   Thirty-one generations; a thousand years of Percys and Pierces 972-1969.   By
Barnard Ledward Colby.   (New London, Conn., 1969)   23 p. 22 cm. Cover title. Page 23 blank for "Notes."
77-82641 MARC.   CS71. P616   1969b

A540   PIND.   Slaegten Pind fra Velds i Ørum sogn.   Om Jens Pedersen (Pind), født 1798, og hustru,
deres forfaedre og efterkommere.   København, Nordisk Slaegtsforskning, 1969.   (108) l. illus. 30 cm.
N. T.   Four fold. geneal. tables inserted. 79-530128.   CS909. P47   1969

PITNER.   See FISHER, 1890 (addenda)

A541   POLHEMUS.   Polhemus family in vertical file.   Ask reference librarian for this material.

A542   POWELL.   Powell genealogy, by Ralph W. Powell.   (Berkeley, Calif., 1970)   83 p. illus., ports.
22 cm. Cover title. Includes bibliographical references. 76-13285 MARC.   CS71. P883   1970

A543   PREBLE.   The memoirs of the Jesse and Elizabeth Preble family.   By Harry Ulyat.   Baltimore, 1967 -   1 v. (loose-leaf) illus., facsims., ports. 23 x 36 cm.   76-21695 MARC.   CS71.P92

A544   PRENDERGAST.   The story of a pioneer family, by A. W. Anderson ... Sponsored and published by Jamestown historical society.   (Jamestown, N. Y.) 1936.   (15) p. illus. 21½ cm.   On cover: A pioneer Chautauqua family.   38-36172.   CS71.P925   1936

PRESCOTT.   See COOK, 1967b (addenda)

A545   PREWITT.   Prewitt-Light, Ringler-Hollowell and allied families.   By Lester Dee Prewitt. Rev. ed.   (Fairfield, Iowa, 1970)   x, 65 p. (p. 65 blank for "Addenda.") geneal. tables, ports. 29 cm.   The 1939 ed. published under title: Notes on the Prewitt-Light, Ringler-Hollowell and allied families.   70-137015 MARC.   CS71.P943   1970

PRICE.   See SCRUGGS, 1912 (addenda)

A546   PRIDGEN.   Stephen Pridgen, 1832-1864; letters, military data, genealogy, and miscellaneous Pridgen records.   By Carolyn Edwards Parker.   Auburn, Ala., 1970.   ix, 122 p. illus., facsims., ports. 24 cm.   Bibliography: p. 110.   74-132525 MARC.   CS71.P9484   1970

A547   PRIEL.   Het nageslacht van Hans Jurriën Priel † 1748, en zijn echtgenote Adriana Schriek, 1709-1787, door A. W. E. Dek.   Den Haag, Drukkerij Vriens, 1962.   208 p. facsims., geneal. tables, ports. 25 cm.   76-11615   CS829.P69   1962

A548   PRINCE.   Line of Hannah Prince (1749-1814) who married Thomas Prince (1749-1840); elder John Prince of Hull, Mass., progenitor.   By Helen (Richardson) Kluegel.   Kaneohe, Hawaii, 1968.   1 v. (various pagings) 29 cm.   "Book 12, family group 15."   74-16013 MARC.   CS71.P955   1968

PROCUNIER.   See BRAGUNIER (addenda)

PROSCH.   See CONKLING, 1909

A549   PYLE.   Colonel John Pyle and his people.   Compiled by C. Homer Pyle.   Edited by Bessie E. Pyle.   Bethany, Mo., BB Engraving and Print. Co., 1970.   40 p. port. 28 cm.   Bibliography: p. 39.   78-18461 MARC.   CS71.P995   1970

———

A550   QUIBELL.   A Quibell family scrapbook ... ; pertaining to the descendants of William Quibell and Ann Bassett of Lincolnshire, England.   By Robert Byron Bird.   Madison, Wis., 1970.   128 l. illus., facsims., maps, ports. 28 cm.   72-18883 MARC.   CS71.Q38   1970

———

A551   RADESTOCK.   Geschichte der Radestock aus Eckartsberga in Thüringen.   Der Bernburger Stamm: Eckartsberga, Bernburg, Ermsleben, Hoym, Magdeburg, Eisleben, Halberstadt, Landsberg (Warthe), Zielenzig, Waldheim (Sachs.).   By Hans-Joachim Radestock.   Hannover (-Kirchrode (Selbstverlag)) 1966.   2 v. (xv, 315 p.) with illus. and maps. 30 cm.   (Familienkundliche Sammlung Radestock, Stück Ca 1, T. 1-2) 70-367334.   CS629.R54   1966

A552   RAMBO.   Genealogy of a branch of the Rambo family and their descendants in the United States, including chart and biographical sketches.   Compiled and drawn by Owen Perry Adkins.   Richard Beale Bahme collaborated.   (Oakland? Calif.) 1959 (i. e. 1967?)   55 l. geneal. tables, map. 29 cm.   Bibliography: leaves 52-54.   75-262004 MARC.   CS71.R175   1967

A553   RANDOLPH.   Randolph family and collateral lines of Parry and Winslow.   By Alexander Du Bin. Philadelphia, Historical Pub. Society, 1946.   16 p. 25 cm.   48-1209*.   CS71.R193   1946a

RANDOLPH. See also ISHAM, 1898 (addenda)

A554 RATHLOFF. The descendants of Conrad and Anna Maria (Preussel) Rathloff: John and Henry Moeller, John Martin families, 1844-1969: and of John Lawrence and Anna J. M. (Molln) Martin, 1864-1969, by Doris F. Brainard. (Iowa Falls, Iowa, Printed by General Pub. and Binding) 1969. 268 p. illus., maps, ports. 22 cm. 74-15765 MARC. CS71.R2345 1969

A555 RAULSTON. The Raulstons, by J. Leonard Raulston. South Pittsburg, Tenn., 1970. 284 p. coat of arms, geneal. table, ports. 22 cm. Bibliography: p. 284. 74-13953 MARC. CS71.R246 1970

A556 RAVENEL. Ravenel records. New ed. with penciled marginal notes and annotations, including a copy of a letter to Capt. Daniel Ravenel, by Benjamin Mazÿck, 29th June, 1776. Dunwoody, Ga., N.S.Berg, 1971. v. 279 p. illus., geneal. tables. ports. 26 cm. First published in 1898. 78-20303 MARC. CS71.R253 1971

A557 RAWDON. The Rawdon papers, consisting of letters on various subjects, literary, political, and ecclesiastical, to and from Dr. John Bramhall, primate of Ireland. Including the correspondence of several most eminent men during the greater part of the seventeenth century. Faithfully printed from the originals; and illustrated with literary and historical notes, by the Rev. Edward Berwick ... London, J. Nichols and son (etc.) 1819. (iii)-vii, 430 p. facsims., fold. tab. 22 cm. Introduction (p.1-14) consists of a biographical sketch of John Bramhall, with a copy of his wills and that of his wife Ellianor Bramhall. 5-5142. DA940.5.R3B5

A558 RAY. A story of the family of William J. Ray (1799-1839), his ancestors and descendants, by L. L. Ray. Eugene, Or. (1970) 72 p. illus., ports. 23 cm. 79-126629 MARC. CS71.R268 1970

READER. See FISHER, 1890 (addenda)

A559 REEVE. Study of the Reeve family of Southold, Long Island, N.Y. and Southold descendants of the Southampton, L.I. Reeves family, and genealogy of said families up to 1800, by Wesley L. Baker. Douglaston, N.Y., 1970. 454 p. illus., facsims. 30 cm. On spine: Reeve-Reeves. 70-13605 MARC. CS71.R331 1970

A560 REITZ. Frutos de imigração: história e genealogia da família Reitz; lista de imigrantes, viagens. By Raulino Reitz. Brusque (Brasil) Azambuja, 1963. 238 p. illus., coats of arms, facsim., geneal. table, ports. 24 cm. Bibliography: p. 238. 75-524803. CS309.R4 1963

A561 RICHMOND. Genealogy of a branch of the Richmond family which came from Rhode Island to Ohio and settled in Amherst Township, Lorain Co., Ohio. By Claude Charles Hamel. Rev. 1955. 10 l. 32 cm. Typescript (carbon copy) Author's address on t.p.: Amherst, Lorain County, Ohio. Bibliography: leaf 10. 74-12022 MARC. CS71.R533 1955

A562 RILANDS. Three hundred years of a family living, being a history of the Rilands of Sutton Coldfield. By the Rev. W. K. Riland Bedford, M.A. Birmingham, Cornish brothers, 1889. 1 p. l., ix, (1), 175, (3) p. incl. geneal. tab. front. (fold. map) 3 port. 26½ cm. "Only fifty copies of this edition have been printed ... No. 28." L.C. COPY REPLACED BY MICROFILM. 2-29111. CS439.R55
Microfilm 22271 CS

A563 ROBBINS. Ancestors of Phyllis Jean (Robbins) Lee ... and Arthur Dale Robbins ... 1970. 11 l. 30 cm. Holograph with typewritten t.p. and bibliography. 75-18873 MARC. CS71.R632 1970

A564 ROBERTS. Roberts families of Roane County, Tennessee, 1794-1969, by Snyder E. Roberts. (Oliver Springs? Tenn., 1968) iv, 323 p. coat of arms, maps, port. 28 cm. 72-16164 MARC. CS71.R64 1968

A565 ROBERTS. Roberts-Wathen and allied families. By Leta Bricken Kirby. (Chamblee? Ga., 1970) A-F, 214 l. illus., coats of arms, ports. 28 cm. 75-19637 MARC. CS71.R64 1970

ROBERTS. See also BUNOT, 1970 (addenda)

A566 ROBINSON. Five pioneer Robinson families in Guernsey County, Ohio; a genealogical study of the families of: Samuel Robinson, Henry Robinson, William Robinson, James Robinson, Mary (Robinson) Thompson. Compiled by Milford E. Barnes, Mary E. (Robinson) Barnes (and) Ross A. Robinson. Iowa City, 1965. 50 l. 28 cm. 77-15921 MARC. CS71.R66 1965

A567   ROGERS.   Descendants of John Rogers and Katherine P. (Johnson) Rogers.   Compiled and published by Orville W. Jones.   Felicity, Ohio (19   v.   30 cm.   Contents. - v.2. - Descendants of James Rogers, 1787-1854, and Susannah (Heim) Rogers. 1793-1864.   70-24098 MARC.   CS71. R73   1971

A568   ROHRBACH.   John R. Rohrbach (Rohrabaugh) 1728-1821: descendants and marriage connections, by James D. Rorabaugh.   Parsons, W. Va., McClain Print. Co., 1966-70.   2 v.   illus., coat of arms, ports. 23 cm.   66-30409.   CS71. R736   1966

A569   ROHRBACH.   Rohrbach genealogy; descendants of nine Rohrbach immigrants to Colonial America, 1709-1754, and more than one hundred Rohrbach immigrants to America 1825-1900.   Philadelphia, Dando-Schaff Print. & Pub. Co., 1970.   615 p.   27 cm.   71-118879 MARC.   CS71. R736   1970

A570   ROOT.   Root.   By Clarice Root Nestor.   (Smithfield? Pa., 1961?)   54 p.   30 cm.   Label on binder: Roote-Root, 1555-1961.   Photocopy of typescript.   70-13593 MARC.   CS71. R782   1961

A571   ROSADO.   Outros dados genealógicos sôbre os Rosado (por) Vingt-un Rosado.   Mossoró, 1966. 116 p.   22 cm.   (Coleção mossoroense.   Série B (Folhetos) no. 90)   At head of title: Prefeitura Municipal de Mossoro.   Secretaria de Educação e Cultura.   74-245327.   CS309. R6   1966

ROSE.   See also COULTER, 1970   (addenda)

A572   ROSE.   One Rose family.   By John William Harrold.   (Largo, Fla., Largo Sentinel Press, 1970)   104 p.   21 cm.   "Approximately one hundred copies have been printed."   Bibliography:p. 89-92   77-21663 MARC.   CS71. R796   1970

A573   ROSENBERGER.   Commemorative narrative of the lives of Robert and Margaret Ann Rosenberger (by Virgil, Carl, Bernice, and Glenn Rosenberger.   Boulder? Colo., 1970?)   ii (8) p.   illus., geneal. table, ports.   28 cm.   78-21406 MARC.   CS71. R813   1970

A574   ROSEWARNE.   The family history of Thomas B. Rosewarne of Cornwall, England & Muskoka, Canada, his ancestors & descendants, 1716-1968, by Pearce & Winnifred Rosewarne.   Ottawa, 1968. x, 151 p.   illus., maps, ports.   28 cm.   Bibliography: p. 147.   79-487831 MARC.   CS90. R62   1968

ROSS.   See DYER, 1970   (addenda)

A575   ROUSE.   Rouse-Stevens ancestry & allied families; Sapp, Blain, Smith, Teter, Graham. By Dolly Bottens.   (Carthage? Mo., 1970)   137 1.   28 cm.   "Continuation of The history of the Robert Lee Smith family ... written by Will Smith."   77-18016 MARC.   CS71. R864   1970

A576   ROUSSIN.   Joseph Roussin, his ancestors and descendants, compiled by David C. Eisenlohr. Alhambra, Calif., 1964.   xii, 82 p.   port.   22 cm.   "An edition of fity copies ... no. 4."   Compiler's letter of transmittal and article, "Origin of the Russian family of Missouri" (Alhambra, California, Genealogical and Historical Committee of the Roussin Family Association of Missouri, 1963): (6) p. inserted after p.(68)   P. 69-72 not used in the pagination.   Bibliography: p.(xi)-xii.   70-14074 MARC.   CS71. R8675   1964

A577   ROWE.   Who are we; how did we get this way? A family record in five parts.   The early families of: Rowe, Gilsdorg, Blackman, Doremus, Ruggles.   Also an account ... of the lives of Adelaide and Milton Rowe.   (1970)   5, 166 p.   geneal. tables.   28 cm.   Introductory letter signed: Sylvania, Ohio, August 1970. Photoreproduction of holograph.   78-22438 MARC.   CS71. R878   1970

A578   RUBINCAM.   New light on the family of Jacob Revercomb.   By Milton Rubincam.   (195-) 18 1.   32 cm.   Caption title.   Typescript (carbon copy)   71-251158 MARC.   CS71. R886   1950z

A579   RUDDIMAN.   The Ruddimans in Scotland; their history and works, by George Harvey Johnston ... Edinburgh and London, Printed by W. & A. K. Johnston, limited, 1901.   xvii, 115 p.   front., illus., plates (1 col.) ports., map, fold. geneal. tables, col. coats of arms.   30 cm.   "Only 21 copies printed of which this is no. 18."   A second and enlarged edition; 1st edition published in 1887 under title "Notes on the Ruddimans."   Contains also pedigrees of the Steuart, Ker, Bradfute and Duncanson families.   "Authorities": p.xiii-xiv.   21-10457.   CS479. R84   1901

A580   RUNDELL.   The genealogy of Elijah Rundell and descendants.   By Onabelle Rundell Hayden. North Newton, Kans., Printed by Mennonite Press, 1970.   xxi, 157 p. illus., facsims., ports. 29 cm. On cover: Rundell genealogy.   71-113174 MARC.   CS71. R94   1970

A581   RUSSEY.   The Russey family in America; a genealogy of James Russey, 1755-1970.   By George Sirrine Russey.   Rev., enl., edited, and published by John Wesley Russey, Jr.   2d ed.   San Antonio, Tex., 1970.   vi, 262 p. illus., facsims., maps. 29 cm. Bibliography: p.245-247. 68-13054 MARC.   1970
                                                                                                      CS71. R967   1970

A582   RUTHERFORD.   A family history for the descendents of Charles Perry Rutherford of Oregon and of Henry John Altnow of Minnesota and Oregon.   By Homer Vincent Rutherford.   Winnipeg, 1970. 146 l. geneal. table. 28 cm. Cover title. Includes bibliographical references. 79-20838 MARC.   CS71. R975   1970

A583   RUTHERFORD.   Rutherford family in vertical file.   Ask reference librarian for this material.

A584   SAMPSON.   Abraham Sampson in America; family genealogy, gathered and compiled 1961-1969 (by) Elizabeth Newman Hutchinson.   (Salt Lake City, Printed by Custom Letter Service, 1970) xiv, 173 p. coat of arms. 30 cm. 70-253532 MARC.   CS71. S189   1970

A585   SANDLIN.   The Sandlin clan, by Dale S. Sandlin.   (Jones Creek, Tex., 1970) 119 l. illus., ports. 29 cm. Cover title. 72-19848 MARC.   CS71. S2194   1970

A586   SANFORD.   President John Sanford of Boston, Massachusetts and Portsmouth, Rhode Island, and descendants with many allied families, 1605-1965.   Also adding the male members given in the "William Sanford of Madison, New York" genealogy by Heman Howes Sanford, 1890, with many families brought up to date.   By Jack Minard Sanford.   Rutland, Vt., Printed by Sharp Printing (1966) xv, 399 p. geneal. table. 24 cm. Cover title: John Sanford genealogy. 66-8695.   CS71. S223   1966

A587   SAPIEHA.   Histoire des Sapieha (1440-1970), essai de généalogie, d'héraldique et d'iconographie (par) D. Labarre de Raillicourt.   Armoiries réalisées par Maria-Teresa Labarre de Raillicourt. Paris, (16ᵉ), l'auteur, 5, square Charles-Dickens, 1970.   iv, 154 p. illus., plates (part fold.) 28 cm. At head of title: Magnats lithuaniens et princes polonais. Half title: Les Sapieha. Illustrated cover. "Il a été tiré de cet ouvrage 205 exemplaires sur papier édition bouffant, numérotés de 1 à 205." No. 52. 72-530023.   CS879. S26   1970

SAPP.   See ROUSE, 1970 (addenda)

SATTERLEE.   See SATTERLY (addenda)

SATTERLEY.   See SATTERLY (addenda)

A588   SATTERLY.   Satterlee-ley-lye & allied families genealogy (by) Goldie Satterlee Moffatt, assisted by John L. Satterlee.   (Middleboro, Mass., Chedwato Service) 1970 (c. 1971)   225 p. illus., coat of arms, map, ports. 27 cm. 74-24100 MARC.   CS71. S255   1971

A589   SCALF.   Chronicles of the Scalf family, by Henry P. Scalf.   (Stanville, Ky.) 1970. 206 p. map. 28 cm. "Research in collaboration with Mrs. Elsie Payne Archer." 71-16074 MARC.   CS71. S282   1970

A590   SCHAEFFER.   Schaeffer family in vertical file.   Ask reference librarian for this material.

A591   SCHEM.   Schem family in vertical file.   Ask reference librarian for this material.

A592   SCHLEGELMILCH.   Schlegelmilch family in vertical file.   Ask reference librarian for this material.

A593   SCOTT.   The arms of Richard Scott, by Richard LeBaron Bowen ... (Providence, R. I., 1939) (12) p. illus. (incl. facsim., col. coat of arms) 23½ cm. "Reprinted from Rhode Island historical society. Collections, vol. XXXII, no.3, July, 1939." 40-32887.   CS71. S43   1939

A594   SCOTT.   Descendants of Thomas Scott (of Muskingum and Coshocton Counties, Ohio).   By Lewis Scott Dayton.   (LaMoille? Ill., 1968) c.1956.   29, (2) l.   30 cm.   A reissue of the 1956 ed. with a few corrections and a "Supplement: corrections and additional data received after publication" (leaves 22-31)   78-16223 MARC.   CS71.S43   1968

A595   SCOTT.   Many generations; a genealogy of the descendants of William H. Scott and Rebecca (Orr) Scott, 1741-1969.   By Martha Blackwell Scott.   (Montgomery, Ala.) 1969.   333 p. illus., ports.   24 cm.   Bibliography: p. 284-286.   77-12824 MARC.   CS71.S43   1969

SCOTT.   See also NELSON, 1969 (addenda)

A596   SCRUGGS.   Scruggs genealogy; with a brief history of the allied families Briscoe, Dial, Dunklin, Leake and Price, comp. by Ethel Hastings Scruggs Dunklin.   New York, Laplante & Dunklin priting company, 1912.   223, xiii p. incl. front. (coat of arms) 20 cm.   Nine blank pages for "Additional notes," following p.223.   CS71.S436   1912

────── Scrugg(e)s, Scroggs, Skrog, Serug, by Margaret Ann Scruggs (Mrs. Carruth).   1970.   (17) l.   geneal. table.   28 cm.   Typescript (carbon copy) 19-20220.   CS71.S436   1912   Suppl.

A597   SEEKINS.   The Seekins genealogy; Aaron Seekins, 1690-1750, of Middleborough, Massachusetts, with most of his descendants.   By Paul Orville Seekins.   Columbus, Ohio, 1970.   xiv, 201 p.   23 cm.   70-19062 MARC.   CS71.S449   1970

A598   SENGLAUB.   Descendants and families of the Senglaub genealogy.   Compiled, edited (and) rev. by Mrs. O. W. Senglaub.   Milwaukee, 1962.   38, 8 l.   28 cm.   65-51581.   CS71.S477   1962

A599   SETZEKORN.   The origin and history of the family Setzekorn, prepared for the descendants of Conrad Wilhelm Setzekorn who immigrated to America in 1858.   By William David Setzekorn.   (1st ed.) Seattle, Goodway Printers, 1970.   86 p.   illus., coat of arms. map, ports.   23 cm.   Includes bibliographical references.   73-19126 MARC.   CS71.S4955   1970

A600   SHARP.   George Sharp(e) of Virginia and Kentucky and some of his descendants in Knox County, Missouri.   By Harold Turk Smutz.   (1970)   11 l.   30 cm.   Photocopy of typescript.   Includes bibliographical references.   71-14699 MARC.   CS71.S53   1970a

SHARP.   See also HOOPER, 1970 (addenda)

A601   SHARPLESS.   The Sharples-Sharpless family.   By Bart Anderson.   Bart Anderson, editor.   West Chester, Pa., 1966.   2 v. (1247 p.) illus., facsims., map, ports.   31 cm.   73-15809 MARC.   CS71.S532   1966

SHEARER.   See GROSS, 1970 (addenda)

A602   SHEILD.   Mary Rooksland Sheild; a Va. genealogy, 871-1965.   By Dollie Hughes Vick.   (Shelburne, Vt., Excelsior Press, 1965?)   159 p. illus., ports. 22 cm.   Cover title.   73-8585 MARC.   CS71.S544   1965

A603   SHELDEN.   Family tree of Edward G. Shelden, born in Ohio, March 1, 1827, died in Illinois, January 22, 1896.   Married Aurenda Stimson, born in New York, January 29, 1829, died in Kansas, December 24, 1917.   1 printed folded table.   In vertical tile.   Ask reference librarian for this material.

A604   SHELDON.   Some descendants of John Sheldon of Rhode Island, compiled by Helen W. Brown.   College Park, Md., 1964.   xiii, 124 p. illus., map. 29 cm.   70-11292 MARC.   CS71.S543   1964

A605   SHEPARDSON.   The Shepardson family.   A record of the line of Zephaniah Shepardson, Guilford, Vermont.   By John Eaton Shepardson.   September 1, 1907.   (Chicago? Ill., 1907)   19 p.   25 cm.   Caption title.   No. 5 of the Shepardson leaflets. cf. p.19.   7-29180.   CS71.S548   1907d

A606   SHERBURNE.   A history of Leagram: the park and the manor, by John Weld ... (Manchester) Printed for the Chetham society, 1913.   4 p. l., (iii)-iv, 168 p. front. (map) 22½ x 17½ cm.   (Added t.-p.: Remains, historical and literary, connected with the palatine counties of Lancs. & Chester. N. s. v. 72. The Shirburne family: p. 28-62.   14-13718.   DA670. L19C5 v. 72

ADDENDA

A607 SHERMAN. Transatlantic Shermans, by Bertha L. Stratton. Staten Island, N.Y. (1969)
iii, 202 p. illus. (part col.) 24 cm. 76-89997 MARC.   CS71.S552   1969

A608 SHERMAN. A New England heritage; the 500-year story of my line of the Sherman and
Mauran families, 1420-1920. by F. Barreda Sherman. San Francisco, Calif., R. F. Publications
(c. 1969)   480 p. illus., facsims., maps, ports. 25 cm. "Limited to 225 copies for private distribution only." Includes bibliographies.
77-15641 MARC.   CS71.S552   1969b

A609 SHIELDS. Research on the East Tennessee Shields families. By Katherine Susong Harmon.
(Greenville, Tenn?) 1968.   164 p. illus., facsims., geneal. tables. 28 cm. 77-12745 MARC.   CS71.S5545   1968b

A610 SHINNICK. Shinnick genealogy. Compiled by Helen Frances Shinnick. (n. p., 1969 or 70)
1 v. (various pagings) illus., geneal. tables, ports. 29 cm. Photocopy of typescript. Includes bibliographical references. 77-19711 MARC.
                                                                        CS71.S5564   1969

        SHIPMAN. See FISHER, 1890 (addenda)

A610a SHIRLEY. Chamblee, Fisher, Grubbs, Hughes, Robinson, Shirley, Speer, and Tribble families of the South. By Ethel Speer Updike. (n. p.) 1969.   301 p. ports. 29 cm. 73-13697 MARC. CS71.S5575   1969

A611 SIAS. The Sias family in America, 1677 to 1952; the first 275 years. From materials
gathered through long and painstaking efforts by many members of the family. By Azariah Boody Sias.
Orlando, Fal., Printed by Florida Press, 1952 (i. e. 1953)-67.   3 v. illus., ports., maps (on lining papers) geneal.
table. 24 cm. Vol. 2: Supplement; v. 3: Supplement 2. Includes bibliographies. 53-32942.   CS71.S569   1953

A612 SKILTON. The teeth of the rake. By George Warner Skilton. Artist: N. William Petersen.
(Farmington? Conn., 1964?)   30 p. (p. 27-30 blank for notes) illus., map. 29 cm. 77-12710 MARC.
                                                                        CS71.S6285   1964

A613 SLADE. Slade-Babcock genealogy; ancestors and descendants of Benjamin and Angeline
(Babcock) Slade of Rensselaer and Saratoga Counties, New York. By Carl Boyer. Newhall, Calif.,
1970.   210 p. ports. 28 cm. Bibliography: p. 169-179. 78-137861 MARC.   CS71.S63   1970

A614 SLEEPER. The Sleeper family of Unity, New Hampshire. Compiled and arr., with additions
from later records, by Aimee Huston Eck.   By Emily Harriet Lewis. 1951. 18, (4) l. 31 cm.
Typescript (carbon copy) On t. p.: Minneapolis, Minn., 1951. Bibliography: leaf (22) 70-15406 MARC.   CS71.S6327   1951

A615 SLOAN. Sloan-Trout; Tom and Tillie's ancestors. Compiled by Walter Reed Sloan.
(McConnellsburg? Pa., 1965?)   125 l. ports. 28 cm. 70-15441 MARC.   CS71.S6334   1965

A616 SMALLWOOD. The Smallwood family of Maryland and Virginia. Compiled by Mildred A.
McDonnell. (n. p., 1970)   188 p. 28 cm. 70-20053 MARC.   CS71.S63614   1970

A617 SMITH. Our family circle. By Annie Elizabeth Miller. Marietta, Ga., Continental Book Co.,
1957 (c. 1931)   552 p. illus., ports., coats of arms. 24 cm. Contents. - House of Landgrave Smith - The "twenty children." - Second
Landgrave Smith and Mary Hyrne. - House of Robert. - House of Bostick. - House of Lawton. - House of Grimball. - House of Erwin. - House of
Daniel. - House of Stafford. - House of Maner. 61-47604.   CS71.S643   1957a

A618 SMITH. Genealogy: Schmidt, Smith, Vrooman, Croman (by Stanley W. Smith. La Salle, Ill.)
1970.   112 p. illus., coats of arms, facsims., ports. 23 cm. Cover title. Label mounted on t. p.: Representative: Charlotte T. Reid.
70-14748 MARC.   CS71.S643   1970

A619 SMITH. A southern neo-colonial home, Houma, Louisiana, and the partial story of its owners:
Mr. and Mrs. C. P. Smith and C. Mildred Smith (by) C. Mildred Smith (and) G. Portre-Bobinski.
(Limited ed. n. p., 1970)   115 p. illus., facsims., maps, ports. 23 cm. At head of title: Louisiana. 77-266068 MARC.
                                                                        CS71.S643   1970b

        SMITH. See also ROUSE, 1970 (addenda)

A620 SMITHSON. The descendants of Horatio Sharp Smithson & A18 Lydia Andrews. Prepared by
Mrs. Forrest Andrews. Knoxville, Tenn. (1968)   14 p. 36 cm. 71-12111 MARC.   CS71.S647   1968

A621 SMOUSE. The history of the Smouse family of America, 1738-1969, by J. Warren Smouse. With revisions and additions by Mary Smouse Yohe. (Havertown? Pa., 1969?) viii, 387 p. illus., coat of arms, ports. 24 cm. 70-16899 MARC. CS71.S654 1969

A622 SNELGROVE. The pioneer Snelgroves of Mississippi, their South Carolina forebears, and vertain pioneer Snelgroves of Georgia and Alabama and their descendants. By Harold Sinclair Snellgrove. State College, Mississippi State University, 1968. iv, 44 l. geneal. table. 28 cm. Includes bibliographical references. 74-628857 MARC. CS71.S6683 1968

A623 SNOWBERGER. Family records of Snowberger and Kegarise, by Hilda Snowberger Chance. (Chester? Pa., 1964) (10), 27 p. illus., geneal. table, ports. 28 cm. Cover title. Bibliography: 1st prelim. page. "Additions and corrections": (6) p. inserted. 64-55585. CS71.S672 1964
—— Snowberger and Kegarise supplement, 1970, with index (by) Hilda Chance. (Liberty? Pa., 1970) 19 l. 28 cm. Cover title. CS71.S672 1964 Suppl.

A624 SOUTER. The Souter family book of remembrance; the story of Andrew Souter and his wife Sarah Elizabeth Harrison with historical, genealogical, and biographical data on their ancestry and descendants. By Jennie Souter Wolgamott. (Salt Lake City, Lithographed by Publishers Press, c. 1968) xvi, 179 p. illus. (part col.), coats of arms, facsims., ports. 29 cm. 72-12792 MARC. CS71.S695 1968

A625 SPENCER. Genealogy of Spencer family of Conn. and Oregon; Champlin of R. I. and Conn.; Davis and Mansfield families of Conn.; Chamberlain of Conn., by Arthur C. Spencer, III. Portland, Or., 1970. 19, 33 l. 28 cm. 72-22360 MARC. CS71.S745 1970

A626 SPRATT. Descendants of Thomas "Kanawha" Spratt. Compiled by A. W. Cockrell, Jr. (Jacksonville? Fla., 1970) 34 l. 29 cm. Originally compiled 1908; brought up to date. 73-17278 MARC. CS71.S7663 1970

A627 SPRINGER. Genealogy of Lorenze Springer family, Sweden, Delaware, Maine. By Edward Perrine Cody. Rev. (Wethersfield? Conn., 1952) geneal. table. 79 x 92 cm. fold. to 43 x 33 cm. Reproduction of original MS. dated March 1952. 52-64164. CS71.S769 1952
—— Springer family. Additions to chart compiled March 1952. (Wethersfield? Conn., 1952) geneal. table. 71 x 89 cm. Reproduction of original MS. dated July 1952. CS71.S769 1952 Suppl.

A628 STAFFORD. A contribution to the genealogy of the Stafford family in America; containing an account of Col. Joab Stafford, and a complete record of his descendants in the male lines. By Henry Marvin Benedict. Albany, J. Munsell, 1870. 27 p. front. (port.) illus., fold. diagr. 25 cm. L. C. COPY REPLACED BY MICROFILM. 9-13800. CS71.S779 1870 Microfilm 22602 CS

A629 STAFFORD. Stafford family in vertical file. Ask reference librarian for this material.

A630 STANSALL. The Stansel family. By Edwin Nathaniel Stansel. (Lake Arrowhead, Calif.?) 1969. 59 l. illus., coats of arms, facsims., geneal. table, map, ports. 31 cm. 76-14747 MARC. CS71.S7878 1969

A631 STANSBURY. The descendants of John Stansbury of Leominster. Comp. by Frederick Howard Wines for the information of the family. Springfield, Ill., the H. W. Rokker printing house, 1895. vii, 55 p. 23½ cm. 12-24994 CS71.S788 1895 Microfilm 19618 CS

A632 STANSFIELD. History of the family of Stansfeld of Stansfield in the parish of Halifax and its numerous branches. By John Stansfeld, Leeds ... Leeds, Goodall and Suddick, printed for private circulation, 1885. 6 p. l., (v)-xii. 459 p. front., illus., plates (1 col.) ports., facsims., geneal. tables (part fold.) coats of arms (part col.) 30 cm. 17-23934. CS439.S85

A633 STARING. The Staring family; records of early generations of hardy pioneers who settled at German Flatts, now Herkimer, 1722-25, by Hubert W. Hess. ... (St. Johnsville, N. Y.) 1929. cover-title, 28 p. 22 cm. "Reprinted from the Enterprise & news, St. Johnsville, N. Y., 1929." 42-31606 rev. CS71.S7945 1929

ADDENDA

A634   STARK.   James Stark, jr. with wife "Cathron" of Virginia.   "Died in the Carolinas".   Genealogical notes and records.   Compiled by Jane H. Abbott.   1928-1929.   (n. p.1929)   71 l. incl. map.
30 cm.   Typewritten.   Includes "Authorities".   34-8468.   CS71.S795   1929

A635   STARR.   A history of the Starr family of New England, from the ancestor, Dr. Comfort Starr
of Ashford, county of Kent, England, who emigrated to Boston, Mass., in 1635; ... by Burgis Pratt
Starr ... Hartford, Conn., The Case, Lockwood & Brainard co., print., 1879.   3 p. l., x, 588, (2) p. front.,
pl., ports., coats of arms. 24 cm. "Supplemental to the Starr family. Hartford, Dec. 1, 1880": 579-588, (2) p. Printed circulars concerning the
Starr family inserted.   20-9253.   L. C. COPY REPLACED BY MICROFILM.   CS71.S7965   1879
                                                                                           Microfilm 18684 CS

A636   STEENROD.   The Steenrod family.   (Compiled by Robert L. Steenrod.   Joplin, Mo., 1969)
206 p. 28 cm.   Cover title.   72-14746 MARC.   CS71.S815   1969

A637   STEENSEN.   Slaegten Steensen fra Engum sogn.   Om Steen Rasmussen, født 1800, og dennes
første hustru, dered forfaedre og efterkommere.   København, Nordisk Slaegtsforskning, 1969.
(69) l. 6 plates. 30 cm. N. T.   Three fold. geneal. tables inserted.   72-530129.   CS909.S74   1969

A638   STEHELIN.   Geschichte der Basler Familie Stehelin und Stähelin.   By Feliz Stahelin.   Basel,
Basler Druck- unde Verlags-Anstalt, 1903.   vii, 130 p. coats of arms. 23 cm. Bibliography: p. (vi)-vii. 73-241270.
                                                                                              CS999.S77   1903

       STENROD.   See STEENROD (addenda)

       STEVENS.   See ROUSE, 1970 (addenda)

A639   STEVENSON.   Early Stevenson history, compiled by Charles S. Stevenson.   (Morris, Man.,
Author, R. R. I., 1966)   99 p. 22 cm.   Cover title.   74-467331 MARC.   CS90.S654   1966

A640   STEWART.   The Stewards of Amite County, and descendants of Robert Edward Stewart and
Elizabeth Callihan Stewart, of Amite County, Mississippi; a family history and family album, by Edsel
Ford Stewart cooperating with Maggie Sanders Duck and Mildred Clark Jenkins.   (New Orleans, 1962)
309 p. illus. 24 cm.   63-28362.   CS71.S93   1962

A641   STICKNEY.   English ancestry of William Stickney of Rowley, Massachusetts, 1938.   By Emily
(Stickney) Spencer.   (Cleveland, Printed by Montgomery Print. Co.) 1970.   23 l. illus., maps. 38 cm.
100 copies printed.   72-16349 MARC.   CS71.S854   1970

A642   STIFFLER.   The descendants of David Stiffler, Senior, and his wife, Magdalene Thomas, with
a sketch of his Stiffler ancestry; a genealogy (by) R. Ewing Stiffler.   (1st ed. Denver, 1957?)
46 p. illus., coat of arms, geneal. tables, col. maps, ports. 30 cm.   "Limited to 50 copies ... copy no. 1."   77-268318 MARC.
                                                                                              CS71.S8553   1957

A643   STOURTON.   The history of the noble house of Stourton, of Stourton, in the county of Wilts.
Comp. from the original official ducments, and other additional sources, under the instructions and
supervision of Charles Botolph Joseph, lord Mowbray, Segrave and Stourton.   London, Priv. print.,
E. Stock, 1899.   2 v. fronts., illus (incl. facsims.) plates, ports., coats of arms. 30 cm. Paged continuously. "One hundred copies
only of this book have been printed. of which this copy is number 22."   21-16267.   DA28.35.S85M7

A644   STOUTENBOROUGH.   Stoutenborough history.   By Marie Fruit Rybolt.   Kenney, Ill., 1968.
94 p. illus., ports. 29 cm. Cover title: Stoutenborough family history. Bibliography: p. 92-94. 68-7905.
                                                                                              CS71.S889   1968

A645   STOWELL.   The Stowell genealogy; a record of the descendants of Samuel Stowell of Hingham,
Mass. By William Henry Harrison Stowell.   (1st Tuttle ed.) Rutland, Vt., C. E. Tuttle Co. (1970)
980 p. illus., ports. 24 cm.   Reprint of the 1922 ed.   78-87789 MARC.   CS71.S893   1970

A646   STRIEBY.   Strieby genealogy and history 1726-1967.   Compiled by Byard B. Strieby, B. Beatrice
Strieby (and) Irene M. Strieby.   Des Moines (1967)   xii, 252 p. coat of arms, facsims., maps. 28 cm. 68-5478.
                                                                                              CS71.S9173   1967

A646 continued: —— Supplement, 1969. Des Moines, Print, Priv, Macdonald Letter Service Co. (1969)   i, 58 p. 28 cm.   CS71.S9173   1967
                                                                                                                                      Suppl.

A647   STRINGFELLOW.   The life of Horace Stringfellow with some instances in the life and work of his descendants, by Lizzie Stringfellow Watkins.   Montgomery, Als., The Paragon press, 1931.
152 p. front., plates, ports., facsim. 24 cm. 31-33599.   BX5995.S85W3

A648   STROUD.   Strode and Stroud families in England and America.   By James Strode Elston. Rutland, Vt., Tuttle Pub. Co. (1949-70) 2 v. illus., facsims., geneal. table, port. 24 cm. Vol. 2 published by Chedwato Service, Middleboro, Mass. Includes bibliographies. 50-344.   CS71.S9255   1949

A649   SVENSSON.   Peter and Cajsa-Maja Svensson; a genealogy of six generations of their descendants.   By Doris L. Roberts.   (South Bend? Ind.) c.1970.   46 l. 30 cm. Cover title: Peter Svensson genealogy. Photocopy of typescript. Includes bibliographical references. 78-148820.   CS71.S969   1970

————————

A650   TAGORE.   The Tagore family; a memoir, by James W. Furrell.   2d ed.   Calcutta, Printed by Thacker, Spink, 1892.   187 p. 19 cm. 75-241146 MARC.   CS1209.T3   1892

A651   TATIAN.   Tatian Gerdastaně.   (Title romanized)   1968   280 p. illus., facsim., ports. 21 cm. Added t.p.: Die Geschichte der Familie Dadian, hrsg. von Ephrem Poghossian. Bibliographical footnotes. 73-232005.   CS1499.T3   1968
                                                                                                                                      Orien Armen

A652   TEAGUE.   The Teague family magazine.   (Winston-Salem, N.C., Teague Family Memorial Association)   v. illus., ports. 23 cm. quarterly. 78-19347.   CS71.T25

A653   TEARMAN.   Genealogy of William Tearman.   Compiled by Arvel W. Crouch (and others) 1970.   1 v. (various pagings) 23 x 30 cm. Typescript (carbon copy) 74-272554 MARC.   CS71.T2545   1970

A654   TEN BROECK.   The Ten Broeck genealogy, being the records and annals of Dirck Wesseles Ten Broeck of Albany and his descendants, compiled by Emma Ten Broeck Runk ... New York, Printed at the De Vinne press, 1897.   x p., 1 l., 277 p. front., plates, ports., facsims. (1 fold.) coats of arms. 23½ cm. "Limited to one hundred copies ... No. 93." 9-14560.   CS71.7289   1897

A655   TEN EYCK.   Ten Eyck family record (by) A. M. Ten Eyck.   (Brodhead? Wis., 1949?) 120 p. illus., coat of arms, ports. 27 cm. Pages 117-120 blank for "Family record." 79-20523 MARC.   CS71.T2894   1949

A656   TERRELL.   The Tirrell, Tirrill-Terrill, Tyrrell book; descendants of William Therrill.   By Robert Wilson Tirrell.   (2d ed.) Englewood, N.J., 1969.   590 p. illus., coat of arms, facsims., maps. 27 cm.
200 copies printed. No.33. Bibliography: p. 529-533. 76-106010 MARC.   CS71.T3   1969

        TESTER.   See ROUSE, 1970 (addenda)

A657   THOMAS.   The Thomas-Thompson genealogist.   Mt. Prospect, Ill. (Genealogist Publications) v. 28 cm. quarterly. 71-12363.   CS71.T455

A658   THORLACIUS.   Thorlacius family in vertical file.   Ask reference librarian for this material.

A659   THÜRINGER.   A few Württemberg families of Grafenberg, Kohlberg, Riederich & Tischardt (ancestry of German-American families) (n.p.) 1956.   21 p. 23 cm. (Annals of German-American families, a genealogical series) 56-36030.   CS719.A2K3

A660   TINGLEY.   The Tingley family revised.   Compiled by Marian McCauley Frye.   1st ed. (Falls Church? Va.) 1970 -   v. port. 24 cm. Contents. - v.1. Being a record of the descendants of Samuel Tingley of Malden, Mass., in both the male and female lines (- 1666) 77-109129 MARC.   CS71.T585   1970

ADDENDA

A661 TITCOMB. Descendants of William Titcomb of Newbury, Massachusetts, 1635. By Gilbert
Merrill Titcomb. (Ann Arbor, Mich., Lithographed by Edwards Brothers, 1969)   vii, 239, xxxiii p.
illus., ports. 24 cm. Bibliographical footnotes. 75-14247 MARC.   CS71. T5984   1969

A662 TOOL. Lineage of Alma Tool Steider. By Alma Tool Steider. Eureka, Ill. (1970)
15 1. 29 cm. Includes bibliographical references. 73-278772 MARC.   CS71. T6645   1970

A663 TOWNSEND. ... The direct ancestry and posterity of Judge Charles Townsend, a pioneer of
Buffalo, N.Y., with biographies of the individuals of the nineteen successive generations thus included,
and other matters of interest to the Townsend family, by Rev. Charles Townsend. Orange, N.J.,
(1897)   62 p. illus. (coats of arms.) fold. geneal. tab. 23½ cm. At head of title: 1375-1897. Authorities: p. 6-7. 18-363.
                                                                                  CS71. T75   1897

A664 TOWNSEND. The Townsend family, 1748-1970. By Peggy Tyner Townsend. (n. p., 1970)
19 1. geneal. table. 28 cm. 70-20998 MARC.   CS71. T75   1970

A665 TRABUE. Trabue family history; ancestry and known descendants of David Trabue Jr., born
Oct. 9, 1768, Manikintown, Virginia, died Apr. 8, 1842, Jessamine Co., Kentucky, by Pauline Trabue
Groves Colwell and Osee Johnson Knouf. (Champaign, Ill.) 1968.   96 1. ports. 28 cm. Includes bibliographical
references. 79-20846 MARC.   CS71. T756   1968

A666 TRAUTMAN. Trautman family in vertical file.   Ask reference librarian for this material.

A667 TRAVERS. The Travis family today and yesterday, by Berdyne D. Travis. Ionia, Mich.,
1969.   63 p. geneal. tables, ports. 23 cm. 73-18303 MARC.   CS71. T78   1969

     TRAVIS. See TRAVERS, 1969 (addenda)

     TREMBLAY. See TREMBLEY. (addenda)

A667a TREMBLEY. Les Trembley de Genève, de 1552 à 1846 (par) Paul-F. Geisendorf. Geneve,
Librairie Alex. Jullien, (1970)   345 p. plates. fold. geneal. table (in pocket) 24 cm. "Il a été tiré de cet ouvrage 225 exemplaires." Includes bibliographical references. 74-543959.   CS71. T7893   1970

     TRESCOT. See TRESCOTT (addenda)

A668 TRESCOTT. An account of the ventures, adventures and misadventures of William Trescott,
1614/15-1699, his descendants and their kin, related against a background of the history of the times
and places where they lived. By Paul Trescott. Charleston, S.C., Printed by Charleston Lithograph-
ing Co., 1970.   iv, 212 p. illus., coat of arms, geneal. table, maps, plan. 22 cm. Bibliography: p. 207-209. 70-116024 MARC.
                                                                                  CS71. T8127   1970

     TROUT. See SLOAN, 1965 (addenda)

A669 TUCKER. Genealogical chart of the descendants of Pleasant Balard Tucker, Jr., 1860-1943;
with an outline of his American ancestors, 1759-1880.   sheet. Consists of a table, dating from about 1931, compiler unknown, showing many of the descendants of John & Jane (Pringle) Buchanan of Scotland, to the generation of P. J. Tucker. Jr., and a table showing the
descendants of P. B. Tucker, Jr., to Feb. 1969, with an index to both tables, by W. M. Guthrey. Photocopy of MS. (Collinsville? Okla., 1969?)
26 x 160 cm. 78-13903 MARC.   CS71. T89   1969

A670 TURBETT. Turbett clan. (Compiled by Ralph C. Turbett. n.p., 1969?)   31 1. 30 cm. Cover
title. 72-19036 MARC.   CS71. T94   1969

A671 TURK. Geschichte der Familie Türk, 1529-1965, von Rudolph Dimpfel. 2. erg. Aufl.
München, Dissertations-Druckerei C. Schön, 1965.   83 p. coat of arms, facsims, geneal. table. 21 cm. 79-238423.
                                                                                  CS629. T84   1965

A672 TWEED. Sketch of the James Tweed family, Wilmington, Mass. By Benj. Walker. Read at a
family reunion, Foster's Pond, Andover, Mass., June 17, 1887. Lowell, Mass., Courier press:
Marden & Rowell, 1887.   30 p. 19 cm. 9-14538.   CS71. T97   1887

A673   ULRIKSEN.   Slaegten Ulriksen fra Hyllerslev.   Om Ulrich Adolph Beck Jensen, født 1824, hans forfaedre og efterkommere.   København, Nordisk Slaegtsforskning, 1969.   (51) l. 5 plates. 30 cm. N. T. Two fold. geneal. tables inserted. 77-530130.   CS909.U43   1969

UPLINGER.   See OBLINGER (addenda)

A674   VADEN.   Genealogy of the Vaden and related families.   Data collected and compiled by Tennie Elizabeth Vaden Winn.   (San Antonio, Schneider Print, Co., 1970)   315 p. illus., facsim., geneal. tables, ports. 24 cm.   Title from p. 22.   71-17753 MARC.   CS71.V125   1970

A675   VALENTINE.   Valentine records.   By Daisy Valentine.   Washington (1970 -   v. 29 cm. 74-253248 MARC.   CS71.V158   1970

A676   VAN BIBBER.   The Van Bibber family, by Josephine Nell Letts, (Mrs. F. Dickinson Letts) (1953?)   34 l. 32 cm. Caption title.   Typescript (carbon copy) Gift of Mrs. F. Dickinson Letts. Apr. 10, 1953. 71-12024 MARC.   CS71.V2196   1953

A677   VANCE.   The Vance family scrapbook, by Joseph H. Vance.   (Lombard, Ill., 1970) 227 p. illus., facsims., ports. 31 cm. 78-15400 MARC.   CS71.V2218   1970

A678   VANDAVEER.   The Vandaveer family of Greene County, Illinois, by Frederick Ewart Vandaveer (and) Kenneth Eugene Vandaveer.   (Fairview Park, Ohio, Printed by West Side Blue) 1970. xi, 197 p. illus., coats of arms, maps, ports. 23 cm. 78-125811 MARC.   CS71.V294   1970

A679   VAN DEUSEN.   The genealogy of Rev. W. H. Van Deusen (son of Jacob Dean Van Deusen and Julia Maria Custer McIntosh Van Deusen) and Custer, Hendrickson, Belton, Chelf, Evans and Stayton families.   By Cherry Laura Van Deusen Pratt.   Rockford, Ohio, Rockford Press (1969)   83 p. illus., ports. 24 cm.   77-11973 MARC.   CS71.V243   1969

A680   VANDEVEER.   The Vandeveers of North Carolina, Kentucky, and Indiana.   By Mable Van Dyke.   Richmond, Whittet & Shepperson, 1960.   xi. 180 p. coat of arms. 24 cm. 60-14806.
                                                                                 CS71.V242   1960

A681   VAN HOUTEN.   The Van Houten family of Bergen, New Jersey.   By Charles L. Demarest Washburn.   (New York, J. J. Little & co.) 1897.   cover-title, 10 p., 1 l. 27½ cm. Reprinted from the New York genealogical and biographical record for October, 1896, and January, 1897.   With ms. notes and corrections signed by author. 9-14794.
                                                                                 CS71.V257   1897

A682   VAN NESS.   A few of the ancestors of Barbara Van Ness and Bartow Van Ness III, compiled from many sources by Bartow Van Ness, Jr. 3d ed., rev. 1967.   37 l. 13 fold. geneal. tables. 33 cm. "Authorities": leaves 30-38. Photocopy of MS. Baltimore? 1968. 78-11838.   CS71.V2693   1967a

A683   VARENNES.   Généalogie de la famille Gaultier de Varennes en Amérique de 1665 à nos jours. By Kathleen (Mennie) de Varennes.   (Québec) Société canadienne de généalogie (Québec), 1970. 399 p. illus., ports. 28 cm. (Société canadienne de généalogie (Québec). Contribution no. 27) Includes bibliographies. 73-518242.
                                                                                 CS80.S58 no. 27

VAUDYN.   See VADEN (addenda)

A684   VERNER.   Verner notes, compiled by Reid W. Stewart.   (Lower Burrell? Pa.) 1969 (c. 1970) xiv, 45, A-36 p. geneal. table, maps, ports. 28 cm.   78-18094 MARC.   CS71.V5295   1969

A685   VINE.   Various Vine families.   By Horace Holmes Wall.   (San Francisco, 1950 - v. in   28 cm. Typescript (carbon copy). corrections in MS. Contents. - pt. 1. Descendants of Robert Vine and Elizabeth Thatcher. - pt. 2. The Wisconsin clan. - pt. 3. Twenty-six immigrants and their descendants. 73-18468 MARC.   CS71.V784   1950

ADDENDA

A686   VON WERL.   Untersuchungen zur Geschichte der Grafen von Werl.   Ein Beitrag zur Geschichte des Hochmittelalters.   By Paul Leidinger.   Verein für Geschichte und Altertumskunde Westfalens, Abt. Paderborn, 1965.   130 p.   24 cm.   (Studien und Quellen zur westfälischen Geschichte, Bd. 5) Based on the author's dissertation.   Münster.   70-493299.   CS629.V65   1965

VROOMAN.   See SMITH, 1970 (addenda)

———

A686a WADDELL.   The name and family of Waddell.   By Charles Wilkin Waddell.   Los Angeles, 1953.
ii, 28 l.   28 cm.   Bibliography: leaf i.   79-14378 MARC.   CS71.W116   1953

A687   WADDINGTON.   Genealogy of the Weddington family, compiled by Andy Simmons-Weddington.
Pulaski, Tenn. (1960)   115 l.   28 cm.   Caption title.   63-59231.   CS71.W118   1960

A687a WALKER.   Genealogy of the descendants of John Walker of Wigton, Scotland, with records of a few allied families.   Also war records and some fragmentary notes pertaining to the history of Virginia.   1600-1902.   By Emma Siggins White ... (Kansas City, Mo.) Press of Tiernan-Dart printing company, 1902.   xxx, 722 p. front., 1 illus., plates, ports., double geneal. tab., col. coat of arms. 24 cm.   CS71.W18   1902
———— Addition.   (Compiled and edited by) Uldric Thompson, III.   (Tampa, Fla., 1967)
(10) p.   24 cm.   Caption title.   2-19111.   CS71.W18   1902
                                                                                       Add.

A688   WALKER.   Henson Walker family record.   (Floyd A. Walker, editor) Pleasant Grove, Utah (1963-67)   xx, 1227 p. illus., facsims., geneal. tables, maps, ports. 23 x 38 cm.   Corrections in MS.   "The Name index" (p. 1155-1227 inserted) was prepared by Milton and Marguerite Noe and published in 1967) Bibliography: p. 1154.   65-5214.   CS71.W18   1965

A689   WALL.   The Walls of Walltown; the known descendents of James Wall of Anson County, North Carolina.   By Anne Wall Thomas.   (Carrboro? N. C., c. 1969)   180 p.   geneal. tables, map, ports. 23 cm.   Includes bibliographical references.   75-12829 MARC.   CS71.W215   1969

WARDE.   See WARD.

A690   WARFIELD.   Warfield records; a collections of records taken from official entries, abstracts of documents, facts of history, conclusions of genealogists, and original research notes on many members of the Warfield family in America and persons associated with them by marriage, business, and geography according to name, location, and chronology beginning with the year 1662.   By Evelyn Ballenger.   Annapolis, Md., T. O. Warfield, 1970.   861 p. col. illus. 28 cm. 75-22125 MARC.   CS71.W274   1970

A691   WARREN.   A family history of the Rev. Robert Smith Warren family, which includes the Smith-Jarratt-Royall-Farrar-Keyser-Morris-Warren-Gurley-Peterson-and Pybas families, also the McAfees and the McCrees.   Compiled by Robert C. Warren.   (Shawnee Mission, Kan., 1970?)   vii, 167 l. ports.
30 cm.   Bibliography.   leaves 165-167.   73-13287 MARC.   CS71.W29   1970

A692   WASHINGTON.   Some colonial mansions and those who lived in them, with genealogies of the various families mentioned, by Thomas Allen Glenn.   2d series.   Philadelphia, H. T. Coates & company, 1900.   12 p., 1 l., 19-503 p. oncl. illus. (incl. coats of arms) plates, ports. front., plates, ports. 24 cm.   Some of the plates accompanied by guard sheets with descriptive letterpress.   "Authorities": p. 329.   Contents. - Mount Vernon and the Washingtons. - The Bowne house at Flushing, L. I. - Laurel Hill and the Rawle family. - Monticello. - The manor of Philipsborough. - Waynesborough. - Preston at Patuxent. - The Schuylers. - Mount Pleasant and the Macphersons.   0-632.   E159.G56

A693   WATERS.   William Watters, his descendants and related families, compiled and edited by Juanita Watters, Nadine Lain (and) Ouida (Watters) Nelson.   Cleburne, Tex., Hallman Print. & Office Supply, 1967.   iv, 388 p. illus. 28 cm. Bibliography: p. 370-373.   67-31849.   CS71.W33   1967
———— Supplement, compiled and edited by Juanita (Jay) Watters, Nadine Lain (and Ouida (Watters) Nelson.   Cleburne, Tex., Hallman Print. & Office Supply, 1968.   387-524 p. 28 cm.   67-31849.
                                                                                  CS71.W33   1967
                                                                                    Suppl.

WATHEN.   See ROBERTS, 1970 (addenda)

A694 WATTS. The family record of John Carroll Watts, containing his Lewis, Gardner, Barber, Kennedy, Teter, and Watts lines. By John Carroll Watts. Troy, N.Y., 1969. iii, 138 p. 28 cm.
70-13289 MARC.   CS71.W35   1969

WAYMAN.   See MARTIN, 1965 (addenda)

WEBER.   See HEINZE, 1970 (addenda)

A695 WEED. One line of Weed ancestry; with connections with Stevens and Disbrow families, 1953, compiled by Frederick J. Simmons. (1953 or 4)   5, 18 l. 32 cm. Typescript (carbon copy) with manuscript additions.
Bibliography: leaf 18. 76-225114 MARC.   CS71.W39   1953

A696 WEMMELUND. Slaegten Wemmelund fra Give sogn. Om Peder Madsen (Wemmelund), født 1789, og hustru, deres forfaedre og efterkommere. København, Nordisk Slaegtsforskning, 1969.
(195) p. 20 plates. 30 cm. N.T. Ten fold. geneal. tables inserted. 70-530131.   CS909.W43   1969

WERL.   See VONWERL (addenda)

A697 WEST. What is in a name? West; the life of a family, a people, their history, their homes, their lands and their hopes, their labors and their courage, their faith, their devotion and their loyalty, their love and their dreams. By Hoke Holland West. Gallatin, Tenn., Quality Print. Co., 1970.
365 p. illus. (part col.), col. coat of arms. maps, plans, ports. 29 cm. 74-21377 MARC.   CS71.W52   1970

A698 WESTERMAN. Westerman family history. By Richard Wilbur Westerman. Scottdale, Pa., 1970.   83 l. 29 cm. 76-22440 MARC.   CS71.W524   1970

WESTERMANN. See WESTERMAN (addenda)

WESTVIG. See WESTWICK.

WESTVIK. See WESTWICK.

A699 WESTWICK. The Westwick tree, including the genealogy of the maternal side of the family. By Russell Enokson. (n.p.1970)   xiv, 270 p. illus., coat of arms, geneal. table, ports. 29 cm. Bibliography: p. 242-243.
72-278729 MARC.   CS71.W536   1970

A700 WETTEROTH. History of the Wetteroth family of Millstadt, Illinois. By Robert Buecher. (Millstadt, 1970?)   (15) l. geneal. table. 30 cm. 71-15811 MARC.   CS71.W544   1970

A701 WEYGANT. Book of Wiant biographies. Co-authors: Rena (Wiant) Prather and Gertrude (Wiant) Stickley. Edited by Rena (Wiant) Prather. (n.p.) 1969.   74 l. 30 cm. 77-19770 MARC.
                                                                                                        CS71.W5487   1969

A702 WEYGANT. Wiant family genealogy, 1782-1970. Co-authors: Rena (Wiant) Prather and Gertrude (Wiant) Stickley. Edited by Rena (Wiant) Prather. (n.p.) 1970.   40, vi l. 30 cm. Bibliography:
leaves i-ii. 72-19769 MARC.   CS71.W5487   1970

A703 WHIPPLE. A partial list of the descendents of Matthew Whipple, the elder, of Bocking, Essex County, England. By Henry Burdette Whipple. High Point, N.C., 1965-69.   2 v. geneal. tables. 28 cm.
Cover title: Matthew Whipple of Bocking, England. & descendants. 66-582.   CS71.W574   1965

A704 WHIPPLE. Genealogy of Whipple, Paddock, Bull families in America, 1620-1970, by Ruth Whipple Kapphahn (and) James Grafton Carter. (Columbus, Ohio, 1969)   69 l. 29 cm. 79-13283 MARC.
                                                                                                        CS71.W574   1969

A705 WHITE. White. By David Kendall Martin. (West Chazy, N.Y., 1965?)   (32) l. 28 cm. Includes
bibliographical references. 70-237839 MARC.   CS71.W585   1965b

A706 WHITE. The White genealogist. Mt. Prospect, Ill. (Genealogist Publications)   v. 28 cm.
quarterly. 78-17318.   CS71.W584

A707   WHITMORE.   Wetmore history and some maternal lines.   By Kathryn Lee Wetmore Stadel. (Ann Arbor, Mich., Printed by Edwards Bros.) 1970.   235 p. illus., ports. 28 cm. 76-21139 MARC.
CS71.W616   1970

A708   WICKLOW.   Case of the Right Honourable Charles Francis Arnold, earl of Wicklow, viscount Wicklow and lord Clonmore, in the peerage of Ireland, on his claiming the right to vote, as Earl of Wicklow, at the election of representative peers of Ireland.   (London, 1869)   34 p. fold. geneal. tab. 28 cm.   Pedigree of the Right Hon, Charles Francis Arnold, earl of Wicklow; fold. geneal. tab.   On verso of last leaf, as filing title: Case of the Right Honourable Charles Francis Arnold, earl of Wicklow, viscount Wicklow, and lord Clonmore.   With this is bound: Gt. Brit. Parliament. House of Lords. Minutes of evidence ... on the Earl of Wicklow's claim to vote for representative peers of Ireland...24-3742.   CS496.W5A5   1869

A709   WICKLOW.   Case on behalf of the infant son of William George Howard and Ellen his wife, claiming to be Earl of Wicklow, lodged pursuant to the order of the Right Honourable the House of Lords, on the 12th day of July 1869 ... (London, 1869)   5 p. 28 cm.   On verso of last leaf, as filing title: case on behalf of the infant son of William George Howard ... 1869. 24-8351.   CS496.W6A5   1869

A710   WIDEMAN.   The Wideman family in Canada and United States; a genealogical record, 1803-1955 (by) Norman E. Wideman (and) Enoch Martin Wideman.   (n. p., 1955)   319 p. 24 cm.   Bibliography: p. 291-292. 74-476781 MARC.   CS90.W56   1955

A711   WILEY.   The Wylie family from Pennsylvania and Ohio.   By Jennie Dwight Wylie.   New York, 1959.   32 p. geneal. table, ports. 22 cm. 73-12212 MARC.   CS71.W675   1959

A712   WILKIE.   The Jonathan tree; or, A Wilkey genealogy.   By Hubert Weldon Wilkey.   (Leitchfield? Ky., 1970?)   159 p. 23 cm. 76-21120 MARC.   CS71.W68   1970

A713   WILLEY.   The avalanche of the White Hills: August 28th, 1826.   (By Isaac McLellan) Boston, Jones' power press office, 1846.   cover-title, (3)-18 p. 23 cm.   Caption title (p.(3) -): Avalanche of the White Hills: and the destruction of the Willey family ... 16-20793 rev.   F41.44.M16

A714   WILLIAMS.   A genealogy of Dan Batchelor and David Neal Williams. By Lyle Keith Williams. (Ft. Worth, Tex., 1968?)   iv, 55 p. 22 cm.   Cover title. 71-11051 MARC.   CS71.W72   1968

A715   WILLIAMS.   Our hill country heritage, by Paul J. Long.   (Oak Ridge? Tenn., 1970) - v. illus., geneal. tables, ports. 28 cm.   Includes bibliographical references.   Contents. - v.1. Williams and related families. 74-13586 MARC.   CS71.W72   1970

A716   WILSON.   My Aunt Louisa and Woodrow Wilson (by) Margaret Axson Elliott.   Chapel Hill, The University of North Carolina press (1944)   vii, 302 p. 22 cm.   An account of the author's life spent in the homes of her aunt and brother-in-law. 44-40197.   E767.3.E4

A717   WILSON.   The Wilson genealogist.   v. 1-   Mar./May 1969 -   v. 28 cm. quarterly. Editor: 1969 -   D. C. Martin. 71-15401.   CS71.W748

A718   WILSON.   Wilsons: England to America, 1600-1970; a genealogy.   By Elva Wilson Nyren. (Red Oak, Iowa, Printed by Express Pub. Co., 1970)   157 p. illus., map, ports. 27 cm.   "Limited edition - 180 copies." 72-126969 MARC.   CS71.W75   1970

A719   WILSON.   Descendants of Wilsons and Garners of Virginia.   By Leola (Wilson) Konopa. (Columbia? S.C., 1970)   31 l. 28 cm.   Cover title. 74-15434 MARC.   CS71.W75   1970b

A720   WILSON.   The Willson (Wilson) family (by) John H. Wilson.   Fort Worth, 1970)   156 p. 28 cm. 71-17824 MARC.   CS71.W75   1970c
——— Willson-Wilson family history, supplement (Fort Worth, 1970)   v. 28 cm.
CS71.W75   1970c
Suppl.

A721   WILT.   Jacob and Sarah Wilt family: history and genealogys 1787-1970, and related familys. Recorded and written by Ralph W. Wilt.   (n. p.) 1970.   61 l. 29 cm. 77-278773 MARC.   CS71.W752   1970

WINCLEBLANK.   See WINKELBLECH (addenda)

A722   WINGFIELD.   Muniments of the ancient Saxon family of Wingfield.   Comp. by Mervyn Edward, seventh viscount Powerscourt ... Privately printed.   London, Mitchell and Hughes, 1894.   viii, 88 p. illus., plates (part col.) ports., facsims., col. diagr,, coats of arms. 41½ cm. Half-title: The family of Wingfield. "The trial, execution, and death of Mary queen of Scots.   Comp, from the original documents, by Charles Dack": p. (57)-63.   L.C. COPY REPLACED BY MICROFILM. 9-32042.
CS439.S58
Microfilm 16939 CS

A723   WINKELBLECH.   Genealogy of the Winkelblech, Winkleblack, Winklepleck family in America, by Aaron M. Winklepleck.   (Connersville? Ind., 1968?)   811 p. illus., facsims., ports. 29 cm. Includes bibliographical references.   72-266892 MARC.
CS71.W774   1968

WINKLEBLACK.   See WINKELBLECH (addenda)

WINKLEPLECK.   See WINKELBLECH (addenda)

A724   WIRTH.   The family register, 1555-1965, compiled by Ed. H. Wirth.   (Belleville, Ill., 1966?) 74 p. 28 cm. Cover title. 79-11987 MARC.
CS71.W795   1966

A725   WITT.   Witt family genealogy (researched and submitted by M. Stewart DeWitt.   1967) 29 l. 30 cm. Caption title. Typescript (part carbon copy) 76-20182 MARC.
CS71.W8274   1967

A726   WOOD.   Henry Wood of Middleborough, Mass., by Nora Bethel Wood and Elijah Francis Atwood.   Sisseton, S.D., Atwood Pub. Co., 1945.   xlviii, 272 l. illus., coats of arms, ports. 27 cm. 70-225115 MARC.
CS71.W875   1945

A727   WOOD.   John Wood of Rhode Island, and his early descendants on the mainland. by Bertha W. Clark.   (n.p., 1966)   x, 113, (40) p. 28 cm. Bibliography compiled by D.W.Ewers: p. (1)-(13) (3d group) 73-11014 MARC.
CS71.W875   1966b

WOODRING.   See BASKIN, 1970 (addenda)

WOOTTEN.   See CARPENTER, 1970 (addenda)

WORTH.   See CLARK, 1970 (addenda)

A728   WRIGHT.   Wright family memorials gathered by Anna E. (Wright) Mathews, for the descendants of her grandfather Justus Wright, of South Hadley, Mass.   Boston, Press of J. A. Crosby, 1886. 1 p. l., 42 p. 19½ cm. Six pages left blank for "Additional notes." L.C. COPY REPLACED BY MICROFILM. 16-5355. CS71.W95   1886
Microfilm 18211 CS

A729   WRIGHT.   Ancestors-descendants, James Wilson Wright, Sr. who married Cynthia Rebecca Jones, Paris, Bourbon County, Kentucky (by W. R. & R. L. McCann.   Hopewell? Va., 1955?) 21 p. 28 cm. 57-39857.
CS71.W94   1955

A730   WYNDHAM.   Felbrigg, the story of a house (by) R. W. Ketton-Cremer.   London, R. Hart-Davis, 1962.   304 p. illus., fold. geneal. table, map, ports. 22 cm. Bibliography: p.292-296. 74-233080.   CS439.W93   1962

———

A731   YAW.   The Yaw-Yeaw family in America.   By Clarence Arthur Phillips.   (n.p., Yaw-Yeaw Family Society) 1962.   211 p. 28 cm. 63-35721.   CS71.Y34   1962
——— 1970 supplement.   (n.p.) Yaw-Yeaw Family Society, 1962 (i.e. 1970)   185-189, 198-254 p.
Cover title.   Includes a revision of chapter 26 of the original work.   CS71.Y34   1962
Suppl.

YOAK.   See YOCK (addenda)

ADDENDA

A732   YOCK.   The Yock - Yoke - Yoak family tree, March 1968 (by Harold R. Yoak.   Clarksburg?
W. Va., c. 1969)   73 1. 28 cm. Caption title. 75-16982 MARC.   CS71. Y5345   1969

A733   YODER.   History of the Yoder family in North Carolina, by Fred Roy Yoder.   (Ann Arbor,
Mich., Lithographed by Edwards Bros., c. 1970)   xi, 158 p. illus., ports. 24 cm. 76-20978 MARC.
                                                                    CS71. Y535   1970

        YOKE.   See YOCK (addenda)

A734   ZAPPI.   Genealogia e cronistoria di una famiglia imolese: gli Zappi. By Alberto Biasi.   Imola,
P. Galeati, 1961.   65, (2) p. illus., geneal. tables, ports. 29 cm. Bibliography: p. (67) 74-227917.   CS769. Z3   1961

A735   ZIEBACH.   Descendants of Bartholomew Ziebach.   By Isabella Coy Smith.   Eugene, Or., 1969.
14 1. geneal. table. 29 cm. Typescript (carbon copy) 79-12716 MARC.   CS71. Z64   1969

A736   ZIEGLER.   The Ziegler family and related families in Pennsylvania.   By Gertrude Mohlin
Ziegler.   Zelienople, Pa., C. Campbell Printing Co., 1970.   iv, 448 p. illus., col. coat of arms, forms, geneal.
table, maps, port. 24 cm. (1st ed.) 70-115646 MARC.   CS71. Z66   1970

961